1,295 Best-Selling Home Plans

Plan # 34150 p. 165
Plan # 34029 p. 242
Plan # 93118 p. 720
Plan # 32095 p. 744
Plan # 94938 p. 223
Plan # 32358 p. 34
Plan # 65465 p. 126
Plan # 99420 p. 3

Table of Contents

Cover plans: Featured plan is number 65138 and may be seen on page 36.
The smaller photos, from left to right, are: Plan number 99459, p. 401; plan number 24245, p. 424; plan number 99491, p. 324; plan number 99434, p. 325; plan number 99450, p. 604.

1295 Best-Selling Home Plans
ISBN: 1-893536-25-4

of Chantilly, VA
Printed in China

CEO & Publisher
Marie L. Galastro

President of Internet Operations and Architecture
D. Jarret Magbee

Editorial/Sales Director
Bruce Arant

The photographed homes may have been modified to suit individual tastes.

Cover photography used through the courtesy of the designers.

Submit all Canadian plan orders to the following address:
Garlinghouse Company, 102 Ellis Street, Penticton, BC V2A 4L5

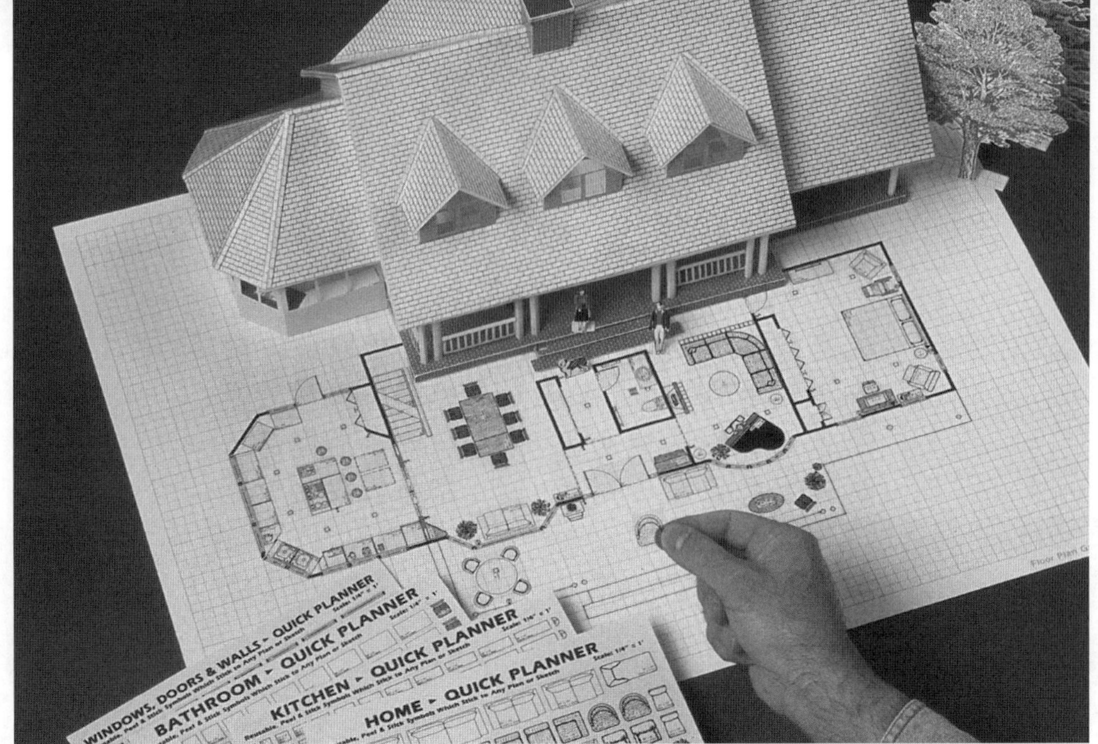
WINDOWS, DOORS & WALLS • QUICK PLANNER
BATHROOM • QUICK PLANNER
KITCHEN • QUICK PLANNER
HOME • QUICK PLANNER

Forget the Aggravation of Complicated Design Software

Design, Build and Decorate Your New Home on Your Kitchen Table

Computers are great, but when it comes to planning your new home, you don't want the frustration of complicated home design software getting between you and your dream. Visualize and test your designs using our proven design systems. Really see how your ideas work with our **3-D Home Kit** and **Home Quick Planner**.

Home Quick Planner

Design and Decorate Your New Home

Our Home Quick Planner comes with 700 pre-cut, reusable peel-and-stick furniture, fixture and architectural symbols that let you design floor plans and make changes instantly. Go ahead! Knock down walls and move cabinets, furniture, appliances, bathroom fixtures, windows and doors—even whole rooms. Includes 1/4-in. scale Floor Plan Grid, stairs, outlets, switches, lights, plus design ideas.

Regularly $22.95 Special Offer: $19.95

3-D Home Kit

"Build" Your New Home

Construct a detailed three-dimensional scale model of your new home. Our kit contains a complete assortment of cardboard building materials—from brick, stone, stucco, clapboards, roofing and decking to windows, doors, skylights, stairs, bathroom fixtures, kitchen cabinets and appliances—to construct a home of up to 3,000 square feet. (For larger homes, order an extra kit.) Includes Floor Plan Grid, interior walls, special Scaled Ruler and Roof Slope Calculator, professional design notes and complete model building instructions.

Regularly $34.95 Special Offer: $29.95

We'll even draw your plans for you.

After you design your dream home using the 3-D Home Kit or the Home Quick Planner, simply mail us a "to-scale" copy of your floor plan layout, and we will give you a custom design price quote.

the Garlinghouse company

To order, call 1-800-235-5700

Monday-Thursday 8:00 am - 7:00 pm; Friday 8:00 am - 6:00 pm
Saturday 10:00 am - 4:00 pm

PHOTOGRAPHY: COURTESY OF THE DESIGNER

above The center gable nicely sets off the gabled garage. The covered porch and triple windows add curb appeal.

compact and PLEASING

design 99420

Units	Single
Price Code	B
Total Finished	1,694 sq. ft.
First Finished	1,298 sq. ft.
Second Finished	396 sq. ft.
Basement Unfinished	1,298 sq. ft.
Garage Unfinished	513 sq. ft.
Dimensions	54'x45'4"
Foundation	Basement
Bedrooms	3
Full Baths	2
Half Baths	1

The main entry leads directly into the formal dining room to the right, past the stairs leading to the second floor, and into the great-room. The breakfast room, with a built-in desk, shares a snack bar with the kitchen, which is almost completely enclosed by its ample counters. The laundry room is a few steps away, beside the door to the spacious garage. In the opposite wing of the first floor is the master suite. The second floor is reserved for two secondary bedrooms and a full bath. A linen closet makes use of what could have been wasted space. This home is designed with a basement foundation. Alternate foundation options available at an additional charge. Please call 1-800-235-5700 for more information.

Please note: The photographed home may have been modified to suit homeowner preferences. If you order plans, have a builder or design professional check them against the photographs to confirm actual construction details.

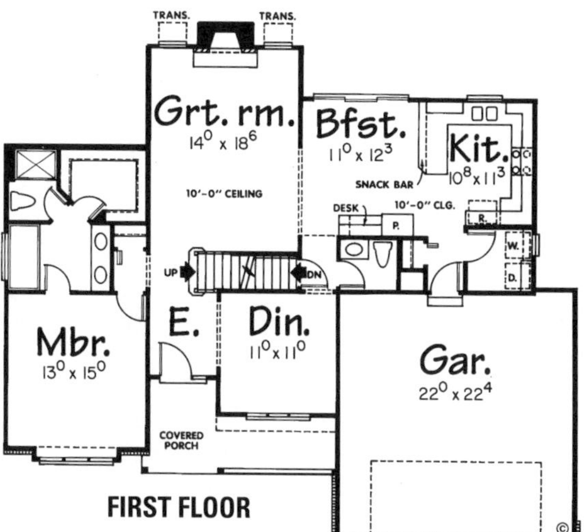

TRANS.
TRANS.
Grt. rm.
14^0 x 18^6
10'-0" CEILING
Bfst.
11^0 x 12^3
Kit.
10^8x11^3
SNACK BAR
DESK
10'-0" CLG.
UP
DN
E.
Din.
11^0x11^0
Mbr.
13^0 x 15^0
Gar.
22^0 x 22^4
COVERED PORCH

FIRST FLOOR

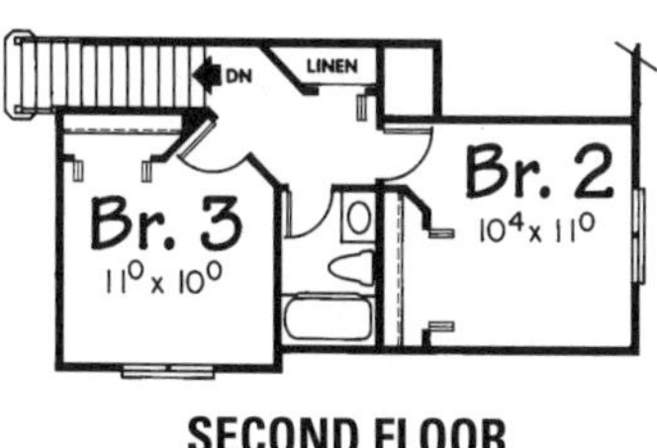

DN
LINEN
Br. 3
11^0 x 10^0
Br. 2
10^4x 11^0

SECOND FLOOR

PHOTOGRAPHY: STEPHEN CRIDLAND

traditional DETAILS

above A mix of clapboard and cedar-shake siding, simple but elegant gables, eave brackets, and tapered pillars establish timeless appeal.

below To the right of the foyer is the formal dining room. Columns on half walls add a touch of elegance to its entry.

Sometimes it's the simple details that make the biggest statement. Such is the case with this house, whose gable roofline, cedar-shake siding accents, and simple but elegant tapered pillars showcase the classic details of traditional design. The living and dining rooms flank the entry. The kitchen features a center island with a cooktop. The second-floor master suite includes a tub, shower, dual-sink vanity, and a walk-in closet. The first floor has 1,211 square feet and the upper level has 867 square feet. This home is designed with a crawlspace foundation.

above The formal living room sits to the left of the foyer, delineated by columns and half walls. Notice the symmetry of the view, including the distant windows and recessed lights.

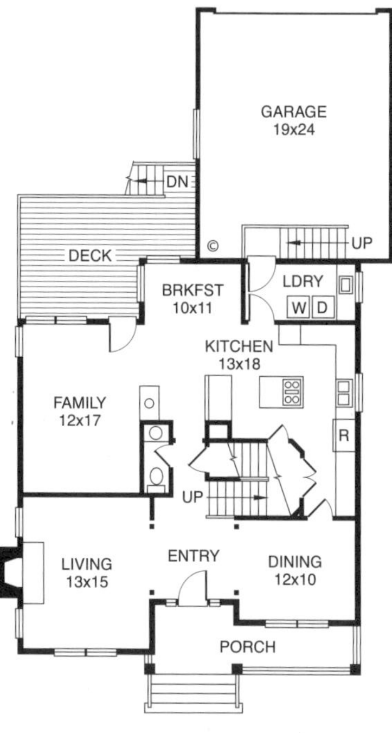
GARAGE
19x24
DN
DECK
UP
BRKFST
10x11
LDRY
W D
KITCHEN
13x18
FAMILY
12x17
R
UP
LIVING
13x15
ENTRY
DINING
12x10
PORCH

FIRST FLOOR

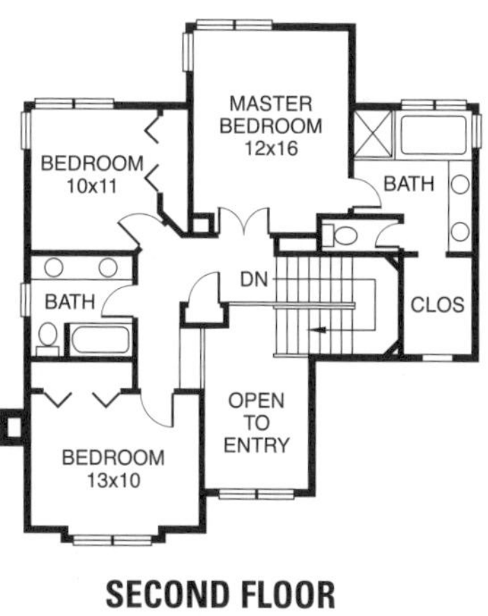
MASTER
BEDROOM
12x16
BEDROOM
10x11
BATH
BATH
DN
CLOS
OPEN
TO
ENTRY
BEDROOM
13x10

SECOND FLOOR

Design Number 32049

Units	Single
Price Code	D
Total Finished	2,078 sq. ft.
First Finished	1,211 sq. ft.
Second Finished	867 sq. ft.
Dimensions	40'6"x65'
Foundation	Crawlspace
Bedrooms	3
Full Baths	2
Half Baths	1

Please note: The photographed home may have been modified to suit homeowner preferences. If you order plans, have a builder or design professional check them against the photographs to confirm actual construction details.

PHOTOGRAPHY: JOHN EHRENCLOU

separate formal SPACES

above A tall gable adds an interesting architectural focal point to this classic design.

The tiled foyer leads to the private dining room on the left and to the isolated living room on the right. Straight ahead is the vast family room, which features a fireplace on one end and built-in bookshelves on the other. Take a left into the window-lined breakfast nook that shares a peninsula snack bar with the efficient kitchen. The handy laundry room is just steps away. On the second floor, two secondary bedrooms, with walk-in closets, share a full bath. The master suite, with two walk-in closets and a full bath with dressing area, fills the right wing. An unfinished area to the left supplies 350 square feet of bonus space. This home is designed with basement, slab, and crawlspace foundation options.

Design Number 34825

Units	Single
Price Code	D
Total Finished	2,242 sq. ft.
First Finished	1,212 sq. ft.
Second Finished	1,030 sq. ft.
Bonus Unfinished	350 sq. ft.
Basement Unfinished	1,212 sq. ft.
Garage Unfinished	521 sq. ft.
Dimensions	55'x34'4"
Foundation	Basement Crawlspace Slab
Bedrooms	3
Full Baths	2
Half Baths	1

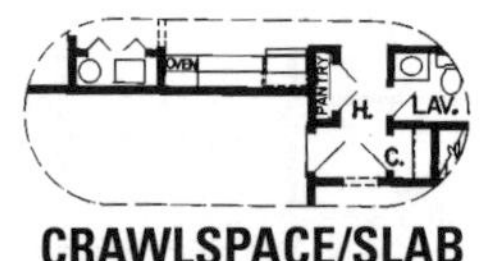
PANTRY
H.
LAV.
C.

CRAWLSPACE/SLAB FOUNDATION OPTION

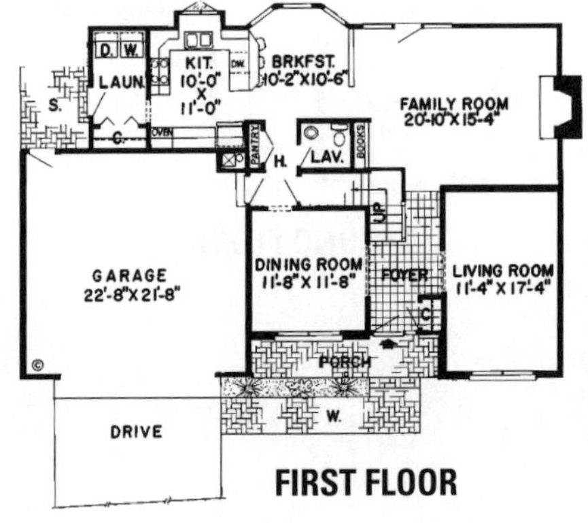
D.W.
LAUN.
KIT. 10'-0" X 11'-0"
BRKFST. 10'-2"X10'-6"
FAMILY ROOM 20'-10"X15'-4"
S.
C.
PANTRY
H.
LAV.
BOOKS
UP
GARAGE 22'-8"X21'-8"
DINING ROOM 11'-8"X11'-8"
FOYER
LIVING ROOM 11'-4"X17'-4"
C.
PORCH
W.
DRIVE

FIRST FLOOR

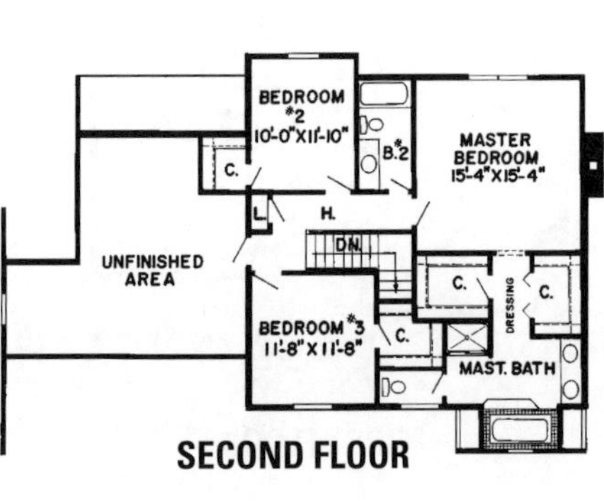
BEDROOM #2 10'-0"X11'-10"
B.#2
MASTER BEDROOM 15'-4"X15'-4"
C.
L.
H.
DN
UNFINISHED AREA
BEDROOM #3 11'-8"X11'-8"
C.
DRESSING
MAST. BATH

SECOND FLOOR

Please note: The photographed home may have been modified to suit homeowner preferences. If you order plans, you may wish to have a builder or design professional check them against the photographs to confirm construction details.

PHOTOGRAPHY: JOHN EHRENCLOU

above An octagonal bay, long, railed porch, and brick facing give this traditional design extra style.

classic DESIGN

This convenient plan is perfect for the modern family with a taste for classic design. Traditional Victorian touches in this three-bedroom beauty include a romantic, railed porch and an intriguing breakfast tower just off the kitchen. The arrangement of the kitchen between the breakfast and formal dining rooms is nothing less than efficient and the wide-open living room, which opens out to the deck, rounds out the common areas.

In the private wing, the master suite enjoys a skylit bath, while two secondary bedrooms boast ample closet space. The third bedroom would also make an ideal den. This home is designed with basement, slab, and crawlspace foundation options.

Please note: The photographed home may have been modified to suit homeowner preferences. If you order plans, have a builder or design professional check them against the photographs to confirm actual construction details.

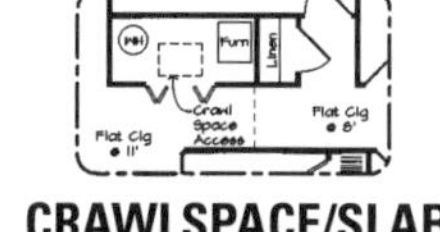

CRAWLSPACE/SLAB FOUNDATION OPTION

Design Number 34043

Units	Single
Price Code	B
Total Finished	1,583 sq. ft.
Main Finished	1,583 sq. ft.
Basement Unfinished	1,573 sq. ft.
Garage Unfinished	484 sq. ft.
Dimensions	70'x46'
Foundation	Basement Crawlspace Slab
Bedrooms	3
Full Baths	2

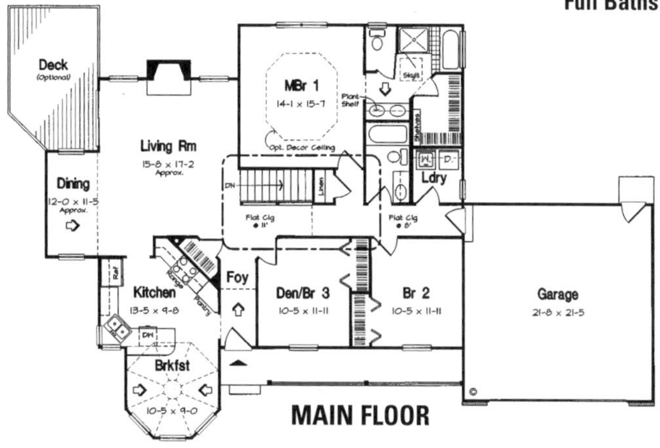
Deck (Optional)
Living Rm
15-8 x 17-2 Approx.
MBr 1
14-1 x 15-7
Dining
12-0 x 11-5 Approx.
Ldry
Kitchen
13-5 x 9-8
Foy
Den/Br 3
10-5 x 11-11
Br 2
10-5 x 11-11
Garage
21-8 x 21-5
Brkfst
10-5 x 9-0

MAIN FLOOR

PHOTOGRAPHY: MARK ENGLUND

homey HABITAT

above Gables, a Palladian window, and a sheltering entry combine to present a welcoming facade on this well-planned design.

Family-friendly describes this design with its open community areas and core of bedrooms. The vaulted ceilings topping the master suite, living, and dining rooms add grand scale. The centralized kitchen boasts ample counter space and easy access to the dining area. Made for the growing family, or one that expects a lot of guests, the design includes a den that can be easily converted into a third bedroom. A corner of windows, a large closet, and a convenient private bath make a comfortable master suite. Meanwhile, a corner of windows and ample closet space spruce up the second bedroom. This home is designed with a basement foundation.

design 51020

Price Code	A
Total Finished	1,252 sq. ft.
Main Finished	1,252 sq. ft.
Basement Unfinished	1,252 sq. ft.
Garage Unfinished	420 sq. ft.
Deck Unfinished	120 sq. ft.
Dimensions	44'8"x50'8"
Foundation	Basement
Bedrooms	3
Full Baths	2

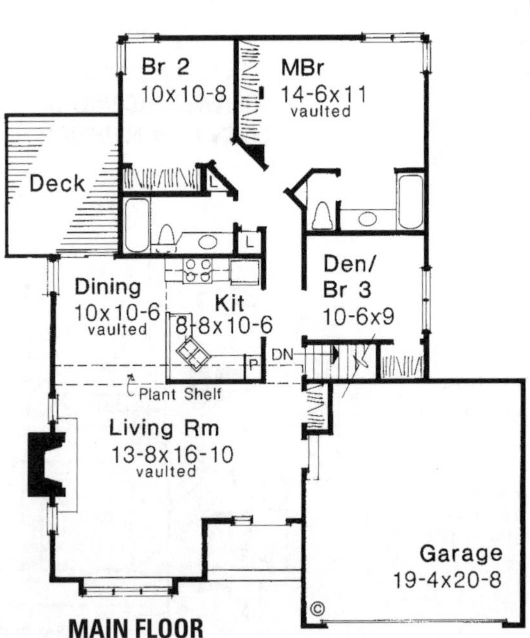

Br 2
10x10-8
MBr
14-6x11
vaulted
Deck
L
L
Dining
10x10-6
vaulted
Kit
8-8x10-6
Den/
Br 3
10-6x9
DN
P
Plant Shelf
Living Rm
13-8x16-10
vaulted
Garage
19-4x20-8
©

MAIN FLOOR

Please note: The photographed home may have been modified to suit homeowner preferences. If you order plans, have a builder or design professional check them against the photographs to confirm actual construction details.

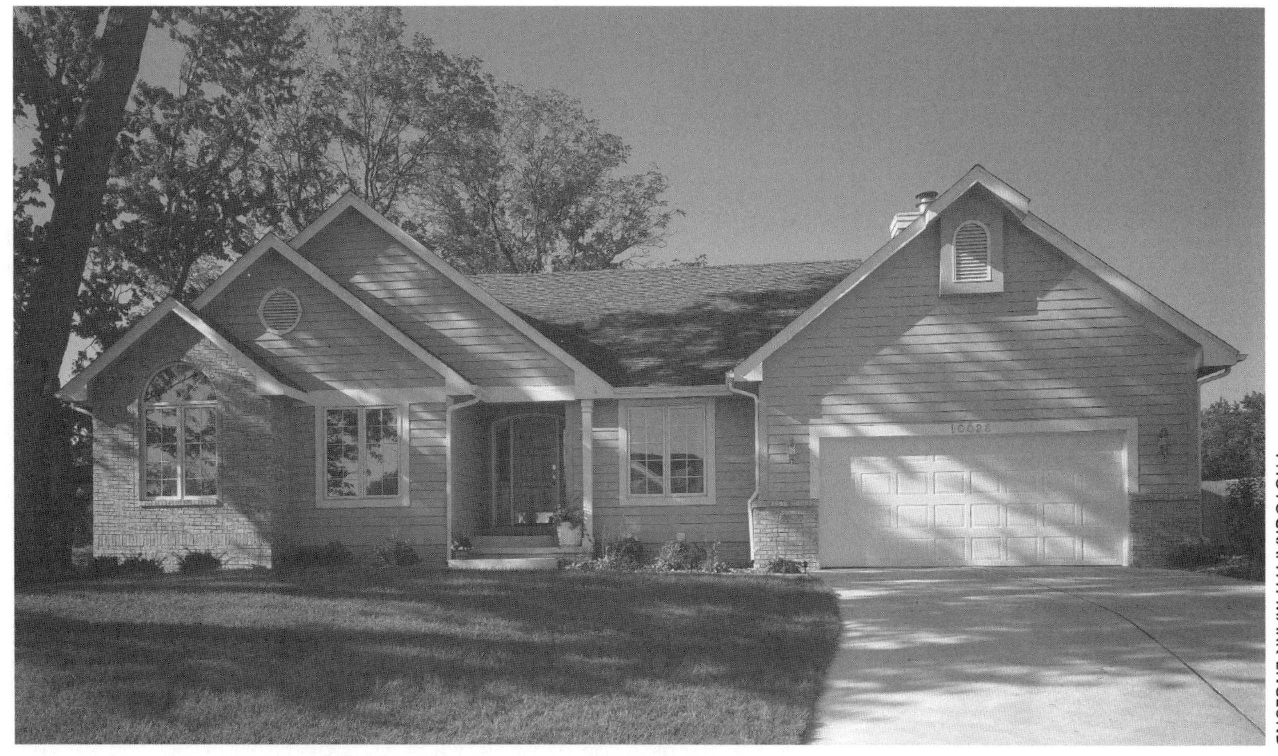

PHOTOGRAPHY: MARK ENGLUND

perfectly DETAILED

above Stacked rooflines and a covered entry add a touch of understated charm to the exterior.

High ceilings, a sunken living room, and built-in plant shelves are just some of the pleasant details embellishing this home's interior. All of these features are highlighted by the abundance of windows that brighten every room.

A fireplace in the living room and one in the country kitchen help create warm and welcoming spaces for family to gather. For quieter times, the bedrooms are isolated in the left wing. A deck completes the plan, extending comfortable living area outdoors. This home is designed with a basement foundation.

design 51017

Units	Single
Price Code	C
Total Finished	1,993 sq. ft.
Main Finished	1,993 sq. ft.
Basement Unfinished	1,993 sq. ft.
Garage Unfinished	521 sq. ft.
Deck Unfinished	180 sq. ft.
Dimensions	60'x48'4"
Foundation	Basement
Bedrooms	3
Full Baths	2

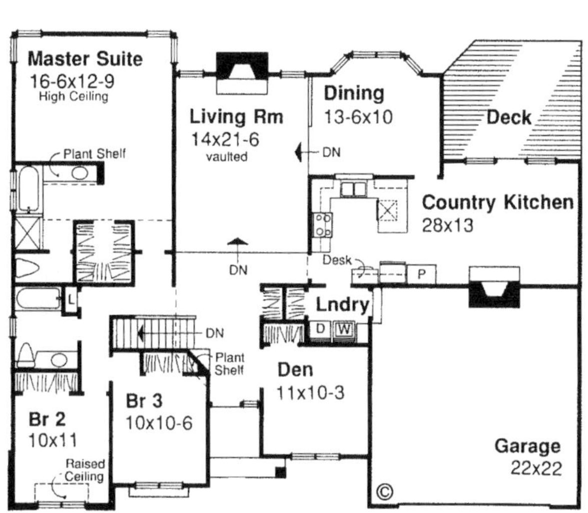
Master Suite
16-6x12-9
High Ceiling
Plant Shelf
Living Rm
14x21-6
vaulted
DN
Dining
13-6x10
Deck
Country Kitchen
28x13
Desk
P
Lndry
D
W
DN
Plant Shelf
Den
11x10-3
Br 3
10x10-6
Br 2
10x11
Raised Ceiling
Garage
22x22
©

MAIN FLOOR

Please note: The photographed home may have been modified to suit homeowner preferences. If you order plans, have a builder or design professional check them against the photographs to confirm actual construction details.

PHOTOGRAPHY: ED GOHLICH

above Efficient zoning of space includes shared, private, and outdoor areas.

cottage DELIGHT

Love of nature and love of home walk side-by-side in this delightful cottage that's perfect for a starter family or empty nesters who still want room for family, friends, or grown children to visit. A deep front porch set into the floor plan is an ideal spot for visiting with neighbors or just watching the world go by. This cottage home provides all the necessary spaces, both private and shared. Its central 340-square-foot living area includes a deep rear bay that's large enough to hold a dining table and chairs. The open living space forms an "L" that wraps around back to enfold the efficient kitchen. A diagonal countertop juts out toward the dining bay and holds the kitchen sink. The door off the back of this space leads to the rear yard. Opposite the kitchen, in its own discrete space, is a laundry facility. The home's two bedrooms are on opposite sides of the house. Each bedroom is large and includes two good-sized closets in the hall that connects to the full bath. Plenty of windows throughout provide all the natural light and views you'll need while exposed rafters and ridges complete the cozy cottage experience. This home is designed with a crawlspace foundation. ⌂

Please note: The photographed home may have been modified to suit homeowner preferences. If you order plans, you may wish to have a builder or design professional check them against the photographs to confirm construction details.

Design Number 32323

Units	Single
Price Code	A
Total Finished	1,200 sq. ft.
Main Finished	1,200 sq. ft.
Porch Unfinished	200 sq. ft.
Dimensions	51'4"x34'
Foundation	Crawlspace
Bedrooms	2
Full Baths	2

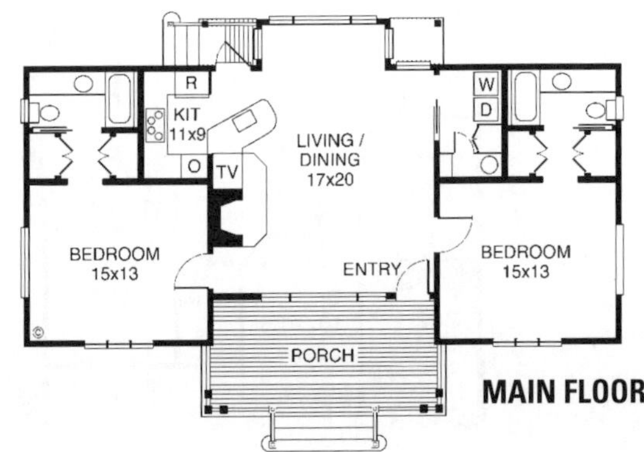
R
KIT
11x9
TV
LIVING /
DINING
17x20
W
D
BEDROOM
15x13
ENTRY
BEDROOM
15x13
PORCH
MAIN FLOOR

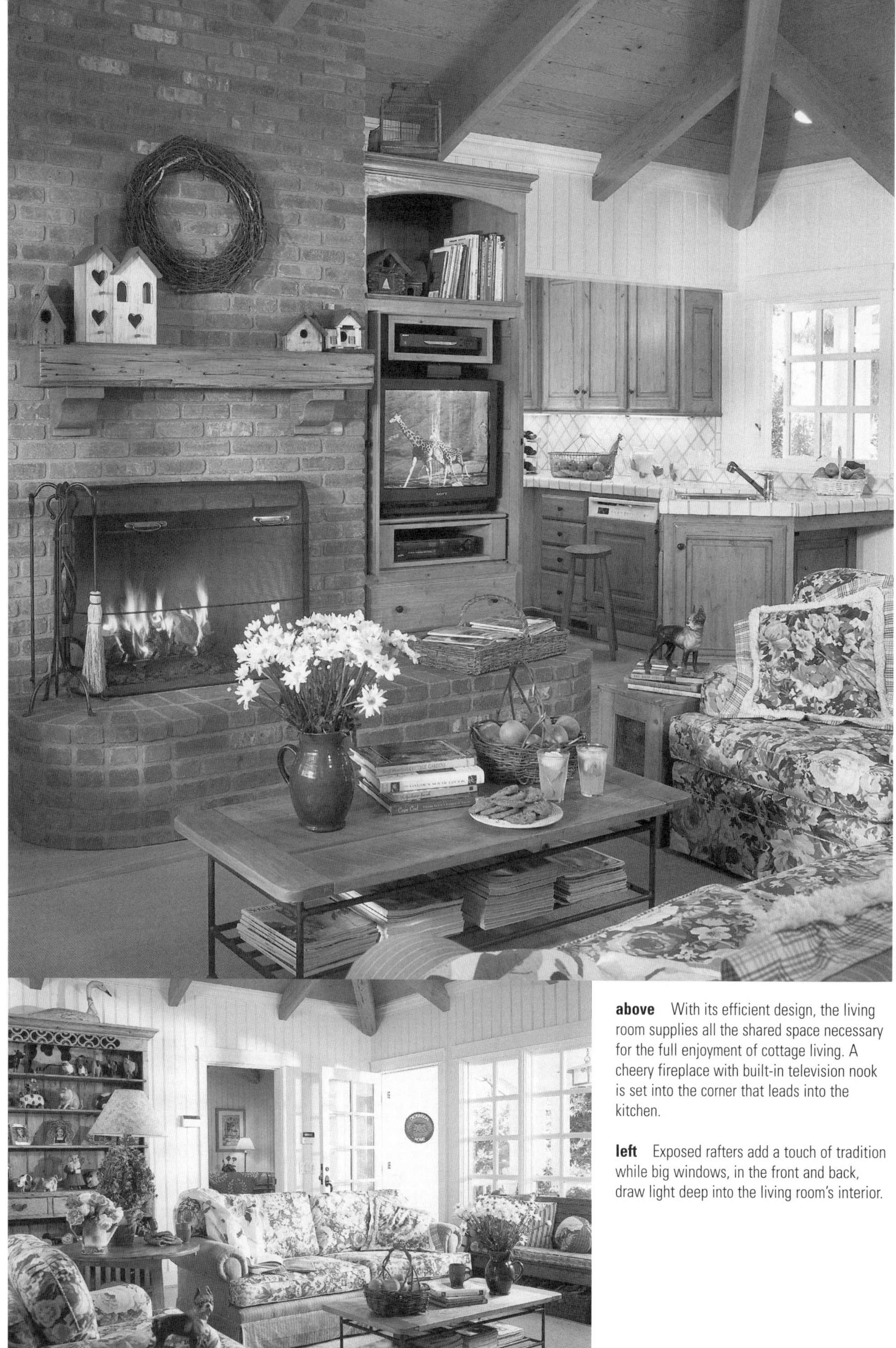

above With its efficient design, the living room supplies all the shared space necessary for the full enjoyment of cottage living. A cheery fireplace with built-in television nook is set into the corner that leads into the kitchen.

left Exposed rafters add a touch of tradition while big windows, in the front and back, draw light deep into the living room's interior.

above In just under 1,000 square feet, this quaint, cottage home exudes a sense of coziness and charm.

cozy Cottage

This home is designed to make the most of its space. The inviting front porch leads the way into the open living area. In the front of the home is the fireplace-warmed living room. It subtly blends into the dining area, which is illumined by a bay window. A cooktop counter distinguishes the efficient kitchen work area. The lower floor is all about utility with a full laundry room and garage. This home is designed with a basement foundation.

design 69030

Units	Single
Price Code	A
Total Finished	914 sq. ft.
Main Finished	914 sq. ft.
Dimensions	28'x28'
Foundation	Basement
Bedrooms	2
Full Baths	1

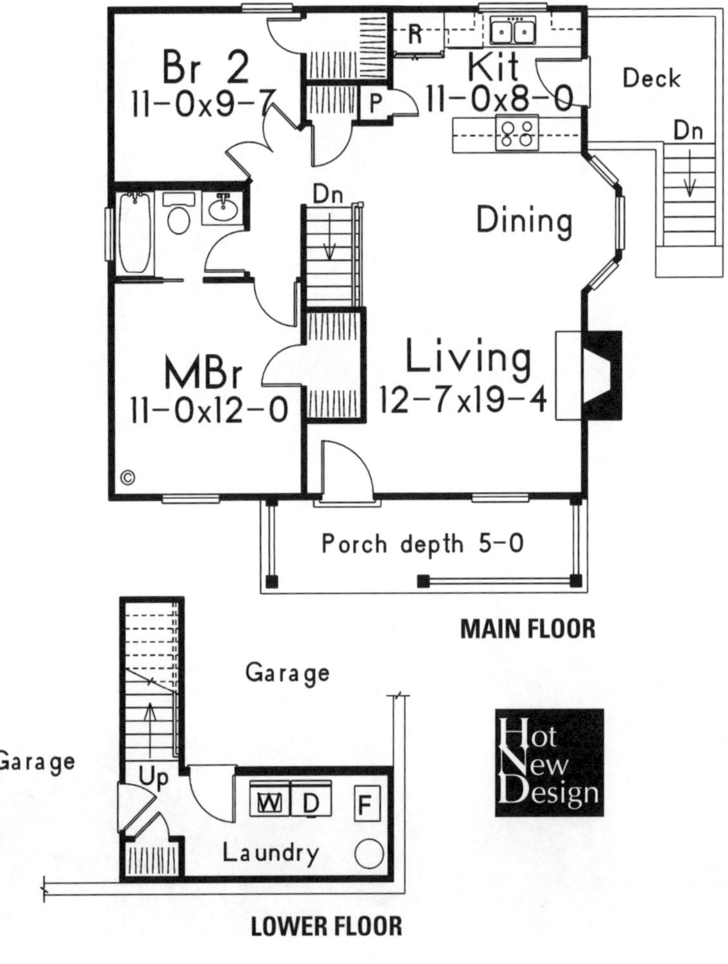
R
Br 2
11-0x9-7
Kit
11-0x8-0
P
Deck
Dn
Dn
Dining
Living
12-7x19-4
MBr
11-0x12-0
Porch depth 5-0
MAIN FLOOR
Garage
Garage
Up
W
D
F
Laundry
LOWER FLOOR
Hot New Design

PHOTOGRAPHY: SUSAN GILMORE

clean LINES

above and below Traditional farmhouse good looks wrap up a carefully laid out interior plan.

design 32056

Units	Single
Price Code	D
Total Finished	1,988 sq. ft.
First Finished	968 sq. ft.
Second Finished	510 sq. ft.
Lower Finished	510 sq. ft.
Basement Unfinished	840 sq. ft.
Garage Unfinished	672 sq. ft.
Dimensions	81'x52'
Foundation	Basement
Bedrooms	3
Full Baths	2

Basic elements of design—one larger rectangle and two smaller rectangles topped by triangular gables—allow this attractive home to be built very cost effectively. Soaring ceilings, open spaces, and carefully positioned windows work together to make this home seem larger than it is. The front porch welcomes guests into an air-lock vestibule, which maintains inside heat during cold weather and air conditioning during hot weather. The vestibule opens to the great-room, which has a cathedral ceiling and a prominent fireplace. The great-room is large enough to accommodate a dining area and opens to the sunroom on one side and kitchen on the other. Stairs lead down from this area to the bedrooms on the walk-out lower level, which also holds a full bath and a walk-in closet. Stairs lead up to the master suite, which includes a private study. This home is designed with a basement foundation. 🏛

Please note: The photographed home may have been modified to suit homeowner preferences. If you order plans, you may wish to have a builder or design professional check them against the photographs to confirm construction details.

BEDROOM
12x11
BEDROOM
12x11
BATH
CLOS
BASEMENT
LOWER FLOOR
MASTER
BEDROOM
12x17
BATH
STUDY
CLOS
SUN-RM
11x13
DN UP
KITCHEN
14x12
GREAT-ROOM
22x17
ENTRY
DN
GARAGE
24x28
FIRST & SECOND FLOOR

PHOTOGRAPHY: JAMES YOCHUM PHOTOGRAPHY

farmhouse FAVORITE

above The covered porch and center gable draw attention to the front of this cozy home.

opposite top This homeowner has chosen the master bath option with the extra closet in the bedroom and double vanity in the bath.

opposite bottom The angled sink sits under two windows, creating a comfortable, well-lit place to work.

All the right spaces in all the right places are packed into this efficient beauty, including formal and informal living spaces, as well as three bedrooms, all in just 1,550 square feet.

A simple footprint makes the design extremely cost efficient to build. The front porch (not shown on the floor plan) leads into the living room, which feels more spacious because it opens to the dining room. The U-shape kitchen maximizes space and seems larger than it is because it opens into the breakfast area and den, which can include a fireplace. A laundry area and powder room complete the 775-square-foot first floor. On the second floor, double doors open to the master suite, which features plenty of closet space. Two secondary bedrooms round out the floor. This home is designed with a basement foundation.

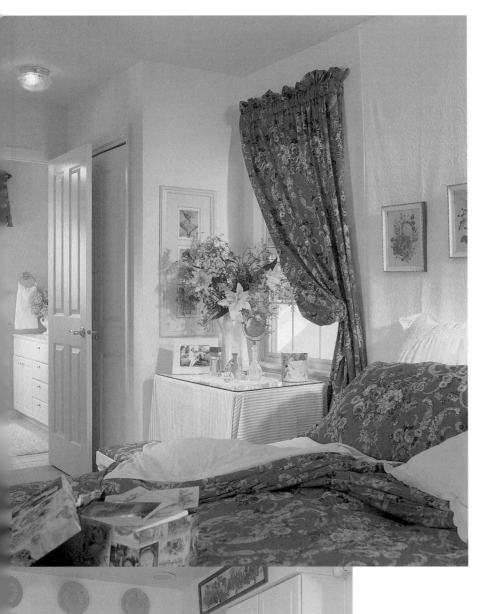

Design Number 32229

Units	Single
Price Code	B
Total Finished	1,550 sq. ft.
First Finished	775 sq. ft.
Second Finished	775 sq. ft.
Basement Unfinished	775 sq. ft.
Deck Unfinished	112 sq. ft.
Porch Unfinished	150 sq. ft.
Dimensions	25'x37'
Foundation	Basement
Bedrooms	3
Full Baths	1
3/4 Baths	1
Half Baths	1
First Ceiling	8'
Second Ceiling	8'
Max Ridge Height	30'3"
Roof Framing	Truss
Exterior Walls	2x4

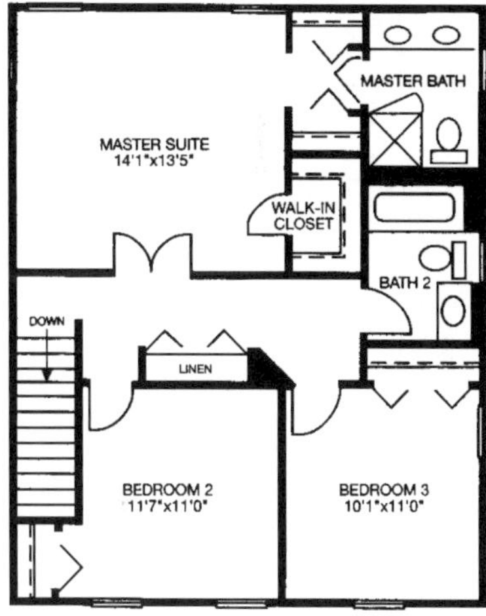
MASTER BATH
MASTER SUITE
14'1"x13'5"
WALK-IN
CLOSET
BATH 2
DOWN
LINEN
BEDROOM 2
11'7"x11'0"
BEDROOM 3
10'1"x11'0"

SECOND FLOOR

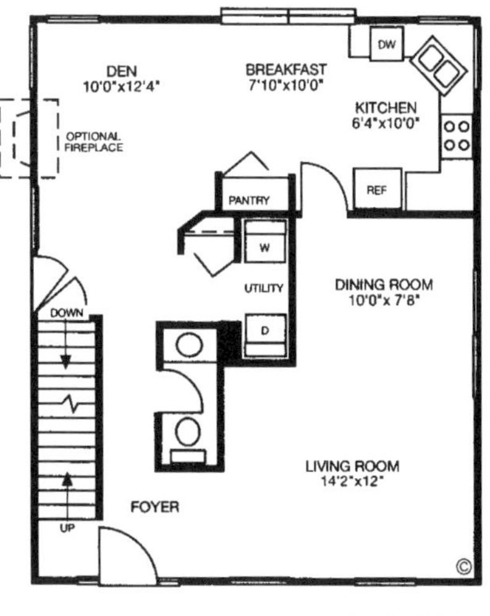
DW
DEN
10'0"x12'4"
BREAKFAST
7'10"x10'0"
KITCHEN
6'4"x10'0"
OPTIONAL
FIREPLACE
PANTRY
REF
W
UTILITY
DINING ROOM
10'0"x 7'8"
DOWN
D
LIVING ROOM
14'2"x12"
FOYER
UP

FIRST FLOOR

Please note: The photographed home may have been modified to suit homeowner preferences. If you order plans, you may wish to have a builder or design professional check them against the photographs to confirm construction details.

above Exquisite detailing wraps this compact home in style that's big enough for a home twice its size.

compact GEM

The foyer of this home contains a convenient coat closet and leads directly into the living room, which opens to the dining area and kitchen. A bay window draws sunlight into the dining area, which divides the open kitchen from the living room area. Counters, an eating area, and a wall of sliding glass doors define the kitchen. The two bedrooms share the left wing of the home and a full bath. Two hall closets add more storage space, while the garage is extra deep for additional storage. This home is designed with a basement foundation.

design 65241

Units	Single
Price Code	A
Total Finished	1,068 sq. ft.
Main Finished	1,068 sq. ft.
Basement Unfinished	1,068 sq. ft.
Garage Unfinished	245 sq. ft.
Dimensions	30'8"x48'
Foundation	Basement
Bedrooms	2
Full Baths	1
Main Ceiling	8'
Max Ridge Height	22'1"
Roof Framing	Truss
Exterior Walls	2x6

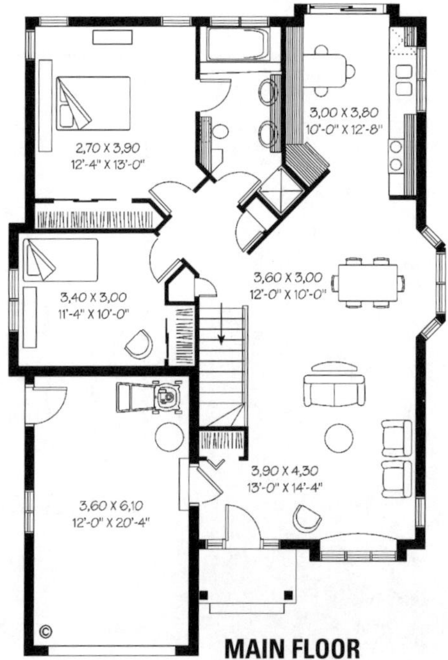
2,70 X 3,90
12'-4" X 13'-0"
3,00 X 3,80
10'-0" X 12'-8"
3,40 X 3,00
11'-4" X 10'-0"
3,60 X 3,00
12'-0" X 10'-0"
3,90 X 4,30
13'-0" X 14'-4"
3,60 X 6,10
12'-0" X 20'-4"

MAIN FLOOR

above White trim, keystones, subtle arches, and clapboard siding add character and appeal.

dollhouse DELIGHT

Design 81037

Units	Single
Price Code	A
Total Finished	1,275 sq. ft.
Main Finished	1,275 sq. ft.
Garage Unfinished	440 sq. ft.
Dimensions	40'x58'
Foundation	Crawlspace
Bedrooms	3
Full Baths	1
3/4 Baths	1
Main Ceiling	9'
Max Ridge Height	26'
Roof Framing	Truss
Exterior Walls	2x6

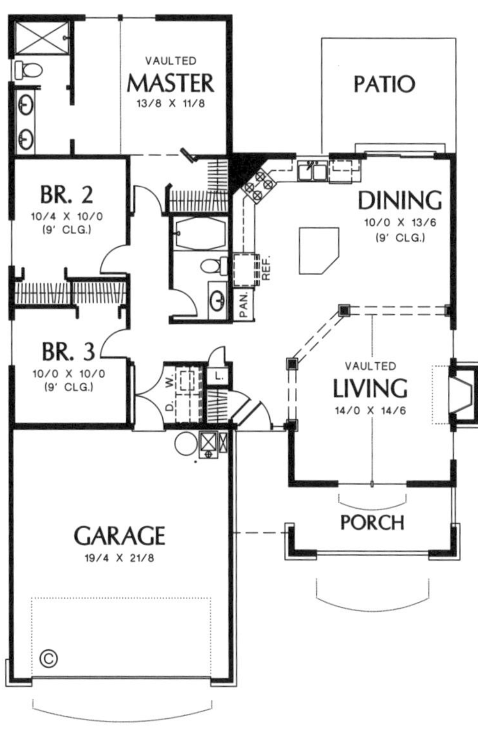
VAULTED
MASTER
13/8 X 11/8
PATIO
BR. 2
10/4 X 10/0
(9' CLG.)
DINING
10/0 X 13/6
(9' CLG.)
REF.
PAN.
BR. 3
10/0 X 10/0
(9' CLG.)
W.
D.
L.
VAULTED
LIVING
14/0 X 14/6
PORCH
GARAGE
19/4 X 21/8

MAIN FLOOR

Victorian detailing sets this home apart in any neighborhood. Reminiscent of the carriage house of old, right down to the stone fireplace and facade base, this home contains all the necessary ingredients for a comfortable lifestyle.

The front porch leads to the formal living room, which is set off by a dramatic vaulted ceiling and angled openings connected by columns. The shared kitchen/dining area is roomy enough for a center island and pantry. In the left wing, two secondary bedrooms share a full hall bath, while the pleasing master suite has a full bath of its own, as well as a walk-in closet. This home is designed with a crawlspace foundation.

PHOTOGRAPHY: COURTESY OF THE DESIGNER

above A quartet of gables topping a covered porch gives this home classic bungalow appeal.

perfect RETREAT

The bungalow-style facade of this home harkens back to the early 20th century when compact four-squares were favored over rambling Victorians and Colonials. Like its predecessors, this floor plan packs a lot of living into its stylish square footage.

Much of the first floor is unobstructed by walls, with arch-and-column configurations serving as the sole delineation for the dining area. The great-room, kitchen, and nook are backed by abundant windows, which allow light to stream in unhindered. French doors and custom built-ins characterize the study.

The second floor features an expansive bonus room over the garage, perfect for games, exercise equipment, or a home office. This home is designed with a crawlspace foundation.

design 81033

Units	Single
Price Code	C
Total Finished	1,946 sq. ft.
First Finished	1,082 sq. ft.
Second Finished	864 sq. ft.
Bonus Unfinished	358 sq. ft.
Garage Unfinished	620 sq. ft.
Porch Unfinished	120 sq. ft.
Dimensions	40'x52'
Foundation	Crawlspace
Bedrooms	3
Full Baths	2
Half Baths	1

Please note: The photographed home may have been modified to suit homeowner preferences. If you order plans, have a builder or design professional check them against the photographs to confirm actual construction details.

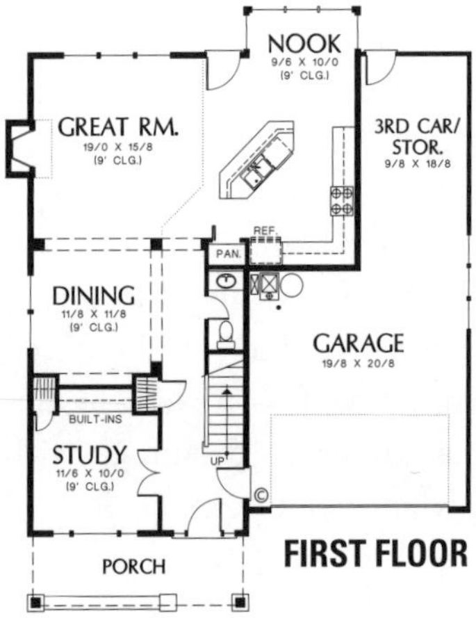

FIRST FLOOR

VAULTED
MASTER
13/8 X 12/0
BONUS
14/6 X 18/0 +
(9' CLG.)
BR. 2
11/4 X 10/0
BR. 3
11/4 X 11/0
DN.
SECOND FLOOR

PHOTOGRAPHY: MIKE MORELAND

above Days and mild nights can be spent enjoying the cool breeze from this home's front porch.

family getaway LODGE

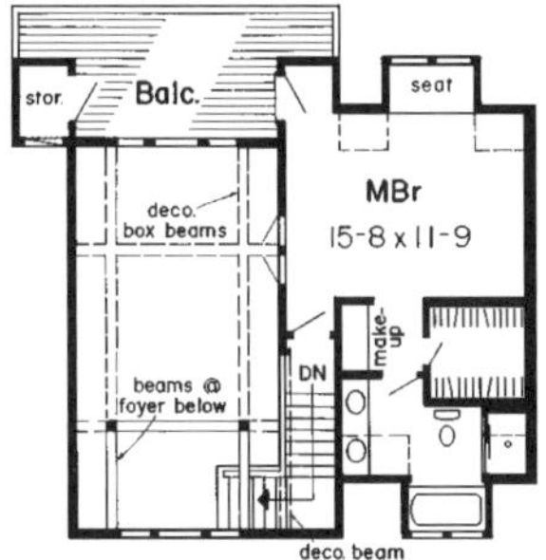

stor.
Balc.
seat
deco. box beams
MBr
15-8 x 11-9
beams @ foyer below
DN
make-up
deco beam

SECOND FLOOR

Design 19422

Units	Single
Price Code	B
Total Finished	1,695 sq. ft.
First Finished	1,290 sq. ft.
Second Finished	405 sq. ft.
Garage Unfinished	513 sq. ft.
Porch Unfinished	152 sq. ft.
Dimensions	50'8"x61'8"
Foundation	Basement Crawlspace
Bedrooms	2
Full Baths	2

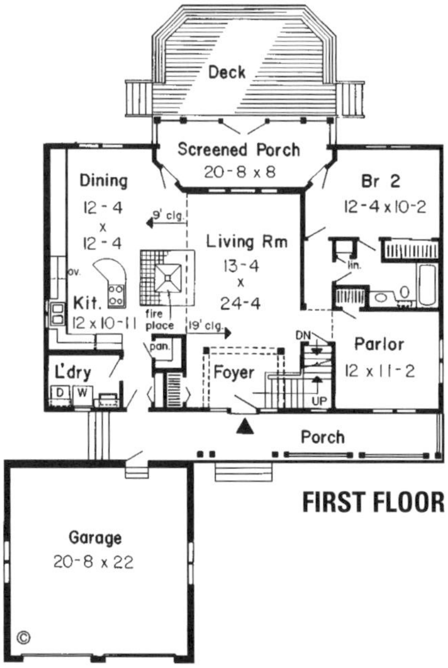

FIRST FLOOR

Please note: The photographed home may have been modified to suit homeowner preferences. If you order plans, you may wish to have a builder or design professional check them against the photographs to confirm construction details.

The features of this plan include a unique fireplace that is centrally located and shared by the living room, kitchen, and dining room. A parlor in the front of the design provides an ideal spot for quieter pursuits and entertaining. For added convenience, a pantry and laundry room help keep the whole family well fed and well organized. A first-floor secondary bedroom, connected to a full bath, rounds out the floor. The second floor is reserved for the master suite, full of amenities including a luxurious bath, makeup area, walk-in closet, and private balcony with a storage closet. This home is designed with basement and crawlspace foundation options.

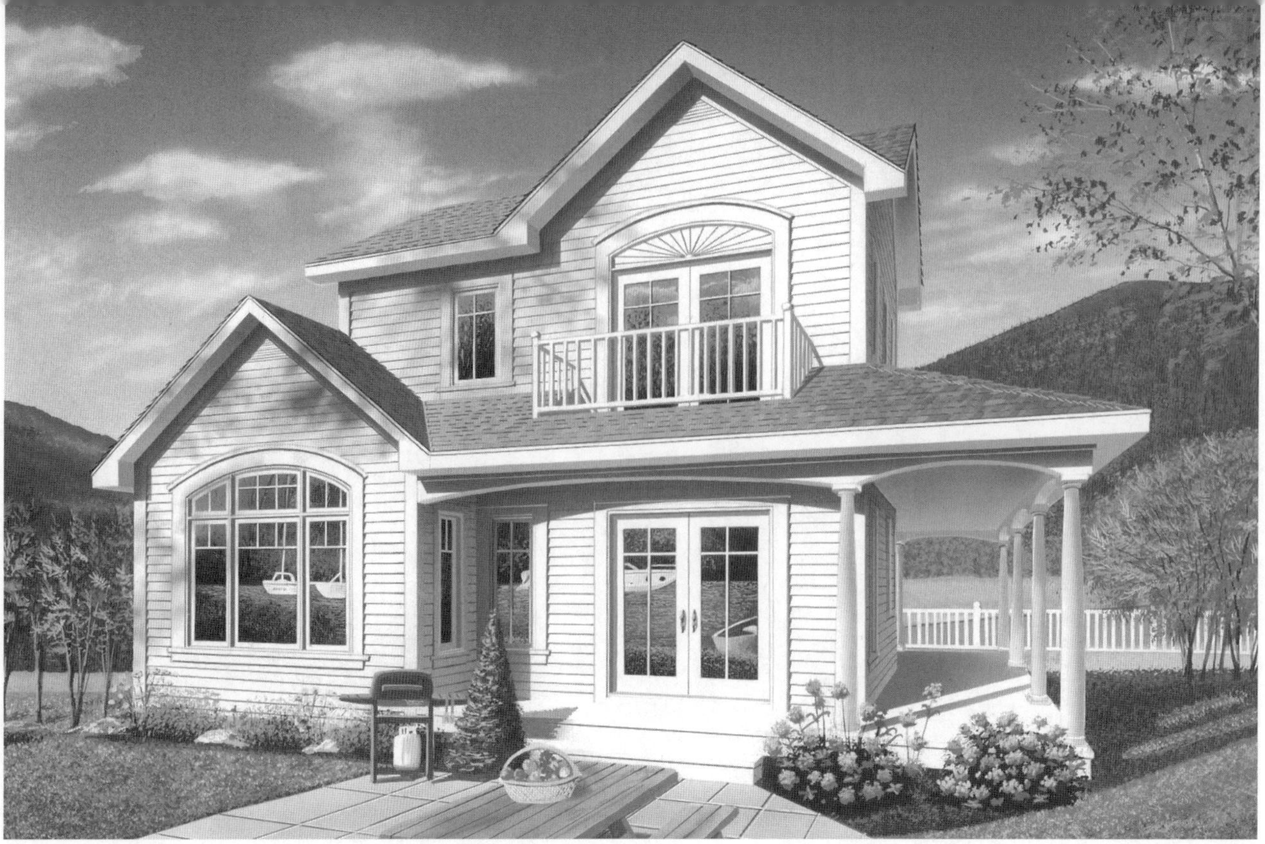

simple CHARM

above A wraparound porch, balcony, decorative windows, and farmhouse gables lend this simple home a taste of the Victorian era.

Decorative columns, glass doors, and arch windows add to the welcoming design of this home and make seeing what's inside hard to resist. The kitchen is brightly lit with natural light, which adds to the ambiance when serving guests at the island snack bar or at the dinner table. Two bedrooms on the second floor share a convenient corner bathroom. The larger bedroom includes a spacious walk-in closet and French doors that open to a small balcony with wooden railing. This home is designed with a basement foundation.

design 65013

Units	Single
Price Code	A
Total Finished	1,298 sq. ft.
First Finished	678 sq. ft.
Second Finished	620 sq. ft.
Basement Unfinished	678 sq. ft.
Garage Unfinished	228 sq. ft.
Porch Unfinished	416 sq. ft.
Dimensions	28'x40'
Foundation	Basement
Bedrooms	2
Full Baths	1
Half Baths	1

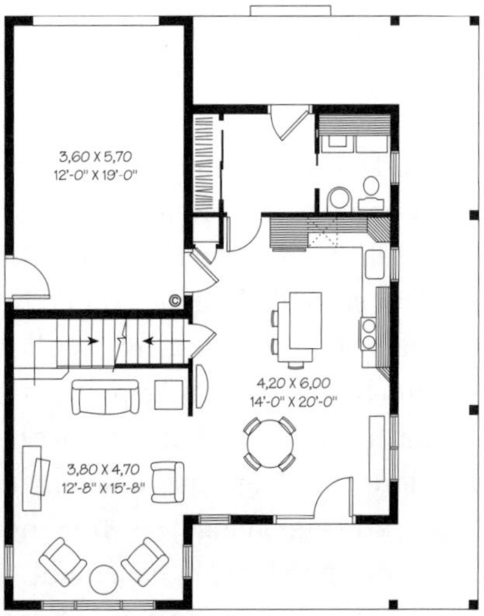

FIRST FLOOR

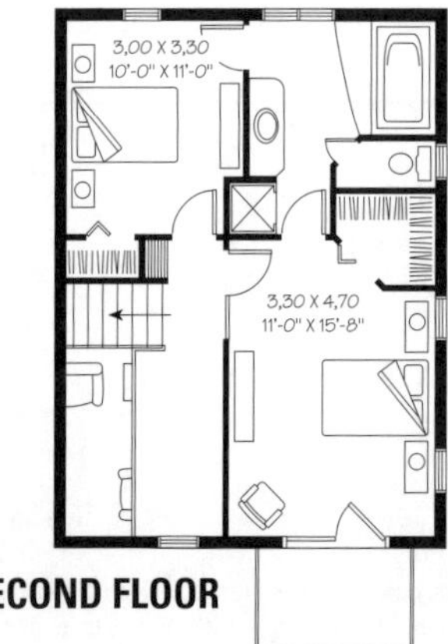
3,00 X 3,30
10'-0" X 11'-0"
3,30 X 4,70
11'-0" X 15'-8"

SECOND FLOOR

above Adorned with Victorian-style millwork and topped with a prominent gable dormer set into a steeply pitched roofline, this home is an immediate attention grabber.

romantic CHARMER

Design 24706

Units	Single
Price Code	A
Total Finished	1,470 sq. ft.
First Finished	1,035 sq. ft.
Second Finished	435 sq. ft.
Basement Unfinished	1,018 sq. ft.
Deck Unfinished	240 sq. ft.
Porch Unfinished	192 sq. ft.
Dimensions	35'x42'
Foundation	Basement Crawlspace Slab
Bedrooms	3
Full Baths	2

The warm glow from the fireplace will comfort you and your guests as you relax in the living room of this storybook home. Two first-floor bedrooms share a bath and the convenience of a nearby kitchen for late night snacks. The upstairs master bedroom is a private haven from the shared spaces downstairs. Set apart from the first floor and accessed through two sets of stairs and a small landing, the master bedroom has its own bathroom and walk-in closet. This home is designed with basement, slab, and crawlspace foundation options.

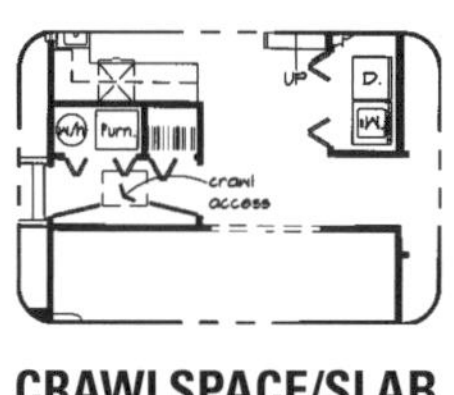
UP
D.
W
Furn.
crawl access

CRAWLSPACE/SLAB OPTION

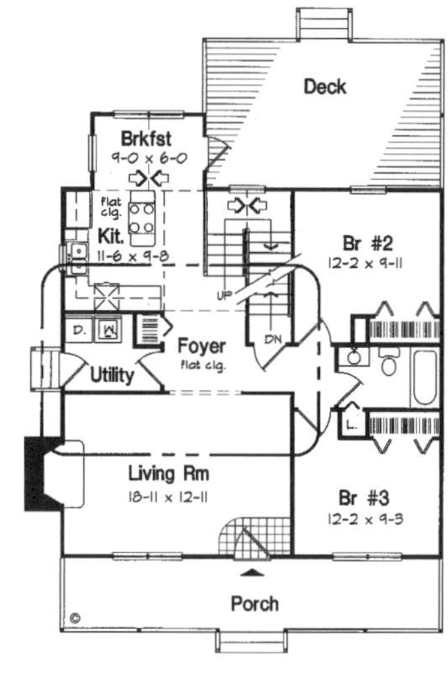
Deck
Brkfst
9-0 x 6-0
Flat clg.
Kit.
11-6 x 9-8
Br #2
12-2 x 9-11
UP
DN
Foyer
Flat clg.
Utility
D.
W
L.
Living Rm
18-11 x 12-11
Br #3
12-2 x 9-3
Porch

FIRST FLOOR

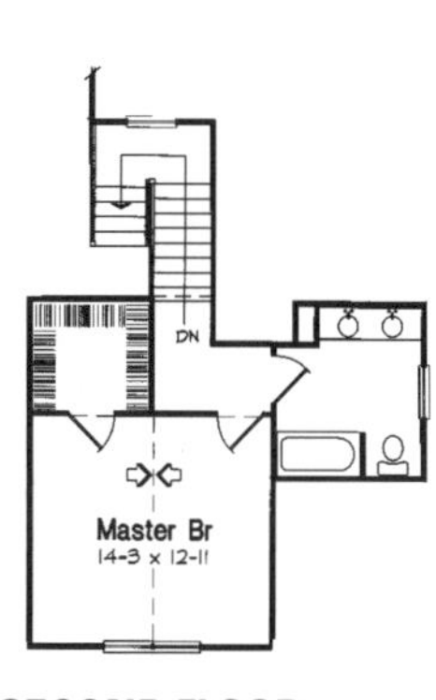
DN
Master Br
14-3 x 12-11

SECOND FLOOR

distinctive SHINGLE & STONE

The shingle and stone exterior, with its angles and peaks and generous porch, sets the stage for an attractively designed interior. The vaulted ceilings in the center rooms, and corner fireplace in the great-room, create a relaxing, welcoming atmosphere. The split-bedroom design allows privacy for every member of the family, while the master bath and shared hall bath offer convenience. This home abounds with convenient features, such as a separate laundry room and plenty of counter space and cabinets in the kitchen. This home is designed with a basement foundation.

above White trim, a shed dormer, arched porch, and mixed siding create a distinctive facade.

design 50021

Units	Single
Price Code	B
Total Finished	1,651 sq. ft.
Main Finished	1,651 sq. ft.
Basement Unfinished	1,651 sq. ft.
Garage Unfinished	430 sq. ft.
Porch Unfinished	212 sq. ft.
Dimensions	60'9"x49'
Foundation	Basement
Bedrooms	3
Full Baths	2

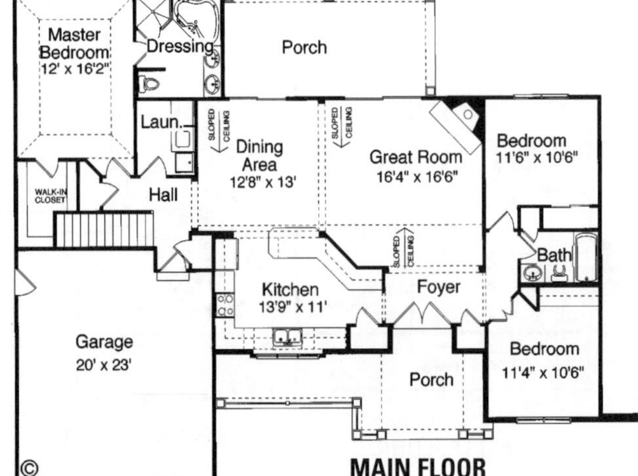
Master Bedroom
12' x 16'2"
Dressing
Porch
Laun.
SLOPED CEILING
Dining Area
12'8" x 13'
SLOPED CEILING
Great Room
16'4" x 16'6"
Bedroom
11'6" x 10'6"
WALK-IN CLOSET
Hall
Bath
SLOPED CEILING
Kitchen
13'9" x 11'
Foyer
Garage
20' x 23'
Bedroom
11'4" x 10'6"
Porch
©

MAIN FLOOR

above Tall windows, an angled porch, and a welcoming gable lend a classic feel.

something for ALL

Design 81036

Units	Single
Price Code	B
Total Finished	1,557 sq. ft.
Main Finished	1,557 sq. ft.
Garage Unfinished	434 sq. ft.
Porch Unfinished	137 sq. ft.
Dimensions	50'x50'
Foundation	Basement Crawlspace Slab
Bedrooms	3
Full Baths	2

The neat front exterior with its tall, elegant windows and front porch provides a warm welcome. This design features vaulted ceilings in the great-room, dining room, and master bedroom, adding space to the generously sized rooms. Ideal for the seasoned chef or the beginner, the wraparound kitchen counter provides ample work area, while the desk and pantry are good for storage and organization. Built-ins and a large closet enhance one secondary bedroom, while the other, an optional den, features an optional French door location as well as its own large closet. This home is designed with basement, slab, and crawlspace foundation options.

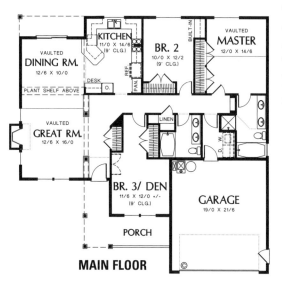

VAULTED DINING RM. 12/6 X 10/0
PLANT SHELF ABOVE
KITCHEN 11/0 X 14/6 (9' CLG.)
DESK
REF
PAN.
BR. 2 10/0 X 12/2 (9' CLG.)
BUILT-IN
VAULTED MASTER 12/0 X 14/6
VAULTED GREAT RM. 12/6 X 16/0
LINEN
W.
D.
BR. 3/ DEN 11/6 X 12/0 +/- (9' CLG.)
GARAGE 19/0 X 21/6
PORCH
©

MAIN FLOOR

PHOTOGRAPHY: JAMES YOCHUM PHOTOGRAPHY

above This home is angled to catch light at every turn, thanks to its ample supply of windows, including the clerestory above the entry.

decked OUTDOORS

This home is a medley of shapes and angles beautifully orchestrated to take advantage of the outdoor splendor that surrounds it. Hundreds of square feet of porch and deck, both covered and open, make it a nature lover's delight. A sense of openness suffuses the 1,213-square-foot first floor. The dining room and kitchen are likewise open and airy, visually open to the living room through the screen porch. The octagonal living room rises up two stories and its wall of windows offers dazzling vistas. The master suite enjoys its own private corner on the first floor, separated from the two upstairs bedrooms, one of which includes a pair of casement windows that opens into the upper regions of the living room. This home is designed with a basement foundation.

design 32109

Units	Single
Price Code	D
Total Finished	2,038 sq. ft.
First Finished	1,213 sq. ft.
Second Finished	825 sq. ft.
Basement Unfinished	1,213 sq. ft.
Deck Unfinished	535 sq. ft.
Porch Unfinished	144 sq. ft.
Dimensions	46'4"x37'8"
Foundation	Basement
Bedrooms	3
Full Baths	1
3/4 Baths	1
Half Baths	1

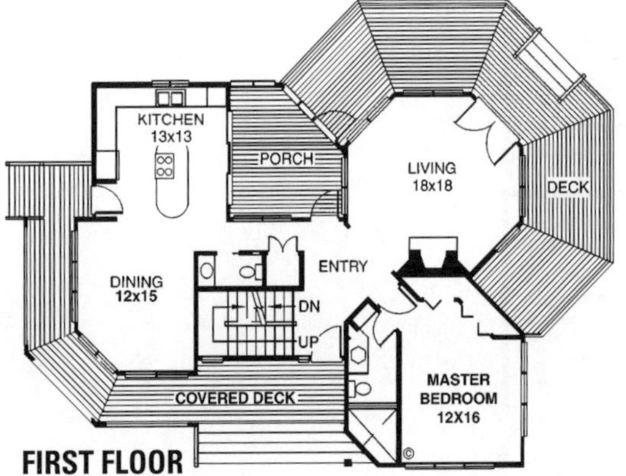
KITCHEN
13x13
PORCH
LIVING
18x18
DECK
DINING
12x15
ENTRY
DN
UP
COVERED DECK
MASTER
BEDROOM
12X16
FIRST FLOOR

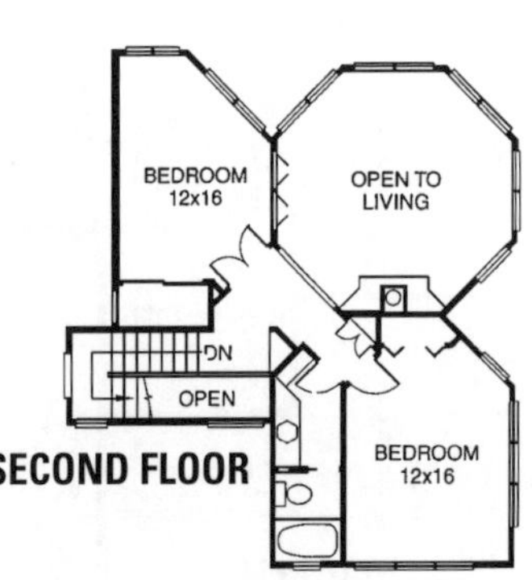
BEDROOM
12x16
OPEN TO
LIVING
DN
OPEN
BEDROOM
12x16
SECOND FLOOR

Please note: The photographed home may have been modified to suit homeowner preferences. If you order plans, have a builder or design professional check them against the photographs to confirm actual construction details.

PHOTOGRAPHY: LAURIE SOLOMON

above A covered porch shades the tall windows that line the dining room and keeps the front entry out of the elements.

a new ANGLE

design 34901

Units	Single
Price Code	C
Total Finished	1,763 sq. ft.
First Finished	909 sq. ft.
Second Finished	854 sq. ft.
Basement Unfinished	899 sq. ft.
Garage Unfinished	491 sq. ft.
Dimensions	48'x44'
Foundation	Basement Crawlspace Slab
Bedrooms	3
Full Baths	1
3/4 Baths	1
Half Baths	1

The appeal of this home begins at the curb, when you get a look at the angled porch, gable, and entryway. The dining room, with a large bump-out window, has a recessed ceiling. The living room includes a large fireplace, which is flanked by a window on one side and a door to the backyard deck on the other. The kitchen has plenty of work space, a pantry, and a double sink overlooking the deck. All three bedrooms are on the second floor. The master suite features a large bath with walk-in closet; the two secondary bedrooms share a bath. This home is designed with basement, slab, and crawlspace foundation options.

Please note: The photographed home may have been modified to suit homeowner preferences. If you order plans, have a builder or design professional check them against the photographs to confirm actual construction details.

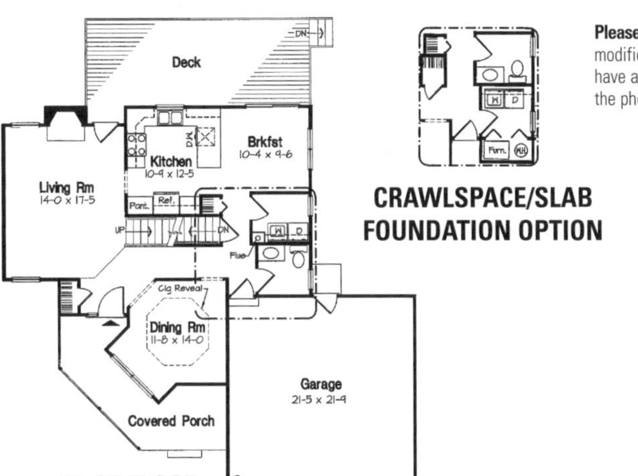

Deck
Living Rm
14-0 x 17-5
Kitchen
Brkfst
Pant.
Ref.
Dining Rm
11-8 x 14-0
Clg Reveal
Garage
21-5 x 21-9
Covered Porch
FIRST FLOOR
CRAWLSPACE/SLAB FOUNDATION OPTION

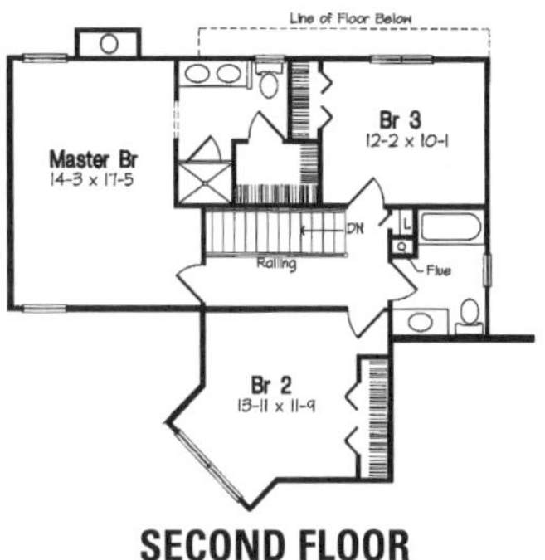

Line of Floor Below
Master Br
14-3 x 17-5
Br 3
12-2 x 10-1
Railing
Br 2
13-11 x 11-9
SECOND FLOOR

PHOTOGRAPHY: BETH SINGER

three GABLES

Roomy and light-filled, this home provides great shared spaces. The 936-square-foot first floor also includes an ample sunroom set just behind the living room.

Exposed trusses in the living room provide evidence of the home's strength and create a subtle lattice work pattern against the tall vaulted ceiling. A lowered ceiling in the dining area and kitchen create a subtle change of mood from the open living room, establishing a clear distinction of function. The comfortable kitchen is fully equipped with storage. The home's laundry is conveniently located behind the kitchen. A detached two-car garage rounds out the home's first floor.

The 916-square-foot second floor holds the master suite, two secondary bedrooms, and a bath. This home is designed with crawlspace and pier/post foundation options. 🏛

above Traditional shingle siding and elegant arched window and door openings provide classic appeal.

below Three gables and a covered porch add visual interest to the rear elevation of this home.

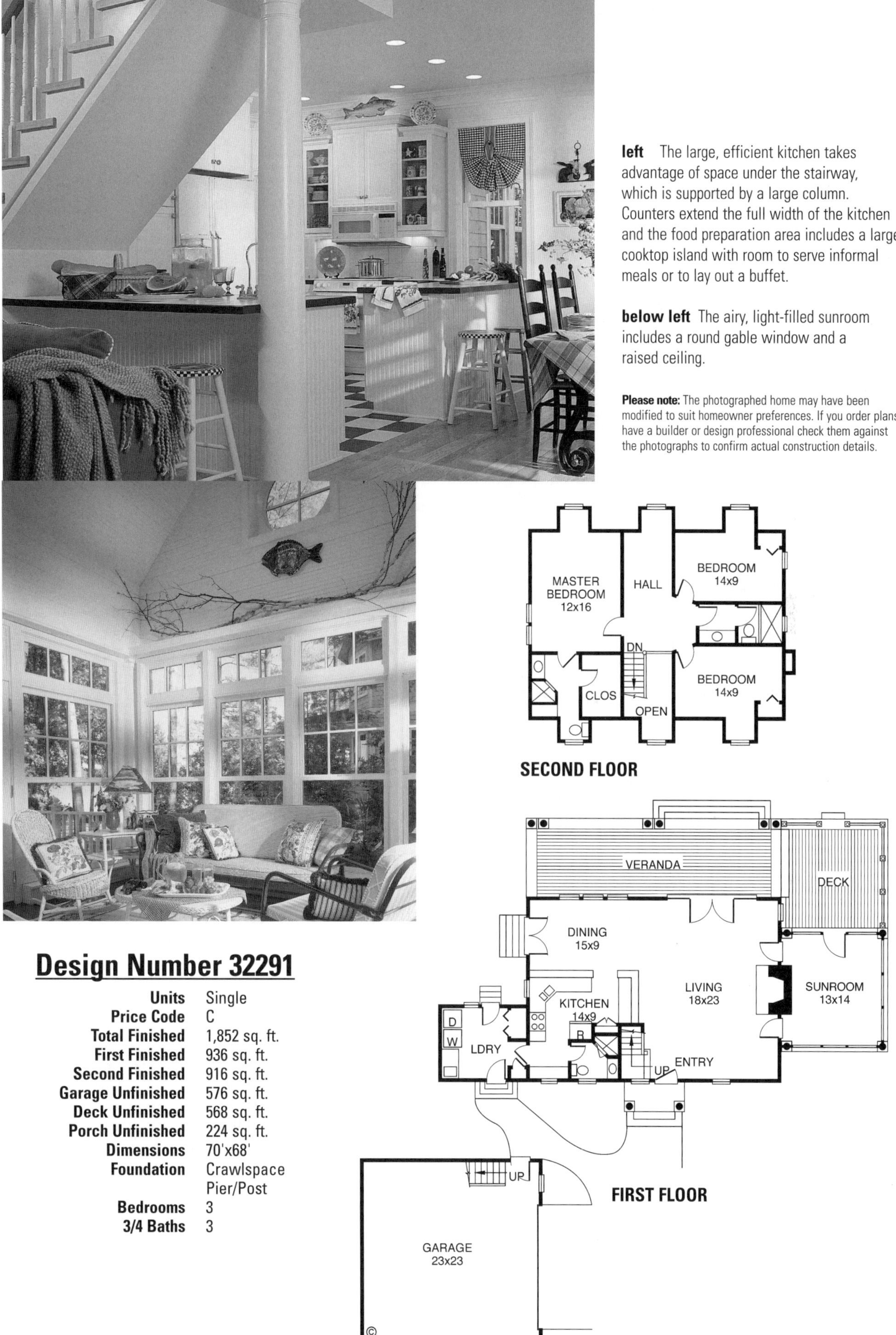
MASTER
BEDROOM
12x16
HALL
BEDROOM
14x9
DN
CLOS
OPEN
BEDROOM
14x9
SECOND FLOOR
VERANDA
DECK
DINING
15x9
KITCHEN
14x9
LIVING
18x23
SUNROOM
13x14
D
W
LDRY
B
UP
ENTRY
UP
GARAGE
23x23
FIRST FLOOR

left The large, efficient kitchen takes advantage of space under the stairway, which is supported by a large column. Counters extend the full width of the kitchen and the food preparation area includes a large cooktop island with room to serve informal meals or to lay out a buffet.

below left The airy, light-filled sunroom includes a round gable window and a raised ceiling.

Please note: The photographed home may have been modified to suit homeowner preferences. If you order plans, have a builder or design professional check them against the photographs to confirm actual construction details.

Design Number 32291

Units	Single
Price Code	C
Total Finished	1,852 sq. ft.
First Finished	936 sq. ft.
Second Finished	916 sq. ft.
Garage Unfinished	576 sq. ft.
Deck Unfinished	568 sq. ft.
Porch Unfinished	224 sq. ft.
Dimensions	70'x68'
Foundation	Crawlspace Pier/Post
Bedrooms	3
3/4 Baths	3

PHOTOGRAPHY: JAMES YOCHUM PHOTOGRAPHY

above The two-story porch lets light into the second floor, but keeps out the sun during the hottest times of the year. Metal roofing and exposed rafter tails suggest the design's tropical roots.

tropical FLAVOR

Created for any climate, but steeped in the regional architecture of Key West, this compact home makes the most of its 1,129 square feet and does it with style. Defining the home is a basic Cape Cod-style shape: a central gable structure with porches front and back. Outside, the home's wide trim, crown moldings, and deep sills create a vintage look. Inside, a sense of spaciousness is projected that reaches beyond the modest-sized home's actual dimensions. To maximize space, hallways are kept at a minimum and the living room, dining area, and kitchen all flow together around a central powder room. Out back is a long screen porch and wraparound deck. On the second floor, a smaller porch leads to a small deck off the rear. The secondary bedroom and master bedroom share the full bath. This home is designed with a crawlspace foundation. 🏛

below Shallow but long, the porch provides just enough space for a group of neighbors to relax.

top Sharing a fireplace (not shown) with the living room and surrounded by windows, the dining area can host both casual and formal meals.

above Nestled into the trees, the first-floor screen porch provides a shaded place to enjoy the backyard in privacy.

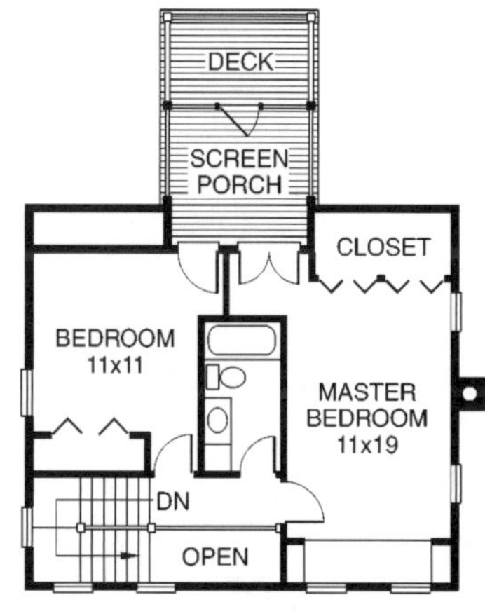

DECK
SCREEN PORCH
CLOSET
BEDROOM 11x11
MASTER BEDROOM 11x19
DN
OPEN

SECOND FLOOR

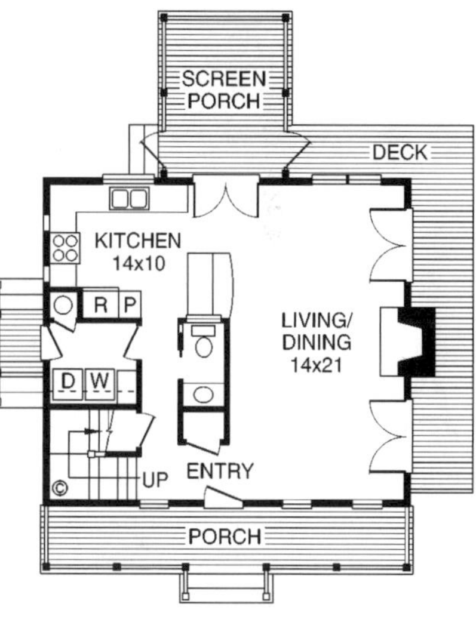

SCREEN PORCH
DECK
KITCHEN 14x10
R P
D W
LIVING/ DINING 14x21
UP
ENTRY
PORCH

FIRST FLOOR

Design Number 32399

Units	Single
Price Code	A
Total Finished	1,129 sq. ft.
First Finished	576 sq. ft.
Second Finished	553 sq. ft.
Deck Unfinished	230 sq. ft.
Porch Unfinished	331 sq. ft.
Dimensions	36'8"x36'
Foundation	Crawlspace
Bedrooms	2
Full Baths	1
Half Baths	1

Please note: The photographed home may have been modified to suit homeowner preferences. If you order plans, have a builder or design professional check them against the photographs to confirm actual construction details.

above Small size doesn't mean lack of style as this well-designed front facade proves.

compact and COZY

A covered porch and a carport add outdoor living area to this home. Inside, the plan packs a lot of living in less than 1,000 square feet. The large, open common area encompasses the family room, kitchen, and dining area. The kitchen makes the most of its space with L-shape counters and a peninsula snack bar. A central pantry is convenient to all three rooms. A closet near the bedrooms is handy for storing linens. The two bedrooms share the right wing with a full bath, which has everything from a window-lined soaking tub to a laundry facility. This home is designed with a basement foundation.

design 65009

Units	Single
Price Code	A
Total Finished	947 sq. ft.
Main Finished	947 sq. ft.
Basement Unfinished	947 sq. ft.
Dimensions	34'x30'
Foundation	Basement
Bedrooms	2
Full Baths	1

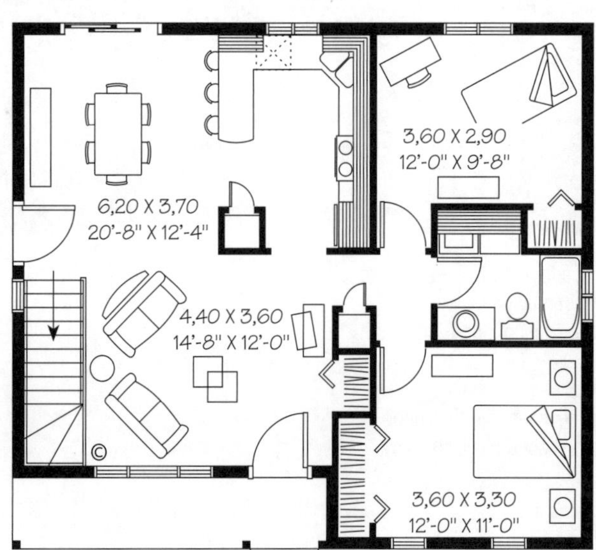

3,60 X 2,90
12'-0" X 9'-8"
6,20 X 3,70
20'-8" X 12'-4"
4,40 X 3,60
14'-8" X 12'-0"
3,60 X 3,30
12'-0" X 11'-0"

MAIN FLOOR

above Outdoor living area is a key element in the design of this home, which includes a large wraparound deck and a balcony.

balcony and PORCHES

design 65004

Units	Single
Price Code	E
Total Finished	2,300 sq. ft.
First Finished	1,067 sq. ft.
Second Finished	1,233 sq. ft.
Basement Unfinished	1,067 sq. ft.
Dimensions	58'x33'
Foundation	Basement
Bedrooms	3
Full Baths	2
Half Baths	1

There are several entrances to this 2,300-square-foot home. From the wraparound porch, you can enter the foyer, the dining room, and the family room. The garage has its own entrance in the rear of the home. Once inside, the foyer hallway opens into the kitchen. The peninsula snack bar is ideal for casual meals, while the nearby dining area is great for more formal times. A step away is the living room, which is just secluded enough to offer privacy. On the second floor are two secondary bedrooms, a full bath, a sitting area, and a luxurious master suite with a fireplace. The balcony, adds outdoor living space to the second floor. This home is designed with a basement foundation.

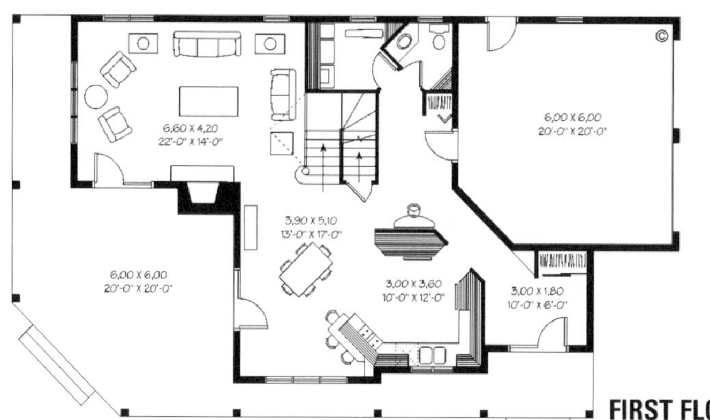
6,60 X 4,20
22'-0" X 14'-0"
6,00 X 6,00
20'-0" X 20'-0"
3,90 X 5,10
13'-0" X 17'-0"
6,00 X 6,00
20'-0" X 20'-0"
3,00 X 3,60
10'-0" X 12'-0"
3,00 X 1,80
10'-0" X 6'-0"

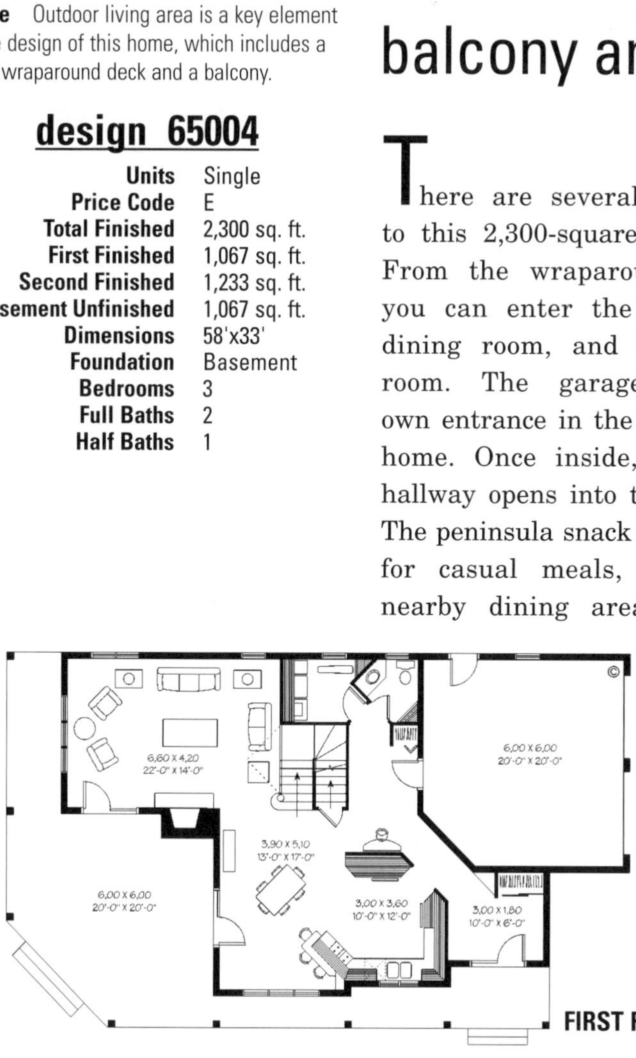

FIRST FLOOR

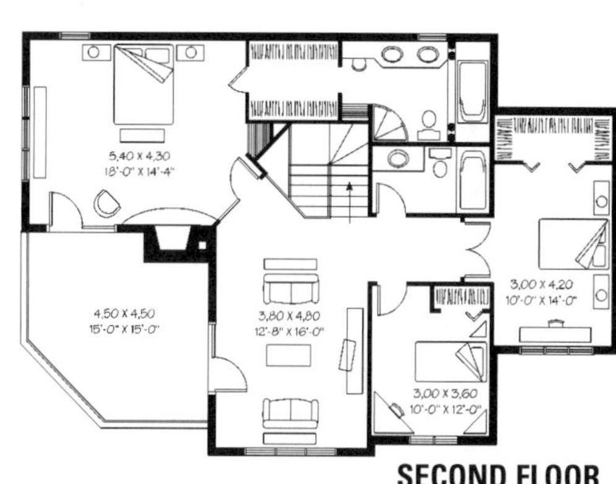
5,40 X 4,30
18'-0" X 14'-4"
4,50 X 4,50
15'-0" X 15'-0"
3,80 X 4,80
12'-8" X 16'-0"
3,00 X 4,20
10'-0" X 14'-0"
3,00 X 3,60
10'-0" X 12'-0"

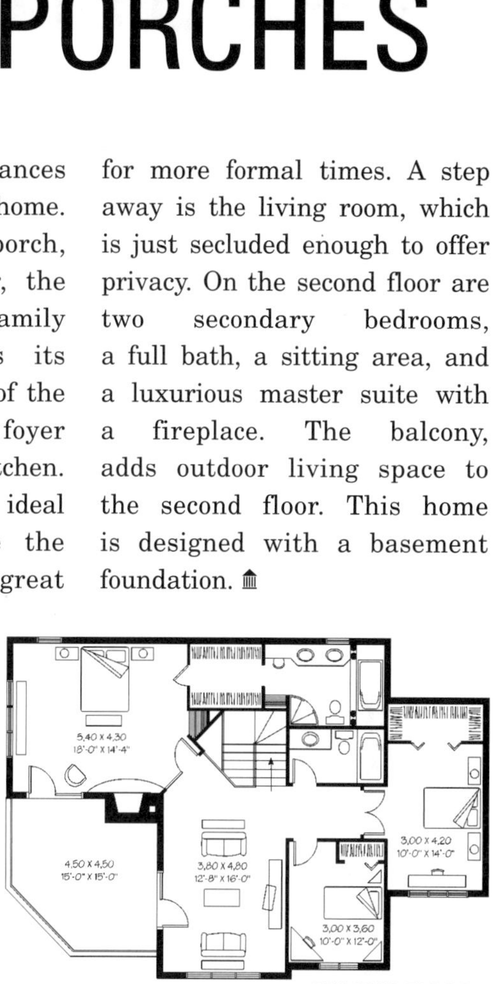

SECOND FLOOR

PHOTOGRAPHY: JOHN EHRENCLOU

above The unique style of this home includes a turret, wraparound porch, and multiple tall gables.

sweet and STYLISH

The charming, classic exterior welcomes family and friends. Inside, the tiled foyer opens into the kitchen/breakfast area to the left, and to a powder room to the right. Straight ahead lie the formal dining room, topped with a decorative ceiling, and the living room, which is warmed by a fireplace and illuminated by skylights. A large center island and abundant built-ins make the kitchen space both attractive and efficient. The second floor was designed with privacy in mind; it contains two secondary bedrooms, which share a full hall bath. The impressive master suite, with private bath and large walk-in closet, rounds out this floor. This home is designed with a basement foundation.

design 20093

Units	Single
Price Code	D
Total Finished	2,001 sq. ft.
First Finished	1,027 sq. ft.
Second Finished	974 sq. ft.
Basement Unfinished	978 sq. ft.
Garage Unfinished	476 sq. ft.
Dimensions	43'x56'
Foundation	Basement
Bedrooms	3
Full Baths	2
Half Baths	1

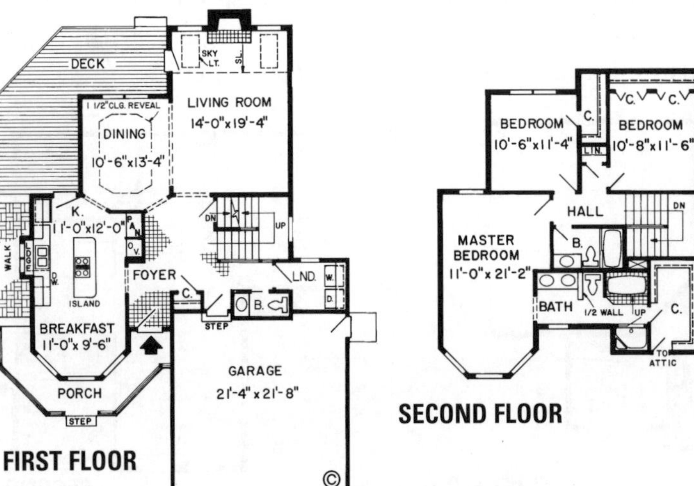
DECK
SKY LT.
LIVING ROOM
14'-0"x19'-4"
1 1/2" CLG. REVEAL
DINING
10'-6"x13'-4"
K.
11'-0"x12'-0"
PAN
OV.
DN
UP
WALK
ISLAND
FOYER
C.
LND.
B.
BREAKFAST
11'-0"x 9'-6"
STEP
PORCH
GARAGE
21'-4" x 21'-8"
FIRST FLOOR
BEDROOM
10'-6"x11'-4"
C.
LIN
BEDROOM
10'-8"x11'-6"
HALL
DN
MASTER BEDROOM
11'-0"x 21'-2"
B.
BATH
1/2 WALL
UP
C.
TO ATTIC
SECOND FLOOR

Please note: The photographed home may have been modified to suit homeowner preferences. If you order plans, have a builder or design professional check them against the photographs to confirm actual construction details.

PHOTOGRAPHY: BETH SINGER

above The basic home style of our colonial ancestors is flawlessly recreated here in this 21st-century update of an early-American saltbox.

colonial PERFECTION

design 32316

Price Code	G
Total Finished	2,752 sq. ft.
First Finished	1,533 sq. ft.
Second Finished	1,219 sq. ft.
Attic Unfinished	988 sq. ft.
Garage Unfinished	828 sq. ft.
Dimensions	74'4"x37'6"
Foundation	Basement
Bedrooms	3
Full Baths	2
Half Baths	1

Please note: The photographed home may have been modified to suit homeowner preferences. If you order plans, have a builder or design professional check them against the photographs to confirm actual construction details.

This saltbox may look like an 18th-century structure, but it's clearly a 21st-century home on the inside. Amenities include an audio room, ample storage, and a three-car garage. The centralized main entry opens to the home's formal spaces, with a living room to the left and a dining room on the right. Toward the rear are the more informal spaces. The keeping room features a fireplace on the interior wall, with triple windows on the opposite. A walk-in pantry and a backyard view enhance the kitchen. The unfinished attic adds 988 square feet. This home is designed with a basement foundation.

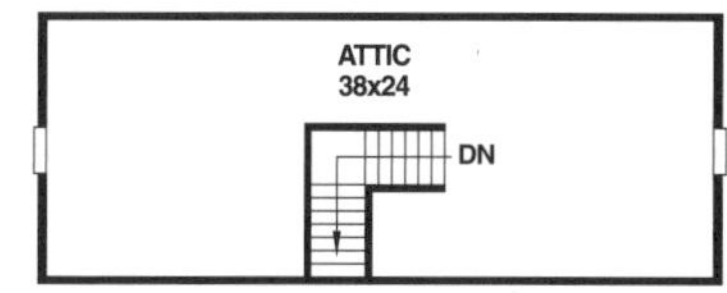
ATTIC
38x24
DN

THIRD FLOOR

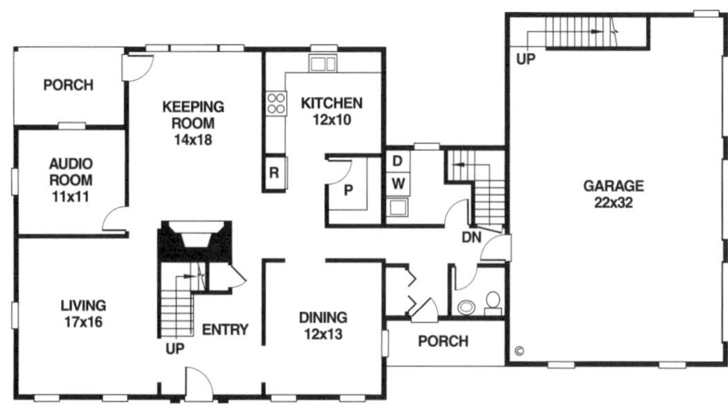
PORCH
KEEPING ROOM
14x18
KITCHEN
12x10
AUDIO ROOM
11x11
R
P
D
W
UP
GARAGE
22x32
DN
LIVING
17x16
ENTRY
UP
DINING
12x13
PORCH

FIRST FLOOR

BATH
CLOSET
BATH
BEDROOM
12x15
CLOSET
DN
MASTER
BEDROOM
15x16
UP
HALL
BEDROOM
12x11

SECOND FLOOR

PHOTOGRAPHY: RICK TAYLOR

casual ELEGANCE

above The mixed siding materials of clapboards and stone create a rich texture. The long, shady porch is a welcoming spot to greet guests and neighbors.

With its wide-open spaces and easy traffic flow, this plan is ideal for entertaining. The front door with sidelights and an arched transom ushers guests inside where they have an immediate view of the formal dining room to the left and straight ahead to the family room. In the kitchen, the cooktop island helps block the view of the food preparation area from the breakfast area. Past the breakfast area, French doors open onto a screen porch. Just off the screen porch, a corner deck offers additional outdoor living space. This home is designed with a basement foundation. 🏛

design 32358

Units	Single
Price Code	I
Total Finished	5,755 sq. ft.
First Finished	2,442 sq. ft.
Second Finished	871 sq. ft.
Lower Finished	2,442 sq. ft.
Bonus Unfinished	480 sq. ft.
Garage Unfinished	935 sq. ft.
Deck Unfinished	307 sq. ft.
Porch Unfinished	442 sq. ft.
Dimensions	72'6"x76'-10"
Foundation	Basement
Bedrooms	3
Full Baths	3
Half Baths	1

Please note: The photographed home may have been modified to suit homeowner preferences. If you order plans, have a builder or design professional check them against the photographs to confirm actual construction details.

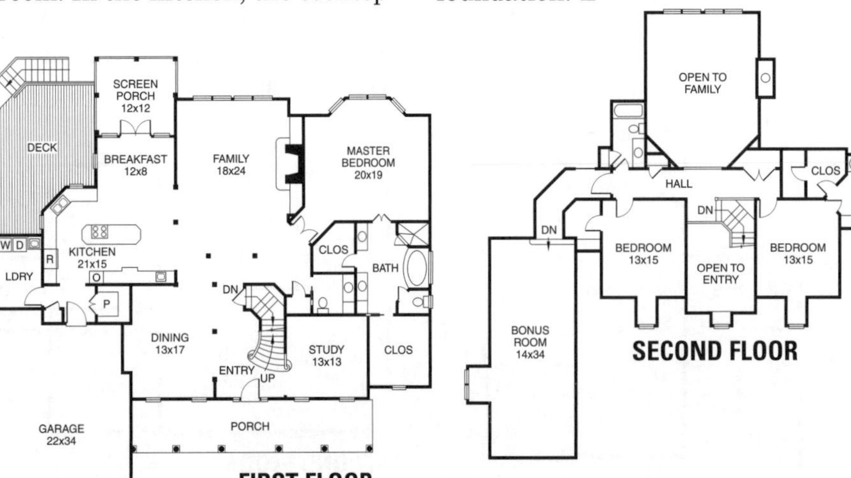

SCREEN PORCH 12x12
DECK
BREAKFAST 12x8
FAMILY 18x24
MASTER BEDROOM 20x19
W D
R
KITCHEN 21x15
LDRY
P
CLOS
BATH
DN
DINING 13x17
ENTRY
UP
STUDY 13x13
CLOS
GARAGE 22x34
PORCH
FIRST FLOOR
OPEN TO FAMILY
HALL
CLOS
BATH
DN
DN
BEDROOM 13x15
OPEN TO ENTRY
BEDROOM 13x15
BONUS ROOM 14x34
SECOND FLOOR

PHOTOGRAPHY: RICK TAYLOR

above A quintet of gables, a rounded dormer that feeds light into the home's interior, mixed siding, and a welcoming entry porch provide lots of curb appeal.

great ROOMS

Spacious and comfortable, open and light, with private and shared spaces, this home rings of entertaining, big family gatherings, and life lived on a large scale. The 2,727 square-foot first floor includes the great-room, family room, dining room, and grand entry as well as first-floor living areas for the grownups of the family. Throw in a powder room, laundry, guest suite with full bath, large rear deck, covered patio, two-car garage, and a wide front porch, and the plan for the first floor alone fills the functional requirements for most lifestyles. Upstairs are 1,168 square feet of additional living space. Two secondary bedrooms share a full bath while a third is a suite, with walk-in closet and a full, private bath, making it ideal for an in-law suite or room for an older child. This home is designed with a basement foundation.

design 32146

Units	Single
Price Code	K
Total Finished	3,895 sq. ft.
First Finished	2,727 sq. ft.
Second Finished	1,168 sq. ft.
Bonus Unfinished	213 sq. ft.
Basement Unfinished	2,250 sq. ft.
Garage Unfinished	984 sq. ft.
Deck Unfinished	230 sq. ft.
Porch Unfinished	402 sq. ft.
Dimensions	73'8"x72'2"
Foundation	Basement
Bedrooms	5
Full Baths	4
Half Baths	1

Please note: The photographed home may have been modified to suit homeowner preferences. If you order plans, have a builder or design professional check them against the photographs to confirm actual construction details.

PATIO
FAMILY
15x19
DECK
BRKFST
12x10
MASTER
BEDROOM
15x18
PORCH
CLOS
UP
GREAT-
ROOM
18x16
KIT
18x14
BATH
CLOS
DN
LDRY
DINING
12x17
ENTRY
GUEST/
STUDY
14x11
UP
GARAGE
20x14
PORCH

FIRST FLOOR

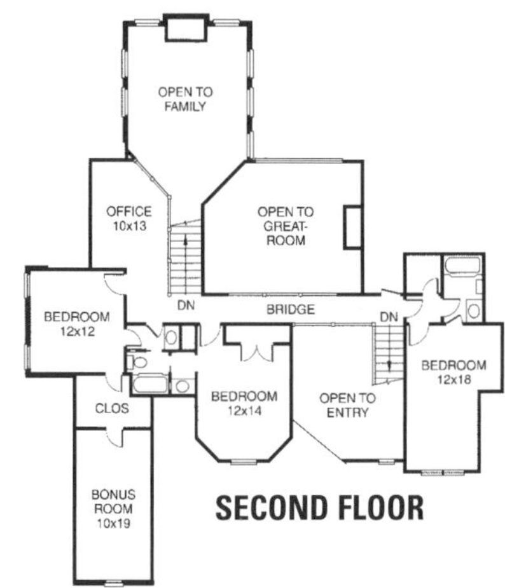
OPEN TO
FAMILY
OFFICE
10x13
OPEN TO
GREAT-
ROOM
BEDROOM
12x12
DN
BRIDGE
DN
BEDROOM
12x18
CLOS
BEDROOM
12x14
OPEN TO
ENTRY
BONUS
ROOM
10x19

SECOND FLOOR

thoughtfully DESIGNED

In just under 2,000 square feet, this home packs in a lot of living space. The first floor houses the common areas, each separate enough for privacy. The second floor holds two bedrooms. This home is designed with a basement foundation.

PHOTOGRAPHY: COURTESY OF THE DESIGNER

design 65431

Units	Single
Price Code	C
Total Finished	1,980 sq. ft.
First Finished	1,980 sq. ft.
Dimensions	43'x53'4"
Foundation	Basement
Bedrooms	2
Full Baths	2

Please note: The photographed home may have been modified to suit homeowner preferences. If you order plans, have a builder or design professional check them against the photographs to confirm actual construction details.

FIRST FLOOR

SECOND FLOOR

elegantly EFFICIENT

This classic Victorian facade houses a world of modern amenities. Formal and informal spaces open to each other, creating an atmosphere for interaction. Private areas rest above. This home is designed with a basement foundation.

PHOTOGRAPHY: COURTESY OF THE DESIGNER

design 65138

Units	Single
Price Code	D
Total Finished	2,257 sq. ft.
First Finished	1,274 sq. ft.
Second Finished	983 sq. ft.
Garage Unfinished	437 sq. ft.
Porch Unfinished	183 sq. ft.
Dimensions	50'x46'
Foundation	Basement
Bedrooms	3
Full Baths	2
Half Baths	1

FIRST FLOOR

SECOND FLOOR

Please note: The photographed home may have been modified to suit homeowner preferences. If you order plans, have a builder or design professional check them against the photographs to confirm actual construction details.

PHOTOGRAPHY: PHIL MUELLER

above Few designs capture the spirit of the country cottage lifestyle better than this elegant home.

forest COTTAGE

design 32063

Units	Single
Price Code	L
Total Finished	4,283 sq. ft.
First Finished	1,642 sq. ft.
Second Finished	1,411 sq. ft.
Lower Finished	1,230 sq. ft.
Basement Unfinished	412 sq. ft.
Deck Unfinished	207 sq. ft.
Porch Unfinished	1,000 sq. ft.
Dimensions	92'x61'
Foundation	Basement
Bedrooms	4
Full Baths	4
Half Baths	1

Please note: The photographed home may have been modified to suit homeowner preferences. If you order plans, have a builder or design professional check them against the photographs to confirm actual construction details.

The exterior of this home exhilarates in the design elements of a storybook cottage, while the interior is all luxurious comfort.

Rooms sprawl openly into each other on the first floor, with only the library/den and the screen porch set apart from the flow. From nearly every space, large windows frame views of nature. A lower floor provides an additional 1,230 square feet, including a guest room, media room, and a playroom among other things. This home is designed with a basement foundation.

FIRST FLOOR

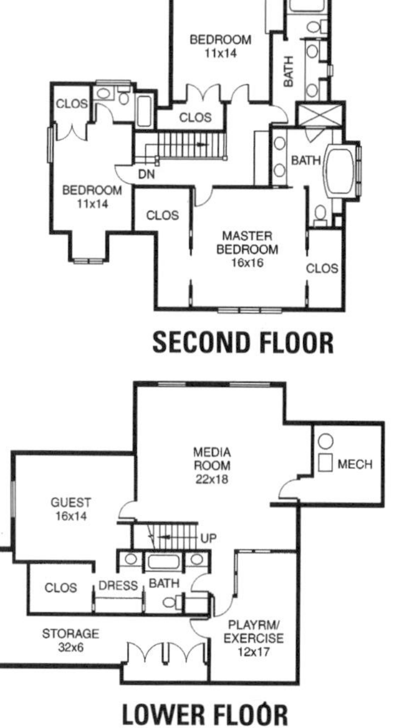

BEDROOM 11x14
BATH
CLOS
CLOS
DN
BEDROOM 11x14
CLOS
BATH
MASTER BEDROOM 16x16
CLOS
MEDIA ROOM 22x18
MECH
GUEST 16x14
UP
CLOS
DRESS
BATH
STORAGE 32x6
PLAYRM/ EXERCISE 12x17

SECOND FLOOR

LOWER FLOOR

Design 65162

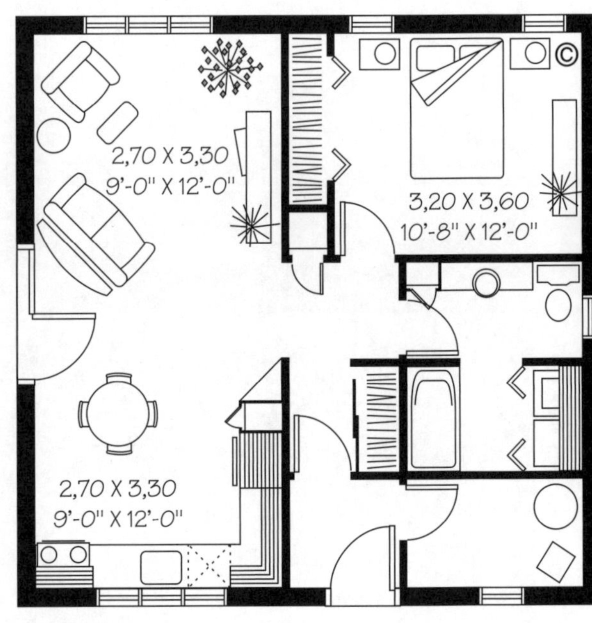
2,70 X 3,30
9'-0" X 12'-0"
3,20 X 3,60
10'-8" X 12'-0"
2,70 X 3,30
9'-0" X 12'-0"

MAIN FLOOR

Units	Single
Price Code	A
Total Finished	784 sq. ft.
Main Finished	784 sq. ft.
Garage Unfinished	46 sq. ft.
Dimensions	28'x28'
Foundation	Slab
Bedrooms	1
Full Baths	1
Main Ceiling	8'
Max Ridge Height	18'
Roof Framing	Truss

Design 99799

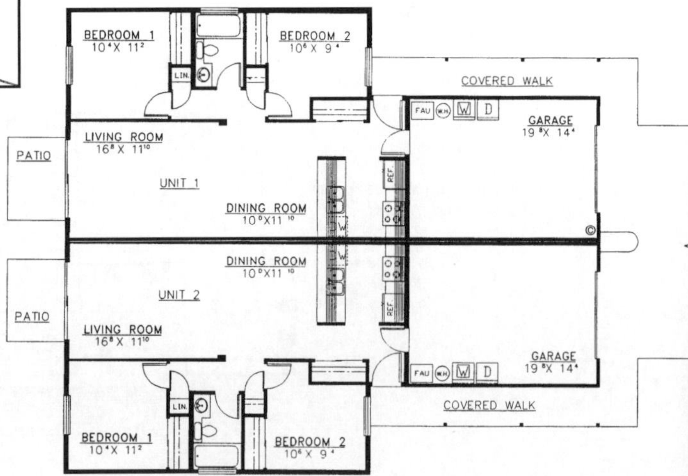
BEDROOM 1
BEDROOM 2
LIN.
COVERED WALK
LIVING ROOM
GARAGE
PATIO
UNIT 1
DINING ROOM
UNIT 2
LIVING ROOM
GARAGE
COVERED WALK
BEDROOM 1
BEDROOM 2

MAIN FLOOR

Units	Duplex
Price Code	G
Total Finished	828 sq. ft.
Main Finished	828 sq. ft.
Dimensions	56'x48'
Foundation	Crawlspace
Bedrooms	4
Full Baths	2
Max Ridge Height	15'
Roof Framing	Stick/Truss
Exterior Walls	2x6

Design 65259

Units	Single
Price Code	A
Total Finished	832 sq. ft.
Main Finished	832 sq. ft.
Dimensions	26'x32'
Foundation	Basement
Bedrooms	2
Full Baths	1
Exterior Walls	2x4

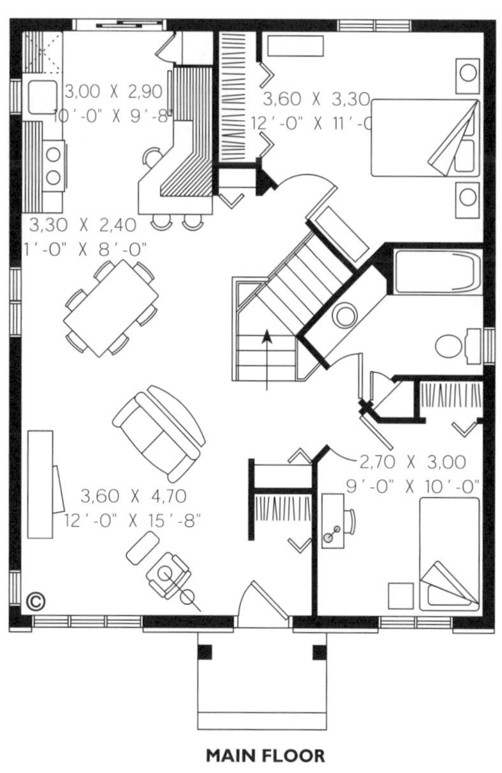
3,00 X 2,90
10'-0" X 9'-8"
3,60 X 3,30
12'-0" X 11'-0
3,30 X 2,40
1'-0" X 8'-0"
2,70 X 3,00
9'-0" X 10'-0"
3,60 X 4,70
12'-0" X 15'-8"
MAIN FLOOR

Design 65263

Units	Single
Price Code	A
Total Finished	840 sq. ft.
Main Finished	840 sq. ft.
Porch Unfinished	466 sq. ft.
Dimensions	33'x31'
Foundation	Basement
Bedrooms	1
Full Baths	1
Main Ceiling	8'
Max Ridge Height	22'11"
Roof Framing	Truss
Exterior Walls	2x6

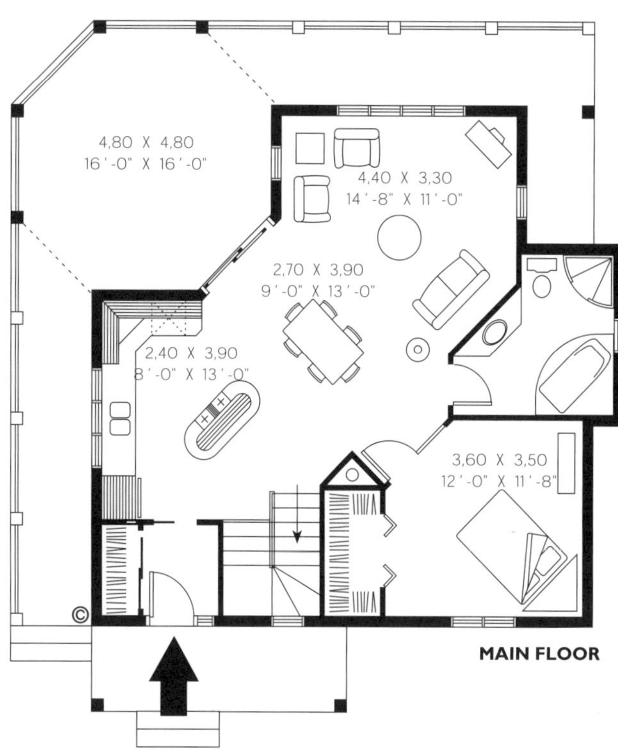
4,80 X 4,80
16'-0" X 16'-0"
4,40 X 3,30
14'-8" X 11'-0"
2,70 X 3,90
9'-0" X 13'-0"
2,40 X 3,90
8'-0" X 13'-0"
3,60 X 3,50
12'-0" X 11'-8"
MAIN FLOOR

Design 65045

Units	Single
Price Code	A
Total Finished	860 sq. ft.
Main Finished	860 sq. ft.
Dimensions	30'x30'
Foundation	Basement
Bedrooms	2
Full Baths	1
Roof Framing	Stick

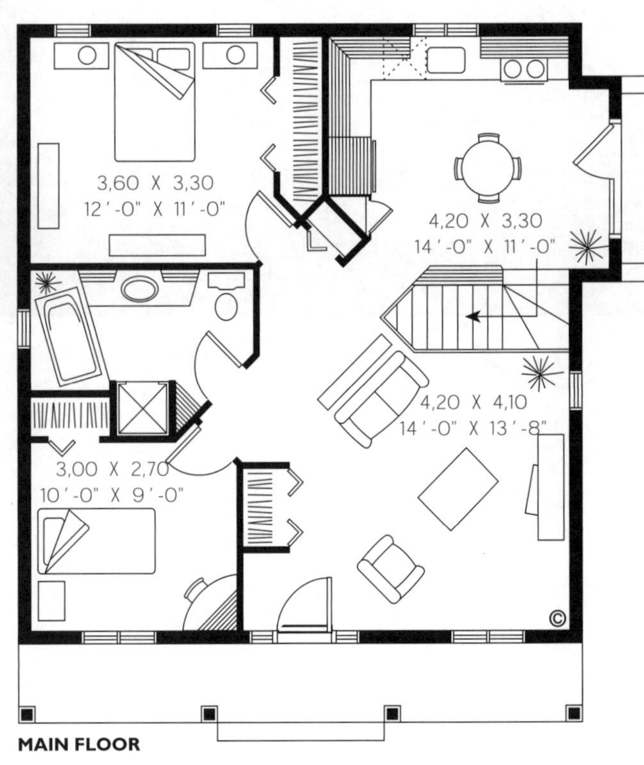

3,60 X 3,30
12'-0" X 11'-0"
4,20 X 3,30
14'-0" X 11'-0"
4,20 X 4,10
14'-0" X 13'-8"
3,00 X 2,70
10'-0" X 9'-0"

MAIN FLOOR

Design 91031

Units	Single
Price Code	A
Total Finished	880 sq. ft.
First Finished	572 sq. ft.
Second Finished	308 sq. ft.
Dimensions	22'x26'
Foundation	Crawlspace
Bedrooms	2
3/4 Baths	1
Max Ridge Height	20'
Roof Framing	Stick
Exterior Walls	2x6

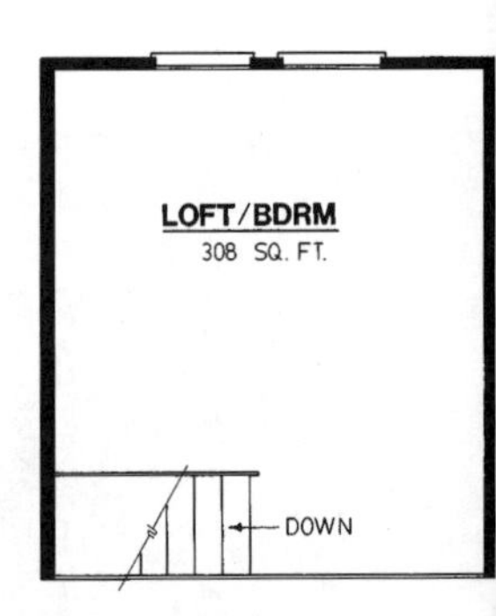

LOFT/BDRM
308 SQ. FT.
DOWN

SECOND FLOOR

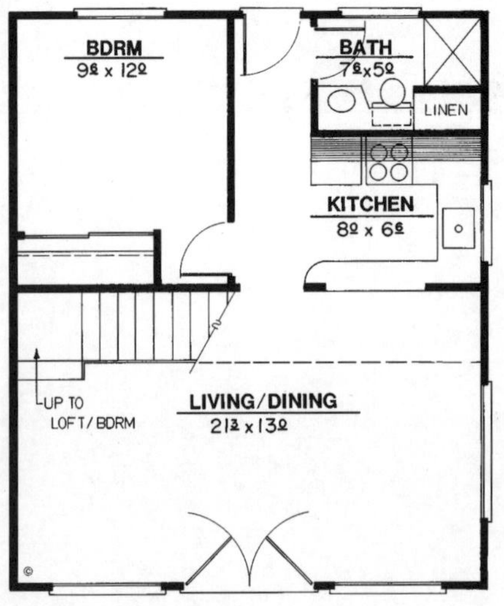

BDRM
9⁰ x 12⁰
BATH
7⁶x5⁰
LINEN
KITCHEN
8⁰ x 6⁶
UP TO
LOFT/BDRM
LIVING/DINING
21⁸ x 13⁰

FIRST FLOOR

Design 90934

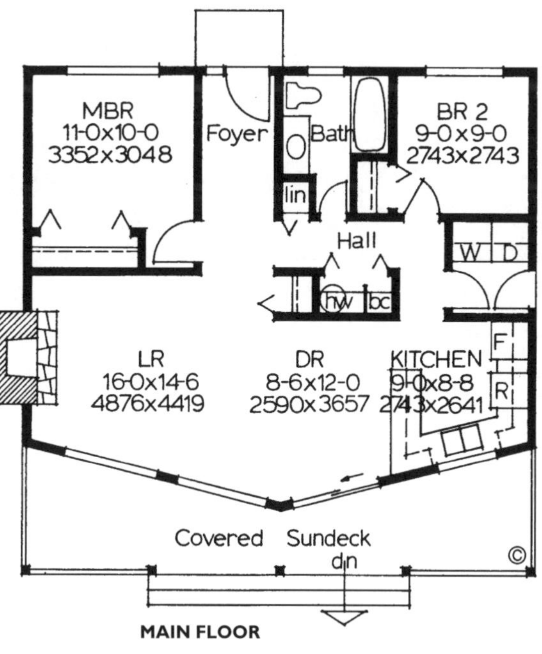
MBR
11-0x10-0
3352x3048
Foyer
Bath
BR 2
9-0x9-0
2743x2743
lin
Hall
W D
hw bc
F
R
LR
16-0x14-6
4876x4419
DR
8-6x12-0
2590x3657
KITCHEN
9-0x8-8
2743x2641
Covered Sundeck
dn
©

MAIN FLOOR

Units	Single
Price Code	A
Total Finished	884 sq. ft.
Main Finished	884 sq. ft.
Dimensions	34'x28'
Foundation	Slab
Bedrooms	2
Full Baths	1
Main Ceiling	8'
Max Ridge Height	15'

Design 24309

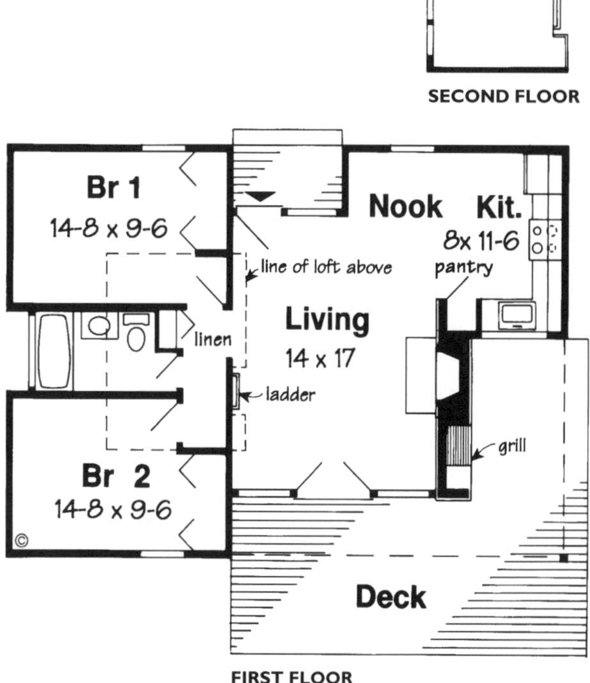
Loft
9 x 12
railing
Br 1
14-8 x 9-6
Nook
Kit.
8x 11-6
pantry
line of loft above
Living
14 x 17
linen
ladder
grill
Br 2
14-8 x 9-6
©
Deck

SECOND FLOOR

FIRST FLOOR

Units	Single
Price Code	A
Total Finished	897 sq. ft.
First Finished	789 sq. ft.
Second Finished	108 sq. ft.
Dimensions	38'x26'
Foundation	Crawlspace
Bedrooms	2
Full Baths	1
First Ceiling	7'9"
Vaulted Ceiling	Loft
Ridge Height	21'
Roof Framing	Stick/Truss
Exterior Walls	2x4

Design 65366

Units	Single
Price Code	A
Total Finished	923 sq. ft.
Main Finished	923 sq. ft.
Basement Unfinished	923 sq. ft.
Dimensions	30'x31'
Foundation	Basement
Bedrooms	2
Full Baths	1
Main Ceiling	8'
Max Ridge Height	22'1"

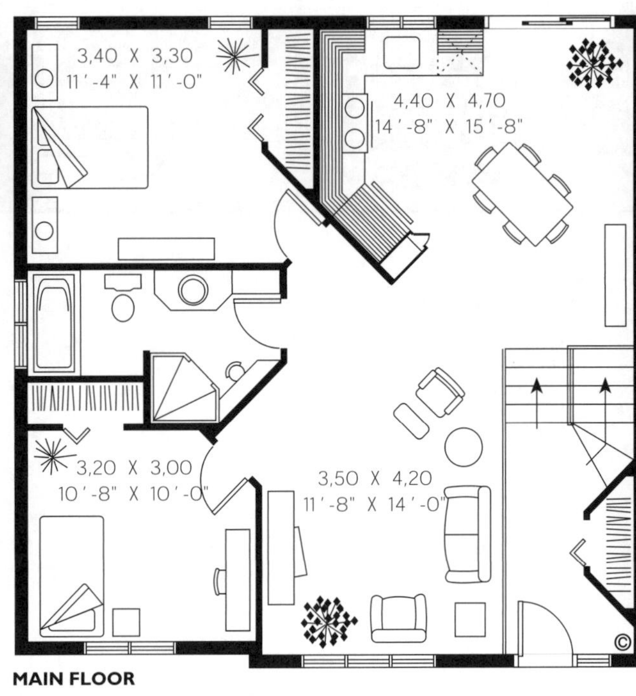
3,40 X 3,30
11'-4" X 11'-0"
4,40 X 4,70
14'-8" X 15'-8"
3,20 X 3,00
10'-8" X 10'-0"
3,50 X 4,20
11'-8" X 14'-0"
©

MAIN FLOOR

Design 90433

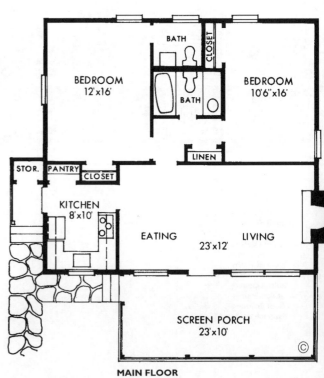

Units	Single
Price Code	A
Total Finished	928 sq. ft.
Main Finished	928 sq. ft.
Porch Unfinished	230 sq. ft.
Dimensions	32'x29'
Foundation	Crawlspace Slab
Bedrooms	2
Full Baths	1
Half Baths	1
Roof Framing	Stick

BATH
CLOSET
BEDROOM 12'x16'
BATH
BEDROOM 10'6"x16'
LINEN
STOR.
PANTRY
CLOSET
KITCHEN 8'x10'
EATING
23'x12'
LIVING
SCREEN PORCH 23'x10'
©

MAIN FLOOR

Design 61093

Units	Single
Price Code	A
Total Finished	930 sq. ft.
Main Finished	930 sq. ft.
Porch Unfinished	102 sq. ft.
Dimensions	35'x28'6"
Foundation	Crawlspace Slab
Bedrooms	3
Full Baths	1
Main Ceiling	8'
Roof Framing	Stick
Exterior Walls	2x4

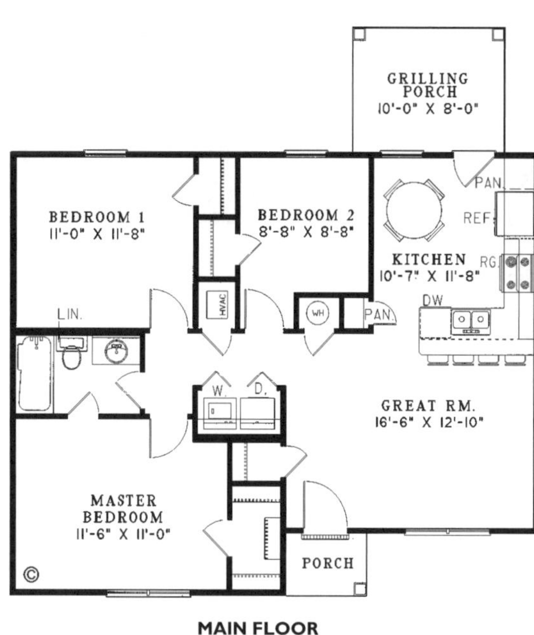
GRILLING PORCH
10'-0" X 8'-0"
BEDROOM 1
11'-0" X 11'-8"
BEDROOM 2
8'-8" X 8'-8"
KITCHEN
10'-7" X 11'-8"
PAN
REF
RG
DW
PAN
WH
HVAC
LIN.
W
D
GREAT RM.
16'-6" X 12'-10"
MASTER BEDROOM
11'-6" X 11'-0"
PORCH

MAIN FLOOR

Design 65387

Units	Single
Price Code	A
Total Finished	948 sq. ft.
Main Finished	948 sq. ft.
Dimensions	30'x34'
Foundation	Basement
Bedrooms	2
Full Baths	1
Roof Framing	Stick

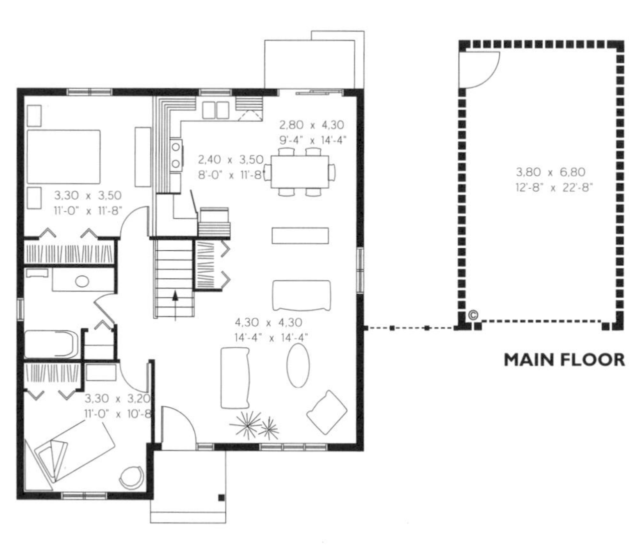
2,80 x 4,30
9'-4" x 14'-4"
2,40 x 3,50
8'-0" x 11'-8"
3,30 x 3,50
11'-0" x 11'-8"
4,30 x 4,30
14'-4" x 14'-4"
3,30 x 3,20
11'-0" x 10'-8"
3,80 x 6,80
12'-8" x 22'-8"

MAIN FLOOR

Design 65005

Units	Single
Price Code	A
Total Finished	972 sq. ft.
Main Finished	972 sq. ft.
Basement Unfinished	972 sq. ft.
Dimensions	30'x35'
Foundation	Basement
Bedrooms	2
Full Baths	1
Main Ceiling	8'2"
Max Ridge Height	17'6"
Exterior Walls	2x6

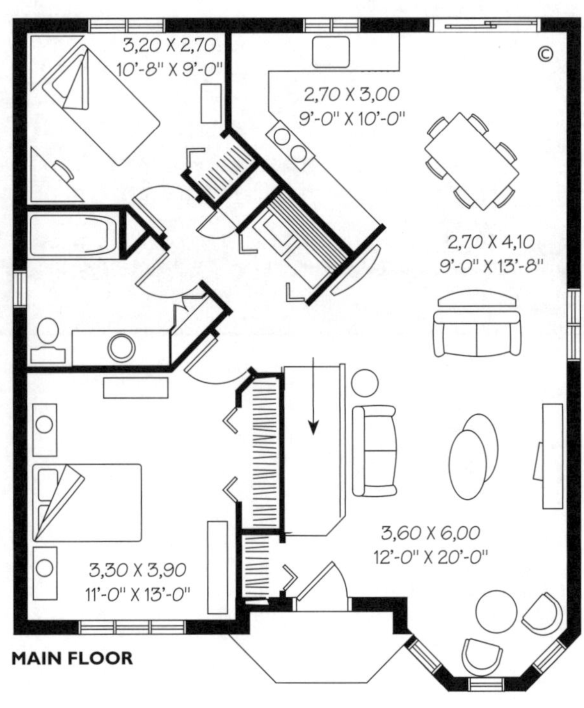

3,20 X 2,70
10'-8" X 9'-0"
2,70 X 3,00
9'-0" X 10'-0"
2,70 X 4,10
9'-0" X 13'-8"
3,60 X 6,00
12'-0" X 20'-0"
3,30 X 3,90
11'-0" X 13'-0"

MAIN FLOOR

Design 91147

Units	Single
Price Code	A
Total Finished	975 sq. ft.
Main Finished	975 sq. ft.
Dimensions	39'4"x31'2"
Foundation	Slab
Bedrooms	3
Full Baths	2

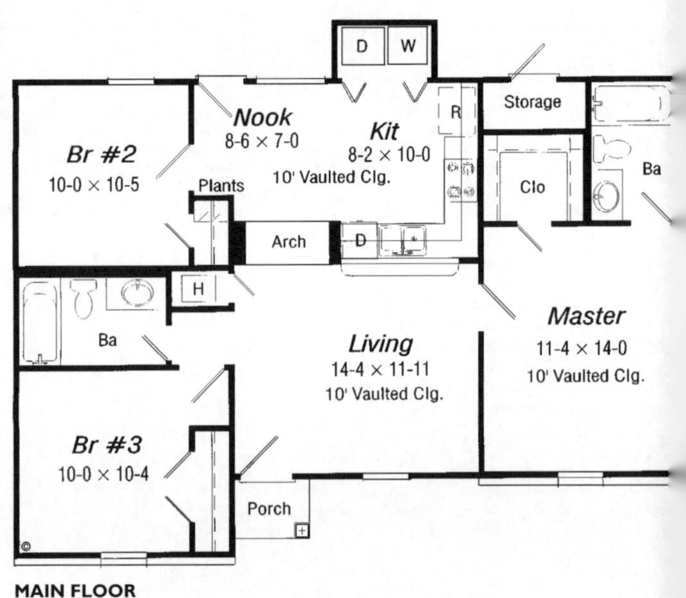

D
W
Nook
8-6 × 7-0
Kit
8-2 × 10-0
10' Vaulted Clg.
Storage
Br #2
10-0 × 10-5
Plants
Clo
Ba
Arch
D
H
Ba
Living
14-4 × 11-11
10' Vaulted Clg.
Master
11-4 × 14-0
10' Vaulted Clg.
Br #3
10-0 × 10-4
Porch

MAIN FLOOR

Design 65003

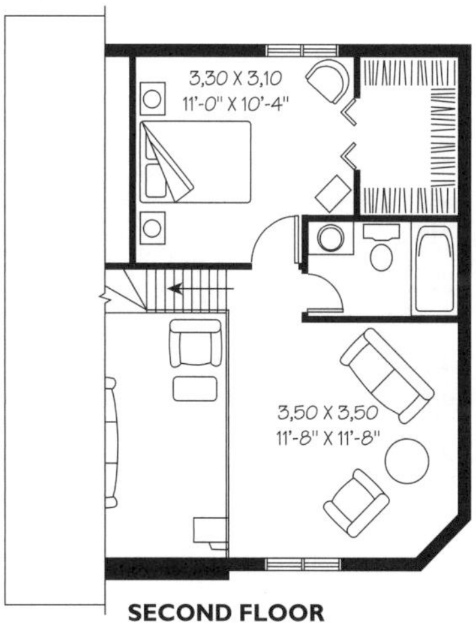

Units	Single
Price Code	A
Total Finished	976 sq. ft.
First Finished	593 sq. ft.
Second Finished	383 sq. ft.
Basement Unfinished	593 sq. ft.
Dimensions	22'8"x26'8"
Foundation	Crawlspace
Bedrooms	2
Full Baths	1
3/4 Baths	1
First Ceiling	8'
Second Ceiling	8'
Max Ridge Height	22'8"
Roof Framing	Truss
Exterior Walls	2x6

2,80 X 3,10
9'-4" X 10'-4"
2,40 X 4,30
8'-0" X 14'-4"
3,90 X 3,60
13'-0" X 12'-0"
3,00 X 7,20
10'-0" X 24'-0"
FIRST FLOOR
3,30 X 3,10
11'-0" X 10'-4"
3,50 X 3,50
11'-8" X 11'-8"
SECOND FLOOR

Design 24303

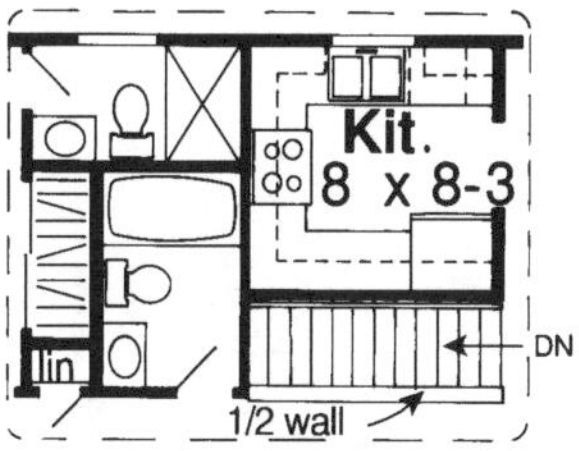

Units	Single
Price Code	A
Total Finished	984 sq. ft.
Main Finished	984 sq. ft.
Basement Unfinished	960 sq. ft.
Garage Unfinished	280 sq. ft.
Dimensions	54'x28'
Foundation	Basement Crawlspace
Bedrooms	3
Full Baths	1
3/4 Baths	1
Max Ridge Height	15'
Roof Framing	Stick
Exterior Walls	2x4

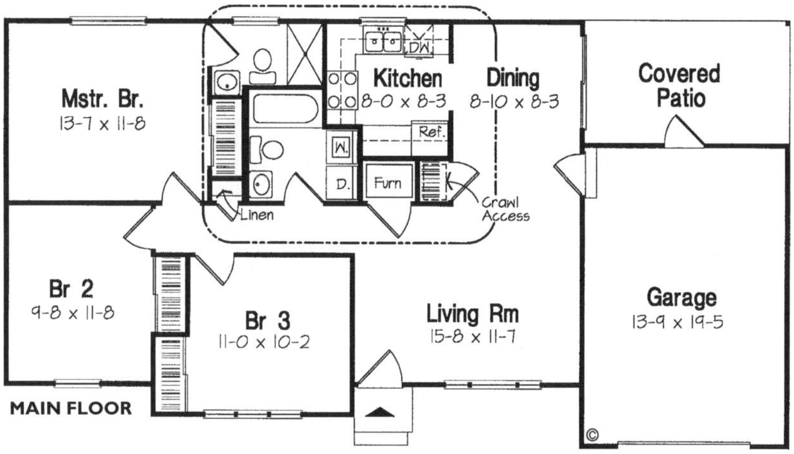

Kit.
8 x 8-3
lin
DN
1/2 wall
OPTIONAL BASEMENT FOUNDATION
Mstr. Br.
13-7 x 11-8
Kitchen
8-0 x 8-3
Dining
8-10 x 8-3
Covered Patio
DW
Ref.
W.
D.
Furn
Linen
Crawl Access
Br 2
9-8 x 11-8
Br 3
11-0 x 10-2
Living Rm
15-8 x 11-7
Garage
13-9 x 19-5
MAIN FLOOR

Design 65643

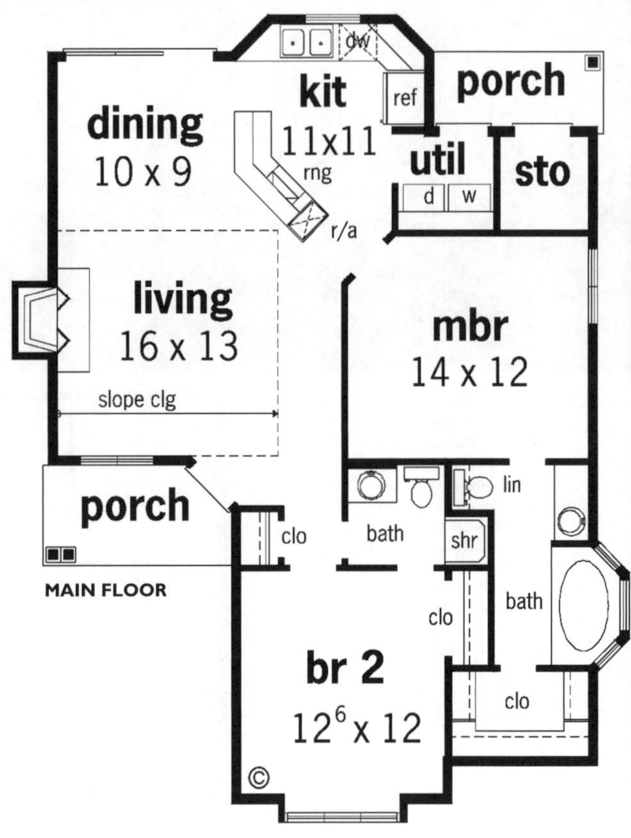

kit
11x11
dw
ref
rng
r/a
porch
dining
10 x 9
util
d
w
sto
living
16 x 13
slope clg
mbr
14 x 12
porch
lin
clo
bath
shr
bath
clo
br 2
12⁶ x 12
clo
MAIN FLOOR

Units	Single
Price Code	A
Total Finished	984 sq. ft.
Main Finished	984 sq. ft.
Dimensions	33'9"x43'
Foundation	Crawlspace Slab
Bedrooms	2
Full Baths	1
3/4 Baths	1
Max Ridge Height	26'
Exterior Walls	2x6

Design 24304

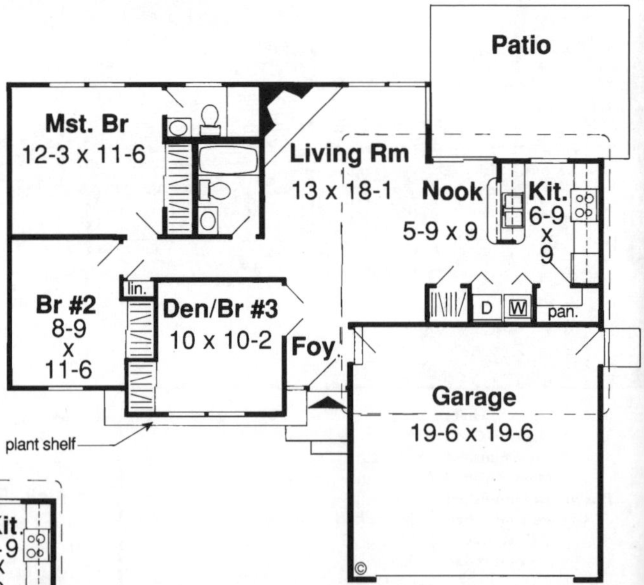

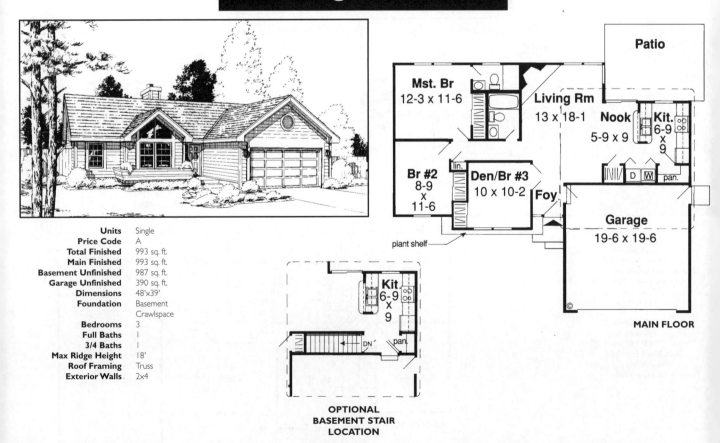

Patio
Mst. Br 12-3 x 11-6
Living Rm 13 x 18-1
Nook 5-9 x 9
Kit. 6-9 x 9
Br #2 8-9 x 11-6
lin.
Den/Br #3 10 x 10-2
Foy
D W pan.
Garage 19-6 x 19-6
plant shelf
MAIN FLOOR

Units	Single
Price Code	A
Total Finished	993 sq. ft.
Main Finished	993 sq. ft.
Basement Unfinished	987 sq. ft.
Garage Unfinished	390 sq. ft.
Dimensions	48'x39'
Foundation	Basement Crawlspace
Bedrooms	3
Full Baths	1
3/4 Baths	1
Max Ridge Height	18'
Roof Framing	Truss
Exterior Walls	2x4

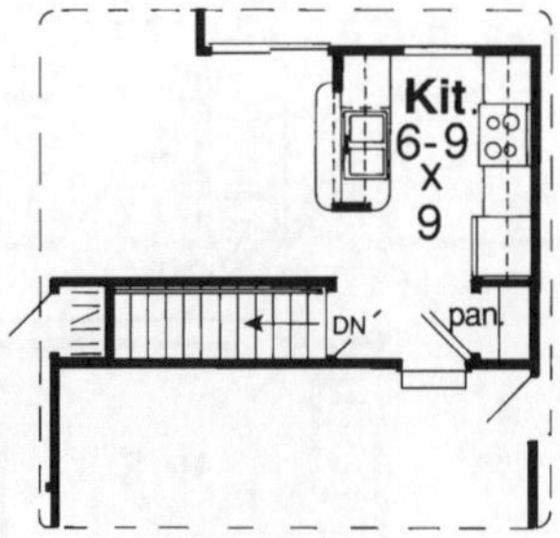

Kit 6-9 x 9
DN
pan.
OPTIONAL BASEMENT STAIR LOCATION

Design 65260

Units	Single
Price Code	A
Total Finished	996 sq. ft.
Main Finished	996 sq. ft.
Dimensions	34'x32'4"
Foundation	Basement
Bedrooms	2
Full Baths	1
Exterior Walls	2x4

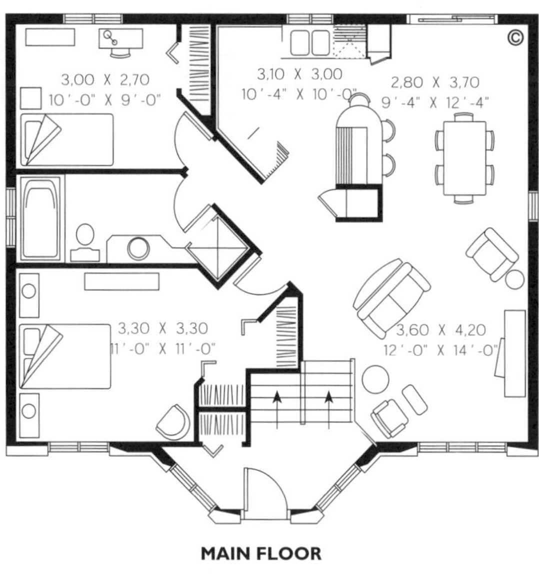
3,00 X 2,70
10'-0" X 9'-0"
3,10 X 3,00
10'-4" X 10'-0"
2,80 X 3,70
9'-4" X 12'-4"
3,30 X 3,30
11'-0" X 11'-0"
3,60 X 4,20
12'-0" X 14'-0"

MAIN FLOOR

Design 65642

Units	Single
Price Code	A
Total Finished	998 sq. ft.
Main Finished	998 sq. ft.
Dimensions	48'x29'
Foundation	Crawlspace Slab
Bedrooms	3
Full Baths	1
Main Ceiling	8'
Max Ridge Height	26'
Roof Framing	Stick
Exterior Walls	2x4

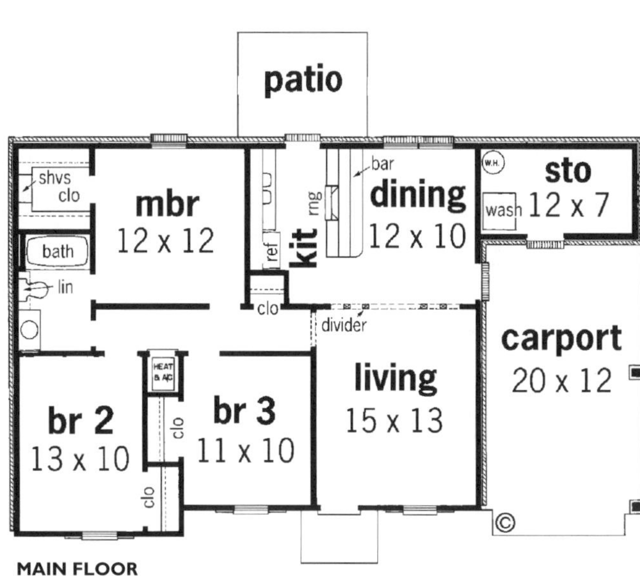
patio
shvs
clo
mbr
12 x 12
bath
lin
rng
ref
kit
bar
dining
12 x 10
W.H.
sto
wash
12 x 7
clo
divider
carport
20 x 12
HEAT & A/C
br 2
13 x 10
br 3
11 x 10
clo
clo
living
15 x 13

MAIN FLOOR

Design 65415

Units	Single
Price Code	A
Total Finished	1,007 sq. ft.
Main Finished	1,007 sq. ft.
Basement Unfinished	1,007 sq. ft.
Garage Unfinished	307 sq. ft.
Deck Unfinished	48 sq. ft.
Porch Unfinished	22 sq. ft.
Dimensions	44'8"x38'
Foundation	Basement
Bedrooms	2
Full Baths	1
Main Ceiling	8'
Max Ridge Height	23'11"
Roof Framing	Truss
Exterior Walls	2x6

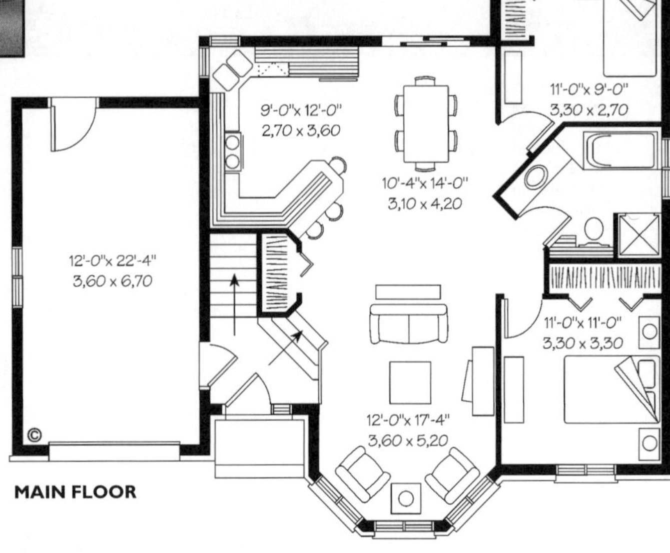
11'-0"x 9'-0"
3,30 x 2,70
9'-0"x 12'-0"
2,70 x 3,60
10'-4"x 14'-0"
3,10 x 4,20
12'-0"x 22'-4"
3,60 x 6,70
11'-0"x 11'-0"
3,30 x 3,30
12'-0"x 17'-4"
3,60 x 5,20
©

MAIN FLOOR

Design 65469

Units	Single
Price Code	A
Total Finished	1,019 sq. ft.
Main Finished	1,019 sq. ft.
Basement Unfinished	1,019 sq. ft.
Garage Unfinished	442 sq. ft.
Porch Unfinished	50 sq. ft.
Dimensions	46'x37'
Foundation	Basement
Bedrooms	2
Full Baths	1
Main Ceiling	8'
Max Ridge Height	23'6"
Roof Framing	Truss
Exterior Walls	2x6

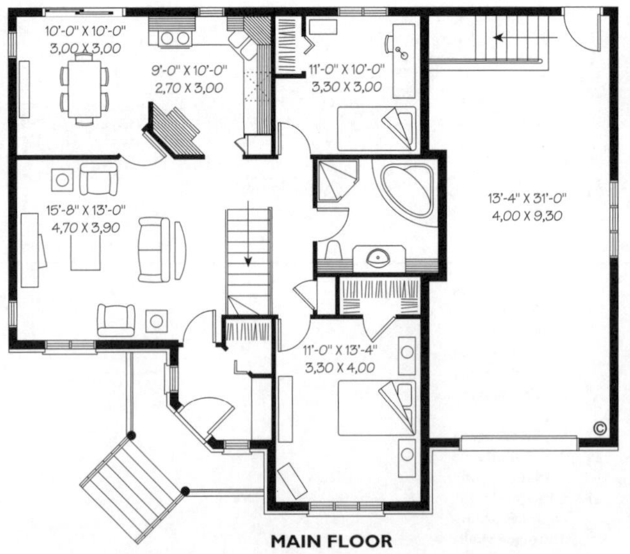
10'-0" X 10'-0"
3,00 X 3,00
9'-0" X 10'-0"
2,70 X 3,00
11'-0" X 10'-0"
3,30 X 3,00
13'-4" X 31'-0"
4,00 X 9,30
15'-8" X 13'-0"
4,70 X 3,90
11'-0" X 13'-4"
3,30 X 4,00
©

MAIN FLOOR

Design 35007

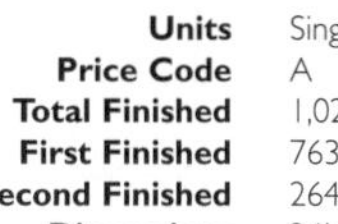

Units	Single
Price Code	A
Total Finished	1,027 sq. ft.
First Finished	763 sq. ft.
Second Finished	264 sq. ft.
Dimensions	24'x32'
Foundation	Basement Crawlspace Slab
Bedrooms	2
Full Baths	1
First Ceiling	8'
Max Ridge Height	24'
Roof Framing	Stick
Exterior Walls	2x4, 2x6

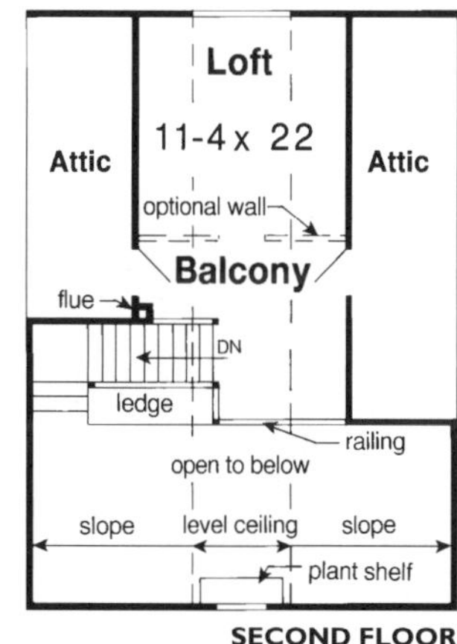
Loft
11-4 x 22
Attic
Attic
optional wall
Balcony
flue
DN
ledge
railing
open to below
slope
level ceiling
slope
plant shelf

SECOND FLOOR

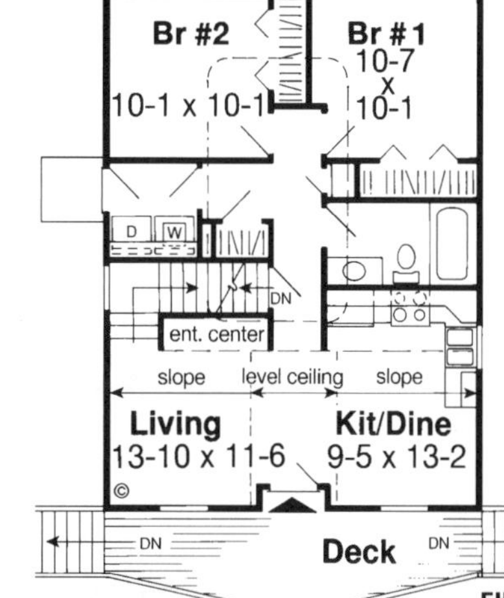
Br #2
10-1 x 10-1
Br #1
10-7 x 10-1
D
W
DN
ent. center
slope
level ceiling
slope
Living
13-10 x 11-6
Kit/Dine
9-5 x 13-2
©
DN
Deck
DN

FIRST FLOOR

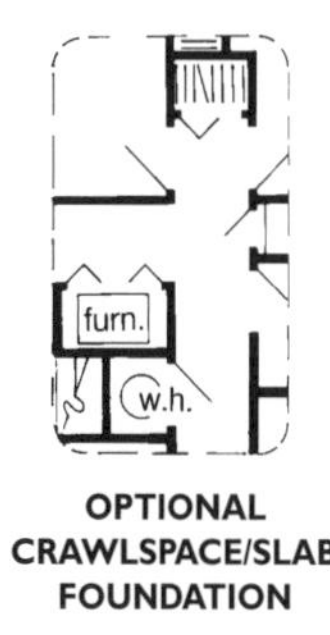
furn.
w.h.

OPTIONAL CRAWLSPACE/SLAB FOUNDATION

Design 98469

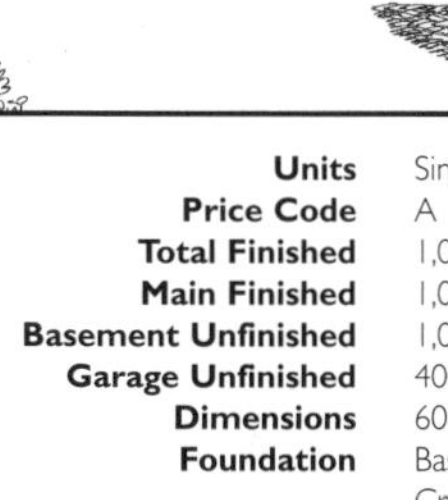

Units	Single
Price Code	A
Total Finished	1,042 sq. ft.
Main Finished	1,042 sq. ft.
Basement Unfinished	1,042 sq. ft.
Garage Unfinished	400 sq. ft.
Dimensions	60'x30'
Foundation	Basement Crawlspace
Bedrooms	3
Full Baths	2
Main Ceiling	9'
Max Ridge Height	22'
Roof Framing	Stick
Exterior Walls	2x4

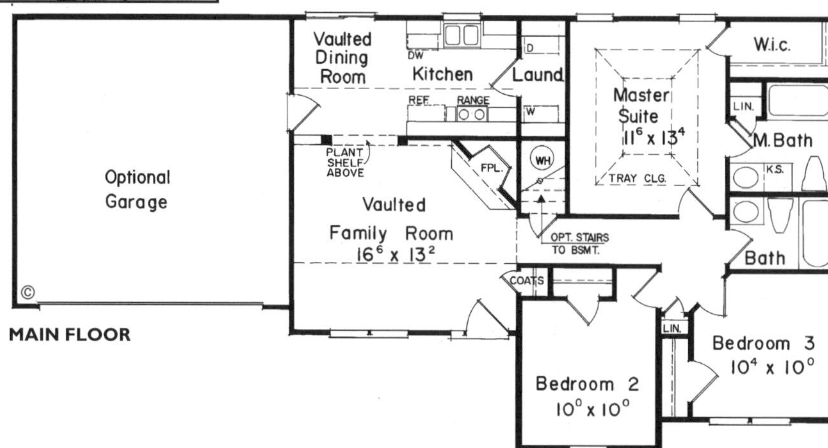
Vaulted
Dining
Room
DW
Kitchen
D
Laund.
REF.
RANGE
W
Master
Suite
11⁶ x 13⁴
TRAY CLG.
W.i.c.
LIN.
M.Bath
K.S.
PLANT SHELF ABOVE
FPL.
WH
Optional
Garage
Vaulted
Family Room
16⁶ x 13²
OPT. STAIRS TO BSMT.
Bath
COATS
©
LIN.
Bedroom 3
10⁴ x 10⁰
Bedroom 2
10⁰ x 10⁰

MAIN FLOOR

Design 92400

Units	Single
Price Code	A
Total Finished	1,050 sq. ft.
Main Finished	1,050 sq. ft.
Garage Unfinished	261 sq. ft.
Dimensions	36'x42'
Foundation	Basement Slab
Bedrooms	3
Full Baths	2
Max Ridge Height	16'
Roof Framing	Stick
Exterior Walls	2x4

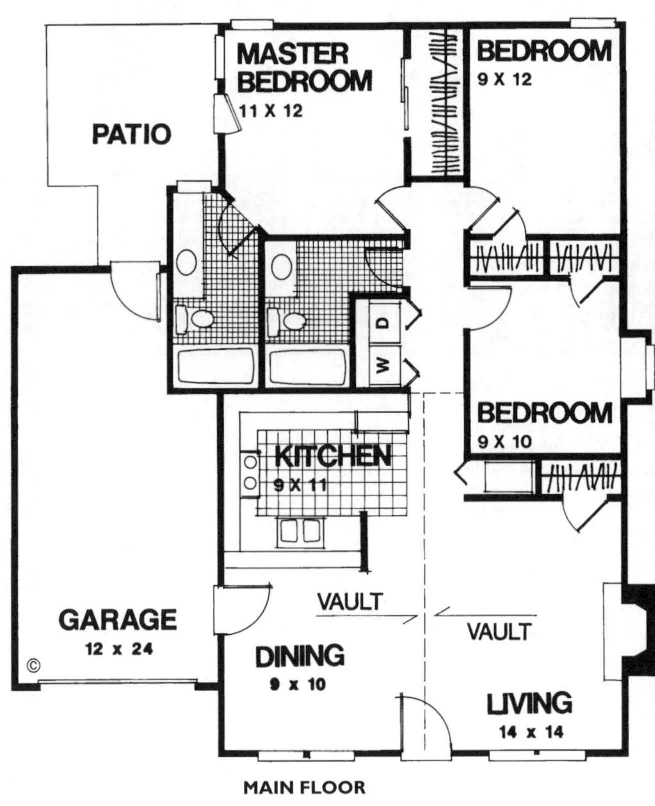

MASTER BEDROOM
11 X 12
BEDROOM
9 X 12
PATIO
BEDROOM
9 X 10
KITCHEN
9 X 11
D
W
VAULT
VAULT
GARAGE
12 x 24
DINING
9 x 10
LIVING
14 x 14
©

MAIN FLOOR

Design 65048

Units	Single
Price Code	A
Total Finished	1,052 sq. ft.
Main Finished	1,052 sq. ft.
Basement Unfinished	1,052 sq. ft.
Dimensions	32'8"x36'
Foundation	Basement
Bedrooms	2
Full Baths	1
Main Ceiling	8'
Max Ridge Height	18'1"
Roof Framing	Truss
Exterior Walls	2x6

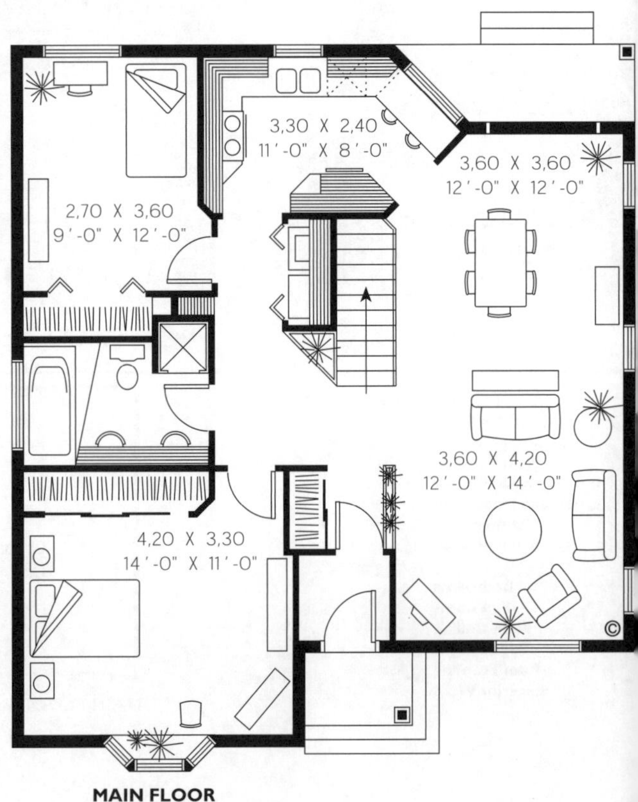

3,30 X 2,40
11'-0" X 8'-0"
3,60 X 3,60
12'-0" X 12'-0"
2,70 X 3,60
9'-0" X 12'-0"
3,60 X 4,20
12'-0" X 14'-0"
4,20 X 3,30
14'-0" X 11'-0"
©

MAIN FLOOR

Design 65036

Units	Single
Price Code	A
Total Finished	1,052 sq. ft.
Main Finished	1,052 sq. ft.
Basement Unfinished	1,052 sq. ft.
Dimensions	32'8"x36'
Foundation	Basement
Bedrooms	2
Full Baths	1
Main Ceiling	8'
Max Ridge Height	17'6"
Roof Framing	Truss
Exterior Walls	2x6

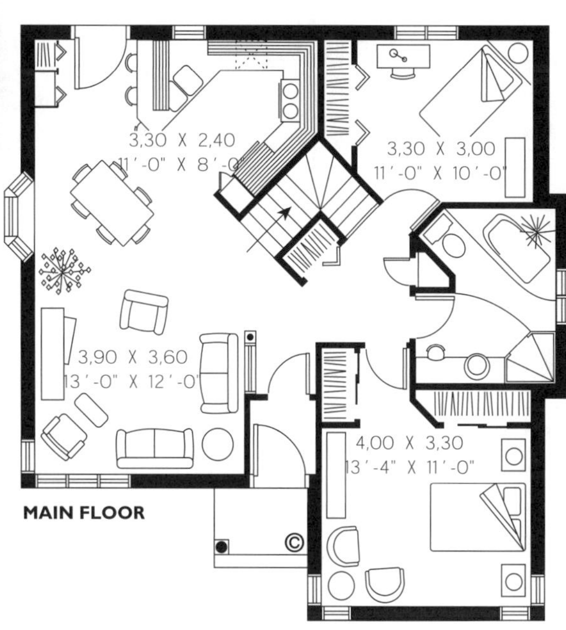
3,30 X 2,40
11'-0" X 8'-0"
3,30 X 3,00
11'-0" X 10'-0"
3,90 X 3,60
13'-0" X 12'-0"
4,00 X 3,30
13'-4" X 11'-0"
MAIN FLOOR

Design 65161

Units	Single
Price Code	A
Total Finished	1,056 sq. ft.
First Finished	576 sq. ft.
Second Finished	480 sq. ft.
Basement Unfinished	576 sq. ft.
Deck Unfinished	315 sq. ft.
Porch Unfinished	45 sq. ft.
Dimensions	24'x30'
Foundation	Basement
Bedrooms	2
Full Baths	1
Half Baths	1
First Ceiling	8'
Second Ceiling	8'
Max Ridge Height	23'
Roof Framing	Truss
Exterior Walls	2x6

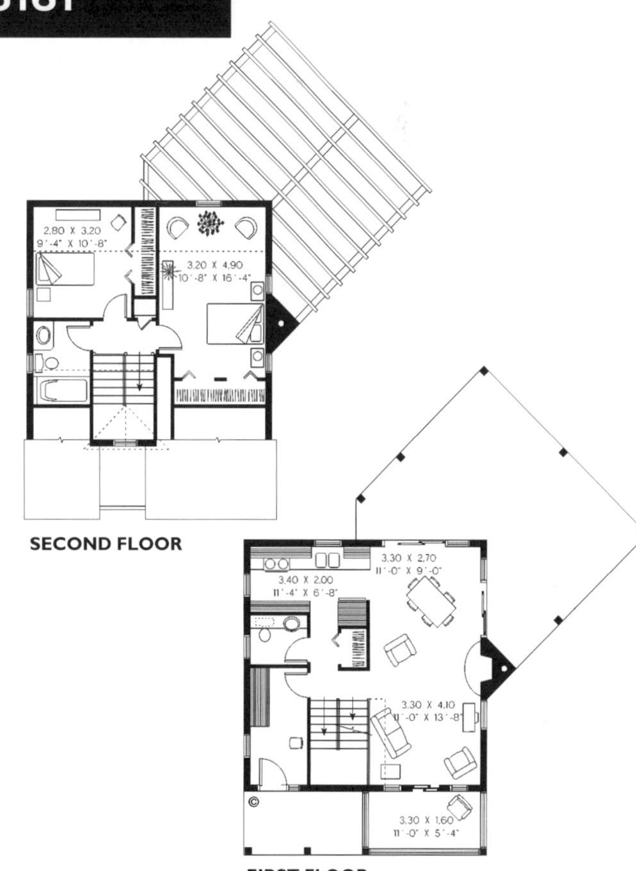
SECOND FLOOR
FIRST FLOOR

Design 65078

Units	Single
Price Code	A
Total Finished	1,059 sq. ft.
Main Finished	1,059 sq. ft.
Garage Unfinished	300 sq. ft.
Dimensions	38'x46'8"
Foundation	Basement
Bedrooms	2
Full Baths	1
Main Ceiling	8'
Max Ridge Height	17'1"
Roof Framing	Truss
Exterior Walls	2x6

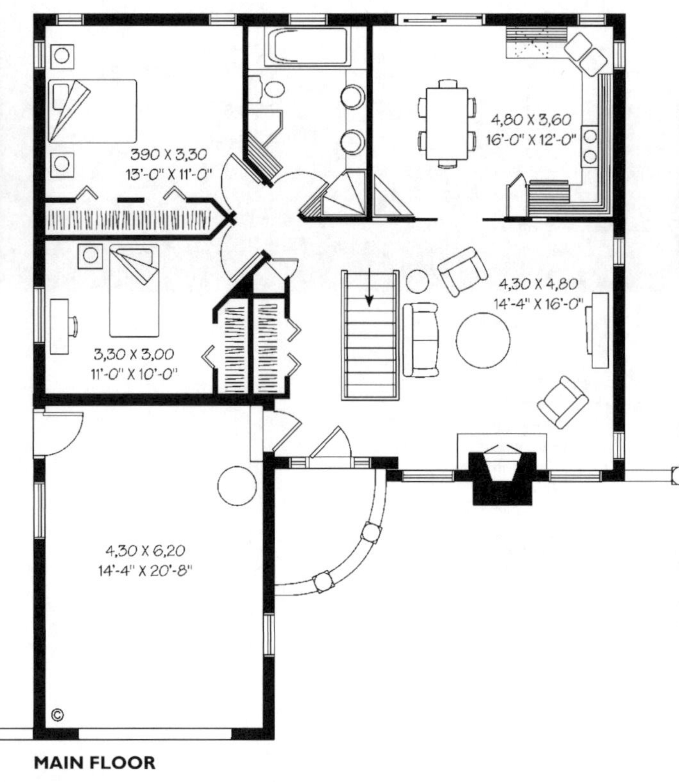
390 X 3,30
13'-0" X 11'-0"
4,80 X 3,60
16'-0" X 12'-0"
3,30 X 3,00
11'-0" X 10'-0"
4,30 X 4,80
14'-4" X 16'-0"
4,30 X 6,20
14'-4" X 20'-8"

MAIN FLOOR

Design 98413

CAD
FILES AVAILABLE
For more information call
800-235-5700

Units	Single
Price Code	A
Total Finished	1,070 sq. ft.
Main Finished	1,070 sq. ft.
Basement Unfinished	1,090 sq. ft.
Garage Unfinished	400 sq. ft.
Dimensions	48'x36'
Foundation	Basement Crawlspace Slab
Bedrooms	3
Full Baths	2
Main Ceiling	9'
Max Ridge Height	22'
Roof Framing	Stick
Exterior Walls	2x4

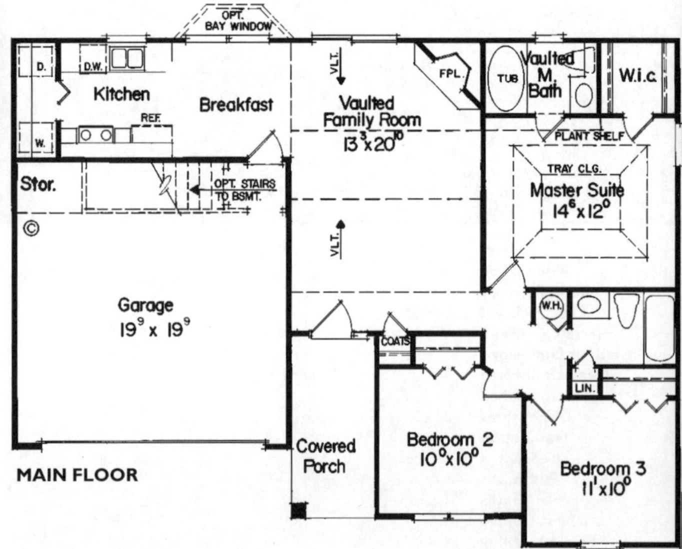
OPT. BAY WINDOW
Kitchen
Breakfast
Vaulted Family Room
13³x20¹⁰
FPL
Vaulted M. Bath
W.i.c.
PLANT SHELF
TRAY CLG.
Master Suite
14⁶x12⁰
Stor.
OPT. STAIRS TO BSMT.
Garage
19⁹ x 19⁹
COATS
Covered Porch
Bedroom 2
10⁰x10⁰
Bedroom 3
11¹x10⁰

MAIN FLOOR

Design 65149

Units	Single
Price Code	A
Total Finished	1,079 sq. ft.
Main Finished	1,079 sq. ft.
Dimensions	34'x34'
Foundation	Basement
Bedrooms	2
Full Baths	1
Max Ridge Height	22'6"
Roof Framing	Truss
Exterior Walls	2x6

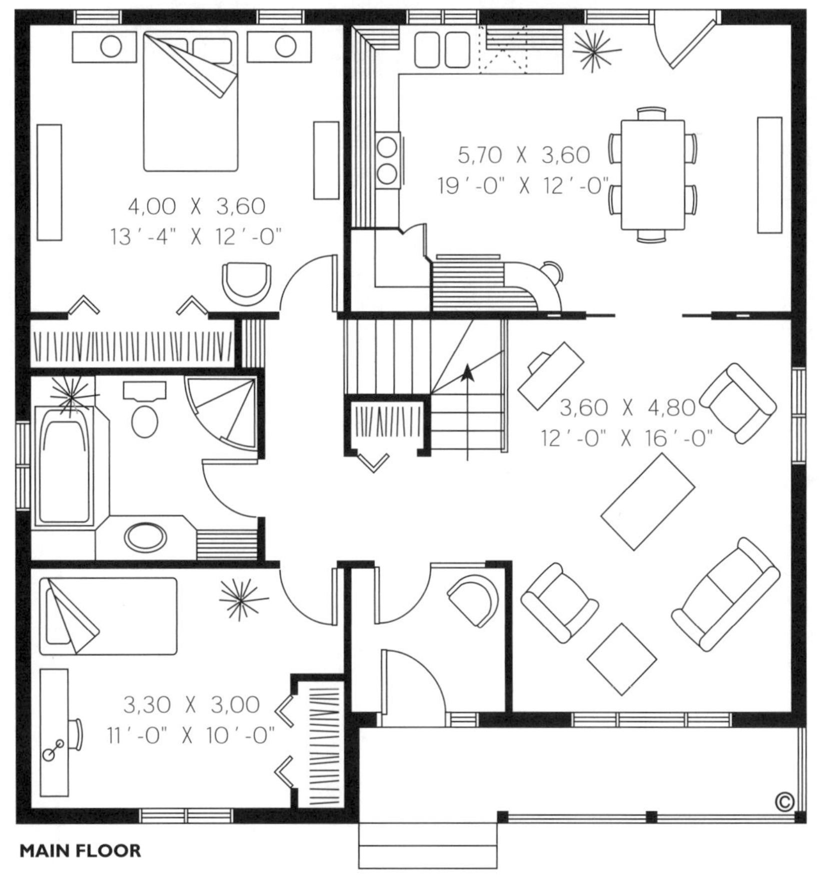
4,00 X 3,60
13'-4" X 12'-0"
5,70 X 3,60
19'-0" X 12'-0"
3,60 X 4,80
12'-0" X 16'-0"
3,30 X 3,00
11'-0" X 10'-0"
©

MAIN FLOOR

Design 65093

Units	Single
Price Code	A
Total Finished	1,087 sq. ft.
Main Finished	1,087 sq. ft.
Dimensions	46'x40'4"
Foundation	Basement
Bedrooms	2
Full Baths	1

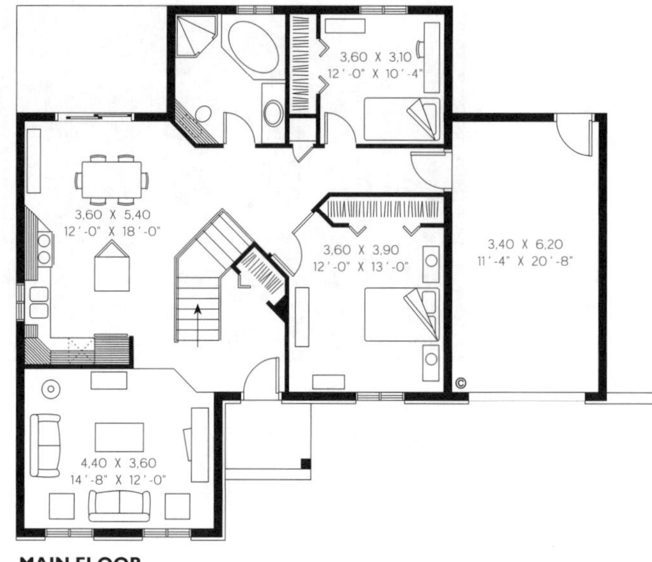

3,60 X 3,10
12'-0" X 10'-4"
3,60 X 5,40
12'-0" X 18'-0"
3,60 X 3,90
12'-0" X 13'-0"
3,40 X 6,20
11'-4" X 20'-8"
4,40 X 3,60
14'-8" X 12'-0"

MAIN FLOOR

Design 65640

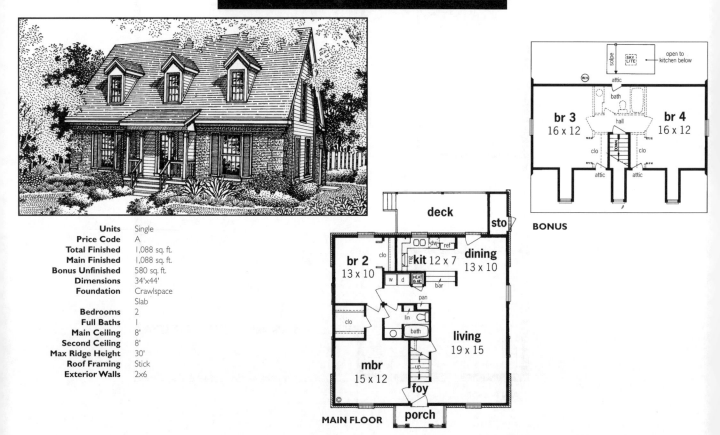

Units	Single
Price Code	A
Total Finished	1,088 sq. ft.
Main Finished	1,088 sq. ft.
Bonus Unfinished	580 sq. ft.
Dimensions	34'x44'
Foundation	Crawlspace Slab
Bedrooms	2
Full Baths	1
Main Ceiling	8'
Second Ceiling	8'
Max Ridge Height	30'
Roof Framing	Stick
Exterior Walls	2x6

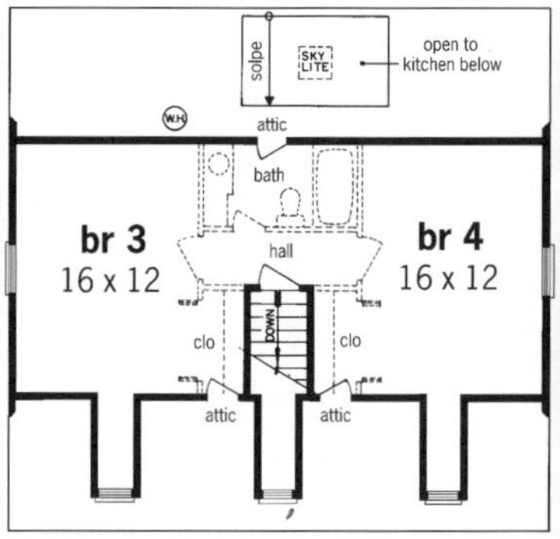

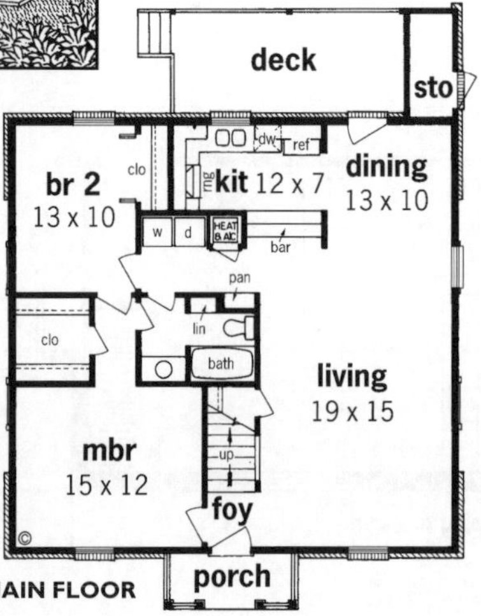

MAIN FLOOR

BONUS

Design 69027

Units	Single
Price Code	A
Total Finished	1,092 sq. ft.
Main Finished	1,092 sq. ft.
Dimensions	39'8"x41'
Foundation	Basement
Bedrooms	3
Full Baths	1
Half Baths	1

Hot
New
Design

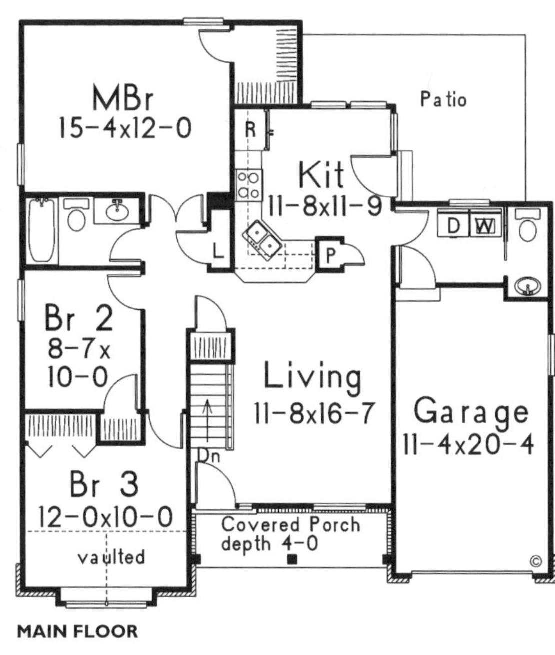
MBr
15-4x12-0
Patio
R
Kit
11-8x11-9
D W
L
P
Br 2
8-7x
10-0
Living
11-8x16-7
Garage
11-4x20-4
Dn
Br 3
12-0x10-0
vaulted
Covered Porch
depth 4-0

MAIN FLOOR

Design 91002

Units	Single
Price Code	A
Total Finished	1,096 sq. ft.
First Finished	808 sq. ft.
Second Finished	288 sq. ft.
Dimensions	24'x32'
Foundation	Crawlspace
Bedrooms	2
Full Baths	1
3/4 Baths	1
Max Ridge Height	25'
Roof Framing	Stick
Exterior Walls	2x6

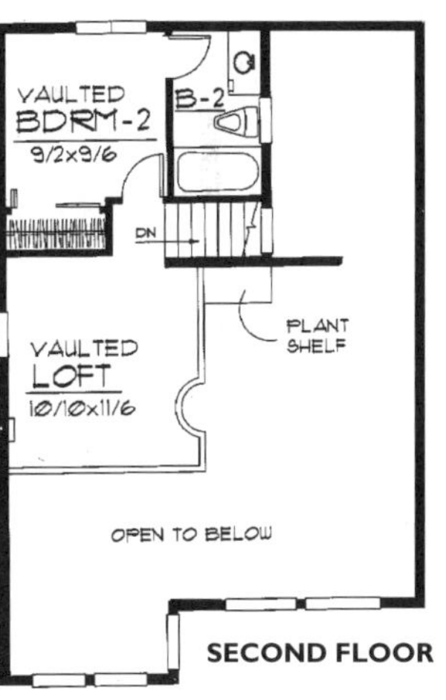
VAULTED
BDRM-2
9/2x9/6
B-2
DN
PLANT
SHELF
VAULTED
LOFT
10/10x11/6
OPEN TO BELOW

SECOND FLOOR

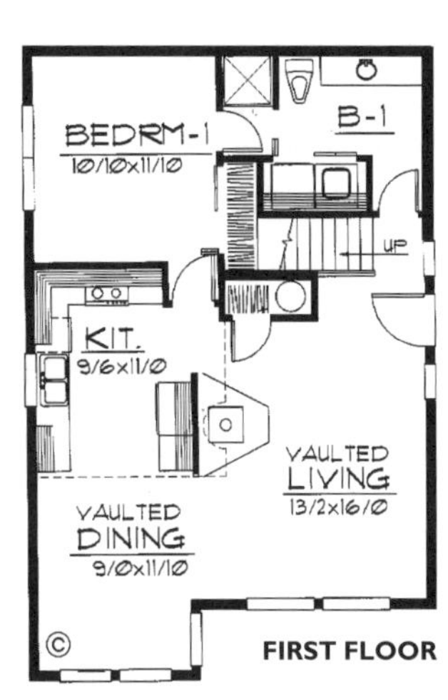
BEDRM-1
10/10x11/10
B-1
UP
KIT.
9/6x11/0
VAULTED
LIVING
13/2x16/0
VAULTED
DINING
9/0x11/10

FIRST FLOOR

Design 98468

Units	Single
Price Code	A
Total Finished	1,104 sq. ft.
Main Finished	1,104 sq. ft.
Basement Unfinished	1,104 sq. ft.
Garage Unfinished	400 sq. ft.
Dimensions	46'6"x41'
Foundation	Basement Crawlspace Slab
Bedrooms	3
Full Baths	2
Main Ceiling	9'
Max Ridge Height	21'
Roof Framing	Stick
Exterior Walls	2x4

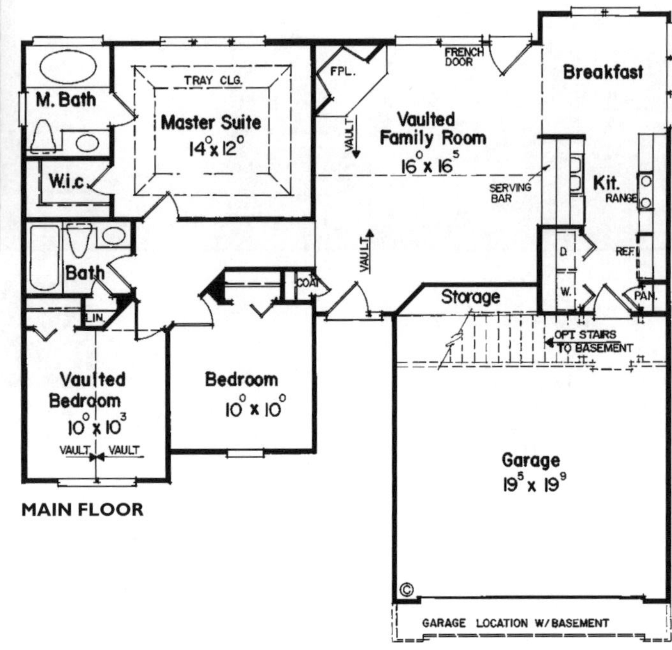

M. Bath
TRAY CLG.
Master Suite
14⁰x12⁰
W.i.c.
FPL.
FRENCH DOOR
Vaulted
Family Room
16⁰ x 16⁵
VAULT
SERVING BAR
Breakfast
Kit.
RANGE
REF
D.
W.
PAN.
Bath
LIN.
COAT
Storage
OPT STAIRS TO BASEMENT
Vaulted
Bedroom
10⁰ x 10³
VAULT
Bedroom
10⁰ x 10⁰
Garage
19⁵ x 19⁹
GARAGE LOCATION W/BASEMENT
MAIN FLOOR

Design 24723

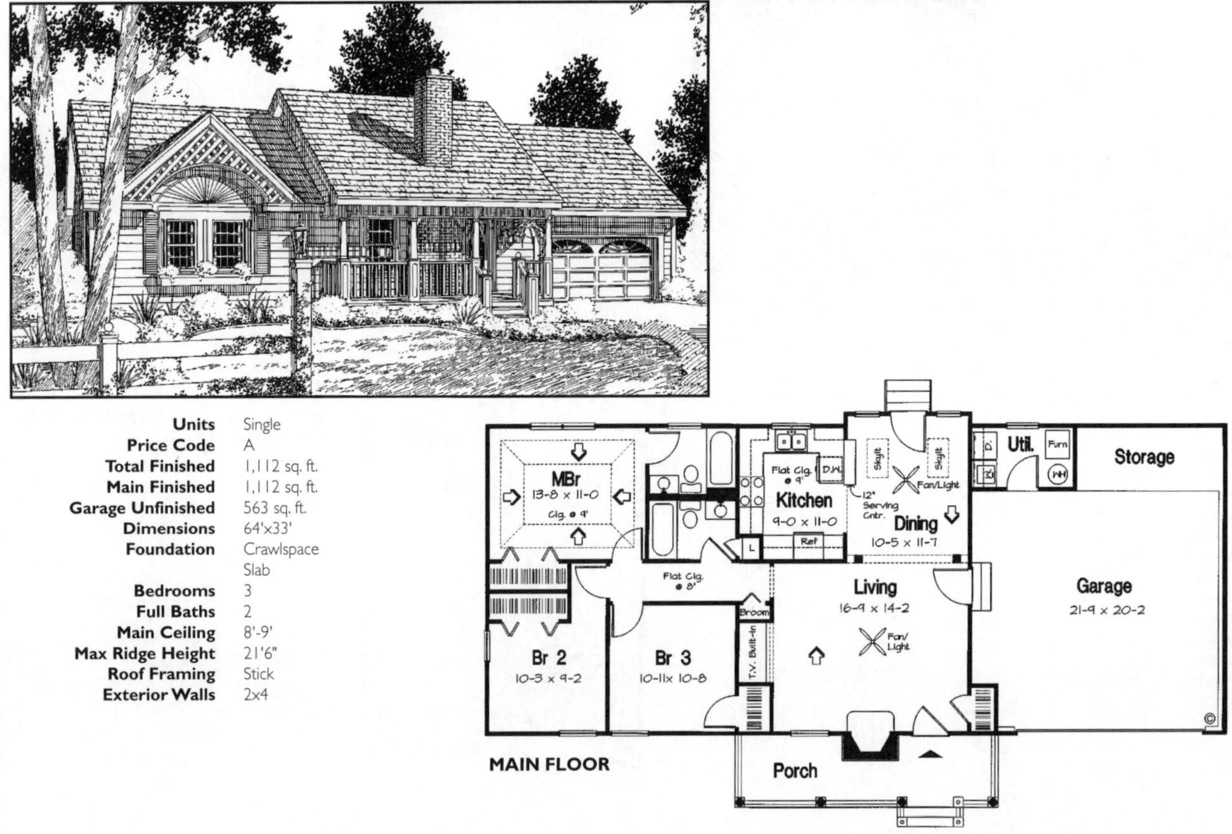

Units	Single
Price Code	A
Total Finished	1,112 sq. ft.
Main Finished	1,112 sq. ft.
Garage Unfinished	563 sq. ft.
Dimensions	64'x33'
Foundation	Crawlspace Slab
Bedrooms	3
Full Baths	2
Main Ceiling	8'-9'
Max Ridge Height	21'6"
Roof Framing	Stick
Exterior Walls	2x4

MBr
13-8 x 11-0
Clg. @ 9'
Flat Clg. @ 9'
D.W.
Kitchen
9-0 x 11-0
Ref
12" Serving Cntr.
Skylt
Fan/Light
Dining
10-5 x 11-7
Util.
Furn
WH
Storage
Flat Clg. @ 8'
Broom
Living
16-9 x 14-2
Fan/Light
T.V. Built-In
Br 2
10-3 x 9-2
Br 3
10-11x 10-8
Garage
21-9 x 20-2
Porch
MAIN FLOOR

Design 26114

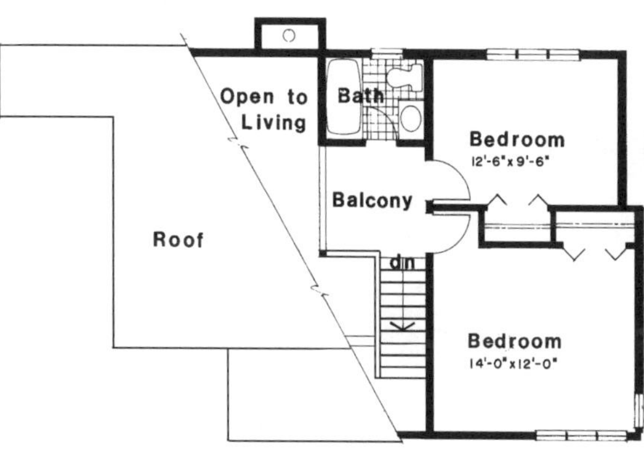
Open to Living
Bath
Bedroom
12'-6"x9'-6"
Balcony
Roof
dn
Bedroom
14'-0"x12'-0"

SECOND FLOOR

Units	Single
Price Code	A
Total Finished	1,112 sq. ft.
First Finished	696 sq. ft.
Second Finished	416 sq. ft.
Basement Unfinished	696 sq. ft.
Dimensions	32'x24'
Foundation	Basement
Bedrooms	3
Full Baths	1
Half Baths	1
Max Ridge Height	32'
Roof Framing	Stick
Exterior Walls	2x6

Storage
Dining
9'-0"x12'-0"
Kitchen
10'-0"x7'-0"
Living
12'-0"x18'-0"
Lav
Deck
dn
up
Bedroom/Den
13'-0"x8'-6"
Entry

FIRST FLOOR

Design 32122

PHOTOGRAPHY: JAMES SALOMON

Please note: The photographed home may have been modified to suit homeowner preferences. If you order plans, have a builder or design professional check them against the photograph to confirm actual construction details.

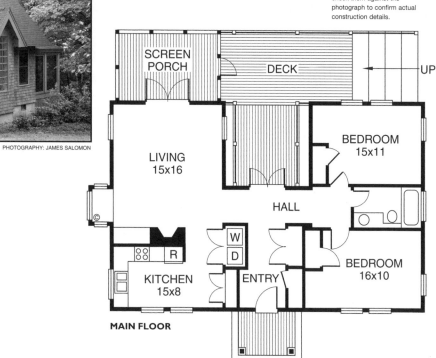

Units	Single
Price Code	A
Total Finished	1,112 sq. ft.
Main Finished	1,112 sq. ft.
Basement Unfinished	484 sq. ft.
Deck Unfinished	280 sq. ft.
Porch Unfinished	152 sq. ft.
Dimensions	47'x45'6"
Foundation	Basement Crawlspace
Bedrooms	2
Full Baths	1
Main Ceiling	9'
Vaulted Ceiling	18'9"
Max Ridge Height	24'9"
Roof Framing	Stick
Exterior Walls	2x6

SCREEN PORCH
DECK
UP
LIVING
15x16
BEDROOM
15x11
HALL
W
D
R
KITCHEN
15x8
ENTRY
BEDROOM
16x10

MAIN FLOOR

Design 63137

Units	Single
Price Code	C
Total Finished	1,118 sq. ft.
Main Finished	1,118 sq. ft.
Dimensions	30'x60'
Foundation	Slab
Bedrooms	3
Full Baths	2
Max Ridge Height	15'11"
Roof Framing	Truss

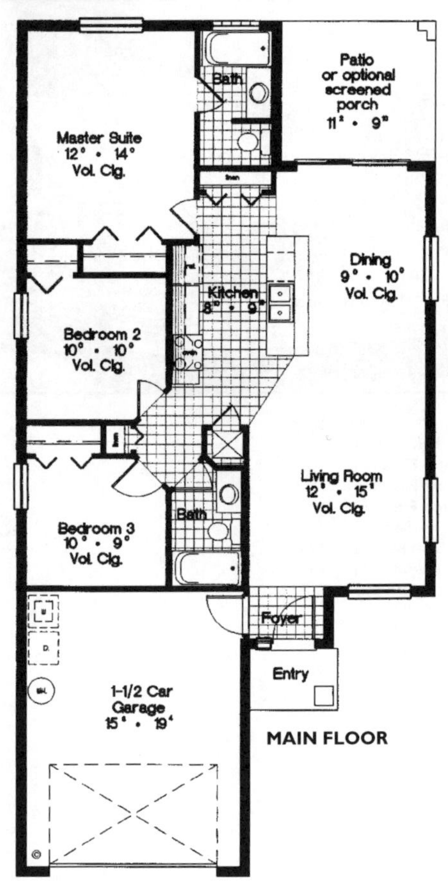

Patio or optional screened porch
11² • 9⁸
Bath
Master Suite
12⁰ • 14⁰
Vol. Clg.
Dining
9⁰ • 10⁰
Vol. Clg.
Kitchen
8⁰ • 9⁸
Bedroom 2
10⁰ • 10⁰
Vol. Clg.
Living Room
12⁸ • 15⁸
Vol. Clg.
Bath
Bedroom 3
10⁰ • 9⁰
Vol. Clg.
Foyer
Entry
1-1/2 Car Garage
15⁶ • 19⁴
MAIN FLOOR

Design 96538

Units	Single
Price Code	A
Total Finished	1,120 sq. ft.
Main Finished	1,120 sq. ft.
Garage Unfinished	288 sq. ft.
Porch Unfinished	150 sq. ft.
Dimensions	52'x34'
Foundation	Slab
Bedrooms	3
Full Baths	2
Main Ceiling	8'
Max Ridge Height	19'
Roof Framing	Stick
Exterior Walls	2x4

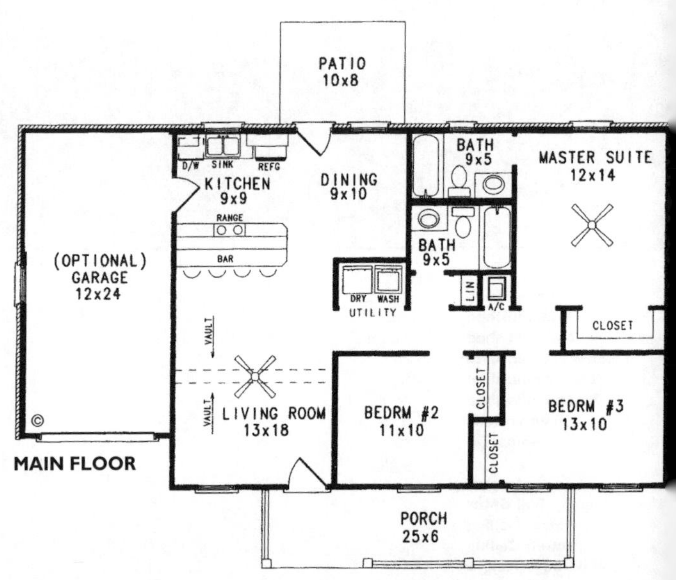

PATIO
10x8
D/W SINK REFG
KITCHEN
9x9
RANGE
BAR
DINING
9x10
BATH
9x5
MASTER SUITE
12x14
BATH
9x5
DRY WASH
UTILITY
LIN
A/C
CLOSET
(OPTIONAL)
GARAGE
12x24
VAULT
VAULT
LIVING ROOM
13x18
BEDRM #2
11x10
CLOSET
CLOSET
BEDRM #3
13x10
MAIN FLOOR
PORCH
25x6

Design 65091

Units	Single
Price Code	A
Total Finished	1,122 sq. ft.
Main Finished	1,122 sq. ft.
Garage Unfinished	294 sq. ft.
Dimensions	32'x48'
Foundation	Basement
Bedrooms	2
Full Baths	1

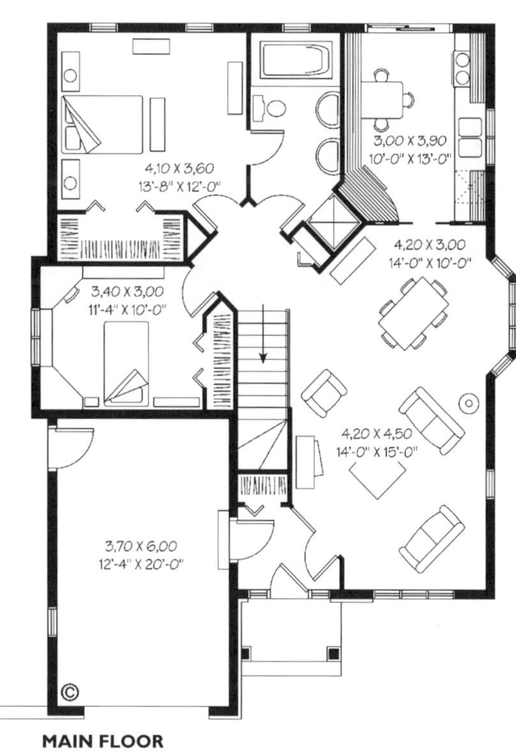
4,10 X 3,60
13'-8" X 12'-0"
3,00 X 3,90
10'-0" X 13'-0"
4,20 X 3,00
14'-0" X 10'-0"
3,40 X 3,00
11'-4" X 10'-0"
4,20 X 4,50
14'-0" X 15'-0"
3,70 X 6,00
12'-4" X 20'-0"
©

MAIN FLOOR

Design 66079

Units	Single
Price Code	A
Total Finished	1,125 sq. ft.
Main Finished	1,125 sq. ft.
Garage Unfinished	440 sq. ft.
Deck Unfinished	110 sq. ft.
Porch Unfinished	40 sq. ft.
Dimensions	45'x45'4"
Foundation	Slab
Bedrooms	3
Full Baths	1
3/4 Baths	1
Max Ridge Height	19'
Roof Framing	Stick
Exterior Walls	2x4

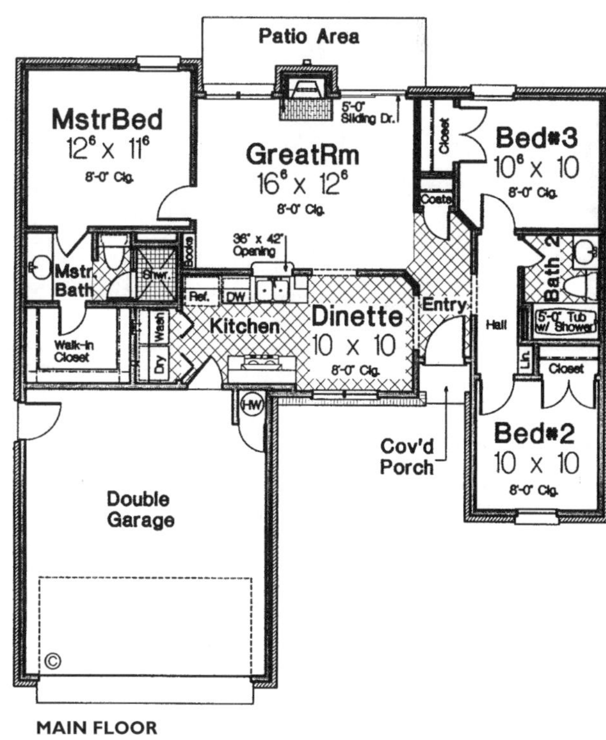
Patio Area
MstrBed
12^{6} x 11^{6}
8'-0" Clg.
5'-0" Sliding Dr.
GreatRm
16^{6} x 12^{6}
8'-0" Clg.
Closet
Bed#3
10^{6} x 10
8'-0" Clg.
Coats
36" x 42" Opening
Mstr Bath
Shwr.
Ref.
DW
Kitchen
Dinette
10 x 10
8'-0" Clg.
Entry
Hall
Bath 2
5'-0" Tub w/ Shower
Wash
Dry
Walk-in Closet
Lin.
Closet
HW
Cov'd Porch
Bed#2
10 x 10
8'-0" Clg.
Double Garage
©

MAIN FLOOR

Design 65414

Units	Single
Price Code	A
Total Finished	1,129 sq. ft.
Main Finished	1,129 sq. ft.
Basement Unfinished	1,129 sq. ft.
Garage Unfinished	317 sq. ft.
Deck Unfinished	48 sq. ft.
Porch Unfinished	22 sq. ft.
Dimensions	49'x37'4"
Foundation	Basement
Bedrooms	2
Full Baths	1
Main Ceiling	8'
Max Ridge Height	29'7"
Roof Framing	Truss
Exterior Walls	2x6

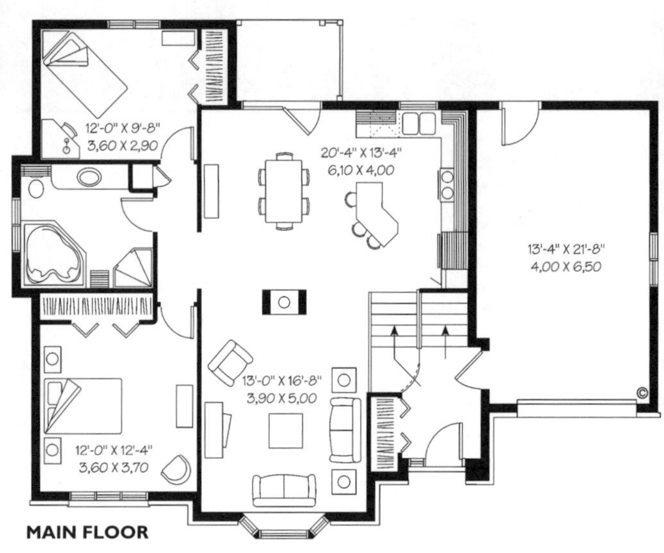

12'-0" X 9'-8"
3,60 X 2,90
20'-4" X 13'-4"
6,10 X 4,00
13'-4" X 21'-8"
4,00 X 6,50
13'-0" X 16'-8"
3,90 X 5,00
12'-0" X 12'-4"
3,60 X 3,70
MAIN FLOOR

Design 98498

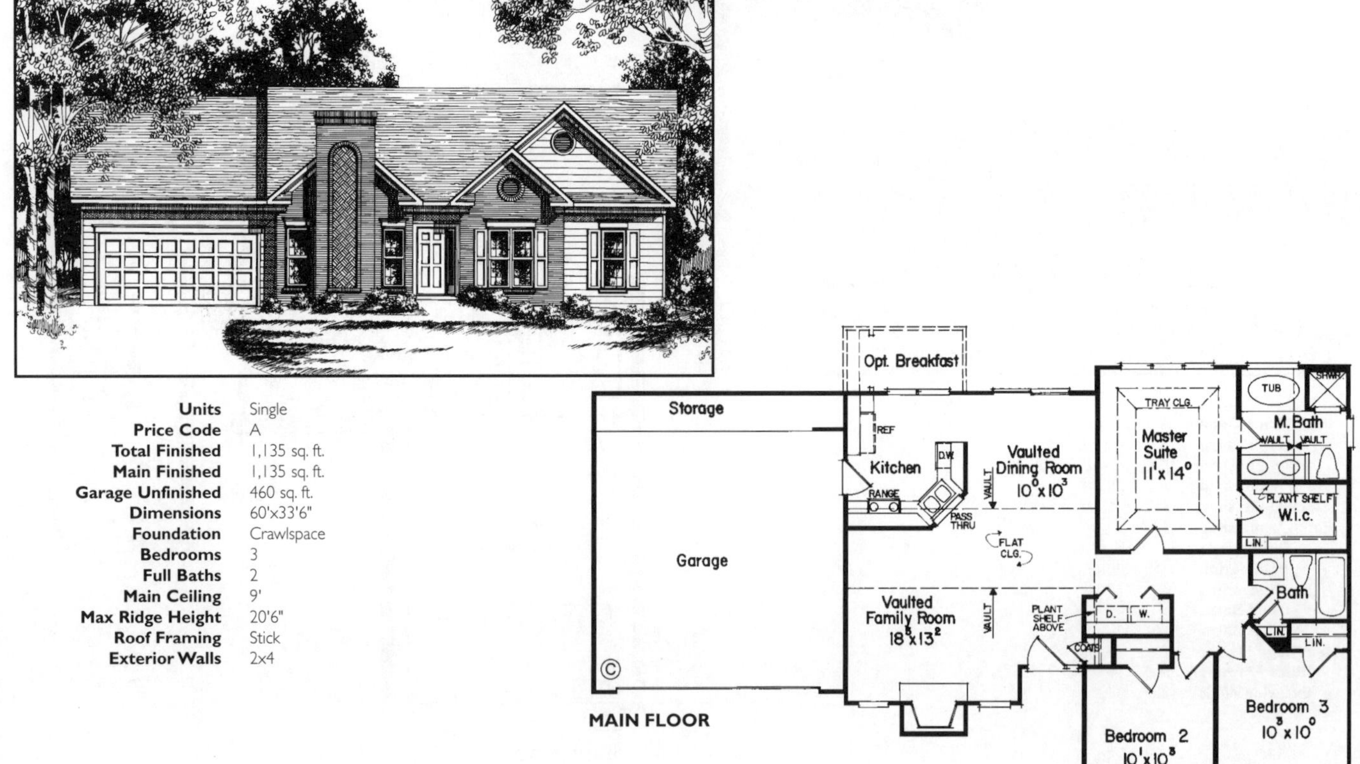

Opt. Breakfast
Storage
REF
Kitchen
D.W.
RANGE
PASS THRU
Vaulted Dining Room
10⁰x10³
VAULT
FLAT CLG.
TRAY CLG.
Master Suite
11¹x14⁰
TUB
SHWR
M. Bath
VAULT
PLANT SHELF
W.i.c.
LIN.
Garage
Vaulted Family Room
18⁵x13²
PLANT SHELF ABOVE
D.
W.
COATS
Bath
LIN.
Bedroom 2
10¹x10³
Bedroom 3
10³x10⁰
MAIN FLOOR

Units	Single
Price Code	A
Total Finished	1,135 sq. ft.
Main Finished	1,135 sq. ft.
Garage Unfinished	460 sq. ft.
Dimensions	60'x33'6"
Foundation	Crawlspace
Bedrooms	3
Full Baths	2
Main Ceiling	9'
Max Ridge Height	20'6"
Roof Framing	Stick
Exterior Walls	2x4

Design 65467

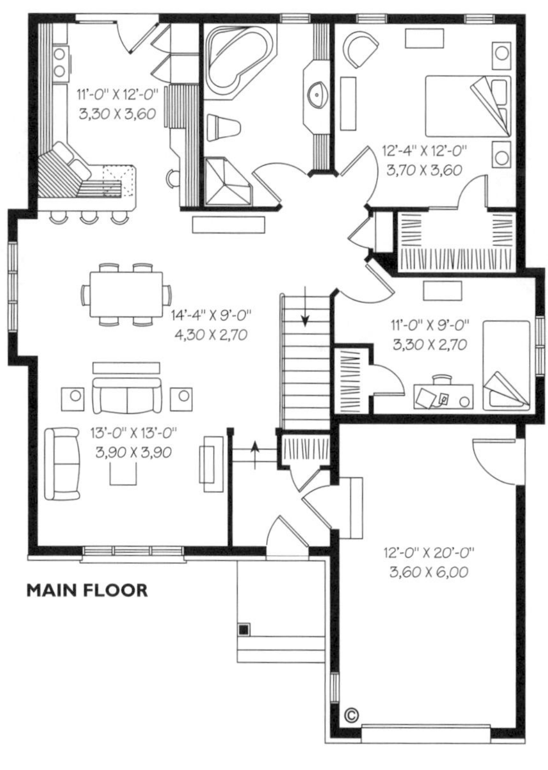
11'-0" X 12'-0"
3,30 X 3,60
12'-4" X 12'-0"
3,70 X 3,60
14'-4" X 9'-0"
4,30 X 2,70
11'-0" X 9'-0"
3,30 X 2,70
13'-0" X 13'-0"
3,90 X 3,90
12'-0" X 20'-0"
3,60 X 6,00
MAIN FLOOR

Units	Single
Price Code	A
Total Finished	1,138 sq. ft.
Main Finished	1,138 sq. ft.
Basement Unfinished	1,138 sq. ft.
Garage Unfinished	278 sq. ft.
Deck Unfinished	40 sq. ft.
Dimensions	34'x48'
Foundation	Basement
Bedrooms	2
Full Baths	1
Main Ceiling	8'
Max Ridge Height	28'2"
Roof Framing	Truss
Exterior Walls	2x6

Design 69026

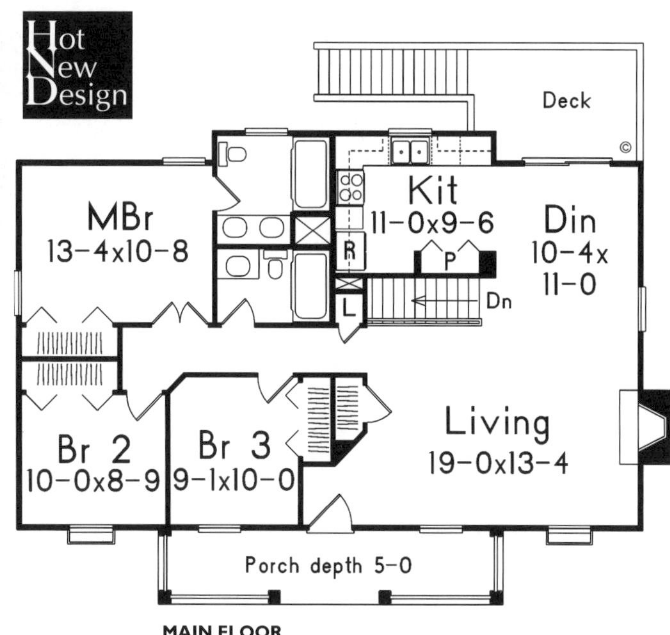
Hot
New
Design
Deck
MBr
13-4x10-8
Kit
11-0x9-6
Din
10-4x
11-0
R
P
L
Dn
Br 2
10-0x8-9
Br 3
9-1x10-0
Living
19-0x13-4
Porch depth 5-0
MAIN FLOOR

Units	Single
Price Code	A
Total Finished	1,140 sq. ft.
Main Finished	1,140 sq. ft.
Dimensions	44'x27'
Foundation	Basement
Bedrooms	3
Full Baths	2

Design 68093

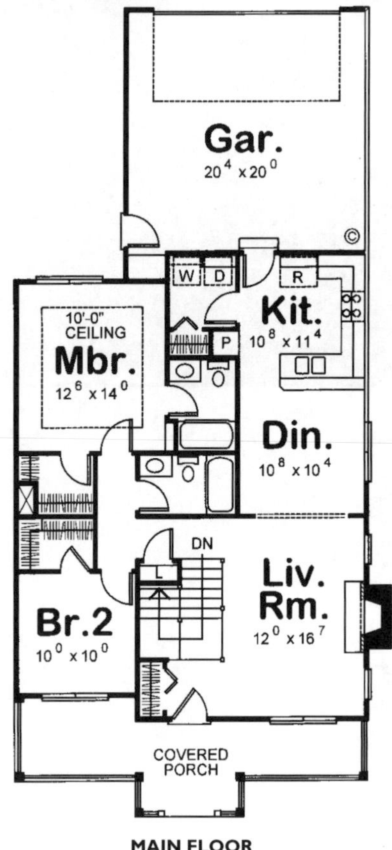

Gar.
20 4 x 20 0
W D
R
Kit.
10 8 x 11 4
P
10'-0" CEILING
Mbr.
12 6 x 14 0
Din.
10 8 x 10 4
DN
L
Liv. Rm.
12 0 x 16 7
Br.2
10 0 x 10 0
COVERED PORCH

MAIN FLOOR

Units	Single
Price Code	A
Total Finished	1,142 sq. ft.
Main Finished	1,142 sq. ft.
Garage Unfinished	435 sq. ft.
Dimensions	30'4"x64'8"
Foundation	Basement
Bedrooms	2
Full Baths	2
Main Ceiling	9'
Max Ridge Height	20'3"
Roof Framing	Stick
Exterior Walls	2x4

* Alternate foundation options available at an additional charge.
Please call 1-800-235-5700 for more information.

Design 34003

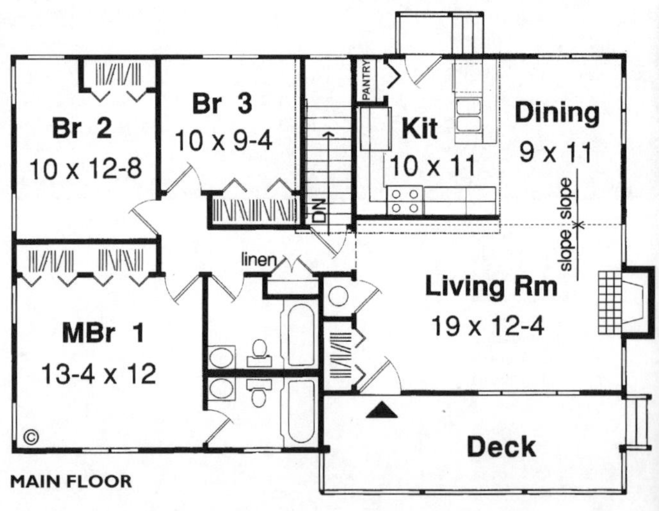

Br 2
10 x 12-8
Br 3
10 x 9-4
PANTRY
Kit
10 x 11
Dining
9 x 11
DN
slope
slope
linen
MBr 1
13-4 x 12
Living Rm
19 x 12-4
Deck

MAIN FLOOR

Units	Single
Price Code	A
Total Finished	1,146 sq. ft.
Main Finished	1,146 sq. ft.
Dimensions	44'x28'
Foundation	Basement Crawlspace Slab
Bedrooms	3
Full Baths	2
Main Ceiling	8'
Max Ridge Height	16'
Roof Framing	Stick
Exterior Walls	2x4, 2x6

Design 99361

Units	Single
Price Code	A
Total Finished	1,146 sq. ft.
Main Finished	1,146 sq. ft.
Dimensions	46'x48'
Foundation	Basement
Bedrooms	3
Full Baths	1
3/4 Baths	1
Max Ridge Height	18'
Roof Framing	Truss
Exterior Walls	2x4

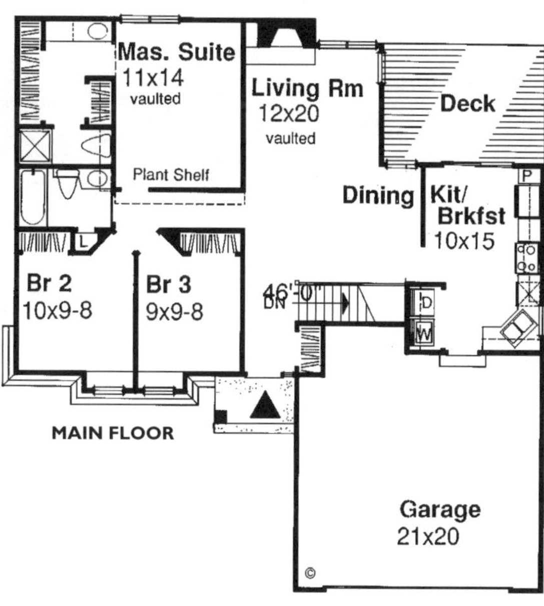
Mas. Suite
11x14
vaulted
Plant Shelf
Living Rm
12x20
vaulted
Deck
Dining
Kit/
Brkfst
10x15
Br 2
10x9-8
Br 3
9x9-8
46'-0"
DN
Garage
21x20
MAIN FLOOR

Design 65014

Units	Single
Price Code	A
Total Finished	1,148 sq. ft.
First Finished	728 sq. ft.
Second Finished	420 sq. ft.
Basement Unfinished	728 sq. ft.
Dimensions	28'x26'
Foundation	Basement
Bedrooms	1
Full Baths	1
Half Baths	1
First Ceiling	8'
Second Ceiling	8'
Max Ridge Height	25'4"
Roof Framing	Truss
Exterior Walls	2x6

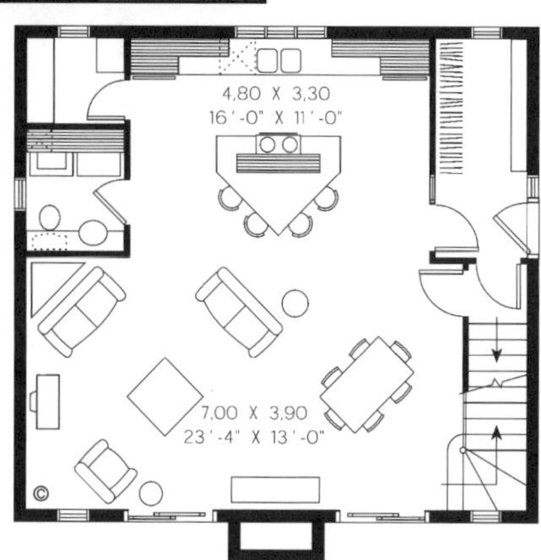
4,80 X 3,30
16'-0" X 11'-0"
7,00 X 3,90
23'-4" X 13'-0"
FIRST FLOOR

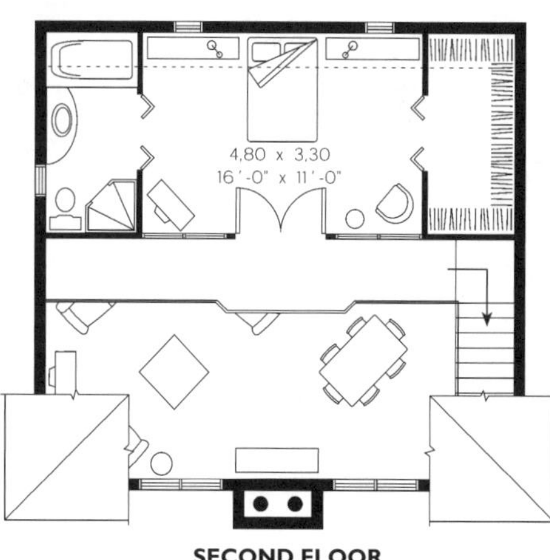
4,80 x 3,30
16'-0" x 11'-0"
SECOND FLOOR

Design 60112

Units	Single
Price Code	A
Total Finished	1,149 sq. ft.
Main Finished	1,149 sq. ft.
Basement Unfinished	1,166 sq. ft.
Garage Unfinished	422 sq. ft.
Dimensions	47'6"x42'4"
Foundation	Basement Crawlspace
Bedrooms	3
Full Baths	2
Main Ceiling	9'
Max Ridge Height	21'10"
Roof Framing	Stick
Exterior Walls	2x4

D.W.
Kitchen
REF.
PANTRY
COATS
STAIRS DN.

OPTIONAL BASEMENT STAIR LOCATION

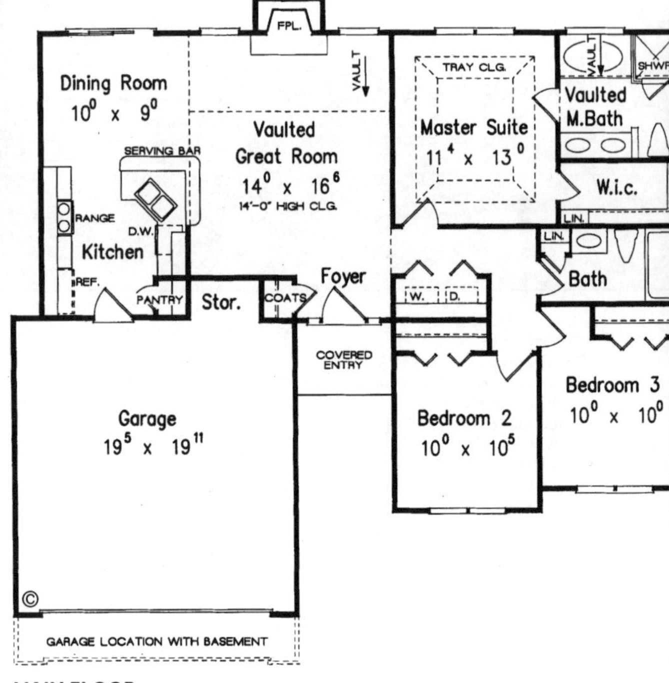
FPL.
Dining Room
10⁰ x 9⁰
VAULT
Vaulted Great Room
14⁰ x 16⁶
14'-0" HIGH CLG.
SERVING BAR
RANGE
D.W.
Kitchen
REF.
PANTRY
Stor.
COATS
Foyer
TRAY CLG.
Master Suite
11⁴ x 13⁰
Vaulted M.Bath
SHWR.
W.i.c.
LIN.
Bath
W.
D.
COVERED ENTRY
Garage
19⁵ x 19¹¹
Bedroom 2
10⁰ x 10⁵
Bedroom 3
10⁰ x 10⁰
GARAGE LOCATION WITH BASEMENT

MAIN FLOOR

Design 65462

Units	Single
Price Code	A
Total Finished	1,163 sq. ft.
Main Finished	1,163 sq. ft.
Basement Unfinished	1,163 sq. ft.
Deck Unfinished	15 sq. ft.
Porch Unfinished	32 sq. ft.
Dimensions	30'x41'
Foundation	Basement
Bedrooms	2
Full Baths	1
Main Ceiling	8'
Max Ridge Height	21'8"
Roof Framing	Truss
Exterior Walls	2x6

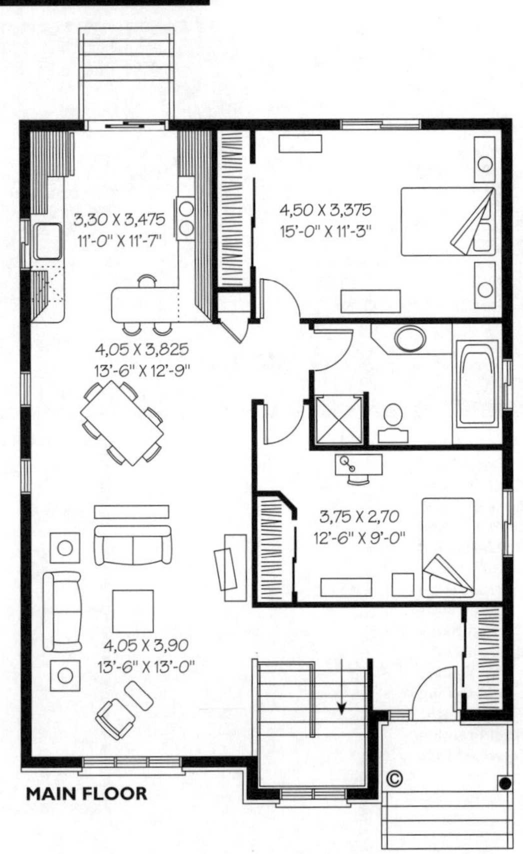
3,30 X 3,475
11'-0" X 11'-7"
4,50 X 3,375
15'-0" X 11'-3"
4,05 X 3,825
13'-6" X 12'-9"
3,75 X 2,70
12'-6" X 9'-0"
4,05 X 3,90
13'-6" X 13'-0"

MAIN FLOOR

Design 93006

Units	Single
Price Code	A
Total Finished	1,163 sq. ft.
Main Finished	1,163 sq. ft.
Garage Unfinished	449 sq. ft.
Porch Unfinished	19 sq. ft.
Dimensions	39'2"x55'10"
Foundation	Slab
Bedrooms	3
Full Baths	1
3/4 Baths	1
Max Ridge Height	19'
Roof Framing	Stick
Exterior Walls	2x4

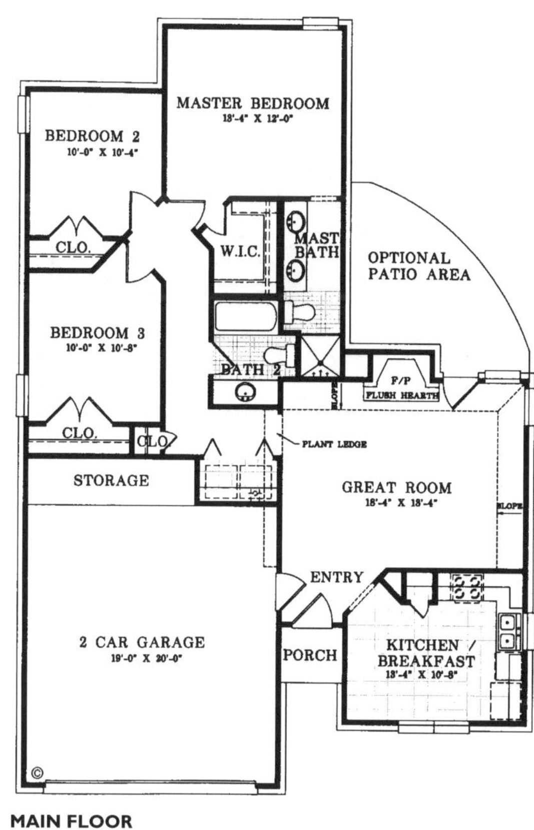
MASTER BEDROOM
13'-4" X 12'-0"
BEDROOM 2
10'-0" X 10'-4"
CLO.
W.I.C.
MAST BATH
OPTIONAL PATIO AREA
BEDROOM 3
10'-0" X 10'-8"
BATH 2
F/P FLUSH HEARTH
CLO.
CLO
PLANT LEDGE
STORAGE
GREAT ROOM
18'-4" X 18'-4"
ENTRY
2 CAR GARAGE
19'-0" X 20'-0"
PORCH
KITCHEN / BREAKFAST
13'-4" X 10'-8"

MAIN FLOOR

Design 97296

Units	Single
Price Code	A
Total Finished	1,166 sq. ft.
Main Finished	1,166 sq. ft.
Basement Unfinished	1,166 sq. ft.
Dimensions	43'4"x34'
Foundation	Basement
Bedrooms	3
Full Baths	2
Max Ridge Height	22'3"
Roof Framing	Stick
Exterior Walls	2x4

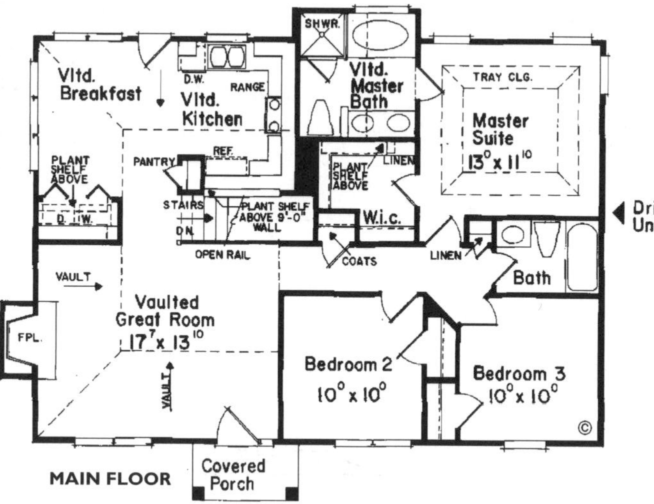
SHWR.
Vltd. Breakfast
D.W.
RANGE
Vltd. Kitchen
Vltd. Master Bath
TRAY CLG.
Master Suite
13⁰ x 11¹⁰
PLANT SHELF ABOVE
PANTRY
REF.
PLANT SHELF ABOVE
LINEN
STAIRS
PLANT SHELF ABOVE 9'-0" WALL
DN
W.i.c.
OPEN RAIL
COATS
LINEN
Drive Under
VAULT
Bath
Vaulted Great Room
17⁷ x 13¹⁰
FPL.
Bedroom 2
10⁰ x 10⁰
Bedroom 3
10⁰ x 10⁰
VAULT
Covered Porch

MAIN FLOOR

Design 98497

Units	Single
Price Code	A
Total Finished	1,169 sq. ft.
Main Finished	1,169 sq. ft.
Basement Unfinished	1,194 sq. ft.
Garage Unfinished	400 sq. ft.
Dimensions	40'x49'6"
Foundation	Basement Crawlspace Slab
Bedrooms	3
Full Baths	2
Main Ceiling	9'
Max Ridge Height	21'
Roof Framing	Stick
Exterior Walls	2x4

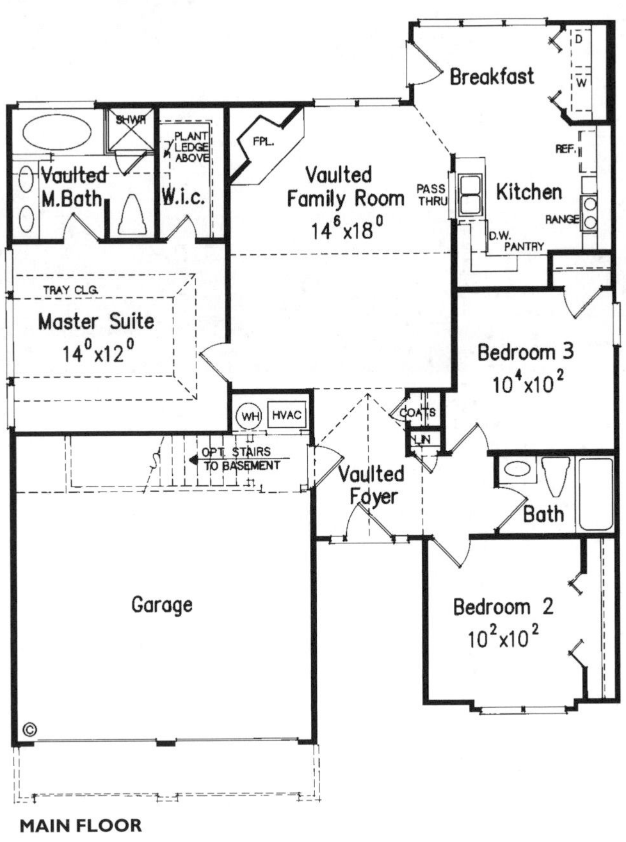
Breakfast
D
W
REF.
Kitchen
RANGE
D.W.
PANTRY
PASS THRU
SHWR
PLANT LEDGE ABOVE
FPL.
Vaulted M.Bath
W.i.c.
Vaulted Family Room
14⁶x18⁰
TRAY CLG.
Master Suite
14⁰x12⁰
Bedroom 3
10⁴x10²
WH
HVAC
COATS
LIN
OPT. STAIRS TO BASEMENT
Vaulted Foyer
Bath
Garage
Bedroom 2
10²x10²
©

MAIN FLOOR

Design 65425

Units	Single
Price Code	A
Total Finished	1,170 sq. ft.
First Finished	585 sq. ft.
Second Finished	585 sq. ft.
Basement Unfinished	585 sq. ft.
Deck Unfinished	32 sq. ft.
Porch Unfinished	43 sq. ft.
Dimensions	24'x24'
Foundation	Basement
Bedrooms	3
Full Baths	1
Half Baths	1
First Ceiling	8'
Second Ceiling	8'
Max Ridge Height	27'6"
Roof Framing	Truss
Exterior Walls	2x6

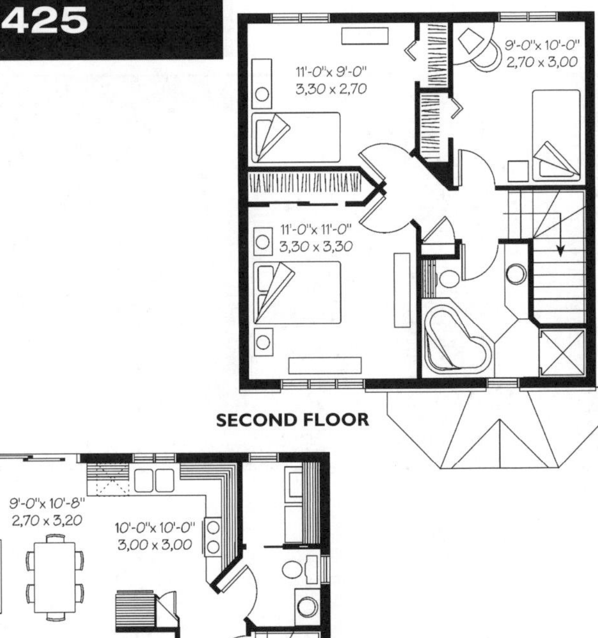
11'-0"x 9'-0"
3,30 x 2,70
9'-0"x 10'-0"
2,70 x 3,00
11'-0"x 11'-0"
3,30 x 3,30
SECOND FLOOR
9'-0"x 10'-8"
2,70 x 3,20
10'-0"x 10'-0"
3,00 x 3,00
13'-0"x 12'-0"
3,90 x 3,60
FIRST FLOOR
©

Design 24241

Units	Single
Price Code	A
Total Finished	1,174 sq. ft.
Main Finished	1,174 sq. ft.
Dimensions	28'x54'
Foundation	Crawlspace
Bedrooms	3
Full Baths	2
Max Ridge Height	21'
Roof Framing	Stick
Exterior Walls	2x4

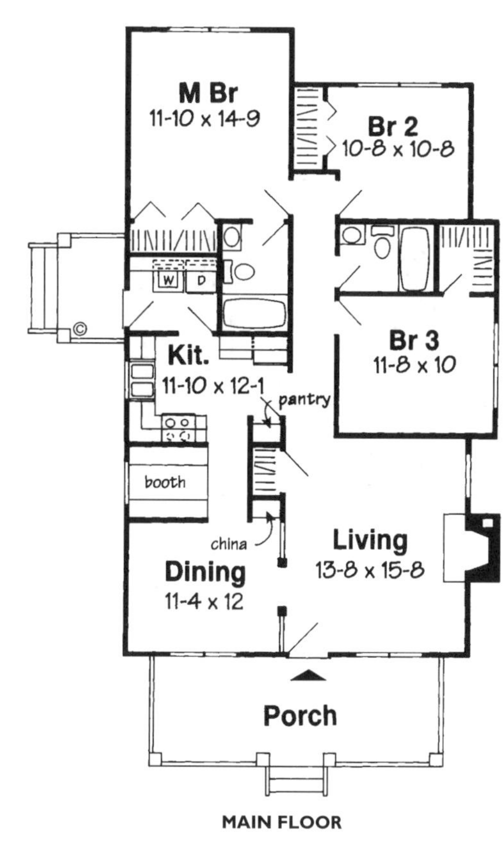
M Br
11-10 x 14-9
Br 2
10-8 x 10-8
W
D
Br 3
11-8 x 10
Kit.
11-10 x 12-1
pantry
booth
china
Living
13-8 x 15-8
Dining
11-4 x 12
Porch

MAIN FLOOR

Design 65075

Units	Single
Price Code	A
Total Finished	1,176 sq. ft.
Main Finished	1,176 sq. ft.
Basement Unfinished	1,176 sq. ft.
Garage Unfinished	401 sq. ft.
Porch Unfinished	110 sq. ft.
Dimensions	58'x28'
Foundation	Basement
Bedrooms	3
Full Baths	1
Max Ridge Height	18'10"
Roof Framing	Truss
Exterior Walls	2x6

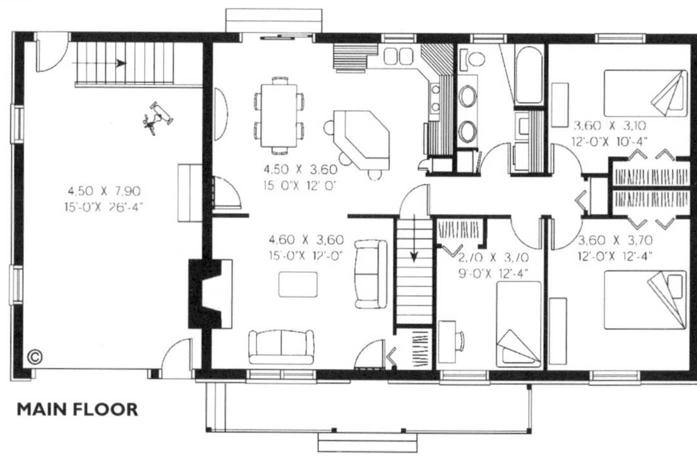
4.50 X 7.90
15'-0"X 26'-4"
4.50 X 3.60
15'0"X 12'0"
4.60 X 3.60
15'-0"X 12'-0"
2.70 X 3.70
9'-0"X 12'-4"
3.60 X 3.10
12'-0"X 10'-4"
3.60 X 3.70
12'-0"X 12'-4"

MAIN FLOOR

Design 98461

Units	Single
Price Code	A
Total Finished	1,185 sq. ft.
Main Finished	1,185 sq. ft.
Basement Unfinished	1,185 sq. ft.
Garage Unfinished	425 sq. ft.
Dimensions	50'x49'4"
Foundation	Basement Crawlspace
Bedrooms	3
Full Baths	2
Max Ridge Height	22'
Roof Framing	Stick
Exterior Walls	2x4

CAD **FILES AVAILABLE** For more information call 800-235-5700

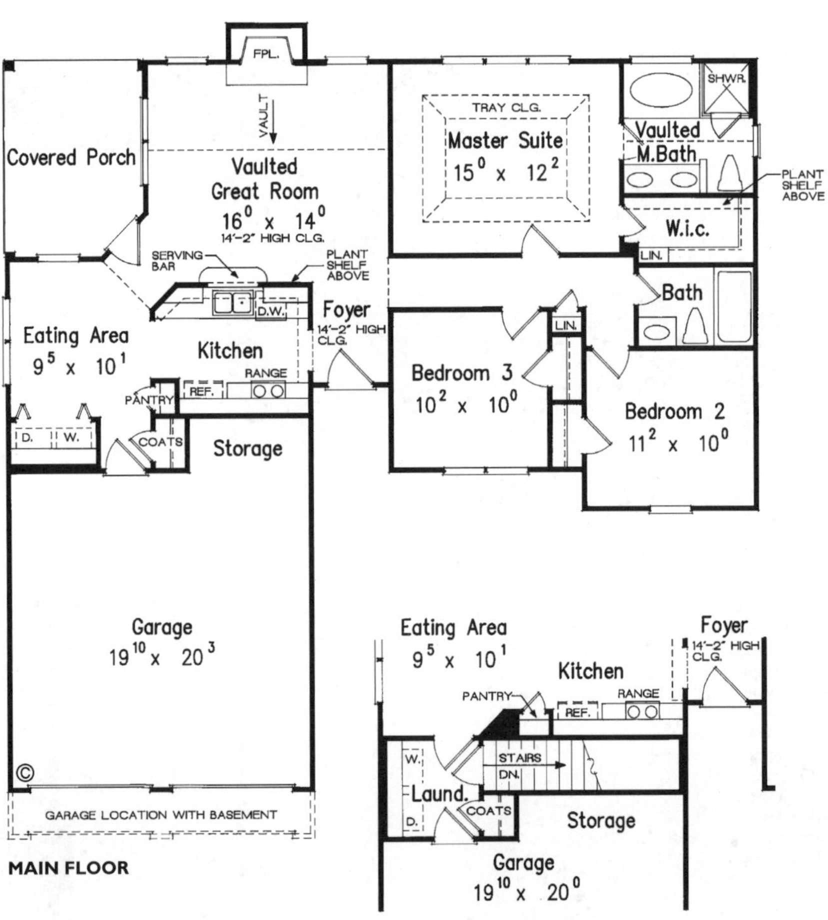

FPL.
VAULT
Covered Porch
Vaulted Great Room
16⁰ x 14⁰
14'-2" HIGH CLG.
TRAY CLG.
Master Suite
15⁰ x 12²
SHWR.
Vaulted M.Bath
PLANT SHELF ABOVE
W.i.c.
LIN.
SERVING BAR
PLANT SHELF ABOVE
D.W.
Foyer
14'-2" HIGH CLG.
Eating Area
9⁵ x 10¹
Kitchen
RANGE
REF.
PANTRY
Bath
LIN.
Bedroom 3
10² x 10⁰
Bedroom 2
11² x 10⁰
D.
W.
COATS
Storage
Garage
19¹⁰ x 20³
GARAGE LOCATION WITH BASEMENT
MAIN FLOOR
Eating Area
9⁵ x 10¹
Foyer
14'-2" HIGH CLG.
Kitchen
PANTRY
RANGE
REF.
STAIRS DN.
W.
Laund.
D.
COATS
Storage
Garage
19¹⁰ x 20⁰
OPTIONAL BASEMENT STAIR LOCATION

Design 97338

Units	Single
Price Code	A
Total Finished	1,186 sq. ft.
Main Finished	1,186 sq. ft.
Basement Unfinished	1,186 sq. ft.
Garage Unfinished	419 sq. ft.
Dimensions	66'4"x32'
Foundation	Basement
Bedrooms	3
Full Baths	1
Main Ceiling	9'
Max Ridge Height	20'8"
Roof Framing	Truss
Exterior Walls	2x6

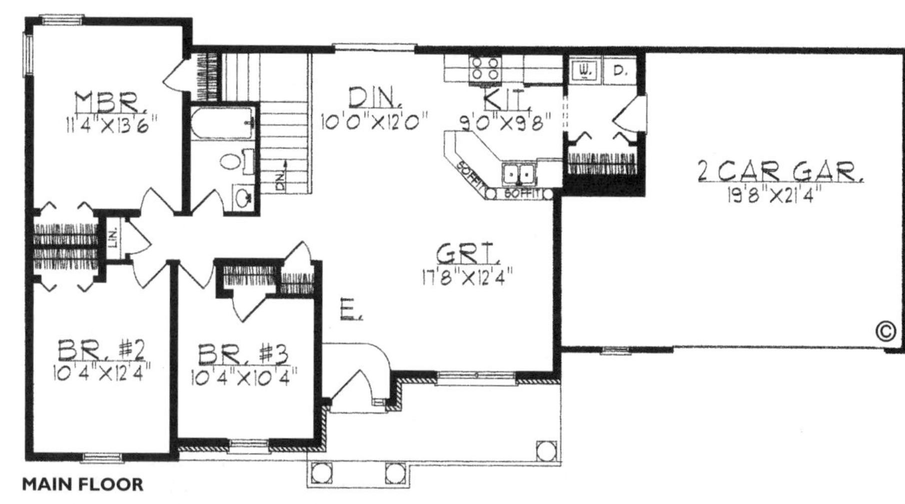
MBR.
11'4"X13'6"
DIN.
10'0"X12'0"
KIT.
9'0"X9'8"
2 CAR GAR.
19'8"X21'4"
GRT.
17'8"X12'4"
E.
BR. #2
10'4"X12'4"
BR. #3
10'4"X10'4"

MAIN FLOOR

Design 65468

Units	Single
Price Code	A
Total Finished	1,191 sq. ft.
Main Finished	1,191 sq. ft.
Basement Unfinished	1,155 sq. ft.
Garage Unfinished	271 sq. ft.
Porch Unfinished	79 sq. ft.
Dimensions	34'8"x48'
Foundation	Basement
Bedrooms	2
Full Baths	1
Main Ceiling	8'
Max Ridge Height	21'3"
Roof Framing	Truss
Exterior Walls	2x6

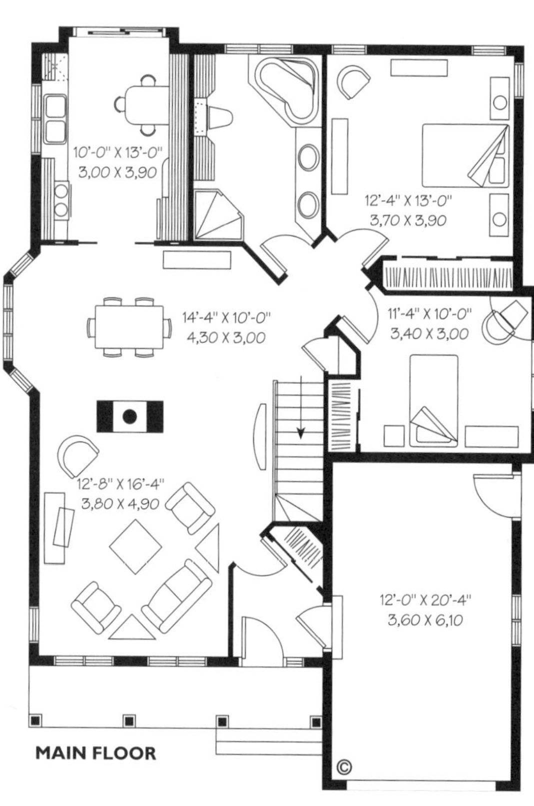
10'-0" X 13'-0"
3,00 X 3,90
12'-4" X 13'-0"
3,70 X 3,90
14'-4" X 10'-0"
4,30 X 3,00
11'-4" X 10'-0"
3,40 X 3,00
12'-8" X 16'-4"
3,80 X 4,90
12'-0" X 20'-4"
3,60 X 6,10

MAIN FLOOR

Design 65648

Units	Single
Price Code	A
Total Finished	1,191 sq. ft.
Main Finished	1,191 sq. ft.
Dimensions	45'x59'
Foundation	Crawlspace Slab
Bedrooms	3
Full Baths	2
Main Ceiling	8'
Max Ridge Height	23'
Roof Framing	Stick
Exterior Walls	2x6

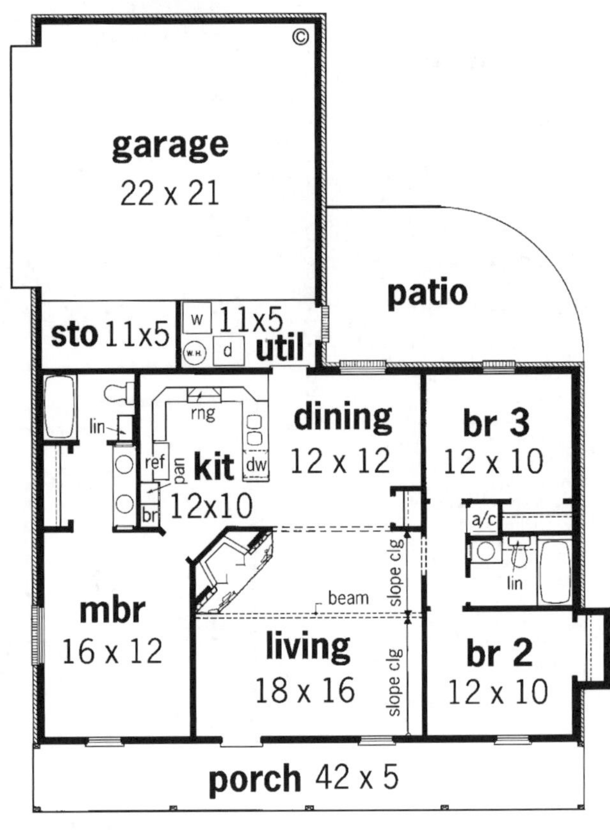

garage
22 x 21
patio
sto 11x5
11x5 util
w
d
dining
12 x 12
br 3
12 x 10
rng
lin
ref
pan
kit
12x10
dw
br
a/c
lin
beam
slope clg
mbr
16 x 12
living
18 x 16
slope clg
br 2
12 x 10
porch 42 x 5

MAIN FLOOR

Design 97467

Units	Single
Price Code	A
Total Finished	1,191 sq. ft.
Main Finished	1,191 sq. ft.
Garage Unfinished	492 sq. ft.
Deck Unfinished	321 sq. ft.
Dimensions	48'4"x43'8"
Foundation	Basement
Bedrooms	3
Full Baths	2
Main Ceiling	9'
Max Ridge Height	23'3"
Roof Framing	Stick
Exterior Walls	2x4

* Alternate foundation options available at an additional charge. Please call 1-800-235-5700 for more information.

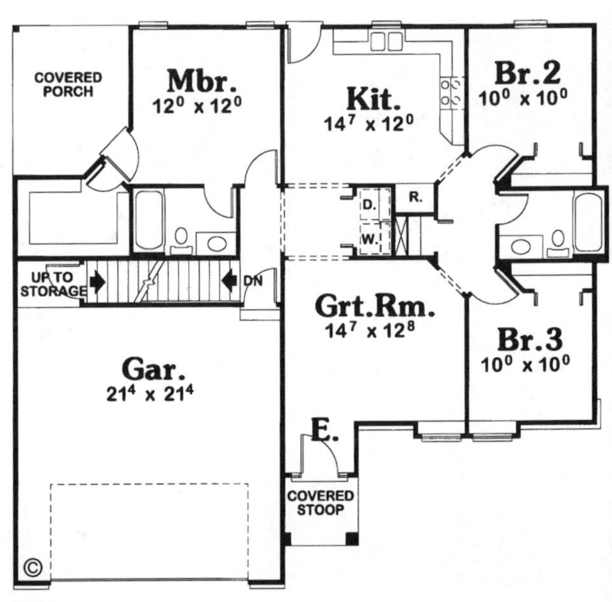

COVERED PORCH
Mbr.
12⁰ x 12⁰
Kit.
14⁷ x 12⁰
Br.2
10⁰ x 10⁰
D.
R.
W.
UP TO STORAGE
DN
Grt.Rm.
14⁷ x 12⁸
Gar.
21⁴ x 21⁴
Br.3
10⁰ x 10⁰
E.
COVERED STOOP

MAIN FLOOR

Design 99919

Units	Single
Price Code	A
Total Finished	1,195 sq. ft.
Main Finished	1,195 sq. ft.
Porch Unfinished	77 sq. ft.
Dimensions	55'x29'6"
Foundation	Crawlspace
Bedrooms	3
Full Baths	1
Half Baths	1
Main Ceiling	8'
Max Ridge Height	14'6"
Roof Framing	Stick
Exterior Walls	2x6

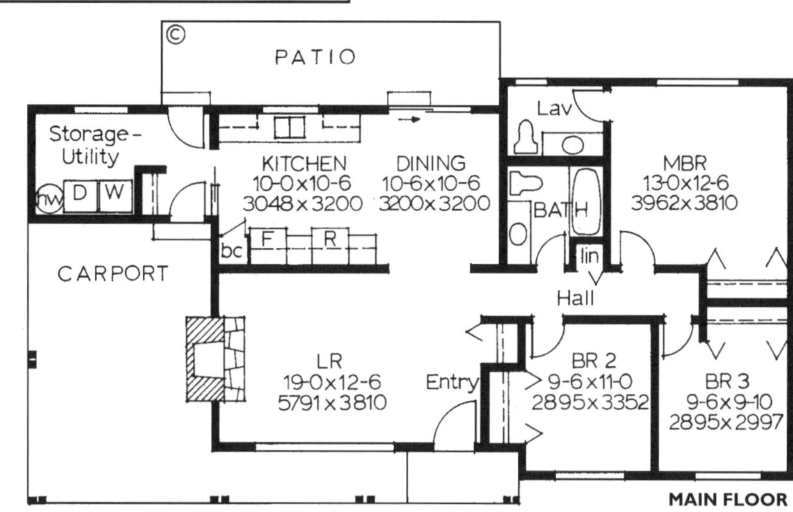
PATIO
Storage-Utility
hw D W
KITCHEN 10-0x10-6 3048x3200
DINING 10-6x10-6 3200x3200
Lav
BATH
lin
MBR 13-0x12-6 3962x3810
bc F R
CARPORT
Hall
LR 19-0x12-6 5791x3810
Entry
BR 2 9-6x11-0 2895x3352
BR 3 9-6x9-10 2895x2997
MAIN FLOOR

Design 92430

Units	Single
Price Code	A
Total Finished	1,197 sq. ft.
Main Finished	1,197 sq. ft.
Garage Unfinished	380 sq. ft.
Porch Unfinished	76 sq. ft.
Dimensions	52'x42'
Foundation	Crawlspace Slab
Bedrooms	3
Full Baths	2
Main Ceiling	8'
Vaulted Ceiling	12'
Max Ridge Height	17'8"
Roof Framing	Truss
Exterior Walls	2x4

OPTIONAL BAY
MASTER BEDROOM 14x12
VAULT
VAULT
FAMILY ROOM 14x18
DINING 10x9
DW
PLANT SHELF
BEDROOM 3 12x11
BEDROOM 2 12x11
MAIN FLOOR
GARAGE 19x20

Design 91107

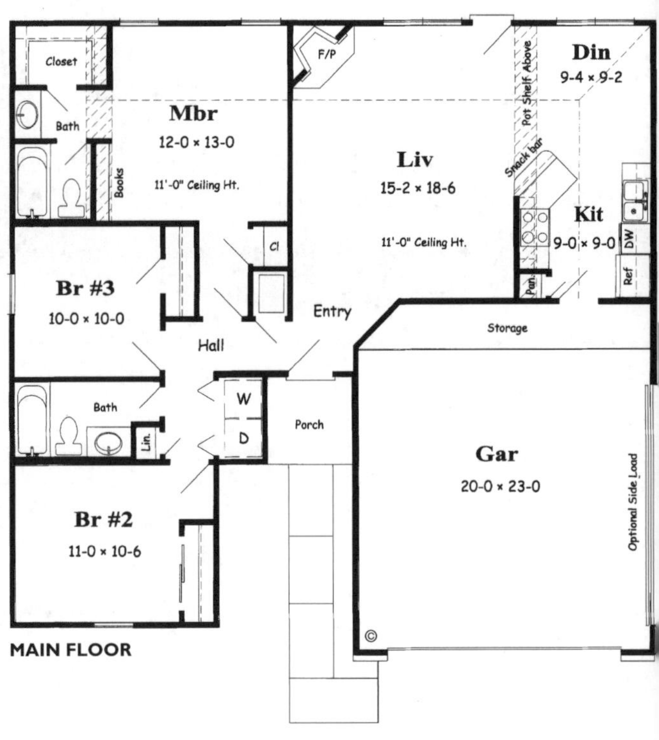

Closet
Bath
Mbr
12-0 × 13-0
11'-0" Ceiling Ht.
Books
F/P
Liv
15-2 × 18-6
11'-0" Ceiling Ht.
Pot Shelf Above
Snack bar
Din
9-4 × 9-2
Kit
9-0 × 9-0
DW
Ref
Pan
Cl
Br #3
10-0 × 10-0
Entry
Hall
Storage
Bath
Lin.
W
D
Porch
Gar
20-0 × 23-0
Optional Side Load
Br #2
11-0 × 10-6
MAIN FLOOR

Units	Single
Price Code	A
Total Finished	1,199 sq. ft.
Main Finished	1,199 sq. ft.
Garage Unfinished	484 sq. ft.
Porch Unfinished	34 sq. ft.
Dimensions	44'2"x42'6¾"
Foundation	Slab
Bedrooms	3
Full Baths	2
Main Ceiling	8'
Vaulted Ceiling	11'
Max Ridge Height	18'
Roof Framing	Stick
Exterior Walls	2x4

Design 93082

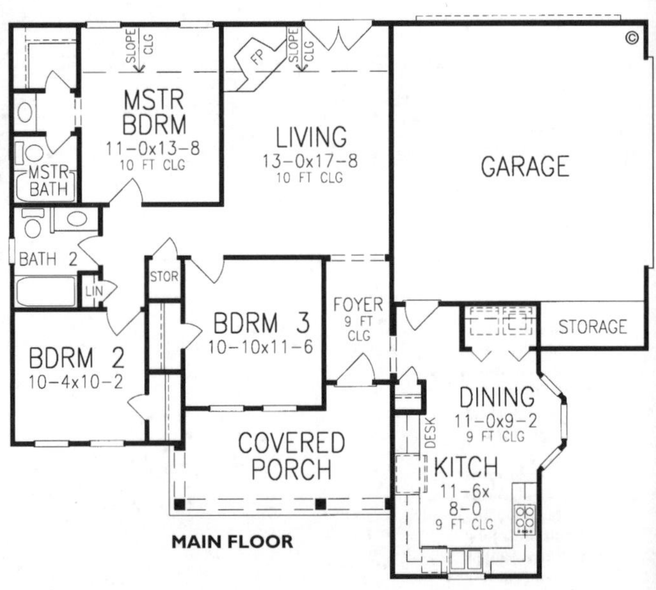

SLOPE CLG
FP
MSTR BDRM
11-0x13-8
10 FT CLG
LIVING
13-0x17-8
10 FT CLG
GARAGE
MSTR BATH
BATH 2
LIN
STOR
BDRM 3
10-10x11-6
FOYER
9 FT CLG
STORAGE
BDRM 2
10-4x10-2
DINING
11-0x9-2
9 FT CLG
DESK
COVERED PORCH
KITCH
11-6x 8-0
9 FT CLG
MAIN FLOOR

Units	Single
Price Code	A
Total Finished	1,202 sq. ft.
Main Finished	1,202 sq. ft.
Garage Unfinished	482 sq. ft.
Porch Unfinished	147 sq. ft.
Dimensions	51'x43'10"
Foundation	Crawlspace Slab
Bedrooms	3
Full Baths	2
Max Ridge Height	21'6"
Roof Framing	Stick
Exterior Walls	2x4

Design 92439

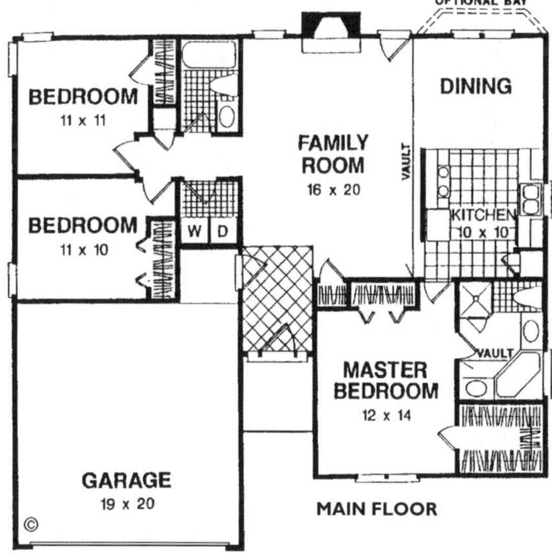
OPTIONAL BAY
BEDROOM
11 x 11
FAMILY ROOM
16 x 20
VAULT
DINING
KITCHEN
10 x 10
W D
BEDROOM
11 x 10
MASTER BEDROOM
12 x 14
VAULT
GARAGE
19 x 20
MAIN FLOOR

Units	Single
Price Code	A
Total Finished	1,205 sq. ft.
Main Finished	1,205 sq. ft.
Dimensions	46'x42'
Foundation	Slab
Bedrooms	3
Full Baths	2
Main Ceiling	8'
Roof Framing	Stick
Exterior Walls	2x4

Design 97341

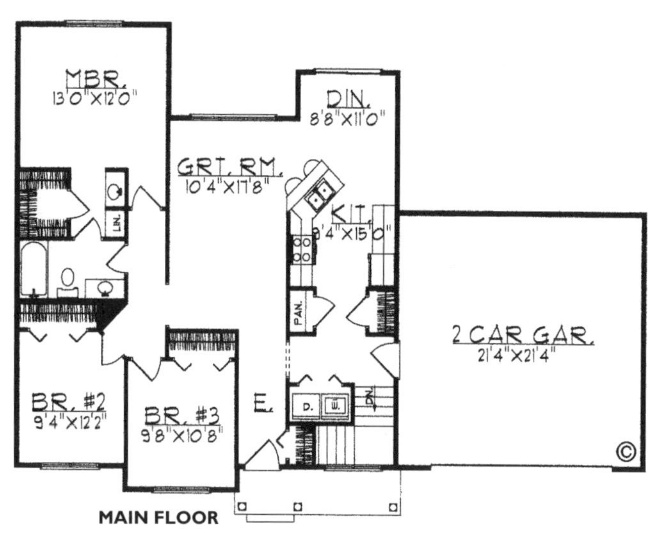
MBR.
13'0"X12'0"
DIN.
8'8"X11'0"
GRT. RM.
10'4"X17'8"
KIT.
9'4"X15'0"
LIN.
PAN.
2 CAR GAR.
21'4"X21'4"
BR. #2
9'4"X12'2"
BR. #3
9'8"X10'8"
E.
D.
W.
DN
MAIN FLOOR

Units	Single
Price Code	A
Total Finished	1,206 sq. ft.
Main Finished	1,206 sq. ft.
Basement Unfinished	1,206 sq. ft.
Garage Unfinished	455 sq. ft.
Dimensions	56'4"x40'
Foundation	Basement
Bedrooms	3
Full Baths	1
Main Ceiling	9'
Max Ridge Height	21'4"
Roof Framing	Truss
Exterior Walls	2x4

Design 91063

Units	Single
Price Code	A
Total Finished	1,207 sq. ft.
Main Finished	1,207 sq. ft.
Garage Unfinished	440 sq. ft.
Dimensions	43'6"x51'
Foundation	Crawlspace
Bedrooms	3
Full Baths	2
Max Ridge Height	18'
Roof Framing	Truss
Exterior Walls	2x6

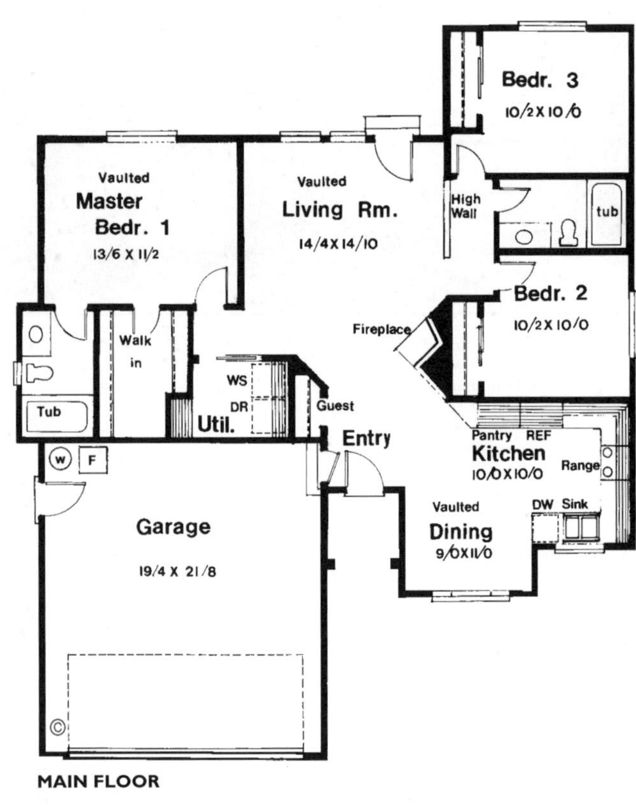
Bedr. 3
10/2 X 10/0
Vaulted
Master
Bedr. 1
13/6 X 11/2
Vaulted
Living Rm.
14/4 X 14/10
High Wall
tub
Bedr. 2
10/2 X 10/0
Fireplace
Walk in
WS
DR
Util.
Guest
Tub
Entry
Pantry REF
Kitchen
10/0 X 10/0
Range
W
F
Garage
19/4 X 21/8
Vaulted
Dining
9/0 X 11/0
DW Sink
MAIN FLOOR

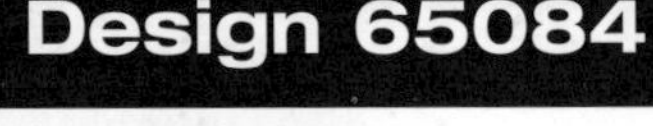

Design 65084

Units	Single
Price Code	A
Total Finished	1,208 sq. ft.
Main Finished	1,208 sq. ft.
Garage Unfinished	278 sq. ft.
Dimensions	41'x45'
Foundation	Basement
Bedrooms	1
Full Baths	2
Main Ceiling	8'
Max Ridge Height	26'22"
Roof Framing	Truss
Exterior Walls	2x6

3,20 X 3,60
10'-8" X 12'-0"
3,50 X 3,90
11'-8" X 13'-0"
3,70 X 6,70
12'-4" X 22'-4"
TWO-BEDROOM OPTION
3,70 X 4,10
12'-4" X 13'-8"
4,20 X 3,90
14'-0" X 13'-0"
3,30 X 3,60
11'-0" X 12'-0"
4,10 X 4,80
13'-8" X 16'-0"
3,70 X 6,70
12'-4" X 22'-4"
MAIN FLOOR

Design 98915

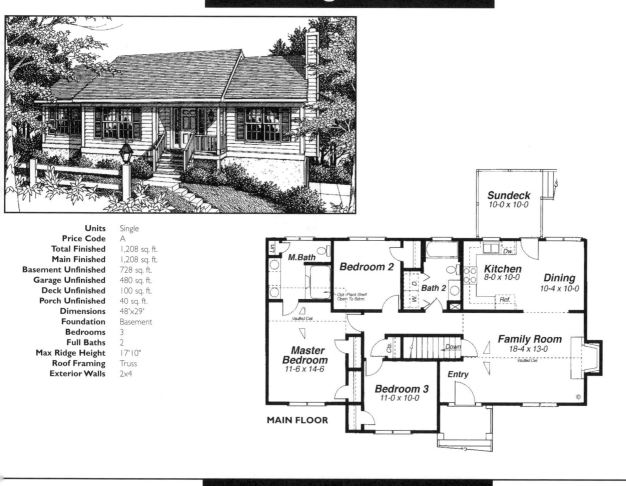

Units	Single
Price Code	A
Total Finished	1,208 sq. ft.
Main Finished	1,208 sq. ft.
Basement Unfinished	728 sq. ft.
Garage Unfinished	480 sq. ft.
Deck Unfinished	100 sq. ft.
Porch Unfinished	40 sq. ft.
Dimensions	48'x29'
Foundation	Basement
Bedrooms	3
Full Baths	2
Max Ridge Height	17'10"
Roof Framing	Truss
Exterior Walls	2x4

Sundeck 10-0 x 10-0
Lin.
M.Bath
Bedroom 2
Opt. Plant Shelf Open To Bdrm.
W. D.
Bath 2
Kitchen 8-0 x 10-0
Dw.
Ref.
Dining 10-4 x 10-0
Vaulted Ceil.
Master Bedroom 11-6 x 14-6
Cls.
Down
Family Room 18-4 x 13-0
Vaulted Ceil.
Entry
Bedroom 3 11-0 x 10-0
©
MAIN FLOOR

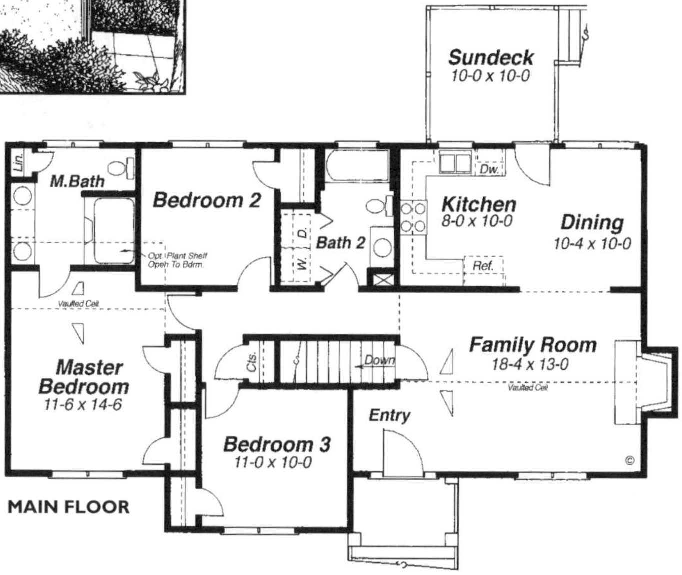

Design 98925

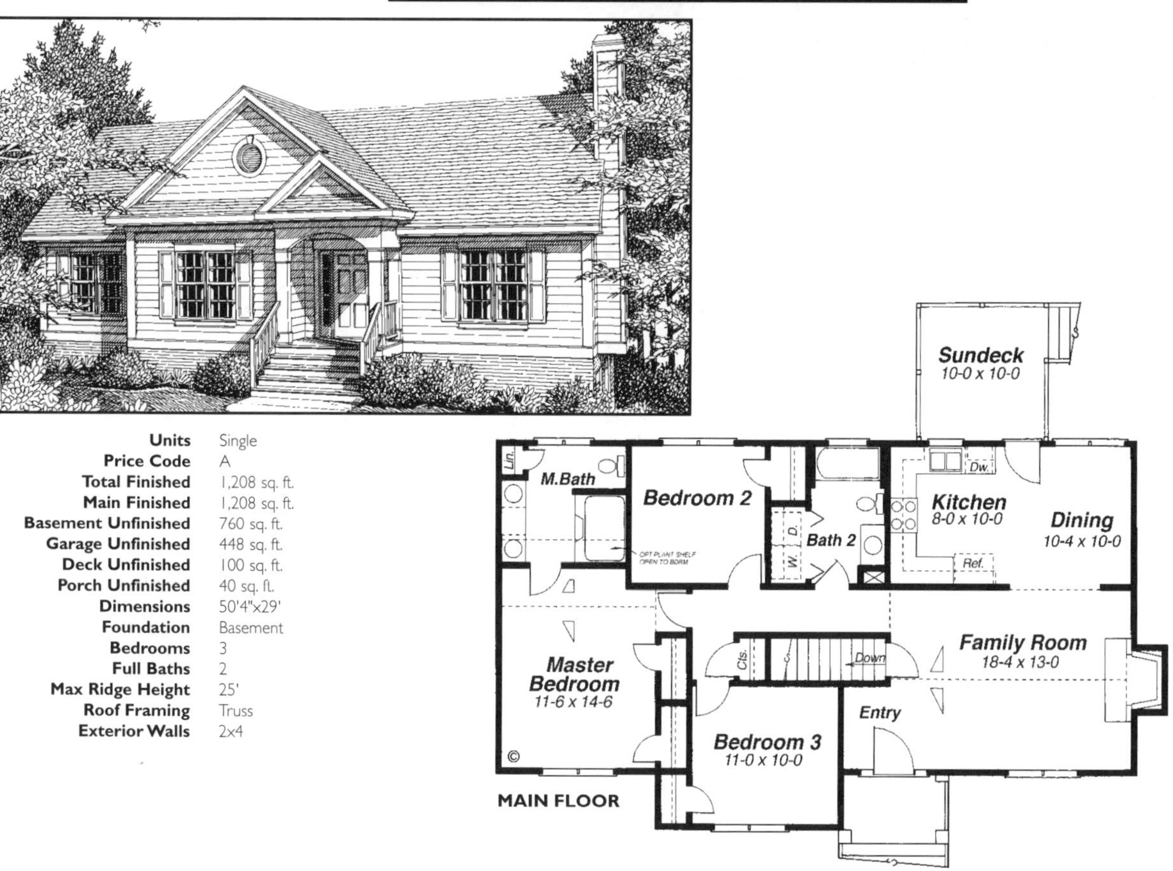
Sundeck
10-0 x 10-0
Lin.
M.Bath
Bedroom 2
OPT PLANT SHELF OPEN TO BDRM
W. D.
Bath 2
Kitchen
8-0 x 10-0
Dw.
Ref.
Dining
10-4 x 10-0
Master Bedroom
11-6 x 14-6
Cls.
Down
Family Room
18-4 x 13-0
Entry
Bedroom 3
11-0 x 10-0
©
MAIN FLOOR

Units	Single
Price Code	A
Total Finished	1,208 sq. ft.
Main Finished	1,208 sq. ft.
Basement Unfinished	760 sq. ft.
Garage Unfinished	448 sq. ft.
Deck Unfinished	100 sq. ft.
Porch Unfinished	40 sq. ft.
Dimensions	50'4"x29'
Foundation	Basement
Bedrooms	3
Full Baths	2
Max Ridge Height	25'
Roof Framing	Truss
Exterior Walls	2x4

Design 94913

Units	Single
Price Code	A
Total Finished	1,212 sq. ft.
Main Finished	1,212 sq. ft.
Basement Unfinished	1,212 sq. ft.
Garage Unfinished	448 sq. ft.
Dimensions	40'x47'8"
Foundation	Basement
Bedrooms	2
Full Baths	1
3/4 Baths	1
Main Ceiling	8'
Max Ridge Height	19'
Roof Framing	Stick
Exterior Walls	2x4

* Alternate foundation options available at an additional charge. Please call 1-800-235-5700 for more information.

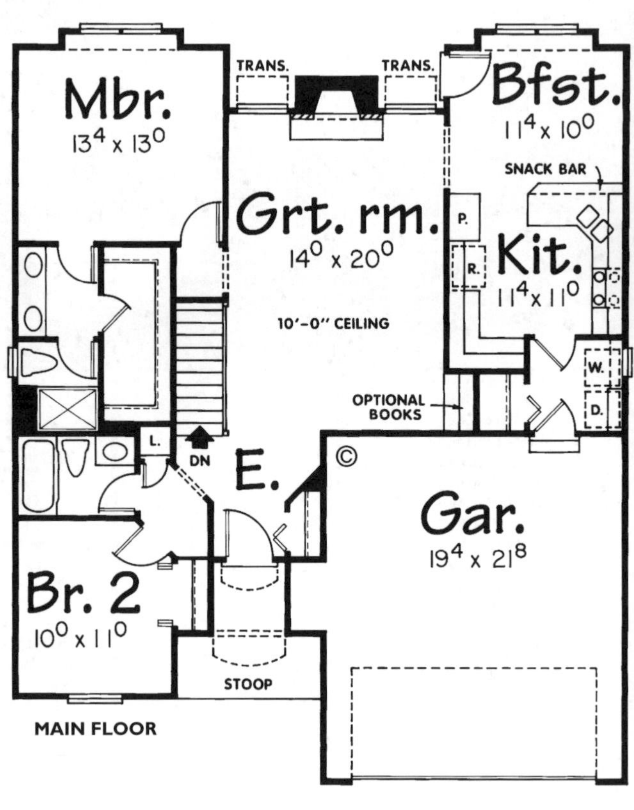

TRANS.
TRANS.
Mbr.
13⁴ x 13⁰
Bfst.
11⁴ x 10⁰
SNACK BAR
Grt. rm.
14⁰ x 20⁰
P.
R.
Kit.
11⁴ x 11⁰
10'-0" CEILING
W.
D.
OPTIONAL BOOKS
L.
DN
E.
©
Gar.
19⁴ x 21⁸
Br. 2
10⁰ x 11⁰
STOOP
MAIN FLOOR

Design 66095

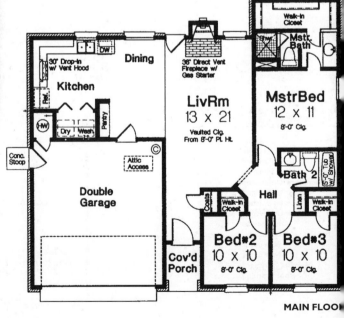

Units	Single
Price Code	A
Total Finished	1,213 sq. ft.
Main Finished	1,213 sq. ft.
Garage Unfinished	412 sq. ft.
Dimensions	44'10"x40'2"
Foundation	Slab
Bedrooms	3
Full Baths	1
3/4 Baths	1
Main Ceiling	8'
Max Ridge Height	21'
Roof Framing	Stick
Exterior Walls	2x4

Walk-in Closet
Mstr. Bath
30" Drop-in w/ Vent Hood
DW
Dining
36" Direct Vent Fireplace w/ Gas Starter
Kitchen
Ref.
LivRm
13 x 21
Vaulted Clg. From 8'-0" Pl. Ht.
MstrBed
12 x 11
8'-0" Clg.
HW
Dry
Wash
Pantry
Conc. Stoop
©
Attic Access
Bath 2
5'-0" Tub w/ Shower
Double Garage
Coats
Walk-in Closet
Hall
Linen
Walk-in Closet
Cov'd Porch
Bed#2
10 x 10
8'-0" Clg.
Bed#3
10 x 10
8'-0" Clg.
MAIN FLOOR

Design 32192

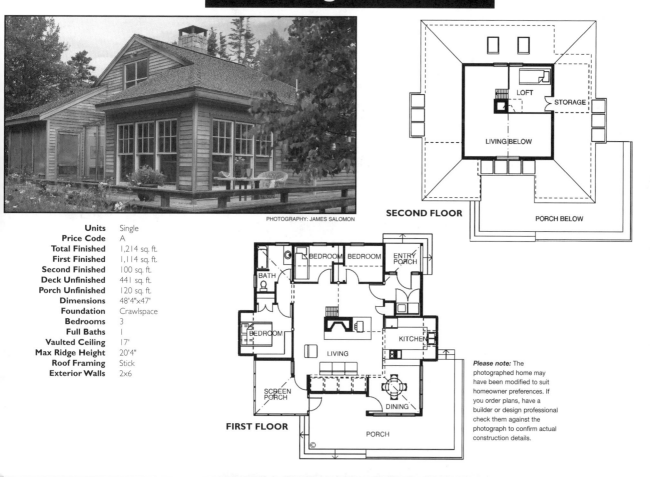

PHOTOGRAPHY: JAMES SALOMON

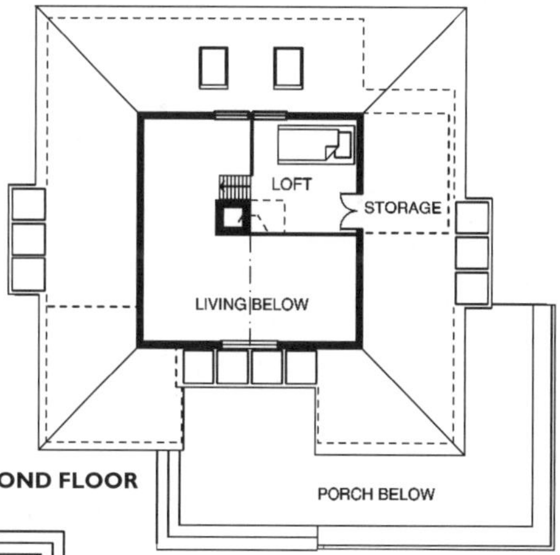

Units	Single
Price Code	A
Total Finished	1,214 sq. ft.
First Finished	1,114 sq. ft.
Second Finished	100 sq. ft.
Deck Unfinished	441 sq. ft.
Porch Unfinished	120 sq. ft.
Dimensions	48'4"x47'
Foundation	Crawlspace
Bedrooms	3
Full Baths	1
Vaulted Ceiling	17'
Max Ridge Height	20'4"
Roof Framing	Stick
Exterior Walls	2x6

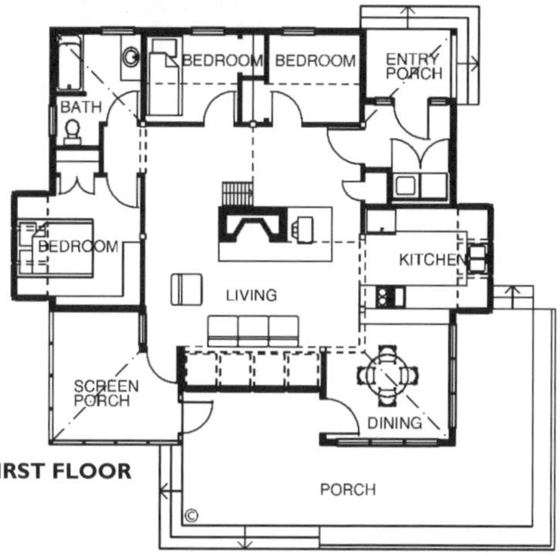

SECOND FLOOR

LOFT
STORAGE
LIVING BELOW
PORCH BELOW

FIRST FLOOR

BATH
BEDROOM
BEDROOM
ENTRY PORCH
BEDROOM
KITCHEN
LIVING
SCREEN PORCH
DINING
PORCH

Please note: The photographed home may have been modified to suit homeowner preferences. If you order plans, have a builder or design professional check them against the photograph to confirm actual construction details.

Design 97836

Units	Single
Price Code	A
Total Finished	1,225 sq. ft.
Main Finished	1,225 sq. ft.
Garage Unfinished	415 sq. ft.
Porch Unfinished	100 sq. ft.
Dimensions	45'x42'
Foundation	Slab
Bedrooms	3
Full Baths	1
3/4 Baths	1
Main Ceiling	8'
Max Ridge Height	17'
Roof Framing	Stick
Exterior Walls	2x4

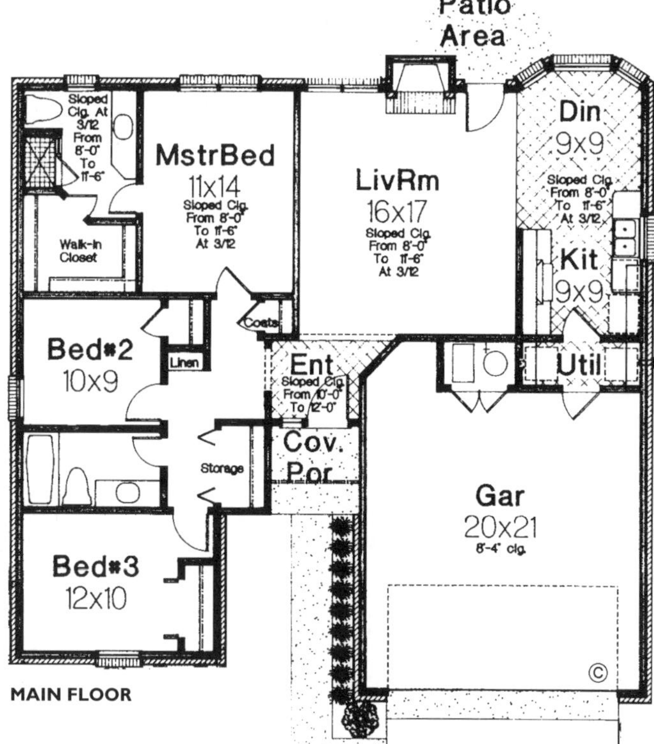
Patio Area
Sloped Clg. At 3/12 From 8'-0" To 11'-6"
MstrBed
11x14
Sloped Clg. From 8'-0" To 11'-6" At 3/12
LivRm
16x17
Sloped Clg. From 8'-0" To 11'-6" At 3/12
Din
9x9
Sloped Clg. From 8'-0" To 11'-6" At 3/12
Walk-In Closet
Kit
9x9
Coats
Bed#2
10x9
Linen
Ent
Sloped Clg. From 10'-0" To 12'-0"
Util
Cov. Por
Storage
Gar
20x21
8'-4" clg.
Bed#3
12x10

MAIN FLOOR

Design 97339

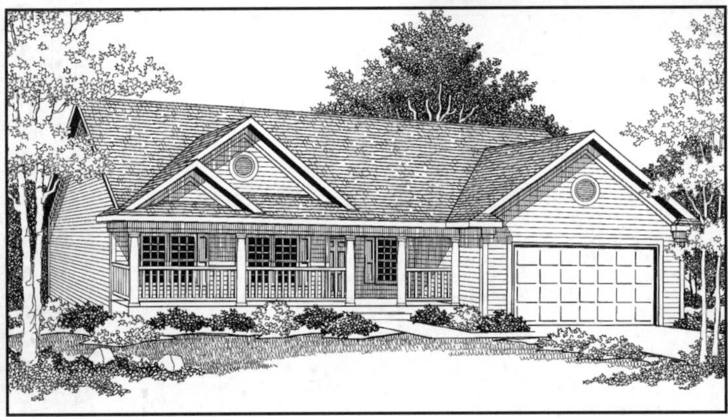

Units	Single
Price Code	A
Total Finished	1,233 sq. ft.
Main Finished	1,233 sq. ft.
Basement Unfinished	1,233 sq. ft.
Garage Unfinished	419 sq. ft.
Dimensions	57'x39'
Foundation	Basement
Bedrooms	3
Full Baths	1
Main Ceiling	9'
Max Ridge Height	23'1"
Roof Framing	Truss
Exterior Walls	2x6

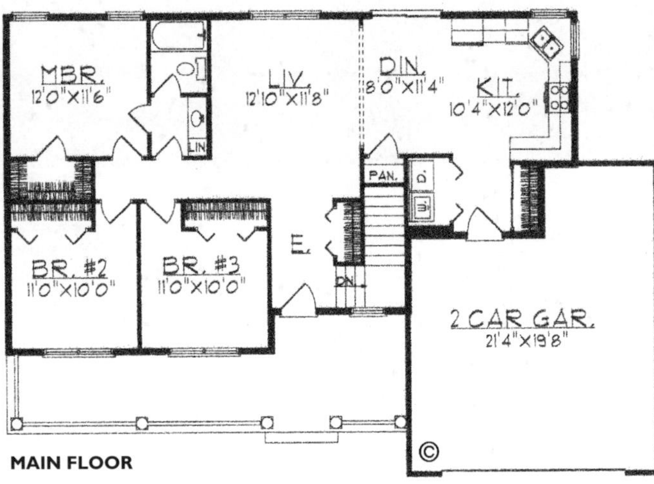
MBR.
12'0"X11'6"
LIV.
12'10"X11'8"
DIN.
8'0"X11'4"
KIT.
10'4"X12'0"
LIN
PAN.
BR. #2
11'0"X10'0"
BR. #3
11'0"X10'0"
E.
DN
2 CAR GAR.
21'4"X19'8"
©
MAIN FLOOR

Design 99428

Units	Duplex
Price Code	G
Total Finished	1,233 sq. ft.
Main Finished	1,233 sq. ft.
Basement Unfinished	1,233 sq. ft.
Garage Unfinished	448 sq. ft.
Dimensions	80'x47'8"
Foundation	Basement
Bedrooms	2
Full Baths	1
3/4 Baths	1
Max Ridge Height	19'
Roof Framing	Stick
Exterior Walls	2x4

* Alternate foundation options available at an additional charge. Please call 1-800-235-5700 for more information.

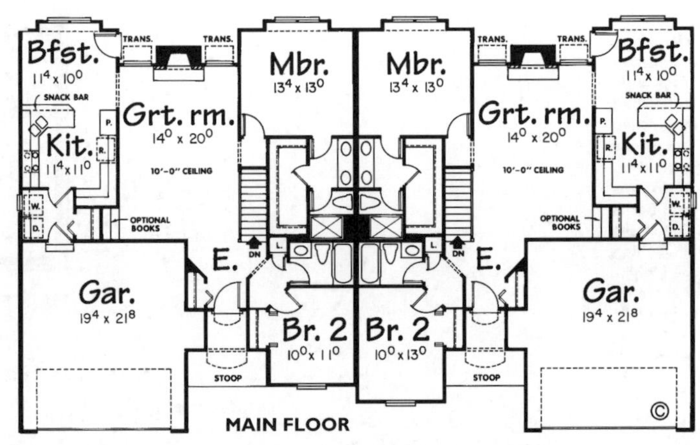
Bfst.
11⁴ x 10⁰
SNACK BAR
Kit.
11⁴x11⁰
Grt. rm.
14⁰ x 20⁰
10'-0" CEILING
TRANS.
TRANS.
OPTIONAL BOOKS
Mbr.
13⁴ x 13⁰
Mbr.
13⁴ x 13⁰
Grt. rm.
14⁰ x 20⁰
Bfst.
11⁴x 10⁰
Kit.
11⁴x11⁰
E.
E.
DN
Gar.
19⁴ x 21⁸
Br. 2
10⁰x 11⁰
Br. 2
10⁰x 13⁰
Gar.
19⁴ x 21⁸
STOOP
STOOP
©
MAIN FLOOR

Design 66075

Units	Single
Price Code	A
Total Finished	1,239 sq. ft.
Main Finished	1,239 sq. ft.
Dimensions	45'x46'16"
Foundation	Slab
Bedrooms	3
Full Baths	2
Main Ceiling	8'-10'
Max Ridge Height	22'
Roof Framing	Stick
Exterior Walls	2x4

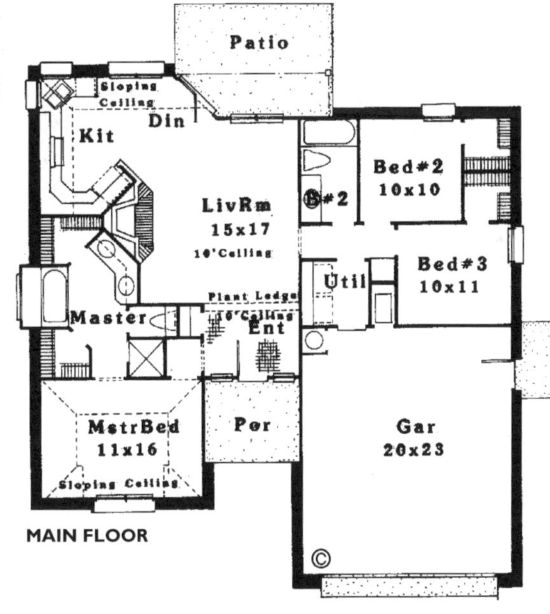
Patio
Sloping Ceiling
Din
Kit
Bed#2
10x10
LivRm
15x17
10'Ceiling
B#2
Util
Bed#3
10x11
Plant Ledge
10'Ceiling
Master
Ent
MstrBed
11x16
Sloping Ceiling
Por
Gar
20x23
©
MAIN FLOOR

Design 90682

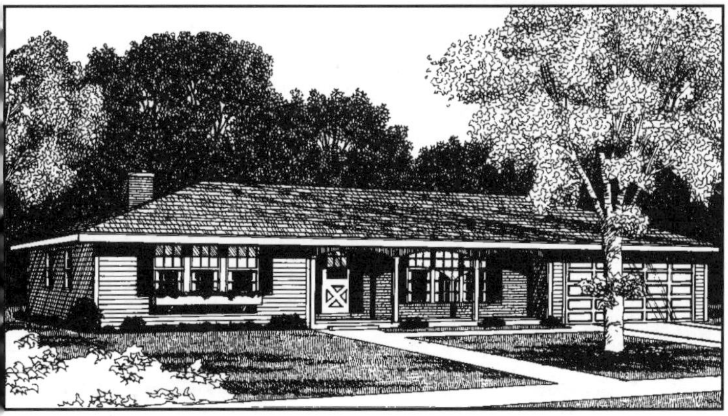

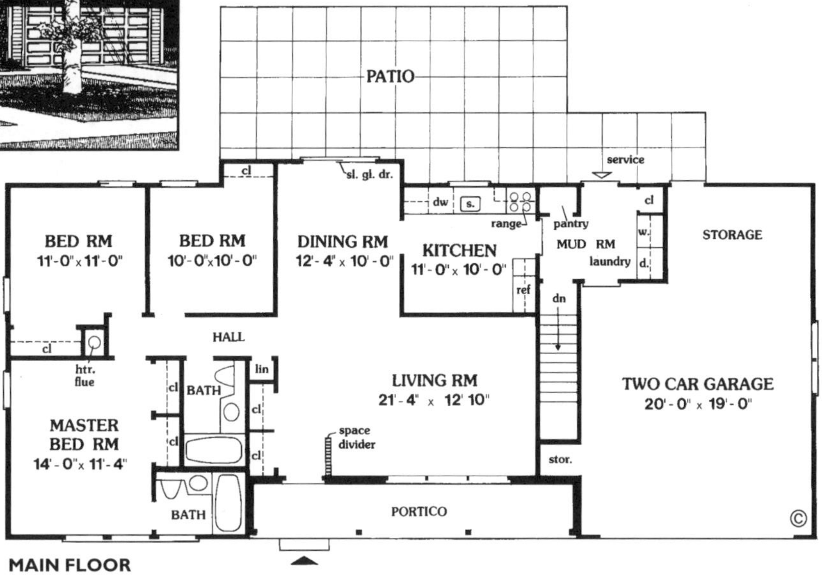

Units	Single
Price Code	A
Total Finished	1,243 sq. ft.
Main Finished	1,243 sq. ft.
Basement Unfinished	1,103 sq. ft.
Garage Unfinished	490 sq. ft.
Dimensions	66'4"x30'4"
Foundation	Basement Slab
Bedrooms	3
Full Baths	2
Max Ridge Height	16'
Roof Framing	Stick
Exterior Walls	2x4

PATIO
BED RM 11'-0" x 11'-0"
BED RM 10'-0" x 10'-0"
DINING RM 12'-4" x 10'-0"
KITCHEN 11'-0" x 10'-0"
MUD RM
STORAGE
HALL
LIVING RM 21'-4" x 12' 10"
MASTER BED RM 14'-0" x 11'-4"
TWO CAR GARAGE 20'-0" x 19'-0"
BATH
BATH
PORTICO
MAIN FLOOR

Design 96519

Units	Single
Price Code	A
Total Finished	1,243 sq. ft.
Main Finished	1,243 sq. ft.
Garage Unfinished	523 sq. ft.
Dimensions	52'x41'
Foundation	Crawlspace Slab
Bedrooms	3
Full Baths	2
Main Ceiling	8'
Vaulted Ceiling	10'
Max Ridge Height	17'
Roof Framing	Stick
Exterior Walls	2x4

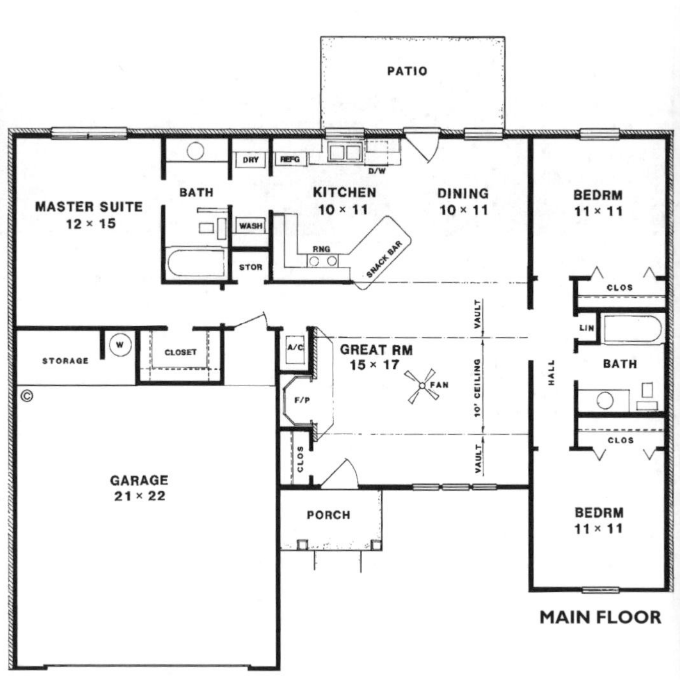
PATIO
MASTER SUITE
12 × 15
BATH
KITCHEN
10 × 11
DINING
10 × 11
BEDRM
11 × 11
STORAGE
CLOSET
GREAT RM
15 × 17
BATH
GARAGE
21 × 22
PORCH
BEDRM
11 × 11
MAIN FLOOR

Design 65638

Units	Single
Price Code	A
Total Finished	1,244 sq. ft.
Main Finished	1,244 sq. ft.
Dimensions	44'x62'
Foundation	Crawlspace Slab
Bedrooms	3
Full Baths	2
Main Ceiling	8'
Max Ridge Height	26'
Roof Framing	Stick
Exterior Walls	2x6

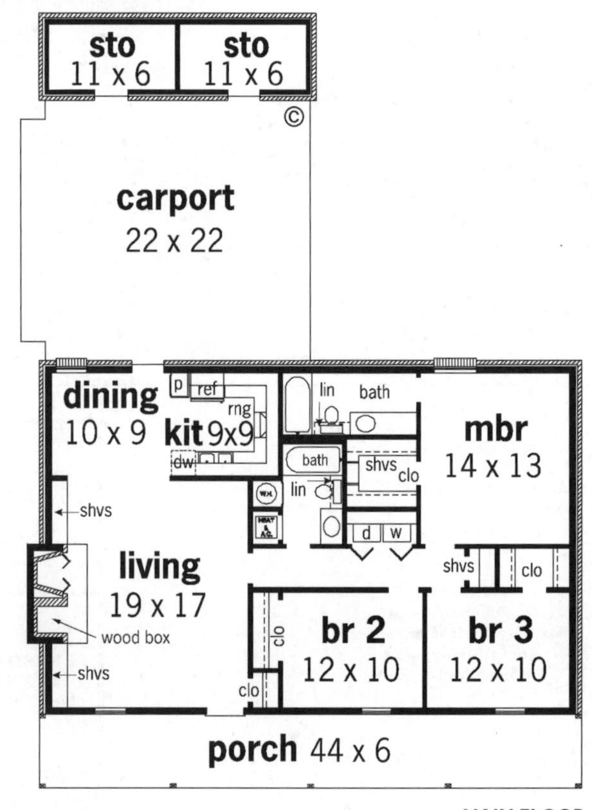
sto
11 x 6
sto
11 x 6
carport
22 x 22
dining
10 x 9
kit 9x9
bath
mbr
14 x 13
living
19 x 17
wood box
br 2
12 x 10
br 3
12 x 10
porch 44 x 6
MAIN FLOOR

Design 96511

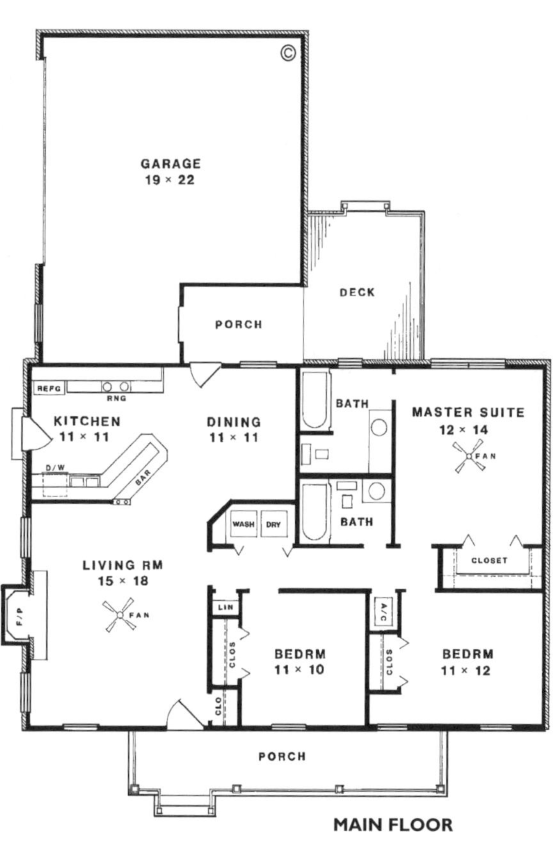

GARAGE
19 × 22
DECK
PORCH
REFG
RNG
KITCHEN
11 × 11
D/W
BAR
DINING
11 × 11
BATH
MASTER SUITE
12 × 14
FAN
WASH
DRY
BATH
CLOSET
LIVING RM
15 × 18
FAN
F/P
LIN
A/C
CLOS
BEDRM
11 × 10
CLOS
BEDRM
11 × 12
CLO
PORCH

MAIN FLOOR

Units	Single
Price Code	A
Total Finished	1,247 sq. ft.
Main Finished	1,247 sq. ft.
Garage Unfinished	512 sq. ft.
Dimensions	43'x60'
Foundation	Crawlspace Slab
Bedrooms	3
Full Baths	2
Main Ceiling	8'
Max Ridge Height	19'
Roof Framing	Stick
Exterior Walls	2x4

Design 91033

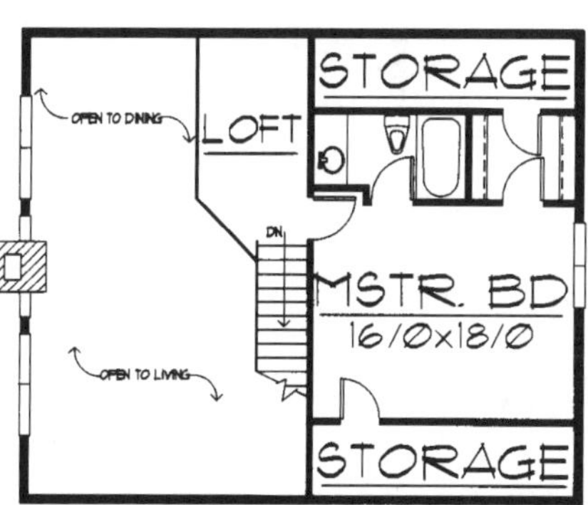

STORAGE
OPEN TO DINING
LOFT
DN
MSTR. BD
16/0x18/0
OPEN TO LIVING
STORAGE

SECOND FLOOR

Units	Single
Price Code	A
Total Finished	1,249 sq. ft.
First Finished	952 sq. ft.
Second Finished	297 sq. ft.
Dimensions	34'x28'
Foundation	Basement Crawlspace
Bedrooms	2
Full Baths	2
First Ceiling	8'
Max Ridge Height	24'
Roof Framing	Stick
Exterior Walls	2x6

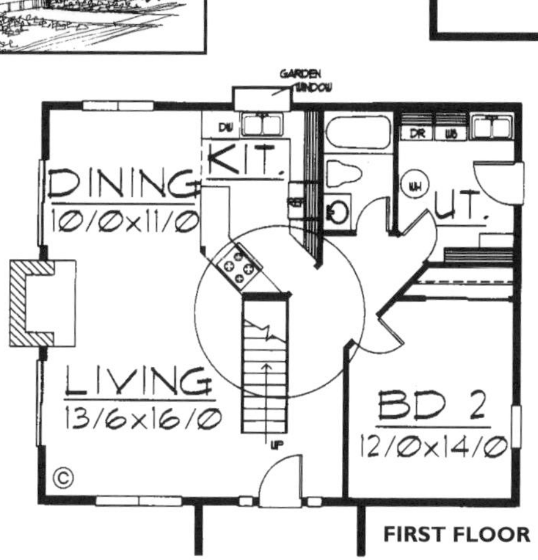

GARDEN WINDOW
DW
KIT.
DINING
10/0x11/0
DR
WH
UT.
LIVING
13/6x16/0
UP
BD 2
12/0x14/0

FIRST FLOOR

OPTIONAL BASEMENT STAIR LOCATION

Design 91120

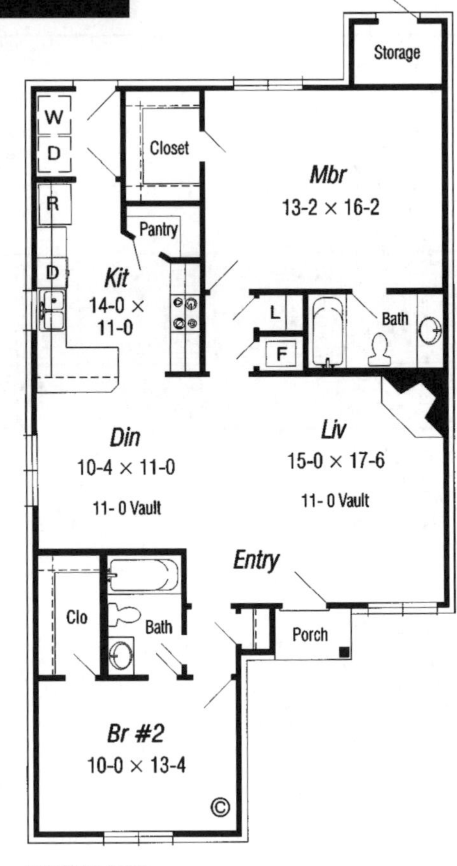
Storage
W
D
Closet
Mbr
13-2 × 16-2
R
Pantry
Kit
14-0 ×
11-0
D
L
Bath
F
Din
10-4 × 11-0
11- 0 Vault
Liv
15-0 × 17-6
11- 0 Vault
Entry
Clo
Bath
Porch
Br #2
10-0 × 13-4
©
MAIN FLOOR

Units	Single
Price Code	A
Total Finished	1,249 sq. ft.
Main Finished	1,249 sq. ft.
Porch Unfinished	23 sq. ft.
Dimensions	29'x54'10"
Foundation	Slab
Bedrooms	2
Full Baths	2
Max Ridge Height	19'3"
Roof Framing	Truss
Exterior Walls	2x4

Design 93023

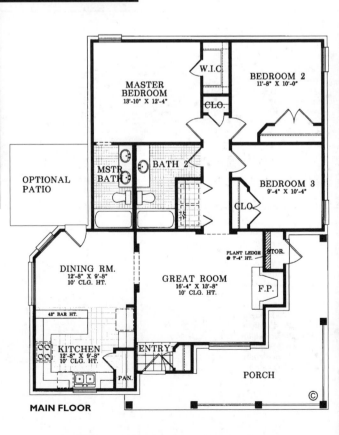

Units	Single
Price Code	A
Total Finished	1,249 sq. ft.
Main Finished	1,249 sq. ft.
Porch Unfinished	263 sq. ft.
Dimensions	38'6"x46'
Foundation	Crawlspace Slab
Bedrooms	3
Full Baths	2
Max Ridge Height	22'
Roof Framing	Stick
Exterior Walls	2x4

W.I.C.
MASTER BEDROOM
13'-10" X 12'-4"
BEDROOM 2
11'-8" X 10'-0"
CLO.
OPTIONAL PATIO
MSTR. BATH
BATH 2
BEDROOM 3
9'-4" X 10'-4"
CLO.
PLANT LEDGE @ 7'-4" HT.
STOR.
DINING RM.
12'-8" X 9'-8"
10' CLG. HT.
GREAT ROOM
16'-4" X 13'-8"
10' CLG. HT.
F.P.
42" BAR HT.
KITCHEN
12'-8" X 9'-8"
10' CLG. HT.
ENTRY
PAN.
PORCH
©
MAIN FLOOR

Design 91091

Units	Single
Price Code	A
Total Finished	1,250 sq. ft.
First Finished	842 sq. ft.
Second Finished	408 sq. ft.
Dimensions	24'x62'
Foundation	Crawlspace
Bedrooms	3
Full Baths	2
Max Ridge Height	24'½"
Roof Framing	Truss
Exterior Walls	2x6

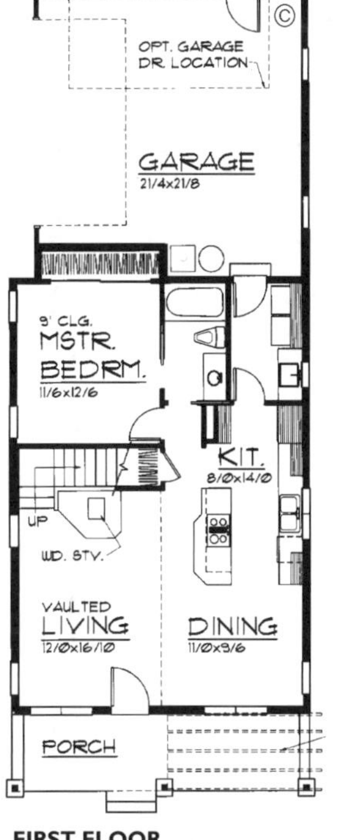
OPT. GARAGE DR. LOCATION
GARAGE
21/4x21/8
9' CLG.
MSTR. BEDRM.
11/6x12/6
KIT.
8/0x14/0
UP
WD. STV.
VAULTED LIVING
12/0x16/10
DINING
11/0x9/6
PORCH

FIRST FLOOR

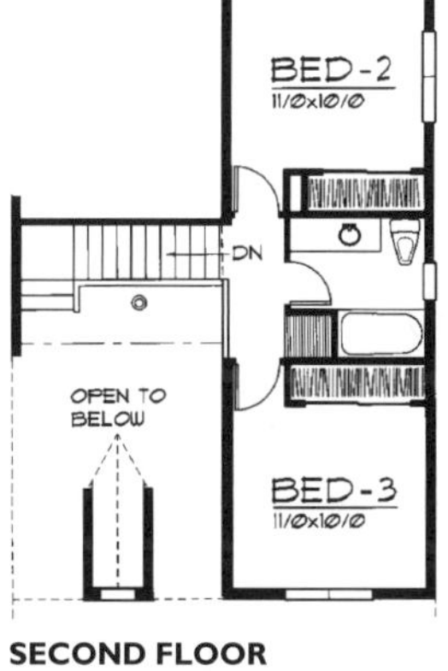
BED-2
11/0x10/0
DN
OPEN TO BELOW
BED-3
11/0x10/0

SECOND FLOOR

Design 93449

Units	Single
Price Code	A
Total Finished	1,253 sq. ft.
Main Finished	1,253 sq. ft.
Garage Unfinished	486 sq. ft.
Porch Unfinished	208 sq. ft.
Dimensions	61'3"x40'6"
Foundation	Crawlspace Slab
Bedrooms	3
Full Baths	2
Main Ceiling	8'
Max Ridge Height	19'6"
Roof Framing	Stick
Exterior Walls	2x4

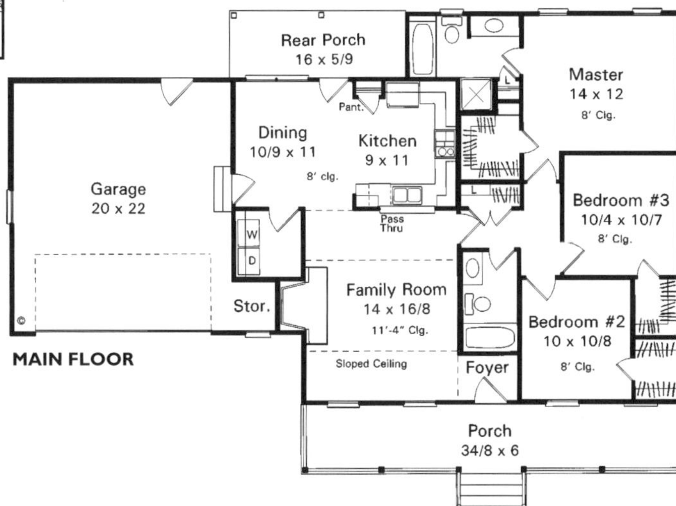
Rear Porch
16 x 5/9
Master
14 x 12
8' Clg.
Pant.
Dining
10/9 x 11
8' clg.
Kitchen
9 x 11
Garage
20 x 22
Bedroom #3
10/4 x 10/7
8' Clg.
Pass Thru
W
D
Family Room
14 x 16/8
11'-4" Clg.
Stor.
Bedroom #2
10 x 10/8
8' Clg.
Sloped Ceiling
Foyer
Porch
34/8 x 6

MAIN FLOOR

Design 65140

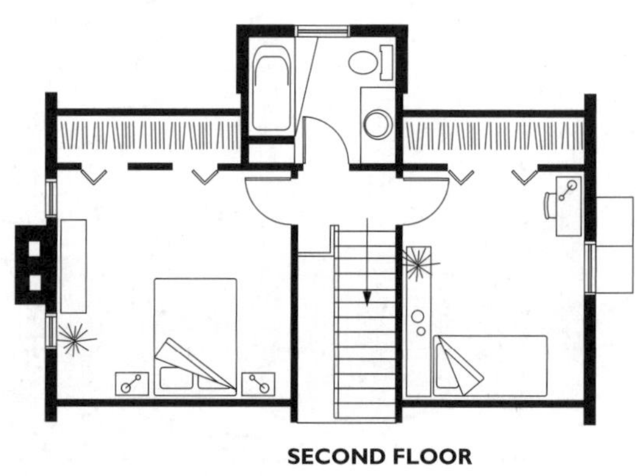

SECOND FLOOR

Units	Single
Price Code	A
Total Finished	1,258 sq. ft.
First Finished	753 sq. ft.
Second Finished	505 sq. ft.
Basement Unfinished	753 sq. ft.
Dimensions	30'x28'
Foundation	Basement
Bedrooms	3
Full Baths	1
Half Baths	1
First Ceiling	8'
Second Ceiling	8'
Max Ridge Height	24'10"
Roof Framing	Truss
Exterior Walls	2x6

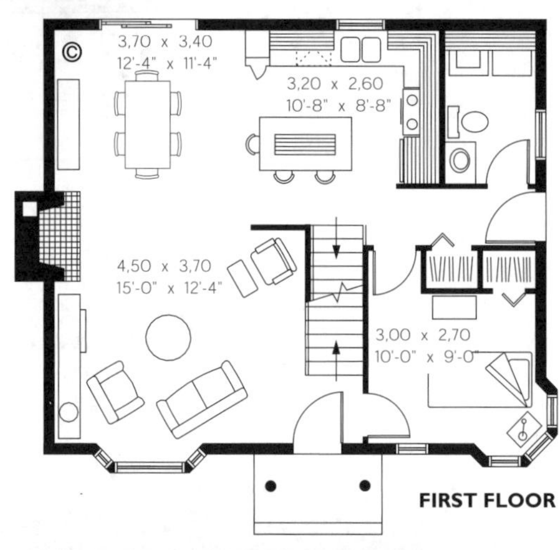
©
3,70 x 3,40
12'-4" x 11'-4"
3,20 x 2,60
10'-8" x 8'-8"
4,50 x 3,70
15'-0" x 12'-4"
3,00 x 2,70
10'-0" x 9'-0"

FIRST FLOOR

Design 97260

CAD FILES AVAILABLE For more information call 800-235-5700

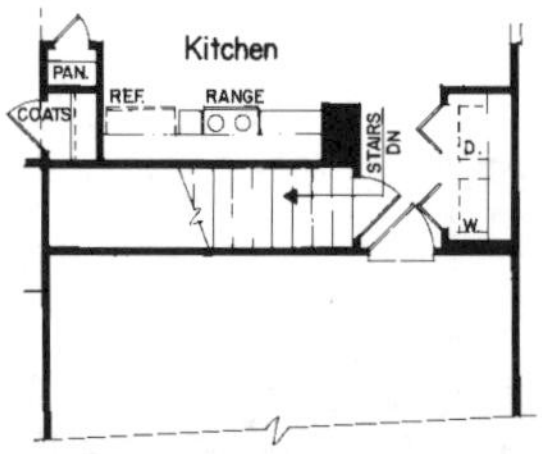

OPTIONAL BASEMENT STAIR LOCATION

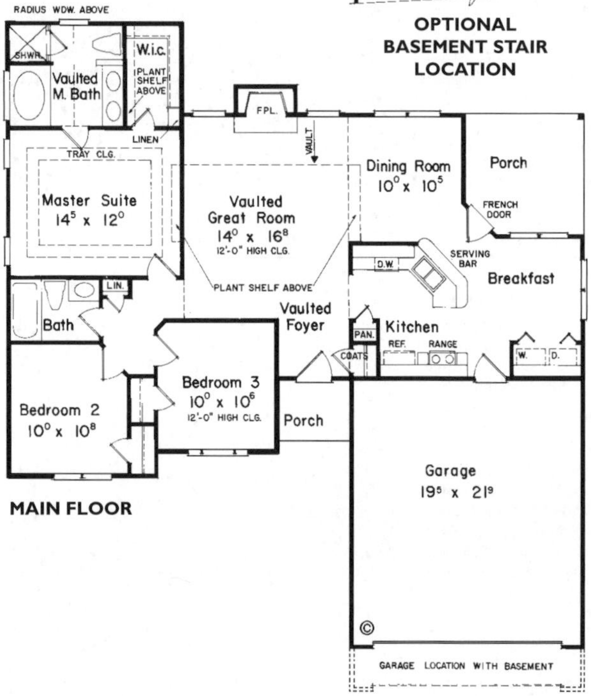

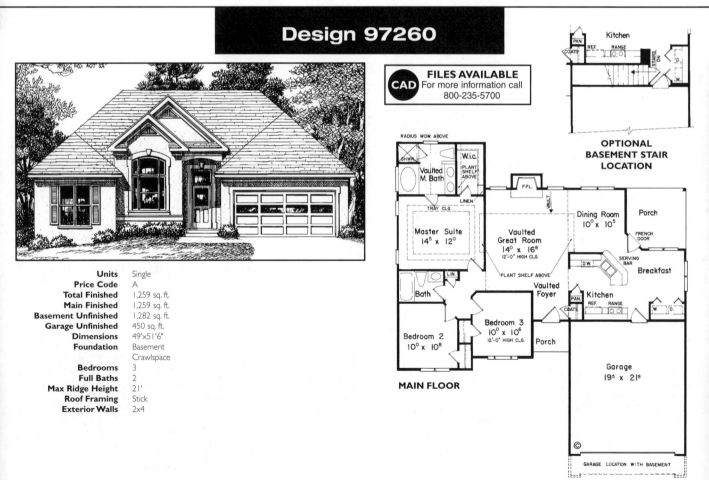

MAIN FLOOR

Units	Single
Price Code	A
Total Finished	1,259 sq. ft.
Main Finished	1,259 sq. ft.
Basement Unfinished	1,282 sq. ft.
Garage Unfinished	450 sq. ft.
Dimensions	49'x51'6"
Foundation	Basement Crawlspace
Bedrooms	3
Full Baths	2
Max Ridge Height	21'
Roof Framing	Stick
Exterior Walls	2x4

Design 90822

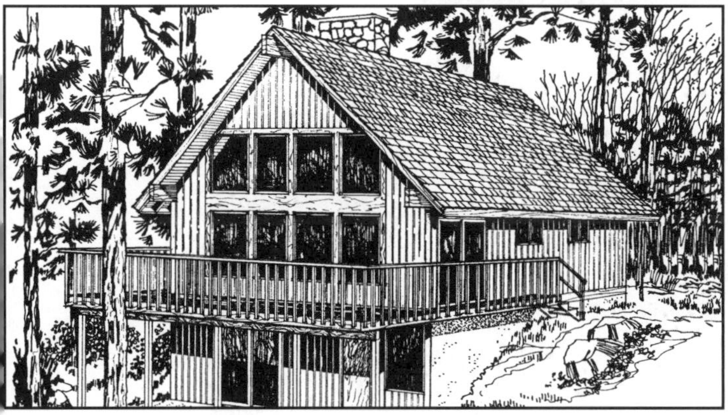

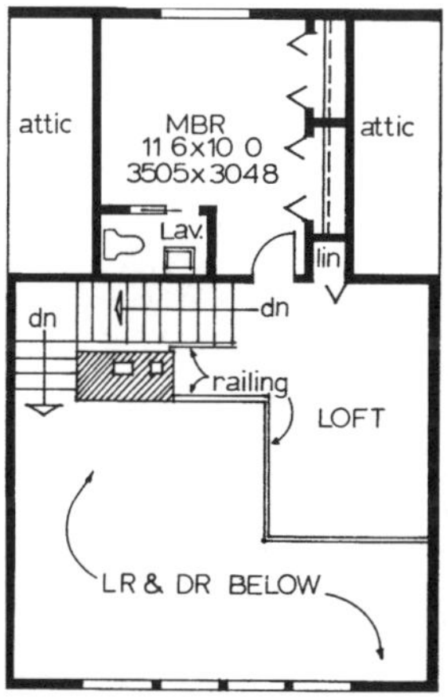

Units	Single
Price Code	A
Total Finished	1,263 sq. ft.
First Finished	925 sq. ft.
Second Finished	338 sq. ft.
Basement Unfinished	864 sq. ft.
Dimensions	33'x47'
Foundation	Basement
Bedrooms	3
Full Baths	1
Half Baths	1
Roof Framing	Stick
Exterior Walls	2x6

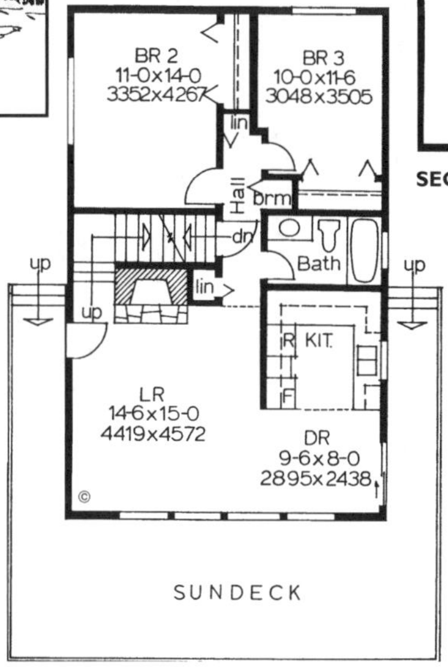

SECOND FLOOR

FIRST FLOOR

Design 69033

Hot
New
Design

Units	Single
Price Code	A
Total Finished	1,268 sq. ft.
Main Finished	1,268 sq. ft.
Dimensions	38'x46'
Foundation	Basement
Bedrooms	3
Full Baths	2

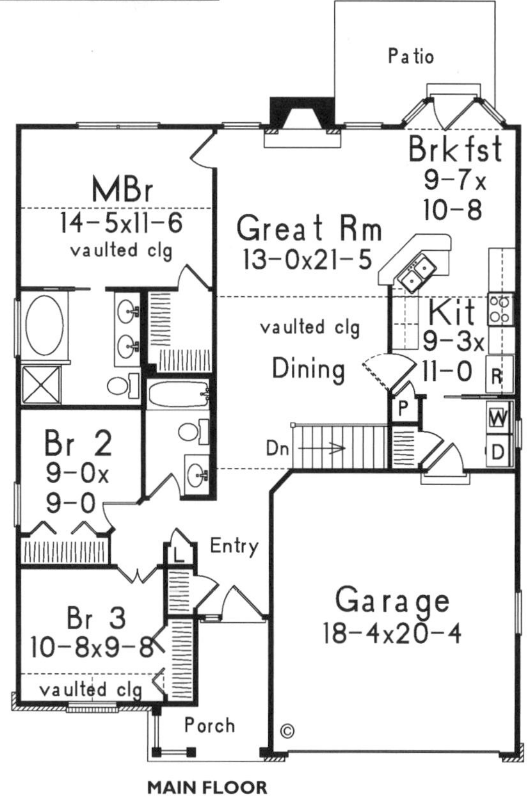
Patio
MBr
14-5x11-6
vaulted clg
Great Rm
13-0x21-5
Brkfst
9-7x
10-8
Kit
9-3x
11-0
vaulted clg
Dining
Br 2
9-0x
9-0
Dn
Entry
Br 3
10-8x9-8
vaulted clg
Garage
18-4x20-4
Porch

MAIN FLOOR

Design 65073

Units	Single
Price Code	A
Total Finished	1,272 sq. ft.
Main Finished	1,272 sq. ft.
Garage Unfinished	274 sq. ft.
Dimensions	42'x42'
Foundation	Basement
Bedrooms	3
Full Baths	1

3,00 X 2,70
10'-0" X 9'-0"

2,60 X 3,60
8'-8" X 12'-0"

3,20 X 2,70
10'-8" X 9'-0"

3,20 X 4,20
10'-8" X 14'-0"

3,60 X 6,80
12'-0" X 22'-8"

4,40 X 3,60
14'-8" X 12'-0"

4,20 X 3,30
14'-0" X 11'-0"

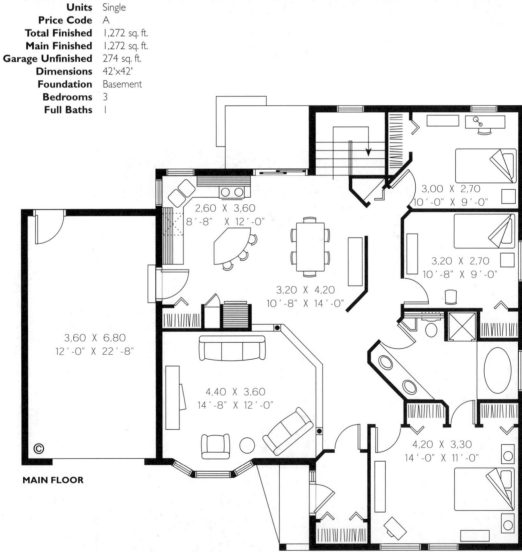

©

MAIN FLOOR

Design 90048

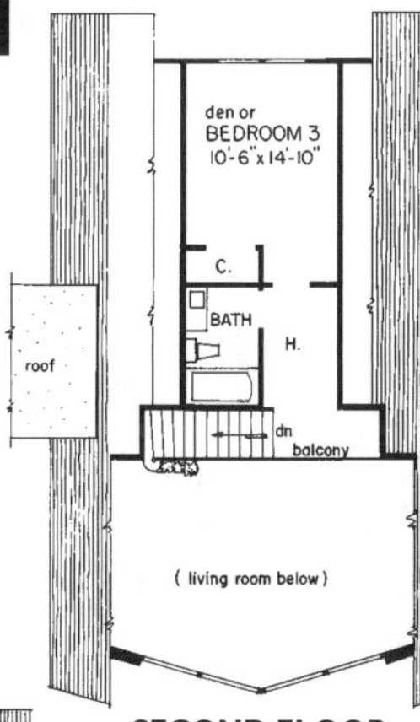

Units	Single
Price Code	A
Total Finished	1,274 sq. ft.
First Finished	974 sq. ft.
Second Finished	300 sq. ft.
Dimensions	23'8"x55'10"
Foundation	Basement
Bedrooms	3
Full Baths	2
Max Ridge Height	23'
Roof Framing	Stick
Exterior Walls	2x4

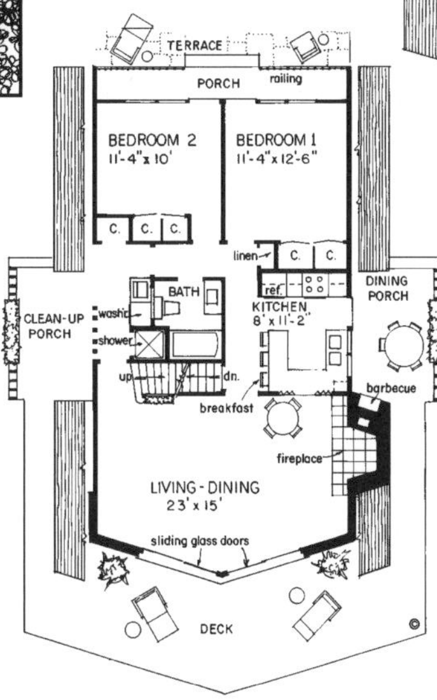

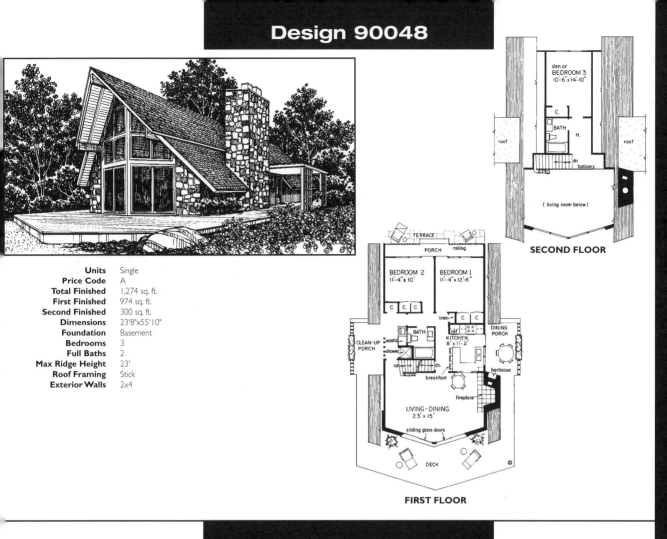

SECOND FLOOR

FIRST FLOOR

Design 97337

Units	Single
Price Code	A
Total Finished	1,274 sq. ft.
Main Finished	1,274 sq. ft.
Basement Unfinished	1,274 sq. ft.
Garage Unfinished	380 sq. ft.
Dimensions	51'x46'
Foundation	Basement
Bedrooms	3
Full Baths	2
Main Ceiling	9'
Second Ceiling	8'
Max Ridge Height	20'2"
Roof Framing	Truss
Exterior Walls	2x6

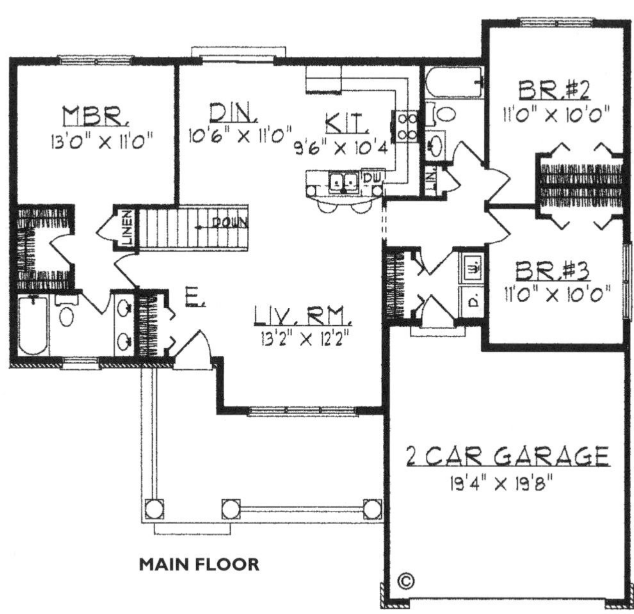
MBR.
13'0" X 11'0"
DIN.
10'6" X 11'0"
KIT.
9'6" X 10'4
BR.#2
11'0" X 10'0"
BR.#3
11'0" X 10'0"
LINEN
DOWN
E.
LIV. RM.
13'2" X 12'2"
2 CAR GARAGE
19'4" X 19'8"

MAIN FLOOR

Design 66066

Units	Single
Price Code	A
Total Finished	1,278 sq. ft.
Main Finished	1,278 sq. ft.
Garage Unfinished	480 sq. ft.
Dimensions	55'x43'6"
Foundation	Slab
Bedrooms	3
Full Baths	1
3/4 Baths	1
Main Ceiling	8'
Max Ridge Height	22'
Roof Framing	Stick
Exterior Walls	2x4

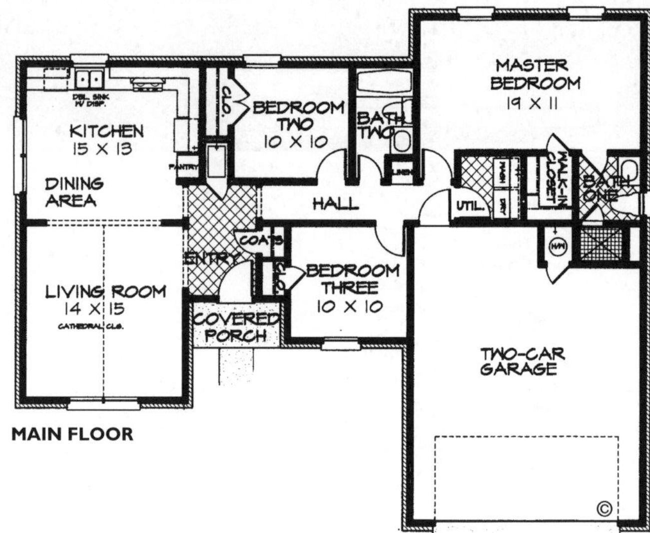
MASTER BEDROOM
19 X 11
KITCHEN
15 X 13
DINING AREA
BEDROOM TWO
10 X 10
BATH TWO
HALL
UTIL.
WALK-IN CLOSET
BATH ONE
ENTRY
COATS
LIVING ROOM
14 X 15
CATHEDRAL CLG.
COVERED PORCH
BEDROOM THREE
10 X 10
TWO-CAR GARAGE
©

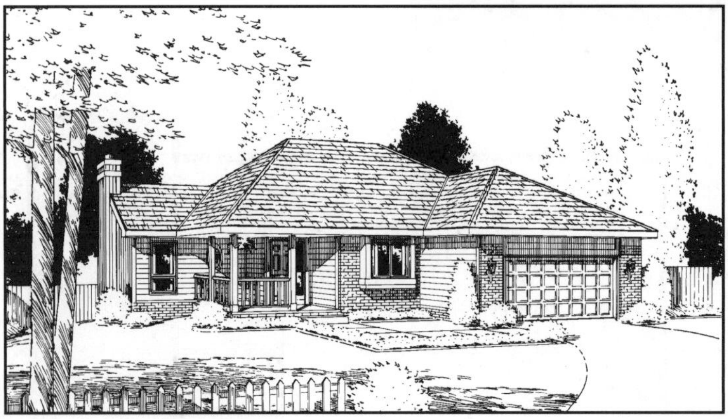

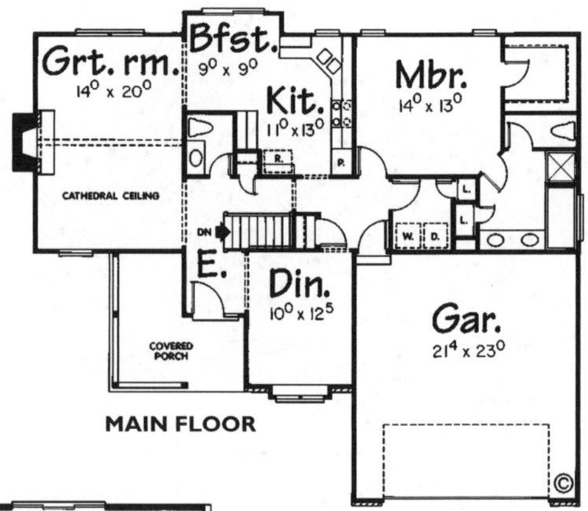

MAIN FLOOR

Design 94985

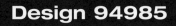

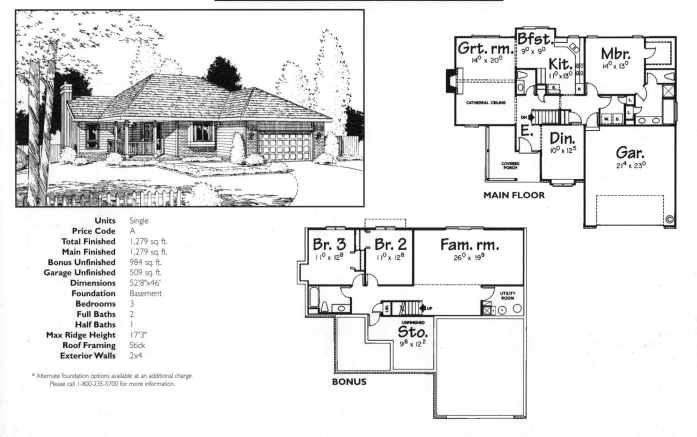

Units	Single
Price Code	A
Total Finished	1,279 sq. ft.
Main Finished	1,279 sq. ft.
Bonus Unfinished	984 sq. ft.
Garage Unfinished	509 sq. ft.
Dimensions	52'8"x46'
Foundation	Basement
Bedrooms	3
Full Baths	2
Half Baths	1
Max Ridge Height	17'3"
Roof Framing	Stick
Exterior Walls	2x4

* Alternate foundation options available at an additional charge. Please call 1-800-235-5700 for more information.

Grt. rm. 14⁰ x 20⁰ · Bfst. 9⁰ x 9⁰ · Kit. 11⁰ x 13⁰ · Mbr. 14⁰ x 13⁰ · CATHEDRAL CEILING · E. · Din. 10⁰ x 12⁵ · Gar. 21⁴ x 23⁰ · COVERED PORCH

MAIN FLOOR

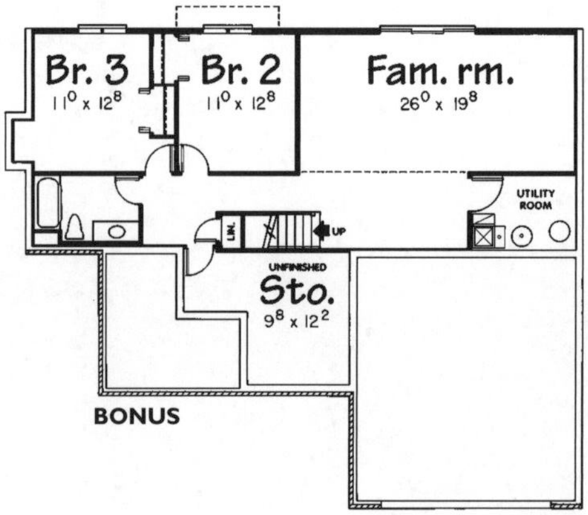

Br. 3 11⁰ x 12⁸ · Br. 2 11⁰ x 12⁸ · Fam. rm. 26⁰ x 19⁸ · UTILITY ROOM · UNFINISHED Sto. 9⁸ x 12²

BONUS

Design 98747

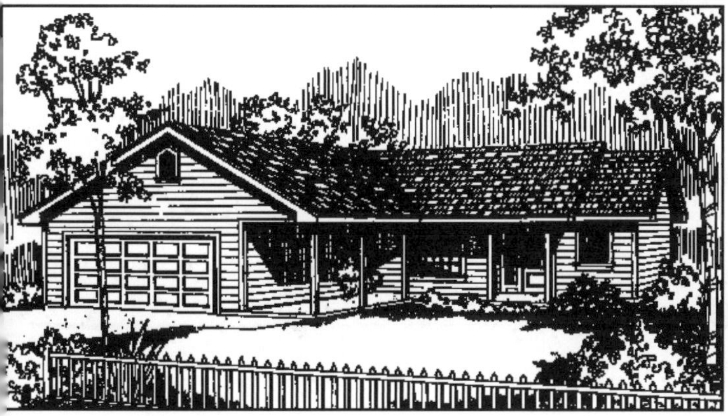

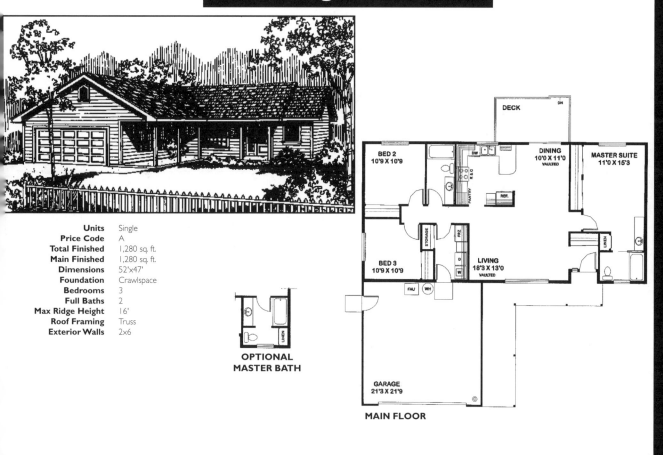

Units	Single
Price Code	A
Total Finished	1,280 sq. ft.
Main Finished	1,280 sq. ft.
Dimensions	52'x47'
Foundation	Crawlspace
Bedrooms	3
Full Baths	2
Max Ridge Height	16'
Roof Framing	Truss
Exterior Walls	2x6

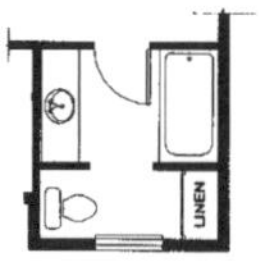

OPTIONAL MASTER BATH

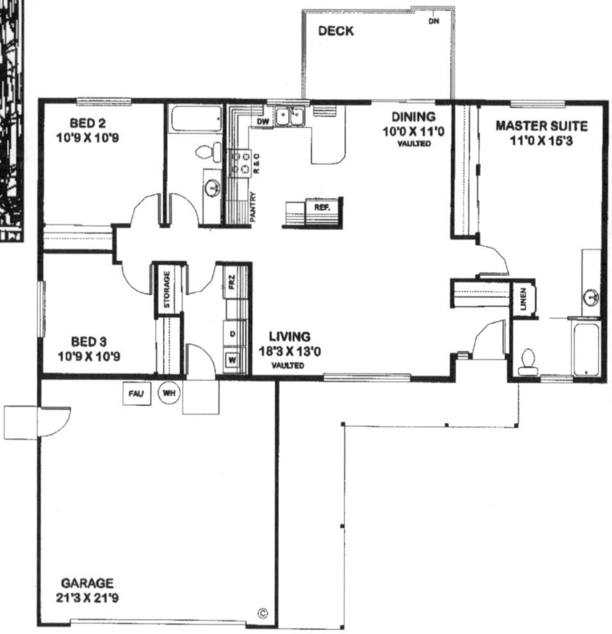

DECK
DN
BED 2 10'9 X 10'9
DINING 10'0 X 11'0 VAULTED
MASTER SUITE 11'0 X 15'3
BED 3 10'9 X 10'9
LIVING 18'3 X 13'0 VAULTED
GARAGE 21'3 X 21'9

MAIN FLOOR

Design 93021

Units	Single
Price Code	A
Total Finished	1,282 sq. ft.
Main Finished	1,282 sq. ft.
Garage Unfinished	501 sq. ft.
Dimensions	48'10"x52'6"
Foundation	Crawlspace Slab
Bedrooms	3
Full Baths	2
Max Ridge Height	20'
Roof Framing	Stick
Exterior Walls	2x4

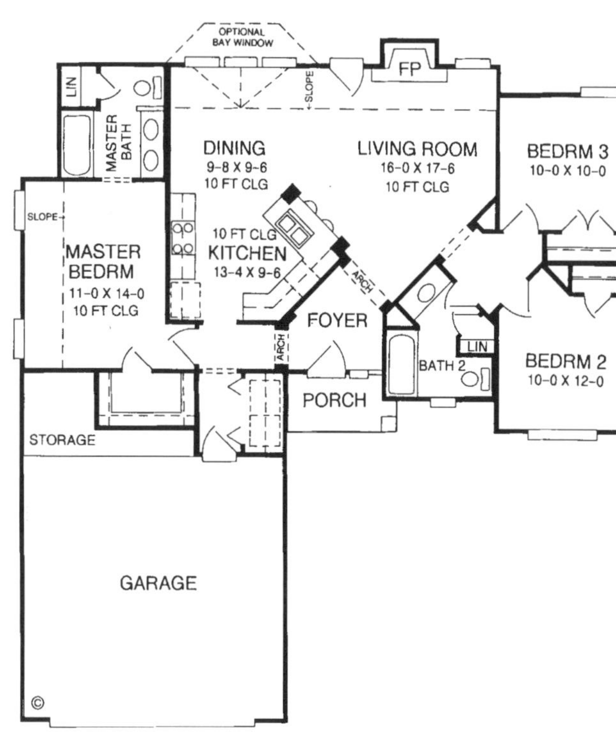
OPTIONAL BAY WINDOW
FP
LIN
MASTER BATH
DINING 9-8 X 9-6 10 FT CLG
LIVING ROOM 16-0 X 17-6 10 FT CLG
BEDRM 3 10-0 X 10-0
SLOPE
MASTER BEDRM 11-0 X 14-0 10 FT CLG
10 FT CLG KITCHEN 13-4 X 9-6
ARCH
FOYER
BATH 2
BEDRM 2 10-0 X 12-0
PORCH
STORAGE
GARAGE

MAIN FLOOR

Design 86011

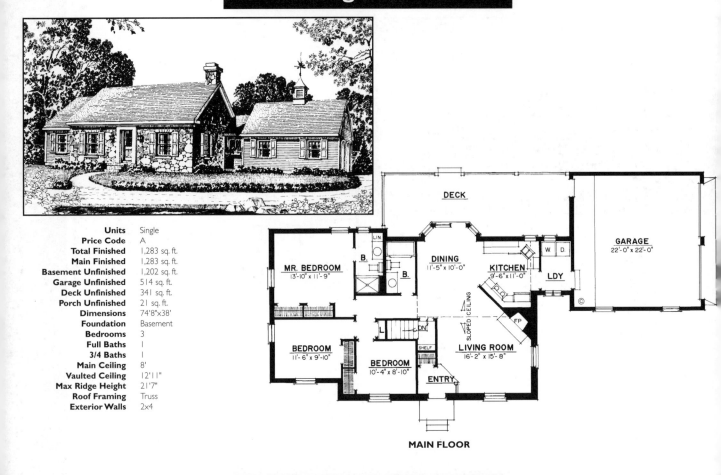

Units	Single
Price Code	A
Total Finished	1,283 sq. ft.
Main Finished	1,283 sq. ft.
Basement Unfinished	1,202 sq. ft.
Garage Unfinished	514 sq. ft.
Deck Unfinished	341 sq. ft.
Porch Unfinished	21 sq. ft.
Dimensions	74'8"x38'
Foundation	Basement
Bedrooms	3
Full Baths	1
3/4 Baths	1
Main Ceiling	8'
Vaulted Ceiling	12'11"
Max Ridge Height	21'7"
Roof Framing	Truss
Exterior Walls	2x4

DECK
GARAGE 22'-0" x 22'-0"
LIN
B.
B.
MR. BEDROOM 13'-10" x 11'-9"
DINING 11'-5" x 10'-0"
KITCHEN 9'-6" x 11'-0"
W D.
LDY
SLOPED CEILING
FP
DN
L
SHELF
BEDROOM 11'-6" x 9'-10"
BEDROOM 10'-4" x 8'-10"
LIVING ROOM 16'-2" x 15'-8"
ENTRY

MAIN FLOOR

Design 97237

Units	Single
Price Code	A
Total Finished	1,283 sq. ft.
Main Finished	1,283 sq. ft.
Basement Unfinished	480 sq. ft.
Garage Unfinished	470 sq. ft.
Dimensions	45'4"x34'
Foundation	Basement
Bedrooms	3
Full Baths	2
Main Ceiling	9'
Max Ridge Height	25'
Roof Framing	Stick
Exterior Walls	2x4

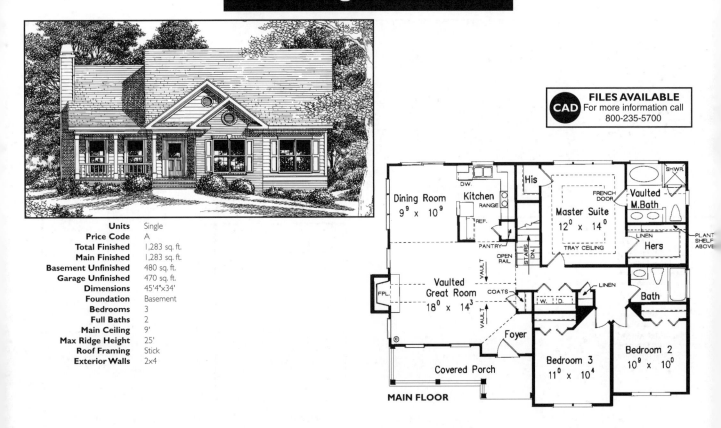

CAD FILES AVAILABLE
For more information call
800-235-5700

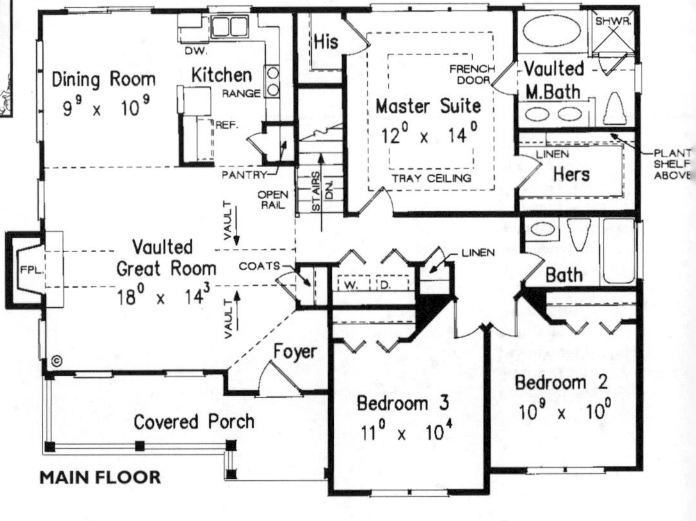

DW.
Dining Room 9^9 x 10^9
Kitchen
RANGE
REF.
PANTRY
OPEN RAIL
STAIRS DN.
His
FRENCH DOOR
Master Suite 12^0 x 14^0
TRAY CEILING
SHWR.
Vaulted M.Bath
LINEN
Hers
PLANT SHELF ABOVE
VAULT
FPL.
Vaulted Great Room 18^0 x 14^3
COATS
W. D.
LINEN
Bath
Foyer
Covered Porch
Bedroom 3 11^0 x 10^4
Bedroom 2 10^9 x 10^0

MAIN FLOOR

Design 10643

Units	Single
Price Code	A
Total Finished	1,285 sq. ft.
Main Finished	1,285 sq. ft.
Garage Unfinished	473 sq. ft.
Dimensions	62'x40'
Foundation	Crawlspace
Bedrooms	3
Full Baths	1
3/4 Baths	1
Max Ridge Height	26'
Roof Framing	Stick
Exterior Walls	2x6

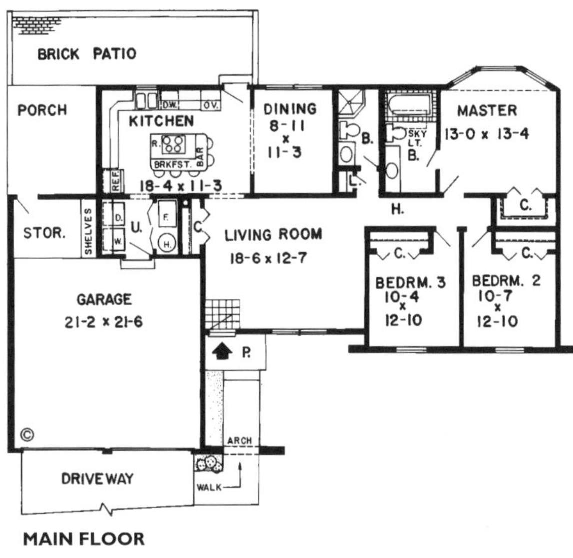
BRICK PATIO
PORCH
KITCHEN
BRKFST. BAR
18-4 x 11-3
DINING
8-11 x 11-3
MASTER
13-0 x 13-4
STOR.
SHELVES
LIVING ROOM
18-6 x 12-7
BEDRM. 3
10-4 x 12-10
BEDRM. 2
10-7 x 12-10
GARAGE
21-2 x 21-6
ARCH
DRIVEWAY
WALK

MAIN FLOOR

Design 97614

Units	Single
Price Code	A
Total Finished	1,287 sq. ft.
Main Finished	1,287 sq. ft.
Bonus Unfinished	312 sq. ft.
Basement Unfinished	1,287 sq. ft.
Garage Unfinished	516 sq. ft.
Dimensions	50'x55'10"
Foundation	Basement Crawlspace
Bedrooms	3
Full Baths	2
Max Ridge Height	24'
Roof Framing	Stick
Exterior Walls	2x4

FILES AVAILABLE
CAD
For more information call
800-235-5700

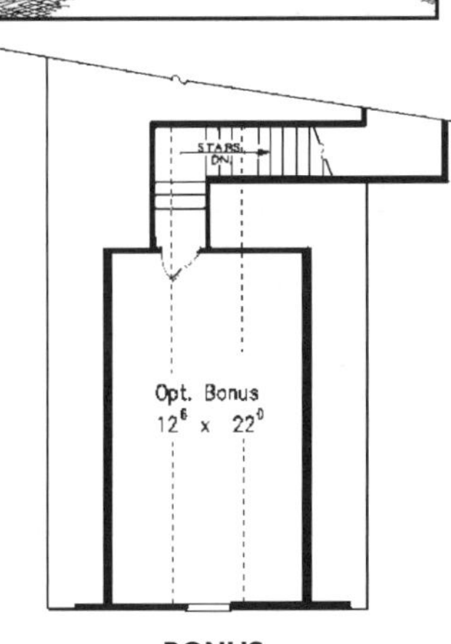
STAIRS DN
Opt. Bonus
12⁶ x 22⁰

BONUS

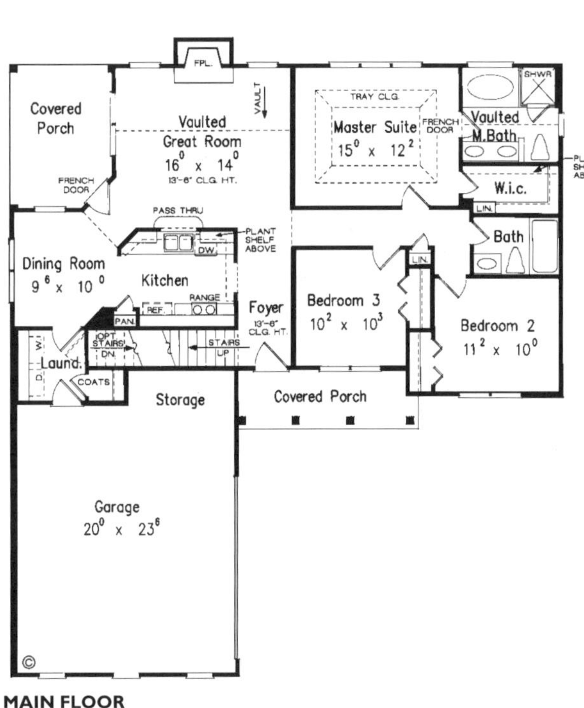
FPL.
Covered Porch
Vaulted Great Room
16⁰ x 14⁰
13'-6" CLG. HT.
FRENCH DOOR
PASS THRU
TRAY CLG.
Master Suite
15⁰ x 12²
Vaulted M.Bath
W.i.c.
PLANT SHELF ABOVE
Bath
Dining Room
9⁶ x 10⁰
Kitchen
Foyer
Bedroom 3
10² x 10³
Bedroom 2
11² x 10⁰
Laund.
COATS
Storage
Covered Porch
Garage
20⁰ x 23⁶

MAIN FLOOR

Design 98444

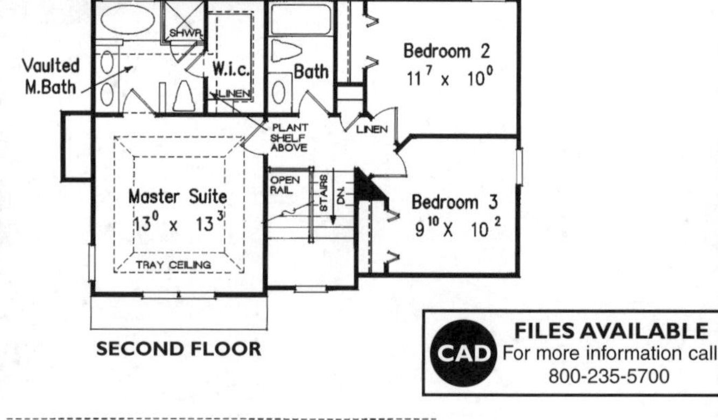
Vaulted M.Bath
SHWR.
W.i.c.
LINEN
Bath
Bedroom 2
11 7 x 10 0
PLANT SHELF ABOVE
LINEN
Master Suite
13 0 x 13 3
TRAY CEILING
OPEN RAIL
STAIRS
DN.
Bedroom 3
9 10 X 10 2
SECOND FLOOR

FILES AVAILABLE
CAD For more information call 800-235-5700

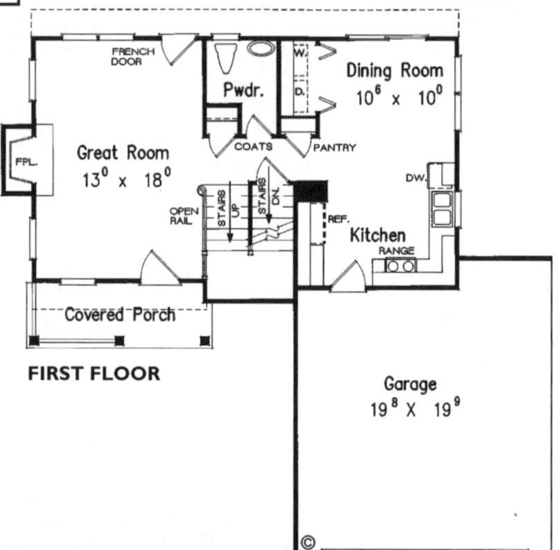
FRENCH DOOR
Pwdr.
Dining Room
10 6 x 10 0
FPL.
Great Room
13 0 x 18 0
COATS
PANTRY
DW.
OPEN RAIL
STAIRS UP
STAIRS DN.
REF.
Kitchen
RANGE
Covered Porch
FIRST FLOOR
Garage
19 8 X 19 9

Units	Single
Price Code	A
Total Finished	1,288 sq. ft.
First Finished	628 sq. ft.
Second Finished	660 sq. ft.
Basement Unfinished	628 sq. ft.
Garage Unfinished	424 sq. ft.
Dimensions	42'10"x39'
Foundation	Basement Crawlspace Slab
Bedrooms	3
Full Baths	2
Half Baths	1
Max Ridge Height	27'
Roof Framing	Stick
Exterior Walls	2x4

Design 93222

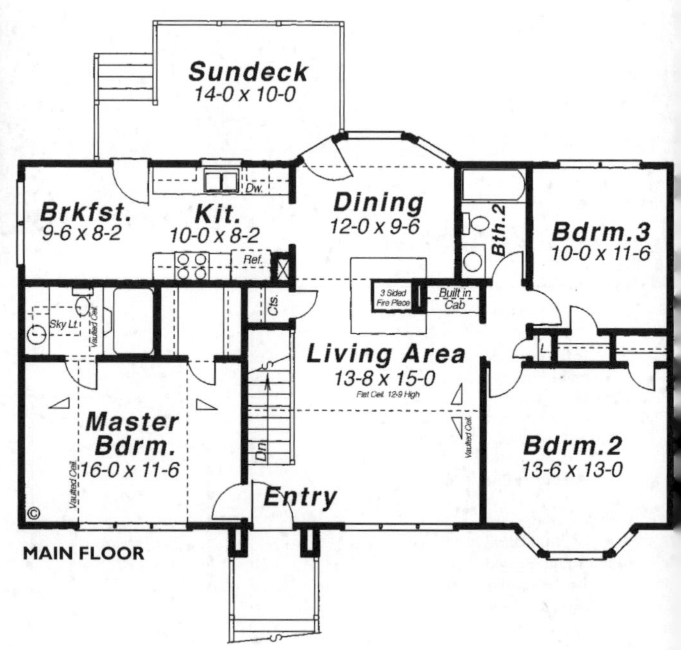
Sundeck
14-0 x 10-0
Brkfst.
9-6 x 8-2
Kit.
10-0 x 8-2
Dw.
Ref.
Dining
12-0 x 9-6
Bth.2
Bdrm.3
10-0 x 11-6
Sky Lt
Cts.
3 Sided Fire Place
Built in Cab
Living Area
13-8 x 15-0
Master Bdrm.
16-0 x 11-6
Dn
Bdrm.2
13-6 x 13-0
Entry
MAIN FLOOR

Units	Single
Price Code	A
Total Finished	1,292 sq. ft.
Main Finished	1,276 sq. ft.
Lower Finished	16 sq. ft.
Basement Unfinished	392 sq. ft.
Garage Unfinished	728 sq. ft.
Dimensions	48'x38'
Foundation	Basement
Bedrooms	3
Full Baths	2
Main Ceiling	8'
Max Ridge Height	16'
Roof Framing	Stick
Exterior Walls	2x4

Design 92523

Units	Single
Price Code	A
Total Finished	1,293 sq. ft.
Main Finished	1,293 sq. ft.
Garage Unfinished	433 sq. ft.
Porch Unfinished	76 sq. ft.
Dimensions	51'10"x40'4"
Foundation	Slab
Bedrooms	3
Full Baths	2
Max Ridge Height	22'
Roof Framing	Stick
Exterior Walls	2x4

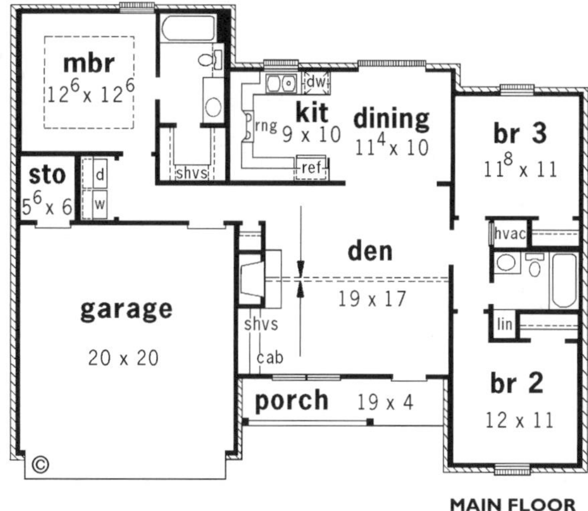
mbr
12⁶ x 12⁶
shvs
dw
kit
9 x 10
rng
ref
dining
11⁴ x 10
br 3
11⁸ x 11
sto
5⁶ x 6
d
w
hvac
den
19 x 17
garage
20 x 20
shvs
cab
lin
porch 19 x 4
br 2
12 x 11
©

MAIN FLOOR

Design 97334

Units	Single
Price Code	A
Total Finished	1,295 sq. ft.
Main Finished	1,295 sq. ft.
Basement Unfinished	1,295 sq. ft.
Garage Unfinished	386 sq. ft.
Dimensions	46'x47'4"
Foundation	Basement
Bedrooms	3
Full Baths	1
3/4 Baths	1
Main Ceiling	9'
Max Ridge Height	19'11"
Roof Framing	Truss
Exterior Walls	2x4

LIN.
MBR.
11'4"X13'4"
LIV.
15'6"X13'4"
DIN.
11'4"X9'8"
EATING BAR
KIT.
11'6"X11'0"
DN.
PAN
LIN.
E.
BR. #3
9'10"X10'0"
BR. #2
9'10"X11'4"
2 CAR GAR.
19'4"X20'0"
©

MAIN FLOOR

Design 92431

Units	Single
Price Code	A
Total Finished	1,296 sq. ft.
Main Finished	1,296 sq. ft.
Basement Unfinished	1,336 sq. ft.
Garage Unfinished	380 sq. ft.
Dimensions	46'x42'
Foundation	Basement Crawlspace Slab
Bedrooms	3
Full Baths	2
Main Ceiling	8'
Vaulted Ceiling	12'
Max Ridge Height	17'6"
Roof Framing	Truss
Exterior Walls	2x4

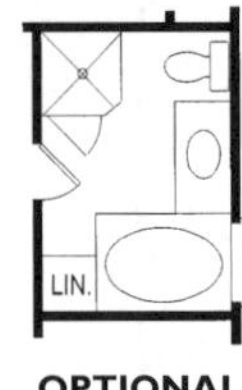
LIN.

OPTIONAL MASTER BATH

OPTIONAL BAY
BEDROOM 2
11x11
DINING
FAMILY ROOM
16x20
VLT.
KITCHEN
10x10
BEDROOM 3
11x10
W
D
12' CEILING
W/H
VLT.
MASTER
BEDROOM
12x14
GARAGE
19x20

MAIN FLOOR

Design 97476

Units	Single
Price Code	A
Total Finished	1,297 sq. ft.
First Finished	603 sq. ft.
Second Finished	694 sq. ft.
Bonus Unfinished	354 sq. ft.
Garage Unfinished	478 sq. ft.
Deck Unfinished	160 sq. ft.
Dimensions	42'x43'
Foundation	Basement
Bedrooms	3
Full Baths	2
Half Baths	1
First Ceiling	9'
Max Ridge Height	25'8"
Exterior Walls	2x4

* Alternate foundation options available at an additional charge. Please call 1-800-235-5700 for more information.

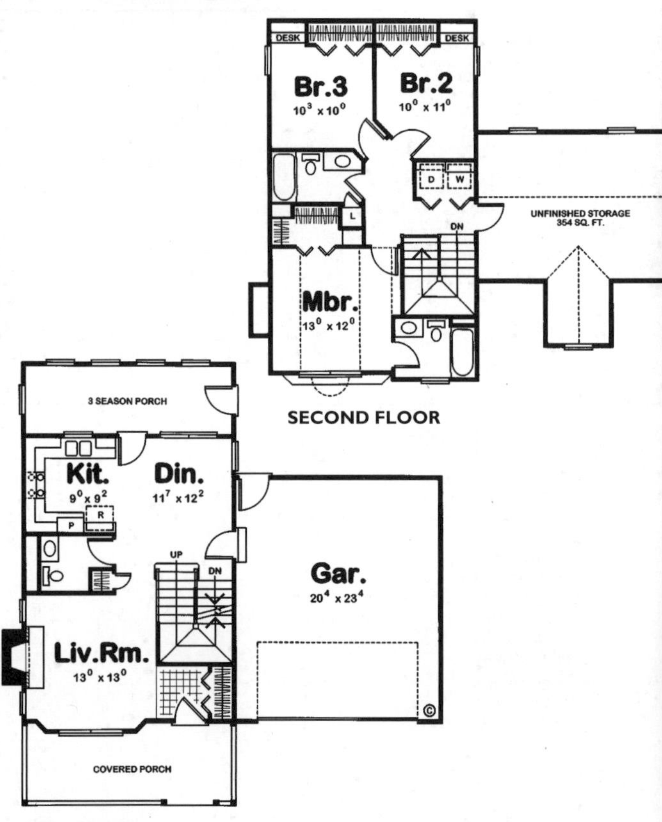
DESK
DESK
Br.3
10³ x 10⁰
Br.2
10⁰ x 11⁰
L
D
W
UNFINISHED STORAGE
354 SQ. FT.
DN
Mbr.
13⁰ x 12⁰
SECOND FLOOR
3 SEASON PORCH
Kit.
9⁰ x 9²
Din.
11⁷ x 12²
R
P
UP
DN
Gar.
20⁴ x 23⁴
Liv.Rm.
13⁰ x 13⁰
COVERED PORCH

SECOND FLOOR

FIRST FLOOR

Design 65134

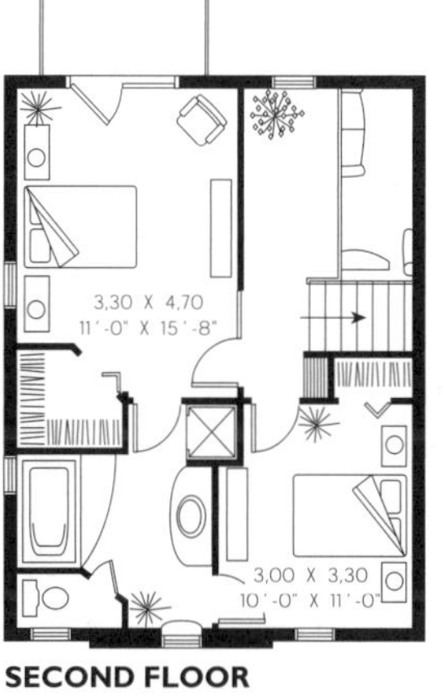
3,30 X 4,70
11'-0" X 15'-8"
3,00 X 3,30
10'-0" X 11'-0"

SECOND FLOOR

Units	Single
Price Code	A
Total Finished	1,304 sq. ft.
First Finished	681 sq. ft.
Second Finished	623 sq. ft.
Garage Unfinished	260 sq. ft.
Dimensions	28'x40'
Foundation	Basement
Bedrooms	2
Full Baths	1
Half Baths	1
First Ceiling	8'
Second Ceiling	8'
Roof Framing	Truss
Exterior Walls	2x6

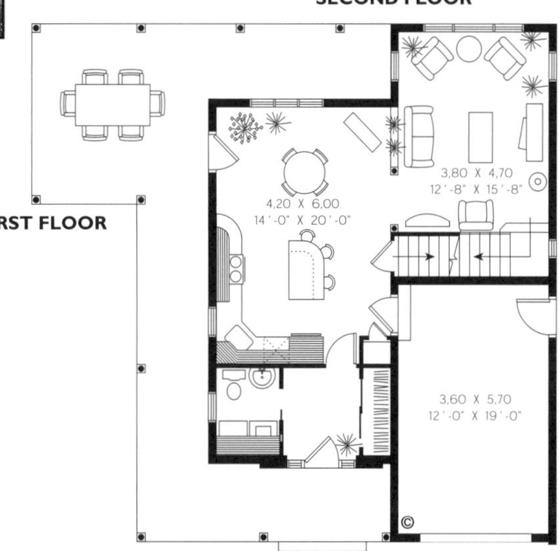
4,20 X 6,00
14'-0" X 20'-0"
3,80 X 4,70
12'-8" X 15'-8"
3,60 X 5,70
12'-0" X 19'-0"

FIRST FLOOR

Design 20161

PHOTOGRAPHY: JOHN EHRENCLOU

Units	Single
Price Code	A
Total Finished	1,307 sq. ft.
Main Finished	1,307 sq. ft.
Basement Unfinished	1,298 sq. ft.
Garage Unfinished	462 sq. ft.
Dimensions	50'x40'
Foundation	Basement Crawlspace Slab
Bedrooms	3
Full Baths	2
Main Ceiling	8'
Max Ridge Height	19'
Roof Framing	Stick
Exterior Walls	2x6

Please note: The photographed home may have been modified to suit homeowner preferences. If you order plans, have a builder or design professional check them against the photograph to confirm actual construction details.

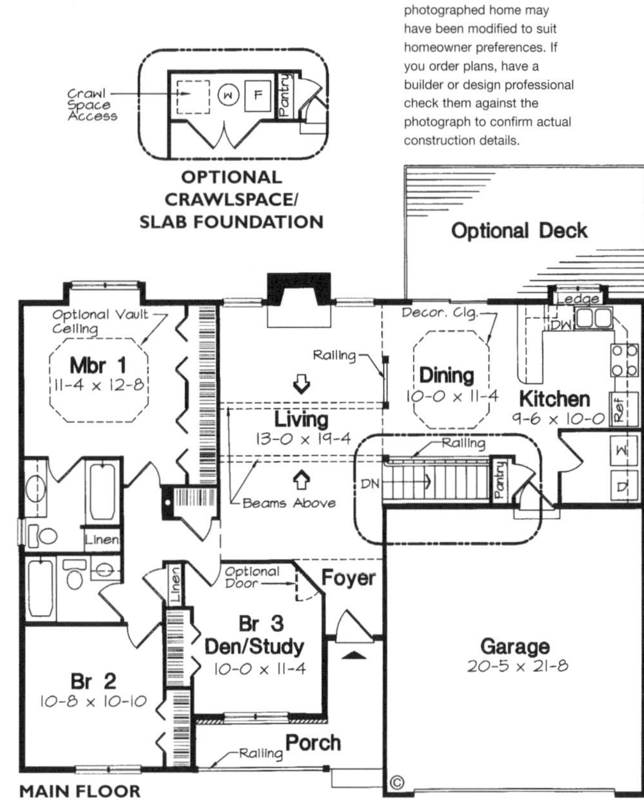
Crawl Space Access
W
F
Pantry
OPTIONAL CRAWLSPACE/ SLAB FOUNDATION
Optional Deck
Optional Vault Ceiling
Mbr 1
11-4 x 12-8
Railing
Decor. Clg.
Ledge
DW
Dining
10-0 x 11-4
Kitchen
9-6 x 10-0
Ref
Living
13-0 x 19-4
Railing
W
D
DN
Pantry
Beams Above
Linen
Linen
Optional Door
Foyer
Br 3
Den/Study
10-0 x 11-4
Br 2
10-8 x 10-10
Garage
20-5 x 21-8
Railing
Porch

MAIN FLOOR

Design 63046

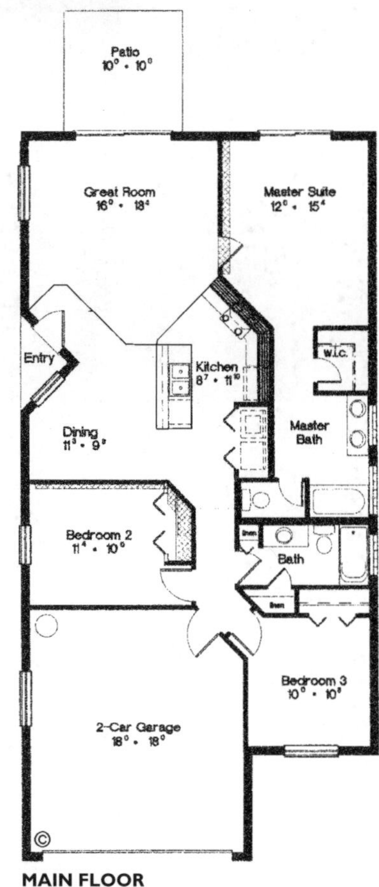

Patio
10⁰ • 10⁰
Great Room
16⁰ • 18⁴
Master Suite
12⁰ • 15⁴
Entry
Kitchen
8⁷ • 11¹⁰
W.I.C.
Dining
11³ • 9⁹
Master Bath
Bedroom 2
11⁴ • 10⁰
Bath
Bedroom 3
10⁰ • 10⁰
2-Car Garage
18⁰ • 18⁰
©

MAIN FLOOR

Units	Single
Price Code	A
Total Finished	1,309 sq. ft.
Main Finished	1,309 sq. ft.
Garage Unfinished	383 sq. ft.
Dimensions	30'x60'
Foundation	Slab
Bedrooms	3
Full Baths	2
Main Ceiling	8'
Vaulted Ceiling	11'10"
Max Ridge Height	15'11"
Roof Framing	Truss

Design 65173

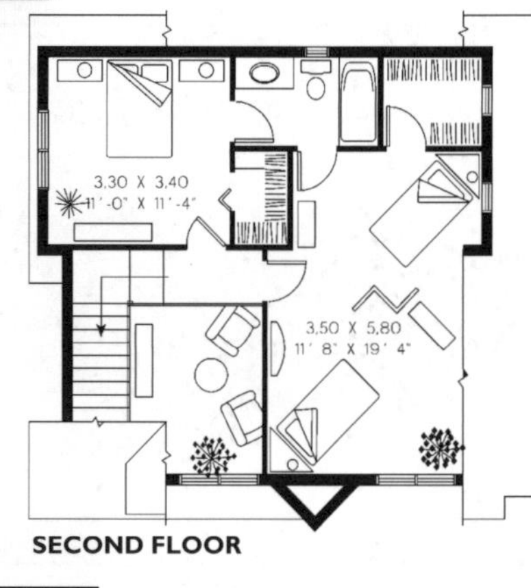

3.30 X 3.40
11'-0" X 11'-4"
3.50 X 5.80
11' 8" X 19' 4"

SECOND FLOOR

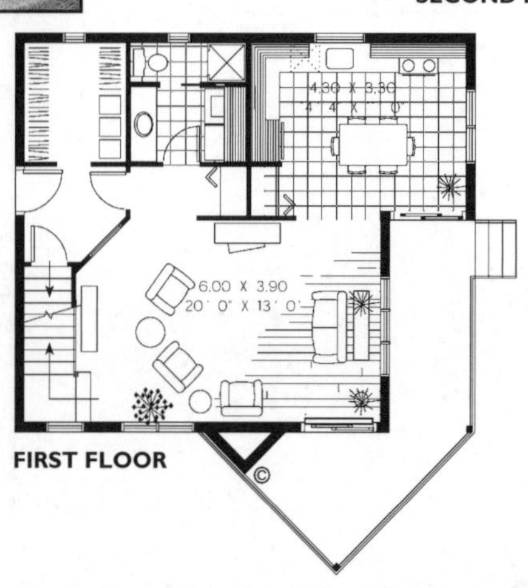

6.00 X 3.90
20' 0" X 13' 0"
©

FIRST FLOOR

Units	Single
Price Code	A
Total Finished	1,311 sq. ft.
First Finished	713 sq. ft.
Second Finished	598 sq. ft.
Basement Unfinished	713 sq. ft.
Porch Unfinished	158 sq. ft.
Dimensions	30'8"x26'
Foundation	Basement
Bedrooms	2
Full Baths	1
3/4 Baths	1
First Ceiling	8'
Second Ceiling	8'
Max Ridge Height	28'4"
Roof Framing	Truss
Exterior Walls	2x6

Design 68096

Units	Single
Price Code	A
Total Finished	1,311 sq. ft.
Main Finished	1,311 sq. ft.
Garage Unfinished	439 sq. ft.
Deck Unfinished	112 sq. ft.
Dimensions	34'8"x58'4"
Foundation	Crawlspace Slab
Bedrooms	3
Full Baths	2
Main Ceiling	9'
Max Ridge Height	22'6"
Exterior Walls	2x4

* Alternate foundation options available at an additional charge. Please call 1-800-235-5700 for more information.

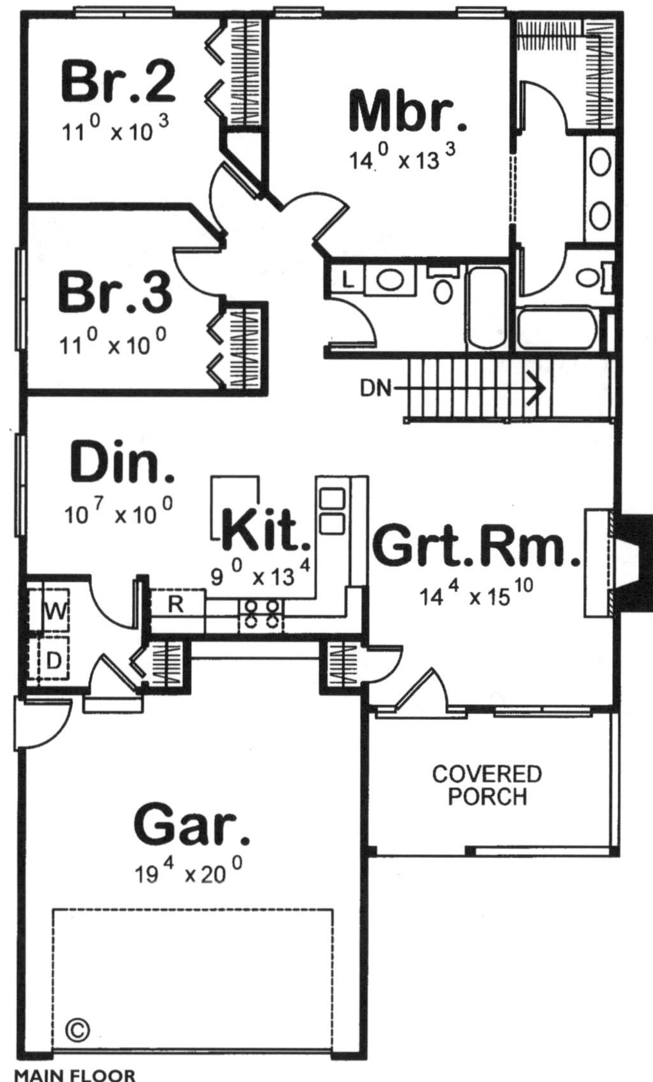
Br.2
11 0 x 10 3
Mbr.
14 0 x 13 3
Br.3
11 0 x 10 0
L
DN
Din.
10 7 x 10 0
Kit.
9 0 x 13 4
Grt.Rm.
14 4 x 15 10
W
D
R
COVERED PORCH
Gar.
19 4 x 20 0
©

MAIN FLOOR

Design 24700

Units	Single
Price Code	A
Total Finished	1,312 sq. ft.
Main Finished	1,312 sq. ft.
Basement Unfinished	1,293 sq. ft.
Garage Unfinished	459 sq. ft.
Deck Unfinished	185 sq. ft.
Porch Unfinished	84 sq. ft.
Dimensions	50'x40'
Foundation	Basement Crawlspace Slab
Bedrooms	3
Full Baths	2
Main Ceiling	8'
Max Ridge Height	20'
Roof Framing	Stick
Exterior Walls	2x6

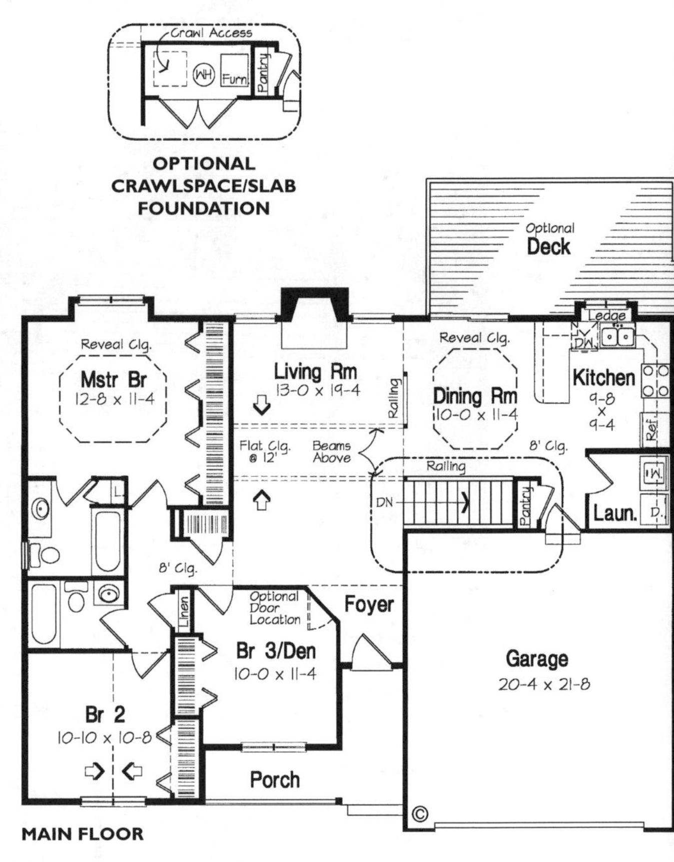
Crawl Access
WH
Furn.
Pantry
OPTIONAL CRAWLSPACE/SLAB FOUNDATION
Optional Deck
Ledge
DW
Reveal Clg.
Mstr Br
12-8 x 11-4
Living Rm
13-0 x 19-4
Railing
Reveal Clg.
Dining Rm
10-0 x 11-4
Kitchen
9-8 x 9-4
Ref.
Flat Clg. @ 12'
Beams Above
8' Clg.
Railing
DN
Pantry
Laun.
8' Clg.
Linen
Optional Door Location
Foyer
Br 3/Den
10-0 x 11-4
Garage
20-4 x 21-8
Br 2
10-10 x 10-8
Porch
MAIN FLOOR

Design 97731

Units	Single
Price Code	A
Total Finished	1,315 sq. ft.
Main Finished	1,315 sq. ft.
Basement Unfinished	1,315 sq. ft.
Garage Unfinished	488 sq. ft.
Porch Unfinished	75 sq. ft.
Dimensions	50'x54'8"
Foundation	Basement
Bedrooms	3
Full Baths	2
Main Ceiling	8'
Max Ridge Height	18'
Roof Framing	Truss
Exterior Walls	2x4

Deck
Master Bedroom
12'-4" x 13'-0"
Great Room
18'-8" x 17'-4"
SLOPE CEIL
Bedroom
11'-4" x 10'-8"
DN 13 RISERS
Bath
Dining
Bath
Kitchen
13'-4" x 9'-11"
SLOPE CEIL
Foyer
Bedroom
12'-4" x 10'-10"
Laun.
Porch
MAIN FLOOR
Garage
20'-0" x 26'-2"

Design 93296

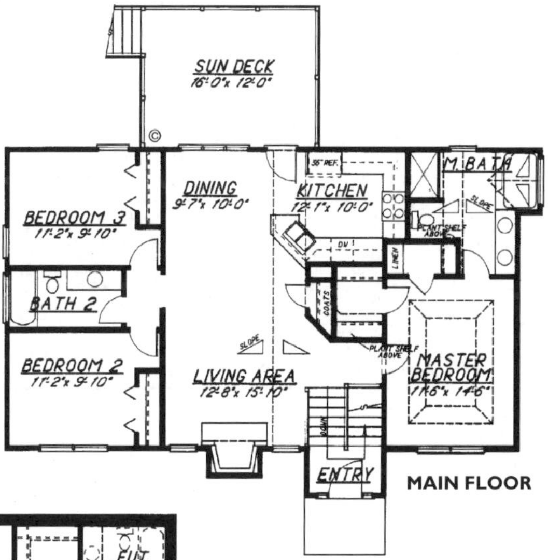

Units	Single
Price Code	A
Total Finished	1,316 sq. ft.
Main Finished	1,237 sq. ft.
Lower Finished	79 sq. ft.
Bonus Unfinished	310 sq. ft.
Deck Unfinished	192 sq. ft.
Dimensions	46'x30'
Foundation	Basement
Bedrooms	3
Full Baths	2
Max Ridge Height	28'
Roof Framing	Stick
Exterior Walls	2x4

SUN DECK 16'-0" x 12'-0"
BEDROOM 3 11'-2" x 9'-10"
DINING 9'-7" x 10'-0"
KITCHEN 12'-1" x 10'-0"
M.BATH
BATH 2
BEDROOM 2 11'-2" x 9'-10"
LIVING AREA 12'-8" x 15'-10"
MASTER BEDROOM 11'-6" x 14'-6"
ENTRY

MAIN FLOOR

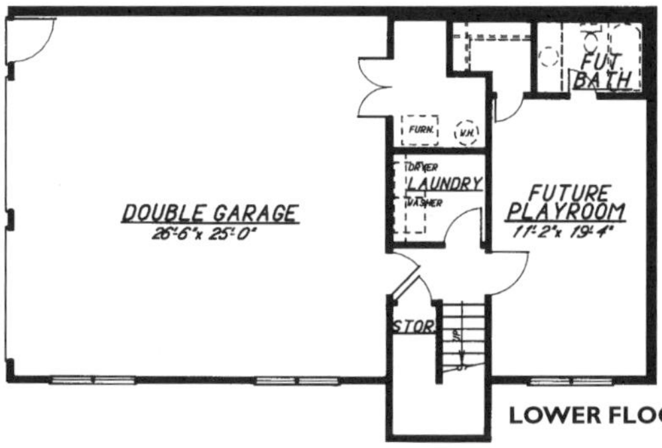

DOUBLE GARAGE 26'-6" x 25'-0"
FUT. BATH
LAUNDRY
FUTURE PLAYROOM 11'-2" x 19'-4"
STOR.

LOWER FLOOR

Design 82044

Units	Single
Price Code	A
Total Finished	1,317 sq. ft.
Main Finished	1,317 sq. ft.
Garage Unfinished	412 sq. ft.
Porch Unfinished	163 sq. ft.
Dimensions	46'x54'10"
Foundation	Basement Crawlspace Slab
Bedrooms	3
Full Baths	2
Main Ceiling	9'
Roof Framing	Stick
Exterior Walls	2x4

GRILLING PORCH
NOOK 7'-0" X 8'-0"
STORAGE
BED RM. 2 11'-0" X 13'-0"
KIT. 10'-4" X 14'-8"
GARAGE 17'-8" X 23'-4"
BED RM. 3 10'-8" X 11'-6"
DINING 10'-0" X 9'-0"
OPT. GAS FIREPLACE
GREAT RM. 14'-0" X 16'-0"
MASTER SUITE 10' BOXED CEILING 13'-0" X 13'-0"
COVERED PORCH 14'-4" X 5'-0"

MAIN FLOOR

Design 66094

Units	Single
Price Code	A
Total Finished	1,319 sq. ft.
Main Finished	1,319 sq. ft.
Garage Unfinished	420 sq. ft.
Dimensions	42'x60'2"
Foundation	Slab
Bedrooms	3
Full Baths	1
3/4 Baths	1
Main Ceiling	8'
Max Ridge Height	23'
Roof Framing	Stick
Exterior Walls	2x4

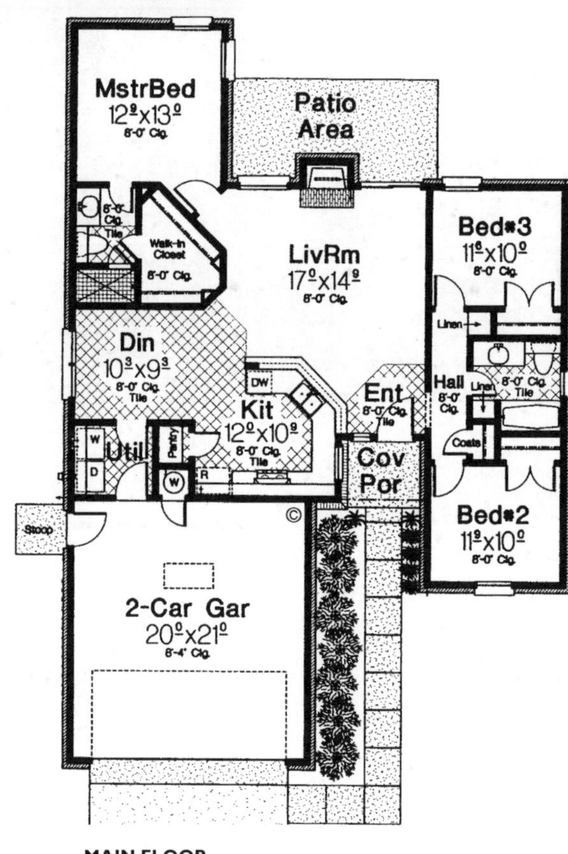
MstrBed
12⁰x13⁰
Patio Area
Walk-in Closet
LivRm
17⁰x14⁹
Bed#3
11⁶x10⁰
Din
10³x9³
Kit
12⁰x10⁹
Ent
Hall
Util
Cov Por
Stoop
2-Car Gar
20⁰x21⁰
Bed#2
11⁹x10⁰
MAIN FLOOR

Design 69157

Units	Single
Price Code	A
Total Finished	1,321 sq. ft.
Main Finished	1,321 sq. ft.
Garage Unfinished	484 sq. ft.
Dimensions	54'x46'
Foundation	Crawlspace
Bedrooms	3
Full Baths	1
3/4 Baths	1
Main Ceiling	8'
Max Ridge Height	17'
Roof Framing	Truss
Exterior Walls	2x6

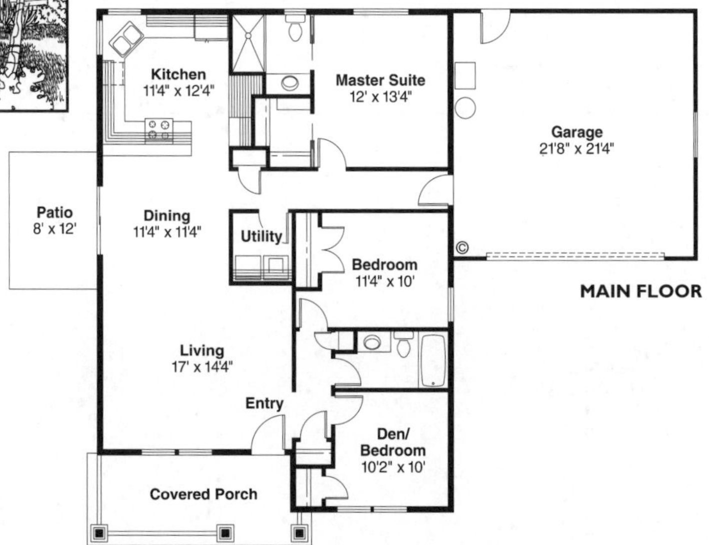
Kitchen
11'4" x 12'4"
Master Suite
12' x 13'4"
Garage
21'8" x 21'4"
Patio
8' x 12'
Dining
11'4" x 11'4"
Utility
Bedroom
11'4" x 10'
Living
17' x 14'4"
Entry
Den/
Bedroom
10'2" x 10'
Covered Porch
MAIN FLOOR

Design 65284

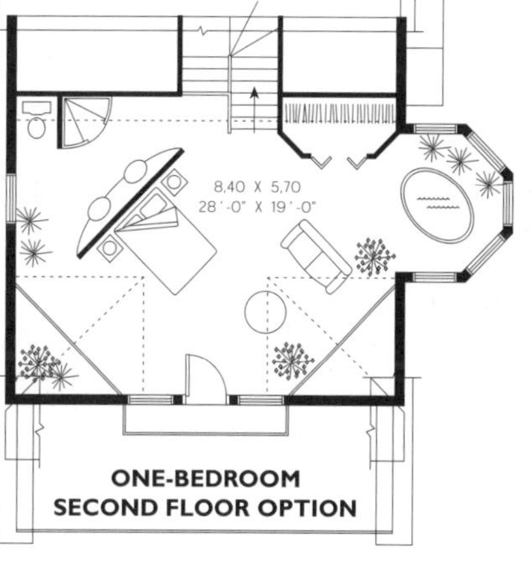
8,40 X 5,70
28'-0" X 19'-0"
ONE-BEDROOM SECOND FLOOR OPTION

Units	Single
Price Code	A
Total Finished	1,324 sq. ft.
First Finished	737 sq. ft.
Second Finished	587 sq. ft.
Dimensions	26'x33'
Foundation	Basement
Bedrooms	1
Full Baths	1
Half Baths	1
First Ceiling	8'
Second Ceiling	8'
Max Ridge Height	34'9"
Roof Framing	Truss
Exterior Walls	2x6

2,40 X 2,70
8'-0" X 9'-0"
3,30 X 5,70
11'-0" X 19'-0"
4,20 X 4,80
14'-0" X 16'-0"
©

FIRST FLOOR

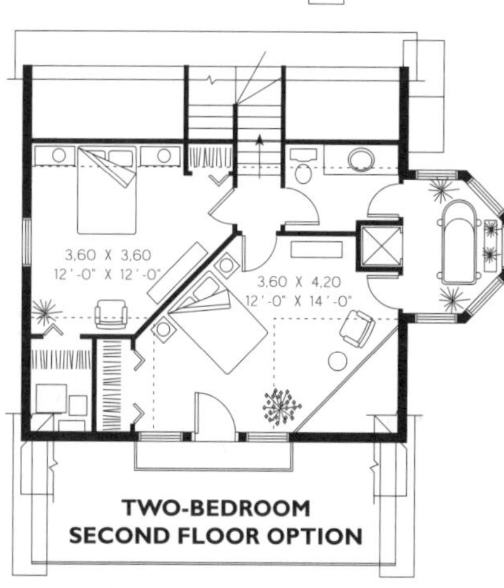
3,60 X 3,60
12'-0" X 12'-0"
3,60 X 4,20
12'-0" X 14'-0"
TWO-BEDROOM SECOND FLOOR OPTION

Design 93265

Sundeck
14-0 x 10-0
Dw.
Dining
10-0 x 9-6
M.Bath
Master Bdrm.
14-0 x 14-0
Kit.
8-0 x 9-6
Bth.2
Ref.
Opt. Plant Shelf Above
Living Area
14-8 x 15-6
Flat Ceil. Line 12-0 High
Vaulted Ceil.
Clo.
Lin.
Up
Dn
Entry
Bdrm.3
9-4 x 11-6
Bdrm.2
10-4 x 9-6

MAIN FLOOR

Units	Single
Price Code	A
Total Finished	1,325 sq. ft.
Main Finished	1,269 sq. ft.
Lower Finished	56 sq. ft.
Bonus Unfinished	382 sq. ft.
Garage Unfinished	598 sq. ft.
Deck Unfinished	140 sq. ft.
Dimensions	45'x36'
Foundation	Basement
Bedrooms	3
Full Baths	2
Max Ridge Height	16'
Roof Framing	Stick/Truss
Exterior Walls	2x4

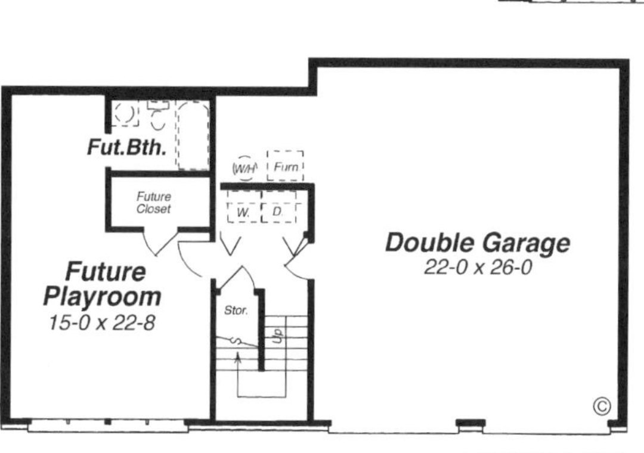
Fut.Bth.
W/H
Furn
Future Closet
W.
D.
Future Playroom
15-0 x 22-8
Stor.
Up
Double Garage
22-0 x 26-0
©
LOWER FLOOR

Design 34600

PHOTOGRAPHY: MICHELE EVANS CHRISTY

Please note: The photographed home may have been modified to suit homeowner preferences. If you order plans, have a builder or design professional check them against the photograph to confirm actual construction details.

SECOND FLOOR

Units	Single
Price Code	A
Total Finished	1,328 sq. ft.
First Finished	1,013 sq. ft.
Second Finished	315 sq. ft.
Basement Unfinished	1,013 sq. ft.
Dimensions	36'x36'
Foundation	Basement Crawlspace Slab
Bedrooms	3
Full Baths	2
First Ceiling	8'
Second Ceiling	7'6"
Max Ridge Height	23'6"
Roof Framing	Stick
Exterior Walls	2x4, 2x6

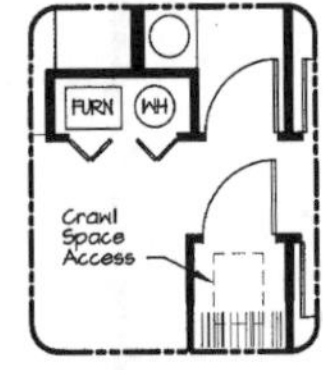
FURN
WH
Crawl Space Access

OPTIONAL CRAWLSPACE/SLAB FOUNDATION

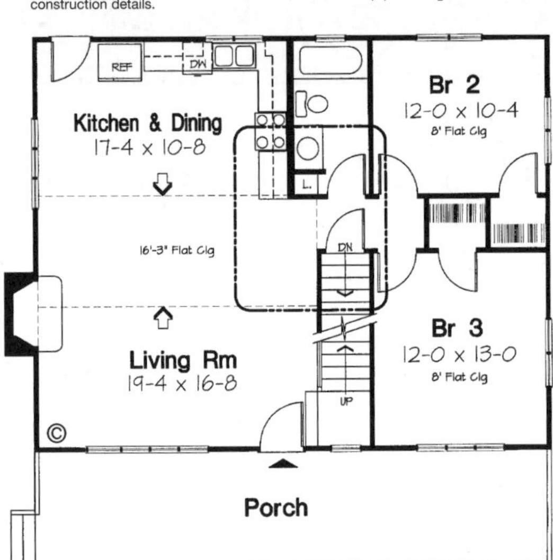
REF
DW
Kitchen & Dining
17-4 x 10-8
16'-3" Flat Clg
Living Rm
19-4 x 16-8
Br 2
12-0 x 10-4
8' Flat Clg
Br 3
12-0 x 13-0
8' Flat Clg
DN
UP
Porch

FIRST FLOOR

Design 90669

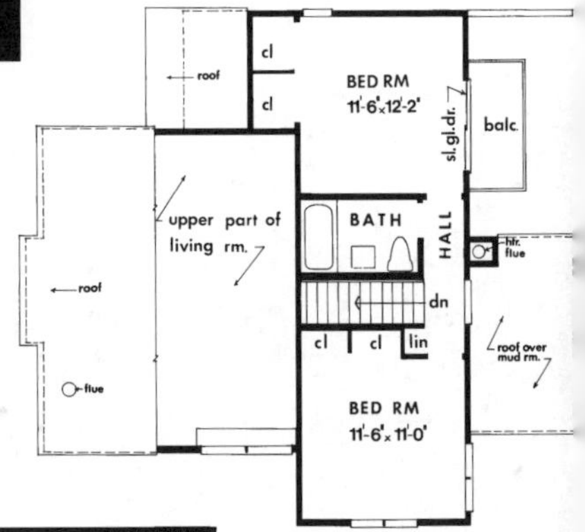

SECOND FLOOR

FIRST FLOOR

Units	Single
Price Code	A
Total Finished	1,332 sq. ft.
First Finished	877 sq. ft.
Second Finished	455 sq. ft.
Dimensions	37'2"x35'
Foundation	Crawlspace
Bedrooms	3
Full Baths	2

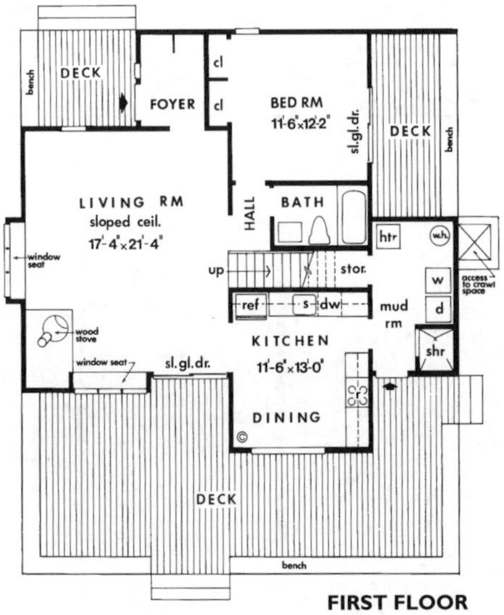

Design 93453

Units	Single
Price Code	A
Total Finished	1,333 sq. ft.
Main Finished	1,333 sq. ft.
Garage Unfinished	520 sq. ft.
Dimensions	55'6"x64'3"
Foundation	Crawlspace Slab
Bedrooms	3
Full Baths	2
Main Ceiling	8'
Max Ridge Height	19'5"
Roof Framing	Stick
Exterior Walls	2x4

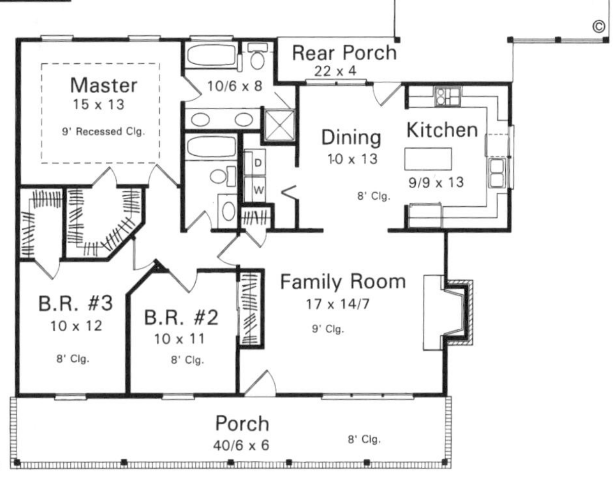
Storage
20 x 6
8' Clg.
Carport
20 x 20
8' Clg.
Rear Porch
22 x 4
Master
15 x 13
9' Recessed Clg.
10/6 x 8
Dining
10 x 13
8' Clg.
Kitchen
9/9 x 13
D
W
Family Room
17 x 14/7
9' Clg.
B.R. #3
10 x 12
8' Clg.
B.R. #2
10 x 11
8' Clg.
Porch
40/6 x 6
8' Clg.

MAIN FLOOR

Design 97332

Units	Single
Price Code	A
Total Finished	1,340 sq. ft.
Main Finished	1,340 sq. ft.
Basement Unfinished	1,340 sq. ft.
Garage Unfinished	419 sq. ft.
Dimensions	51'x40'
Foundation	Basement
Bedrooms	3
Full Baths	1
3/4 Baths	1
Main Ceiling	9'
Max Ridge Height	19'11"
Roof Framing	Truss
Exterior Walls	2x4

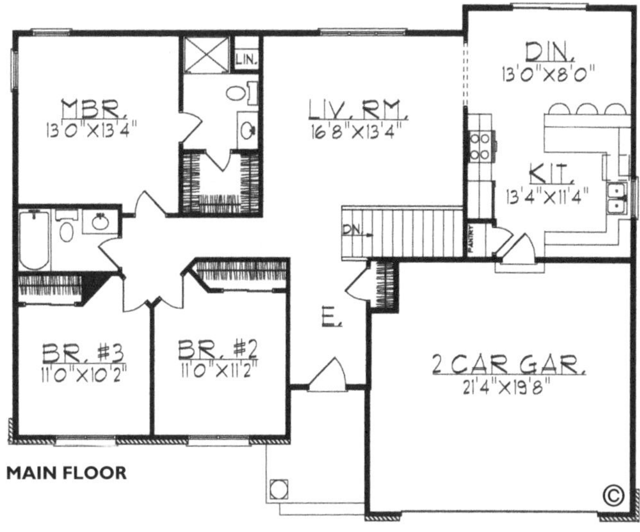
LIN.
MBR.
13'0"X13'4"
LIV. RM.
16'8"X13'4"
DIN.
13'0"X8'0"
KIT.
13'4"X11'4"
DN.
E.
BR. #3
11'0"X10'2"
BR. #2
11'0"X11'2"
2 CAR GAR.
21'4"X19'8"

MAIN FLOOR

Design 26111

Bedroom
12'-0"x 13'-0"
Cl
Bath
Cl
dn
Skylights
Balcony
Bedroom
12'-0"x 20'-0"
Open to Living
Cl
SECOND FLOOR

Units	Single
Price Code	A
Total Finished	1,341 sq. ft.
First Finished	769 sq. ft.
Second Finished	572 sq. ft.
Basement Unfinished	546 sq. ft.
Dimensions	30'x32'
Foundation	Basement
Bedrooms	3
Full Baths	1
3/4 Baths	1
Max Ridge Height	33'
Roof Framing	Stick
Exterior Walls	2x4, 2x6

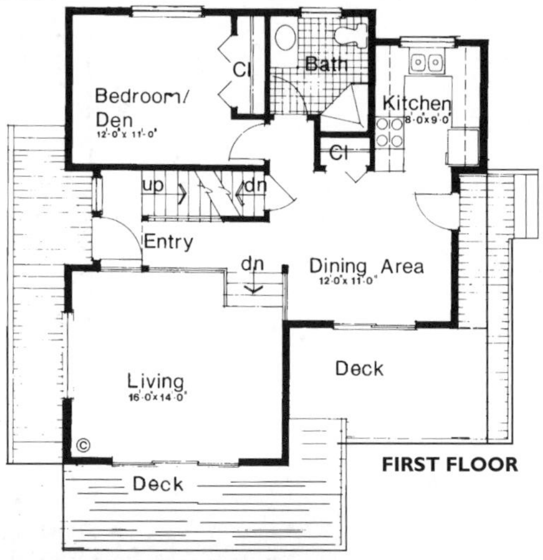
Bedroom/
Den
12'-0"x 11'-0"
Cl
Bath
Kitchen
8'-0"x9'-0"
Cl
up
dn
Entry
dn
Dining Area
12'-0"x 11'-0"
Deck
Living
16'-0"x14'-0"
Deck
FIRST FLOOR

Design 97331

Units	Single
Price Code	A
Total Finished	1,342 sq. ft.
Main Finished	1,342 sq. ft.
Basement Unfinished	1,342 sq. ft.
Garage Unfinished	416 sq. ft.
Dimensions	57'x45'
Foundation	Basement
Bedrooms	3
Full Baths	2
Main Ceiling	9'
Max Ridge Height	23'5"
Roof Framing	Truss
Exterior Walls	2x6

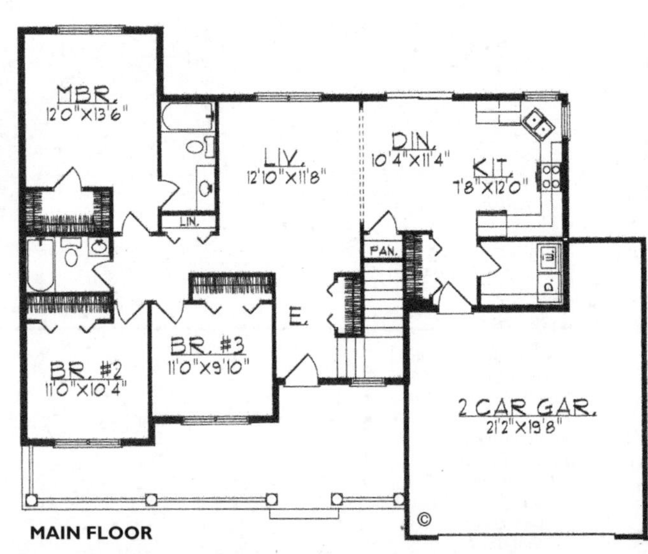
MBR.
12'0"X13'6"
LIV.
12'10"X11'8"
DIN.
10'4"X11'4"
KIT.
7'8"X12'0"
LIN.
PAN.
E.
BR. #2
11'0"X10'4"
BR. #3
11'0"X9'10"
2 CAR GAR.
21'2"X19'8"
MAIN FLOOR

Design 99186

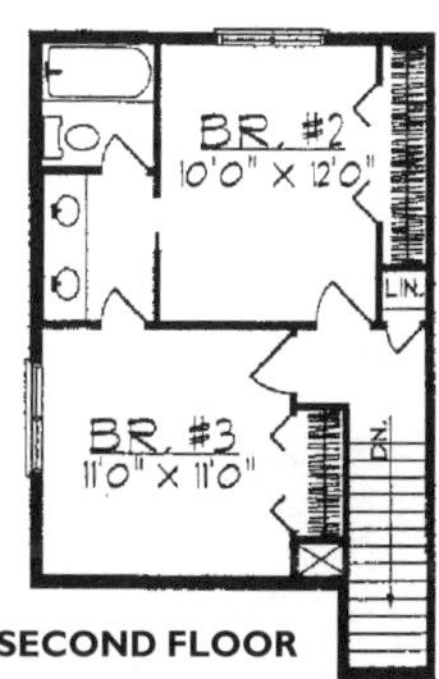
BR. #2
10'0" X 12'0"
LIN.
BR. #3
11'0" X 11'0"
DN.

SECOND FLOOR

Units	Single
Price Code	A
Total Finished	1,342 sq. ft.
First Finished	927 sq. ft.
Second Finished	415 sq. ft.
Basement Unfinished	927 sq. ft.
Garage Unfinished	440 sq. ft.
Dimensions	42'x44'
Foundation	Basement
Bedrooms	3
Full Baths	1
3/4 Baths	1
Half Baths	1
First Ceiling	8'
Second Ceiling	8'
Max Ridge Height	25'6"
Roof Framing	Truss
Exterior Walls	2x6

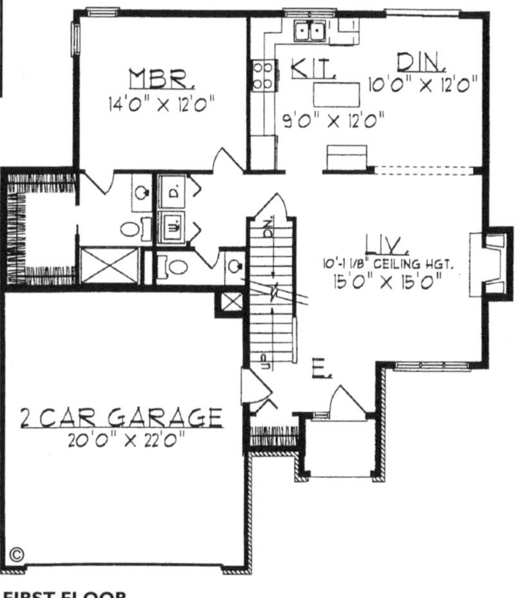
MBR.
14'0" X 12'0"
KIT.
9'0" X 12'0"
DIN.
10'0" X 12'0"
LIV.
10'-1 1/8" CEILING HGT.
15'0" X 15'0"
E.
UP
DN.
2 CAR GARAGE
20'0" X 22'0"

FIRST FLOOR

Design 97202

Units	Single
Price Code	A
Total Finished	1,344 sq. ft.
Main Finished	1,344 sq. ft.
Basement Unfinished	1,363 sq. ft.
Garage Unfinished	409 sq. ft.
Dimensions	48'x44'10"
Foundation	Basement Crawlspace Slab
Bedrooms	3
Full Baths	2
Main Ceiling	9'
Max Ridge Height	22'6"
Roof Framing	Stick
Exterior Walls	2x4

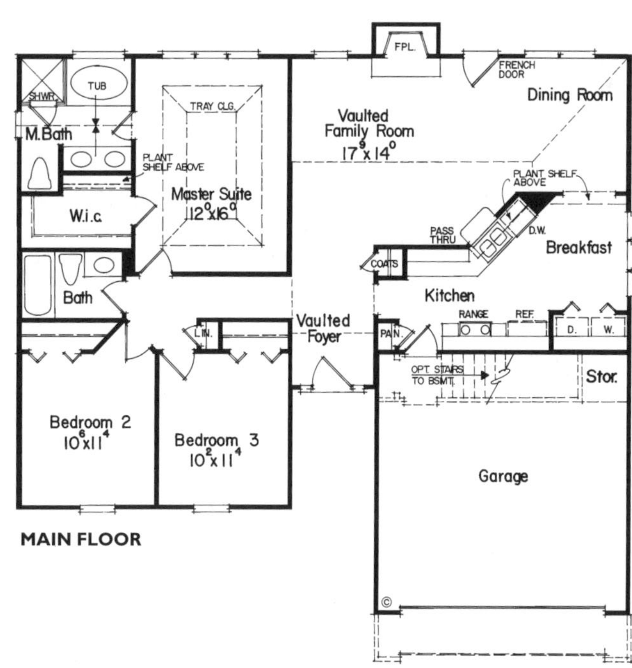
FPL.
FRENCH DOOR
Dining Room
SHWR.
TUB
M.Bath
TRAY CLG.
Vaulted
Family Room
17⁹x14⁰
PLANT SHELF ABOVE
Master Suite
12⁰x16⁰
PLANT SHELF ABOVE
W.i.c.
PASS THRU
D.W.
Breakfast
COATS
Bath
Kitchen
RANGE
REF.
Vaulted
Foyer
LIN.
PAN.
D.
W.
OPT STAIRS TO BSMT.
Stor.
Bedroom 2
10⁶x11⁴
Bedroom 3
10²x11⁴
Garage

MAIN FLOOR

Design 91342

Units	Single
Price Code	A
Total Finished	1,345 sq. ft.
Main Finished	1,345 sq. ft.
Dimensions	47'8"x56'
Foundation	Crawlspace Slab
Bedrooms	3
Full Baths	2
Max Ridge Height	19"
Roof Framing	Stick/Truss
Exterior Walls	2x4

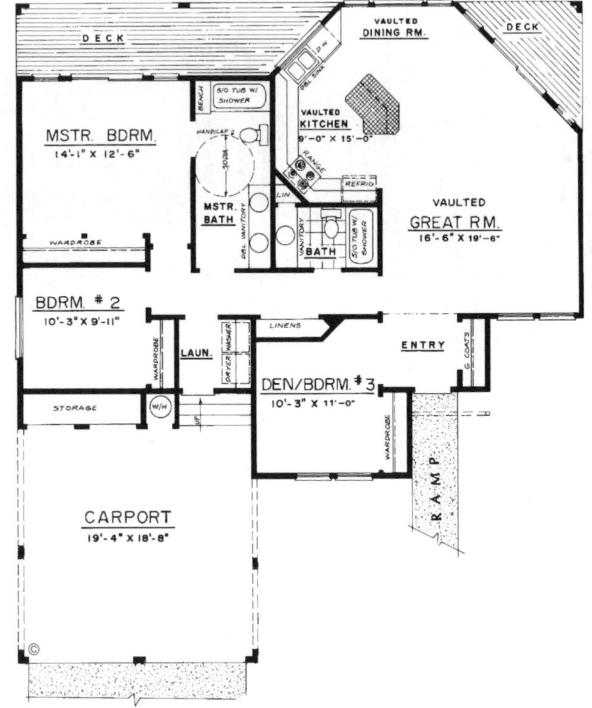
DECK
VAULTED
DINING RM.
DECK
MSTR. BDRM.
14'-1" X 12'-6"
VAULTED
KITCHEN
9'-0" X 15'-0"
MSTR.
BATH
VAULTED
GREAT RM.
16'-6" X 19'-6"
BATH
BDRM. # 2
10'-3" X 9'-11"
LAUN.
LINENS
ENTRY
DEN/BDRM. # 3
10'-3" X 11'-0"
STORAGE
CARPORT
19'-4" X 18'-8"
RAMP

MAIN FLOOR

Design 98912

Units	Single
Price Code	A
Total Finished	1,345 sq. ft.
Main Finished	1,325 sq. ft.
Lower Finished	20 sq. ft.
Basement Unfinished	556 sq. ft.
Garage Unfinished	724 sq. ft.
Deck Unfinished	157 sq. ft.
Porch Unfinished	216 sq. ft.
Dimensions	52'x42'
Foundation	Basement
Bedrooms	3
Full Baths	2
Main Ceiling	8'
Max Ridge Height	19'
Roof Framing	Stick
Exterior Walls	2x4

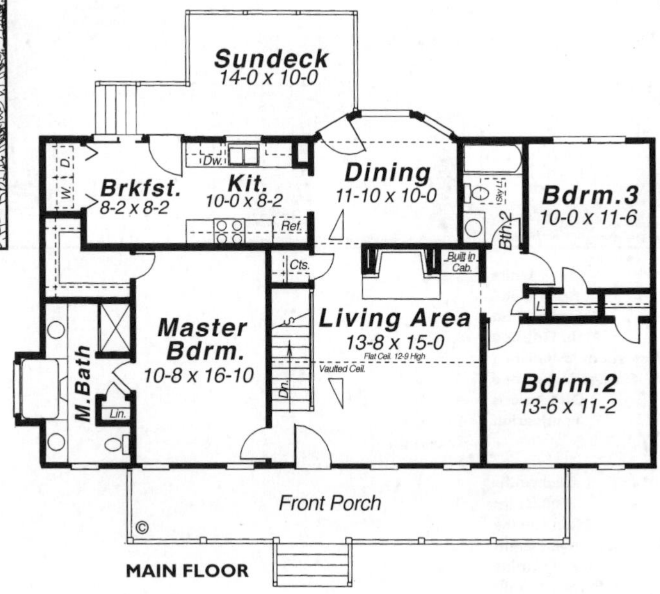
Sundeck
14-0 x 10-0
Brkfst.
8-2 x 8-2
Kit.
10-0 x 8-2
Dining
11-10 x 10-0
Bdrm.3
10-0 x 11-6
Master
Bdrm.
10-8 x 16-10
Living Area
13-8 x 15-0
Bdrm.2
13-6 x 11-2
M.Bath
Front Porch

MAIN FLOOR

Design 65644

Units	Single
Price Code	A
Total Finished	1,346 sq. ft.
Main Finished	1,346 sq. ft.
Dimensions	54'x44'6"
Foundation	Crawlspace Slab
Bedrooms	3
Full Baths	2
Main Ceiling	8'
Max Ridge Height	25'
Roof Framing	Stick
Exterior Walls	2x4

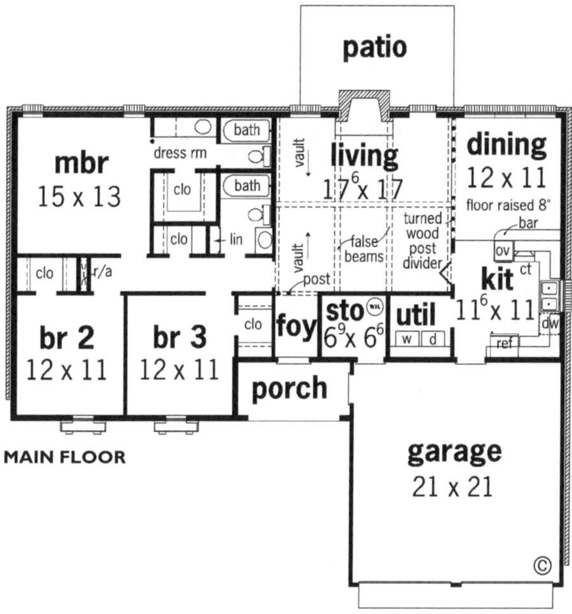

patio
mbr
15 x 13
dress rm
bath
clo
bath
lin
clo
clo
r/a
vault
living
17^6x 17
false beams
turned wood post divider
vault
post
dining
12 x 11
floor raised 8"
bar
ov
ct
kit
11^6x 11
dw
ref
br 2
12 x 11
br 3
12 x 11
clo
foy
sto
6^9x 6^6
util
w
d
porch
garage
21 x 21
MAIN FLOOR

Design 98434

Units	Single
Price Code	A
Total Finished	1,346 sq. ft.
Main Finished	1,346 sq. ft.
Basement Unfinished	1,358 sq. ft.
Garage Unfinished	395 sq. ft.
Dimensions	39'x51'
Foundation	Basement Crawlspace Slab
Bedrooms	3
Full Baths	2
Max Ridge Height	21'6"
Roof Framing	Stick
Exterior Walls	2x4

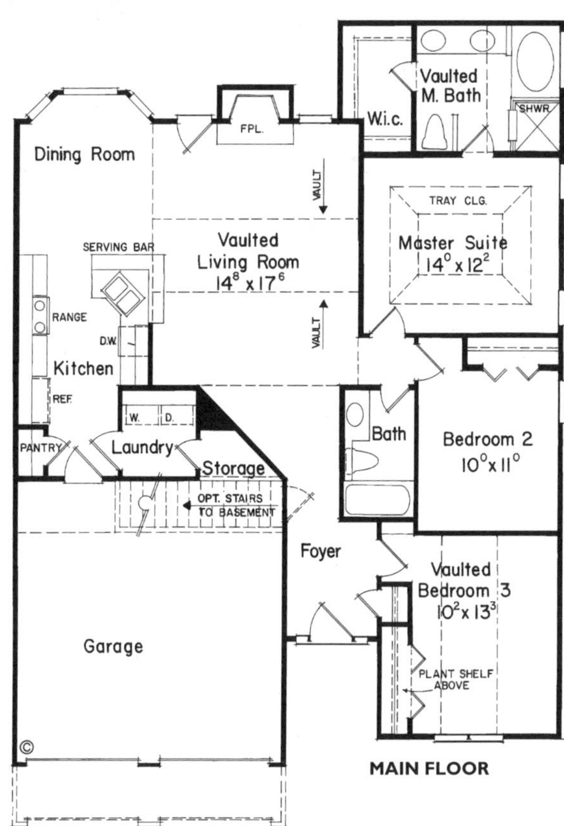

W.i.c.
Vaulted
M. Bath
SHWR
Dining Room
FPL.
VAULT
TRAY CLG.
Master Suite
14^0 x 12^2
SERVING BAR
Vaulted
Living Room
14^8 x 17^6
RANGE
D.W.
VAULT
Kitchen
REF
W.
D.
Laundry
PANTRY
Storage
OPT. STAIRS
TO BASEMENT
Bath
Bedroom 2
10^0 x 11^0
Foyer
Vaulted
Bedroom 3
10^2 x 13^3
Garage
PLANT SHELF
ABOVE
MAIN FLOOR

Design 91171

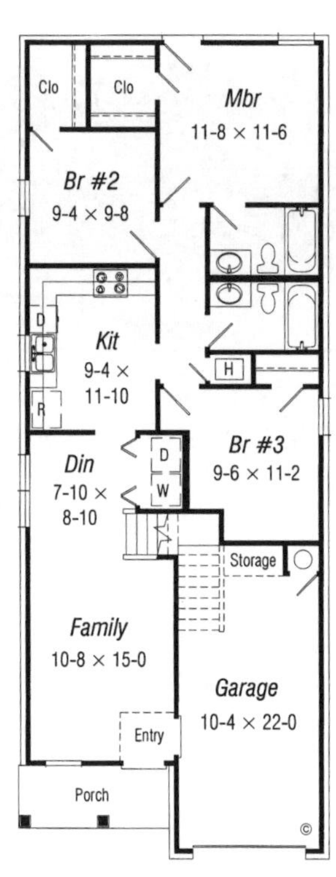

Clo
Clo
Mbr
11-8 × 11-6
Br #2
9-4 × 9-8
Kit
9-4 ×
11-10
D
R
H
Din
7-10 ×
8-10
D
W
Br #3
9-6 × 11-2
Storage
Family
10-8 × 15-0
Garage
10-4 × 22-0
Entry
Porch
©

FIRST FLOOR

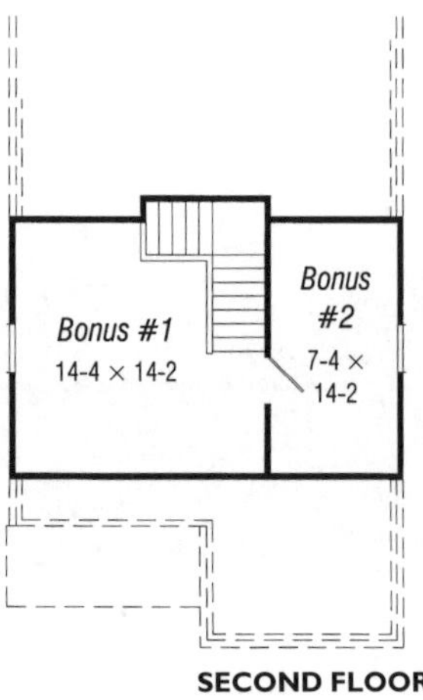

Bonus #1
14-4 × 14-2
Bonus
#2
7-4 ×
14-2

SECOND FLOOR

Units	Single
Price Code	A
Total Finished	1,347 sq. ft.
First Finished	1,040 sq. ft.
Second Finished	307 sq. ft.
Garage Unfinished	263 sq. ft.
Porch Unfinished	48 sq. ft.
Dimensions	22'9½"x60'1½"
Foundation	Slab
Bedrooms	3
Full Baths	2
First Ceiling	8'1⅛"
Second Ceiling	8'1⅛"
Roof Framing	Stick
Exterior Walls	2x4

Design 90356

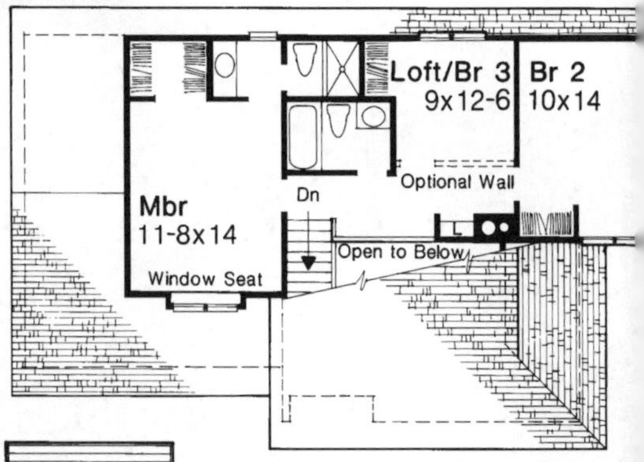

Loft/Br 3
9x12-6
Br 2
10x14
Optional Wall
Dn
Mbr
11-8x14
Open to Below
Window Seat

SECOND FLOOR

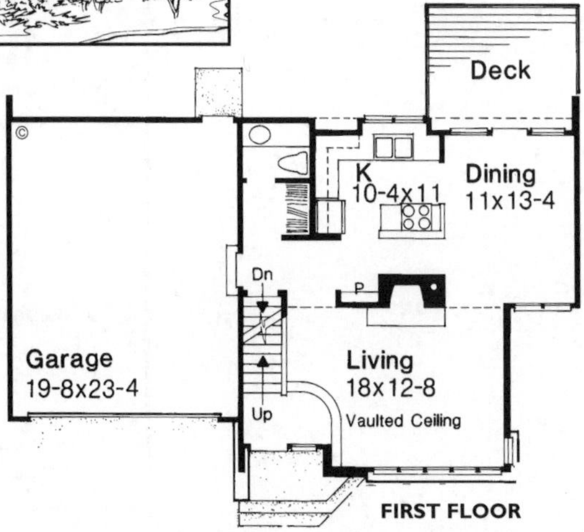

Deck
K
10-4x11
Dining
11x13-4
Dn
P
Garage
19-8x23-4
Living
18x12-8
Vaulted Ceiling
Up

FIRST FLOOR

Units	Single
Price Code	A
Total Finished	1,351 sq. ft.
First Finished	674 sq. ft.
Second Finished	677 sq. ft.
Basement Unfinished	674 sq. ft.
Dimensions	48'x30'2"
Foundation	Basement
Bedrooms	3
Full Baths	1
3/4 Baths	1
Half Baths	1
Max Ridge Height	25'
Roof Framing	Stick/Truss
Exterior Walls	2x4

Design 65176

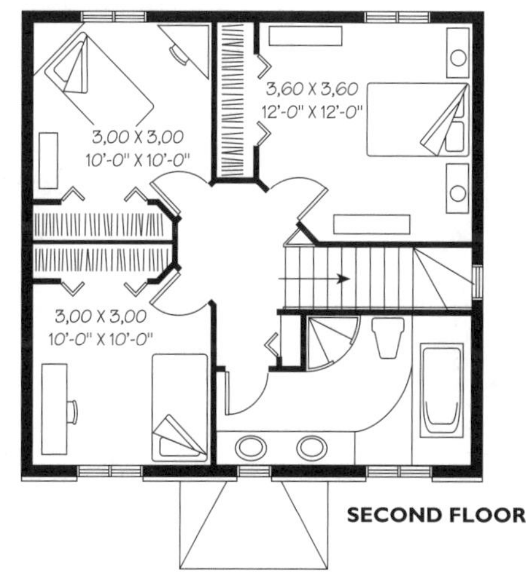
3,60 X 3,60
12'-0" X 12'-0"
3,00 X 3,00
10'-0" X 10'-0"
3,00 X 3,00
10'-0" X 10'-0"

SECOND FLOOR

Units	Single
Price Code	A
Total Finished	1,352 sq. ft.
First Finished	676 sq. ft.
Second Finished	676 sq. ft.
Basement Unfinished	676 sq. ft.
Deck Unfinished	32 sq. ft.
Dimensions	26'x26'
Foundation	Basement
Bedrooms	3
Full Baths	1
3/4 Baths	1
First Ceiling	8'
Second Ceiling	8'
Max Ridge Height	28'1"
Roof Framing	Truss
Exterior Walls	2x6

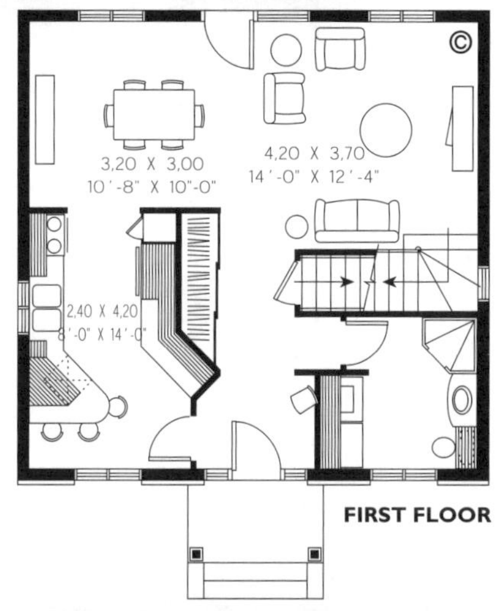
3,20 X 3,00
10'-8" X 10"-0"
4,20 X 3,70
14'-0" X 12'-4"
2,40 X 4,20
8'-0' X 14'-0"

FIRST FLOOR

Design 50035

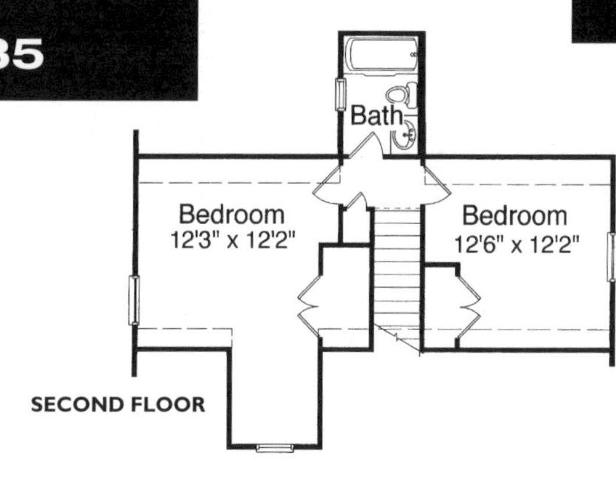
Bath
Bedroom
12'3" x 12'2"
Bedroom
12'6" x 12'2"

SECOND FLOOR

Units	Single
Price Code	A
Total Finished	1,354 sq. ft.
First Finished	873 sq. ft.
Second Finished	481 sq. ft.
Basement Unfinished	873 sq. ft.
Garage Unfinished	253 sq. ft.
Porch Unfinished	95 sq. ft.
Dimensions	51'6"x31'8"
Foundation	Basement
Bedrooms	3
Full Baths	2
First Ceiling	8'
Second Ceiling	8'
Max Ridge Height	23'
Roof Framing	Stick
Exterior Walls	2x4

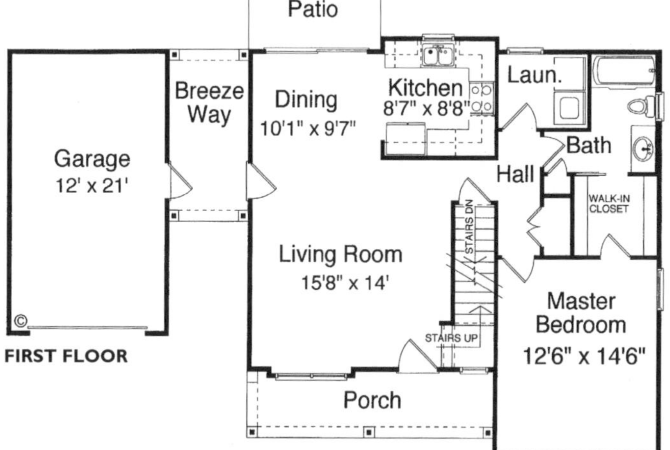
Patio
Garage
12' x 21'
Breeze Way
Dining
10'1" x 9'7"
Kitchen
8'7" x 8'8"
Laun.
Bath
Hall
WALK-IN CLOSET
Living Room
15'8" x 14'
STAIRS DN
STAIRS UP
Master Bedroom
12'6" x 14'6"
Porch

FIRST FLOOR

Design 91026

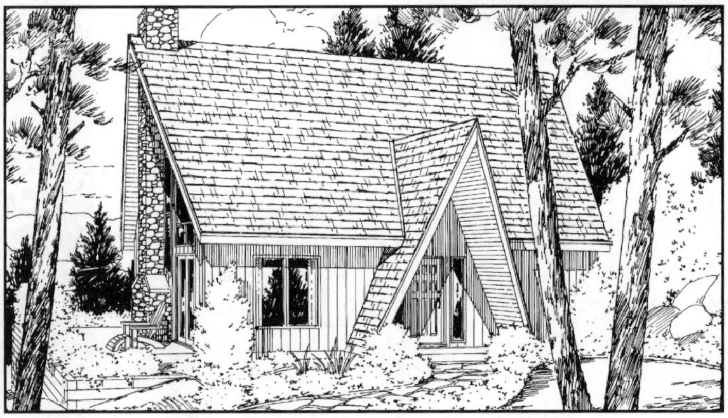

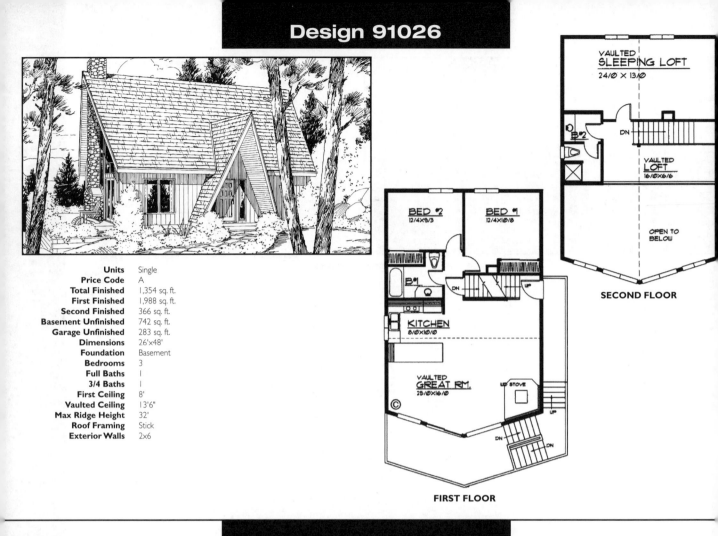

SLEEPING LOFT
24/0 X 13/0
VAULTED LOFT
16/0X6/6
OPEN TO BELOW
SECOND FLOOR

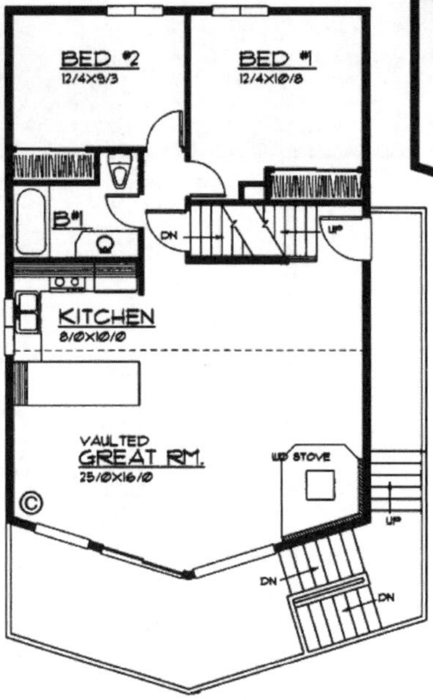

BED #2
12/4X9/3
BED #1
12/4X10/8
KITCHEN
8/0X10/0
VAULTED GREAT RM.
25/0X16/0
FIRST FLOOR

Units	Single
Price Code	A
Total Finished	1,354 sq. ft.
First Finished	1,988 sq. ft.
Second Finished	366 sq. ft.
Basement Unfinished	742 sq. ft.
Garage Unfinished	283 sq. ft.
Dimensions	26'x48'
Foundation	Basement
Bedrooms	3
Full Baths	1
3/4 Baths	1
First Ceiling	8'
Vaulted Ceiling	13'6"
Max Ridge Height	32'
Roof Framing	Stick
Exterior Walls	2x6

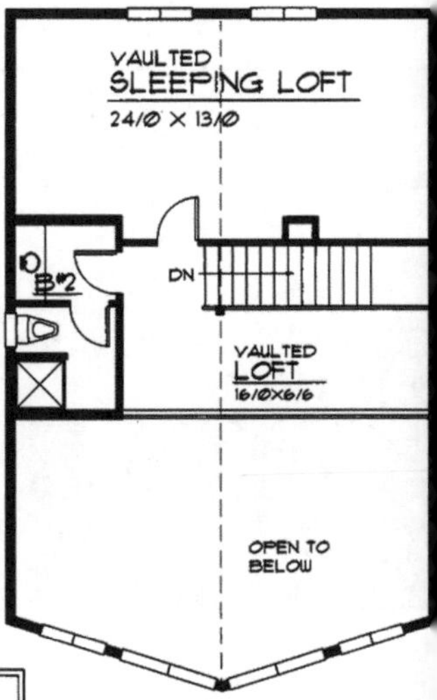

Design 97272

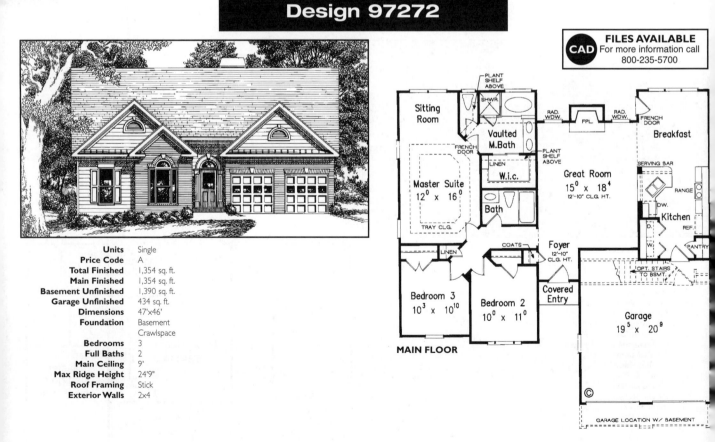

CAD FILES AVAILABLE
For more information call
800-235-5700

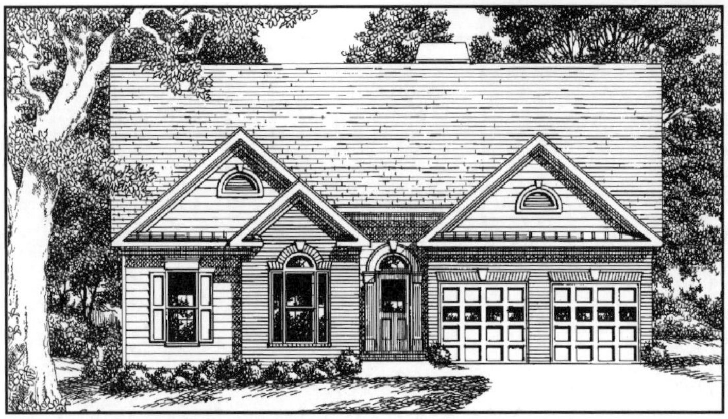

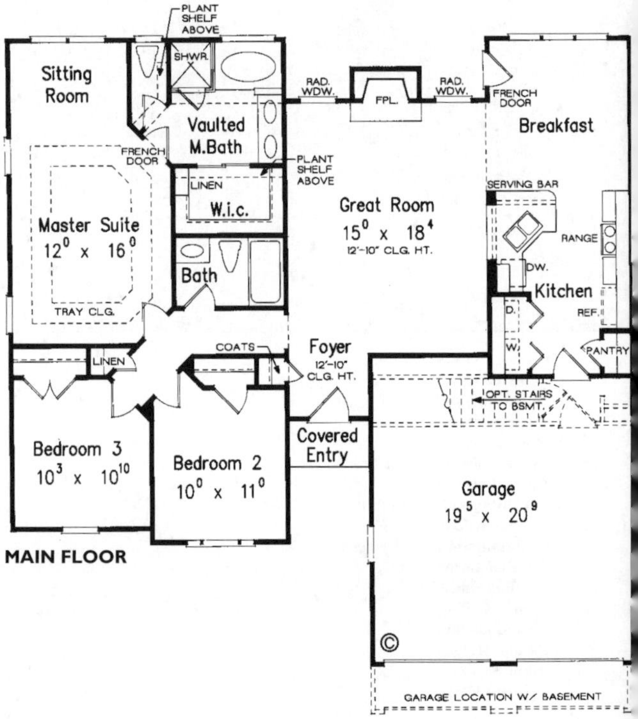

Sitting Room
Vaulted M.Bath
Master Suite
12^0 x 16^0
W.i.c.
Bath
Great Room
15^0 x 18^4
12'-10" CLG. HT.
Breakfast
Kitchen
Foyer
12'-10" CLG. HT.
Covered Entry
Bedroom 3
10^3 x 10^{10}
Bedroom 2
10^0 x 11^0
Garage
19^5 x 20^9
GARAGE LOCATION W/ BASEMENT
MAIN FLOOR

Units	Single
Price Code	A
Total Finished	1,354 sq. ft.
Main Finished	1,354 sq. ft.
Basement Unfinished	1,390 sq. ft.
Garage Unfinished	434 sq. ft.
Dimensions	47'x46'
Foundation	Basement Crawlspace
Bedrooms	3
Full Baths	2
Main Ceiling	9'
Max Ridge Height	24'9"
Roof Framing	Stick
Exterior Walls	2x4

Design 97678

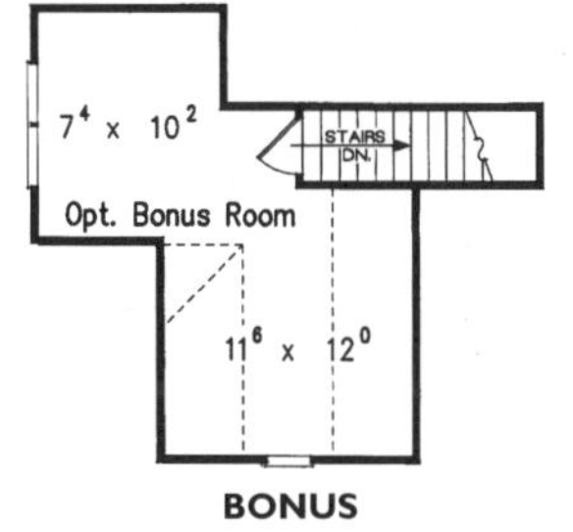

7⁴ x 10²
STAIRS DN.
Opt. Bonus Room
11⁶ x 12⁰
BONUS

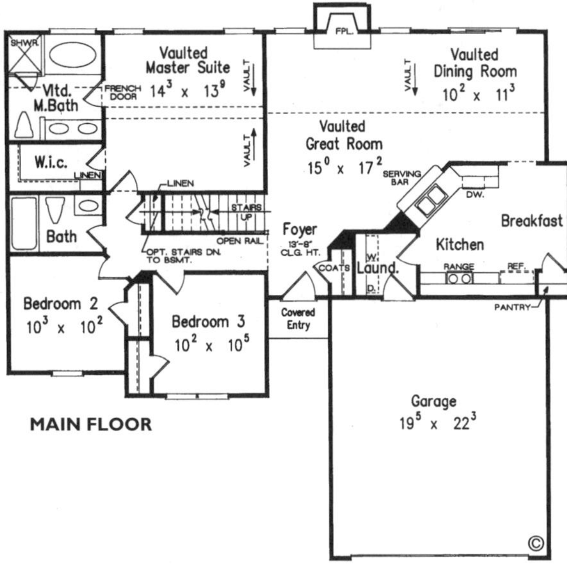

SHWR.
Vaulted Master Suite 14³ x 13⁹
Vltd. M.Bath
FRENCH DOOR
VAULT
FPL.
Vaulted Dining Room 10² x 11³
Vaulted Great Room 15⁰ x 17²
SERVING BAR
W.i.c.
LINEN
STAIRS UP
OPEN RAIL
OPT. STAIRS DN. TO BSMT.
Bath
Foyer 13'-8" CLG. HT.
COATS
W. Laund. D.
Kitchen
DW.
Breakfast
RANGE
REF.
PANTRY
Bedroom 2 10³ x 10²
Bedroom 3 10² x 10⁵
Covered Entry
Garage 19⁵ x 22³
MAIN FLOOR

Units	Single
Price Code	A
Total Finished	1,354 sq. ft.
Main Finished	1,354 sq. ft.
Bonus Unfinished	246 sq. ft.
Basement Unfinished	1,354 sq. ft.
Garage Unfinished	450 sq. ft.
Dimensions	51'x48'4"
Foundation	Basement Crawlspace
Bedrooms	3
Full Baths	2
Main Ceiling	8'
Second Ceiling	8'
Max Ridge Height	22'
Roof Framing	Stick
Exterior Walls	2x4

Design 10519

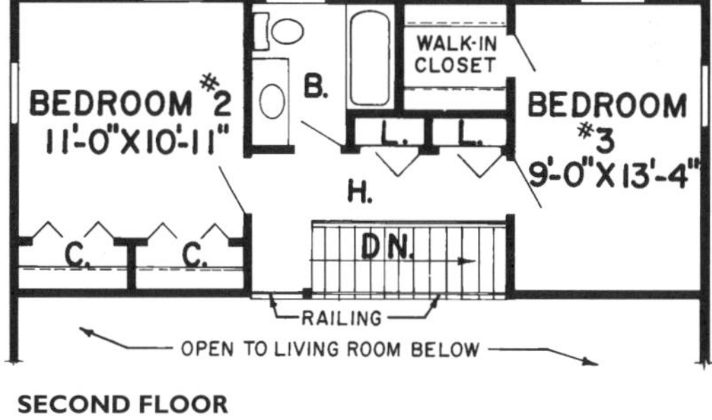

BEDROOM #2 11'-0"X10'-11"
B.
WALK-IN CLOSET
BEDROOM #3 9'-0"X13'-4"
L.
L.
H.
C.
C.
DN.
RAILING
OPEN TO LIVING ROOM BELOW
SECOND FLOOR

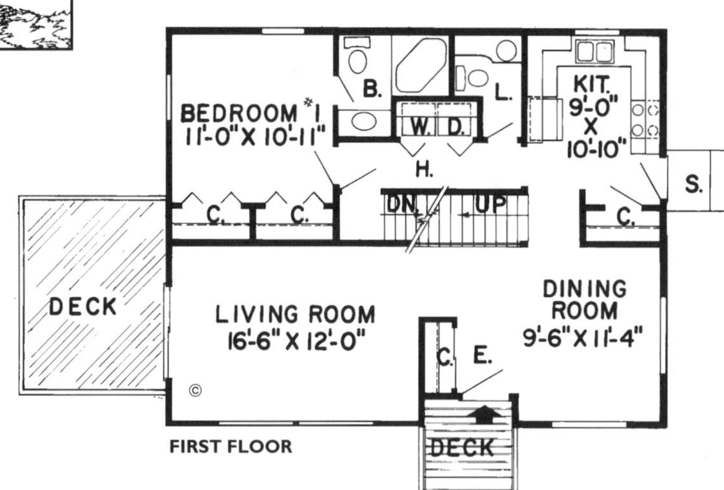

B.
L.
BEDROOM #1 11'-0"X 10'-11"
W. D.
KIT. 9'-0" X 10'-10"
H.
S.
C.
C.
DN.
UP
C.
DECK
LIVING ROOM 16'-6" X 12'-0"
DINING ROOM 9'-6"X11'-4"
C.
E.
DECK
FIRST FLOOR

Units	Single
Price Code	A
Total Finished	1,355 sq. ft.
First Finished	872 sq. ft.
Second Finished	483 sq. ft.
Dimensions	34'x26'
Foundation	Basement
Bedrooms	3
Full Baths	2
Half Baths	1
Max Ridge Height	23'
Roof Framing	Stick
Exterior Walls	2x6

Design 97336

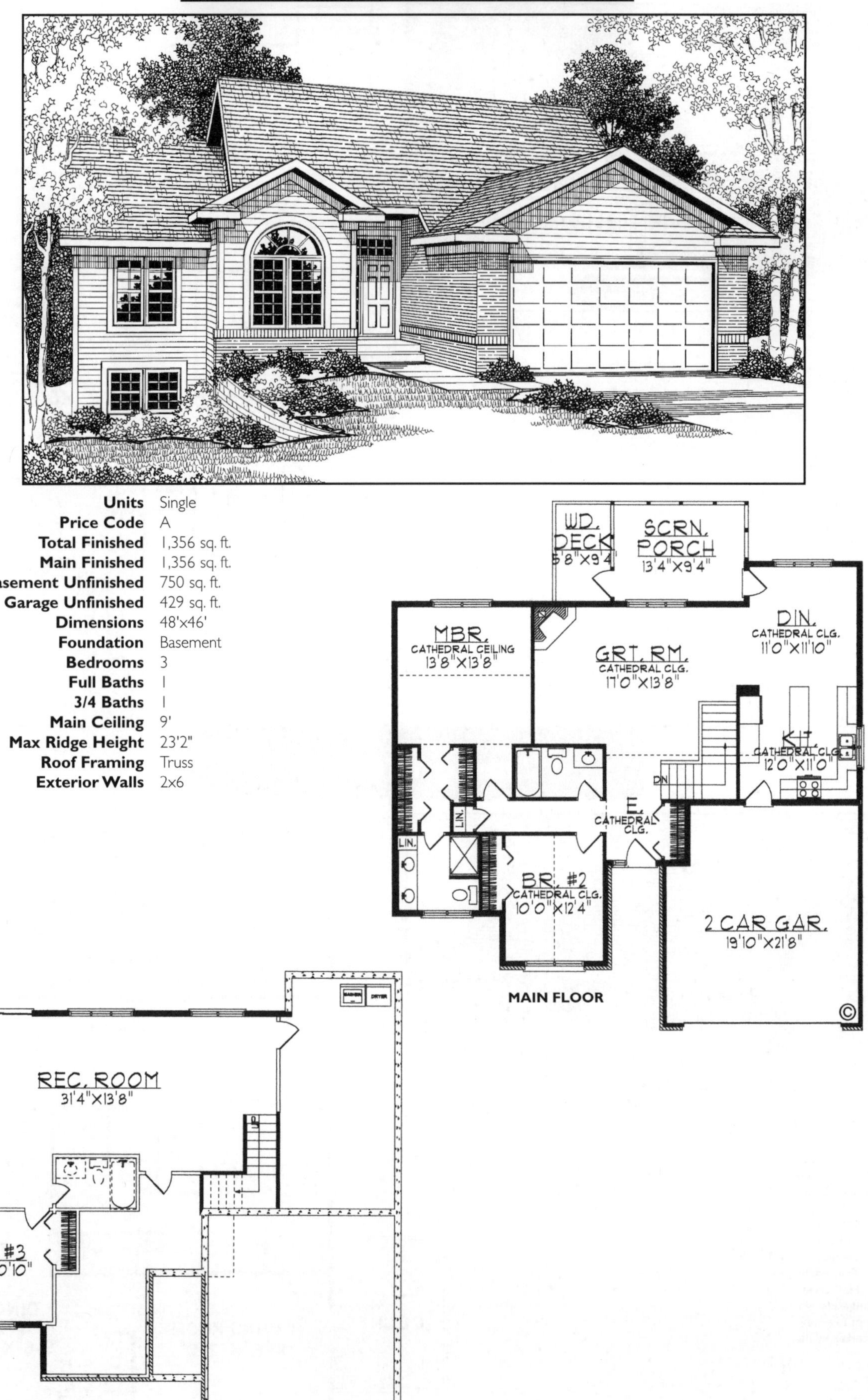

WD. DECK 5'8"X9'4"
SCRN. PORCH 13'4"X9'4"
MBR. CATHEDRAL CEILING 13'8"X13'8"
GRT. RM. CATHEDRAL CLG. 17'0"X13'8"
DIN. CATHEDRAL CLG. 11'0"X11'10"
KIT. CATHEDRAL CLG. 12'0"X11'0"
DN
LIN.
LIN.
E. CATHEDRAL CLG.
BR. #2 CATHEDRAL CLG. 10'0"X12'4"
2 CAR GAR. 19'10"X21'8"
MAIN FLOOR
REC. ROOM 31'4"X13'8"
BR. #3 11'8"X10'10"
LOWER FLOOR

Units	Single
Price Code	A
Total Finished	1,356 sq. ft.
Main Finished	1,356 sq. ft.
Basement Unfinished	750 sq. ft.
Garage Unfinished	429 sq. ft.
Dimensions	48'x46'
Foundation	Basement
Bedrooms	3
Full Baths	1
3/4 Baths	1
Main Ceiling	9'
Max Ridge Height	23'2"
Roof Framing	Truss
Exterior Walls	2x6

Design 98443

Units	Single
Price Code	A
Total Finished	1,359 sq. ft.
Main Finished	1,359 sq. ft.
Garage Unfinished	439 sq. ft.
Dimensions	49'x53'
Foundation	Crawlspace Slab
Bedrooms	3
Full Baths	2
Max Ridge Height	19'6"
Roof Framing	Stick
Exterior Walls	2x4

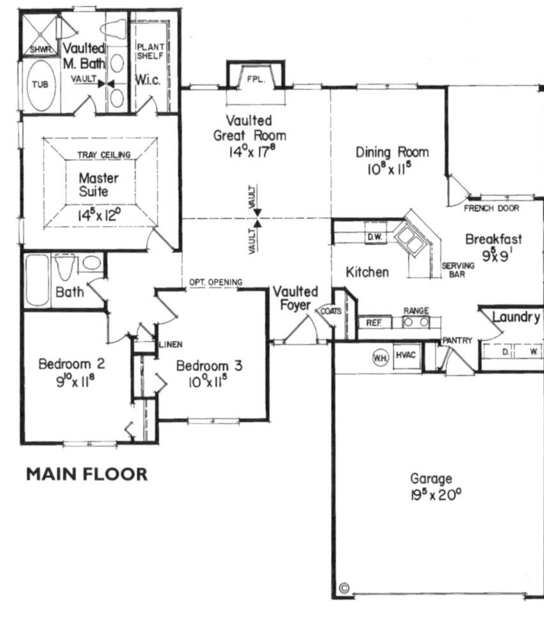
SHWR.
TUB
Vaulted M. Bath
VAULT
PLANT SHELF
W.i.c.
FPL.
Vaulted Great Room 14⁰x 17⁸
Dining Room 10⁸x 11⁵
TRAY CEILING
Master Suite 14⁵x 12⁰
VAULT
FRENCH DOOR
Breakfast 9⁵x 9¹
D.W.
Kitchen
SERVING BAR
Bath
OPT. OPENING
Vaulted Foyer
COATS
REF
RANGE
Laundry
PANTRY
LINEN
W.H.
HVAC
D.
W.
Bedroom 2 9¹⁰x 11⁸
Bedroom 3 10⁰x 11⁵
Garage 19⁵x 20⁰

MAIN FLOOR

Design 65015

Units	Single
Price Code	A
Total Finished	1,360 sq. ft.
First Finished	858 sq. ft.
Second Finished	502 sq. ft.
Basement Unfinished	858 sq. ft.
Dimensions	35'x29'8"
Foundation	Basement
Bedrooms	3
Full Baths	2
First Ceiling	8'
Second Ceiling	8'
Max Ridge Height	26'6"
Roof Framing	Truss
Exterior Walls	2x6

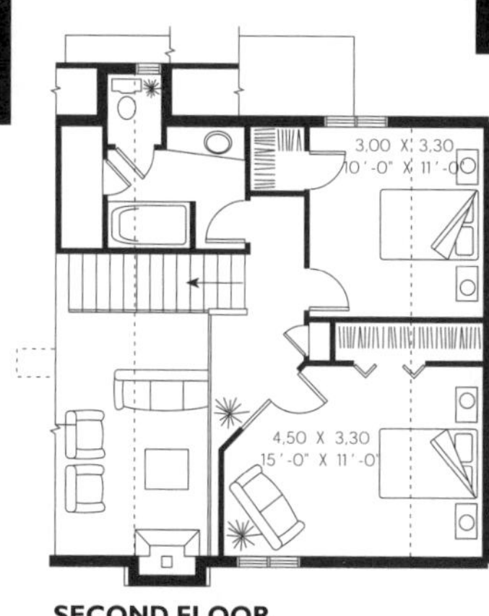
3,00 X 3,30
10'-0" X 11'-0"
4,50 X 3,30
15'-0" X 11'-0"

SECOND FLOOR

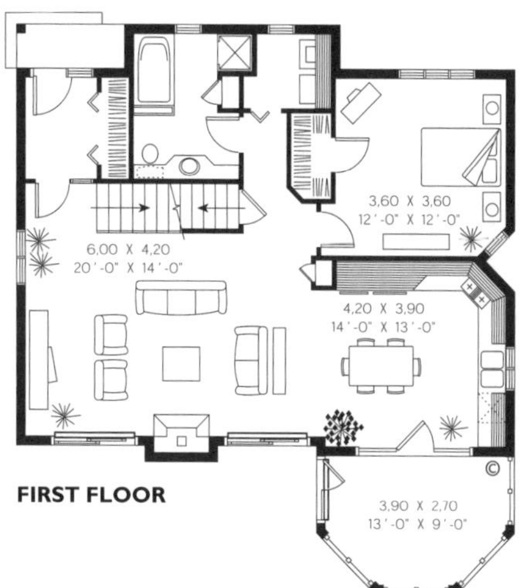
3,60 X 3,60
12'-0" X 12'-0"
6,00 X 4,20
20'-0" X 14'-0"
4,20 X 3,90
14'-0" X 13'-0"
3,90 X 2,70
13'-0" X 9'-0"

FIRST FLOOR

Design 69022

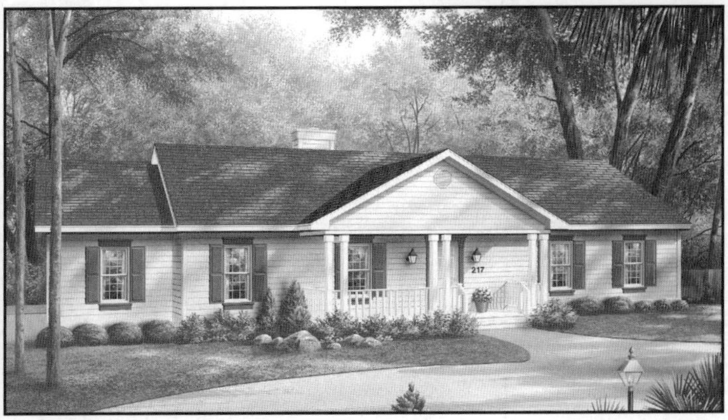

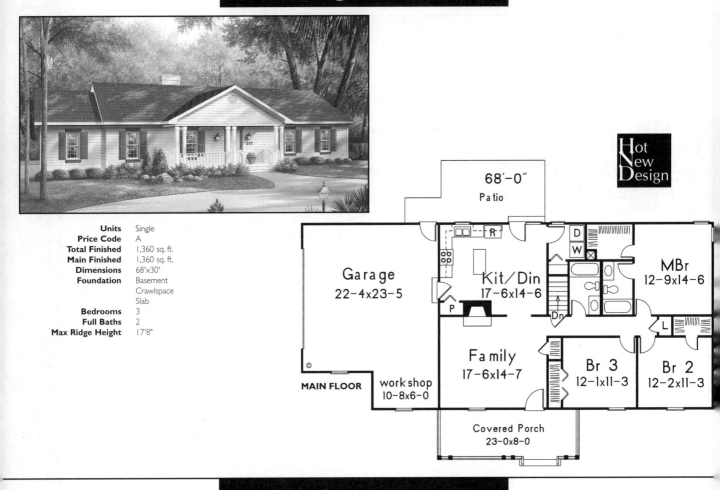

Hot New Design

Units	Single
Price Code	A
Total Finished	1,360 sq. ft.
Main Finished	1,360 sq. ft.
Dimensions	68'x30'
Foundation	Basement Crawlspace Slab
Bedrooms	3
Full Baths	2
Max Ridge Height	17'8"

68'-0"
Patio
Garage 22-4x23-5
Kit/Din 17-6x14-6
MBr 12-9x14-6
Family 17-6x14-7
Br 3 12-1x11-3
Br 2 12-2x11-3
workshop 10-8x6-0
Covered Porch 23-0x8-0

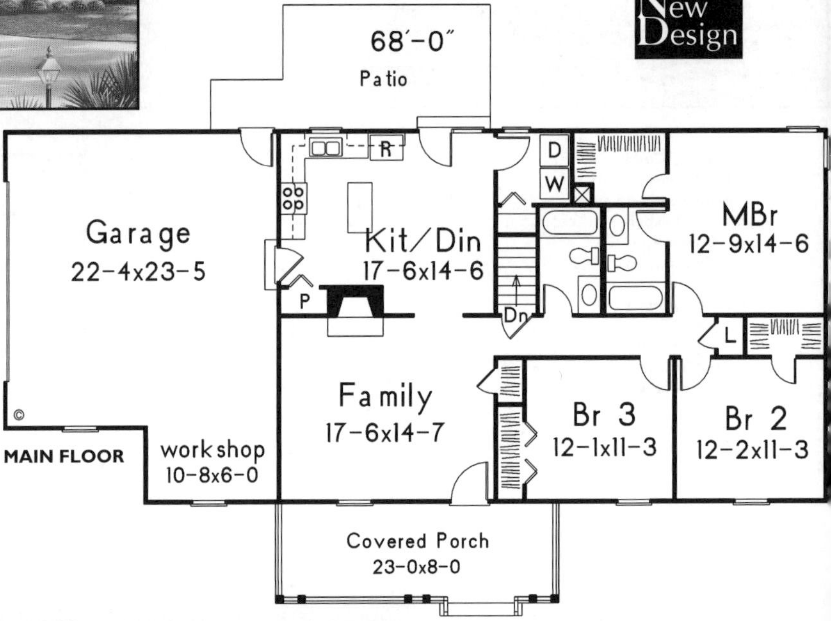

MAIN FLOOR

Design 92281

Units	Single
Price Code	A
Total Finished	1,360 sq. ft.
Main Finished	1,360 sq. ft.
Garage Unfinished	380 sq. ft.
Deck Unfinished	82 sq. ft.
Porch Unfinished	18 sq. ft.
Dimensions	40'x49'10"
Foundation	Slab
Bedrooms	3
Full Baths	2
Max Ridge Height	21'
Roof Framing	Stick
Exterior Walls	2x4

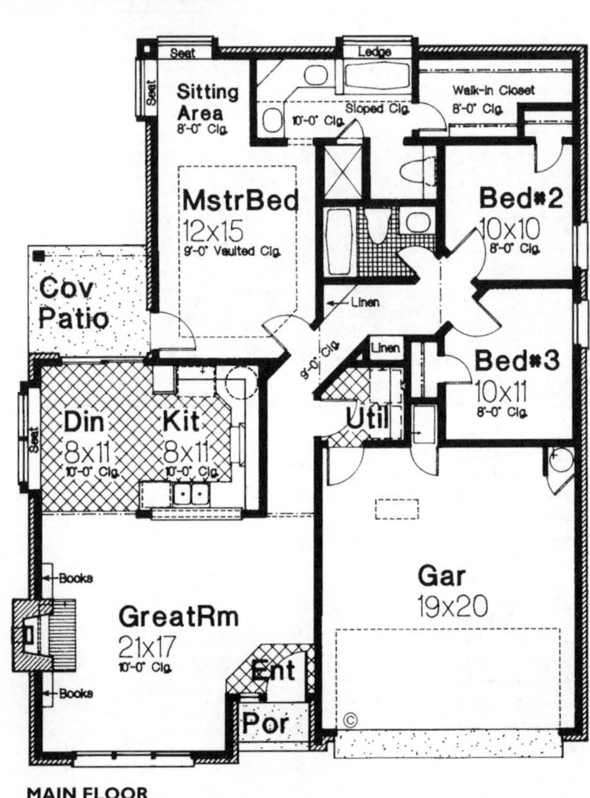
Seat
Ledge
Sitting Area
8'-0" Clg.
10'-0" Clg.
Sloped Clg.
Walk-in Closet
8'-0" Clg.
MstrBed
12x15
9'-0" Vaulted Clg.
Bed#2
10x10
8'-0" Clg.
Cov Patio
Linen
9'-0" Clg.
Bed#3
10x11
8'-0" Clg.
Din
8x11
10'-0" Clg.
Kit
8x11
10'-0" Clg.
Util
Books
GreatRm
21x17
10'-0" Clg.
Gar
19x20
Ent
Por
MAIN FLOOR

Design 94982

Units	Single
Price Code	A
Total Finished	1,360 sq. ft.
Main Finished	1,360 sq. ft.
Garage Unfinished	544 sq. ft.
Dimensions	52'x46'
Foundation	Basement
Bedrooms	3
Full Baths	2
Max Ridge Height	18'
Roof Framing	Stick
Exterior Walls	2x4

* Alternate foundation options available at an additional charge. Please call 1-800-235-5700 for more information.

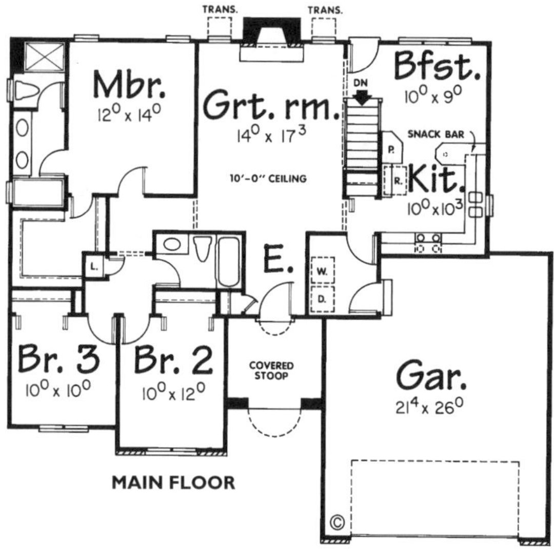

TRANS.
TRANS.
Mbr.
12⁰ x 14⁰
Grt. rm.
14⁰ x 17³
10'-0" CEILING
DN
Bfst.
10⁰ x 9⁰
SNACK BAR
Kit.
10⁰ x 10³
E.
W.
D.
L.
Br. 3
10⁰ x 10⁰
Br. 2
10⁰ x 12⁰
COVERED STOOP
Gar.
21⁴ x 26⁰

MAIN FLOOR

Design 97224

Units	Single
Price Code	A
Total Finished	1,363 sq. ft.
Main Finished	1,363 sq. ft.
Basement Unfinished	715 sq. ft.
Garage Unfinished	677 sq. ft.
Dimensions	47'x35'4"
Foundation	Basement
Bedrooms	3
Full Baths	2
Main Ceiling	9'
Max Ridge Height	22'4"
Roof Framing	Stick
Exterior Walls	2x4

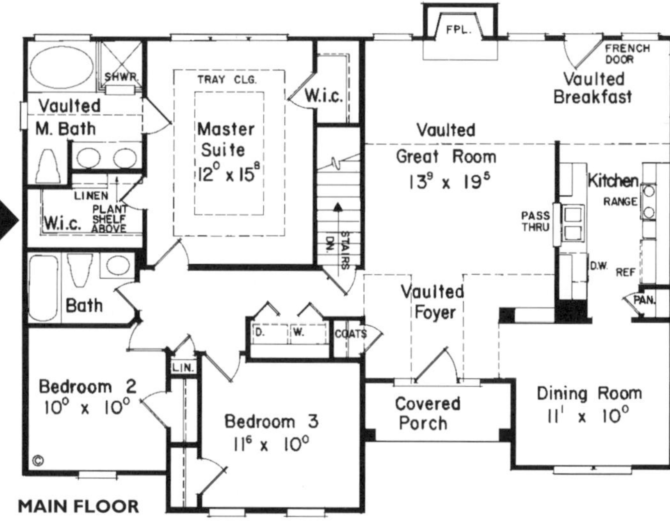

DRIVE UNDER
SHWR
Vaulted M. Bath
TRAY CLG.
Master Suite
12⁰ x 15⁸
W.i.c.
LINEN
PLANT SHELF ABOVE
W.i.c.
FPL.
FRENCH DOOR
Vaulted Breakfast
Vaulted Great Room
13⁹ x 19⁵
Kitchen
RANGE
PASS THRU
D.W.
REF
PAN.
DN
STAIRS
Bath
D.
W.
COATS
Vaulted Foyer
LIN.
Bedroom 2
10⁰ x 10⁰
Bedroom 3
11⁶ x 10⁰
Covered Porch
Dining Room
11¹ x 10⁰

MAIN FLOOR

Design 65427

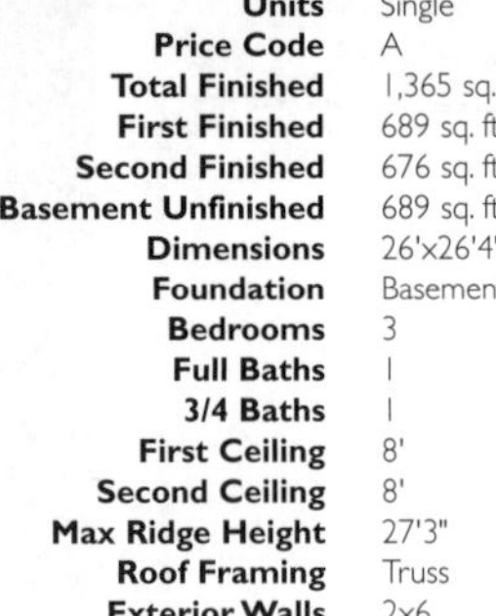

Units	Single
Price Code	A
Total Finished	1,365 sq. ft.
First Finished	689 sq. ft.
Second Finished	676 sq. ft.
Basement Unfinished	689 sq. ft.
Dimensions	26'x26'4"
Foundation	Basement
Bedrooms	3
Full Baths	1
3/4 Baths	1
First Ceiling	8'
Second Ceiling	8'
Max Ridge Height	27'3"
Roof Framing	Truss
Exterior Walls	2x6

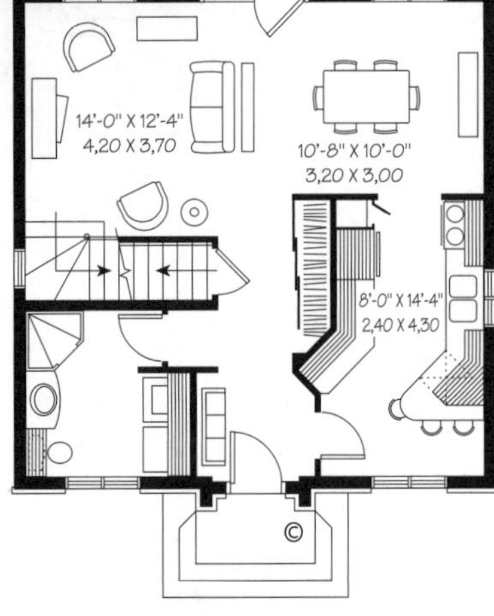
14'-0" X 12'-4"
4,20 X 3,70
10'-8" X 10'-0"
3,20 X 3,00
8'-0" X 14'-4"
2,40 X 4,30

FIRST FLOOR

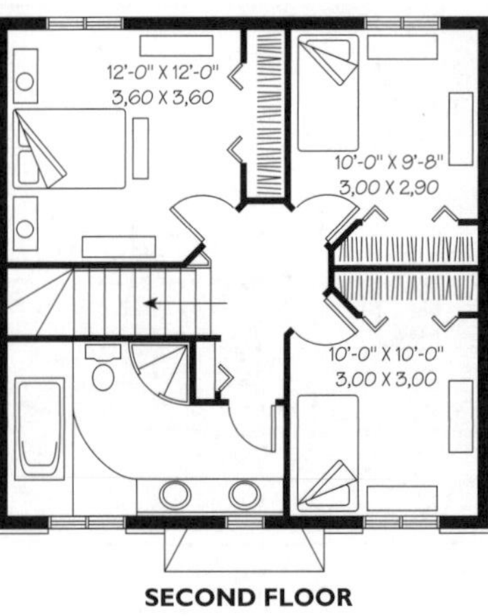
12'-0" X 12'-0"
3,60 X 3,60
10'-0" X 9'-8"
3,00 X 2,90
10'-0" X 10'-0"
3,00 X 3,00

SECOND FLOOR

Design 98985

Units	Single
Price Code	A
Total Finished	1,365 sq. ft.
Main Finished	1,365 sq. ft.
Garage Unfinished	407 sq. ft.
Dimensions	37'x53'
Foundation	Basement Slab
Bedrooms	3
Full Baths	2
Main Ceiling	8'
Max Ridge Height	19'10"
Roof Framing	Stick
Exterior Walls	2x4

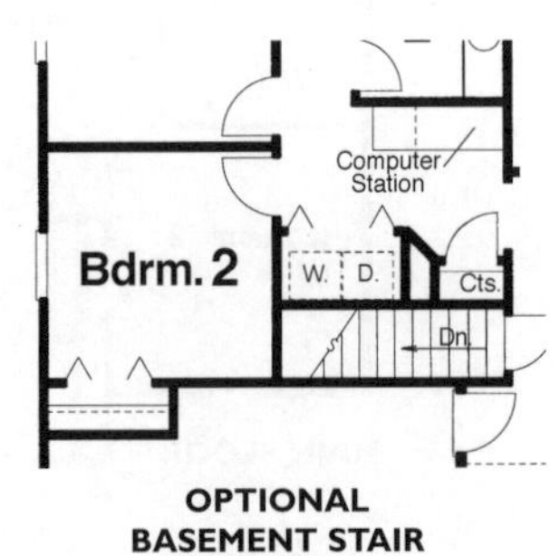
Computer Station
Bdrm. 2
W.
D.
Cts.
Dn.

OPTIONAL BASEMENT STAIR LOCATION

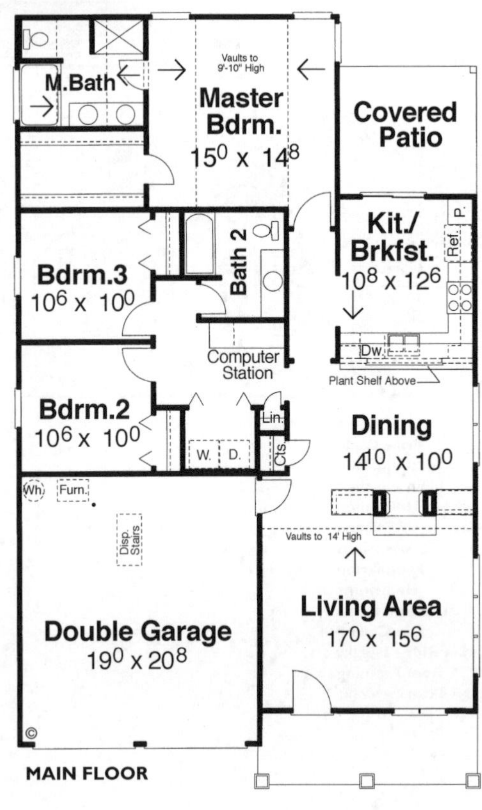
M.Bath
Vaults to 9'-10" High
Master Bdrm.
15^{0} x 14^{8}
Covered Patio
Kit./ Brkfst.
10^{8} x 12^{6}
Ref.
P.
Dw.
Bath 2
Bdrm.3
10^{6} x 10^{0}
Computer Station
Plant Shelf Above
Bdrm.2
10^{6} x 10^{0}
Lin.
Cts.
W.
D.
Dining
14^{10} x 10^{0}
Wh.
Furn.
Disp. Stairs
Vaults to 14' High
Living Area
17^{0} x 15^{6}
Double Garage
19^{0} x 20^{8}

MAIN FLOOR

Design 60013

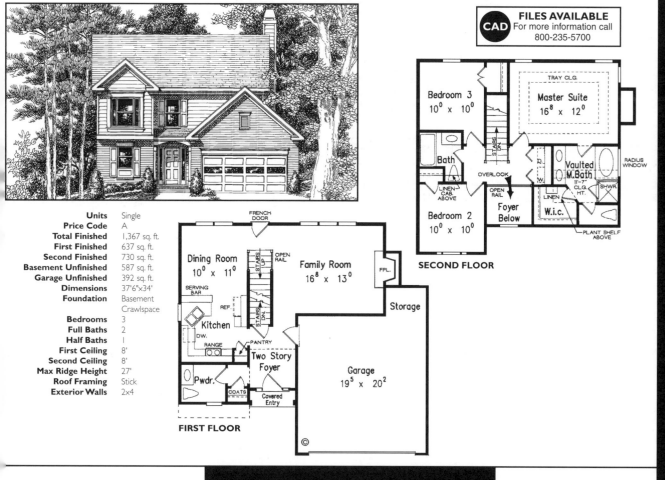

Units	Single
Price Code	A
Total Finished	1,367 sq. ft.
First Finished	637 sq. ft.
Second Finished	730 sq. ft.
Basement Unfinished	587 sq. ft.
Garage Unfinished	392 sq. ft.
Dimensions	37'6"x34'
Foundation	Basement Crawlspace
Bedrooms	3
Full Baths	2
Half Baths	1
First Ceiling	8'
Second Ceiling	8'
Max Ridge Height	27'
Roof Framing	Stick
Exterior Walls	2x4

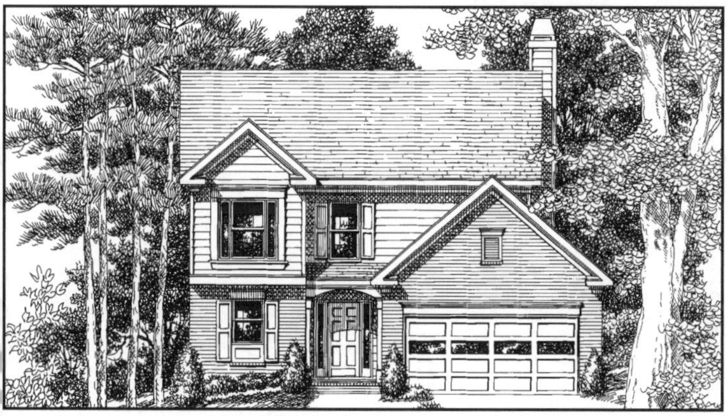

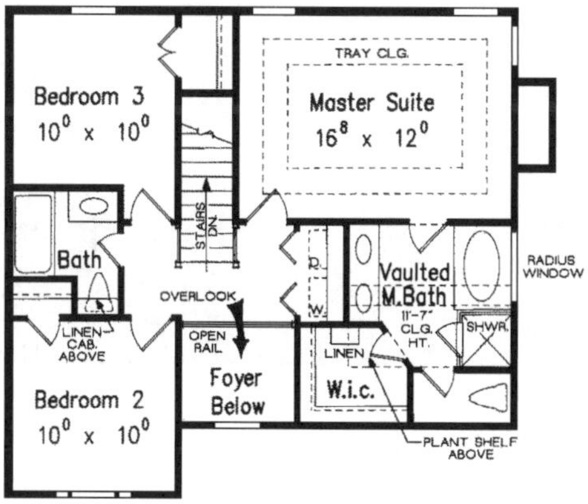

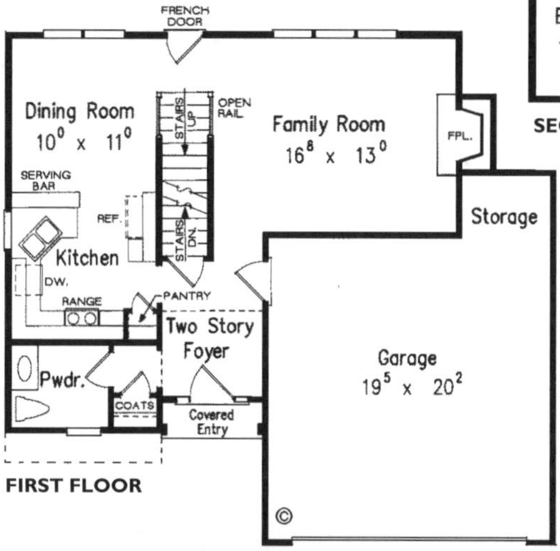

FIRST FLOOR: French Door; Dining Room $10^0 \times 11^0$; Open Rail; Family Room $16^8 \times 13^0$; FPL.; Serving Bar; Ref.; Kitchen; DW.; Range; Pantry; Stairs Up; Stairs Dn.; Two Story Foyer; Storage; Garage $19^5 \times 20^2$; Pwdr.; Coats; Covered Entry

SECOND FLOOR: Bedroom 3 $10^0 \times 10^0$; Tray Clg.; Master Suite $16^8 \times 12^0$; Bath; Stairs Dn.; Overlook; Linen Cab. Above; Open Rail; Foyer Below; Vaulted M.Bath 11'-7" Clg. Ht.; Radius Window; Shwr.; Linen; W.i.c.; Bedroom 2 $10^0 \times 10^0$; Plant Shelf Above

Design 99639

Units	Single
Price Code	A
Total Finished	1,367 sq. ft.
Main Finished	1,367 sq. ft.
Basement Unfinished	1,267 sq. ft.
Garage Unfinished	431 sq. ft.
Dimensions	71'4"x33'10"
Foundation	Basement Slab
Bedrooms	3
Full Baths	2
Main Ceiling	8'
Vaulted Ceiling	11'
Max Ridge Height	20'
Roof Framing	Stick
Exterior Walls	2x6

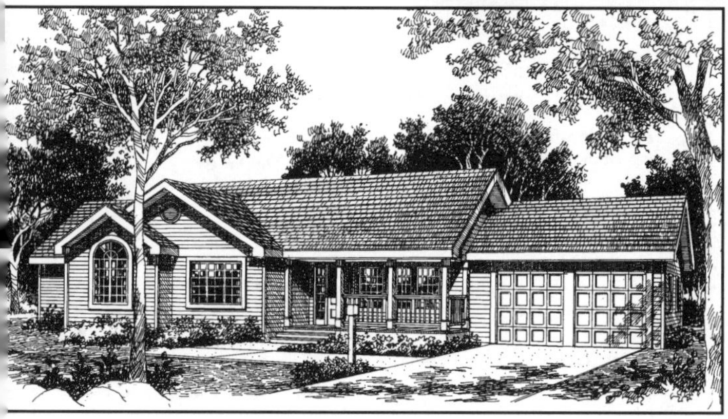

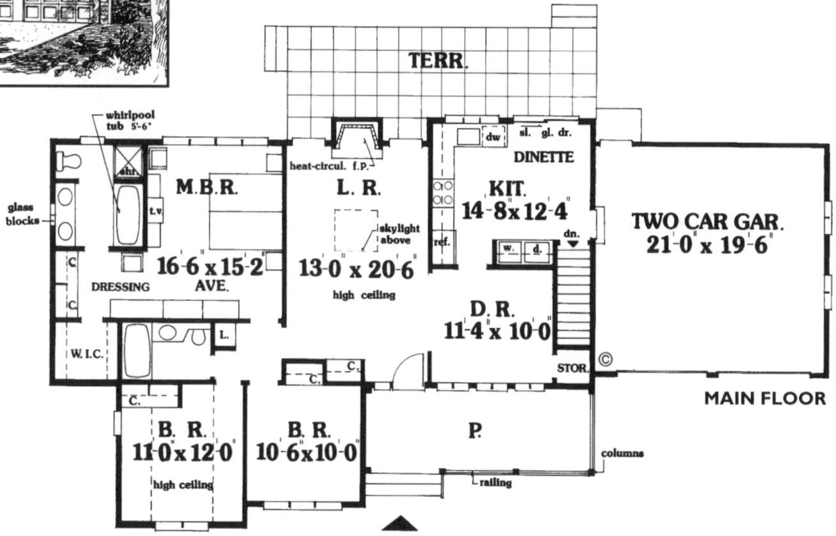

MAIN FLOOR: TERR.; whirlpool tub 5'-6"; glass blocks; shr.; t.v.; M.B.R. 16'6" x 15'2"; Dressing; Ave.; W.I.C.; heat-circul. f.p.; L. R. 13'0" x 20'6"; skylight above; high ceiling; dw; sl. gl. dr.; Dinette; KIT. 14'8" x 12'4"; ref.; w.; d.; dn.; D.R. 11'4" x 10'0"; Stor.; TWO CAR GAR. 21'0" x 19'6"; B.R. 11'0" x 12'0" high ceiling; B.R. 10'6" x 10'0"; P.; columns; railing

Design 51018

PHOTOGRAPHY: COURTESY OF THE DESIGNER

Units	Single
Price Code	A
Total Finished	1,368 sq. ft.
Main Finished	1,368 sq. ft.
Basement Unfinished	1,368 sq. ft.
Deck Unfinished	32 sq. ft.
Dimensions	48'4"x48'4"
Foundation	Basement
Bedrooms	3
Full Baths	2
Main Ceiling	8'
Max Ridge Height	20'6"
Roof Framing	Truss
Exterior Walls	2x4

Please note: The photographed home may have been modified to suit homeowner preferences. If you order plans, have a builder or design professional check them against the photograph to confirm actual construction details.

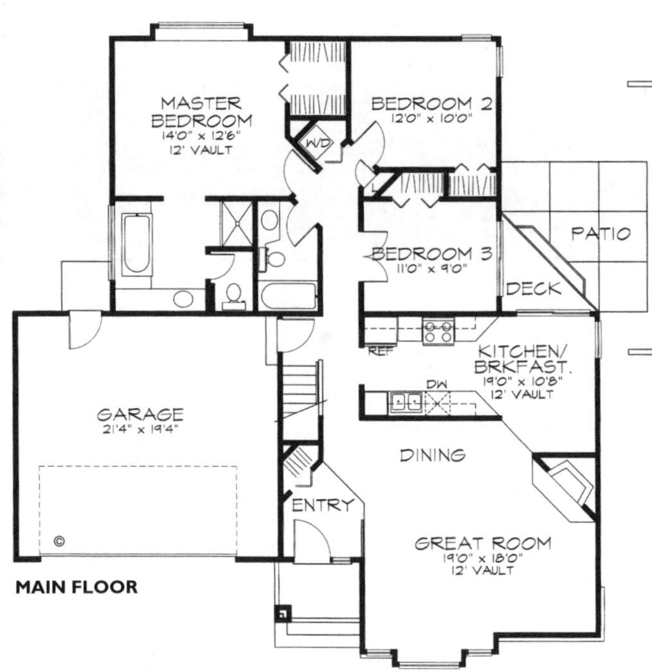
MASTER BEDROOM
14'0" x 12'6"
12' VAULT
W/D
BEDROOM 2
12'0" x 10'0"
BEDROOM 3
11'0" x 9'0"
PATIO
DECK
REF
KITCHEN/ BRKFAST.
19'0" x 10'8"
12' VAULT
DW
GARAGE
21'4" x 19'4"
DINING
ENTRY
GREAT ROOM
19'0" x 18'0"
12' VAULT
MAIN FLOOR

Design 99930

Units	Single
Price Code	A
Total Finished	1,368 sq. ft.
Main Finished	1,368 sq. ft.
Basement Unfinished	1,360 sq. ft.
Garage Unfinished	462 sq. ft.
Deck Unfinished	80 sq. ft.
Porch Unfinished	128 sq. ft.
Dimensions	46'x54'
Foundation	Basement
Bedrooms	3
Full Baths	2
Main Ceiling	8'
Tray Ceiling	11'6"
Max Ridge Height	19'
Roof Framing	Truss
Exterior Walls	2x6

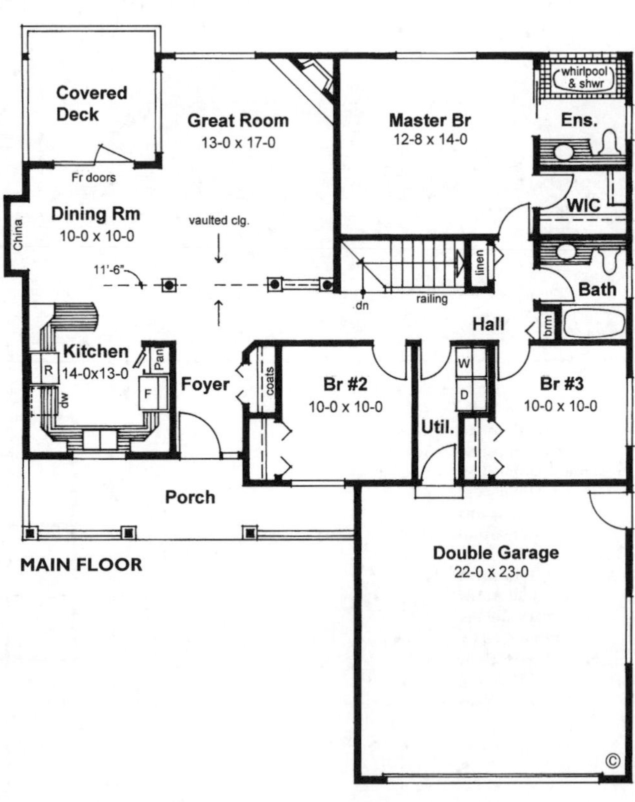
Covered Deck
Great Room
13-0 x 17-0
Master Br
12-8 x 14-0
whirlpool & shwr
Ens.
Fr doors
Dining Rm
10-0 x 10-0
vaulted clg.
China
11'-6"
WIC
linen
Bath
railing
dn
Hall
brm
Kitchen
14-0x13-0
Pan
R
dw
F
Foyer
coats
Br #2
10-0 x 10-0
W
D
Util.
Br #3
10-0 x 10-0
Porch
Double Garage
22-0 x 23-0
MAIN FLOOR

Design 99321

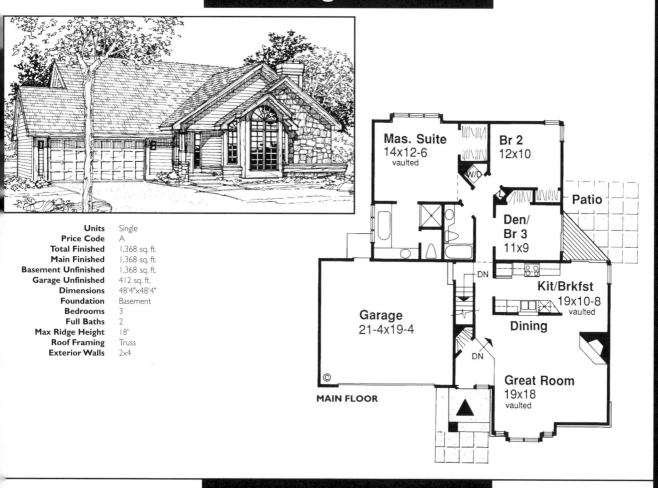

Units	Single
Price Code	A
Total Finished	1,368 sq. ft.
Main Finished	1,368 sq. ft.
Basement Unfinished	1,368 sq. ft.
Garage Unfinished	412 sq. ft.
Dimensions	48'4"x48'4"
Foundation	Basement
Bedrooms	3
Full Baths	2
Max Ridge Height	18'
Roof Framing	Truss
Exterior Walls	2x4

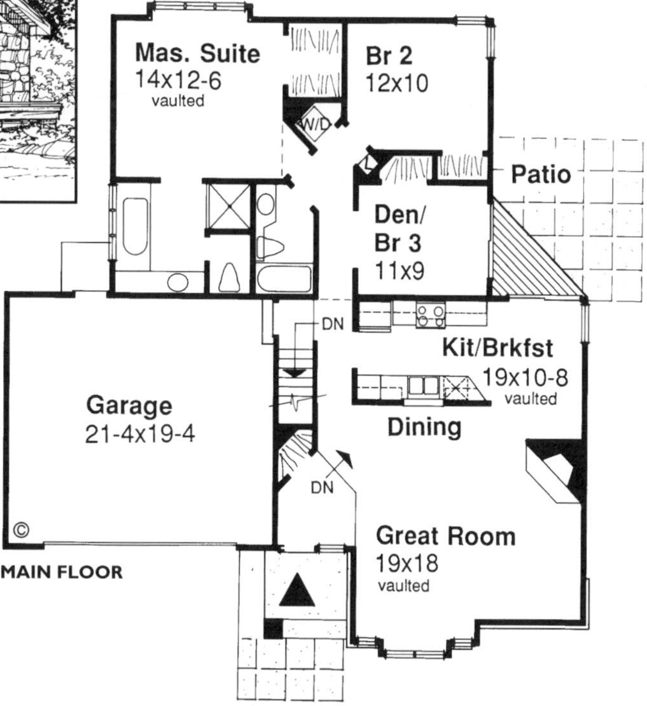

Mas. Suite 14x12-6 vaulted
Br 2 12x10
W/D
Patio
Den/ Br 3 11x9
DN
Kit/Brkfst 19x10-8 vaulted
Garage 21-4x19-4
Dining
DN
Great Room 19x18 vaulted
©

MAIN FLOOR

Design 96510

Units	Single
Price Code	A
Total Finished	1,372 sq. ft.
Main Finished	1,372 sq. ft.
Garage Unfinished	465 sq. ft.
Porch Unfinished	136 sq. ft.
Dimensions	38'x65'
Foundation	Crawlspace Slab
Bedrooms	3
Full Baths	2
Main Ceiling	8'
Max Ridge Height	19'
Roof Framing	Stick
Exterior Walls	2x4

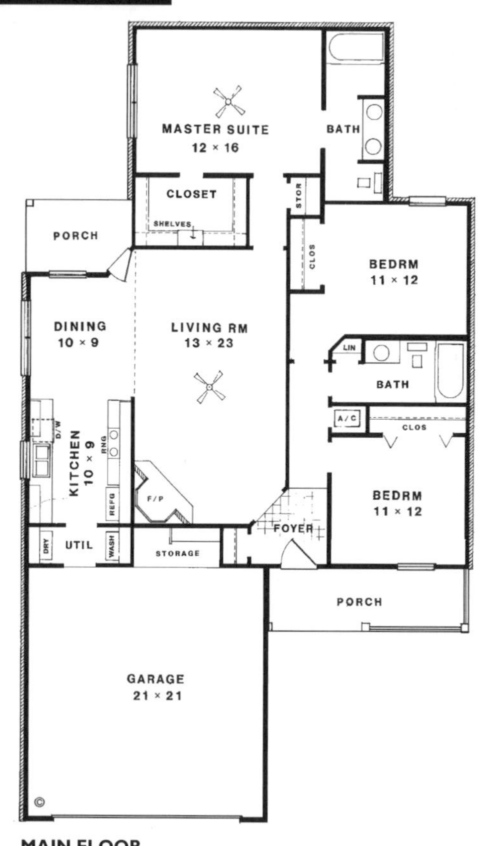
MASTER SUITE
12 × 16
BATH
CLOSET
SHELVES
STOR
PORCH
CLOS
BEDRM
11 × 12
DINING
10 × 9
LIVING RM
13 × 23
LIN
BATH
A/C
CLOS
KITCHEN
10 × 9
D/W
RNG
REFG
F/P
BEDRM
11 × 12
FOYER
DRY
UTIL
WASH
STORAGE
PORCH
GARAGE
21 × 21

MAIN FLOOR

Design 97638

FILES AVAILABLE
CAD
For more information call
800-235-5700

Units	Single
Price Code	A
Total Finished	1,374 sq. ft.
Main Finished	1,374 sq. ft.
Basement Unfinished	1,391 sq. ft.
Garage Unfinished	460 sq. ft.
Dimensions	50'4"x46'
Foundation	Basement Crawlspace
Bedrooms	3
Full Baths	2
Main Ceiling	9'
Max Ridge Height	24'
Roof Framing	Stick
Exterior Walls	2x4

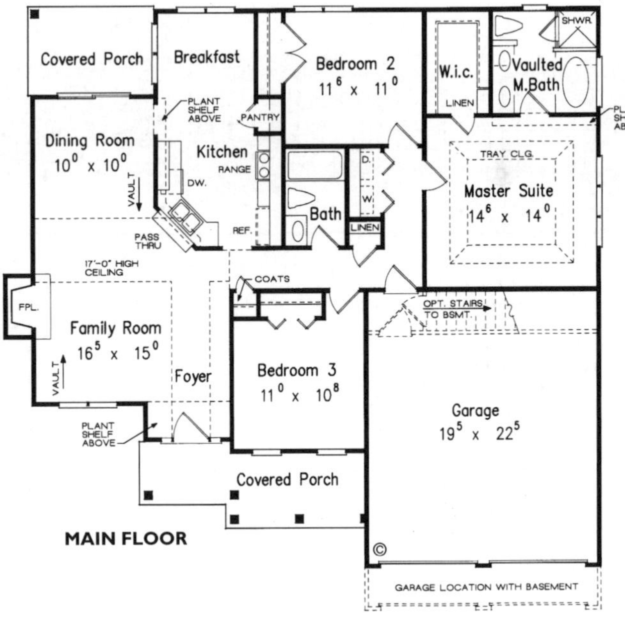
Covered Porch
Breakfast
Bedroom 2
11 6 x 11 0
W.i.c.
Vaulted M.Bath
SHWR
LINEN
PLANT SHELF ABOVE
PANTRY
Dining Room
10 0 x 10 0
Kitchen
RANGE
DW.
VAULT
TRAY CLG.
Master Suite
14 6 x 14 0
Bath
D.
W.
LINEN
REF.
PASS THRU
17'-0" HIGH CEILING
COATS
FPL.
Family Room
16 5 x 15 0
OPT. STAIRS TO BSMT.
Foyer
Bedroom 3
11 0 x 10 8
Garage
19 5 x 22 5
Covered Porch
GARAGE LOCATION WITH BASEMENT

MAIN FLOOR

Design 65600

Units	Single
Price Code	A
Total Finished	1,375 sq. ft.
Main Finished	1,375 sq. ft.
Garage Unfinished	525 sq. ft.
Porch Unfinished	105 sq. ft.
Dimensions	61'x35'
Foundation	Slab
Bedrooms	3
Full Baths	2
Main Ceiling	8'
Max Ridge Height	20'
Roof Framing	Stick
Exterior Walls	2x4

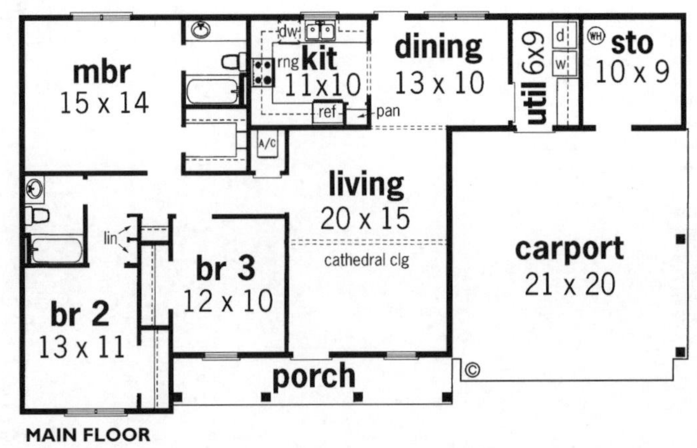
mbr
15 x 14
dw
rng
kit
11x10
ref
pan
dining
13 x 10
util 6x9
d
w
WH
sto
10 x 9
A/C
living
20 x 15
cathedral clg
lin
br 3
12 x 10
carport
21 x 20
br 2
13 x 11
porch

MAIN FLOOR

Design 65617

Units	Single
Price Code	A
Total Finished	1,375 sq. ft.
Main Finished	1,375 sq. ft.
Dimensions	61'x35'
Foundation	Crawlspace Slab
Bedrooms	3
Full Baths	2
Main Ceiling	8'
Max Ridge Height	24'
Roof Framing	Stick
Exterior Walls	2x4

patio
mbr 15 x 14
kit
dw
rng
pan
ref
dining 13 x 10
util
d
w
sto 9 x 10
WH
clo
shvs
HEAT & A/C
living 20 x 15
beam
cathedral ceiling
carport 21 x 20
LINEN
LINEN
clo
br 3 12 x 10
br 2 13 x 11
clo
porch
©

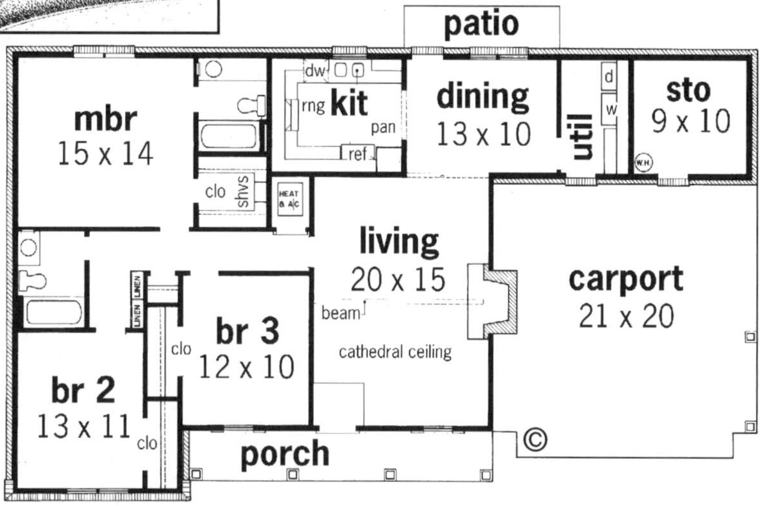

MAIN FLOOR

Design 66076

Units	Single
Price Code	A
Total Finished	1,377 sq. ft.
Main Finished	1,377 sq. ft.
Garage Unfinished	410 sq. ft.
Dimensions	45'x54'1"
Foundation	Crawlspace Slab
Bedrooms	3
Full Baths	2
Main Ceiling	8'
Max Ridge Height	22'
Roof Framing	Stick
Exterior Walls	2x4

Mstr
Sloping Ceiling
MstrBed 13x16
Bed#3 10x14
Patio
Kit 8x11
Din 10x11
9'Ceiling
Bed#2 10x11
B#2
Plant Ledge
Cathedral Ceiling
Util
Ent
LivRm 14x20
Gar 20x22
Por
©

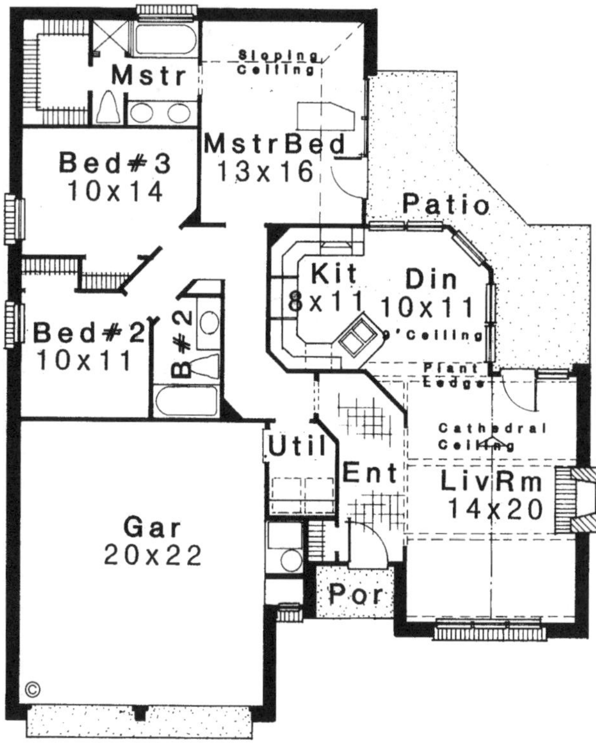

MAIN FLOOR

Design 94304

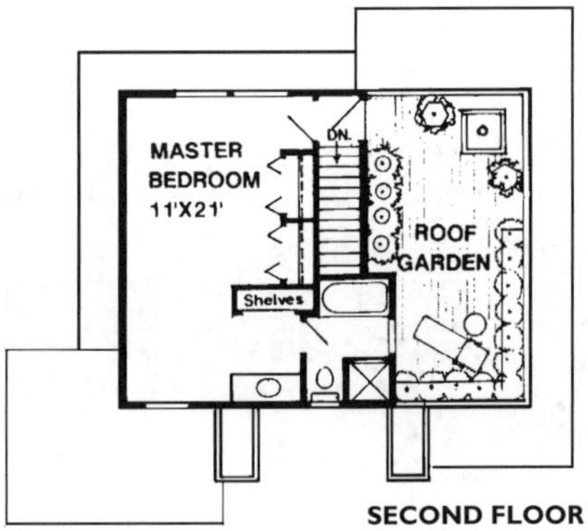

MASTER BEDROOM 11'X21'
DN.
ROOF GARDEN
Shelves

SECOND FLOOR

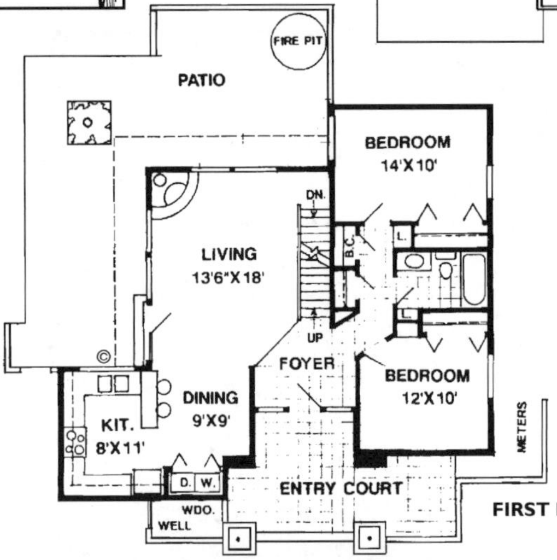

FIRE PIT
PATIO
BEDROOM 14'X10'
DN.
B.C.
LIVING 13'6"X18'
UP
FOYER
BEDROOM 12'X10'
DINING 9'X9'
KIT. 8'X11'
D. W.
METERS
ENTRY COURT
WDO. WELL

FIRST FLOOR

Units	Single
Price Code	A
Total Finished	1,377 sq. ft.
First Finished	981 sq. ft.
Second Finished	396 sq. ft.
Dimensions	40'x50'
Foundation	Basement
Bedrooms	3
Full Baths	2
First Ceiling	8'
Second Ceiling	8'
Roof Framing	Truss
Exterior Walls	2x4

Design 82003

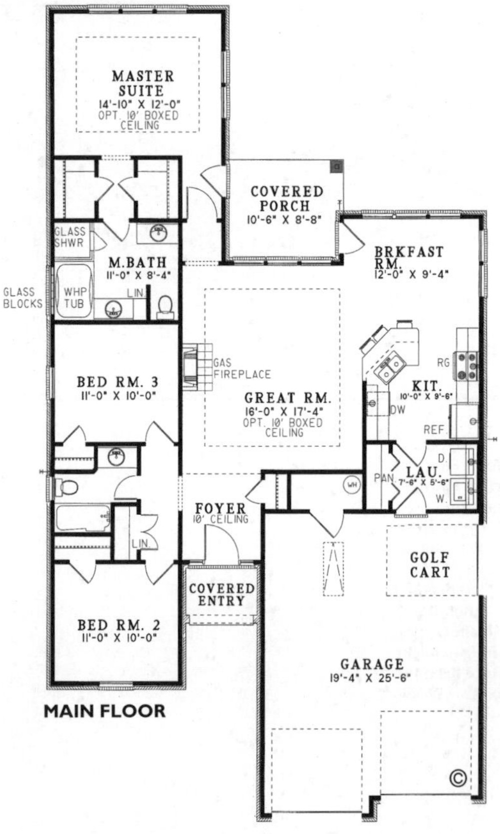

MASTER SUITE 14'-10" X 12'-0" OPT. 10' BOXED CEILING
COVERED PORCH 10'-6" X 8'-8"
GLASS SHWR
M.BATH 11'-0" X 8'-4"
GLASS BLOCKS
WHP TUB
LIN
BRKFAST RM. 12'-0" X 9'-4"
GAS FIREPLACE
GREAT RM. 16'-0" X 17'-4" OPT. 10' BOXED CEILING
BED RM. 3 11'-0" X 10'-0"
KIT. 10'-0" X 9'-6"
RG
DW
REF
LAU. 7'-6" X 5'-6"
PAN
WH
D
W
FOYER 10' CEILING
LIN.
COVERED ENTRY
GOLF CART
BED RM. 2 11'-0" X 10'-0"
GARAGE 19'-4" X 25'-6"

MAIN FLOOR

Units	Single
Price Code	A
Total Finished	1,379 sq. ft.
Main Finished	1,379 sq. ft.
Garage Unfinished	493 sq. ft.
Porch Unfinished	142 sq. ft.
Dimensions	38'4"x68'6"
Foundation	Crawlspace Slab
Bedrooms	3
Full Baths	2
Main Ceiling	9'
Roof Framing	Stick
Exterior Walls	2x4

Design 99673

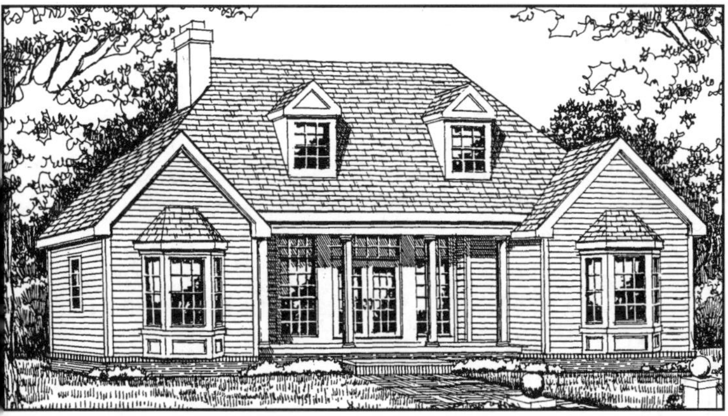

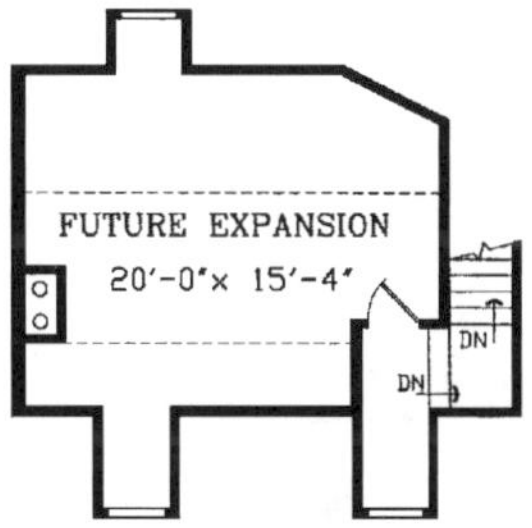

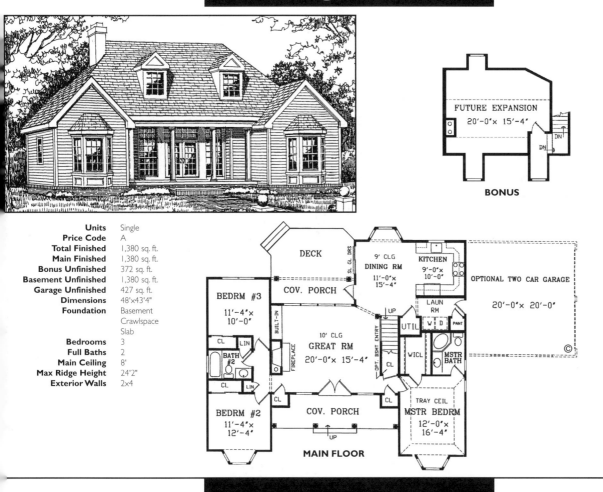

FUTURE EXPANSION
20'-0"x 15'-4"
DN
BONUS

Units	Single
Price Code	A
Total Finished	1,380 sq. ft.
Main Finished	1,380 sq. ft.
Bonus Unfinished	372 sq. ft.
Basement Unfinished	1,380 sq. ft.
Garage Unfinished	427 sq. ft.
Dimensions	48'x43'4"
Foundation	Basement Crawlspace Slab
Bedrooms	3
Full Baths	2
Main Ceiling	8'
Max Ridge Height	24'2"
Exterior Walls	2x4

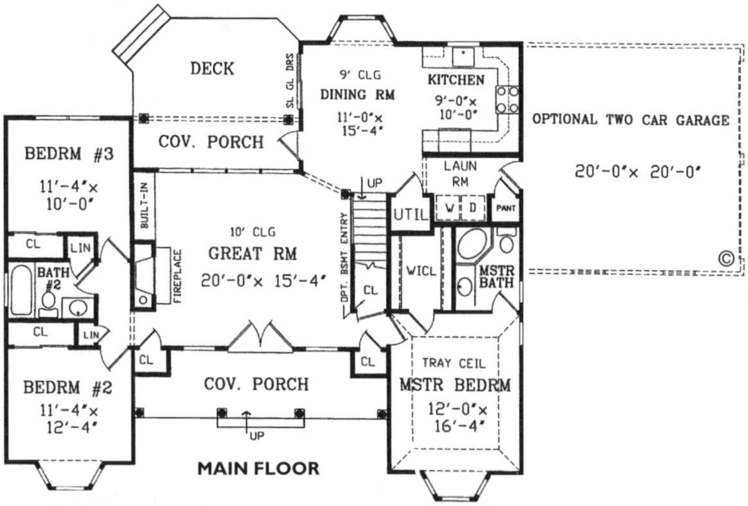

DECK
9' CLG DINING RM 11'-0"x 15'-4"
KITCHEN 9'-0"x 10'-0"
OPTIONAL TWO CAR GARAGE 20'-0"x 20'-0"
BEDRM #3 11'-4"x 10'-0"
COV. PORCH
10' CLG GREAT RM 20'-0"x 15'-4"
LAUN RM
UTIL
WICL
MSTR BATH
BATH #2
TRAY CEIL MSTR BEDRM 12'-0"x 16'-4"
BEDRM #2 11'-4"x 12'-4"
COV. PORCH
MAIN FLOOR

Design 69036

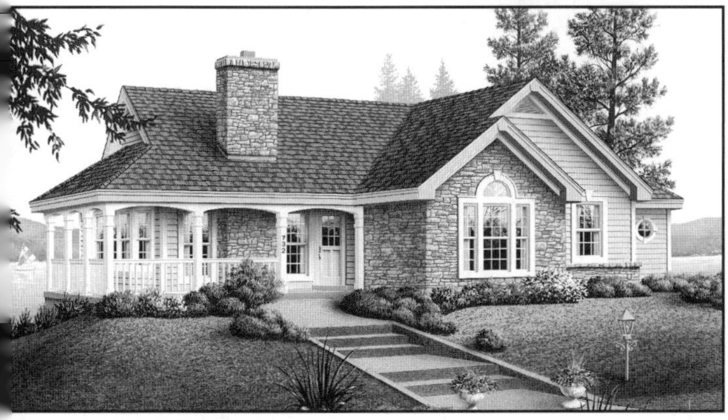

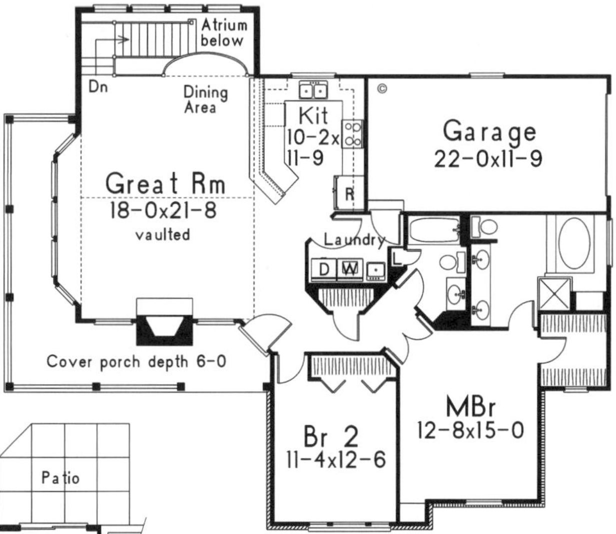

Units	Single
Price Code	A
Total Finished	1,384 sq. ft.
Main Finished	1,384 sq. ft.
Bonus Unfinished	611 sq. ft.
Dimensions	55'8"x46'
Foundation	Basement
Bedrooms	2
Full Baths	2
Roof Framing	Stick

Hot New Design

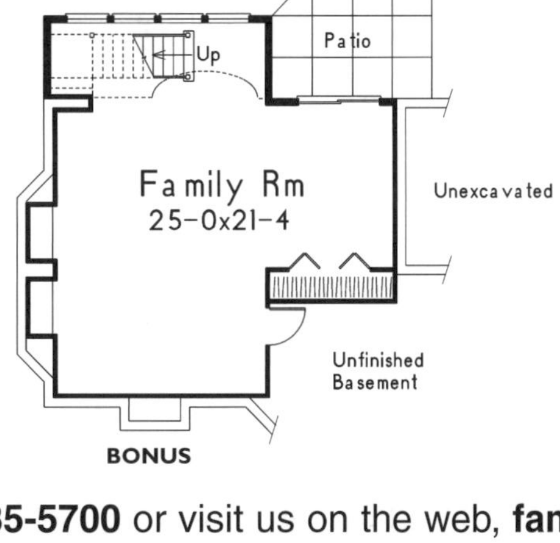

Atrium below
Dining Area
Kit 10-2x11-9
Garage 22-0x11-9
Great Rm 18-0x21-8 vaulted
Laundry
Cover porch depth 6-0
Br 2 11-4x12-6
MBr 12-8x15-0
MAIN FLOOR

Patio
Family Rm 25-0x21-4
Unexcavated
Unfinished Basement
BONUS

Design 93279

Units	Single
Price Code	A
Total Finished	1,388 sq. ft.
Main Finished	1,388 sq. ft.
Garage Unfinished	400 sq. ft.
Dimensions	48'x46'
Foundation	Crawlspace Slab
Bedrooms	3
Full Baths	2
Main Ceiling	8'
Max Ridge Height	18'
Roof Framing	Truss
Exterior Walls	2x4

Patio 12-0 x 10-0
Dining 10-0 x 11-0
Brkfst. Bar
Living Area 13-8 x 17-6
Pass Thru Fire Place
Vaulted Ceil.
Master Bdrm. 13-6 x 12-2
Opt. Plant Shelf Above
Kitchen 10-0 x 12-6
Dw.
Ref.
Pant.
Bth.2
W. D.
Clo.
Lnd.
Stor.
Foyer
WH
Furn.
M.Bath
Lin.
Bdrm.3 10-0 x 10-0
Bdrm.2 11-0 x 10-8
Double Garage 19-4 x 19-4
©

MAIN FLOOR

Design 92557

Units	Single
Price Code	A
Total Finished	1,390 sq. ft.
Main Finished	1,390 sq. ft.
Garage Unfinished	590 sq. ft.
Porch Unfinished	66 sq. ft.
Dimensions	67'4"x32'10"
Foundation	Crawlspace Slab
Bedrooms	3
Full Baths	2
Main Ceiling	9'
Max Ridge Height	22'6"
Roof Framing	Stick
Exterior Walls	2x4

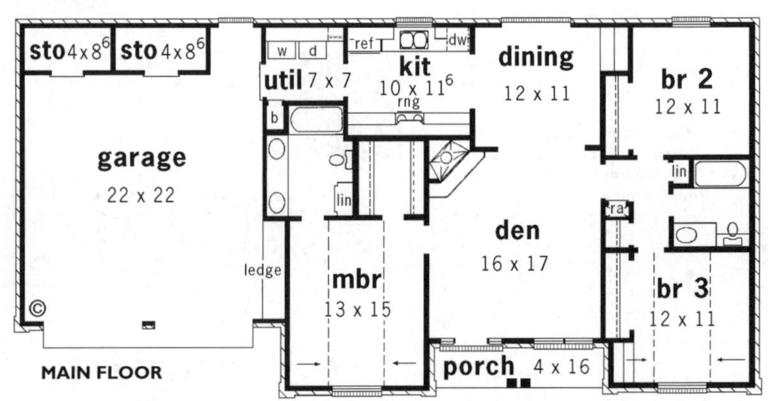
sto 4 x 8⁶
sto 4 x 8⁶
w d
util 7 x 7
ref
dw
kit 10 x 11⁶
rng
dining 12 x 11
br 2 12 x 11
garage 22 x 22
b
lin
lin
ra
den 16 x 17
ledge
mbr 13 x 15
br 3 12 x 11
porch 4 x 16
©

MAIN FLOOR

Design 92441

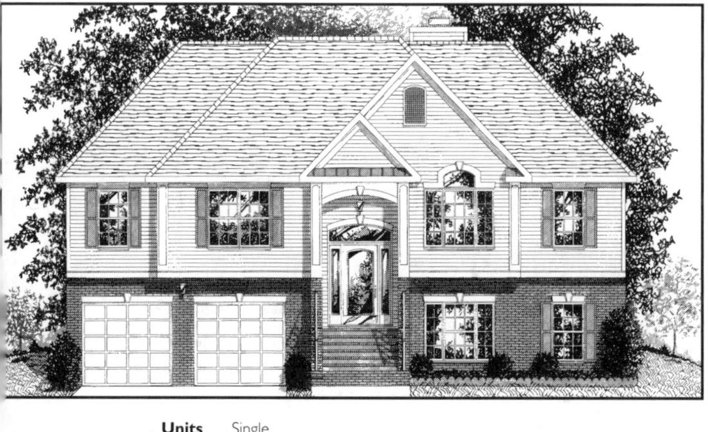

DECK
DECK
TRAY CEILING
BEDROOM 2
11 X 10
SUNROOM
9 X 10
MSTR. BEDROOM
14 X 13
FAMILY ROOM
14 X 17
15'-6" HIGH CEILING
KIT.
9 X 10
VAULT
COATS
DN
UP
BEDROOM 3
12 X 10
DINING
10 X 12
BRKFST.
9 X 9
MAIN FLOOR

Units	Single
Price Code	A
Total Finished	1,459 sq. ft.
Main Finished	1,391 sq. ft.
Lower Finished	68 sq. ft.
Bonus Unfinished	520 sq. ft.
Garage Unfinished	595 sq. ft.
Dimensions	49'x27'
Foundation	Combo Crawlspace/ Slab
Bedrooms	3
Full Baths	2
Max Ridge Height	29'
Roof Framing	Stick
Exterior Walls	2x4

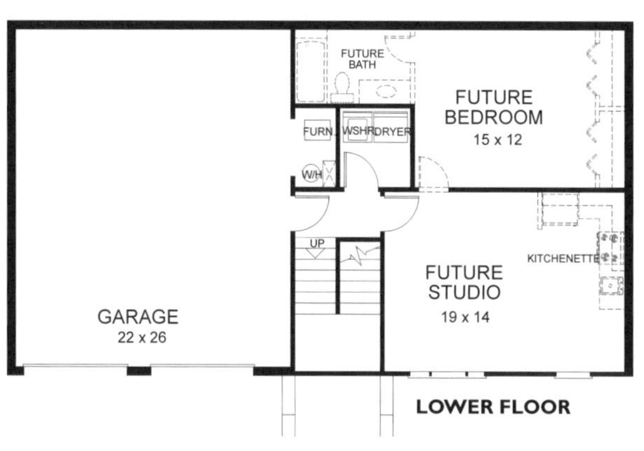
FUTURE BATH
FURN.
WSHR
DRYER
W/H
FUTURE BEDROOM
15 x 12
UP
KITCHENETTE
FUTURE STUDIO
19 x 14
GARAGE
22 x 26
LOWER FLOOR

Design 93469

Units	Single
Price Code	A
Total Finished	1,391 sq. ft.
Main Finished	1,391 sq. ft.
Garage Unfinished	528 sq. ft.
Deck Unfinished	99 sq. ft.
Porch Unfinished	89 sq. ft.
Dimensions	64'x61'4"
Foundation	Crawlspace Slab
Bedrooms	3
Full Baths	2
Main Ceiling	8'
Vaulted Ceiling	11'
Tray Ceiling	12'8"
Max Ridge Height	21'6"
Roof Framing	Stick
Exterior Walls	2x4

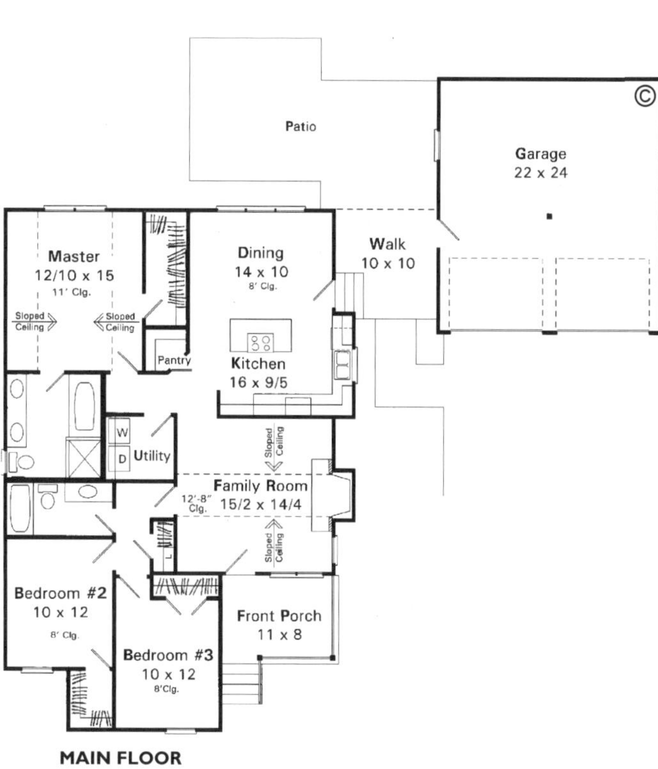
Patio
Garage
22 x 24
Master
12/10 x 15
11' Clg.
Sloped Ceiling
Sloped Ceiling
Dining
14 x 10
8' Clg.
Walk
10 x 10
Pantry
Kitchen
16 x 9/5
W
D
Utility
Sloped Ceiling
Family Room
12'-8" Clg.
15/2 x 14/4
Sloped Ceiling
Bedroom #2
10 x 12
8' Clg.
Bedroom #3
10 x 12
8'Clg.
Front Porch
11 x 8
MAIN FLOOR

Design 97604

Units	Single
Price Code	A
Total Finished	1,392 sq. ft.
Main Finished	1,392 sq. ft.
Basement Unfinished	1,414 sq. ft.
Garage Unfinished	415 sq. ft.
Dimensions	49'x49'4"
Foundation	Basement Crawlspace
Bedrooms	3
Full Baths	2
Main Ceiling	9'
Max Ridge Height	23'
Roof Framing	Stick
Exterior Walls	2x4

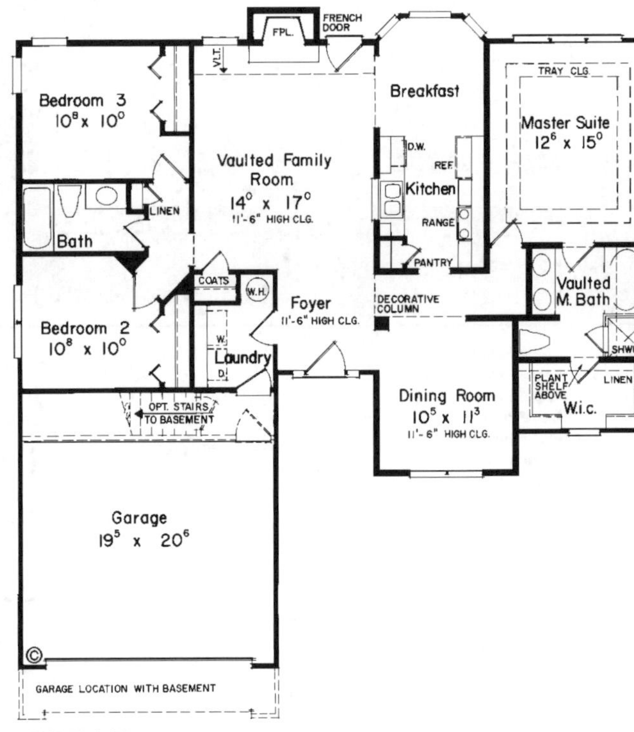
FPL.
FRENCH DOOR
Bedroom 3
10⁸ x 10⁰
Breakfast
TRAY CLG.
Master Suite
12⁶ x 15⁰
Vaulted Family Room
14⁰ x 17⁰
11'-6" HIGH CLG.
D.W.
REF.
Kitchen
RANGE
LINEN
Bath
PANTRY
COATS
W.H.
Foyer
11'-6" HIGH CLG.
DECORATIVE COLUMN
Vaulted M. Bath
Bedroom 2
10⁸ x 10⁰
Laundry
SHWR.
PLANT SHELF ABOVE
LINEN
W.i.c.
OPT. STAIRS TO BASEMENT
Dining Room
10⁵ x 11³
11'-6" HIGH CLG.
Garage
19⁵ x 20⁶
GARAGE LOCATION WITH BASEMENT

MAIN FLOOR

Design 65465

Units	Single
Price Code	A
Total Finished	1,393 sq. ft.
Main Finished	1,393 sq. ft.
Basement Unfinished	1,393 sq. ft.
Garage Unfinished	319 sq. ft.
Deck Unfinished	40 sq. ft.
Porch Unfinished	32 sq. ft.
Dimensions	36'x56'
Foundation	Basement
Bedrooms	3
Full Baths	1
Main Ceiling	9'
Max Ridge Height	23'10"
Roof Framing	Truss
Exterior Walls	2x6

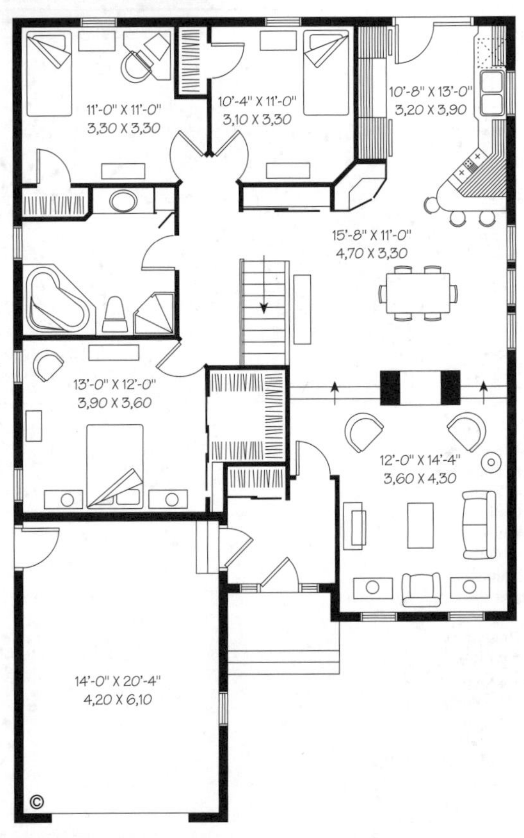
11'-0" X 11'-0"
3,30 X 3,30
10'-4" X 11'-0"
3,10 X 3,30
10'-8" X 13'-0"
3,20 X 3,90
15'-8" X 11'-0"
4,70 X 3,30
13'-0" X 12'-0"
3,90 X 3,60
12'-0" X 14'-4"
3,60 X 4,30
14'-0" X 20'-4"
4,20 X 6,10

MAIN FLOOR

Design 90680

Units	Single
Price Code	A
Total Finished	1,393 sq. ft.
Main Finished	1,393 sq. ft.
Basement Unfinished	1,393 sq. ft.
Garage Unfinished	542 sq. ft.
Porch Unfinished	195 sq. ft.
Dimensions	72'4"x36'8"
Foundation	Basement Slab
Bedrooms	3
Full Baths	2

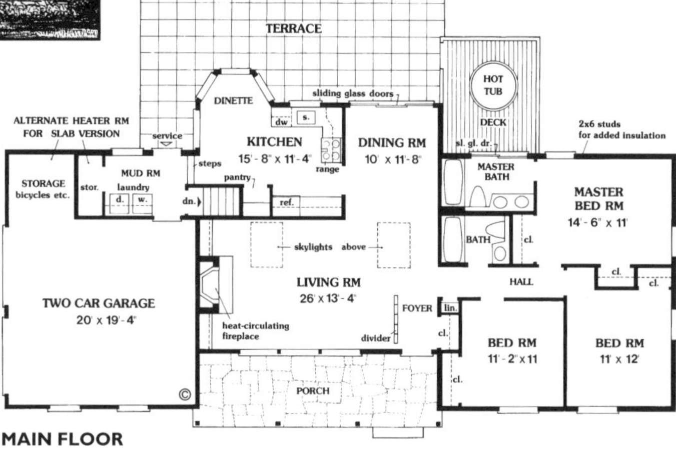
TERRACE
HOT TUB
DECK
ALTERNATE HEATER RM FOR SLAB VERSION
DINETTE
sliding glass doors
2x6 studs for added insulation
KITCHEN
15'-8" x 11'-4"
DINING RM
10' x 11'-8"
MASTER BATH
MASTER BED RM
14'-6" x 11'
STORAGE bicycles etc.
MUD RM laundry
pantry
skylights above
LIVING RM
26' x 13'-4"
TWO CAR GARAGE
20' x 19'-4"
heat-circulating fireplace
FOYER
HALL
BED RM
11'-2" x 11'
BED RM
11' x 12'
PORCH

MAIN FLOOR

Design 96803

Units	Single
Price Code	A
Total Finished	1,399 sq. ft.
First Finished	732 sq. ft.
Second Finished	667 sq. ft.
Basement Unfinished	732 sq. ft.
Garage Unfinished	406 sq. ft.
Dimensions	46'9"x43'6"
Foundation	Basement Crawlspace Slab
Bedrooms	3
Full Baths	1
Half Baths	1
First Ceiling	9'
Second Ceiling	8'2"
Max Ridge Height	25'9"
Roof Framing	Truss
Exterior Walls	2x4

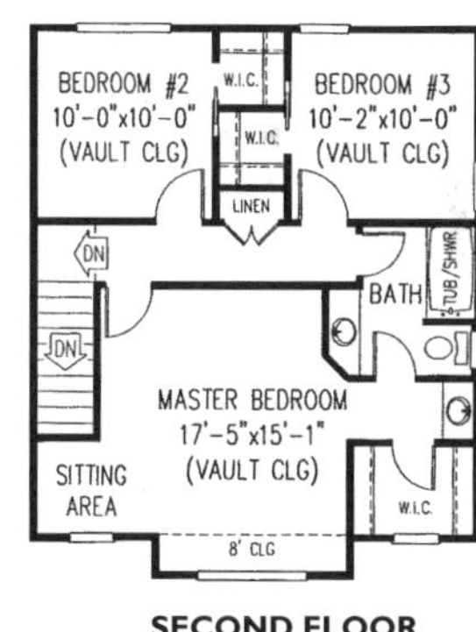
BEDROOM #2
10'-0"x10'-0"
(VAULT CLG)
BEDROOM #3
10'-2"x10'-0"
(VAULT CLG)
LINEN
BATH
MASTER BEDROOM
17'-5"x15'-1"
(VAULT CLG)
SITTING AREA
8' CLG

SECOND FLOOR

9' WIDE COVERED PORCH
CANTILEVERED 2nd FLOOR
SHOP/ STORAGE 7'-7"x11'-9"
LNDRY 1/2 BATH
DINING 10'-3x10'-5" (9' CLG)
KITCHEN 10'-6x10'-5" (9' CLG)
ARCH OVER COLUMNS
LIVING ROOM 20'-9"x15'-6" (9' CLG)
VENTLESS GAS FIREPLACE
8' WIDE COVERED PORCH
OPTIONAL TWO CAR GARAGE
GARAGE 14'-0"x22'-2"
10' OVERHEAD DOOR
8' WIDE COVERED PORCH

FIRST FLOOR

Design 34054

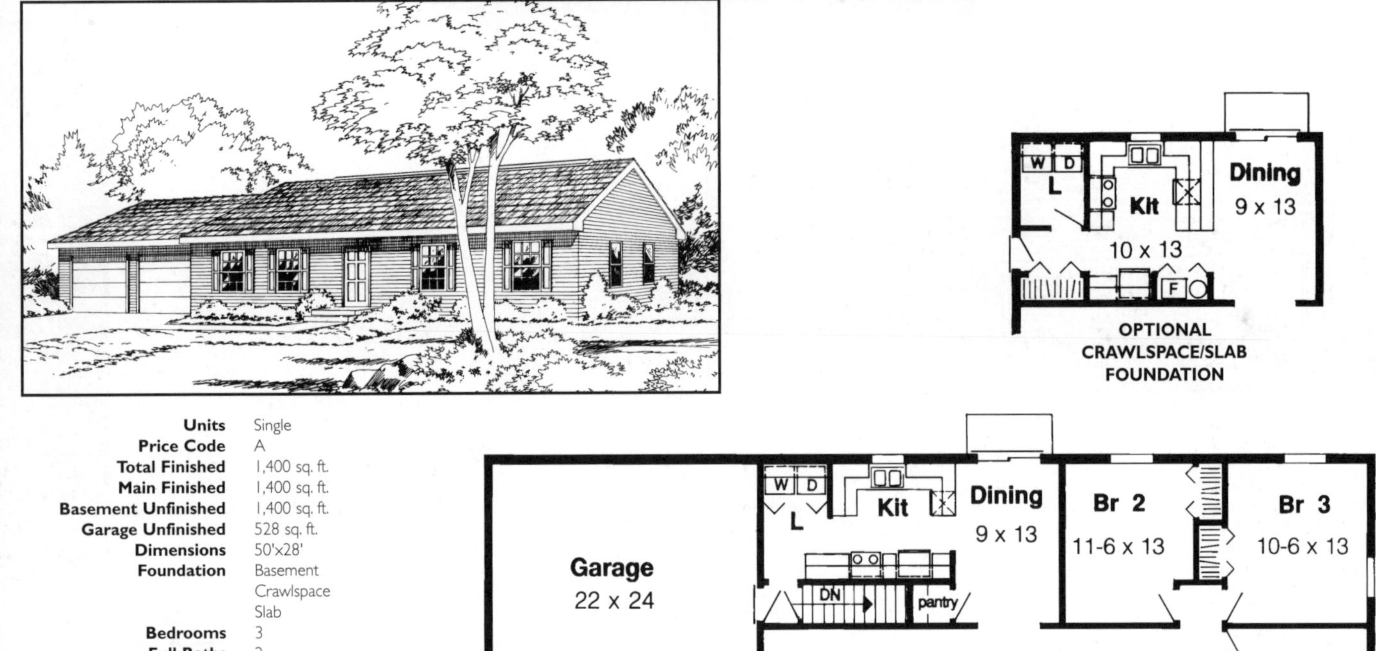
W D
L
Kit
Dining
9 x 13
10 x 13
F
OPTIONAL
CRAWLSPACE/SLAB
FOUNDATION

Units	Single
Price Code	A
Total Finished	1,400 sq. ft.
Main Finished	1,400 sq. ft.
Basement Unfinished	1,400 sq. ft.
Garage Unfinished	528 sq. ft.
Dimensions	50'x28'
Foundation	Basement Crawlspace Slab
Bedrooms	3
Full Baths	2
Main Ceiling	8'
Max Ridge Height	17'
Roof Framing	Stick
Exterior Walls	2x4, 2x6

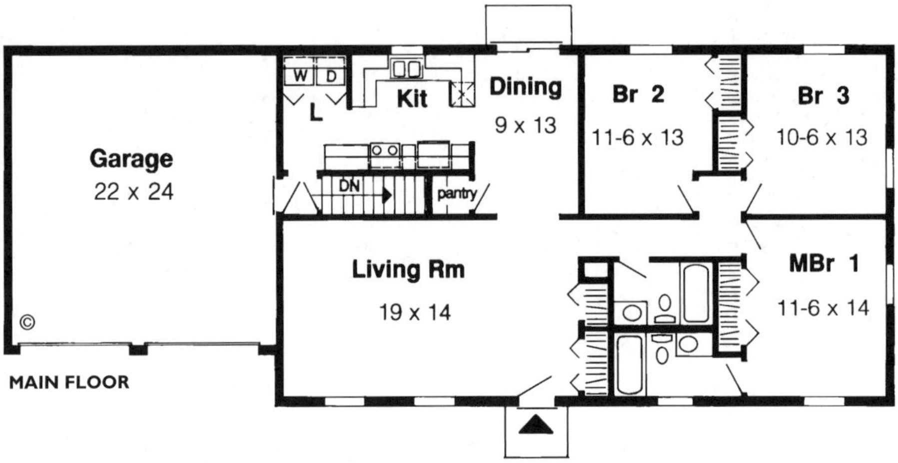

Garage 22 x 24
W D L
Kit
Dining 9 x 13
DN pantry
Br 2 11-6 x 13
Br 3 10-6 x 13
Living Rm 19 x 14
MBr 1 11-6 x 14
©
MAIN FLOOR

Design 69031

Hot New Design

Units	Single
Price Code	A
Total Finished	1,400 sq. ft.
Main Finished	1,400 sq. ft.
Dimensions	72'x28'
Foundation	Basement Crawlspace
Bedrooms	3
Full Baths	2

Patio
Br 2 11-8x11-7
Dining 10-11x11-7
Kit 10-6x 11-7
R
D W
Utility 11-10x6-0
P
storage area
Dn
L
Garage 21-8x27-4
Br 3 13-0x9-11
Living 19-11x15-5 vaulted
MBr 13-6x13-0 vaulted
©
MAIN FLOOR
Covered Porch depth 6-0

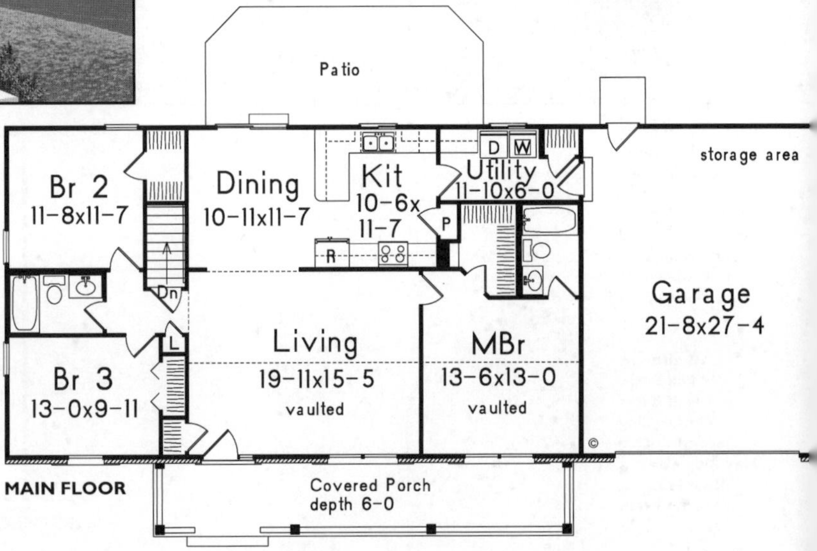

Design 99255

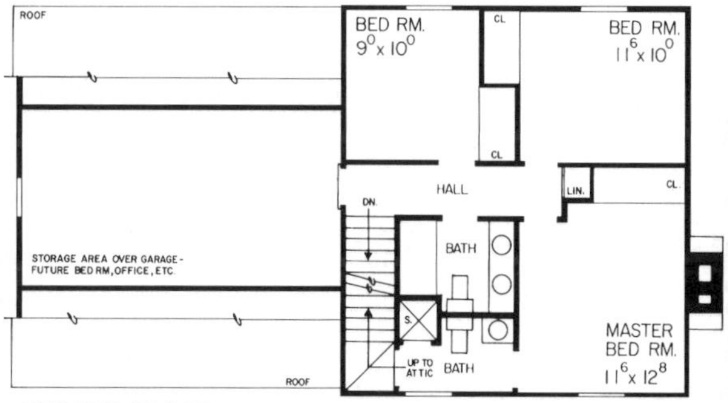

Units	Single
Price Code	A
Total Finished	1,400 sq. ft.
First Finished	700 sq. ft.
Second Finished	700 sq. ft.
Garage Unfinished	510 sq. ft.
Dimensions	46'x26'
Foundation	Basement
Bedrooms	3
Full Baths	1
3/4 Baths	1
Half Baths	1
Max Ridge Height	30'
Roof Framing	Stick
Exterior Walls	2x4

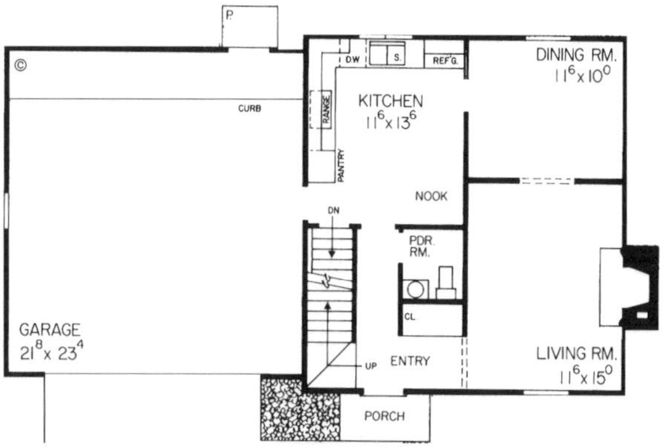

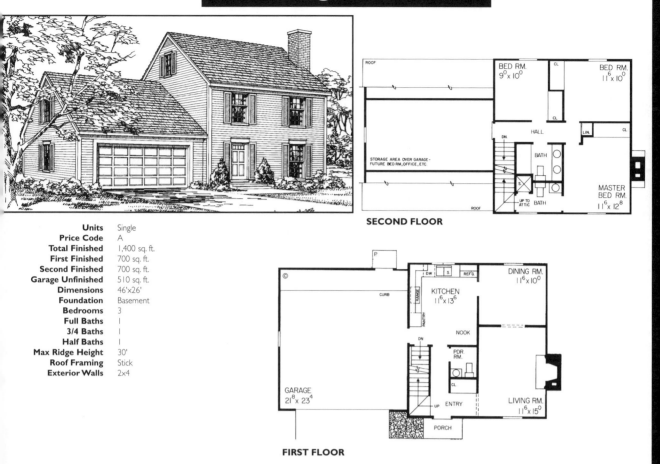

SECOND FLOOR

FIRST FLOOR

Design 62024

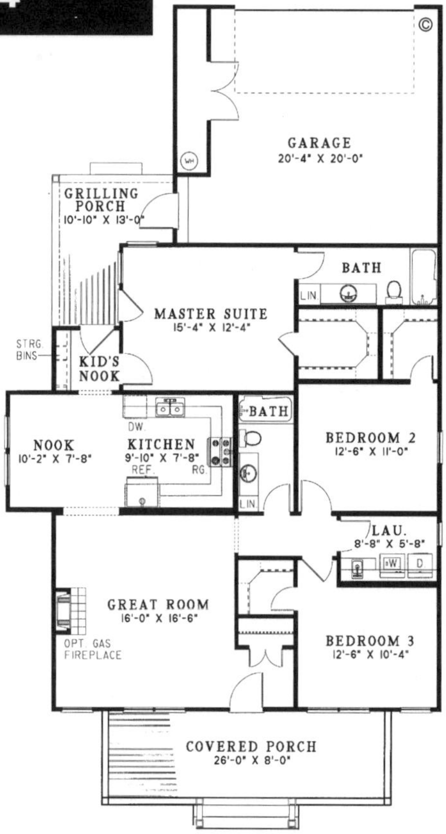

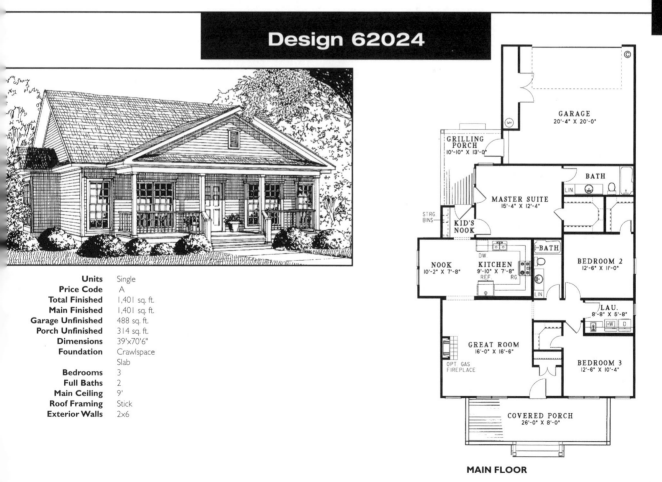

Units	Single
Price Code	A
Total Finished	1,401 sq. ft.
Main Finished	1,401 sq. ft.
Garage Unfinished	488 sq. ft.
Porch Unfinished	314 sq. ft.
Dimensions	39'x70'6"
Foundation	Crawlspace Slab
Bedrooms	3
Full Baths	2
Main Ceiling	9'
Roof Framing	Stick
Exterior Walls	2x6

MAIN FLOOR

Design 69147

Units	Single
Price Code	A
Total Finished	1,401 sq. ft.
Main Finished	1,401 sq. ft.
Garage Unfinished	462 sq. ft.
Dimensions	50'x53'
Foundation	Crawlspace
Bedrooms	3
Full Baths	2
Main Ceiling	8'
Vaulted Ceiling	11'
Max Ridge Height	18'2"
Roof Framing	Truss
Exterior Walls	2x6

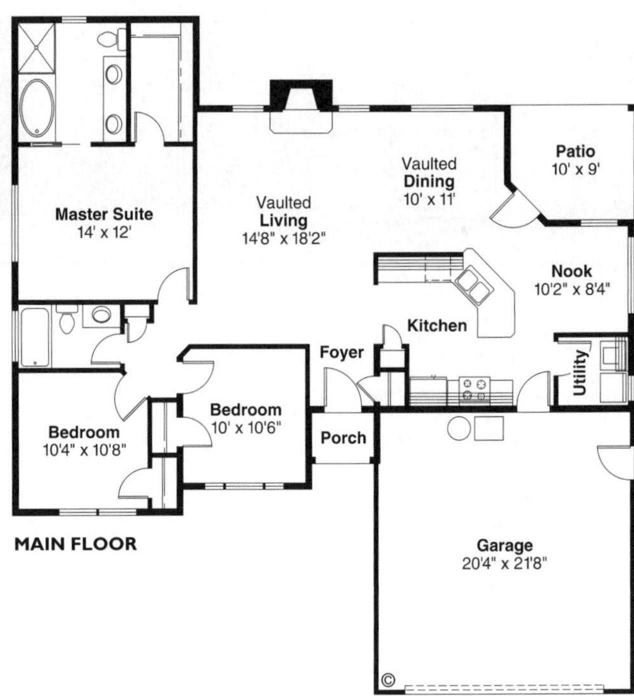
Master Suite
14' x 12'
Vaulted
Living
14'8" x 18'2"
Vaulted
Dining
10' x 11'
Patio
10' x 9'
Nook
10'2" x 8'4"
Kitchen
Foyer
Utility
Bedroom
10' x 10'6"
Bedroom
10'4" x 10'8"
Porch
Garage
20'4" x 21'8"
MAIN FLOOR

Design 94690

Units	Single
Price Code	A
Total Finished	1,401 sq. ft.
Main Finished	1,401 sq. ft.
Porch Unfinished	137 sq. ft.
Dimensions	30'x59'10"
Foundation	Slab
Bedrooms	3
Full Baths	2
Main Ceiling	9'
Max Ridge Height	20'6"
Roof Framing	Stick
Exterior Walls	2x4

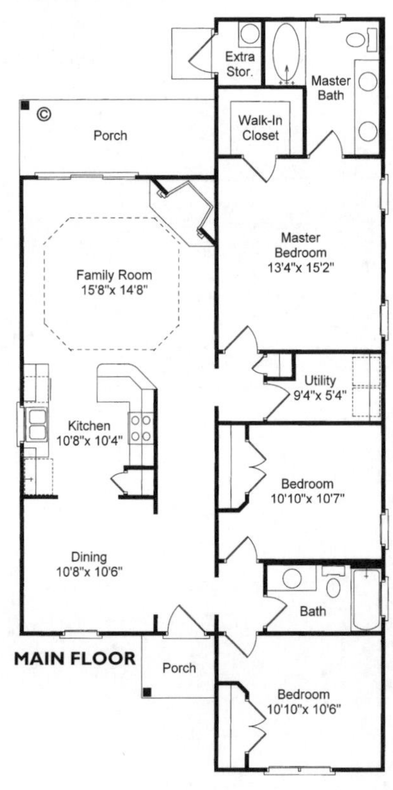
Extra
Stor.
Master
Bath
Porch
Walk-In
Closet
Master
Bedroom
13'4"x 15'2"
Family Room
15'8"x 14'8"
Utility
9'4"x 5'4"
Kitchen
10'8"x 10'4"
Bedroom
10'10"x 10'7"
Dining
10'8"x 10'6"
Bath
MAIN FLOOR
Porch
Bedroom
10'10"x 10'6"

Design 94689

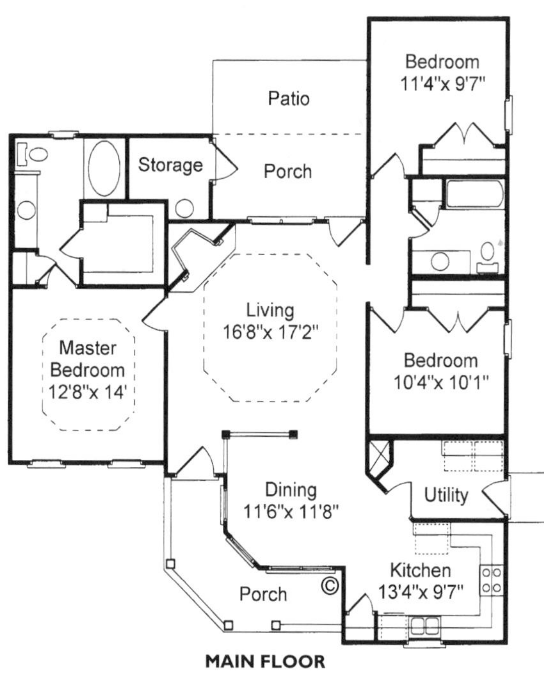
Bedroom
11'4"x 9'7"
Patio
Storage
Porch
Living
16'8"x 17'2"
Master
Bedroom
12'8"x 14'
Bedroom
10'4"x 10'1"
Dining
11'6"x 11'8"
Utility
Kitchen
13'4"x 9'7"
Porch
©

MAIN FLOOR

Units	Single
Price Code	A
Total Finished	1,405 sq. ft.
Main Finished	1,405 sq. ft.
Dimensions	42'x51'
Foundation	Slab
Bedrooms	3
Full Baths	2
Main Ceiling	8'
Max Ridge Height	19'4"
Roof Framing	Stick
Exterior Walls	2x4

Design 98505

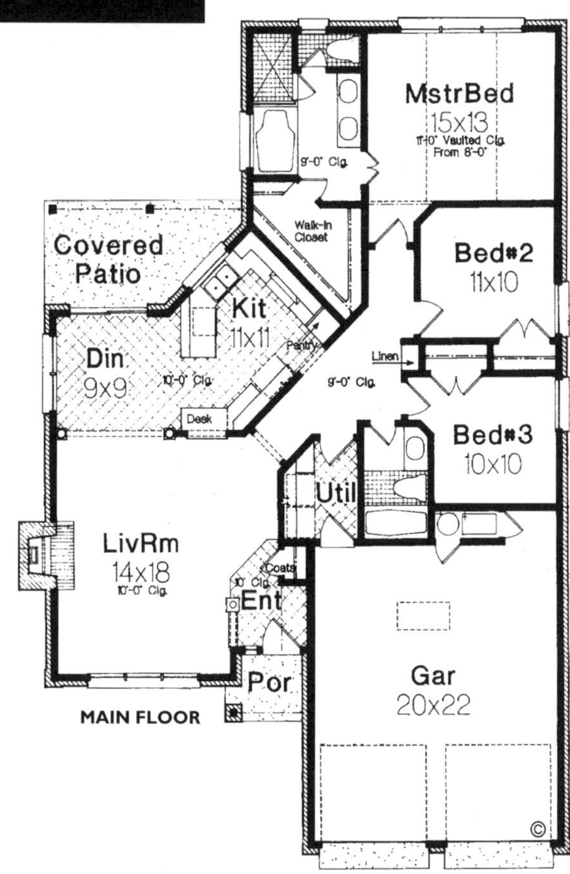
MstrBed
15x13
11'-0" Vaulted Clg.
From 8'-0"
9'-0" Clg.
Walk-In
Closet
Covered
Patio
Bed#2
11x10
Kit
11x11
Pantry
Linen
Din
9x9
10'-0" Clg.
9'-0" Clg.
Deck
Bed#3
10x10
Util
LivRm
14x18
10'-0" Clg.
Coats
10' Clg.
Ent
Por
Gar
20x22
©

MAIN FLOOR

Units	Single
Price Code	A
Total Finished	1,405 sq. ft.
Main Finished	1,405 sq. ft.
Garage Unfinished	440 sq. ft.
Deck Unfinished	160 sq. ft.
Porch Unfinished	28 sq. ft.
Dimensions	40'x60'
Foundation	Slab
Bedrooms	3
Full Baths	2
Max Ridge Height	21'3"
Roof Framing	Stick
Exterior Walls	2x4

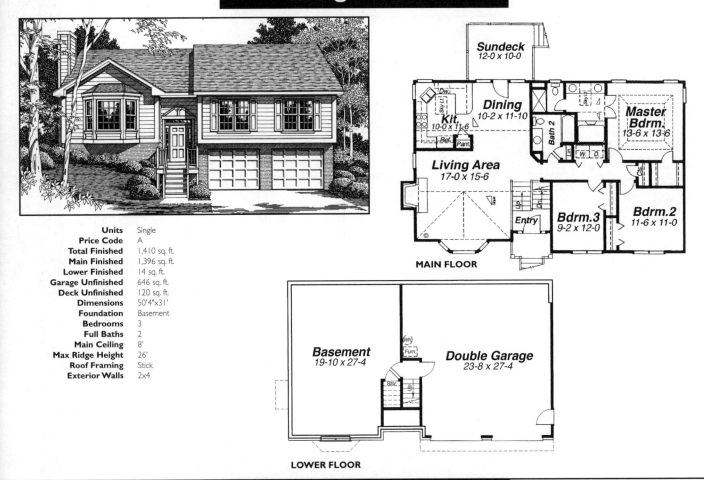

Design 98970

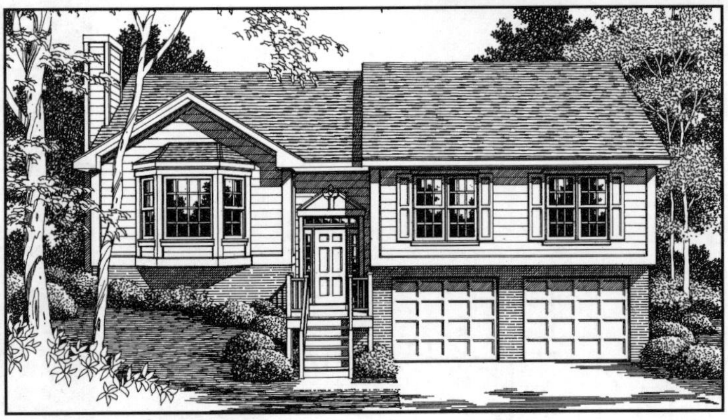

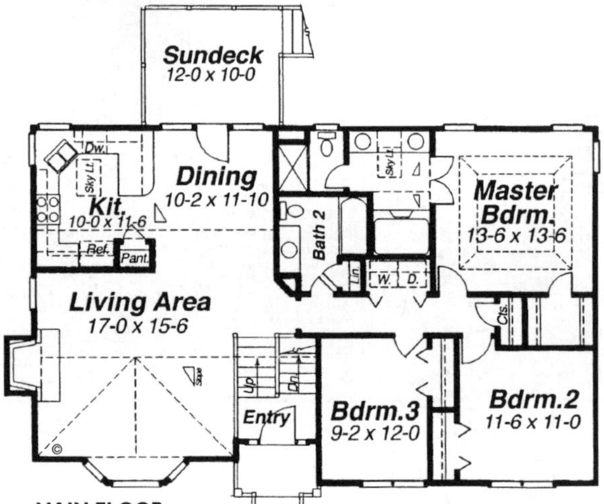

Units	Single
Price Code	A
Total Finished	1,410 sq. ft.
Main Finished	1,396 sq. ft.
Lower Finished	14 sq. ft.
Garage Unfinished	646 sq. ft.
Deck Unfinished	120 sq. ft.
Dimensions	50'4"x31'
Foundation	Basement
Bedrooms	3
Full Baths	2
Main Ceiling	8'
Max Ridge Height	26'
Roof Framing	Stick
Exterior Walls	2x4

Sundeck 12-0 x 10-0
Dining 10-2 x 11-10
Kit. 10-0 x 11-6
Master Bdrm. 13-6 x 13-6
Bath 2
Living Area 17-0 x 15-6
Entry
Bdrm.3 9-2 x 12-0
Bdrm.2 11-6 x 11-0
MAIN FLOOR

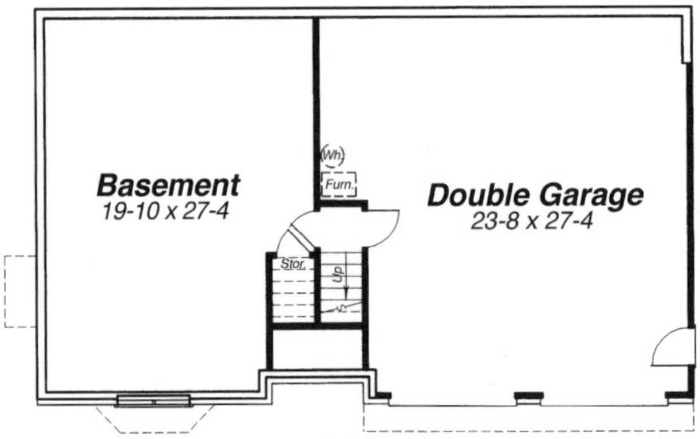

Basement 19-10 x 27-4
Double Garage 23-8 x 27-4
LOWER FLOOR

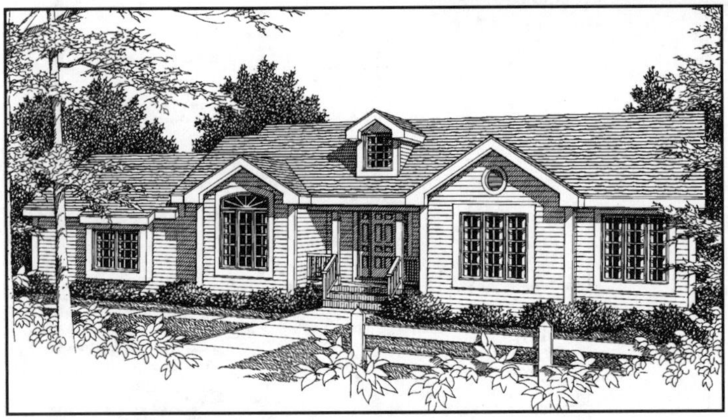

Design 99669

Units	Single
Price Code	A
Total Finished	1,412 sq. ft.
Main Finished	1,412 sq. ft.
Basement Unfinished	1,412 sq. ft.
Garage Unfinished	441 sq. ft.
Deck Unfinished	370 sq. ft.
Porch Unfinished	65 sq. ft.
Dimensions	72'x30'8"
Foundation	Basement Slab
Bedrooms	3
Full Baths	2
Main Ceiling	8'
Vaulted Ceiling	11'
Max Ridge Height	18'
Roof Framing	Stick
Exterior Walls	2x4

WOOD DECK
DINING RM 10'-4" X 10' HIGH CLG.
SKYLIGHT ABOVE
WHIRLPOOL TUB
GREAT RM 13'-4" X 19'-4" HIGH CLG.
MASTER SUITE 12' X 16'
W. I. C.
2-CAR GARAGE 20' X 21'
KITCH. 10' X 10'-4"
BAR
HALL
BED RM-3 10' X 10'
PORCH
BED RM-2 11' X 10'
DINETTE 10' X 9'
MAIN FLOOR

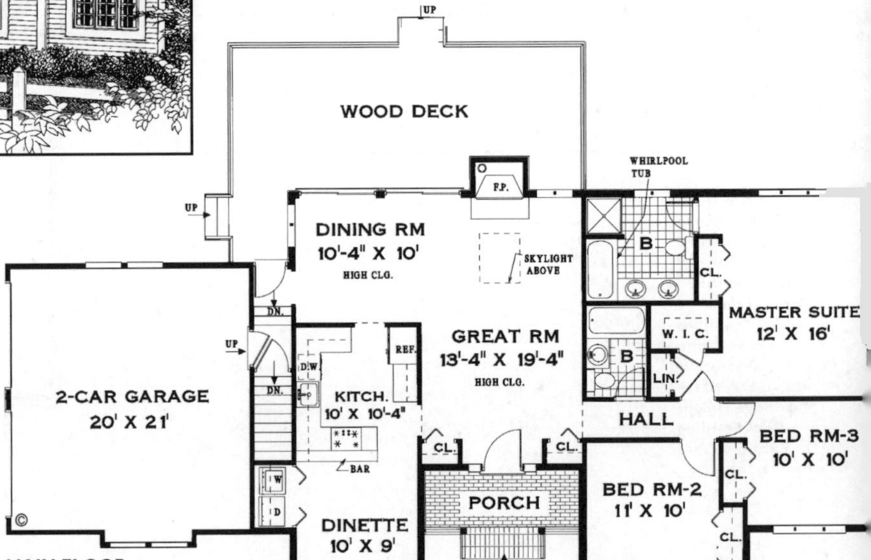

Design 34601

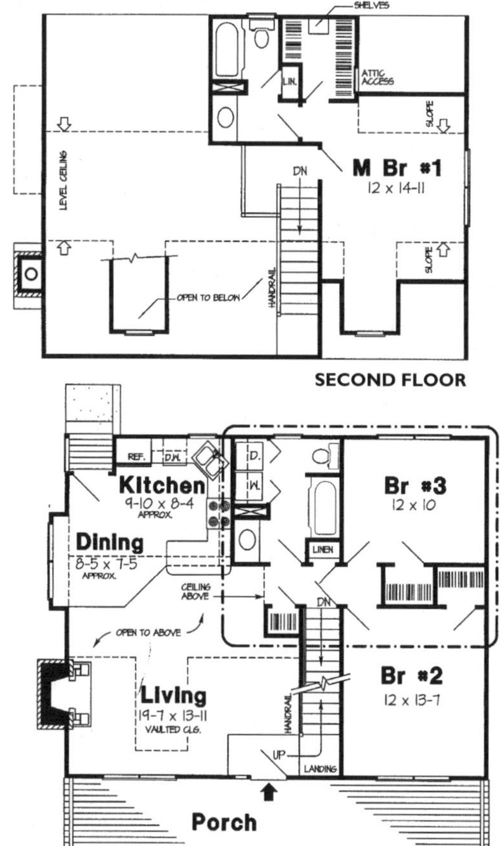
SHELVES
LIN.
ATTIC ACCESS
SLOPE
LEVEL CEILING
DN
M Br #1
12 x 14-11
OPEN TO BELOW
HANDRAIL
SLOPE
REF.
D.W.
Kitchen
9-10 x 8-4
APPROX.
Dining
8-5 x 7-5
APPROX.
CEILING ABOVE
OPEN TO ABOVE
Living
19-7 x 13-11
VAULTED CLG.
D.
W.
LINEN
DN
Br #3
12 x 10
Br #2
12 x 13-7
HANDRAIL
UP
LANDING
Porch

SECOND FLOOR

FIRST FLOOR

Units	Single
Price Code	A
Total Finished	1,415 sq. ft.
First Finished	1,007 sq. ft.
Second Finished	408 sq. ft.
Basement Unfinished	1,007 sq. ft.
Porch Unfinished	300 sq. ft.
Dimensions	38'4"x36'
Foundation	Basement Crawlspace Slab
Bedrooms	3
Full Baths	2
First Ceiling	8'
Second Ceiling	8'
Max Ridge Height	24'6"
Roof Framing	Stick
Exterior Walls	2x4, 2x6

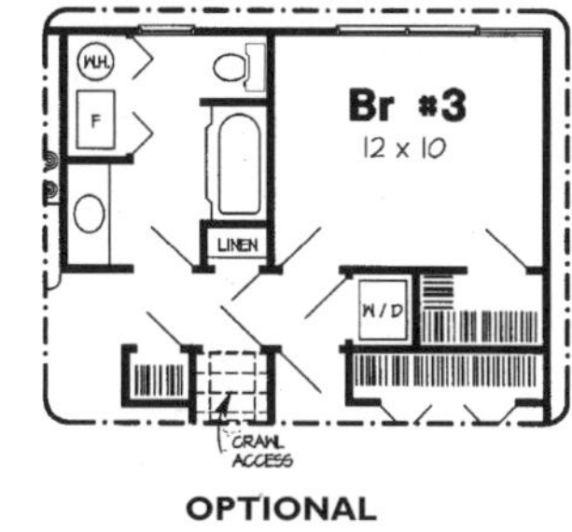
W.H.
F
LINEN
Br #3
12 x 10
W/D
CRAWL ACCESS

OPTIONAL CRAWLSPACE/SLAB FOUNDATION

Design 65618

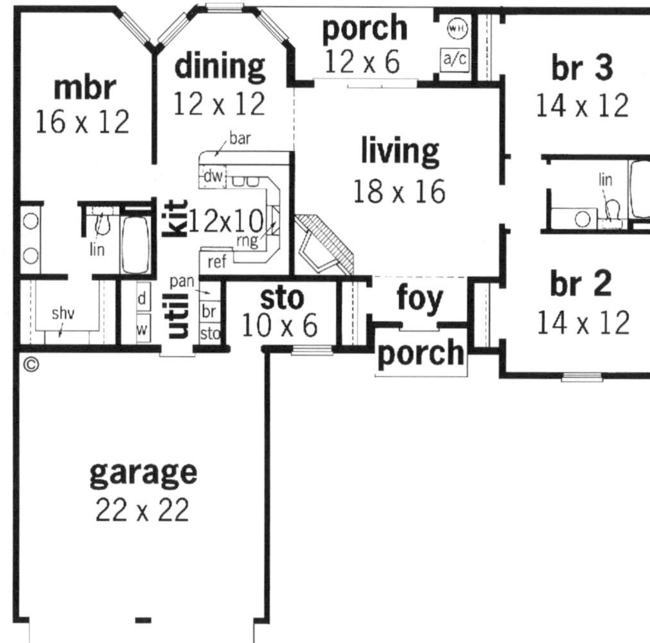
porch
12 x 6
WH
a/c
mbr
16 x 12
dining
12 x 12
br 3
14 x 12
bar
dw
living
18 x 16
lin
kit 12x10
rng
ref
lin
pan
br 2
14 x 12
shv
d
w
util
br
sto
sto
10 x 6
foy
porch
garage
22 x 22

MAIN FLOOR

Units	Single
Price Code	A
Total Finished	1,415 sq. ft.
Main Finished	1,415 sq. ft.
Dimensions	56'x50'
Foundation	Crawlspace Slab
Bedrooms	3
Full Baths	2
Main Ceiling	8'
Max Ridge Height	26'
Roof Framing	Stick
Exterior Walls	2x6

Design 97113

Units	Single
Price Code	A
Total Finished	1,416 sq. ft.
Main Finished	1,416 sq. ft.
Basement Unfinished	1,416 sq. ft.
Dimensions	48'x55'4"
Foundation	Basement
Bedrooms	3
Full Baths	2
Max Ridge Height	21'8"
Roof Framing	Truss
Exterior Walls	2x6

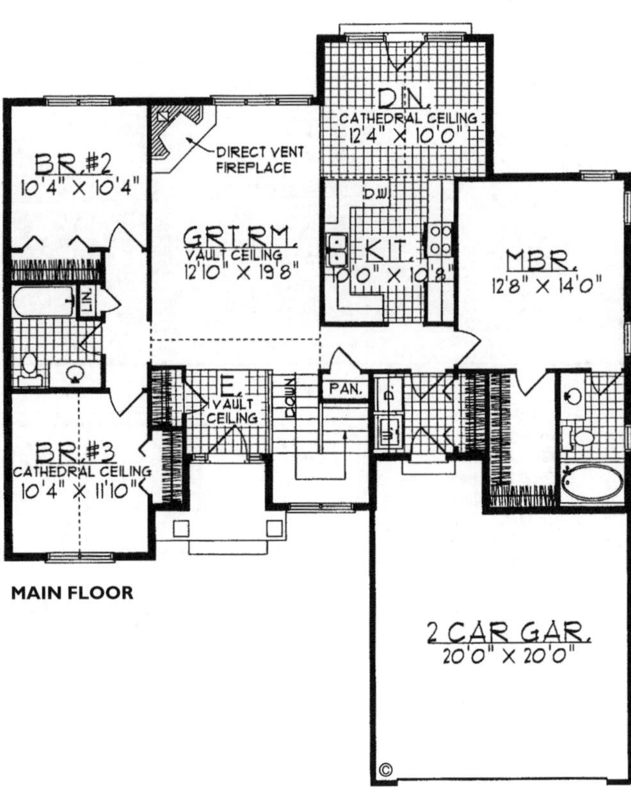

DN.
CATHEDRAL CEILING
12'4" X 10'0"
BR.#2
10'4" X 10'4"
DIRECT VENT FIREPLACE
GRT.RM.
VAULT CEILING
12'10" X 19'8"
DW
KIT.
10'0" X 10'8"
MBR.
12'8" X 14'0"
LIN.
E.
VAULT CEILING
DOWN
PAN.
BR.#3
CATHEDRAL CEILING
10'4" X 11'10"
2 CAR GAR.
20'0" X 20'0"

MAIN FLOOR

Design 69158

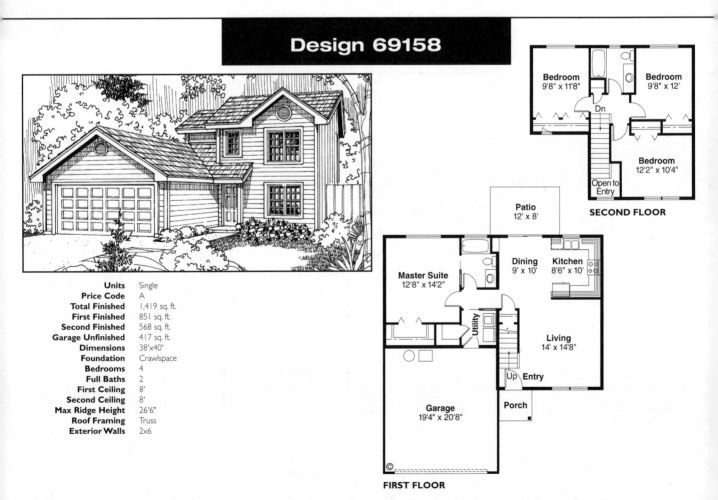

Units	Single
Price Code	A
Total Finished	1,419 sq. ft.
First Finished	851 sq. ft.
Second Finished	568 sq. ft.
Garage Unfinished	417 sq. ft.
Dimensions	38'x40'
Foundation	Crawlspace
Bedrooms	4
Full Baths	2
First Ceiling	8'
Second Ceiling	8'
Max Ridge Height	26'6"
Roof Framing	Truss
Exterior Walls	2x6

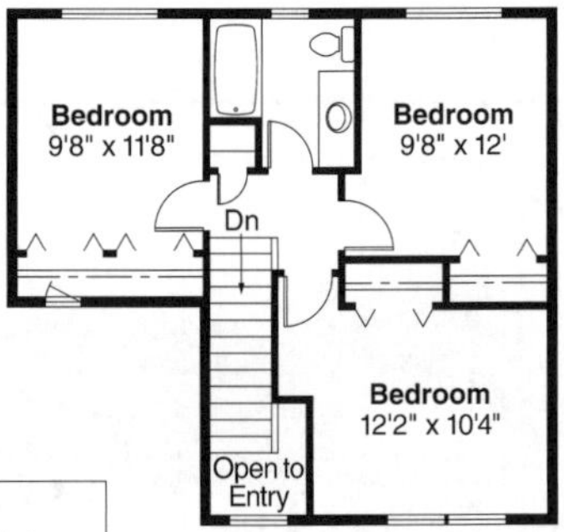

Bedroom 9'8" x 11'8"
Bedroom 9'8" x 12'
Dn
Bedroom 12'2" x 10'4"
Open to Entry

SECOND FLOOR

Patio 12' x 8'
Master Suite 12'8" x 14'2"
Dining 9' x 10'
Kitchen 8'6" x 10'
Utility
Living 14' x 14'8"
Up Entry
Porch
Garage 19'4" x 20'8"

FIRST FLOOR

Design 65636

Units	Single
Price Code	A
Total Finished	1,420 sq. ft.
Main Finished	1,420 sq. ft.
Dimensions	52'x56'
Foundation	Crawlspace Slab
Bedrooms	3
Full Baths	2
Max Ridge Height	28'
Roof Framing	Stick
Exterior Walls	2x6

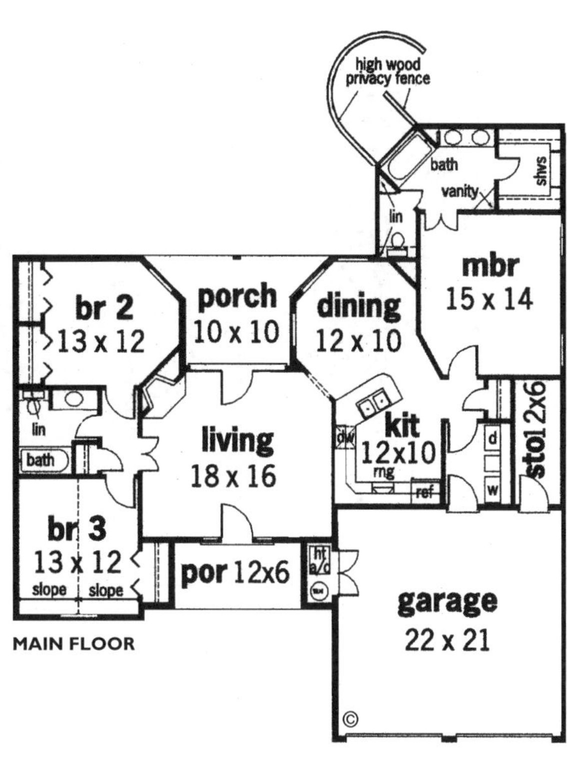
high wood privacy fence
bath
vanity
shvs
lin
mbr
15 x 14
br 2
13 x 12
porch
10 x 10
dining
12 x 10
sto 12x6
lin
bath
living
18 x 16
kit
12x10
dw
rng
ref
d
w
br 3
13 x 12
slope
slope
por 12x6
ht a/c
wh
garage
22 x 21
MAIN FLOOR

Design 10567

Units	Single
Price Code	A
Total Finished	1,421 sq. ft.
First Finished	1,046 sq. ft.
Second Finished	375 sq. ft.
Basement Unfinished	1,046 sq. ft.
Garage Unfinished	472 sq. ft.
Dimensions	50'x48'
Foundation	Basement
Bedrooms	3
Full Baths	2
Max Ridge Height	26'
Roof Framing	Stick
Exterior Walls	2x6

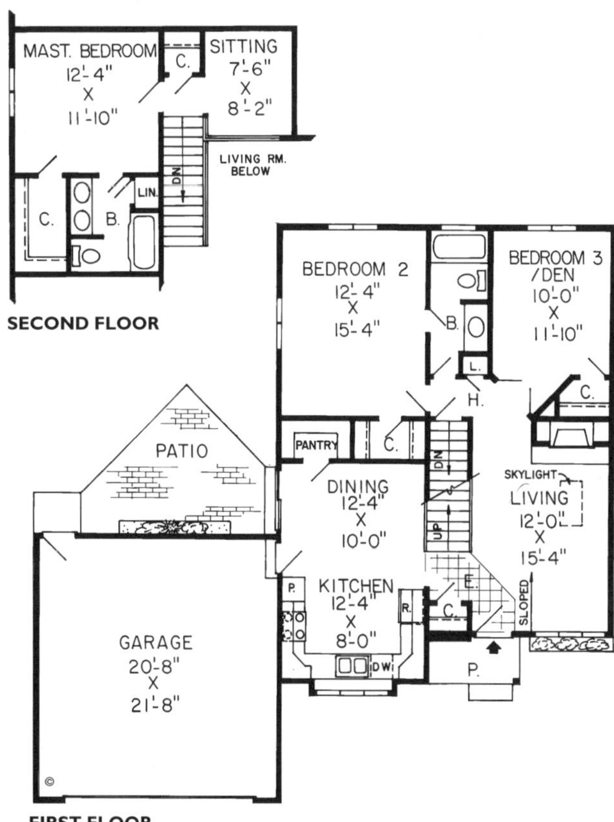
MAST. BEDROOM
12'-4" X 11'-10"
C.
SITTING
7'-6" X 8'-2"
LIVING RM. BELOW
DN
LIN.
C.
B.
SECOND FLOOR
BEDROOM 2
12'-4" X 15'-4"
B.
BEDROOM 3 /DEN
10'-0" X 11'-10"
L.
H.
C.
PATIO
PANTRY
C.
DINING
12'-4" X 10'-0"
DN
UP
SKYLIGHT
LIVING
12'-0" X 15'-4"
KITCHEN
12'-4" X 8'-0"
P.
R.
E.
C.
SLOPED
DW
P.
GARAGE
20'-8" X 21'-8"
FIRST FLOOR

Design 97493

Units	Single
Price Code	A
Total Finished	1,422 sq. ft.
Main Finished	1,422 sq. ft.
Garage Unfinished	566 sq. ft.
Dimensions	50'x58'
Foundation	Basement
Bedrooms	3
Full Baths	2
Main Ceiling	8'
Max Ridge Height	21'3"
Roof Framing	Stick
Exterior Walls	2x4

* Alternate foundation options available at an additional charge. Please call 1-800-235-5700 for more information.

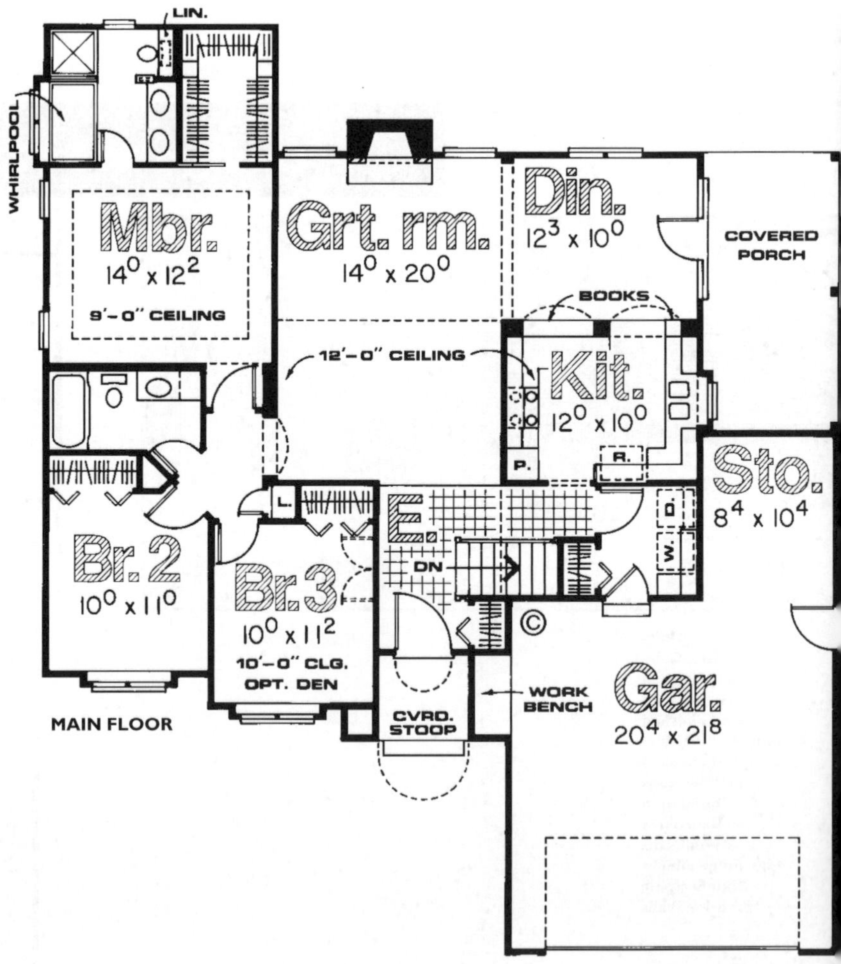
LIN.
WHIRLPOOL
Mbr.
14⁰ x 12²
9'-0" CEILING
Grt. rm.
14⁰ x 20⁰
Din.
12³ x 10⁰
COVERED PORCH
BOOKS
12'-0" CEILING
Kit.
12⁰ x 10⁰
P.
R.
Sto.
8⁴ x 10⁴
D.
W.
L.
E.
DN
Br. 2
10⁰ x 11⁰
Br. 3
10⁰ x 11²
10'-0" CLG.
OPT. DEN
©
WORK BENCH
Gar.
20⁴ x 21⁸
CVRD. STOOP
MAIN FLOOR

Design 90990

Units	Single
Price Code	A
Total Finished	1,423 sq. ft.
Main Finished	1,423 sq. ft.
Basement Unfinished	1,423 sq. ft.
Garage Unfinished	399 sq. ft.
Dimensions	54'x49'
Foundation	Basement
Bedrooms	3
Full Baths	1
3/4 Baths	1
Exterior Walls	2x6

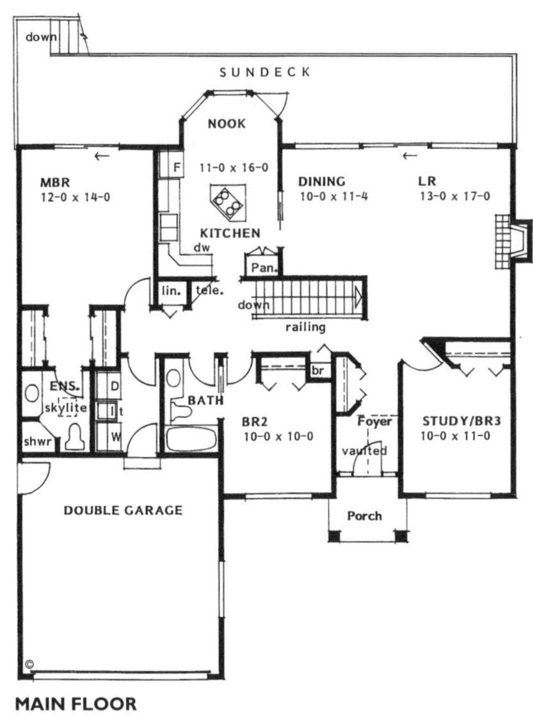
down
SUNDECK
NOOK
11-0 x 16-0
MBR
12-0 x 14-0
KITCHEN
DINING
10-0 x 11-4
LR
13-0 x 17-0
Pan.
lin.
tele.
down
railing
ENS.
skylite
shwr
BATH
BR2
10-0 x 10-0
br
Foyer
vaulted
STUDY/BR3
10-0 x 11-0
DOUBLE GARAGE
Porch

MAIN FLOOR

Design 82043

Units	Single
Price Code	A
Total Finished	1,425 sq. ft.
Main Finished	1,425 sq. ft.
Garage Unfinished	353 sq. ft.
Porch Unfinished	137 sq. ft.
Dimensions	45'x64'10"
Foundation	Basement Crawlspace Slab
Bedrooms	3
Full Baths	2
Main Ceiling	9'
Roof Framing	Stick
Exterior Walls	2x4

WHP TUB
SHWR
LIN
GRILLING PORCH
11'-8" X 6'-0"
HEARTH RM.
11'-4" X 12'-0"
OPT. GAS FIREPLACE
MASTER SUITE
14'-8" X 13'-8"
10' BOXED CEILING
GARAGE
17'-8" X 20'-0"
KIT.
11'-4" X 11'-2"
DW
RG
REF
BEDROOM 2
11'-4" X 11'-0"
GREAT RM.
14'-8" X 16'-6"
10' BOXED CEILING
GAS FIREPLACE
BATH
COVERED PORCH
15'-0" X 8'-0"
10" COLUMNS
BEDROOM 3 / STUDY
11'-4" X 12'-0"

MAIN FLOOR

Design 92056

Units	Single
Price Code	A
Total Finished	1,425 sq. ft.
Main Finished	1,425 sq. ft.
Basement Unfinished	1,425 sq. ft.
Dimensions	50'x47'
Foundation	Basement
Bedrooms	3
Full Baths	1
3/4 Baths	1
Max Ridge Height	18'6"
Roof Framing	Stick
Exterior Walls	2x4

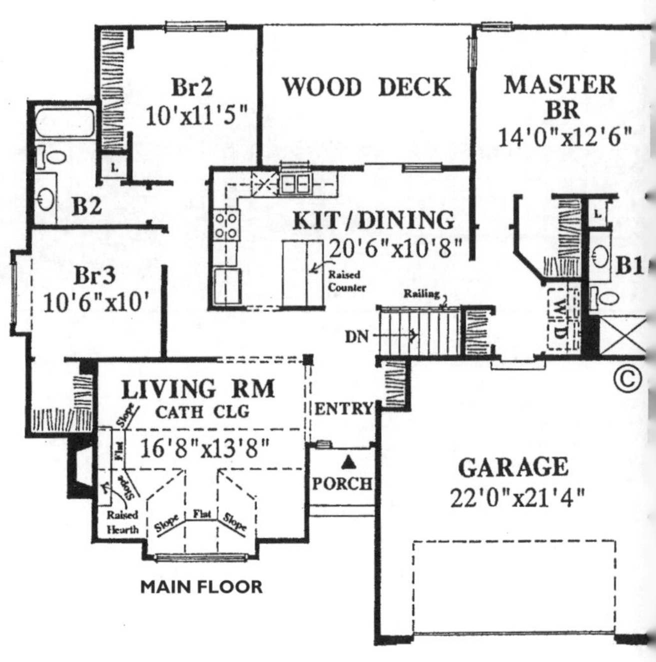
Br2
10'x11'5"
WOOD DECK
MASTER BR
14'0"x12'6"
B2
KIT/DINING
20'6"x10'8"
Raised Counter
Railing
B1
Br3
10'6"x10'
DN
W/D
LIVING RM
CATH CLG
16'8"x13'8"
ENTRY
PORCH
Slope
Flat
Raised Hearth
GARAGE
22'0"x21'4"
©
MAIN FLOOR

Design 97652

Units	Single
Price Code	A
Total Finished	1,425 sq. ft.
Main Finished	1,425 sq. ft.
Basement Unfinished	1,425 sq. ft.
Garage Unfinished	394 sq. ft.
Dimensions	40'x53'
Foundation	Basement Crawlspace
Bedrooms	3
Full Baths	2
Main Ceiling	8'
Max Ridge Height	24'
Roof Framing	Stick
Exterior Walls	2x4

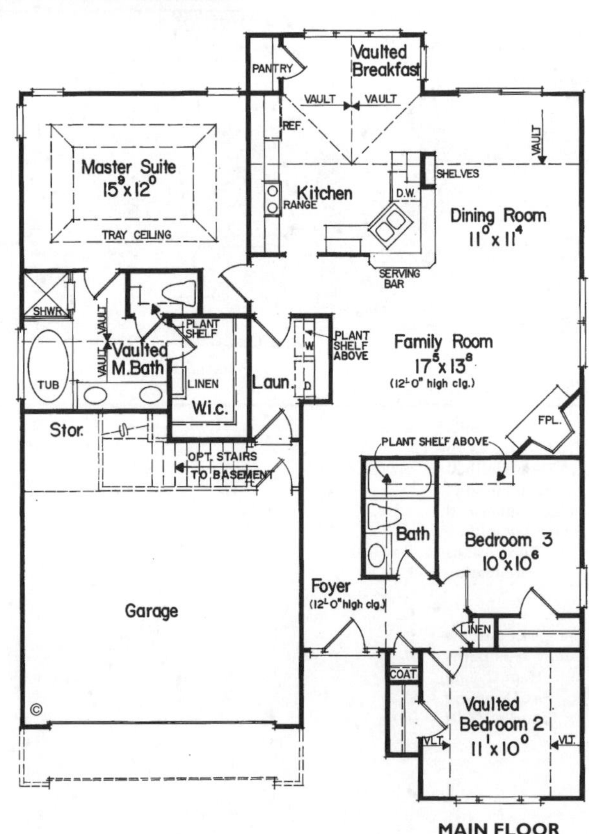
PANTRY
Vaulted Breakfast
VAULT
VAULT
REF.
Master Suite
15⁹x12⁰
TRAY CEILING
Kitchen
RANGE
D.W.
SHELVES
Dining Room
11⁰x11⁴
SERVING BAR
SHWR.
VAULT
Vaulted M.Bath
PLANT SHELF
PLANT SHELF ABOVE
Family Room
17⁵x13⁸
(12'-0" high clg.)
TUB
LINEN
W.i.c.
Laun.
FPL.
Stor.
OPT. STAIRS TO BASEMENT
PLANT SHELF ABOVE
Bath
Bedroom 3
10⁰x10⁶
Foyer
(12'-0" high clg.)
Garage
LINEN
COAT
Vaulted Bedroom 2
11¹x10⁰
VLT.
©
MAIN FLOOR

Design 65059

Units	Single
Price Code	A
Total Finished	1,426 sq. ft.
Main Finished	1,426 sq. ft.
Dimensions	41'4"x42'
Foundation	Basement
Bedrooms	3
Full Baths	1
Main Ceiling	8'
Exterior Walls	2x6

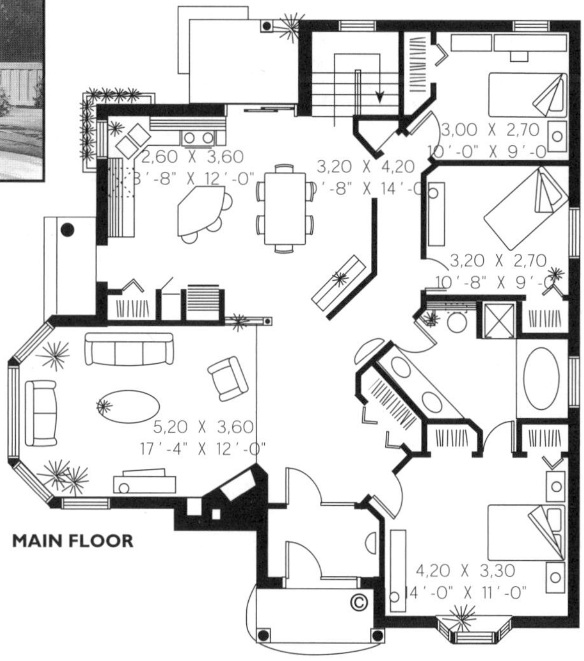

2,60 X 3,60
8'-8" X 12'-0"
3,20 X 4,20
10'-8" X 14'-0"
3,00 X 2,70
10'-0" X 9'-0"
3,20 X 2,70
10'-8" X 9'-0"
5,20 X 3,60
17'-4" X 12'-0"
4,20 X 3,30
14'-0" X 11'-0"
MAIN FLOOR

Design 69124

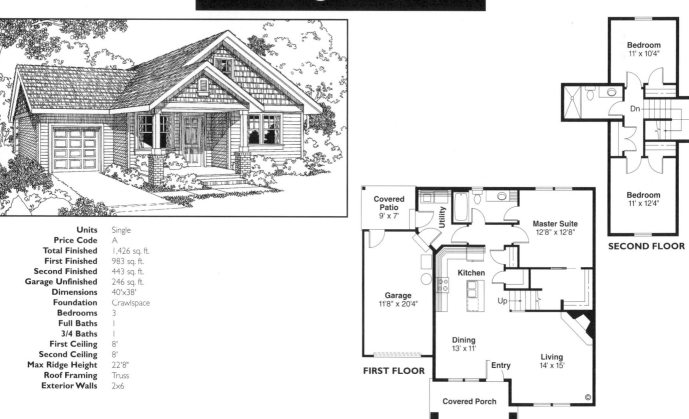

Units	Single
Price Code	A
Total Finished	1,426 sq. ft.
First Finished	983 sq. ft.
Second Finished	443 sq. ft.
Garage Unfinished	246 sq. ft.
Dimensions	40'x38'
Foundation	Crawlspace
Bedrooms	3
Full Baths	1
3/4 Baths	1
First Ceiling	8'
Second Ceiling	8'
Max Ridge Height	22'8"
Roof Framing	Truss
Exterior Walls	2x6

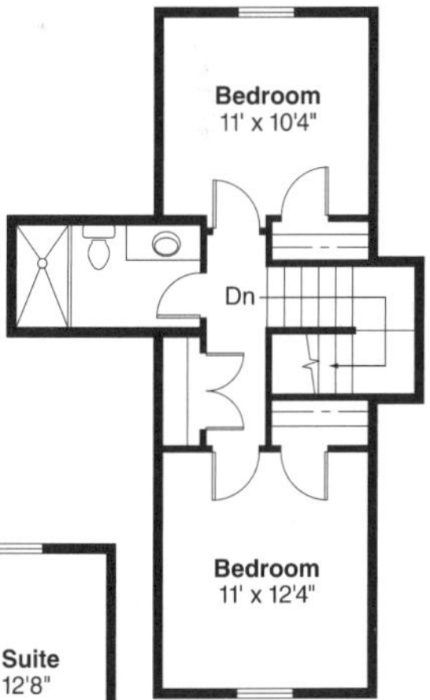

Bedroom
11' x 10'4"
Dn
Bedroom
11' x 12'4"
SECOND FLOOR 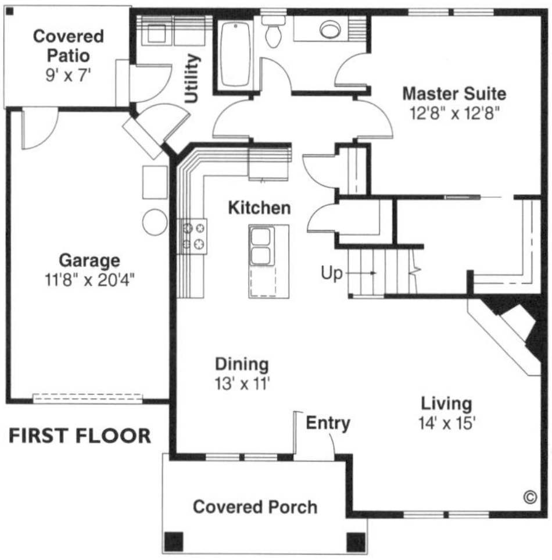
Covered Patio
9' x 7'
Utility
Master Suite
12'8" x 12'8"
Kitchen
Garage
11'8" x 20'4"
Up
Dining
13' x 11'
Living
14' x 15'
Entry
FIRST FLOOR
Covered Porch

Design 91473

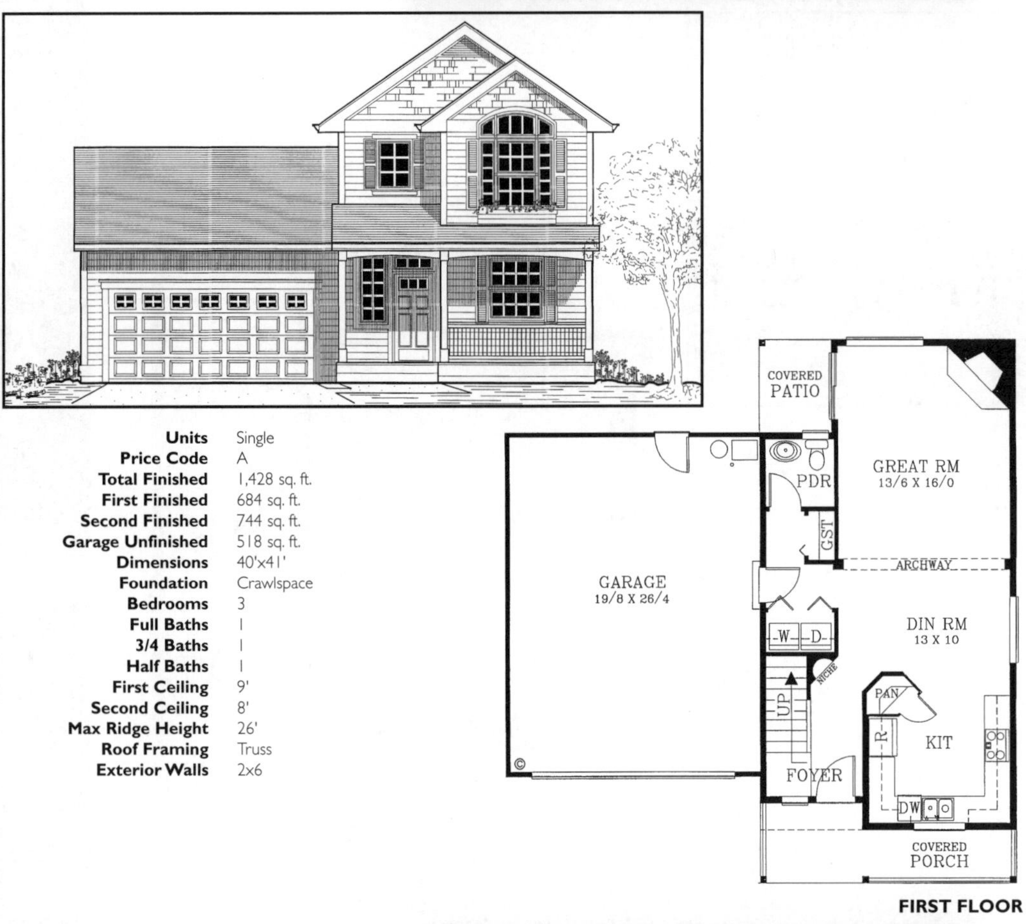
COVERED PATIO
GREAT RM 13/6 X 16/0
PDR
GST
ARCHWAY
GARAGE 19/8 X 26/4
DIN RM 13 X 10
W
D
NICHE
UP
PAN
R
KIT
DW
FOYER
COVERED PORCH

FIRST FLOOR

Units	Single
Price Code	A
Total Finished	1,428 sq. ft.
First Finished	684 sq. ft.
Second Finished	744 sq. ft.
Garage Unfinished	518 sq. ft.
Dimensions	40'x41'
Foundation	Crawlspace
Bedrooms	3
Full Baths	1
3/4 Baths	1
Half Baths	1
First Ceiling	9'
Second Ceiling	8'
Max Ridge Height	26'
Roof Framing	Truss
Exterior Walls	2x6

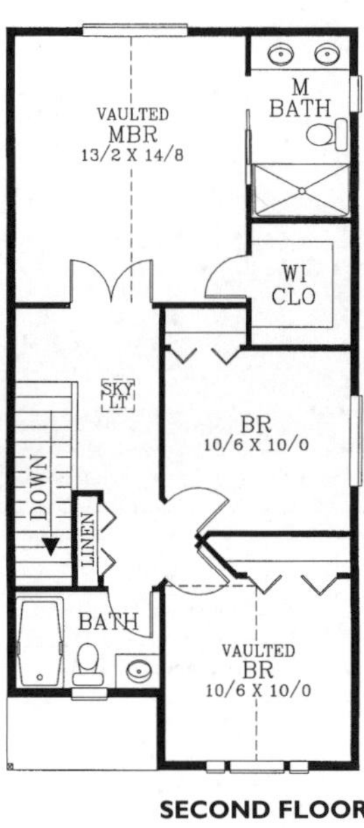
VAULTED MBR 13/2 X 14/8
M BATH
WI CLO
SKY LT
BR 10/6 X 10/0
DOWN
LINEN
BATH
VAULTED BR 10/6 X 10/0

SECOND FLOOR

Design 91478

Units	Single
Price Code	A
Total Finished	1,428 sq. ft.
First Finished	684 sq. ft.
Second Finished	744 sq. ft.
Dimensions	20'x41'
Foundation	Crawlspace
Bedrooms	3
Full Baths	1
3/4 Baths	1
Half Baths	1
First Ceiling	9'
Second Ceiling	8'
Max Ridge Height	26'
Roof Framing	Truss
Exterior Walls	2x6

GREAT RM 13/8 X 16/0
COVERED PATIO
PDR
MECH
ARCHWAY
DIN RM 13/8 X 10/0
W
D
NICHE
PAN
R
UP
KIT
DW
FOYER
COVERED PORCH

FIRST FLOOR

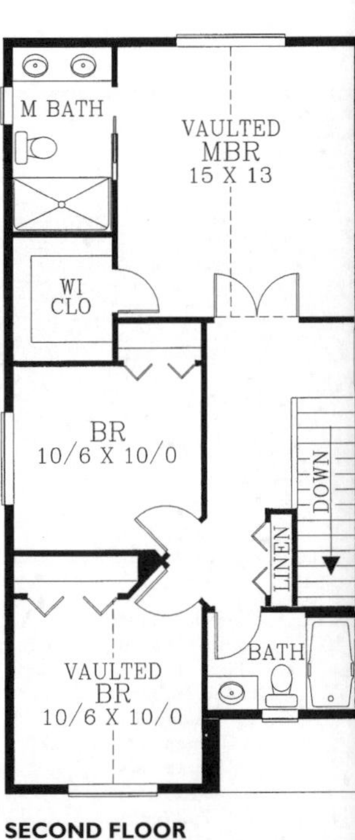
M BATH
VAULTED MBR 15 X 13
WI CLO
BR 10/6 X 10/0
DOWN
LINEN
VAULTED BR 10/6 X 10/0
BATH

SECOND FLOOR

Design 92440

Units	Single
Price Code	A
Total Finished	1,428 sq. ft.
Main Finished	1,428 sq. ft.
Dimensions	48'x30'
Foundation	Basement
Bedrooms	3
Full Baths	2
Main Ceiling	8'
Roof Framing	Stick
Exterior Walls	2x4

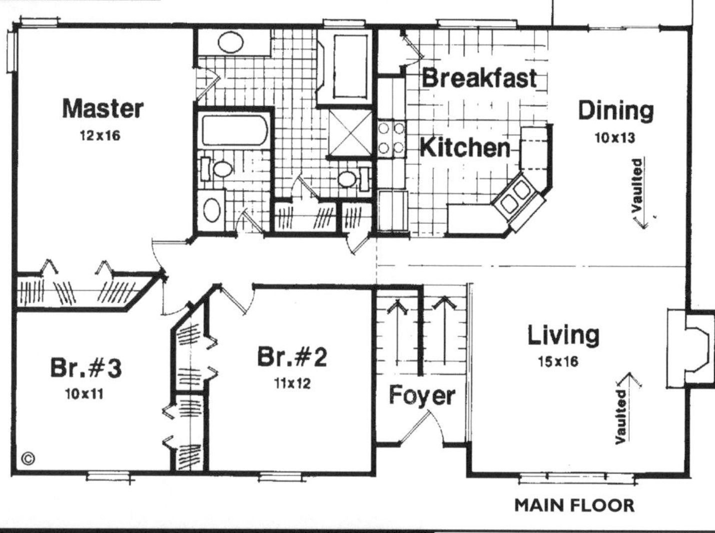
Deck
Master
12x16
Breakfast
Kitchen
Dining
10x13
Vaulted
Br.#3
10x11
Br.#2
11x12
Foyer
Living
15x16
Vaulted

MAIN FLOOR

Design 98415

CAD FILES AVAILABLE For more information call 800-235-5700

Units	Single
Price Code	A
Total Finished	1,429 sq. ft.
Main Finished	1,429 sq. ft.
Basement Unfinished	1,472 sq. ft.
Garage Unfinished	438 sq. ft.
Dimensions	49'x53'
Foundation	Basement Crawlspace Slab
Bedrooms	3
Full Baths	2
Main Ceiling	8'
Max Ridge Height	23'
Roof Framing	Stick
Exterior Walls	2x4

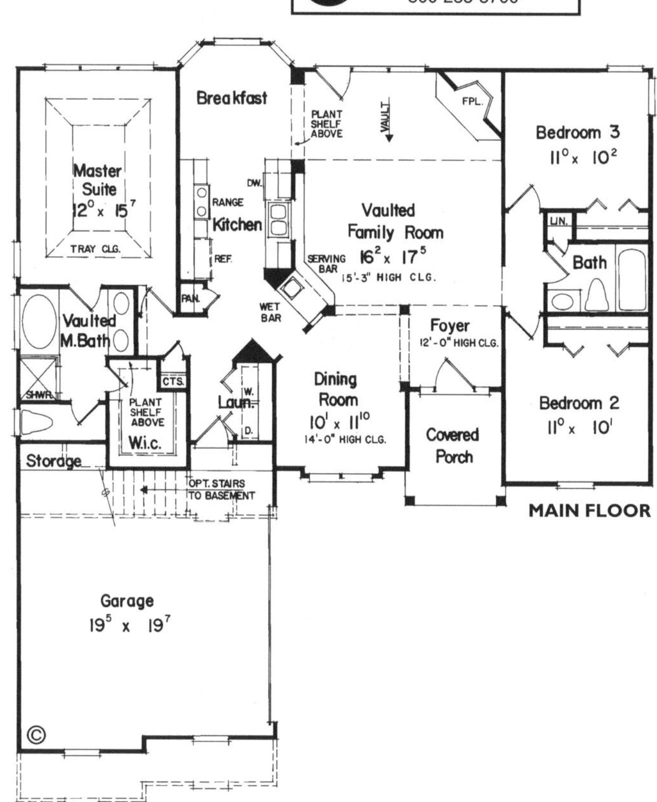
Breakfast
PLANT SHELF ABOVE
VAULT
FPL.
Bedroom 3
11^{0} x 10^{2}
Master Suite
12^{0} x 15^{7}
TRAY CLG.
DW.
RANGE
Kitchen
REF.
Vaulted Family Room
16^{2} x 17^{5}
SERVING BAR
15'-3" HIGH CLG.
LIN.
Bath
PAN.
WET BAR
Vaulted M.Bath
Foyer
12'-0" HIGH CLG.
SHWR.
PLANT SHELF ABOVE
W.i.c.
CTS.
Laun.
W.
D.
Dining Room
10^{1} x 11^{10}
14'-0" HIGH CLG.
Covered Porch
Bedroom 2
11^{0} x 10^{1}
Storage
OPT. STAIRS TO BASEMENT
Garage
19^{5} x 19^{7}

MAIN FLOOR

Design 93470

Units	Single
Price Code	A
Total Finished	1,430 sq. ft.
Main Finished	1,430 sq. ft.
Garage Unfinished	528 sq. ft.
Deck Unfinished	95 sq. ft.
Porch Unfinished	79 sq. ft.
Dimensions	64'x60'
Foundation	Crawlspace Slab
Bedrooms	3
Full Baths	2
Main Ceiling	9'
Vaulted Ceiling	12'
Tray Ceiling	10'
Max Ridge Height	22'5"
Roof Framing	Stick
Exterior Walls	2x4

Patio
Garage
22 x 24
Walk
8/8 x 10
Dining
13/8 x 10
9' Clg.
Master
12/10 x 15
Recessed Clg. 10'
Pantry
Kitchen
15/10 x 10
Utility
W
D
Family Room
17/2 x 14/8
12' Clg.
Sloped Ceiling
Sloped
Porch
13 x 6
Bedroom #3
10 x 12/8
9' Clg
Bedroom #2
10 x 11/8
9' Clg

MAIN FLOOR

Design 97609

CAD
FILES AVAILABLE
For more information call
800-235-5700

Units	Single
Price Code	A
Total Finished	1,430 sq. ft.
Main Finished	1,430 sq. ft.
Basement Unfinished	1,510 sq. ft.
Garage Unfinished	400 sq. ft.
Dimensions	47'x52'4"
Foundation	Basement Crawlspace Slab
Bedrooms	3
Full Baths	2
Max Ridge Height	23'6"
Roof Framing	Stick
Exterior Walls	2x4

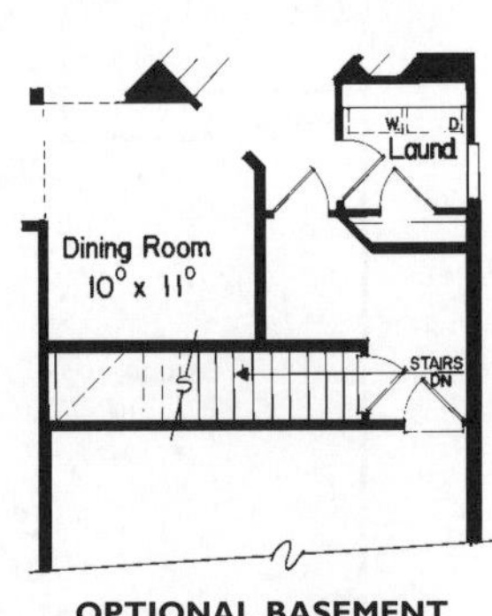
Laund.
W. D.
Dining Room
10° x 11°
STAIRS DN

OPTIONAL BASEMENT STAIR LOCATION

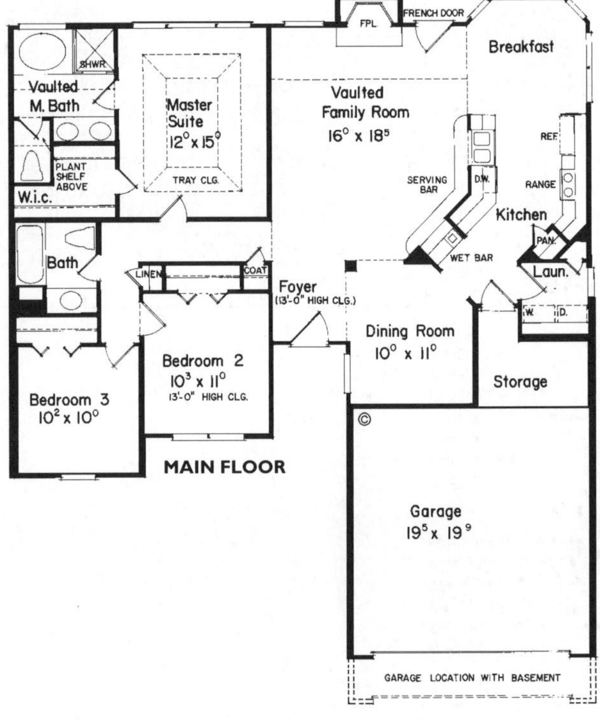
FPL
FRENCH DOOR
Breakfast
Vaulted M. Bath
SHWR
Master Suite
12° x 15°
TRAY CLG.
Vaulted Family Room
16° x 18⁵
PLANT SHELF ABOVE
W.i.c.
SERVING BAR
REF.
RANGE
D.W.
Kitchen
WET BAR
PAN.
Laun.
Bath
LINEN
COAT
Foyer
(13'-0" HIGH CLG.)
Bedroom 2
10³ x 11°
13'-0" HIGH CLG.
Dining Room
10° x 11°
Storage
Bedroom 3
10² x 10°
Garage
19⁵ x 19⁹
GARAGE LOCATION WITH BASEMENT

MAIN FLOOR

Design 98354

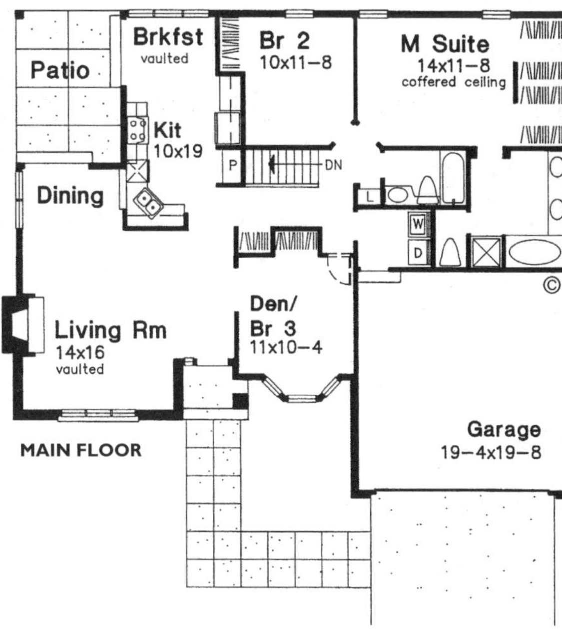
Patio
Brkfst
vaulted
Br 2
10x11–8
M Suite
14x11–8
coffered ceiling
Kit
10x19
DN
P
L
W
D
Dining
Living Rm
14x16
vaulted
Den/
Br 3
11x10–4
Garage
19–4x19–8
MAIN FLOOR

Units	Single
Price Code	A
Total Finished	1,431 sq. ft.
Main Finished	1,431 sq. ft.
Basement Unfinished	1,431 sq. ft.
Garage Unfinished	410 sq. ft.
Dimensions	53'x43'8"
Foundation	Basement
Bedrooms	3
Full Baths	2
Main Ceiling	8'
Max Ridge Height	21'
Roof Framing	Truss
Exterior Walls	2x6

Design 98549

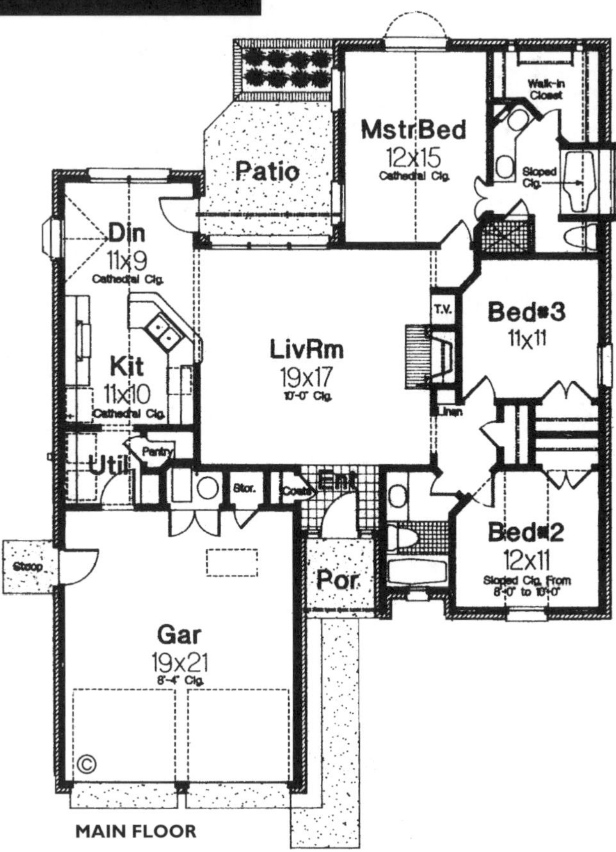
Patio
MstrBed
12x15
Cathedral Clg.
Walk-in
Closet
Sloped
Clg.
Din
11x9
Cathedral Clg.
Kit
11x10
Cathedral Clg.
LivRm
19x17
10'-0" Clg.
T.V.
Bed#3
11x11
Linen
Util
Pantry
Stor.
Coats
Ent
Bed#2
12x11
Sloped Clg. From
8'-0" to 10'-0"
Stoop
Por
Gar
19x21
8'-4" Clg.
MAIN FLOOR

Units	Single
Price Code	A
Total Finished	1,431 sq. ft.
Main Finished	1,431 sq. ft.
Garage Unfinished	410 sq. ft.
Deck Unfinished	110 sq. ft.
Dimensions	44'x57'1"
Foundation	Slab
Bedrooms	3
Full Baths	2
Max Ridge Height	23'2"
Roof Framing	Stick
Exterior Walls	2x4

Design 65181

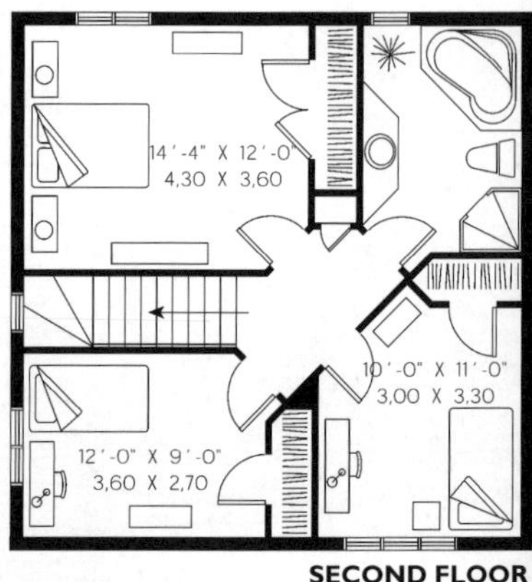
14'-4" X 12'-0"
4,30 X 3,60
10'-0" X 11'-0"
3,00 X 3,30
12'-0" X 9'-0"
3,60 X 2,70
SECOND FLOOR

Units	Single
Price Code	A
Total Finished	1,432 sq. ft.
First Finished	756 sq. ft.
Second Finished	676 sq. ft.
Basement Unfinished	657 sq. ft.
Porch Unfinished	148 sq. ft.
Dimensions	26'x32'
Foundation	Basement
Bedrooms	3
Full Baths	1
3/4 Baths	1
First Ceiling	8'
Second Ceiling	8'
Roof Framing	Truss
Exterior Walls	2x6

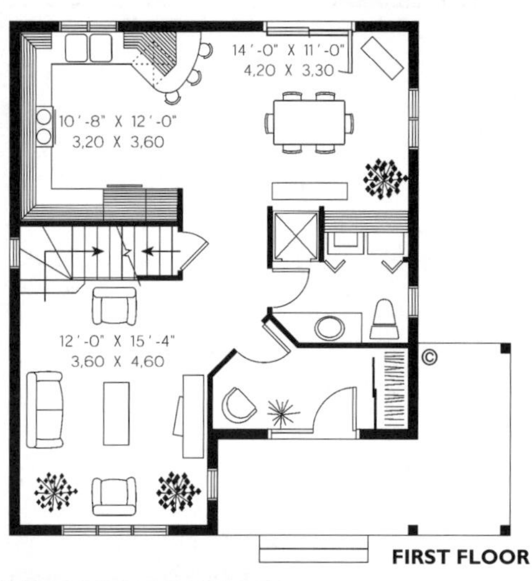
14'-0" X 11'-0"
4,20 X 3,30
10'-8" X 12'-0"
3,20 X 3,60
12'-0" X 15'-4"
3,60 X 4,60
FIRST FLOOR

Design 65418

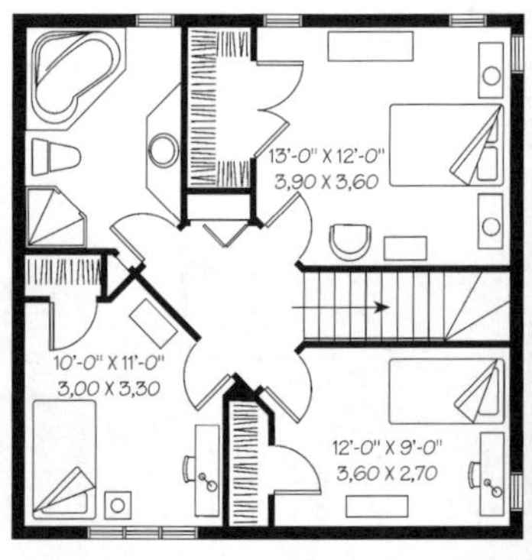
13'-0" X 12'-0"
3,90 X 3,60
10'-0" X 11'-0"
3,00 X 3,30
12'-0" X 9'-0"
3,60 X 2,70
SECOND FLOOR

Units	Single
Price Code	A
Total Finished	1,432 sq. ft.
First Finished	756 sq. ft.
Second Finished	676 sq. ft.
Basement Unfinished	756 sq. ft.
Garage Unfinished	330 sq. ft.
Deck Unfinished	40 sq. ft.
Porch Unfinished	148 sq. ft.
Dimensions	38'8"x32'
Foundation	Basement Slab
Bedrooms	3
Full Baths	1
3/4 Baths	1
First Ceiling	8'
Second Ceiling	8'
Max Ridge Height	30'1"
Roof Framing	Truss
Exterior Walls	2x6

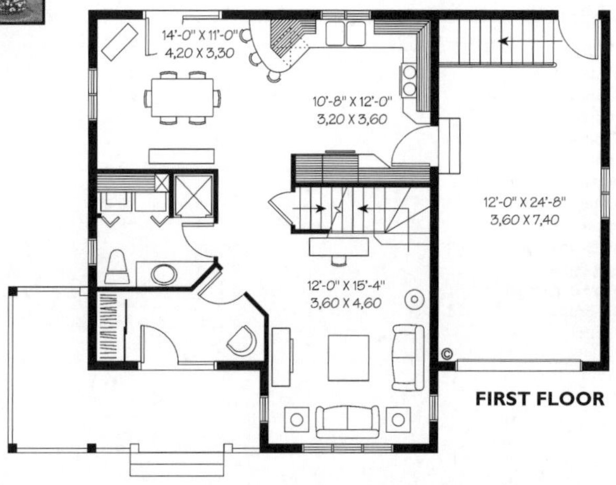
14'-0" X 11'-0"
4,20 X 3,30
10'-8" X 12'-0"
3,20 X 3,60
12'-0" X 24'-8"
3,60 X 7,40
12'-0" X 15'-4"
3,60 X 4,60
FIRST FLOOR

Design 92259

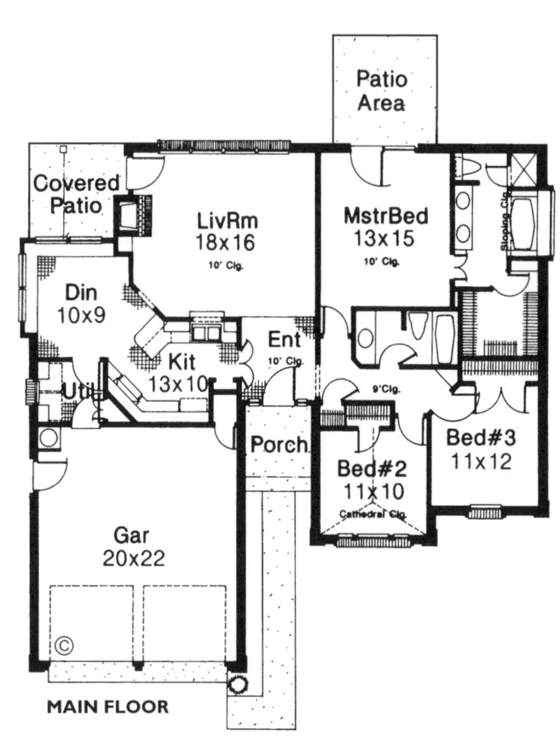
Patio Area
Covered Patio
LivRm 18x16
10' Clg.
MstrBed 13x15
10' Clg.
Din 10x9
Kit 13x10
Ent
10' Clg.
9'Clg.
Util
Porch
Bed#2 11x10
Cathedral Clg.
Bed#3 11x12
Gar 20x22
MAIN FLOOR

Units	Single
Price Code	A
Total Finished	1,432 sq. ft.
Main Finished	1,432 sq. ft.
Garage Unfinished	409 sq. ft.
Porch Unfinished	42 sq. ft.
Dimensions	50'x49'2"
Foundation	Slab
Bedrooms	3
Full Baths	2
Max Ridge Height	21'
Roof Framing	Stick
Exterior Walls	2x4

Design 97274

CAD FILES AVAILABLE
For more information call
800-235-5700

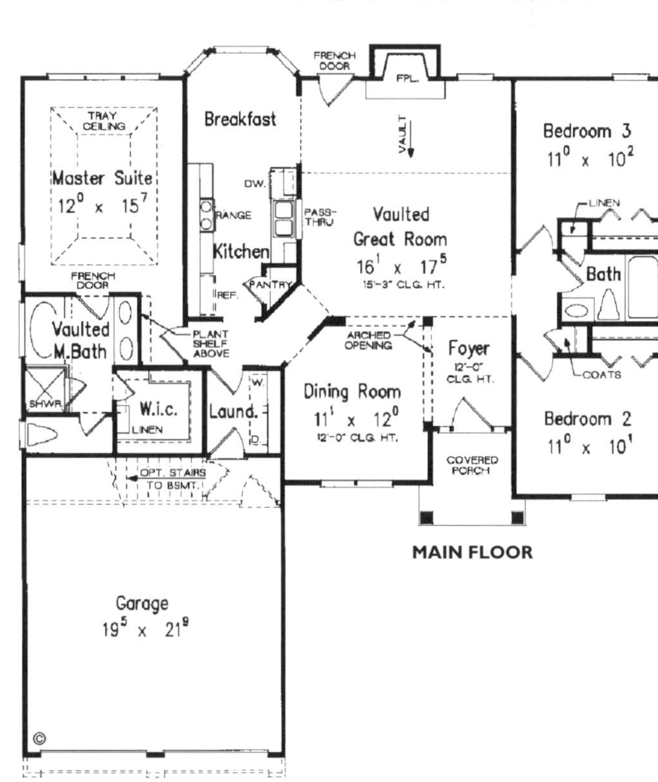
FRENCH DOOR
FPL.
TRAY CEILING
Breakfast
VAULT
Bedroom 3 11⁰ x 10²
Master Suite 12⁰ x 15⁷
DW.
RANGE
PASS-THRU
Vaulted Great Room 16¹ x 17⁵
15'-3" CLG. HT.
LINEN
Kitchen
PANTRY
REF.
Bath
FRENCH DOOR
Vaulted M.Bath
PLANT SHELF ABOVE
ARCHED OPENING
Foyer
12'-0" CLG. HT.
COATS
SHWR.
W.i.c.
LINEN
Laund.
Dining Room 11¹ x 12⁰
12'-0" CLG. HT.
Bedroom 2 11⁰ x 10¹
COVERED PORCH
OPT. STAIRS TO BSMT.
MAIN FLOOR
Garage 19⁵ x 21⁹
GARAGE LOCATION WITH BASEMENT

Units	Single
Price Code	A
Total Finished	1,432 sq. ft.
Main Finished	1,432 sq. ft.
Basement Unfinished	1,454 sq. ft.
Garage Unfinished	440 sq. ft.
Dimensions	49'x52'4"
Foundation	Basement Crawlspace
Bedrooms	3
Full Baths	2
Max Ridge Height	24'2"
Roof Framing	Stick
Exterior Walls	2x4

Design 96802

Units	Single
Price Code	A
Total Finished	1,433 sq. ft.
Main Finished	1,433 sq. ft.
Basement Unfinished	1,433 sq. ft.
Garage Unfinished	456 sq. ft.
Dimensions	54'x41'
Foundation	Basement Crawlspace Slab
Bedrooms	3
Full Baths	2
Main Ceiling	8'
Vaulted Ceiling	11'9"
Max Ridge Height	19'9"
Roof Framing	Truss
Exterior Walls	2x4

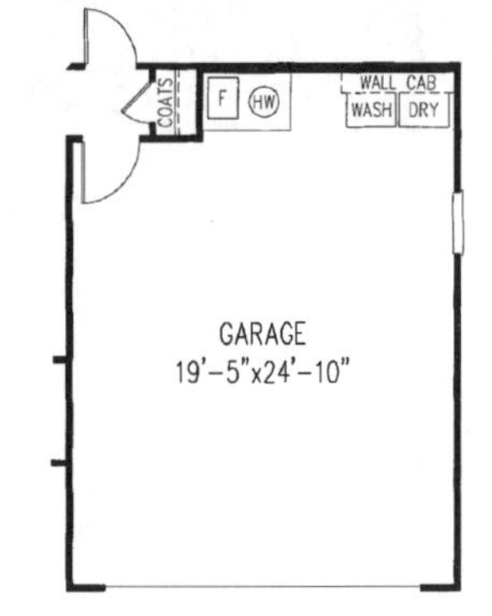

COATS
F
HW
WALL CAB
WASH
DRY
GARAGE
19'-5"x24'-10"

OPTIONAL CRAWLSPACE/ SLAB FOUNDATION

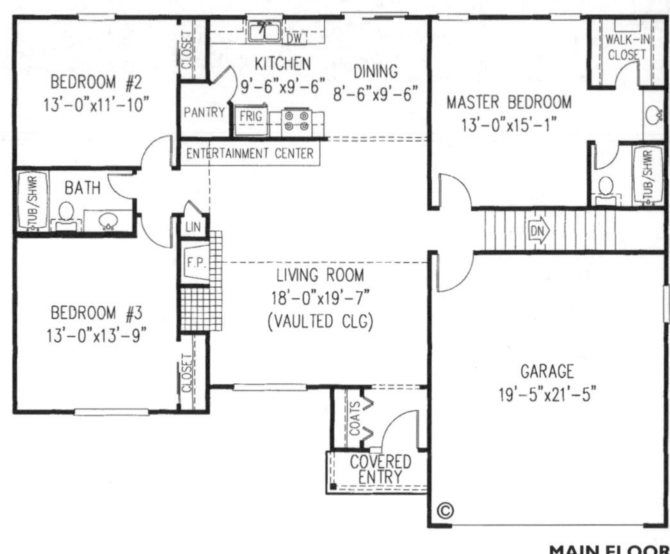

BEDROOM #2
13'-0"x11'-10"
CLOSET
DW
KITCHEN
9'-6"x9'-6"
DINING
8'-6"x9'-6"
WALK-IN CLOSET
MASTER BEDROOM
13'-0"x15'-1"
PANTRY
FRIG
ENTERTAINMENT CENTER
TUB/SHWR
BATH
LIN
DN
F.P.
LIVING ROOM
18'-0"x19'-7"
(VAULTED CLG)
BEDROOM #3
13'-0"x13'-9"
CLOSET
COATS
GARAGE
19'-5"x21'-5"
COVERED ENTRY
©

MAIN FLOOR

Design 97443

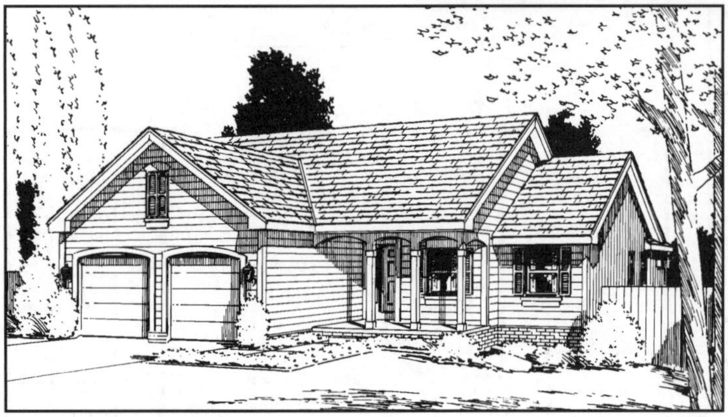

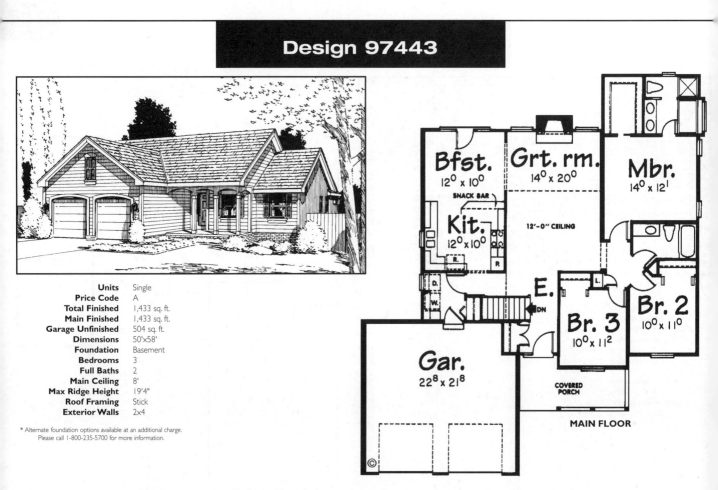

Units	Single
Price Code	A
Total Finished	1,433 sq. ft.
Main Finished	1,433 sq. ft.
Garage Unfinished	504 sq. ft.
Dimensions	50'x58'
Foundation	Basement
Bedrooms	3
Full Baths	2
Main Ceiling	8'
Max Ridge Height	19'4"
Roof Framing	Stick
Exterior Walls	2x4

* Alternate foundation options available at an additional charge. Please call 1-800-235-5700 for more information.

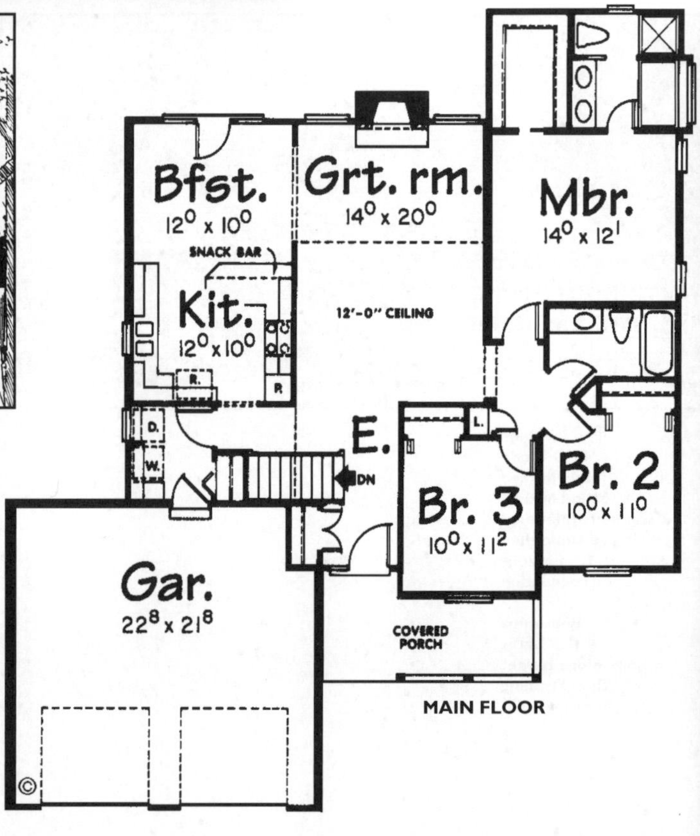

MAIN FLOOR

Design 24711

Units	Single
Price Code	A
Total Finished	1,434 sq. ft.
First Finished	1,018 sq. ft.
Second Finished	416 sq. ft.
Basement Unfinished	1,008 sq. ft.
Garage Unfinished	624 sq. ft.
Porch Unfinished	288 sq. ft.
Dimensions	73'x36'
Foundation	Basement Crawlspace Slab
Bedrooms	3
Full Baths	2
Max Ridge Height	24'6"
Roof Framing	Stick
Exterior Walls	2x4

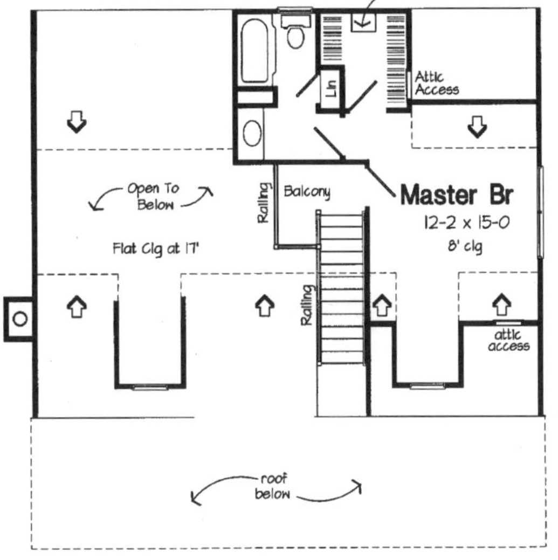
Shelves
Lin
Attic Access
Open To Below
Flat Clg at 17'
Railing
Balcony
Master Br
12-2 x 15-0
8' clg
Railing
attic access
roof below

SECOND FLOOR

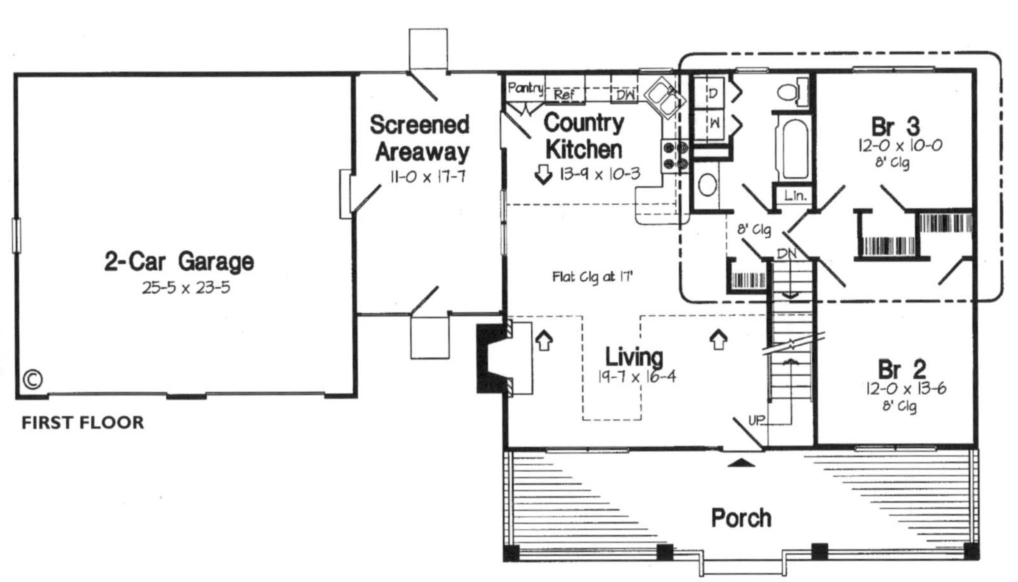
Screened Areaway
11-0 x 17-7
Pantry
Ref
DW
Country Kitchen
13-9 x 10-3
2-Car Garage
25-5 x 23-5
Flat Clg at 17'
8' Clg
Lin.
DN
Br 3
12-0 x 10-0
8' Clg
Living
19-7 x 16-4
UP
Br 2
12-0 x 13-6
8' Clg
Porch

FIRST FLOOR

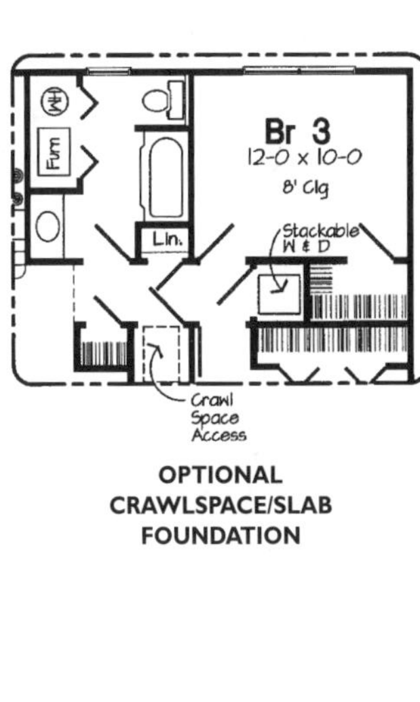
Br 3
12-0 x 10-0
8' Clg
Lin.
Stackable W & D
Crawl Space Access

OPTIONAL CRAWLSPACE/SLAB FOUNDATION

Design 96509

Units	Single
Price Code	A
Total Finished	1,438 sq. ft.
Main Finished	1,438 sq. ft.
Garage Unfinished	486 sq. ft.
Deck Unfinished	282 sq. ft.
Porch Unfinished	126 sq. ft.
Dimensions	54'x57'
Foundation	Crawlspace Slab
Bedrooms	3
Full Baths	2
Max Ridge Height	19'
Roof Framing	Stick
Exterior Walls	2x4

GARAGE 22 × 22
DECK
PANTRY
REFG
DINING 12 × 11
KITCHEN 12 × 10
RNG
D/W
SHWR
BATH
MASTER SUITE 13 × 15
WASH DRY
BATH
SHELVES
STOR
CLOSET
GREAT RM 17 × 18
F/P
A/C
CLOS
BEDRM 14 × 11
CLOS
BEDRM 11 × 13
CLOS
FOYER
PORCH

MAIN FLOOR

Design 65095

Units	Single
Price Code	A
Total Finished	1,440 sq. ft.
Main Finished	1,440 sq. ft.
Basement Unfinished	1,440 sq. ft.
Garage Unfinished	332 sq. ft.
Dimensions	58'x36'
Foundation	Basement
Bedrooms	3
Full Baths	1
Main Ceiling	8'
Max Ridge Height	26'
Roof Framing	Truss
Exterior Walls	2x6

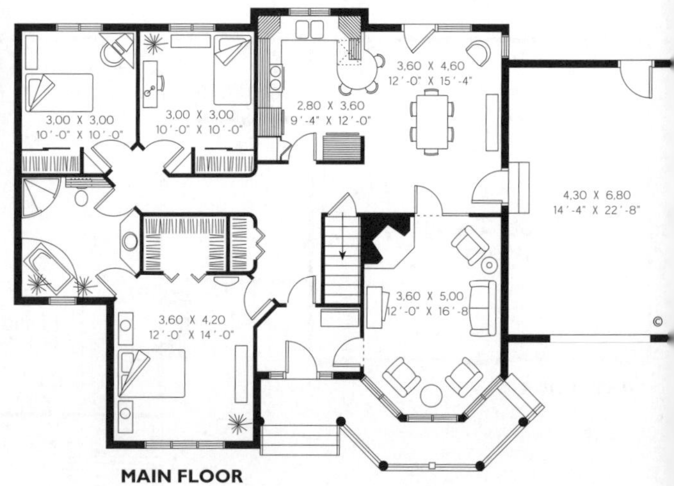
3,00 X 3,00
10'-0" X 10'-0"
3,00 X 3,00
10'-0" X 10'-0"
2,80 X 3,60
9'-4" X 12'-0"
3,60 X 4,60
12'-0" X 15'-4"
4,30 X 6,80
14'-4" X 22'-8"
3,60 X 5,00
12'-0" X 16'-8"
3,60 X 4,20
12'-0" X 14'-0"

MAIN FLOOR

Design 62025

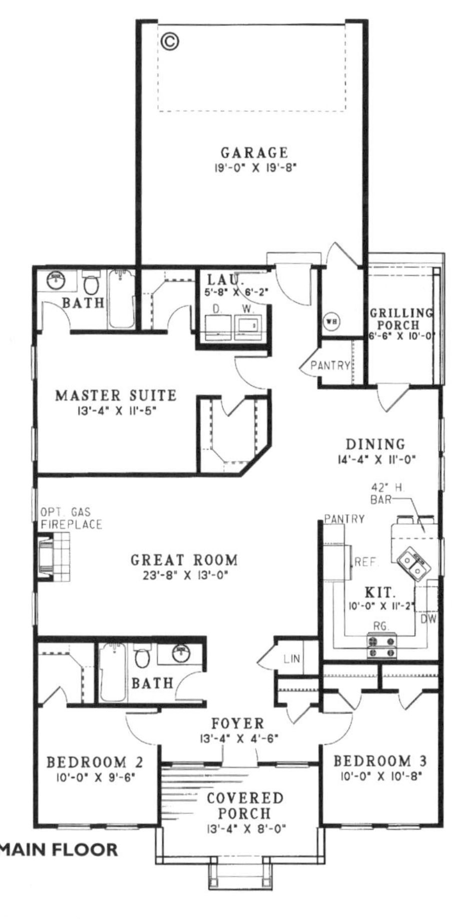

GARAGE
19'-0" X 19'-8"
BATH
LAU.
5'-8" X 8'-2"
D W
WH
GRILLING PORCH
6'-6" X 10'-0"
PANTRY
MASTER SUITE
13'-4" X 11'-5"
DINING
14'-4" X 11'-0"
42" H. BAR
OPT. GAS FIREPLACE
PANTRY
GREAT ROOM
23'-8" X 13'-0"
REF
KIT.
10'-0" X 11'-2"
DW
RG
LIN
BATH
FOYER
13'-4" X 4'-6"
BEDROOM 2
10'-0" X 9'-6"
BEDROOM 3
10'-0" X 10'-8"
COVERED PORCH
13'-4" X 8'-0"
MAIN FLOOR

Units	Single
Price Code	A
Total Finished	1,442 sq. ft.
Main Finished	1,442 sq. ft.
Garage Unfinished	417 sq. ft.
Porch Unfinished	172 sq. ft.
Dimensions	34'8"x71'
Foundation	Crawlspace Slab
Bedrooms	3
Full Baths	2
Main Ceiling	9'
Exterior Walls	2x4

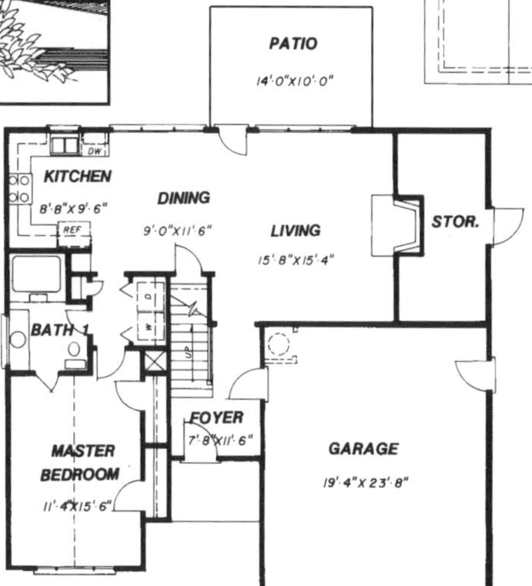

Design 93226

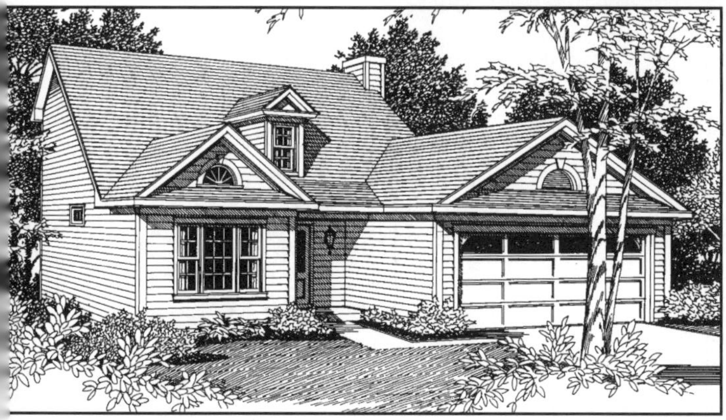

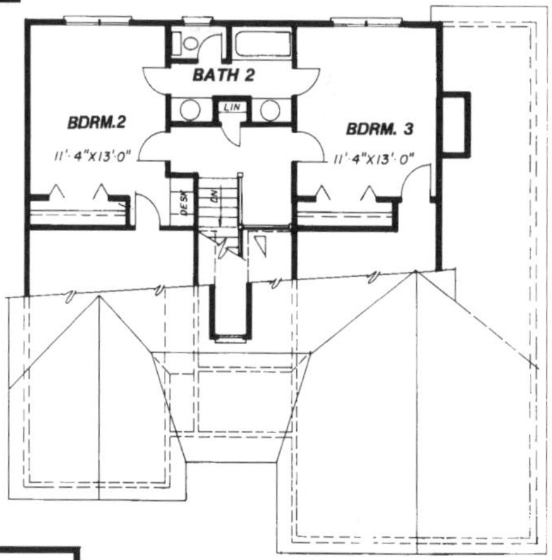

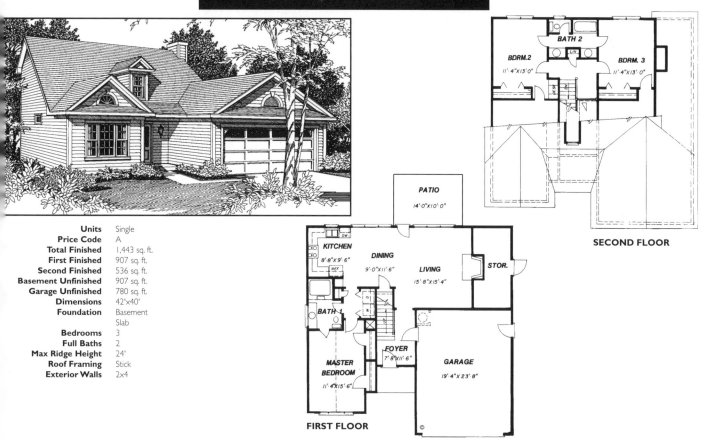

Units	Single
Price Code	A
Total Finished	1,443 sq. ft.
First Finished	907 sq. ft.
Second Finished	536 sq. ft.
Basement Unfinished	907 sq. ft.
Garage Unfinished	780 sq. ft.
Dimensions	42'x40'
Foundation	Basement Slab
Bedrooms	3
Full Baths	2
Max Ridge Height	24'
Roof Framing	Stick
Exterior Walls	2x4

SECOND FLOOR

FIRST FLOOR

Design 82049

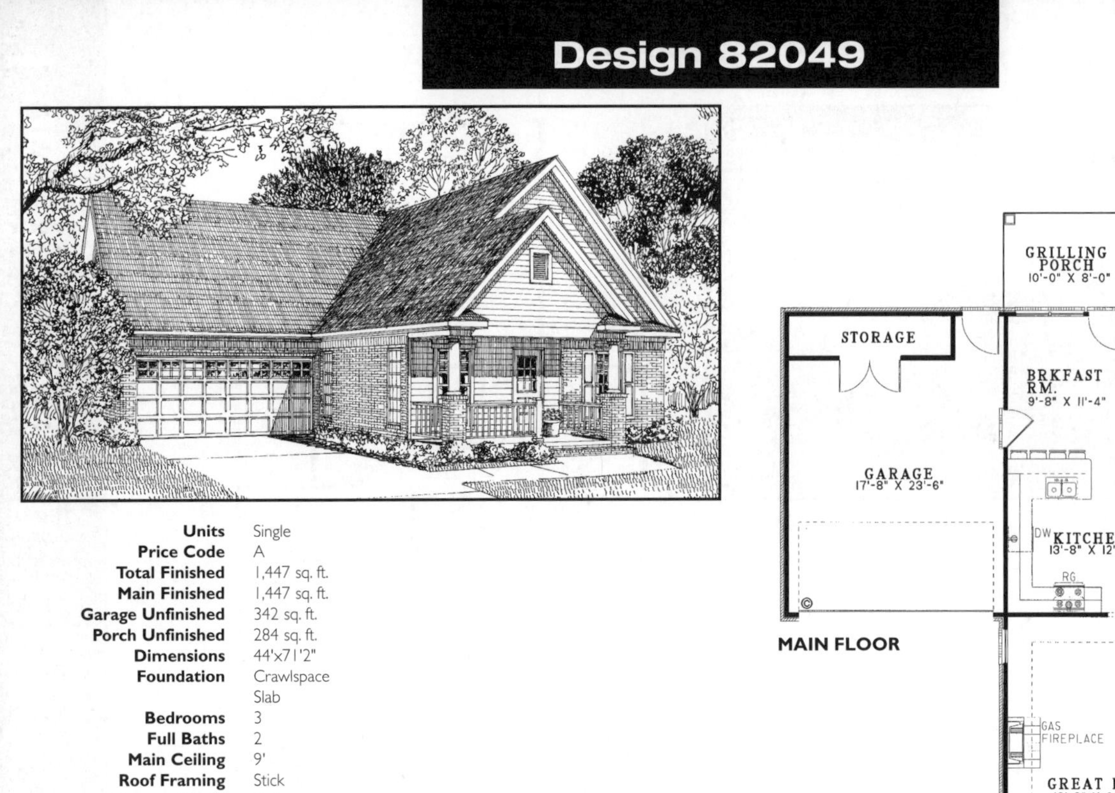
WHP TUB
MASTER BATH 15'-4" X 10'-6"
LIN
GRILLING PORCH 10'-0" X 8'-0"
MASTER SUITE 15'-4" X 13'-0" 10' BOXED CEILING
STORAGE
BRKFAST RM. 9'-8" X 11'-4"
GARAGE 17'-8" X 23'-6"
BED RM. 2 11'-4" X 12'-0"
DW KITCHEN 13'-8" X 12'-2"
REF
RG
PAN.
BATH
LIN
GAS FIREPLACE
OPTIONAL CLOSET
OFFICE / BED RM. 3 11'-0" X 14'-4"
GREAT RM. 13'-8" X 20'-0" 10' BOXED CEILING
8" COLUMNS
COVERED PORCH 15'-0" X 8'-0"
MAIN FLOOR

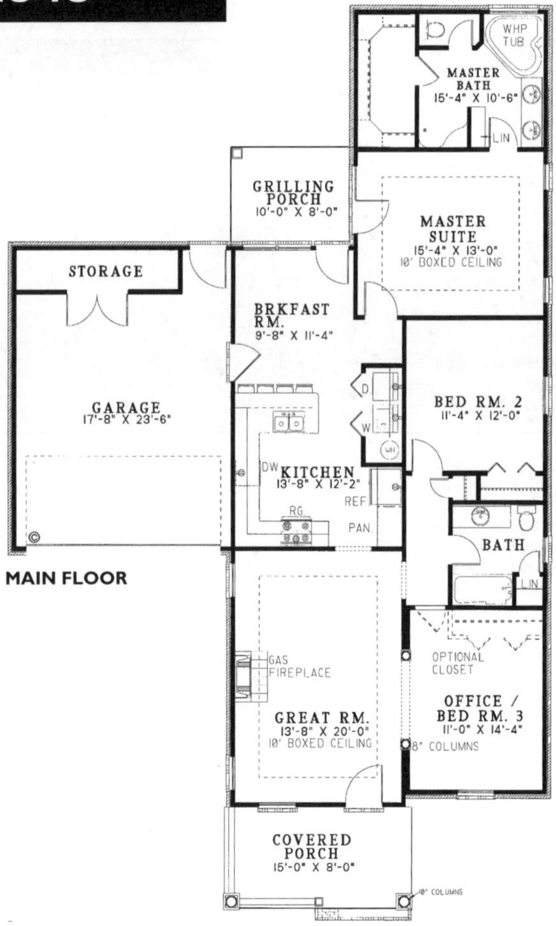

Units	Single
Price Code	A
Total Finished	1,447 sq. ft.
Main Finished	1,447 sq. ft.
Garage Unfinished	342 sq. ft.
Porch Unfinished	284 sq. ft.
Dimensions	44'x71'2"
Foundation	Crawlspace Slab
Bedrooms	3
Full Baths	2
Main Ceiling	9'
Roof Framing	Stick
Exterior Walls	2x4

Design 97201

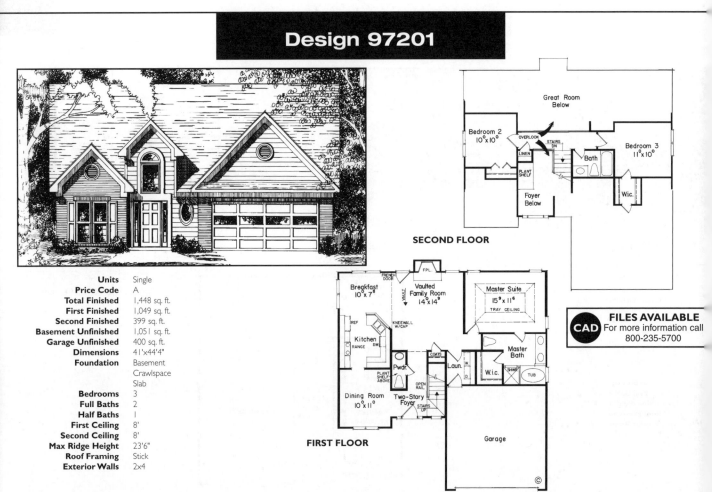

Units	Single
Price Code	A
Total Finished	1,448 sq. ft.
First Finished	1,049 sq. ft.
Second Finished	399 sq. ft.
Basement Unfinished	1,051 sq. ft.
Garage Unfinished	400 sq. ft.
Dimensions	41'x44'4"
Foundation	Basement Crawlspace Slab
Bedrooms	3
Full Baths	2
Half Baths	1
First Ceiling	8'
Second Ceiling	8'
Max Ridge Height	23'6"
Roof Framing	Stick
Exterior Walls	2x4

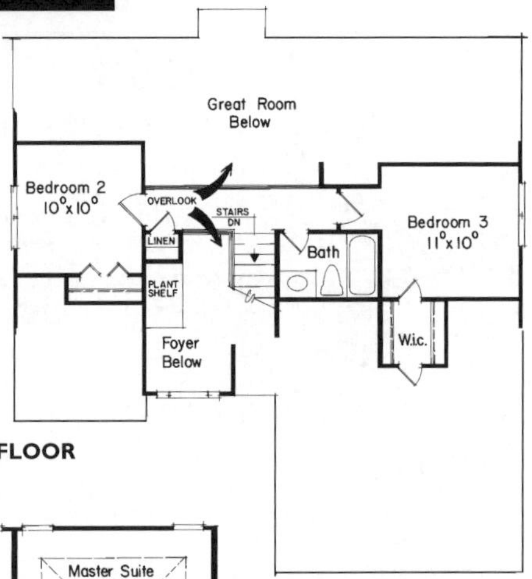

SECOND FLOOR

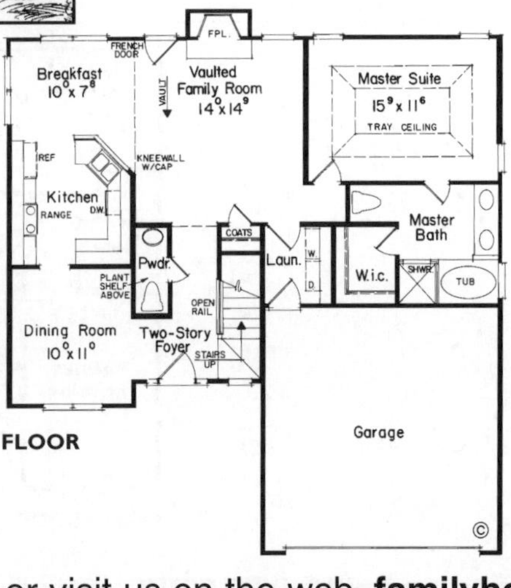

FIRST FLOOR

CAD FILES AVAILABLE For more information call 800-235-5700

Design 65179

Units	Single
Price Code	A
Total Finished	1,450 sq. ft.
First Finished	918 sq. ft.
Second Finished	532 sq. ft.
Basement Unfinished	918 sq. ft.
Dimensions	26'4"x37'
Foundation	Basement
Bedrooms	3
Full Baths	1
3/4 Baths	1
First Ceiling	8'
Second Ceiling	8'
Max Ridge Height	27'4"
Roof Framing	Truss
Exterior Walls	2x6

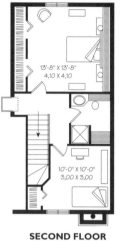

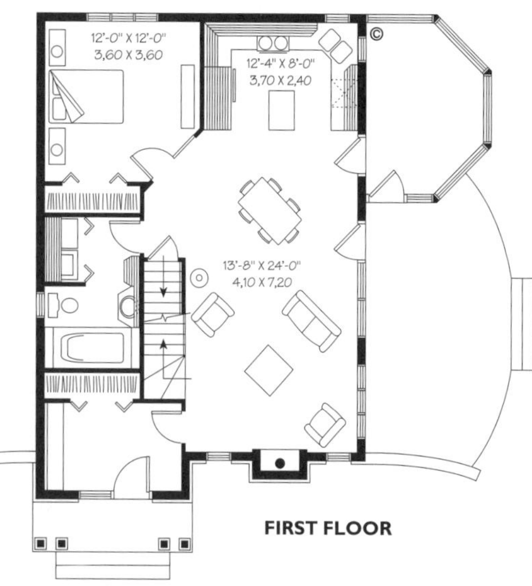
12'-0" X 12'-0"
3,60 X 3,60
12'-4" X 8'-0"
3,70 X 2,40
13'-8" X 24'-0"
4,10 X 7,20
FIRST FLOOR

13'-8" X 13'-8"
4,10 X 4,10

10'-0" X 10'-0"
3,00 X 3,00

SECOND FLOOR

Design 24718

Units	Single
Price Code	A
Total Finished	1,452 sq. ft.
Main Finished	1,452 sq. ft.
Garage Unfinished	584 sq. ft.
Deck Unfinished	158 sq. ft.
Porch Unfinished	89 sq. ft.
Dimensions	67'x47'
Foundation	Crawlspace Slab
Bedrooms	3
Full Baths	2
Main Ceiling	8'
Max Ridge Height	21'
Roof Framing	Stick
Exterior Walls	2x4

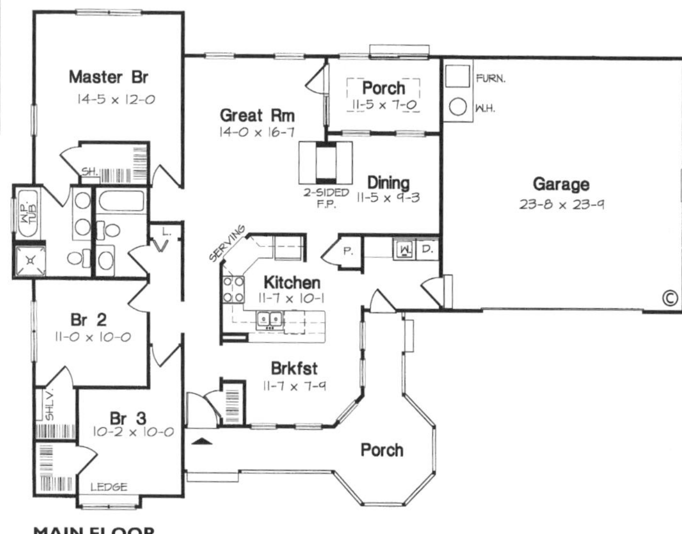
Master Br
14-5 x 12-0
Great Rm
14-0 x 16-7
Porch
11-5 x 7-0
FURN.
W.H.
Garage
23-8 x 23-9
2-SIDED F.P.
Dining
11-5 x 9-3
SERVING
Kitchen
11-7 x 10-1
Br 2
11-0 x 10-0
Brkfst
11-7 x 7-9
Br 3
10-2 x 10-0
Porch
LEDGE
MAIN FLOOR

Design 94914

Units	Single
Price Code	A
Total Finished	1,453 sq. ft.
Main Finished	1,453 sq. ft.
Basement Unfinished	1,453 sq. ft.
Garage Unfinished	481 sq. ft.
Dimensions	48'8"x44'
Foundation	Basement
Bedrooms	3
Full Baths	2
Main Ceiling	8'
Max Ridge Height	18'6"
Roof Framing	Stick
Exterior Walls	2x4

* Alternate foundation options available at an additional charge. Please call 1-800-235-5700 for more information.

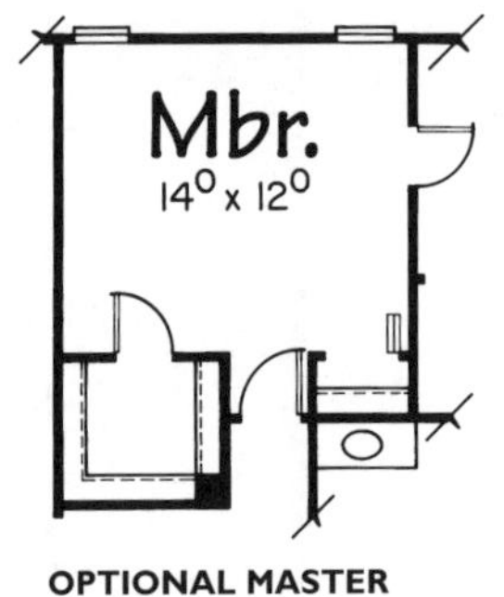

Mbr.
14^{0} x 12^{0}

OPTIONAL MASTER BEDROOM

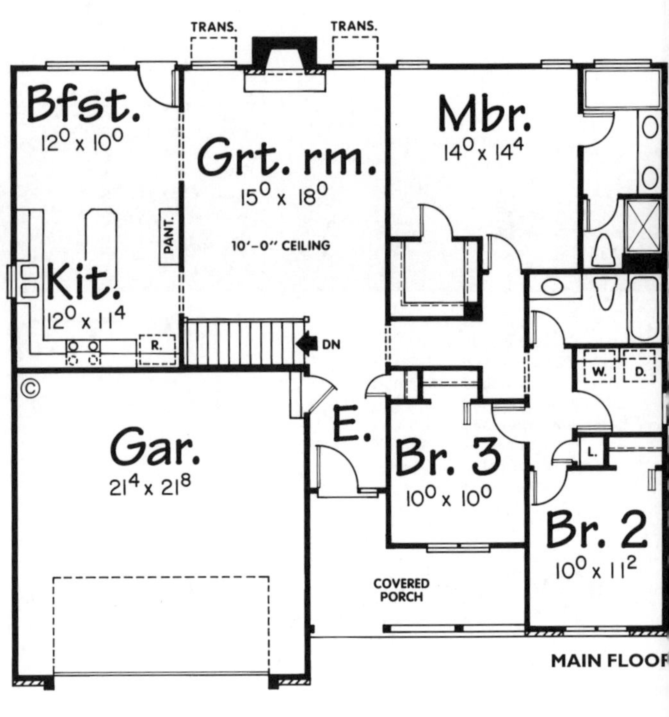

TRANS.
TRANS.
Bfst.
12^{0} x 10^{0}
Grt. rm.
15^{0} x 18^{0}
10'-0" CEILING
Mbr.
14^{0} x 14^{4}
PANT.
Kit.
12^{0} x 11^{4}
R.
DN
W.
D.
Gar.
21^{4} x 21^{8}
E.
Br. 3
10^{0} x 10^{0}
L.
Br. 2
10^{0} x 11^{2}
COVERED PORCH
MAIN FLOOR

Design 90412

Units	Single
Price Code	A
Total Finished	1,454 sq. ft.
Main Finished	1,454 sq. ft.
Dimensions	67'x34'10"
Foundation	Basement Crawlspace Slab
Bedrooms	3
Full Baths	2
Max Ridge Height	16'2"
Roof Framing	Stick
Exterior Walls	2x4

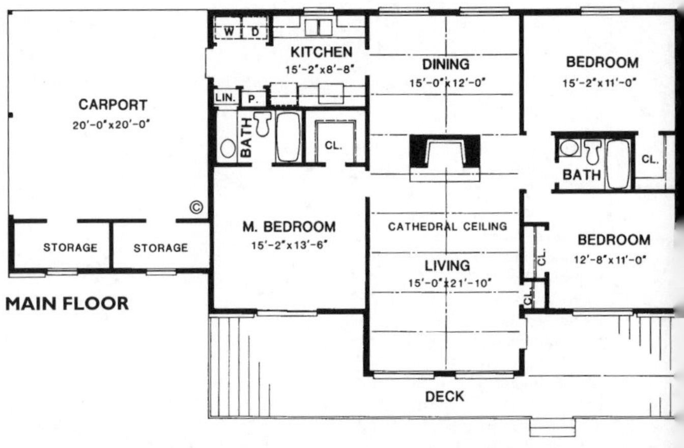

W
D
KITCHEN
15'-2"x8'-8"
DINING
15'-0"x12'-0"
BEDROOM
15'-2"x11'-0"
CARPORT
20'-0"x20'-0"
LIN.
P.
BATH
CL.
BATH
CL.
STORAGE
STORAGE
M. BEDROOM
15'-2"x13'-6"
CATHEDRAL CEILING
LIVING
15'-0"x21'-10"
BEDROOM
12'-8"x11'-0"
CL.
CL.
DECK

MAIN FLOOR

Design 20164

PHOTOGRAPHY: GAUTHIER ROOFING AND SIDING

Units	Single
Price Code	A
Total Finished	1,456 sq. ft.
Main Finished	1,456 sq. ft.
Basement Unfinished	1,448 sq. ft.
Garage Unfinished	452 sq. ft.
Dimensions	50'x45'4"
Foundation	Basement Crawlspace Slab
Bedrooms	3
Full Baths	2
Main Ceiling	8'
Max Ridge Height	19'
Roof Framing	Stick
Exterior Walls	2x6

Please note: The photographed home may have been modified to suit homeowner preferences. If you order plans, have a builder or design professional check them against the photograph to confirm actual construction details.

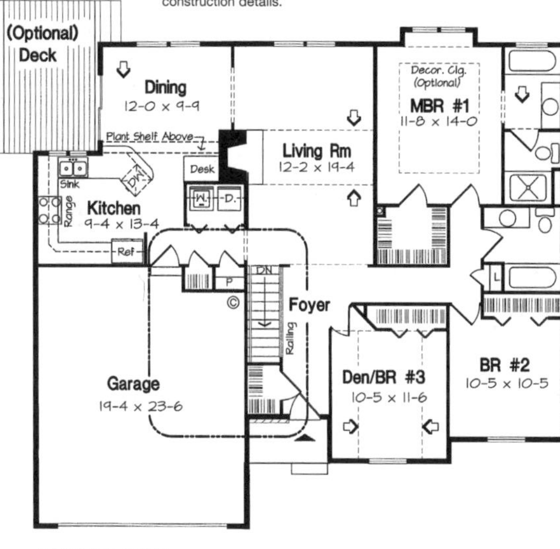
(Optional) Deck
Dining 12-0 x 9-9
Plant Shelf Above
Living Rm 12-2 x 14-4
Decor. Clg. (Optional)
MBR #1 11-8 x 14-0
Kitchen 9-4 x 13-4
Desk
Foyer
Garage 19-4 x 23-6
Den/BR #3 10-5 x 11-6
BR #2 10-5 x 10-5

MAIN FLOOR

Garage

OPTIONAL CRAWLSPACE/SLAB FOUNDATION

Design 96516

Units	Single
Price Code	A
Total Finished	1,458 sq. ft.
Main Finished	1,458 sq. ft.
Garage Unfinished	452 sq. ft.
Dimensions	67'x40'
Foundation	Crawlspace Slab
Bedrooms	3
Full Baths	2
Max Ridge Height	19'
Roof Framing	Stick
Exterior Walls	2x4

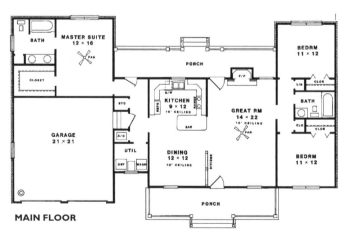

BATH · MASTER SUITE 12 × 16 · CLOSET · PORCH · BEDRM 11 × 12 · KITCHEN 9 × 12 10' CEILING · GREAT RM 14 × 22 10' CEILING · BATH · GARAGE 21 × 21 · UTIL · DINING 12 × 12 10' CEILING · BEDRM 11 × 12 · PORCH

MAIN FLOOR

Design 97137

Units	Single
Price Code	A
Total Finished	1,461 sq. ft.
Main Finished	1,461 sq. ft.
Garage Unfinished	458 sq. ft.
Deck Unfinished	200 sq. ft.
Dimensions	56'x42'
Foundation	Basement
Bedrooms	3
Full Baths	2
Main Ceiling	8'
Max Ridge Height	21'5"
Roof Framing	Truss
Exterior Walls	2x6

WOOD DECK 20'0" X 10'0"
MBR. 12'10" X 15'0"
GRT. RM. CATHEDRAL CEILING 14'6" X 19'0"
DIN. CATH. CLG. 10'6" X 11'4"
KIT. CATH. CLG. 11'0" X 11'4"
BR. #2/ DEN 11'0" X 11'0"
OPTIONAL DOOR
BR. #3 10'0" X 10'6"
2 CAR GARAGE 19'8" X 23'4"

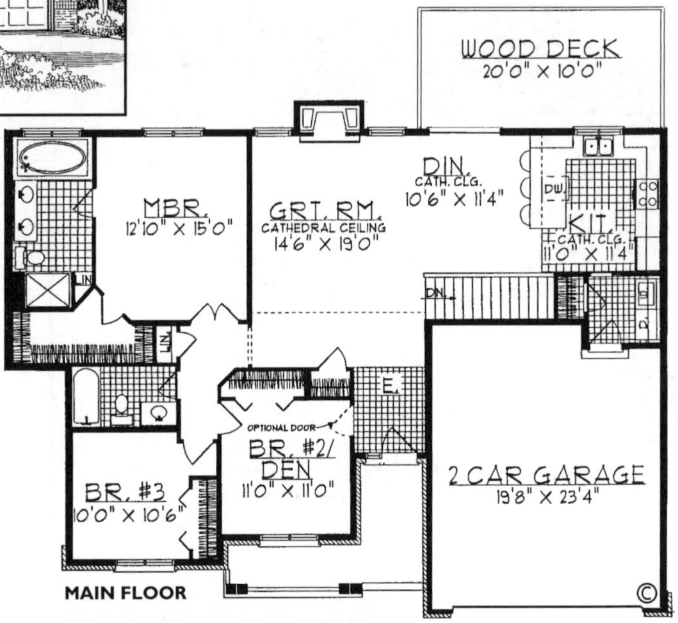

MAIN FLOOR

Design 97176

Units	Single
Price Code	A
Total Finished	1,462 sq. ft.
Main Finished	1,462 sq. ft.
Basement Unfinished	1,462 sq. ft.
Garage Unfinished	400 sq. ft.
Dimensions	52'x46'
Foundation	Basement
Bedrooms	3
Full Baths	2
Main Ceiling	8'
Max Ridge Height	24'10"
Roof Framing	Truss
Exterior Walls	2x6

BR. #3 10'0" X 12'8"
BR. #2 10'0" X 12'8"
MBR. 14'8" X 13'8"
GRT. RM. CATHEDRAL CEILING 18'0" X 14'0"
KIT. 11'0" X 12'8"
DIN. 11'0" X 9'10"
2 CAR GAR. 20'0" X 20'0"

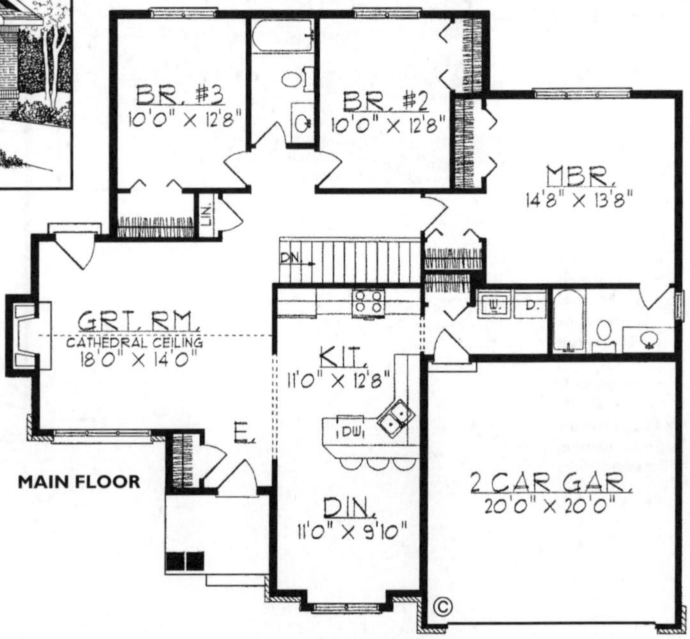

MAIN FLOOR

Design 99926

Units	Single
Price Code	A
Total Finished	1,463 sq. ft.
Main Finished	1,463 sq. ft.
Basement Unfinished	1,446 sq. ft.
Garage Unfinished	390 sq. ft.
Deck Unfinished	100 sq. ft.
Porch Unfinished	40 sq. ft.
Dimensions	40'x60'
Foundation	Basement
Bedrooms	3
Full Baths	2
Main Ceiling	8'
Vaulted Ceiling	11'
Max Ridge Height	18'6"
Roof Framing	Truss
Exterior Walls	2x6

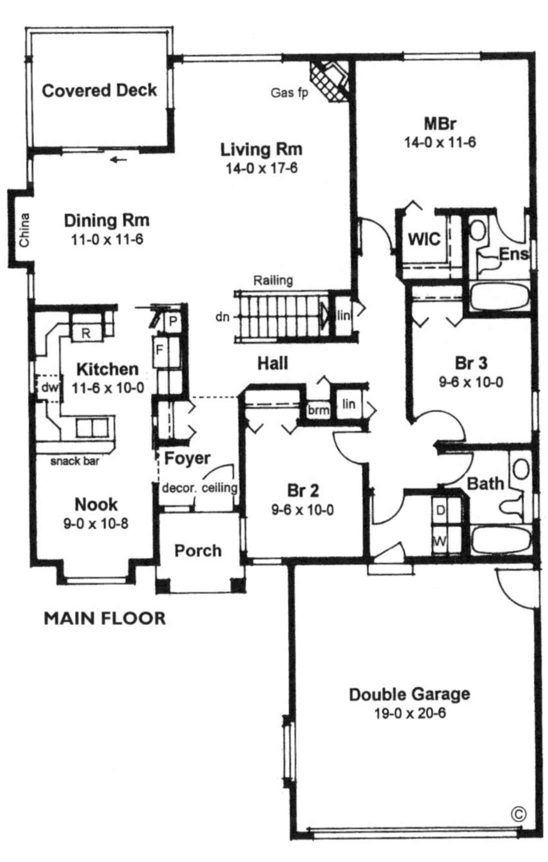
Covered Deck
Gas fp
Living Rm
14-0 x 17-6
MBr
14-0 x 11-6
China
Dining Rm
11-0 x 11-6
WIC
Ens
Railing
dn
lin
R
P
F
Kitchen
11-6 x 10-0
dw
Hall
Br 3
9-6 x 10-0
brm
lin
snack bar
Foyer
decor. ceiling
Nook
9-0 x 10-8
Br 2
9-6 x 10-0
Bath
D
W
Porch
MAIN FLOOR
Double Garage
19-0 x 20-6

Design 91554

Units	Single
Price Code	A
Total Finished	1,467 sq. ft.
Main Finished	1,467 sq. ft.
Garage Unfinished	400 sq. ft.
Dimensions	49'x43'
Foundation	Crawlspace
Bedrooms	3
Full Baths	2
Main Ceiling	8'1"
Vaulted Ceiling	13'
Max Ridge Height	20'6"
Roof Framing	Truss
Exterior Walls	2x6

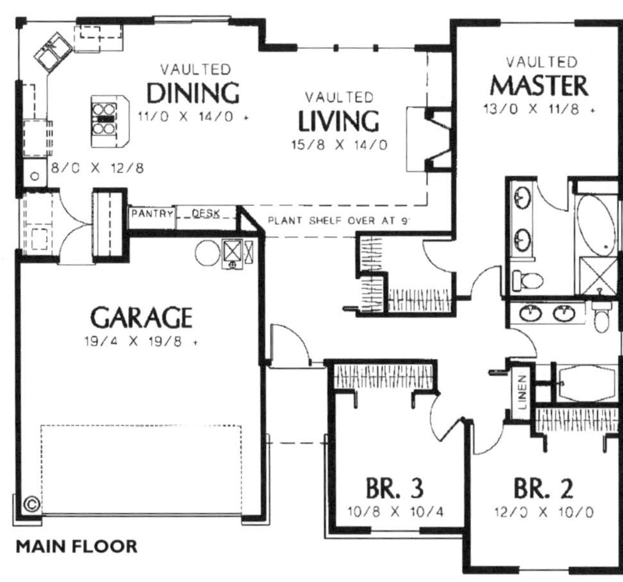
VAULTED
DINING
11/0 X 14/0
VAULTED
LIVING
15/8 X 14/0
VAULTED
MASTER
13/0 X 11/8
8/0 X 12/8
PANTRY
DESK
PLANT SHELF OVER AT 9'
GARAGE
19/4 X 19/8
LINEN
BR. 3
10/8 X 10/4
BR. 2
12/0 X 10/0
MAIN FLOOR

Design 65000

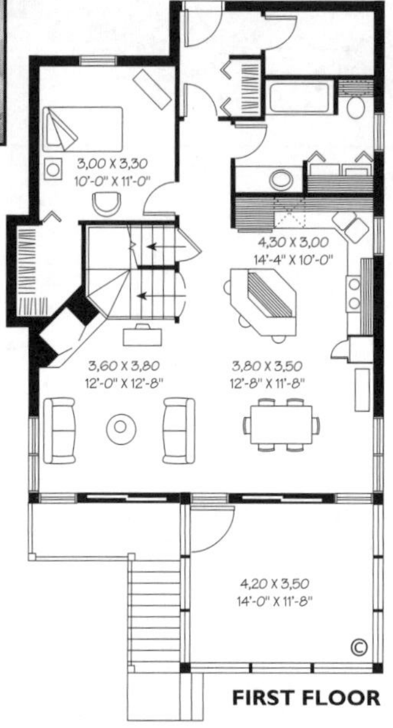

3,00 X 3,30
10'-0" X 11'-0"
4,30 X 3,00
14'-4" X 10'-0"
3,60 X 3,80
12'-0" X 12'-8"
3,80 X 3,50
12'-8" X 11'-8"
4,20 X 3,50
14'-0" X 11'-8"
©

FIRST FLOOR

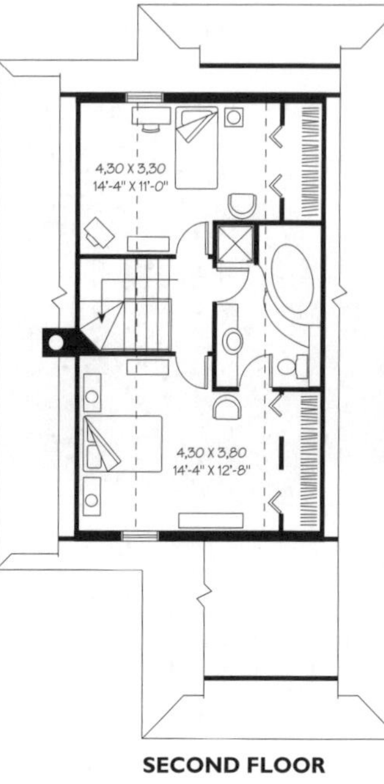

4,30 X 3,30
14'-4" X 11'-0"
4,30 X 3,80
14'-4" X 12'-8"

SECOND FLOOR

Units	Single
Price Code	A
Total Finished	1,471 sq. ft.
First Finished	895 sq. ft.
Second Finished	576 sq. ft.
Basement Unfinished	895 sq. ft.
Dimensions	26'x36'
Foundation	Basement
Bedrooms	3
Full Baths	2
First Ceiling	8'2"
Second Ceiling	8'2"
Max Ridge Height	23'8"
Roof Framing	Truss
Exterior Walls	2x6

Design 93165

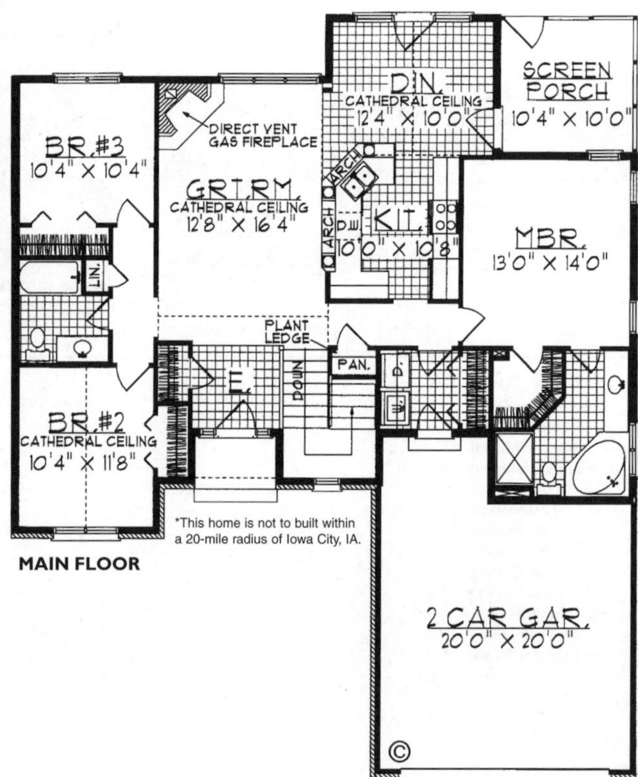

BR.#3
10'4" X 10'4"
DIRECT VENT
GAS FIREPLACE
GRT.RM.
CATHEDRAL CEILING
12'8" X 16'4"
DIN.
CATHEDRAL CEILING
12'4" X 10'0"
SCREEN
PORCH
10'4" X 10'0"
ARCH
ARCH
D.W.
KIT.
10'0" X 10'8"
MBR.
13'0" X 14'0"
LIN.
PLANT
LEDGE
PAN.
E.
DOWN
BR.#2
CATHEDRAL CEILING
10'4" X 11'8"
2 CAR GAR.
20'0" X 20'0"
©

*This home is not to built within a 20-mile radius of Iowa City, IA.

MAIN FLOOR

Units	Single
Price Code	A
Total Finished	1,472 sq. ft.
Main Finished	1,472 sq. ft.
Basement Unfinished	1,472 sq. ft.
Garage Unfinished	424 sq. ft.
Dimensions	48'x56'4"
Foundation	Basement
Bedrooms	3
Full Baths	2
Max Ridge Height	19'8"
Roof Framing	Stick
Exterior Walls	2x6

Design 93416

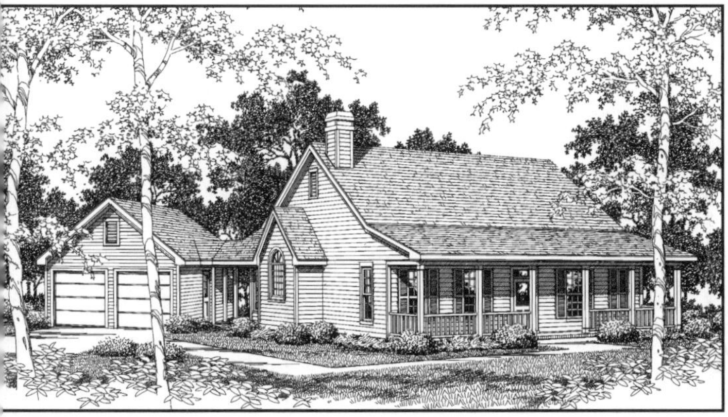

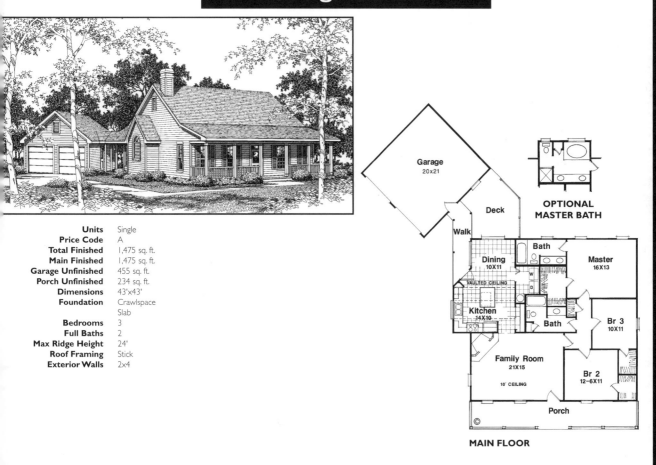

Units	Single
Price Code	A
Total Finished	1,475 sq. ft.
Main Finished	1,475 sq. ft.
Garage Unfinished	455 sq. ft.
Porch Unfinished	234 sq. ft.
Dimensions	43'x43'
Foundation	Crawlspace Slab
Bedrooms	3
Full Baths	2
Max Ridge Height	24'
Roof Framing	Stick
Exterior Walls	2x4

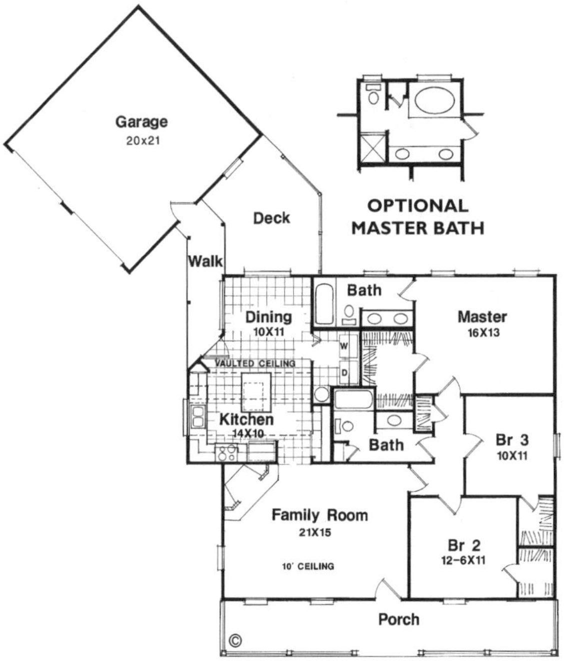

Garage 20x21
Deck
Walk
Dining 10X11
VAULTED CEILING
Kitchen 14X10
Bath
Master 16X13
Bath
Br 3 10X11
Family Room 21X15
10' CEILING
Br 2 12-6X11
Porch

OPTIONAL MASTER BATH

MAIN FLOOR

Design 90689

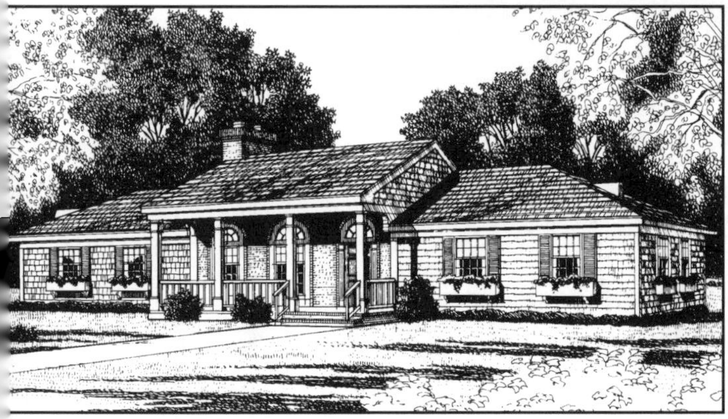

Units	Single
Price Code	A
Total Finished	1,476 sq. ft.
Main Finished	1,476 sq. ft.
Basement Unfinished	1,361 sq. ft.
Garage Unfinished	548 sq. ft.
Dimensions	75'9"x34'6"
Foundation	Basement Slab
Bedrooms	3
Full Baths	2
Max Ridge Height	19'
Roof Framing	Stick
Exterior Walls	2x6

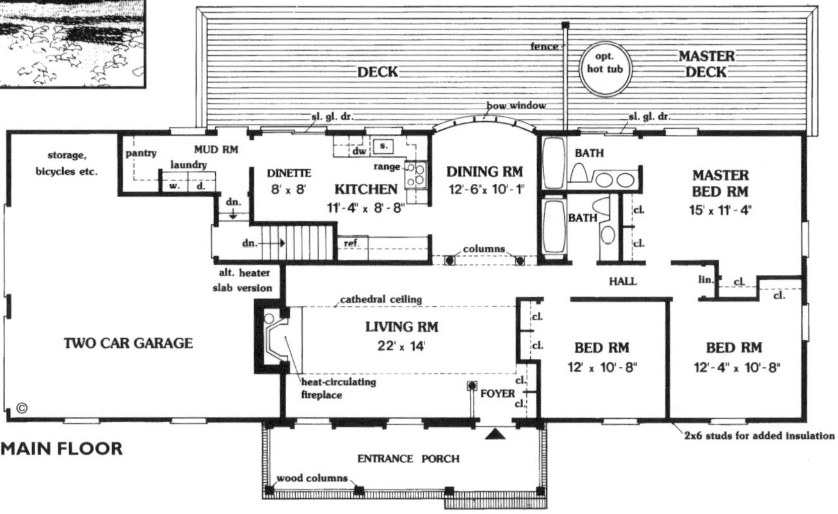

DECK
fence
opt. hot tub
MASTER DECK
bow window
sl. gl. dr.
storage, bicycles etc.
pantry
MUD RM
laundry
DINETTE 8' x 8'
KITCHEN 11'-4" x 8'-8"
DINING RM 12'-6"x 10'-1"
BATH
MASTER BED RM 15' x 11'-4"
alt. heater slab version
TWO CAR GARAGE
cathedral ceiling
LIVING RM 22' x 14'
heat-circulating fireplace
FOYER
HALL
BED RM 12' x 10'-8"
BED RM 12'-4" x 10'-8"
2x6 studs for added insulation
ENTRANCE PORCH
wood columns

MAIN FLOOR

Design 60084

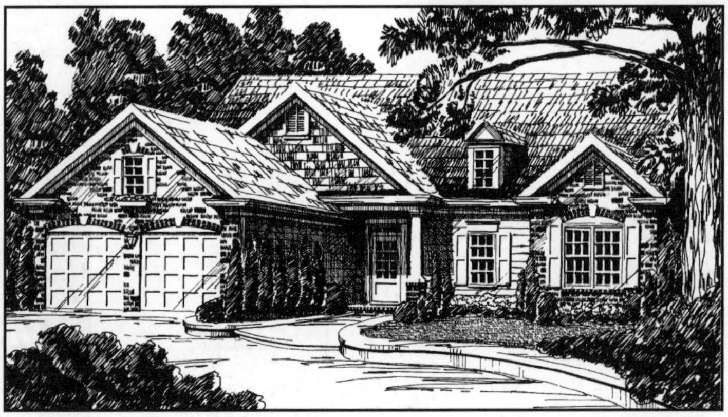

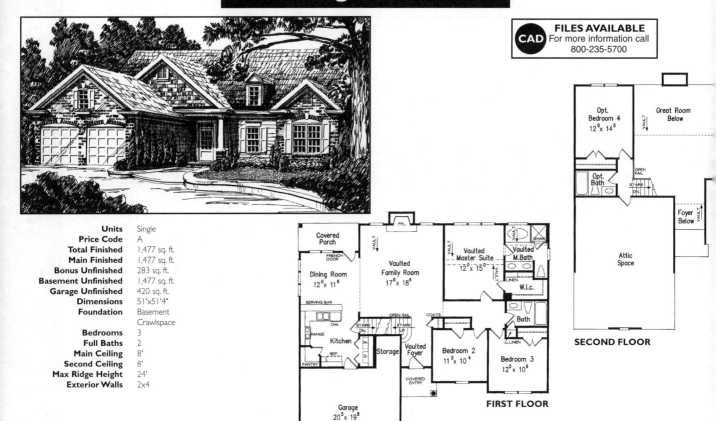

FILES AVAILABLE
CAD For more information call
800-235-5700

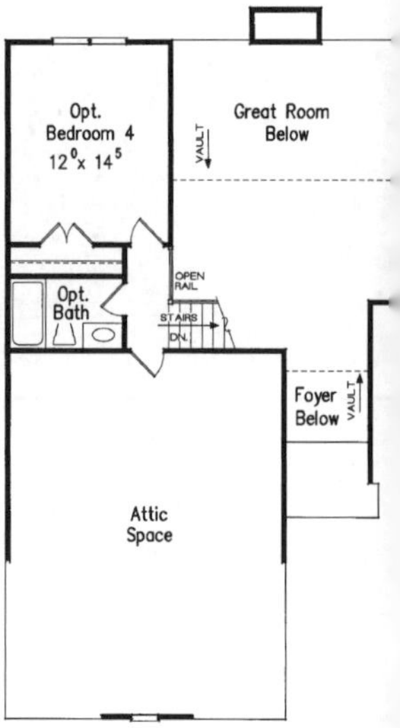

SECOND FLOOR

FIRST FLOOR

Units	Single
Price Code	A
Total Finished	1,477 sq. ft.
Main Finished	1,477 sq. ft.
Bonus Unfinished	283 sq. ft.
Basement Unfinished	1,477 sq. ft.
Garage Unfinished	420 sq. ft.
Dimensions	51'x51'4"
Foundation	Basement Crawlspace
Bedrooms	3
Full Baths	2
Main Ceiling	8'
Second Ceiling	8'
Max Ridge Height	24'
Exterior Walls	2x4

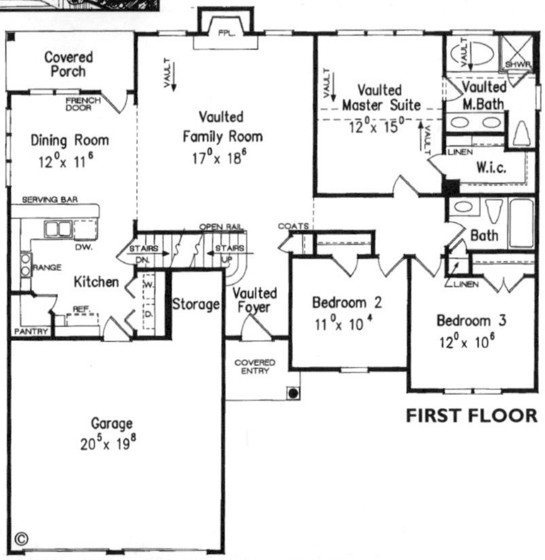

Design 91847

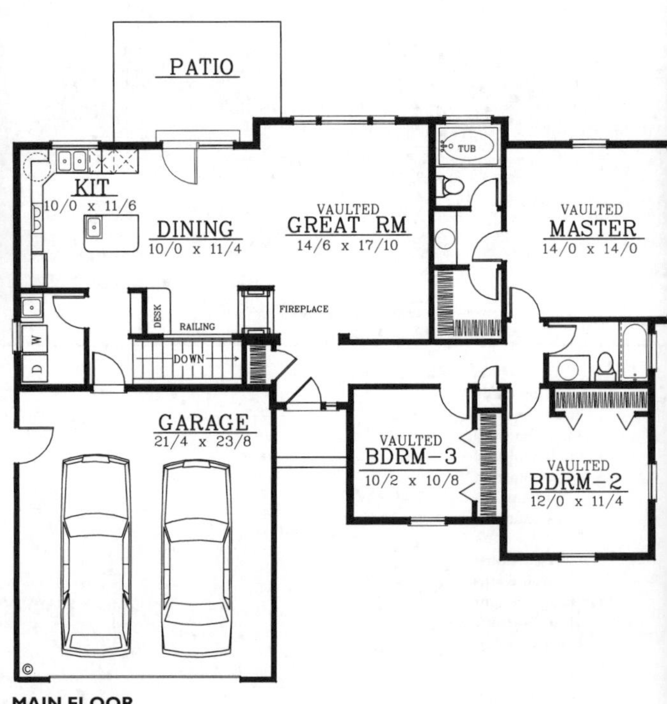
PATIO
KIT
10/0 x 11/6
DINING
10/0 x 11/4
VAULTED
GREAT RM
14/6 x 17/10
TUB
VAULTED
MASTER
14/0 x 14/0
DESK
RAILING
FIREPLACE
DOWN
GARAGE
21/4 x 23/8
VAULTED
BDRM-3
10/2 x 10/8
VAULTED
BDRM-2
12/0 x 11/4

MAIN FLOOR

Units	Single
Price Code	A
Total Finished	1,479 sq. ft.
Main Finished	1,479 sq. ft.
Basement Unfinished	1,430 sq. ft.
Garage Unfinished	528 sq. ft.
Dimensions	56'x46'6"
Foundation	Basement Crawlspace Slab
Bedrooms	3
Full Baths	2
Main Ceiling	8'
Max Ridge Height	19'4"
Roof Framing	Truss
Exterior Walls	2x6

Design 99490

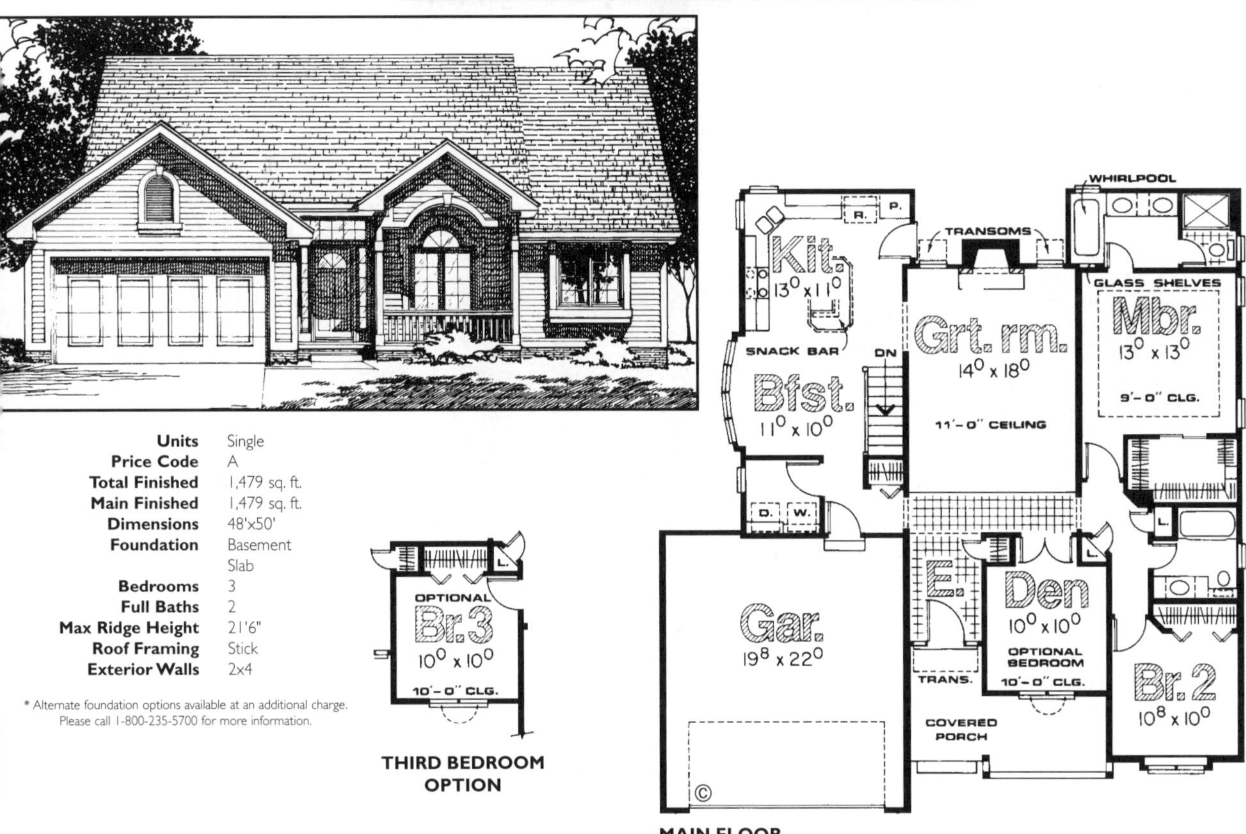
WHIRLPOOL
TRANSOMS
R.
P.
Kit.
13⁰ x 11⁰
GLASS SHELVES
SNACK BAR
DN
Grt. rm.
14⁰ x 18⁰
Mbr.
13⁰ x 13⁰
9'-0" CLG.
Bfst.
11⁰ x 10⁰
11'-0" CEILING
D.
W.
L.
OPTIONAL
Br. 3
10⁰ x 10⁰
10'-0" CLG.
THIRD BEDROOM OPTION
Gar.
19⁸ x 22⁰
E.
Den
10⁰ x 10⁰
OPTIONAL BEDROOM
10'-0" CLG.
TRANS.
COVERED PORCH
Br. 2
10⁸ x 10⁰
MAIN FLOOR

Units	Single
Price Code	A
Total Finished	1,479 sq. ft.
Main Finished	1,479 sq. ft.
Dimensions	48'x50'
Foundation	Basement Slab
Bedrooms	3
Full Baths	2
Max Ridge Height	21'6"
Roof Framing	Stick
Exterior Walls	2x4

* Alternate foundation options available at an additional charge. Please call 1-800-235-5700 for more information.

Design 65001

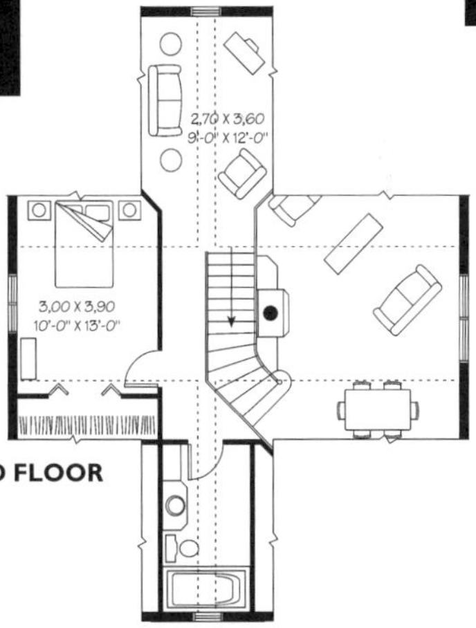

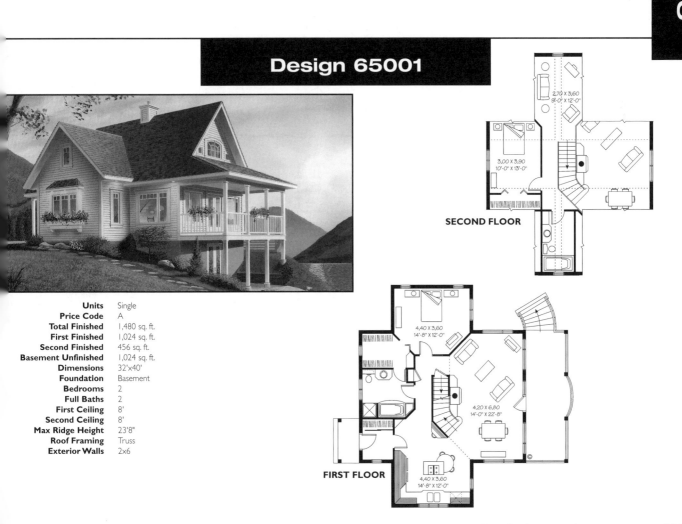

2,70 X 3,60
9'-0" X 12'-0"

3,00 X 3,90
10'-0" X 13'-0"

SECOND FLOOR

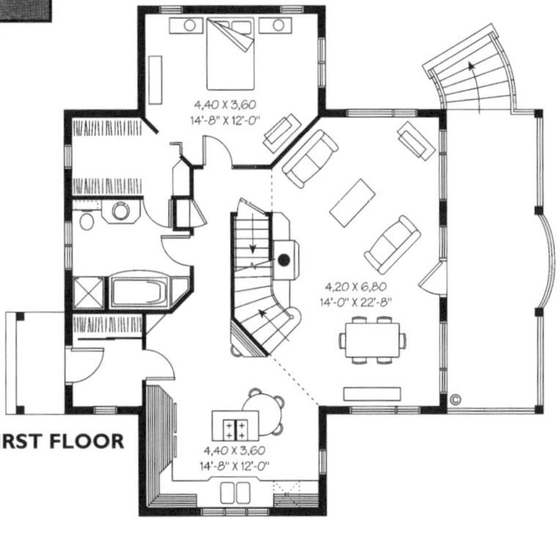

4,40 X 3,60
14'-8" X 12'-0"

4,20 X 6,80
14'-0" X 22'-8"

4,40 X 3,60
14'-8" X 12'-0"

FIRST FLOOR

Units	Single
Price Code	A
Total Finished	1,480 sq. ft.
First Finished	1,024 sq. ft.
Second Finished	456 sq. ft.
Basement Unfinished	1,024 sq. ft.
Dimensions	32'x40'
Foundation	Basement
Bedrooms	2
Full Baths	2
First Ceiling	8'
Second Ceiling	8'
Max Ridge Height	23'8"
Roof Framing	Truss
Exterior Walls	2x6

Design 96508

Units	Single
Price Code	A
Total Finished	1,481 sq. ft.
Main Finished	1,481 sq. ft.
Garage Unfinished	477 sq. ft.
Porch Unfinished	40 sq. ft.
Dimensions	54'x44'
Foundation	Crawlspace Slab
Bedrooms	3
Full Baths	2
Main Ceiling	9'
Max Ridge Height	26'
Roof Framing	Stick
Exterior Walls	2x4

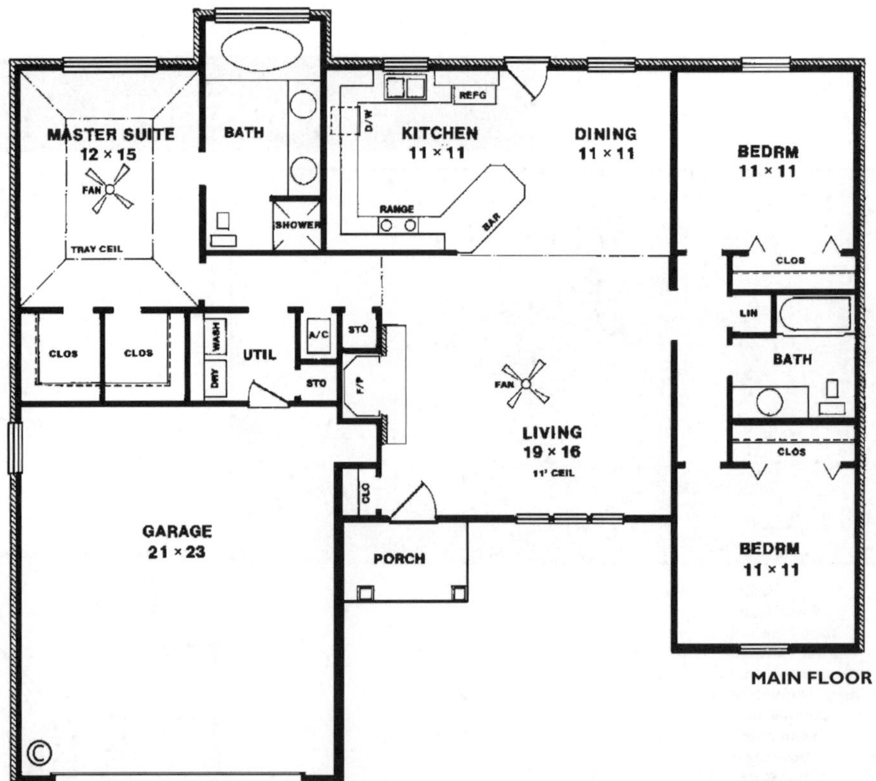
MASTER SUITE
12 × 15
FAN
TRAY CEIL
BATH
SHOWER
KITCHEN
11 × 11
D/W
REFG
RANGE
BAR
DINING
11 × 11
BEDRM
11 × 11
CLOS
LIN
BATH
CLOS
CLOS
UTIL
WASH
DRY
A/C
STO
STO
F/P
FAN
LIVING
19 × 16
11' CEIL
CLO
GARAGE
21 × 23
PORCH
BEDRM
11 × 11
©

MAIN FLOOR

Design 61032

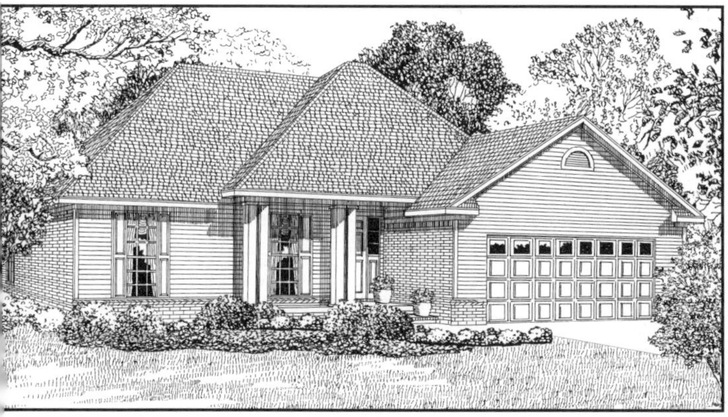

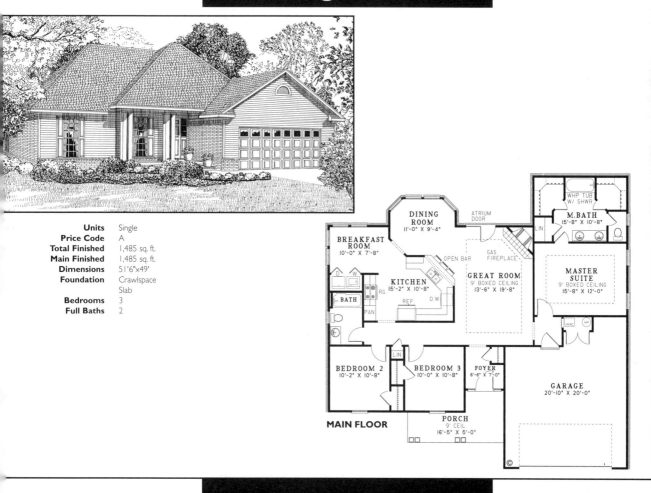

Units	Single
Price Code	A
Total Finished	1,485 sq. ft.
Main Finished	1,485 sq. ft.
Dimensions	51'6"x49'
Foundation	Crawlspace Slab
Bedrooms	3
Full Baths	2

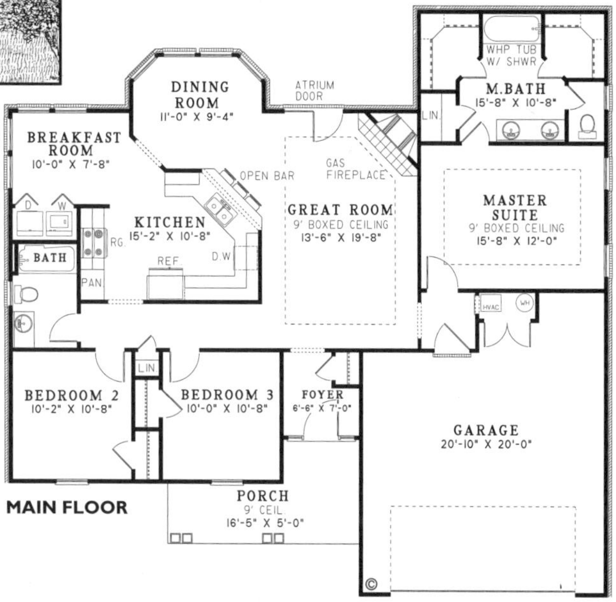

MAIN FLOOR

Design 61033

Units	Single
Price Code	A
Total Finished	1,485 sq. ft.
Main Finished	1,485 sq. ft.
Dimensions	51'6"x49'10"
Foundation	Crawlspace Slab
Bedrooms	3
Full Baths	2

WHP TUB
M.BATH
15'-8" X 10'-8"
LIN
COVERED PORCH
24'-10" X 9'-8"
ATRIUM DOOR
DINING ROOM
11'-0" X 9'-6"
GRILLING PATIO
10'-4" X 9'-8"
BRKFAST ROOM
10'-0" X 8'-0"
COMPUTER DESK
GAS FIREPLACE
OPEN BAR
MASTER SUITE
15'-8" X 12'-0"
9' BOXED CEILING
GREAT ROOM
13'-6" X 19'-8"
9' BOXED CEILING
KITCHEN
15'-2" X 10'-8"
DW
REF.
RG.
BATH
WH
D.
W
LAU.
6'-4" X 5'-6"
OPT DOOR
FOYER
6'-6" X 7'-0"
LIN
BEDROOM 3 / STUDY
10'-0" X 10'-8"
BEDROOM 2
10'-2" X 10'-8"
GARAGE
20'-10" X 20'-0"
COVERED PORCH
16'-5" X 5'-0"

MAIN FLOOR

Design 82026

Units	Single
Price Code	A
Total Finished	1,485 sq. ft.
Main Finished	1,485 sq. ft.
Garage Unfinished	415 sq. ft.
Porch Unfinished	180 sq. ft.
Dimensions	51'6"x49'10"
Foundation	Crawlspace Slab
Bedrooms	3
Full Baths	2
Main Ceiling	9'
Roof Framing	Stick
Exterior Walls	2x4

GLASS BLOCKS
10" BOXED COLUMNS
GRILLING PORCH 10'-5" X 9'-2"
COVERED PORCH 13'-2" X 9'-2"
WHP TUB
M.BATH 16'-0" X 12'-0"
DINING ROOM 11'-0" X 9'-6"
BRKFAST ROOM 10'-0" X 8'-0"
GAS FIREPLACE
OPEN BAR
COMPUTER DESK
KITCHEN 15'-2" X 11'-0"
RG
REF
DW
PANTRY
GREAT ROOM 13'-6" X 19'-8"
MASTER SUITE 15'-8" X 12'-0"
9' BOXED CEILING
9' BOXED CEILING
D
W
WH
LIN
OPT DOOR
FOYER
BEDROOM 2 10'-2" X 10'-8"
BEDROOM 3 / STUDY 10'-0" X 10'-8"
GARAGE 20'-10" X 20'-0"
COVERED PORCH 16'-6" X 5'-0"
10" BOXED COLUMNS

MAIN FLOOR

Design 91797

Units	Single
Price Code	A
Total Finished	1,485 sq. ft.
Main Finished	1,485 sq. ft.
Garage Unfinished	701 sq. ft.
Dimensions	51'6"x63'
Foundation	Crawlspace
Bedrooms	3
Full Baths	2
Max Ridge Height	22'
Roof Framing	Stick/Truss
Exterior Walls	2x6

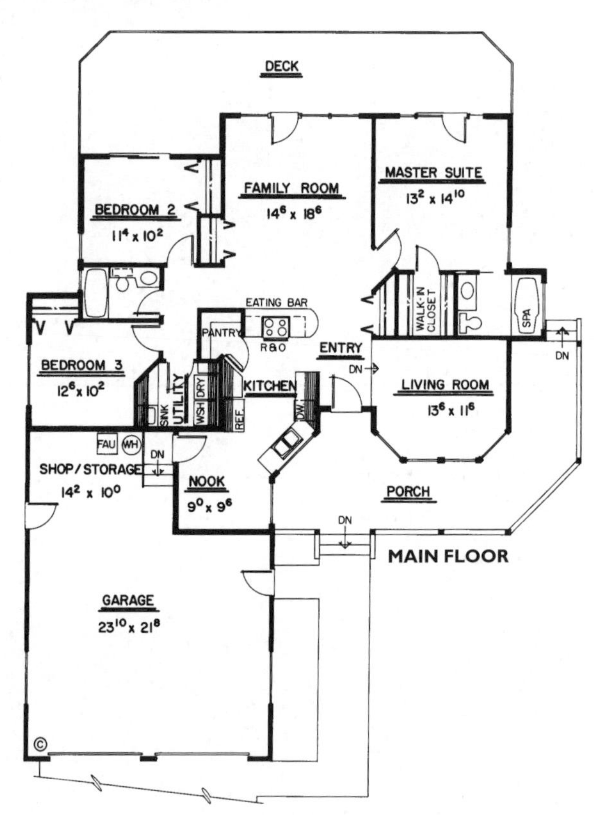
DECK
FAMILY ROOM
14^6 x 18^6
MASTER SUITE
13^2 x 14^{10}
BEDROOM 2
11^4 x 10^2
EATING BAR
PANTRY
R&O
WALK-IN CLOSET
SPA
ENTRY
DN
DN
BEDROOM 3
12^6 x 10^2
SINK
UTILITY
WSH
DRY
REF.
KITCHEN
DW
LIVING ROOM
13^6 x 11^6
FAU
WH
DN
SHOP / STORAGE
14^2 x 10^0
NOOK
9^0 x 9^6
PORCH
DN
GARAGE
23^{10} x 21^8

MAIN FLOOR

Design 26112

PHOTOGRAPHY: BETH SINGER

Units	Single
Price Code	A
Total Finished	1,487 sq. ft.
First Finished	911 sq. ft.
Second Finished	576 sq. ft.
Basement Unfinished	911 sq. ft.
Dimensions	32'x34'
Foundation	Basement
Bedrooms	3
Full Baths	1
Half Baths	1
First Ceiling	9'
Second Ceiling	8'
Max Ridge Height	29'
Roof Framing	Stick
Exterior Walls	2x6

Cl
Bath
Cl Cl
Bedroom 12'-0"x12'-0"
dn
Bedroom 13'-0"x14'-0"
Balcony
Deck
Open to Living
Skylights

SECOND FLOOR

Please note: The photographed home may have been modified to suit homeowner preferences. If you order plans, have a builder or design professional check them against the photograph to confirm actual construction details.

Vest.
Entry
up
Kitchen
Cl
Lav
Dining 13'-0"x10'-0"
Bedroom/Den 12'-0"x12'-0"
dn
Deck
Living 20'-0"x16'-0"
Deck

FIRST FLOOR

Design 98807

Units	Single
Price Code	A
Total Finished	1,487 sq. ft.
Main Finished	1,487 sq. ft.
Basement Unfinished	1,480 sq. ft.
Garage Unfinished	427 sq. ft.
Dimensions	46'x50'
Foundation	Basement
Bedrooms	2
Full Baths	2
Main Ceiling	8'
Max Ridge Height	19'11"
Roof Framing	Truss
Exterior Walls	2x6

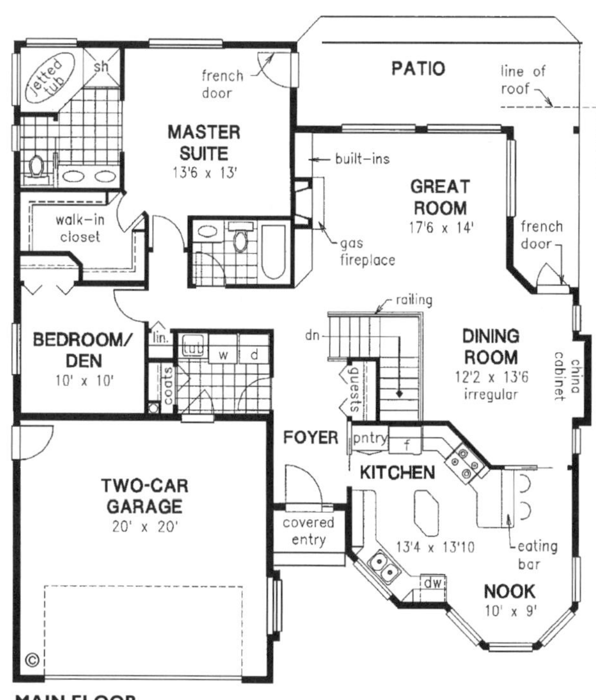
jetted tub
sh
french door
MASTER SUITE
13'6 x 13'
PATIO
line of roof
built-ins
GREAT ROOM
17'6 x 14'
walk-in closet
gas fireplace
french door
railing
dn
BEDROOM/ DEN
10' x 10'
lin.
tub
w d
coats
guests
DINING ROOM
12'2 x 13'6
irregular
china cabinet
FOYER
pntry
f
KITCHEN
TWO-CAR GARAGE
20' x 20'
covered entry
13'4 x 13'10
eating bar
dw
NOOK
10' x 9'

MAIN FLOOR

Design 97241

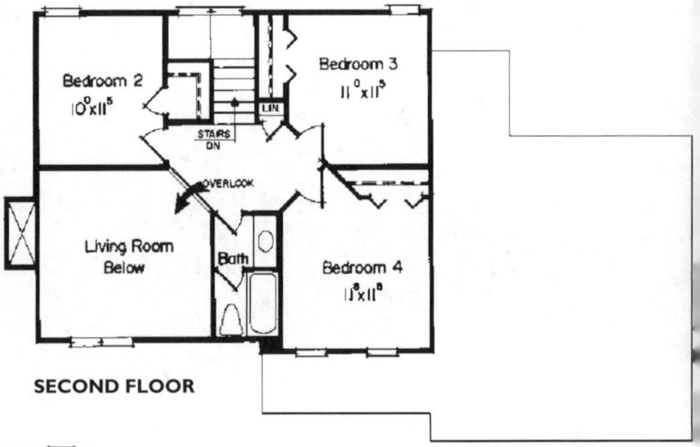

Bedroom 2
10⁰x11⁵
Bedroom 3
11⁰x11³
LIN
STAIRS DN
OVERLOOK
Living Room Below
Bath
Bedroom 4
11⁸x11⁸

SECOND FLOOR

Units	Single
Price Code	A
Total Finished	1,489 sq. ft.
First Finished	906 sq. ft.
Second Finished	583 sq. ft.
Basement Unfinished	906 sq. ft.
Garage Unfinished	460 sq. ft.
Dimensions	53'4"x33'6"
Foundation	Basement Crawlspace Slab
Bedrooms	4
Full Baths	2
Half Baths	1
Max Ridge Height	27'6"
Roof Framing	Stick
Exterior Walls	2x4

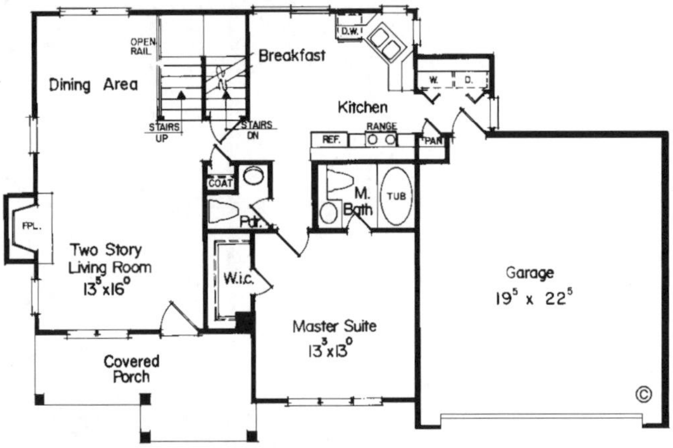

OPEN RAIL
Dining Area
Breakfast
D.W.
W. D.
Kitchen
STAIRS UP
STAIRS DN
REF.
RANGE
PAN
COAT
Pdr.
M. Bath
TUB
FPL.
Two Story Living Room
13⁵x16⁰
W.i.c.
Master Suite
13³x13⁰
Garage
19⁵ x 22⁵
©
Covered Porch

FIRST FLOOR

Design 61035

Units	Single
Price Code	A
Total Finished	1,490 sq. ft.
Main Finished	1,490 sq. ft.
Garage Unfinished	386 sq. ft.
Porch Unfinished	20 sq. ft.
Dimensions	31'6"x72'10"
Foundation	Crawlspace Slab
Bedrooms	3
Full Baths	2
Main Ceiling	9'
Exterior Walls	2x4

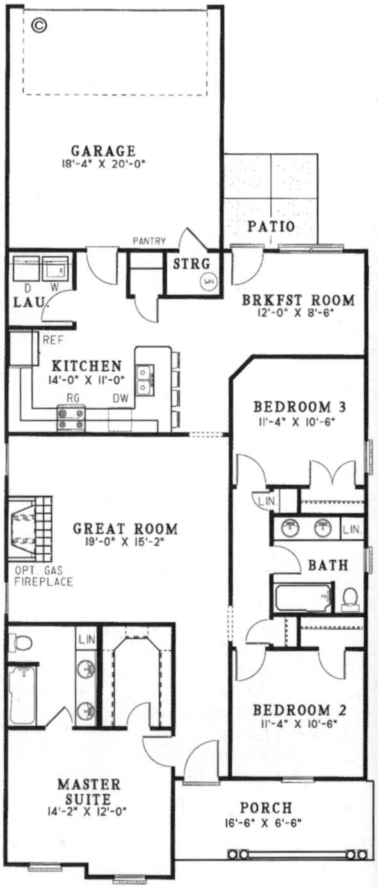

©
GARAGE
18'-4" X 20'-0"
PATIO
PANTRY
STRG
WH
D W
LAU.
BRKFST ROOM
12'-0" X 8'-6"
REF
KITCHEN
14'-0" X 11'-0"
RG DW
BEDROOM 3
11'-4" X 10'-6"
LIN
GREAT ROOM
19'-0" X 15'-2"
OPT. GAS FIREPLACE
LIN
BATH
LIN
BEDROOM 2
11'-4" X 10'-6"
MASTER SUITE
14'-2" X 12'-0"
PORCH
16'-6" X 6'-6"

MAIN FLOOR

Design 34150

PHOTOGRAPHY: JOHN EHRENCLOU

Units	Single
Price Code	A
Total Finished	1,492 sq. ft.
Main Finished	1,492 sq. ft.
Basement Unfinished	1,486 sq. ft.
Garage Unfinished	462 sq. ft.
Dimensions	56'x48'
Foundation	Basement Crawlspace Slab
Bedrooms	3
Full Baths	2
Main Ceiling	8'
Vaulted Ceiling	13'
Max Ridge Height	19'
Roof Framing	Stick
Exterior Walls	2x4, 2x6

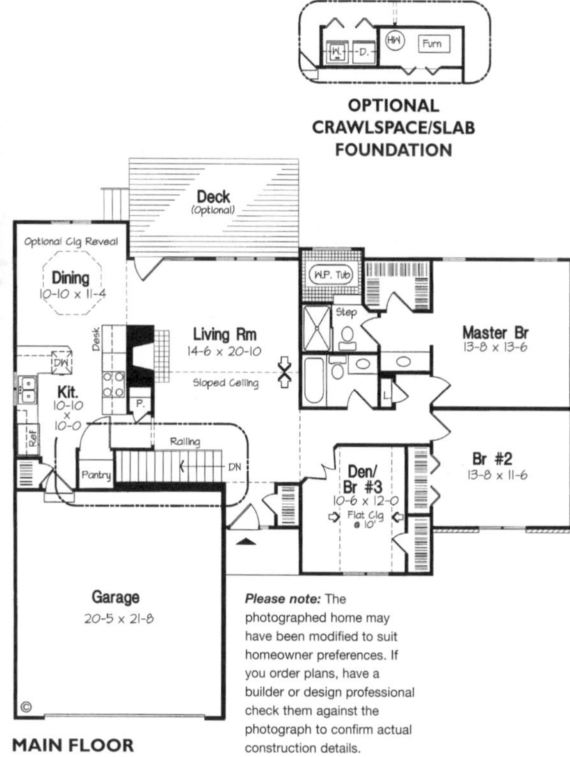
OPTIONAL CRAWLSPACE/SLAB FOUNDATION
Deck (Optional)
Optional Clg Reveal
Dining 10-10 x 11-4
Living Rm 14-6 x 20-10
Sloped Ceiling
Kit. 10-10 x 10-0
Pantry
Railing
DN
Master Br 13-8 x 13-6
Br #2 13-8 x 11-6
Den/ Br #3 10-6 x 12-0
Flat Clg @ 10'
Garage 20-5 x 21-8
MAIN FLOOR

Please note: The photographed home may have been modified to suit homeowner preferences. If you order plans, have a builder or design professional check them against the photograph to confirm actual construction details.

Design 65275

Units	Single
Price Code	A
Total Finished	1,492 sq. ft.
First Finished	856 sq. ft.
Second Finished	636 sq. ft.
Dimensions	44'x26'
Foundation	Basement
Bedrooms	3
Full Baths	1
Half Baths	1
Max Ridge Height	31'9"
Roof Framing	Stick
Exterior Walls	2x6

3,40 X 2,80
11'-4" X 9'-4"
4,80 X 3,80
16'-0" X 12'-8"
OPEN TO BELOW
SECOND FLOOR

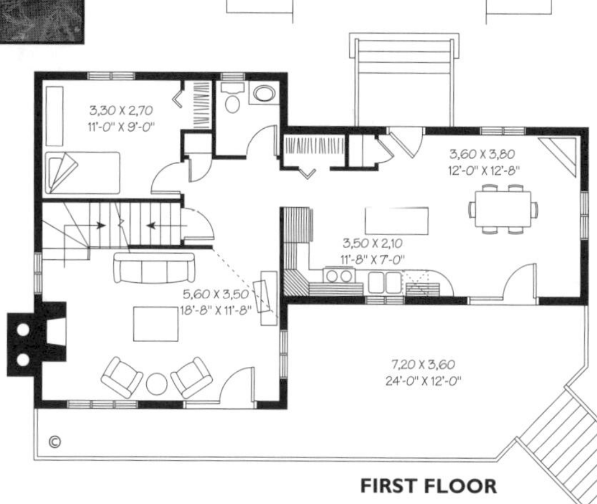
3,30 X 2,70
11'-0" X 9'-0"
3,60 X 3,80
12'-0" X 12'-8"
3,50 X 2,10
11'-8" X 7'-0"
5,60 X 3,50
18'-8" X 11'-8"
7,20 X 3,60
24'-0" X 12'-0"
FIRST FLOOR

Design 90692

Units	Single
Price Code	A
Total Finished	1,492 sq. ft.
Main Finished	1,492 sq. ft.
Dimensions	67'10"x28'4"
Foundation	Basement Slab
Bedrooms	3
Full Baths	2

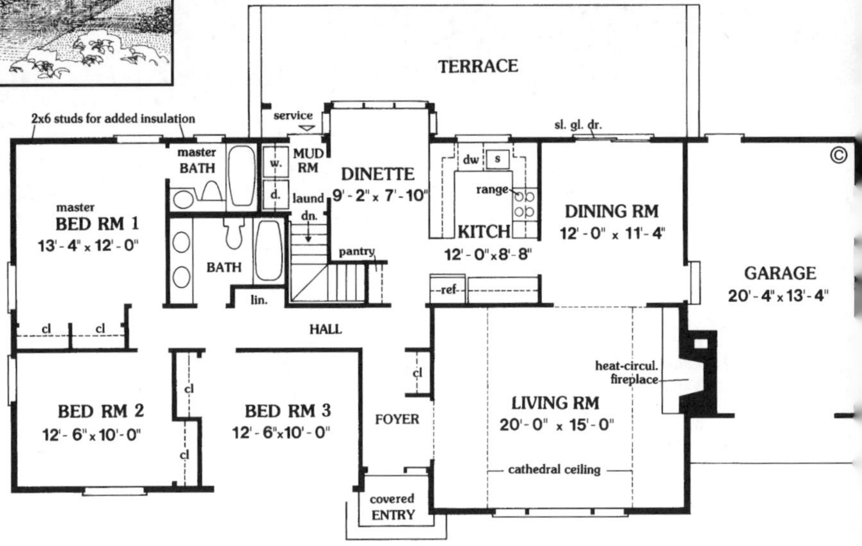

TERRACE
2x6 studs for added insulation
service
sl. gl. dr.
master BATH
MUD RM
w.
d.
laund
dn.
DINETTE 9'-2" x 7'-10"
dw
s
range
KITCH 12'-0"x8'-8"
DINING RM 12'-0" x 11'-4"
GARAGE 20'-4"x13'-4"
master BED RM 1 13'-4" x 12'-0"
BATH
lin.
pantry
ref
HALL
cl
heat-circul. fireplace
BED RM 2 12'-6"x10'-0"
BED RM 3 12'-6"x10'-0"
FOYER
LIVING RM 20'-0" x 15'-0"
cathedral ceiling
covered ENTRY

MAIN FLOOR

Design 98472

Units	Single
Price Code	A
Total Finished	1,492 sq. ft.
Main Finished	1,492 sq. ft.
Garage Unfinished	465 sq. ft.
Dimensions	56'x49'10"
Foundation	Basement Crawlspace
Bedrooms	3
Full Baths	2
Main Ceiling	9'
Max Ridge Height	27'6"
Roof Framing	Stick
Exterior Walls	2x4

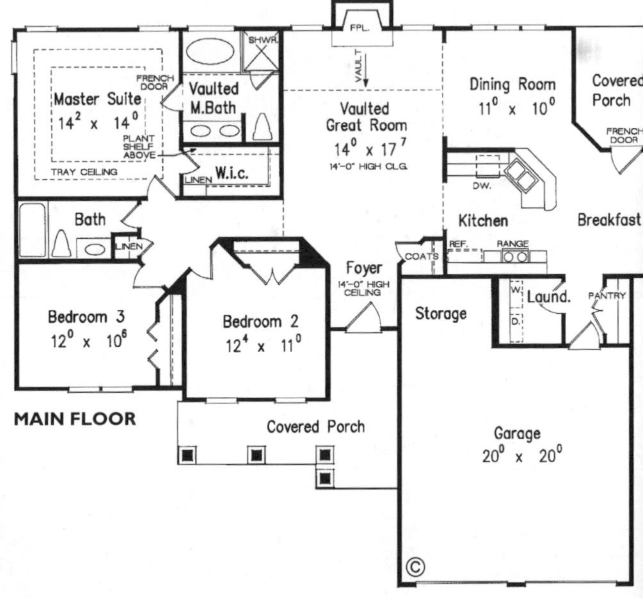
FPL.
VAULT
Master Suite 14^2 x 14^0
FRENCH DOOR
PLANT SHELF ABOVE
TRAY CEILING
SHWR
Vaulted M.Bath
W.i.c.
LINEN
Vaulted Great Room 14^0 x 17^7
14'-0" HIGH CLG.
Dining Room 11^0 x 10^0
Covered Porch
FRENCH DOOR
DW.
Kitchen
Breakfast
REF.
RANGE
COATS
Bath
LINEN
Foyer
14'-0" HIGH CEILING
Bedroom 3 12^0 x 10^6
Bedroom 2 12^4 x 11^0
Storage
W.
D.
Laund.
PANTRY
Covered Porch
Garage 20^0 x 20^0
©

MAIN FLOOR

Design 99922

Units	Single
Price Code	A
Total Finished	1,493 sq. ft.
Main Finished	1,493 sq. ft.
Basement Unfinished	1,493 sq. ft.
Garage Unfinished	441 sq. ft.
Deck Unfinished	140 sq. ft.
Porch Unfinished	30 sq. ft.
Dimensions	48'x58'
Foundation	Basement
Bedrooms	3
Full Baths	2
Main Ceiling	8'
Vaulted Ceiling	10'6"
Max Ridge Height	20'
Roof Framing	Truss
Exterior Walls	2x6

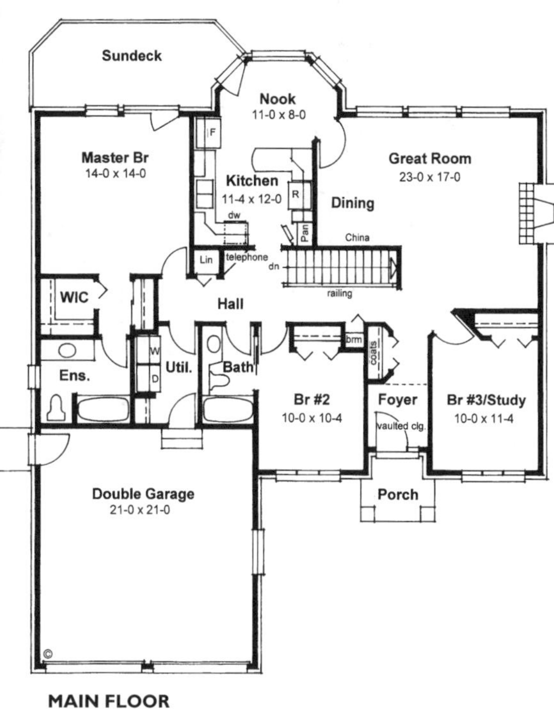
Sundeck
Nook
11-0 x 8-0
Master Br
14-0 x 14-0
Kitchen
11-4 x 12-0
Dining
Great Room
23-0 x 17-0
China
telephone
railing
WIC
Hall
Ens.
Util.
Bath
Br #2
10-0 x 10-4
Foyer
vaulted clg.
Br #3/Study
10-0 x 11-4
Double Garage
21-0 x 21-0
Porch

MAIN FLOOR

Design 99106

Units	Single
Price Code	A
Total Finished	1,495 sq. ft.
Main Finished	1,495 sq. ft.
Basement Unfinished	1,495 sq. ft.
Dimensions	48'x58'8"
Foundation	Basement
Bedrooms	3
Full Baths	2
Max Ridge Height	20'6"
Roof Framing	Truss
Exterior Walls	2x4

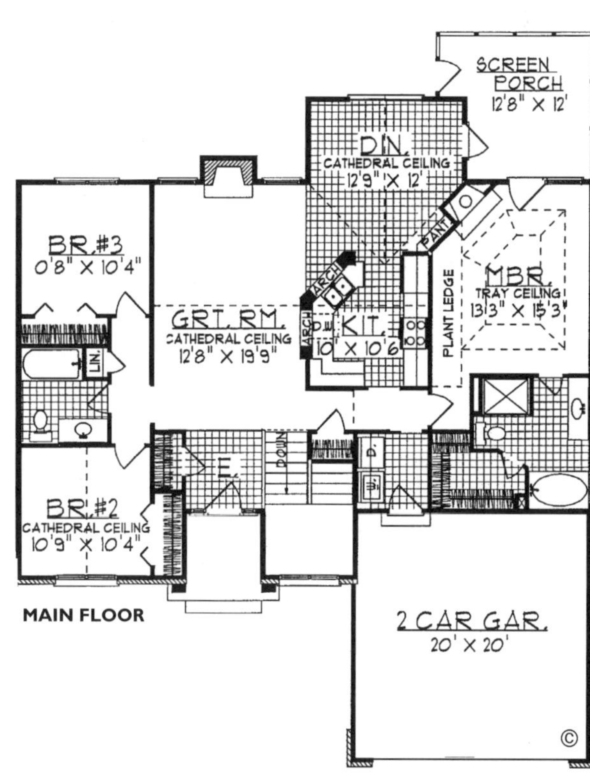
SCREEN PORCH
12'8" X 12'
DIN.
CATHEDRAL CEILING
12'9" X 12'
BR.#3
10'8" X 10'4"
GRT. RM.
CATHEDRAL CEILING
12'8" X 19'9"
KIT.
10' X 10'6
PLANT LEDGE
MBR.
TRAY CEILING
13'3" X 15'3"
BR.#2
CATHEDRAL CEILING
10'9" X 10'4"
2 CAR GAR.
20' X 20'

MAIN FLOOR

Design 97999

Units	Single
Price Code	A
Total Finished	1,499 sq. ft.
Main Finished	1,499 sq. ft.
Garage Unfinished	493 sq. ft.
Dimensions	42'x54'
Foundation	Basement Crawlspace Slab
Bedrooms	2
Full Baths	2
Max Ridge Height	19'7"
Roof Framing	Stick
Exterior Walls	2x4, 2x6

* Alternate foundation options available at an additional charge. Please call 1-800-235-5700 for more information.

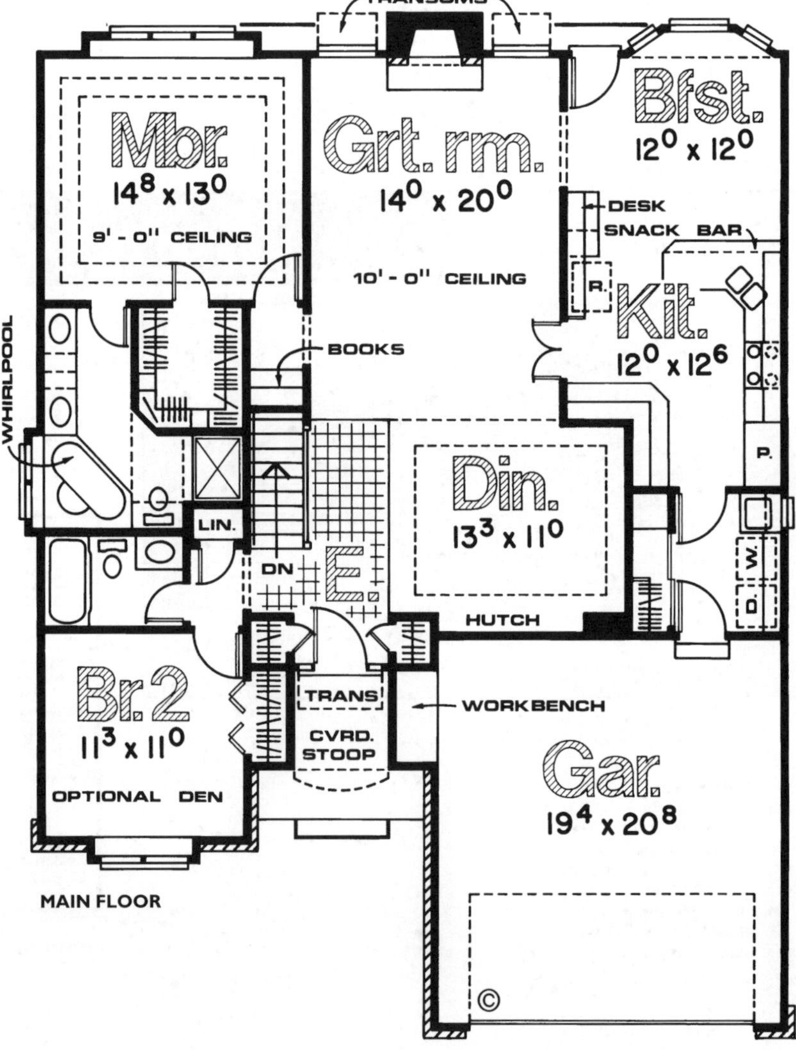

TRANSOMS
Mbr.
14^8 x 13^0
9' - 0" CEILING
Grt. rm.
14^0 x 20^0
10' - 0" CEILING
Bfst.
12^0 x 12^0
DESK
SNACK BAR
R.
Kit.
12^0 x 12^6
P.
BOOKS
WHIRLPOOL
LIN.
Din.
13^3 x 11^0
HUTCH
DN
E.
W.
D.
Br. 2
11^3 x 11^0
OPTIONAL DEN
TRANS
CVRD. STOOP
WORKBENCH
Gar.
19^4 x 20^8
©
MAIN FLOOR

Design 69024

Units	Single
Price Code	A
Total Finished	1,501 sq. ft.
Main Finished	1,501 sq. ft.
Dimensions	48'x64'
Foundation	Basement Crawlspace Slab
Bedrooms	3
Full Baths	2

Hot New Design

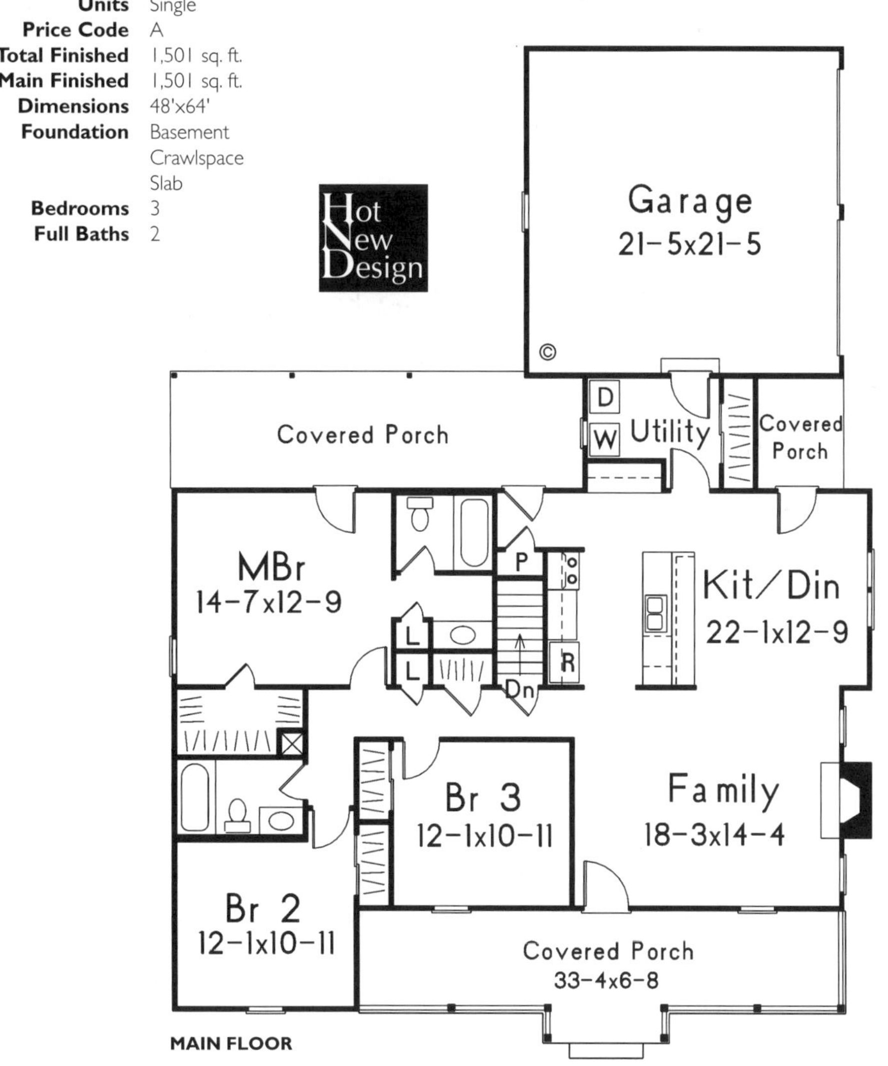
Garage
21-5x21-5
©
Covered Porch
D
W
Utility
Covered Porch
MBr
14-7x12-9
P
Kit/Din
22-1x12-9
L
L
R
Dn
Br 3
12-1x10-11
Family
18-3x14-4
Br 2
12-1x10-11
Covered Porch
33-4x6-8

MAIN FLOOR

Design 98441

FILES AVAILABLE
CAD
For more information call
800-235-5700

Units	Single
Price Code	B
Total Finished	1,502 sq. ft.
Main Finished	1,502 sq. ft.
Basement Unfinished	1,555 sq. ft.
Garage Unfinished	448 sq. ft.
Dimensions	51'x50'6"
Foundation	Basement Crawlspace
Bedrooms	3
Full Baths	2
Max Ridge Height	24'9"
Roof Framing	Stick
Exterior Walls	2x4

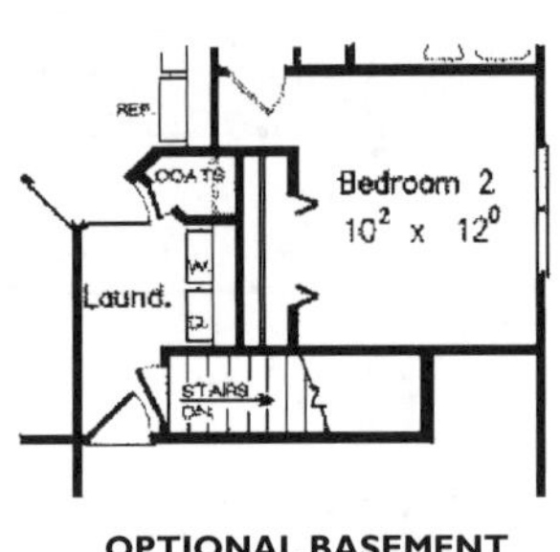
Bedroom 2
10² x 12⁰
COATS
Laund.
STAIRS DN.

OPTIONAL BASEMENT STAIR LOCATION

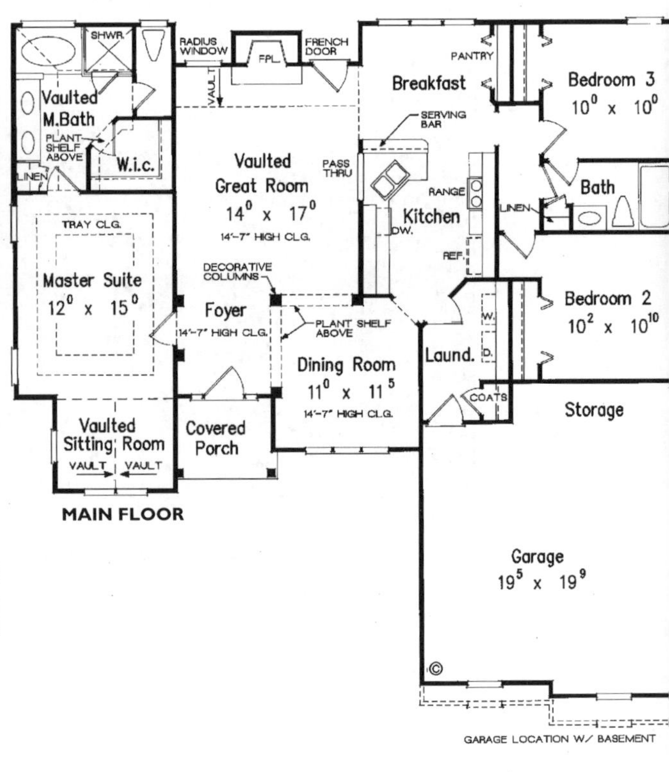
SHWR.
RADIUS WINDOW
FRENCH DOOR
FPL.
VAULT
PANTRY
Breakfast
Bedroom 3
10⁰ x 10⁰
Vaulted M.Bath
PLANT SHELF ABOVE
W.i.c.
LINEN
Vaulted Great Room
14⁰ x 17⁰
14'-7" HIGH CLG.
SERVING BAR
PASS THRU
RANGE
Kitchen
DW.
Bath
LINEN
REF.
TRAY CLG.
Master Suite
12⁰ x 15⁰
DECORATIVE COLUMNS
Foyer
14'-7" HIGH CLG.
PLANT SHELF ABOVE
Dining Room
11⁰ x 11⁵
14'-7" HIGH CLG.
Laund.
Bedroom 2
10² x 10¹⁰
COATS
Storage
Vaulted Sitting Room
VAULT
VAULT
Covered Porch
MAIN FLOOR
Garage
19⁵ x 19⁹
GARAGE LOCATION W/ BASEMENT

Design 24326

Units	Single
Price Code	B
Total Finished	1,505 sq. ft.
First Finished	692 sq. ft.
Second Finished	813 sq. ft.
Basement Unfinished	699 sq. ft.
Garage Unfinished	484 sq. ft.
Dimensions	42'x34'4"
Foundation	Basement Crawlspace Slab
Bedrooms	4
Full Baths	1
3/4 Baths	1
Half Baths	1
First Ceiling	8'
Second Ceiling	8'
Max Ridge Height	26'
Roof Framing	Stick
Exterior Walls	2x6

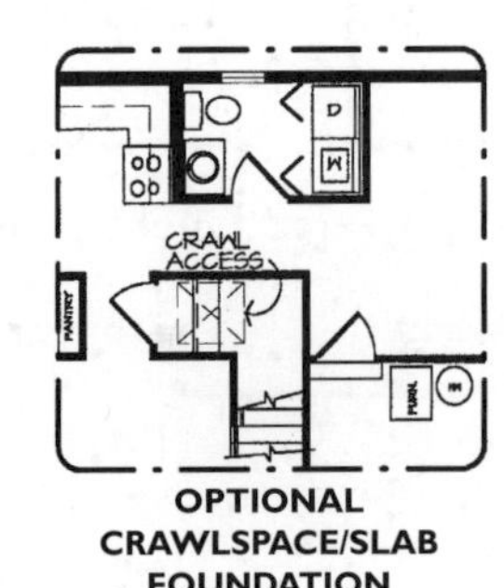
CRAWL ACCESS
PANTRY

OPTIONAL CRAWLSPACE/SLAB FOUNDATION

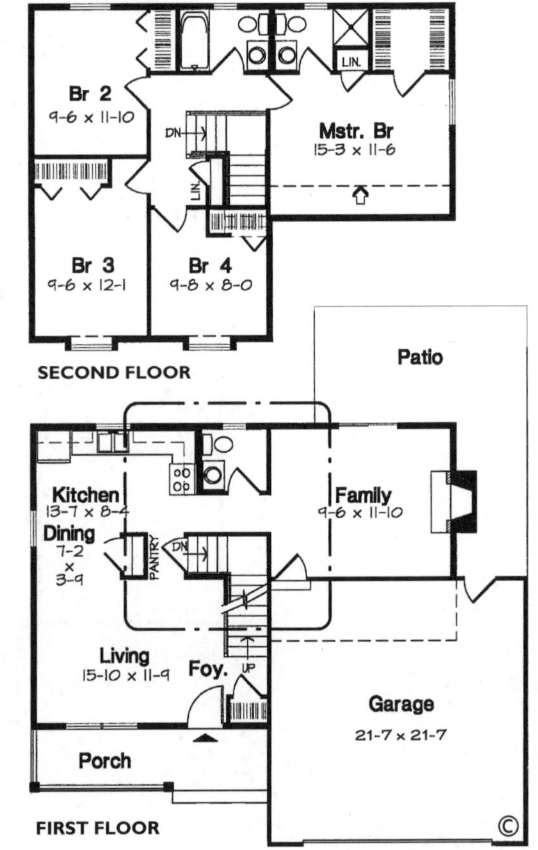
LIN.
Br 2
9-6 x 11-10
DN
Mstr. Br
15-3 x 11-6
LIN.
Br 3
9-6 x 12-1
Br 4
9-8 x 8-0
SECOND FLOOR
Patio
Kitchen
13-7 x 8-4
Family
9-6 x 11-10
Dining
7-2 x 3-9
PANTRY
DN
Living
15-10 x 11-9
Foy.
UP
Garage
21-7 x 21-7
Porch
FIRST FLOOR

Design 98463

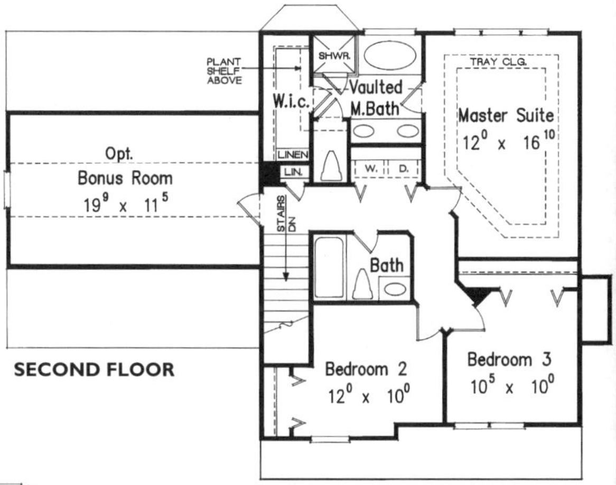

SECOND FLOOR

FIRST FLOOR

Units	Single
Price Code	B
Total Finished	1,505 sq. ft.
First Finished	767 sq. ft.
Second Finished	738 sq. ft.
Bonus Unfinished	240 sq. ft.
Basement Unfinished	767 sq. ft.
Garage Unfinished	480 sq. ft.
Dimensions	47'10"x36'
Foundation	Basement Crawlspace
Bedrooms	3
Full Baths	2
Half Baths	1
Max Ridge Height	29'5"
Roof Framing	Stick
Exterior Walls	2x4

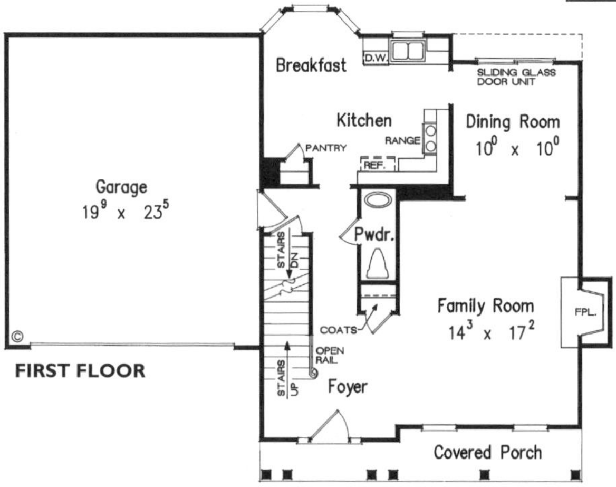

Design 92442

Units	Single
Price Code	B
Total Finished	1,507 sq. ft.
Main Finished	1,507 sq. ft.
Dimensions	50'x30'
Foundation	Basement
Bedrooms	3
Full Baths	2
Roof Framing	Stick
Exterior Walls	2x4

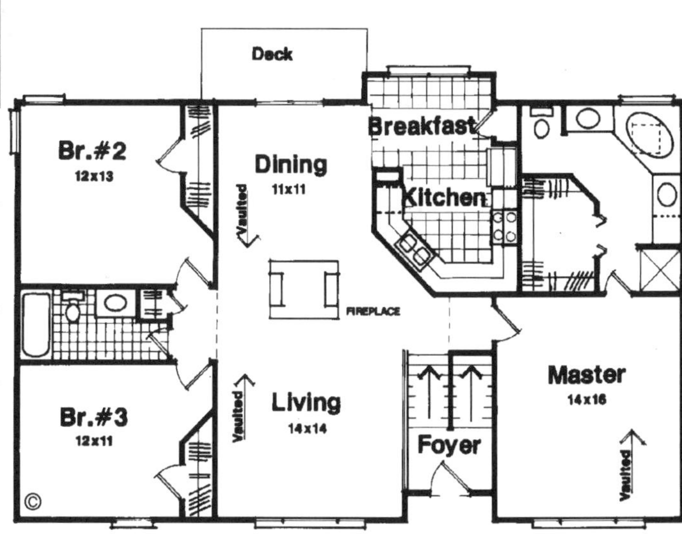
Deck
Br.#2
12x13
Dining
11x11
Vaulted
Breakfast
Kitchen
FIREPLACE
Br.#3
12x11
Living
14x14
Vaulted
Foyer
Master
14x16
Vaulted

MAIN FLOOR

Design 92649

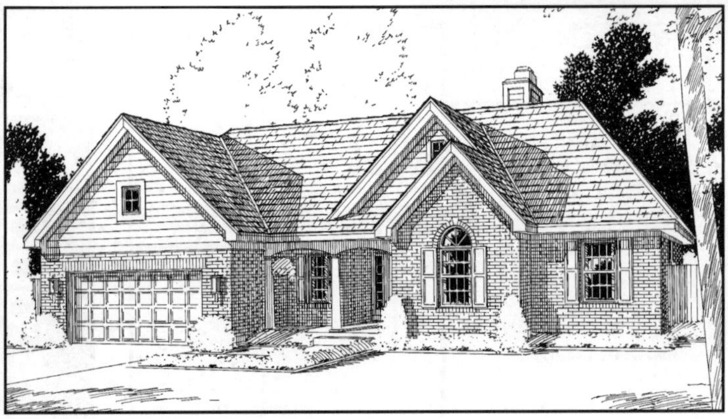

Units	Single
Price Code	B
Total Finished	1,508 sq. ft.
Main Finished	1,508 sq. ft.
Basement Unfinished	1,439 sq. ft.
Garage Unfinished	440 sq. ft.
Dimensions	60'x47'
Foundation	Basement
Bedrooms	3
Full Baths	2
Main Ceiling	8'
Max Ridge Height	21'9"
Roof Framing	Truss
Exterior Walls	2x4

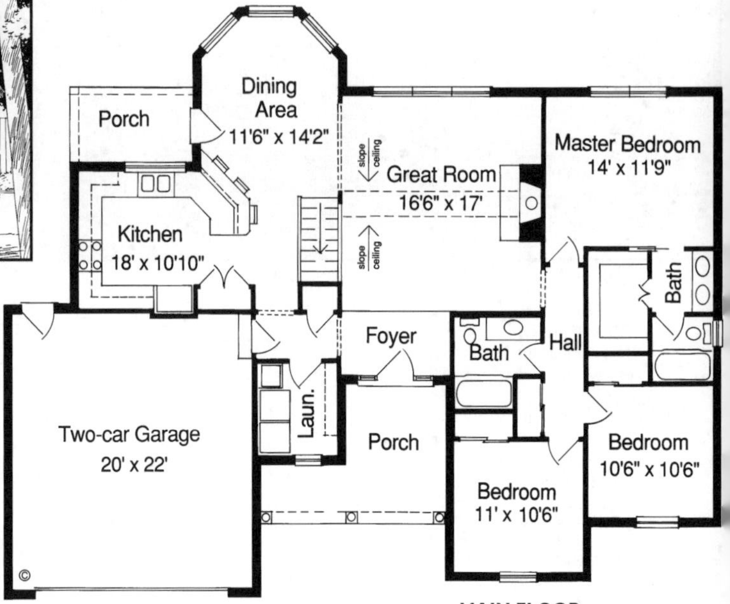

Porch
Dining Area 11'6" x 14'2"
Great Room 16'6" x 17'
Master Bedroom 14' x 11'9"
Kitchen 18' x 10'10"
Bath
Foyer
Bath
Hall
Laun.
Two-car Garage 20' x 22'
Porch
Bedroom 10'6" x 10'6"
Bedroom 11' x 10'6"

MAIN FLOOR

Design 91474

Units	Single
Price Code	B
Total Finished	1,512 sq. ft.
Main Finished	1,512 sq. ft.
Garage Unfinished	476 sq. ft.
Dimensions	40'x57'10"
Foundation	Crawlspace
Bedrooms	3
Full Baths	1
3/4 Baths	1
Main Ceiling	8'
Max Ridge Height	21'6"
Roof Framing	Truss
Exterior Walls	2x6

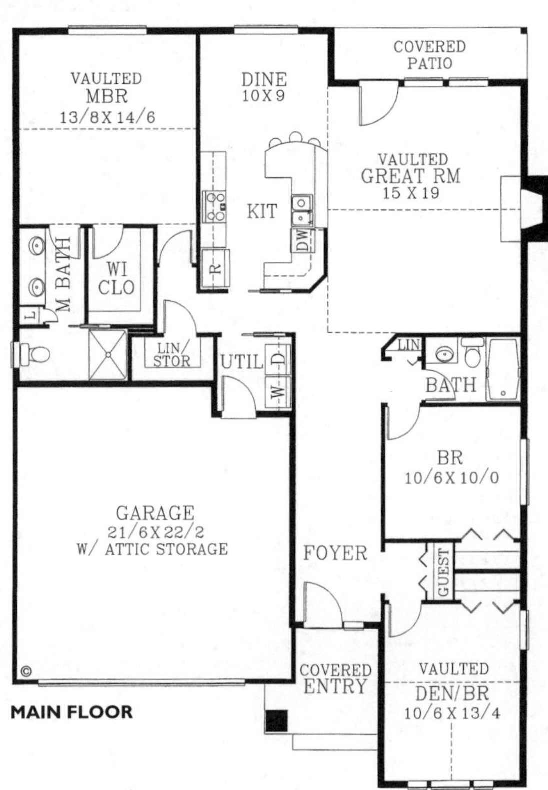
VAULTED MBR 13/8X14/6
DINE 10X9
COVERED PATIO
VAULTED GREAT RM 15 X 19
KIT
M BATH
WI CLO
LIN/STOR
UTIL
LIN
BATH
BR 10/6X10/0
GARAGE 21/6X22/2 W/ ATTIC STORAGE
FOYER
GUEST
COVERED ENTRY
VAULTED DEN/BR 10/6X13/4

MAIN FLOOR

Design 98984

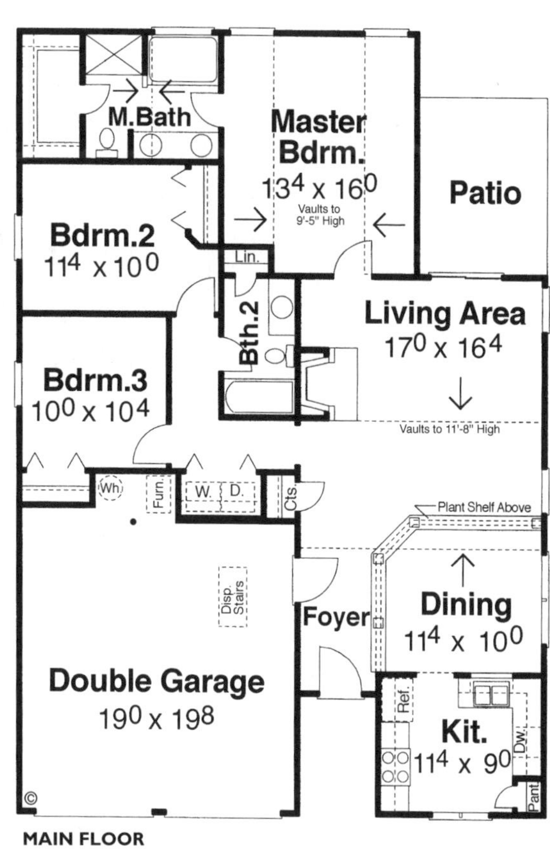
M.Bath
Master Bdrm.
13⁴ x 16⁰
Vaults to 9'-5" High
Patio
Bdrm.2
11⁴ x 10⁰
Lin.
Bth.2
Living Area
17⁰ x 16⁴
Vaults to 11'-8" High
Bdrm.3
10⁰ x 10⁴
Wh.
Furn.
W.
D.
Cts.
Plant Shelf Above
Disp. Stairs
Foyer
Dining
11⁴ x 10⁰
Double Garage
19⁰ x 19⁸
Ref.
Kit.
11⁴ x 9⁰
Dw.
Pant
MAIN FLOOR

Units	Single
Price Code	B
Total Finished	1,514 sq. ft.
Main Finished	1,514 sq. ft.
Garage Unfinished	406 sq. ft.
Dimensions	37'x61'
Foundation	Basement Slab
Bedrooms	3
Full Baths	2
Main Ceiling	8'
Max Ridge Height	25'
Roof Framing	Stick
Exterior Walls	2x4

Design 65198

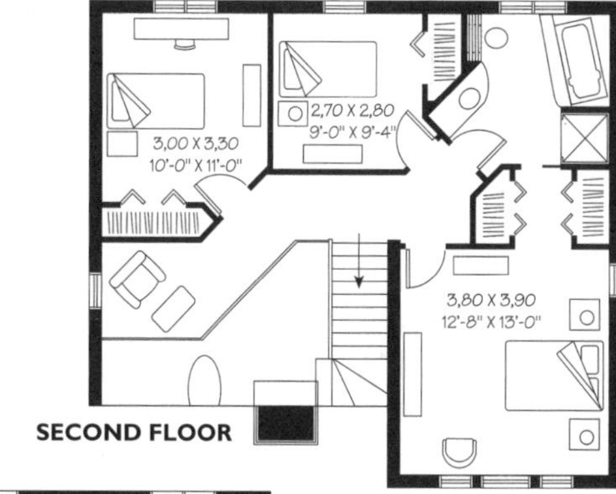
3,00 X 3,30
10'-0" X 11'-0"
2,70 X 2,80
9'-0" X 9'-4"
3,80 X 3,90
12'-8" X 13'-0"
SECOND FLOOR

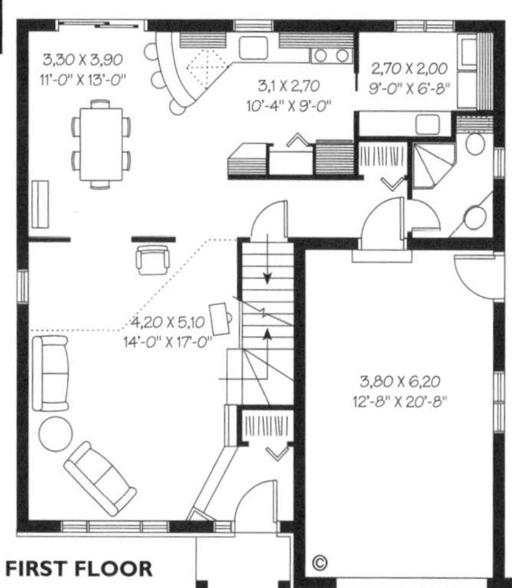
3,30 X 3,90
11'-0" X 13'-0"
3,1 X 2,70
10'-4" X 9'-0"
2,70 X 2,00
9'-0" X 6'-8"
4,20 X 5,10
14'-0" X 17'-0"
3,80 X 6,20
12'-8" X 20'-8"
FIRST FLOOR

Units	Single
Price Code	B
Total Finished	1,519 sq. ft.
First Finished	788 sq. ft.
Second Finished	731 sq. ft.
Garage Unfinished	266 sq. ft.
Dimensions	32'x36'
Foundation	Basement
Bedrooms	3
Full Baths	1
3/4 Baths	1

Design 94650

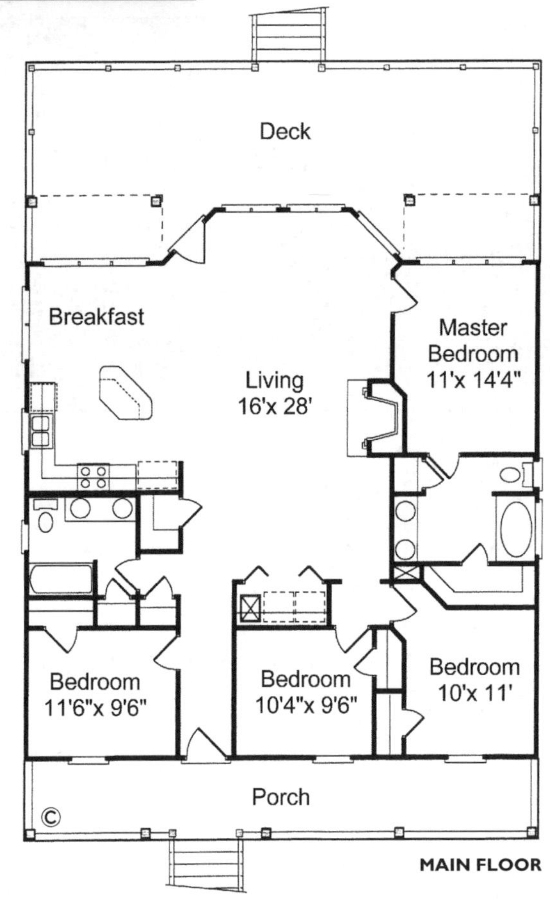

Deck
Breakfast
Living
16'x 28'
Master Bedroom
11'x 14'4"
Bedroom
11'6"x 9'6"
Bedroom
10'4"x 9'6"
Bedroom
10'x 11'
Porch
©
MAIN FLOOR

Units	Single
Price Code	B
Total Finished	1,520 sq. ft.
Main Finished	1,520 sq. ft.
Dimensions	40'x59'
Foundation	Pier/Post
Bedrooms	4
Full Baths	2
Main Ceiling	9'
Max Ridge Height	32'
Roof Framing	Stick
Exterior Walls	2x4

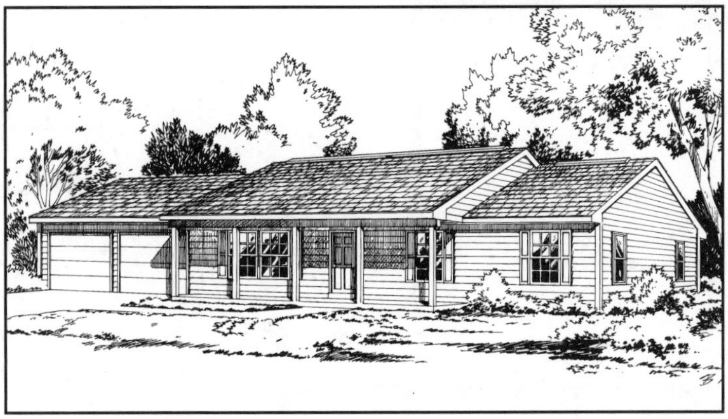

Design 34055

Dining
11-6 x 13-6
pantry
Br 4
12 x 11-2
F

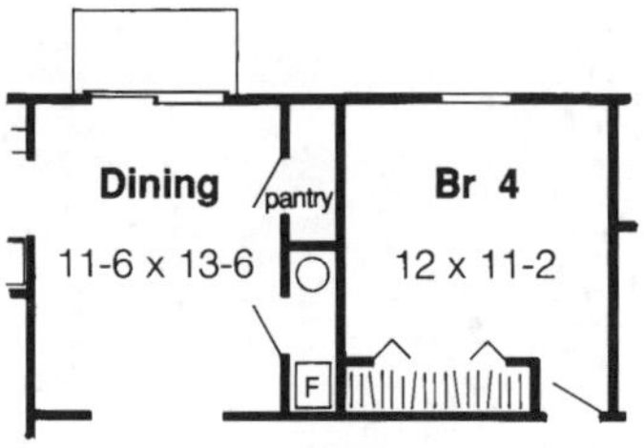

OPTIONAL CRAWLSPACE/ SLAB FOUNDATION

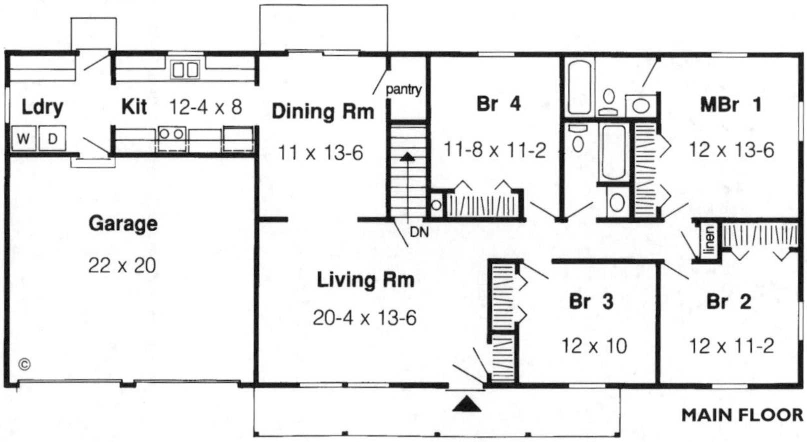

Units	Single
Price Code	B
Total Finished	1,527 sq. ft.
Main Finished	1,527 sq. ft.
Basement Unfinished	1,344 sq. ft.
Garage Unfinished	425 sq. ft.
Dimensions	70'x28'
Foundation	Basement Crawlspace Slab
Bedrooms	4
Full Baths	2
Max Ridge Height	18'
Roof Framing	Stick
Exterior Walls	2x4, 2x6

Ldry
W D
Kit 12-4 x 8
Dining Rm
11 x 13-6
pantry
Br 4
11-8 x 11-2
MBr 1
12 x 13-6
linen
Garage
22 x 20
DN
Living Rm
20-4 x 13-6
Br 3
12 x 10
Br 2
12 x 11-2
©

MAIN FLOOR

Design 69142

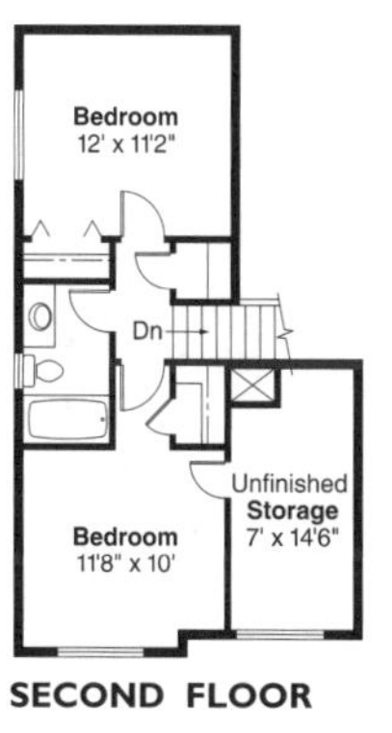
Bedroom
12' x 11'2"
Dn
Unfinished
Storage
7' x 14'6"
Bedroom
11'8" x 10'

SECOND FLOOR

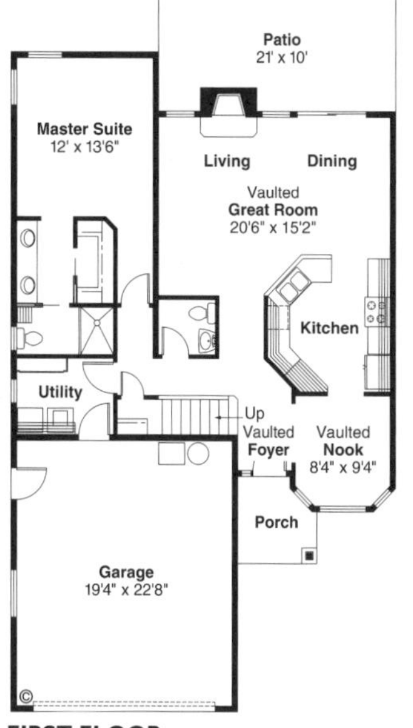
Patio
21' x 10'
Master Suite
12' x 13'6"
Living
Dining
Vaulted
Great Room
20'6" x 15'2"
Kitchen
Utility
Up
Vaulted
Foyer
Vaulted
Nook
8'4" x 9'4"
Porch
Garage
19'4" x 22'8"

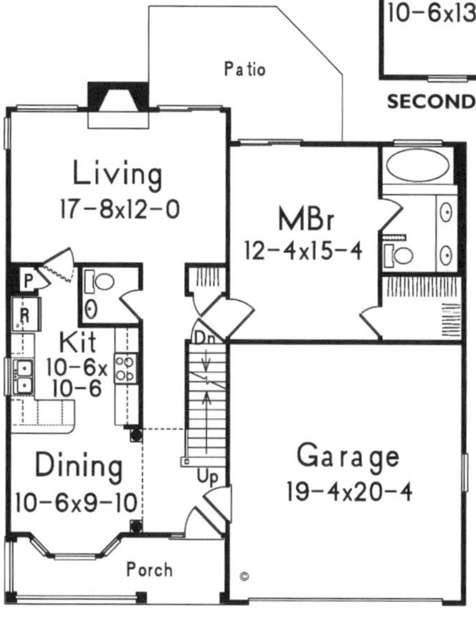

FIRST FLOOR

Units	Single
Price Code	B
Total Finished	1,528 sq. ft.
First Finished	1,095 sq. ft.
Second Finished	433 sq. ft.
Bonus Unfinished	116 sq. ft.
Garage Unfinished	458 sq. ft.
Dimensions	34'x56'
Foundation	Crawlspace
Bedrooms	3
Full Baths	1
3/4 Baths	1
Half Baths	1
First Ceiling	8'
Max Ridge Height	23'
Roof Framing	Truss
Exterior Walls	2x6

Design 69029

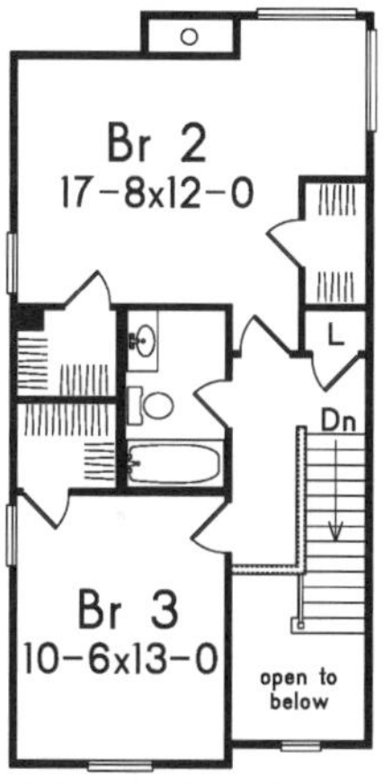

Units	Single
Price Code	B
Total Finished	1,524 sq. ft.
First Finished	951 sq. ft.
Second Finished	573 sq. ft.
Dimensions	38'x39'4"
Foundation	Basement
Bedrooms	3
Full Baths	2
Half Baths	1

Hot New Design

Br 2
17-8x12-0
L
Dn
Br 3
10-6x13-0
open to below

SECOND FLOOR

Patio
Living
17-8x12-0
MBr
12-4x15-4
P
R
Kit
10-6x
10-6
Dn
Garage
19-4x20-4
Dining
10-6x9-10
Up
Porch

FIRST FLOOR

Design 82033

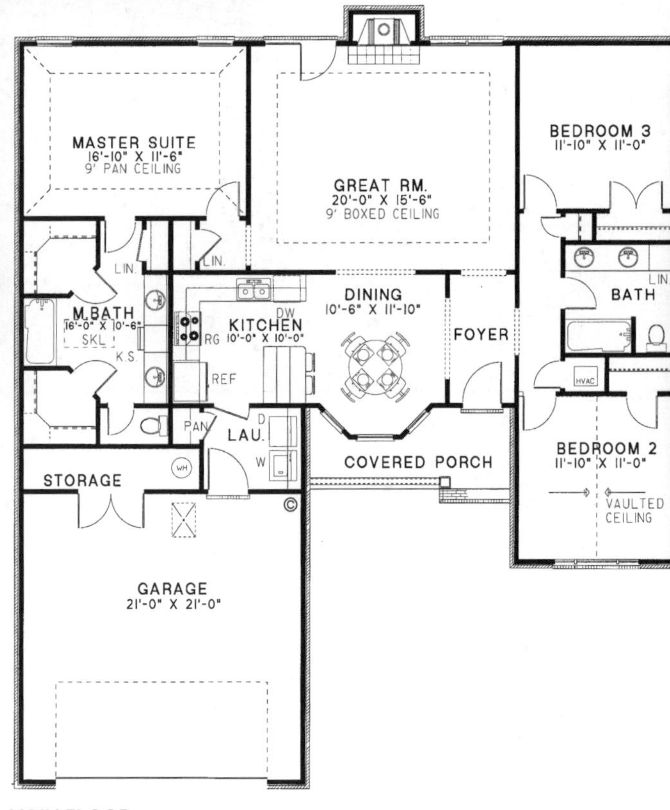
MASTER SUITE
16'-10" X 11'-6"
9' PAN CEILING
GREAT RM.
20'-0" X 15'-6"
9' BOXED CEILING
BEDROOM 3
11'-10" X 11'-0"
LIN.
M.BATH
16'-0" X 10'-6"
SKL
K.S.
KITCHEN
10'-0" X 10'-0"
RG
DW
REF
DINING
10'-6" X 11'-10"
FOYER
BATH
HVAC
PAN
LAU.
D
W
WH
STORAGE
COVERED PORCH
BEDROOM 2
11'-10" X 11'-0"
VAULTED CEILING
GARAGE
21'-0" X 21'-0"

MAIN FLOOR

Units	Single
Price Code	B
Total Finished	1,538 sq. ft.
Main Finished	1,538 sq. ft.
Garage Unfinished	441 sq. ft.
Porch Unfinished	142 sq. ft.
Dimensions	50'x56'
Foundation	Basement Crawlspace Slab
Bedrooms	3
Full Baths	2
Main Ceiling	8'
Roof Framing	Stick
Exterior Walls	2x4

Design 97261

Breakfast
FPL.
FRENCH DOOR
TUB
M.Bath
TRAY CLG.
Master Suite
12^3x16^0
SERVING BAR
RANGE
Kitchen
D.W.
REF.
PANTRY
VAULT
Vaulted Family Room
13^0x 17^6
Bath
LINEN
W.i.c.
OPEN RAIL
COATS
Dining Room
11^6x 12^8
STAIRS DN
STAIRS UP
Foyer
Bedroom 2
11^0x10^0
Bedroom 3
11^3x10^6

MAIN FLOOR

Units	Single
Price Code	B
Total Finished	1,538 sq. ft.
Main Finished	1,466 sq. ft.
Lower Finished	72 sq. ft.
Basement Unfinished	902 sq. ft.
Garage Unfinished	495 sq. ft.
Dimensions	44'x36'6"
Foundation	Basement
Bedrooms	3
Full Baths	2
Main Ceiling	8'
Max Ridge Height	24'
Roof Framing	Stick
Exterior Walls	2x4

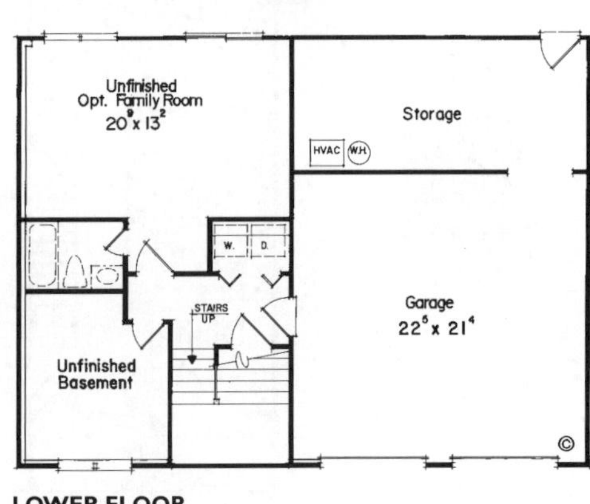
Unfinished
Opt. Family Room
20^9x 13^2
Storage
HVAC
W.H.
W.
D.
STAIRS UP
Unfinished Basement
Garage
22^5x 21^4

LOWER FLOOR

Design 24721

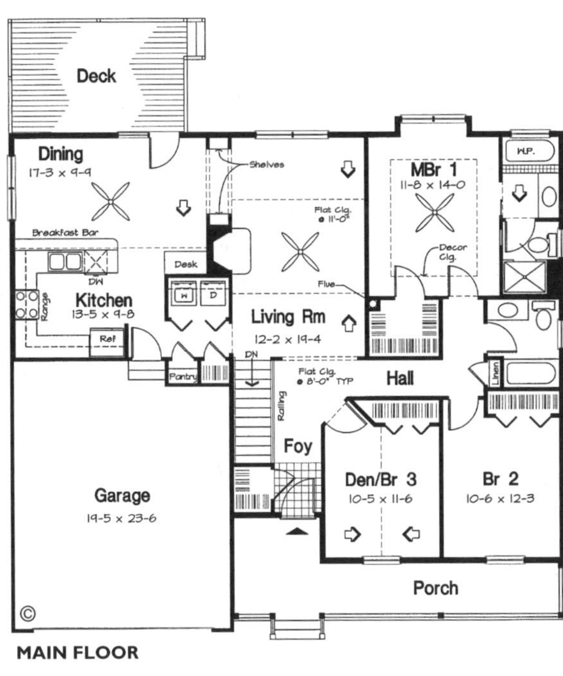
Deck
Dining
17-3 x 9-9
Breakfast Bar
DW
Kitchen
13-5 x 9-8
Range
Ref
Desk
W
D
Pantry
Shelves
Flat Clg. @ 11'-0"
Flue
Living Rm
12-2 x 19-4
Flat Clg. @ 8'-0" TYP
DN
Railing
Foy
MBr 1
11-8 x 14-0
Decor Clg.
W.P.
Linen
Hall
Den/Br 3
10-5 x 11-6
Br 2
10-6 x 12-3
Garage
19-5 x 23-6
Porch
©
MAIN FLOOR

Units	Single
Price Code	B
Total Finished	1,539 sq. ft.
Main Finished	1,539 sq. ft.
Basement Unfinished	1,530 sq. ft.
Garage Unfinished	460 sq. ft.
Deck Unfinished	160 sq. ft.
Porch Unfinished	182 sq. ft.
Dimensions	50'x45'4"
Foundation	Basement Crawlspace Slab
Bedrooms	3
Full Baths	2
Main Ceiling	8'
Max Ridge Height	21'
Roof Framing	Stick
Exterior Walls	2x6

Design 10748

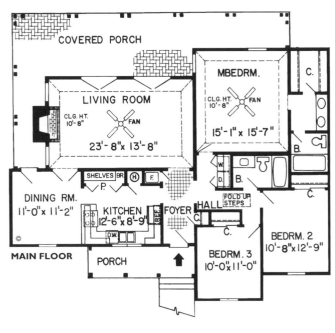

Units	Single
Price Code	B
Total Finished	1,540 sq. ft.
Main Finished	1,540 sq. ft.
Porch Unfinished	530 sq. ft.
Dimensions	52'x45'
Foundation	Slab Post/Pier
Bedrooms	3
Full Baths	2
Max Ridge Height	21'
Roof Framing	Stick
Exterior Walls	2x6

COVERED PORCH
LIVING ROOM
CLG. HT. 10'-8"
FAN
23'-8"x 13'-8"
MBEDRM.
CLG. HT. 10'-8"
FAN
15'-1" x 15'-7"
C.
B.
W.
D.
SHELVES
BR.
P.
H
F.
DINING RM.
11'-0"x 11'-2"
KITCHEN
12'-6"x 8'-9"
REF.
D.W.
FOYER
HALL
FOLD UP STEPS
C.
BEDRM. 2
10'-8"x 12'-9"
BEDRM. 3
10'-0"x 11'-0"
PORCH
©
MAIN FLOOR

Design 93161

Units	Single
Price Code	B
Total Finished	1,540 sq. ft.
Main Finished	1,540 sq. ft.
Basement Unfinished	1,540 sq. ft.
Dimensions	60'4"x46'
Foundation	Basement
Bedrooms	3
Full Baths	2
Main Ceiling	8'
Vaulted Ceiling	12'6"
Max Ridge Height	21'4"
Roof Framing	Stick
Exterior Walls	2x6

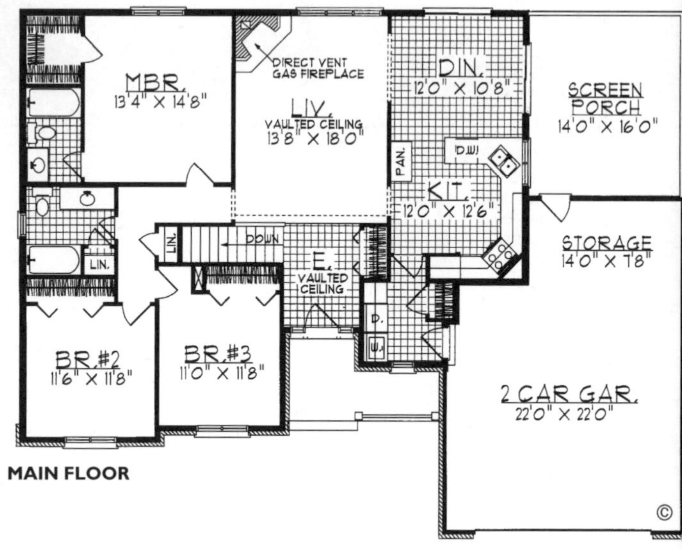

MBR.
13'4" X 14'8"
DIRECT VENT GAS FIREPLACE
LIV.
VAULTED CEILING
13'8" X 18'0"
DIN.
12'0" X 10'8"
SCREEN PORCH
14'0" X 16'0"
D.W.
PAN.
KIT.
12'0" X 12'6"
STORAGE
14'0" X 7'8"
LIN.
DOWN
E.
VAULTED CEILING
BR.#2
11'6" X 11'8"
BR.#3
11'0" X 11'8"
2 CAR GAR.
22'0" X 22'0"

MAIN FLOOR

Design 98460

CAD **FILES AVAILABLE** For more information call 800-235-5700

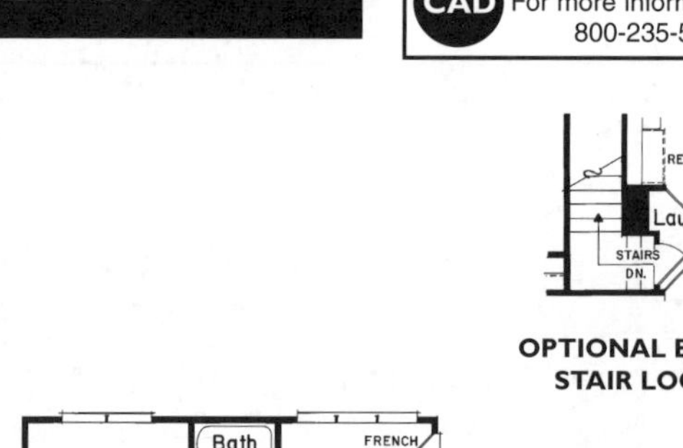

REF.
Laund.
W.
D.
PANTRY
STAIRS DN.

OPTIONAL BASEMENT STAIR LOCATION

Units	Single
Price Code	B
Total Finished	1,544 sq. ft.
Main Finished	1,544 sq. ft.
Bonus Unfinished	284 sq. ft.
Basement Unfinished	1,544 sq. ft.
Garage Unfinished	440 sq. ft.
Dimensions	54'x47'6"
Foundation	Basement Crawlspace
Bedrooms	3
Full Baths	2
Main Ceiling	9'2"
Second Ceiling	8'2"
Max Ridge Height	26'6"
Roof Framing	Stick
Exterior Walls	2x4

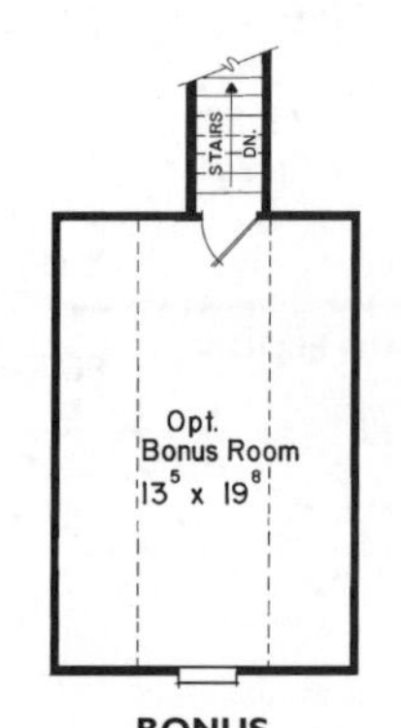

STAIRS DN.
Opt. Bonus Room
13^5 x 19^8

BONUS

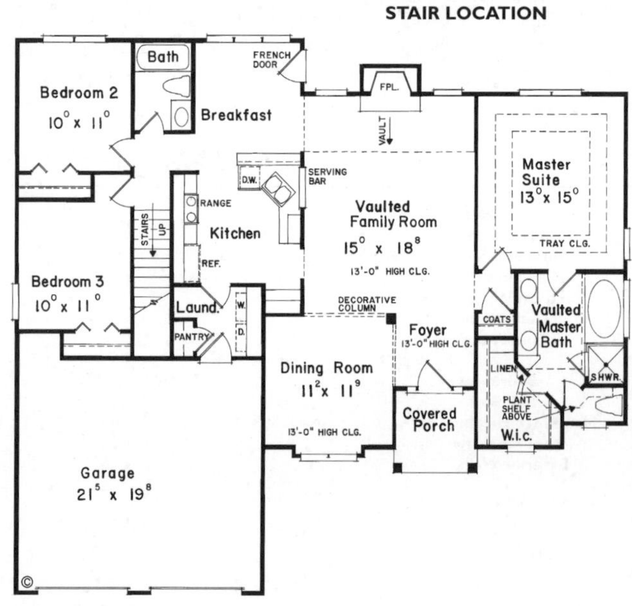

Bath
FRENCH DOOR
Bedroom 2
10^0 x 11^0
Breakfast
FPL.
VAULT
SERVING BAR
D.W.
RANGE
Kitchen
STAIRS UP
REF.
Vaulted Family Room
15^0 x 18^8
13'-0" HIGH CLG.
Master Suite
13^0x 15^0
TRAY CLG.
Bedroom 3
10^0 x 11^0
Laund.
W.
D.
PANTRY
DECORATIVE COLUMN
Foyer
13'-0" HIGH CLG.
COATS
Vaulted Master Bath
LINEN
SHWR.
PLANT SHELF ABOVE
W.i.c.
Dining Room
11^2x 11^9
13'-0" HIGH CLG.
Covered Porch
Garage
21^5 x 19^8

MAIN FLOOR

Design 94116

Units	Single
Price Code	B
Total Finished	1,546 sq. ft.
Main Finished	1,546 sq. ft.
Basement Unfinished	1,530 sq. ft.
Garage Unfinished	440 sq. ft.
Dimensions	60'x43'
Foundation	Basement
Bedrooms	3
Full Baths	1
3/4 Baths	1
Main Ceiling	9'2"
Max Ridge Height	23'
Roof Framing	Truss
Exterior Walls	2x4

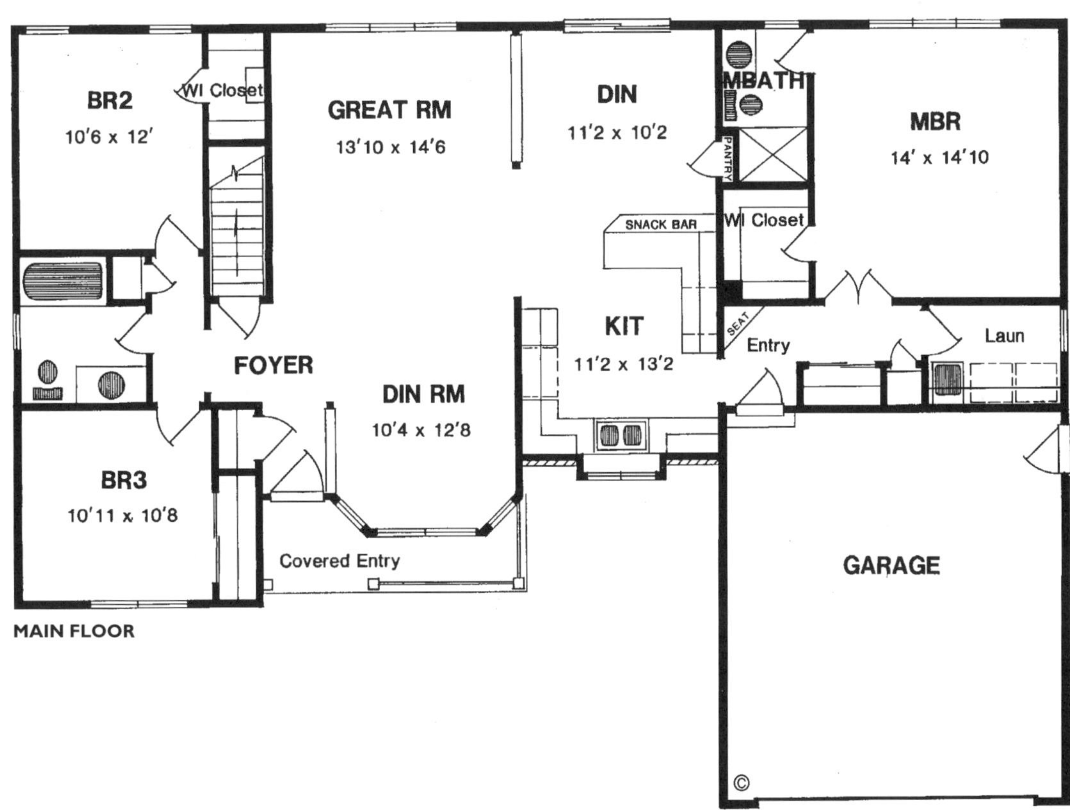
BR2
10'6 x 12'
WI Closet
GREAT RM
13'10 x 14'6
DIN
11'2 x 10'2
MBATH
PANTRY
MBR
14' x 14'10
SNACK BAR
WI Closet
KIT
11'2 x 13'2
SEAT
Entry
Laun
FOYER
DIN RM
10'4 x 12'8
BR3
10'11 x 10'8
Covered Entry
GARAGE
©

MAIN FLOOR

Design 93175

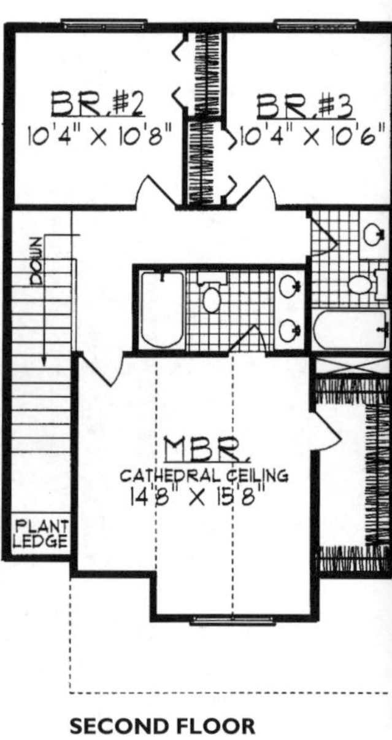
BR.#2
10'4" X 10'8"
BR.#3
10'4" X 10'6"
DOWN
MBR.
CATHEDRAL CEILING
14'8" X 15'8"
PLANT LEDGE

SECOND FLOOR

*This plan is not to be built within a 20-mile radius of Iowa City, IA.

Units	Single
Price Code	B
Total Finished	1,550 sq. ft.
First Finished	804 sq. ft.
Second Finished	746 sq. ft.
Basement Unfinished	804 sq. ft.
Dimensions	38'x38'4"
Foundation	Basement
Bedrooms	3
Full Baths	2
Half Baths	1
Max Ridge Height	26'6"
Roof Framing	Stick
Exterior Walls	2x6

DIN.
9'-1 1/8" TRAY CEILING
11'8" X 11'8"
KIT.
9'-1 1/8" TRAY CEILING
12'0" X 11'4"
DW
DIRECT VENT GAS FIREPLACE
GRT.RM.
CATHEDRAL CEILING
13'4" X 19'4"
DOWN
UP
W.
D.
PLANT BOX
PLANT BOX
E.
PLANT LEDGE ABOVE
2 CAR GAR.
20'4" X 20'0"
©

FIRST FLOOR

Design 93455

Units	Single
Price Code	B
Total Finished	1,550 sq. ft.
Main Finished	1,550 sq. ft.
Garage Unfinished	548 sq. ft.
Dimensions	68'3"x73'8"
Foundation	Crawlspace Slab
Bedrooms	3
Full Baths	2
Max Ridge Height	19'9"
Roof Framing	Stick
Exterior Walls	2x4

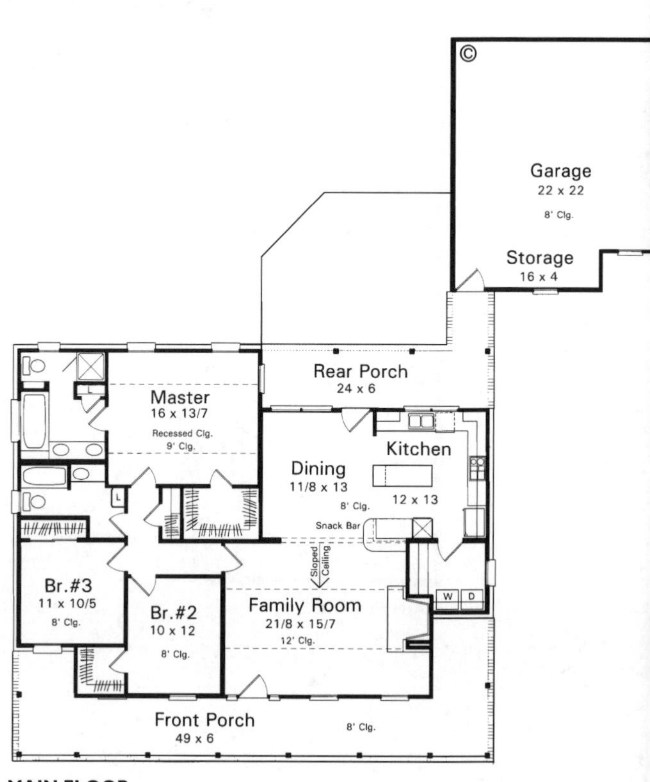
©
Garage
22 x 22
8' Clg.
Storage
16 x 4
Rear Porch
24 x 6
Master
16 x 13/7
Recessed Clg.
9' Clg.
Kitchen
12 x 13
Dining
11/8 x 13
8' Clg.
Snack Bar
Sloped Ceiling
Br.#3
11 x 10/5
8' Clg.
Br.#2
10 x 12
8' Clg.
Family Room
21/8 x 15/7
12' Clg.
W
D
Front Porch
49 x 6
8' Clg.

MAIN FLOOR

Design 90844

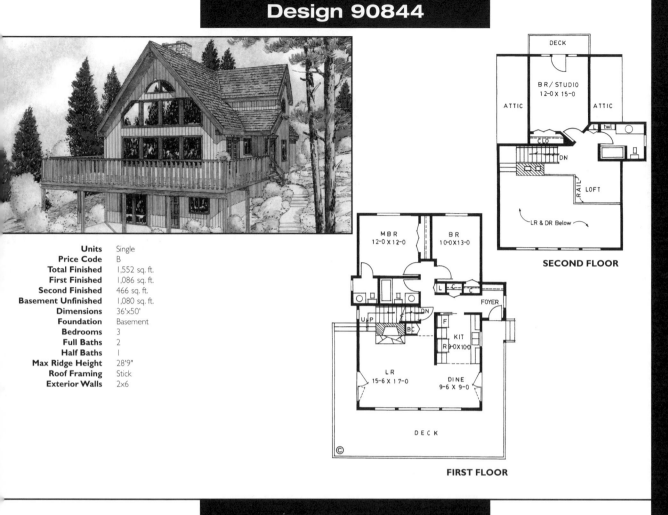

Units	Single
Price Code	B
Total Finished	1,552 sq. ft.
First Finished	1,086 sq. ft.
Second Finished	466 sq. ft.
Basement Unfinished	1,080 sq. ft.
Dimensions	36'x50'
Foundation	Basement
Bedrooms	3
Full Baths	2
Half Baths	1
Max Ridge Height	28'9"
Roof Framing	Stick
Exterior Walls	2x6

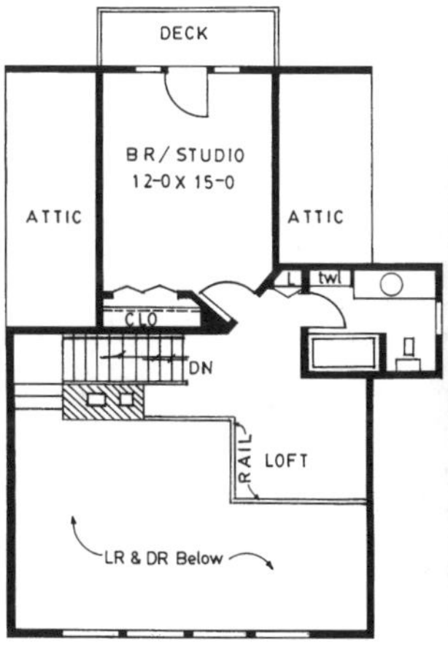

SECOND FLOOR

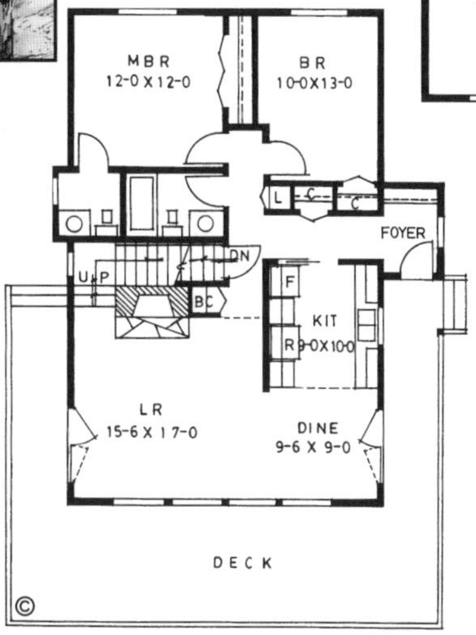

FIRST FLOOR

Design 24654

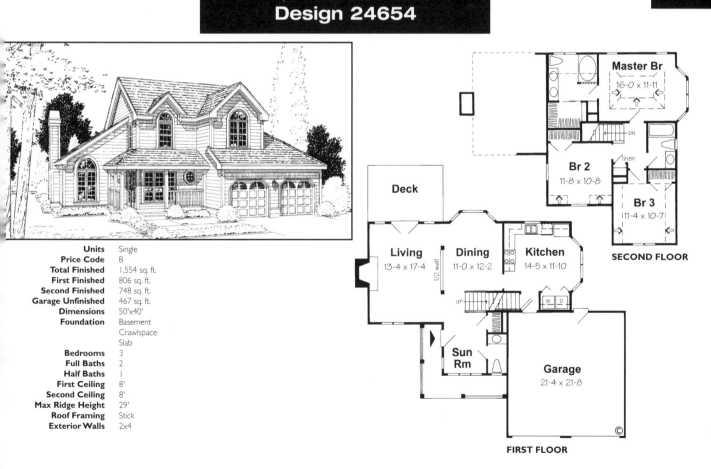

Units	Single
Price Code	B
Total Finished	1,554 sq. ft.
First Finished	806 sq. ft.
Second Finished	748 sq. ft.
Garage Unfinished	467 sq. ft.
Dimensions	50'x40'
Foundation	Basement Crawlspace Slab
Bedrooms	3
Full Baths	2
Half Baths	1
First Ceiling	8'
Second Ceiling	8'
Max Ridge Height	29'
Roof Framing	Stick
Exterior Walls	2x4

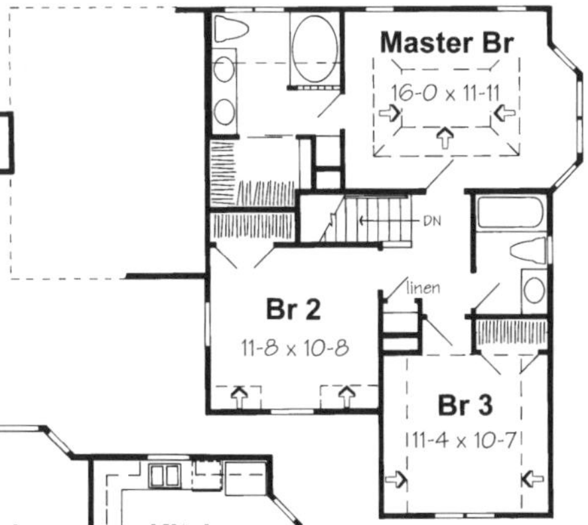

SECOND FLOOR

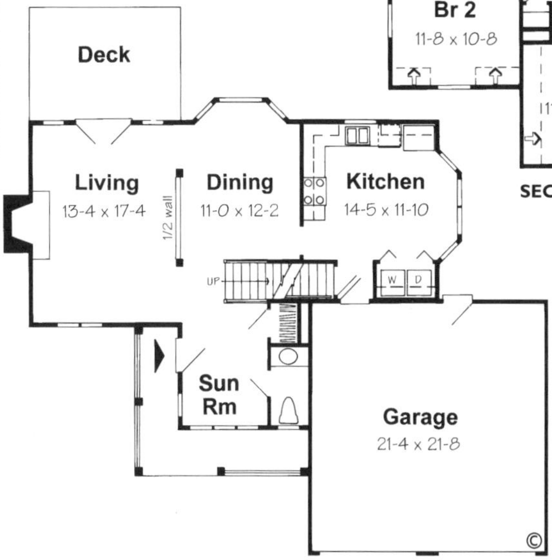

FIRST FLOOR

Design 94920

Units	Single
Price Code	B
Total Finished	1,554 sq. ft.
Main Finished	1,554 sq. ft.
Basement Unfinished	1,554 sq. ft.
Garage Unfinished	464 sq. ft.
Dimensions	50'x52'8"
Foundation	Basement
Bedrooms	2
Full Baths	2
Main Ceiling	8'
Max Ridge Height	24'
Roof Framing	Stick
Exterior Walls	2x4

* Alternate foundation options available at an additional charge. Please call 1-800-235-5700 for more information.

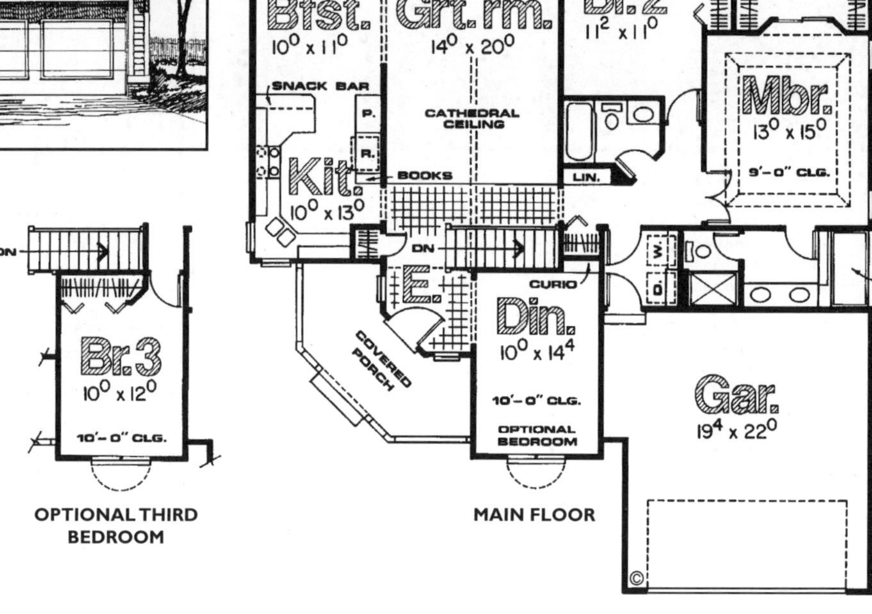

DN
Br. 3
10⁰ x 12⁰
10'-0" CLG.
OPTIONAL THIRD BEDROOM
Bfst.
10⁰ x 11⁰
SNACK BAR
P.
R.
Kit.
10⁰ x 13⁰
Grt. rm.
14⁰ x 20⁰
CATHEDRAL CEILING
BOOKS
DN
E.
COVERED PORCH
CURIO
Din.
10⁰ x 14⁴
10'-0" CLG.
OPTIONAL BEDROOM
Br. 2
11² x 11⁰
LIN.
Mbr.
13⁰ x 15⁰
9'-0" CLG.
W
D
Gar.
19⁴ x 22⁰
MAIN FLOOR

Design 92556

Units	Single
Price Code	B
Total Finished	1,556 sq. ft.
Main Finished	1,556 sq. ft.
Bonus Unfinished	282 sq. ft.
Garage Unfinished	565 sq. ft.
Porch Unfinished	108 sq. ft.
Dimensions	66'10"x50'10"
Foundation	Crawlspace Slab
Bedrooms	3
Full Baths	2
Max Ridge Height	22'6"
Roof Framing	Stick
Exterior Walls	2x4

bonus rm
12 x 16
BONUS

mbr
14 x 14
shr
lin
util 6 x 8
d w b
eating
9 x 11
por 4 x 19
br 3
12 x 11
garage
22 x 23
kit
11x11
ref
rng
dw
den
16 x 15
sto
8 x 6
dining
11 x 11
foy
por
8 x 4
br 2
11 x 11
lin
MAIN FLOOR

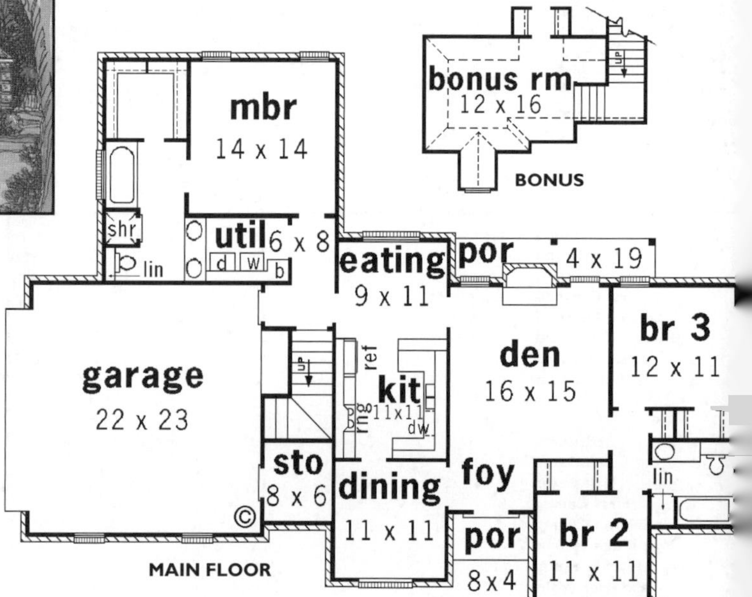

Design 99168

BR. #2
10'10" X 12'0"
LIN.
BR. #3
12'2" X 10'8"
DN

SECOND FLOOR

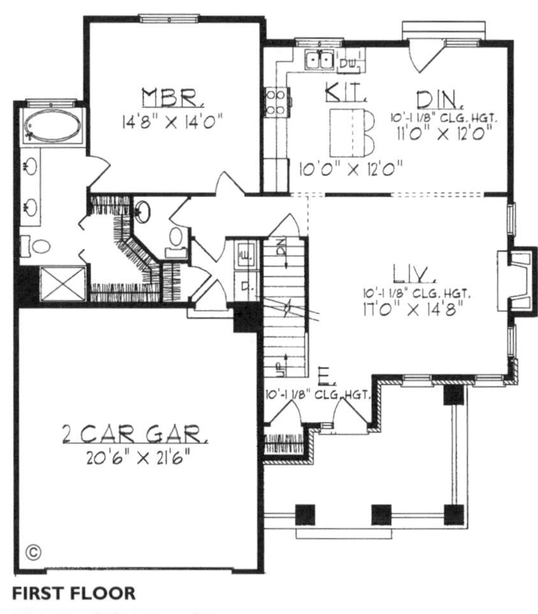

MBR.
14'8" X 14'0"
DW
KIT.
DIN.
10'-1 1/8" CLG. HGT.
11'0" X 12'0"
10'0" X 12'0"
LIV.
10'-1 1/8" CLG. HGT.
17'0" X 14'8"
E.
10'-1 1/8" CLG. HGT.
2 CAR GAR.
20'6" X 21'6"

FIRST FLOOR

Units	Single
Price Code	B
Total Finished	1,556 sq. ft.
First Finished	1,126 sq. ft.
Second Finished	430 sq. ft.
Basement Unfinished	1,126 sq. ft.
Garage Unfinished	469 sq. ft.
Dimensions	45'x46'
Foundation	Basement
Bedrooms	3
Full Baths	2
Half Baths	1
Max Ridge Height	29'8"
Roof Framing	Truss
Exterior Walls	2x6

Design 99152

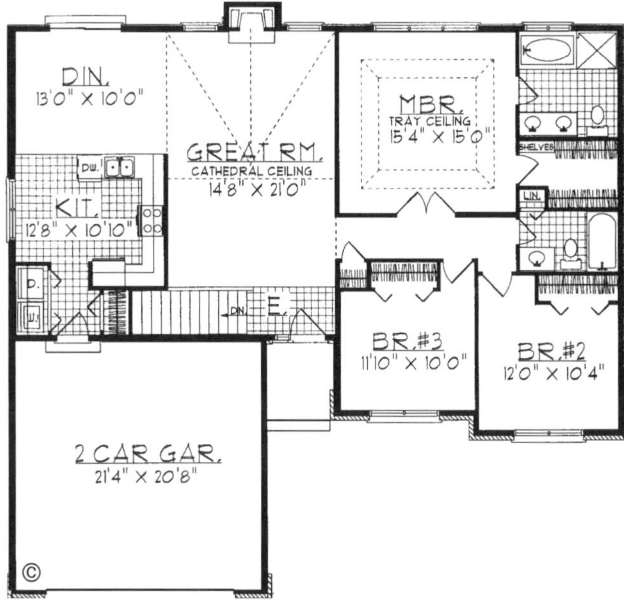

DIN.
13'0" X 10'0"
GREAT RM.
CATHEDRAL CEILING
14'8" X 21'0"
MBR.
TRAY CEILING
15'4" X 15'0"
SHELVES
LIN.
DW
KIT.
12'8" X 10'10"
DN
E.
BR.#3
11'10" X 10'0"
BR.#2
12'0" X 10'4"
2 CAR GAR.
21'4" X 20'8"

MAIN FLOOR

Units	Single
Price Code	B
Total Finished	1,557 sq. ft.
Main Finished	1,557 sq. ft.
Basement Unfinished	1,557 sq. ft.
Garage Unfinished	440 sq. ft.
Dimensions	53'x49'
Foundation	Basement
Bedrooms	3
Full Baths	2
Max Ridge Height	21'
Roof Framing	Truss
Exterior Walls	2x4

Design 63088

Units	Single
Price Code	B
Total Finished	1,558 sq. ft.
Main Finished	1,558 sq. ft.
Garage Unfinished	413 sq. ft.
Dimensions	50'x45'
Foundation	Slab
Bedrooms	3
Full Baths	2
Main Ceiling	10'-14'6"
Max Ridge Height	21'
Roof Framing	Truss
Exterior Walls	2x4

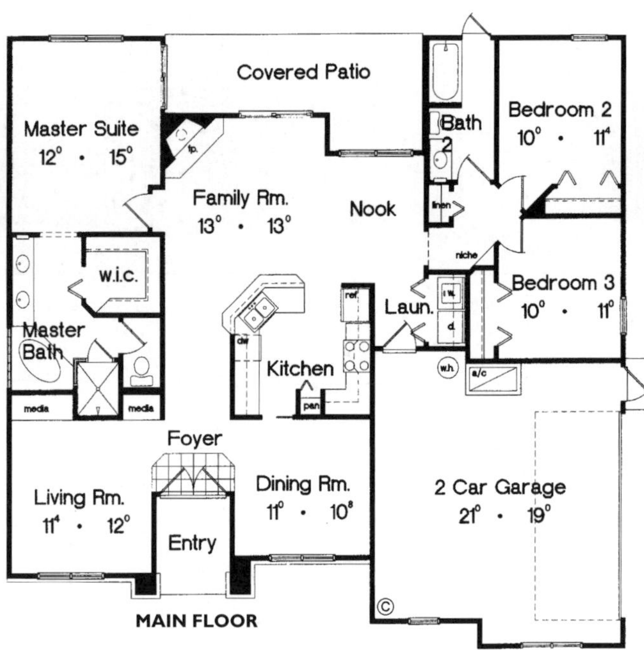

Covered Patio
Master Suite
12^{0} · 15^{0}
fp.
Family Rm.
13^{0} · 13^{0}
Nook
Bath 2
Bedroom 2
10^{0} · 11^{4}
linen
niche
Bedroom 3
10^{0} · 11^{0}
w.i.c.
Master Bath
media
media
dw
Kitchen
ref.
pan
Laun.
w.h.
a/c
Foyer
Living Rm.
11^{4} · 12^{0}
Entry
Dining Rm.
11^{0} · 10^{8}
2 Car Garage
21^{0} · 19^{0}
©

MAIN FLOOR

Design 34602

Units	Single
Price Code	B
Total Finished	1,560 sq. ft.
First Finished	1,061 sq. ft.
Second Finished	499 sq. ft.
Basement Unfinished	1,061 sq. ft.
Porch Unfinished	339 sq. ft.
Dimensions	44'x34'
Foundation	Basement Crawlspace Slab
Bedrooms	3
Full Baths	2
Half Baths	1
First Ceiling	8'
Second Ceiling	8'
Max Ridge Height	26'
Roof Framing	Stick
Exterior Walls	2x4, 2x6

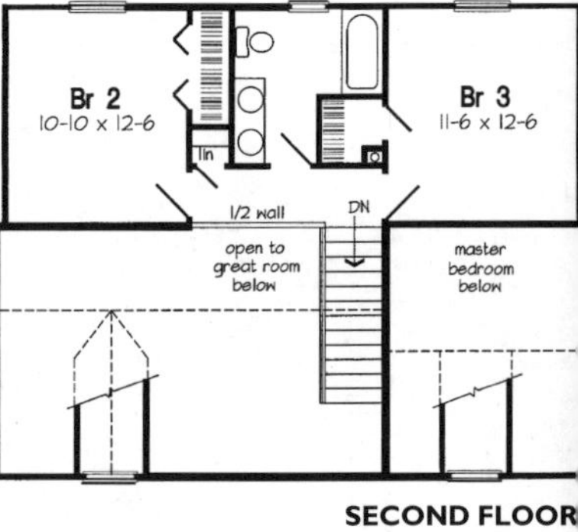

Br 2
10-10 x 12-6
Br 3
11-6 x 12-6
lin
1/2 wall
DN
open to great room below
master bedroom below

SECOND FLOOR

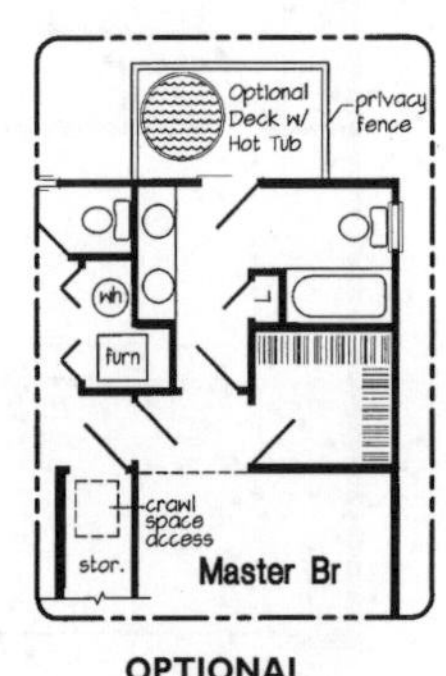

Optional Deck w/ Hot Tub
privacy fence
wh
furn
crawl space access
stor.
Master Br

OPTIONAL CRAWLSPACE/SLAB FOUNDATION

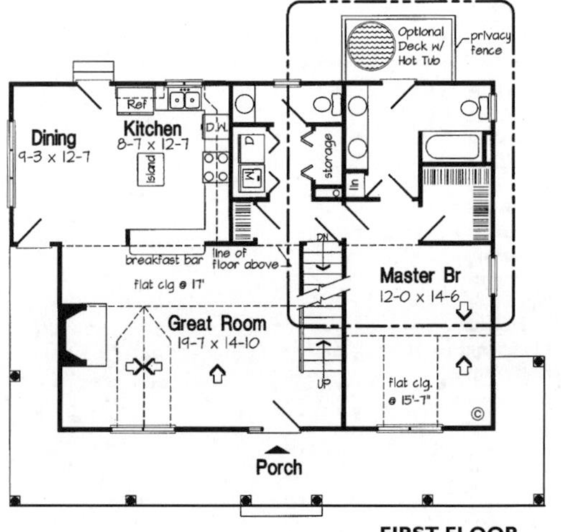

Optional Deck w/ Hot Tub
privacy fence
Ref
Dining
9-3 x 12-7
Kitchen
8-7 x 12-7
island
storage
lin
breakfast bar
line of floor above
Flat clg @ 17'
Great Room
19-7 x 14-10
Master Br
12-0 x 14-6
DN
UP
Flat clg. @ 15'-7"
Porch
©

FIRST FLOOR

 To order blueprints, call **800-235-5700** or visit us on the web, **familyhomeplans.com**

Design 24705

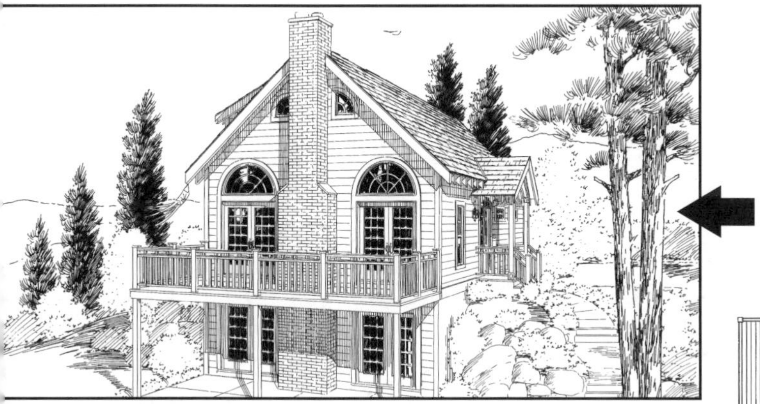

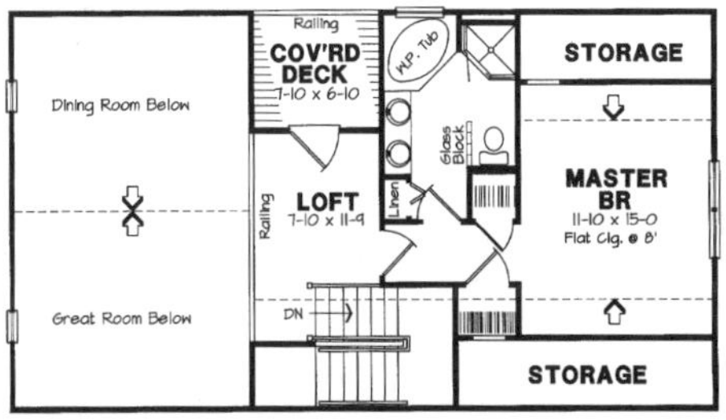

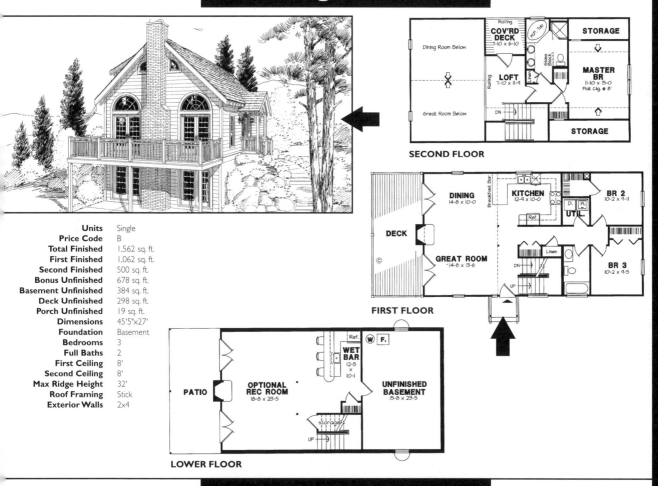

SECOND FLOOR

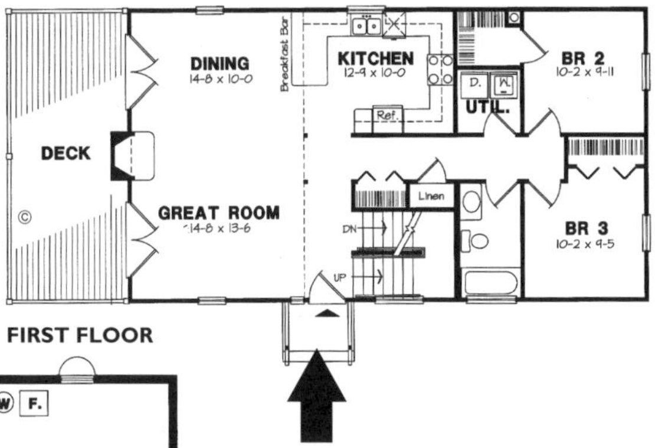

FIRST FLOOR

LOWER FLOOR

Units	Single
Price Code	B
Total Finished	1,562 sq. ft.
First Finished	1,062 sq. ft.
Second Finished	500 sq. ft.
Bonus Unfinished	678 sq. ft.
Basement Unfinished	384 sq. ft.
Deck Unfinished	298 sq. ft.
Porch Unfinished	19 sq. ft.
Dimensions	45'5"x27'
Foundation	Basement
Bedrooms	3
Full Baths	2
First Ceiling	8'
Second Ceiling	8'
Max Ridge Height	32'
Roof Framing	Stick
Exterior Walls	2x4

Design 66080

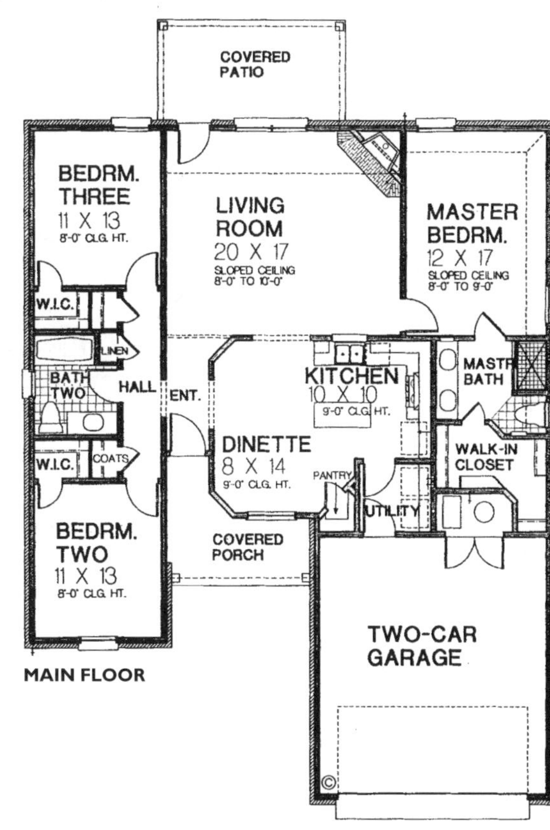
COVERED PATIO
BEDRM. THREE 11 X 13 8'-0" CLG. HT.
LIVING ROOM 20 X 17 SLOPED CEILING 8'-0" TO 10'-0"
MASTER BEDRM. 12 X 17 SLOPED CEILING 8'-0" TO 9'-0"
W.I.C.
LINEN
BATH TWO
HALL
ENT.
KITCHEN 10 X 10 9'-0" CLG. HT.
MASTR BATH
DINETTE 8 X 14 9'-0" CLG. HT.
WALK-IN CLOSET
W.I.C.
COATS
PANTRY
UTILITY
BEDRM. TWO 11 X 13 8'-0" CLG. HT.
COVERED PORCH
TWO-CAR GARAGE

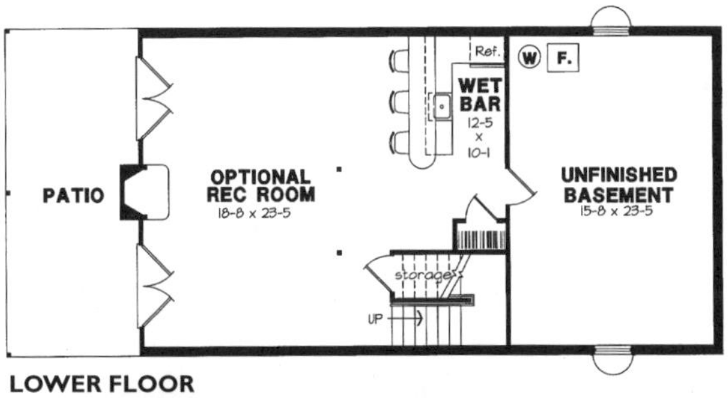

MAIN FLOOR

Units	Single
Price Code	B
Total Finished	1,563 sq. ft.
Main Finished	1,563 sq. ft.
Garage Unfinished	240 sq. ft.
Deck Unfinished	160 sq. ft.
Porch Unfinished	125 sq. ft.
Dimensions	45'x55'
Foundation	Slab
Bedrooms	3
Full Baths	1
3/4 Baths	1
Max Ridge Height	24'
Roof Framing	Stick
Exterior Walls	2x4

Design 92405

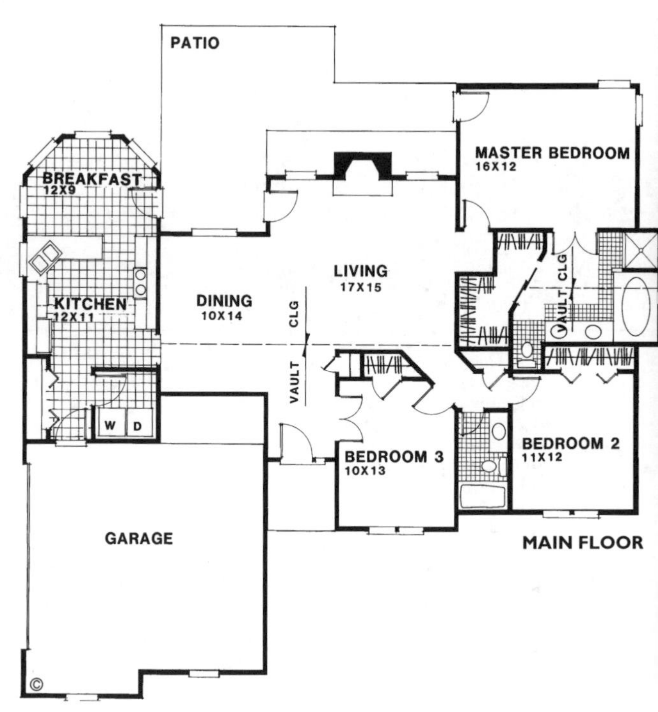

PATIO
BREAKFAST
12X9
MASTER BEDROOM
16X12
LIVING
17X15
KITCHEN
12X11
DINING
10X14
CLG
VAULT
VAULT CLG
W
D
BEDROOM 3
10X13
BEDROOM 2
11X12
GARAGE
MAIN FLOOR

Units	Single
Price Code	B
Total Finished	1,564 sq. ft.
Main Finished	1,564 sq. ft.
Garage Unfinished	476 sq. ft.
Dimensions	55'x46'
Foundation	Slab
Bedrooms	3
Full Baths	2
Max Ridge Height	18'
Roof Framing	Stick
Exterior Walls	2x4

Design 99641

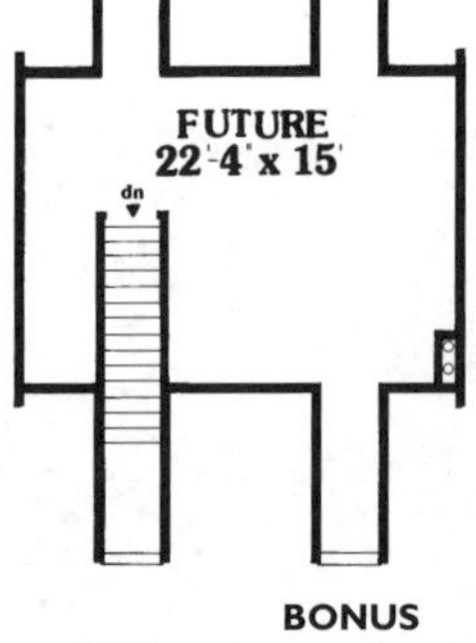

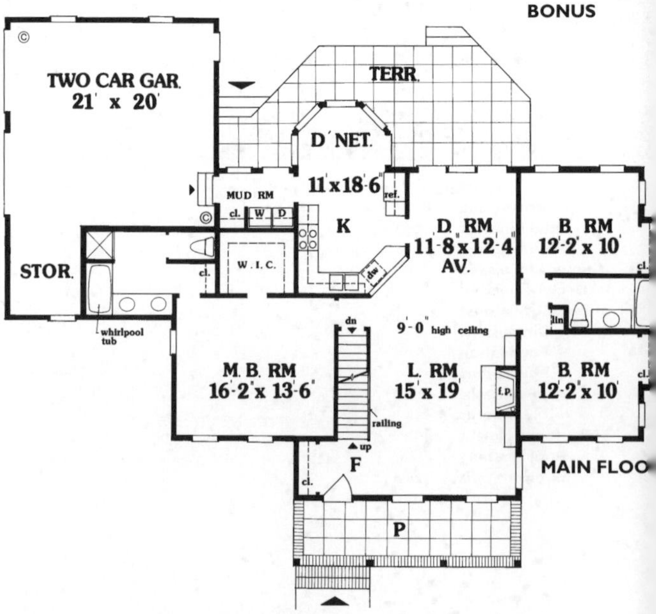

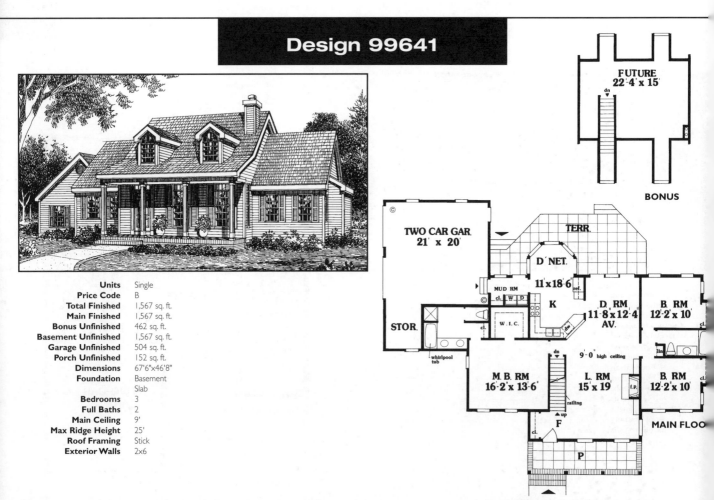

FUTURE
22'-4" x 15'
BONUS

TWO CAR GAR.
21' x 20'
TERR.
D'NET.
11' x 18'-6"
MUD RM
K
D. RM
11'-8" x 12'-4"
AV.
B. RM
12'-2" x 10'
STOR.
W. I. C.
whirlpool tub
9'-0" high ceiling
M. B. RM
16'-2" x 13'-6"
L. RM
15' x 19'
f.p.
B. RM
12'-2" x 10'
railing
F
P
MAIN FLOO

Units	Single
Price Code	B
Total Finished	1,567 sq. ft.
Main Finished	1,567 sq. ft.
Bonus Unfinished	462 sq. ft.
Basement Unfinished	1,567 sq. ft.
Garage Unfinished	504 sq. ft.
Porch Unfinished	152 sq. ft.
Dimensions	67'6"x46'8"
Foundation	Basement Slab
Bedrooms	3
Full Baths	2
Main Ceiling	9'
Max Ridge Height	25'
Roof Framing	Stick
Exterior Walls	2x6

Design 63084

Units	Single
Price Code	B
Total Finished	1,571 sq. ft.
Main Finished	1,571 sq. ft.
Garage Unfinished	381 sq. ft.
Porch Unfinished	123 sq. ft.
Dimensions	40'x55'
Foundation	Slab
Bedrooms	3
Full Baths	2
Max Ridge Height	20'
Roof Framing	Truss
Exterior Walls	2x4

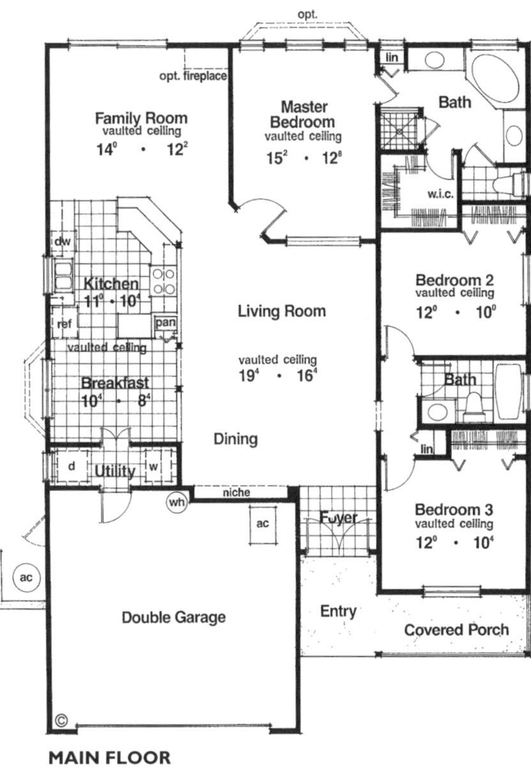
opt.
opt. fireplace
Family Room
vaulted ceiling
14⁰ · 12²
Master
Bedroom
vaulted ceiling
15² · 12⁸
lin
Bath
w.i.c.
dw
Kitchen
11⁰ · 10⁴
ref
pan
vaulted ceiling
Living Room
vaulted ceiling
19⁴ · 16⁴
Bedroom 2
vaulted ceiling
12⁰ · 10⁰
Breakfast
10⁴ · 8⁴
Bath
Dining
lin
d
Utility
w
wh
niche
ac
Foyer
Bedroom 3
vaulted ceiling
12⁰ · 10⁴
ac
Double Garage
Entry
Covered Porch

MAIN FLOOR

Design 63089

Units	Single
Price Code	B
Total Finished	1,571 sq. ft.
Main Finished	1,571 sq. ft.
Garage Unfinished	381 sq. ft.
Dimensions	40'x55'
Foundation	Slab
Bedrooms	3
Full Baths	2
Max Ridge Height	20'
Roof Framing	Truss
Exterior Walls	2x4

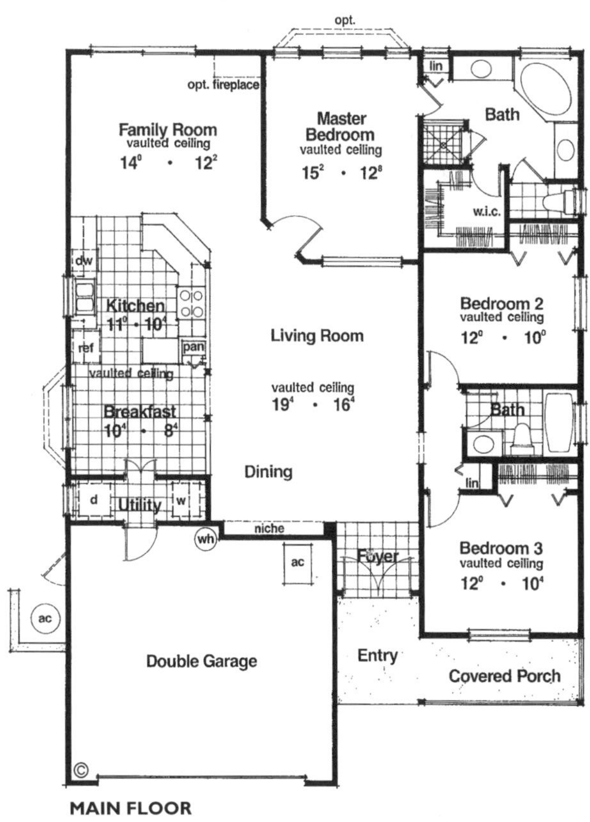
opt.
opt. fireplace
Family Room
vaulted ceiling
14⁰ · 12²
Master
Bedroom
vaulted ceiling
15² · 12⁸
lin
Bath
w.i.c.
dw
Kitchen
11⁰ · 10⁴
ref
pan
vaulted ceiling
Living Room
vaulted ceiling
19⁴ · 16⁴
Bedroom 2
vaulted ceiling
12⁰ · 10⁰
Breakfast
10⁴ · 8⁴
Bath
Dining
lin
d
Utility
w
wh
niche
ac
Foyer
Bedroom 3
vaulted ceiling
12⁰ · 10⁴
ac
Double Garage
Entry
Covered Porch

MAIN FLOOR

Design 66044

Units	Single
Price Code	B
Total Finished	1,573 sq. ft.
Main Finished	1,573 sq. ft.
Dimensions	48'x51'
Foundation	Slab
Bedrooms	3
Full Baths	2
Main Ceiling	8-10'
Max Ridge Height	24'
Roof Framing	Stick
Exterior Walls	2x4

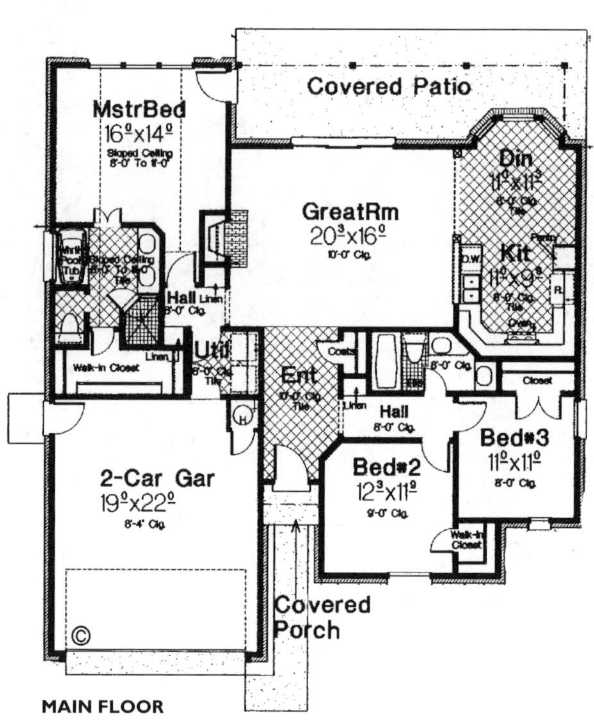
Covered Patio
MstrBed
16⁰x14⁰
Sloped Ceiling 8'-0" To 11'-0"
GreatRm
20³x16⁰
10'-0" Clg.
Din
11⁰x11²
Kit
11⁰x9⁸
Hall
Util
Walk-in Closet
Ent
Hall
8'-0" Clg.
Closet
Bed#3
11⁰x11⁰
8'-0" Clg.
Bed#2
12³x11⁰
9'-0" Clg.
2-Car Gar
19⁰x22⁰
8'-4" Clg.
Walk-in Closet
Covered Porch
©
MAIN FLOOR

Design 20083

Units	Single
Price Code	B
Total Finished	1,575 sq. ft.
Main Finished	1,575 sq. ft.
Basement Unfinished	1,575 sq. ft.
Garage Unfinished	475 sq. ft.
Dimensions	60'x40'4"
Foundation	Basement Crawlspace Slab
Bedrooms	3
Full Baths	2
Main Ceiling	8'-10'
Max Ridge Height	19'6"
Roof Framing	Stick
Exterior Walls	2x4, 2x6

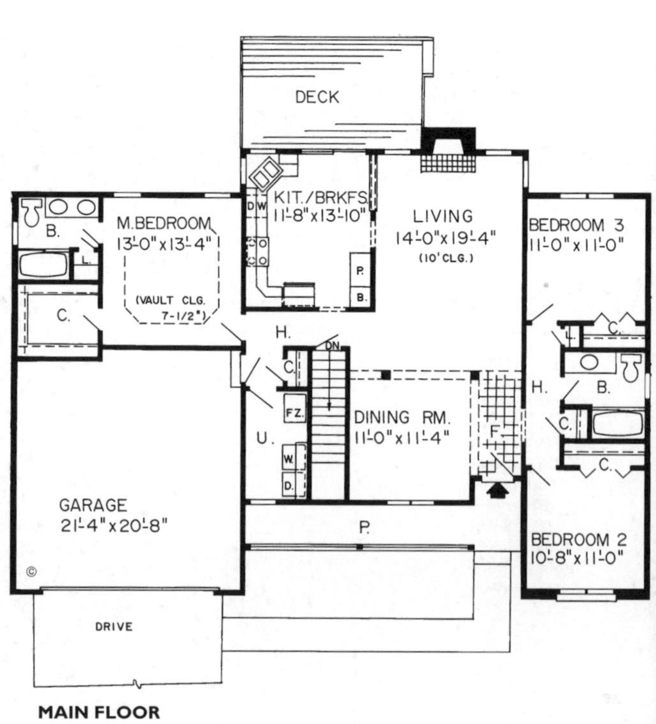
DECK
KIT./BRKFS.
11'-8"x13'-10"
LIVING
14'-0"x19'-4"
(10' CLG.)
M.BEDROOM
13'-0"x13'-4"
(VAULT CLG. 7-1/2")
BEDROOM 3
11'-0"x11'-0"
DINING RM.
11'-0"x11'-4"
GARAGE
21'-4"x20'-8"
P.
BEDROOM 2
10'-8"x11'-0"
DRIVE
©
MAIN FLOOR

Design 93062

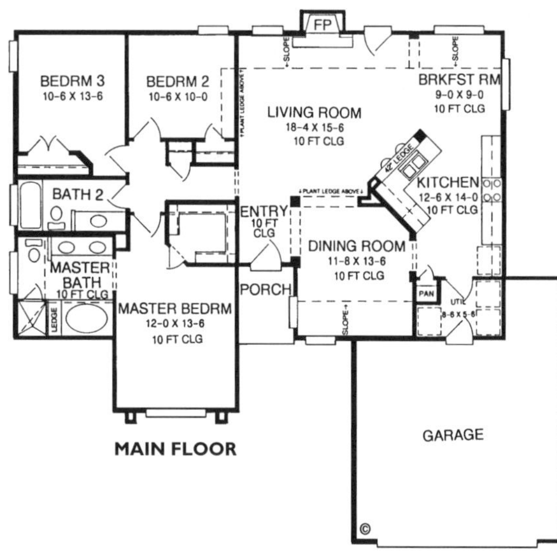
FP
BEDRM 3
10-6 X 13-6
BEDRM 2
10-6 X 10-0
LIVING ROOM
18-4 X 15-6
10 FT CLG
BRKFST RM
9-0 X 9-0
10 FT CLG
KITCHEN
12-6 X 14-0
10 FT CLG
BATH 2
ENTRY
10 FT
CLG
DINING ROOM
11-8 X 13-6
10 FT CLG
MASTER
BATH
10 FT CLG
PORCH
PAN
UTIL
8-6 X 5-6
MASTER BEDRM
12-0 X 13-6
10 FT CLG
GARAGE
©

MAIN FLOOR

Units	Single
Price Code	B
Total Finished	1,575 sq. ft.
Main Finished	1,575 sq. ft.
Garage Unfinished	474 sq. ft.
Porch Unfinished	41 sq. ft.
Dimensions	55'6"x52'
Foundation	Crawlspace Slab
Bedrooms	3
Full Baths	2
Main Ceiling	10'
Max Ridge Height	20'
Roof Framing	Truss
Exterior Walls	2x4

Design 97712

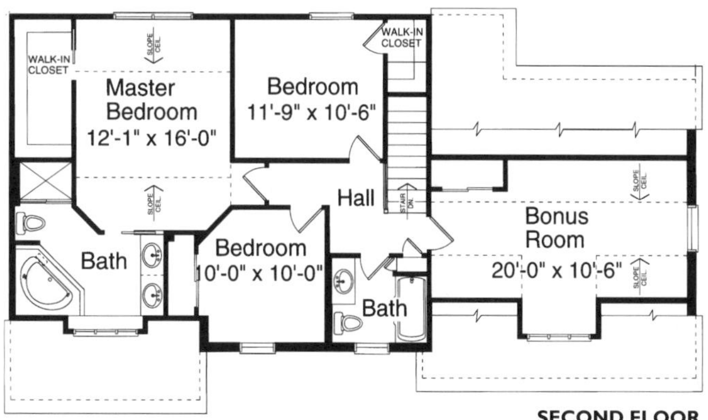
WALK-IN
CLOSET
Master
Bedroom
12'-1" x 16'-0"
Bedroom
11'-9" x 10'-6"
WALK-IN
CLOSET
Hall
Bath
Bedroom
10'-0" x 10'-0"
Bath
Bonus
Room
20'-0" x 10'-6"

SECOND FLOOR

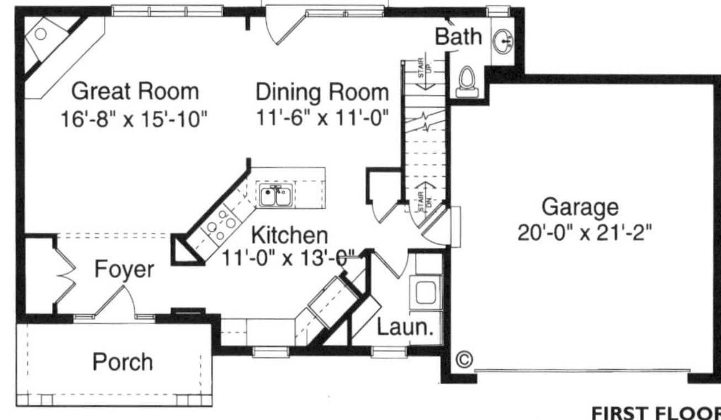
Bath
Great Room
16'-8" x 15'-10"
Dining Room
11'-6" x 11'-0"
Kitchen
11'-0" x 13'-6"
Garage
20'-0" x 21'-2"
Foyer
Laun.
Porch
©

FIRST FLOOR

Units	Single
Price Code	B
Total Finished	1,575 sq. ft.
First Finished	798 sq. ft.
Second Finished	777 sq. ft.
Bonus Unfinished	242 sq. ft.
Basement Unfinished	798 sq. ft.
Porch Unfinished	88 sq. ft.
Dimensions	53'6"x27'4"
Foundation	Basement
Bedrooms	3
Full Baths	2
Half Baths	1
Max Ridge Height	26'
Roof Framing	Truss
Exterior Walls	2x4

Design 97786

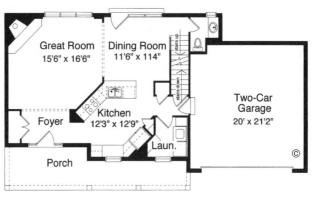

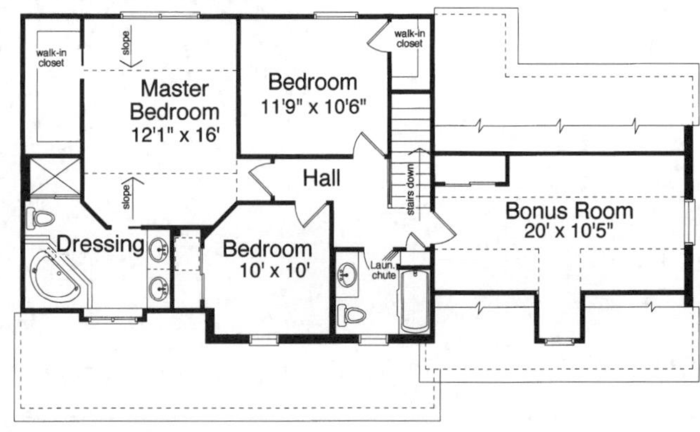
walk-in closet
Master Bedroom 12'1" x 16'
Bedroom 11'9" x 10'6"
walk-in closet
Hall
Bonus Room 20' x 10'5"
Dressing
Bedroom 10' x 10'
Laun. chute
stairs down
SECOND FLOOR
Great Room 15'6" x 16'6"
Dining Room 11'6" x 114"
Kitchen 12'3" x 12'9"
Foyer
Laun.
Porch
Two-Car Garage 20' x 21'2"
FIRST FLOOR

Units	Single
Price Code	B
Total Finished	1,575 sq. ft.
First Finished	798 sq. ft.
Second Finished	777 sq. ft.
Bonus Unfinished	242 sq. ft.
Basement Unfinished	798 sq. ft.
Dimensions	53'6"x27'4"
Foundation	Basement
Bedrooms	3
Full Baths	2
Half Baths	1
First Ceiling	8'
Second Ceiling	8'
Max Ridge Height	26'
Roof Framing	Truss
Exterior Walls	2x4

Design 69018

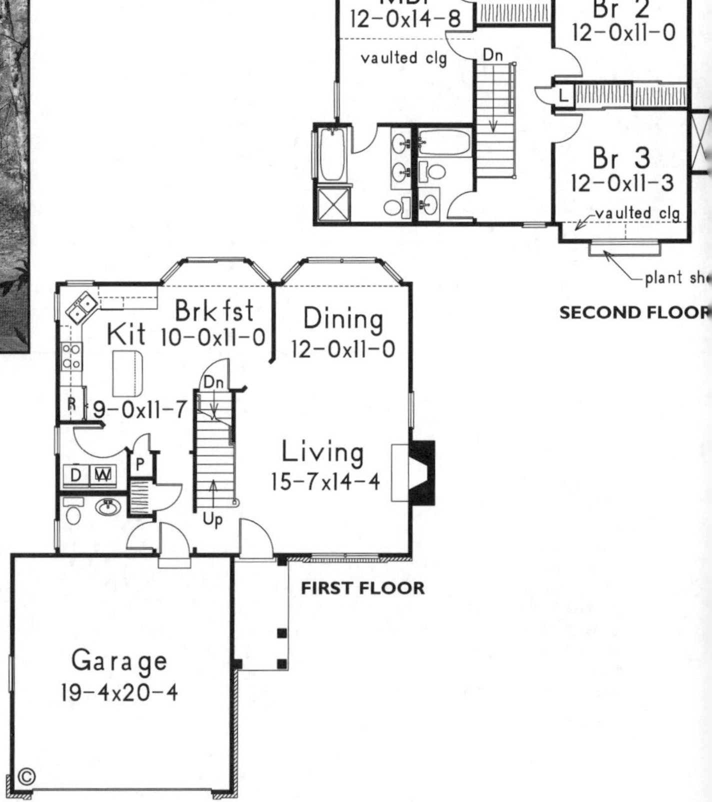
MBr 12-0x14-8
vaulted clg
Dn
Br 2 12-0x11-0
L
Br 3 12-0x11-3
vaulted clg
plant sh
SECOND FLOOR
Brkfst 10-0x11-0
Dining 12-0x11-0
Kit 9-0x11-7
Dn
R
Living 15-7x14-4
D W
P
Up
FIRST FLOOR
Garage 19-4x20-4

Units	Single
Price Code	B
Total Finished	1,575 sq. ft.
First Finished	802 sq. ft.
Second Finished	773 sq. ft.
Dimensions	38'x47'
Foundation	Basement
Bedrooms	3
Full Baths	2
Half Baths	1
First Ceiling	8'
Second Ceiling	8'
Max Ridge Height	26'6"
Roof Framing	Truss
Exterior Walls	2x4

Design 24708

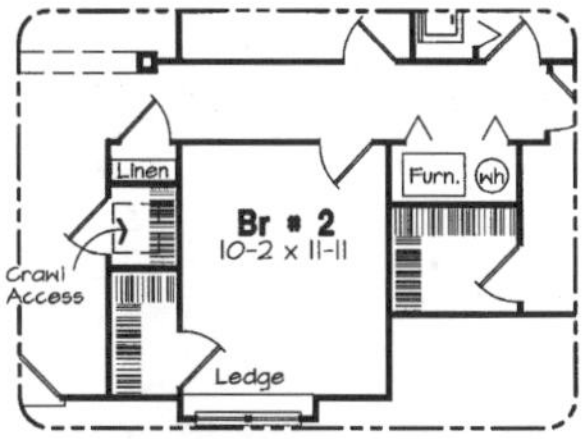

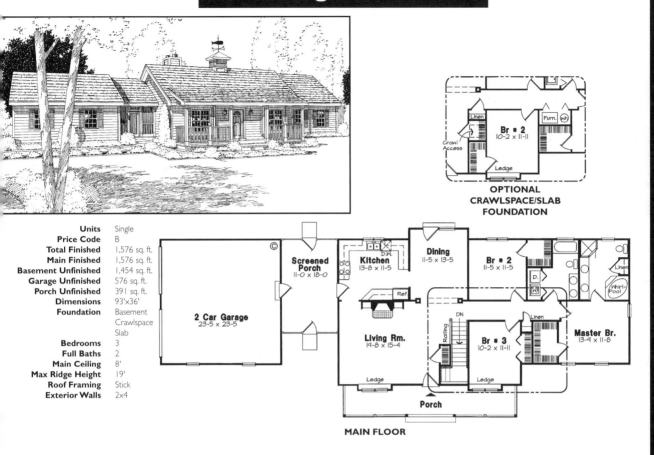

OPTIONAL CRAWLSPACE/SLAB FOUNDATION

Linen
Br # 2
10-2 x 11-11
Furn.
wh
Crawl Access
Ledge

Units	Single
Price Code	B
Total Finished	1,576 sq. ft.
Main Finished	1,576 sq. ft.
Basement Unfinished	1,454 sq. ft.
Garage Unfinished	576 sq. ft.
Porch Unfinished	391 sq. ft.
Dimensions	93'x36'
Foundation	Basement Crawlspace Slab
Bedrooms	3
Full Baths	2
Main Ceiling	8'
Max Ridge Height	19'
Roof Framing	Stick
Exterior Walls	2x4

2 Car Garage
23-5 x 23-5
Screened Porch
11-0 x 18-0
Kitchen
13-8 x 11-5
D.W.
Ref
Dining
11-5 x 13-5
Br # 2
11-5 x 11-5
D.
W.
Linen
Whirl-Pool
Living Rm.
14-8 x 15-4
DN
Railing
Br # 3
10-2 x 11-11
Linen
Master Br.
13-9 x 11-8
Ledge
Ledge
Porch

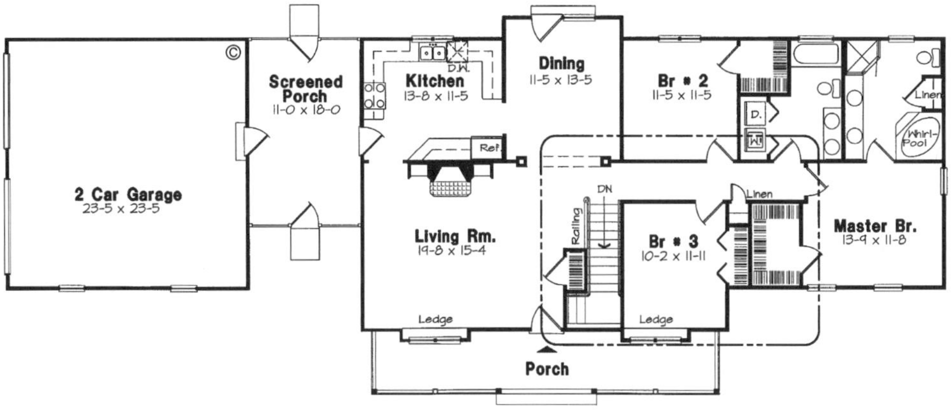

MAIN FLOOR

Design 97464

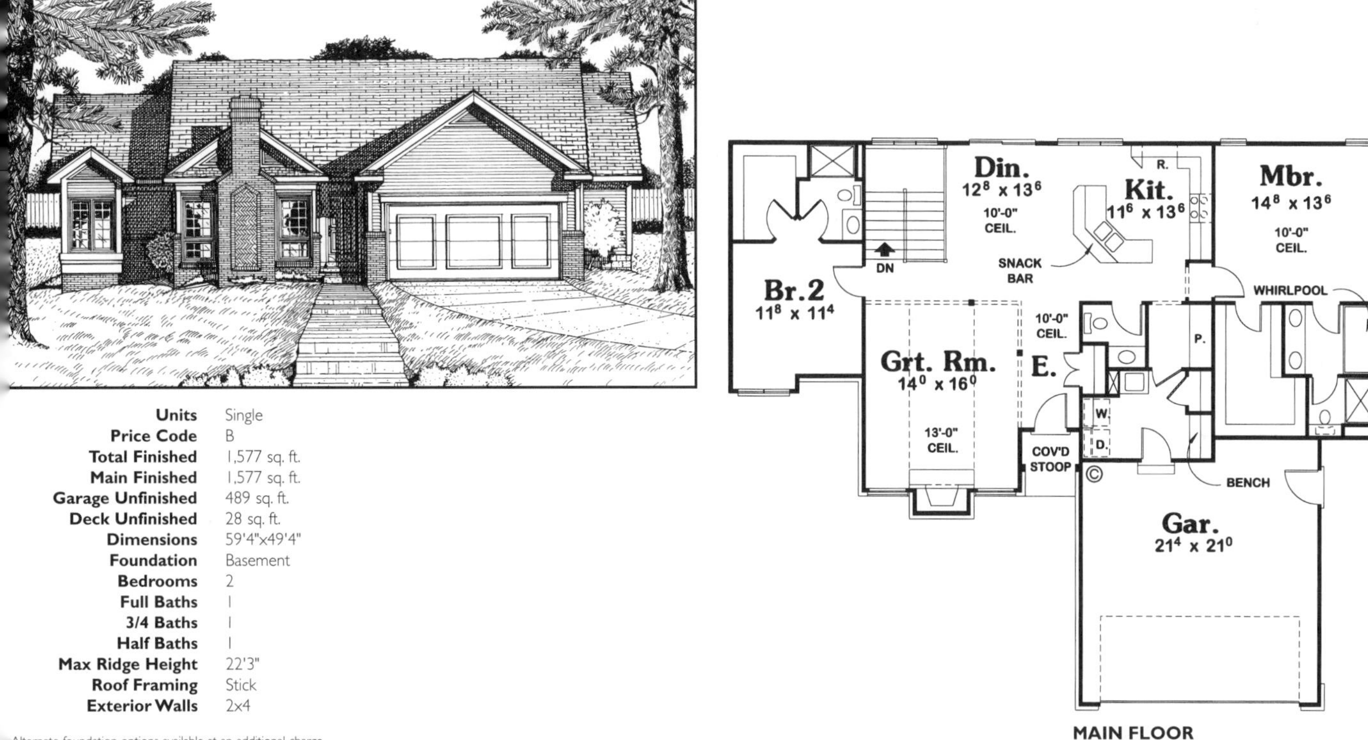
Din.
12^8 x 13^6
10'-0" CEIL.
Kit.
11^6 x 13^6
R.
SNACK BAR
Mbr.
14^8 x 13^6
10'-0" CEIL.
WHIRLPOOL
DN
Br.2
11^8 x 11^4
10'-0" CEIL.
Grt. Rm.
14^0 x 16^0
13'-0" CEIL.
E.
P.
W.
D.
COV'D STOOP
BENCH
Gar.
21^4 x 21^0
MAIN FLOOR

Units	Single
Price Code	B
Total Finished	1,577 sq. ft.
Main Finished	1,577 sq. ft.
Garage Unfinished	489 sq. ft.
Deck Unfinished	28 sq. ft.
Dimensions	59'4"x49'4"
Foundation	Basement
Bedrooms	2
Full Baths	1
3/4 Baths	1
Half Baths	1
Max Ridge Height	22'3"
Roof Framing	Stick
Exterior Walls	2x4

Alternate foundation options available at an additional charge.
Please call 1-800-235-5700 for more information.

Design 98983

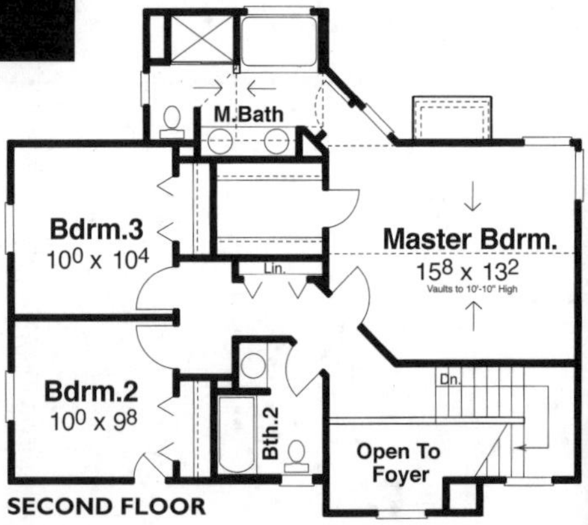

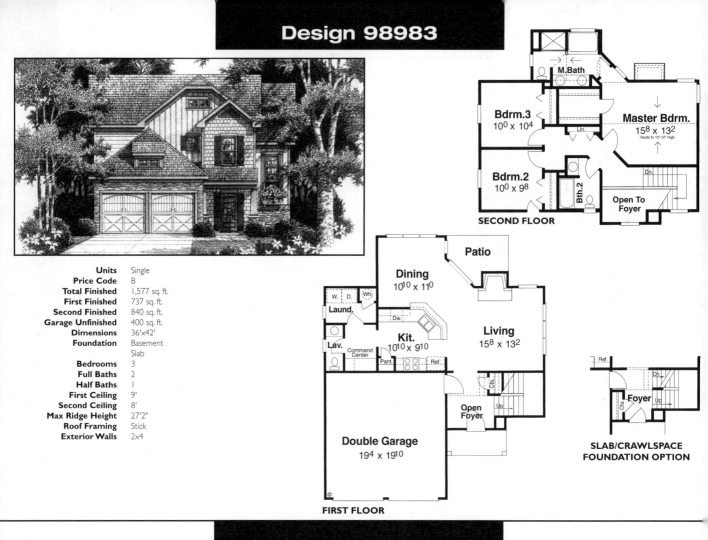

Units	Single
Price Code	B
Total Finished	1,577 sq. ft.
First Finished	737 sq. ft.
Second Finished	840 sq. ft.
Garage Unfinished	400 sq. ft.
Dimensions	36'x42'
Foundation	Basement Slab
Bedrooms	3
Full Baths	2
Half Baths	1
First Ceiling	9'
Second Ceiling	8'
Max Ridge Height	27'2"
Roof Framing	Stick
Exterior Walls	2x4

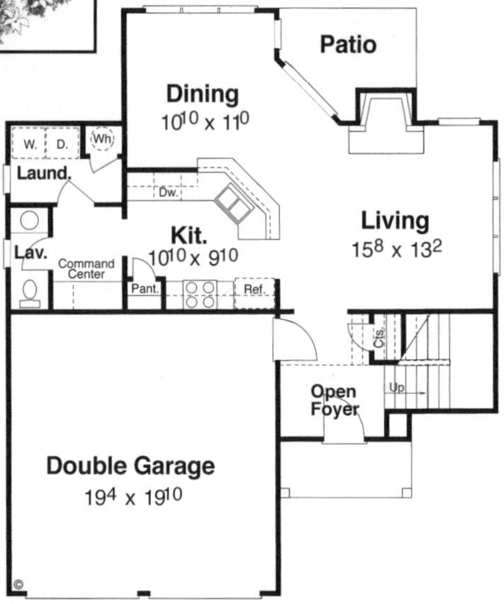

M.Bath
Bdrm.3 10^0 x 10^4
Master Bdrm. 15^8 x 13^2 Vaults to 10'-10" High
Lin.
Bdrm.2 10^0 x 9^8
Bth.2
Open To Foyer
Dn.

SECOND FLOOR

Patio
Dining 10^{10} x 11^0
W. D. Wh.
Laund.
Dw.
Kit. 10^{10} x 9^{10}
Living 15^8 x 13^2
Lav.
Command Center
Pant.
Ref.
Cts.
Up
Open Foyer
Double Garage 19^4 x 19^{10}

FIRST FLOOR

Ref.
Dn.
Foyer
Cts.
Up

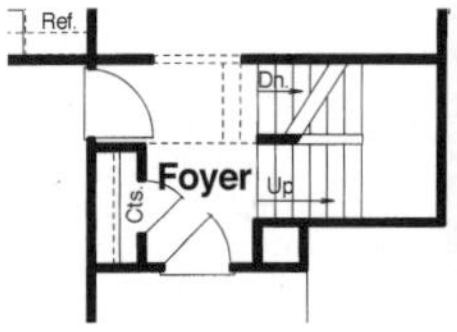

SLAB/CRAWLSPACE FOUNDATION OPTION

Design 99771

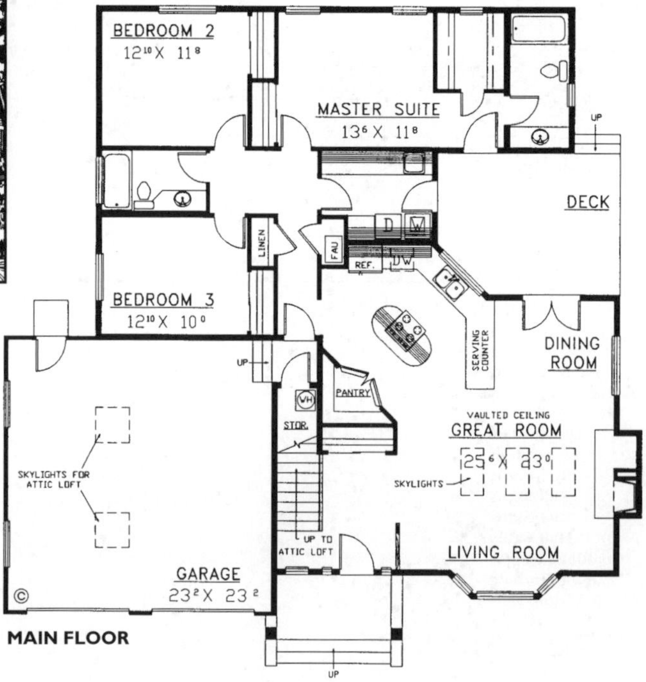

Units	Single
Price Code	B
Total Finished	1,578 sq. ft.
Main Finished	1,578 sq. ft.
Bonus Unfinished	724 sq. ft.
Garage Unfinished	658 sq. ft.
Dimensions	56'x52'
Foundation	Crawlspace
Bedrooms	3
Full Baths	2
Max Ridge Height	27'
Roof Framing	Stick/Truss
Exterior Walls	2x6

BEDROOM 2 12^{10}X 11^8
MASTER SUITE 13^6X 11^8
UP
DECK
LINEN
FAU
D W
REF.
DW
BEDROOM 3 12^{10}X 10^0
SERVING COUNTER
DINING ROOM
UP
VH
PANTRY
STOR.
VAULTED CEILING GREAT ROOM 25^6X 23^0
SKYLIGHTS FOR ATTIC LOFT
SKYLIGHTS
UP TO ATTIC LOFT
LIVING ROOM
GARAGE 23^2X 23^2
UP

MAIN FLOOR

Design 65420

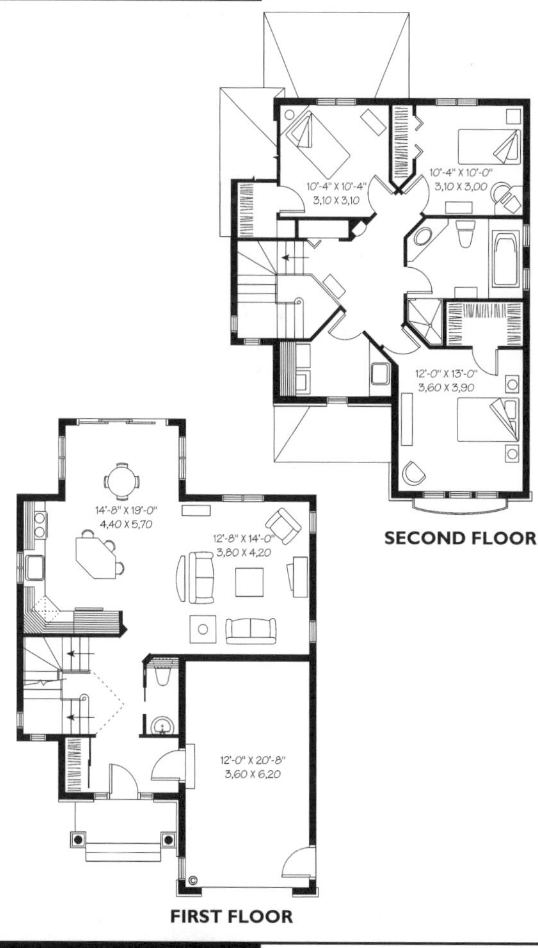
10'-4" X 10'-4"
3,10 X 3,10
10'-4" X 10'-0"
3,10 X 3,00
12'-0" X 13'-0"
3,60 X 3,90
SECOND FLOOR
14'-8" X 19'-0"
4,40 X 5,70
12'-8" X 14'-0"
3,80 X 4,20
12'-0" X 20'-8"
3,60 X 6,20
FIRST FLOOR

Units	Single
Price Code	B
Total Finished	1,579 sq. ft.
First Finished	709 sq. ft.
Second Finished	870 sq. ft.
Basement Unfinished	709 sq. ft.
Garage Unfinished	284 sq. ft.
Porch Unfinished	35 sq. ft.
Dimensions	29'x44'
Foundation	Basement
Bedrooms	3
Full Baths	1
Half Baths	1
First Ceiling	8'
Second Ceiling	8'
Max Ridge Height	32'10"
Roof Framing	Truss
Exterior Walls	2x6

Design 94823

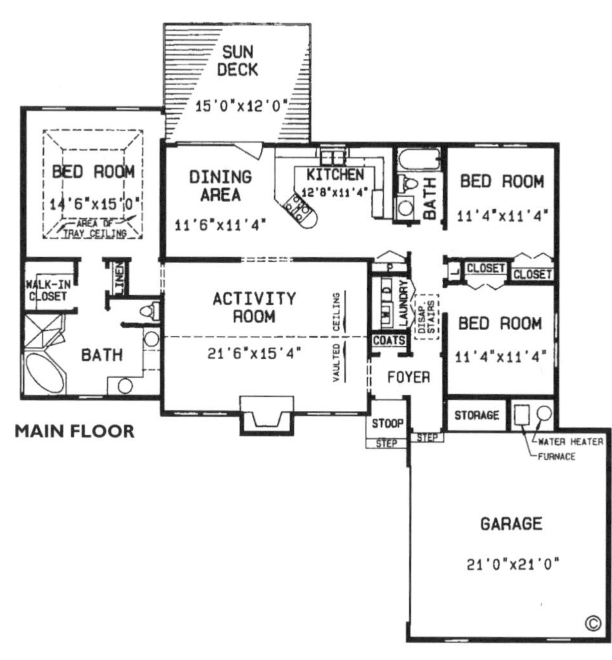
SUN DECK
15'0"x12'0"
BED ROOM
14'6"x15'0"
AREA OF TRAY CEILING
DINING AREA
11'6"x11'4"
KITCHEN
12'8"x11'4"
BATH
BED ROOM
11'4"x11'4"
WALK-IN CLOSET
LINEN
CLOSET
CLOSET
ACTIVITY ROOM
21'6"x15'4"
VAULTED CEILING
LAUNDRY
DISAP. STAIRS
COATS
BED ROOM
11'4"x11'4"
BATH
FOYER
STOOP
STEP
STEP
STORAGE
WATER HEATER
FURNACE
MAIN FLOOR
GARAGE
21'0"x21'0"

Units	Single
Price Code	B
Total Finished	1,580 sq. ft.
Main Finished	1,580 sq. ft.
Garage Unfinished	479 sq. ft.
Deck Unfinished	180 sq. ft.
Dimensions	62'2"x50'8"
Foundation	Crawlspace Slab
Bedrooms	3
Full Baths	2
Main Ceiling	8'
Max Ridge Height	22'
Roof Framing	Stick
Exterior Walls	2x4

Design 86014

Units	Single
Price Code	B
Total Finished	1,582 sq. ft.
First Finished	949 sq. ft.
Second Finished	633 sq. ft.
Porch Unfinished	415 sq. ft.
Dimensions	40'3"x40'6"
Foundation	Crawlspace
Bedrooms	3
Full Baths	2
First Ceiling	9'
Second Ceiling	8'
Max Ridge Height	30'10"
Roof Framing	Stick
Exterior Walls	2x4

SCREENED PORCH
9'-10"x9'-8"
PORCH
FP
INFORMAL DINING
8'-0"x8'-0"
LIVING ROOM
13'-8"x14'-4"
BEDROOM
12'-1"x11'-0"
KITCHEN
14'-0"x8'-4"
WIC
LIN.
ENTRY
W
D
BATH
F
WH
UP
DINING
10'-4"x10'-9"
PORCH

FIRST FLOOR

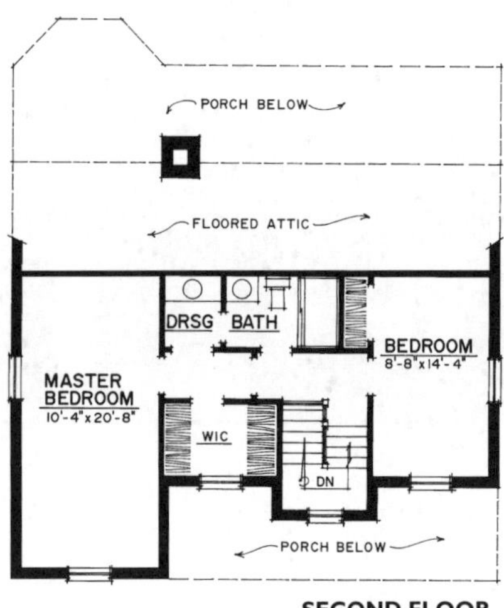
PORCH BELOW
FLOORED ATTIC
DRSG
BATH
BEDROOM
8'-8"x14'-4"
MASTER BEDROOM
10'-4"x20'-8"
WIC
DN
PORCH BELOW

SECOND FLOOR

Design 63083

Units	Single
Price Code	B
Total Finished	1,589 sq. ft.
Main Finished	1,589 sq. ft.
Garage Unfinished	480 sq. ft.
Dimensions	43'x59'
Foundation	Slab
Bedrooms	3
Full Baths	2
Main Ceiling	11'
Vaulted Ceiling	13'
Max Ridge Height	19'
Roof Framing	Truss

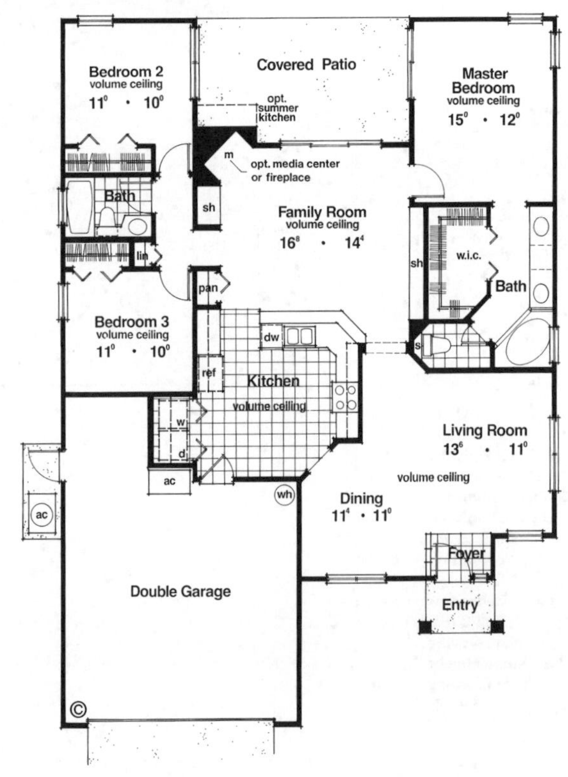
Bedroom 2
volume ceiling
11⁰ · 10⁰
Covered Patio
opt. summer kitchen
Master Bedroom
volume ceiling
15⁰ · 12⁰
opt. media center or fireplace
Bath
sh
Family Room
volume ceiling
16⁸ · 14⁴
w.i.c.
sh
Bath
lin
pan
Bedroom 3
volume ceiling
11⁰ · 10⁰
dw
ref
Kitchen
volume ceiling
w
d
ac
wh
Living Room
13⁶ · 11⁰
volume ceiling
Dining
11⁴ · 11⁰
Foyer
Double Garage
Entry

MAIN FLOOR

Design 98959

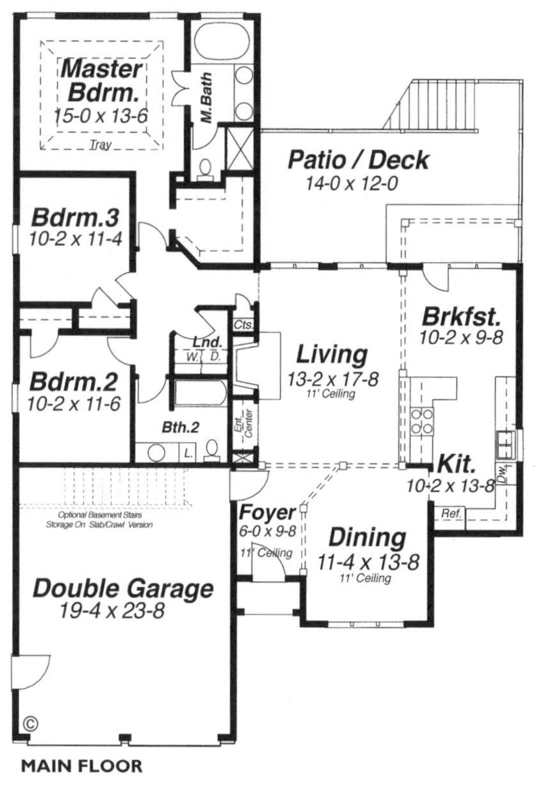

Master Bdrm.
15-0 x 13-6
Tray
M.Bath
Patio / Deck
14-0 x 12-0
Bdrm.3
10-2 x 11-4
Brkfst.
10-2 x 9-8
Cts.
Lnd.
W. D.
Living
13-2 x 17-8
11' Ceiling
Bdrm.2
10-2 x 11-6
Ent. Center
Bth.2
Kit.
10-2 x 13-8
Optional Basement Stairs
Storage On Slab/Crawl Version
Foyer
6-0 x 9-8
11' Ceiling
Dining
11-4 x 13-8
11' Ceiling
Ref.
Double Garage
19-4 x 23-8

MAIN FLOOR

Units	Single
Price Code	B
Total Finished	1,591 sq. ft.
Main Finished	1,591 sq. ft.
Garage Unfinished	480 sq. ft.
Deck Unfinished	280 sq. ft.
Dimensions	46'x64'
Foundation	Basement
Bedrooms	3
Full Baths	2
Main Ceiling	9'
Max Ridge Height	20'
Roof Framing	Stick
Exterior Walls	2x4

Design 69139

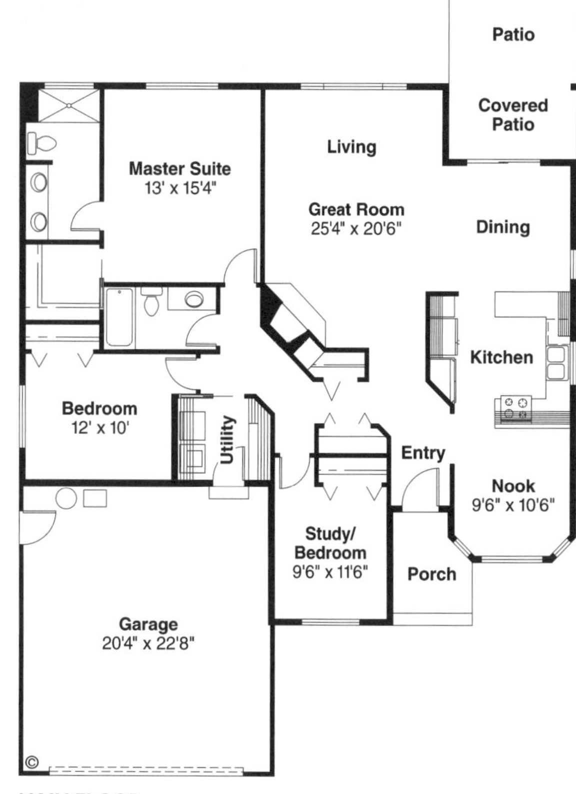

Patio
Covered Patio
Living
Master Suite
13' x 15'4"
Great Room
25'4" x 20'6"
Dining
Kitchen
Bedroom
12' x 10'
Utility
Entry
Nook
9'6" x 10'6"
Study/ Bedroom
9'6" x 11'6"
Porch
Garage
20'4" x 22'8"

MAIN FLOOR

Units	Single
Price Code	B
Total Finished	1,592 sq. ft.
Main Finished	1,592 sq. ft.
Garage Unfinished	477 sq. ft.
Dimensions	46'x55'
Foundation	Crawlspace
Bedrooms	3
Full Baths	1
3/4 Baths	1
Main Ceiling	8'
Max Ridge Height	19'4"
Roof Framing	Truss
Exterior Walls	2x6

Design 67014

Units	Single
Price Code	B
Total Finished	1,593 sq. ft.
Main Finished	1,593 sq. ft.
Garage Unfinished	486 sq. ft.
Dimensions	64'4"x41'9"
Foundation	Slab
Bedrooms	3
Full Baths	2
Main Ceiling	8'
Roof Framing	Stick
Exterior Walls	2x4

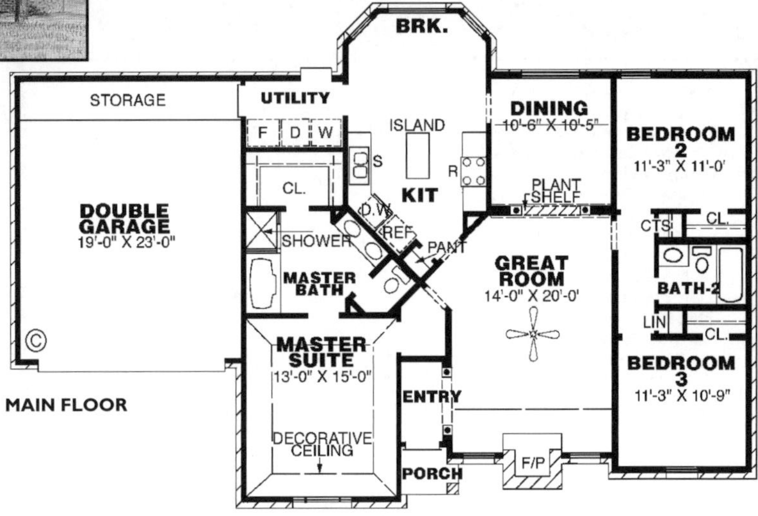
BRK.
STORAGE
UTILITY
F D W
ISLAND
DINING
10'-6" X 10'-5"
BEDROOM 2
11'-3" X 11'-0'
S
R
KIT
PLANT SHELF
DOUBLE GARAGE
19'-0" X 23'-0"
CL.
D.W.
REF
CTS
CL.
SHOWER
PANT
GREAT ROOM
14'-0" X 20'-0'
MASTER BATH
BATH-2
LIN
CL.
MASTER SUITE
13'-0" X 15'-0"
BEDROOM 3
11'-3" X 10'-9"
ENTRY
DECORATIVE CEILING
F/P
PORCH
MAIN FLOOR

Design 97740

Units	Single
Price Code	B
Total Finished	1,593 sq. ft.
Main Finished	1,593 sq. ft.
Basement Unfinished	1,593 sq. ft.
Garage Unfinished	550 sq. ft.
Porch Unfinished	104 sq. ft.
Dimensions	60'x48'10"
Foundation	Basement
Bedrooms	3
Full Baths	2
Main Ceiling	8'
Vaulted Ceiling	11'6"
Tray Ceiling	9'
Max Ridge Height	21'6"
Roof Framing	Truss
Exterior Walls	2x4

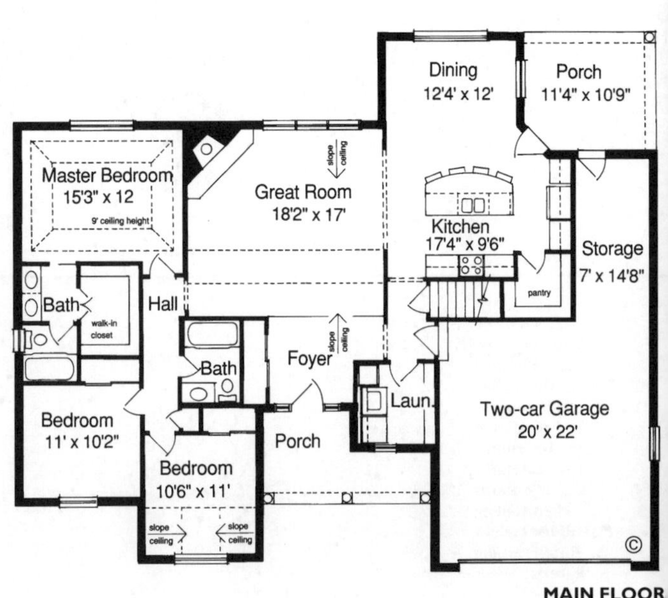
Dining
12'4' x 12'
Porch
11'4" x 10'9"
Master Bedroom
15'3" x 12
9' ceiling height
Great Room
18'2" x 17'
slope ceiling
Kitchen
17'4" x 9'6"
Storage
7' x 14'8"
pantry
Bath
walk-in closet
Hall
Bath
Foyer
slope ceiling
Laun.
Two-car Garage
20' x 22'
Bedroom
11' x 10'2"
Porch
Bedroom
10'6" x 11'
slope ceiling
slope ceiling
MAIN FLOOR

Design 96542

Units	Single
Price Code	B
Total Finished	1,594 sq. ft.
Main Finished	1,594 sq. ft.
Garage Unfinished	525 sq. ft.
Porch Unfinished	284 sq. ft.
Dimensions	79'x45'
Foundation	Crawlspace Slab
Bedrooms	3
Full Baths	2
Main Ceiling	9'
Max Ridge Height	26'6"
Roof Framing	Stick
Exterior Walls	2x4

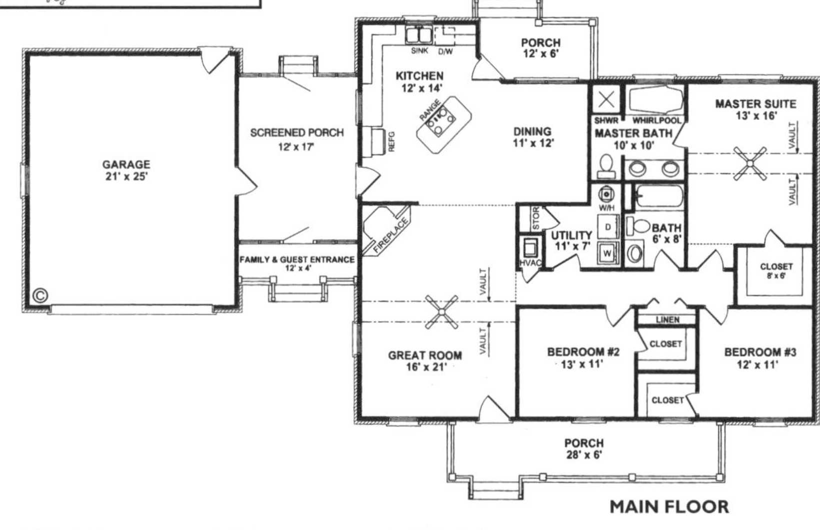

PORCH 12' x 6'
SINK
D/W
KITCHEN 12' x 14'
RANGE
REFG
DINING 11' x 12'
GARAGE 21' x 25'
SCREENED PORCH 12' x 17'
FAMILY & GUEST ENTRANCE 12' x 4'
FIREPLACE
SHWR
WHIRLPOOL
MASTER BATH 10' x 10'
MASTER SUITE 13' x 16'
VAULT
STOR
UTILITY 11' x 7'
HVAC
W/H
D
W
BATH 6' x 8'
CLOSET 8' x 6'
LINEN
CLOSET
GREAT ROOM 16' x 21'
BEDROOM #2 13' x 11'
BEDROOM #3 12' x 11'
PORCH 28' x 6'

MAIN FLOOR

Design 97762

Units	Single
Price Code	B
Total Finished	1,594 sq. ft.
Main Finished	1,594 sq. ft.
Basement Unfinished	1,594 sq. ft.
Garage Unfinished	512 sq. ft.
Deck Unfinished	328 sq. ft.
Porch Unfinished	125 sq. ft.
Dimensions	52'8"x55'5"
Foundation	Basement
Bedrooms	3
Full Baths	2
Main Ceiling	8'
Vaulted Ceiling	10'
Max Ridge Height	23'6"
Roof Framing	Truss
Exterior Walls	2x4

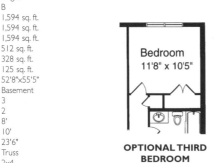

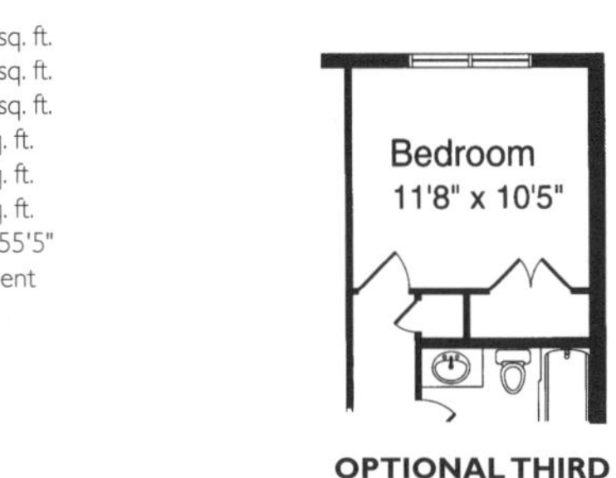

Bedroom 11'8" x 10'5"

OPTIONAL THIRD BEDROOM

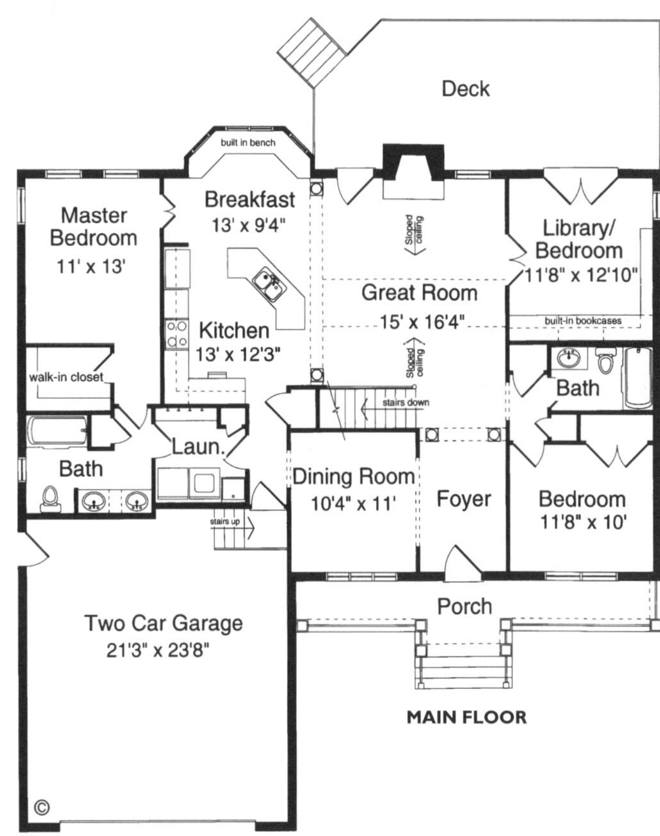

Deck
built in bench
Master Bedroom 11' x 13'
Breakfast 13' x 9'4"
Sloped ceiling
Library/ Bedroom 11'8" x 12'10"
Great Room 15' x 16'4"
built-in bookcases
Kitchen 13' x 12'3"
walk-in closet
Bath
stairs down
Laun.
Bath
Dining Room 10'4" x 11'
Foyer
Bedroom 11'8" x 10'
stairs up
Porch
Two Car Garage 21'3" x 23'8"

MAIN FLOOR

Design 93419

Units	Single
Price Code	B
Total Finished	1,595 sq. ft.
Main Finished	1,595 sq. ft.
Garage Unfinished	470 sq. ft.
Porch Unfinished	196 sq. ft.
Dimensions	59'x55'
Foundation	Crawlspace Slab
Bedrooms	3
Full Baths	2
Main Ceiling	9'
Max Ridge Height	26'
Roof Framing	Stick
Exterior Walls	2x4

Deck
GARAGE
Drive
MASTER
12x16
DINING
10x12
KITCHEN
Desk
Laundry
STOR.
BR.#2
10x12
BR.#3
10x12
FAMILY ROOM
14x20
11'CLG.
FOYER
PORCH
MAIN FLOOR

Design 94827

Units	Single
Price Code	B
Total Finished	1,595 sq. ft.
Main Finished	1,595 sq. ft.
Basement Unfinished	1,595 sq. ft.
Garage Unfinished	491 sq. ft.
Dimensions	63'x50'6"
Foundation	Basement Crawlspace Slab
Bedrooms	3
Full Baths	2
Max Ridge Height	22'
Roof Framing	Stick
Exterior Walls	2x4

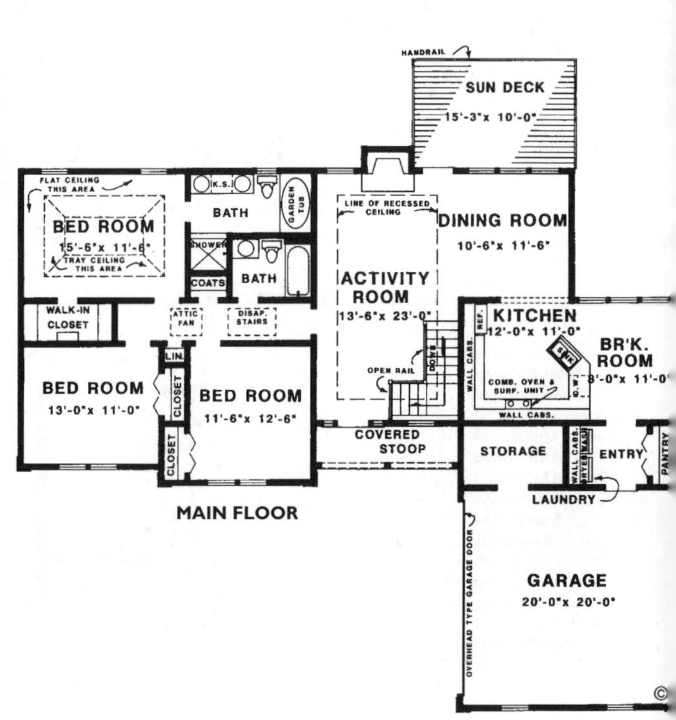
HANDRAIL
SUN DECK
15'-3"x 10'-0"
FLAT CEILING THIS AREA
BED ROOM
15'-6"x 11'-6"
TRAY CEILING THIS AREA
BATH
BATH
COATS
WALK-IN CLOSET
ATTIC FAN
DISAP. STAIRS
LINE OF RECESSED CEILING
ACTIVITY ROOM
13'-6"x 23'-0"
OPEN RAIL
DINING ROOM
10'-6"x 11'-6"
KITCHEN
12'-0"x 11'-0"
COMB. OVEN & SURF. UNIT
WALL CABS.
BR'K. ROOM
BED ROOM
13'-0"x 11'-0"
BED ROOM
11'-6"x 12'-6"
CLOSET
CLOSET
COVERED STOOP
STORAGE
ENTRY
PANTRY
LAUNDRY
MAIN FLOOR
GARAGE
20'-0"x 20'-0"
OVERHEAD TYPE GARAGE DOOR

Design 97489

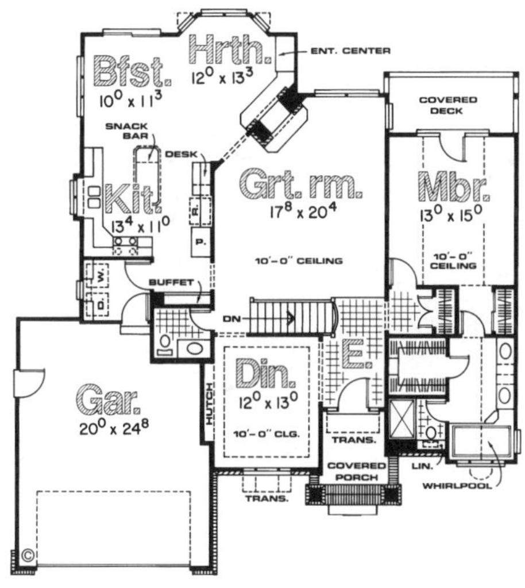

Units	Single
Price Code	B
Total Finished	1,595 sq. ft.
Main Finished	1,595 sq. ft.
Basement Unfinished	790 sq. ft.
Garage Unfinished	476 sq. ft.
Dimensions	52'x56'
Foundation	Basement
Bedrooms	3
Full Baths	2
Half Baths	1
Main Ceiling	8'
Max Ridge Height	20'9"
Roof Framing	Stick
Exterior Walls	2x4

* Alternate foundation options available at an additional charge. Please call 1-800-235-5700 for more information.

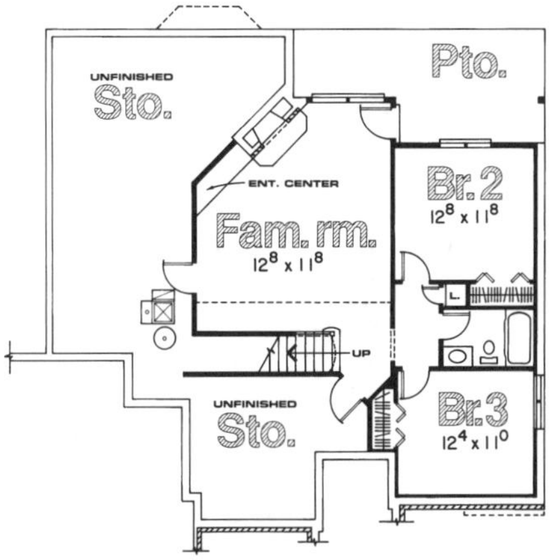

LOWER FLOOR

MAIN FLOOR

Design 97763

Units	Single
Price Code	B
Total Finished	1,595 sq. ft.
Main Finished	1,595 sq. ft.
Basement Unfinished	1,589 sq. ft.
Garage Unfinished	409 sq. ft.
Deck Unfinished	279 sq. ft.
Dimensions	48'x51'4"
Foundation	Basement
Bedrooms	3
Full Baths	2
Main Ceiling	8'
Vaulted Ceiling	14'
Max Ridge Height	24'6"
Roof Framing	Truss
Exterior Walls	2x4

Deck
Master Bedroom
16'3" x 15'3"
Bath
Great Room
15'6" x 17'10"
Dining
8'10" x 13'6"
walk-in closet
Kitchen
8'10" x 16'6"
Hall
Bath
Laun.
Bedroom
11'6" x 11'
Bedroom /Library
10'1" x 12'
Foyer
Two-car Garage
19'2" x 22'
Porch

MAIN FLOOR

Design 99682

Units	Single
Price Code	B
Total Finished	1,595 sq. ft.
Main Finished	1,595 sq. ft.
Basement Unfinished	1,595 sq. ft.
Garage Unfinished	548 sq. ft.
Dimensions	70'x37'4"
Foundation	Basement
Bedrooms	3
Full Baths	2
Main Ceiling	9'1"
Vaulted Ceiling	10'9"
Tray Ceiling	14'
Max Ridge Height	22'
Roof Framing	Stick
Exterior Walls	2x4

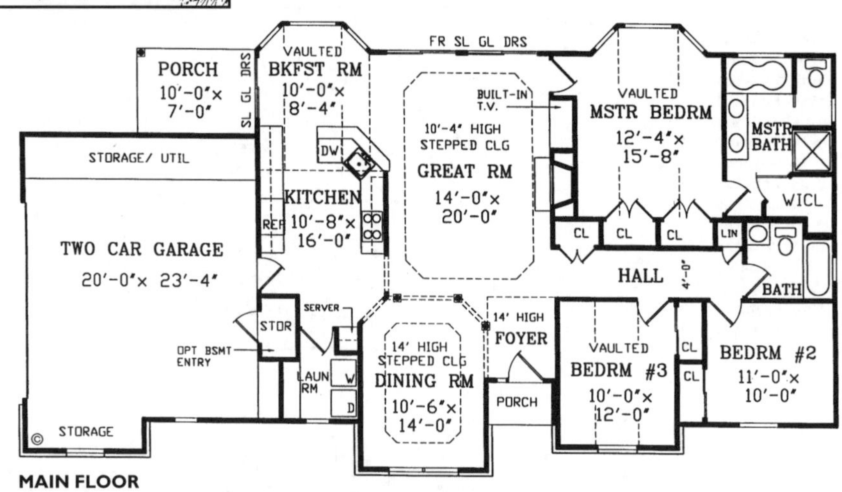

PORCH 10'-0"x 7'-0"
SL GL DRS
VAULTED BKFST RM 10'-0"x 8'-4"
FR SL GL DRS
BUILT-IN T.V.
10'-4" HIGH STEPPED CLG
GREAT RM 14'-0"x 20'-0"
VAULTED MSTR BEDRM 12'-4"x 15'-8"
MSTR BATH
WICL
STORAGE/ UTIL
DW
KITCHEN 10'-8"x 16'-0"
REF
TWO CAR GARAGE 20'-0"x 23'-4"
CL
CL
CL
LIN
HALL
BATH
STOR
SERVER
14' HIGH FOYER
OPT BSMT ENTRY
14' HIGH STEPPED CLG
DINING RM 10'-6"x 14'-0"
LAUN RM
PORCH
VAULTED BEDRM #3 10'-0"x 12'-0"
CL
CL
BEDRM #2 11'-0"x 10'-0"
STORAGE

MAIN FLOOR

Design 98560

Units	Single
Price Code	B
Total Finished	1,596 sq. ft.
First Finished	1,192 sq. ft.
Second Finished	404 sq. ft.
Garage Unfinished	410 sq. ft.
Dimensions	50'x39'11"
Foundation	Basement Crawlspace Slab
Bedrooms	3
Full Baths	2
Half Baths	1
Max Ridge Height	23'6"
Roof Framing	Stick
Exterior Walls	2x6

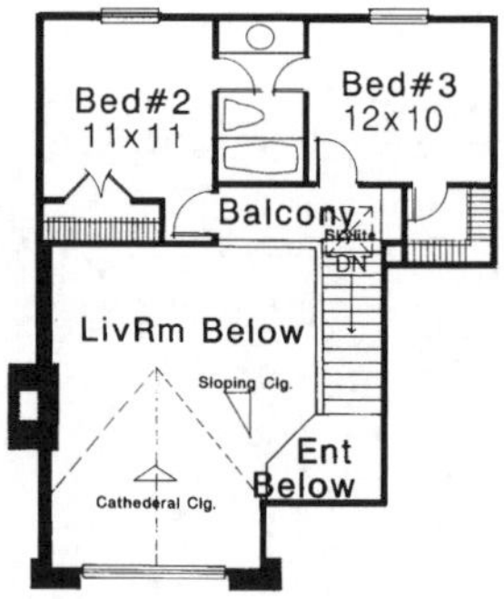

Bed#2 11x11

Bed#3 12x10

Balcony

DN

LivRm Below

Sloping Clg.

Ent Below

Cathedral Clg.

SECOND FLOOR

Patio

Covered Patio

Kit

8'Clg.

Din 10x12

Pantry

MstrBed 14x14

8'to 10'Flat Clg.

Laundry

LivRm 14x20

Sloping Clg.

UP

Cathedral Clg.

Ent

Pwdr

Gar 20x20

Por

FIRST FLOOR

Design 62086

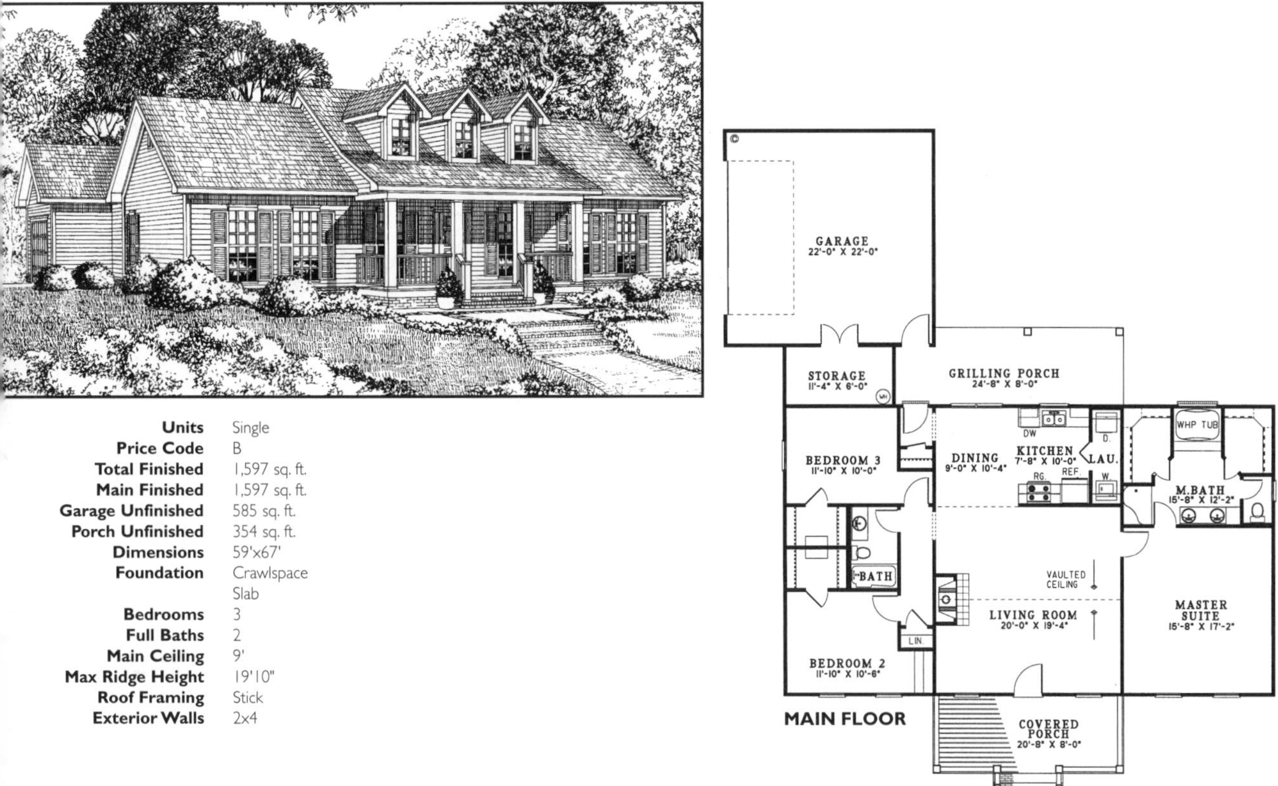

GARAGE
22'-0" X 22'-0"
STORAGE
11'-4" X 6'-0"
GRILLING PORCH
24'-8" X 8'-0"
BEDROOM 3
11'-10" X 10'-0"
DINING
9'-0" X 10'-4"
KITCHEN
7'-8" X 10'-0"
LAU.
WHP TUB
M.BATH
15'-8" X 12'-2"
BATH
VAULTED CEILING
LIVING ROOM
20'-0" X 19'-4"
MASTER SUITE
15'-8" X 17'-2"
LIN.
BEDROOM 2
11'-10" X 10'-6"
MAIN FLOOR
COVERED PORCH
20'-8" X 8'-0"

Units	Single
Price Code	B
Total Finished	1,597 sq. ft.
Main Finished	1,597 sq. ft.
Garage Unfinished	585 sq. ft.
Porch Unfinished	354 sq. ft.
Dimensions	59'x67'
Foundation	Crawlspace Slab
Bedrooms	3
Full Baths	2
Main Ceiling	9'
Max Ridge Height	19'10"
Roof Framing	Stick
Exterior Walls	2x4

Design 90697

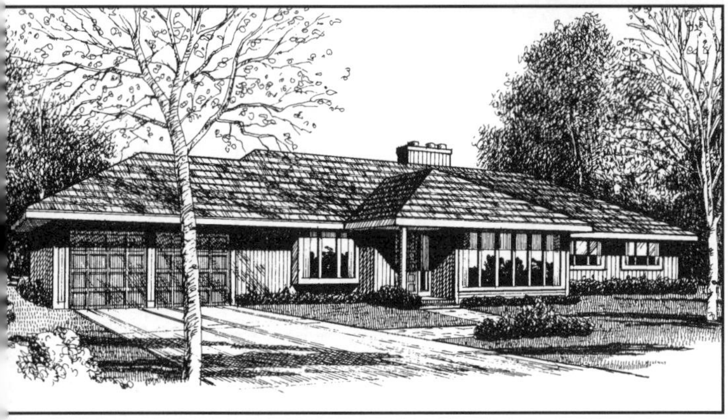

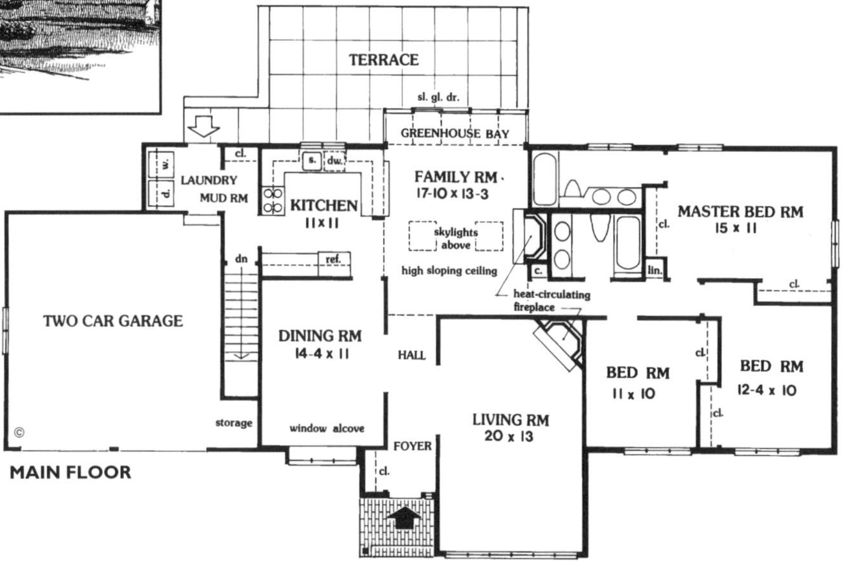

Units	Single
Price Code	B
Total Finished	1,597 sq. ft.
Main Finished	1,597 sq. ft.
Basement Unfinished	1,512 sq. ft.
Garage Unfinished	380 sq. ft.
Dimensions	75'4"x38'8"
Foundation	Basement Slab
Bedrooms	3
Full Baths	2

MAIN FLOOR

Design 50007

Units	Single
Price Code	B
Total Finished	1,598 sq. ft.
Main Finished	1,598 sq. ft.
Basement Unfinished	1,598 sq. ft.
Garage Unfinished	478 sq. ft.
Porch Unfinished	161 sq. ft.
Dimensions	59'4"x45'6"
Foundation	Basement
Bedrooms	3
Full Baths	1
3/4 Baths	1
Main Ceiling	8'
Max Ridge Height	18'8"
Roof Framing	Truss
Exterior Walls	2x4

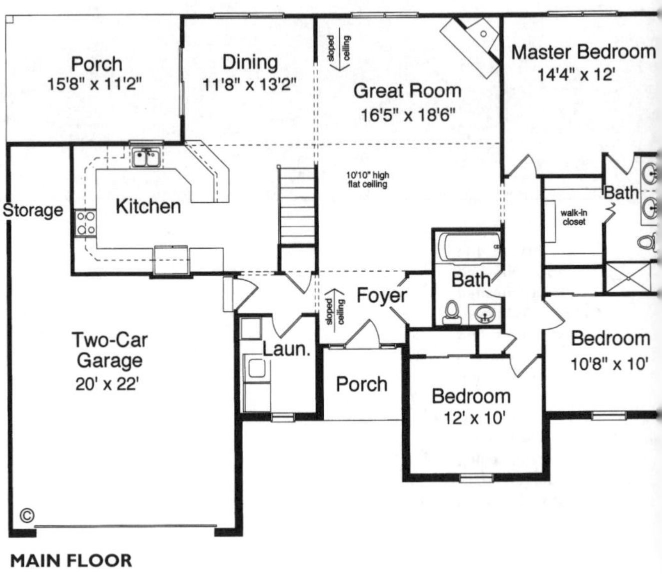
Porch
15'8" x 11'2"
Dining
11'8" x 13'2"
Great Room
16'5" x 18'6"
Master Bedroom
14'4" x 12'
Storage
Kitchen
Bath
walk-in closet
Two-Car Garage
20' x 22'
Laun.
Foyer
Bath
Porch
Bedroom
12' x 10'
Bedroom
10'8" x 10'

MAIN FLOOR

Design 92424

Units	Single
Price Code	B
Total Finished	1,598 sq. ft.
First Finished	812 sq. ft.
Second Finished	786 sq. ft.
Garage Unfinished	560 sq. ft.
Dimensions	52'x28'
Foundation	Crawlspace Slab
Bedrooms	3
Full Baths	2
Half Baths	1
First Ceiling	8'
Second Ceiling	8'
Vaulted Ceiling	15'
Max Ridge Height	25'10"
Roof Framing	Truss
Exterior Walls	2x4

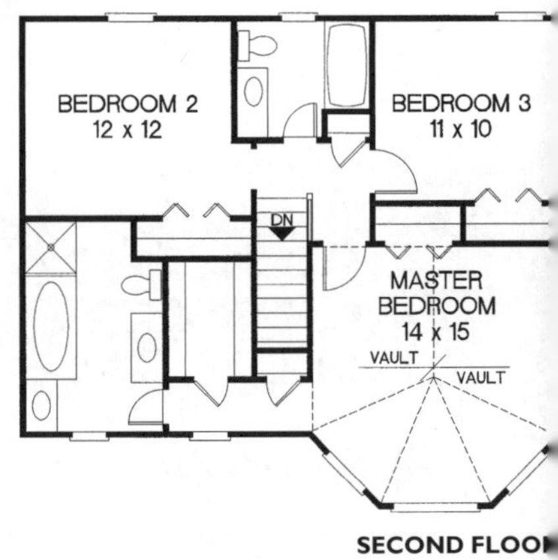
BEDROOM 2
12 x 12
BEDROOM 3
11 x 10
DN
MASTER BEDROOM
14 x 15
VAULT
VAULT

SECOND FLOOR

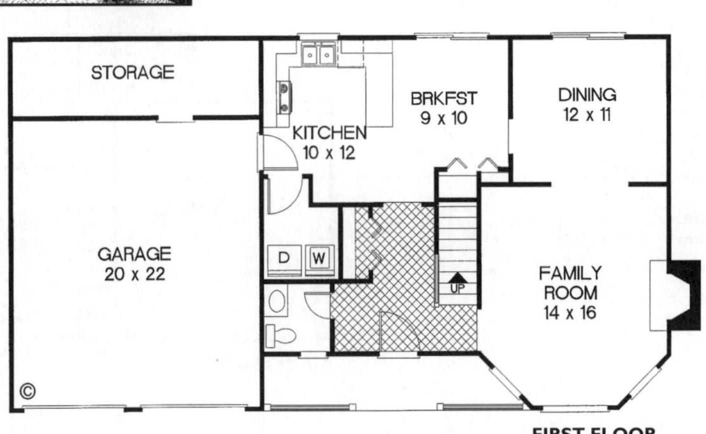
STORAGE
KITCHEN
10 x 12
BRKFST
9 x 10
DINING
12 x 11
GARAGE
20 x 22
D
W
UP
FAMILY ROOM
14 x 16

FIRST FLOOR

Design 10674

Units	Single
Price Code	B
Total Finished	1,600 sq. ft.
Main Finished	1,600 sq. ft.
Garage Unfinished	465 sq. ft.
Dimensions	58'x51'
Foundation	Slab
Bedrooms	3
Full Baths	2
Max Ridge Height	15'
Roof Framing	Stick
Exterior Walls	2x6

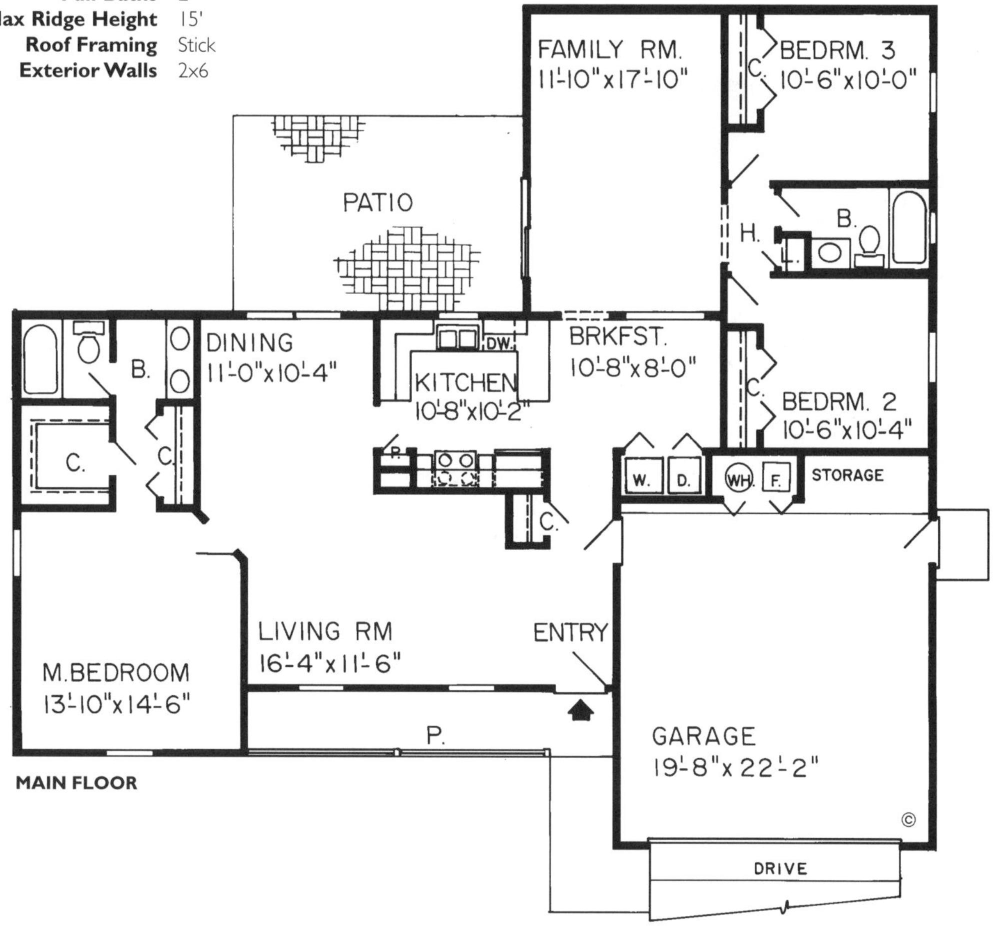

FAMILY RM.
11'-10"x17'-10"

BEDRM. 3
10'-6"x10'-0"

C.

PATIO

H.

B.

L.

B.

DINING
11'-0"x10'-4"

DW.

KITCHEN
10'-8"x10'-2"

BRKFST.
10'-8"x8'-0"

C.

BEDRM. 2
10'-6"x10'-4"

C.

C.

R.

W.

D.

WH.

F.

STORAGE

C.

LIVING RM
16'-4"x11'-6"

ENTRY

M.BEDROOM
13'-10"x14'-6"

P.

GARAGE
19'-8"x22'-2"

©

MAIN FLOOR

DRIVE

Design 98406

CAD
FILES AVAILABLE
For more information call
800-235-5700

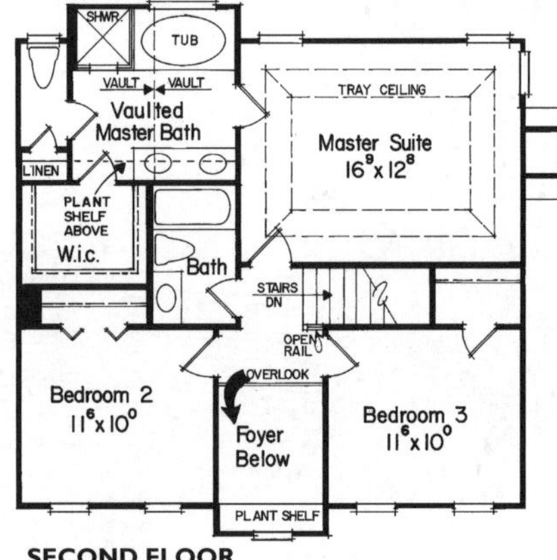

SHWR.
TUB
VAULT
VAULT
Vaulted
Master Bath
TRAY CEILING
Master Suite
16^{9}x12^{8}
LINEN
PLANT SHELF ABOVE
W.i.c.
Bath
STAIRS DN
OPEN RAIL
OVERLOOK
Bedroom 2
11^{6}x10^{0}
Foyer Below
Bedroom 3
11^{6}x10^{0}
PLANT SHELF
SECOND FLOOR

Units	Single
Price Code	B
Total Finished	1,600 sq. ft.
First Finished	828 sq. ft.
Second Finished	772 sq. ft.
Basement Unfinished	828 sq. ft.
Garage Unfinished	473 sq. ft.
Dimensions	52'4"x34'
Foundation	Basement Crawlspace Slab
Bedrooms	3
Full Baths	2
Half Baths	1
First Ceiling	9'
Second Ceiling	8'
Max Ridge Height	28'
Roof Framing	Stick
Exterior Walls	2x4

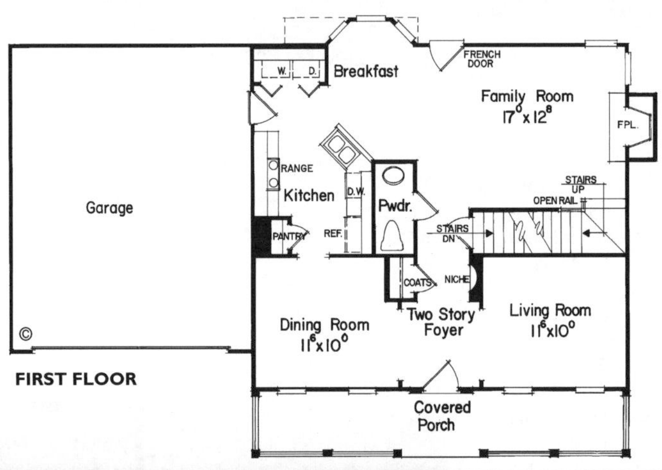

W.
D.
Breakfast
FRENCH DOOR
Family Room
17^{0}x12^{8}
FPL.
Garage
RANGE
Kitchen
D.W.
Pwdr.
STAIRS UP
OPEN RAIL
PANTRY
REF.
STAIRS DN
COATS
NICHE
Dining Room
11^{6}x10^{0}
Two Story Foyer
Living Room
11^{6}x10^{0}
FIRST FLOOR
Covered Porch

Design 99163

Units	Single
Price Code	B
Total Finished	1,600 sq. ft.
Main Finished	1,600 sq. ft.
Basement Unfinished	1,600 sq. ft.
Garage Unfinished	406 sq. ft.
Deck Unfinished	118 sq. ft.
Dimensions	54'8"x45'
Foundation	Basement
Bedrooms	3
Full Baths	2
Max Ridge Height	25'
Roof Framing	Truss
Exterior Walls	2x4

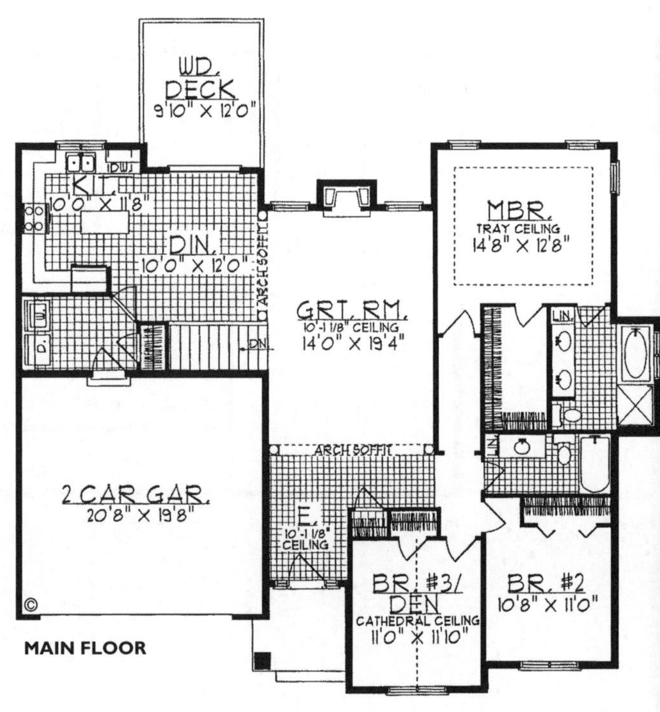

WD. DECK
9'10" X 12'0"
KIT.
10'0" X 11'8"
DW
DIN.
10'0" X 12'0"
ARCH SOFFIT
GRT. RM.
10'-1 1/8" CEILING
14'0" X 19'4"
DN.
MBR.
TRAY CEILING
14'8" X 12'8"
LIN.
ARCH SOFFIT
2 CAR GAR.
20'8" X 19'8"
E.
10'-1 1/8" CEILING
BR. #3/ DEN
CATHEDRAL CEILING
11'0" X 11'10"
BR. #2
10'8" X 11'0"
MAIN FLOOR

Design 62058

GARAGE 21'-0" X 20'-0"
GRILLING PORCH
LAU.
STOR.
PATIO
KITCHEN 12'-4" X 10'-10"
M.BATH 7'-10" X 19'-8"
MASTER SUITE 12'-0" X 16'-8"
10' BOXED CEILING
DINING 17'-8" X 10'-0"
COMP CENTER
W.I.C.
8' COLUMNS
BATH
GREAT ROOM 14'-10" X 19'-9"
10' BOXED CEILING
BEDROOM 3 11'-0" X 12'-6"
FOYER
OPT BOOK SHELVES
COVERED PORCH 20'-8" X 8'-0"
BEDROOM 2 / STUDY 12'-0" X 13'-8"

MAIN FLOOR

Units	Single
Price Code	C
Total Finished	1,601 sq. ft.
Main Finished	1,601 sq. ft.
Garage Unfinished	771 sq. ft.
Porch Unfinished	279 sq. ft.
Dimensions	39'x77'2"
Foundation	Crawlspace Slab
Bedrooms	3
Full Baths	2
Main Ceiling	9'
Max Ridge Height	22'
Roof Framing	Stick
Exterior Walls	2x4

Design 69145

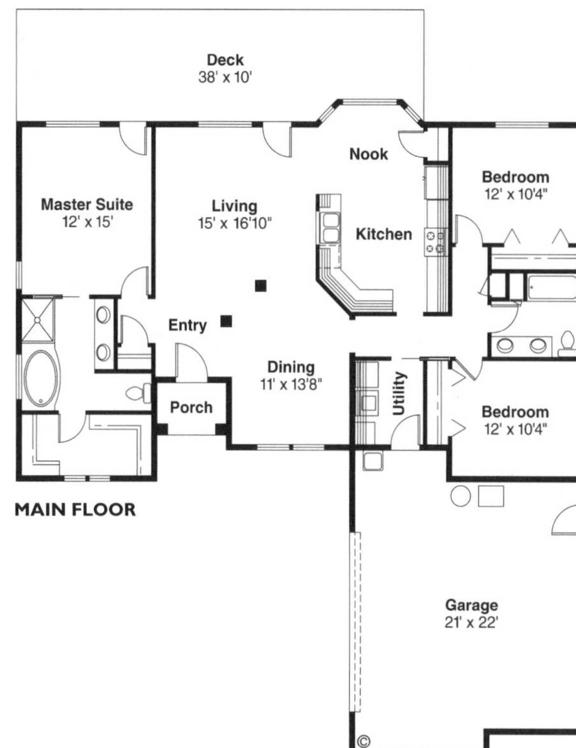
Deck
38' x 10'
Nook
Master Suite
12' x 15'
Living
15' x 16'10"
Kitchen
Bedroom
12' x 10'4"
Entry
Dining
11' x 13'8"
Porch
Utility
Bedroom
12' x 10'4"
Garage
21' x 22'

MAIN FLOOR

Units	Single
Price Code	B
Total Finished	1,605 sq. ft.
Main Finished	1,605 sq. ft.
Garage Unfinished	547 sq. ft.
Dimensions	53'x58'
Foundation	Crawlspace
Bedrooms	3
Full Baths	2
Main Ceiling	9'
Vaulted Ceiling	12'
Max Ridge Height	22'
Roof Framing	Truss
Exterior Walls	2x6

Design 20191

Units	Single
Price Code	B
Total Finished	1,606 sq. ft.
Main Finished	1,606 sq. ft.
Basement Unfinished	1,575 sq. ft.
Garage Unfinished	545 sq. ft.
Dimensions	60'x46'
Foundation	Basement
Bedrooms	3
Full Baths	2
Main Ceiling	8'
Max Ridge Height	20'
Roof Framing	Stick
Exterior Walls	2x6

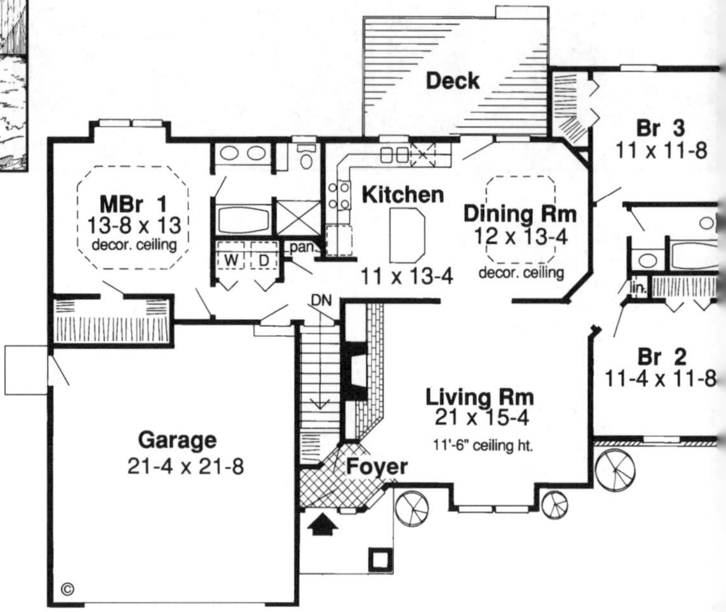

MAIN FLOOR

Design 91172

Units	Single
Price Code	B
Total Finished	1,607 sq. ft.
Main Finished	1,607 sq. ft.
Garage Unfinished	410 sq. ft.
Porch Unfinished	27 sq. ft.
Dimensions	39'11½"x62'7½"
Foundation	Slab
Bedrooms	3
Full Baths	2
Main Ceiling	8'1⅛"
Max Ridge Height	18'
Roof Framing	Stick
Exterior Walls	2x4

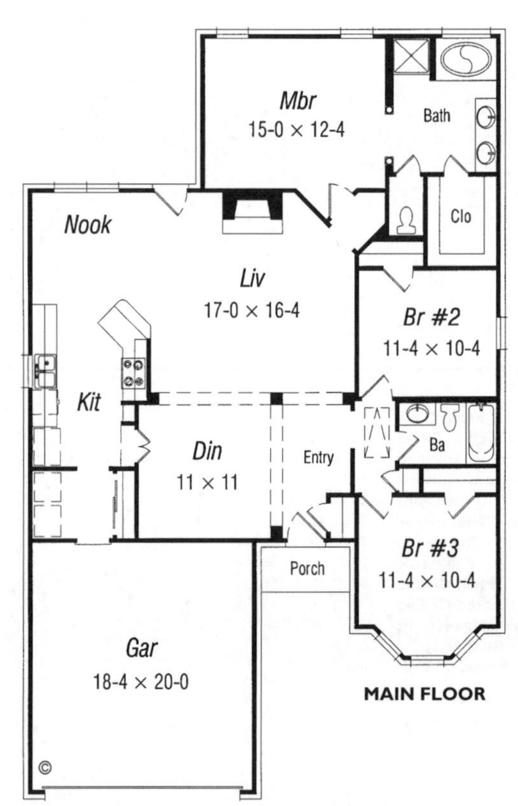
Mbr
15-0 × 12-4
Bath
Clo
Nook
Liv
17-0 × 16-4
Br #2
11-4 × 10-4
Kit
Din
11 × 11
Entry
Ba
Br #3
11-4 × 10-4
Porch
Gar
18-4 × 20-0
©

MAIN FLOOR

Design 35001

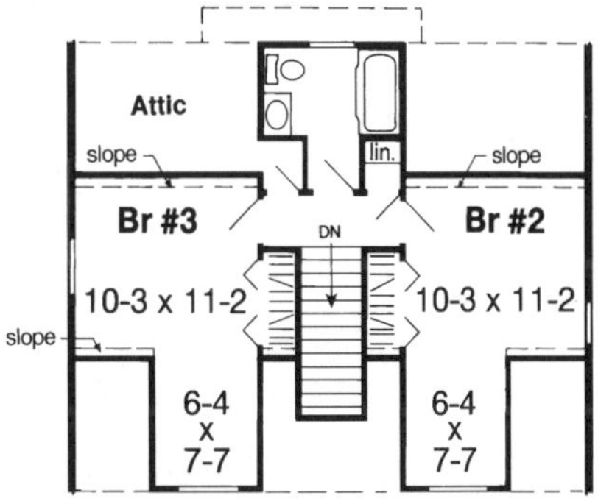

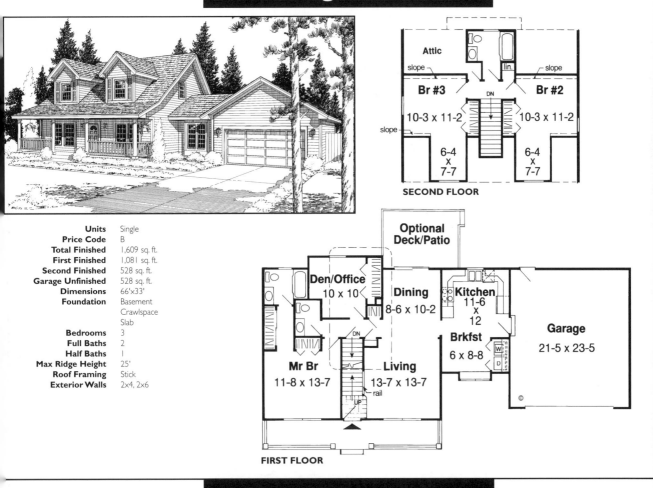

Attic
slope
lin.
slope
Br #3
10-3 x 11-2
DN
Br #2
10-3 x 11-2
slope
6-4 x 7-7
6-4 x 7-7

SECOND FLOOR

Units	Single
Price Code	B
Total Finished	1,609 sq. ft.
First Finished	1,081 sq. ft.
Second Finished	528 sq. ft.
Garage Unfinished	528 sq. ft.
Dimensions	66'x33'
Foundation	Basement Crawlspace Slab
Bedrooms	3
Full Baths	2
Half Baths	1
Max Ridge Height	25'
Roof Framing	Stick
Exterior Walls	2x4, 2x6

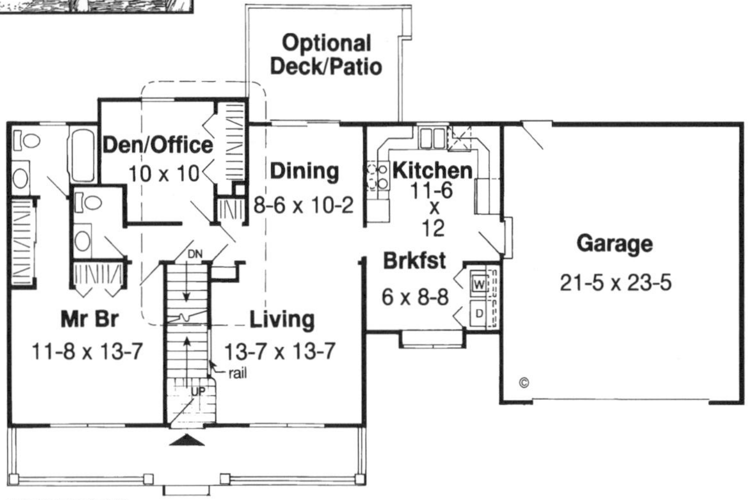

Optional Deck/Patio
Den/Office
10 x 10
Dining
8-6 x 10-2
Kitchen
11-6 x 12
Brkfst
6 x 8-8
Garage
21-5 x 23-5
DN
Mr Br
11-8 x 13-7
Living
13-7 x 13-7
rail
UP
W
D

FIRST FLOOR

Design 91115

Units	Single
Price Code	B
Total Finished	1,611 sq. ft.
Main Finished	1,611 sq. ft.
Garage Unfinished	501 sq. ft.
Dimensions	53'10"x50'4"
Foundation	Slab
Bedrooms	3
Full Baths	2
Max Ridge Height	21'
Roof Framing	Stick
Exterior Walls	2x4

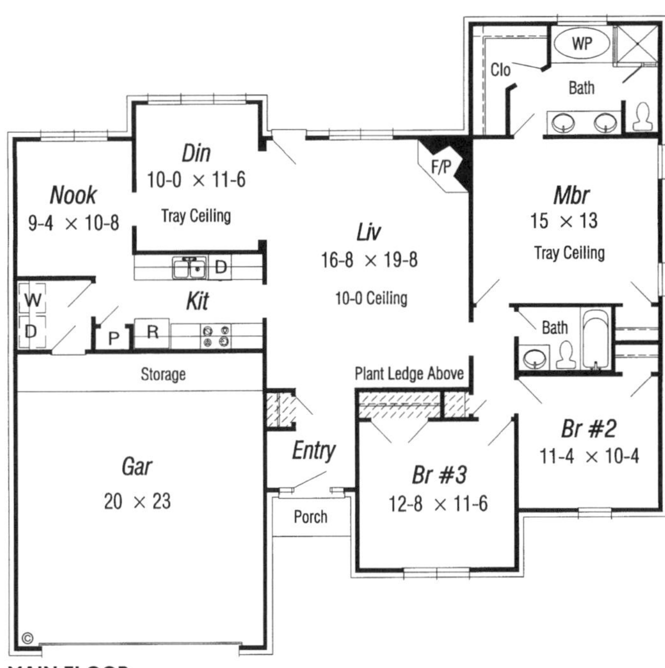
WP
Clo
Bath
Din
10-0 × 11-6
Tray Ceiling
F/P
Nook
9-4 × 10-8
Liv
16-8 × 19-8
10-0 Ceiling
Mbr
15 × 13
Tray Ceiling
W
D
Kit
P
R
D
Bath
Storage
Plant Ledge Above
Gar
20 × 23
Entry
Br #3
12-8 × 11-6
Br #2
11-4 × 10-4
Porch

MAIN FLOOR

Design 97759

Units	Single
Price Code	B
Total Finished	1,611 sq. ft.
Main Finished	1,611 sq. ft.
Basement Unfinished	1,611 sq. ft.
Garage Unfinished	430 sq. ft.
Deck Unfinished	228 sq. ft.
Porch Unfinished	163 sq. ft.
Dimensions	67'x44'4"
Foundation	Basement
Bedrooms	3
Full Baths	2
Main Ceiling	8'
Vaulted Ceiling	10'
Tray Ceiling	10'
Max Ridge Height	22'6"
Roof Framing	Truss
Exterior Walls	2x4

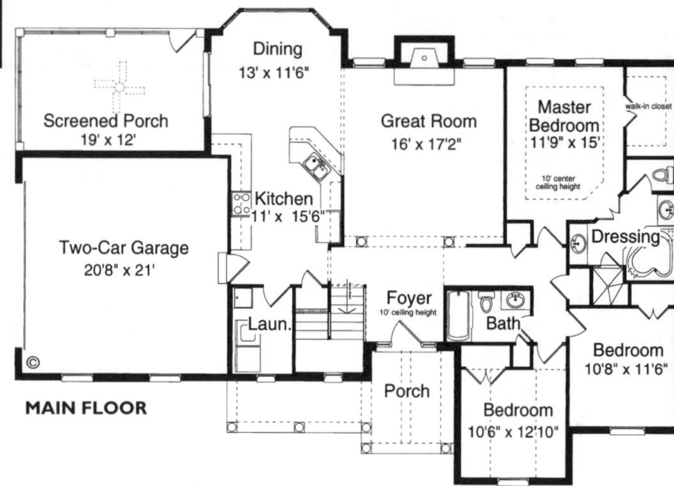

Dining
13' x 11'6"
Screened Porch
19' x 12'
Great Room
16' x 17'2"
Master Bedroom
11'9" x 15'
walk-in closet
10' center ceiling height
Kitchen
11' x 15'6"
Two-Car Garage
20'8" x 21'
Dressing
Foyer
10' ceiling height
Laun.
Bath
Bedroom
10'8" x 11'6"
Porch
Bedroom
10'6" x 12'10"
MAIN FLOOR

Design 97760

Units	Single
Price Code	B
Total Finished	1,611 sq. ft.
Main Finished	1,611 sq. ft.
Garage Unfinished	430 sq. ft.
Deck Unfinished	228 sq. ft.
Porch Unfinished	163 sq. ft.
Dimensions	66'4"x43'10"
Foundation	Basement
Bedrooms	3
Full Baths	2
Main Ceiling	8'
Vaulted Ceiling	10'
Tray Ceiling	10'
Max Ridge Height	22'6"
Roof Framing	Truss
Exterior Walls	2x4

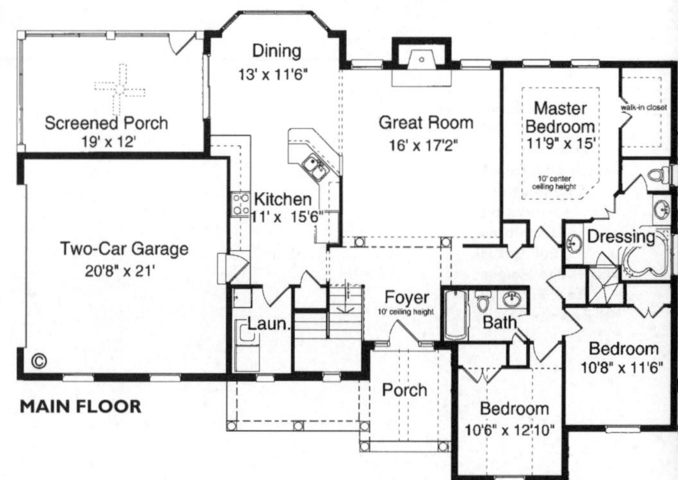

Dining
13' x 11'6"
Screened Porch
19' x 12'
Great Room
16' x 17'2"
Master Bedroom
11'9" x 15'
walk-in closet
10' center ceiling height
Kitchen
11' x 15'6"
Two-Car Garage
20'8" x 21'
Dressing
Foyer
10' ceiling height
Laun.
Bath
Bedroom
10'8" x 11'6"
Porch
Bedroom
10'6" x 12'10"
MAIN FLOOR

Design 93465

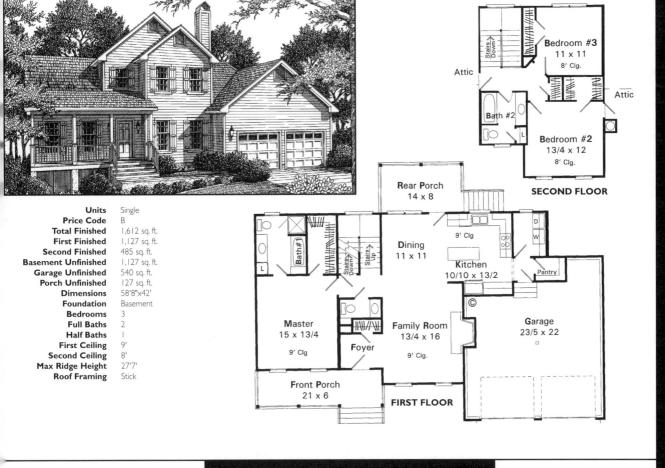

Rear Porch
14 x 8
Bedroom #3
11 x 11
8' Clg.
Stairs Down
Attic
Attic
Bath #2
Bedroom #2
13/4 x 12
8' Clg.
SECOND FLOOR
Bath#1
Stairs Down
Stairs Up
Dining
11 x 11
9' Clg
Kitchen
10/10 x 13/2
D
W
Pantry
Master
15 x 13/4
9' Clg
Foyer
Family Room
13/4 x 16
9' Clg.
Garage
23/5 x 22
Front Porch
21 x 6
FIRST FLOOR

Units	Single
Price Code	B
Total Finished	1,612 sq. ft.
First Finished	1,127 sq. ft.
Second Finished	485 sq. ft.
Basement Unfinished	1,127 sq. ft.
Garage Unfinished	540 sq. ft.
Porch Unfinished	127 sq. ft.
Dimensions	58'8"x42'
Foundation	Basement
Bedrooms	3
Full Baths	2
Half Baths	1
First Ceiling	9'
Second Ceiling	8'
Max Ridge Height	27'7'
Roof Framing	Stick

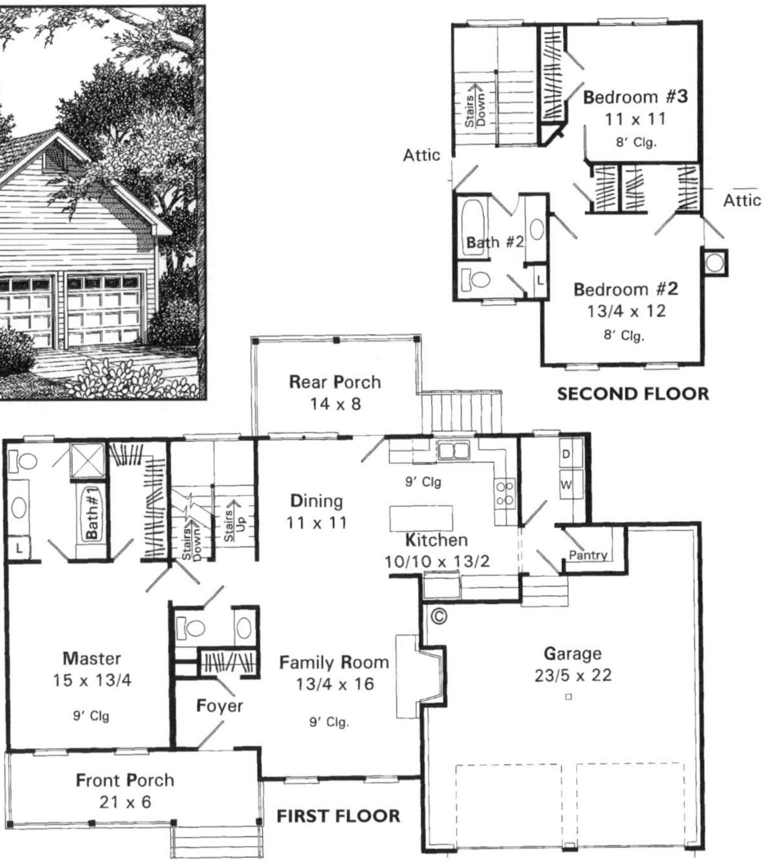

Design 94624

Units	Single
Price Code	B
Total Finished	1,615 sq. ft.
Main Finished	1,615 sq. ft.
Garage Unfinished	451 sq. ft.
Porch Unfinished	145 sq. ft.
Dimensions	38'x62'5"
Foundation	Slab
Bedrooms	3
Full Baths	2
Main Ceiling	9'
Max Ridge Height	23'1"
Roof Framing	Stick
Exterior Walls	2x4

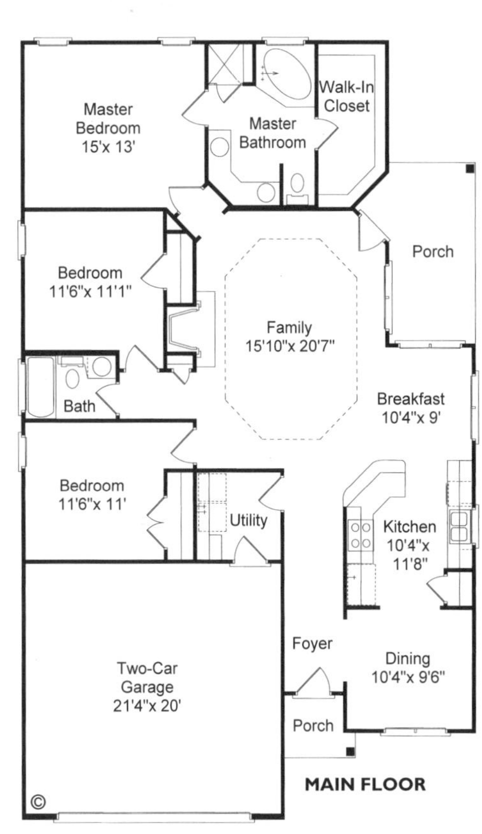
Master Bedroom
15'x 13'
Master Bathroom
Walk-In Closet
Porch
Bedroom
11'6"x 11'1"
Family
15'10"x 20'7"
Bath
Breakfast
10'4"x 9'
Bedroom
11'6"x 11'
Utility
Kitchen
10'4"x
11'8"
Foyer
Two-Car Garage
21'4"x 20'
Dining
10'4"x 9'6"
Porch
MAIN FLOOR

Design 64196

Units	Single
Price Code	G
Total Finished	1,616 sq. ft.
Main Finished	1,616 sq. ft.
Bonus Unfinished	362 sq. ft.
Garage Unfinished	534 sq. ft.
Dimensions	64'x54'6"
Foundation	Crawlspace
Bedrooms	3
Full Baths	2
Max Ridge Height	23'2"
Exterior Walls	2x6

* Alternate foundation options available at an additional charge. Please call 1-800-235-5700 for more information.

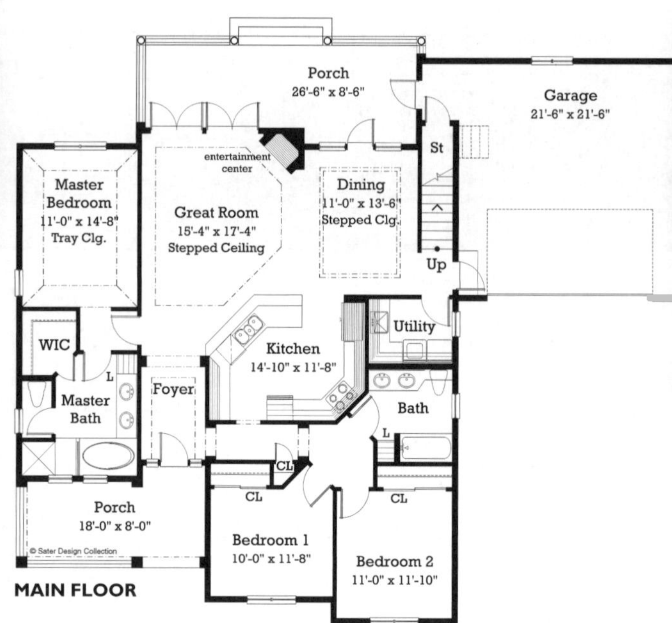

Porch
26'-6" x 8'-6"
Garage
21'-6" x 21'-6"
St
entertainment center
Master Bedroom
11'-0" x 14'-8"
Tray Clg.
Great Room
15'-4" x 17'-4"
Stepped Ceiling
Dining
11'-0" x 13'-6"
Stepped Clg.
Up
WIC
Utility
Kitchen
14'-10" x 11'-8"
Master Bath
Foyer
Bath
CL
Porch
18'-0" x 8'-0"
Bedroom 1
10'-0" x 11'-8"
Bedroom 2
11'-0" x 11'-10"
© Sater Design Collection
MAIN FLOOR

Design 98924

Units	Single
Price Code	B
Total Finished	1,617 sq. ft.
Main Finished	1,617 sq. ft.
Garage Unfinished	524 sq. ft.
Deck Unfinished	233 sq. ft.
Porch Unfinished	133 sq. ft.
Dimensions	53'x38'
Foundation	Combo Basement Crawlspace
Bedrooms	3
Full Baths	2
Main Ceiling	8'
Max Ridge Height	27'
Roof Framing	Stick
Exterior Walls	2x4

Sundeck
23-6 x 12-0
Brkfst.
11-6 x 7-4
Pantry
Master Bedroom
11-6 x 17-4
M.Bath
Linen
Kitchen
11-6 x 8-2
Dining
11-0 x 11-6
Ref.
Bath 2
Down
W. D.
Plant Shelf Above
Linen
Up
Living Area
22-10 x 15-6
Cts.
Bedroom 2
11-6 x 10-2
Bedroom 3
11-6 x 10-2
©
MAIN FLOOR

Design 98416

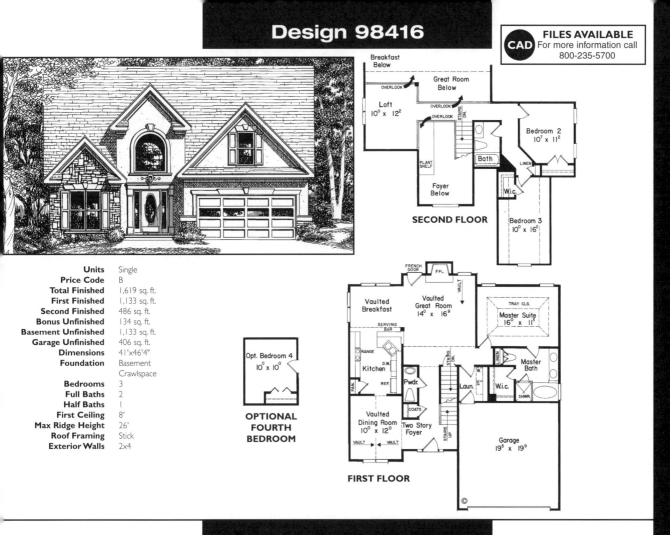

CAD FILES AVAILABLE
For more information call
800-235-5700

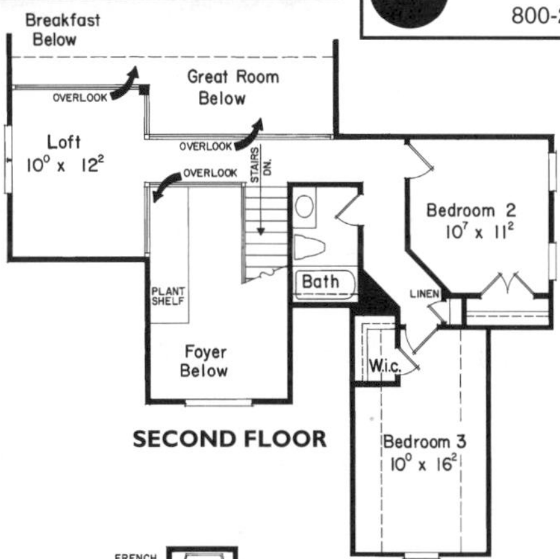

1,501-2,000 sq.ft. HOME PLANS

Units	Single
Price Code	B
Total Finished	1,619 sq. ft.
First Finished	1,133 sq. ft.
Second Finished	486 sq. ft.
Bonus Unfinished	134 sq. ft.
Basement Unfinished	1,133 sq. ft.
Garage Unfinished	406 sq. ft.
Dimensions	41'x46'4"
Foundation	Basement Crawlspace
Bedrooms	3
Full Baths	2
Half Baths	1
First Ceiling	8'
Max Ridge Height	26'
Roof Framing	Stick
Exterior Walls	2x4

SECOND FLOOR

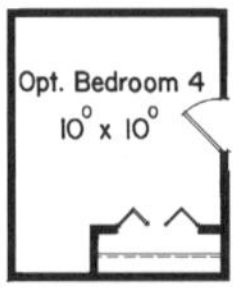

OPTIONAL FOURTH BEDROOM

FIRST FLOOR

Design 24317

Units	Single
Price Code	B
Total Finished	1,620 sq. ft.
Main Finished	1,620 sq. ft.
Dimensions	50'x55'8"
Foundation	Basement Crawlspace
Bedrooms	3
Full Baths	1
3/4 Baths	1
Max Ridge Height	23'
Roof Framing	Stick
Exterior Walls	2x4

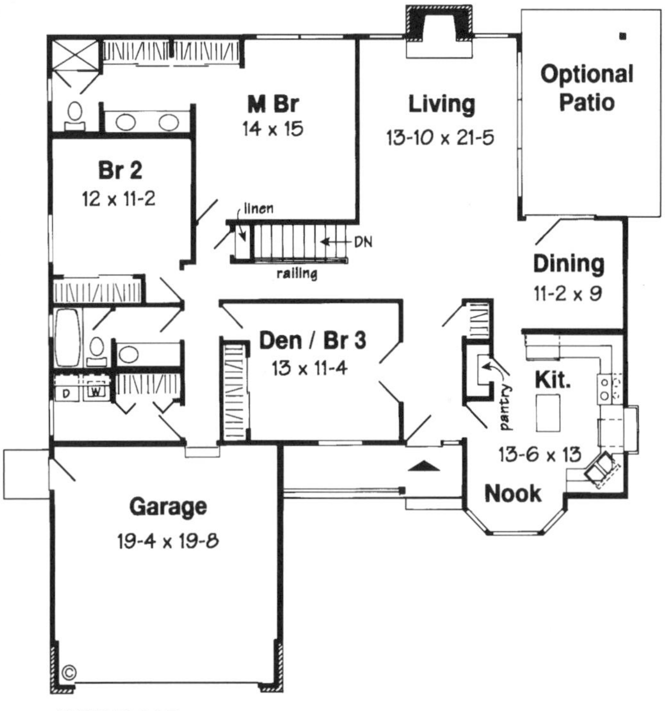

MAIN FLOOR

Design 97495

Units	Single
Price Code	B
Total Finished	1,622 sq. ft.
Main Finished	1,622 sq. ft.
Garage Unfinished	469 sq. ft.
Dimensions	51'x52'
Foundation	Basement
Bedrooms	3
Full Baths	2
Main Ceiling	8'
Max Ridge Height	20'6"
Roof Framing	Stick
Exterior Walls	2x4

* Alternate foundation options available at an additional charge. Please call 1-800-235-5700 for more information.

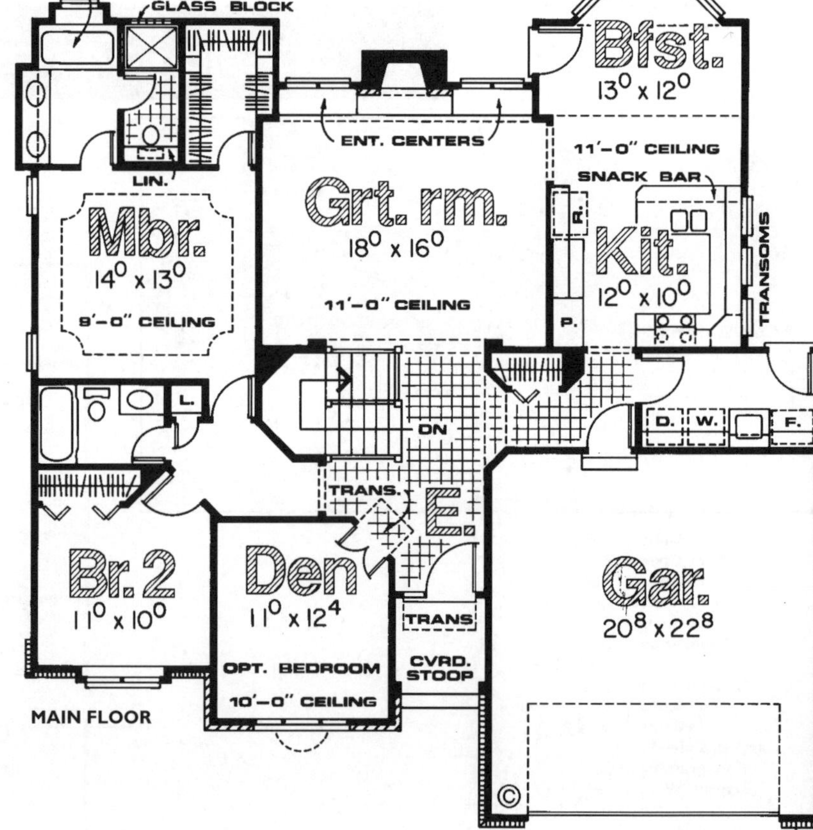
WHIRLPOOL
GLASS BLOCK
LIN.
Mbr.
14⁰ x 13⁰
9'-0" CEILING
ENT. CENTERS
Grt. rm.
18⁰ x 16⁰
11'-0" CEILING
Bfst.
13⁰ x 12⁰
11'-0" CEILING
SNACK BAR
R.
Kit.
12⁰ x 10⁰
P.
TRANSOMS
L.
DN
D. W. F.
TRANS.
E.
Br. 2
11⁰ x 10⁰
Den
11⁰ x 12⁴
OPT. BEDROOM
10'-0" CEILING
TRANS
CVRD. STOOP
Gar.
20⁸ x 22⁸
MAIN FLOOR

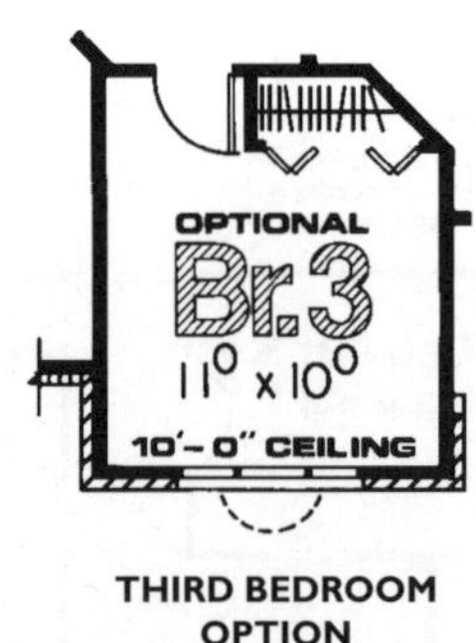
OPTIONAL
Br. 3
11⁰ x 10⁰
10'-0" CEILING

THIRD BEDROOM OPTION

Design 64017

Units	Single
Price Code	B
Total Finished	1,624 sq. ft.
Main Finished	1,624 sq. ft.
Bonus Unfinished	142 sq. ft.
Garage Unfinished	462 sq. ft.
Dimensions	60'x48'
Foundation	Crawlspace Slab
Bedrooms	3
Full Baths	2
Main Ceiling	8'
Roof Framing	Stick
Exterior Walls	2x4

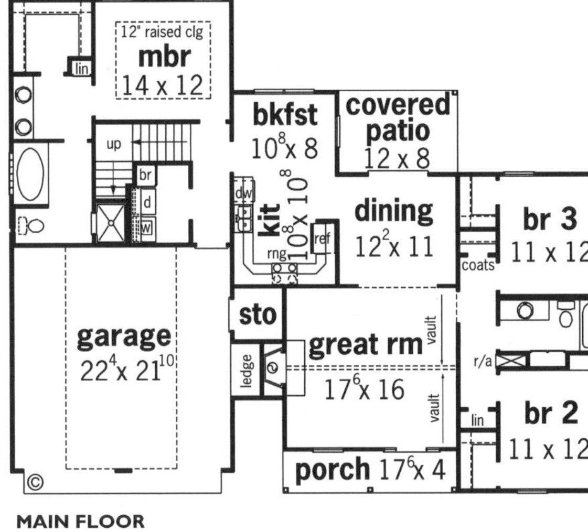
12" raised clg
mbr
14 x 12
lin
up
br
d
w
bkfst
10⁸x 8
covered
patio
12 x 8
dw
kit
10⁸x 10⁸
rng
ref
dining
12²x 11
br 3
11 x 12
coats
sto
garage
22⁴x 21¹⁰
great rm
17⁶x 16
vault
vault
r/a
ledge
lin
br 2
11 x 12
porch 17⁶x 4

MAIN FLOOR

Design 24701

Units	Single
Price Code	B
Total Finished	1,625 sq. ft.
Main Finished	1,625 sq. ft.
Basement Unfinished	1,625 sq. ft.
Garage Unfinished	455 sq. ft.
Dimensions	54'x48'4"
Foundation	Basement Crawlspace Slab
Bedrooms	3
Full Baths	2
Main Ceiling	8'-9'
Max Ridge Height	22'
Roof Framing	Stick
Exterior Walls	2x4, 2x6

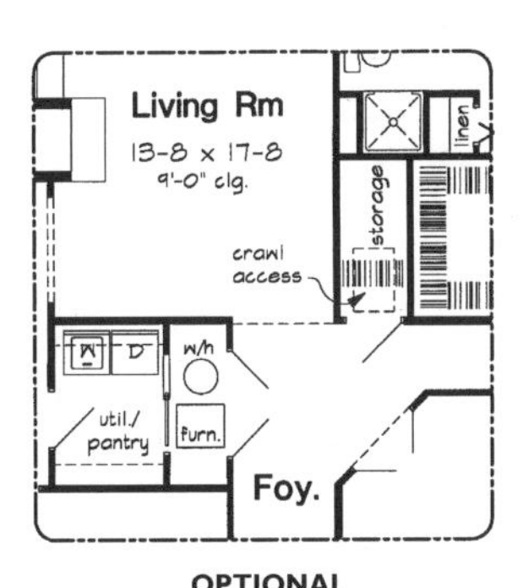
Living Rm
13-8 x 17-8
9'-0" clg.
linen
storage
crawl access
w/h
util./ pantry
furn.
Foy.

OPTIONAL CRAWLSPACE/SLAB FOUNDATION

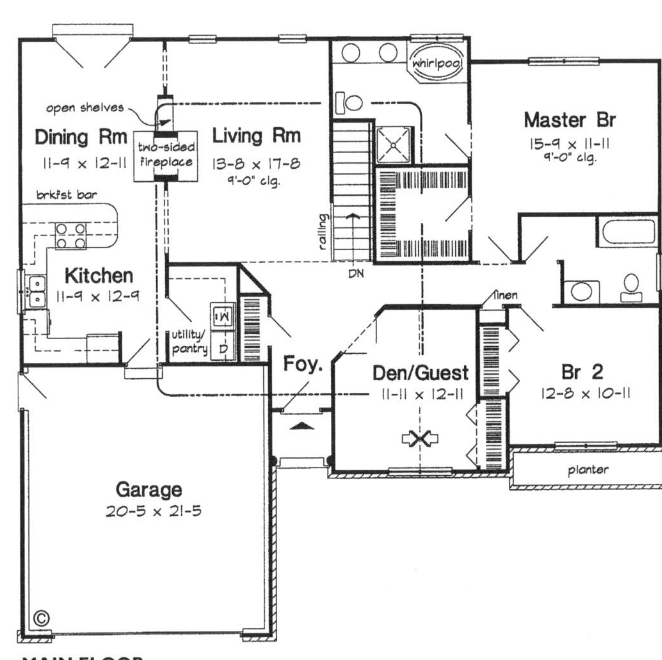
open shelves
Dining Rm
11-9 x 12-11
two-sided fireplace
Living Rm
13-8 x 17-8
9'-0" clg.
whirlpool
Master Br
15-9 x 11-11
9'-0" clg.
brkfst bar
railing
DN
Kitchen
11-9 x 12-9
utility/ pantry
linen
Foy.
Den/Guest
11-11 x 12-11
Br 2
12-8 x 10-11
planter
Garage
20-5 x 21-5

MAIN FLOOR

Design 63091

Units	Single
Price Code	B
Total Finished	1,627 sq. ft.
Main Finished	1,627 sq. ft.
Garage Unfinished	420 sq. ft.
Dimensions	46'x70'
Foundation	Slab
Bedrooms	3
Full Baths	2
Main Ceiling	10'
Max Ridge Height	25'8"
Exterior Walls	2x4

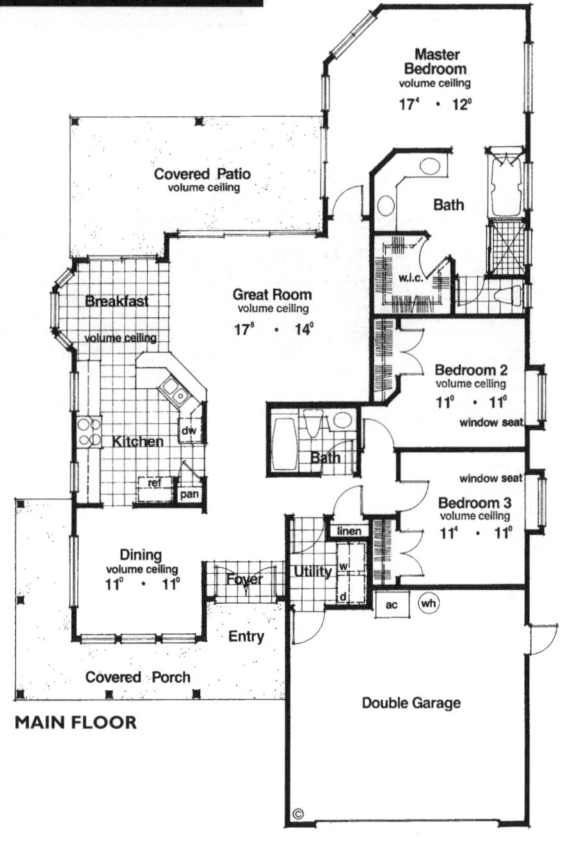
Master Bedroom
volume ceiling
17⁴ • 12⁰
Covered Patio
volume ceiling
Bath
w.i.c.
Great Room
volume ceiling
17⁸ • 14⁰
Breakfast
volume ceiling
Bedroom 2
volume ceiling
11⁰ • 11⁰
window seat
Kitchen
dw
Bath
ref
pan
window seat
Bedroom 3
volume ceiling
11⁴ • 11⁰
linen
Dining
volume ceiling
11⁰ • 11⁰
Foyer
Utility
w
d
ac
wh
Entry
Covered Porch
Double Garage
MAIN FLOOR

Design 96805

Units	Single
Price Code	B
Total Finished	1,627 sq. ft.
Main Finished	1,627 sq. ft.
Garage Unfinished	480 sq. ft.
Dimensions	52'x53'
Foundation	Crawlspace Slab
Bedrooms	3
Full Baths	2
Main Ceiling	8'2"
Vaulted Ceiling	13'9"
Max Ridge Height	20'8"
Roof Framing	Truss
Exterior Walls	2x4

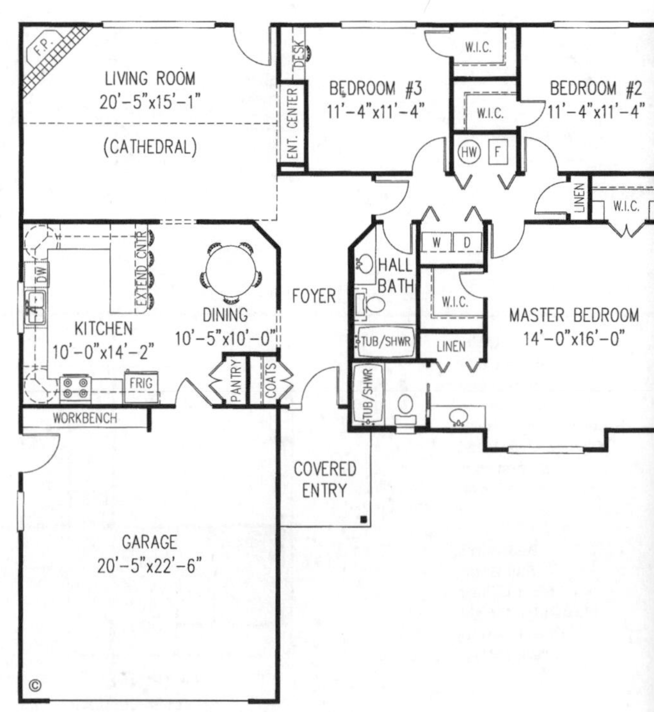
F.P.
LIVING ROOM
20'-5"x15'-1"
(CATHEDRAL)
ENT. CENTER
DESK
BEDROOM #3
11'-4"x11'-4"
W.I.C.
W.I.C.
BEDROOM #2
11'-4"x11'-4"
HW
F
LINEN
W.I.C.
EXTEND CNTR
DW
KITCHEN
10'-0"x14'-2"
DINING
10'-5"x10'-0"
FRIG
PANTRY
COATS
FOYER
W
D
HALL BATH
W.I.C.
MASTER BEDROOM
14'-0"x16'-0"
TUB/SHWR
LINEN
TUB/SHWR
WORKBENCH
COVERED ENTRY
GARAGE
20'-5"x22'-6"
MAIN FLOOR

Design 90398

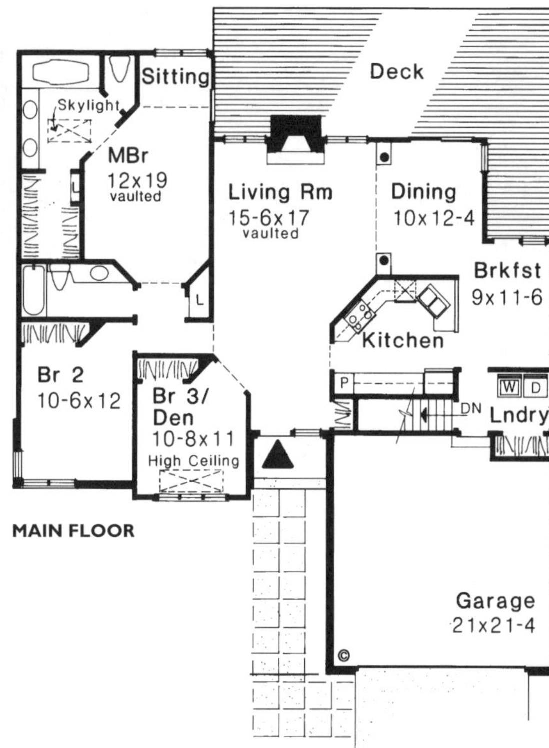
Sitting
Deck
Skylight
MBr
12x19
vaulted
Living Rm
15-6x17
vaulted
Dining
10x12-4
Brkfst
9x11-6
Kitchen
Br 2
10-6x12
Br 3/
Den
10-8x11
High Ceiling
P
DN
Lndry
W D
Garage
21x21-4

MAIN FLOOR

Units	Single
Price Code	B
Total Finished	1,630 sq. ft.
Main Finished	1,630 sq. ft.
Dimensions	52'4"x57'4"
Foundation	Basement
Bedrooms	2
Full Baths	2
Exterior Walls	2x4

Design 93418

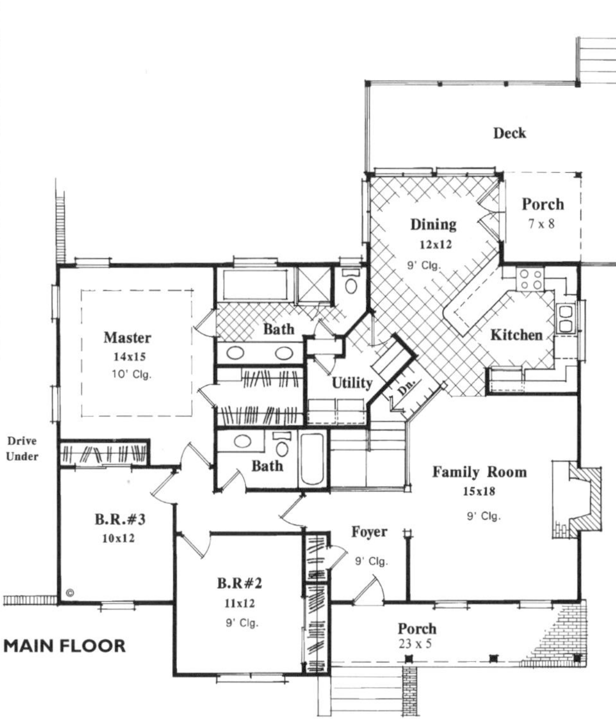
Deck
Dining
12x12
9' Clg.
Porch
7 x 8
Master
14x15
10' Clg.
Bath
Kitchen
Utility
Dn.
Drive
Under
Bath
Family Room
15x18
9' Clg.
B.R.#3
10x12
Foyer
9' Clg.
B.R#2
11x12
9' Clg.
Porch
23 x 5

MAIN FLOOR

Units	Single
Price Code	B
Total Finished	1,631 sq. ft.
Main Finished	1,631 sq. ft.
Basement Unfinished	1,015 sq. ft.
Garage Unfinished	616 sq. ft.
Porch Unfinished	115 sq. ft.
Dimensions	48'x44'
Foundation	Basement
Bedrooms	3
Full Baths	2
Max Ridge Height	26'
Roof Framing	Stick
Exterior Walls	2x4

Design 97115

Units	Single
Price Code	B
Total Finished	1,633 sq. ft.
Main Finished	1,633 sq. ft.
Basement Unfinished	1,633 sq. ft.
Dimensions	53'x52'
Foundation	Basement
Bedrooms	3
Full Baths	2
Max Ridge Height	20'
Roof Framing	Truss
Exterior Walls	2x6

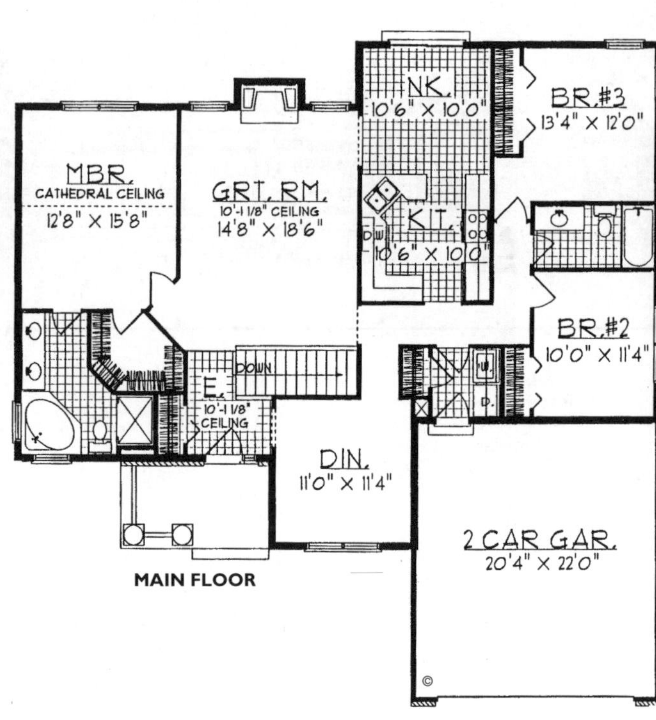

NK.
10'6" X 10'0"
BR.#3
13'4" X 12'0"
MBR.
CATHEDRAL CEILING
12'8" X 15'8"
GRT. RM.
10'-1 1/8" CEILING
14'8" X 18'6"
KIT.
10'6" X 10'0"
BR.#2
10'0" X 11'4"
DOWN
E.
10'-1 1/8" CEILING
DIN.
11'0" X 11'4"
2 CAR GAR.
20'4" X 22'0"
MAIN FLOOR

Design 69149

Units	Single
Price Code	B
Total Finished	1,634 sq. ft.
Main Finished	1,634 sq. ft.
Garage Unfinished	476 sq. ft.
Dimensions	68'x40'
Foundation	Crawlspace
Bedrooms	3
Full Baths	1
3/4 Baths	1
Main Ceiling	8'
Max Ridge Height	26'6"
Roof Framing	Truss
Exterior Walls	2x6

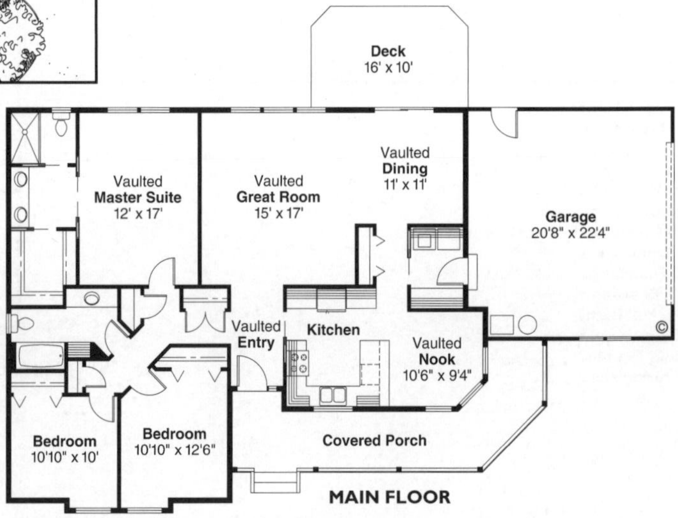

Deck 16' x 10'
Vaulted Master Suite 12' x 17'
Vaulted Great Room 15' x 17'
Vaulted Dining 11' x 11'
Garage 20'8" x 22'4"
Vaulted Entry
Kitchen
Vaulted Nook 10'6" x 9'4"
Bedroom 10'10" x 10'
Bedroom 10'10" x 12'6"
Covered Porch
MAIN FLOOR

Design 68079

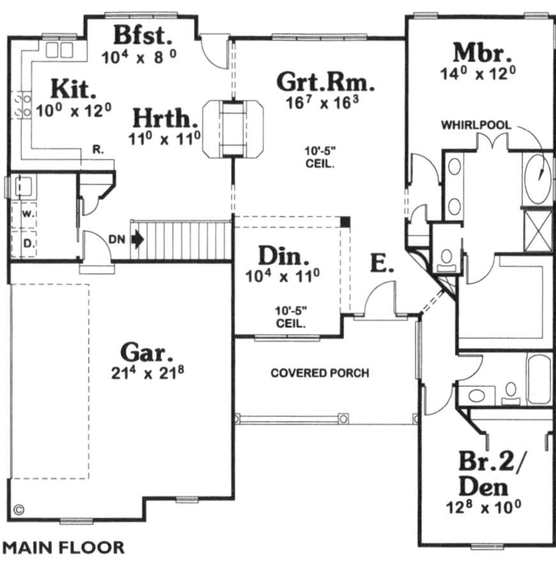
Bfst.
10⁴ x 8⁰
Kit.
10⁰ x 12⁰
Hrth.
11⁰ x 11⁰
R.
Grt.Rm.
16⁷ x 16³
10'-5" CEIL.
Mbr.
14⁰ x 12⁰
WHIRLPOOL
W.
D.
DN
Din.
10⁴ x 11⁰
10'-5" CEIL.
E.
Gar.
21⁴ x 21⁸
COVERED PORCH
Br.2/ Den
12⁸ x 10⁰
MAIN FLOOR

Units	Single
Price Code	B
Total Finished	1,636 sq. ft.
Main Finished	1,636 sq. ft.
Basement Unfinished	1,636 sq. ft.
Garage Unfinished	508 sq. ft.
Deck Unfinished	158 sq. ft.
Dimensions	53'4"x49'4"
Foundation	Basement Crawlspace Slab
Bedrooms	2
Full Baths	2
Main Ceiling	9'
Max Ridge Height	24'3"
Roof Framing	Stick
Exterior Walls	2x4

* Alternate foundation options available at an additional charge.
Please call 1-800-235-5700 for more information.

Design 97455

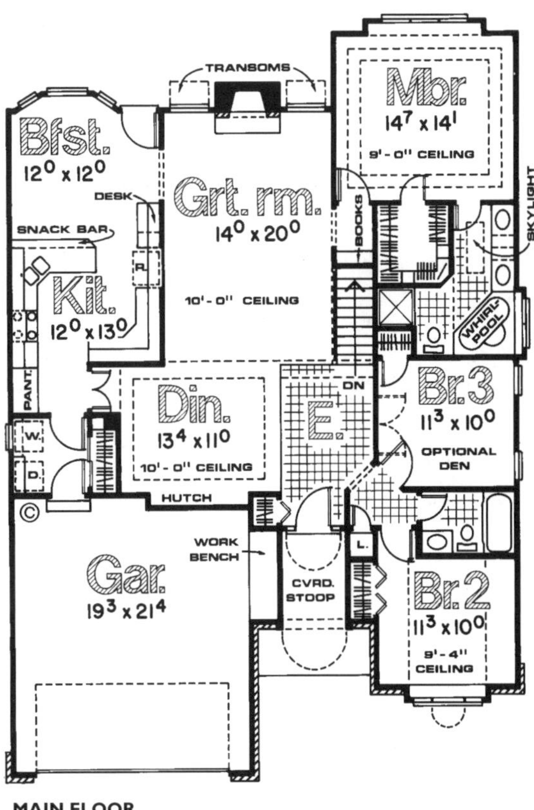
TRANSOMS
Bfst.
12⁰ x 12⁰
DESK
SNACK BAR
Grt. rm.
14⁰ x 20⁰
10'-0" CEILING
Mbr.
14⁷ x 14¹
9'-0" CEILING
BOOKS
SKYLIGHT
WHIRLPOOL
Kit.
12⁰ x 13⁰
R.
PANT.
W.
D.
Din.
13⁴ x 11⁰
10'-0" CEILING
HUTCH
E.
DN
Br.3
11³ x 10⁰
OPTIONAL DEN
WORK BENCH
Gar.
19³ x 21⁴
CVRD. STOOP
L.
Br.2
11³ x 10⁰
9'-4" CEILING
MAIN FLOOR

Units	Single
Price Code	B
Total Finished	1,636 sq. ft.
Main Finished	1,636 sq. ft.
Garage Unfinished	448 sq. ft.
Dimensions	42'x59'8"
Foundation	Basement
Bedrooms	3
Full Baths	2
Main Ceiling	8'
Max Ridge Height	21'
Roof Framing	Stick
Exterior Walls	2x4, 2x6

* Alternate foundation options available at an additional charge.
Please call 1-800-235-5700 for more information.

Design 92242

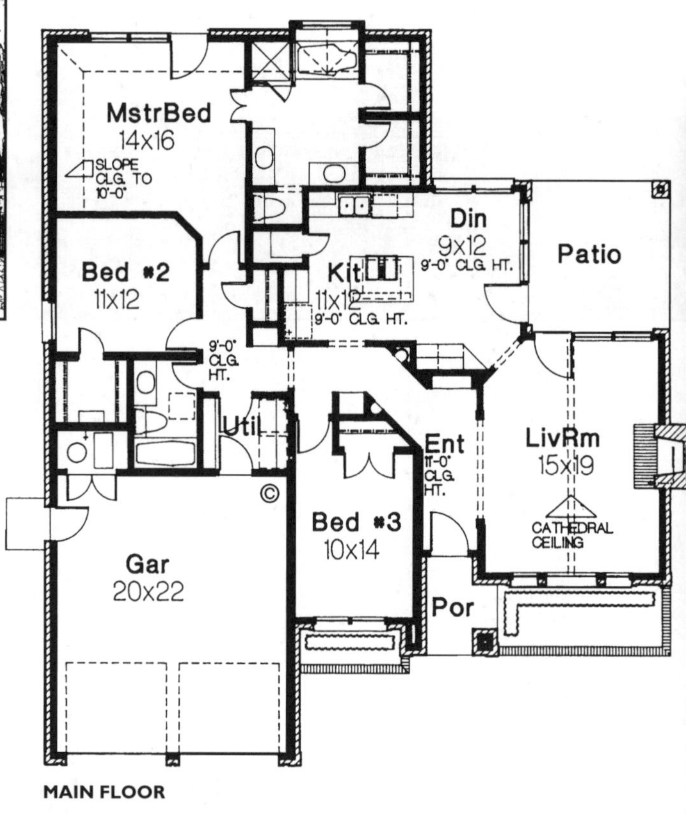
MstrBed
14x16
SLOPE CLG. TO 10'-0"
Bed #2
11x12
Din
9x12
9'-0" CLG. HT.
Kit
11x12
9'-0" CLG. HT.
Patio
9'-0" CLG. HT.
Util
Ent
11'-0" CLG. HT.
LivRm
15x19
CATHEDRAL CEILING
Bed #3
10x14
Gar
20x22
Por
MAIN FLOOR

Units	Single
Price Code	B
Total Finished	1,639 sq. ft.
Main Finished	1,639 sq. ft.
Garage Unfinished	442 sq. ft.
Deck Unfinished	145 sq. ft.
Porch Unfinished	52 sq. ft.
Dimensions	49'10"x57'1"
Foundation	Slab
Bedrooms	3
Full Baths	2
Main Ceiling	8'
Second Ceiling	10'
Vaulted Ceiling	10'
Max Ridge Height	24'6"
Roof Framing	Stick
Exterior Walls	2x4

Design 91471

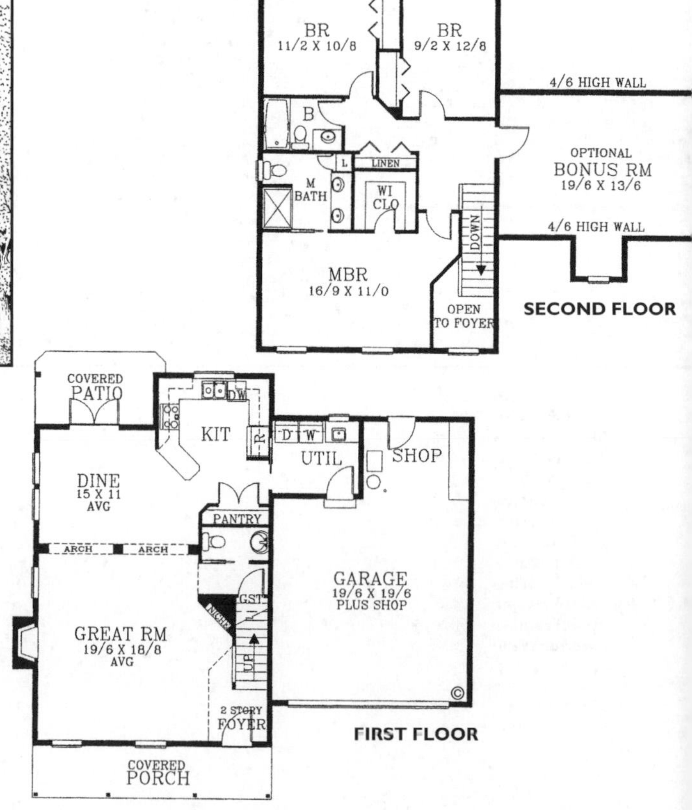
BR
11/2 X 10/8
BR
9/2 X 12/8
4/6 HIGH WALL
B
M BATH
LINEN
WI CLO
OPTIONAL BONUS RM
19/6 X 13/6
4/6 HIGH WALL
DOWN
MBR
16/9 X 11/0
OPEN TO FOYER
SECOND FLOOR
COVERED PATIO
KIT
DW
UTIL
SHOP
DINE
15 X 11
AVG
PANTRY
ARCH
ARCH
GARAGE
19/6 X 19/6
PLUS SHOP
GST
NICHE
GREAT RM
19/6 X 18/8
AVG
UP
2 STORY FOYER
FIRST FLOOR
COVERED PORCH

Units	Single
Price Code	C
Total Finished	1,640 sq. ft.
First Finished	865 sq. ft.
Second Finished	775 sq. ft.
Bonus Unfinished	315 sq. ft.
Garage Unfinished	380 sq. ft.
Dimensions	44'x41'
Foundation	Crawlspace
Bedrooms	3
Full Baths	1
3/4 Baths	1
Half Baths	1
First Ceiling	8'
Second Ceiling	8'
Max Ridge Height	29'
Roof Framing	Truss
Exterior Walls	2x6

Design 98580

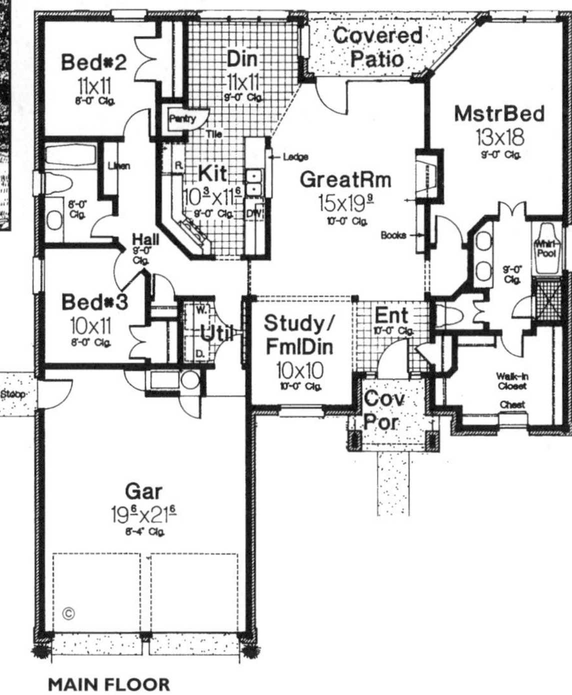
Bed#2
11x11
8'-0" Clg.
Din
11x11
9'-0" Clg.
Covered
Patio
MstrBed
13x18
9'-0" Clg.
Pantry
Tile
Linen
Kit
10³x11⁶
9'-0" Clg.
Ledge
GreatRm
15x19⁹
10'-0" Clg.
DW
Books
Whirl-Pool
Hall
9'-0" Clg.
Bed#3
10x11
8'-0" Clg.
Util
Study/
FmlDin
10x10
10'-0" Clg.
Ent
10'-0" Clg.
Walk-in
Closet
Chest
Stoop
Cov
Por
Gar
19⁶x21⁶
8'-4" Clg.
MAIN FLOOR

Units	Single
Price Code	B
Total Finished	1,640 sq. ft.
Main Finished	1,640 sq. ft.
Garage Unfinished	408 sq. ft.
Deck Unfinished	72 sq. ft.
Porch Unfinished	60 sq. ft.
Dimensions	50'x56'4"
Foundation	Slab
Bedrooms	3
Full Baths	2
Max Ridge Height	24'2"
Roof Framing	Stick
Exterior Walls	2x4

Design 24717

OPTIONAL BASEMENT STAIR LOCATION

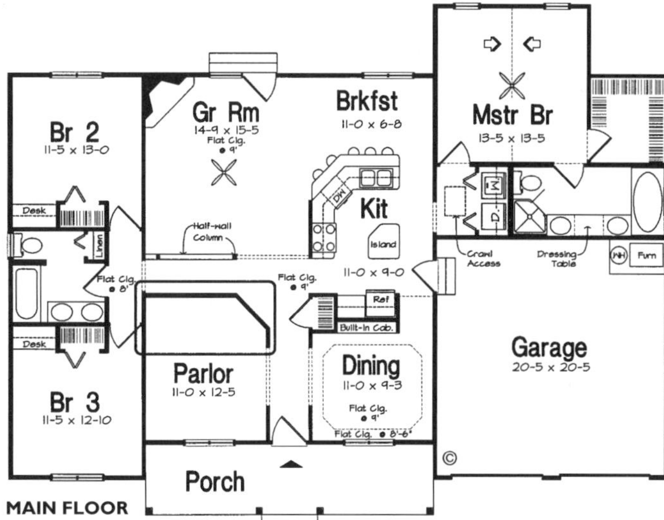
Br 2
11-5 x 13-0
Desk
Gr Rm
14-9 x 15-5
Flat Clg.
@ 9'
Brkfst
11-0 x 6-8
Mstr Br
13-5 x 13-5
Half-wall
Column
Kit
Island
11-0 x 9-0
Crawl
Access
Dressing
Table
Furn
Linen
Flat Clg. @ 8'
Flat Clg. @ 9'
Ref
Built-in Cab.
Parlor
11-0 x 12-5
Dining
11-0 x 9-3
Flat Clg. @ 9'
Flat Clg. @ 8'-6"
Garage
20-5 x 20-5
Br 3
11-5 x 12-10
Porch
MAIN FLOOR

Units	Single
Price Code	B
Total Finished	1,642 sq. ft.
Main Finished	1,642 sq. ft.
Basement Unfinished	1,642 sq. ft.
Garage Unfinished	430 sq. ft.
Porch Unfinished	156 sq. ft.
Dimensions	59'x44'
Foundation	Basement Crawlspace Slab
Bedrooms	3
Full Baths	2
Main Ceiling	9'
Vaulted Ceiling	13'6"
Max Ridge Height	24'
Roof Framing	Stick
Exterior Walls	2x4

Design 93171

Units	Single
Price Code	B
Total Finished	1,642 sq. ft.
Main Finished	1,642 sq. ft.
Basement Unfinished	1,642 sq. ft.
Porch Unfinished	192 sq. ft.
Dimensions	59'x66'
Foundation	Basement
Bedrooms	3
Full Baths	1
3/4 Baths	1
Half Baths	1
Max Ridge Height	22'
Roof Framing	Stick
Exterior Walls	2x6

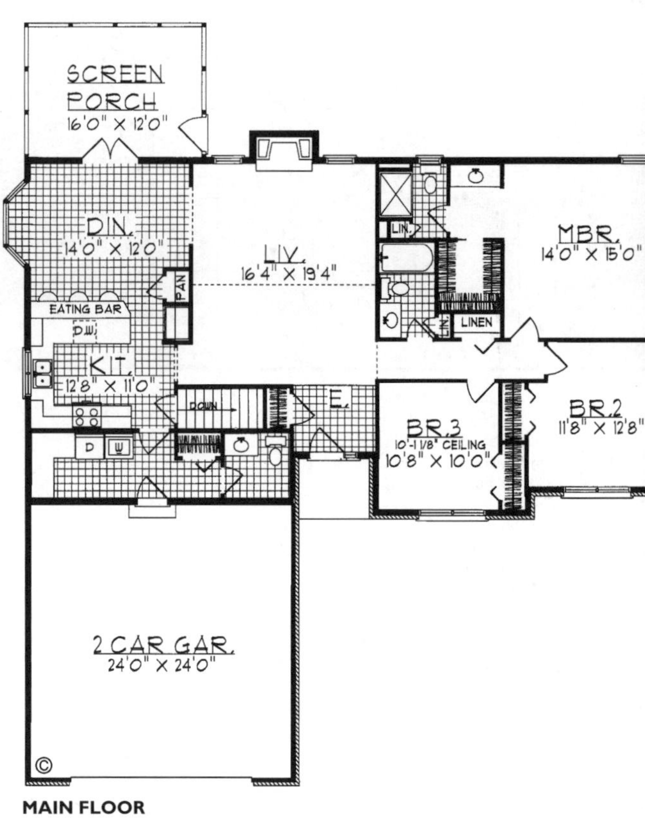

SCREEN PORCH
16'0" X 12'0"
DIN.
14'0" X 12'0"
LIV.
16'4" X 19'4"
MBR.
14'0" X 15'0"
LIN.
LINEN
PAN
EATING BAR
DW
KIT.
12'8" X 11'0"
DOWN
E.
BR.3
10'-1 1/8" CEILING
10'8" X 10'0"
BR.2
11'8" X 12'8"
D
W
2 CAR GAR.
24'0" X 24'0"
©

MAIN FLOOR

Design 92423

Units	Single
Price Code	B
Total Finished	1,643 sq. ft.
First Finished	1,064 sq. ft.
Second Finished	579 sq. ft.
Dimensions	38'x34'
Foundation	Basement
Bedrooms	3
Full Baths	2
Half Baths	1
First Ceiling	8'
Second Ceiling	8'
Vaulted Ceiling	14'
Max Ridge Height	21'6"
Exterior Walls	2x4

STORAGE
BEDROOM 3
15X12
DN
OPEN TO BELOW
BEDROOM 2
15X12

SECOND FLOOR

SKYLIGHT
DINING
12x12
KITCHEN
10x12
VAULT
COATS
D
W
DN
VAULT
UP
MASTER BEDRM
15x13
FAMILY ROOM
18x15
©

FIRST FLOOR

Design 92422

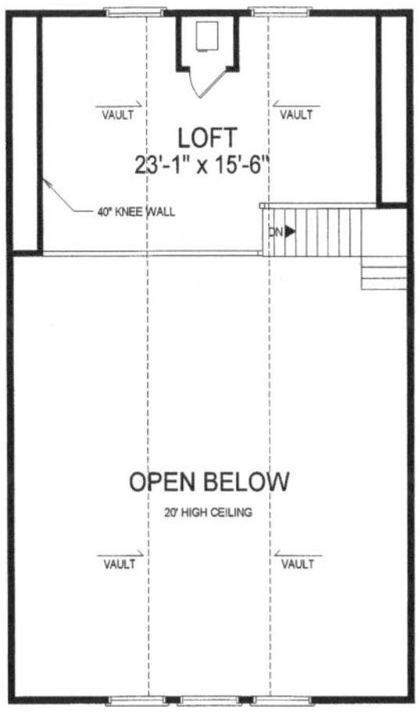

Units	Single
Price Code	B
Total Finished	1,647 sq. ft.
First Finished	1,288 sq. ft.
Second Finished	359 sq. ft.
Dimensions	28'x46'
Foundation	Slab
Bedrooms	2
Full Baths	1
First Ceiling	8'
Second Ceiling	11'
Vaulted Ceiling	20'
Max Ridge Height	25'3"
Roof Framing	Stick
Exterior Walls	2x4

FIRST FLOOR

SECOND FLOOR

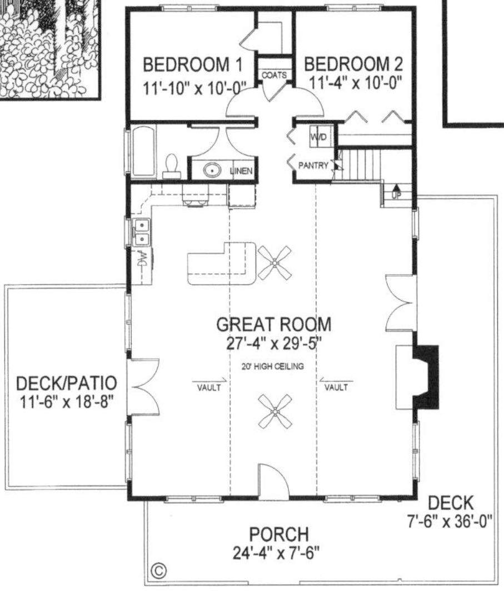

Design 96507

Units	Single
Price Code	B
Total Finished	1,647 sq. ft.
Main Finished	1,647 sq. ft.
Garage Unfinished	528 sq. ft.
Porch Unfinished	187 sq. ft.
Dimensions	51'x70'
Foundation	Crawlspace Slab
Bedrooms	3
Full Baths	2
Main Ceiling	9'
Max Ridge Height	23'
Roof Framing	Stick
Exterior Walls	2x4

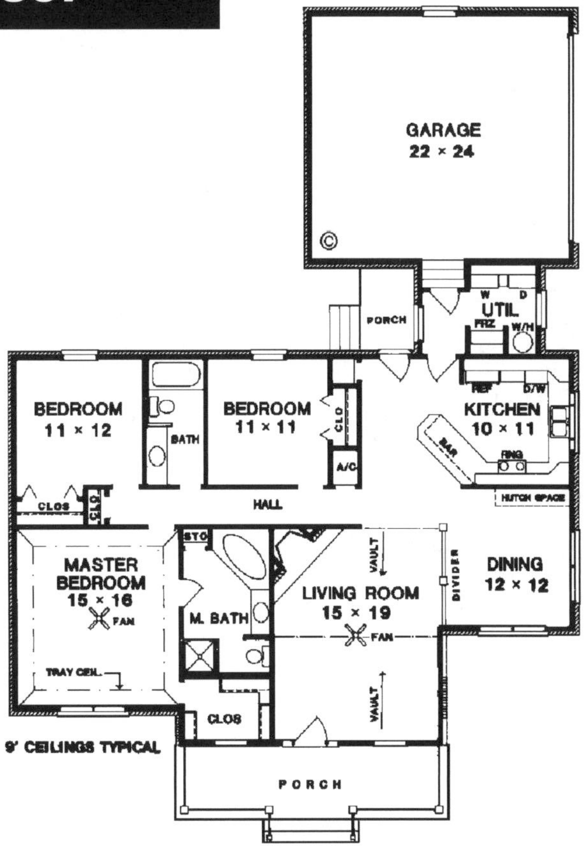

MAIN FLOOR

Design 96513

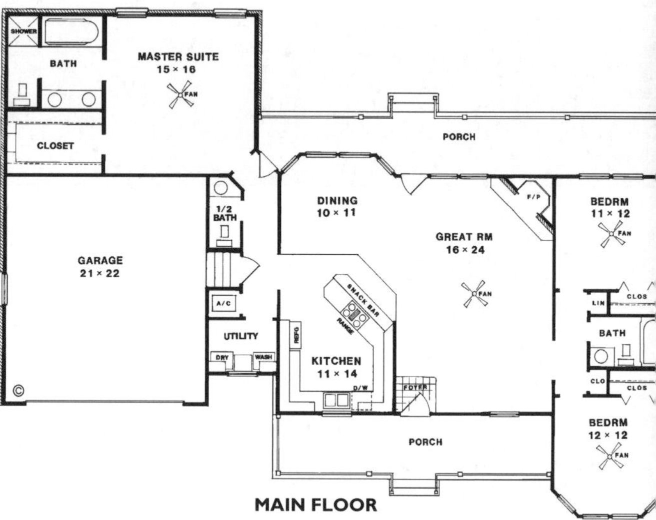
SHOWER
BATH
MASTER SUITE
15 × 16
FAN
CLOSET
PORCH
GARAGE
21 × 22
1/2 BATH
A/C
UTILITY
DRY
WASH
DINING
10 × 11
F/P
GREAT RM
16 × 24
SNACK BAR
RANGE
REFG
KITCHEN
11 × 14
D/W
FOYER
PORCH
BEDRM
11 × 12
LIN
CLOS
BATH
CLO
CLOS
BEDRM
12 × 12
MAIN FLOOR

Units	Single
Price Code	B
Total Finished	1,648 sq. ft.
Main Finished	1,648 sq. ft.
Garage Unfinished	479 sq. ft.
Dimensions	68'x50'
Foundation	Crawlspace Slab
Bedrooms	3
Full Baths	2
Half Baths	1
Main Ceiling	9'
Max Ridge Height	20'
Roof Framing	Stick
Exterior Walls	2x4

Design 94651

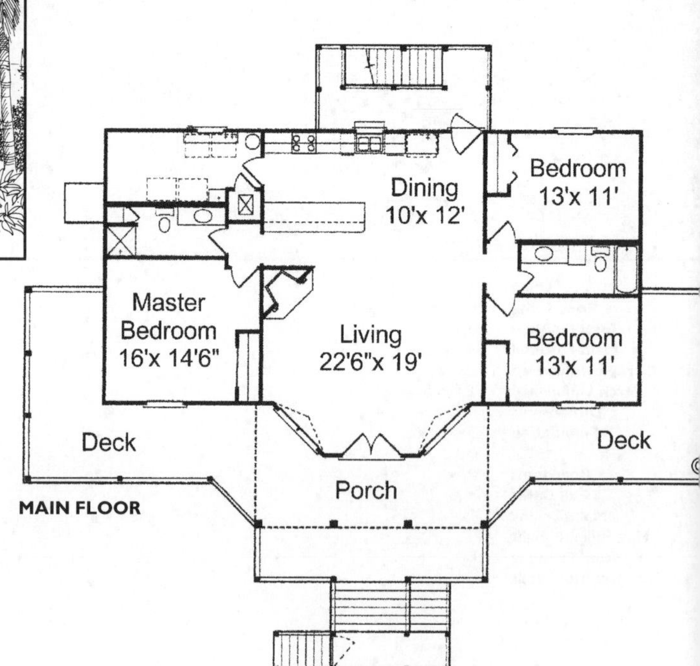
Dining
10'x 12'
Bedroom
13'x 11'
Master
Bedroom
16'x 14'6"
Living
22'6"x 19'
Bedroom
13'x 11'
Deck
Deck
Porch
MAIN FLOOR

Units	Single
Price Code	B
Total Finished	1,649 sq. ft.
Main Finished	1,649 sq. ft.
Dimensions	72'x55'
Foundation	Pier/Post
Bedrooms	3
Full Baths	1
3/4 Baths	1
Main Ceiling	8'
Max Ridge Height	28'
Roof Framing	Stick
Exterior Walls	2x4

Design 94938

PHOTOGRAPHY: COURTESY OF THE DESIGNER

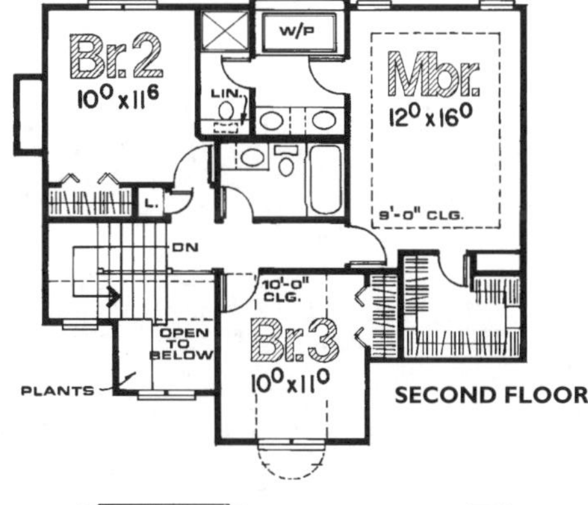
W/P
Br. 2
10^0 x 11^6
LIN.
Mbr.
12^0 x 16^0
9'-0" CLG.
L.
DN
10'-0" CLG.
OPEN TO BELOW
Br. 3
10^0 x 11^0
PLANTS
SECOND FLOOR

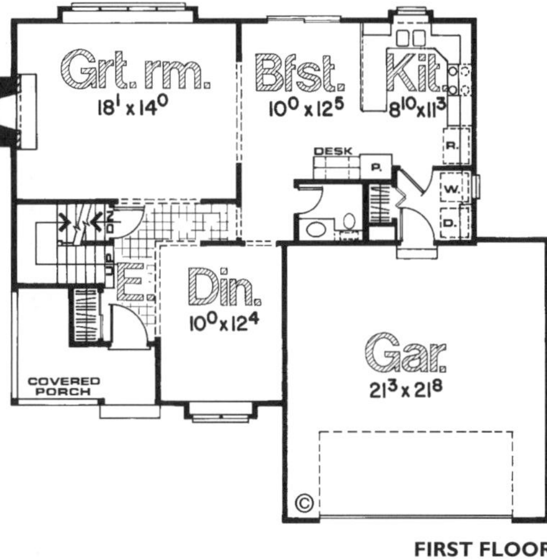
Grt. rm.
18^1 x 14^0
Bfst.
10^0 x 12^5
Kit.
8^{10} x 11^3
DESK
P.
R.
W.
D.
E.
Din.
10^0 x 12^4
Gar.
21^3 x 21^8
COVERED PORCH
FIRST FLOOR

Units	Single
Price Code	B
Total Finished	1,650 sq. ft.
First Finished	891 sq. ft.
Second Finished	759 sq. ft.
Basement Unfinished	891 sq. ft.
Garage Unfinished	484 sq. ft.
Dimensions	44'x40'
Foundation	Basement
Bedrooms	3
Full Baths	2
Half Baths	1
Max Ridge Height	25'6"
Roof Framing	Stick
Exterior Walls	2x4

* Alternate foundation options available at an additional charge. Please call 1-800-235-5700 for more information.

Please note: The photographed home may have been modified to suit homeowner preferences. If you order plans, have a builder or design professional check them against the photograph to confirm actual construction details.

Design 94921

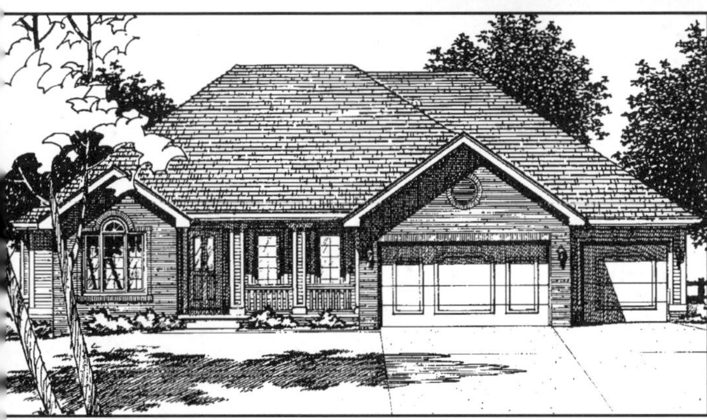

Units	Single
Price Code	B
Total Finished	1,651 sq. ft.
Main Finished	1,651 sq. ft.
Basement Unfinished	1,651 sq. ft.
Garage Unfinished	480 sq. ft.
Dimensions	62'x56'
Foundation	Basement
Bedrooms	3
Full Baths	2
Max Ridge Height	24'
Roof Framing	Stick
Exterior Walls	2x4

Alternate foundation options available at an additional charge. Please call 1-800-235-5700 for more information.

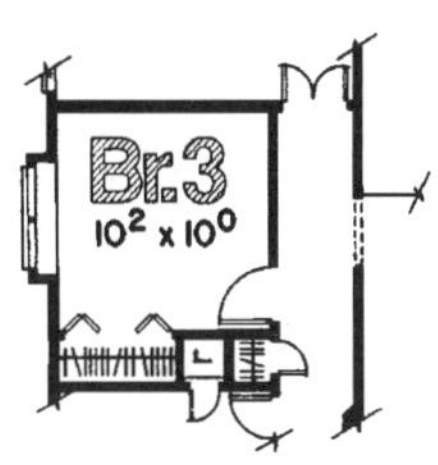
Br. 3
10^2 x 10^0
L

OPTIONAL THIRD BEDROOM

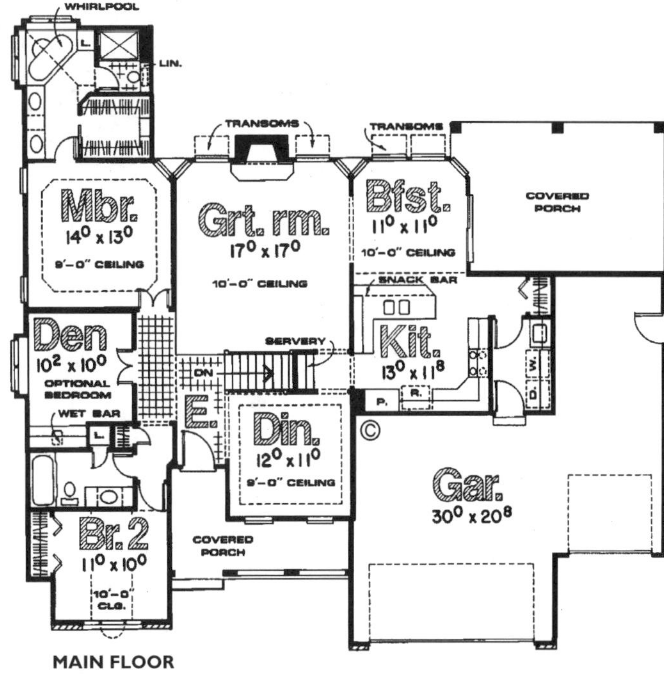
WHIRLPOOL
LIN.
TRANSOMS
TRANSOMS
Mbr.
14^0 x 13^0
9'-0" CEILING
Grt. rm.
17^0 x 17^0
10'-0" CEILING
Bfst.
11^0 x 11^0
10'-0" CEILING
COVERED PORCH
SNACK BAR
Den
10^2 x 10^0
OPTIONAL BEDROOM
WET BAR
SERVERY
DN
Kit.
13^0 x 11^8
P.
R.
W.
D.
E.
Din.
12^0 x 11^0
9'-0" CEILING
Gar.
30^0 x 20^8
Br. 2
11^0 x 10^0
10'-0" CLG.
COVERED PORCH
MAIN FLOOR

Design 96523

Units	Single
Price Code	B
Total Finished	1,652 sq. ft.
Main Finished	1,652 sq. ft.
Garage Unfinished	497 sq. ft.
Porch Unfinished	368 sq. ft.
Dimensions	72'x40'
Foundation	Crawlspace Slab
Bedrooms	3
Full Baths	2
Max Ridge Height	22'
Roof Framing	Stick
Exterior Walls	2x4

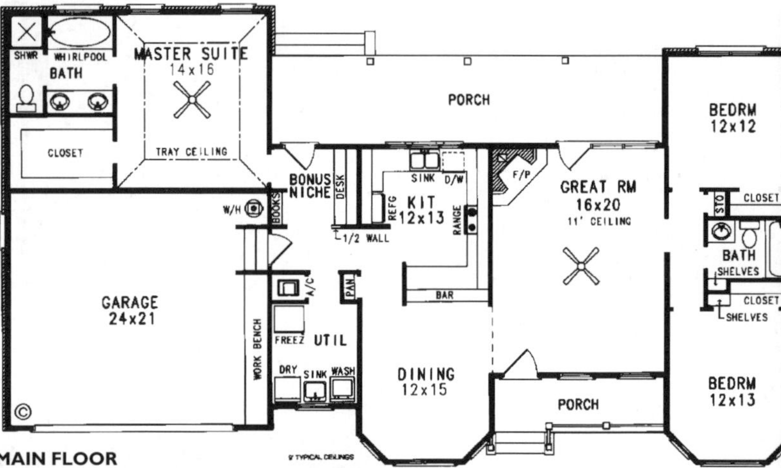
SHWR
WHIRLPOOL
BATH
MASTER SUITE
14x16
CLOSET
TRAY CEILING
PORCH
BEDRM
12x12
BONUS NICHE
DESK
SINK
D/W
KIT
12x13
REFG
RANGE
1/2 WALL
F/P
GREAT RM
16x20
11' CEILING
STO
CLOSET
BATH
SHELVES
CLOSET
SHELVES
W/H
BOOKS
GARAGE
24x21
A/C
PAN
BAR
WORK BENCH
FREEZ
UTIL
DRY
SINK
WASH
DINING
12x15
PORCH
BEDRM
12x13
MAIN FLOOR
9' TYPICAL CEILINGS

Design 96506

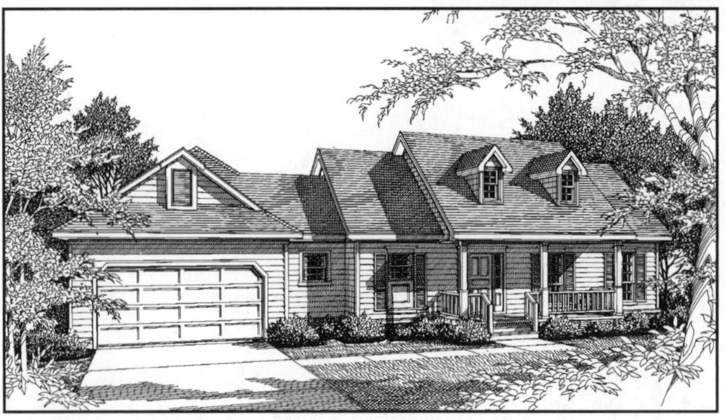

Units	Single
Price Code	B
Total Finished	1,654 sq. ft.
Main Finished	1,654 sq. ft.
Garage Unfinished	480 sq. ft.
Porch Unfinished	401 sq. ft.
Dimensions	68'x46'
Foundation	Crawlspace Slab
Bedrooms	3
Full Baths	2
Half Baths	1
Main Ceiling	9'
Max Ridge Height	21'
Roof Framing	Stick
Exterior Walls	2x4

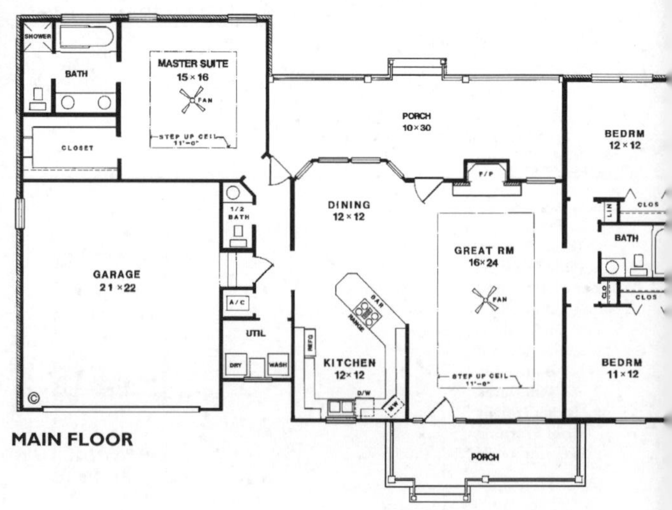
SHOWER
BATH
CLOSET
MASTER SUITE
15×16
FAN
STEP UP CEIL 11'-0"
PORCH
10×30
BEDRM
12×12
F/P
DINING
12×12
1/2 BATH
GARAGE
21×22
GREAT RM
16×24
FAN
CLOS
LIN
BATH
CLOS
A/C
UTIL
BAR
RANGE
REFG
KITCHEN
12×12
D/W
DRY
WASH
STEP UP CEIL 11'-0"
BEDRM
11×12
PORCH
MAIN FLOOR

Design 65635

PHOTOGRAPHY: COURTESY OF THE DESIGNER

Units	Single
Price Code	B
Total Finished	1,655 sq. ft.
Main Finished	1,655 sq. ft.
Dimensions	52'x66'
Foundation	Crawlspace Slab
Bedrooms	3
Full Baths	2
Max Ridge Height	26'
Roof Framing	Stick
Exterior Walls	2x6

Please note: The photographed home may have been modified to suit homeowner preferences. If you order plans, have a builder or design professional check them against the photograph to confirm actual construction details.

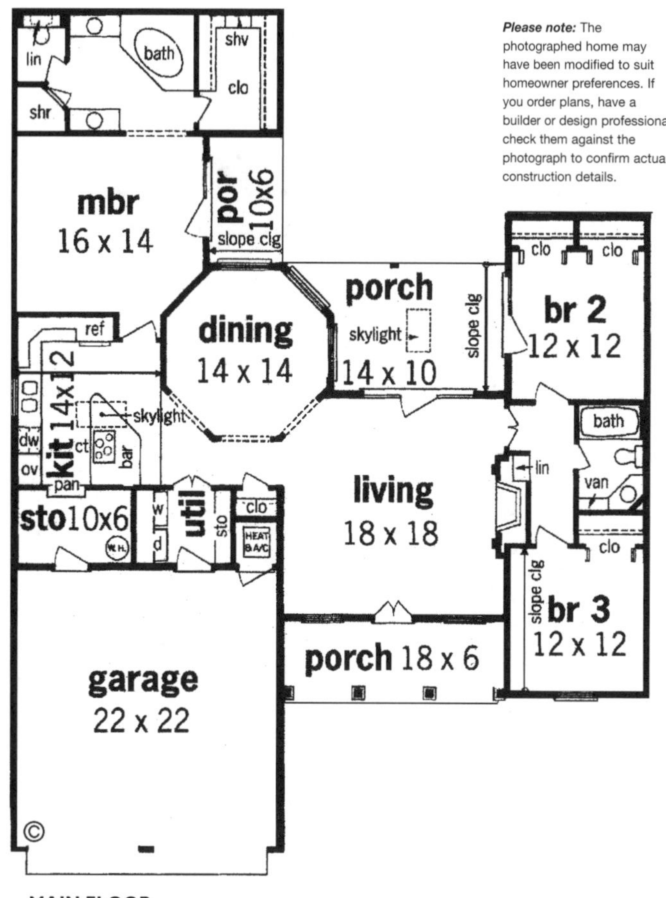
lin
bath
shv
clo
shr
mbr
16 x 14
por
10x6
slope clg
porch
dining
14 x 14
skylight
14 x 10
slope clg
clo
clo
br 2
12 x 12
ref
kit 14x12
skylight
bar
ct
dw
ov
pan
bath
lin
living
18 x 18
van
sto10x6
W.H.
w
d
util
sto
clo
HEAT A/C
clo
slope clg
br 3
12 x 12
porch 18 x 6
garage
22 x 22
©

MAIN FLOOR

Design 92560

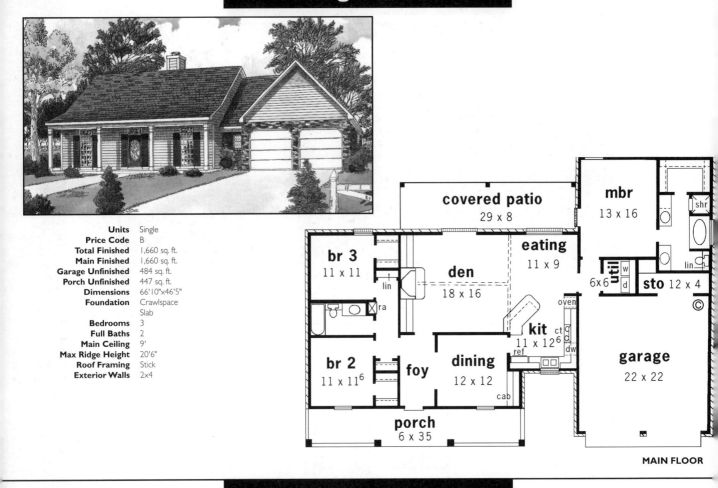

Units	Single
Price Code	B
Total Finished	1,660 sq. ft.
Main Finished	1,660 sq. ft.
Garage Unfinished	484 sq. ft.
Porch Unfinished	447 sq. ft.
Dimensions	66'10"x46'5"
Foundation	Crawlspace Slab
Bedrooms	3
Full Baths	2
Main Ceiling	9'
Max Ridge Height	20'6"
Roof Framing	Stick
Exterior Walls	2x4

covered patio 29 x 8
mbr 13 x 16
shr
lin
eating 11 x 9
br 3 11 x 11
lin
den 18 x 16
util 6x6
w
d
sto 12 x 4
ra
oven
kit 11 x 12⁶
ct
dw
ref
br 2 11 x 11⁶
foy
dining 12 x 12
cab
garage 22 x 22
porch 6 x 35
©

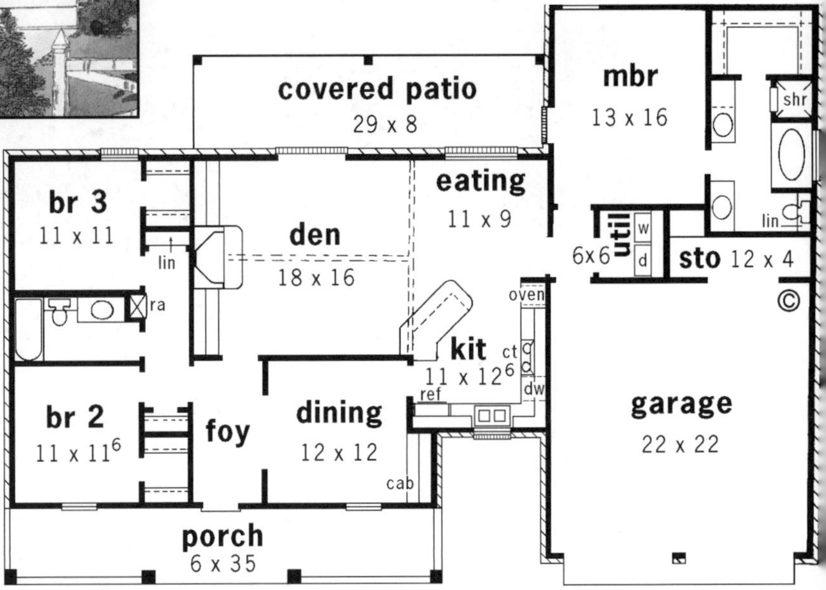

MAIN FLOOR

Design 24725

Units	Single
Price Code	B
Total Finished	1,661 sq. ft.
Main Finished	1,661 sq. ft.
Basement Unfinished	1,642 sq. ft.
Garage Unfinished	546 sq. ft.
Deck Unfinished	194 sq. ft.
Porch Unfinished	40 sq. ft.
Dimensions	56'x46'
Foundation	Basement Crawlspace Slab
Bedrooms	3
Full Baths	2
Main Ceiling	8'
Tray Ceiling	10'
Max Ridge Height	23'
Roof Framing	Stick
Exterior Walls	2x4

LAUN.
Garage
Foyer

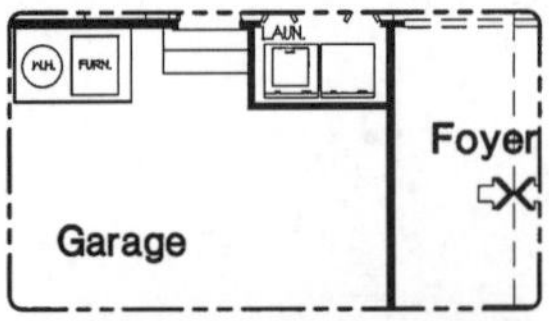

OPTIONAL CRAWLSPACE/
SLAB FOUNDATION

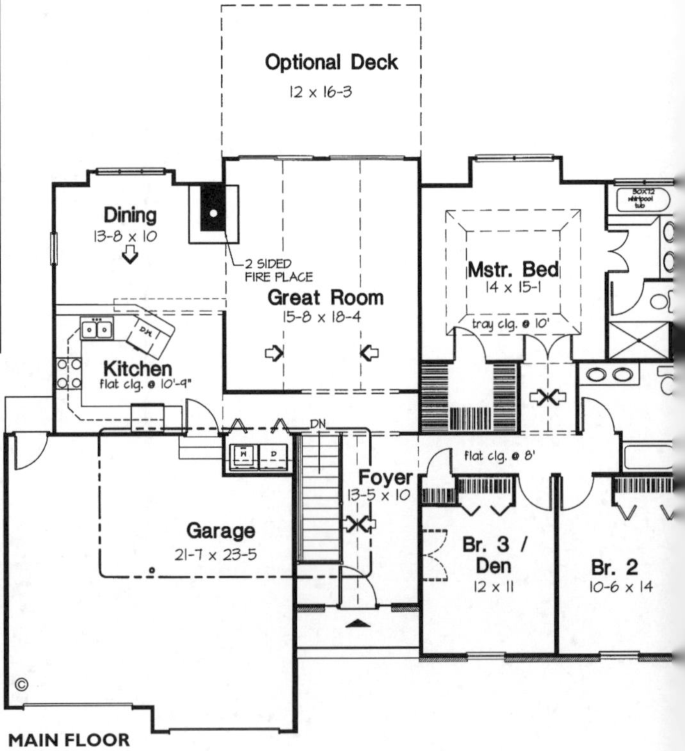

Optional Deck 12 x 16-3
Dining 13-8 x 10
2 SIDED FIRE PLACE
Great Room 15-8 x 18-4
Mstr. Bed 14 x 15-1
tray clg. @ 10'
Kitchen Flat clg. @ 10'-4"
DN
Flat clg. @ 8'
Foyer 13-5 x 10
Garage 21-7 x 23-5
Br. 3 / Den 12 x 11
Br. 2 10-6 x 14
©

MAIN FLOOR

Design 65463

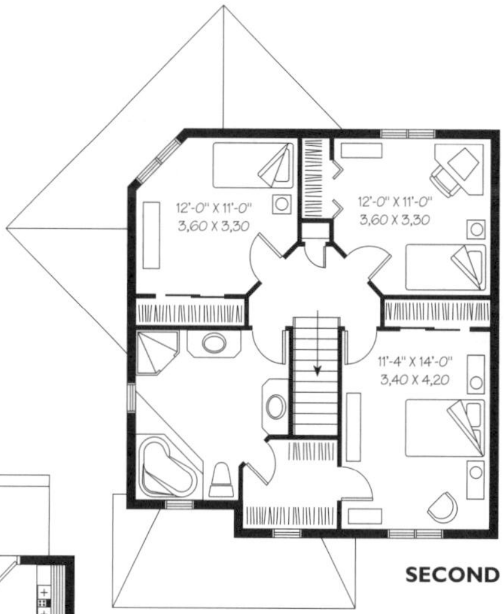

Units	Single
Price Code	B
Total Finished	1,662 sq. ft.
First Finished	884 sq. ft.
Second Finished	778 sq. ft.
Basement Unfinished	884 sq. ft.
Deck Unfinished	50 sq. ft.
Porch Unfinished	80 sq. ft.
Dimensions	34'8"x36'
Foundation	Basement
Bedrooms	3
Full Baths	1
3/4 Baths	1
First Ceiling	8'
Second Ceiling	8'
Max Ridge Height	28'7"
Roof Framing	Truss
Exterior Walls	2x6

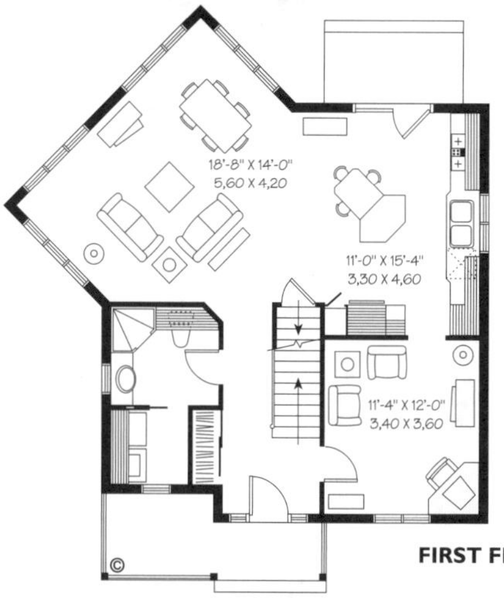

12'-0" X 11'-0" 3,60 X 3,30
12'-0" X 11'-0" 3,60 X 3,30
11'-4" X 14'-0" 3,40 X 4,20

SECOND FLOOR

18'-8" X 14'-0" 5,60 X 4,20
11'-0" X 15'-4" 3,30 X 4,60
11'-4" X 12'-0" 3,40 X 3,60

FIRST FLOOR

Design 98478

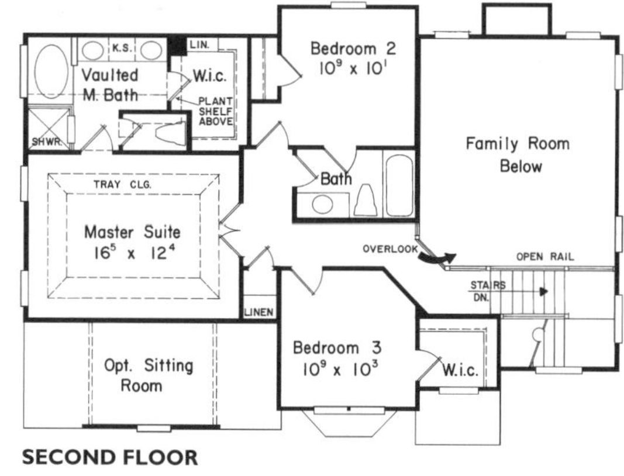
K.S.
LIN.
Vaulted M. Bath
W.i.c.
PLANT SHELF ABOVE
SHWR.
Bedroom 2 10⁹ x 10¹
Family Room Below
Bath
TRAY CLG.
Master Suite 16⁵ x 12⁴
OVERLOOK
OPEN RAIL
STAIRS DN.
LINEN
Bedroom 3 10⁹ x 10³
W.i.c.
Opt. Sitting Room

SECOND FLOOR

Units	Single
Price Code	B
Total Finished	1,663 sq. ft.
First Finished	840 sq. ft.
Second Finished	823 sq. ft.
Bonus Unfinished	80 sq. ft.
Basement Unfinished	840 sq. ft.
Garage Unfinished	494 sq. ft.
Dimensions	46'6"x32'10"
Foundation	Basement Crawlspace
Bedrooms	3
Full Baths	2
Half Baths	1
Max Ridge Height	29'6"
Roof Framing	Stick
Exterior Walls	2x6

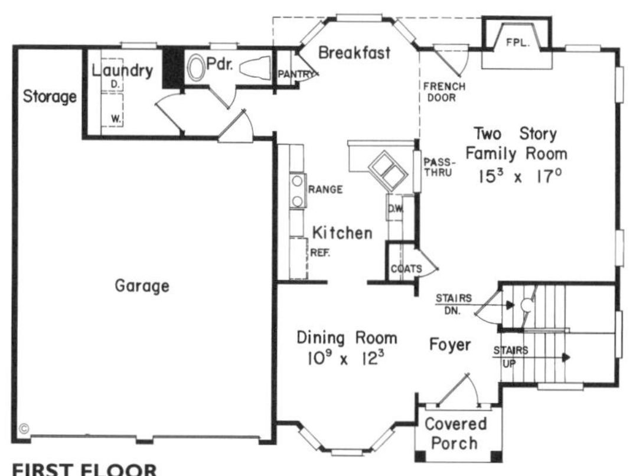
Storage
Laundry
D.
W.
Pdr.
PANTRY
Breakfast
FPL.
FRENCH DOOR
Two Story Family Room 15³ x 17⁰
PASS-THRU
RANGE
D.W.
Kitchen
REF.
COATS
Garage
STAIRS DN.
Dining Room 10⁹ x 12³
Foyer
STAIRS UP
Covered Porch

FIRST FLOOR

Design 92238

Units	Single
Price Code	B
Total Finished	1,664 sq. ft.
Main Finished	1,664 sq. ft.
Basement Unfinished	1,600 sq. ft.
Garage Unfinished	440 sq. ft.
Dimensions	48'x63'
Foundation	Basement Crawlspace Slab
Bedrooms	3
Full Baths	2
Max Ridge Height	22'6"
Roof Framing	Stick
Exterior Walls	2x4

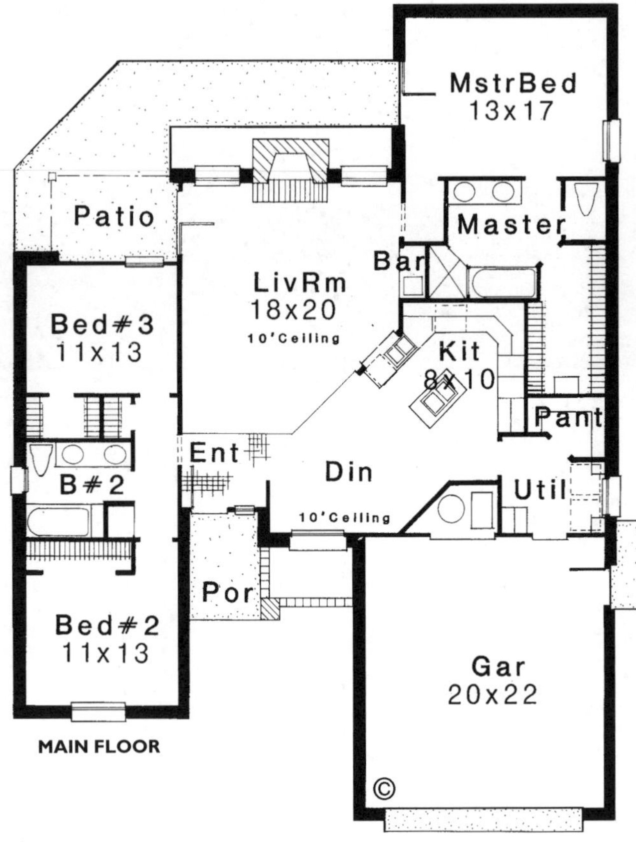
MstrBed
13x17
Patio
Master
Bar
LivRm
18x20
10'Ceiling
Bed#3
11x13
Kit
8x10
Pant
Ent
B#2
Din
Util
10'Ceiling
Por
Bed#2
11x13
Gar
20x22
©

MAIN FLOOR

Design 91418

Units	Single
Price Code	B
Total Finished	1,665 sq. ft.
Main Finished	1,665 sq. ft.
Dimensions	44'x65'
Foundation	Basement Crawlspace Slab
Bedrooms	3
Full Baths	2
Max Ridge Height	21'
Roof Framing	Stick/Truss
Exterior Walls	2x6

UTIL
D
W

OPTIONAL BASEMENT STAIR LOCATION

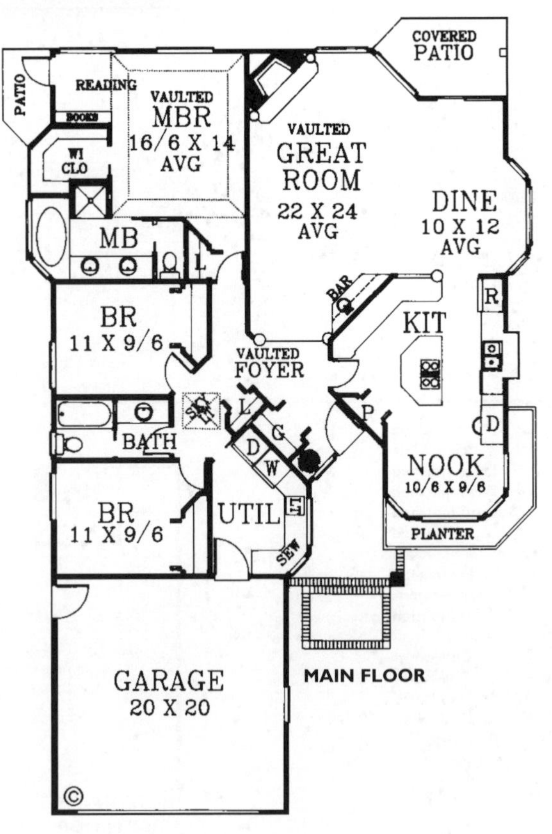
COVERED
PATIO
PATIO
READING
BOOKS
VAULTED
MBR
16/6 X 14
AVG
WI
CLO
VAULTED
GREAT
ROOM
22 X 24
AVG
DINE
10 X 12
AVG
MB
L
BAR
R
KIT
BR
11 X 9/6
VAULTED
FOYER
L
G
P
D
BATH
D
W
NOOK
10/6 X 9/6
BR
11 X 9/6
UTIL
SEW
PLANTER
GARAGE
20 X 20
©

MAIN FLOOR

Design 94655

PHOTOGRAPHY: COURTESY OF THE DESIGNER

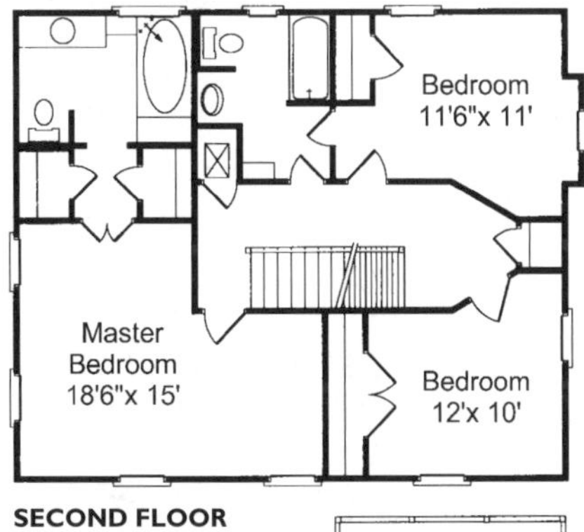
Bedroom
11'6"x 11'
Master
Bedroom
18'6"x 15'
Bedroom
12'x 10'
SECOND FLOOR

Units	Single
Price Code	C
Total Finished	1,804 sq. ft.
First Finished	731 sq. ft.
Second Finished	935 sq. ft.
Third Finished	138 sq. ft.
Dimensions	35'x38'
Foundation	Pier/Post
Bedrooms	3
Full Baths	3
First Ceiling	9'
Second Ceiling	8'
Max Ridge Height	39'
Roof Framing	Stick
Exterior Walls	2x4

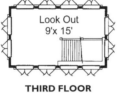

Look Out
9'x 15'

THIRD FLOOR

Please note: The photographed home may have been modified to suit homeowner preferences. If you order plans, have a builder or design professional check them against the photograph to confirm actual construction details.

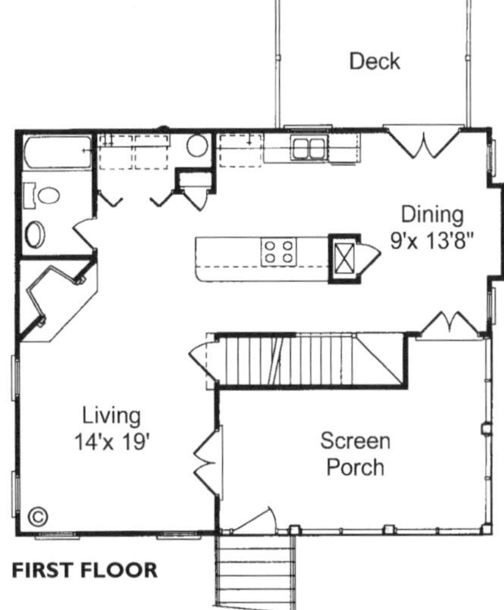
Deck
Dining
9'x 13'8"
Living
14'x 19'
Screen
Porch
FIRST FLOOR

Design 94923

PHOTOGRAPHY: COURTESY OF THE DESIGNER

Units	Single
Price Code	B
Total Finished	1,666 sq. ft.
Main Finished	1,666 sq. ft.
Basement Unfinished	1,666 sq. ft.
Garage Unfinished	496 sq. ft.
Dimensions	55'4"x48'
Foundation	Basement
Bedrooms	3
Full Baths	2
Max Ridge Height	22'9"
Roof Framing	Stick
Exterior Walls	2x4

* Alternate foundation options available at an additional charge. Please call 1-800-235-5700 for more information.

Please note: The photographed home may have been modified to suit homeowner preferences. If you order plans, have a builder or design professional check them against the photograph to confirm actual construction details.

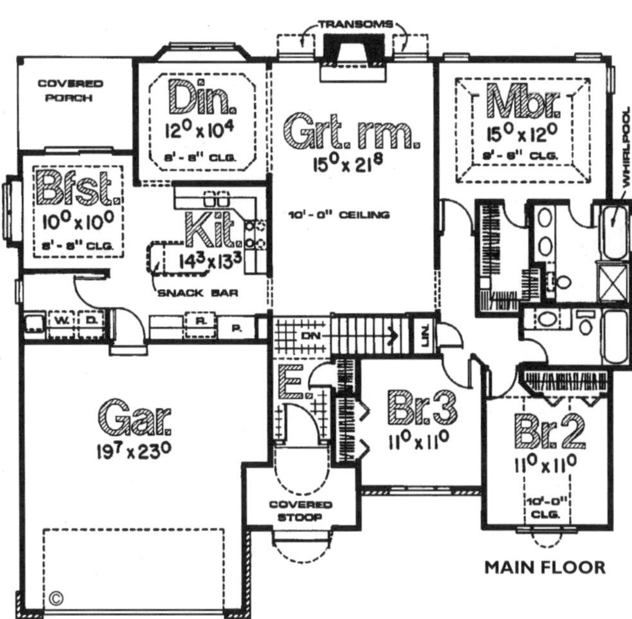
TRANSOMS
COVERED PORCH
Din.
12⁰ x 10⁴
8'-8" CLG.
Grt. rm.
15⁰ x 21⁸
10'-0" CEILING
Mbr.
15⁰ x 12⁰
8'-8" CLG.
WHIRLPOOL
Bfst.
10⁰ x 10⁰
8'-8" CLG.
Kit.
14³ x 13³
SNACK BAR
W. D.
DN
LIN.
E.
Br.3
11⁰ x 11⁰
Br.2
11⁰ x 11⁰
10'-0" CLG.
Gar.
19⁷ x 23⁰
COVERED STOOP
MAIN FLOOR

Design 93219

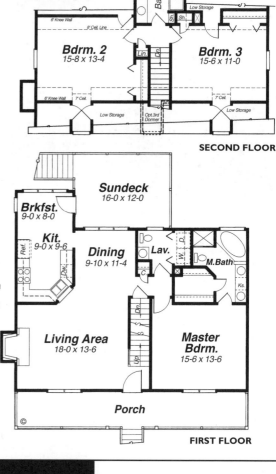

PHOTOGRAPHY: JOHN EHRENCLOU

Units	Single
Price Code	B
Total Finished	1,668 sq. ft.
First Finished	1,057 sq. ft.
Second Finished	611 sq. ft.
Basement Unfinished	511 sq. ft.
Garage Unfinished	546 sq. ft.
Dimensions	40'4"x38'
Foundation	Basement
Bedrooms	3
Full Baths	2
Half Baths	1
First Ceiling	8'
Second Ceiling	8'
Max Ridge Height	23'
Roof Framing	Stick
Exterior Walls	2x4

Please note: The photographed home may have been modified to suit homeowner preferences. If you order plans, have a builder or design professional check them against the photograph to confirm actual construction details.

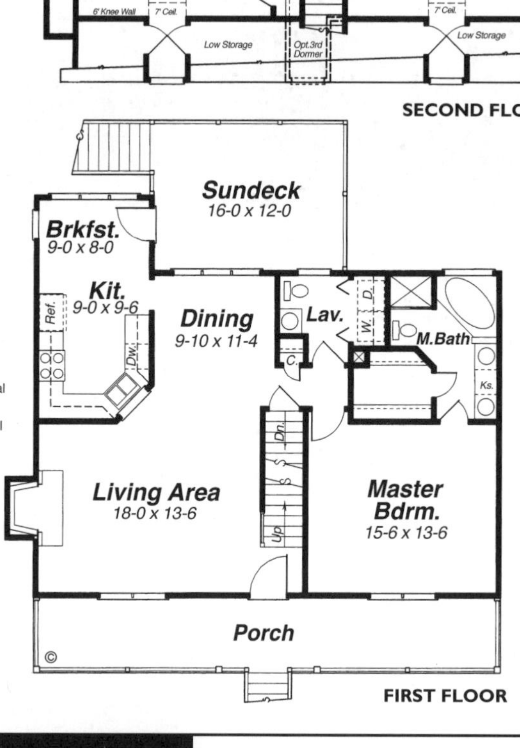

Bath 2
Low Storage
6' Knee Wall
8' Ceil. Line
Bdrm. 2
15-8 x 13-4
Bdrm. 3
15-6 x 11-0
Lin.
Dn.
6' Knee Wall
7' Ceil.
7' Ceil.
Low Storage
Opt.3rd Dormer
Low Storage
SECOND FLOOR
Sundeck
16-0 x 12-0
Brkfst.
9-0 x 8-0
Kit.
9-0 x 9-6
Ref.
Dw.
Dining
9-10 x 11-4
Lav.
W.
D.
M.Bath
C.
Ks.
Dn.
Living Area
18-0 x 13-6
Up
Master
Bdrm.
15-6 x 13-6
Porch
FIRST FLOOR

Design 67007

Units	Single
Price Code	B
Total Finished	1,670 sq. ft.
Main Finished	1,670 sq. ft.
Bonus Unfinished	350 sq. ft.
Garage Unfinished	474 sq. ft.
Porch Unfinished	10 sq. ft.
Dimensions	53'x55'9"
Foundation	Slab
Bedrooms	3
Full Baths	2
Main Ceiling	8'
Vaulted Ceiling	11'
Tray Ceiling	13'
Max Ridge Height	24'9"
Roof Framing	Truss

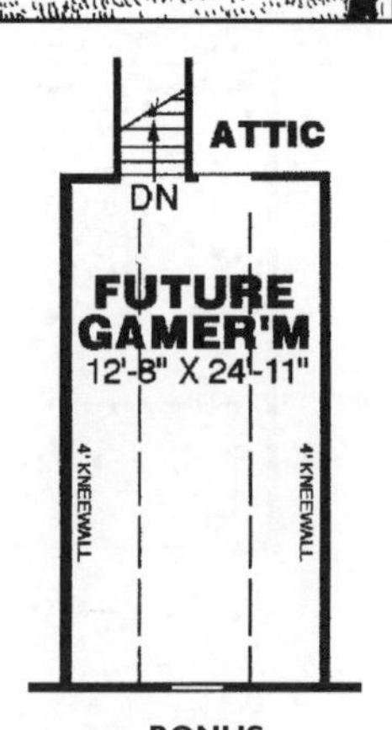

ATTIC
DN
FUTURE
GAMER'M
12'-8" X 24'-11"
4' KNEEWALL
4' KNEEWALL
BONUS

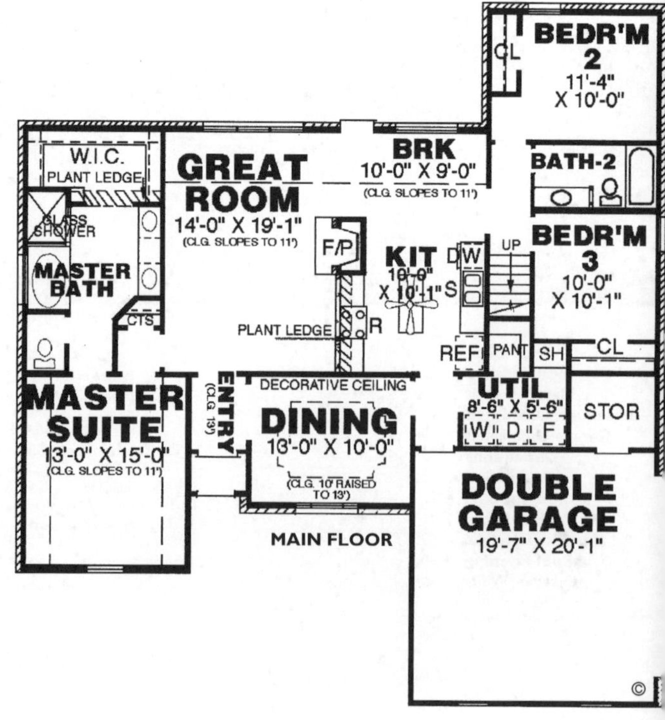

BEDR'M
2
11'-4"
X 10'-0"
CL
W.I.C.
PLANT LEDGE
GREAT
ROOM
14'-0" X 19'-1"
(CLG. SLOPES TO 11')
BRK
10'-0" X 9'-0"
(CLG. SLOPES TO 11')
BATH-2
GLASS SHOWER
MASTER BATH
F/P
KIT
DW
UP
S
R
BEDR'M
3
10'-0"
X 10'-1"
CTS
PLANT LEDGE
REF
PANT
SH
CL
MASTER
SUITE
13'-0" X 15'-0"
(CLG. SLOPES TO 11')
ENTRY
(CLG. 13')
DECORATIVE CEILING
DINING
13'-0" X 10'-0"
(CLG. 10' RAISED TO 13')
UTIL
8'-6" X 5'-6"
W D F
STOR
DOUBLE
GARAGE
19'-7" X 20'-1"
MAIN FLOOR

Design 98432

FILES AVAILABLE
CAD For more information call
800-235-5700

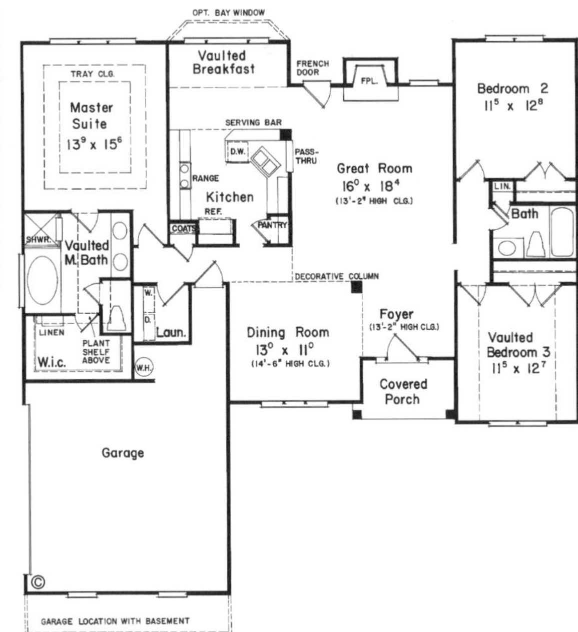

OPT. BAY WINDOW
Vaulted Breakfast
FRENCH DOOR
FPL.
TRAY CLG.
Master Suite
13^{9} x 15^{6}
SERVING BAR
D.W.
PASS-THRU
RANGE
Kitchen
REF.
Great Room
16^{0} x 18^{4}
($13'$-$2''$ HIGH CLG.)
Bedroom 2
11^{5} x 12^{8}
LIN.
Bath
COATS
PANTRY
SHWR.
Vaulted M. Bath
DECORATIVE COLUMN
W.
D.
Laun.
LINEN
PLANT SHELF ABOVE
W.i.c.
W.H.
Dining Room
13^{0} x 11^{0}
($14'$-$6''$ HIGH CLG.)
Foyer
($13'$-$2''$ HIGH CLG.)
Vaulted Bedroom 3
11^{5} x 12^{7}
Covered Porch
Garage
©
GARAGE LOCATION WITH BASEMENT

MAIN FLOOR

Units	Single
Price Code	B
Total Finished	1,670 sq. ft.
Main Finished	1,670 sq. ft.
Garage Unfinished	240 sq. ft.
Dimensions	54'x52'
Foundation	Basement Crawlspace Slab
Bedrooms	3
Full Baths	2
Main Ceiling	9'
Max Ridge Height	24'6"
Roof Framing	Stick
Exterior Walls	2x4

Design 98423

FILES AVAILABLE
CAD For more information call
800-235-5700

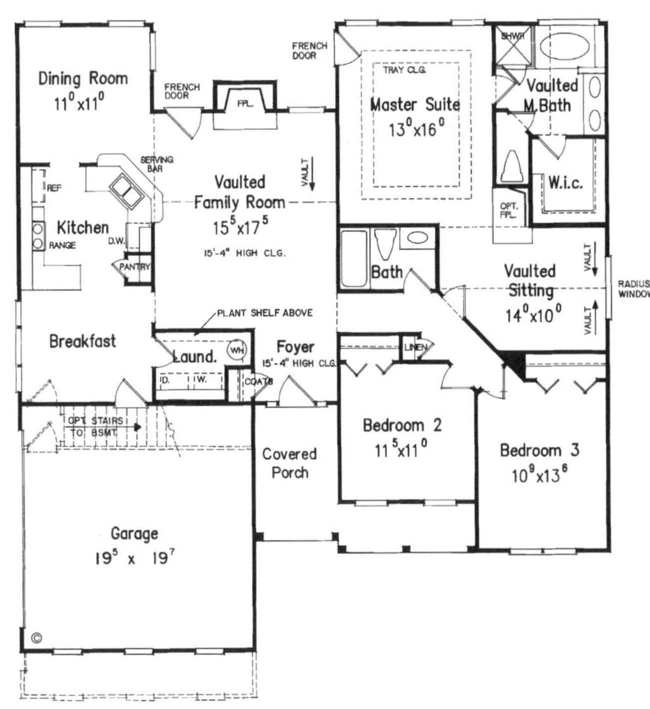

FRENCH DOOR
Dining Room
11^{0}x11^{0}
FRENCH DOOR
FPL.
TRAY CLG.
Master Suite
13^{0}x16^{0}
SHWR.
Vaulted M.Bath
W.i.c.
SERVING BAR
REF
Vaulted Family Room
15^{5}x17^{5}
$15'$-$4''$ HIGH CLG.
VAULT
Kitchen
RANGE
D.W.
PANTRY
OPT. FPL.
Bath
Vaulted Sitting
14^{0}x10^{0}
RADIUS WINDOW
PLANT SHELF ABOVE
Breakfast
Laund.
WH
D. W.
Foyer
$15'$-$4''$ HIGH CLG.
COATS
LINEN
OPT. STAIRS TO BSMT.
Covered Porch
Bedroom 2
11^{5}x11^{0}
Bedroom 3
10^{9}x13^{6}
Garage
19^{5} x 19^{7}
©

MAIN FLOOR

Units	Single
Price Code	B
Total Finished	1,671 sq. ft.
Main Finished	1,671 sq. ft.
Basement Unfinished	1,685 sq. ft.
Garage Unfinished	400 sq. ft.
Dimensions	50'x51'
Foundation	Basement Crawlspace Slab
Bedrooms	3
Full Baths	2
Main Ceiling	9'
Max Ridge Height	22'6"
Roof Framing	Stick
Exterior Walls	2x4

Design 98476

CAD
FILES AVAILABLE
For more information call
800-235-5700

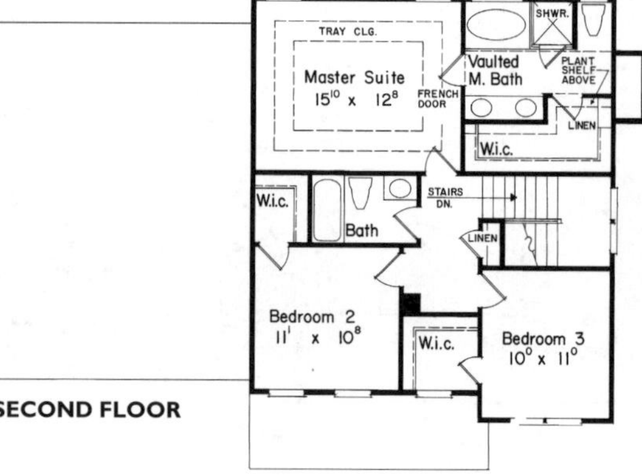

TRAY CLG.
Master Suite
15^{10} x 12^{8}
FRENCH DOOR
SHWR.
Vaulted M. Bath
PLANT SHELF ABOVE
LINEN
W.i.c.
W.i.c.
Bath
STAIRS DN.
LINEN
Bedroom 2
11^{1} x 10^{8}
W.i.c.
Bedroom 3
10^{0} x 11^{0}
SECOND FLOOR

Units	Single
Price Code	B
Total Finished	1,671 sq. ft.
First Finished	887 sq. ft.
Second Finished	784 sq. ft.
Bonus Unfinished	406 sq. ft.
Basement Unfinished	887 sq. ft.
Garage Unfinished	490 sq. ft.
Dimensions	50'4"x35'
Foundation	Basement Crawlspace
Bedrooms	3
Full Baths	2
Half Baths	1
First Ceiling	9'
Second Ceiling	8'
Max Ridge Height	31'6"
Roof Framing	Stick
Exterior Walls	2x4

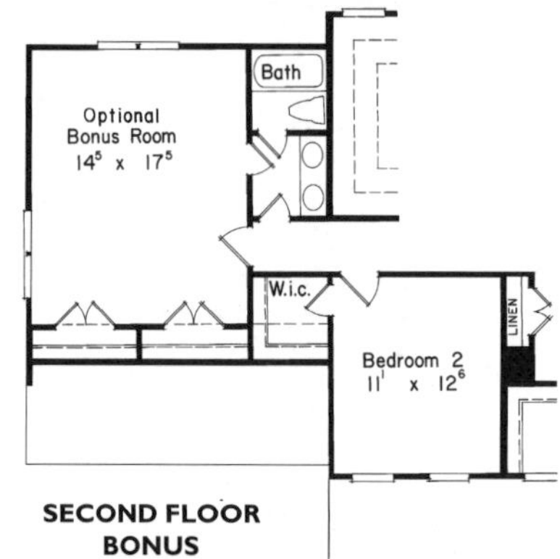

Optional Bonus Room
14^{5} x 17^{5}
Bath
W.i.c.
LINEN
Bedroom 2
11^{1} x 12^{6}
SECOND FLOOR BONUS

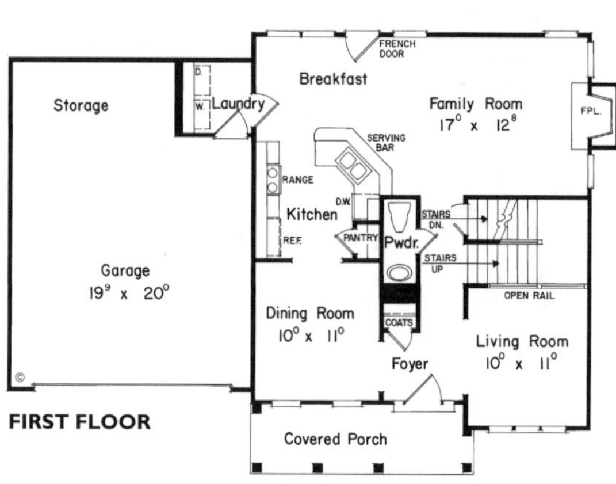

Storage
Laundry
FRENCH DOOR
Breakfast
Family Room
17^{0} x 12^{8}
FPL.
SERVING BAR
RANGE
D.W.
Kitchen
REF.
PANTRY
Pwdr.
STAIRS DN.
STAIRS UP
COATS
Garage
19^{9} x 20^{0}
OPEN RAIL
Dining Room
10^{0} x 11^{0}
Living Room
10^{0} x 11^{0}
Foyer
Covered Porch
FIRST FLOOR

Design 34011

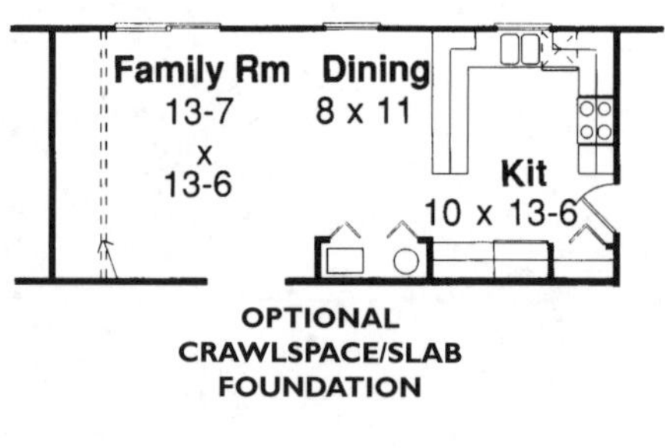

Family Rm
13-7
x
13-6
Dining
8 x 11
Kit
10 x 13-6
OPTIONAL CRAWLSPACE/SLAB FOUNDATION

Units	Single
Price Code	B
Total Finished	1,672 sq. ft.
Main Finished	1,672 sq. ft.
Garage Unfinished	566 sq. ft.
Dimensions	80'x32'
Foundation	Basement Crawlspace Slab
Bedrooms	3
Full Baths	2
Max Ridge Height	19'
Roof Framing	Stick
Exterior Walls	2x4, 2x6

MBr 1
12 x 13-6
Family Rm
10-1
x
13-6
Dining
8 x 11
Kit
10 x 13-6
Garage
24 x 24
W D
Ldry
DN
Living Rm
18-8 x 13-6
Entry
linen
Br 2
11-8 x 11-8
Br 3
11-8 x 11-8
©

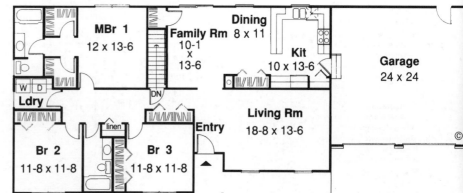

MAIN FLOOR

Design 62028

Units	Single
Price Code	B
Total Finished	1,672 sq. ft.
First Finished	1,140 sq. ft.
Second Finished	532 sq. ft.
Porch Unfinished	328 sq. ft.
Dimensions	27'x54'
Foundation	Crawlspace Slab
Bedrooms	3
Full Baths	2
Half Baths	1
First Ceiling	9'
Second Ceiling	8'
Exterior Walls	2x4

ATTIC STORAGE
DN.
COMP DESK
LIN.
BATH
LIN
BEDROOM 2
11'-8" X 12'-0"
BEDROOM 3
12'-0" X 13'-5"
PORCH
14'-8" X 8'-0"
SECOND FLOOR
WHP TUB
GLASS SHWR
MASTER SUITE
13'-8" X 14'-0"
10' BOXED CEILING
D.
W
KID'S NOOK
BENCH / STORAGE HANGING
REF.
UP
KITCHEN
10'-0" X 14'-2"
DW
RG
LIVING RM.
14'-0" X 14'-4"
8" COLUMNS
DINING
10'-0" X 13'-0"
COVERED PORCH
14'-0" X 8'-0"
FIRST FLOOR

Design 90486

Units	Single
Price Code	B
Total Finished	1,672 sq. ft.
Main Finished	1,672 sq. ft.
Garage Unfinished	650 sq. ft.
Porch Unfinished	320 sq. ft.
Dimensions	52'10"x66'9"
Foundation	Crawlspace Slab
Bedrooms	3
Full Baths	2
Max Ridge Height	22'10"
Roof Framing	Stick
Exterior Walls	2x4

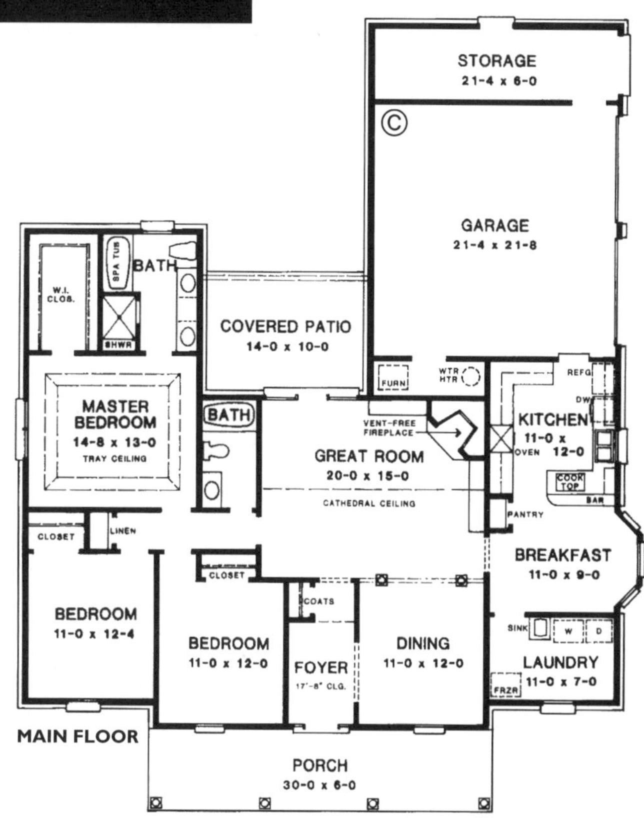
STORAGE
21-4 x 6-0
GARAGE
21-4 x 21-8
W.I. CLOS.
SPA TUB
BATH
SHWR
COVERED PATIO
14-0 x 10-0
FURN
WTR HTR
REFG
DW
MASTER BEDROOM
14-8 x 13-0
TRAY CEILING
BATH
VENT-FREE FIREPLACE
GREAT ROOM
20-0 x 15-0
CATHEDRAL CEILING
KITCHEN
11-0 x 12-0
OVEN
COOK TOP
BAR
PANTRY
CLOSET
LINEN
CLOSET
COATS
BREAKFAST
11-0 x 9-0
BEDROOM
11-0 x 12-4
BEDROOM
11-0 x 12-0
FOYER
17'-8" CLG.
DINING
11-0 x 12-0
SINK
W
D
LAUNDRY
11-0 x 7-0
FRZR
MAIN FLOOR
PORCH
30-0 x 6-0

Design 20061

Units	Single
Price Code	B
Total Finished	1,674 sq. ft.
Main Finished	1,674 sq. ft.
Basement Unfinished	1,656 sq. ft.
Garage Unfinished	472 sq. ft.
Dimensions	50'x50'6"
Foundation	Basement
Bedrooms	3
Full Baths	2
Max Ridge Height	23'
Roof Framing	Stick
Exterior Walls	2x6

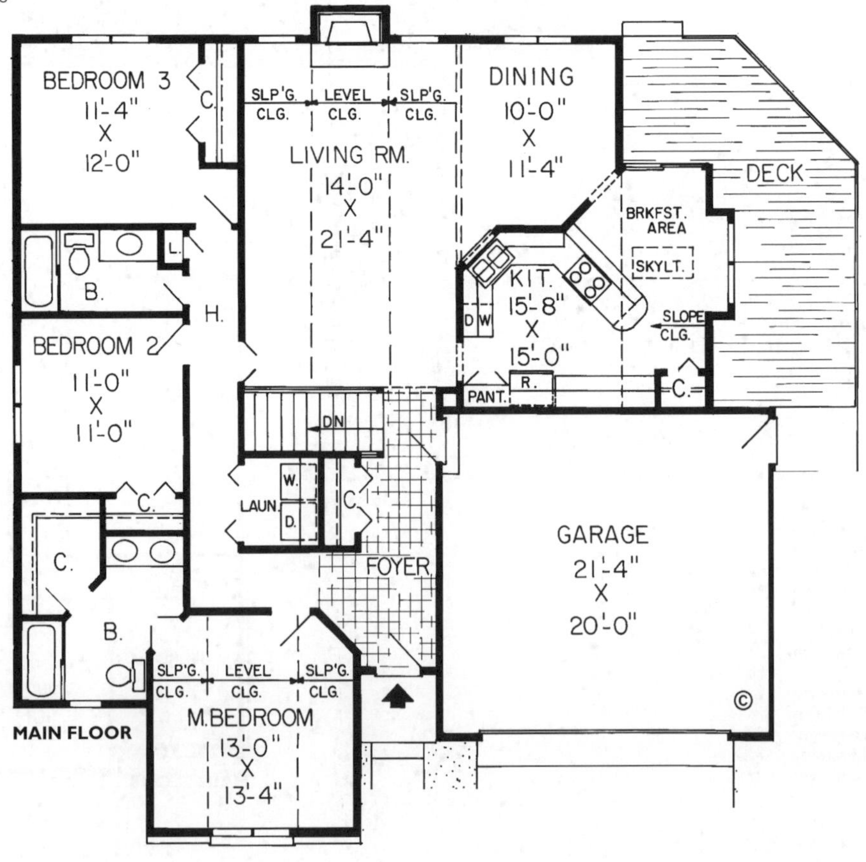

BEDROOM 3
11'-4" X 12'-0"
C.
SLP'G. CLG.
LEVEL CLG.
SLP'G. CLG.
LIVING RM.
14'-0" X 21'-4"
DINING
10'-0" X 11'-4"
DECK
BRKFST. AREA
SKYLT.
L.
B.
H.
KIT.
15'-8" X 15'-0"
DW
SLOPE CLG.
BEDROOM 2
11'-0" X 11'-0"
PANT.
R.
C.
DN
W.
D.
LAUN.
C.
C.
GARAGE
21'-4" X 20'-0"
C.
FOYER
B.
SLP'G. CLG.
LEVEL CLG.
SLP'G. CLG.
M.BEDROOM
13'-0" X 13'-4"
©

MAIN FLOOR

Design 97263

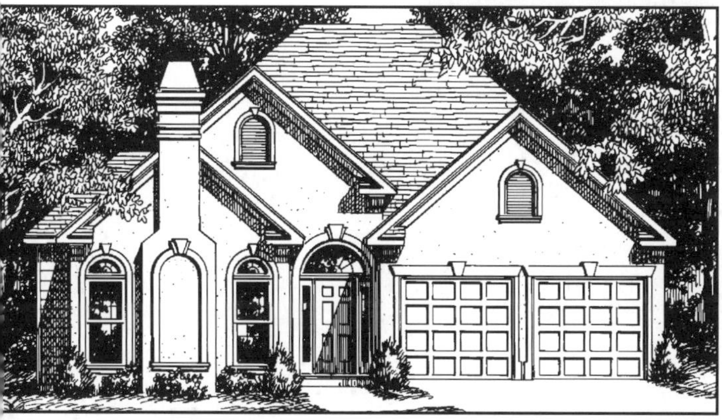

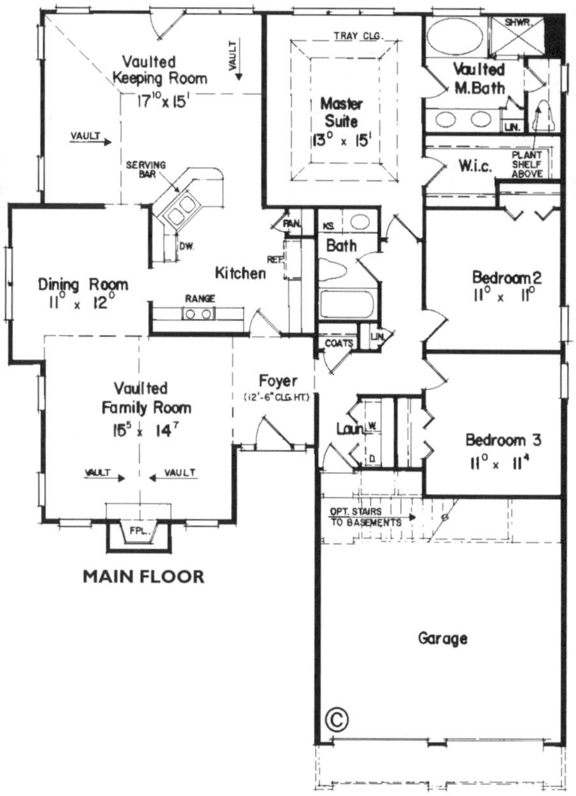

Units	Single
Price Code	B
Total Finished	1,674 sq. ft.
Main Finished	1,674 sq. ft.
Basement Unfinished	1,703 sq. ft.
Garage Unfinished	410 sq. ft.
Dimensions	45'6"x58'
Foundation	Basement Crawlspace
Bedrooms	3
Full Baths	2
Max Ridge Height	25'
Roof Framing	Stick
Exterior Walls	2x4

MAIN FLOOR

Vaulted Keeping Room 17¹⁰ x 15' · Master Suite 13⁰ x 15' · Vaulted M.Bath · W.i.c. · Dining Room 11⁰ x 12⁰ · Kitchen · Bath · Bedroom 2 11⁰ x 11⁰ · Vaulted Family Room 15⁵ x 14⁷ · Foyer (12'-6" CLG. HT.) · Laun. · Bedroom 3 11⁰ x 11⁴ · Garage

Design 98431

CAD FILES AVAILABLE For more information call 800-235-5700

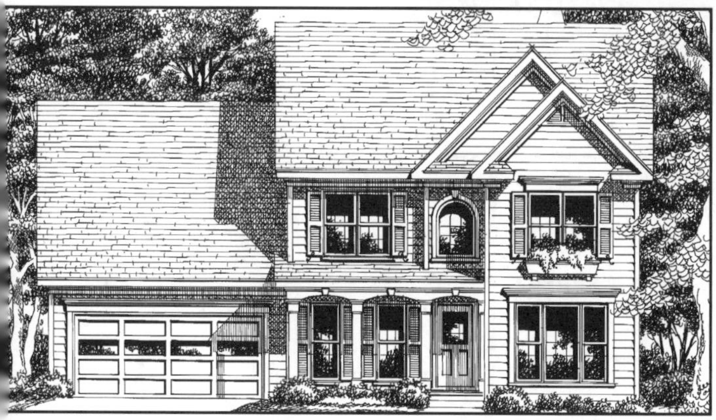

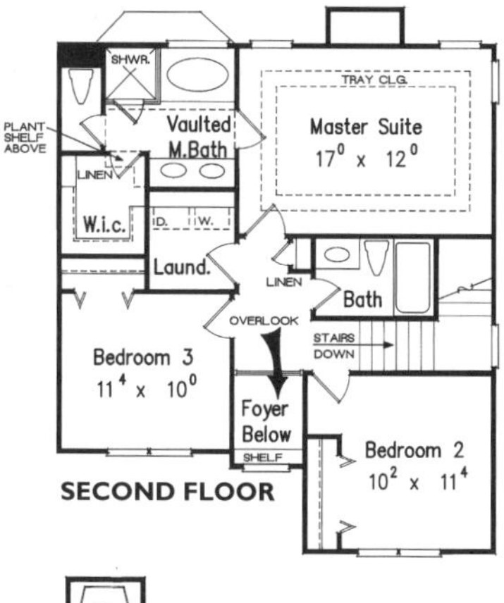

Units	Single
Price Code	B
Total Finished	1,675 sq. ft.
First Finished	882 sq. ft.
Second Finished	793 sq. ft.
Bonus Unfinished	416 sq. ft.
Basement Unfinished	882 sq. ft.
Garage Unfinished	510 sq. ft.
Dimensions	49'6"x35'4"
Foundation	Basement Crawlspace Slab
Bedrooms	3
Full Baths	2
Half Baths	1
First Ceiling	8'
Second Ceiling	8'
Max Ridge Height	29'6"
Roof Framing	Stick
Exterior Walls	2x4

SECOND FLOOR

Vaulted M.Bath · Master Suite 17⁰ x 12⁰ · W.i.c. · Laund. · Bath · Bedroom 3 11⁴ x 10⁰ · Foyer Below · Bedroom 2 10² x 11⁴

FIRST FLOOR

Breakfast · Family Room 17⁴ x 12⁰ · Garage 19⁹ x 25⁰ · Kitchen · Pwdr. · Dining Room 11⁴ x 10⁰ · Two Story Foyer · Living Room 12⁵ x 11⁴ · Covered Porch

SECOND FLOOR BONUS

Opt. Bonus Room 15⁵ x 20³ · W.i.c. · Vaulted M.Bath · Bedroom 3 11⁴ x 10⁰

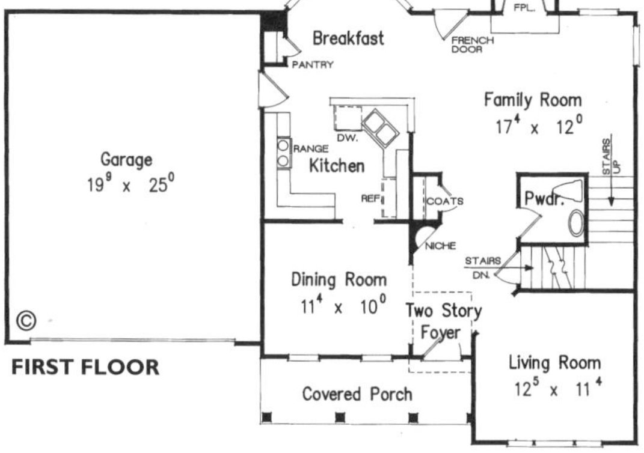

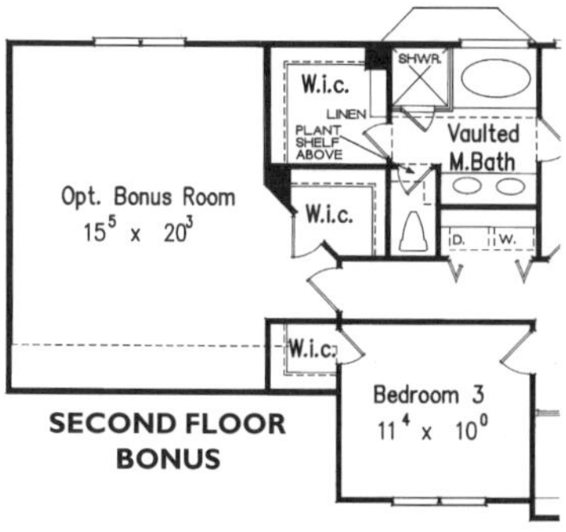

Design 10760

Units	Single
Price Code	B
Total Finished	1,676 sq. ft.
Main Finished	1,676 sq. ft.
Basement Unfinished	592 sq. ft.
Garage Unfinished	697 sq. ft.
Dimensions	55'2"x32'
Foundation	Basement
Bedrooms	3
Full Baths	2
Max Ridge Height	26'
Roof Framing	Stick
Exterior Walls	2x6

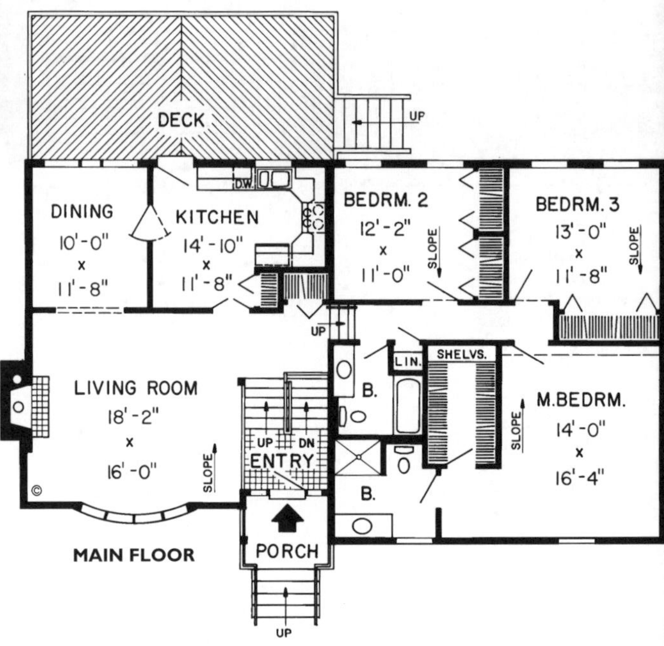
DECK
DINING 10'-0" x 11'-8"
KITCHEN 14'-10" x 11'-8"
BEDRM. 2 12'-2" x 11'-0"
BEDRM. 3 13'-0" x 11'-8"
LIVING ROOM 18'-2" x 16'-0"
ENTRY
PORCH
M.BEDRM. 14'-0" x 16'-4"
SHELVS.
LIN.
B.
B.
SLOPE
UP
DN
MAIN FLOOR

Design 98960

Units	Single
Price Code	B
Total Finished	1,676 sq. ft.
Main Finished	1,676 sq. ft.
Garage Unfinished	552 sq. ft.
Deck Unfinished	192 sq. ft.
Porch Unfinished	89 sq. ft.
Dimensions	56'x62'
Foundation	Basement
Bedrooms	3
Full Baths	2
Main Ceiling	9'
Max Ridge Height	23'
Roof Framing	Stick
Exterior Walls	2x4

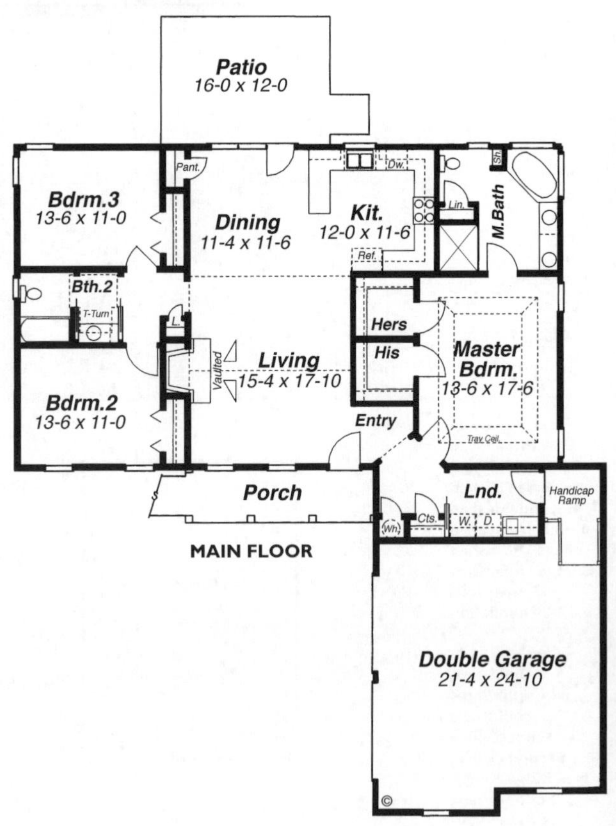
Patio 16-0 x 12-0
Bdrm.3 13-6 x 11-0
Dining 11-4 x 11-6
Kit. 12-0 x 11-6
M.Bath
Bth.2
Living 15-4 x 17-10
Hers
His
Master Bdrm. 13-6 x 17-6
Bdrm.2 13-6 x 11-0
Entry
Porch
Lnd.
Handicap Ramp
Double Garage 21-4 x 24-10
MAIN FLOOR

Design 98968

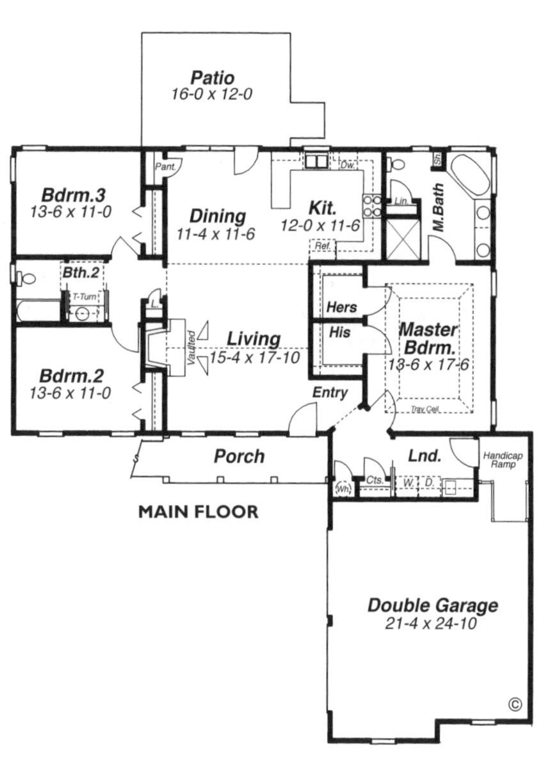
Patio
16-0 x 12-0
Bdrm.3
13-6 x 11-0
Pant.
Dining
11-4 x 11-6
Kit.
12-0 x 11-6
Ref.
Lin.
M.Bath
Bth.2
T-Turn
Hers
His
Master
Bdrm.
13-6 x 17-6
Vaulted
Living
15-4 x 17-10
Bdrm.2
13-6 x 11-0
Entry
Porch
Lnd.
Handicap
Ramp
Cts.
W D
MAIN FLOOR
Double Garage
21-4 x 24-10

Units	Single
Price Code	B
Total Finished	1,676 sq. ft.
Main Finished	1,676 sq. ft.
Garage Unfinished	522 sq. ft.
Deck Unfinished	192 sq. ft.
Porch Unfinished	89 sq. ft.
Dimensions	56'x62'
Foundation	Crawlspace Slab
Bedrooms	3
Full Baths	2
Main Ceiling	9'
Max Ridge Height	23'
Roof Framing	Stick
Exterior Walls	2x4

Design 69023

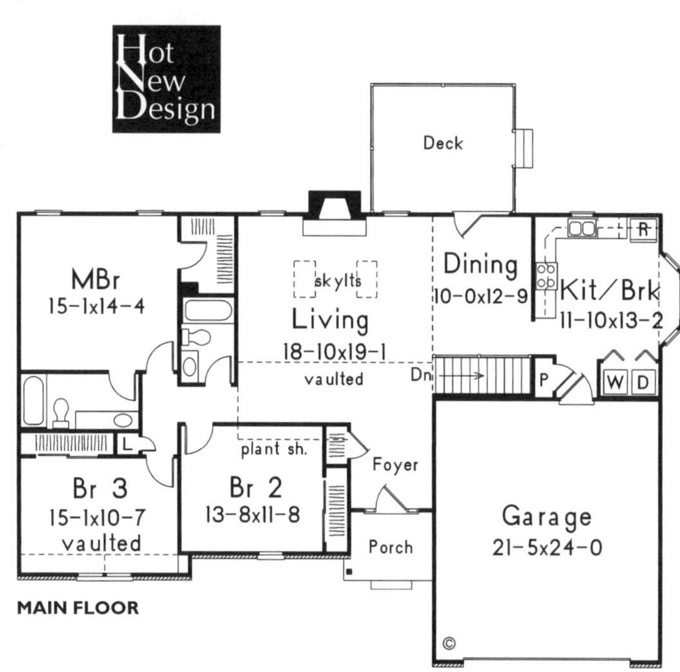
Hot
New
Design
Deck
MBr
15-1x14-4
skylts
Living
18-10x19-1
vaulted
Dining
10-0x12-9
Kit/Brk
11-10x13-2
Dn
P
W D
plant sh.
Foyer
Br 3
15-1x10-7
vaulted
Br 2
13-8x11-8
Porch
Garage
21-5x24-0
MAIN FLOOR

Units	Single
Price Code	B
Total Finished	1,676 sq. ft.
Main Finished	1,676 sq. ft.
Dimensions	64'x43'8"
Foundation	Basement Crawlspace Slab
Bedrooms	3
Full Baths	2

Design 99914

Units	Single
Price Code	B
Total Finished	1,677 sq. ft.
First Finished	1,064 sq. ft.
Second Finished	613 sq. ft.
Deck Unfinished	474 sq. ft.
Porch Unfinished	32 sq. ft.
Dimensions	28'x40'
Foundation	Basement Crawlspace
Bedrooms	2
Full Baths	2
First Ceiling	8'
Second Ceiling	8'
Vaulted Ceiling	22'
Max Ridge Height	26'6"
Roof Framing	Stick
Exterior Walls	2x6

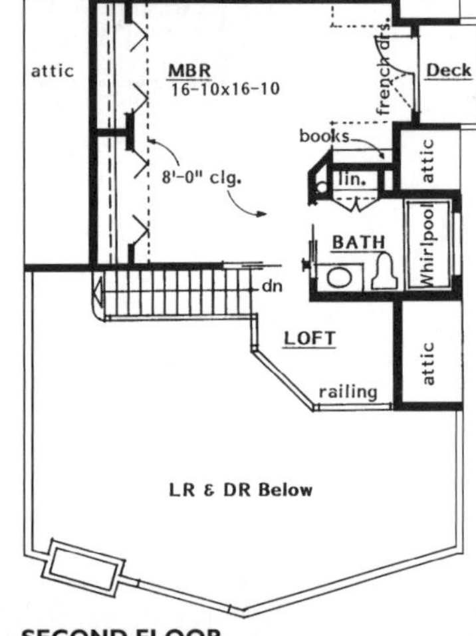

attic
MBR
16-10x16-10
french drs.
Deck
books
lin.
attic
8'-0" clg.
BATH
Whirlpool
dn
LOFT
attic
railing
LR & DR Below

SECOND FLOOR

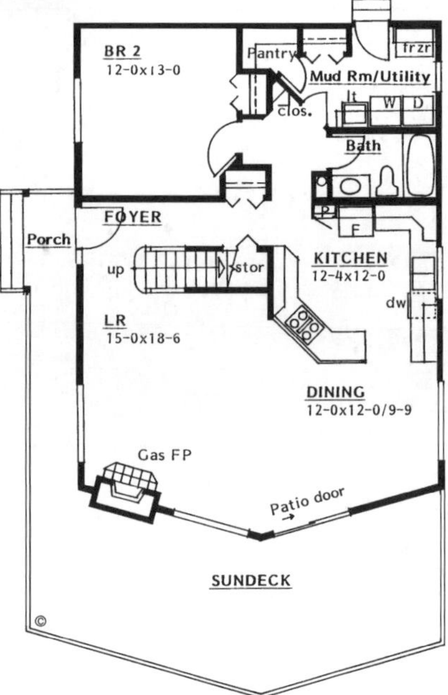

BR 2
12-0x13-0
Pantry
frzr
Mud Rm/Utility
clos.
W
D
Bath
Porch
FOYER
up
stor
KITCHEN
12-4x12-0
dw
LR
15-0x18-6
DINING
12-0x12-0/9-9
Gas FP
Patio door
SUNDECK
©

FIRST FLOOR

Design 67021

Units	Single
Price Code	B
Total Finished	1,680 sq. ft.
Main Finished	1,680 sq. ft.
Dimensions	50'x45'
Foundation	Slab
Bedrooms	4
Full Baths	2
Roof Framing	Stick
Exterior Walls	2x4

MASTER SUITE
12'-0" X 14'-5"
(VAULTED)
GREAT ROOM
23'-7" X 13'-6"
(VAULTED)
WET BAR
PANT
BRK/KIT
REF
MASTER BATH
F/P
R
S
DW
CL
CL
CL
EATING BAR
DINING
13'-4" X 10'-1"
BEDR'M 2
10'-0" X 10'-9"
LIN
D
W
OPT. DOOR
CL
PLANT LEDGE ABOVE
BATH
BEDR'M/ STUDY
10'-0" X 10'-0"
ENTRY
DOUBLE GARAGE
19'-0" X 19'-6"
BEDR'M 3
11'-4" X 10'-0"
CL
PORCH
©

MAIN FLOOR

Design 92563

Units	Single
Price Code	B
Total Finished	1,680 sq. ft.
Main Finished	1,680 sq. ft.
Garage Unfinished	538 sq. ft.
Porch Unfinished	24 sq. ft.
Dimensions	66'10"x44'10"
Foundation	Crawlspace Slab
Bedrooms	3
Full Baths	2
Main Ceiling	9'
Max Ridge Height	20'6"
Roof Framing	Stick
Exterior Walls	2x4

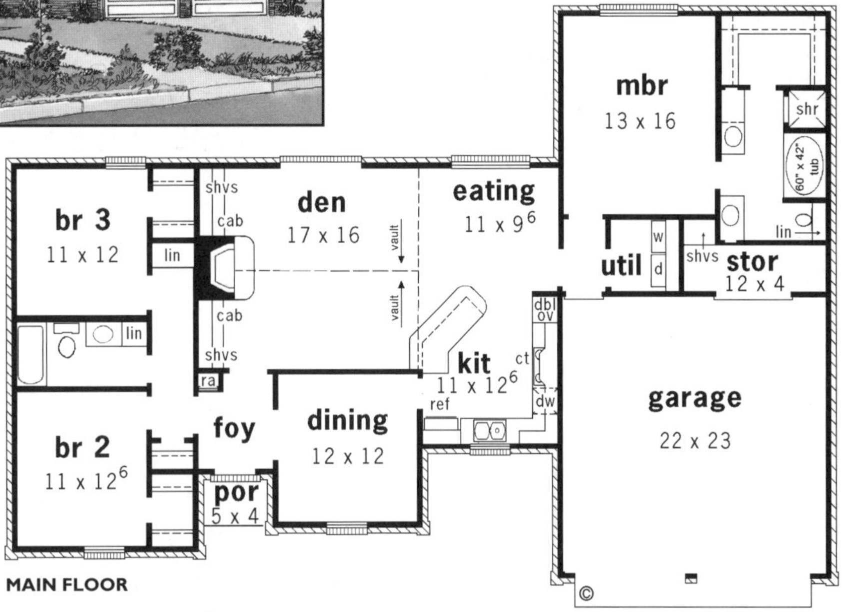

MAIN FLOOR

Design 96543

Units	Single
Price Code	B
Total Finished	1,680 sq. ft.
Main Finished	1,680 sq. ft.
Garage Unfinished	592 sq. ft.
Porch Unfinished	259 sq. ft.
Dimensions	54'x61'
Foundation	Crawlspace Slab
Bedrooms	3
Full Baths	2
Main Ceiling	9'
Vaulted Ceiling	14'
Tray Ceiling	12'
Max Ridge Height	23'
Roof Framing	Stick
Exterior Walls	2x4

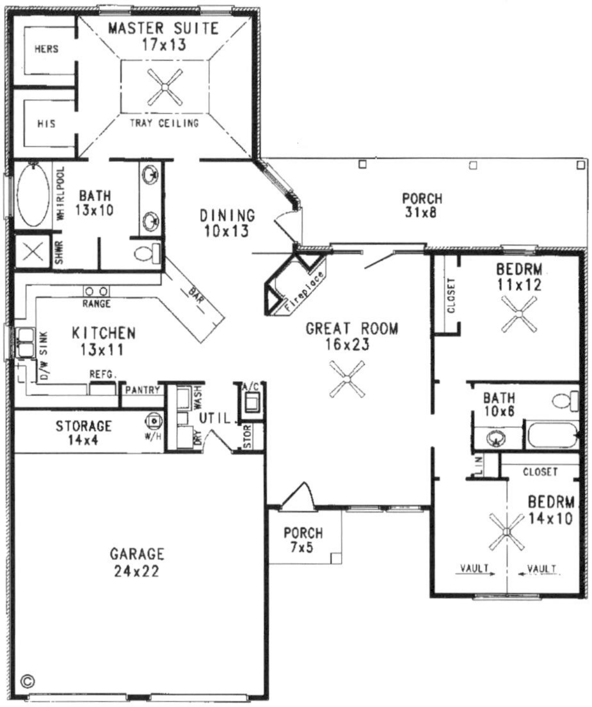

MAIN FLOOR

Design 92434

Units	Single
Price Code	B
Total Finished	1,681 sq. ft.
Main Finished	1,681 sq. ft.
Garage Unfinished	427 sq. ft.
Dimensions	55'8"x53'2"
Foundation	Slab
Bedrooms	3
Full Baths	2
Main Ceiling	9'
Vaulted Ceiling	11'
Tray Ceiling	11'
Max Ridge Height	21'8"
Roof Framing	Stick

TRAY CEILING
SITTING
MASTER BDRM
21'-4" x 15'-0"
DECK
17'-4" x 13'-6"
LINEN
FAMILY
18'-0" x 16'-2"
11' HIGH CEILING
BEDROOM 3
13'-0" x 11'-0"
BREAKFAST BAR
BRKFST
9'-7" x 11'-0"
KITCHEN
11'-9" x 11'-0"
SERVING BAR
PLANT SHELF
PANTRY
DESK
SQUARE COLUMNS
ENTRY
11' HIGH CEILING
COATS
DINING
11'-0" x 12'-0"
BEDROOM 2
13'-0" x 11'-0"
GARAGE
21'-4" x 20'-0"
MAIN FLOOR

Design 93464

Units	Single
Price Code	B
Total Finished	1,681 sq. ft.
Main Finished	1,681 sq. ft.
Basement Unfinished	1,681 sq. ft.
Garage Unfinished	484 sq. ft.
Porch Unfinished	79 sq. ft.
Dimensions	58'x58'
Foundation	Basement
Bedrooms	3
Full Baths	2
Main Ceiling	8'
Vaulted Ceiling	11'9"
Tray Ceiling	10'
Max Ridge Height	18'7"
Roof Framing	Stick
Exterior Walls	2x4

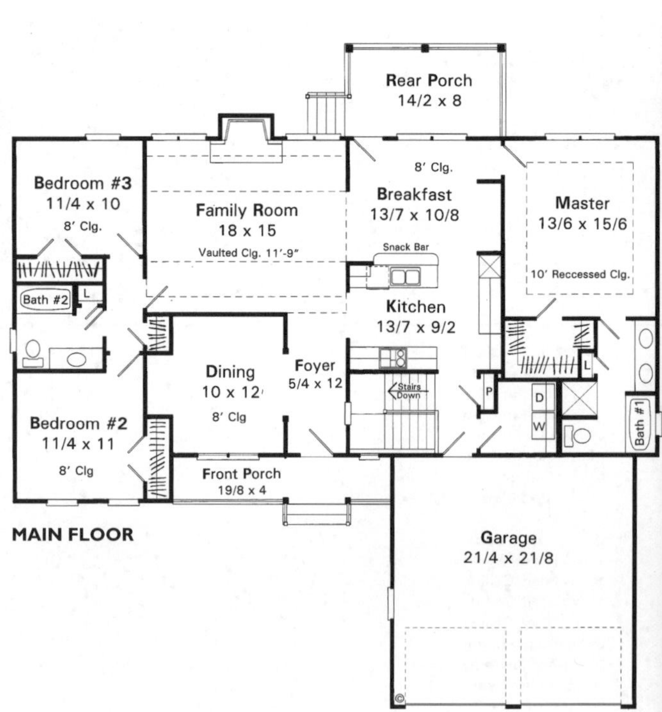
Rear Porch
14/2 x 8
Bedroom #3
11/4 x 10
8' Clg.
Family Room
18 x 15
Vaulted Clg. 11'-9"
8' Clg.
Breakfast
13/7 x 10/8
Snack Bar
Master
13/6 x 15/6
10' Recessed Clg.
Bath #2
Kitchen
13/7 x 9/2
Dining
10 x 12
8' Clg
Foyer
5/4 x 12
Stairs Down
Bedroom #2
11/4 x 11
8' Clg
Bath #1
Front Porch
19/8 x 4
MAIN FLOOR
Garage
21/4 x 21/8

Design 82010

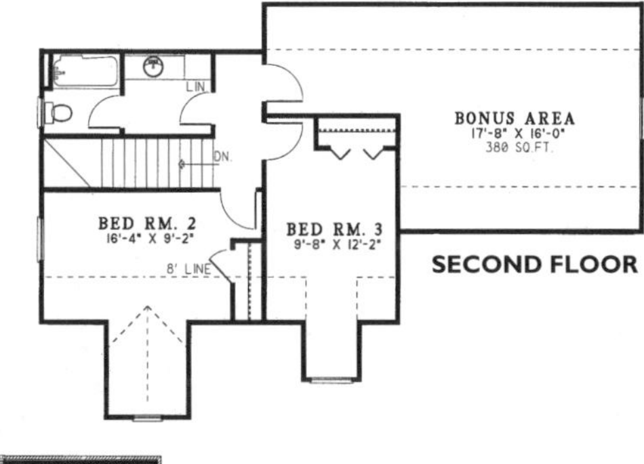
BONUS AREA
17'-8" X 16'-0"
380 SQ.FT.
LIN.
DN.
BED RM. 2
16'-4" X 9'-2"
8' LINE
BED RM. 3
9'-8" X 12'-2"
SECOND FLOOR

WHP TUB
LIN.
MASTER BATH
GRILLING PORCH
14'-0" X 6'-0"
KITCHEN
11'-0" X 10'-0"
DW
RG.
REF.
ISLAND
NOOK
7'-0" X 9'-0"
LAU.
STORAGE
10'-0" X 6'-0"
MASTER SUITE
11'-6" X 14'-0"
GARAGE
19'-8" X 19'-4"
UP
8" COLUMNS
DINING
10'-2" X 14'-0"
GREAT RM.
15'-6" X 16'-0"
FIRST FLOOR
FOYER
PRCH

Units	Single
Price Code	B
Total Finished	1,684 sq. ft.
First Finished	1,155 sq. ft.
Second Finished	529 sq. ft.
Bonus Unfinished	380 sq. ft.
Garage Unfinished	400 sq. ft.
Porch Unfinished	164 sq. ft.
Dimensions	47'x50'
Foundation	Basement Crawlspace Slab
Bedrooms	3
Full Baths	2
Half Baths	1
First Ceiling	9'
Second Ceiling	8'
Roof Framing	Stick
Exterior Walls	2x4

Design 93468

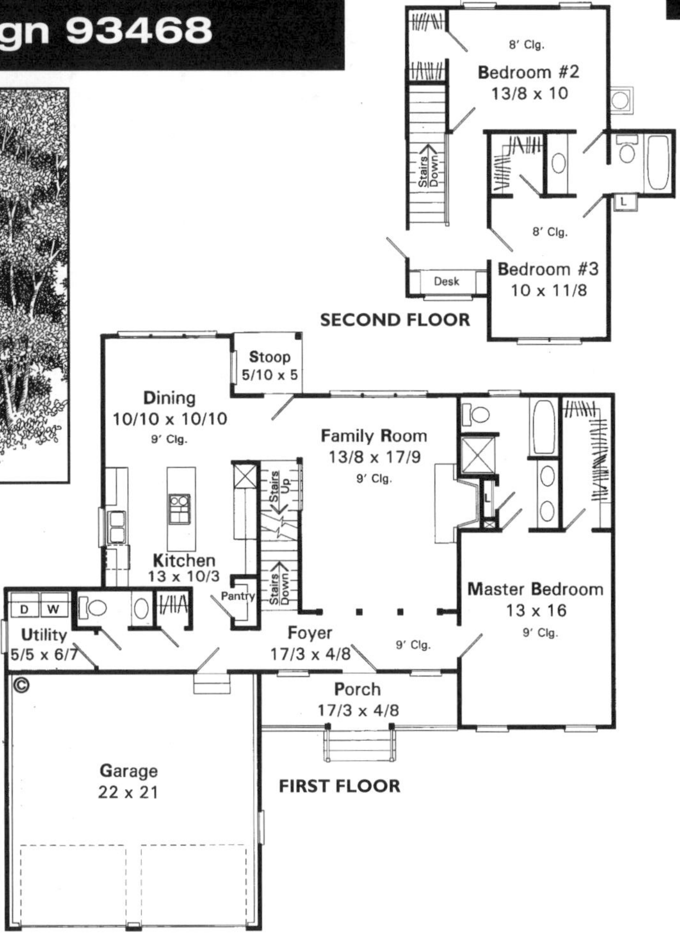

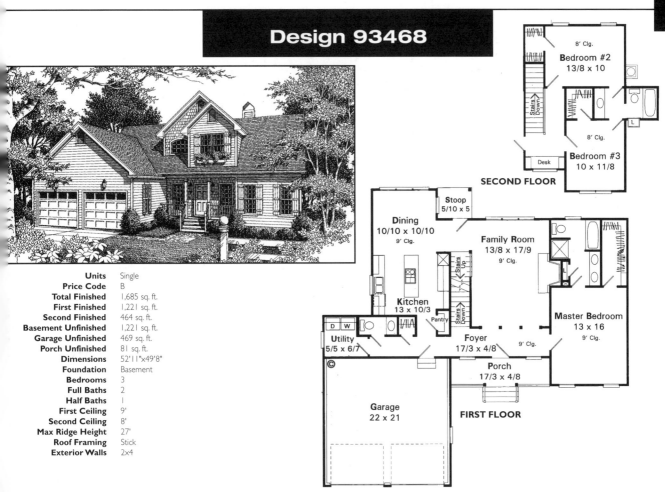

8' Clg.
Bedroom #2
13/8 x 10
Stairs Down
8' Clg.
Bedroom #3
10 x 11/8
Desk
SECOND FLOOR

Stoop
5/10 x 5
Dining
10/10 x 10/10
9' Clg.
Family Room
13/8 x 17/9
9' Clg.
Stairs Up
Kitchen
13 x 10/3
Pantry
Stairs Down
Master Bedroom
13 x 16
9' Clg.
D W
Utility
5/5 x 6/7
Foyer
17/3 x 4/8
9' Clg.
Porch
17/3 x 4/8
Garage
22 x 21
FIRST FLOOR

Units	Single
Price Code	B
Total Finished	1,685 sq. ft.
First Finished	1,221 sq. ft.
Second Finished	464 sq. ft.
Basement Unfinished	1,221 sq. ft.
Garage Unfinished	469 sq. ft.
Porch Unfinished	81 sq. ft.
Dimensions	52'11"x49'8"
Foundation	Basement
Bedrooms	3
Full Baths	2
Half Baths	1
First Ceiling	9'
Second Ceiling	8'
Max Ridge Height	27'
Roof Framing	Stick
Exterior Walls	2x4

Design 34029

PHOTOGRAPHY: CHARLES BROOKS

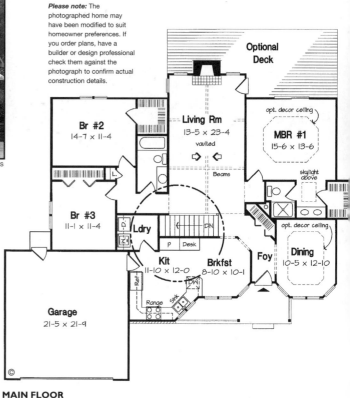

Please note: The photographed home may have been modified to suit homeowner preferences. If you order plans, have a builder or design professional check them against the photograph to confirm actual construction details.

Units	Single
Price Code	B
Total Finished	1,686 sq. ft.
Main Finished	1,686 sq. ft.
Basement Unfinished	1,676 sq. ft.
Garage Unfinished	484 sq. ft.
Dimensions	61'x54'
Foundation	Basement Crawlspace Slab
Bedrooms	3
Full Baths	1
3/4 Baths	1
Main Ceiling	8'
Max Ridge Height	23'
Roof Framing	Stick
Exterior Walls	2x4, 2x6

Crawl Space Access
Furn
WH
P
Desk

OPTIONAL CRAWLSPACE/SLAB FOUNDATION

Optional Deck
Living Rm 13-5 x 23-4 vaulted
Beams
Br #2 14-7 x 11-4
MBR #1 15-6 x 13-6
opt. decor ceiling
skylight above
Br #3 11-1 x 11-4
L.
Ldry
D
W
DN
P
Desk
Kit 11-10 x 12-0
Brkfst 8-10 x 10-1
Foy
Dining 10-5 x 12-10
opt. decor ceiling
Ref
Range
Sink
DW
Garage 21-5 x 21-9
©

MAIN FLOOR

Design 97617

CAD
FILES AVAILABLE
For more information call
800-235-5700

Units	Single
Price Code	B
Total Finished	1,688 sq. ft.
Main Finished	1,688 sq. ft.
Basement Unfinished	1,702 sq. ft.
Garage Unfinished	402 sq. ft.
Dimensions	50'x51'
Foundation	Basement Crawlspace Slab
Bedrooms	4
Full Baths	2
Max Ridge Height	24'6"
Roof Framing	Stick
Exterior Walls	2x4

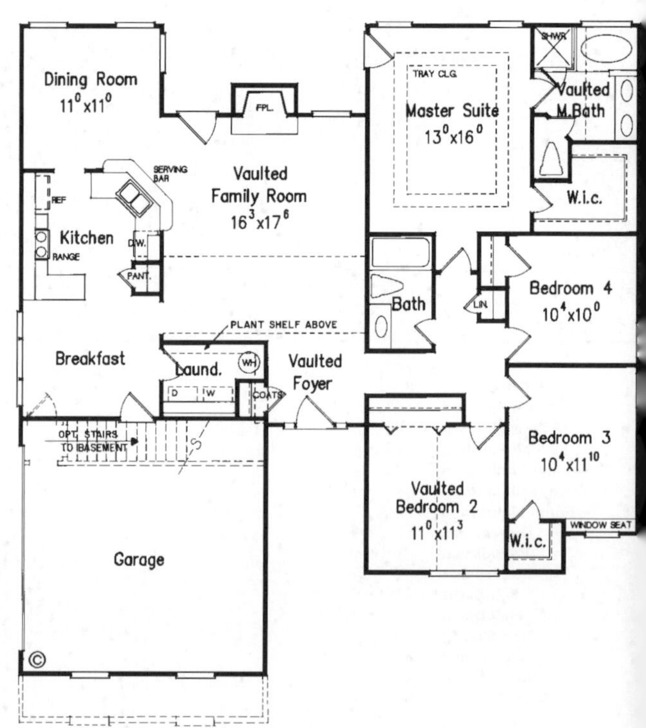
Dining Room
11^0x11^0
FPL.
SERVING BAR
Vaulted Family Room
16^3x17^6
REF
Kitchen
RANGE
D.W.
PANT.
TRAY CLG.
Master Suite
13^0x16^0
SHWR.
Vaulted M.Bath
W.i.c.
Bath
LIN.
Bedroom 4
10^4x10^0
PLANT SHELF ABOVE
Breakfast
Laund.
WH
D
W
COATS
Vaulted Foyer
OPT. STAIRS TO BASEMENT
Bedroom 3
10^4x11^{10}
Vaulted Bedroom 2
11^0x11^3
W.i.c.
WINDOW SEAT
Garage
©

MAIN FLOOR

Design 97207

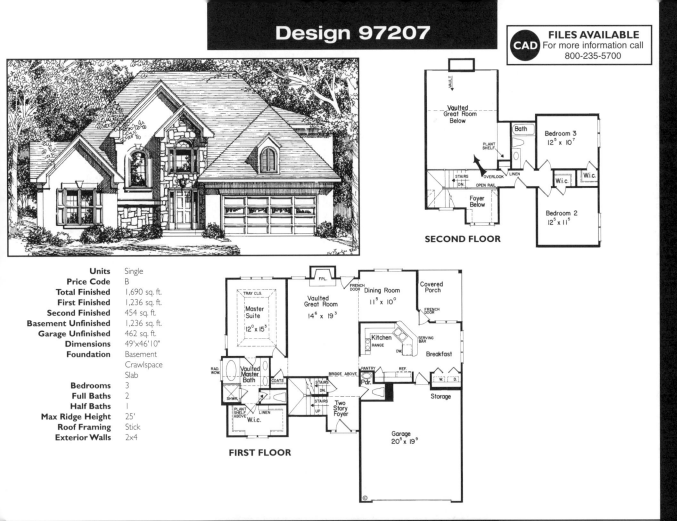

Units	Single
Price Code	B
Total Finished	1,690 sq. ft.
First Finished	1,236 sq. ft.
Second Finished	454 sq. ft.
Basement Unfinished	1,236 sq. ft.
Garage Unfinished	462 sq. ft.
Dimensions	49'x46'10"
Foundation	Basement Crawlspace Slab
Bedrooms	3
Full Baths	2
Half Baths	1
Max Ridge Height	25'
Roof Framing	Stick
Exterior Walls	2x4

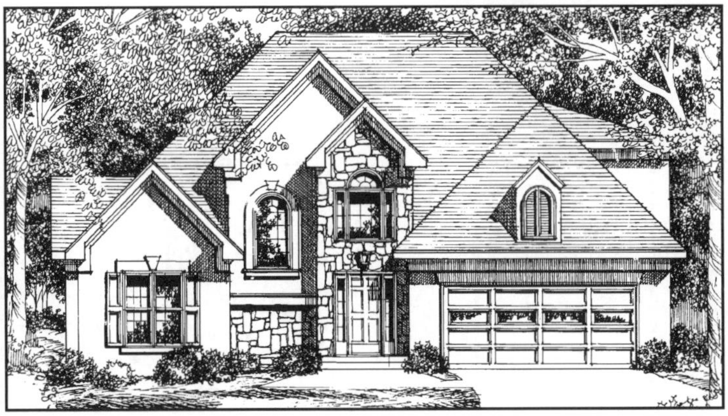

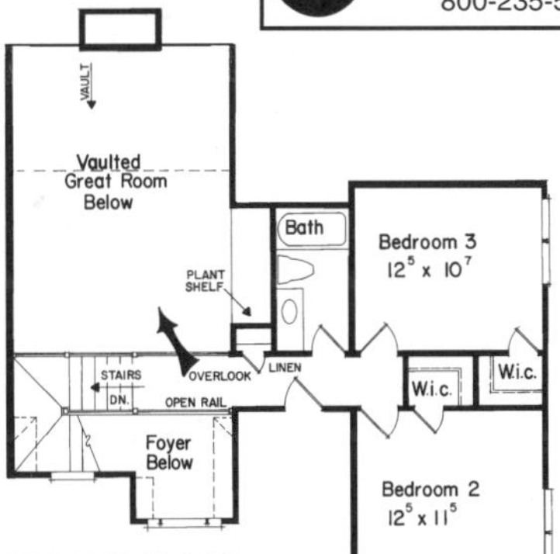

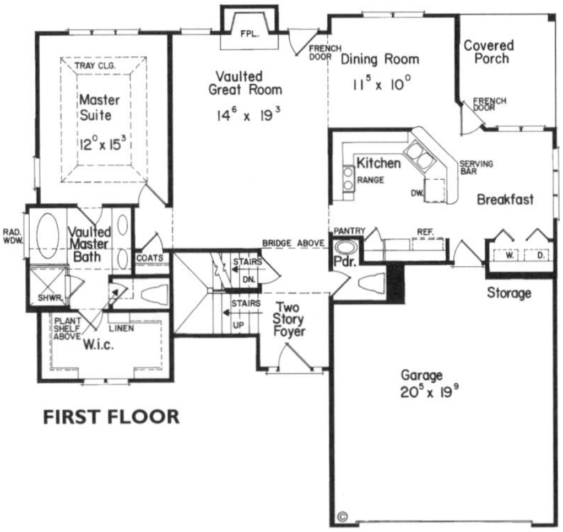

SECOND FLOOR

FIRST FLOOR

Design 99180

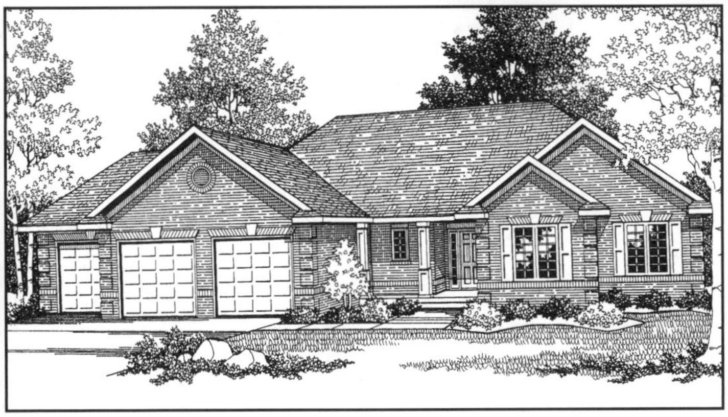

Units	Single
Price Code	B
Total Finished	1,690 sq. ft.
Main Finished	1,690 sq. ft.
Basement Unfinished	1,690 sq. ft.
Garage Unfinished	959 sq. ft.
Deck Unfinished	231 sq. ft.
Dimensions	74'4"x48'
Foundation	Basement
Bedrooms	3
Full Baths	1
3/4 Baths	1
Max Ridge Height	23'8"
Roof Framing	Truss
Exterior Walls	2x6

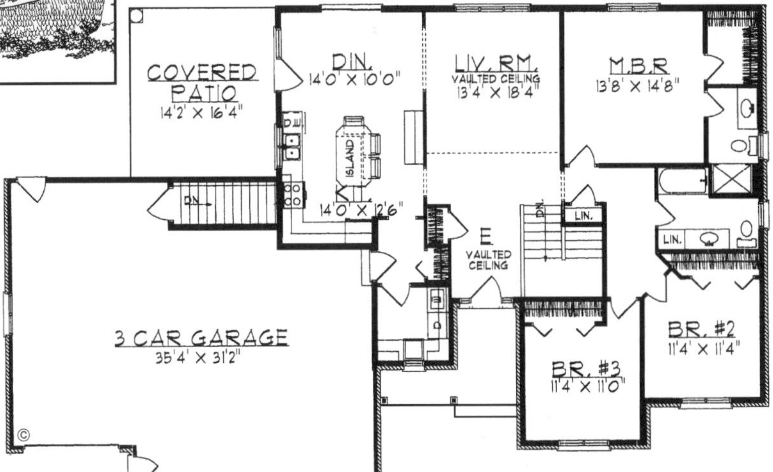

MAIN FLOOR

Design 97254

CAD
FILES AVAILABLE
For more information call
800-235-5700

Units	Single
Price Code	B
Total Finished	1,692 sq. ft.
Main Finished	1,692 sq. ft.
Bonus Unfinished	358 sq. ft.
Basement Unfinished	1,705 sq. ft.
Garage Unfinished	472 sq. ft.
Dimensions	54'x56'6"
Foundation	Basement Crawlspace
Bedrooms	3
Full Baths	2
Max Ridge Height	27'
Roof Framing	Stick
Exterior Walls	2x4

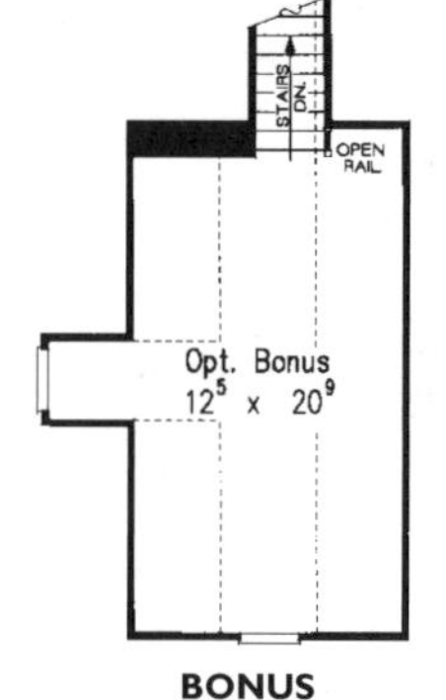
STAIRS DN
OPEN RAIL
Opt. Bonus
12⁵ x 20⁹

BONUS

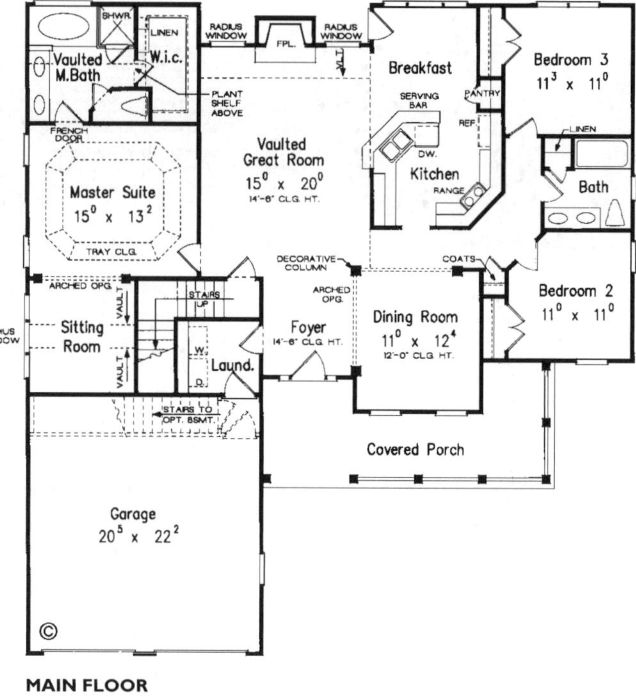
SHWR.
LINEN
Vaulted M.Bath
W.i.c.
RADIUS WINDOW
FPL.
RADIUS WINDOW
Breakfast
Bedroom 3
11³ x 11⁰
PLANT SHELF ABOVE
SERVING BAR
PANTRY
REF.
LINEN
FRENCH DOOR
Vaulted Great Room
15⁰ x 20⁰
14'-6" CLG. HT.
DW.
Kitchen
RANGE
Bath
Master Suite
15⁰ x 13²
TRAY CLG.
DECORATIVE COLUMN
COATS
ARCHED OPG.
STAIRS UP
ARCHED OPG.
Bedroom 2
11⁰ x 11⁰
RADIUS WINDOW
Sitting Room
VAULT
Foyer
14'-6" CLG. HT.
Dining Room
11⁰ x 12⁴
12'-0" CLG. HT.
W.
D.
Laund.
STAIRS TO OPT. BSMT.
Covered Porch
Garage
20⁵ x 22²
©

MAIN FLOOR

Design 98994

Units	Single
Price Code	B
Total Finished	1,695 sq. ft.
Main Finished	1,632 sq. ft.
Lower Finished	63 sq. ft.
Basement Unfinished	1,548 sq. ft.
Garage Unfinished	700 sq. ft.
Porch Unfinished	120 sq. ft.
Dimensions	45'x48'
Foundation	Basement
Bedrooms	3
Full Baths	2
Main Ceiling	8'
Max Ridge Height	22'
Roof Framing	Stick
Exterior Walls	2x4

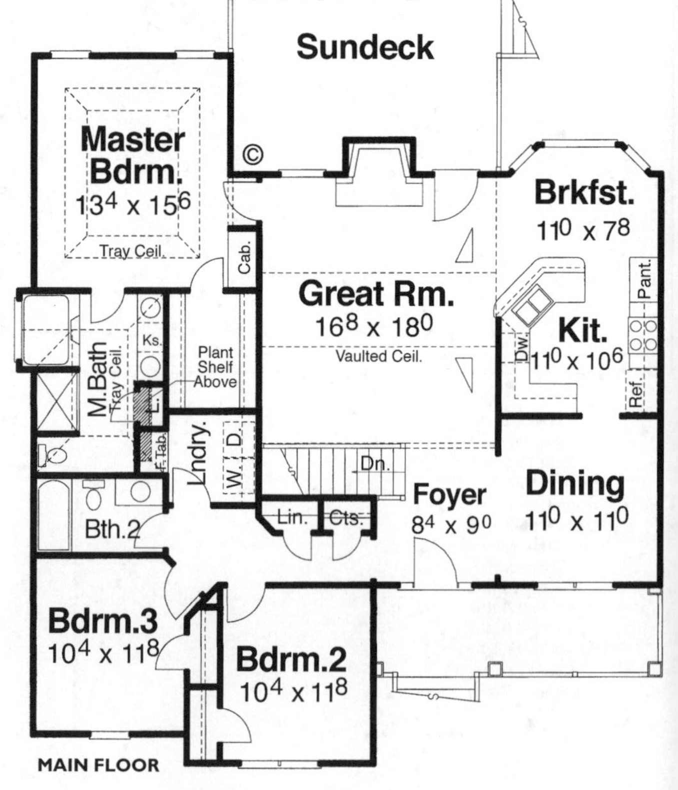
Sundeck
Master Bdrm.
13⁴ x 15⁶
Tray Ceil.
©
Brkfst.
11⁰ x 7⁸
Cab.
Great Rm.
16⁸ x 18⁰
Vaulted Ceil.
Pant.
Kit.
11⁰ x 10⁶
Dw
Ref.
M.Bath
Tray Ceil.
Ks.
Plant Shelf Above
L.
F.Tab.
Lndry.
W.
D.
Dn.
Foyer
8⁴ x 9⁰
Dining
11⁰ x 11⁰
Bth.2
Lin.
Cts.
Bdrm.3
10⁴ x 11⁸
Bdrm.2
10⁴ x 11⁸

MAIN FLOOR

Design 92290

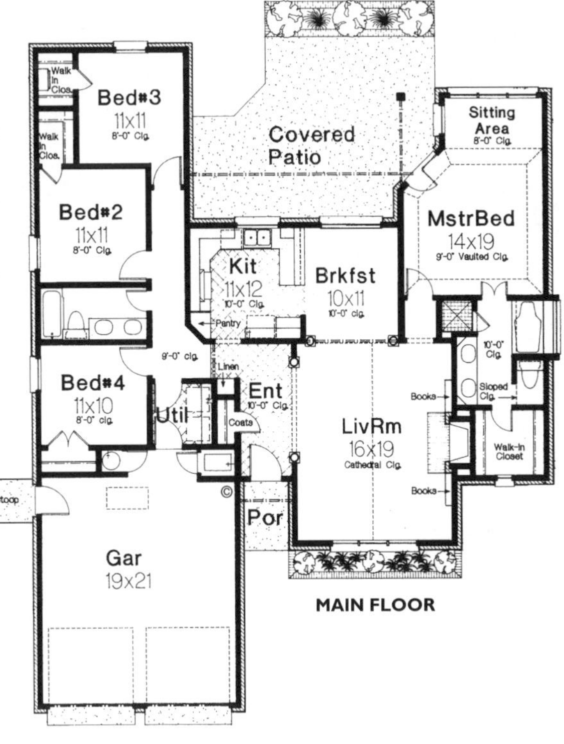
Covered Patio
Sitting Area
8'-0" Clg.
Bed#3
11x11
8'-0" Clg.
Walk In Clos.
Bed#2
11x11
8'-0" Clg.
Kit
11x12
10'-0" Clg.
Pantry
Brkfst
10x11
10'-0" clg.
MstrBed
14x19
9'-0" Vaulted Clg.
10'-0" Clg.
Sloped Clg.
Walk-In Closet
9'-0" clg.
Linen
Bed#4
11x10
8'-0" clg.
Util
Ent
10'-0" Clg.
Coats
LivRm
16x19
Cathedral Clg.
Books
Stoop
Por
Gar
19x21
MAIN FLOOR

Units	Single
Price Code	B
Total Finished	1,696 sq. ft.
Main Finished	1,696 sq. ft.
Garage Unfinished	389 sq. ft.
Deck Unfinished	200 sq. ft.
Porch Unfinished	30 sq. ft.
Dimensions	50'x62'2"
Foundation	Slab
Bedrooms	4
Full Baths	2
Max Ridge Height	22'
Roof Framing	Stick
Exterior Walls	2x4

Design 50013

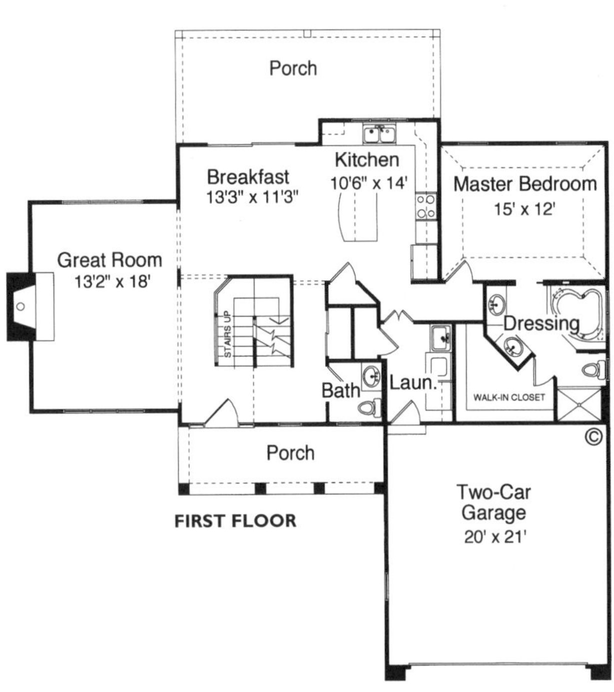
Porch
Breakfast
13'3" x 11'3"
Kitchen
10'6" x 14'
Master Bedroom
15' x 12'
Great Room
13'2" x 18'
STAIRS UP
Dressing
Bath
Laun.
WALK-IN CLOSET
Porch
Two-Car Garage
20' x 21'
FIRST FLOOR

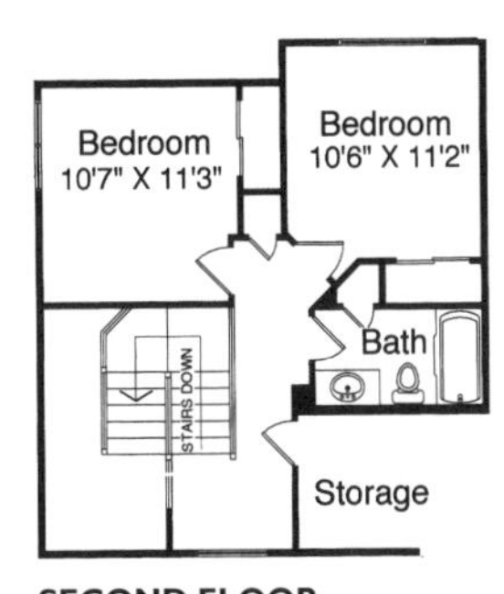
Bedroom
10'7" X 11'3"
Bedroom
10'6" X 11'2"
Bath
STAIRS DOWN
Storage
SECOND FLOOR

Units	Single
Price Code	B
Total Finished	1,697 sq. ft.
First Finished	1,263 sq. ft.
Second Finished	434 sq. ft.
Basement Unfinished	1,263 sq. ft.
Garage Unfinished	393 sq. ft.
Porch Unfinished	111 sq. ft.
Dimensions	55'2"x57'3"
Foundation	Basement
Bedrooms	3
Full Baths	2
Half Baths	1
First Ceiling	8'
Second Ceiling	8'
Max Ridge Height	24'6"
Roof Framing	Truss
Exterior Walls	2x4

Design 94925

Units	Single
Price Code	B
Total Finished	1,697 sq. ft.
Main Finished	1,697 sq. ft.
Basement Unfinished	1,697 sq. ft.
Garage Unfinished	470 sq. ft.
Dimensions	54'x54'
Foundation	Basement
Bedrooms	3
Full Baths	2
Main Ceiling	8'-10'
Max Ridge Height	20'4"
Roof Framing	Stick
Exterior Walls	2x4

* Alternate foundation options available at an additional charge. Please call 1-800-235-5700 for more information.

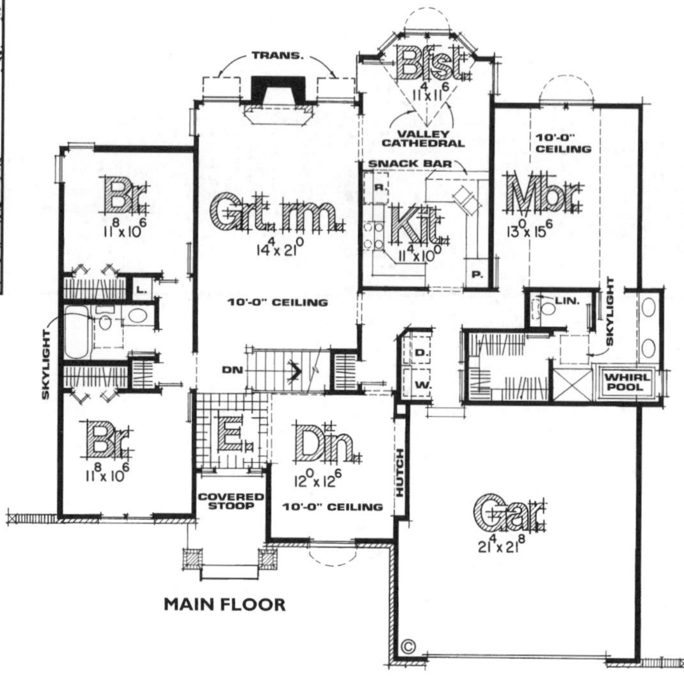
TRANS.
Bfst. 11⁴x11⁶
VALLEY CATHEDRAL
SNACK BAR
10'-0" CEILING
Br. 11⁸x10⁶
Grt.rm. 14⁴x21⁰
Kit. 11⁴x10⁰
Mbr. 13⁰x15⁶
10'-0" CEILING
LIN.
SKYLIGHT
DN
D.
W.
WHIRL POOL
E.
Br. 11⁸x10⁶
Din. 12⁰x12⁶
HUTCH
COVERED STOOP
10'-0" CEILING
Gar. 21⁴x21⁸
MAIN FLOOR

Design 81011

Units	Single
Price Code	B
Total Finished	1,698 sq. ft.
First Finished	951 sq. ft.
Second Finished	747 sq. ft.
Bonus Unfinished	254 sq. ft.
Garage Unfinished	703 sq. ft.
Dimensions	50'x44'6"
Foundation	Crawlspace
Bedrooms	3
Full Baths	2
3/4 Baths	1
First Ceiling	9'
Second Ceiling	8'
Max Ridge Height	28'
Exterior Walls	2x6

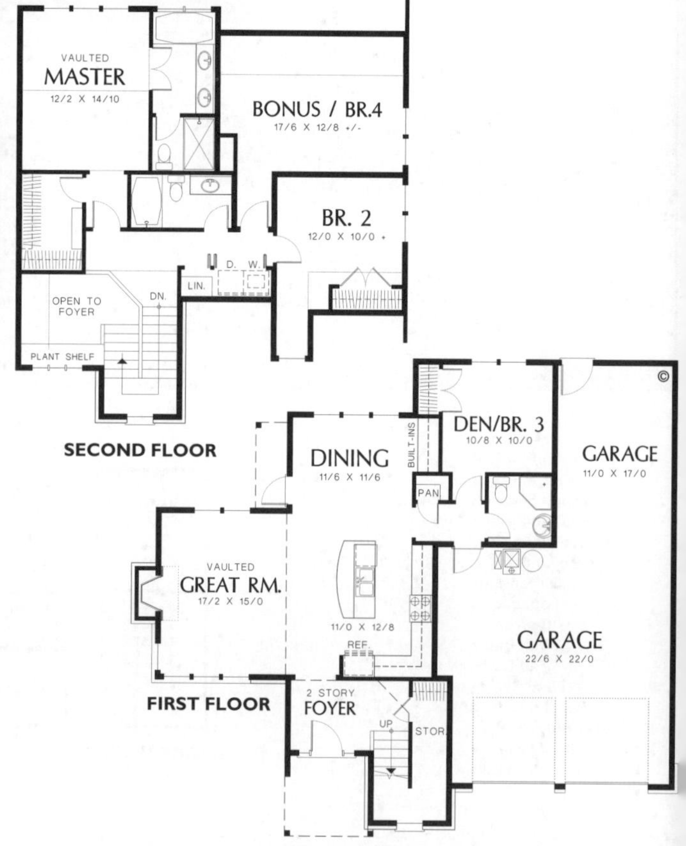
VAULTED MASTER 12/2 X 14/10
BONUS / BR.4 17/6 X 12/8 +/-
BR. 2 12/0 X 10/0 +
D. W.
LIN.
OPEN TO FOYER
DN.
PLANT SHELF
SECOND FLOOR
DINING 11/6 X 11/6
BUILT-INS
DEN/BR. 3 10/8 X 10/0
GARAGE 11/0 X 17/0
PAN
VAULTED GREAT RM. 17/2 X 15/0
11/0 X 12/8
REF.
GARAGE 22/6 X 22/0
FIRST FLOOR
2 STORY FOYER
UP
STOR.

Design 67012

Units	Single
Price Code	B
Total Finished	1,699 sq. ft.
Main Finished	1,699 sq. ft.
Bonus Unfinished	260 sq. ft.
Garage Unfinished	498 sq. ft.
Porch Unfinished	22 sq. ft.
Dimensions	56'9"x57'8"
Foundation	Slab
Bedrooms	3
Full Baths	2
Main Ceiling	8'
Max Ridge Height	21'5"
Roof Framing	Stick
Exterior Walls	2x4

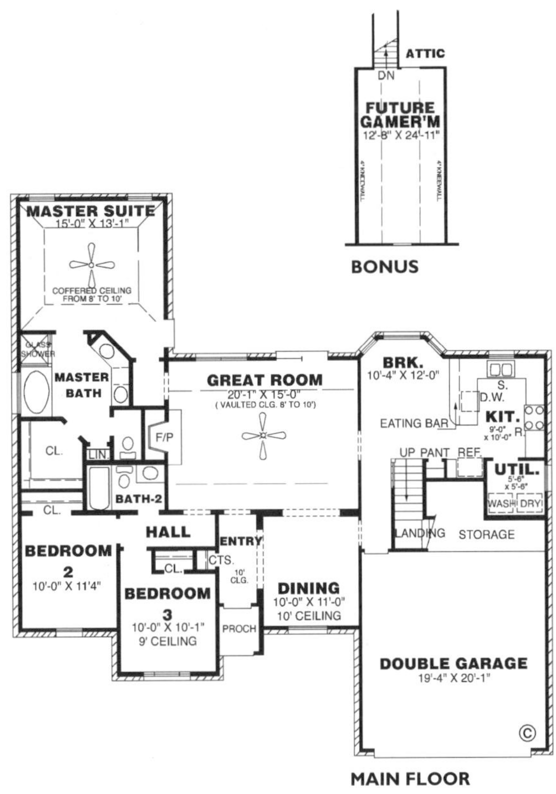
ATTIC
DN
FUTURE GAMER'M
12'-8" X 24'-11"
BONUS
MASTER SUITE
15'-0" X 13'-1"
COFFERED CEILING FROM 8' TO 10'
MASTER BATH
CL.
LIN
BATH-2
CL.
F/P
GREAT ROOM
20'-1" X 15'-0"
(VAULTED CLG. 8' TO 10')
BRK.
10'-4" X 12'-0"
EATING BAR
S.
D.W.
KIT.
UP
PANT
REF.
UTIL.
WASH
DRY
LANDING
STORAGE
HALL
ENTRY
CTS.
CL.
BEDROOM 2
10'-0" X 11'4"
BEDROOM 3
10'-0" X 10'-1"
9' CEILING
PROCH
DINING
10'-0" X 11'-0"
10' CEILING
DOUBLE GARAGE
19'-4" X 20'-1"
MAIN FLOOR

Design 81010

Units	Single
Price Code	B
Total Finished	1,699 sq. ft.
Main Finished	1,699 sq. ft.
Dimensions	50'x51'
Foundation	Crawlspace
Bedrooms	3
Full Baths	2
Main Ceiling	9'
Max Ridge Height	23'
Roof Framing	Truss
Exterior Walls	2x6

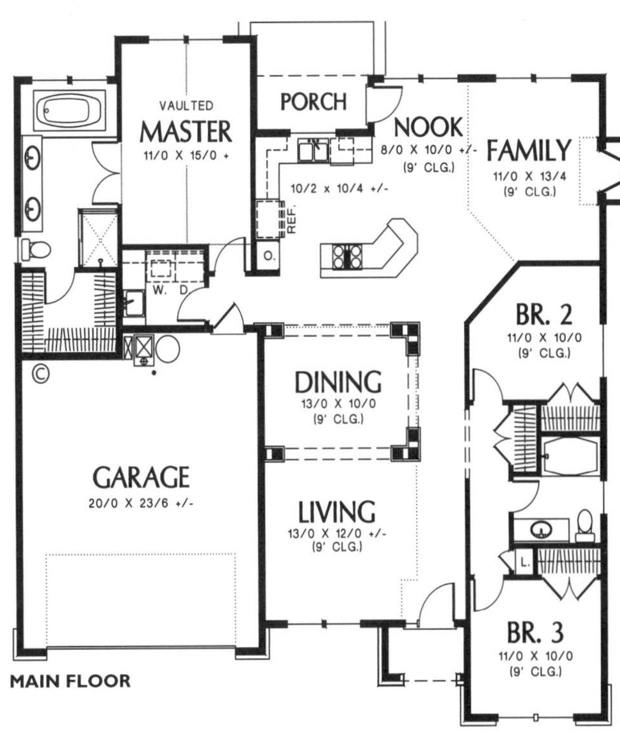
VAULTED
MASTER
11/0 X 15/0 +
PORCH
NOOK
8/0 X 10/0 +/-
(9' CLG.)
FAMILY
11/0 X 13/4
(9' CLG.)
10/2 x 10/4 +/-
REF.
W. D
BR. 2
11/0 X 10/0
(9' CLG.)
DINING
13/0 X 10/0
(9' CLG.)
GARAGE
20/0 X 23/6 +/-
LIVING
13/0 X 12/0 +/-
(9' CLG.)
BR. 3
11/0 X 10/0
(9' CLG.)
MAIN FLOOR

Design 64504

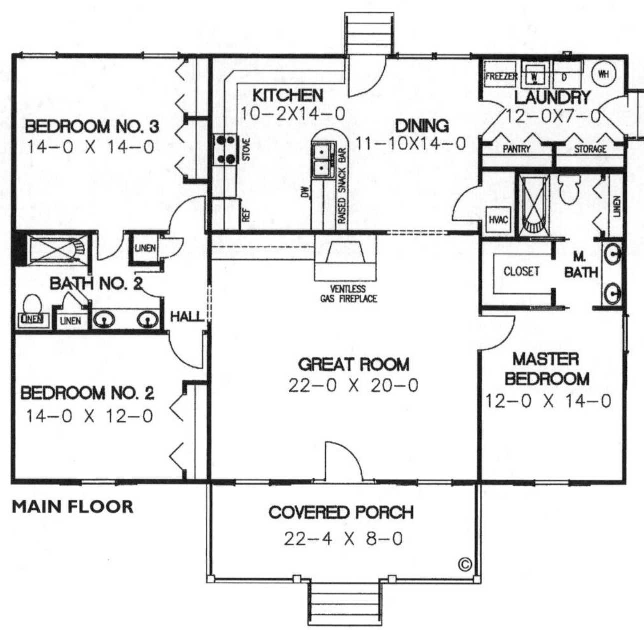

KITCHEN
10–2X14–0
DINING
11–10X14–0
LAUNDRY
12–0X7–0
FREEZER
W
D
WH
PANTRY
STORAGE
BEDROOM NO. 3
14–0 X 14–0
STOVE
DW
RAISED SNACK BAR
REF
HVAC
LINEN
LINEN
BATH NO. 2
LINEN
LINEN
HALL
VENTLESS GAS FIREPLACE
CLOSET
M. BATH
GREAT ROOM
22–0 X 20–0
MASTER BEDROOM
12–0 X 14–0
BEDROOM NO. 2
14–0 X 12–0
MAIN FLOOR
COVERED PORCH
22–4 X 8–0
©

Units	Single
Price Code	D
Total Finished	1,700 sq. ft.
Main Finished	1,700 sq. ft.
Dimensions	50'x42'
Foundation	Crawlspace
Bedrooms	3
Full Baths	2
Main Ceiling	9'
Max Ridge Height	24'
Roof Framing	Truss
Exterior Walls	2x4

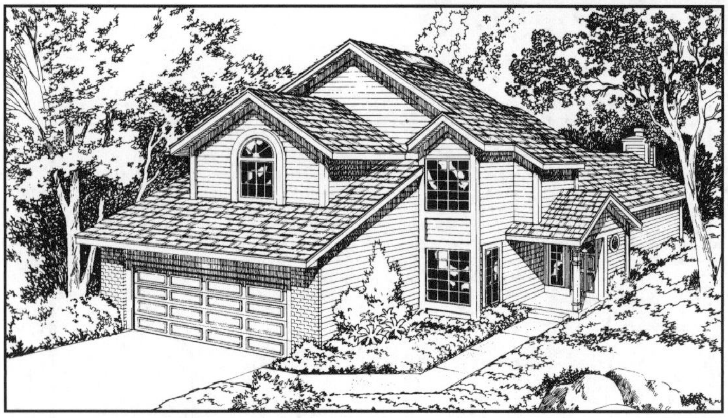

Design 20055

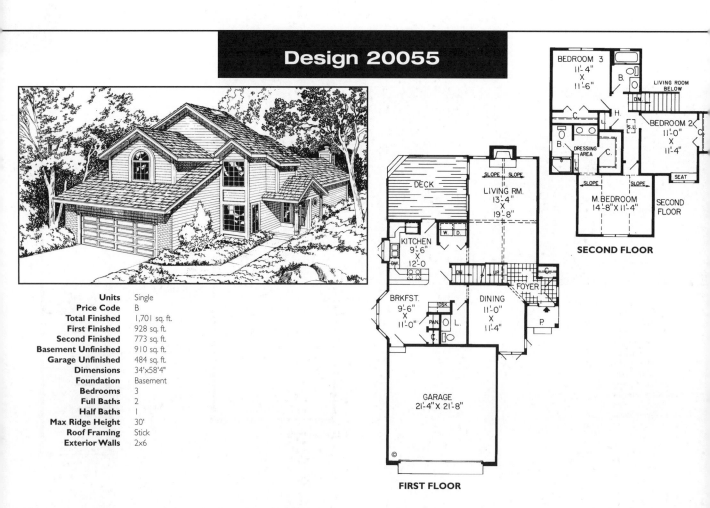

Units	Single
Price Code	B
Total Finished	1,701 sq. ft.
First Finished	928 sq. ft.
Second Finished	773 sq. ft.
Basement Unfinished	910 sq. ft.
Garage Unfinished	484 sq. ft.
Dimensions	34'x58'4"
Foundation	Basement
Bedrooms	3
Full Baths	2
Half Baths	1
Max Ridge Height	30'
Roof Framing	Stick
Exterior Walls	2x6

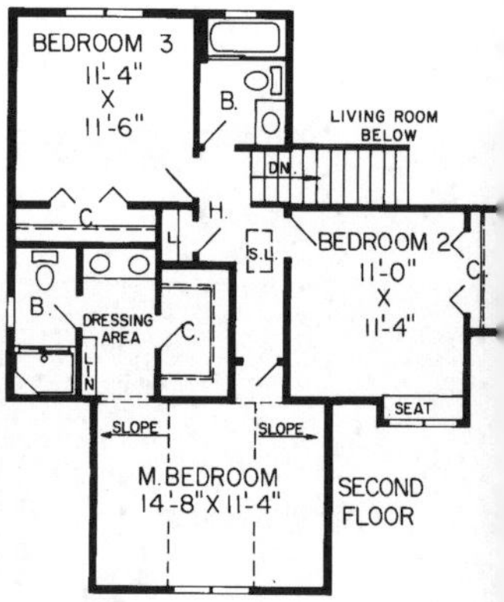

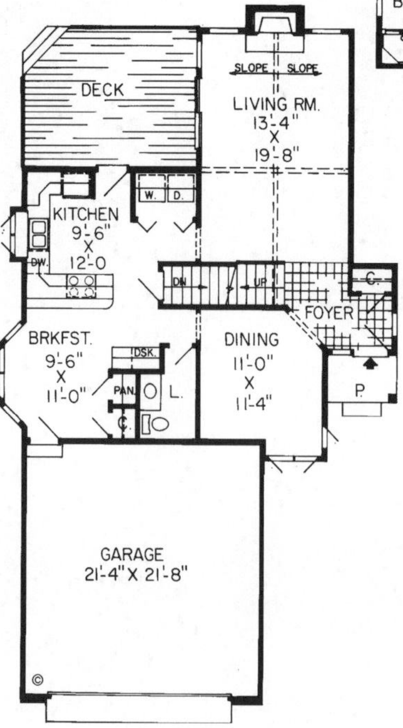

FIRST FLOOR

SECOND FLOOR

Design 90930

Units	Single
Price Code	B
Total Finished	1,702 sq. ft.
First Finished	1,238 sq. ft.
Second Finished	464 sq. ft.
Basement Unfinished	1,175 sq. ft.
Dimensions	34'x56'
Foundation	Basement
Bedrooms	3
Full Baths	1
3/4 Baths	1
Max Ridge Height	26'6"
Roof Framing	Stick
Exterior Walls	2x6

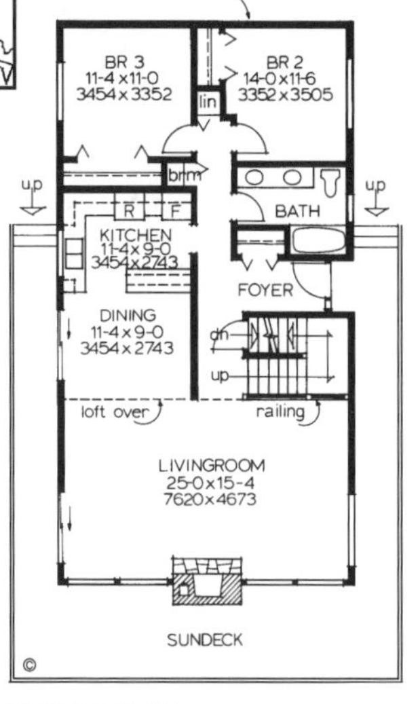
Full Basement under
BR 3
11-4 x 11-0
3454 x 3352
BR 2
14-0 x 11-6
3352 x 3505
lin
b.rm
up
BATH
KITCHEN
11-4 x 9-0
3454 x 2743
R
F
FOYER
DINING
11-4 x 9-0
3454 x 2743
dn
up
loft over
railing
LIVINGROOM
25-0 x 15-4
7620 x 4673
SUNDECK
©

FIRST FLOOR

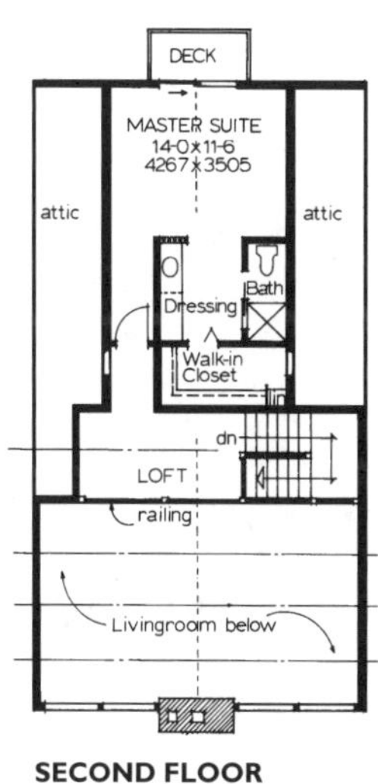
DECK
MASTER SUITE
14-0 x 11-6
4267 x 3505
attic
attic
Bath
Dressing
Walk-in Closet
dn
LOFT
railing
Livingroom below

SECOND FLOOR

Design 96524

Units	Single
Price Code	B
Total Finished	1,705 sq. ft.
First Finished	1,056 sq. ft.
Second Finished	649 sq. ft.
Garage Unfinished	562 sq. ft.
Porch Unfinished	162 sq. ft.
Dimensions	45'x45'
Foundation	Crawlspace Slab
Bedrooms	4
Full Baths	2
Half Baths	1
First Ceiling	8'
Second Ceiling	8'
Max Ridge Height	25'
Exterior Walls	2x4

BED RM.
12x11
CLOSET
BATH
BED RM.
12x11
LANDING
A/C
CLOSET
BED RM.
13x11
CLOSET
DOWN
ACCESS

SECOND FLOOR

PORCH
REFG
D/W
SINK
KITCHEN
10x11
RANGE
SHWR
WHIRLPOOL
BATH
MASTER SUITE
13x14
DINING
12x11
PANT
BATH
CLOSET
GREAT RM.
15x18
STOR
A/C
WASH
DRY
W/H
STORAGE
FIREPLACE
FOYER
GARAGE
23x23
PORCH
©

FIRST FLOOR

Design 69016

Units	Single
Price Code	B
Total Finished	1,708 sq. ft.
Main Finished	1,708 sq. ft.
Dimensions	80'x42'
Foundation	Basement Crawlspace
Bedrooms	3
Full Baths	2
Main Ceiling	8'
Max Ridge Height	21'6"
Roof Framing	Truss
Exterior Walls	2x4

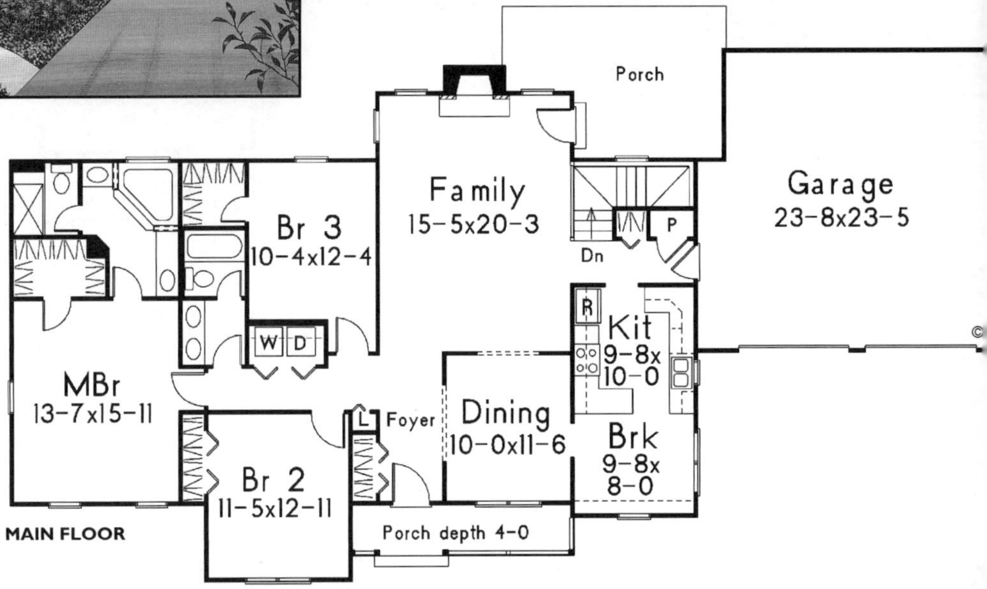

Porch
Family 15-5x20-3
Garage 23-8x23-5
Br 3 10-4x12-4
Dn
P
W D
R
Kit 9-8x 10-0
MBr 13-7x15-11
Foyer
Dining 10-0x11-6
Brk 9-8x 8-0
Br 2 11-5x12-11
Porch depth 4-0

MAIN FLOOR

Design 94250

Units	Single
Price Code	F
Total Finished	1,706 sq. ft.
First Finished	906 sq. ft.
Second Finished	714 sq. ft.
Lower Finished	86 sq. ft.
Basement Unfinished	155 sq. ft.
Garage Unfinished	950 sq. ft.
Deck Unfinished	116 sq. ft.
Porch Unfinished	471 sq. ft.
Dimensions	40'x37'
Foundation	Pier/Post
Bedrooms	2
Full Baths	2
Half Baths	1
First Ceiling	8'
Second Ceiling	8'
Max Ridge Height	47'6"
Roof Framing	Stick/Truss
Exterior Walls	2x6

* Alternate foundation options available at an additional charge.
Please call 1-800-235-5700 for more information.

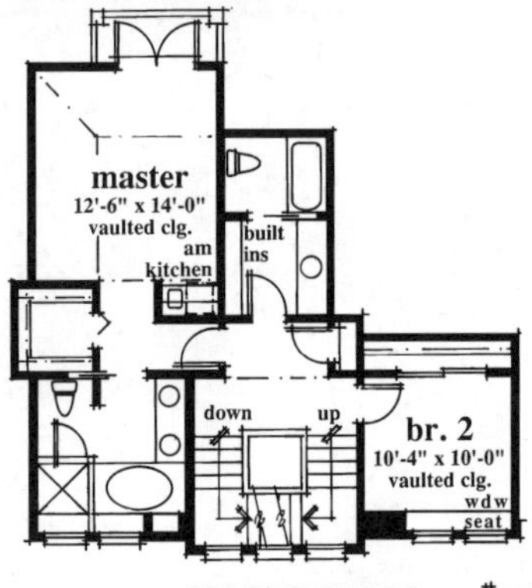

master 12'-6" x 14'-0" vaulted clg.
am kitchen
built ins
down
up
br. 2 10'-4" x 10'-0" vaulted clg.
wdw seat

SECOND FLOOR

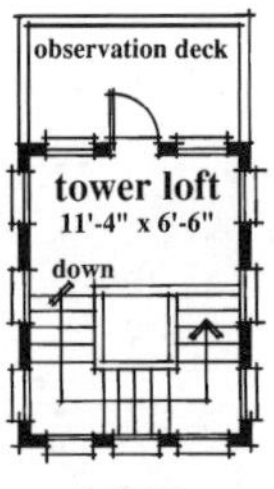

observation deck
tower loft 11'-4" x 6'-6"
down

LOFT

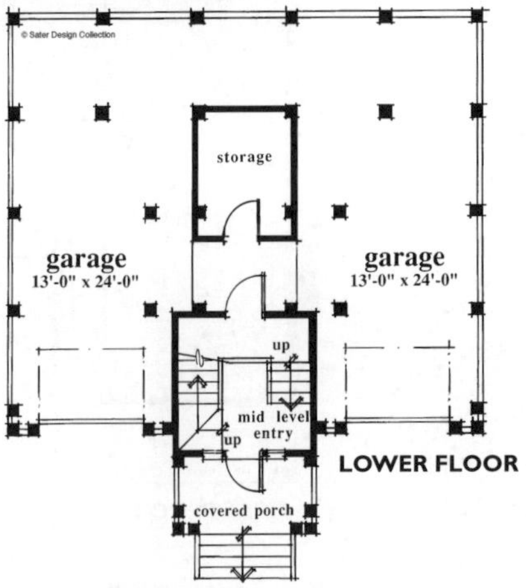

storage
garage 13'-0" x 24'-0"
garage 13'-0" x 24'-0"
up
mid level entry
up
covered porch

LOWER FLOOR

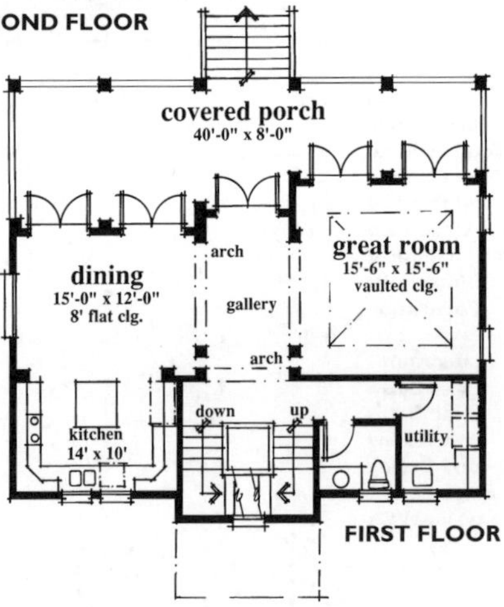

covered porch 40'-0" x 8'-0"
dining 15'-0" x 12'-0" 8' flat clg.
arch
gallery
arch
great room 15'-6" x 15'-6" vaulted clg.
kitchen 14' x 10'
down
up
utility

FIRST FLOOR

Design 24319

PHOTOGRAPHY: JOHN EHRENCLOU

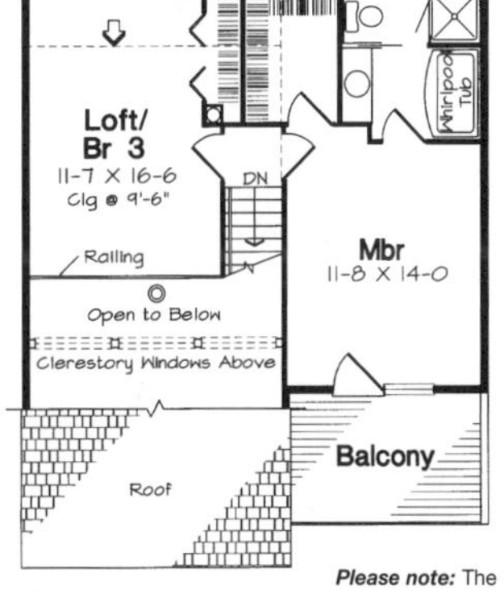
Loft/
Br 3
11-7 X 16-6
Clg @ 9'-6"
DN
Railing
Mbr
11-8 X 14-0
Open to Below
Clerestory Windows Above
Whirlpool Tub
Balcony
Roof

SECOND FLOOR

Please note: The photographed home may have been modified to suit homeowner preferences. If you order plans, have a builder or design professional check them against the photograph to confirm actual construction details.

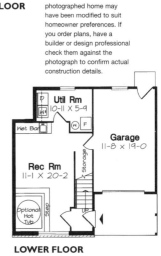

Units	Single
Price Code	B
Total Finished	1,710 sq. ft.
First Finished	728 sq. ft.
Second Finished	573 sq. ft.
Lower Finished	409 sq. ft.
Garage Unfinished	244 sq. ft.
Dimensions	28'x32'
Foundation	Basement
Bedrooms	3
Full Baths	2
First Ceiling	8'
Second Ceiling	8'
Max Ridge Height	33'
Roof Framing	Stick
Exterior Walls	2x4, 2x6

FIRST FLOOR

LOWER FLOOR

Design 94922

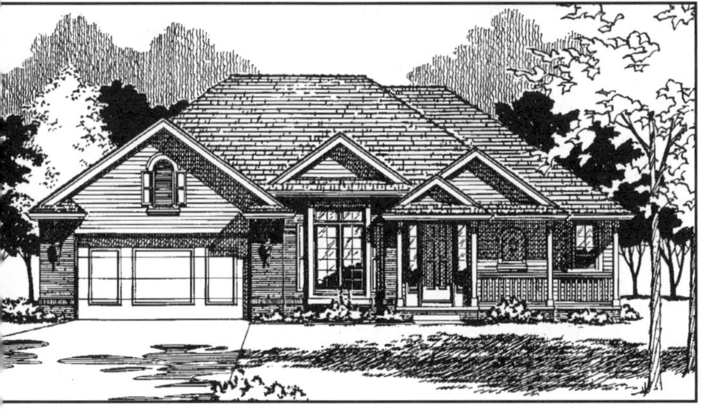

Units	Single
Price Code	B
Total Finished	1,710 sq. ft.
Main Finished	1,710 sq. ft.
Basement Unfinished	1,710 sq. ft.
Garage Unfinished	480 sq. ft.
Dimensions	53'4"x54'10"
Foundation	Basement
Bedrooms	3
Full Baths	2
Max Ridge Height	20'3"
Roof Framing	Stick
Exterior Walls	2x4

Alternate foundation options available at an additional charge. Please call 1-800-235-5700 for more information.

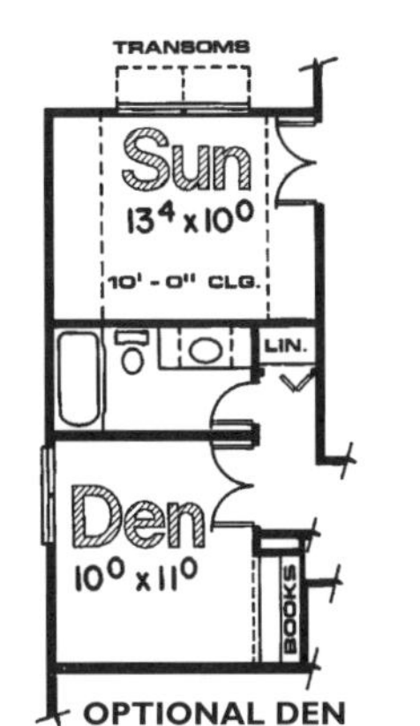
TRANSOMS
Sun
13⁴ x 10⁰
10' - 0" CLG.
LIN.
Den
10⁰ x 11⁰
BOOKS

OPTIONAL DEN

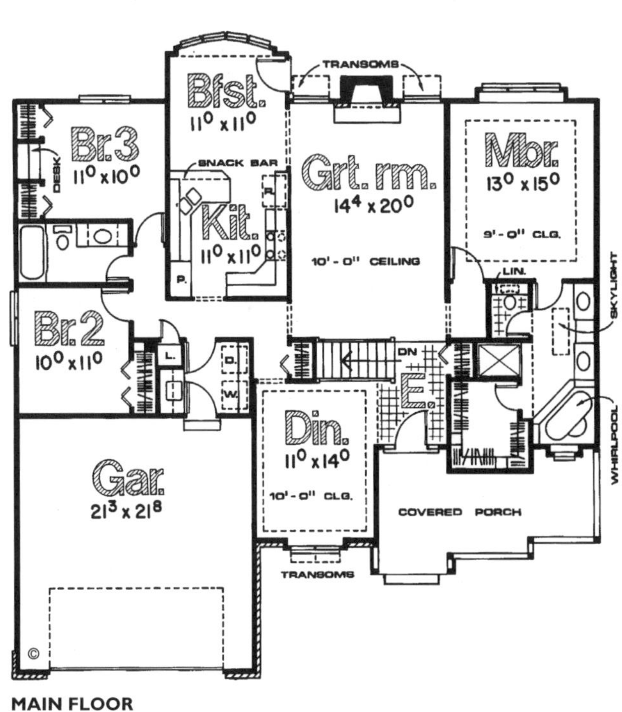
TRANSOMS
Bfst.
11⁰ x 11⁰
Br.3
11⁰ x 10⁰
DESK
SNACK BAR
Grt. rm.
14⁴ x 20⁰
10' - 0" CEILING
Kit.
11⁰ x 11⁰
Mbr.
13⁰ x 15⁰
9' - 0" CLG.
LIN.
SKYLIGHT
Br.2
10⁰ x 11⁰
DN
E.
WHIRLPOOL
Din.
11⁰ x 14⁰
10' - 0" CLG.
Gar.
21³ x 21⁸
COVERED PORCH
TRANSOMS

MAIN FLOOR

Units	Single
Price Code	B
Total Finished	1,711 sq. ft.
First Finished	990 sq. ft.
Second Finished	721 sq. ft.
Basement Unfinished	934 sq. ft.
Garage Unfinished	429 sq. ft.
Dimensions	45'x36'
Foundation	Basement
Bedrooms	3
Full Baths	2
Half Baths	1
Max Ridge Height	27'
Roof Framing	Truss
Exterior Walls	2x6

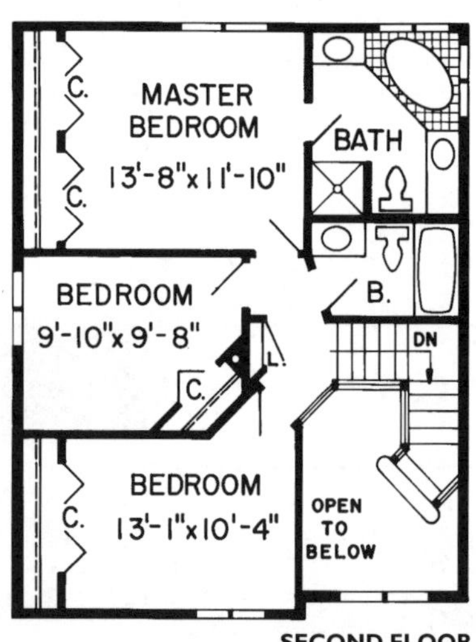
MASTER BEDROOM
13'-8"x11'-10"
BATH
C.
C.
BEDROOM
9'-10"x 9'-8"
B.
DN
L.
C.
BEDROOM
13'-1"x10'-4"
C.
OPEN TO BELOW

SECOND FLOOR

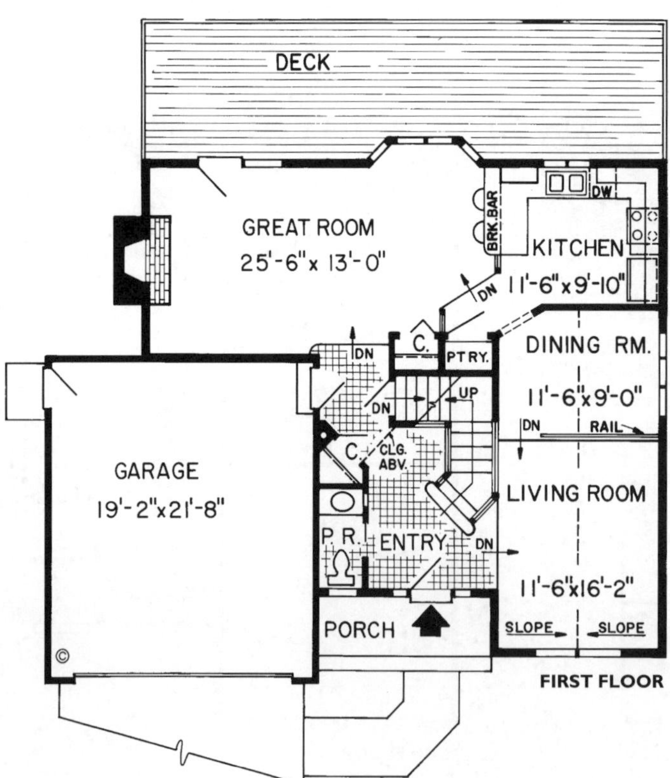
DECK
GREAT ROOM
25'-6" x 13'-0"
BRK.BAR
KITCHEN
11'-6"x9'-10"
DW
DN
C.
PTRY.
DINING RM.
11'-6"x9'-0"
DN
UP
DN
RAIL
GARAGE
19'-2"x21'-8"
C.
CLG. ABV.
LIVING ROOM
P.R.
ENTRY
DN
11'-6"x16'-2"
PORCH
SLOPE
SLOPE
©

FIRST FLOOR

Design 97222

FPL.
Vaulted Sitting
FRENCH DOOR
PLANT SHELF ABOVE
Vaulted Breakfast
VAULT
SERVING BAR
Vaulted Family Room
18^0 x 16^1
LIN.
SHWR.
Vaulted M. Bath
Master Suite
13^0 x 16^2
TRAY CLG.
K.S.
PLANT SHELF ABOVE
D.W.
PASS THRU
RANGE
Kitchen
REF
Bath
W.i.c.
Vaulted Foyer
Dining Room
12^3 x 11^4
COATS
PANTRY
W.
D.
LIN.
Stor.
Bedroom 2
11^1 x 11^3
Bedroom 3
12^1 x 11^0
Garage
GARAGE LOCATION WITH BASEMENT

MAIN FLOOR

Units	Single
Price Code	B
Total Finished	1,712 sq. ft.
Main Finished	1,712 sq. ft.
Basement Unfinished	1,760 sq. ft.
Garage Unfinished	400 sq. ft.
Dimensions	55'x55'
Foundation	Basement Crawlspace
Bedrooms	3
Full Baths	2
Main Ceiling	9'
Max Ridge Height	21'6"
Roof Framing	Stick
Exterior Walls	2x4

STAIR DN
W.
D.
Dining Room
PANTRY
Stor.

OPTIONAL BASEMENT STAIR LOCATION

Design 91465

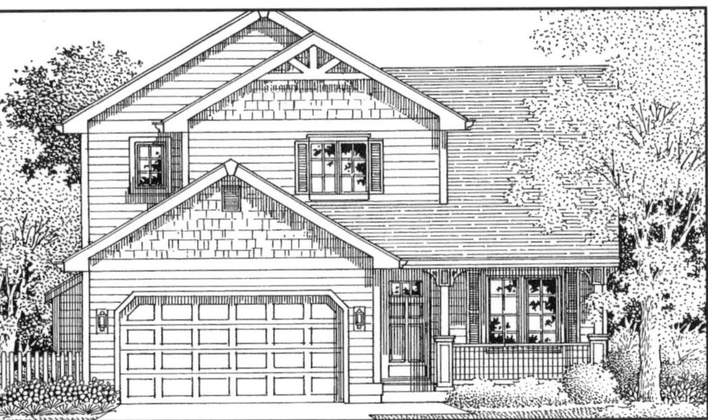

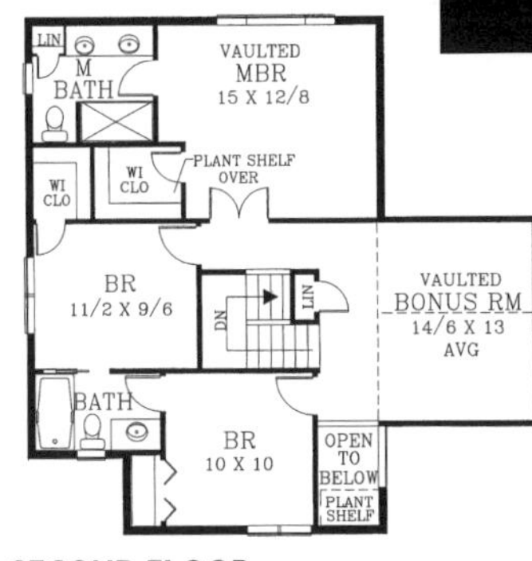
LIN
M BATH
VAULTED MBR
15 X 12/8
WI CLO
WI CLO
PLANT SHELF OVER
BR
11/2 X 9/6
DN
LIN
VAULTED BONUS RM
14/6 X 13 AVG
BATH
BR
10 X 10
OPEN TO BELOW
PLANT SHELF

SECOND FLOOR

PATIO
GREAT RM
23/6 X 14
VAULTED NOOK
10/6 X 8/2
KIT
DW
R
W
D
UP
GST
P
VAULTED FOYER
VAULTED DIN RM
10 X 11
GARAGE
19/4 X 21/2
COVERED PORCH

FIRST FLOOR

Units	Single
Price Code	B
Total Finished	1,713 sq. ft.
First Finished	870 sq. ft.
Second Finished	843 sq. ft.
Garage Unfinished	409 sq. ft.
Dimensions	35'x43'
Foundation	Crawlspace
Bedrooms	3
Full Baths	1
3/4 Baths	1
Half Baths	1
First Ceiling	14'
Second Ceiling	11'
Max Ridge Height	24'6"
Roof Framing	Truss
Exterior Walls	2x6

Design 98456

CAD **FILES AVAILABLE** For more information call 800-235-5700

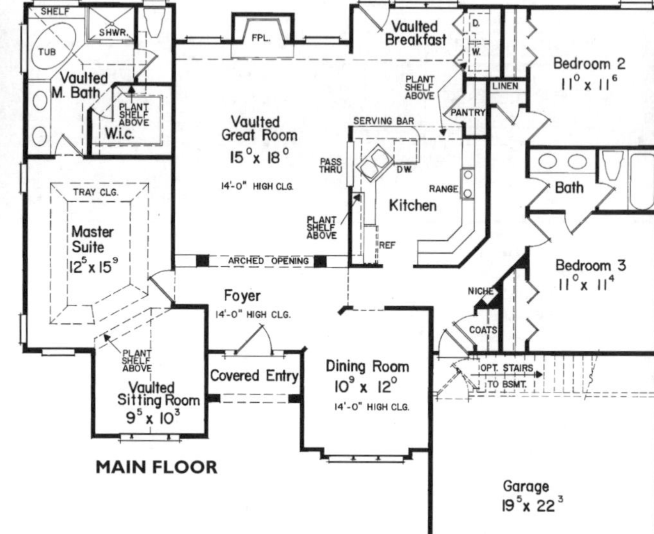

SHELF
SHWR.
TUB
Vaulted M. Bath
PLANT SHELF ABOVE
W.i.c.
FPL.
FRENCH DOOR
Vaulted Breakfast
D.
W.
PLANT SHELF ABOVE
PANTRY
LINEN
Bedroom 2
11⁰ x 11⁶
Vaulted Great Room
15⁰ x 18⁰
14'-0" HIGH CLG.
SERVING BAR
PASS THRU
DW.
RANGE
Kitchen
PLANT SHELF ABOVE
REF
Bath
TRAY CLG.
Master Suite
12⁵ x 15⁹
ARCHED OPENING
Foyer
14'-0" HIGH CLG.
NICHE
Bedroom 3
11⁰ x 11⁴
COATS
PLANT SHELF ABOVE
Vaulted Sitting Room
9⁵ x 10³
Covered Entry
Dining Room
10⁹ x 12⁰
14'-0" HIGH CLG.
OPT. STAIRS TO BSMT.
MAIN FLOOR
Garage
19⁵ x 22³
©

Units	Single
Price Code	B
Total Finished	1,715 sq. ft.
Main Finished	1,715 sq. ft.
Basement Unfinished	1,715 sq. ft.
Garage Unfinished	450 sq. ft.
Dimensions	55'x51'6"
Foundation	Basement Crawlspace Slab
Bedrooms	3
Full Baths	2
Main Ceiling	9'1"
Max Ridge Height	25'
Roof Framing	Stick
Exterior Walls	2x4

Design 98981

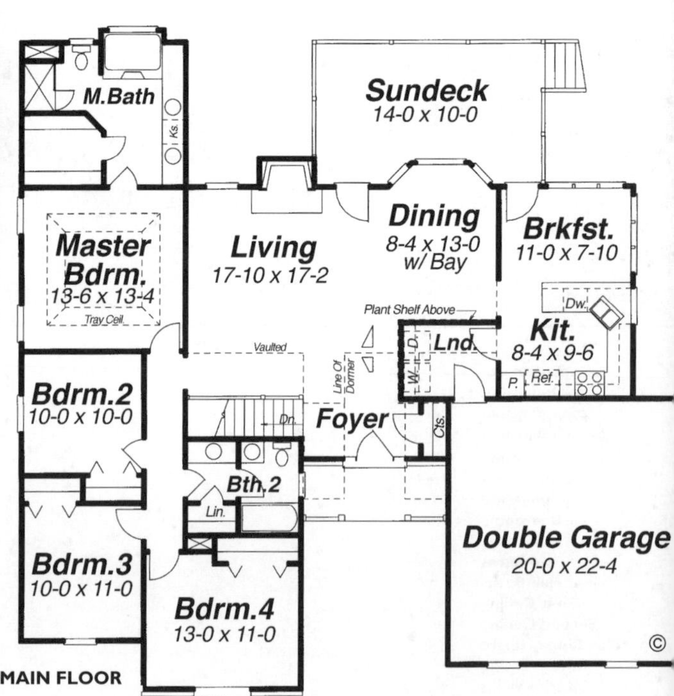

M.Bath
Ks.
Sundeck
14-0 x 10-0
Master Bdrm.
13-6 x 13-4
Tray Ceil.
Living
17-10 x 17-2
Dining
8-4 x 13-0 w/ Bay
Brkfst.
11-0 x 7-10
Plant Shelf Above
Dw.
Kit.
8-4 x 9-6
Vaulted
Line Of Dormer
Lnd.
D.
W.
P.
Ref.
Bdrm.2
10-0 x 10-0
Dn.
Foyer
Cts.
Bth.2
Lin.
Double Garage
20-0 x 22-4
Bdrm.3
10-0 x 11-0
Bdrm.4
13-0 x 11-0
MAIN FLOOR
©

Units	Single
Price Code	B
Total Finished	1,716 sq. ft.
Main Finished	1,716 sq. ft.
Dimensions	56'x55'
Foundation	Crawlspace Slab
Bedrooms	4
Full Baths	2
Main Ceiling	8'
Max Ridge Height	20'
Roof Framing	Stick
Exterior Walls	2x4

Design 69140

Units	Single
Price Code	B
Total Finished	1,719 sq. ft.
Main Finished	1,719 sq. ft.
Garage Unfinished	576 sq. ft.
Dimensions	60'x54'
Foundation	Crawlspace
Bedrooms	3
Full Baths	2
Half Baths	1
Main Ceiling	9'
Vaulted Ceiling	10'
Max Ridge Height	16'9"
Roof Framing	Truss
Exterior Walls	2x6

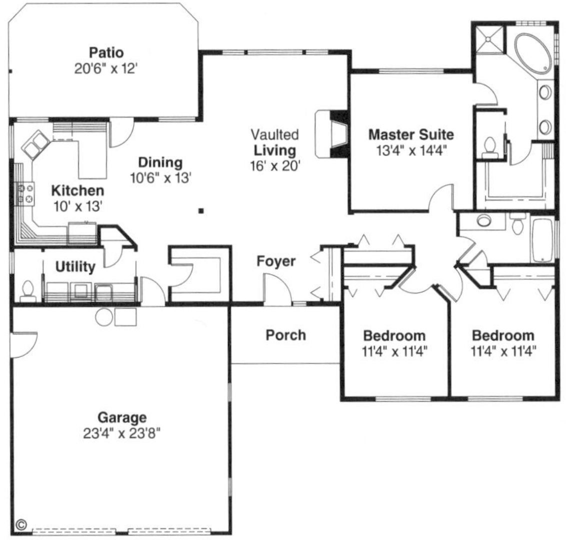
Patio
20'6" x 12'
Kitchen
10' x 13'
Dining
10'6" x 13'
Vaulted
Living
16' x 20'
Master Suite
13'4" x 14'4"
Utility
Foyer
Porch
Bedroom
11'4" x 11'4"
Bedroom
11'4" x 11'4"
Garage
23'4" x 23'8"

MAIN FLOOR

Design 98989

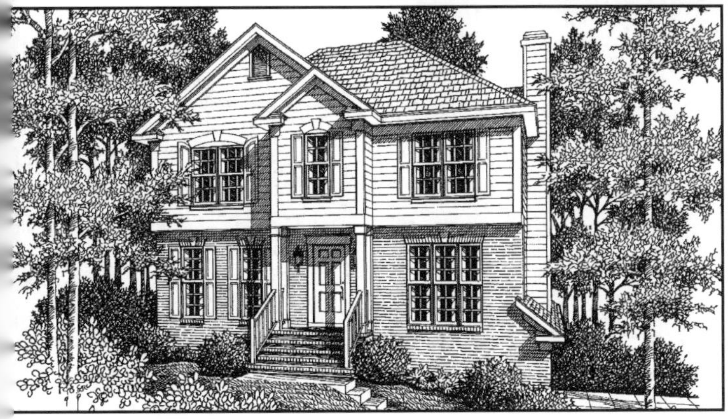

Units	Single
Price Code	C
Total Finished	1,719 sq. ft.
Main Finished	830 sq. ft.
Second Finished	889 sq. ft.
Dimensions	36'4"x29'6"
Foundation	Basement
Bedrooms	3
Full Baths	2
Half Baths	1
Main Ceiling	8'
Max Ridge Height	27'6"
Roof Framing	Stick
Exterior Walls	2x4

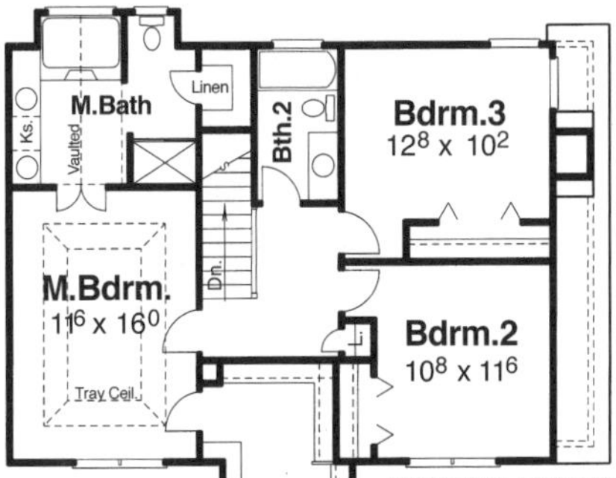

M.Bath
Linen
Bth.2
Bdrm.3
12^8 x 10^2
M.Bdrm.
11^6 x 16^0
Tray Ceil.
Bdrm.2
10^8 x 11^6

SECOND FLOOR

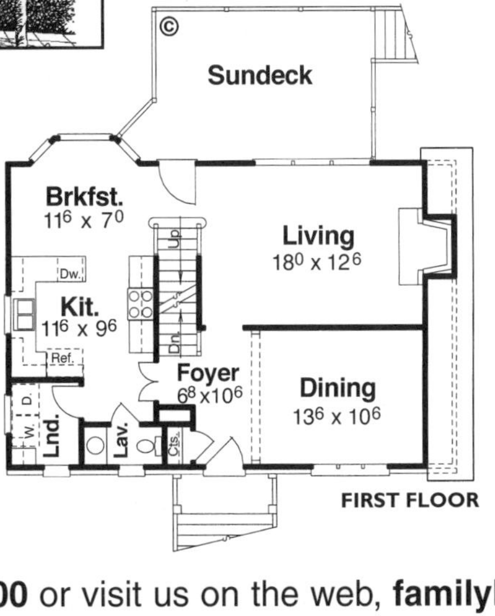

Sundeck
Brkfst.
11^6 x 7^0
Living
18^0 x 12^6
Kit.
11^6 x 9^6
Foyer
6^8 x 10^6
Dining
13^6 x 10^6
Lnd.
Lav.

FIRST FLOOR

Design 69014

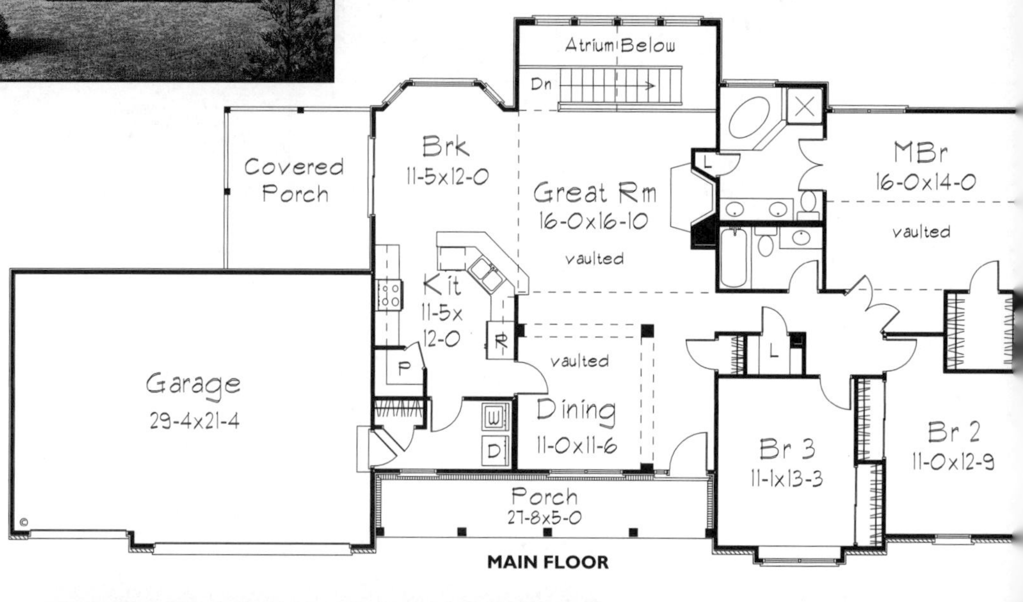

Atrium Below
Dn
Covered Porch
Brk
11-5x12-0
Great Rm
16-0x16-10
vaulted
MBr
16-0x14-0
vaulted
L
Kit
11-5x
12-0
R
P
vaulted
Dining
11-0x11-6
W
D
Garage
29-4x21-4
L
Br 3
11-1x13-3
Br 2
11-0x12-9
Porch
27-8x5-0
MAIN FLOOR

Units	Single
Price Code	B
Total Finished	1,721 sq. ft.
Main Finished	1,721 sq. ft.
Dimensions	83'x42'
Foundation	Basement Crawlspace Slab
Bedrooms	3
Full Baths	2
Main Ceiling	8'
Max Ridge Height	22'
Roof Framing	Truss
Exterior Walls	2x4

Design 65421

12'-4" X 15'-0"
3,70 X 4,50

10'-4" X 11'-8"
3,10 X 3,50

12'-4" X 13'-0"
3,70 X 3,90

SECOND FLOOR

11'-0" X 15'-0"
3,30 X 4,50
11'-8" X 11'-8"
3,50 X 3,50
13'-4" X 17'-4"
4,00 X 5,20
12'-0" X 21'-0"
3,60 X 6,30
FIRST FLOOR

Units	Single
Price Code	C
Total Finished	1,722 sq. ft.
First Finished	804 sq. ft.
Second Finished	918 sq. ft.
Basement Unfinished	804 sq. ft.
Garage Unfinished	285 sq. ft.
Deck Unfinished	40 sq. ft.
Porch Unfinished	23 sq. ft.
Dimensions	36'x38'
Foundation	Basement
Bedrooms	3
Full Baths	1
3/4 Baths	1
Half Baths	1
First Ceiling	8'
Second Ceiling	8'
Max Ridge Height	32'2"
Roof Framing	Truss
Exterior Walls	2x6

Design 66089

Units	Single
Price Code	B
Total Finished	1,724 sq. ft.
Main Finished	1,724 sq. ft.
Garage Unfinished	552 sq. ft.
Deck Unfinished	220 sq. ft.
Dimensions	74'10"x38'10"
Foundation	Slab
Bedrooms	3
Full Baths	2
Half Baths	1
Main Ceiling	8'-10'
Max Ridge Height	28'
Roof Framing	Stick
Exterior Walls	2x4

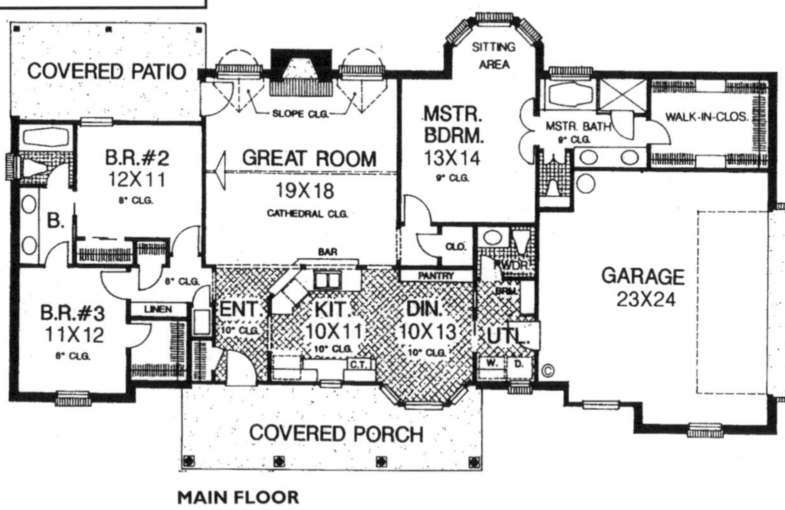
COVERED PATIO
SITTING AREA
SLOPE CLG.
B.R.#2
12X11
8" CLG.
GREAT ROOM
19X18
CATHEDRAL CLG.
MSTR. BDRM.
13X14
9" CLG.
MSTR. BATH
9" CLG.
WALK-IN-CLOS.
B.
CLO.
BAR
PANTRY
PWDR
8" CLG.
B.R.#3
11X12
8" CLG.
LINEN
ENT.
10" CLG.
KIT.
10X11
10" CLG.
DIN.
10X13
10" CLG.
C.T.
BRM.
UTL.
W.
D.
GARAGE
23X24
COVERED PORCH

MAIN FLOOR

Design 97933

Units	Single
Price Code	B
Total Finished	1,724 sq. ft.
Main Finished	1,724 sq. ft.
Garage Unfinished	460 sq. ft.
Dimensions	50'x50'
Foundation	Basement
Bedrooms	3
Full Baths	2
Main Ceiling	9'
Max Ridge Height	24'4"
Roof Framing	Stick
Exterior Walls	2x4

Alternate foundation options available at an additional charge.
Please call 1-800-235-5700 for more information.

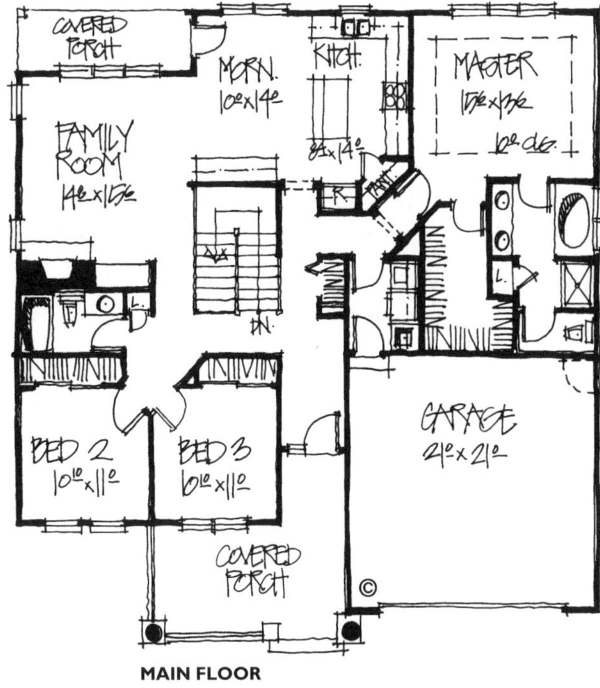
COVERED PORCH
MORN.
KITCH.
MASTER
FAMILY ROOM
DN.
BED 2
BED 3
GARAGE
COVERED PORCH

MAIN FLOOR

Design 93079

Units	Single
Price Code	B
Total Finished	1,725 sq. ft.
Main Finished	1,725 sq. ft.
Garage Unfinished	496 sq. ft.
Dimensions	56'4"x72'8"
Foundation	Crawlspace Slab
Bedrooms	3
Full Baths	2
Max Ridge Height	23'
Roof Framing	Stick
Exterior Walls	2x4

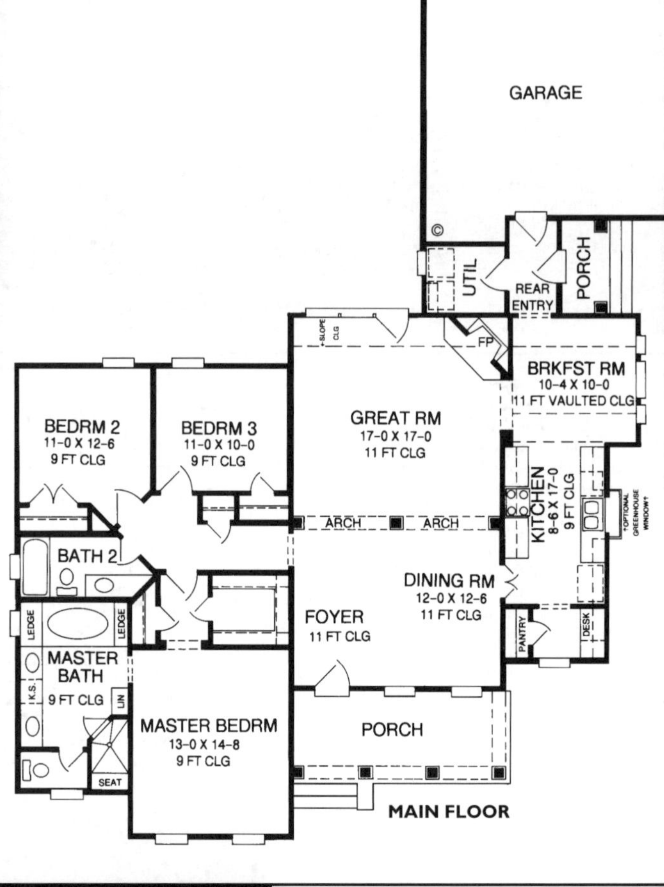
GARAGE
UTIL
REAR ENTRY
PORCH
FP
BRKFST RM
10-4 X 10-0
11 FT VAULTED CLG
GREAT RM
17-0 X 17-0
11 FT CLG
BEDRM 2
11-0 X 12-6
9 FT CLG
BEDRM 3
11-0 X 10-0
9 FT CLG
KITCHEN
8-6 X 17-0
9 FT CLG
ARCH
ARCH
BATH 2
DINING RM
12-0 X 12-6
11 FT CLG
FOYER
11 FT CLG
LEDGE
LEDGE
MASTER BATH
9 FT CLG
PANTRY
DESK
MASTER BEDRM
13-0 X 14-8
9 FT CLG
PORCH
SEAT
MAIN FLOOR

Design 97773

Units	Single
Price Code	B
Total Finished	1,727 sq. ft.
First Finished	939 sq. ft.
Second Finished	788 sq. ft.
Bonus Unfinished	210 sq. ft.
Basement Unfinished	939 sq. ft.
Garage Unfinished	401 sq. ft.
Porch Unfinished	65 sq. ft.
Dimensions	34'x52'2"
Foundation	Basement
Bedrooms	3
Full Baths	1
3/4 Baths	1
Half Baths	1
First Ceiling	8'
Second Ceiling	8'
Max Ridge Height	27'10"
Roof Framing	Truss
Exterior Walls	2x4

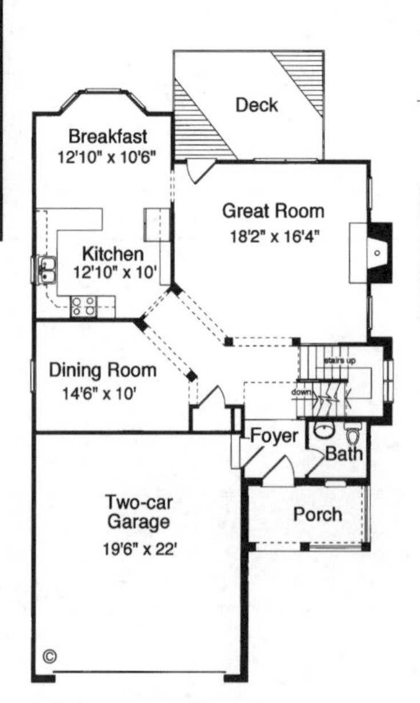
Deck
Breakfast
12'10" x 10'6"
Great Room
18'2" x 16'4"
Kitchen
12'10" x 10'
Dining Room
14'6" x 10'
Foyer
Bath
Two-car Garage
19'6" x 22'
Porch
FIRST FLOOR

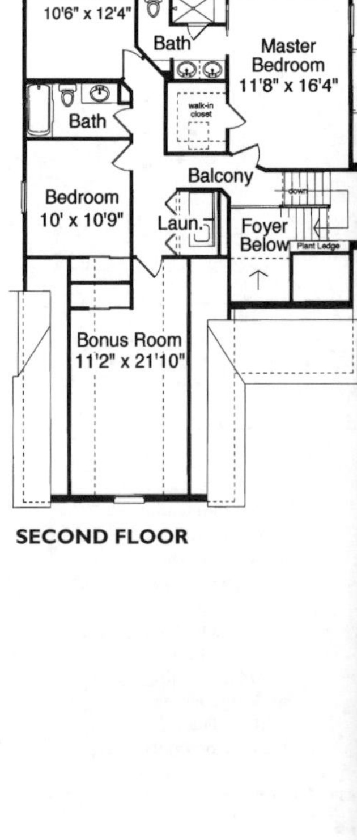
Bedroom
10'6" x 12'4"
Bath
Master Bedroom
11'8" x 16'4"
Bath
Balcony
Bedroom
10' x 10'9"
Laun.
Foyer Below
Bonus Room
11'2" x 21'10"
SECOND FLOOR

Design 90986

Units	Single
Price Code	B
Total Finished	1,731 sq. ft.
Main Finished	1,731 sq. ft.
Basement Unfinished	1,715 sq. ft.
Garage Unfinished	888 sq. ft.
Dimensions	74'x45'
Foundation	Basement Crawlspace
Bedrooms	3
Full Baths	2
Half Baths	1
Main Ceiling	8'
Max Ridge Height	18'6"
Roof Framing	Truss
Exterior Walls	2x6

GREAT ROOM
BATH
railing
down
STUDY/BR3
10-0x11-6

OPTIONAL BASEMNT STAIR LOCATION

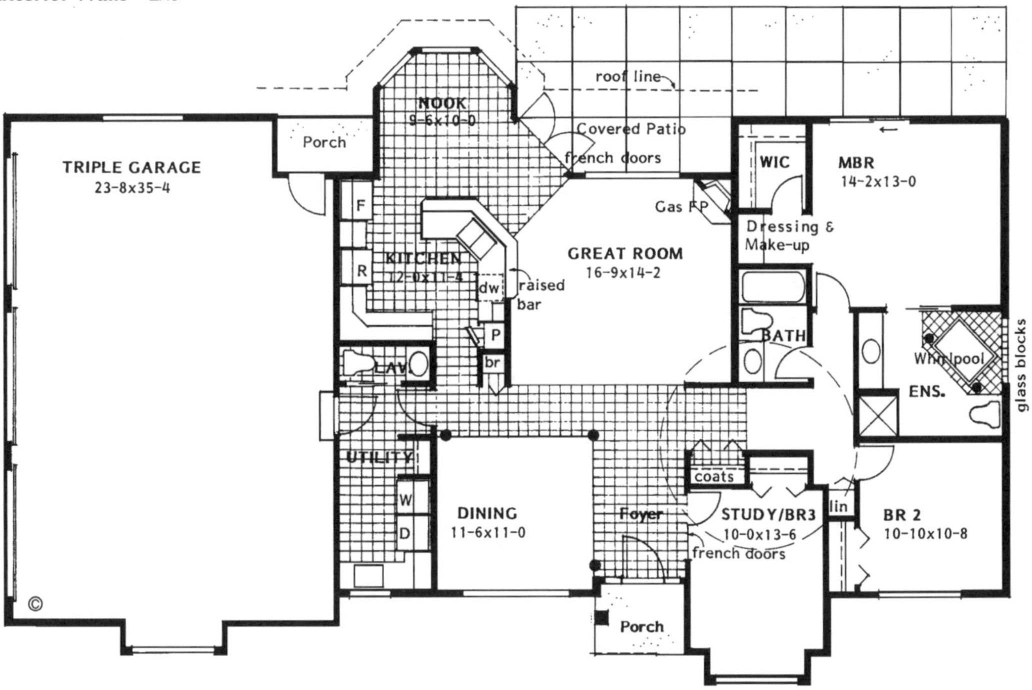

roof line
NOOK
9-6x10-0
Covered Patio
french doors
Porch
TRIPLE GARAGE
23-8x35-4
F
R
KITCHEN
12-0x11-4
dw
raised bar
P
br
GREAT ROOM
16-9x14-2
Gas FP
WIC
MBR
14-2x13-0
Dressing & Make-up
BATH
Whirlpool
ENS.
glass blocks
LAV
UTILITY
W
D
DINING
11-6x11-0
Foyer
coats
STUDY/BR3
10-0x13-6
french doors
lin
BR 2
10-10x10-8
Porch
©

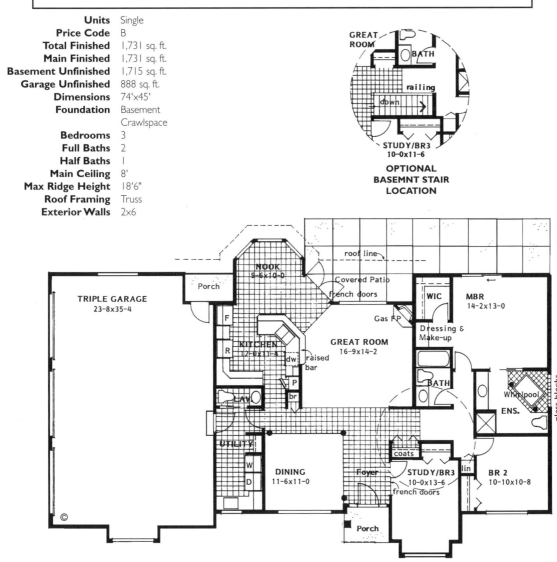

MAIN FLOOR

Design 99923

Units	Single
Price Code	B
Total Finished	1,734 sq. ft.
Main Finished	1,734 sq. ft.
Basement Unfinished	1,842 sq. ft.
Garage Unfinished	528 sq. ft.
Deck Unfinished	252 sq. ft.
Porch Unfinished	132 sq. ft.
Dimensions	66'x48'
Foundation	Basement
Bedrooms	3
Full Baths	2
Half Baths	1
Main Ceiling	8'
Vaulted Ceiling	10'
Max Ridge Height	22'
Roof Framing	Truss
Exterior Walls	2x6

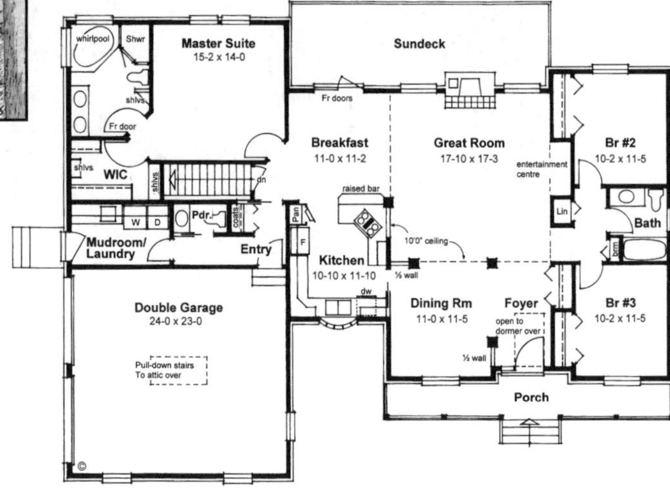
whirlpool
Shwr
Master Suite
15-2 x 14-0
Sundeck
shlvs
Fr door
Fr doors
shlvs
WIC
shlvs
dn
Breakfast
11-0 x 11-2
Great Room
17-10 x 17-3
entertainment centre
Br #2
10-2 x 11-5
raised bar
W
D
Pdr.
coats
Pan
Lin
Bath
Mudroom/
Laundry
Entry
F
Kitchen
10-10 x 11-10
10'0" ceiling
½ wall
brm
dw
Dining Rm
11-0 x 11-5
Foyer
open to dormer over
Br #3
10-2 x 11-5
Double Garage
24-0 x 23-0
Pull-down stairs
To attic over
½ wall
Porch

MAIN FLOOR

Design 65422

Units	Single
Price Code	C
Total Finished	1,735 sq. ft.
First Finished	813 sq. ft.
Second Finished	922 sq. ft.
Basement Unfinished	813 sq. ft.
Garage Unfinished	288 sq. ft.
Deck Unfinished	40 sq. ft.
Porch Unfinished	21 sq. ft.
Dimensions	36'x38'
Foundation	Basement
Bedrooms	3
Full Baths	1
3/4 Baths	1
Half Baths	1;
First Ceiling	8'
Second Ceiling	8'
Max Ridge Height	32'
Roof Framing	Truss
Exterior Walls	2x6

11'-0" X 15'-0"
3,30 X 4,50
11'-8" X 11'-8"
3,50 X 3,50
13'-4" X 17-4"
4,00 X 5,20
12'-0" X 21'-0"
3,60 X 6,30

FIRST FLOOR

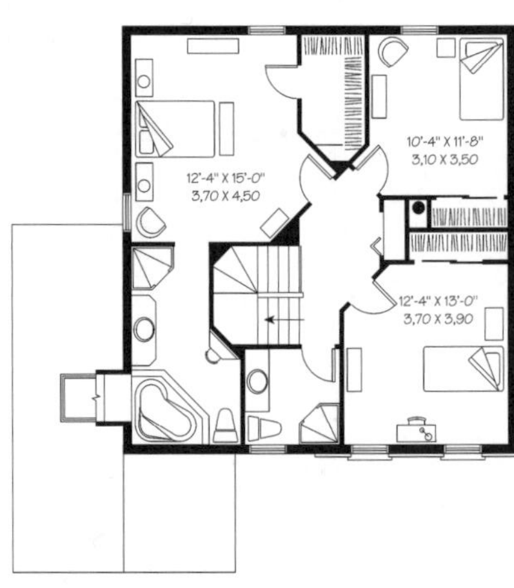
10'-4" X 11'-8"
3,10 X 3,50
12'-4" X 15'-0"
3,70 X 4,50
12'-4" X 13'-0"
3,70 X 3,90

SECOND FLOOR

Design 93269

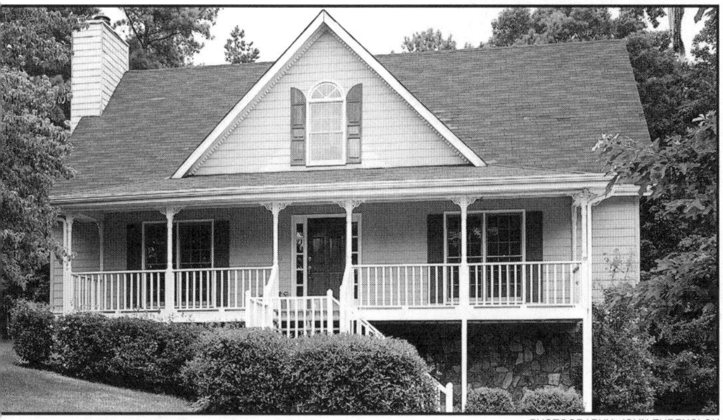

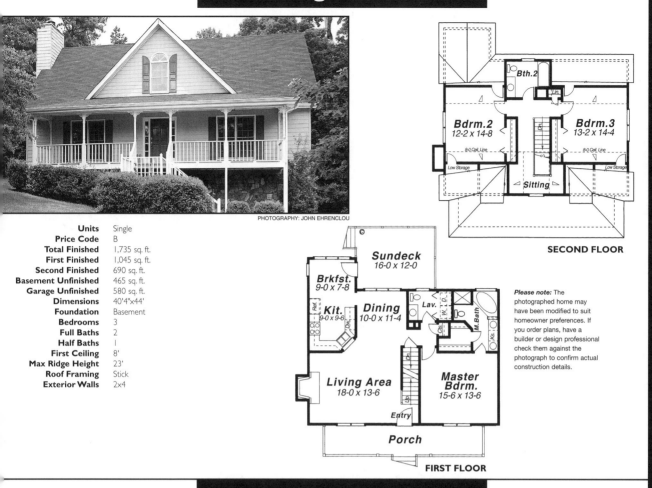

PHOTOGRAPHY: JOHN EHRENCLOU

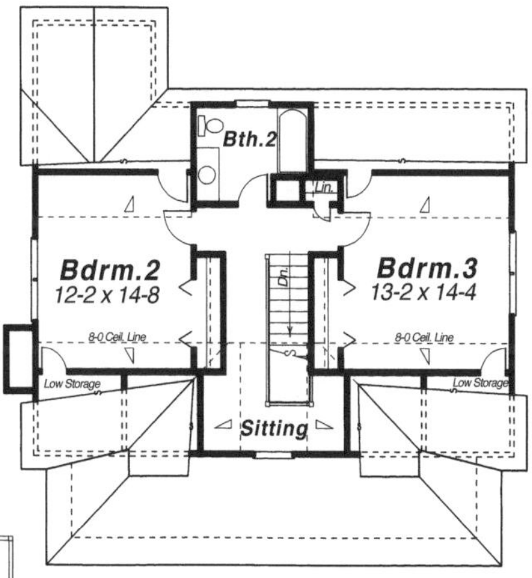

Units	Single
Price Code	B
Total Finished	1,735 sq. ft.
First Finished	1,045 sq. ft.
Second Finished	690 sq. ft.
Basement Unfinished	465 sq. ft.
Garage Unfinished	580 sq. ft.
Dimensions	40'4"x44'
Foundation	Basement
Bedrooms	3
Full Baths	2
Half Baths	1
First Ceiling	8'
Max Ridge Height	23'
Roof Framing	Stick
Exterior Walls	2x4

Bth.2
Bdrm.2
12-2 x 14-8
Bdrm.3
13-2 x 14-4
Low Storage
Sitting

SECOND FLOOR

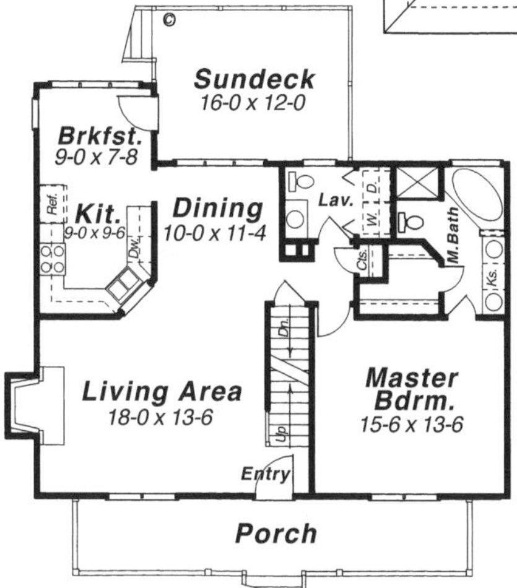

Sundeck
16-0 x 12-0
Brkfst.
9-0 x 7-8
Kit.
9-0 x 9-6
Dining
10-0 x 11-4
Lav.
M.Bath
Living Area
18-0 x 13-6
Master Bdrm.
15-6 x 13-6
Entry
Porch

FIRST FLOOR

Please note: The photographed home may have been modified to suit homeowner preferences. If you order plans, have a builder or design professional check them against the photograph to confirm actual construction details.

Design 93467

Units	Single
Price Code	B
Total Finished	1,735 sq. ft.
First Finished	1,189 sq. ft.
Second Finished	546 sq. ft.
Bonus Unfinished	355 sq. ft.
Basement Unfinished	1,189 sq. ft.
Garage Unfinished	539 sq. ft.
Porch Unfinished	280 sq. ft.
Dimensions	44'x60'5"
Foundation	Crawlspace
Bedrooms	3
Full Baths	2
Half Baths	1
First Ceiling	9'
Second Ceiling	8'
Max Ridge Height	26'5"
Roof Framing	Stick
Exterior Walls	2x4

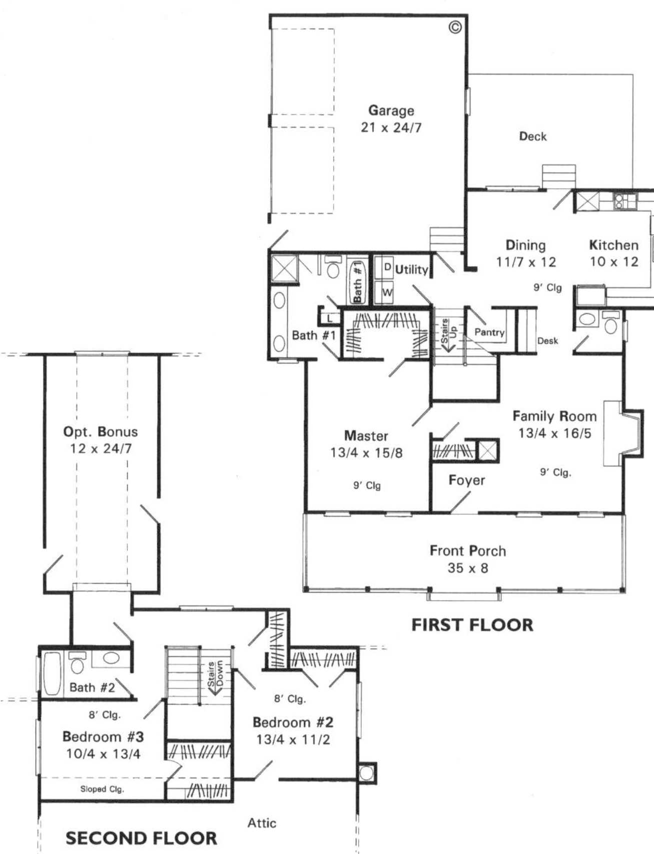
Garage
21 x 24/7
Deck
Dining
11/7 x 12
Kitchen
10 x 12
9' Clg
Utility
Bath #1
Pantry
Desk
Master
13/4 x 15/8
9' Clg
Family Room
13/4 x 16/5
9' Clg.
Foyer
Front Porch
35 x 8
Opt. Bonus
12 x 24/7
Bath #2
8' Clg.
Bedroom #3
10/4 x 13/4
Sloped Clg.
Bedroom #2
13/4 x 11/2
Attic

FIRST FLOOR

SECOND FLOOR

Design 97352

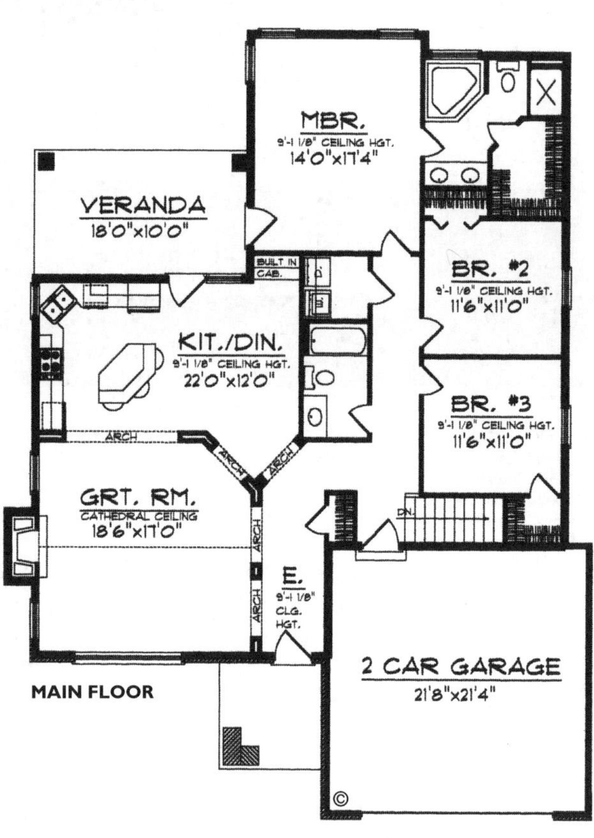
MBR.
9'-1 1/8" CEILING HGT.
14'0"x17'4"
VERANDA
18'0"x10'0"
BUILT IN CAB.
BR. #2
9'-1 1/8" CEILING HGT.
11'6"x11'0"
KIT./DIN.
9'-1 1/8" CEILING HGT.
22'0"x12'0"
ARCH
BR. #3
9'-1 1/8" CEILING HGT.
11'6"x11'0"
GRT. RM.
CATHEDRAL CEILING
18'6"x17'0"
DN.
E.
9'-1 1/8" CLG. HGT.
2 CAR GARAGE
21'8"x21'4"
MAIN FLOOR

Units	Single
Price Code	C
Total Finished	1,735 sq. ft.
Main Finished	1,735 sq. ft.
Basement Unfinished	1,314 sq. ft.
Dimensions	49'4"x63'8"
Foundation	Basement
Bedrooms	3
Full Baths	2
Main Ceiling	9'
Max Ridge Height	24'3"
Roof Framing	Truss
Exterior Walls	2x6

Design 20100

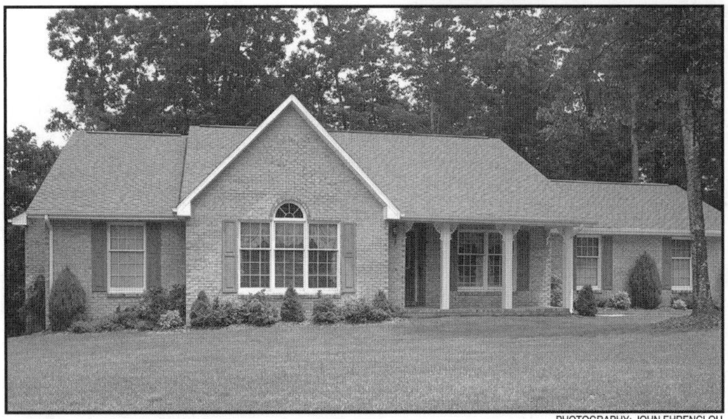

PHOTOGRAPHY: JOHN EHRENCLOU

Units	Single
Price Code	B
Total Finished	1,737 sq. ft.
Main Finished	1,737 sq. ft.
Basement Unfinished	1,727 sq. ft.
Garage Unfinished	484 sq. ft.
Dimensions	72'4"x43'
Foundation	Basement Crawlspace Slab
Bedrooms	3
Full Baths	2
Main Ceiling	8'
Max Ridge Height	21'
Roof Framing	Stick
Exterior Walls	2x6

Please note: The photographed home may have been modified to suit homeowner preferences. If you order plans, have a builder or design professional check them against the photograph to confirm actual construction details.

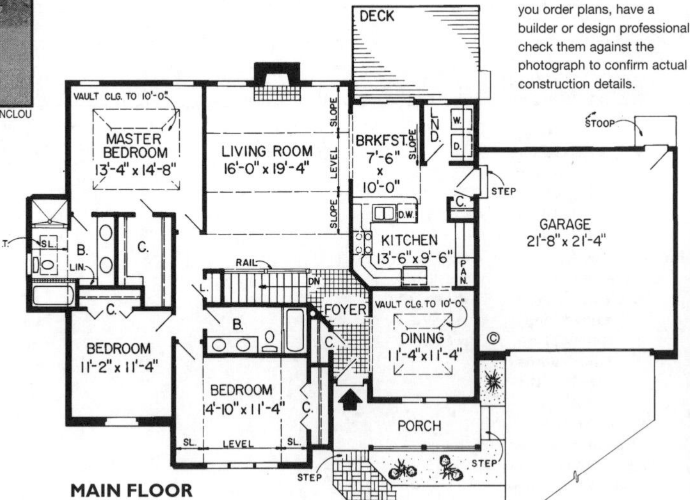

DECK
VAULT CLG. TO 10'-0"
MASTER BEDROOM 13'-4" x 14'-8"
LIVING ROOM 16'-0" x 19'-4"
BRKFST. 7'-6" x 10'-0"
KITCHEN 13'-6" x 9'-6"
GARAGE 21'-8" x 21'-4"
STOOP
STEP
FOYER
VAULT CLG. TO 10'-0"
DINING 11'-4" x 11'-4"
BEDROOM 11'-2" x 11'-4"
BEDROOM 14'-10" x 11'-4"
PORCH
MAIN FLOOR

Design 91479

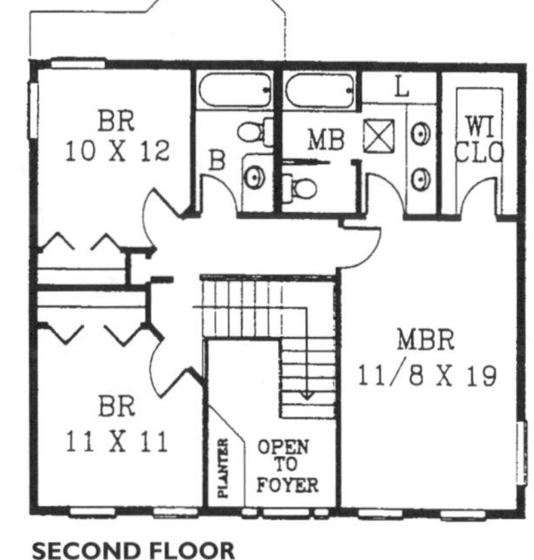
BR
10 X 12
B
MB
L
WI
CLO
BR
11 X 11
PLANTER
OPEN
TO
FOYER
MBR
11/8 X 19

SECOND FLOOR

Units	Single
Price Code	B
Total Finished	1,737 sq. ft.
First Finished	963 sq. ft.
Second Finished	774 sq. ft.
Garage Unfinished	462 sq. ft.
Dimensions	54'6"x33'
Foundation	Crawlspace
Bedrooms	3
Full Baths	2
Half Baths	1
First Ceiling	8'
Second Ceiling	8'
Max Ridge Height	23'
Roof Framing	Truss
Exterior Walls	2x6

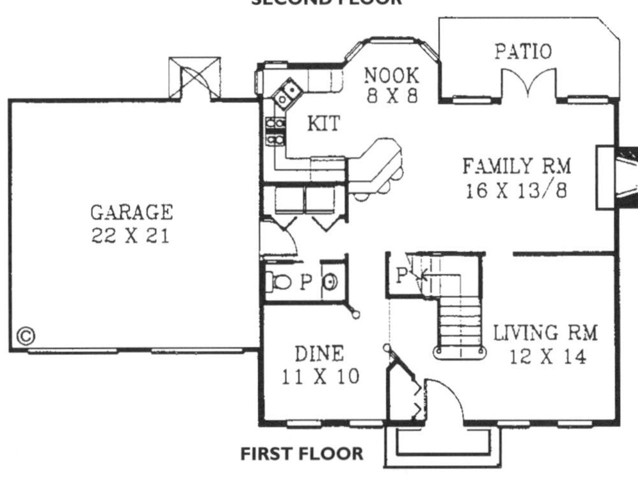
PATIO
NOOK
8 X 8
KIT
FAMILY RM
16 X 13/8
GARAGE
22 X 21
P
P
DINE
11 X 10
LIVING RM
12 X 14

FIRST FLOOR

Design 93149

Units	Single
Price Code	B
Total Finished	1,739 sq. ft.
Main Finished	1,739 sq. ft.
Basement Unfinished	1,739 sq. ft.
Dimensions	54'x48'
Foundation	Basement
Bedrooms	3
Full Baths	2
Half Baths	1
Max Ridge Height	22'6"
Roof Framing	Stick
Exterior Walls	2x6

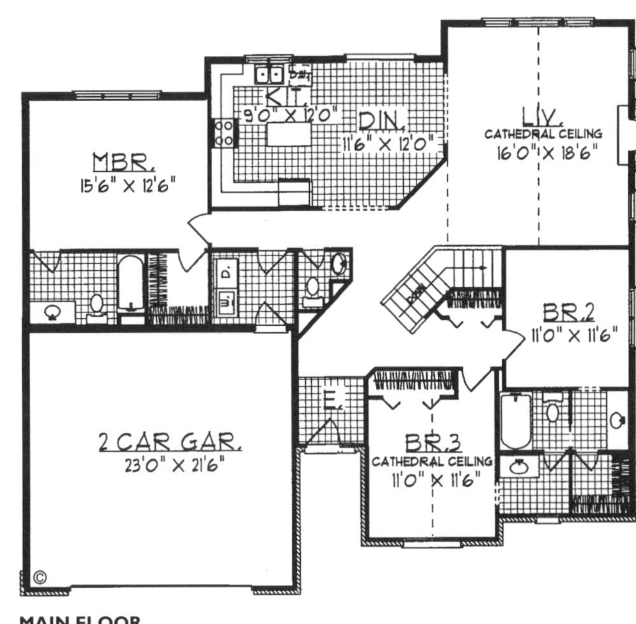
KIT.
9'0" X 12'0"
DIN.
11'6" X 12'0"
LIV.
CATHEDRAL CEILING
16'0" X 18'6"
MBR.
15'6" X 12'6"
BR.2
11'0" X 11'6"
E.
2 CAR GAR.
23'0" X 21'6"
BR.3
CATHEDRAL CEILING
11'0" X 11'6"

MAIN FLOOR

Design 10596

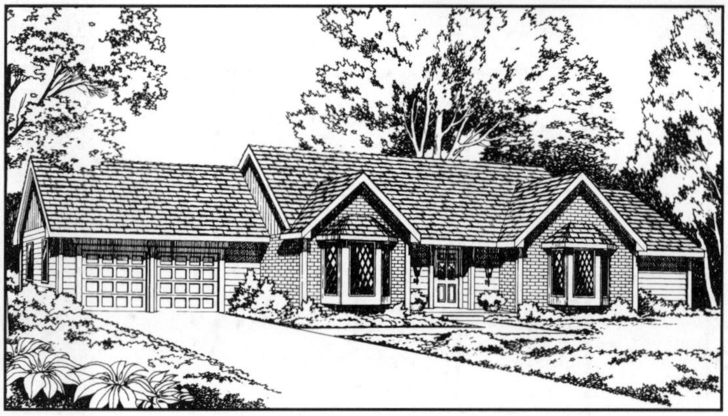

Units	Single
Price Code	B
Total Finished	1,740 sq. ft.
Main Finished	1,740 sq. ft.
Basement Unfinished	1,377 sq. ft.
Garage Unfinished	480 sq. ft.
Dimensions	74'x36'8"
Foundation	Basement
Bedrooms	3
Full Baths	2
Max Ridge Height	19'
Roof Framing	Stick
Exterior Walls	2x6

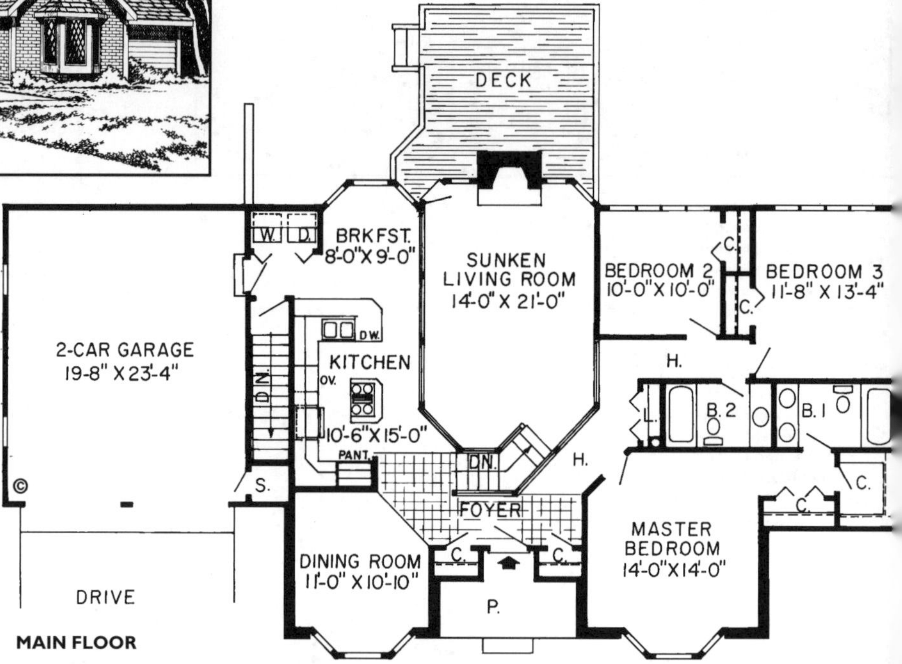

DECK
BRKFST. 8'-0"X 9'-0"
SUNKEN LIVING ROOM 14'-0" X 21'-0"
BEDROOM 2 10'-0" X 10'-0"
BEDROOM 3 11'-8" X 13'-4"
2-CAR GARAGE 19-8" X 23'-4"
KITCHEN 10'-6" X 15'-0"
DINING ROOM 11'-0" X 10'-10"
FOYER
MASTER BEDROOM 14'-0" X 14'-0"
DRIVE
P.

MAIN FLOOR

Design 24249

Units	Single
Price Code	B
Total Finished	1,741 sq. ft.
Main Finished	1,741 sq. ft.
Basement Unfinished	957 sq. ft.
Garage Unfinished	789 sq. ft.
Dimensions	61'x36'
Foundation	Basement
Bedrooms	3
Full Baths	2
Max Ridge Height	28'
Roof Framing	Stick
Exterior Walls	2x4

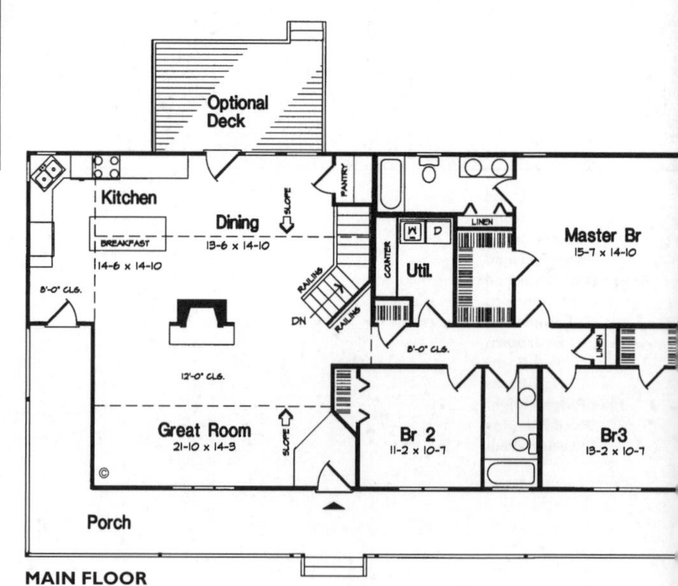
Optional Deck
Kitchen
Breakfast 14-6 x 14-10
Dining 13-6 x 14-10
Util.
Master Br 15-7 x 14-10
Great Room 21-10 x 14-3
Br 2 11-2 x 10-7
Br3 13-2 x 10-7
Porch

MAIN FLOOR

Design 93061

Units	Single
Price Code	B
Total Finished	1,742 sq. ft.
Main Finished	1,742 sq. ft.
Garage Unfinished	566 sq. ft.
Porch Unfinished	14 sq. ft.
Dimensions	78'10"x40'10"
Foundation	Crawlspace Slab
Bedrooms	3
Full Baths	2
Max Ridge Height	22'
Roof Framing	Truss
Exterior Walls	2x4

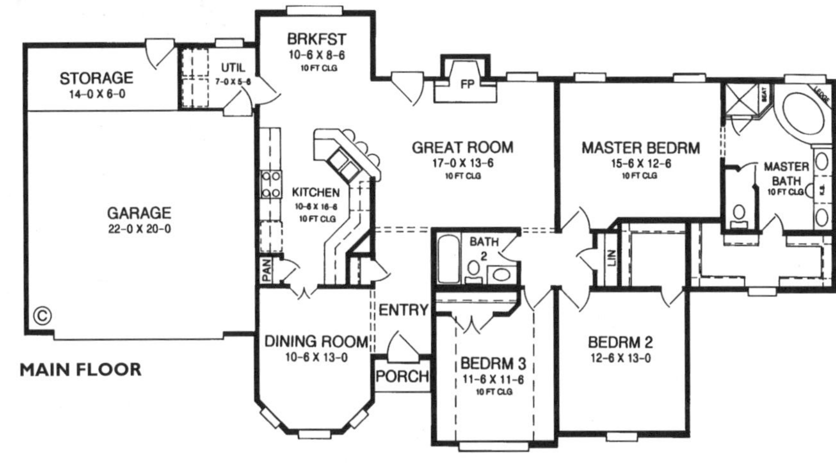

BRKFST
10-6 X 8-6
10 FT CLG
STORAGE
14-0 X 6-0
UTIL
7-0 X 5-6
FP
GREAT ROOM
17-0 X 13-6
10 FT CLG
MASTER BEDRM
15-6 X 12-6
10 FT CLG
MASTER BATH
10 FT CLG
KITCHEN
10-6 X 16-6
10 FT CLG
GARAGE
22-0 X 20-0
BATH 2
LIN
PAN
ENTRY
DINING ROOM
10-6 X 13-0
BEDRM 3
11-6 X 11-6
10 FT CLG
BEDRM 2
12-6 X 13-0
PORCH
MAIN FLOOR

Design 97233

Units	Single
Price Code	B
Total Finished	1,743 sq. ft.
Main Finished	1,743 sq. ft.
Basement Unfinished	998 sq. ft.
Garage Unfinished	763 sq. ft.
Dimensions	53'6"x39'4"
Foundation	Basement
Bedrooms	3
Full Baths	2
Max Ridge Height	22'8"
Roof Framing	Stick
Exterior Walls	2x4

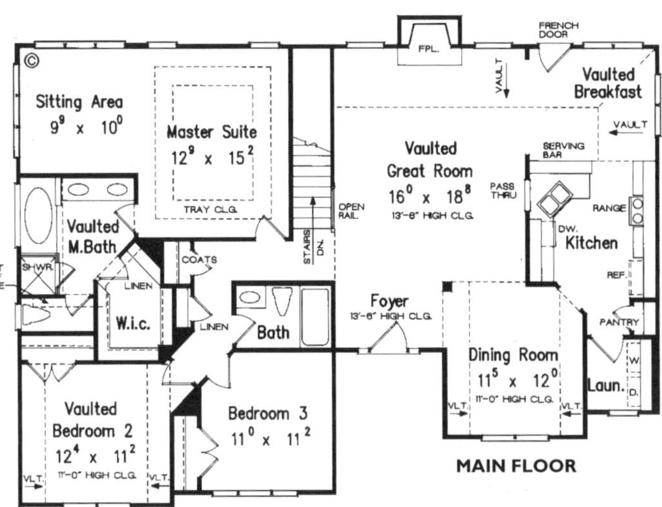

FPL.
FRENCH DOOR
Vaulted Breakfast
Sitting Area
9⁹ x 10⁰
Master Suite
12⁹ x 15²
TRAY CLG.
Vaulted Great Room
16⁰ x 18⁸
13'-6" HIGH CLG.
SERVING BAR
PASS THRU
RANGE
DW.
Kitchen
REF.
PANTRY
Vaulted M.Bath
PLANT SHELF ABOVE
SHWR.
LINEN
COATS
W.i.c.
OPEN RAIL
Foyer
13'-6" HIGH CLG.
Bath
Dining Room
11⁵ x 12⁰
11'-0" HIGH CLG.
Laun.
Vaulted Bedroom 2
12⁴ x 11²
11'-0" HIGH CLG.
Bedroom 3
11⁰ x 11²
MAIN FLOOR

Design 67006

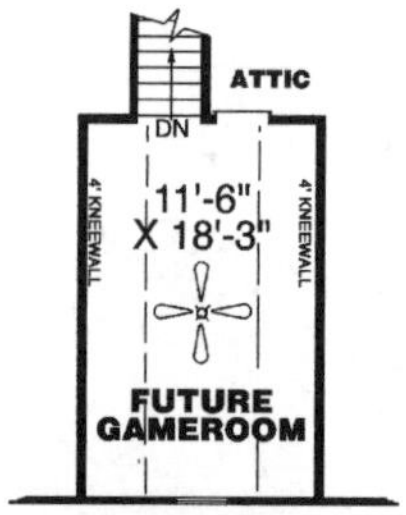

Units	Single
Price Code	B
Total Finished	1,744 sq. ft.
Main Finished	1,744 sq. ft.
Bonus Unfinished	264 sq. ft.
Garage Unfinished	487 sq. ft.
Porch Unfinished	24 sq. ft.
Dimensions	51'x63'
Foundation	Slab
Bedrooms	3
Full Baths	2
First Ceiling	8'
Vaulted Ceiling	13'6"
Roof Framing	Stick
Exterior Walls	2x4

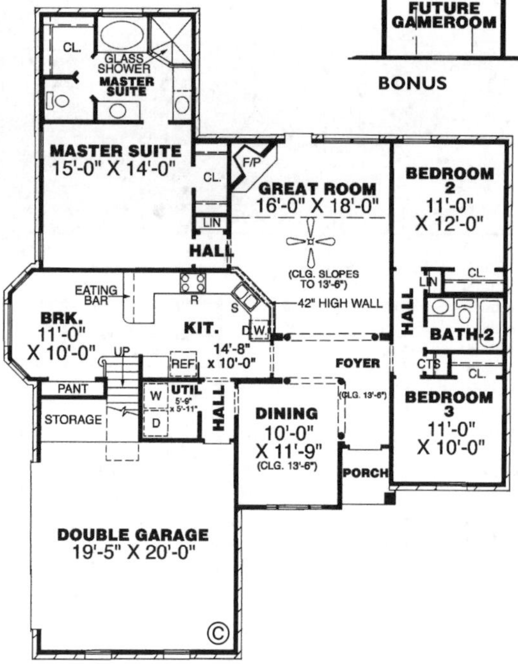

BONUS

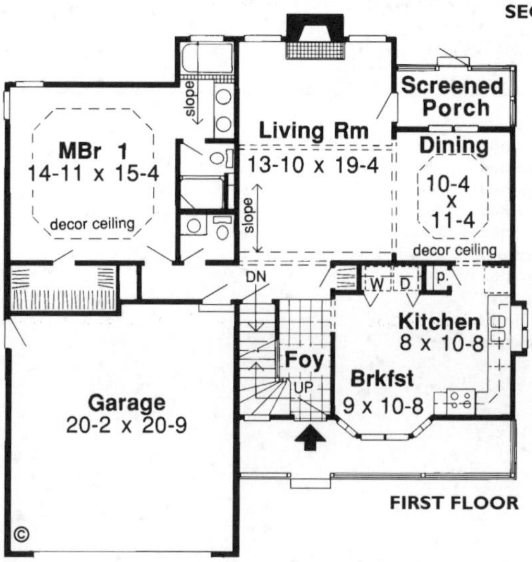

MAIN FLOOR

Design 20203

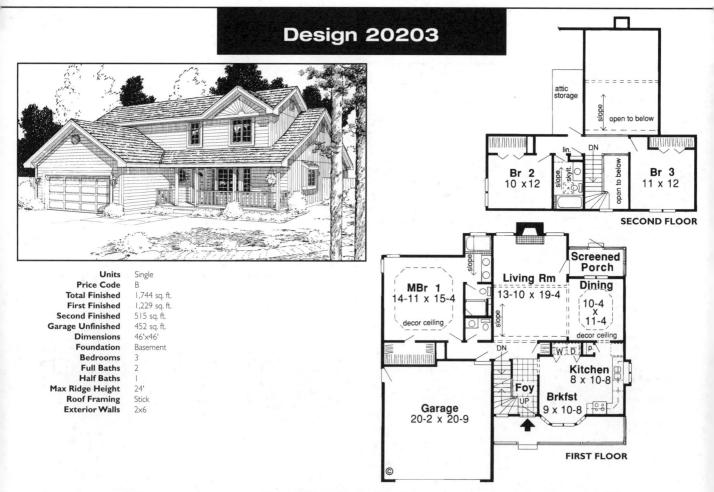

Units	Single
Price Code	B
Total Finished	1,744 sq. ft.
First Finished	1,229 sq. ft.
Second Finished	515 sq. ft.
Garage Unfinished	452 sq. ft.
Dimensions	46'x46'
Foundation	Basement
Bedrooms	3
Full Baths	2
Half Baths	1
Max Ridge Height	24'
Roof Framing	Stick
Exterior Walls	2x6

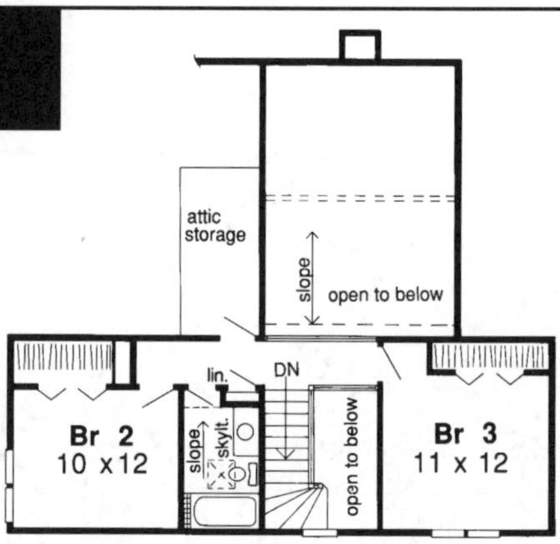

SECOND FLOOR

FIRST FLOOR

Design 98474

CAD
FILES AVAILABLE
For more information call
800-235-5700

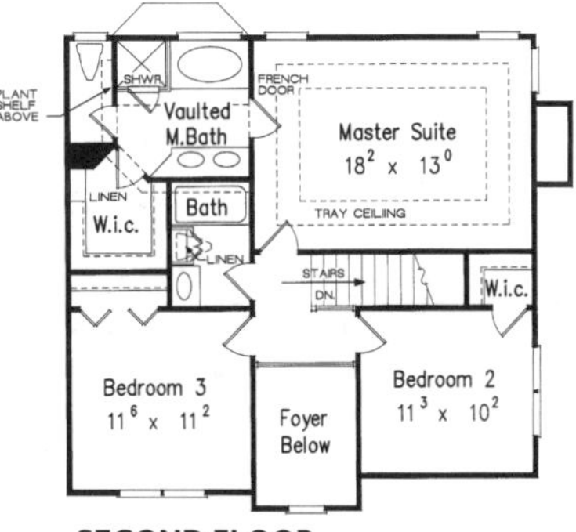
PLANT SHELF ABOVE
SHWR
Vaulted M.Bath
FRENCH DOOR
Master Suite
18^2 x 13^0
LINEN
W.i.c.
Bath
TRAY CEILING
LINEN
STAIRS DN.
W.i.c.
Bedroom 3
11^6 x 11^2
Foyer Below
Bedroom 2
11^3 x 10^2

SECOND FLOOR

Units	Single
Price Code	B
Total Finished	1,744 sq. ft.
First Finished	972 sq. ft.
Second Finished	772 sq. ft.
Bonus Unfinished	358 sq. ft.
Basement Unfinished	972 sq. ft.
Garage Unfinished	520 sq. ft.
Dimensions	52'10"x37'6"
Foundation	Basement Crawlspace
Bedrooms	4
Full Baths	3
First Ceiling	9'
Second Ceiling	8'
Max Ridge Height	31'
Roof Framing	Stick
Exterior Walls	2x4

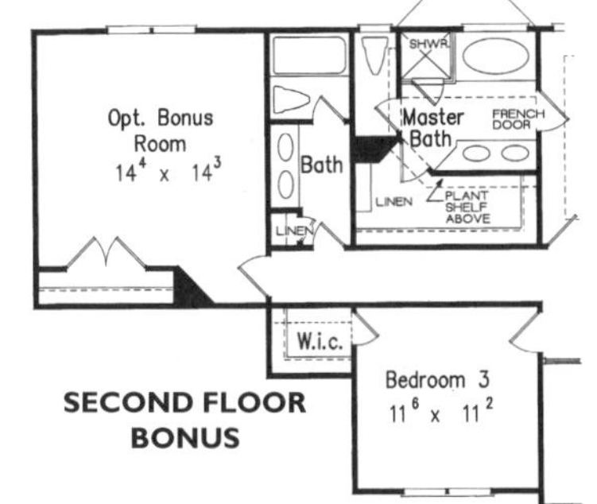
Opt. Bonus Room
14^4 x 14^3
SHWR
Master Bath
FRENCH DOOR
Bath
LINEN
PLANT SHELF ABOVE
LINEN
W.i.c.
Bedroom 3
11^6 x 11^2

SECOND FLOOR BONUS

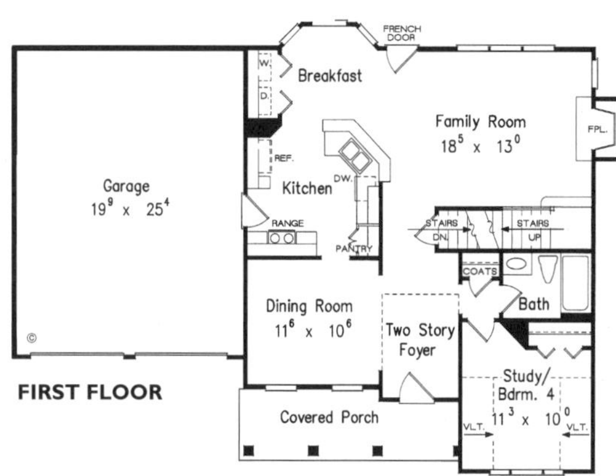
FRENCH DOOR
Breakfast
W.
D.
Family Room
18^5 x 13^0
FPL.
Garage
19^9 x 25^4
REF.
DW.
Kitchen
RANGE
PANTRY
STAIRS DN.
STAIRS UP
COATS
Bath
Dining Room
11^6 x 10^6
Two Story Foyer
Study/ Bdrm. 4
11^3 x 10^0
VLT.
VLT.
Covered Porch

FIRST FLOOR

Design 82050

Units	Single
Price Code	B
Total Finished	1,746 sq. ft.
Main Finished	1,746 sq. ft.
Garage Unfinished	491 sq. ft.
Porch Unfinished	596 sq. ft.
Dimensions	67'x54'10"
Foundation	Basement Crawlspace Slab
Bedrooms	3
Full Baths	2
Main Ceiling	9'
Roof Framing	Stick
Exterior Walls	2x4

MASTER SUITE
10' BOXED CEILING
12'-8" X 18'-0"
M.BATH
8'-4" X 11'-8"
FRENCH DOORS
WHP TUB
GLASS BLOCKS
BED RM. 2
13'-0" X 11'-0"
SCREENED PORCH
17'-0" X 10'-0"
BRKFAST RM.
13'-0" X 8'-8"
LAU.
8'-0" X 5'-6"
STORAGE
9'-4" X 5'-6"
ISLAND
KITCHEN
13'-0" X 10'-10"
GREAT RM.
11' BOXED CEILING
17'-0" X 16'-4"
10' CEILING
GARAGE
22'-4" X 22'-0"
OPTIONAL SIDE LOAD GARAGE
DINING RM.
10' BOXED CEILING
13'-0" X 11'-6"
BED RM. 3
13'-0" X 11'-0"
FOYER
10' CEILING
17'-0" X 4'-0"
COVERED PORCH
44'-10" X 8'-0"

MAIN FLOOR

Design 92625

Units	Single
Price Code	B
Total Finished	1,746 sq. ft.
Main Finished	1,746 sq. ft.
Basement Unfinished	1,560 sq. ft.
Garage Unfinished	455 sq. ft.
Dimensions	65'10"x56'
Foundation	Basement
Bedrooms	3
Full Baths	2
Max Ridge Height	21'9"
Roof Framing	Truss
Exterior Walls	2x4

Patio
Breakfast 10'10" x12'
Great Room 16'2" x 18'4"
Master Bedroom 15' x12'10"
Bath
walk-in closet
Kitchen 11'8" x 14' 4"
Dining Room 11' x 9'2"
Foyer
Hall
Bath
Bedroom 11' x 12'6"
Bedroom 12'6"x11'11"
Porch
Laun.
Two-car Garage 22' x 20'8"

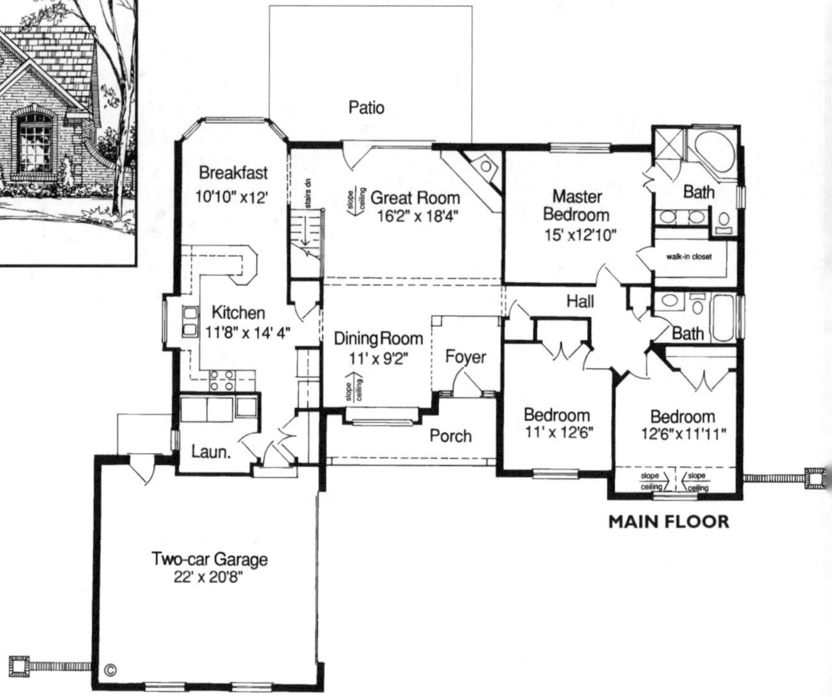

MAIN FLOOR

Design 92655

Units	Single
Price Code	B
Total Finished	1,746 sq. ft.
Main Finished	1,746 sq. ft.
Basement Unfinished	1,697 sq. ft.
Garage Unfinished	480 sq. ft.
Porch Unfinished	111 sq. ft.
Dimensions	65'10"x56'
Foundation	Basement
Bedrooms	3
Full Baths	2
Max Ridge Height	21'6"
Roof Framing	Truss
Exterior Walls	2x4

Patio
Breakfast 10'10" x12'
Great Room 16'2" x 18'4"
Master Bedroom 15' x12'10"
Bath
walk-in closet
Kitchen 11'8" x 14' 4"
Dining Room 11' x 9'2"
Foyer
Hall
Bath
Bedroom 11' x 12'6"
Bedroom 12'6"x11'11"
Porch
Laun.
Two-car Garage 22' x 20'8"

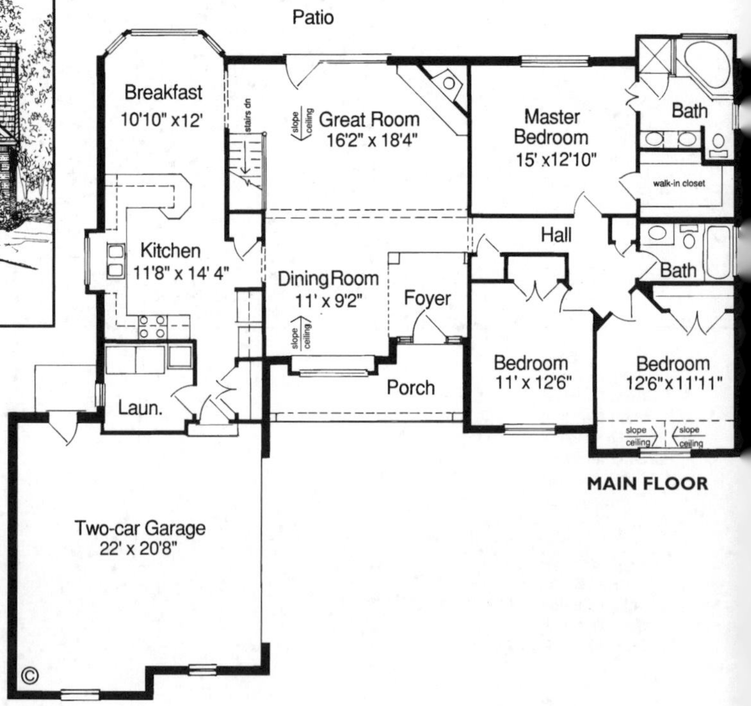

MAIN FLOOR

 To order blueprints, call **800-235-5700** or visit us on the web, **familyhomeplans.com**

Design 69144

Units	Single
Price Code	B
Total Finished	1,749 sq. ft.
First Finished	1,280 sq. ft.
Second Finished	469 sq. ft.
Dimensions	32'x48'
Foundation	Crawlspace
Bedrooms	3
Full Baths	2
3/4 Baths	1
First Ceiling	8'
Max Ridge Height	24'7"
Roof Framing	Stick
Exterior Walls	2x6

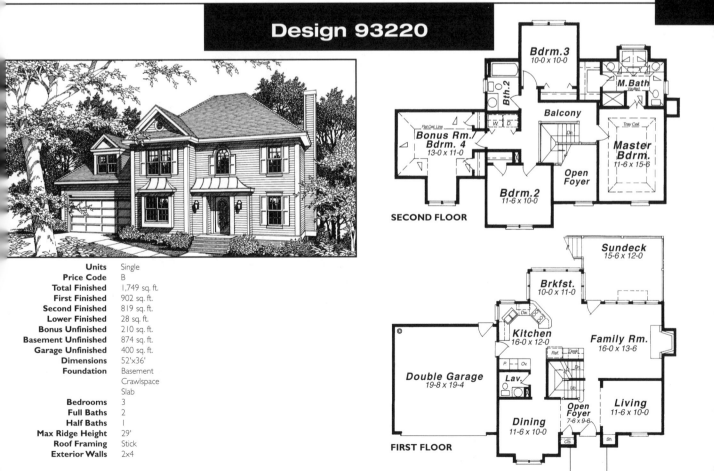

Vaulted
Loft
18'10" x 22'2"
Dn
Open to Great Room Below

SECOND FLOOR

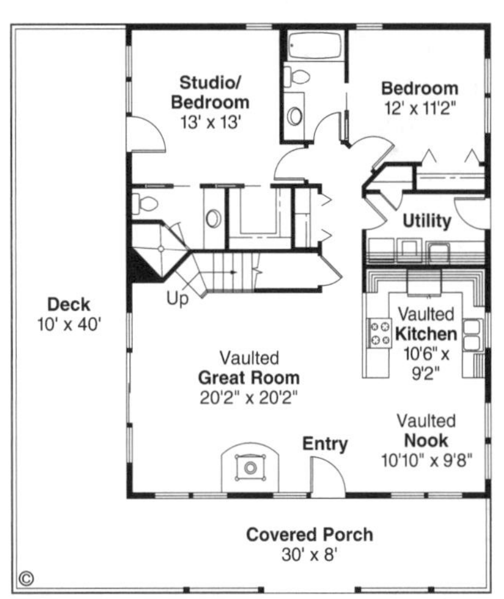
Studio/
Bedroom
13' x 13'
Bedroom
12' x 11'2"
Utility
Up
Deck
10' x 40'
Vaulted
Kitchen
10'6" x
9'2"
Vaulted
Great Room
20'2" x 20'2"
Vaulted
Nook
10'10" x 9'8"
Entry
Covered Porch
30' x 8'

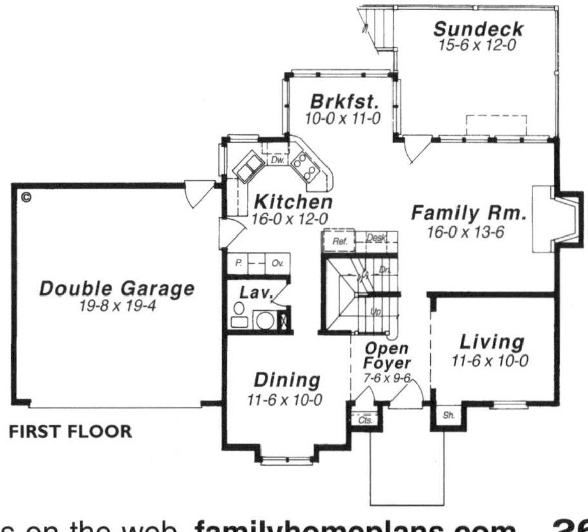

FIRST FLOOR

Design 93220

Units	Single
Price Code	B
Total Finished	1,749 sq. ft.
First Finished	902 sq. ft.
Second Finished	819 sq. ft.
Lower Finished	28 sq. ft.
Bonus Unfinished	210 sq. ft.
Basement Unfinished	874 sq. ft.
Garage Unfinished	400 sq. ft.
Dimensions	52'x36'
Foundation	Basement Crawlspace Slab
Bedrooms	3
Full Baths	2
Half Baths	1
Max Ridge Height	29'
Roof Framing	Stick
Exterior Walls	2x4

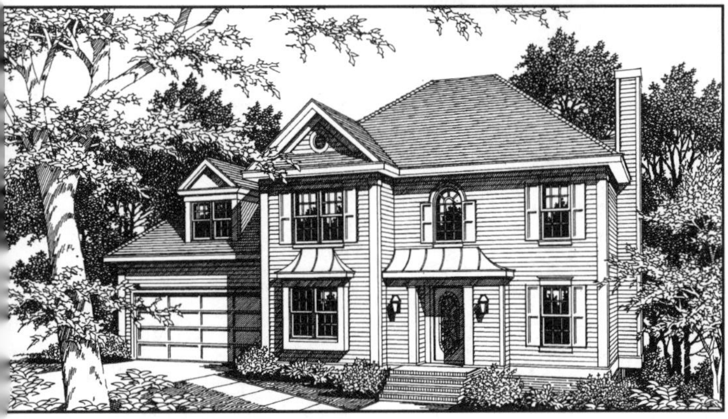

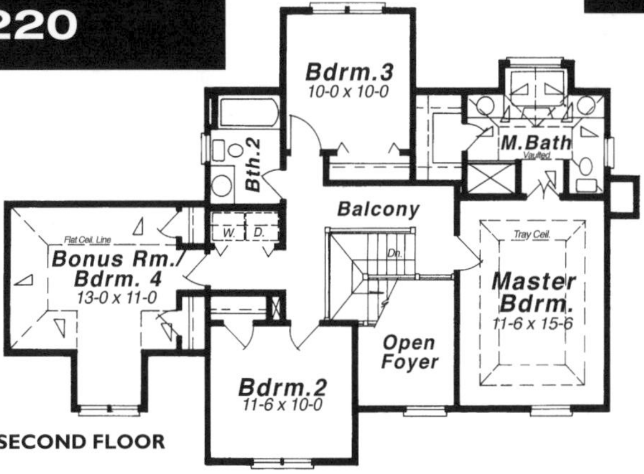

SECOND FLOOR

FIRST FLOOR

Design 10839

PHOTOGRAPHY: JOHN EHRENCLOU

Units	Single
Price Code	B
Total Finished	1,750 sq. ft.
Main Finished	1,750 sq. ft.
Basement Unfinished	1,083 sq. ft.
Garage Unfinished	796 sq. ft.
Porch Unfinished	100 sq. ft.
Dimensions	66'x50'
Foundation	Basement Crawlspace Slab
Bedrooms	2
Full Baths	2
Main Ceiling	8'
Max Ridge Height	24'6"
Roof Framing	Stick
Exterior Walls	2x4, 2x6

Please note: The photographed home may have been modified to suit homeowner preferences. If you order plans, have a builder or design professional check them against the photograph to confirm actual construction details.

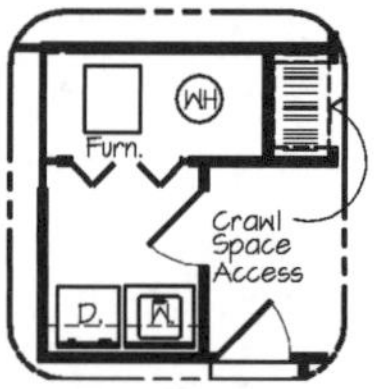

WH
Furn.
Crawl Space Access
D
W

OPTIONAL CRAWLSPACE/SLAB FOUNDATION

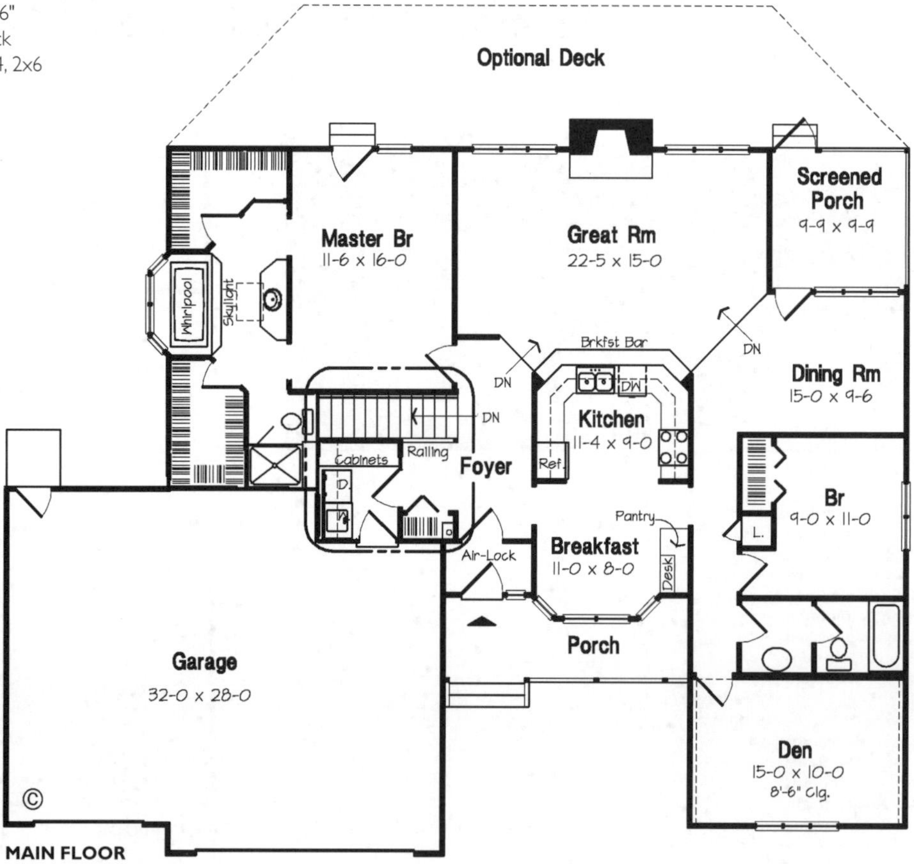

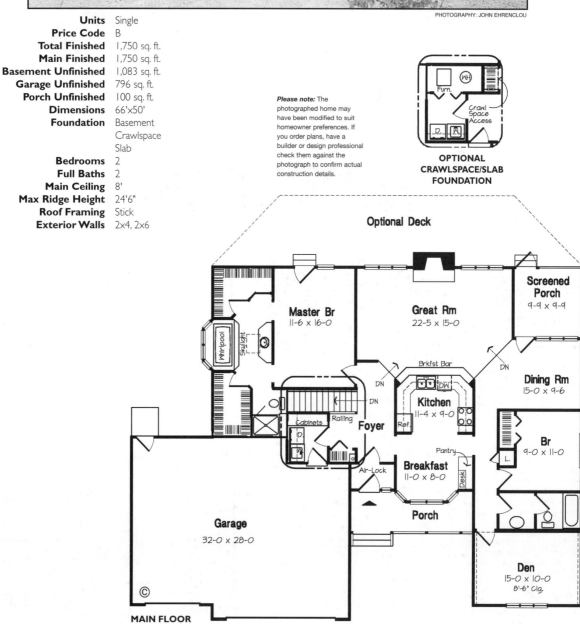

Optional Deck
Master Br 11-6 x 16-0
Whirlpool
Skylight
Great Rm 22-5 x 15-0
Screened Porch 9-9 x 9-9
Brkfst Bar
DW
DN
Kitchen 11-4 x 9-0
Ref.
Dining Rm 15-0 x 9-6
Cabinets
Railing
D
W
Foyer
Br 9-0 x 11-0
L.
Pantry
Breakfast 11-0 x 8-0
Desk
Air-Lock
Porch
Garage 32-0 x 28-0
Den 15-0 x 10-0 8'-6" Clg.
©

MAIN FLOOR

Design 98224

Units	Single
Price Code	C
Total Finished	1,751 sq. ft.
Main Finished	1,751 sq. ft.
Dimensions	64'x40'6"
Foundation	Basement Crawlspace
Bedrooms	3
Full Baths	2
Half Baths	1
Main Ceiling	9'
Vaulted Ceiling	12'
Tray Ceiling	12'
Max Ridge Height	16'
Roof Framing	Stick
Exterior Walls	2x4

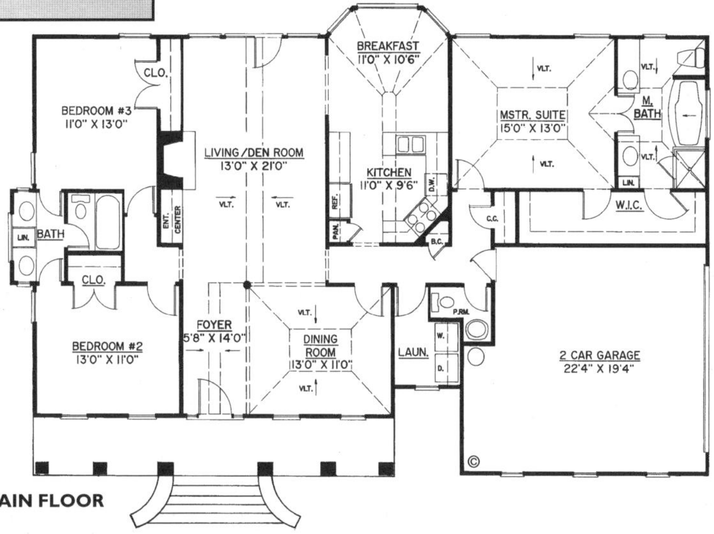

MAIN FLOOR

Design 50011

Units	Single
Price Code	B
Total Finished	1,754 sq. ft.
First Finished	889 sq. ft.
Second Finished	865 sq. ft.
Basement Unfinished	889 sq. ft.
Garage Unfinished	474 sq. ft.
Porch Unfinished	91 sq. ft.
Dimensions	40'10"x50'
Foundation	Basement
Bedrooms	3
Full Baths	2
Half Baths	1
First Ceiling	9'
Second Ceiling	8'
Max Ridge Height	26'8"
Roof Framing	Truss
Exterior Walls	2x4

SECOND FLOOR

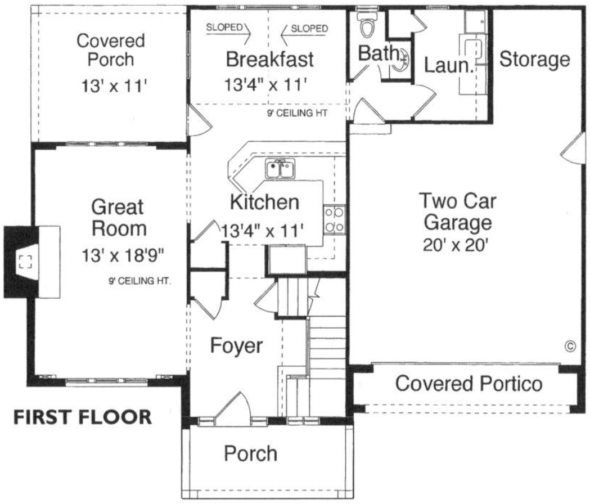

FIRST FLOOR

Design 92531

Units	Single
Price Code	C
Total Finished	1,754 sq. ft.
Main Finished	1,754 sq. ft.
Garage Unfinished	552 sq. ft.
Porch Unfinished	236 sq. ft.
Dimensions	69'10"x53'5"
Foundation	Crawlspace Slab
Bedrooms	3
Full Baths	2
Max Ridge Height	22'
Roof Framing	Stick
Exterior Walls	2x4

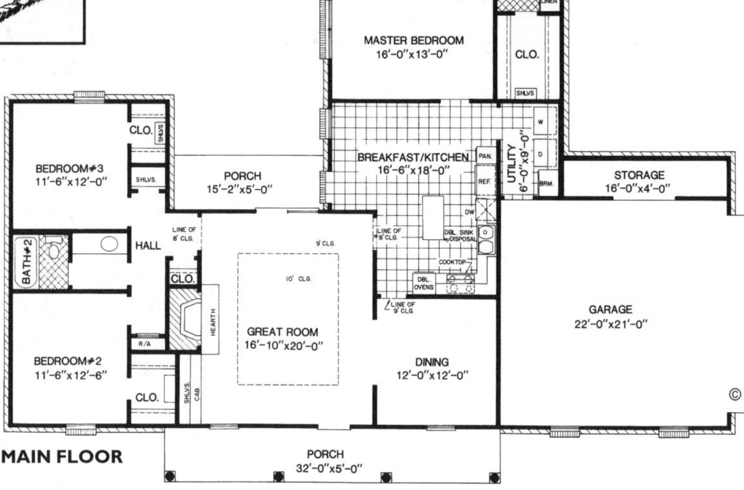

MASTER BATH
MASTER BEDROOM
16'-0"x13'-0"
CLO.
BEDROOM#3
11'-6"x12'-0"
CLO.
PORCH
15'-2"x5'-0"
BREAKFAST/KITCHEN
16'-6"x18'-0"
UTILITY
6'-0"x9'-0"
STORAGE
16'-0"x4'-0"
HALL
BATH#2
CLO.
GREAT ROOM
16'-10"x20'-0"
GARAGE
22'-0"x21'-0"
BEDROOM#2
11'-6"x12'-6"
CLO.
DINING
12'-0"x12'-0"
MAIN FLOOR
PORCH
32'-0"x5'-0"

Design 91176

Units	Single
Price Code	C
Total Finished	1,755 sq. ft.
First Finished	858 sq. ft.
Second Finished	897 sq. ft.
Bonus Unfinished	242 sq. ft.
Garage Unfinished	498 sq. ft.
Dimensions	45'11½"x31'9"
Foundation	Slab
Bedrooms	3
Full Baths	2
Half Baths	1
First Ceiling	8'1⅛"
Second Ceiling	8'1⅛"
Max Ridge Height	28'
Roof Framing	Stick
Exterior Walls	2x4

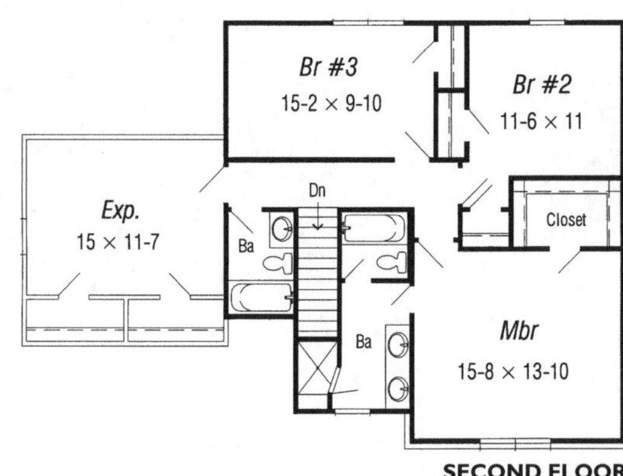

Br #3
15-2 × 9-10
Br #2
11-6 × 11
Exp.
15 × 11-7
Dn
Ba
Closet
Ba
Mbr
15-8 × 13-10
SECOND FLOOR

Stor 7 × 7 · Util · W D F · Kit 11-6 × 12 · Din 10-6 × 13 · 2-car Gar 20 × 20-6 · Liv 20-10 × 16 · Ent · Up

FIRST FLOOR

Design 97757

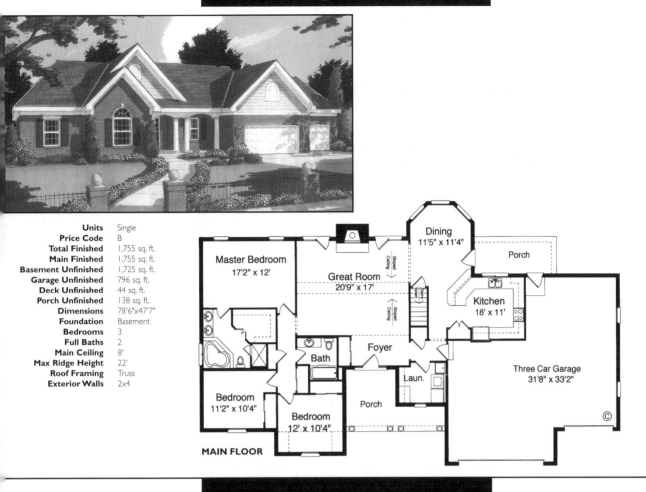

Units	Single
Price Code	B
Total Finished	1,755 sq. ft.
Main Finished	1,755 sq. ft.
Basement Unfinished	1,725 sq. ft.
Garage Unfinished	796 sq. ft.
Deck Unfinished	44 sq. ft.
Porch Unfinished	138 sq. ft.
Dimensions	78'6"x47'7"
Foundation	Basement
Bedrooms	3
Full Baths	2
Main Ceiling	8'
Max Ridge Height	22'
Roof Framing	Truss
Exterior Walls	2x4

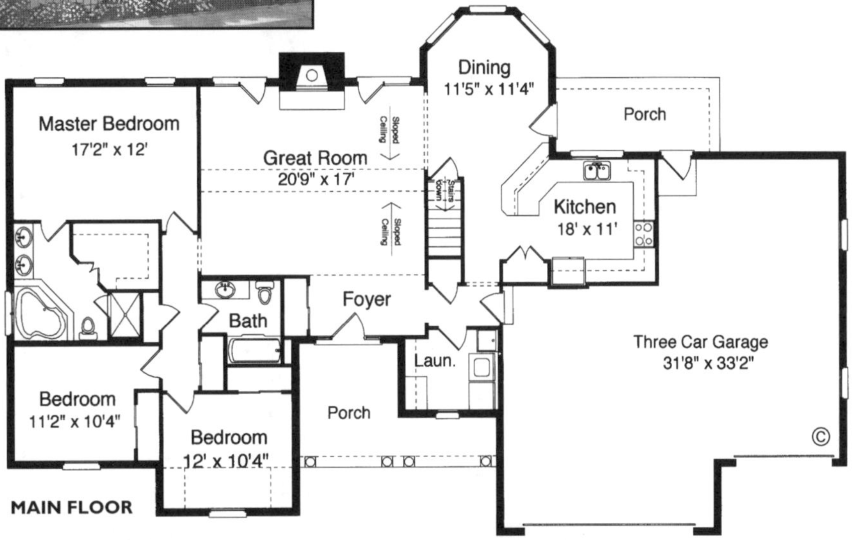

Dining 11'5" x 11'4"
Porch
Master Bedroom 17'2" x 12'
Great Room 20'9" x 17'
Sloped Ceiling
Kitchen 18' x 11'
Foyer
Bath
Laun.
Three Car Garage 31'8" x 33'2"
Bedroom 11'2" x 10'4"
Porch
Bedroom 12' x 10'4"
©

MAIN FLOOR

Design 99185

Units	Single
Price Code	C
Total Finished	1,755 sq. ft.
Main Finished	1,755 sq. ft.
Basement Unfinished	1,755 sq. ft.
Porch Unfinished	164 sq. ft.
Dimensions	70'x64'
Foundation	Basement
Bedrooms	3
Full Baths	1
3/4 Baths	1
Half Baths	1
Main Ceiling	9'-10'
Max Ridge Height	24'8"
Roof Framing	Truss
Exterior Walls	2x6

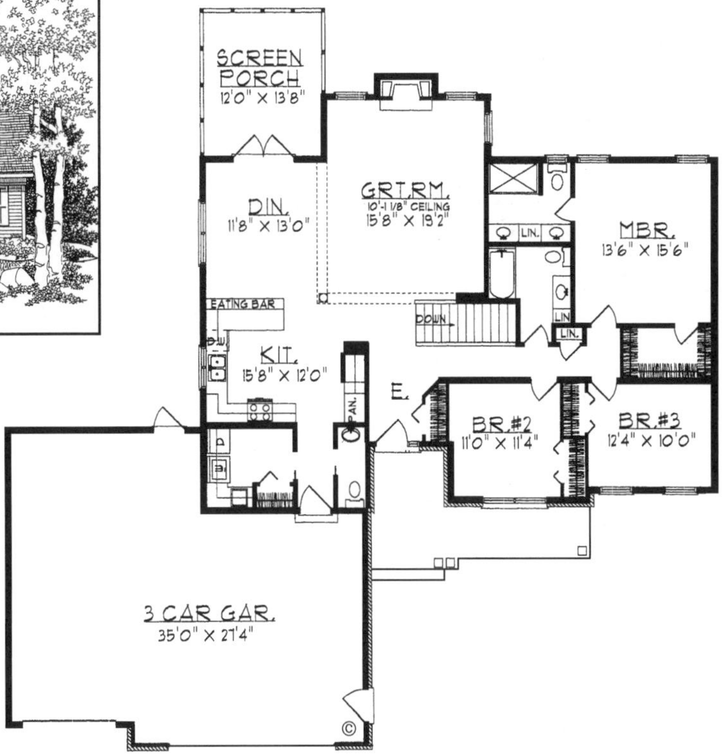

SCREEN PORCH 12'0" X 13'8"
DIN. 11'8" X 13'0"
GRT.RM. 10'-1 1/8" CEILING 15'8" X 19'2"
MBR. 13'6" X 15'6"
LIN.
EATING BAR
KIT. 15'8" X 12'0"
DOWN
E.
PAN.
BR.#2 11'0" X 11'4"
BR.#3 12'4" X 10'0"
3 CAR GAR. 35'0" X 27'4"
©

MAIN FLOOR

Design 93104

Units	Single
Price Code	C
Total Finished	1,756 sq. ft.
Main Finished	1,756 sq. ft.
Basement Unfinished	1,756 sq. ft.
Garage Unfinished	536 sq. ft.
Dimensions	58'x55'
Foundation	Basement
Bedrooms	3
Full Baths	2
Max Ridge Height	23'
Roof Framing	Truss
Exterior Walls	2x6

DINING ROOM
15'-0"X 12'-0"
GREAT ROOM
16'-0"X 22'-0"
BEDROOM #2
13'-0"X 11'-0"
MASTER BEDROOM
14'-0"X 16'-0"
KITCHEN
15'-0"X 11'-0"
FOYER
BEDROOM #3
12'-0"X 11'-0"
MAIN FLOOR
2 CAR GARAGE
22'-0"X 24'-0"
©

Design 93191

Units	Single
Price Code	C
Total Finished	1,756 sq. ft.
Main Finished	1,756 sq. ft.
Basement Unfinished	1,756 sq. ft.
Dimensions	59'x58'
Foundation	Basement
Bedrooms	3
Full Baths	2
Max Ridge Height	21'10"
Roof Framing	Truss
Exterior Walls	2x6

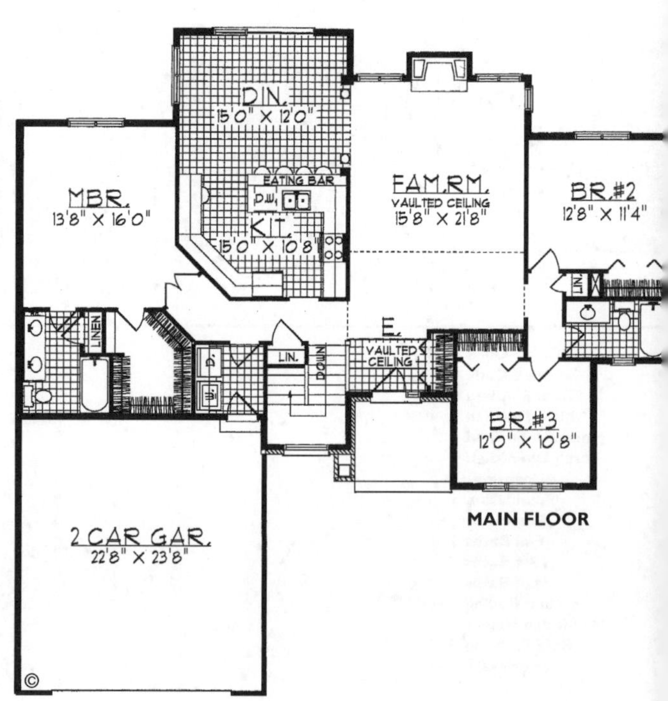
DIN.
15'0" X 12'0"
EATING BAR
D.W.
KIT.
15'0" X 10'8"
FAM.RM.
VAULTED CEILING
15'8" X 21'8"
MBR.
13'8" X 16'0"
BR.#2
12'8" X 11'4"
LIN.
LINEN
DOWN
E.
VAULTED CEILING
BR.#3
12'0" X 10'8"
MAIN FLOOR
2 CAR GAR.
22'8" X 23'8"
©

Design 34077

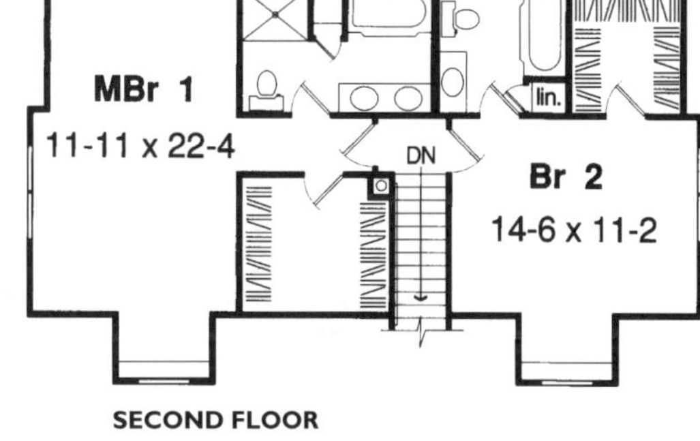
MBr 1
11-11 x 22-4
DN
Br 2
14-6 x 11-2
lin.
SECOND FLOOR

Units	Single
Price Code	C
Total Finished	1,757 sq. ft.
First Finished	957 sq. ft.
Second Finished	800 sq. ft.
Dimensions	40'x24'
Foundation	Basement Crawlspace Slab
Bedrooms	4
Full Baths	3
Max Ridge Height	25'
Roof Framing	Stick
Exterior Walls	2x4

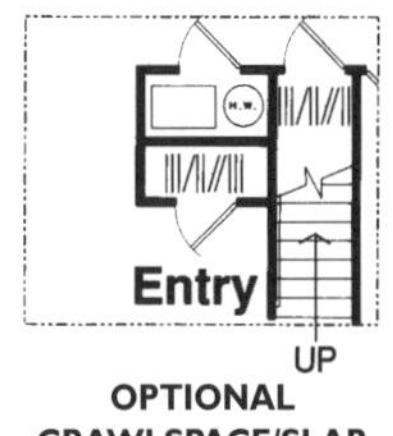
Entry
UP

OPTIONAL CRAWLSPACE/SLAB FOUNDATION

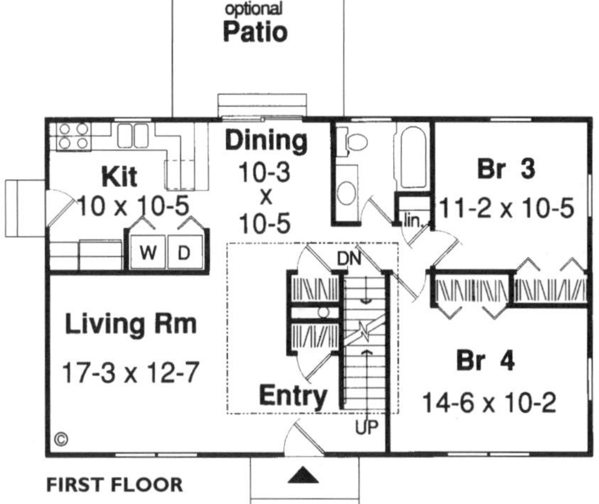
optional
Patio
Kit
10 x 10-5
Dining
10-3
x
10-5
Br 3
11-2 x 10-5
lin.
DN
W D
Living Rm
17-3 x 12-7
Entry
Br 4
14-6 x 10-2
UP
FIRST FLOOR

Design 91830

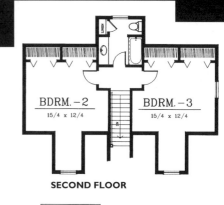

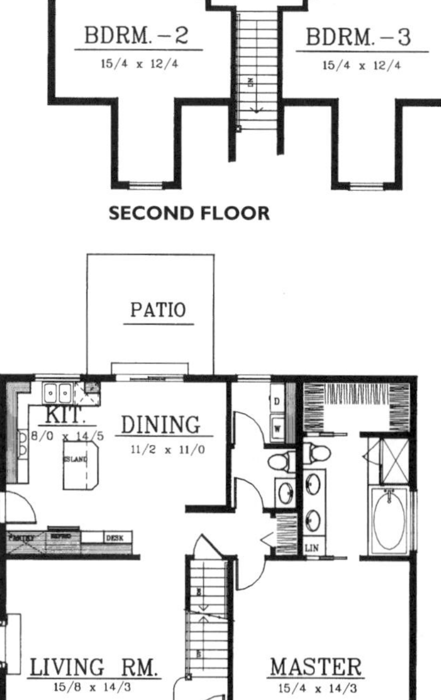
BDRM. -2
15/4 x 12/4
BDRM. -3
15/4 x 12/4
SECOND FLOOR
PATIO
KIT.
8/0 x 14/5
DINING
11/2 x 11/0
GARAGE
23/8 x 23/4
LIN
LIVING RM.
15/8 x 14/3
MASTER
15/4 x 14/3
PORCH
FIRST FLOOR

Units	Single
Price Code	C
Total Finished	1,757 sq. ft.
First Finished	1,080 sq. ft.
Second Finished	677 sq. ft.
Basement Unfinished	1,080 sq. ft.
Garage Unfinished	576 sq. ft.
Porch Unfinished	192 sq. ft.
Dimensions	60'x36'
Foundation	Crawlspace
Bedrooms	3
Full Baths	2
Half Baths	1
First Ceiling	8'
Second Ceiling	8'
Max Ridge Height	22'6"
Roof Framing	Stick
Exterior Walls	2x6

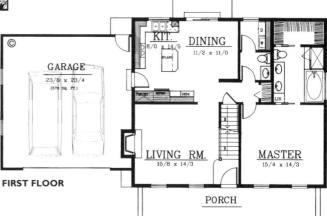

Design 63090

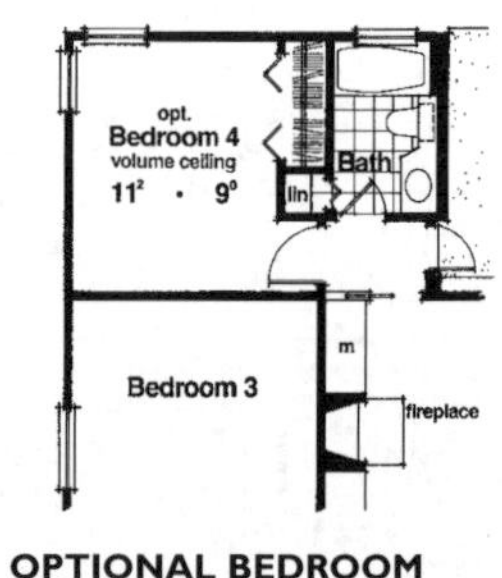

opt.
Bedroom 4
volume ceiling
Bath
lin
m
Bedroom 3
fireplace

OPTIONAL BEDROOM

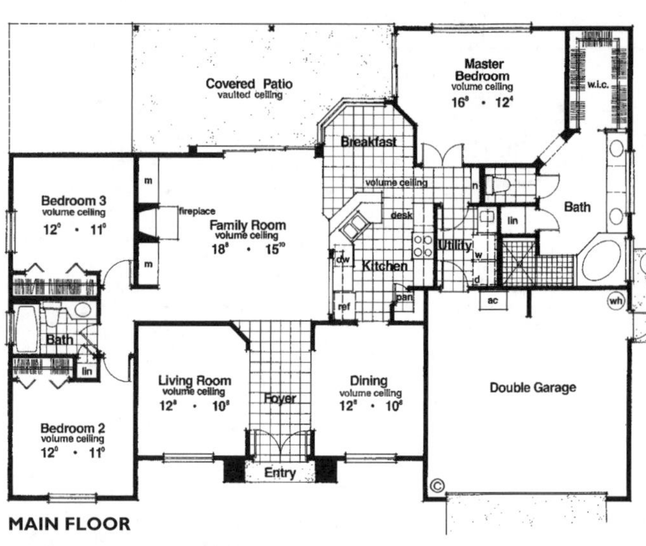

Covered Patio
vaulted ceiling
Master Bedroom
volume ceiling
w.i.c.
Breakfast
volume ceiling
Bath
lin
Bedroom 3
volume ceiling
fireplace
Family Room
volume ceiling
m
desk
Utility
Kitchen
dw
ref
pan
ac
wh
Bath
lin
Living Room
volume ceiling
Foyer
Dining
volume ceiling
Double Garage
Bedroom 2
volume ceiling
Entry

MAIN FLOOR

Units	Single
Price Code	C
Total Finished	1,758 sq. ft.
Main Finished	1,758 sq. ft.
Garage Unfinished	409 sq. ft.
Dimensions	60'x45'
Foundation	Slab
Bedrooms	3
Full Baths	2
Main Ceiling	10'
Max Ridge Height	20'8"
Roof Framing	Truss
Exterior Walls	2x4

Design 97456

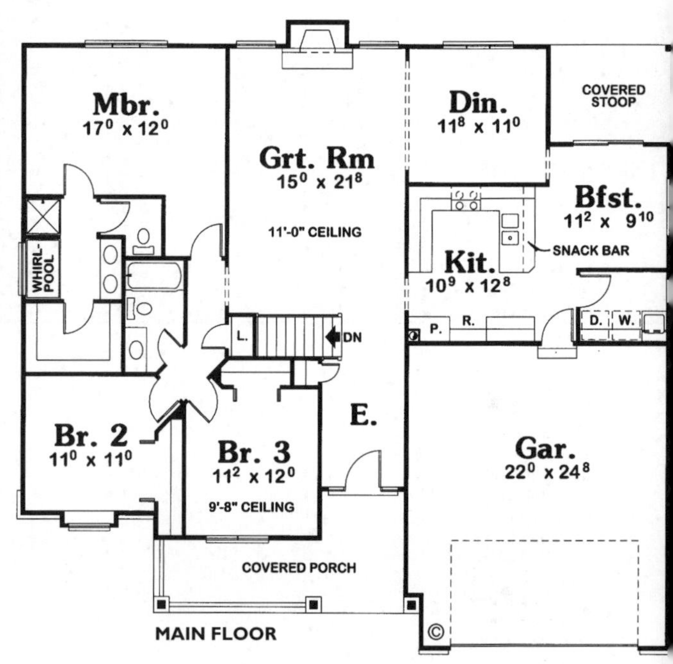

Mbr.
17^0 x 12^0
Grt. Rm
15^0 x 21^8
11'-0" CEILING
Din.
11^8 x 11^0
COVERED STOOP
Bfst.
11^2 x 9^{10}
SNACK BAR
Kit.
10^9 x 12^8
WHIRLPOOL
L.
DN
P.
R.
D.
W.
E.
Br. 2
11^0 x 11^0
Br. 3
11^2 x 12^0
9'-8" CEILING
Gar.
22^0 x 24^8
COVERED PORCH

MAIN FLOOR

Units	Single
Price Code	C
Total Finished	1,758 sq. ft.
Main Finished	1,758 sq. ft.
Garage Unfinished	494 sq. ft.
Dimensions	55'4"x49'8"
Foundation	Basement
Bedrooms	3
Full Baths	2
Main Ceiling	9'
Max Ridge Height	26'
Roof Framing	Stick
Exterior Walls	2x4

* Alternate foundation options available at an additional charge. Please call 1-800-235-5700 for more information.

Design 69035

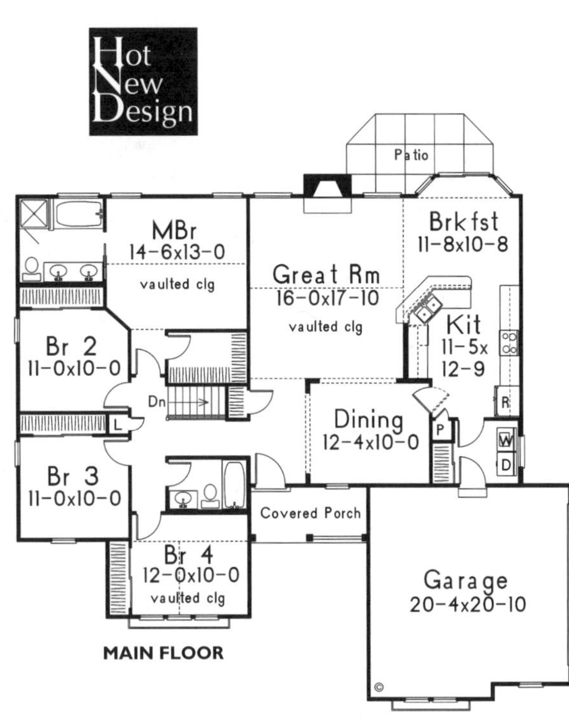
Hot
New
Design
Patio
MBr
14-6x13-0
vaulted clg
Great Rm
16-0x17-10
vaulted clg
Brkfst
11-8x10-8
Kit
11-5x
12-9
Br 2
11-0x10-0
Dn
L
P
W
D
R
Dining
12-4x10-0
Br 3
11-0x10-0
Covered Porch
Br 4
12-0x10-0
vaulted clg
Garage
20-4x20-10
MAIN FLOOR

Units	Single
Price Code	C
Total Finished	1,761 sq. ft.
Main Finished	1,761 sq. ft.
Dimensions	57'x52'2"
Foundation	Basement
Bedrooms	4
Full Baths	2

Design 99498

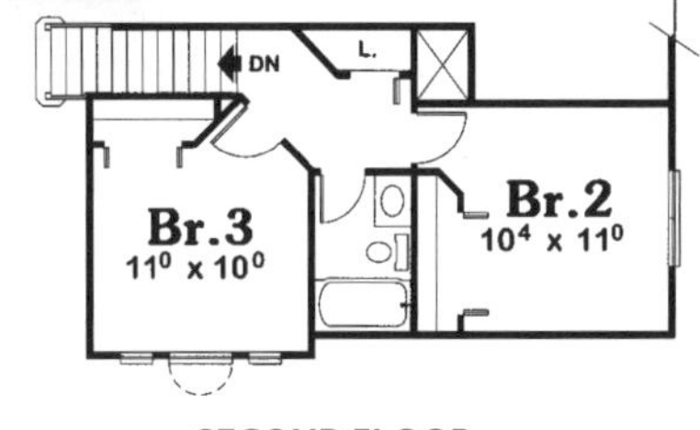
DN
L.
Br.3
11⁰ x 10⁰
Br.2
10⁴ x 11⁰
SECOND FLOOR

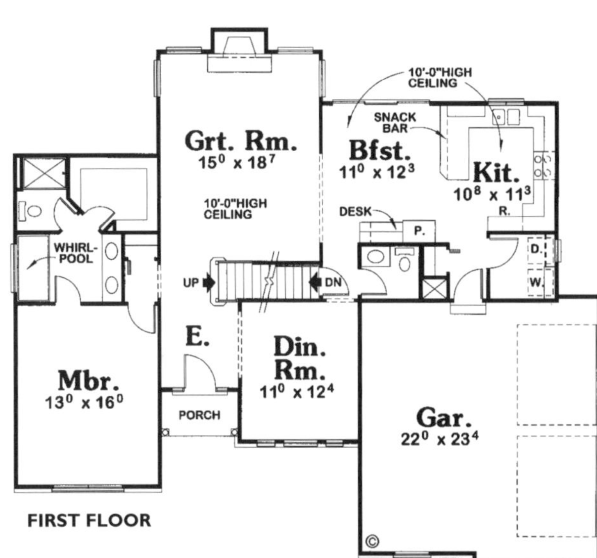
10'-0"HIGH CEILING
SNACK BAR
Grt. Rm.
15⁰ x 18⁷
10'-0"HIGH CEILING
Bfst.
11⁰ x 12³
Kit.
10⁸ x 11³
R.
DESK
P.
D.
W.
WHIRL-POOL
UP
DN
E.
Mbr.
13⁰ x 16⁰
PORCH
Din. Rm.
11⁰ x 12⁴
Gar.
22⁰ x 23⁴
FIRST FLOOR

Units	Single
Price Code	C
Total Finished	1,762 sq. ft.
First Finished	1,363 sq. ft.
Second Finished	399 sq. ft.
Garage Unfinished	524 sq. ft.
Dimensions	55'x46'4"
Foundation	Basement
Bedrooms	3
Full Baths	2
Half Baths	1
First Ceiling	9'
Max Ridge Height	27'
Roof Framing	Stick
Exterior Walls	2x4

* Alternate foundation options available at an additional charge.
Please call 1-800-235-5700 for more information.

Design 93133

Units	Single
Price Code	C
Total Finished	1,763 sq. ft.
Main Finished	1,763 sq. ft.
Basement Unfinished	1,763 sq. ft.
Garage Unfinished	658 sq. ft.
Dimensions	67'8"x42'8"
Foundation	Basement
Bedrooms	3
Full Baths	2
Main Ceiling	8'
Vaulted Ceiling	14'
Max Ridge Height	22'
Roof Framing	Truss
Exterior Walls	2x6

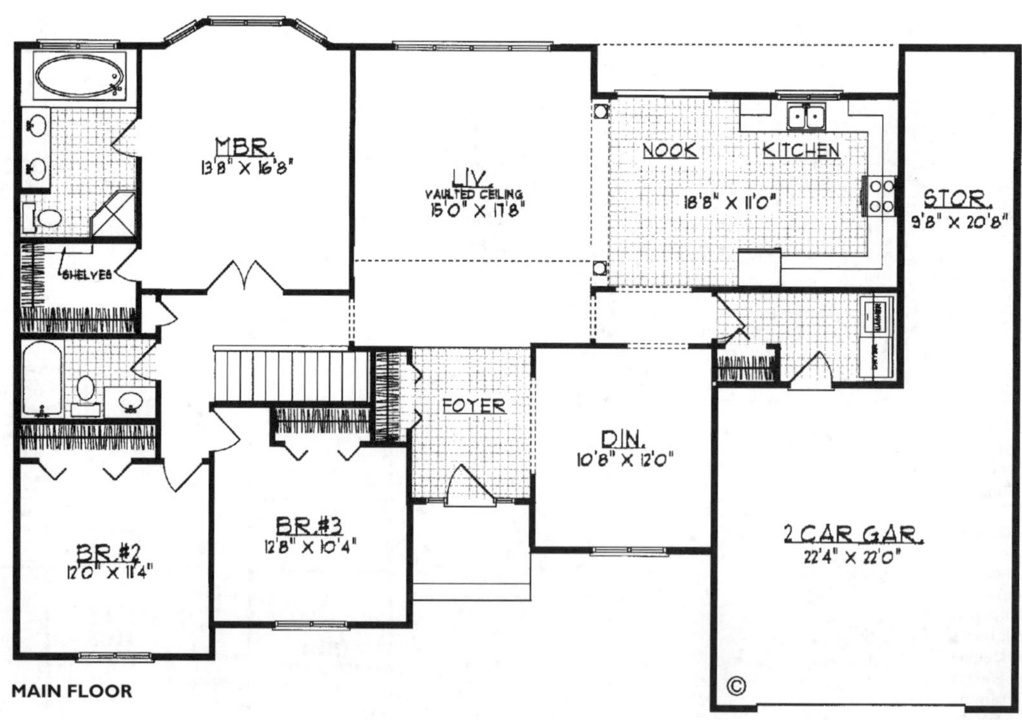
MBR.
13'8" X 16'8"
LIV.
VAULTED CEILING
15'0" X 17'8"
NOOK
KITCHEN
18'8" X 11'0"
STOR.
9'8" X 20'8"
SHELVES
FOYER
DIN.
10'8" X 12'0"
2 CAR GAR.
22'4" X 22'0"
BR.#2
12'0" X 11'4"
BR.#3
12'8" X 10'4"
©

MAIN FLOOR

Design 93230

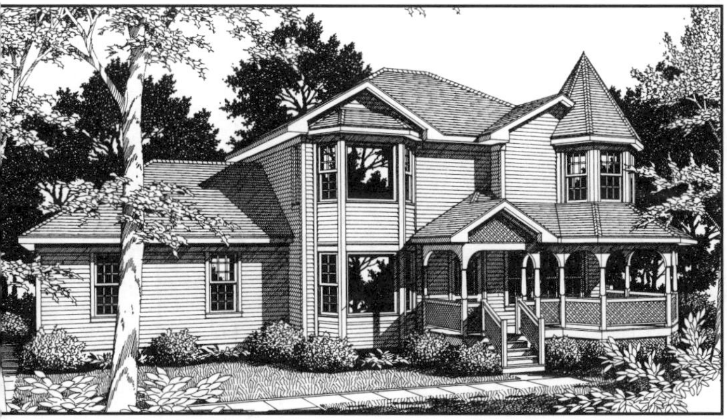

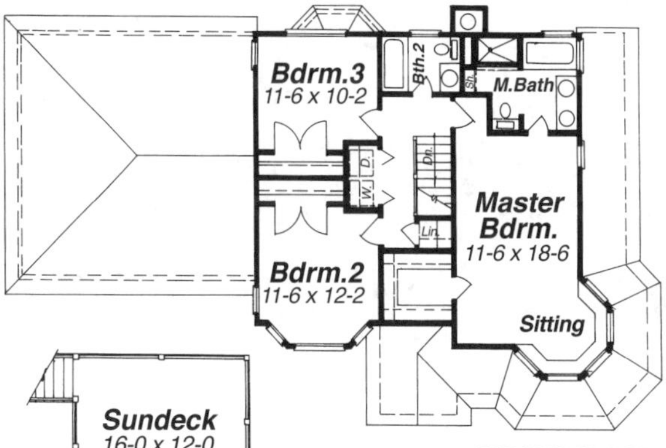

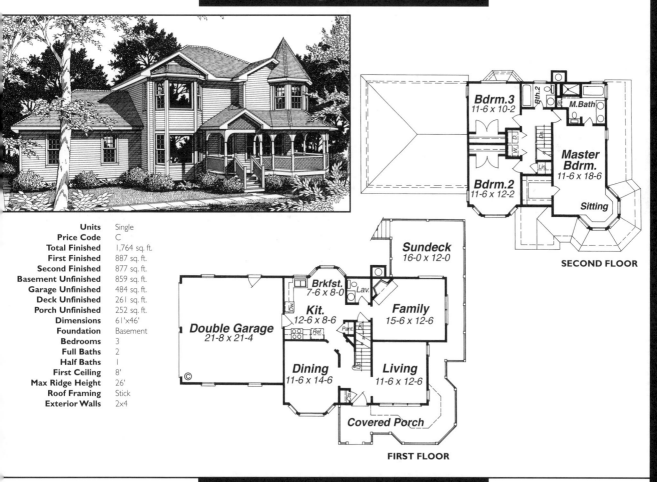

SECOND FLOOR

Units	Single
Price Code	C
Total Finished	1,764 sq. ft.
First Finished	887 sq. ft.
Second Finished	877 sq. ft.
Basement Unfinished	859 sq. ft.
Garage Unfinished	484 sq. ft.
Deck Unfinished	261 sq. ft.
Porch Unfinished	252 sq. ft.
Dimensions	61'x46'
Foundation	Basement
Bedrooms	3
Full Baths	2
Half Baths	1
First Ceiling	8'
Max Ridge Height	26'
Roof Framing	Stick
Exterior Walls	2x4

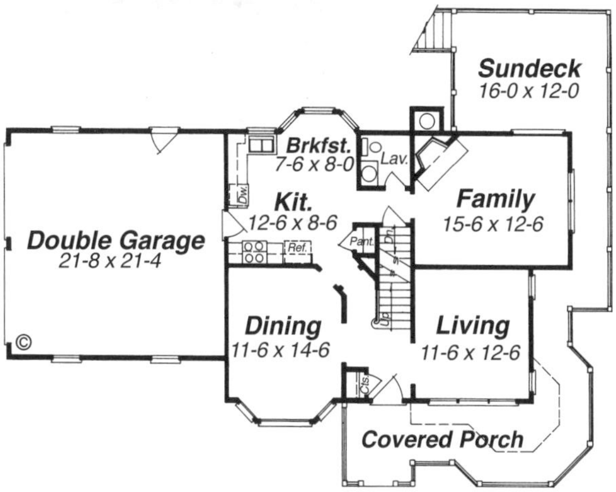

FIRST FLOOR

Design 94204

PHOTOGRAPHY: COURTESY OF THE DESIGNER

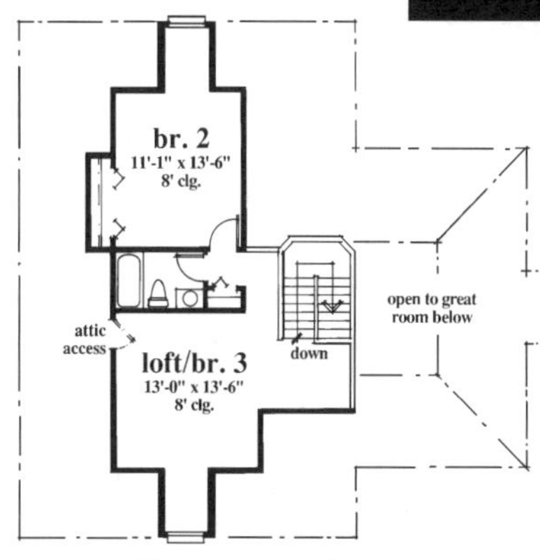
br. 2
11'-1" x 13'-6"
8' clg.
attic access
loft/br. 3
13'-0" x 13'-6"
8' clg.
down
open to great room below

SECOND FLOOR

Please note: The photographed home may have been modified to suit homeowner preferences. If you order plans, have a builder or design professional check them against the photograph to confirm actual construction details.

Units	Single
Price Code	C
Total Finished	1,764 sq. ft.
First Finished	1,189 sq. ft.
Second Finished	575 sq. ft.
Bonus Unfinished	581 sq. ft.
Garage Unfinished	658 sq. ft.
Dimensions	46'x44'6"
Foundation	Post
Bedrooms	3
Full Baths	2
Half Baths	1
Max Ridge Height	36'
Roof Framing	Stick/Truss
Exterior Walls	2x6

Alternate foundation options available at an additional charge. Please call 1-800-235-5700 for more information.

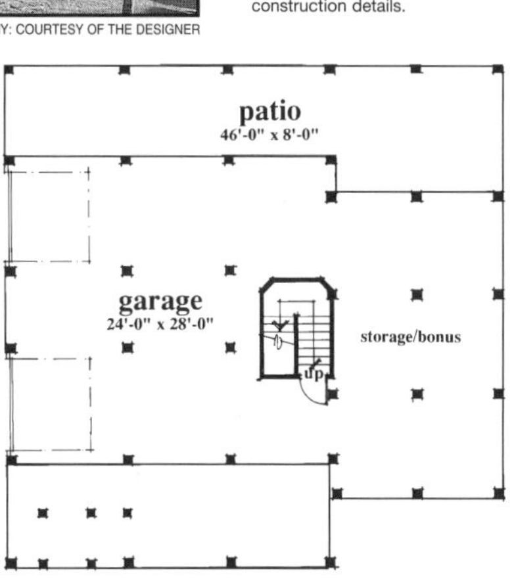
patio
46'-0" x 8'-0"
garage
24'-0" x 28'-0"
storage/bonus
up

LOWER FLOOR

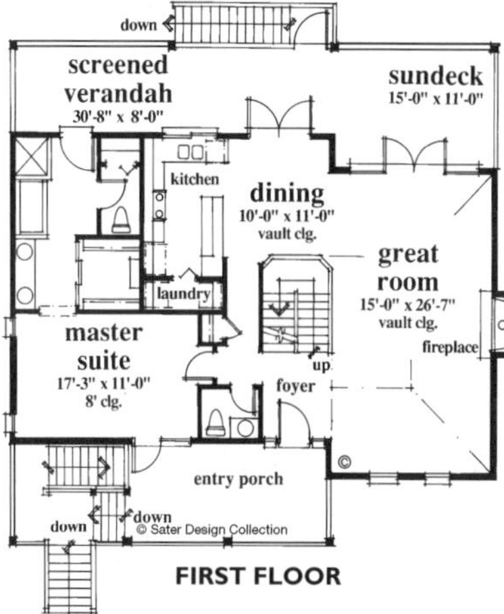
down
screened verandah
30'-8" x 8'-0"
sundeck
15'-0" x 11'-0"
kitchen
dining
10'-0" x 11'-0"
vault clg.
great room
15'-0" x 26'-7"
vault clg.
fireplace
laundry
master suite
17'-3" x 11'-0"
8' clg.
foyer
up
entry porch
down
down
© Sater Design Collection

FIRST FLOOR

Design 63048

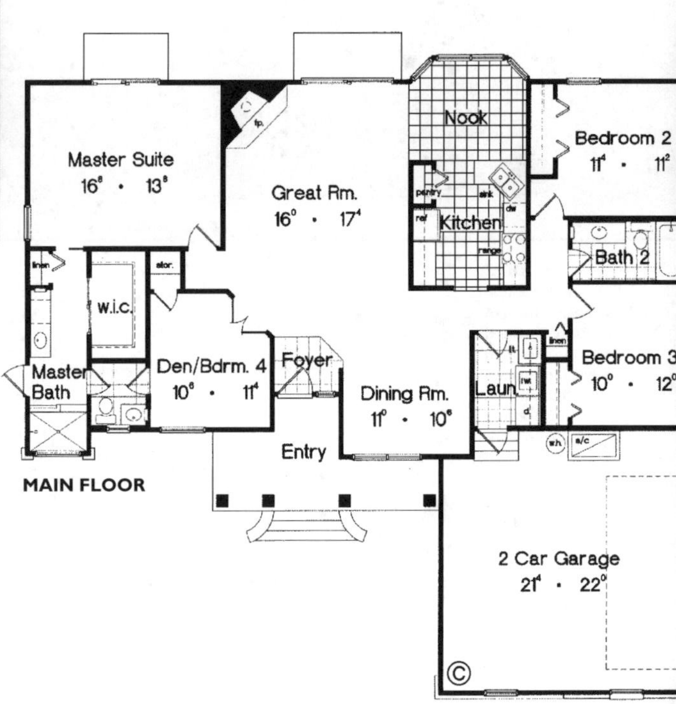

Master Suite
16⁸ · 13⁸
Great Rm.
16⁰ · 17⁴
Nook
Kitchen
Bedroom 2
11⁴ · 11²
Bath 2
w.i.c.
Master Bath
Den/Bdrm. 4
10⁶ · 11⁴
Foyer
Dining Rm.
11⁰ · 10⁶
Laun.
Bedroom 3
10⁰ · 12⁰
Entry
MAIN FLOOR
2 Car Garage
21⁴ · 22⁰

Units	Single
Price Code	B
Total Finished	1,765 sq. ft.
Main Finished	1,765 sq. ft.
Deck Unfinished	90 sq. ft.
Porch Unfinished	130 sq. ft.
Dimensions	58'x54'
Foundation	Slab
Bedrooms	4
Full Baths	1
3/4 Baths	1
Main Ceiling	8'
Max Ridge Height	20'
Roof Framing	Truss

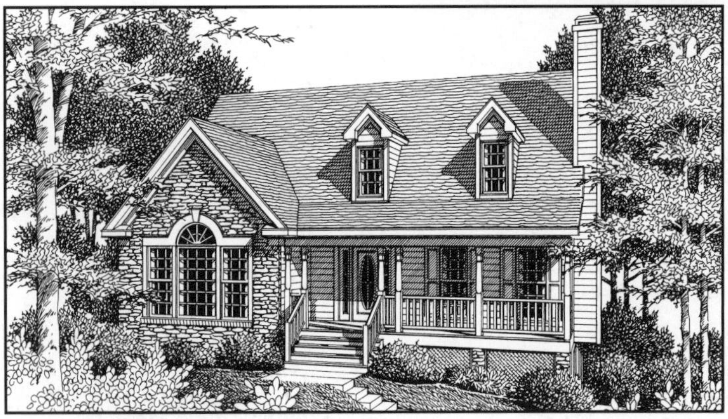

Design 98931

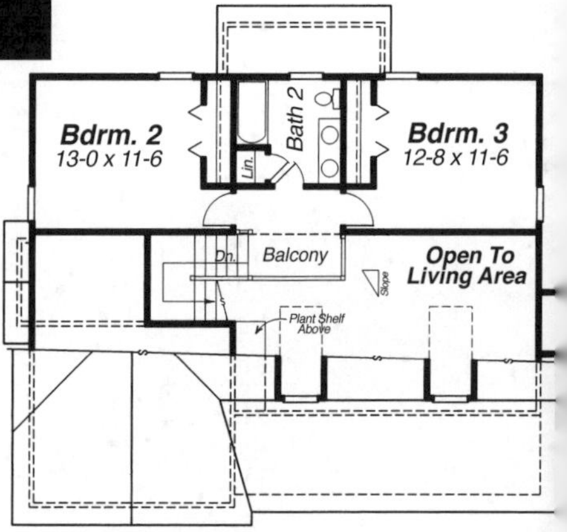

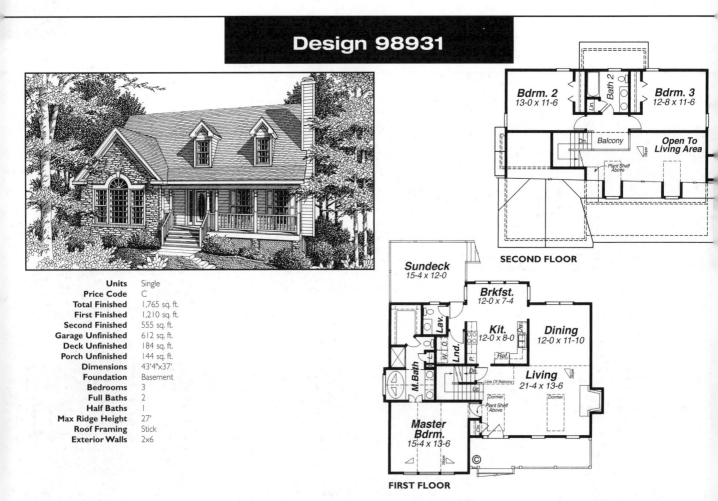

Bdrm. 2
13-0 x 11-6
Bath 2
Bdrm. 3
12-8 x 11-6
Balcony
Open To Living Area
SECOND FLOOR

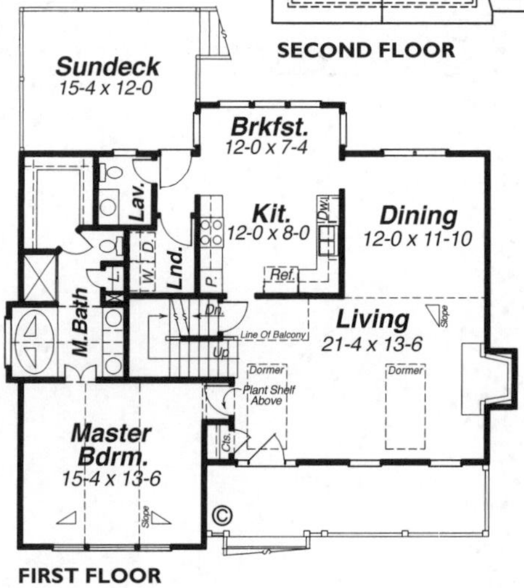

Sundeck
15-4 x 12-0
Brkfst.
12-0 x 7-4
Kit.
12-0 x 8-0
Dining
12-0 x 11-10
Living
21-4 x 13-6
M.Bath
Master Bdrm.
15-4 x 13-6
FIRST FLOOR

Units	Single
Price Code	C
Total Finished	1,765 sq. ft.
First Finished	1,210 sq. ft.
Second Finished	555 sq. ft.
Garage Unfinished	612 sq. ft.
Deck Unfinished	184 sq. ft.
Porch Unfinished	144 sq. ft.
Dimensions	43'4"x37'
Foundation	Basement
Bedrooms	3
Full Baths	2
Half Baths	1
Max Ridge Height	27'
Roof Framing	Stick
Exterior Walls	2x6

Design 91055

Units	Single
Price Code	C
Total Finished	1,766 sq. ft.
First Finished	805 sq. ft.
Second Finished	961 sq. ft.
Garage Unfinished	540 sq. ft.
Dimensions	37'x38'
Foundation	Crawlspace
Bedrooms	3
Full Baths	2
Half Baths	1
Max Ridge Height	26'
Roof Framing	Stick
Exterior Walls	2x6

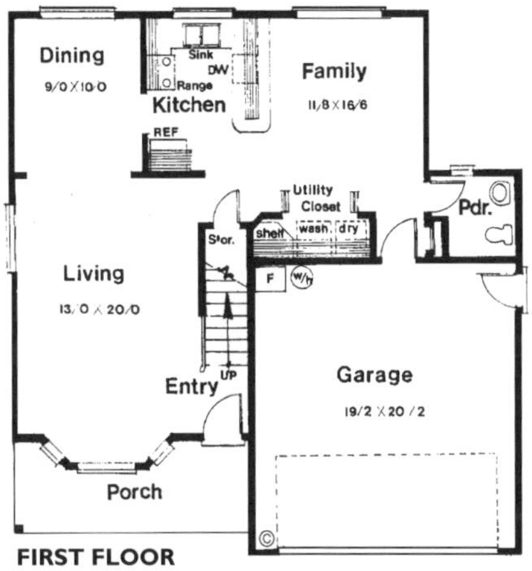

walk in
TUB
TUB
Bedr. 2
10/0 X 10/3
lin.
D.N
Master
Bedr. 1
13/0 x 14/8
Playroom
16/2 X 9/0
UP
Bedr. 3
13/0 X 12/0
SECOND FLOOR
Dining
9/0 X 10-0
Sink
DW
Range
Kitchen
REF
Family
11/8 X 16/6
Utility Closet
wash dry
shelf
Stor.
Pdr.
Living
13/0 X 20/0
F
W/H
Entry
UP
Garage
19/2 X 20/2
Porch
FIRST FLOOR 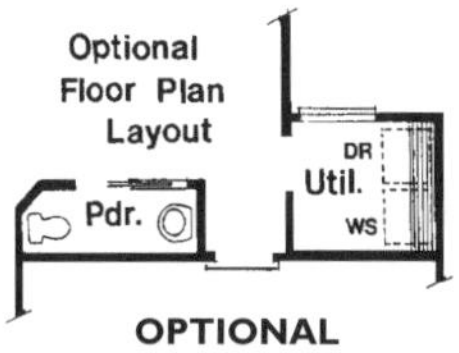
Optional
Floor Plan
Layout
DR
Util.
WS
Pdr.
OPTIONAL
LAUNDRY/HALF BATH
LOCATION

Design 99045

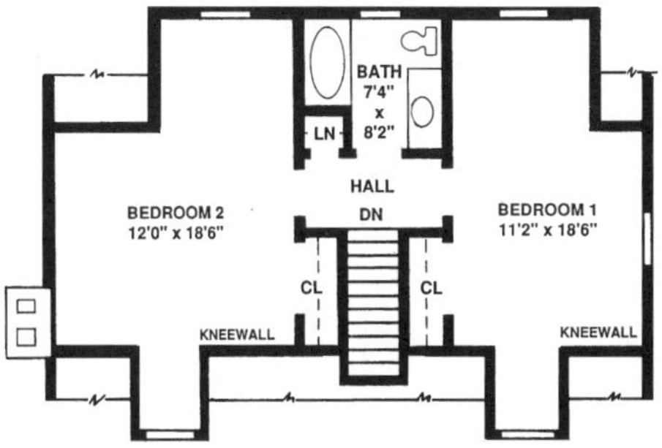

Units	Single
Price Code	C
Total Finished	1,767 sq. ft.
First Finished	1,108 sq. ft.
Second Finished	659 sq. ft.
Basement Unfinished	875 sq. ft.
Porch Unfinished	145 sq. ft.
Dimensions	67'x30'
Foundation	Basement
Bedrooms	3
Full Baths	2
Half Baths	1
Max Ridge Height	21'
Roof Framing	Truss
Exterior Walls	2x4

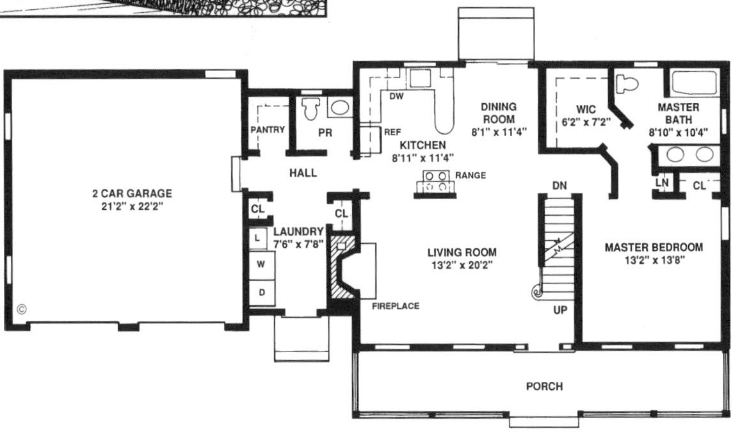

BATH
7'4" x 8'2"
LN
HALL
DN
BEDROOM 2
12'0" x 18'6"
BEDROOM 1
11'2" x 18'6"
CL
CL
KNEEWALL
KNEEWALL
SECOND FLOOR
2 CAR GARAGE
21'2" x 22'2"
PANTRY
PR
HALL
CL
CL
LAUNDRY
7'6" x 7'8"
L
W
D
DW
REF
KITCHEN
8'11" x 11'4"
RANGE
DINING ROOM
8'1" x 11'4"
LIVING ROOM
13'2" x 20'2"
FIREPLACE
DN
UP
WIC
6'2" x 7'2"
MASTER BATH
8'10" x 10'4"
LN
CL
MASTER BEDROOM
13'2" x 13'8"
PORCH
FIRST FLOOR

Design 63086

Units	Single
Price Code	C
Total Finished	1,768 sq. ft.
Main Finished	1,768 sq. ft.
Garage Unfinished	338 sq. ft.
Dimensions	40'x60'
Foundation	Slab
Bedrooms	3
Full Baths	2
Max Ridge Height	21'4"
Roof Framing	Truss
Exterior Walls	2x4

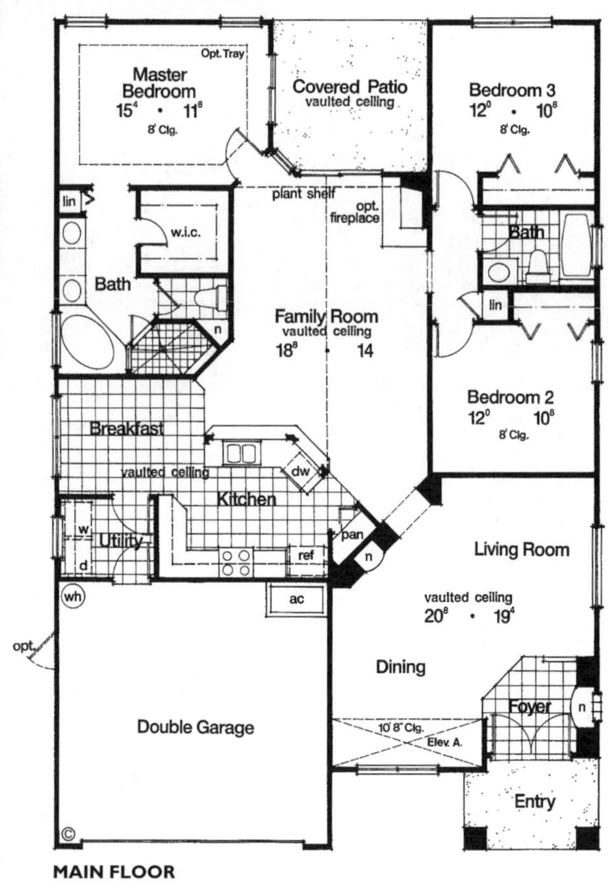
Master Bedroom
15^{4} • 11^{8}
8' Clg.
Opt. Tray
Covered Patio
vaulted ceiling
Bedroom 3
12^{0} • 10^{8}
8' Clg.
plant shelf
opt. fireplace
lin
w.i.c.
Bath
Family Room
vaulted ceiling
18^{8} 14
n
Bath
lin
Bedroom 2
12^{0} 10^{8}
8' Clg.
Breakfast
vaulted ceiling
dw
Kitchen
w
Utility
d
pan
n
ref
wh
ac
Living Room
vaulted ceiling
20^{8} • 19^{4}
opt.
Dining
Foyer
n
Double Garage
10'8" Clg.
Elev. A.
Entry
©

MAIN FLOOR

Design 94907

PHOTOGRAPHY: COURTESY OF THE DESIGNER

Please note: The photographed home may have been modified to suit homeowner preferences. If you order plans, have a builder or design professional check them against the photograph to confirm actual construction details.

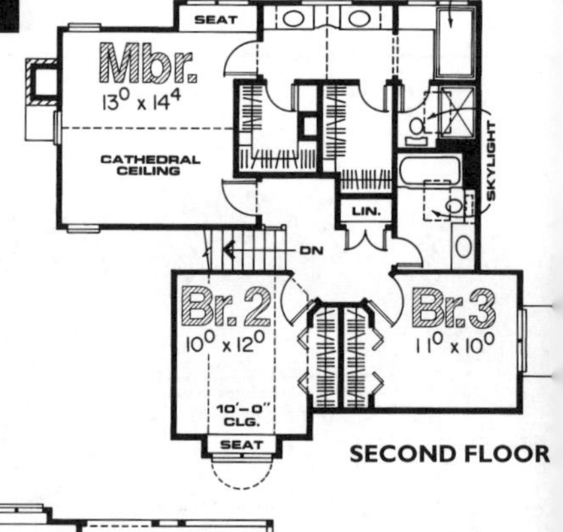
SEAT
WHIRLPOOL
Mbr.
13^{0} x 14^{4}
CATHEDRAL CEILING
SKYLIGHT
LIN.
DN
Br. 2
10^{0} x 12^{0}
Br. 3
11^{0} x 10^{0}
10'-0" CLG.
SEAT

SECOND FLOOR

Units	Single
Price Code	C
Total Finished	1,768 sq. ft.
First Finished	905 sq. ft.
Second Finished	863 sq. ft.
Basement Unfinished	905 sq. ft.
Garage Unfinished	487 sq. ft.
Dimensions	40'8"x46'
Foundation	Basement
Bedrooms	3
Full Baths	2
Half Baths	1
First Ceiling	8'
Max Ridge Height	30'6"
Roof Framing	Stick
Exterior Walls	2x4

* Alternate foundation options available at an additional charge. Please call 1-800-235-5700 for more information.

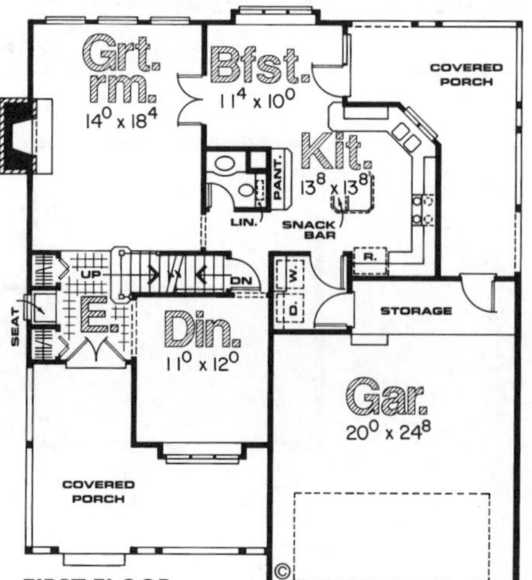
Grt. rm.
14^{0} x 18^{4}
Bfst.
11^{4} x 10^{0}
COVERED PORCH
Kit.
13^{8} x 13^{8}
PANT.
LIN.
SNACK BAR
R.
UP
DN
W.
D.
STORAGE
SEAT
E.
Din.
11^{0} x 12^{0}
Gar.
20^{0} x 24^{8}
COVERED PORCH
©

FIRST FLOOR

Design 65664

Units	Single
Price Code	C
Total Finished	1,770 sq. ft.
Main Finished	1,770 sq. ft.
Dimensions	64'x48'
Foundation	Crawlspace Slab
Bedrooms	3
Full Baths	2
Main Ceiling	8'-12'
Max Ridge Height	29'
Roof Framing	Stick
Exterior Walls	2x6

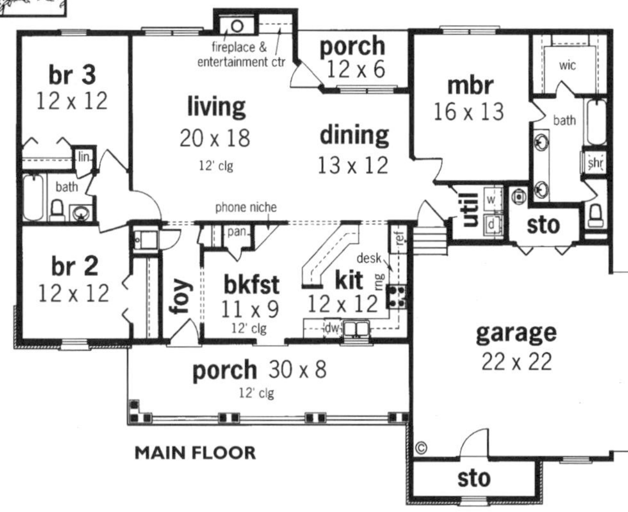
br 3
12 x 12
fireplace & entertainment ctr
porch
12 x 6
living
20 x 18
12' clg
dining
13 x 12
mbr
16 x 13
wic
bath
shr
lin
bath
phone niche
pan.
util
w
d
sto
br 2
12 x 12
foy
bkfst
11 x 9
12' clg
desk
kit
12 x 12
ref
dw
garage
22 x 22
porch 30 x 8
12' clg
sto

MAIN FLOOR

Design 69028

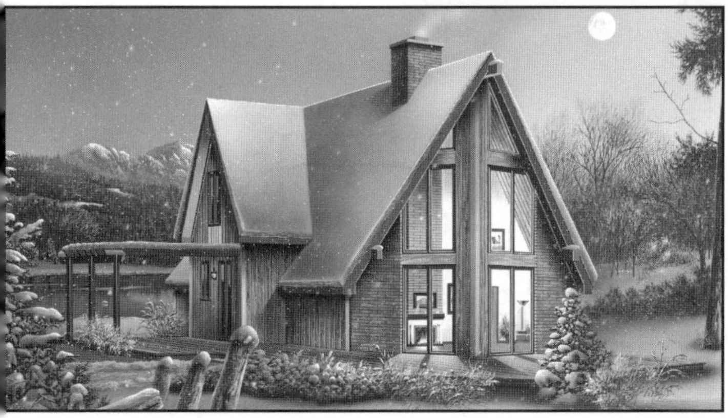

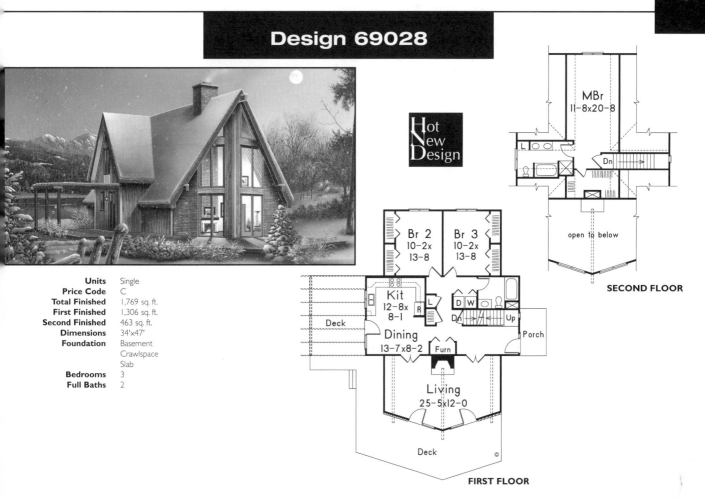

Hot New Design

Units	Single
Price Code	C
Total Finished	1,769 sq. ft.
First Finished	1,306 sq. ft.
Second Finished	463 sq. ft.
Dimensions	34'x47'
Foundation	Basement Crawlspace Slab
Bedrooms	3
Full Baths	2

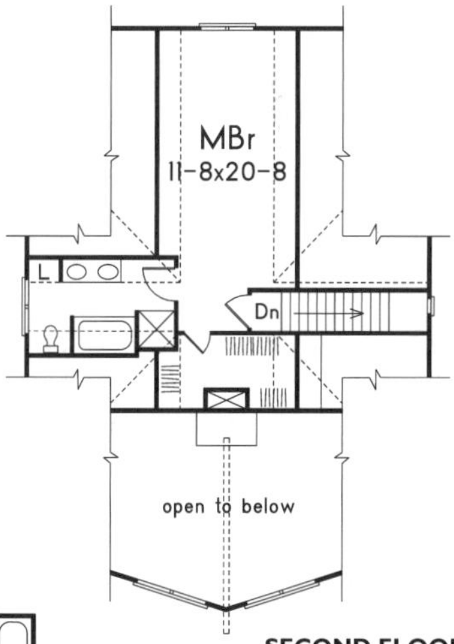

SECOND FLOOR

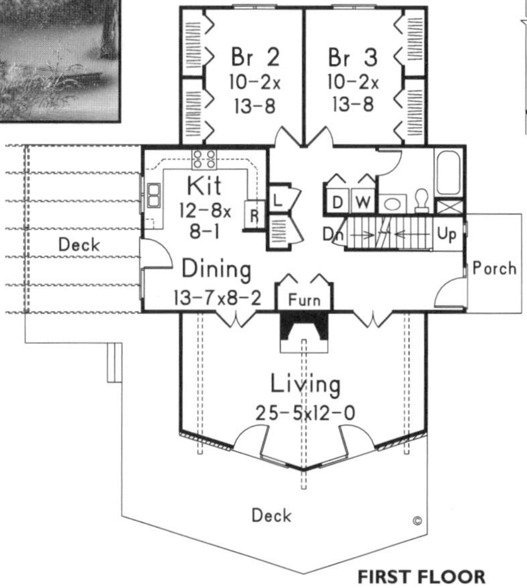

FIRST FLOOR

Design 24714

Crawl Space Access

OPTIONAL CRAWLSPACE/SLAB FOUNDATION

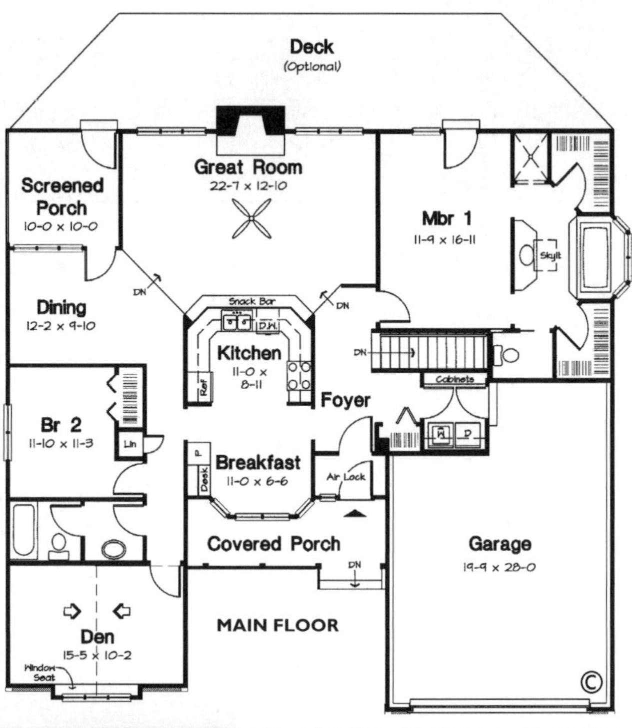
Deck
(Optional)
Screened Porch
10-0 x 10-0
Great Room
22-7 x 12-10
Mbr 1
11-9 x 16-11
Skylt
Dining
12-2 x 9-10
DN
Snack Bar
Kitchen
11-0 x 8-11
Ref
Foyer
Cabinets
Br 2
11-10 x 11-3
Lin
Breakfast
11-0 x 6-6
Deck
Air Lock
Covered Porch
Garage
19-9 x 28-0
Den
15-5 x 10-2
Window Seat
MAIN FLOOR

Units Single
Price Code C
Total Finished 1,771 sq. ft.
Main Finished 1,771 sq. ft.
Basement Unfinished 1,194 sq. ft.
Garage Unfinished 517 sq. ft.
Porch Unfinished 106 sq. ft.
Dimensions 54'x50'
Foundation Crawlspace
Slab
Bedrooms 2
Full Baths 2
Main Ceiling 8'
Vaulted Ceiling 13'6"
Max Ridge Height 23'6"
Roof Framing Stick
Exterior Walls 2x4

Design 63087

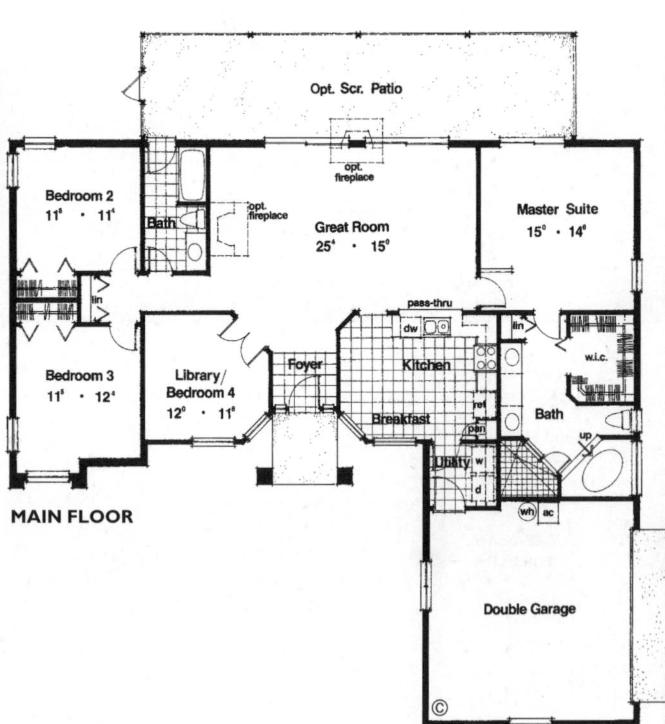
Opt. Scr. Patio
opt. fireplace
Bedroom 2
11⁰ · 11⁴
Bath
Great Room
25⁴ · 15⁰
Master Suite
15⁰ · 14⁸
lin
pass-thru
Bedroom 3
11⁸ · 12⁴
Library/ Bedroom 4
12⁰ · 11⁶
Foyer
Kitchen
w.i.c.
Breakfast
Bath
Utility
wh
ac
Double Garage
MAIN FLOOR

Units Single
Price Code C
Total Finished 1,771 sq. ft.
Main Finished 1,771 sq. ft.
Garage Unfinished 394 sq. ft.
Dimensions 60'x54'4"
Foundation Slab
Bedrooms 4
Full Baths 2
Max Ridge Height 18'2"
Roof Framing Truss

Design 10394

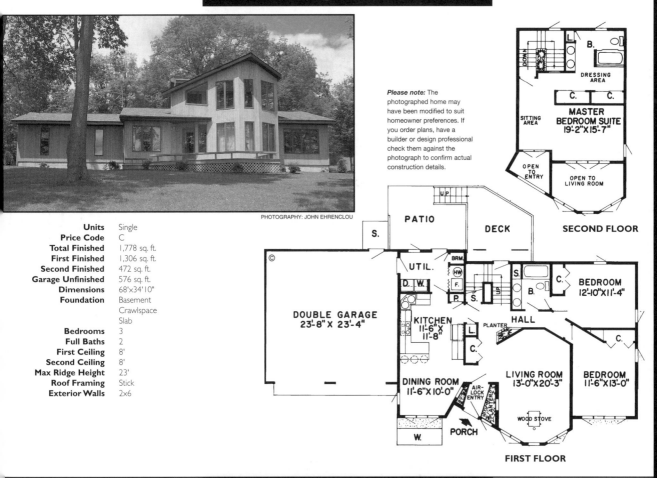

PHOTOGRAPHY: JOHN EHRENCLOU

Please note: The photographed home may have been modified to suit homeowner preferences. If you order plans, have a builder or design professional check them against the photograph to confirm actual construction details.

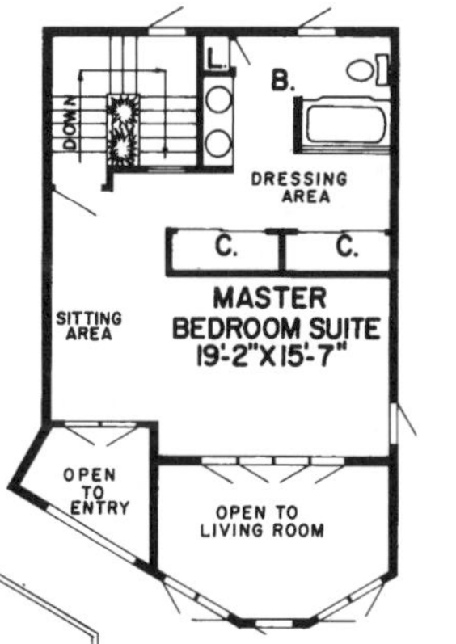

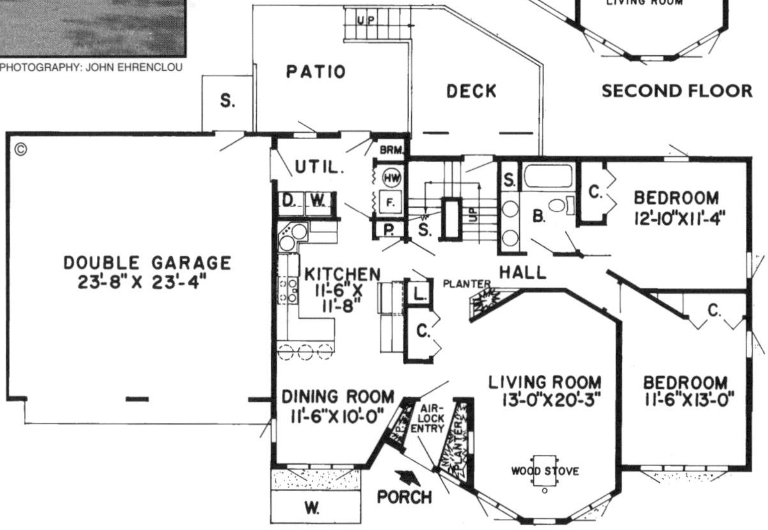

Units	Single
Price Code	C
Total Finished	1,778 sq. ft.
First Finished	1,306 sq. ft.
Second Finished	472 sq. ft.
Garage Unfinished	576 sq. ft.
Dimensions	68'x34'10"
Foundation	Basement Crawlspace Slab
Bedrooms	3
Full Baths	2
First Ceiling	8'
Second Ceiling	8'
Max Ridge Height	23'
Roof Framing	Stick
Exterior Walls	2x6

SECOND FLOOR

FIRST FLOOR

Design 93261

Units	Single
Price Code	C
Total Finished	1,778 sq. ft.
Main Finished	1,778 sq. ft.
Basement Unfinished	1,008 sq. ft.
Garage Unfinished	728 sq. ft.
Dimensions	62'x28'
Foundation	Basement
Bedrooms	3
Full Baths	2
Main Ceiling	8'
Vaulted Ceiling	10'4"
Max Ridge Height	26'
Roof Framing	Stick/Truss
Exterior Walls	2x4

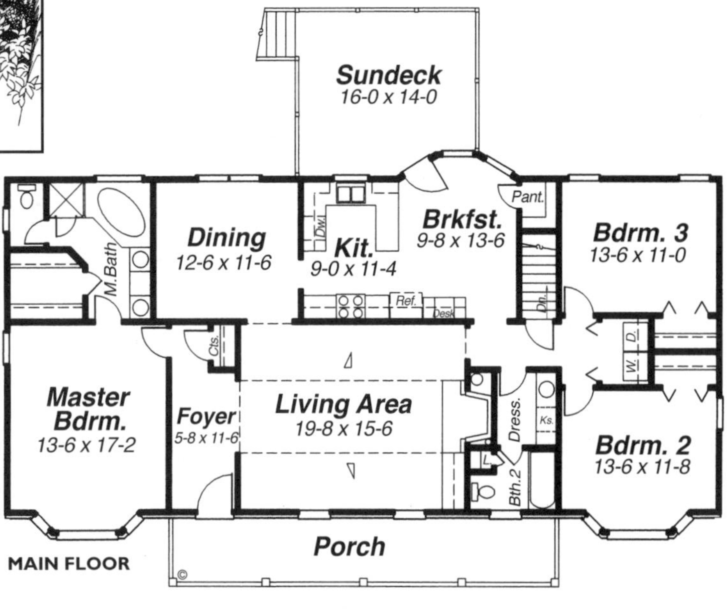

MAIN FLOOR

Design 98464

CAD FILES AVAILABLE For more information call 800-235-5700

Units	Single
Price Code	C
Total Finished	1,779 sq. ft.
Main Finished	1,779 sq. ft.
Basement Unfinished	1,818 sq. ft.
Garage Unfinished	499 sq. ft.
Dimensions	57'x56'4"
Foundation	Basement Crawlspace
Bedrooms	3
Full Baths	2
Main Ceiling	9'
Max Ridge Height	24'6"
Roof Framing	Stick
Exterior Walls	2x4

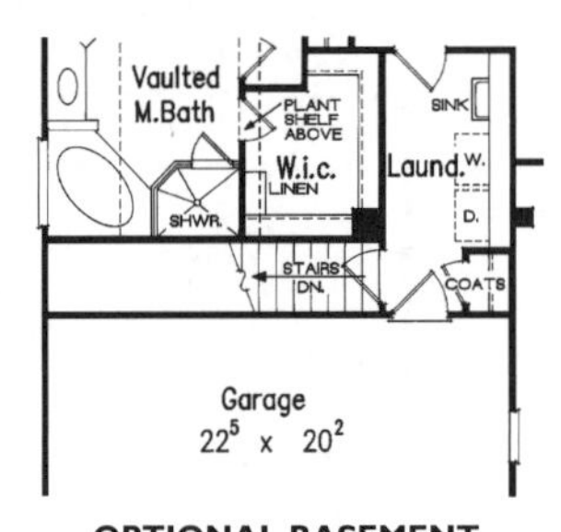
Vaulted M.Bath
PLANT SHELF ABOVE
W.i.c.
LINEN
SHWR.
Laund.
SINK
W.
D.
STAIRS DN.
COATS
Garage
22⁵ x 20²

OPTIONAL BASEMENT STAIR LOCATION

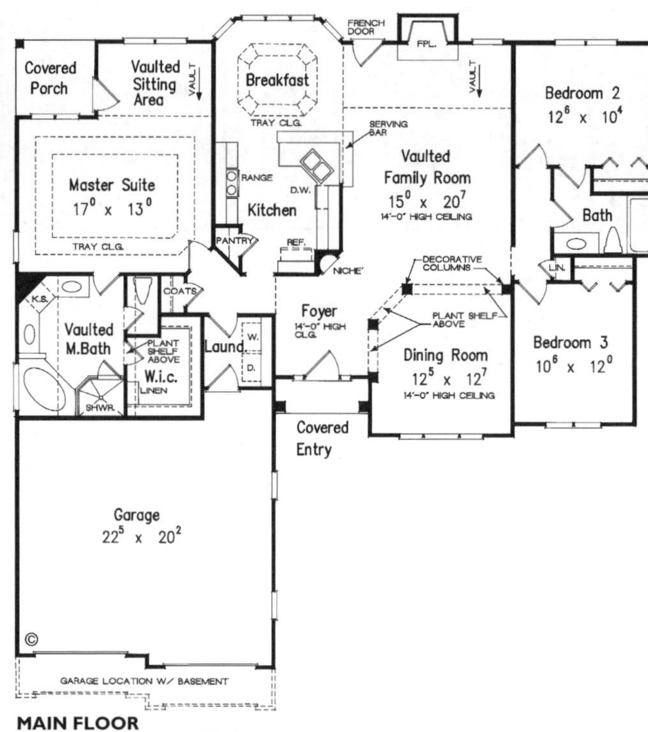
Covered Porch
Vaulted Sitting Area
VAULT
Breakfast
TRAY CLG.
FRENCH DOOR
FPL.
VAULT
SERVING BAR
Bedroom 2
12⁶ x 10⁴
Master Suite
17⁰ x 13⁰
TRAY CLG.
RANGE
D.W.
Kitchen
PANTRY
REF.
NICHE
Vaulted Family Room
15⁰ x 20⁷
14'-0" HIGH CEILING
Bath
LIN.
K.S.
Vaulted M.Bath
SHWR.
COATS
PLANT SHELF ABOVE
W.i.c.
LINEN
Laund.
W.
D.
Foyer
14'-0" HIGH CLG.
DECORATIVE COLUMNS
PLANT SHELF ABOVE
Dining Room
12⁵ x 12⁷
14'-0" HIGH CEILING
Bedroom 3
10⁶ x 12⁰
Covered Entry
Garage
22⁵ x 20²
©
GARAGE LOCATION W/ BASEMENT

MAIN FLOOR

Design 91466

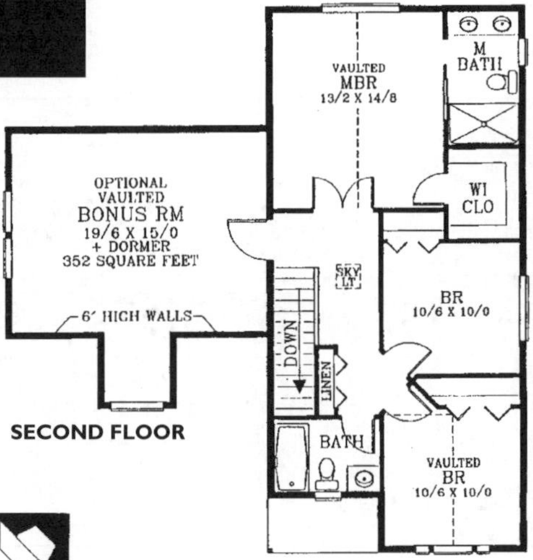

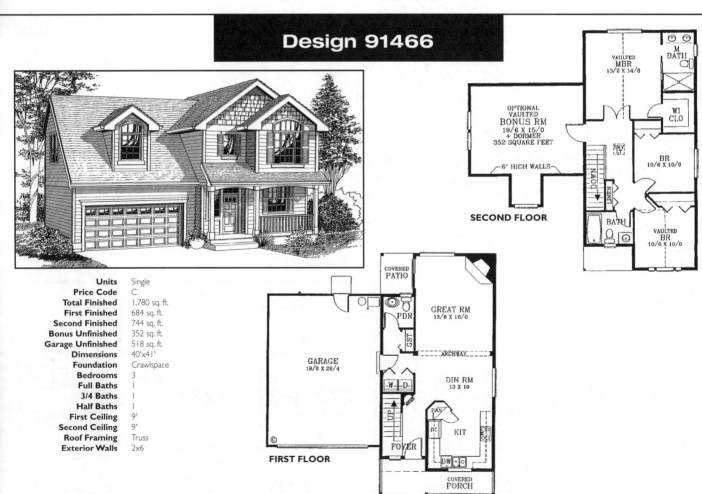

Units	Single
Price Code	C
Total Finished	1,780 sq. ft.
First Finished	684 sq. ft.
Second Finished	744 sq. ft.
Bonus Unfinished	352 sq. ft.
Garage Unfinished	518 sq. ft.
Dimensions	40'x41'
Foundation	Crawlspace
Bedrooms	3
Full Baths	1
3/4 Baths	1
Half Baths	1
First Ceiling	9'
Second Ceiling	9'
Roof Framing	Truss
Exterior Walls	2x6

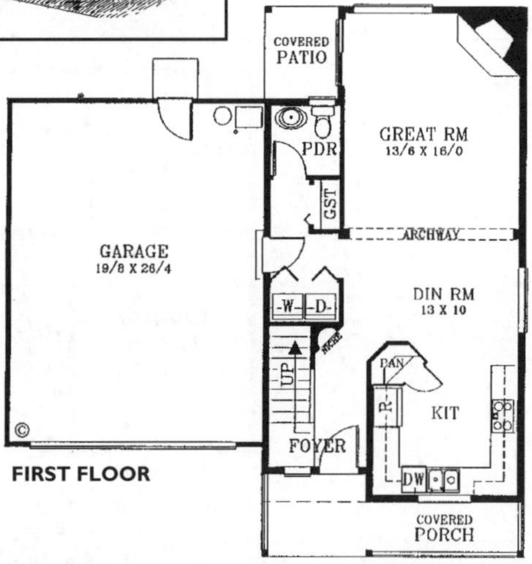

OPTIONAL VAULTED BONUS RM 19/6 X 15/0 + DORMER 352 SQUARE FEET
6' HIGH WALLS
VAULTED MBR 13/2 X 14/8
M BATH
WI CLO
SKY LT
BR 10/6 X 10/0
DOWN
LINEN
BATH
VAULTED BR 10/6 X 10/0

SECOND FLOOR

COVERED PATIO
PDR
GST
GREAT RM 13/6 X 16/0
ARCHWAY
GARAGE 19/8 X 26/4
W
D
DIN RM 13 X 10
UP
PAN
R
KIT
DW
FOYER
COVERED PORCH
©

FIRST FLOOR

Design 63111

Units	Single
Price Code	C
Total Finished	1,782 sq. ft.
Main Finished	1,782 sq. ft.
Bonus Unfinished	262 sq. ft.
Garage Unfinished	394 sq. ft.
Dimensions	40'x61'
Foundation	Slab
Bedrooms	3
Full Baths	2
Main Ceiling	8'
Max Ridge Height	20'4"
Roof Framing	Truss

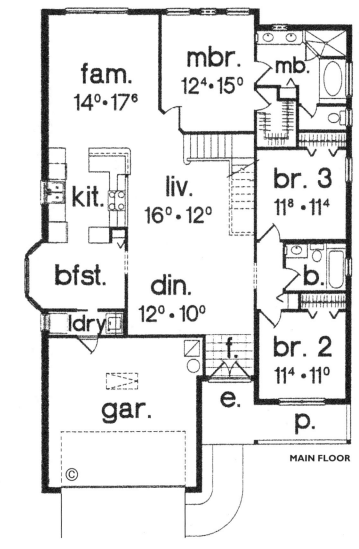

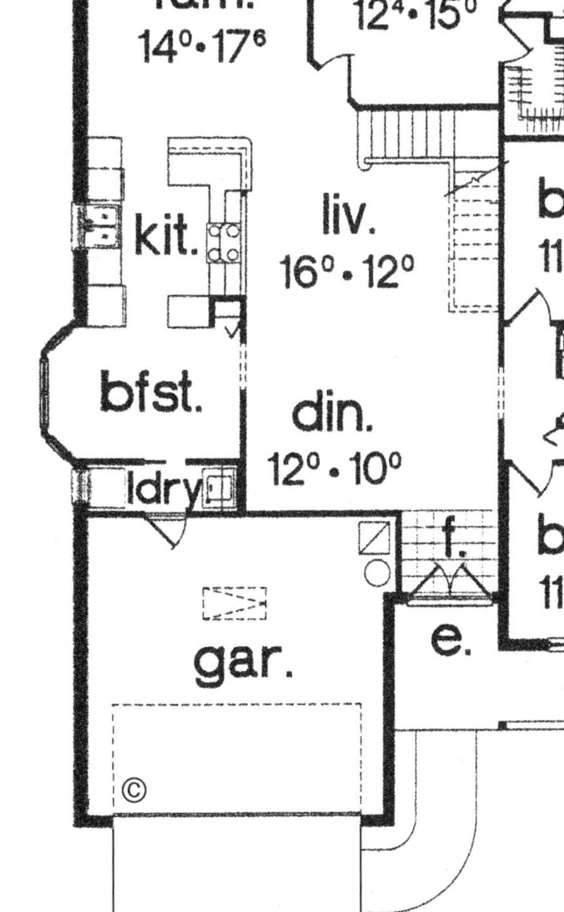
fam.
14⁰•17⁶
mbr.
12⁴•15⁰
mb.
kit.
liv.
16⁰•12⁰
br. 3
11⁸•11⁴
bfst.
din.
12⁰•10⁰
b.
ldry
f.
br. 2
11⁴•11⁰
e.
gar.
p.

MAIN FLOOR

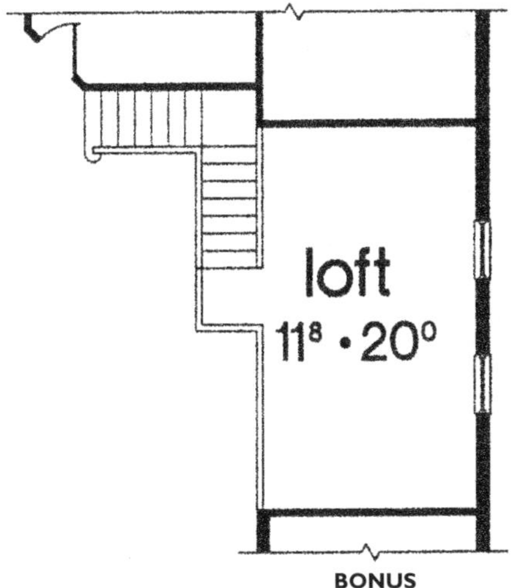
loft
11⁸•20⁰

BONUS

Design 92630

PHOTOGRAPHY: DONNA AND RON KOLB, EXPOSURES UNLIMITED

Units	Single
Price Code	C
Total Finished	1,782 sq. ft.
Main Finished	1,782 sq. ft.
Basement Unfinished	1,735 sq. ft.
Garage Unfinished	407 sq. ft.
Dimensions	67'2"x47'
Foundation	Basement
Bedrooms	3
Full Baths	2
Max Ridge Height	20'
Roof Framing	Truss
Exterior Walls	2x4

Please note: The photographed home may have been modified to suit homeowner preferences. If you order plans, have a builder or design professional check them against the photograph to confirm actual construction details.

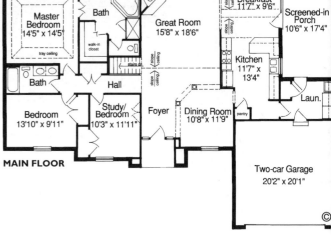

Master Bedroom 14'5" x 14'5"
tray ceiling
Bath
walk-in closet
Great Room 15'8" x 18'6"
Breakfast 11'7" x 9'6"
Screened-in Porch 10'6" x 17'4"
Kitchen 11'7" x 13'4"
Bath
Hall
stairs dn
Laun.
Bedroom 13'10" x 9'11"
Study/ Bedroom 10'3" x 11'11"
Foyer
Dining Room 10'8" x 11'9"
pantry
Two-car Garage 20'2" x 20'1"
MAIN FLOOR
©

Design 94917

Units	Single
Price Code	C
Total Finished	1,782 sq. ft.
Main Finished	1,782 sq. ft.
Basement Unfinished	1,782 sq. ft.
Garage Unfinished	466 sq. ft.
Dimensions	52'x59'4"
Foundation	Basement Slab
Bedrooms	3
Full Baths	2
Max Ridge Height	21'
Roof Framing	Stick
Exterior Walls	2x4

* Alternate foundation options available at an additional charge. Please call 1-800-235-5700 for more information.

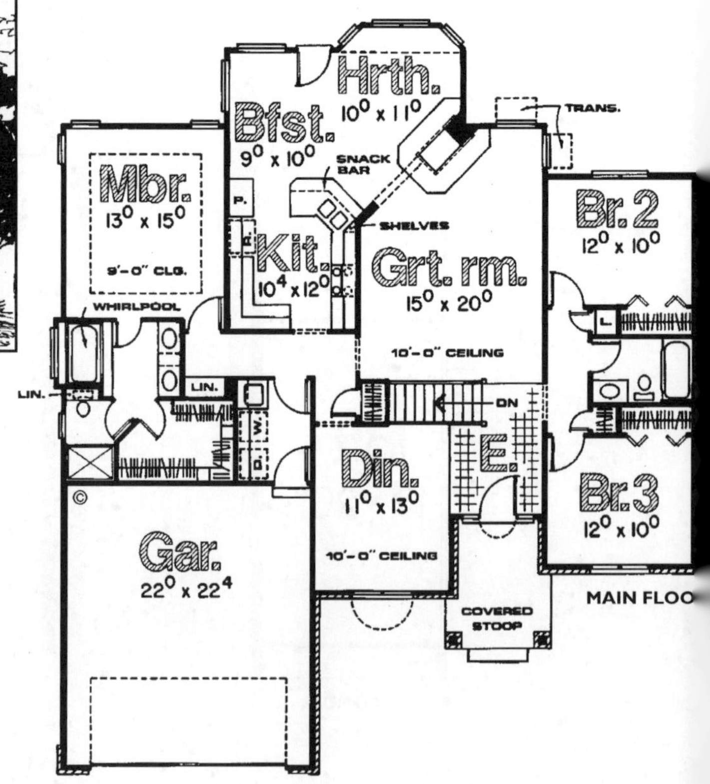
Hrth. 10⁰ x 11⁰
Bfst. 9⁰ x 10⁰
TRANS.
SNACK BAR
Mbr. 13⁰ x 15⁰
9'-0" CLG.
P.
SHELVES
Br. 2 12⁰ x 10⁰
Kit. 10⁴ x 12⁰
Grt. rm. 15⁰ x 20⁰
WHIRLPOOL
10'-0" CEILING
LIN.
LIN.
DN
W.
D.
E.
Din. 11⁰ x 13⁰
Br. 3 12⁰ x 10⁰
©
Gar. 22⁰ x 22⁴
10'-0" CEILING
COVERED STOOP
MAIN FLOO

Design 10274

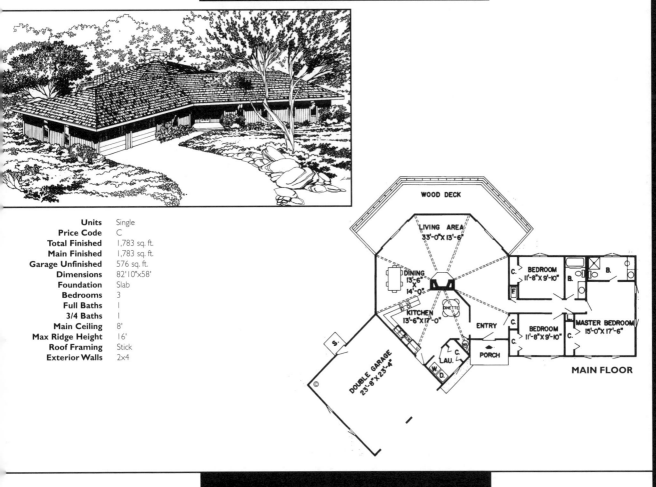

Units	Single
Price Code	C
Total Finished	1,783 sq. ft.
Main Finished	1,783 sq. ft.
Garage Unfinished	576 sq. ft.
Dimensions	82'10"x58'
Foundation	Slab
Bedrooms	3
Full Baths	1
3/4 Baths	1
Main Ceiling	8'
Max Ridge Height	16'
Roof Framing	Stick
Exterior Walls	2x4

WOOD DECK
LIVING AREA 33'-0"X 13'-6"
DINING 13'-6" X 14'-0"
KITCHEN 13'-6"X 17'-0"
DINETTE
BEDROOM 11'-8"X 9'-10"
BEDROOM 11'-8"X 9'-10"
MASTER BEDROOM 15'-0"X 17'-6"
ENTRY
PORCH
LAU.
DOUBLE GARAGE 23'-8"X 23'-4"

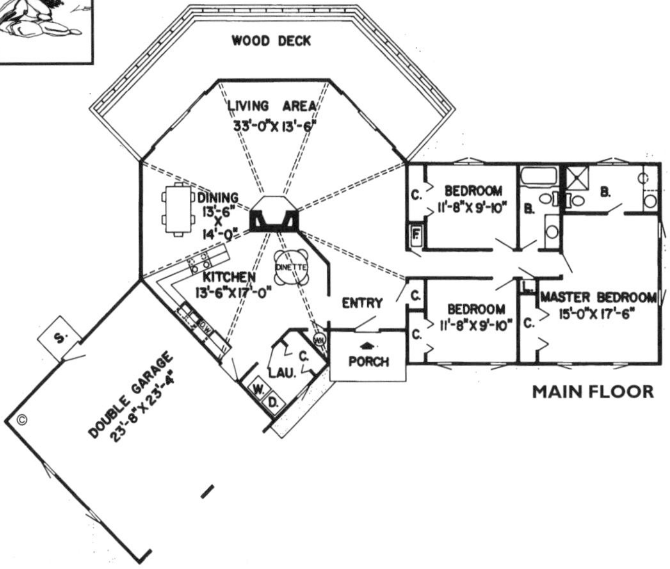

MAIN FLOOR

Design 34800

Units	Single
Price Code	C
Total Finished	1,784 sq. ft.
First Finished	1,187 sq. ft.
Second Finished	597 sq. ft.
Basement Unfinished	1,169 sq. ft.
Garage Unfinished	484 sq. ft.
Dimensions	46'x46'4"
Foundation	Basement Crawlspace Slab
Bedrooms	3
Full Baths	2
Half Baths	1
Max Ridge Height	24'
Roof Framing	Stick
Exterior Walls	2x4

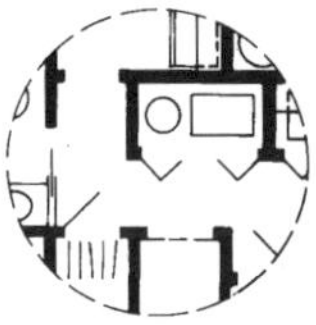

OPTIONAL CRAWLSPACE/ SLAB FOUNDATION

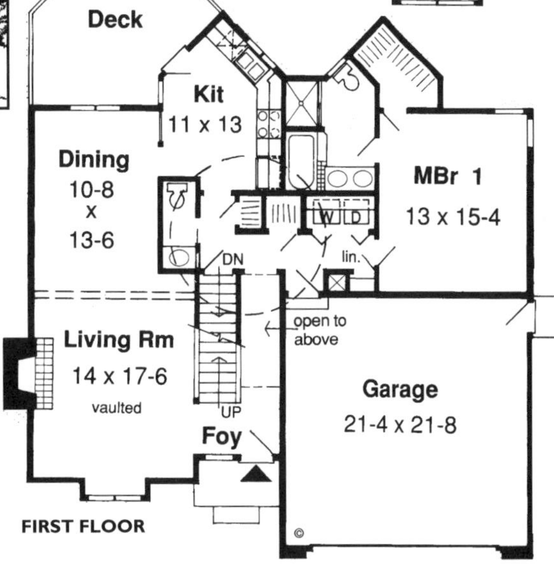

Br 2 11 x 13-4
Br 3 11 x 15-4
skylight
linen
DN
open to below

SECOND FLOOR

Deck
Kit 11 x 13
Dining 10-8 x 13-6
MBr 1 13 x 15-4
Living Rm 14 x 17-6 vaulted
open to above
Garage 21-4 x 21-8
Foy

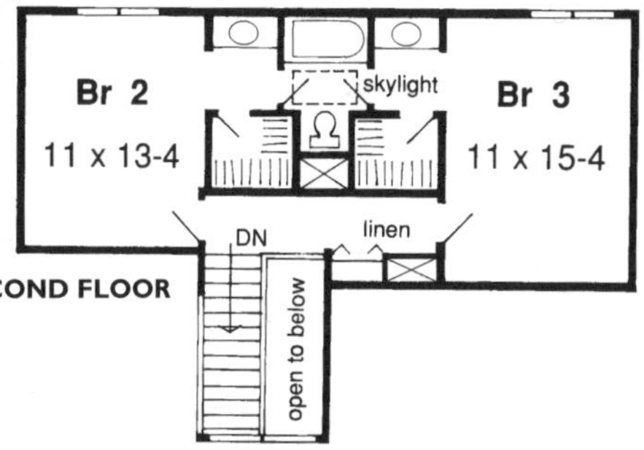

FIRST FLOOR

Design 24610

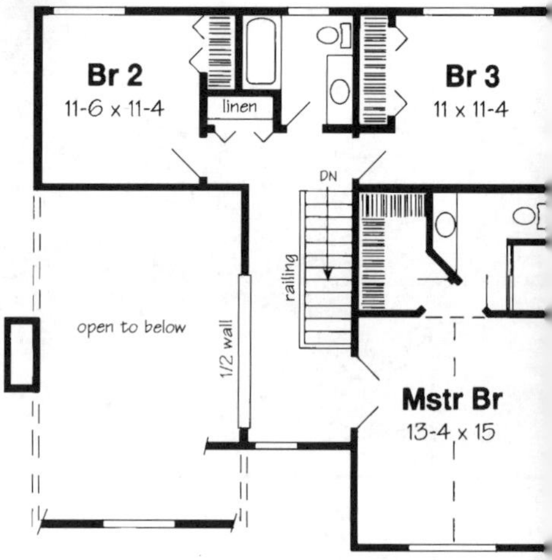

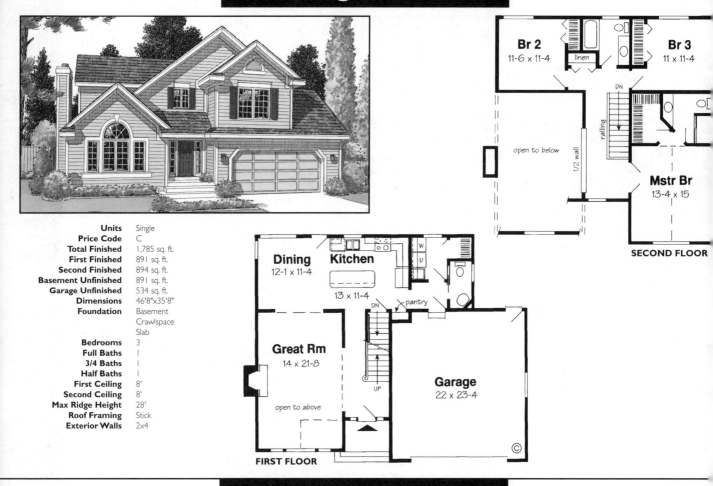

Br 2
11-6 x 11-4
linen
Br 3
11 x 11-4
DN
railing
open to below
1/2 wall
Mstr Br
13-4 x 15
SECOND FLOOR

Units	Single
Price Code	C
Total Finished	1,785 sq. ft.
First Finished	891 sq. ft.
Second Finished	894 sq. ft.
Basement Unfinished	891 sq. ft.
Garage Unfinished	534 sq. ft.
Dimensions	46'8"x35'8"
Foundation	Basement Crawlspace Slab
Bedrooms	3
Full Baths	1
3/4 Baths	1
Half Baths	1
First Ceiling	8'
Second Ceiling	8'
Max Ridge Height	28'
Roof Framing	Stick
Exterior Walls	2x4

Dining
12-1 x 11-4
Kitchen
13 x 11-4
W
D
pantry
DN
Great Rm
14 x 21-8
open to above
UP
Garage
22 x 23-4
©
FIRST FLOOR

Design 64500

Units	Single
Price Code	C
Total Finished	1,785 sq. ft.
Main Finished	1,785 sq. ft.
Basement Unfinished	1,785 sq. ft.
Garage Unfinished	528 sq. ft.
Porch Unfinished	334 sq. ft.
Dimensions	56'x32'
Foundation	Basement Crawlspace Slab
Bedrooms	3
Full Baths	2
3/4 Baths	1
Main Ceiling	9'
Max Ridge Height	24'
Roof Framing	Stick
Exterior Walls	2x4

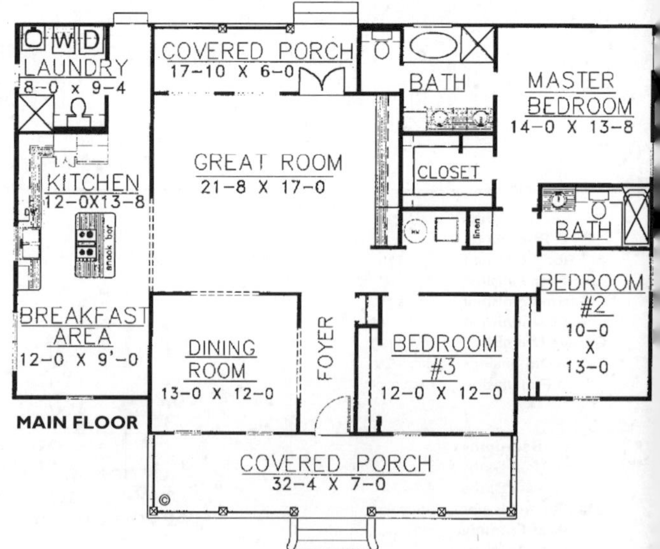
W D
LAUNDRY
8-0 x 9-4
COVERED PORCH
17-10 X 6-0
BATH
MASTER
BEDROOM
14-0 X 13-8
GREAT ROOM
21-8 X 17-0
CLOSET
KITCHEN
12-0X13-8
snack bar
linen
BATH
BEDROOM
#2
10-0
X
13-0
BREAKFAST
AREA
12-0 X 9'-0
DINING
ROOM
13-0 X 12-0
FOYER
BEDROOM
#3
12-0 X 12-0
MAIN FLOOR
COVERED PORCH
32-4 X 7-0
©

Design 65464

Units	Single
Price Code	C
Total Finished	1,785 sq. ft.
First Finished	889 sq. ft.
Second Finished	896 sq. ft.
Basement Unfinished	889 sq. ft.
Deck Unfinished	40 sq. ft.
Dimensions	32'x28'
Foundation	Basement
Bedrooms	4
Full Baths	1
3/4 Baths	1
First Ceiling	8'
Second Ceiling	8'
Max Ridge Height	29'
Roof Framing	Truss
Exterior Walls	2x6

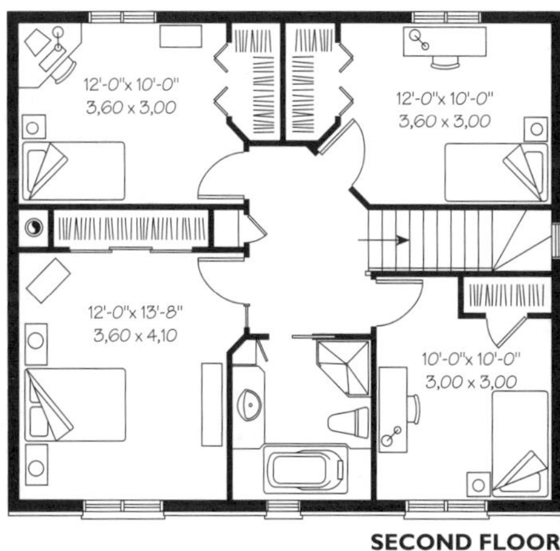
12'-0"x 10'-0"
3,60 x 3,00
12'-0"x 10'-0"
3,60 x 3,00
12'-0"x 13'-8"
3,60 x 4,10
10'-0"x 10'-0"
3,00 x 3,00

SECOND FLOOR

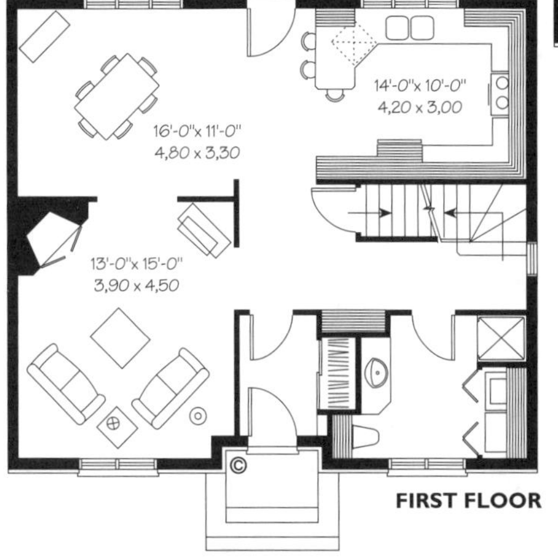
16'-0"x 11'-0"
4,80 x 3,30
14'-0"x 10'-0"
4,20 x 3,00
13'-0"x 15'-0"
3,90 x 4,50

FIRST FLOOR

Design 93166

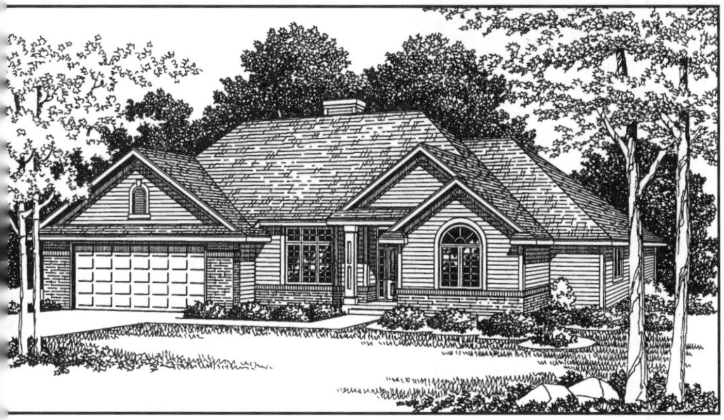

Units	Single
Price Code	C
Total Finished	1,785 sq. ft.
Main Finished	1,785 sq. ft.
Basement Unfinished	1,785 sq. ft.
Dimensions	63'x46'
Foundation	Basement
Bedrooms	3
Full Baths	2
Half Baths	1
Max Ridge Height	23'
Roof Framing	Stick
Exterior Walls	2x6

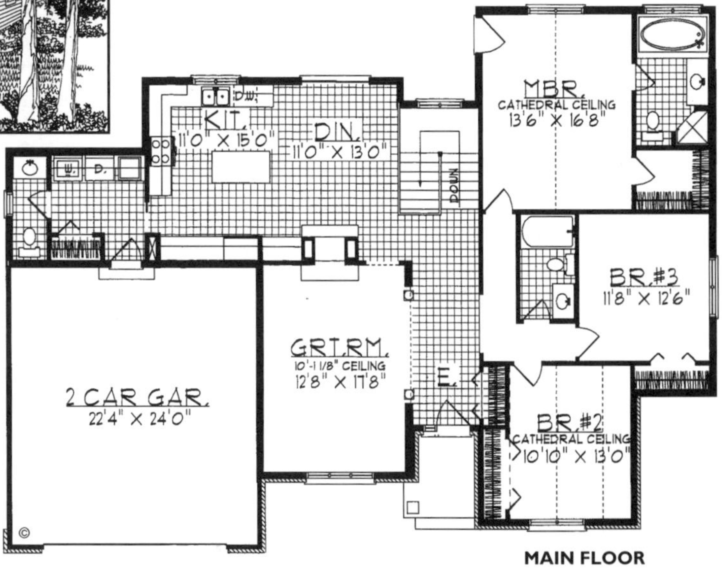

MAIN FLOOR

Design 60020

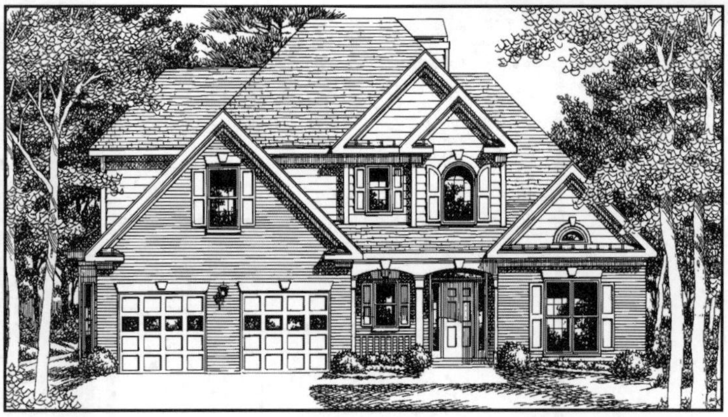

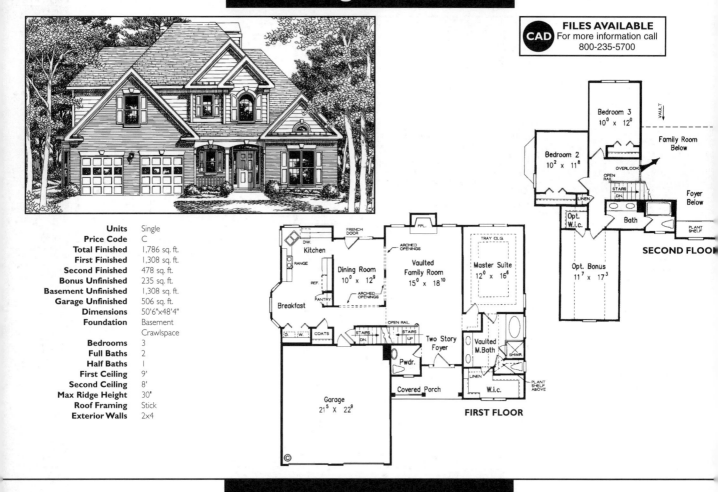

FILES AVAILABLE
CAD For more information call
800-235-5700

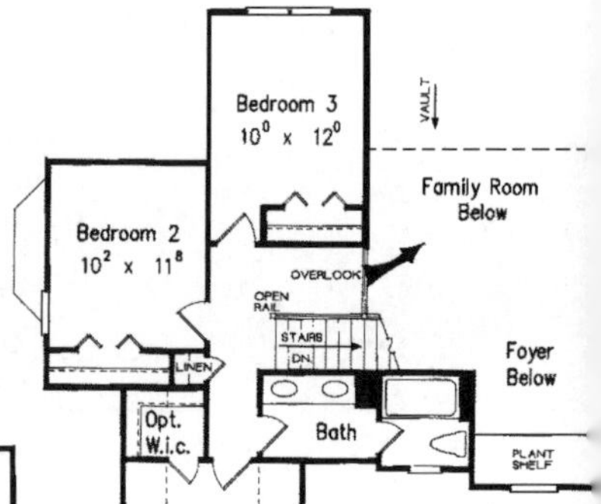

Units	Single
Price Code	C
Total Finished	1,786 sq. ft.
First Finished	1,308 sq. ft.
Second Finished	478 sq. ft.
Bonus Unfinished	235 sq. ft.
Basement Unfinished	1,308 sq. ft.
Garage Unfinished	506 sq. ft.
Dimensions	50'6"x48'4"
Foundation	Basement Crawlspace
Bedrooms	3
Full Baths	2
Half Baths	1
First Ceiling	9'
Second Ceiling	8'
Max Ridge Height	30'
Roof Framing	Stick
Exterior Walls	2x4

Kitchen
Dining Room 10^0 x 12^9
Vaulted Family Room 15^0 x 18^{10}
Master Suite 12^0 x 16^6
Breakfast
Two Story Foyer
Vaulted M.Bath
Pwdr.
W.i.c.
Covered Porch
Garage 21^5 x 22^9

FIRST FLOOR

Bedroom 3 10^0 x 12^0
Bedroom 2 10^2 x 11^8
Family Room Below
Foyer Below
Opt. W.i.c.
Bath
Opt. Bonus 11^7 x 17^3

SECOND FLOOR

Design 92420

Units	Single
Price Code	B
Total Finished	1,787 sq. ft.
Main Finished	1,787 sq. ft.
Bonus Unfinished	263 sq. ft.
Basement Unfinished	1,787 sq. ft.
Dimensions	55'8"x56'6"
Foundation	Basement Crawlspace
Bedrooms	3
Full Baths	2
Main Ceiling	9'
Vaulted Ceiling	11'
Tray Ceiling	11'
Max Ridge Height	21'
Roof Framing	Stick
Exterior Walls	2x4

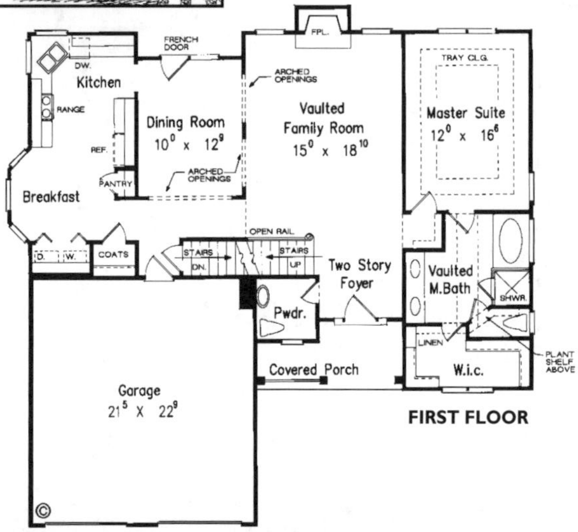

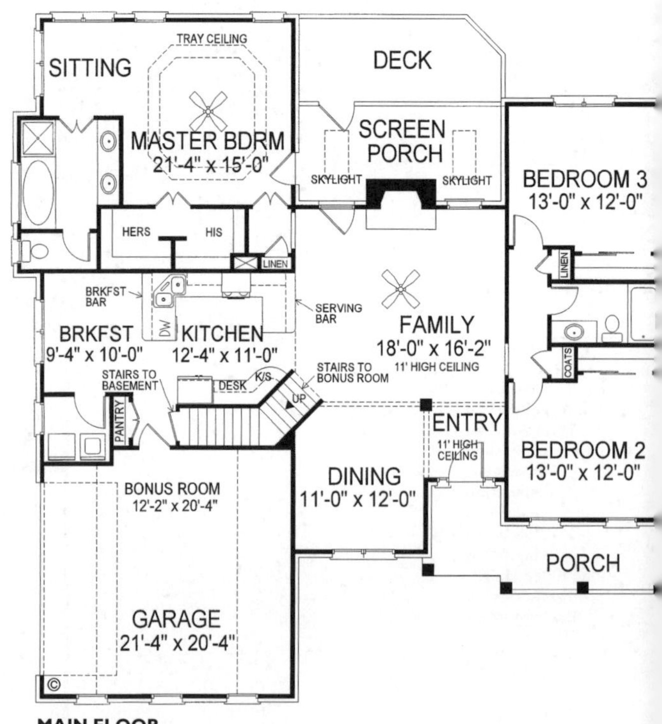
SITTING
TRAY CEILING
MASTER BDRM
21'-4" x 15'-0"
DECK
SCREEN PORCH
SKYLIGHT
SKYLIGHT
BEDROOM 3
13'-0" x 12'-0"
HERS
HIS
LINEN
BRKFST BAR
SERVING BAR
BRKFST
9'-4" x 10'-0"
KITCHEN
12'-4" x 11'-0"
FAMILY
18'-0" x 16'-2"
11' HIGH CEILING
STAIRS TO BASEMENT
DESK
STAIRS TO BONUS ROOM
PANTRY
ENTRY
11' HIGH CEILING
BEDROOM 2
13'-0" x 12'-0"
BONUS ROOM
12'-2" x 20'-4"
DINING
11'-0" x 12'-0"
PORCH
GARAGE
21'-4" x 20'-4"

MAIN FLOOR

Design 69015

Units	Single
Price Code	C
Total Finished	1,787 sq. ft.
Main Finished	1,787 sq. ft.
Dimensions	59'x37'8"
Foundation	Basement
Bedrooms	3
Full Baths	2

Hot
New
Design

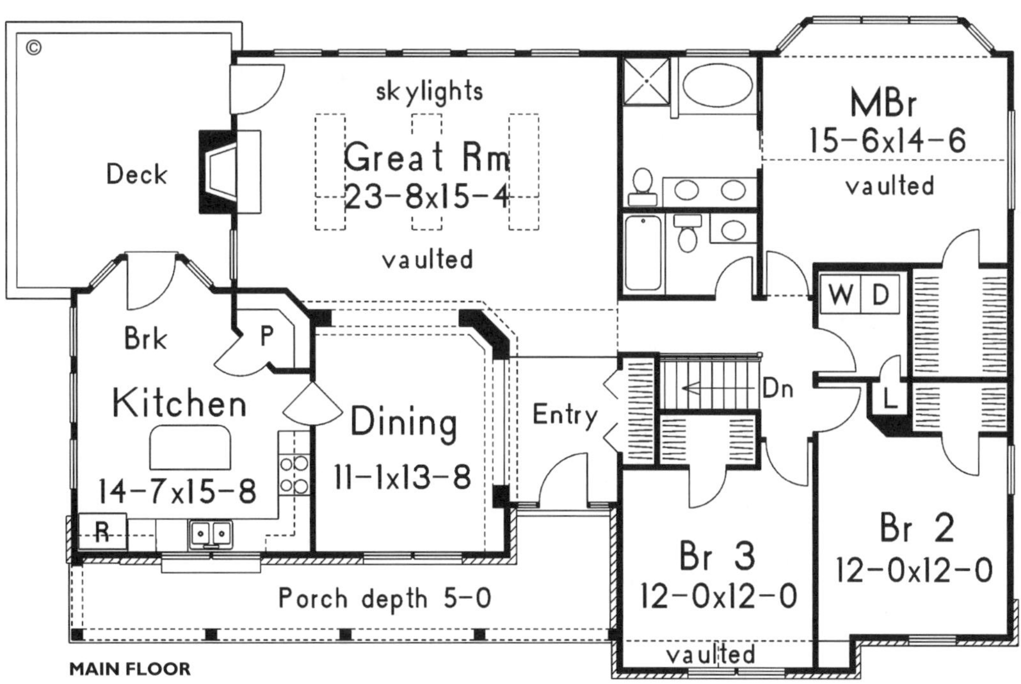
Deck
skylights
Great Rm
23-8x15-4
vaulted
MBr
15-6x14-6
vaulted
W D
Brk
P
Kitchen
14-7x15-8
Dining
11-1x13-8
Entry
Dn
L
R
Br 3
12-0x12-0
Br 2
12-0x12-0
Porch depth 5-0
vaulted

MAIN FLOOR

Design 50025

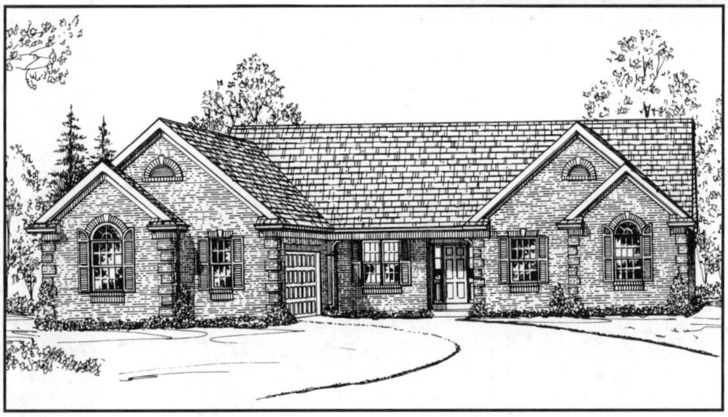

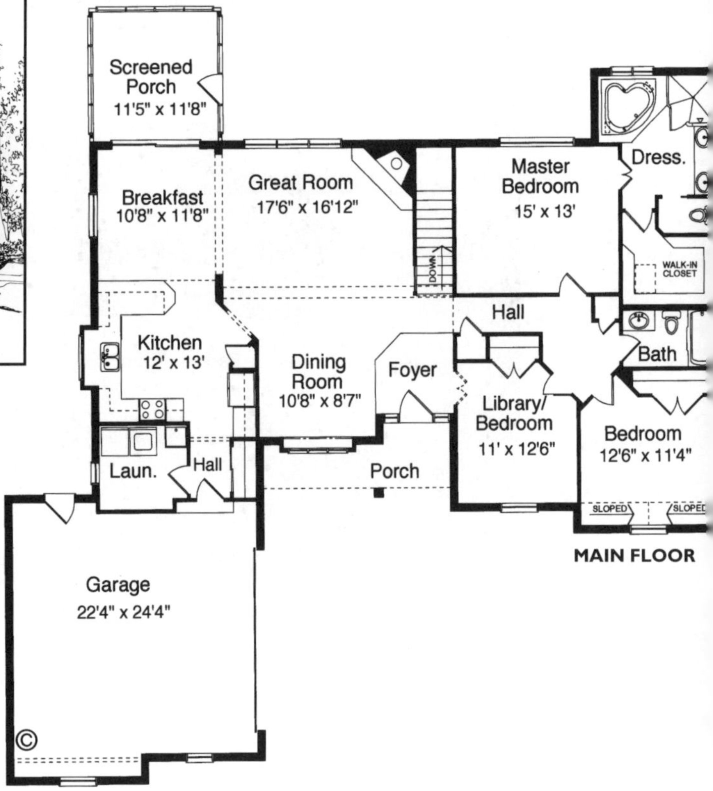

Units	Single
Price Code	C
Total Finished	1,788 sq. ft.
Main Finished	1,788 sq. ft.
Basement Unfinished	1,788 sq. ft.
Garage Unfinished	496 sq. ft.
Porch Unfinished	130 sq. ft.
Dimensions	66'x63'4"
Foundation	Basement
Bedrooms	3
Full Baths	2
Main Ceiling	8'1"
Max Ridge Height	21'
Roof Framing	Truss
Exterior Walls	2x4

Design 69017

Units	Single
Price Code	C
Total Finished	1,791 sq. ft.
Main Finished	1,791 sq. ft.
Dimensions	67'4"x48'4"
Foundation	Basement
Bedrooms	4
Full Baths	2
Main Ceiling	8'
Max Ridge Height	22'
Roof Framing	Truss
Exterior Walls	2x4

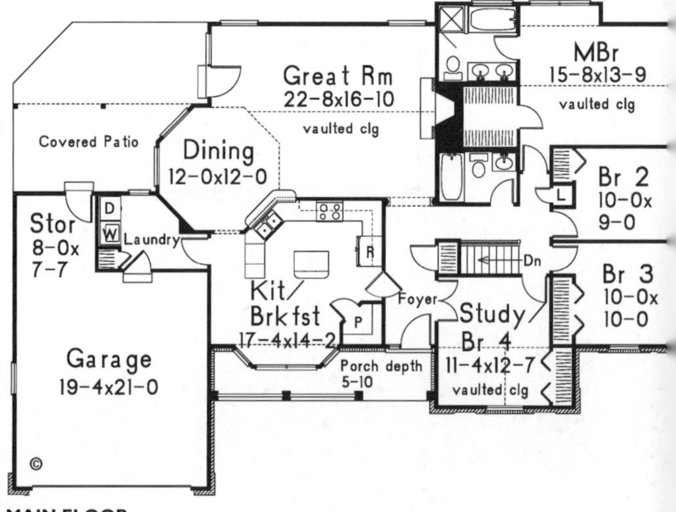
Great Rm
22-8x16-10
vaulted clg
MBr
15-8x13-9
vaulted clg
Covered Patio
Dining
12-0x12-0
Br 2
10-0x
9-0
Stor
8-0x
7-7
Laundry
Dn
Br 3
10-0x
10-0
Kit/
Brkfst
17-4x14-2
Foyer
Study/
Br 4
11-4x12-7
vaulted clg
Porch depth
5-10
Garage
19-4x21-0
MAIN FLOOR

Design 20198

Units	Single
Price Code	C
Total Finished	1,792 sq. ft.
Main Finished	1,792 sq. ft.
Basement Unfinished	818 sq. ft.
Garage Unfinished	857 sq. ft.
Porch Unfinished	336 sq. ft.
Dimensions	56'x32'
Foundation	Basement
Bedrooms	3
Full Baths	2
Main Ceiling	8'
Max Ridge Height	25'
Roof Framing	Stick
Exterior Walls	2x4, 2x6

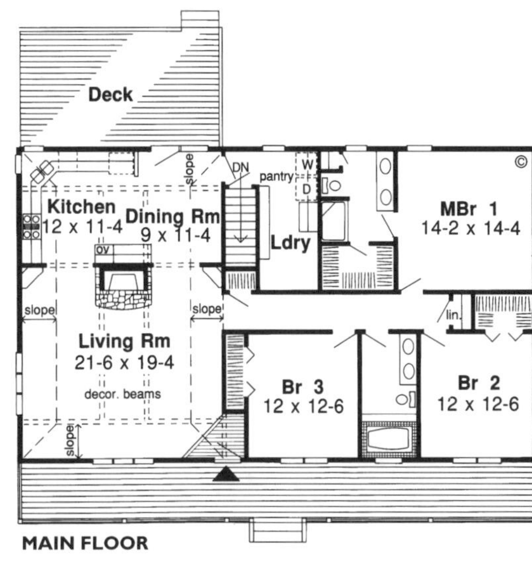
Deck
Kitchen
12 x 11-4
Dining Rm
9 x 11-4
pantry
DN
Ldry
MBr 1
14-2 x 14-4
Living Rm
21-6 x 19-4
decor. beams
slope
lin.
Br 3
12 x 12-6
Br 2
12 x 12-6
MAIN FLOOR

Design 69032

Units	Single
Price Code	C
Total Finished	1,791 sq. ft.
Main Finished	1,791 sq. ft.
Dimensions	67'4"x48'
Foundation	Basement
Bedrooms	4
Full Baths	2

Hot New Design

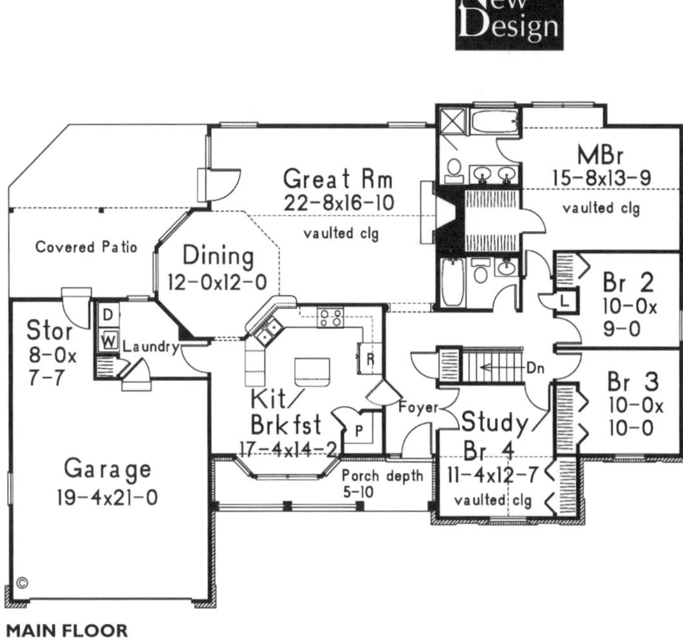
Great Rm
22-8x16-10
vaulted clg
MBr
15-8x13-9
vaulted clg
Covered Patio
Dining
12-0x12-0
Br 2
10-0x
9-0
Stor
8-0x
7-7
Laundry
Dn
Br 3
10-0x
10-0
Kit/
Brkfst
17-4x14-2
Foyer
Study/
Br 4
11-4x12-7
vaulted clg
Porch depth
5-10
Garage
19-4x21-0
MAIN FLOOR

Design 97108

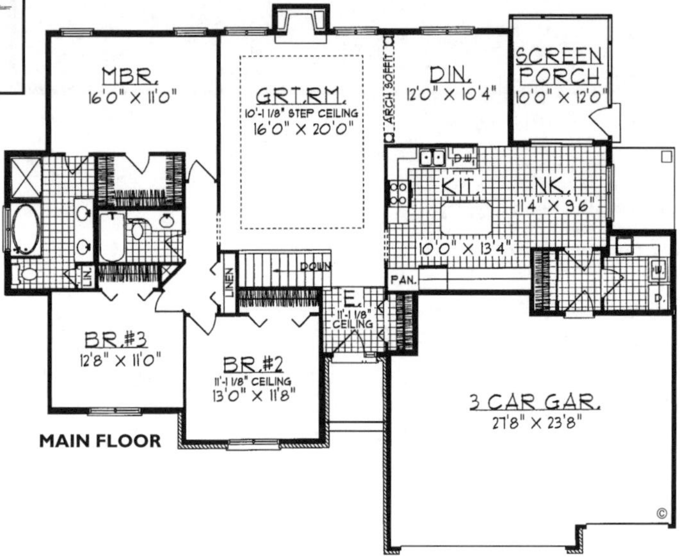

Units	Single
Price Code	C
Total Finished	1,794 sq. ft.
Main Finished	1,794 sq. ft.
Basement Unfinished	1,794 sq. ft.
Dimensions	65'4"x51'4"
Foundation	Basement
Bedrooms	3
Full Baths	2
Max Ridge Height	26'2"
Roof Framing	Truss
Exterior Walls	2x6

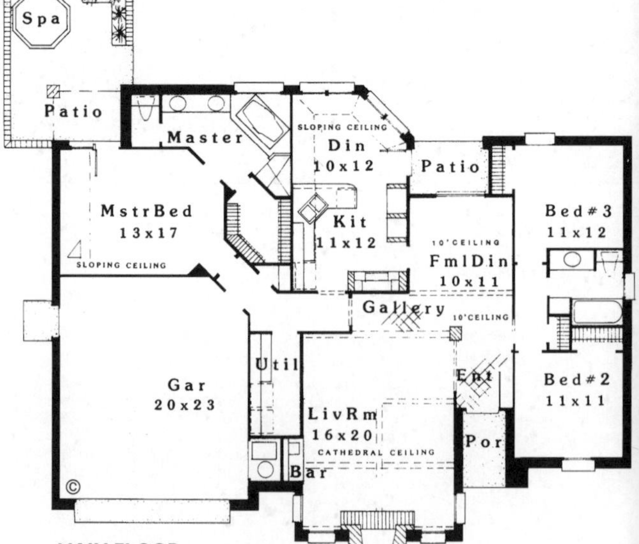

MAIN FLOOR

Design 98561

Units	Single
Price Code	C
Total Finished	1,794 sq. ft.
Main Finished	1,794 sq. ft.
Garage Unfinished	460 sq. ft.
Deck Unfinished	102 sq. ft.
Dimensions	60'x45'4"
Foundation	Crawlspace Slab
Bedrooms	3
Full Baths	2
Main Ceiling	8'-10'
Max Ridge Height	30'6"
Roof Framing	Stick
Exterior Walls	2x4

MAIN FLOOR

Design 93176

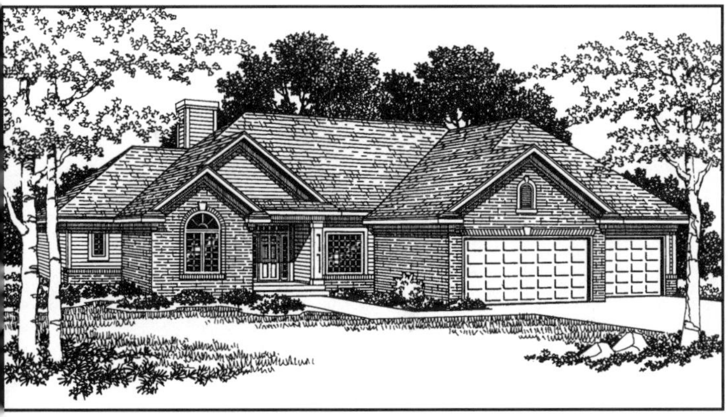

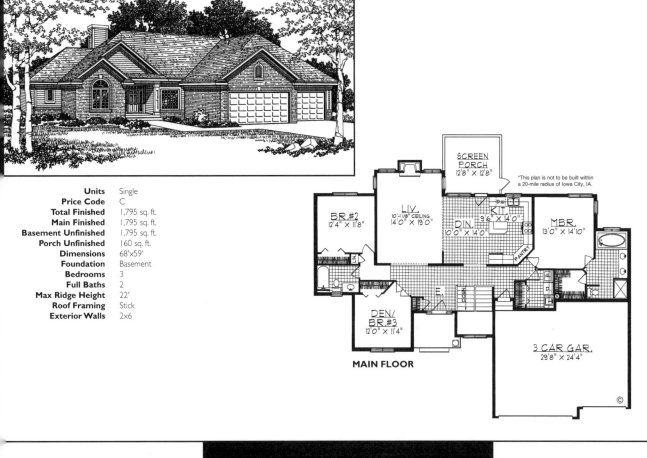

Units	Single
Price Code	C
Total Finished	1,795 sq. ft.
Main Finished	1,795 sq. ft.
Basement Unfinished	1,795 sq. ft.
Porch Unfinished	160 sq. ft.
Dimensions	68'x59'
Foundation	Basement
Bedrooms	3
Full Baths	2
Max Ridge Height	22'
Roof Framing	Stick
Exterior Walls	2x6

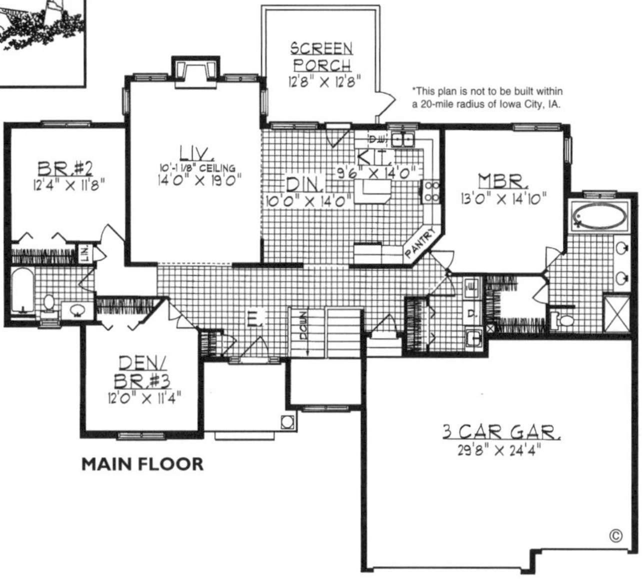

*This plan is not to be built within a 20-mile radius of Iowa City, IA.

SCREEN PORCH 12'8" X 12'8"
BR.#2 12'4" X 11'8"
LIV. 10'-1 1/8" CEILING 14'0" X 19'0"
KIT. 9'6" X 14'0"
DIN. 10'0" X 14'0"
MBR. 13'0" X 14'10"
PANTRY
E.
DEN/ BR.#3 12'0" X 11'4"
3 CAR GAR. 29'8" X 24'4"

MAIN FLOOR

Design 61048

Units	Single
Price Code	C
Total Finished	1,798 sq. ft.
Main Finished	1,798 sq. ft.
Garage Unfinished	417 sq. ft.
Porch Unfinished	196 sq. ft.
Dimensions	54'2"x56'2"
Foundation	Basement Crawlspace Slab
Bedrooms	3
Full Baths	2
Main Ceiling	8'
Roof Framing	Stick
Exterior Walls	2x4

BRKFAST RM.
10'-0" X 10'-4"
MASTER SUITE
14'-6" X 14'-0"
9' BOXED CEILING
GRILLING PORCH
12'-4" X 7'-0"
REF.
RG
DW
KITCHEN
10'-0" X 12'-8"
GREAT RM.
16'-0" X 20'-8"
9' BOXED CEILING
BED RM. 2
12'-0" X 11'-0"
M.BATH
10'-8" X 15'-2"
GLASS BLOCKS
WHP TUB
8" BOXED COLUMNS
LIN.
BATH
STORAGE
10'-8" X 3'-0"
WH
W
LAU.
D
DINING RM.
12'-8" X 11'-0"
10' CEILING
FOYER
HVAC
PORCH
10" RND COL.
BED RM. 1
12'-0" X 13'-4"
GARAGE
20'-10" X 20'-0"

MAIN FLOOR

Design 65621

Units	Single
Price Code	C
Total Finished	1,800 sq. ft.
Main Finished	1,800 sq. ft.
Dimensions	80'x40'
Foundation	Crawlspace Slab
Bedrooms	3
Full Baths	2
Main Ceiling	8'
Vaulted Ceiling	12'
Max Ridge Height	25'
Roof Framing	Stick
Exterior Walls	2x4

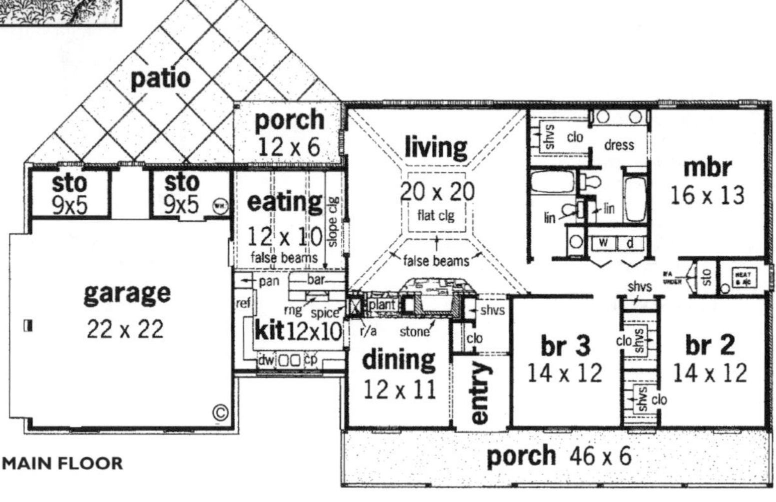
patio
porch 12 x 6
living 20 x 20 flat clg
false beams
mbr 16 x 13
shvs
clo
dress
lin
w d
sto 9x5
sto 9x5
eating 12 x 10
slope clg
garage 22 x 22
pan
bar
ref
rng
spice
kit 12x10
dw
cp
plant
r/a
stone
dining 12 x 11
entry
shvs
clo
br 3 14 x 12
br 2 14 x 12
sto
porch 46 x 6

MAIN FLOOR

Design 65622

Units	Single
Price Code	C
Total Finished	1,800 sq. ft.
Main Finished	1,800 sq. ft.
Dimensions	66'x40'
Foundation	Basement Crawlspace Slab
Bedrooms	3
Full Baths	2
Main Ceiling	8'
Max Ridge Height	29'
Roof Framing	Stick
Exterior Walls	2x6

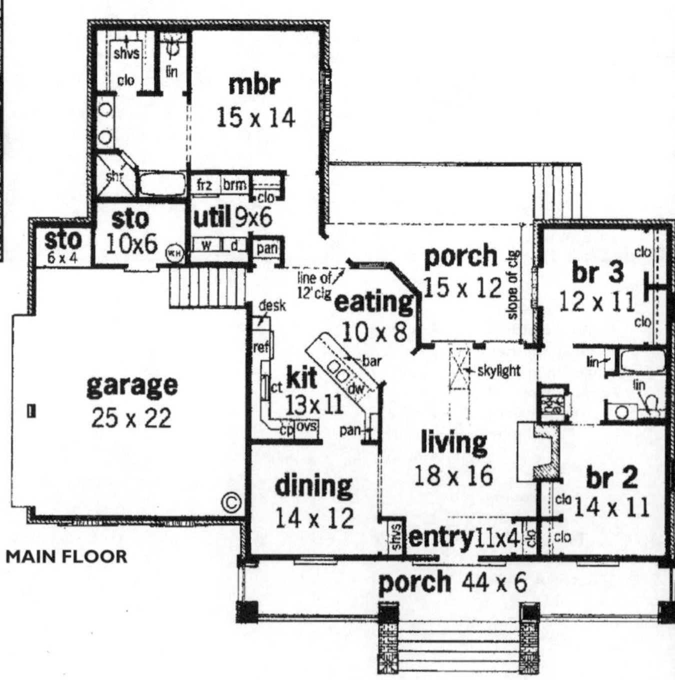
shvs
clo
lin
mbr 15 x 14
sh
frz
brm
clo
sto 6 x 4
sto 10x6
util 9x6
w d
pan
line of 12' clg
eating 10 x 8
porch 15 x 12
slope of clg
br 3 12 x 11
desk
ref
kit 13x11
bar
dw
ovs
pan
skylight
lin
garage 25 x 22
living 18 x 16
dining 14 x 12
br 2 14 x 11
shvs
entry 11x4
clo
porch 44 x 6

MAIN FLOOR

Design 65623

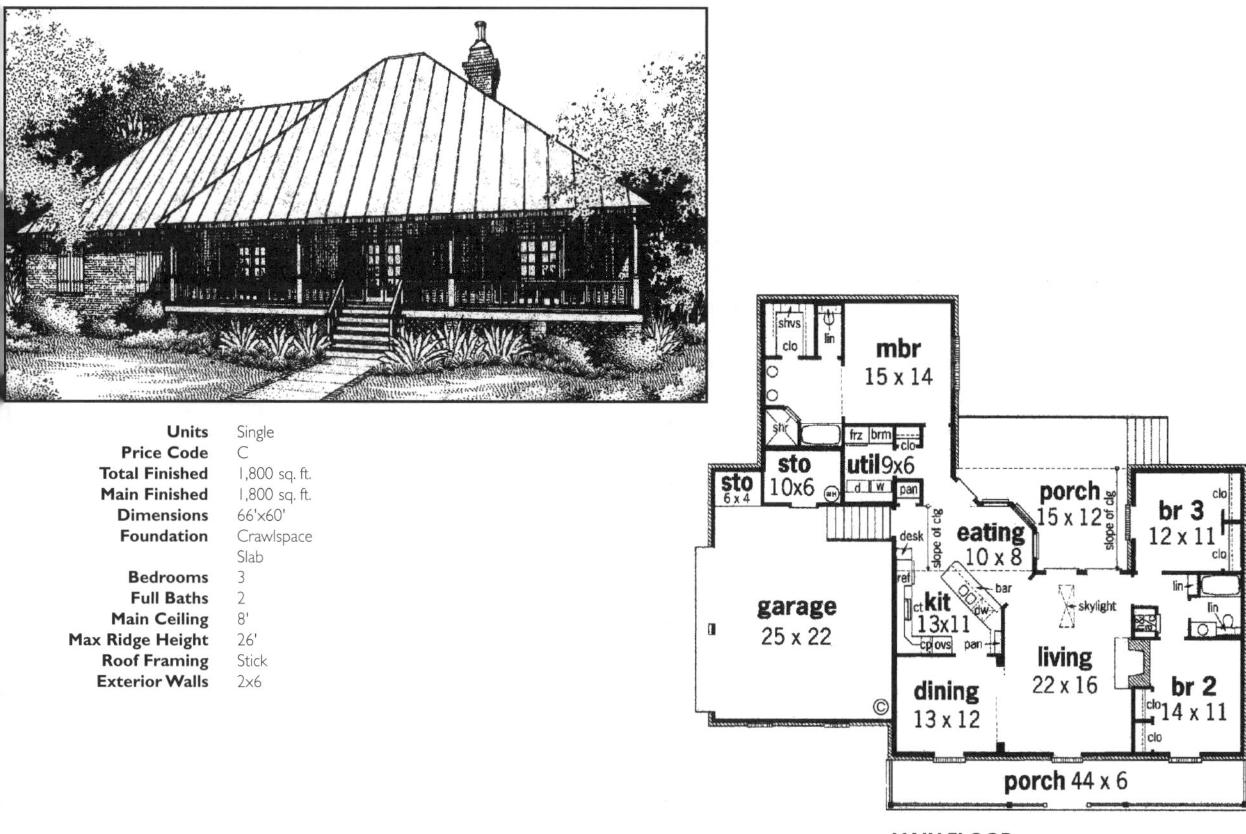
shvs
clo
lin
mbr
15 x 14
shr
frz brm
clo
sto
10x6
util 9x6
d w pan
sto
6 x 4
porch
15 x 12
slope of clg
br 3
12 x 11
clo
desk
eating
10 x 8
ref
kit
13x11
bar
dw
ct
cp ovs
pan
skylight
lin
garage
25 x 22
living
22 x 16
br 2
14 x 11
dining
13 x 12
clo
porch 44 x 6

MAIN FLOOR

Units	Single
Price Code	C
Total Finished	1,800 sq. ft.
Main Finished	1,800 sq. ft.
Dimensions	66'x60'
Foundation	Crawlspace Slab
Bedrooms	3
Full Baths	2
Main Ceiling	8'
Max Ridge Height	26'
Roof Framing	Stick
Exterior Walls	2x6

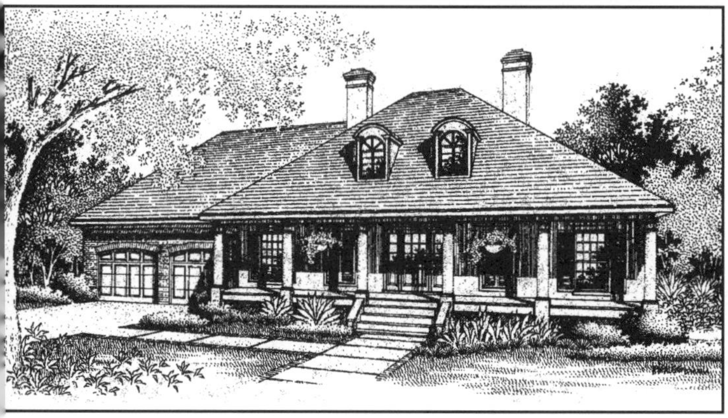

Design 65625

Units	Single
Price Code	C
Total Finished	1,800 sq. ft.
Main Finished	1,800 sq. ft.
Dimensions	66'x60'
Foundation	Crawlspace Slab
Bedrooms	3
Full Baths	2
Main Ceiling	8'
Max Ridge Height	26'
Roof Framing	Stick
Exterior Walls	2x6

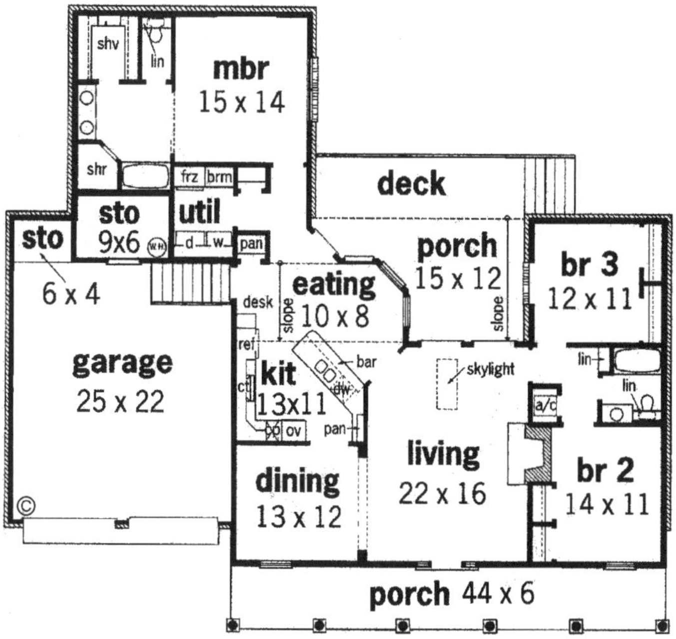

MAIN FLOOR

Design 97610

CAD
FILES AVAILABLE
For more information call
800-235-5700

Units	Single
Price Code	C
Total Finished	1,800 sq. ft.
First Finished	1,378 sq. ft.
Second Finished	422 sq. ft.
Bonus Unfinished	244 sq. ft.
Basement Unfinished	1,378 sq. ft.
Dimensions	48'x45'10"
Foundation	Basement Crawlspace
Bedrooms	3
Full Baths	2
Half Baths	1
Max Ridge Height	27'
Roof Framing	Stick
Exterior Walls	2x4

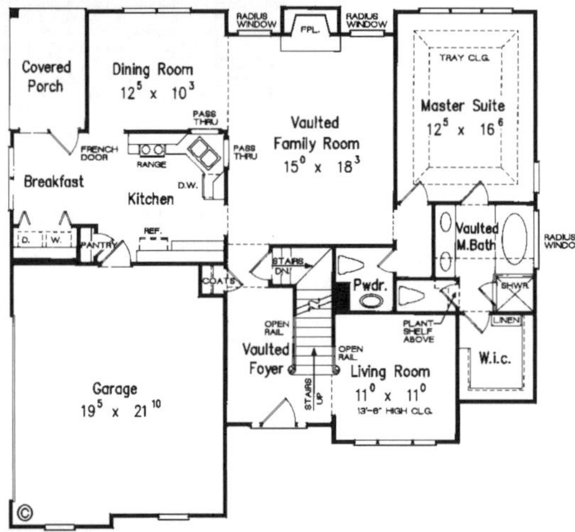

Covered Porch
Dining Room 12⁵ x 10³
RADIUS WINDOW
FPL.
RADIUS WINDOW
Master Suite 12⁵ x 16⁶
TRAY CLG.
PASS THRU
Vaulted Family Room 15⁰ x 18³
FRENCH DOOR
RANGE
Breakfast
Kitchen
D.W.
D.
W.
PANTRY
REF.
STAIRS DN.
Pwdr.
Vaulted M.Bath
RADIUS WINDOW
COATS
SHWR
LINEN
PLANT SHELF ABOVE
OPEN RAIL
Vaulted Foyer
OPEN RAIL
Living Room 11⁰ x 11⁰
13'-6" HIGH CLG.
W.i.c.
STAIRS UP
Garage 19⁵ x 21¹⁰
FIRST FLOOR

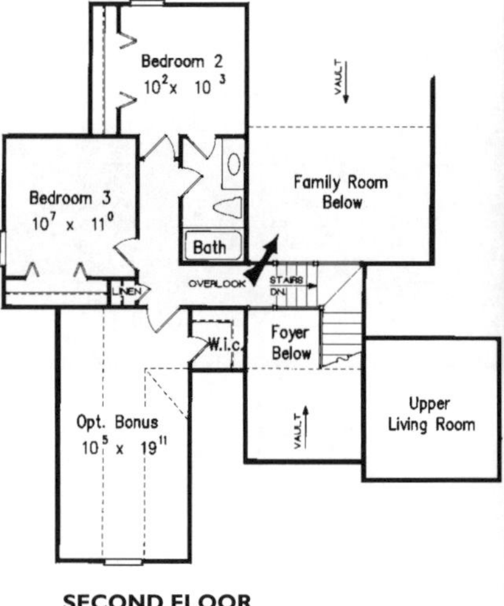

Bedroom 2 10² x 10³
VAULT
Bedroom 3 10⁷ x 11⁰
Family Room Below
Bath
LINEN
OVERLOOK
STAIRS DN.
W.i.c.
Foyer Below
Opt. Bonus 10⁵ x 19¹¹
VAULT
Upper Living Room
SECOND FLOOR

Design 99055

Units	Single
Price Code	C
Total Finished	1,800 sq. ft.
Main Finished	1,800 sq. ft.
Basement Unfinished	1,780 sq. ft.
Garage Unfinished	400 sq. ft.
Porch Unfinished	186 sq. ft.
Dimensions	87'x65'8"
Foundation	Basement
Bedrooms	4
Full Baths	2
3/4 Baths	1
Max Ridge Height	15'
Roof Framing	Stick
Exterior Walls	2x4

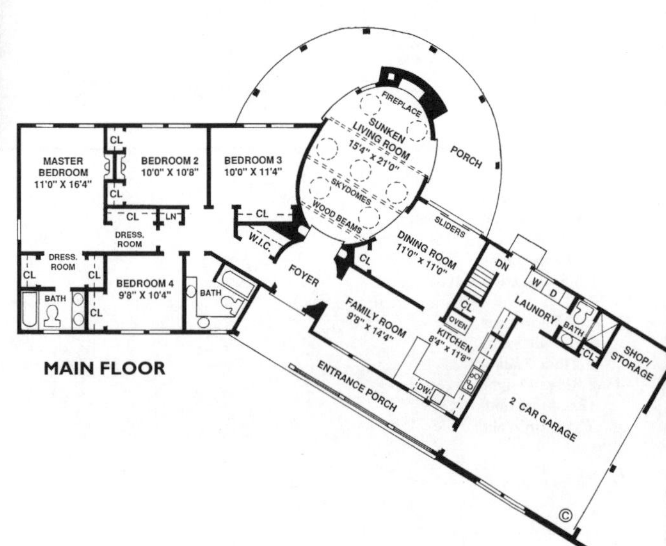

FIREPLACE
SUNKEN LIVING ROOM 15'4" x 21'0"
PORCH
SKYDOMES
WOOD BEAMS
MASTER BEDROOM 11'0" X 16'4"
CL
BEDROOM 2 10'0" X 10'8"
BEDROOM 3 10'0" X 11'4"
CL
LN
DRESS. ROOM
W.I.C.
DRESS. ROOM
BEDROOM 4 9'8" X 10'4"
BATH
BATH
FOYER
DINING ROOM 11'0" x 11'0"
SLIDERS
DN
FAMILY ROOM 9'8" x 14'4"
KITCHEN 8'4" x 11'8"
OVEN
LAUNDRY
W
D
BATH
SHOP/ STORAGE
DW
ENTRANCE PORCH
2 CAR GARAGE
MAIN FLOOR

Design 90476

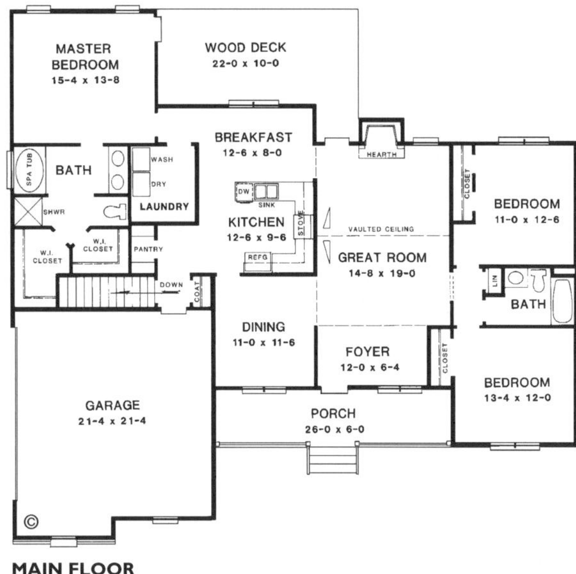

MASTER BEDROOM 15-4 x 13-8
WOOD DECK 22-0 x 10-0
BREAKFAST 12-6 x 8-0
HEARTH
BATH
SPA TUB
SHWR
W.I. CLOSET
W.I. CLOSET
WASH
DRY
LAUNDRY
PANTRY
DW
SINK
KITCHEN 12-6 x 9-6
STOVE
REFG
VAULTED CEILING
GREAT ROOM 14-8 x 19-0
CLOSET
BEDROOM 11-0 x 12-6
LIN
BATH
DOWN
COAT
DINING 11-0 x 11-6
FOYER 12-0 x 6-4
CLOSET
BEDROOM 13-4 x 12-0
GARAGE 21-4 x 21-4
PORCH 26-0 x 6-0
©

MAIN FLOOR

Units	Single
Price Code	C
Total Finished	1,804 sq. ft.
Main Finished	1,804 sq. ft.
Basement Unfinished	1,804 sq. ft.
Garage Unfinished	506 sq. ft.
Deck Unfinished	220 sq. ft.
Porch Unfinished	156 sq. ft.
Dimensions	62'x55'8"
Foundation	Basement Crawlspace Slab
Bedrooms	3
Full Baths	2
Main Ceiling	8'
Max Ridge Height	22'1"
Roof Framing	Stick
Exterior Walls	2x4

Design 63054

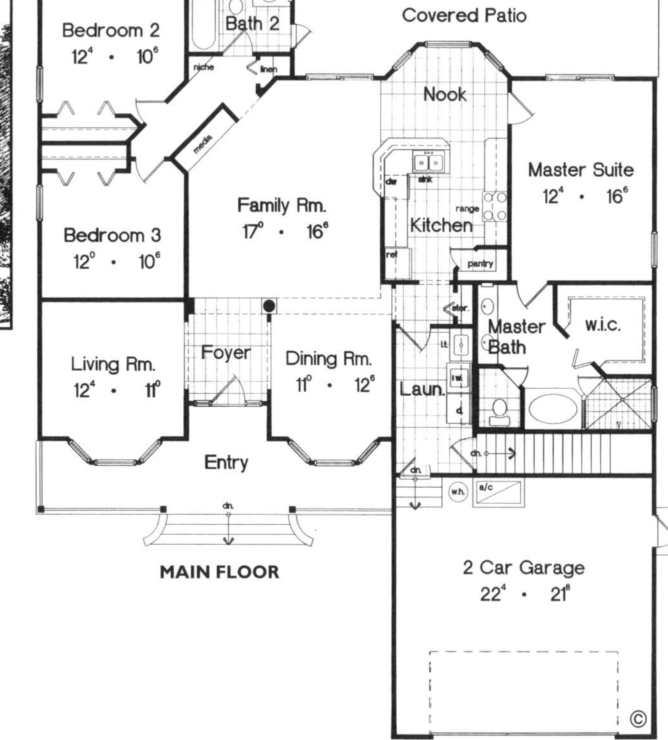

Bedroom 2 12⁴ • 10⁶
Bath 2
niche
linen
Covered Patio
Nook
media
Family Rm. 17⁰ • 16⁶
Kitchen
dw
sink
range
ref
pantry
Master Suite 12⁴ • 16⁶
Bedroom 3 12⁰ • 10⁶
Living Rm. 12⁴ • 11⁰
Foyer
Dining Rm. 11⁰ • 12⁶
Laun.
Master Bath
w.i.c.
Entry
dn.
dn.
dn.
w.h.
a/c
2 Car Garage 22⁴ • 21⁸
©

MAIN FLOOR

Units	Single
Price Code	C
Total Finished	1,806 sq. ft.
Main Finished	1,806 sq. ft.
Garage Unfinished	491 sq. ft.
Porch Unfinished	216 sq. ft.
Dimensions	54'x58'8"
Foundation	Slab
Bedrooms	3
Full Baths	2
Main Ceiling	8'
Vaulted Ceiling	13'6"
Max Ridge Height	18'
Roof Framing	Truss

Design 65412

Units	Single
Price Code	C
Total Finished	1,806 sq. ft.
First Finished	917 sq. ft.
Second Finished	889 sq. ft.
Basement Unfinished	917 sq. ft.
Garage Unfinished	408 sq. ft.
Deck Unfinished	58 sq. ft.
Porch Unfinished	43 sq. ft.
Dimensions	40'x40'
Foundation	Basement
Bedrooms	3
Full Baths	1
3/4 Baths	1
Half Baths	1
First Ceiling	9'
Second Ceiling	8'
Max Ridge Height	31'8"
Roof Framing	Truss
Exterior Walls	2x6

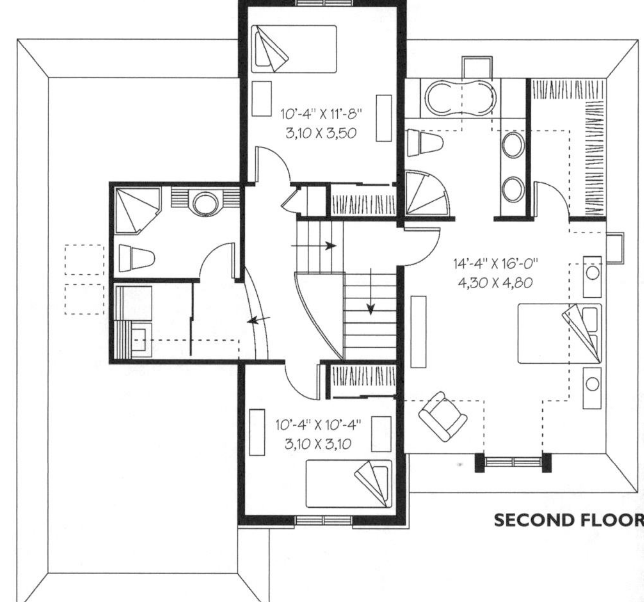
10'-4" X 11'-8"
3,10 X 3,50
14'-4" X 16'-0"
4,30 X 4,80
10'-4" X 10'-4"
3,10 X 3,10

SECOND FLOOR

11'-0" X 9'-0"
3,30 X 2,70
13'-0" X 10'-0"
3,90 X 3,00
13'-0" X 10'-0"
3,90 X 3,00
14'-0" X 26'-4"
4,20 X 7,90
13'-0" X 14'-0"
3,90 X 4,20

FIRST FLOOR

Design 66083

Units	Single
Price Code	C
Total Finished	1,806 sq. ft.
Main Finished	1,806 sq. ft.
Dimensions	52'x59'4"
Foundation	Slab
Bedrooms	4
Full Baths	2
Main Ceiling	8'
Max Ridge Height	23'6"
Roof Framing	Stick
Exterior Walls	2x4

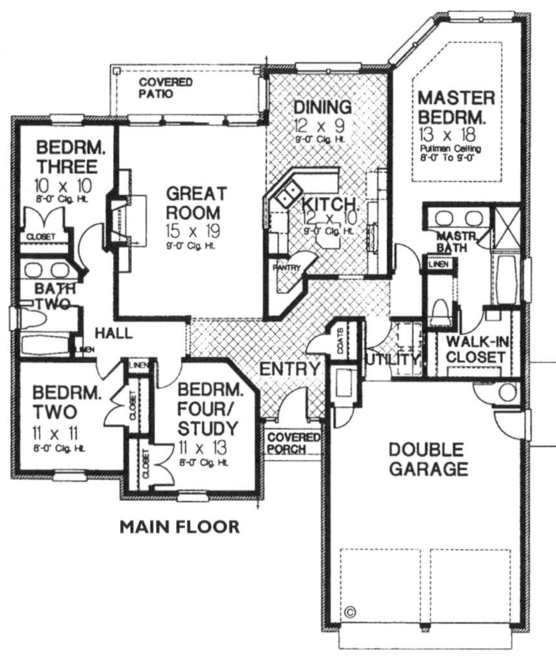
COVERED PATIO
DINING
12 x 9
9'-0" Clg. Ht.
MASTER BEDRM.
13 x 18
Pullman Ceiling 8'-0" To 9'-0"
BEDRM. THREE
10 x 10
8'-0" Clg. Ht.
GREAT ROOM
15 x 19
9'-0" Clg. Ht.
KITCH.
12 x 10
9'-0" Clg. Ht.
CLOSET
PANTRY
MASTR. BATH
LINEN
BATH TWO
HALL
COATS
WALK-IN CLOSET
UTILITY
ENTRY
BEDRM. TWO
11 x 11
8'-0" Clg. Ht.
BEDRM. FOUR/ STUDY
11 x 13
8'-0" Clg. Ht.
COVERED PORCH
DOUBLE GARAGE

MAIN FLOOR

Design 66105

Units	Single
Price Code	C
Total Finished	1,806 sq. ft.
Main Finished	1,806 sq. ft.
Bonus Unfinished	351 sq. ft.
Garage Unfinished	704 sq. ft.
Dimensions	75'x44'8"
Foundation	Slab
Bedrooms	3
Full Baths	2
Half Baths	1
Main Ceiling	8'-9'
Max Ridge Height	22'
Roof Framing	Stick
Exterior Walls	2x4

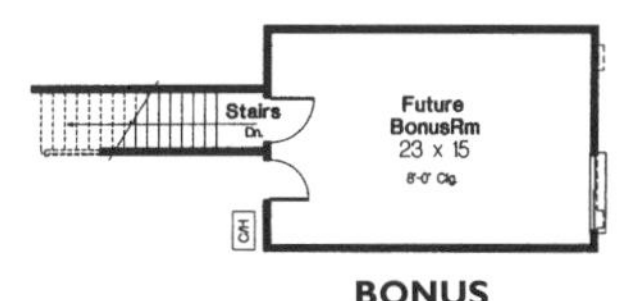
Stairs
Future BonusRm
23 x 15
8'-0" Clg.

BONUS

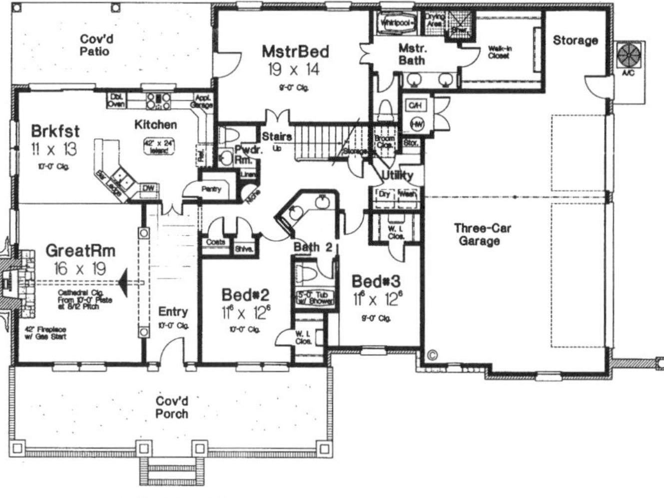
Cov'd Patio
MstrBed
19 x 14
9'-0" Clg.
Mstr. Bath
Storage
Brkfst
11 x 13
Kitchen
Stairs
Pwdr. Rm.
Utility
GreatRm
16 x 19
Entry
Bed#2
Bath 2
Bed#3
Three-Car Garage
Cov'd Porch

MAIN FLOOR

Design 97462

Units	Single
Price Code	B
Total Finished	1,806 sq. ft.
Main Finished	1,806 sq. ft.
Garage Unfinished	655 sq. ft.
Dimensions	65'4"x56'
Foundation	Basement
Bedrooms	3
Full Baths	2
Main Ceiling	9'
Max Ridge Height	21'
Roof Framing	Stick
Exterior Walls	2x4

* Alternate foundation options available at an additional charge. Please call 1-800-235-5700 for more information.

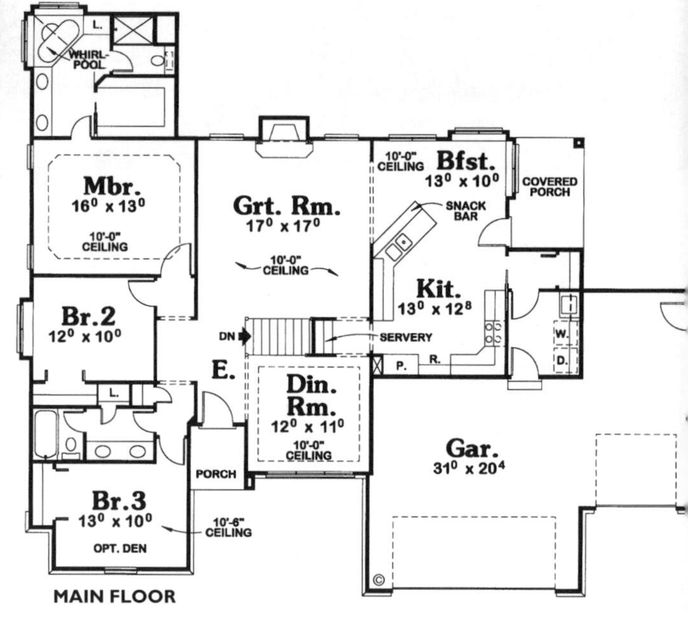

WHIRL-POOL
L.
Mbr.
16⁰ x 13⁰
10'-0" CEILING
Grt. Rm.
17⁰ x 17⁰
10'-0" CEILING
10'-0" CEILING
Bfst.
13⁰ x 10⁰
COVERED PORCH
SNACK BAR
Kit.
13⁰ x 12⁸
SERVERY
P.
R.
W.
D.
Br.2
12⁰ x 10⁰
DN
E.
Din. Rm.
12⁰ x 11⁰
10'-0" CEILING
L
Gar.
31⁰ x 20⁴
PORCH
Br.3
13⁰ x 10⁰
OPT. DEN
10'-6" CEILING
©

MAIN FLOOR

Design 93413

Units	Single
Price Code	C
Total Finished	1,808 sq. ft.
First Finished	1,271 sq. ft.
Second Finished	537 sq. ft.
Basement Unfinished	1,271 sq. ft.
Garage Unfinished	555 sq. ft.
Dimensions	44'4"x73'2"
Foundation	Basement
Bedrooms	3
Full Baths	2
Half Baths	1
Max Ridge Height	28'
Roof Framing	Stick
Exterior Walls	2x4

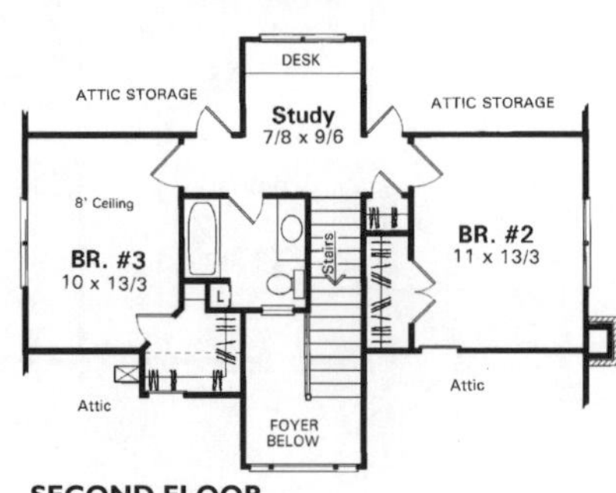

DESK
ATTIC STORAGE
Study
7/8 x 9/6
ATTIC STORAGE
8' Ceiling
BR. #3
10 x 13/3
Stairs
BR. #2
11 x 13/3
L
Attic
Attic
FOYER BELOW

SECOND FLOOR

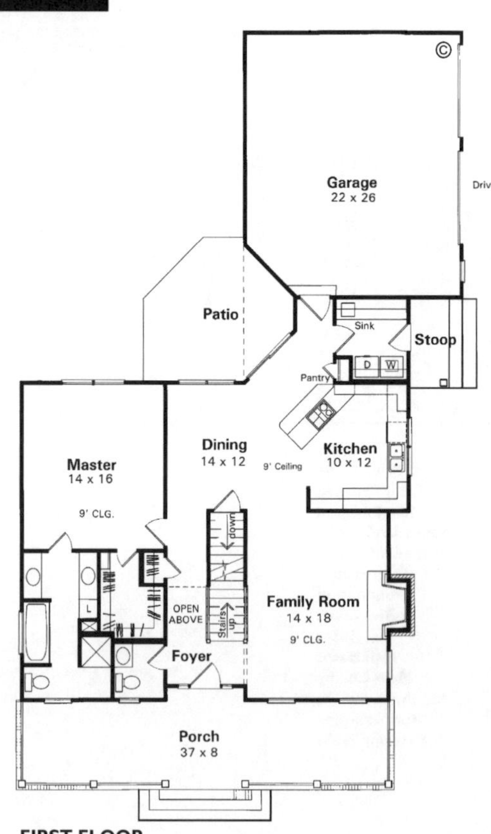

©
Garage
22 x 26
Drive
Patio
Sink
Stoop
Pantry
D
W
Dining
14 x 12
9' Ceiling
Kitchen
10 x 12
Master
14 x 16
9' CLG.
Down
L
OPEN ABOVE
Stairs up
Family Room
14 x 18
9' CLG.
Foyer
Porch
37 x 8

FIRST FLOOR

Design 94928

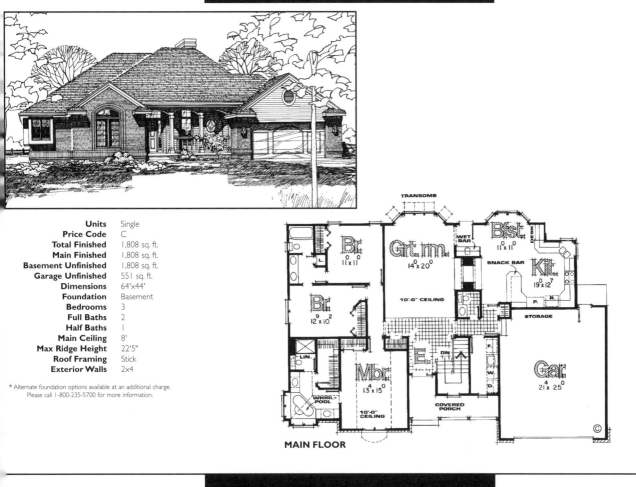

Units	Single
Price Code	C
Total Finished	1,808 sq. ft.
Main Finished	1,808 sq. ft.
Basement Unfinished	1,808 sq. ft.
Garage Unfinished	551 sq. ft.
Dimensions	64'x44'
Foundation	Basement
Bedrooms	3
Full Baths	2
Half Baths	1
Main Ceiling	8'
Max Ridge Height	22'5"
Roof Framing	Stick
Exterior Walls	2x4

* Alternate foundation options available at an additional charge. Please call 1-800-235-5700 for more information.

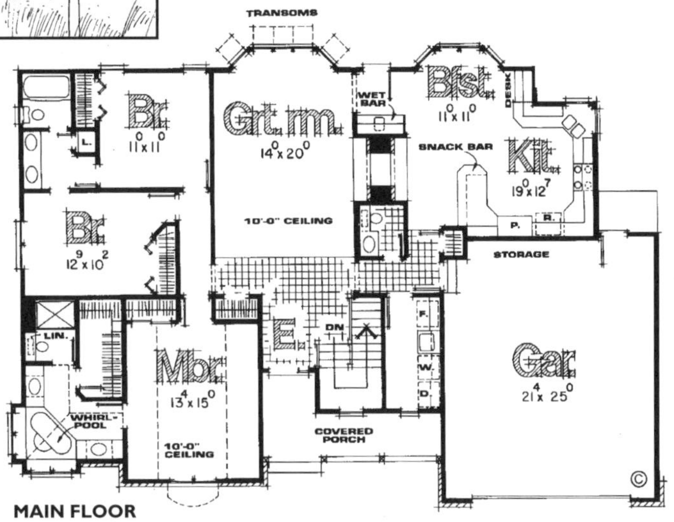

MAIN FLOOR

Design 90441

Units	Single
Price Code	C
Total Finished	1,811 sq. ft.
Main Finished	1,811 sq. ft.
Basement Unfinished	1,811 sq. ft.
Garage Unfinished	484 sq. ft.
Deck Unfinished	336 sq. ft.
Porch Unfinished	390 sq. ft.
Dimensions	89'6"x44'4"
Foundation	Basement Crawlspace Slab
Bedrooms	3
Full Baths	2
Main Ceiling	8'
Max Ridge Height	16'4"
Roof Framing	Stick
Exterior Walls	2x4

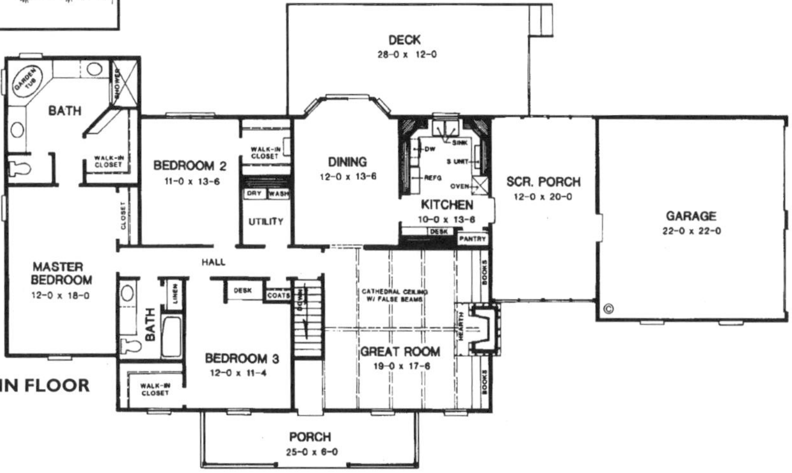

MAIN FLOOR

Design 91457

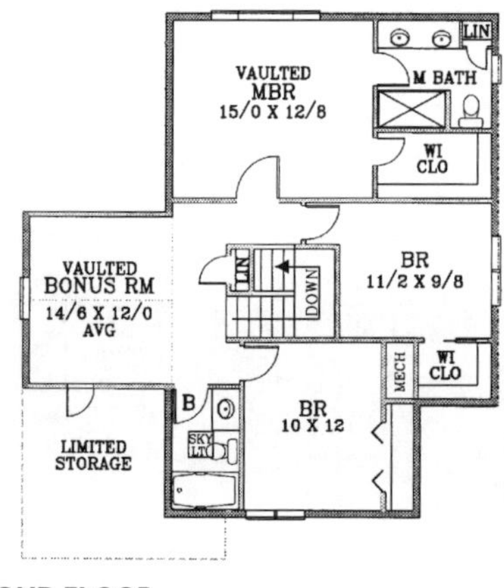

VAULTED MBR 15/0 X 12/8
M BATH
LIN
WI CLO
VAULTED BONUS RM 14/6 X 12/0 AVG
BR 11/2 X 9/8
LIN
DOWN
MECH
WI CLO
B
SKY LT
BR 10 X 12
LIMITED STORAGE

SECOND FLOOR

Units	Single
Price Code	C
Total Finished	1,812 sq. ft.
First Finished	895 sq. ft.
Second Finished	917 sq. ft.
Garage Unfinished	409 sq. ft.
Dimensions	35'x43'
Foundation	Crawlspace
Bedrooms	3
Full Baths	1
3/4 Baths	1
Half Baths	1
First Ceiling	8'
Second Ceiling	8'
Max Ridge Height	25'
Roof Framing	Truss
Exterior Walls	2x6

PATIO
VAULTED DIN RM 10/6 X 9/2
GREAT RM 23/6 X 14/0
KIT
DW
R
UP
GST
W D
PDR
OPTION RM 10 X 11
FOYER
GARAGE 19/4 X 21/2
COVERED PORCH

FIRST FLOOR

Design 62084

Units	Single
Price Code	C
Total Finished	1,813 sq. ft.
Main Finished	1,813 sq. ft.
Garage Unfinished	426 sq. ft.
Dimensions	5'8"x57'
Foundation	Crawlspace Slab
Full Baths	2
Bedrooms	3
Main Ceiling	9'
Max Ridge Height	23'10"
Roof Framing	Stick
Exterior Walls	2x4

MAIN FLOOR

Design 97300

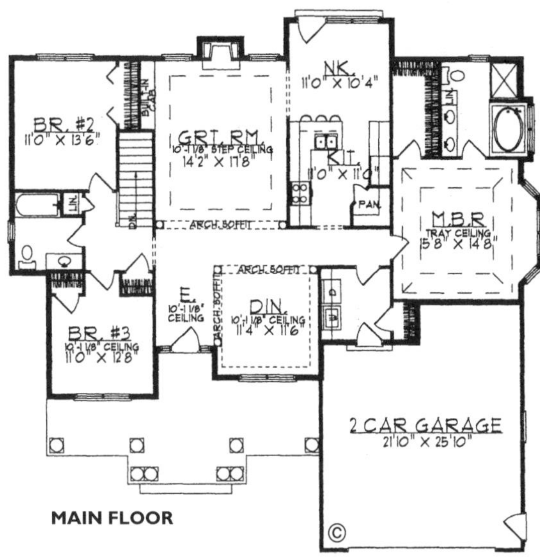
BR. #2
11'0" X 13'6"
GRT. RM.
10'-1 1/8" STEP CEILING
14'2" X 17'8"
NK.
11'0" X 10'4"
KIT.
11'0" X 11'0"
PAN.
M.B.R.
TRAY CEILING
15'8" X 14'8"
ARCH. SOFFIT
E.
10'-1 1/8" CEILING
DIN.
10'-1 1/8" CEILING
11'4" X 11'6"
BR. #3
10'-1 1/8" CEILING
11'0" X 12'8"
2 CAR GARAGE
21'10" X 25'10"

MAIN FLOOR

Units	Single
Price Code	C
Total Finished	1,814 sq. ft.
Main Finished	1,814 sq. ft.
Basement Unfinished	1,814 sq. ft.
Dimensions	58'x56'
Foundation	Basement
Bedrooms	3
Full Baths	2
Main Ceiling	9'1/8"
Max Ridge Height	27'8"
Roof Framing	Truss
Exterior Walls	2x6

Design 63112

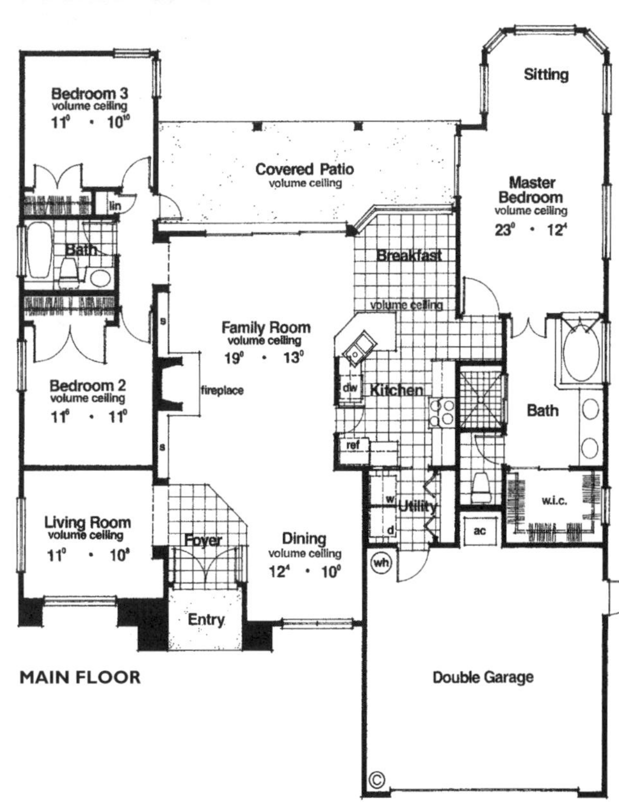
Bedroom 3
volume ceiling
$11^{0} \cdot 10^{10}$
Covered Patio
volume ceiling
Sitting
Master Bedroom
volume ceiling
$23^{0} \cdot 12^{4}$
lin
Bath
Breakfast
volume ceiling
Family Room
volume ceiling
$19^{0} \cdot 13^{0}$
fireplace
Bedroom 2
volume ceiling
$11^{6} \cdot 11^{0}$
dw
Kitchen
ref
Bath
Utility
w.i.c.
ac
Living Room
volume ceiling
$11^{0} \cdot 10^{8}$
Foyer
Dining
volume ceiling
$12^{4} \cdot 10^{0}$
wh
Entry
Double Garage

MAIN FLOOR

Units	Single
Price Code	C
Total Finished	1,817 sq. ft.
Main Finished	1,817 sq. ft.
Garage Unfinished	420 sq. ft.
Dimensions	50'x63'
Foundation	Slab
Bedrooms	3
Full Baths	2
Main Ceiling	10'
Max Ridge Height	26'5"
Roof Framing	Truss
Exterior Walls	2x4

Design 93155

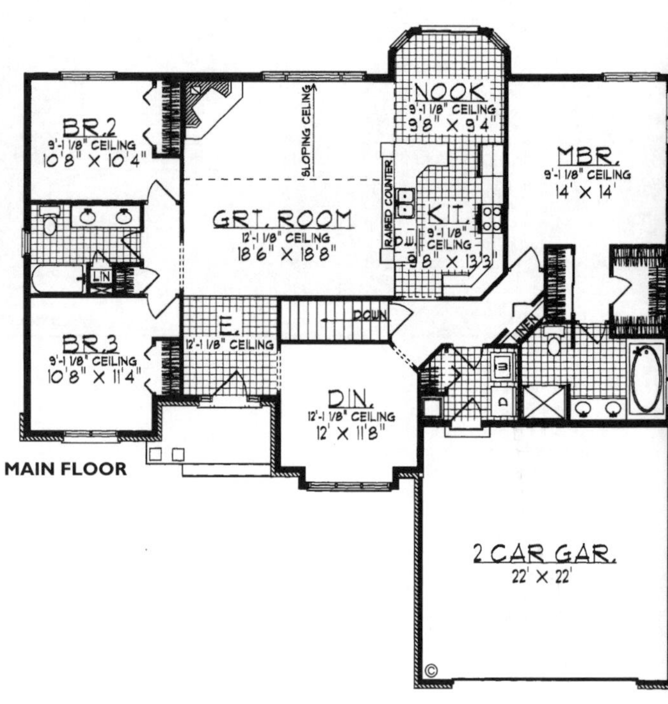

BR.2
9'-1 1/8" CEILING
10'8" X 10'4"
SLOPING CEILING
NOOK
9'-1 1/8" CEILING
9'8" X 9'4"
MBR.
9'-1 1/8" CEILING
14' X 14'
GRT. ROOM
12'-1 1/8" CEILING
18'6" X 18'8"
RAISED COUNTER
KIT.
9'-1 1/8" CEILING
9'8" X 13'3"
LIN
BR.3
9'-1 1/8" CEILING
10'8" X 11'4"
E.
12'-1 1/8" CEILING
DOWN
LINEN
DIN.
12'-1 1/8" CEILING
12' X 11'8"
2 CAR GAR.
22' X 22'

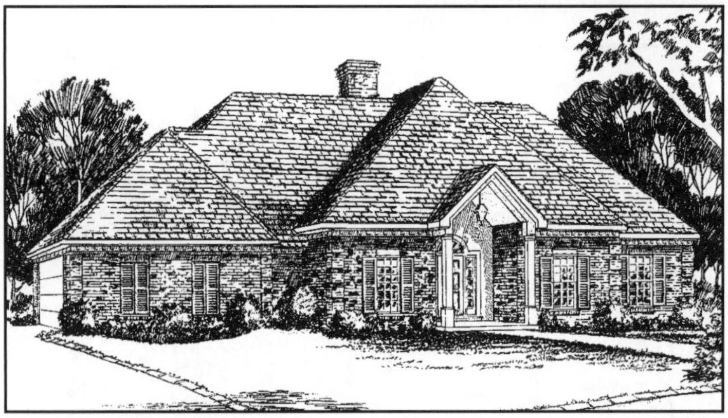

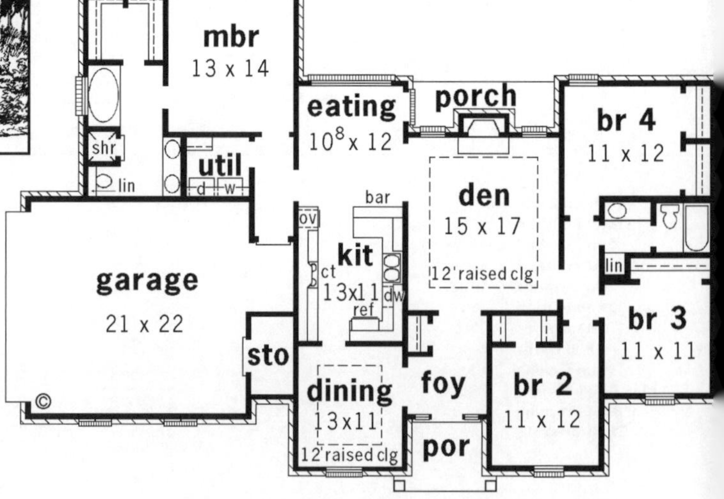

MAIN FLOOR

Units	Single
Price Code	C
Total Finished	1,817 sq. ft.
Main Finished	1,817 sq. ft.
Basement Unfinished	1,817 sq. ft.
Dimensions	57'x56'
Foundation	Basement
Bedrooms	3
Full Baths	2
Max Ridge Height	22'
Roof Framing	Stick
Exterior Walls	2x6

Design 92551

Units	Single
Price Code	C
Total Finished	1,818 sq. ft.
Main Finished	1,818 sq. ft.
Garage Unfinished	522 sq. ft.
Dimensions	67'10"x48'5"
Foundation	Crawlspace Slab
Bedrooms	4
Full Baths	2
Main Ceiling	9'
Max Ridge Height	22'
Roof Framing	Stick
Exterior Walls	2x4

MAIN FLOOR

Design 97611

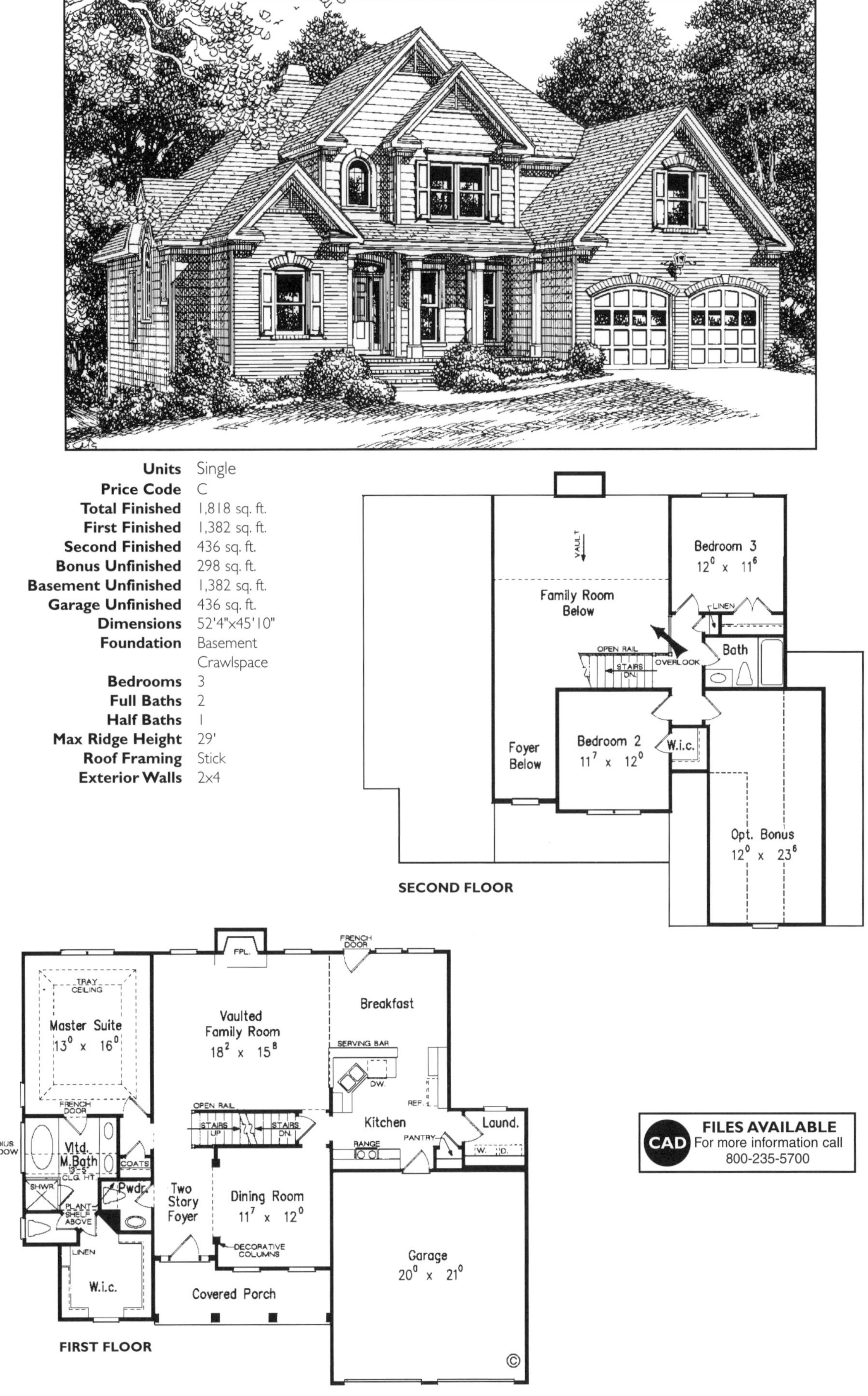

SECOND FLOOR
Bedroom 3
12⁰ x 11⁶
VAULT
Family Room
Below
LINEN
OPEN RAIL
STAIRS DN.
OVERLOOK
Bath
Foyer
Below
Bedroom 2
11⁷ x 12⁰
W.i.c.
Opt. Bonus
12⁰ x 23⁶
FIRST FLOOR
TRAY CEILING
Master Suite
13⁰ x 16⁰
FRENCH DOOR
RADIUS WINDOW
Vltd. M.Bath
9'-8" CLG. HT.
SHWR
PLANT SHELF ABOVE
LINEN
W.i.c.
COATS
Pwdr.
Two Story Foyer
FPL.
Vaulted
Family Room
18² x 15⁸
OPEN RAIL
STAIRS UP
STAIRS DN.
Dining Room
11⁷ x 12⁰
DECORATIVE COLUMNS
Covered Porch
FRENCH DOOR
Breakfast
SERVING BAR
DW.
REF.
Kitchen
RANGE
PANTRY
Laund.
W.
D.
Garage
20⁰ x 21⁰
©

Units	Single
Price Code	C
Total Finished	1,818 sq. ft.
First Finished	1,382 sq. ft.
Second Finished	436 sq. ft.
Bonus Unfinished	298 sq. ft.
Basement Unfinished	1,382 sq. ft.
Garage Unfinished	436 sq. ft.
Dimensions	52'4"x45'10"
Foundation	Basement Crawlspace
Bedrooms	3
Full Baths	2
Half Baths	1
Max Ridge Height	29'
Roof Framing	Stick
Exterior Walls	2x4

CAD **FILES AVAILABLE**
For more information call
800-235-5700

Design 64132

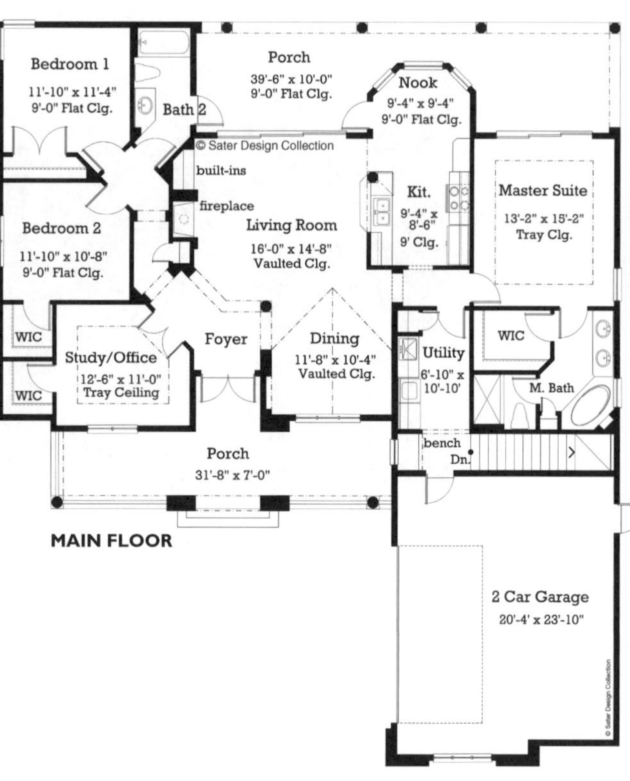

Bedroom 1
11'-10" x 11'-4"
9'-0" Flat Clg.
Bath 2
Porch
39'-6" x 10'-0"
9'-0" Flat Clg.
Nook
9'-4" x 9'-4"
9'-0" Flat Clg.
© Sater Design Collection
built-ins
fireplace
Kit.
9'-4" x 8'-6"
9' Clg.
Master Suite
13'-2" x 15'-2"
Tray Clg.
Bedroom 2
11'-10" x 10'-8"
9'-0" Flat Clg.
Living Room
16'-0" x 14'-8"
Vaulted Clg.
WIC
Study/Office
12'-6" x 11'-0"
Tray Ceiling
WIC
Foyer
Dining
11'-8" x 10'-4"
Vaulted Clg.
Utility
6'-10" x 10'-10'
WIC
M. Bath
bench
Dn.
Porch
31'-8" x 7'-0"
MAIN FLOOR
2 Car Garage
20'-4' x 23'-10"
© Sater Design Collection

Units	Single
Price Code	G
Total Finished	1,822 sq. ft.
Main Finished	1,822 sq. ft.
Garage Unfinished	537 sq. ft.
Dimensions	58'x67'2"
Foundation	Basement
Bedrooms	3
Full Baths	2
Max Ridge Height	26'10"
Roof Framing	Stick
Exterior Walls	2x6

* Alternate foundation options available at an additional charge. Please call 1-800-235-5700 for more information.

Design 65471

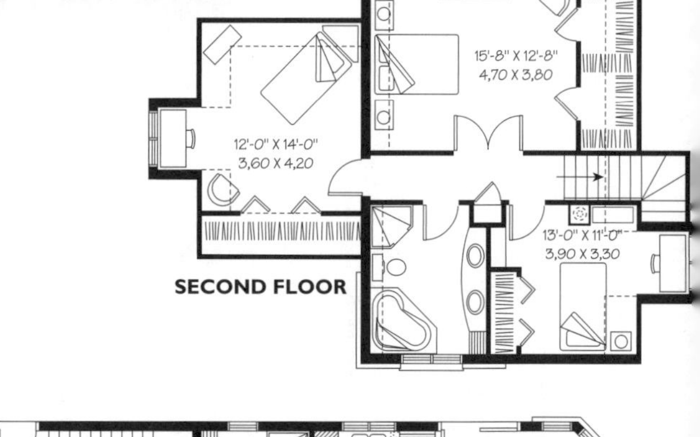

15'-8" X 12'-8"
4,70 X 3,80
12'-0" X 14'-0"
3,60 X 4,20
13'-0" X 11'-0"
3,90 X 3,30
SECOND FLOOR

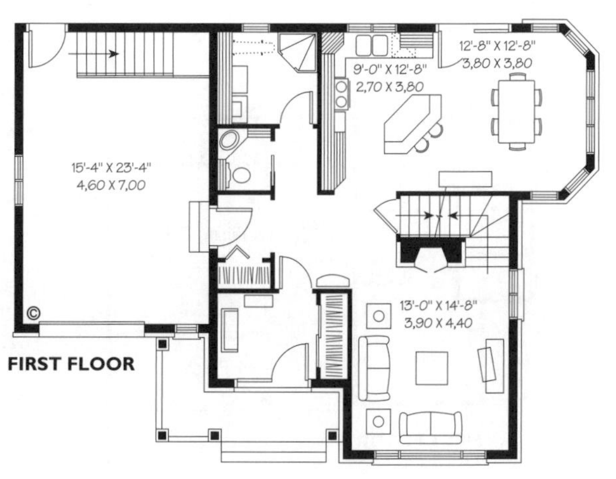

12'-8" X 12'-8"
3,80 X 3,80
9'-0" X 12'-8"
2,70 X 3,80
15'-4" X 23'-4"
4,60 X 7,00
13'-0" X 14'-8"
3,90 X 4,40
FIRST FLOOR

Units	Single
Price Code	C
Total Finished	1,826 sq. ft.
First Finished	918 sq. ft.
Second Finished	908 sq. ft.
Basement Unfinished	918 sq. ft.
Garage Unfinished	400 sq. ft.
Deck Unfinished	40 sq. ft.
Porch Unfinished	77 sq. ft.
Dimensions	48'x35'4"
Foundation	Basement
Bedrooms	3
Full Baths	1
3/4 Baths	1
First Ceiling	8'
Second Ceiling	8'
Max Ridge Height	32'2"
Roof Framing	Truss
Exterior Walls	2x6

Design 50009

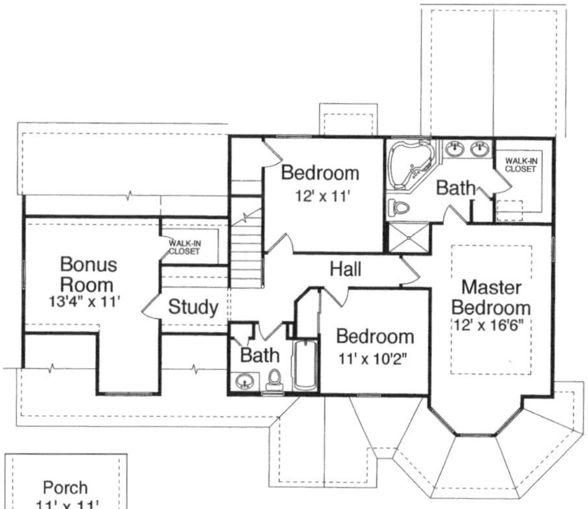

Units	Single
Price Code	C
Total Finished	1,827 sq. ft.
First Finished	949 sq. ft.
Second Finished	878 sq. ft.
Bonus Unfinished	282 sq. ft.
Basement Unfinished	949 sq. ft.
Garage Unfinished	498 sq. ft.
Dimensions	55'8"x34'4"
Foundation	Basement
Bedrooms	3
Full Baths	2
Half Baths	1
First Ceiling	8'
Second Ceiling	8'
Tray Ceiling	9'
Max Ridge Height	26'10"
Roof Framing	Truss
Exterior Walls	2x4

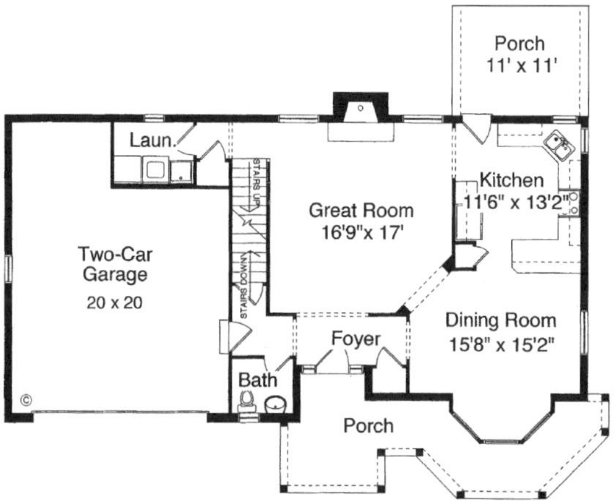

Bedroom 12' x 11'
Bath
Walk-in Closet
Bonus Room 13'4" x 11'
Walk-in Closet
Hall
Study
Master Bedroom 12' x 16'6"
Bath
Bedroom 11' x 10'2"

SECOND FLOOR

Porch 11' x 11'
Laun.
Kitchen 11'6" x 13'2"
Great Room 16'9" x 17'
Two-Car Garage 20 x 20
Dining Room 15'8" x 15'2"
Foyer
Bath
Porch

FIRST FLOOR

Design 93423

Units	Single
Price Code	C
Total Finished	1,829 sq. ft.
First Finished	1,339 sq. ft.
Second Finished	490 sq. ft.
Bonus Unfinished	145 sq. ft.
Garage Unfinished	491 sq. ft.
Porch Unfinished	173 sq. ft.
Dimensions	57'x60'
Foundation	Basement
Bedrooms	3
Full Baths	2
Half Baths	1
First Ceiling	9'
Second Ceiling	8'
Max Ridge Height	29'
Roof Framing	Stick
Exterior Walls	2x4

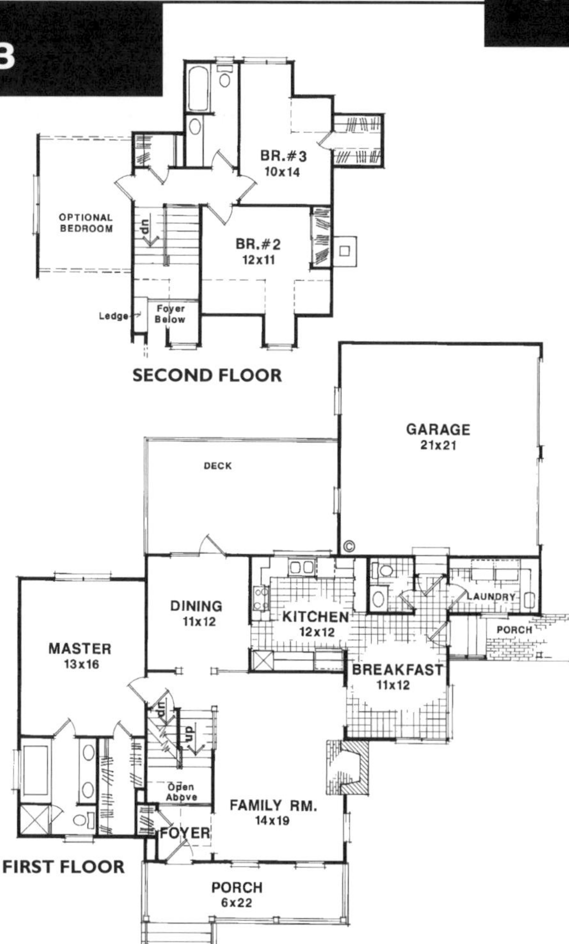
BR.#3 10x14
OPTIONAL BEDROOM
BR.#2 12x11
Ledge
Foyer Below
SECOND FLOOR
GARAGE 21x21
DECK
DINING 11x12
KITCHEN 12x12
LAUNDRY
PORCH
MASTER 13x16
BREAKFAST 11x12
Open Above
FAMILY RM. 14x19
FOYER
FIRST FLOOR
PORCH 6x22

Design 90007

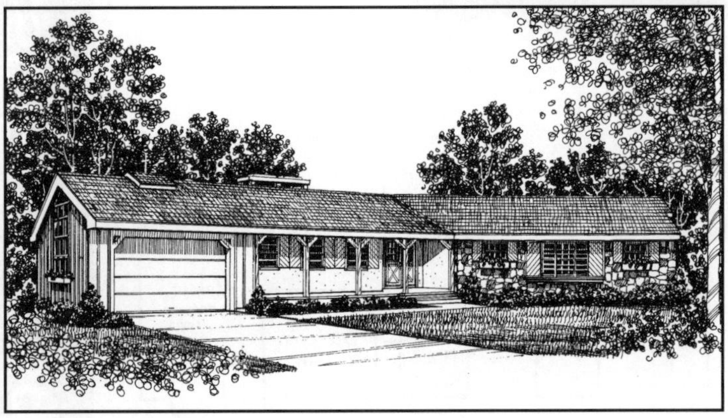

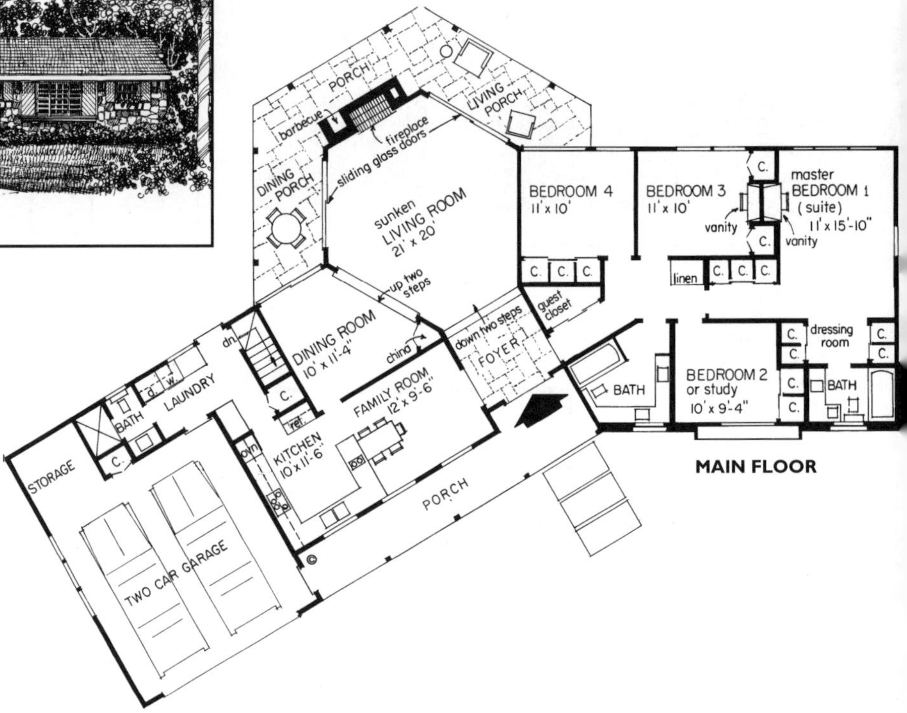

Units	Single
Price Code	C
Total Finished	1,830 sq. ft.
Main Finished	1,830 sq. ft.
Basement Unfinished	1,830 sq. ft.
Garage Unfinished	540 sq. ft.
Dimensions	86'x65'
Foundation	Basement
Bedrooms	4
Full Baths	2
3/4 Baths	1
Max Ridge Height	18'
Roof Framing	Stick
Exterior Walls	2x4

PORCH
barbecue
fireplace
sliding glass doors
LIVING PORCH
DINING PORCH
sunken LIVING ROOM 21' x 20'
up two steps
BEDROOM 4 11' x 10'
BEDROOM 3 11' x 10'
master BEDROOM 1 (suite) 11' x 15'-10"
vanity
vanity
linen
guest closet
dressing room
DINING ROOM 10' x 11'-4"
china
down two steps
FOYER
FAMILY ROOM 12' x 9'-6"
BATH
BEDROOM 2 or study 10' x 9'-4"
BATH
LAUNDRY
BATH
KITCHEN 10' x 11'-6"
STORAGE
PORCH
TWO CAR GARAGE
MAIN FLOOR

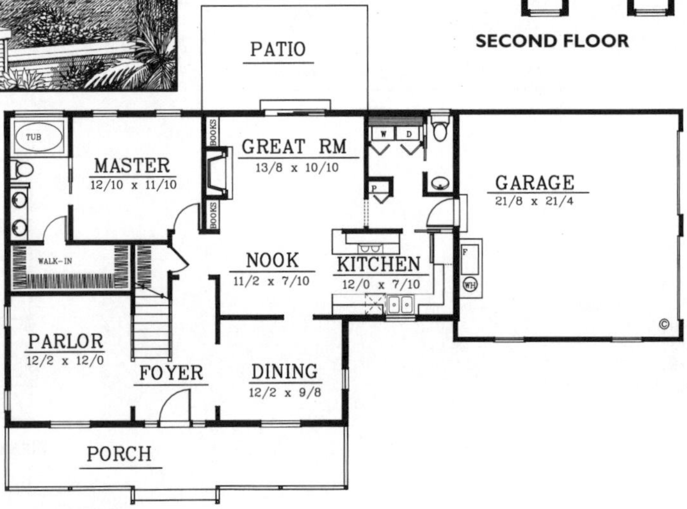

Design 91835

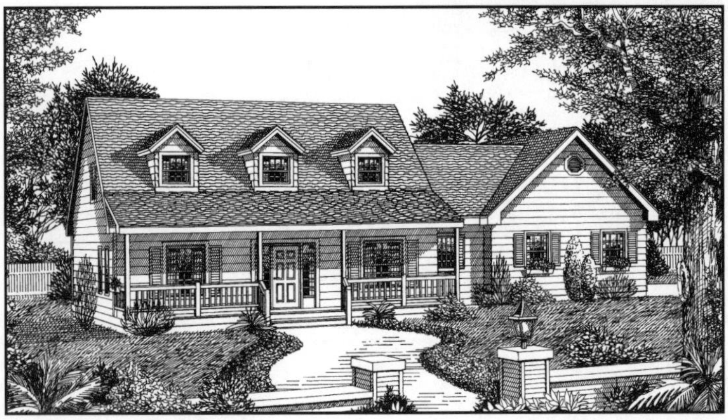

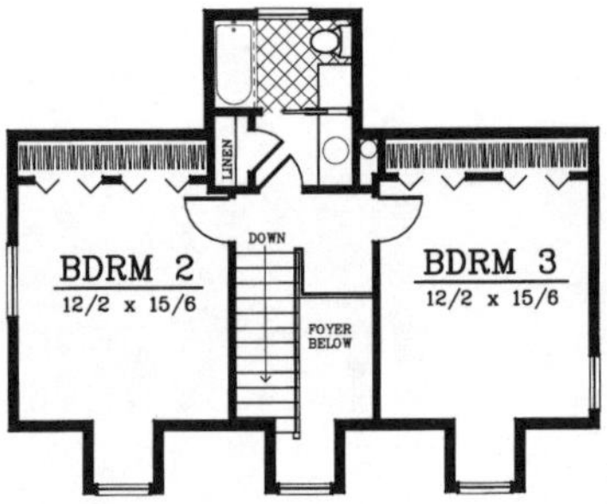

Units	Single
Price Code	C
Total Finished	1,830 sq. ft.
First Finished	1,240 sq. ft.
Second Finished	590 sq. ft.
Garage Unfinished	485 sq. ft.
Dimensions	67'x36'
Foundation	Crawlspace
Bedrooms	3
Full Baths	2
Half Baths	1
First Ceiling	8'
Max Ridge Height	23'3"
Roof Framing	Stick/Truss
Exterior Walls	2x6

BDRM 2 12/2 x 15/6
DOWN
FOYER BELOW
BDRM 3 12/2 x 15/6
SECOND FLOOR
PATIO
MASTER 12/10 x 11/10
GREAT RM 13/8 x 10/10
GARAGE 21/8 x 21/4
WALK-IN
NOOK 11/2 x 7/10
KITCHEN 12/0 x 7/10
PARLOR 12/2 x 12/0
FOYER
DINING 12/2 x 9/8
PORCH
FIRST FLOOR

Design 92220

Units	Single
Price Code	C
Total Finished	1,830 sq. ft.
Main Finished	1,830 sq. ft.
Garage Unfinished	759 sq. ft.
Deck Unfinished	315 sq. ft.
Porch Unfinished	390 sq. ft.
Dimensions	75'x52'3"
Foundation	Basement Crawlspace Slab
Bedrooms	3
Full Baths	2
Max Ridge Height	27'3"
Roof Framing	Stick
Exterior Walls	2x4

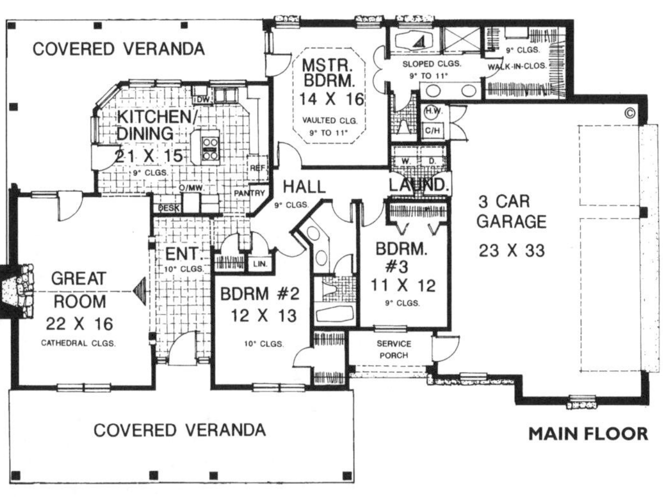
COVERED VERANDA
MSTR. BDRM. 14 X 16
VAULTED CLG. 9' TO 11'
SLOPED CLGS. 9' TO 11'
9' CLGS.
WALK-IN-CLOS.
KITCHEN/ DINING 21 X 15
9' CLGS.
DW
REF.
PANTRY
O/MW
DESK
HALL
9' CLGS.
H.W.
C/H
W
D.
LAUND.
3 CAR GARAGE 23 X 33
ENT.
10' CLGS.
LIN.
BDRM. #3 11 X 12
9' CLGS.
GREAT ROOM 22 X 16
CATHEDRAL CLGS.
BDRM #2 12 X 13
10' CLGS.
SERVICE PORCH
COVERED VERANDA
MAIN FLOOR

Design 98957

Units	Single
Price Code	C
Total Finished	1,830 sq. ft.
Main Finished	1,830 sq. ft.
Garage Unfinished	390 sq. ft.
Dimensions	49'x64'
Foundation	Basement Crawlspace Slab
Bedrooms	3
Full Baths	2
Main Ceiling	8'
Max Ridge Height	21'
Roof Framing	Stick
Exterior Walls	2x4

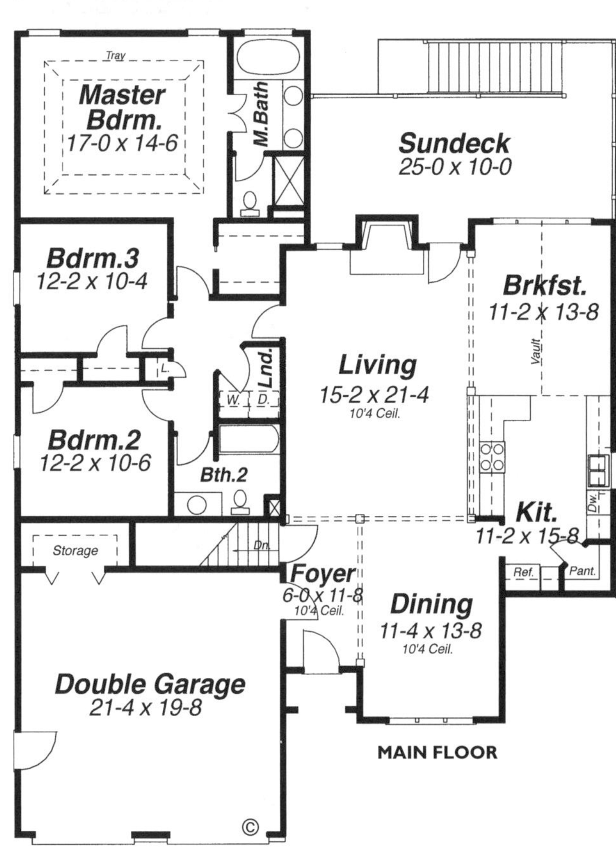
Tray
Master Bdrm. 17-0 x 14-6
M.Bath
Sundeck 25-0 x 10-0
Bdrm.3 12-2 x 10-4
Brkfst. 11-2 x 13-8
Vault
L
Lnd.
W.
D.
Living 15-2 x 21-4
10'4 Ceil.
Bdrm.2 12-2 x 10-6
Bth.2
Kit. 11-2 x 15-8
Dw
Storage
Dn.
Foyer 6-0 x 11-8
10'4 Ceil.
Ref.
Pant.
Dining 11-4 x 13-8
10'4 Ceil.
Double Garage 21-4 x 19-8
MAIN FLOOR

Design 99208

Units	Single
Price Code	C
Total Finished	1,830 sq. ft.
Main Finished	1,830 sq. ft.
Basement Unfinished	1,830 sq. ft.
Dimensions	75'x43'5"
Foundation	Basement
Bedrooms	3
Full Baths	2
Max Ridge Height	25'
Roof Framing	Truss
Exterior Walls	2x6

TERRACE
MASTER BEDROOM
GATHERING RM
DINING RM
BATH
DRESS RM
KITCHEN
GARAGE
BATH
FOYER
BRKFST RM
COVERED PORCH
BEDROOM
STUDY/ BEDROOM
STORAGE

MAIN FLOOR

Design 34031

OPTIONAL CRAWLSPACE/ SLAB FOUNDATION

Units	Single
Price Code	C
Total Finished	1,831 sq. ft.
Main Finished	1,831 sq. ft.
Basement Unfinished	1,831 sq. ft.
Garage Unfinished	484 sq. ft.
Dimensions	60'x52'
Foundation	Basement Crawlspace Slab
Bedrooms	3
Full Baths	2
Half Baths	1
Main Ceiling	8'
Max Ridge Height	22'
Roof Framing	Stick
Exterior Walls	2x4, 2x6

BRKFST.
BEDROOM 3 11'-6" X 11'-8"
DINING 11'-0" X 11'-6"
KITCHEN 10'-6" X 11'-6"
DESK
MAST. BEDROOM 14'-0" X 15'-4"
LIVING ROOM 21'-4" X 13'-6" (12' CEIL.)
DESK
BEDROOM 2 11'-6" X 11'-8"
U.
GARAGE 21'-4" X 21'-8"

MAIN FLOOR

Design 65380

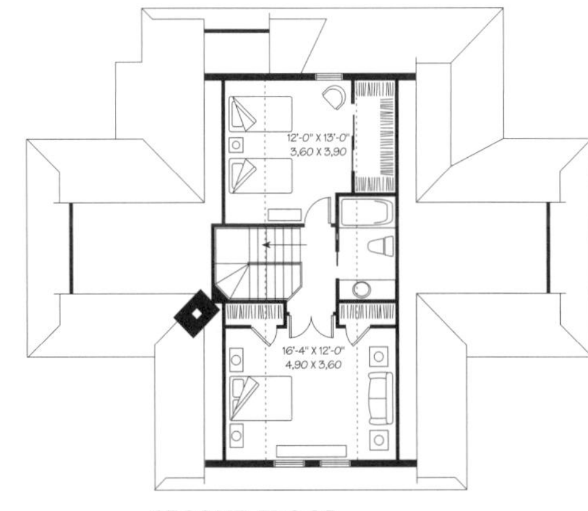

SECOND FLOOR

Units	Single
Price Code	C
Total Finished	1,832 sq. ft.
First Finished	1,212 sq. ft.
Second Finished	620 sq. ft.
Basement Unfinished	1,212 sq. ft.
Dimensions	38'x40'
Foundation	Basement
Bedrooms	3
Full Baths	2
First Ceiling	8'
Max Ridge Height	26'4"

FIRST FLOOR

Design 98467

Units	Single
Price Code	C
Total Finished	1,832 sq. ft.
Main Finished	1,832 sq. ft.
Bonus Unfinished	68 sq. ft.
Basement Unfinished	1,832 sq. ft.
Garage Unfinished	451 sq. ft.
Dimensions	59'6"x52'6"
Foundation	Basement Crawlspace
Bedrooms	3
Full Baths	2
Half Baths	1
Main Ceiling	9'
Max Ridge Height	26'
Roof Framing	Stick
Exterior Walls	2x4

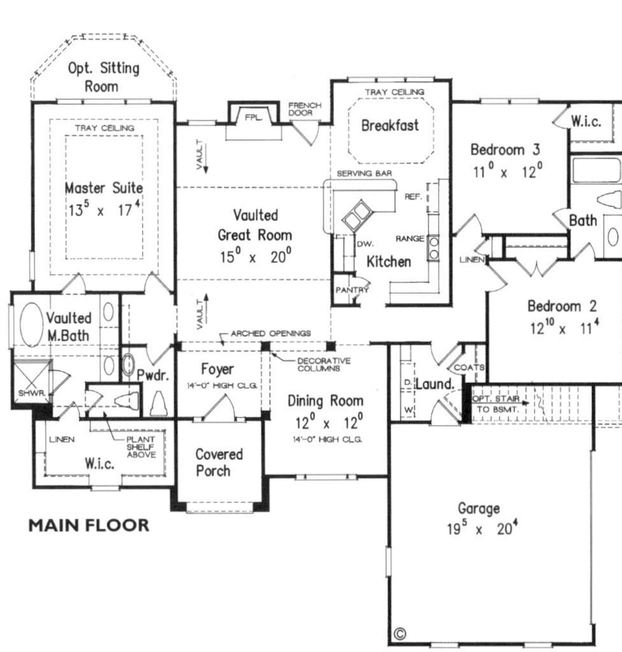
Opt. Sitting Room
TRAY CEILING
Master Suite
13⁵ x 17⁴
FPL.
FRENCH DOOR
TRAY CEILING
Breakfast
Bedroom 3
11⁰ x 12⁰
W.i.c.
Vaulted Great Room
15⁰ x 20⁰
SERVING BAR
REF.
RANGE
DW.
Kitchen
PANTRY
Bath
LINEN
Bedroom 2
12¹⁰ x 11⁴
Vaulted M.Bath
ARCHED OPENINGS
DECORATIVE COLUMNS
Foyer
14'-0" HIGH CLG.
Pwdr.
Dining Room
12⁰ x 12⁰
14'-0" HIGH CLG.
Laund.
COATS
OPT. STAIR TO BSMT.
SHWR.
LINEN
PLANT SHELF ABOVE
W.i.c.
Covered Porch
Garage
19⁵ x 20⁴

MAIN FLOOR

Design 63027

Units Single
Price Code C
Total Finished 1,833 sq. ft.
Main Finished 1,833 sq. ft.
Garage Unfinished 392 sq. ft.
Dimensions 59'4"x48'8"
Foundation Slab
Bedrooms 3
Full Baths 2
Main Ceiling 10'
Max Ridge Height 19'6"
Roof Framing Truss
Exterior Walls 2x4

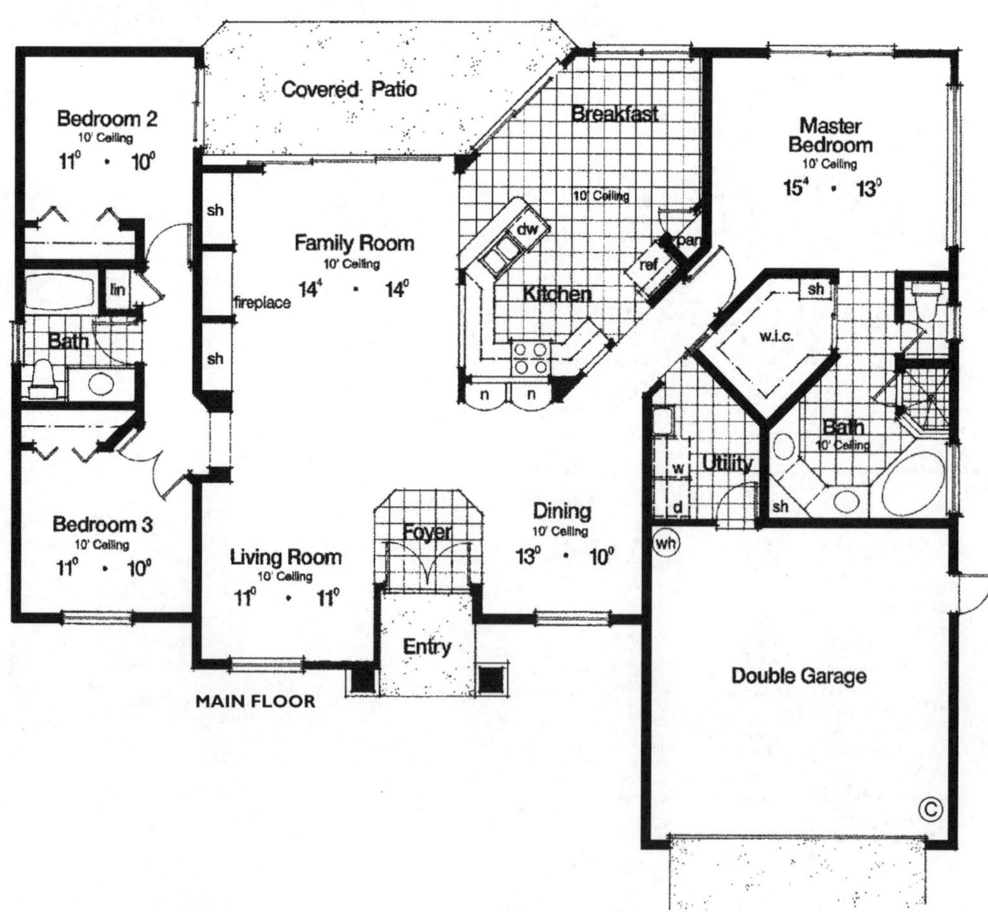

Covered Patio
Breakfast
10' Ceiling
Master Bedroom
10' Ceiling
15⁴ · 13⁰
Bedroom 2
10' Ceiling
11⁰ · 10⁰
sh
Family Room
10' Ceiling
14⁴ · 14⁰
fireplace
dw
ref
pan
Kitchen
sh
w.i.c.
lin
Bath
sh
n
n
Bath
10' Ceiling
Utility
w
d
sh
Bedroom 3
10' Ceiling
11⁰ · 10⁰
Living Room
10' Ceiling
11⁰ · 11⁰
Foyer
Dining
10' Ceiling
13⁰ · 10⁰
wh
Entry
Double Garage
MAIN FLOOR

Design 93432

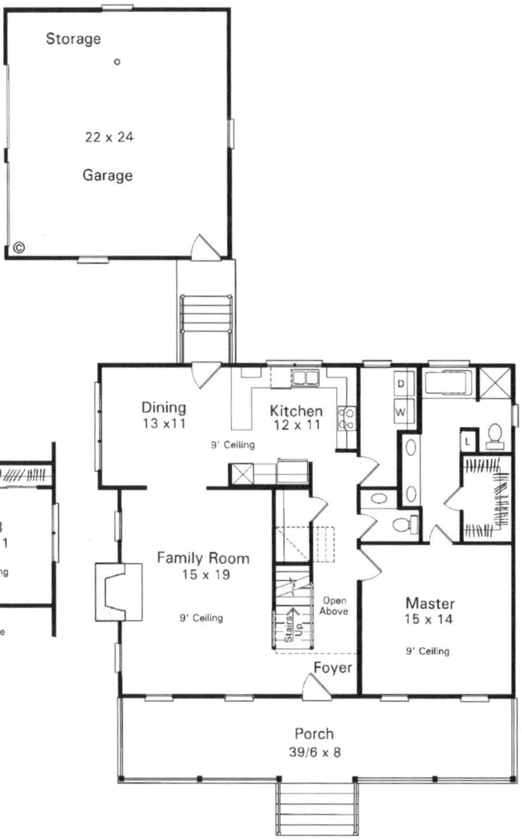

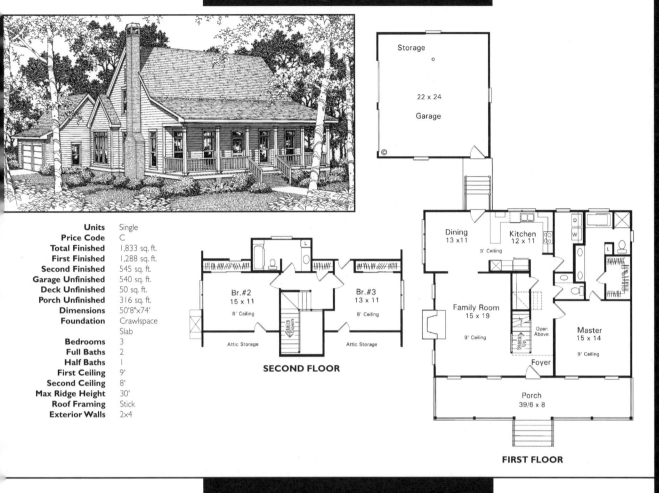

Units	Single
Price Code	C
Total Finished	1,833 sq. ft.
First Finished	1,288 sq. ft.
Second Finished	545 sq. ft.
Garage Unfinished	540 sq. ft.
Deck Unfinished	50 sq. ft.
Porch Unfinished	316 sq. ft.
Dimensions	50'8"x74'
Foundation	Crawlspace Slab
Bedrooms	3
Full Baths	2
Half Baths	1
First Ceiling	9'
Second Ceiling	8'
Max Ridge Height	30'
Roof Framing	Stick
Exterior Walls	2x4

Storage
22 x 24
Garage

Br.#2
15 x 11
8' Ceiling

Br.#3
13 x 11
8' Ceiling

Attic Storage
Attic Storage

SECOND FLOOR

Dining
13 x11

Kitchen
12 x 11
9' Ceiling

Family Room
15 x 19
9' Ceiling

Open Above

Master
15 x 14
9' Ceiling

Foyer

Porch
39/6 x 8

FIRST FLOOR

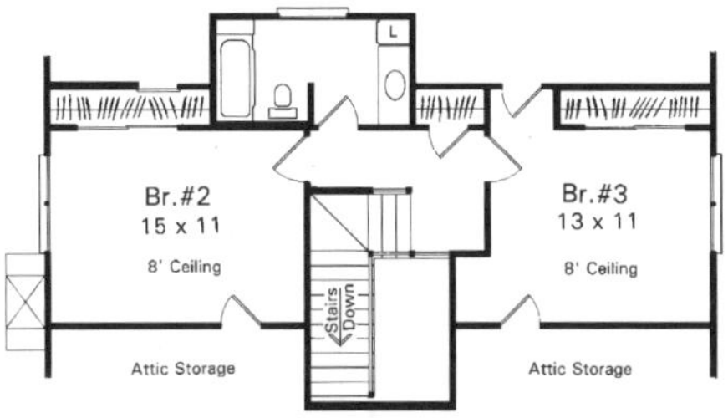

Design 99918

Units	Single
Price Code	C
Total Finished	1,833 sq. ft.
Main Finished	1,833 sq. ft.
Basement Unfinished	1,815 sq. ft.
Garage Unfinished	506 sq. ft.
Porch Unfinished	39 sq. ft.
Dimensions	48'x59'
Foundation	Basement
Bedrooms	3
Full Baths	2
Main Ceiling	8'
Vaulted Ceiling	11'
Max Ridge Height	20'
Roof Framing	Truss
Exterior Walls	2x6

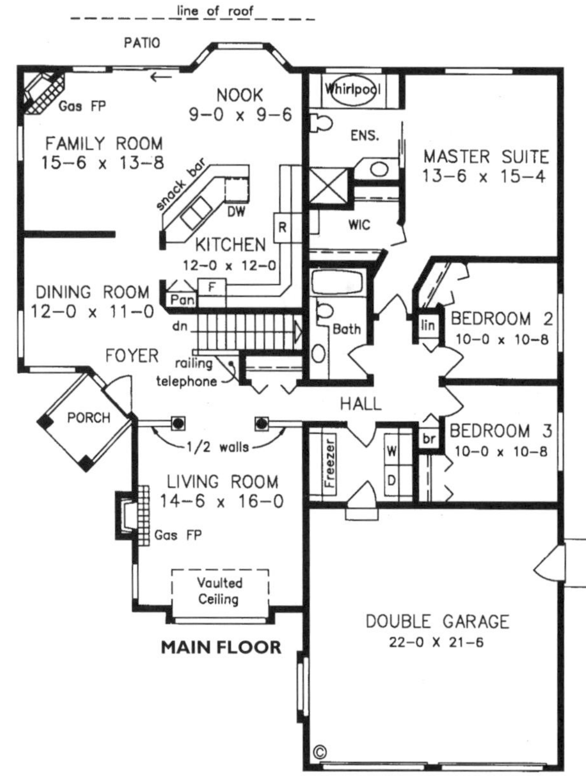
line of roof
PATIO
Gas FP
NOOK
9-0 x 9-6
FAMILY ROOM
15-6 x 13-8
snack bar
DW
KITCHEN
12-0 x 12-0
Whirlpool
ENS.
MASTER SUITE
13-6 x 15-4
WIC
DINING ROOM
12-0 x 11-0
Pan
dn
FOYER
railing
telephone
Bath
lin
BEDROOM 2
10-0 x 10-8
HALL
PORCH
1/2 walls
br
BEDROOM 3
10-0 x 10-8
Freezer
LIVING ROOM
14-6 x 16-0
Gas FP
Vaulted Ceiling
DOUBLE GARAGE
22-0 X 21-6

MAIN FLOOR

Design 32228

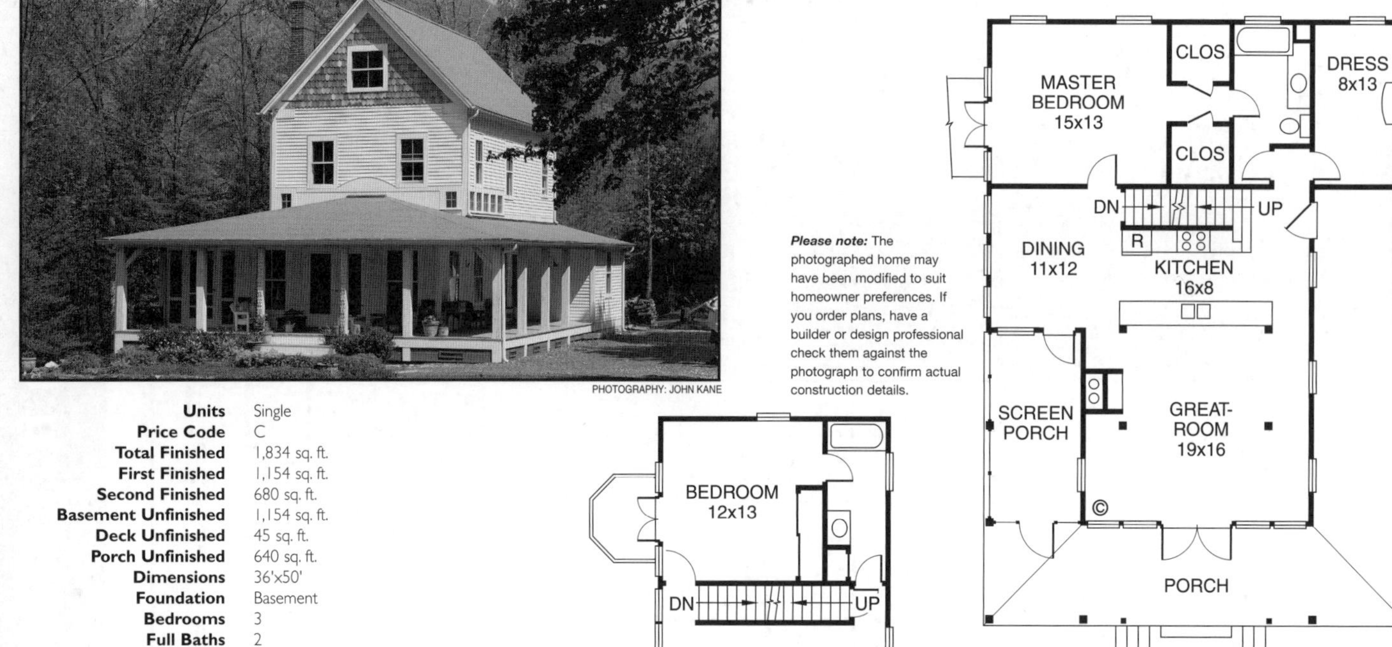
MASTER BEDROOM 15x13
CLOS
CLOS
DRESS 8x13
DN
UP
R
DINING 11x12
KITCHEN 16x8
SCREEN PORCH
GREAT-ROOM 19x16
PORCH
FIRST FLOOR
BEDROOM 12x13
DN
UP
OPEN
LOFT/ BEDROOM 14x11
railing
OPEN
SECOND FLOOR

PHOTOGRAPHY: JOHN KANE

Please note: The photographed home may have been modified to suit homeowner preferences. If you order plans, have a builder or design professional check them against the photograph to confirm actual construction details.

Units	Single
Price Code	C
Total Finished	1,834 sq. ft.
First Finished	1,154 sq. ft.
Second Finished	680 sq. ft.
Basement Unfinished	1,154 sq. ft.
Deck Unfinished	45 sq. ft.
Porch Unfinished	640 sq. ft.
Dimensions	36'x50'
Foundation	Basement
Bedrooms	3
Full Baths	2
First Ceiling	9'
Second Ceiling	8'
Vaulted Ceiling	19'
Max Ridge Height	36'8"
Roof Framing	Stick
Exterior Walls	2x4

Design 97764

Units	Single
Price Code	C
Total Finished	1,834 sq. ft.
Main Finished	1,834 sq. ft.
Basement Unfinished	1,834 sq. ft.
Garage Unfinished	485 sq. ft.
Porch Unfinished	140 sq. ft.
Dimensions	66'9"x50'7"
Foundation	Basement
Bedrooms	3
Full Baths	2
Main Ceiling	8'
Vaulted Ceiling	10'
Max Ridge Height	22'3"
Roof Framing	Truss
Exterior Walls	2x4

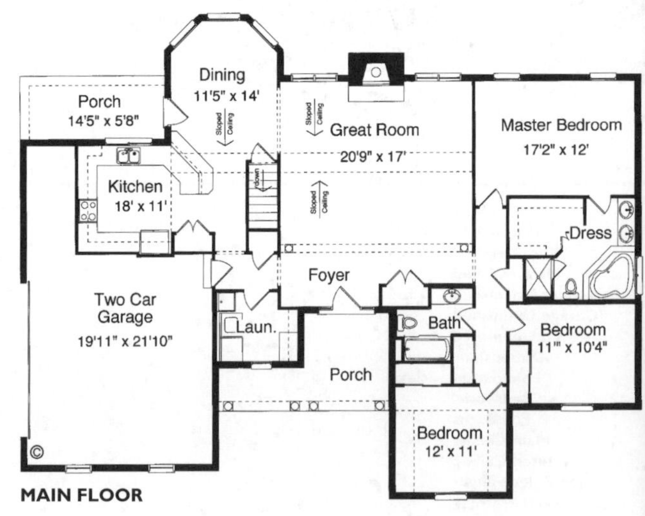
Dining 11'5" x 14'
Porch 14'5" x 5'8"
Great Room 20'9" x 17'
Master Bedroom 17'2" x 12'
Kitchen 18' x 11'
Dress
Foyer
Two Car Garage 19'11" x 21'10"
Laun.
Bath
Bedroom 11'" x 10'4"
Porch
Bedroom 12' x 11'
MAIN FLOOR

Design 91704

Units	Single
Price Code	C
Total Finished	1,837 sq. ft.
First Finished	1,448 sq. ft.
Second Finished	389 sq. ft.
Garage Unfinished	312 sq. ft.
Dimensions	54'x44'
Foundation	Crawlspace
Bedrooms	2
Full Baths	1
3/4 Baths	2
Max Ridge Height	28'
Roof Framing	Stick
Exterior Walls	2x6

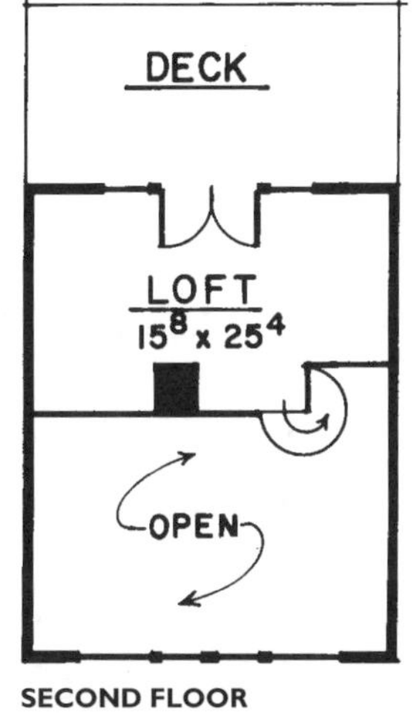
DECK
LOFT
15⁸ x 25⁴
OPEN

SECOND FLOOR

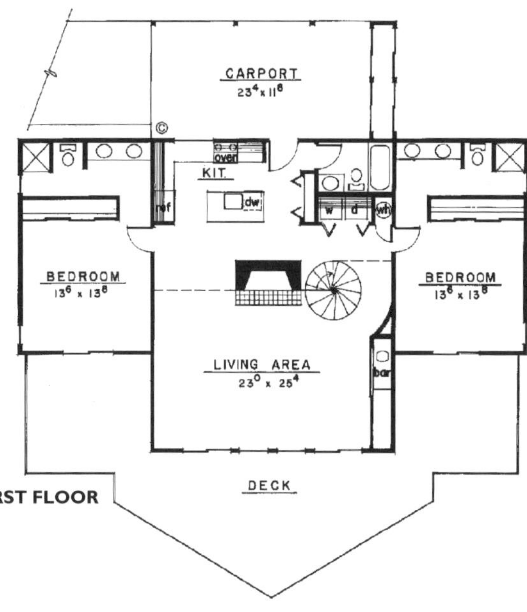
CARPORT
23⁴ x 11⁶
KIT.
oven
dw
ref
w
d
wh
BEDROOM
13⁶ x 13⁶
BEDROOM
13⁶ x 13⁶
LIVING AREA
23⁰ x 25⁴
bar
DECK

FIRST FLOOR

Design 91122

Units	Single
Price Code	C
Total Finished	1,838 sq. ft.
Main Finished	1,838 sq. ft.
Garage Unfinished	452 sq. ft.
Dimensions	48'6"x59'10"
Foundation	Slab
Bedrooms	3
Full Baths	2
Max Ridge Height	35'
Roof Framing	Stick
Exterior Walls	2x4

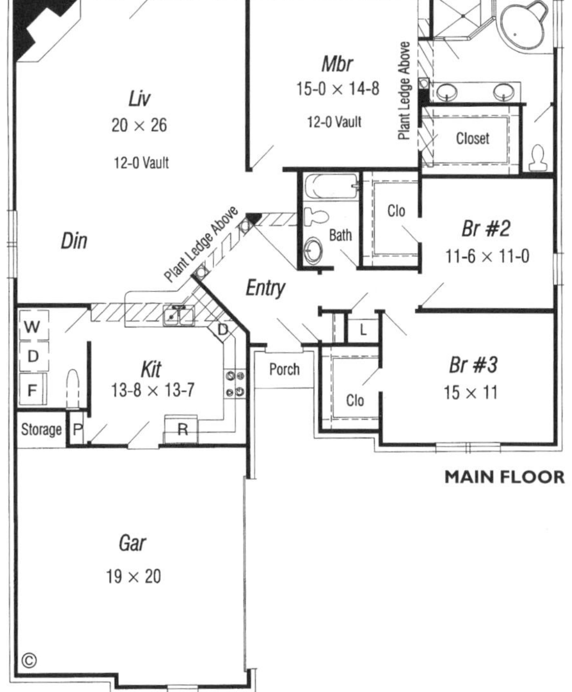
Liv
20 × 26
12-0 Vault
Mbr
15-0 × 14-8
12-0 Vault
Plant Ledge Above
Closet
Din
Plant Ledge Above
Bath
Clo
Br #2
11-6 × 11-0
Entry
W
D
F
Kit
13-8 × 13-7
D
Porch
L
Clo
Br #3
15 × 11
Storage
P
R
Gar
19 × 20

MAIN FLOOR

Design 96819

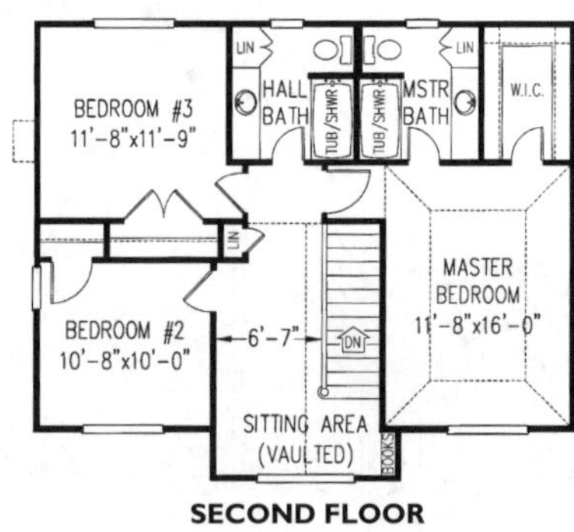
BEDROOM #3
11'-8"x11'-9"
LIN
HALL BATH
TUB/SHWR
TUB/SHWR
MSTR BATH
LIN
W.I.C.
LIN
MASTER BEDROOM
11'-8"x16'-0"
BEDROOM #2
10'-8"x10'-0"
6'-7"
DN
SITTING AREA
(VAULTED)
BOOKS

SECOND FLOOR

Units	Single
Price Code	C
Total Finished	1,840 sq. ft.
First Finished	1,014 sq. ft.
Second Finished	826 sq. ft.
Garage Unfinished	690 sq. ft.
Dimensions	62'7"x45'
Foundation	Basement Crawlspace Slab
Bedrooms	4
Full Baths	2
Half Baths	1
First Ceiling	9'
Roof Framing	Stick
Exterior Walls	2x4

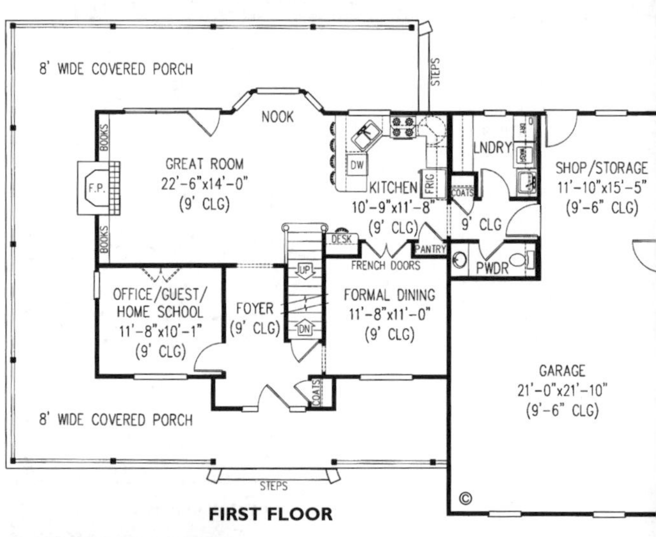
8' WIDE COVERED PORCH
STEPS
NOOK
BOOKS
F.P.
BOOKS
GREAT ROOM
22'-6"x14'-0"
(9' CLG)
DW
KITCHEN
10'-9"x11'-8"
(9' CLG)
FRIG
COATS
LNDRY
9' CLG
SHOP/STORAGE
11'-10"x15'-5"
(9'-6" CLG)
DESK
PANTRY
FRENCH DOORS
PWDR
UP
DN
OFFICE/GUEST/
HOME SCHOOL
11'-8"x10'-1"
(9' CLG)
FOYER
(9' CLG)
FORMAL DINING
11'-8"x11'-0"
(9' CLG)
COATS
GARAGE
21'-0"x21'-10"
(9'-6" CLG)
8' WIDE COVERED PORCH
STEPS
©

FIRST FLOOR

Design 68164

Units	Single
Price Code	B
Total Finished	1,842 sq. ft.
Main Finished	1,842 sq. ft.
Bonus Unfinished	386 sq. ft.
Dimensions	54'x63'
Foundation	Crawlspace Slab
Bedrooms	3
Full Baths	2
Main Ceiling	9'
Max Ridge Height	30'
Exterior Walls	2x4

* Alternate foundation options available at an additional charge. Please call 1-800-235-5700 for more information.

DN
OPTIONAL GAMEROOM
20'4" X 16'

BONUS

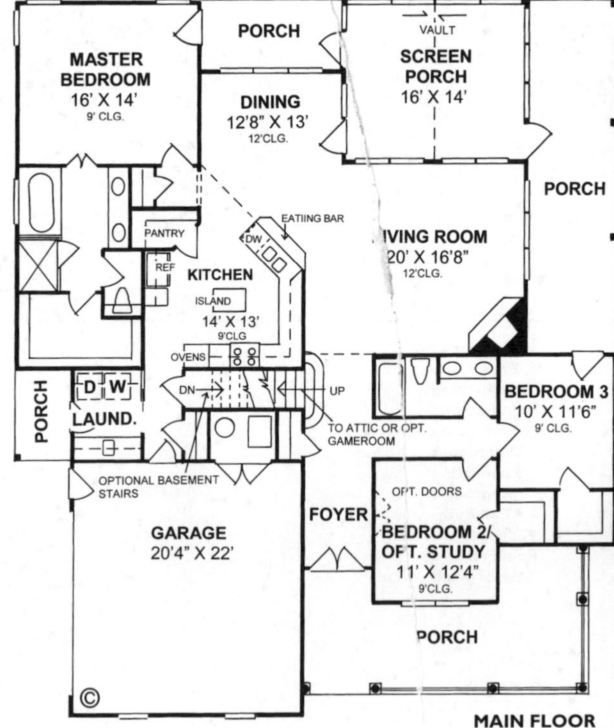
MASTER BEDROOM
16' X 14'
9' CLG.
PORCH
DINING
12'8" X 13'
12'CLG.
VAULT
SCREEN PORCH
16' X 14'
PORCH
PANTRY
EATIING BAR
DW
REF
KITCHEN
ISLAND
14' X 13'
9'CLG
IVING ROOM
20' X 16'8"
12'CLG.
OVENS
DN
UP
PORCH
D W
LAUND.
TO ATTIC OR OPT. GAMEROOM
BEDROOM 3
10' X 11'6"
9' CLG.
OPTIONAL BASEMENT STAIRS
GARAGE
20'4" X 22'
FOYER
OPT. DOORS
BEDROOM 2/
OPT. STUDY
11' X 12'4"
9'CLG.
PORCH
©

MAIN FLOOR

Design 93425

Units	Single
Price Code	C
Total Finished	1,842 sq. ft.
Main Finished	1,842 sq. ft.
Garage Unfinished	507 sq. ft.
Dimensions	56'4"x68'6"
Foundation	Crawlspace Slab
Bedrooms	3
Full Baths	2
Main Ceiling	9'
Vaulted Ceiling	12'
Max Ridge Height	20'6"
Roof Framing	Stick
Exterior Walls	2x4

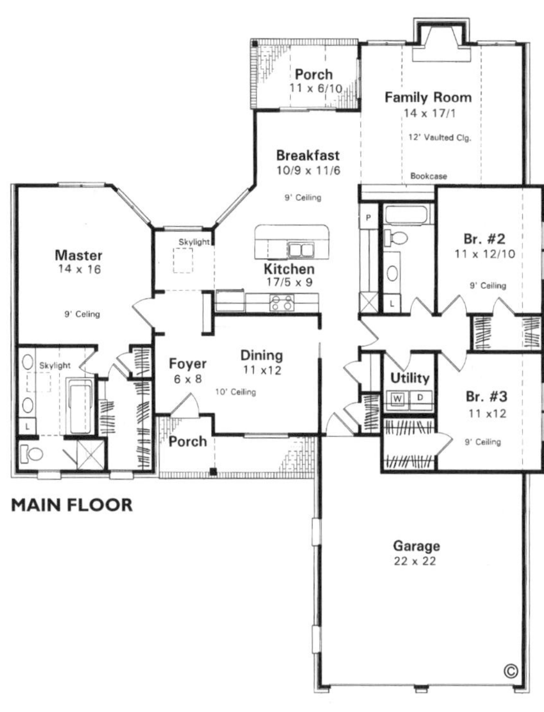
Porch
11 x 6/10
Family Room
14 x 17/1
12' Vaulted Clg.
Bookcase
Breakfast
10/9 x 11/6
9' Ceiling
Master
14 x 16
9' Ceiling
Skylight
Kitchen
17/5 x 9
Br. #2
11 x 12/10
9' Ceiling
Skylight
Foyer
6 x 8
Dining
11 x12
10' Ceiling
Utility
W
D
Br. #3
11 x12
9' Ceiling
Porch
Garage
22 x 22
©

MAIN FLOOR

Design 97416

Units	Single
Price Code	C
Total Finished	1,842 sq. ft.
Main Finished	1,842 sq. ft.
Garage Unfinished	498 sq. ft.
Dimensions	62'x48'
Foundation	Basement
Bedrooms	[illegible]
Full Baths	[illegible]
Half Baths	[illegible]
Max Ridge Height	20'9"
Roof Framing	Stick

Alternate foundation options available at an additional charge. Please call 1-800-235-5700 for more information.

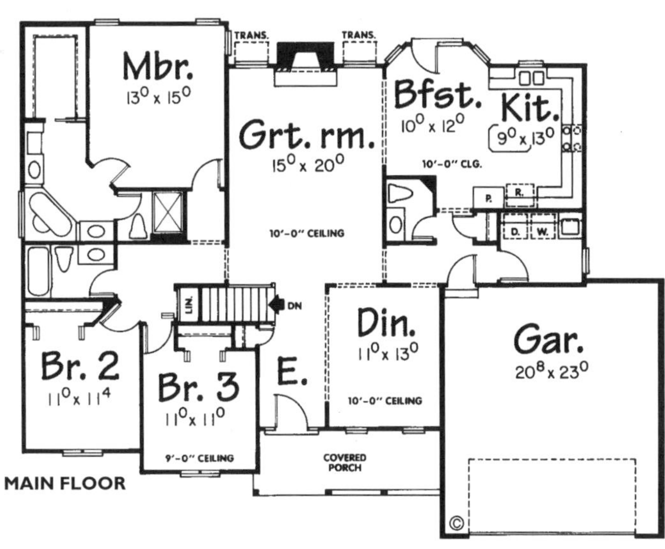
TRANS.
TRANS.
Mbr.
13^0 x 15^0
Grt. rm.
15^0 x 20^0
10'-0" CEILING
Bfst.
10^0 x 12^0
Kit.
9^0 x 13^0
10'-0" CLG.
P.
R.
D.
W.
LIN.
DN
Br. 2
11^0 x 11^4
Br. 3
11^0 x 11^0
9'-0" CEILING
E.
Din.
11^0 x 13^0
10'-0" CEILING
COVERED PORCH
Gar.
20^8 x 23^0
©

MAIN FLOOR

Design 67000

Units	Single
Price Code	C
Total Finished	1,843 sq. ft.
Main Finished	1,843 sq. ft.
Garage Unfinished	534 sq. ft.
Porch Unfinished	225 sq. ft.
Dimensions	60'11"x67'9"
Foundation	Slab
Bedrooms	3
Full Baths	2
Main Ceiling	8'
Max Ridge Height	24'
Roof Framing	Stick
Exterior Walls	2x4

DOUBLE GARAGE
21'-0" X 21'-0"
STOR
UTIL
D
W
UP
LANDING
CL
MASTER BATH
LIN
MASTER SUITE
16'-0" X 13'-0"
BRK
10'-0" X 10'-0"
EATING BAR
KIT
S
R
DW
REF
PANT
F/P
GREAT ROOM
14'-0" X 21'-0"
BEDR'M 3
12'-0" X 10'-9"
BATH-2
BEDR'M 2
12'-0" X 11'-0"
DINING
13'-6" X 11'-0"
CTS
ENTRY
PORCH

MAIN FLOOR

Design 90466

Units	Single
Price Code	C
Total Finished	1,843 sq. ft.
Main Finished	1,843 sq. ft.
Garage Unfinished	534 sq. ft.
Porch Unfinished	225 sq. ft.
Dimensions	60'11"x67'9"
Foundation	Slab
Bedrooms	3
Full Baths	2
Half Baths	1
Main Ceiling	8'
Max Ridge Height	24'
Roof Framing	Stick
Exterior Walls	2x4

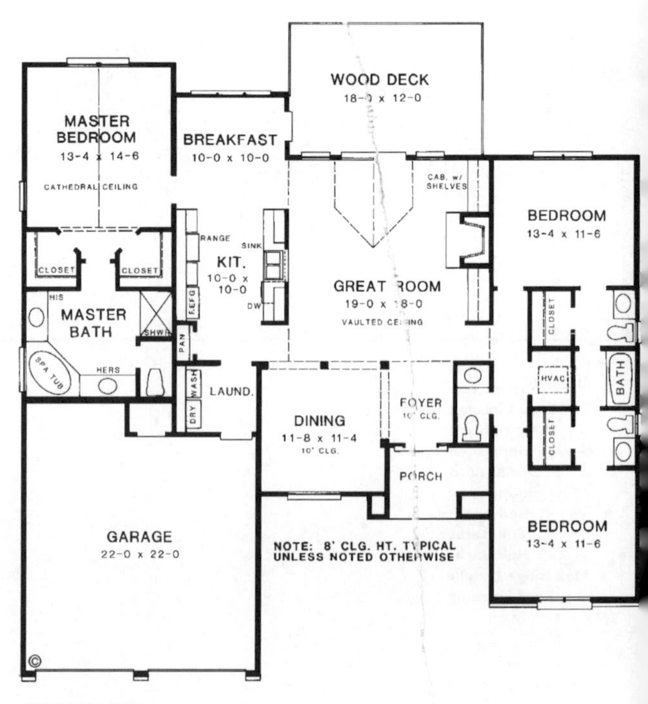
WOOD DECK
18-0 x 12-0
MASTER BEDROOM
CATHEDRAL CEILING
BREAKFAST
10-0 x 10-0
CAB. w/ SHELVES
BEDROOM
13-4 x 11-6
CLOSET
CLOSET
RANGE
SINK
KIT.
10-0 x 10-0
DW
GREAT ROOM
VAULTED CEILING
MASTER BATH
HIS
HERS
SPA TUB
SHWR
PAN
WASH
DRY
LAUND.
DINING
11-8 x 11-4
FOYER
PORCH
HVAC
BATH
BEDROOM
13-4 x 11-6
GARAGE
22-0 x 22-0
NOTE: 8' CLG. HT. TYPICAL UNLESS NOTED OTHERWISE

MAIN FLOOR

Design 97284

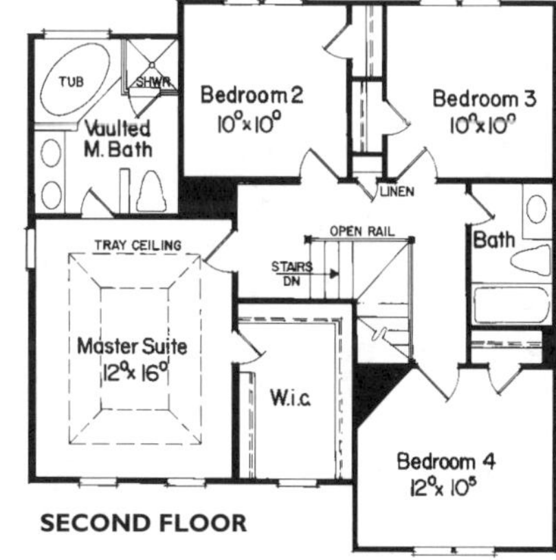
TUB
SHWR.
Vaulted M.Bath
Bedroom 2 10⁰x10⁰
Bedroom 3 10⁰x10⁰
LINEN
OPEN RAIL
Bath
TRAY CEILING
STAIRS DN
Master Suite 12⁰x16⁰
W.i.c.
Bedroom 4 12⁰x10⁵
SECOND FLOOR

Units	Single
Price Code	C
Total Finished	1,845 sq. ft.
First Finished	954 sq. ft.
Second Finished	891 sq. ft.
Basement Unfinished	954 sq. ft.
Garage Unfinished	460 sq. ft.
Dimensions	54'4"x36'
Foundation	Basement Crawlspace Slab
Bedrooms	4
Full Baths	2
Half Baths	1
Max Ridge Height	26'6"
Roof Framing	Stick
Exterior Walls	2x4

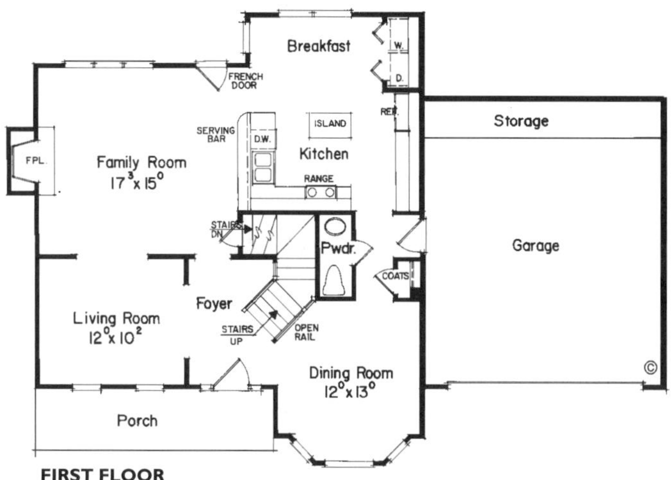
Breakfast
W.
D.
FRENCH DOOR
SERVING BAR
D.W.
ISLAND
REF.
Storage
FPL.
Family Room 17³x15⁰
Kitchen
RANGE
STAIRS DN
Pwdr.
Garage
COATS
Foyer
Living Room 12⁰x10²
STAIRS UP
OPEN RAIL
Dining Room 12⁰x13⁰
Porch
FIRST FLOOR

Design 98425

CAD
FILES AVAILABLE
For more information call
800-235-5700

Units	Single
Price Code	C
Total Finished	1,845 sq. ft.
Main Finished	1,845 sq. ft.
Bonus Unfinished	409 sq. ft.
Basement Unfinished	1,845 sq. ft.
Garage Unfinished	529 sq. ft.
Dimensions	56'x60'
Foundation	Basement Crawlspace
Bedrooms	3
Full Baths	2
Half Baths	1
Main Ceiling	9'
Max Ridge Height	26'6"
Roof Framing	Stick
Exterior Walls	2x4

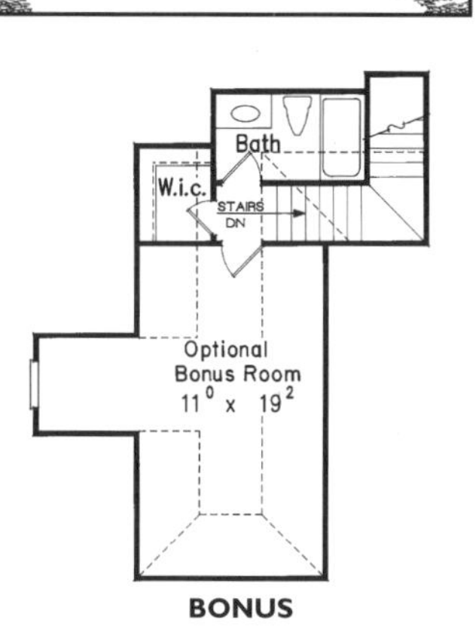
Bath
W.i.c.
STAIRS DN
Optional Bonus Room 11⁰ x 19²
BONUS

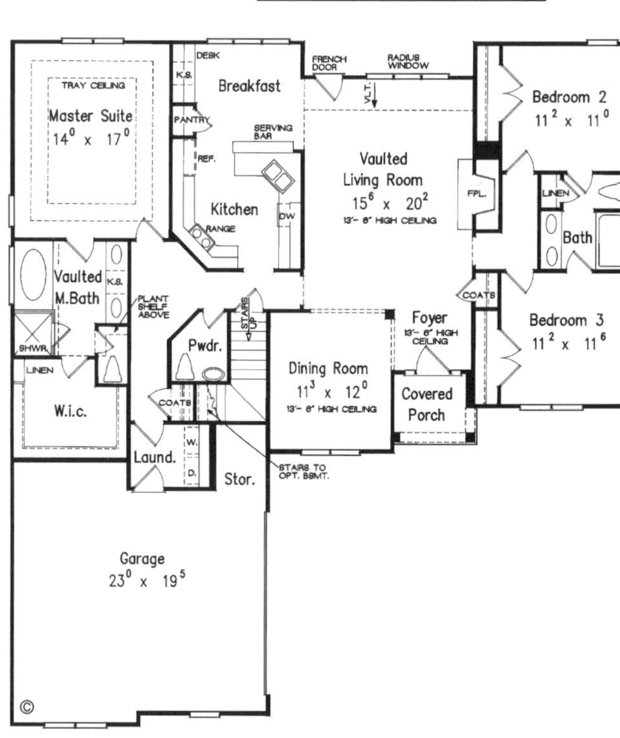
DESK
K.S.
Breakfast
FRENCH DOOR
RADIUS WINDOW
TRAY CEILING
Master Suite 14⁰ x 17⁰
PANTRY
SERVING BAR
REF.
Vaulted Living Room 15⁶ x 20²
13'- 8" HIGH CEILING
Bedroom 2 11² x 11⁰
FPL.
LINEN
Kitchen
RANGE
DW
Bath
Vaulted M.Bath
K.S.
PLANT SHELF ABOVE
STAIRS UP
Pwdr.
Foyer
13'- 8" HIGH CEILING
COATS
Bedroom 3 11² x 11⁶
SHWR.
LINEN
W.i.c.
COATS
Dining Room 11³ x 12⁰
13'- 8" HIGH CEILING
Covered Porch
Laund.
W.
D.
Stor.
STAIRS TO OPT. BSMT.
Garage 23⁰ x 19⁵
MAIN FLOOR

Design 99491

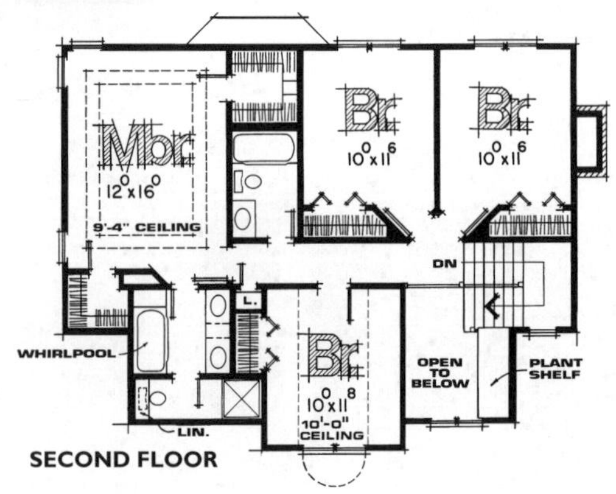

Mbr
12⁰x16⁰
9'-4" CEILING
Br
10⁰x11⁶
Br
10⁰x11⁶
DN
L.
WHIRLPOOL
Br
10⁰x11⁸
10'-0" CEILING
LIN.
OPEN TO BELOW
PLANT SHELF
SECOND FLOOR

Units	Single
Price Code	C
Total Finished	1,846 sq. ft.
First Finished	919 sq. ft.
Second Finished	927 sq. ft.
Garage Unfinished	414 sq. ft.
Dimensions	44'x40'
Foundation	Basement Slab
Bedrooms	4
Full Baths	2
Half Baths	1
Max Ridge Height	26'10"
Roof Framing	Stick
Exterior Walls	2x4

* Alternate foundation options available at an additional charge. Please call 1-800-235-5700 for more information.

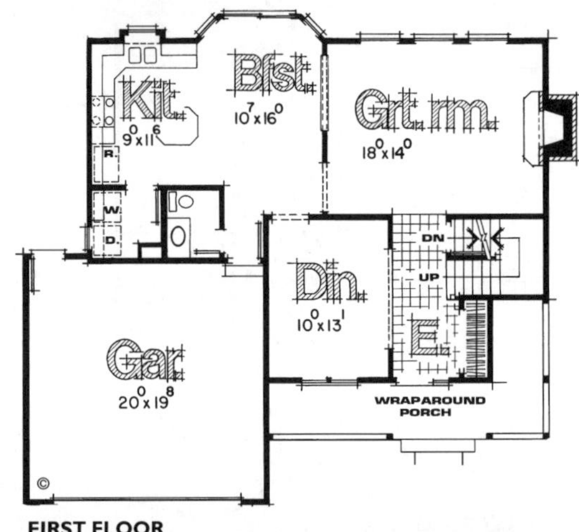

Kit
9⁰x11⁶
Bfst
10⁷x16⁰
Grt rm
18⁰x14⁰
R.
W.
D.
DN
UP
Din
10⁰x13¹
E
Gar
20⁰x19⁸
WRAPAROUND PORCH
FIRST FLOOR

Design 94692

Units	Single
Price Code	C
Total Finished	1,847 sq. ft.
Main Finished	1,847 sq. ft.
Garage Unfinished	593 sq. ft.
Porch Unfinished	528 sq. ft.
Dimensions	49'6"x72'5"
Foundation	Slab
Bedrooms	3
Full Baths	2
Max Ridge Height	24'8"
Roof Framing	Stick
Exterior Walls	2x4

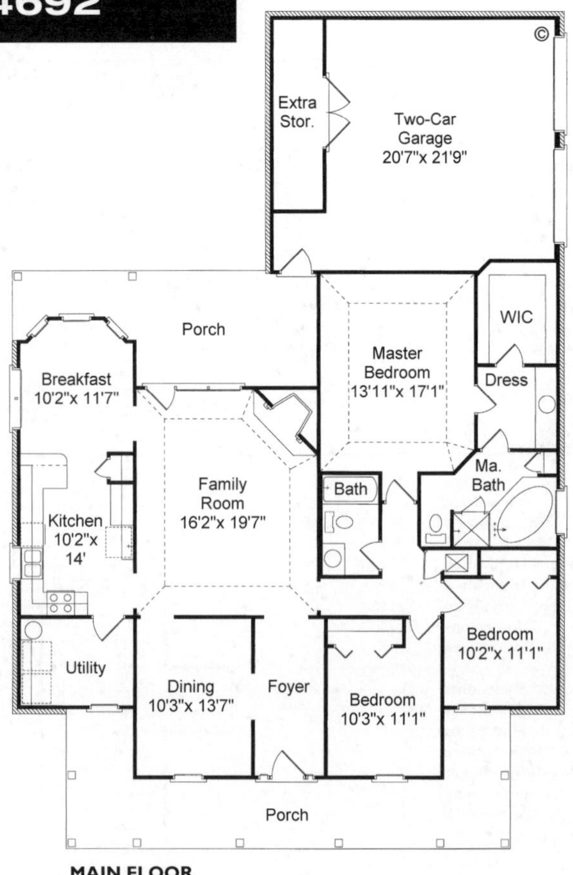

Extra Stor.
Two-Car Garage
20'7"x 21'9"
Porch
WIC
Master Bedroom
13'11"x 17'1"
Dress
Breakfast
10'2"x 11'7"
Ma. Bath
Bath
Family Room
16'2"x 19'7"
Kitchen
10'2"x 14'
Bedroom
10'2"x 11'1"
Utility
Dining
10'3"x 13'7"
Foyer
Bedroom
10'3"x 11'1"
Porch
MAIN FLOOR

Design 97295

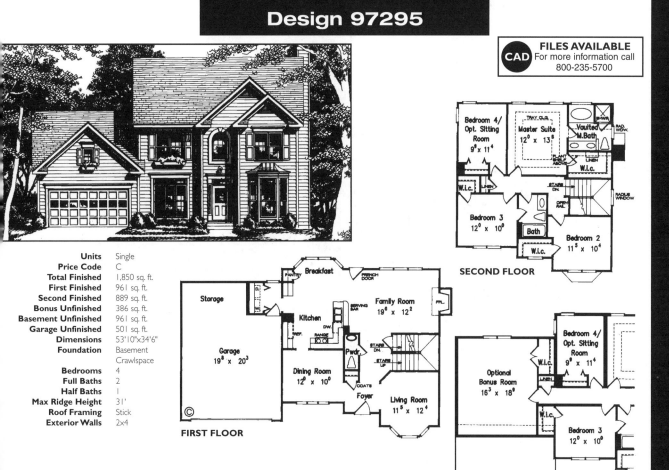

Units	Single
Price Code	C
Total Finished	1,850 sq. ft.
First Finished	961 sq. ft.
Second Finished	889 sq. ft.
Bonus Unfinished	386 sq. ft.
Basement Unfinished	961 sq. ft.
Garage Unfinished	501 sq. ft.
Dimensions	53'10"x34'6"
Foundation	Basement Crawlspace
Bedrooms	4
Full Baths	2
Half Baths	1
Max Ridge Height	31'
Roof Framing	Stick
Exterior Walls	2x4

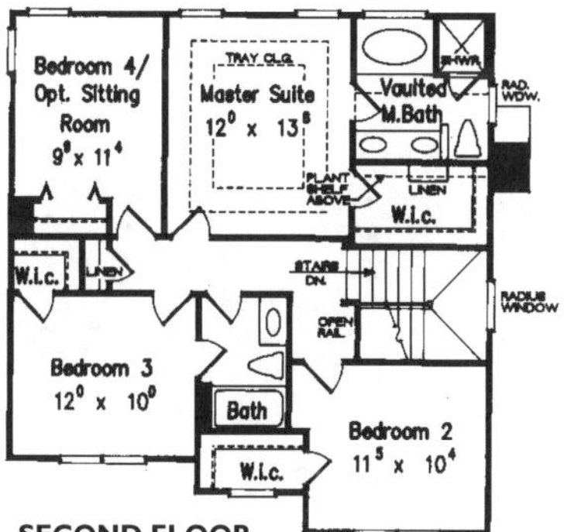

SECOND FLOOR

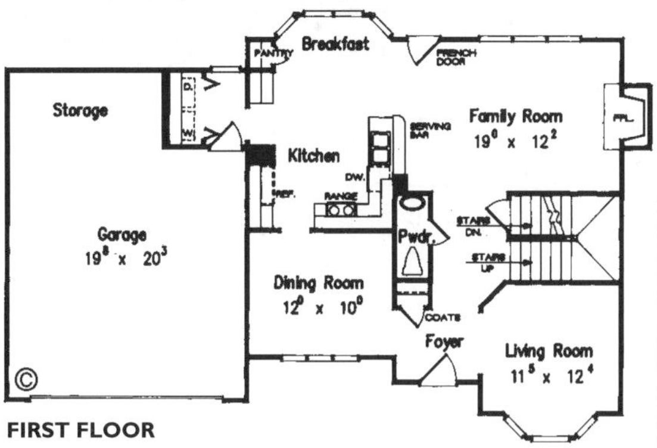

FIRST FLOOR

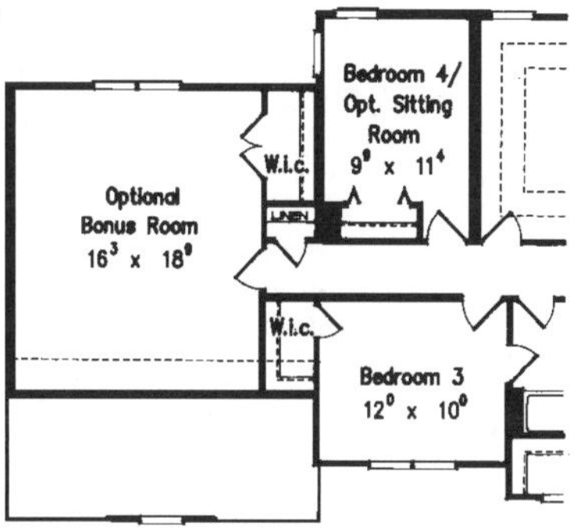

SECOND FLOOR BONUS

Design 99434

Units	Single
Price Code	C
Total Finished	1,850 sq. ft.
Main Finished	1,850 sq. ft.
Garage Unfinished	487 sq. ft.
Dimensions	62'x48'
Foundation	Basement
Bedrooms	3
Full Baths	2
Main Ceiling	8'
Max Ridge Height	20'
Roof Framing	Stick
Exterior Walls	2x4

* Alternate foundation options available at an additional charge.
Please call 1-800-235-5700 for more information.

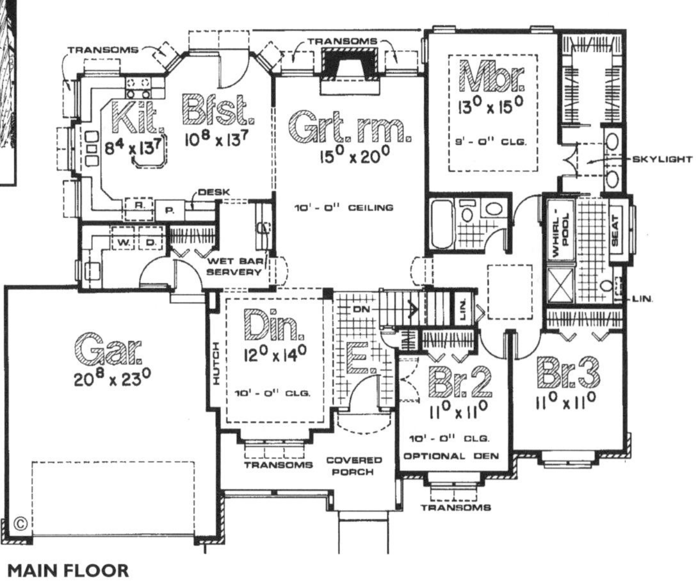

MAIN FLOOR

Design 81008

Units	Single
Price Code	C
Total Finished	1,852 sq. ft.
Main Finished	1,852 sq. ft.
Garage Unfinished	757 sq. ft.
Dimensions	70'x45'
Foundation	Crawlspace
Bedrooms	3
Full Baths	2

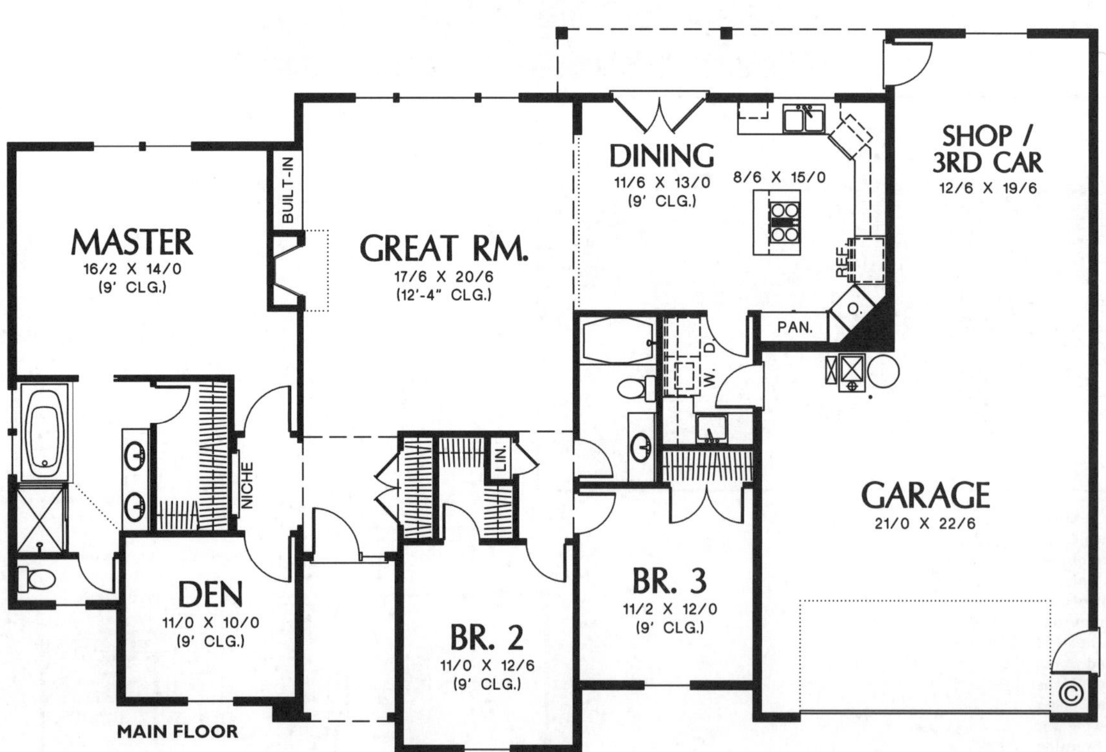

MASTER
16/2 X 14/0
(9' CLG.)
BUILT-IN
GREAT RM.
17/6 X 20/6
(12'-4" CLG.)
DINING
11/6 X 13/0
(9' CLG.)
8/6 X 15/0
REF.
O.
PAN.
W.
D.
SHOP /
3RD CAR
12/6 X 19/6
GARAGE
21/0 X 22/6
NICHE
LIN.
DEN
11/0 X 10/0
(9' CLG.)
BR. 2
11/0 X 12/6
(9' CLG.)
BR. 3
11/2 X 12/0
(9' CLG.)
MAIN FLOOR

Design 94248

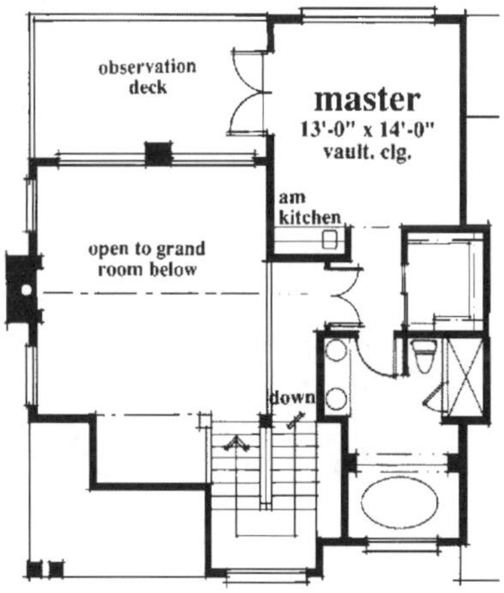

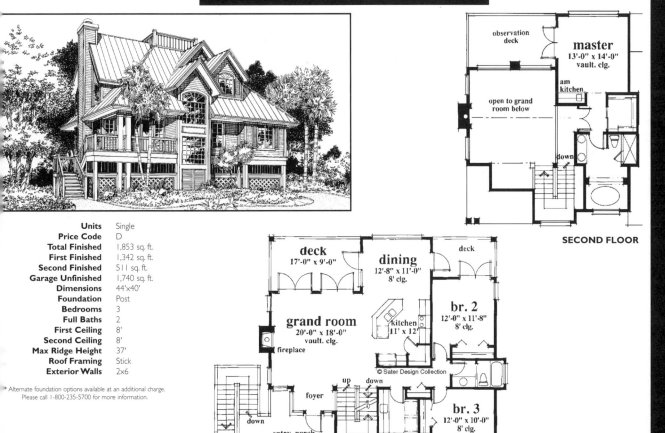

observation deck
master 13'-0" x 14'-0" vault. clg.
am kitchen
open to grand room below
down
SECOND FLOOR

Units	Single
Price Code	D
Total Finished	1,853 sq. ft.
First Finished	1,342 sq. ft.
Second Finished	511 sq. ft.
Garage Unfinished	1,740 sq. ft.
Dimensions	44'x40'
Foundation	Post
Bedrooms	3
Full Baths	2
First Ceiling	8'
Second Ceiling	8'
Max Ridge Height	37'
Roof Framing	Stick
Exterior Walls	2x6

* Alternate foundation options available at an additional charge. Please call 1-800-235-5700 for more information.

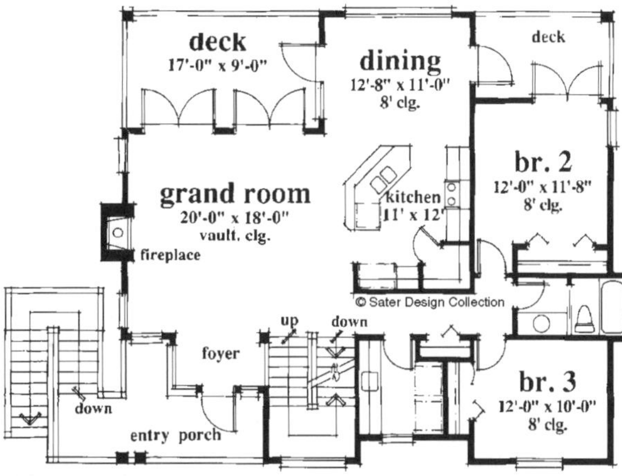

deck 17'-0" x 9'-0"
dining 12'-8" x 11'-0" 8' clg.
deck
grand room 20'-0" x 18'-0" vault. clg.
fireplace
kitchen 11' x 12'
br. 2 12'-0" x 11'-8" 8' clg.
© Sater Design Collection
up down
foyer
down
entry porch
br. 3 12'-0" x 10'-0" 8' clg.
FIRST FLOOR

Design 98986

Units	Single
Price Code	C
Total Finished	1,854 sq. ft.
Main Finished	1,854 sq. ft.
Garage Unfinished	424 sq. ft.
Dimensions	65'x56'5"
Foundation	Basement
Bedrooms	3
Full Baths	2
Half Baths	1
Main Ceiling	8'
Max Ridge Height	24'
Roof Framing	Stick
Exterior Walls	2x4

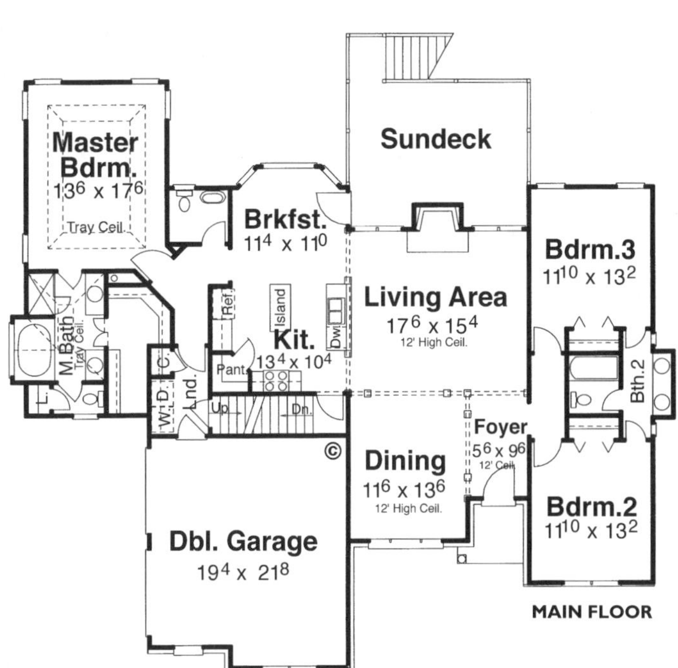
Sundeck
Master Bdrm. 13⁶ x 17⁶
Tray Ceil.
Brkfst. 11⁴ x 11⁰
Bdrm.3 11¹⁰ x 13²
Living Area 17⁶ x 15⁴
12' High Ceil.
Ref.
Island
Dw
Kit. 13⁴ x 10⁴
Pant.
M.Bath
Tray Ceil.
W. D.
Lnd.
Up
Dn.
Bth.2
Foyer 5⁶ x 9⁶
12' Ceil.
Dining 11⁶ x 13⁶
12' High Ceil.
Bdrm.2 11¹⁰ x 13²
Dbl. Garage 19⁴ x 21⁸
©

MAIN FLOOR

Design 24704

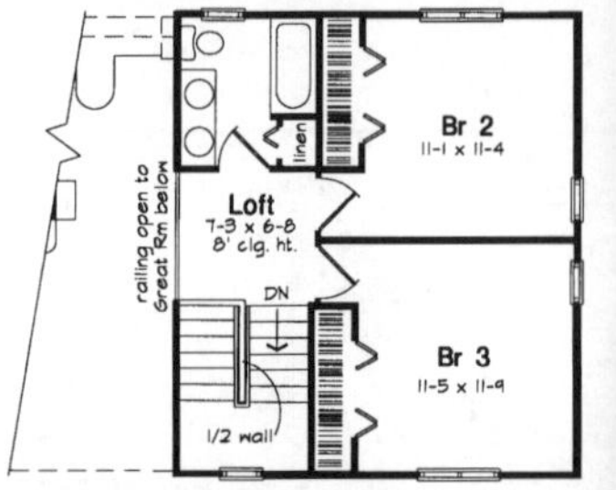

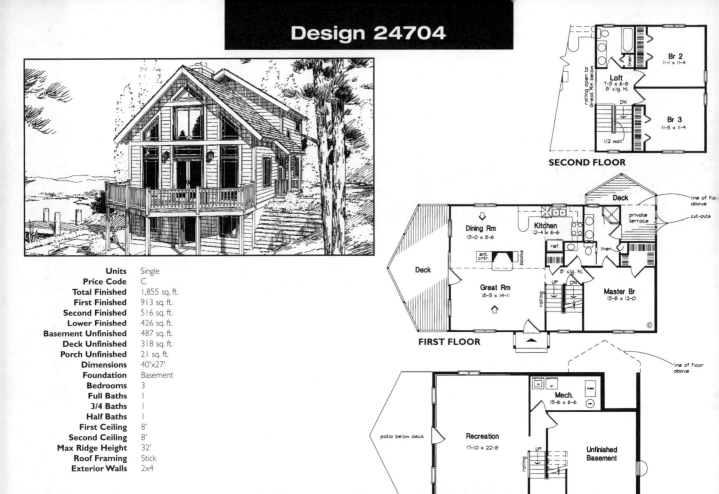

SECOND FLOOR

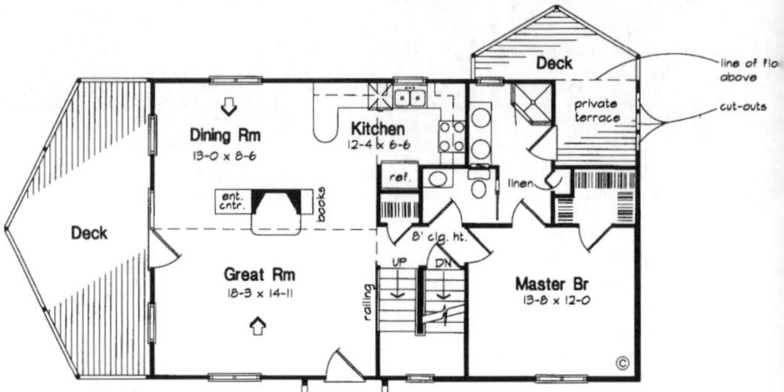

FIRST FLOOR

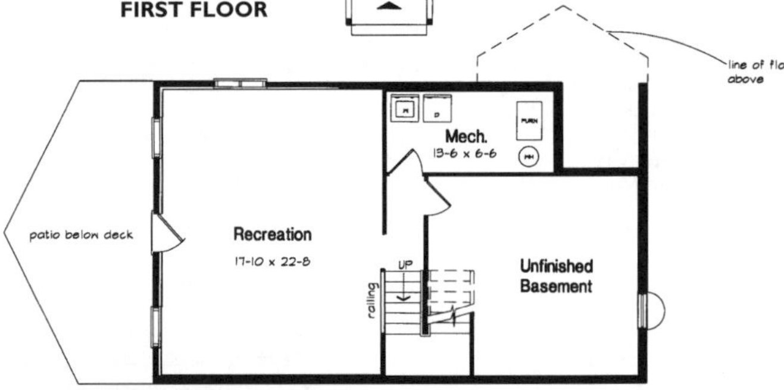

LOWER FLOOR

Units	Single
Price Code	C
Total Finished	1,855 sq. ft.
First Finished	913 sq. ft.
Second Finished	516 sq. ft.
Lower Finished	426 sq. ft.
Basement Unfinished	487 sq. ft.
Deck Unfinished	318 sq. ft.
Porch Unfinished	21 sq. ft.
Dimensions	40'x27'
Foundation	Basement
Bedrooms	3
Full Baths	1
3/4 Baths	1
Half Baths	1
First Ceiling	8'
Second Ceiling	8'
Max Ridge Height	32'
Roof Framing	Stick
Exterior Walls	2x4

Design 97719

Units	Single
Price Code	C
Total Finished	1,855 sq. ft.
Main Finished	1,855 sq. ft.
Dimensions	66'3"x48'2"
Foundation	Basement
Bedrooms	3
Full Baths	2
Max Ridge Height	22'
Roof Framing	Stick
Exterior Walls	2x4

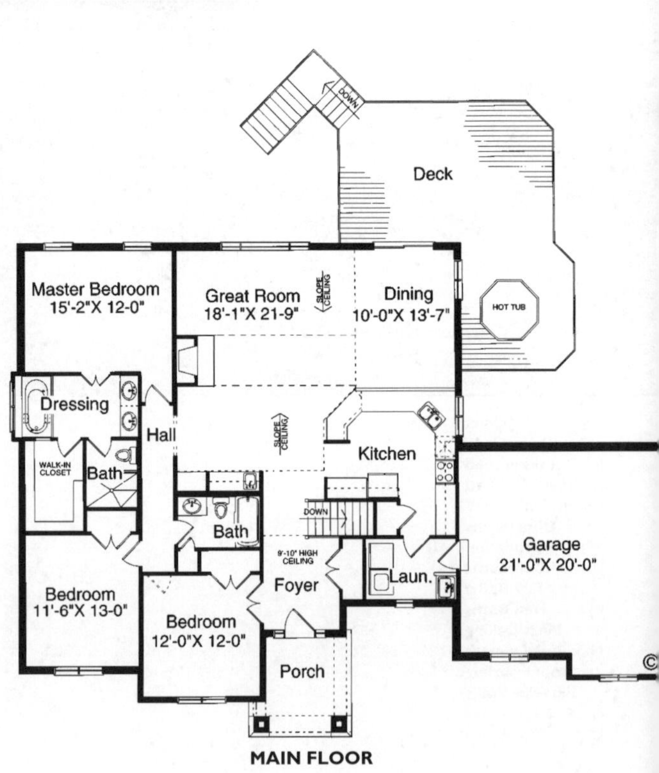
Deck
Master Bedroom
15'-2"X 12-0"
Great Room
18'-1"X 21-9"
Dining
10'-0"X 13'-7"
HOT TUB
Dressing
Hall
Kitchen
WALK-IN CLOSET
Bath
Bath
Foyer
Laun.
Garage
21'-0"X 20'-0"
Bedroom
11'-6"X 13-0"
Bedroom
12'-0"X 12-0"
Porch

MAIN FLOOR

Design 97909

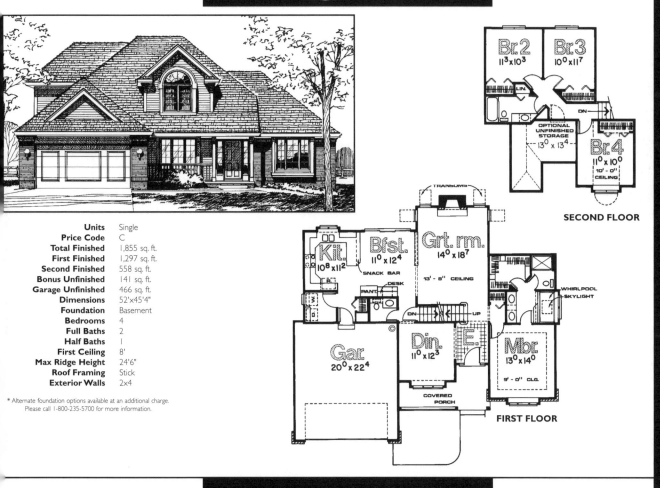

Units	Single
Price Code	C
Total Finished	1,855 sq. ft.
First Finished	1,297 sq. ft.
Second Finished	558 sq. ft.
Bonus Unfinished	141 sq. ft.
Garage Unfinished	466 sq. ft.
Dimensions	52'x45'4"
Foundation	Basement
Bedrooms	4
Full Baths	2
Half Baths	1
First Ceiling	8'
Max Ridge Height	24'6"
Roof Framing	Stick
Exterior Walls	2x4

* Alternate foundation options available at an additional charge. Please call 1-800-235-5700 for more information.

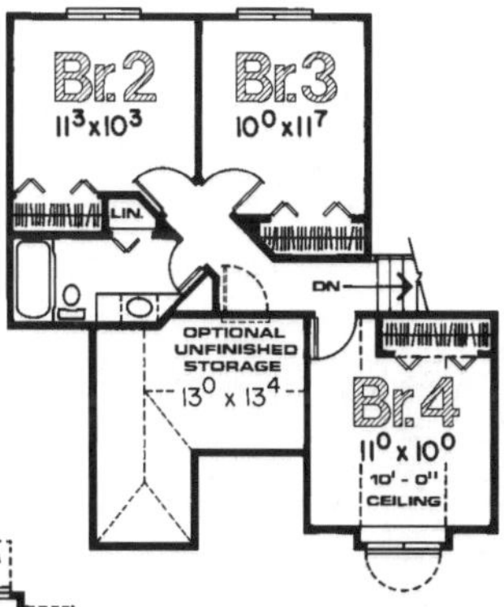

Br.2 11³x10³
Br.3 10⁰x11⁷
LIN.
DN
OPTIONAL UNFINISHED STORAGE 13⁰ x 13⁴
Br.4 11⁰x10⁰ 10'-0" CEILING

SECOND FLOOR

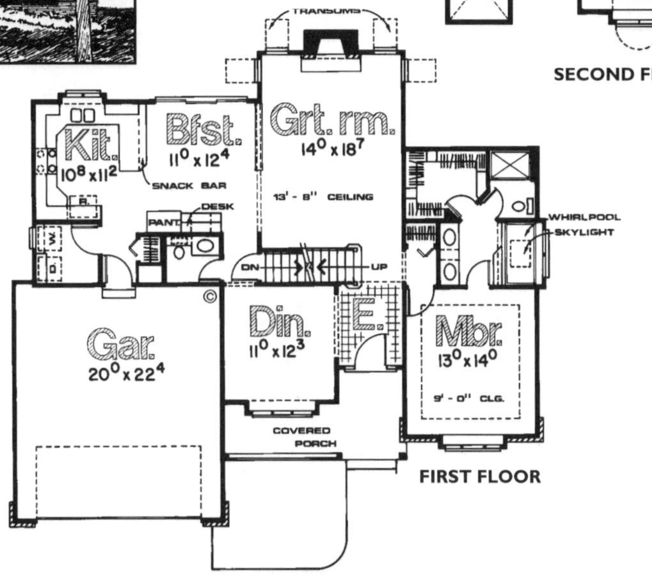

TRANSOMS
Kit. 10⁸x11²
Bfst. 11⁰x12⁴
SNACK BAR
DESK
PANT.
Grt. rm. 14⁰x18⁷
13'-8" CEILING
DN
UP
WHIRLPOOL
SKYLIGHT
Gar. 20⁰x22⁴
Din. 11⁰x12³
E.
Mbr. 13⁰x14⁰
9'-0" CLG.
COVERED PORCH

FIRST FLOOR

Design 97707

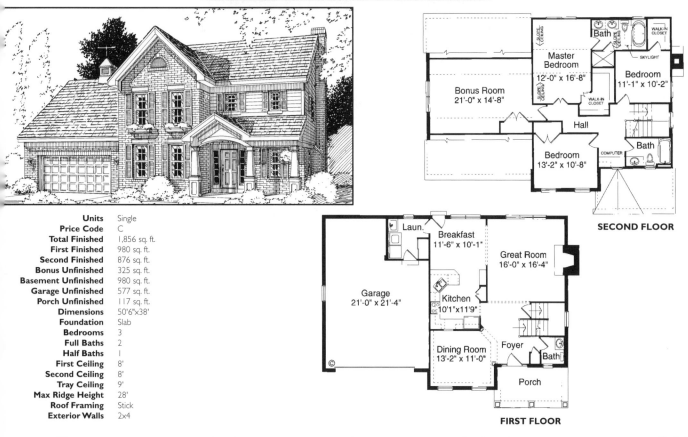

Units	Single
Price Code	C
Total Finished	1,856 sq. ft.
First Finished	980 sq. ft.
Second Finished	876 sq. ft.
Bonus Unfinished	325 sq. ft.
Basement Unfinished	980 sq. ft.
Garage Unfinished	577 sq. ft.
Porch Unfinished	117 sq. ft.
Dimensions	50'6"x38'
Foundation	Slab
Bedrooms	3
Full Baths	2
Half Baths	1
First Ceiling	8'
Second Ceiling	8'
Tray Ceiling	9'
Max Ridge Height	28'
Roof Framing	Stick
Exterior Walls	2x4

SLOPE CEILING
Bath
WALK-IN CLOSET
SKYLIGHT
Master Bedroom 12'-0" x 16'-8"
Bedroom 11'-1" x 10'-2"
Bonus Room 21'-0" x 14'-8"
WALK-IN CLOSET
Hall
Bedroom 13'-2" x 10'-8"
COMPUTER
Bath

SECOND FLOOR

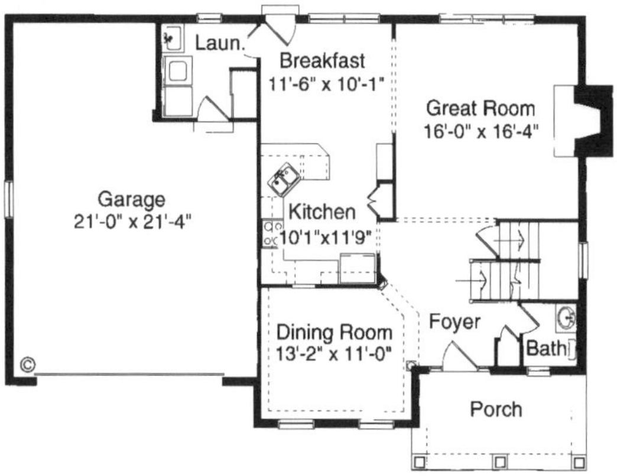

Laun.
Breakfast 11'-6" x 10'-1"
Great Room 16'-0" x 16'-4"
Garage 21'-0" x 21'-4"
Kitchen 10'1"x11'9"
Dining Room 13'-2" x 11'-0"
Foyer
Bath
Porch

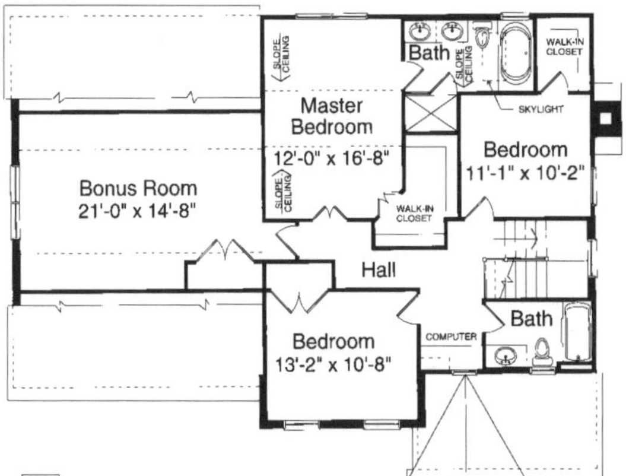

FIRST FLOOR

Design 98408

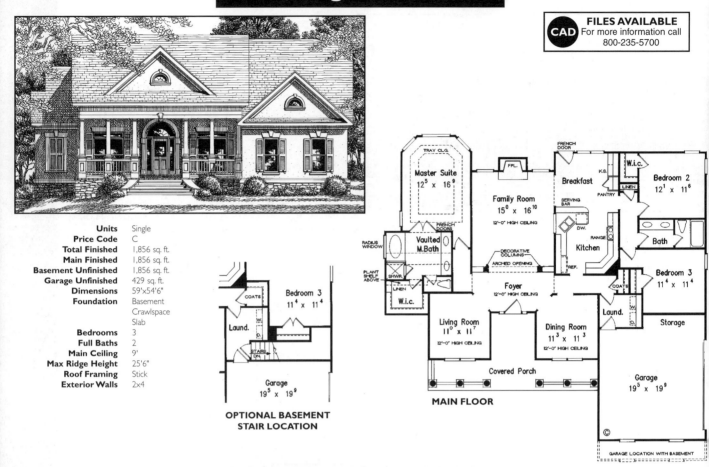

CAD FILES AVAILABLE
For more information call
800-235-5700

Units	Single
Price Code	C
Total Finished	1,856 sq. ft.
Main Finished	1,856 sq. ft.
Basement Unfinished	1,856 sq. ft.
Garage Unfinished	429 sq. ft.
Dimensions	59'x54'6"
Foundation	Basement Crawlspace Slab
Bedrooms	3
Full Baths	2
Main Ceiling	9'
Max Ridge Height	25'6"
Roof Framing	Stick
Exterior Walls	2x4

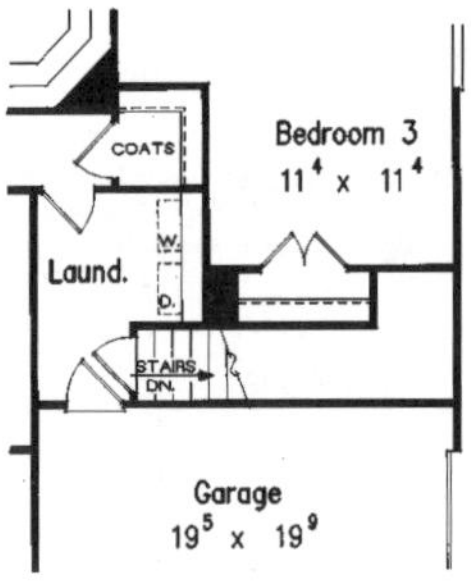

Bedroom 3
11⁴ x 11⁴
COATS
Laund.
W.
D.
STAIRS DN.
Garage
19⁵ x 19⁹

OPTIONAL BASEMENT STAIR LOCATION

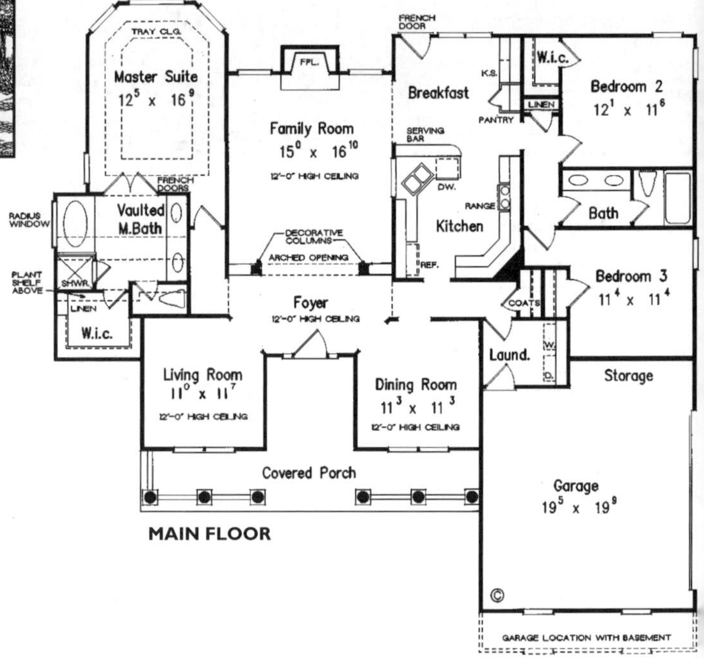

TRAY CLG.
Master Suite
12⁵ x 16⁹
FPL.
Family Room
15⁰ x 16¹⁰
12'-0" HIGH CEILING
FRENCH DOOR
Breakfast
K.S.
PANTRY
W.i.c.
LINEN
Bedroom 2
12¹ x 11⁶
SERVING BAR
DW.
RANGE
Kitchen
REF.
Bath
FRENCH DOORS
RADIUS WINDOW
Vaulted M.Bath
DECORATIVE COLUMNS
ARCHED OPENING
PLANT SHELF ABOVE
SHWR.
LINEN
W.i.c.
Foyer
12'-0" HIGH CEILING
COATS
Bedroom 3
11⁴ x 11⁴
Living Room
11⁰ x 11⁷
12'-0" HIGH CEILING
Dining Room
11³ x 11³
12'-0" HIGH CEILING
Laund.
W.
D.
Storage
Covered Porch
Garage
19⁵ x 19⁹
GARAGE LOCATION WITH BASEMENT

MAIN FLOOR

Design 94623

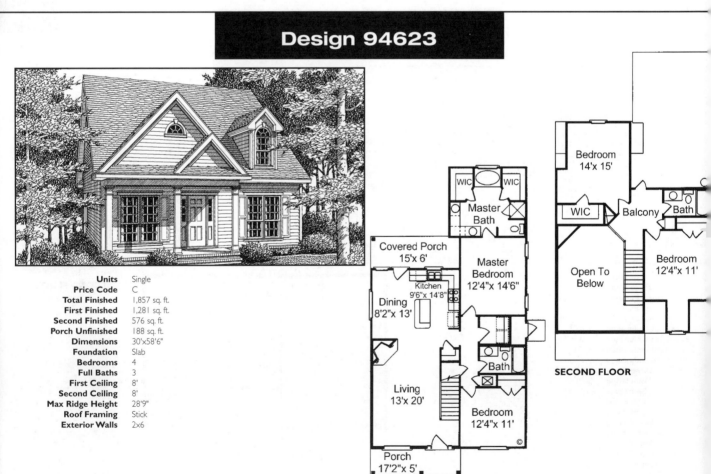

Units	Single
Price Code	C
Total Finished	1,857 sq. ft.
First Finished	1,281 sq. ft.
Second Finished	576 sq. ft.
Porch Unfinished	188 sq. ft.
Dimensions	30'x58'6"
Foundation	Slab
Bedrooms	4
Full Baths	3
First Ceiling	8'
Second Ceiling	8'
Max Ridge Height	28'9"
Roof Framing	Stick
Exterior Walls	2x6

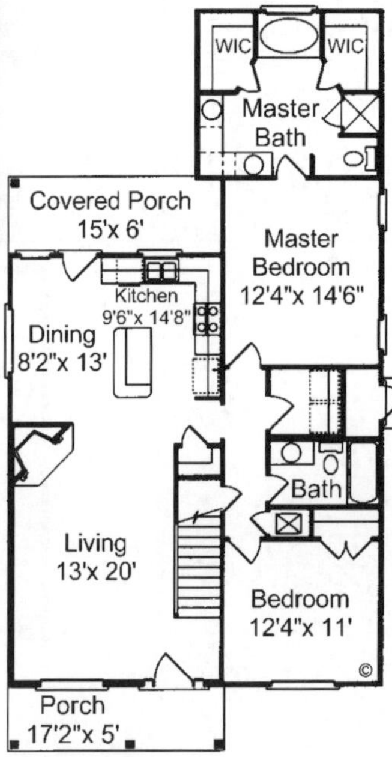

WIC
WIC
Master Bath
Covered Porch
15'x 6'
Master Bedroom
12'4"x 14'6"
Kitchen
9'6"x 14'8"
Dining
8'2"x 13'
Bath
Living
13'x 20'
Bedroom
12'4"x 11'
Porch
17'2"x 5'

FIRST FLOOR

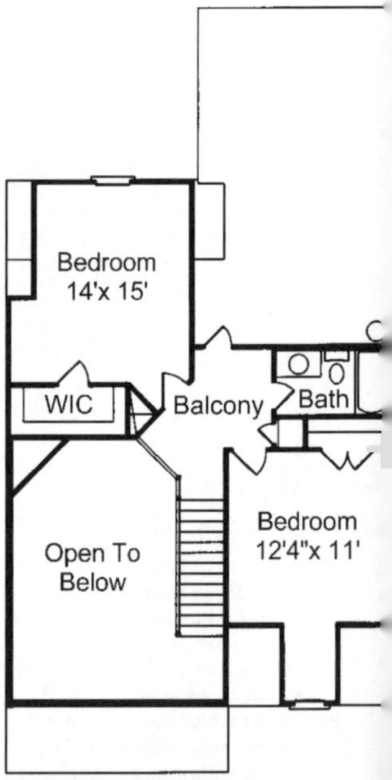

Bedroom
14'x 15'
WIC
Balcony
Bath
Open To Below
Bedroom
12'4"x 11'

SECOND FLOOR

Design 94119

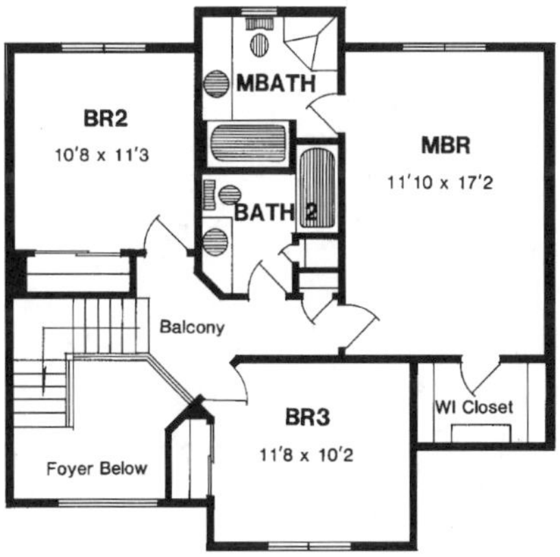

BR2
10'8 x 11'3
MBATH
MBR
11'10 x 17'2
BATH 2
Balcony
BR3
11'8 x 10'2
WI Closet
Foyer Below

SECOND FLOOR

DIN
9'8 x 11'6
KIT
10' x 13'8
Lav
Laun
Entry
GREAT RM
15'2 x 19'
cath cl'g
plus bay
Two-Story
FOYER
DIN RM
11'8 x 11'2
plus bay
GARAGE
21'8 x 21'8
Covered Entry

FIRST FLOOR

Units	Single
Price Code	C
Total Finished	1,859 sq. ft.
First Finished	1,070 sq. ft.
Second Finished	789 sq. ft.
Basement Unfinished	1,050 sq. ft.
Garage Unfinished	484 sq. ft.
Dimensions	61'4"x36'
Foundation	Basement
Bedrooms	3
Full Baths	2
Half Baths	1
Max Ridge Height	29'
Exterior Walls	2x4

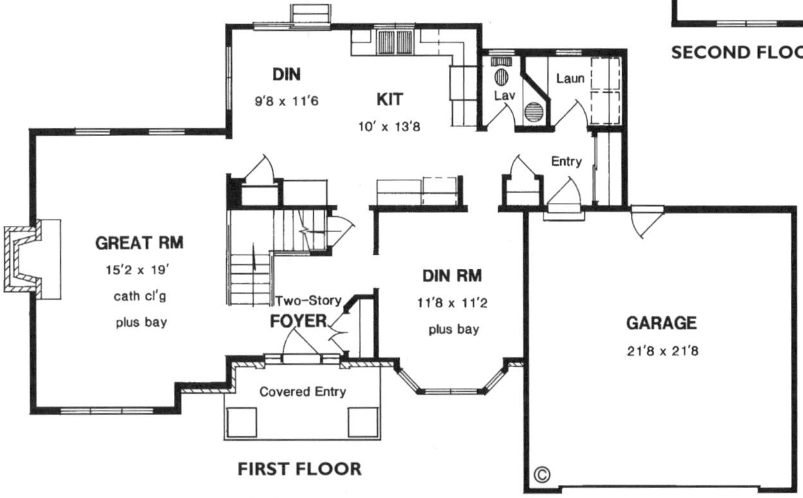

Design 99174

Units	Single
Price Code	C
Total Finished	1,859 sq. ft.
Main Finished	1,859 sq. ft.
Basement Unfinished	1,859 sq. ft.
Garage Unfinished	750 sq. ft.
Dimensions	69'8"x43'
Foundation	Basement
Bedrooms	3
Full Baths	2
Half Baths	1
Main Ceiling	8'2"
Max Ridge Height	23'7"
Roof Framing	Truss
Exterior Walls	2x6

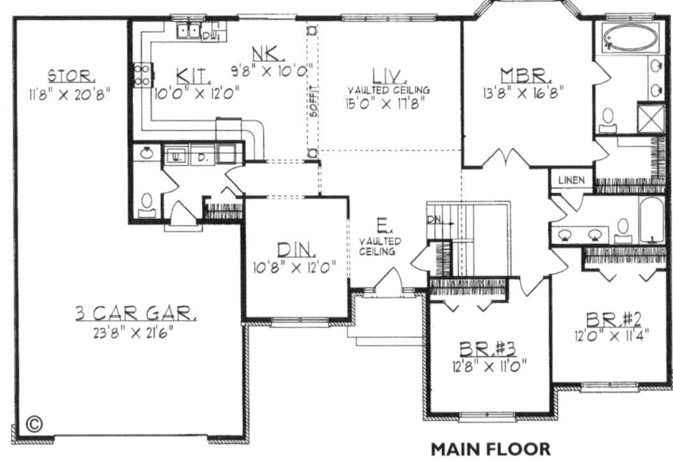
STOR.
11'8" X 20'8"
NK.
9'8" X 10'0"
KIT.
10'0" X 12'0"
LIV.
VAULTED CEILING
15'0" X 17'8"
MBR.
13'8" X 16'8"
SOFFIT
LINEN
DIN.
10'8" X 12'0"
E.
VAULTED CEILING
3 CAR GAR.
23'8" X 21'6"
BR.#3
12'8" X 11'0"
BR.#2
12'0" X 11'4"

MAIN FLOOR

Design 50032

PHOTOGRAPHY: COURTESY OF THE DESIGNER

Please note: The photographed home may have been modified to suit homeowner preferences. If you order plans, have a builder or design professional check them against the photograph to confirm actual construction details.

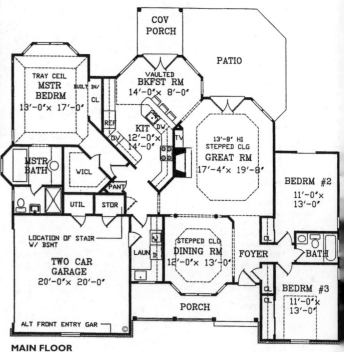

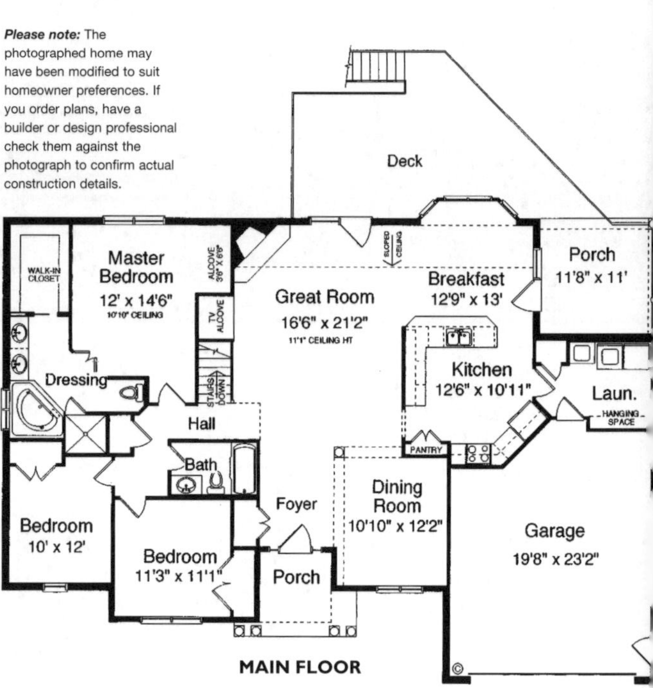

Deck
Master Bedroom
12' x 14'6"
10'10" CEILING
WALK-IN CLOSET
ALCOVE 3'6" X 6'8"
TV ALCOVE
Great Room
16'6" x 21'2"
11'1" CEILING HT
SLOPED CEILING
Breakfast
12'9" x 13'
Porch
11'8" x 11'
Dressing
Kitchen
12'6" x 10'11"
Laun.
HANGING SPACE
STAIRS DOWN
Hall
Bath
PANTRY
Foyer
Dining Room
10'10" x 12'2"
Bedroom
10' x 12'
Bedroom
11'3" x 11'1"
Porch
Garage
19'8" x 23'2"

MAIN FLOOR

Units	Single
Price Code	C
Total Finished	1,860 sq. ft.
Main Finished	1,860 sq. ft.
Basement Unfinished	1,860 sq. ft.
Porch Unfinished	69 sq. ft.
Dimensions	64'2"x44'2"
Foundation	Basement
Bedrooms	3
Full Baths	2
Max Ridge Height	23'
Roof Framing	Truss
Exterior Walls	2x4

Design 99679

Units	Single
Price Code	C
Total Finished	1,860 sq. ft.
Main Finished	1,860 sq. ft.
Basement Unfinished	1,860 sq. ft.
Garage Unfinished	434 sq. ft.
Dimensions	57'4"x49'8"
Foundation	Basement Crawlspace Slab
Bedrooms	3
Full Baths	2
Main Ceiling	8'
Vaulted Ceiling	13'8"
Tray Ceiling	11'6"
Max Ridge Height	18'
Roof Framing	Stick
Exterior Walls	2x4

COV PORCH
PATIO
TRAY CEIL MSTR BEDRM 13'-0"x 17'-0"
BUILT IN/ CL
VAULTED BKFST RM 14'-0"x 8'-0"
REF
DW
KIT 12'-0"x 14'-0"
TV
13'-8" HI STEPPED CLG GREAT RM 17'-4"x 19'-8"
MSTR BATH
WICL
PANT
UTIL
STOR
BEDRM #2 11'-0"x 13'-0"
LOCATION OF STAIR W/ BSMT
TWO CAR GARAGE 20'-0"x 20'-0"
LAUN
STEPPED CLG DINING RM 12'-0"x 13'-0"
FOYER
CL
BATH
BEDRM #3 11'-0"x 13'-0"
PORCH
ALT FRONT ENTRY GAR

MAIN FLOOR

Design 97616

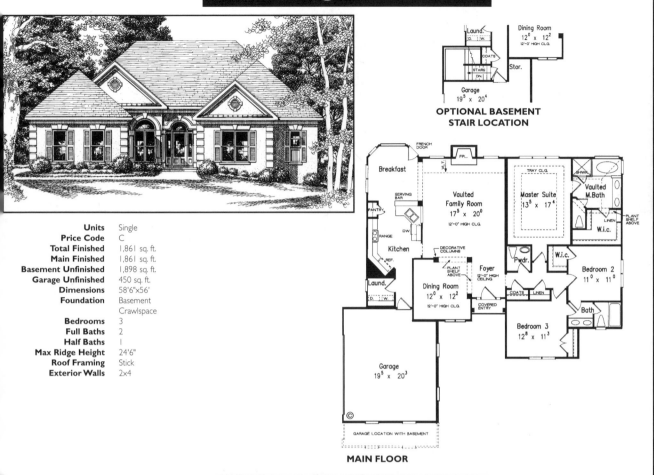

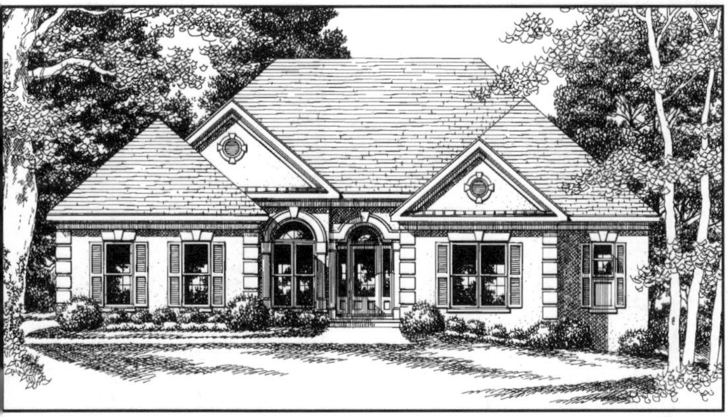

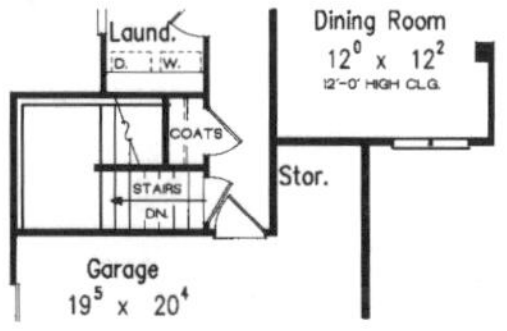

Units	Single
Price Code	C
Total Finished	1,861 sq. ft.
Main Finished	1,861 sq. ft.
Basement Unfinished	1,898 sq. ft.
Garage Unfinished	450 sq. ft.
Dimensions	58'6"x56'
Foundation	Basement Crawlspace
Bedrooms	3
Full Baths	2
Half Baths	1
Max Ridge Height	24'6"
Roof Framing	Stick
Exterior Walls	2x4

Laund. Dining Room 12^0 x 12^2 12'-0" HIGH CLG. Stor. Garage 19^5 x 20^4

OPTIONAL BASEMENT STAIR LOCATION

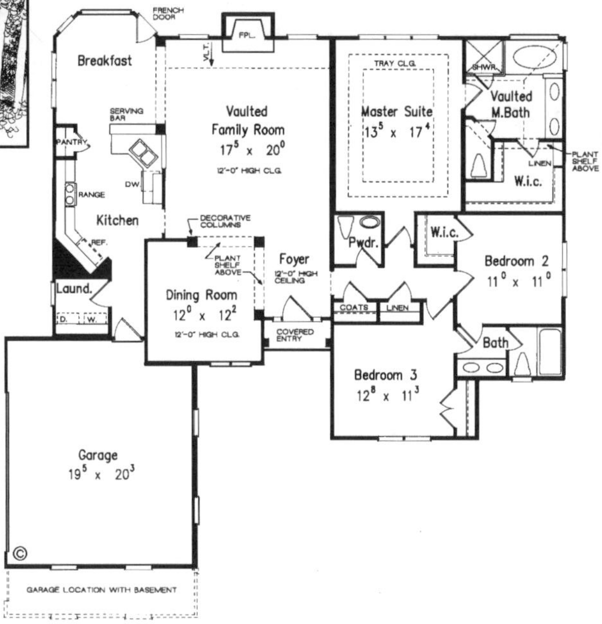

Breakfast · Vaulted Family Room 17^5 x 20^0 12'-0" HIGH CLG. · Master Suite 13^5 x 17^4 · Vaulted M.Bath · W.i.c. · Kitchen · Pwdr. · Laund. · Dining Room 12^0 x 12^2 12'-0" HIGH CLG. · Foyer · Bedroom 2 11^0 x 11^0 · Bath · Bedroom 3 12^8 x 11^3 · Garage 19^5 x 20^3 · GARAGE LOCATION WITH BASEMENT

MAIN FLOOR

Design 97777

Units	Single
Price Code	C
Total Finished	1,861 sq. ft.
Main Finished	1,861 sq. ft.
Basement Unfinished	1,861 sq. ft.
Garage Unfinished	433 sq. ft.
Deck Unfinished	120 sq. ft.
Porch Unfinished	21 sq. ft.
Dimensions	50'8"x59'10"
Foundation	Basement
Bedrooms	3
Full Baths	2
Main Ceiling	9'
Tray Ceiling	10'
Max Ridge Height	23'
Roof Framing	Truss
Exterior Walls	2x4

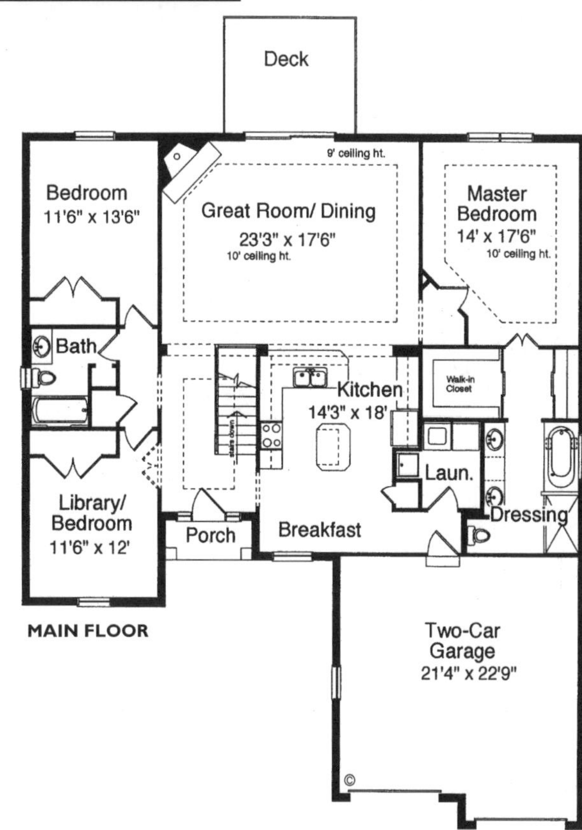
Deck
9' ceiling ht.
Bedroom 11'6" x 13'6"
Great Room/ Dining 23'3" x 17'6" 10' ceiling ht.
Master Bedroom 14' x 17'6" 10' ceiling ht.
Bath
Kitchen 14'3" x 18'
Walk-in Closet
Laun.
Library/ Bedroom 11'6" x 12'
Porch
Breakfast
Dressing
Two-Car Garage 21'4" x 22'9"

MAIN FLOOR

Design 66101

Units	Single
Price Code	C
Total Finished	1,862 sq. ft.
Main Finished	1,862 sq. ft.
Garage Unfinished	495 sq. ft.
Deck Unfinished	180 sq. ft.
Dimensions	50'x66'4"
Foundation	Slab
Bedrooms	3
Full Baths	2
Main Ceiling	9'
Max Ridge Height	24'
Roof Framing	Stick
Exterior Walls	2x4

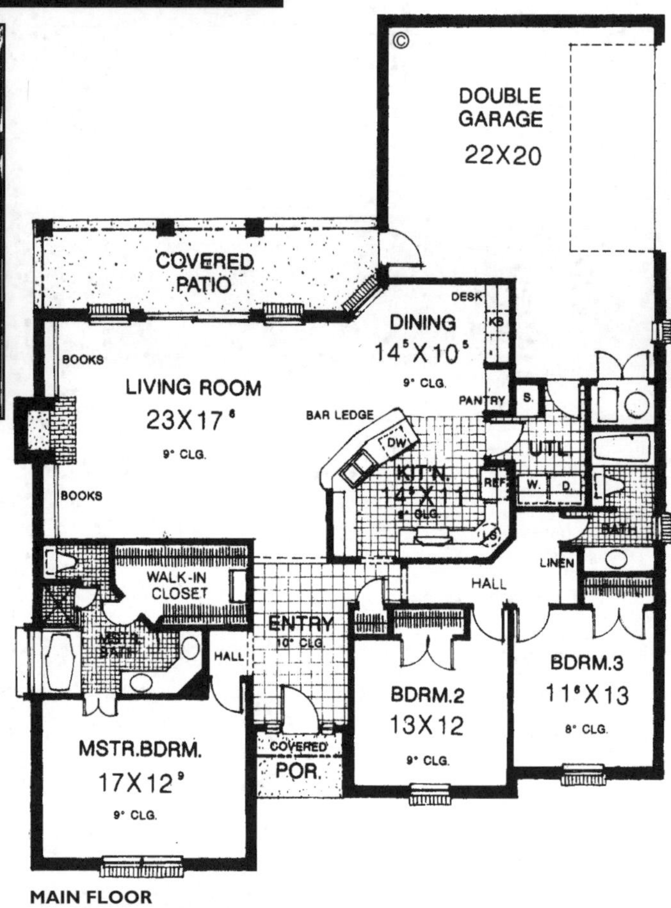
DOUBLE GARAGE
22X20
COVERED PATIO
DESK
DINING
14⁵X10⁵
9" CLG.
BOOKS
LIVING ROOM
23X17⁶
9" CLG.
BAR LEDGE
PANTRY
UTL.
W.
D.
BATH
BOOKS
WALK-IN CLOSET
ENTRY
10" CLG.
HALL
LINEN
HALL
BDRM.2
13X12
9" CLG.
BDRM.3
11⁶X13
8" CLG.
COVERED POR.
MSTR.BDRM.
17X12⁹
9" CLG.

MAIN FLOOR

Design 91157

Units	Single
Price Code	C
Total Finished	1,862 sq. ft.
Main Finished	1,862 sq. ft.
Garage Unfinished	495 sq. ft.
Deck Unfinished	180 sq. ft.
Dimensions	50'x66'4"
Foundation	Slab
Bedrooms	3
Full Baths	2
Main Ceiling	9'
Max Ridge Height	24'
Roof Framing	Stick
Exterior Walls	2x4

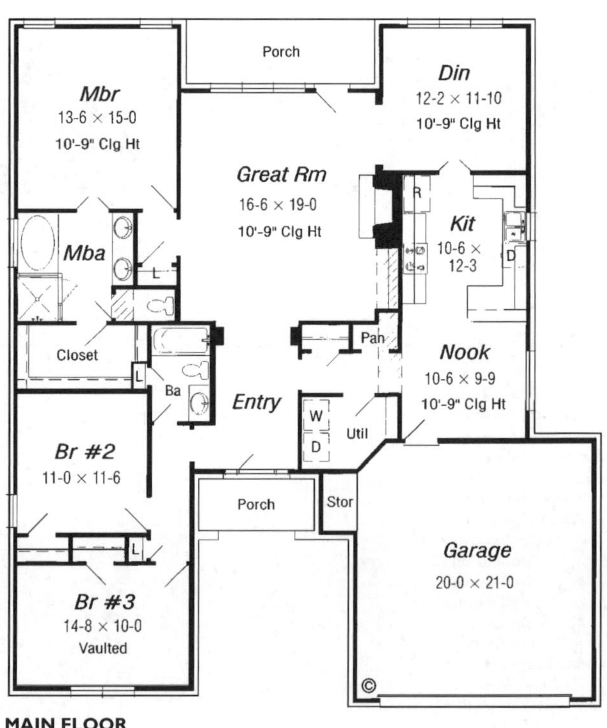
Porch
Din
12-2 × 11-10
10'-9" Clg Ht
Mbr
13-6 × 15-0
10'-9" Clg Ht
Great Rm
16-6 × 19-0
10'-9" Clg Ht
Kit
10-6 × 12-3
Mba
Closet
Pan
Nook
10-6 × 9-9
10'-9" Clg Ht
Ba
Entry
W
D
Util
Br #2
11-0 × 11-6
Porch
Stor
Garage
20-0 × 21-0
Br #3
14-8 × 10-0
Vaulted

MAIN FLOOR

Design 66052

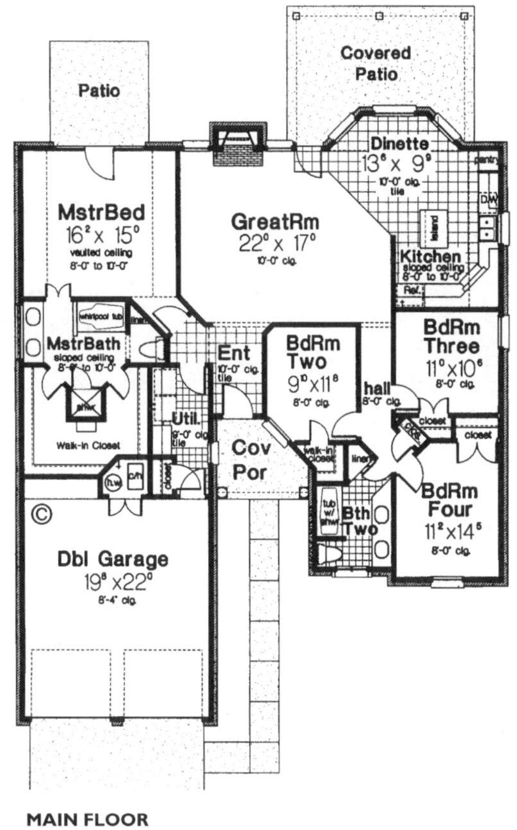
Covered Patio
Patio
Dinette
13⁶ x 9⁹
MstrBed
16² x 15⁰
vaulted ceiling
8'-0" to 10'-0"
GreatRm
22⁰ x 17⁰
10'-0" clg.
Kitchen
sloped ceiling
8'-0" to 10'-0"
MstrBath
sloped ceiling
8'-0" to 10'-0"
Ent
BdRm Two
9¹⁰ x 11⁸
8'-0" clg.
hall
BdRm Three
11⁰ x 10⁶
8'-0" clg.
Walk-in Closet
Util.
Cov Por
Bth Two
BdRm Four
11² x 14⁵
8'-0" clg.
Dbl Garage
19⁸ x 22⁰
8'-4" clg.

MAIN FLOOR

Units	Single
Price Code	C
Total Finished	1,863 sq. ft.
Main Finished	1,863 sq. ft.
Garage Unfinished	442 sq. ft.
Deck Unfinished	162 sq. ft.
Dimensions	50'x61'2"
Foundation	Slab
Bedrooms	4
Full Baths	2
Max Ridge Height	28'6"
Roof Framing	Stick
Exterior Walls	2x4

Design 65207

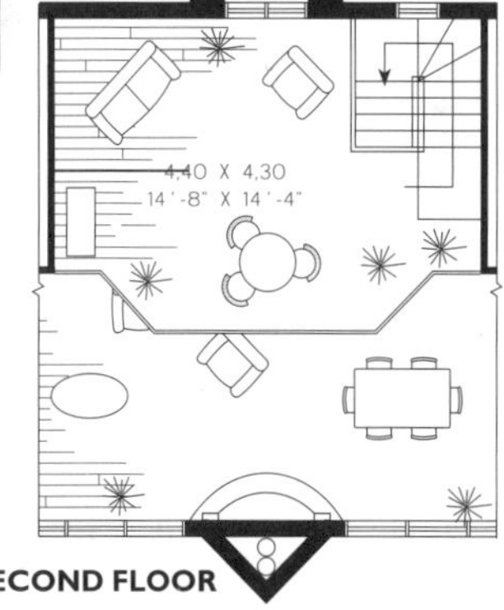
4,40 X 4,30
14'-8" X 14'-4"

SECOND FLOOR

Units	Single
Price Code	C
Total Finished	1,864 sq. ft.
First Finished	790 sq. ft.
Second Finished	287 sq. ft.
Lower Finished	787 sq. ft.
Dimensions	32'4"x24'4"
Foundation	Basement
Bedrooms	3
Full Baths	1
3/4 Baths	1
Max Ridge Height	29'6"
Roof Framing	Truss

2,70 X 3,30
9'-0" X 11'-0"
2,30 X 3,30
7'-8" X 11'-0"
3,90 X 2,70
13'-0" X 9'-0"
5,10 X 3,30
17'-0" X 11'-0"

LOWER FLOOR

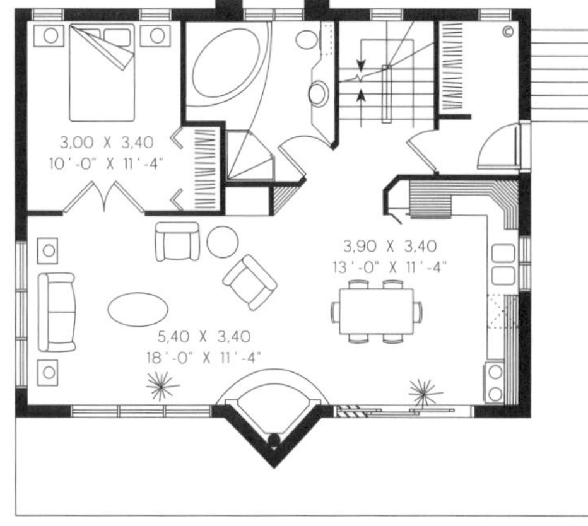
3,00 X 3,40
10'-0" X 11'-4"
3,90 X 3,40
13'-0" X 11'-4"
5,40 X 3,40
18'-0" X 11'-4"

FIRST FLOOR

Design 65645

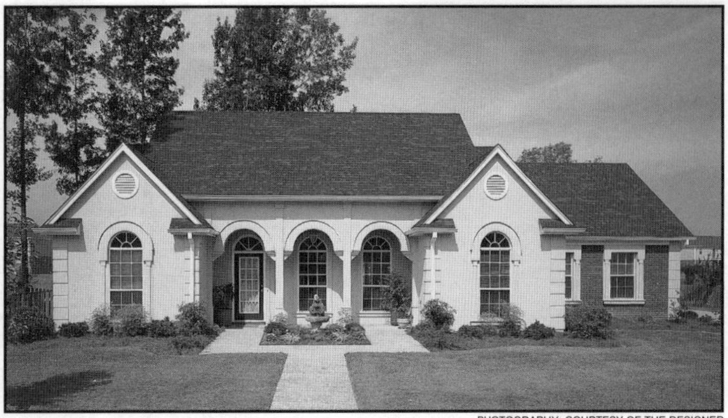

PHOTOGRAPHY: COURTESY OF THE DESIGNER

Please note: The photographed home may have been modified to suit homeowner preferences. If you order plans, have a builder or design professional check them against the photograph to confirm actual construction details.

Units	Single
Price Code	C
Total Finished	1,865 sq. ft.
Main Finished	1,865 sq. ft.
Dimensions	62'x64'
Foundation	Crawlspace Slab
Bedrooms	3
Full Baths	2
Main Ceiling	8'
Max Ridge Height	27'
Roof Framing	Stick
Exterior Walls	2x6

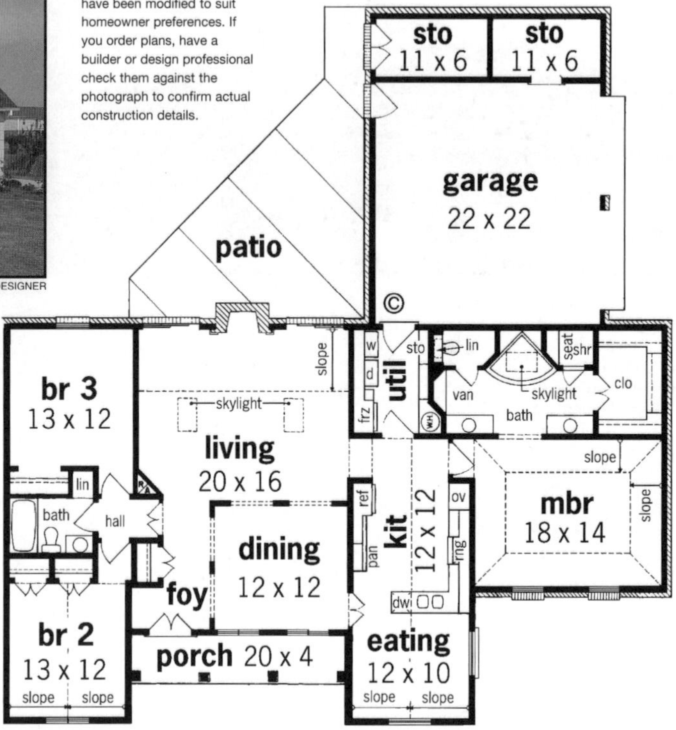

sto 11 x 6
sto 11 x 6
garage 22 x 22
patio
br 3 13 x 12
living 20 x 16
skylight
slope
util
sto
lin
van
bath
skylight
clo
seat
shr
frz
mbr 18 x 14
kit 12 x 12
dining 12 x 12
bath
hall
lin
foy
br 2 13 x 12
porch 20 x 4
eating 12 x 10
ref
pan
ov
rng
dw

MAIN FLOOR

Design 63114

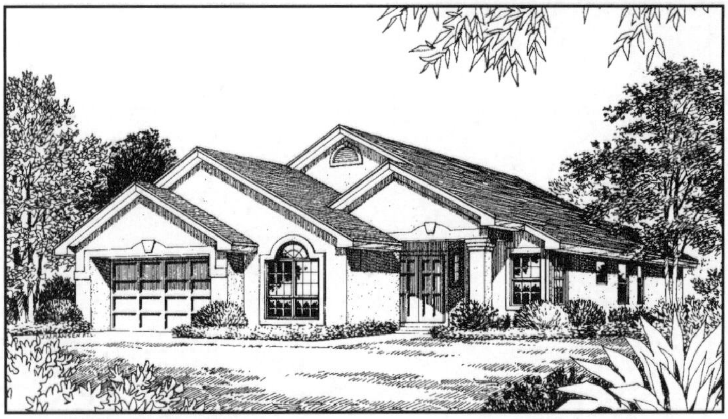

Units	Single
Price Code	C
Total Finished	1,868 sq. ft.
Main Finished	1,868 sq. ft.
Garage Unfinished	400 sq. ft.
Dimensions	45'x66'
Foundation	Slab
Bedrooms	4
Full Baths	2
Max Ridge Height	19'10"
Roof Framing	Truss

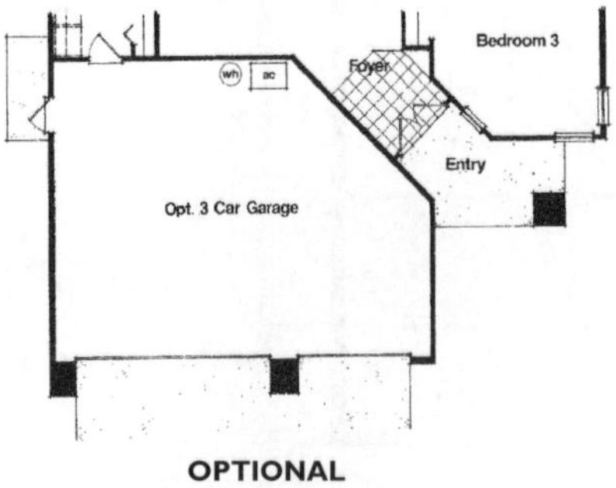

Bedroom 3
Foyer
Entry
Opt. 3 Car Garage

OPTIONAL THREE-CAR GARAGE

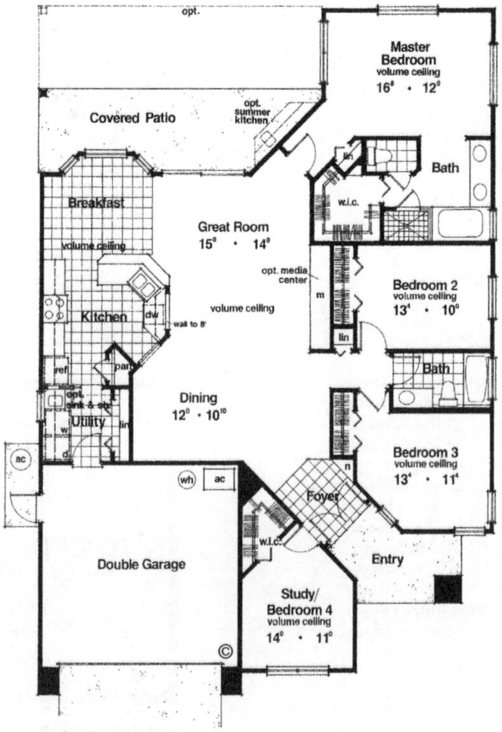

opt.
Master Bedroom volume ceiling 16' · 12'
Covered Patio
opt. summer kitchen
Bath
w.i.c.
Breakfast
volume ceiling
Great Room 15' · 14'
opt. media center
Bedroom 2 volume ceiling 13' · 10'
Kitchen
volume ceiling
Bath
Dining 12' · 10'
Utility
Bedroom 3 volume ceiling 13' · 11'
Foyer
Double Garage
Entry
Study/ Bedroom 4 volume ceiling 14' · 11'

MAIN FLOOR

Design 93107

Units	Single
Price Code	C
Total Finished	1,868 sq. ft.
Main Finished	1,868 sq. ft.
Basement Unfinished	1,868 sq. ft.
Garage Unfinished	782 sq. ft.
Dimensions	72'x42'4"
Foundation	Basement
Bedrooms	3
Full Baths	2
Main Ceiling	8'
Max Ridge Height	25'6"
Roof Framing	Stick/Truss
Exterior Walls	2x6

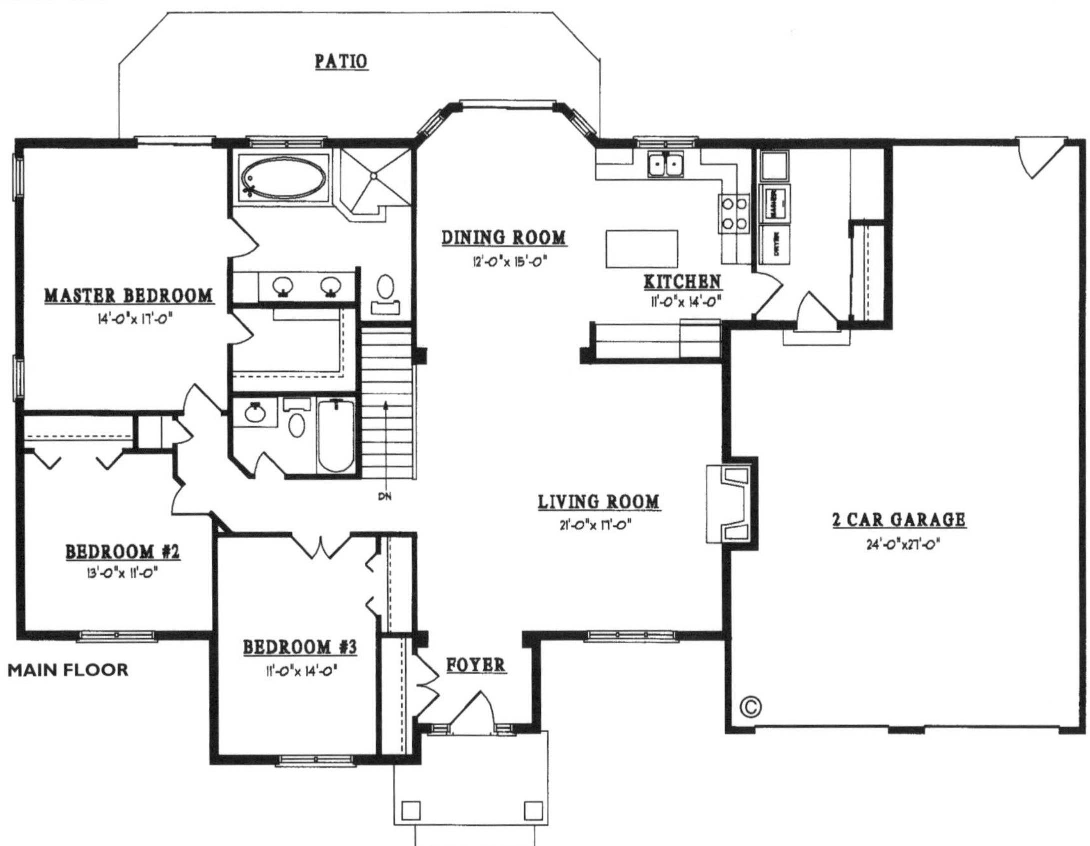
PATIO
DINING ROOM
12'-0"x 15'-0"
KITCHEN
11'-0"x 14'-0"
MASTER BEDROOM
14'-0"x 17'-0"
DN
LIVING ROOM
21'-0"x 17'-0"
2 CAR GARAGE
24'-0"x27'-0"
BEDROOM #2
13'-0"x 11'-0"
BEDROOM #3
11'-0"x 14'-0"
FOYER
©
MAIN FLOOR

Design 93192

Units	Single
Price Code	C
Total Finished	1,868 sq. ft.
Main Finished	1,868 sq. ft.
Basement Unfinished	1,868 sq. ft.
Dimensions	72'x41'8"
Foundation	Basement
Bedrooms	3
Full Baths	2
Half Baths	1
Max Ridge Height	21'8"
Roof Framing	Truss
Exterior Walls	2x6

MBR. 13'8" X 17'0"
DIN. 12'0" X 14'4"
KIT. 10'8" X 13'0"
STORAGE 12'4" X 12'0"
LIN
SHELVES
SOFFIT
DN
LIV. 10'-1 1/8" CEILING 20'8" X 17'8"
2 CAR GAR. 23'4" X 27'4"
BR.#2 13'0" X 11'8"
BR.#3 10'4" X 13'8"
CATHEDRAL CEILING

MAIN FLOOR

Design 63115

Units	Single
Price Code	C
Total Finished	1,869 sq. ft.
Main Finished	1,869 sq. ft.
Garage Unfinished	470 sq. ft.
Dimensions	61'8"x53'
Foundation	Slab
Bedrooms	3
Full Baths	2
Main Ceiling	10'
Max Ridge Height	20'
Roof Framing	Truss
Exterior Walls	2x4

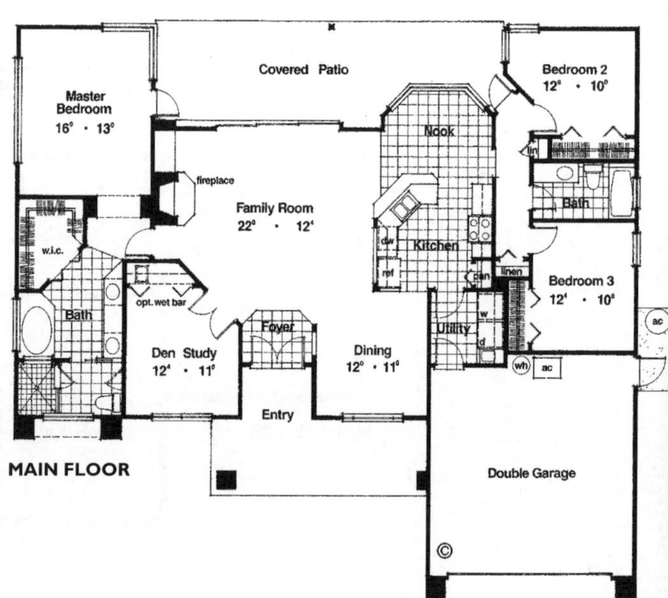

Covered Patio
Master Bedroom 16⁰ · 13⁰
Bedroom 2 12⁴ · 10⁰
Nook
fireplace
Family Room 22⁰ · 12⁴
w.i.c.
Bath
Kitchen
opt. wet bar
Foyer
Den Study 12⁴ · 11⁰
Dining 12⁰ · 11⁶
Entry
Utility
Bedroom 3 12⁴ · 10⁰
Double Garage
MAIN FLOOR

Design 91467

Units	Single
Price Code	D
Total Finished	1,869 sq. ft.
First Finished	945 sq. ft.
Second Finished	924 sq. ft.
Bonus Unfinished	330 sq. ft.
Garage Unfinished	409 sq. ft.
Dimensions	38'x43'
Bedrooms	3
Full Baths	1
3/4 Baths	1
Half Baths	1
Second Ceiling	8'9"
Max Ridge Height	29'
Roof Framing	Truss
Exterior Walls	2x6

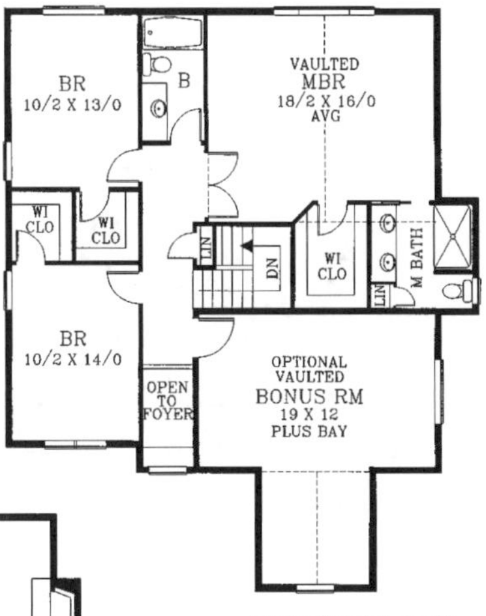

BR 10/2 X 13/0
B
VAULTED MBR 18/2 X 16/0 AVG
WI CLO
WI CLO
LIN
DN
WI CLO
M BATH
LIN
BR 10/2 X 14/0
OPEN TO FOYER
OPTIONAL VAULTED BONUS RM 19 X 12 PLUS BAY

SECOND FLOOR

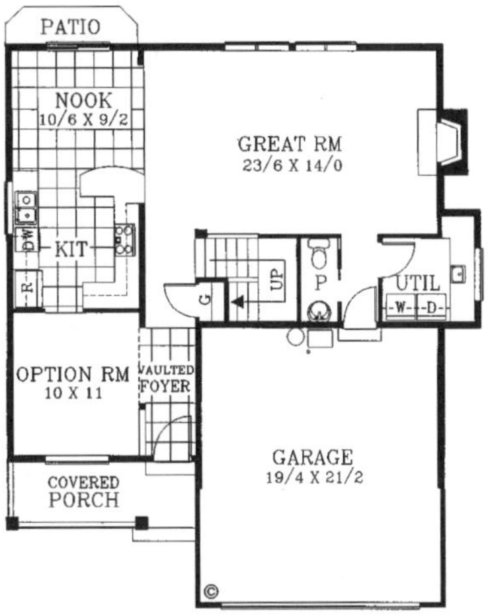

PATIO
NOOK 10/6 X 9/2
GREAT RM 23/6 X 14/0
DW
KIT
R
UP
P
UTIL
W
D
G
OPTION RM 10 X 11
VAULTED FOYER
GARAGE 19/4 X 21/2
COVERED PORCH

FIRST FLOOR

Design 92536

Units	Single
Price Code	C
Total Finished	1,869 sq. ft.
Main Finished	1,869 sq. ft.
Garage Unfinished	561 sq. ft.
Dimensions	74'10"x40'4"
Foundation	Crawlspace Slab
Bedrooms	3
Full Baths	2
Main Ceiling	9'
Max Ridge Height	21'
Roof Framing	Stick
Exterior Walls	2x4

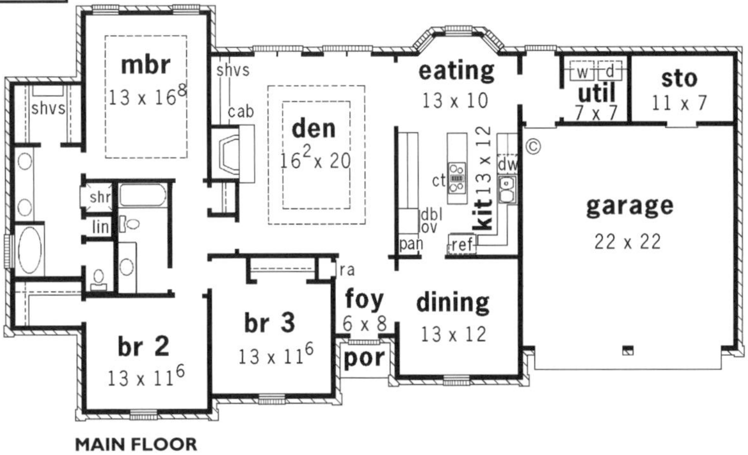

mbr 13 x 16^8
shvs
shvs
cab
den 16^2 x 20
eating 13 x 10
w d
util 7 x 7
sto 11 x 7
shr
lin
ct
dbl ov
pan
kit 13 x 12
dw
ref
garage 22 x 22
ra
foy 6 x 8
dining 13 x 12
br 3 13 x 11^6
br 2 13 x 11^6
por

MAIN FLOOR

Design 94989

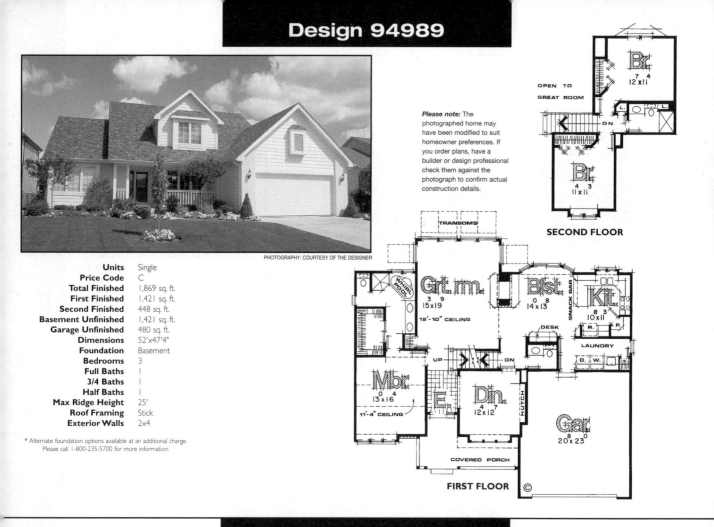

PHOTOGRAPHY: COURTESY OF THE DESIGNER

Units	Single
Price Code	C
Total Finished	1,869 sq. ft.
First Finished	1,421 sq. ft.
Second Finished	448 sq. ft.
Basement Unfinished	1,421 sq. ft.
Garage Unfinished	480 sq. ft.
Dimensions	52'x47'4"
Foundation	Basement
Bedrooms	3
Full Baths	1
3/4 Baths	1
Half Baths	1
Max Ridge Height	25'
Roof Framing	Stick
Exterior Walls	2x4

* Alternate foundation options available at an additional charge. Please call 1-800-235-5700 for more information.

Please note: The photographed home may have been modified to suit homeowner preferences. If you order plans, have a builder or design professional check them against the photograph to confirm actual construction details.

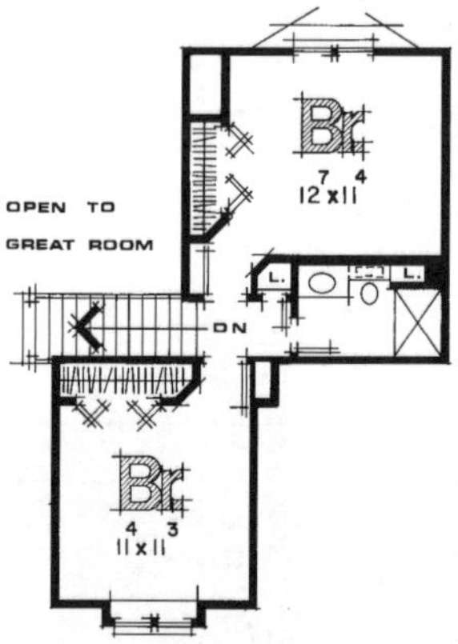

SECOND FLOOR

FIRST FLOOR

Design 98956

Units	Single
Price Code	C
Total Finished	1,869 sq. ft.
Main Finished	1,869 sq. ft.
Garage Unfinished	505 sq. ft.
Dimensions	54'x60'
Foundation	Basement Crawlspace Slab
Bedrooms	3
Full Baths	2
Main Ceiling	8'
Max Ridge Height	24'
Roof Framing	Stick
Exterior Walls	2x4

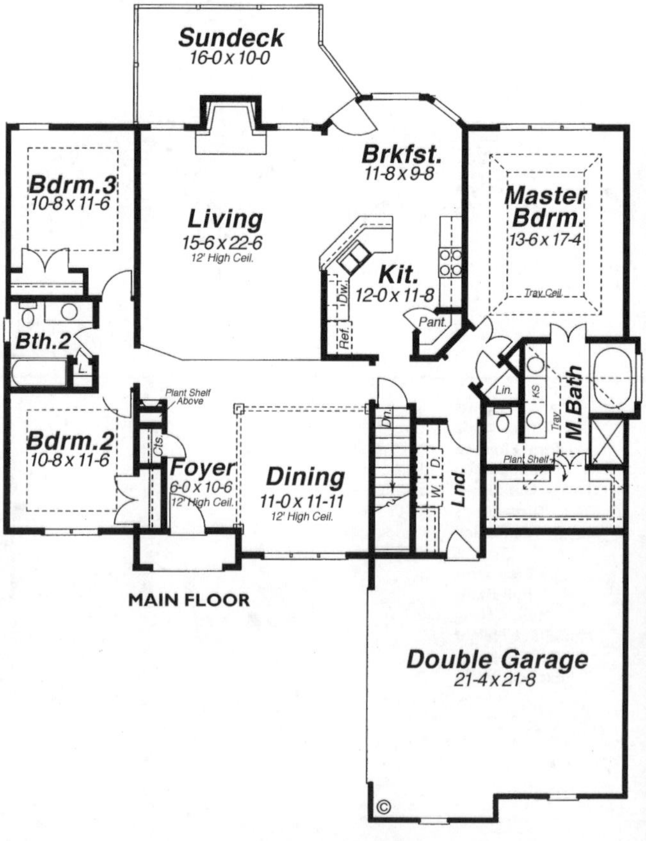

MAIN FLOOR

Design 63116

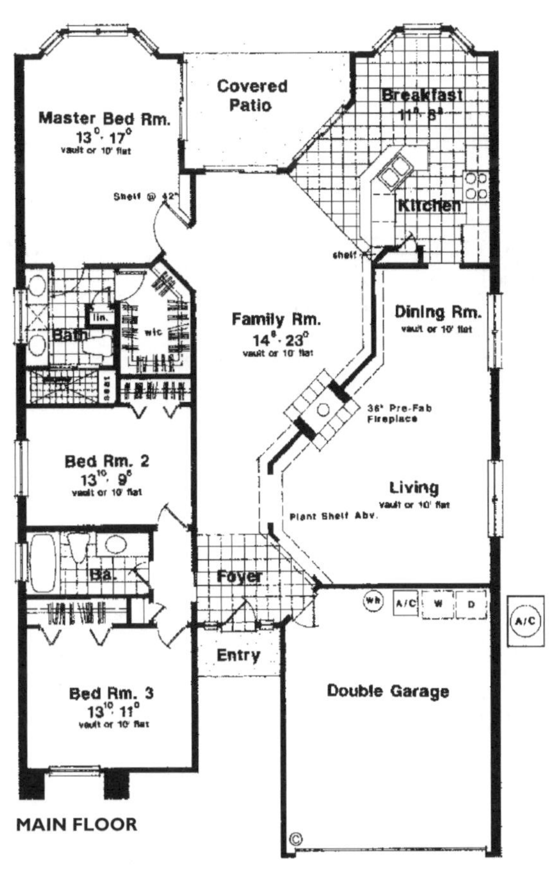
Master Bed Rm.
13⁰· 17⁰
vault or 10' flat
Covered Patio
Breakfast
Kitchen
Family Rm.
14⁸· 23⁰
vault or 10' flat
Dining Rm.
vault or 10' flat
36" Pre-Fab Fireplace
Bath
wic
Bed Rm. 2
13¹⁰· 9⁶
vault or 10' flat
Living
vault or 10' flat
Plant Shelf Abv.
Ba.
Foyer
Entry
A/C
W
D
Double Garage
Bed Rm. 3
13¹⁰· 11⁰
vault or 10' flat
MAIN FLOOR

Units	Single
Price Code	C
Total Finished	1,872 sq. ft.
Main Finished	1,872 sq. ft.
Garage Unfinished	398 sq. ft.
Dimensions	40'x66'8"
Foundation	Slab
Bedrooms	3
Full Baths	1
3/4 Baths	1
Max Ridge Height	18'3"
Roof Framing	Truss

Design 91124

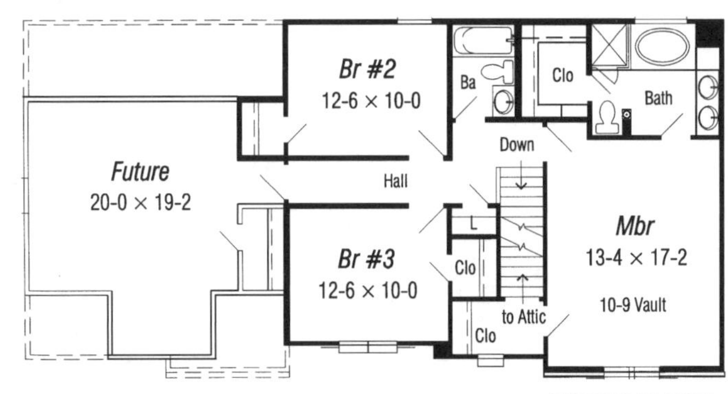
Br #2
12-6 × 10-0
Ba
Clo
Bath
Down
Future
20-0 × 19-2
Hall
Br #3
12-6 × 10-0
L
Clo
Mbr
13-4 × 17-2
10-9 Vault
to Attic
Clo
SECOND FLOOR

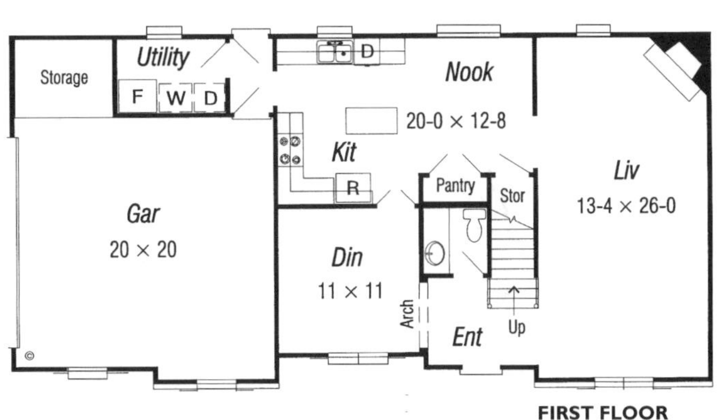
Storage
Utility
F
W
D
Nook
20-0 × 12-8
Kit
R
Pantry
Stor
Liv
13-4 × 26-0
Gar
20 × 20
Din
11 × 11
Arch
Ent
Up
FIRST FLOOR

Units	Single
Price Code	C
Total Finished	1,874 sq. ft.
First Finished	967 sq. ft.
Second Finished	907 sq. ft.
Bonus Unfinished	327 sq. ft.
Garage Unfinished	458 sq. ft.
Dimensions	54'8"x27'1"
Foundation	Slab
Bedrooms	3
Full Baths	2
Half Baths	1
First Ceiling	8'
Second Ceiling	8'
Max Ridge Height	31'3"
Roof Framing	Stick
Exterior Walls	2x4

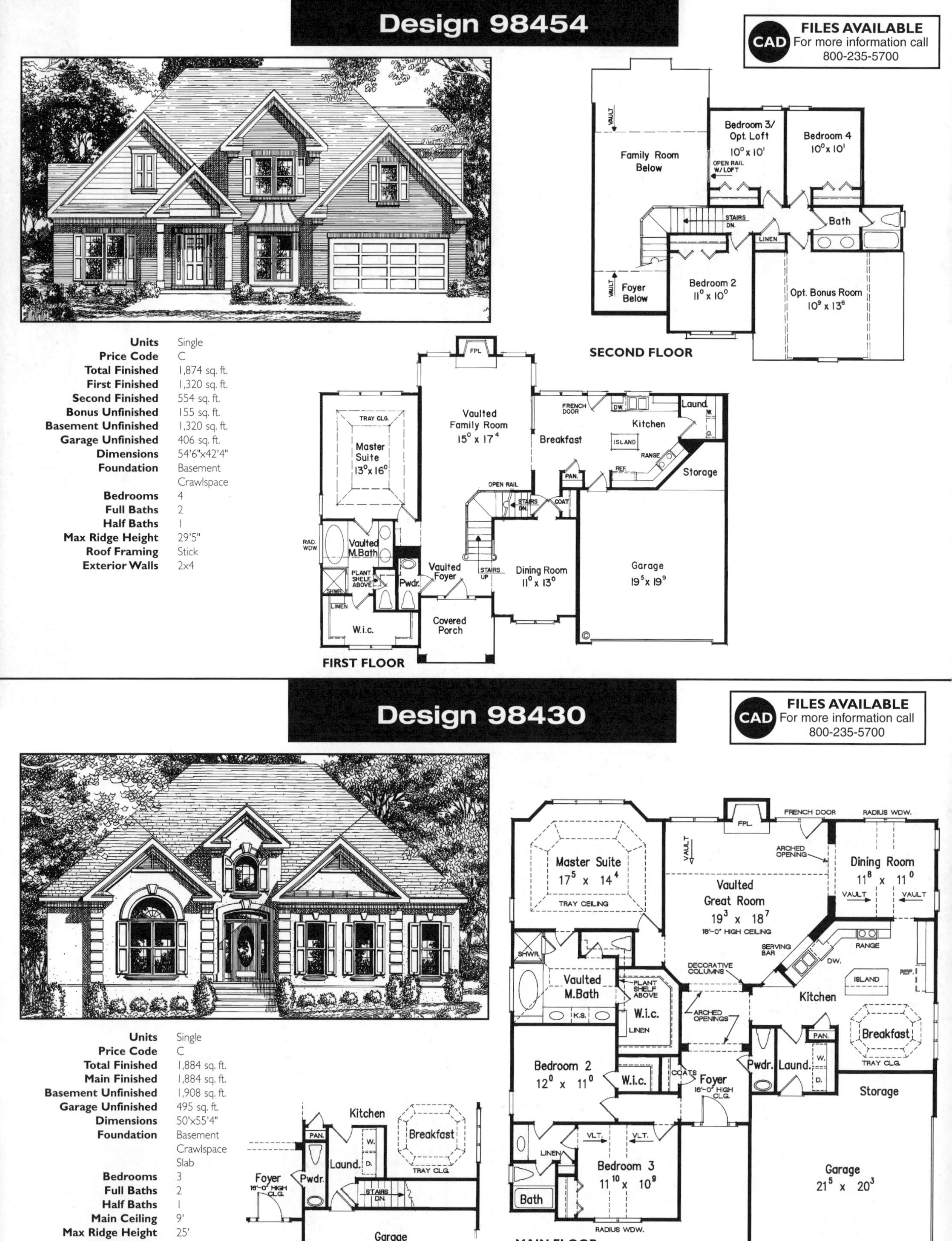

Design 98454
CAD FILES AVAILABLE For more information call 800-235-5700
Units Single
Price Code C
Total Finished 1,874 sq. ft.
First Finished 1,320 sq. ft.
Second Finished 554 sq. ft.
Bonus Unfinished 155 sq. ft.
Basement Unfinished 1,320 sq. ft.
Garage Unfinished 406 sq. ft.
Dimensions 54'6"x42'4"
Foundation Basement
Crawlspace
Bedrooms 4
Full Baths 2
Half Baths 1
Max Ridge Height 29'5"
Roof Framing Stick
Exterior Walls 2x4
Family Room Below
Bedroom 3/ Opt. Loft 10⁰x10'
Bedroom 4 10⁰x10'
OPEN RAIL W/LOFT
STAIRS DN.
LINEN
Bath
Foyer Below
Bedroom 2 11⁰x10⁰
Opt. Bonus Room 10⁹x13⁶
SECOND FLOOR
FPL
Vaulted Family Room 15⁰x17⁴
TRAY CLG.
Master Suite 13⁰x16⁰
FRENCH DOOR
DW.
Laund.
Kitchen
Breakfast
ISLAND
RANGE
REF.
PAN.
Storage
OPEN RAIL
STAIRS DN.
COAT
RAD. WDW.
Vaulted M.Bath
PLANT SHELF ABOVE
SHWR.
Pwdr.
Vaulted Foyer
STAIRS UP
Dining Room 11⁰x13⁰
Garage 19⁵x19⁹
LINEN
W.i.c.
Covered Porch
FIRST FLOOR
Design 98430
CAD FILES AVAILABLE For more information call 800-235-5700
Units Single
Price Code C
Total Finished 1,884 sq. ft.
Main Finished 1,884 sq. ft.
Basement Unfinished 1,908 sq. ft.
Garage Unfinished 495 sq. ft.
Dimensions 50'x55'4"
Foundation Basement
Crawlspace
Slab
Bedrooms 3
Full Baths 2
Half Baths 1
Main Ceiling 9'
Max Ridge Height 25'
Roof Framing Stick
Exterior Walls 2x4
Kitchen
Breakfast
PAN.
W.
D.
Laund.
TRAY CLG.
Foyer 16'-0" HIGH CLG.
Pwdr.
STAIRS DN.
Garage 21⁵x20⁰
OPTIONAL BASEMENT STAIR LOCATION
Master Suite 17⁵x14⁴
TRAY CEILING
FPL.
FRENCH DOOR
RADIUS WDW.
ARCHED OPENING
Dining Room 11⁸x11⁰
VAULT
Vaulted Great Room 19³x18⁷
16'-0" HIGH CEILING
SERVING BAR
RANGE
DECORATIVE COLUMNS
DW.
ISLAND
REF.
SHWR.
Vaulted M.Bath
K.S.
PLANT SHELF ABOVE
W.i.c.
LINEN
ARCHED OPENINGS
Kitchen
Breakfast
PAN.
TRAY CLG.
Bedroom 2 12⁰x11⁰
W.i.c.
COATS
Foyer 16'-0" HIGH CLG.
Pwdr.
Laund.
W.
D.
Storage
VLT.
LINEN
Bedroom 3 11¹⁰x10⁹
Bath
RADIUS WDW.
Garage 21⁵x20³
MAIN FLOOR
GARAGE LOCATION W/ BASEMENT

Design 94107

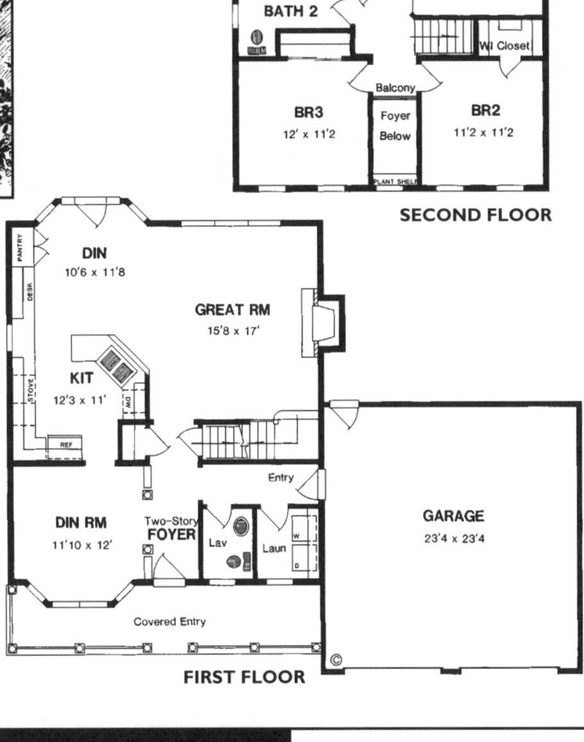
MBATH
MBR
14'8 x 17'
WI Closet
BATH 2
WI Closet
Balcony
BR3
12' x 11'2
Foyer
Below
BR2
11'2 x 11'2
PLANT SHELF
SECOND FLOOR
PANTRY
DESK
DIN
10'6 x 11'8
GREAT RM
15'8 x 17'
STOVE
KIT
12'3 x 11'
MO
REF
Entry
GARAGE
23'4 x 23'4
DIN RM
11'10 x 12'
Two-Story
FOYER
Lav
Laun
W
D
Covered Entry
FIRST FLOOR

Units	Single
Price Code	C
Total Finished	1,887 sq. ft.
First Finished	961 sq. ft.
Second Finished	926 sq. ft.
Basement Unfinished	928 sq. ft.
Garage Unfinished	548 sq. ft.
Dimensions	52'8"x40'
Foundation	Basement
Bedrooms	3
Full Baths	2
Half Baths	1
Max Ridge Height	32'
Roof Framing	Stick/Truss
Exterior Walls	2x4, 2x6

Design 93080

Units	Single
Price Code	C
Total Finished	1,890 sq. ft.
Main Finished	1,890 sq. ft.
Garage Unfinished	565 sq. ft.
Porch Unfinished	241 sq. ft.
Dimensions	65'10"x53'5"
Foundation	Crawlspace Slab
Bedrooms	3
Full Baths	2
Main Ceiling	10'
Max Ridge Height	21'6"
Roof Framing	Stick
Exterior Walls	2x4

SEAT
MASTER BATH
PORCH
BRKFST RM
10-8 X 11-8
10 FT CLG
UTIL
8-0 X 5-8
STORAGE
STORAGE
MASTER BEDRM
14-4 X 15-6
10 FT CLG
BUILT INS
FP
LIVING ROOM
17-4 X 15-8
10 FT CLG
KITCHEN
10-8 X 13-6
10 FT CLG
GARAGE
PAN
BATH 2
LIN
ARCH
FOYER
10 FT CLG
DINING ROOM
11-0 X 13-0
10 FT COFFERED CLG
BEDROOM 2
12-6 X 11-6
BEDROOM 3
12-0 X 13-4
10 FT CLG
PORCH
MAIN FLOOR

Design 96601

Units	Single
Price Code	C
Total Finished	1,890 sq. ft.
Main Finished	1,890 sq. ft.
Garage Unfinished	565 sq. ft.
Porch Unfinished	241 sq. ft.
Dimensions	65'10"x53'5"
Foundation	Crawlspace Slab
Bedrooms	3
Full Baths	2
Max Ridge Height	21'4"
Roof Framing	Stick
Exterior Walls	2x4

MASTER BATH
PORCH
BRKFST RM 10-8 X 11-8 10 FT CLG
UTIL 8-0 X 5-8
STORAGE
STORAGE
MASTER BEDRM 14-4 X 15-6 10 FT CLG
BUILT INS
FP
LIVING ROOM 17-4 X 15-8 10 FT CLG
KITCHEN 10-8 X 13-6 10 FT CLG
GARAGE
BATH 2
LIN
PAN
BEDROOM 2 12-6 X 11-6
BEDROOM 3 12-0 X 13-4 10 FT CLG
FOYER 10 FT CLG
DINING ROOM 11-0 X 13-0 10 FT COFFERED CLG
PORCH
©
MAIN FLOOR

Design 65624

Units	Single
Price Code	C
Total Finished	1,891 sq. ft.
Main Finished	1,891 sq. ft.
Dimensions	49'x64'
Foundation	Crawlspace Slab
Bedrooms	2
Full Baths	2
Main Ceiling	9'
Vaulted Ceiling	12'
Max Ridge Height	24'
Roof Framing	Stick
Exterior Walls	2x4

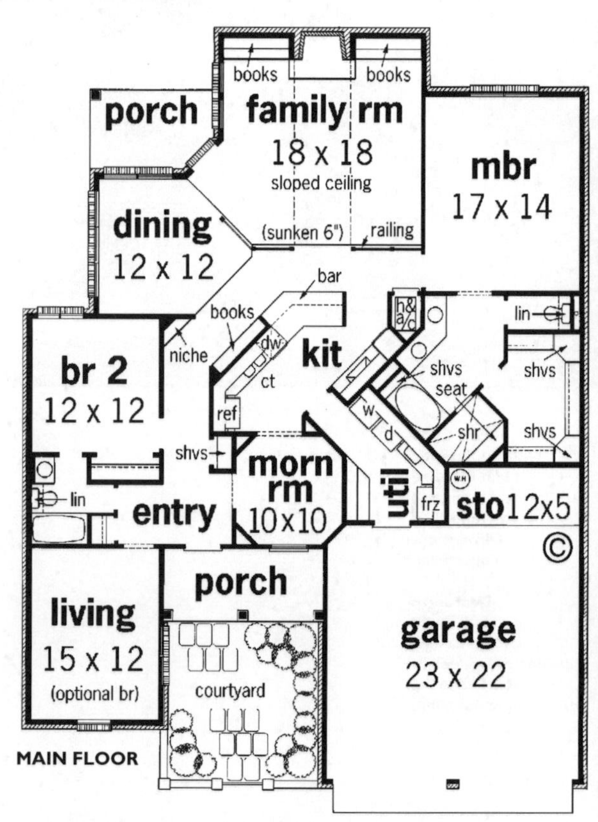
books
books
porch
family rm
18 x 18
sloped ceiling
(sunken 6")
railing
mbr
17 x 14
dining
12 x 12
bar
books
niche
dw
kit
ct
ref
h a/c
lin
shvs
seat
shvs
shr
shvs
br 2
12 x 12
shvs
w
d
lin
entry
morn rm
10x10
util
frz
sto 12x5
©
porch
living
15 x 12
(optional br)
courtyard
garage
23 x 22
MAIN FLOOR

Design 66082

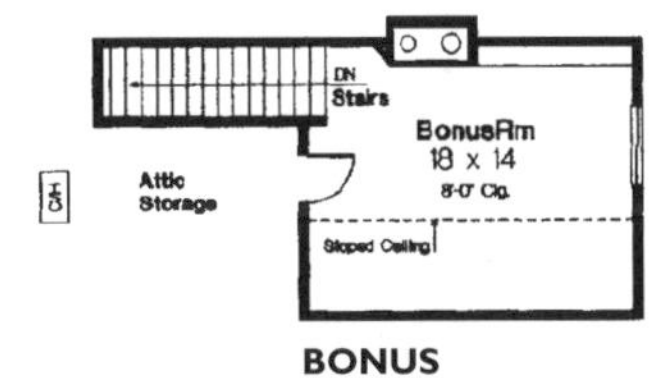
DN Stairs
BonusRm 18 x 14 8'-0" Clg.
Attic Storage
Sloped Ceiling
BONUS

Units	Single
Price Code	B
Total Finished	1,892 sq. ft.
Main Finished	1,892 sq. ft.
Bonus Unfinished	252 sq. ft.
Garage Unfinished	560 sq. ft.
Deck Unfinished	140 sq. ft.
Porch Unfinished	190 sq. ft.
Dimensions	75'10"x44'4"
Foundation	Slab
Bedrooms	3
Full Baths	2
Half Baths	1
Main Ceiling	10'
Max Ridge Height	26'
Roof Framing	Stick
Exterior Walls	2x4

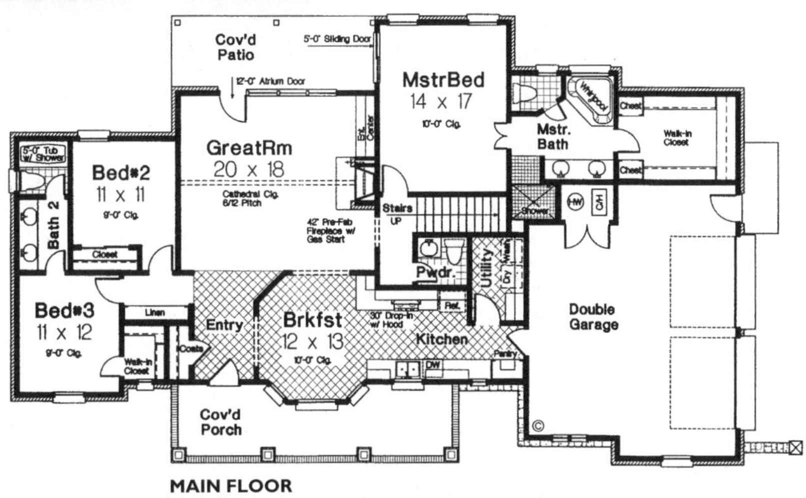
Cov'd Patio
5'-0" Sliding Door
12'-0" Atrium Door
GreatRm 20 x 18
Cathedral Clg. 6/12 Pitch
42" Pre-Fab Fireplace w/ Gas Start
MstrBed 14 x 17
10'-0" Clg.
Mstr. Bath
Whirlpool
Chest
Walk-in Closet
Shower
5'-0" Tub w/ Shower
Bath 2
Bed#2 11 x 11
9'-0" Clg.
Closet
Stairs UP
Pwdr.
Utility
Wash
Dry
Double Garage
Bed#3 11 x 12
9'-0" Clg.
Linen
Entry
Coats
Walk-in Closet
Brkfst 12 x 13
10'-0" Clg.
30" Drop-In w/ Hood
Ref.
Kitchen
Pantry
DW
Cov'd Porch
MAIN FLOOR

Design 81034

Units	Single
Price Code	C
Total Finished	1,893 sq. ft.
First Finished	1,087 sq. ft.
Second Finished	806 sq. ft.
Garage Unfinished	636 sq. ft.
Dimensions	40'x45'
Foundation	Crawlspace
Bedrooms	3
Full Baths	2
Half Baths	1
First Ceiling	9'
Max Ridge Height	29'
Roof Framing	Stick
Exterior Walls	2x6

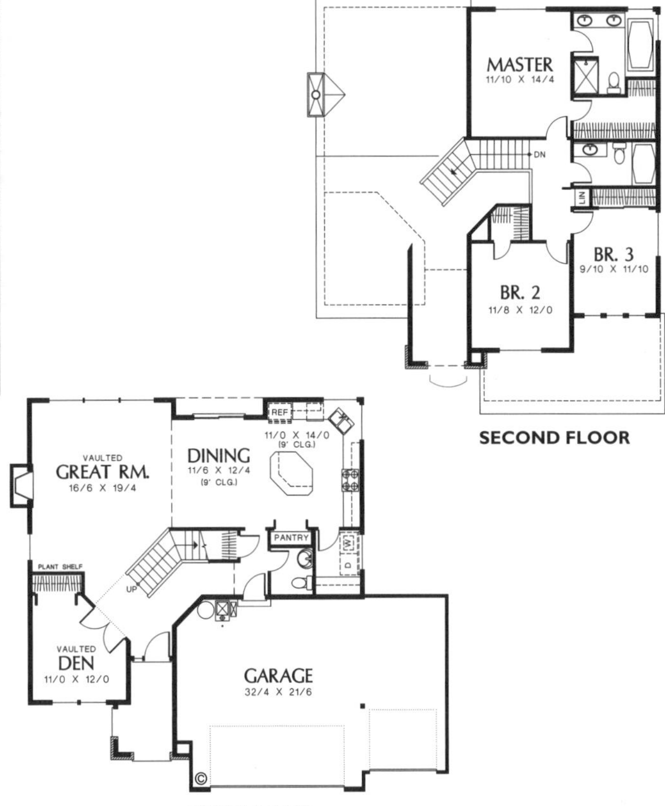
MASTER 11/10 X 14/4
DN
LIN
BR. 3 9/10 X 11/10
BR. 2 11/8 X 12/0
SECOND FLOOR
VAULTED GREAT RM. 16/6 X 19/4
DINING 11/6 X 12/4 (9' CLG.)
11/0 X 14/0 (9' CLG.)
REF
PANTRY
PLANT SHELF
UP
VAULTED DEN 11/0 X 12/0
GARAGE 32/4 X 21/6
FIRST FLOOR

Units	Single
Price Code	C
Total Finished	1,901 sq. ft.
Main Finished	1,901 sq. ft.
Garage Unfinished	484 sq. ft.
Porch Unfinished	383 sq. ft.
Dimensions	62'x53'8"
Foundation	Slab
Bedrooms	3
Full Baths	2
Main Ceiling	8'
Max Ridge Height	20'
Roof Framing	Truss

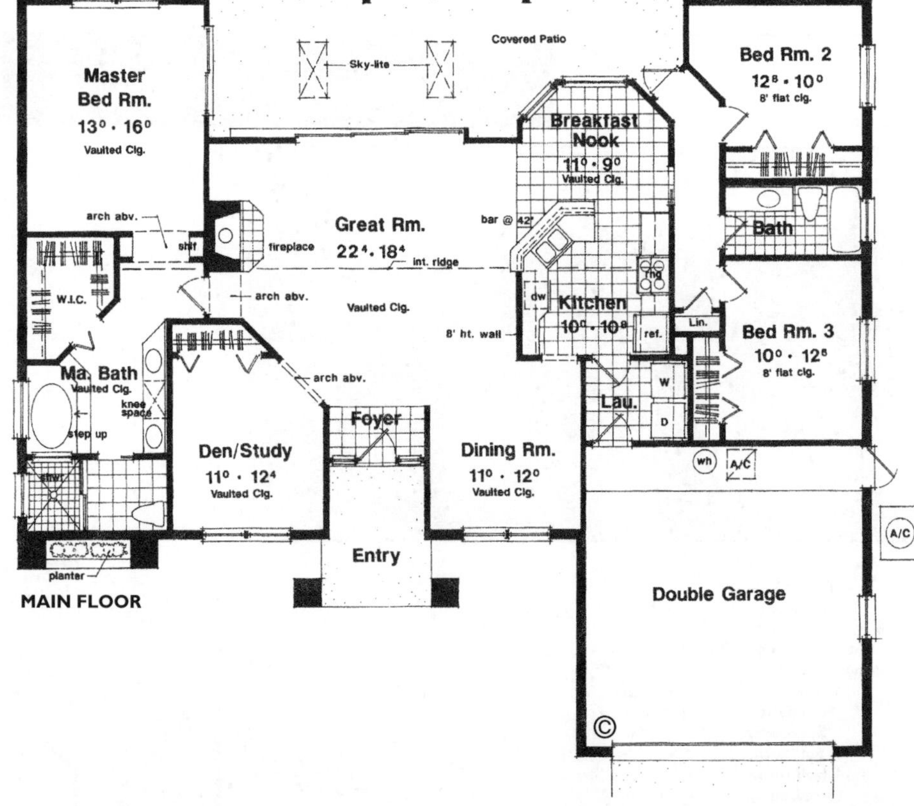
Covered Patio
Sky-lite
Master Bed Rm.
$13^{0} \cdot 16^{0}$
Vaulted Clg.
Bed Rm. 2
$12^{8} \cdot 10^{0}$
8' flat clg.
Breakfast Nook
$11^{0} \cdot 9^{0}$
Vaulted Clg.
Great Rm.
$22^{4} \cdot 18^{4}$
fireplace
int. ridge
bar @ 42"
arch abv.
shlf
W.I.C.
arch abv.
Vaulted Clg.
8' ht. wall
Kitchen
$10^{0} \cdot 10^{8}$
ref.
dw
Bath
Lin.
Bed Rm. 3
$10^{0} \cdot 12^{8}$
8' flat clg.
Ma. Bath
Vaulted Clg.
knee space
step up
shwr.
arch abv.
Den/Study
$11^{0} \cdot 12^{4}$
Vaulted Clg.
Foyer
Dining Rm.
$11^{0} \cdot 12^{0}$
Vaulted Clg.
Lau.
W
D
wh
A/C
A/C
Entry
planter
Double Garage
©

MAIN FLOOR

Design 98589

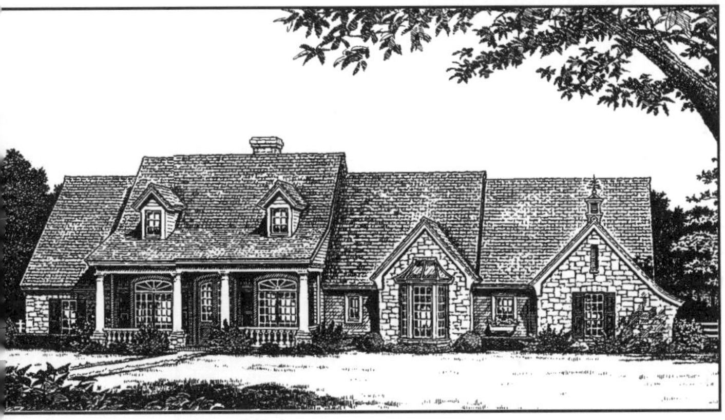

Units	Single
Price Code	C
Total Finished	1,902 sq. ft.
Main Finished	1,902 sq. ft.
Garage Unfinished	636 sq. ft.
Deck Unfinished	210 sq. ft.
Porch Unfinished	185 sq. ft.
Dimensions	84'7"x34'5"
Foundation	Slab
Bedrooms	3
Full Baths	2
Half Baths	1
Roof Framing	Stick
Exterior Walls	2x4

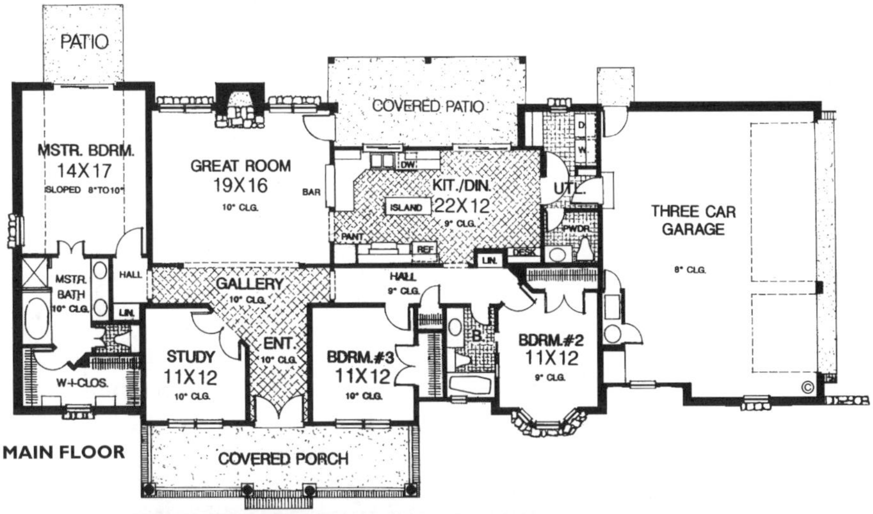

MAIN FLOOR

PATIO
MSTR. BDRM. 14X17 SLOPED 8"TO10"
GREAT ROOM 19X16 10" CLG.
BAR
COVERED PATIO
KIT./DIN. 22X12 9" CLG.
ISLAND
UTL.
THREE CAR GARAGE 8" CLG.
MSTR. BATH 10" CLG.
HALL
GALLERY 10" CLG.
HALL 9" CLG.
W-I-CLOS.
STUDY 11X12 10" CLG.
ENT. 10" CLG.
BDRM.#3 11X12 10" CLG.
BDRM.#2 11X12 9" CLG.
COVERED PORCH

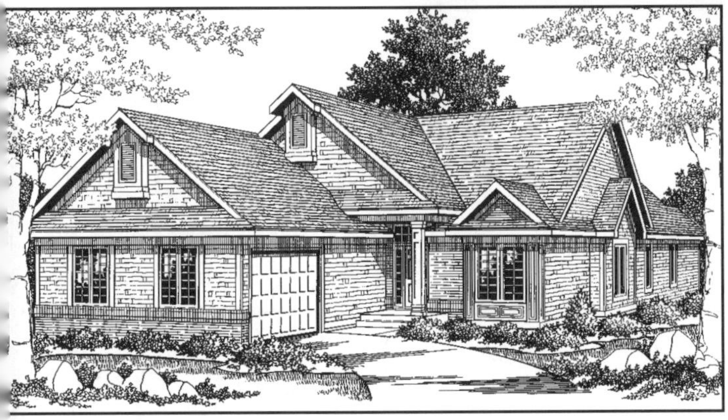

Design 97177

Units	Single
Price Code	C
Total Finished	1,904 sq. ft.
Main Finished	1,904 sq. ft.
Basement Unfinished	1,904 sq. ft.
Garage Unfinished	612 sq. ft.
Dimensions	98'x42'
Foundation	Basement
Bedrooms	2
Full Baths	2
Main Ceiling	11'
Max Ridge Height	24'8"
Roof Framing	Stick
Exterior Walls	2x6

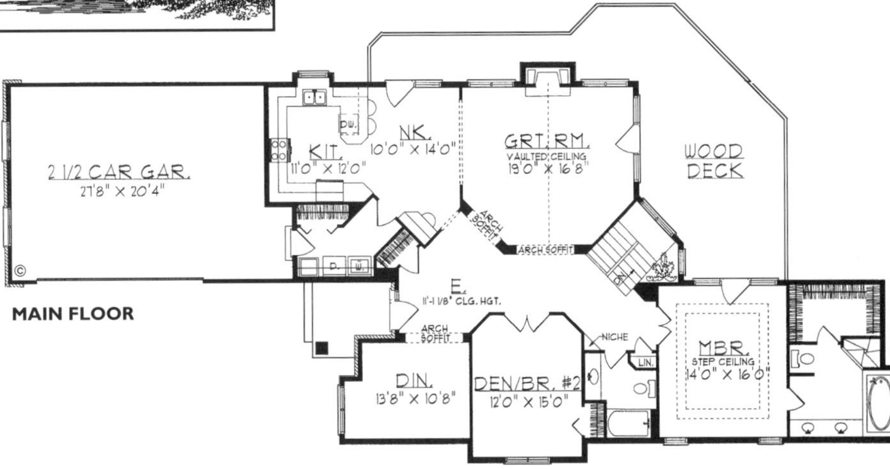

MAIN FLOOR

2 1/2 CAR GAR. 27'8" X 20'4"
KIT. 11'0" X 12'0"
NK. 10'0" X 14'0"
GRT. RM. VAULTED CEILING 19'0" X 16'8"
WOOD DECK
E. 11'-1 1/8" CLG. HGT.
DIN. 13'8" X 10'8"
DEN/BR. #2 12'0" X 15'0"
MBR. STEP CEILING 14'0" X 16'0"

Design 63141

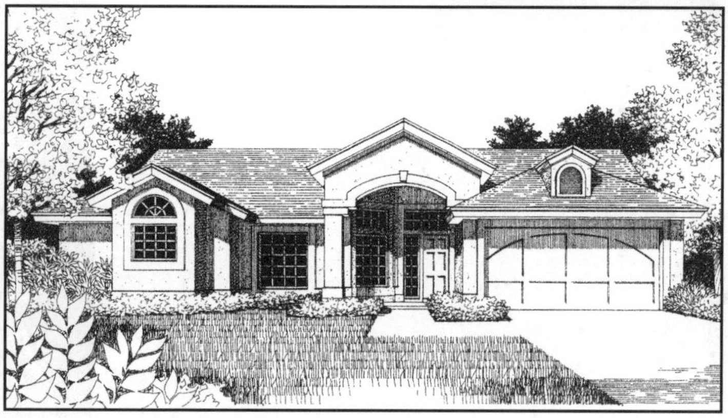

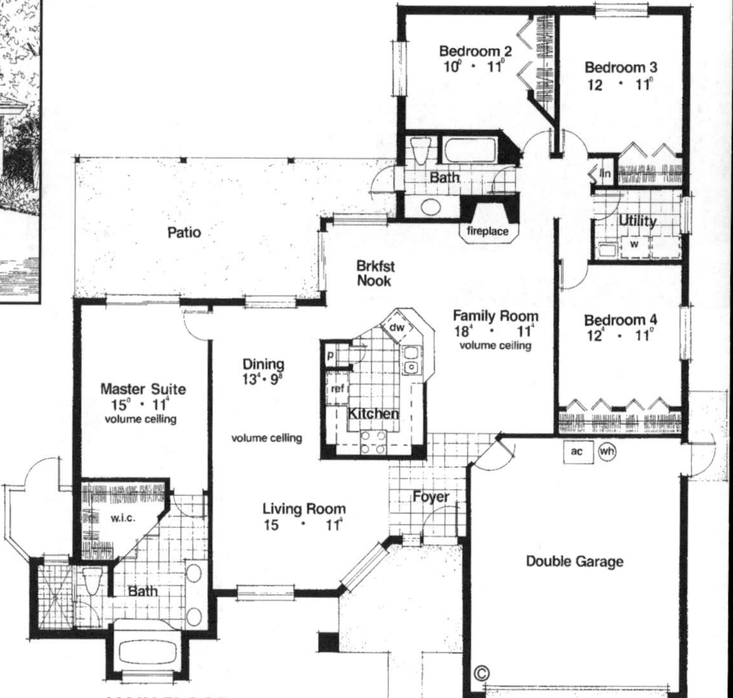

Units	Single
Price Code	C
Total Finished	1,906 sq. ft.
Main Finished	1,906 sq. ft.
Garage Unfinished	444 sq. ft.
Dimensions	58'2"x59'10"
Foundation	Slab
Bedrooms	4
Full Baths	2
Main Ceiling	8'
Max Ridge Height	18'5"
Roof Framing	Truss

Bedroom 2 10⁰ · 11⁰
Bedroom 3 12 · 11⁰
Bath
fireplace
Utility
Patio
Brkfst Nook
Family Room 18⁴ · 11⁴ volume ceiling
Bedroom 4 12⁴ · 11⁰
Master Suite 15⁰ · 11⁴ volume ceiling
Dining 13⁴ · 9⁸
volume ceiling
Kitchen
w.i.c.
Bath
Living Room 15 · 11⁴
Foyer
Double Garage

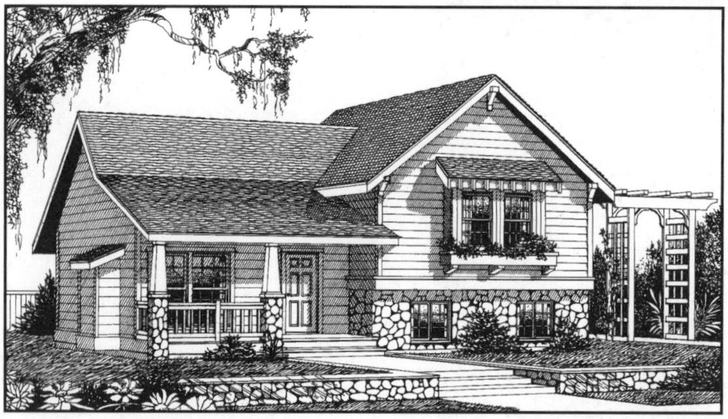

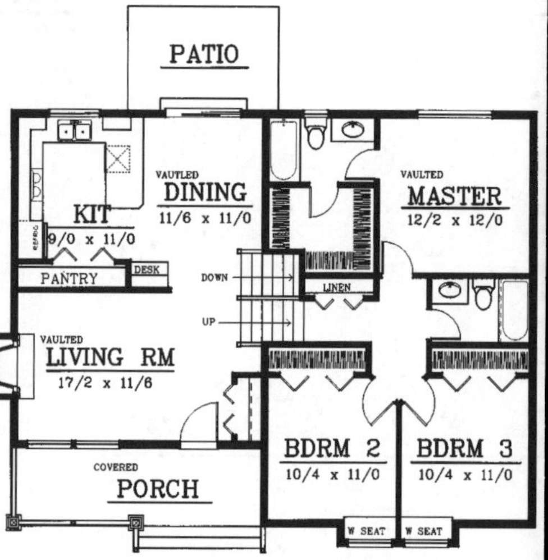

MAIN FLOOR

Design 91839

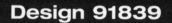

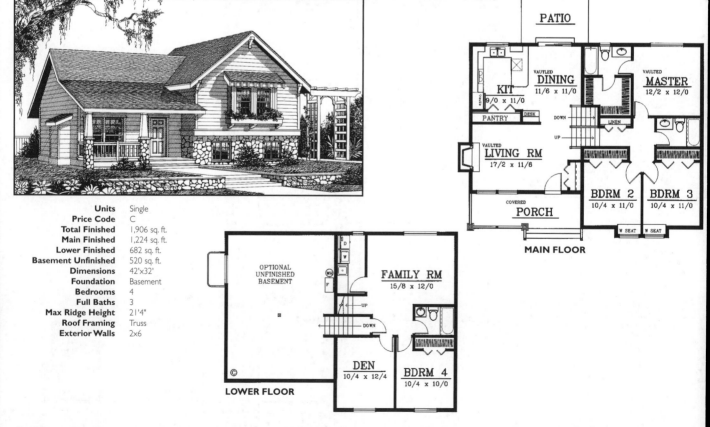

Units	Single
Price Code	C
Total Finished	1,906 sq. ft.
Main Finished	1,224 sq. ft.
Lower Finished	682 sq. ft.
Basement Unfinished	520 sq. ft.
Dimensions	42'x32'
Foundation	Basement
Bedrooms	4
Full Baths	3
Max Ridge Height	21'4"
Roof Framing	Truss
Exterior Walls	2x6

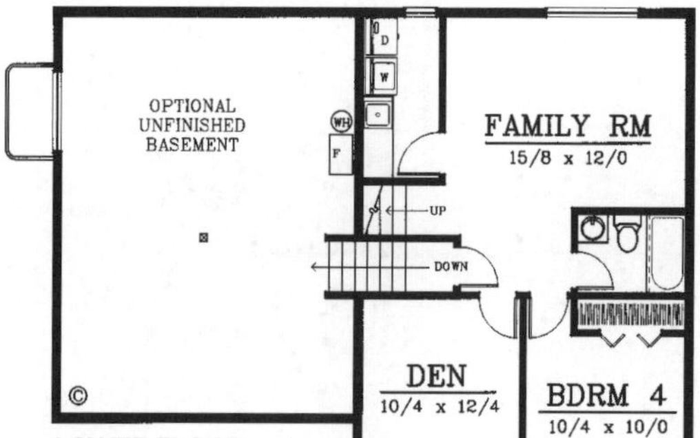

PATIO
KIT 9/0 x 11/0
VAULTED DINING 11/6 x 11/0
VAULTED MASTER 12/2 x 12/0
PANTRY
DESK
LINEN
VAULTED LIVING RM 17/2 x 11/6
COVERED PORCH
BDRM 2 10/4 x 11/0
BDRM 3 10/4 x 11/0
W SEAT
W SEAT

MAIN FLOOR

OPTIONAL UNFINISHED BASEMENT
FAMILY RM 15/8 x 12/0
DEN 10/4 x 12/4
BDRM 4 10/4 x 10/0

LOWER FLOOR

Design 99113

Units	Single
Price Code	C
Total Finished	1,906 sq. ft.
Main Finished	1,906 sq. ft.
Basement Unfinished	1,906 sq. ft.
Dimensions	72'x44'8"
Foundation	Basement
Bedrooms	3
Full Baths	2
Half Baths	1
Max Ridge Height	12'4"
Roof Framing	Truss
Exterior Walls	2x6

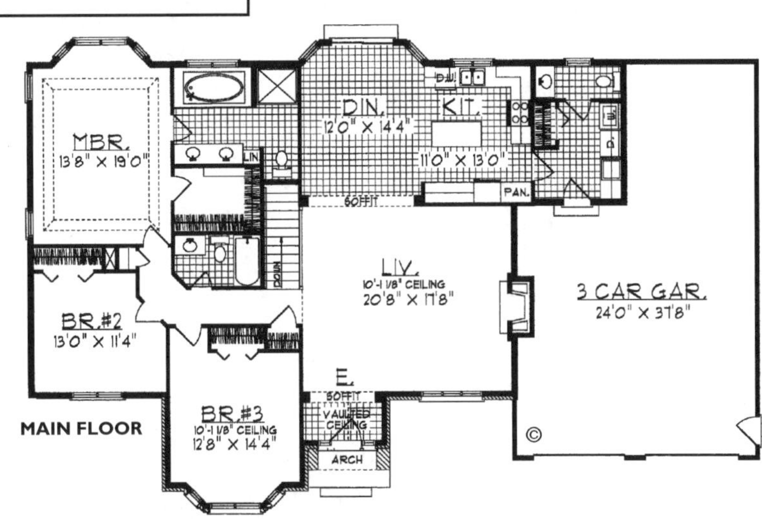
MBR.
13'8" X 19'0"
DIN.
12'0" X 14'4"
KIT.
11'0" X 13'0"
PAN.
SOFFIT
LIV.
10'-1 1/8" CEILING
20'8" X 17'8"
3 CAR GAR.
24'0" X 37'8"
BR.#2
13'0" X 11'4"
BR.#3
10'-1 1/8" CEILING
12'8" X 14'4"
E.
SOFFIT
VAULTED CEILING
ARCH

MAIN FLOOR

Design 10785

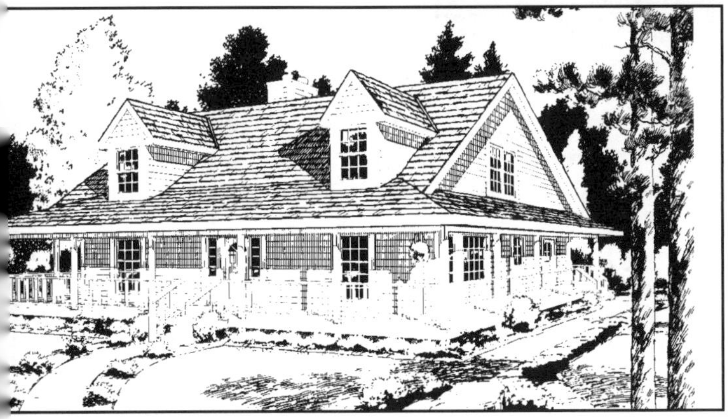

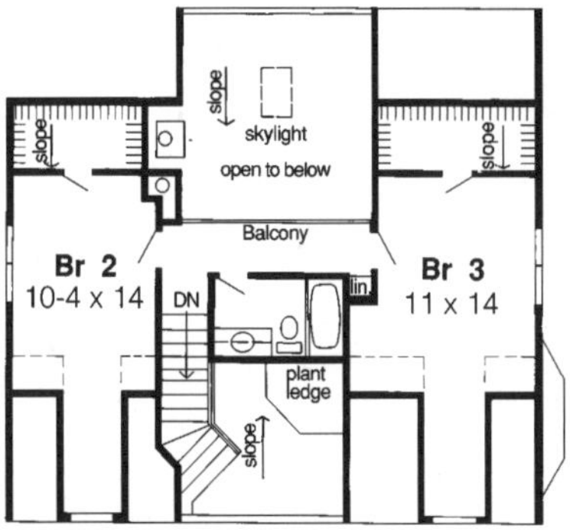

Units	Single
Price Code	C
Total Finished	1,907 sq. ft.
First Finished	1,269 sq. ft.
Second Finished	638 sq. ft.
Basement Unfinished	1,269 sq. ft.
Dimensions	47'x39'
Foundation	Basement Crawlspace Slab
Bedrooms	3
Full Baths	2
Half Baths	1
First Ceiling	8'
Second Ceiling	8'
Max Ridge Height	24'
Roof Framing	Stick
Exterior Walls	2x6

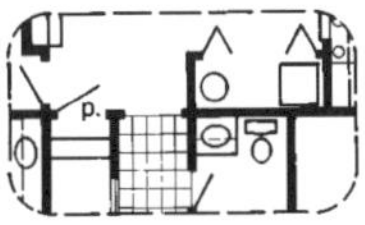

OPTIONAL CRAWLSPACE/ SLAB FOUNDATION

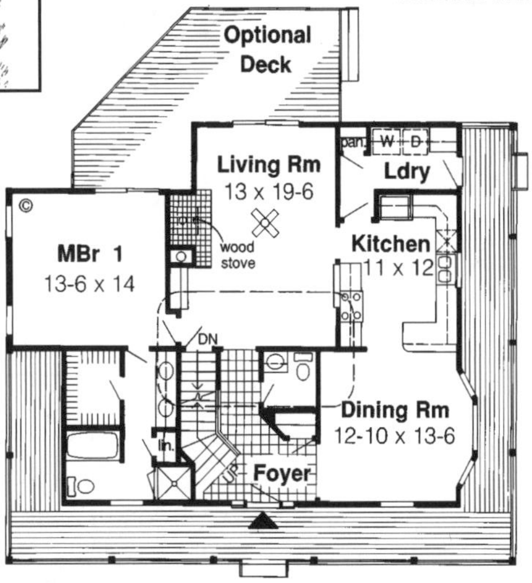

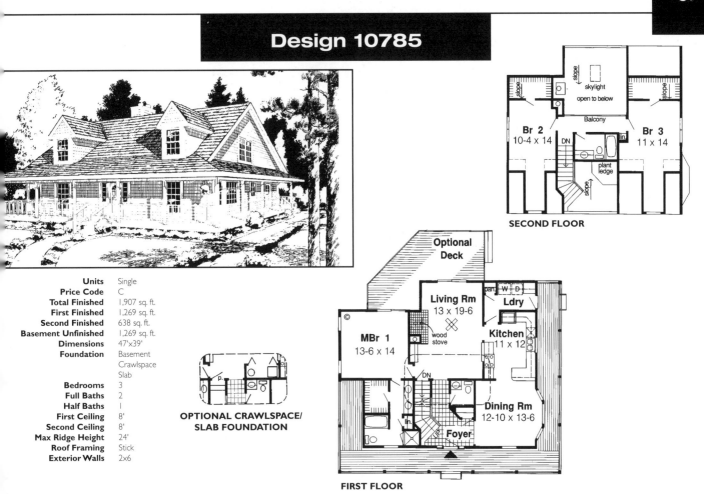

SECOND FLOOR

FIRST FLOOR

Design 66084

Units	Single
Price Code	C
Total Finished	1,907 sq. ft.
Main Finished	1,907 sq. ft.
Bonus Unfinished	369 sq. ft.
Garage Unfinished	430 sq. ft.
Deck Unfinished	160 sq. ft.
Porch Unfinished	85 sq. ft.
Dimensions	52'x59'9"
Foundation	Slab
Bedrooms	3
Full Baths	2
Max Ridge Height	26'
Roof Framing	Stick
Exterior Walls	2x4

BONUS

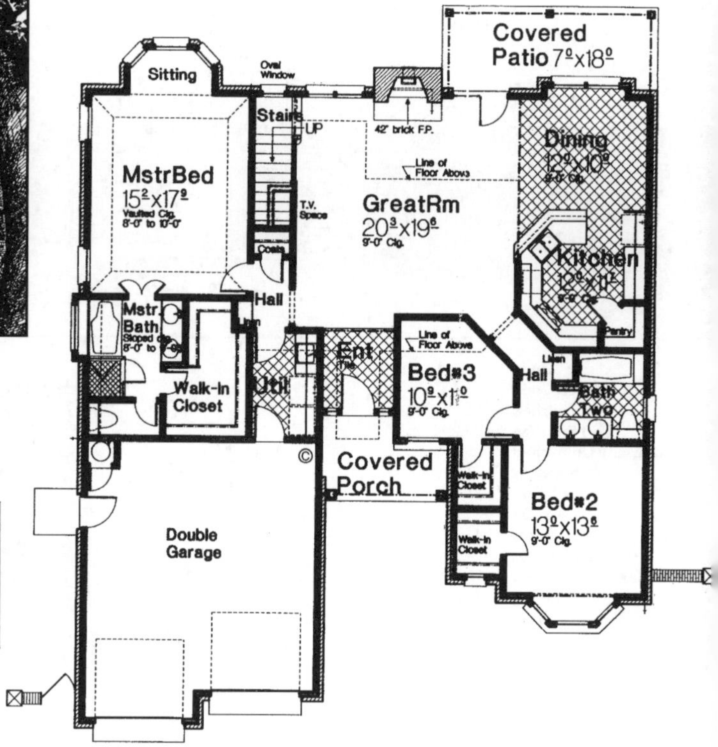

MAIN FLOOR

Design 60073

Units	Single
Price Code	C
Total Finished	1,911 sq. ft.
First Finished	1,391 sq. ft.
Second Finished	520 sq. ft.
Bonus Unfinished	99 sq. ft.
Basement Unfinished	1,391 sq. ft.
Garage Unfinished	450 sq. ft.
Dimensions	57'x38'4"
Foundation	Basement Crawlspace
Bedrooms	3
Full Baths	2
Half Baths	1
First Ceiling	9'
Second Ceiling	8'
Max Ridge Height	26'6"
Roof Framing	Stick
Exterior Walls	2x6

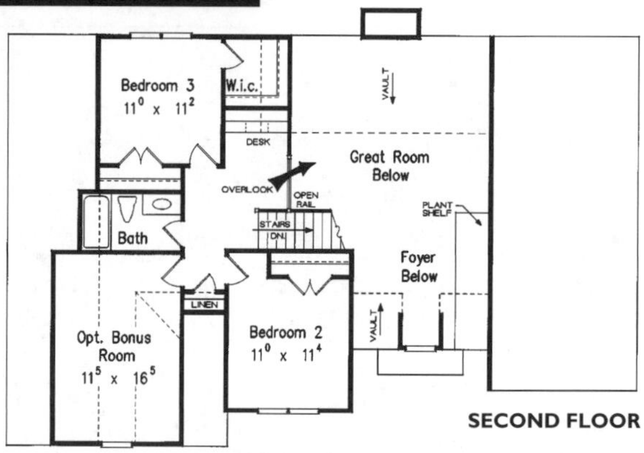

SECOND FLOOR

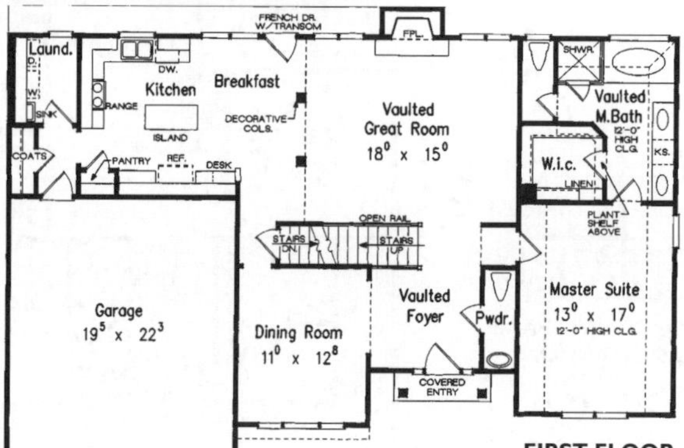

FIRST FLOOR

CAD FILES AVAILABLE
For more information call
800-235-5700

Design 94966

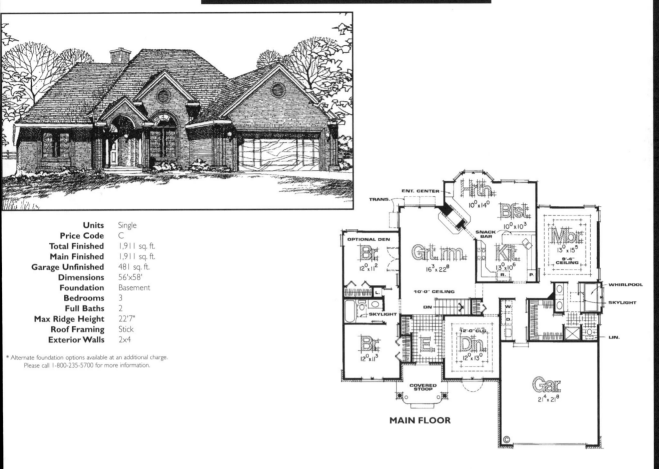

Units	Single
Price Code	C
Total Finished	1,911 sq. ft.
Main Finished	1,911 sq. ft.
Garage Unfinished	481 sq. ft.
Dimensions	56'x58'
Foundation	Basement
Bedrooms	3
Full Baths	2
Max Ridge Height	22'7"
Roof Framing	Stick
Exterior Walls	2x4

* Alternate foundation options available at an additional charge. Please call 1-800-235-5700 for more information.

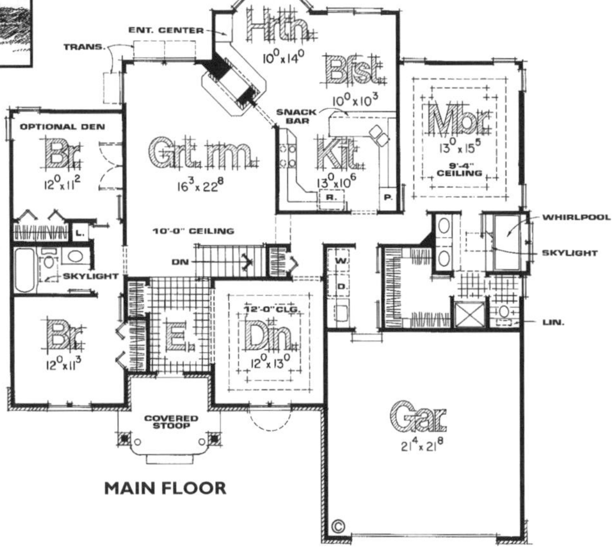

ENT. CENTER
TRANS.
Hrth. 10^0x14^0
Bfst. 10^0x10^3
SNACK BAR
OPTIONAL DEN
Br. 12^0x11^2
Grt. rm. 16^3x22^8
Kit. 13^0x10^6
Mbr. 13^0x15^5
9'-4" CEILING
WHIRLPOOL
SKYLIGHT
10'-0" CEILING
DN
SKYLIGHT
12'-0" CLG.
Br. 12^0x11^3
E.
Dn. 12^0x13^0
LIN.
COVERED STOOP
Gar. 21^4x21^8

MAIN FLOOR

Design 98445

CAD FILES AVAILABLE For more information call 800-235-5700

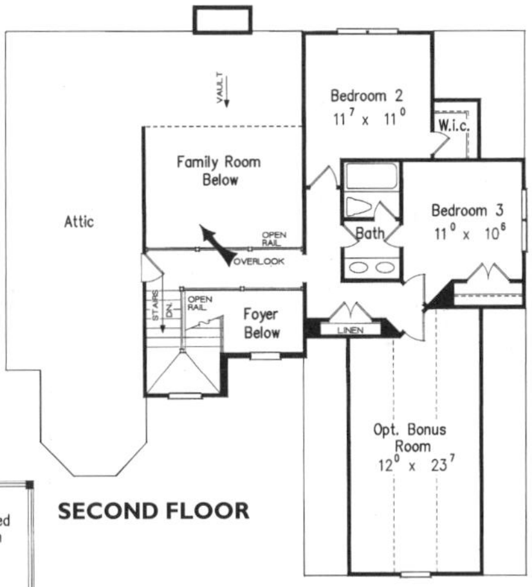

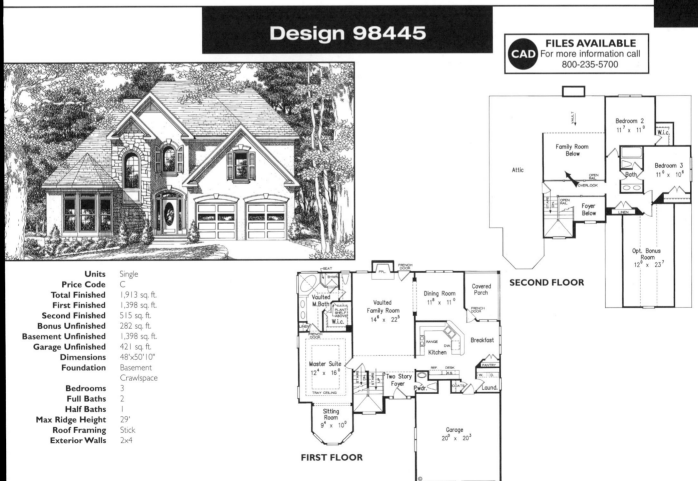

Units	Single
Price Code	C
Total Finished	1,913 sq. ft.
First Finished	1,398 sq. ft.
Second Finished	515 sq. ft.
Bonus Unfinished	282 sq. ft.
Basement Unfinished	1,398 sq. ft.
Garage Unfinished	421 sq. ft.
Dimensions	48'x50'10"
Foundation	Basement Crawlspace
Bedrooms	3
Full Baths	2
Half Baths	1
Max Ridge Height	29'
Roof Framing	Stick
Exterior Walls	2x4

Vault
Bedroom 2 11^7 x 11^0
W.i.c.
Family Room Below
Attic
Bedroom 3 11^0 x 10^8
Bath
Open Rail Overlook
Foyer Below
Linen
Opt. Bonus Room 12^0 x 23^7

SECOND FLOOR

Seat
French Door
Vaulted M.Bath
Plant Shelf Above
W.i.c.
Vaulted Family Room 14^6 x 22^5
Dining Room 11^8 x 11^0
Covered Porch
French Door
Range
DW.
Kitchen
Breakfast
French Door
Master Suite 12^4 x 16^0
Tray Ceiling
Pantry
Two Story Foyer
Pwdr.
Coats
Laund.
Sitting Room 9^4 x 10^0
Garage 20^0 x 20^3

FIRST FLOOR

Design 97618

CAD
FILES AVAILABLE
For more information call
800-235-5700

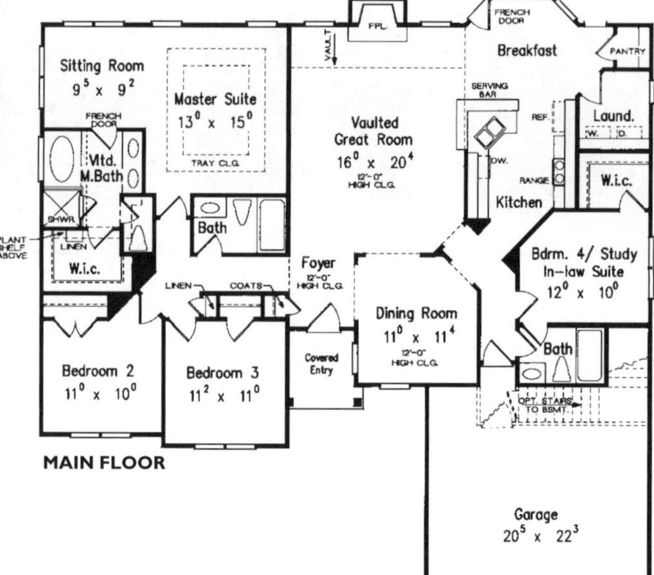
Sitting Room
9⁵ x 9²
Master Suite
13⁰ x 15⁰
TRAY CLG.
FRENCH DOOR
Vltd. M.Bath
SHWR.
LINEN
W.i.c.
PLANT SHELF ABOVE
Bath
LINEN
COATS
Bedroom 2
11⁰ x 10⁰
Bedroom 3
11² x 11⁰
FPL.
VAULT
Vaulted Great Room
16⁰ x 20⁴
12'-0" HIGH CLG.
Foyer
12'-0" HIGH CLG.
Covered Entry
Dining Room
11⁰ x 11⁴
12'-0" HIGH CLG.
FRENCH DOOR
Breakfast
PANTRY
SERVING BAR
REF.
DW.
RANGE
Kitchen
Laund.
W.
D.
W.i.c.
Bdrm. 4/ Study In-law Suite
12⁰ x 10⁰
Bath
OPT. STAIRS TO BSMT.
Garage
20⁵ x 22³
GARAGE LOCATION WITH BASEMENT
MAIN FLOOR

Units	Single
Price Code	C
Total Finished	1,915 sq. ft.
Main Finished	1,915 sq. ft.
Basement Unfinished	1,932 sq. ft.
Garage Unfinished	489 sq. ft.
Dimensions	56'6"x57'6"
Foundation	Basement Crawlspace
Bedrooms	4
Full Baths	3
Max Ridge Height	22'6"
Roof Framing	Stick
Exterior Walls	2x4

Design 90480

Units	Single
Price Code	C
Total Finished	1,918 sq. ft.
Main Finished	1,918 sq. ft.
Bonus Unfinished	264 sq. ft.
Basement Unfinished	1,904 sq. ft.
Garage Unfinished	484 sq. ft.
Deck Unfinished	268 sq. ft.
Porch Unfinished	192 sq. ft.
Dimensions	67'x60'
Foundation	Basement Crawlspace Slab
Bedrooms	3
Full Baths	2
Max Ridge Height	21'8"
Roof Framing	Stick
Exterior Walls	2x4

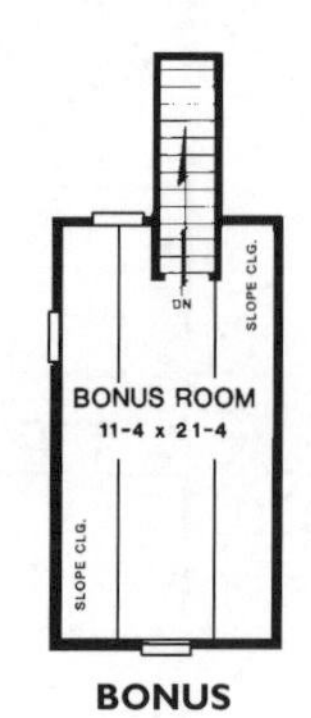
DN
SLOPE CLG.
BONUS ROOM
11-4 x 21-4
SLOPE CLG.
BONUS

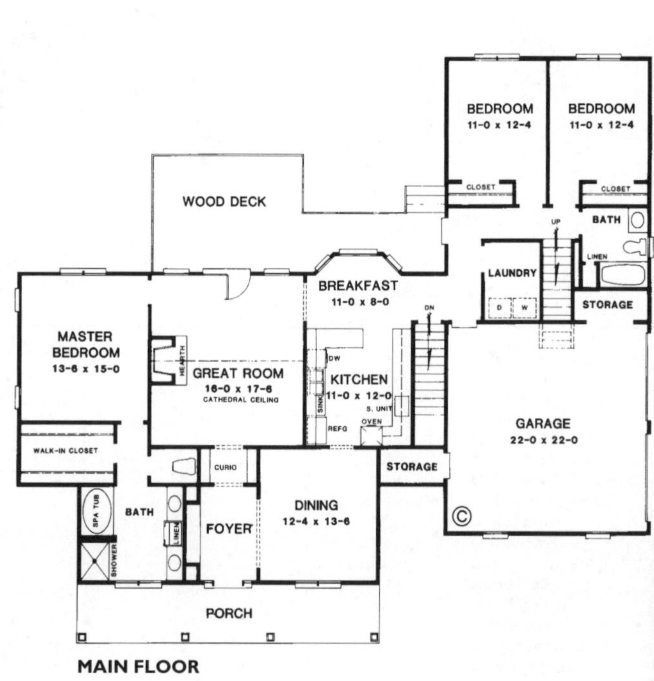
BEDROOM
11-0 x 12-4
BEDROOM
11-0 x 12-4
CLOSET
CLOSET
BATH
LINEN
WOOD DECK
BREAKFAST
11-0 x 8-0
UP
DN
LAUNDRY
STORAGE
MASTER BEDROOM
13-6 x 15-0
HEARTH
GREAT ROOM
16-0 x 17-6
CATHEDRAL CEILING
DW
KITCHEN
11-0 x 12-0
S. UNIT
OVEN
REFG
SINK
GARAGE
22-0 x 22-0
WALK-IN CLOSET
CURIO
STORAGE
SPA TUB
BATH
SHOWER
LINEN
FOYER
DINING
12-4 x 13-6
PORCH
MAIN FLOOR

Design 63001

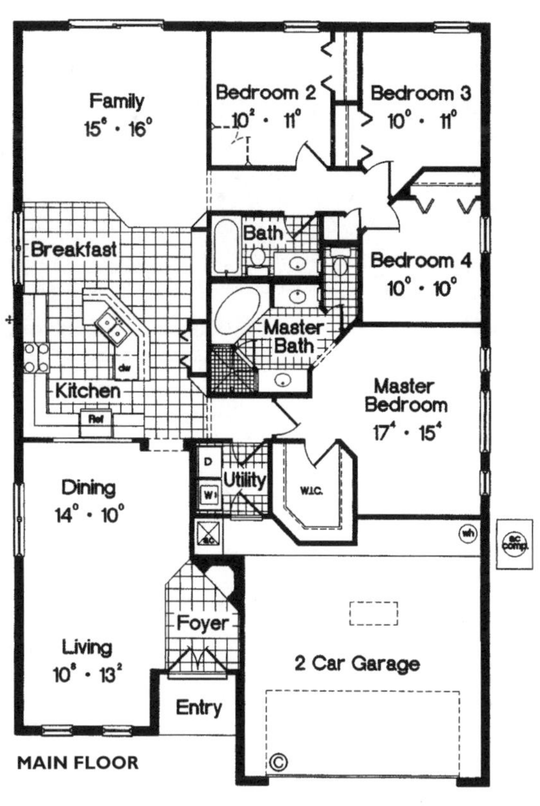

Family
15⁶ · 16⁰
Bedroom 2
10² · 11⁰
Bedroom 3
10⁰ · 11⁰
Breakfast
Bath
Bedroom 4
10⁰ · 10⁰
Master Bath
Kitchen
Master Bedroom
17⁴ · 15⁴
Dining
14⁰ · 10⁰
Utility
W.I.C.
Foyer
Living
10⁶ · 13²
2 Car Garage
Entry
MAIN FLOOR

Units	Single
Price Code	C
Total Finished	1,919 sq. ft.
Main Finished	1,919 sq. ft.
Garage Unfinished	454 sq. ft.
Dimensions	40'x62'
Foundation	Slab
Bedrooms	4
Full Baths	2
Main Ceiling	8'
Max Ridge Height	18'6"
Roof Framing	Stick

Design 67010

F/P
HEARTH ROOM
14'-0"
X 11'-0"
11' CEILING
BRK
12'-6"
X 10'-0"
11' CEILING
EATING BAR
W.I.C.
PLANT LEDGE
GREAT ROOM
14'-0"
X 17'-0"
11' CEILING
BEDROOM 2
11'-2"
X 10'-0"
MASTER BATH
(VAULTED)
KIT
LIN
CL
BATH-2
MASTER SUITE
13'-0"
X 14'-0"
FOYER
DINING
11'-0"
X 11'-9"
UTIL
BEDROOM 3
10'-0"
X 11'-0"
PORCH
UP
STOR
MAIN FLOOR
DOUBLE GARAGE
19'-6" X 20'-0"

Units	Single
Price Code	C
Total Finished	1,919 sq. ft.
Main Finished	1,919 sq. ft.
Bonus Unfinished	281 sq. ft.
Garage Unfinished	456 sq. ft.
Porch Unfinished	111 sq. ft.
Dimensions	53'4"x66'3"
Foundation	Crawlspace
Bedrooms	3
Full Baths	2
Main Ceiling	8'
Vaulted Ceiling	11'
Max Ridge Height	23'3"
Roof Framing	Stick
Exterior Walls	2x4

Design 99117

Units	Single
Price Code	C
Total Finished	1,919 sq. ft.
Main Finished	1,919 sq. ft.
Basement Unfinished	1,919 sq. ft.
Dimensions	60'x58'
Foundation	Basement
Bedrooms	3
Full Baths	2
Max Ridge Height	20'10"
Roof Framing	Truss
Exterior Walls	2x6

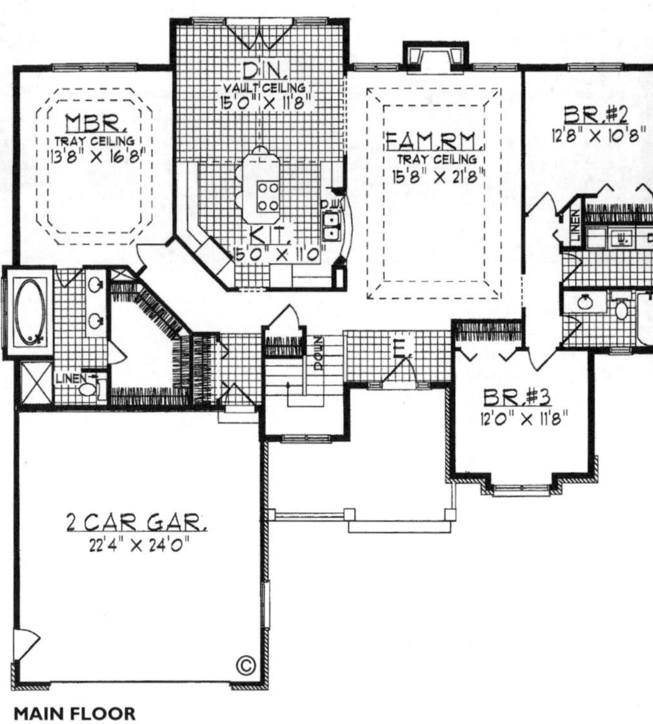

DIN.
VAULT CEILING
15'0" X 11'8"
MBR.
TRAY CEILING
13'8" X 16'8"
FAM.RM.
TRAY CEILING
15'8" X 21'8"
BR.#2
12'8" X 10'8"
KIT.
15'0" X 11'0"
LINEN
DOWN
BR.#3
12'0" X 11'8"
2 CAR GAR.
22'4" X 24'0"

MAIN FLOOR

Design 97870

Units	Single
Price Code	C
Total Finished	1,920 sq. ft.
Main Finished	1,920 sq. ft.
Garage Unfinished	483 sq. ft.
Deck Unfinished	150 sq. ft.
Porch Unfinished	42 sq. ft.
Dimensions	61'x48'7"
Foundation	Slab
Bedrooms	3
Full Baths	2
Half Baths	1
Main Ceiling	8'-10'
Max Ridge Height	30'
Roof Framing	Stick
Exterior Walls	2x4

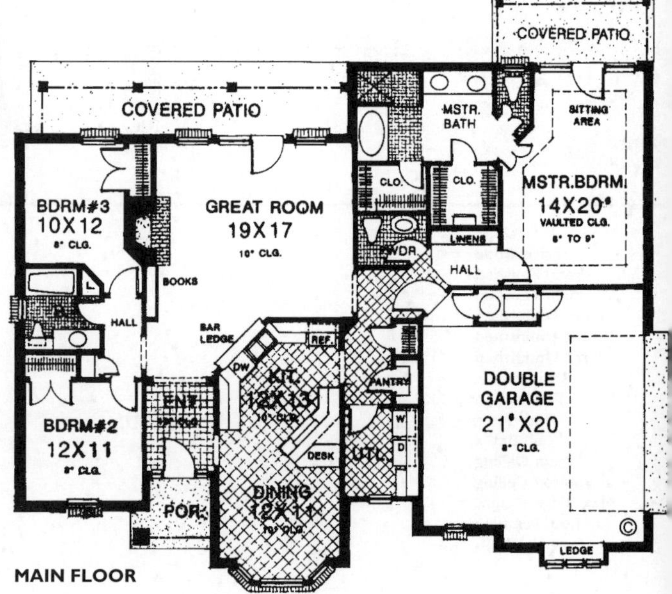

COVERED PATIO
COVERED PATIO
MSTR. BATH
SITTING AREA
BDRM#3
10X12
GREAT ROOM
19X17
CLO.
CLO.
MSTR.BDRM.
LINENS
PWDR
HALL
BOOKS
HALL
BAR LEDGE
REF
KIT.
12X13
PANTRY
DOUBLE GARAGE
BDRM#2
12X11
DESK
UTL.
DINING
12X11
POR.
LEDGE

MAIN FLOOR

Design 65157

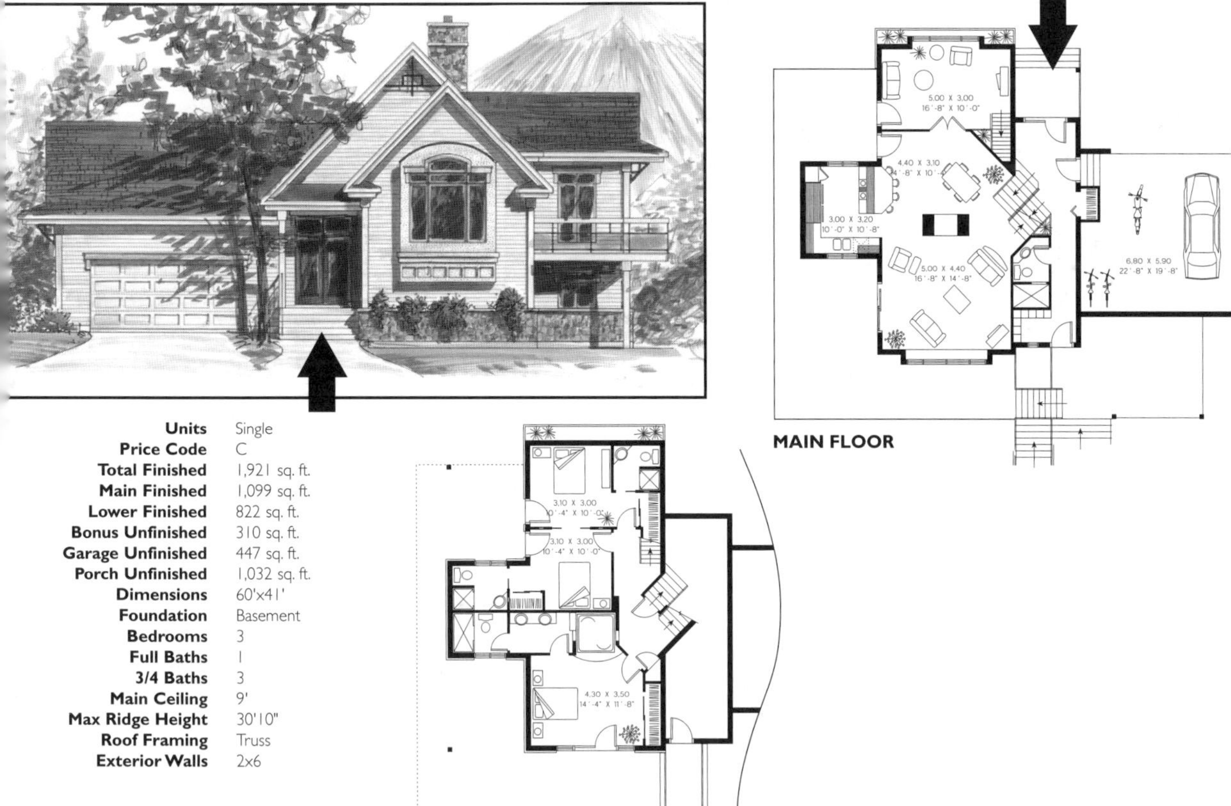
MAIN FLOOR
LOWER FLOOR

Units	Single
Price Code	C
Total Finished	1,921 sq. ft.
Main Finished	1,099 sq. ft.
Lower Finished	822 sq. ft.
Bonus Unfinished	310 sq. ft.
Garage Unfinished	447 sq. ft.
Porch Unfinished	1,032 sq. ft.
Dimensions	60'x41'
Foundation	Basement
Bedrooms	3
Full Baths	1
3/4 Baths	3
Main Ceiling	9'
Max Ridge Height	30'10"
Roof Framing	Truss
Exterior Walls	2x6

Design 82051

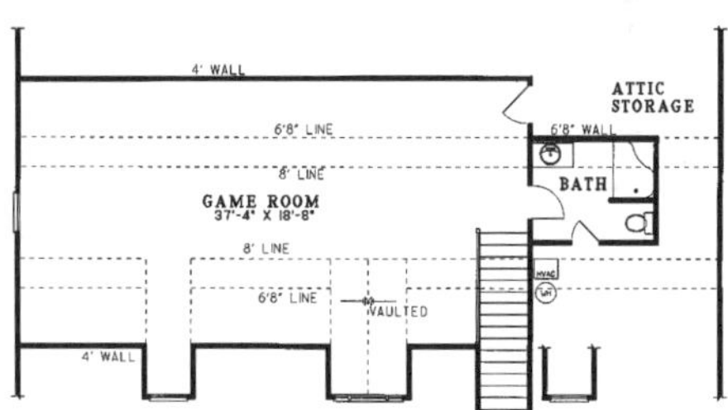
ATTIC STORAGE
GAME ROOM
BATH
BONUS

Units	Single
Price Code	C
Total Finished	1,921 sq. ft.
Main Finished	1,921 sq. ft.
Bonus Unfinished	812 sq. ft.
Garage Unfinished	505 sq. ft.
Porch Unfinished	959 sq. ft.
Dimensions	84'x55'6"
Foundation	Basement Crawlspace Slab
Bedrooms	3
Full Baths	2
Main Ceiling	8'
Roof Framing	Stick
Exterior Walls	2x4

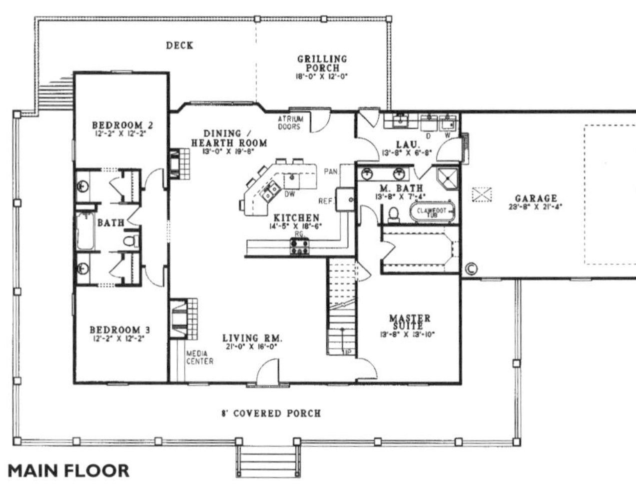
DECK
GRILLING PORCH
BEDROOM 2
DINING / HEARTH ROOM
KITCHEN
LAU.
M. BATH
GARAGE
BATH
BEDROOM 3
LIVING RM.
MASTER SUITE
8' COVERED PORCH
MAIN FLOOR

Design 91827

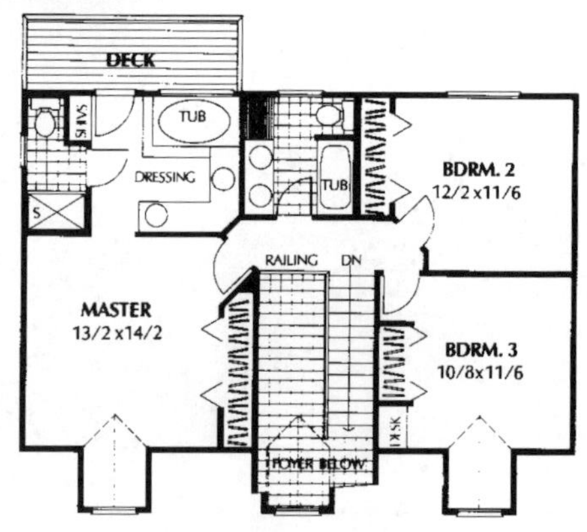
DECK
TUB
DRESSING
TUB
BDRM. 2
12/2x11/6
RAILING
DN
MASTER
13/2x14/2
BDRM. 3
10/8x11/6
FOYER BELOW

SECOND FLOOR

Units	Single
Price Code	C
Total Finished	1,921 sq. ft.
First Finished	1,064 sq. ft.
Second Finished	857 sq. ft.
Basement Unfinished	1,064 sq. ft.
Dimensions	62'x34'
Foundation	Basement Crawlspace Slab
Bedrooms	3
Full Baths	2
Half Baths	1
First Ceiling	8'
Second Ceiling	8'
Max Ridge Height	26'4"
Roof Framing	Stick
Exterior Walls	2x6

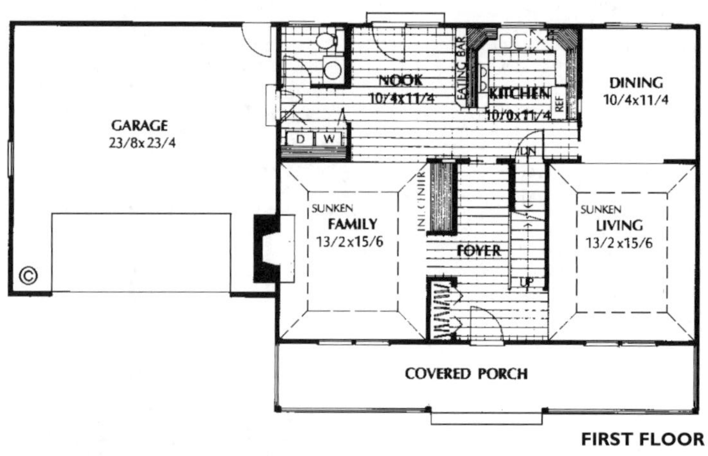
GARAGE
23/8x23/4
NOOK
10/4x11/4
EATING BAR
KITCHEN
10/0x11/4
REF
DINING
10/4x11/4
D
W
DN
SUNKEN
FAMILY
13/2x15/6
FOYER
UP
SUNKEN
LIVING
13/2x15/6
COVERED PORCH

FIRST FLOOR

Design 99192

Units	Single
Price Code	C
Total Finished	1,921 sq. ft.
Main Finished	1,921 sq. ft.
Basement Unfinished	1,921 sq. ft.
Garage Unfinished	486 sq. ft.
Dimensions	53'8"x59'
Foundation	Basement
Bedrooms	3
Full Baths	2
Main Ceiling	9'
Tray Ceiling	11'
Max Ridge Height	25'3"
Roof Framing	Truss
Exterior Walls	2x4

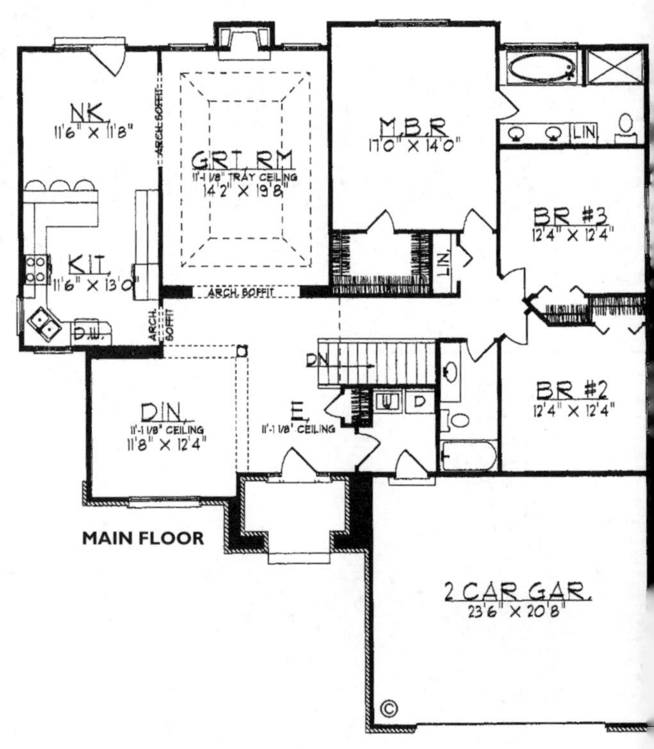
NK
11'6" X 11'8"
ARCH. SOFFIT
GRT RM
11'-1 1/8" TRAY CEILING
14'2" X 19'8"
M.B.R
17'0" X 14'0"
LIN
BR #3
12'4" X 12'4"
KIT
11'6" X 13'0"
ARCH. SOFFIT
D.W.
DN
DIN
11'-1 1/8" CEILING
11'8" X 12'4"
E
11'-1 1/8" CEILING
W
D
BR #2
12'4" X 12'4"
2 CAR GAR
23'6" X 20'8"

MAIN FLOOR

Design 65012

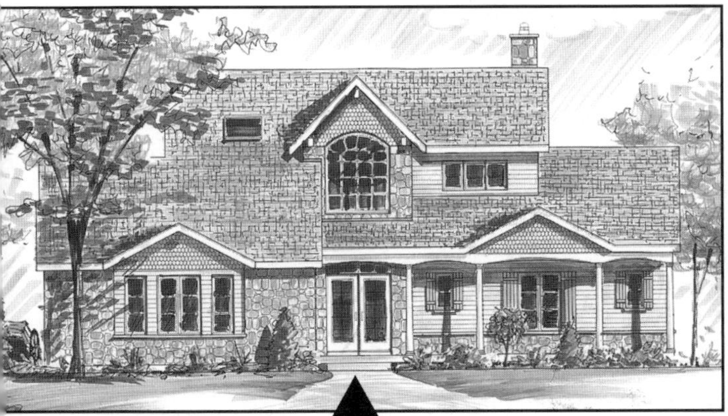

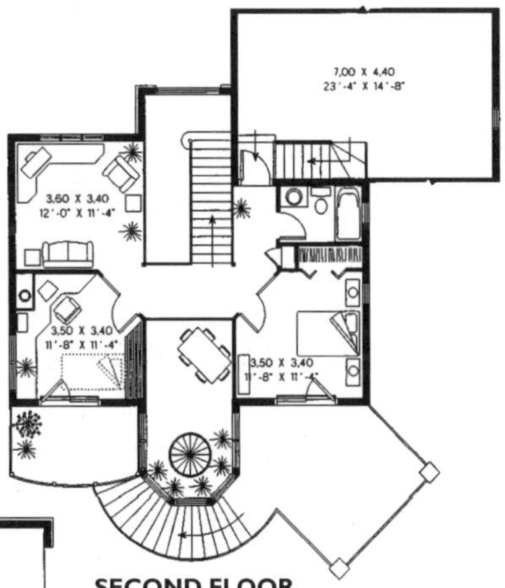

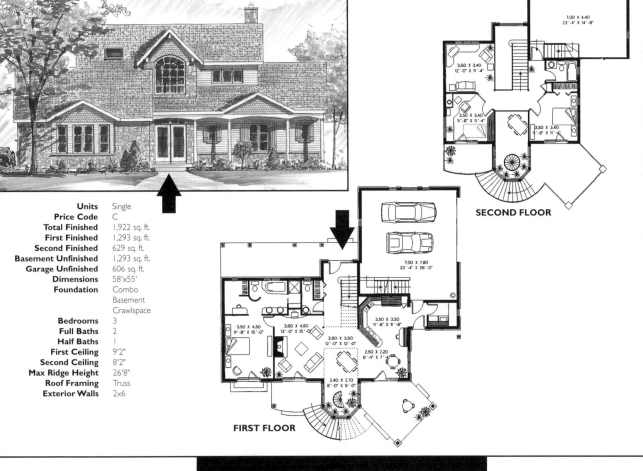

SECOND FLOOR

FIRST FLOOR

Units	Single
Price Code	C
Total Finished	1,922 sq. ft.
First Finished	1,293 sq. ft.
Second Finished	629 sq. ft.
Basement Unfinished	1,293 sq. ft.
Garage Unfinished	606 sq. ft.
Dimensions	58'x55'
Foundation	Combo Basement Crawlspace
Bedrooms	3
Full Baths	2
Half Baths	1
First Ceiling	9'2"
Second Ceiling	8'2"
Max Ridge Height	26'8"
Roof Framing	Truss
Exterior Walls	2x6

Design 97330

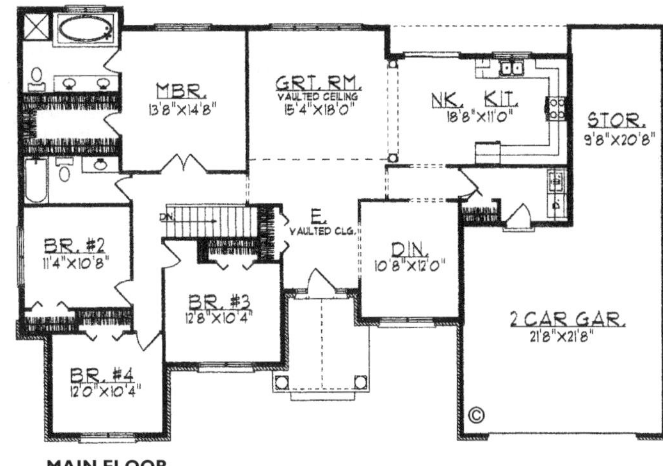

MBR.
13'8"X14'8"
GRT. RM.
VAULTED CEILING
15'4"X18'0"
NK. KIT.
18'8"X11'0"
STOR.
9'8"X20'8"
BR. #2
11'4"X10'8"
E.
VAULTED CLG.
DIN.
10'8"X12'0"
BR. #3
12'8"X10'4"
2 CAR GAR.
21'8"X21'8"
BR. #4
12'0"X10'4"

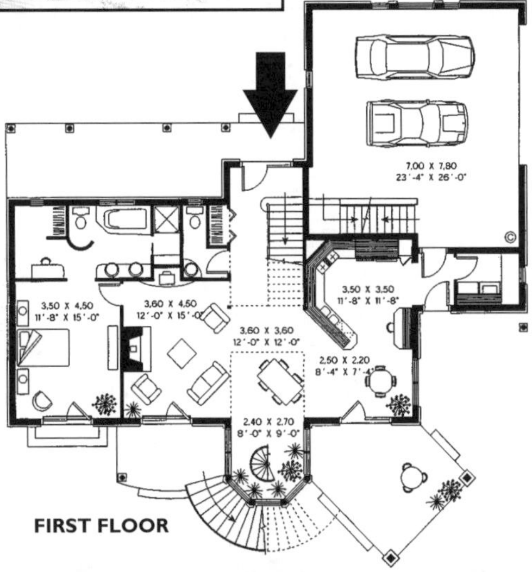

MAIN FLOOR

Units	Single
Price Code	C
Total Finished	1,923 sq. ft.
Main Finished	1,923 sq. ft.
Basement Unfinished	1,923 sq. ft.
Garage Unfinished	668 sq. ft.
Dimensions	70'8"x45'
Foundation	Basement
Bedrooms	4
Full Baths	2
Main Ceiling	21'4"
Max Ridge Height	21'4"
Roof Framing	Truss
Exterior Walls	2x6

Design 65672

Units	Single
Price Code	C
Total Finished	1,925 sq. ft.
Main Finished	1,925 sq. ft.
Dimensions	78'x52'
Foundation	Crawlspace Slab
Bedrooms	3
Full Baths	2
Main Ceiling	9'
Max Ridge Height	30'
Roof Framing	Stick
Exterior Walls	2x6

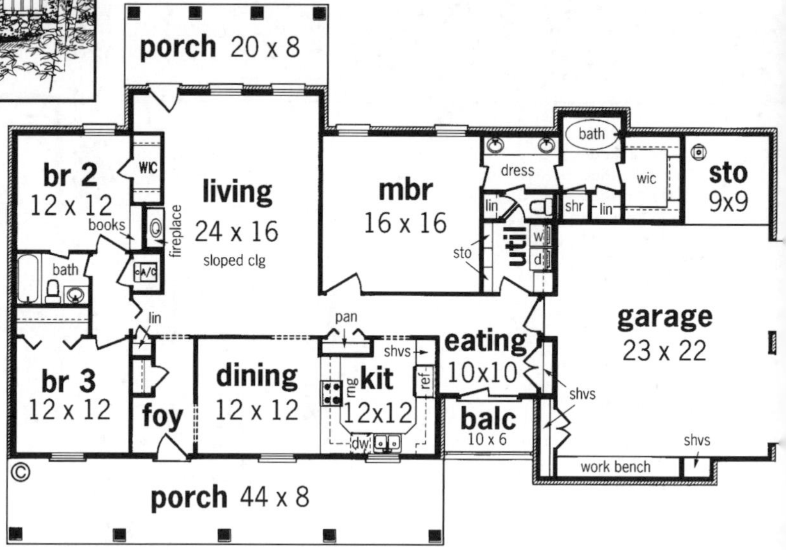

porch 20 x 8
br 2 12 x 12
WIC
books
living 24 x 16 sloped clg
fireplace
mbr 16 x 16
dress
bath
wic
sto 9x9
lin
shr
util
sto
A/C
bath
lin
pan
shvs
eating 10x10
garage 23 x 22
br 3 12 x 12
foy
dining 12 x 12
rng
kit 12x12
ref
dw
balc 10 x 6
shvs
work bench
©
porch 44 x 8

MAIN FLOOR

Design 96544

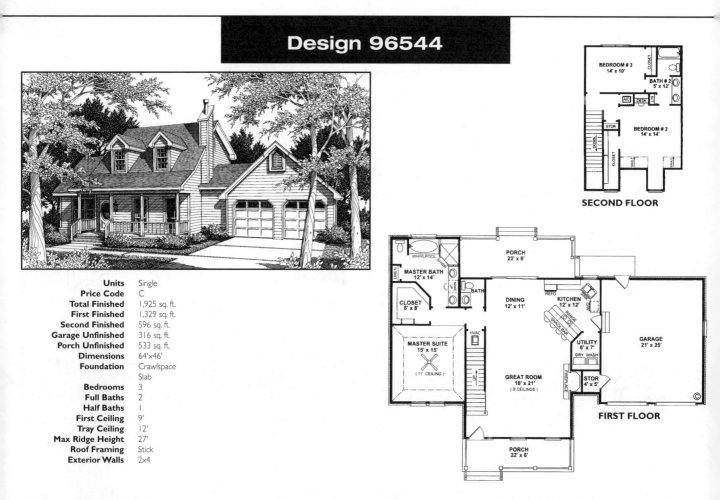

Units	Single
Price Code	C
Total Finished	1,925 sq. ft.
First Finished	1,329 sq. ft.
Second Finished	596 sq. ft.
Garage Unfinished	316 sq. ft.
Porch Unfinished	533 sq. ft.
Dimensions	64'x46'
Foundation	Crawlspace Slab
Bedrooms	3
Full Baths	2
Half Baths	1
First Ceiling	9'
Tray Ceiling	12'
Max Ridge Height	27'
Roof Framing	Stick
Exterior Walls	2x4

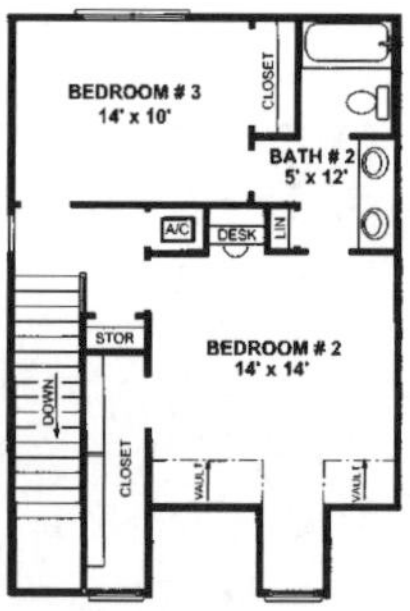

BEDROOM # 3 14' x 10'
CLOSET
BATH # 2 5' x 12'
A/C
DESK
LIN
STOR
BEDROOM # 2 14' x 14'
DOWN
CLOSET

SECOND FLOOR

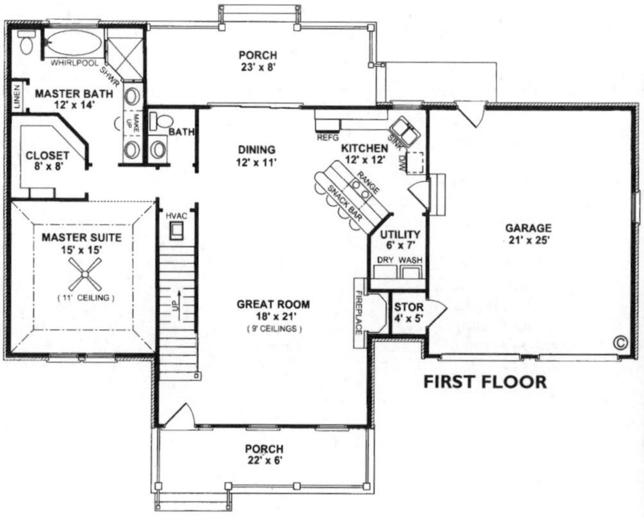

WHIRLPOOL
SHWR
PORCH 23' x 8'
LINEN
MASTER BATH 12' x 14'
BATH
DINING 12' x 11'
REFG
KITCHEN 12' x 12'
CLOSET 8' x 8'
RANGE
SNACK BAR
HVAC
MASTER SUITE 15' x 15'
(11' CEILING)
UTILITY 6' x 7'
DRY WASH
GARAGE 21' x 25'
UP
GREAT ROOM 18' x 21' (9' CEILINGS)
FIREPLACE
STOR 4' x 5'
©
PORCH 22' x 6'

FIRST FLOOR

Design 97277

Units	Single
Price Code	C
Total Finished	1,927 sq. ft.
Main Finished	1,927 sq. ft.
Bonus Unfinished	424 sq. ft.
Basement Unfinished	1,927 sq. ft.
Garage Unfinished	494 sq. ft.
Dimensions	55'6"x64'
Foundation	Basement Crawlspace
Bedrooms	3
Full Baths	2
Main Ceiling	9'
Second Ceiling	8'
Max Ridge Height	28'2"
Roof Framing	Stick
Exterior Walls	2x4

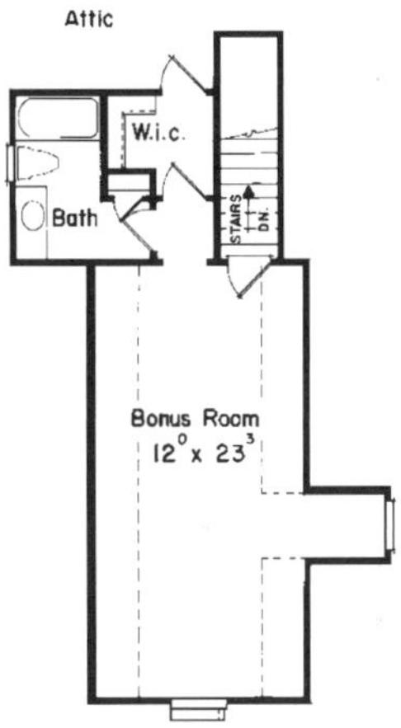

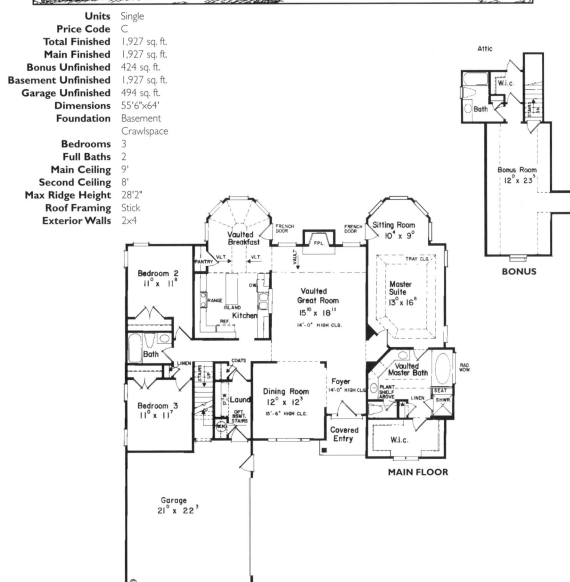

Attic
W.i.c.
Bath
STAIRS DN.
Bonus Room
12^{0} x 23^{3}

BONUS

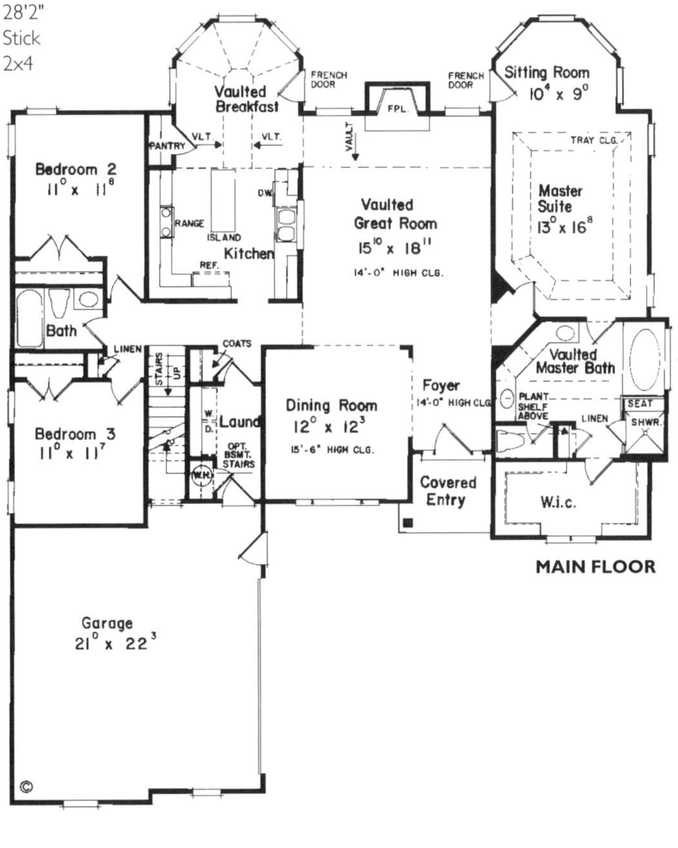

Vaulted Breakfast
FRENCH DOOR
FPL.
FRENCH DOOR
Sitting Room
10^{4} x 9^{0}
PANTRY
VLT.
VLT.
VAULT
TRAY CLG.
Bedroom 2
11^{0} x 11^{6}
DW.
RANGE
ISLAND
Kitchen
REF.
Vaulted Great Room
15^{10} x 18^{11}
14'-0" HIGH CLG.
Master Suite
13^{0} x 16^{8}
Bath
LINEN
STAIRS UP
COATS
Vaulted Master Bath
RAD WDW.
Foyer
14'-0" HIGH CLG.
PLANT SHELF ABOVE
SEAT
LINEN
SHWR.
Dining Room
12^{0} x 12^{3}
15'-6" HIGH CLG.
W. D.
Laund
OPT. BSMT. STAIRS
W.H.
Bedroom 3
11^{0} x 11^{7}
Covered Entry
W.i.c.

MAIN FLOOR

Garage
21^{0} x 22^{3}

©

Design 97335

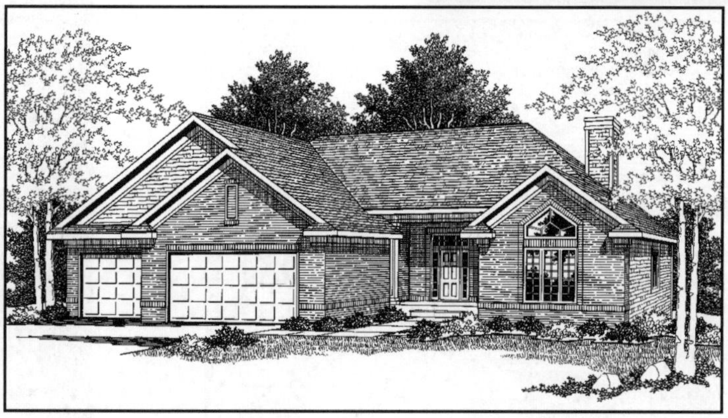

Units	Single
Price Code	C
Total Finished	1,927 sq. ft.
Main Finished	1,927 sq. ft.
Basement Unfinished	1,927 sq. ft.
Garage Unfinished	911 sq. ft.
Dimensions	62'x56'
Foundation	Basement
Bedrooms	3
Full Baths	2
Half Baths	1
Main Ceiling	9'
Max Ridge Height	22'11"
Roof Framing	Truss
Exterior Walls	2x6

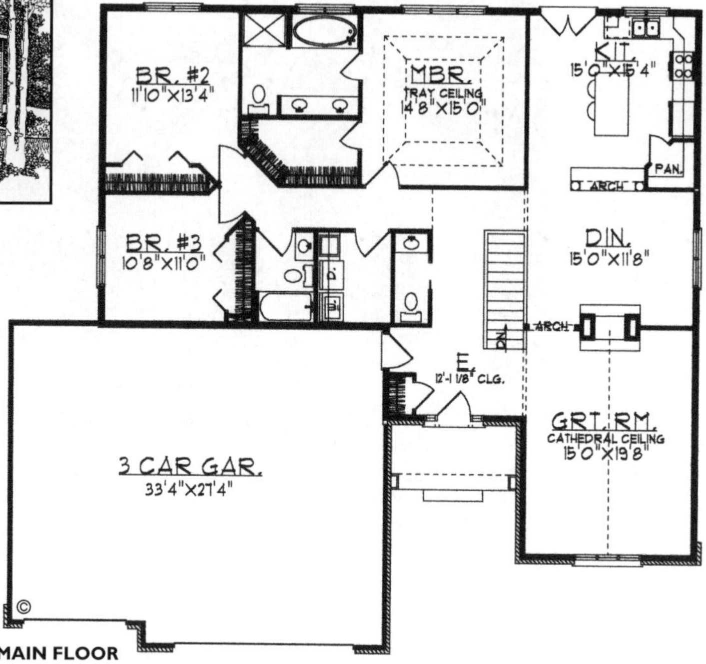

MAIN FLOOR

Design 98238

Units	Single
Price Code	C
Total Finished	1,928 sq. ft.
Main Finished	1,928 sq. ft.
Bonus Unfinished	160 sq. ft.
Garage Unfinished	400 sq. ft.
Porch Unfinished	315 sq. ft.
Dimensions	58'x47'
Foundation	Slab
Bedrooms	4
Full Baths	2
Main Ceiling	9'
Max Ridge Height	24'
Roof Framing	Stick
Exterior Walls	2x4

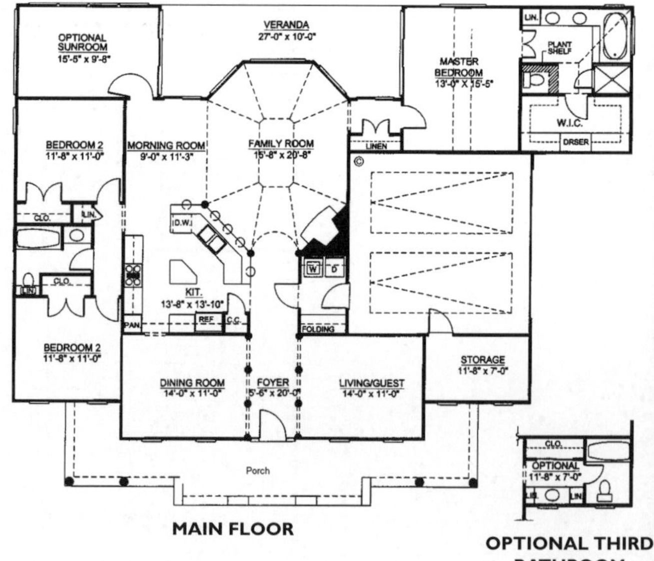
OPTIONAL SUNROOM
15'-5" x 9'-8"
VERANDA
27'-0" x 10'-0"
MASTER BEDROOM
13'-0" X 15'-5"
BEDROOM 2
11'-8" x 11'-0"
MORNING ROOM
9'-0" x 11'-3"
FAMILY ROOM
15'-8" x 20'-8"
KIT.
13'-8" x 13'-10"
BEDROOM 2
11'-8" x 11'-0"
DINING ROOM
14'-0" x 11'-0"
FOYER
5'-6" x 20'-0"
LIVING/GUEST
14'-0" x 11'-0"
STORAGE
11'-8" x 7'-0"
Porch
OPTIONAL
11'-8" x 7'-0"

MAIN FLOOR

OPTIONAL THIRD BATHROOM

Design 97353

Units	Single
Price Code	C
Total Finished	1,929 sq. ft.
Main Finished	1,929 sq. ft.
Dimensions	68'x49'
Foundation	Basement
Bedrooms	3
Full Baths	2
Max Ridge Height	23'8"
Roof Framing	Truss
Exterior Walls	2x6

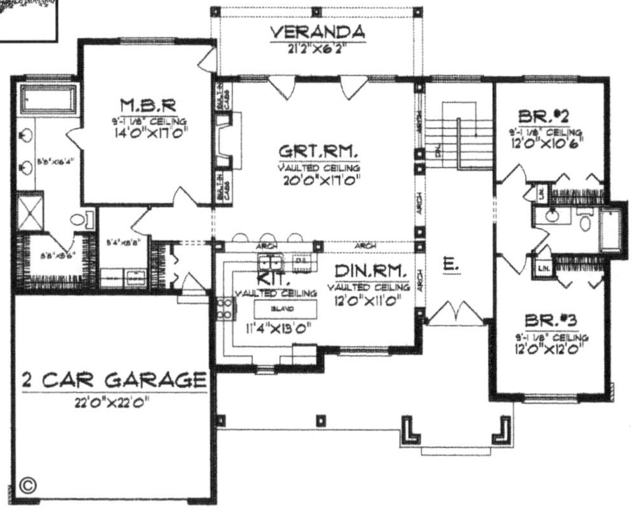

VERANDA 21'2"X6'2"
M.B.R 9'-1 1/8" CEILING 14'0"X17'0"
GRT.RM. VAULTED CEILING 20'0"X17'0"
BR.#2 9'-1 1/8" CEILING 12'0"X10'6"
KIT. VAULTED CEILING 11'4"X13'0"
DIN.RM. VAULTED CEILING 12'0"X11'0"
BR.#3 9'-1 1/8" CEILING 12'0"X12'0"
2 CAR GARAGE 22'0"X22'0"

MAIN FLOOR

Design 34851

Units	Single
Price Code	C
Total Finished	1,930 sq. ft.
First Finished	1,056 sq. ft.
Second Finished	874 sq. ft.
Basement Unfinished	1,023 sq. ft.
Garage Unfinished	430 sq. ft.
Dimensions	44'10"x38'
Foundation	Basement Crawlspace Slab
Bedrooms	3
Full Baths	2
Half Baths	1
Max Ridge Height	26'
Roof Framing	Stick
Exterior Walls	2x4, 2x6

Br 2 10 x 12-8
Br 3 10 x 11
MBr 1 14-4 x 15
open to below

SECOND FLOOR

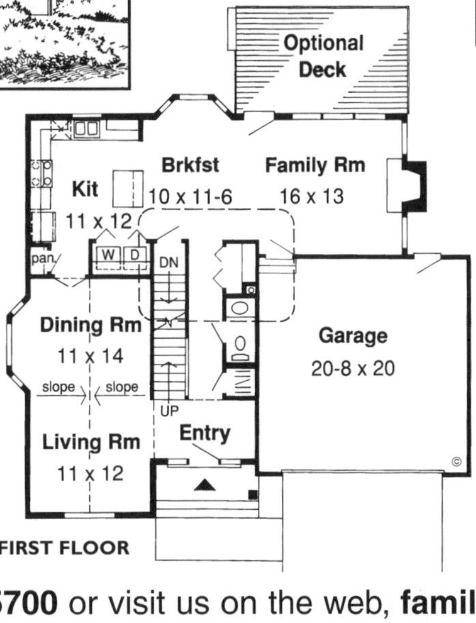

Optional Deck
Kit 11 x 12
Brkfst 10 x 11-6
Family Rm 16 x 13
Dining Rm 11 x 14
Garage 20-8 x 20
Living Rm 11 x 12
Entry

FIRST FLOOR

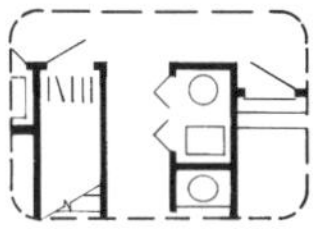

OPTIONAL CRAWLSPACE/ SLAB FOUNDATION

Design 62053

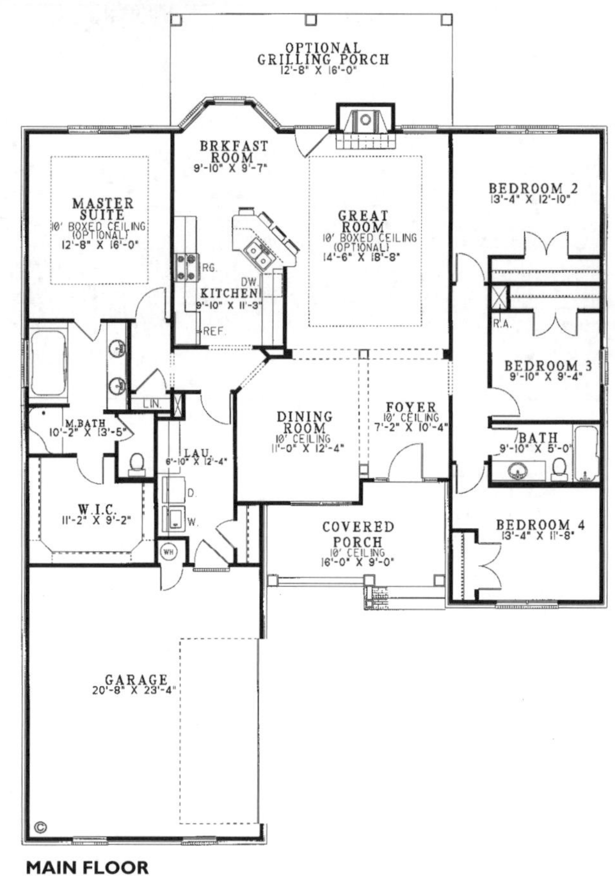
OPTIONAL GRILLING PORCH
12'-8" X 16'-0"
BRKFAST ROOM
9'-10" X 9'-7"
MASTER SUITE
10' BOXED CEILING (OPTIONAL)
12'-8" X 16'-0"
GREAT ROOM
10' BOXED CEILING (OPTIONAL)
14'-6" X 18'-8"
BEDROOM 2
13'-4" X 12'-10"
KITCHEN
9'-10" X 11'-3"
RG.
DW
REF.
R.A.
BEDROOM 3
9'-10" X 9'-4"
LIN.
M.BATH
10'-2" X 13'-5"
LAU.
6'-10" X 12'-4"
DINING ROOM
10' CEILING
11'-0" X 12'-4"
FOYER
10' CEILING
7'-2" X 10'-4"
BATH
9'-10" X 5'-0"
W.I.C.
11'-2" X 9'-2"
D.
W.
WH
COVERED PORCH
10' CEILING
16'-0" X 9'-0"
BEDROOM 4
13'-4" X 11'-8"
GARAGE
20'-8" X 23'-4"

MAIN FLOOR

Units	Single
Price Code	C
Total Finished	1,930 sq. ft.
Main Finished	1,930 sq. ft.
Garage Unfinished	509 sq. ft.
Porch Unfinished	357 sq. ft.
Dimensions	52'x71'6"
Foundation	Slab
Bedrooms	4
Full Baths	2
Main Ceiling	8'
Max Ridge Height	26'8"
Roof Framing	Truss
Exterior Walls	2x4, 2x6

Design 94902

PHOTOGRAPHY: ROB LOWE

Units	Single
Price Code	C
Total Finished	1,931 sq. ft.
First Finished	944 sq. ft.
Second Finished	987 sq. ft.
Basement Unfinished	944 sq. ft.
Garage Unfinished	557 sq. ft.
Dimensions	54'x42'
Foundation	Basement
Bedrooms	4
Full Baths	2
Half Baths	1
First Ceiling	8'
Max Ridge Height	29'
Roof Framing	Stick
Exterior Walls	2x4

* Alternate foundation options available at an additional charge. Please call 1-800-235-5700 for more information.

Please note: The photographed home may have been modified to suit homeowner preferences. If you order plans, have a builder or design professional check them against the photograph to confirm actual construction details.

Br.3
$10^0 \times 11^0$
Br.4
$10^0 \times 11^0$
DN
Mbr.
$14^8 \times 13^5$
9'-0" CEILING
OPEN TO BELOW
LIN.
Br.2
$11^0 \times 11^3$
10'-0" CEILING
TRANSOM
L.
10'-0" CEILING
W/P

SECOND FLOOR

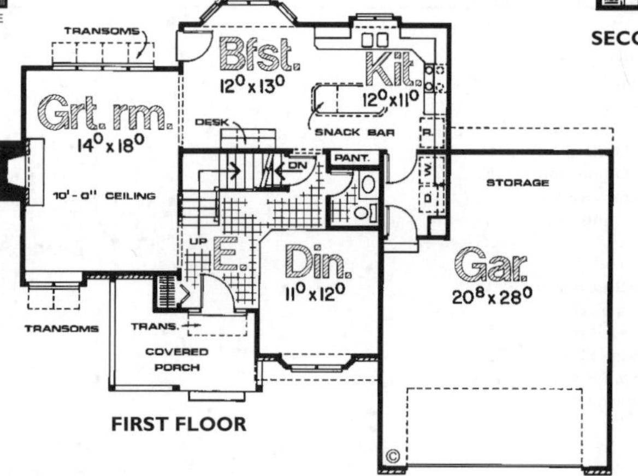
TRANSOMS
Bfst.
$12^0 \times 13^0$
Kit.
$12^0 \times 11^0$
Grt. rm.
$14^0 \times 18^0$
DESK
SNACK BAR
10'-0" CEILING
DN
PANT.
STORAGE
UP
E.
Din.
$11^0 \times 12^0$
Gar.
$20^8 \times 28^0$
TRANSOMS
TRANS.
COVERED PORCH

FIRST FLOOR

Design 60098

CAD
FILES AVAILABLE
For more information call
800-235-5700

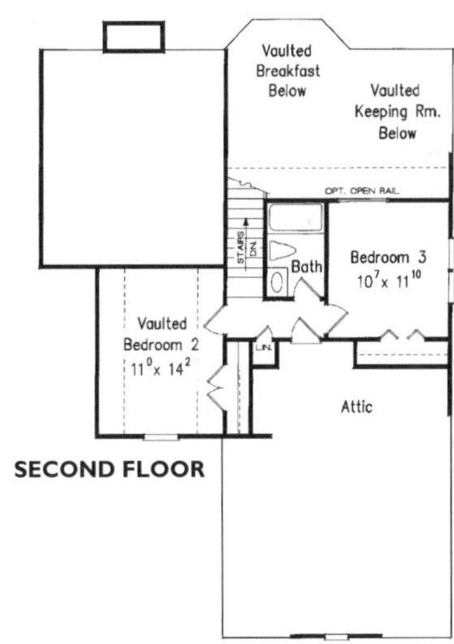
Vaulted Breakfast Below
Vaulted Keeping Rm. Below
OPT. OPEN RAIL
Bath
Bedroom 3
10⁷x 11¹⁰
Vaulted Bedroom 2
11⁰x 14²
Attic
SECOND FLOOR

Units	Single
Price Code	C
Total Finished	1,932 sq. ft.
First Finished	1,506 sq. ft.
Second Finished	426 sq. ft.
Basement Unfinished	1,506 sq. ft.
Garage Unfinished	457 sq. ft.
Dimensions	50'x52'6"
Foundation	Basement Crawlspace
Bedrooms	3
Full Baths	2
Half Baths	1
First Ceiling	9'
Second Ceiling	8'
Max Ridge Height	25'3'
Roof Framing	Stick
Exterior Walls	2x4

TRAY CEILING
Master Suite
13⁵x 16⁰
Vaulted Family Room
16⁰x 18⁰
Vaulted Breakfast
FRENCH DOOR
Vaulted Keeping Room
10⁰X 12⁵
SERVING BAR
ISLAND
DW
Kitchen
PANTRY
RANGE
RADIUS WINDOW
Vaulted M.Bath
SHWR.
LINEN
W.i.c.
Pwdr.
Foyer
Dining Room
11⁴x 11⁵
Laund.
COATS
Storage
Covered Porch
Garage
19⁵x 19⁹
FIRST FLOOR

Design 65647

Units	Single
Price Code	C
Total Finished	1,932 sq. ft.
Main Finished	1,932 sq. ft.
Bonus Unfinished	342 sq. ft.
Garage Unfinished	1,340 sq. ft.
Dimensions	66'x72'
Foundation	Crawlspace Slab
Bedrooms	3
Full Baths	2
Main Ceiling	9'
Second Ceiling	9'
Max Ridge Height	30'
Roof Framing	Stick
Exterior Walls	2x6

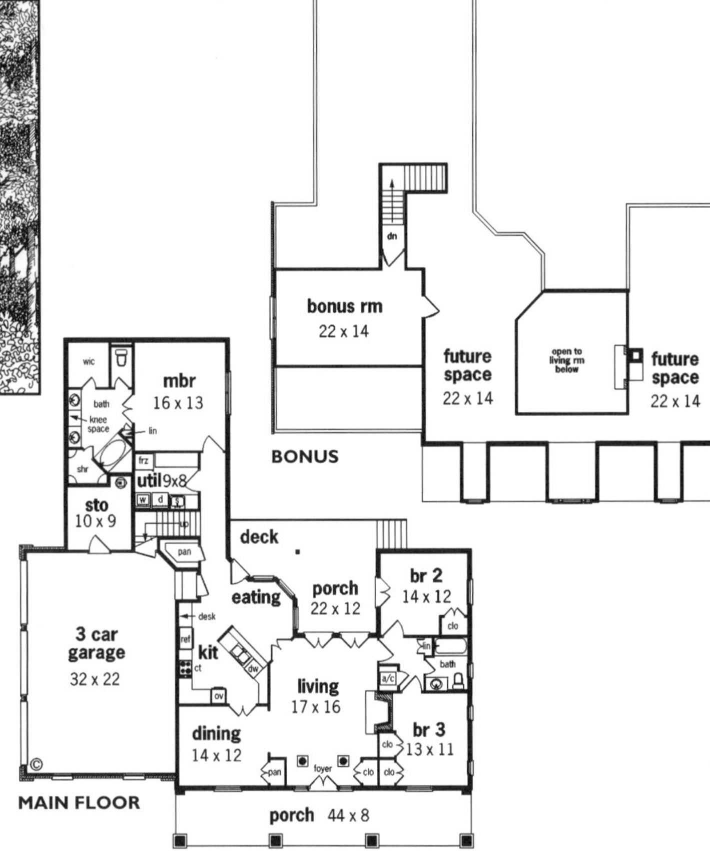
dn
bonus rm
22 x 14
future space
22 x 14
open to living rm below
future space
22 x 14
BONUS
wic
bath
knee space
shr
mbr
16 x 13
lin
frz
util 9x8
sto
10 x 9
deck
pan
3 car garage
32 x 22
eating
porch
22 x 12
br 2
14 x 12
desk
kit
living
17 x 16
bath
br 3
13 x 11
dining
14 x 12
foyer
MAIN FLOOR
porch 44 x 8

Design 93098

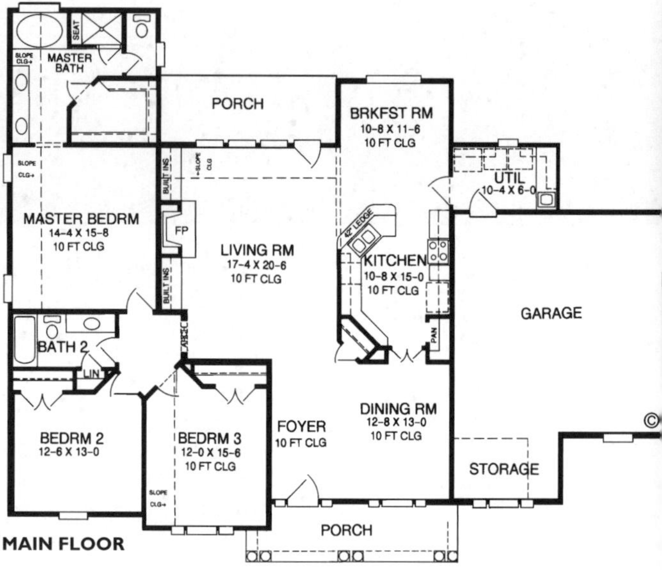

MASTER BATH
SEAT
SLOPE CLG+
PORCH
BRKFST RM
10-8 X 11-6
10 FT CLG
UTIL
10-4 X 6-0
MASTER BEDRM
14-4 X 15-8
10 FT CLG
FP
BUILT INS
LIVING RM
17-4 X 20-6
10 FT CLG
42" LEDGE
KITCHEN
10-8 X 15-0
10 FT CLG
PAN
GARAGE
BATH 2
LIN
DINING RM
12-8 X 13-0
10 FT CLG
BEDRM 2
12-6 X 13-0
BEDRM 3
12-0 X 15-6
10 FT CLG
FOYER
10 FT CLG
STORAGE
PORCH
MAIN FLOOR

Units	Single
Price Code	C
Total Finished	1,932 sq. ft.
Main Finished	1,932 sq. ft.
Garage Unfinished	552 sq. ft.
Deck Unfinished	225 sq. ft.
Dimensions	65'10"x53'5"
Foundation	Crawlspace Slab
Bedrooms	3
Full Baths	2
Max Ridge Height	22'4"
Roof Framing	Stick
Exterior Walls	2x4

Design 94944

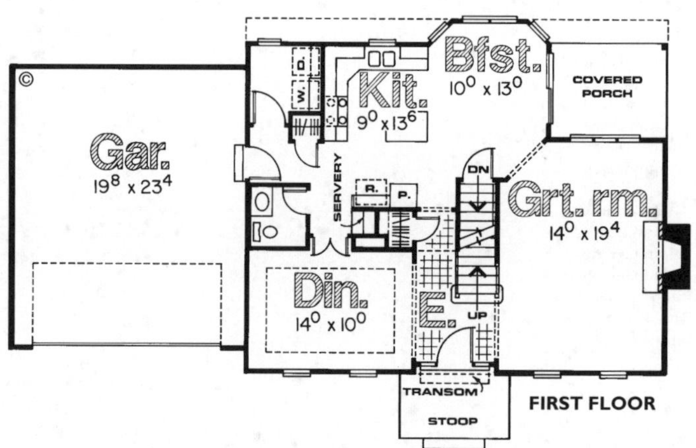

WHIRLPOOL
Mbr.
14^0 x 13^0
9'-0" CEILING
Br. 2
10^3 x 11^0
LIN.
DN
Br. 3
11^7 x 10^0
OPEN TO BELOW
Br. 4
11^7 x 10^0
PLANT SHELF
SECOND FLOOR
Gar.
19^8 x 23^4
W. D.
Kit.
9^0 x 13^6
Bfst.
10^0 x 13^0
COVERED PORCH
SERVERY
R.
P.
DN
Grt. rm.
14^0 x 19^4
Din.
14^0 x 10^0
E.
UP
TRANSOM
STOOP
FIRST FLOOR

Units	Single
Price Code	C
Total Finished	1,933 sq. ft.
First Finished	941 sq. ft.
Second Finished	992 sq. ft.
Basement Unfinished	941 sq. ft.
Garage Unfinished	480 sq. ft.
Dimensions	56'x30'
Foundation	Basement Slab
Bedrooms	4
Full Baths	2
Half Baths	1
Max Ridge Height	28'
Roof Framing	Stick
Exterior Walls	2x4

* Alternate foundation options available at an additional charge. Please call 1-800-235-5700 for more information.

Design 91472

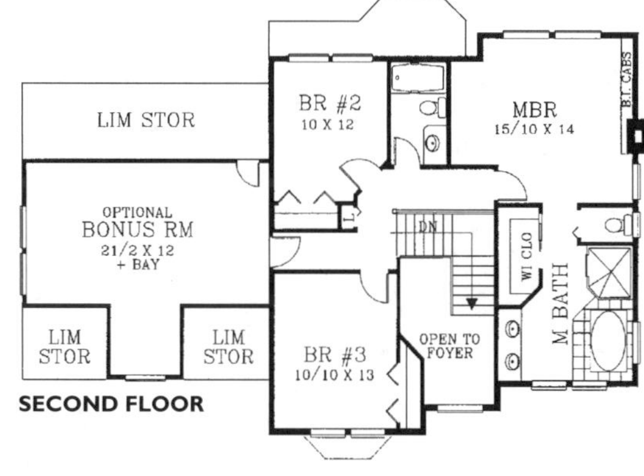
LIM STOR
BR #2
10 X 12
MBR
15/10 X 14
B.I. CABS
OPTIONAL
BONUS RM
21/2 X 12
+ BAY
DN
WI CLO
M BATH
LIM STOR
LIM STOR
BR #3
10/10 X 13
OPEN TO
FOYER
SECOND FLOOR

Units	Single
Price Code	E
Total Finished	1,934 sq. ft.
First Finished	1,066 sq. ft.
Second Finished	868 sq. ft.
Bonus Unfinished	320 sq. ft.
Garage Unfinished	511 sq. ft.
Dimensions	55'x41'
Foundation	Crawlspace
Bedrooms	3
Full Baths	2
Half Baths	1
First Ceiling	8'
Second Ceiling	8'
Roof Framing	Stick/Truss
Exterior Walls	2x6

FIRST FLOOR: VAULTED NOOK 9/2 X 10/2; PATIO; KIT; DW; R; FAM RM 19 X 12/8 AVG; OPT. DOORS; SHOP/STOR; F; W/H; D; W; S; UTIL; GARAGE 21 X 24/6; GST; UP; P; LIV RM 12 X 14; VAULTED FOYER; DIN RM 13/2 X 12 AVG + BAY; COVERED PORCH

Design 65670

Units	Single
Price Code	C
Total Finished	1,936 sq. ft.
Main Finished	1,936 sq. ft.
Dimensions	62'x68'
Foundation	Crawlspace Slab
Bedrooms	3
Full Baths	2
Main Ceiling	8'
Max Ridge Height	26'
Roof Framing	Stick
Exterior Walls	2x6

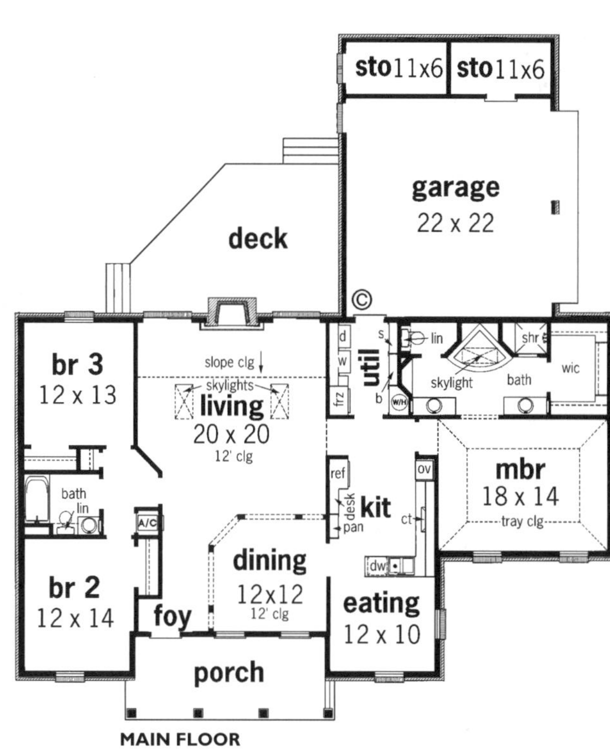
sto 11x6
sto 11x6
garage
22 x 22
deck
br 3
12 x 13
slope clg
skylights
living
20 x 20
12' clg
util
lin
shr
skylight
bath
wic
bath
lin
A/C
ref
desk
pan
kit
ct
ov
mbr
18 x 14
tray clg
br 2
12 x 14
foy
dining
12x12
12' clg
dw
eating
12 x 10
porch
MAIN FLOOR

Design 82034

COVERED PORCH 18'-5" X 4'-0"
BREAKFAST ROOM 9'-4" X 10'-11"
MASTER SUITE 15'-0" X 15'-0" 9' PAN CEILING
GREAT ROOM 9' BOX CEILING 15'-0" X 19'-6"
BEDROOM 4 13'-6" X 14'-6"
BATH
BEDROOM 3 10'-0" X 10'-4"
KITCHEN 9'-11" X 12'-7"
RG.
DW
REF.
PAN
BUILT-INS
KNEE SPACE
M.BATH 15'-0" X 11'-8"
WHP TUB
LAU.
DINING ROOM 11'-6" X 9'-8"
FOYER 7'-0" X 7'-0"
LIN
STORAGE
BEDROOM 2 12'-4" X 10'-6"
10" RND COL W/ BASE
4' PORCH
GARAGE 20'-10" X 20'-0"

MAIN FLOOR

Units	Single
Price Code	C
Total Finished	1,940 sq. ft.
Main Finished	1,940 sq. ft.
Garage Unfinished	417 sq. ft.
Porch Unfinished	188 sq. ft.
Dimensions	58'x54'10"
Foundation	Crawlspace Slab
Bedrooms	4
Full Baths	2
Main Ceiling	8'
Roof Framing	Stick
Exterior Walls	2x4

Design 92132

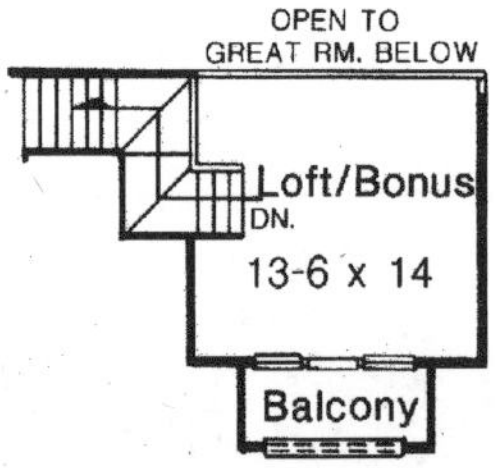

OPEN TO GREAT RM. BELOW
Loft/Bonus
DN.
13-6 x 14
Balcony

BONUS

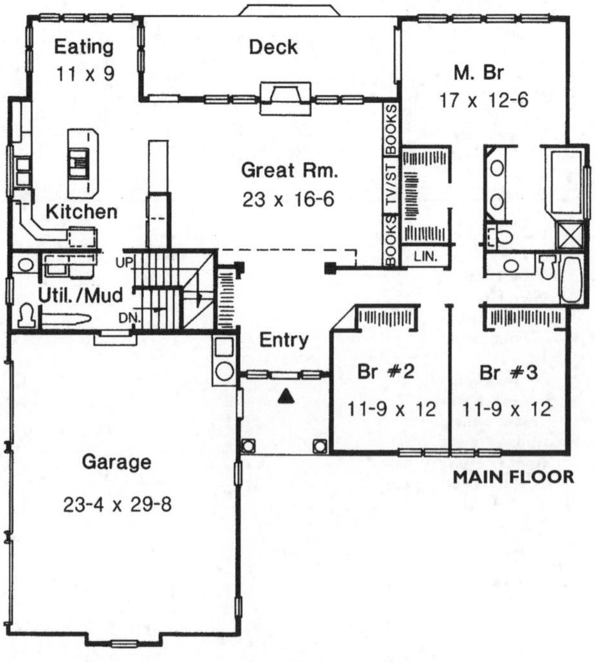

Eating 11 x 9
Deck
M. Br 17 x 12-6
Kitchen
Great Rm. 23 x 16-6
BOOKS
TV/ST
BOOKS
LIN.
UP
Util./Mud
DN.
Entry
Br #2 11-9 x 12
Br #3 11-9 x 12
Garage 23-4 x 29-8

MAIN FLOOR

Units	Single
Price Code	C
Total Finished	1,941 sq. ft.
Main Finished	1,941 sq. ft.
Bonus Unfinished	200 sq. ft.
Basement Unfinished	1,592 sq. ft.
Garage Unfinished	720 sq. ft.
Deck Unfinished	204 sq. ft.
Porch Unfinished	54 sq. ft.
Dimensions	60'x62'
Foundation	Basement Slab
Bedrooms	3
Full Baths	2
Half Baths	1
Main Ceiling	9'
Vaulted Ceiling	17'
Max Ridge Height	23'
Roof Framing	Stick/Truss
Exterior Walls	2x6

Design 24665

Units	Single
Price Code	C
Total Finished	1,944 sq. ft.
First Finished	988 sq. ft.
Second Finished	956 sq. ft.
Bonus Unfinished	144 sq. ft.
Basement Unfinished	976 sq. ft.
Garage Unfinished	532 sq. ft.
Dimensions	50'4"x47'
Foundation	Basement Crawlspace Slab
Bedrooms	3
Full Baths	2
Half Baths	1
First Ceiling	8'
Second Ceiling	8'
Max Ridge Height	27'
Roof Framing	Stick
Exterior Walls	2x4

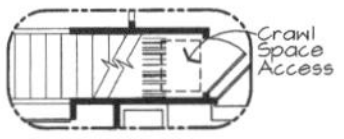

OPTIONAL CRAWLSPACE/SLAB FOUNDATION

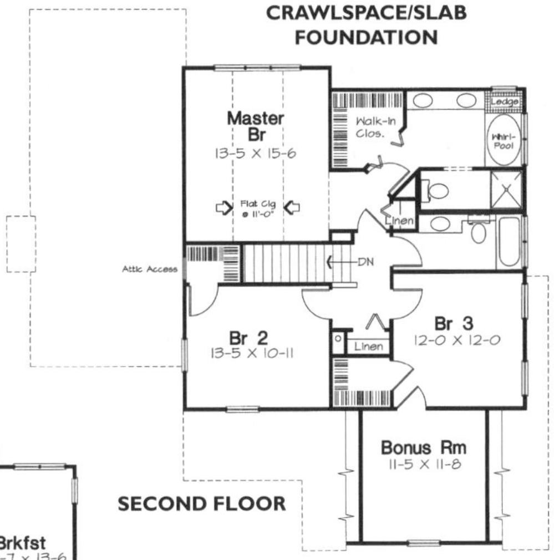

FIRST FLOOR

SECOND FLOOR

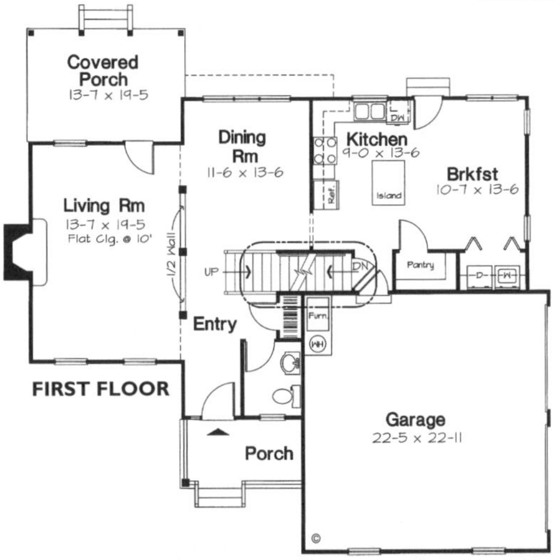

Design 98435

FILES AVAILABLE
CAD For more information call 800-235-5700

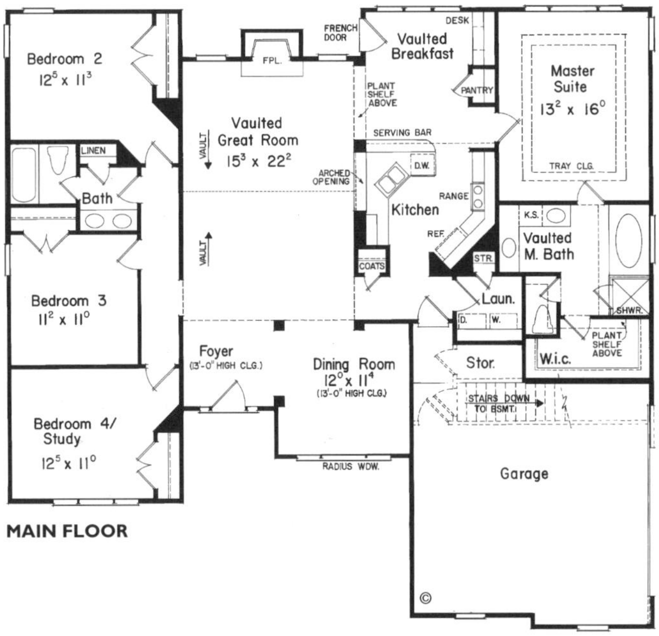

Units	Single
Price Code	C
Total Finished	1,945 sq. ft.
Main Finished	1,945 sq. ft.
Dimensions	56'6"x52'6"
Foundation	Basement Crawlspace
Bedrooms	4
Full Baths	2
Main Ceiling	9'
Max Ridge Height	26'4"
Roof Framing	Stick
Exterior Walls	2x4

MAIN FLOOR

Design 99115

Units	Single
Price Code	C
Total Finished	1,947 sq. ft.
Main Finished	1,947 sq. ft.
Basement Unfinished	1,947 sq. ft.
Dimensions	69'8"x46'
Foundation	Basement
Bedrooms	3
Full Baths	2
Half Baths	1
Main Ceiling	8'
Max Ridge Height	22'4"
Roof Framing	Truss
Exterior Walls	2x6

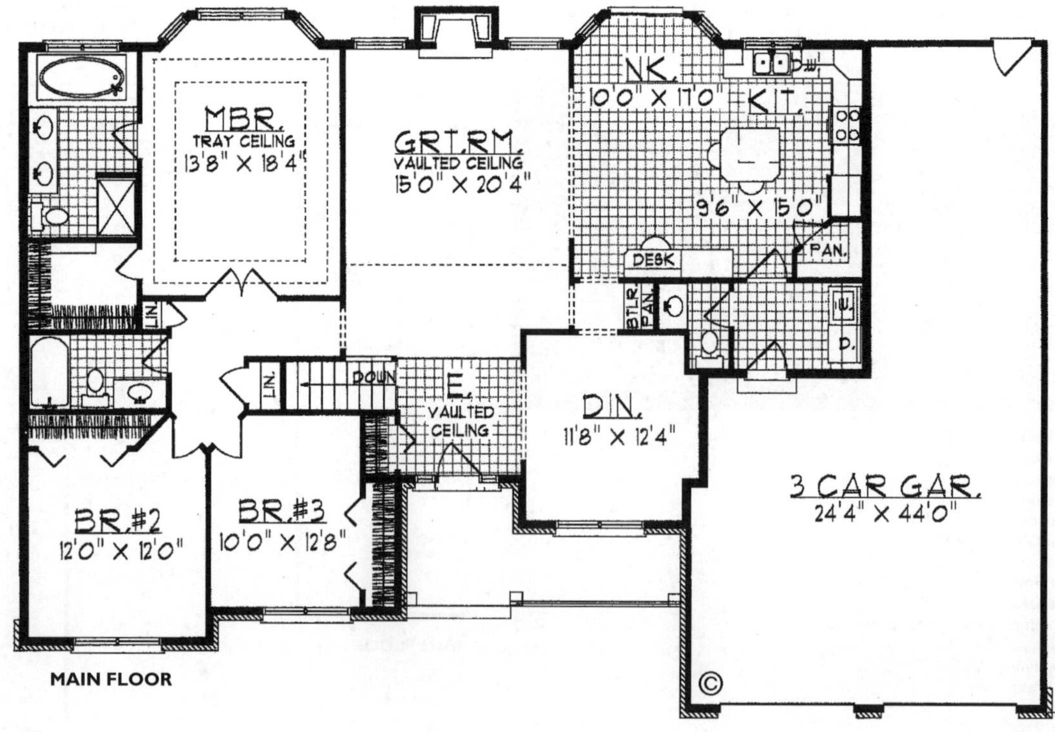
MBR.
TRAY CEILING
13'8" X 18'4"
GRT.RM.
VAULTED CEILING
15'0" X 20'4"
NK.
10'0" X 11'0"
KIT.
9'6" X 15'0"
PAN.
DESK
BTR.
PAN
W.
D.
LIN.
LIN.
DOWN
E.
VAULTED
CEILING
DIN.
11'8" X 12'4"
3 CAR GAR.
24'4" X 44'0"
BR.#2
12'0" X 12'0"
BR.#3
10'0" X 12'8"
©

MAIN FLOOR

Design 97993

Units	Single
Price Code	C
Total Finished	1,948 sq. ft.
Main Finished	1,948 sq. ft.
Basement Unfinished	1,948 sq. ft.
Garage Unfinished	517 sq. ft.
Dimensions	64'x52'
Foundation	Basement Crawlspace Slab
Bedrooms	3
Full Baths	2
Half Baths	1
Main Ceiling	8'
Max Ridge Height	20'
Roof Framing	Stick
Exterior Walls	2x4

* Alternate foundation options available at an additional charge. Please call 1-800-235-5700 for more information.

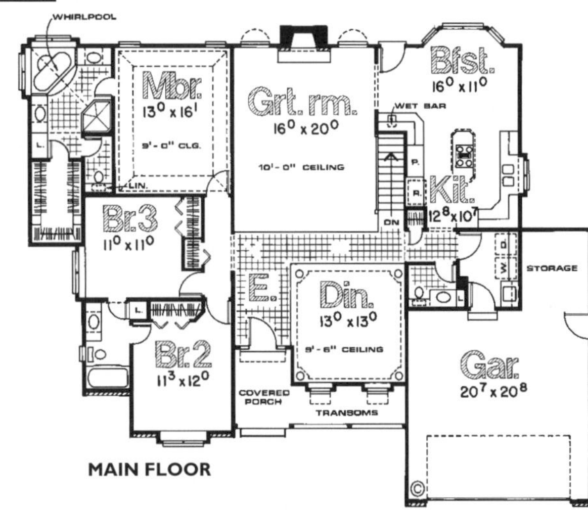
WHIRLPOOL
Mbr.
13^0 x 16^1
9'-0" CLG.
LIN.
Grt. rm.
16^0 x 20^0
10'-0" CEILING
WET BAR
Bfst.
16^0 x 11^0
Kit.
12^8 x 10^7
DN
Br.3
11^0 x 11^0
E.
Din.
13^0 x 13^0
9'-6" CEILING
STORAGE
Br.2
11^3 x 12^0
COVERED PORCH
TRANSOMS
Gar.
20^7 x 20^8

MAIN FLOOR

Design 96902

Units	Single
Price Code	C
Total Finished	1,950 sq. ft.
Main Finished	1,950 sq. ft.
Bonus Unfinished	255 sq. ft.
Basement Unfinished	1,287 sq. ft.
Garage Unfinished	466 sq. ft.
Porch Unfinished	35 sq. ft.
Dimensions	59'4"x61'4"
Foundation	Basement Crawlspace
Bedrooms	3
Full Baths	2
Half Baths	1
Max Ridge Height	26'6"
Roof Framing	Stick
Exterior Walls	2x4

OPTIONAL BONUS ROOM 12'-4" x 16'-8"

BONUS

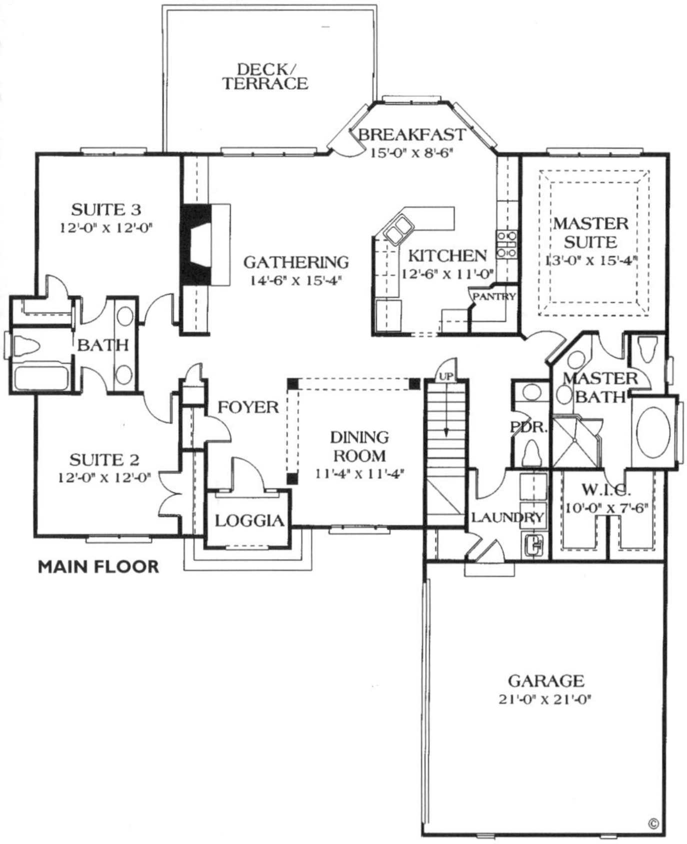

DECK/TERRACE

BREAKFAST 15'-0" x 8'-6"

SUITE 3 12'-0" x 12'-0"

GATHERING 14'-6" x 15'-4"

KITCHEN 12'-6" x 11'-0"

PANTRY

MASTER SUITE 13'-0" x 15'-4"

BATH

MASTER BATH

FOYER

DINING ROOM 11'-4" x 11'-4"

PDR.

SUITE 2 12'-0" x 12'-0"

LOGGIA

LAUNDRY

W.I.C. 10'-0" x 7'-6"

GARAGE 21'-0" x 21'-0"

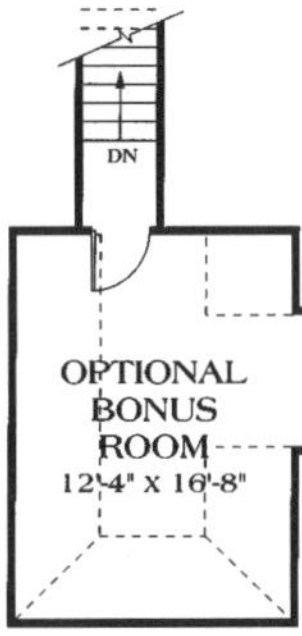

MAIN FLOOR

Design 96811

Units	Single
Price Code	C
Total Finished	1,954 sq. ft.
Main Finished	1,954 sq. ft.
Garage Unfinished	411 sq. ft.
Porch Unfinished	325 sq. ft.
Dimensions	74'6"x43'
Foundation	Crawlspace Slab
Bedrooms	3
Full Baths	2
Half Baths	1
Main Ceiling	8'
Max Ridge Height	23'4"
Roof Framing	Truss
Exterior Walls	2x4

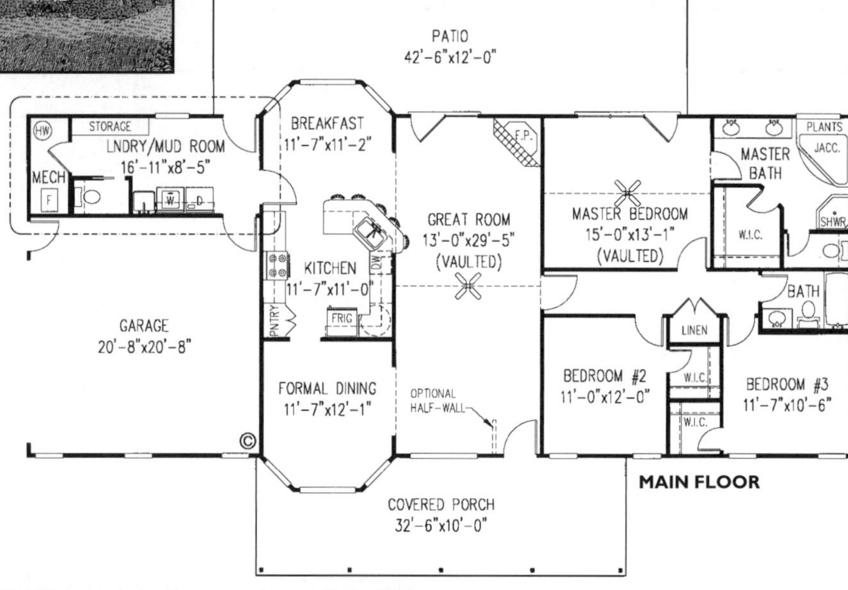
PATIO
42'-6"x12'-0"
STORAGE
LNDRY/MUD ROOM
16'-11"x8'-5"
MECH
BREAKFAST
11'-7"x11'-2"
F.P.
GREAT ROOM
13'-0"x29'-5"
(VAULTED)
MASTER BEDROOM
15'-0"x13'-1"
(VAULTED)
MASTER BATH
PLANTS
JACC.
SHWR
W.I.C.
KITCHEN
11'-7"x11'-0"
PNTRY
FRIG
GARAGE
20'-8"x20'-8"
BATH
LINEN
BEDROOM #2
11'-0"x12'-0"
BEDROOM #3
11'-7"x10'-6"
FORMAL DINING
11'-7"x12'-1"
OPTIONAL HALF-WALL
COVERED PORCH
32'-6"x10'-0"

MAIN FLOOR

Design 93031

Units	Single
Price Code	C
Total Finished	1,955 sq. ft.
Main Finished	1,955 sq. ft.
Bonus Unfinished	240 sq. ft.
Garage Unfinished	561 sq. ft.
Porch Unfinished	215 sq. ft.
Dimensions	60'10"x65'
Foundation	Crawlspace Slab
Bedrooms	3
Full Baths	2
Max Ridge Height	24'
Roof Framing	Stick
Exterior Walls	2x4

BATH 2
BEDRM 2
14-0 X 11-4
UTIL
GARAGE

OPTIONAL BEDROOM/GARAGE LAYOUT W/ STAIR TO BONUS

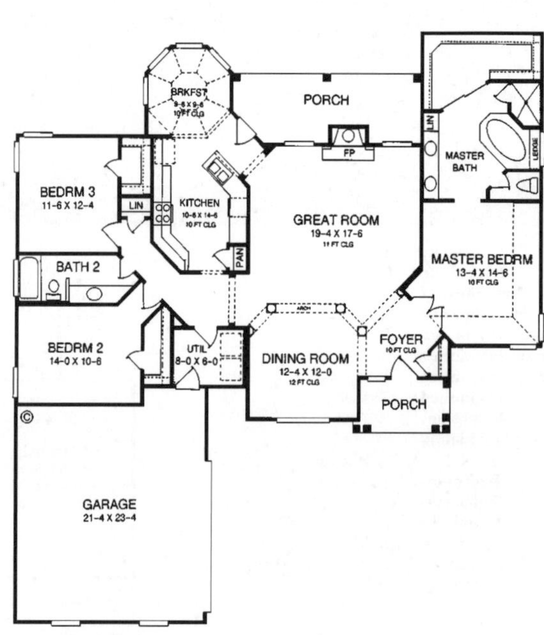
BRKFST
PORCH
FP
MASTER BATH
BEDRM 3
11-6 X 12-4
LIN
KITCHEN
GREAT ROOM
19-4 X 17-6
MASTER BEDRM
13-4 X 14-6
BATH 2
BEDRM 2
14-0 X 10-8
UTIL
8-0 X 6-0
DINING ROOM
12-4 X 12-0
FOYER
PORCH
GARAGE
21-4 X 23-4

MAIN FLOOR

Design 93085

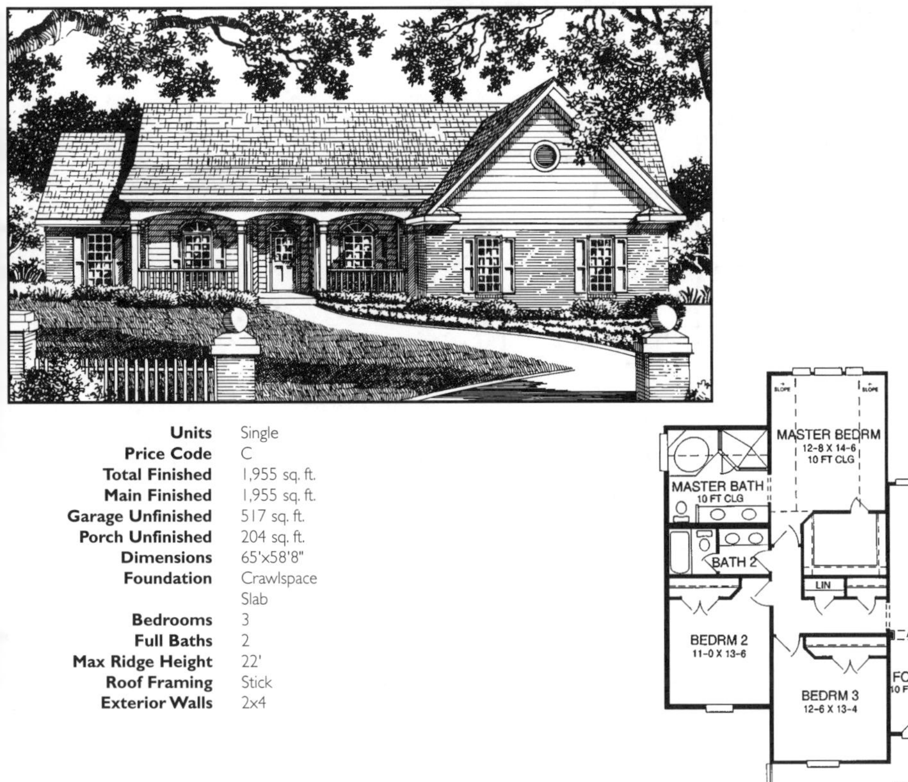

MAIN FLOOR

Units	Single
Price Code	C
Total Finished	1,955 sq. ft.
Main Finished	1,955 sq. ft.
Garage Unfinished	517 sq. ft.
Porch Unfinished	204 sq. ft.
Dimensions	65'x58'8"
Foundation	Crawlspace Slab
Bedrooms	3
Full Baths	2
Max Ridge Height	22'
Roof Framing	Stick
Exterior Walls	2x4

Design 90663

BED RM
12'-0"x11'-4"
BED RM
10'-0"x8'-0"
BATH
walk-in closet
dress
balcony
rail
lin.
dn
open
MASTER BED RM
16'-0"x11'-4"
BED RM
12'-4"x10'-0"
cl
BATH

SECOND FLOOR

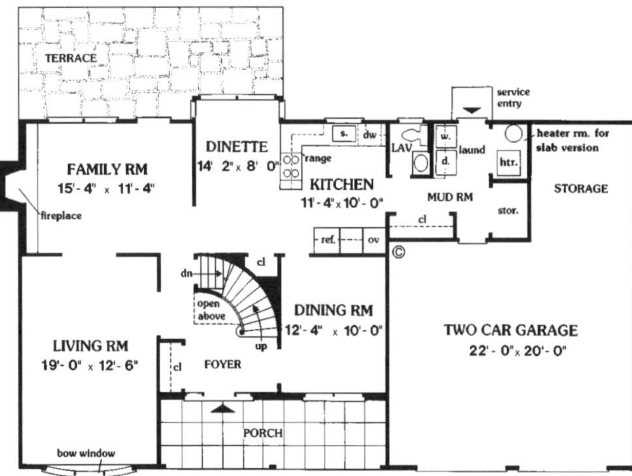
TERRACE
service entry
FAMILY RM
15'-4" x 11'-4"
fireplace
DINETTE
14'2"x8'0"
range
dw
KITCHEN
11'-4"x10'-0"
LAV
laund
htr.
heater rm. for slab version
STORAGE
MUD RM
stor.
cl
ref.
ov
dn
open above
up
DINING RM
12'-4" x 10'-0"
TWO CAR GARAGE
22'-0"x20'-0"
LIVING RM
19'-0" x 12'-6"
FOYER
PORCH
bow window

FIRST FLOOR

Units	Single
Price Code	C
Total Finished	1,956 sq. ft.
First Finished	1,119 sq. ft.
Second Finished	837 sq. ft.
Basement Unfinished	1,080 sq. ft.
Dimensions	60'6"x33'4"
Foundation	Basement Slab
Bedrooms	4
Full Baths	1
3/4 Baths	1
Half Baths	1
Max Ridge Height	23'6"

Design 82078

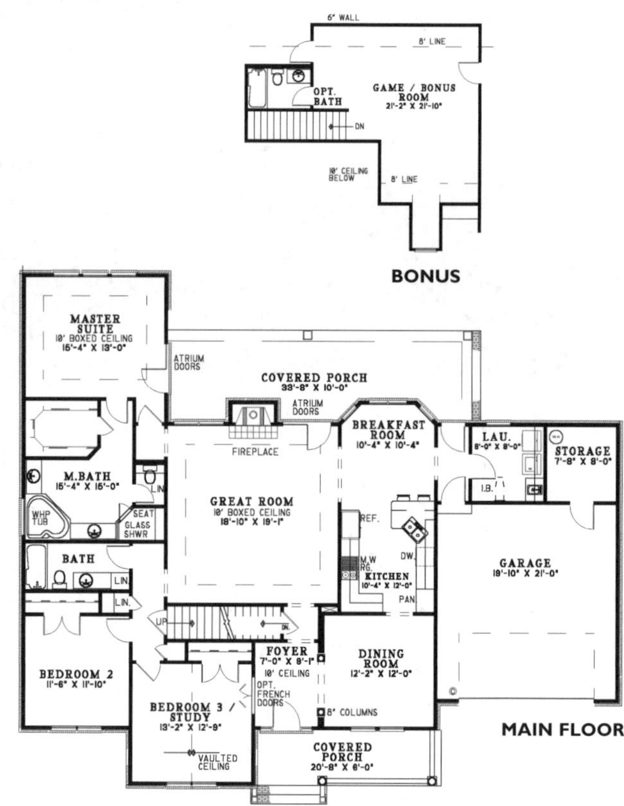

6' WALL
8' LINE
OPT. BATH
GAME / BONUS ROOM
21'-2" X 21'-10"
DN
10' CEILING BELOW
8' LINE
BONUS
MASTER SUITE
10' BOXED CEILING
16'-4" X 13'-0"
ATRIUM DOORS
COVERED PORCH
33'-8" X 10'-0"
ATRIUM DOORS
BREAKFAST ROOM
10'-4" X 10'-4"
LAU.
8'-0" X 8'-0"
STORAGE
7'-8" X 8'-0"
FIREPLACE
M.BATH
16'-4" X 16'-0"
GREAT ROOM
10' BOXED CEILING
18'-10" X 19'-1"
REF.
WHP TUB
SEAT GLASS SHWR
BATH
DW
KITCHEN
10'-4" X 12'-0"
GARAGE
19'-10" X 21'-0"
LIN
PAN
UP
DN
BEDROOM 2
11'-6" X 11'-10"
FOYER
7'-0" X 9'-1"
10' CEILING
DINING ROOM
12'-2" X 12'-0"
BEDROOM 3 / STUDY
13'-2" X 12'-9"
OPT. FRENCH DOORS
8" COLUMNS
VAULTED CEILING
COVERED PORCH
20'-8" X 6'-0"
MAIN FLOOR

Units	Single
Price Code	C
Total Finished	1,957 sq. ft.
Main Finished	1,957 sq. ft.
Bonus Unfinished	479 sq. ft.
Garage Unfinished	417 sq. ft.
Porch Unfinished	203 sq. ft.
Dimensions	66'x55'
Foundation	Basement Crawlspace Slab
Bedrooms	3
Full Baths	2
Exterior Walls	2x4

Design 94906

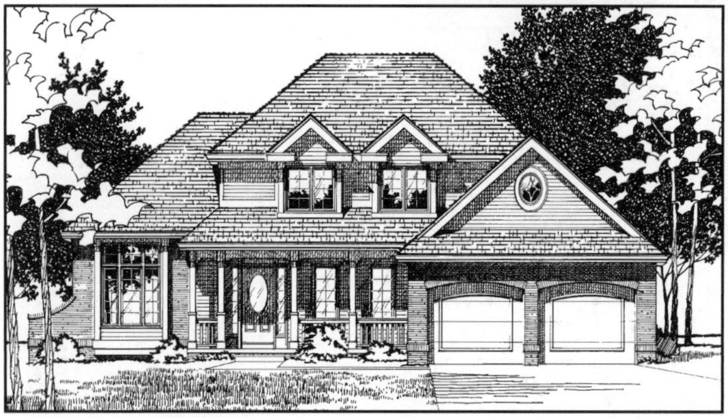

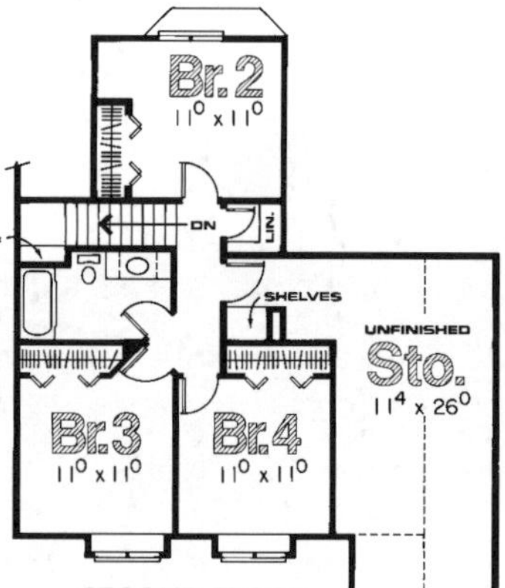

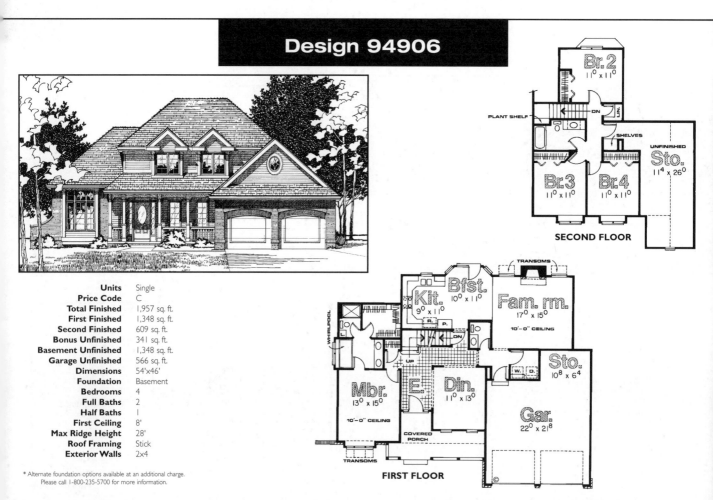

SECOND FLOOR

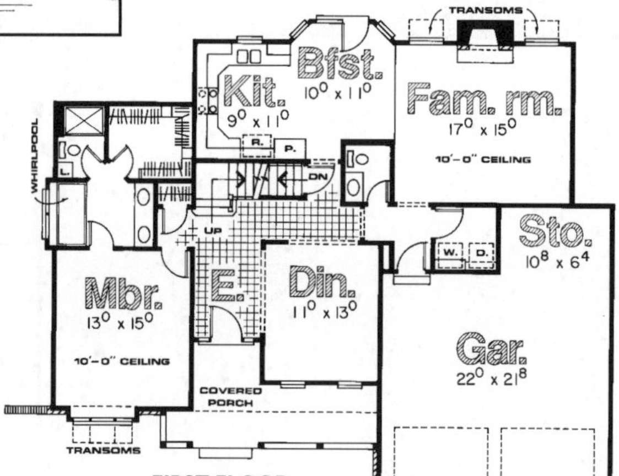

FIRST FLOOR

Units	Single
Price Code	C
Total Finished	1,957 sq. ft.
First Finished	1,348 sq. ft.
Second Finished	609 sq. ft.
Bonus Unfinished	341 sq. ft.
Basement Unfinished	1,348 sq. ft.
Garage Unfinished	566 sq. ft.
Dimensions	54'x46'
Foundation	Basement
Bedrooms	4
Full Baths	2
Half Baths	1
First Ceiling	8'
Max Ridge Height	28'
Roof Framing	Stick
Exterior Walls	2x4

* Alternate foundation options available at an additional charge. Please call 1-800-235-5700 for more information.

Design 68171

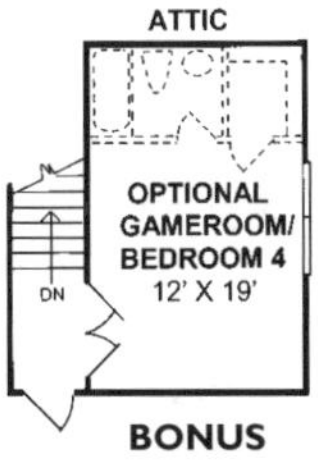

ATTIC
OPTIONAL GAMEROOM/ BEDROOM 4 12' X 19'
DN
BONUS

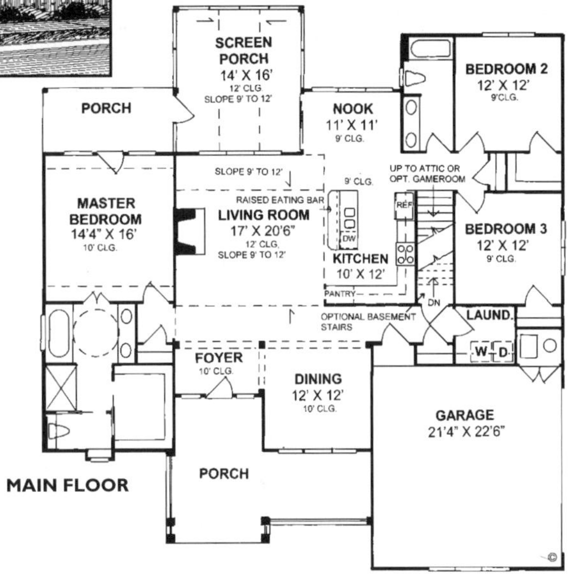

SCREEN PORCH 14' X 16' 12' CLG. SLOPE 9' TO 12'
PORCH
NOOK 11' X 11' 9' CLG.
BEDROOM 2 12' X 12' 9'CLG.
SLOPE 9' TO 12'
9' CLG.
UP TO ATTIC OR OPT. GAMEROOM
MASTER BEDROOM 14'4" X 16' 10' CLG.
RAISED EATING BAR
LIVING ROOM 17' X 20'6" 12' CLG. SLOPE 9' TO 12'
REF
DW
KITCHEN 10' X 12'
BEDROOM 3 12' X 12' 9' CLG.
PANTRY
DN
OPTIONAL BASEMENT STAIRS
LAUND.
W D
FOYER 10' CLG.
DINING 12' X 12' 10' CLG.
GARAGE 21'4" X 22'6"
PORCH
MAIN FLOOR

Units	Single
Price Code	C
Total Finished	1,958 sq. ft.
Main Finished	1,958 sq. ft.
Bonus Unfinished	276 sq. ft.
Deck Unfinished	600 sq. ft.
Dimensions	59'x62'
Foundation	Crawlspace Slab
Bedrooms	3
Full Baths	2
Main Ceiling	9'
Max Ridge Height	26'
Exterior Walls	2x4

* Alternate foundation options available at an additional charge. Please call 1-800-235-5700 for more information.

Design 82015

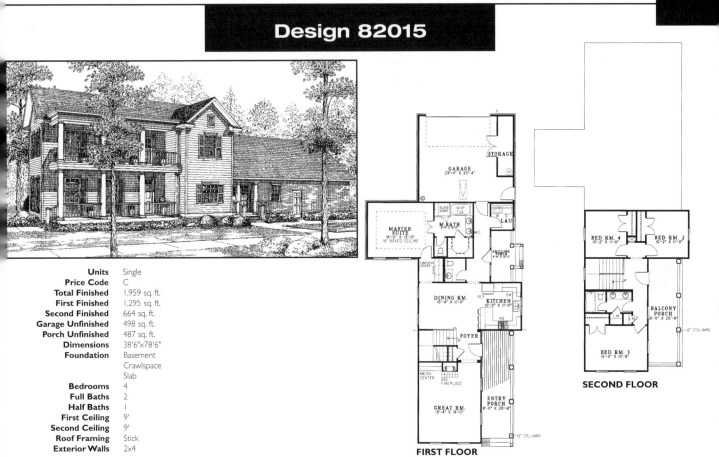

STORAGE
GARAGE 23'-4" X 20'-4"
GLASS SHWR
WHP TUB
W D
LAU
MASTER SUITE 16'-0" X 13'-0" 10' BOXED CEILING
M.BATH
W.C.
GRILLING PORCH
COMPUTER CENTER
DINING RM. 15'-4" X 11'-0"
REF
DW
KITCHEN 10'-0" X 11'-0"
RG
FOYER
MEDIA CENTER
GAS FIREPLACE
GREAT RM. 15'-4" X 18'-0"
ENTRY PORCH 8'-0" X 25'-8"
12" COLUMNS
FIRST FLOOR

BED RM. 4 10'-2" X 11'-0"
BED RM. 2 10'-2" X 11'-0"
LIN
LIN
BALCONY PORCH 8'-0" X 26'-8"
12" COLUMNS
BED RM. 3 15'-4" X 10'-8"
SECOND FLOOR

Units	Single
Price Code	C
Total Finished	1,959 sq. ft.
First Finished	1,295 sq. ft.
Second Finished	664 sq. ft.
Garage Unfinished	498 sq. ft.
Porch Unfinished	487 sq. ft.
Dimensions	38'6"x78'6"
Foundation	Basement Crawlspace Slab
Bedrooms	4
Full Baths	2
Half Baths	1
First Ceiling	9'
Second Ceiling	9'
Roof Framing	Stick
Exterior Walls	2x4

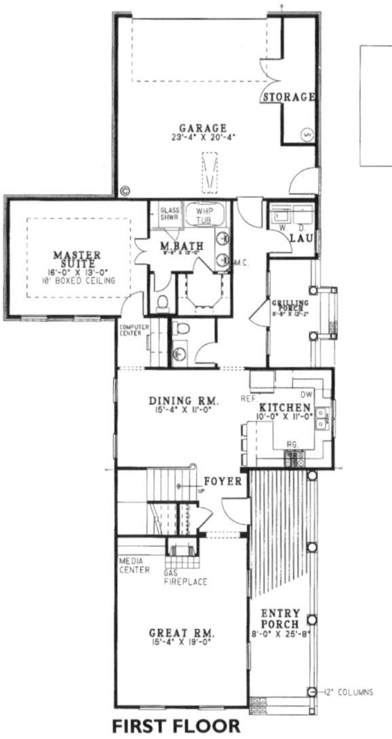

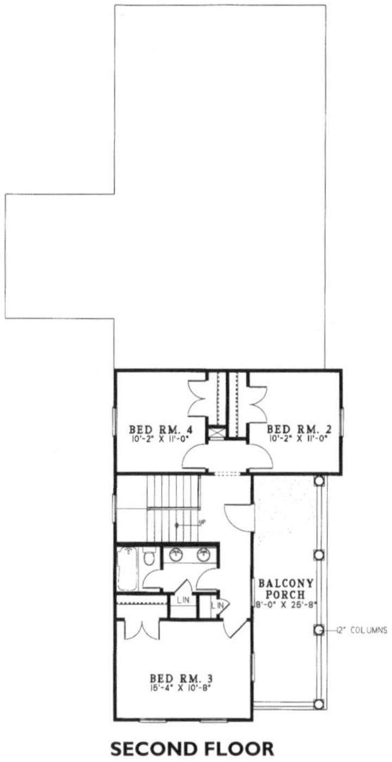

Design 34027

PHOTOGRAPHY: JOHN EHRENCLOU

Please note: The photographed home may have been modified to suit homeowner preferences. If you order plans, have a builder or design professional check them against the photograph to confirm actual construction details.

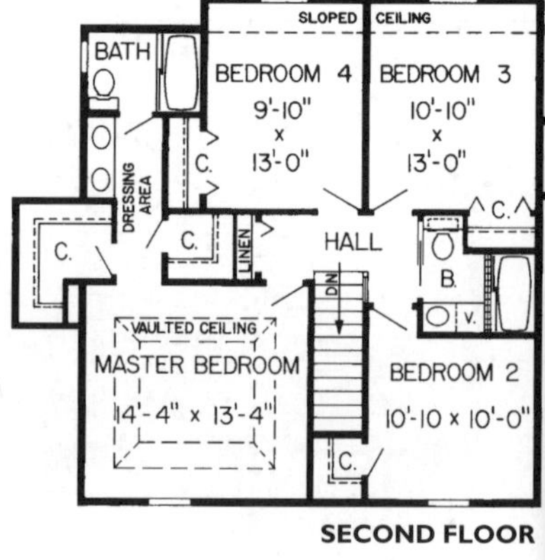

SLOPED CEILING
BATH
BEDROOM 4
9'-10" x 13'-0"
BEDROOM 3
10'-10" x 13'-0"
DRESSING AREA
C.
LINEN
HALL
DN
B.
V.
VAULTED CEILING
MASTER BEDROOM
14'-4" x 13'-4"
BEDROOM 2
10'-10 x 10'-0"

SECOND FLOOR

Units	Single
Price Code	C
Total Finished	1,960 sq. ft.
First Finished	955 sq. ft.
Second Finished	1,005 sq. ft.
Basement Unfinished	930 sq. ft.
Garage Unfinished	484 sq. ft.
Dimensions	52'x31'
Foundation	Basement Crawlspace Slab
Bedrooms	4
Full Baths	2
Half Baths	1
Max Ridge Height	28'
Roof Framing	Stick
Exterior Walls	2x4, 2x6

OPT. PATIO
STEP
DW
KITCHEN
14'-4" x 9'-6"
FAMILY ROOM
14'-4" x 15'-4"
PAN.
GARAGE
21'-8" x 21'-4"
UTIL.
W
D
P.R.
C.
DN
DINING ROOM
10'-10" x 13'-4"
LIVING ROOM
10'-10" x 13'-4"
FOYER
UP
PORCH

FIRST FLOOR

OPTIONAL CRAWLSPACE/SLAB FOUNDATION

Design 97227

Units	Single
Price Code	C
Total Finished	1,960 sq. ft.
Main Finished	1,960 sq. ft.
Basement Unfinished	1,993 sq. ft.
Garage Unfinished	476 sq. ft.
Dimensions	59'x62'
Foundation	Basement Crawlspace
Bedrooms	4
Full Baths	3
Main Ceiling	9'1⅛
Max Ridge Height	24'
Roof Framing	Stick
Exterior Walls	2x4

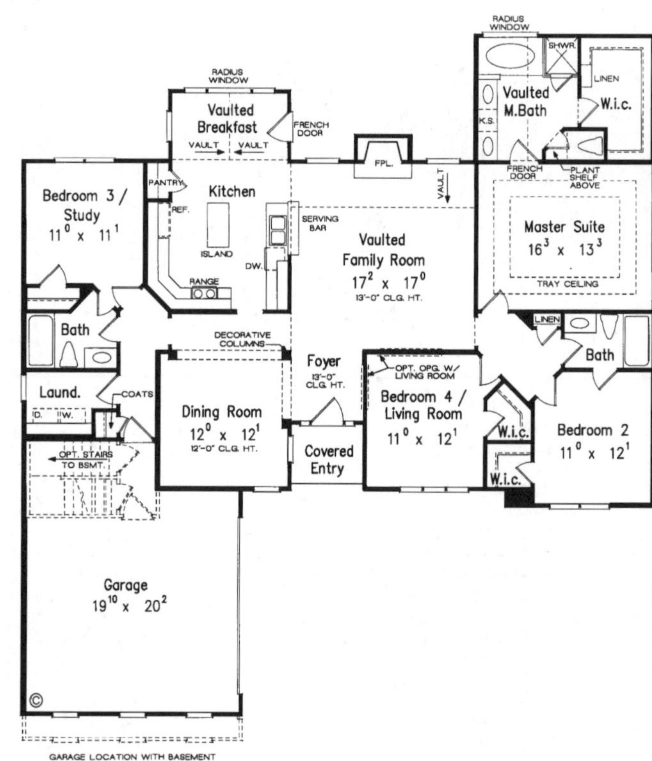

RADIUS WINDOW
Vaulted Breakfast
VAULT
FRENCH DOOR
SHWR.
LINEN
Vaulted M.Bath
W.i.c.
K.S.
FPL.
VAULT
FRENCH DOOR
PLANT SHELF ABOVE
Bedroom 3 / Study
11⁰ x 11¹
PANTRY
Kitchen
REF.
ISLAND
RANGE
DW.
SERVING BAR
Vaulted Family Room
17² x 17⁰
13'-0" CLG. HT.
Master Suite
16³ x 13³
TRAY CEILING
Bath
DECORATIVE COLUMNS
Foyer
13'-0" CLG. HT.
OPT. OPG. W/ LIVING ROOM
Bedroom 4 / Living Room
11⁰ x 12¹
Bath
Laund.
COATS
Dining Room
12⁰ x 12¹
12'-0" CLG. HT.
Covered Entry
W.i.c.
Bedroom 2
11⁰ x 12¹
W.i.c.
OPT. STAIRS TO BSMT.
Garage
19¹⁰ x 20²
GARAGE LOCATION WITH BASEMENT

MAIN FLOOR

Design 91462

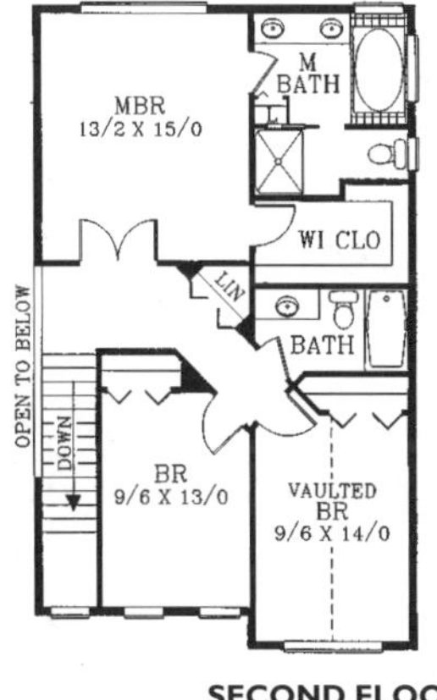
M BATH
MBR
13/2 X 15/0
WI CLO
LIN
BATH
OPEN TO BELOW
DOWN
BR
9/6 X 13/0
VAULTED BR
9/6 X 14/0
SECOND FLOOR

Units	Single
Price Code	C
Total Finished	1,962 sq. ft.
First Finished	1,118 sq. ft.
Second Finished	844 sq. ft.
Dimensions	40'x45'8"
Foundation	Crawlspace
Bedrooms	3
Full Baths	2
Half Baths	1
First Ceiling	8'
Second Ceiling	8'
Max Ridge Height	27'
Roof Framing	Truss
Exterior Walls	2x6

COVERED PATIO
DIN RM
13 X 11
KIT
ARCHWAY
DW
R
PAN
VAULTED GREAT RM
15/6 X 19/3
B.I. HUTCH
GST
W
D
PDR
UTIL
STOR
OPT PLANT SHELF OVER
OPT DOOR
UP
GARAGE
19/4 X 20/2
VAULTED OPTION RM
11/0 X 13/8
VAULTED FOYER
COVERED PORCH

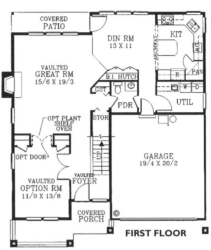

FIRST FLOOR

Design 69103

Rear Elevation

Units	Single
Price Code	C
Total Finished	1,965 sq. ft.
Main Finished	1,965 sq. ft.
Garage Unfinished	440 sq. ft.
Dimensions	71'x68'1"
Foundation	Crawlspace
Bedrooms	3
Full Baths	1
3/4 Baths	1
Main Ceiling	10'
Vaulted Ceiling	14'2"
Max Ridge Height	21'
Roof Framing	Truss
Exterior Walls	2x6

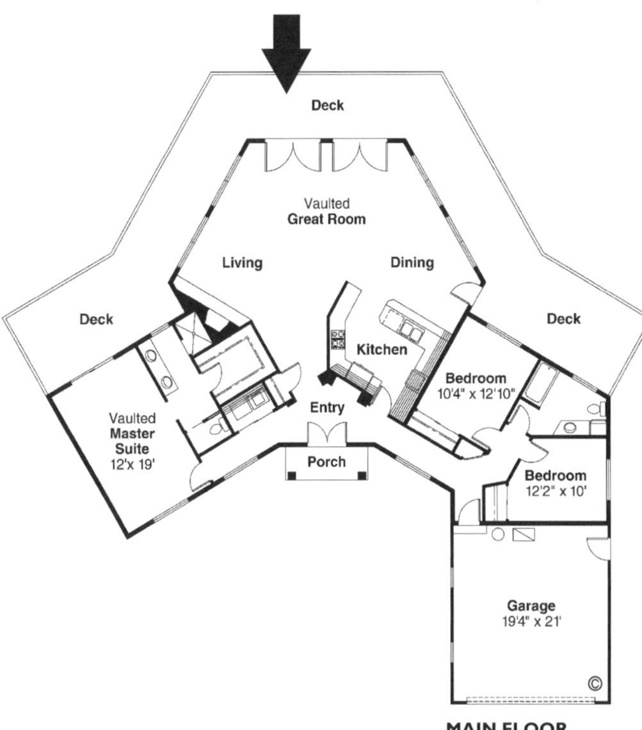
Deck
Vaulted
Great Room
Living
Dining
Deck
Deck
Kitchen
Bedroom
10'4" x 12'10"
Vaulted
Master
Suite
12'x 19'
Entry
Porch
Bedroom
12'2" x 10'
Garage
19'4" x 21'
MAIN FLOOR

Design 92696

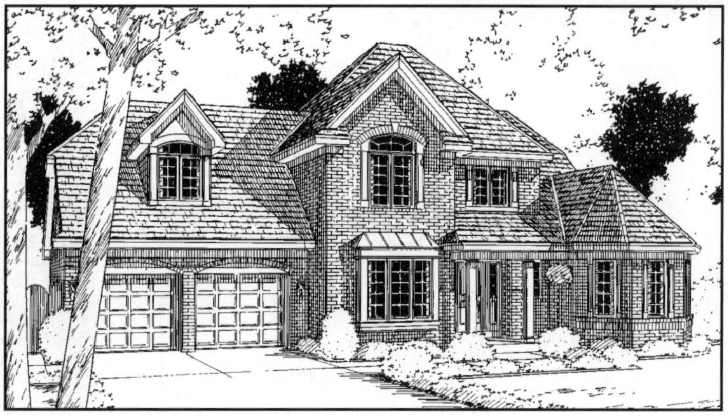

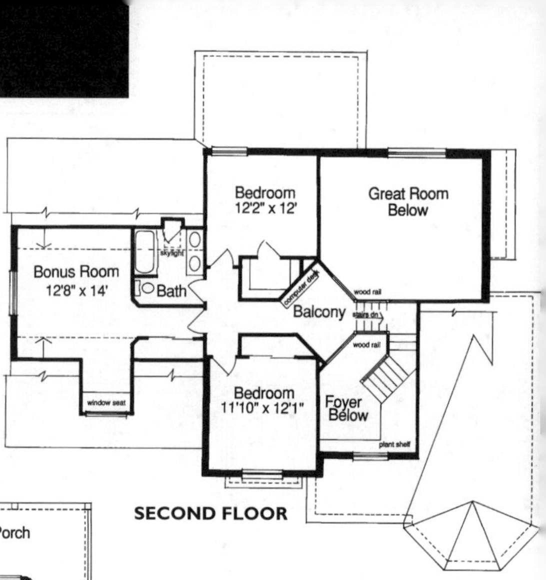

Units	Single
Price Code	C
Total Finished	1,969 sq. ft.
First Finished	1,420 sq. ft.
Second Finished	549 sq. ft.
Bonus Unfinished	268 sq. ft.
Basement Unfinished	1,420 sq. ft.
Garage Unfinished	532 sq. ft.
Porch Unfinished	57 sq. ft.
Dimensions	58'x44'4"
Foundation	Basement
Bedrooms	3
Full Baths	2
Half Baths	1
Max Ridge Height	29'6"
Roof Framing	Truss
Exterior Walls	2x4

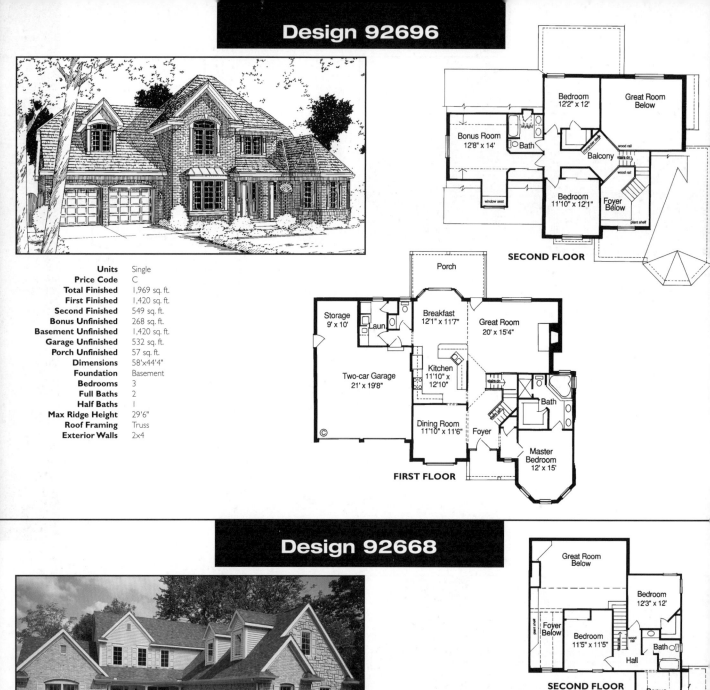

SECOND FLOOR

Bedroom 12'2" x 12'
Great Room Below
Bonus Room 12'8" x 14'
Bath
Balcony
Bedroom 11'10" x 12'1"
Foyer Below

FIRST FLOOR

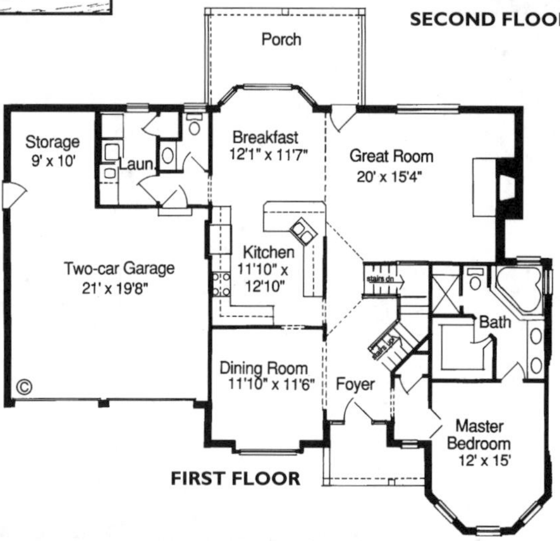

Porch
Storage 9' x 10'
Laun.
Breakfast 12'1" x 11'7"
Great Room 20' x 15'4"
Two-car Garage 21' x 19'8"
Kitchen 11'10" x 12'10"
Bath
Dining Room 11'10" x 11'6"
Foyer
Master Bedroom 12' x 15'

Design 92668

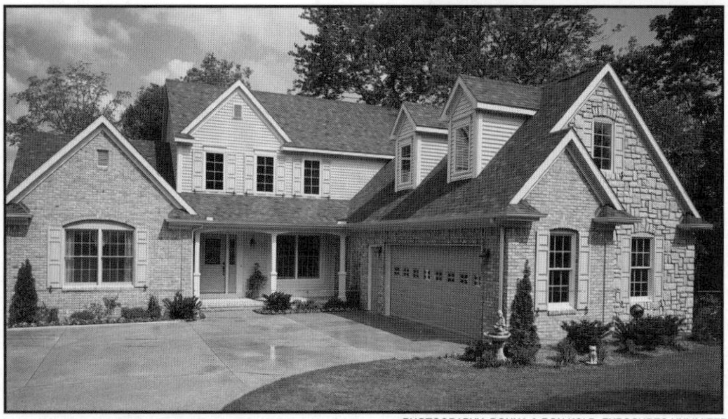

PHOTOGRAPHY: DONNA & RON KOLB, EXPOSURES UNLIMITED

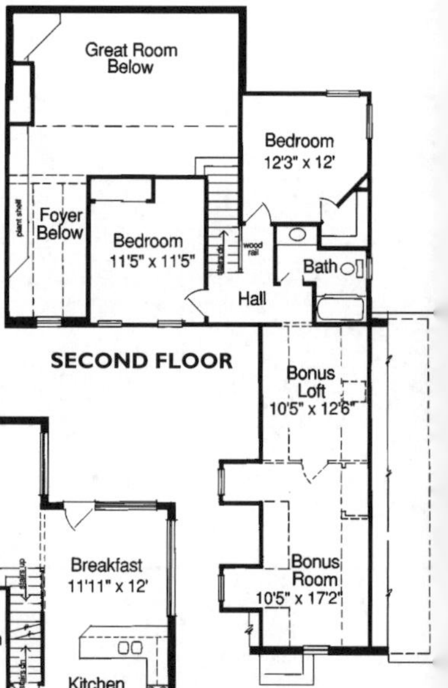

Units	Single
Price Code	C
Total Finished	1,970 sq. ft.
First Finished	1,497 sq. ft.
Second Finished	473 sq. ft.
Bonus Unfinished	401 sq. ft.
Basement Unfinished	1,420 sq. ft.
Garage Unfinished	468 sq. ft.
Porch Unfinished	91 sq. ft.
Dimensions	55'x63'6"
Foundation	Basement
Bedrooms	3
Full Baths	2
Half Baths	1
First Ceiling	8'
Second Ceiling	8'
Vaulted Ceiling	18'
Tray Ceiling	9'
Max Ridge Height	27'2"
Roof Framing	Truss
Exterior Walls	2x4

SECOND FLOOR

Great Room Below
Bedroom 12'3" x 12'
Foyer Below
Bedroom 11'5" x 11'5"
Bath
Hall
Bonus Loft 10'5" x 12'6"
Bonus Room 10'5" x 17'2"

FIRST FLOOR

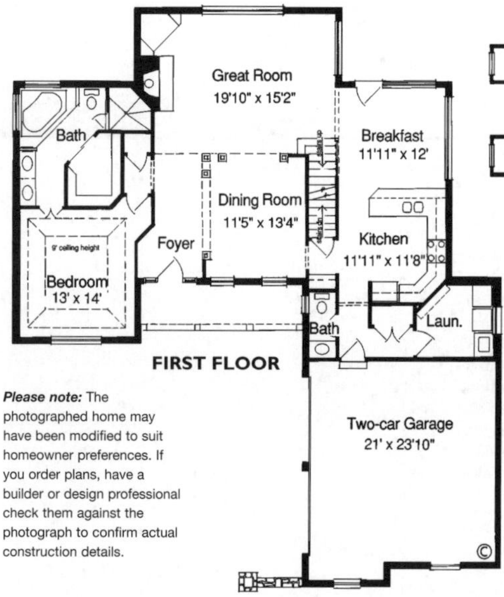

Great Room 19'10" x 15'2"
Bath
Breakfast 11'11" x 12'
Dining Room 11'5" x 13'4"
Foyer
Kitchen 11'11" x 11'8"
Bedroom 13' x 14'
Bath
Laun.
Two-car Garage 21' x 23'10"

Please note: The photographed home may have been modified to suit homeowner preferences. If you order plans, have a builder or design professional check them against the photograph to confirm actual construction details.

Design 93077

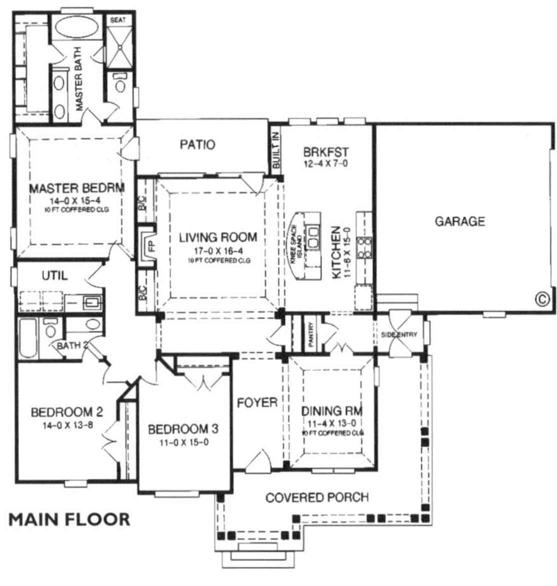
SEAT
MASTER BATH
PATIO
BUILT IN
BRKFST
12-4 X 7-0
MASTER BEDRM
14-0 X 15-4
10 FT COFFERED CLG
LIVING ROOM
17-0 X 16-4
10 FT COFFERED CLG
KITCHEN
11-8 X 15-0
GARAGE
UTIL
BATH 2
PANTRY
SIDE ENTRY
BEDROOM 2
14-0 X 13-8
BEDROOM 3
11-0 X 15-0
FOYER
DINING RM
11-4 X 13-0
COVERED PORCH
MAIN FLOOR

Units	Single
Price Code	C
Total Finished	1,971 sq. ft.
Main Finished	1,971 sq. ft.
Garage Unfinished	498 sq. ft.
Porch Unfinished	373 sq. ft.
Dimensions	66'2"x62'4"
Foundation	Crawlspace
Bedrooms	3
Full Baths	2
Max Ridge Height	20'
Roof Framing	Stick
Exterior Walls	2x4

Design 65210

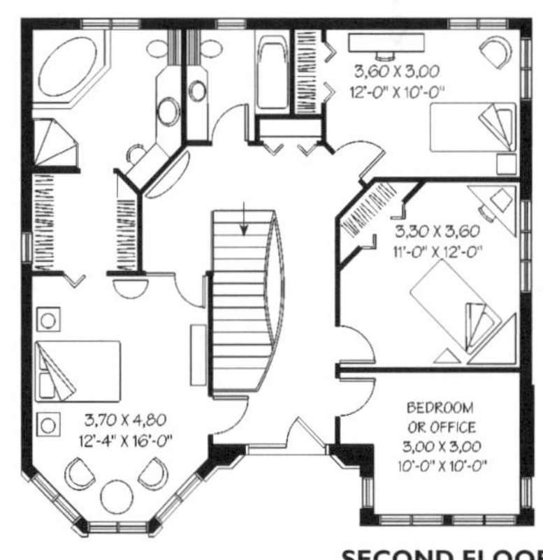
3,60 X 3,00
12'-0" X 10'-0"
3,30 X 3,60
11'-0" X 12'-0"
3,70 X 4,80
12'-4" X 16'-0"
BEDROOM OR OFFICE
3,00 X 3,00
10'-0" X 10'-0"
SECOND FLOOR

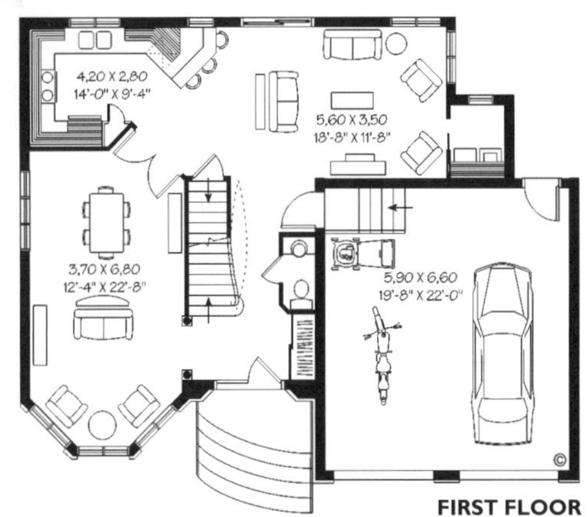
4,20 X 2,80
14'-0" X 9'-4"
5,60 X 3,50
18'-8" X 11'-8"
3,70 X 6,80
12'-4" X 22'-8"
5,90 X 6,60
19'-8" X 22'-0"
FIRST FLOOR

Units	Single
Price Code	C
Total Finished	1,976 sq. ft.
First Finished	924 sq. ft.
Second Finished	1,052 sq. ft.
Basement Unfinished	1,067 sq. ft.
Garage Unfinished	388 sq. ft.
Porch Unfinished	596 sq. ft.
Dimensions	44'8'x36'
Foundation	Basement
Bedrooms	4
Full Baths	2
Half Baths	1
First Ceiling	9'
Second Ceiling	8'
Max Ridge Height	33'5"
Roof Framing	Truss
Exterior Walls	2x6

Design 69037

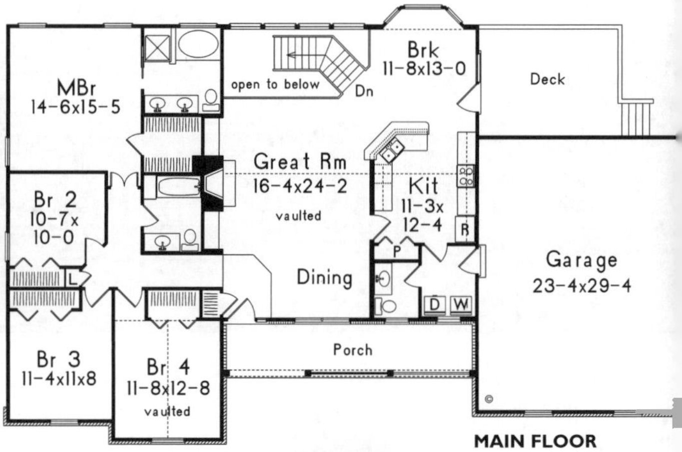

MAIN FLOOR

BONUS

Hot New Design

Units	Single
Price Code	C
Total Finished	1,977 sq. ft.
Main Finished	1,977 sq. ft.
Bonus Unfinished	1,416 sq. ft.
Dimensions	76'x45'
Foundation	Basement
Bedrooms	4
Full Baths	2
Half Baths	1

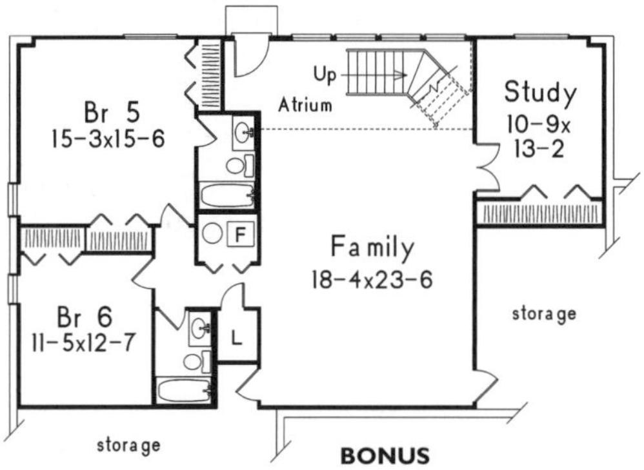

Design 10514

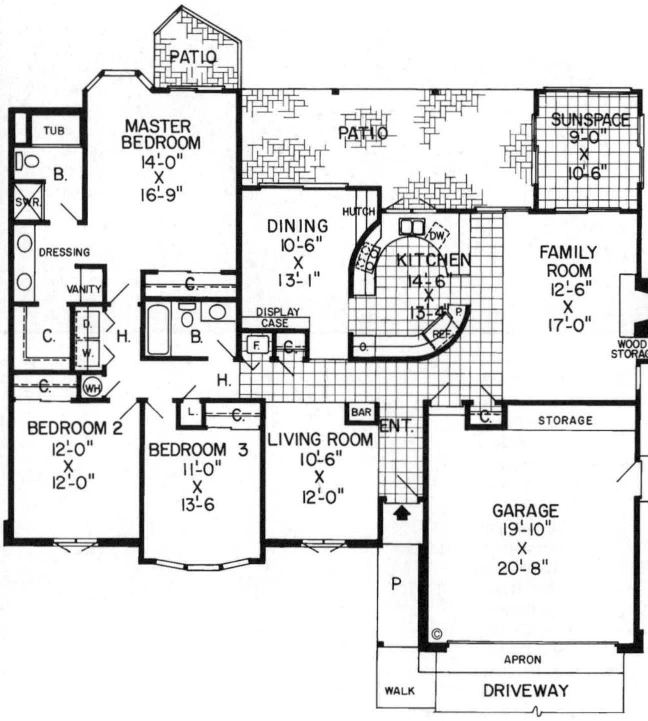

MAIN FLOOR

Units	Single
Price Code	C
Total Finished	1,980 sq. ft.
Main Finished	1,980 sq. ft.
Garage Unfinished	434 sq. ft.
Dimensions	60'x51'
Foundation	Crawlspace
Bedrooms	3
Full Baths	2
Max Ridge Height	20'
Roof Framing	Stick
Exterior Walls	2x6

Design 19299

PHOTOGRAPHY: STEVE GRAHAM

Units	Single
Price Code	C
Total Finished	1,980 sq. ft.
Main Finished	1,980 sq. ft.
Garage Unfinished	484 sq. ft.
Dimensions	64'8"x55'
Foundation	Combo Basement/ Crawlspace
Bedrooms	3
Full Baths	2
Half Baths	1
Main Ceiling	8'
Max Ridge Height	21'
Roof Framing	Stick
Exterior Walls	2x4

DECK
DECK
BRKFST 10½x9½
FAMILY 15x19½
BATH
MASTER BEDRM 13½x17½
KIT 12½x10
CLOS
BATH
W D
LAV
DINING 13x12
ENTRY
BEDRM 11x11
BEDRM 10½x13½
PORCH
GARAGE 21x21

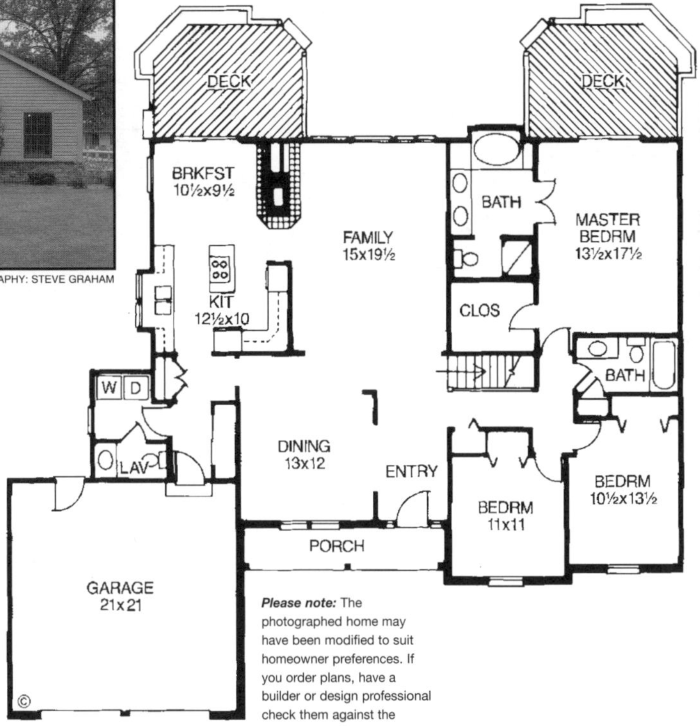

MAIN FLOOR

Please note: The photographed home may have been modified to suit homeowner preferences. If you order plans, have a builder or design professional check them against the photograph to confirm actual construction details.

Design 24724

Units	Single
Price Code	C
Total Finished	1,982 sq. ft.
First Finished	999 sq. ft.
Second Finished	983 sq. ft.
Basement Unfinished	840 sq. ft.
Porch Unfinished	516 sq. ft.
Dimensions	51'x36'
Foundation	Crawlspace Slab
Bedrooms	4
Full Baths	2
Half Baths	1
First Ceiling	8'
Second Ceiling	8'
Max Ridge Height	31'6"
Roof Framing	Stick
Exterior Walls	2x4

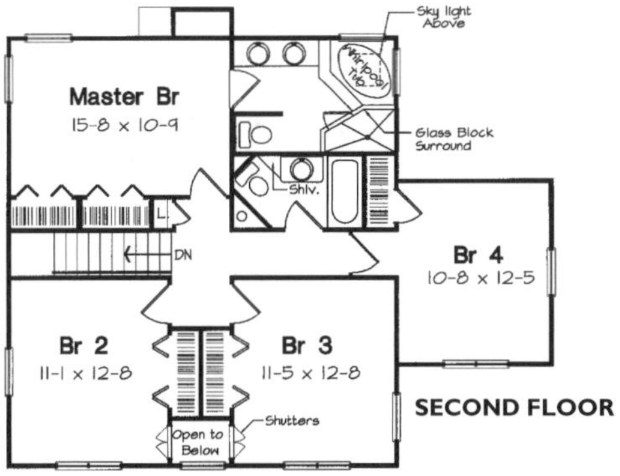

Sky light Above
Master Br 15-8 x 10-9
Whirlpool Tub
Glass Block Surround
Shlv.
DN
Br 4 10-8 x 12-5
Br 2 11-1 x 12-8
Br 3 11-5 x 12-8
Open to Below
Shutters

SECOND FLOOR

Crawl Space Access
Furn.
W.H.

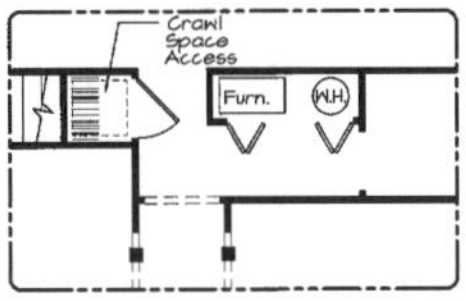

OPTIONAL CRAWLSPACE/SLAB FOUNDATION

Wood Box
Ent. Center
Brkfst 7-8 x 7-0
Screened Porch 10-8 x 9-8
Sky light Above
Great Rm 19-5 x 13-1
UP
DN
Kitchen 10-8 x 12-5
Ref
DW
Decor Clg
Parlor 11-5 x 12-8
Dining 11-5 x 10-2

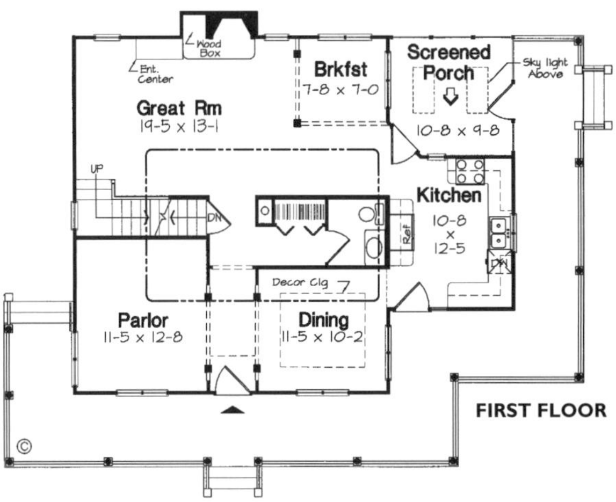

FIRST FLOOR

Design 92427

Units	Single
Price Code	C
Total Finished	1,982 sq. ft.
Main Finished	1,982 sq. ft.
Bonus Unfinished	386 sq. ft.
Basement Unfinished	1,982 sq. ft.
Dimensions	63'x58'
Foundation	Basement Crawlspace
Bedrooms	3
Full Baths	2
Half Baths	1
Main Ceiling	9'
Vaulted Ceiling	14'4"
Tray Ceiling	12'4"
Max Ridge Height	21'10"
Roof Framing	Stick
Exterior Walls	2x4

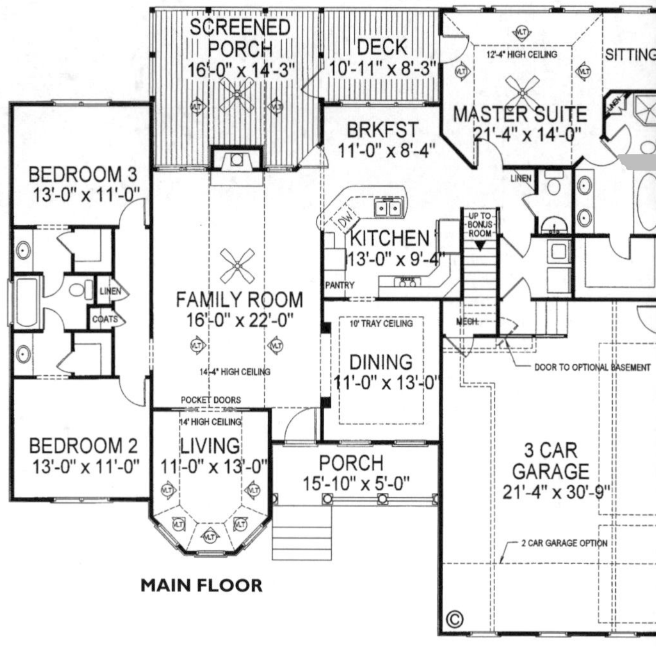
SCREENED PORCH
16'-0" x 14'-3"
DECK
10'-11" x 8'-3"
MASTER SUITE
21'-4" x 14'-0"
12'-4" HIGH CEILING
SITTING
BRKFST
11'-0" x 8'-4"
BEDROOM 3
13'-0" x 11'-0"
LINEN
COATS
UP TO BONUS ROOM
KITCHEN
13'-0" x 9'-4"
PANTRY
FAMILY ROOM
16'-0" x 22'-0"
14'-4" HIGH CEILING
10' TRAY CEILING
DINING
11'-0" x 13'-0"
MECH.
DOOR TO OPTIONAL BASEMENT
POCKET DOORS
14' HIGH CEILING
BEDROOM 2
13'-0" x 11'-0"
LIVING
11'-0" x 13'-0"
PORCH
15'-10" x 5'-0"
3 CAR GARAGE
21'-4" x 30'-9"
2 CAR GARAGE OPTION
MAIN FLOOR

Design 97355

Units	Single
Price Code	C
Total Finished	1,982 sq. ft.
Main Finished	1,982 sq. ft.
Lower Unfinished	1,484 sq. ft.
Dimensions	60'x61'
Foundation	Basement
Bedrooms	3
Full Baths	2
Half Baths	1
Roof Framing	Stick
Exterior Walls	2x4

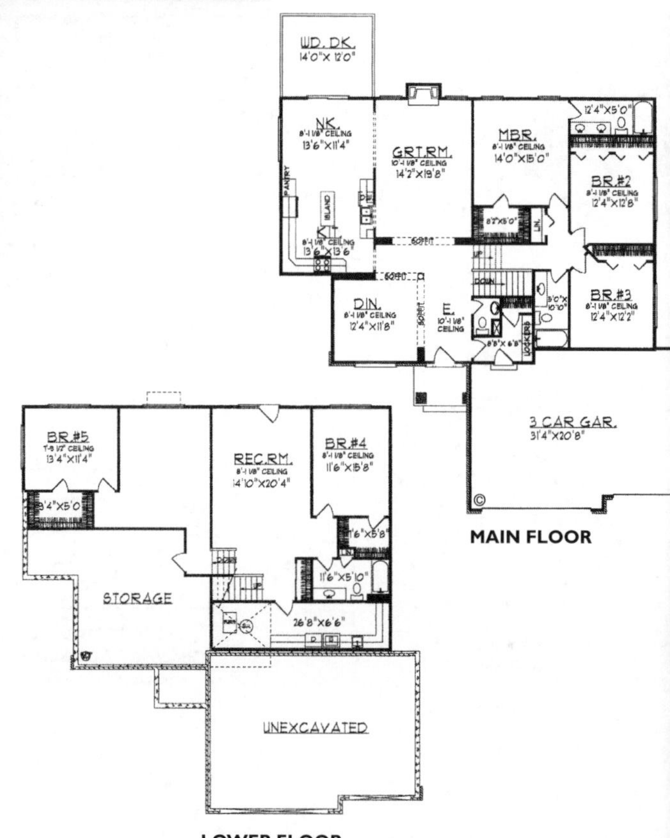
WD. DK.
14'0"X 12'0"
NK.
13'6"X11'4"
GRT.RM.
14'2"X19'8"
MBR.
14'0"X15'0"
BR.#2
12'4"X12'8"
BR.#3
12'4"X12'2"
DIN.
12'4"X11'8"
E.
3 CAR GAR.
31'4"X20'8"
MAIN FLOOR
BR.#5
13'4"X11'4"
REC.RM.
14'10"X20'4"
BR.#4
11'6"X15'8"
STORAGE
UNEXCAVATED
LOWER FLOOR

Design 93466

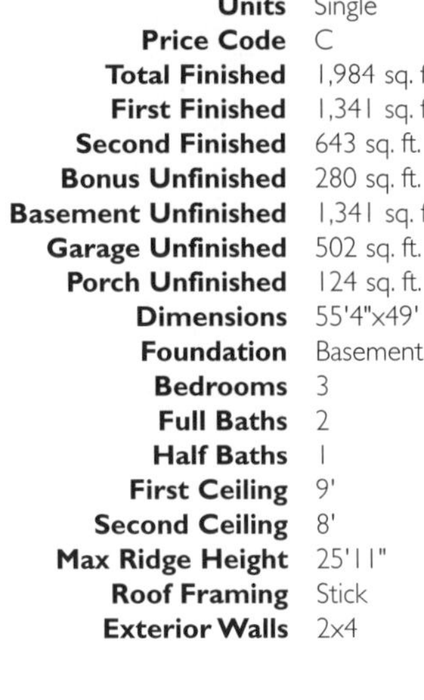

Units	Single
Price Code	C
Total Finished	1,984 sq. ft.
First Finished	1,341 sq. ft.
Second Finished	643 sq. ft.
Bonus Unfinished	280 sq. ft.
Basement Unfinished	1,341 sq. ft.
Garage Unfinished	502 sq. ft.
Porch Unfinished	124 sq. ft.
Dimensions	55'4"x49'
Foundation	Basement
Bedrooms	3
Full Baths	2
Half Baths	1
First Ceiling	9'
Second Ceiling	8'
Max Ridge Height	25'11"
Roof Framing	Stick
Exterior Walls	2x4

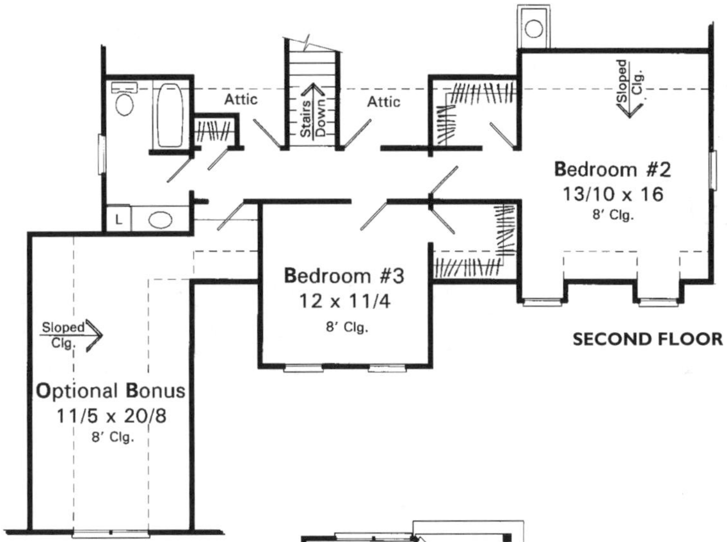

Attic
Stairs Down
Attic
Sloped Clg.
Bedroom #2
13/10 x 16
8' Clg.
L
Bedroom #3
12 x 11/4
8' Clg.
Sloped Clg.
Optional Bonus
11/5 x 20/8
8' Clg.

SECOND FLOOR

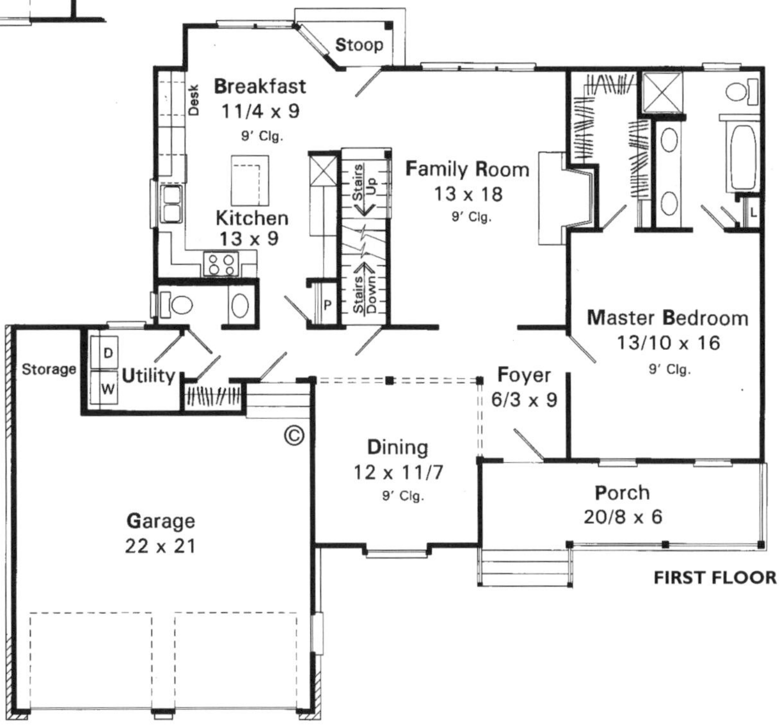

Stoop
Desk
Breakfast
11/4 x 9
9' Clg.
Stairs Up
Family Room
13 x 18
9' Clg.
L
Kitchen
13 x 9
P
Stairs Down
Master Bedroom
13/10 x 16
9' Clg.
D
W
Storage
Utility
Foyer
6/3 x 9
©
Dining
12 x 11/7
9' Clg.
Porch
20/8 x 6
Garage
22 x 21

FIRST FLOOR

Design 93010

Units	Single
Price Code	C
Total Finished	1,985 sq. ft.
Main Finished	1,985 sq. ft.
Dimensions	71'10"x57'
Foundation	Crawlspace Slab
Bedrooms	3
Full Baths	2
Max Ridge Height	22'
Roof Framing	Stick
Exterior Walls	2x4

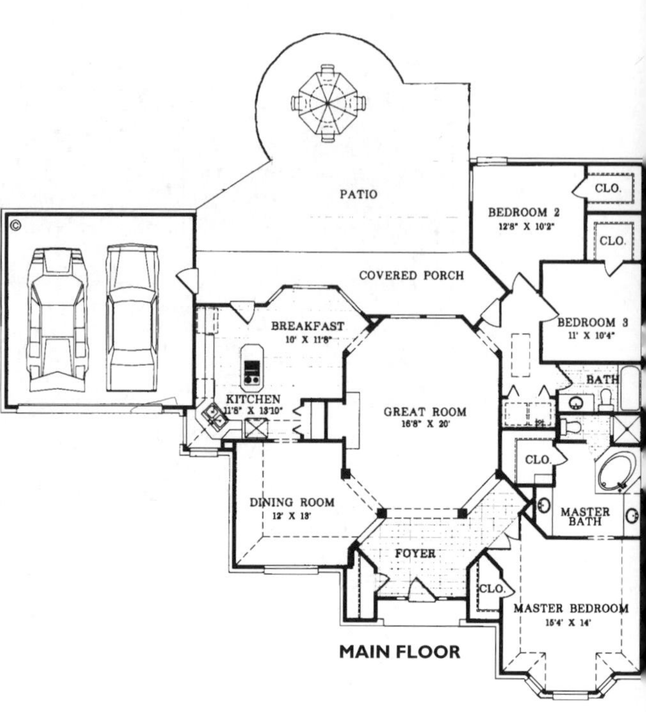

PATIO
BEDROOM 2
12'8" X 10'2"
CLO.
CLO.
COVERED PORCH
BEDROOM 3
11' X 10'4"
BREAKFAST
10' X 11'8"
KITCHEN
11'8" X 13'10"
GREAT ROOM
16'8" X 20'
BATH
CLO.
MASTER BATH
DINING ROOM
12' X 13'
FOYER
CLO.
MASTER BEDROOM
15'4" X 14'

MAIN FLOOR

Design 91464

Units	Single
Price Code	C
Total Finished	1,986 sq. ft.
First Finished	1,010 sq. ft.
Second Finished	976 sq. ft.
Garage Unfinished	455 sq. ft.
Dimensions	54'6"x33'
Foundation	Basement
Bedrooms	4
Full Baths	1
3/4 Baths	1
Half Baths	1
First Ceiling	8'
Second Ceiling	8'
Max Ridge Height	26'
Roof Framing	Stick
Exterior Walls	2x4

BR 2
10/0 X 15/0
MASTER
13/0 X 13/8
M BATH
WI CLO
STOR
BATH
DN
OPEN TO BELOW
LIN
BR 3
11/10 X 10/0
BR 4
10/10 X 9/10
WI CLO

SECOND FLOOR

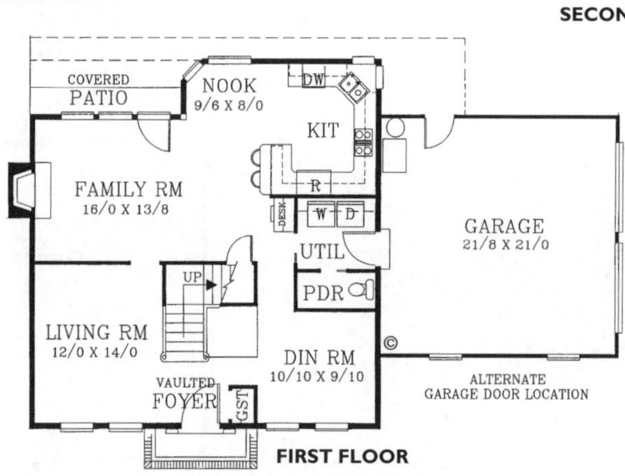

COVERED PATIO
NOOK
9/6 X 8/0
DW
KIT
R
FAMILY RM
16/0 X 13/8
DESK
W D
UTIL
GARAGE
21/8 X 21/0
UP
PDR
LIVING RM
12/0 X 14/0
DIN RM
10/10 X 9/10
ALTERNATE GARAGE DOOR LOCATION
VAULTED FOYER
GST

FIRST FLOOR

Design 92544

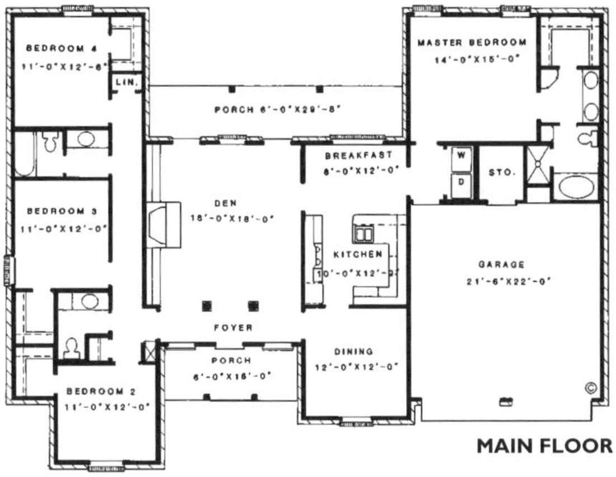

MAIN FLOOR

Units	Single
Price Code	C
Total Finished	1,987 sq. ft.
Main Finished	1,987 sq. ft.
Garage Unfinished	515 sq. ft.
Porch Unfinished	274 sq. ft.
Dimensions	67'x49'
Foundation	Crawlspace Slab
Bedrooms	4
Full Baths	2
Half Baths	1
Main Ceiling	9'
Max Ridge Height	22'
Roof Framing	Truss
Exterior Walls	2x4

Design 93215

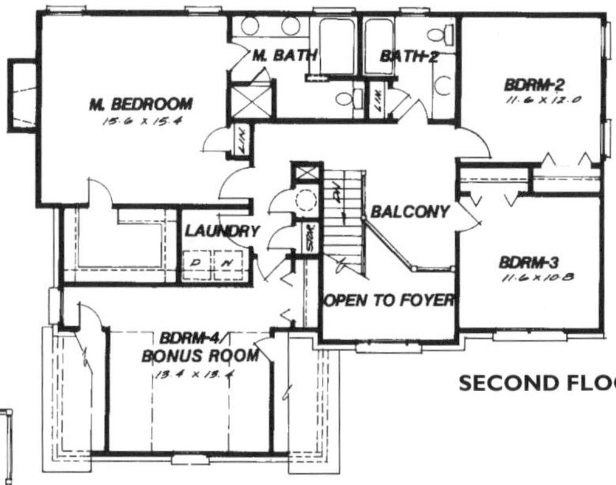

SECOND FLOOR

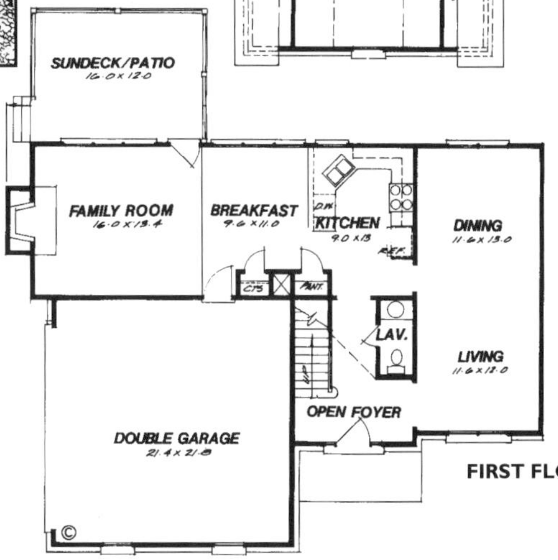

FIRST FLOOR

Units	Single
Price Code	C
Total Finished	1,987 sq. ft.
First Finished	949 sq. ft.
Second Finished	1,038 sq. ft.
Bonus Unfinished	232 sq. ft.
Basement Unfinished	949 sq. ft.
Garage Unfinished	484 sq. ft.
Deck Unfinished	192 sq. ft.
Dimensions	47'4"x36'5"
Foundation	Basement Crawlspace Slab
Bedrooms	3
Full Baths	2
Half Baths	1
Max Ridge Height	29'
Roof Framing	Stick
Exterior Walls	2x4

Design 64173

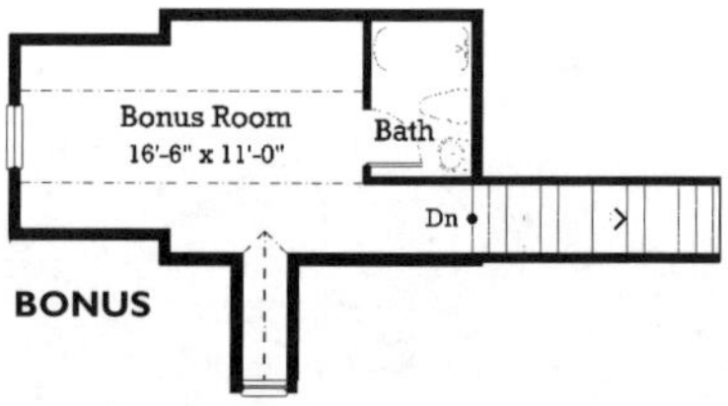

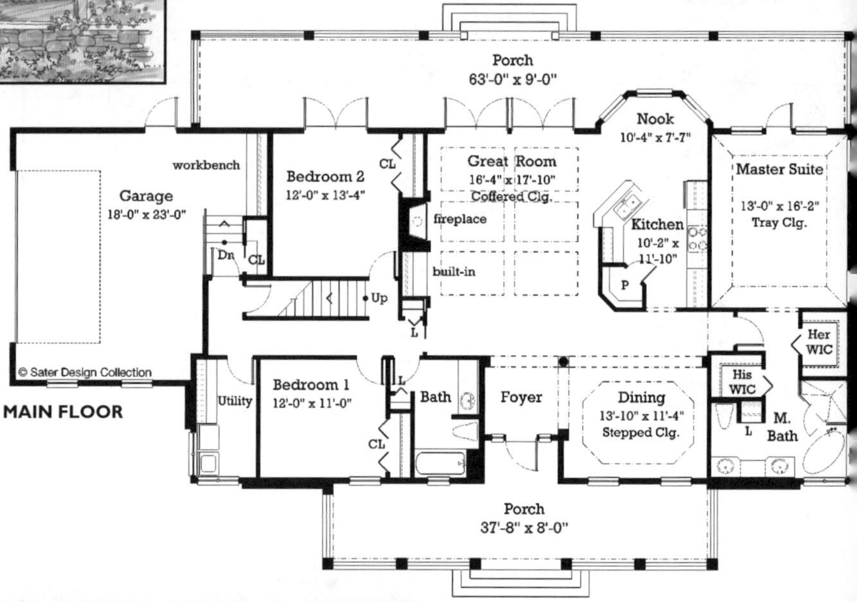

BONUS

Units	Single
Price Code	H
Total Finished	1,989 sq. ft.
Main Finished	1,989 sq. ft.
Bonus Unfinished	274 sq. ft.
Garage Unfinished	525 sq. ft.
Dimensions	81'x50'
Foundation	Crawlspace
Bedrooms	3
Full Baths	2
Max Ridge Height	27'
Roof Framing	Stick/Truss
Exterior Walls	2x6

* Alternate foundation options available at an additional charge. Please call 1-800-235-5700 for more information.

MAIN FLOOR

© Sater Design Collection

Design 82052

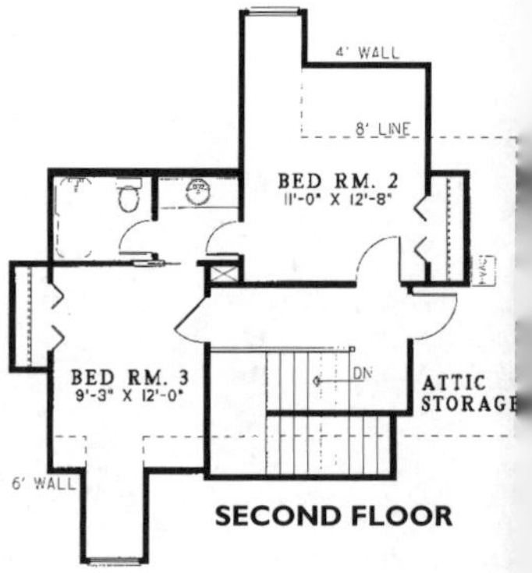

Units	Single
Price Code	C
Total Finished	1,990 sq. ft.
First Finished	1,515 sq. ft.
Second Finished	475 sq. ft.
Garage Unfinished	405 sq. ft.
Porch Unfinished	72 sq. ft.
Dimensions	49'x46'
Foundation	Crawlspace Slab
Bedrooms	3
Full Baths	2
Half Baths	1
First Ceiling	9'
Second Ceiling	8'
Roof Framing	Stick
Exterior Walls	2x4

SECOND FLOOR

FIRST FLOOR

Design 90465

Units	Single
Price Code	C
Total Finished	1,990 sq. ft.
Main Finished	1,990 sq. ft.
Basement Unfinished	1,415 sq. ft.
Garage Unfinished	484 sq. ft.
Deck Unfinished	416 sq. ft.
Porch Unfinished	36 sq. ft.
Dimensions	64'10"x57'4"
Foundation	Basement Crawlspace
Bedrooms	3
Full Baths	2
Main Ceiling	9'
Max Ridge Height	27'6"
Roof Framing	Stick
Exterior Walls	2x4

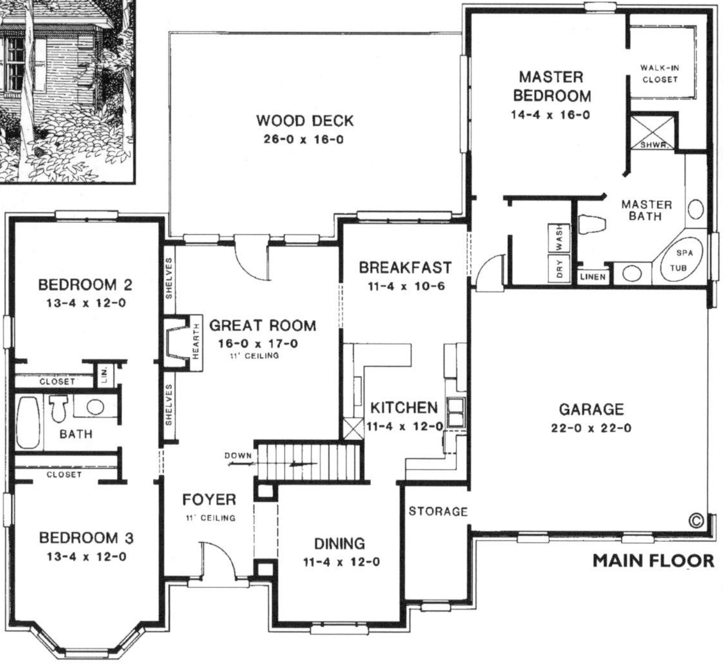

MAIN FLOOR

Design 98980

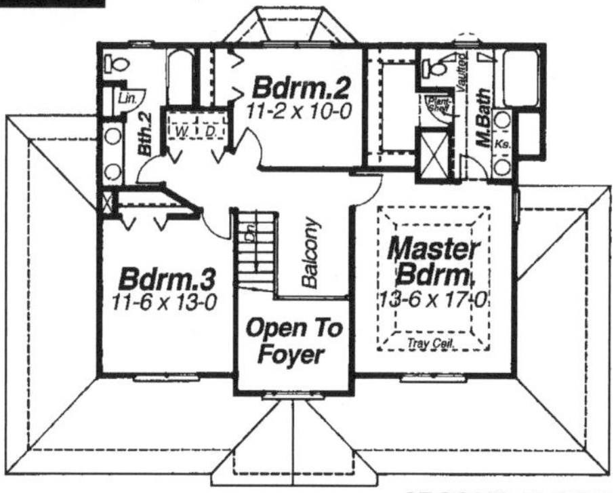

Units	Single
Price Code	C
Total Finished	1,990 sq. ft.
First Finished	1,035 sq. ft.
Second Finished	955 sq. ft.
Dimensions	48'x48'
Foundation	Basement
Bedrooms	3
Full Baths	2
Half Baths	1
Max Ridge Height	35'
Exterior Walls	2x4

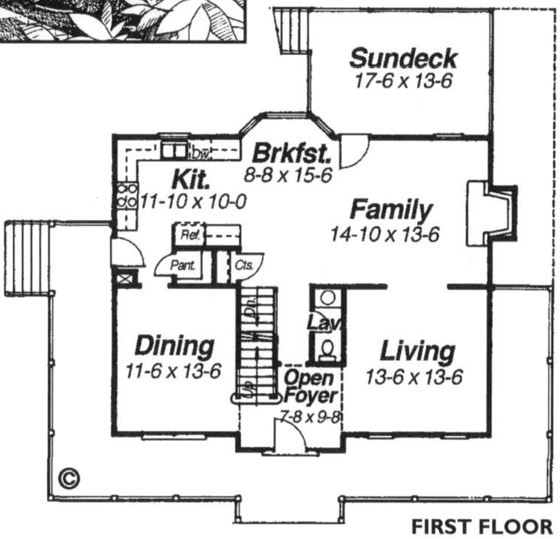

SECOND FLOOR

FIRST FLOOR

Design 90616

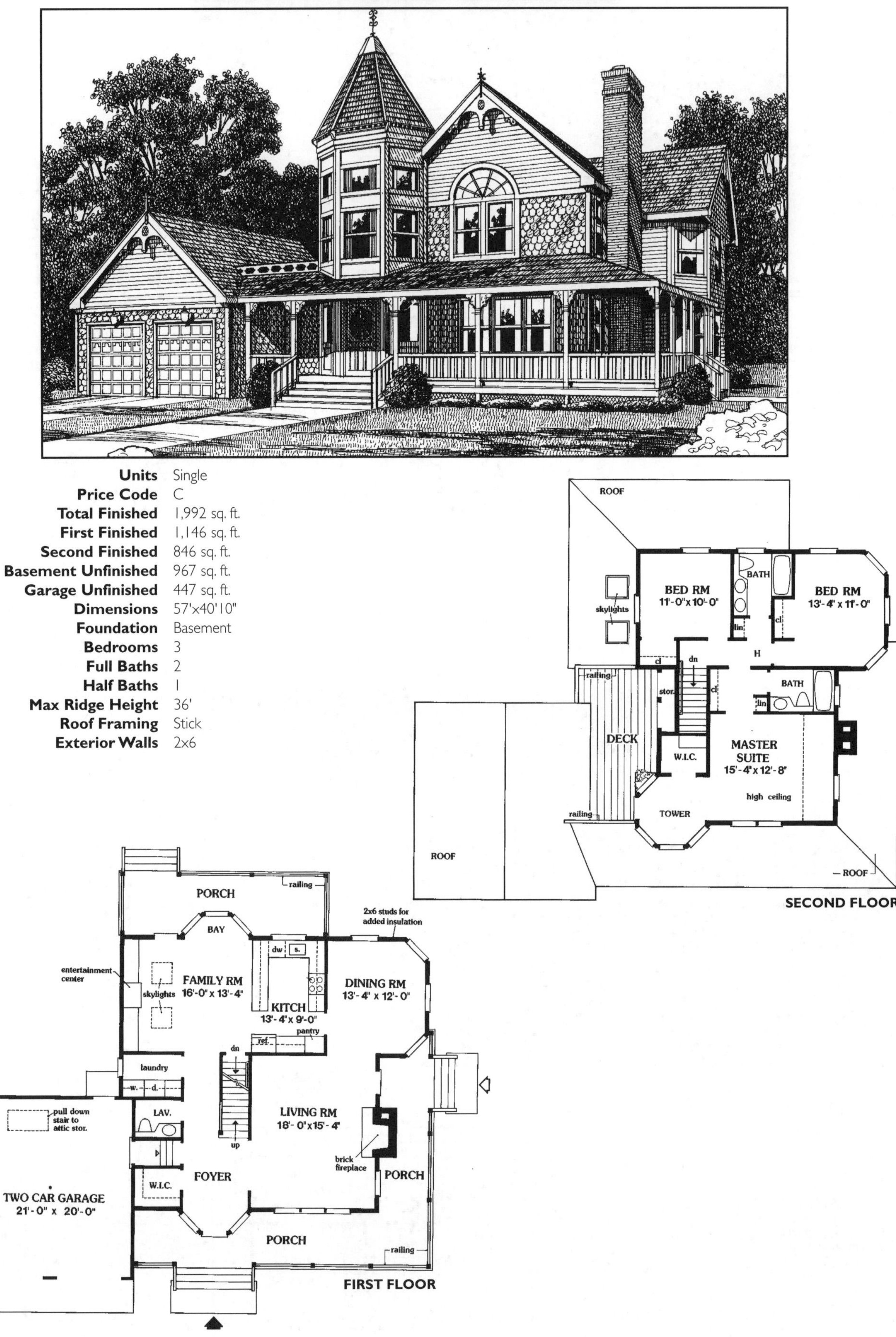
ROOF
BED RM
11'-0"x10'-0"
BATH
BED RM
13'-4" x 11'-0"
skylights
cl
lin
dn
H
cl
railing
stor.
cl
BATH
lin
DECK
W.I.C.
MASTER
SUITE
15'-4"x 12'-8"
high ceiling
railing
TOWER
ROOF
ROOF
SECOND FLOOR
PORCH
railing
2x6 studs for
added insulation
BAY
dw
s.
entertainment
center
FAMILY RM
16'-0" x 13'-4"
skylights
KITCH
13'-4" x 9'-0"
DINING RM
13'-4" x 12'-0"
pantry
ref.
dn
laundry
w.
d.
pull down
stair to
attic stor.
LAV.
LIVING RM
18'-0"x15'-4"
up
brick
fireplace
FOYER
PORCH
W.I.C.
TWO CAR GARAGE
21'-0" x 20'-0"
PORCH
railing
FIRST FLOOR

Units	Single
Price Code	C
Total Finished	1,992 sq. ft.
First Finished	1,146 sq. ft.
Second Finished	846 sq. ft.
Basement Unfinished	967 sq. ft.
Garage Unfinished	447 sq. ft.
Dimensions	57'x40'10"
Foundation	Basement
Bedrooms	3
Full Baths	2
Half Baths	1
Max Ridge Height	36'
Roof Framing	Stick
Exterior Walls	2x6

Design 92421

SCREENED PORCH
15'4" x 13'10"
DECK
11'0" x 7'6"
SITTING
MASTER SUITE
21'4" x 15'0"
BRKFST
11'0" x 10'10"
BEDROOM 3
13'0" x 11'0"
FAMILY ROOM
16'0" x 24'1"
KITCHEN
13'8" x 9'6"
PANTRY
LINEN
COATS
OPTIONAL STAIRS TO BASEMENT
10' CEILING
DINING
11'0" x 12'0"
TRAY CEILING
9' CEILING
BEDROOM 2
13'0" x 11'0"
LIVING
11'0" x 12'0"
PORCH
15'4" x 5'4"
3 CAR GARAGE
21'4" x 29'10"
2 CAR GARAGE OPTION

MAIN FLOOR

Units	Single
Price Code	C
Total Finished	1,992 sq. ft.
Main Finished	1,992 sq. ft.
Dimensions	63'x57'2"
Foundation	Basement Crawlspace Slab
Bedrooms	3
Full Baths	2
Half Baths	1
Main Ceiling	9'
Vaulted Ceiling	13'10"
Tray Ceiling	12'
Max Ridge Height	20'

Design 92446

Units	Single
Price Code	C
Total Finished	1,992 sq. ft.
Main Finished	1,992 sq. ft.
Bonus Unfinished	247 sq. ft.
Garage Unfinished	609 sq. ft.
Dimensions	66'2"x62'
Foundation	Basement Slab
Bedrooms	4
Full Baths	3
Main Ceiling	9'
Max Ridge Height	24'
Roof Framing	Stick
Exterior Walls	2x4

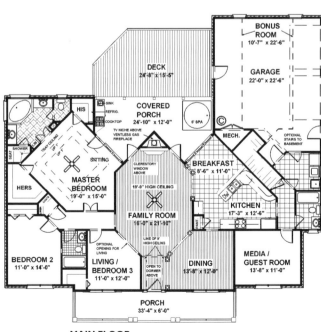

BONUS ROOM
10'-7" x 22'-6"
GARAGE
22'-0" x 22'-6"
DECK
24'-8" x 15'-5"
HIS
COVERED PORCH
24'-10" x 12'-0"
5' SPA
MECH.
OPTIONAL STAIRS TO BASEMENT
TV NICHE ABOVE VENTLESS GAS FIREPLACE
SITTING
SHOWER
HERS
MASTER BEDROOM
19'-0" x 15'-0"
CLERESTORY WINDOW ABOVE
19'-9" HIGH CEILING
BREAKFAST
8'-6" x 11'-0"
FAMILY ROOM
15'-0" x 21'-10"
KITCHEN
17'-3" x 12'-6"
LINE OF 9' HIGH CEILING
OPTIONAL OPENING FOR LIVING
BEDROOM 2
11'-0" x 14'-0"
LIVING / BEDROOM 3
11'-0" x 12'-0"
OPEN TO DORMER ABOVE
DINING
13'-8" x 12'-0"
MEDIA / GUEST ROOM
13'-8" x 11'-0"
PORCH
33'-4" x 6'-0"

MAIN FLOOR

Design 34679

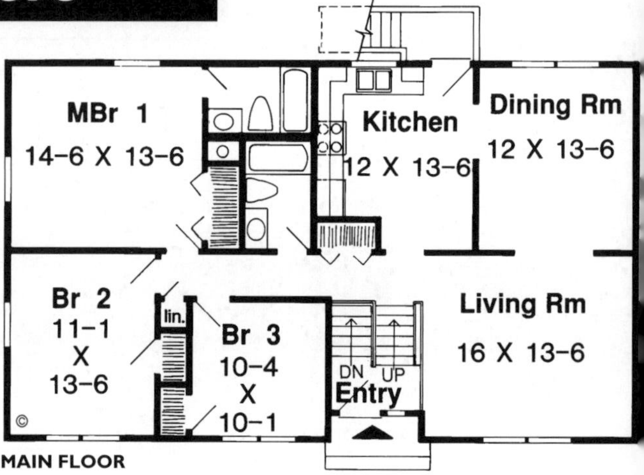

MBr 1
14-6 X 13-6
Kitchen
12 X 13-6
Dining Rm
12 X 13-6
Br 2
11-1 X 13-6
Br 3
10-4 X 10-1
Living Rm
16 X 13-6
Entry

MAIN FLOOR

Units	Single
Price Code	C
Total Finished	1,994 sq. ft.
Main Finished	1,331 sq. ft.
Lower Finished	663 sq. ft.
Garage Unfinished	584 sq. ft.
Dimensions	48'x28'
Foundation	Basement
Bedrooms	3
Full Baths	2
Half Baths	1
Main Ceiling	8'
Max Ridge Height	22'
Roof Framing	Stick
Exterior Walls	2x4, 2x6

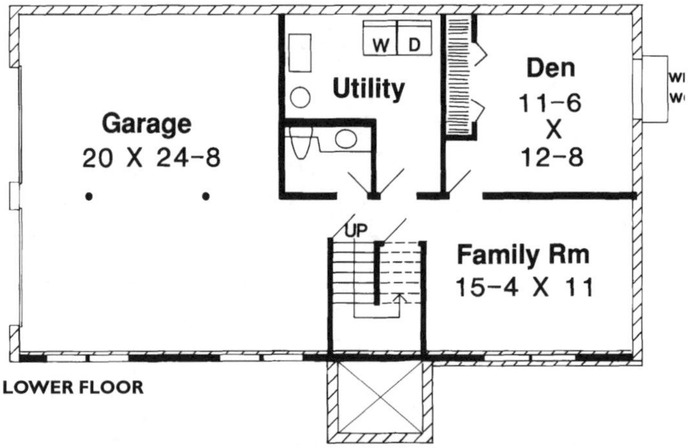

Garage
20 X 24-8
Utility
Den
11-6 X 12-8
Family Rm
15-4 X 11

LOWER FLOOR

Design 82080

Units	Single
Price Code	C
Total Finished	1,994 sq. ft.
Main Finished	1,994 sq. ft.
Garage Unfinished	417 sq. ft.
Porch Unfinished	118 sq. ft.
Dimensions	65'2"x63'
Foundation	Basement Crawlspace Slab
Bedrooms	3
Full Baths	2
Roof Framing	Stick
Exterior Walls	2x4

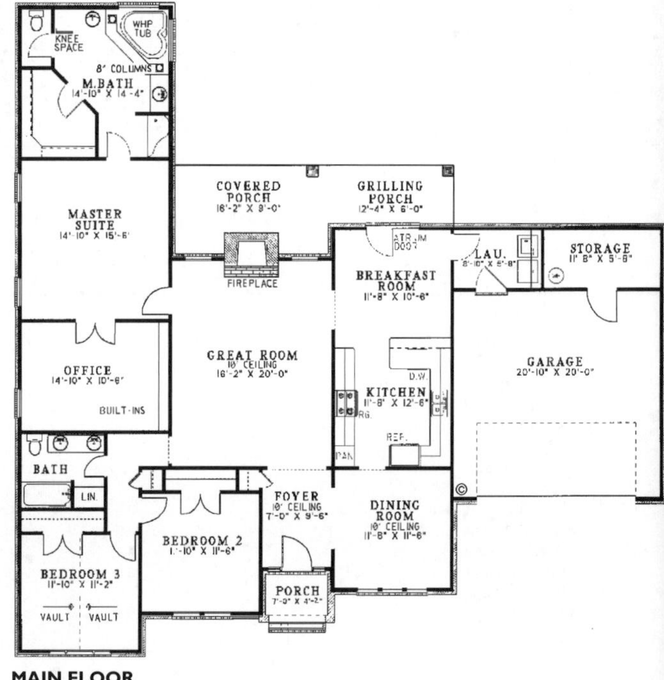
M.BATH
MASTER SUITE
COVERED PORCH
GRILLING PORCH
STORAGE
LAU.
BREAKFAST ROOM
FIREPLACE
GREAT ROOM
OFFICE
KITCHEN
GARAGE
BATH
FOYER
DINING ROOM
BEDROOM 2
BEDROOM 3
PORCH

MAIN FLOOR

Design 20230

Bedroom #2
10-11 x 13-0
(Open to Below)
1/2 Wall
Dn
Lin.
1/2 Hall
Bedroom #3
11-0 x 10-8
Bedroom #4
10-5 x 11-4
SECOND FLOOR

Units	Single
Price Code	C
Total Finished	1,995 sq. ft.
First Finished	1,365 sq. ft.
Second Finished	630 sq. ft.
Basement Unfinished	1,419 sq. ft.
Garage Unfinished	426 sq. ft.
Porch Unfinished	89 sq. ft.
Dimensions	44'x54'
Foundation	Basement Crawlspace Slab
Bedrooms	4
Full Baths	2
Half Baths	1
First Ceiling	9'
Second Ceiling	8'
Max Ridge Height	25'6"
Roof Framing	Truss
Exterior Walls	2x4

SLAB/CRAWLSPACE

OPTIONAL CRAWLSPACE/SLAB FOUNDATION

Nook
10-11 x 10-0
Great Room
18-6 x 15-6
(Open to Above)
Master Bedroom
13-5 x 13-0
Kitchen
10-11 x 15-11
Up
Dn
M. Bath
Dining Room
10-11 x 12-0
Covered Porch
Garage
19-5 x 21-11

FIRST FLOOR

Design 65234

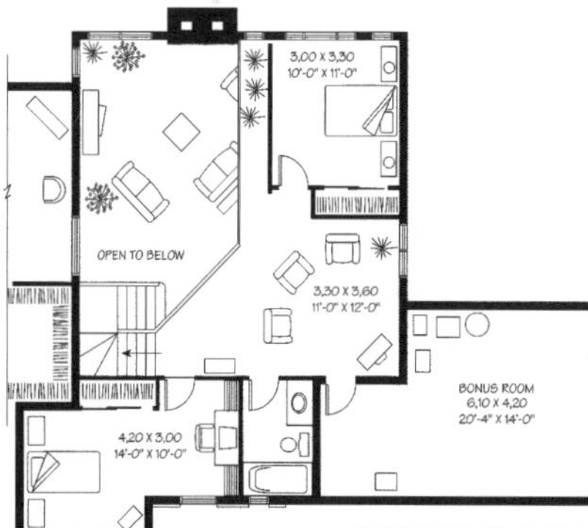

3,00 X 3,30
10'-0" X 11'-0"
OPEN TO BELOW
3,30 X 3,60
11'-0" X 12'-0"
BONUS ROOM
6,10 X 4,20
20'-4" X 14'-0"
4,20 X 3,00
14'-0" X 10'-0"

SECOND FLOOR

Units	Single
Price Code	E
Total Finished	1,995 sq. ft.
First Finished	1,525 sq. ft.
Second Finished	470 sq. ft.
Basement Unfinished	1,525 sq. ft.
Garage Unfinished	596 sq. ft.
Dimensions	56'x53'2"
Foundation	Basement
Bedrooms	3
Full Baths	2
Half Baths	1
First Ceiling	9'
Second Ceiling	8'
Max Ridge Height	29'9"
Roof Framing	Truss
Exterior Walls	2x6

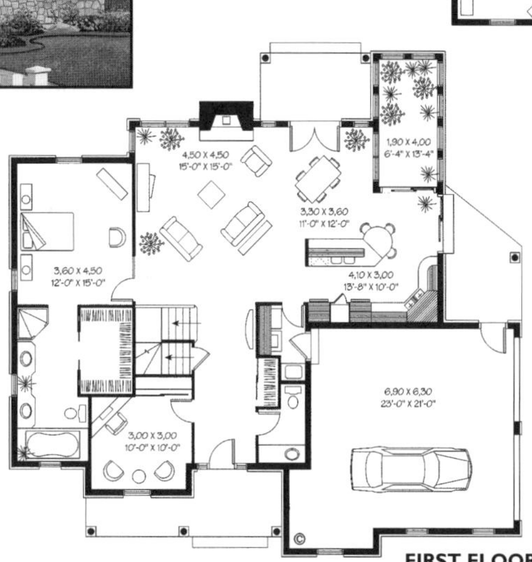

4,50 X 4,50
15'-0" X 15'-0"
1,90 X 4,00
6'-4" X 13'-4"
3,30 X 3,60
11'-0" X 12'-0"
3,60 X 4,50
12'-0" X 15'-0"
4,10 X 3,00
13'-8" X 10'-0"
6,90 X 6,30
23'-0" X 21'-0"
3,00 X 3,00
10'-0" X 10'-0"

FIRST FLOOR

Design 69127

Units	Single
Price Code	C
Total Finished	1,995 sq. ft.
First Finished	1,007 sq. ft.
Second Finished	988 sq. ft.
Garage Unfinished	493 sq. ft.
Dimensions	56'x44'8"
Foundation	Crawlspace
Bedrooms	3
Full Baths	2
Half Baths	1
First Ceiling	8'
Max Ridge Height	24'
Roof Framing	Truss
Exterior Walls	2x6

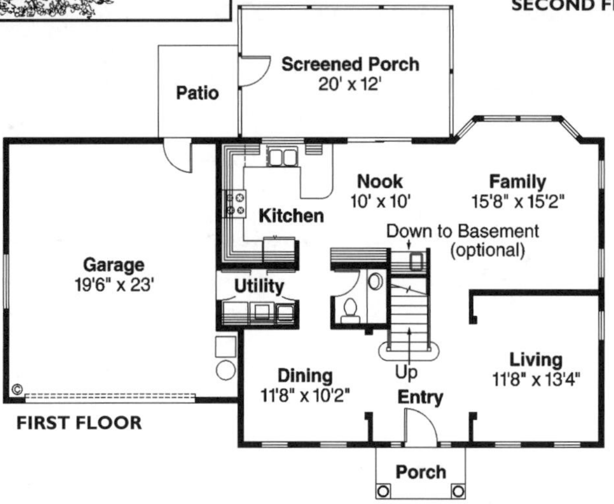

Bedroom
10' x 13'
Dn
Bedroom
13'4" x 11'
Master Suite
19'4" x 15'
Sitting
Balcony
SECOND FLOOR

Patio
Screened Porch
20' x 12'
Garage
19'6" x 23'
Kitchen
Nook
10' x 10'
Family
15'8" x 15'2"
Down to Basement
(optional)
Utility
Dining
11'8" x 10'2"
Up
Entry
Living
11'8" x 13'4"
Porch
FIRST FLOOR

Design 91125

Units	Single
Price Code	C
Total Finished	1,995 sq. ft.
Main Finished	1,995 sq. ft.
Garage Unfinished	469 sq. ft.
Porch Unfinished	24 sq. ft.
Dimensions	43'x67'8"
Foundation	Slab
Bedrooms	3
Full Baths	2
Max Ridge Height	20'9"
Roof Framing	Stick
Exterior Walls	2x4

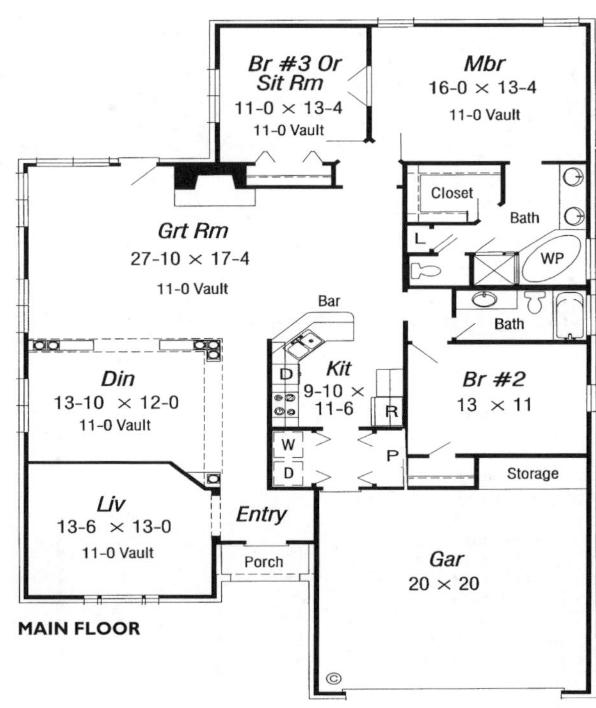
Br #3 Or
Sit Rm
11-0 × 13-4
11-0 Vault
Mbr
16-0 × 13-4
11-0 Vault
Closet
Bath
WP
Grt Rm
27-10 × 17-4
11-0 Vault
Bar
Bath
Din
13-10 × 12-0
11-0 Vault
Kit
9-10 ×
11-6
Br #2
13 × 11
Storage
Liv
13-6 × 13-0
11-0 Vault
Entry
Porch
Gar
20 × 20
MAIN FLOOR

Design 97912

Units	Single
Price Code	C
Total Finished	1,995 sq. ft.
Main Finished	1,995 sq. ft.
Bonus Unfinished	308 sq. ft.
Basement Unfinished	1,995 sq. ft.
Dimensions	56'x62'
Foundation	Basement
Bedrooms	3
Full Baths	2
Main Ceiling	9'
Max Ridge Height	26'
Roof framing	Stick/Truss
Exterior Walls	2x4

* Alternate foundation options available at an additional charge. Please call 1-800-235-5700 for more information.

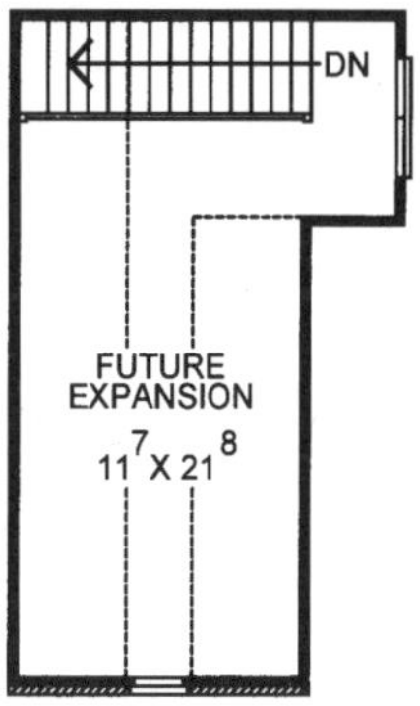

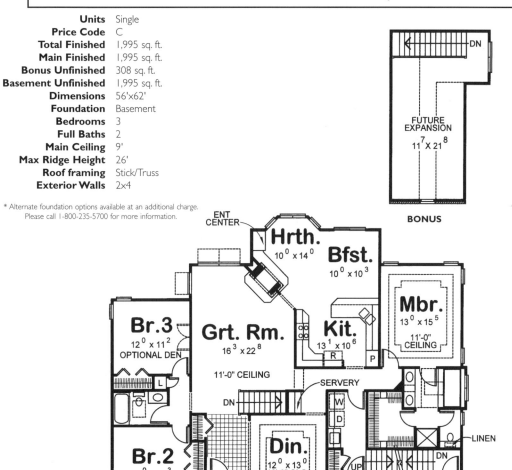

DN
FUTURE EXPANSION
11^{7} X 21^{8}

BONUS

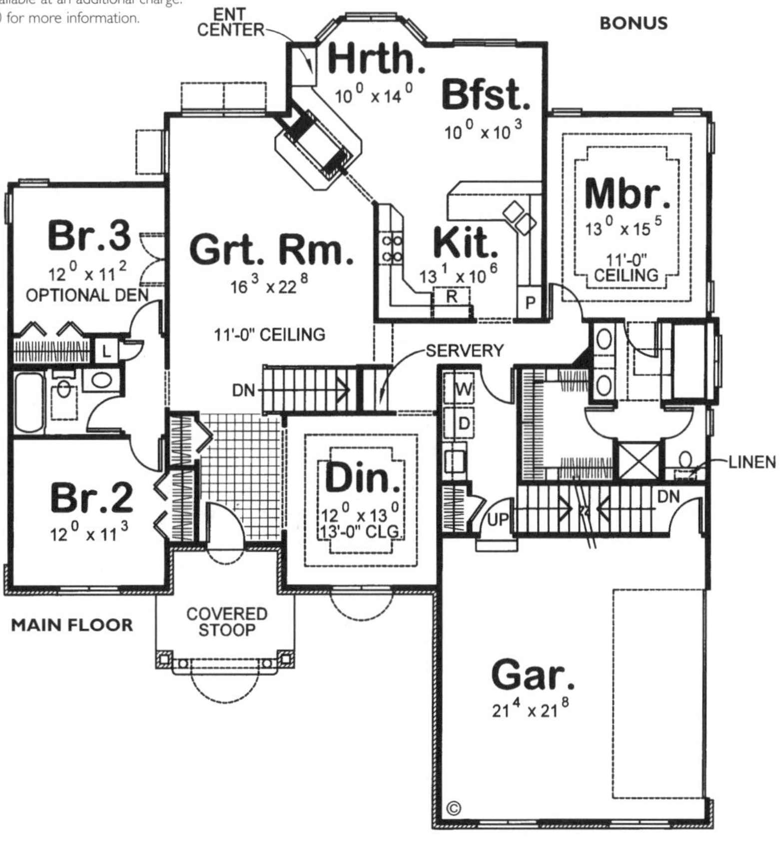

ENT CENTER
Hrth. 10^{0} x 14^{0}
Bfst. 10^{0} x 10^{3}
Mbr. 13^{0} x 15^{5} 11'-0" CEILING
Br.3 12^{0} x 11^{2} OPTIONAL DEN
Grt. Rm. 16^{3} x 22^{8} 11'-0" CEILING
Kit. 13^{1} x 10^{6}
R
P
L
SERVERY
W
D
DN
LINEN
DN
UP
Br.2 12^{0} x 11^{3}
Din. 12^{0} x 13^{0} 13'-0" CLG.
Gar. 21^{4} x 21^{8}
©
COVERED STOOP

MAIN FLOOR

Design 94926

Units	Single
Price Code	C
Total Finished	1,996 sq. ft.
Main Finished	1,996 sq. ft.
Garage Unfinished	683 sq. ft.
Dimensions	64'x50'
Foundation	Basement
Bedrooms	3
Full Baths	2
Main Ceiling	10'
Max Ridge Height	21'9"
Roof Framing	Stick
Exterior Walls	2x4

* Alternate foundation options available at an additional charge. Please call 1-800-235-5700 for more information.

TRANSOMS
Bfst. 13^8 x 12^0
10'-0" CEILING
SNACK BAR
DESK
Grt. rm. 16^7 x 18^9
10'-0" CEILING
BOOKS
Mbr. 15^2 x 13^6
10'-0" CEILING
TANDEM DRIVE-THRU
Kit. 13^8 x 9^10
R.
P.
DN
L.
D. W.
LAUNDRY
9'-0" CLG.
12'-0" CLG.
W/P
SKYLIGHT
HUTCH
Din. 12^0 x 13^0
11'-0" CEILING
E.
Gar. 20^0 x 42^0
OPT. BEDROOM
Liv. rm. 13^4 x 13^8
10'-0" CEILING
Br. 11^8 x 12^0
CVRD. STOOP

MAIN FLOOR

Design 63049

Units	Single
Price Code	C
Total Finished	1,997 sq. ft.
Main Finished	1,997 sq. ft.
Bonus Unfinished	310 sq. ft.
Garage Unfinished	502 sq. ft.
Dimensions	64'x57'
Foundation	Basement
Bedrooms	2
Full Baths	2
Half Baths	1
Main Ceiling	10'
Max Ridge Height	23'
Roof Framing	Truss
Exterior Walls	2x4

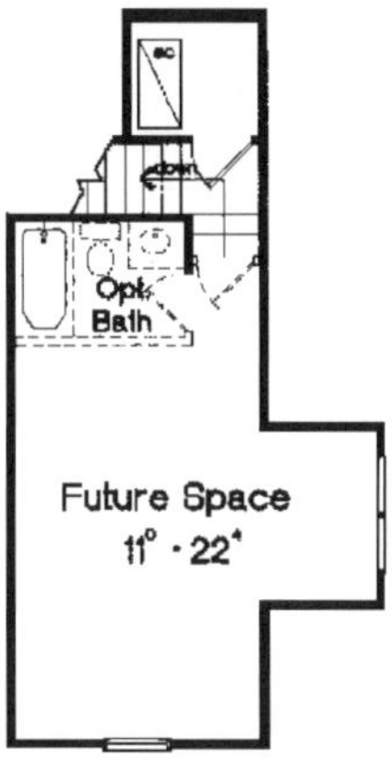

Opt. Bath
Future Space
11⁰ · 22⁴

BONUS

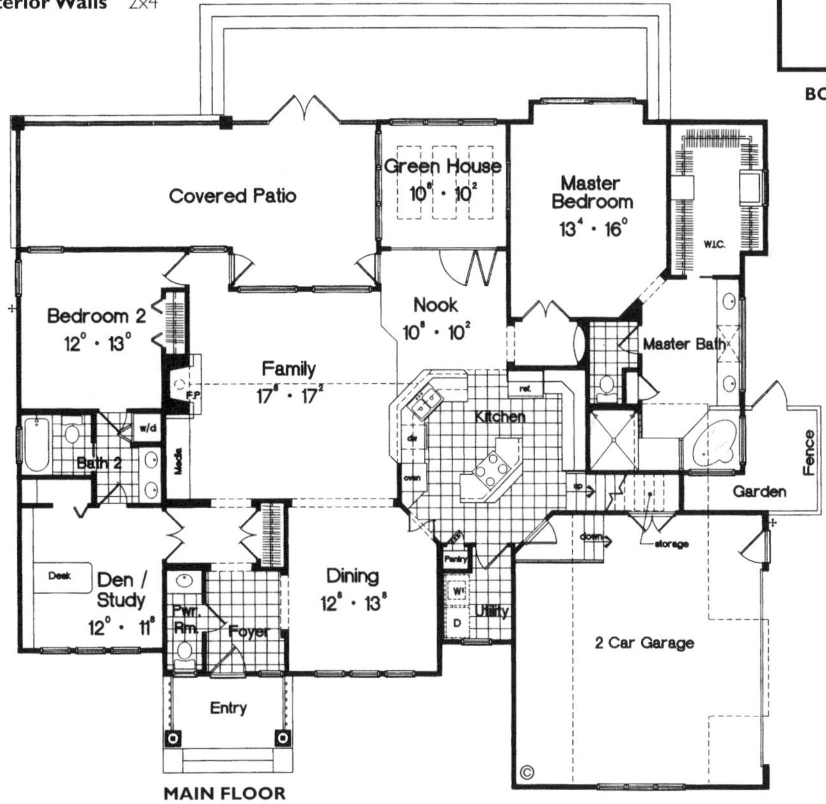

Covered Patio
Green House 10⁸ · 10²
Master Bedroom 13⁴ · 16⁰
W.I.C.
Bedroom 2 12⁰ · 13⁰
Nook 10⁸ · 10²
Family 17⁸ · 17²
Master Bath
Kitchen
Bath 2
Garden
Fence
Den / Study 12⁰ · 11⁸
Dining 12⁸ · 13⁸
Pwr. Rm.
Foyer
Utility
storage
2 Car Garage
Entry

MAIN FLOOR

Design 94904

PHOTOGRAPHY: COURTESY OF THE DESIGNER

Units	Single
Price Code	C
Total Finished	1,998 sq. ft.
First Finished	1,093 sq. ft.
Second Finished	905 sq. ft.
Basement Unfinished	1,093 sq. ft.
Garage Unfinished	527 sq. ft.
Dimensions	55'4"x37'8"
Foundation	Basement
Bedrooms	3
Full Baths	2
Half Baths	1
First Ceiling	8'
Second Ceiling	8'
Max Ridge Height	29'
Roof Framing	Stick
Exterior Walls	2x4

* Alternate foundation options available at an additional charge. Please call 1-800-235-5700 for more information.

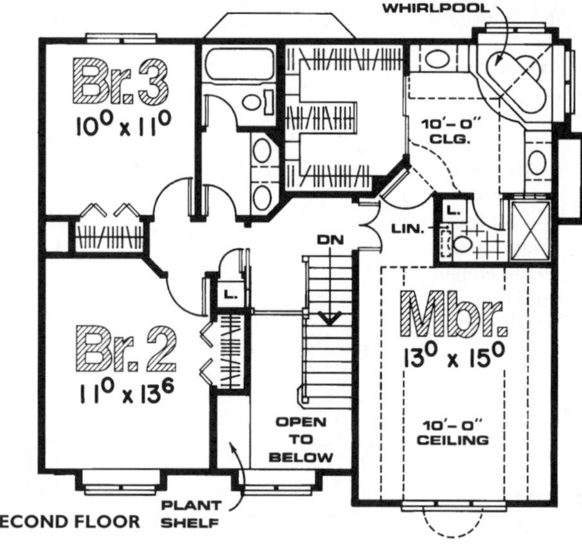
WHIRLPOOL
Br. 3
10⁰ x 11⁰
10'-0" CLG.
LIN.
L.
DN
Br. 2
11⁰ x 13⁶
Mbr.
13⁰ x 15⁰
OPEN TO BELOW
10'-0" CEILING
SECOND FLOOR
PLANT SHELF

Please note: The photographed home may have been modified to suit homeowner preferences. If you order plans, have a builder or design professional check them against the photograph to confirm actual construction details.

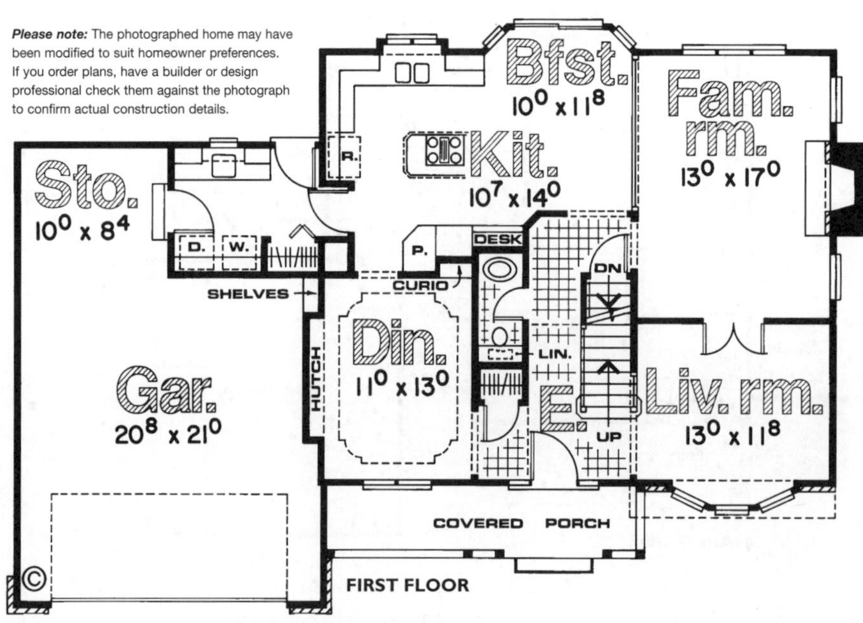
Bfst.
10⁰ x 11⁸
Fam. rm.
13⁰ x 17⁰
Sto.
10⁰ x 8⁴
R.
Kit.
10⁷ x 14⁰
D.
W.
P.
DESK
SHELVES
CURIO
DN
Din.
11⁰ x 13⁰
HUTCH
LIN.
Gar.
20⁸ x 21⁰
E.
UP
Liv. rm.
13⁰ x 11⁸
COVERED PORCH
FIRST FLOOR

Design 94900

Units	Single
Price Code	C
Total Finished	1,999 sq. ft.
First Finished	1,421 sq. ft.
Second Finished	578 sq. ft.
Basement Unfinished	1,421 sq. ft.
Garage Unfinished	480 sq. ft.
Dimensions	52'x47'4"
Foundation	Basement
Bedrooms	4
Full Baths	2
Half Baths	1
First Ceiling	8'
Max Ridge Height	28'3"
Roof Framing	Stick
Exterior Walls	2x4

* Alternate foundation options available at an additional charge. Please call 1-800-235-5700 for more information.

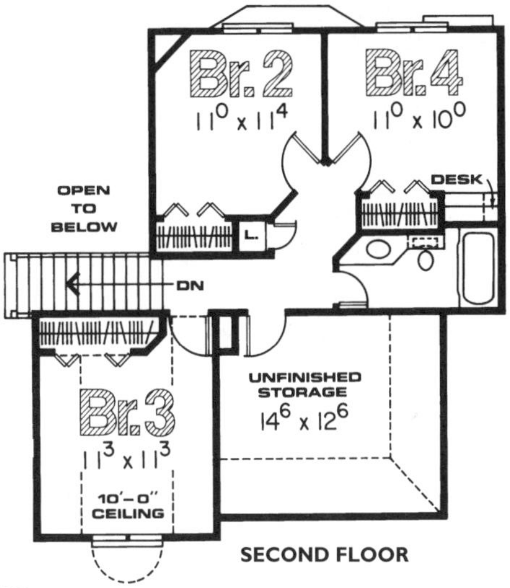

Br. 2 11⁰ x 11⁴ · Br. 4 11⁰ x 10⁰ · DESK · OPEN TO BELOW · L. · DN · Br. 3 11³ x 11³ · 10'-0" CEILING · UNFINISHED STORAGE 14⁶ x 12⁶

SECOND FLOOR

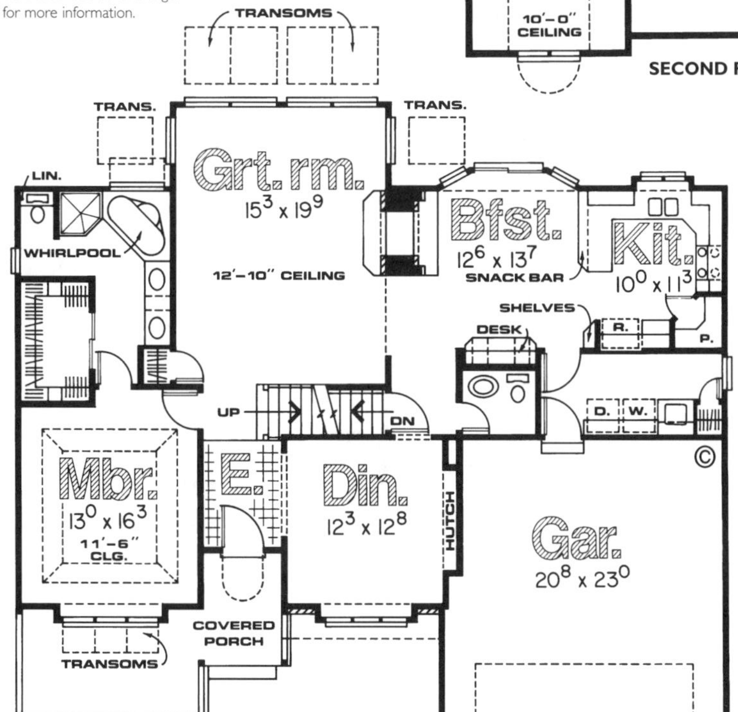

TRANSOMS · TRANS. · TRANS. · LIN. · WHIRLPOOL · Grt. rm. 15³ x 19⁹ · 12'-10" CEILING · Bfst. 12⁶ x 13⁷ · SNACK BAR · Kit. 10⁰ x 11³ · SHELVES · DESK · R. · P. · D. · W. · UP · DN · Mbr. 13⁰ x 16³ · 11'-6" CLG. · E. · Din. 12³ x 12⁸ · HUTCH · Gar. 20⁸ x 23⁰ · COVERED PORCH · TRANSOMS · BENCH · ©

FIRST FLOOR

Design 63055

Units	Single
Price Code	C
Total Finished	2,000 sq. ft.
First Finished	1,667 sq. ft.
Second Finished	333 sq. ft.
Garage Unfinished	777 sq. ft.
Dimensions	60'8"x70'4"
Foundation	Slab
Bedrooms	3
Full Baths	2
3/4 Baths	1
First Ceiling	8'
Max Ridge Height	26'6"
Roof Framing	Truss

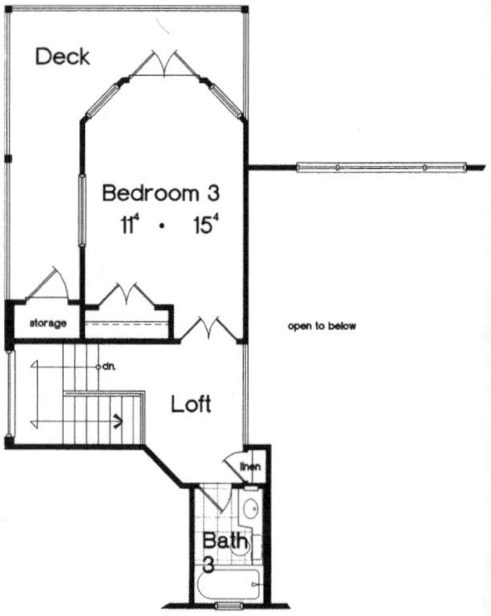

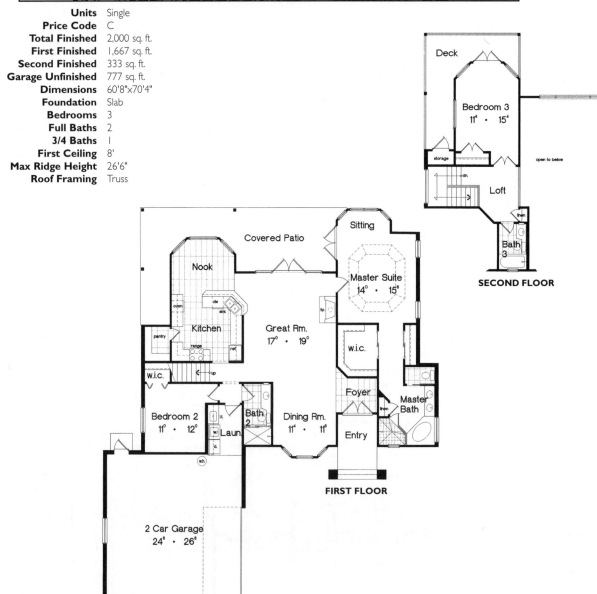

Deck
Bedroom 3
$11^{4} \cdot 15^{4}$
storage
open to below
dn.
Loft
linen
Bath 3

SECOND FLOOR

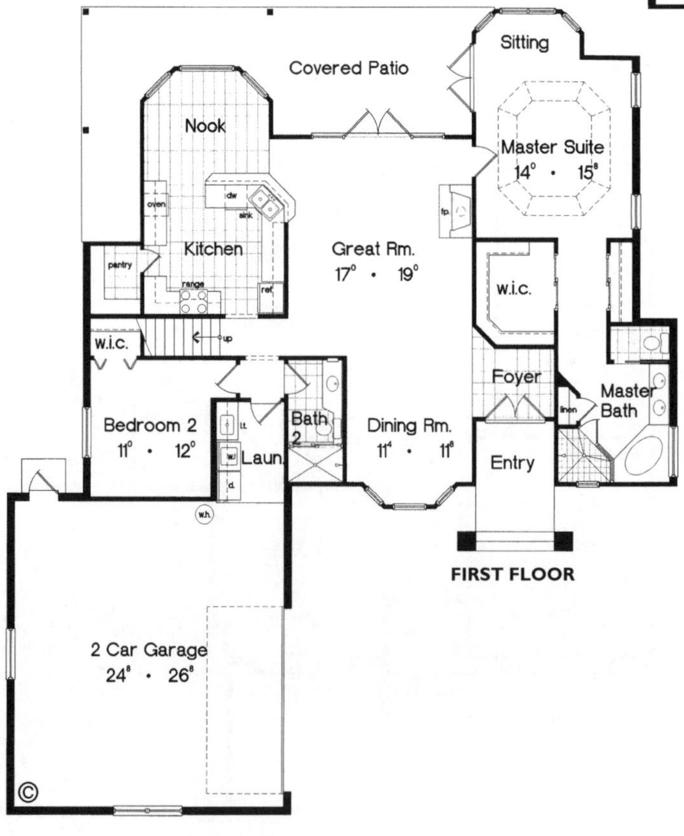

Covered Patio
Sitting
Nook
Master Suite
$14^{0} \cdot 15^{8}$
dw
sink
oven
fp.
Kitchen
Great Rm.
$17^{0} \cdot 19^{0}$
pantry
range
ref.
w.i.c.
W.i.C.
up
Foyer
Bedroom 2
$11^{0} \cdot 12^{0}$
lt.
Bath 2
Master Bath
linen
w.
Laun.
Dining Rm.
$11^{4} \cdot 11^{8}$
Entry
d.
w.h.

FIRST FLOOR

2 Car Garage
$24^{8} \cdot 26^{8}$
©

Design 65630

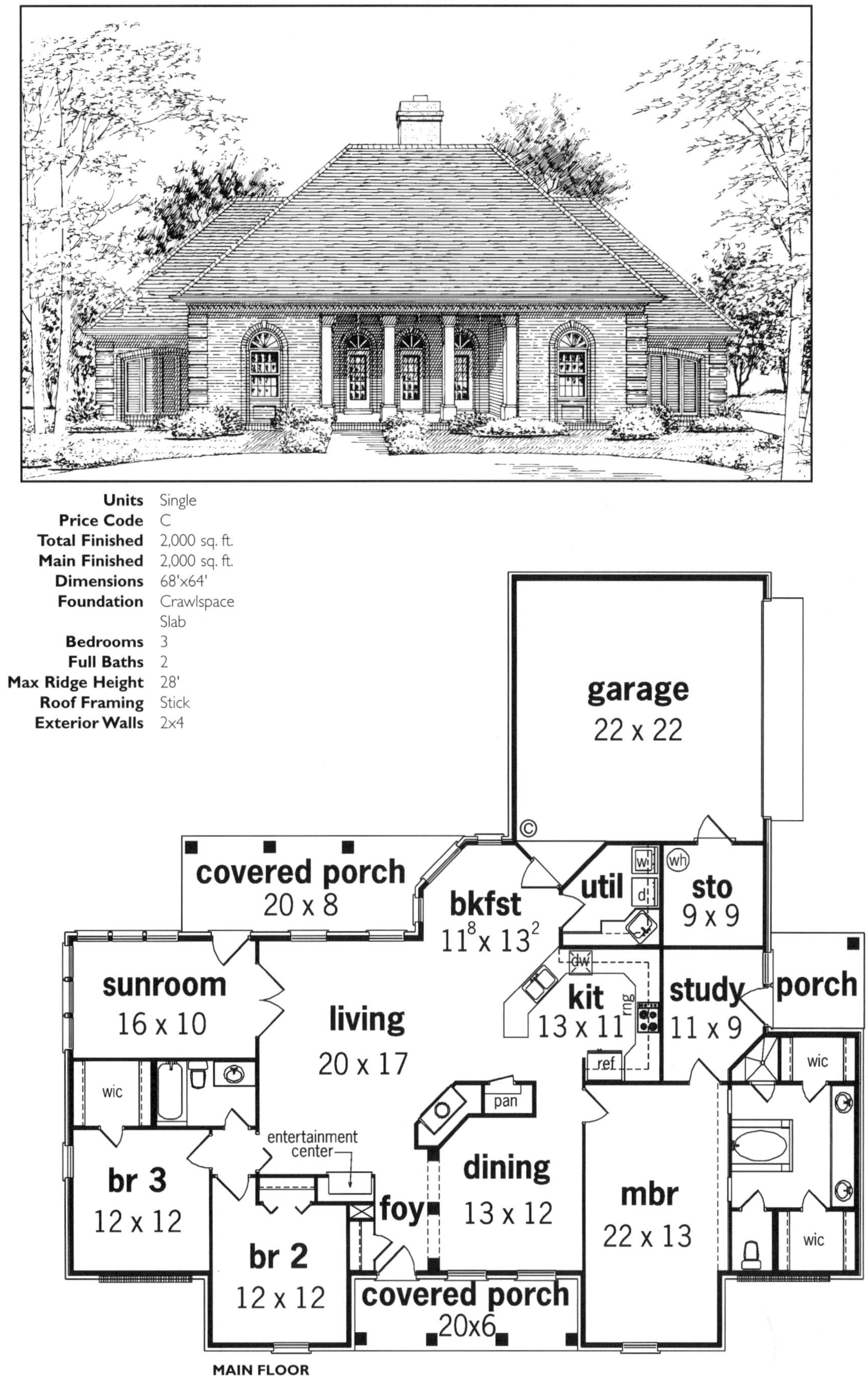

garage
22 x 22
covered porch
20 x 8
bkfst
11⁸ x 13²
util
w
d
wh
sto
9 x 9
sunroom
16 x 10
living
20 x 17
dw
kit
13 x 11
rng
ref
study
11 x 9
porch
wic
pan
entertainment center
br 3
12 x 12
dining
13 x 12
foy
mbr
22 x 13
br 2
12 x 12
covered porch
20x6
MAIN FLOOR

Units	Single
Price Code	C
Total Finished	2,000 sq. ft.
Main Finished	2,000 sq. ft.
Dimensions	68'x64'
Foundation	Crawlspace Slab
Bedrooms	3
Full Baths	2
Max Ridge Height	28'
Roof Framing	Stick
Exterior Walls	2x4

Design 86019

Units	Single
Price Code	D
Total Finished	2,001 sq. ft.
Main Finished	2,001 sq. ft.
Basement Unfinished	979 sq. ft.
Garage Unfinished	455 sq. ft.
Deck Unfinished	220 sq. ft.
Porch Unfinished	21 sq. ft.
Dimensions	39'6"x84'10"
Bedrooms	3
Full Baths	2
Main Ceiling	8'
Max Ridge Height	27'7"
Roof Framing	Stick
Exterior Walls	2x4

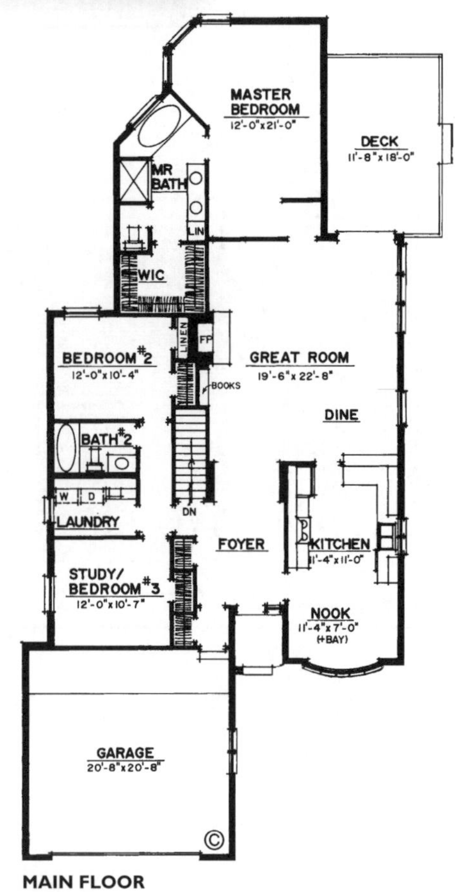
MASTER BEDROOM
12'-0"x21'-0"
DECK
11'-8"x18'-0"
MR BATH
LIN
WIC
LINEN
FP
BEDROOM #2
12'-0"x10'-4"
GREAT ROOM
19'-6"x22'-8"
BOOKS
DINE
BATH #2
W
D
LAUNDRY
DN
FOYER
KITCHEN
11'-4"x11'-0"
STUDY/
BEDROOM #3
12'-0"x10'-7"
NOOK
11'-4"x7'-0"
(+BAY)
GARAGE
20'-8"x20'-8"
©

MAIN FLOOR

Design 65626

Units	Single
Price Code	D
Total Finished	2,002 sq. ft.
Main Finished	2,002 sq. ft.
Dimensions	66'x60'
Foundation	Crawlspace Slab
Bedrooms	3
Full Baths	2
Main Ceiling	8'
Max Ridge Height	29'
Roof Framing	Stick
Exterior Walls	2x6

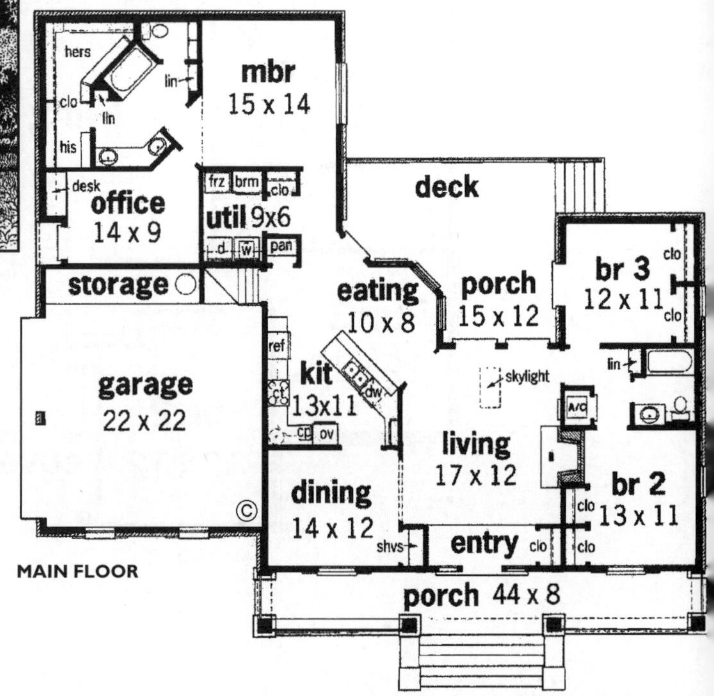
hers
lin
clo
fln
his
mbr
15 x 14
desk
office
14 x 9
frz
brm
clo
util 9x6
d
w
pan
deck
storage
eating
10 x 8
porch
15 x 12
br 3
12 x 11
clo
clo
lin
ref
kit
13x11
dw
skylight
A/C
garage
22 x 22
cp
ov
living
17 x 12
br 2
13 x 11
dining
14 x 12
clo
clo
shvs
entry
clo
porch 44 x 8
©

MAIN FLOOR

Design 63125

Units	Single
Price Code	D
Total Finished	2,005 sq. ft.
Main Finished	2,005 sq. ft.
Garage Unfinished	466 sq. ft.
Dimensions	58'x60'
Foundation	Slab
Bedrooms	3
Full Baths	2
Main Ceiling	10'
Max Ridge Height	20'10"
Roof Framing	Truss

Covered Patio
Master Bedroom
volume ceiling
16⁰ · 12⁰
Bedroom 2
volume ceiling
13¹⁰ · 12⁰
Breakfast
Great Room
vaulted ceiling
20⁰ · 18⁰
vaulted ceiling
Bath
w.i.c.
Bath
Kitchen
Bedroom 3
volume ceiling
12⁰ · 11⁶
opt. fireplace
Living Room
volume ceiling
15⁰ · 12⁰
Foyer
Dining
vaulted ceiling
12⁴ · 12⁰
Utility
Entry
Double Garage
MAIN FLOOR

Design 92445

Units	Single
Price Code	D
Total Finished	2,006 sq. ft.
Main Finished	2,006 sq. ft.
Dimensions	66'x54'
Foundation	Basement Slab
Bedrooms	3
Full Baths	2
Main Ceiling	9'
Roof Framing	Stick
Exterior Walls	2x4

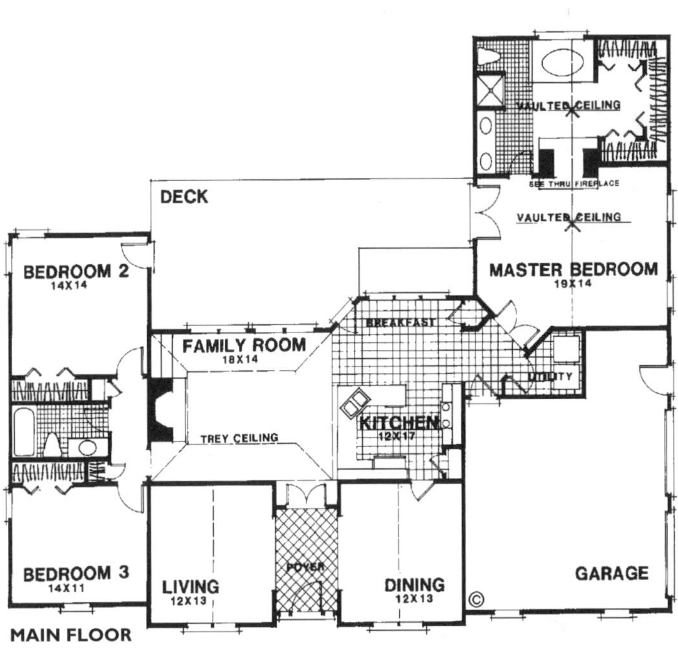
VAULTED CEILING
SEE THRU FIREPLACE
VAULTED CEILING
DECK
MASTER BEDROOM
19X14
BEDROOM 2
14X14
BREAKFAST
FAMILY ROOM
18X14
UTILITY
KITCHEN
12X17
TREY CEILING
FOYER
BEDROOM 3
14X11
LIVING
12X13
DINING
12X13
GARAGE
MAIN FLOOR

Design 98594

Units	Single
Price Code	D
Total Finished	2,006 sq. ft.
Main Finished	2,006 sq. ft.
Garage Unfinished	651 sq. ft.
Deck Unfinished	220 sq. ft.
Porch Unfinished	240 sq. ft.
Dimensions	72'x41'4"
Foundation	Crawlspace Slab
Bedrooms	3
Full Baths	2
Half Baths	1
Max Ridge Height	26'6"
Roof Framing	Stick
Exterior Walls	2x4

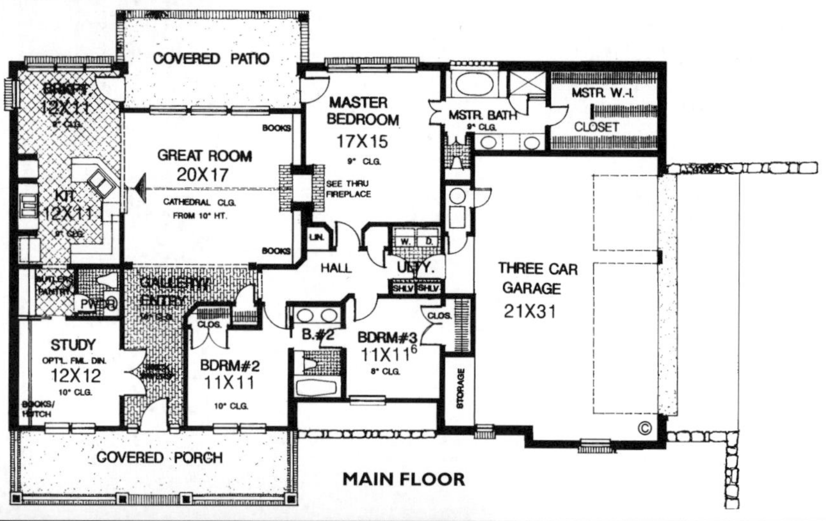
COVERED PATIO
BRKFT. 12X11
KIT. 12X11
GREAT ROOM 20X17
CATHEDRAL CLG. FROM 10" HT.
MASTER BEDROOM 17X15
9" CLG.
MSTR. BATH
MSTR. W.-I. CLOSET
SEE THRU FIREPLACE
HALL
UTLY.
THREE CAR GARAGE 21X31
GALLERY/ ENTRY
STUDY
OPT'L. FML. DIN.
12X12
10" CLG.
BDRM#2 11X11
10" CLG.
B.#2
BDRM#3 11X11
STORAGE
COVERED PORCH

MAIN FLOOR

Design 97151

Units	Single
Price Code	D
Total Finished	2,007 sq. ft.
Main Finished	2,007 sq. ft.
Deck Unfinished	144 sq. ft.
Dimensions	67'x53'
Foundation	Basement
Bedrooms	3
Full Baths	2
Max Ridge Height	24'
Roof Framing	Truss
Exterior Walls	2x6

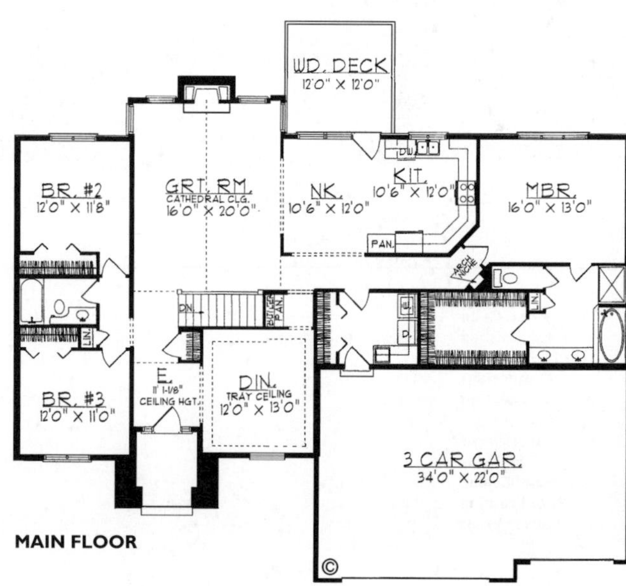
WD. DECK
12'0" X 12'0"
BR. #2
12'0" X 11'8"
GRT. RM.
CATHEDRAL CLG.
16'0" X 20'0"
NK.
10'6" X 12'0"
KIT.
10'6" X 12'0"
MBR.
16'0" X 13'0"
PAN.
BR. #3
12'0" X 11'0"
E.
11' 1-1/8" CEILING HGT.
DIN.
TRAY CEILING
12'0" X 13'0"
3 CAR GAR.
34'0" X 22'0"

MAIN FLOOR

Design 65423

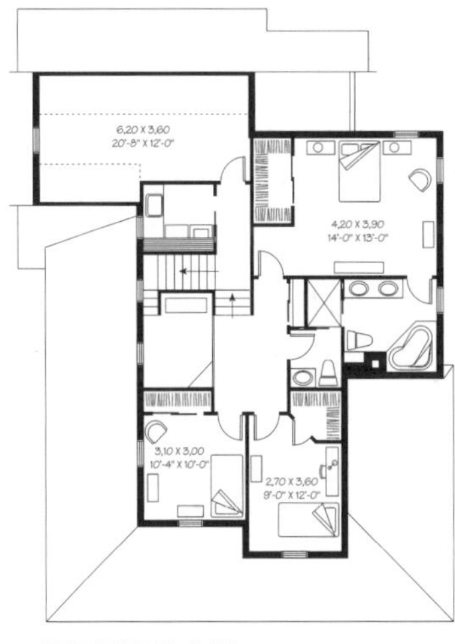

SECOND FLOOR

Units	Single
Price Code	D
Total Finished	2,008 sq. ft.
First Finished	1,080 sq. ft.
Second Finished	928 sq. ft.
Bonus Unfinished	249 sq. ft.
Basement Unfinished	1,080 sq. ft.
Garage Unfinished	468 sq. ft.
Porch Unfinished	457 sq. ft.
Dimensions	40'8"x51'
Foundation	Basement
Bedrooms	3
Full Baths	1
3/4 Baths	1
Half Baths	1
First Ceiling	9'
Second Ceiling	8'
Max Ridge Height	32'2"
Roof Framing	Truss
Exterior Walls	2x6

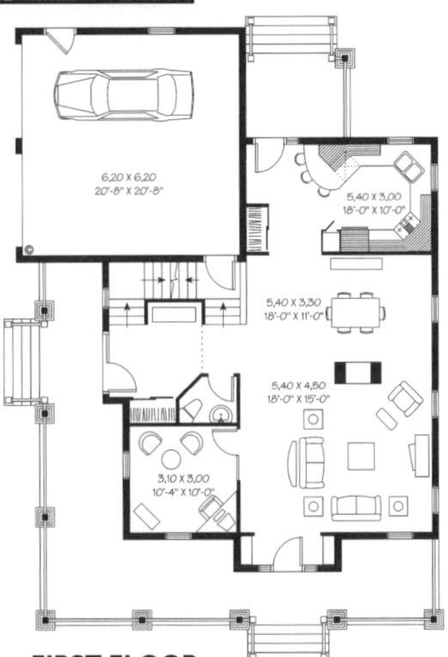

FIRST FLOOR

Design 65125

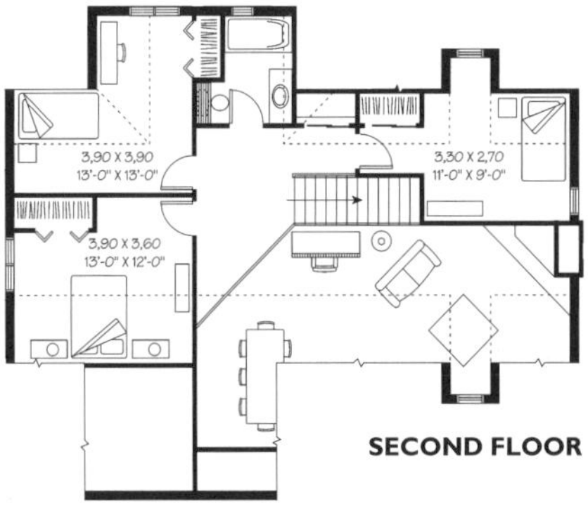

SECOND FLOOR

Units	Single
Price Code	D
Total Finished	2,012 sq. ft.
First Finished	1,324 sq. ft.
Second Finished	688 sq. ft.
Basement Unfinished	1,324 sq. ft.
Garage Unfinished	425 sq. ft.
Dimensions	56'x41'
Foundation	Basement
Bedrooms	4
Full Baths	2
First Ceiling	8'
Second Ceiling	8'
Max Ridge Height	25'
Roof Framing	Truss
Exterior Walls	2x6

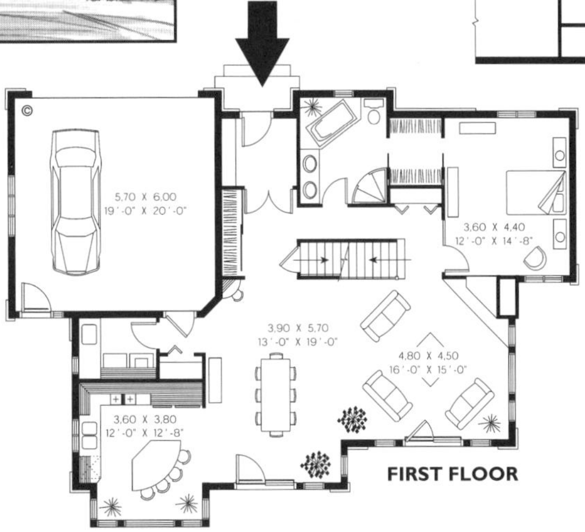

FIRST FLOOR

Design 91174

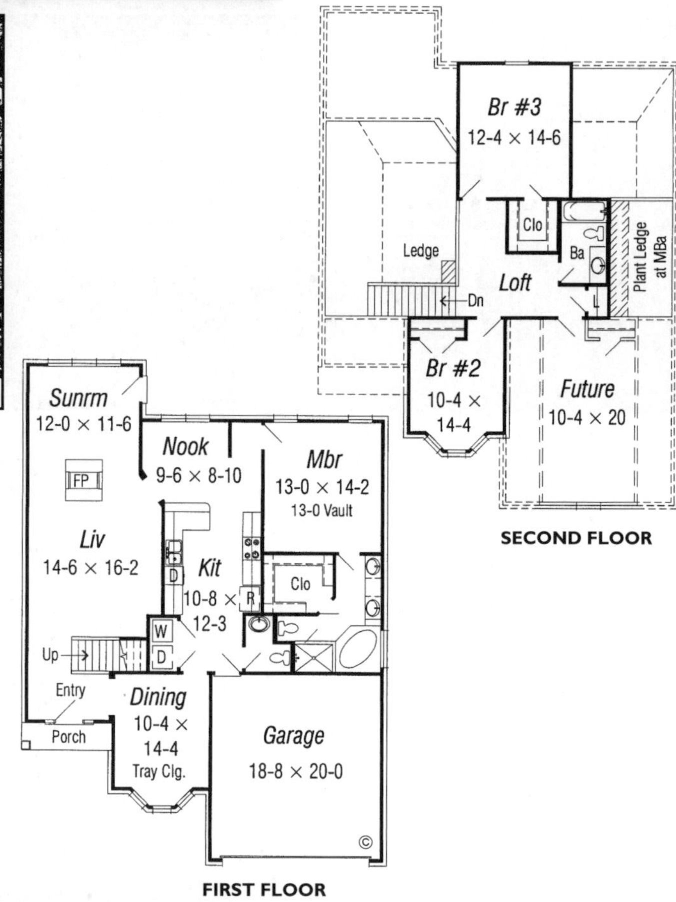
Br #3
12-4 × 14-6
Clo
Ba
Plant Ledge at MBa
Ledge
Loft
Dn
Br #2
10-4 × 14-4
Future
10-4 × 20
SECOND FLOOR
Sunrm
12-0 × 11-6
FP
Nook
9-6 × 8-10
Mbr
13-0 × 14-2
13-0 Vault
Liv
14-6 × 16-2
Kit
10-8 × 12-3
Clo
D
R
W
D
Up
Entry
Dining
10-4 × 14-4
Tray Clg.
Porch
Garage
18-8 × 20-0
FIRST FLOOR

Units	Single
Price Code	D
Total Finished	2,012 sq. ft.
First Finished	1,427 sq. ft.
Second Finished	585 sq. ft.
Bonus Unfinished	228 sq. ft.
Garage Unfinished	407 sq. ft.
Porch Unfinished	30 sq. ft.
Dimensions	40'3½"x54'1½"
Foundation	Slab
Bedrooms	3
Full Baths	2
Half Baths	1
First Ceiling	8'1⅛"
Second Ceiling	8' 1⅛"
Max Ridge Height	26'
Roof Framing	Stick
Exterior Walls	2x4

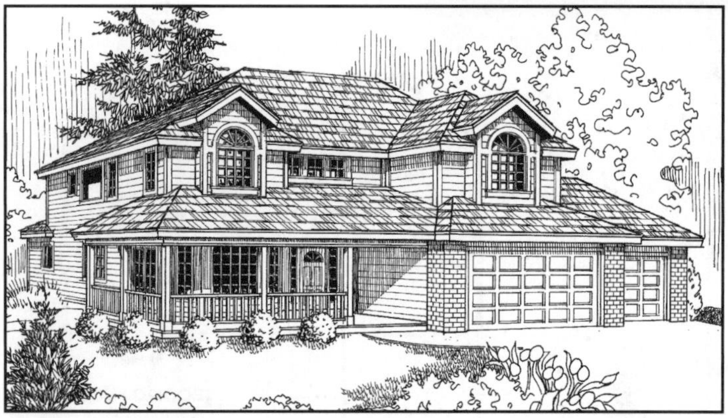

Design 69148

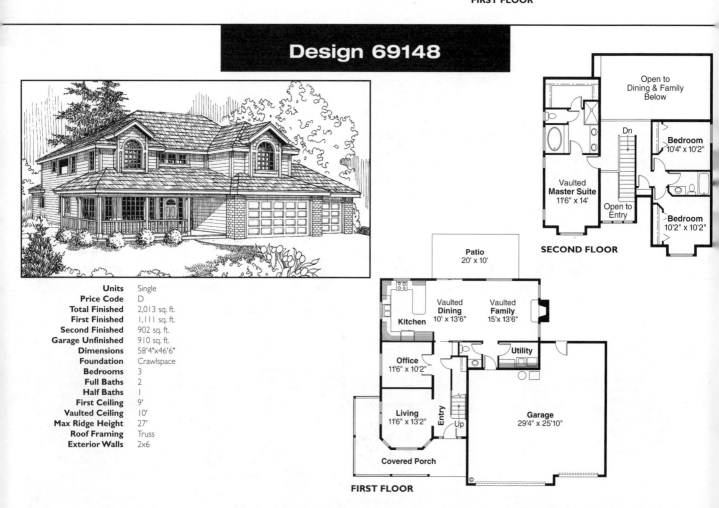

Units	Single
Price Code	D
Total Finished	2,013 sq. ft.
First Finished	1,111 sq. ft.
Second Finished	902 sq. ft.
Garage Unfinished	910 sq. ft.
Dimensions	58'4"x46'6"
Foundation	Crawlspace
Bedrooms	3
Full Baths	2
Half Baths	1
First Ceiling	9'
Vaulted Ceiling	10'
Max Ridge Height	27'
Roof Framing	Truss
Exterior Walls	2x6

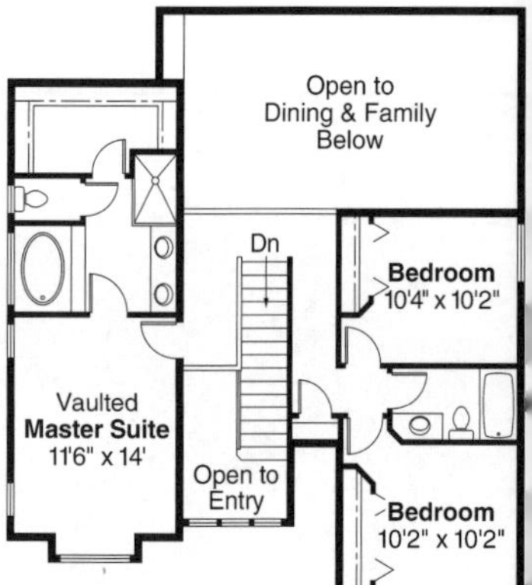

SECOND FLOOR

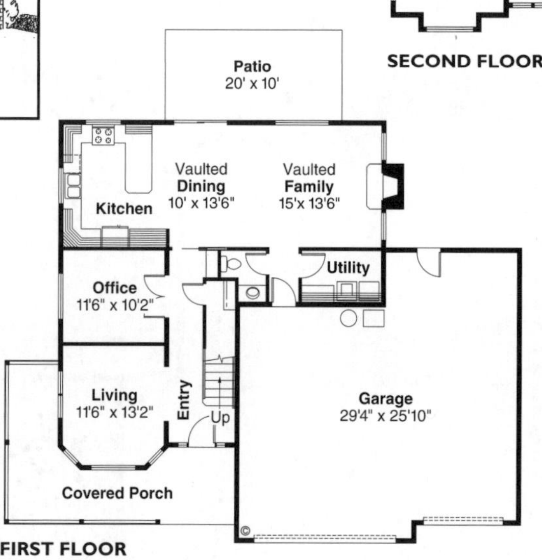

FIRST FLOOR

Design 10515

PHOTOGRAPHY: JOHN EHRENCLOU

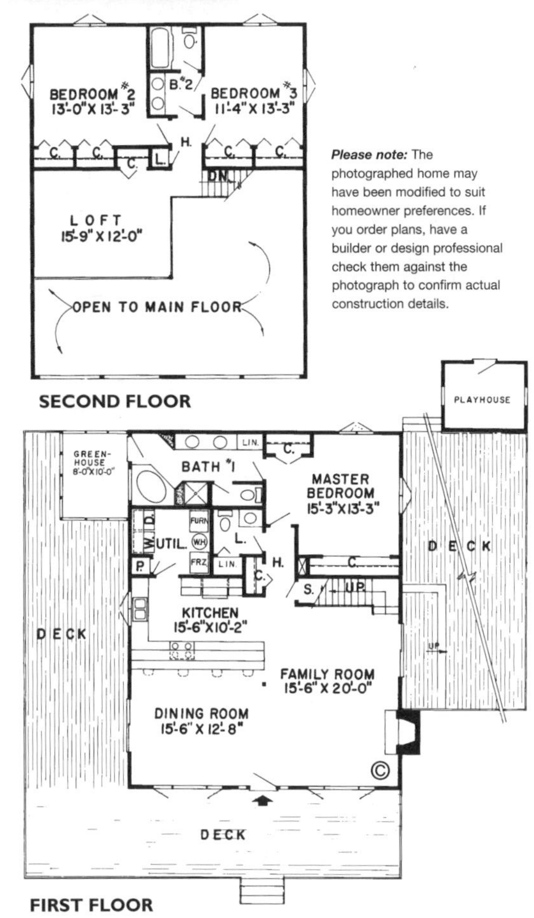
BEDROOM #2
13'-0" X 13'-3"
B.#2
BEDROOM #3
11'-4" X 13'-3"
LOFT
15'-9" X 12'-0"
OPEN TO MAIN FLOOR
SECOND FLOOR
PLAYHOUSE
GREEN-HOUSE
8'-0"X10'-0"
BATH #1
MASTER BEDROOM
15'-3"X13'-3"
UTIL.
KITCHEN
15'-6"X10'-2"
FAMILY ROOM
15'-6" X 20'-0"
DINING ROOM
15'-6" X 12'-8"
DECK
FIRST FLOOR

Please note: The photographed home may have been modified to suit homeowner preferences. If you order plans, have a builder or design professional check them against the photograph to confirm actual construction details.

Units	Single
Price Code	D
Total Finished	2,015 sq. ft.
First Finished	1,280 sq. ft.
Second Finished	735 sq. ft.
Porch Unfinished	80 sq. ft.
Dimensions	32'x40'
Foundation	Crawlspace
Bedrooms	3
Full Baths	2
Half Baths	1
First Ceiling	8'
Second Ceiling	8'
Max Ridge Height	32'
Roof Framing	Stick
Exterior Walls	2x6

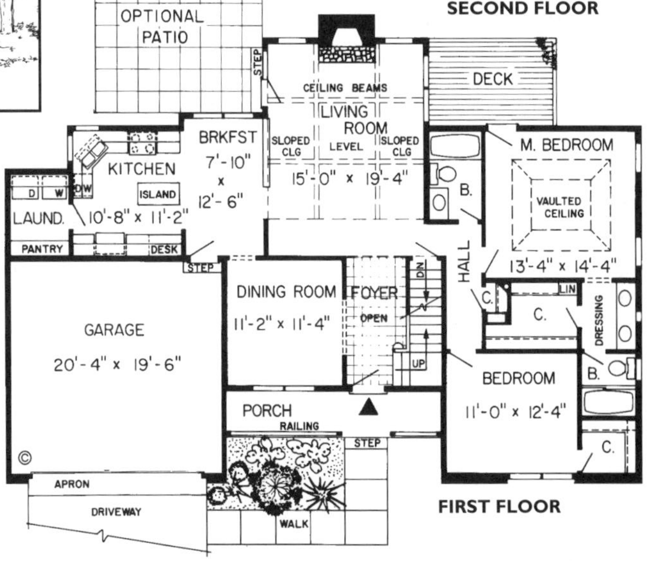

Design 34049

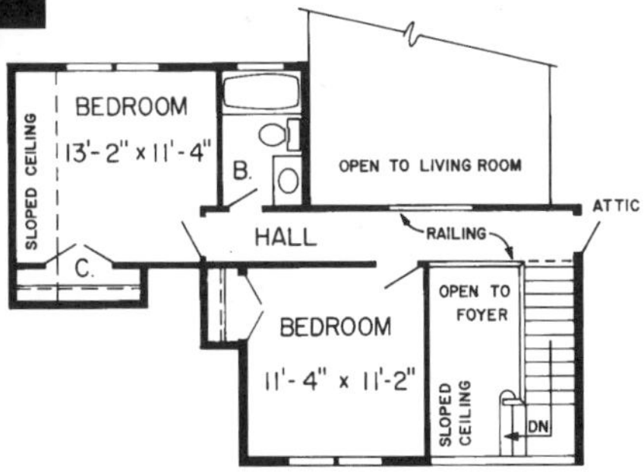

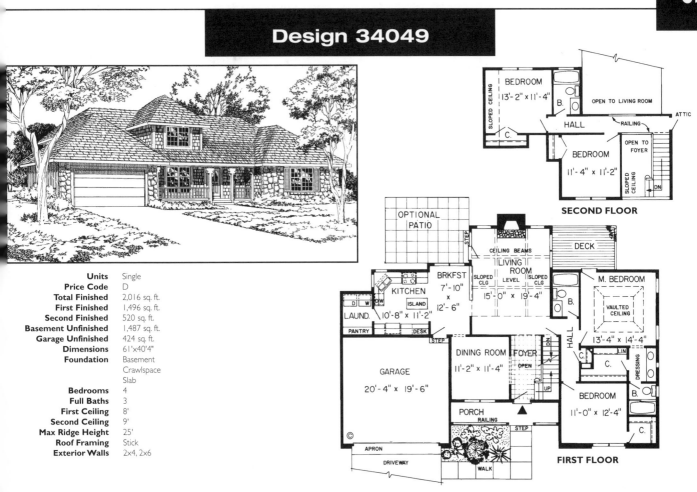

Units	Single
Price Code	D
Total Finished	2,016 sq. ft.
First Finished	1,496 sq. ft.
Second Finished	520 sq. ft.
Basement Unfinished	1,487 sq. ft.
Garage Unfinished	424 sq. ft.
Dimensions	61'x40'4"
Foundation	Basement Crawlspace Slab
Bedrooms	4
Full Baths	3
First Ceiling	8'
Second Ceiling	9'
Max Ridge Height	25'
Roof Framing	Stick
Exterior Walls	2x4, 2x6

Design 92697

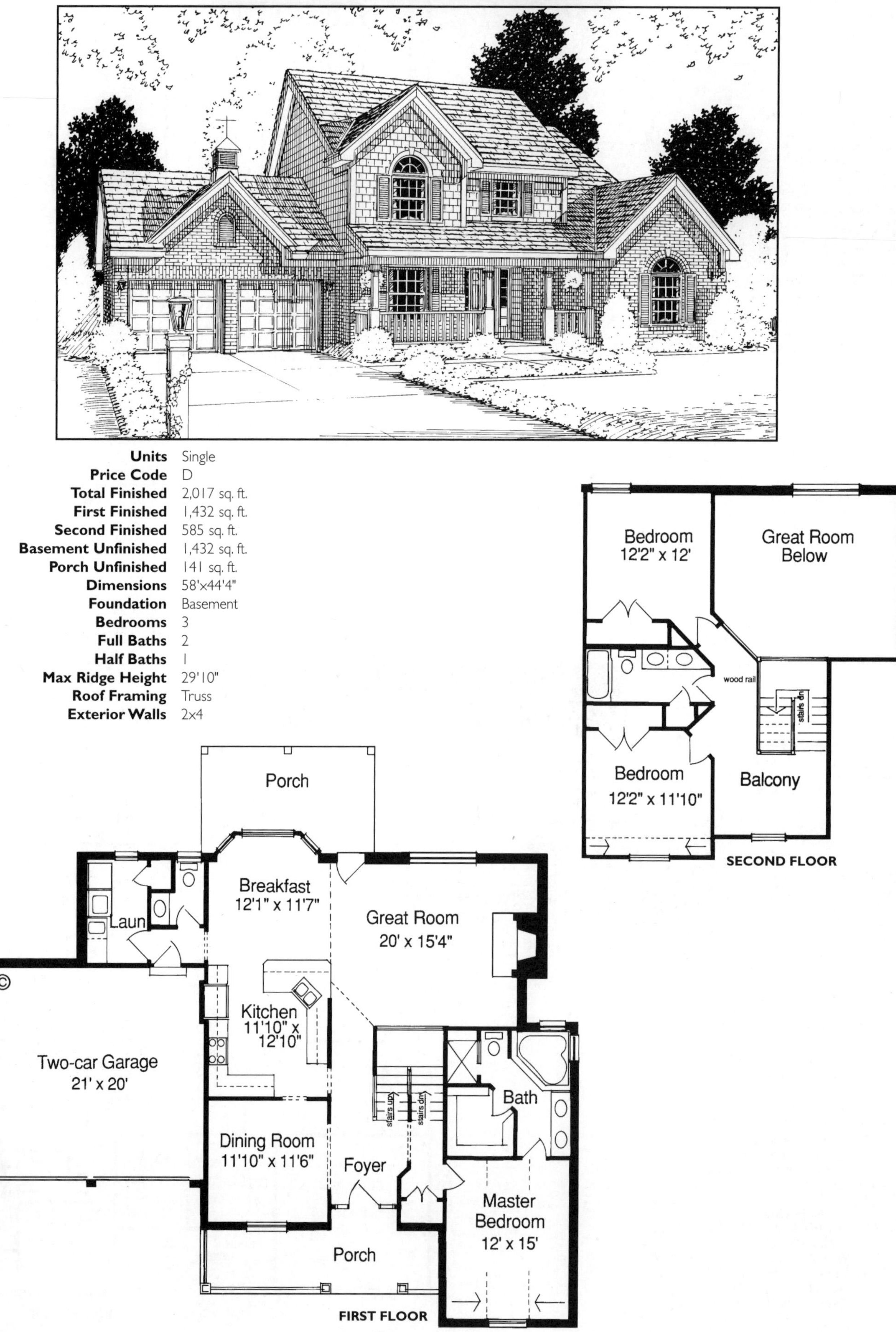

Porch
Breakfast
12'1" x 11'7"
Great Room
20' x 15'4"
Laun
©
Kitchen
11'10" x
12'10"
Two-car Garage
21' x 20'
stairs up
stairs dn
Bath
Dining Room
11'10" x 11'6"
Foyer
Master
Bedroom
12' x 15'
Porch
FIRST FLOOR
Bedroom
12'2" x 12'
Great Room
Below
wood rail
stairs dn
Bedroom
12'2" x 11'10"
Balcony
SECOND FLOOR

Units	Single
Price Code	D
Total Finished	2,017 sq. ft.
First Finished	1,432 sq. ft.
Second Finished	585 sq. ft.
Basement Unfinished	1,432 sq. ft.
Porch Unfinished	141 sq. ft.
Dimensions	58'x44'4"
Foundation	Basement
Bedrooms	3
Full Baths	2
Half Baths	1
Max Ridge Height	29'10"
Roof Framing	Truss
Exterior Walls	2x4

Design 97308

Units	Single
Price Code	D
Total Finished	2,017 sq. ft.
Main Finished	2,017 sq. ft.
Garage Unfinished	912 sq. ft.
Dimensions	81'x51'4"
Foundation	Basement
Bedrooms	3
Full Baths	2
Half Baths	1
Main Ceiling	9'1⅛"
Max Ridge Height	24'8"
Roof Framing	Truss
Exterior Walls	2x6

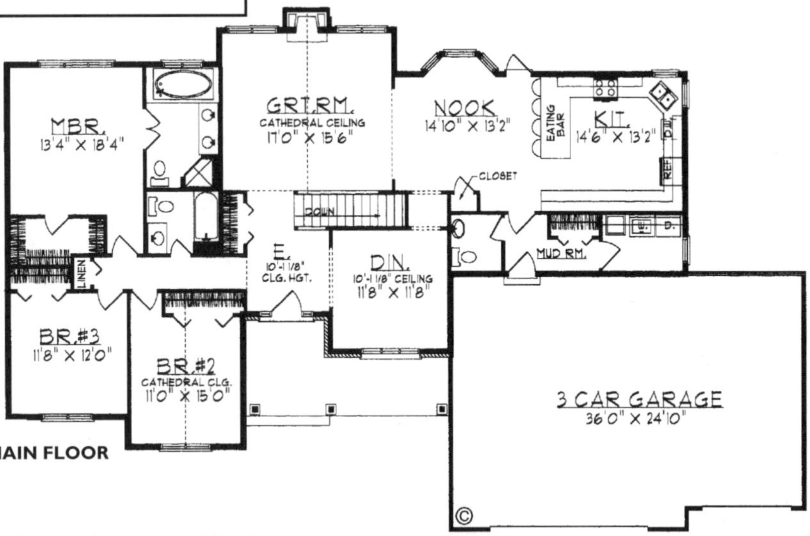

MAIN FLOOR

Design 98714

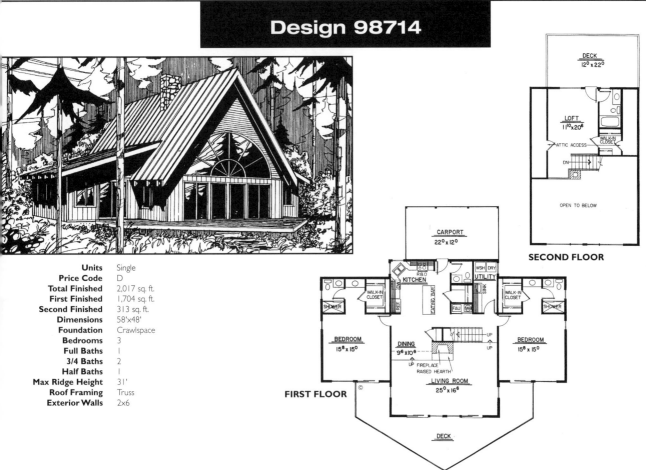

Units	Single
Price Code	D
Total Finished	2,017 sq. ft.
First Finished	1,704 sq. ft.
Second Finished	313 sq. ft.
Dimensions	58'x48'
Foundation	Crawlspace
Bedrooms	3
Full Baths	1
3/4 Baths	2
Half Baths	1
Max Ridge Height	31'
Roof Framing	Truss
Exterior Walls	2x6

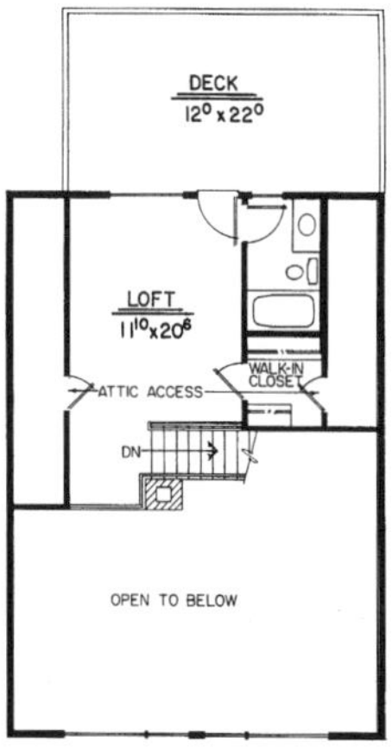

SECOND FLOOR

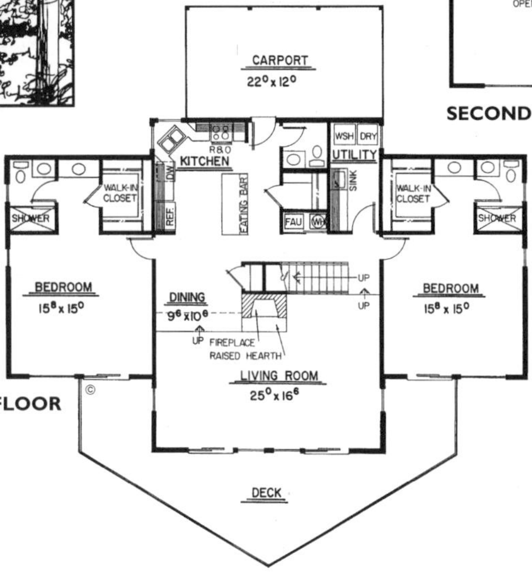

FIRST FLOOR

Design 92629

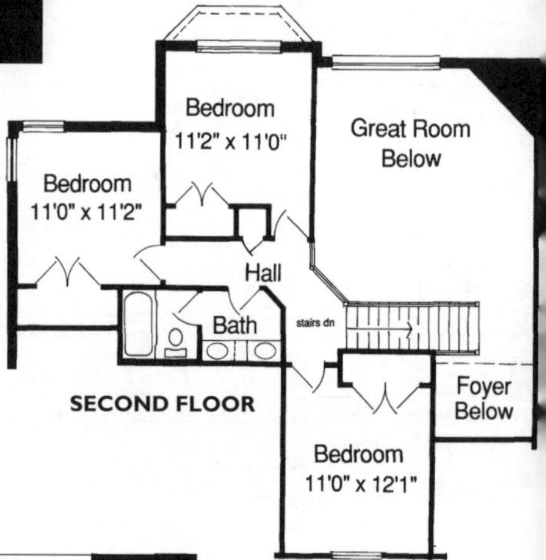

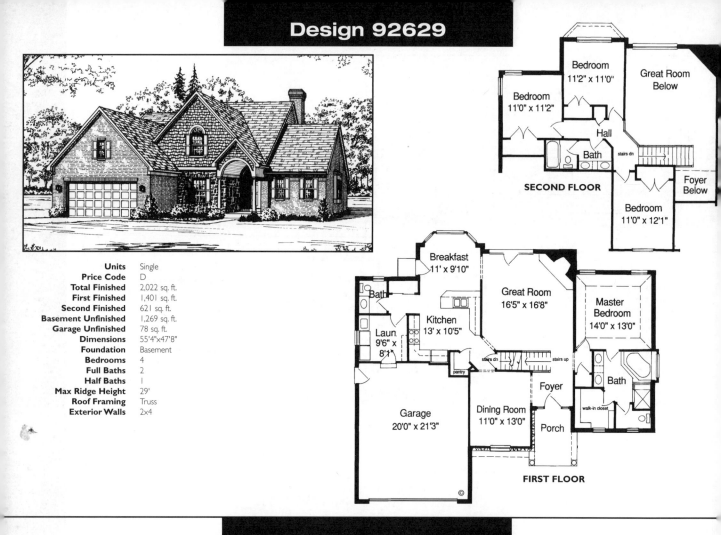

Units	Single
Price Code	D
Total Finished	2,022 sq. ft.
First Finished	1,401 sq. ft.
Second Finished	621 sq. ft.
Basement Unfinished	1,269 sq. ft.
Garage Unfinished	78 sq. ft.
Dimensions	55'4"x47'8"
Foundation	Basement
Bedrooms	4
Full Baths	2
Half Baths	1
Max Ridge Height	29'
Roof Framing	Truss
Exterior Walls	2x4

Bedroom 11'2" x 11'0"
Great Room Below
Bedroom 11'0" x 11'2"
Hall
Bath
stairs dn
Foyer Below
Bedroom 11'0" x 12'1"

SECOND FLOOR

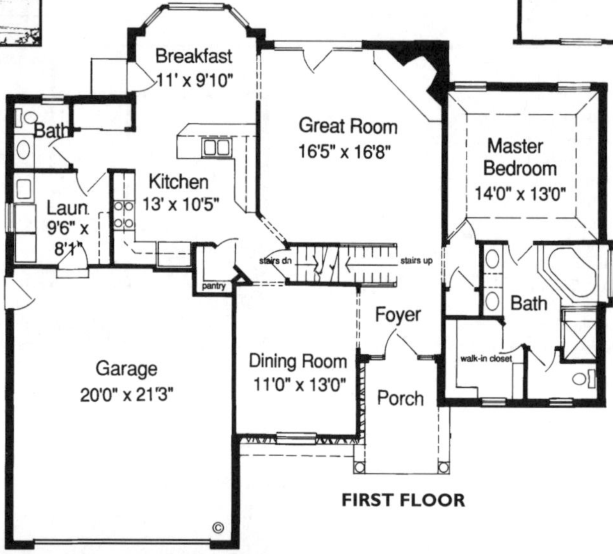

Breakfast 11' x 9'10"
Bath
Great Room 16'5" x 16'8"
Master Bedroom 14'0" x 13'0"
Kitchen 13' x 10'5"
Laun. 9'6" x 8'1"
stairs dn
stairs up
pantry
Bath
Foyer
walk-in closet
Garage 20'0" x 21'3"
Dining Room 11'0" x 13'0"
Porch

FIRST FLOOR

Design 65674

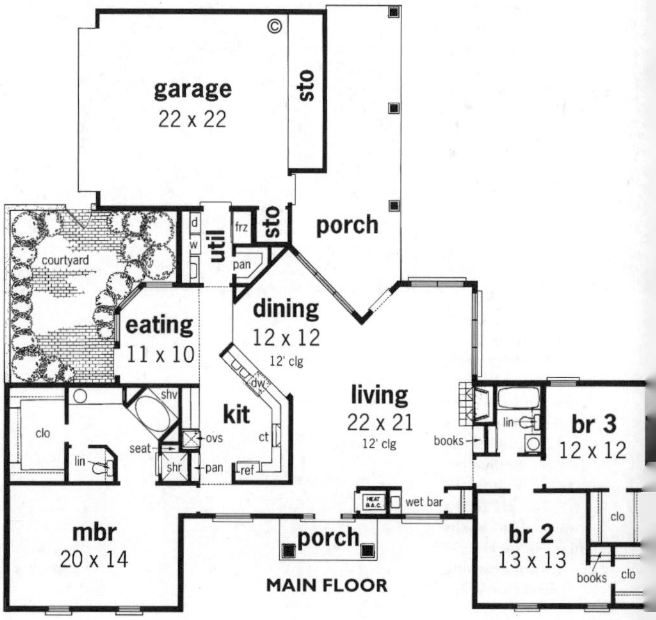

Units	Single
Price Code	D
Total Finished	2,023 sq. ft.
Main Finished	2,023 sq. ft.
Dimensions	73'x66'
Foundation	Crawlspace Slab
Bedrooms	3
Full Baths	2
Main Ceiling	8'
Max Ridge Height	28'
Roof Framing	Stick
Exterior Walls	2x6

garage 22 x 22
sto
sto
porch
util
frz
pan
courtyard
eating 11 x 10
dining 12 x 12
12' clg
living 22 x 21
12' clg
dw
kit
ovs
ct
pan
ref
shr
seat
shv
clo
lin
lin
books
br 3 12 x 12
wet bar
mbr 20 x 14
porch
br 2 13 x 13
books
clo
clo

MAIN FLOOR

Design 98361

Units	Single
Price Code	D
Total Finished	2,029 sq. ft.
Main Finished	2,029 sq. ft.
Basement Unfinished	2,029 sq. ft.
Garage Unfinished	704 sq. ft.
Dimensions	76'x71'4"
Foundation	Basement
Bedrooms	3
Full Baths	2
Half Baths	1
Max Ridge Height	24'
Roof Framing	Truss
Exterior Walls	2x6

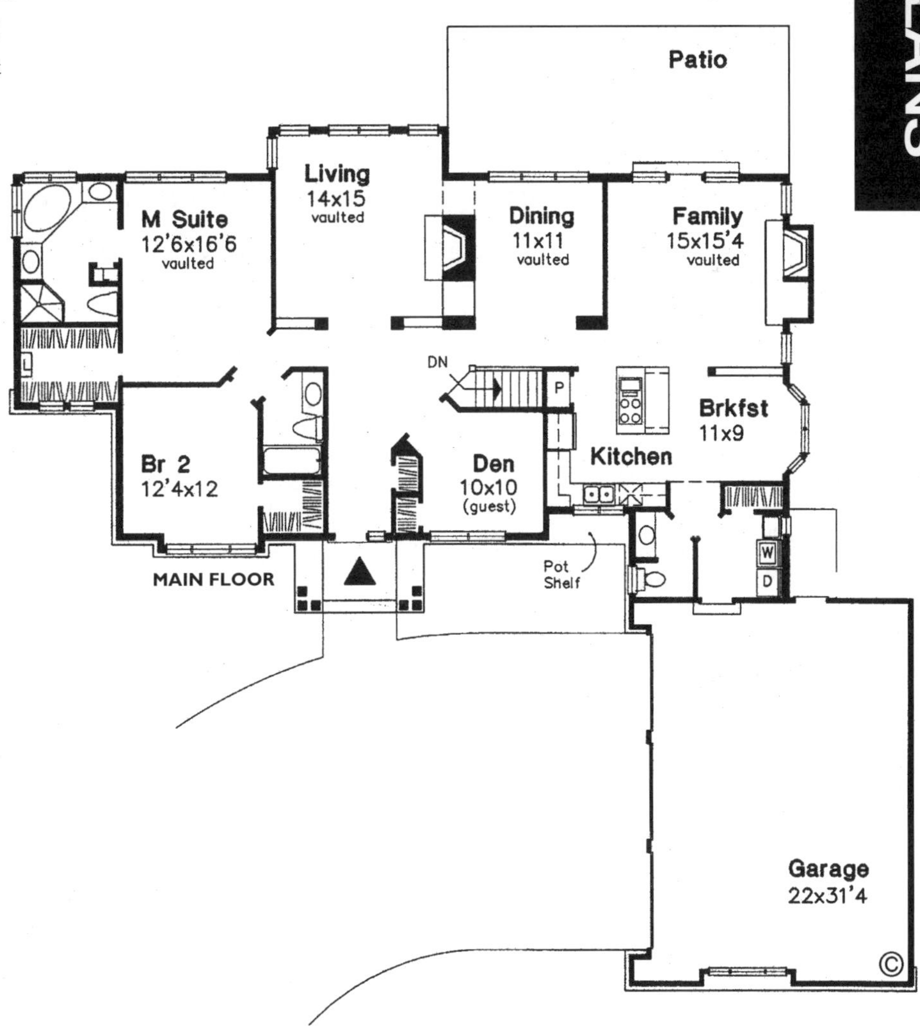
Patio
Living
14x15
vaulted
M Suite
12'6x16'6
vaulted
Dining
11x11
vaulted
Family
15x15'4
vaulted
DN
P
Brkfst
11x9
Kitchen
Br 2
12'4x12
Den
10x10
(guest)
W
D
Pot
Shelf
MAIN FLOOR
Garage
22x31'4
©

Design 69019

Units	Single
Price Code	D
Total Finished	2,029 sq. ft.
Main Finished	2,029 sq. ft.
Dimensions	61'x51'
Foundation	Basement
Bedrooms	3
Full Baths	2
Main Ceiling	9'
Max Ridge Height	23'6"
Roof Framing	Truss
Exterior Walls	2x4

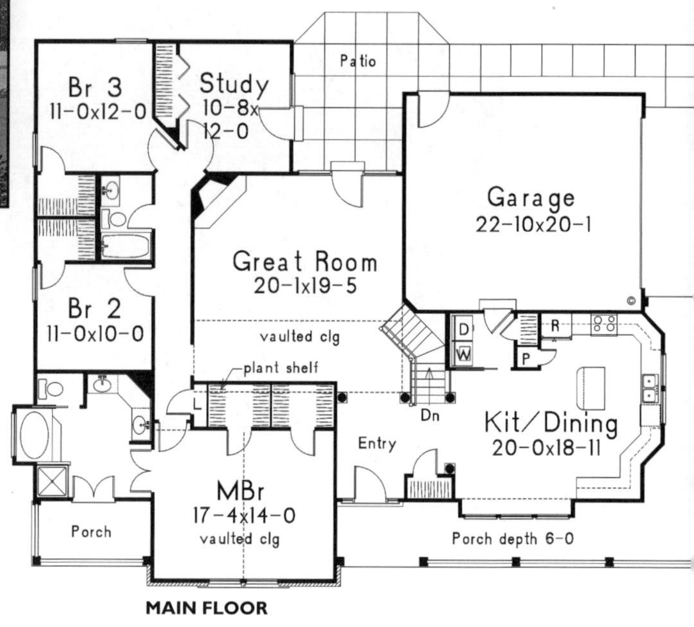
Patio
Br 3
11-0x12-0
Study
10-8x
12-0
Garage
22-10x20-1
Great Room
20-1x19-5
vaulted clg
Br 2
11-0x10-0
plant shelf
Dn
Entry
Kit/Dining
20-0x18-11
MBr
17-4x14-0
vaulted clg
Porch
Porch depth 6-0

MAIN FLOOR

Design 97619

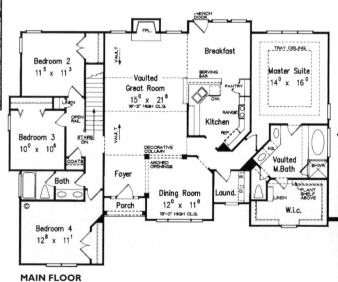

Units	Single
Price Code	D
Total Finished	2,032 sq. ft.
Main Finished	2,032 sq. ft.
Basement Unfinished	1,471 sq. ft.
Garage Unfinished	561 sq. ft.
Dimensions	58'6"x43'1"
Foundation	Basement
Bedrooms	4
Full Baths	2
Main Ceiling	9'
Max Ridge Height	24'
Roof Framing	Stick
Exterior Walls	2x4

MAIN FLOOR

Design 69105

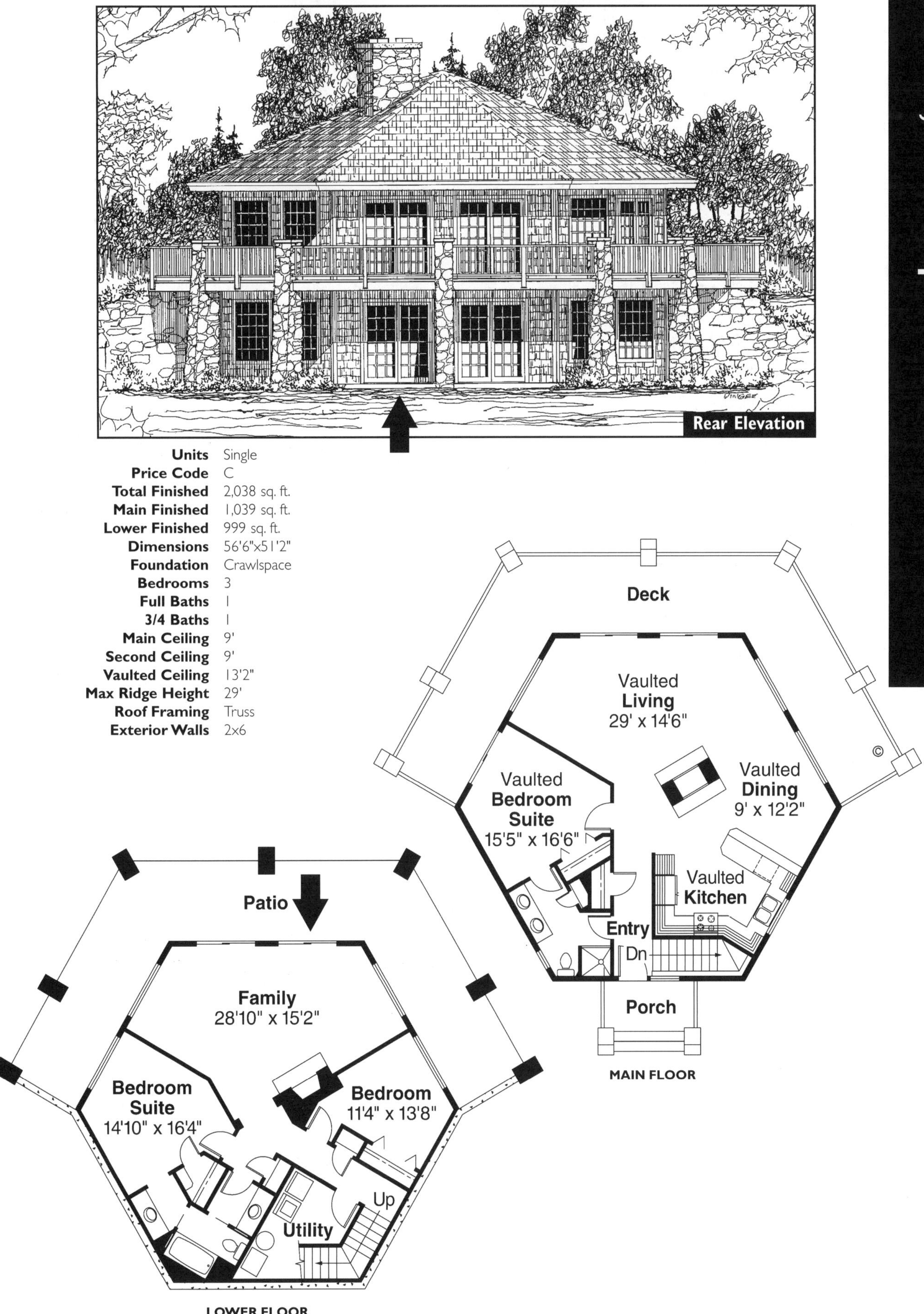
Rear Elevation
Deck
Vaulted
Living
29' x 14'6"
Vaulted
Bedroom
Suite
15'5" x 16'6"
Vaulted
Dining
9' x 12'2"
Vaulted
Kitchen
Entry
Dn
Porch
MAIN FLOOR
Patio
Family
28'10" x 15'2"
Bedroom
Suite
14'10" x 16'4"
Bedroom
11'4" x 13'8"
Utility
Up
LOWER FLOOR

Units	Single
Price Code	C
Total Finished	2,038 sq. ft.
Main Finished	1,039 sq. ft.
Lower Finished	999 sq. ft.
Dimensions	56'6"x51'2"
Foundation	Crawlspace
Bedrooms	3
Full Baths	1
3/4 Baths	1
Main Ceiling	9'
Second Ceiling	9'
Vaulted Ceiling	13'2"
Max Ridge Height	29'
Roof Framing	Truss
Exterior Walls	2x6

Design 69141

Units	Single
Price Code	D
Total Finished	2,038 sq. ft.
Main Finished	2,038 sq. ft.
Garage Unfinished	685 sq. ft.
Dimensions	68'x55'6"
Foundation	Crawlspace
Bedrooms	3
Full Baths	1
3/4 Baths	1
Main Ceiling	9'
Max Ridge Height	23'
Roof Framing	Stick
Exterior Walls	2x6

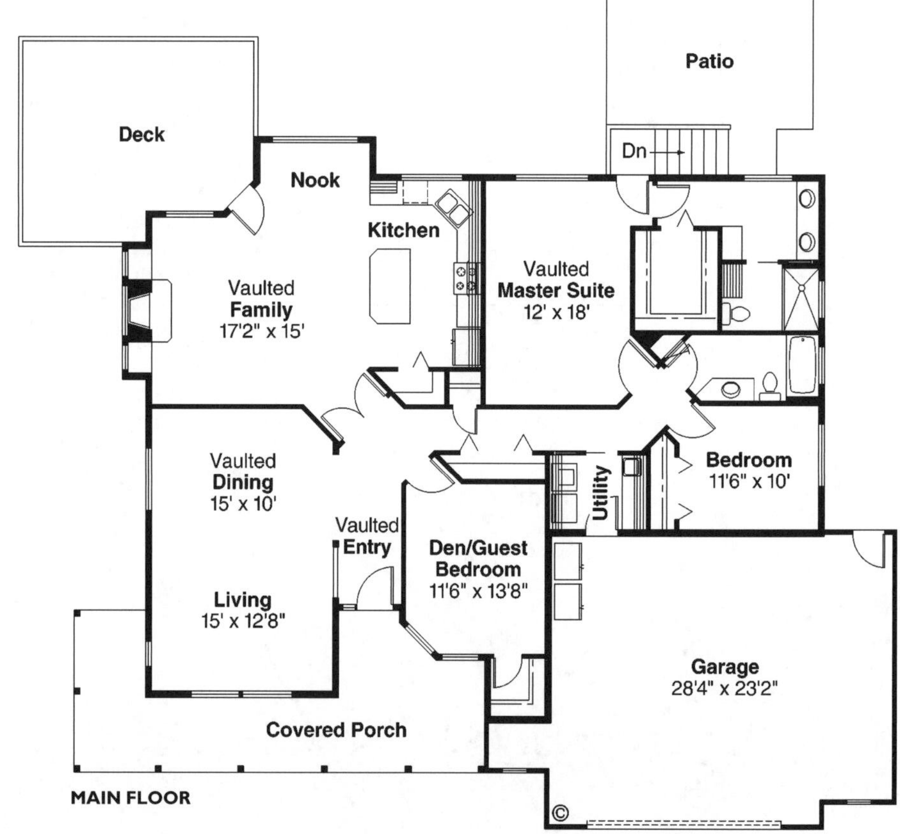

Patio
Deck
Dn
Nook
Kitchen
Vaulted
Master Suite
12' x 18'
Vaulted
Family
17'2" x 15'
Vaulted
Dining
15' x 10'
Utility
Bedroom
11'6" x 10'
Vaulted
Entry
Den/Guest
Bedroom
11'6" x 13'8"
Living
15' x 12'8"
Garage
28'4" x 23'2"
Covered Porch
MAIN FLOOR
©

Design 97406

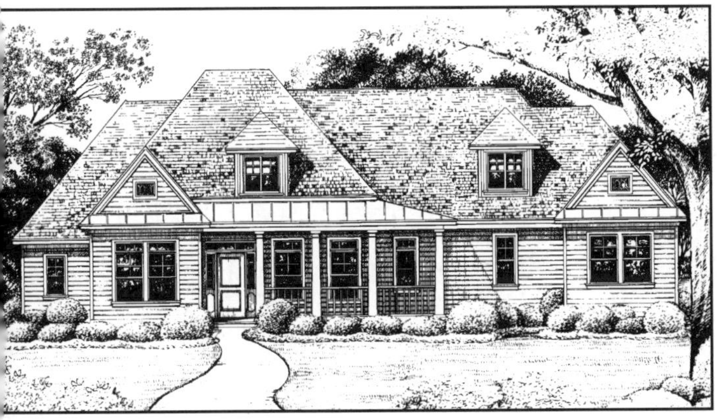

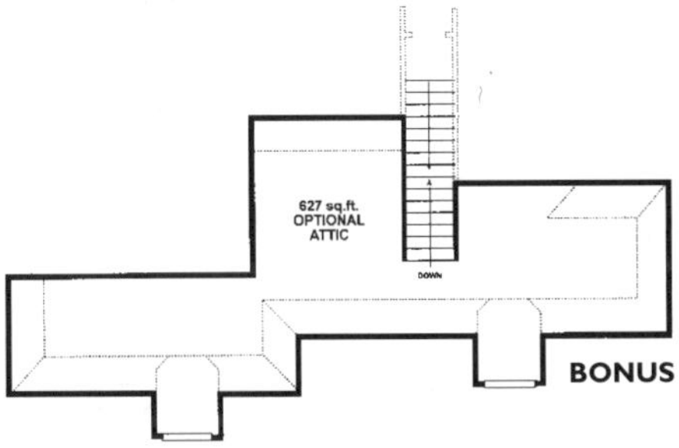

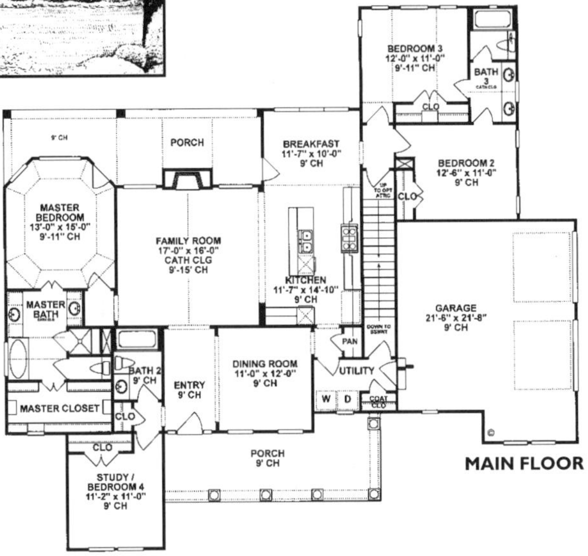

Units	Single
Price Code	D
Total Finished	2,040 sq. ft.
Main Finished	2,040 sq. ft.
Dimensions	69'5"x63'6"
Foundation	Slab
Bedrooms	4
Full Baths	3
Max Ridge Height	28'
Roof Framing	Stick
Exterior Walls	2x4

* Alternate foundation options available at an additional charge. Please call 1-800-235-5700 for more information.

BONUS

MAIN FLOOR

Design 63050

Units	Single
Price Code	D
Total Finished	2,041 sq. ft.
Main Finished	2,041 sq. ft.
Garage Unfinished	452 sq. ft.
Porch Unfinished	340 sq. ft.
Dimensions	60'4"x56'
Foundation	Slab
Bedrooms	4
Full Baths	2
Max Ridge Height	19'
Roof Framing	Truss
Exterior Walls	2x4

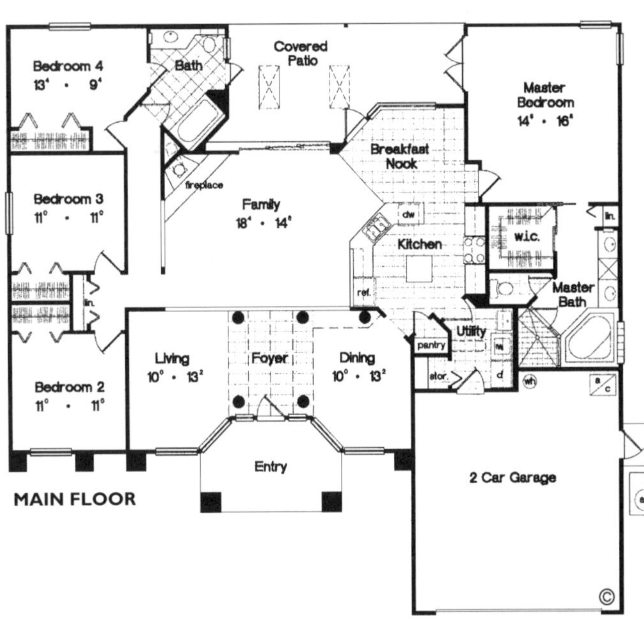
Bedroom 4
13' · 9'
Bath
Covered Patio
Master Bedroom
14' · 16'
Breakfast Nook
Bedroom 3
11' · 11'
fireplace
Family
18' · 14'
dw
Kitchen
w.i.c.
ref.
Master Bath
Utility
pantry
Living
10' · 13'
Foyer
Dining
10' · 13'
Bedroom 2
11' · 11'
Entry
2 Car Garage
MAIN FLOOR

Design 92688

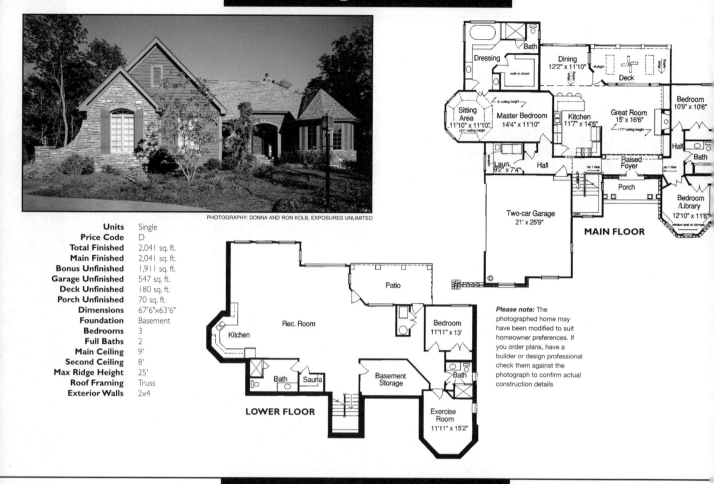

PHOTOGRAPHY: DONNA AND RON KOLB, EXPOSURES UNLIMITED

Units	Single
Price Code	D
Total Finished	2,041 sq. ft.
Main Finished	2,041 sq. ft.
Bonus Unfinished	1,911 sq. ft.
Garage Unfinished	547 sq. ft.
Deck Unfinished	180 sq. ft.
Porch Unfinished	70 sq. ft.
Dimensions	67'6"x63'6"
Foundation	Basement
Bedrooms	3
Full Baths	2
Main Ceiling	9'
Second Ceiling	8'
Max Ridge Height	25'
Roof Framing	Truss
Exterior Walls	2x4

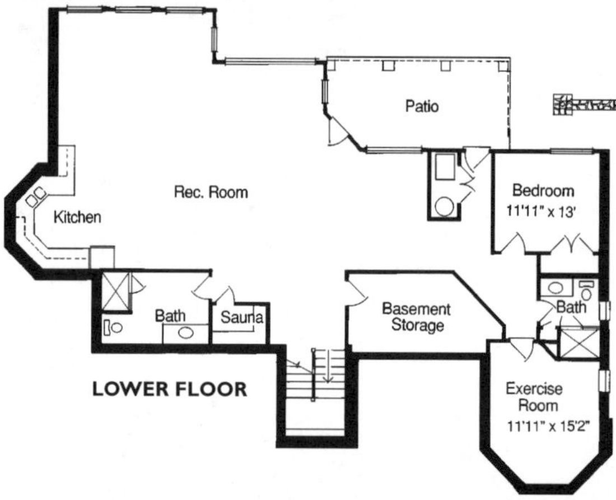

Bath
Dressing
walk-in closet
Dining 12'2" x 11'10"
Deck
Sitting Area 11'10" x 11'10"
Master Bedroom 14'4" x 11'10"
Kitchen 11'7" x 14'6"
Great Room 15' x 16'6"
Bedroom 10'9" x 10'6"
Hall
Bath
Laun. 9'2" x 7'4"
Hall
Raised Foyer
Porch
Bedroom /Library 12'10" x 11'6"
Two-car Garage 21' x 25'9"

MAIN FLOOR

Patio
Kitchen
Rec. Room
Bedroom 11'11" x 13'
Bath
Sauna
Basement Storage
Bath
Exercise Room 11'11" x 15'2"

LOWER FLOOR

Please note: The photographed home may have been modified to suit homeowner preferences. If you order plans, have a builder or design professional check them against the photograph to confirm actual construction details

Design 94984

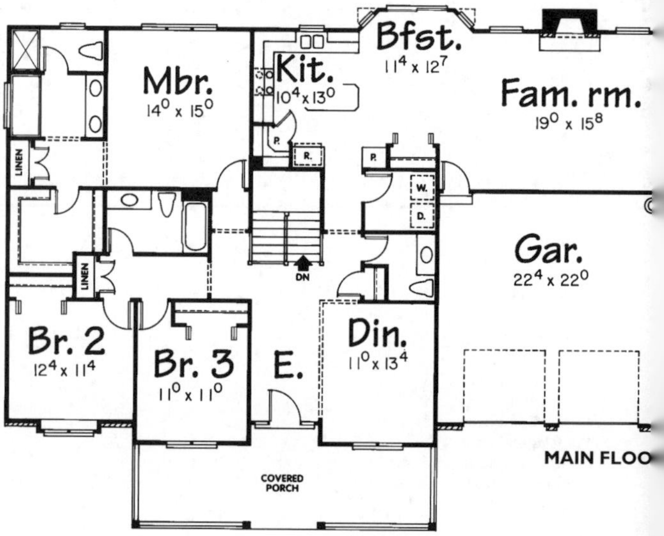

Units	Single
Price Code	D
Total Finished	2,042 sq. ft.
Main Finished	2,042 sq. ft.
Garage Unfinished	506 sq. ft.
Dimensions	65'4"x42'
Foundation	Basement
Bedrooms	3
Full Baths	2
Half Baths	1
Main Ceiling	8'
Max Ridge Height	19'
Roof Framing	Stick
Exterior Walls	2x4

* Alternate foundation options available at an additional charge. Please call 1-800-235-5700 for more information.

Mbr. 14^0 x 15^0
Kit. 10^4 x 13^0
Bfst. 11^4 x 12^7
Fam. rm. 19^0 x 15^8
Gar. 22^4 x 22^0
Br. 2 12^4 x 11^4
Br. 3 11^0 x 11^0
E.
Din. 11^0 x 13^4
COVERED PORCH

MAIN FLOO

Design 24736

Units	Single
Price Code	D
Total Finished	2,044 sq. ft.
First Finished	1,403 sq. ft.
Second Finished	641 sq. ft.
Basement Unfinished	1,394 sq. ft.
Garage Unfinished	680 sq. ft.
Deck Unfinished	156 sq. ft.
Porch Unfinished	231 sq. ft.
Dimensions	68'x47'
Foundation	Basement Crawlspace Slab
Bedrooms	3
Full Baths	2
Half Baths	1
First Ceiling	9'
Second Ceiling	8'
Vaulted Ceiling	12'9"
Roof Framing	Truss
Exterior Walls	2x4

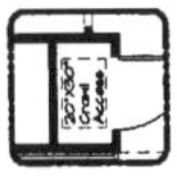

OPTIONAL CRAWLSPACE/SLAB FOUNDATION

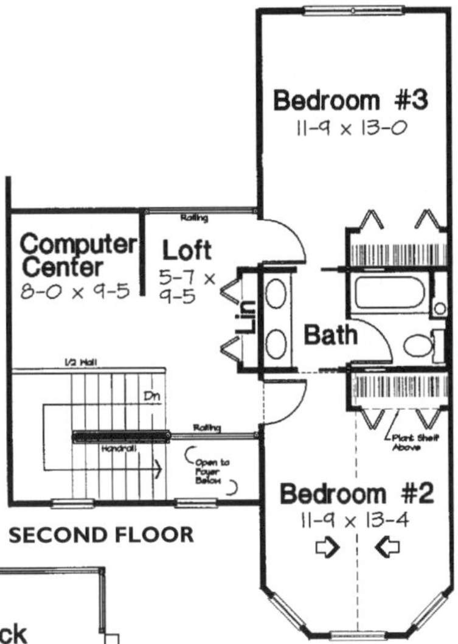

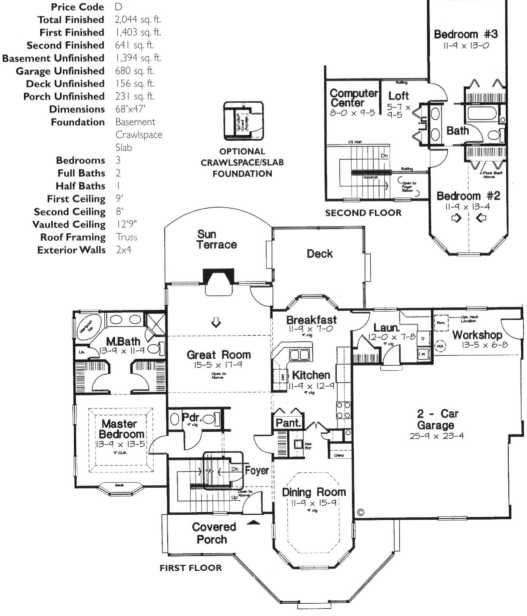

Bedroom #3
11-9 x 13-0
Computer Center
8-0 x 9-5
Loft
5-7 x 9-5
Lin
Bath
Dn
Bedroom #2
11-9 x 13-4

SECOND FLOOR

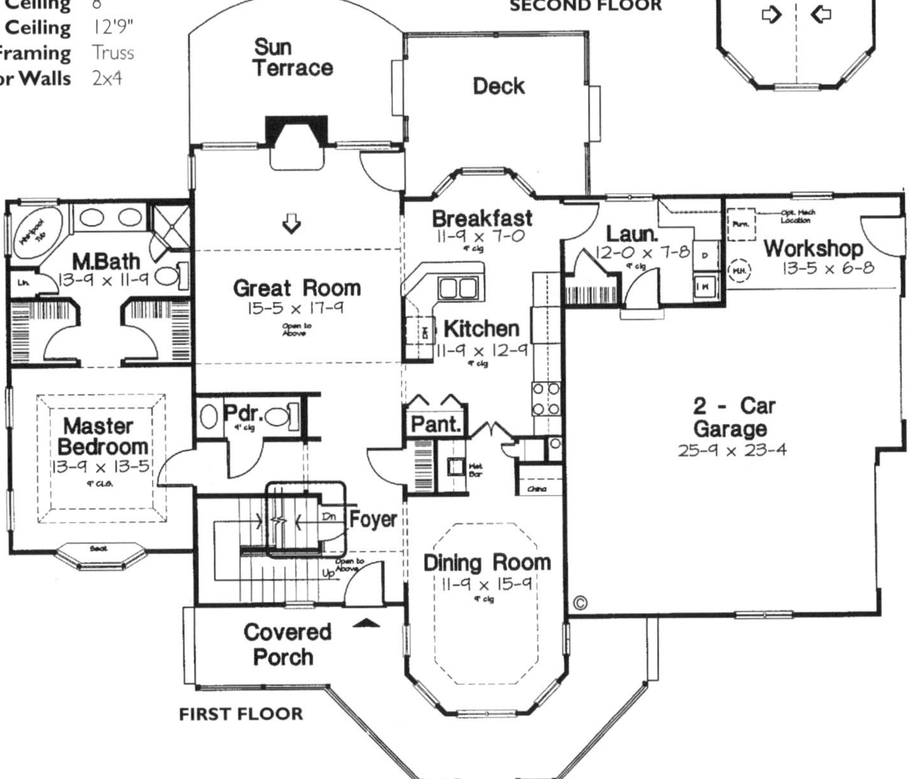

Sun Terrace
Deck
Breakfast
11-9 x 7-0
Laun.
12-0 x 7-8
Workshop
13-5 x 6-8
M.Bath
13-9 x 11-9
Great Room
15-5 x 17-9
Kitchen
11-9 x 12-9
2 - Car Garage
25-9 x 23-4
Master Bedroom
13-9 x 13-5
Pdr.
Pant.
Foyer
Dining Room
11-9 x 15-9
Covered Porch

FIRST FLOOR

Design 67003

Units	Single
Price Code	D
Total Finished	2,044 sq. ft.
First Finished	1,203 sq. ft.
Second Finished	841 sq. ft.
Garage Unfinished	462 sq. ft.
Porch Unfinished	323 sq. ft.
Dimensions	56'x44'5"
Foundation	Slab
Bedrooms	3
Full Baths	2
Half Baths	1
First Ceiling	8'
Second Ceiling	8'
Vaulted Ceiling	16'
Max Ridge Height	28'9"
Roof Framing	Stick
Exterior Walls	2x4

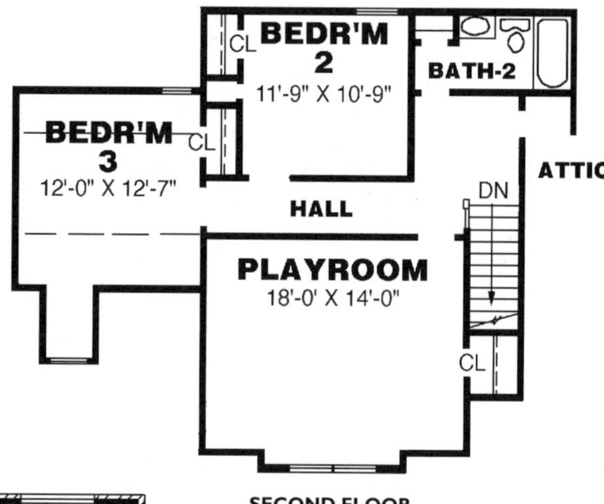

CL
BEDR'M 2
11'-9" X 10'-9"
BATH-2
BEDR'M 3
CL
12'-0" X 12'-7"
ATTIC
DN
HALL
PLAYROOM
18'-0' X 14'-0"
CL

SECOND FLOOR

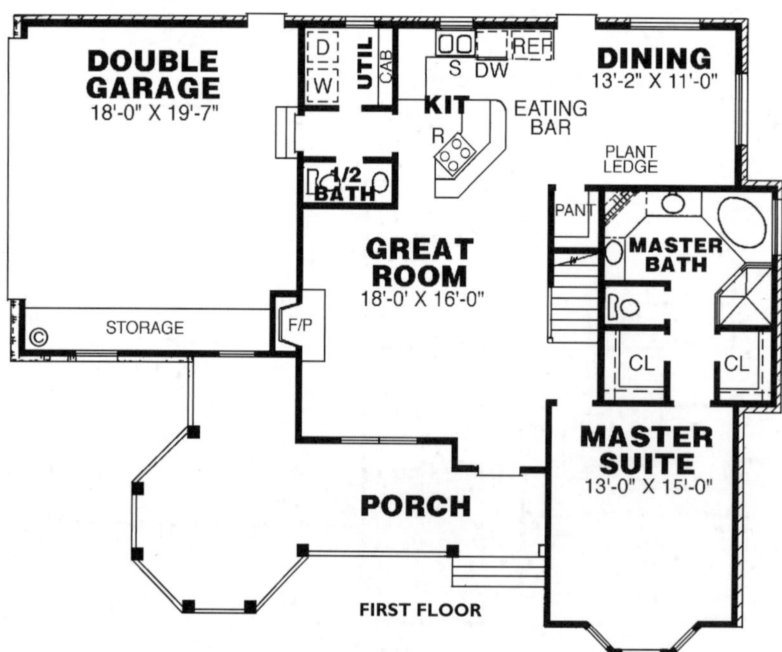

DOUBLE GARAGE
18'-0" X 19'-7"
D
W
UTIL
CAB
S
DW
REF
DINING
13'-2" X 11'-0"
KIT
EATING BAR
R
PLANT LEDGE
1/2 BATH
PANT
MASTER BATH
GREAT ROOM
18'-0' X 16'-0"
STORAGE
F/P
CL
CL
MASTER SUITE
13'-0" X 15'-0"
PORCH

FIRST FLOOR

Design 68013

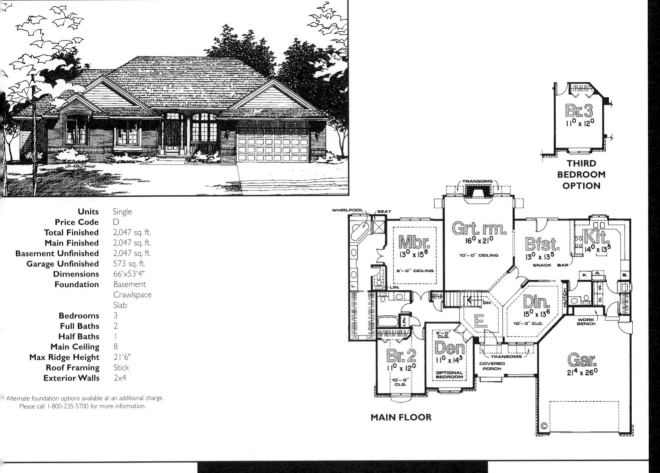

Units	Single
Price Code	D
Total Finished	2,047 sq. ft.
Main Finished	2,047 sq. ft.
Basement Unfinished	2,047 sq. ft.
Garage Unfinished	573 sq. ft.
Dimensions	66'x53'4"
Foundation	Basement Crawlspace Slab
Bedrooms	3
Full Baths	2
Half Baths	1
Main Ceiling	8
Max Ridge Height	21'6"
Roof Framing	Stick
Exterior Walls	2x4

* Alternate foundation options available at an additional charge. Please call 1-800-235-5700 for more information.

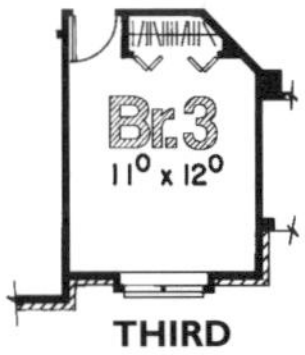

Br. 3 11⁰ x 12⁰
THIRD BEDROOM OPTION

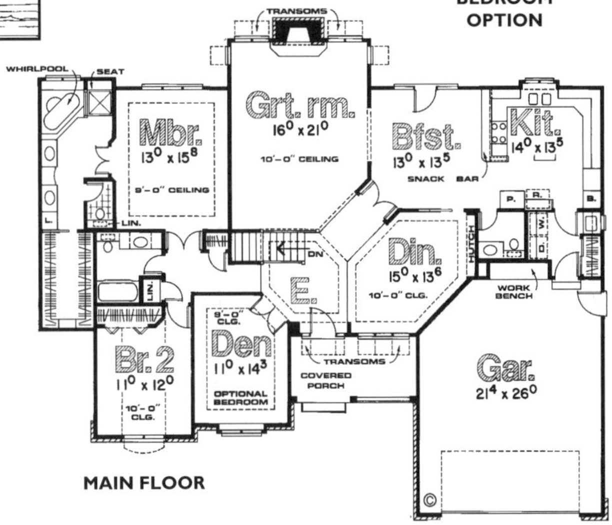

TRANSOMS
WHIRLPOOL SEAT
Mbr. 13⁰ x 15⁸ 9'-0" CEILING
Grt. rm. 16⁰ x 21⁰ 10'-0" CEILING
Bfst. 13⁰ x 13⁵ SNACK BAR
Kit. 14⁰ x 13⁵
LIN.
DN
E.
Din. 15⁰ x 13⁶ 10'-0" CLG.
HUTCH
WORK BENCH
Br. 2 11⁰ x 12⁰ 10'-0" CLG.
Den 11⁰ x 14³ 9'-0" CLG. OPTIONAL BEDROOM
TRANSOMS
COVERED PORCH
Gar. 21⁴ x 26⁰
MAIN FLOOR

Design 69154

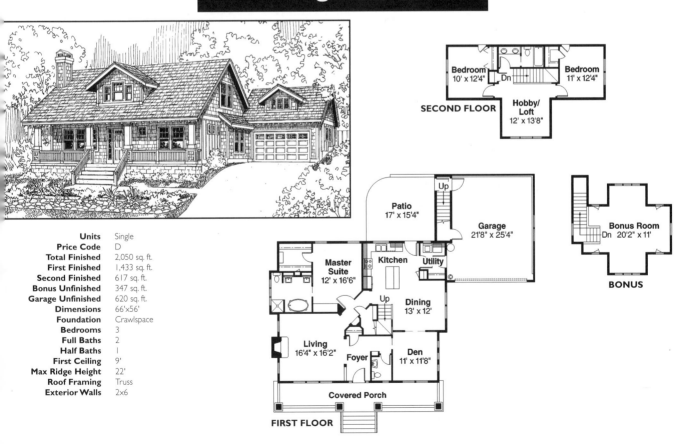

Units	Single
Price Code	D
Total Finished	2,050 sq. ft.
First Finished	1,433 sq. ft.
Second Finished	617 sq. ft.
Bonus Unfinished	347 sq. ft.
Garage Unfinished	620 sq. ft.
Dimensions	66'x56'
Foundation	Crawlspace
Bedrooms	3
Full Baths	2
Half Baths	1
First Ceiling	9'
Max Ridge Height	22'
Roof Framing	Truss
Exterior Walls	2x6

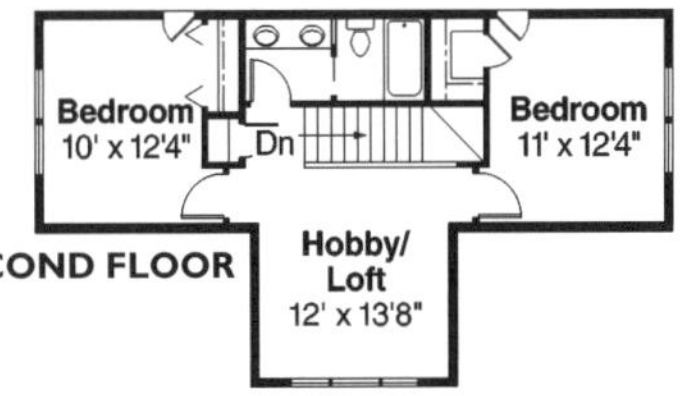

Bedroom 10' x 12'4"
Dn
Bedroom 11' x 12'4"
Hobby/ Loft 12' x 13'8"
SECOND FLOOR

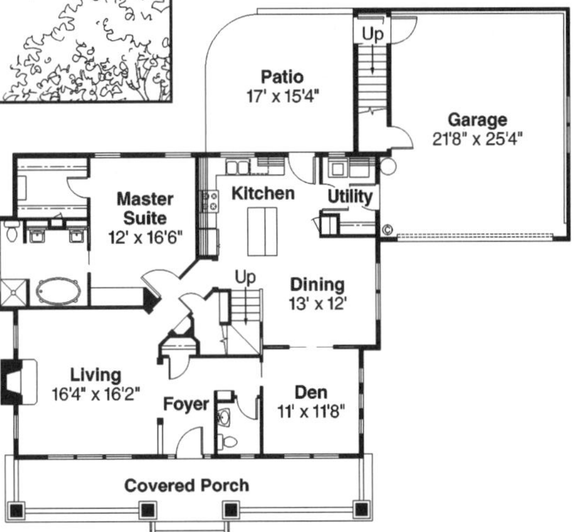

Up
Patio 17' x 15'4"
Garage 21'8" x 25'4"
Master Suite 12' x 16'6"
Kitchen
Utility
Up
Dining 13' x 12'
Living 16'4" x 16'2"
Foyer
Den 11' x 11'8"
Covered Porch
FIRST FLOOR

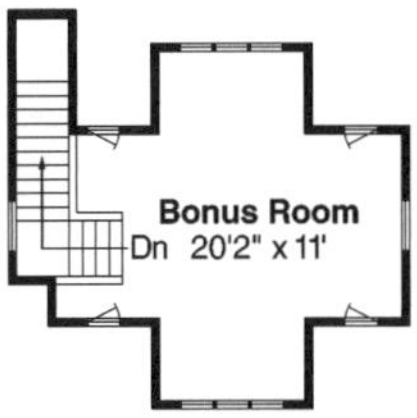

Bonus Room Dn 20'2" x 11'
BONUS

Design 94141

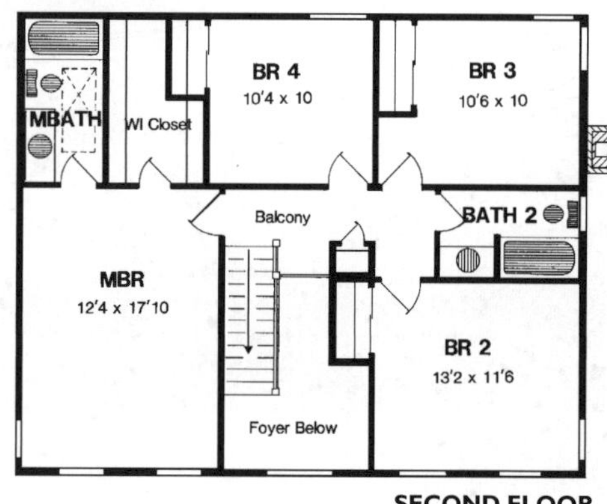

MBATH
WI Closet
BR 4
10'4 x 10
BR 3
10'6 x 10
Balcony
BATH 2
MBR
12'4 x 17'10
BR 2
13'2 x 11'6
Foyer Below
SECOND FLOOR

Units	Single
Price Code	D
Total Finished	2,050 sq. ft.
First Finished	1,108 sq. ft.
Second Finished	942 sq. ft.
Basement Unfinished	1,108 sq. ft.
Garage Unfinished	455 sq. ft.
Dimensions	66'x32'
Foundation	Basement
Bedrooms	4
Full Baths	2
Half Baths	1
First Ceiling	8'1⅛"
Second Ceiling	8'1⅛"
Max Ridge Height	28'
Roof Framing	Truss
Exterior Walls	2x4

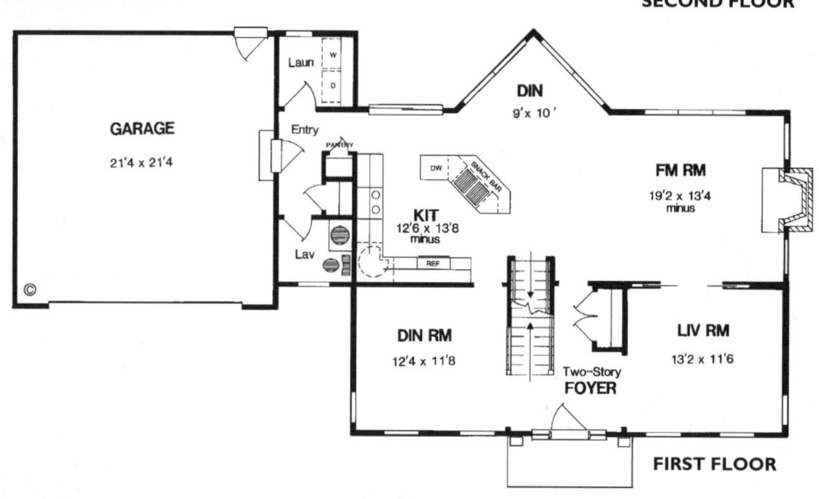

GARAGE
21'4 x 21'4
Laun
Entry
PANTRY
DIN
9' x 10'
DW
SNACK BAR
KIT
12'6 x 13'8
minus
REF
FM RM
19'2 x 13'4
minus
Lav
DIN RM
12'4 x 11'8
Two-Story
FOYER
LIV RM
13'2 x 11'6
FIRST FLOOR

Design 98427

CAD
FILES AVAILABLE
For more information call
800-235-5700

Units	Single
Price Code	D
Total Finished	2,051 sq. ft.
Main Finished	2,051 sq. ft.
Basement Unfinished	2,051 sq. ft.
Garage Unfinished	441 sq. ft.
Dimensions	56'x60'6"
Foundation	Basement Crawlspace Slab
Bedrooms	3
Full Baths	2
Main Ceiling	9'
Max Ridge Height	27'5"
Roof Framing	Stick
Exterior Walls	2x4

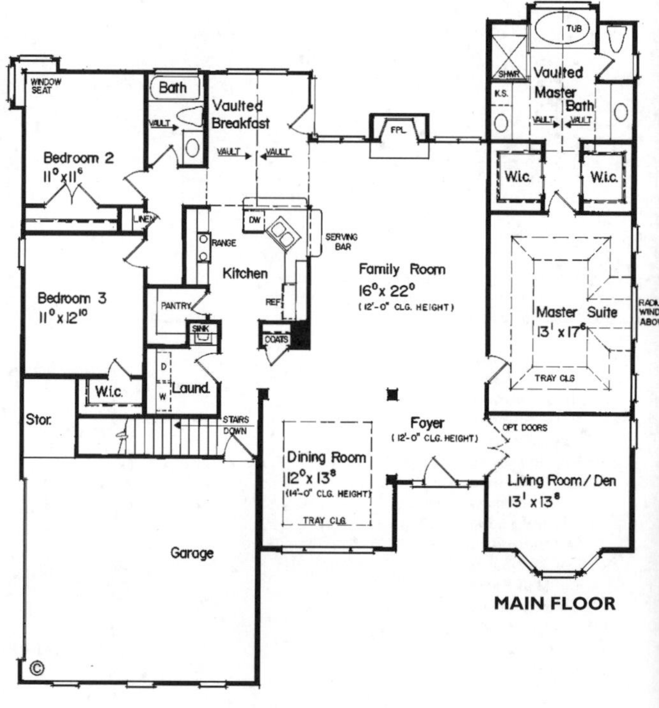

WINDOW SEAT
Bath
Vaulted Breakfast
FPL
TUB
Vaulted Master Bath
Bedroom 2
11⁰ x 11⁶
W.i.c.
W.i.c.
DW
SERVING BAR
RANGE
Kitchen
Family Room
16⁰ x 22⁰
(12'-0" CLG. HEIGHT)
Bedroom 3
11⁰ x 12¹⁰
PANTRY
REF
SINK
COATS
Master Suite
13¹ x 17⁶
TRAY CLG
W.i.c.
Laund.
Stor.
STAIRS DOWN
Foyer
(12'-0" CLG. HEIGHT)
OPT. DOORS
Dining Room
12⁰ x 13⁸
(14'-0" CLG. HEIGHT)
TRAY CLG.
Living Room/Den
13¹ x 13⁸
Garage
MAIN FLOOR

Design 98407

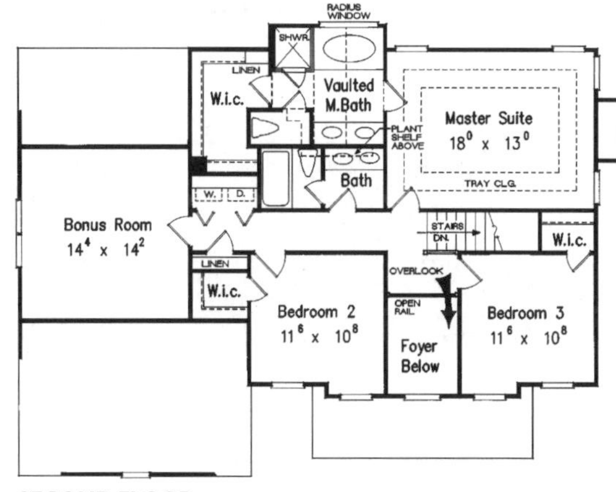
RADIUS WINDOW
SHWR.
LINEN
W.i.c.
Vaulted M.Bath
Master Suite
18⁰ x 13⁰
PLANT SHELF ABOVE
TRAY CLG.
Bath
W. D.
Bonus Room
14⁴ x 14²
STAIRS DN.
W.i.c.
LINEN
W.i.c.
OVERLOOK
Bedroom 2
11⁶ x 10⁸
OPEN RAIL
Foyer Below
Bedroom 3
11⁶ x 10⁸

SECOND FLOOR

Units	Single
Price Code	D
Total Finished	2,052 sq. ft.
First Finished	1,135 sq. ft.
Second Finished	917 sq. ft.
Bonus Unfinished	216 sq. ft.
Basement Unfinished	1,135 sq. ft.
Garage Unfinished	452 sq. ft.
Dimensions	52'4"x37'6"
Foundation	Basement Crawlspace Slab
Bedrooms	4
Full Baths	3
First Ceiling	9'2"
Second Ceiling	8'2"
Max Ridge Height	31'
Roof Framing	Stick
Exterior Walls	2x4

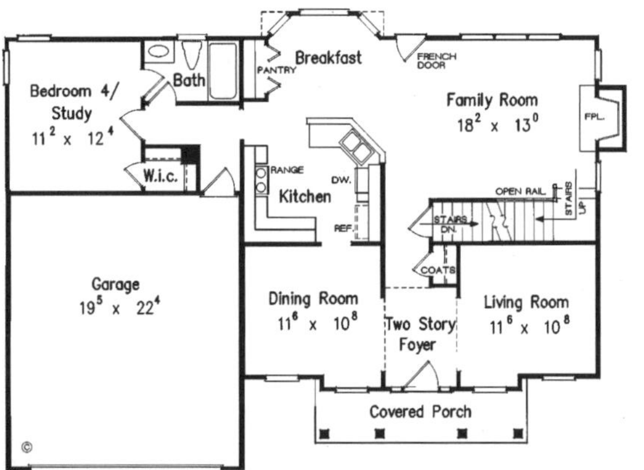
Breakfast
PANTRY
FRENCH DOOR
Bedroom 4/ Study
11² x 12⁴
Bath
Family Room
18² x 13⁰
FPL.
W.i.c.
RANGE
DW.
Kitchen
REF.
OPEN RAIL
STAIRS DN.
STAIRS UP
COATS
Garage
19⁵ x 22⁴
Dining Room
11⁶ x 10⁸
Two Story Foyer
Living Room
11⁶ x 10⁸
Covered Porch

FIRST FLOOR

CAD FILES AVAILABLE For more information call 800-235-5700

Design 63120

Units	Single
Price Code	D
Total Finished	2,060 sq. ft.
Main Finished	2,060 sq. ft.
Garage Unfinished	478 sq. ft.
Dimensions	60'4"x56'
Foundation	Slab
Bedrooms	4
Full Baths	2
Main Ceiling	10'
Max Ridge Height	24'
Roof Framing	Truss
Exterior Walls	2x4

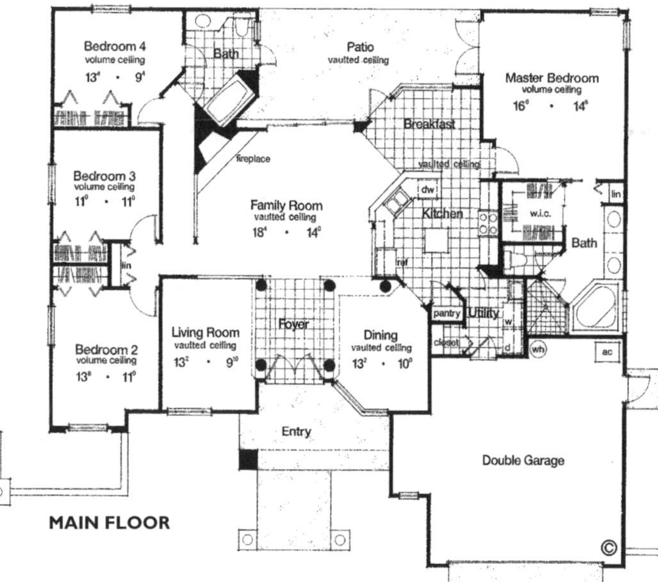
Bedroom 4
volume ceiling
Bath
Patio
vaulted ceiling
Master Bedroom
volume ceiling
Breakfast
fireplace
Bedroom 3
volume ceiling
vaulted ceiling
Family Room
vaulted ceiling
dw
Kitchen
lin
w.i.c.
Bath
lin
ref
Foyer
pantry
Utility
Living Room
vaulted ceiling
Dining
vaulted ceiling
Bedroom 2
volume ceiling
closet
wh
ac
Entry
Double Garage

MAIN FLOOR

Design 99427

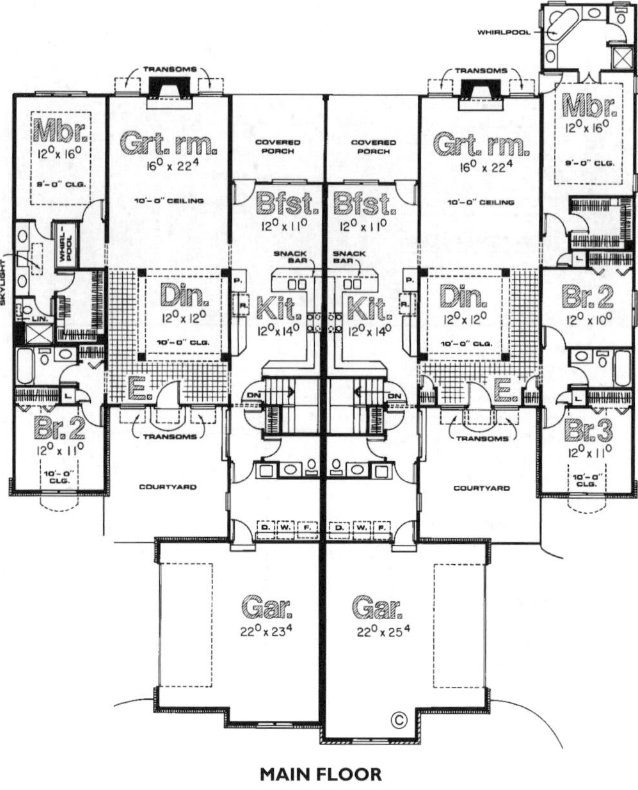
WHIRLPOOL
TRANSOMS
Mbr.
Grt. rm.
COVERED PORCH
Bfst.
SNACK BAR
Din.
Kit.
Br. 2
Br. 3
E.
COURTYARD
Gar.
SKYLIGHT
MAIN FLOOR

Units	Duplex
Price Code	G
Total Finished	2,060 sq. ft.
Main Finished	2,060 sq. ft.
Basement Unfinished	2,060 sq. ft.
Garage Unfinished	530 sq. ft.
Dimensions	82'8"x96'
Foundation	Basement
Bedrooms	2 or 3
Full Baths	2
Half Baths	1
Roof Framing	Stick
Exterior Walls	2x4

* Alternate foundation options available at an additional charge.
Please call 1-800-235-5700 for more information.

Design 63085

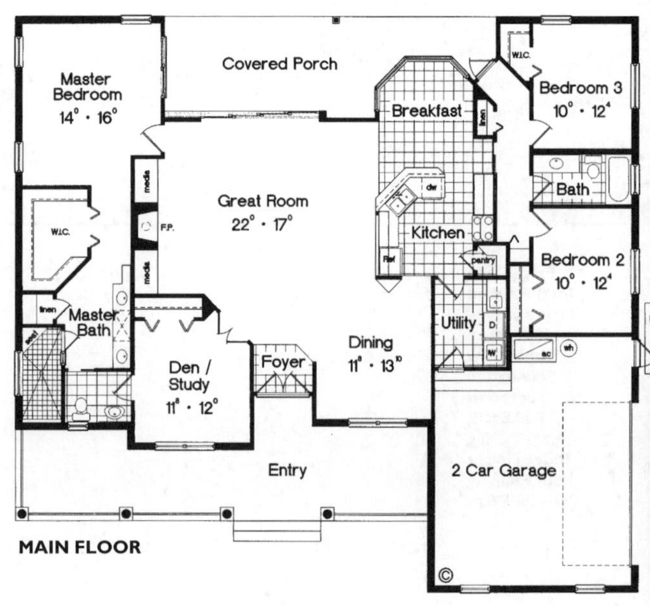
Master Bedroom
14° · 16°
Covered Porch
Breakfast
Bedroom 3
10° · 12⁴
Great Room
22° · 17°
Bath
Kitchen
Bedroom 2
10° · 12⁴
Master Bath
Utility
Den / Study
11⁸ · 12°
Foyer
Dining
11⁸ · 13¹⁰
Entry
2 Car Garage
MAIN FLOOR

Units	Single
Price Code	D
Total Finished	2,062 sq. ft.
Main Finished	2,062 sq. ft.
Garage Unfinished	514 sq. ft.
Porch Unfinished	647 sq. ft.
Dimensions	63'x56'8"
Foundation	Slab
Bedrooms	3
Full Baths	1
3/4 Baths	1
Max Ridge Height	25'4"
Roof Framing	Truss

Design 66103

Units	Single
Price Code	D
Total Finished	2,065 sq. ft.
Main Finished	2,065 sq. ft.
Dimensions	50'x70'
Foundation	Slab
Bedrooms	4
Full Baths	3
Main Ceiling	8'-10'
Max Ridge Height	25'
Roof Framing	Stick
Exterior Walls	2x4

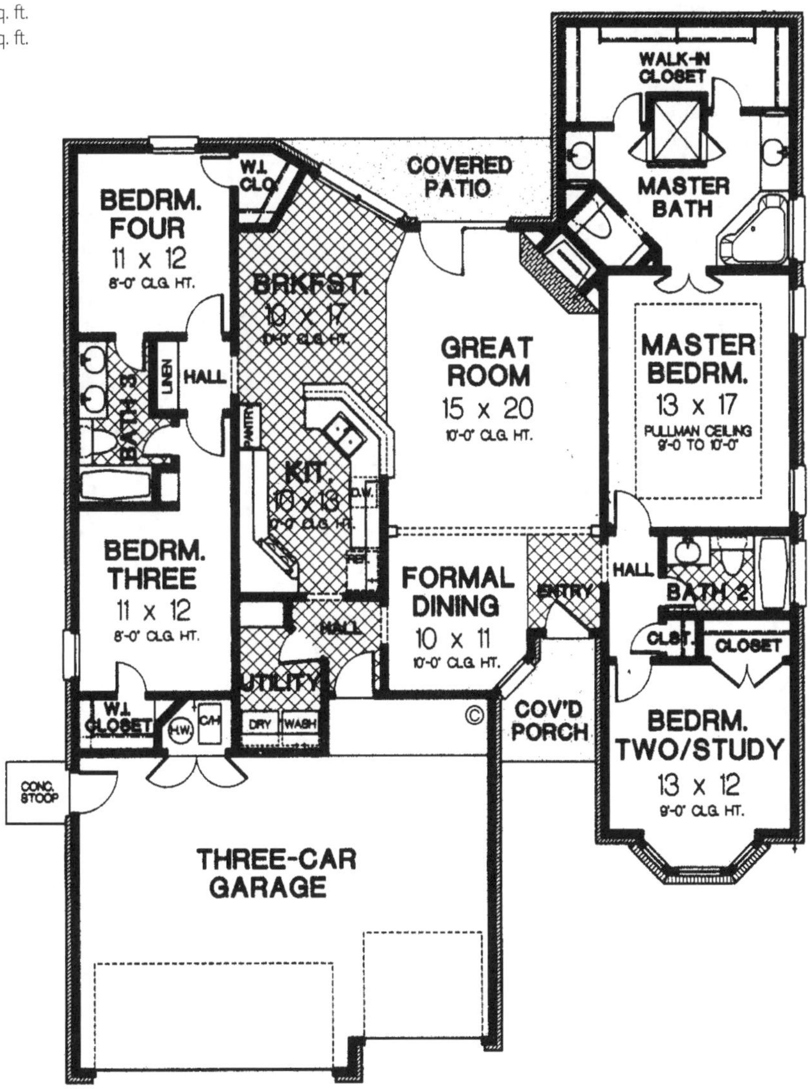

WALK-IN CLOSET
COVERED PATIO
MASTER BATH
W.I. CLO.
BEDRM. FOUR 11 x 12 8'-0" CLG. HT.
BRKFST. 10 x 17 10'-0" CLG. HT.
GREAT ROOM 15 x 20 10'-0" CLG. HT.
MASTER BEDRM. 13 x 17 PULLMAN CEILING 9'-0 TO 10'-0"
LINEN
HALL
BATH 3
PANTRY
KIT 10 x 13
D.W.
BEDRM. THREE 11 x 12 8'-0" CLG. HT.
FORMAL DINING 10 x 11 10'-0" CLG. HT.
ENTRY
HALL
BATH 2
CLST.
CLOSET
HALL
UTILITY
DRY WASH
W.I. CLOSET
H.W.
C/H
COV'D PORCH
BEDRM. TWO/STUDY 13 x 12 9'-0" CLG. HT.
CONC. STOOP
THREE-CAR GARAGE

MAIN FLOOR

Design 94260

Units	Single
Price Code	F
Total Finished	2,068 sq. ft.
Main Finished	2,068 sq. ft.
Lower Unfinished	1,402 sq. ft.
Garage Unfinished	560 sq. ft.
Deck Unfinished	594 sq. ft.
Porch Unfinished	696 sq. ft.
Dimensions	54'x58'
Foundation	Post
Bedrooms	3
Full Baths	2
Max Ridge Height	37'
Roof Framing	Truss
Exterior Walls	2x6

* Alternate foundation options available at an additional charge.
Please call 1-800-235-5700 for more information.

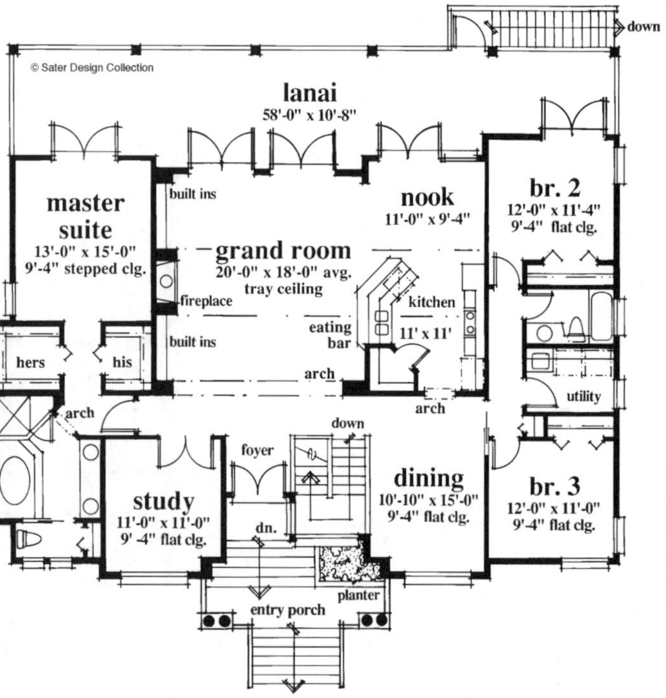

© Sater Design Collection

down
lanai
58'-0" x 10'-8"
master suite
13'-0" x 15'-0"
9'-4" stepped clg.
built ins
nook
11'-0" x 9'-4"
br. 2
12'-0" x 11'-4"
9'-4" flat clg.
grand room
20'-0" x 18'-0" avg.
tray ceiling
fireplace
kitchen
11' x 11'
eating bar
built ins
hers
his
arch
arch
arch
utility
down
foyer
study
11'-0" x 11'-0"
9'-4" flat clg.
dining
10'-10" x 15'-0"
9'-4" flat clg.
br. 3
12'-0" x 11'-0"
9'-4" flat clg.
dn.
planter
entry porch

MAIN FLOOR

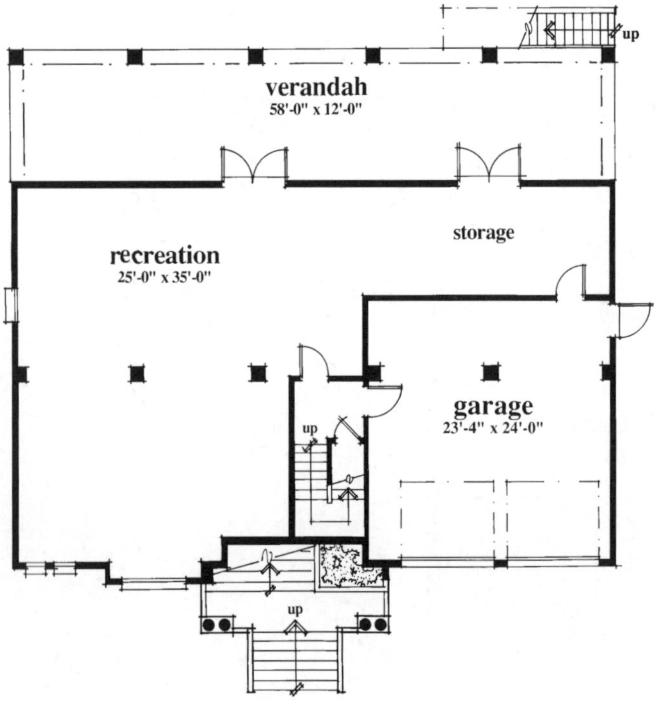

up
verandah
58'-0" x 12'-0"
storage
recreation
25'-0" x 35'-0"
garage
23'-4" x 24'-0"
up
up

LOWER FLOOR

Design 96505

Units	Single
Price Code	D
Total Finished	2,069 sq. ft.
Main Finished	2,069 sq. ft.
Garage Unfinished	481 sq. ft.
Porch Unfinished	374 sq. ft.
Dimensions	70'x58'
Foundation	Crawlspace Slab
Bedrooms	3
Full Baths	2
Half Baths	1
Main Ceiling	9'
Max Ridge Height	23'
Exterior Walls	2x4

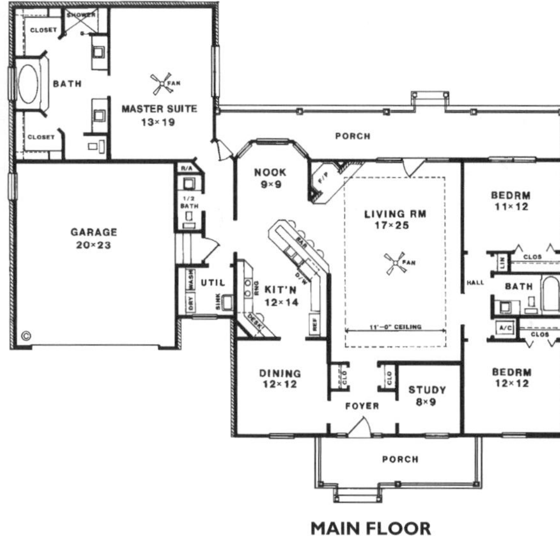
CLOSET
SHOWER
BATH
CLOSET
MASTER SUITE
13×19
FAN
PORCH
NOOK
9×9
LIVING RM
17×25
BEDRM
11×12
GARAGE
20×23
1/2 BATH
UTIL
KIT'N
12×14
CLOS
HALL
BATH
11'-0" CEILING
DINING
12×12
STUDY
8×9
FOYER
BEDRM
12×12
PORCH

MAIN FLOOR

Design 22004

Units	Single
Price Code	D
Total Finished	2,070 sq. ft.
Main Finished	2,070 sq. ft.
Garage Unfinished	474 sq. ft.
Dimensions	52'x68'6"
Foundation	Slab
Bedrooms	4
Full Baths	2
3/4 Baths	1
Max Ridge Height	21'
Roof Framing	Stick
Exterior Walls	2x4

GARAGE
20'-6"X21'-2"
BATH
UTILITY
PATIO
NOOK
11'-0"X10'-6"
MASTER BEDROOM
14'-8" X 13'-8"
KITCHEN
FAMILY ROOM
23'-2" X 15'-4"
BATH
BATH
P
BAR
ENTRY
DINING
11'-0"X12'-0"
BEDROOM
12'-0"X11'-0"
PORCH
BEDROOM
10'-6"X12'-6"
BEDROOM
11'-0"X11'-6"

MAIN FLOOR

Design 94936

PHOTOGRAPHY: COURTESY OF THE DESIGNER

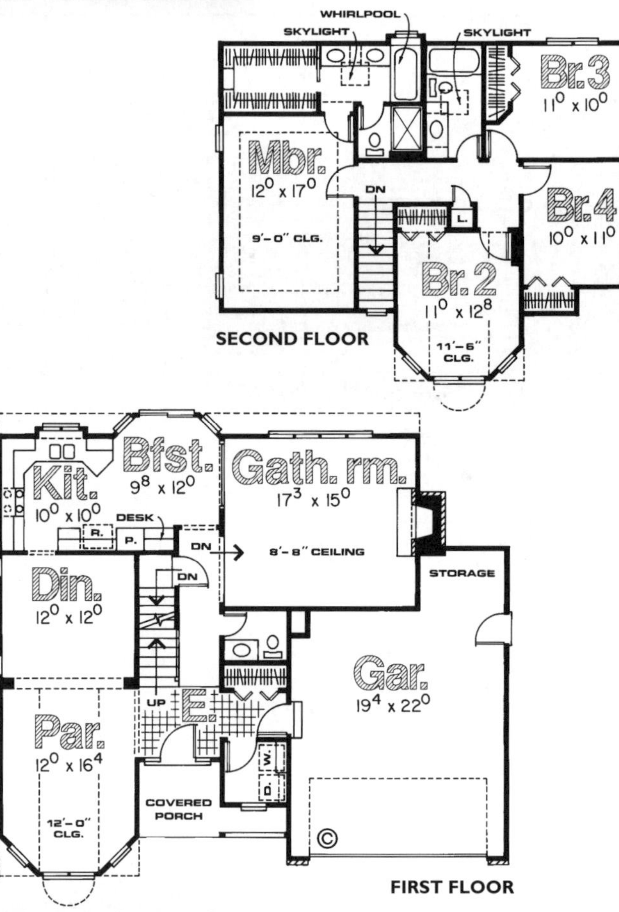
WHIRLPOOL
SKYLIGHT
SKYLIGHT
Br.3
11⁰ x 10⁰
Mbr.
12⁰ x 17⁰
9'-0" CLG.
DN
L.
Br.4
10⁰ x 11⁰
Br.2
11⁰ x 12⁸
11'-6" CLG.
SECOND FLOOR
Bfst.
9⁸ x 12⁰
Kit.
10⁰ x 10⁰
DESK
R.
P.
Gath. rm.
17³ x 15⁰
8'-8" CEILING
DN
STORAGE
Din.
12⁰ x 12⁰
Gar.
19⁴ x 22⁰
UP
E.
Par.
12⁰ x 16⁴
12'-0" CLG.
COVERED PORCH
FIRST FLOOR

Units	Single
Price Code	D
Total Finished	2,078 sq. ft.
First Finished	1,113 sq. ft.
Second Finished	965 sq. ft.
Basement Unfinished	1,113 sq. ft.
Garage Unfinished	486 sq. ft.
Dimensions	46'x41'5"
Foundation	Basement
Bedrooms	4
Full Baths	2
Half Baths	1
First Ceiling	8'
Second Ceiling	8'
Max Ridge Height	25'5"
Roof Framing	Stick
Exterior Walls	2x4

* Alternate foundation options available at an additional charge. Please call 1-800-235-5700 for more information.

Please note: The photographed home may have been modified to suit homeowner preferences. If you order plans, have a builder or design professional check them against the photograph to confirm actual construction details.

Design 98583

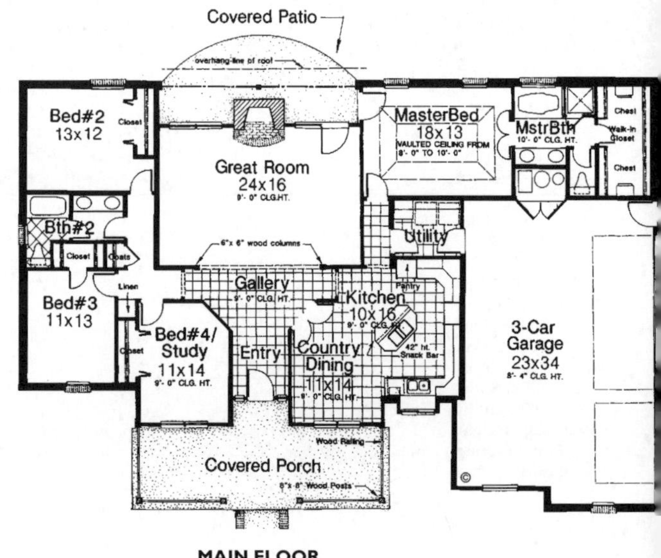
Covered Patio
Bed#2
13x12
Great Room
24x16
MasterBed
18x13
MstrBth
Bth#2
Utility
Gallery
Kitchen
10x16
Bed#3
11x13
Bed#4/
Study
11x14
Entry
Country
Dining
11x14
3-Car
Garage
23x34
Covered Porch
MAIN FLOOR

Units	Single
Price Code	D
Total Finished	2,078 sq. ft.
Main Finished	2,078 sq. ft.
Garage Unfinished	734 sq. ft.
Deck Unfinished	140 sq. ft.
Porch Unfinished	240 sq. ft.
Dimensions	75'x47'10"
Foundation	Crawlspace Slab
Bedrooms	4
Full Baths	2
Max Ridge Height	27'
Roof Framing	Stick
Exterior Walls	2x4

Design 63052

Units	Single
Price Code	E
Total Finished	2,081 sq. ft.
Main Finished	2,081 sq. ft.
Garage Unfinished	559 sq. ft.
Porch Unfinished	219 sq. ft.
Dimensions	58'x66'8"
Foundation	Slab
Bedrooms	3
Full Baths	2
Main Ceiling	10'-12'
Max Ridge Height	24'
Roof Framing	Truss

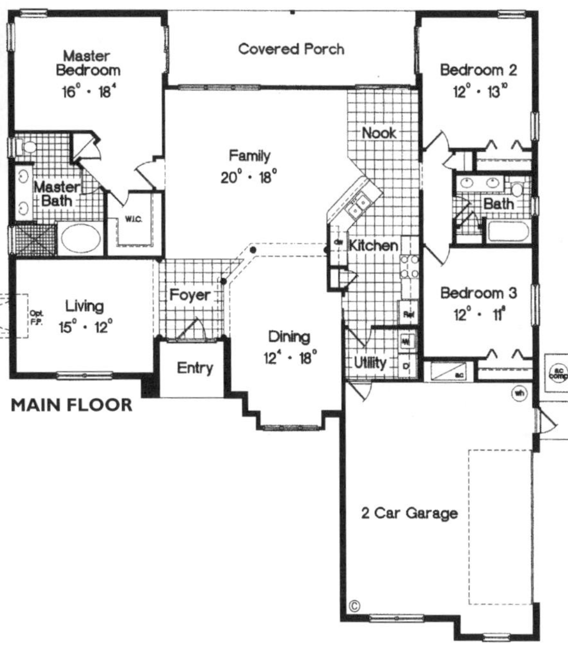
Covered Porch
Master Bedroom
16⁰ · 18⁴
Bedroom 2
12⁰ · 13¹⁰
Nook
Family
20⁰ · 18⁰
Master Bath
W.I.C.
Bath
Kitchen
Living
15⁰ · 12⁰
Foyer
Bedroom 3
12⁰ · 11⁸
Dining
12⁴ · 18⁰
Entry
Utility
MAIN FLOOR
2 Car Garage

Design 98559

Units	Single
Price Code	D
Total Finished	2,081 sq. ft.
Main Finished	2,081 sq. ft.
Garage Unfinished	422 sq. ft.
Porch Unfinished	240 sq. ft.
Dimensions	55'x57'10"
Foundation	Slab
Bedrooms	3
Full Baths	2
3/4 Baths	1
Max Ridge Height	24'6"
Roof Framing	Stick
Exterior Walls	2x4

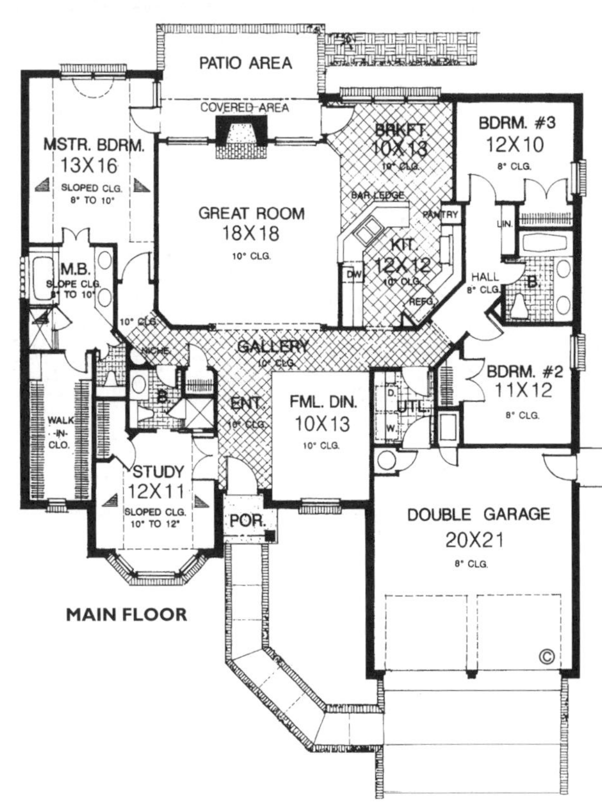
PATIO AREA
COVERED AREA
MSTR. BDRM.
13X16
SLOPED CLG.
8" TO 10"
BRKFT.
10X13
BDRM. #3
12X10
8" CLG.
GREAT ROOM
18X18
10" CLG.
PANTRY
KIT.
12X12
M.B.
SLOPE CLG.
TO 10"
HALL
8" CLG.
GALLERY
BDRM. #2
11X12
8" CLG.
WALK-IN-CLO.
ENT.
FML. DIN.
10X13
10" CLG.
UTL.
STUDY
12X11
SLOPED CLG.
10" TO 12"
POR.
DOUBLE GARAGE
20X21
8" CLG.
MAIN FLOOR

Design 92642

PHOTOGRAPHY: DONNA AND RON KOLB, EXPOSURES UNLIMITED

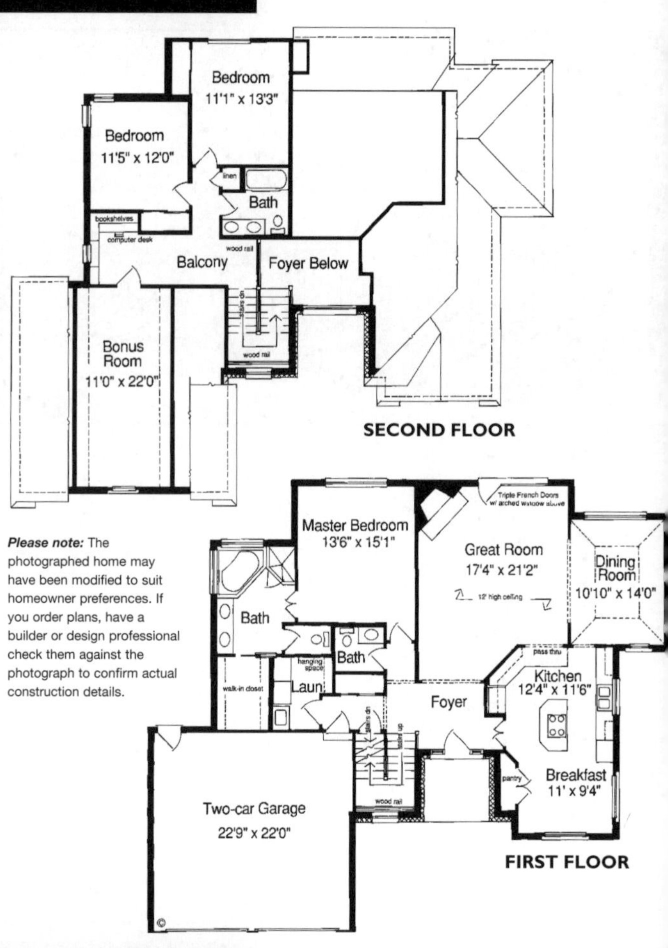

Bedroom
11'1" x 13'3"
Bedroom
11'5" x 12'0"
Bath
Balcony
Foyer Below
Bonus Room
11'0" x 22'0"
SECOND FLOOR
Master Bedroom
13'6" x 15'1"
Great Room
17'4" x 21'2"
Dining Room
10'10" x 14'0"
Bath
Bath
Laun
Kitchen
12'4" x 11'6"
Foyer
Breakfast
11' x 9'4"
Two-car Garage
22'9" x 22'0"
FIRST FLOOR

Units	Single
Price Code	D
Total Finished	2,082 sq. ft.
First Finished	1,524 sq. ft.
Second Finished	558 sq. ft.
Bonus Unfinished	267 sq. ft.
Basement Unfinished	1,460 sq. ft.
Dimensions	60'x50'4"
Foundation	Basement
Bedrooms	3
Full Baths	2
Half Baths	1
First Ceiling	8'
Second Ceiling	8'
Max Ridge Height	26'
Roof Framing	Truss
Exterior Walls	2x4

Please note: The photographed home may have been modified to suit homeowner preferences. If you order plans, have a builder or design professional check them against the photograph to confirm actual construction details.

Design 24245

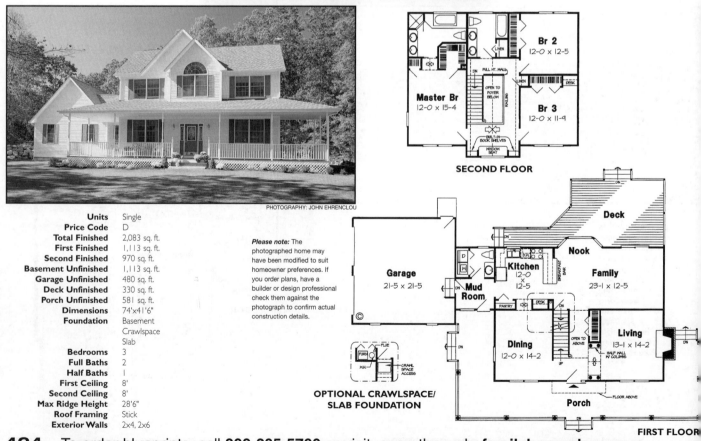

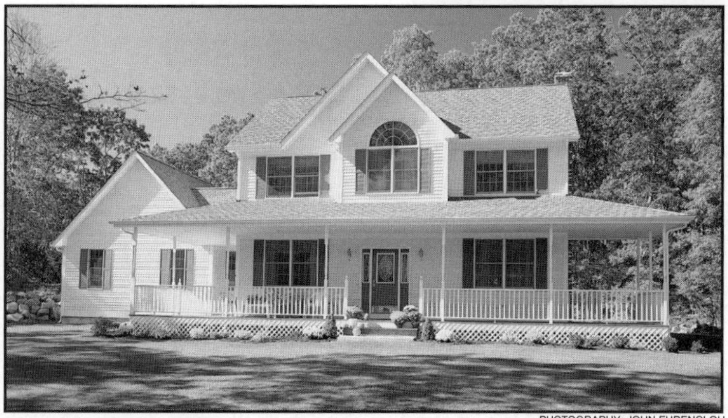

PHOTOGRAPHY: JOHN EHRENCLOU

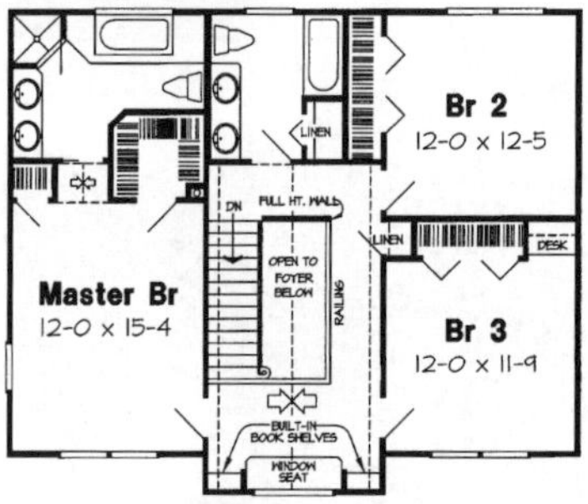

Units	Single
Price Code	D
Total Finished	2,083 sq. ft.
First Finished	1,113 sq. ft.
Second Finished	970 sq. ft.
Basement Unfinished	1,113 sq. ft.
Garage Unfinished	480 sq. ft.
Deck Unfinished	330 sq. ft.
Porch Unfinished	581 sq. ft.
Dimensions	74'x41'6"
Foundation	Basement Crawlspace Slab
Bedrooms	3
Full Baths	2
Half Baths	1
First Ceiling	8'
Second Ceiling	8'
Max Ridge Height	28'6"
Roof Framing	Stick
Exterior Walls	2x4, 2x6

Please note: The photographed home may have been modified to suit homeowner preferences. If you order plans, have a builder or design professional check them against the photograph to confirm actual construction details.

Master Br 12-0 x 15-4
Br 2 12-0 x 12-5
Br 3 12-0 x 11-9

SECOND FLOOR

Garage 21-5 x 21-5
Mud Room
Kitchen 12-0 x 12-5
Nook
Deck
Family 23-1 x 12-5
Dining 12-0 x 14-2
Living 13-1 x 14-2
Porch

OPTIONAL CRAWLSPACE/ SLAB FOUNDATION

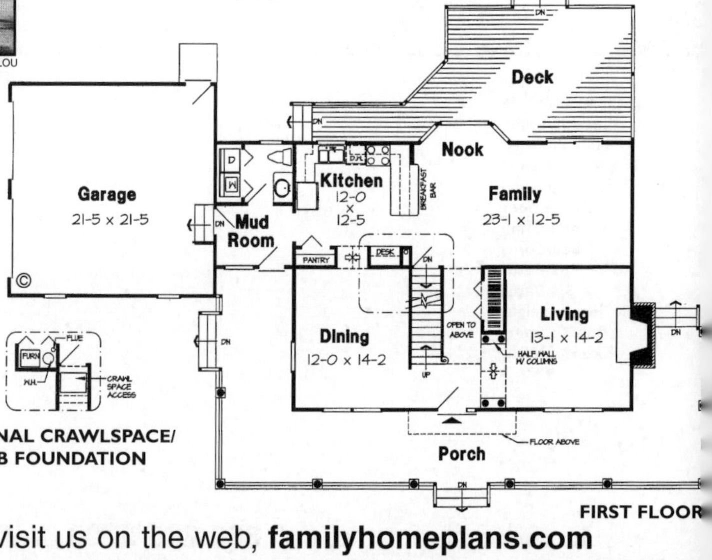

FIRST FLOOR

Design 69115

Units	Single
Price Code	D
Total Finished	2,083 sq. ft.
Main Finished	2,083 sq. ft.
Garage Unfinished	533 sq. ft.
Dimensions	84'x43'9"
Foundation	Crawlspace
Bedrooms	3
Full Baths	1
3/4 Baths	1
Main Ceiling	9'
Max Ridge Height	20'10"
Roof Framing	Truss
Exterior Walls	2x6

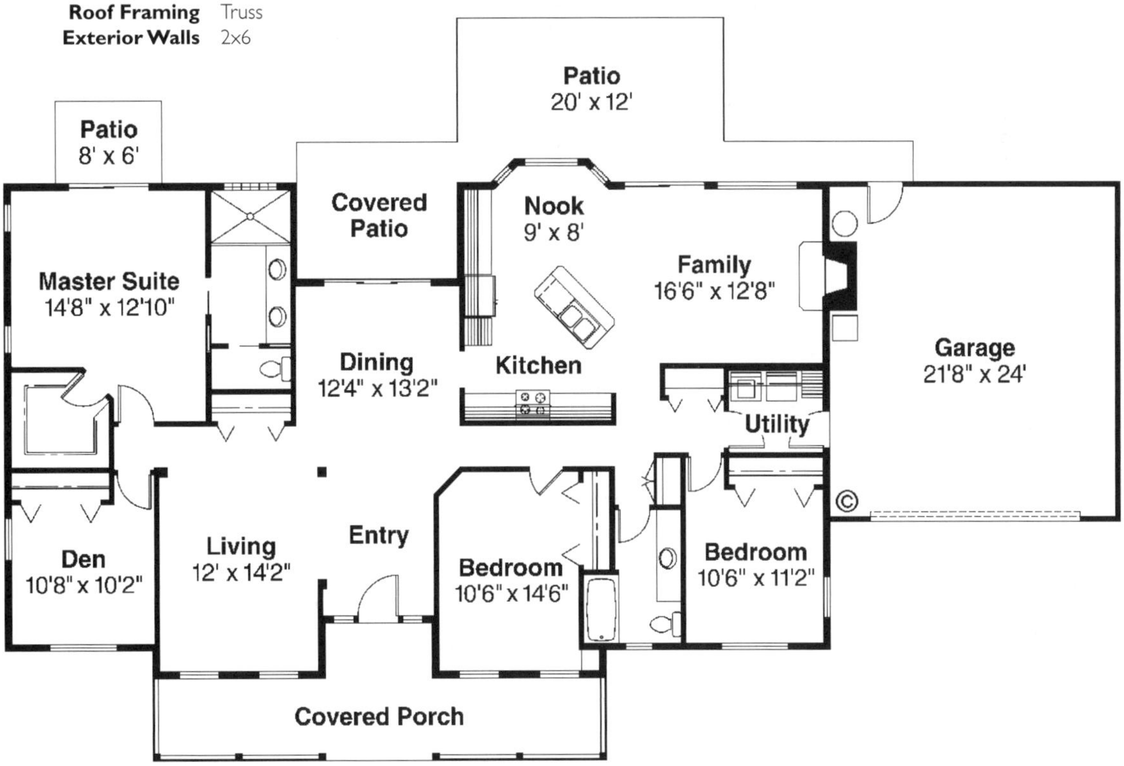

Patio 20' x 12'

Patio 8' x 6'

Covered Patio

Nook 9' x 8'

Master Suite 14'8" x 12'10"

Family 16'6" x 12'8"

Dining 12'4" x 13'2"

Kitchen

Garage 21'8" x 24'

Utility

Den 10'8" x 10'2"

Living 12' x 14'2"

Entry

Bedroom 10'6" x 14'6"

Bedroom 10'6" x 11'2"

Covered Porch

MAIN FLOOR

Design 93213

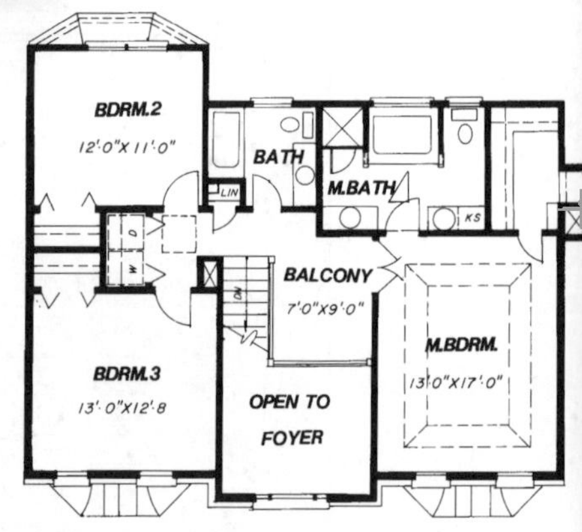
BDRM.2
12'-0"X11'-0"
BATH
LIN
M.BATH
KS
BALCONY
7'-0"X9'-0"
M.BDRM.
13'-0"X17'-0"
BDRM.3
13'-0"X12'-8
OPEN TO
FOYER
SECOND FLOOR

Units	Single
Price Code	D
Total Finished	2,085 sq. ft.
First Finished	1,126 sq. ft.
Second Finished	959 sq. ft.
Basement Unfinished	458 sq. ft.
Garage Unfinished	627 sq. ft.
Dimensions	40'4"x35'
Foundation	Basement Slab
Bedrooms	3
Full Baths	2
Half Baths	1
First Ceiling	8'
Max Ridge Height	29'
Roof Framing	Stick
Exterior Walls	2x4

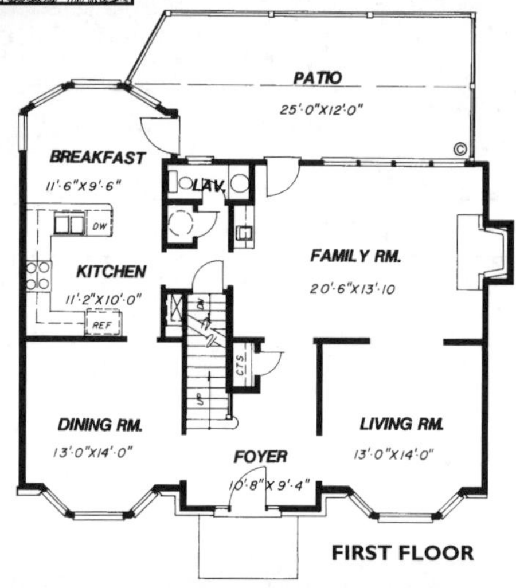
PATIO
25'-0"X12'-0"
BREAKFAST
11'-6"X9'-6"
LAV.
DW
KITCHEN
11'-2"X10'-0"
REF
FAMILY RM.
20'-6"X13'-10
CTS.
DINING RM.
13'-0"X14'-0"
FOYER
10'-8"X9'-4"
LIVING RM.
13'-0"X14'-0"
FIRST FLOOR

Design 92435

Units	Single
Price Code	D
Total Finished	2,088 sq. ft.
Main Finished	2,088 sq. ft.
Bonus Unfinished	282 sq. ft.
Basement Unfinished	2,088 sq. ft.
Dimensions	68'x53'
Foundation	Basement Crawlspace Slab
Bedrooms	3
Full Baths	2
Half Baths	1
Main Ceiling	9'
Vaulted Ceiling	14'
Tray Ceiling	11'
Max Ridge Height	22'
Roof Framing	Stick
Exterior Walls	2x4

DECK
MORNING
PORCH
11' CEILING
MASTER
BEDROOM
16X15
BEDROOM 3
14X11
BRKFST
11X9
11' CEILING
14' CEILING
FAMILY ROOM
17X19
KITCHEN
13X12
11' CEILING
STORAGE
BEDROOM 2
14X11
LIVING
11X12
FOYER
DINING
13X11
11' CEILING
BONUS ROOM ABOVE
GARAGE
23X20
MAIN FLOOR

Design 63056

Units	Single
Price Code	C
Total Finished	2,089 sq. ft.
Main Finished	2,089 sq. ft.
Garage Unfinished	415 sq. ft.
Deck Unfinished	359 sq. ft.
Dimensions	61'8"x49'11"
Foundation	Slab
Bedrooms	4
Full Baths	3
Main Ceiling	10'
Max Ridge Height	20'10"
Exterior Walls	2x4

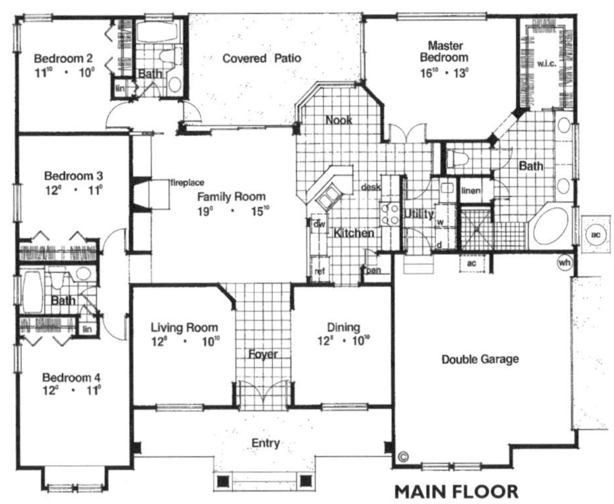
Bedroom 2
Bath
lin
Covered Patio
Master Bedroom
w.i.c.
Nook
Bath
Bedroom 3
fireplace
Family Room
desk
Utility
linen
Kitchen
ac
wh
Bath
lin
Living Room
Dining
Foyer
Double Garage
Bedroom 4
Entry

MAIN FLOOR

Design 65135

Units	Single
Price Code	D
Total Finished	2,089 sq. ft.
First Finished	1,146 sq. ft.
Second Finished	943 sq. ft.
Bonus Unfinished	313 sq. ft.
Basement Unfinished	483 sq. ft.
Porch Unfinished	168 sq. ft.
Dimensions	56'x38'
Foundation	Basement
Bedrooms	3
Full Baths	2
Half Baths	1
First Ceiling	9'
Second Ceiling	8'
Max Ridge Height	31'3"
Roof Framing	Truss
Exterior Walls	2x6

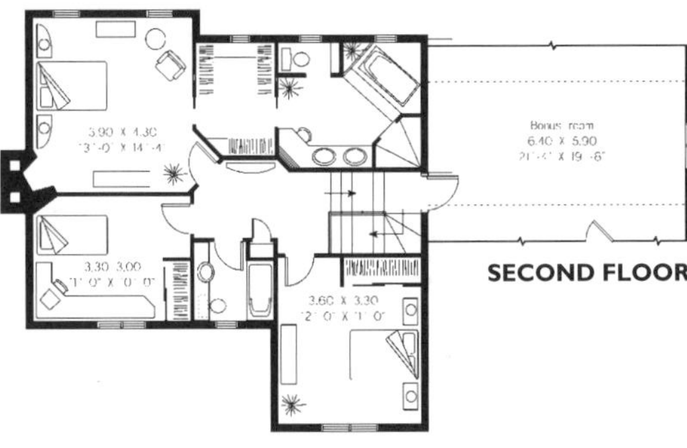

SECOND FLOOR

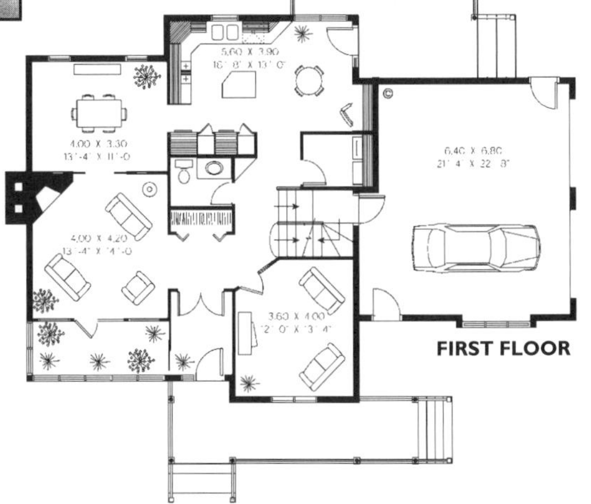

FIRST FLOOR

Design 96529

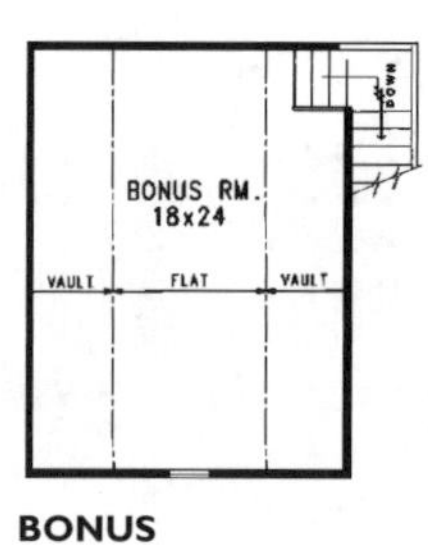
BONUS RM.
18x24
VAULT
FLAT
VAULT
DOWN

BONUS

Units	Single
Price Code	D
Total Finished	2,089 sq. ft.
Main Finished	2,089 sq. ft.
Bonus Unfinished	497 sq. ft.
Garage Unfinished	541 sq. ft.
Dimensions	79'x52'
Foundation	Crawlspace Slab
Bedrooms	3
Full Baths	2
Half Baths	1
Main Ceiling	9'
Max Ridge Height	22'
Roof Framing	Stick
Exterior Walls	2x4

MASTER SUITE 13x19
BATH
PORCH
PANTRY
KITCHEN 12x15
GREAT RM. 18x19
BED RM. 13x13
UTILITY
GARAGE 26x24
BATH
DINING 12x13
FOYER
STUDY 11x9
PORCH
BED RM. 13x14

MAIN FLOOR

Design 93212

Study 11-2 x 11-0
Bdrm.2 13-6 x 13-4
Bdrm.3 12-0 x 13-4
Bth.2
Bonus Rm. 11-8 x 21-10

SECOND FLOOR

Units	Single
Price Code	D
Total Finished	2,091 sq. ft.
First Finished	1,362 sq. ft.
Second Finished	729 sq. ft.
Bonus Unfinished	384 sq. ft.
Basement Unfinished	988 sq. ft.
Garage Unfinished	559 sq. ft.
Porch Unfinished	396 sq. ft.
Dimensions	78'x38'
Foundation	Basement Crawlspace Slab
Bedrooms	3
Full Baths	2
Half Baths	1
Max Ridge Height	23'
Roof Framing	Stick
Exterior Walls	2x4

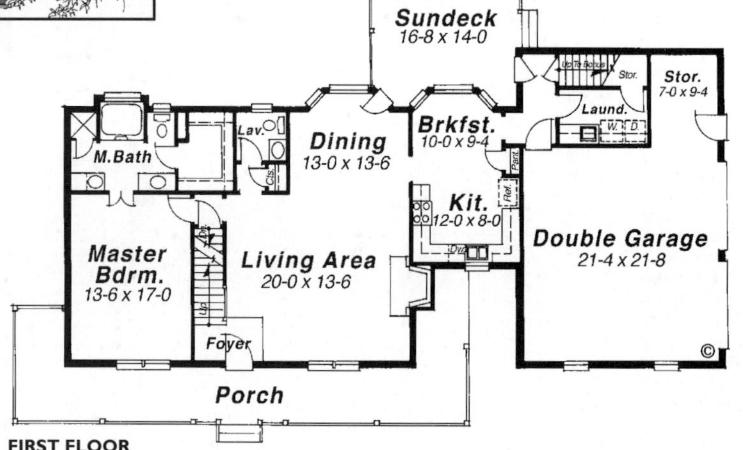
Sundeck 16-8 x 14-0
M.Bath
Lav.
Dining 13-0 x 13-6
Brkfst. 10-0 x 9-4
Stor. 7-0 x 9-4
Laund.
Kit. 12-0 x 8-0
Master Bdrm. 13-6 x 17-0
Living Area 20-0 x 13-6
Double Garage 21-4 x 21-8
Foyer
Porch

FIRST FLOOR

Design 67004

Units	Single
Price Code	D
Total Finished	2,093 sq. ft.
First Finished	1,713 sq. ft.
Second Finished	381 sq. ft.
Bonus Unfinished	327 sq. ft.
Garage Unfinished	480 sq. ft.
Porch Unfinished	271 sq. ft.
Dimensions	62'4"x60'
Foundation	Crawlspace Slab
Bedrooms	3
Full Baths	2
Half Baths	1
First Ceiling	8
Second Ceiling	8
Max Ridge Height	20'
Roof Framing	Stick
Exterior Walls	2x4

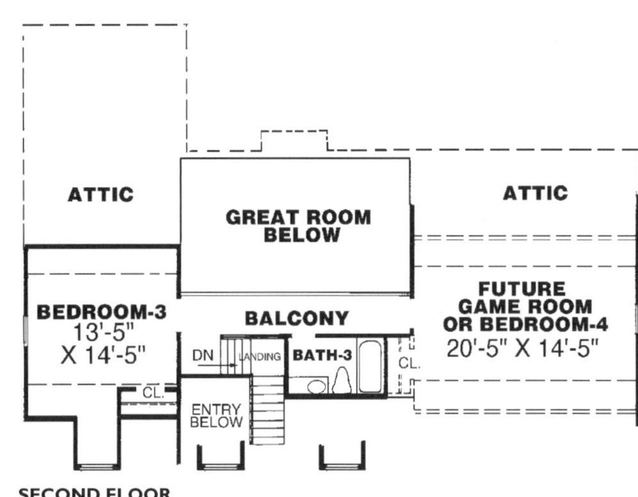
ATTIC
GREAT ROOM BELOW
ATTIC
BEDROOM-3
13'-5"
X 14'-5"
BALCONY
FUTURE GAME ROOM OR BEDROOM-4
20'-5" X 14'-5"
DN
LANDING
BATH-3
CL.
CL.
ENTRY BELOW

SECOND FLOOR

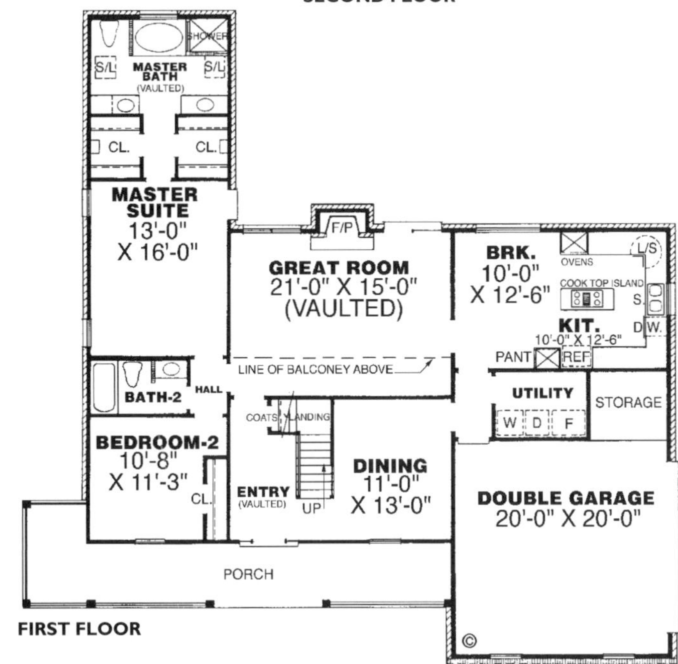
SHOWER
S/L
MASTER BATH
(VAULTED)
S/L
CL.
CL.
MASTER SUITE
13'-0"
X 16'-0"
F/P
GREAT ROOM
21'-0" X 15'-0"
(VAULTED)
BRK.
10'-0"
X 12'-6"
OVENS
COOK TOP ISLAND
L/S
S.
KIT.
10'-0" X 12'-6"
D.W.
PANT
REF
LINE OF BALCONEY ABOVE
BATH-2
HALL
UTILITY
W D F
STORAGE
COATS
LANDING
BEDROOM-2
10'-8"
X 11'-3"
CL.
ENTRY
(VAULTED)
UP
DINING
11'-0"
X 13'-0"
DOUBLE GARAGE
20'-0" X 20'-0"
PORCH
©

FIRST FLOOR

Design 93158

Units	Single
Price Code	D
Total Finished	2,095 sq. ft.
Main Finished	2,095 sq. ft.
Basement Unfinished	2,095 sq. ft.
Dimensions	67'x58'
Foundation	Basement
Bedrooms	3
Full Baths	2
Max Ridge Height	24'9"
Roof Framing	Stick
Exterior Walls	2x6

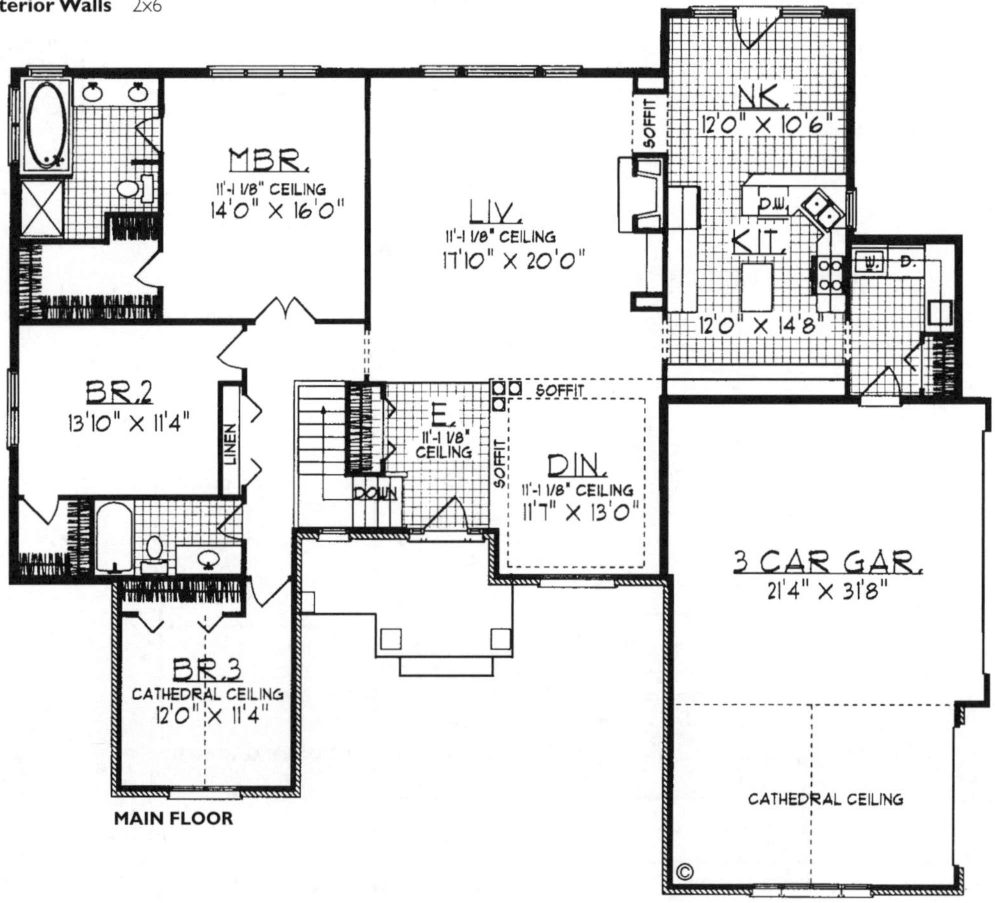
NK.
12'0" X 10'6"
SOFFIT
MBR.
11'-1 1/8" CEILING
14'0" X 16'0"
LIV.
11'-1 1/8" CEILING
17'10" X 20'0"
DW.
KIT.
12'0" X 14'8"
D.
BR.2
13'10" X 11'4"
LINEN
E.
11'-1 1/8" CEILING
DOWN
SOFFIT
DIN.
11'-1 1/8" CEILING
11'7" X 13'0"
3 CAR GAR.
21'4" X 31'8"
BR.3
CATHEDRAL CEILING
12'0" X 11'4"
CATHEDRAL CEILING
MAIN FLOOR

Design 97279

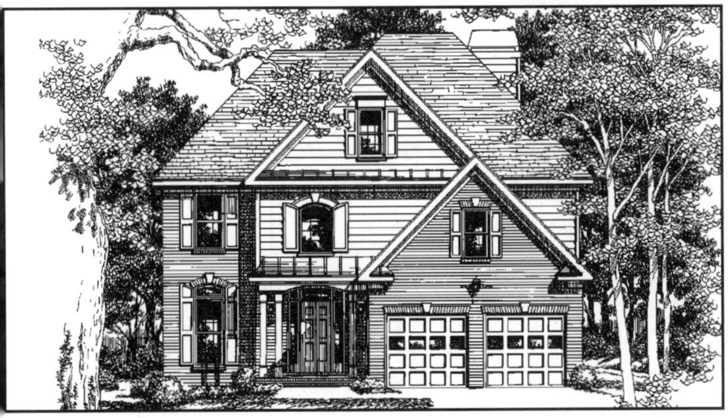

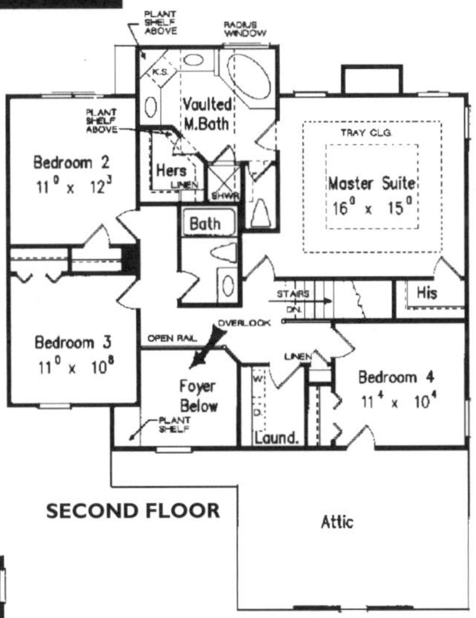

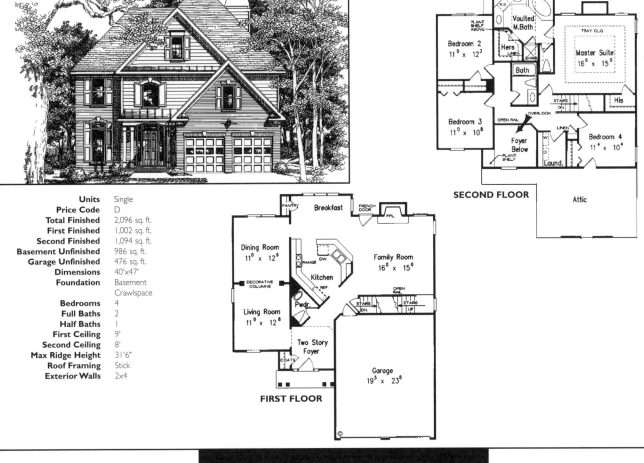

Units	Single
Price Code	D
Total Finished	2,096 sq. ft.
First Finished	1,002 sq. ft.
Second Finished	1,094 sq. ft.
Basement Unfinished	986 sq. ft.
Garage Unfinished	476 sq. ft.
Dimensions	40'x47'
Foundation	Basement Crawlspace
Bedrooms	4
Full Baths	2
Half Baths	1
First Ceiling	9'
Second Ceiling	8'
Max Ridge Height	31'6"
Roof Framing	Stick
Exterior Walls	2x4

FIRST FLOOR

SECOND FLOOR

Design 92444

Units	Single
Price Code	D
Total Finished	2,097 sq. ft.
Main Finished	2,097 sq. ft.
Bonus Unfinished	452 sq. ft.
Garage Unfinished	721 sq. ft.
Dimensions	70'2"x59'
Foundation	Slab
Bedrooms	3
Full Baths	3
Main Ceiling	9'
Max Ridge Height	24'
Roof Framing	Stick
Exterior Walls	2x4

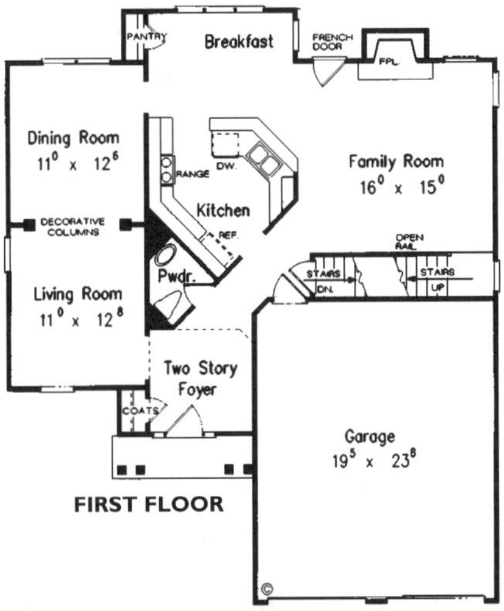

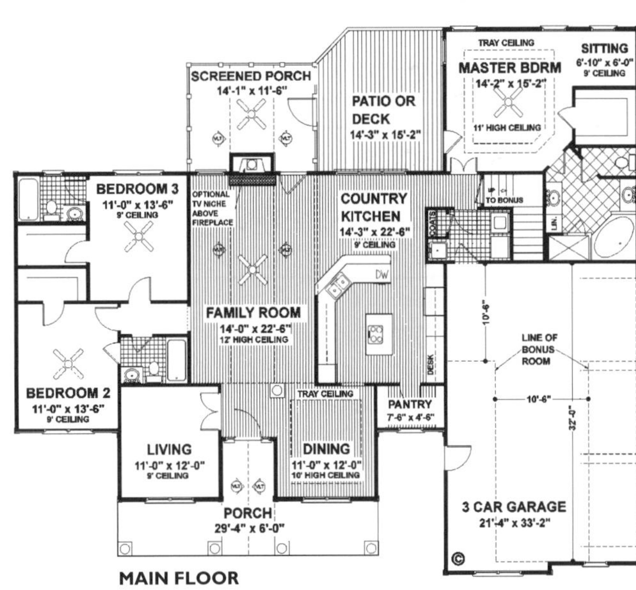
SCREENED PORCH
14'-1" x 11'-6"
PATIO OR DECK
14'-3" x 15'-2"
TRAY CEILING
MASTER BDRM
14'-2" x 15'-2"
11' HIGH CEILING
SITTING
6'-10" x 6'-0"
9' CEILING
BEDROOM 3
11'-0" x 13'-6"
9' CEILING
OPTIONAL TV NICHE ABOVE FIREPLACE
COUNTRY KITCHEN
14'-3" x 22'-6"
9' CEILING
TO BONUS
FAMILY ROOM
14'-0" x 22'-6"
12' HIGH CEILING
LINE OF BONUS ROOM
BEDROOM 2
11'-0" x 13'-6"
9' CEILING
TRAY CEILING
PANTRY
7'-6" x 4'-6"
LIVING
11'-0" x 12'-0"
9' CEILING
DINING
11'-0" x 12'-0"
10' HIGH CEILING
PORCH
29'-4" x 6'-0"
3 CAR GARAGE
21'-4" x 33'-2"

MAIN FLOOR

Design 96539

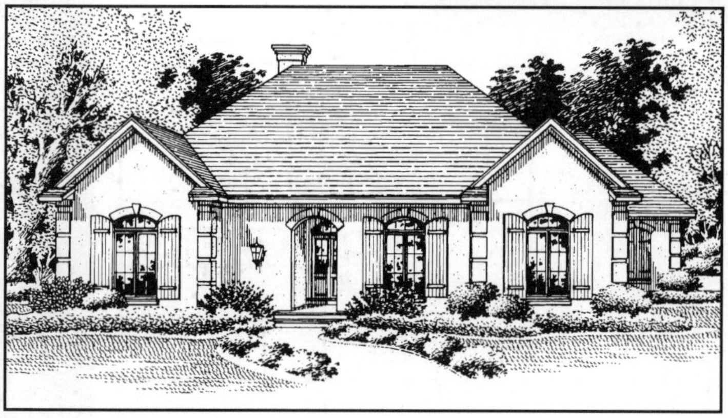

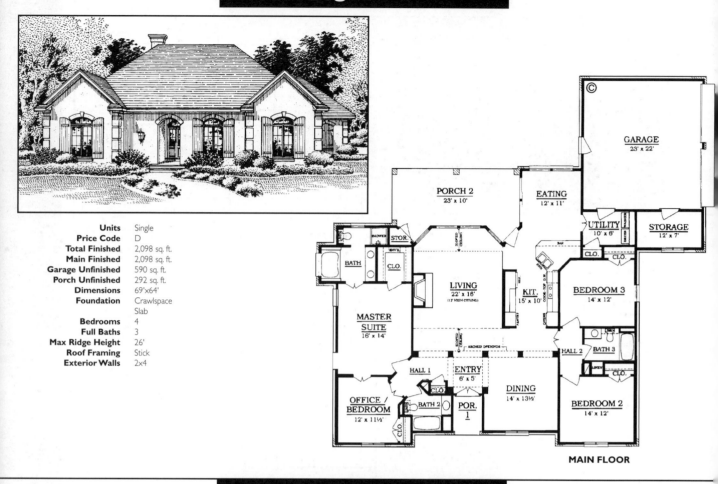

Units	Single
Price Code	D
Total Finished	2,098 sq. ft.
Main Finished	2,098 sq. ft.
Garage Unfinished	590 sq. ft.
Porch Unfinished	292 sq. ft.
Dimensions	69'x64'
Foundation	Crawlspace Slab
Bedrooms	4
Full Baths	3
Max Ridge Height	26'
Roof Framing	Stick
Exterior Walls	2x4

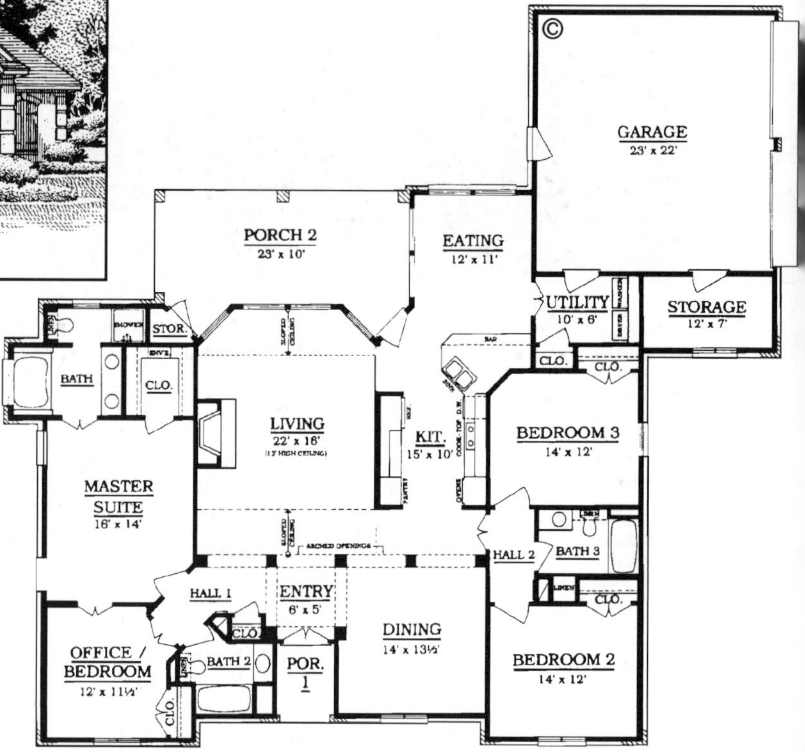

GARAGE 23' x 22'
PORCH 2 23' x 10'
EATING 12' x 11'
UTILITY 10' x 6'
STORAGE 12' x 7'
BATH
STOR.
CLO.
LIVING 22' x 16'
KIT. 15' x 10'
BEDROOM 3 14' x 12'
MASTER SUITE 16' x 14'
BATH 3
HALL 2
HALL 1
ENTRY 6' x 5'
DINING 14' x 13½'
BEDROOM 2 14' x 12'
OFFICE / BEDROOM 12' x 11½'
BATH 2
POR. 1

MAIN FLOOR

Design 91053

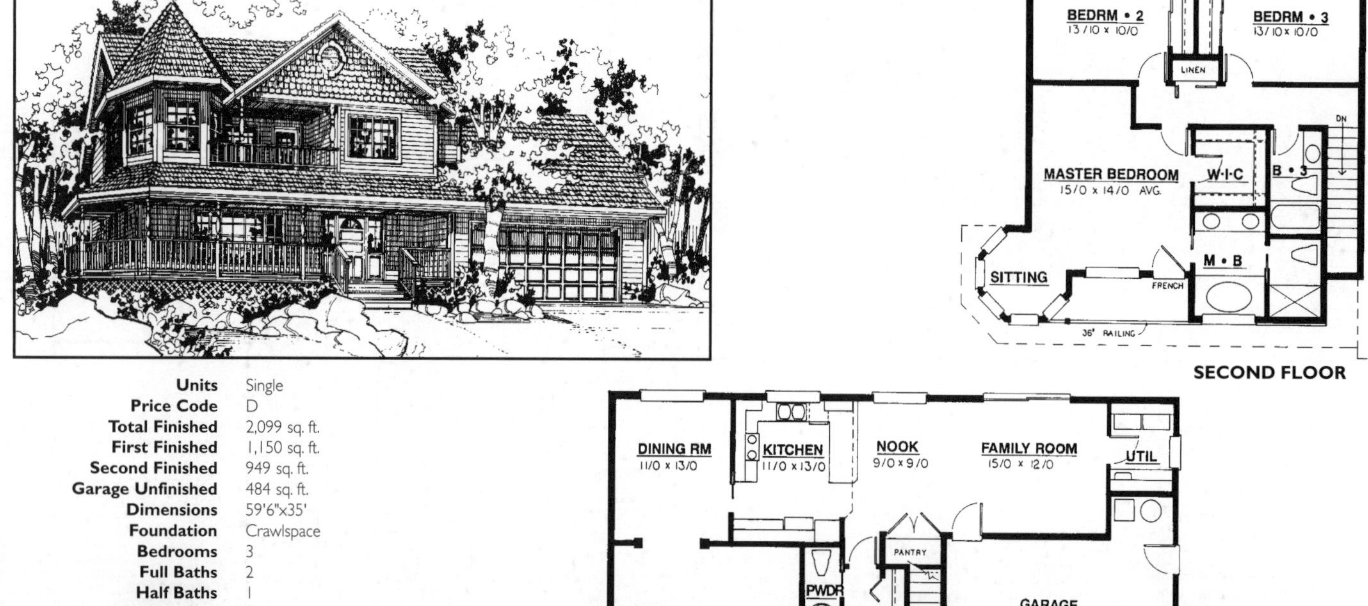
BEDRM • 2
13/10 x 10/0
BEDRM • 3
13/10 x 10/0
LINEN
MASTER BEDROOM
15/0 x 14/0 AVG.
W-I-C
B • 3
SITTING
M • B
FRENCH
36" RAILING
SECOND FLOOR
DINING RM
11/0 x 13/0
KITCHEN
11/0 x 13/0
NOOK
9/0 x 9/0
FAMILY ROOM
15/0 x 12/0
UTIL
PANTRY
PWDR
LIVING RM
17/6 x 13/8
GARAGE
21/4 x 24/8

Units	Single
Price Code	D
Total Finished	2,099 sq. ft.
First Finished	1,150 sq. ft.
Second Finished	949 sq. ft.
Garage Unfinished	484 sq. ft.
Dimensions	59'6"x35'
Foundation	Crawlspace
Bedrooms	3
Full Baths	2
Half Baths	1
First Ceiling	8'
Max Ridge Height	26'
Roof Framing	Truss
Exterior Walls	2x6

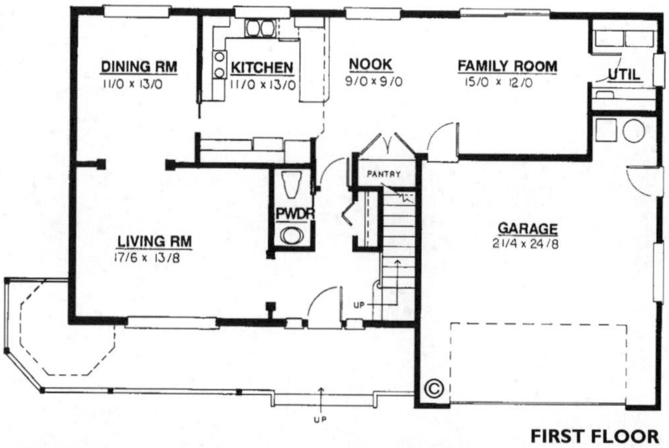

FIRST FLOOR

Design 65470

SECOND FLOOR

FIRST FLOOR

Units	Single
Price Code	D
Total Finished	2,100 sq. ft.
First Finished	1,405 sq. ft.
Second Finished	695 sq. ft.
Basement Unfinished	1,405 sq. ft.
Garage Unfinished	479 sq. ft.
Deck Unfinished	415 sq. ft.
Porch Unfinished	32 sq. ft.
Dimensions	60'x46'
Foundation	Basement
Bedrooms	3
Full Baths	2
Half Baths	1
First Ceiling	8'
Second Ceiling	8'
Max Ridge Height	26'9"
Roof Framing	Truss
Exterior Walls	2x6

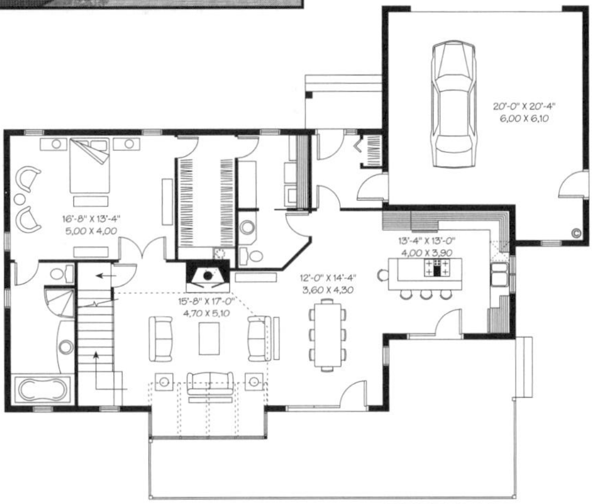

Design 92610

PHOTOGRAPHY: COURTESY OF DONNA AND RON KOLB, EXPOSURES UNLIMITED

Units	Single
Price Code	D
Total Finished	2,101 sq. ft.
First Finished	1,626 sq. ft.
Second Finished	475 sq. ft.
Basement Unfinished	1,512 sq. ft.
Garage Unfinished	438 sq. ft.
Dimensions	59'x60'8"
Foundation	Basement
Bedrooms	3
Full Baths	2
Half Baths	1
First Ceiling	8'
Second Ceiling	8'
Max Ridge Height	31'
Roof Framing	Truss
Exterior Walls	2x4

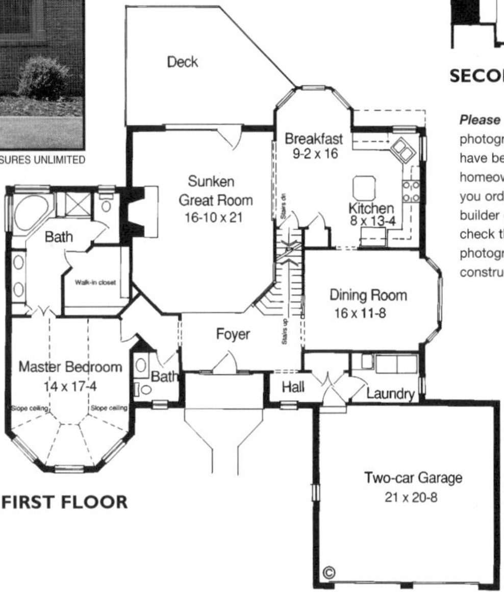

SECOND FLOOR

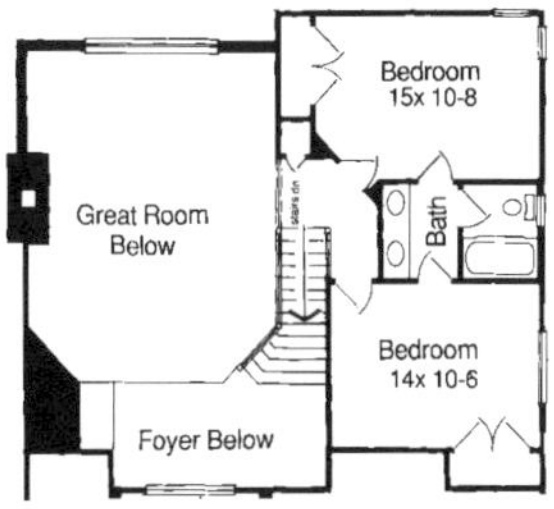

FIRST FLOOR

Please note: The photographed home may have been modified to suit homeowner preferences. If you order plans, have a builder or design professional check them against the photograph to confirm actual construction details.

Design 93354

Units	Single
Price Code	D
Total Finished	2,102 sq. ft.
First Finished	1,110 sq. ft.
Second Finished	992 sq. ft.
Basement Unfinished	1,110 sq. ft.
Garage Unfinished	530 sq. ft.
Porch Unfinished	32 sq. ft.
Dimensions	59'4"x37'4"
Foundation	Basement
Bedrooms	4
Full Baths	2
Half Baths	1
First Ceiling	8'
Second Ceiling	8'
Max Ridge Height	29'
Roof Framing	Stick
Exterior Walls	2x4

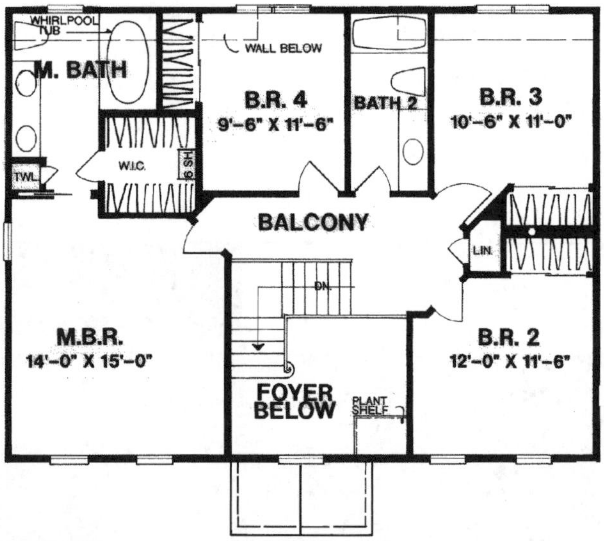

WHIRLPOOL TUB
M. BATH
WALL BELOW
B.R. 4
9'-6" X 11'-6"
BATH 2
B.R. 3
10'-6" X 11'-0"
W.I.C.
TWL.
BALCONY
LIN.
DN.
M.B.R.
14'-0" X 15'-0"
B.R. 2
12'-0" X 11'-6"
FOYER BELOW
PLANT SHELF

SECOND FLOOR

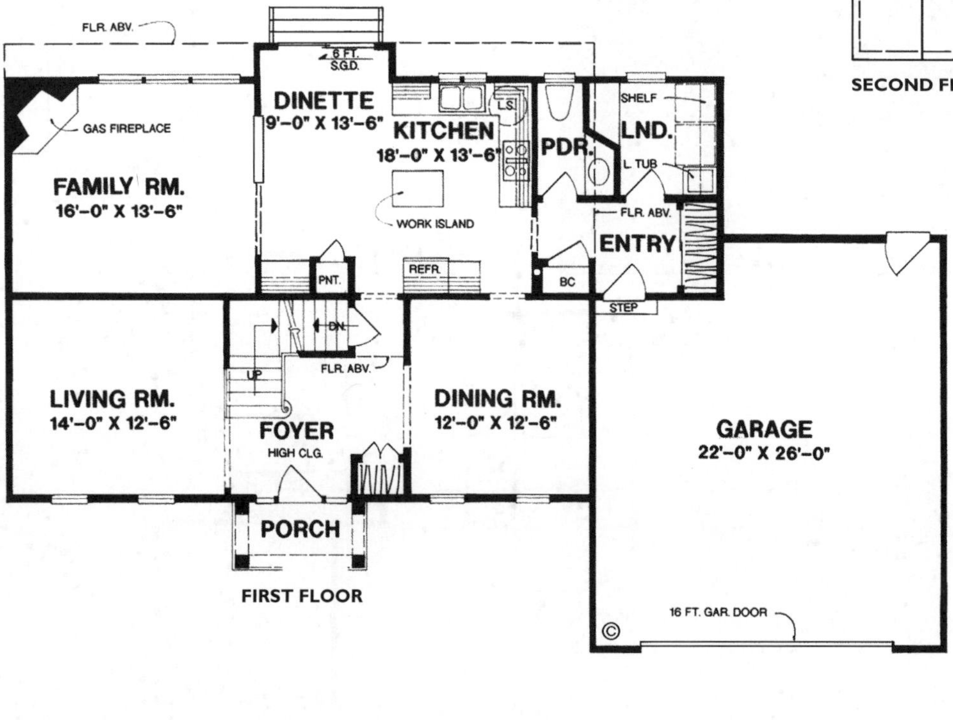

FLR. ABV.
6 FT. S.G.D.
DINETTE
9'-0" X 13'-6"
KITCHEN
18'-0" X 13'-6"
L.S.
PDR.
SHELF
LND.
L. TUB
GAS FIREPLACE
FAMILY RM.
16'-0" X 13'-6"
WORK ISLAND
FLR. ABV.
ENTRY
PNT.
REFR.
BC
STEP
DN.
UP
FLR. ABV.
LIVING RM.
14'-0" X 12'-6"
FOYER
HIGH CLG.
DINING RM.
12'-0" X 12'-6"
GARAGE
22'-0" X 26'-0"
PORCH
16 FT. GAR. DOOR
©

FIRST FLOOR

Design 65428

14'-8" X 12'-8"
4,40 X 3,80
12'-8" X 10'-8"
3,80 X 3,20
9'-4" X 20'-4"
2,80 X 6,10
SECOND FLOOR

Units	Single
Price Code	D
Total Finished	2,104 sq. ft.
First Finished	1,558 sq. ft.
Second Finished	546 sq. ft.
Bonus Unfinished	233 sq. ft.
Basement Unfinished	1,558 sq. ft.
Garage Unfinished	384 sq. ft.
Deck Unfinished	90 sq. ft.
Porch Unfinished	36 sq. ft.
Dimensions	48'x52'
Foundation	Basement
Bedrooms	3
Full Baths	2
Half Baths	1
Max Ridge Height	31'4"
Roof Framing	Truss

10'-0" X 18'-4"
3,00 X 5,50
12'-0" X 12'-8"
3,60 X 3,80
15'-0" X 16'-8"
4,50 X 5,00
12'-0" X 15'-0"
3,60 X 4,50
10'-0" X 12'-8"
3,00 X 3,80
16'-4" X 20'-4"
4,90 X 6,10
FIRST FLOOR

Design 96550

Units	Single
Price Code	D
Total Finished	2,104 sq. ft.
Main Finished	2,104 sq. ft.
Garage Unfinished	564 sq. ft.
Porch Unfinished	305 sq. ft.
Dimensions	75'x56'
Foundation	Crawlspace Slab
Bedrooms	3
Full Baths	2
Half Baths	1
Main Ceiling	9'
Max Ridge Height	24'6"
Roof Framing	Stick
Exterior Walls	2x4

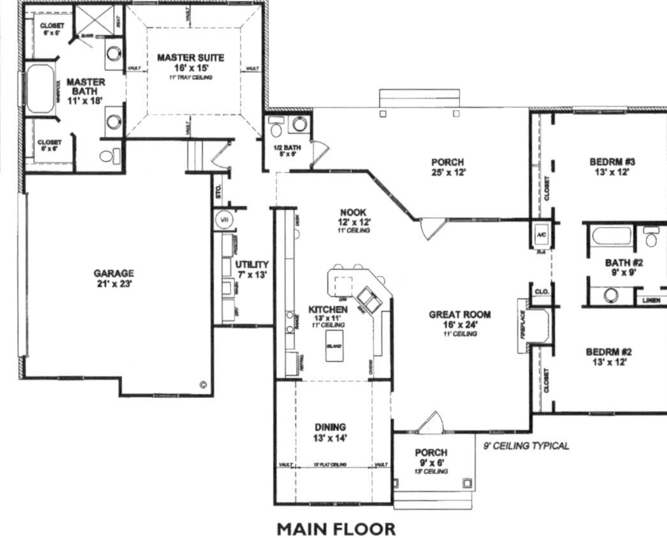
MASTER SUITE
16' x 15'
MASTER BATH
11' x 18'
GARAGE
21' x 23'
PORCH
25' x 12'
NOOK
12' x 12'
UTILITY
7' x 13'
KITCHEN
13' x 11'
GREAT ROOM
16' x 24'
BEDRM #3
13' x 12'
BATH #2
9' x 9'
BEDRM #2
13' x 12'
DINING
13' x 14'
PORCH
9' x 6'
9' CEILING TYPICAL
MAIN FLOOR

Design 32162

PHOTOGRAPHY: JAMES YOCHUM PHOTOGRAPHY

Please note: The photographed home may have been modified to suit homeowner preferences. If you order plans, have a builder or design professional check them against the photograph to confirm actual construction details

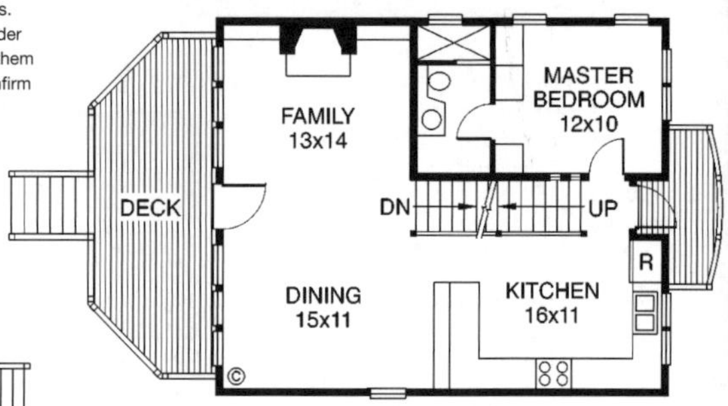

Units	Single
Price Code	D
Total Finished	2,107 sq. ft.
First Finished	827 sq. ft.
Second Finished	453 sq. ft.
Lower Finished	827 sq. ft.
Deck Unfinished	319 sq. ft.
Dimensions	26'x50'
Foundation	Basement
Bedrooms	4
3/4 Baths	3
First Ceiling	9
Vaulted Ceiling	10'4"
Max Ridge Height	33'8"
Roof Framing	Stick
Exterior Walls	2x6

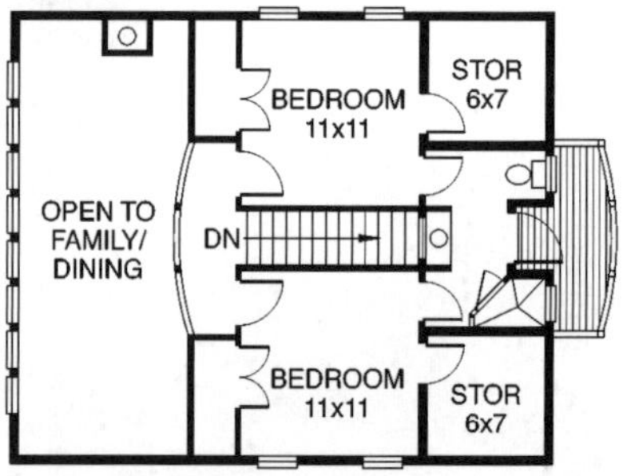

OPEN TO FAMILY/ DINING
DN
BEDROOM 11x11
STOR 6x7
BEDROOM 11x11
STOR 6x7

SECOND FLOOR

DECK
FAMILY 13x14
MASTER BEDROOM 12x10
DN
UP
R
DINING 15x11
KITCHEN 16x11

FIRST FLOOR

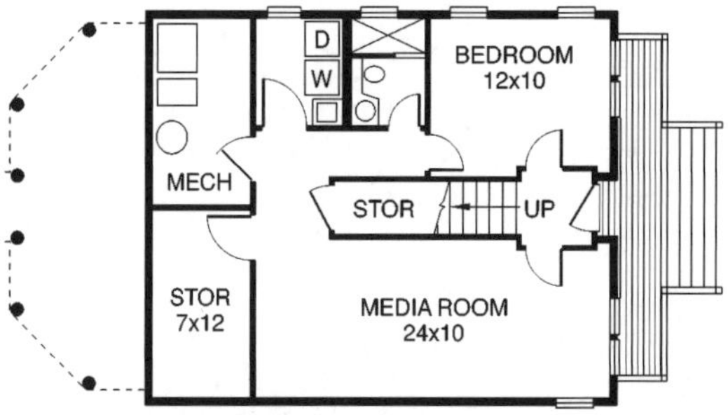

D
W
BEDROOM 12x10
MECH
STOR
UP
STOR 7x12
MEDIA ROOM 24x10

LOWER FLOOR

Design 10012

Units	Single
Price Code	D
Total Finished	2,108 sq. ft.
Main Finished	1,198 sq. ft.
Lower Finished	910 sq. ft.
Garage Unfinished	288 sq. ft.
Dimensions	32'x36'
Foundation	Basement
Bedrooms	3
Full Baths	2
Half Baths	1
Exterior Walls	2x4

BEDROOM 14'-0"X13'-0"
C.
BEDROOM 14'-8"X13'-0"
C.
H.
C.
C.
B.
C.
S.
LIVING ROOM 13'-0"X19'-0"
B.
LAU.
DN
KITCHEN 15'-0"X10'-4"
DECK
DN

MAIN FLOOR

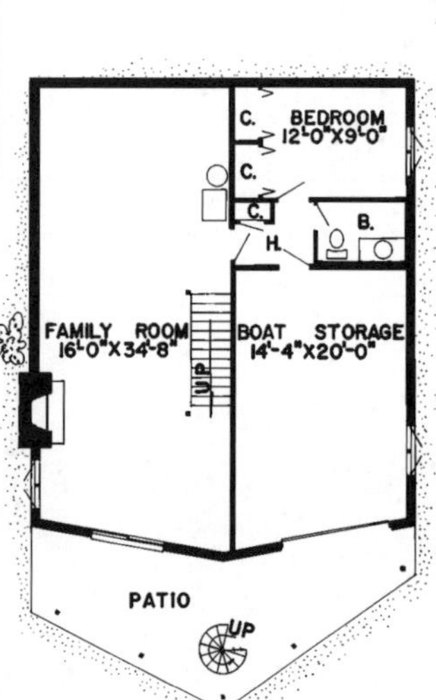
C.
BEDROOM 12'-0"X9'-0"
C.
C.
B.
H.
FAMILY ROOM 16'-0"X34'-8"
UP
BOAT STORAGE 14'-4"X20'-0"
PATIO
UP

LOWER FLOOR

Design 24256

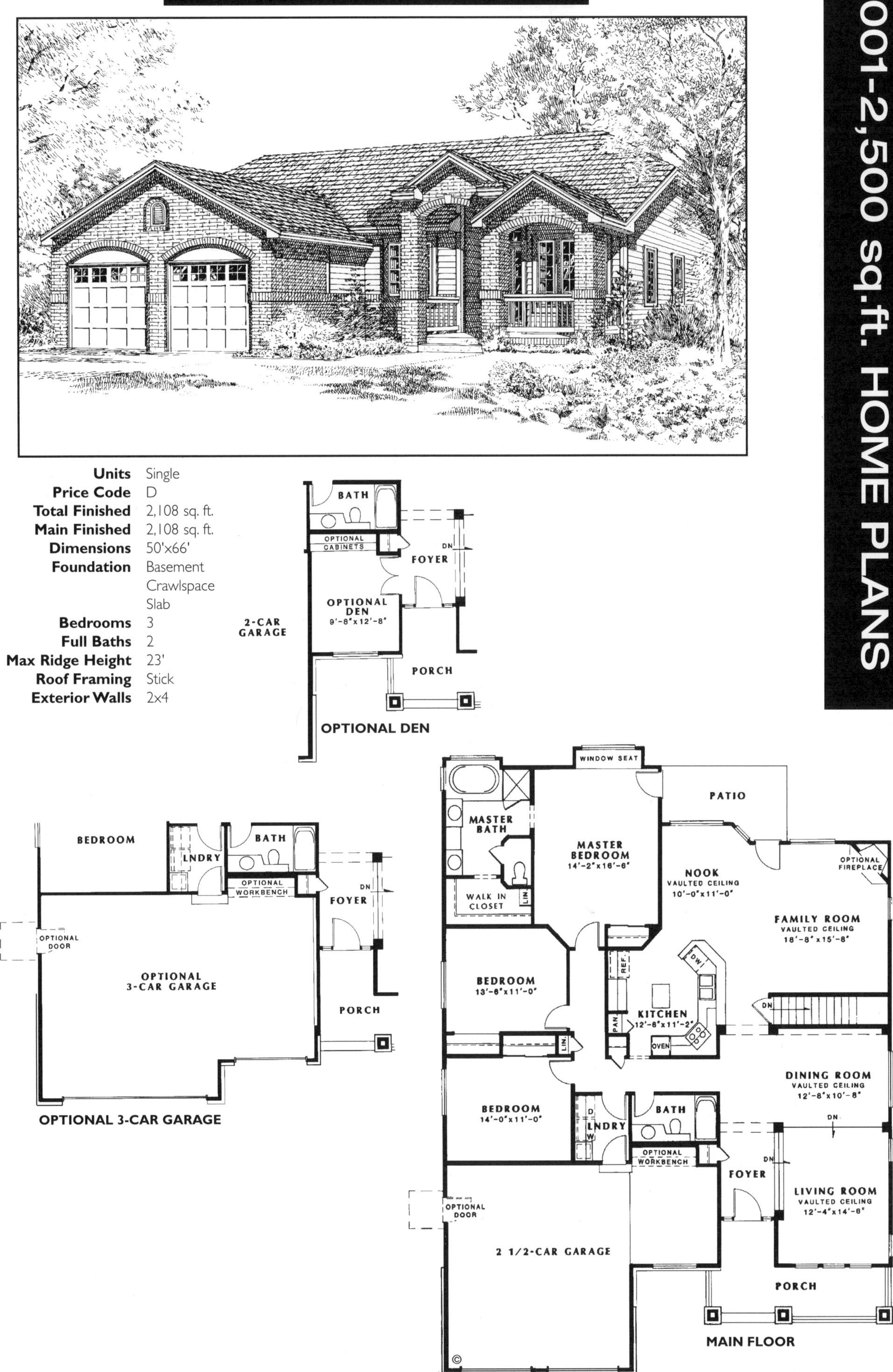

BATH
OPTIONAL CABINETS
DN
FOYER
OPTIONAL DEN 9'-8"x12'-8"
2-CAR GARAGE
PORCH
OPTIONAL DEN
BEDROOM
LNDRY
BATH
OPTIONAL WORKBENCH
DN
FOYER
OPTIONAL DOOR
OPTIONAL 3-CAR GARAGE
PORCH
OPTIONAL 3-CAR GARAGE
WINDOW SEAT
PATIO
MASTER BATH
MASTER BEDROOM 14'-2"x16'-6"
WALK IN CLOSET
LIN
NOOK VAULTED CEILING 10'-0"x11'-0"
OPTIONAL FIREPLACE
FAMILY ROOM VAULTED CEILING 18'-8"x15'-8"
BEDROOM 13'-6"x11'-0"
REF
DW
KITCHEN 12'-6"x11'-2"
PAN
OVEN
DN
LIN
DINING ROOM VAULTED CEILING 12'-8"x10'-8"
BEDROOM 14'-0"x11'-0"
D
W
LNDRY
BATH
OPTIONAL WORKBENCH
DN
FOYER
LIVING ROOM VAULTED CEILING 12'-4"x14'-8"
OPTIONAL DOOR
2 1/2-CAR GARAGE
PORCH
MAIN FLOOR
©

Units	Single
Price Code	D
Total Finished	2,108 sq. ft.
Main Finished	2,108 sq. ft.
Dimensions	50'x66'
Foundation	Basement Crawlspace Slab
Bedrooms	3
Full Baths	2
Max Ridge Height	23'
Roof Framing	Stick
Exterior Walls	2x4

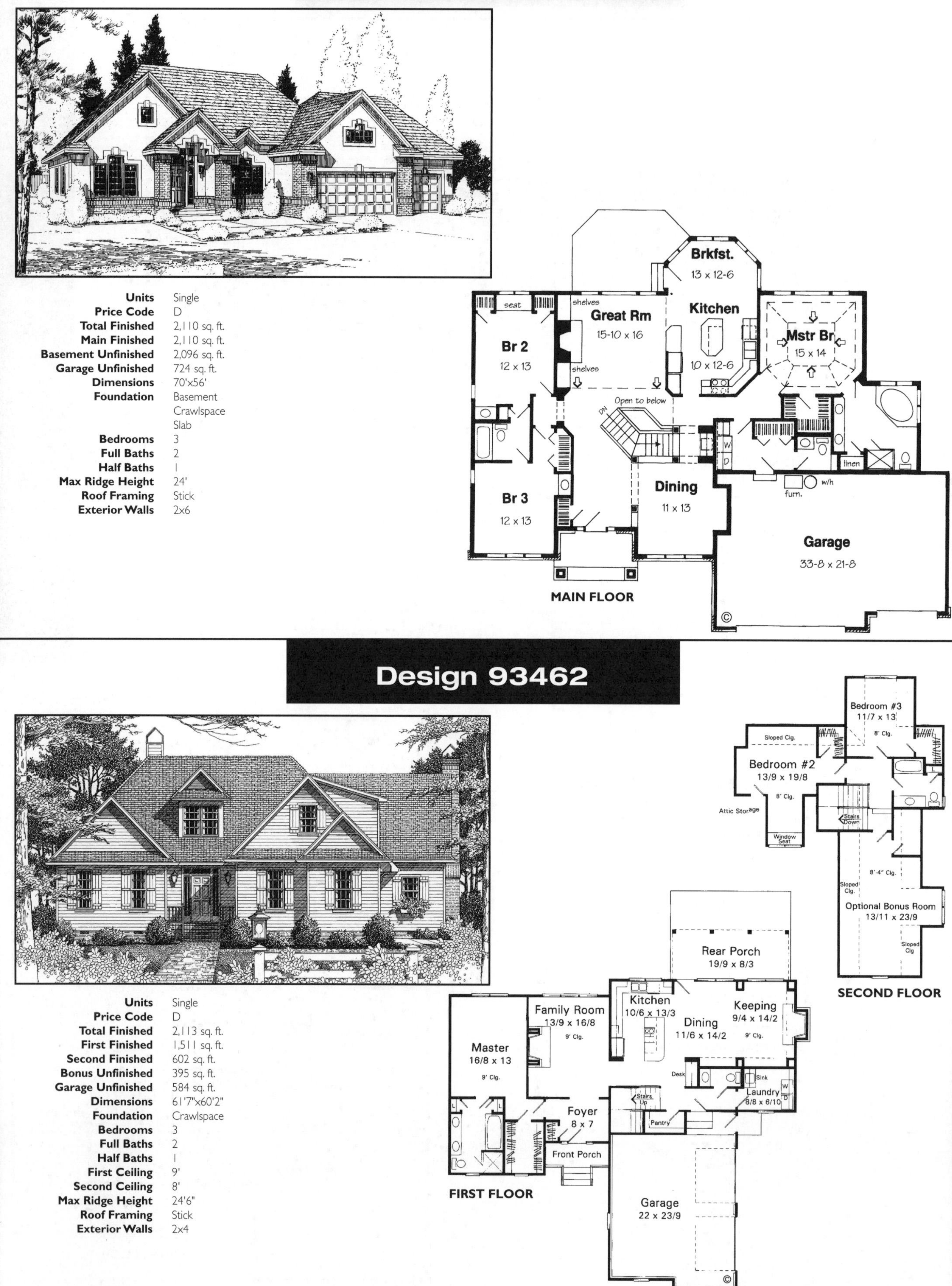
Design 24557
Units Single
Price Code D
Total Finished 2,110 sq. ft.
Main Finished 2,110 sq. ft.
Basement Unfinished 2,096 sq. ft.
Garage Unfinished 724 sq. ft.
Dimensions 70'x56'
Foundation Basement
Crawlspace
Slab
Bedrooms 3
Full Baths 2
Half Baths 1
Max Ridge Height 24'
Roof Framing Stick
Exterior Walls 2x6
Brkfst.
13 x 12-6
Kitchen
10 x 12-6
Great Rm
15-10 x 16
shelves
seat
Br 2
12 x 13
Br 3
12 x 13
Mstr Br
15 x 14
Open to below
DN
Dining
11 x 13
w/h
furn.
linen
Garage
33-8 x 21-8
MAIN FLOOR
Design 93462
Units Single
Price Code D
Total Finished 2,113 sq. ft.
First Finished 1,511 sq. ft.
Second Finished 602 sq. ft.
Bonus Unfinished 395 sq. ft.
Garage Unfinished 584 sq. ft.
Dimensions 61'7"x60'2"
Foundation Crawlspace
Bedrooms 3
Full Baths 2
Half Baths 1
First Ceiling 9'
Second Ceiling 8'
Max Ridge Height 24'6"
Roof Framing Stick
Exterior Walls 2x4
Bedroom #3
11/7 x 13
8' Clg.
Sloped Clg.
Bedroom #2
13/9 x 19/8
8' Clg.
Attic Storage
Window Seat
Stairs Down
8'-4" Clg.
Sloped Clg.
Optional Bonus Room
13/11 x 23/9
Sloped Clg
SECOND FLOOR
Rear Porch
19/9 x 8/3
Family Room
13/9 x 16/8
9' Clg.
Kitchen
10/6 x 13/3
Dining
11/6 x 14/2
Keeping
9/4 x 14/2
9' Clg.
Master
16/8 x 13
9' Clg.
Desk
Sink
Laundry
8/8 x 6/10
Stairs Up
Pantry
Foyer
8 x 7
Front Porch
Garage
22 x 23/9
FIRST FLOOR

Design 69135

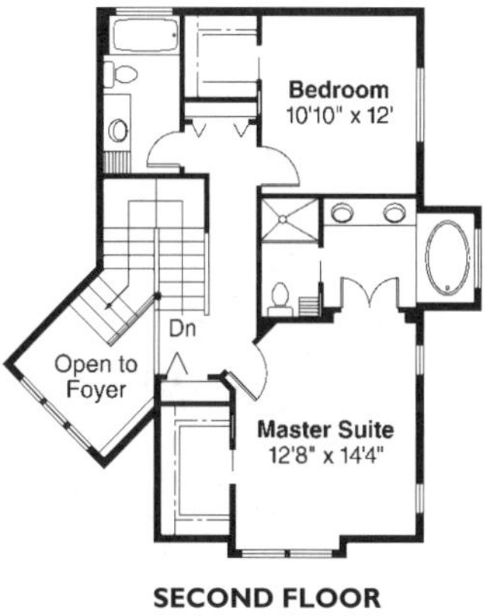
Bedroom
10'10" x 12'
Open to
Foyer
Dn
Master Suite
12'8" x 14'4"
SECOND FLOOR

Units	Single
Price Code	D
Total Finished	2,117 sq. ft.
First Finished	1,386 sq. ft.
Second Finished	731 sq. ft.
Dimensions	73'x41'
Foundation	Crawlspace
Bedrooms	2
Full Baths	2
3/4 Baths	1
First Ceiling	9'
Second Ceiling	8'
Max Ridge Height	23'5"
Roof Framing	Truss
Exterior Walls	2x6

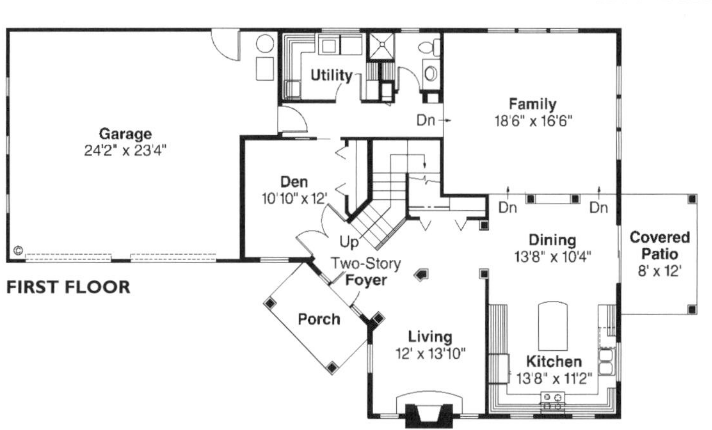
Garage
24'2" x 23'4"
Utility
Dn
Family
18'6" x 16'6"
Den
10'10" x 12'
Dn
Dn
Up
Two-Story
Foyer
Dining
13'8" x 10'4"
Covered
Patio
8' x 12'
Porch
Living
12' x 13'10"
Kitchen
13'8" x 11'2"
FIRST FLOOR

Design 22014

Units	Single
Price Code	D
Total Finished	2,118 sq. ft.
Main Finished	2,118 sq. ft.
Garage Unfinished	448 sq. ft.
Dimensions	54'x68'4"
Foundation	Slab
Bedrooms	3
Full Baths	2
Half Baths	1
Max Ridge Height	21'
Roof Framing	Stick
Exterior Walls	2x4

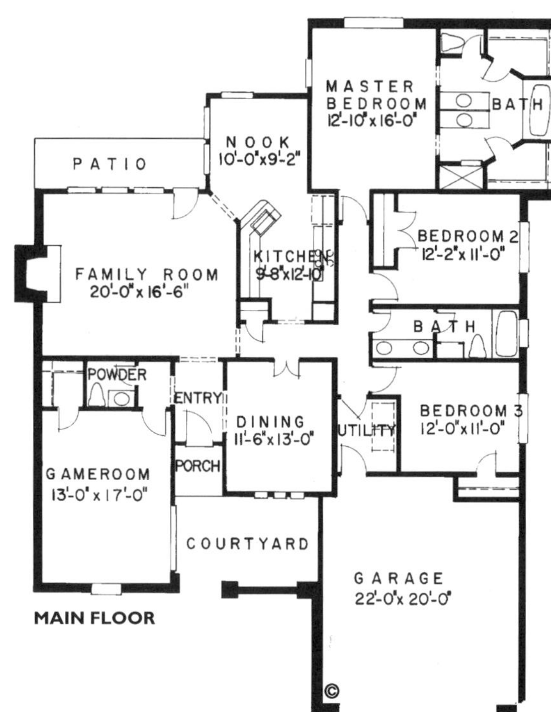
MASTER
BEDROOM
12'-10"x16'-0"
BATH
NOOK
10'-0"x9'-2"
PATIO
BEDROOM 2
12'-2"x11'-0"
FAMILY ROOM
20'-0"x16'-6"
KITCHEN
9'-8"x12'-10"
BATH
POWDER
ENTRY
DINING
11'-6"x13'-0"
UTILITY
BEDROOM 3
12'-0"x11'-0"
GAMEROOM
13'-0"x17'-0"
PORCH
COURTYARD
GARAGE
22'-0"x20'-0"
MAIN FLOOR

Design 63047

Units	Single
Price Code	D
Total Finished	2,118 sq. ft.
Main Finished	2,118 sq. ft.
Garage Unfinished	483 sq. ft.
Dimensions	58'x62'
Foundation	Slab
Bedrooms	3
Full Baths	2
Main Ceiling	9'4"
Max Ridge Height	20'9"
Roof Framing	Truss

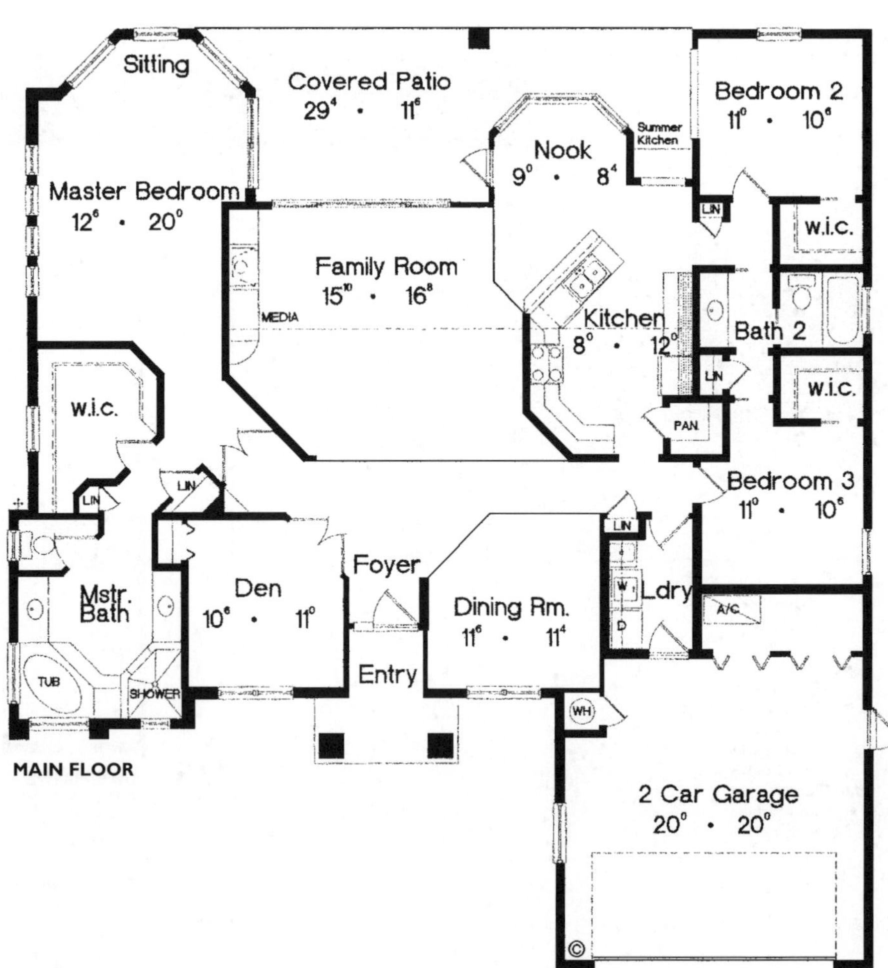
Sitting
Covered Patio
29⁴ • 11⁶
Bedroom 2
11⁰ • 10⁶
Summer Kitchen
Nook
9⁰ • 8⁴
Master Bedroom
12⁶ • 20⁰
LIN
w.i.c.
Family Room
15¹⁰ • 16⁸
MEDIA
Kitchen
8⁰ • 12⁰
Bath 2
LIN
w.i.c.
w.i.c.
PAN
Bedroom 3
11⁰ • 10⁶
LIN
LIN
LIN
Foyer
Mstr. Bath
Den
10⁶ • 11⁰
Dining Rm.
11⁶ • 11⁴
Ldry
A/C
TUB
SHOWER
Entry
WH
2 Car Garage
20⁰ • 20⁰

MAIN FLOOR

Design 97890

Units	Single
Price Code	D
Total Finished	2,118 sq. ft.
Main Finished	2,118 sq. ft.
Garage Unfinished	660 sq. ft.
Deck Unfinished	260 sq. ft.
Porch Unfinished	304 sq. ft.
Dimensions	73'4"x49'1"
Foundation	Slab
Bedrooms	4
Full Baths	2
Half Baths	1
Main Ceiling	9'-10'
Max Ridge Height	27'
Roof Framing	Stick
Exterior Walls	2x4

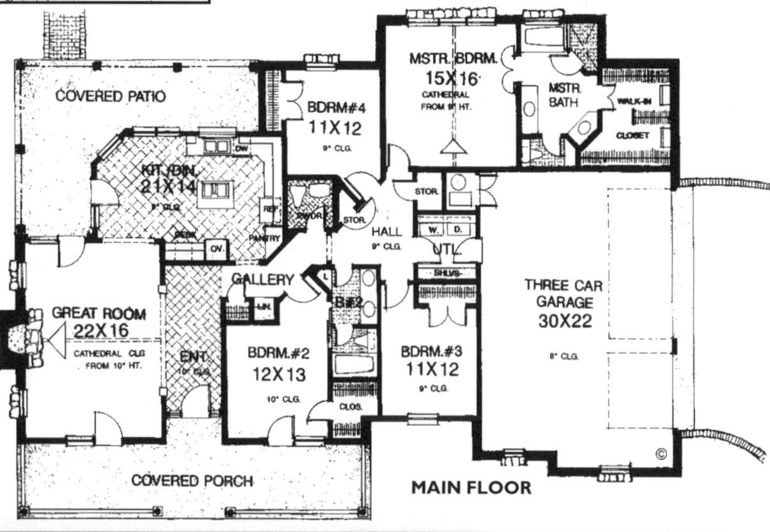
COVERED PATIO
BDRM#4
11X12
MSTR. BDRM.
15X16
CATHEDRAL FROM 9' HT.
MSTR. BATH
WALK-IN CLOSET
KIT/DIN.
21X14
HALL
GALLERY
GREAT ROOM
22X16
CATHEDRAL CLG FROM 10' HT.
ENT.
BDRM.#2
12X13
BDRM.#3
11X12
THREE CAR GARAGE
30X22
COVERED PORCH

MAIN FLOOR

Design 20108

Units	Single
Price Code	D
Total Finished	2,120 sq. ft.
Main Finished	2,120 sq. ft.
Basement Unfinished	2,120 sq. ft.
Garage Unfinished	576 sq. ft.
Dimensions	68'x63'
Foundation	Basement
Bedrooms	3
Full Baths	2
Half Baths	1
Max Ridge Height	22'
Roof Framing	Stick
Exterior Walls	2x6

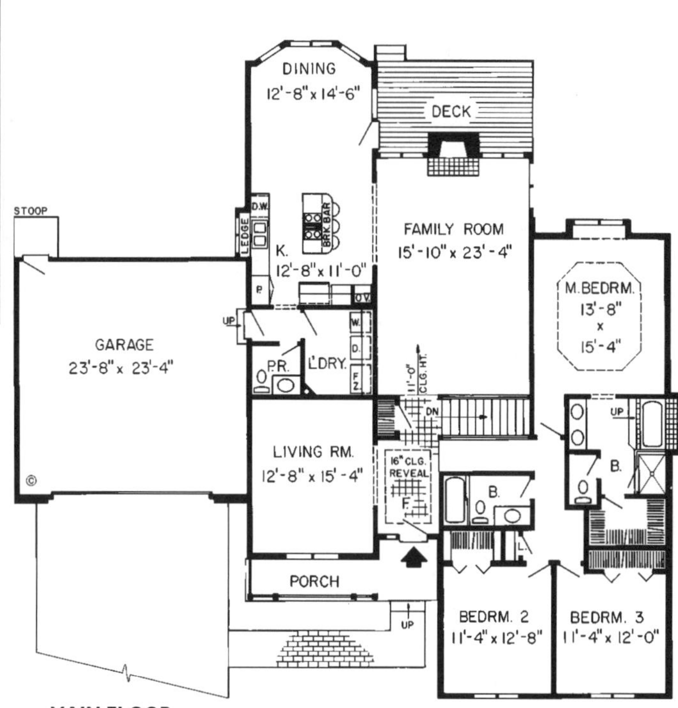
DINING
12'-8" x 14'-6"
DECK
STOOP
FAMILY ROOM
15'-10" x 23'-4"
K.
12'-8" x 11'-0"
M.BEDRM.
13'-8" x 15'-4"
GARAGE
23'-8" x 23'-4"
PR.
L'DRY.
LIVING RM.
12'-8" x 15'-4"
PORCH
BEDRM. 2
11'-4" x 12'-8"
BEDRM. 3
11'-4" x 12'-0"

MAIN FLOOR

Design 97100

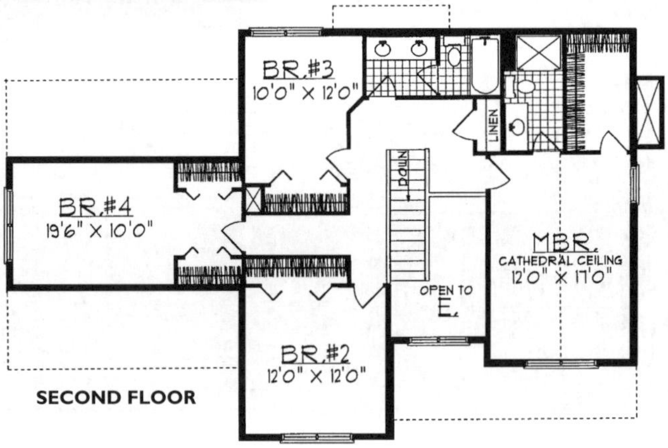

SECOND FLOOR

FIRST FLOOR

Units	Single
Price Code	D
Total Finished	2,120 sq. ft.
First Finished	995 sq. ft.
Second Finished	1,125 sq. ft.
Basement Unfinished	995 sq. ft.
Dimensions	56'4"x35'8"
Foundation	Basement
Bedrooms	4
Full Baths	1
Half Baths	1
3/4 Baths	1
Max Ridge Height	28'4"
Roof Framing	Truss
Exterior Walls	2x6

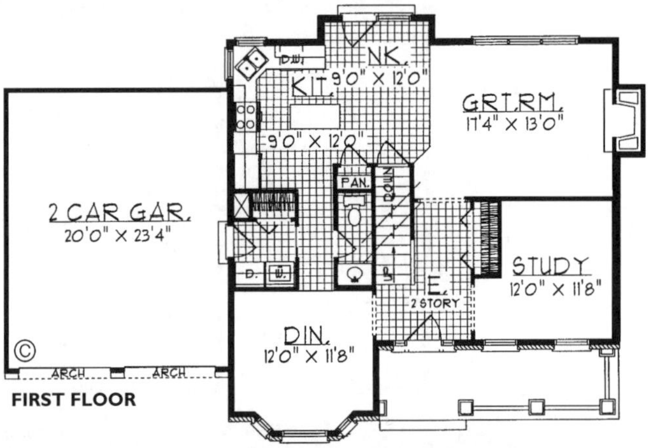

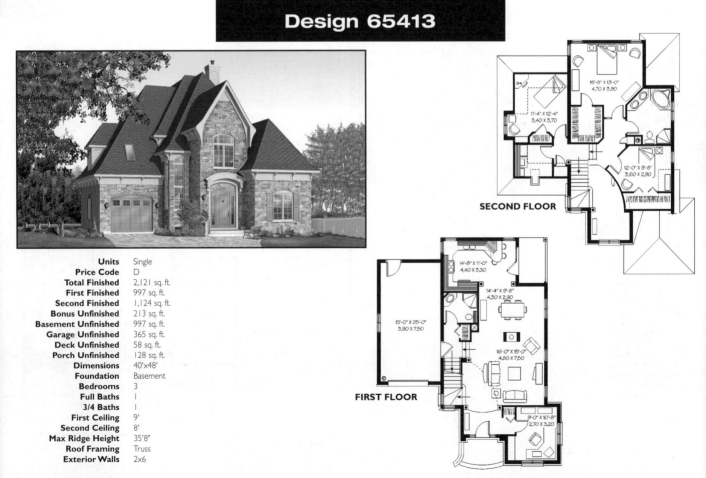

Design 65413

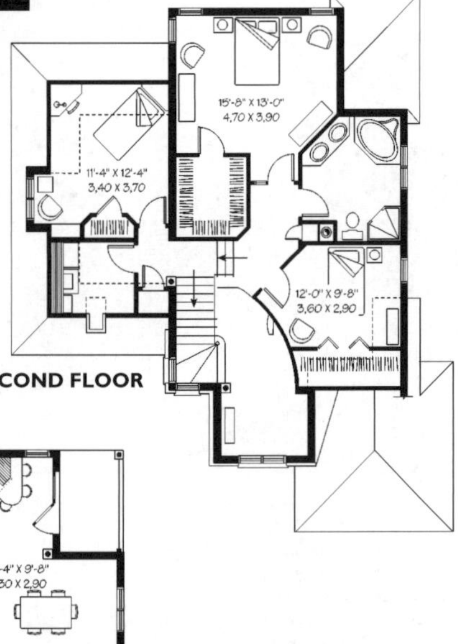

SECOND FLOOR

FIRST FLOOR

Units	Single
Price Code	D
Total Finished	2,121 sq. ft.
First Finished	997 sq. ft.
Second Finished	1,124 sq. ft.
Bonus Unfinished	213 sq. ft.
Basement Unfinished	997 sq. ft.
Garage Unfinished	365 sq. ft.
Deck Unfinished	58 sq. ft.
Porch Unfinished	128 sq. ft.
Dimensions	40'x48'
Foundation	Basement
Bedrooms	3
Full Baths	1
3/4 Baths	1
First Ceiling	9'
Second Ceiling	8'
Max Ridge Height	35'8"
Roof Framing	Truss
Exterior Walls	2x6

Design 68152

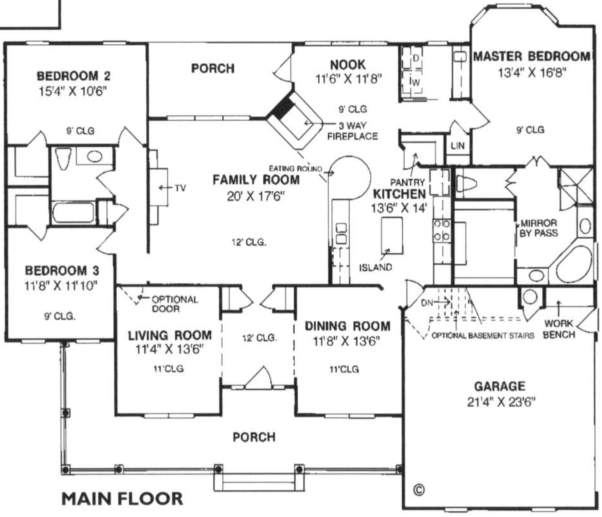

Units	Single
Price Code	D
Total Finished	2,126 sq. ft.
Main Finished	2,126 sq. ft.
Garage Unfinished	528 sq. ft.
Deck Unfinished	428 sq. ft.
Dimensions	66'x54'
Foundation	Basement Crawlspace Slab
Bedrooms	3
Full Baths	2
Main Ceiling	9'
Max Ridge Height	24'
Exterior Walls	2x4

* Alternate foundation options available at an additional charge. Please call 1-800-235-5700 for more information.

BEDROOM 2 15'4" X 10'6" 9' CLG
PORCH
NOOK 11'6" X 11'8" 9' CLG
3 WAY FIREPLACE
MASTER BEDROOM 13'4" X 16'8" 9' CLG
W D
LIN
TV
EATING ROUND
FAMILY ROOM 20' X 17'6" 12' CLG.
PANTRY
KITCHEN 13'6" X 14'
ISLAND
MIRROR BY PASS
BEDROOM 3 11'8" X 11'10" 9' CLG.
OPTIONAL DOOR
DN
OPTIONAL BASEMENT STAIRS
WORK BENCH
LIVING ROOM 11'4" X 13'6" 11'CLG
12' CLG.
DINING ROOM 11'8" X 13'6" 11'CLG
GARAGE 21'4" X 23'6"
PORCH
©

MAIN FLOOR

Design 98485

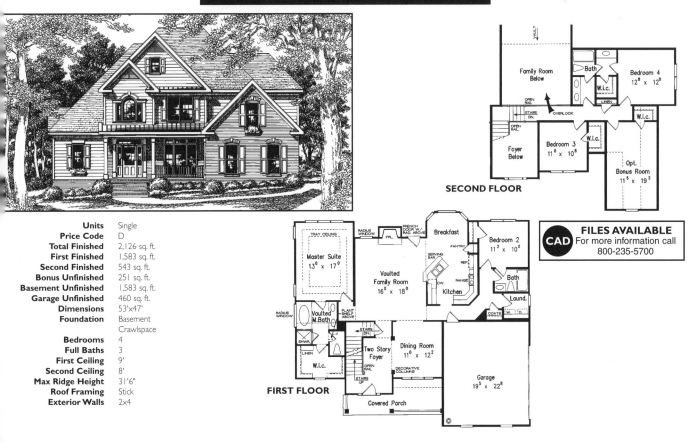

Units	Single
Price Code	D
Total Finished	2,126 sq. ft.
First Finished	1,583 sq. ft.
Second Finished	543 sq. ft.
Bonus Unfinished	251 sq. ft.
Basement Unfinished	1,583 sq. ft.
Garage Unfinished	460 sq. ft.
Dimensions	53'x47'
Foundation	Basement Crawlspace
Bedrooms	4
Full Baths	3
First Ceiling	9'
Second Ceiling	8'
Max Ridge Height	31'6"
Roof Framing	Stick
Exterior Walls	2x4

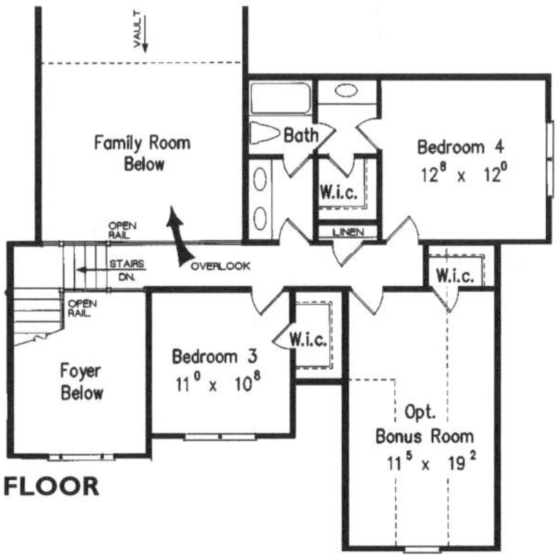

VAULT
Family Room Below
Bath
Bedroom 4 12^8 x 12^0
W.i.c.
LINEN
OPEN RAIL
STAIRS DN.
OVERLOOK
W.i.c.
OPEN RAIL
W.i.c.
Foyer Below
Bedroom 3 11^0 x 10^8
Opt. Bonus Room 11^5 x 19^2

SECOND FLOOR

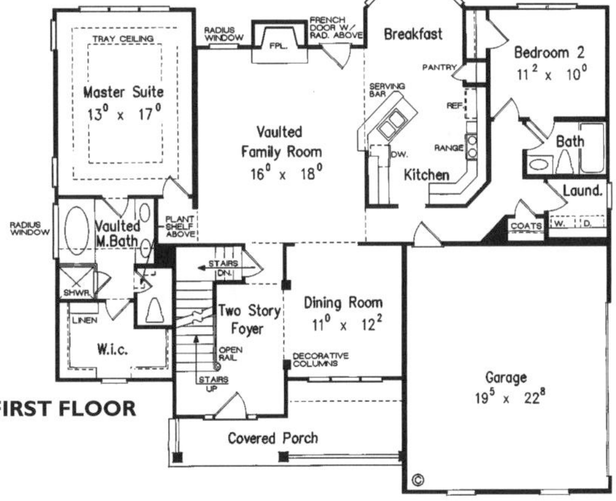

RADIUS WINDOW
FPL.
FRENCH DOOR W/ RAD. ABOVE
Breakfast
TRAY CEILING
Master Suite 13^0 x 17^0
PANTRY
SERVING BAR
REF.
Bedroom 2 11^2 x 10^0
Vaulted Family Room 16^0 x 18^0
RANGE
D.W.
Kitchen
Bath
Laund.
RADIUS WINDOW
Vaulted M.Bath
PLANT SHELF ABOVE
COATS
W. D.
STAIRS DN.
SHWR.
LINEN
W.i.c.
Two Story Foyer
OPEN RAIL
Dining Room 11^0 x 12^2
DECORATIVE COLUMNS
STAIRS UP
Garage 19^5 x 22^8
Covered Porch
©

FIRST FLOOR

CAD **FILES AVAILABLE** For more information call 800-235-5700

Design 97219

FILES AVAILABLE
CAD For more information call
800-235-5700

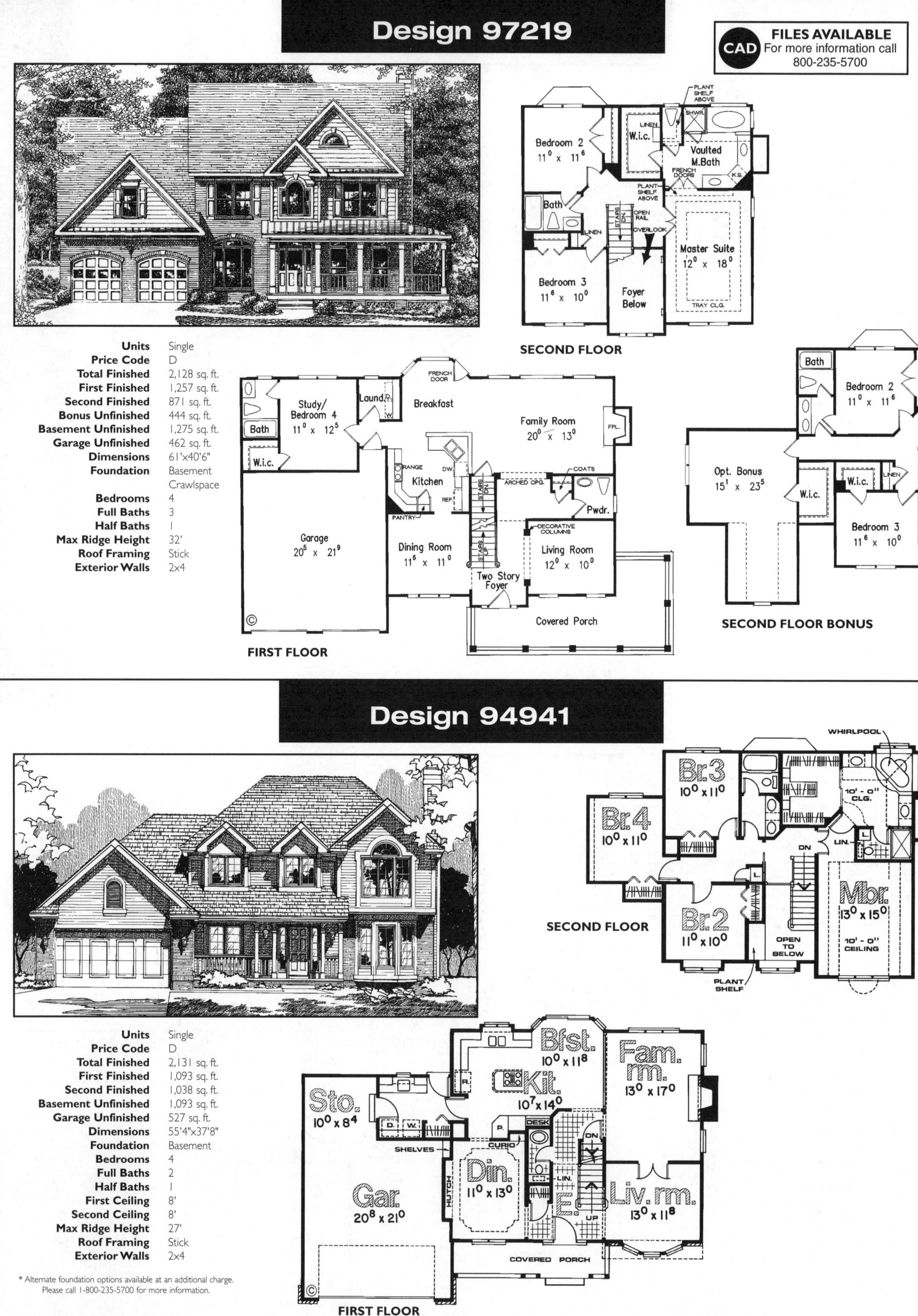

PLANT SHELF ABOVE
Bedroom 2 11⁰ x 11⁶
LINEN
W.i.c.
SHWR.
Vaulted M.Bath
FRENCH DOORS
K.S.
PLANT SHELF ABOVE
Bath
STAIRS DN
OPEN RAIL
OVERLOOK
LINEN
Master Suite 12⁰ x 18⁰
Bedroom 3 11⁶ x 10⁰
Foyer Below
TRAY CLG.
SECOND FLOOR
FRENCH DOOR
Bath
Study/ Bedroom 4 11⁰ x 12⁵
Laund.
Breakfast
Family Room 20⁰ x 13⁰
FPL.
W.i.c.
RANGE
DW.
Kitchen
REF.
STAIRS DN
ARCHED OPG.
COATS
PANTRY
Pwdr.
DECORATIVE COLUMNS
Garage 20⁵ x 21⁹
Dining Room 11⁶ x 11⁰
STAIRS UP
Living Room 12⁰ x 10⁰
Two Story Foyer
Covered Porch
FIRST FLOOR
Bath
Bedroom 2 11⁰ x 11⁶
Opt. Bonus 15¹ x 23⁵
W.i.c.
W.i.c.
LINEN
Bedroom 3 11⁶ x 10⁰
SECOND FLOOR BONUS

Units	Single
Price Code	D
Total Finished	2,128 sq. ft.
First Finished	1,257 sq. ft.
Second Finished	871 sq. ft.
Bonus Unfinished	444 sq. ft.
Basement Unfinished	1,275 sq. ft.
Garage Unfinished	462 sq. ft.
Dimensions	61'x40'6"
Foundation	Basement Crawlspace
Bedrooms	4
Full Baths	3
Half Baths	1
Max Ridge Height	32'
Roof Framing	Stick
Exterior Walls	2x4

Design 94941

WHIRLPOOL
Br.3 10⁰ x 11⁰
Br.4 10⁰ x 11⁰
10' - 0" CLG.
DN
L.
LIN.
L.
Mbr. 13⁰ x 15⁰
10' - 0" CEILING
Br.2 11⁰ x 10⁰
OPEN TO BELOW
PLANT SHELF
SECOND FLOOR
Bfst. 10⁰ x 11⁸
Fam. rm. 13⁰ x 17⁰
R.
Kit. 10⁷ x 14⁰
Sto. 10⁰ x 8⁴
D. W.
P.
DESK
SHELVES
CURIO
DN
Din. 11⁰ x 13⁰
HUTCH
LIN.
Gar. 20⁸ x 21⁰
E.
UP
Liv. rm. 13⁰ x 11⁸
COVERED PORCH
FIRST FLOOR

Units	Single
Price Code	D
Total Finished	2,131 sq. ft.
First Finished	1,093 sq. ft.
Second Finished	1,038 sq. ft.
Basement Unfinished	1,093 sq. ft.
Garage Unfinished	527 sq. ft.
Dimensions	55'4"x37'8"
Foundation	Basement
Bedrooms	4
Full Baths	2
Half Baths	1
First Ceiling	8'
Second Ceiling	8'
Max Ridge Height	27'
Roof Framing	Stick
Exterior Walls	2x4

* Alternate foundation options available at an additional charge. Please call 1-800-235-5700 for more information.

Design 92280

Units	Single
Price Code	D
Total Finished	2,132 sq. ft.
Main Finished	2,132 sq. ft.
Garage Unfinished	644 sq. ft.
Deck Unfinished	352 sq. ft.
Porch Unfinished	10 sq. ft.
Dimensions	60'x62'1"
Foundation	Slab
Bedrooms	4
Full Baths	3
Main Ceiling	8'-10'
Max Ridge Height	25'
Roof Framing	Stick
Exterior Walls	2x4

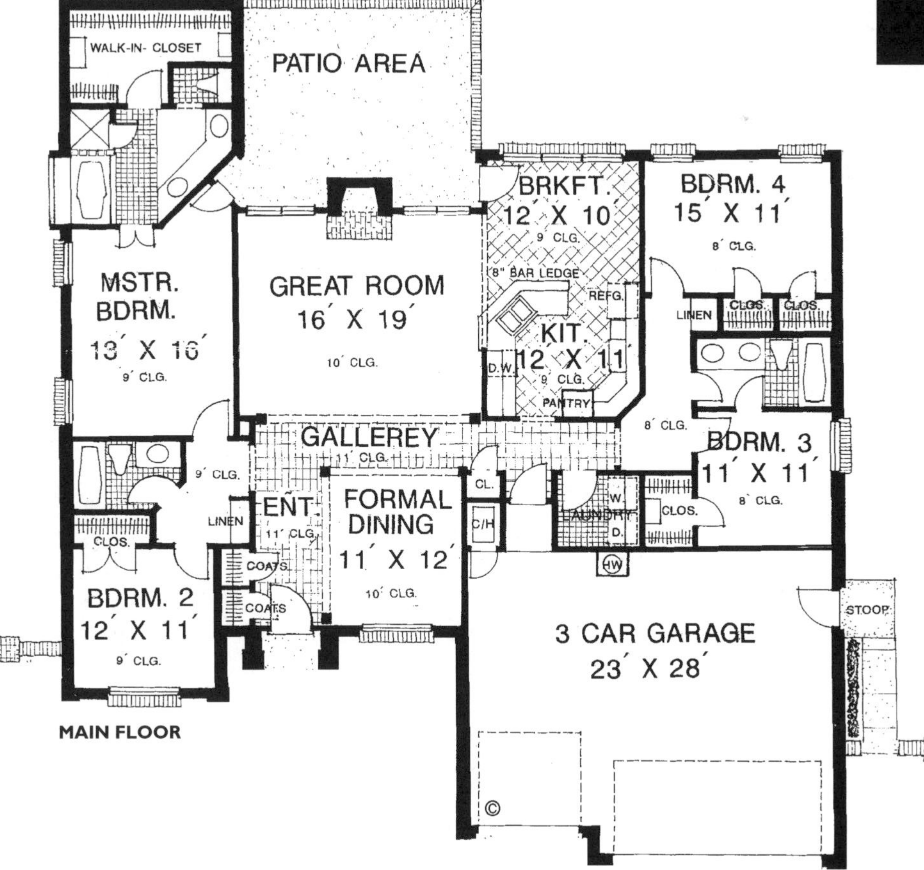
WALK-IN- CLOSET
PATIO AREA
BRKFT.
12' X 10'
9' CLG.
BDRM. 4
15' X 11'
8' CLG.
8" BAR LEDGE
REFG.
MSTR.
BDRM.
13' X 16'
9' CLG.
GREAT ROOM
16' X 19'
10' CLG.
KIT.
12' X 11'
9' CLG.
D.W.
PANTRY
LINEN
CLOS.
CLOS.
8' CLG.
GALLEREY
11' CLG.
BDRM. 3
11' X 11'
8' CLG.
9' CLG.
ENT.
11' CLG.
FORMAL
DINING
11' X 12'
10' CLG.
CL.
C/H
W.
LAUNDRY
D.
CLOS.
LINEN
CLOS.
COATS
COATS
HW
STOOP
BDRM. 2
12' X 11'
9' CLG.
3 CAR GARAGE
23' X 28'
MAIN FLOOR

Design 97488

Units	Single
Price Code	D
Total Finished	2,132 sq. ft.
Main Finished	2,132 sq. ft.
Garage Unfinished	763 sq. ft.
Dimensions	72'x58'
Foundation	Basement
Bedrooms	3
Full Baths	2
Main Ceiling	8'
Max Ridge Height	22'
Exterior Walls	2x4

* Alternate foundation options available at an additional charge.
Please call 1-800-235-5700 for more information.

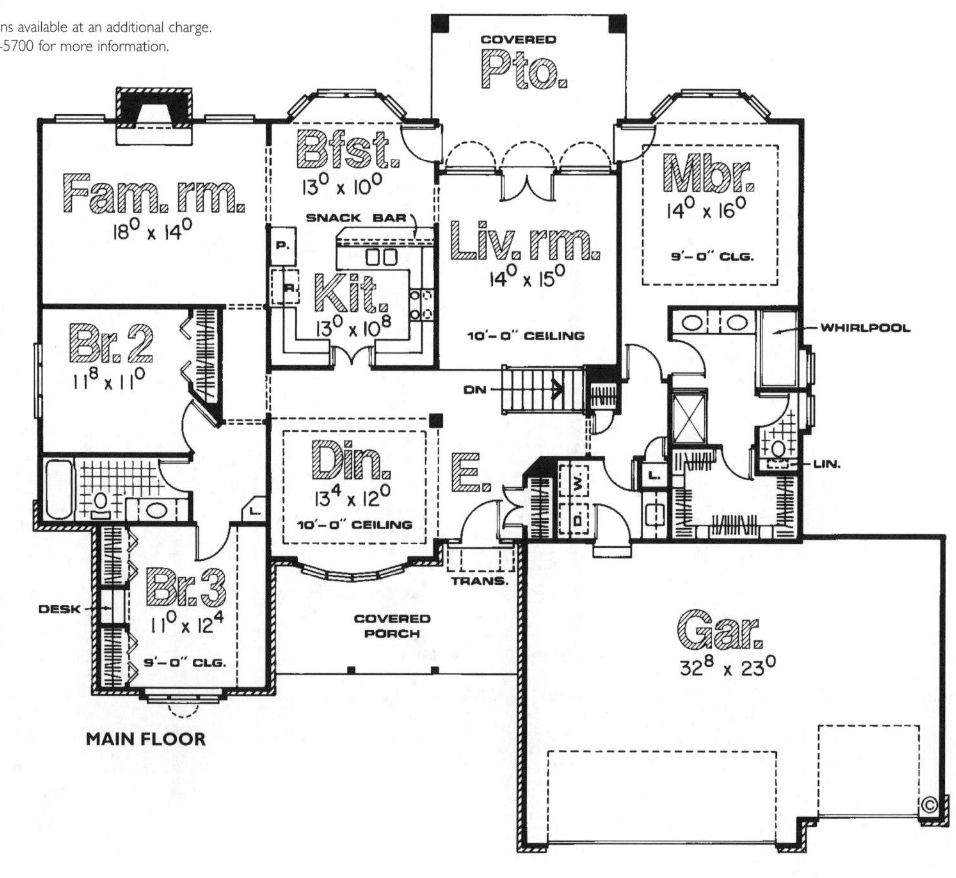

COVERED
Pto.
Bfst.
13⁰ x 10⁰
Fam. rm.
18⁰ x 14⁰
SNACK BAR
P.
R.
Kit.
13⁰ x 10⁸
Liv. rm.
14⁰ x 15⁰
10'-0" CEILING
Mbr.
14⁰ x 16⁰
9'-0" CLG.
WHIRLPOOL
Br. 2
11⁸ x 11⁰
DN
Din.
13⁴ x 12⁰
10'-0" CEILING
E.
W.
D.
L.
LIN.
TRANS.
DESK
Br. 3
11⁰ x 12⁴
9'-0" CLG.
COVERED
PORCH
Gar.
32⁸ x 23⁰
MAIN FLOOR

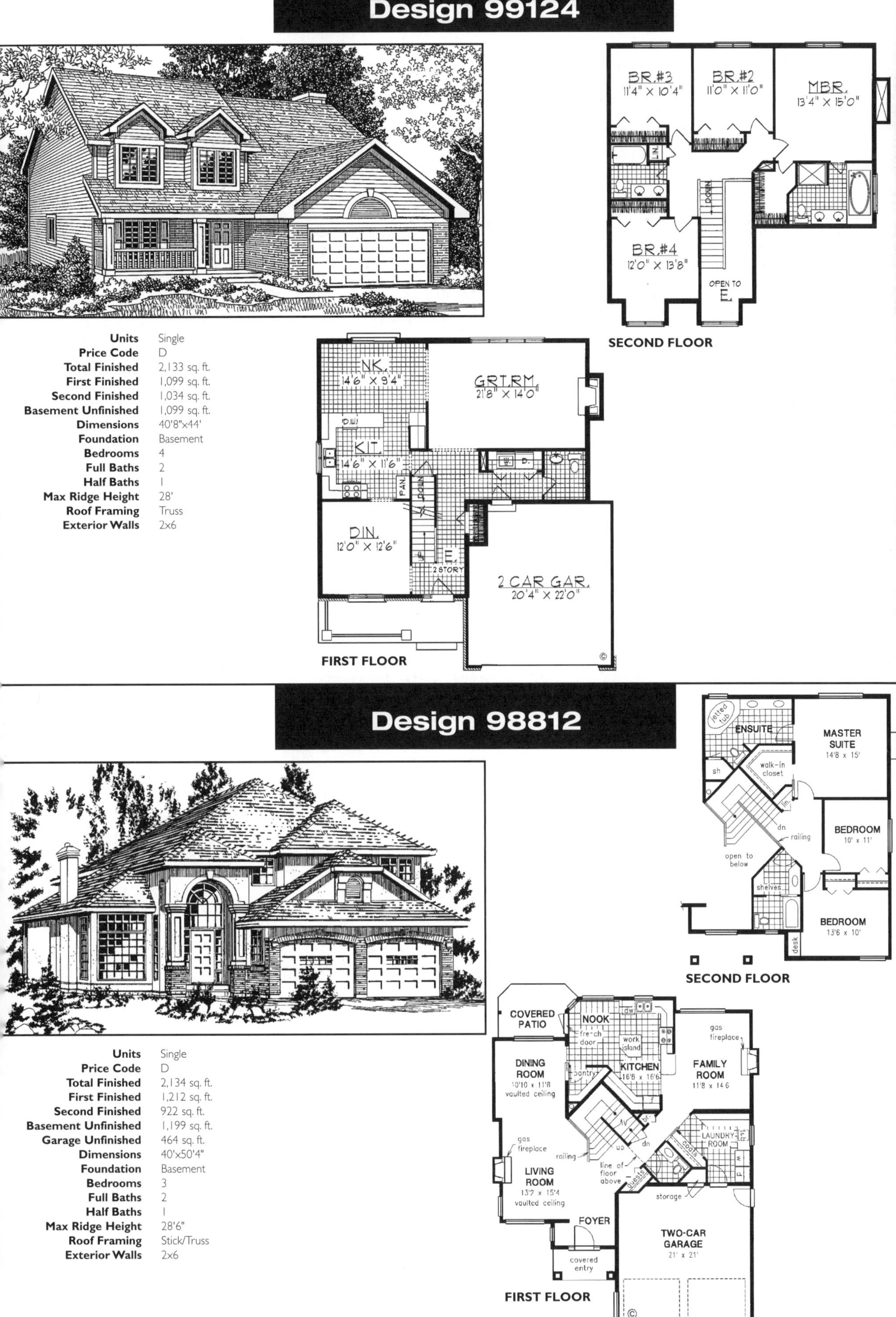
BR.#3
11'4" x 10'4"
BR.#2
11'0" x 11'0"
MBR.
13'4" x 15'0"
BR.#4
12'0" x 13'8"
OPEN TO E.
SECOND FLOOR
NK.
14'6" x 9'4"
GRT.RM.
21'8" x 14'0"
KIT.
14'6" x 11'6"
DIN.
12'0" x 12'6"
2 CAR GAR.
20'4" x 22'0"
2 STORY
FIRST FLOOR
ENSUITE
MASTER SUITE
14'8 x 15'
walk-in closet
BEDROOM
10' x 11'
BEDROOM
13'6 x 10'
open to below
SECOND FLOOR
COVERED PATIO
NOOK
KITCHEN
16'8 x 16'6
FAMILY ROOM
11'8 x 14'6
DINING ROOM
10'10 x 11'8
vaulted ceiling
LIVING ROOM
13'2 x 15'4
vaulted ceiling
FOYER
covered entry
LAUNDRY ROOM
TWO-CAR GARAGE
21' x 21'
FIRST FLOOR

Design 99124

Units	Single
Price Code	D
Total Finished	2,133 sq. ft.
First Finished	1,099 sq. ft.
Second Finished	1,034 sq. ft.
Basement Unfinished	1,099 sq. ft.
Dimensions	40'8"x44'
Foundation	Basement
Bedrooms	4
Full Baths	2
Half Baths	1
Max Ridge Height	28'
Roof Framing	Truss
Exterior Walls	2x6

Design 98812

Units	Single
Price Code	D
Total Finished	2,134 sq. ft.
First Finished	1,212 sq. ft.
Second Finished	922 sq. ft.
Basement Unfinished	1,199 sq. ft.
Garage Unfinished	464 sq. ft.
Dimensions	40'x50'4"
Foundation	Basement
Bedrooms	3
Full Baths	2
Half Baths	1
Max Ridge Height	28'6"
Roof Framing	Stick/Truss
Exterior Walls	2x6

Design 91179

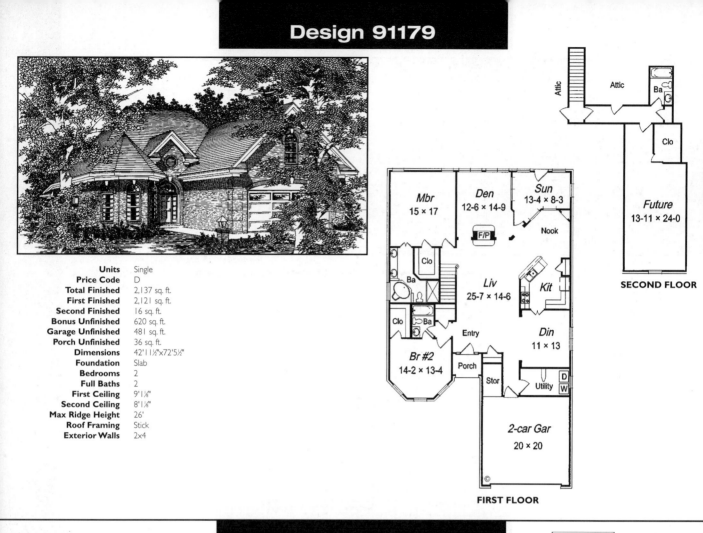

Units	Single
Price Code	D
Total Finished	2,137 sq. ft.
First Finished	2,121 sq. ft.
Second Finished	16 sq. ft.
Bonus Unfinished	620 sq. ft.
Garage Unfinished	481 sq. ft.
Porch Unfinished	36 sq. ft.
Dimensions	42'11½"x72'5½"
Foundation	Slab
Bedrooms	2
Full Baths	2
First Ceiling	9'1⅛"
Second Ceiling	8'1⅛"
Max Ridge Height	26'
Roof Framing	Stick
Exterior Walls	2x4

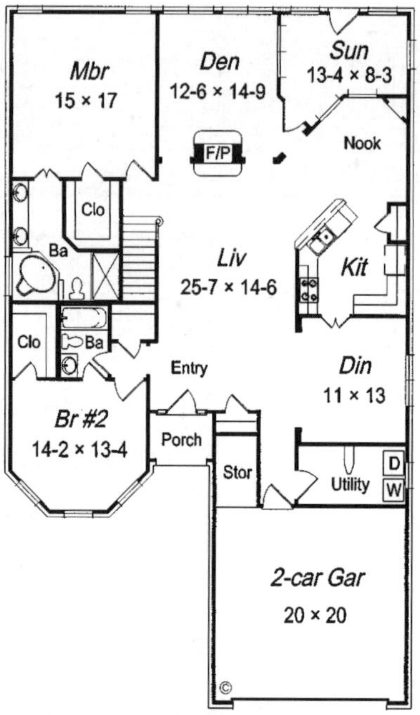

SECOND FLOOR

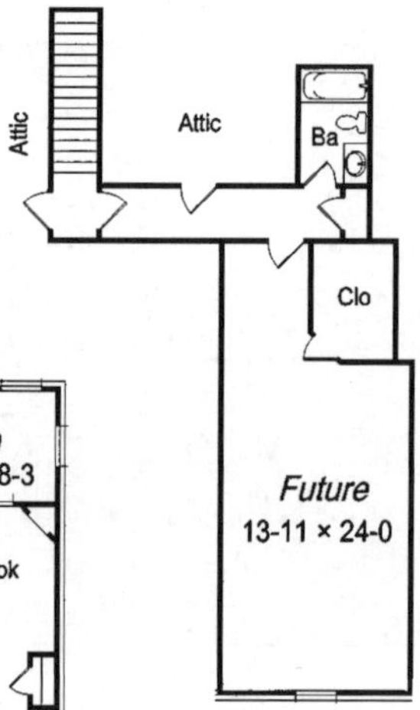

FIRST FLOOR

Design 65419

Units	Single
Price Code	D
Total Finished	2,138 sq. ft.
First Finished	1,134 sq. ft.
Second Finished	1,004 sq. ft.
Basement Unfinished	1,134 sq. ft.
Garage Unfinished	325 sq. ft.
Deck Unfinished	60 sq. ft.
Porch Unfinished	153 sq. ft.
Dimensions	38'x54'
Foundation	Basement
Bedrooms	3
Full Baths	1
Half Baths	1
First Ceiling	9'
Second Ceiling	8'
Max Ridge Height	34'5"
Roof Framing	Truss
Exterior Walls	2x6

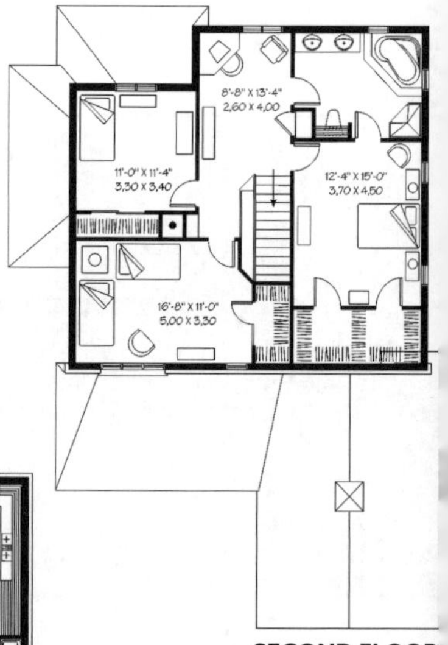

SECOND FLOOR

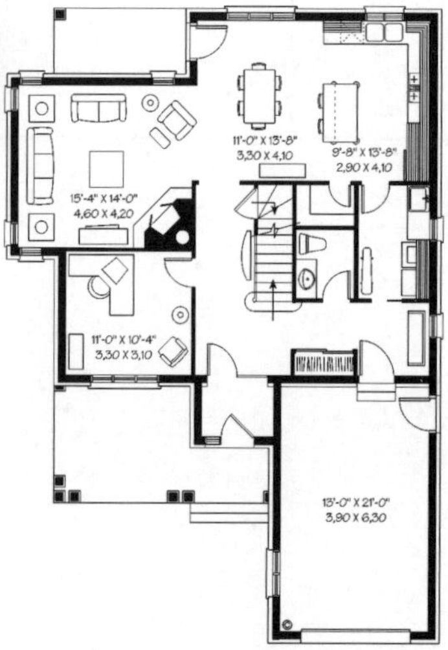

FIRST FLOOR

Design 91411

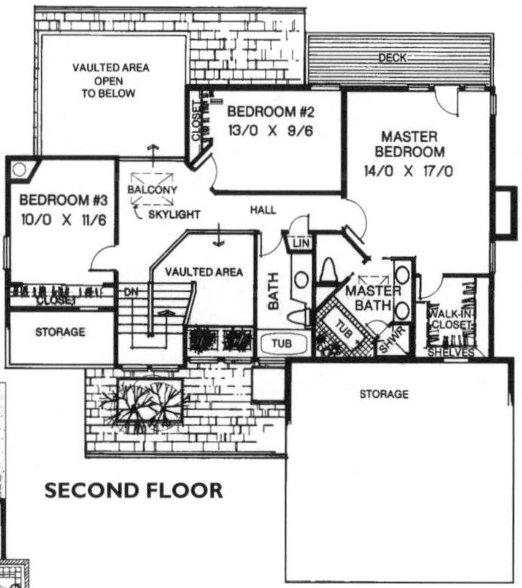

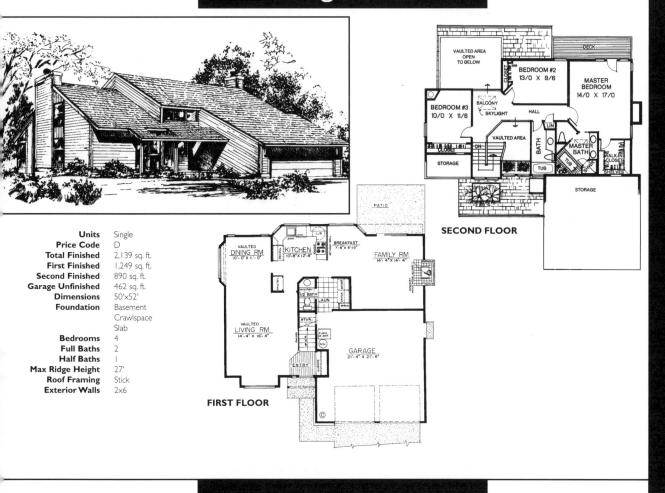

Units	Single
Price Code	D
Total Finished	2,139 sq. ft.
First Finished	1,249 sq. ft.
Second Finished	890 sq. ft.
Garage Unfinished	462 sq. ft.
Dimensions	50'x52'
Foundation	Basement Crawlspace Slab
Bedrooms	4
Full Baths	2
Half Baths	1
Max Ridge Height	27'
Roof Framing	Stick
Exterior Walls	2x6

FIRST FLOOR

SECOND FLOOR

Design 61095

Units	Single
Price Code	D
Total Finished	2,140 sq. ft.
Main Finished	2,140 sq. ft.
Garage Unfinished	394 sq. ft.
Porch Unfinished	235 sq. ft.
Dimensions	40'x84'4"
Foundation	Basement
Bedrooms	3
Main Ceiling	9'
Roof Framing	Stick
Exterior Walls	2x6

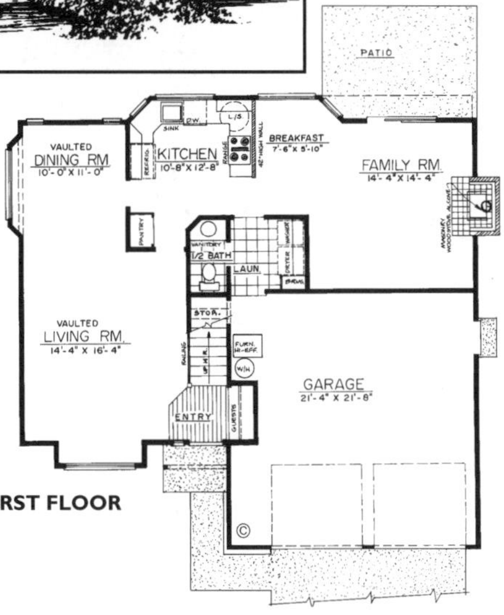

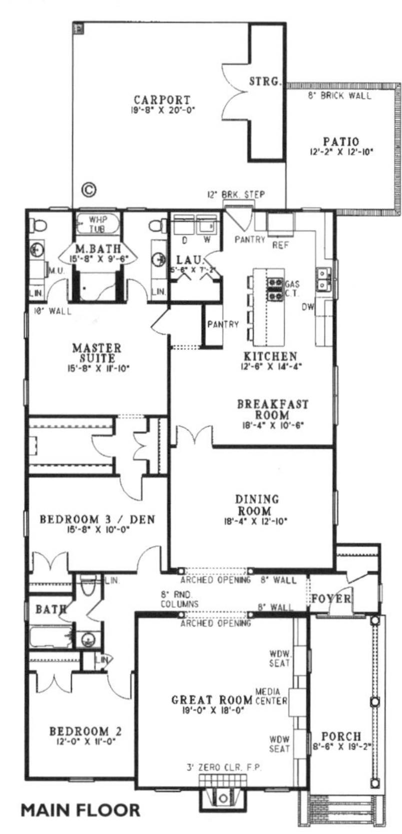
CARPORT
19'-8" X 20'-0"
STRG.
PATIO
12'-2" X 12'-10"
M.BATH
15'-8" X 9'-6"
MASTER SUITE
15'-8" X 11'-10"
KITCHEN
12'-6" X 14'-4"
BREAKFAST ROOM
18'-4" X 10'-6"
DINING ROOM
18'-4" X 12'-10"
BEDROOM 3 / DEN
15'-8" X 10'-0"
FOYER
GREAT ROOM
19'-0" X 18'-0"
BEDROOM 2
12'-0" X 11'-0"
PORCH
8'-6" X 19'-2"

MAIN FLOOR

Design 65391

Units	Single
Price Code	D
Total Finished	2,140 sq. ft.
Main Finished	2,140 sq. ft.
Garage Unfinished	428 sq. ft.
Dimensions	64'x44'4"
Foundation	Basement
Bedrooms	4
Full Baths	2

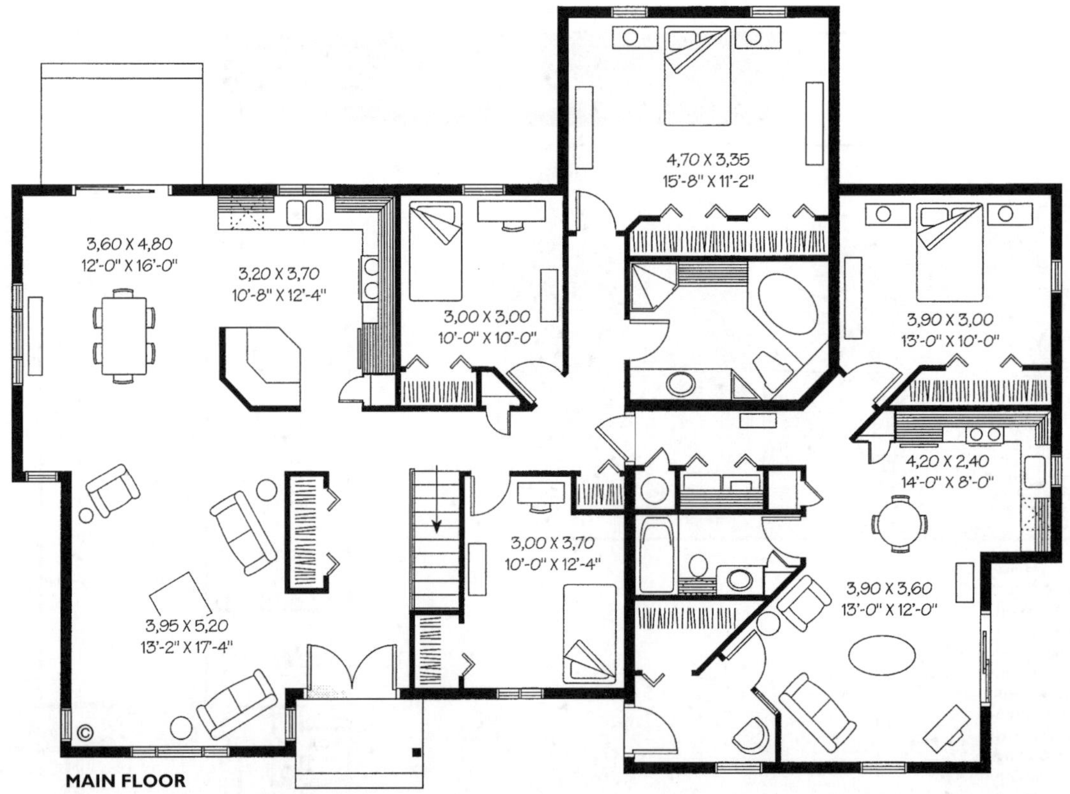

3,60 X 4,80
12'-0" X 16'-0"
3,20 X 3,70
10'-8" X 12'-4"
3,00 X 3,00
10'-0" X 10'-0"
4,70 X 3,35
15'-8" X 11'-2"
3,90 X 3,00
13'-0" X 10'-0"
4,20 X 2,40
14'-0" X 8'-0"
3,00 X 3,70
10'-0" X 12'-4"
3,95 X 5,20
13'-2" X 17'-4"
3,90 X 3,60
13'-0" X 12'-0"
©

MAIN FLOOR

Design 69129

Units	Single
Price Code	D
Total Finished	2,140 sq. ft.
Main Finished	2,140 sq. ft.
Bonus Unfinished	403 sq. ft.
Garage Unfinished	547 sq. ft.
Dimensions	59'x70'
Foundation	Crawlspace
Bedrooms	3
Full Baths	2
Half Baths	1
Main Ceiling	9'
Second Ceiling	8'
Max Ridge Height	26'
Roof Framing	Truss
Exterior Walls	2x6

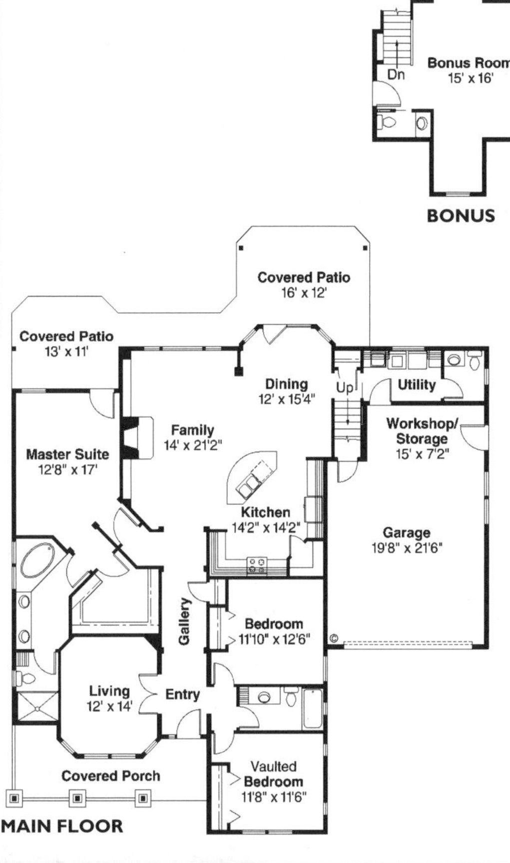

Bonus Room 15' x 16'
Dn
BONUS
Covered Patio 16' x 12'
Covered Patio 13' x 11'
Dining 12' x 15'4"
Up
Utility
Family 14' x 21'2"
Master Suite 12'8" x 17'
Workshop/ Storage 15' x 7'2"
Kitchen 14'2" x 14'2"
Garage 19'8" x 21'6"
Gallery
Bedroom 11'10" x 12'6"
Living 12' x 14'
Entry
Covered Porch
Vaulted Bedroom 11'8" x 11'6"
MAIN FLOOR

Design 92251

Units	Single
Price Code	D
Total Finished	2,140 sq. ft.
Main Finished	2,140 sq. ft.
Garage Unfinished	409 sq. ft.
Dimensions	65'x54'7"
Foundation	Crawlspace Slab
Bedrooms	3
Full Baths	2
Max Ridge Height	27'
Roof Framing	Stick
Exterior Walls	2x4

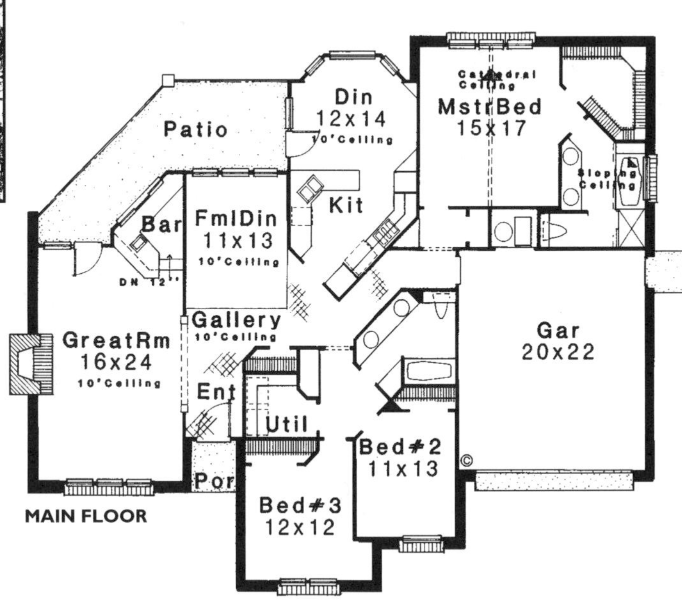

Patio
Din 12x14 10'Ceiling
Cathedral Ceiling
MstrBed 15x17
Sloping Ceiling
Bar
FmlDin 11x13 10'Ceiling
Kit
DN 12"
GreatRm 16x24 10'Ceiling
Gallery 10'Ceiling
Gar 20x22
Ent
Util
Bed#2 11x13
Por
Bed#3 12x12
MAIN FLOOR

Design 20179

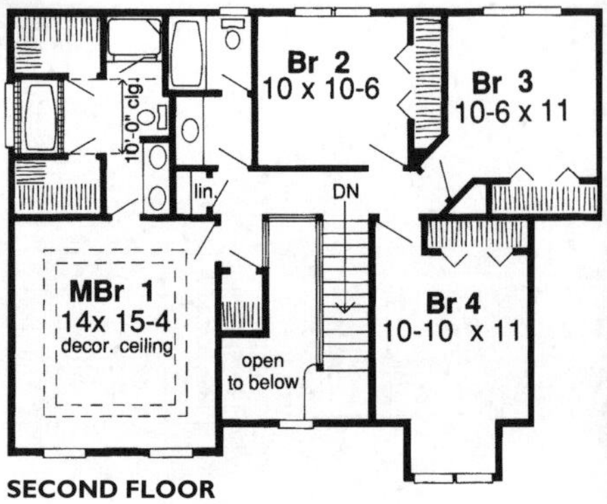

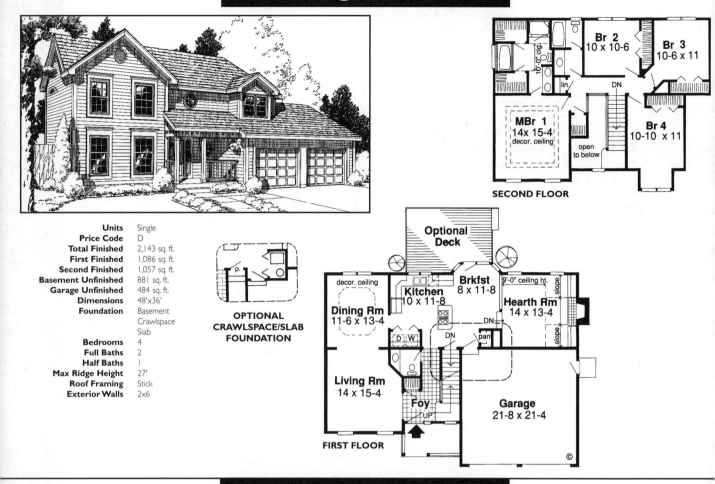

Units	Single
Price Code	D
Total Finished	2,143 sq. ft.
First Finished	1,086 sq. ft.
Second Finished	1,057 sq. ft.
Basement Unfinished	881 sq. ft.
Garage Unfinished	484 sq. ft.
Dimensions	48'x36'
Foundation	Basement Crawlspace Slab
Bedrooms	4
Full Baths	2
Half Baths	1
Max Ridge Height	27'
Roof Framing	Stick
Exterior Walls	2x6

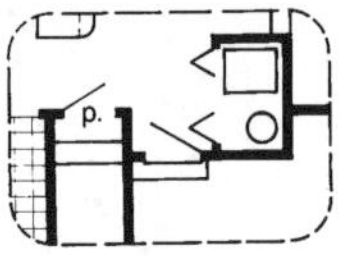

Br 2
10 x 10-6
Br 3
10-6 x 11
10'-0" clg.
lin.
DN
MBr 1
14x 15-4
decor. ceiling
open to below
Br 4
10-10 x 11
SECOND FLOOR
Optional Deck
decor. ceiling
Brkfst
8 x 11-8
9'-0" ceiling ht.
Kitchen
10 x 11-8
Dining Rm
11-6 x 13-4
Hearth Rm
14 x 13-4
slope
DN
D W
pan
Living Rm
14 x 15-4
Foy
UP
Garage
21-8 x 21-4
FIRST FLOOR
p.
OPTIONAL CRAWLSPACE/SLAB FOUNDATION

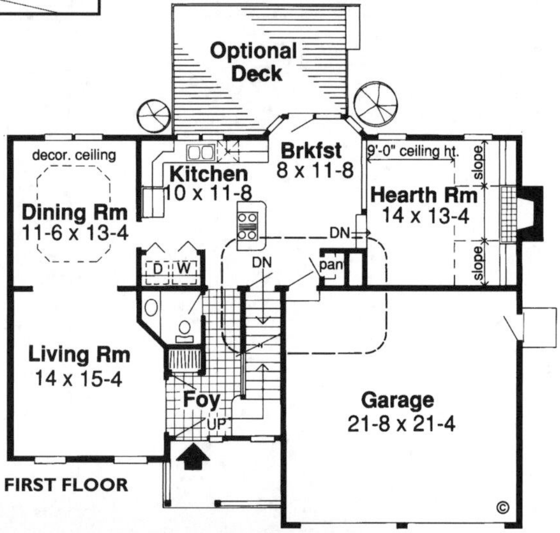

Design 50037

Units	Single
Price Code	D
Total Finished	2,143 sq. ft.
Main Finished	2,143 sq. ft.
Basement Unfinished	2,143 sq. ft.
Garage Unfinished	529 sq. ft.
Porch Unfinished	217 sq. ft.
Dimensions	76'8"x44'
Foundation	Basement
Bedrooms	3
Full Baths	2
Main Ceiling	9'
Max Ridge Height	26'
Roof Framing	Truss
Exterior Walls	2x4

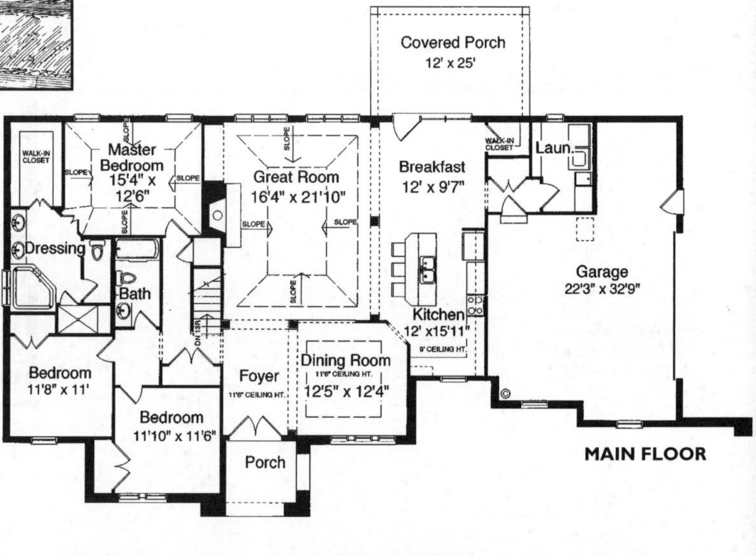

Covered Porch
12' x 25'
WALK-IN CLOSET
Master Bedroom
15'4" x 12'6"
SLOPE
Great Room
16'4" x 21'10"
Breakfast
12' x 9'7"
WALK-IN CLOSET
Laun.
Dressing
Bath
Garage
22'3" x 32'9"
Kitchen
12' x15'11"
9' CEILING HT.
Bedroom
11'8" x 11'
Foyer
11'6" CEILING HT.
Dining Room
11'6" CEILING HT.
12'5" x 12'4"
Bedroom
11'10" x 11'6"
Porch
MAIN FLOOR

Design 91184

Units	Single
Price Code	D
Total Finished	2,143 sq. ft.
First Finished	1,563 sq. ft.
Second Finished	580 sq. ft.
Bonus Unfinished	630 sq. ft.
Garage Unfinished	469 sq. ft.
Porch Unfinished	158 sq. ft.
Dimensions	32'10½"x68'10½"
Foundation	Slab
Bedrooms	3
Full Baths	2
Half Baths	1
First Ceiling	8'
Max Ridge Height	28'
Roof Framing	Stick
Exterior Walls	2x4

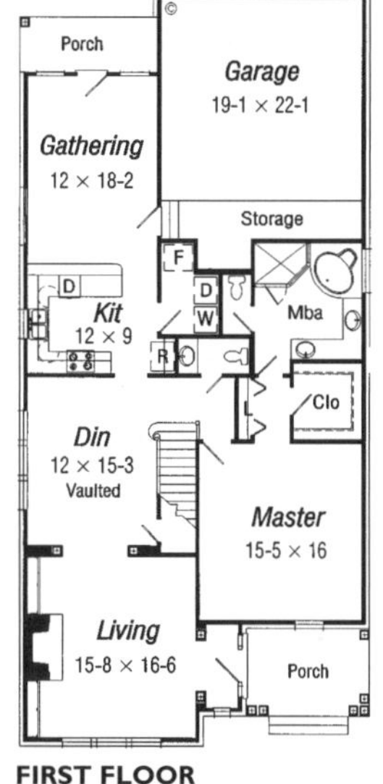
Porch
Garage
19-1 × 22-1
Gathering
12 × 18-2
Storage
Kit
12 × 9
Mba
Clo
Din
12 × 15-3
Vaulted
Master
15-5 × 16
Living
15-8 × 16-6
Porch

FIRST FLOOR

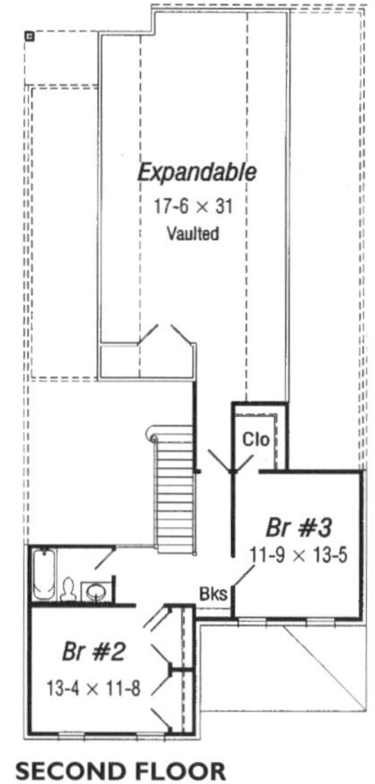
Expandable
17-6 × 31
Vaulted
Clo
Br #3
11-9 × 13-5
Bks
Br #2
13-4 × 11-8

SECOND FLOOR

Design 10465

Units	Single
Price Code	D
Total Finished	2,144 sq. ft.
Main Finished	2,144 sq. ft.
Garage Unfinished	483 sq. ft.
Dimensions	57'4"x65'
Foundation	Slab
Bedrooms	4
Full Baths	3
Max Ridge Height	25
Roof Framing	Stick
Exterior Walls	2x6

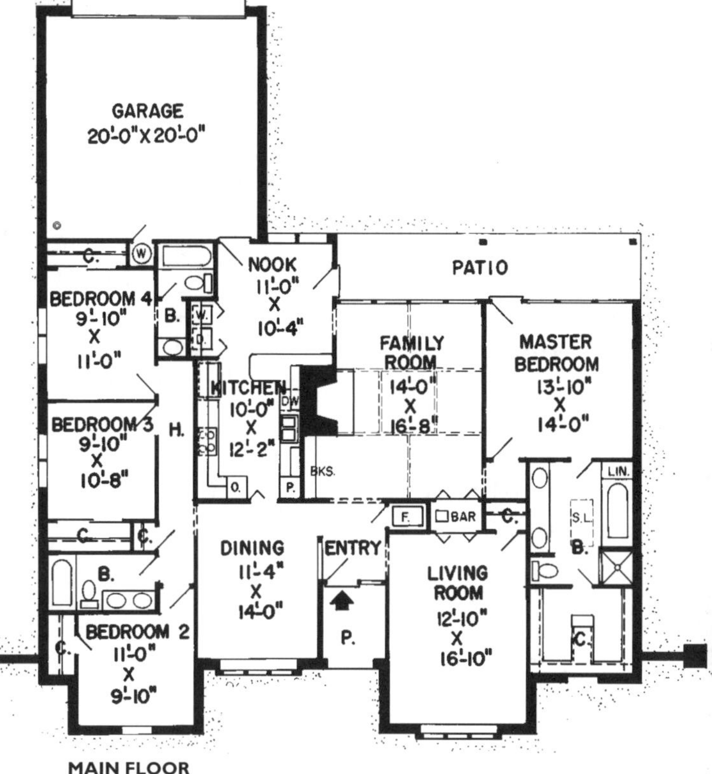
GARAGE
20'-0"X20'-0"
NOOK
11'-0"
X
10'-4"
PATIO
BEDROOM 4
9'-10"
X
11'-0"
FAMILY
ROOM
14'-0"
X
16'-8"
MASTER
BEDROOM
13'-10"
X
14'-0"
KITCHEN
10'-0"
X
12'-2"
BEDROOM 3
9'-10"
X
10'-8"
BKS.
BAR
LIN.
DINING
11'-4"
X
14'-0"
ENTRY
LIVING
ROOM
12'-10"
X
16'-10"
BEDROOM 2
11'-0"
X
9'-10"

MAIN FLOOR

Design 94983

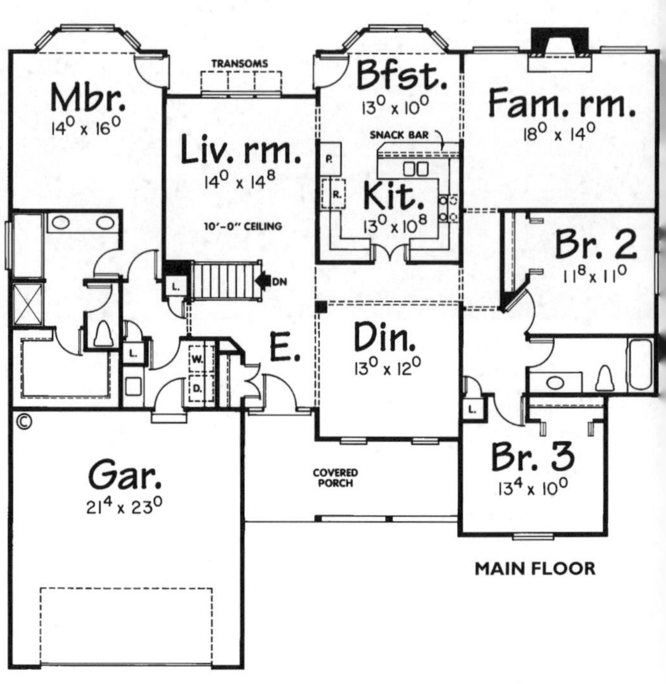

TRANSOMS
Mbr.
$14^0 \times 16^0$
Liv. rm.
$14^0 \times 14^8$
10'-0" CEILING
Bfst.
$13^0 \times 10^0$
SNACK BAR
Kit.
$13^0 \times 10^8$
Fam. rm.
$18^0 \times 14^0$
Br. 2
$11^8 \times 11^0$
DN
E.
Din.
$13^0 \times 12^0$
Gar.
$21^4 \times 23^0$
COVERED PORCH
Br. 3
$13^4 \times 10^0$
MAIN FLOOR

Units	Single
Price Code	D
Total Finished	2,144 sq. ft.
Main Finished	2,144 sq. ft.
Garage Unfinished	513 sq. ft.
Dimensions	60'8"x58'
Foundation	Basement
Bedrooms	3
Full Baths	2
Max Ridge Height	19'10"
Roof Framing	Stick
Exterior Walls	2x4

* Alternate foundation options available at an additional charge. Please call 1-800-235-5700 for more information.

Design 69104

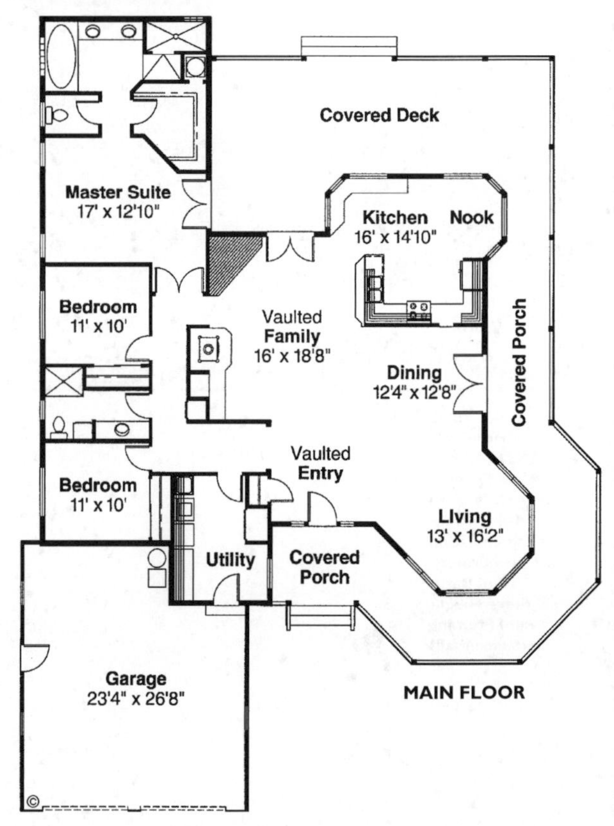

Covered Deck
Master Suite
17' x 12'10"
Kitchen
Nook
16' x 14'10"
Bedroom
11' x 10'
Vaulted
Family
16' x 18'8"
Dining
12'4" x 12'8"
Covered Porch
Vaulted
Entry
Bedroom
11' x 10'
Living
13' x 16'2"
Utility
Covered
Porch
Garage
23'4" x 26'8"
MAIN FLOOR

Units	Single
Price Code	D
Total Finished	2,145 sq. ft.
Main Finished	2,145 sq. ft.
Garage Unfinished	647 sq. ft.
Dimensions	60'11"x83'
Foundation	Crawlspace
Bedrooms	3
Full Baths	1
3/4 Baths	1
Main Ceiling	9'
Vaulted Ceiling	18'2"
Max Ridge Height	25'8"
Roof Framing	Truss
Exterior Walls	2x6

Design 62083

Units	Single
Price Code	D
Total Finished	2,146 sq. ft.
First Finished	1,654 sq. ft.
Second Finished	492 sq. ft.
Garage Unfinished	464 sq. ft.
Porch Unfinished	324 sq. ft.
Dimensions	38'10"x70'4'
Foundation	Crawlspace Slab
Bedrooms	3
Full Baths	2
Half Baths	1
First Ceiling	9'
Second Ceiling	8'
Max Ridge Height	28'10"
Roof Framing	Stick
Exterior Walls	2x4

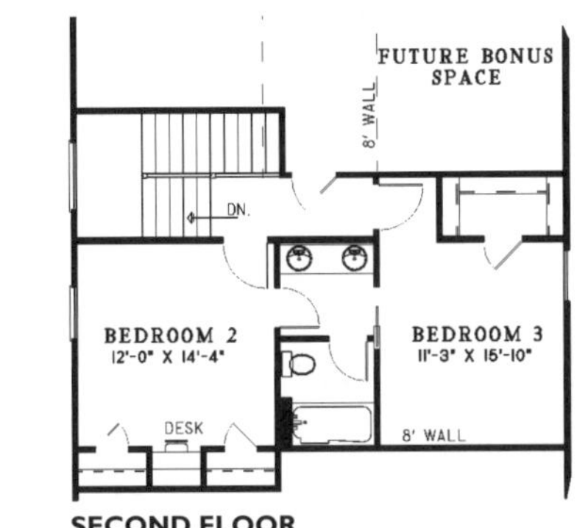
FUTURE BONUS SPACE
8' WALL
DN.
BEDROOM 2
12'-0" X 14'-4"
DESK
BEDROOM 3
11'-3" X 15'-10"
8' WALL

SECOND FLOOR

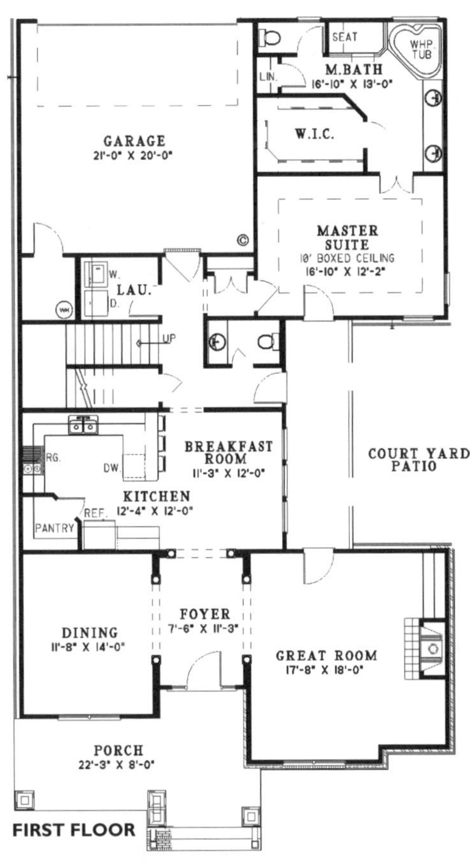
SEAT
WHP TUB
M.BATH
16'-10" X 13'-0"
LIN.
W.I.C.
GARAGE
21'-0" X 20'-0"
MASTER SUITE
10' BOXED CEILING
16'-10" X 12'-2"
W.
LAU.
D.
UP
BREAKFAST ROOM
11'-3" X 12'-0"
RG.
DW
KITCHEN
12'-4" X 12'-0"
REF.
PANTRY
COURT YARD PATIO
DINING
11'-8" X 14'-0"
FOYER
7'-6" X 11'-3"
GREAT ROOM
17'-8" X 18'-0"
PORCH
22'-3" X 8'-0"

FIRST FLOOR

Design 61096

Units	Single
Price Code	D
Total Finished	2,148 sq. ft.
Main Finished	2,148 sq. ft.
Garage Unfinished	477 sq. ft.
Porch Unfinished	190 sq. ft.
Dimensions	63'x52'8"
Foundation	Crawlspace Slab
Bedrooms	4
Full Baths	2
Main Ceiling	9'
Roof Framing	Stick
Exterior Walls	2x4

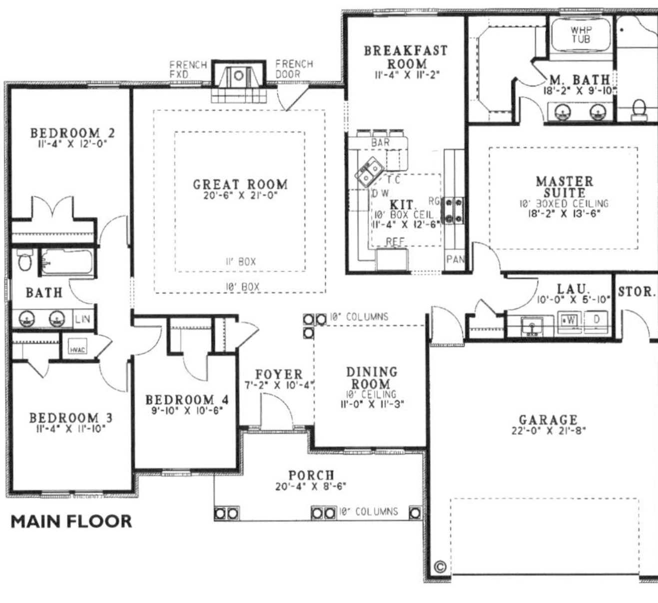
FRENCH FXD
FRENCH DOOR
BREAKFAST ROOM
11'-4" X 11'-2"
WHP TUB
M. BATH
18'-2" X 9'-10"
BEDROOM 2
11'-4" X 12'-0"
GREAT ROOM
20'-6" X 21'-0"
BAR
KIT.
10' BOX CEIL.
11'-4" X 12'-6"
REF.
MASTER SUITE
10' BOXED CEILING
18'-2" X 13'-6"
11' BOX
10' BOX
BATH
LIN
HVAC
10" COLUMNS
LAU.
10'-0" X 5'-10"
STOR.
FOYER
7'-2" X 10'-4"
DINING ROOM
10' CEILING
11'-0" X 11'-3"
BEDROOM 4
9'-10" X 10'-6"
BEDROOM 3
11'-4" X 11'-10"
GARAGE
22'-0" X 21'-8"
PORCH
20'-4" X 8'-6"
10" COLUMNS

MAIN FLOOR

Design 69155

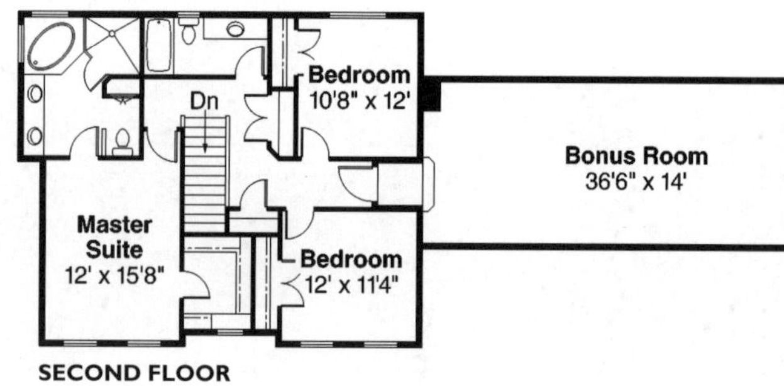
Bedroom
10'8" x 12'
Dn
Bonus Room
36'6" x 14'
Master
Suite
12' x 15'8"
Bedroom
12' x 11'4"

SECOND FLOOR

Units	Single
Price Code	D
Total Finished	2,148 sq. ft.
First Finished	1,195 sq. ft.
Second Finished	953 sq. ft.
Bonus Unfinished	570 sq. ft.
Garage Unfinished	959 sq. ft.
Dimensions	77'x45'
Foundation	Crawlspace
Bedrooms	3
Full Baths	2
Half Baths	1
First Ceiling	9'
Second Ceiling	9'
Max Ridge Height	28'
Roof Framing	Truss
Exterior Walls	2x6

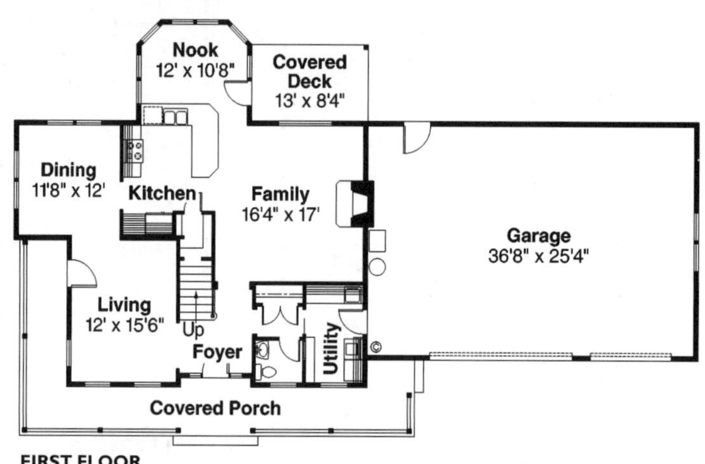
Nook
12' x 10'8"
Covered
Deck
13' x 8'4"
Dining
11'8" x 12'
Kitchen
Family
16'4" x 17'
Garage
36'8" x 25'4"
Living
12' x 15'6"
Up
Foyer
Utility
Covered Porch

FIRST FLOOR

Design 93442

Br.#2
13 x 10/3
Br.#3
11 x 12
SECOND FLOOR
Opt. Bonus
12 x 23/5

SECOND FLOOR

Units	Single
Price Code	D
Total Finished	2,148 sq. ft.
First Finished	1,626 sq. ft.
Second Finished	522 sq. ft.
Bonus Unfinished	336 sq. ft.
Basement Unfinished	1,626 sq. ft.
Garage Unfinished	522 sq. ft.
Porch Unfinished	71 sq. ft.
Dimensions	54'7"x62'8"
Foundation	Basement
Bedrooms	3
Full Baths	2
Half Baths	1
First Ceiling	9'
Second Ceiling	8'
Vaulted Ceiling	14'
Tray Ceiling	10'
Max Ridge Height	27'11"
Roof Framing	Stick
Exterior Walls	2x4

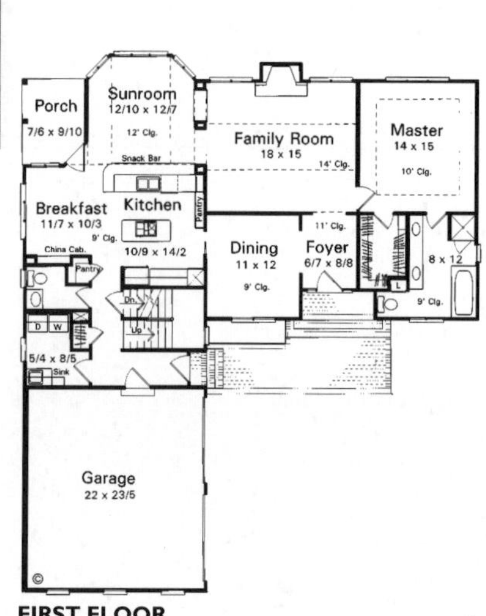
Porch
7/6 x 9/10
Sunroom
12/10 x 12/7
Family Room
18 x 15
Master
14 x 15
Breakfast
11/7 x 10/3
Kitchen
10/9 x 14/2
Dining
11 x 12
Foyer
6/7 x 8/8
8 x 12
Garage
22 x 23/5

FIRST FLOOR

Design 63028

Units	Single
Price Code	D
Total Finished	2,153 sq. ft.
Main Finished	2,153 sq. ft.
Garage Unfinished	434 sq. ft.
Dimensions	61'8"x62'
Foundation	Slab
Bedrooms	4
Full Baths	2
Main Ceiling	10'
Vaulted Ceiling	12'
Max Ridge Height	21'6"
Roof Framing	Truss
Exterior Walls	2x4

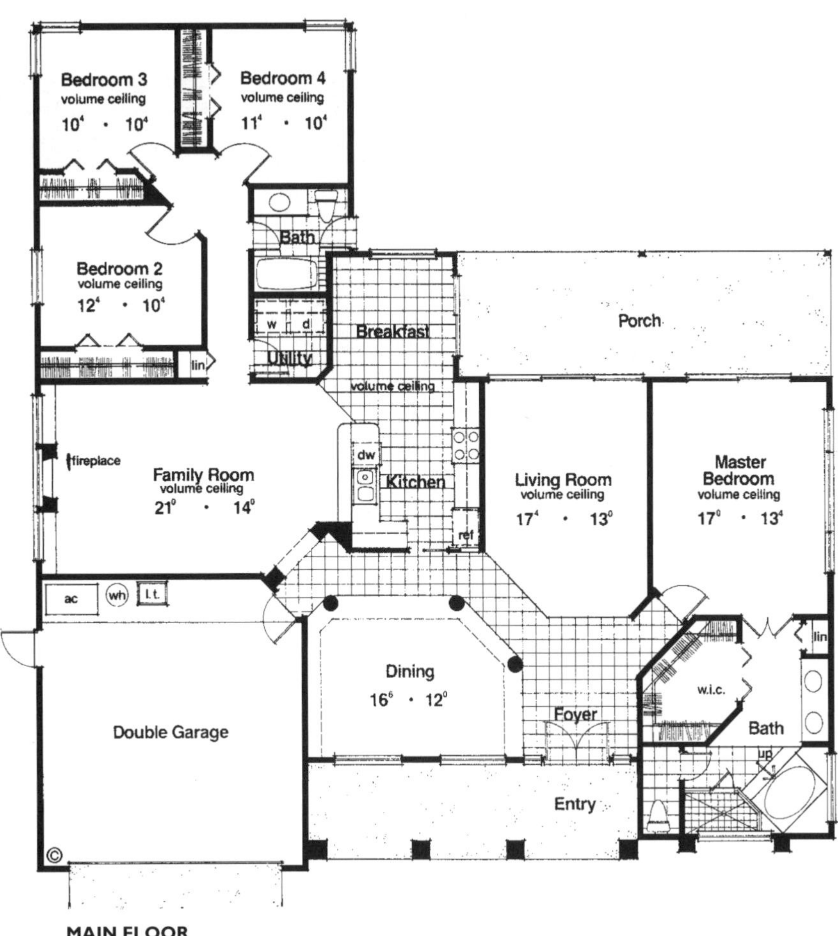
Bedroom 3
volume ceiling
10⁴ · 10⁴
Bedroom 4
volume ceiling
11⁴ · 10⁴
Bath
Bedroom 2
volume ceiling
12⁴ · 10⁴
lin
w d
Utility
Breakfast
volume ceiling
Porch
fireplace
Family Room
volume ceiling
21⁰ · 14⁰
dw
Kitchen
ref
Living Room
volume ceiling
17⁴ · 13⁰
Master
Bedroom
volume ceiling
17⁰ · 13⁴
ac
wh
l.t.
Dining
16⁶ · 12⁰
Foyer
w.i.c.
lin
Bath
up
Double Garage
Entry

MAIN FLOOR

Design 97150

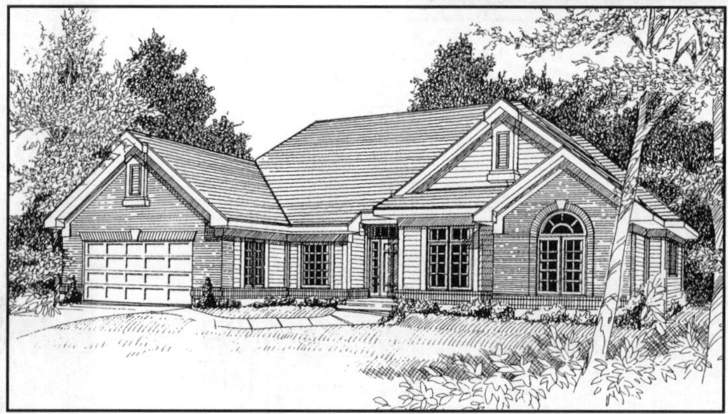

Units	Single
Price Code	D
Total Finished	2,153 sq. ft.
Main Finished	2,153 sq. ft.
Basement Unfinished	2,153 sq. ft.
Garage Unfinished	573 sq. ft.
Dimensions	65'x54'
Foundation	Basement
Bedrooms	3
Full Baths	2
Main Ceiling	9'1⅛"
Max Ridge Height	24'
Roof Framing	Truss
Exterior Walls	2x6

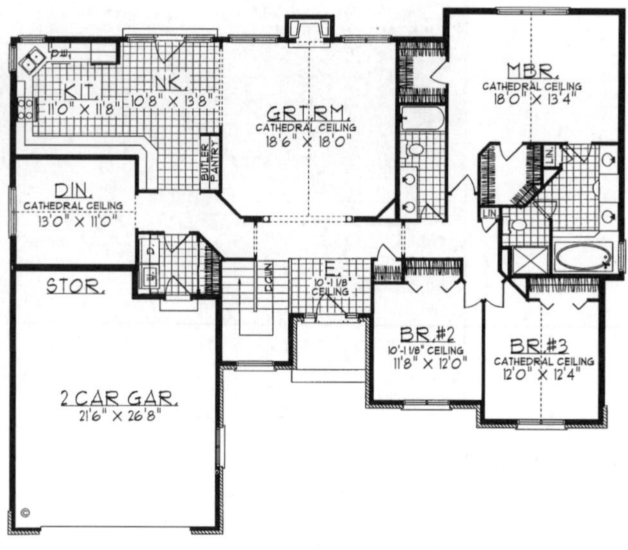
KIT.
11'0" X 11'8"
NK.
10'8" X 13'8"
GRT.RM.
CATHEDRAL CEILING
18'6" X 18'0"
MBR.
CATHEDRAL CEILING
18'0" X 13'4"
DIN.
CATHEDRAL CEILING
13'0" X 11'0"
BUTLER PANTRY
STOR.
DOWN
E.
10'-1 1/8" CEILING
BR.#2
10'-1 1/8" CEILING
11'8" X 12'0"
BR.#3
CATHEDRAL CEILING
12'0" X 12'4"
2 CAR GAR.
21'6" X 26'8"

MAIN FLOOR

Design 91548

Units	Single
Price Code	D
Total Finished	2,155 sq. ft.
Main Finished	2,155 sq. ft.
Dimensions	60'x79'
Foundation	Crawlspace
Bedrooms	3
Full Baths	2
Half Baths	1
Max Ridge Height	22'
Roof Framing	Truss
Exterior Walls	2x6

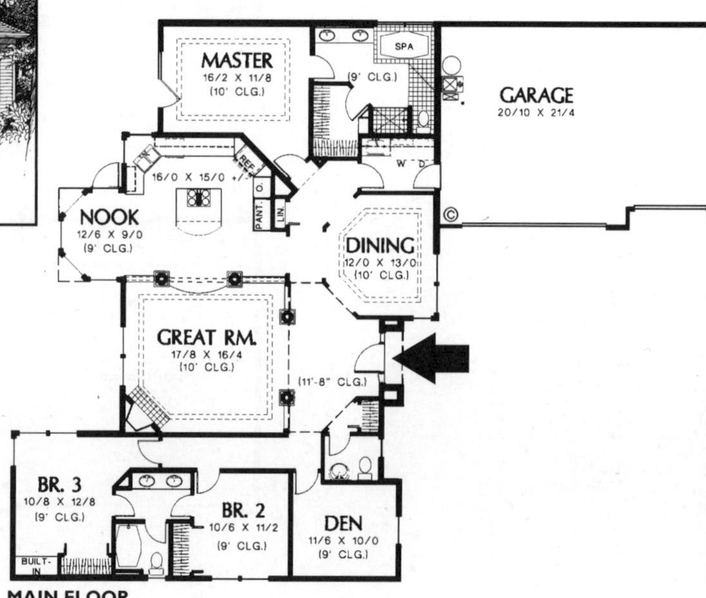
MASTER
16/2 X 11/8
(10' CLG.)
SPA
(9' CLG.)
GARAGE
20/10 X 21/4
16/0 X 15/0
NOOK
12/6 X 9/0
(9' CLG.)
DINING
12/0 X 13/0
(10' CLG.)
GREAT RM.
17/8 X 16/4
(10' CLG.)
(11'-8" CLG.)
BR. 3
10/8 X 12/8
(9' CLG.)
BR. 2
10/6 X 11/2
(9' CLG.)
DEN
11/6 X 10/0
(9' CLG.)
BUILT-IN

MAIN FLOOR

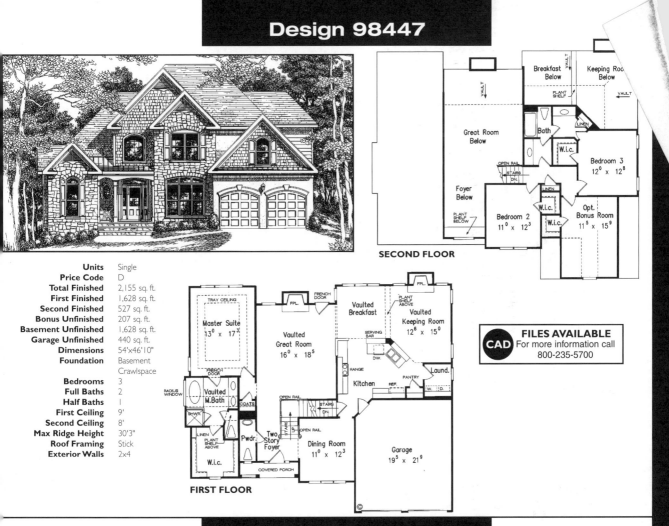

Design 98447

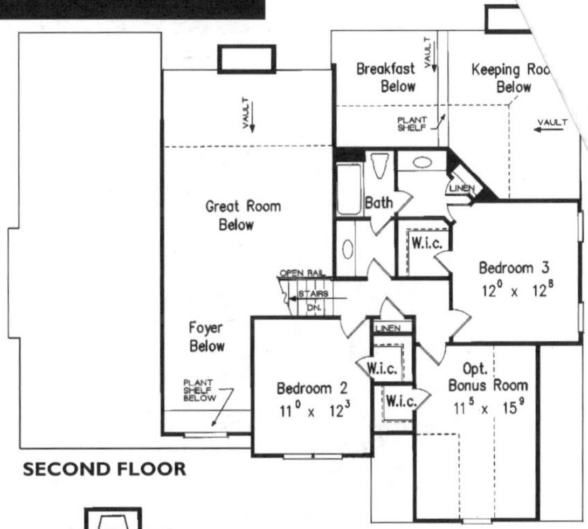

Units	Single
Price Code	D
Total Finished	2,155 sq. ft.
First Finished	1,628 sq. ft.
Second Finished	527 sq. ft.
Bonus Unfinished	207 sq. ft.
Basement Unfinished	1,628 sq. ft.
Garage Unfinished	440 sq. ft.
Dimensions	54'x46'10"
Foundation	Basement Crawlspace
Bedrooms	3
Full Baths	2
Half Baths	1
First Ceiling	9'
Second Ceiling	8'
Max Ridge Height	30'3"
Roof Framing	Stick
Exterior Walls	2x4

SECOND FLOOR

FIRST FLOOR

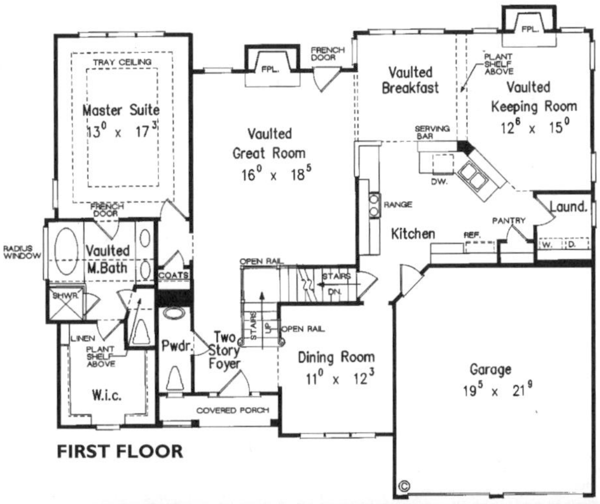

CAD FILES AVAILABLE For more information call 800-235-5700

Design 20160

PHOTOGRAPHY: JOHN EHRENCLOU

Please note: The photographed home may have been modified to suit homeowner preferences. If you order plans, have a builder or design professional check them against the photograph to confirm actual construction details.

Units	Single
Price Code	D
Total Finished	2,157 sq. ft.
First Finished	1,590 sq. ft.
Second Finished	567 sq. ft.
Basement Unfinished	1,576 sq. ft.
Garage Unfinished	456 sq. ft.
Dimensions	54'x46'
Foundation	Basement Crawlspace Slab
Bedrooms	3
Full Baths	2
Half Baths	1
Max Ridge Height	28'
Roof Framing	Stick
Exterior Walls	2x4, 2x6

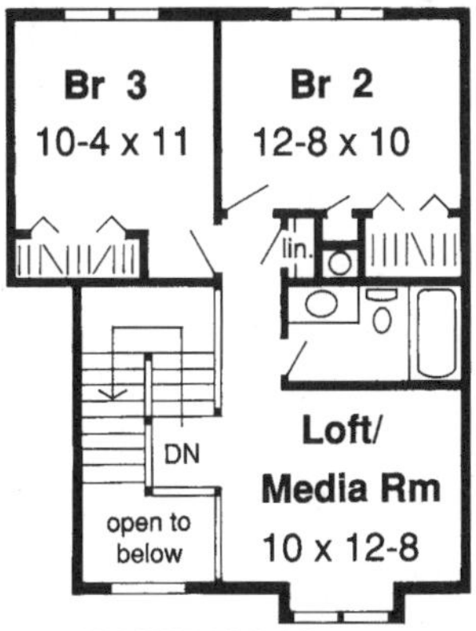

SECOND FLOOR

FIRST FLOOR

Design 97294

Units	Single
Price Code	D
Total Finished	2,158 sq. ft.
Main Finished	2,158 sq. ft.
Basement Unfinished	2,190 sq. ft.
Garage Unfinished	485 sq. ft.
Dimensions	63'x63'6"
Foundation	Basement Crawlspace
Bedrooms	4
Full Baths	3
Max Ridge Height	25'
Roof Framing	Stick
Exterior Walls	2x4

CAD FILES AVAILABLE For more information call 800-235-5700

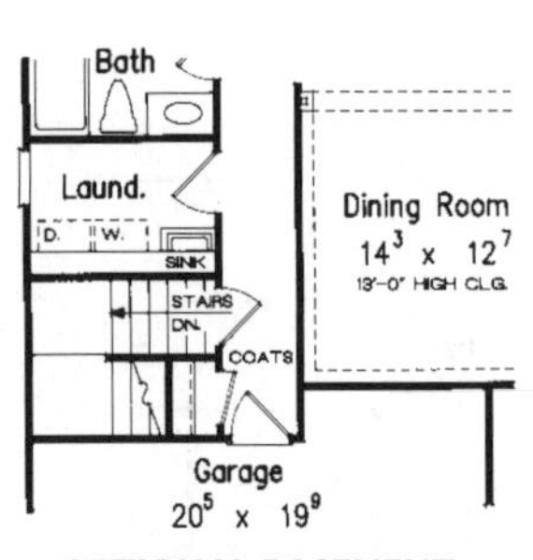

Bath
Laund.
D. W.
SINK
STAIRS DN.
COATS
Dining Room
14³ x 12⁷
13'-0" HIGH CLG.
Garage
20⁵ x 19⁹

OPTIONAL BASEMENT STAIR LOCATION

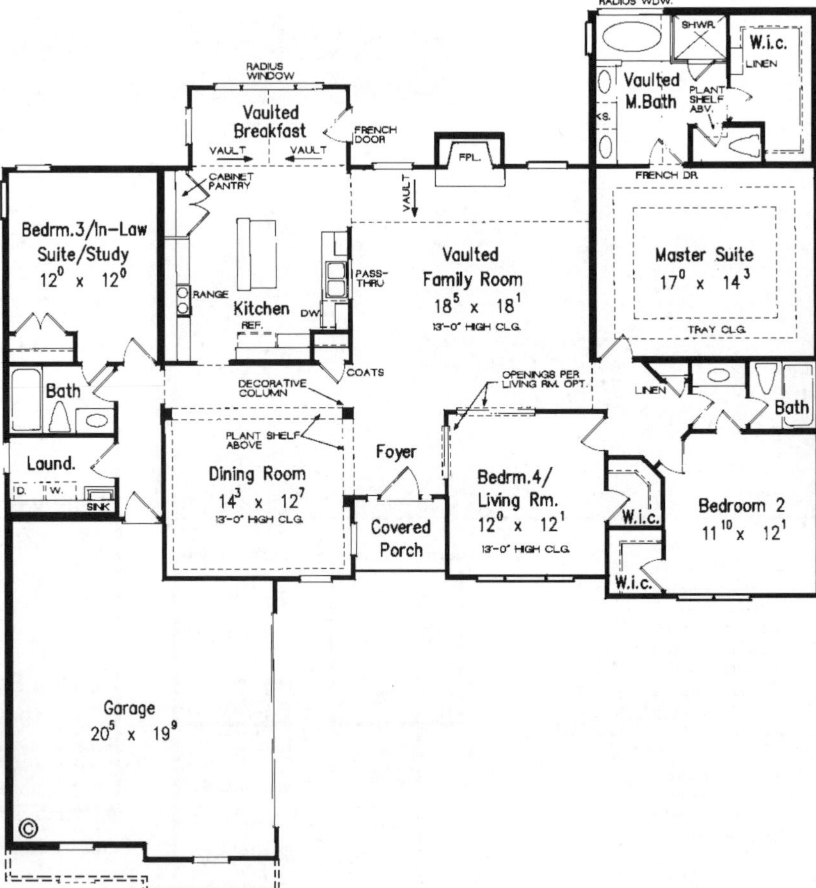

RADIUS WDW.
SHWR.
W.i.c.
LINEN
Vaulted M.Bath
PLANT SHELF ABV.
RADIUS WINDOW
Vaulted Breakfast
VAULT
FRENCH DOOR
FPL.
FRENCH DR.
CABINET PANTRY
Bedrm.3/In-Law Suite/Study
12⁰ x 12⁰
RANGE
Kitchen
REF.
DW
PASS-THRU
Vaulted Family Room
18⁵ x 18¹
13'-0" HIGH CLG.
Master Suite
17⁰ x 14³
TRAY CLG.
Bath
COATS
DECORATIVE COLUMN
OPENINGS PER LIVING RM. OPT.
LINEN
Bath
PLANT SHELF ABOVE
Laund.
D. W.
SINK
Dining Room
14³ x 12⁷
13'-0" HIGH CLG.
Foyer
Bedrm.4/ Living Rm.
12⁰ x 12¹
13'-0" HIGH CLG.
W.i.c.
Bedroom 2
11¹⁰ x 12¹
Covered Porch
W.i.c.
Garage
20⁵ x 19⁹
©
GARAGE LOCATION W/ BASEMENT

MAIN FLOOR

Design 91461

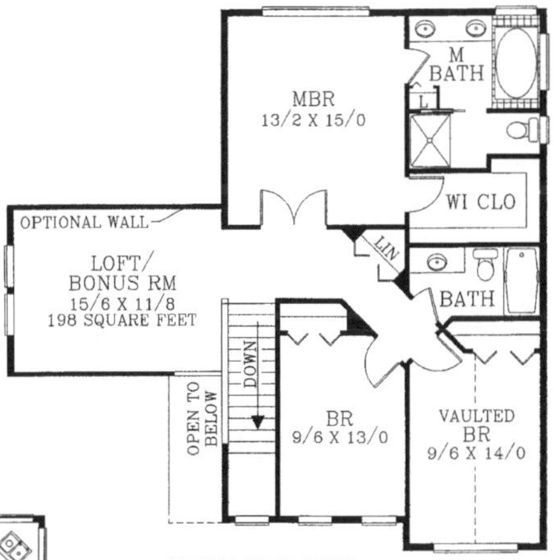

Units	Single
Price Code	D
Total Finished	2,160 sq. ft.
First Finished	1,118 sq. ft.
Second Finished	844 sq. ft.
Bonus Unfinished	198 sq. ft.
Garage Unfinished	390 sq. ft.
Dimensions	40'x45'8"
Foundation	Crawlspace
Bedrooms	3
Full Baths	2
Half Baths	1
First Ceiling	8'
Second Ceiling	8'
Max Ridge Height	27'
Roof Framing	Stick/Truss
Exterior Walls	2x6

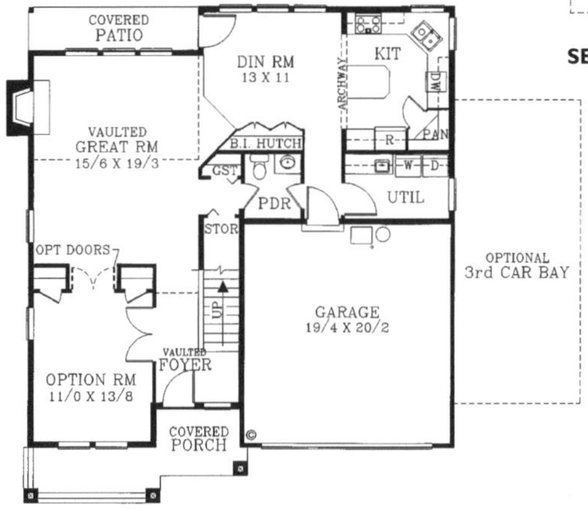

MBR 13/2 X 15/0
M BATH
WI CLO
OPTIONAL WALL
LOFT/ BONUS RM 15/6 X 11/8 198 SQUARE FEET
LIN
BATH
DOWN
OPEN TO BELOW
BR 9/6 X 13/0
VAULTED BR 9/6 X 14/0

SECOND FLOOR

COVERED PATIO
DIN RM 13 X 11
KIT
ARCHWAY
DW
R
PAN
W D
VAULTED GREAT RM 15/6 X 19/3
B.I. HUTCH
GST
PDR
UTIL
STOR
OPT DOORS
UP
OPTIONAL 3rd CAR BAY
GARAGE 19/4 X 20/2
VAULTED FOYER
OPTION RM 11/0 X 13/8
COVERED PORCH

FIRST FLOOR

Design 91343

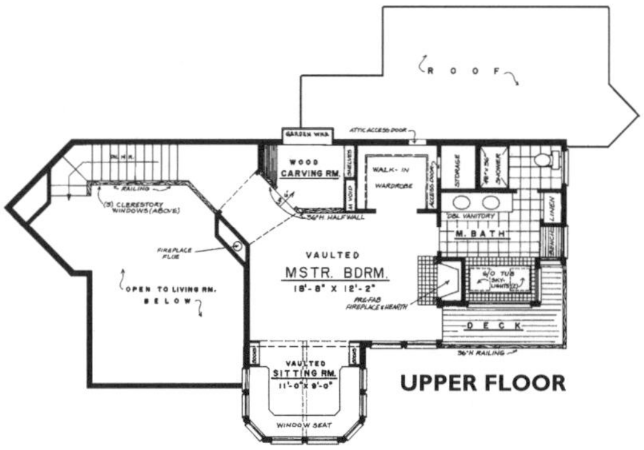

Units	Single
Price Code	D
Total Finished	2,162 sq. ft.
First Finished	1,338 sq. ft.
Second Finished	763 sq. ft.
Lower Finished	61 sq. ft.
Garage Unfinished	779 sq. ft.
Deck Unfinished	360 sq. ft.
Dimensions	67'x41'
Bedrooms	3
Full Baths	2
Half Baths	1
Max Ridge Height	31'6"
Roof Framing	Stick
Exterior Walls	2x6

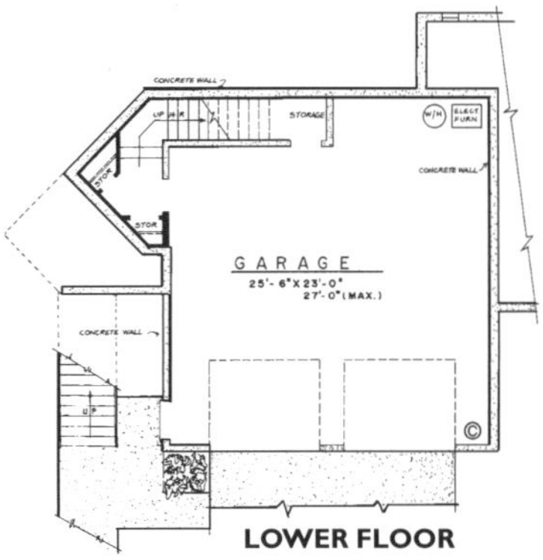

ROOF
WOOD CARVING RM.
WALK-IN WARDROBE
VAULTED MSTR. BDRM. 18'-8" X 12'-2"
M. BATH
OPEN TO LIVING RM. BELOW
DECK
VAULTED SITTING RM. 11'-0" X 9'-0"
WINDOW SEAT

UPPER FLOOR

GARAGE 25'-6" X 23'-0" 27'-0" (MAX.)
STORAGE
CONCRETE WALL

LOWER FLOOR

BDRM. #2 15'-8" X 9'-10"
BATH
UTIL
WARDROBE
BDRM. #3 11'-8" X 10'-6"
KITCHEN 16'-0" X 13'-2"
VAULTED ENTRY
DECK
VAULTED LIVING RM. 15'-4" X 18'-8"
DINING RM. 11'-0" X 11'-0"
DECK

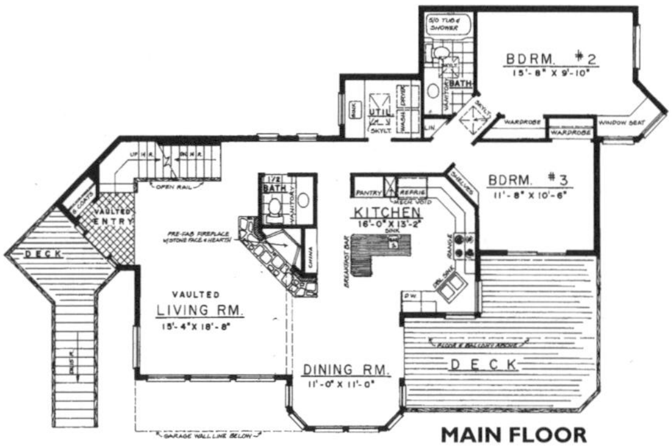

MAIN FLOOR

Design 96504

Units	Single
Price Code	D
Total Finished	2,162 sq. ft.
Main Finished	2,162 sq. ft.
Garage Unfinished	498 sq. ft.
Porch Unfinished	343 sq. ft.
Dimensions	70'x50'
Foundation	Crawlspace Slab
Bedrooms	3
Full Baths	2
Main Ceiling	8'
Tray Ceiling	10'
Max Ridge Height	25'
Roof Framing	Stick
Exterior Walls	2x4

MAIN FLOOR

Design 90484

Units	Single
Price Code	D
Total Finished	2,167 sq. ft.
Main Finished	2,167 sq. ft.
Basement Unfinished	2,167 sq. ft.
Garage Unfinished	491 sq. ft.
Deck Unfinished	184 sq. ft.
Dimensions	59'x59'10"
Foundation	Basement Crawlspace Slab
Bedrooms	3
Full Baths	2
Max Ridge Height	26'
Roof Framing	Stick
Exterior Walls	2x4

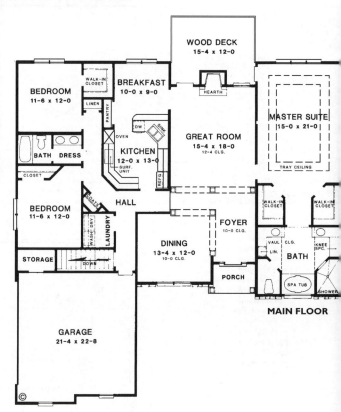

MAIN FLOOR

Design 98512

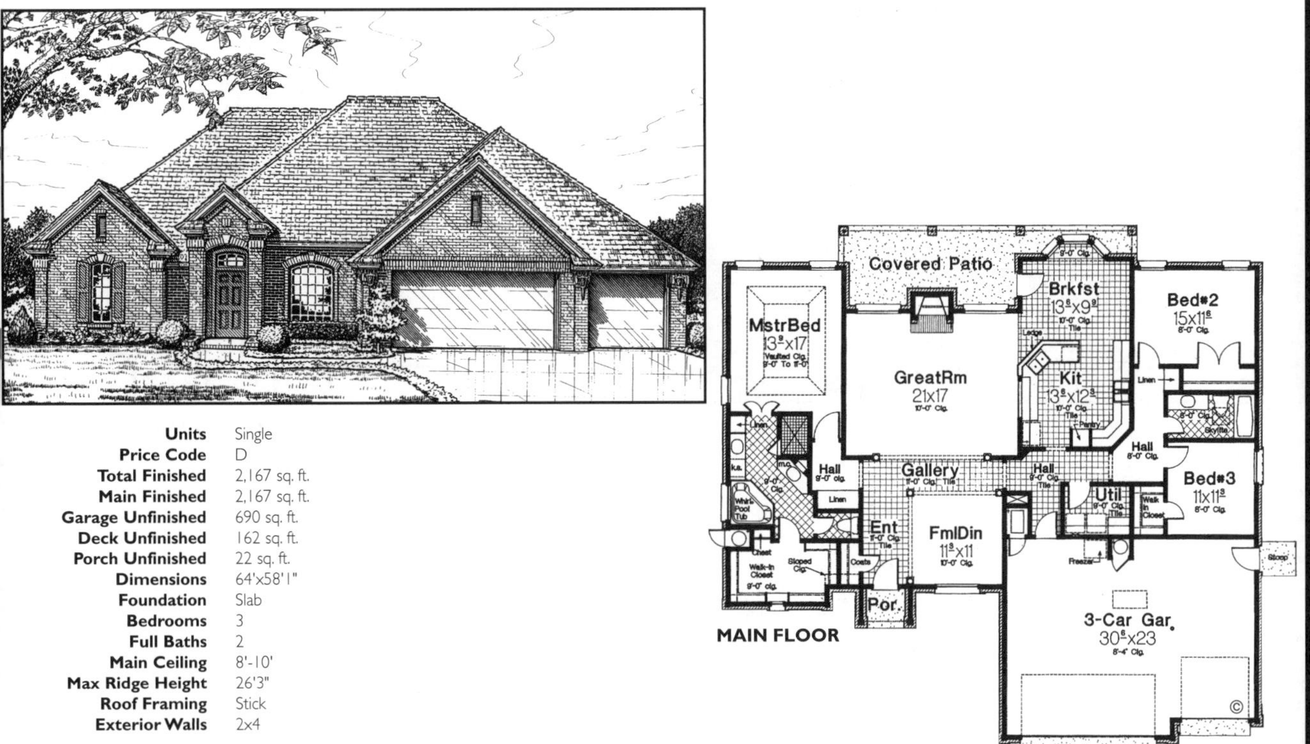
Covered Patio
Brkfst
13^8x9^8
Bed#2
15x11^6
MstrBed
13^8x17
GreatRm
21x17
Kit
13^8x12^8
Gallery
Hall
Util
Bed#3
11x11^8
Ent
FmlDin
11^8x11
Por.
3-Car Gar.
30^6x23
MAIN FLOOR

Units	Single
Price Code	D
Total Finished	2,167 sq. ft.
Main Finished	2,167 sq. ft.
Garage Unfinished	690 sq. ft.
Deck Unfinished	162 sq. ft.
Porch Unfinished	22 sq. ft.
Dimensions	64'x58'1"
Foundation	Slab
Bedrooms	3
Full Baths	2
Main Ceiling	8'-10'
Max Ridge Height	26'3"
Roof Framing	Stick
Exterior Walls	2x4

Design 66050

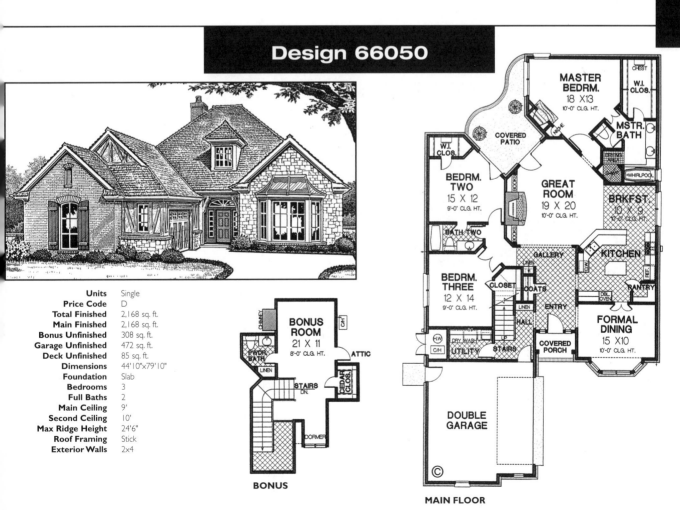

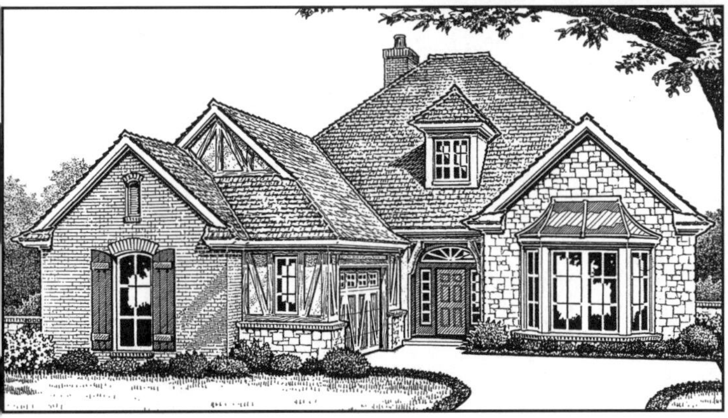

Units	Single
Price Code	D
Total Finished	2,168 sq. ft.
Main Finished	2,168 sq. ft.
Bonus Unfinished	308 sq. ft.
Garage Unfinished	472 sq. ft.
Deck Unfinished	85 sq. ft.
Dimensions	44'10"x79'10"
Foundation	Slab
Bedrooms	3
Full Baths	2
Main Ceiling	9'
Second Ceiling	10'
Max Ridge Height	24'6"
Roof Framing	Stick
Exterior Walls	2x4

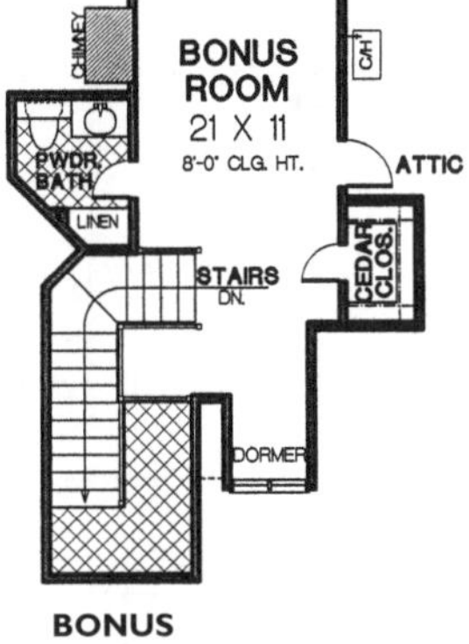

BONUS ROOM 21 X 11 8'-0" CLG. HT.

BONUS

MASTER BEDRM. 18 X13 10'-0" CLG. HT.
COVERED PATIO
BEDRM. TWO 15 X 12 9'-0" CLG. HT.
GREAT ROOM 19 X 20 10'-0" CLG. HT.
BRKFST. 10 X 9
KITCHEN
BEDRM. THREE 12 X 14 9'-0" CLG. HT.
FORMAL DINING 15 X10 10'-0" CLG. HT.
COVERED PORCH
DOUBLE GARAGE

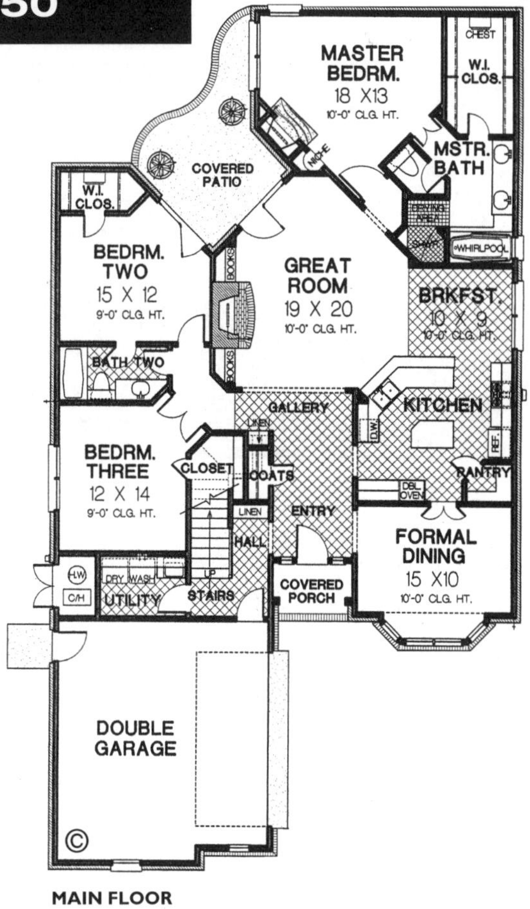

MAIN FLOOR

Design 64171

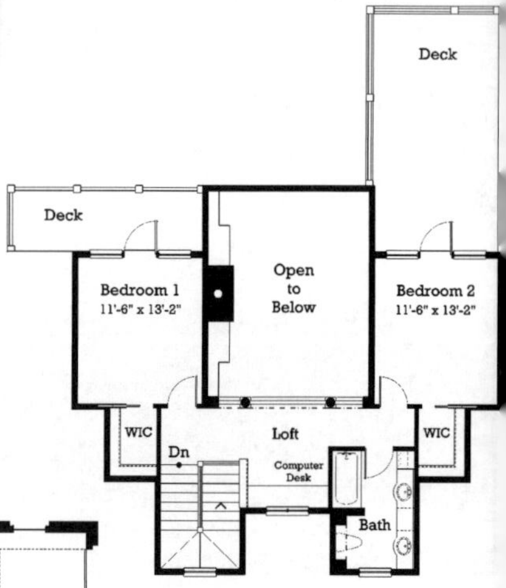

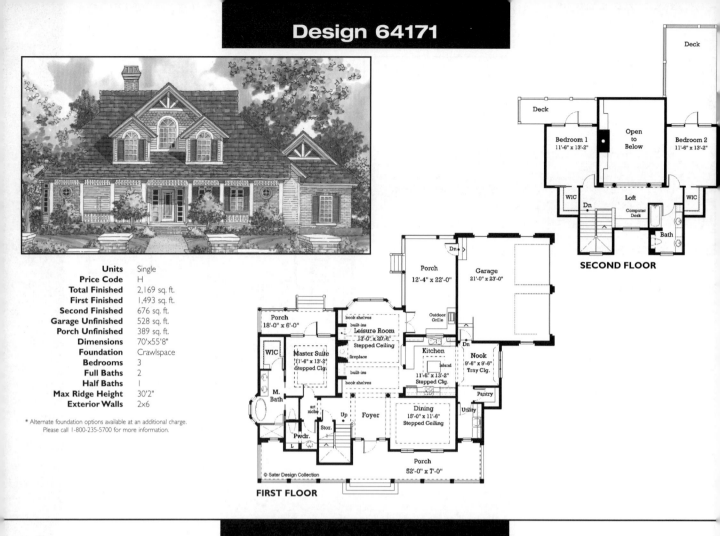

Units	Single
Price Code	H
Total Finished	2,169 sq. ft.
First Finished	1,493 sq. ft.
Second Finished	676 sq. ft.
Garage Unfinished	528 sq. ft.
Porch Unfinished	389 sq. ft.
Dimensions	70'x55'8"
Foundation	Crawlspace
Bedrooms	3
Full Baths	2
Half Baths	1
Max Ridge Height	30'2"
Exterior Walls	2x6

* Alternate foundation options available at an additional charge. Please call 1-800-235-5700 for more information.

Deck
Deck
Bedroom 1
11'-6" x 13'-2"
Open to Below
Bedroom 2
11'-6" x 13'-2"
WIC
Loft
WIC
Dn
Computer Desk
Bath

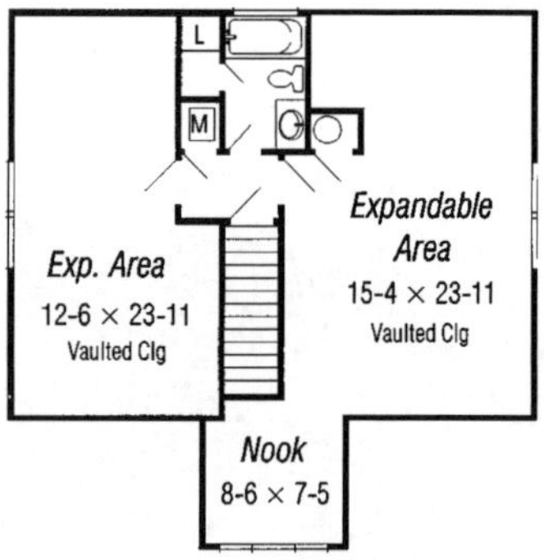

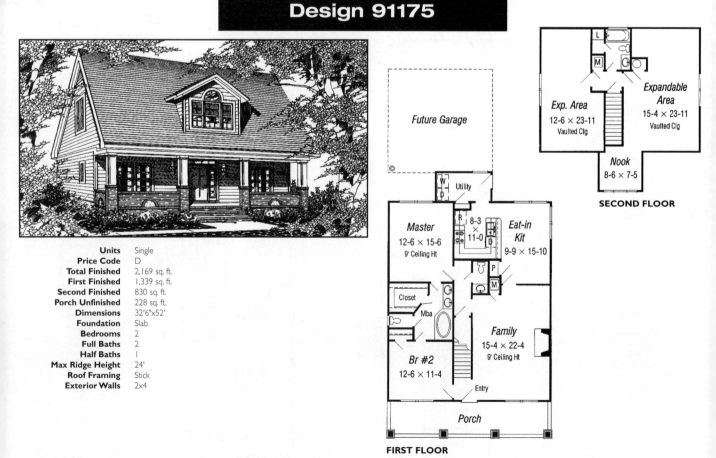

SECOND FLOOR

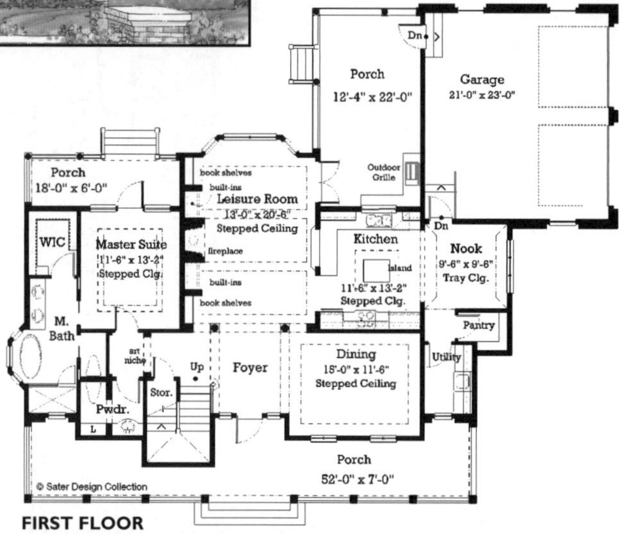

Porch
12'-4" x 22'-0"
Dn
Garage
21'-0" x 23'-0"
Porch
18'-0" x 6'-0"
book shelves
built-ins
Leisure Room
13'-0" x 20'-6"
Stepped Ceiling
Outdoor Grille
WIC
Master Suite
11'-6" x 13'-2"
Stepped Clg.
fireplace
built-ins
book shelves
Kitchen
island
11'-6" x 13'-2"
Stepped Clg.
Dn
Nook
9'-6" x 9'-6"
Tray Clg.
Pantry
M. Bath
art niche
Up
Foyer
Dining
15'-0" x 11'-6"
Stepped Ceiling
Utility
Stor.
Pwdr.
Porch
52'-0" x 7'-0"
© Sater Design Collection

FIRST FLOOR

Design 91175

Units	Single
Price Code	D
Total Finished	2,169 sq. ft.
First Finished	1,339 sq. ft.
Second Finished	830 sq. ft.
Porch Unfinished	228 sq. ft.
Dimensions	32'6"x52'
Foundation	Slab
Bedrooms	2
Full Baths	2
Half Baths	1
Max Ridge Height	24'
Roof Framing	Stick
Exterior Walls	2x4

Exp. Area
12-6 × 23-11
Vaulted Clg
Expandable Area
15-4 × 23-11
Vaulted Clg
Nook
8-6 × 7-5

SECOND FLOOR

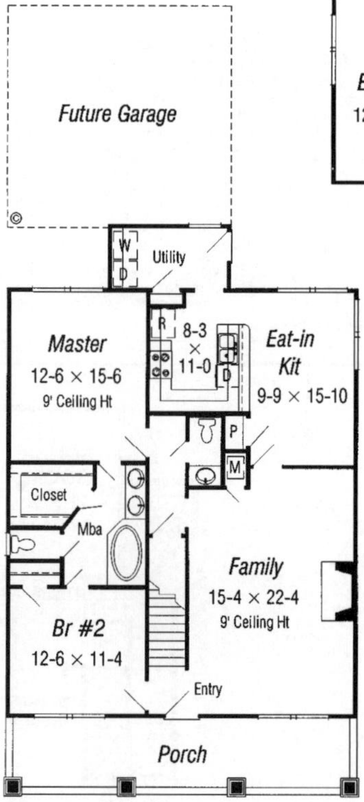

Future Garage
Utility
Master
12-6 × 15-6
9' Ceiling Ht
8-3 × 11-0
Eat-in Kit
9-9 × 15-10
Closet
Mba
Family
15-4 × 22-4
9' Ceiling Ht
Br #2
12-6 × 11-4
Entry
Porch

FIRST FLOOR

Design 98554

Units	Single
Price Code	D
Total Finished	2,169 sq. ft.
Main Finished	2,169 sq. ft.
Garage Unfinished	542 sq. ft.
Deck Unfinished	160 sq. ft.
Dimensions	76'6"x44'4"
Foundation	Slab
Bedrooms	4
Full Baths	3
Main Ceiling	8'-10'
Max Ridge Height	24'6"
Roof Framing	Stick
Exterior Walls	2x4

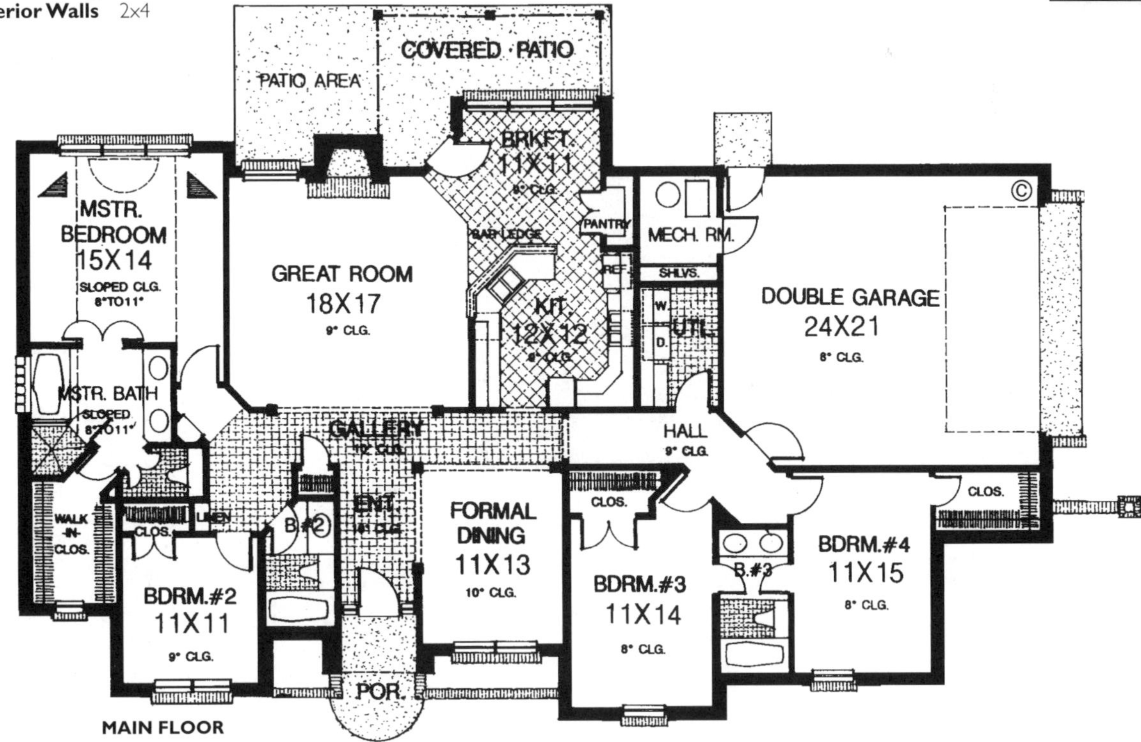

COVERED PATIO
PATIO AREA
BRKFT. 11X11
PANTRY
MECH. RM.
MSTR. BEDROOM 15X14
SLOPED CLG. 8"TO11"
GREAT ROOM 18X17
9" CLG.
BAR LEDGE
REF.
SHLVS.
KIT. 12X12
UTL.
DOUBLE GARAGE 24X21
8" CLG.
MSTR. BATH
GALLERY
HALL
9" CLG.
WALK-IN-CLOS.
CLOS.
LINEN
B.#2
ENT.
FORMAL DINING 11X13
10" CLG.
CLOS.
BDRM.#3 11X14
8" CLG.
B.#3
BDRM.#4 11X15
8" CLG.
BDRM.#2 11X11
9" CLG.
POR.

MAIN FLOOR

Design 98470

CAD FILES AVAILABLE
For more information call
800-235-5700

Units	Single
Price Code	D
Total Finished	2,170 sq. ft.
Main Finished	2,170 sq. ft.
Basement Unfinished	2,184 sq. ft.
Garage Unfinished	484 sq. ft.
Dimensions	63'6"x61'
Foundation	Basement Crawlspace
Bedrooms	3
Full Baths	2
Half Baths	1
Main Ceiling	9'
Max Ridge Height	27'
Roof Framing	Stick
Exterior Walls	2x4

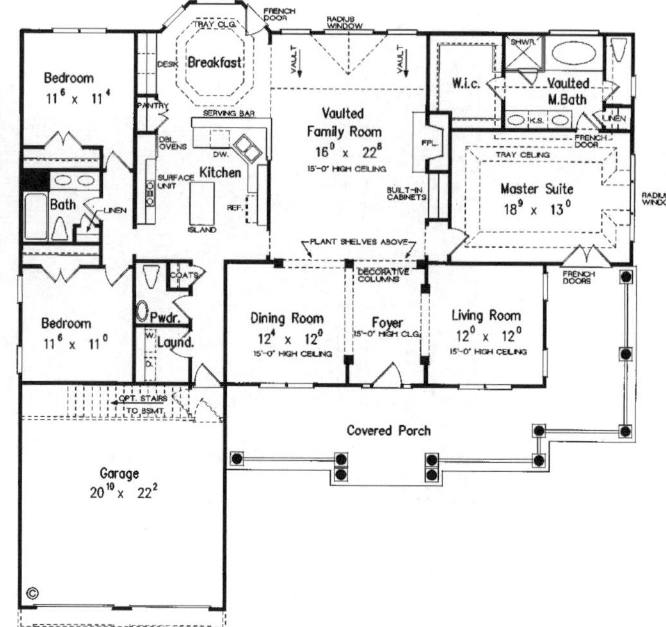
FRENCH DOOR
RADIUS WINDOW
TRAY CLG.
DESK
Breakfast
Bedroom
11^{6} x 11^{4}
PANTRY
SERVING BAR
Vaulted
Family Room
16^{0} x 22^{8}
15'-0" HIGH CEILING
VAULT
VAULT
W.i.c.
SHWR.
Vaulted
M.Bath
K.S.
LINEN
FRENCH DOOR
TRAY CEILING
Master Suite
18^{9} x 13^{0}
RADIUS WINDOW
DBL. OVENS
DW.
Kitchen
SURFACE UNIT
REF.
ISLAND
FPL.
BUILT-IN CABINETS
Bath
LINEN
PLANT SHELVES ABOVE
COATS
DECORATIVE COLUMNS
FRENCH DOORS
Bedroom
11^{6} x 11^{0}
Pwdr.
Laund.
Dining Room
12^{4} x 12^{0}
15'-0" HIGH CEILING
Foyer
15'-0" HIGH CLG.
Living Room
12^{0} x 12^{0}
15'-0" HIGH CEILING
OPT. STAIRS TO BSMT.
Covered Porch
Garage
20^{10} x 22^{2}
GARAGE LOCATION W/ BASEMENT

MAIN FLOOR

Design 24751

Units	Single
Price Code	D
Total Finished	2,172 sq. ft.
Main Finished	2,172 sq. ft.
Basement Unfinished	2,172 sq. ft.
Garage Unfinished	623 sq. ft.
Porch Unfinished	151 sq. ft.
Dimensions	64'6"x56'10"
Foundation	Basement Crawlspace Slab
Bedrooms	3
Full Baths	2
Main Ceiling	9'
Max Ridge Height	27'6"
Roof Framing	Stick
Exterior Walls	2x4

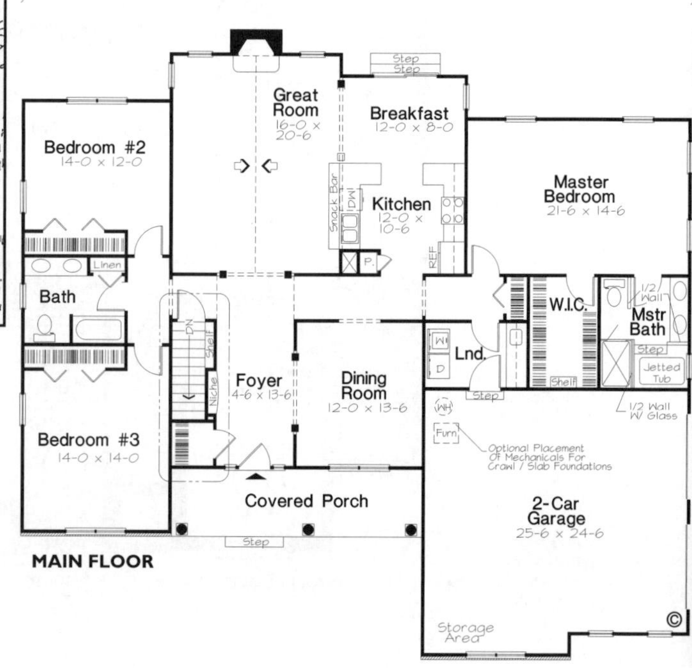
Step
Step
Great Room
16-0 x 20-6
Breakfast
12-0 x 8-0
Bedroom #2
14-0 x 12-0
Snack Bar
DW
Kitchen
12-0 x 10-6
REF
Master Bedroom
21-6 x 14-6
Linen
Bath
Dn
Shelf
Niche
Foyer
4-6 x 13-6
Dining Room
12-0 x 13-6
Lnd.
W.I.C.
Shelf
1/2 Wall
Mstr Bath
Step
Jetted Tub
Step
1/2 Wall W/ Glass
Bedroom #3
14-0 x 14-0
WH
Furn
Optional Placement Of Mechanicals For Crawl / Slab Foundations
Covered Porch
Step
2-Car Garage
25-6 x 24-6
Storage Area

MAIN FLOOR

Design 65131

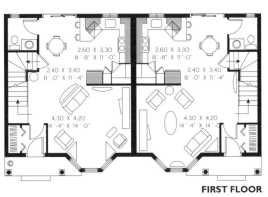

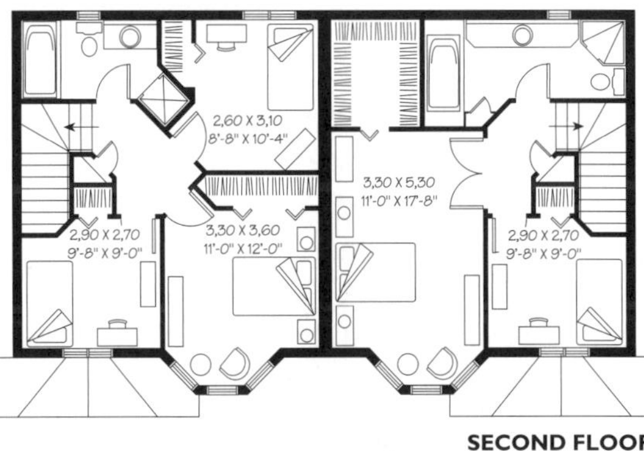
2,60 X 3,10
8'-8" X 10'-4"
3,30 X 5,30
11'-0" X 17'-8"
2,90 X 2,70
9'-8" X 9'-0"
3,30 X 3,60
11'-0" X 12'-0"
2,90 X 2,70
9'-8" X 9'-0"

SECOND FLOOR

Units	Duplex
Price Code	D
Total Finished	2,172 sq. ft.
First Finished	1,086 sq. ft.
Second Finished	1,086 sq. ft.
Dimensions	44'x28'8"
Foundation	Basement
Bedrooms	3
Full Baths	1
Half Baths	1
First Ceiling	8'
Second Ceiling	8'
Max Ridge Height	25'11"
Roof Framing	Truss
Exterior Walls	2x6

FIRST FLOOR

Design 94971

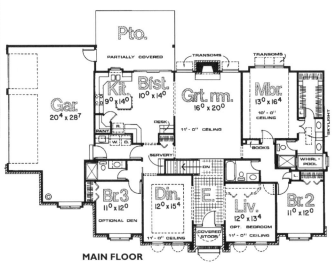

Units	Single
Price Code	D
Total Finished	2,172 sq. ft.
Main Finished	2,172 sq. ft.
Garage Unfinished	680 sq. ft.
Dimensions	76'x46'
Foundation	Basement
Bedrooms	3
Full Baths	2
3/4 Baths	1
Max Ridge Height	21'6"
Roof Framing	Stick
Exterior Walls	2x4

MAIN FLOOR

* Alternate foundation options available at an additional charge.
Please call 1-800-235-5700 for more information.

Design 93145

Units	Single
Price Code	D
Total Finished	2,174 sq. ft.
Main Finished	2,174 sq. ft.
Basement Unfinished	2,174 sq. ft.
Dimensions	67'x54'
Foundation	Basement
Bedrooms	3
Full Baths	2
Max Ridge Height	23'
Roof Framing	Truss
Exterior Walls	2x6

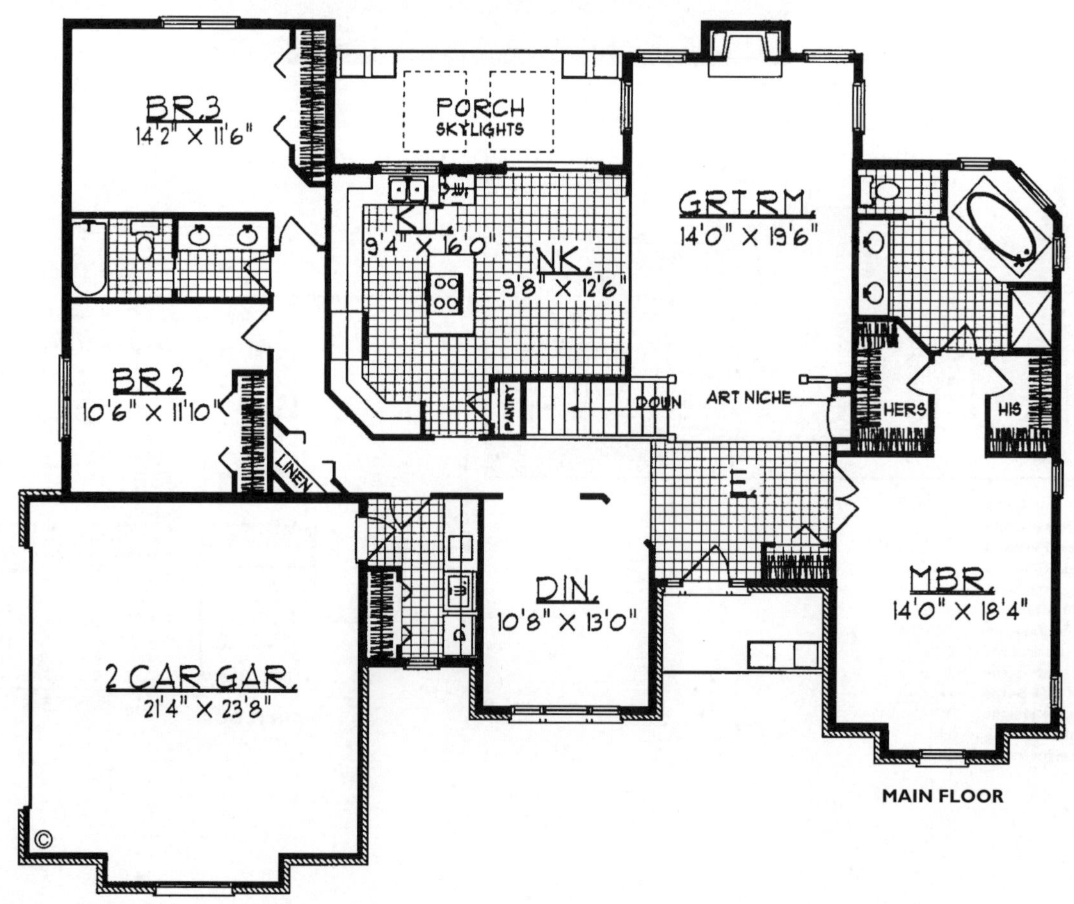
BR.3
14'2" X 11'6"
PORCH
SKYLIGHTS
GRT.RM.
14'0" X 19'6"
KIT.
9'4" X 16'0"
NK.
9'8" X 12'6"
BR.2
10'6" X 11'10"
PANTRY
DOWN
ART NICHE
HERS
HIS
LINEN
E.
MBR.
14'0" X 18'4"
DIN.
10'8" X 13'0"
2 CAR GAR.
21'4" X 23'8"
©
MAIN FLOOR

Design 19410

PHOTOGRAPHY: MIKE MORELAND

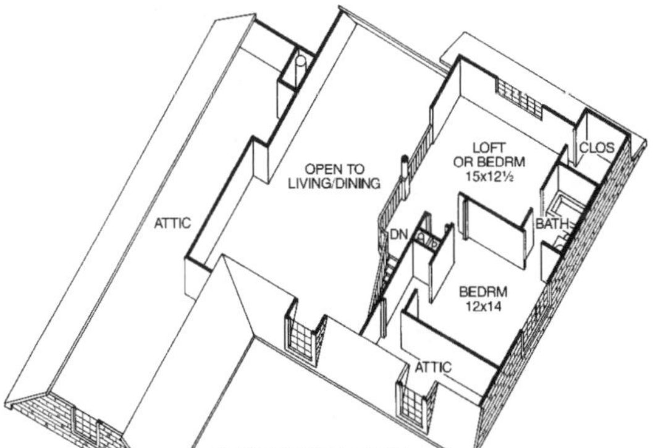

Units	Single
Price Code	D
Total Finished	2,175 sq. ft.
First Finished	1,600 sq. ft.
Second Finished	575 sq. ft.
Basement Unfinished	1,509 sq. ft.
Garage Unfinished	413 sq. ft.
Dimensions	48'4"x60'
Foundation	Basement
Bedrooms	3
Full Baths	2
Half Baths	1
First Ceiling	8'4"
Second Ceiling	8'4"
Roof Framing	Stick
Exterior Walls	2x4

Please note: The photographed home may have been modified to suit homeowner preferences. If you order plans, have a builder or design professional check them against the photograph to confirm actual construction details.

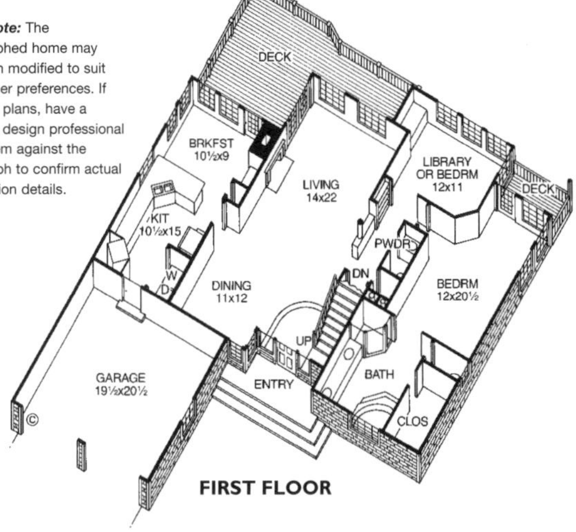

ATTIC
OPEN TO LIVING/DINING
LOFT OR BEDRM 15x12½
CLOS
BATH
DN
BEDRM 12x14
ATTIC
SECOND FLOOR

DECK
BRKFST 10½x9
LIVING 14x22
LIBRARY OR BEDRM 12x11
DECK
KIT 10½x15
W
D
DINING 11x12
PWDR
DN
BEDRM 12x20½
UP
GARAGE 19½x20½
ENTRY
BATH
CLOS
©
FIRST FLOOR

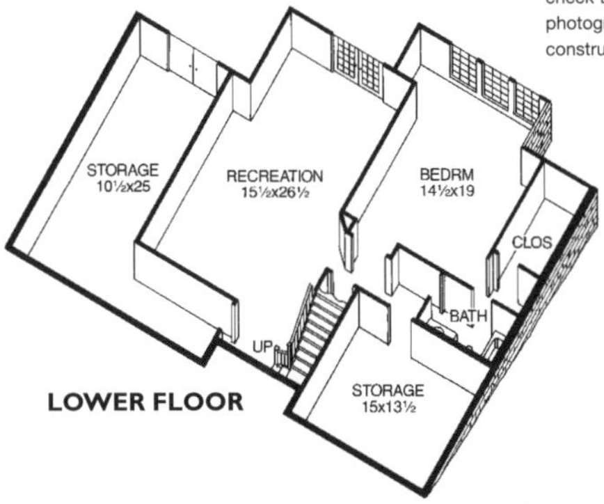

STORAGE 10½x25
RECREATION 15½x26½
BEDRM 14½x19
CLOS
BATH
UP
STORAGE 15x13½
LOWER FLOOR

Design 98517

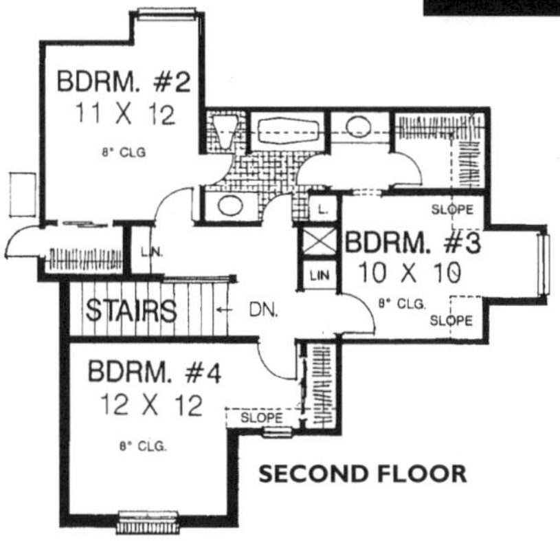

Units	Single
Price Code	D
Total Finished	2,175 sq. ft.
First Finished	1,472 sq. ft.
Second Finished	703 sq. ft.
Garage Unfinished	540 sq. ft.
Deck Unfinished	144 sq. ft.
Porch Unfinished	36 sq. ft.
Dimensions	58'x39'10"
Foundation	Slab
Bedrooms	4
Full Baths	2
Half Baths	1
First Ceiling	9'
Second Ceiling	8'
Max Ridge Height	25'
Roof Framing	Stick
Exterior Walls	2x4

BDRM. #2 11 X 12 8" CLG.
L.
SLOPE
BDRM. #3 10 X 10 8" CLG.
LIN
LIN.
STAIRS
DN.
SLOPE
BDRM. #4 12 X 12 8" CLG.
SLOPE
SECOND FLOOR

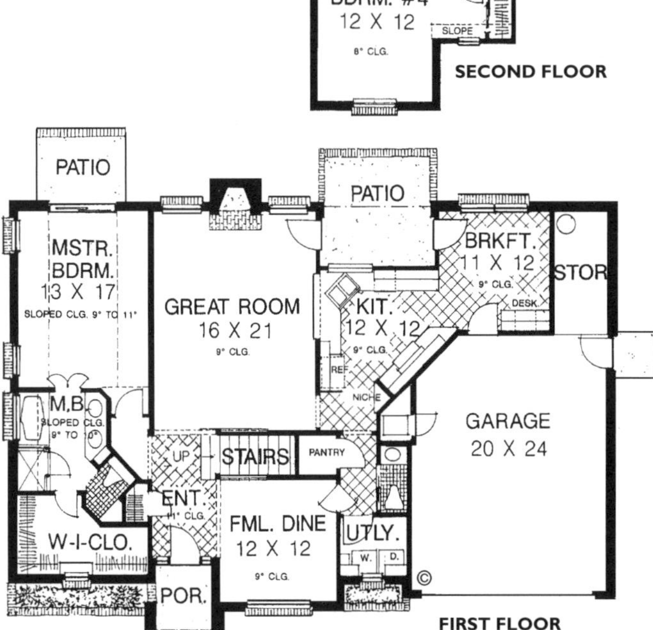
PATIO
PATIO
MSTR. BDRM. 13 X 17
SLOPED CLG. 9" TO 11"
GREAT ROOM 16 X 21
9" CLG.
BRKFT. 11 X 12
9" CLG.
STOR
DESK
KIT. 12 X 12
9" CLG.
REF
NICHE
GARAGE 20 X 24
M.B.
SLOPED CLG. 9" TO
UP
STAIRS
PANTRY
ENT.
FML. DINE 12 X 12
9" CLG.
UTLY.
W.
D.
W-I-CLO.
POR.
©
FIRST FLOOR

Design 10555

PHOTOGRAPHY: JOHN EHRENCLOU

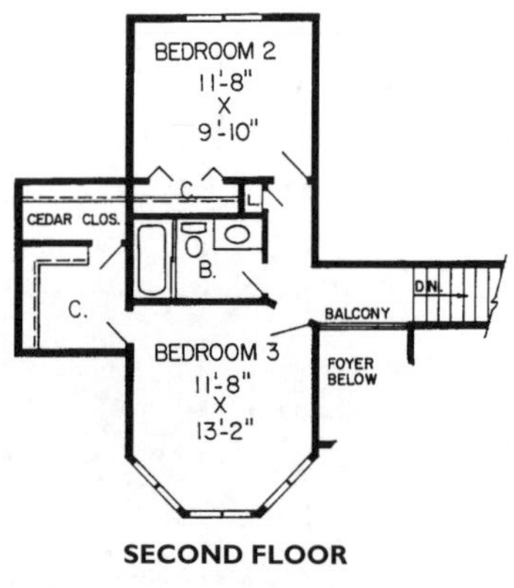
BEDROOM 2
11'-8" X 9'-10"
CEDAR CLOS.
C.
B.
L.
BALCONY
DN.
BEDROOM 3
11'-8" X 13'-2"
FOYER BELOW
SECOND FLOOR

Please note: The photographed home may have been modified to suit homeowner preferences. If you order plans, have a builder or design professional check them against the photograph to confirm actual construction details.

Units	Single
Price Code	D
Total Finished	2,176 sq. ft.
First Finished	1,671 sq. ft.
Second Finished	505 sq. ft.
Basement Unfinished	1,661 sq. ft.
Garage Unfinished	604 sq. ft.
Porch Unfinished	114 sq. ft.
Dimensions	77'x41'6"
Foundation	Basement Crawlspace Slab
Bedrooms	3
Full Baths	2
Half Baths	1
First Ceiling	8'
Second Ceiling	8'
Max Ridge Height	28'
Roof Framing	Stick
Exterior Walls	2x4, 2x6

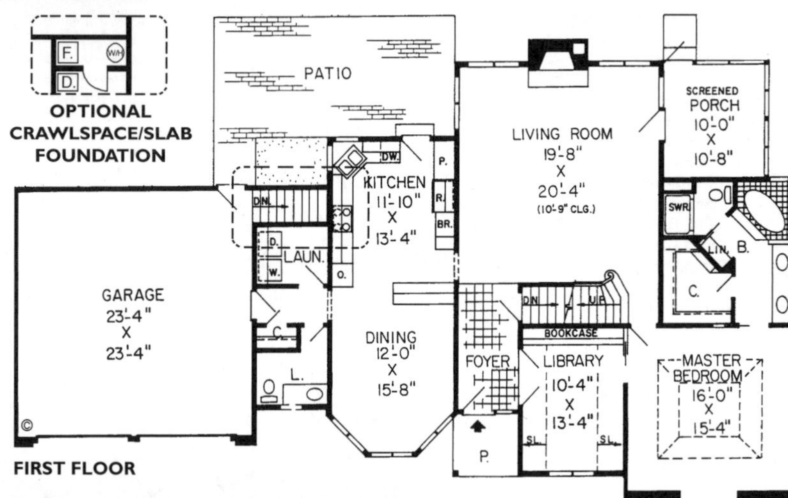
OPTIONAL CRAWLSPACE/SLAB FOUNDATION
PATIO
KITCHEN 11'-10" X 13'-4"
LIVING ROOM 19'-8" X 20'-4" (10'-9" CLG.)
SCREENED PORCH 10'-0" X 10'-8"
GARAGE 23'-4" X 23'-4"
LAUN.
DINING 12'-0" X 15'-8"
FOYER
LIBRARY 10'-4" X 13'-4"
BOOKCASE
MASTER BEDROOM 16'-0" X 15'-4"
FIRST FLOOR

Design 65649

Units	Single
Price Code	D
Total Finished	2,177 sq. ft.
Main Finished	2,177 sq. ft.
Dimensions	61'x77'
Foundation	Basement Crawlspace Slab
Bedrooms	3
Full Baths	2
Main Ceiling	9'
Max Ridge Height	28'
Roof Framing	Stick
Exterior Walls	2x4

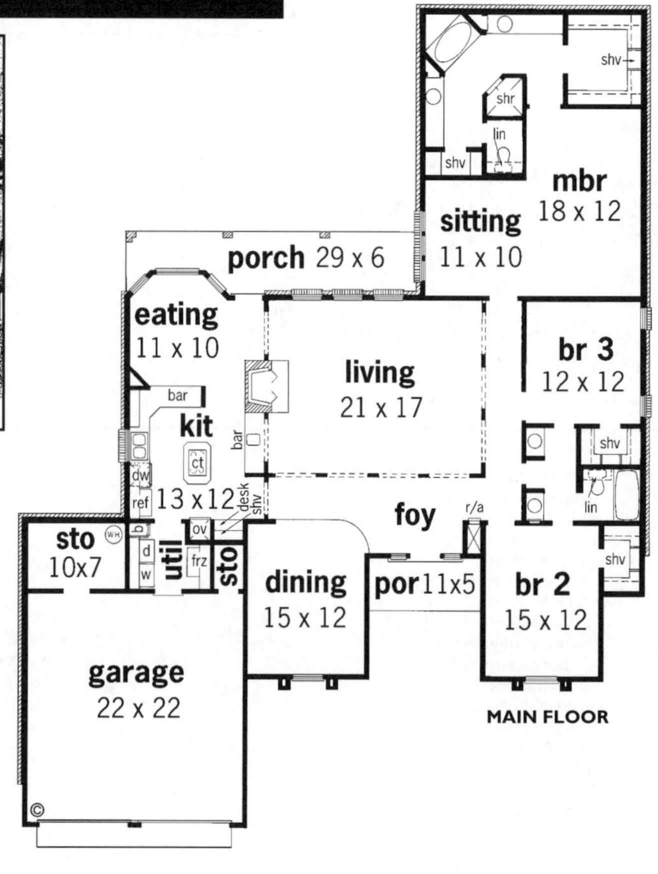
mbr 18 x 12
sitting 11 x 10
porch 29 x 6
eating 11 x 10
living 21 x 17
br 3 12 x 12
kit 13 x 12
foy
sto 10x7
util
dining 15 x 12
por 11x5
br 2 15 x 12
garage 22 x 22
MAIN FLOOR

Design 69006

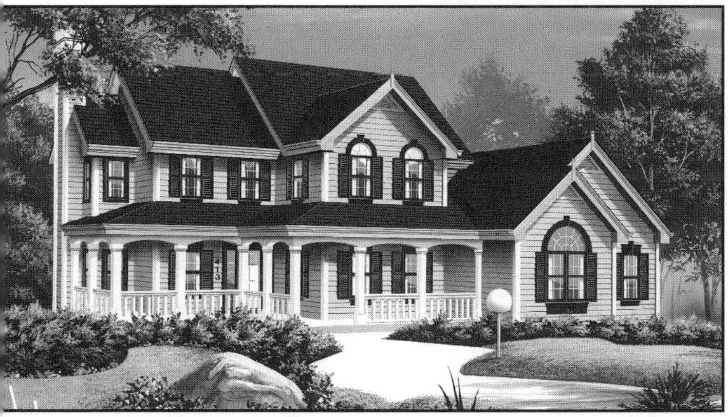

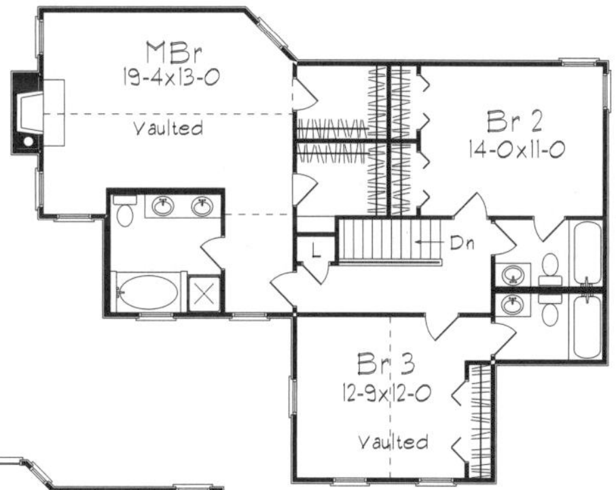

Units	Single
Price Code	D
Total Finished	2,182 sq. ft.
First Finished	1,112 sq. ft.
Second Finished	1,070 sq. ft.
Dimensions	51'x48'8"
Foundation	Basement
Bedrooms	3
Full Baths	3
Half Baths	1

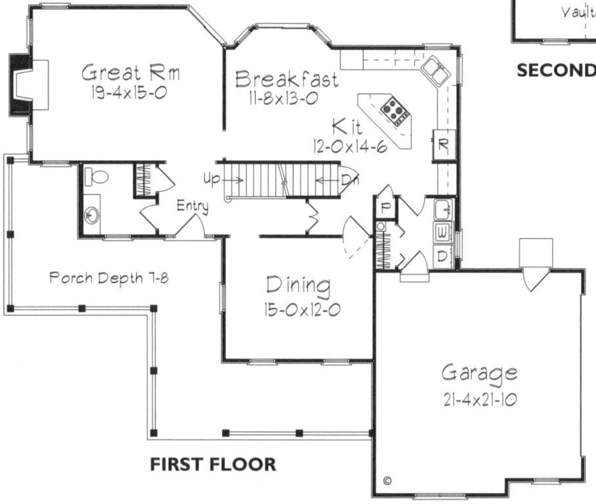

MBr 19-4x13-0 Vaulted
Br 2 14-0x11-0
Br 3 12-9x12-0 Vaulted

SECOND FLOOR

Great Rm 19-4x15-0
Breakfast 11-8x13-0
Kit 12-0x14-6
Entry
Porch Depth 7-8
Dining 15-0x12-0
Garage 21-4x21-10

FIRST FLOOR

Design 92443

Units	Single
Price Code	D
Total Finished	2,184 sq. ft.
Main Finished	2,184 sq. ft.
Garage Unfinished	548 sq. ft.
Dimensions	71'2"x58'1"
Foundation	Basement Slab
Bedrooms	3
Full Baths	3
Main Ceiling	9'
Max Ridge Height	24'
Exterior Walls	2x4

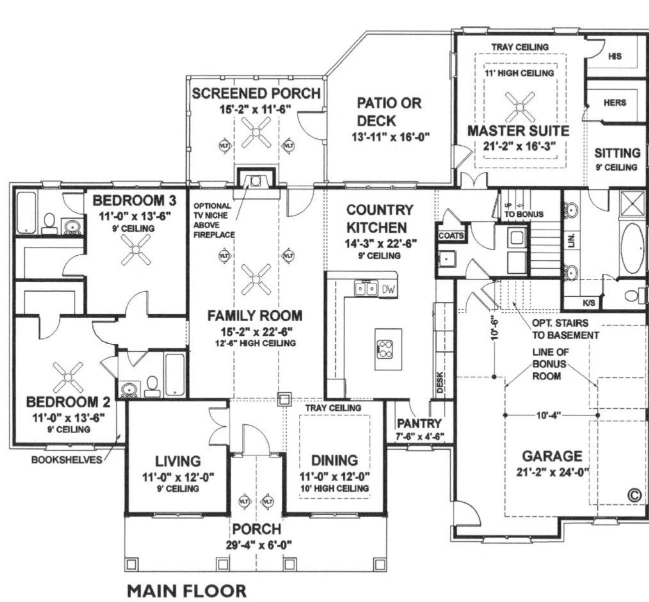
SCREENED PORCH 15'-2" x 11'-6"
PATIO OR DECK 13'-11" x 16'-0"
TRAY CEILING
11' HIGH CEILING
MASTER SUITE 21'-2" x 16'-3"
HIS
HERS
SITTING 9' CEILING
BEDROOM 3 11'-0" x 13'-6" 9' CEILING
OPTIONAL TV NICHE ABOVE FIREPLACE
COUNTRY KITCHEN 14'-3" x 22'-6" 9' CEILING
TO BONUS
COATS
FAMILY ROOM 15'-2" x 22'-6" 12'-6" HIGH CEILING
OPT. STAIRS TO BASEMENT
LINE OF BONUS ROOM
BEDROOM 2 11'-0" x 13'-6" 9' CEILING
TRAY CEILING
PANTRY 7'-6" x 4'-6"
GARAGE 21'-2" x 24'-0"
BOOKSHELVES
LIVING 11'-0" x 12'-0" 9' CEILING
DINING 11'-0" x 12'-0" 10' HIGH CEILING
PORCH 29'-4" x 6'-0"

MAIN FLOOR

Design 97494

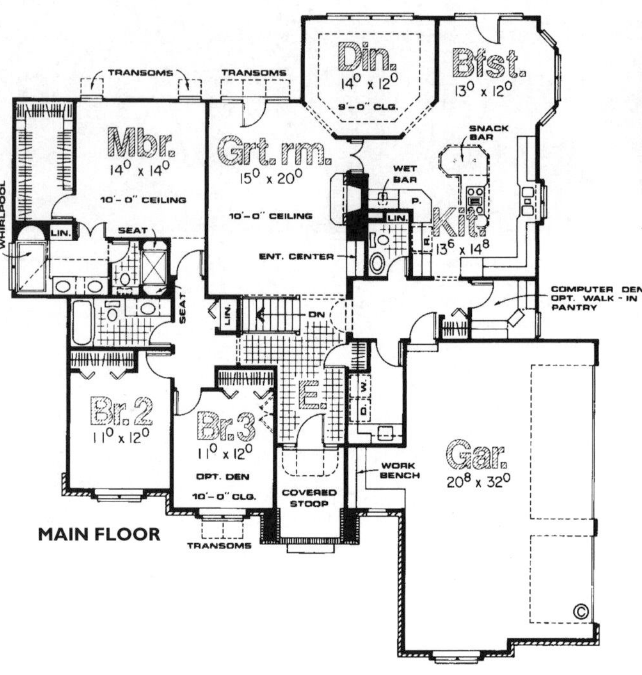

TRANSOMS
TRANSOMS
Din.
14⁰ x 12⁰
9'-0" CLG.
Bfst.
13⁰ x 12⁰
SNACK BAR
Mbr.
14⁰ x 14⁰
10'-0" CEILING
Grt. rm.
15⁰ x 20⁰
10'-0" CEILING
WET BAR
P.
Kit.
13⁶ x 14⁸
WHIRLPOOL
LIN.
SEAT
ENT. CENTER
LIN.
R.
COMPUTER DEN/ OPT. WALK - IN PANTRY
SEAT
LIN.
DN
Br. 2
11⁰ x 12⁰
Br. 3
11⁰ x 12⁰
OPT. DEN
10'-0" CLG.
E.
W.
D.
WORK BENCH
Gar.
20⁸ x 32⁰
COVERED STOOP
MAIN FLOOR
TRANSOMS

Units	Single
Price Code	D
Total Finished	2,186 sq. ft.
Main Finished	2,186 sq. ft.
Garage Unfinished	720 sq. ft.
Dimensions	64'x66'
Foundation	Basement
Bedrooms	3
Full Baths	2
Half Baths	1
Main Ceiling	8'
Max Ridge Height	25'
Roof Framing	Stick
Exterior Walls	2x4

* Alternate foundation options available at an additional charge. Please call 1-800-235-5700 for more information.

Design 97278

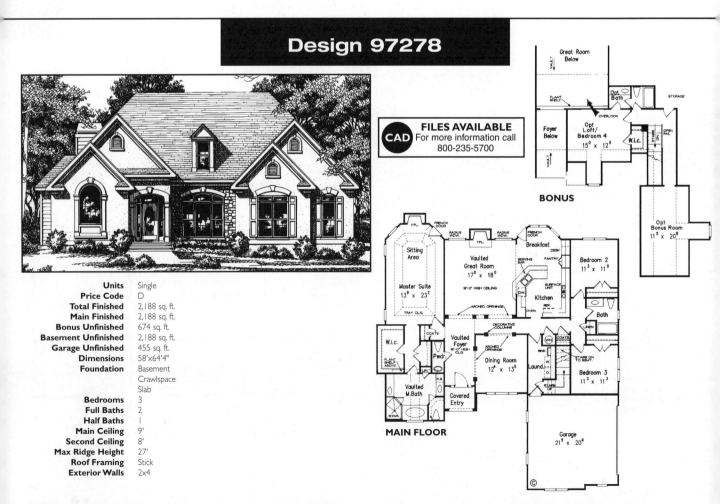

CAD FILES AVAILABLE
For more information call 800-235-5700

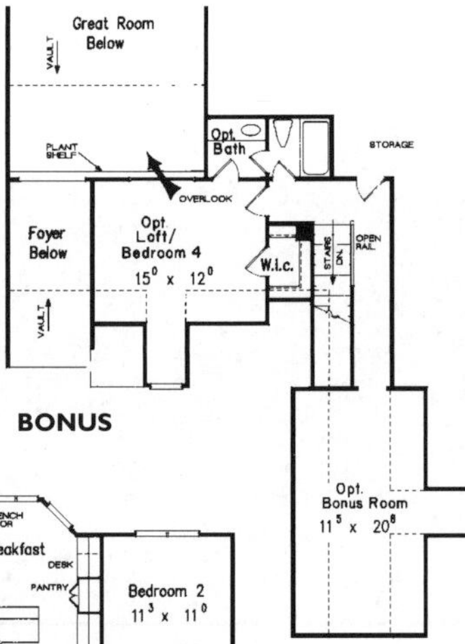

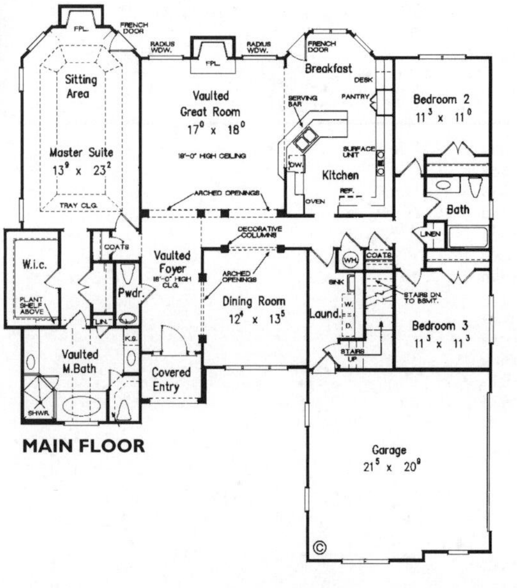

BONUS

MAIN FLOOR

Units	Single
Price Code	D
Total Finished	2,188 sq. ft.
Main Finished	2,188 sq. ft.
Bonus Unfinished	674 sq. ft.
Basement Unfinished	2,188 sq. ft.
Garage Unfinished	455 sq. ft.
Dimensions	58'x64'4"
Foundation	Basement Crawlspace Slab
Bedrooms	3
Full Baths	2
Half Baths	1
Main Ceiling	9'
Second Ceiling	8'
Max Ridge Height	27'
Roof Framing	Stick
Exterior Walls	2x4

Design 97470

Units	Single
Price Code	D
Total Finished	2,188 sq. ft.
Main Finished	2,188 sq. ft.
Garage Unfinished	704 sq. ft.
Deck Unfinished	269 sq. ft.
Dimensions	74'x49'4"
Foundation	Basement
Bedrooms	3
Full Baths	2
Main Ceiling	9'
Max Ridge Height	28'10"
Roof Framing	Stick
Exterior Walls	2x4

* Alternate foundation options available at an additional charge.
Please call 1-800-235-5700 for more information.

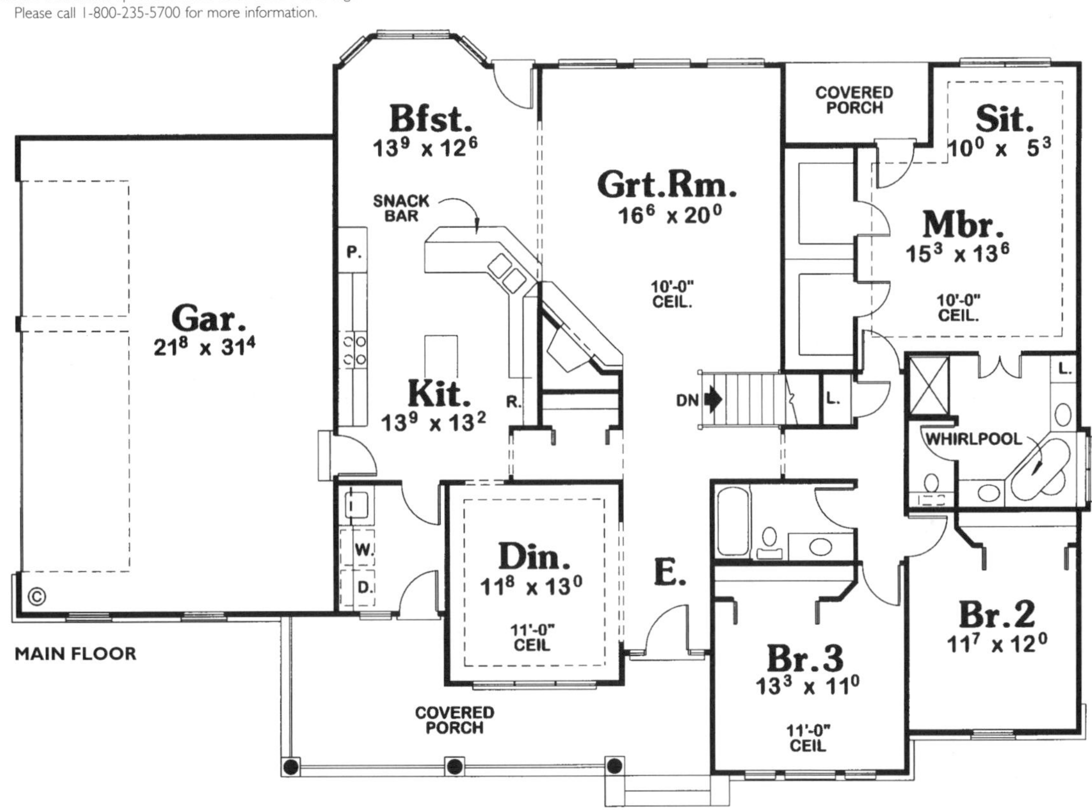
Bfst.
13⁹ x 12⁶
SNACK BAR
Grt.Rm.
16⁶ x 20⁰
10'-0" CEIL.
COVERED PORCH
Sit.
10⁰ x 5³
Mbr.
15³ x 13⁶
10'-0" CEIL.
P.
Gar.
21⁸ x 31⁴
Kit.
13⁹ x 13²
R.
DN
L.
WHIRLPOOL
W.
D.
Din.
11⁸ x 13⁰
11'-0" CEIL
E.
Br.3
13³ x 11⁰
11'-0" CEIL
Br.2
11⁷ x 12⁰
COVERED PORCH
MAIN FLOOR

Design 64513

Units	Single
Price Code	D
Total Finished	2,189 sq. ft.
Main Finished	2,189 sq. ft.
Porch Unfinished	360 sq. ft.
Dimensions	62'x40'
Foundation	Crawlspace Slab
Bedrooms	3
Full Baths	2
Half Baths	1
Main Ceiling	8'
Max Ridge Height	24'
Roof Framing	Stick
Exterior Walls	2x4

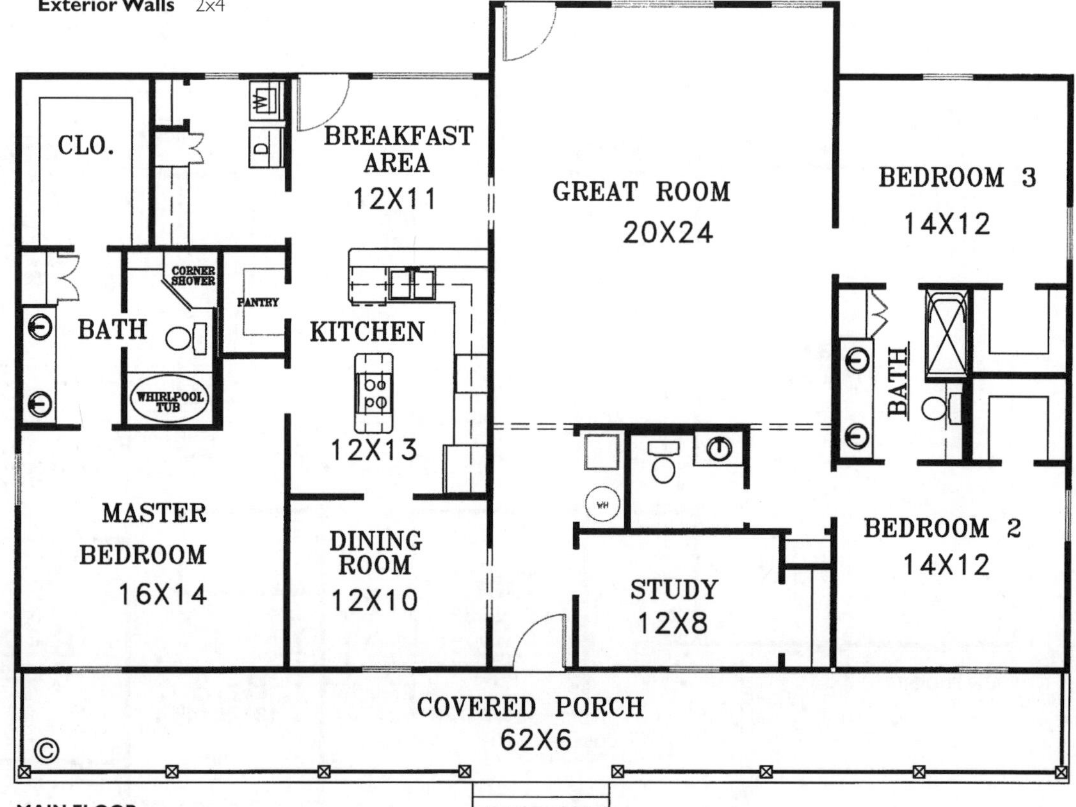
CLO.
BREAKFAST AREA 12X11
GREAT ROOM 20X24
BEDROOM 3 14X12
CORNER SHOWER
PANTRY
BATH
KITCHEN
WHIRLPOOL TUB
12X13
BATH
MASTER BEDROOM 16X14
DINING ROOM 12X10
STUDY 12X8
BEDROOM 2 14X12
COVERED PORCH 62X6
©

MAIN FLOOR

Design 97825

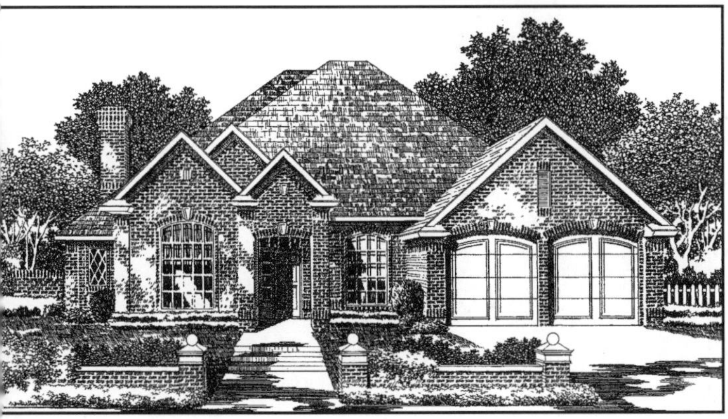

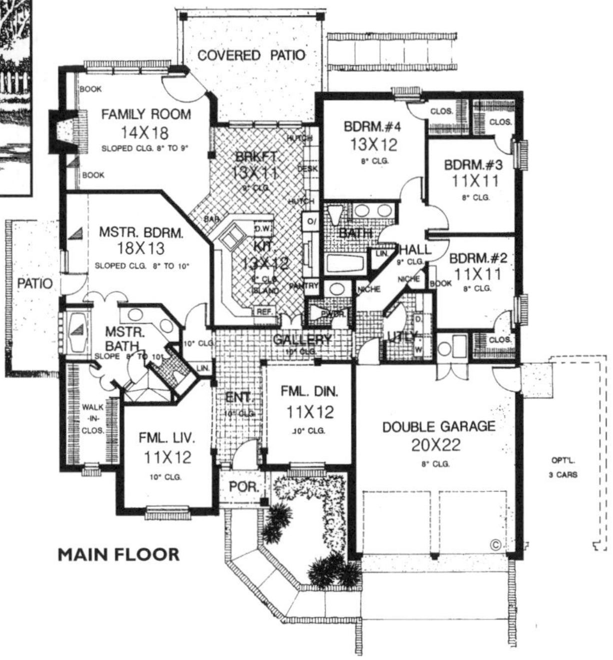

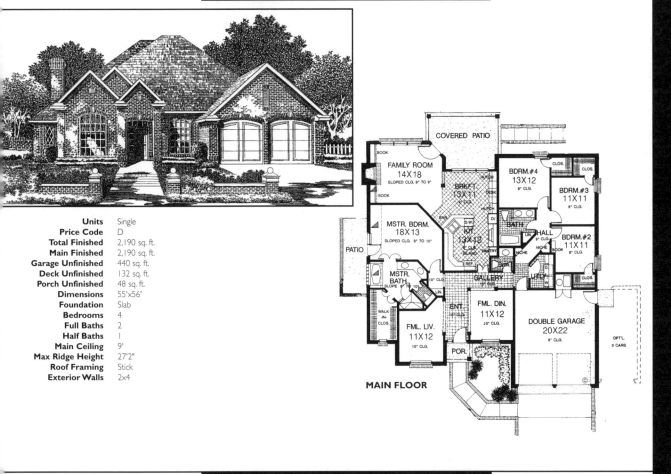

Units	Single
Price Code	D
Total Finished	2,190 sq. ft.
Main Finished	2,190 sq. ft.
Garage Unfinished	440 sq. ft.
Deck Unfinished	132 sq. ft.
Porch Unfinished	48 sq. ft.
Dimensions	55'x56'
Foundation	Slab
Bedrooms	4
Full Baths	2
Half Baths	1
Main Ceiling	9'
Max Ridge Height	27'2"
Roof Framing	Stick
Exterior Walls	2x4

MAIN FLOOR

Design 98555

Units	Single
Price Code	D
Total Finished	2,190 sq. ft.
Main Finished	2,190 sq. ft.
Garage Unfinished	642 sq. ft.
Deck Unfinished	122 sq. ft.
Dimensions	65'x63'
Foundation	Slab
Bedrooms	4
Full Baths	2
Half Baths	1
Max Ridge Height	24'2"
Roof Framing	Stick
Exterior Walls	2x4

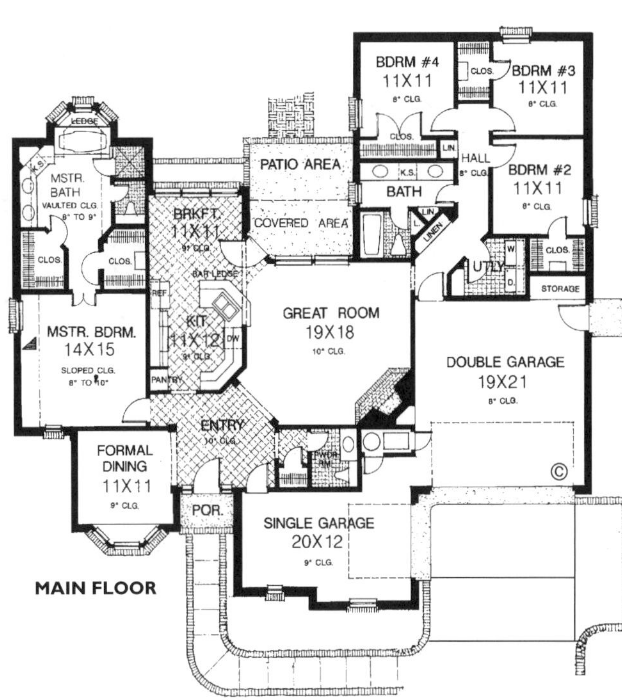
BDRM #4
11X11
BDRM #3
11X11
MSTR. BATH
VAULTED CLG. 8" TO 9"
PATIO AREA
HALL
BDRM #2
11X11
BATH
BRKFT.
11X11
COVERED AREA
MSTR. BDRM.
14X15
SLOPED CLG. 8" TO 10"
KIT
11X12
GREAT ROOM
19X18
10" CLG.
DOUBLE GARAGE
19X21
ENTRY
FORMAL DINING
11X11
POR.
SINGLE GARAGE
20X12
MAIN FLOOR

Design 69143

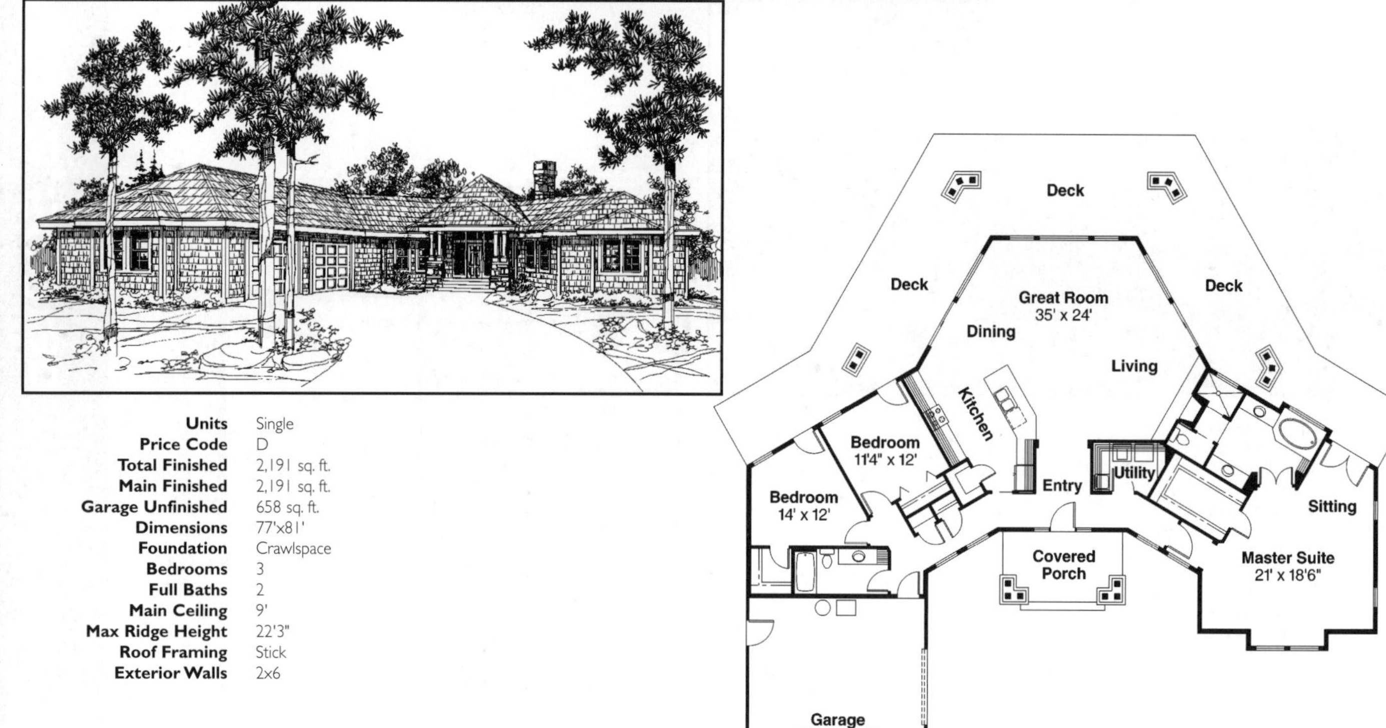
Deck
Deck
Great Room
35' x 24'
Deck
Dining
Living
Kitchen
Bedroom
11'4" x 12'
Bedroom
14' x 12'
Entry
Utility
Sitting
Covered
Porch
Master Suite
21' x 18'6"
Garage
21'4" x 30'8"
MAIN FLOOR

Units	Single
Price Code	D
Total Finished	2,191 sq. ft.
Main Finished	2,191 sq. ft.
Garage Unfinished	658 sq. ft.
Dimensions	77'x81'
Foundation	Crawlspace
Bedrooms	3
Full Baths	2
Main Ceiling	9'
Max Ridge Height	22'3"
Roof Framing	Stick
Exterior Walls	2x6

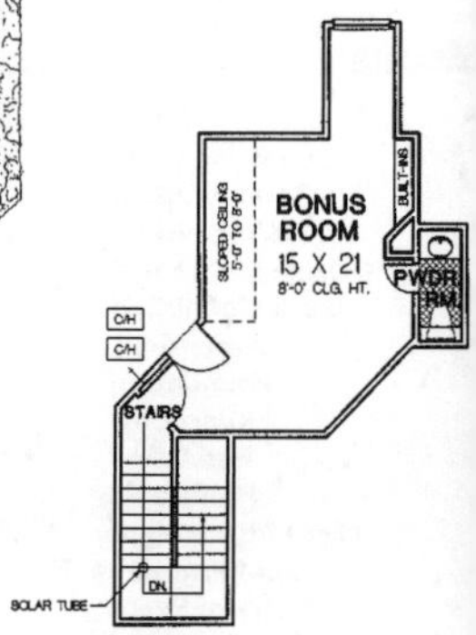

Design 66054

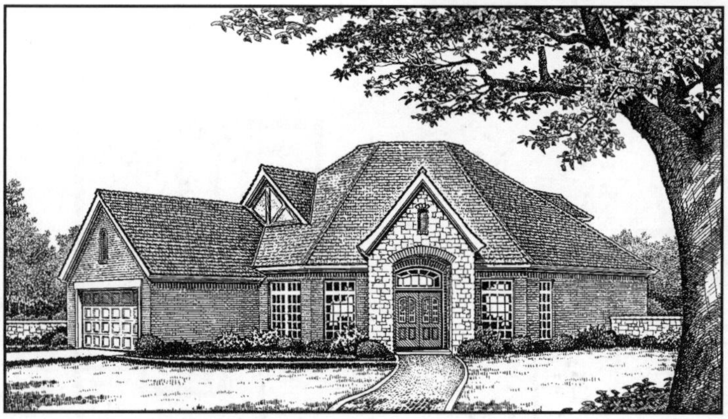

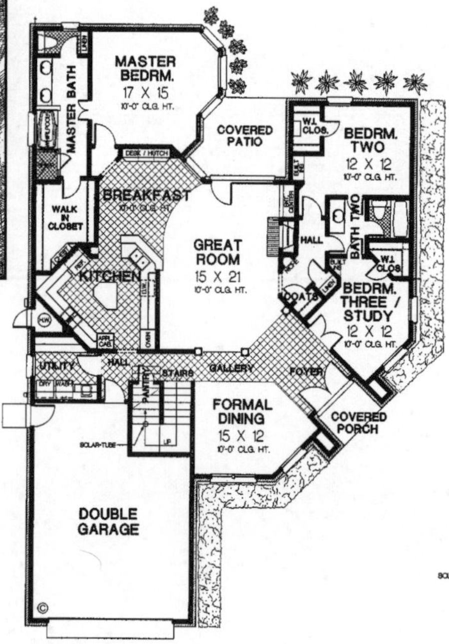

Units	Single
Price Code	D
Total Finished	2,168 sq. ft.
Main Finished	2,168 sq. ft.
Bonus Unfinished	308 sq. ft.
Garage Unfinished	472 sq. ft.
Deck Unfinished	85 sq. ft.
Dimensions	44'10"x79'10"
Foundation	Slab
Bedrooms	3
Full Baths	2
Main Ceiling	9'
Second Ceiling	10'
Max Ridge Height	24'6"
Roof Framing	Stick
Exterior Walls	2x4

MAIN FLOOR

BONUS

Design 97847

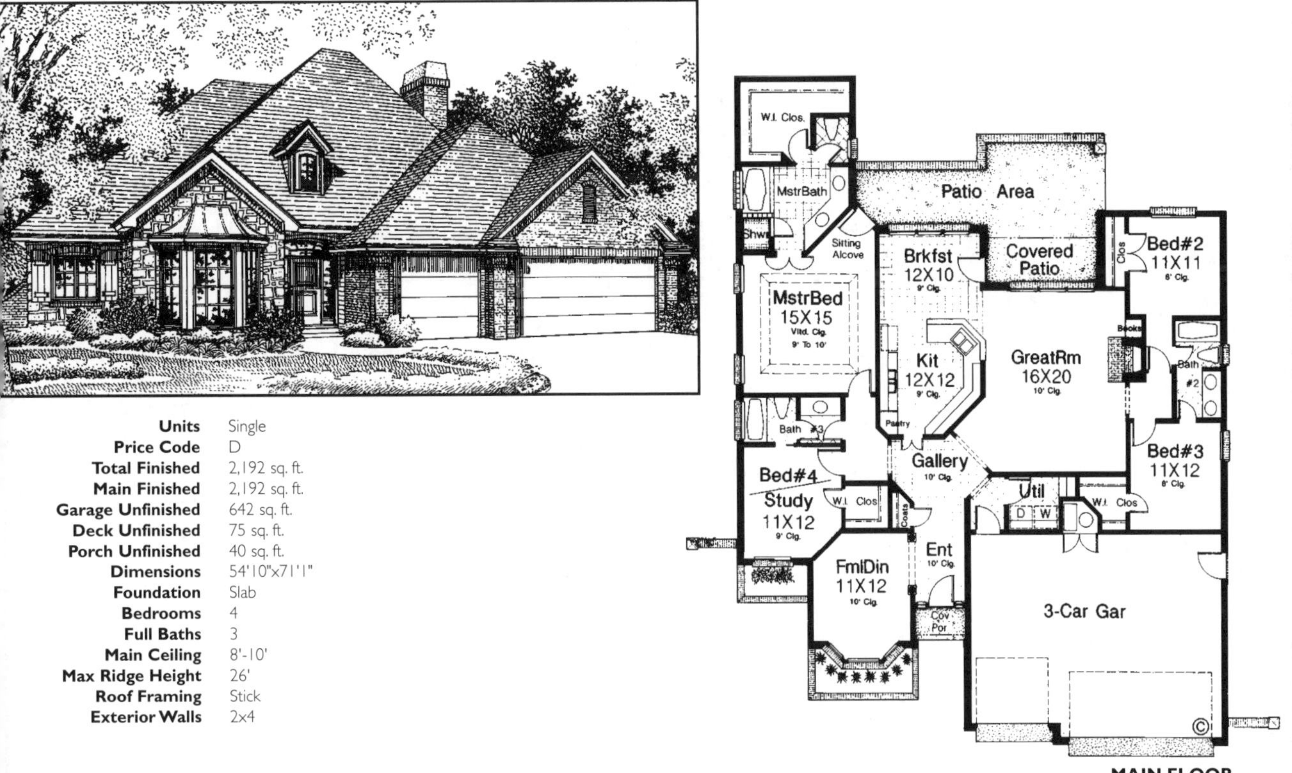
W.I. Clos.
MstrBath
Patio Area
Shwr
Sitting Alcove
Brkfst 12X10
Covered Patio
Bed#2 11X11
MstrBed 15X15
Kit 12X12
GreatRm 16X20
Bath #3
Bath #2
Bed#4 Study 11X12
Gallery
Bed#3 11X12
Util
W.I. Clos
FmlDin 11X12
Ent
Cov Por
3-Car Gar

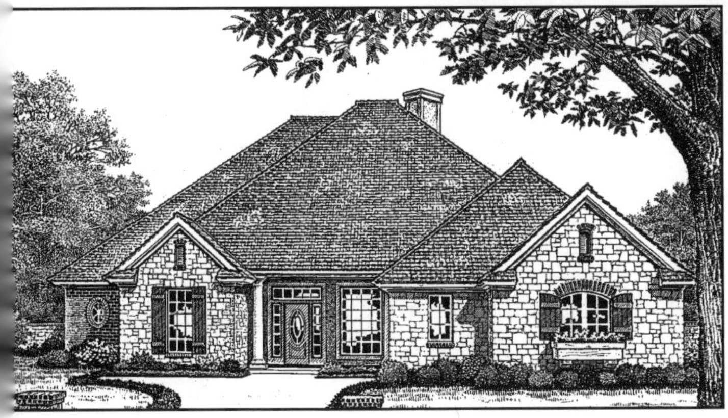

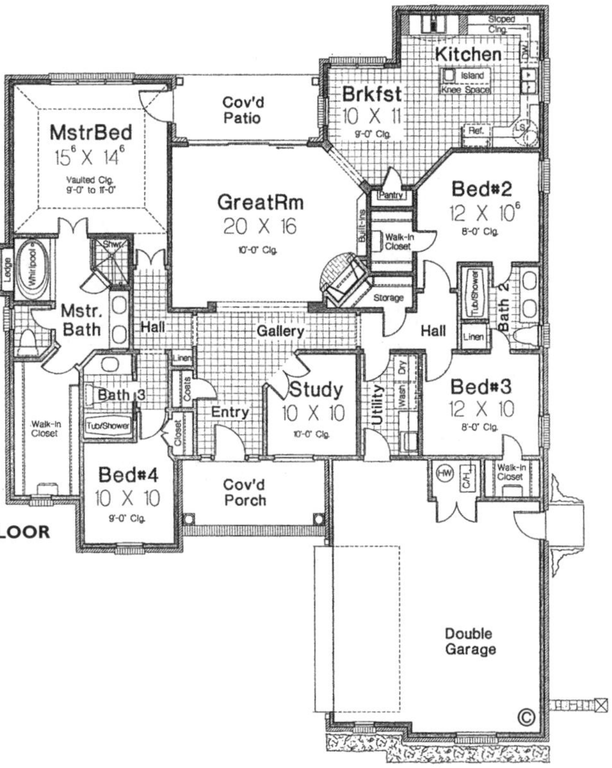

MAIN FLOOR

Units	Single
Price Code	D
Total Finished	2,192 sq. ft.
Main Finished	2,192 sq. ft.
Garage Unfinished	642 sq. ft.
Deck Unfinished	75 sq. ft.
Porch Unfinished	40 sq. ft.
Dimensions	54'10"x71'1"
Foundation	Slab
Bedrooms	4
Full Baths	3
Main Ceiling	8'-10'
Max Ridge Height	26'
Roof Framing	Stick
Exterior Walls	2x4

Design 66055

Units	Single
Price Code	D
Total Finished	2,193 sq. ft.
Main Finished	2,193 sq. ft.
Garage Unfinished	560 sq. ft.
Deck Unfinished	185 sq. ft.
Dimensions	55'x70'10"
Foundation	Slab
Bedrooms	4
Full Baths	3
Max Ridge Height	28'
Roof Framing	Stick
Exterior Walls	2x4

MAIN FLOOR

Design 98466

CAD
FILES AVAILABLE
For more information call
800-235-5700

Units	Single
Price Code	D
Total Finished	2,193 sq. ft.
Main Finished	2,193 sq. ft.
Bonus Unfinished	400 sq. ft.
Basement Unfinished	2,193 sq. ft.
Garage Unfinished	522 sq. ft.
Dimensions	64'6"x59'
Foundation	Basement Crawlspace Slab
Bedrooms	4
Full Baths	2
Main Ceiling	9'
Second Ceiling	8'
Max Ridge Height	27'
Roof Framing	Stick
Exterior Walls	2x4

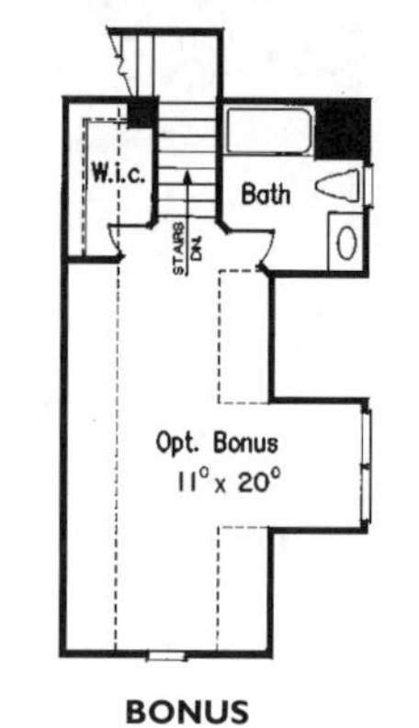

W.i.c.
Bath
Opt. Bonus
11° x 20°

BONUS

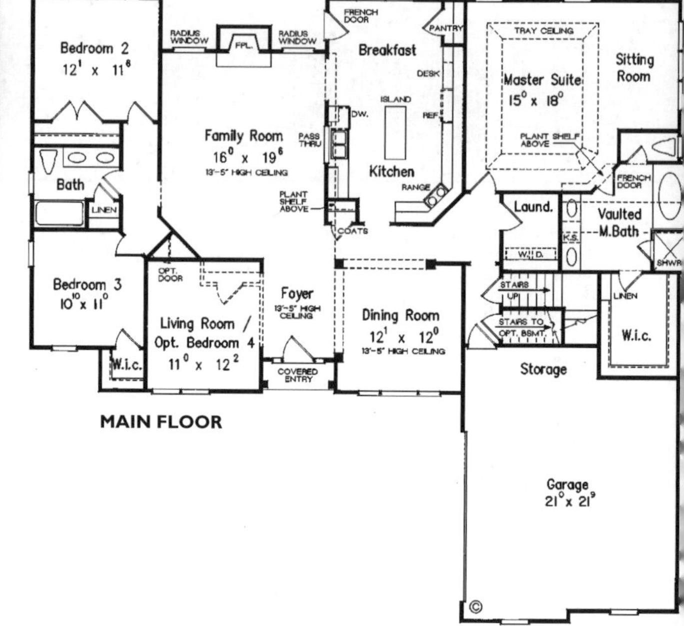

Bedroom 2
Bath
Bedroom 3
Family Room
Breakfast
Kitchen
Master Suite
Sitting Room
Laund.
Vaulted M.Bath
Living Room / Opt. Bedroom 4
Foyer
Dining Room
Storage
W.i.c.
Garage

MAIN FLOOR

Design 10507

Units	Single
Price Code	D
Total Finished	2,194 sq. ft.
Main Finished	2,194 sq. ft.
Garage Unfinished	576 sq. ft.
Dimensions	76'x75'
Foundation	Crawlspace
Bedrooms	3
Full Baths	1
3/4 Baths	1
Main Ceiling	8'
Max Ridge Height	15'
Roof Framing	Stick
Exterior Walls	2x6

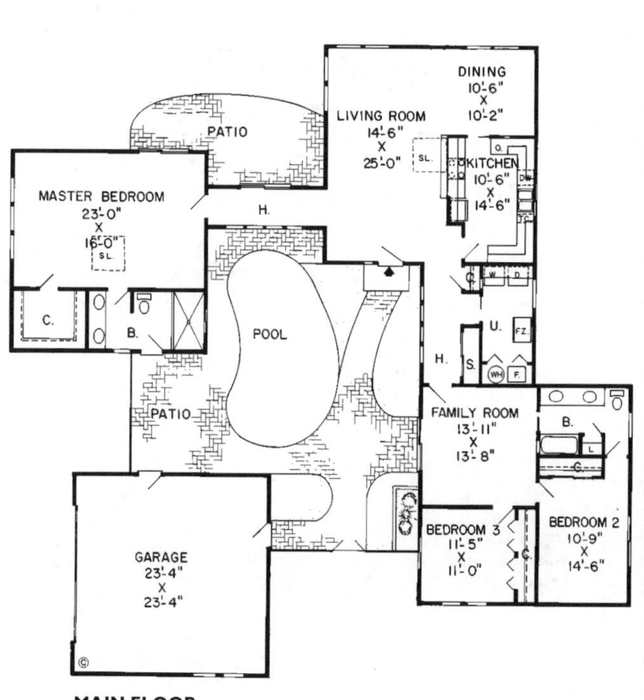

DINING
LIVING ROOM
PATIO
MASTER BEDROOM
KITCHEN
POOL
PATIO
FAMILY ROOM
BEDROOM 3
BEDROOM 2
GARAGE

MAIN FLOOR

Design 93190

Units	Single
Price Code	D
Total Finished	2,196 sq. ft.
Main Finished	2,196 sq. ft.
Basement Unfinished	2,196 sq. ft.
Dimensions	73'x58'8"
Foundation	Basement
Bedrooms	3
Full Baths	2
Half Baths	1
Max Ridge Height	23'6"
Roof Framing	Truss
Exterior Walls	2x6

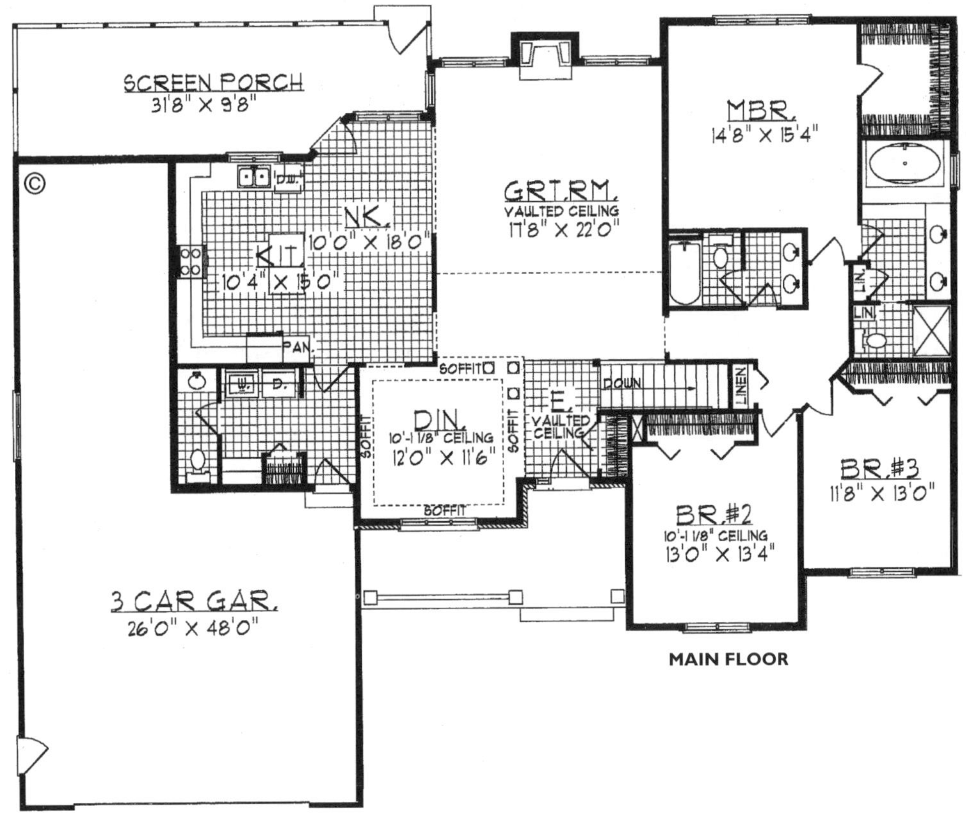
SCREEN PORCH
31'8" X 9'8"
MBR.
14'8" X 15'4"
GRT.RM.
VAULTED CEILING
17'8" X 22'0"
NK.
10'0" X 18'0"
KIT.
10'4" X 15'0"
PAN.
SOFFIT
DOWN
LINEN
LIN.
E.
VAULTED CEILING
DIN.
10'-1 1/8" CEILING
12'0" X 11'6"
BR.#3
11'8" X 13'0"
BR.#2
10'-1 1/8" CEILING
13'0" X 13'4"
3 CAR GAR.
26'0" X 48'0"

MAIN FLOOR

Design 97708

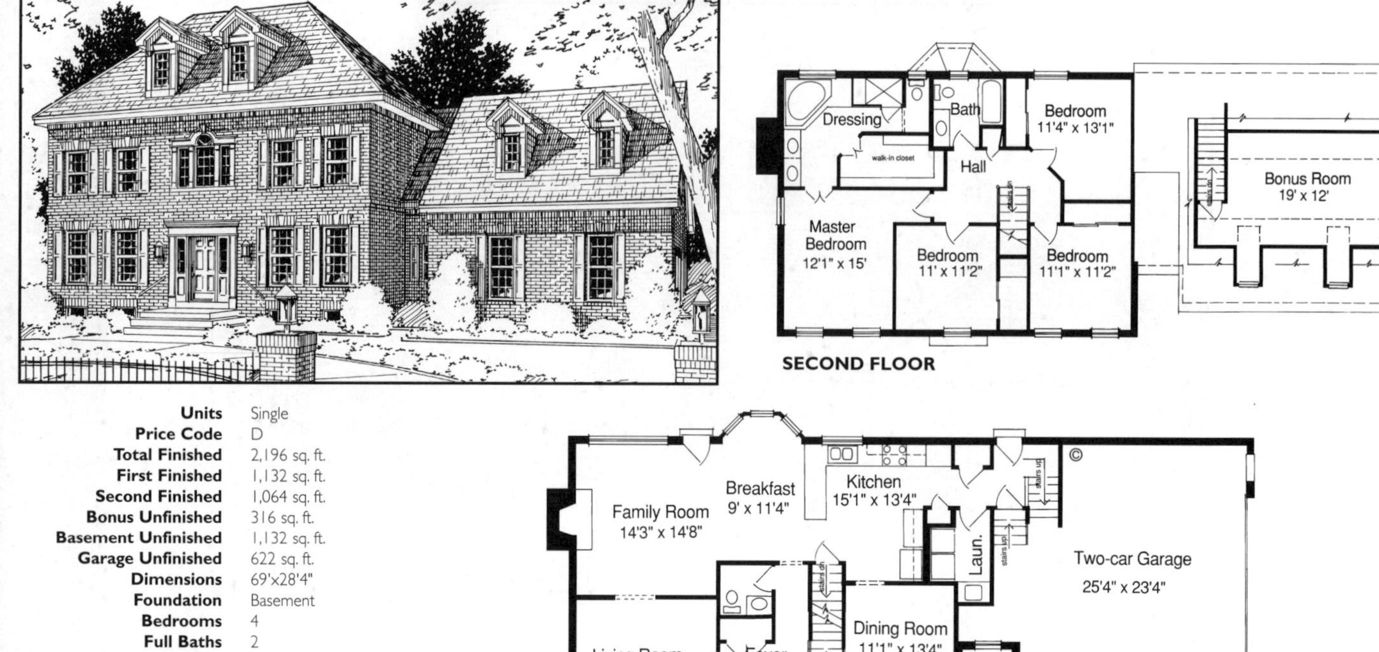

Dressing
walk-in closet
Bath
Bedroom
11'4" x 13'1"
Hall
Bonus Room
19' x 12'
Master
Bedroom
12'1" x 15'
Bedroom
11' x 11'2"
Bedroom
11'1" x 11'2"
SECOND FLOOR

Units	Single
Price Code	D
Total Finished	2,196 sq. ft.
First Finished	1,132 sq. ft.
Second Finished	1,064 sq. ft.
Bonus Unfinished	316 sq. ft.
Basement Unfinished	1,132 sq. ft.
Garage Unfinished	622 sq. ft.
Dimensions	69'x28'4"
Foundation	Basement
Bedrooms	4
Full Baths	2
Half Baths	1
First Ceiling	9'
Second Ceiling	9'
Max Ridge Height	33'½"
Roof Framing	Truss
Exterior Walls	2x4

Breakfast
9' x 11'4"
Kitchen
15'1" x 13'4"
Family Room
14'3" x 14'8"
Laun.
Two-car Garage
25'4" x 23'4"
Dining Room
11'1" x 13'4"
Living Room
14'3" x 12'1"
Foyer

FIRST FLOOR

Design 97303

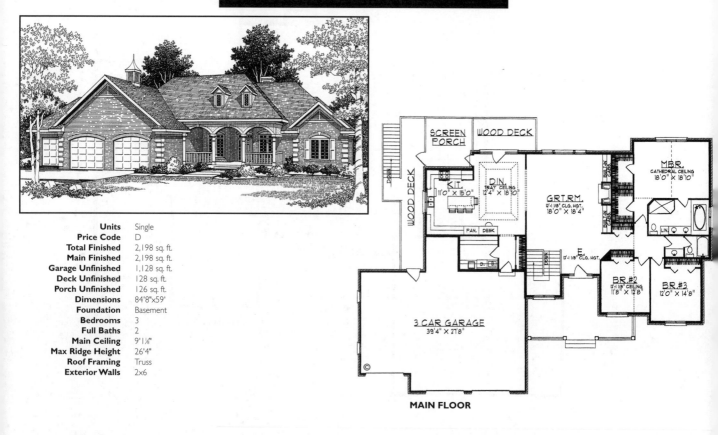

Units	Single
Price Code	D
Total Finished	2,198 sq. ft.
Main Finished	2,198 sq. ft.
Garage Unfinished	1,128 sq. ft.
Deck Unfinished	128 sq. ft.
Porch Unfinished	126 sq. ft.
Dimensions	84'8"x59'
Foundation	Basement
Bedrooms	3
Full Baths	2
Main Ceiling	9'1⅛"
Max Ridge Height	26'4"
Roof Framing	Truss
Exterior Walls	2x6

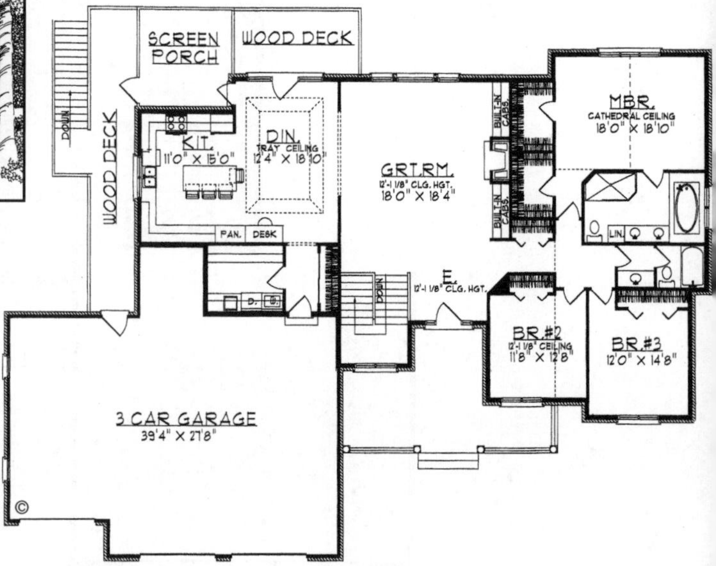

SCREEN PORCH
WOOD DECK
WOOD DECK
KIT.
11'0" X 15'0"
DIN.
TRAY CEILING
12'4" X 18'0"
GRT.RM.
12'-1 1/8" CLG. HGT.
18'0" X 18'4"
MBR.
CATHEDRAL CEILING
18'0" X 18'10"
PAN. DESK
12'-1 1/8" CLG. HGT.
BR.#2
12'-1 1/8" CEILING
11'8" X 12'8"
BR.#3
12'0" X 14'8"
3 CAR GARAGE
39'4" X 27'8"

MAIN FLOOR

Design 97710

Bedroom
15' x 10'7"
Great Room
Below
Bath
Bedroom
13'10" x 10'7"
Foyer Below
SECOND FLOOR

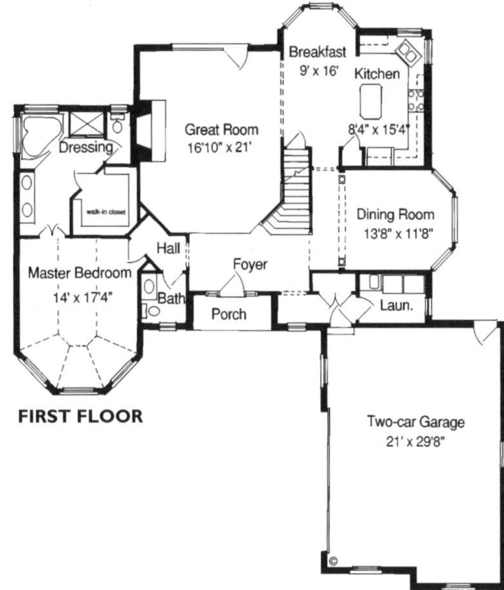
Breakfast
9' x 16'
Kitchen
8'4" x 15'4"
Great Room
16'10" x 21'
Dressing
Dining Room
13'8" x 11'8"
Hall
Foyer
Master Bedroom
14' x 17'4"
Bath
Porch
Laun.
FIRST FLOOR
Two-car Garage
21' x 29'8"

Units	Single
Price Code	D
Total Finished	2,198 sq. ft.
First Finished	1,706 sq. ft.
Second Finished	492 sq. ft.
Basement Unfinished	1,706 sq. ft.
Deck Unfinished	175 sq. ft.
Porch Unfinished	38 sq. ft.
Dimensions	59'4"x65'
Foundation	Basement
Bedrooms	3
Full Baths	2
Half Baths	1
Max Ridge Height	31'
Roof Framing	Truss
Exterior Walls	2x4

Design 60066

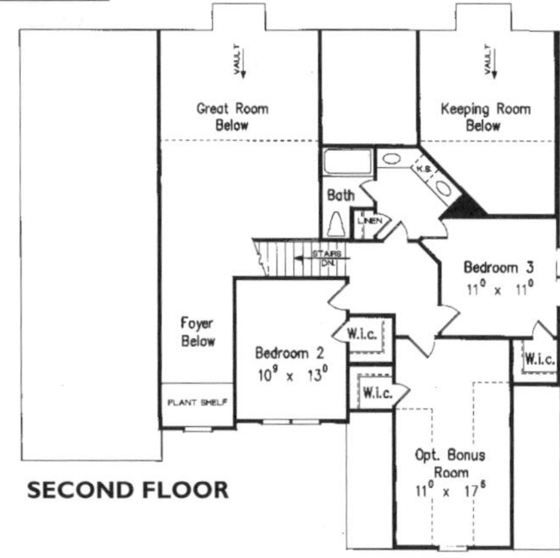
Great Room
Below
Keeping Room
Below
Bath
Bedroom 3
11⁰ x 11⁰
Foyer
Below
Bedroom 2
10⁹ x 13⁰
W.I.c.
W.I.c.
W.I.c.
Opt. Bonus
Room
11⁰ x 17⁶
SECOND FLOOR

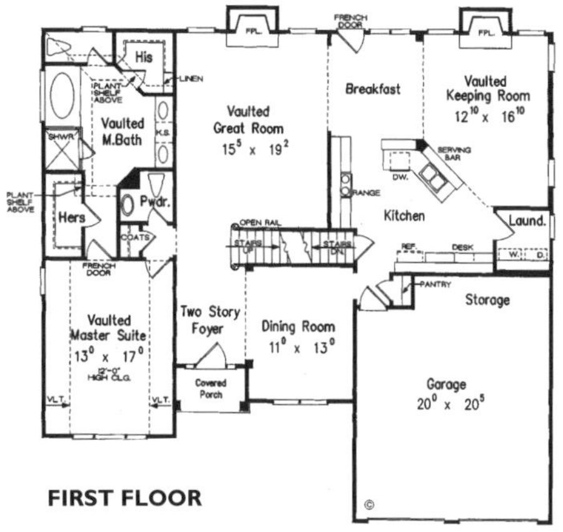
His
Vaulted
M.Bath
Vaulted
Great Room
15⁵ x 19²
Breakfast
Vaulted
Keeping Room
12¹⁰ x 16¹⁰
Hers
Pwdr.
Kitchen
Laund.
Storage
Vaulted
Master Suite
13⁰ x 17⁰
Two Story
Foyer
Dining Room
11⁰ x 13⁰
Covered
Porch
Garage
20⁰ x 20⁵
FIRST FLOOR

Units	Single
Price Code	D
Total Finished	2,200 sq. ft.
First Finished	1,688 sq. ft.
Second Finished	512 sq. ft.
Bonus Unfinished	238 sq. ft.
Basement Unfinished	1,688 sq. ft.
Garage Unfinished	471 sq. ft.
Dimensions	52'x48'
Foundation	Basement Crawlspace
Bedrooms	3
Full Baths	2
Half Baths	1
First Ceiling	9'
Second Ceiling	8'
Max Ridge Height	29'6"
Roof Framing	Stick
Exterior Walls	2x4

CAD
FILES AVAILABLE
For more information call
800-235-5700

Design 65666

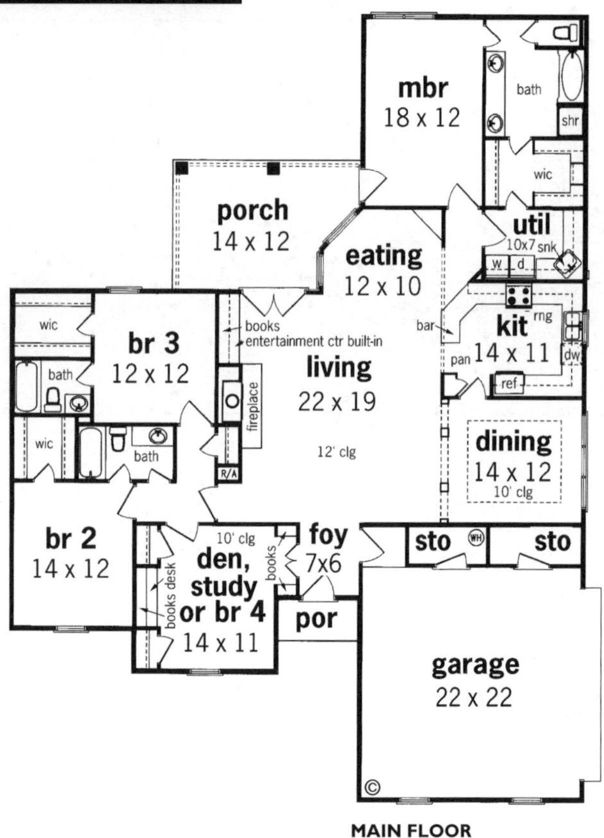
mbr
18 x 12
bath
shr
wic
porch
14 x 12
eating
12 x 10
util
10x7
snk
w
d
br 3
12 x 12
wic
books
entertainment ctr built-in
bar
kit
14 x 11
rng
dw
pan
ref
bath
living
22 x 19
fireplace
wic
bath
12' clg
dining
14 x 12
10' clg
R/A
br 2
14 x 12
10' clg
den,
study
or br 4
14 x 11
books desk
books
foy
7x6
sto
WH
sto
por
garage
22 x 22
MAIN FLOOR

Units	Single
Price Code	D
Total Finished	2,200 sq. ft.
Main Finished	2,200 sq. ft.
Dimensions	56'x74'
Foundation	Crawlspace Slab
Bedrooms	4
Full Baths	3
Main Ceiling	8'
Max Ridge Height	8'
Roof Framing	Stick
Exterior Walls	2x4

Design 94676

PHOTOGRAPHY: CHRIS A. LITTLE

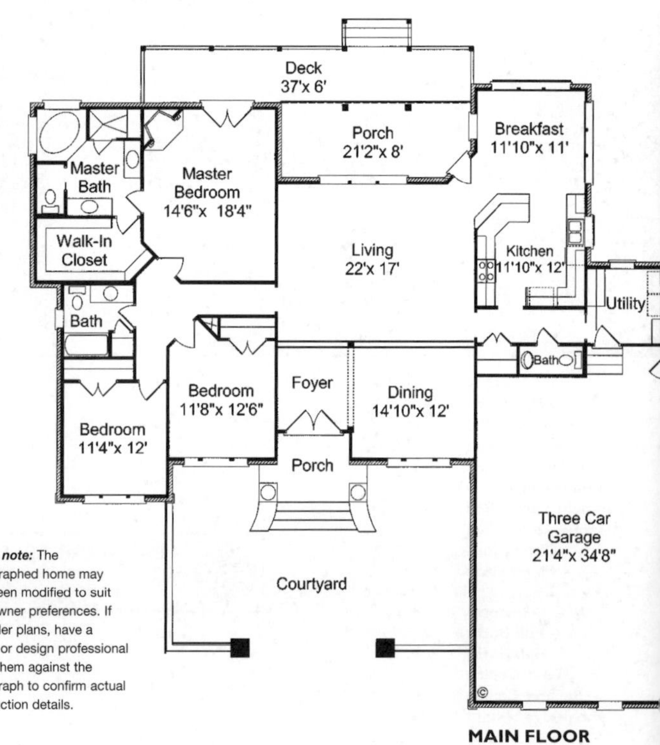
Deck
37'x 6'
Porch
21'2"x 8'
Breakfast
11'10"x 11'
Master
Bath
Master
Bedroom
14'6"x 18'4"
Walk-In
Closet
Living
22'x 17'
Kitchen
11'10"x 12'
Utility
Bath
Bath
Bedroom
11'8"x 12'6"
Foyer
Dining
14'10"x 12'
Bedroom
11'4"x 12'
Porch
Three Car
Garage
21'4"x 34'8"
Courtyard
MAIN FLOOR

Units	Single
Price Code	D
Total Finished	2,201 sq. ft.
Main Finished	2,201 sq. ft.
Garage Unfinished	853 sq. ft.
Deck Unfinished	222 sq. ft.
Porch Unfinished	240 sq. ft.
Dimensions	71'10"x66'10"
Foundation	Crawlspace
Bedrooms	3
Full Baths	2
Half Baths	1
Main Ceiling	9'
Max Ridge Height	30'9"
Roof Framing	Stick
Exterior Walls	2x4

Please note: The photographed home may have been modified to suit homeowner preferences. If you order plans, have a builder or design professional check them against the photograph to confirm actual construction details.

Design 97228

Units	Single
Price Code	D
Total Finished	2,201 sq. ft.
Main Finished	2,201 sq. ft.
Basement Unfinished	2,201 sq. ft.
Garage Unfinished	452 sq. ft.
Dimensions	59'6"x62'
Foundation	Basement Crawlspace
Bedrooms	3
Full Baths	2
Half Baths	1
Max Ridge Height	25'
Roof Framing	Stick
Exterior Walls	2x4

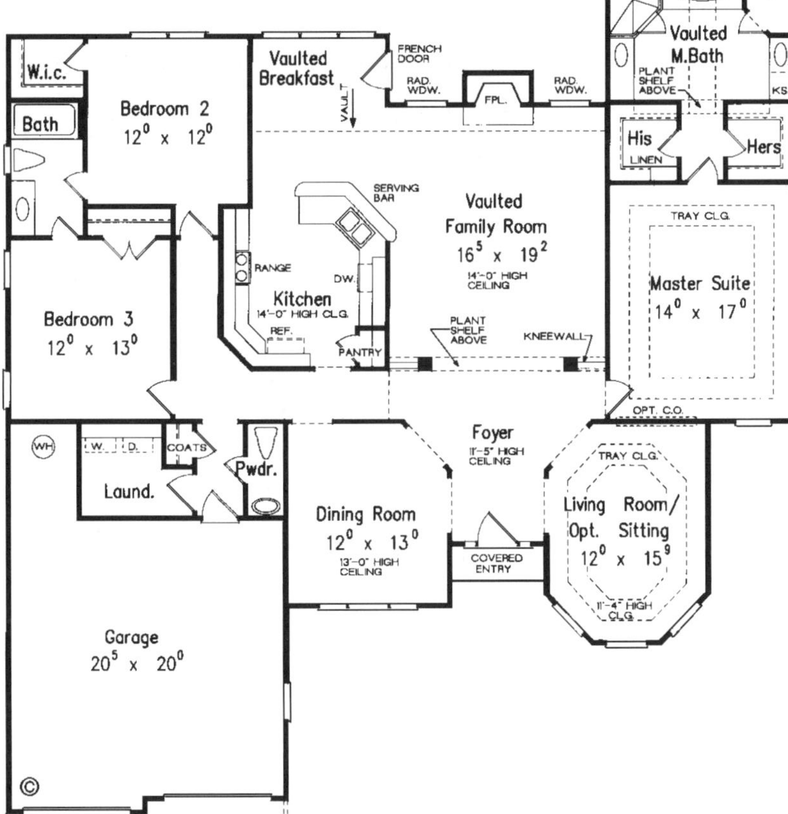

RADIUS WINDOW
SHWR.
Vaulted M.Bath
PLANT SHELF ABOVE
KS.
His
LINEN
Hers
W.i.c.
Bath
Bedroom 2 12^0 x 12^0
Vaulted Breakfast
FRENCH DOOR
VAULT
RAD. WDW.
FPL.
RAD. WDW.
SERVING BAR
Vaulted Family Room 16^5 x 19^2
14'-0" HIGH CEILING
RANGE
DW.
Kitchen
14'-0" HIGH CLG.
REF.
PANTRY
PLANT SHELF ABOVE
KNEEWALL
TRAY CLG.
Master Suite 14^0 x 17^0
OPT. C.O.
Bedroom 3 12^0 x 13^0
WH
W. D.
COATS
Laund.
Pwdr.
Foyer
11'-5" HIGH CEILING
Dining Room 12^0 x 13^0
13'-0" HIGH CEILING
COVERED ENTRY
TRAY CLG.
Living Room/ Opt. Sitting 12^0 x 15^9
11'-4" HIGH CLG.
Garage 20^5 x 20^0
GARAGE LOCATION W/ BASEMENT

MAIN FLOOR

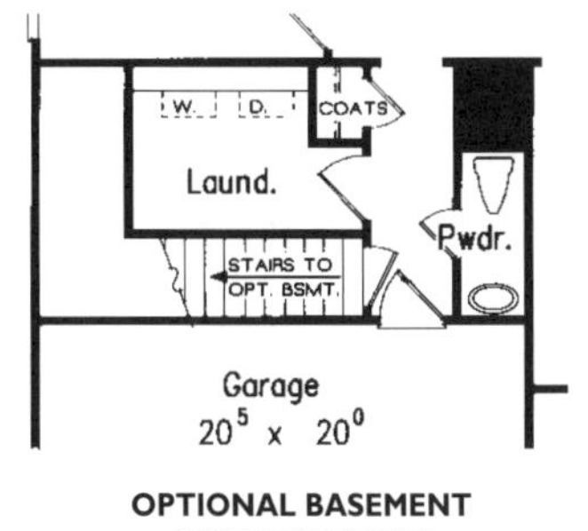

W. D.
COATS
Laund.
STAIRS TO OPT. BSMT.
Pwdr.
Garage 20^5 x 20^0

OPTIONAL BASEMENT STAIR LOCATION

Design 65426

Units	Single
Price Code	D
Total Finished	2,204 sq. ft.
First Finished	1,618 sq. ft.
Second Finished	586 sq. ft.
Bonus Unfinished	334 sq. ft.
Garage Unfinished	534 sq. ft.
Deck Unfinished	370 sq. ft.
Porch Unfinished	185 sq. ft.
Dimensions	65'x44'
Foundation	Basement
Bedrooms	3
Full Baths	2
Half Baths	1
First Ceiling	9'
Second Ceiling	8'
Max Ridge Height	29'9"
Roof Framing	Stick
Exterior Walls	2x6

SECOND FLOOR

FIRST FLOOR

Design 99130

Units	Single
Price Code	D
Total Finished	2,204 sq. ft.
Main Finished	2,204 sq. ft.
Basement Unfinished	2,204 sq. ft.
Dimensions	64'x56'
Foundation	Basement
Bedrooms	3
Full Baths	2
Max Ridge Height	23'8"
Roof Framing	Truss
Exterior Wall	2x6

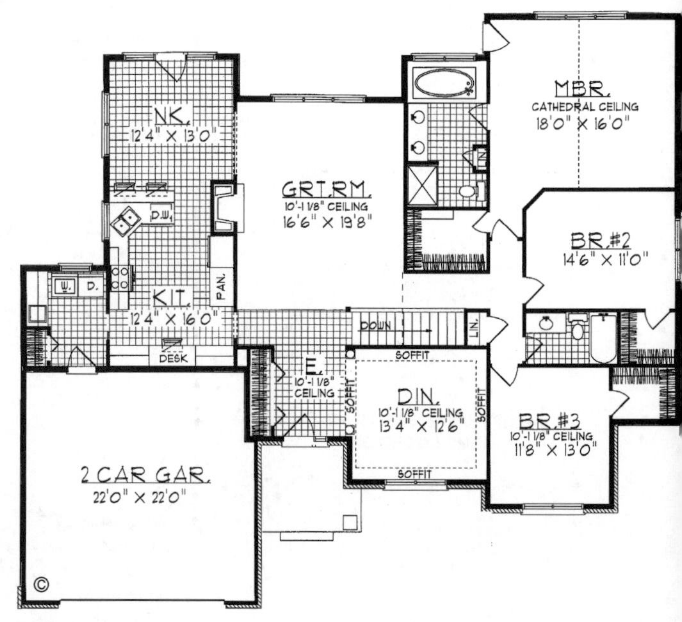
NK.
12'4" X 13'0"
GRT.RM.
10'-1 1/8" CEILING
16'6" X 19'8"
MBR.
CATHEDRAL CEILING
18'0" X 16'0"
BR.#2
14'6" X 11'0"
KIT.
12'4" X 16'0"
P.W.
PAN.
DESK
DOWN
LIN.
E.
10'-1 1/8" CEILING
SOFFIT
DIN.
10'-1 1/8" CEILING
13'4" X 12'6"
BR.#3
10'-1 1/8" CEILING
11'8" X 13'0"
2 CAR GAR.
22'0" X 22'0"
MAIN FLOOR

Design 94658

PHOTOGRAPHY: COURTESY OF THE DESIGNER

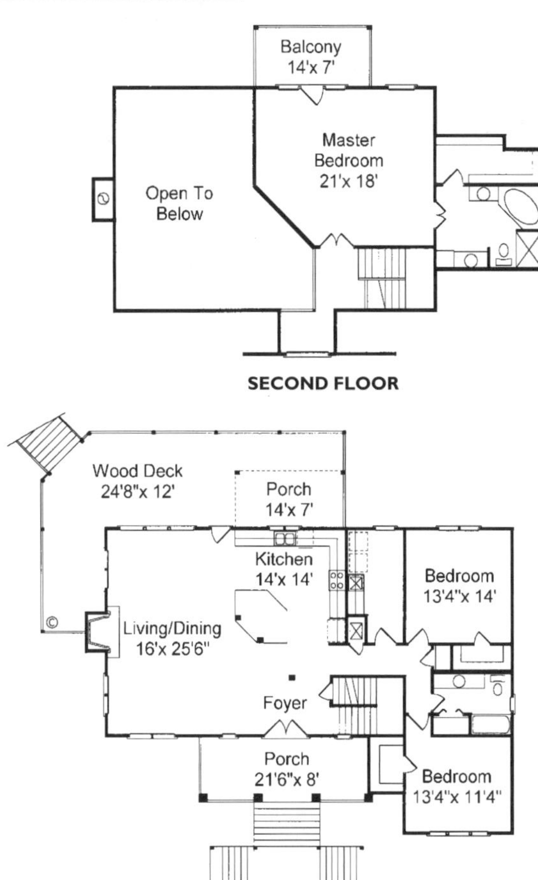
Balcony
14'x 7'
Master
Bedroom
21'x 18'
Open To
Below
SECOND FLOOR
Wood Deck
24'8"x 12'
Porch
14'x 7'
Kitchen
14'x 14'
Bedroom
13'4"x 14'
Living/Dining
16'x 25'6"
Foyer
Porch
21'6"x 8'
Bedroom
13'4"x 11'4"
FIRST FLOOR

Units	Single
Price Code	D
Total Finished	2,205 sq. ft.
First Finished	1,552 sq. ft.
Second Finished	653 sq. ft.
Dimensions	60'x50'
Foundation	Pier/Post
Bedrooms	3
Full Baths	2
First Ceiling	9'
Second Ceiling	9'
Max Ridge Height	37'10"
Roof Framing	Stick
Exterior Walls	2x4

Please note: The photographed home may have been modified to suit homeowner preferences. If you order plans, have a builder or design professional check them against the photograph to confirm actual construction details.

Design 92643

Great Room
Below
Study
10'3" x 13'6"
Bedroom
13'10" x 10'8"
Hall
Bath
Bedroom
11'0" x 13'0"
Bonus
Room
11'1" x 20'
SECOND FLOOR

Units	Single
Price Code	D
Total Finished	2,209 sq. ft.
First Finished	1,542 sq. ft.
Second Finished	667 sq. ft.
Bonus Unfinished	236 sq. ft.
Basement Unfinished	1,470 sq. ft.
Garage Unfinished	420 sq. ft.
Dimensions	58'6"x49'
Foundation	Basement
Bedrooms	3
Full Baths	2
Half Baths	1
First Ceiling	8'
Second Ceiling	8'
Max Ridge Height	26'
Roof Framing	Truss
Exterior Walls	2x4

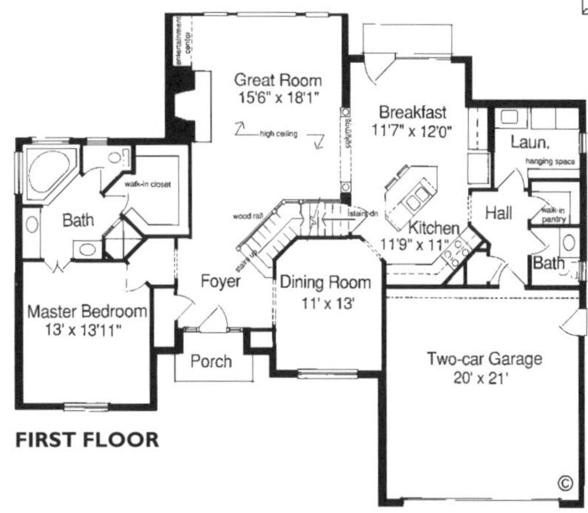
Great Room
15'6" x 18'1"
Breakfast
11'7" x 12'0"
Laun.
Bath
Hall
Kitchen
11'9" x 11'
Bath
Foyer
Dining Room
11' x 13'
Master Bedroom
13' x 13'11"
Porch
Two-car Garage
20' x 21'
FIRST FLOOR

Design 93437

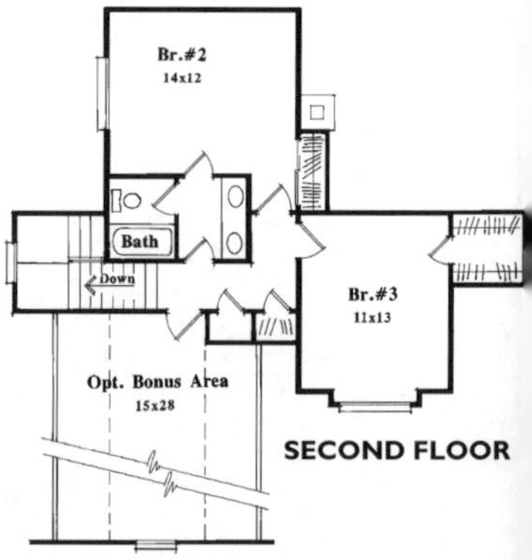

Units	Single
Price Code	D
Total Finished	2,210 sq. ft.
First Finished	1,670 sq. ft.
Second Finished	540 sq. ft.
Bonus Unfinished	455 sq. ft.
Basement Unfinished	1,677 sq. ft.
Garage Unfinished	594 sq. ft.
Dimensions	54'x61'
Foundation	Basement
Bedrooms	3
Full Baths	2
Half Baths	1
Max Ridge Height	31'
Roof Framing	Stick
Exterior Walls	2x4

Br.#2 14x12
Bath
Down
Br.#3 11x13
Opt. Bonus Area 15x28
SECOND FLOOR

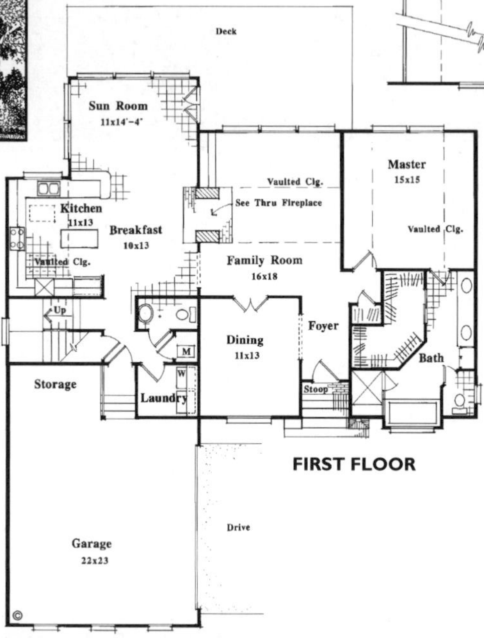

Deck
Sun Room 11x14'-4"
Kitchen 11x13
Breakfast 10x13
Vaulted Clg.
Vaulted Clg.
See Thru Fireplace
Master 15x15
Vaulted Clg.
Family Room 16x18
Up
Dining 11x13
Foyer
Storage
Laundry
Stoop
Bath
FIRST FLOOR
Drive
Garage 22x23

Design 91901

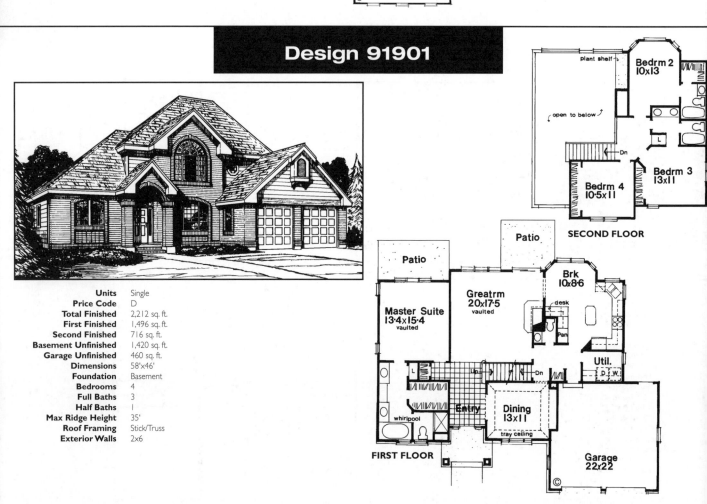

Units	Single
Price Code	D
Total Finished	2,212 sq. ft.
First Finished	1,496 sq. ft.
Second Finished	716 sq. ft.
Basement Unfinished	1,420 sq. ft.
Garage Unfinished	460 sq. ft.
Dimensions	58'x46'
Foundation	Basement
Bedrooms	4
Full Baths	3
Half Baths	1
Max Ridge Height	35'
Roof Framing	Stick/Truss
Exterior Walls	2x6

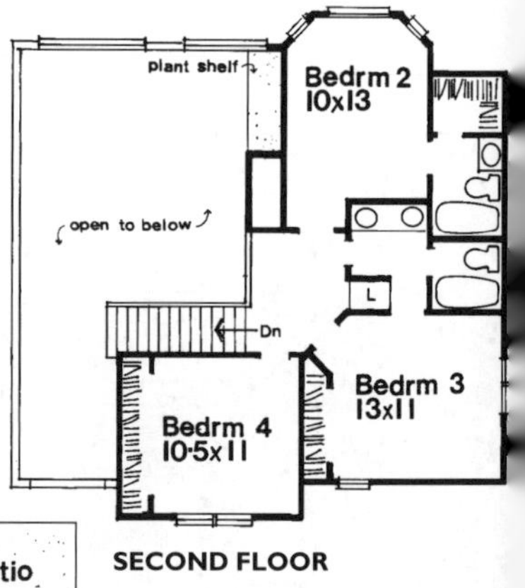

plant shelf
Bedrm 2 10x13
open to below
Dn
Bedrm 3 13x11
Bedrm 4 10·5x11
SECOND FLOOR

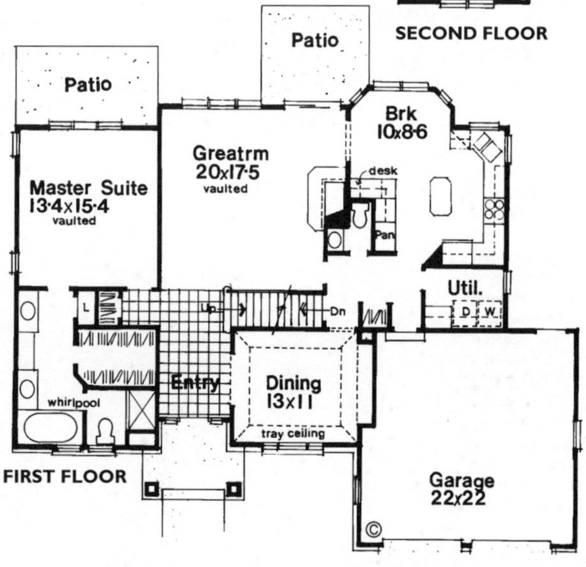

Patio
Patio
Brk 10x8·6
Greatrm 20x17·5 vaulted
desk
Pan
Master Suite 13·4x15·4 vaulted
Util.
Up
Dn
Entry
Dining 13x11
tray ceiling
whirlpool
FIRST FLOOR
Garage 22x22

 To order blueprints, call **800-235-5700** or visit us on the web, **familyhomeplans.com**

Design 91463

Units	Single
Price Code	D
Total Finished	2,214 sq. ft.
Main Finished	2,214 sq. ft.
Garage Unfinished	498 sq. ft.
Dimensions	58'6"x53'6"
Foundation	Basement
Bedrooms	3
Full Baths	2
Half Baths	1
Main Ceiling	9'
Second Ceiling	9'
Max Ridge Height	25'
Roof Framing	Truss
Exterior Walls	2x6

PATIO
WI CLO
M BATH
LINEN
NOOK
12/0 X 11/6
B. I. CAB'S
FAMILY RM
17 X 19
MASTER BR
16/4 X 16/0
BR
11/2 X 11/6
KIT
DW
B. I. CAB'S
P
SKYLT
B
R
PAN
ARCH
SKYLT
DIN RM
15/4 X 12/0
GUEST
D
W
UTIL
BR
12 X 10
ARCH
DEN/BR
11/0 X 14/2
ARCH
FOYER
VAULTED
LIV RM
15/4 X 17/6
COVR'D
PORCH
3 CAR GARAGE
35 X 23
COURTYARD
©
MAIN FLOOR

Design 97858

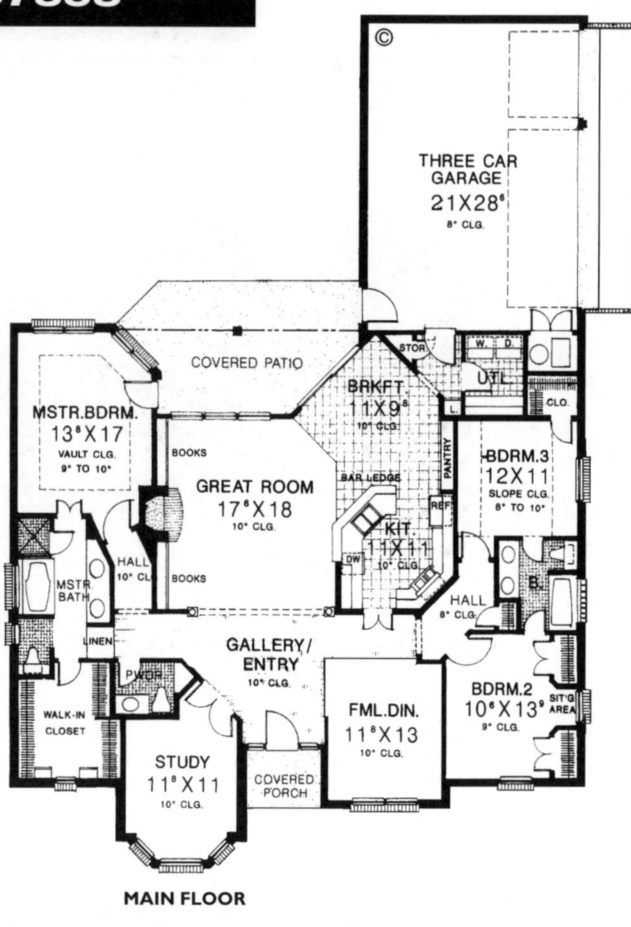

THREE CAR GARAGE
21X28⁶
8" CLG.
COVERED PATIO
MSTR.BDRM.
13⁸X17
VAULT CLG.
9" TO 10"
BRKFT.
11X9⁸
10" CLG.
BDRM.3
12X11
SLOPE CLG.
8" TO 10"
STOR
W. D.
UTL
CLO.
PANTRY
BOOKS
GREAT ROOM
17⁶X18
10" CLG.
BAR LEDGE
REF
KIT.
11X11
10" CLG.
DW
HALL
10" CLG
MSTR. BATH
LINEN
HALL
8" CLG.
B.
GALLERY/ ENTRY
10" CLG.
PWDR
WALK-IN CLOSET
FML.DIN.
11⁸X13
10" CLG.
BDRM.2
10⁶X13⁹
9" CLG.
SIT'G AREA
STUDY
11⁸X11
10" CLG.
COVERED PORCH
MAIN FLOOR

Units	Single
Price Code	D
Total Finished	2,214 sq. ft.
Main Finished	2,214 sq. ft.
Garage Unfinished	599 sq. ft.
Deck Unfinished	136 sq. ft.
Porch Unfinished	42 sq. ft.
Dimensions	55'x77'11"
Foundation	Slab
Bedrooms	3
Full Baths	2
Half Baths	1
Main Ceiling	9'-10'
Max Ridge Height	27'
Roof Framing	Stick
Exterior Walls	2x4

Design 90454

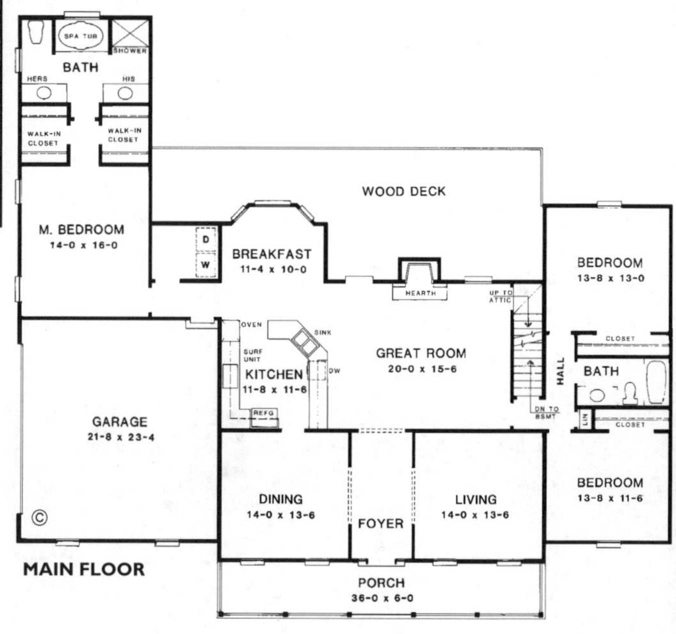

SPA TUB
SHOWER
BATH
HERS
HIS
WALK-IN CLOSET
WALK-IN CLOSET
WOOD DECK
M. BEDROOM
14-0 x 16-0
D
W
BREAKFAST
11-4 x 10-0
HEARTH
UP TO ATTIC
BEDROOM
13-8 x 13-0
OVEN
SINK
SURF UNIT
KITCHEN
11-8 x 11-6
DW
REFG
GREAT ROOM
20-0 x 15-6
CLOSET
HALL
BATH
DN TO BSMT
LIN
CLOSET
GARAGE
21-8 x 23-4
DINING
14-0 x 13-6
FOYER
LIVING
14-0 x 13-6
BEDROOM
13-8 x 11-6
PORCH
36-0 x 6-0
MAIN FLOOR

Units	Single
Price Code	D
Total Finished	2,218 sq. ft.
Main Finished	2,218 sq. ft.
Basement Unfinished	1,658 sq. ft.
Garage Unfinished	528 sq. ft.
Deck Unfinished	342 sq. ft.
Porch Unfinished	216 sq. ft.
Dimensions	72'x64'
Foundation	Basement Crawlspace
Bedrooms	3
Full Baths	2
Main Ceiling	9'
Max Ridge Height	20'10"
Roof Framing	Stick
Exterior Walls	2x4

Design 94659

PHOTOGRAPHY: COURTESY OF THE DESIGNER

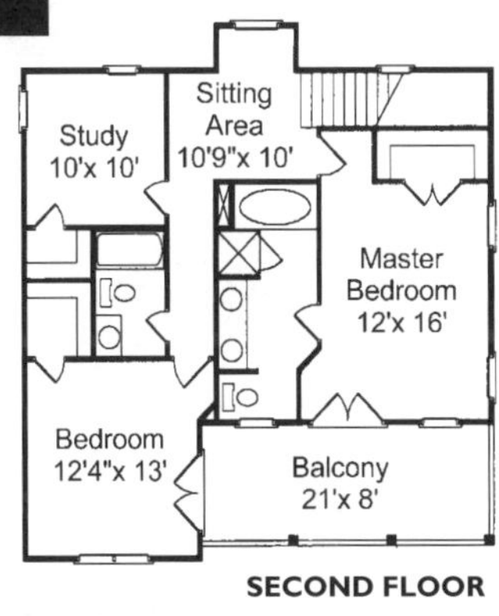
Study
10'x 10'
Sitting Area
10'9"x 10'
Master Bedroom
12'x 16'
Bedroom
12'4"x 13'
Balcony
21'x 8'

SECOND FLOOR

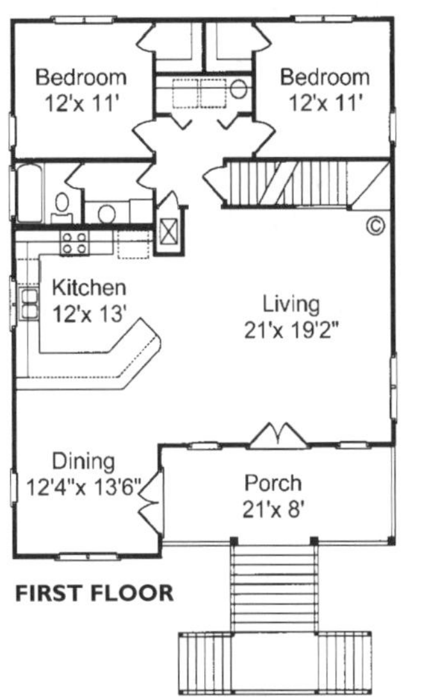
Bedroom
12'x 11'
Bedroom
12'x 11'
Kitchen
12'x 13'
Living
21'x 19'2"
Dining
12'4"x 13'6"
Porch
21'x 8'

FIRST FLOOR

Units	Single
Price Code	D
Total Finished	2,221 sq. ft.
First Finished	1,307 sq. ft.
Second Finished	914 sq. ft.
Dimensions	34'x44'
Foundation	Post
Bedrooms	4
Full Baths	3
First Ceiling	9'
Second Ceiling	8'
Max Ridge Height	41'
Roof Framing	Stick
Exterior Walls	2x4

Please note: The photographed home may have been modified to suit homeowner preferences. If you order plans, have a builder or design professional check them against the photograph to confirm actual construction details.

Design 34705

Br 4
11-4 x 10-8
MBr 1
13-8 x 15-6
Br 2
11-8 x 16
Br 3
11-4 x 10-8

SECOND FLOOR

Garage
21-8 x 23-4
Kitchen
10-4 x 12-6
Brkfst
10-8 x 10-2
Family Rm
20 x 12-6
Dining Rm
13-8 x 12-6
Living
15 x 12-6

FIRST FLOOR

OPTIONAL BASEMENT STAIR LOCATION

Units	Single
Price Code	D
Total Finished	2,224 sq. ft.
First Finished	1,090 sq. ft.
Second Finished	1,134 sq. ft.
Basement Unfinished	1,090 sq. ft.
Garage Unfinished	576 sq. ft.
Dimensions	66'x27'
Foundation	Basement Crawlspace Slab
Bedrooms	4
Full Baths	2
Half Baths	1
Max Ridge Height	27'
Roof Framing	Stick
Exterior Walls	2x4, 2x6

Design 63100

Units	Single
Price Code	D
Total Finished	2,224 sq. ft.
Main Finished	2,224 sq. ft.
Garage Unfinished	554 sq. ft.
Dimensions	58'6"x72'
Foundation	Slab
Bedrooms	4
Full Baths	2
3/4 Baths	1
Max Ridge Height	25'10"
Roof Framing	Truss

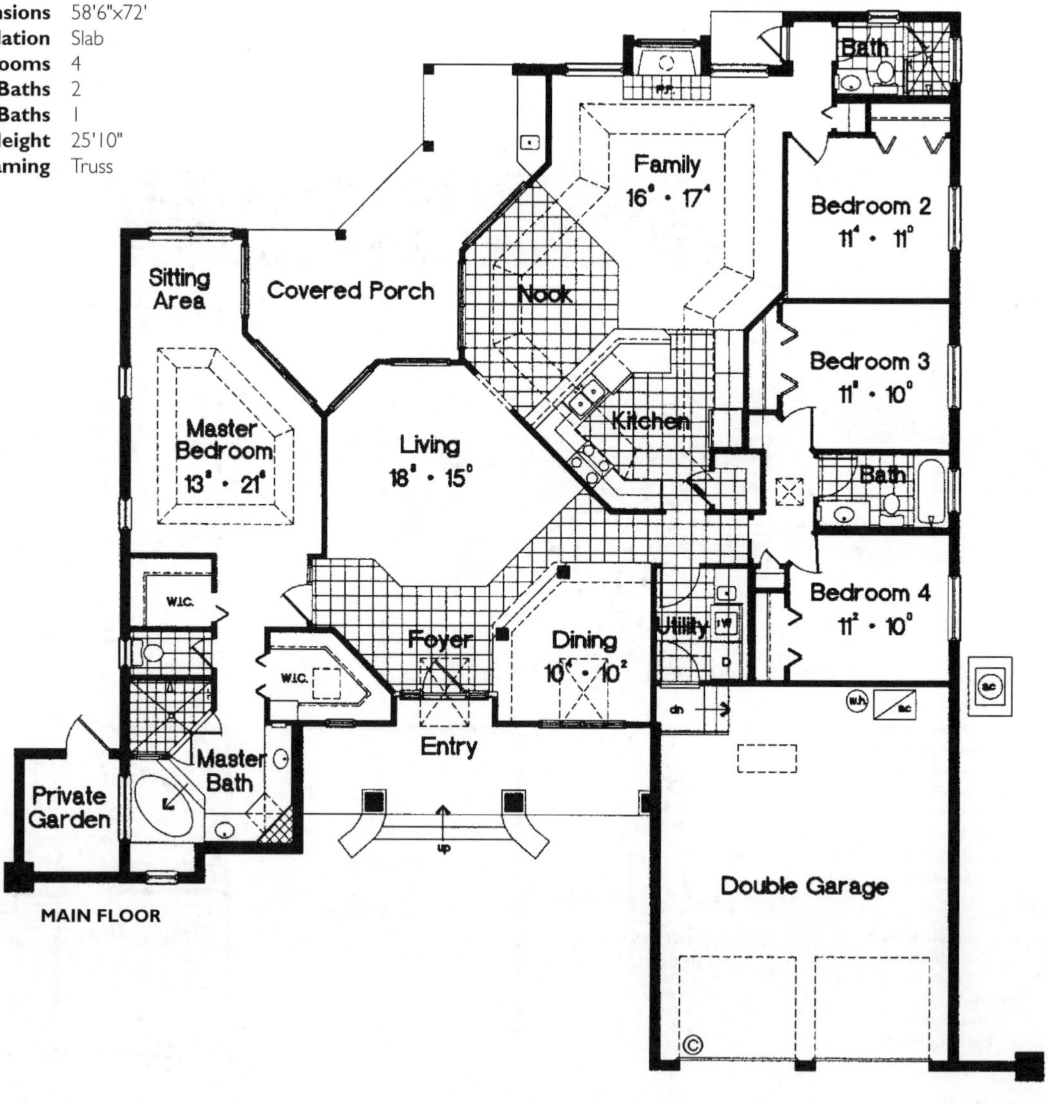

Bath
Family $16^6 \cdot 17^4$
Bedroom 2 $11^4 \cdot 11^0$
Sitting Area
Covered Porch
Nook
Bedroom 3 $11^8 \cdot 10^0$
Kitchen
Master Bedroom $13^8 \cdot 21^6$
Living $18^8 \cdot 15^0$
Bath
W.I.C.
Bedroom 4 $11^2 \cdot 10^0$
Foyer
Dining $10^4 \cdot 10^2$
Utility
W.I.C.
dn
Entry
Master Bath
Private Garden
up
Double Garage

MAIN FLOOR

Design 91591

Units	Single
Price Code	D
Total Finished	2,225 sq. ft.
Main Finished	2,225 sq. ft.
Garage Unfinished	420 sq. ft.
Dimensions	45'x73'
Foundation	Crawlspace
Bedrooms	3
Full Baths	2
Max Ridge Height	28'
Roof Framing	Stick
Exterior Walls	2x6

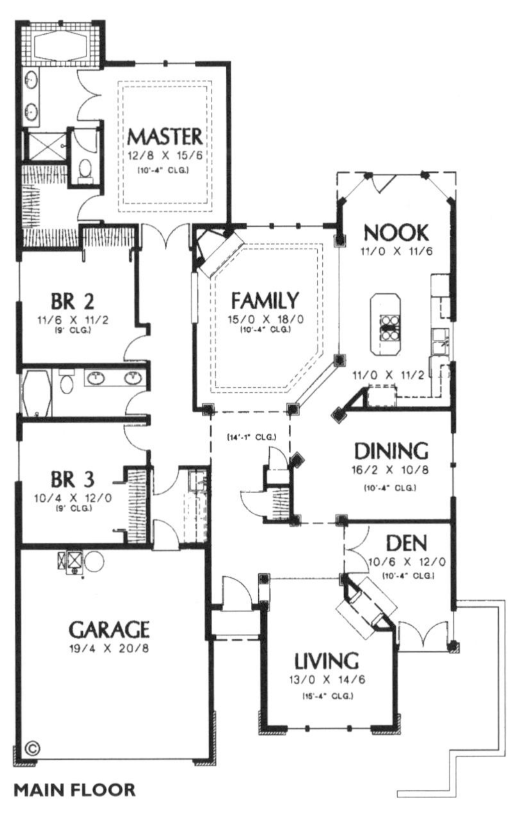
MASTER
12/8 X 15/6
(10'-4" CLG.)
NOOK
11/0 X 11/6
BR 2
11/6 X 11/2
(9' CLG.)
FAMILY
15/0 X 18/0
(10'-4" CLG.)
11/0 X 11/2
(14'-1" CLG.)
DINING
16/2 X 10/8
(10'-4" CLG.)
BR 3
10/4 X 12/0
(9' CLG.)
DEN
10/6 X 12/0
(10'-4" CLG.)
GARAGE
19/4 X 20/8
LIVING
13/0 X 14/6
(15'-4" CLG.)
©

MAIN FLOOR

Design 10396

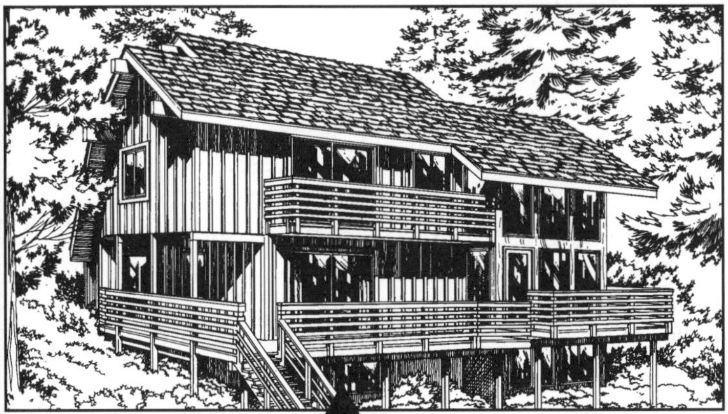

Units	Single
Price Code	D
Total Finished	2,228 sq. ft.
First Finished	886 sq. ft.
Second Finished	456 sq. ft.
Lower Finished	886 sq. ft.
Dimensions	38'x40'
Foundation	Basement
Bedrooms	3
Full Baths	3
Max Ridge Height	31'
Roof Framing	Stick
Exterior Walls	2x6

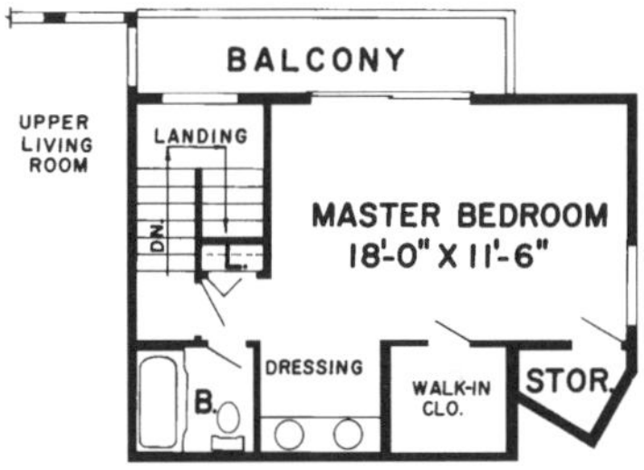

SECOND FLOOR

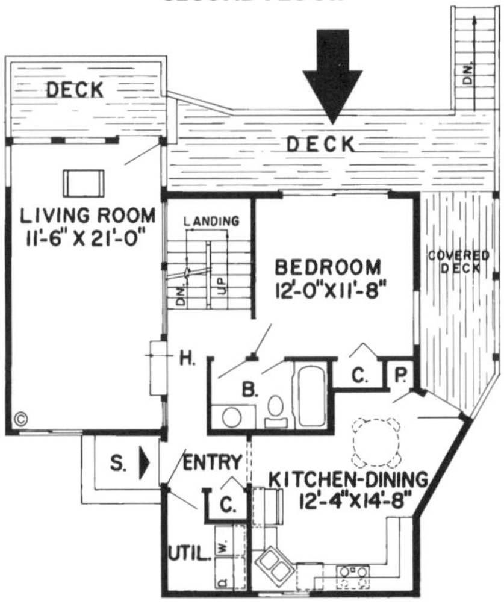

FIRST FLOOR

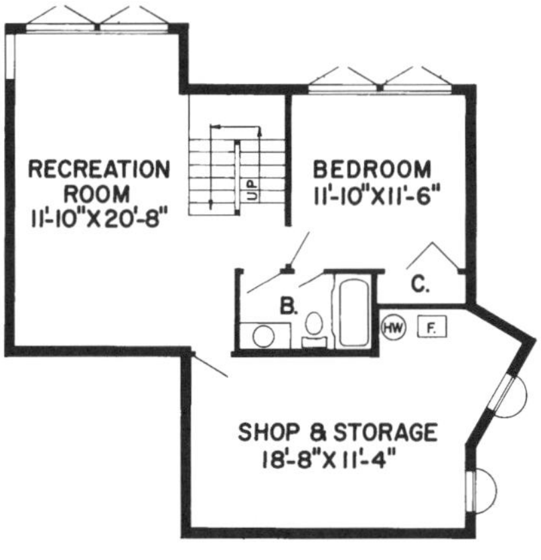

LOWER FLOOR

Design 97774

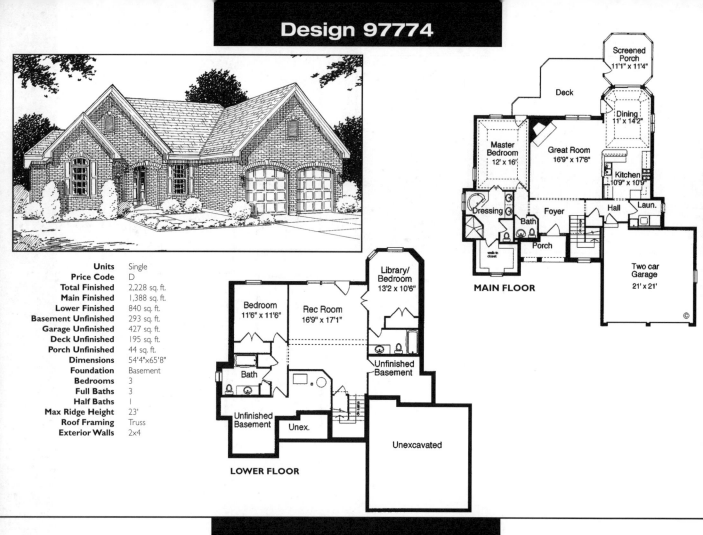

Units	Single
Price Code	D
Total Finished	2,228 sq. ft.
Main Finished	1,388 sq. ft.
Lower Finished	840 sq. ft.
Basement Unfinished	293 sq. ft.
Garage Unfinished	427 sq. ft.
Deck Unfinished	195 sq. ft.
Porch Unfinished	44 sq. ft.
Dimensions	54'4"x65'8"
Foundation	Basement
Bedrooms	3
Full Baths	3
Half Baths	1
Max Ridge Height	23'
Roof Framing	Truss
Exterior Walls	2x4

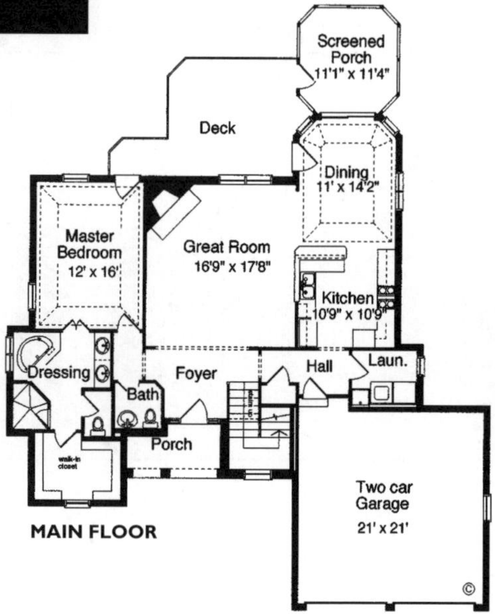

Design 98329

Units	Single
Price Code	D
Total Finished	2,228 sq. ft.
Main Finished	2,228 sq. ft.
Deck Unfinished	130 sq. ft.
Porch Unfinished	48 sq. ft.
Dimensions	58'4"x61'4"
Foundation	Slab
Bedrooms	3
Full Baths	2
Main Ceiling	10'
Max Ridge Height	22'6"
Roof Framing	Stick
Exterior Walls	2x6

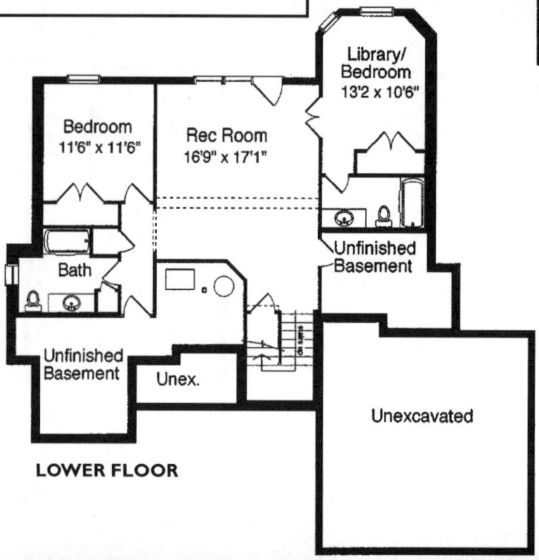

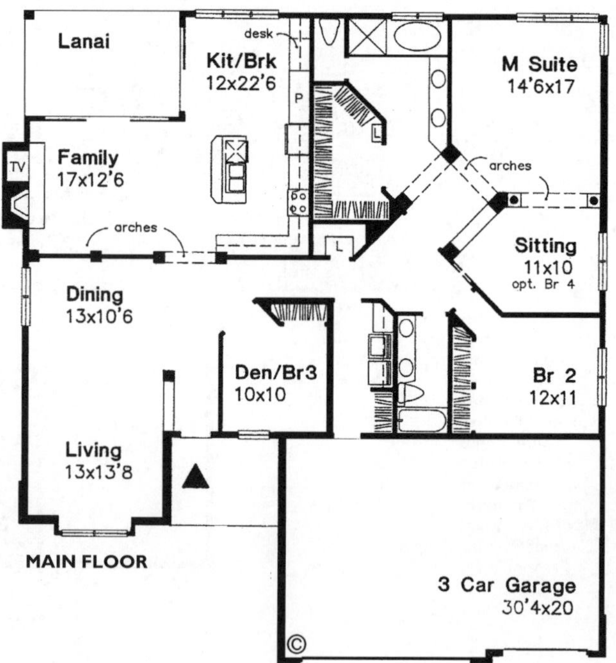
Lanai
desk
Kit/Brk
12x22'6
M Suite
14'6x17
Family
17x12'6
TV
arches
arches
Sitting
11x10
opt. Br 4
Dining
13x10'6
Den/Br3
10x10
Br 2
12x11
Living
13x13'8
MAIN FLOOR
3 Car Garage
30'4x20

Design 97135

Units	Single
Price Code	D
Total Finished	2,229 sq. ft.
Main Finished	2,229 sq. ft.
Basement Unfinished	2,229 sq. ft.
Garage Unfinished	551 sq. ft.
Dimensions	65'x56'
Foundation	Basement
Bedrooms	3
Full Baths	2
Max Ridge Height	26'
Roof Framing	Truss
Exterior Walls	2x6

NK.
10'4" X 10'4"
DIN.
TRAY CEILING
11'4" X 12'6"
GRT.RM.
CATHEDRAL CEILING
18'6" X 19'0"
MBR.
CATHEDRAL CEILING
18'0" X 13'4"
LIN.
KIT.
12'8" X 15'8"
PANTRY
OVEN
E.
LIN.
BR.2
11'2" X 12'8"
BR.3
12'8" X 12'4"
2 CAR GAR.
21'6" X 25'8"

MAIN FLOOR

Design 94673

Units	Single
Price Code	D
Total Finished	2,232 sq. ft.
Main Finished	2,232 sq. ft.
Dimensions	57'6"x37'10"
Foundation	Slab
Bedrooms	3
Full Baths	2
Roof Framing	Stick

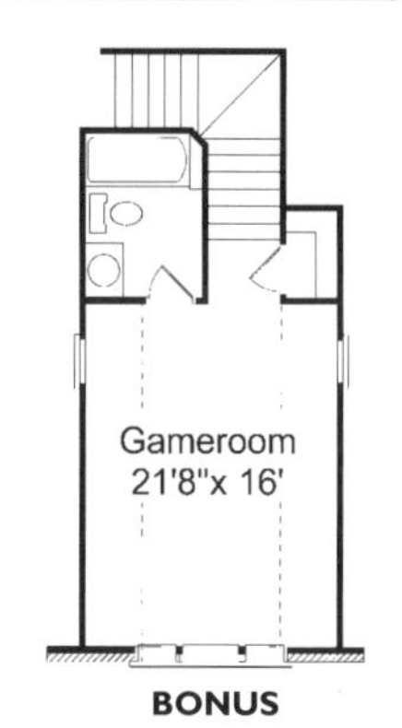

Gameroom
21'8"x 16'

BONUS

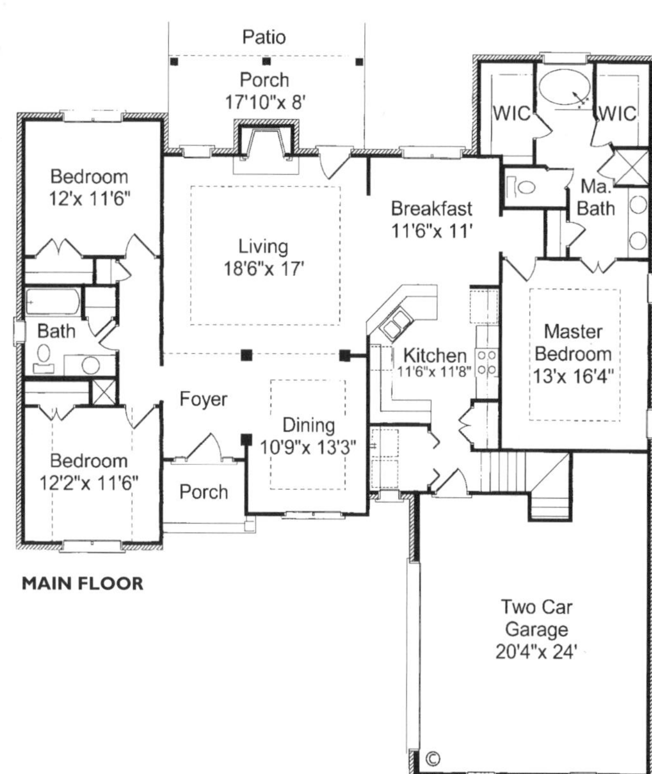

Patio
Porch
17'10"x 8'
WIC
WIC
Ma.
Bath
Bedroom
12'x 11'6"
Breakfast
11'6"x 11'
Living
18'6"x 17'
Bath
Kitchen
11'6"x 11'8"
Master
Bedroom
13'x 16'4"
Foyer
Dining
10'9"x 13'3"
Bedroom
12'2"x 11'6"
Porch
Two Car
Garage
20'4"x 24'

MAIN FLOOR

Design 69108

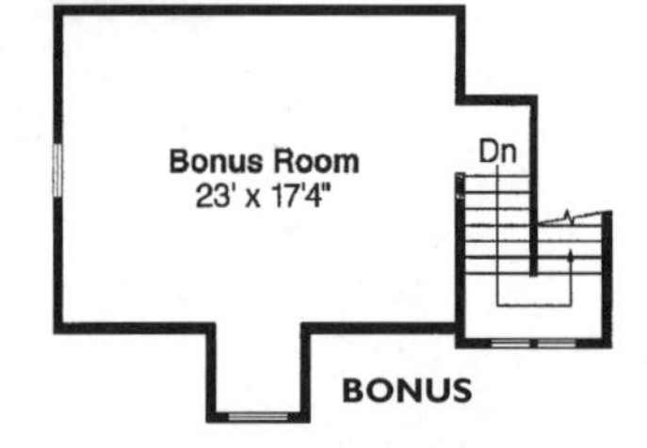
Bonus Room
23' x 17'4"
Dn
BONUS

Patio
12' x 26'
Shop/Storage
23'4" x 10'4"
Utility
Vaulted
Dining
12' x 14'4"
Vaulted
Family
16'4" x 19'8"
Bedroom
12' x 12'
Dn
Up
Kitchen
15'10" x 13'
Garage
23'4" x 21'
Bedroom
11' x 14'
Vaulted
Entry
Living/Den/
Library
14' x 13'8"
Vaulted
Master Suite
14' x 15'8"
Covered Porch
MAIN FLOOR

Units	Single
Price Code	D
Total Finished	2,234 sq. ft.
Main Finished	2,234 sq. ft.
Bonus Unfinished	489 sq. ft.
Garage Unfinished	755 sq. ft.
Dimensions	76'x56'4"
Foundation	Crawlspace
Bedrooms	3
Full Baths	2
Main Ceiling	9'
Second Ceiling	8'
Vaulted Ceiling	18'
Max Ridge Height	26'
Roof Framing	Truss
Exterior Walls	2x6

Design 93151

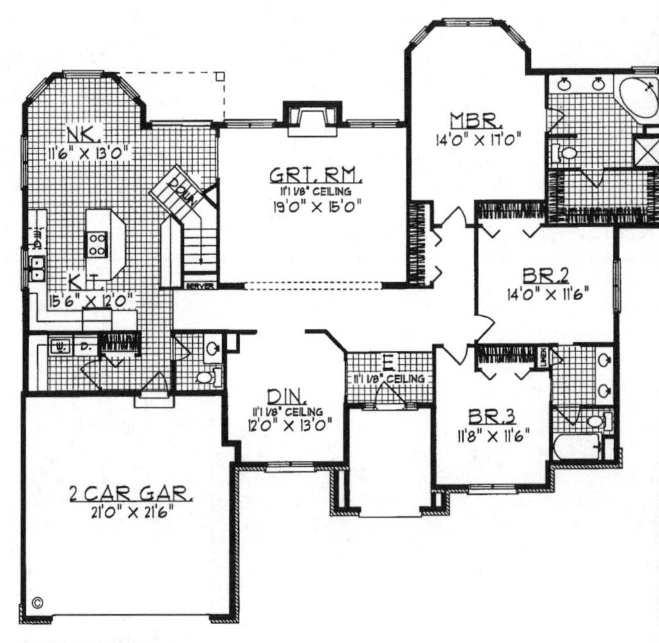
NK.
11'6" X 13'0"
GRT. RM.
11'1 1/8" CEILING
19'0" X 15'0"
MBR.
14'0" X 17'0"
KT.
15'6" X 12'0"
BR.2
14'0" X 11'6"
DIN.
11'1 1/8" CEILING
12'0" X 13'0"
E
11'1 1/8" CEILING
BR.3
11'8" X 11'6"
2 CAR GAR.
21'0" X 21'6"

MAIN FLOOR

Units	Single
Price Code	D
Total Finished	2,234 sq. ft.
Main Finished	2,234 sq. ft.
Basement Unfinished	2,234 sq. ft.
Dimensions	66'x59'
Foundation	Basement
Bedrooms	3
Full Baths	2
Half Baths	1
Max Ridge Height	22'6"
Roof Framing	Stick
Exterior Walls	2x6

Design 98424

Units	Single
Price Code	D
Total Finished	2,236 sq. ft.
Main Finished	2,236 sq. ft.
Basement Unfinished	2,236 sq. ft.
Garage Unfinished	517 sq. ft.
Dimensions	63'x67'
Foundation	Basement Crawlspace
Bedrooms	3
Full Baths	2
Half Baths	1
Max Ridge Height	25'5"
Roof Framing	Stick
Exterior Walls	2x4

CAD
FILES AVAILABLE
For more information call
800-235-5700

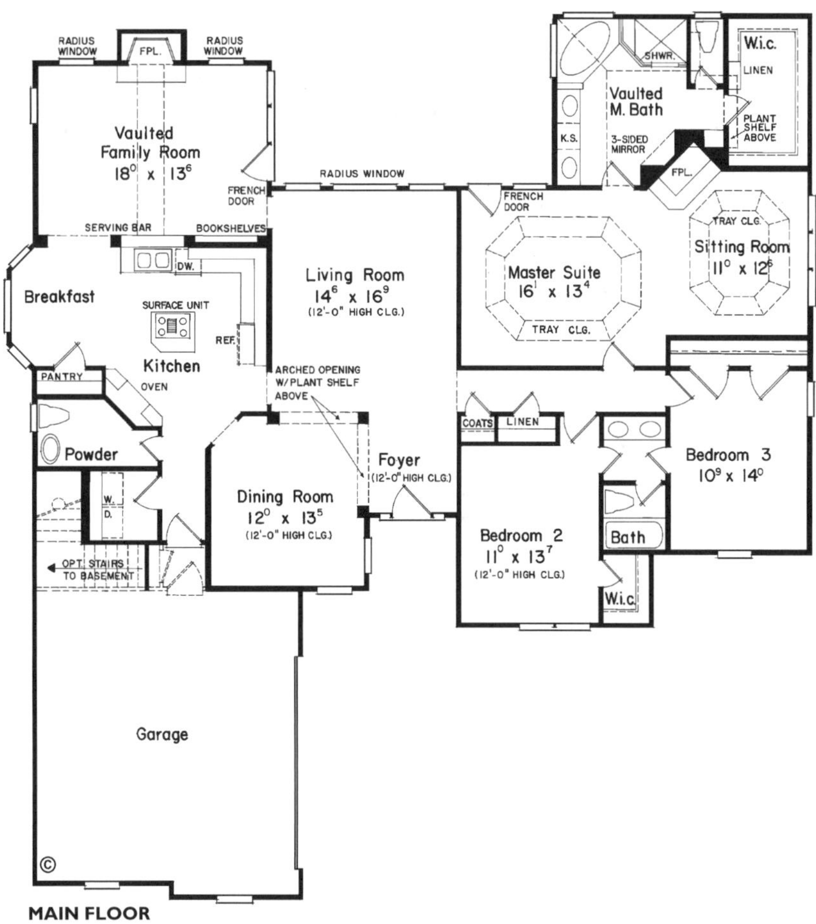
RADIUS WINDOW
FPL.
RADIUS WINDOW
Vaulted Family Room
18^0 x 13^6
FRENCH DOOR
SERVING BAR
BOOKSHELVES
RADIUS WINDOW
Breakfast
DW.
SURFACE UNIT
REF.
Kitchen
OVEN
PANTRY
Powder
W. D.
OPT. STAIRS TO BASEMENT
Living Room
14^6 x 16^9
(12'-0" HIGH CLG.)
ARCHED OPENING W/PLANT SHELF ABOVE
Dining Room
12^0 x 13^5
(12'-0" HIGH CLG.)
Foyer
(12'-0" HIGH CLG.)
Garage
SHWR.
W.i.c.
LINEN
Vaulted M. Bath
PLANT SHELF ABOVE
K.S.
3-SIDED MIRROR
FPL.
FRENCH DOOR
Master Suite
16^1 x 13^4
TRAY CLG.
TRAY CLG.
Sitting Room
11^0 x 12^6
COATS
LINEN
Bedroom 3
10^9 x 14^0
Bedroom 2
11^0 x 13^7
(12'-0" HIGH CLG.)
Bath
W.i.c.
©

MAIN FLOOR

Design 98544

Units	Single
Price Code	D
Total Finished	2,238 sq. ft.
Main Finished	2,238 sq. ft.
Dimensions	60'x61'1"
Foundation	Slab
Bedrooms	4
Full Baths	3
Max Ridge Height	24'
Roof Framing	Stick
Exterior Walls	2x4

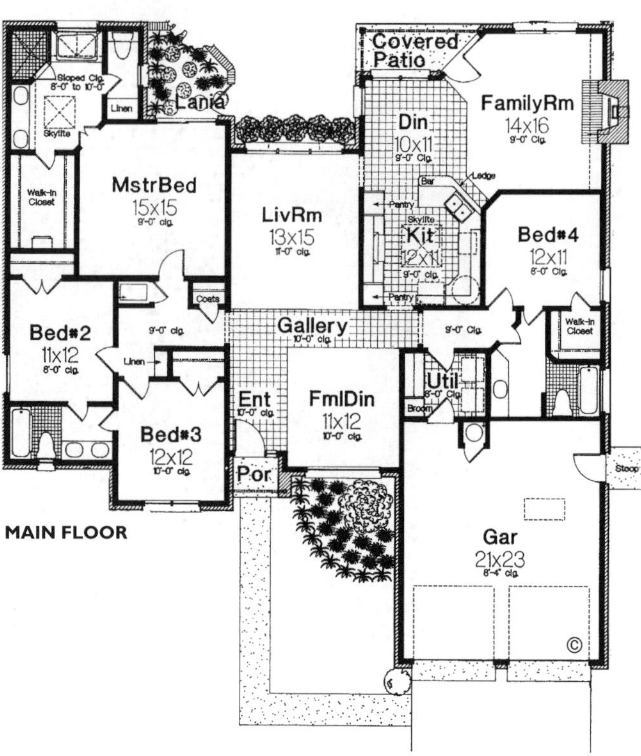

Covered Patio
FamilyRm 14x16 9'-0" Clg.
Din 10x11 9'-0" Clg.
Lania
MstrBed 15x15 9'-0" clg.
LivRm 13x15 11'-0" clg.
Kit 12x11 9'-0" clg.
Bed#4 12x11 8'-0" Clg.
Walk-In Closet
Linen
Skylite
Bed#2 11x12 8'-0" clg.
Gallery 10'-0" clg.
Ent 10'-0" clg.
FmlDin 11x12 10'-0" clg.
Util
Bed#3 12x12 10'-0" clg.
Por
Gar 21x23 8'-4" clg.
Stoop
MAIN FLOOR

Design 24964

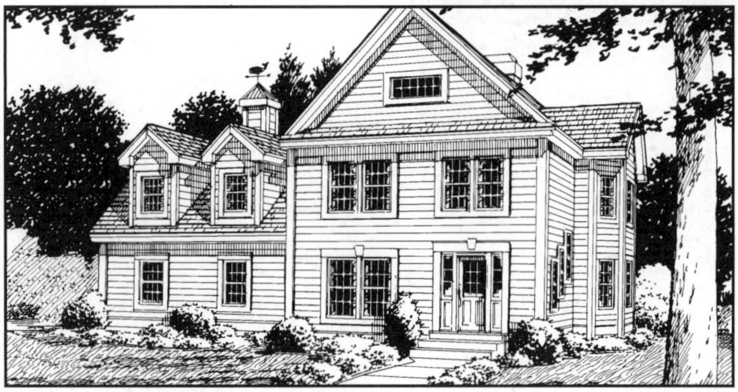

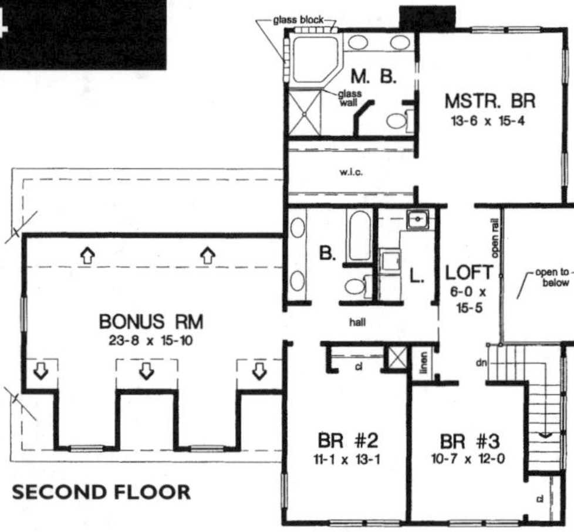

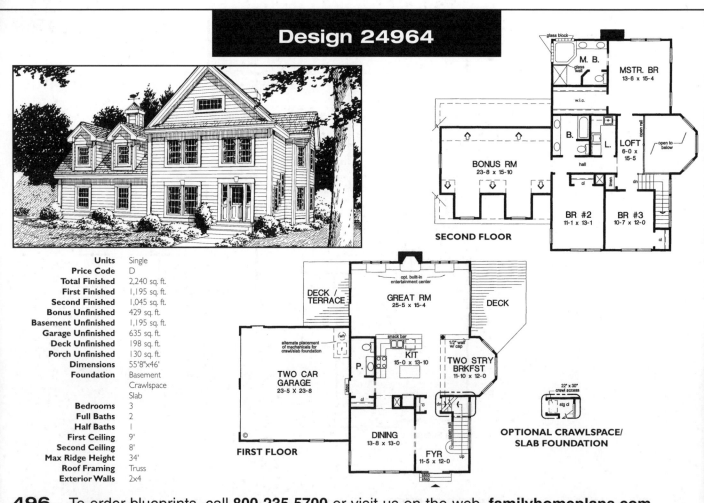

Units	Single
Price Code	D
Total Finished	2,240 sq. ft.
First Finished	1,195 sq. ft.
Second Finished	1,045 sq. ft.
Bonus Unfinished	429 sq. ft.
Basement Unfinished	1,195 sq. ft.
Garage Unfinished	635 sq. ft.
Deck Unfinished	198 sq. ft.
Porch Unfinished	130 sq. ft.
Dimensions	55'8"x46'
Foundation	Basement Crawlspace Slab
Bedrooms	3
Full Baths	2
Half Baths	1
First Ceiling	9'
Second Ceiling	8'
Max Ridge Height	34'
Roof Framing	Truss
Exterior Walls	2x4

M. B.
MSTR. BR 13-6 x 15-4
BONUS RM 23-8 x 15-10
LOFT 6-0 x 15-5
BR #2 11-1 x 13-1
BR #3 10-7 x 12-0

SECOND FLOOR

DECK / TERRACE
GREAT RM 25-5 x 15-4
DECK
KIT 15-0 x 13-10
TWO STRY BRKFST 11-10 x 12-0
TWO CAR GARAGE 23-5 X 23-8
DINING 13-8 x 13-0
FYR 11-5 x 12-0

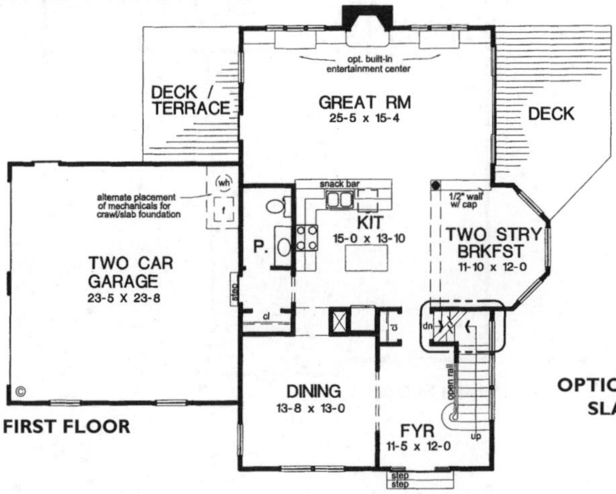

FIRST FLOOR

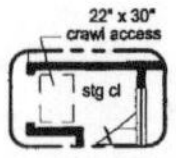

OPTIONAL CRAWLSPACE/ SLAB FOUNDATION

Design 34827

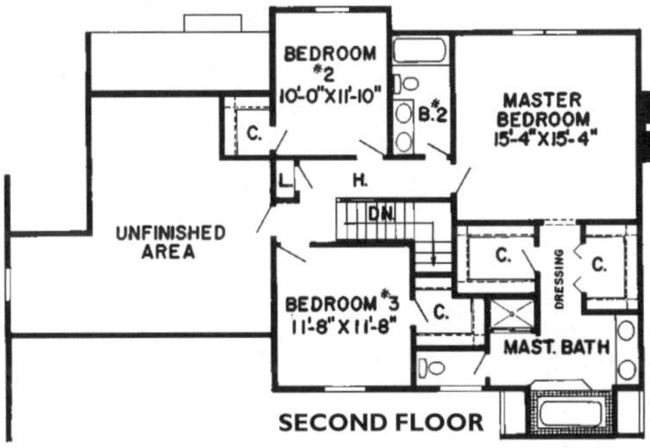

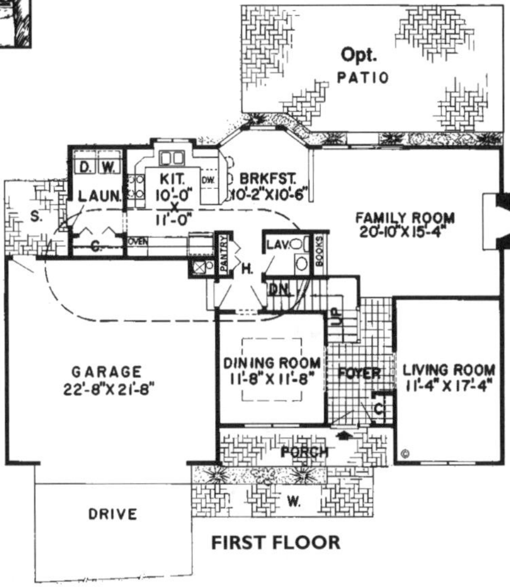

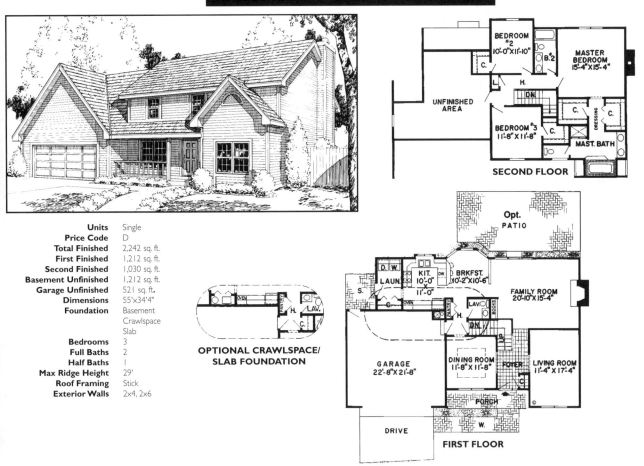

SECOND FLOOR

FIRST FLOOR

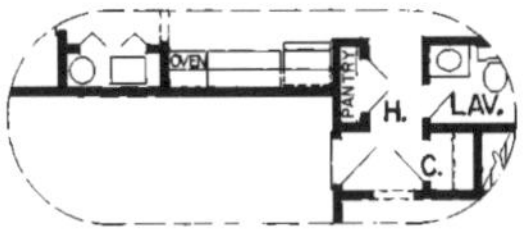

OPTIONAL CRAWLSPACE/ SLAB FOUNDATION

Units	Single
Price Code	D
Total Finished	2,242 sq. ft.
First Finished	1,212 sq. ft.
Second Finished	1,030 sq. ft.
Basement Unfinished	1,212 sq. ft.
Garage Unfinished	521 sq. ft.
Dimensions	55'x34'4"
Foundation	Basement Crawlspace Slab
Bedrooms	3
Full Baths	2
Half Baths	1
Max Ridge Height	29'
Roof Framing	Stick
Exterior Walls	2x4, 2x6

Design 68068

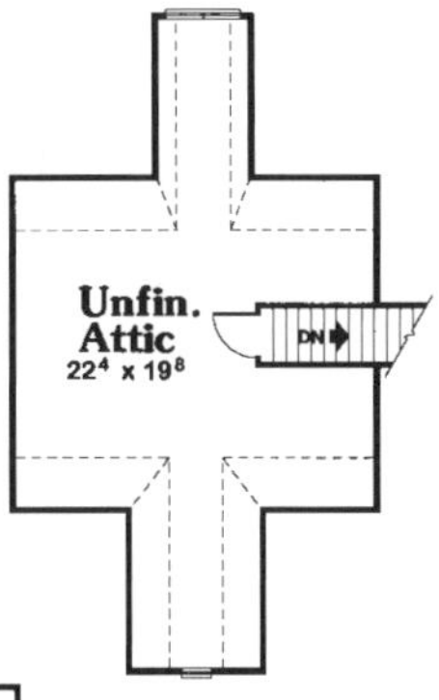

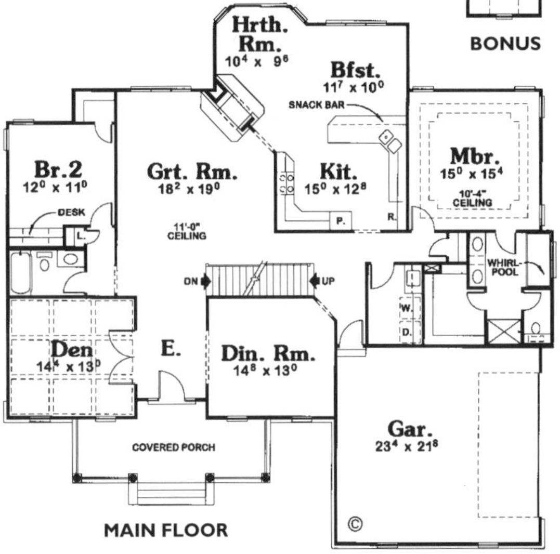

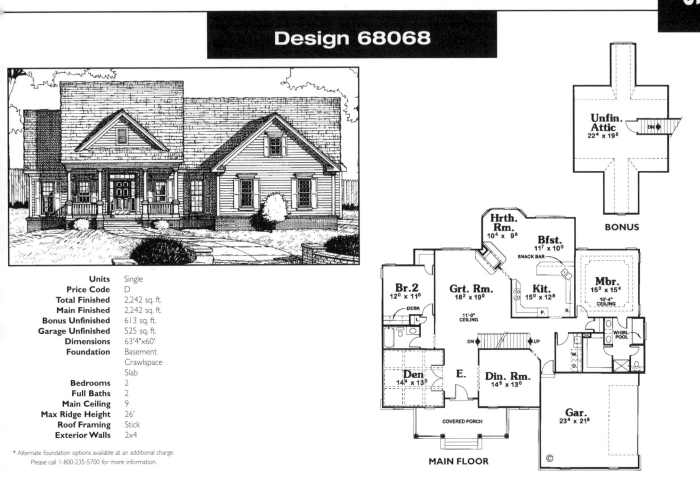

BONUS

MAIN FLOOR

Units	Single
Price Code	D
Total Finished	2,242 sq. ft.
Main Finished	2,242 sq. ft.
Bonus Unfinished	613 sq. ft.
Garage Unfinished	525 sq. ft.
Dimensions	63'4"x60'
Foundation	Basement Crawlspace Slab
Bedrooms	2
Full Baths	2
Main Ceiling	9
Max Ridge Height	26'
Roof Framing	Stick
Exterior Walls	2x4

* Alternate foundation options available at an additional charge. Please call 1-800-235-5700 for more information.

Design 24268

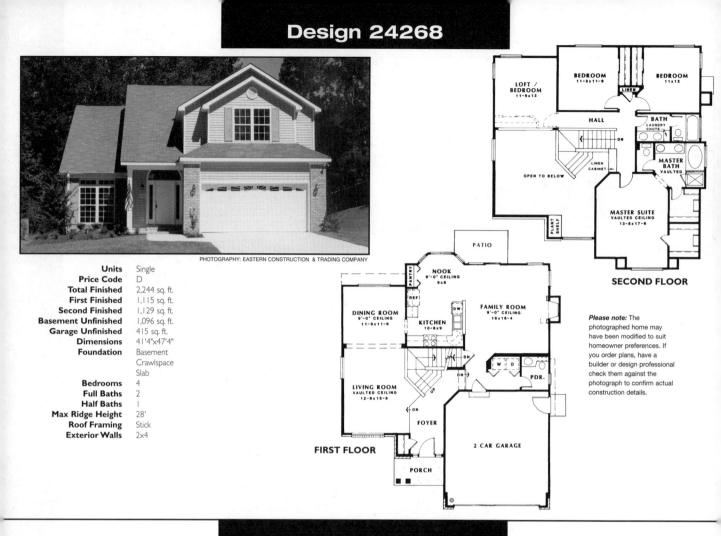

PHOTOGRAPHY: EASTERN CONSTRUCTION & TRADING COMPANY

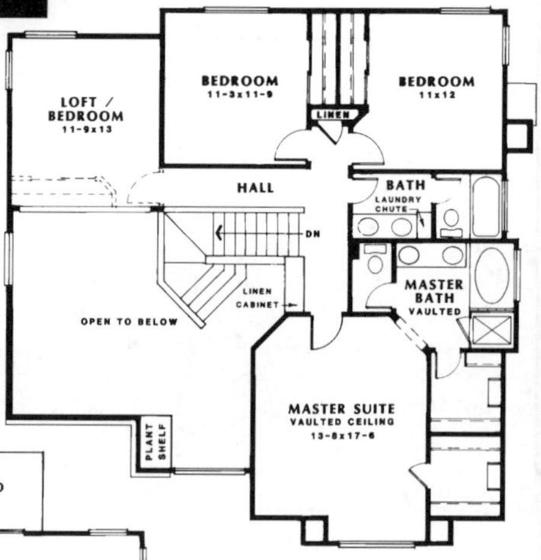

Units	Single
Price Code	D
Total Finished	2,244 sq. ft.
First Finished	1,115 sq. ft.
Second Finished	1,129 sq. ft.
Basement Unfinished	1,096 sq. ft.
Garage Unfinished	415 sq. ft.
Dimensions	41'4"x47'4"
Foundation	Basement Crawlspace Slab
Bedrooms	4
Full Baths	2
Half Baths	1
Max Ridge Height	28'
Roof Framing	Stick
Exterior Walls	2x4

SECOND FLOOR

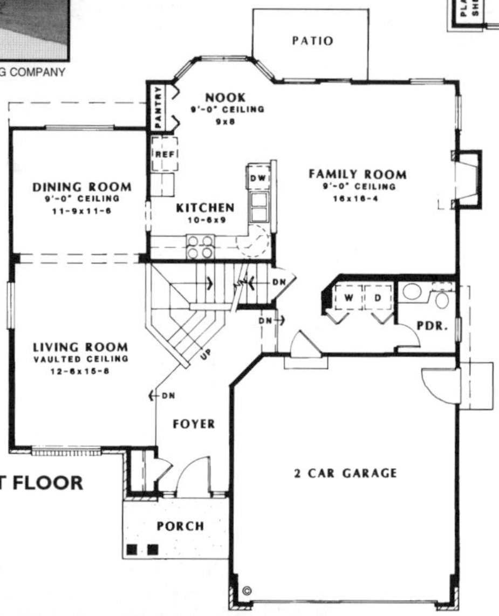

FIRST FLOOR

Please note: The photographed home may have been modified to suit homeowner preferences. If you order plans, have a builder or design professional check them against the photograph to confirm actual construction details.

Design 94610

Units	Single
Price Code	D
Total Finished	2,246 sq. ft.
Main Finished	2,246 sq. ft.
Garage Unfinished	546 sq. ft.
Porch Unfinished	195 sq. ft.
Dimensions	61'10"x65'5"
Foundation	Crawlspace Slab
Bedrooms	4
Full Baths	2
Half Baths	1
Main Ceiling	9'
Max Ridge Height	24'
Roof Framing	Truss
Exterior Walls	2x4, 2x6

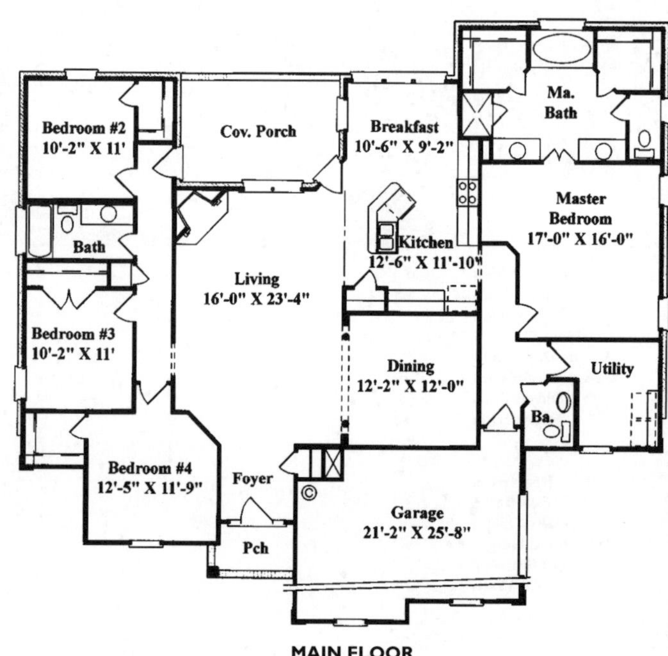
Bedroom #2
10'-2" X 11'
Cov. Porch
Breakfast
10'-6" X 9'-2"
Ma.
Bath
Bath
Kitchen
12'-6" X 11'-10"
Master
Bedroom
17'-0" X 16'-0"
Living
16'-0" X 23'-4"
Bedroom #3
10'-2" X 11'
Dining
12'-2" X 12'-0"
Utility
Ba.
Bedroom #4
12'-5" X 11'-9"
Foyer
Garage
21'-2" X 25'-8"
Pch

MAIN FLOOR

Design 65667

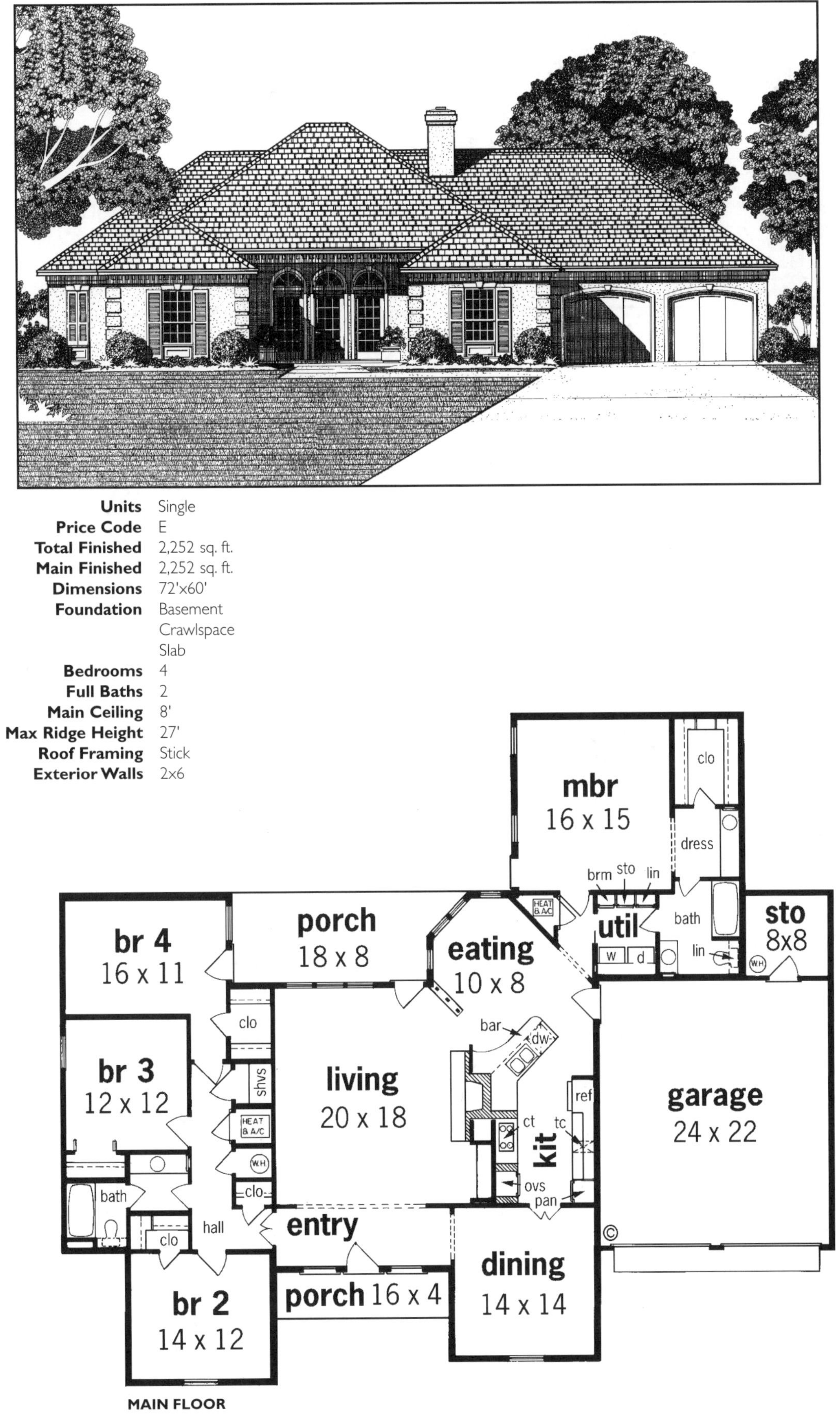
mbr
16 x 15
clo
dress
brm
sto
lin
HEAT B.A/C
util
w
d
bath
lin
W.H.
sto
8x8
porch
18 x 8
eating
10 x 8
br 4
16 x 11
clo
bar
dw
br 3
12 x 12
shvs
HEAT B.A/C
W.H.
living
20 x 18
ref
ct
tc
kit
garage
24 x 22
bath
clo
ovs
pan
clo
hall
entry
porch 16 x 4
dining
14 x 14
br 2
14 x 12
MAIN FLOOR

Units	Single
Price Code	E
Total Finished	2,252 sq. ft.
Main Finished	2,252 sq. ft.
Dimensions	72'x60'
Foundation	Basement Crawlspace Slab
Bedrooms	4
Full Baths	2
Main Ceiling	8'
Max Ridge Height	27'
Roof Framing	Stick
Exterior Walls	2x6

Design 68162

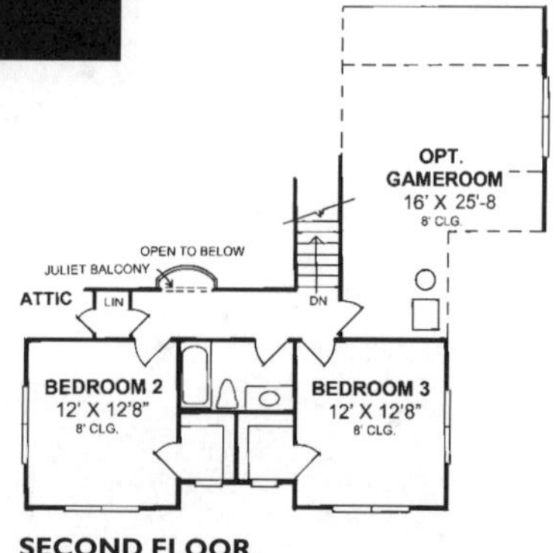

OPT. GAMEROOM
16' X 25'-8
8' CLG.
OPEN TO BELOW
JULIET BALCONY
ATTIC
LIN
DN
BEDROOM 2
12' X 12'8"
8' CLG.
BEDROOM 3
12' X 12'8"
8' CLG.
SECOND FLOOR

Units	Single
Price Code	E
Total Finished	2,252 sq. ft.
First Finished	1,736 sq. ft.
Second Finished	516 sq. ft.
Bonus Unfinished	242 sq. ft.
Garage Unfinished	638 sq. ft.
Porch Unfinished	1,223 sq. ft.
Dimensions	80'x59'
Foundation	Slab
Bedrooms	4
Full Baths	3
First Ceiling	9'
Max Ridge Height	30'
Exterior Walls	2x4

* Alternate foundation options available at an additional charge. Please call 1-800-235-5700 for more information.

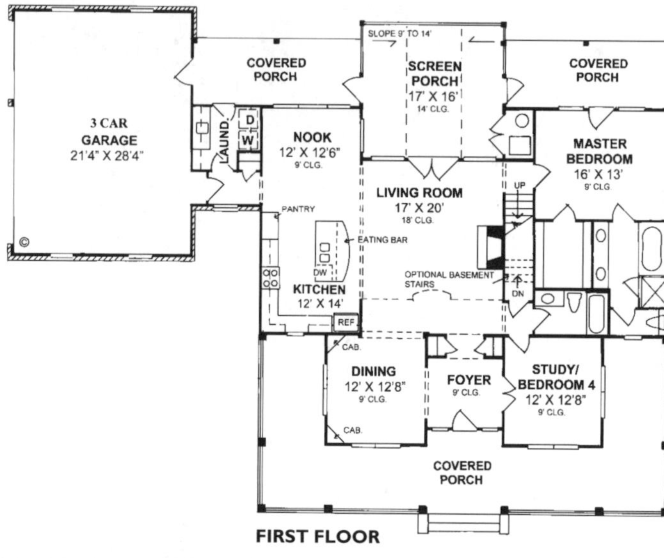

3 CAR GARAGE
21'4" X 28'4"
COVERED PORCH
SLOPE 9' TO 14'
SCREEN PORCH
17' X 16'
14' CLG.
COVERED PORCH
LAUND.
D
W
NOOK
12' X 12'6"
9' CLG.
MASTER BEDROOM
16' X 13'
9' CLG.
LIVING ROOM
17' X 20'
18' CLG.
UP
PANTRY
EATING BAR
DW
OPTIONAL BASEMENT STAIRS
DN
KITCHEN
12' X 14'
REF.
CAB.
DINING
12' X 12'8"
9' CLG.
FOYER
9' CLG.
STUDY/ BEDROOM 4
12' X 12'8"
9' CLG.
CAB.
COVERED PORCH
FIRST FLOOR

Design 97850

Units	Single
Price Code	E
Total Finished	2,253 sq. ft.
Main Finished	2,253 sq. ft.
Garage Unfinished	602 sq. ft.
Deck Unfinished	205 sq. ft.
Porch Unfinished	110 sq. ft.
Dimensions	63'x60'3"
Foundation	Slab
Bedrooms	4
Full Baths	2
3/4 Baths	1
Main Ceiling	8'-10'
Max Ridge Height	26'
Roof Framing	Stick
Exterior Walls	2x4

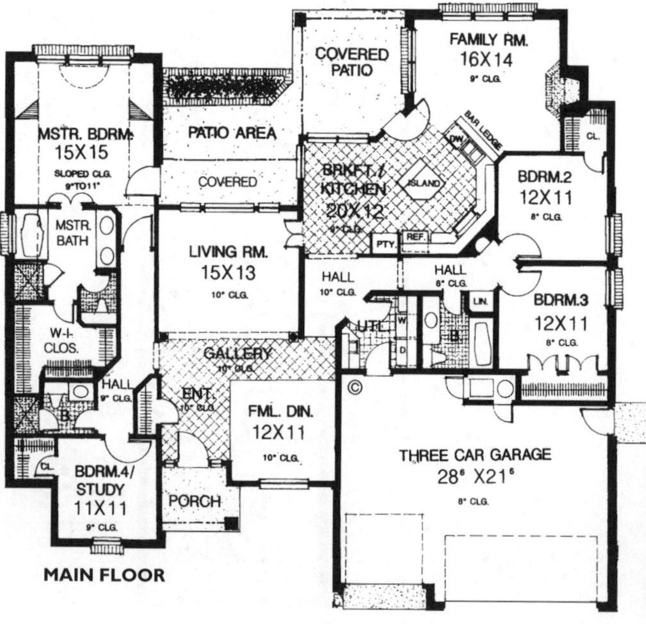

COVERED PATIO
FAMILY RM.
16X14
9' CLG.
MSTR. BDRM.
15X15
SLOPED CLG.
9'TO11'
PATIO AREA
COVERED
BAR LEDGE
DW
BRKFT./ KITCHEN
20X12
ISLAND
CL.
BDRM.2
12X11
8' CLG.
MSTR. BATH
PTY.
REF.
LIVING RM.
15X13
10' CLG.
HALL
10' CLG.
HALL
8' CLG.
LIN.
BDRM.3
12X11
8' CLG.
W-I-CLOS.
UTL.
GALLERY
10' CLG.
HALL
9' CLG.
ENT.
10' CLG.
FML. DIN.
12X11
10' CLG.
THREE CAR GARAGE
28⁶ X21⁶
8' CLG.
CL.
BDRM.4/ STUDY
11X11
9' CLG.
PORCH
MAIN FLOOR

Design 66090

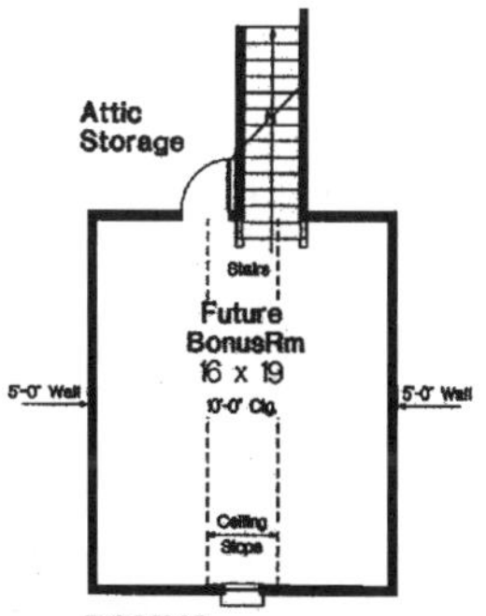

Units	Single
Price Code	F
Total Finished	2,255 sq. ft.
Main Finished	2,255 sq. ft.
Bonus Unfinished	324 sq. ft.
Garage Unfinished	660 sq. ft.
Dimensions	55'x70'
Foundation	Slab
Bedrooms	4
Full Baths	2
3/4 Baths	1
Main Ceiling	8'
Max Ridge Height	24'6"
Roof Framing	Stick
Exterior Walls	2x4

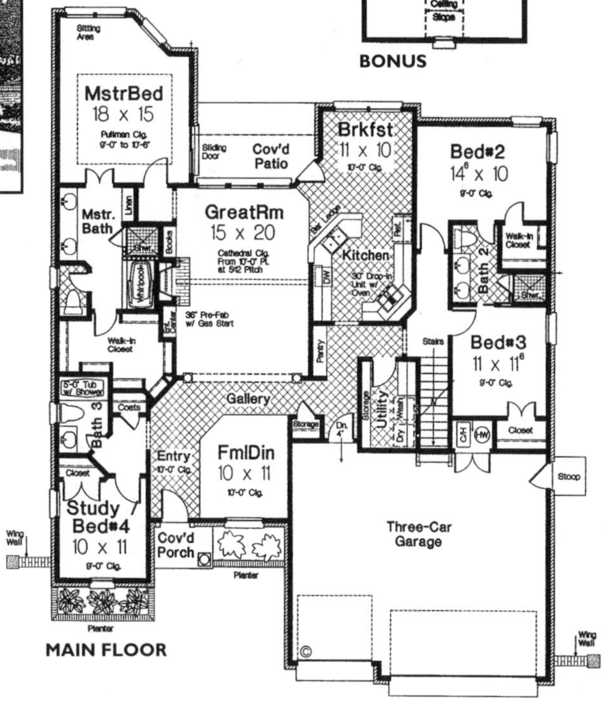

BONUS

MAIN FLOOR

Design 99459

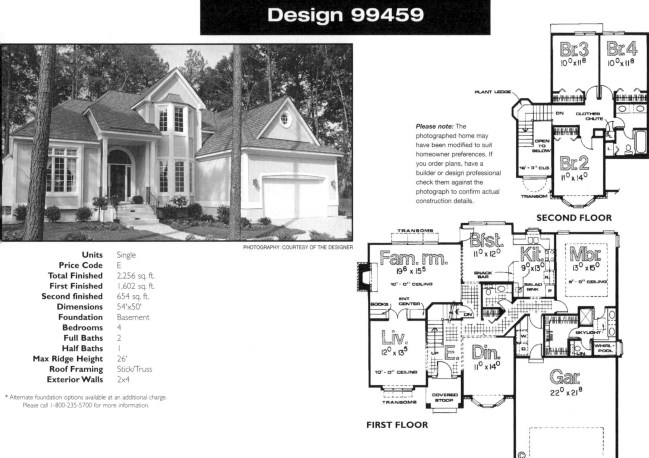

PHOTOGRAPHY: COURTESY OF THE DESIGNER

Units	Single
Price Code	E
Total Finished	2,256 sq. ft.
First Finished	1,602 sq. ft.
Second finished	654 sq. ft.
Dimensions	54'x50'
Foundation	Basement
Bedrooms	4
Full Baths	2
Half Baths	1
Max Ridge Height	26'
Roof Framing	Stick/Truss
Exterior Walls	2x4

* Alternate foundation options available at an additional charge. Please call 1-800-235-5700 for more information.

Please note: The photographed home may have been modified to suit homeowner preferences. If you order plans, have a builder or design professional check them against the photograph to confirm actual construction details.

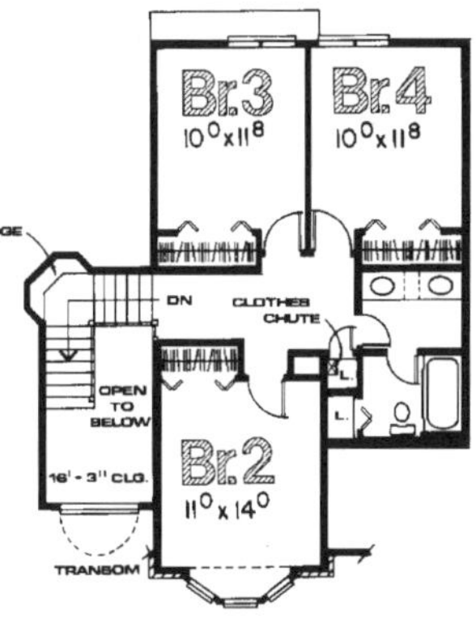

SECOND FLOOR

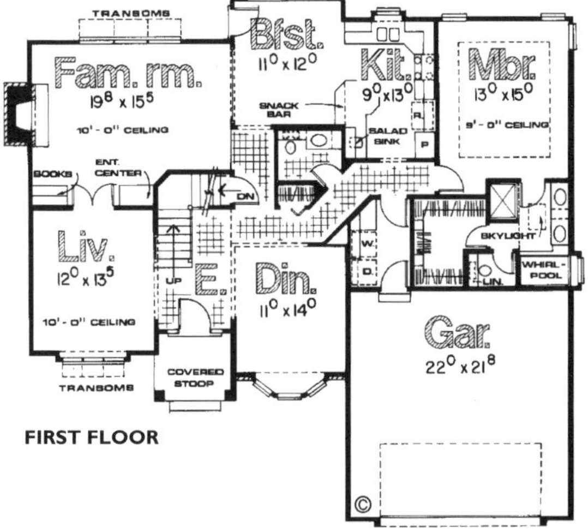

FIRST FLOOR

Design 20231

Units	Single
Price Code	E
Total Finished	2,257 sq. ft.
First Finished	1,540 sq. ft.
Second Finished	717 sq. ft.
Basement Unfinished	1,545 sq. ft.
Garage Unfinished	503 sq. ft.
Porch Unfinished	144 sq. ft.
Dimensions	57'x56'8"
Foundation	Basement Crawlspace Slab
Bedrooms	4
Full Baths	2
Half Baths	1
First Ceiling	9'
Second Ceiling	8'
Max Ridge Height	33'6"
Roof Framing	Truss

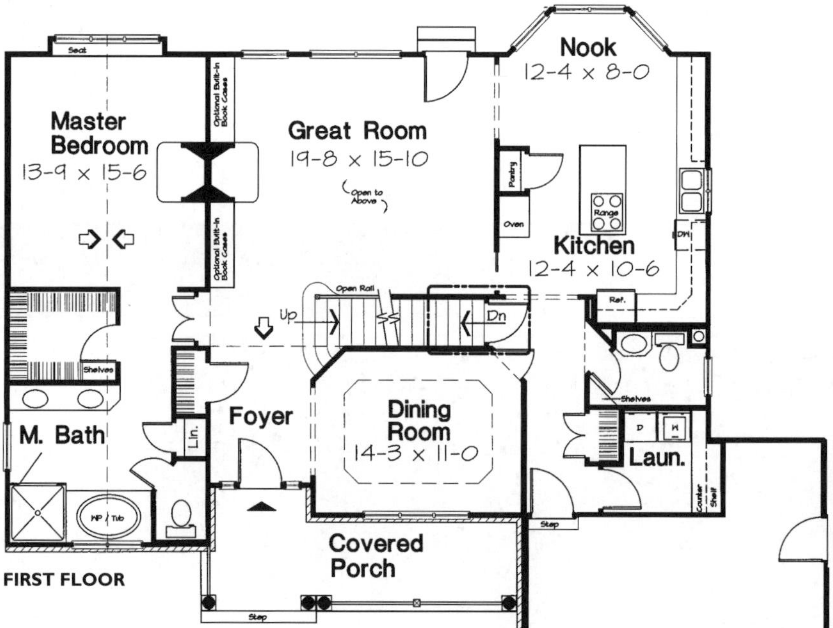

Master Bedroom 13-9 x 15-6
Great Room 19-8 x 15-10 (Open to Above)
Nook 12-4 x 8-0
Kitchen 12-4 x 10-6
M. Bath
Foyer
Dining Room 14-3 x 11-0
Laun.
Covered Porch
Garage 20-7 x 21-8

FIRST FLOOR

OPTIONAL CRAWLSPACE/ SLAB FOUNDATION

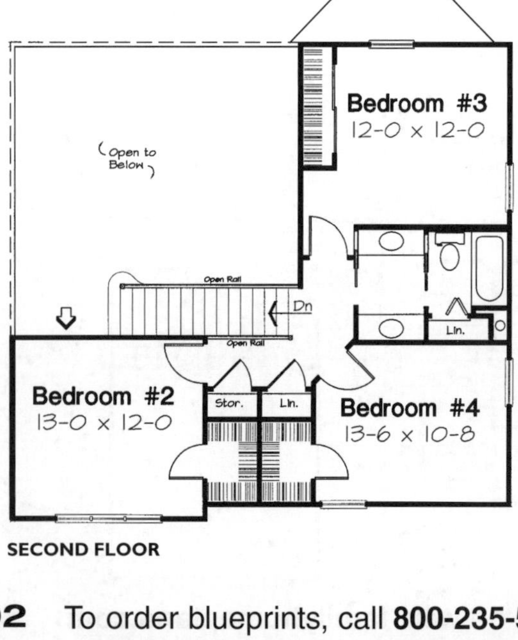

(Open to Below)
Bedroom #3 12-0 x 12-0
Bedroom #2 13-0 x 12-0
Bedroom #4 13-6 x 10-8

SECOND FLOOR

Design 98548

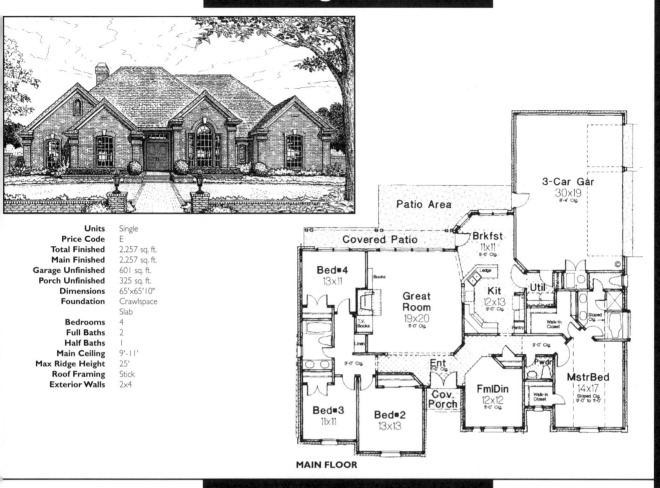

Units	Single
Price Code	E
Total Finished	2,257 sq. ft.
Main Finished	2,257 sq. ft.
Garage Unfinished	601 sq. ft.
Porch Unfinished	325 sq. ft.
Dimensions	65'x65'10"
Foundation	Crawlspace Slab
Bedrooms	4
Full Baths	2
Half Baths	1
Main Ceiling	9'-11'
Max Ridge Height	25'
Roof Framing	Stick
Exterior Walls	2x4

3-Car Gar 30x19 8'-4" Clg.
Patio Area
Covered Patio
Brkfst 11x11 9'-0" Clg.
Bed#4 13x11
Great Room 19x20 11'-0" Clg.
Kit 12x13 9'-0" Clg.
Util
Walk-in Closet
MstrBed 14x17 Sloped Clg. 9'-0" to 11'-0"
Ent 11'-0" Clg.
Pwdr
Cov. Porch
FmlDin 12x12 11'-0" Clg.
Bed#3 11x11
Bed#2 13x13

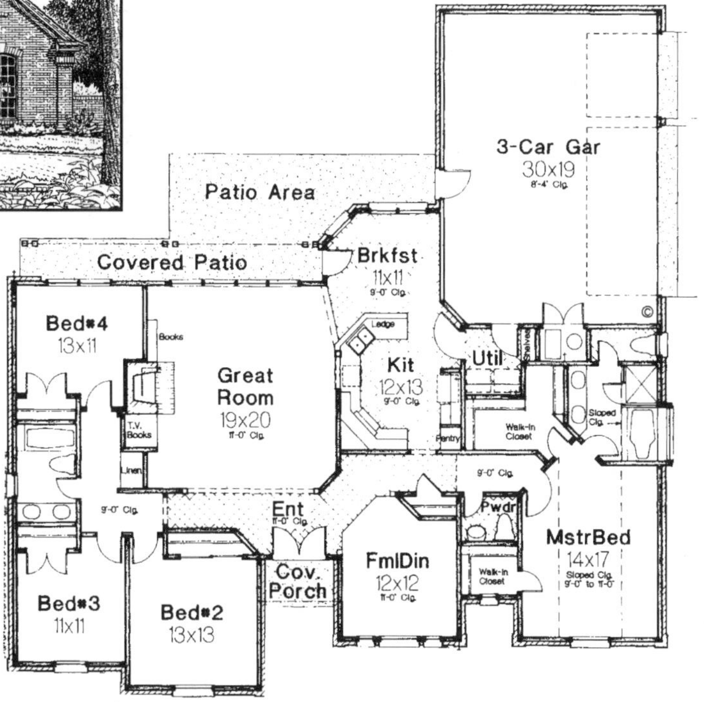

MAIN FLOOR

Design 98557

Units	Single
Price Code	E
Total Finished	2,257 sq. ft.
Main Finished	2,257 sq. ft.
Garage Unfinished	528 sq. ft.
Dimensions	64'7"x77'10"
Foundation	Slab
Bedrooms	3
Full Baths	2
Half Baths	1
Main Ceiling	9'-10'
Max Ridge Height	26'6"
Roof Framing	Stick
Exterior Walls	2x4

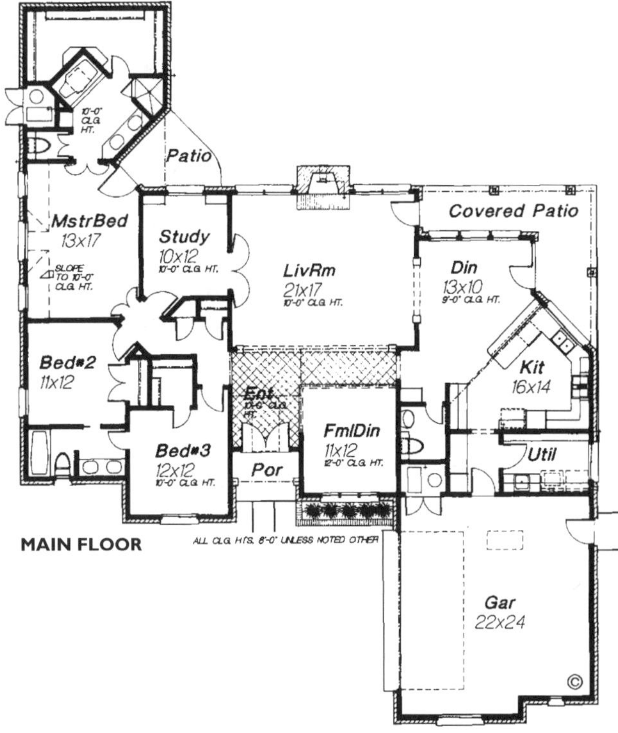
Patio
Covered Patio
MstrBed 13x17
Study 10x12 10'-0" CLG. HT.
LivRm 21x17 10'-0" CLG. HT.
Din 13x10 9'-0" CLG. HT.
Kit 16x14
Bed#2 11x12
Ent
FmlDin 11x12 12'-0" CLG. HT.
Bed#3 12x12 10'-0" CLG. HT.
Por
Util
MAIN FLOOR
ALL CLG. HTS. 8'-0" UNLESS NOTED OTHER
Gar 22x24

Design 65668

Units	Single
Price Code	E
Total Finished	2,259 sq. ft.
Main Finished	2,259 sq. ft.
Dimensions	56'x93'
Foundation	Crawlspace Slab
Bedrooms	3
Full Baths	2
Half Baths	1
Max Ridge Height	32'
Roof Framing	Stick
Exterior Walls	2x6

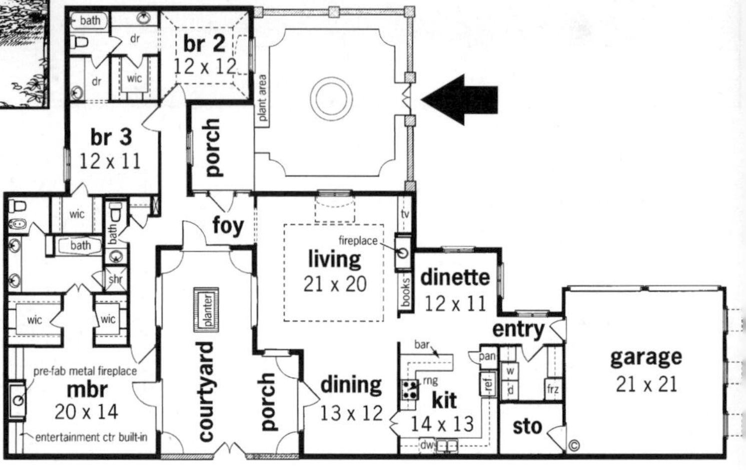

bath
dr
br 2
12 x 12
dr
wic
plant area
br 3
12 x 11
porch
wic
bath
foy
bath
fireplace
living
21 x 20
books
tv
dinette
12 x 11
shr
wic
wic
planter
entry
bar
pan
garage
21 x 21
prefab metal fireplace
mbr
20 x 14
courtyard
porch
dining
13 x 12
rng
kit
14 x 13
ref
w
d
frz
sto
entertainment ctr built-in
dw

MAIN FLOOR

Design 24732

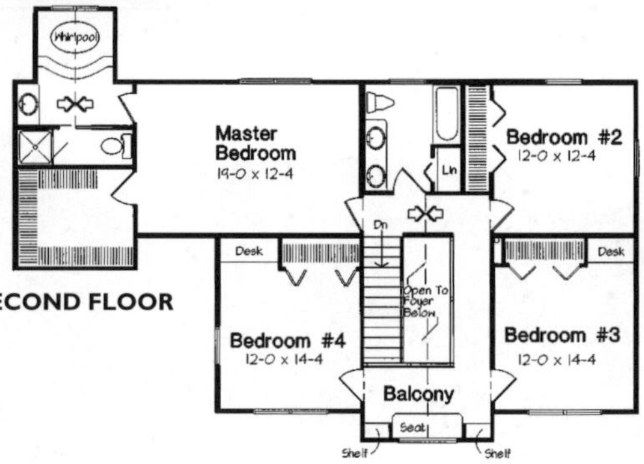

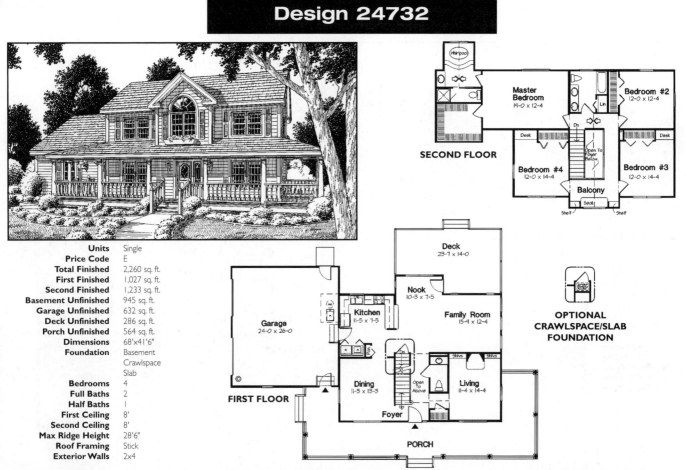

Units	Single
Price Code	E
Total Finished	2,260 sq. ft.
First Finished	1,027 sq. ft.
Second Finished	1,233 sq. ft.
Basement Unfinished	945 sq. ft.
Garage Unfinished	632 sq. ft.
Deck Unfinished	286 sq. ft.
Porch Unfinished	564 sq. ft.
Dimensions	68'x41'6"
Foundation	Basement Crawlspace Slab
Bedrooms	4
Full Baths	2
Half Baths	1
First Ceiling	8'
Second Ceiling	8'
Max Ridge Height	28'6"
Roof Framing	Stick
Exterior Walls	2x4

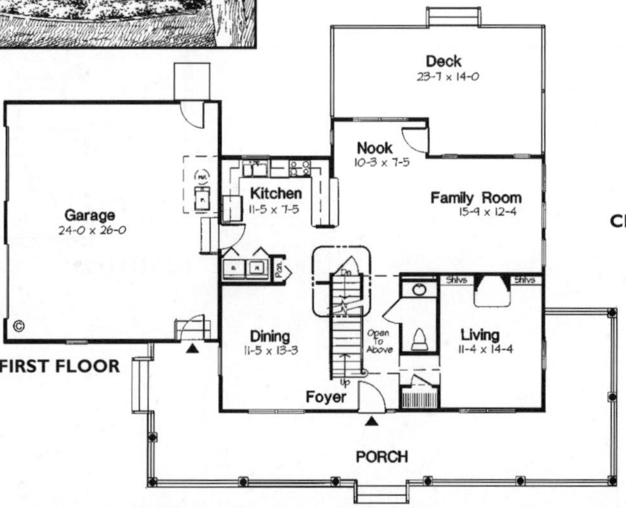

Whirlpool
Master Bedroom
14-0 x 12-4
Bedroom #2
12-0 x 12-4
Lin
Dn
Desk
Desk
Open To Foyer Below
Bedroom #4
12-0 x 14-4
Bedroom #3
12-0 x 14-4
Balcony
Seat
Shelf
Shelf

SECOND FLOOR

Deck
23-7 x 14-0
Nook
10-3 x 7-5
Kitchen
11-5 x 7-5
Family Room
15-4 x 12-4
Garage
24-0 x 26-0
Pan.
Shlvs
Shlvs
Dining
11-5 x 13-3
Open To Above
Living
11-4 x 14-4
Up
Foyer
PORCH

FIRST FLOOR

OPTIONAL CRAWLSPACE/SLAB FOUNDATION

Design 92284

Units	Single
Price Code	E
Total Finished	2,261 sq. ft.
Main Finished	2,261 sq. ft.
Garage Unfinished	640 sq. ft.
Deck Unfinished	124 sq. ft.
Porch Unfinished	280 sq. ft.
Dimensions	82'x54'
Foundation	Basement Slab
Bedrooms	4
Full Baths	2
Half Baths	1
Main Ceiling	10'
Vaulted Ceiling	9'-11'
Max Ridge Height	28'
Roof Framing	Stick
Exterior Walls	2x4

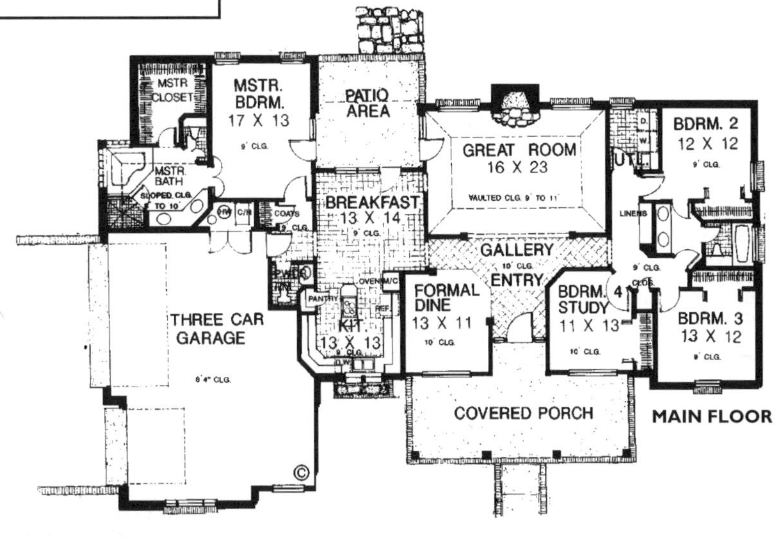
MSTR. CLOSET
MSTR. BDRM. 17 X 13
9' CLG.
PATIO AREA
MSTR BATH
SLOPED CLG. TO 10'
BREAKFAST 13 X 14
9' CLG.
COATS
GREAT ROOM 16 X 23
VAULTED CLG. 9' TO 11'
BDRM. 2 12 X 12
9' CLG.
LINENS
GALLERY
10' CLG.
ENTRY
FORMAL DINE 13 X 11
10' CLG.
BDRM. 4 STUDY 11 X 13
10' CLG.
BDRM. 3 13 X 12
9' CLG.
THREE CAR GARAGE
8'4" CLG.
PANTRY
OVEN/M/C
REF.
KIT 13 X 13
9' CLG.
COVERED PORCH

MAIN FLOOR

Design 90458

Units	Single
Price Code	E
Total Finished	2,263 sq. ft.
First Finished	1,125 sq. ft.
Second Finished	1,138 sq. ft.
Basement Unfinished	1,125 sq. ft.
Porch Unfinished	936 sq. ft.
Dimensions	51'4"x40'
Foundation	Basement Crawlspace
Bedrooms	3
Full Baths	2
Half Baths	1
First Ceiling	8'
Second Ceiling	8'
Max Ridge Height	26'4"
Roof Framing	Stick
Exterior Walls	2x4

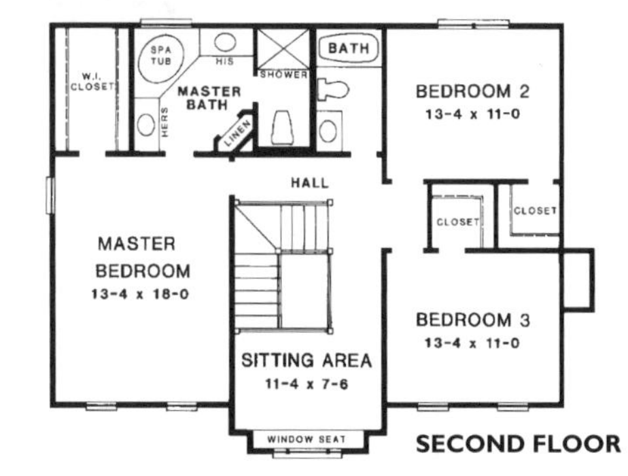
W.I. CLOSET
SPA TUB
HIS
HERS
MASTER BATH
LINEN
SHOWER
BATH
BEDROOM 2
13-4 x 11-0
HALL
CLOSET
CLOSET
MASTER BEDROOM
13-4 x 18-0
BEDROOM 3
13-4 x 11-0
SITTING AREA
11-4 x 7-6
WINDOW SEAT

SECOND FLOOR

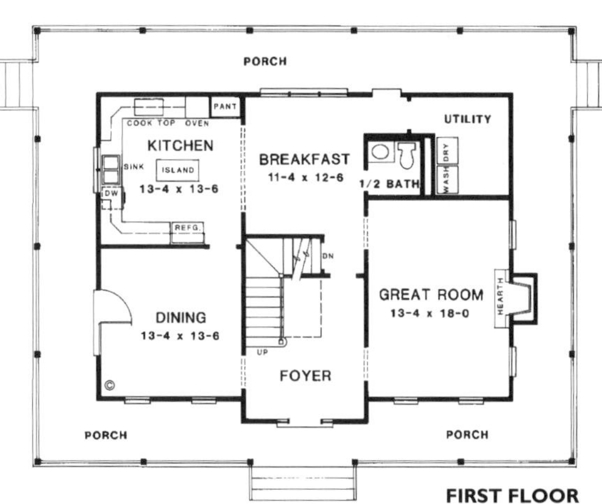
PORCH
PANT
COOK TOP
OVEN
UTILITY
KITCHEN
SINK
ISLAND
13-4 x 13-6
DW
REFG.
BREAKFAST
11-4 x 12-6
1/2 BATH
WASH DRY
DN
DINING
13-4 x 13-6
UP
GREAT ROOM
13-4 x 18-0
HEARTH
FOYER
PORCH
PORCH

FIRST FLOOR

Design 24713

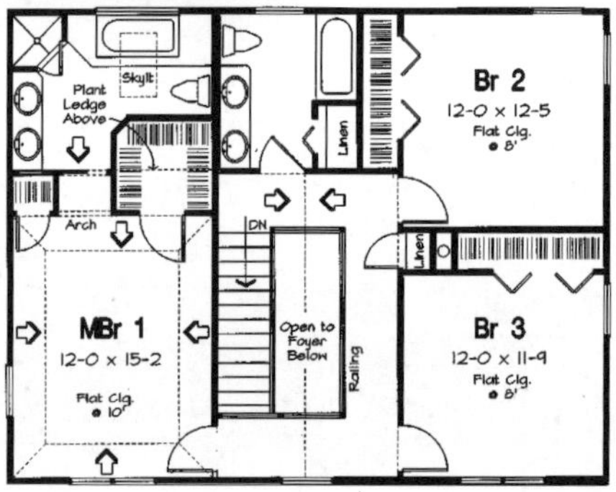

Units	Single
Price Code	E
Total Finished	2,269 sq. ft.
First Finished	1,279 sq. ft.
Second Finished	990 sq. ft.
Basement Unfinished	1,122 sq. ft.
Garage Unfinished	572 sq. ft.
Porch Unfinished	408 sq. ft.
Dimensions	68'x41'6"
Foundation	Basement
Bedrooms	4
Full Baths	3
First Ceiling	8'
Second Ceiling	8'
Vaulted Ceiling	9'
Tray Ceiling	10'
Max Ridge Height	28'9"
Roof Framing	Stick
Exterior Walls	2x4

SECOND FLOOR

FIRST FLOOR

Design 99457

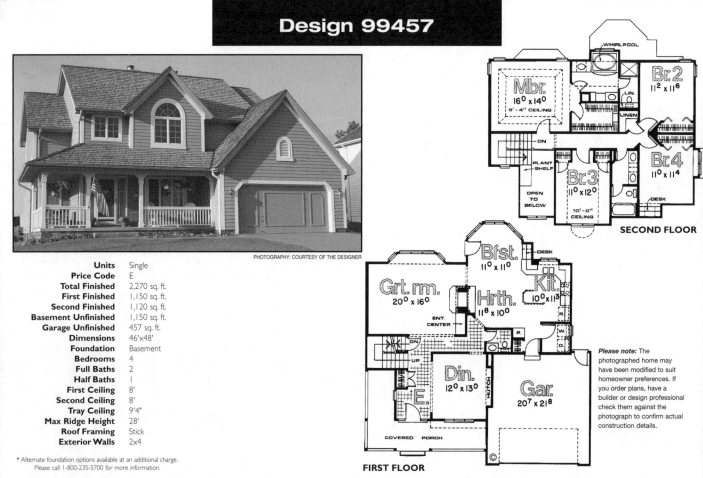

PHOTOGRAPHY: COURTESY OF THE DESIGNER

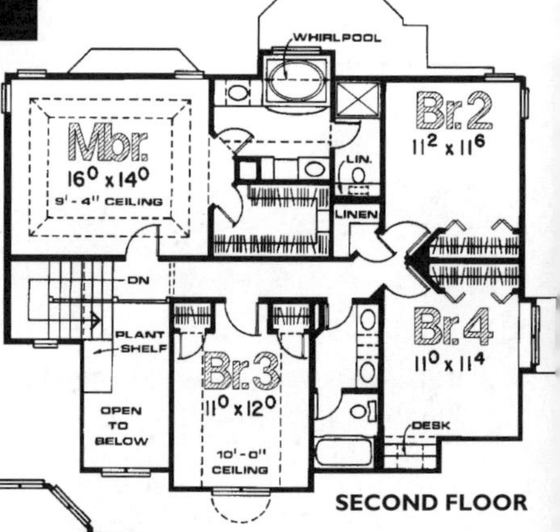

Units	Single
Price Code	E
Total Finished	2,270 sq. ft.
First Finished	1,150 sq. ft.
Second Finished	1,120 sq. ft.
Basement Unfinished	1,150 sq. ft.
Garage Unfinished	457 sq. ft.
Dimensions	46'x48'
Foundation	Basement
Bedrooms	4
Full Baths	2
Half Baths	1
First Ceiling	8'
Second Ceiling	8'
Tray Ceiling	9'4"
Max Ridge Height	28'
Roof Framing	Stick
Exterior Walls	2x4

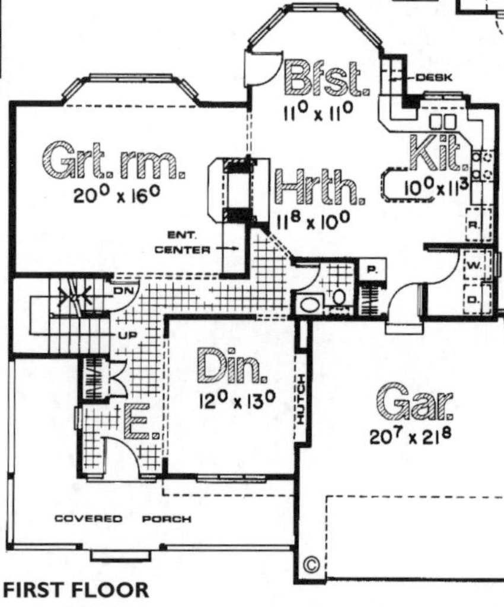

SECOND FLOOR

FIRST FLOOR

Please note: The photographed home may have been modified to suit homeowner preferences. If you order plans, have a builder or design professional check them against the photograph to confirm actual construction details.

* Alternate foundation options available at an additional charge. Please call 1-800-235-5700 for more information.

Design 90485

Units	Single
Price Code	E
Total Finished	2,271 sq. ft.
Main Finished	2,271 sq. ft.
Garage Unfinished	484 sq. ft.
Dimensions	61'6"x57'10"
Foundation	Basement Crawlspace Slab
Bedrooms	4
Full Baths	2
Max Ridge Height	25'4"
Roof Framing	Stick
Exterior	Walls

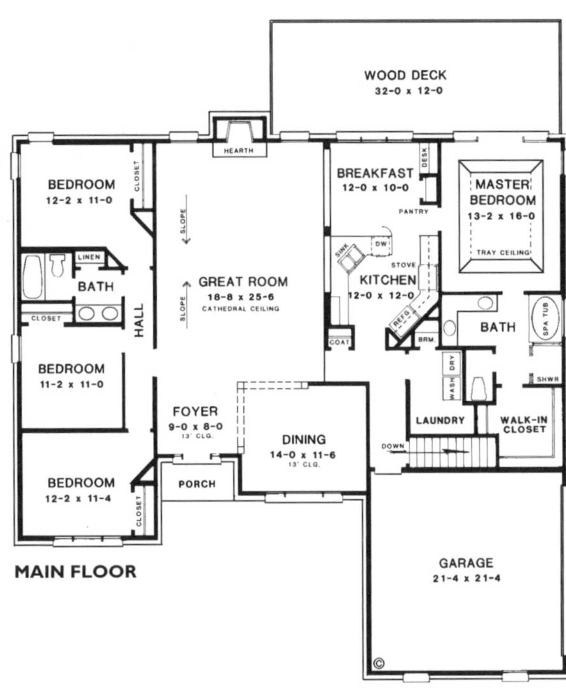
WOOD DECK
32-0 x 12-0
HEARTH
BEDROOM
12-2 x 11-0
CLOSET
BREAKFAST
12-0 x 10-0
DESK
MASTER BEDROOM
13-2 x 16-0
PANTRY
TRAY CEILING
SLOPE
LINEN
BATH
GREAT ROOM
18-8 x 25-6
CATHEDRAL CEILING
SINK
DW
STOVE
KITCHEN
12-0 x 12-0
CLOSET
HALL
REFG
BRM
BATH
SPA TUB
COAT
BEDROOM
11-2 x 11-0
DRY
WASH
SHWR
FOYER
9-0 x 8-0
13' CLG.
LAUNDRY
WALK-IN CLOSET
DINING
14-0 x 11-6
13' CLG.
DOWN
BEDROOM
12-2 x 11-4
PORCH
GARAGE
21-4 x 21-4

MAIN FLOOR

Design 93172

Units	Single
Price Code	E
Total Finished	2,274 sq. ft.
Main Finished	2,274 sq. ft.
Basement Unfinished	2,274 sq. ft.
Porch Unfinished	232 sq. ft.
Dimensions	77'8"x56'
Foundation	Basement
Bedrooms	3
Full Baths	2
Max Ridge Height	24'6"
Roof Framing	Stick
Exterior Walls	2x6

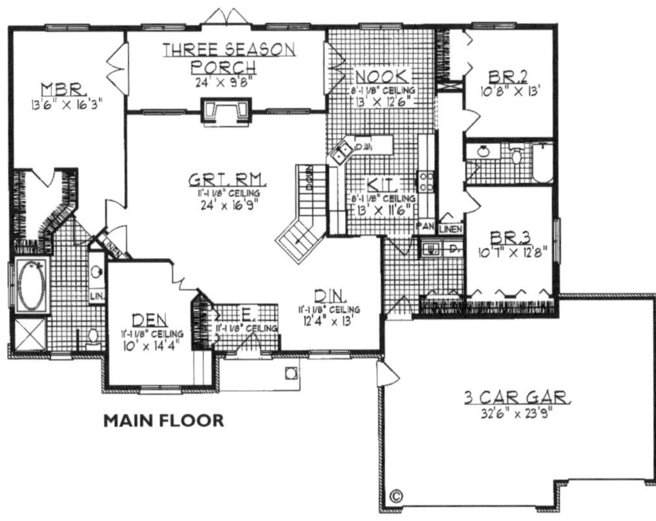
THREE SEASON PORCH
24' x 9'8"
NOOK
8'-1 1/8" CEILING
13' x 12'6"
BR.2
10'8" x 13'
MBR.
13'6" x 16'3"
GRT. RM.
11'-1 1/8" CEILING
24' x 16'9"
KIT.
8'-1 1/8" CEILING
13' x 11'6"
PAN
LINEN
BR.3
10'1" x 12'8"
LIN
DIN.
11'-1 1/8" CEILING
12'4" x 13'
DEN
11'-1 1/8" CEILING
10' x 14'4"
E.
11'-1 1/8" CEILING
3 CAR GAR.
32'6" x 23'9"

MAIN FLOOR

Design 92404

Units	Single
Price Code	E
Total Finished	2,275 sq. ft.
Main Finished	2,275 sq. ft.
Basement Unfinished	2,207 sq. ft.
Garage Unfinished	512 sq. ft.
Dimensions	62'x60'
Foundation	Basement
Bedrooms	3
Full Baths	2
Max Ridge Height	22'
Roof Framing	Stick
Exterior Walls	2x4

DECK
BR.#2 14x11
BREAKFAST
MASTER 14x18
KITCHEN 10x10
FAMILY ROOM 16X18
BR.#3 13x12
DINING 12x13
FOYER
LIVING 13x13
UTILITY
WORKSHOP
GARAGE 22x19

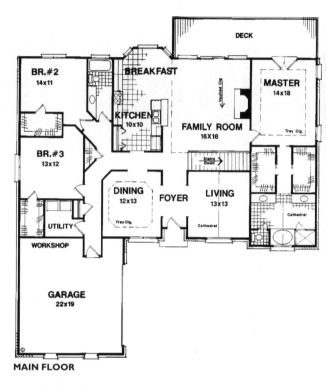

MAIN FLOOR

Design 97737

Units	Single
Price Code	E
Total Finished	2,278 sq. ft.
Main Finished	2,278 sq. ft.
Basement Unfinished	2,278 sq. ft.
Garage Unfinished	540 sq. ft.
Porch Unfinished	41 sq. ft.
Dimensions	59'x57'
Foundation	Basement
Bedrooms	3
Full Baths	1
3/4 Baths	1
Main Ceiling	9'
Max Ridge Height	25'
Roof Framing	Truss
Exterior Walls	2x4

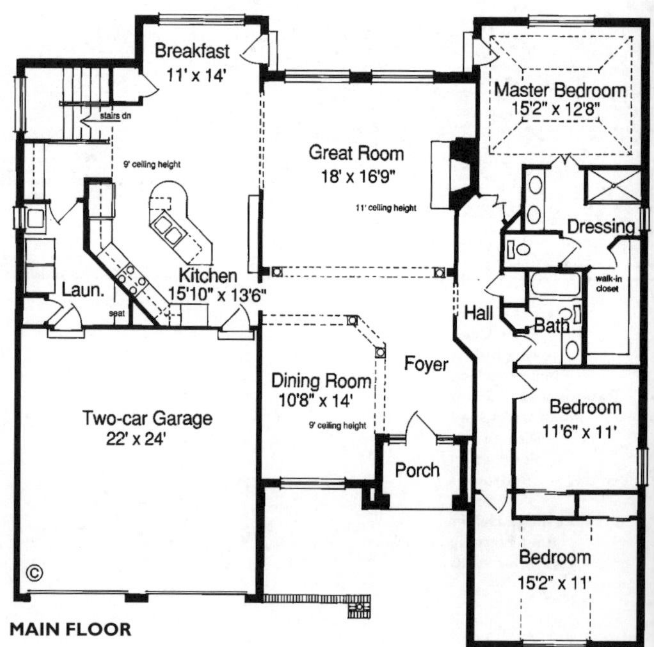
Breakfast 11' x 14'
Master Bedroom 15'2" x 12'8"
Great Room 18' x 16'9"
Dressing
Kitchen 15'10" x 13'6"
Laun.
Hall
Bath
Foyer
Dining Room 10'8" x 14'
Two-car Garage 22' x 24'
Bedroom 11'6" x 11'
Porch
Bedroom 15'2" x 11'

MAIN FLOOR

Design 97833

Units	Single
Price Code	E
Total Finished	2,279 sq. ft.
Main Finished	2,279 sq. ft.
Garage Unfinished	588 sq. ft.
Deck Unfinished	120 sq. ft.
Dimensions	60'x63'7"
Foundation	Slab
Bedrooms	4
Full Baths	2
Half Baths	1
Main Ceiling	8'
Max Ridge Height	27'
Roof Framing	Stick
Exterior Walls	2x4

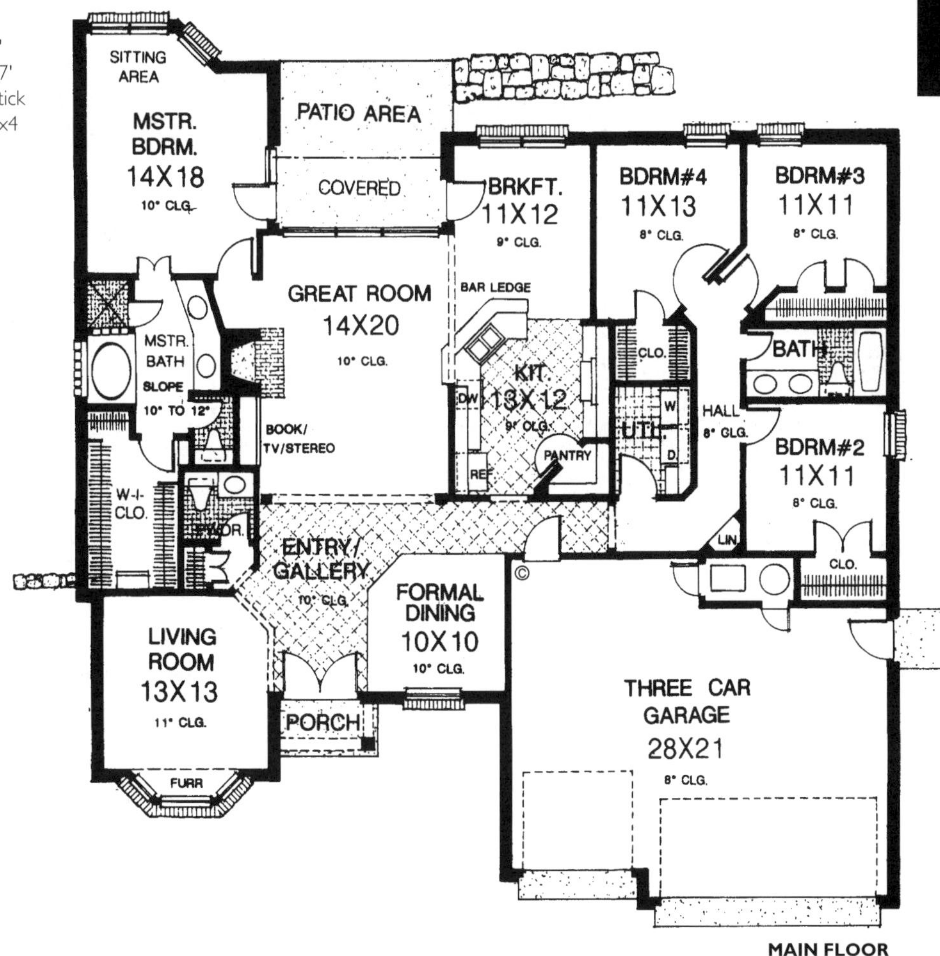
SITTING AREA
MSTR. BDRM. 14X18 10° CLG.
PATIO AREA
COVERED
BRKFT. 11X12 9° CLG.
BDRM#4 11X13 8° CLG.
BDRM#3 11X11 8° CLG.
GREAT ROOM 14X20 10° CLG.
BAR LEDGE
MSTR. BATH SLOPE 10° TO 12°
KIT 13X12 9° CLG.
DW
REF
PANTRY
CLO.
UTIL.
W
D
HALL 8° CLG.
BATH
BDRM#2 11X11 8° CLG.
BOOK/ TV/STEREO
W-I-CLO.
LIN.
ENTRY/ GALLERY 10° CLG.
FORMAL DINING 10X10 10° CLG.
CLO.
LIVING ROOM 13X13 11° CLG.
PORCH
FURR
THREE CAR GARAGE 28X21 8° CLG.

MAIN FLOOR

Design 91796

Units	Single
Price Code	E
Total Finished	2,280 sq. ft.
Main Finished	2,280 sq. ft.
Garage Unfinished	440 sq. ft.
Dimensions	99'6"x66'
Foundation	Basement
Bedrooms	3
Full Baths	1
3/4 Baths	1
Max Ridge Height	17'
Roof Framing	Stick/Truss
Exterior Walls	2x6

MAIN FLOOR

Design 10690

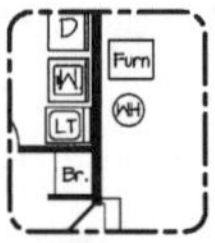

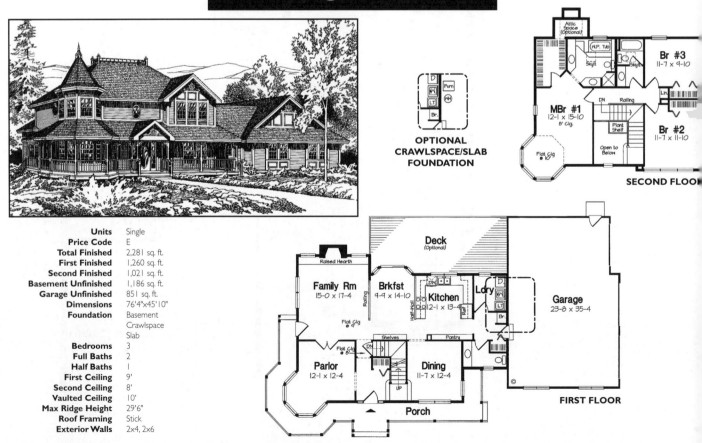

Units	Single
Price Code	E
Total Finished	2,281 sq. ft.
First Finished	1,260 sq. ft.
Second Finished	1,021 sq. ft.
Basement Unfinished	1,186 sq. ft.
Garage Unfinished	851 sq. ft.
Dimensions	76'4"x45'10"
Foundation	Basement Crawlspace Slab
Bedrooms	3
Full Baths	2
Half Baths	1
First Ceiling	9'
Second Ceiling	8'
Vaulted Ceiling	10'
Max Ridge Height	29'6"
Roof Framing	Stick
Exterior Walls	2x4, 2x6

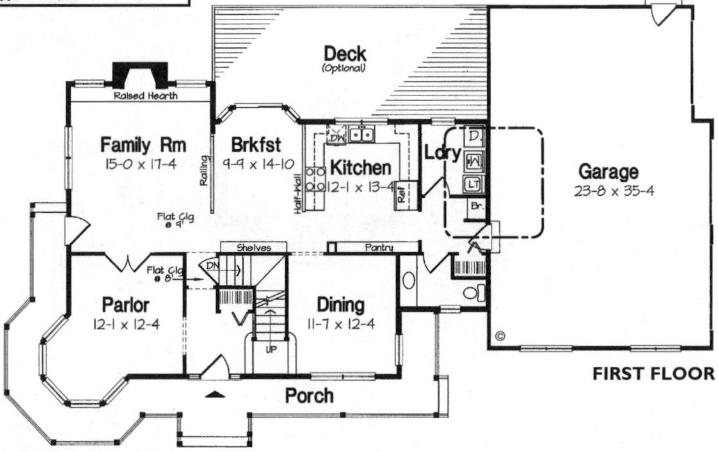

OPTIONAL CRAWLSPACE/SLAB FOUNDATION

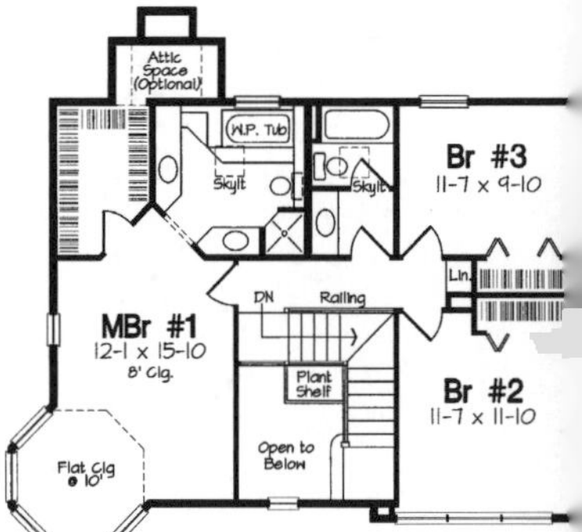

SECOND FLOOR

FIRST FLOOR

Design 69020

Br 4 10-2x 10-8
Br 3 11-7x10-8
MBr 12-8x15-11 vaulted
open to below
Br 2 12-4x10-8
Dn L

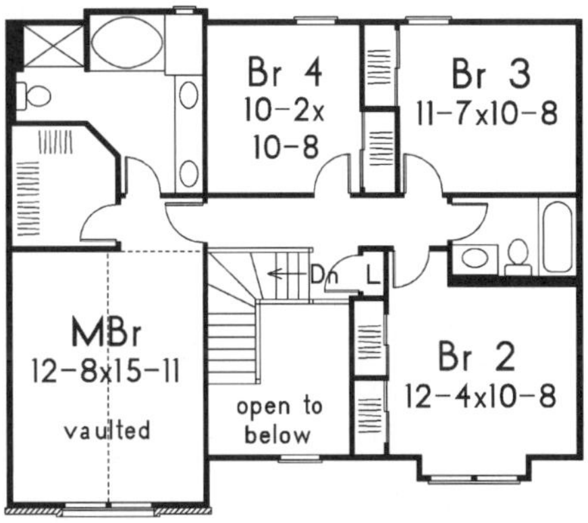

SECOND FLOOR

Hot New Design

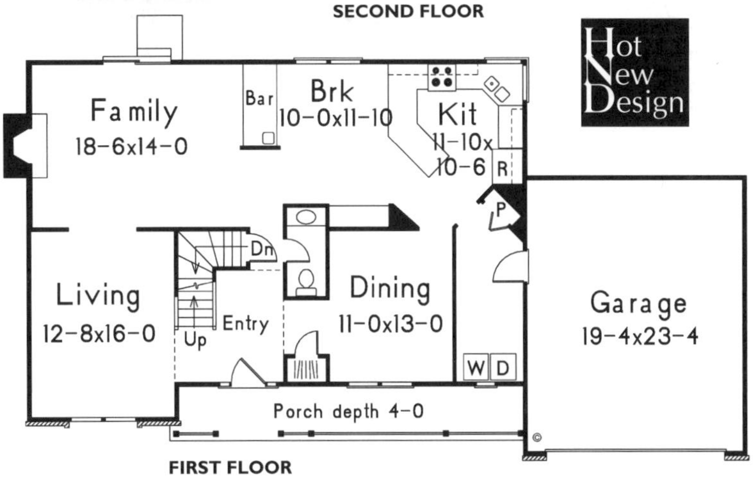

Family 18-6x14-0
Bar
Brk 10-0x11-10
Kit 11-10x 10-6
R
P
Living 12-8x16-0
Dn
Up
Entry
Dining 11-0x13-0
W D
Garage 19-4x23-4
Porch depth 4-0

FIRST FLOOR

Units	Single
Price Code	E
Total Finished	2,286 sq. ft.
First Finished	1,283 sq. ft.
Second Finished	1,003 sq. ft.
Dimensions	64'x34'
Foundation	Basement Crawlspace Slab
Bedrooms	4
Full Baths	2
Half Baths	1
First Ceiling	8'
Second Ceiling	8'
Max Ridge Height	25'6"
Roof Framing	Stick
Exterior Walls	2x4

Design 92449

Units	Single
Price Code	E
Total Finished	2,288 sq. ft.
Main Finished	2,288 sq. ft.
Bonus Unfinished	271 sq. ft.
Garage Unfinished	525 sq. ft.
Dimensions	69'4"x62'9"
Foundation	Basement Crawlspace
Bedrooms	3
Full Baths	2
Half Baths	1
Main Ceiling	9'
Max Ridge Height	22'6"
Exterior Walls	2x4

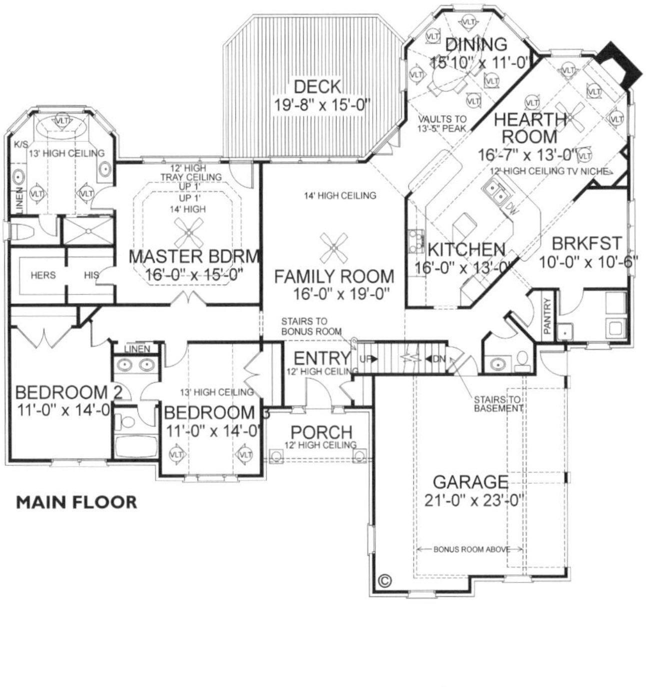

DECK 19'-8" x 15'-0"
DINING 15'10" x 11'-0"
VAULTS TO 13'-5" PEAK
HEARTH ROOM 16'-7" x 13'-0"
12' HIGH CEILING TV NICHE
13' HIGH CEILING
12' HIGH TRAY CEILING UP 1' UP 1' 14' HIGH
MASTER BDRM 16'-0" x 15'-0"
HERS HIS
14' HIGH CEILING
FAMILY ROOM 16'-0" x 19'-0"
KITCHEN 16'-0" x 13'-0"
BRKFST 10'-0" x 10'-6"
PANTRY
STAIRS TO BONUS ROOM
LINEN
ENTRY 12' HIGH CEILING
UP DN
BEDROOM 2 11'-0" x 14'-0"
13' HIGH CEILING
BEDROOM 3 11'-0" x 14'-0"
PORCH 12' HIGH CEILING
STAIRS TO BASEMENT
GARAGE 21'-0" x 23'-0"
BONUS ROOM ABOVE

MAIN FLOOR

Design 96530

Units	Single
Price Code	E
Total Finished	2,289 sq. ft.
Main Finished	2,289 sq. ft.
Garage Unfinished	758 sq. ft.
Dimensions	66'x77'
Foundation	Crawlspace Slab
Bedrooms	3
Full Baths	3
Main Ceiling	8'
Max Ridge Height	22'
Roof Framing	Stick
Exterior Walls	2x4

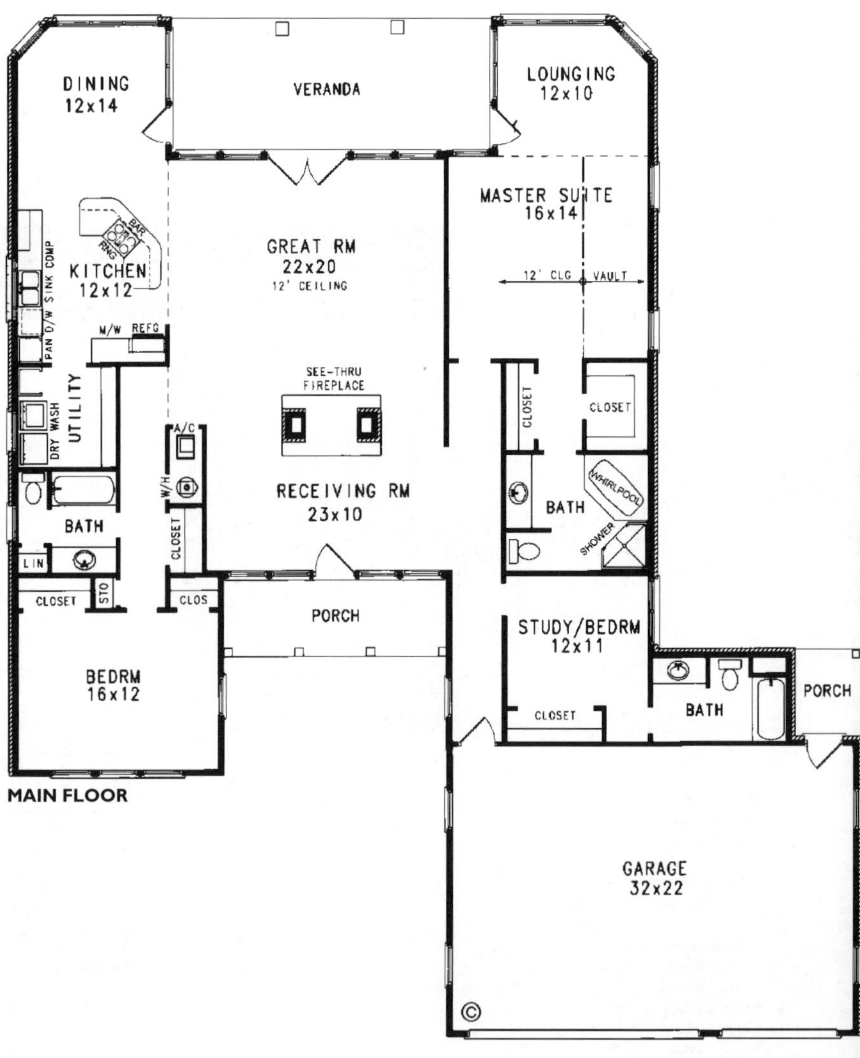
DINING
12x14
VERANDA
LOUNGING
12x10
MASTER SUITE
16x14
GREAT RM
22x20
12' CEILING
KITCHEN
12x12
BAR
RNG
PAN D/W SINK COMP
M/W REFG
UTILITY
DRY WASH
12' CLG VAULT
SEE-THRU
FIREPLACE
CLOSET
CLOSET
A/C
W/H
RECEIVING RM
23x10
WHIRLPOOL
BATH
SHOWER
BATH
LIN
CLOSET
CLOSET
STO
CLOS
PORCH
STUDY/BEDRM
12x11
BEDRM
16x12
BATH
PORCH
CLOSET
GARAGE
32x22
MAIN FLOOR

Design 97234

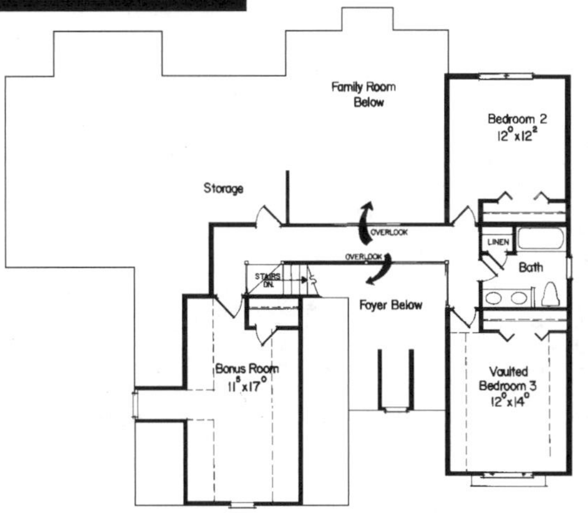

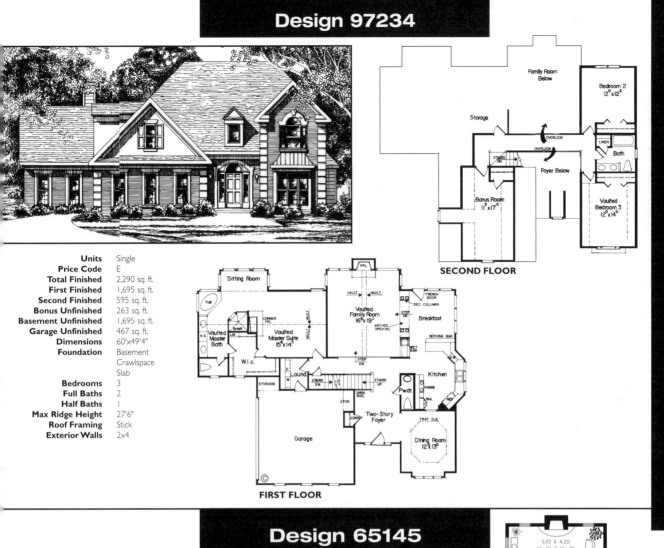

Family Room Below
Bedroom 2 12^0x12^2
Storage
OVERLOOK
LINEN
Bath
STAIRS DN.
Foyer Below
Bonus Room 11^8x17^0
Vaulted Bedroom 3 12^0x14^0

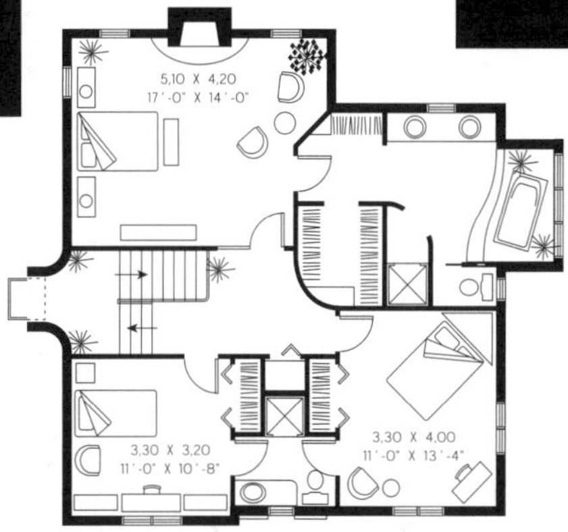

SECOND FLOOR

Units	Single
Price Code	E
Total Finished	2,290 sq. ft.
First Finished	1,695 sq. ft.
Second Finished	595 sq. ft.
Bonus Unfinished	263 sq. ft.
Basement Unfinished	1,695 sq. ft.
Garage Unfinished	467 sq. ft.
Dimensions	60'x49'4"
Foundation	Basement Crawlspace Slab
Bedrooms	3
Full Baths	2
Half Baths	1
Max Ridge Height	27'6"
Roof Framing	Stick
Exterior Walls	2x4

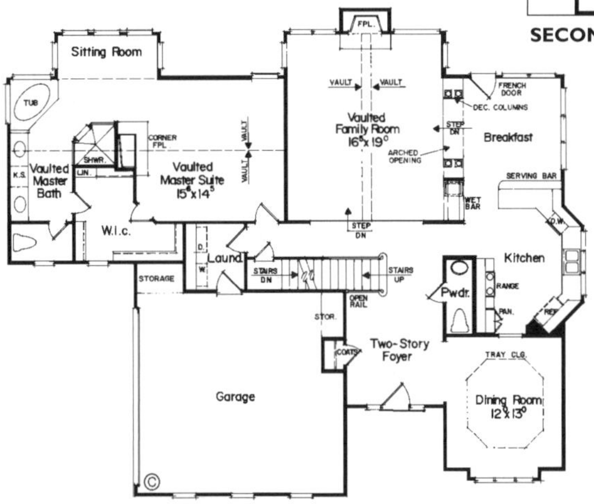

Sitting Room
FPL.
Vaulted Family Room 16^5x19^0
Vaulted Master Suite 15^0x14^5
Vaulted Master Bath
CORNER FPL
Breakfast
Kitchen
W.I.c.
Laund.
STORAGE
STAIRS DN
STAIRS UP
Pwdr.
Two-Story Foyer
Dining Room 12^0x13^0
Garage

FIRST FLOOR

Design 65145

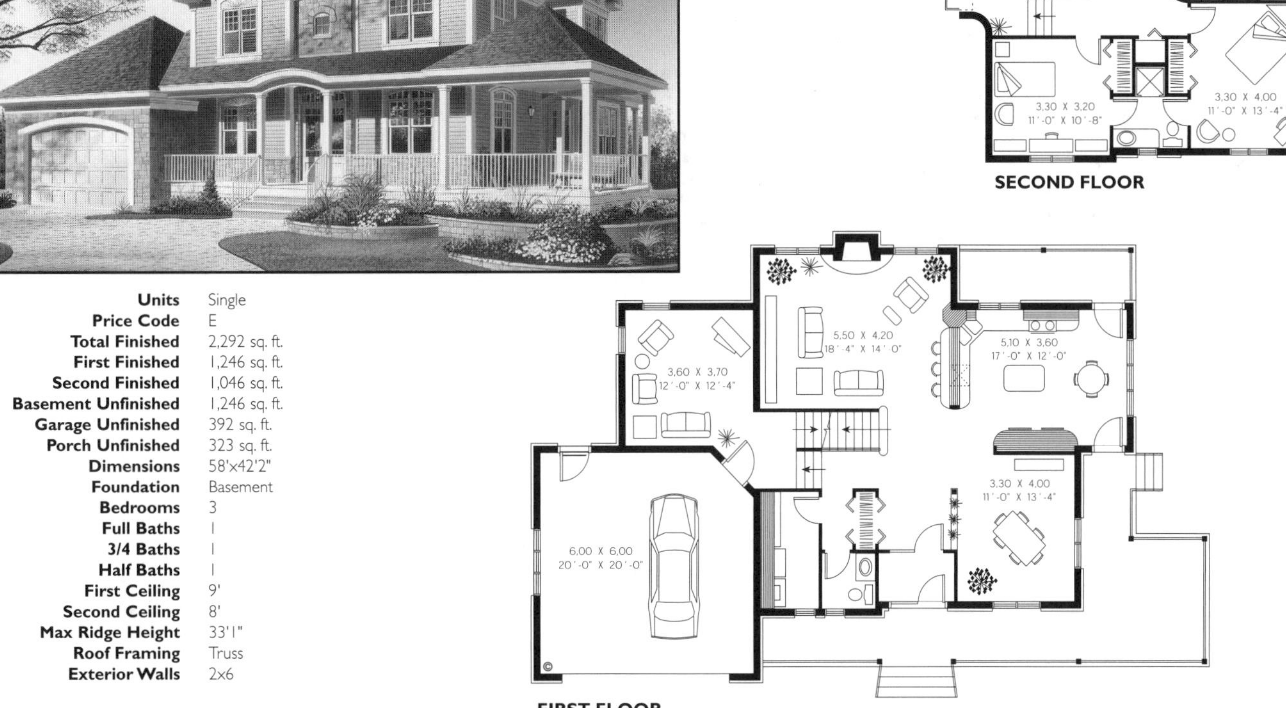
5,50 X 4,20
18'-4" X 14'-0"
3,60 X 3,70
12'-0" X 12'-4"
5,10 X 3,60
17'-0" X 12'-0"
3,30 X 4,00
11'-0" X 13'-4"
6,00 X 6,00
20'-0" X 20'-0"

Units	Single
Price Code	E
Total Finished	2,292 sq. ft.
First Finished	1,246 sq. ft.
Second Finished	1,046 sq. ft.
Basement Unfinished	1,246 sq. ft.
Garage Unfinished	392 sq. ft.
Porch Unfinished	323 sq. ft.
Dimensions	58'x42'2"
Foundation	Basement
Bedrooms	3
Full Baths	1
3/4 Baths	1
Half Baths	1
First Ceiling	9'
Second Ceiling	8'
Max Ridge Height	33'1"
Roof Framing	Truss
Exterior Walls	2x6

5,10 X 4,20
17'-0" X 14'-0"
3,30 X 3,20
11'-0" X 10'-8"
3,30 X 4,00
11'-0" X 13'-4"

SECOND FLOOR

FIRST FLOOR

Design 93049

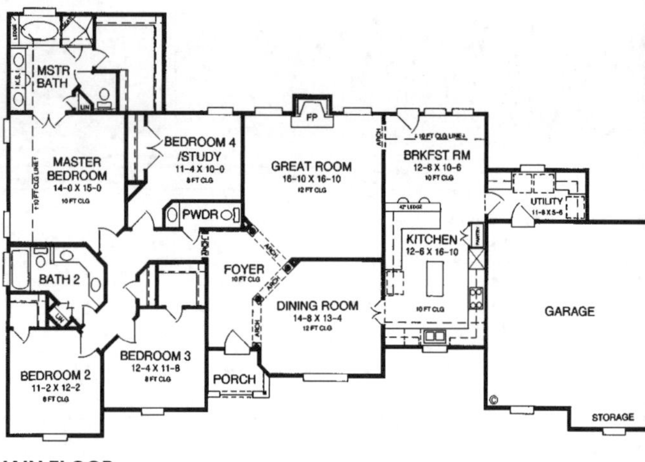

MSTR BATH
MASTER BEDROOM
14-0 X 15-0
10 FT CLG
BEDROOM 4 /STUDY
11-4 X 10-0
8 FT CLG
GREAT ROOM
15-10 X 16-10
12 FT CLG
FP
BRKFST RM
12-6 X 10-6
10 FT CLG
UTILITY
PWDR
KITCHEN
12-6 X 16-10
BATH 2
FOYER
10 FT CLG
DINING ROOM
14-8 X 13-4
12 FT CLG
GARAGE
BEDROOM 3
12-4 X 11-8
8 FT CLG
BEDROOM 2
11-2 X 12-2
8 FT CLG
PORCH
STORAGE

MAIN FLOOR

Units	Single
Price Code	E
Total Finished	2,292 sq. ft.
Main Finished	2,292 sq. ft.
Garage Unfinished	526 sq. ft.
Dimensions	80'7"x50'6"
Foundation	Crawlspace Slab
Bedrooms	4
Full Baths	2
Half Baths	1
Max Ridge Height	22'
Roof Framing	Stick
Exterior Walls	2x4

Design 66109

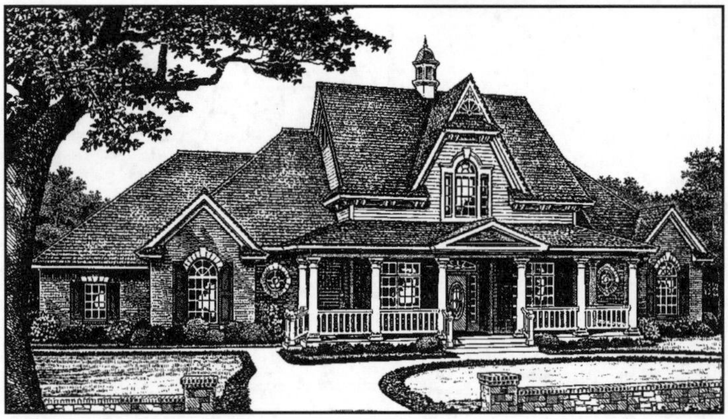

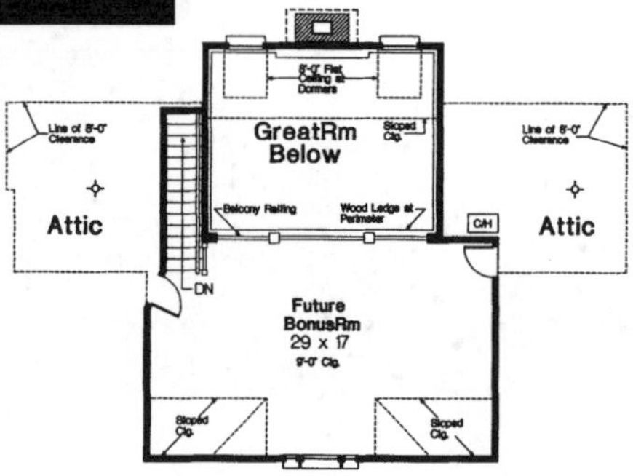

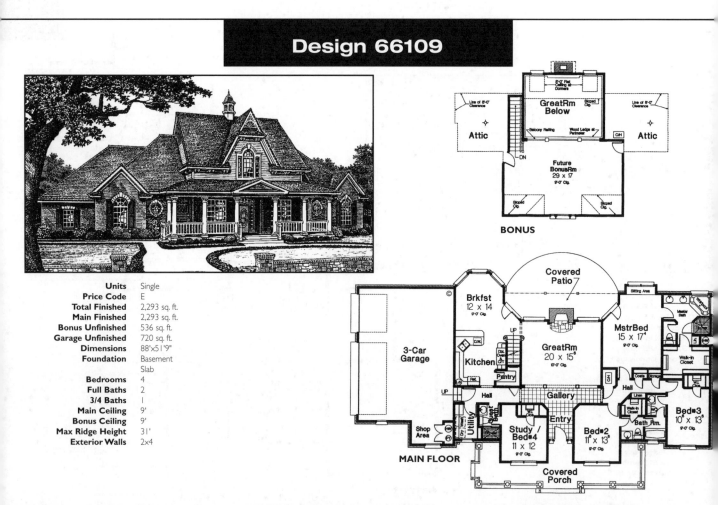

BONUS

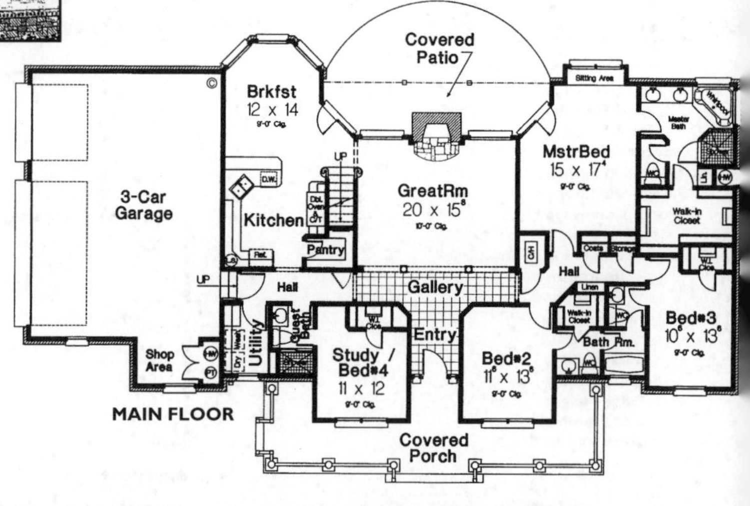

MAIN FLOOR

Units	Single
Price Code	E
Total Finished	2,293 sq. ft.
Main Finished	2,293 sq. ft.
Bonus Unfinished	536 sq. ft.
Garage Unfinished	720 sq. ft.
Dimensions	88'x51'9"
Foundation	Basement Slab
Bedrooms	4
Full Baths	2
3/4 Baths	1
Main Ceiling	9'
Bonus Ceiling	9'
Max Ridge Height	31'
Exterior Walls	2x4

Design 96551

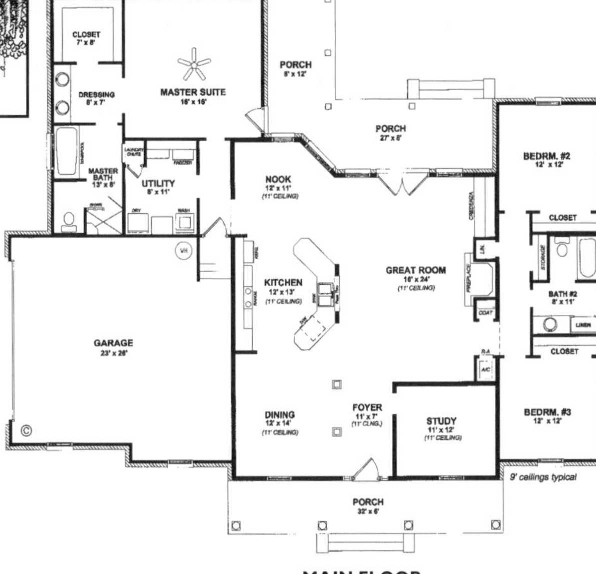
CLOSET
7' x 8'
DRESSING
8' x 7'
MASTER SUITE
16' x 16'
PORCH
8' x 12'
PORCH
27' x 8'
MASTER BATH
13' x 8'
UTILITY
8' x 11'
NOOK
12' x 11'
(11' CEILING)
BEDRM. #2
12' x 12'
CLOSET
KITCHEN
12' x 13'
(11' CEILING)
GREAT ROOM
16' x 24'
(11' CEILING)
BATH #2
8' x 11'
LINEN
CLOSET
GARAGE
23' x 26'
DINING
12' x 14'
(11' CEILING)
FOYER
11' x 7'
(11' CLNG.)
STUDY
11' x 12'
(11' CEILING)
BEDRM. #3
12' x 12'
9' ceilings typical
PORCH
32' x 6'

MAIN FLOOR

Units	Single
Price Code	E
Total Finished	2,296 sq. ft.
Main Finished	2,296 sq. ft.
Garage Unfinished	641 sq. ft.
Porch Unfinished	483 sq. ft.
Dimensions	70'x61'
Foundation	Crawlspace Slab
Bedrooms	3
Full Baths	2
Main Ceiling	9'
Max Ridge Height	26'8"
Roof Framing	Stick
Exterior Walls	2x4, 2x6

Design 65612

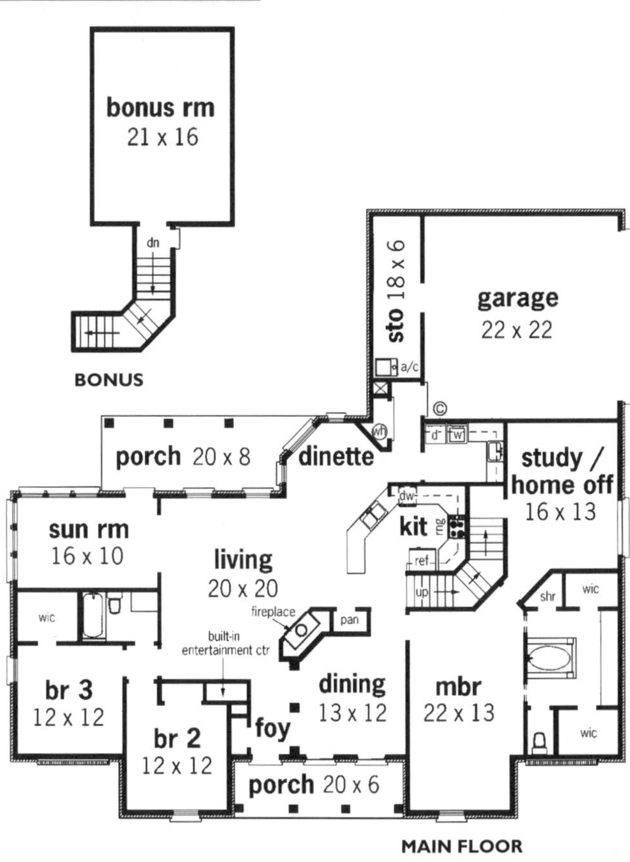
bonus rm
21 x 16
dn
BONUS
sto 18 x 6
garage
22 x 22
a/c
porch 20 x 8
dinette
study / home off
16 x 13
sun rm
16 x 10
kit
living
20 x 20
fireplace
pan
built-in entertainment ctr
wic
shr
wic
br 3
12 x 12
br 2
12 x 12
foy
dining
13 x 12
mbr
22 x 13
wic
porch 20 x 6

MAIN FLOOR

Units	Single
Price Code	E
Total Finished	2,299 sq. ft.
Main Finished	2,299 sq. ft.
Bonus Unfinished	352 sq. ft.
Garage Unfinished	1,040 sq. ft.
Dimensions	68'x64'
Foundation	Basement Crawlspace Slab
Bedrooms	3
Full Baths	2
Main Ceiling	9'-12'
Max Ridge Height	26'
Roof Framing	Stick
Exterior Walls	2x4

Design 90444

UPPER GREAT ROOM
STORAGE
BATH
RAIL
LOFT
21-4 x 12-0
STORAGE
VAULTED CEILING
SECOND FLOOR
GARAGE
21-4 x 22-0
SCREENED PORCH
21-8 x 12-0
UTILITY
DRY
WASH
FREEZ
STORAGE
FURN
HEARTH
REFG.
DW
RANGE
FALSE BEAMS
BREAKFAST
9-8 x 9-6
KITCHEN
11-0 x 13-0
BAR
WET BAR
S.L.
S.L.
GREAT ROOM
21-4 x 17-0
VAULTED CEILING
BEDROOM 2
12-6 x 12-0
DESK
WALK-IN CLOSET
LINEN
PANTRY
GARDEN TUB
BATH
HALL
BATH
DN
UP
LIN.
MASTER BEDROOM
14-4 x 16-0
COATS
WALK-IN CLOSET
BEDROOM 3
12-6 x 12-0
WALK-IN CLOSET
DINING ROOM
12-8 x 12-6
FOYER
HUTCH
DESK
FIRST FLOOR
PORCH

Units	Single
Price Code	E
Total Finished	2,301 sq. ft.
First Finished	1,996 sq. ft.
Second Finished	305 sq. ft.
Dimensions	63'x64'6"
Foundation	Basement Crawlspace
Bedrooms	3
Full Baths	3
Max Ridge Height	22'10"
Roof Framing	Stick
Exterior Walls	2x4

Design 94674

Units	Single
Price Code	E
Total Finished	2,306 sq. ft.
Main Finished	2,306 sq. ft.
Garage Unfinished	538 sq. ft.
Dimensions	57'4"x77'9"
Foundation	Slab
Bedrooms	4
Full Baths	3
Main Ceiling	9'
Max Ridge Height	25'11"
Roof Framing	Stick
Exterior Walls	2x4

Two-Car Garage 21'8"x 23'
Utility
Patio 13'6"x 9'6"
WIC
WIC
Master Bath
Porch 23'6"x 5'6"
Breakfast 13'11"x 10'
Master Bedroom 18'x 13'11"
Living 19'3"x 18'6"
Kitchen 13'11"x 10'
Bath
Bath
WIC
Dining 10'11"x 14'
Foyer
Bedroom 11'x 11'6"
Bedroom 11'x 12'7"
Bedroom 11'4"x 11'
Porch

MAIN FLOOR

Design 94947

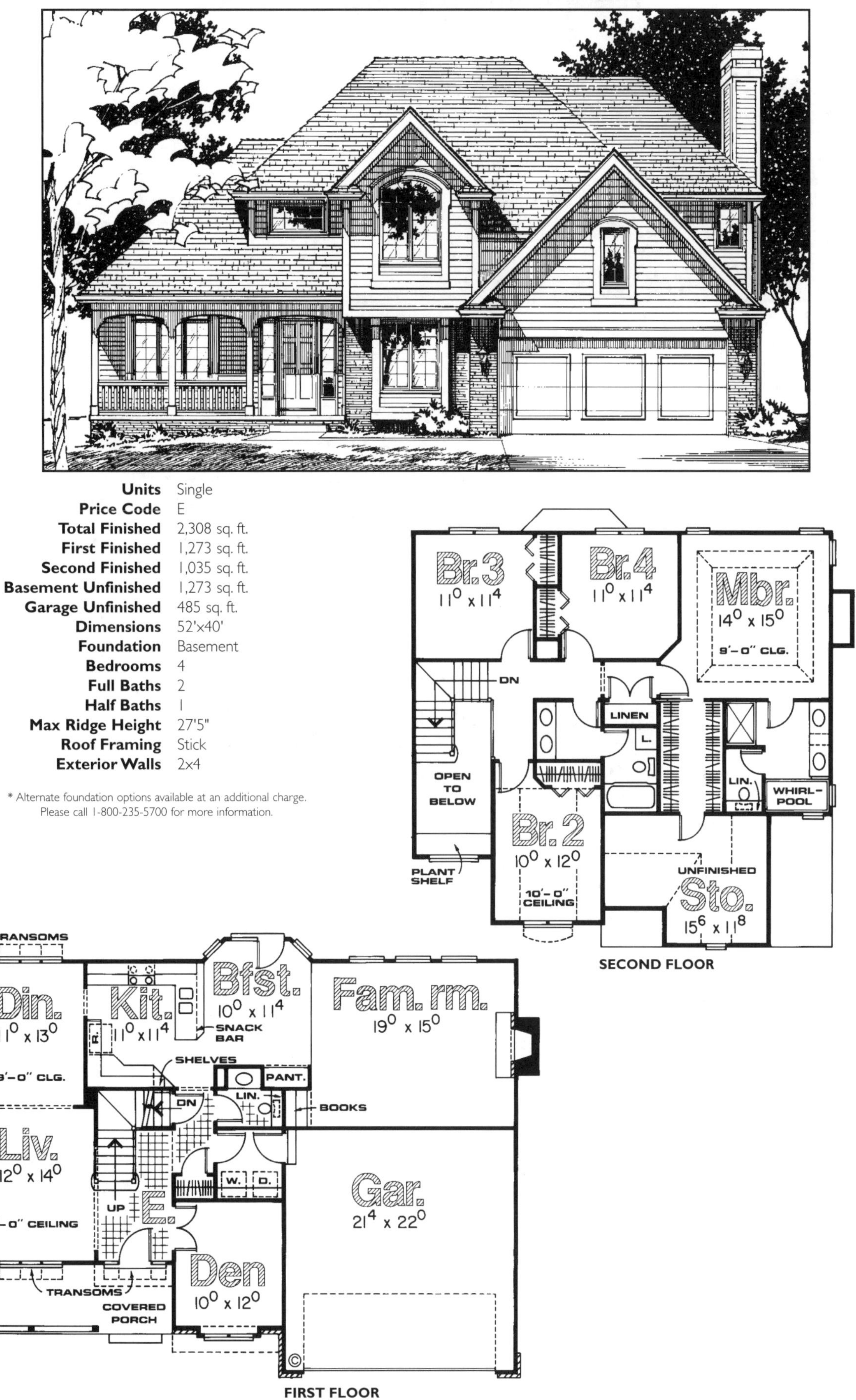
Br.3
11^0 x 11^4
Br.4
11^0 x 11^4
Mbr.
14^0 x 15^0
9'-0" CLG.
DN
LINEN
L
LIN.
WHIRL-POOL
OPEN TO BELOW
PLANT SHELF
Br.2
10^0 x 12^0
10'-0" CEILING
UNFINISHED
Sto.
15^6 x 11^8
SECOND FLOOR
TRANSOMS
Din.
11^0 x 13^0
9'-0" CLG.
HUTCH
Kit.
11^0 x 11^4
R.
Bfst.
10^0 x 11^4
SNACK BAR
Fam. rm.
19^0 x 15^0
SHELVES
PANT.
DN
LIN.
BOOKS
Liv.
12^0 x 14^0
9'-0" CEILING
UP
E.
W.
D.
Gar.
21^4 x 22^0
TRANSOMS
COVERED PORCH
Den
10^0 x 12^0
FIRST FLOOR

Units	Single
Price Code	E
Total Finished	2,308 sq. ft.
First Finished	1,273 sq. ft.
Second Finished	1,035 sq. ft.
Basement Unfinished	1,273 sq. ft.
Garage Unfinished	485 sq. ft.
Dimensions	52'x40'
Foundation	Basement
Bedrooms	4
Full Baths	2
Half Baths	1
Max Ridge Height	27'5"
Roof Framing	Stick
Exterior Walls	2x4

* Alternate foundation options available at an additional charge. Please call 1-800-235-5700 for more information.

Design 65416

Units	Single
Price Code	E
Total Finished	2,310 sq. ft.
First Finished	1,255 sq. ft.
Second Finished	1,055 sq. ft.
Basement Unfinished	1,255 sq. ft.
Garage Unfinished	452 sq. ft.
Deck Unfinished	60 sq. ft.
Porch Unfinished	24 sq. ft.
Dimensions	55'x43'
Foundation	Basement
Bedrooms	3
Full Baths	1
3/4 Baths	1
First Ceiling	9'
Second Ceiling	8'
Max Ridge Height	33'10"
Roof Framing	Truss
Exterior Walls	2x6

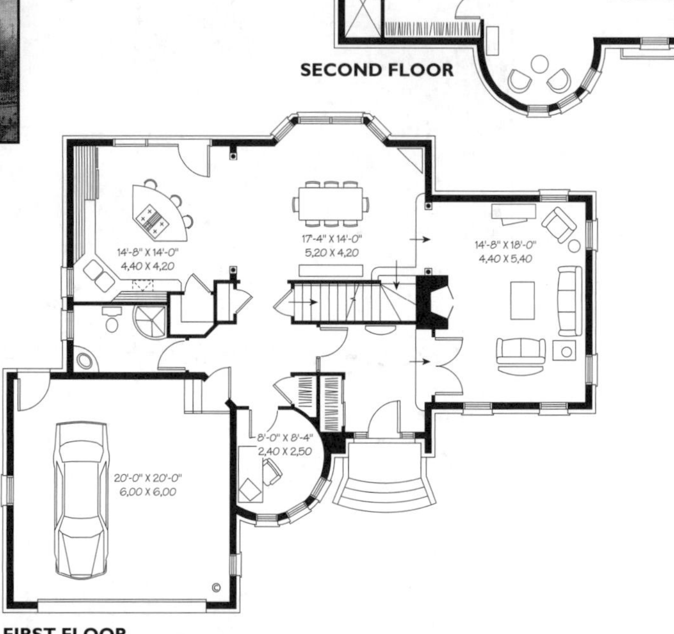
11'-0" X 12'-0"
3,30 X 3,60
11'-0" X 12'-0"
3,30 X 3,60
19'-8" X 14'-0"
5,90 X 4,20
SECOND FLOOR
14'-8" X 14'-0"
4,40 X 4,20
17'-4" X 14'-0"
5,20 X 4,20
14'-8" X 18'-0"
4,40 X 5,40
8'-0" X 8'-4"
2,40 X 2,50
20'-0" X 20'-0"
6,00 X 6,00
FIRST FLOOR

Design 97503

Units	Single
Price Code	E
Total Finished	2,310 sq. ft.
Main Finished	2,310 sq. ft.
Garage Unfinished	638 sq. ft.
Dimensions	54'6"x97'7"
Foundation	Slab
Bedrooms	3
Full Baths	2
Half Baths	1
Max Ridge Height	25'10"
Roof Framing	Stick
Exterior Walls	2x4

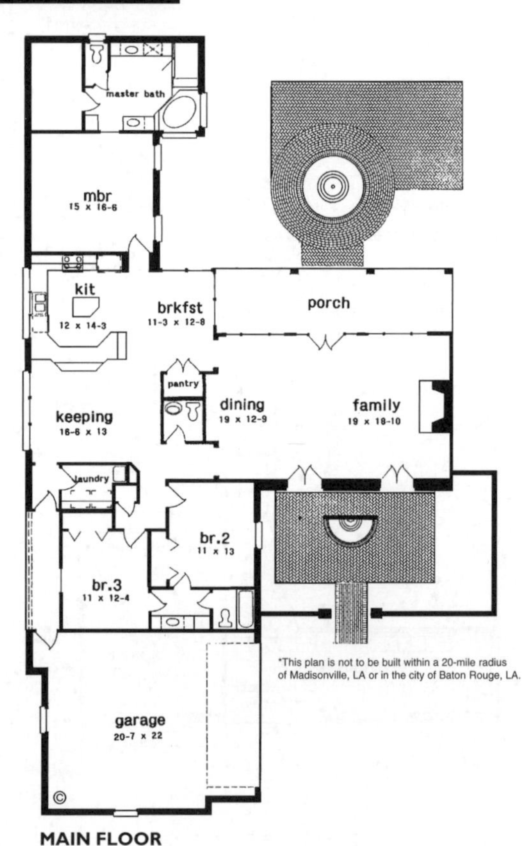
master bath
mbr
15 x 16-6
kit
12 x 14-3
brkfst
11-3 x 12-8
porch
pantry
dining
19 x 12-9
family
19 x 18-10
keeping
16-6 x 13
laundry
br.2
11 x 13
br.3
11 x 12-4
*This plan is not to be built within a 20-mile radius of Madisonville, LA or in the city of Baton Rouge, LA.
garage
20-7 x 22
MAIN FLOOR

Design 97246

Units	Single
Price Code	E
Total Finished	2,311 sq. ft.
Main Finished	2,311 sq. ft.
Bonus Unfinished	425 sq. ft.
Basement Unfinished	2,311 sq. ft.
Garage Unfinished	500 sq. ft.
Dimensions	61'x65'4"
Foundation	Basement Crawlspace
Bedrooms	4
Full Baths	2
Half Baths	1
Main Ceiling	9'
Second Ceiling	8'
Max Ridge Height	26'8"
Roof Framing	Stick
Exterior Walls	2x4

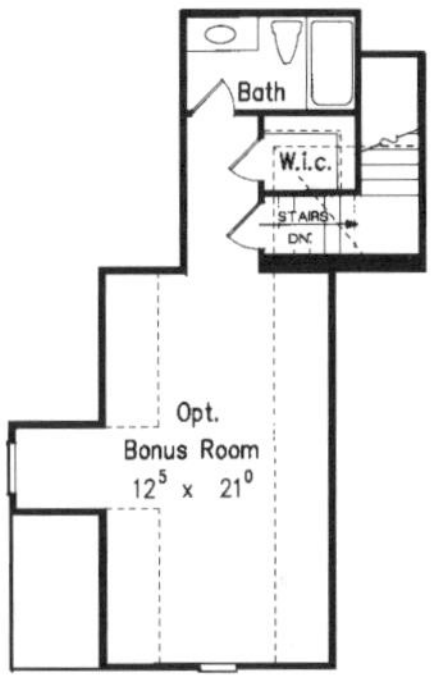

BONUS

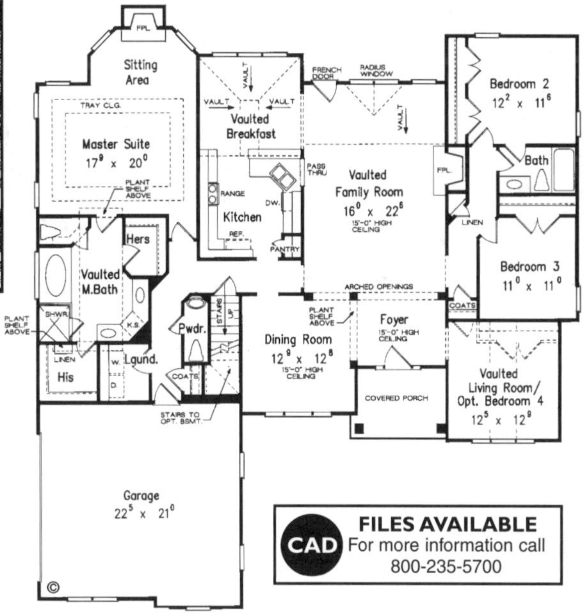

MAIN FLOOR

CAD FILES AVAILABLE
For more information call
800-235-5700

Design 98571

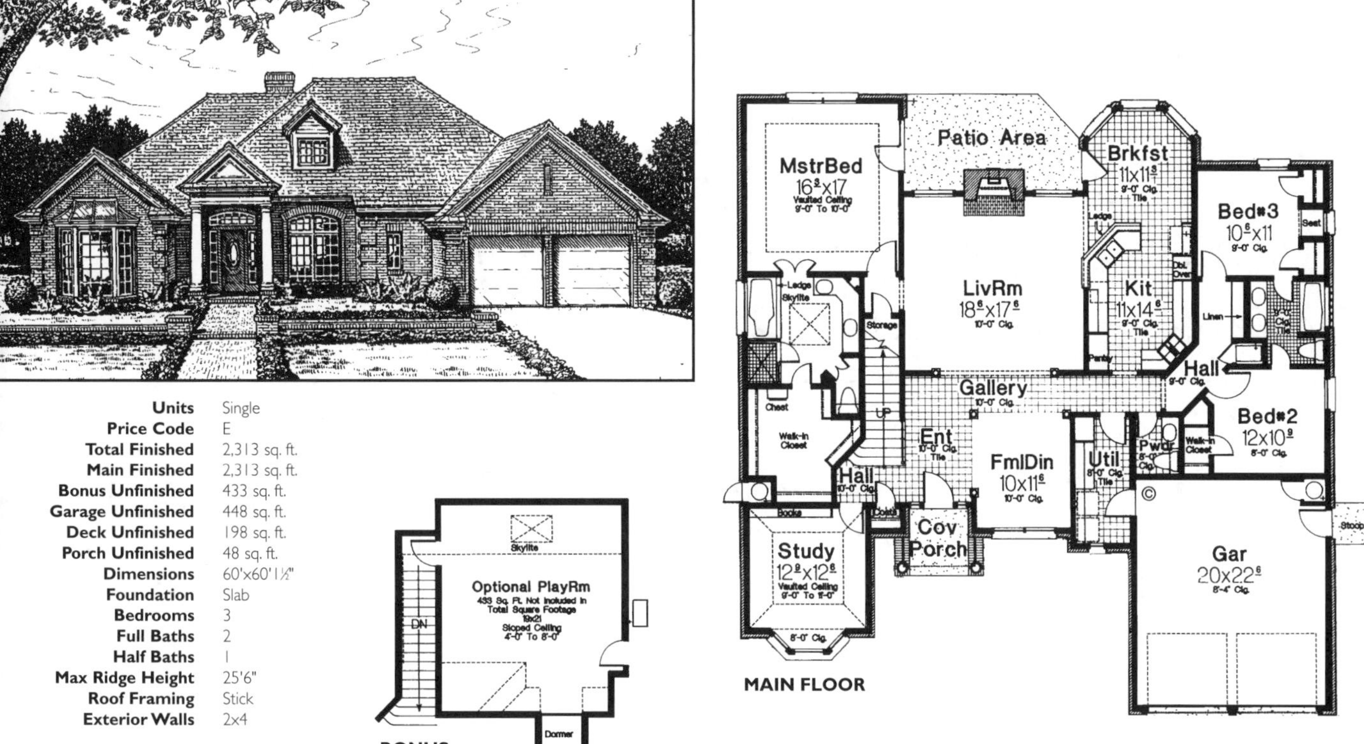

MstrBed
16⁸x17
Patio Area
Brkfst
11x11⁸
Bed#3
10⁸x11
LivRm
18⁸x17⁶
Kit
11x14⁶
Gallery
Hall
Bed#2
12x10⁹
Ent
FmlDin
10x11⁶
Util
Pwdr
Study
12⁸x12⁶
Cov Porch
Gar
20x22⁶
Optional PlayRm

Units	Single
Price Code	E
Total Finished	2,313 sq. ft.
Main Finished	2,313 sq. ft.
Bonus Unfinished	433 sq. ft.
Garage Unfinished	448 sq. ft.
Deck Unfinished	198 sq. ft.
Porch Unfinished	48 sq. ft.
Dimensions	60'x60'1½"
Foundation	Slab
Bedrooms	3
Full Baths	2
Half Baths	1
Max Ridge Height	25'6"
Roof Framing	Stick
Exterior Walls	2x4

BONUS

MAIN FLOOR

Design 92646

Units	Single
Price Code	E
Total Finished	2,320 sq. ft.
First Finished	1,595 sq. ft.
Second Finished	725 sq. ft.
Basement Unfinished	1,471 sq. ft.
Garage Unfinished	409 sq. ft.
Dimensions	61'x41'8"
Foundation	Basement
Bedrooms	4
Full Baths	2
Half Baths	1
First Ceiling	8'
Second Ceiling	8'
Max Ridge Height	29'3"
Roof Framing	Truss
Exterior Walls	2x4

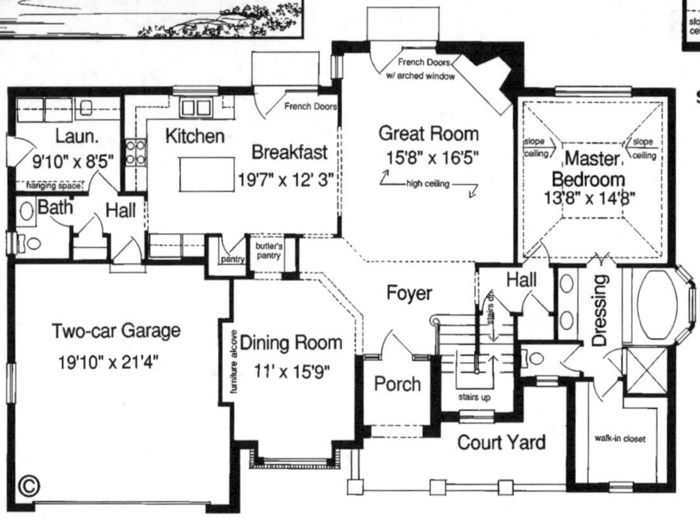

SECOND FLOOR

FIRST FLOOR

Design 97504

Units	Single
Price Code	E
Total Finished	2,322 sq. ft.
Main Finished	2,322 sq. ft.
Garage Unfinished	484 sq. ft.
Porch Unfinished	100 sq. ft.
Dimensions	68'11"x74'
Foundation	Slab
Bedrooms	4
Full Baths	2
Half Baths	1
Main Ceiling	9'-12'
Max Ridge Height	30'
Roof Framing	Stick
Exterior Walls	2x4

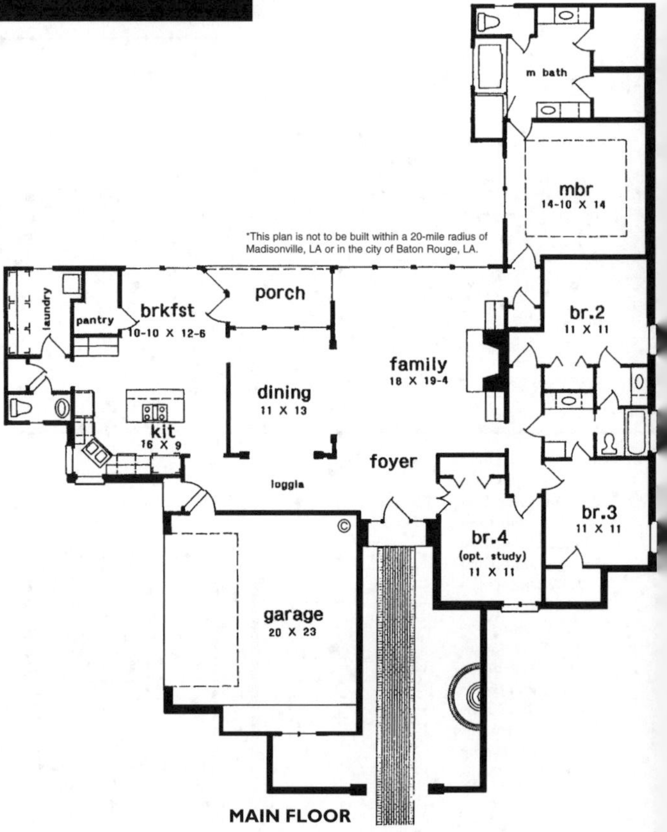

*This plan is not to be built within a 20-mile radius of Madisonville, LA or in the city of Baton Rouge, LA.

MAIN FLOOR

Design 97621

Units	Single
Price Code	E
Total Finished	2,322 sq. ft.
Main Finished	2,322 sq. ft.
Basement Unfinished	2,322 sq. ft.
Garage Unfinished	453 sq. ft.
Dimensions	62'x61'
Foundation	Basement Crawlspace Slab
Bedrooms	3
Full Baths	2
Half Baths	1
Main Ceiling	9'
Max Ridge Height	30'
Roof Framing	Stick
Exterior Walls	2x4

CAD FILES AVAILABLE
For more information call
800-235-5700

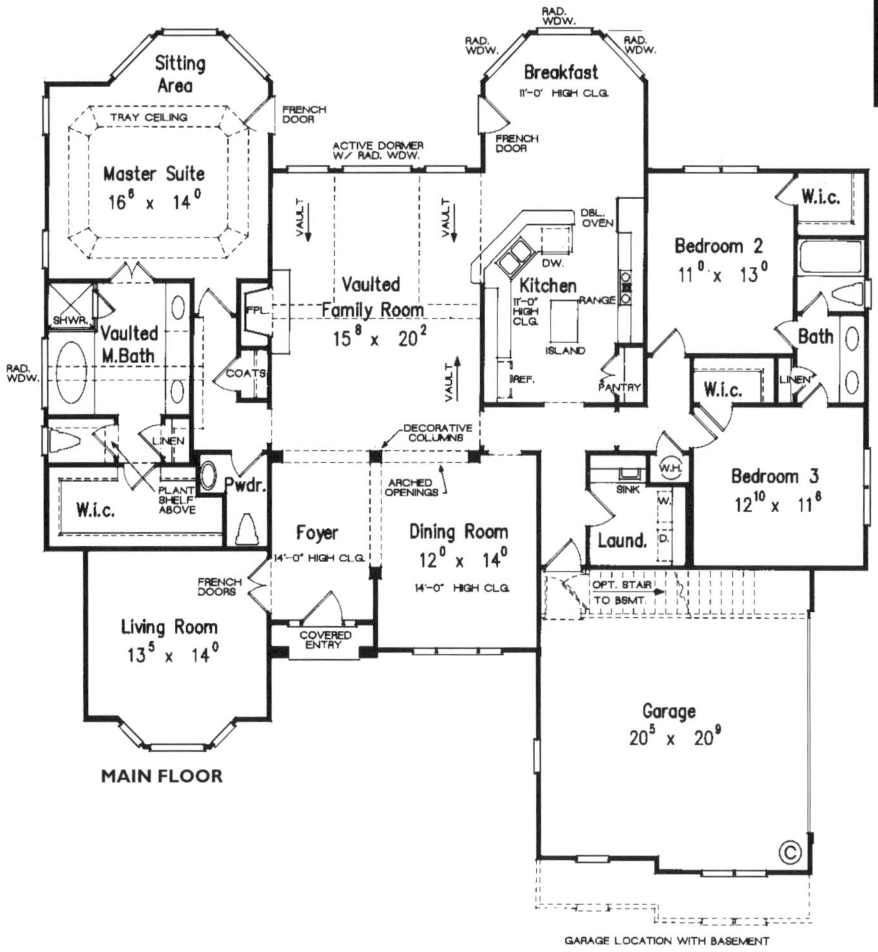

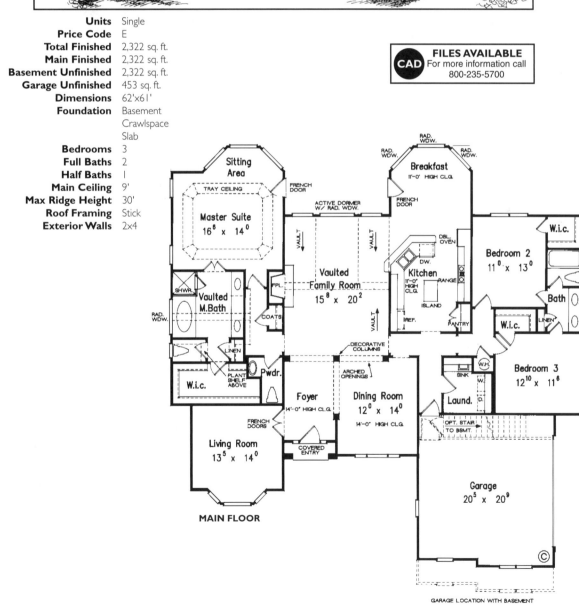

Sitting Area
Master Suite 16^6 x 14^0
TRAY CEILING
FRENCH DOOR
Vaulted M.Bath
SHWR.
RAD. WDW.
LINEN
W.i.c.
PLANT SHELF ABOVE
Pwdr.
COATS
FPL.
ACTIVE DORMER W/ RAD. WDW.
Vaulted Family Room 15^8 x 20^2
VAULT
DECORATIVE COLUMNS
Breakfast 11'-0" HIGH CLG.
RAD. WDW.
FRENCH DOOR
Kitchen 11'-0" HIGH CLG.
DBL. OVEN
DW.
RANGE
ISLAND
REF.
PANTRY
Bedroom 2 11^0 x 13^0
W.i.c.
Bath
LINEN
W.i.c.
Bedroom 3 12^{10} x 11^8
W.H.
SINK
Laund.
OPT. STAIR TO BSMT.
Foyer 14'-0" HIGH CLG.
ARCHED OPENINGS
Dining Room 12^0 x 14^0 14'-0" HIGH CLG.
FRENCH DOORS
Living Room 13^5 x 14^0
COVERED ENTRY
Garage 20^5 x 20^9
GARAGE LOCATION WITH BASEMENT

MAIN FLOOR

Design 69138

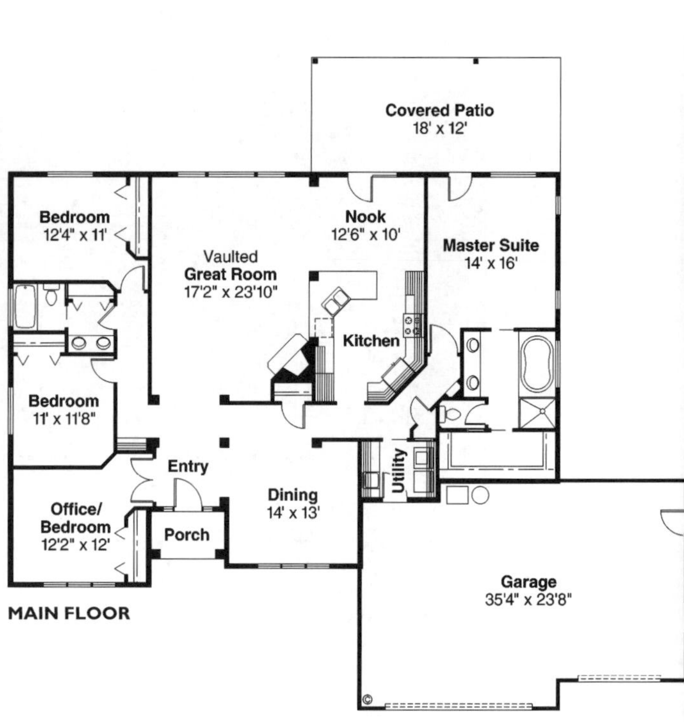
Covered Patio
18' x 12'
Bedroom
12'4" x 11'
Vaulted
Great Room
17'2" x 23'10"
Nook
12'6" x 10'
Master Suite
14' x 16'
Kitchen
Bedroom
11' x 11'8"
Entry
Utility
Dining
14' x 13'
Office/
Bedroom
12'2" x 12'
Porch
Garage
35'4" x 23'8"
MAIN FLOOR

Units	Single
Price Code	E
Total Finished	2,326 sq. ft.
Main Finished	2,326 sq. ft.
Garage Unfinished	808 sq. ft.
Dimensions	74'x69'
Foundation	Crawlspace
Bedrooms	4
Full Baths	2
Main Ceiling	9'
Vaulted Ceiling	15'
Max Ridge Height	21'
Roof Framing	Truss
Exterior Walls	2x6

Design 94633

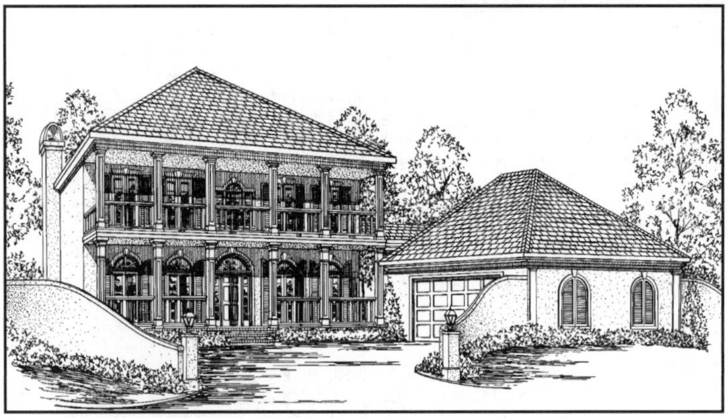

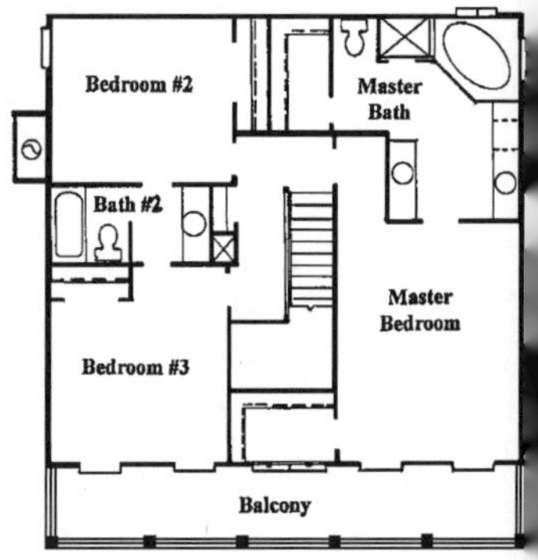

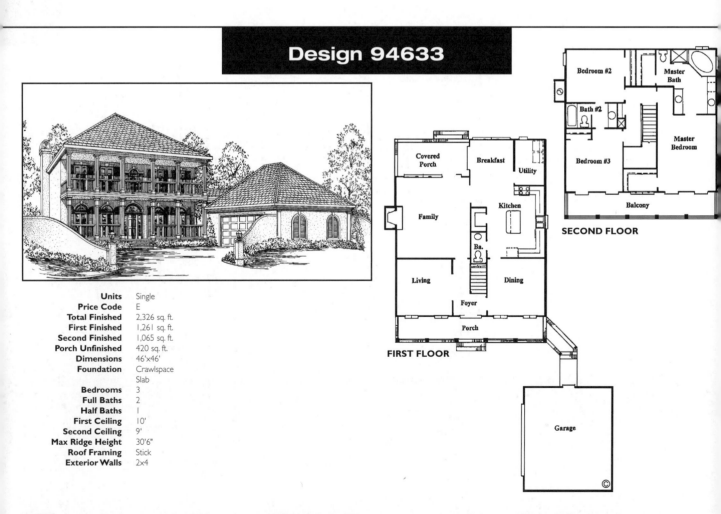

SECOND FLOOR

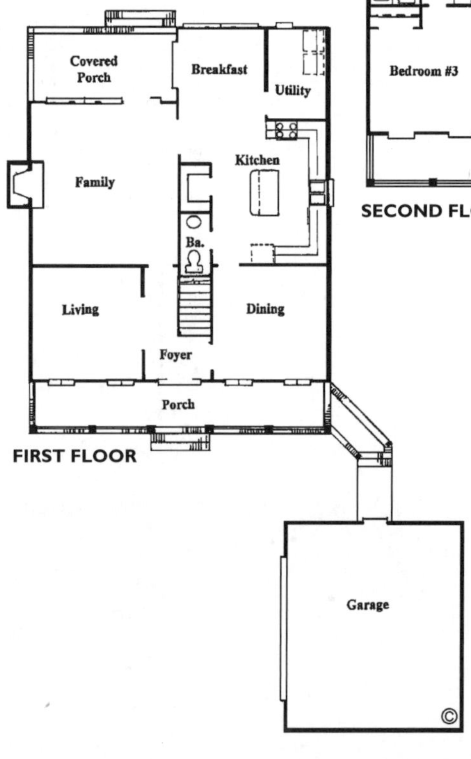

FIRST FLOOR

Units	Single
Price Code	E
Total Finished	2,326 sq. ft.
First Finished	1,261 sq. ft.
Second Finished	1,065 sq. ft.
Porch Unfinished	420 sq. ft.
Dimensions	46'x46'
Foundation	Crawlspace Slab
Bedrooms	3
Full Baths	2
Half Baths	1
First Ceiling	10'
Second Ceiling	9'
Max Ridge Height	30'6"
Roof Framing	Stick
Exterior Walls	2x4

Design 96820

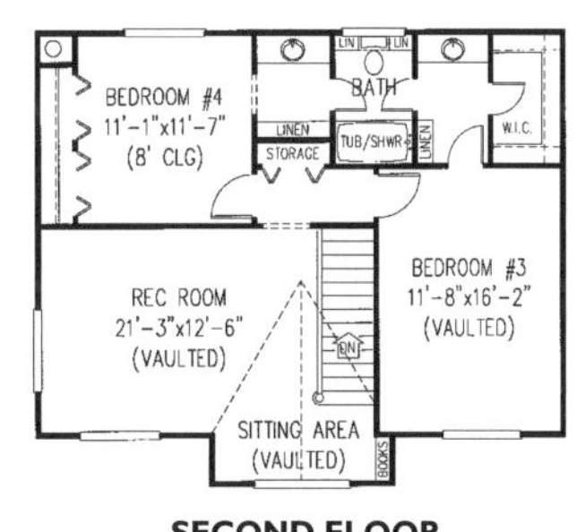
BEDROOM #4
11'-1"x11'-7"
(8' CLG)
BATH
LINEN
STORAGE
TUB/SHWR
W.I.C.
REC ROOM
21'-3"x12'-6"
(VAULTED)
BEDROOM #3
11'-8"x16'-2"
(VAULTED)
SITTING AREA
(VAULTED)

SECOND FLOOR

Units	Single
Price Code	E
Total Finished	2,327 sq. ft.
First Finished	1,484 sq. ft.
Second Finished	843 sq. ft.
Basement Unfinished	1,484 sq. ft.
Garage Unfinished	652 sq. ft.
Porch Unfinished	320 sq. ft.
Dimensions	68'10"x51'2"
Foundation	Basement Crawlspace Slab
Bedrooms	4
Full Baths	2
Half Baths	1
First Ceiling	9'
Roof Framing	Stick
Exterior Walls	2x4

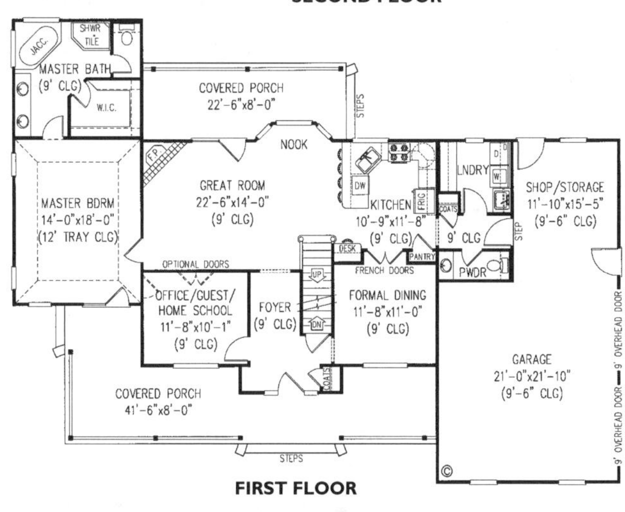
MASTER BATH
(9' CLG)
W.I.C.
COVERED PORCH
22'-6"x8'-0"
STEPS
NOOK
MASTER BDRM
14'-0"x18'-0"
(12' TRAY CLG)
GREAT ROOM
22'-6"x14'-0"
(9' CLG)
KITCHEN
10'-9"x11'-8"
(9' CLG)
LNDRY
9' CLG
SHOP/STORAGE
11'-10"x15'-5"
(9'-6" CLG)
PANTRY
PWDR
FRENCH DOORS
OPTIONAL DOORS
OFFICE/GUEST/
HOME SCHOOL
11'-8"x10'-1"
(9' CLG)
FOYER
(9' CLG)
FORMAL DINING
11'-8"x11'-0"
(9' CLG)
GARAGE
21'-0"x21'-10"
(9'-6" CLG)
9' OVERHEAD DOOR
COVERED PORCH
41'-6"x8'-0"
STEPS

FIRST FLOOR

Design 64165

Units	Single
Price Code	H
Total Finished	2,329 sq. ft.
Main Finished	2,329 sq. ft.
Garage Unfinished	528 sq. ft.
Porch Unfinished	215 sq. ft.
Dimensions	72'x73'
Foundation	Crawlspace
Bedrooms	3
Full Baths	2
Half Baths	1
Max Ridge Height	25'4"
Exterior Walls	2x6

* Alternate foundation options available at an additional charge. Please call 1-800-235-5700 for more information.

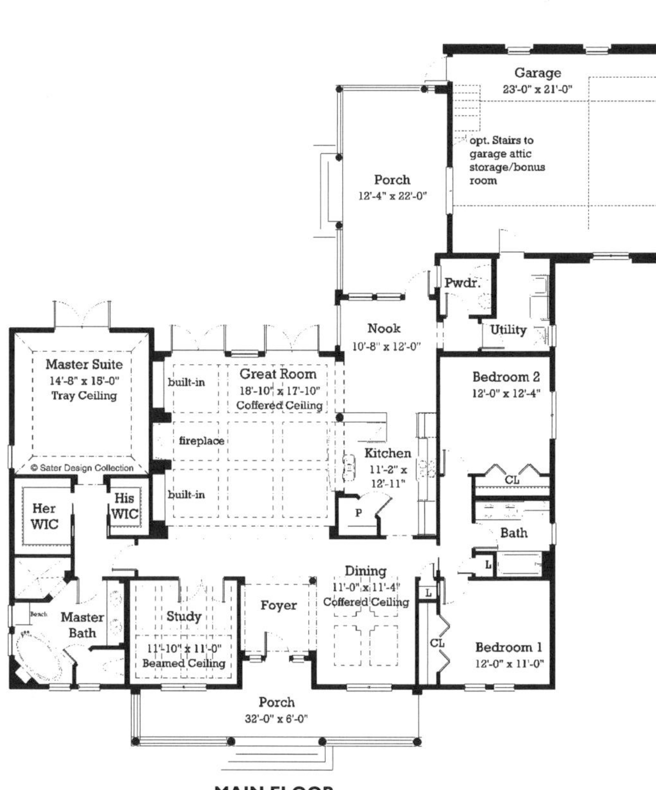
Garage
23'-0" x 21'-0"
opt. Stairs to garage attic storage/bonus room
Porch
12'-4" x 22'-0"
Pwdr.
Utility
Nook
10'-8" x 12'-0"
Master Suite
14'-8" x 15'-0"
Tray Ceiling
Great Room
18'-10" x 17'-10"
Coffered Ceiling
built-in
fireplace
built-in
Bedroom 2
12'-0" x 12'-4"
Kitchen
11'-2" x
12'-11"
© Sater Design Collection
Her WIC
His WIC
CL
Bath
Dining
11'-0" x 11'-4"
Coffered Ceiling
Master Bath
Study
11'-10" x 11'-0"
Beamed Ceiling
Foyer
Bedroom 1
12'-0" x 11'-0"
Porch
32'-0" x 6'-0"

MAIN FLOOR

Design 98233

Units	Single
Price Code	E
Total Finished	2,330 sq. ft.
Main Finished	2,330 sq. ft.
Basement Unfinished	2,330 sq. ft.
Garage Unfinished	416 sq. ft.
Deck Unfinished	196 sq. ft.
Dimensions	50'x70'
Foundation	Crawlspace
Bedrooms	3
Full Baths	3
Main Ceiling	9'
Tray Ceiling	14'
Max Ridge Height	32'
Roof Framing	Stick
Exterior Walls	2x4

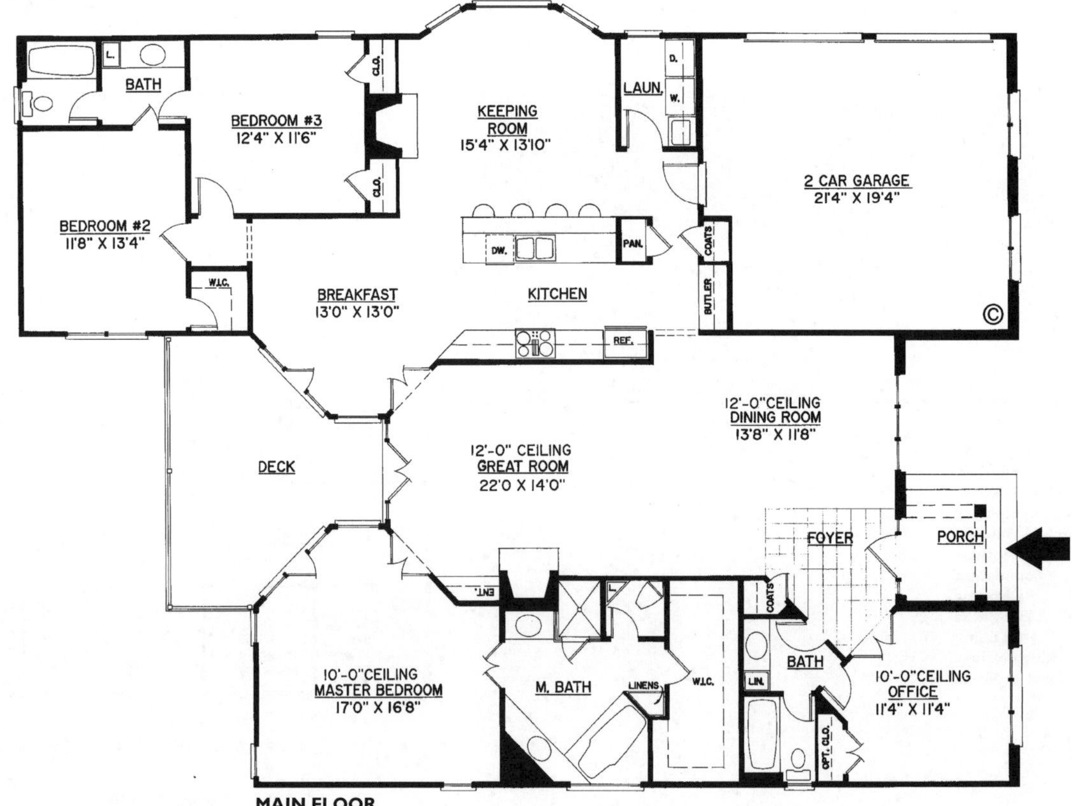
BATH
BEDROOM #3
12'4" X 11'6"
KEEPING ROOM
15'4" X 13'10"
LAUN.
2 CAR GARAGE
21'4" X 19'4"
BEDROOM #2
11'8" X 13'4"
W.I.C.
BREAKFAST
13'0" X 13'0"
KITCHEN
PAN.
COATS
BUTLER
REF.
12'-0"CEILING
DINING ROOM
13'8" X 11'8"
DECK
12'-0" CEILING
GREAT ROOM
22'0 X 14'0"
FOYER
PORCH
ENT.
10'-0"CEILING
MASTER BEDROOM
17'0" X 16'8"
M. BATH
LINENS
W.I.C.
BATH
LIN.
OPT. CLO.
10'-0"CEILING
OFFICE
11'4" X 11'4"

MAIN FLOOR

Design 50023

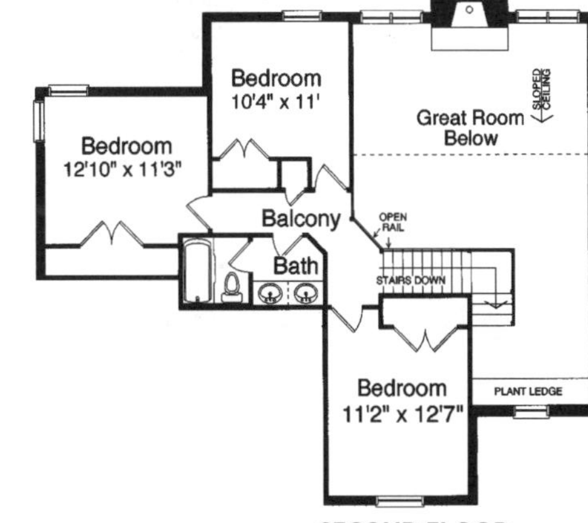
Bedroom
10'4" x 11'
Bedroom
12'10" x 11'3"
Great Room
Below
SLOPED CEILING
Balcony
OPEN RAIL
Bath
STAIRS DOWN
Bedroom
11'2" x 12'7"
PLANT LEDGE
SECOND FLOOR

Units	Single
Price Code	E
Total Finished	2,332 sq. ft.
First Finished	1,680 sq. ft.
Second Finished	652 sq. ft.
Basement Unfinished	1,680 sq. ft.
Garage Unfinished	510 sq. ft.
Dimensions	58'8"x46'8"
Foundation	Basement
Bedrooms	4
Full Baths	2
Half Baths	1
First Ceiling	8'
Second Ceiling	8'
Max Ridge Height	29'6"
Roof Framing	Truss
Exterior Walls	2x4

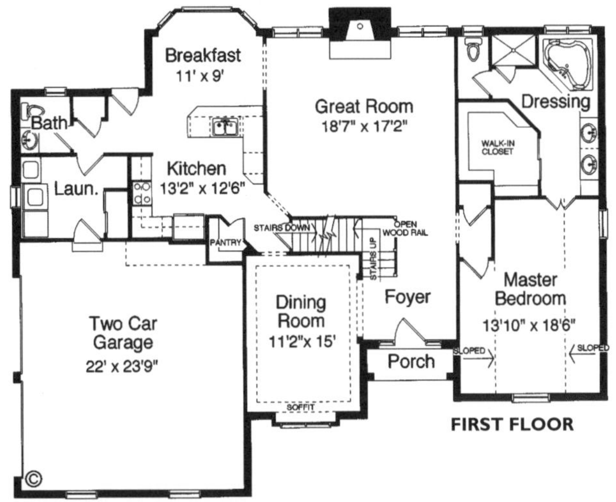
Breakfast
11' x 9'
Great Room
18'7" x 17'2"
Dressing
Bath
WALK-IN CLOSET
Kitchen
13'2" x 12'6"
Laun.
STAIRS DOWN
PANTRY
OPEN WOOD RAIL
STAIRS UP
Dining
Room
11'2"x 15'
Foyer
Master
Bedroom
13'10" x 18'6"
Two Car
Garage
22' x 23'9"
Porch
SLOPED
SLOPED
SOFFIT
FIRST FLOOR

Design 97427

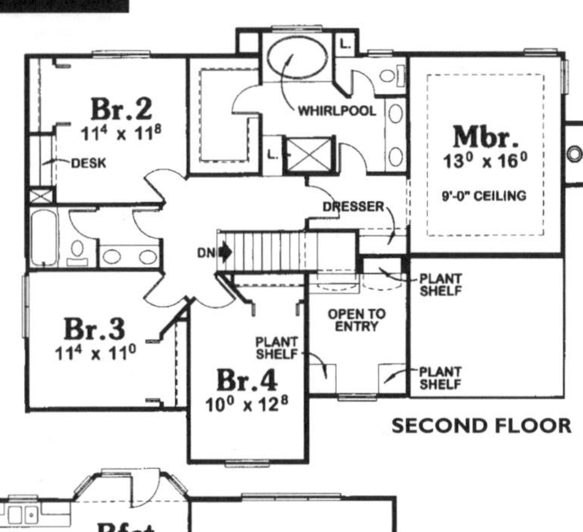
Br. 2
11⁴ x 11⁸
DESK
WHIRLPOOL
L.
L.
Mbr.
13⁰ x 16⁰
9'-0" CEILING
DRESSER
DN
Br. 3
11⁴ x 11⁰
PLANT SHELF
Br. 4
10⁰ x 12⁸
OPEN TO ENTRY
PLANT SHELF
PLANT SHELF
SECOND FLOOR

Units	Single
Price Code	E
Total Finished	2,332 sq. ft.
First Finished	1,214 sq. ft.
Second Finished	1,118 sq. ft.
Garage Unfinished	511 sq. ft.
Dimensions	54'x43'4"
Foundation	Basement
Bedrooms	4
Full Baths	2
Half Baths	1
Max Ridge Height	26'3"
Roof Framing	Stick
Exterior Walls	2x4

* Alternate foundation options available at an additional charge. Please call 1-800-235-5700 for more information.

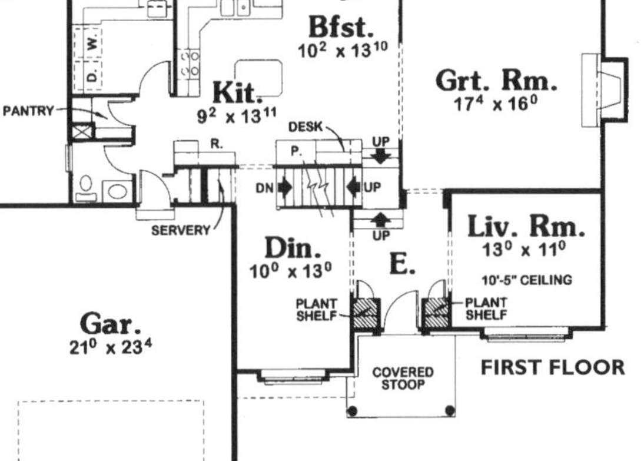
Bfst.
10² x 13¹⁰
Grt. Rm.
17⁴ x 16⁰
Kit.
9² x 13¹¹
PANTRY
DESK
R.
P.
UP
DN
UP
UP
SERVERY
Din.
10⁰ x 13⁰
E.
Liv. Rm.
13⁰ x 11⁰
10'-5" CEILING
PLANT SHELF
PLANT SHELF
Gar.
21⁰ x 23⁴
COVERED STOOP
FIRST FLOOR

Design 97857

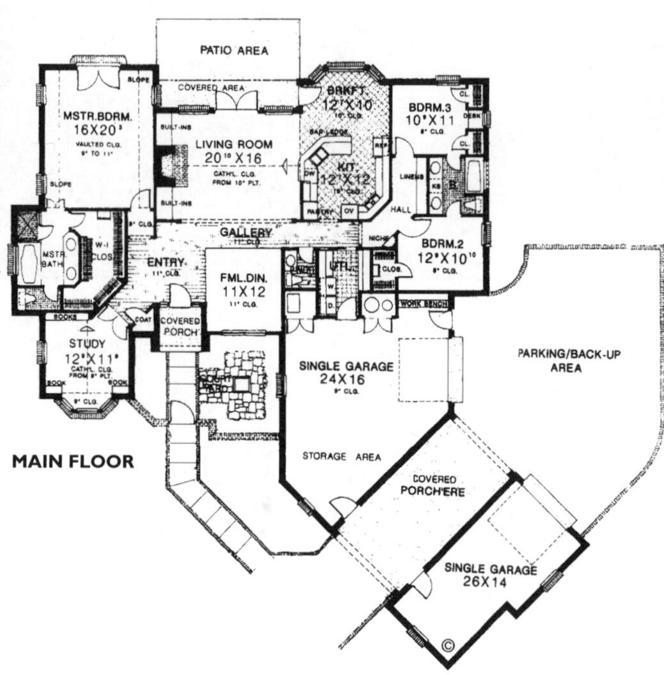

PATIO AREA
COVERED AREA
MSTR.BDRM.
16X20
VAULTED CLG.
LIVING ROOM
20 X16
BRKFT.
12 X10
BDRM.3
10 X11
KIT.
12 X12
GALLERY
BDRM.2
12 X10
ENTRY
FML.DIN.
11X12
MSTR BATH
W-I CLOS
UTIL.
STUDY
12 X11
COVERED PORCH
SINGLE GARAGE
24X16
PARKING/BACK-UP AREA
STORAGE AREA
COVERED PORCHERE
SINGLE GARAGE
26X14
MAIN FLOOR

Units	Single
Price Code	E
Total Finished	2,332 sq. ft.
Main Finished	2,332 sq. ft.
Garage Unfinished	620 sq. ft.
Deck Unfinished	80 sq. ft.
Porch Unfinished	48 sq. ft.
Dimensions	82'3"x86'6"
Foundation	Slab
Bedrooms	3
Full Baths	2
Half Baths	1
Main Ceiling	9'-10'
Max Ridge Height	29'
Roof Framing	Stick
Exterior Walls	2x4

Design 65316

3,00 X 3,10
10'-0" X 10'-4"
2,80 X 3,90
9'-4" X 13'-0"
3,30 X 3,40
11'-0" X 11'-4"
3,90 X 4,30
13'-0" X 14'-4"
SECOND FLOOR
3,90 X 4,30
13'-0" X 14'-4"
3,50 X 3,90
11'-8" X 13'-0"
3,60 X 4,40
12'-0" X 14'-8"
2,20 X 4,40
7'-4" X 14'-8"
6,30 X 6,60
21'-0" X 22'-0"
3,90 X 4,30
13'-0" X 14'-4"
FIRST FLOOR

Units	Single
Price Code	E
Total Finished	2,333 sq. ft.
First Finished	1,472 sq. ft.
Second Finished	861 sq. ft.
Basement Unfinished	1,472 sq. ft.
Dimensions	52'8"x51'
Foundation	Basement
Bedrooms	4
Full Baths	2
First Ceiling	9'
Second Ceiling	8'
Max Ridge Height	31'6"
Roof Framing	Truss
Exterior Walls	2x6

Design 64128

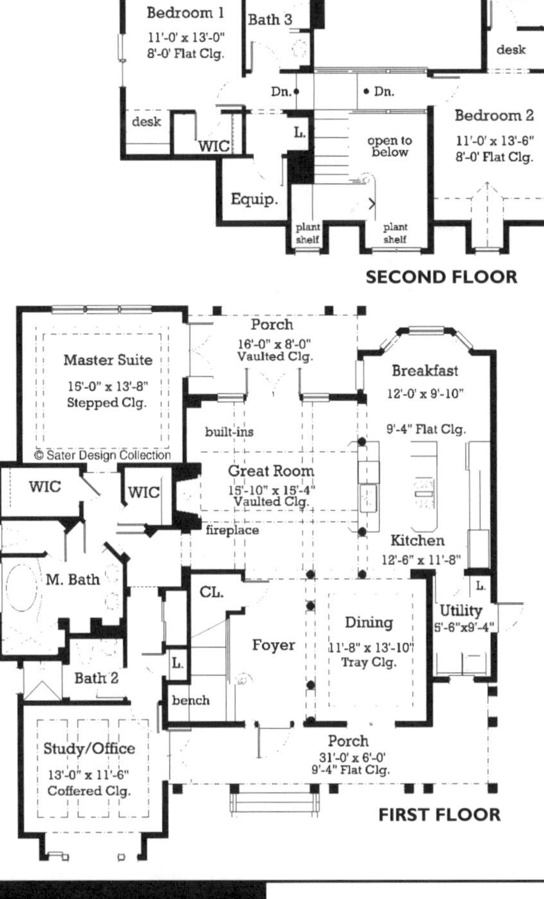
Bedroom 1
11'-0' x 13'-0"
8'-0' Flat Clg.
Bath 3
open to below
WIC
desk
Dn.
Dn.
desk
WIC
L.
open to below
Bedroom 2
11'-0' x 13'-6"
8'-0' Flat Clg.
Equip.
plant shelf
plant shelf
SECOND FLOOR
Master Suite
15'-0" x 13'-8"
Stepped Clg.
Porch
16'-0" x 8'-0"
Vaulted Clg.
Breakfast
12'-0' x 9'-10"
9'-4" Flat Clg.
built-ins
© Sater Design Collection
Great Room
15'-10" x 15'-4"
Vaulted Clg.
WIC
WIC
fireplace
Kitchen
12'-6" x 11'-8"
M. Bath
CL.
Foyer
Dining
11'-8" x 13'-10"
Tray Clg.
L.
Utility
5'-6"x9'-4"
L.
Bath 2
bench
Study/Office
13'-0" x 11'-6"
Coffered Clg.
Porch
31'-0' x 6'-0'
9'-4" Flat Clg.
FIRST FLOOR

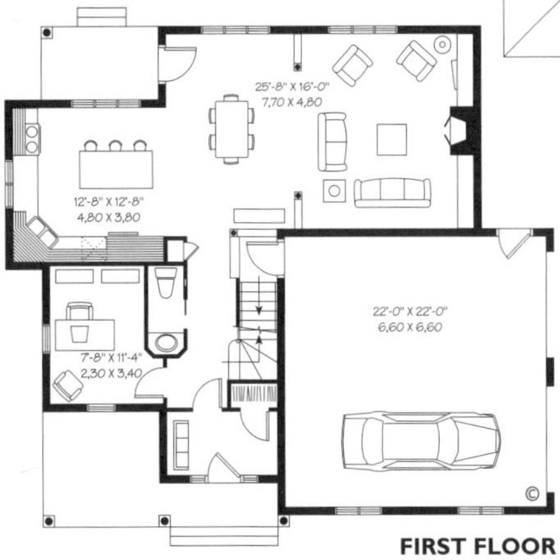

Units	Single
Price Code	H
Total Finished	2,334 sq. ft.
First Finished	1,716 sq. ft.
Second Finished	618 sq. ft.
Deck Unfinished	210 sq. ft.
Porch Unfinished	128 sq. ft.
Dimensions	47'x50'
Foundation	Slab
Bedrooms	3
Full Baths	2
3/4 Baths	1
Max Ridge Height	29'2"
Roof Framing	Stick/Truss
Exterior Walls	2x6

* Alternate foundation options available at an additional charge. Please call 1-800-235-5700 for more information.

Design 65430

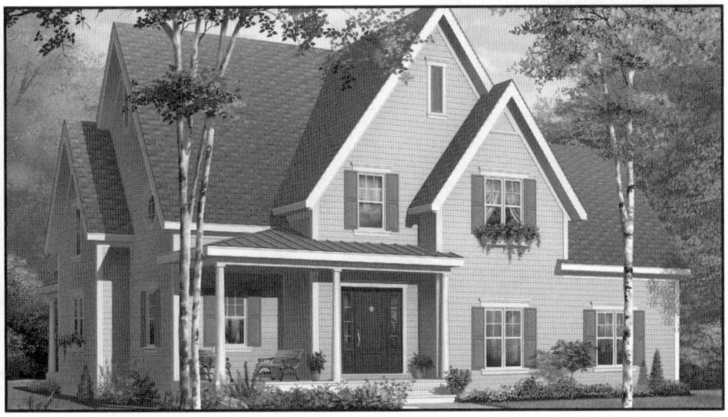

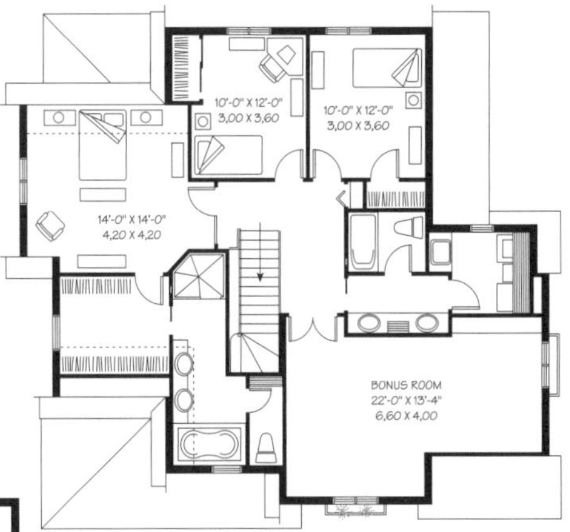

Units	Single
Price Code	E
Total Finished	2,339 sq. ft.
First Finished	971 sq. ft.
Second Finished	1,368 sq. ft.
Garage Unfinished	520 sq. ft.
Porch Unfinished	128 sq. ft.
Dimensions	36'x40'
Foundation	Basement
Bedrooms	3
Full Baths	2
Half Baths	1
First Ceiling	8'
Second Ceiling	8'
Max Ridge Height	31'10"
Roof Framing	Truss
Exterior Walls	2x6

SECOND FLOOR

FIRST FLOOR

Design 81003

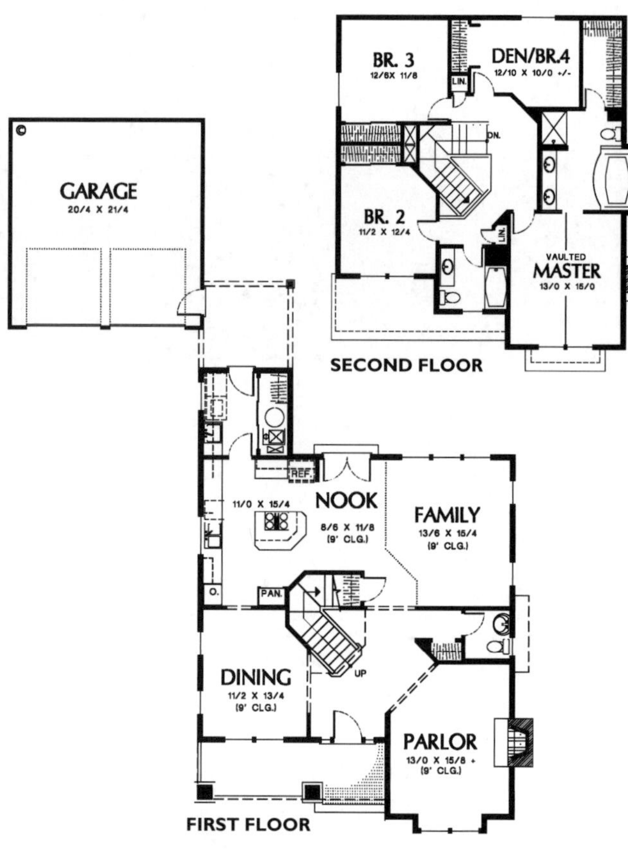

GARAGE
20/4 X 21/4
BR. 3
12/6X 11/8
DEN/BR.4
12/10 X 10/0 +/-
BR. 2
11/2 X 12/4
VAULTED
MASTER
13/0 X 18/0
SECOND FLOOR
11/0 X 15/4
NOOK
8/6 X 11/8
(9' CLG.)
FAMILY
13/6 X 15/4
(9' CLG.)
DINING
11/2 X 13/4
(9' CLG.)
PARLOR
13/0 X 15/8 +
(9' CLG.)
FIRST FLOOR

Units	Single
Price Code	E
Total Finished	2,342 sq. ft.
First Finished	1,234 sq. ft.
Second Finished	1,108 sq. ft.
Dimensions	56'x74'6"
Foundation	Crawlspace
Bedrooms	4
Full Baths	2
Half Baths	1
First Ceiling	9'
Second Ceiling	8'
Max Ridge Height	34'6"
Roof Framing	Truss
Exterior Walls	2x6

Design 94639

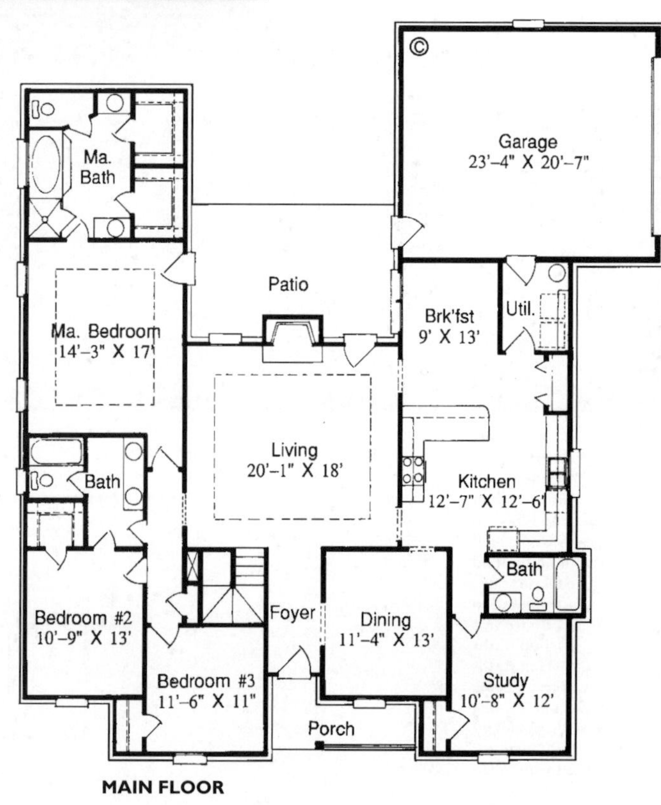

Ma. Bath
Garage
23'-4" X 20'-7"
Patio
Ma. Bedroom
14'-3" X 17'
Brk'fst
9' X 13'
Util.
Living
20'-1" X 18'
Bath
Kitchen
12'-7" X 12'-6'
Bath
Bedroom #2
10'-9" X 13'
Foyer
Dining
11'-4" X 13'
Bedroom #3
11'-6" X 11"
Study
10'-8" X 12'
Porch
MAIN FLOOR

Units	Single
Price Code	E
Total Finished	2,345 sq. ft.
Main Finished	2,345 sq. ft.
Garage Unfinished	510 sq. ft.
Porch Unfinished	62 sq. ft.
Dimensions	59'10"x66'3"
Foundation	Slab
Bedrooms	3
Full Baths	3
Max Ridge Height	23'
Roof Framing	Stick
Exterior Walls	2x4

Design 52103

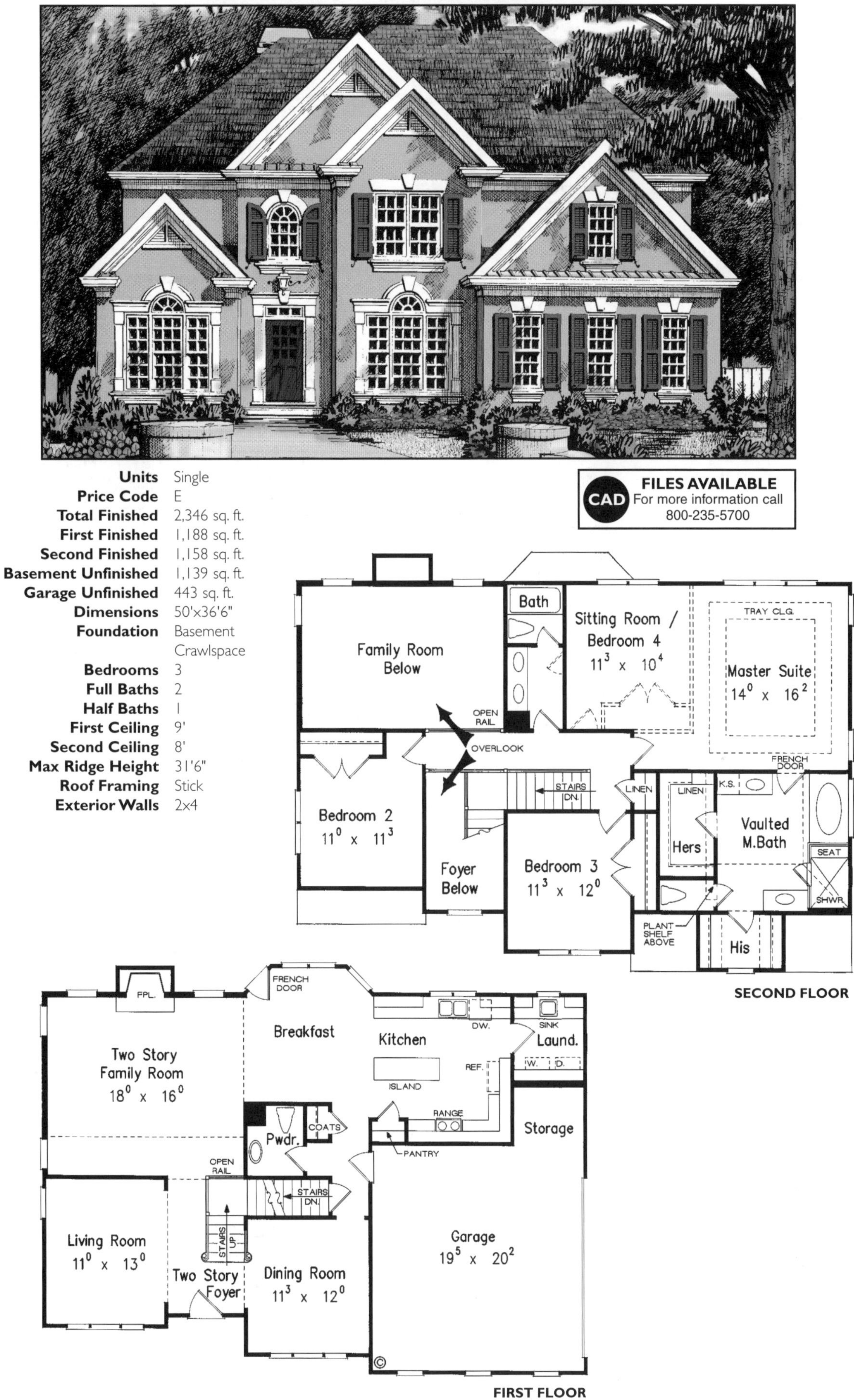

SECOND FLOOR
Family Room Below
Bath
Sitting Room / Bedroom 4
11^3 x 10^4
TRAY CLG.
Master Suite
14^0 x 16^2
OPEN RAIL
OVERLOOK
FRENCH DOOR
Bedroom 2
11^0 x 11^3
STAIRS DN.
LINEN
LINEN
K.S.
Hers
Vaulted M.Bath
SEAT
SHWR.
Foyer Below
Bedroom 3
11^3 x 12^0
PLANT SHELF ABOVE
His
FIRST FLOOR
FPL.
FRENCH DOOR
Breakfast
Kitchen
DW.
SINK
Laund.
W.
D.
Two Story Family Room
18^0 x 16^0
REF.
ISLAND
RANGE
Storage
COATS
Pwdr.
PANTRY
OPEN RAIL
STAIRS DN.
STAIRS UP
Garage
19^5 x 20^2
Living Room
11^0 x 13^0
Two Story Foyer
Dining Room
11^3 x 12^0

Units	Single
Price Code	E
Total Finished	2,346 sq. ft.
First Finished	1,188 sq. ft.
Second Finished	1,158 sq. ft.
Basement Unfinished	1,139 sq. ft.
Garage Unfinished	443 sq. ft.
Dimensions	50'x36'6"
Foundation	Basement Crawlspace
Bedrooms	3
Full Baths	2
Half Baths	1
First Ceiling	9'
Second Ceiling	8'
Max Ridge Height	31'6"
Roof Framing	Stick
Exterior Walls	2x4

CAD **FILES AVAILABLE**
For more information call
800-235-5700

Design 98455

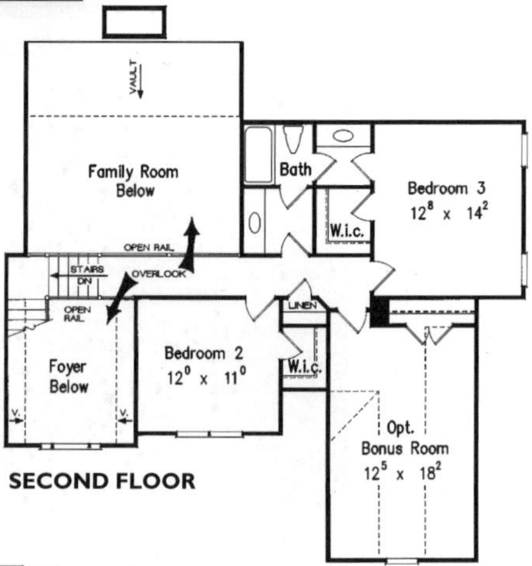

Units	Single
Price Code	E
Total Finished	2,349 sq. ft.
First Finished	1,761 sq. ft.
Second Finished	588 sq. ft.
Bonus Unfinished	267 sq. ft.
Basement Unfinished	1,761 sq. ft.
Garage Unfinished	435 sq. ft.
Dimensions	56'x47'6"
Foundation	Basement Crawlspace
Bedrooms	4
Full Baths	3
First Ceiling	9'
Second Ceiling	8'
Max Ridge Height	31'6"
Roof Framing	Stick
Exterior Walls	2x4

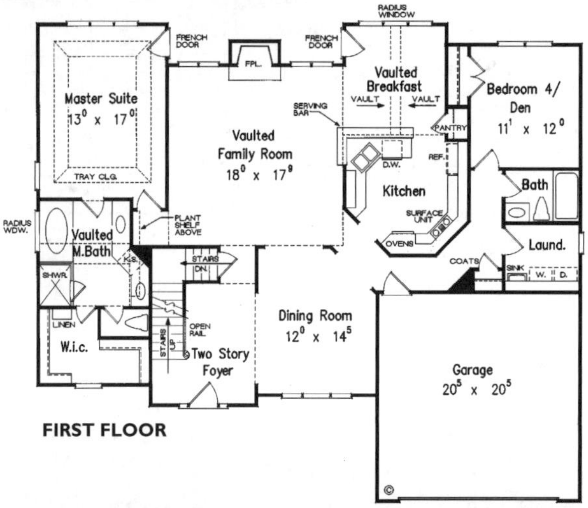

SECOND FLOOR

FIRST FLOOR

FILES AVAILABLE
CAD For more information call
800-235-5700

Design 10619

Units	Single
Price Code	E
Total Finished	2,352 sq. ft.
Main Finished	2,352 sq. ft.
Basement Unfinished	2,352 sq. ft.
Garage Unfinished	696 sq. ft.
Dimensions	93'6"x48'
Foundation	Basement
Bedrooms	3
Full Baths	2
3/4 Baths	1
Max Ridge Height	20'
Roof Framing	Stick
Exterior Walls	2x6

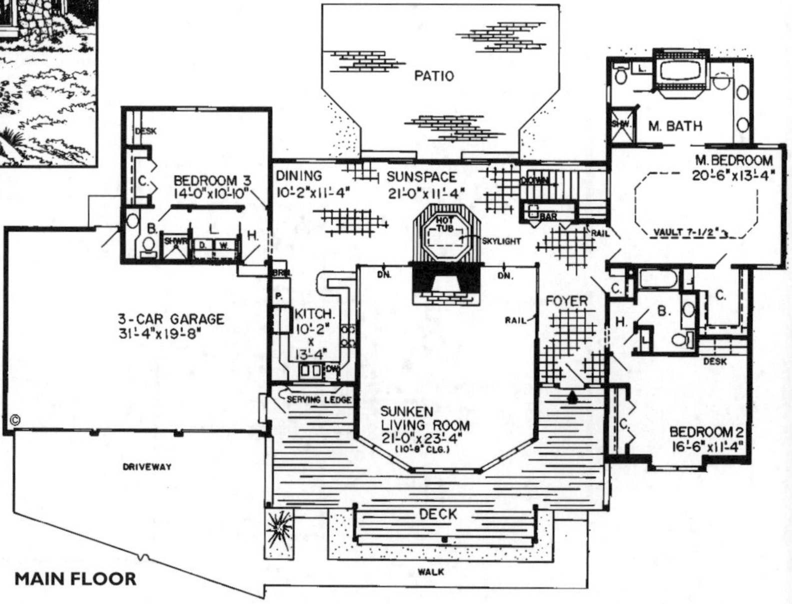

MAIN FLOOR

Design 66048

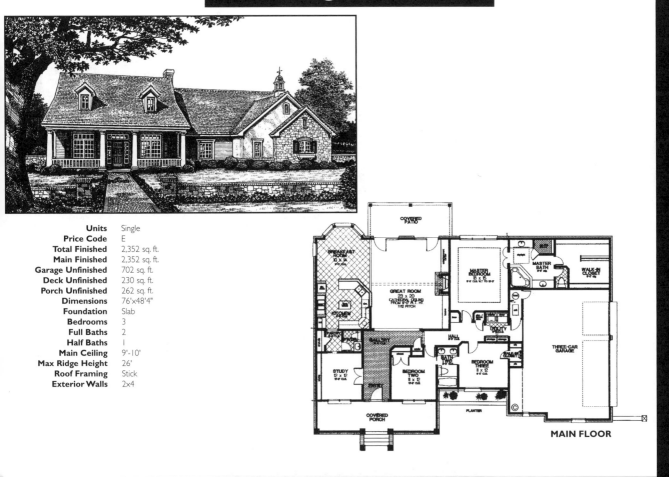

Units	Single
Price Code	E
Total Finished	2,352 sq. ft.
Main Finished	2,352 sq. ft.
Garage Unfinished	702 sq. ft.
Deck Unfinished	230 sq. ft.
Porch Unfinished	262 sq. ft.
Dimensions	76'x48'4"
Foundation	Slab
Bedrooms	3
Full Baths	2
Half Baths	1
Main Ceiling	9'-10'
Max Ridge Height	26'
Roof Framing	Stick
Exterior Walls	2x4

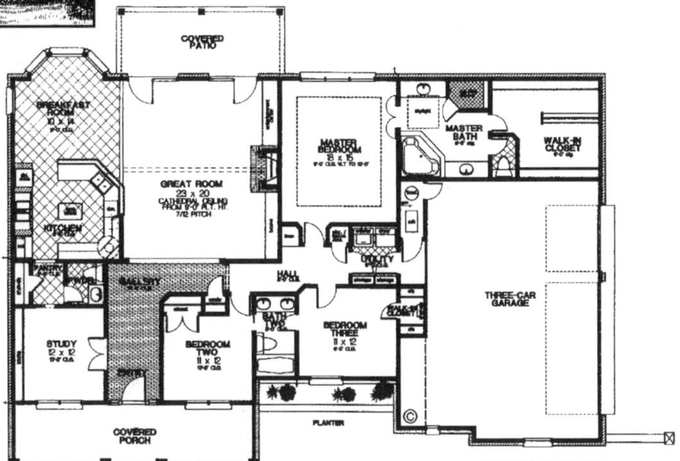

MAIN FLOOR

Design 66051

Units	Single
Price Code	E
Total Finished	2,352 sq. ft.
Main Finished	2,352 sq. ft.
Garage Unfinished	726 sq. ft.
Deck Unfinished	210 sq. ft.
Dimensions	77'6"x53'2"
Foundation	Crawlspace Slab
Bedrooms	4
Full Baths	3
Main Ceiling	9'-10'
Max Ridge Height	25'
Roof Framing	Stick
Exterior Walls	2x4

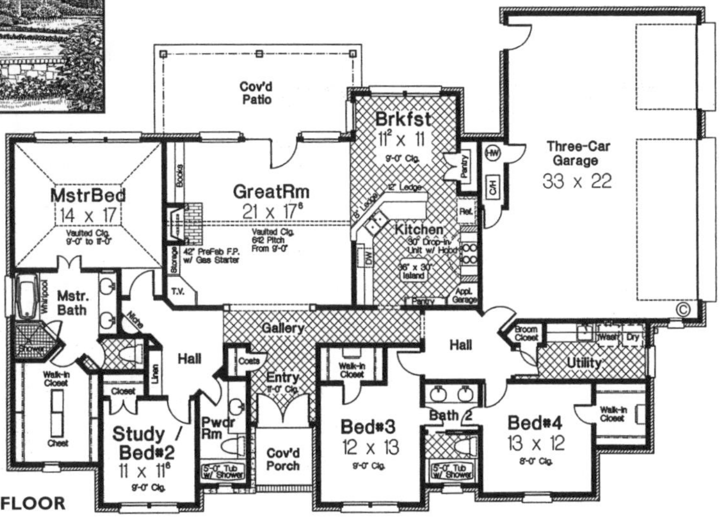

MAIN FLOOR

Design 66047

Units Single
Price Code E
Total Finished 2,353 sq. ft.
Main Finished 2,353 sq. ft.
Garage Unfinished 650 sq. ft.
Deck Unfinished 150 sq. ft.
Dimensions 55'x70'7¼"
Foundation Slab
Bedrooms 4
Full Baths 3
Main Ceiling 9'
Max Ridge Height 27'6"
Roof Framing Stick
Exterior Walls 2x4

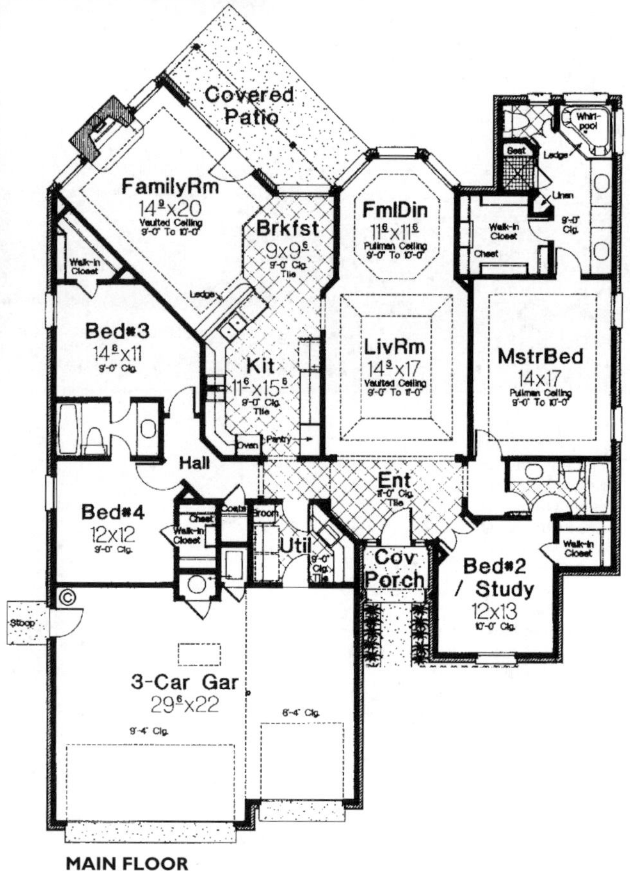

Covered Patio
FamilyRm
14^{8}x20
Brkfst
9x9^{6}
FmlDin
11^{6}x11^{6}
Bed#3
14^{8}x11
Kit
11^{6}x15^{6}
LivRm
14^{8}x17
MstrBed
14x17
Hall
Ent
Bed#4
12x12
Util
Cov Porch
Bed#2 / Study
12x13
Stoop
3-Car Gar
29^{6}x22
MAIN FLOOR

Design 94967

Units Single
Price Code E
Total Finished 2,355 sq. ft.
Main Finished 2,355 sq. ft.
Garage Unfinished 673 sq. ft.
Dimensions 70'x62'
Foundation Basement
Bedrooms 3
Full Baths 2
Half Baths 1
Max Ridge Height 20'3"
Roof Framing Stick
Exterior Walls 2x4

* Alternate foundation options available at an additional charge. Please call 1-800-235-5700 for more information.

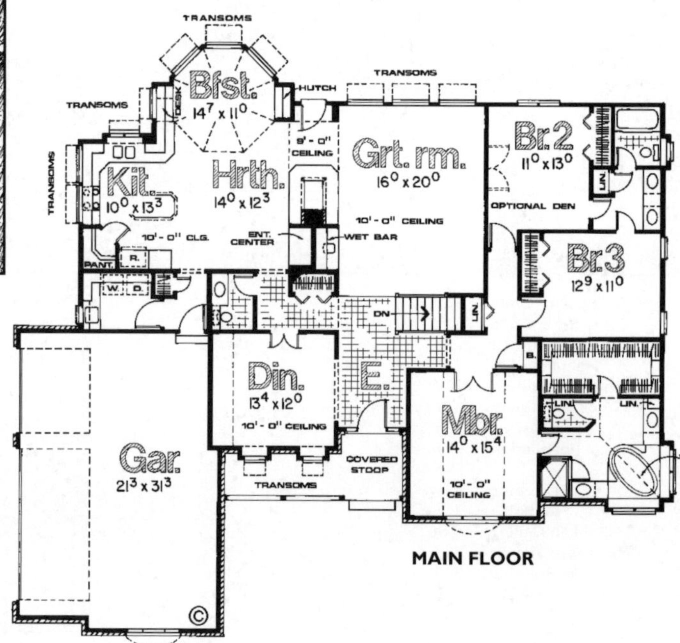

TRANSOMS
Bfst.
14^{7} x 11^{0}
HUTCH
TRANSOMS
Kit.
10^{0} x 13^{3}
Hrth.
14^{0} x 12^{3}
Grt. rm.
16^{0} x 20^{0}
10'-0" CEILING
WET BAR
ENT. CENTER
Br. 2
11^{0} x 13^{0}
OPTIONAL DEN
Br. 3
12^{9} x 11^{0}
Din.
13^{4} x 12^{0}
E.
Mbr.
14^{0} x 15^{4}
COVERED STOOP
Gar.
21^{3} x 31^{3}
MAIN FLOOR

Design 24404

Units	Single
Price Code	E
Total Finished	2,356 sq. ft.
First Finished	1,236 sq. ft.
Second Finished	1,120 sq. ft.
Dimensions	68'8½"x42'
Foundation	Basement Crawlspace Slab
Bedrooms	4
Full Baths	2
3/4 Baths	1
First Ceiling	9'
Second Ceiling	8'
Max Ridge Height	28'
Roof Framing	Stick
Exterior Walls	2x4

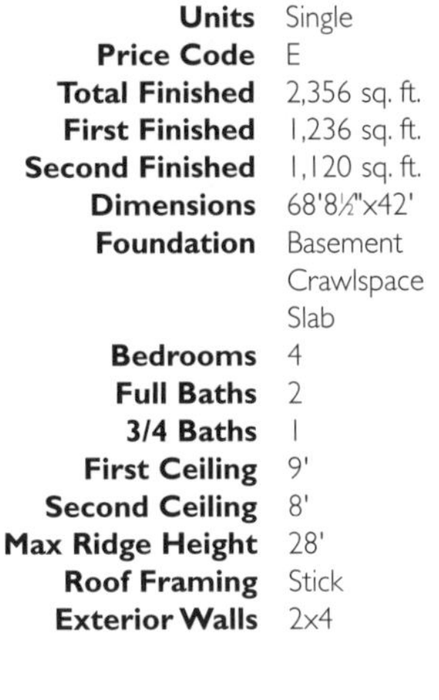
wh
furn
Workshop
14-5 x 14-5

OPTIONAL CRAWLSPACE/ SLAB FOUNDATION

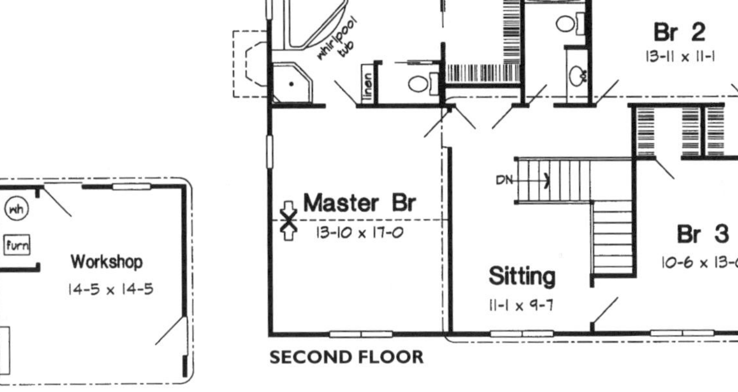
whirlpool tub
linen
Br 2
13-11 x 11-1
DN
Master Br
13-10 x 17-0
Br 3
10-6 x 13-0
Sitting
11-1 x 9-7

SECOND FLOOR

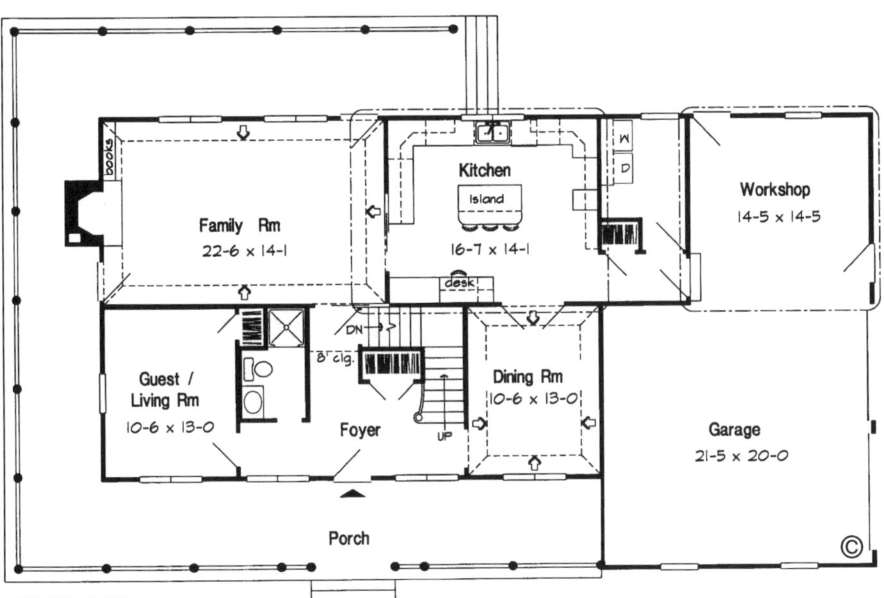
books
Family Rm
22-6 x 14-1
Kitchen
Island
16-7 x 14-1
desk
W
D
Workshop
14-5 x 14-5
Guest /
Living Rm
10-6 x 13-0
8' clg.
DN
Foyer
UP
Dining Rm
10-6 x 13-0
Garage
21-5 x 20-0
Porch
©

FIRST FLOOR

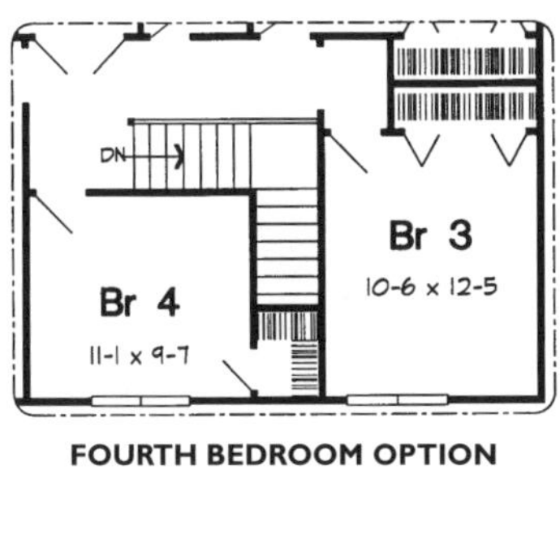
DN
Br 3
10-6 x 12-5
Br 4
11-1 x 9-7

FOURTH BEDROOM OPTION

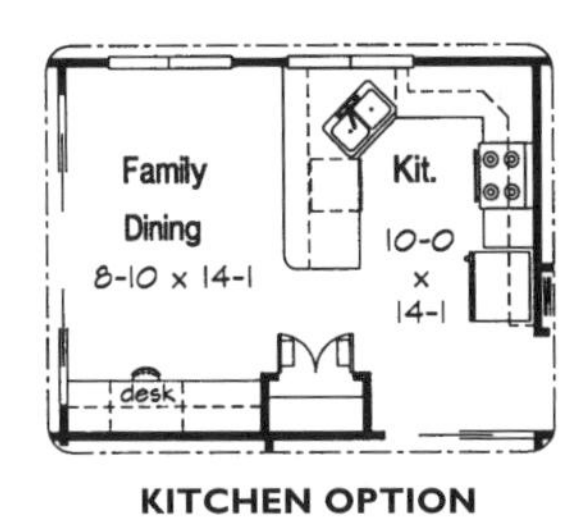
Family
Dining
8-10 x 14-1
Kit.
10-0
x
14-1
desk

KITCHEN OPTION

Design 91480

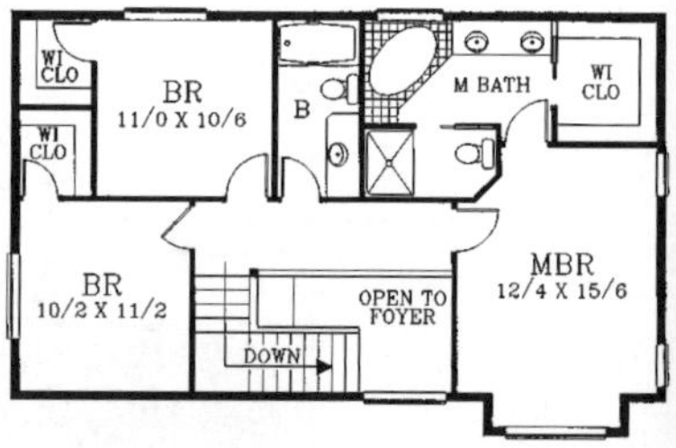

Units	Single
Price Code	E
Total Finished	2,356 sq. ft.
First Finished	1,027 sq. ft.
Second Finished	804 sq. ft.
Bonus Unfinished	525 sq. ft.
Garage Unfinished	490 sq. ft.
Dimensions	39'8"x55'
Foundation	Crawlspace
Bedrooms	3
Full Baths	2
Half Baths	1
First Ceiling	8'
Second Ceiling	8'
Max Ridge Height	27'
Roof Framing	Truss
Exterior Walls	2x6

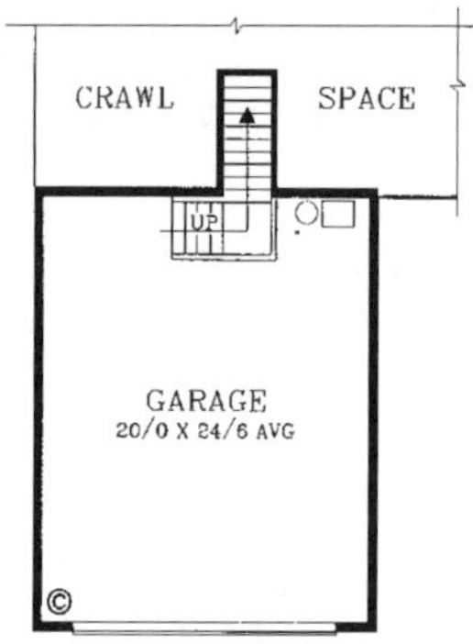

WI CLO
BR 11/0 X 10/6
B
M BATH
WI CLO
WI CLO
BR 10/2 X 11/2
OPEN TO FOYER
DOWN
MBR 12/4 X 15/6

SECOND FLOOR

PATIO
NOOK 9 X 8 AVG
KIT
DW
FAM RM 18/6 X 16/8 AVG
DIN RM 10 X 10 AVG
PAN
R
PDR
LIV RM 12/8 X 12/0 AVG
2 STORY FOYER
GST
UTIL
W D
DOWN
UP
STOR
COVERED PORCH
DOWN
VAULTED BONUS RM 20/0 X 24/8
OPT. VIEW DECK

FIRST FLOOR

CRAWL SPACE
UP
GARAGE 20/0 X 24/6 AVG
©

GARAGE

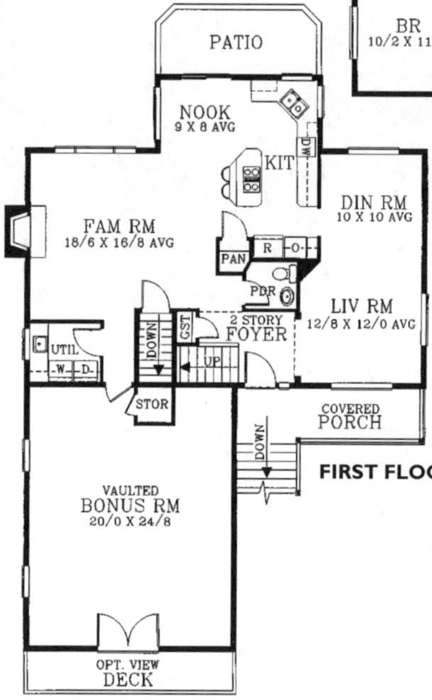

Design 94613

Units	Single
Price Code	E
Total Finished	2,357 sq. ft.
First Finished	1,492 sq. ft.
Second Finished	865 sq. ft.
Bonus Unfinished	303 sq. ft.
Garage Unfinished	574 sq. ft.
Porch Unfinished	440 sq. ft.
Dimensions	66'10"x49'7"
Foundation	Crawlspace Slab
Bedrooms	4
Full Baths	3
Half Baths	1
First Ceiling	9'
Second Ceiling	8'
Max Ridge Height	29'
Roof Framing	Truss
Exterior Walls	2x4, 2x6

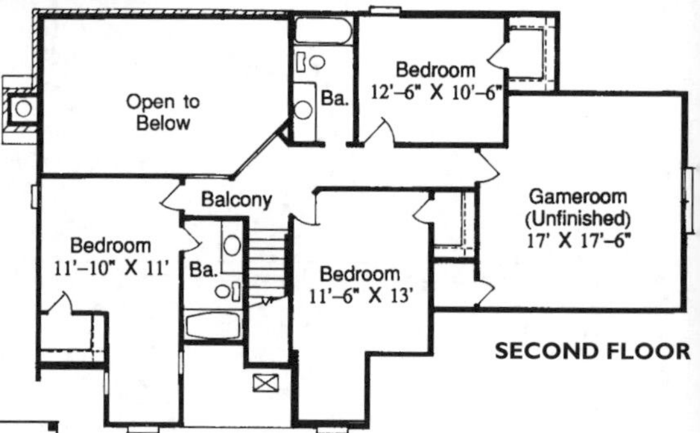

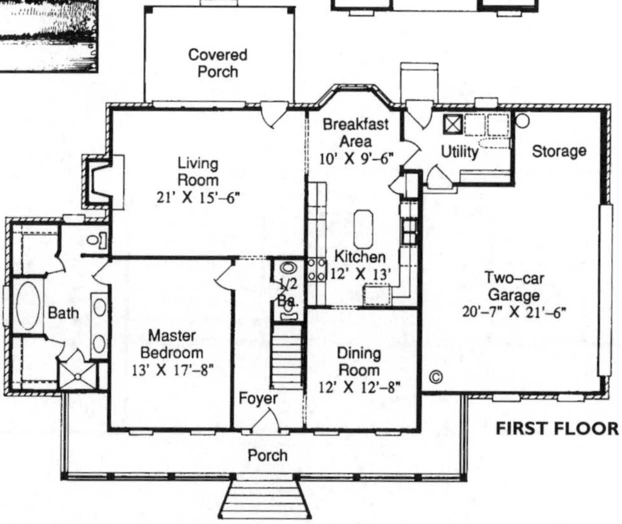

Open to Below
Ba.
Bedroom 12'-6" X 10'-6"
Balcony
Gameroom (Unfinished) 17' X 17'-6"
Bedroom 11'-10" X 11'
Ba.
Bedroom 11'-6" X 13'

SECOND FLOOR

Covered Porch
Breakfast Area 10' X 9'-6"
Utility
Storage
Living Room 21' X 15'-6"
Kitchen 12' X 13'
Bath
1/2 Ba.
Two-car Garage 20'-7" X 21'-6"
Master Bedroom 13' X 17'-8"
Dining Room 12' X 12'-8"
Foyer
©
Porch

FIRST FLOOR

Design 93440

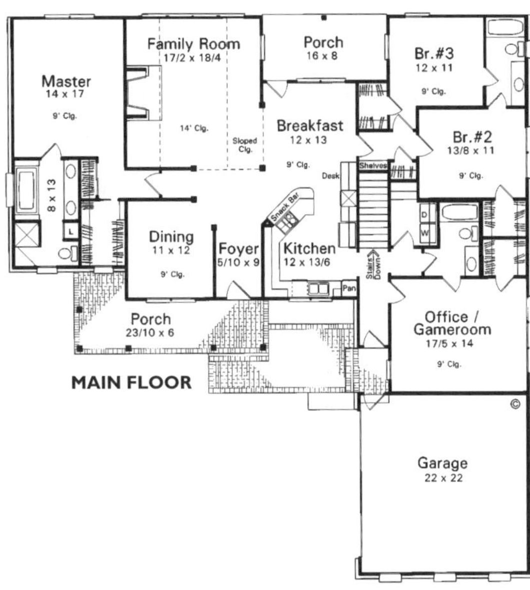
Family Room
17/2 x 18/4
Porch
16 x 8
Br.#3
12 x 11
9' Clg.
Master
14 x 17
9' Clg.
14' Clg.
Sloped Clg.
Breakfast
12 x 13
9' Clg.
Desk
Shelves
Br.#2
13/8 x 11
9' Clg.
8 x 13
L
Snack Bar
D
W
Dining
11 x 12
9' Clg.
Foyer
5/10 x 9
Kitchen
12 x 13/6
Stairs Down
Pan
Porch
23/10 x 6
Office /
Gameroom
17/5 x 14
9' Clg.
MAIN FLOOR
Garage
22 x 22

Units	Single
Price Code	E
Total Finished	2,361 sq. ft.
Main Finished	2,361 sq. ft.
Basement Unfinished	2,361 sq. ft.
Garage Unfinished	490 sq. ft.
Deck Unfinished	128 sq. ft.
Porch Unfinished	168 sq. ft.
Dimensions	67'x69'6"
Foundation	Basement
Bedrooms	3
Full Baths	3
Main Ceiling	9'
Vaulted Ceiling	14'
Max Ridge Height	22'5"
Roof Framing	Stick
Exterior Walls	2x4

Design 69107

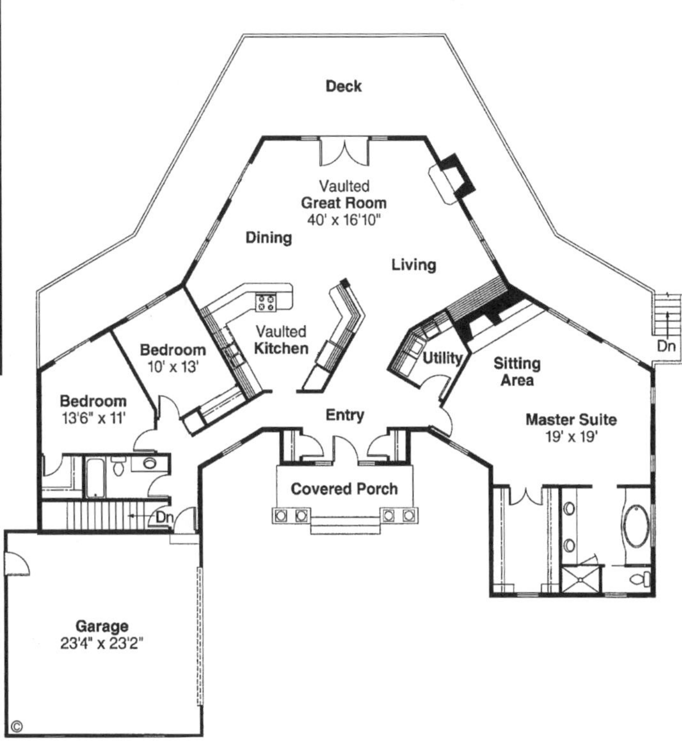
Deck
Vaulted
Great Room
40' x 16'10"
Dining
Living
Vaulted
Kitchen
Bedroom
10' x 13'
Bedroom
13'6" x 11'
Utility
Sitting
Area
Dn
Entry
Master Suite
19' x 19'
Covered Porch
Dn
Garage
23'4" x 23'2"
MAIN FLOOR

Units	Single
Price Code	E
Total Finished	2,365 sq. ft.
Main Finished	2,365 sq. ft.
Basement Unfinished	2,365 sq. ft.
Garage Unfinished	566 sq. ft.
Dimensions	79'x70'6"
Foundation	Crawlspace
Bedrooms	3
Full Baths	2
Main Ceiling	10'
Second Ceiling	8'
Vaulted Ceiling	21'
Max Ridge Height	24'
Roof Framing	Truss
Exterior Walls	2x6

Design 94632

Units Single
Price Code E
Total Finished 2,365 sq. ft.
Main Finished 2,365 sq. ft.
Dimensions 67'6"x73'
Foundation Crawlspace
Slab
Bedrooms 4
Full Baths 2
Main Ceiling 9'
Max Ridge Height 31'6"
Roof Framing Stick
Exterior Walls 2x4

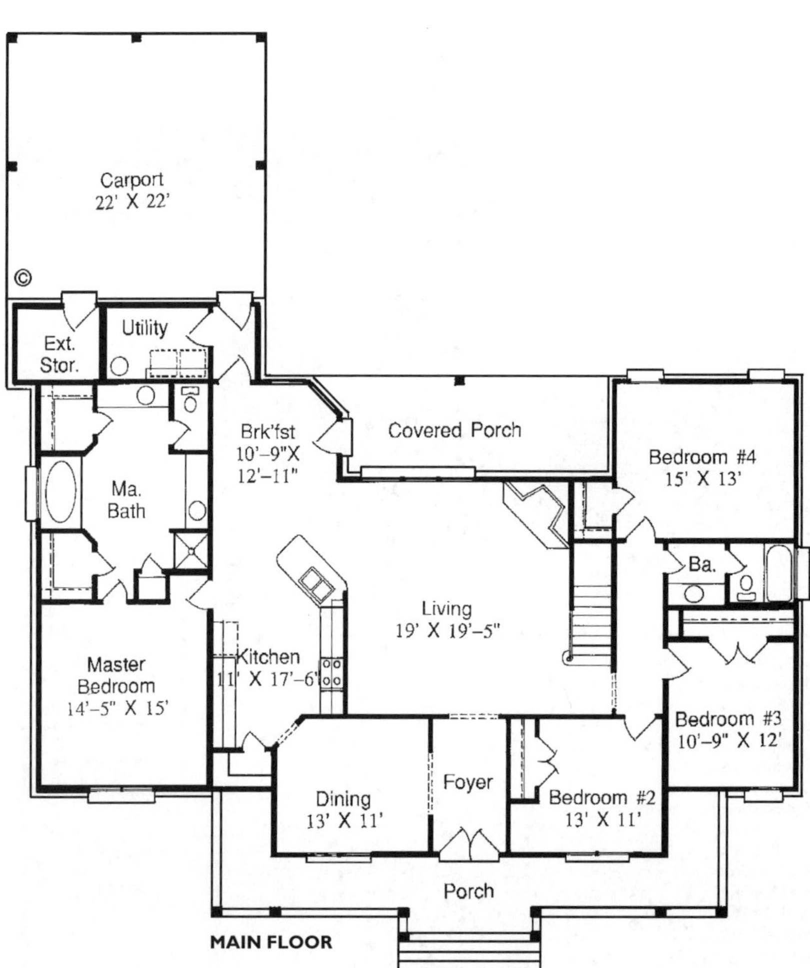

Carport
22' X 22'
©
Ext.
Stor.
Utility
Brk'fst
10'-9"X
12'-11"
Covered Porch
Bedroom #4
15' X 13'
Ma.
Bath
Ba.
Living
19' X 19'-5"
Master
Bedroom
14'-5" X 15'
Kitchen
11' X 17'-6"
Bedroom #3
10'-9" X 12'
Dining
13' X 11'
Foyer
Bedroom #2
13' X 11'
Porch
MAIN FLOOR

Design 98988

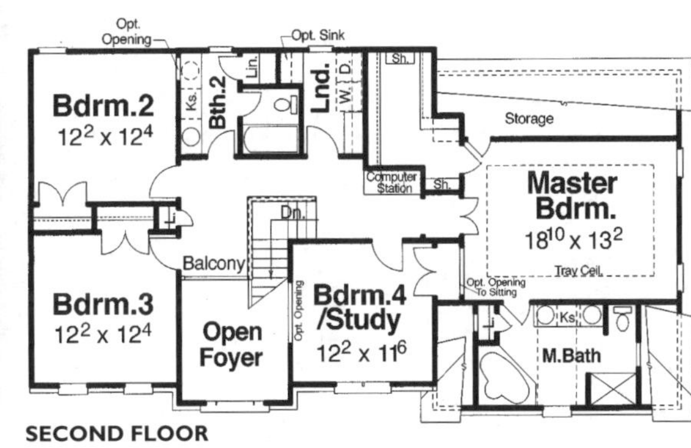
Opt. Opening
Opt. Sink
Bdrm.2
12^2 x 12^4
Bth.2
Lnd.
Storage
Master Bdrm.
18^{10} x 13^2
Tray Ceil.
Computer Station
Dn.
Balcony
Bdrm.3
12^2 x 12^4
Open Foyer
Bdrm.4 /Study
12^2 x 11^6
Opt. Opening To Sitting
M.Bath

SECOND FLOOR

Units	Single
Price Code	E
Total Finished	2,367 sq. ft.
First Finished	1,025 sq. ft.
Second Finished	1,342 sq. ft.
Dimensions	58'4"x30'
Foundation	Basement
Bedrooms	4
Full Baths	2
Half Baths	1
First Ceiling	9'
Second Ceiling	8'
Roof Framing	Stick
Exterior Walls	2x4

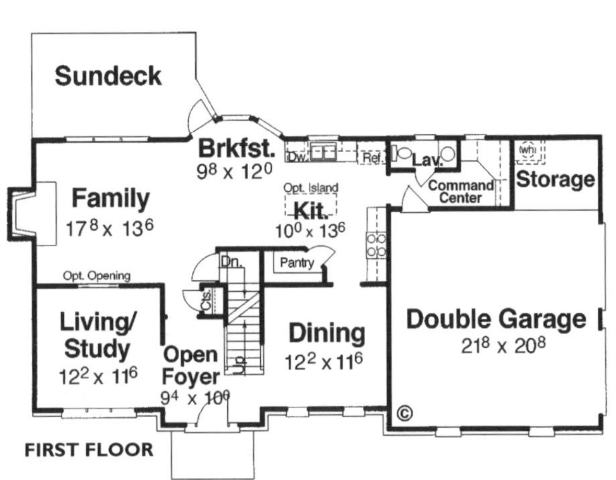
Sundeck
Brkfst.
9^8 x 12^0
Lav.
Storage
Command Center
Family
17^8 x 13^6
Opt. Island
Kit.
10^0 x 13^6
Pantry
Dn.
Opt. Opening
Living/ Study
12^2 x 11^6
Open Foyer
9^4 x 10^0
Dining
12^2 x 11^6
Double Garage
21^8 x 20^8

FIRST FLOOR

Design 98409

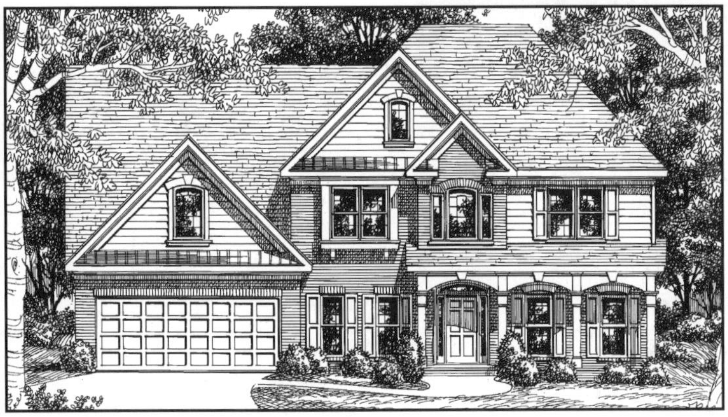

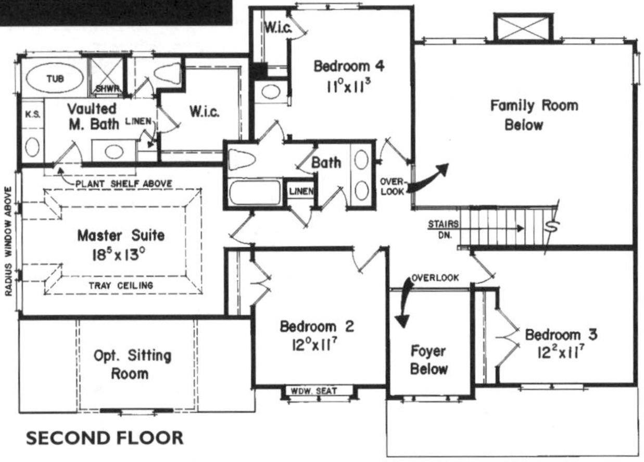

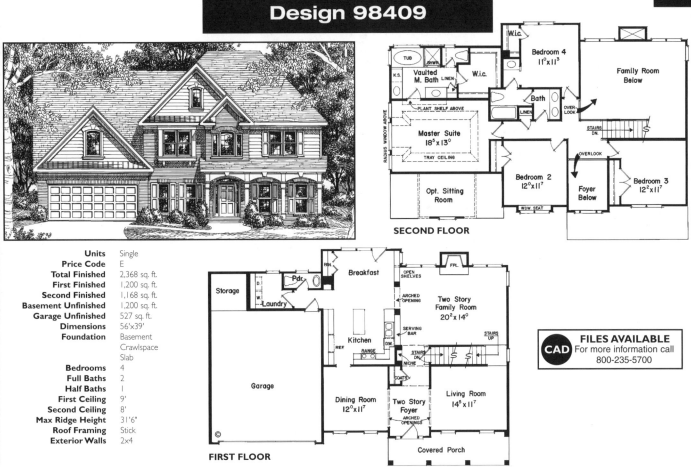

SECOND FLOOR

Units	Single
Price Code	E
Total Finished	2,368 sq. ft.
First Finished	1,200 sq. ft.
Second Finished	1,168 sq. ft.
Basement Unfinished	1,200 sq. ft.
Garage Unfinished	527 sq. ft.
Dimensions	56'x39'
Foundation	Basement Crawlspace Slab
Bedrooms	4
Full Baths	2
Half Baths	1
First Ceiling	9'
Second Ceiling	8'
Max Ridge Height	31'6"
Roof Framing	Stick
Exterior Walls	2x4

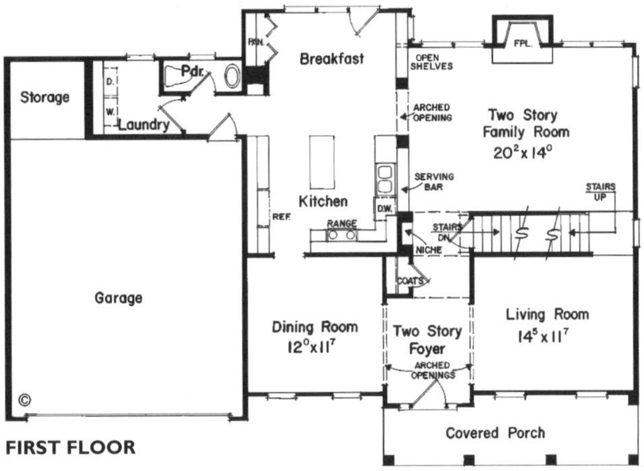

FIRST FLOOR

CAD FILES AVAILABLE For more information call 800-235-5700

Design 98572

Units	Single
Price Code	E
Total Finished	2,370 sq. ft.
Main Finished	2,370 sq. ft.
Garage Unfinished	638 sq. ft.
Deck Unfinished	132 sq. ft.
Porch Unfinished	30 sq. ft.
Dimensions	55'x63'10"
Foundation	Slab
Bedrooms	4
Full Baths	2
Half Baths	1
Max Ridge Height	26'8"
Roof Framing	Stick
Exterior Walls	2x4

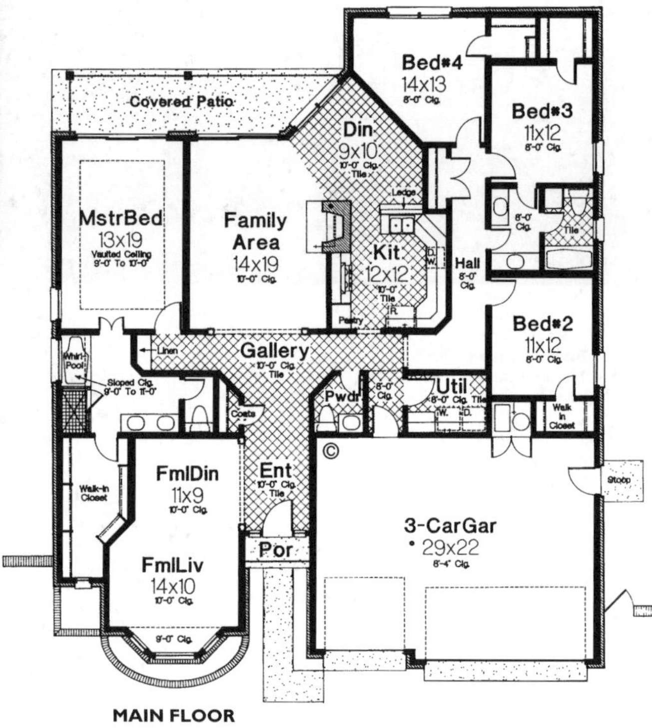

Covered Patio
Bed#4
14x13
Bed#3
11x12
Din
9x10
MstrBed
13x19
Vaulted Ceiling
Family
Area
14x19
Kit
12x12
Hall
Bed#2
11x12
Gallery
Linen
Pwdr
Util
Walk in Closet
Coats
FmlDin
11x9
Ent
Por
3-CarGar
29x22
FmlLiv
14x10

MAIN FLOOR

Design 20368

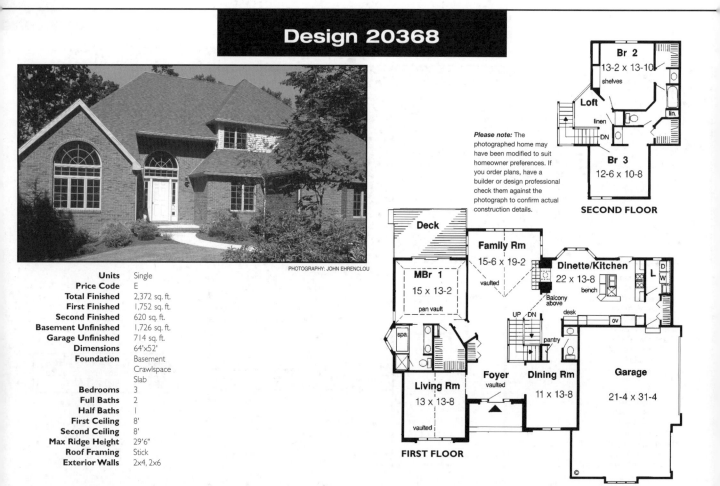

PHOTOGRAPHY: JOHN EHRENCLOU

Units	Single
Price Code	E
Total Finished	2,372 sq. ft.
First Finished	1,752 sq. ft.
Second Finished	620 sq. ft.
Basement Unfinished	1,726 sq. ft.
Garage Unfinished	714 sq. ft.
Dimensions	64'x52'
Foundation	Basement Crawlspace Slab
Bedrooms	3
Full Baths	2
Half Baths	1
First Ceiling	8'
Second Ceiling	8'
Max Ridge Height	29'6"
Roof Framing	Stick
Exterior Walls	2x4, 2x6

Please note: The photographed home may have been modified to suit homeowner preferences. If you order plans, have a builder or design professional check them against the photograph to confirm actual construction details.

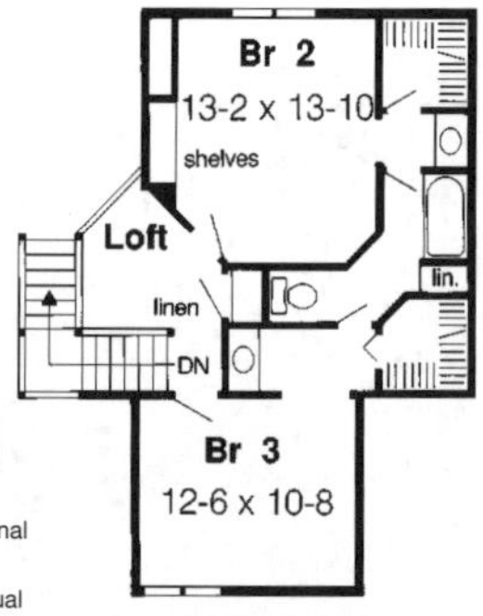

Br 2
13-2 x 13-10
shelves
Loft
linen
DN
Br 3
12-6 x 10-8

SECOND FLOOR

Deck
Family Rm
15-6 x 19-2
vaulted
Dinette/Kitchen
22 x 13-8
bench
MBr 1
15 x 13-2
pan vault
Balcony above
UP DN
desk
pantry
spa
Foyer
vaulted
Dining Rm
11 x 13-8
Garage
21-4 x 31-4
Living Rm
13 x 13-8
vaulted

FIRST FLOOR

Design 91460

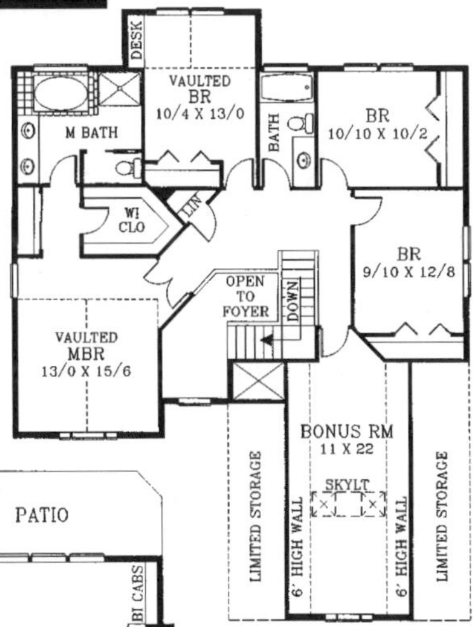

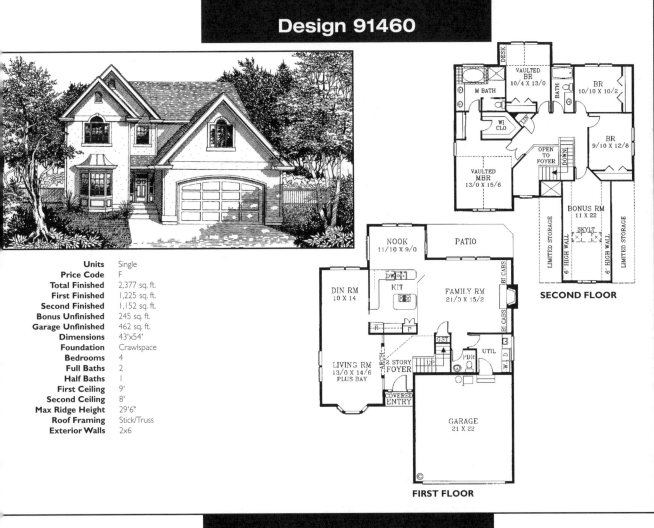

Units	Single
Price Code	F
Total Finished	2,377 sq. ft.
First Finished	1,225 sq. ft.
Second Finished	1,152 sq. ft.
Bonus Unfinished	245 sq. ft.
Garage Unfinished	462 sq. ft.
Dimensions	43'x54'
Foundation	Crawlspace
Bedrooms	4
Full Baths	2
Half Baths	1
First Ceiling	9'
Second Ceiling	8'
Max Ridge Height	29'6"
Roof Framing	Stick/Truss
Exterior Walls	2x6

DESK
VAULTED BR 10/4 X 13/0
M BATH
BATH
BR 10/10 X 10/2
WI CLO
LIN
BR 9/10 X 12/8
OPEN TO FOYER
DOWN
VAULTED MBR 13/0 X 15/6
BONUS RM 11 X 22
SKYLT
LIMITED STORAGE
6' HIGH WALL
6' HIGH WALL
LIMITED STORAGE

SECOND FLOOR

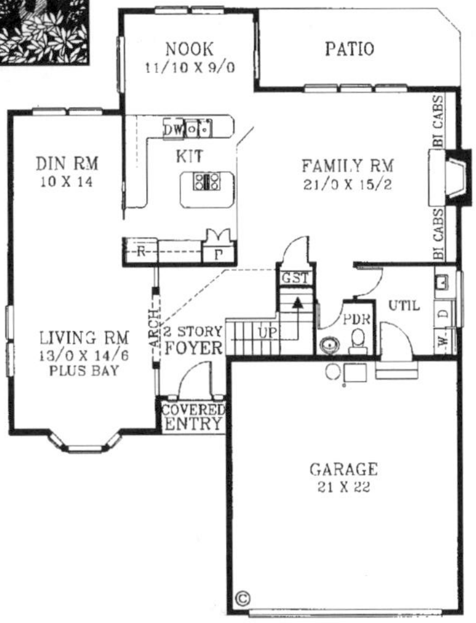

NOOK 11/10 X 9/0
PATIO
DW
KIT
BI CABS
DIN RM 10 X 14
FAMILY RM 21/0 X 15/2
BI CABS
R
P
GST
UTIL
W
D
ARCH
LIVING RM 13/0 X 14/6 PLUS BAY
2 STORY FOYER
UP
PDR
COVERED ENTRY
GARAGE 21 X 22

FIRST FLOOR

Design 62062

Units	Single
Price Code	E
Total Finished	2,379 sq. ft.
Main Finished	2,379 sq. ft.
Bonus Unfinished	754 sq. ft.
Garage Unfinished	576 sq. ft.
Porch Unfinished	405 sq. ft.
Dimensions	66'10"x73'4"
Foundation	Crawlspace Slab
Bedrooms	4
Full Baths	3
Main Ceiling	9'
Second Ceiling	8'
Max Ridge Height	28'1"
Roof Framing	Stick
Exterior Walls	2x4

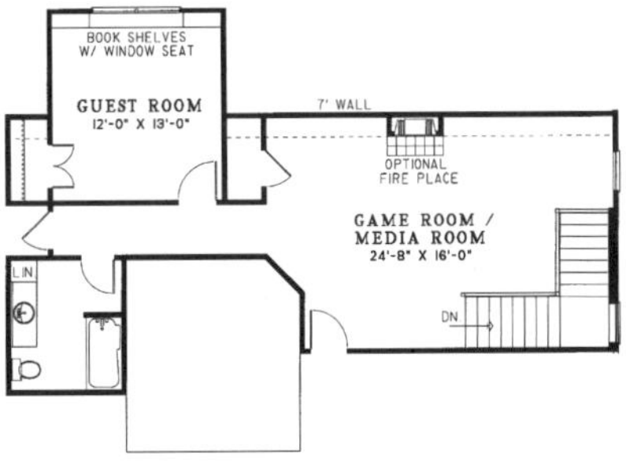

GRILLING PORCH 25'-10" X 8'-0"
WHP TUB
LIN
M. BATH 12'-6" X 15'-4"
MASTER SUITE 10' BOXED CEILING 13'-6" X 15'-4"
GREAT ROOM 14'-0" X 19'-0"
BREAKFAST ROOM 9'-0" X 9'-8"
HEARTH ROOM 15'-0" X 16'-4"
W.I.C.
REF.
D.W.
KITCHEN 11'-7" X 12'-3"
PAN
RG
UP
BATH 11'-0" X 5'-0"
LIN
FOYER 7'-6" X 9'-9"
8" RND COL.
D W
LAU.
KID'S NOOK
DINING ROOM 10' CEILING 12'-4" X 13'-4"
BEDROOM 3 11'-0" X 13'-0"
BEDROOM 2 / STUDY 11'-2" X 11'-2"
TEENAGE / GUEST ROOM 12'-0" X 11'-9"
BATH
COVERED PORCH 10' CEILING 21'-6" X 8'-0"
STRG.
GARAGE 22'-0" X 23'-6"

MAIN FLOOR

BOOK SHELVES W/ WINDOW SEAT
GUEST ROOM 12'-0" X 13'-0"
7' WALL
OPTIONAL FIRE PLACE
GAME ROOM / MEDIA ROOM 24'-8" X 16'-0"
LIN
DN

BONUS

Design 91503

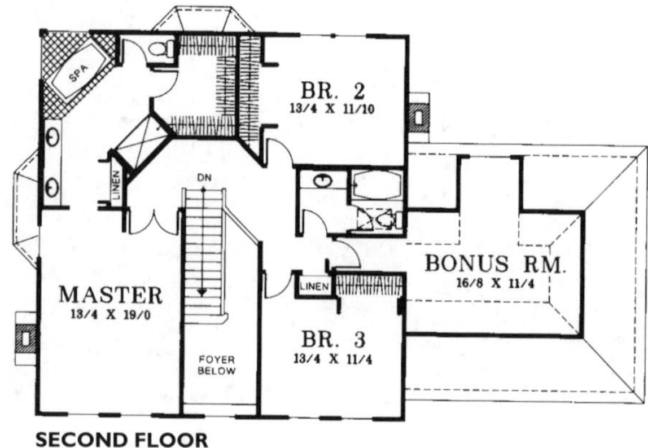
SPA
BR. 2
13/4 X 11/10
LINEN
DN
BONUS RM.
16/8 X 11/4
MASTER
13/4 X 19/0
LINEN
BR. 3
13/4 X 11/4
FOYER BELOW

SECOND FLOOR

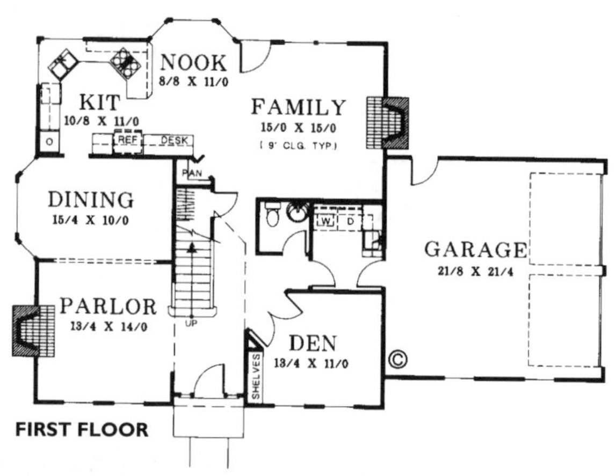
NOOK
8/8 X 11/0
KIT
10/8 X 11/0
FAMILY
15/0 X 15/0
(9' CLG. TYP.)
REF
DESK
PLAN
DINING
15/4 X 10/0
GARAGE
21/8 X 21/4
PARLOR
13/4 X 14/0
UP
DEN
13/4 X 11/0
SHELVES

FIRST FLOOR

Units	Single
Price Code	E
Total Finished	2,385 sq. ft.
First Finished	1,285 sq. ft.
Second Finished	1,100 sq. ft.
Bonus Unfinished	238 sq. ft.
Dimensions	59'x38'
Foundation	Basement Crawlspace
Bedrooms	3
Full Baths	2
Half Baths	1
Max Ridge Height	31'
Roof Framing	Stick
Exterior Walls	2x4

Design 98486

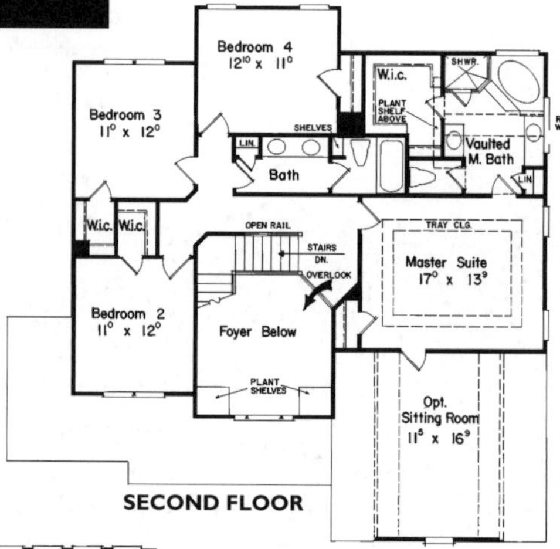

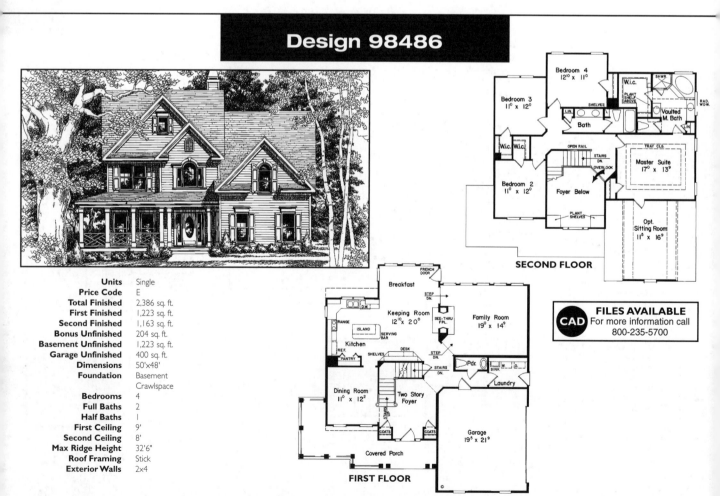

SECOND FLOOR

FIRST FLOOR

Units	Single
Price Code	E
Total Finished	2,386 sq. ft.
First Finished	1,223 sq. ft.
Second Finished	1,163 sq. ft.
Bonus Unfinished	204 sq. ft.
Basement Unfinished	1,223 sq. ft.
Garage Unfinished	400 sq. ft.
Dimensions	50'x48'
Foundation	Basement Crawlspace
Bedrooms	4
Full Baths	2
Half Baths	1
First Ceiling	9'
Second Ceiling	8'
Max Ridge Height	32'6"
Roof Framing	Stick
Exterior Walls	2x4

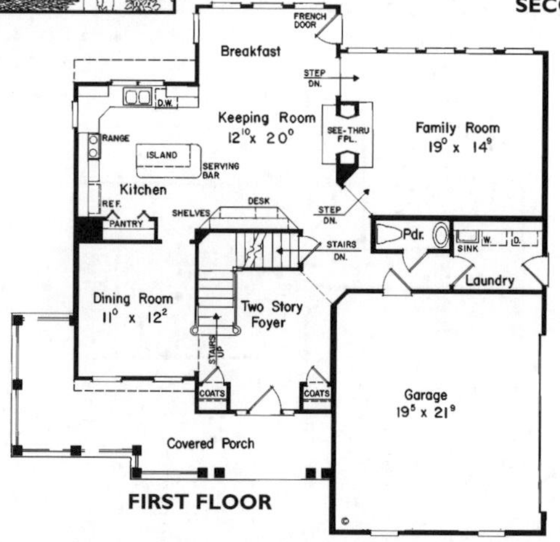

Design 20209

Units	Single
Price Code	E
Total Finished	2,387 sq. ft.
Main Finished	1,861 sq. ft.
Lower Finished	526 sq. ft.
Basement Unfinished	874 sq. ft.
Garage Unfinished	574 sq. ft.
Dimensions	54'x50'
Foundation	Basement
Bedrooms	3
Full Baths	2
Half Baths	1
Max Ridge Height	26'
Roof Framing	Stick
Exterior Walls	2x4

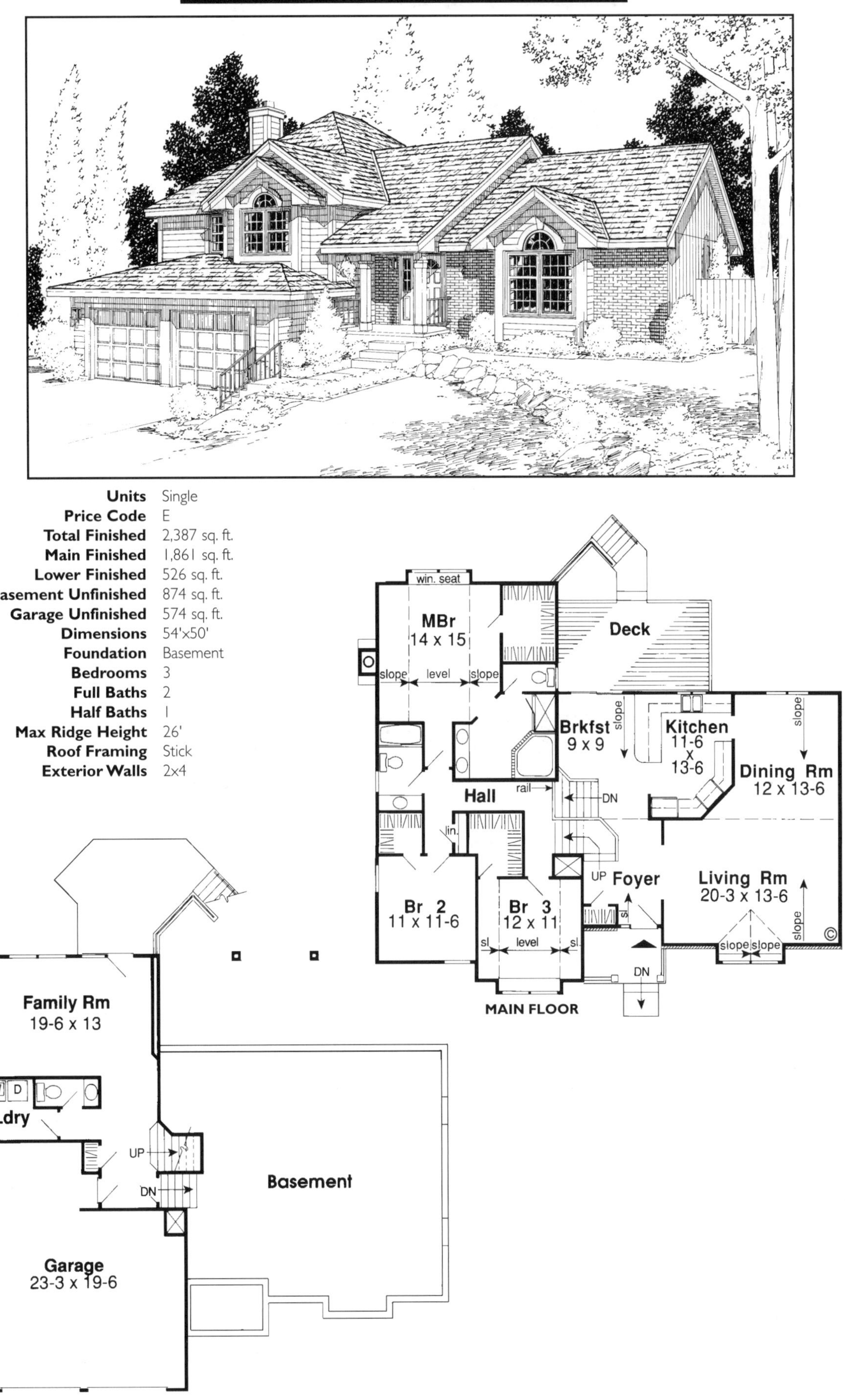
win. seat
MBr
14 x 15
slope
level
slope
Deck
Brkfst
9 x 9
slope
Kitchen
11-6
x
13-6
slope
Dining Rm
12 x 13-6
Hall
rail
DN
lin.
UP
Foyer
Living Rm
20-3 x 13-6
Br 2
11 x 11-6
Br 3
12 x 11
sl
level
sl
slope
slope
slope
DN
MAIN FLOOR
books
Family Rm
19-6 x 13
books
W
D
Ldry
UP
DN
Basement
Garage
23-3 x 19-6
LOWER FLOOR

Design 92546

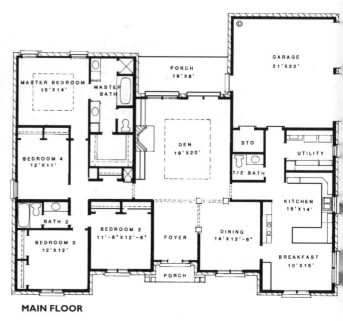

Units	Single
Price Code	E
Total Finished	2,387 sq. ft.
Main Finished	2,387 sq. ft.
Garage Unfinished	505 sq. ft.
Porch Unfinished	194 sq. ft.
Dimensions	64'10"x54'10"
Foundation	Crawlspace Slab
Bedrooms	4
Full Baths	2
Half Baths	1
Main Ceiling	9'
Max Ridge Height	28'
Roof Framing	Truss
Exterior Walls	2x4

MASTER BEDROOM 15'X14'
MASTER BATH
PORCH 19'X8'
GARAGE 21'X22'
BEDROOM 4 12'X11'
DEN 19'X20'
STO
UTILITY
1/2 BATH
KITCHEN 15'X14'
BATH 2
BEDROOM 2 11'-6"X12'-6"
FOYER
DINING 14'X12'-6"
BEDROOM 3 12'X12'
BREAKFAST 10'X15'
PORCH

MAIN FLOOR

Design 93033

Units	Single
Price Code	E
Total Finished	2,389 sq. ft.
Main Finished	2,389 sq. ft.
Garage Unfinished	543 sq. ft.
Porch Unfinished	208 sq. ft.
Dimensions	75'2"x61'4"
Foundation	Crawlspace Slab
Bedrooms	4
Full Baths	2
Half Baths	1
Max Ridge Height	22'
Roof Framing	Stick
Exterior Walls	2x4

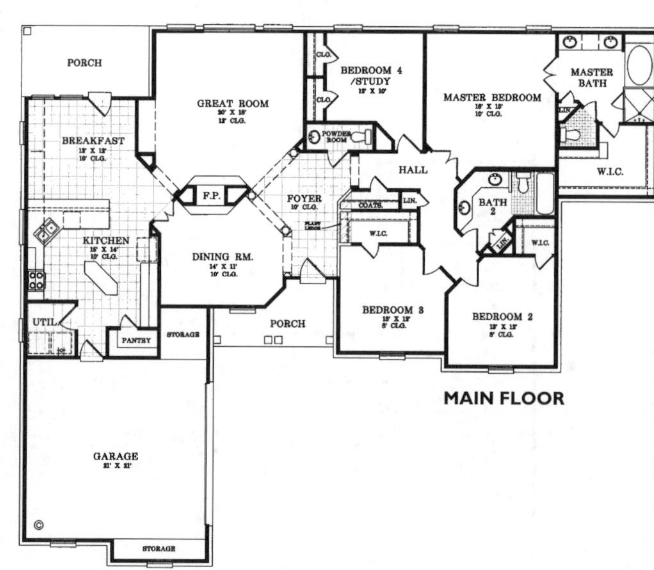
PORCH
GREAT ROOM
BEDROOM 4 /STUDY
MASTER BEDROOM
MASTER BATH
BREAKFAST
HALL
W.I.C.
F.P.
FOYER
BATH 2
KITCHEN
DINING RM.
BEDROOM 3
BEDROOM 2
UTIL.
PANTRY
STORAGE
PORCH
GARAGE
STORAGE

MAIN FLOOR

Design 98410

Vaulted M.Bath
SHWR
W.i.c.
Family Room Below
PLANT SHELF ABOVE
Bedroom 3 11^0 x 11^0
Bath
LINEN
OVERLOOK
OPEN RAIL
TRAY CLG.
Master Suite 13^5 x 18^5
STAIRS DN
PLANT SHELF BELOW
Foyer Below
Bedroom 2 11^1 x 11^0
SECOND FLOOR

Units	Single
Price Code	E
Total Finished	2,389 sq. ft.
First Finished	1,428 sq. ft.
Second Finished	961 sq. ft.
Bonus Unfinished	472 sq. ft.
Basement Unfinished	1,428 sq. ft.
Garage Unfinished	507 sq. ft.
Dimensions	61'x37'10"
Foundation	Basement Crawlspace
Bedrooms	4
Full Baths	3
First Ceiling	9'
Second Ceiling	8'
Max Ridge Height	31'6"
Roof Framing	Stick
Exterior Walls	2x4

FIRST FLOOR: Den / Bedroom 4 13^5 x 11^0; Two Story Family Room 14^6 x 18^2; Breakfast; Laund.; Storage; Kitchen; Bath; Garage 20^9 x 20^6; Living Room 13^5 x 14^0; Two Story Foyer; Dining Room 13^5 x 11^0

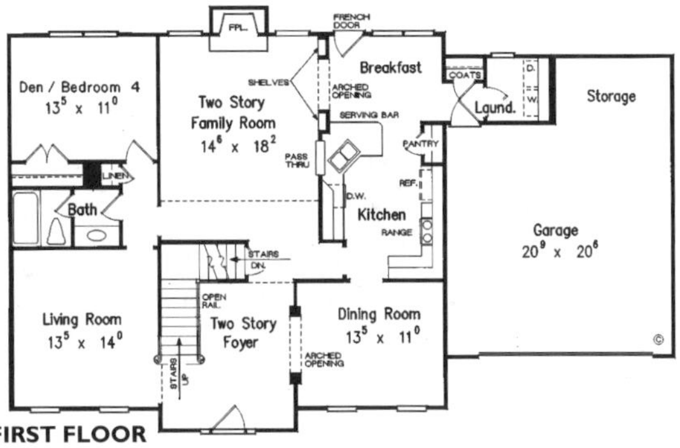

BONUS: Bedroom 3 11^0 x 12^4; Bath; Bonus Room 12^{10} x 20^5; Bedroom 2 13^5 x 12^3

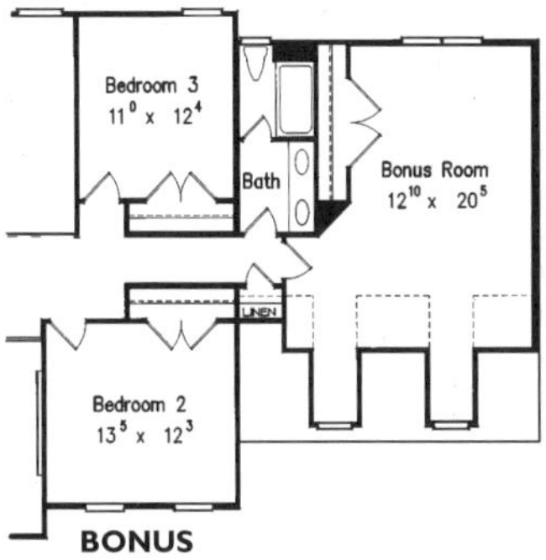

Design 98992

SECOND FLOOR: Bdrm.2 11^6 x 11^{10}; Bth.2; Lnd.; Master Bdrm. 13^6 x 17^6; Tray Ceil.; Plant Shelf Above; Bdrm.4 10^0 x 10^4; Open To Foyer; Bdrm.3 10^8 x 12^4; M.Bath Vaulted Ceil.

Units	Single
Price Code	G
Total Finished	2,389 sq. ft.
First Finished	1,067 sq. ft.
Second Finished	1,322 sq. ft.
Dimensions	48'x36'
Foundation	Basement
Bedrooms	4
Full Baths	2
Half Baths	1
First Ceiling	9'
Roof Framing	Stick
Exterior Walls	2x4

FIRST FLOOR: Sundeck; Living Area 19^{10} x 15^6; Brkfst. 10^0 x 13^0; Kit. 9^4 x 13^4; Island; Pant.; Ref.; Lav.; Library 10^0 x 12^4 w/ Bay; Open Foyer 6^4 x 11^2; Dining 10^8 x 11^2; Double Garage 19^4 x 21^8

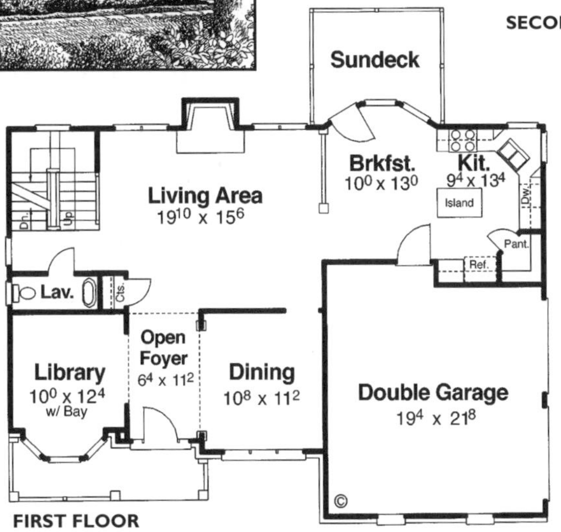

Design 66039

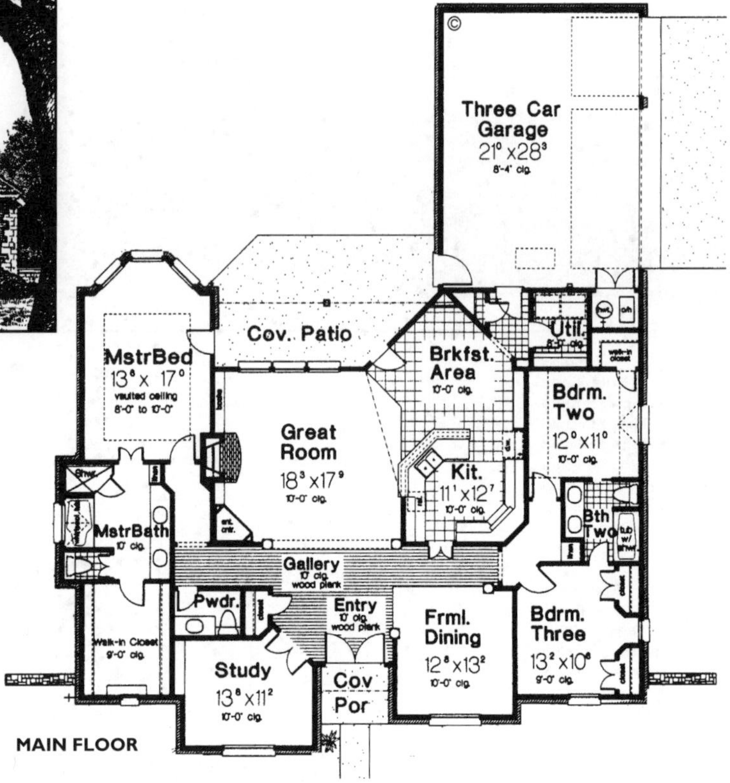

Units	Single
Price Code	E
Total Finished	2,390 sq. ft.
Main Finished	2,390 sq. ft.
Garage Unfinished	602 sq. ft.
Deck Unfinished	202 sq. ft.
Dimensions	60'x76'
Foundation	Slab
Bedrooms	3
Full Baths	2
Half Baths	1
Main Ceiling	9'/10'
Max Ridge Height	27'6"
Roof Framing	Stick
Exterior Walls	2x4

MAIN FLOOR

Design 65629

PHOTOGRAPHY: COURTESY OF THE DESIGNER

Units	Single
Price Code	E
Total Finished	2,396 sq. ft.
Main Finished	2,396 sq. ft.
Dimensions	72'x60'
Foundation	Basement Crawlspace Slab
Bedrooms	4
Full Baths	2
Main Ceiling	9'
Max Ridge Height	28'
Roof Framing	Stick
Exterior Walls	2x6

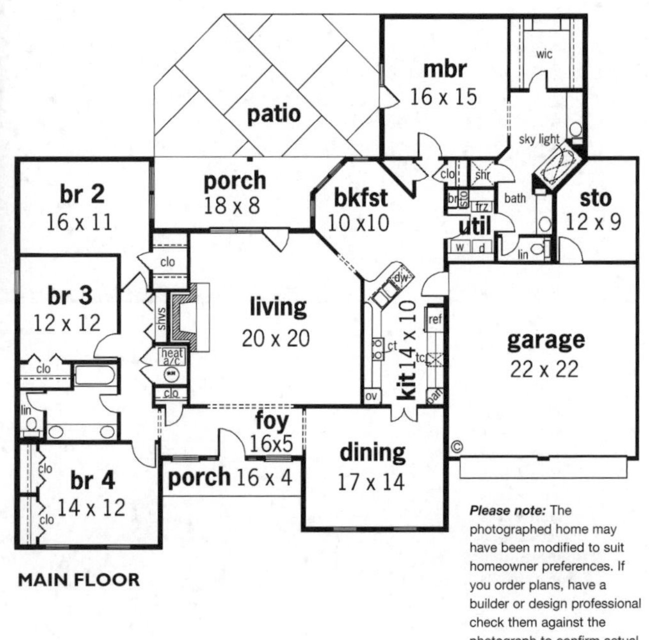
patio
mbr
16 x 15
wic
sky light
br 2
16 x 11
porch
18 x 8
bkfst
10 x 10
bath
util
sto
12 x 9
br 3
12 x 12
living
20 x 20
kit 14 x 10
garage
22 x 22
foy
16x5
dining
17 x 14
porch 16 x 4
br 4
14 x 12
MAIN FLOOR

Please note: The photographed home may have been modified to suit homeowner preferences. If you order plans, have a builder or design professional check them against the photograph to confirm actual construction details.

Design 63108

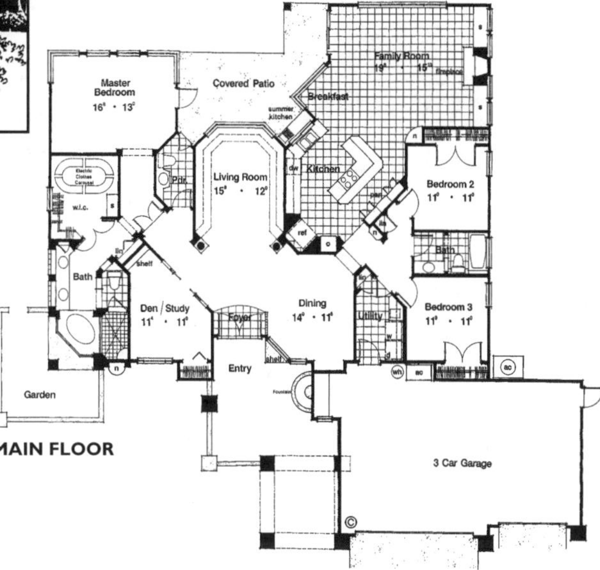
Master Bedroom
Covered Patio
Family Room
Fireplace
Breakfast
summer kitchen
Living Room
Kitchen
Bedroom 2
Bath
Den/Study
Foyer
Dining
Utility
Bedroom 3
Entry
Garden
3 Car Garage

MAIN FLOOR

Units	Single
Price Code	E
Total Finished	2,397 sq. ft.
Main Finished	2,397 sq. ft.
Garage Unfinished	473 sq. ft.
Dimensions	73'2"x73'2"
Foundation	Slab
Bedrooms	3
Full Baths	2
Half Baths	1
Main Ceiling	10'
Tray Ceiling	13'4"
Max Ridge Height	22'8"
Roof Framing	Truss
Exterior Walls	2x4

Design 90450

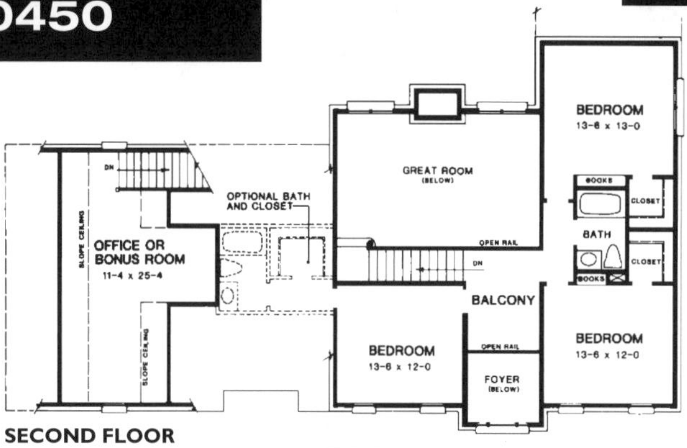

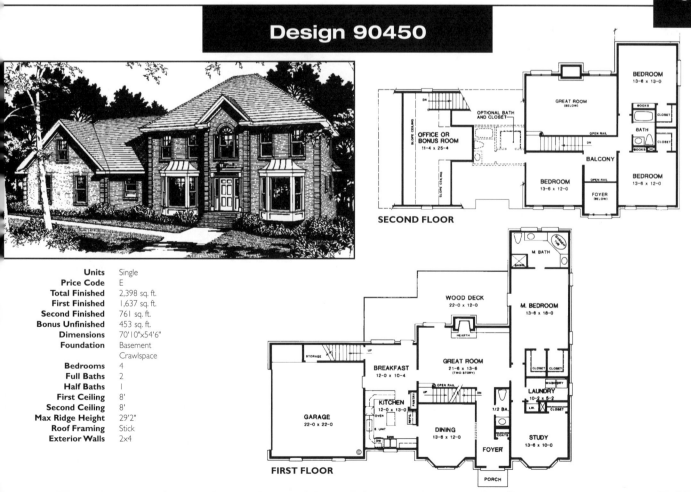

SECOND FLOOR

FIRST FLOOR

Units	Single
Price Code	E
Total Finished	2,398 sq. ft.
First Finished	1,637 sq. ft.
Second Finished	761 sq. ft.
Bonus Unfinished	453 sq. ft.
Dimensions	70'10"x54'6"
Foundation	Basement Crawlspace
Bedrooms	4
Full Baths	2
Half Baths	1
First Ceiling	8'
Second Ceiling	8'
Max Ridge Height	29'2"
Roof Framing	Stick
Exterior Walls	2x4

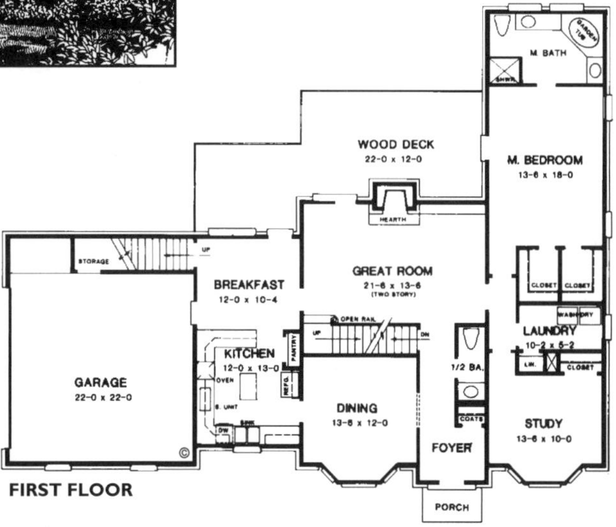

Design 68046

Units	Single
Price Code	E
Total Finished	2,399 sq. ft.
Main Finished	2,399 sq. ft.
Garage Unfinished	723 sq. ft.
Dimensions	72'8"x64'6"
Foundation	Basement Crawlspace Slab
Bedrooms	3
Full Baths	2
Half Baths	1
Main Ceiling	8'
Max Ridge Height	21'
Roof Framing	Stick
Exterior Walls	2x6

* Alternate foundation options available at an additional charge.
Please call 1-800-235-5700 for more information.

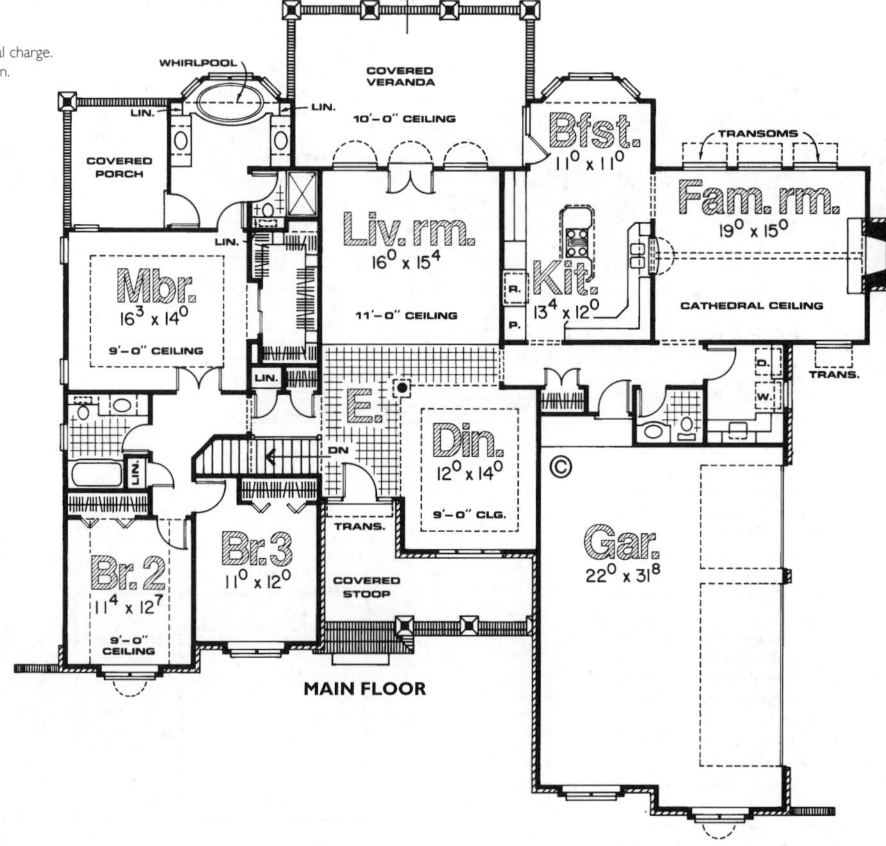
WHIRLPOOL
COVERED VERANDA
10'-0" CEILING
LIN.
COVERED PORCH
Bfst.
11^{0} x 11^{0}
TRANSOMS
Fam. rm.
19^{0} x 15^{0}
CATHEDRAL CEILING
Liv. rm.
16^{0} x 15^{4}
11'-0" CEILING
Mbr.
16^{3} x 14^{0}
9'-0" CEILING
Kit.
13^{4} x 12^{0}
R.
P.
D.
W.
TRANS.
E.
Din.
12^{0} x 14^{0}
9'-0" CLG.
DN
Gar.
22^{0} x 31^{8}
Br. 2
11^{4} x 12^{7}
9'-0" CEILING
Br. 3
11^{0} x 12^{0}
COVERED STOOP
MAIN FLOOR

Design 92651

PHOTOGRAPHY: DOMENIC CENTOFANTI

Units	Single
Price Code	E
Total Finished	2,403 sq. ft.
First Finished	1,710 sq. ft.
Second Finished	693 sq. ft.
Basement Unfinished	1,620 sq. ft.
Garage Unfinished	467 sq. ft.
Porch Unfinished	43 sq. ft.
Dimensions	63'4"x48'
Foundation	Basement Slab
Bedrooms	4
Full Baths	3
Half Baths	1
First Ceiling	8'
Second Ceiling	8'
Vaulted Ceiling	11'
Tray Ceiling	17'
Max Ridge Height	20'
Roof Framing	Truss
Exterior Walls	2x4

Great Room Below
high glass
high ceiling
plant shelf
Bath
Bedroom 11'4" x 12'6"
Hall
linen
Bedroom 10' x 13'10"
Bath
walk-in closet
Bedroom 12' x 10'6"
slope ceiling
slope ceiling

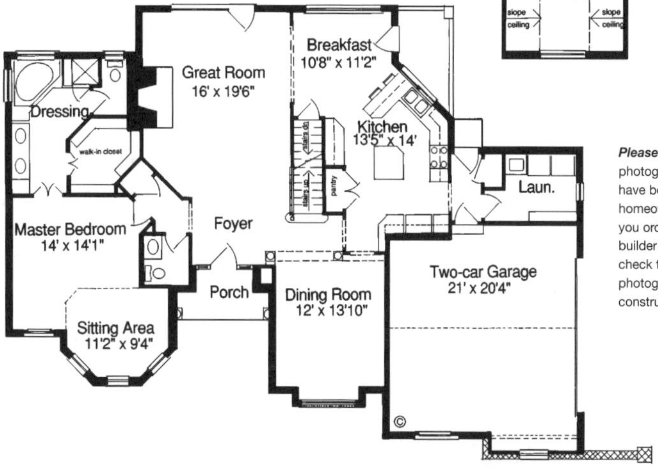

Dressing
walk-in closet
Great Room 16' x 19'6"
Breakfast 10'8" x 11'2"
Kitchen 13'5" x 14'
pantry
Laun.
Master Bedroom 14' x 14'1"
Foyer
Porch
Sitting Area 11'2" x 9'4"
Dining Room 12' x 13'10"
Two-car Garage 21' x 20'4"

Please note: The photographed home may have been modified to suit homeowner preferences. If you order plans, have a builder or design professional check them against the photograph to confirm actual construction details.

Design 91700

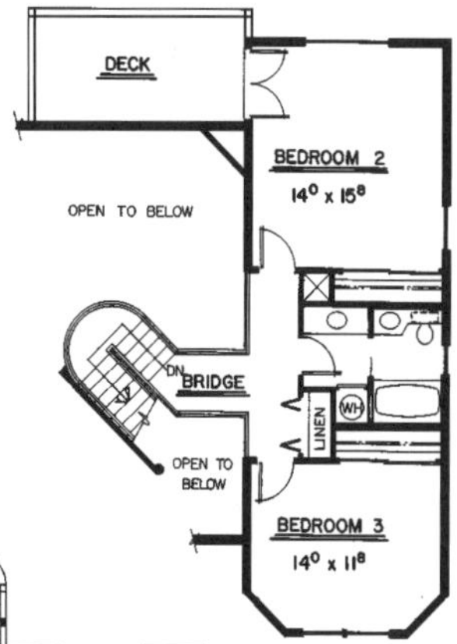

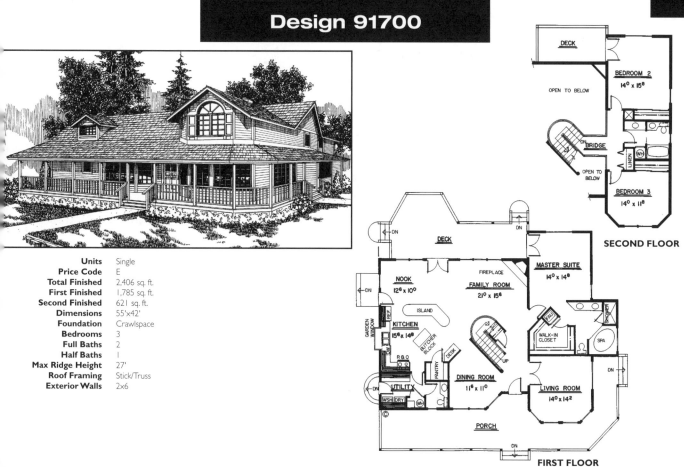

Units	Single
Price Code	E
Total Finished	2,406 sq. ft.
First Finished	1,785 sq. ft.
Second Finished	621 sq. ft.
Dimensions	55'x42'
Foundation	Crawlspace
Bedrooms	3
Full Baths	2
Half Baths	1
Max Ridge Height	27'
Roof Framing	Stick/Truss
Exterior Walls	2x6

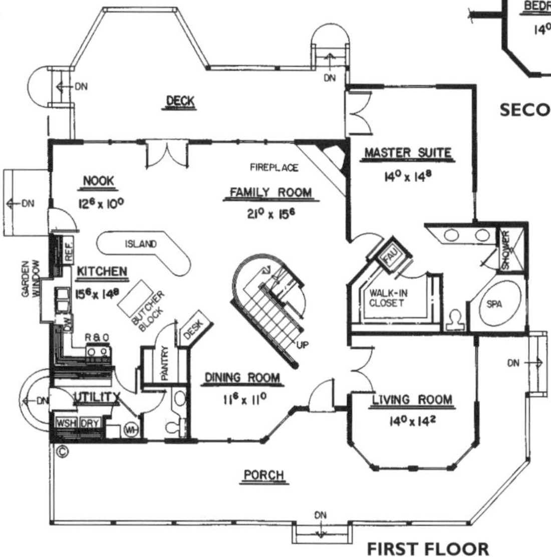

DECK
BEDROOM 2 $14^0 \times 15^6$
OPEN TO BELOW
BRIDGE
OPEN TO BELOW
LINEN
BEDROOM 3 $14^0 \times 11^8$
SECOND FLOOR

DECK
NOOK $12^6 \times 10^0$
FIREPLACE
FAMILY ROOM $21^0 \times 15^6$
MASTER SUITE $14^0 \times 14^8$
ISLAND
GARDEN WINDOW
KITCHEN $15^6 \times 14^8$
BUTCHER BLOCK
WALK-IN CLOSET
SHOWER
SPA
PANTRY
DESK
DINING ROOM $11^6 \times 11^0$
LIVING ROOM $14^0 \times 14^2$
UTILITY
WSH DRY
PORCH
FIRST FLOOR

Design 24950

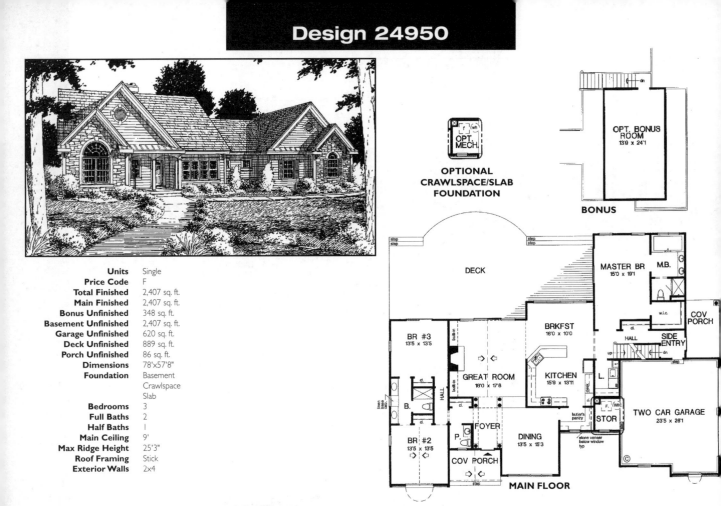

OPTIONAL CRAWLSPACE/SLAB FOUNDATION

BONUS

MAIN FLOOR

Units	Single
Price Code	F
Total Finished	2,407 sq. ft.
Main Finished	2,407 sq. ft.
Bonus Unfinished	348 sq. ft.
Basement Unfinished	2,407 sq. ft.
Garage Unfinished	620 sq. ft.
Deck Unfinished	889 sq. ft.
Porch Unfinished	86 sq. ft.
Dimensions	78'x57'8"
Foundation	Basement Crawlspace Slab
Bedrooms	3
Full Baths	2
Half Baths	1
Main Ceiling	9'
Max Ridge Height	25'3"
Roof Framing	Stick
Exterior Walls	2x4

Design 52067

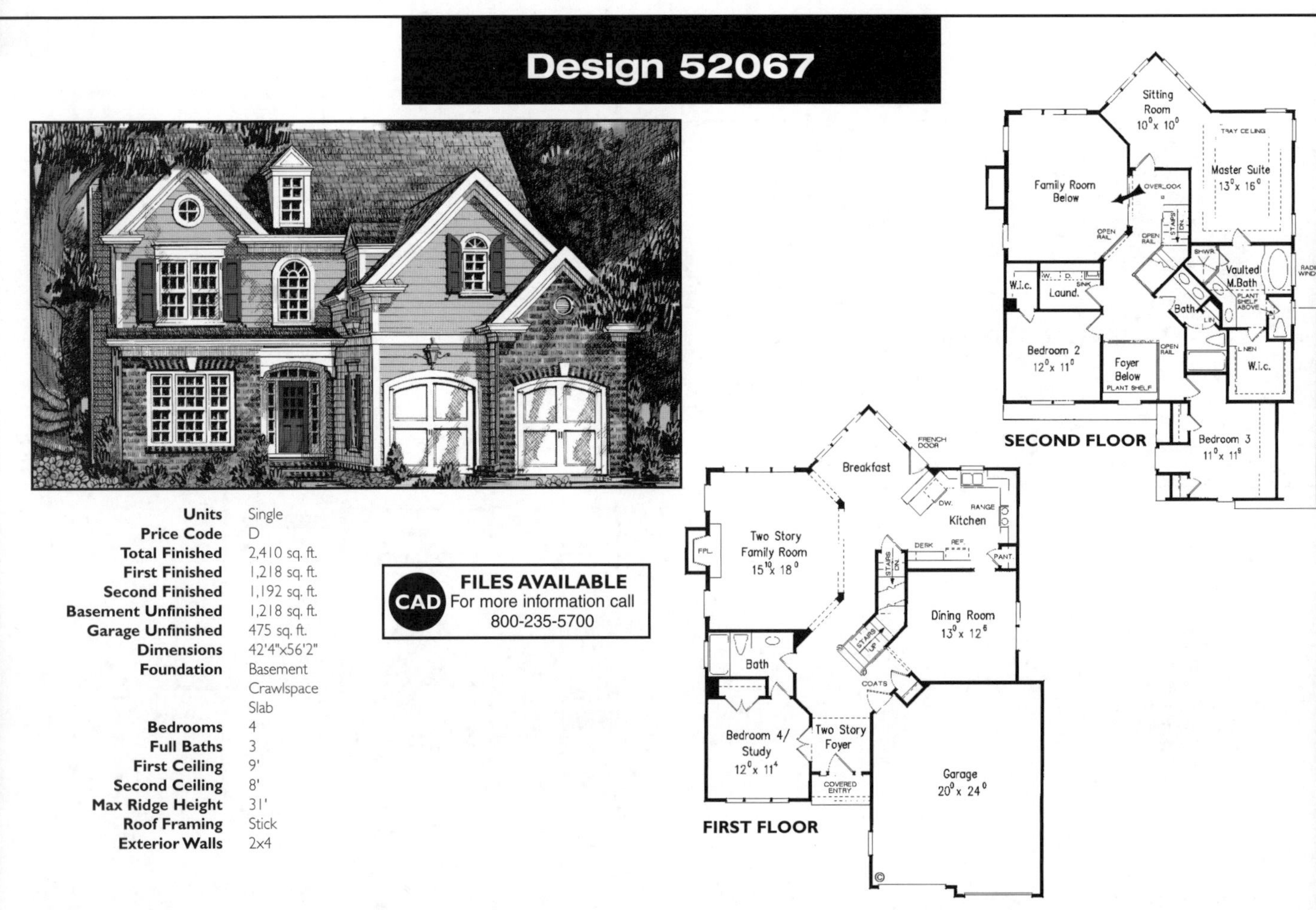

Sitting Room 10⁰x 10⁰
Family Room Below
Master Suite 13⁰x 16⁰
Vaulted M.Bath
Laund.
Bedroom 2 12⁰x 11⁰
Foyer Below
Bedroom 3 11⁰x 11⁶
Breakfast
Kitchen
Two Story Family Room 15¹⁰x 18⁰
Dining Room 13⁰x 12⁶
Bath
Bedroom 4/ Study 12⁰x 11⁴
Two Story Foyer
Garage 20⁰x 24⁰

SECOND FLOOR

FIRST FLOOR

Units	Single
Price Code	D
Total Finished	2,410 sq. ft.
First Finished	1,218 sq. ft.
Second Finished	1,192 sq. ft.
Basement Unfinished	1,218 sq. ft.
Garage Unfinished	475 sq. ft.
Dimensions	42'4"x56'2"
Foundation	Basement Crawlspace Slab
Bedrooms	4
Full Baths	3
First Ceiling	9'
Second Ceiling	8'
Max Ridge Height	31'
Roof Framing	Stick
Exterior Walls	2x4

Design 24262

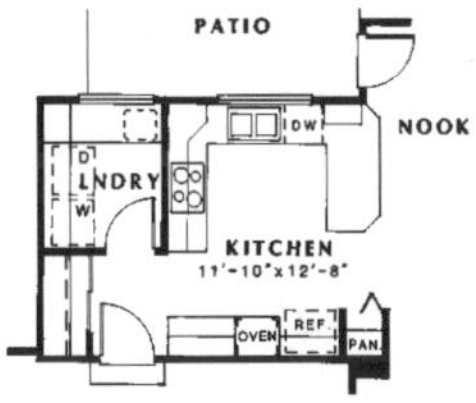

Units	Single
Price Code	E
Total Finished	2,411 sq. ft.
First Finished	1,241 sq. ft.
Second Finished	1,170 sq. ft.
Basement Unfinished	1,241 sq. ft.
Garage Unfinished	500 sq. ft.
Dimensions	52'x43'
Foundation	Basement Crawlspace Slab
Bedrooms	4
Full Baths	2
Half Baths	1
Max Ridge Height	27'
Roof Framing	Stick
Exterior Walls	2x4

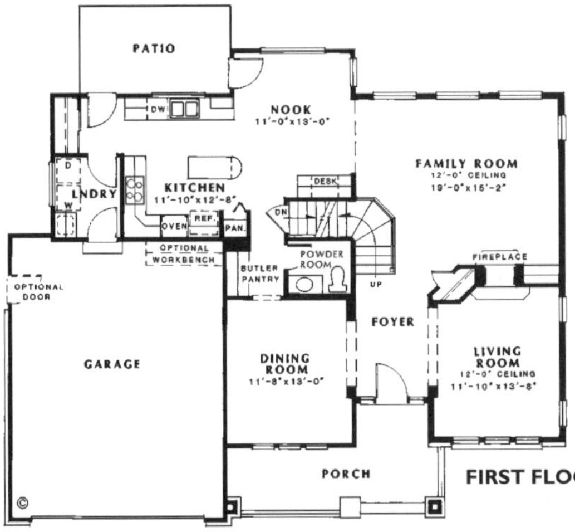

OPTIONAL KITCHEN

OPTIONAL RETREAT

FIRST FLOOR

SECOND FLOOR

Design 93602

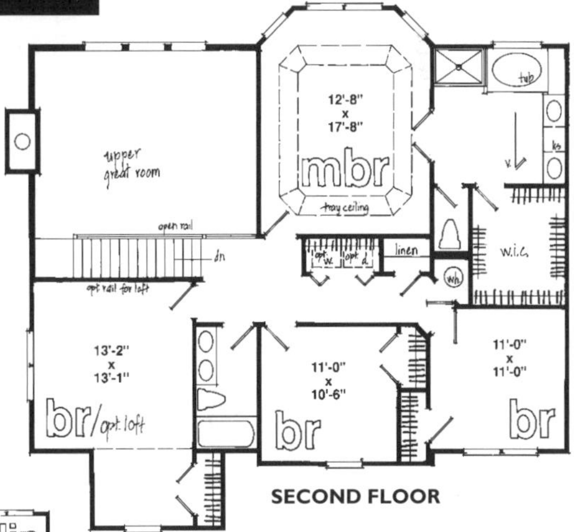

Units	Single
Price Code	E
Total Finished	2,411 sq. ft.
First Finished	1,209 sq. ft.
Second Finished	1,202 sq. ft.
Basement Unfinished	1,209 sq. ft.
Garage Unfinished	370 sq. ft.
Dimensions	46'x41'
Foundation	Basement Slab
Bedrooms	4
Full Baths	2
Half Baths	1
Max Ridge Height	30'
Roof Framing	Truss
Exterior Walls	2x4

SECOND FLOOR

FIRST FLOOR

Design 24735

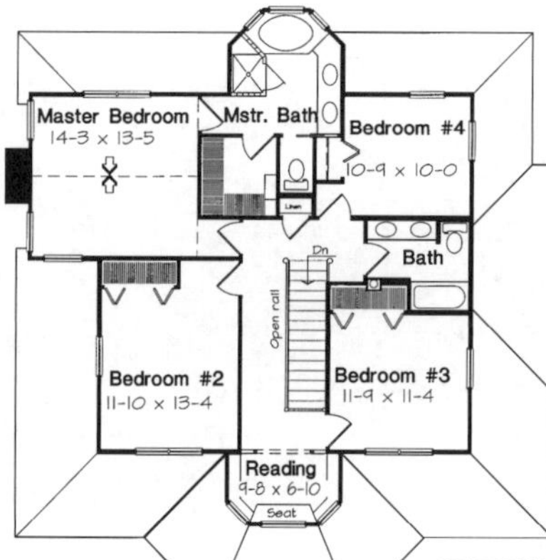

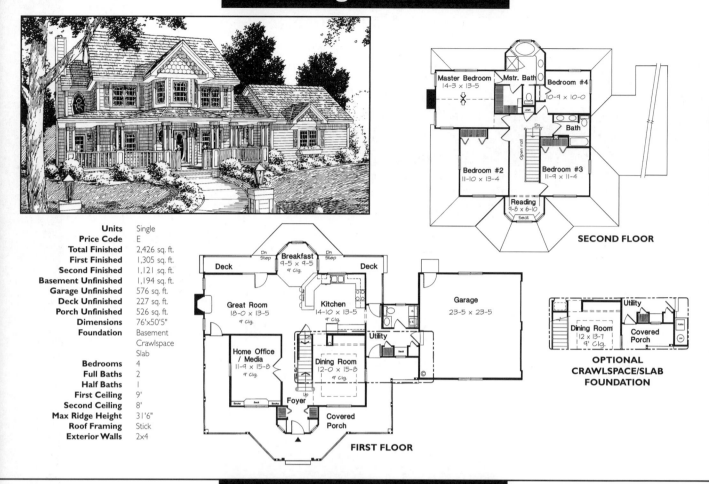

Units	Single
Price Code	E
Total Finished	2,426 sq. ft.
First Finished	1,305 sq. ft.
Second Finished	1,121 sq. ft.
Basement Unfinished	1,194 sq. ft.
Garage Unfinished	576 sq. ft.
Deck Unfinished	227 sq. ft.
Porch Unfinished	526 sq. ft.
Dimensions	76'x50'5"
Foundation	Basement Crawlspace Slab
Bedrooms	4
Full Baths	2
Half Baths	1
First Ceiling	9'
Second Ceiling	8'
Max Ridge Height	31'6"
Roof Framing	Stick
Exterior Walls	2x4

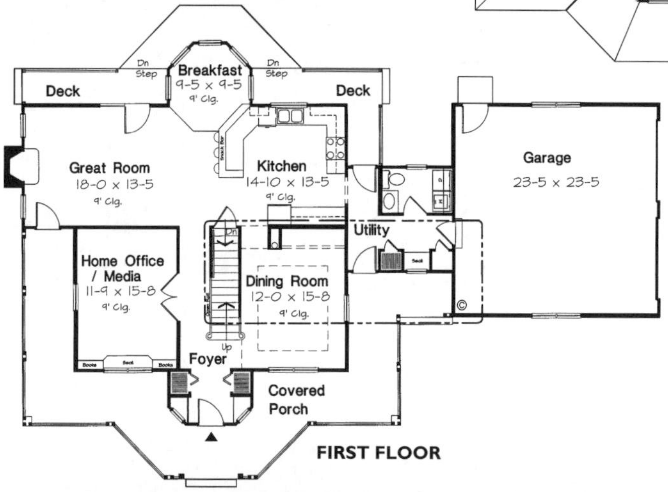

SECOND FLOOR

FIRST FLOOR

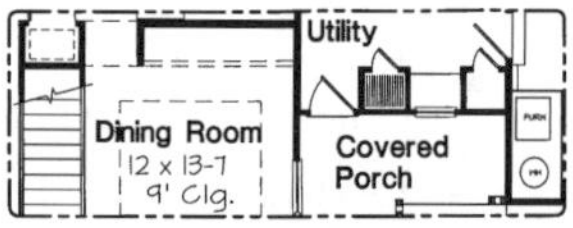

OPTIONAL CRAWLSPACE/SLAB FOUNDATION

Design 24567

PHOTOGRAPHY: SUSAN GILMORE

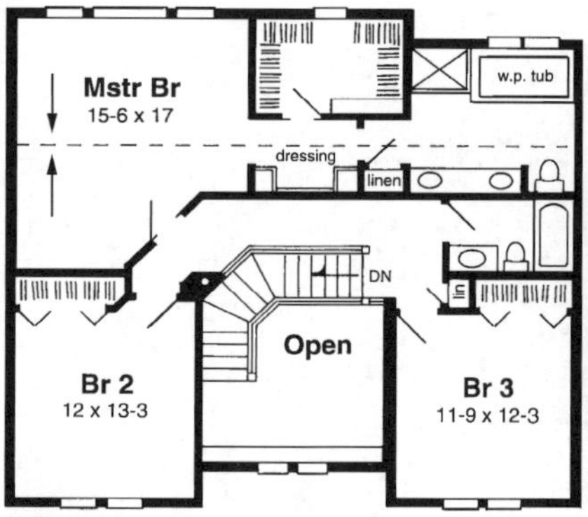

Units	Single
Price Code	E
Total Finished	2,432 sq. ft.
First Finished	1,332 sq. ft.
Second Finished	1,100 sq. ft.
Basement Unfinished	1,293 sq. ft.
Garage Unfinished	686 sq. ft.
Dimensions	72'x36'8"
Foundation	Basement Crawlspace Slab
Bedrooms	3
Full Baths	2
Half Baths	1
First Ceiling	9'
Second Ceiling	8'
Max Ridge Height	31'
Roof Framing	Stick
Exterior Walls	2x6

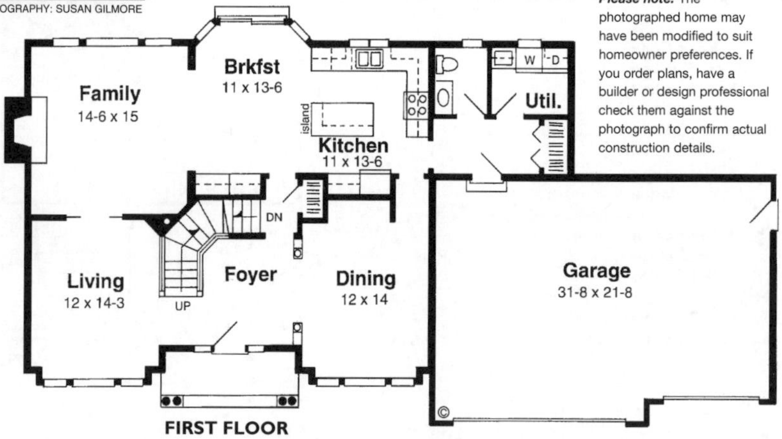

SECOND FLOOR

FIRST FLOOR

Please note: The photographed home may have been modified to suit homeowner preferences. If you order plans, have a builder or design professional check them against the photograph to confirm actual construction details.

Design 69131

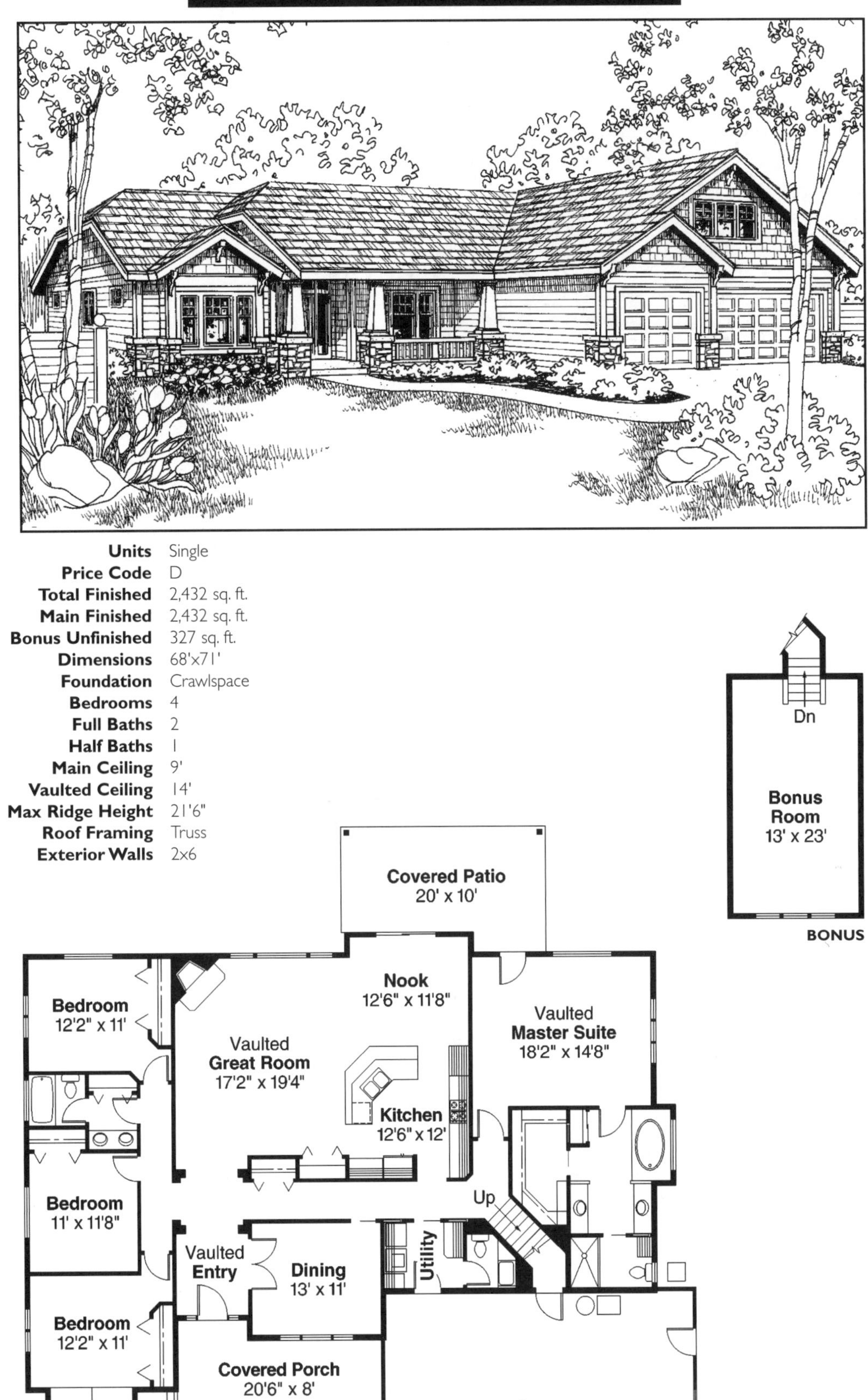
Covered Patio
20' x 10'
Nook
12'6" x 11'8"
Bedroom
12'2" x 11'
Vaulted
Great Room
17'2" x 19'4"
Vaulted
Master Suite
18'2" x 14'8"
Kitchen
12'6" x 12'
Bedroom
11' x 11'8"
Up
Vaulted
Entry
Dining
13' x 11'
Utility
Bedroom
12'2" x 11'
Covered Porch
20'6" x 8'
Garage
31'4" x 23'2"
MAIN FLOOR
Dn
Bonus
Room
13' x 23'
BONUS

Units	Single
Price Code	D
Total Finished	2,432 sq. ft.
Main Finished	2,432 sq. ft.
Bonus Unfinished	327 sq. ft.
Dimensions	68'x71'
Foundation	Crawlspace
Bedrooms	4
Full Baths	2
Half Baths	1
Main Ceiling	9'
Vaulted Ceiling	14'
Max Ridge Height	21'6"
Roof Framing	Truss
Exterior Walls	2x6

Design 96813

Units	Single
Price Code	E
Total Finished	2,437 sq. ft.
Main Finished	2,437 sq. ft.
Garage Unfinished	646 sq. ft.
Porch Unfinished	213 sq. ft.
Dimensions	64'9"x59'
Foundation	Basement Crawlspace Slab
Bedrooms	3
Full Baths	2
Main Ceiling	9'
Max Ridge Height	26'
Roof Framing	Stick
Exterior Walls	2x4

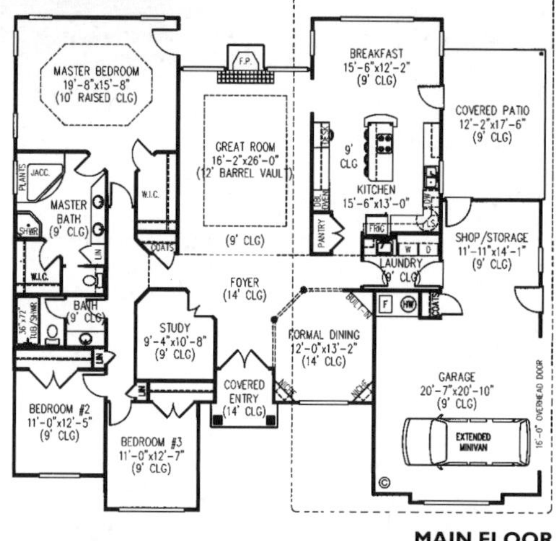
MASTER BEDROOM
19'-8"x15'-8"
(10' RAISED CLG)
F.P.
GREAT ROOM
16'-2"x26'-0"
(12' BARREL VAULT)
BREAKFAST
15'-6"x12'-2"
(9' CLG)
COVERED PATIO
12'-2"x17'-6"
(9' CLG)
MASTER BATH
(9' CLG)
W.I.C.
KITCHEN
15'-6"x13'-0"
(9' CLG)
PANTRY
LAUNDRY
(9' CLG)
SHOP/STORAGE
11'-11"x14'-1"
(9' CLG)
FOYER
(14' CLG)
BATH
(9' CLG)
STUDY
9'-4"x10'-8"
(9' CLG)
FORMAL DINING
12'-0"x13'-2"
(14' CLG)
GARAGE
20'-7"x20'-10"
(9' CLG)
COVERED ENTRY
(14' CLG)
BEDROOM #2
11'-0"x12'-5"
(9' CLG)
BEDROOM #3
11'-0"x12'-7"
(9' CLG)
EXTENDED MINIVAN
16'-0" OVERHEAD DOOR

MAIN FLOOR

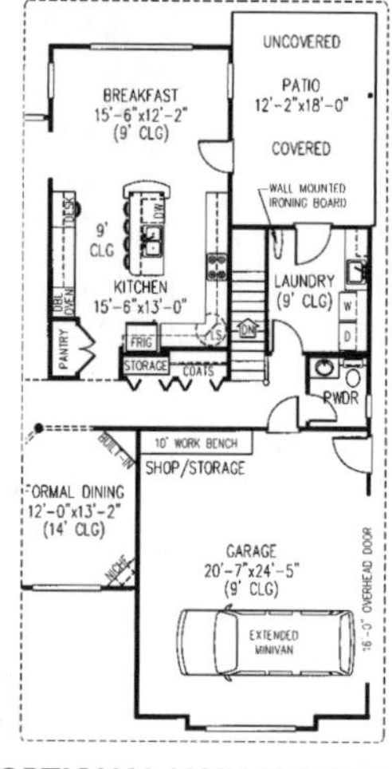
UNCOVERED
PATIO
12'-2"x18'-0"
COVERED
BREAKFAST
15'-6"x12'-2"
(9' CLG)
WALL MOUNTED IRONING BOARD
KITCHEN
15'-6"x13'-0"
LAUNDRY
(9' CLG)
PANTRY
STORAGE
COATS
PWDR
10' WORK BENCH
SHOP/STORAGE
FORMAL DINING
12'-0"x13'-2"
(14' CLG)
GARAGE
20'-7"x24'-5"
(9' CLG)
EXTENDED MINIVAN
16'-0" OVERHEAD DOOR

OPTIONAL MAIN FLOOR W/ BASEMENT FOUNDATION

Design 96919

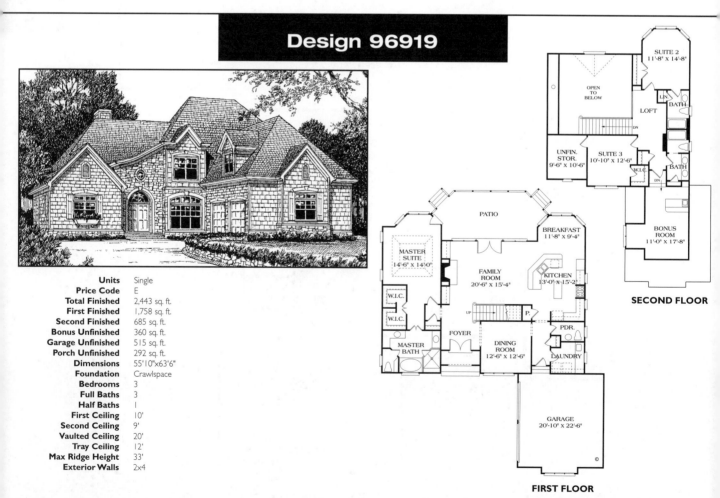

Units	Single
Price Code	E
Total Finished	2,443 sq. ft.
First Finished	1,758 sq. ft.
Second Finished	685 sq. ft.
Bonus Unfinished	360 sq. ft.
Garage Unfinished	515 sq. ft.
Porch Unfinished	292 sq. ft.
Dimensions	55'10"x63'6"
Foundation	Crawlspace
Bedrooms	3
Full Baths	3
Half Baths	1
First Ceiling	10'
Second Ceiling	9'
Vaulted Ceiling	20'
Tray Ceiling	12'
Max Ridge Height	33'
Exterior Walls	2x4

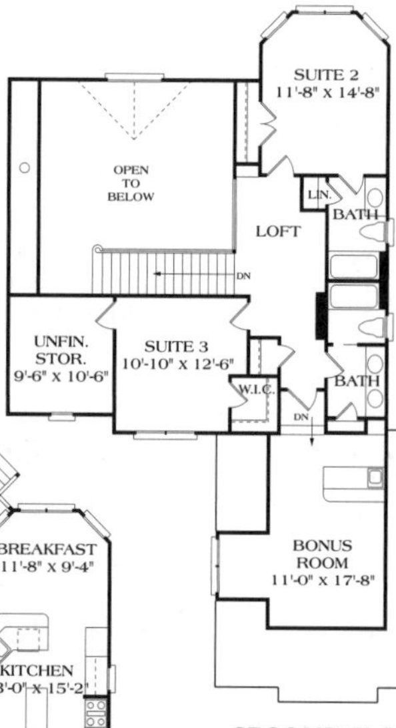

SECOND FLOOR

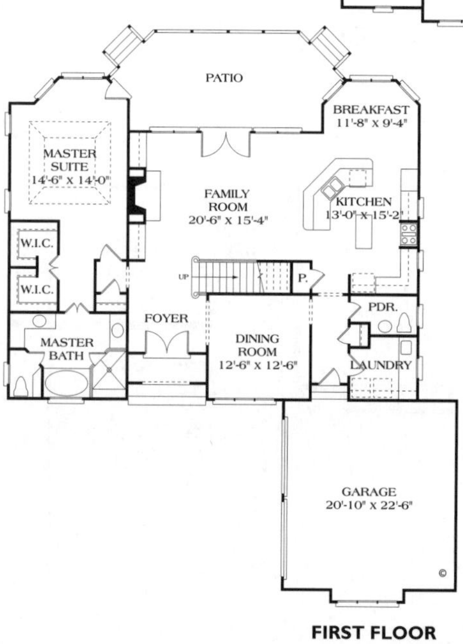

FIRST FLOOR

Design 98511

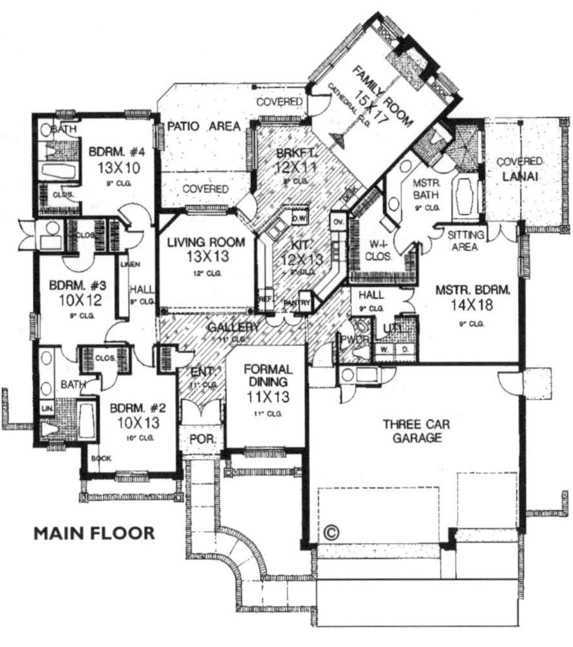
BATH
BDRM. #4
13X10
PATIO AREA
COVERED
FAMILY ROOM
15X17
BRKFT.
12X11
MSTR. BATH
COVERED LANAI
LIVING ROOM
13X13
KIT.
12X13
W-I-CLOS.
SITTING AREA
BDRM. #3
10X12
HALL
MSTR. BDRM.
14X18
GALLERY
PANTRY
PWDR.
UTIL.
BATH
CLOS.
BDRM. #2
10X13
ENT.
FORMAL DINING
11X13
POR.
THREE CAR GARAGE

MAIN FLOOR

Units	Single
Price Code	E
Total Finished	2,445 sq. ft.
Main Finished	2,445 sq. ft.
Garage Unfinished	630 sq. ft.
Deck Unfinished	234 sq. ft.
Porch Unfinished	32 sq. ft.
Dimensions	65'x68'8"
Foundation	Crawlspace Slab
Bedrooms	4
Full Baths	3
Half Baths	1
Main Ceiling	9'-12'
Max Ridge Height	32'
Roof Framing	Stick
Exterior Walls	2x4

Design 50012

Units	Single
Price Code	D
Total Finished	2,449 sq. ft.
First Finished	1,925 sq. ft.
Second Finished	524 sq. ft.
Basement Unfinished	1,925 sq. ft.
Garage Unfinished	489 sq. ft.
Porch Unfinished	106 sq. ft.
Dimensions	56'4"x53'4"
Foundation	Basement
Bedrooms	3
Full Baths	2
Half Baths	1
First Ceiling	9'
Second Ceiling	8'
Roof Framing	Truss
Exterior Walls	2x4

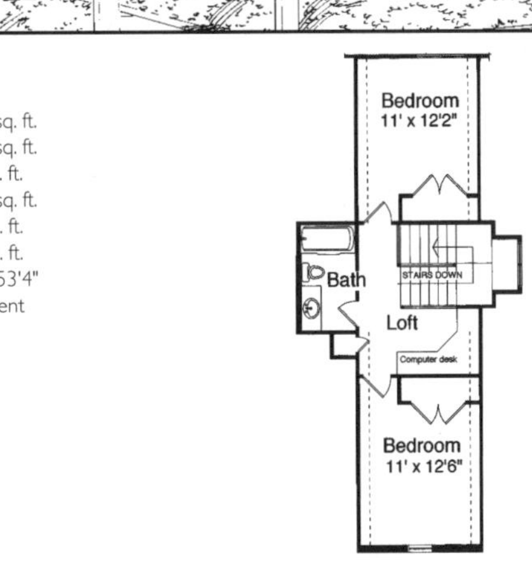
Bedroom
11' x 12'2"
Bath
STAIRS DOWN
Loft
Computer desk
Bedroom
11' x 12'6"

SECOND FLOOR

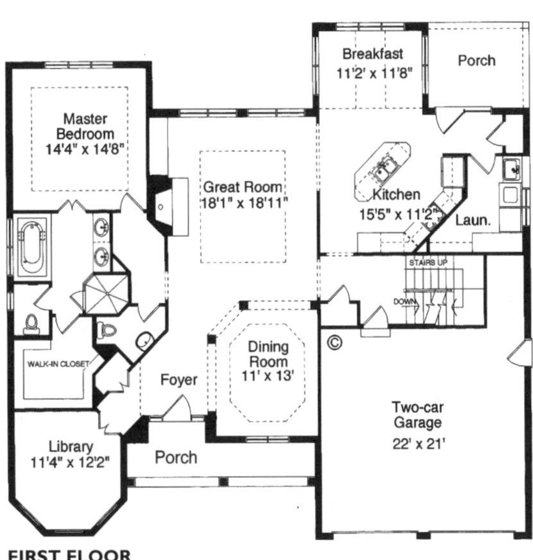
Breakfast
11'2' x 11'8"
Porch
Master Bedroom
14'4" x 14'8"
Great Room
18'1" x 18'11"
Kitchen
15'5" x 11'2"
Laun.
STAIRS UP
DOWN
WALK-IN CLOSET
Dining Room
11' x 13'
Foyer
Two-car Garage
22' x 21'
Library
11'4" x 12'2"
Porch

FIRST FLOOR

Design 10570

Units Single
Price Code E
Total Finished 2,450 sq. ft.
Main Finished 2,450 sq. ft.
Basement Unfinished 2,450 sq. ft.
Garage Unfinished 739 sq. ft.
Dimensions 96'x60'6"
Foundation Basement
Bedrooms 4
Full Baths 2
Max Ridge Height 21'
Roof Framing Stick
Exterior Walls 2x6

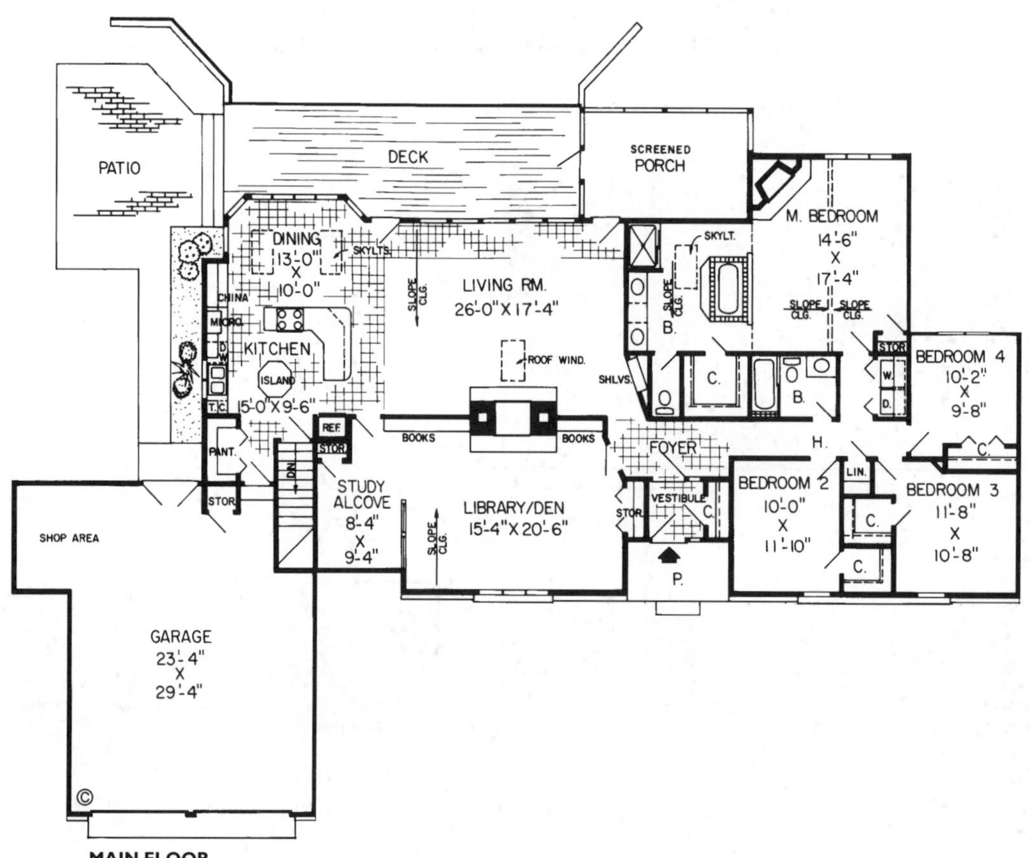
PATIO
DECK
SCREENED PORCH
M. BEDROOM
14'-6" X 17'-4"
DINING
13'-0" X 10'-0"
SKYLTS.
LIVING RM.
26'-0"X17'-4"
SLOPE CLG.
SKYLT.
CHINA
MICRO
KITCHEN
ISLAND
15'-0"X9'-6"
T.C
ROOF WIND.
SHLVS.
B.
C.
BEDROOM 4
10'-2" X 9'-8"
STOR
W.
D.
REF
STOR
BOOKS
BOOKS
FOYER
H.
LIN.
PANT.
STOR
DN
STUDY ALCOVE
8'-4" X 9'-4"
LIBRARY/DEN
15'-4"X20'-6"
STOR.
VESTIBULE
BEDROOM 2
10'-0" X 11'-10"
BEDROOM 3
11'-8" X 10'-8"
P.
SHOP AREA
GARAGE
23'-4" X 29'-4"
©

MAIN FLOOR

Design 64194

Units	Single
Price Code	H
Total Finished	2,454 sq. ft.
Main Finished	2,454 sq. ft.
Bonus Unfinished	256 sq. ft.
Garage Unfinished	547 sq. ft.
Porch Unfinished	165 sq. ft.
Dimensions	80'6"x66'6"
Foundation	Crawlspace
Bedrooms	3
Full Baths	2
Max Ridge Height	24'2"
Exterior Walls	2x6

* Alternate foundation options available at an additional charge. Please call 1-800-235-5700 for more information.

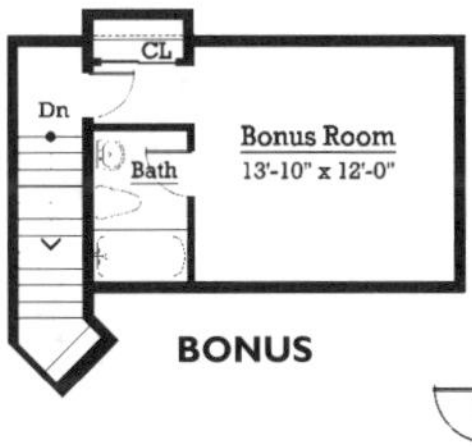

CL
Dn
Bath
Bonus Room 13'-10" x 12'-0"
BONUS

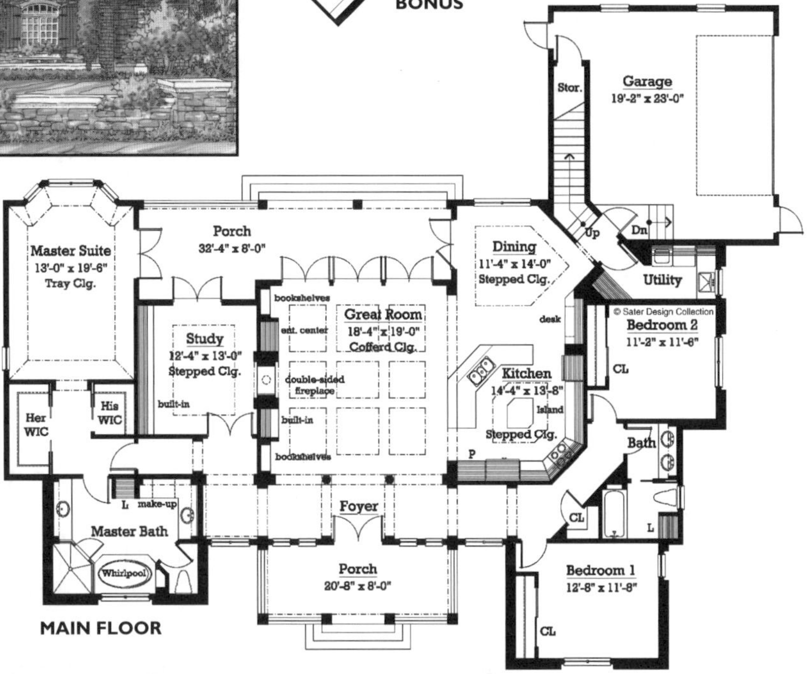

Garage 19'-2" x 23'-0"
Stor.
Up
Dn
Utility
Porch 32'-4" x 8'-0"
Master Suite 13'-0" x 19'-6" Tray Clg.
Dining 11'-4" x 14'-0" Stepped Clg.
bookshelves
Great Room 18'-4" x 19'-0" Cofferd Clg.
ent. center
Study 12'-4" x 13'-0" Stepped Clg.
desk
© Sater Design Collection
Bedroom 2 11'-2" x 11'-6"
CL
double-sided fireplace
Kitchen 14'-4" x 13'-8"
island
built-in
Her WIC
His WIC
built-in
Stepped Clg.
bookshelves
P
Bath
L
make-up
Foyer
CL
Master Bath
Whirlpool
L
Porch 20'-8" x 8'-0"
Bedroom 1 12'-8" x 11'-8"
CL
MAIN FLOOR

Design 32189

PHOTOGRAPHY: JAMES SALOMON

Units	Single
Price Code	E
Total Finished	2,455 sq. ft.
First Finished	1,508 sq. ft.
Second Finished	947 sq. ft.
Basement Unfinished	1,508 sq. ft.
Garage Unfinished	735 sq. ft.
Dimensions	60'4"x60'
Foundation	Basement
Bedrooms	3
Full Baths	1
3/4 Baths	2
Half Baths	1
First Ceiling	8'
Second Ceiling	8'
Vaulted Ceiling	10'
Max Ridge Height	30'
Roof Framing	Stick
Exterior Walls	2x6

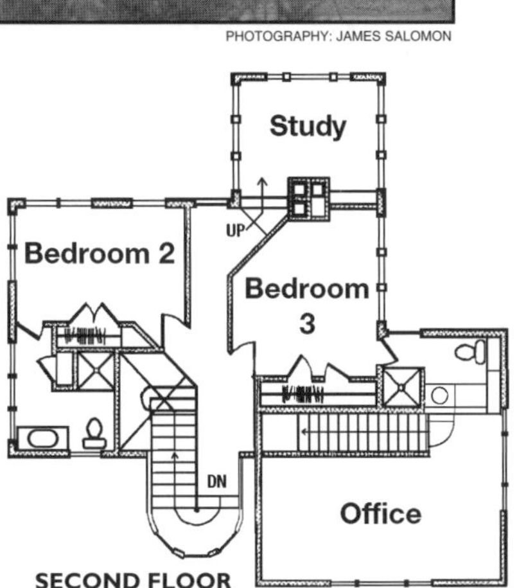
Study
Bedroom 2
UP
Bedroom 3
DN
Office
SECOND FLOOR

Please note: The photographed home may have been modified to suit homeowner preferences. If you order plans, have a builder or design professional check them against the photograph to confirm actual construction details.

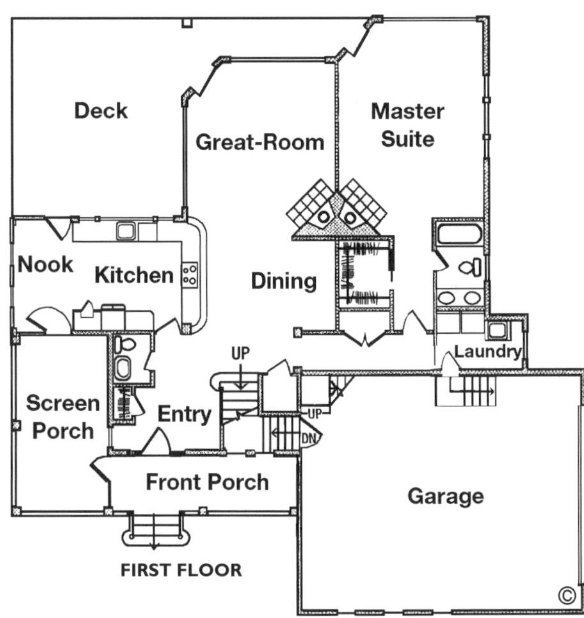
Deck
Great-Room
Master Suite
Nook
Kitchen
Dining
UP
Laundry
Screen Porch
Entry
UP
DN
Front Porch
Garage
FIRST FLOOR
©

Design 98518

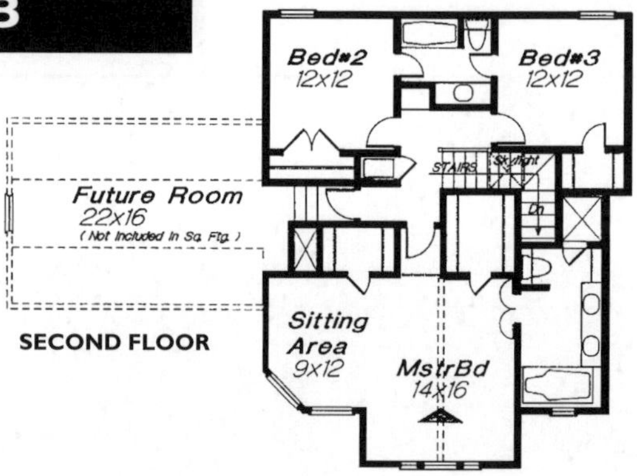

Units	Single
Price Code	E
Total Finished	2,455 sq. ft.
First Finished	1,447 sq. ft.
Second Finished	1,008 sq. ft.
Bonus Unfinished	352 sq. ft.
Garage Unfinished	756 sq. ft.
Deck Unfinished	220 sq. ft.
Porch Unfinished	210 sq. ft.
Dimensions	65'x37'11"
Foundation	Basement Slab
Bedrooms	3
Full Baths	2
Half Baths	1
First Ceiling	9'
Second Ceiling	8'
Max Ridge Height	30'
Roof Framing	Stick
Exterior Walls	2x4

SECOND FLOOR

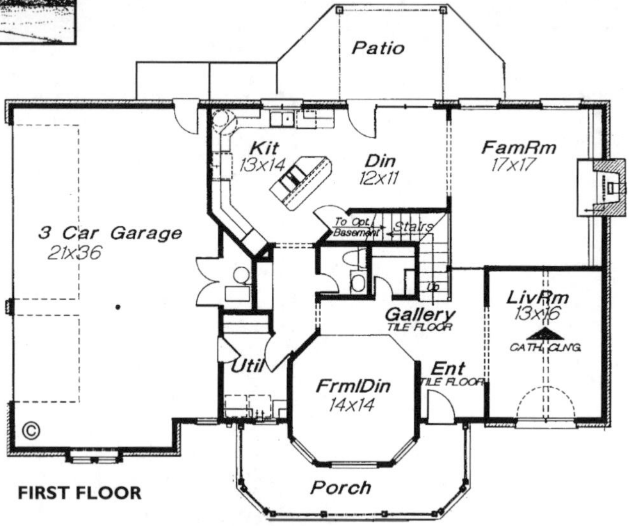

FIRST FLOOR

Design 52203

Units	Single
Price Code	E
Total Finished	2,461 sq. ft.
Main Finished	2,461 sq. ft.
Bonus Unfinished	284 sq. ft.
Basement Unfinished	2,461 sq. ft.
Garage Unfinished	536 sq. ft.
Dimensions	65'4"x66'
Foundation	Basement Crawlspace
Bedrooms	4
Full Baths	3
Max Ridge Height	24'6"
Roof Framing	Stick
Exterior Walls	2x4

BONUS

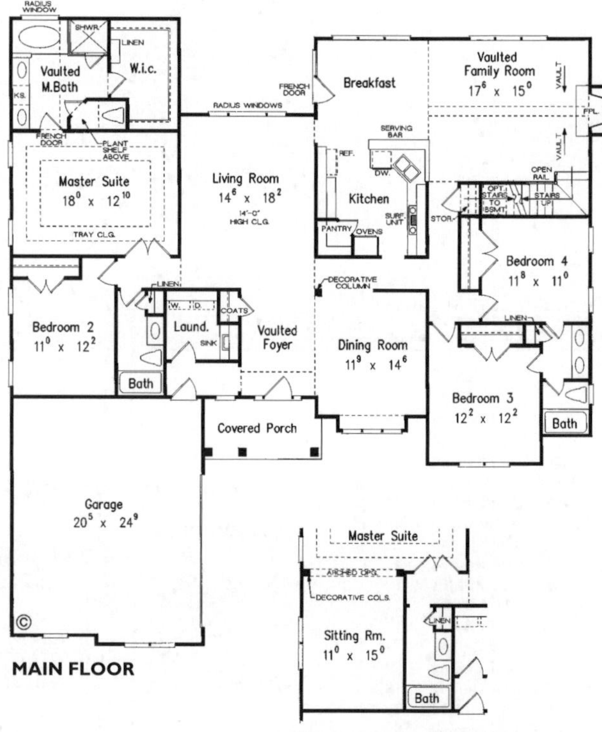
Vaulted M.Bath
W.i.c.
Master Suite
18⁰ x 12¹⁰
Living Room
14⁶ x 18²
Breakfast
Vaulted Family Room
17⁶ x 15⁰
Kitchen
Bedroom 4
11⁸ x 11⁰
Bedroom 2
11⁰ x 12²
Laund.
Vaulted Foyer
Dining Room
11⁹ x 14⁶
Bedroom 3
12² x 12²
Bath
Covered Porch
Garage
20⁵ x 24⁹

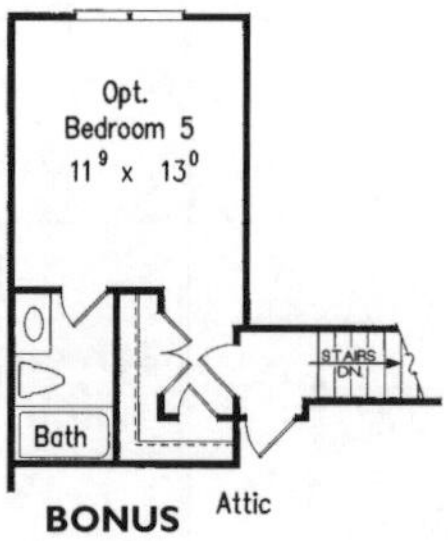

MAIN FLOOR

OPTIONAL SITTING ROOM

Design 97842

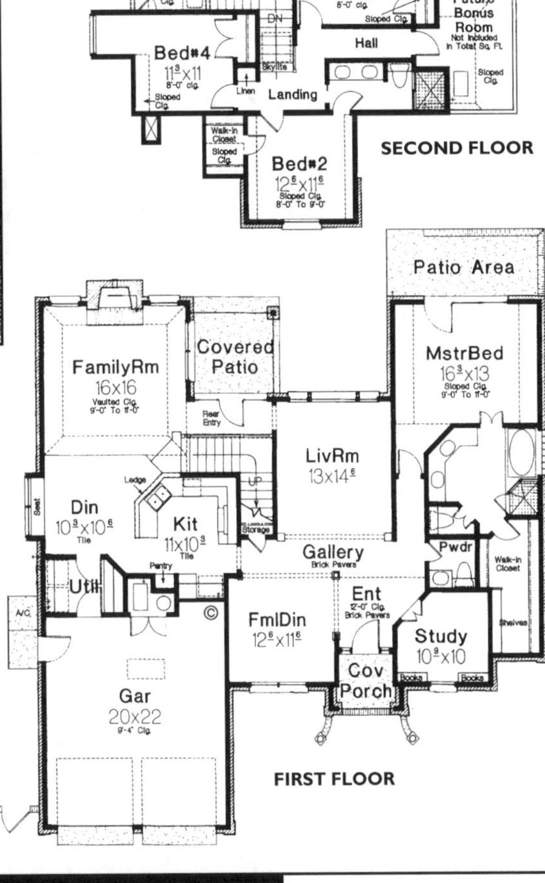
Optional Bath
Bed#3
Future Bonus Room
Bed#4
Hall
Landing
Bed#2
SECOND FLOOR
Patio Area
FamilyRm
Covered Patio
MstrBed
LivRm
Din
Kit
Gallery
Pwdr
Util
Ent
FmlDin
Study
Cov Porch
Gar
FIRST FLOOR

Units	Single
Price Code	E
Total Finished	2,466 sq. ft.
First Finished	1,815 sq. ft.
Second Finished	651 sq. ft.
Bonus Unfinished	185 sq. ft.
Garage Unfinished	440 sq. ft.
Deck Unfinished	120 sq. ft.
Porch Unfinished	64 sq. ft.
Dimensions	55'x55'7"
Foundation	Slab
Bedrooms	4
Full Baths	1
3/4 Baths	1
Half Baths	1
First Ceiling	9'
Second Ceiling	8'
Roof Framing	Stick
Exterior Walls	2x4

Design 99640

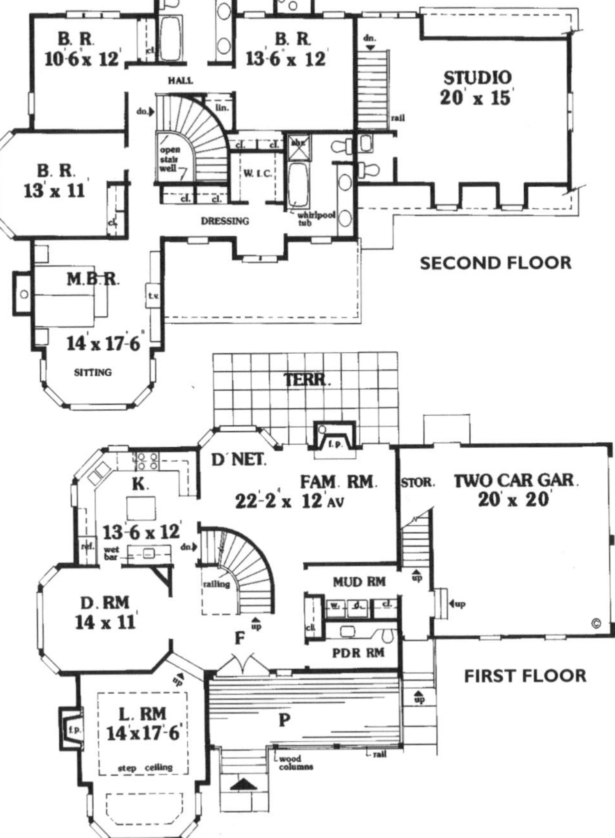
B. R.
B. R.
STUDIO 20' x 15'
B. R. 13' x 11'
DRESSING
M.B.R. 14' x 17'6"
SITTING
SECOND FLOOR
TERR.
D'NET.
FAM. RM.
K.
TWO CAR GAR. 20' x 20'
D. RM 14 x 11
MUD RM
PDR RM
L. RM 14'x17'6"
P
FIRST FLOOR

Units	Single
Price Code	E
Total Finished	2,466 sq. ft.
First Finished	1,217 sq. ft.
Second Finished	1,249 sq. ft.
Bonus Unfinished	496 sq. ft.
Basement Unfinished	1,217 sq. ft.
Garage Unfinished	431 sq. ft.
Dimensions	65'x44'6"
Foundation	Basement Slab
Bedrooms	4
Full Baths	2
Half Baths	2
Max Ridge Height	30'
Roof Framing	Stick
Exterior Walls	2x6

Design 97258

Units	Single
Price Code	E
Total Finished	2,472 sq. ft.
First Finished	1,860 sq. ft.
Second Finished	612 sq. ft.
Bonus Unfinished	244 sq. ft.
Basement Unfinished	1,860 sq. ft.
Garage Unfinished	460 sq. ft.
Dimensions	54'6"x56'4"
Foundation	Basement Crawlspace
Bedrooms	4
Full Baths	3
First Ceiling	9'
Second Ceiling	8'
Max Ridge Height	31'
Roof Framing	Stick
Exterior Walls	2x4

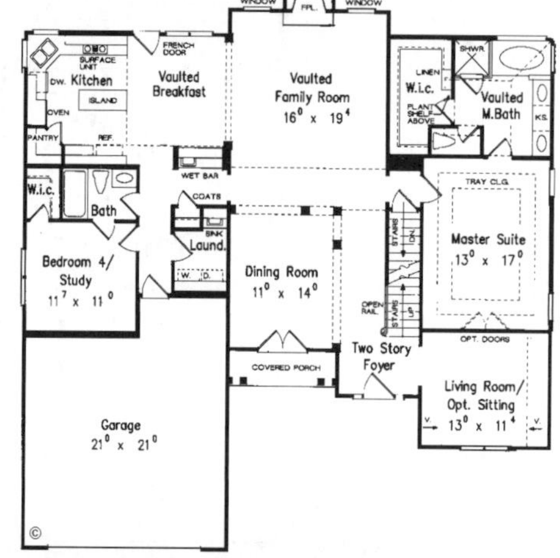
Kitchen
Vaulted Breakfast
Vaulted Family Room 16⁰ x 19⁴
Vaulted M.Bath
Master Suite 13⁰ x 17⁰
Bedroom 4/ Study 11⁷ x 11⁰
Bath
Dining Room 11⁰ x 14⁰
Two Story Foyer
Living Room/ Opt. Sitting 13⁰ x 11⁴
Garage 21⁰ x 21⁰

FIRST FLOOR

Breakfast Below
Family Room Below
Attic
Bedroom 2 13⁰ x 11⁴
Bedroom 3 11⁰ x 13¹⁰
Bath
W.i.c.
Foyer Below
Opt. Bonus 11⁰ x 20⁸

SECOND FLOOR

Design 91706

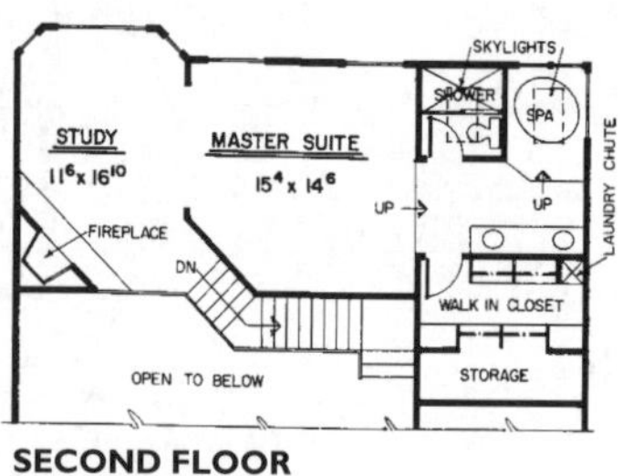
STUDY 11⁶x 16¹⁰
MASTER SUITE 15⁴x 14⁶
SKYLIGHTS
SPA
FIREPLACE
WALK IN CLOSET
STORAGE
OPEN TO BELOW

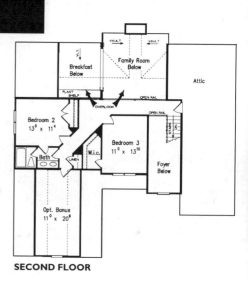

SECOND FLOOR

Units	Single
Price Code	E
Total Finished	2,474 sq. ft.
First Finished	1,856 sq. ft.
Second Finished	618 sq. ft.
Garage Unfinished	704 sq. ft.
Dimensions	86'x42'
Foundation	Crawlspace
Bedrooms	3
Full Baths	2
Half Baths	1
Max Ridge Height	24'
Roof Framing	Stick/Truss
Exterior Walls	2x6

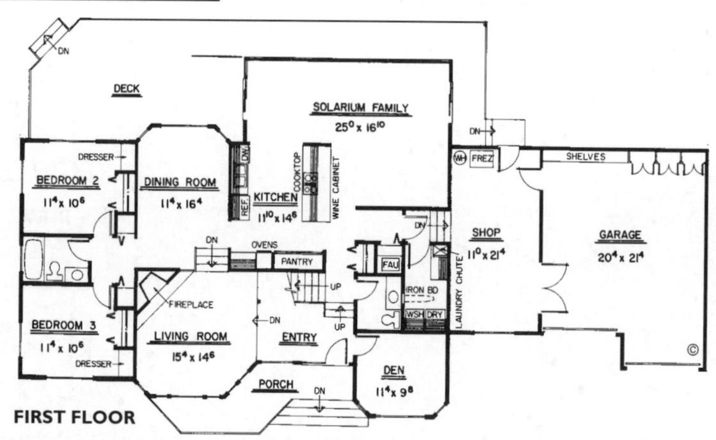
DECK
SOLARIUM FAMILY 25⁰x 16¹⁰
BEDROOM 2 11⁴x 10⁶
DINING ROOM 11⁴x 16⁴
KITCHEN 11¹⁰x 14⁶
SHOP 11⁰x 21⁴
GARAGE 20⁴x 21⁴
BEDROOM 3 11⁴x 10⁶
LIVING ROOM 15⁴x 14⁶
ENTRY
PORCH
DEN 11⁴x 9⁸

FIRST FLOOR

Design 91168

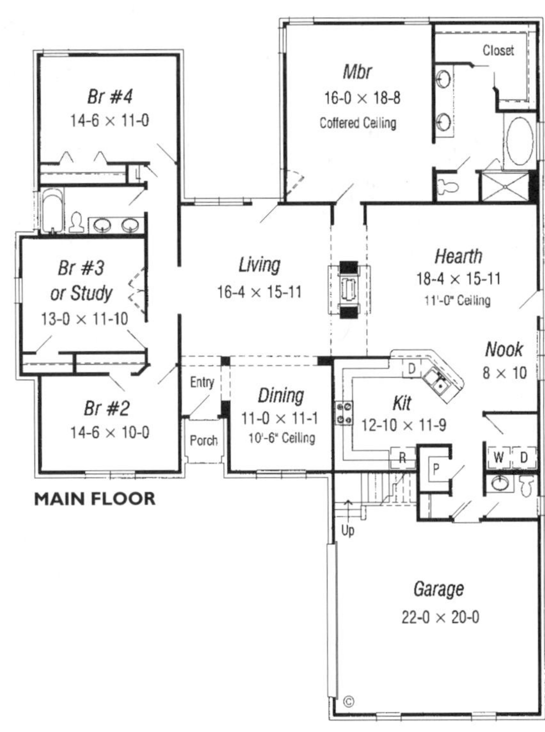

Br #4
14-6 × 11-0
Mbr
16-0 × 18-8
Coffered Ceiling
Closet
Br #3
or Study
13-0 × 11-10
Living
16-4 × 15-11
Hearth
18-4 × 15-11
11'-0" Ceiling
Nook
8 × 10
Entry
Dining
11-0 × 11-1
10'-6" Ceiling
Kit
12-10 × 11-9
Br #2
14-6 × 10-0
Porch
Up
Garage
22-0 × 20-0

MAIN FLOOR

Units	Single
Price Code	E
Total Finished	2,478 sq. ft.
Main Finished	2,478 sq. ft.
Garage Unfinished	535 sq. ft.
Porch Unfinished	20 sq. ft.
Dimensions	56'2"x73'9.5"
Foundation	Slab
Bedrooms	4
Full Baths	2
Half Baths	1
Main Ceiling	8'1⅛"
Vaulted Ceiling	11'1⅛"
Max Ridge Height	22'
Roof Framing	Stick
Exterior Walls	2x4

Design 91475

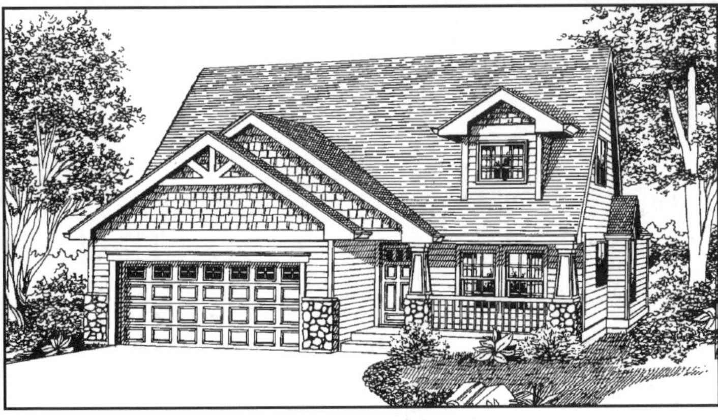

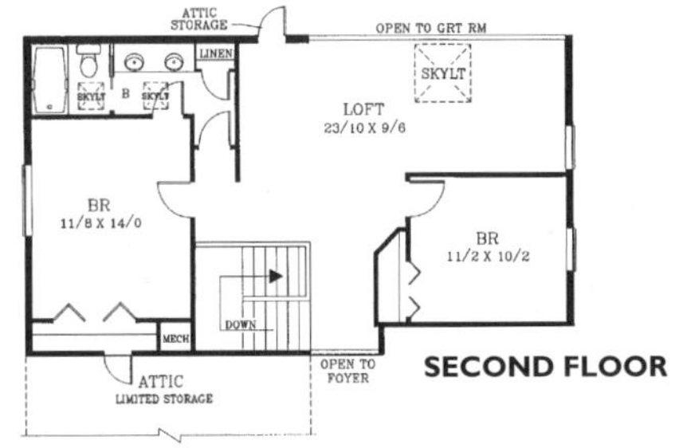

ATTIC STORAGE
OPEN TO GRT RM
LINEN
SKYLT
LOFT
23/10 X 9/6
BR
11/8 X 14/0
BR
11/2 X 10/2
DOWN
MECH
OPEN TO FOYER
ATTIC
LIMITED STORAGE

SECOND FLOOR

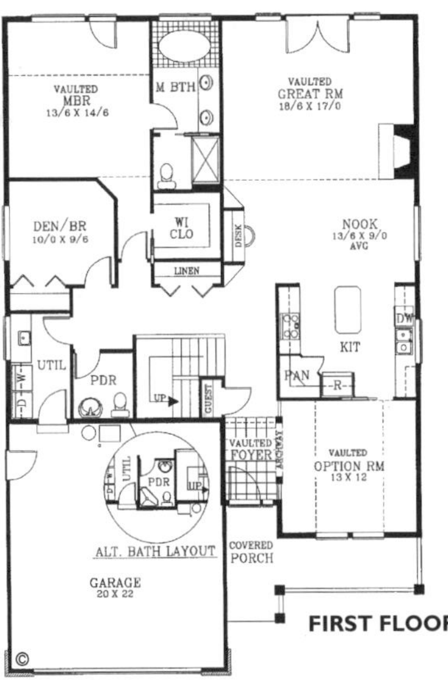

VAULTED
MBR
13/6 X 14/6
M BTH
VAULTED
GREAT RM
18/6 X 17/0
DEN/BR
10/0 X 9/6
WI
CLO
LINEN
DESK
NOOK
13/6 X 9/0
AVG
KIT
UTIL
PDR
UP
PAN
VAULTED
FOYER
VAULTED
OPTION RM
13 X 12
ALT. BATH LAYOUT
COVERED
PORCH
GARAGE
20 X 22

FIRST FLOOR

Units	Single
Price Code	E
Total Finished	2,479 sq. ft.
First Finished	1,675 sq. ft.
Second Finished	804 sq. ft.
Garage Unfinished	440 sq. ft.
Dimensions	40'x60'
Foundation	Crawlspace
Bedrooms	4
Full Baths	2
Half Baths	1
First Ceiling	8'
Second Ceiling	8'
Max Ridge Height	24'
Roof Framing	Stick
Exterior Walls	2x6

Design 94940

WHIRLPOOL
Mbr.
14⁰ x 17⁰
9' - 4" CEILING
Br.3
11⁰ x 11⁶
LIN.
Br.4
11⁰ x 11⁰
DN
LIN.
OPEN TO BELOW
Br.2
11⁰ x 12⁴
9' - 0" CLG.
SECOND FLOOR
TRANSOMS
Din.
12⁰ x 13⁰
10' - 0" CLG.
Kit.
11⁰ x 12⁸
Bfst.
13⁰ x 11⁰
DN
Fam. rm.
14⁰ x 19⁰
9' - 0" CEILING
DESK
W.
D.
B.
P.
R.
Liv.
12⁰ x 14⁸
10' - 0" CLG.
DN
UP
E.
BOOKS
Den
11⁰ x 12⁰
COVERED STOOP
Gar.
31³ x 22⁰
FIRST FLOOR

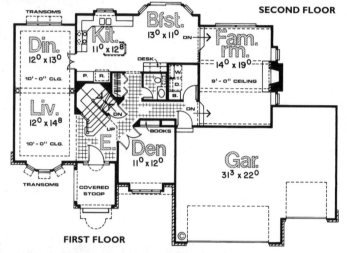

Units	Single
Price Code	E
Total Finished	2,480 sq. ft.
First Finished	1,369 sq. ft.
Second Finished	1,111 sq. ft.
Basement Unfinished	1,369 sq. ft.
Garage Unfinished	716 sq. ft.
Dimensions	64'x46'
Foundation	Basement Slab
Bedrooms	4
Full Baths	2
Half Baths	1
First Ceiling	8'
Second Ceiling	8'
Max Ridge Height	28'3"
Roof Framing	Stick
Exterior Walls	2x4

* Alternate foundation options available at an additional charge. Please call 1-800-235-5700 for more information.

Design 69034

Units	Single
Price Code	E
Total Finished	2,483 sq. ft.
Main Finished	2,483 sq. ft.
Dimensions	69'x53'8"
Foundation	Basement
Bedrooms	3
Full Baths	2

Hot
New
Design

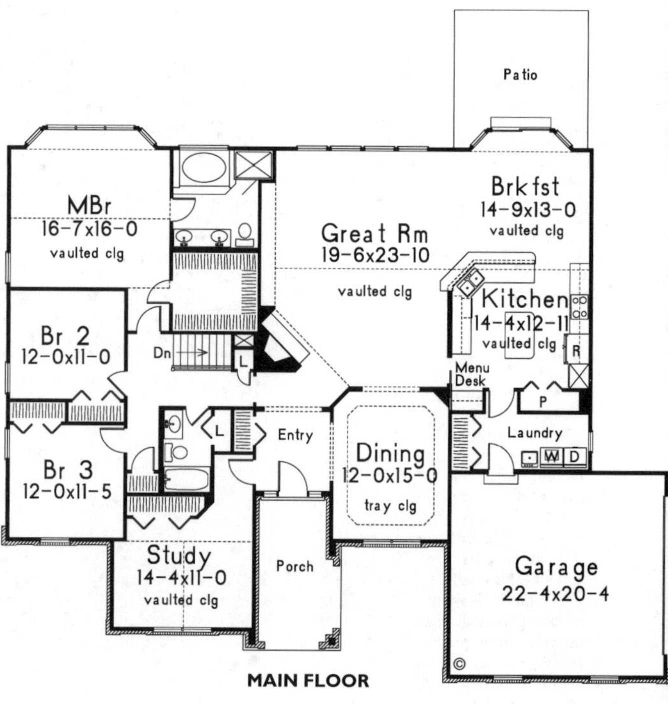

Patio
MBr
16-7x16-0
vaulted clg
Great Rm
19-6x23-10
vaulted clg
Brkfst
14-9x13-0
vaulted clg
Kitchen
14-4x12-11
vaulted clg
Menu Desk
Br 2
12-0x11-0
Dn
Br 3
12-0x11-5
Entry
Dining
12-0x15-0
tray clg
Laundry
Study
14-4x11-0
vaulted clg
Porch
Garage
22-4x20-4
MAIN FLOOR

Design 20134

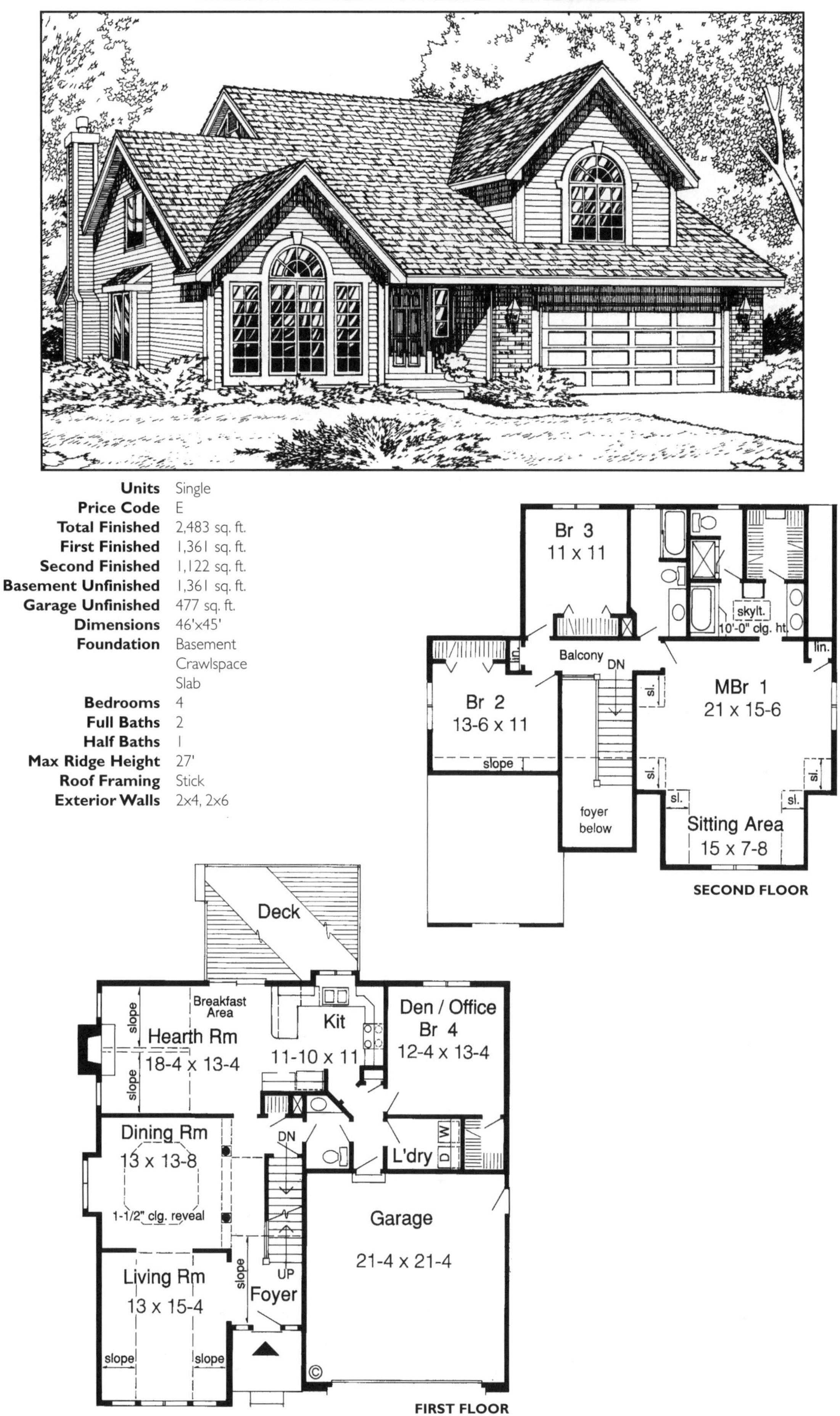
Br 3
11 x 11
skylt.
10'-0" clg. ht.
lin.
Balcony
DN
MBr 1
21 x 15-6
Br 2
13-6 x 11
sl.
slope
foyer
below
Sitting Area
15 x 7-8
SECOND FLOOR
Deck
Breakfast Area
Hearth Rm
18-4 x 13-4
Kit
11-10 x 11
Den / Office
Br 4
12-4 x 13-4
Dining Rm
13 x 13-8
1-1/2" clg. reveal
DN
L'dry
W
D
Garage
21-4 x 21-4
Living Rm
13 x 15-4
UP
Foyer
FIRST FLOOR

Units	Single
Price Code	E
Total Finished	2,483 sq. ft.
First Finished	1,361 sq. ft.
Second Finished	1,122 sq. ft.
Basement Unfinished	1,361 sq. ft.
Garage Unfinished	477 sq. ft.
Dimensions	46'x45'
Foundation	Basement Crawlspace Slab
Bedrooms	4
Full Baths	2
Half Baths	1
Max Ridge Height	27'
Roof Framing	Stick
Exterior Walls	2x4, 2x6

Design 90461

Units	Single
Price Code	E
Total Finished	2,485 sq. ft.
Main Finished	2,485 sq. ft.
Basement Unfinished	2,485 sq. ft.
Garage Unfinished	484 sq. ft.
Deck Unfinished	328 sq. ft.
Porch Unfinished	320 sq. ft.
Dimensions	84'x55'8"
Foundation	Basement Crawlspace
Bedrooms	3
Full Baths	2
Half Baths	1
First Ceiling	9'
Max Ridge Height	24'8"
Roof Framing	Stick
Exterior Walls	2x4

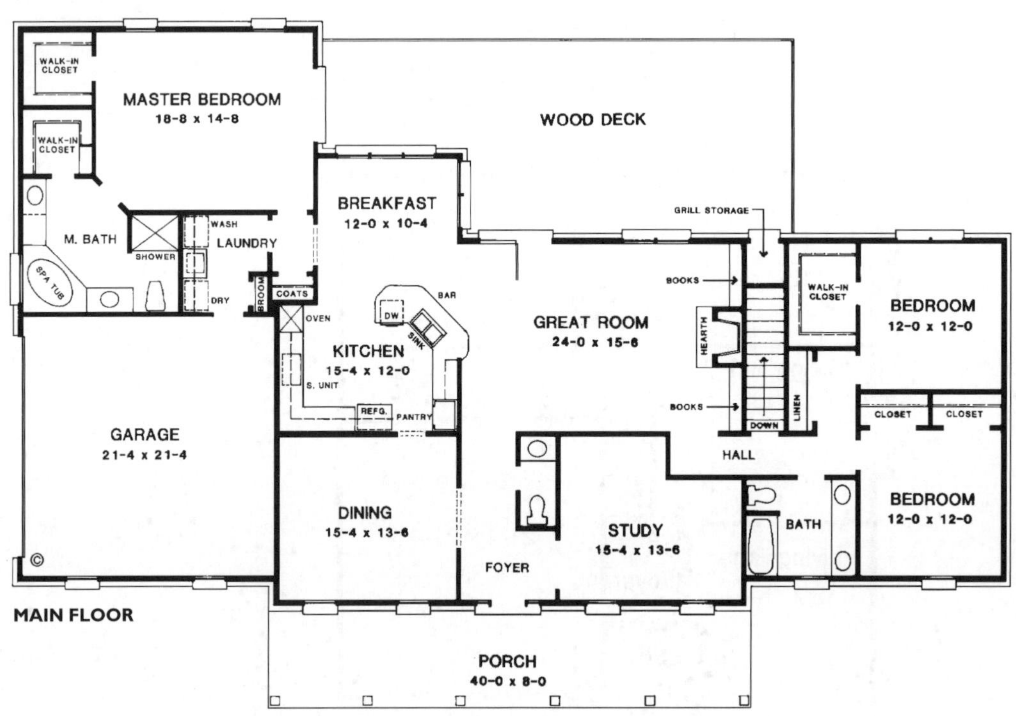
WALK-IN CLOSET
MASTER BEDROOM
18-8 x 14-8
WOOD DECK
WALK-IN CLOSET
BREAKFAST
12-0 x 10-4
GRILL STORAGE
M. BATH
WASH
LAUNDRY
SHOWER
SPA TUB
DRY
BROOM
COATS
BAR
DW
SINK
OVEN
BOOKS
GREAT ROOM
24-0 x 15-6
HEARTH
WALK-IN CLOSET
BEDROOM
12-0 x 12-0
KITCHEN
15-4 x 12-0
S. UNIT
REFG.
PANTRY
BOOKS
LINEN
DOWN
CLOSET
CLOSET
GARAGE
21-4 x 21-4
HALL
DINING
15-4 x 13-6
STUDY
15-4 x 13-6
BATH
BEDROOM
12-0 x 12-0
FOYER
MAIN FLOOR
PORCH
40-0 x 8-0

Design 94998

Units	Single
Price Code	E
Total Finished	2,486 sq. ft.
First Finished	1,829 sq. ft.
Second Finished	657 sq. ft.
Basement Unfinished	1,829 sq. ft.
Garage Unfinished	658 sq. ft.
Dimensions	68'8"x47'8"
Foundation	Basement
Bedrooms	4
Full Baths	2
Half Baths	1
Max Ridge Height	26'9"
Roof Framing	Stick
Exterior Walls	2x4

* Alternate foundation options available at an additional charge.
Please call 1-800-235-5700 for more information.

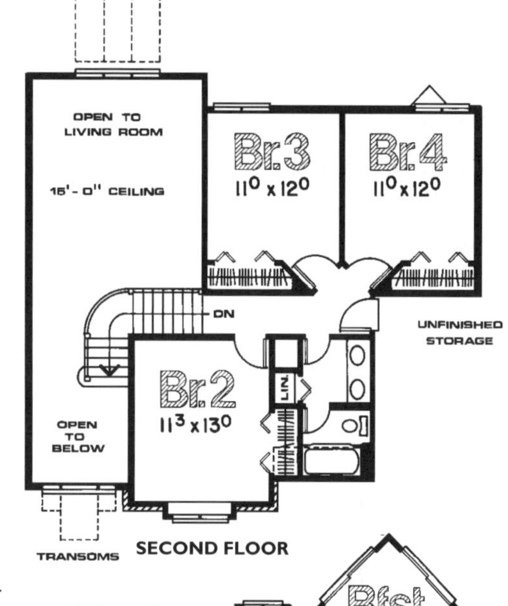
TRANSOMS
OPEN TO LIVING ROOM
15'-0" CEILING
Br.3
11^{0} x 12^{0}
Br.4
11^{0} x 12^{0}
DN
UNFINISHED STORAGE
Br.2
11^{3} x 13^{0}
LIN.
OPEN TO BELOW
TRANSOMS

SECOND FLOOR

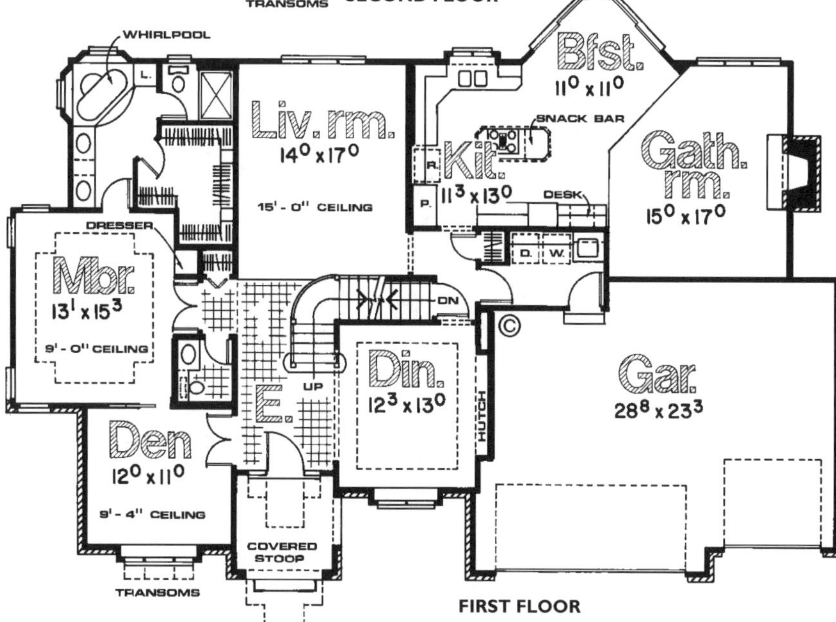
WHIRLPOOL
L.
Bfst.
11^{0} x 11^{0}
Liv. rm.
14^{0} x 17^{0}
15'-0" CEILING
SNACK BAR
Kit.
11^{3} x 13^{0}
R.
P.
DESK
Gath. rm.
15^{0} x 17^{0}
D.
W.
DRESSER
Mbr.
13^{1} x 15^{3}
9'-0" CEILING
DN
Din.
12^{3} x 13^{0}
HUTCH
Gar.
28^{8} x 23^{3}
UP
E.
Den
12^{0} x 11^{0}
9'-4" CEILING
COVERED STOOP
TRANSOMS

FIRST FLOOR

Design 91856

Units	Single
Price Code	B
Total Finished	2,487 sq. ft.
First Finished	1,624 sq. ft.
Second Finished	863 sq. ft.
Bonus Unfinished	407 sq. ft.
Basement Unfinished	1,624 sq. ft.
Dimensions	68'x50'
Foundation	Basement
Bedrooms	4
Full Baths	2
Half Baths	1
First Ceiling	8'
Max Ridge Height	26'5"
Roof Framing	Stick/Truss
Exterior Walls	2x6

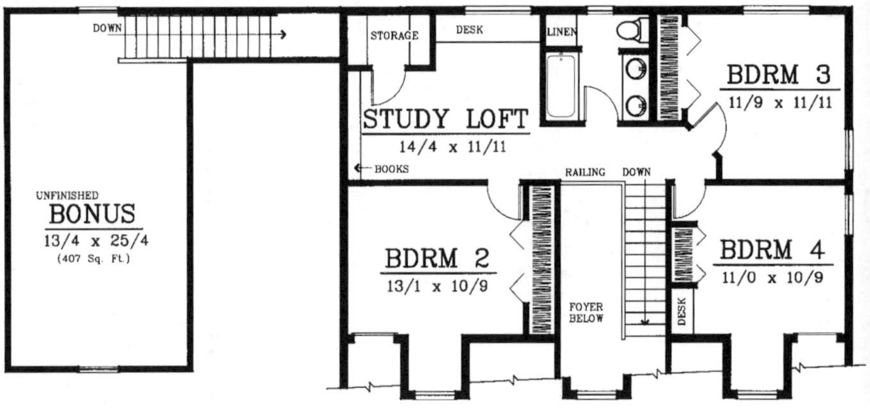

DOWN
UNFINISHED
BONUS
13/4 x 25/4
(407 Sq. Ft.)
STORAGE
DESK
LINEN
STUDY LOFT
14/4 x 11/11
BOOKS
BDRM 3
11/9 x 11/11
RAILING
DOWN
BDRM 2
13/1 x 10/9
FOYER BELOW
BDRM 4
11/0 x 10/9
DESK

SECOND FLOOR

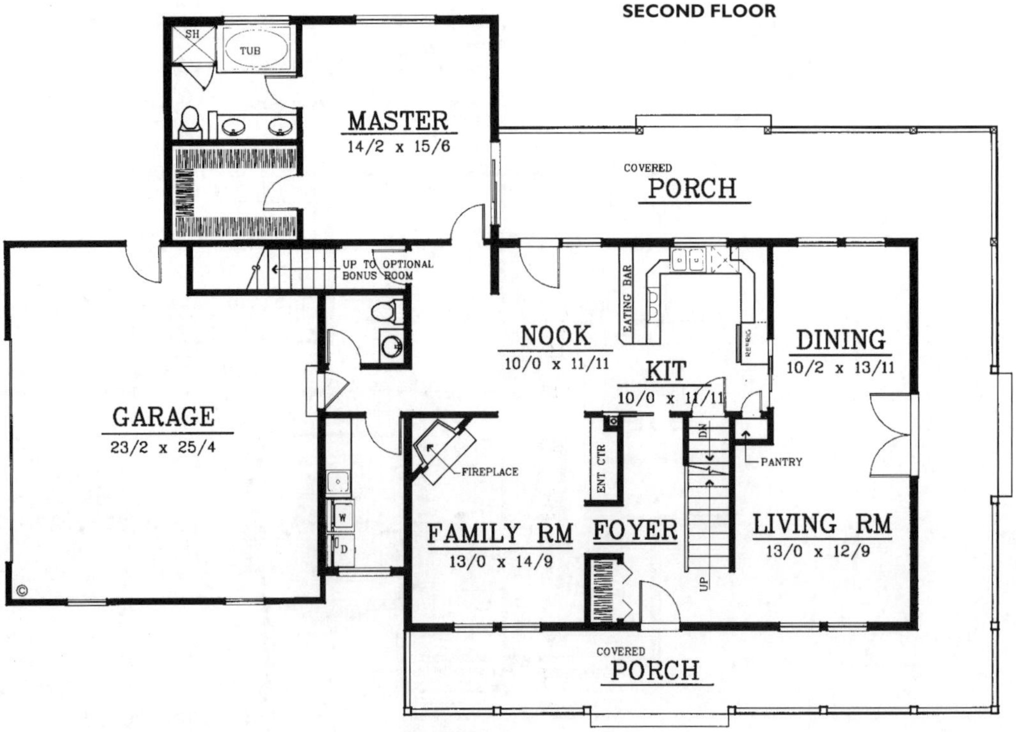

SH
TUB
MASTER
14/2 x 15/6
COVERED
PORCH
UP TO OPTIONAL BONUS ROOM
EATING BAR
NOOK
10/0 x 11/11
KIT
10/0 x 11/11
REFRIG
DINING
10/2 x 13/11
GARAGE
23/2 x 25/4
DN
PANTRY
FIREPLACE
ENT CTR
W
D
FAMILY RM
13/0 x 14/9
FOYER
LIVING RM
13/0 x 12/9
UP
COVERED
PORCH

FIRST FLOOR

Design 92549

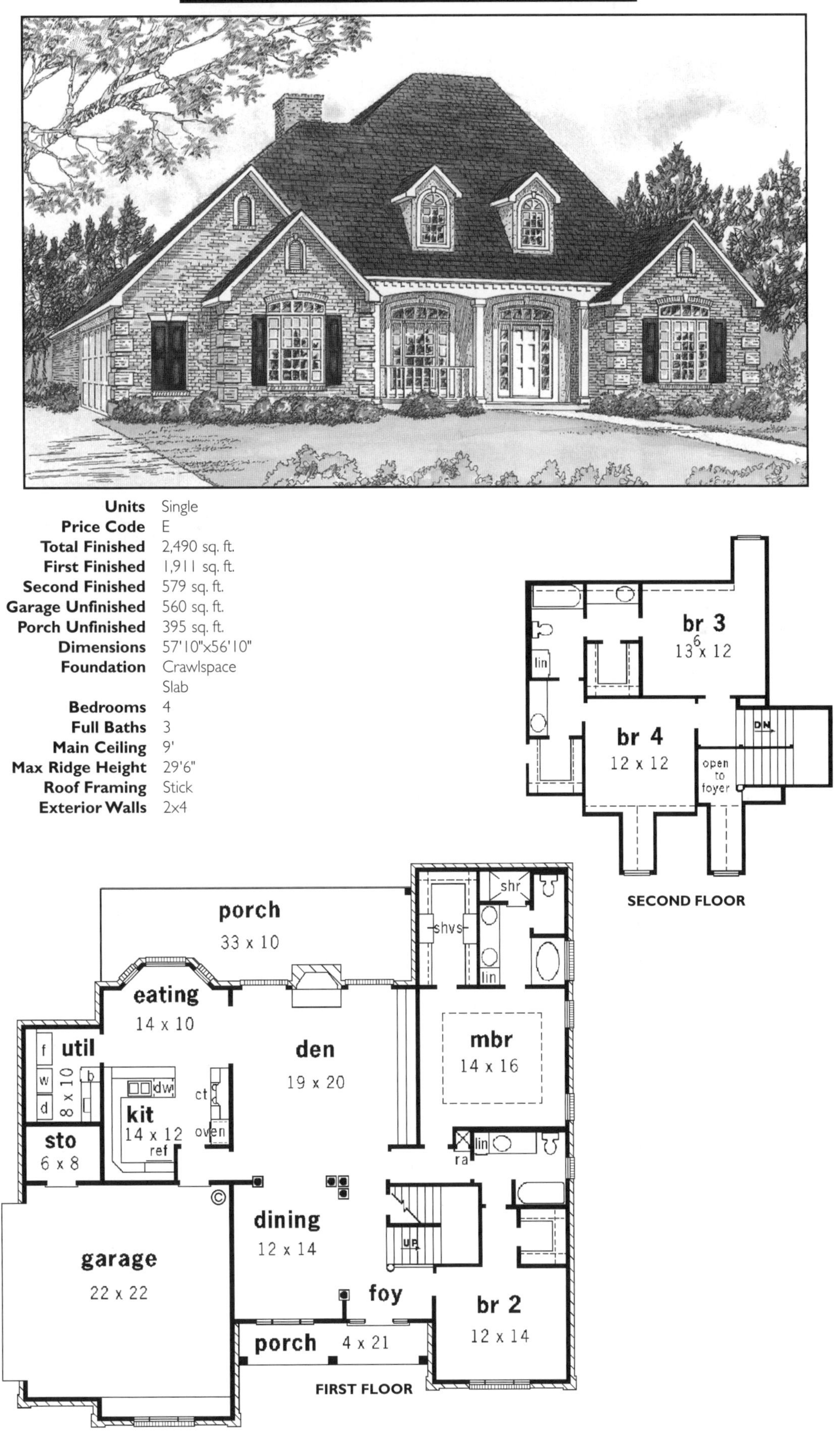
br 3
13⁶ x 12
lin
br 4
12 x 12
open to foyer
DN
SECOND FLOOR
porch
33 x 10
shvs
shr
lin
eating
14 x 10
den
19 x 20
mbr
14 x 16
util
8 x 10
f
w
d
b
dw
ct
kit
14 x 12
oven
ref
sto
6 x 8
lin
ra
dining
12 x 14
UP
garage
22 x 22
foy
br 2
12 x 14
porch
4 x 21
FIRST FLOOR

Units	Single
Price Code	E
Total Finished	2,490 sq. ft.
First Finished	1,911 sq. ft.
Second Finished	579 sq. ft.
Garage Unfinished	560 sq. ft.
Porch Unfinished	395 sq. ft.
Dimensions	57'10"x56'10"
Foundation	Crawlspace Slab
Bedrooms	4
Full Baths	3
Main Ceiling	9'
Max Ridge Height	29'6"
Roof Framing	Stick
Exterior Walls	2x4

Design 97299

Units	Single
Price Code	E
Total Finished	2,491 sq. ft.
Main Finished	2,491 sq. ft.
Bonus Unfinished	588 sq. ft.
Basement Unfinished	2,491 sq. ft.
Garage Unfinished	522 sq. ft.
Dimensions	64'x72'4"
Foundation	Basement Crawlspace
Bedrooms	3
Full Baths	2
Half Baths	1
Max Ridge Height	28'
Roof Framing	Stick
Exterior Walls	2x4

CAD
FILES AVAILABLE
For more information call
800-235-5700

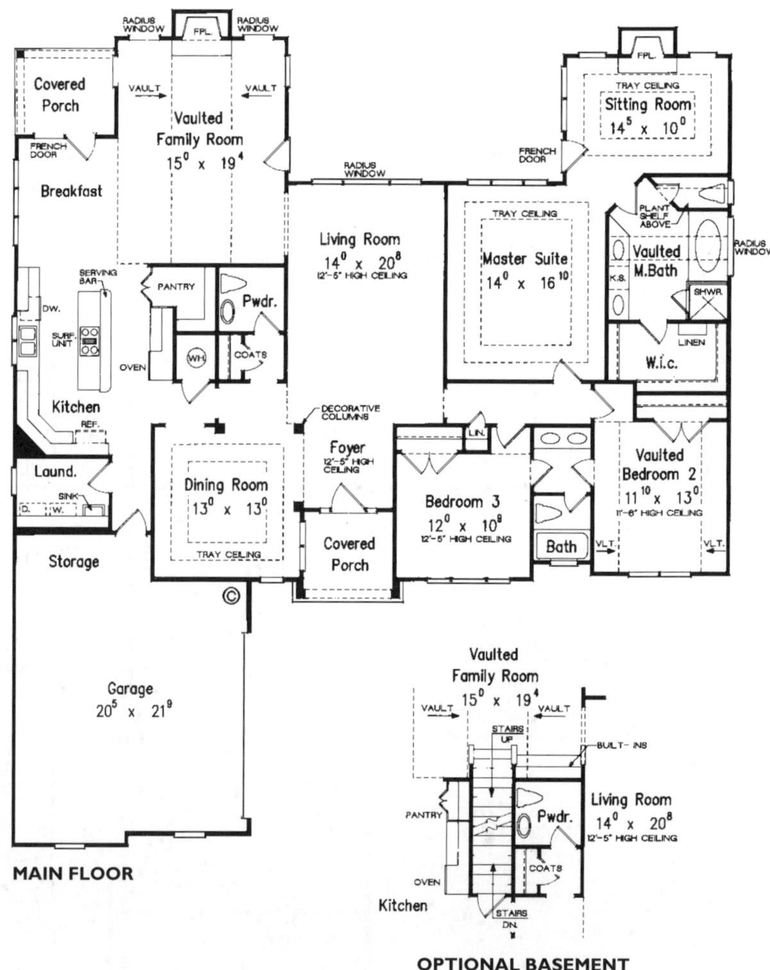
Covered Porch
Vaulted Family Room
15^0 x 19^4
RADIUS WINDOW
FPL.
VAULT
FRENCH DOOR
Breakfast
SERVING BAR
PANTRY
Pwdr.
DW.
SURF. UNIT
OVEN
WH.
COATS
Kitchen
REF.
Laund.
SINK
D.
W.
Storage
Dining Room
13^0 x 13^0
TRAY CEILING
DECORATIVE COLUMNS
Foyer
12'-5" HIGH CEILING
Covered Porch
Garage
20^5 x 21^9
Living Room
14^0 x 20^8
12'-5" HIGH CEILING
Sitting Room
14^5 x 10^0
Master Suite
14^0 x 16^{10}
PLANT SHELF ABOVE
Vaulted M.Bath
K.S.
SHWR.
LINEN
W.i.c.
LIN.
Bedroom 3
12^0 x 10^8
12'-5" HIGH CEILING
Bath
Vaulted Bedroom 2
11^{10} x 13^0
11'-6" HIGH CEILING
VLT.
STAIRS UP
BUILT-INS
STAIRS DN.

MAIN FLOOR

OPTIONAL BASEMENT STAIR LOCATION

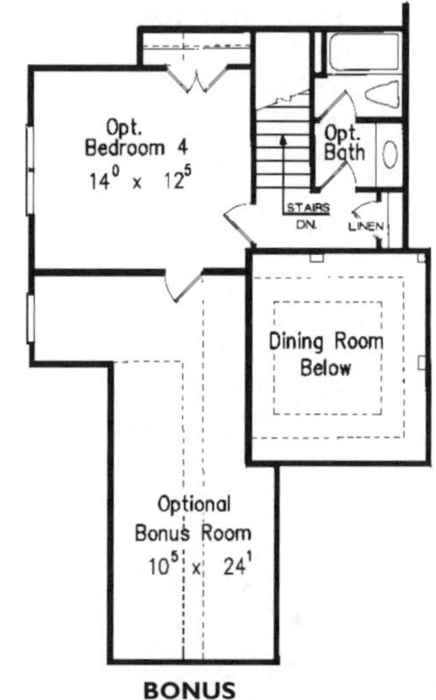
Opt. Bedroom 4
14^0 x 12^5
Opt. Bath
STAIRS DN.
LINEN
Dining Room Below
Optional Bonus Room
10^5 x 24^1

BONUS

Design 92453

Units	Single
Price Code	E
Total Finished	2,499 sq. ft.
Main Finished	2,499 sq. ft.
Dimensions	70'x69'
Foundation	Basement Crawlspace Slab
Bedrooms	4
Full Baths	2
Half Baths	1
Main Ceiling	9'
Roof Framing	Stick
Exterior Walls	2x4

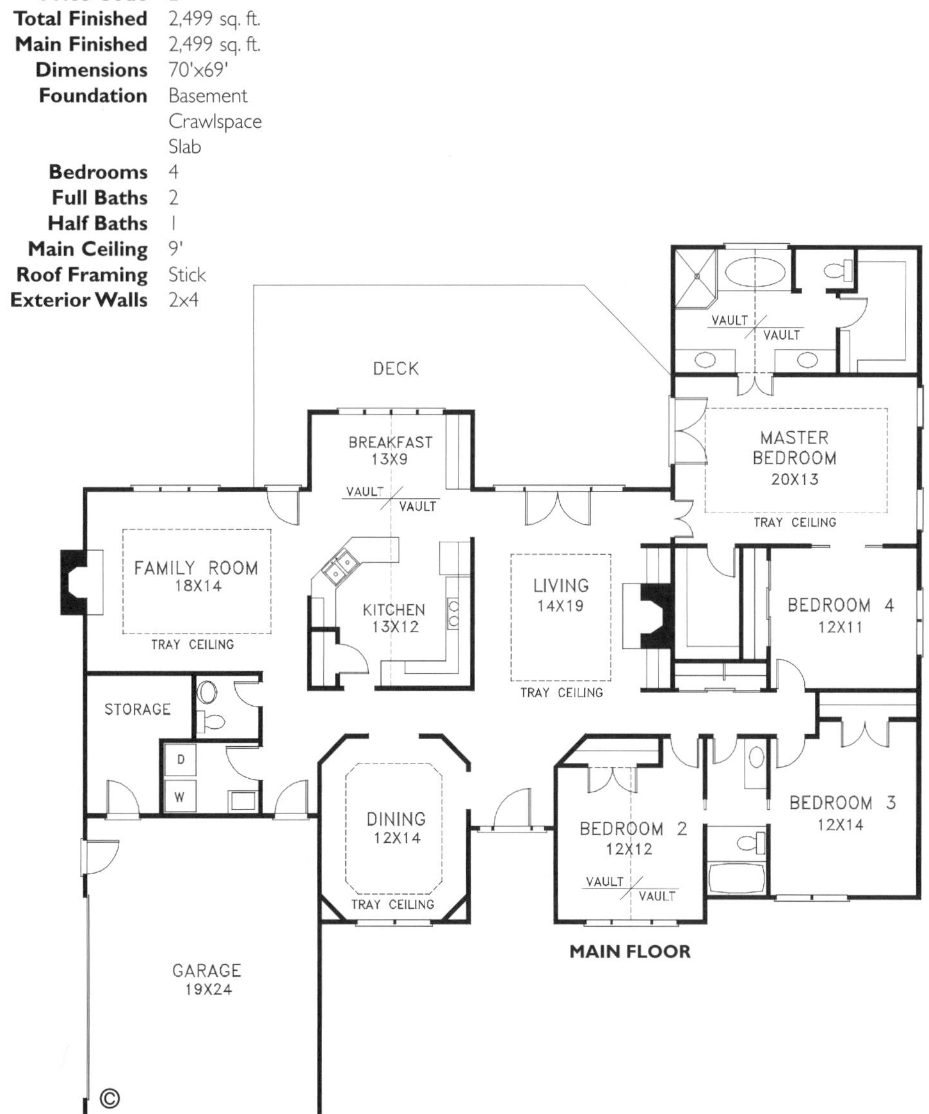

DECK
VAULT
VAULT
MASTER BEDROOM 20X13
TRAY CEILING
BREAKFAST 13X9
VAULT
VAULT
FAMILY ROOM 18X14
TRAY CEILING
KITCHEN 13X12
LIVING 14X19
TRAY CEILING
BEDROOM 4 12X11
STORAGE
D
W
DINING 12X14
TRAY CEILING
BEDROOM 2 12X12
VAULT
VAULT
BEDROOM 3 12X14
GARAGE 19X24
©

MAIN FLOOR

OPTIONAL BATHROOM

Design 69025

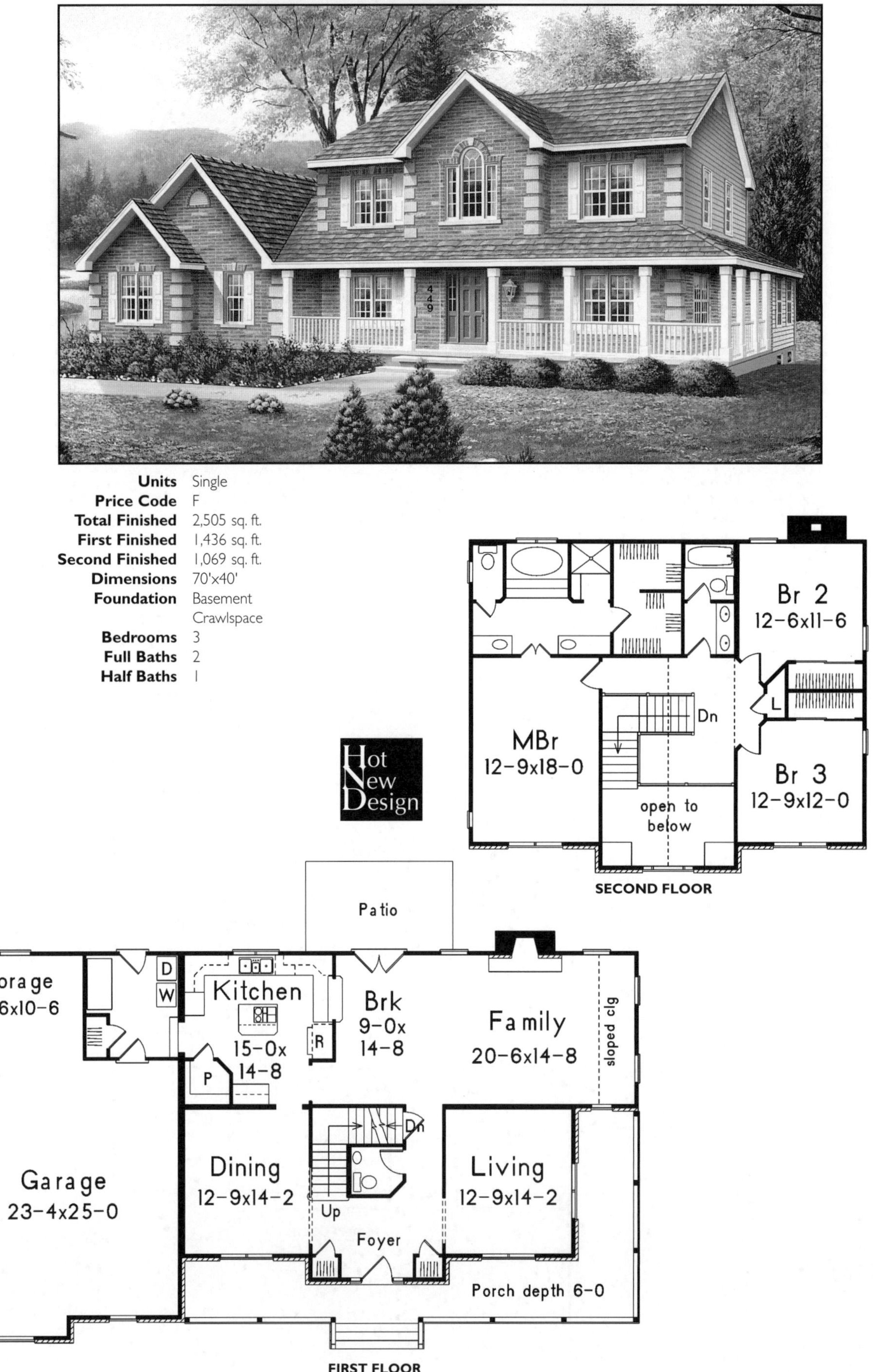

4
4
9
Hot
New
Design
Br 2
12-6x11-6
L
Dn
MBr
12-9x18-0
Br 3
12-9x12-0
open to
below
SECOND FLOOR
Patio
Storage
13-6x10-6
D
W
Kitchen
15-0x
14-8
R
P
Brk
9-0x
14-8
Family
20-6x14-8
sloped clg
Dn
Garage
23-4x25-0
Dining
12-9x14-2
Up
Foyer
Living
12-9x14-2
Porch depth 6-0
©
FIRST FLOOR

Units	Single
Price Code	F
Total Finished	2,505 sq. ft.
First Finished	1,436 sq. ft.
Second Finished	1,069 sq. ft.
Dimensions	70'x40'
Foundation	Basement Crawlspace
Bedrooms	3
Full Baths	2
Half Baths	1

Design 82096

Units	Single
Price Code	F
Total Finished	2,502 sq. ft.
Main Finished	2,502 sq. ft.
Garage Unfinished	770 sq. ft.
Porch Unfinished	434 sq. ft.
Dimensions	72'10"x67'
Foundation	Basement Crawlspace Slab
Bedrooms	4
Full Baths	2
Main Ceiling	9'
Exterior Walls	2x4

COVERED PORCH 15'-0" X 6'-0"
BRKFAST RM. 13'-0" X 12'-0"
COVERED PORCH 23'-8" X 6'-0"
BED RM. 4 16'-0" X 12'-0"
GREAT RM. 19'-10" X 17'-2"
KITCHEN 13'-0" X 15'-8"
M.BED RM. 13'-8" X 17'-10"
M.BATH
BATH
LAU./HOBBY
STOR.
BED RM. 2 / STUDY 12'-4" X 12'-8"
FOYER
DINING RM. 14'-8" X 12'-8"
BED RM. 3 11'-8" X 14'-8"
OPTIONAL GOLF CART
COVERED PORCH 20'-10" X 5'-0"
GARAGE 23'-4" X 33'-0"

MAIN FLOOR

Design 69137

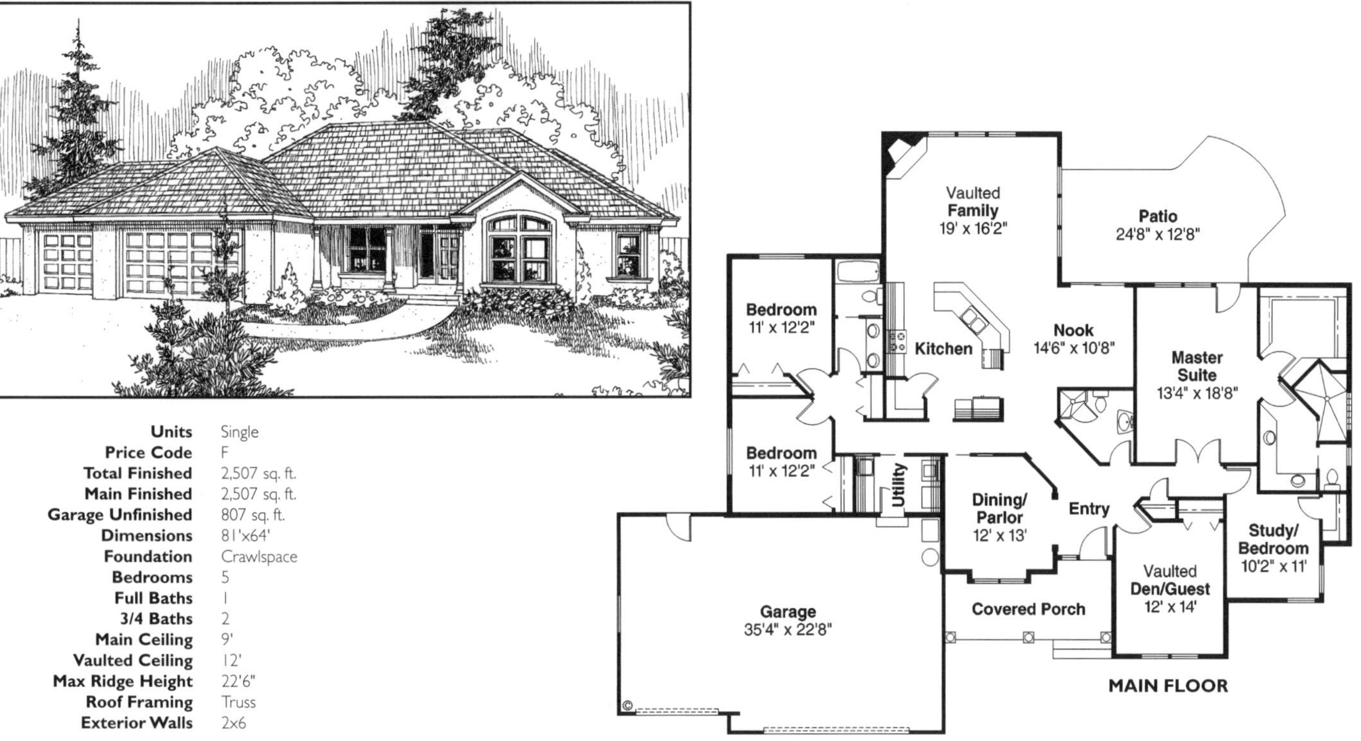
Vaulted Family 19' x 16'2"
Patio 24'8" x 12'8"
Bedroom 11' x 12'2"
Kitchen
Nook 14'6" x 10'8"
Master Suite 13'4" x 18'8"
Bedroom 11' x 12'2"
Utility
Dining/ Parlor 12' x 13'
Entry
Study/ Bedroom 10'2" x 11'
Vaulted Den/Guest 12' x 14'
Garage 35'4" x 22'8"
Covered Porch
MAIN FLOOR

Units	Single
Price Code	F
Total Finished	2,507 sq. ft.
Main Finished	2,507 sq. ft.
Garage Unfinished	807 sq. ft.
Dimensions	81'x64'
Foundation	Crawlspace
Bedrooms	5
Full Baths	1
3/4 Baths	2
Main Ceiling	9'
Vaulted Ceiling	12'
Max Ridge Height	22'6"
Roof Framing	Truss
Exterior Walls	2x6

Design 93056

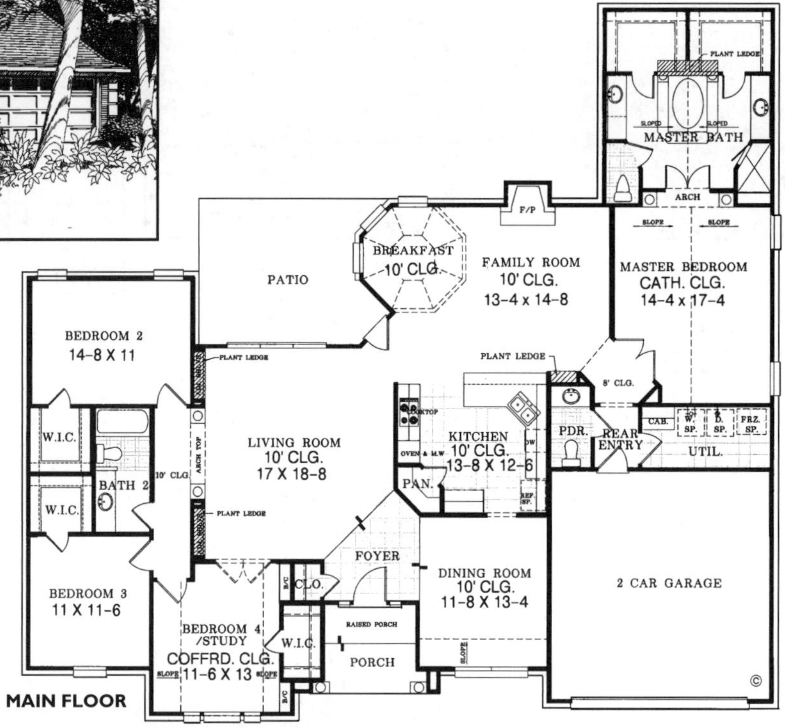

Units	Single
Price Code	F
Total Finished	2,517 sq. ft.
Main Finished	2,517 sq. ft.
Garage Unfinished	443 sq. ft.
Porch Unfinished	72 sq. ft.
Dimensions	69'x63'6"
Foundation	Crawlspace Slab
Bedrooms	4
Full Baths	2
Half Baths	1
Max Ridge Height	23'6"
Roof Framing	Truss
Exterior Walls	2x4

MAIN FLOOR

Design 97486

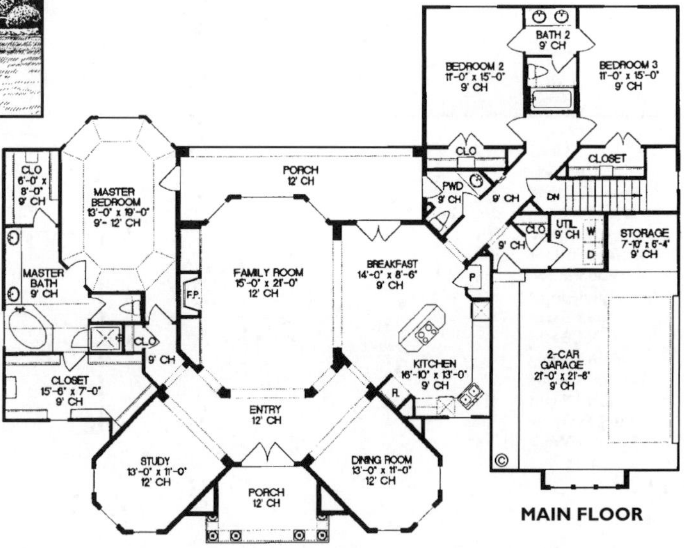

Units	Single
Price Code	F
Total Finished	2,517 sq. ft.
Main Finished	2,517 sq. ft.
Garage Unfinished	617 sq. ft.
Deck Unfinished	101 sq. ft.
Dimensions	77'x59'
Foundation	Slab
Bedrooms	3
Full Baths	2
Half Baths	1
Main Ceiling	9'
Max Ridge Height	27'4"
Exterior Walls	2x4

* Alternate foundation options available at an additional charge.
Please call 1-800-235-5700 for more information.

MAIN FLOOR

Design 98519

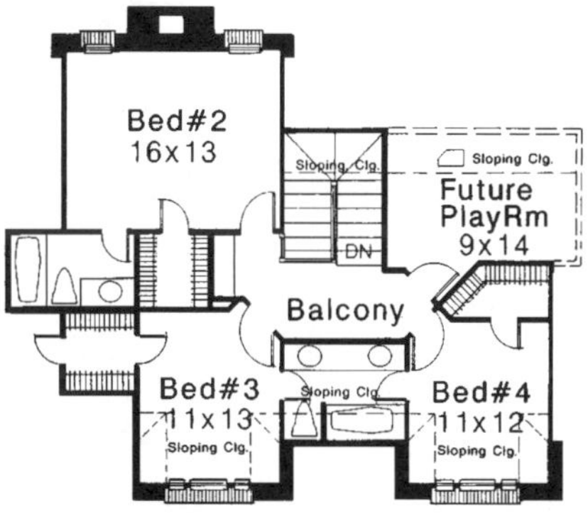

SECOND FLOOR

FIRST FLOOR

Units	Single
Price Code	F
Total Finished	2,524 sq. ft.
First Finished	1,735 sq. ft.
Second Finished	789 sq. ft.
Bonus Unfinished	132 sq. ft.
Garage Unfinished	482 sq. ft.
Deck Unfinished	89 sq. ft.
Porch Unfinished	80 sq. ft.
Dimensions	65'x51'1"
Foundation	Slab
Bedrooms	4
Full Baths	3
Half Baths	1
First Ceiling	9'
Second Ceiling	8'
Max Ridge Height	26'
Roof Framing	Stick
Exterior Walls	2x4

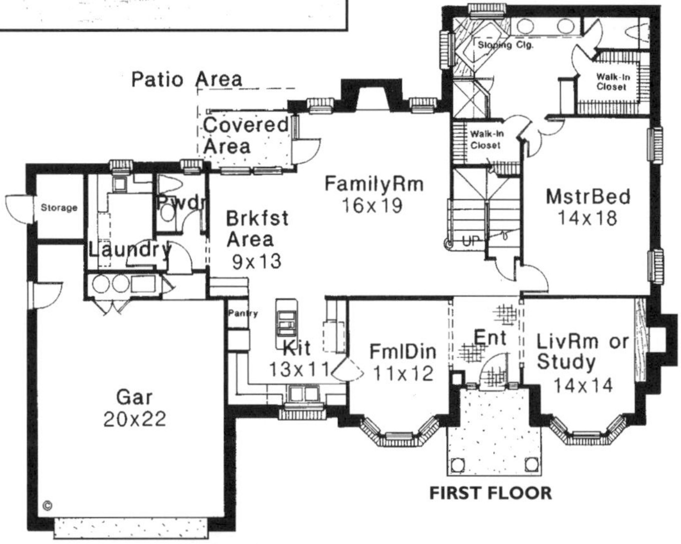

2,501-3,000 sq.ft. HOME PLANS

Design 34926

PHOTOGRAPHY: JOHN EHRENCLOU

Please note: The photographed home may have been modified to suit homeowner preferences. If you order plans, have a builder or design professional check them against the photograph to confirm actual construction details.

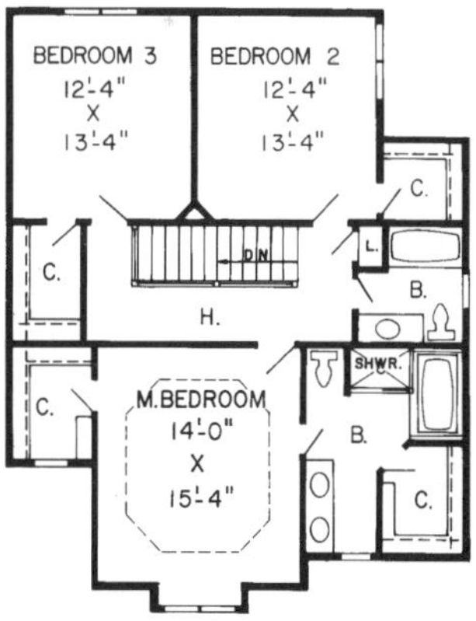

SECOND FLOOR

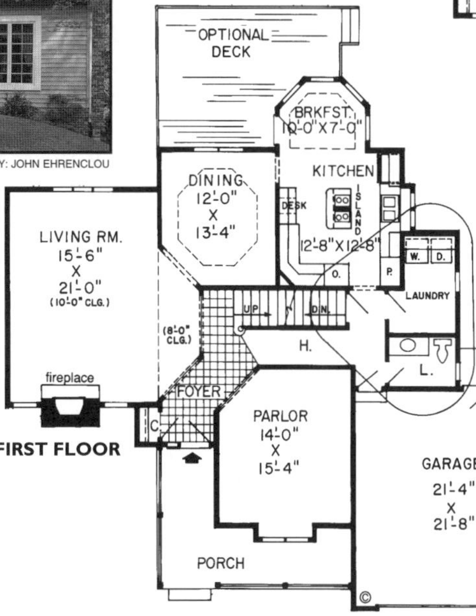

FIRST FLOOR

OPTIONAL CRAWLSPACE/SLAB FOUNDATION

Units	Single
Price Code	F
Total Finished	2,525 sq. ft.
First Finished	1,409 sq. ft.
Second Finished	1,116 sq. ft.
Basement Unfinished	1,409 sq. ft.
Garage Unfinished	483 sq. ft.
Dimensions	58'4"x53'
Foundation	Basement Crawlspace Slab
Bedrooms	3
Full Baths	2
Half Baths	1
Max Ridge Height	31'
Roof Framing	Stick
Exterior Walls	2x4, 2x6

Design 50028

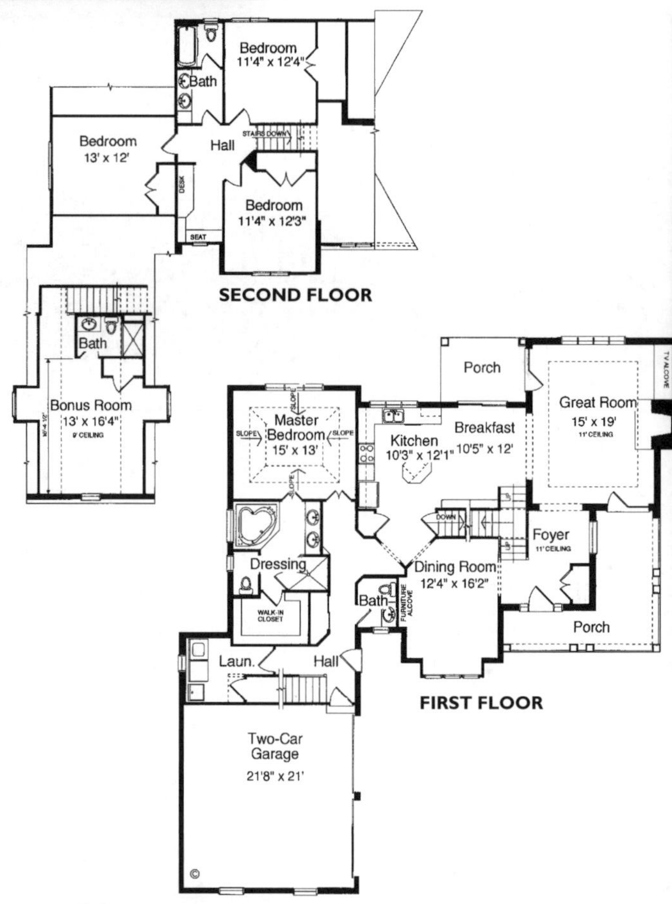

Bedroom
11'4" x 12'4"
Bath
Bedroom
13' x 12'
Hall
STAIRS DOWN
DESK
Bedroom
11'4" x 12'3"
SEAT
SECOND FLOOR
Bath
Bonus Room
13' x 16'4"
9' CEILING
Porch
Master
Bedroom
15' x 13'
SLOPE
Kitchen
10'3" x 12'1"
Breakfast
10'5" x 12'
Great Room
15' x 19'
11' CEILING
TV ALCOVE
DOWN
Foyer
11' CEILING
Dressing
WALK-IN CLOSET
Dining Room
12'4" x 16'2"
Bath
FURNITURE ALCOVE
Porch
Laun.
Hall
FIRST FLOOR
Two-Car
Garage
21'8" x 21'

Units	Single
Price Code	F
Total Finished	2,537 sq. ft.
First Finished	1,772 sq. ft.
Second Finished	765 sq. ft.
Bonus Unfinished	380 sq. ft.
Basement Unfinished	1,772 sq. ft.
Garage Unfinished	460 sq. ft.
Porch Unfinished	189 sq. ft.
Dimensions	61'8'x66'4"
Foundation	Basement
Bedrooms	4
Full Baths	2
Half Baths	1
First Ceiling	8'
Second Ceiling	8'
Max Ridge Height	31'
Roof Framing	Truss
Exterior Walls	2x4

Design 97408

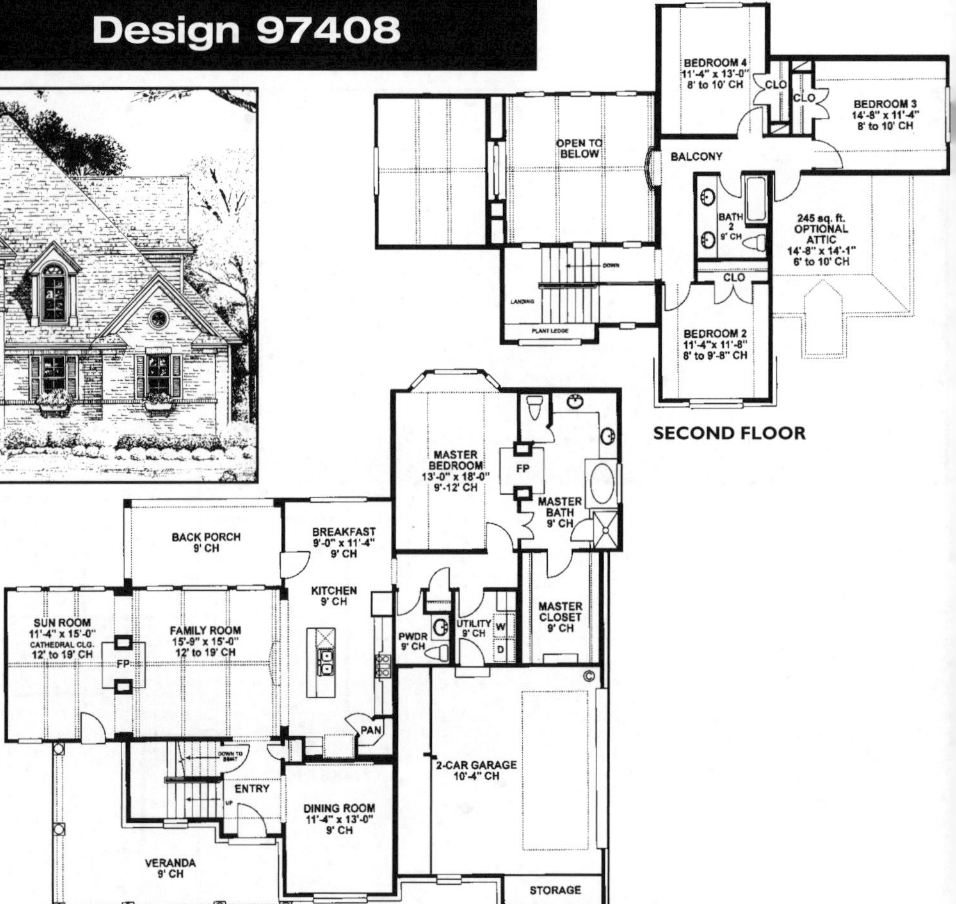

BEDROOM 4
11'-4" x 13'-0"
8' to 10' CH
CLO
CLO
BEDROOM 3
14'-8" x 11'-4"
8' to 10' CH
OPEN TO BELOW
BALCONY
BATH 2
9' CH
245 sq. ft.
OPTIONAL ATTIC
14'-8" x 14'-1"
6' to 10' CH
DOWN
LANDING
PLANT LEDGE
CLO
BEDROOM 2
11'-4" x 11'-8"
8' to 9'-8" CH
SECOND FLOOR

MASTER BEDROOM
13'-0" x 18'-0"
9'-12' CH
FP
MASTER BATH
9' CH
BACK PORCH
9' CH
BREAKFAST
9'-0" x 11'-4"
9' CH
KITCHEN
9' CH
PWDR
9' CH
UTILITY
9' CH
W
D
MASTER CLOSET
9' CH
SUN ROOM
11'-4" x 15'-0"
CATHEDRAL CLG.
12' to 19' CH
FAMILY ROOM
15'-9" x 15'-0"
12' to 19' CH
FP
PAN
DOWN TO BSMT
UP
ENTRY
DINING ROOM
11'-4" x 13'-0"
9' CH
2-CAR GARAGE
10'-4" CH
VERANDA
9' CH
STORAGE
FIRST FLOOR

Units	Single
Price Code	F
Total Finished	2,537 sq. ft.
First Finished	1,794 sq. ft.
Second Finished	743 sq. ft.
Dimensions	66'x55'11½"
Foundation	Slab
Bedrooms	4
Full Baths	2
Half Baths	1
Max Ridge Height	33'
Roof Framing	Stick
Exterior Walls	2x4

* Alternate foundation options available at an additional charge. Please call 1-800-235-5700 for more information.

Design 99469

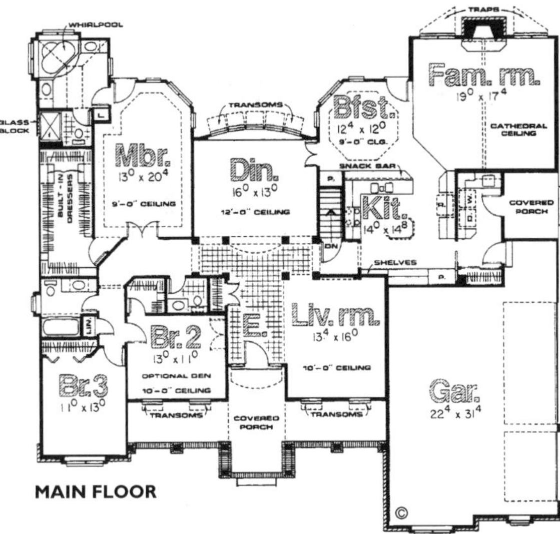
WHIRLPOOL
GLASS BLOCK
BUILT-IN DRESSERS
Mbr.
$13^0 \times 20^4$
9'-0" CEILING
TRANSOMS
Din.
$16^0 \times 13^0$
12'-0" CEILING
Bfst.
$12^4 \times 12^0$
9'-0" CLG.
SNACK BAR
Kit.
$14^0 \times 14^8$
TRAPS
Fam. rm.
$19^0 \times 17^4$
CATHEDRAL CEILING
COVERED PORCH
SHELVES
Br. 2
$13^0 \times 11^0$
OPTIONAL DEN
10'-0" CEILING
E.
Liv. rm.
$13^4 \times 16^0$
10'-0" CEILING
Br. 3
$11^0 \times 13^0$
TRANSOMS
COVERED PORCH
TRANSOMS
Gar.
$22^4 \times 31^4$
MAIN FLOOR

Units	Single
Price Code	F
Total Finished	2,538 sq. ft.
Main Finished	2,538 sq. ft.
Garage Unfinished	755 sq. ft.
Dimensions	68'8"x64'8"
Foundation	Basement
Bedrooms	3
Full Baths	2
Half Baths	1
Main Ceiling	8'
Max Ridge Height	24'6"
Roof Framing	Stick
Exterior Walls	2x4

* Alternate foundation options available at an additional charge. Please call 1-800-235-5700 for more information.

Design 20176

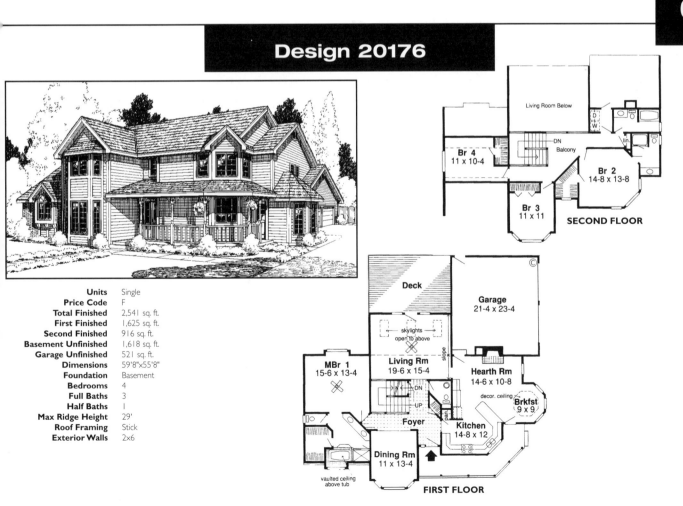

Living Room Below
DN
Balcony
Br 4
11 x 10-4
Br 2
14-8 x 13-8
Br 3
11 x 11
SECOND FLOOR

Deck
Garage
21-4 x 23-4
skylights
open to above
Living Rm
19-6 x 15-4
MBr 1
15-6 x 13-4
Hearth Rm
14-6 x 10-8
decor. ceiling
Brkfst
9 x 9
Foyer
Kitchen
14-8 x 12
Dining Rm
11 x 13-4
vaulted ceiling above tub
FIRST FLOOR

Units	Single
Price Code	F
Total Finished	2,541 sq. ft.
First Finished	1,625 sq. ft.
Second Finished	916 sq. ft.
Basement Unfinished	1,618 sq. ft.
Garage Unfinished	521 sq. ft.
Dimensions	59'8"x55'8"
Foundation	Basement
Bedrooms	4
Full Baths	3
Half Baths	1
Max Ridge Height	29'
Roof Framing	Stick
Exterior Walls	2x6

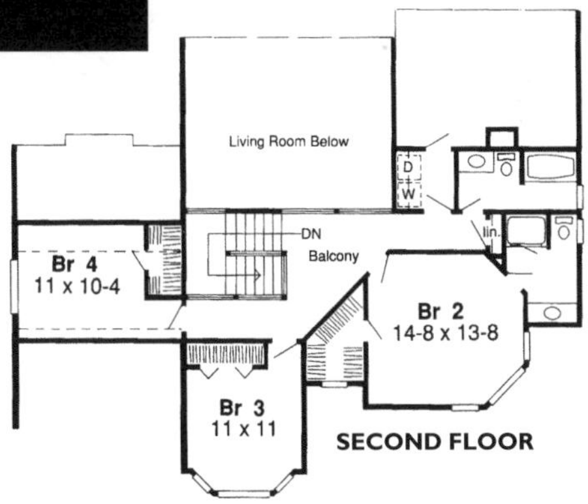

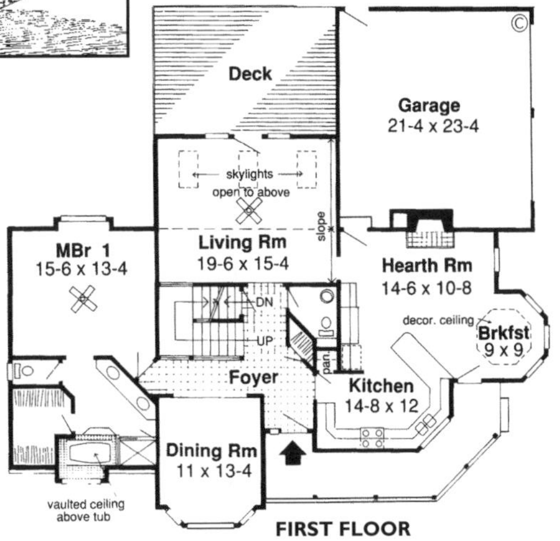

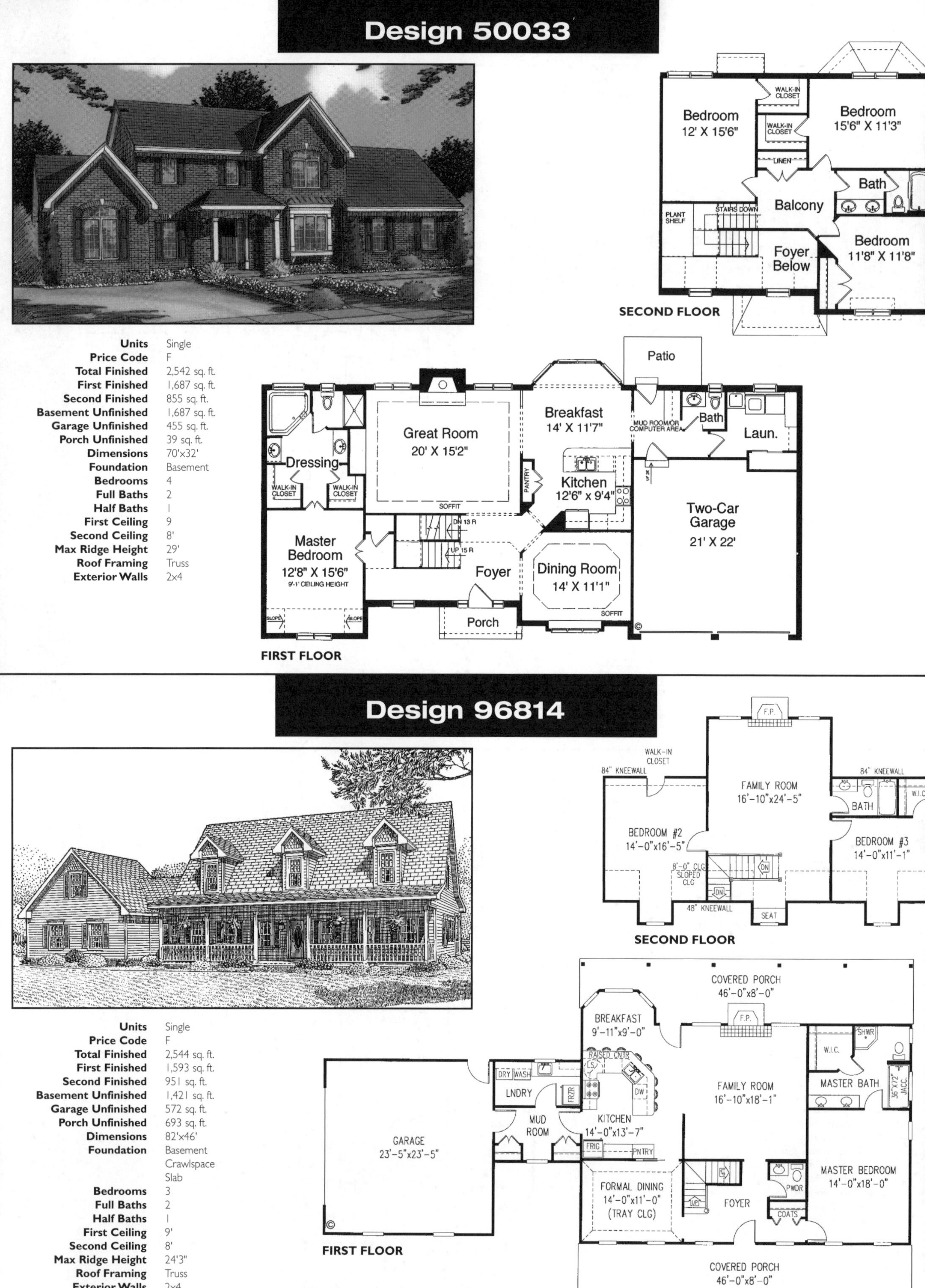
SECOND FLOOR
Bedroom 12' X 15'6"
WALK-IN CLOSET
WALK-IN CLOSET
Bedroom 15'6" X 11'3"
LINEN
Bath
Balcony
PLANT SHELF
STAIRS DOWN
Foyer Below
Bedroom 11'8" X 11'8"
Patio
Great Room 20' X 15'2"
SOFFIT
Breakfast 14' X 11'7"
MUD ROOM/OR COMPUTER AREA
Bath
Laun.
Dressing
WALK-IN CLOSET
WALK-IN CLOSET
PANTRY
Kitchen 12'6" x 9'4"
Two-Car Garage 21' X 22'
DN 13 R
UP 15 R
Master Bedroom 12'8" X 15'6"
9'-1' CEILING HEIGHT
Foyer
Dining Room 14' X 11'1"
SLOPE
SLOPE
Porch
SOFFIT
FIRST FLOOR
F.P.
WALK-IN CLOSET
84" KNEEWALL
84" KNEEWALL
FAMILY ROOM 16'-10"x24'-5"
BATH
W.I.C.
BEDROOM #2 14'-0"x16'-5"
BEDROOM #3 14'-0"x11'-1"
8'-0" CLG
SLOPED CLG
DN
DN
48" KNEEWALL
SEAT
SECOND FLOOR
COVERED PORCH 46'-0"x8'-0"
BREAKFAST 9'-11"x9'-0"
F.P.
RAISED CNTR
SHWR
W.I.C.
DRY
WASH
LNDRY
FRZR
DW
FAMILY ROOM 16'-10"x18'-1"
MASTER BATH
36"X72" JACC.
MUD ROOM
KITCHEN 14'-0"x13'-7"
GARAGE 23'-5"x23'-5"
FRIG
PNTRY
FORMAL DINING 14'-0"x11'-0" (TRAY CLG)
UP
FOYER
PWDR
COATS
MASTER BEDROOM 14'-0"x18'-0"
FIRST FLOOR
COVERED PORCH 46'-0"x8'-0"

Design 50033

Units	Single
Price Code	F
Total Finished	2,542 sq. ft.
First Finished	1,687 sq. ft.
Second Finished	855 sq. ft.
Basement Unfinished	1,687 sq. ft.
Garage Unfinished	455 sq. ft.
Porch Unfinished	39 sq. ft.
Dimensions	70'x32'
Foundation	Basement
Bedrooms	4
Full Baths	2
Half Baths	1
First Ceiling	9
Second Ceiling	8'
Max Ridge Height	29'
Roof Framing	Truss
Exterior Walls	2x4

Design 96814

Units	Single
Price Code	F
Total Finished	2,544 sq. ft.
First Finished	1,593 sq. ft.
Second Finished	951 sq. ft.
Basement Unfinished	1,421 sq. ft.
Garage Unfinished	572 sq. ft.
Porch Unfinished	693 sq. ft.
Dimensions	82'x46'
Foundation	Basement Crawlspace Slab
Bedrooms	3
Full Baths	2
Half Baths	1
First Ceiling	9'
Second Ceiling	8'
Max Ridge Height	24'3"
Roof Framing	Truss
Exterior Walls	2x4

Design 96552

Units	Single
Price Code	F
Total Finished	2,545 sq. ft.
Main Finished	2,545 sq. ft.
Garage Unfinished	603 sq. ft.
Porch Unfinished	354 sq. ft.
Dimensions	78'x58'
Foundation	Crawlspace Slab
Bedrooms	4
Full Baths	3
Half Baths	1
Main Ceiling	9'
Max Ridge Height	27'4"
Roof Framing	Stick
Exterior Walls	2x4

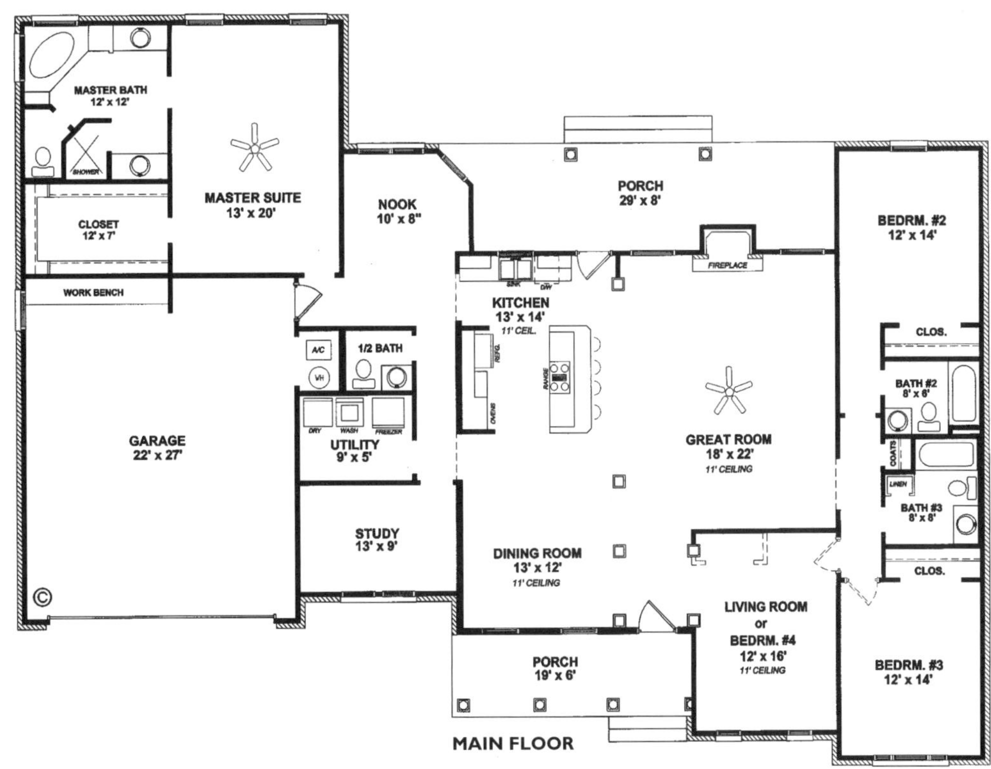
MASTER BATH
12' x 12'
SHOWER
MASTER SUITE
13' x 20'
CLOSET
12' x 7'
WORK BENCH
NOOK
10' x 8"
PORCH
29' x 8'
BEDRM. #2
12' x 14'
FIREPLACE
KITCHEN
13' x 14'
11' CEIL.
A/C
WH
1/2 BATH
CLOS.
BATH #2
8' x 6'
GARAGE
22' x 27'
DRY
WASH
FREEZER
UTILITY
9' x 5'
GREAT ROOM
18' x 22'
11' CEILING
COATS
LINEN
BATH #3
8' x 8'
STUDY
13' x 9'
DINING ROOM
13' x 12'
11' CEILING
CLOS.
LIVING ROOM
or
BEDRM. #4
12' x 16'
11' CEILING
PORCH
19' x 6'
BEDRM. #3
12' x 14'
©

MAIN FLOOR

Design 91518

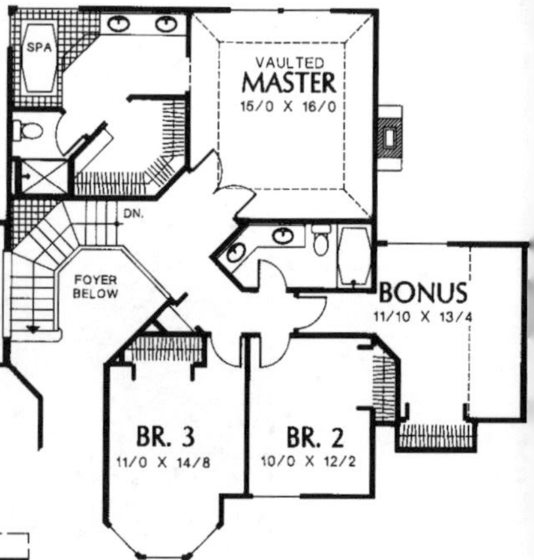

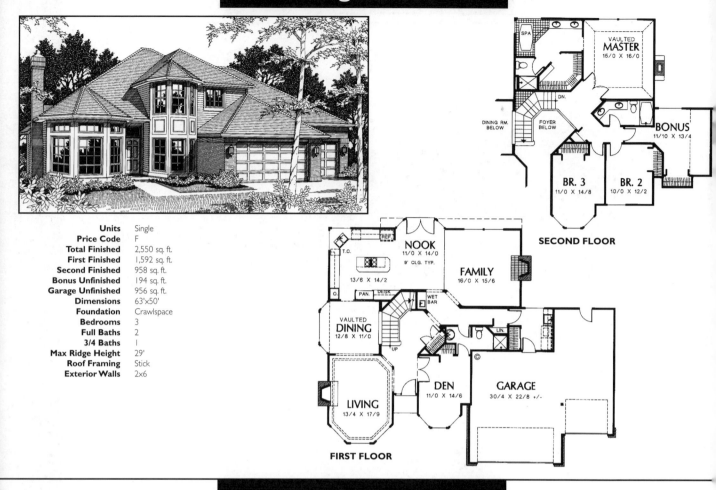

Units	Single
Price Code	F
Total Finished	2,550 sq. ft.
First Finished	1,592 sq. ft.
Second Finished	958 sq. ft.
Bonus Unfinished	194 sq. ft.
Garage Unfinished	956 sq. ft.
Dimensions	63'x50'
Foundation	Crawlspace
Bedrooms	3
Full Baths	2
3/4 Baths	1
Max Ridge Height	29'
Roof Framing	Stick
Exterior Walls	2x6

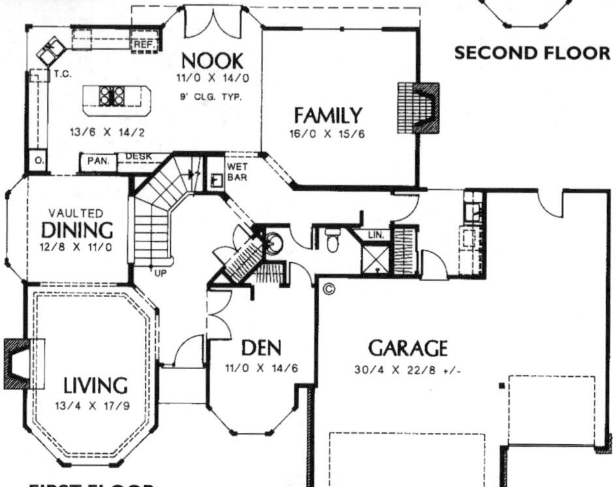

SECOND FLOOR

FIRST FLOOR

Design 97837

Units	Single
Price Code	F
Total Finished	2,551 sq. ft.
Main Finished	2,551 sq. ft.
Garage Unfinished	642 sq. ft.
Deck Unfinished	310 sq. ft.
Porch Unfinished	48 sq. ft.
Dimensions	97'10"x52'4"
Foundation	Slab
Bedrooms	3
Full Baths	2
Half Baths	1
Max Ridge Height	29'
Roof Framing	Stick
Exterior Walls	2x4

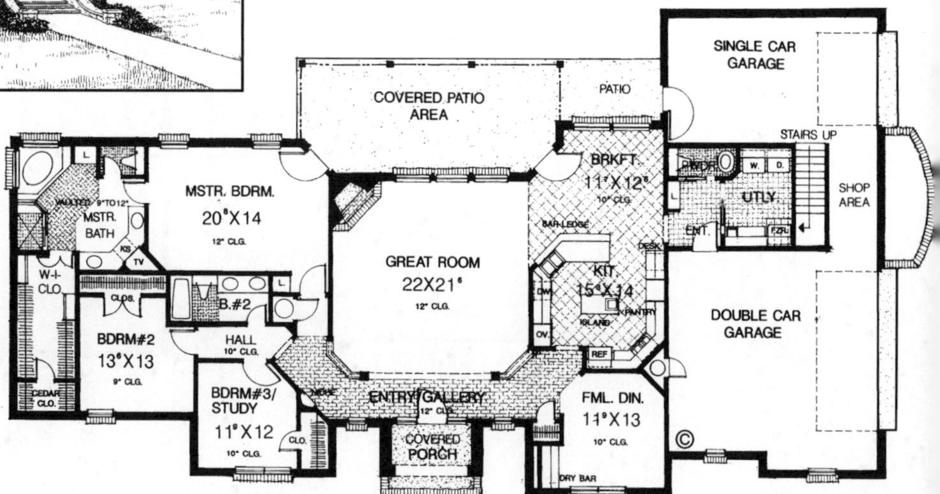

MAIN FLOOR

Design 98201

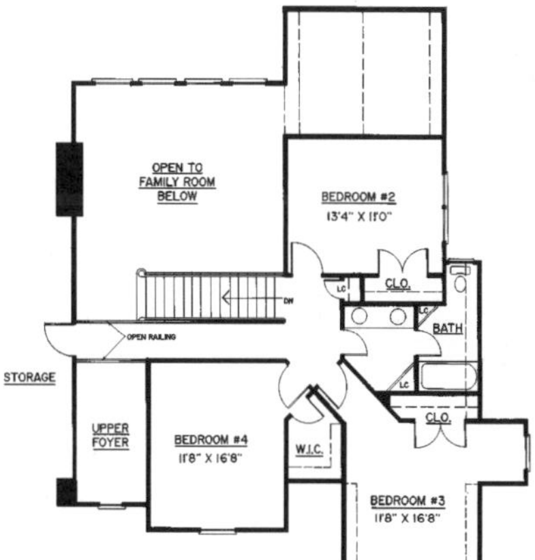

Units	Single
Price Code	F
Total Finished	2,551 sq. ft.
First Finished	1,803 sq. ft.
Second Finished	748 sq. ft.
Basement Unfinished	1,803 sq. ft.
Dimensions	60'6"x53'4"
Foundation	Basement
Bedrooms	4
Full Baths	2
Half Baths	1
First Ceiling	9'
Second Ceiling	8'
Max Ridge Height	33'6"
Roof Framing	Stick
Exterior Walls	2x4

FIRST FLOOR

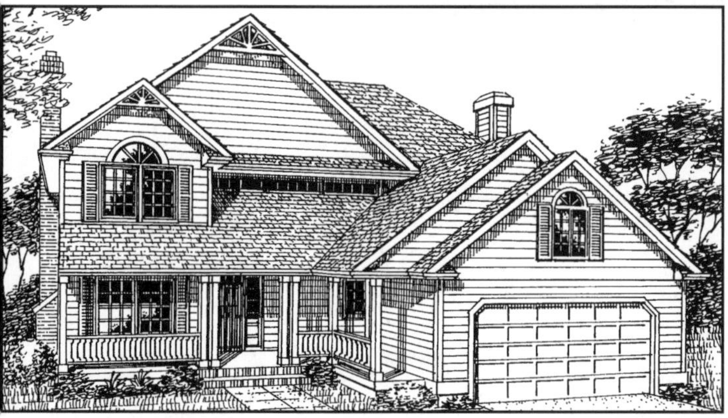

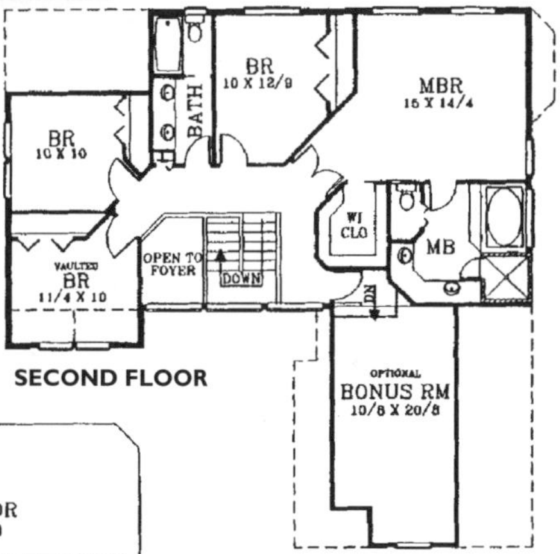

SECOND FLOOR

Design 91481

Units	Single
Price Code	F
Total Finished	2,552 sq. ft.
First Finished	1,275 sq. ft.
Second Finished	1,046 sq. ft.
Bonus Unfinished	231 sq. ft.
Garage Unfinished	420 sq. ft.
Dimensions	49'x47'
Foundation	Crawlspace
Bedrooms	5
Full Baths	2
3/4 Baths	1
First Ceiling	8'
Second Ceiling	8'
Max Ridge Height	30'
Roof Framing	Stick/Truss
Exterior Walls	2x6

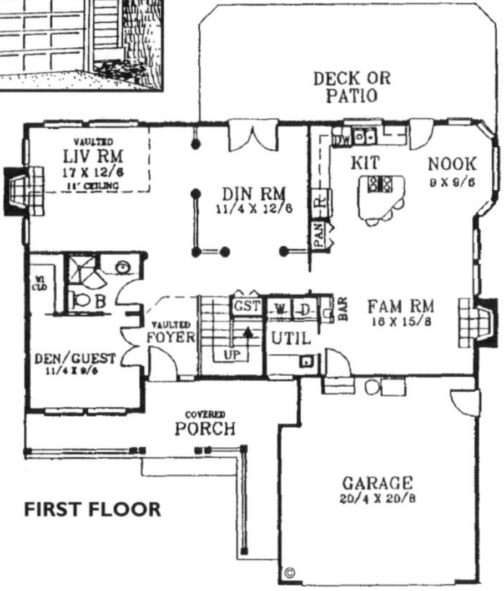

SECOND FLOOR

FIRST FLOOR

Design 94640

Units	Single
Price Code	F
Total Finished	2,558 sq. ft.
Main Finished	2,558 sq. ft.
Garage Unfinished	549 sq. ft.
Porch Unfinished	151 sq. ft.
Dimensions	63'6"x71'6"
Foundation	Crawlspace Slab
Bedrooms	4
Full Baths	3
Main Ceiling	9'
Max Ridge Height	21'6"
Roof Framing	Stick
Exterior Walls	2x4

Two-car Garage 21'-4" X 22'-2"
Bath
Storage
Utility
Master Bedroom 17'-10" X 14'
Covered Porch
Breakfast 12'-4" X 12'
Bedroom 11' X 12'-6"
Family Room 20' X 17'-6"
Ba.
Kitchen 12'-4" X 12'-6"
Ba.
Bedroom 12'-2" X 13'
Foyer
Dining Room 13'-4" X 12'
Bedroom 12'-1" X 12'
Living Room 13'-4" X 14'-6"
Porch

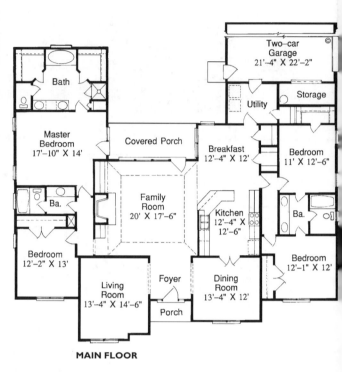

MAIN FLOOR

Design 50022

Units	Single
Price Code	F
Total Finished	2,560 sq. ft.
First Finished	1,770 sq. ft.
Second Finished	790 sq. ft.
Basement Unfinished	1,770 sq. ft.
Garage Unfinished	120 sq. ft.
Porch Unfinished	95 sq. ft.
Dimensions	59'8'x46'6"
Foundation	Basement
Bedrooms	4
Full Baths	2
Half Baths	1
First Ceiling	9'
Second Ceiling	8'
Max Ridge Height	23'
Roof Framing	Stick/Truss
Exterior Walls	2x4

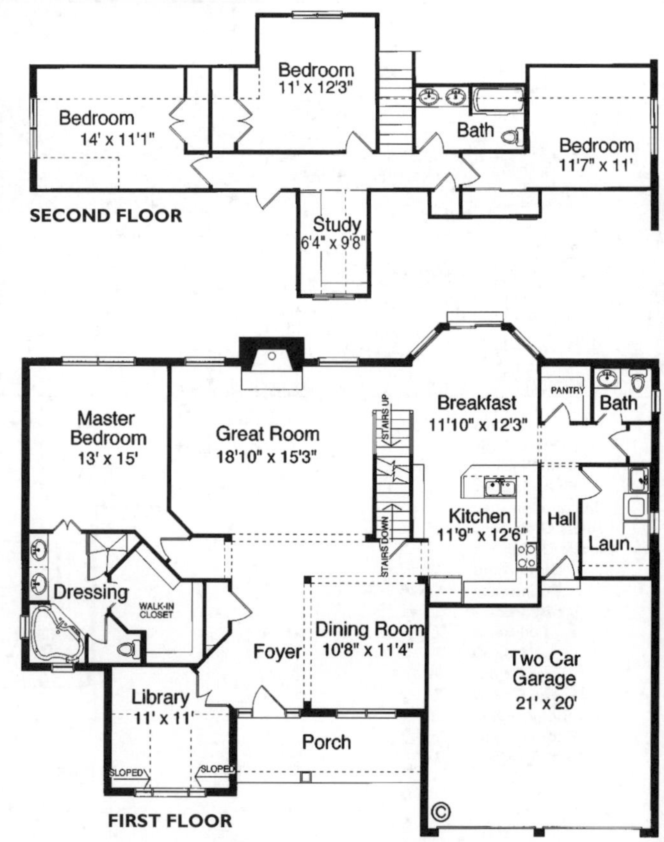

Bedroom 11' x 12'3"
Bedroom 14' x 11'1"
Bath
Bedroom 11'7" x 11'
SECOND FLOOR
Study 6'4" x 9'8"
Master Bedroom 13' x 15'
Great Room 18'10" x 15'3"
STAIRS UP
Breakfast 11'10" x 12'3"
PANTRY
Bath
Kitchen 11'9" x 12'6"
Hall
Laun.
STAIRS DOWN
Dressing
WALK-IN CLOSET
Dining Room 10'8" x 11'4"
Foyer
Two Car Garage 21' x 20'
Library 11' x 11'
Porch
SLOPED
SLOPED
FIRST FLOOR

Design 69146

Units	Single
Price Code	F
Total Finished	2,561 sq. ft.
Main Finished	2,561 sq. ft.
Garage Unfinished	739 sq. ft.
Dimensions	64'x63'
Foundation	Crawlspace
Bedrooms	3
Full Baths	2
Half Baths	1
Main Ceiling	9'
Vaulted Ceiling	10'
Max Ridge Height	24'
Roof Framing	Truss
Exterior Walls	2x6

Patio
30'8" x 13'
Master Suite
19' x 14'
Sun Room
12'4" x 10'
Vaulted
Nook
14' x 10'
Vaulted
Living
17' x 21'8"
Dining
12' x 12'
Kitchen
Utility
Bedroom
12'8" x 11'
Vaulted
Den
11' x 14'
Vaulted
Foyer
Garage
32'4" x 23'8"
Porch
Vaulted
Bedroom
12'8" x 11'

MAIN FLOOR

Design 50018

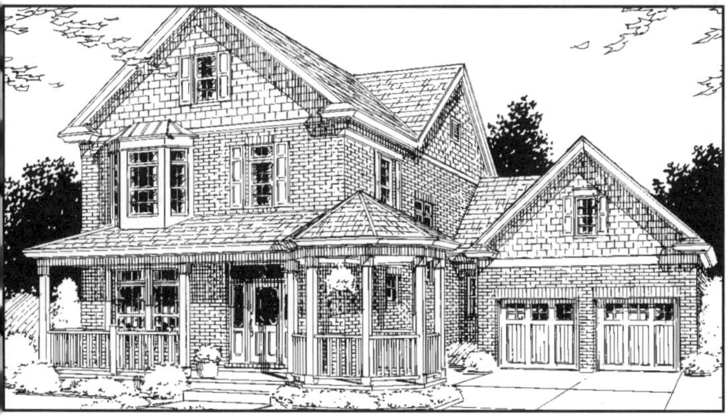

Units	Single
Price Code	F
Total Finished	2,562 sq. ft.
First Finished	1,304 sq. ft.
Second Finished	1,258 sq. ft.
Basement Unfinished	1,304 sq. ft.
Garage Unfinished	437 sq. ft.
Deck Unfinished	344 sq. ft.
Porch Unfinished	223 sq. ft.
Dimensions	56'6"x56'9"
Foundation	Basement
Bedrooms	3
Full Baths	2
Half Baths	1
First Ceiling	9'
Second Ceiling	9'
Max Ridge Height	32'
Roof Framing	Truss
Exterior Walls	2x4

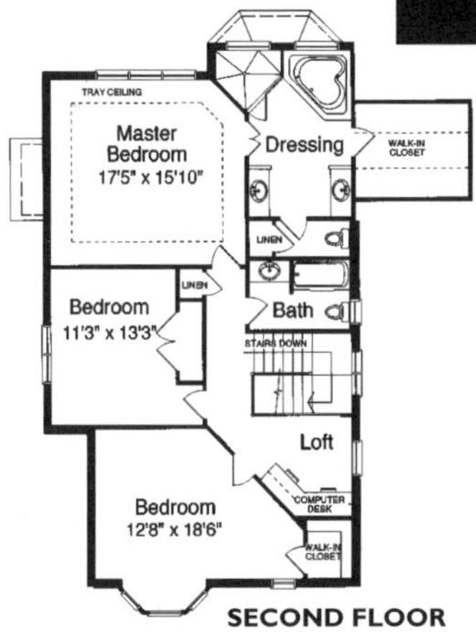

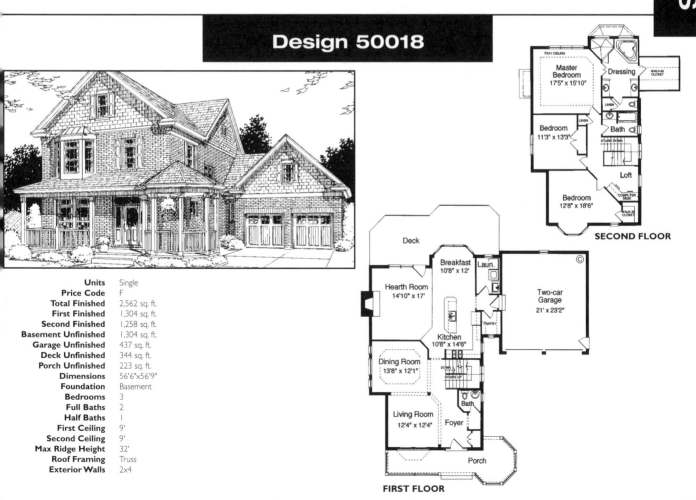

SECOND FLOOR

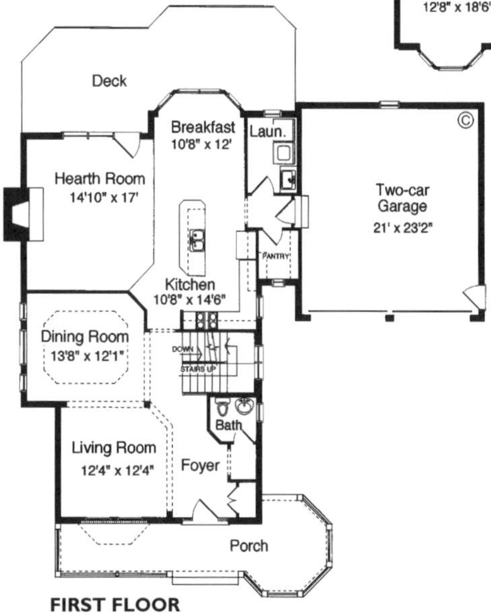

FIRST FLOOR

Design 66012

Units	Single
Price Code	G
Total Finished	2,569 sq. ft.
Main Finished	2,569 sq. ft.
Dimensions	90'6"x62'11"
Foundation	Crawlspace Slab
Bedrooms	3
Full Baths	2
Half Baths	1
Main Ceiling	10'
Max Ridge Height	28
Roof Framing	Stick
Exterior Walls	2x4

MAIN FLOOR

Design 66087

Units	Single
Price Code	F
Total Finished	2,569 sq. ft.
Main Finished	2,569 sq. ft.
Bonus Unfinished	352 sq. ft.
Garage Unfinished	702 sq. ft.
Deck Unfinished	132 sq. ft.
Porch Unfinished	62 sq. ft.
Dimensions	68'10"x74'7"
Foundation	Slab
Bedrooms	4
Full Baths	3
Main Ceiling	10'
Max Ridge Height	31'6"
Roof Framing	Stick
Exterior Walls	2x4

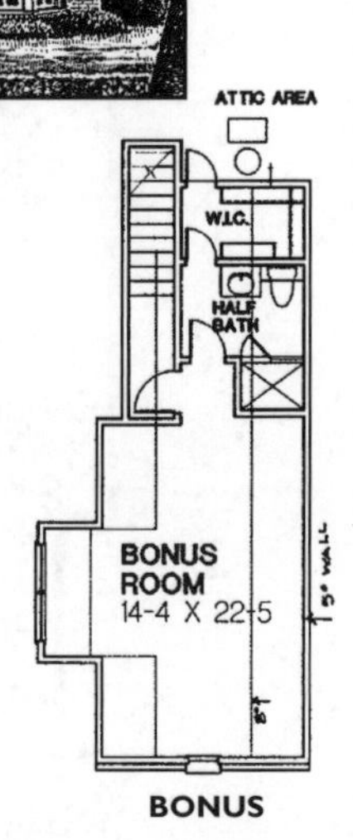
ATTIC AREA
W.I.C.
HALF BATH
BONUS ROOM
14-4 X 22-5

BONUS

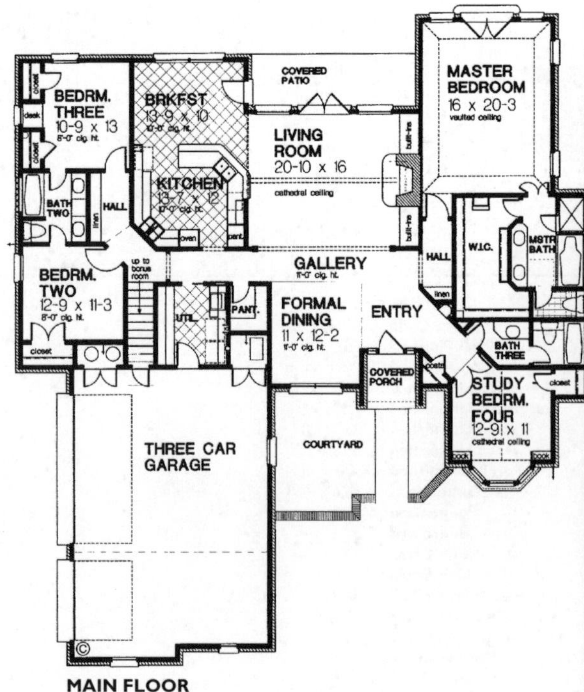
BEDRM. THREE
10-9 x 13
BRKFST
13-9 x 10
COVERED PATIO
LIVING ROOM
20-10 x 16
cathedral ceiling
MASTER BEDROOM
16 x 20-3
vaulted ceiling
KITCHEN
BATH TWO
HALL
W.I.C.
MSTR BATH
BEDRM. TWO
12-9 x 11-3
GALLERY
FORMAL DINING
11 x 12-2
ENTRY
UTIL
PANT.
BATH THREE
COVERED PORCH
STUDY BEDRM. FOUR
12-9 x 11
cathedral ceiling
COURTYARD
THREE CAR GARAGE

MAIN FLOOR

Design 93708

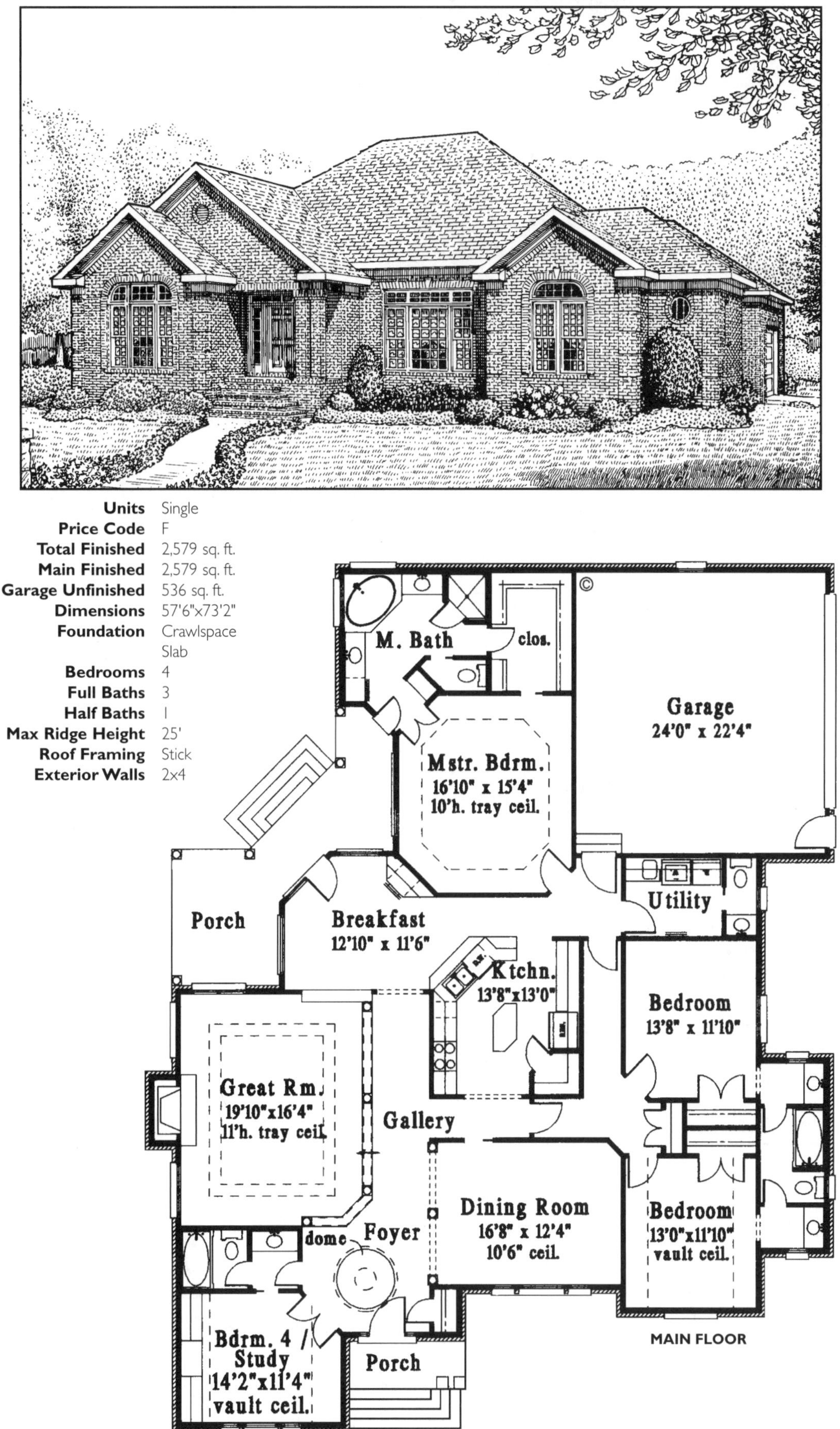
M. Bath
clos.
Garage
24'0" x 22'4"
Mstr. Bdrm.
16'10" x 15'4"
10'h. tray ceil.
Porch
Breakfast
12'10" x 11'6"
Utility
Ktchn.
13'8"x13'0"
Bedroom
13'8" x 11'10"
Great Rm.
19'10"x16'4"
11'h. tray ceil.
Gallery
Dining Room
16'8" x 12'4"
10'6" ceil.
Bedroom
13'0"x11'10"
vault ceil.
dome
Foyer
Bdrm. 4 /
Study
14'2"x11'4"
vault ceil.
Porch
MAIN FLOOR

Units Single
Price Code F
Total Finished 2,579 sq. ft.
Main Finished 2,579 sq. ft.
Garage Unfinished 536 sq. ft.
Dimensions 57'6"x73'2"
Foundation Crawlspace
Slab
Bedrooms 4
Full Baths 3
Half Baths 1
Max Ridge Height 25'
Roof Framing Stick
Exterior Walls 2x4

Design 91173

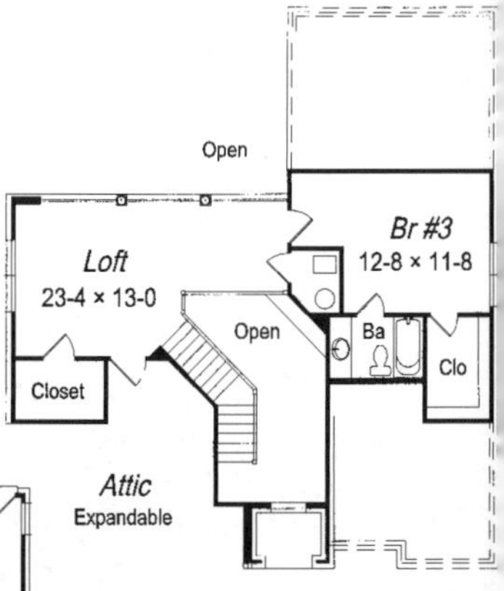

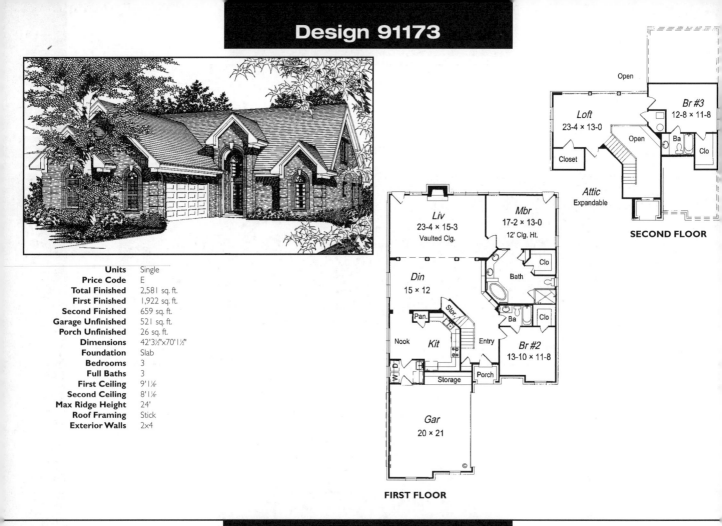

Units	Single
Price Code	E
Total Finished	2,581 sq. ft.
First Finished	1,922 sq. ft.
Second Finished	659 sq. ft.
Garage Unfinished	521 sq. ft.
Porch Unfinished	26 sq. ft.
Dimensions	42'3½"x70'1½"
Foundation	Slab
Bedrooms	3
Full Baths	3
First Ceiling	9'1⅛"
Second Ceiling	8'1⅛"
Max Ridge Height	24'
Roof Framing	Stick
Exterior Walls	2x4

Open
Loft 23-4 × 13-0
Br #3 12-8 × 11-8
Open
Ba
Clo
Closet
Attic Expandable

SECOND FLOOR

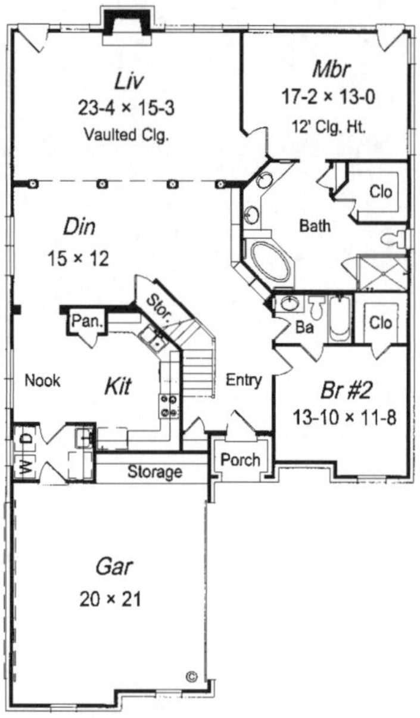

Liv 23-4 × 15-3 Vaulted Clg.
Mbr 17-2 × 13-0 12' Clg. Ht.
Clo
Din 15 × 12
Bath
Stor.
Pan.
Ba
Clo
Nook
Kit
Entry
Br #2 13-10 × 11-8
W D
Storage
Porch
Gar 20 × 21
©

FIRST FLOOR

Design 50008

Units	Single
Price Code	F
Total Finished	2,584 sq. ft.
First Finished	1,391 sq. ft.
Second Finished	1,193 sq. ft.
Basement Unfinished	1,391 sq. ft.
Garage Unfinished	437 sq. ft.
Porch Unfinished	109 sq. ft.
Dimensions	54'6"x39'6"
Foundation	Basement
Bedrooms	4
Full Baths	2
Half Baths	1
First Ceiling	8'
Second Ceiling	8'
Max Ridge Height	28'
Roof Framing	Truss
Exterior Walls	2x4

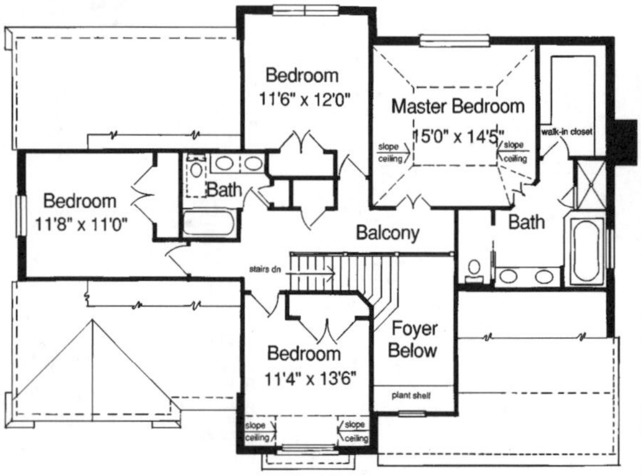

Bedroom 11'6" x 12'0"
Master Bedroom 15'0" x 14'5"
slope ceiling
walk-in closet
Bedroom 11'8" x 11'0"
Bath
Balcony
Bath
stairs dn
Bedroom 11'4" x 13'6"
Foyer Below
plant shelf
slope ceiling

SECOND FLOOR

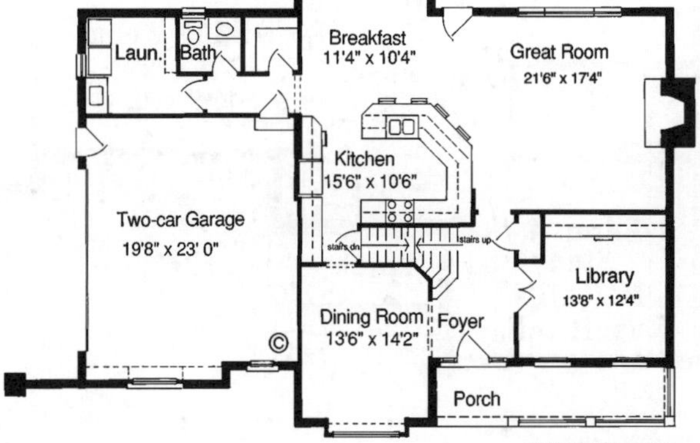

Laun.
Bath
Breakfast 11'4" x 10'4"
Great Room 21'6" x 17'4"
Kitchen 15'6" x 10'6"
Two-car Garage 19'8" x 23' 0"
stairs dn
stairs up
Library 13'8" x 12'4"
Dining Room 13'6" x 14'2"
Foyer
©
Porch

FIRST FLOOR

Design 96938

Units	Single
Price Code	F
Total Finished	2,585 sq. ft.
Main Finished	2,585 sq. ft.
Bonus Unfinished	519 sq. ft.
Basement Unfinished	2,609 sq. ft.
Garage Unfinished	607 sq. ft.
Dimensions	61'x80'
Foundation	Basement Crawlspace
Bedrooms	3
Full Baths	2
Half Baths	1
Main Ceiling	9'
Vaulted Ceiling	12'
Tray Ceiling	10'6"
Max Ridge Height	31'
Roof Framing	Stick
Exterior Walls	2x4

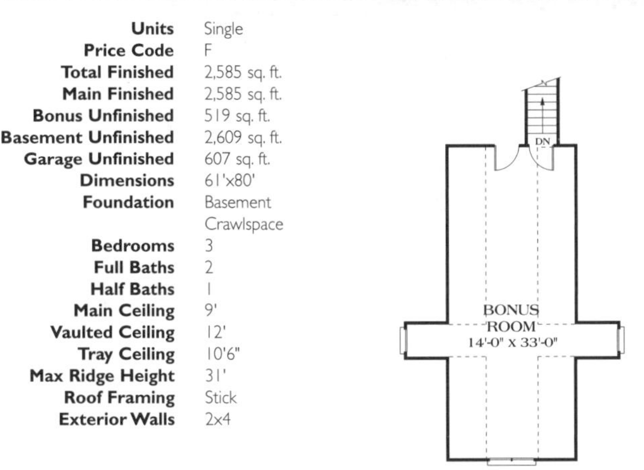
DN
BONUS ROOM
14'-0" X 33'-0"

BONUS

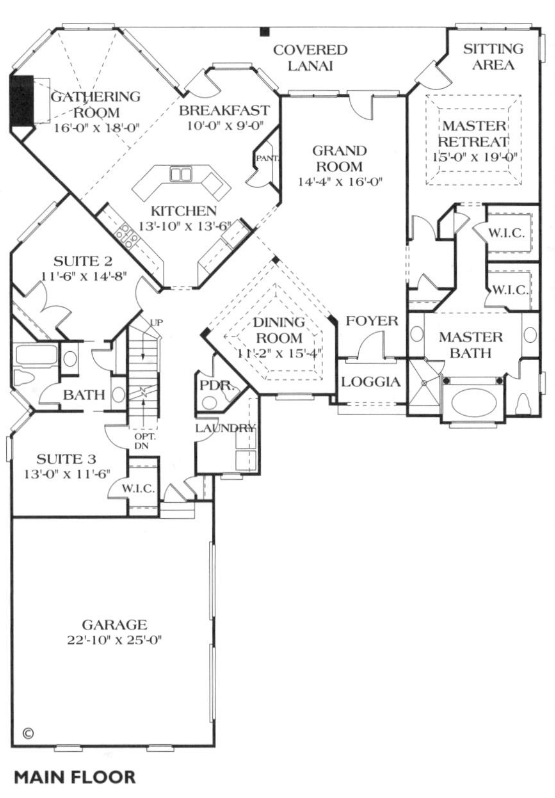
COVERED LANAI
SITTING AREA
GATHERING ROOM
16'-0" X 18'-0"
BREAKFAST
10'-0" X 9'-0"
PANT
GRAND ROOM
14'-4" X 16'-0"
MASTER RETREAT
15'-0" X 19'-0"
KITCHEN
13'-10" X 13'-6"
W.I.C.
W.I.C.
SUITE 2
11'-6" X 14'-8"
UP
DINING ROOM
11'-2" X 15'-4"
FOYER
MASTER BATH
BATH
PDR.
LOGGIA
OPT. DN
LAUNDRY
SUITE 3
13'-0" X 11'-6"
W.I.C.
GARAGE
22'-10" X 25'-0"
©

MAIN FLOOR

Design 93094

Units	Single
Price Code	F
Total Finished	2,586 sq. ft.
First Finished	2,028 sq. ft.
Second Finished	558 sq. ft.
Bonus Unfinished	272 sq. ft.
Garage Unfinished	551 sq. ft.
Porch Unfinished	223 sq. ft.
Dimensions	64'10"x61'
Foundation	Basement Crawlspace Slab
Bedrooms	4
Full Baths	3
Max Ridge Height	29'
Roof Framing	Stick
Exterior Walls	2x4

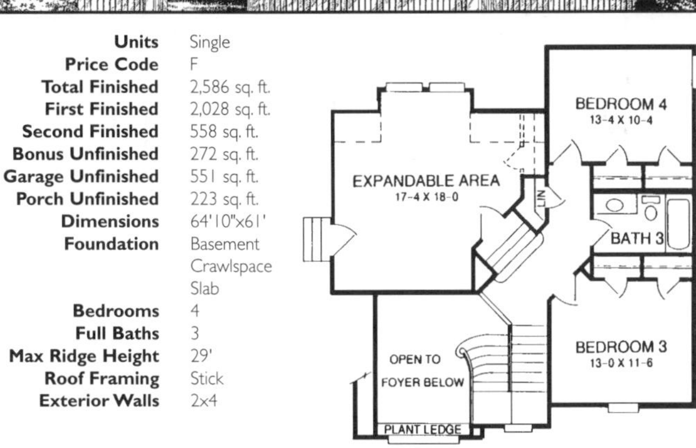
BEDROOM 4
13-4 X 10-4
EXPANDABLE AREA
17-4 X 18-0
LIN
BATH 3
BEDROOM 3
13-0 X 11-6
OPEN TO
FOYER BELOW
PLANT LEDGE

SECOND FLOOR

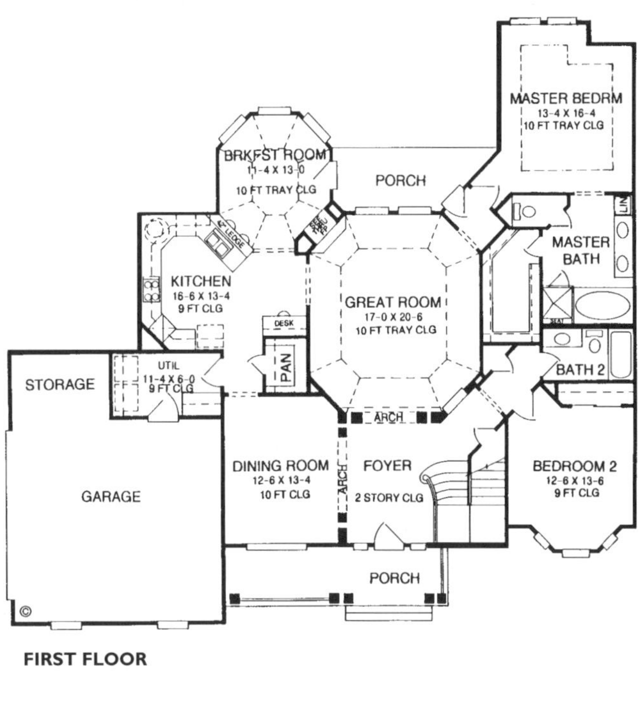
MASTER BEDRM
13-4 X 16-4
10 FT TRAY CLG
BRKFST ROOM
11-4 X 13-0
10 FT TRAY CLG
PORCH
LIN
MASTER BATH
KITCHEN
16-6 X 13-4
9 FT CLG
LEDGE
GREAT ROOM
17-0 X 20-6
10 FT TRAY CLG
DESK
PAN
STORAGE
UTIL
11-4 X 6-0
9 FT CLG
BATH 2
ARCH
GARAGE
DINING ROOM
12-6 X 13-4
10 FT CLG
ARCH
FOYER
2 STORY CLG
BEDROOM 2
12-6 X 13-6
9 FT CLG
PORCH
©

FIRST FLOOR

Design 91469

Units	Single
Price Code	E
Total Finished	2,591 sq. ft.
Main Finished	2,591 sq. ft.
Garage Unfinished	445 sq. ft.
Dimensions	65'x66'
Foundation	Crawlspace
Bedrooms	3
Full Baths	2
Half Baths	1
Main Ceiling	8'
Max Ridge Height	28'
Roof Framing	Stick
Exterior Walls	2x6

COFFERED MBR 19/8 X 14/8
NOOK 12 X 10
COVERED PORCH
BI CABS
BR 13 X 11
M BATH
WI CLO
DW
COFFERED FAMILY RM 15/8 X 19/2
KIT
BATH
BOOKS
DEN 12/6 X 11/0
GUEST
PAN
R
LIN
ARCH
GALLERY HALL
UTIL
BR 11/6 X 12/0
COFFERED DIN RM 13 X 14
FOYER
COFFERED LIV RM 12 X 14
W
D
BRM
PDR
GARAGE 19/8 X 22/8
COVERED PORCH

MAIN FLOOR

Design 69153

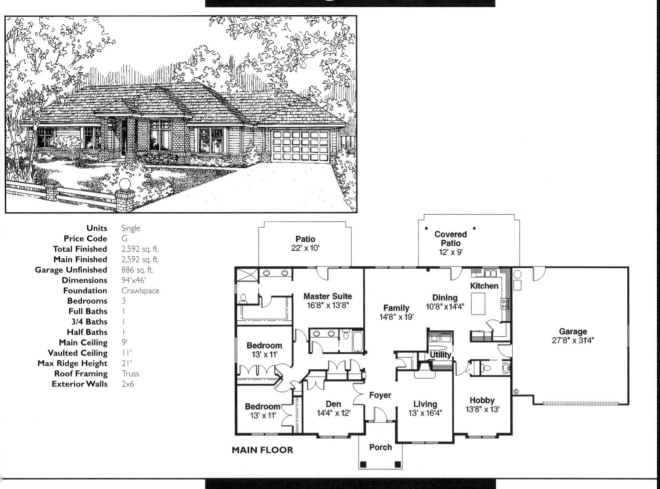

Units	Single
Price Code	G
Total Finished	2,592 sq. ft.
Main Finished	2,592 sq. ft.
Garage Unfinished	886 sq. ft.
Dimensions	94'x46'
Foundation	Crawlspace
Bedrooms	3
Full Baths	1
3/4 Baths	1
Half Baths	1
Main Ceiling	9'
Vaulted Ceiling	11'
Max Ridge Height	21'
Roof Framing	Truss
Exterior Walls	2x6

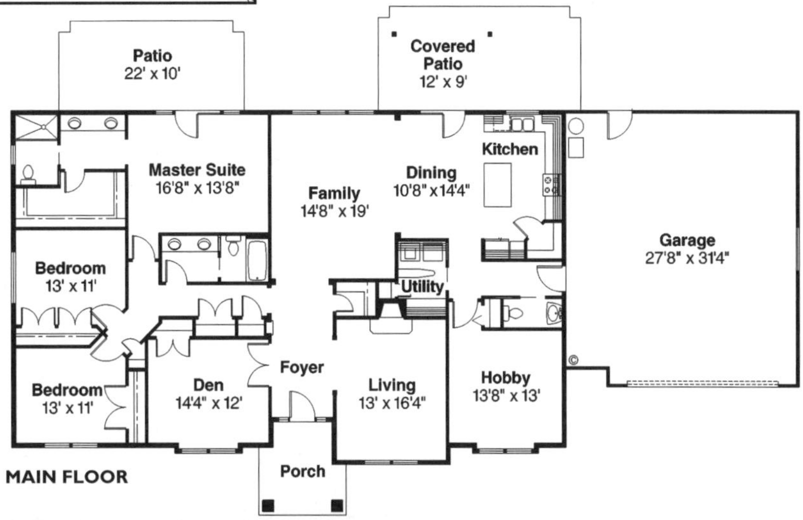

Patio 22' x 10'
Covered Patio 12' x 9'
Master Suite 16'8" x 13'8"
Family 14'8" x 19'
Dining 10'8" x 14'4"
Kitchen
Garage 27'8" x 31'4"
Bedroom 13' x 11'
Utility
Bedroom 13' x 11'
Den 14'4" x 12'
Foyer
Living 13' x 16'4"
Hobby 13'8" x 13'
Porch

MAIN FLOOR

Design 63106

Units	Single
Price Code	F
Total Finished	2,593 sq. ft.
Main Finished	2,593 sq. ft.
Garage Unfinished	508 sq. ft.
Dimensions	70'x70'
Foundation	Slab
Bedrooms	3
Full Baths	2
3/4 Baths	1
Main Ceiling	10'
Tray Ceiling	12'
Max Ridge Height	20'4"
Roof Framing	Truss

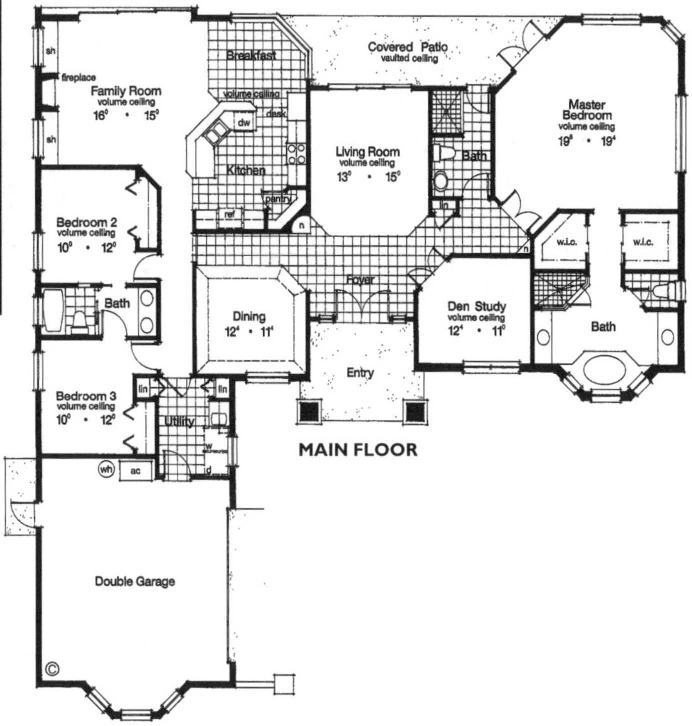

Breakfast
Covered Patio vaulted ceiling
Family Room volume ceiling 16° • 15°
Kitchen
Living Room volume ceiling 13° • 15°
Master Bedroom volume ceiling 19° • 19⁴
Bath
Bedroom 2 volume ceiling 10° • 12°
Bath
Foyer
Dining 12⁴ • 11¹
Den Study volume ceiling 12⁴ • 11⁰
Entry
Bath
Bedroom 3 volume ceiling 10° • 12°
Utility
Double Garage

MAIN FLOOR

Design 94932

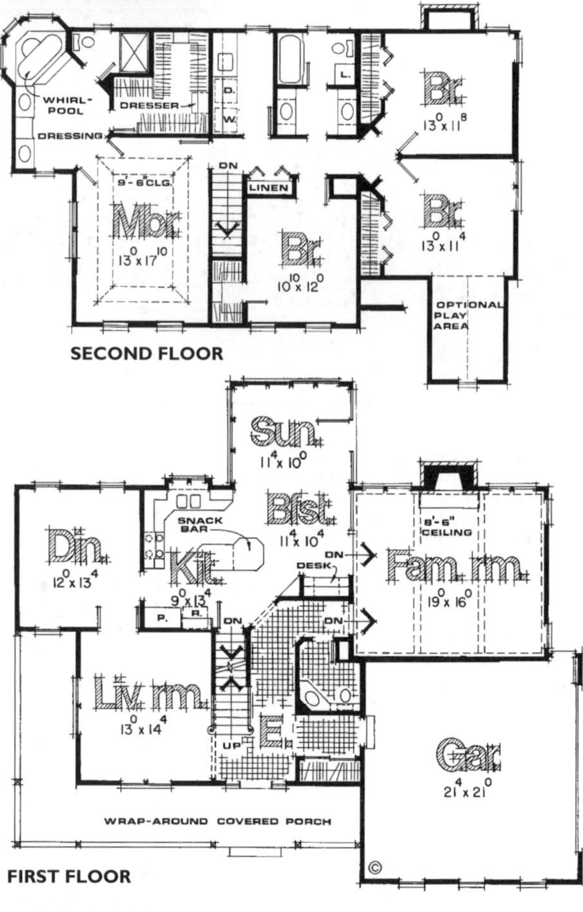

WHIRL-POOL
DRESSER
DRESSING
D.
W.
L.
Br. 13⁰ x 11⁸
9'-6" CLG.
Mbr. 13⁰ x 17¹⁰
DN
LINEN
Br. 10¹⁰ x 12⁰
Br. 13⁰ x 11⁴
OPTIONAL PLAY AREA
SECOND FLOOR
Sun. 11⁴ x 10⁰
SNACK BAR
Bfst. 11⁴ x 10⁴
8'-6" CEILING
Din. 12⁰ x 13⁴
Kit. 9⁰ x 13⁴
DN
DESK
Fam. rm. 19⁰ x 16⁰
P.
R.
DN
Liv. rm. 13⁰ x 14⁴
UP
E.
Gar. 21⁴ x 21⁰
WRAP-AROUND COVERED PORCH
FIRST FLOOR

Units	Single
Price Code	F
Total Finished	2,594 sq. ft.
First Finished	1,322 sq. ft.
Second Finished	1,272 sq. ft.
Bonus Unfinished	80 sq. ft.
Basement Unfinished	1,322 sq. ft.
Garage Unfinished	468 sq. ft.
Dimensions	56'x48'
Foundation	Basement
Bedrooms	4
Full Baths	2
Half Baths	1
First Ceiling	8'
Second Ceiling	8'
Max Ridge Height	27'
Roof Framing	Stick
Exterior Walls	2x4

* Alternate foundation options available at an additional charge. Please call 1-800-235-5700 for more information.

Design 32090

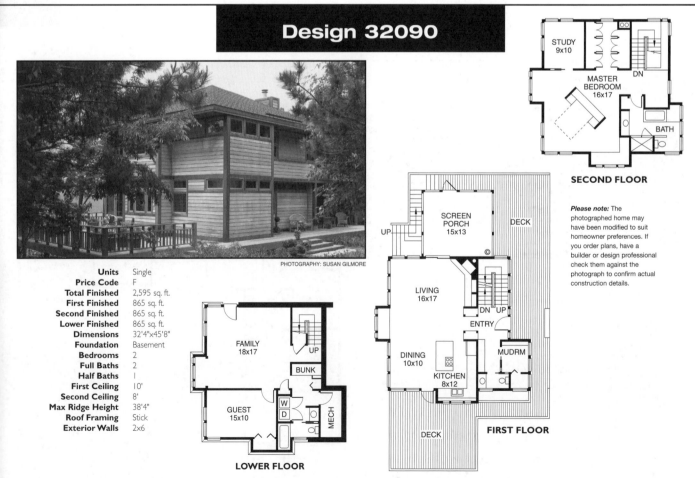

PHOTOGRAPHY: SUSAN GILMORE

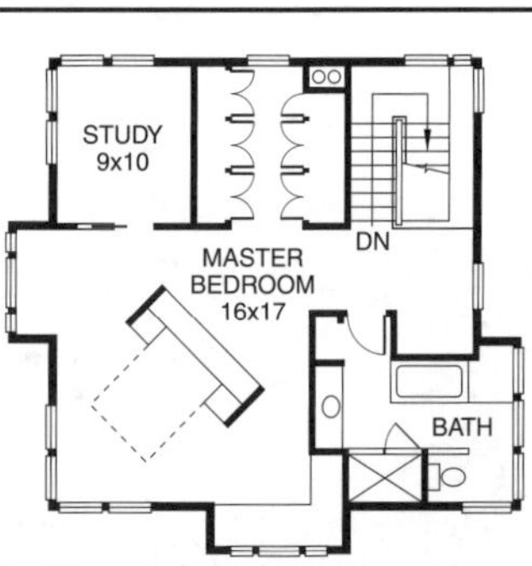

Units	Single
Price Code	F
Total Finished	2,595 sq. ft.
First Finished	865 sq. ft.
Second Finished	865 sq. ft.
Lower Finished	865 sq. ft.
Dimensions	32'4"x45'8"
Foundation	Basement
Bedrooms	2
Full Baths	2
Half Baths	1
First Ceiling	10'
Second Ceiling	8'
Max Ridge Height	38'4"
Roof Framing	Stick
Exterior Walls	2x6

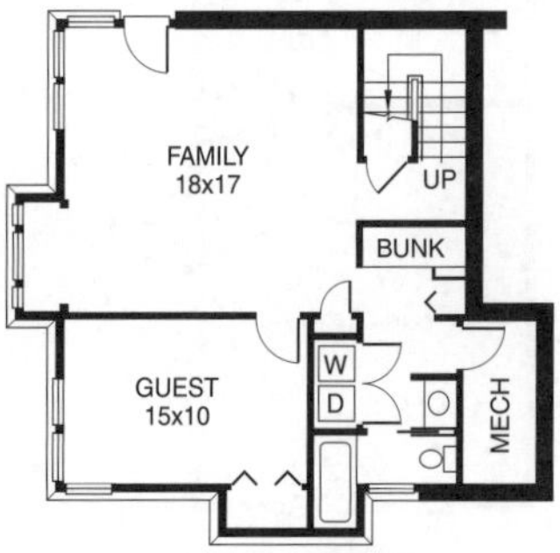

FAMILY 18x17
UP
BUNK
GUEST 15x10
W
D
MECH
LOWER FLOOR

SCREEN PORCH 15x13
UP
DECK
LIVING 16x17
DN UP
ENTRY
DINING 10x10
MUDRM
KITCHEN 8x12
DECK
FIRST FLOOR

STUDY 9x10
DN
MASTER BEDROOM 16x17
BATH
SECOND FLOOR

Please note: The photographed home may have been modified to suit homeowner preferences. If you order plans, have a builder or design professional check them against the photograph to confirm actual construction details.

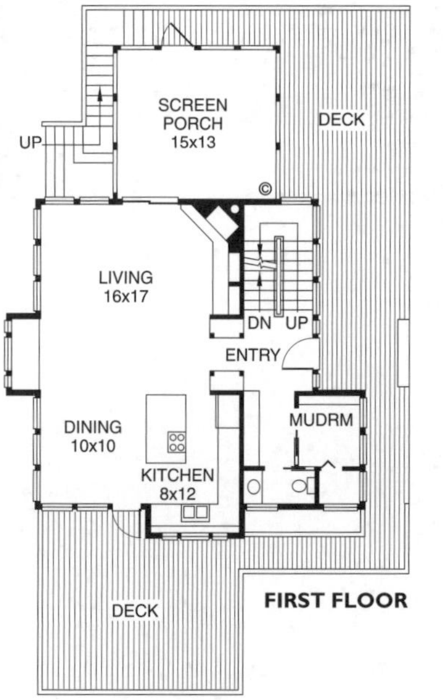

Design 69003

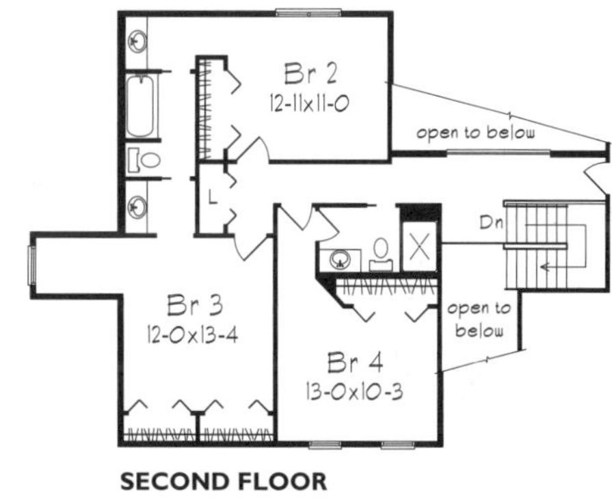
Br 2
12-11x11-0
open to below
Dn
Br 3
12-0x13-4
open to below
Br 4
13-0x10-3

SECOND FLOOR

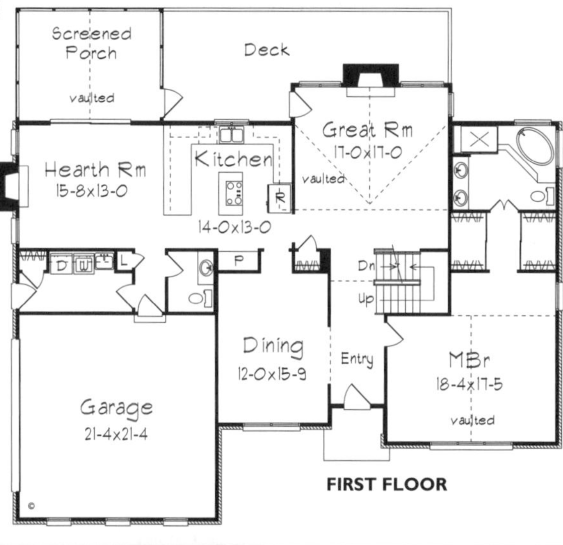
Screened Porch
vaulted
Deck
Great Rm
17-0x17-0
vaulted
Hearth Rm
15-8x13-0
Kitchen
14-0x13-0
R
P
Dn
Up
Dining
12-0x15-9
Entry
MBr
18-4x17-5
vaulted
Garage
21-4x21-4

FIRST FLOOR

Units	Single
Price Code	F
Total Finished	2,597 sq. ft.
First Finished	1,742 sq. ft.
Second Finished	855 sq. ft.
Dimensions	61'4"x48'
Foundation	Basement Crawlspace Slab
Bedrooms	4
Full Baths	2
3/4 Baths	1
Half Baths	1

Design 97210

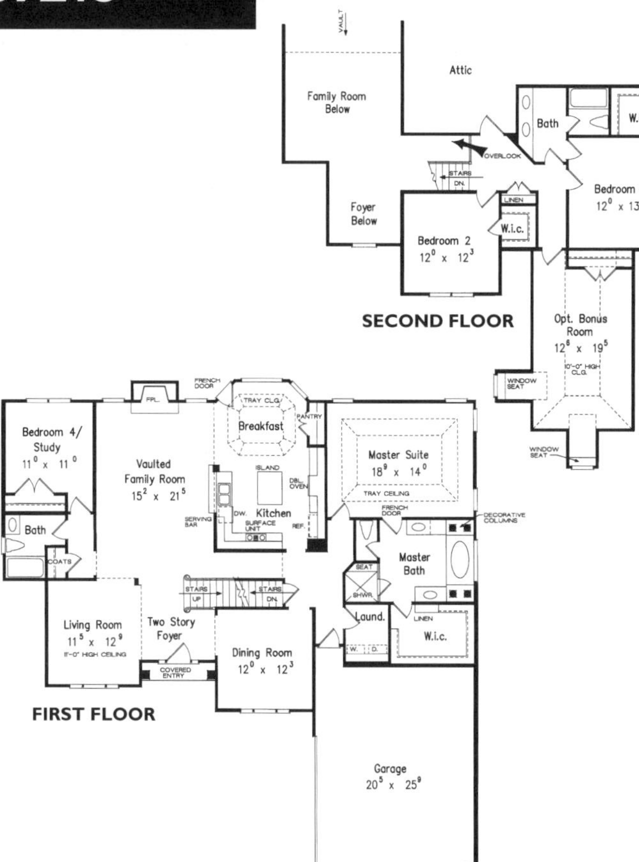
Family Room
Below
Attic
Bath
W.i.c.
Overlook
Foyer
Below
Bedroom 2
12^{0} x 12^{3}
W.i.c.
Bedroom 3
12^{0} x 13^{8}
SECOND FLOOR
Opt. Bonus
Room
12^{8} x 19^{5}
Window Seat
Bedroom 4/
Study
11^{0} x 11^{0}
Vaulted
Family Room
15^{2} x 21^{5}
Breakfast
Kitchen
Master Suite
18^{9} x 14^{0}
Tray Ceiling
Bath
Coats
Master
Bath
Laund.
W.i.c.
Living Room
11^{5} x 12^{9}
Two Story
Foyer
Covered Entry
Dining Room
12^{0} x 12^{3}
Garage
20^{5} x 25^{9}

FIRST FLOOR

Units	Single
Price Code	F
Total Finished	2,601 sq. ft.
First Finished	2,003 sq. ft.
Second Finished	598 sq. ft.
Bonus Unfinished	321 sq. ft.
Basement Unfinished	2,003 sq. ft.
Garage Unfinished	546 sq. ft.
Dimensions	60'x61'
Foundation	Basement Crawlspace Slab
Bedrooms	4
Full Baths	3
Max Ridge Height	31'6"
Roof Framing	Stick
Exterior Walls	2x4

CAD FILES AVAILABLE
For more information call
800-235-5700

Design 69130

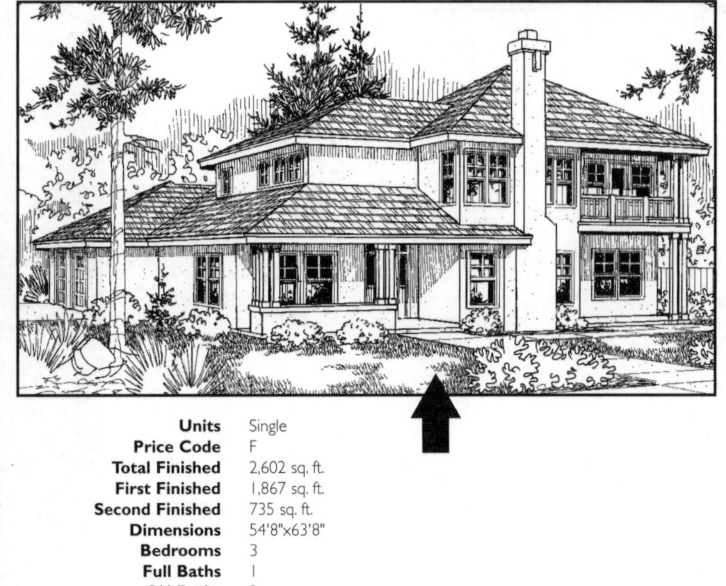

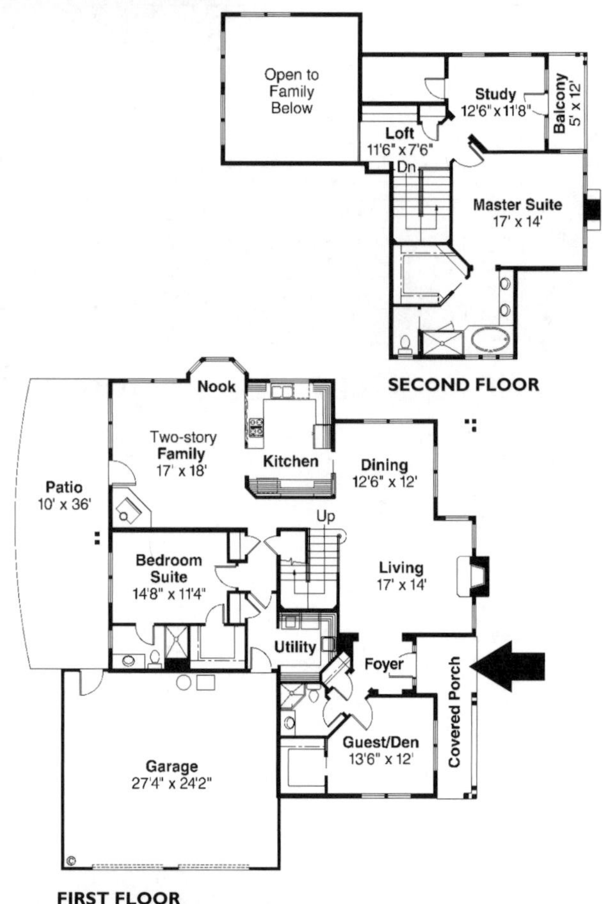
Open to Family Below
Study 12'6" x 11'8"
Balcony 5' x 12'
Loft 11'6" x 7'6"
Dn
Master Suite 17' x 14'
SECOND FLOOR
Nook
Two-story Family 17' x 18'
Kitchen
Dining 12'6" x 12'
Patio 10' x 36'
Up
Living 17' x 14'
Bedroom Suite 14'8" x 11'4"
Utility
Foyer
Covered Porch
Guest/Den 13'6" x 12'
Garage 27'4" x 24'2"
FIRST FLOOR

Units	Single
Price Code	F
Total Finished	2,602 sq. ft.
First Finished	1,867 sq. ft.
Second Finished	735 sq. ft.
Dimensions	54'8"x63'8"
Bedrooms	3
Full Baths	1
3/4 Baths	2
First Ceiling	9'
Second Ceiling	9'
Vaulted Ceiling	18'
Max Ridge Height	27'2"
Roof Framing	Truss
Exterior Walls	2x6

Design 64508

Units	Single
Price Code	F
Total Finished	2,605 sq. ft.
Main Finished	2,605 sq. ft.
Basement Unfinished	2,605 sq. ft.
Garage Unfinished	480 sq. ft.
Porch Unfinished	508 sq. ft.
Dimensions	78'x51'
Foundation	Basement Crawlspace Slab
Bedrooms	4
Full Baths	3
Half Baths	1
Main Ceiling	9'
Max Ridge Height	25'
Roof Framing	Stick/Truss
Exterior Walls	2x4

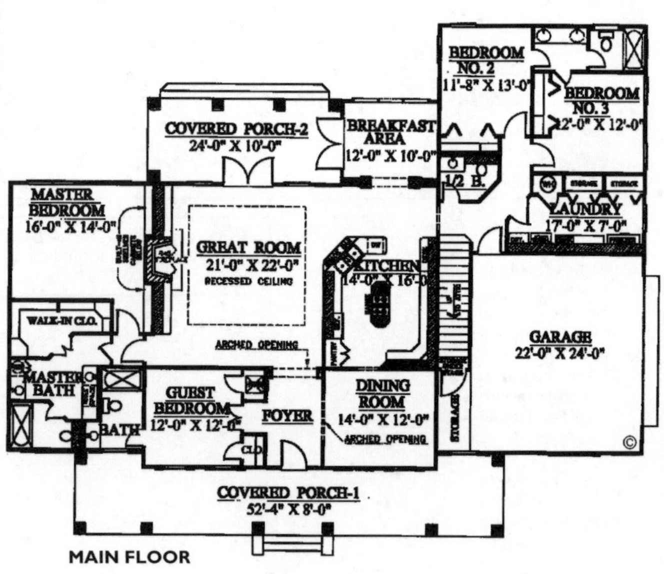
BEDROOM NO. 2 11'-8" X 13'-0"
BEDROOM NO. 3 12'-0" X 12'-0"
COVERED PORCH-2 24'-0" X 10'-0"
BREAKFAST AREA 12'-0" X 10'-0"
1/2 B.
LAUNDRY 17'-0" X 7'-0"
MASTER BEDROOM 16'-0" X 14'-0"
GREAT ROOM 21'-0" X 22'-0" RECESSED CEILING
KITCHEN 14'-0" X 16'-0"
WALK-IN CLO.
ARCHED OPENING
GARAGE 22'-0" X 24'-0"
MASTER BATH
GUEST BEDROOM 12'-0" X 12'-0"
FOYER
DINING ROOM 14'-0" X 12'-0"
ARCHED OPENING
BATH
CLO.
STORAGE
COVERED PORCH-1 52'-4" X 8'-0"
MAIN FLOOR

Design 92156

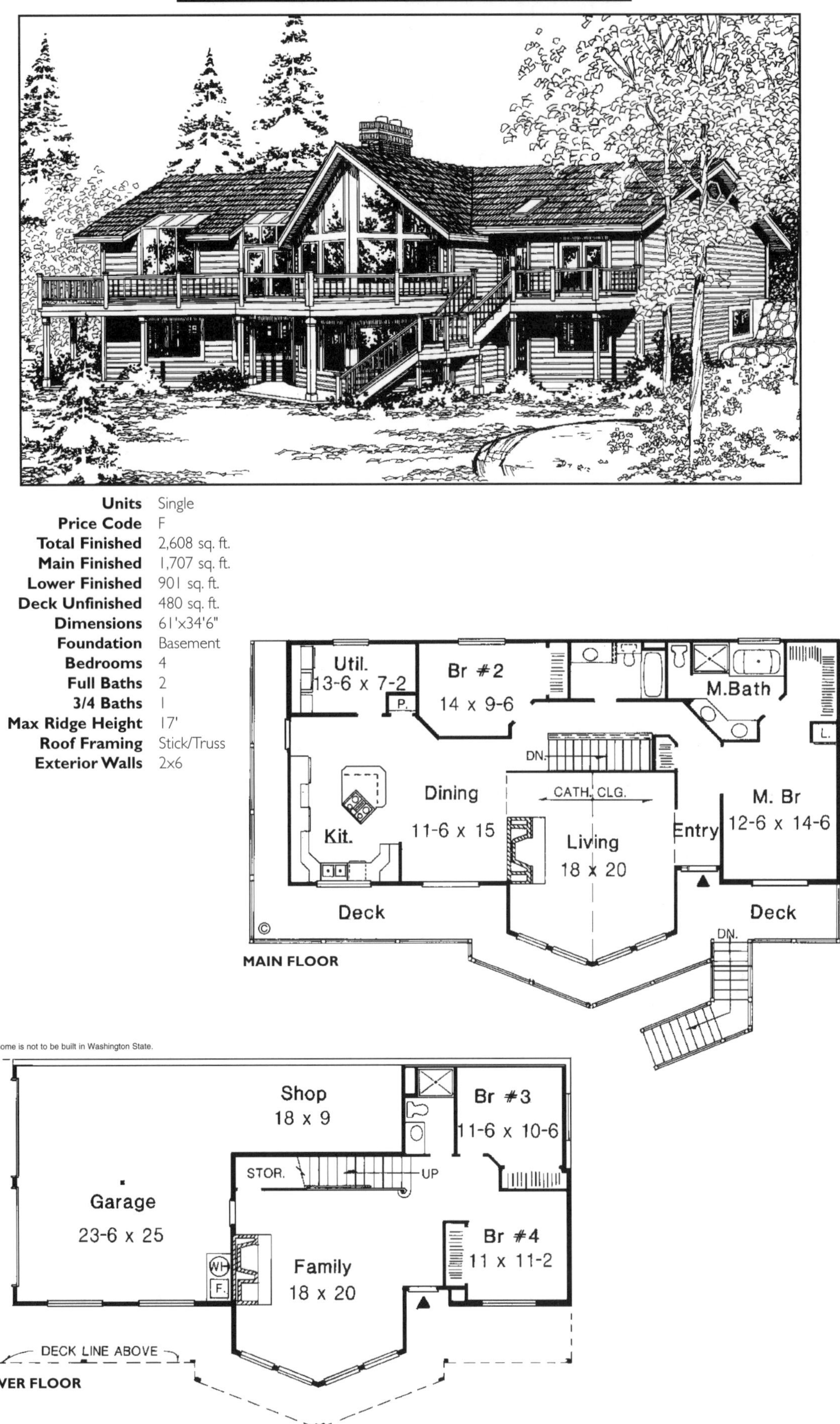
Util.
13-6 x 7-2
P.
Br #2
14 x 9-6
M.Bath
L.
DN.
CATH. CLG.
Dining
11-6 x 15
Kit.
Living
18 x 20
Entry
M. Br
12-6 x 14-6
Deck
Deck
DN.
©
MAIN FLOOR
*This home is not to be built in Washington State.
Shop
18 x 9
Br #3
11-6 x 10-6
STOR.
UP
Garage
23-6 x 25
WH
F.
Family
18 x 20
Br #4
11 x 11-2
DECK LINE ABOVE
LOWER FLOOR

Units	Single
Price Code	F
Total Finished	2,608 sq. ft.
Main Finished	1,707 sq. ft.
Lower Finished	901 sq. ft.
Deck Unfinished	480 sq. ft.
Dimensions	61'x34'6"
Foundation	Basement
Bedrooms	4
Full Baths	2
3/4 Baths	1
Max Ridge Height	17'
Roof Framing	Stick/Truss
Exterior Walls	2x6

Design 97216

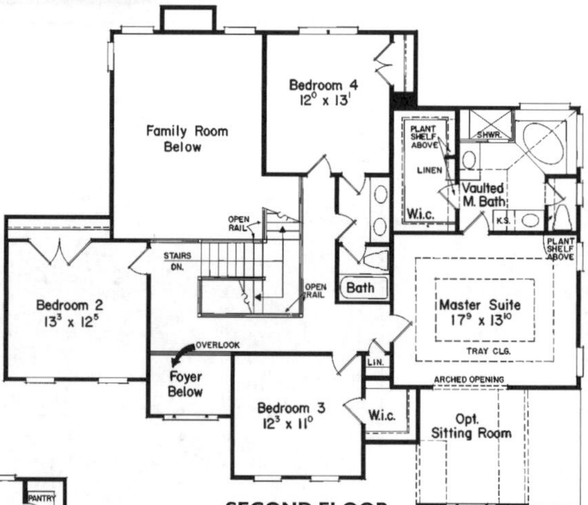

Units	Single
Price Code	F
Total Finished	2,608 sq. ft.
First Finished	1,351 sq. ft.
Second Finished	1,257 sq. ft.
Bonus Unfinished	115 sq. ft.
Basement Unfinished	1,351 sq. ft.
Garage Unfinished	511 sq. ft.
Dimensions	60'x46'4"
Foundation	Basement
Bedrooms	4
Full Baths	2
Half Baths	1
Max Ridge Height	36'
Roof Framing	Stick
Exterior Walls	2x4

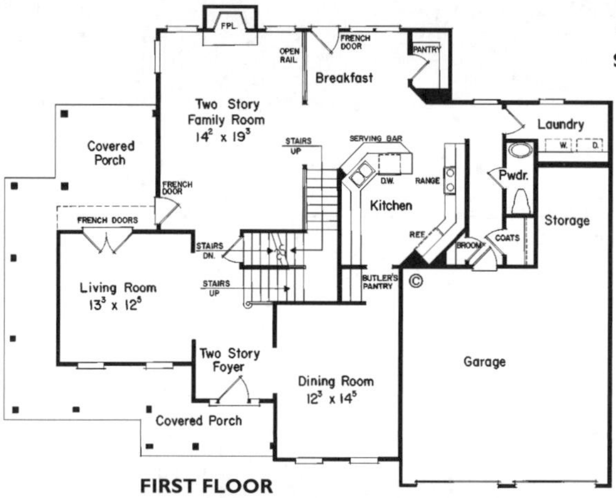

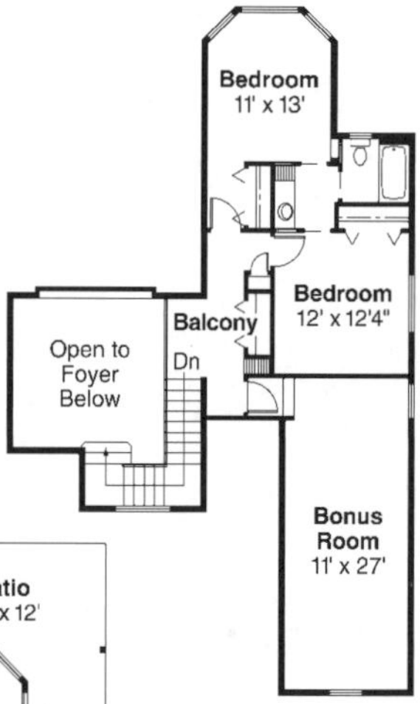

SECOND FLOOR

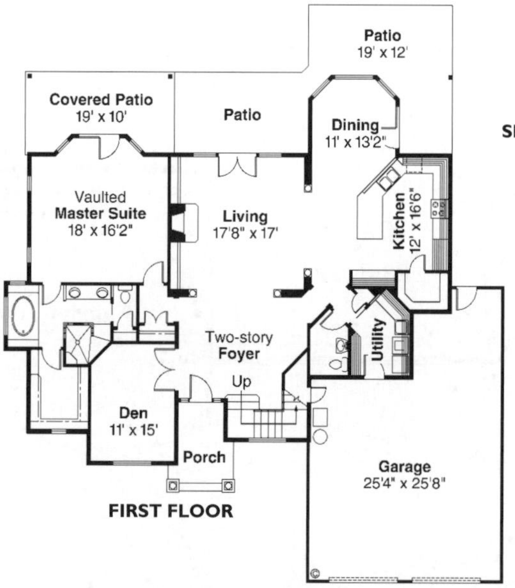

FIRST FLOOR

Design 69152

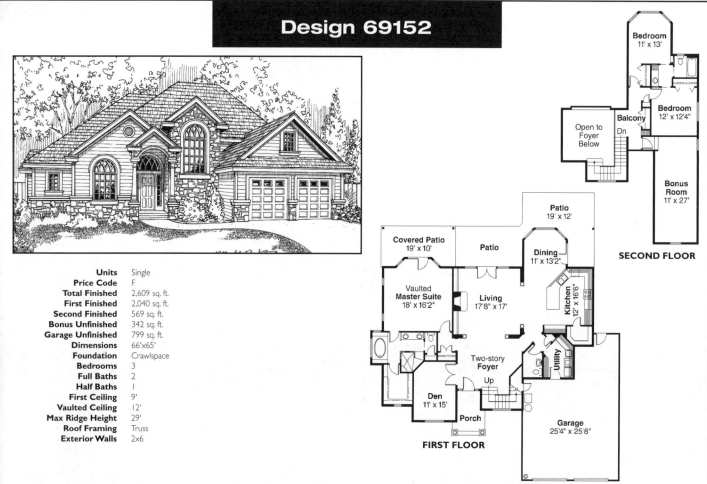

Units	Single
Price Code	F
Total Finished	2,609 sq. ft.
First Finished	2,040 sq. ft.
Second Finished	569 sq. ft.
Bonus Unfinished	342 sq. ft.
Garage Unfinished	799 sq. ft.
Dimensions	66'x65'
Foundation	Crawlspace
Bedrooms	3
Full Baths	2
Half Baths	1
First Ceiling	9'
Vaulted Ceiling	12'
Max Ridge Height	29'
Roof Framing	Truss
Exterior Walls	2x6

SECOND FLOOR

FIRST FLOOR

Design 91458

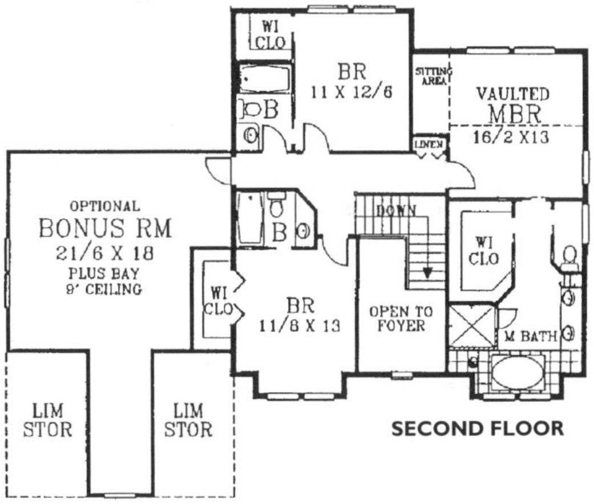

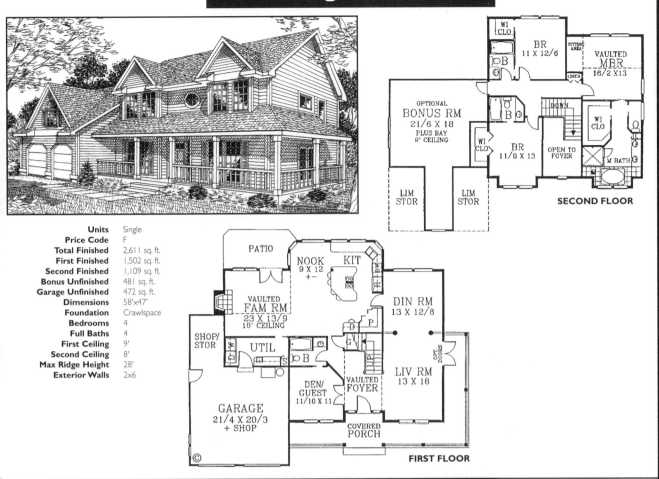

SECOND FLOOR

FIRST FLOOR

Units	Single
Price Code	F
Total Finished	2,611 sq. ft.
First Finished	1,502 sq. ft.
Second Finished	1,109 sq. ft.
Bonus Unfinished	481 sq. ft.
Garage Unfinished	472 sq. ft.
Dimensions	58'x47'
Foundation	Crawlspace
Bedrooms	4
Full Baths	4
First Ceiling	9'
Second Ceiling	8'
Max Ridge Height	28'
Exterior Walls	2x6

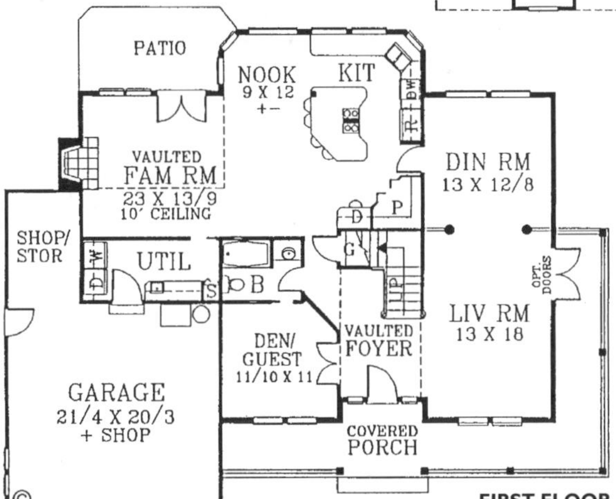

Design 99499

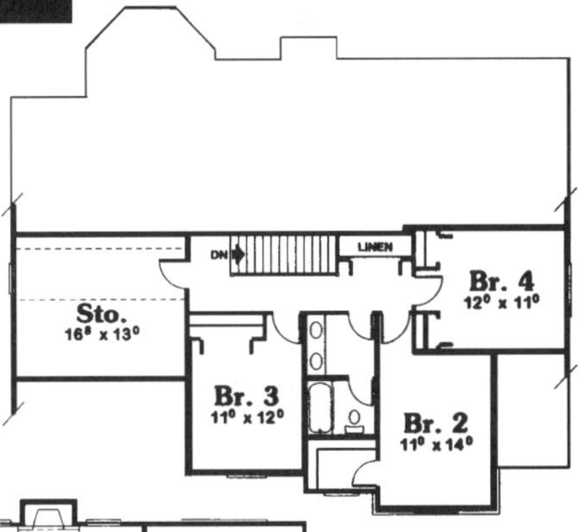

SECOND FLOOR

FIRST FLOOR

Units	Single
Price Code	F
Total Finished	2,613 sq. ft.
First Finished	1,847 sq. ft.
Second Finished	766 sq. ft.
Bonus Unfinished	232 sq. ft.
Garage Unfinished	719 sq. ft.
Dimensions	60'x59'4"
Foundation	Basement
Bedrooms	4
Full Baths	2
Half Baths	1
First Ceiling	9'
Max Ridge Height	29'5"
Roof Framing	Stick
Exterior Walls	2x4

* Alternate foundation options available at an additional charge. Please call 1-800-235-5700 for more information.

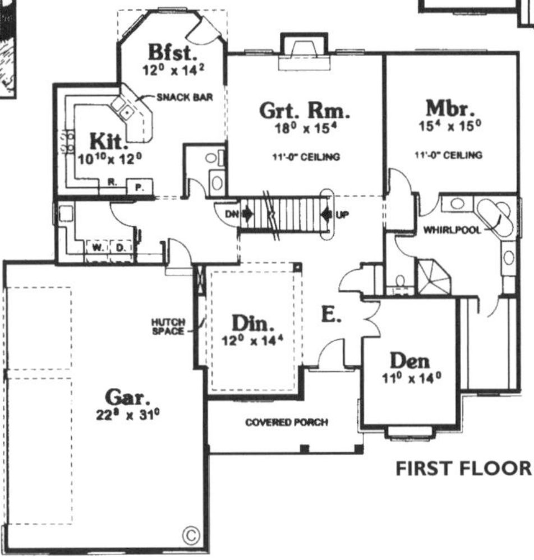

Design 66053

Units	Single
Price Code	F
Total Finished	2,617 sq. ft.
Main Finished	2,617 sq. ft.
Bonus Unfinished	467 sq. ft.
Dimensions	74'6"x75'7"
Foundation	Slab
Bedrooms	3
Full Baths	2
Half Baths	1
Main Ceiling	10'
Second Ceiling	8'
Max Ridge Height	30'
Roof Framing	Stick
Exterior Walls	2x4

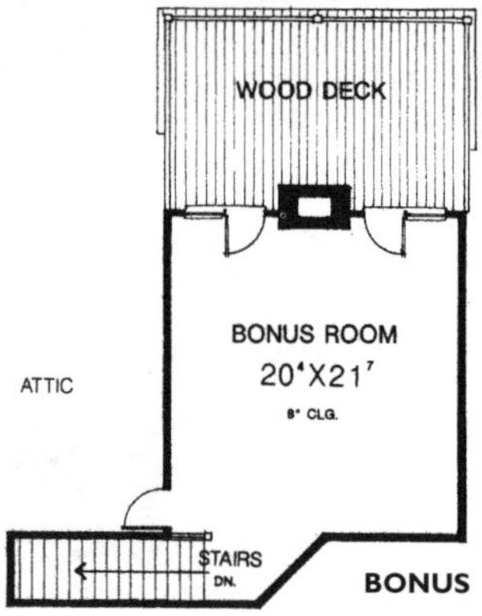

WOOD DECK
BONUS ROOM 20⁴X21⁷ 9' CLG.
ATTIC
STAIRS DN.
BONUS

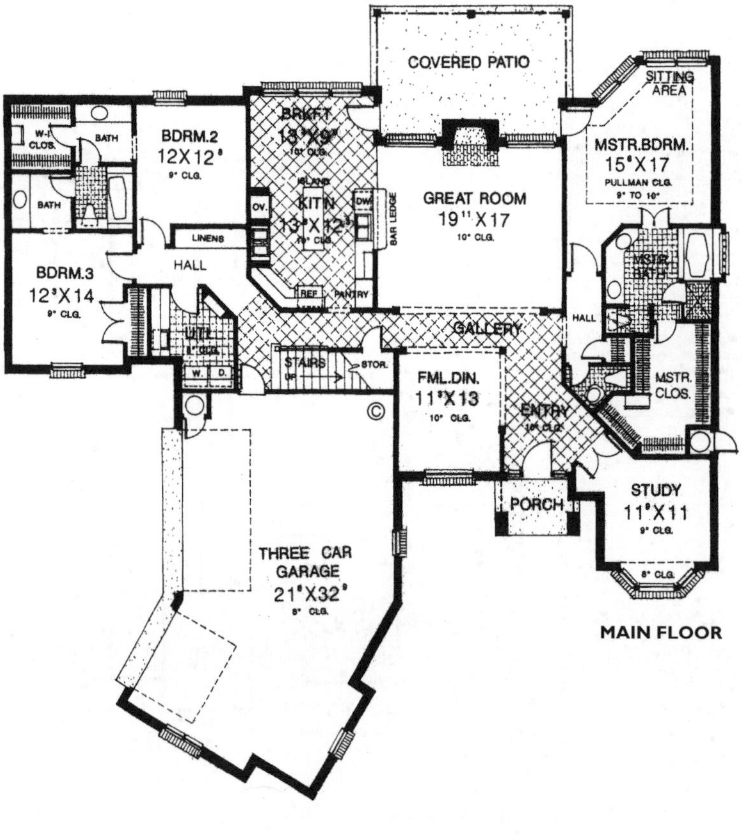

COVERED PATIO
SITTING AREA
MSTR.BDRM. 15⁶X17 PULLMAN CLG. 9' TO 10'
BRKFT 13⁶X9⁶ 10' CLG.
GREAT ROOM 19¹¹X17 10' CLG.
KIT'N 13⁶X12⁵ 10' CLG.
BDRM.2 12X12⁶ 9' CLG.
W-I CLOS.
BATH
BATH
LINENS
HALL
BDRM.3 12³X14 9' CLG.
UTIL.
W. D.
STAIRS UP
STOR.
GALLERY
HALL
MSTR. BATH
MSTR. CLOS.
FML.DIN. 11⁹X13 10' CLG.
ENTRY 10' CLG.
PORCH
STUDY 11⁹X11 9' CLG.
8' CLG.
THREE CAR GARAGE 21⁸X32⁹ 8' CLG.
MAIN FLOOR

Design 84066

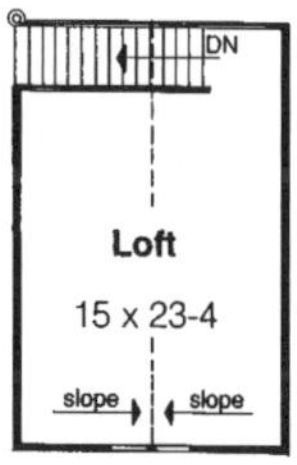

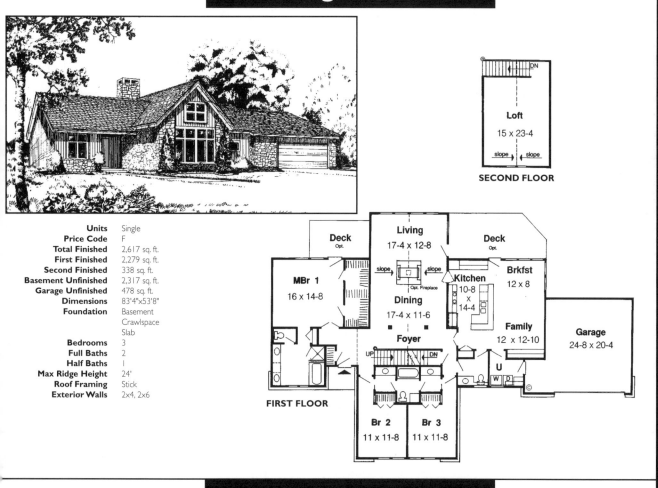

Loft
15 x 23-4
slope
slope
DN

SECOND FLOOR

Deck
Opt.
Living
17-4 x 12-8
Deck
Opt.
MBr 1
16 x 14-8
slope
slope
Opt. Fireplace
Kitchen
10-8 x 14-4
Brkfst
12 x 8
Dining
17-4 x 11-6
Family
12 x 12-10
Garage
24-8 x 20-4
Foyer
UP
DN
U
W D
Br 2
11 x 11-8
Br 3
11 x 11-8

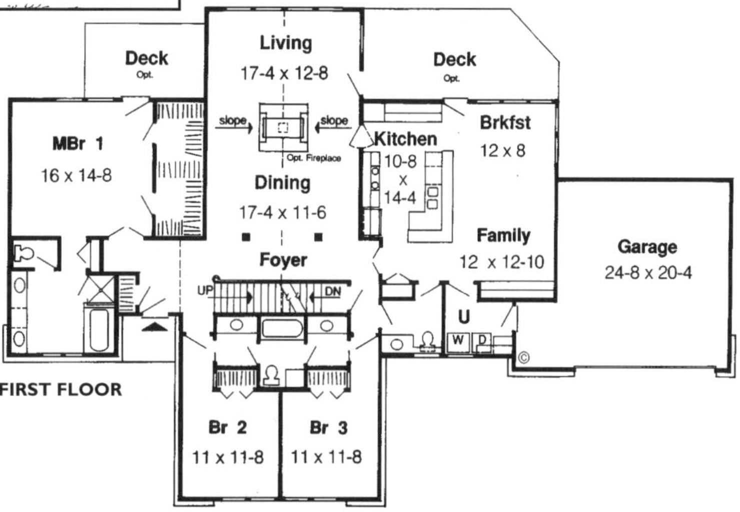

FIRST FLOOR

Units	Single
Price Code	F
Total Finished	2,617 sq. ft.
First Finished	2,279 sq. ft.
Second Finished	338 sq. ft.
Basement Unfinished	2,317 sq. ft.
Garage Unfinished	478 sq. ft.
Dimensions	83'4"x53'8"
Foundation	Basement Crawlspace Slab
Bedrooms	3
Full Baths	2
Half Baths	1
Max Ridge Height	24'
Roof Framing	Stick
Exterior Walls	2x4, 2x6

Design 97505

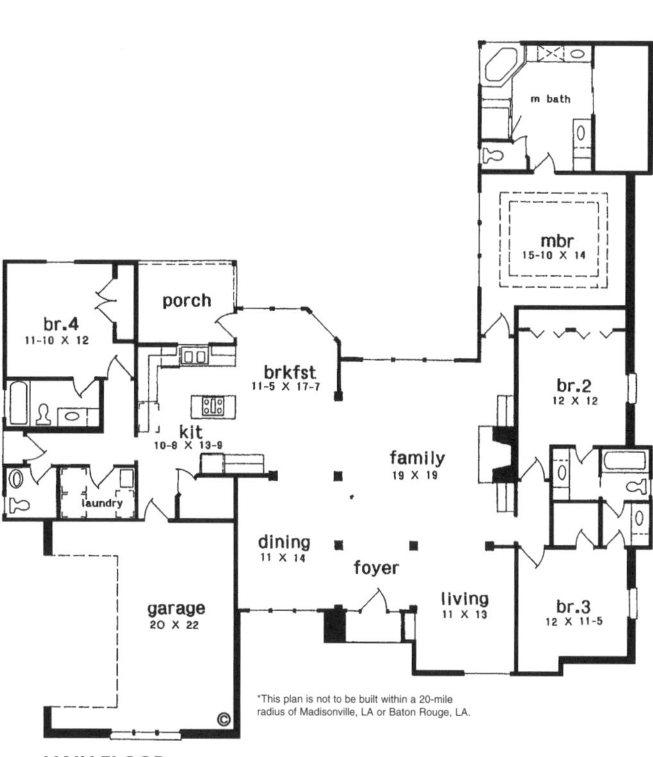
m bath
mbr
15-10 X 14
br.4
11-10 X 12
porch
brkfst
11-5 X 17-7
br.2
12 X 12
kit
10-8 X 13-9
family
19 X 19
laundry
dining
11 X 14
foyer
living
11 X 13
br.3
12 X 11-5
garage
20 X 22
*This plan is not to be built within a 20-mile radius of Madisonville, LA or Baton Rouge, LA.

MAIN FLOOR

Units	Single
Price Code	F
Total Finished	2,618 sq. ft.
Main Finished	2,618 sq. ft.
Garage Unfinished	482 sq. ft.
Porch Unfinished	128 sq. ft.
Dimensions	71'x74'
Foundation	Slab
Bedrooms	4
Full Baths	3
Half Baths	1
Max Ridge Height	29'6"
Roof Framing	Stick
Exterior Walls	2x4

Design 94137

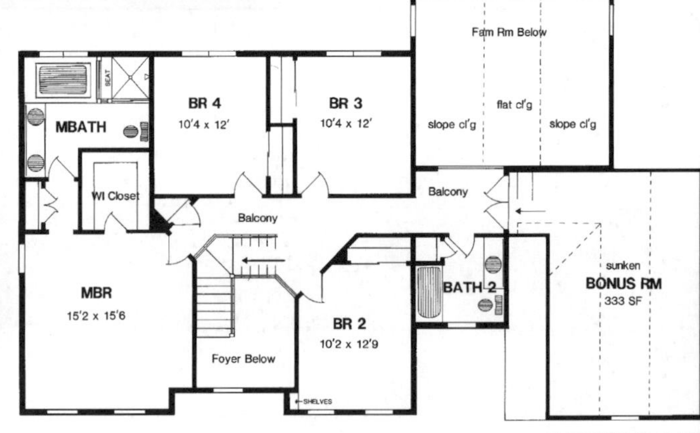

Fam Rm Below
BR 4
10'4 x 12'
BR 3
10'4 x 12'
slope cl'g
flat cl'g
slope cl'g
MBATH
WI Closet
Balcony
Balcony
MBR
15'2 x 15'6
BR 2
10'2 x 12'9
Foyer Below
BATH 2
sunken
BONUS RM
333 SF
SHELVES

SECOND FLOOR

Units	Single
Price Code	F
Total Finished	2,620 sq. ft.
First Finished	1,431 sq. ft.
Second Finished	1,189 sq. ft.
Bonus Unfinished	333 sq. ft.
Basement Unfinished	1,431 sq. ft.
Garage Unfinished	476 sq. ft.
Porch Unfinished	204 sq. ft.
Dimensions	66'x41'
Foundation	Basement
Bedrooms	4
Full Baths	2
3/4 Baths	1
Max Ridge Height	30'6"
Roof Framing	Stick/Truss
Exterior Walls	2x6

cath cl'g
FAM RM
17'6 x 15'
DIN
10'6 x 13'4
KIT
12'9 x 11'4
step cl'g
DIN RM
11'8 x 13'
PANTRY
REF
BATH 3
Entry
LIV RM
15'2 x 13'2
Two Story
FOYER
STUDY
10'2 x 9'
Laun
Covered Porch
GARAGE
21'4 x 21'4
Covered Entry

FIRST FLOOR

Design 69038

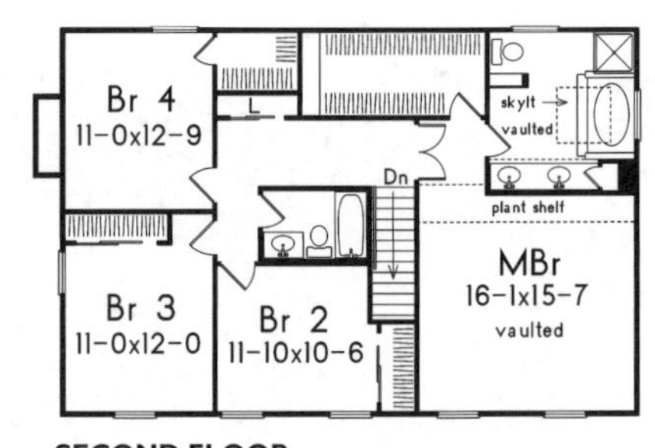

Hot
New
Design
Br 4
11-0x12-9
skylt
vaulted
Dn
plant shelf
MBr
16-1x15-7
vaulted
Br 3
11-0x12-0
Br 2
11-10x10-6

SECOND FLOOR

Units	Single
Price Code	F
Total Finished	2,727 sq. ft.
First Finished	1,523 sq. ft.
Second Finished	1,204 sq. ft.
Dimensions	81'x28'
Foundation	Basement
Bedrooms	4
Full Baths	2
Half Baths	1

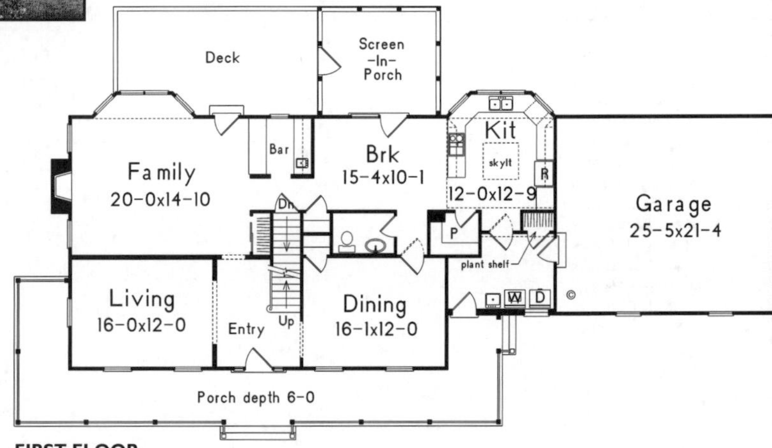

Deck
Screen
-In-
Porch
Family
20-0x14-10
Bar
Brk
15-4x10-1
Kit
skylt
12-0x12-9
Garage
25-5x21-4
Dn
P
plant shelf
Living
16-0x12-0
Entry
Up
Dining
16-1x12-0
W
D
Porch depth 6-0

FIRST FLOOR

Design 66108

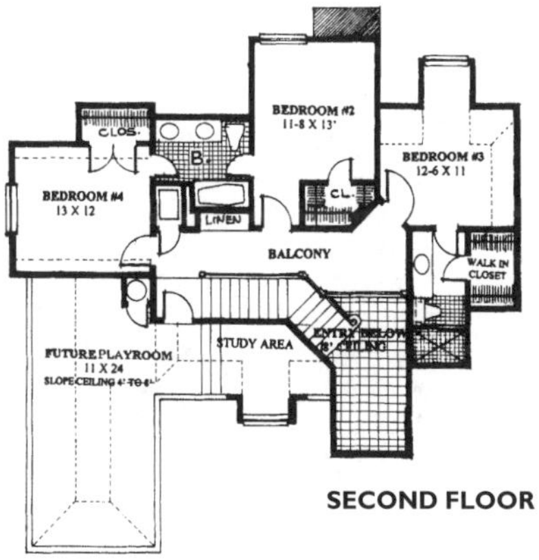

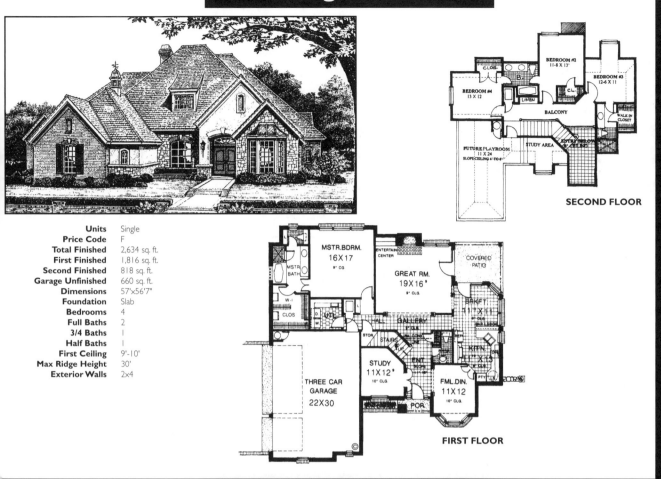

Units	Single
Price Code	F
Total Finished	2,634 sq. ft.
First Finished	1,816 sq. ft.
Second Finished	818 sq. ft.
Garage Unfinished	660 sq. ft.
Dimensions	57'x56'7"
Foundation	Slab
Bedrooms	4
Full Baths	2
3/4 Baths	1
Half Baths	1
First Ceiling	9'-10'
Max Ridge Height	30'
Exterior Walls	2x4

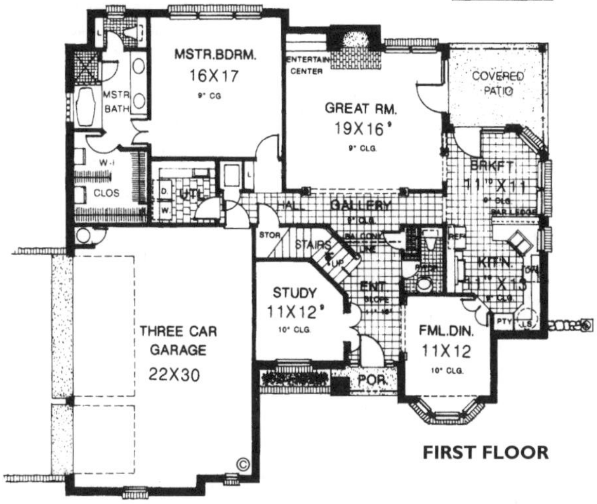

BEDROOM #2
11-8 X 13'
BEDROOM #3
12-6 X 11
BEDROOM #4
13 X 12
CLOS.
LINEN
CL.
BALCONY
WALK IN CLOSET
FUTURE PLAYROOM
11 X 24
STUDY AREA

SECOND FLOOR

MSTR.BDRM.
16X17
MSTR BATH
CLOS
GREAT RM.
19X16
ENTERTAIN CENTER
COVERED PATIO
BRKFT.
HALL
GALLERY
STOR
STAIRS
KIT'N.
STUDY
11X12
THREE CAR GARAGE
22X30
FML.DIN.
11X12
POR.
PTY

FIRST FLOOR

Design 93372

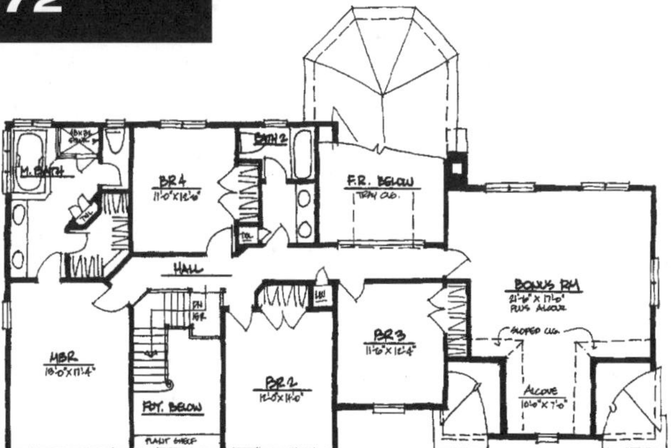

Units	Single
Price Code	F
Total Finished	2,634 sq. ft.
First Finished	1,489 sq. ft.
Second Finished	1,145 sq. ft.
Bonus Unfinished	440 sq. ft.
Basement Unfinished	1,489 sq. ft.
Garage Unfinished	528 sq. ft.
Dimensions	67'8"x42'
Foundation	Basement
Bedrooms	4
Full Baths	2
Half Baths	1
First Ceiling	9'
Second Ceiling	8'
Vaulted Ceiling	17'6"
Max Ridge Height	29'
Roof Framing	Stick/Truss
Exterior Walls	2x6

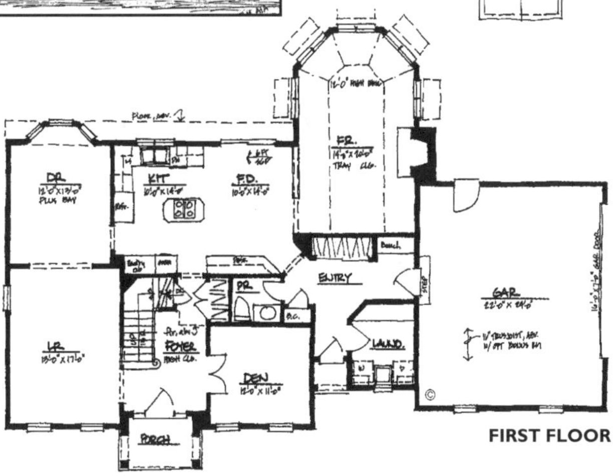

M. BATH
BR 4
BATH 2
F.R. BELOW
HALL
BONUS RM
MBR
BR 2
BR 3
ALCOVE
FOY. BELOW

SECOND FLOOR

DR
KIT
F.D.
F.R.
ENTRY
PR
LR
FOYER
DEN
LAUND.
GAR.
PORCH

FIRST FLOOR

Design 99473

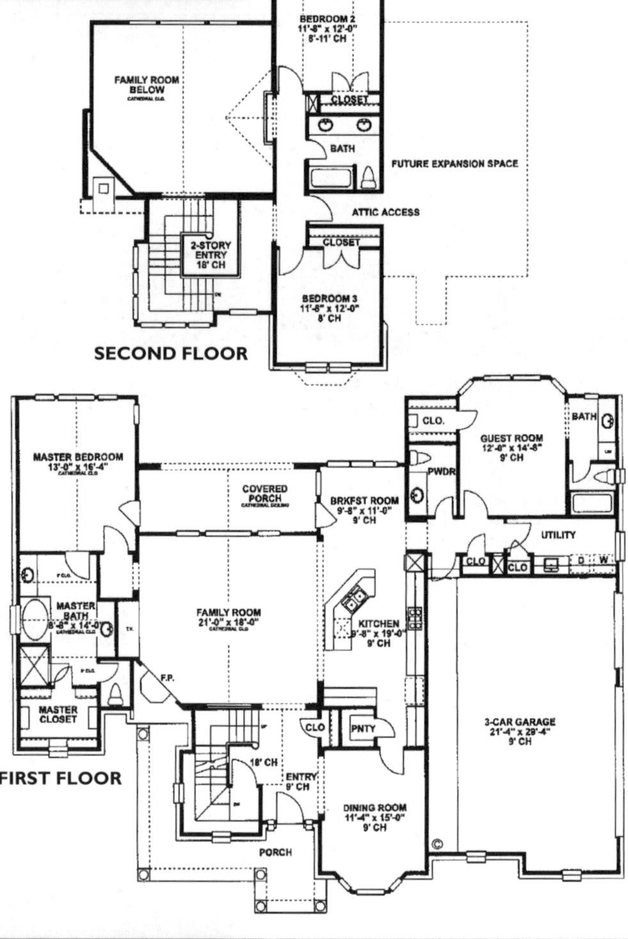

FAMILY ROOM BELOW
BEDROOM 2 11'-8" x 12'-0" 8'-11' CH
CLOSET
BATH
FUTURE EXPANSION SPACE
ATTIC ACCESS
2-STORY ENTRY 18' CH
CLOSET
BEDROOM 3 11'-8" x 12'-0" 8' CH
MASTER BEDROOM 13'-0" x 16'-4"
COVERED PORCH
BRKFST ROOM 9'-8" x 11'-0" 9' CH
CLO.
PWDR
GUEST ROOM 12'-0" x 14'-8" 9' CH
BATH
UTILITY
CLO
CLO
MASTER BATH
FAMILY ROOM 21'-0" x 18'-0"
KITCHEN 9'-8" x 19'-0" 9' CH
F.P.
MASTER CLOSET
CLO
PNTY
3-CAR GARAGE 21'-4" x 29'-4" 9' CH
18' CH
ENTRY 9' CH
DINING ROOM 11'-4" x 15'-0" 9' CH
PORCH

SECOND FLOOR

FIRST FLOOR

Units	Single
Price Code	F
Total Finished	2,639 sq. ft.
First Finished	2,087 sq. ft.
Second Finished	552 sq. ft.
Basement Unfinished	2,087 sq. ft.
Garage Unfinished	673 sq. ft.
Dimensions	68'7"x57'4"
Foundation	Basement Slab
Bedrooms	4
Full Baths	3
Half Baths	1
First Ceiling	9'
Second Ceiling	8'
Max Ridge Height	30'9"
Roof Framing	Stick
Exterior Walls	2x4

* Alternate foundation options available at an additional charge.
Please call 1-800-235-5700 for more information.

Design 94946

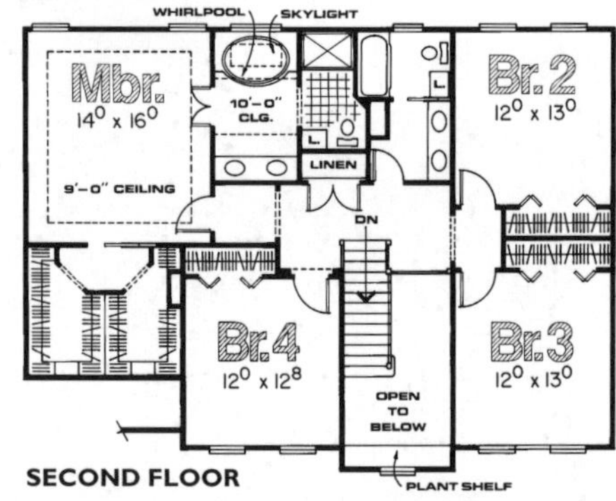

WHIRLPOOL
SKYLIGHT
Mbr. 14⁰ x 16⁰
10'-0" CLG.
9'-0" CEILING
LINEN
Br. 2 12⁰ x 13⁰
DN
Br. 4 12⁰ x 12⁸
OPEN TO BELOW
Br. 3 12⁰ x 13⁰
PLANT SHELF

SECOND FLOOR

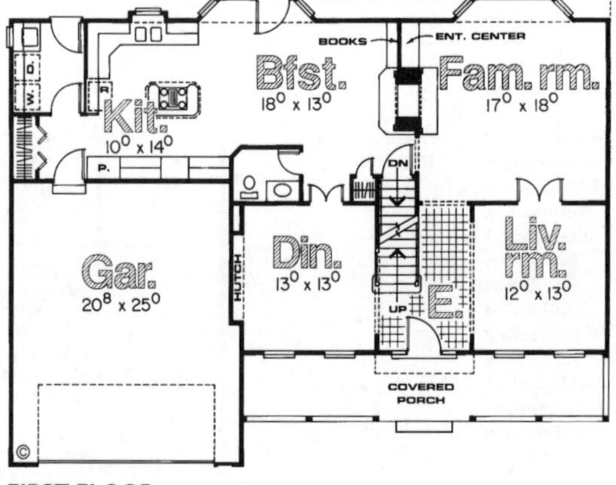

BOOKS
ENT. CENTER
Bfst. 18⁰ x 13⁰
Fam. rm. 17⁰ x 18⁰
Kit. 10⁰ x 14⁰
P.
DN
Gar. 20⁸ x 25⁰
HUTCH
Din. 13⁰ x 13⁰
Liv. rm. 12⁰ x 13⁰
UP
E.
COVERED PORCH

FIRST FLOOR

Units	Single
Price Code	F
Total Finished	2,644 sq. ft.
First Finished	1,366 sq. ft.
Second Finished	1,278 sq. ft.
Basement Unfinished	1,366 sq. ft.
Garage Unfinished	523 sq. ft.
Dimensions	54'8"x42'
Foundation	Basement Slab
Bedrooms	4
Full Baths	2
Half Baths	1
Max Ridge Height	28'5"
Roof Framing	Stick
Exterior Walls	2x4

* Alternate foundation options available at an additional charge.
Please call 1-800-235-5700 for more information.

Design 97506

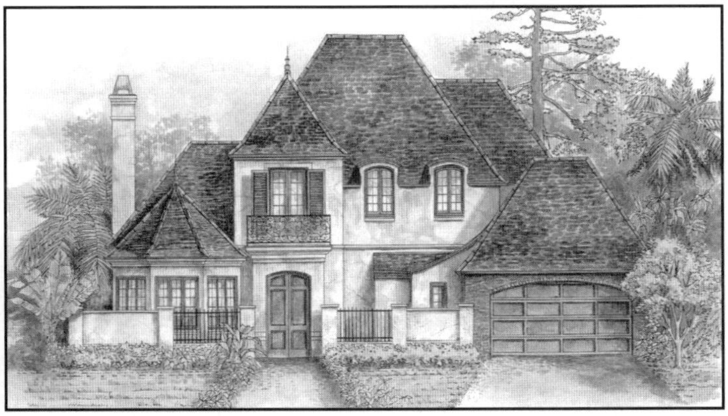

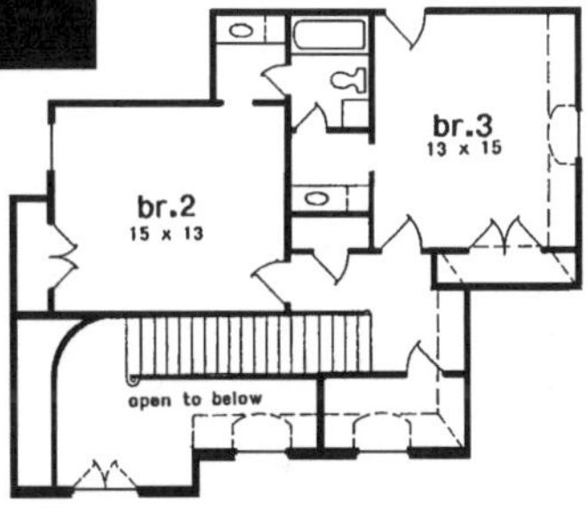

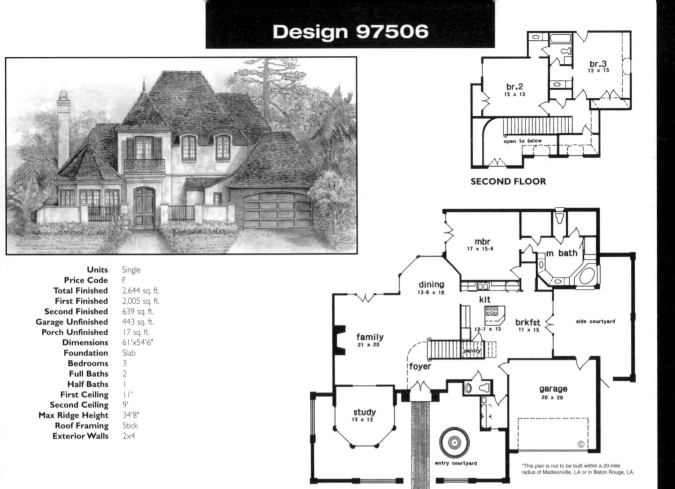

Units	Single
Price Code	F
Total Finished	2,644 sq. ft.
First Finished	2,005 sq. ft.
Second Finished	639 sq. ft.
Garage Unfinished	443 sq. ft.
Porch Unfinished	17 sq. ft.
Dimensions	61'x54'6"
Foundation	Slab
Bedrooms	3
Full Baths	2
Half Baths	1
First Ceiling	11'
Second Ceiling	9'
Max Ridge Height	34'8"
Roof Framing	Stick
Exterior Walls	2x4

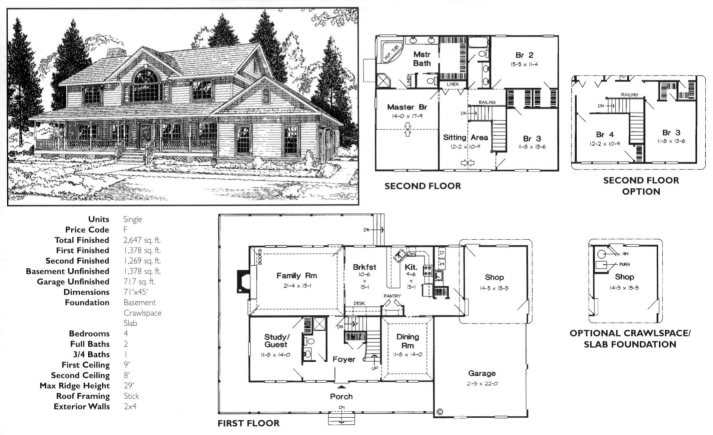

br.2 15 x 13
br.3 13 x 15
open to below

SECOND FLOOR

mbr 17 x 15-4
m bath
dining 13-8 x 18
kit 13-7 x 13
brkfst 11 x 15
side courtyard
family 21 x 20
pantry
foyer
garage 20 x 20
study 13 x 13
entry courtyard

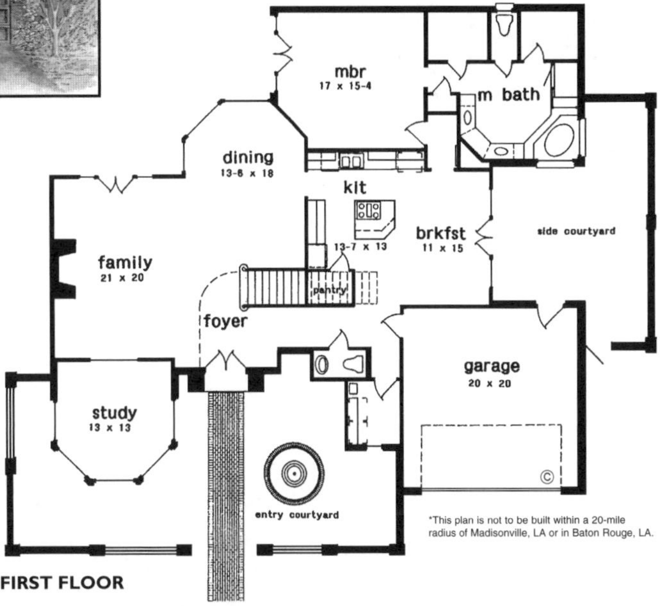

*This plan is not to be built within a 20-mile radius of Madisonville, LA or in Baton Rouge, LA.

FIRST FLOOR

Design 24403

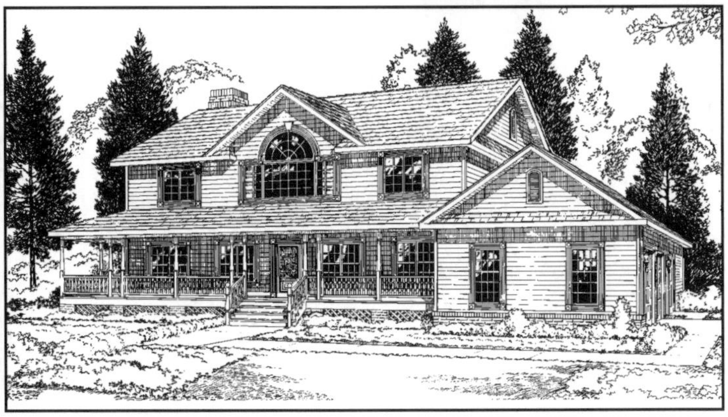

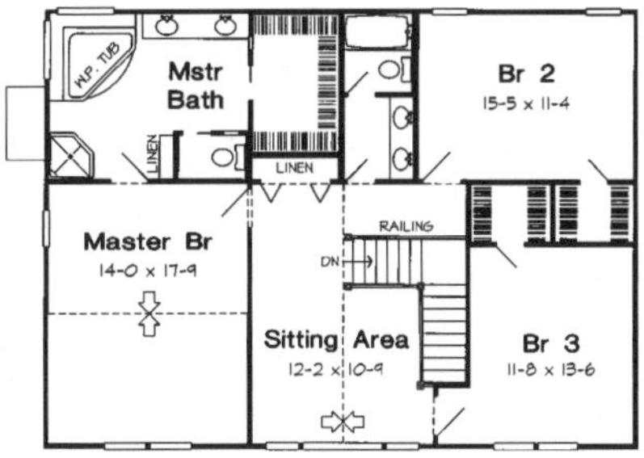

Units	Single
Price Code	F
Total Finished	2,647 sq. ft.
First Finished	1,378 sq. ft.
Second Finished	1,269 sq. ft.
Basement Unfinished	1,378 sq. ft.
Garage Unfinished	717 sq. ft.
Dimensions	71'x45'
Foundation	Basement Crawlspace Slab
Bedrooms	4
Full Baths	2
3/4 Baths	1
First Ceiling	9'
Second Ceiling	8'
Max Ridge Height	29'
Roof Framing	Stick
Exterior Walls	2x4

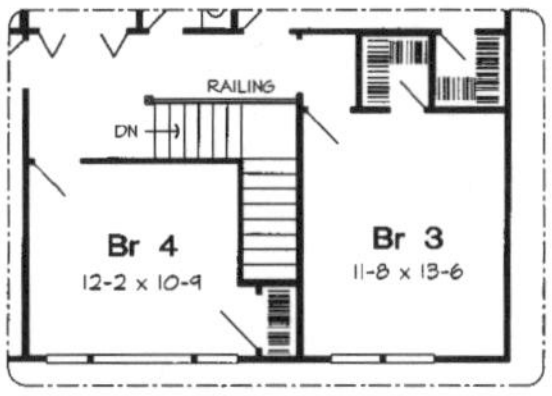

Mstr Bath
Br 2 15-5 x 11-4
Master Br 14-0 x 17-9
Sitting Area 12-2 x 10-9
Br 3 11-8 x 13-6

SECOND FLOOR

Br 4 12-2 x 10-9
Br 3 11-8 x 13-6

SECOND FLOOR OPTION

Family Rm 21-4 x 15-1
Brkfst 10-6 x 15-1
Kit. 9-6 x 15-1
Shop 14-5 x 15-5
Study/ Guest 11-8 x 14-0
Foyer
Dining Rm 11-8 x 14-0
Garage 21-5 x 22-0
Porch

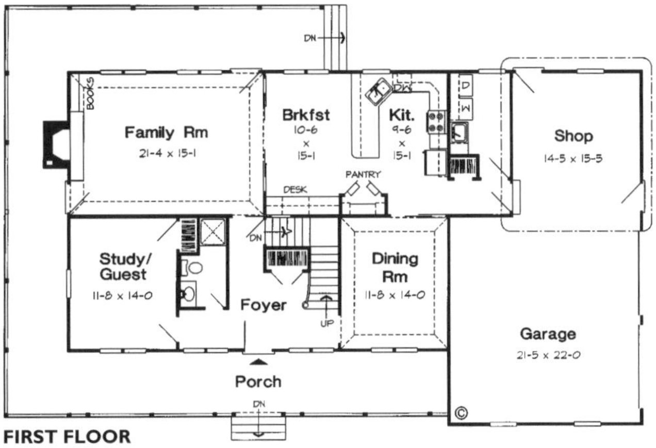

FIRST FLOOR

Shop 14-5 x 15-5

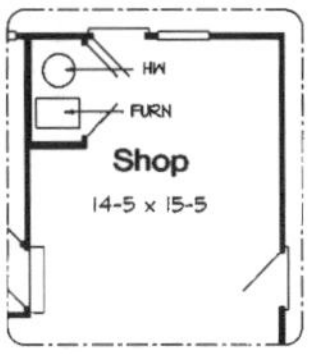

OPTIONAL CRAWLSPACE/ SLAB FOUNDATION

Design 92623

PHOTOGRAPHY: COURTESY OF THE DESIGNER

Please note: The photographed home may have been modified to suit homeowner preferences. If you order plans, have a builder or design professional check them against the photograph to confirm actual construction details.

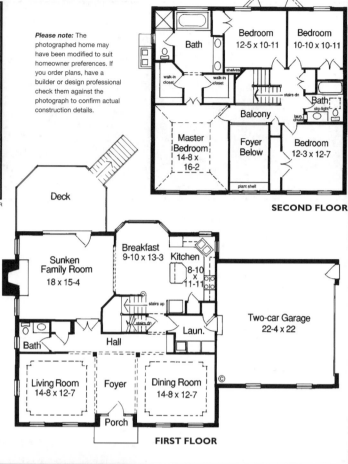

Units	Single
Price Code	F
Total Finished	2,653 sq. ft.
First Finished	1,365 sq. ft.
Second Finished	1,288 sq. ft.
Basement Unfinished	1,217 sq. ft.
Garage Unfinished	491 sq. ft.
Dimensions	61'x37'6"
Foundation	Basement
Bedrooms	4
Full Baths	2
Half Baths	1
Max Ridge Height	34'9"
Roof Framing	Truss
Exterior Walls	2x4

Bath
Bedroom 12-5 x 10-11
Bedroom 10-10 x 10-11
walk-in closet
walk-in closet
shelves
stairs dn
Bath
sky-light
Balcony
laun. chute
Master Bedroom 14-8 x 16-2
Foyer Below
Bedroom 12-3 x 12-7
plant shelf

SECOND FLOOR

Deck
Sunken Family Room 18 x 15-4
Breakfast 9-10 x 13-3
Kitchen 8-10 x 11-11
stairs up
stairs dn
Two-car Garage 22-4 x 22
Bath
Hall
Laun.
Living Room 14-8 x 12-7
Foyer
Dining Room 14-8 x 12-7
Porch
©

FIRST FLOOR

Design 99424

Units	Single
Price Code	F
Total Finished	2,655 sq. ft.
First Finished	1,906 sq. ft.
Second Finished	749 sq. ft.
Basement Unfinished	1,906 sq. ft.
Garage Unfinished	682 sq. ft.
Dimensions	65'3"x57'1½"
Foundation	Basement Slab
Bedrooms	4
Full Baths	2
Half Baths	1
First Ceiling	9'
Second Ceiling	8'
Max Ridge Height	29'9"
Roof Framing	Stick
Exterior Walls	2x4

* Alternate foundation options available at an additional charge. Please call 1-800-235-5700 for more information.

PORCH
MASTER BEDROOM 13'-0" X 17'-0" 9' C.H.
BREAKFAST 11'-0" X 12'-0" 9' C.H.
FP
MASTER BATH
FAMILY ROOM 19'-0" X 15'-0" 11'-19' C.H.
UTILITY
PWDR
KITCHEN 13'-4" X 15'-0" 11'-19' C.H.
SERV. ENTRY
PANT
MASTER CLOSET
DN
GALLERY 9' C.H.
BUTLER'S
UP
ENTRY 18' C.H.
DINING ROOM 11'-0" X 13'-0" 9' C.H.
STUDY 12'-6" X 13'-0" 9' C.H.
PORCH
3-CAR GARAGE 9' C.H.
BEDROOM 2 13'-0" X 11'-0" 8' C.H.
W.I.C.
LIN
LIN
BATH
OPEN TO FAMILY ROOM
OPEN TO KITCHEN
©
FIRST FLOOR
DN
BALCONY
ATTIC
OPEN TO BELOW
BEDROOM 4 11'-0" X 11'-0" 8' C.H.
BEDROOM 3 12'-6" X 11'-0" 8' C.H.
SECOND FLOOR

Design 97507

Units	Single
Price Code	F
Total Finished	2,659 sq. ft.
Main Finished	2,659 sq. ft.
Garage Unfinished	517 sq. ft.
Porch Unfinished	189 sq. ft.
Dimensions	69'4"x84'8"
Foundation	Slab
Bedrooms	4
Full Baths	3
Max Ridge Height	28'8"
Roof Framing	Stick
Exterior Walls	2x4

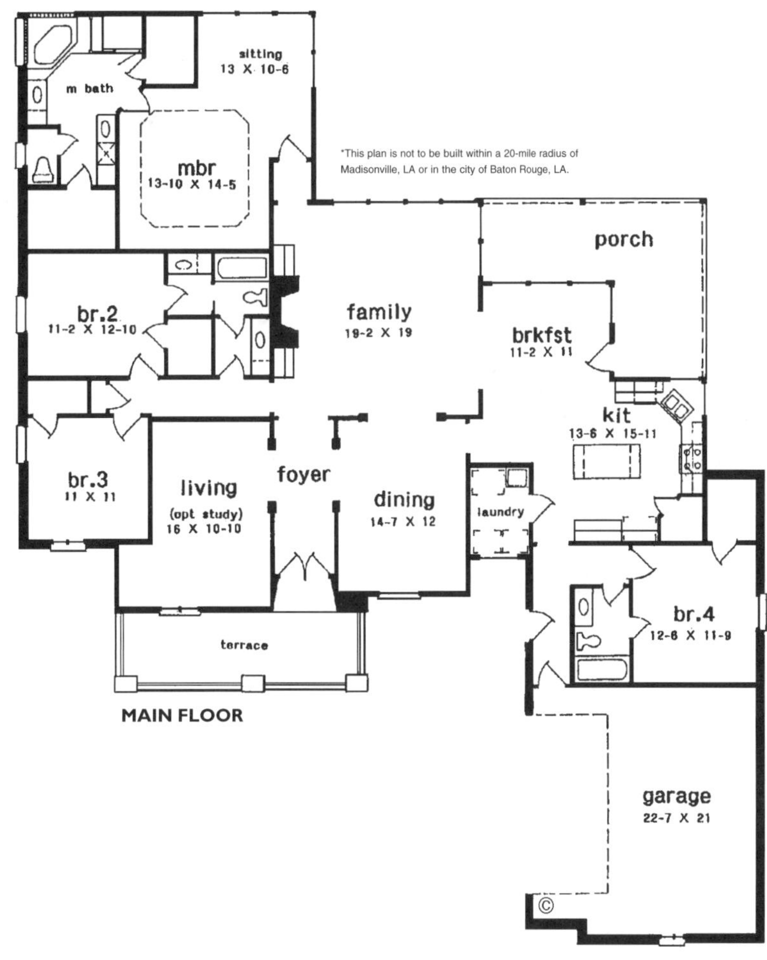
sitting
13 X 10-6
m bath
mbr
13-10 X 14-5
*This plan is not to be built within a 20-mile radius of Madisonville, LA or in the city of Baton Rouge, LA.
porch
family
19-2 X 19
br.2
11-2 X 12-10
brkfst
11-2 X 11
kit
13-6 X 15-11
br.3
11 X 11
living
(opt study)
16 X 10-10
foyer
dining
14-7 X 12
laundry
br.4
12-6 X 11-9
terrace
MAIN FLOOR
garage
22-7 X 21

Design 97192

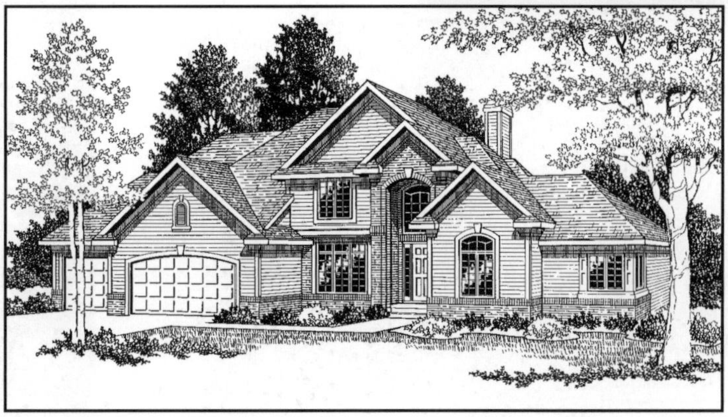

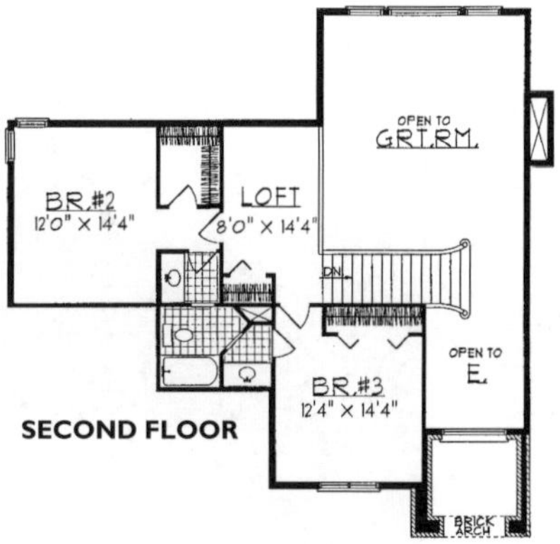

Units	Single
Price Code	F
Total Finished	2,673 sq. ft.
First Finished	2,018 sq. ft.
Second Finished	655 sq. ft.
Basement Unfinished	2,018 sq. ft.
Porch Unfinished	224 sq. ft.
Dimensions	81'x53'
Foundation	Basement
Bedrooms	3
Full Baths	2
Half Baths	1
Max Ridge Height	30'
Roof Framing	Truss
Exterior Walls	2x6

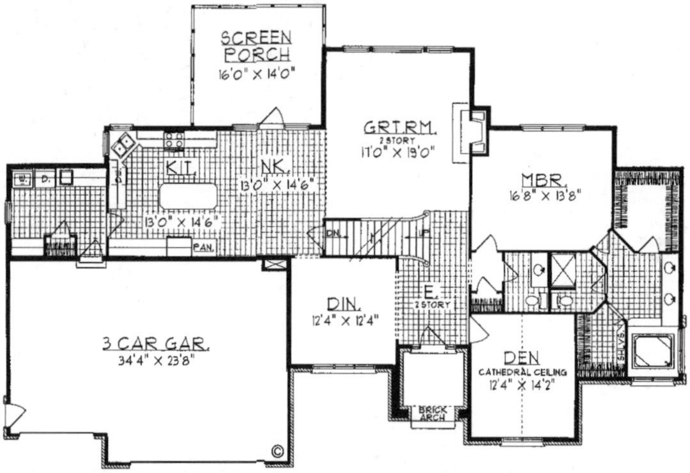

SCREEN PORCH 16'0" x 14'0"
GRT.RM. 2 STORY 17'0" x 19'0"
KIT. NK. 13'0" x 14'6"
MBR. 16'8" x 13'8"
DIN. 12'4" x 12'4"
E. 2 STORY
3 CAR GAR. 34'4" x 23'8"
DEN CATHEDRAL CEILING 12'4" x 14'2"
BRICK ARCH

FIRST FLOOR

BR.#2 12'0" x 14'4"
LOFT 8'0" x 14'4"
OPEN TO GRT.RM.
BR.#3 12'4" x 14'4"
OPEN TO E.

SECOND FLOOR

Design 34047

Units	Single
Price Code	F
Total Finished	2,674 sq. ft.
First Finished	1,511 sq. ft.
Second Finished	1,163 sq. ft.
Basement Unfinished	1,511 sq. ft.
Garage Unfinished	765 sq. ft.
Dimensions	67'x51'
Foundation	Basement Crawlspace Slab
Bedrooms	3
Full Baths	2
Half Baths	1
First Ceiling	8'
Second Ceiling	8'
Max Ridge Height	33'
Roof Framing	Stick
Exterior Walls	2x4, 2x6

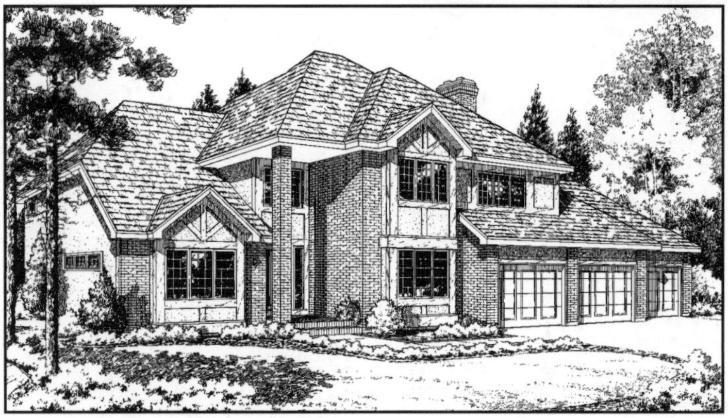

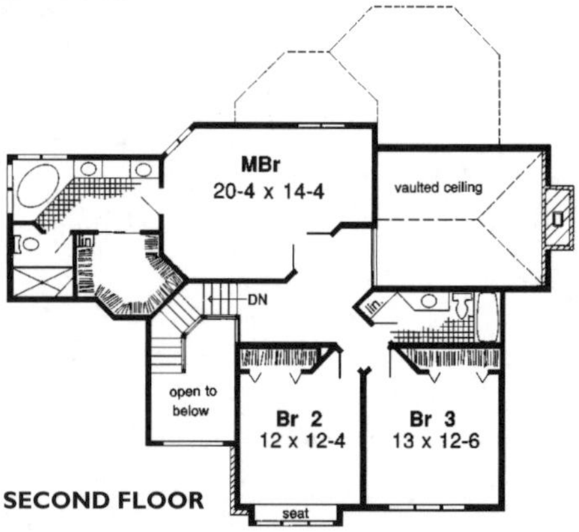

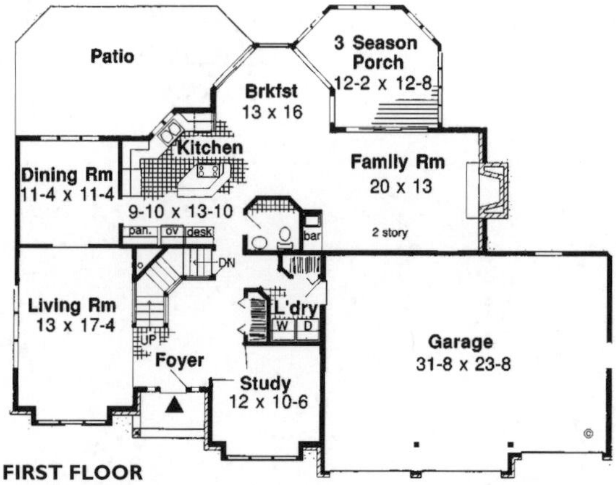

MBr 20-4 x 14-4
vaulted ceiling
open to below
Br 2 12 x 12-4
Br 3 13 x 12-6
seat

SECOND FLOOR

Patio
3 Season Porch 12-2 x 12-8
Brkfst 13 x 16
Kitchen 9-10 x 13-10
Dining Rm 11-4 x 11-4
Family Rm 20 x 13
2 story
Living Rm 13 x 17-4
L'dry
Foyer
Study 12 x 10-6
Garage 31-8 x 23-8

FIRST FLOOR

Design 92275

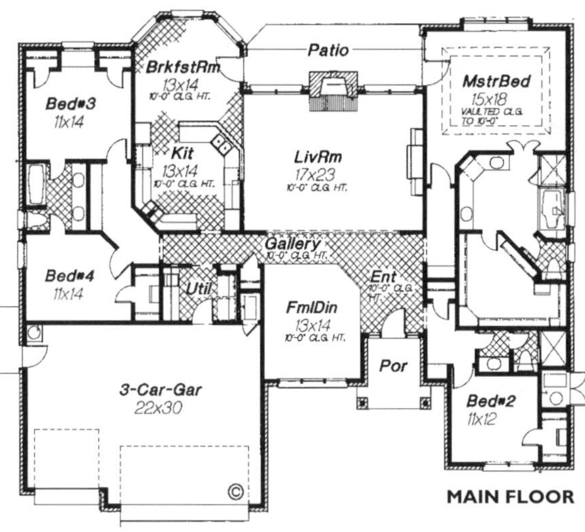
Patio
BrkfstRm
13x14
10'-0" CLG. HT.
MstrBed
15x18
VAULTED CLG. TO 10'-0"
Bed#3
11x14
Kit
13x14
10'-0" CLG. HT.
LivRm
17x23
10'-0" CLG. HT.
Gallery
10'-0" CLG. HT.
Bed#4
11x14
Util
Ent
10'-0" CLG. HT.
FmlDin
13x14
10'-0" CLG. HT.
Por
3-Car-Gar
22x30
Bed#2
11x12
MAIN FLOOR

Units	Single
Price Code	F
Total Finished	2,675 sq. ft.
Main Finished	2,675 sq. ft.
Garage Unfinished	638 sq. ft.
Dimensions	69'x59'10"
Foundation	Slab
Bedrooms	4
Full Baths	2
3/4 Baths	1
Max Ridge Height	28'
Roof Framing	Stick
Exterior Walls	2x4

Design 98418

CAD FILES AVAILABLE
For more information call
800-235-5700

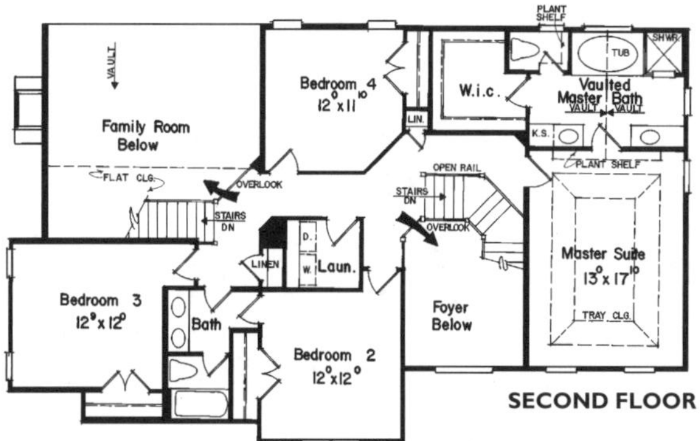

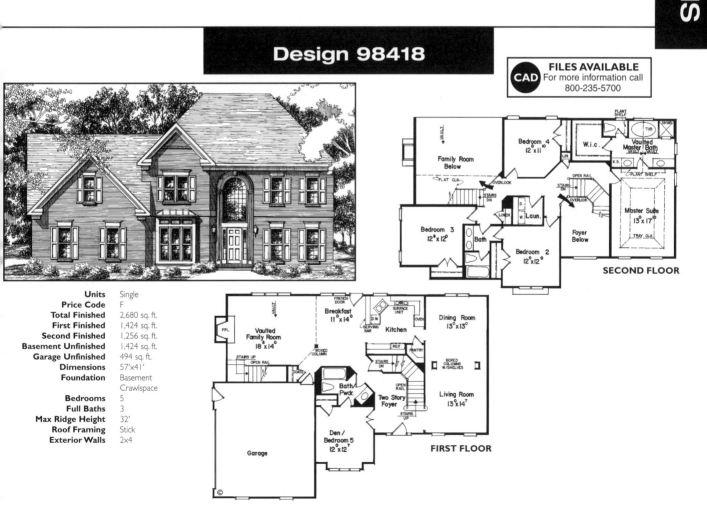

SECOND FLOOR

FIRST FLOOR

Units	Single
Price Code	F
Total Finished	2,680 sq. ft.
First Finished	1,424 sq. ft.
Second Finished	1,256 sq. ft.
Basement Unfinished	1,424 sq. ft.
Garage Unfinished	494 sq. ft.
Dimensions	57'x41'
Foundation	Basement Crawlspace
Bedrooms	5
Full Baths	3
Max Ridge Height	32'
Roof Framing	Stick
Exterior Walls	2x4

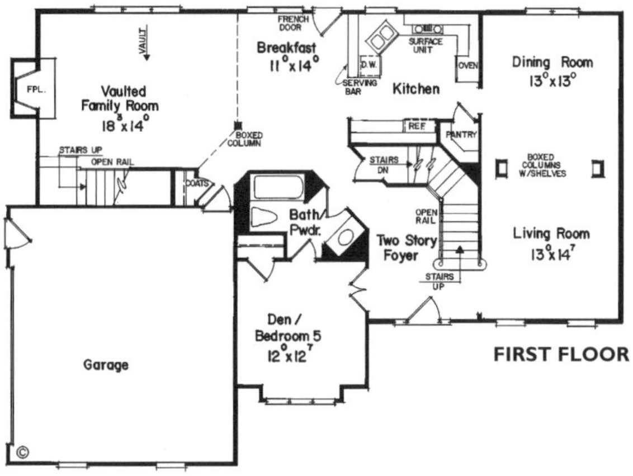

Design 90838

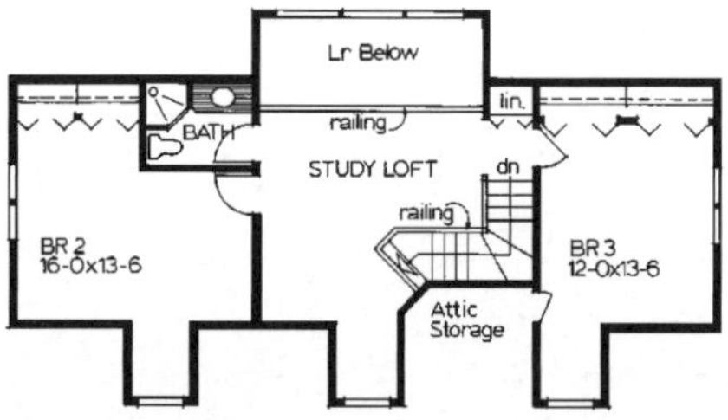

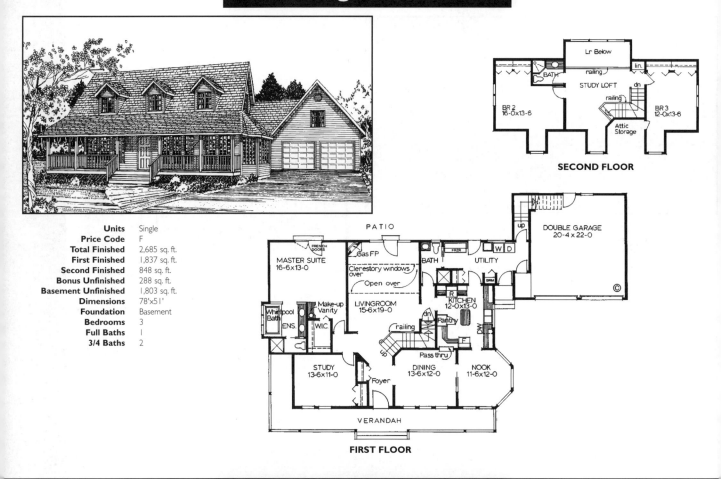

Units	Single
Price Code	F
Total Finished	2,685 sq. ft.
First Finished	1,837 sq. ft.
Second Finished	848 sq. ft.
Bonus Unfinished	288 sq. ft.
Basement Unfinished	1,803 sq. ft.
Dimensions	78'x51'
Foundation	Basement
Bedrooms	3
Full Baths	1
3/4 Baths	2

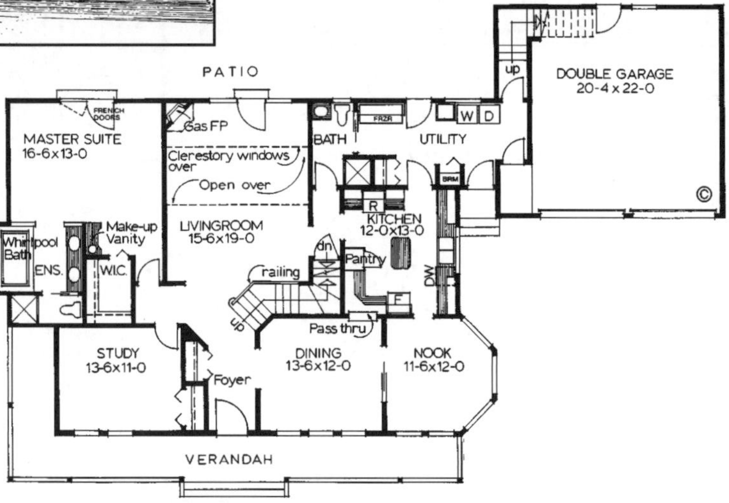

SECOND FLOOR

FIRST FLOOR

Design 97249

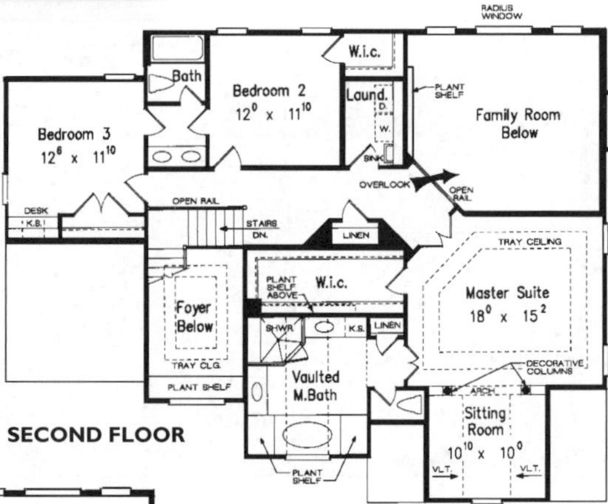

Units	Single
Price Code	F
Total Finished	2,685 sq. ft.
First Finished	1,374 sq. ft.
Second Finished	1,311 sq. ft.
Basement Unfinished	1,374 sq. ft.
Garage Unfinished	560 sq. ft.
Dimensions	57'4"x42'
Foundation	Basement Crawlspace
Bedrooms	4
Full Baths	3
Max Ridge Height	33'
Roof Framing	Stick
Exterior Walls	2x4

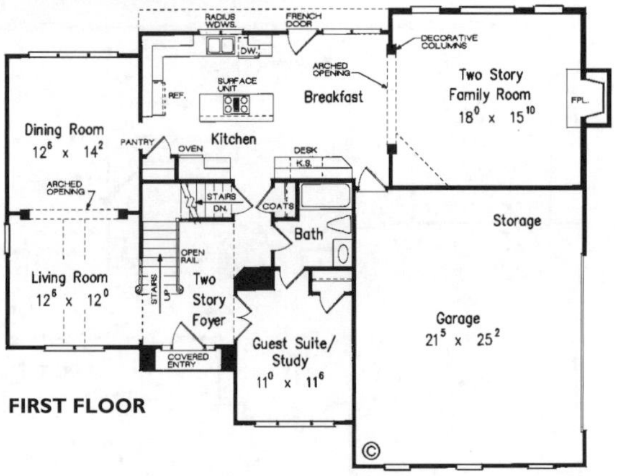

SECOND FLOOR

FIRST FLOOR

Design 98457

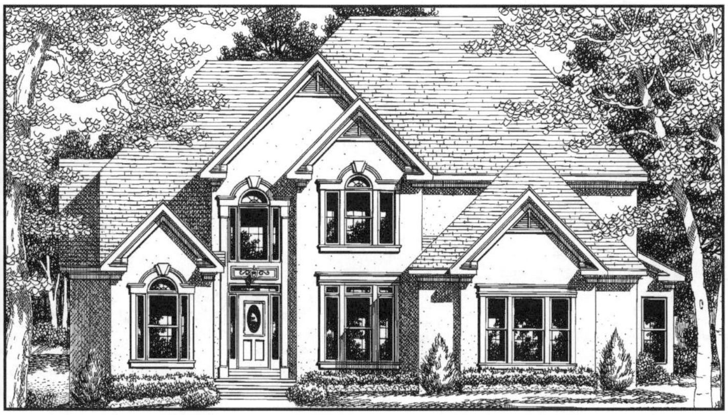

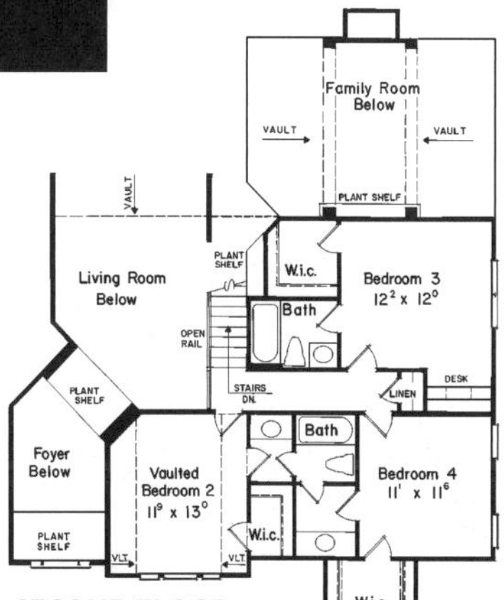

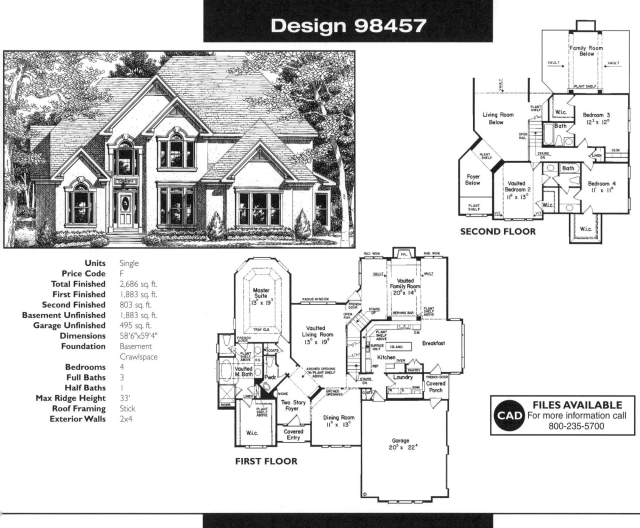

Units	Single
Price Code	F
Total Finished	2,686 sq. ft.
First Finished	1,883 sq. ft.
Second Finished	803 sq. ft.
Basement Unfinished	1,883 sq. ft.
Garage Unfinished	495 sq. ft.
Dimensions	58'6"x59'4"
Foundation	Basement Crawlspace
Bedrooms	4
Full Baths	3
Half Baths	1
Max Ridge Height	33'
Roof Framing	Stick
Exterior Walls	2x4

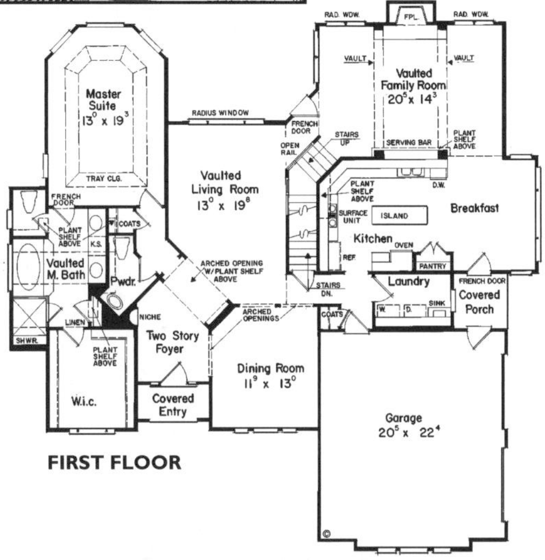

SECOND FLOOR

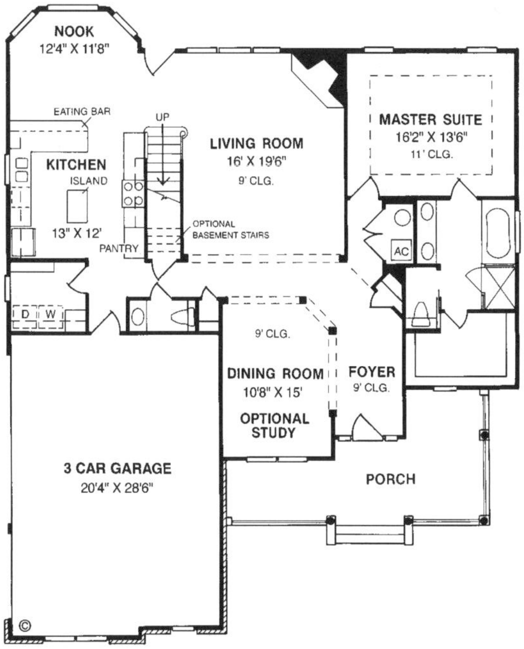

FIRST FLOOR

Design 97946

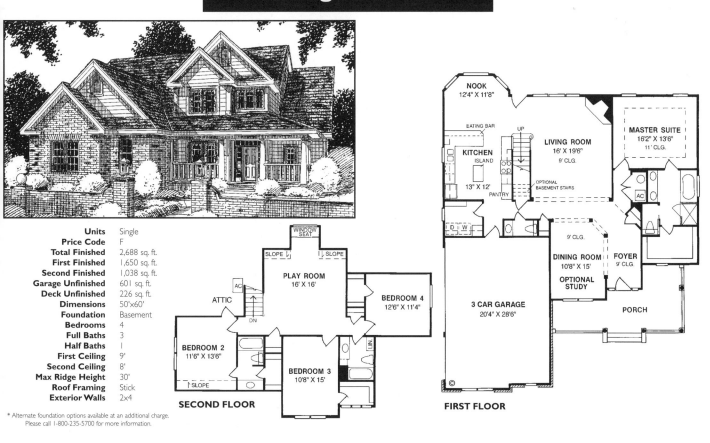

Units	Single
Price Code	F
Total Finished	2,688 sq. ft.
First Finished	1,650 sq. ft.
Second Finished	1,038 sq. ft.
Garage Unfinished	601 sq. ft.
Deck Unfinished	226 sq. ft.
Dimensions	50'x60'
Foundation	Basement
Bedrooms	4
Full Baths	3
Half Baths	1
First Ceiling	9'
Second Ceiling	8'
Max Ridge Height	30'
Roof Framing	Stick
Exterior Walls	2x4

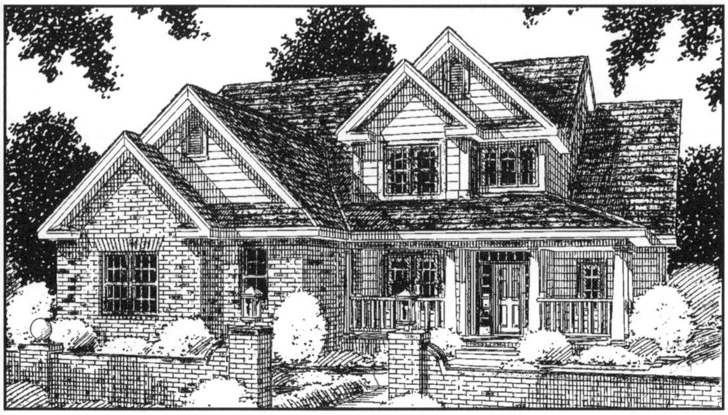

* Alternate foundation options available at an additional charge. Please call 1-800-235-5700 for more information.

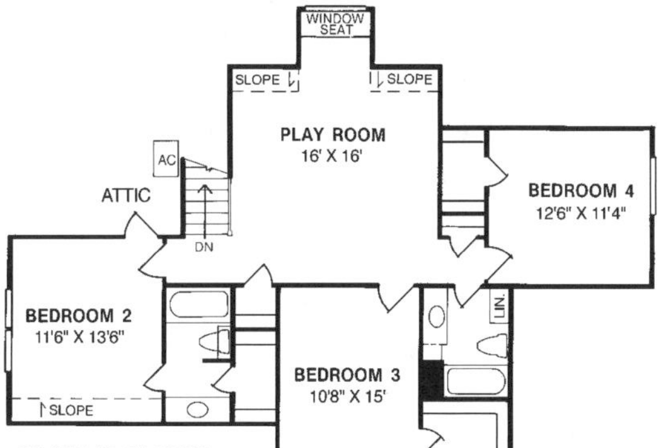

SECOND FLOOR

FIRST FLOOR

Design 66098

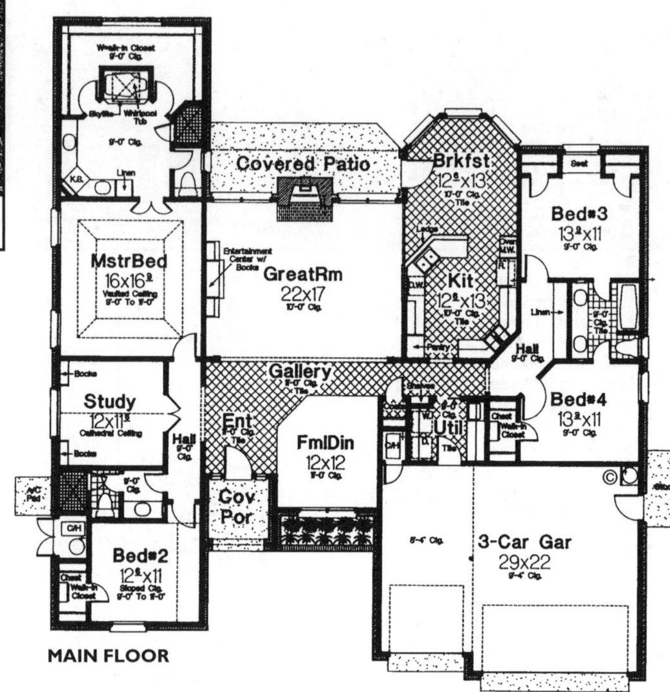

Walk-in Closet
Skylite
Whirlpool Tub
Linen
Covered Patio
Brkfst
12⁸x13
Bed#3
13⁸x11
MstrBed
16x16⁸
Vaulted Ceiling
GreatRm
22x17
Kit
12⁸x13
Hall
Gallery
Bed#4
13⁸x11
Study
12x11⁸
Cathedral Ceiling
Ent
FmlDin
12x12
Util
Cov Por
3-Car Gar
29x22
Bed#2
12⁸x11
Sloped Clg.

MAIN FLOOR

Units	Single
Price Code	F
Total Finished	2,689 sq. ft.
Main Finished	2,689 sq. ft.
Garage Unfinished	638 sq. ft.
Dimensions	65'x68'4"
Foundation	Slab
Bedrooms	4
Full Baths	2
3/4 Baths	1
Main Ceiling	9'
Max Ridge Height	27'
Roof Framing	Stick
Exterior Walls	2x4

Design 99450

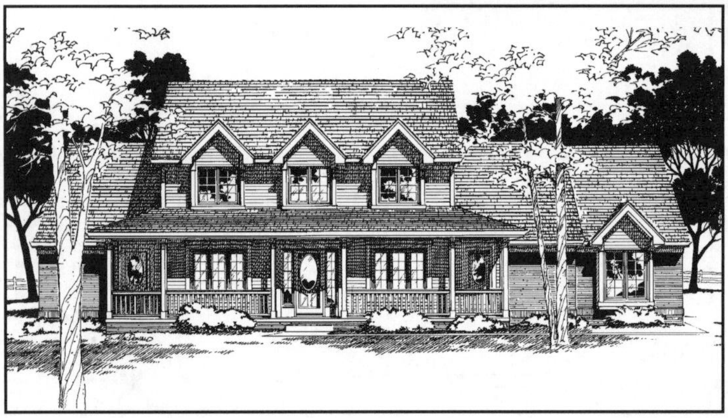

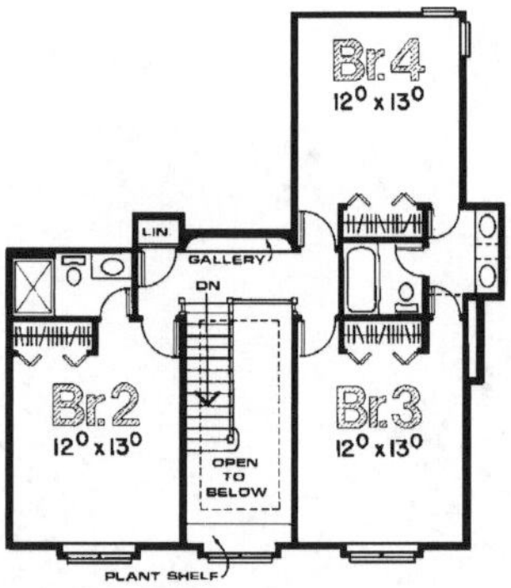

Br. 4
12⁰ x 13⁰
LIN
GALLERY
DN
Br. 2
12⁰ x 13⁰
OPEN TO BELOW
Br. 3
12⁰ x 13⁰
PLANT SHELF

SECOND FLOOR

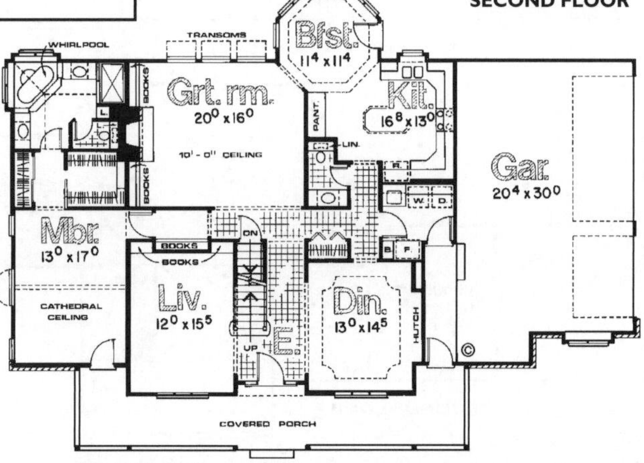

WHIRLPOOL
TRANSOMS
Bfst.
11⁴ x 11⁴
Grt. rm.
20⁰ x 16⁰
10'-0" CEILING
Kit.
16⁸ x 13⁰
Gar.
20⁴ x 30⁰
Mbr.
13⁰ x 17⁰
CATHEDRAL CEILING
BOOKS
Liv.
12⁰ x 15⁵
E.
Din.
13⁰ x 14⁵
HUTCH
COVERED PORCH

FIRST FLOOR

Units	Single
Price Code	F
Total Finished	2,695 sq. ft.
First Finished	1,881 sq. ft.
Second Finished	814 sq. ft.
Basement Unfinished	1,881 sq. ft.
Garage Unfinished	534 sq. ft.
Dimensions	72'x45'4"
Foundation	Basement Slab
Bedrooms	4
Full Baths	2
3/4 Baths	1
Half Baths	1
First Ceiling	8'
Second Ceiling	8'
Max Ridge Height	27'6"
Roof Framing	Stick
Exterior Walls	2x4

* Alternate foundation options available at an additional charge. Please call 1-800-235-5700 for more information.

Design 91022

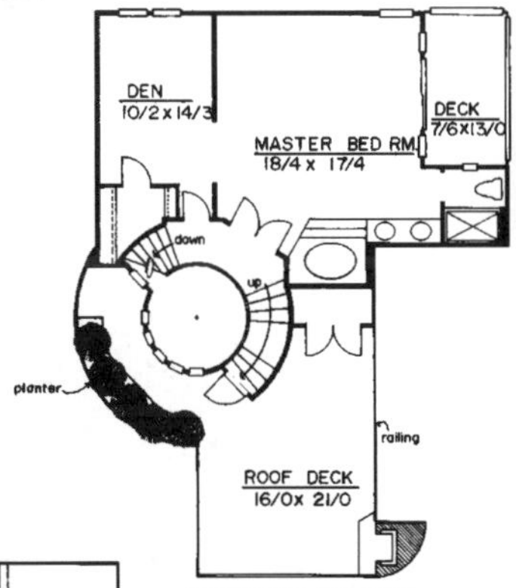

SECOND FLOOR

FIRST FLOOR

Units	Single
Price Code	F
Total Finished	2,700 sq. ft.
First Finished	1,985 sq. ft.
Second Finished	715 sq. ft.
Basement Unfinished	1,985 sq. ft.
Garage Unfinished	608 sq. ft.
Dimensions	70'3"x64'
Foundation	Basement Crawlspace Slab
Bedrooms	3
Full Baths	2
Half Baths	1
Max Ridge Height	26'
Roof Framing	Stick
Exterior Walls	2x6

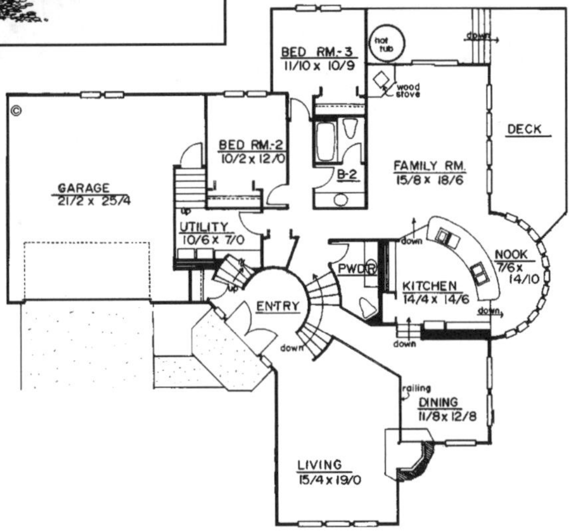

Design 62006

SECOND FLOOR

FIRST FLOOR

Units	Single
Price Code	F
Total Finished	2,701 sq. ft.
First Finished	2,352 sq. ft.
Second Finished	349 sq. ft.
Garage Unfinished	697 sq. ft.
Porch Unfinished	724 sq. ft.
Dimensions	69'x69'10"
Foundation	Basement Crawlspace Slab
Bedrooms	3
Full Baths	2
3/4 Baths	2
Half Baths	1
First Ceiling	9'
Second Ceiling	8'
Roof Framing	Stick
Exterior Walls	2x4

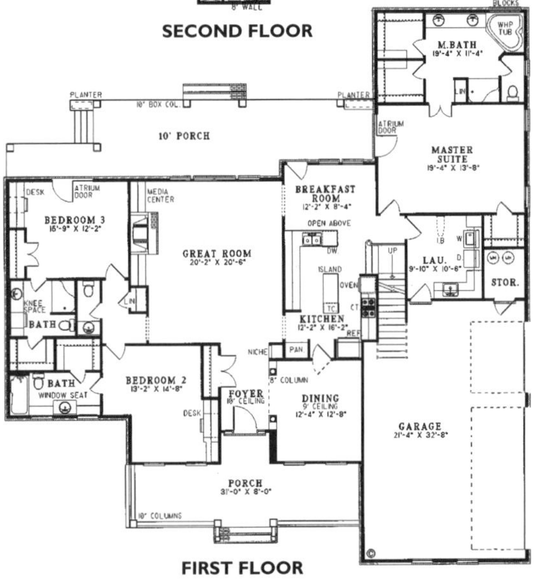

Design 93332

Units	Single
Price Code	F
Total Finished	2,707 sq. ft.
First Finished	1,484 sq. ft.
Second Finished	1,223 sq. ft.
Basement Unfinished	1,484 sq. ft.
Dimensions	82'x48'8"
Foundation	Basement
Bedrooms	3
Full Baths	2
Half Baths	1
First Ceiling	9'
Second Ceiling	8'
Max Ridge Height	32'
Roof Framing	Stick
Exterior Walls	2x4

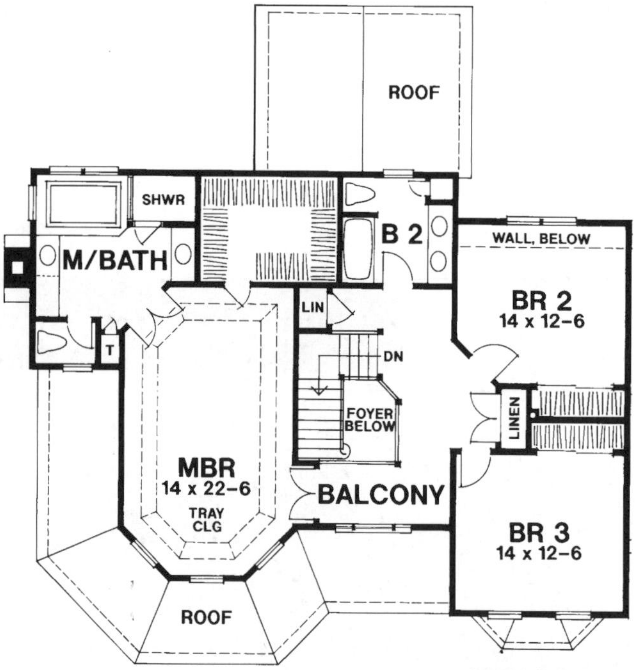

ROOF
SHWR
M/BATH
T
B 2
LIN
WALL, BELOW
BR 2
14 x 12-6
DN
FOYER BELOW
LINEN
MBR
14 x 22-6
TRAY CLG
BALCONY
BR 3
14 x 12-6
ROOF

SECOND FLOOR

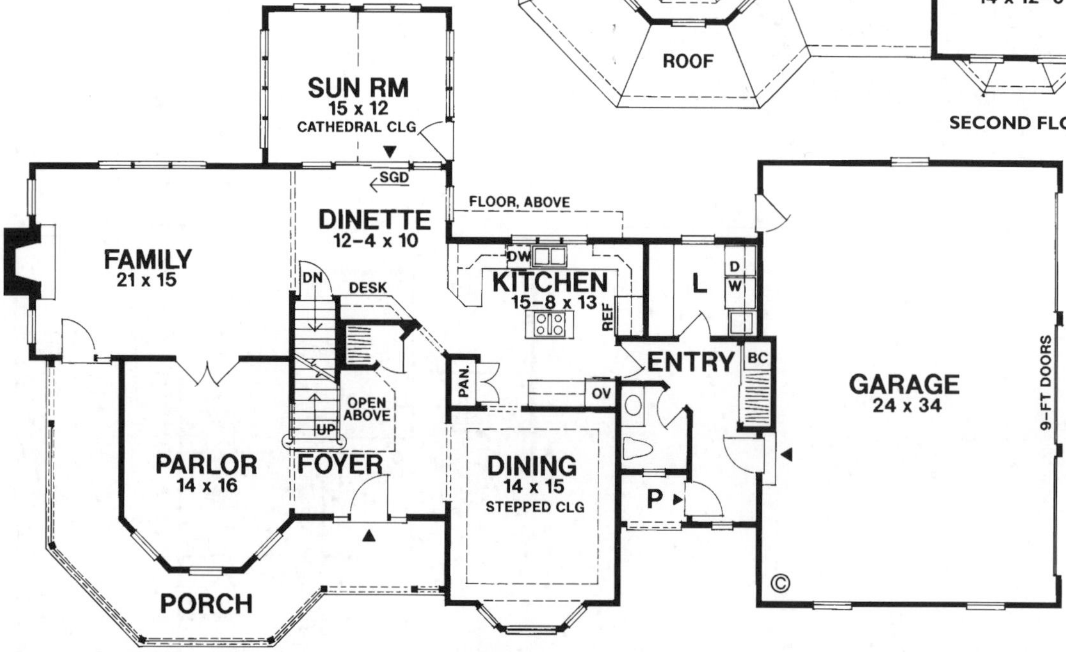

SUN RM
15 x 12
CATHEDRAL CLG
SGD
FAMILY
21 x 15
DINETTE
12-4 x 10
FLOOR, ABOVE
DW
KITCHEN
15-8 x 13
REF
L
D
W
DN
DESK
PAN.
OV
ENTRY
BC
OPEN ABOVE
UP
PARLOR
14 x 16
FOYER
DINING
14 x 15
STEPPED CLG
P
GARAGE
24 x 34
9-FT DOORS
©
PORCH

FIRST FLOOR

Design 34073

PHOTOGRAPHY: JOHN EHRENCLOU

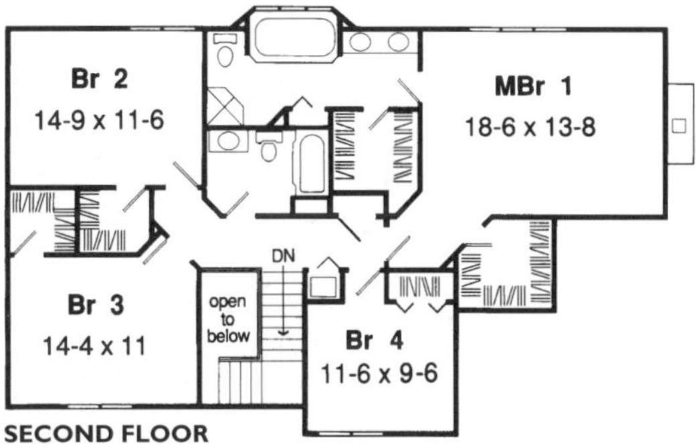

SECOND FLOOR

Br 2 14-9 x 11-6
MBr 1 18-6 x 13-8
Br 3 14-4 x 11
open to below
DN
Br 4 11-6 x 9-6

FIRST FLOOR

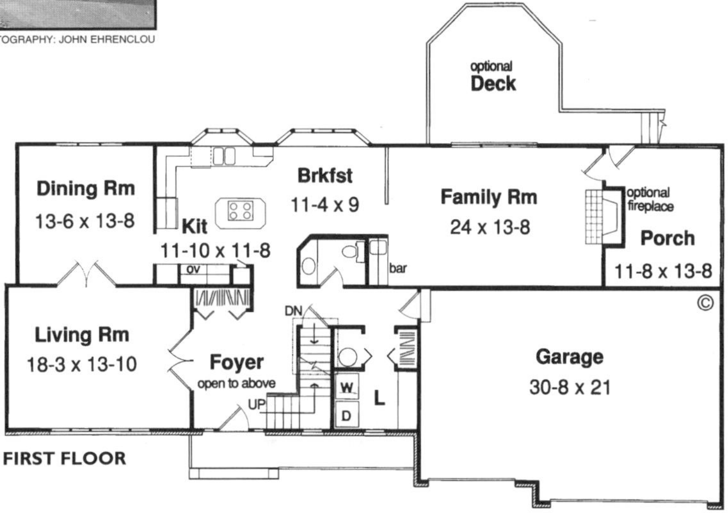

optional Deck
Dining Rm 13-6 x 13-8
Brkfst 11-4 x 9
Kit 11-10 x 11-8
ov
Family Rm 24 x 13-8
bar
optional fireplace
Porch 11-8 x 13-8
Living Rm 18-3 x 13-10
Foyer open to above
DN
UP
W
D
L
Garage 30-8 x 21
©

Units	Single
Price Code	F
Total Finished	2,710 sq. ft.
First Finished	1,469 sq. ft.
Second Finished	1,241 sq. ft.
Dimensions	73'x35'6"
Foundation	Basement Crawlspace Slab
Bedrooms	4
Full Baths	2
Half Baths	1
Max Ridge Height	36'
Roof Framing	Stick
Exterior Walls	2x4, 2x6

OPTIONAL CRAWLSPACE/SLAB FOUNDATION

Please note: The photographed home may have been modified to suit homeowner preferences. If you order plans, have a builder or design professional check them against the photograph to confirm actual construction details.

Design 69126

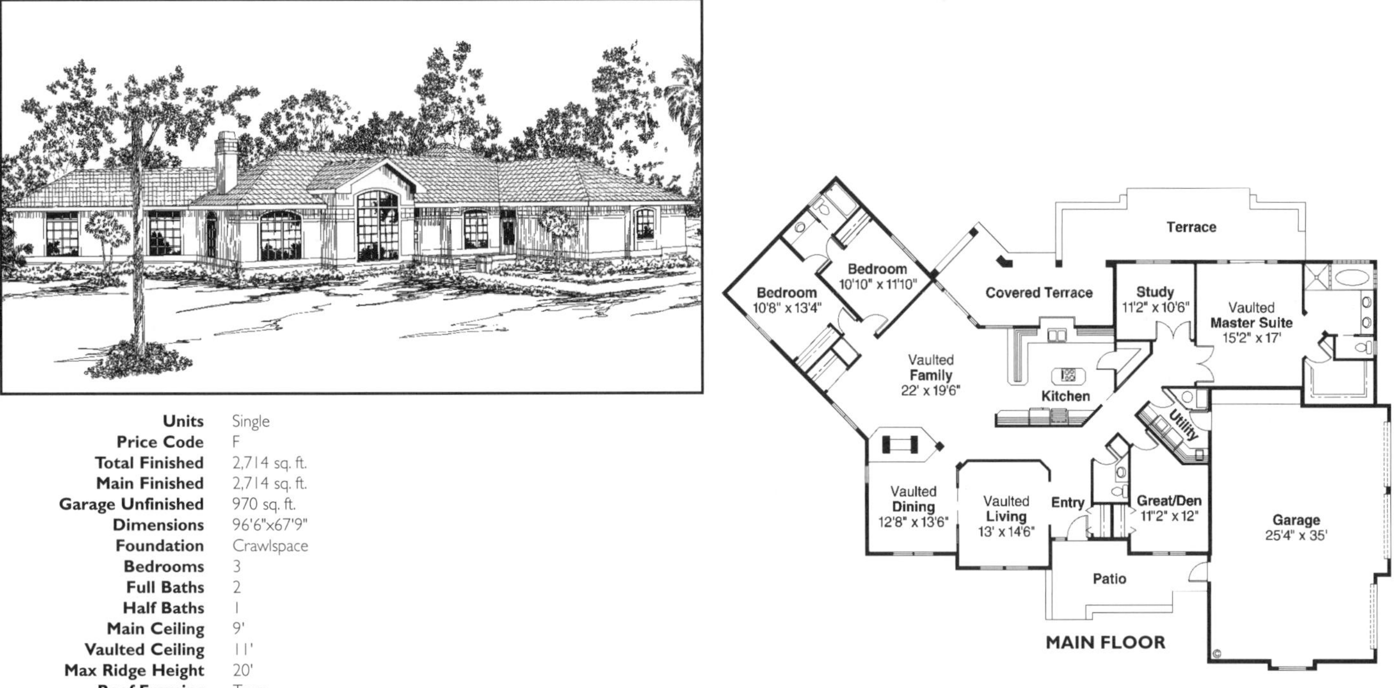
Terrace
Bedroom 10'10" x 11'10"
Bedroom 10'8" x 13'4"
Covered Terrace
Study 11'2" x 10'6"
Vaulted Master Suite 15'2" x 17'
Vaulted Family 22' x 19'6"
Kitchen
Utility
Vaulted Dining 12'8" x 13'6"
Vaulted Living 13' x 14'6"
Entry
Great/Den 11'2" x 12"
Garage 25'4" x 35'
Patio
MAIN FLOOR

Units	Single
Price Code	F
Total Finished	2,714 sq. ft.
Main Finished	2,714 sq. ft.
Garage Unfinished	970 sq. ft.
Dimensions	96'6"x67'9"
Foundation	Crawlspace
Bedrooms	3
Full Baths	2
Half Baths	1
Main Ceiling	9'
Vaulted Ceiling	11'
Max Ridge Height	20'
Roof Framing	Truss
Exterior Walls	2x6

Design 90470

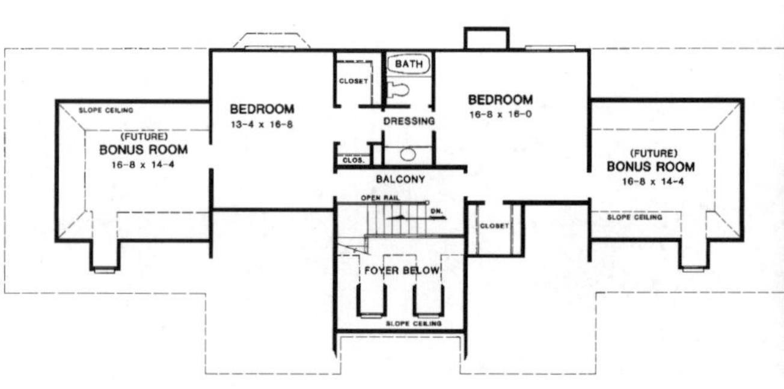

BEDROOM
13-4 x 16-8
BEDROOM
16-8 x 16-0
BATH
CLOSET
DRESSING
(FUTURE)
BONUS ROOM
16-8 x 14-4
(FUTURE)
BONUS ROOM
16-8 x 14-4
BALCONY
OPEN RAIL
FOYER BELOW
SLOPE CEILING

SECOND FLOOR

Units	Single
Price Code	F
Total Finished	2,714 sq. ft.
First Finished	1,997 sq. ft.
Second Finished	717 sq. ft.
Bonus Unfinished	541 sq. ft.
Basement Unfinished	1,997 sq. ft.
Garage Unfinished	575 sq. ft.
Deck Unfinished	264 sq. ft.
Porch Unfinished	48 sq. ft.
Dimensions	86'10"x34'10"
Foundation	Basement Crawlspace
Bedrooms	3
Full Baths	2
Half Baths	1
First Ceiling	9'
Second Ceiling	8'
Max Ridge Height	25'4"
Roof Framing	Stick
Exterior Walls	2x4

WOOD DECK
22-0 x 12-0
HEARTH
BREAKFAST
13-4 x 11-0
LAUNDRY
GARAGE
21-8 x 24-8
GREAT ROOM
22-0 x 15-6
BATH
CLOSET
HALL
KITCHEN
13-4 x 12-0
MEDIA CENTER
MASTER BEDROOM
18-0 x 14-0
FOYER
DINING
13-4 x 12-0
LIVING
13-4 x 14-0
PORCH

FIRST FLOOR

Design 94965

MASTER BEDROOM
13'-4" X 17'-4"
8'-10" C.H.
BATH
BEDROOM 2
15'-4" X 11'-4"
8' C.H.
MASTER BATH
W.I.C.
W.I.C.
DN
OPEN TO FAMILY ROOM
BATH
BEDROOM 4
11'-0" X 12'-8"
8'-10" C.H.
BEDROOM 3
11'-4" X 12'-4"
8'-10" C.H.

SECOND FLOOR

Units	Single
Price Code	F
Total Finished	2,715 sq. ft.
First Finished	1,400 sq. ft.
Second Finished	1,315 sq. ft.
Basement Unfinished	1,400 sq. ft.
Garage Unfinished	631 sq. ft.
Porch Unfinished	253 sq. ft.
Dimensions	75'1.5"x38'
Foundation	Basement Slab
Bedrooms	4
Full Baths	3
Half Baths	1
First Ceiling	9'
Second Ceiling	8'
Max Ridge Height	30'6"
Roof Framing	Stick
Exterior Walls	2x4

3-CAR GARAGE
9' C.H.
UTILITY
BREAKFAST
12'-0" X 11'-4"
9' C.H.
PORCH
KITCHEN
15'-4" X 15'-0"
9' C.H.
PWDR
PANTRY
DN
UP
FP
FAMILY ROOM
15'-4" X 19'-4"
12'-19' C.H.
DINING ROOM
13'-4" X 14'-0"
9' C.H.
ENTRY
9' C.H.
LIVING ROOM
13'-4" X 12'-8"
9' C.H.
PORCH
UP

FIRST FLOOR

* Alternate foundation options available at an additional charge.
Please call 1-800-235-5700 for more information.

 To order blueprints, call **800-235-5700** or visit us on the web, **familyhomeplans.com**

Design 24550

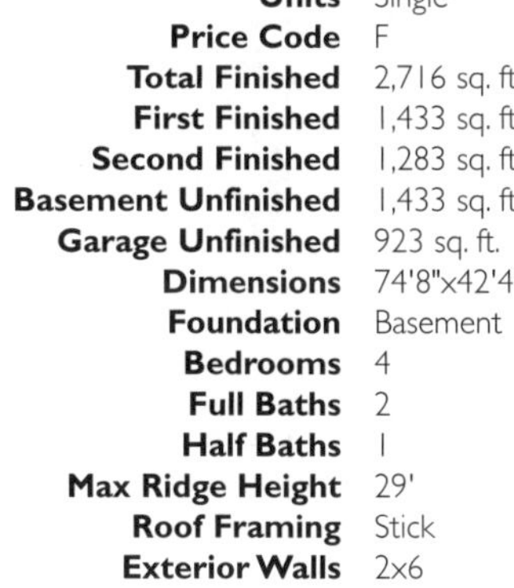

Units	Single
Price Code	F
Total Finished	2,716 sq. ft.
First Finished	1,433 sq. ft.
Second Finished	1,283 sq. ft.
Basement Unfinished	1,433 sq. ft.
Garage Unfinished	923 sq. ft.
Dimensions	74'8"x42'4"
Foundation	Basement
Bedrooms	4
Full Baths	2
Half Baths	1
Max Ridge Height	29'
Roof Framing	Stick
Exterior Walls	2x6

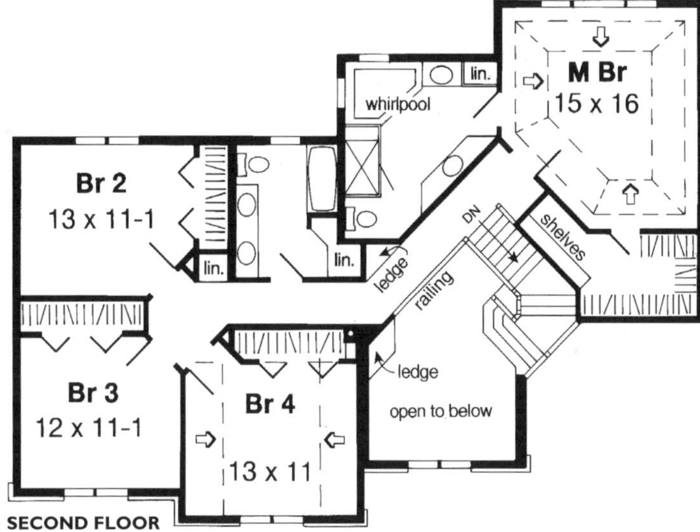
M Br
15 x 16
lin.
whirlpool
Br 2
13 x 11-1
lin.
lin.
ledge
railing
DN
shelves
Br 3
12 x 11-1
Br 4
13 x 11
ledge
open to below

SECOND FLOOR

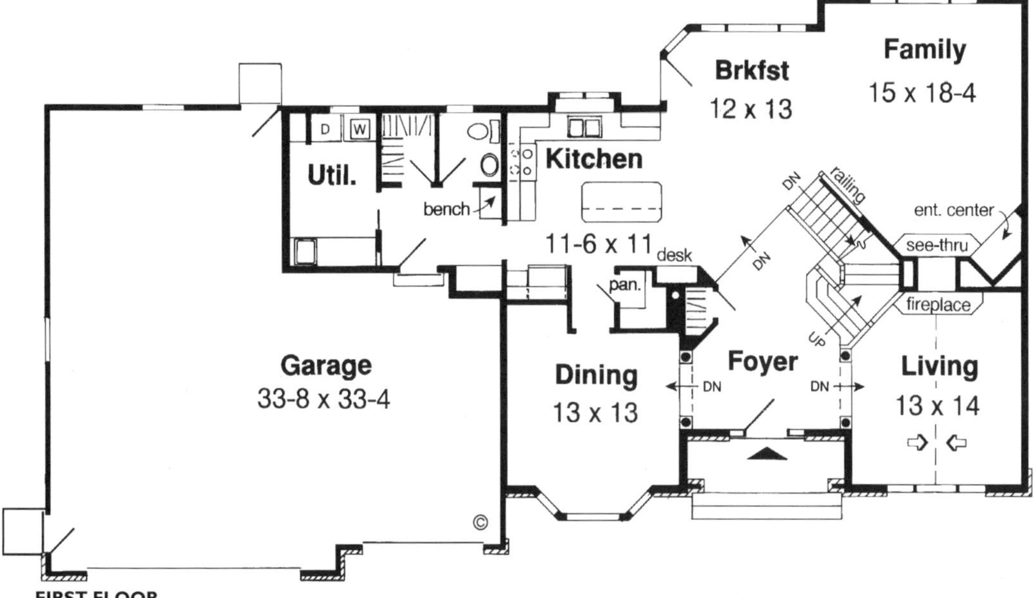
Brkfst
12 x 13
Family
15 x 18-4
D
W
Util.
bench
Kitchen
11-6 x 11
desk
pan.
DN
railing
DN
ent. center
see-thru
fireplace
UP
Garage
33-8 x 33-4
Dining
13 x 13
DN
Foyer
DN
Living
13 x 14

FIRST FLOOR

Design 94145

Units	Single
Price Code	F
Total Finished	2,721 sq. ft.
First Finished	1,845 sq. ft.
Second Finished	876 sq. ft.
Basement Unfinished	1,832 sq. ft.
Garage Unfinished	512 sq. ft.
Porch Unfinished	279 sq. ft.
Dimensions	75'6"x45'4"
Foundation	Basement
Bedrooms	4
Full Baths	3
Half Baths	2
First Ceiling	8'1⅛"
Second Ceiling	8'1⅛"
Max Ridge Height	30'6"
Roof Framing	Stick/Truss
Exterior Walls	2x6

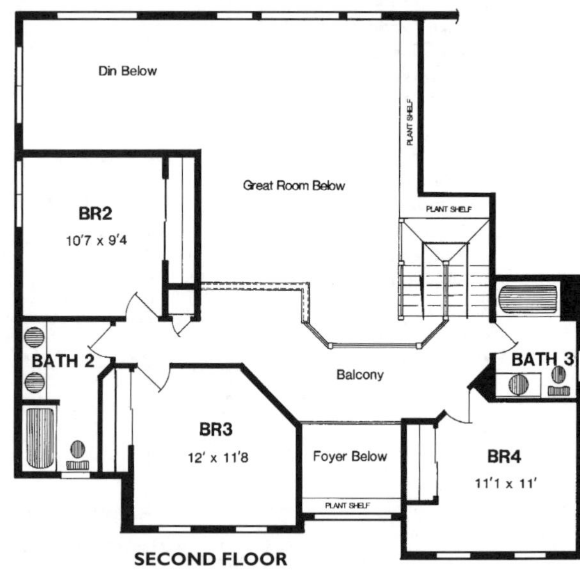

Din Below
Great Room Below
PLANT SHELF
PLANT SHELF
BR2
10'7 x 9'4
BATH 2
Balcony
BATH 3
BR3
12' x 11'8
Foyer Below
PLANT SHELF
BR4
11'1 x 11'

SECOND FLOOR

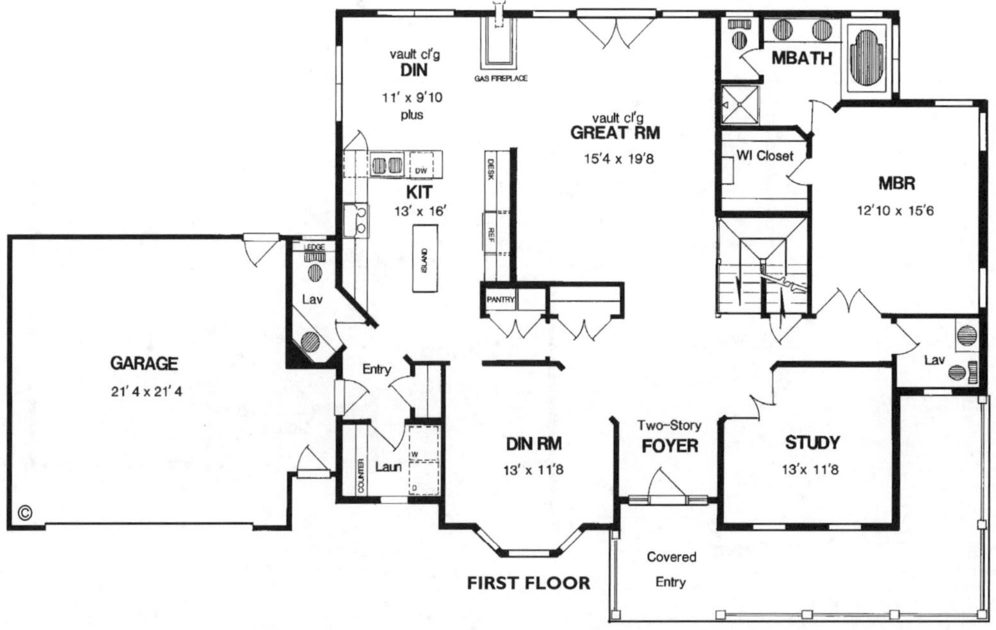

vault cl'g
DIN
11' x 9'10
plus
GAS FIREPLACE
vault cl'g
GREAT RM
15'4 x 19'8
MBATH
WI Closet
MBR
12'10 x 15'6
KIT
13' x 16'
DW
DESK
REF
ISLAND
PANTRY
LEDGE
Lav
GARAGE
21' 4 x 21' 4
Entry
Lav
Laun
COUNTER
W
D
DIN RM
13' x 11'8
Two-Story
FOYER
STUDY
13'x 11'8
Covered
Entry

FIRST FLOOR

Design 92501

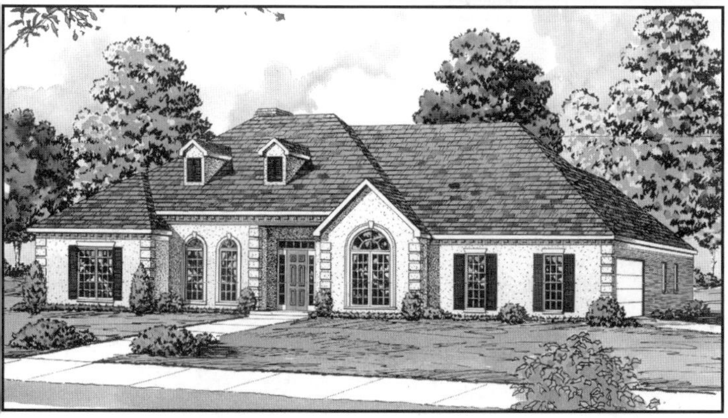

Units	Single
Price Code	F
Total Finished	2,727 sq. ft.
Main Finished	2,727 sq. ft.
Garage Unfinished	569 sq. ft.
Porch Unfinished	190 sq. ft.
Dimensions	70'10"x64'5"
Foundation	Crawlspace Slab
Bedrooms	4
Full Baths	3
Half Baths	1
Main Ceiling	9'
Vaulted Ceiling	11'
Tray Ceiling	10'
Max Ridge Height	24'
Roof Framing	Stick
Exterior Walls	2x4

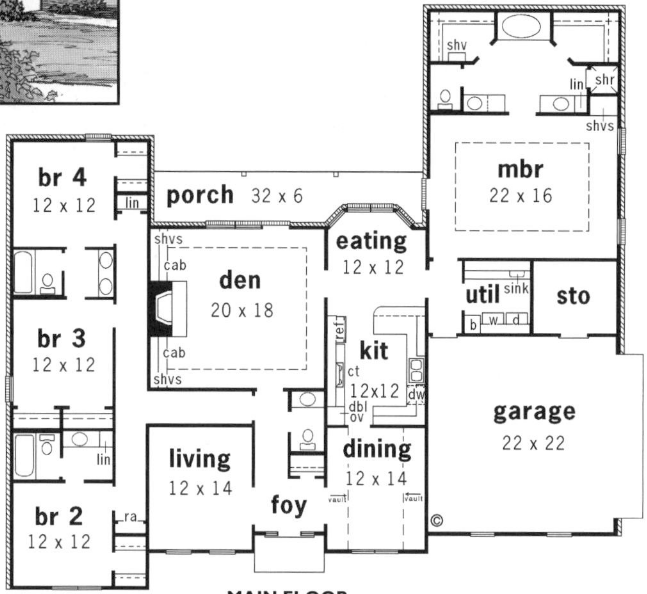

MAIN FLOOR

Design 99162

Units	Single
Price Code	F
Total Finished	2,730 sq. ft.
Main Finished	2,730 sq. ft.
Basement Unfinished	2,730 sq. ft.
Garage Unfinished	707 sq. ft.
Dimensions	72'x81'8"
Foundation	Basement
Bedrooms	3
Full Baths	2
Half Baths	1
Max Ridge Height	26'
Roof Framing	Truss
Exterior Walls	2x6

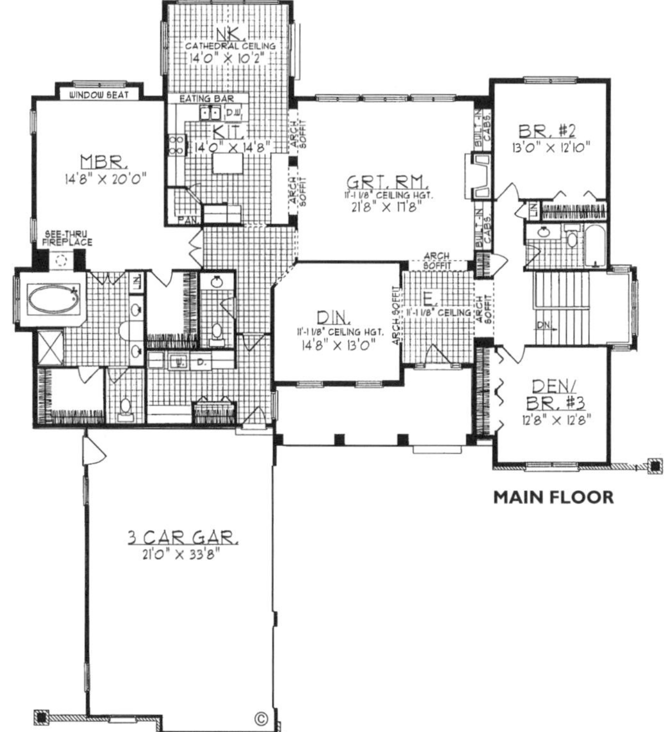
NK.
CATHEDRAL CEILING
14'0" X 10'2"
EATING BAR
KIT.
14'0" X 14'8"
WINDOW SEAT
MBR.
14'8" X 20'0"
SEE-THRU FIREPLACE
GRT. RM.
21'8" X 17'8"
BR. #2
13'0" X 12'10"
DIN.
14'8" X 13'0"
E.
ARCH SOFFIT
DEN/
BR. #3
12'8" X 12'8"
3 CAR GAR.
21'0" X 33'8"

MAIN FLOOR

Design 92538

Units	Single
Price Code	F
Total Finished	2,733 sq. ft.
Main Finished	2,733 sq. ft.
Garage Unfinished	569 sq. ft.
Dimensions	70'10"x67'4"
Foundation	Crawlspace Slab
Bedrooms	4
Full Baths	3
Main Ceiling	9'
Max Ridge Height	28'
Roof Framing	Stick
Exterior Walls	2x4

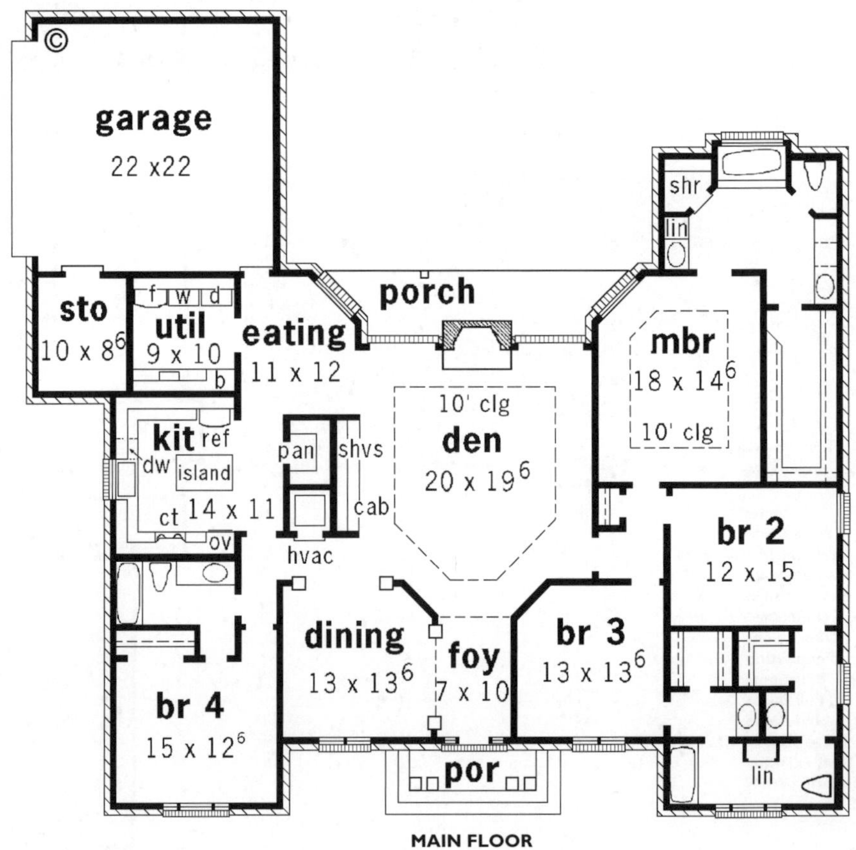

©
garage
22 x22
shr
lin
porch
sto
10 x 8⁶
f w d
util
9 x 10
b
eating
11 x 12
mbr
18 x 14⁶
10' clg
10' clg
den
20 x 19⁶
kit ref
dw
island
ct 14 x 11
ov
pan
shvs
cab
hvac
br 2
12 x 15
dining
13 x 13⁶
foy
7 x 10
br 3
13 x 13⁶
br 4
15 x 12⁶
por
lin

MAIN FLOOR

Design 94112

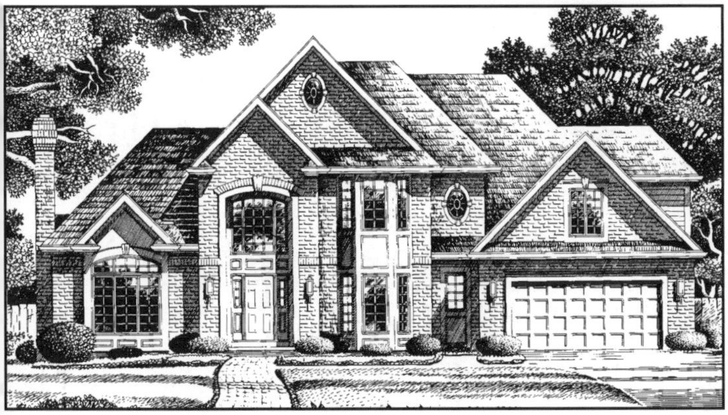

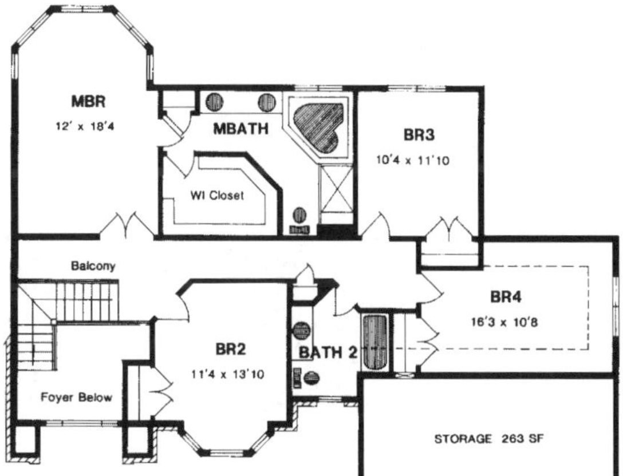

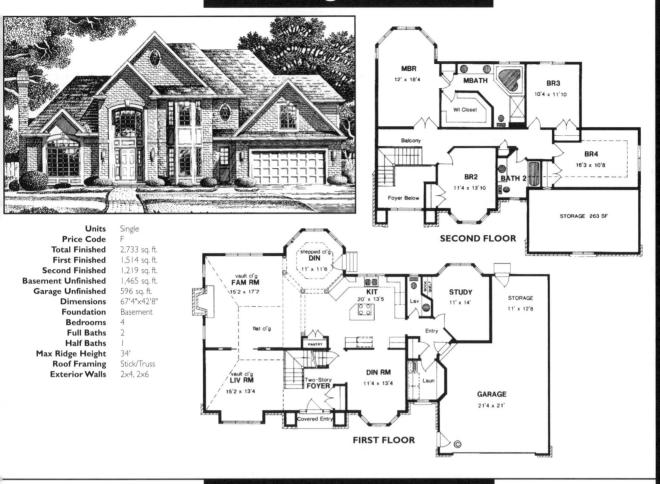

Units	Single
Price Code	F
Total Finished	2,733 sq. ft.
First Finished	1,514 sq. ft.
Second Finished	1,219 sq. ft.
Basement Unfinished	1,465 sq. ft.
Garage Unfinished	596 sq. ft.
Dimensions	67'4"x42'8"
Foundation	Basement
Bedrooms	4
Full Baths	2
Half Baths	1
Max Ridge Height	34'
Roof Framing	Stick/Truss
Exterior Walls	2x4, 2x6

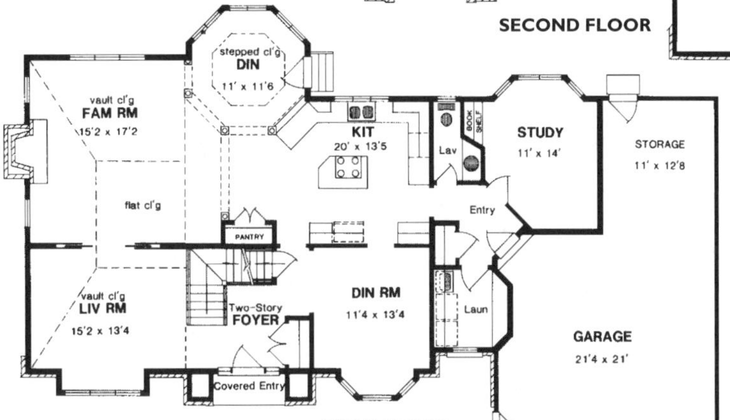

Design 96912

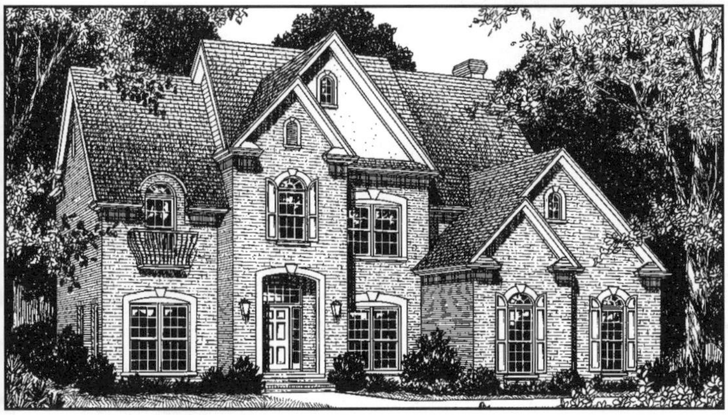

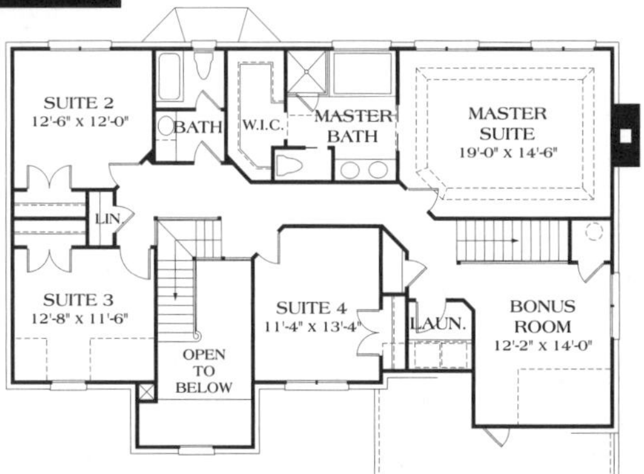

Units	Single
Price Code	F
Total Finished	2,741 sq. ft.
First Finished	1,426 sq. ft.
Second Finished	1,315 sq. ft.
Bonus Unfinished	200 sq. ft.
Garage Unfinished	508 sq. ft.
Deck Unfinished	223 sq. ft.
Porch Unfinished	44 sq. ft.
Dimensions	57'8"x44'10"
Foundation	Crawlspace
Bedrooms	4
Full Baths	2
Half Baths	1
Max Ridge Height	35'
Roof Framing	Stick
Exterior Walls	2x4

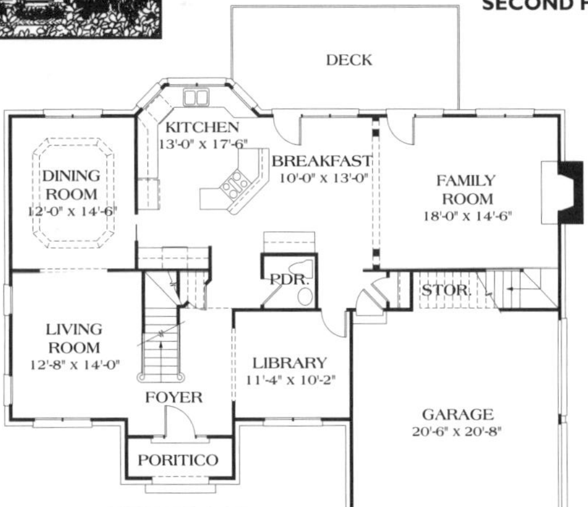

Design 65652

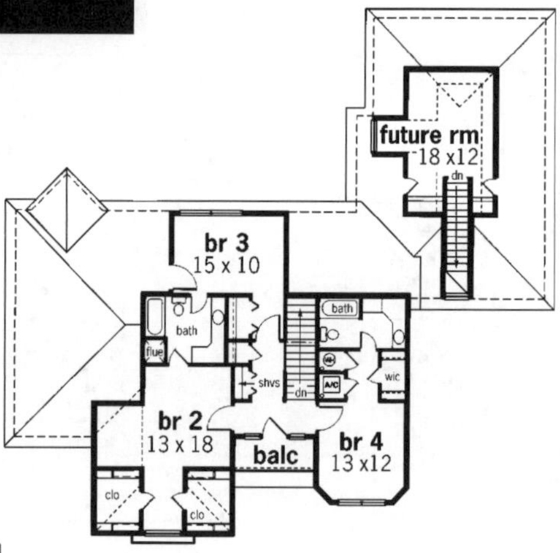

Units	Single
Price Code	F
Total Finished	2,743 sq. ft.
First Finished	1,707 sq. ft.
Second Finished	1,036 sq. ft.
Dimensions	67'x64'
Foundation	Crawlspace Slab
Bedrooms	4
Full Baths	3
Half Baths	1
First Ceiling	9'
Second Ceiling	9'
Max Ridge Height	32'
Roof Framing	Stick
Exterior Walls	2x6

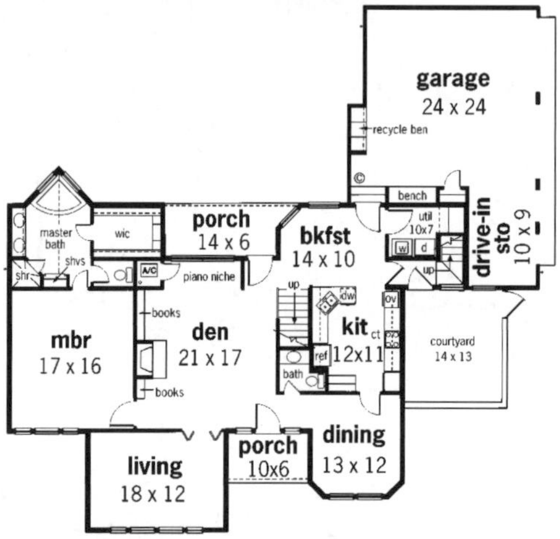

SECOND FLOOR

FIRST FLOOR

Design 66102

Units	Single
Price Code	F
Total Finished	2,744 sq. ft.
Main Finished	2,744 sq. ft.
Garage Unfinished	690 sq. ft.
Dimensions	66'6"x74'6"
Foundation	Slab
Bedrooms	3
Full Baths	2
Main Ceiling	9'-11'
Max Ridge Height	34'
Roof Framing	Stick
Exterior Walls	2x4

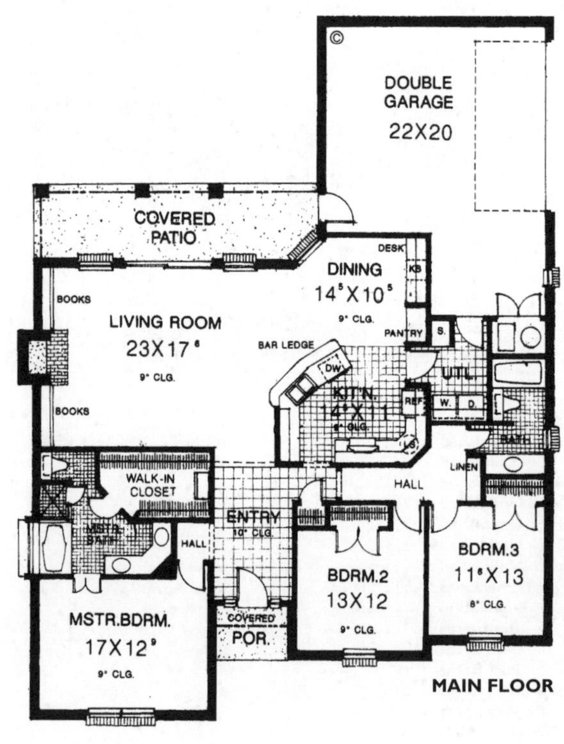
DOUBLE GARAGE
22X20
COVERED PATIO
DINING
LIVING ROOM
23X17
BOOKS
BAR LEDGE
PANTRY
UTL
HALL
LINEN
WALK-IN CLOSET
ENTRY
10' CLG.
BDRM.2
13X12
BDRM.3
MSTR.BDRM.
COVERED POR.

MAIN FLOOR

Design 93629

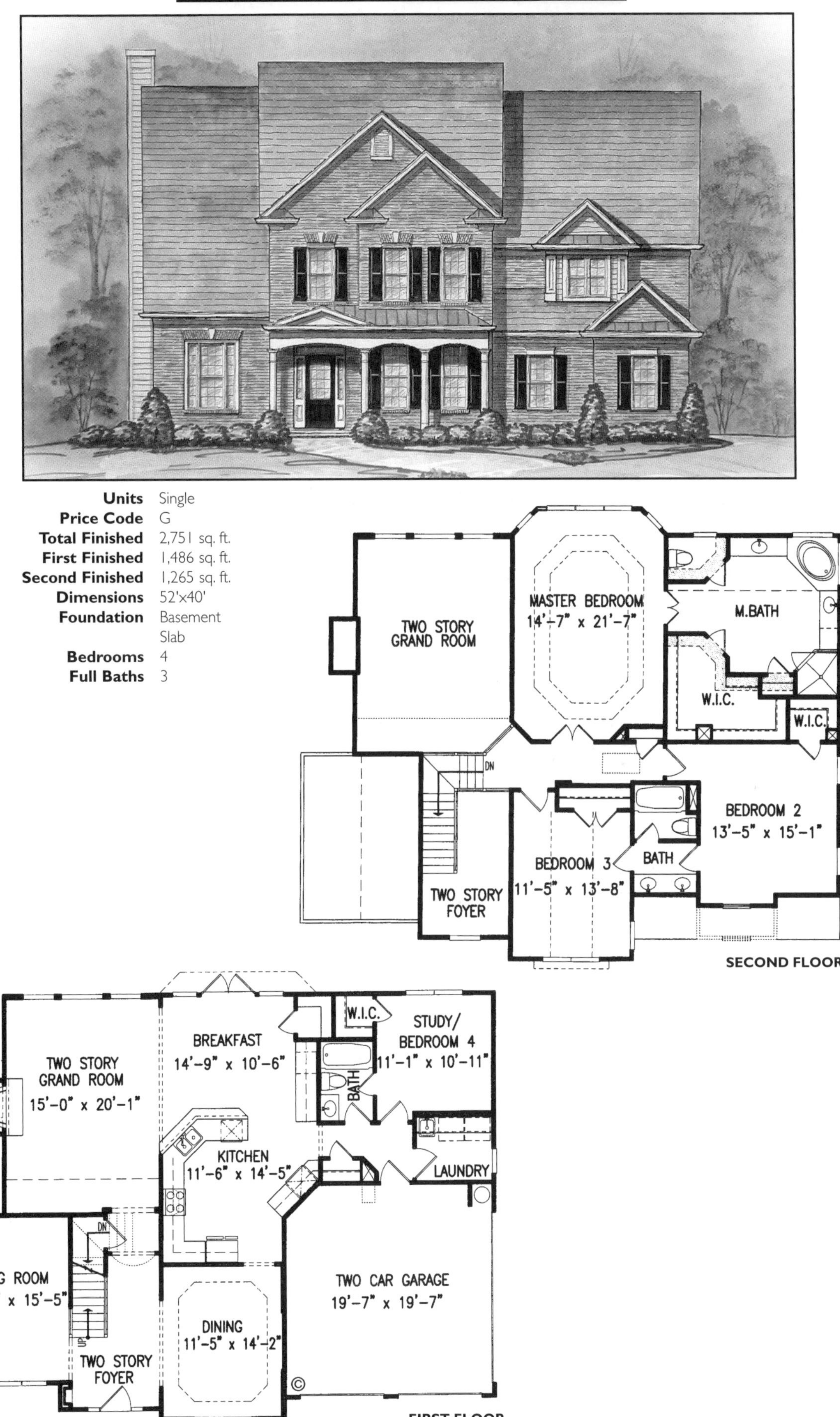
TWO STORY
GRAND ROOM
MASTER BEDROOM
14'-7" x 21'-7"
M.BATH
W.I.C.
W.I.C.
DN
BEDROOM 2
13'-5" x 15'-1"
BATH
BEDROOM 3
11'-5" x 13'-8"
TWO STORY
FOYER
SECOND FLOOR
BREAKFAST
14'-9" x 10'-6"
W.I.C.
STUDY/
BEDROOM 4
11'-1" x 10'-11"
BATH
TWO STORY
GRAND ROOM
15'-0" x 20'-1"
KITCHEN
11'-6" x 14'-5"
LAUNDRY
DN
LIVING ROOM
11'-1" x 15'-5"
UP
TWO STORY
FOYER
DINING
11'-5" x 14'-2"
TWO CAR GARAGE
19'-7" x 19'-7"
FIRST FLOOR

Units	Single
Price Code	G
Total Finished	2,751 sq. ft.
First Finished	1,486 sq. ft.
Second Finished	1,265 sq. ft.
Dimensions	52'x40'
Foundation	Basement Slab
Bedrooms	4
Full Baths	3

Design 63018

Units	Single
Price Code	G
Total Finished	2,755 sq. ft.
Main Finished	2,755 sq. ft.
Bonus Unfinished	440 sq. ft.
Garage Unfinished	724 sq. ft.
Porch Unfinished	419 sq. ft.
Dimensions	73'x82'8"
Foundation	Slab
Bedrooms	4
Full Baths	2
3/4 Baths	1
Max Ridge Height	22'
Roof Framing	Truss

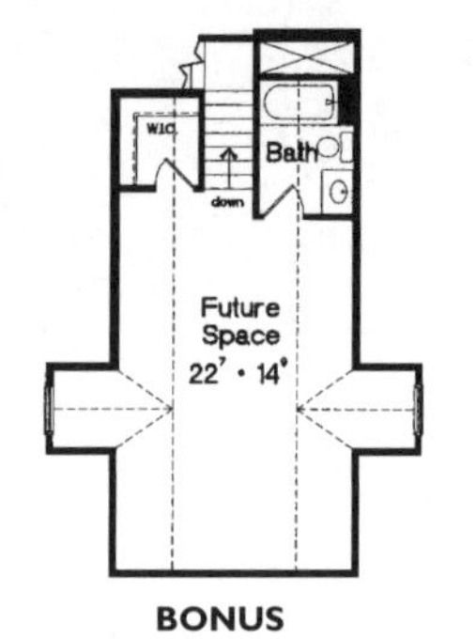

W.I.C.
Bath
down
Future Space
22' • 14'

BONUS

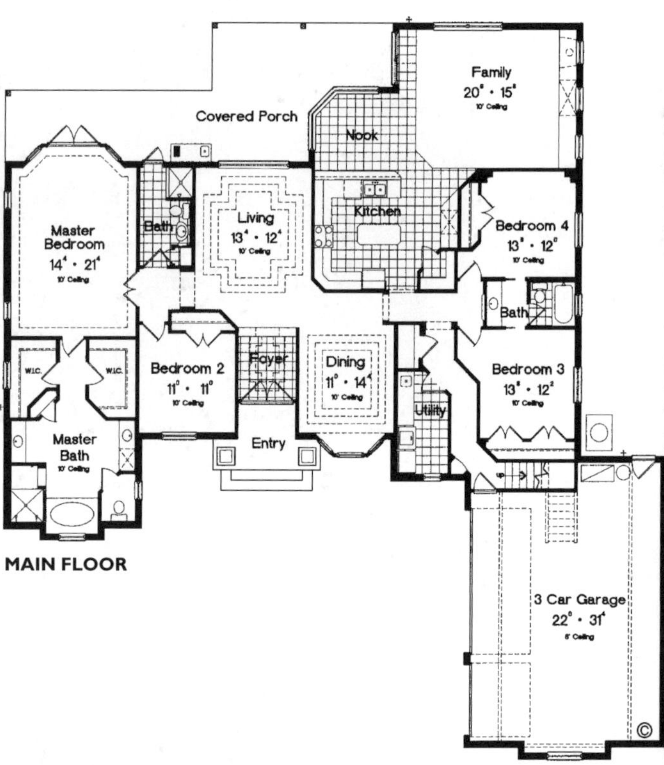

Family
20' • 15'
Covered Porch
Nook
Kitchen
Living
13' • 12'
Bath
Master Bedroom
14' • 21'
Bedroom 4
13' • 12'
Bath
Bedroom 3
13' • 12'
Dining
11' • 14'
Foyer
Bedroom 2
11' • 11'
W.I.C.
W.I.C.
Master Bath
Entry
Utility
3 Car Garage
22' • 31'

MAIN FLOOR

Design 94660

Units	Single
Price Code	G
Total Finished	2,763 sq. ft.
Main Finished	2,763 sq. ft.
Dimensions	64'4"x72'11"
Foundation	Slab
Bedrooms	4
Full Baths	3
Main Ceiling	9'
Roof Framing	Stick
Exterior Walls	2x4

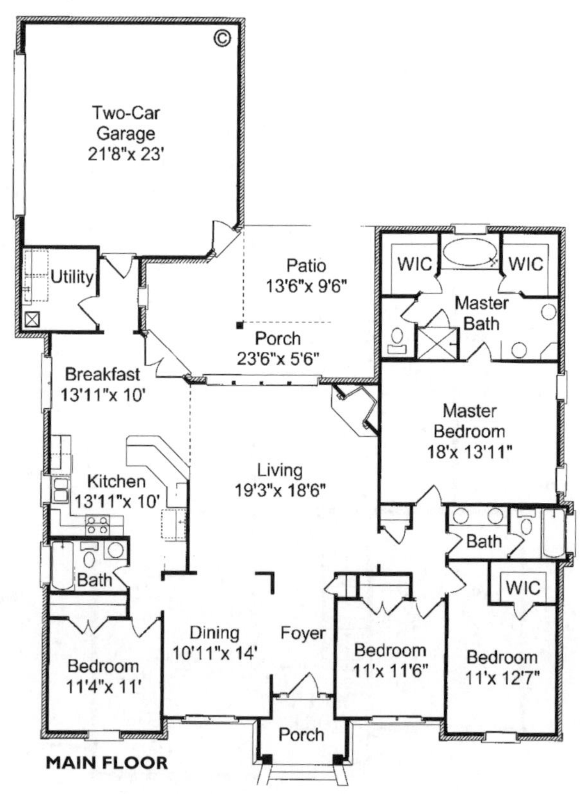

Two-Car Garage
21'8"x 23'
Utility
Patio
13'6"x 9'6"
WIC
WIC
Master Bath
Porch
23'6"x 5'6"
Breakfast
13'11"x 10'
Master Bedroom
18'x 13'11"
Kitchen
13'11"x 10'
Living
19'3"x 18'6"
Bath
Bath
WIC
Dining
10'11"x 14'
Foyer
Bedroom
11'4"x 11'
Bedroom
11'x 11'6"
Bedroom
11'x 12'7"
Porch

MAIN FLOOR

Design 98987

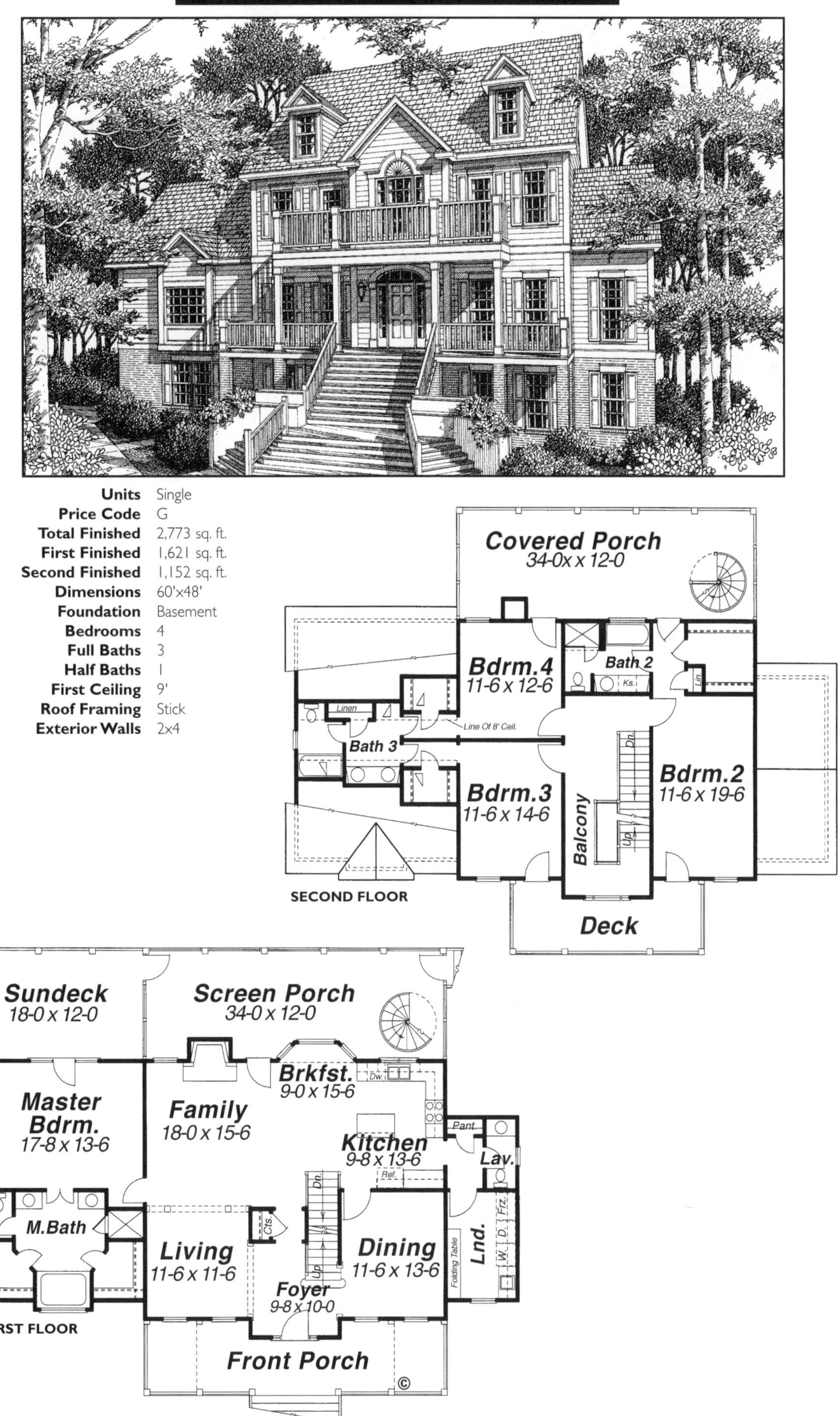
Covered Porch
34-0x x 12-0
Bdrm.4
11-6 x 12-6
Bath 2
Ks.
Lin.
Linen
Line Of 8' Ceil.
Bath 3
Dn.
Bdrm.3
11-6 x 14-6
Bdrm.2
11-6 x 19-6
Balcony
Up
SECOND FLOOR
Deck
Sundeck
18-0 x 12-0
Screen Porch
34-0 x 12-0
Brkfst.
9-0 x 15-6
Dw.
Master
Bdrm.
17-8 x 13-6
Family
18-0 x 15-6
Kitchen
9-8 x 13-6
Pant.
Lav.
Ref.
M.Bath
Cts.
Dn.
Up
Living
11-6 x 11-6
Dining
11-6 x 13-6
Folding Table
Lnd.
W.
D.
Frz.
Foyer
9-8 x 10-0
FIRST FLOOR
Front Porch
©

Units	Single
Price Code	G
Total Finished	2,773 sq. ft.
First Finished	1,621 sq. ft.
Second Finished	1,152 sq. ft.
Dimensions	60'x48'
Foundation	Basement
Bedrooms	4
Full Baths	3
Half Baths	1
First Ceiling	9'
Roof Framing	Stick
Exterior Walls	2x4

Design 96910

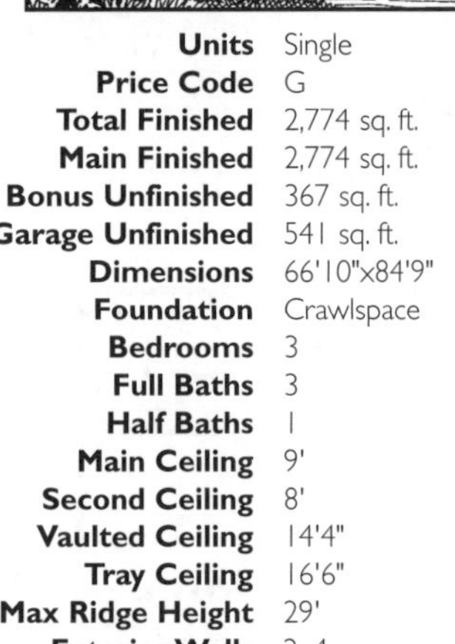

Units	Single
Price Code	G
Total Finished	2,774 sq. ft.
Main Finished	2,774 sq. ft.
Bonus Unfinished	367 sq. ft.
Garage Unfinished	541 sq. ft.
Dimensions	66'10"x84'9"
Foundation	Crawlspace
Bedrooms	3
Full Baths	3
Half Baths	1
Main Ceiling	9'
Second Ceiling	8'
Vaulted Ceiling	14'4"
Tray Ceiling	16'6"
Max Ridge Height	29'
Exterior Walls	2x4

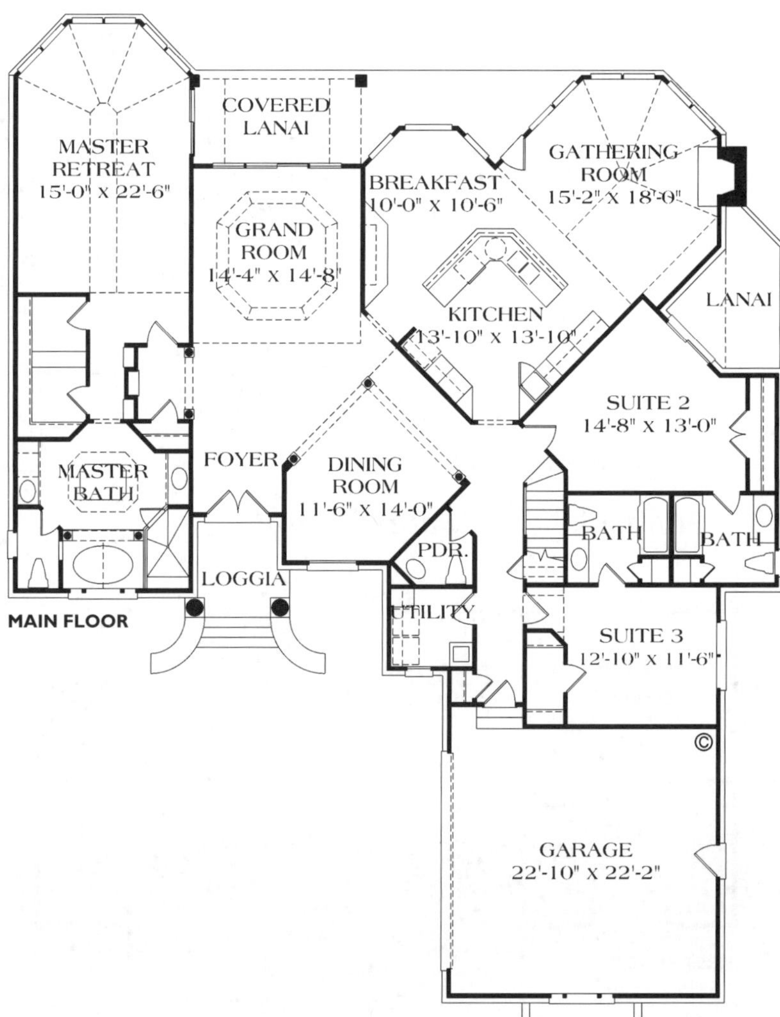

COVERED LANAI
MASTER RETREAT 15'-0" x 22'-6"
GRAND ROOM 14'-4" x 14'-8"
BREAKFAST 10'-0" x 10'-6"
GATHERING ROOM 15'-2" x 18'-0"
KITCHEN 13'-10" x 13'-10"
LANAI
SUITE 2 14'-8" x 13'-0"
FOYER
DINING ROOM 11'-6" x 14'-0"
MASTER BATH
BATH
BATH
PDR.
LOGGIA
UTILITY
SUITE 3 12'-10" x 11'-6"
GARAGE 22'-10" x 22'-2"
MAIN FLOOR

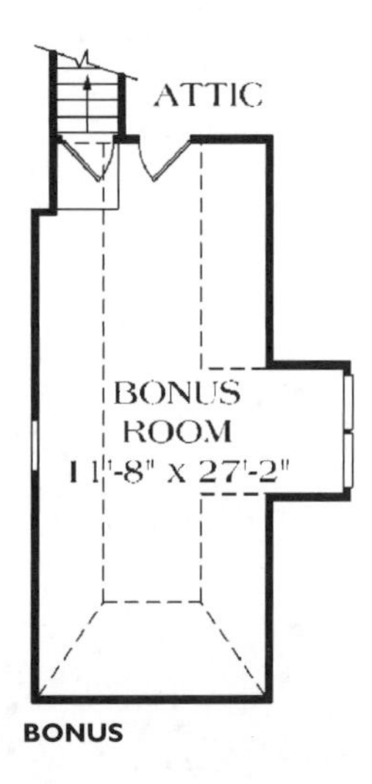

ATTIC
BONUS ROOM 11'-8" x 27'-2"
BONUS

Design 99446

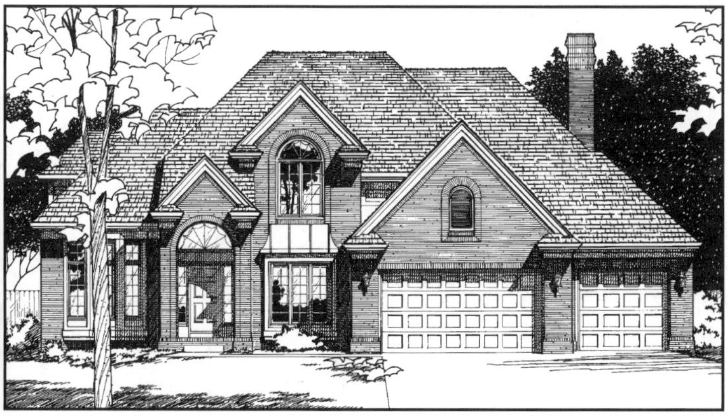

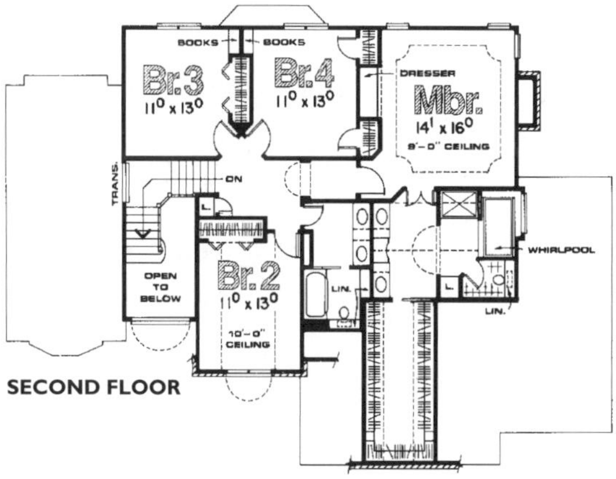

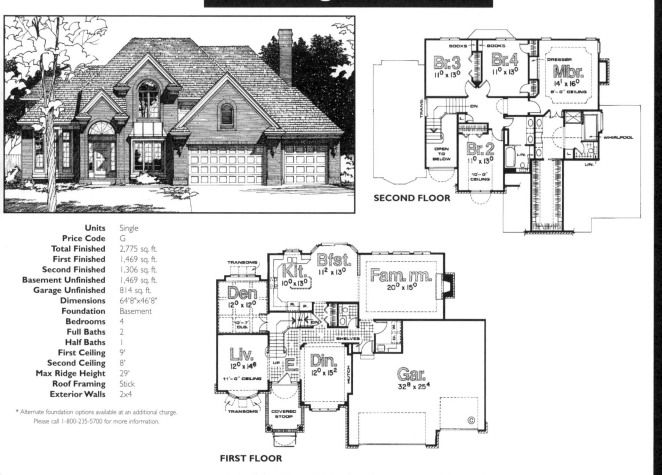

SECOND FLOOR

FIRST FLOOR

Units	Single
Price Code	G
Total Finished	2,775 sq. ft.
First Finished	1,469 sq. ft.
Second Finished	1,306 sq. ft.
Basement Unfinished	1,469 sq. ft.
Garage Unfinished	814 sq. ft.
Dimensions	64'8"x46'8"
Foundation	Basement
Bedrooms	4
Full Baths	2
Half Baths	1
First Ceiling	9'
Second Ceiling	8'
Max Ridge Height	29'
Roof Framing	Stick
Exterior Walls	2x4

* Alternate foundation options available at an additional charge. Please call 1-800-235-5700 for more information.

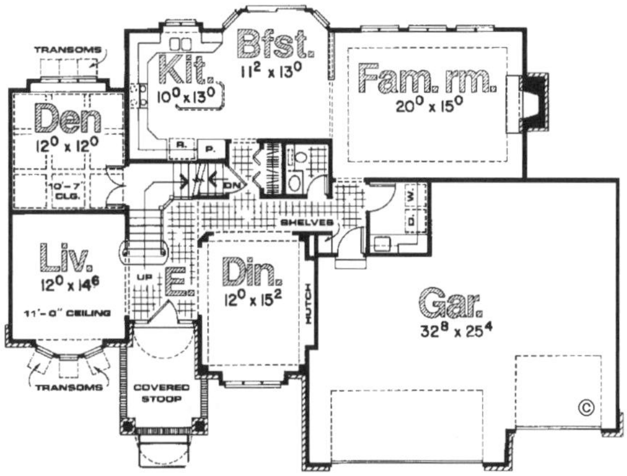

Design 10805

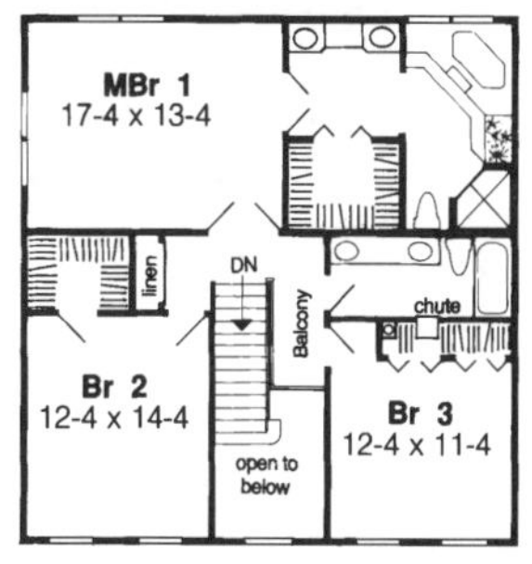
MBr 1
17-4 x 13-4
DN
linen
Balcony
chute
Br 2
12-4 x 14-4
Br 3
12-4 x 11-4
open to below

SECOND FLOOR

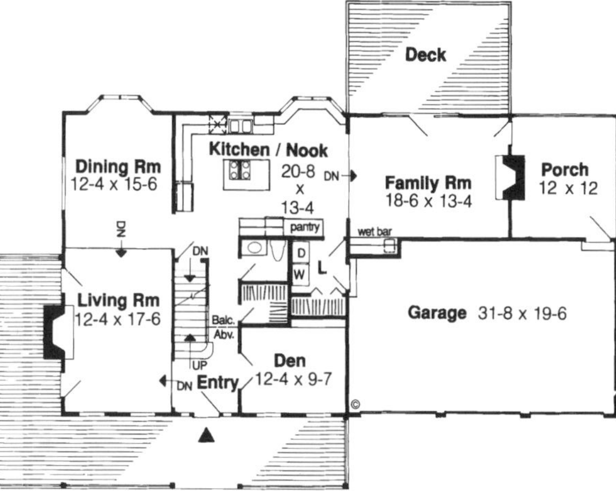
Deck
Dining Rm
12-4 x 15-6
Kitchen / Nook
20-8 x 13-4
DN
pantry
Family Rm
18-6 x 13-4
Porch
12 x 12
wet bar
D
W
Living Rm
12-4 x 17-6
Balc. Abv.
Garage 31-8 x 19-6
Den
12-4 x 9-7
UP
DN
Entry

FIRST FLOOR

Units	Single
Price Code	G
Total Finished	2,778 sq. ft.
First Finished	1,622 sq. ft.
Second Finished	1,156 sq. ft.
Dimensions	74'x43'6"
Foundation	Basement
Bedrooms	3
Full Baths	2
Half Baths	1
First Ceiling	8'
Second Ceiling	8'
Max Ridge Height	28'
Roof Framing	Truss
Exterior Walls	2x6

Design 60052

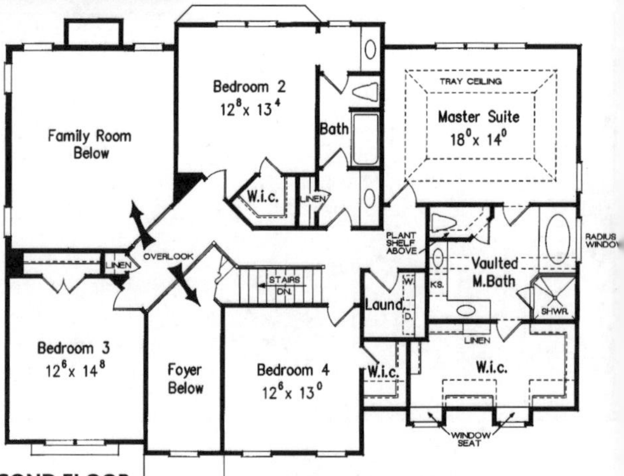

Units	Single
Price Code	G
Total Finished	2,778 sq. ft.
First Finished	1,279 sq. ft.
Second Finished	1,499 sq. ft.
Bonus Unfinished	240 sq. ft.
Basement Unfinished	1,279 sq. ft.
Garage Unfinished	660 sq. ft.
Dimensions	53'x46'6"
Foundation	Basement Crawlspace
Bedrooms	4
Full Baths	2
Half Baths	1
First Ceiling	9'
Second Ceiling	8'
Exterior Walls	2x4

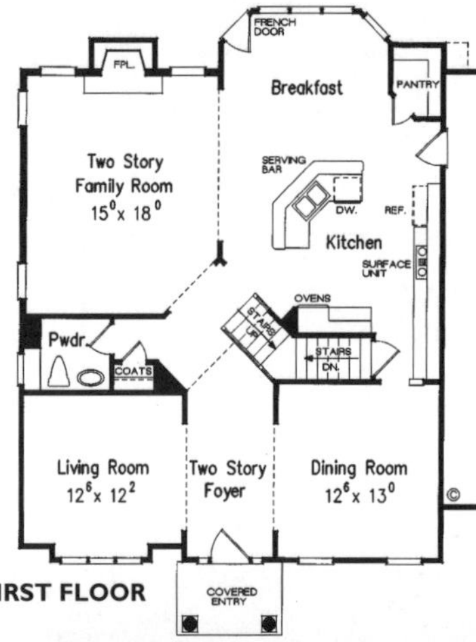

SECOND FLOOR

CAD FILES AVAILABLE For more information call 800-235-5700

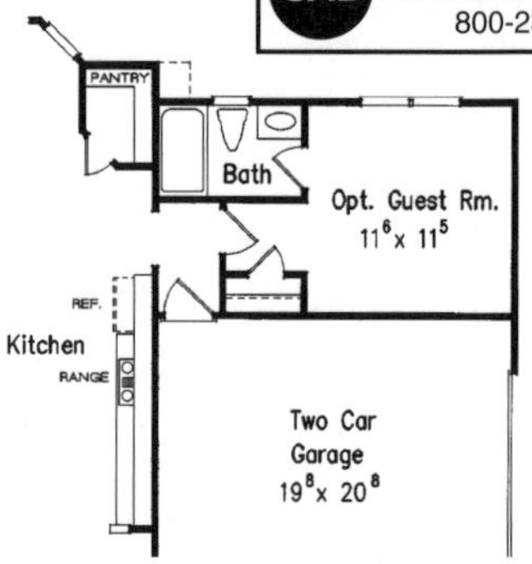

FIRST FLOOR

OPTIONAL FIFTH BEDROOM WITH TWO-CAR GARAGE

Design 32145

PHOTOGRAPHY: RICHARD SEXTON

Units	Single
Price Code	G
Total Finished	2,780 sq. ft.
Main Finished	2,780 sq. ft.
Basement Unfinished	523 sq. ft.
Dimensions	67'x71'
Foundation	Slab
Bedrooms	3
Full Baths	2
Half Baths	1
Main Ceiling	10'
Vaulted Ceiling	18'6"
Max Ridge Height	21'6"
Roof Framing	Stick
Exterior Walls	2x4

Please note: The photographed home may have been modified to suit homeowner preferences. If you order plans, have a builder or design professional check them against the photograph to confirm actual construction details.

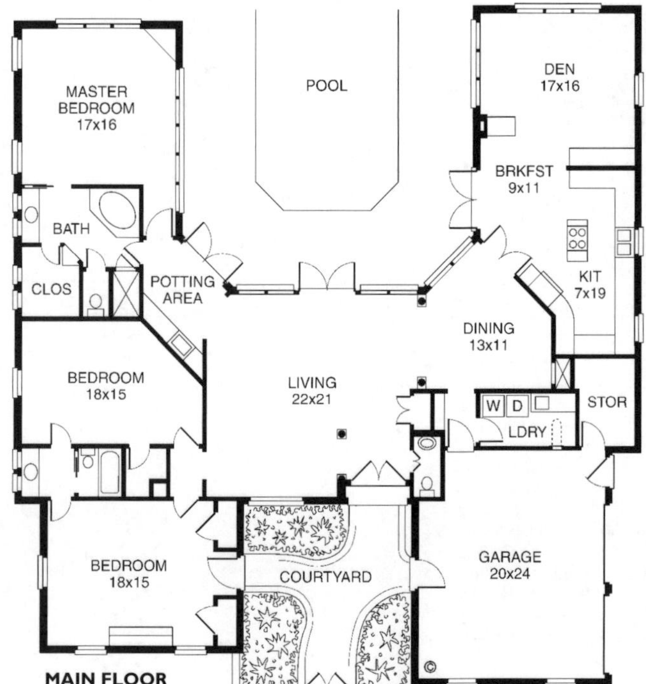
MASTER BEDROOM 17x16
POOL
DEN 17x16
BRKFST 9x11
BATH
KIT 7x19
CLOS
POTTING AREA
DINING 13x11
BEDROOM 18x15
LIVING 22x21
STOR
LDRY
BEDROOM 18x15
COURTYARD
GARAGE 20x24

MAIN FLOOR

Design 91855

Units	Single
Price Code	G
Total Finished	2,781 sq. ft.
First Finished	1,370 sq. ft.
Second Finished	1,411 sq. ft.
Bonus Unfinished	410 sq. ft.
Basement Unfinished	850 sq. ft.
Garage Unfinished	808 sq. ft.
Deck Unfinished	321 sq. ft.
Porch Unfinished	96 sq. ft.
Dimensions	52'x40'
Foundation	Basement
Bedrooms	4
Full Baths	2
Half Baths	1
First Ceiling	9'
Max Ridge Height	37'9"
Roof Framing	Truss
Exterior Walls	2x4

BDRM 3
12/0 x 12/4
BDRM 2
11/8 x 12/8
SHOWER
VANITY
TUB
LIN
DOWN
BDRM 4
13/1 x 12/6
LAUNDRY
SITTING
8/7 x 10/5
MASTER
13/4 x 15/0

SECOND FLOOR

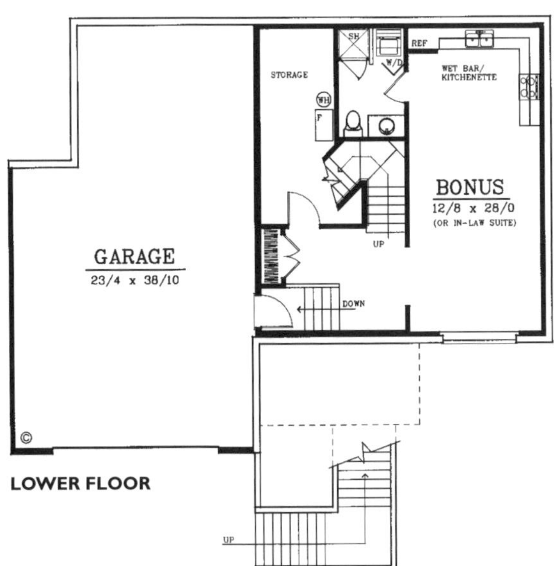
SH
REF
STORAGE
WH
W/D
WET BAR/
KITCHENETTE
BONUS
12/8 x 28/0
(OR IN-LAW SUITE)
UP
GARAGE
23/4 x 38/10
DOWN
UP

LOWER FLOOR

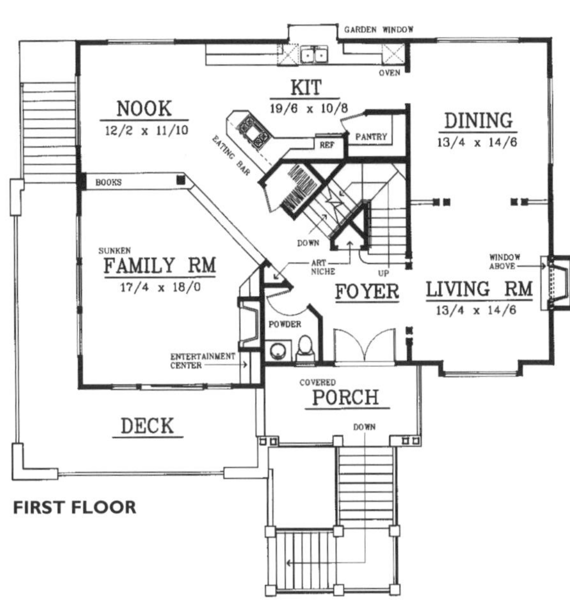
GARDEN WINDOW
OVEN
NOOK
12/2 x 11/10
KIT
19/6 x 10/8
EATING BAR
REF
PANTRY
DINING
13/4 x 14/6
BOOKS
SUNKEN
FAMILY RM
17/4 x 18/0
DOWN
ART
NICHE
UP
WINDOW
ABOVE
FOYER
LIVING RM
13/4 x 14/6
POWDER
ENTERTAINMENT
CENTER
COVERED
PORCH
DOWN
DECK

FIRST FLOOR

Design 93339

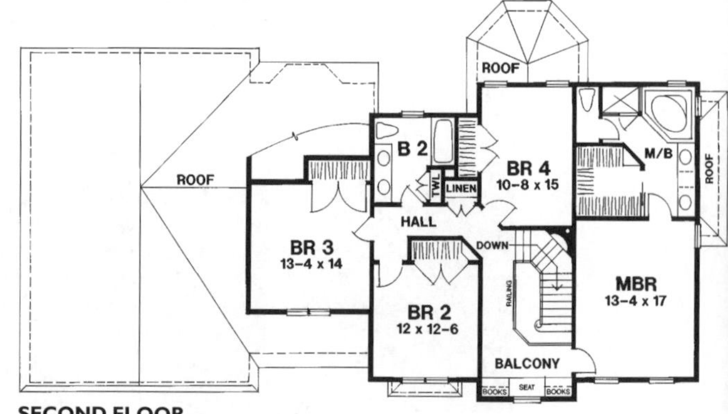
ROOF
ROOF
B 2
BR 4
10-8 x 15
M/B
ROOF
TWL
LINEN
HALL
BR 3
13-4 x 14
DOWN
BR 2
12 x 12-6
MBR
13-4 x 17
RAILING
BALCONY
BOOKS
SEAT
BOOKS

SECOND FLOOR

Units	Single
Price Code	G
Total Finished	2,781 sq. ft.
First Finished	1,536 sq. ft.
Second Finished	1,245 sq. ft.
Dimensions	75'x42'6"
Foundation	Basement
Bedrooms	4
Full Baths	2
Half Baths	1
Max Ridge Height	31'
Roof Framing	Stick
Exterior Walls	2x6

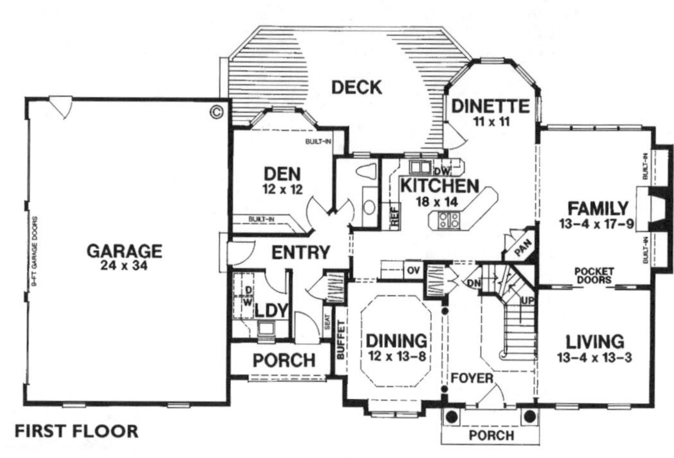
DECK
DINETTE
11 x 11
DEN
12 x 12
BUILT-IN
DW
KITCHEN
18 x 14
REF
FAMILY
13-4 x 17-9
BUILT-IN
GARAGE
24 x 34
9-FT GARAGE DOORS
ENTRY
PAN
OV
DN
POCKET DOORS
D W
LDY
SEAT
BUFFET
DINING
12 x 13-8
UP
LIVING
13-4 x 13-3
PORCH
FOYER
PORCH

FIRST FLOOR

Design 91134

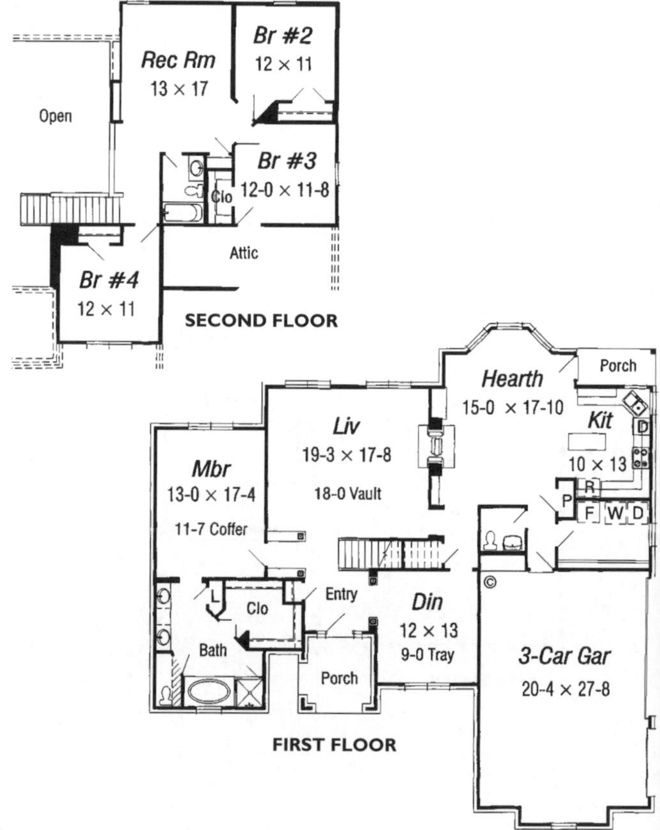
Rec Rm
13 × 17
Br #2
12 × 11
Open
Br #3
12-0 × 11-8
Clo
Attic
Br #4
12 × 11
Porch
Hearth
15-0 × 17-10
Liv
19-3 × 17-8
18-0 Vault
Kit
10 × 13
Mbr
13-0 × 17-4
11-7 Coffer
R
P
F
W
D
Entry
Clo
Din
12 × 13
9-0 Tray
Bath
Porch
3-Car Gar
20-4 × 27-8

SECOND FLOOR

FIRST FLOOR

Units	Single
Price Code	G
Total Finished	2,786 sq. ft.
First Finished	1,893 sq. ft.
Second Finished	893 sq. ft.
Garage Unfinished	632 sq. ft.
Porch Unfinished	120 sq. ft.
Dimensions	60'8"x59'8"
Foundation	Slab
Bedrooms	4
Full Baths	2
Half Baths	1
Max Ridge Height	29'10"
Roof Framing	Stick
Exterior Walls	2x4

Design 91476

Units	Single
Price Code	G
Total Finished	2,786 sq. ft.
Main Finished	2,786 sq. ft.
Garage Unfinished	445 sq. ft.
Dimensions	65'x75'
Foundation	Crawlspace
Bedrooms	3
Full Baths	2
Half Baths	1
Max Ridge Height	27'9"
Roof Framing	Truss
Exterior Walls	2x6

VAULTED MBR 19/8 X 15/0
WI CLO
WI CLO
M BATH
NOOK 12 X 10
COVERED PORCH
BI CABS
COFFERED FAM RM 15/8 X 19/2
BR 13 X 11
KIT
DW
BI CABS
BATH
DEN 12/6 X 11/0
PAN
R
LIN
GST
GALLERY HALL
BR 11/6 X 12/0
UTIL
W
D
ST
PDR
COFFERED DIN RM 13 X 14
FOYER
COFFERED LIV RM 12 X 14
GARAGE 19/8 X 22/8
COVERED PORCH

MAIN FLOOR

Design 91468

Units	Single
Price Code	G
Total Finished	2,800 sq. ft.
Main Finished	1,841 sq. ft.
Lower Finished	959 sq. ft.
Garage Unfinished	439 sq. ft.
Dimensions	55'x58'
Foundation	Basement
Bedrooms	4
Full Baths	3
Main Ceiling	9'
Second Ceiling	8'
Max Ridge Height	22'
Roof Framing	Stick
Exterior Walls	2x6

VIEW DECK
SITTING AREA
COFFERED GREAT RM 22 X 15/6
BRKFST ROOM 9 X 10
COFFERED MBR 16/6 X 13 AVG INC SITTING AREA
COLONADE
HER WI CLO
HIS WI CLO
SPA
M BATH
NICHE
PAN
KIT
GRDN WDW
GST
DOWN
PDR
VAULTED FOYER
UTIL
STORAGE
COFFERED DEN/BR 11 X 12
DIN RM 11 X 12
SHOP
LOGGIA
GARAGE 19/6 X 22/6 INC SHOP

MAIN FLOOR

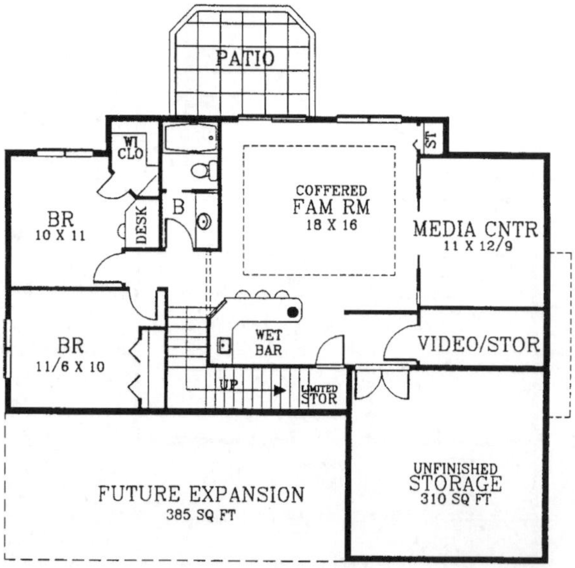

PATIO
WI CLO
BR 10 X 11
DESK
B
COFFERED FAM RM 18 X 16
MEDIA CNTR 11 X 12/9
BR 11/6 X 10
WET BAR
VIDEO/STOR
UP
LIMITED STOR
FUTURE EXPANSION 385 SQ FT
UNFINISHED STORAGE 310 SQ FT

LOWER FLOOR

Design 32044

PHOTOGRAPHY: JAMES YOCHUM PHOTOGRAPHY

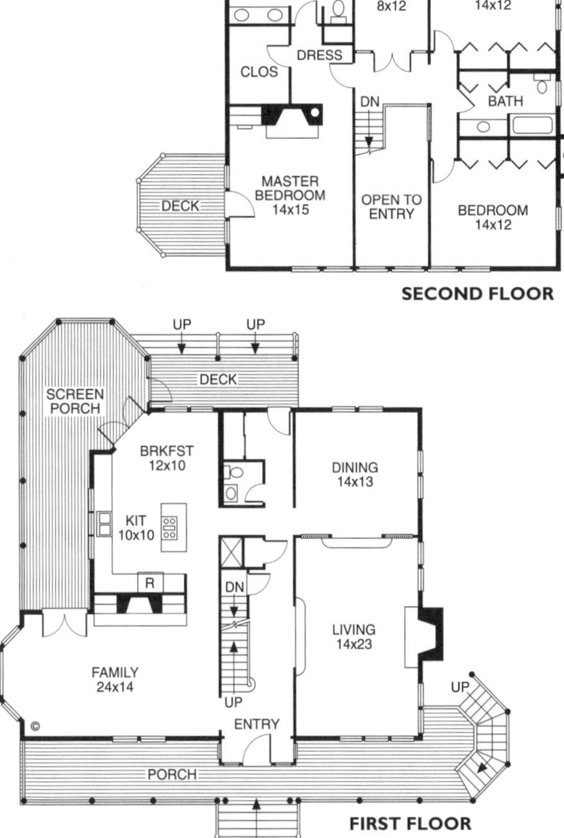
BATH
LIBRARY 8x12
BEDROOM 14x12
DRESS
CLOS
DN
BATH
DECK
MASTER BEDROOM 14x15
OPEN TO ENTRY
BEDROOM 14x12
SECOND FLOOR
UP
UP
DECK
SCREEN PORCH
BRKFST 12x10
DINING 14x13
KIT 10x10
R
DN
LIVING 14x23
FAMILY 24x14
UP
ENTRY
UP
PORCH
FIRST FLOOR

Units	Single
Price Code	G
Total Finished	2,804 sq. ft.
First Finished	1,615 sq. ft.
Second Finished	1,189 sq. ft.
Dimensions	58'6"x70'6"
Foundation	Basement
Bedrooms	3
Full Baths	2
Half Baths	1
Max Ridge Height	36'
Roof Framing	Stick
Exterior Walls	2x6

Please note: The photographed home may have been modified to suit homeowner preferences. If you order plans, have a builder or design professional check them against the photograph to confirm actual construction details.

Design 69011

Hot New Design

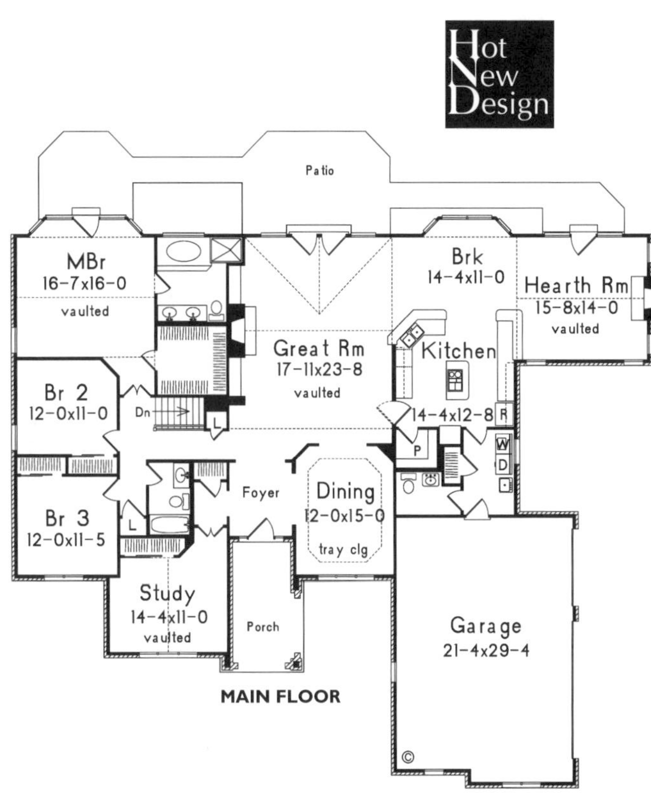
Patio
MBr 16-7x16-0 vaulted
Brk 14-4x11-0
Hearth Rm 15-8x14-0 vaulted
Great Rm 17-11x23-8 vaulted
Kitchen 14-4x12-8
Br 2 12-0x11-0
Dn
Foyer
Dining 12-0x15-0 tray clg
Br 3 12-0x11-5
Study 14-4x11-0 vaulted
Porch
Garage 21-4x29-4
MAIN FLOOR

Units	Single
Price Code	F
Total Finished	2,723 sq. ft.
Main Finished	2,723 sq. ft.
Dimensions	79'x64'2"
Foundation	Basement
Bedrooms	3
Full Baths	2
Half Baths	1

Design 66093

Units	Single
Price Code	F
Total Finished	2,828 sq. ft.
Main Finished	2,828 sq. ft.
Garage Unfinished	862 sq. ft.
Deck Unfinished	72 sq. ft.
Porch Unfinished	72 sq. ft.
Dimensions	74'x82'4"
Foundation	Slab
Bedrooms	4
Full Baths	2
3/4 Baths	1
Half Baths	1
Main Ceiling	9'
Max Ridge Height	32'
Roof Framing	Stick
Exterior Walls	2x4

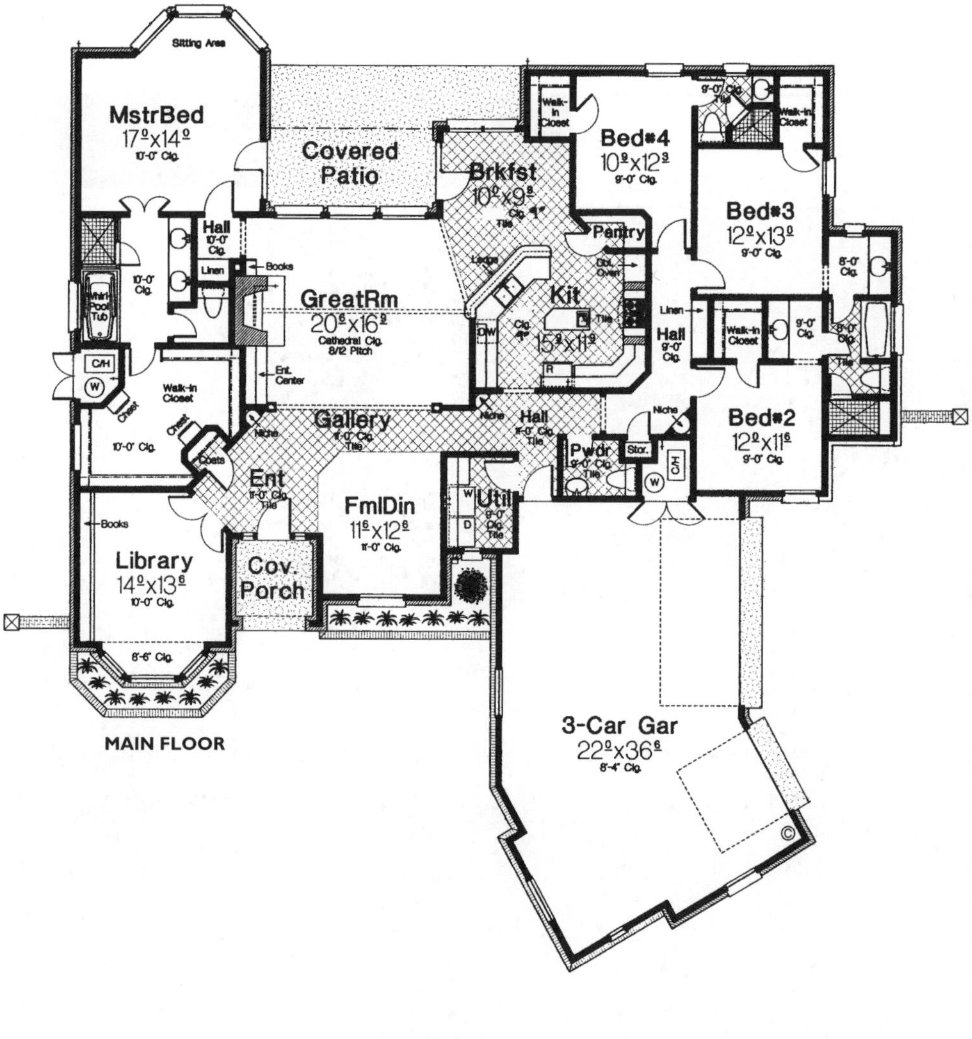

Sitting Area
MstrBed 17^{0}x14^{0} 10'-0" Clg.
Covered Patio
Brkfst 10^{0}x9^{8}
Bed#4 10^{0}x12^{3} 9'-0" Clg.
Bed#3 12^{0}x13^{0} 9'-0" Clg.
GreatRm 20^{8}x16^{2} Cathedral Clg. 8/12 Pitch
Kit 15^{9}x11^{0}
Pantry
Gallery
Hall
Bed#2 12^{0}x11^{6} 9'-0" Clg.
Ent
Pwdr
Util
FmlDin 11^{6}x12^{6} 11'-0" Clg.
Library 14^{0}x13^{6} 10'-0" Clg.
Cov. Porch
3-Car Gar 22^{0}x36^{6} 8'-4" Clg.

MAIN FLOOR

 To order blueprints, call **800-235-5700** or visit us on the web, **familyhomeplans.com**

Design 69005

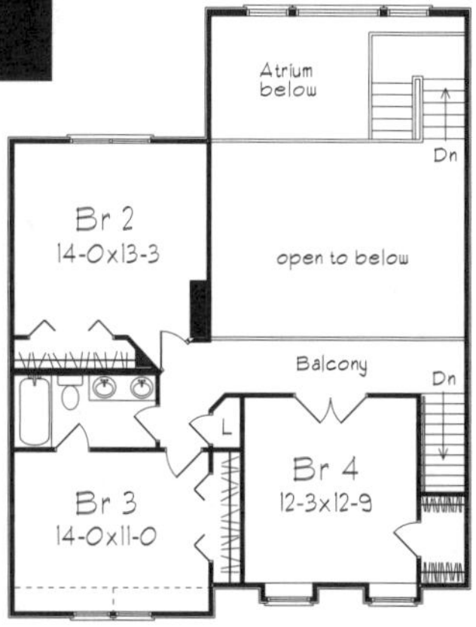

Units	Single
Price Code	G
Total Finished	2,806 sq. ft.
First Finished	1,473 sq. ft.
Second Finished	785 sq. ft.
Lower Finished	548 sq. ft.
Dimensions	54'8"x51'
Foundation	Basement
Bedrooms	4
Full Baths	2
Half Baths	1

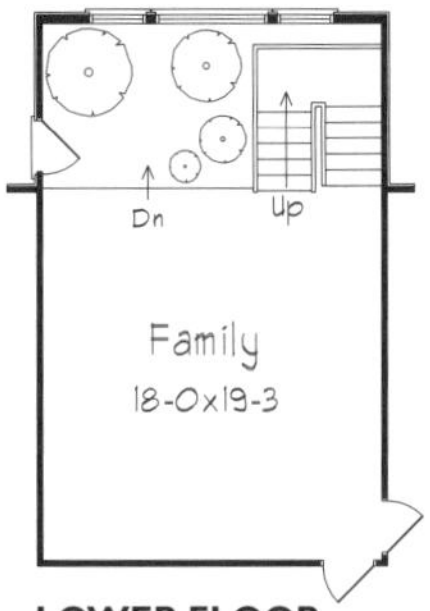

Atrium below
Dn
Br 2
14-0x13-3
open to below
Balcony
Dn
Br 3
14-0x11-0
Br 4
12-3x12-9
SECOND FLOOR
Atrium below
Deck
Dn
Dining
10-2x13-3
Kit
11-0x
13-3
Great Rm
18-0x19-10
vaulted
vaulted
Bar
MBr
14-0x16-9
Foyer
Up
Garage
21-4x21-4
Porch
FIRST FLOOR
Dn
Up
Family
18-0x19-3
LOWER FLOOR

Design 93034

PHOTOGRAPHY: COURTESY OF THE DESIGNER

Units	Single
Price Code	G
Total Finished	2,838 sq. ft.
First Finished	1,966 sq. ft.
Second Finished	872 sq. ft.
Garage Unfinished	569 sq. ft.
Dimensions	79'10"x63'10"
Foundation	Basement Crawlspace Slab
Bedrooms	5
Full Baths	3
First Ceiling	9'
Second Ceiling	8'
Max Ridge Height	29'6"
Roof Framing	Stick
Exterior Walls	2x4

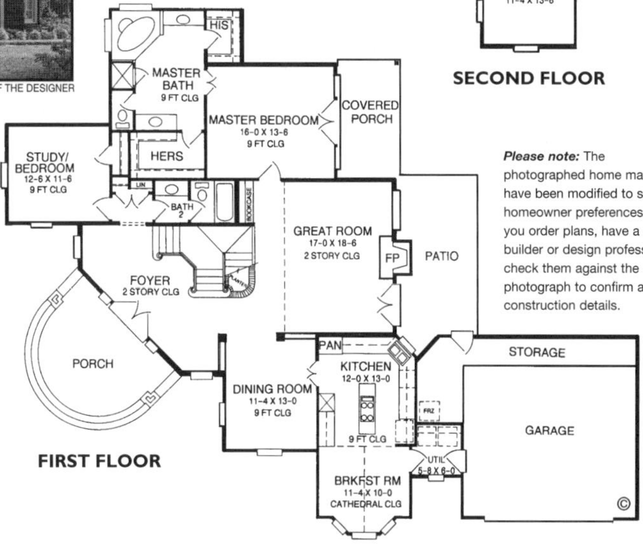

BEDROOM 3
12-6 X 12-6
BEDROOM 2
12-6 X 11-6
BATH 3
LIN
BALCONY
BALCONY
OPEN TO GREAT ROOM BELOW
OPEN TO FOYER BELOW
ATTIC
BEDROOM 4
11-4 X 13-6
SECOND FLOOR
HIS
MASTER BATH
9 FT CLG
MASTER BEDROOM
16-0 X 13-6
9 FT CLG
COVERED PORCH
HERS
STUDY/ BEDROOM
12-6 X 11-6
9 FT CLG
LIN
BATH 2
BOOKCASE
GREAT ROOM
17-0 X 18-6
2 STORY CLG
FP
PATIO
FOYER
2 STORY CLG
PORCH
PAN
KITCHEN
12-0 X 13-0
DINING ROOM
11-4 X 13-0
9 FT CLG
STORAGE
GARAGE
FRZ
9 FT CLG
UTIL
5-8 X 6-0
BRKFST RM
11-4 X 10-0
CATHEDRAL CLG
FIRST FLOOR

Please note: The photographed home may have been modified to suit homeowner preferences. If you order plans, have a builder or design professional check them against the photograph to confirm actual construction details.

Design 69007

Units	Single
Price Code	G
Total Finished	2,828 sq. ft.
First Finished	2,006 sq. ft.
Second Finished	822 sq. ft.
Dimensions	70'6"x55'6"
Foundation	Basement
Bedrooms	5
Full Baths	3
Half Baths	1

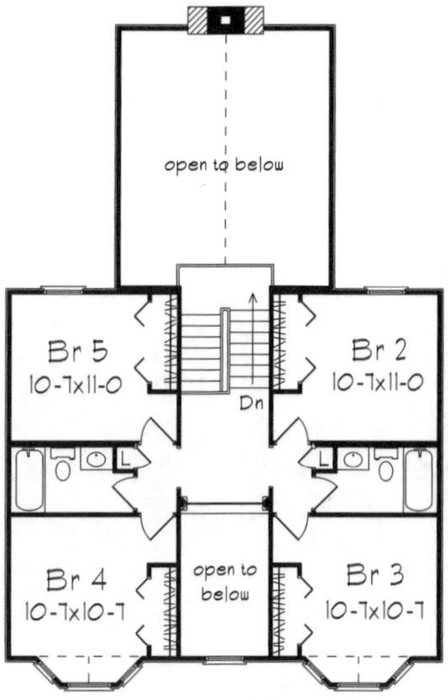

open to below
Br 5 10-7x11-0
Br 2 10-7x11-0
Dn
Br 4 10-7x10-7
open to below
Br 3 10-7x10-7

SECOND FLOOR

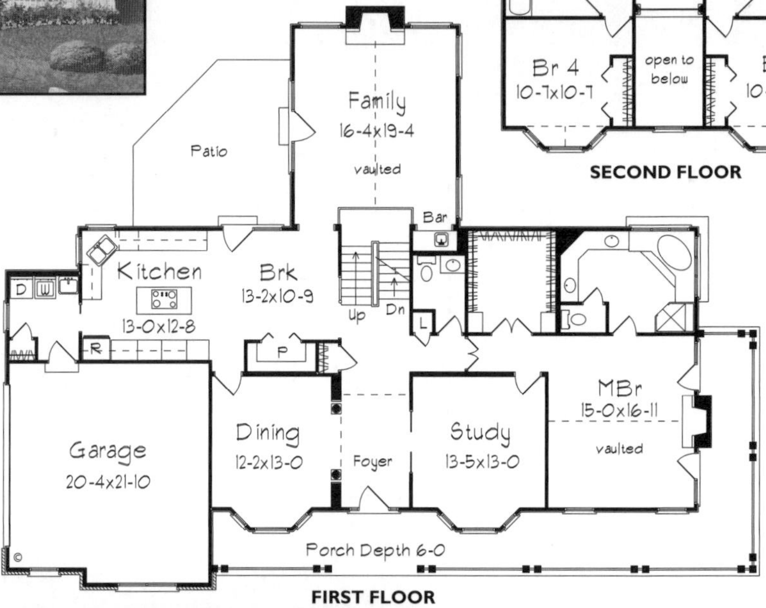

Family 16-4x19-4 vaulted
Patio
Bar
Kitchen 13-0x12-8
Brk 13-2x10-9
D W
R
P
Up Dn
L
Garage 20-4x21-10
Dining 12-2x13-0
Foyer
Study 13-5x13-0
MBr 15-0x16-11 vaulted
Porch Depth 6-0

FIRST FLOOR

Design 91169

Units	Single
Price Code	G
Total Finished	2,845 sq. ft.
First Finished	2,307 sq. ft.
Second Finished	538 sq. ft.
Garage Unfinished	486 sq. ft.
Porch Unfinished	430 sq. ft.
Dimensions	69'9½"x69'7½"
Bedrooms	4
Full Baths	3
Half Baths	1
First Ceiling	8'1⅛"
Second Ceiling	8'1⅛"
Max Ridge Height	26'
Exterior Walls	2x4

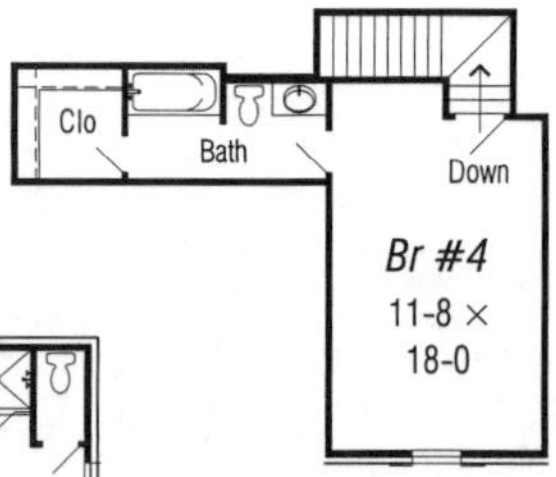

Clo
Bath
Down
Br #4 11-8 × 18-0

SECOND FLOOR

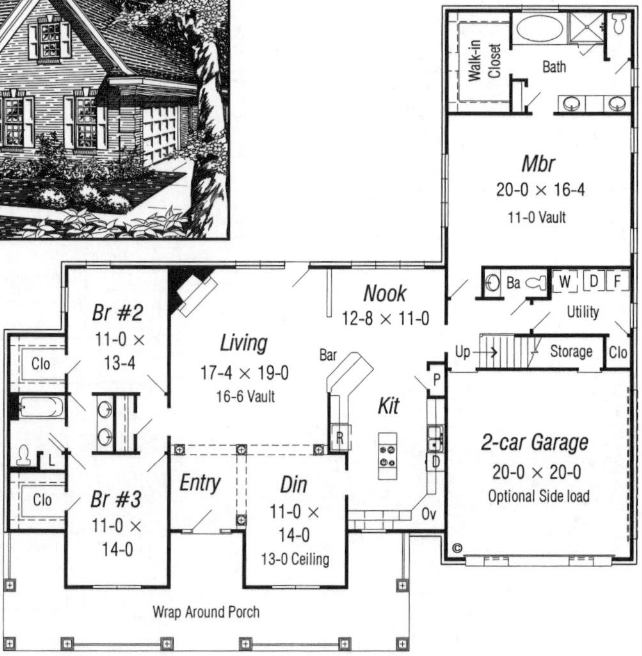

Walk-in Closet
Bath
Mbr 20-0 × 16-4 11-0 Vault
Br #2 11-0 × 13-4
Living 17-4 × 19-0 16-6 Vault
Nook 12-8 × 11-0
Ba W D F
Utility
Bar
Up
Storage
Clo
Kit
P
R
D
2-car Garage 20-0 × 20-0 Optional Side load
Clo
L
Br #3 11-0 × 14-0
Entry
Din 11-0 × 14-0 13-0 Ceiling
Ov
Wrap Around Porch

FIRST FLOOR

Design 20090

SECOND FLOOR
BEDROOM 11'-8"x15'-0"
BALCONY
RAILING
DN
LINEN
SKY LT.
B.
BEDROOM 11'-0" 13'-4"
C.
OPEN TO FOYER BELOW
SLOPE
BEDROOM 12'-4" 13'-4"
ATTIC ACCESS
FIRST FLOOR
Opt. DECK
MASTER BEDROOM 14'-10 x 15'-4"
7-1/2" CLG. RECESS
FAMILY ROOM 16'-8"x 23'-4"
10'-0" CEILING HEIGHT
BRKFST. 9'-0"x10'-6"
SKY LTS.
WALK
KITCHEN 13'-4"x 14'-0"
LAUN.
BALCONY ABOVE
P.R.
UP
DN
BOOKCASE
LIBRARY/ PARLOR 12'-6"x15'-4"
11'-0" CLG. HEIGHT
FOYER
DINING ROOM 12'-6"x 13'-4"
3-1/2" CLG. RECESS
GARAGE 22'-0"x22'-0"
PORCH
DRIVE
WALK

PHOTOGRAPHY: COURTESY OF THE DESIGNER

Units	Single
Price Code	G
Total Finished	2,851 sq. ft.
First Finished	1,933 sq. ft.
Second Finished	918 sq. ft.
Basement Unfinished	1,888 sq. ft.
Garage Unfinished	475 sq. ft.
Dimensions	62'8"x50'
Foundation	Basement Crawlspace Slab
Bedrooms	4
Full Baths	2
Half Baths	1
Max Ridge Height	32'
Roof Framing	Stick
Exterior Walls	2x6

Please note: The photographed home may have been modified to suit homeowner preferences. If you order plans, have a builder or design professional check them against the photograph to confirm actual construction details.

KITCHEN
LAUN.
OV.
W. D.
P.

OPTIONAL CRAWLSPACE/SLAB FOUNDATION

Design 94630

Units	Single
Price Code	G
Total Finished	2,852 sq. ft.
First Finished	1,730 sq. ft.
Second Finished	1,122 sq. ft.
Bonus Unfinished	270 sq. ft.
Porch Unfinished	553 sq. ft.
Dimensions	60'x67'6"
Foundation	Crawlspace Slab
Bedrooms	4
Full Baths	3
Half Baths	1
Max Ridge Height	32'10"
Roof Framing	Stick
Exterior Walls	2x4

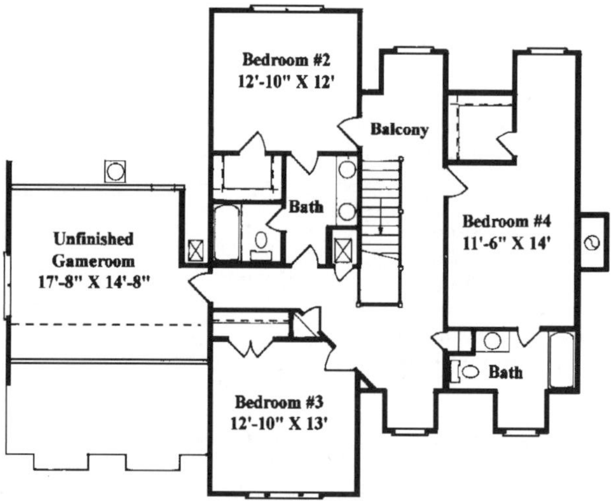

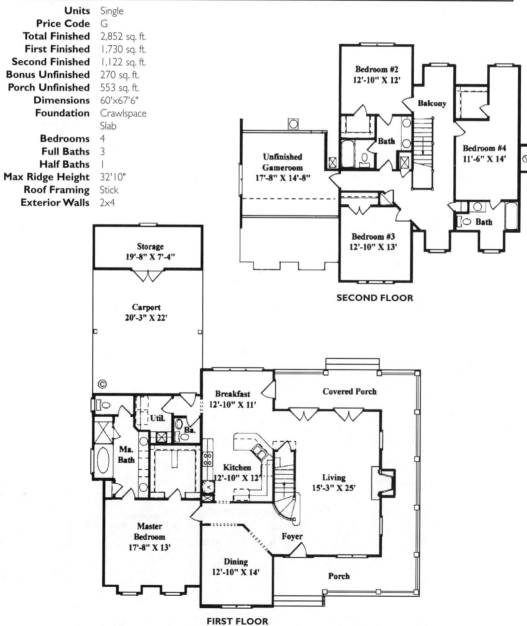

Bedroom #2
12'-10" X 12'

Balcony

Bath

Unfinished
Gameroom
17'-8" X 14'-8"

Bedroom #4
11'-6" X 14'

Bath

Bedroom #3
12'-10" X 13'

SECOND FLOOR

Storage
19'-8" X 7'-4"

Carport
20'-3" X 22'

Breakfast
12'-10" X 11'

Covered Porch

Util.

Ba.

Ma.
Bath

Kitchen
12'-10" X 12'

Living
15'-3" X 25'

Master
Bedroom
17'-8" X 13'

Foyer

Dining
12'-10" X 14'

Porch

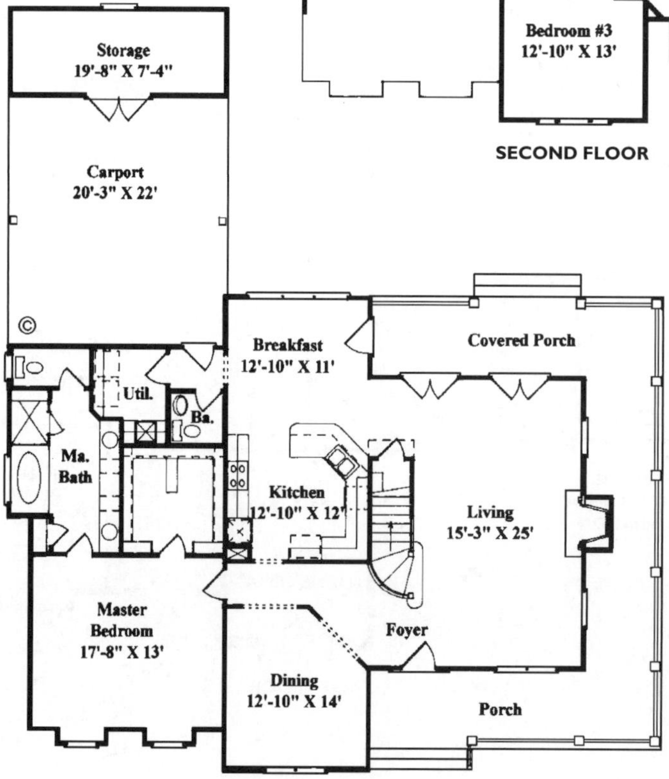

FIRST FLOOR

Design 97978

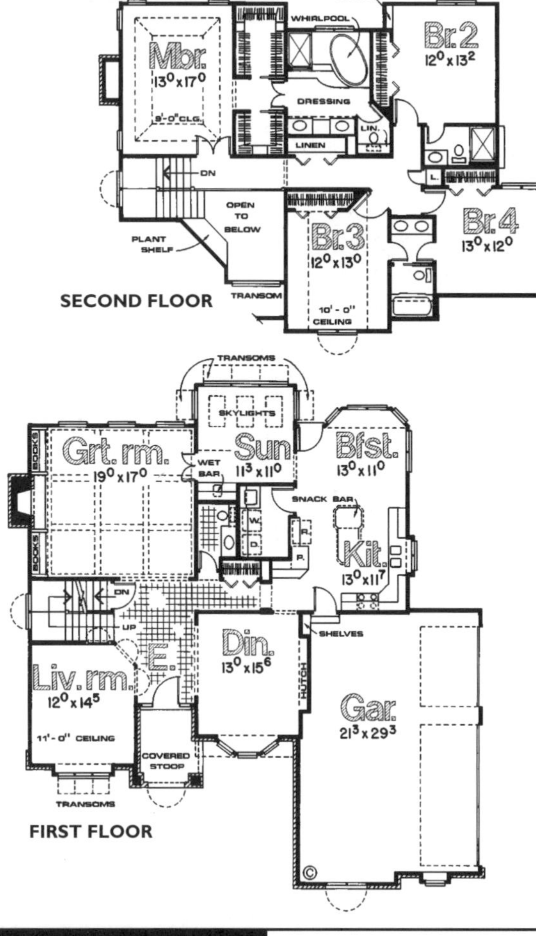
BOOKS
WHIRLPOOL
Mbr.
13^0x17^0
9'-0" CLG.
Br.2
12^0x13^2
DRESSING
LINEN
LIN.
DN
OPEN TO BELOW
Br.3
12^0x13^0
Br.4
13^0x12^0
PLANT SHELF
TRANSOM
10'-0" CEILING
SECOND FLOOR
TRANSOMS
SKYLIGHTS
Grt. rm.
19^0x17^0
WET BAR
Sun
11^3x11^0
Bfst.
13^0x11^0
SNACK BAR
Kit.
13^0x11^7
DN
UP
SHELVES
Din.
13^0x15^6
HUTCH
E.
Liv. rm.
12^0x14^5
11'-0" CEILING
COVERED STOOP
Gar.
21^3x29^3
TRANSOMS
FIRST FLOOR

Units	Single
Price Code	G
Total Finished	2,854 sq. ft.
First Finished	1,520 sq. ft.
Second Finished	1,334 sq. ft.
Garage Unfinished	649 sq. ft.
Dimensions	53'4"x56'8"
Foundation	Basement Crawlspace Slab
Bedrooms	4
Full Baths	2
3/4 Baths	1
Half Baths	1
First Ceiling	9'
Max Ridge Height	30'
Roof Framing	Stick
Exterior Walls	2x4

* Alternate foundation options available at an additional charge.
Please call 1-800-235-5700 for more information.

Design 52068

FILES AVAILABLE
CAD
For more information call
800-235-5700

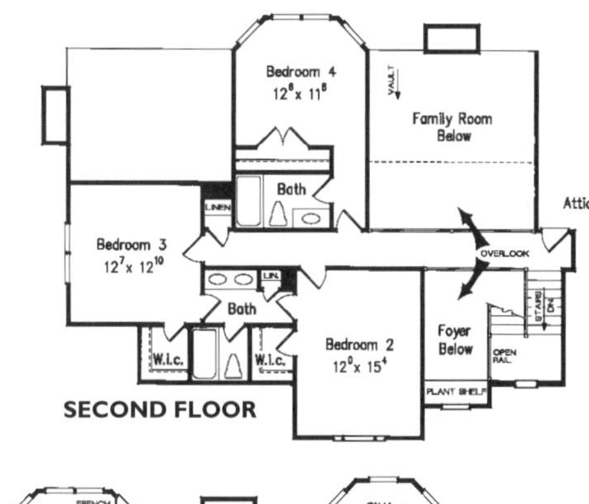
Bedroom 4
12^6 x 11^8
VAULT
Family Room Below
Bath
LINEN
Attic
Bedroom 3
12^7 x 12^{10}
OVERLOOK
Bath
LIN.
Bedroom 2
12^0 x 15^4
Foyer Below
W.I.c.
W.I.c.
PLANT SHELF
OPEN RAIL
SECOND FLOOR

FRENCH DOOR
Sitting
Vaulted Keeping Room
15^8 x 12^0
FP.
Breakfast
FP.
Vaulted Family Room
16^0 x 19^{10}
TRAY CEILING
Master Suite
13^0 x 19^4
SERVING BAR
OVENS
DW.
SURFACE UNIT
Kitchen
W.I.c.
Bath
FRENCH DOOR
COATS
SHWR.
DECORATIVE COLUMN
PANTRY
REF.
Bedroom 5
12^0 x 10^{10}
Laund.
Two Story Foyer
Vaulted M.Bath
Dining Room
12^0 x 12^{10}
LIN.
W.I.c.
Garage
21^6 x 21^9
Covered Porch
FIRST FLOOR

Units	Single
Price Code	F
Total Finished	2,858 sq. ft.
First Finished	1,967 sq. ft.
Second Finished	891 sq. ft.
Basement Unfinished	1,967 sq. ft.
Garage Unfinished	463 sq. ft.
Dimensions	60'10"x55'
Foundation	Combo/ Basement Crawlspace
Bedrooms	5
Full Baths	4
First Ceiling	9'
Second Ceiling	8'
Max Ridge Height	28'
Roof Framing	Stick
Exterior Walls	2x4

Design 92576

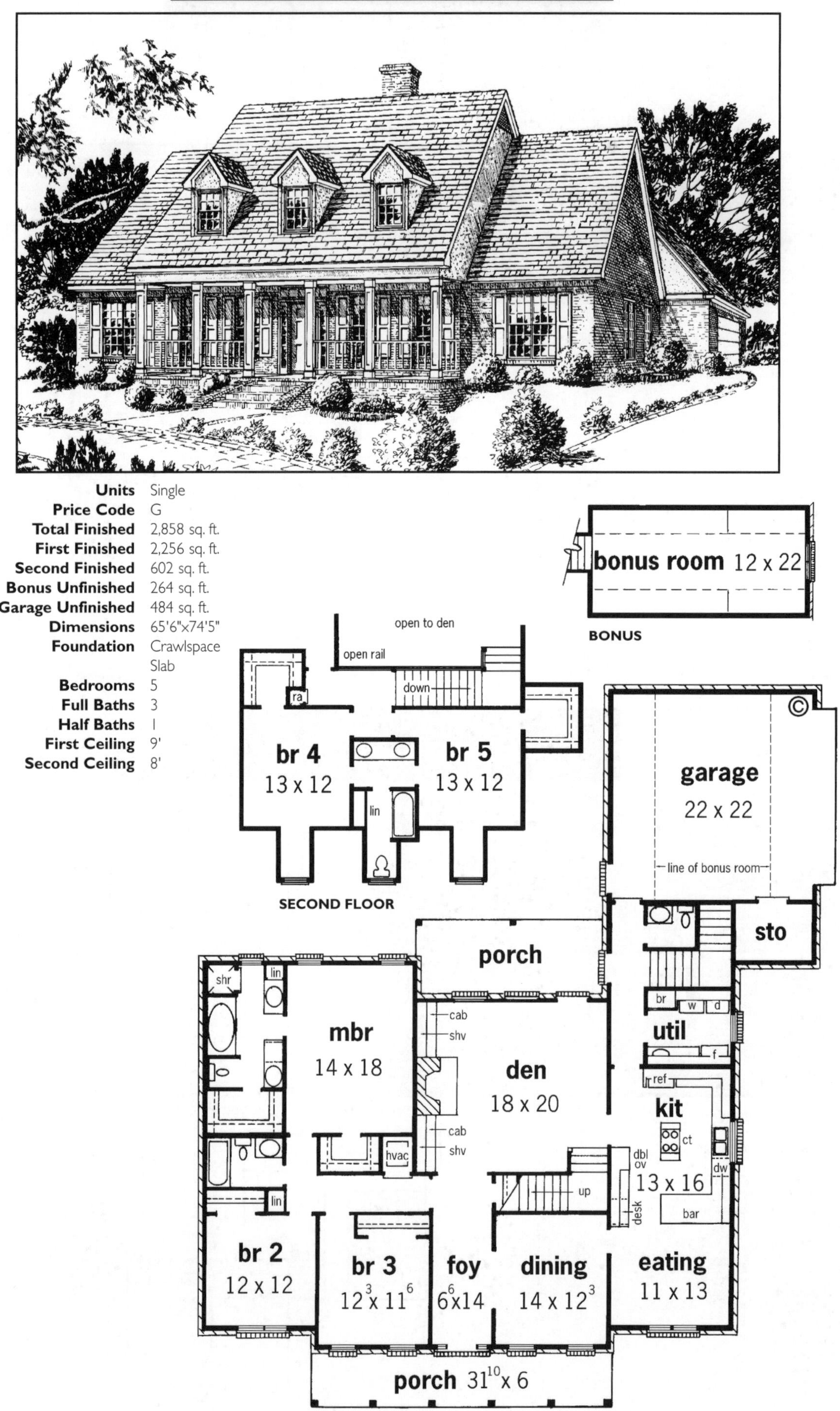

bonus room 12 x 22
BONUS
open to den
open rail
down
ra
br 4
13 x 12
br 5
13 x 12
lin
SECOND FLOOR
garage
22 x 22
line of bonus room
sto
porch
shr
lin
mbr
14 x 18
cab
shv
den
18 x 20
br
w
d
util
f
ref
kit
ct
dbl ov
13 x 16
dw
up
desk
bar
hvac
lin
br 2
12 x 12
br 3
12³ x 11⁶
foy
6⁶x14
dining
14 x 12³
eating
11 x 13
porch 31¹⁰ x 6
FIRST FLOOR

Units	Single
Price Code	G
Total Finished	2,858 sq. ft.
First Finished	2,256 sq. ft.
Second Finished	602 sq. ft.
Bonus Unfinished	264 sq. ft.
Garage Unfinished	484 sq. ft.
Dimensions	65'6"x74'5"
Foundation	Crawlspace Slab
Bedrooms	5
Full Baths	3
Half Baths	1
First Ceiling	9'
Second Ceiling	8'

Design 24702

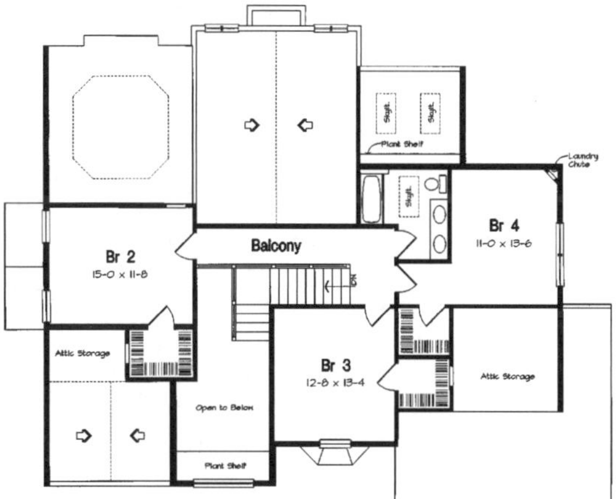

SECOND FLOOR

FIRST FLOOR

Units	Single
Price Code	G
Total Finished	2,859 sq. ft.
First Finished	1,939 sq. ft.
Second Finished	920 sq. ft.
Basement Unfinished	1,939 sq. ft.
Garage Unfinished	736 sq. ft.
Porch Unfinished	36 sq. ft.
Dimensions	62'8"x63'6"
Foundation	Basement Crawlspace Slab
Bedrooms	4
Full Baths	2
Half Baths	1
First Ceiling	9'
Second Ceiling	8'
Vaulted Ceiling	14'
Max Ridge Height	32'6"
Roof Framing	Stick
Exterior Walls	2x6

Br 2
15-0 x 11-8

Balcony

Br 4
11-0 x 13-6

Br 3
12-8 x 13-4

Attic Storage

Open to Below

Attic Storage

Plant Shelf

MBr
14-10 x 15-4

Family Rm
16-8 x 14-10

Breakfast
10-6 x 9-0

Kitchen
14-4 x 13-6

Lndry

Dining
12-6 x 13-4

Library/Parlor
12-6 x 13-6

Foyer

3 Car Garage
21-8 x 33-0

Design 98946

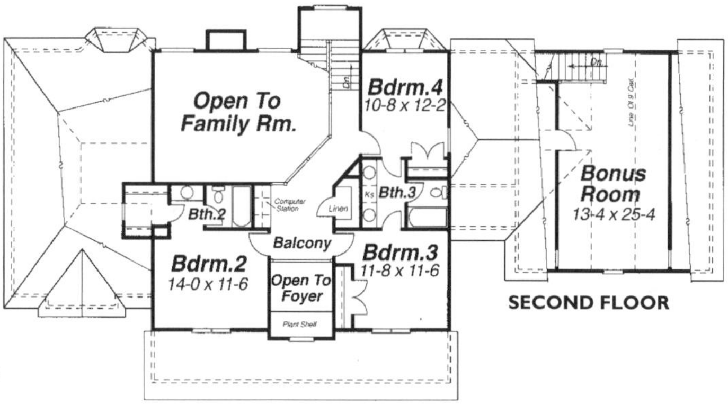

SECOND FLOOR

Open To Family Rm.

Bdrm.4
10-8 x 12-2

Bonus Room
13-4 x 25-4

Bth.2

Bth.3

Bdrm.2
14-0 x 11-6

Balcony

Open To Foyer

Bdrm.3
11-8 x 11-6

FIRST FLOOR

Units	Single
Price Code	G
Total Finished	2,859 sq. ft.
First Finished	1,912 sq. ft.
Second Finished	947 sq. ft.
Bonus Unfinished	364 sq. ft.
Basement Unfinished	1,872 sq. ft.
Garage Unfinished	619 sq. ft.
Deck Unfinished	256 sq. ft.
Porch Unfinished	237 sq. ft.
Dimensions	86'x51'
Foundation	Basement Crawlspace Slab
Bedrooms	4
Full Baths	3
Half Baths	1
First Ceiling	9'
Second Ceiling	8'
Max Ridge Height	32'
Roof Framing	Stick
Exterior Walls	2x4

Sundeck
20-6 x 12-6

Master Bdrm.
16-8 x 16-0 + Bay

Two Story Family Rm.
21-6 x 15-2

Brkfst.
10-8 x 11-8 + Bay

Lnd.

Kitchen
14-0 x 10-10

Double Garage
23-4 x 25-4

M. Bath

Living/Office
14-0 x 11-6

Lav.

Open Foyer
7-8 x 12-6

Dining
14-0 x 11-6

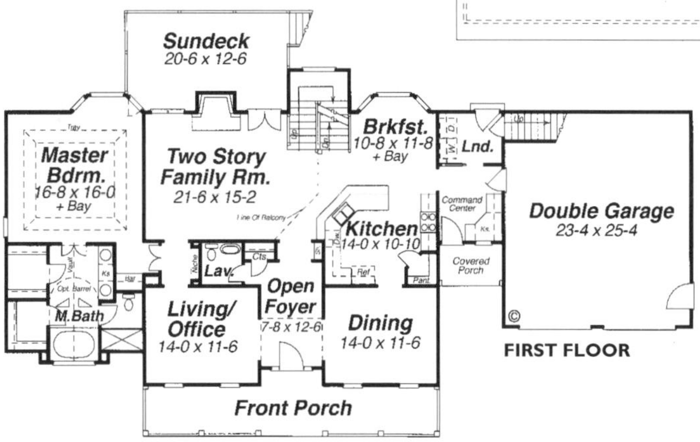

Design 94247

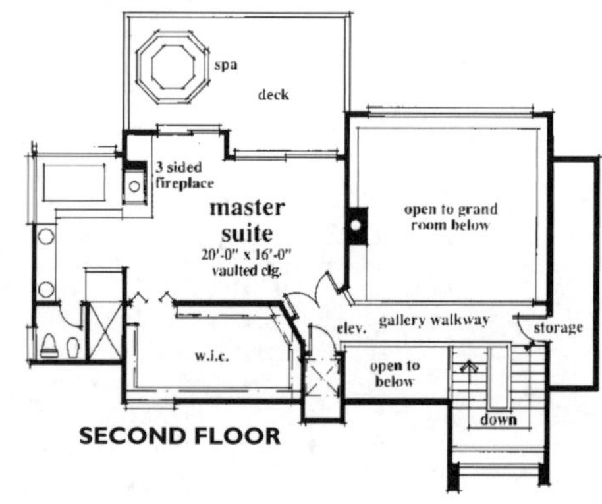
spa
deck
3 sided fireplace
master suite
20'-0" x 16'-0"
vaulted clg.
open to grand room below
gallery walkway
storage
elev.
w.i.c.
open to below
down

SECOND FLOOR

Units	Single
Price Code	J
Total Finished	2,875 sq. ft.
First Finished	2,066 sq. ft.
Second Finished	809 sq. ft.
Lower Unfinished	1,260 sq. ft.
Garage Unfinished	798 sq. ft.
Dimensions	64'x45'
Foundation	Pier/Post
Bedrooms	3
Full Baths	2
3/4 Baths	1
Half Baths	1
First Ceiling	8'6"
Second Ceiling	9'
Vaulted Ceiling	19'
Max Ridge Height	40'
Roof Framing	Truss
Exterior Walls	2x6

* Alternate foundation options available at an additional charge. Please call 1-800-235-5700 for more information.

deck
50'-0" x 12'-0"
bonus
bonus
36'-0" x 17'-0"
garage
25'-0" x 27'-0"
opt. elev.
storage
up
bonus

LOWER FLOOR

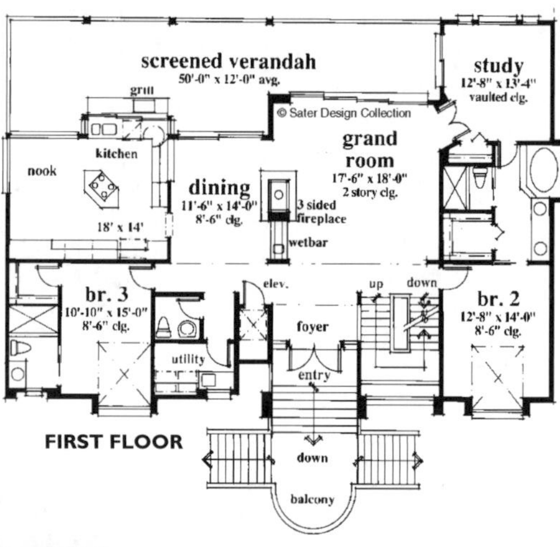
screened verandah
50'-0" x 12'-0" avg.
study
12'-8" x 13'-4"
vaulted clg.
grill
© Sater Design Collection
nook
kitchen
grand room
17'-6" x 18'-0"
2 story clg.
dining
11'-6" x 14'-0"
8'-6" clg.
3 sided fireplace
18' x 14'
wetbar
br. 3
10'-10" x 15'-0"
8'-6" clg.
elev.
up
down
br. 2
12'-8" x 14'-0"
8'-6" clg.
foyer
utility
entry
down
balcony

FIRST FLOOR

Design 69000

Units	Single
Price Code	G
Total Finished	2,874 sq. ft.
Main Finished	2,874 sq. ft.
Dimensions	83'x50'4"
Foundation	Basement
Bedrooms	4
Full Baths	2
Half Baths	1
Main Ceiling	8'
Max Ridge Height	22'3"
Roof Framing	Stick
Exterior Walls	2x4

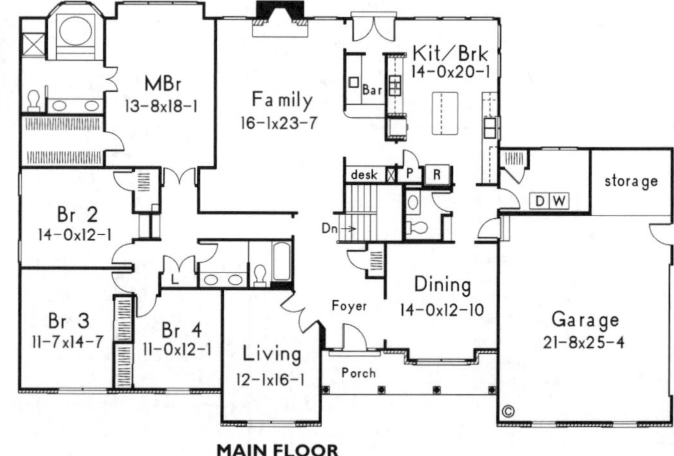
MBr
13-8x18-1
Family
16-1x23-7
Kit/Brk
14-0x20-1
Bar
desk
P
R
storage
DW
Br 2
14-0x12-1
Dn
Dining
14-0x12-10
Br 3
11-7x14-7
Br 4
11-0x12-1
Foyer
Living
12-1x16-1
Porch
Garage
21-8x25-4
©

MAIN FLOOR

Design 66107

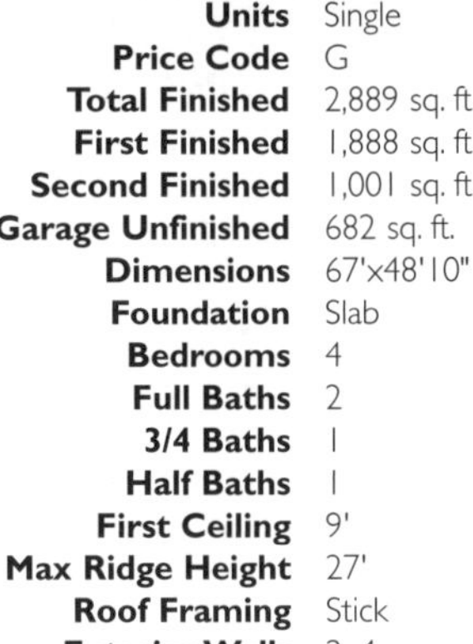

Units	Single
Price Code	G
Total Finished	2,889 sq. ft.
First Finished	1,888 sq. ft.
Second Finished	1,001 sq. ft.
Garage Unfinished	682 sq. ft.
Dimensions	67'x48'10"
Foundation	Slab
Bedrooms	4
Full Baths	2
3/4 Baths	1
Half Baths	1
First Ceiling	9'
Max Ridge Height	27'
Roof Framing	Stick
Exterior Walls	2x4

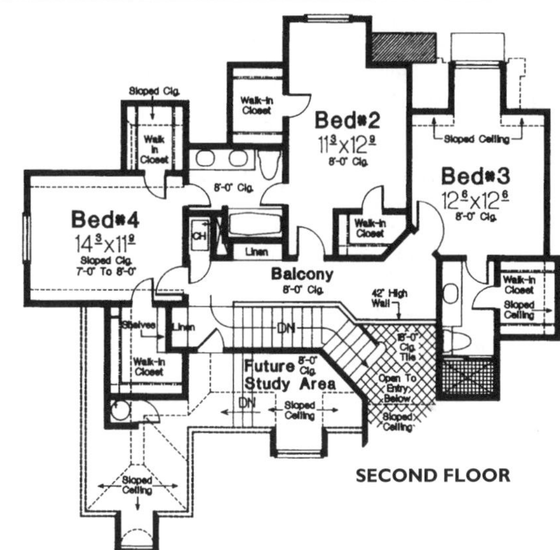
Bed#2
Bed#3
Bed#4
Balcony
Future Study Area
Walk-in Closet
Sloped Ceiling
Linen
DN

SECOND FLOOR

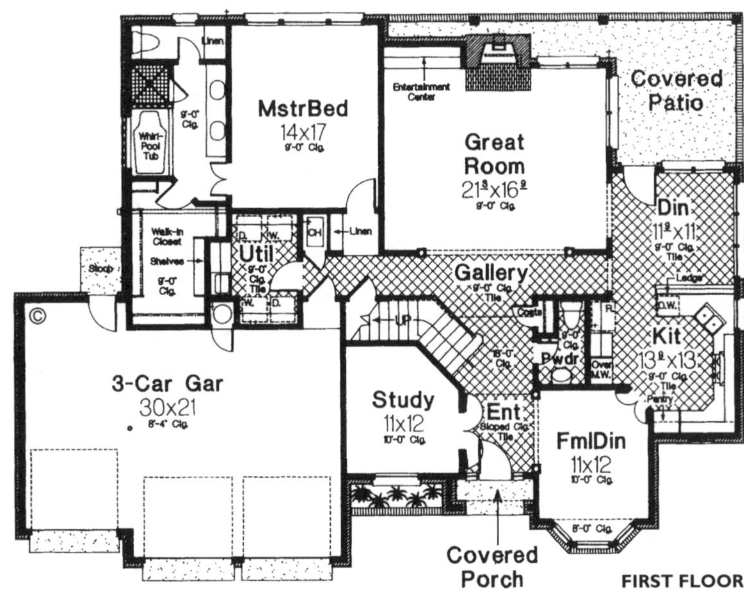
MstrBed
14x17
Great Room
Covered Patio
Din
Util
Gallery
Kit
Pwdr
Study
11x12
Ent
FmlDin
11x12
3-Car Gar
30x21
Covered Porch
Walk-in Closet
Whirl-Pool Tub
Entertainment Center
UP

FIRST FLOOR

Design 94231

Units	Single
Price Code	H
Total Finished	2,891 sq. ft.
First Finished	2,181 sq. ft.
Second Finished	710 sq. ft.
Garage Unfinished	658 sq. ft.
Deck Unfinished	251 sq. ft.
Porch Unfinished	426 sq. ft.
Dimensions	66'4"x79'
Foundation	Basement Slab
Bedrooms	3
Full Baths	2
3/4 Baths	1
First Ceiling	10'
Second Ceiling	9'4"
Tray Ceiling	13'
Max Ridge Height	33'4"
Roof Framing	Truss

* Alternate foundation options available at an additional charge. Please call 1-800-235-5700 for more information.

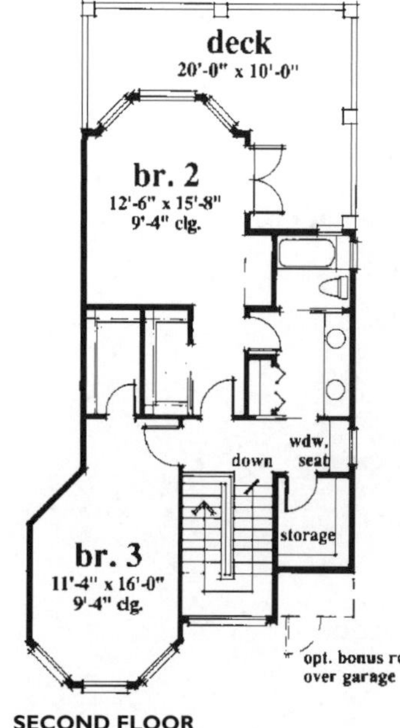

deck
20'-0" x 10'-0"
br. 2
12'-6" x 15'-8"
9'-4" clg.
wdw. seat
down
storage
br. 3
11'-4" x 16'-0"
9'-4" clg.
opt. bonus room over garage

SECOND FLOOR

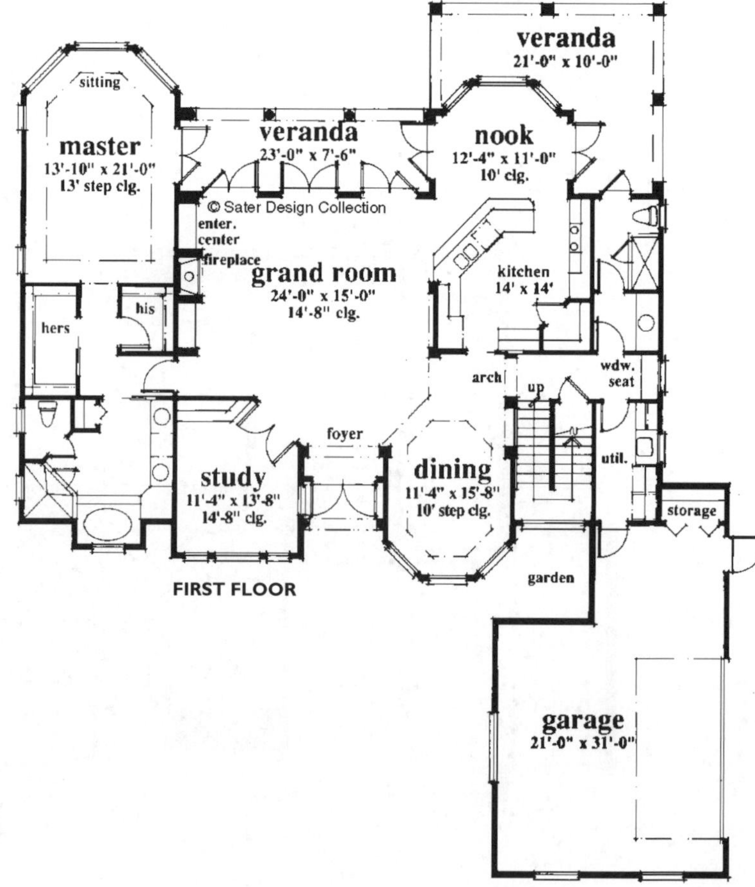

veranda
21'-0" x 10'-0"
sitting
master
13'-10" x 21'-0"
13' step clg.
veranda
23'-0" x 7'-6"
nook
12'-4" x 11'-0"
10' clg.
© Sater Design Collection
enter. center
fireplace
grand room
24'-0" x 15'-0"
14'-8" clg.
kitchen
14' x 14'
his
hers
arch
up
wdw. seat
util.
foyer
study
11'-4" x 13'-8"
14'-8" clg.
dining
11'-4" x 15'-8"
10' step clg.
storage
garden
garage
21'-0" x 31'-0"

FIRST FLOOR

Design 97220

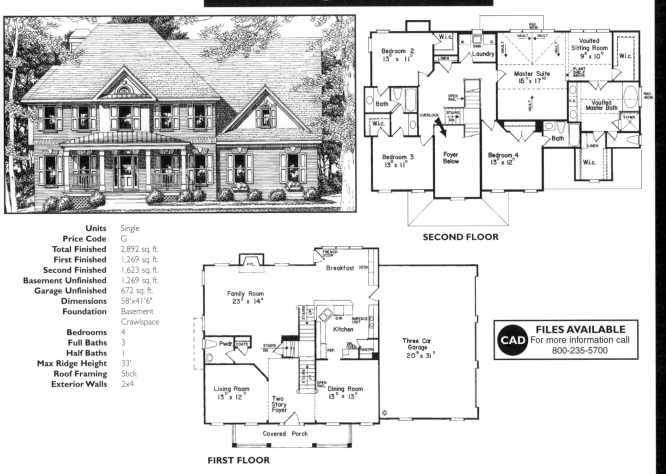

Units	Single
Price Code	G
Total Finished	2,892 sq. ft.
First Finished	1,269 sq. ft.
Second Finished	1,623 sq. ft.
Basement Unfinished	1,269 sq. ft.
Garage Unfinished	672 sq. ft.
Dimensions	58'x41'6"
Foundation	Basement Crawlspace
Bedrooms	4
Full Baths	3
Half Baths	1
Max Ridge Height	33'
Roof Framing	Stick
Exterior Walls	2x4

SECOND FLOOR

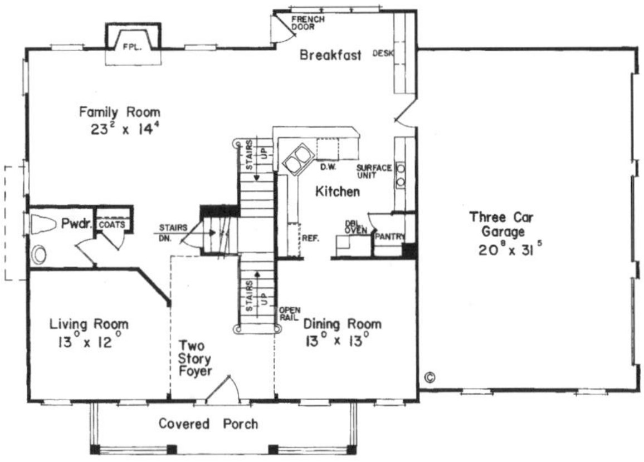

FIRST FLOOR

CAD FILES AVAILABLE
For more information call
800-235-5700

Design 66099

Units	Single
Price Code	G
Total Finished	2,896 sq. ft.
First Finished	2,387 sq. ft.
Second Finished	509 sq. ft.
Garage Unfinished	821 sq. ft.
Dimensions	82'3"x86'6"
Foundation	Slab
Bedrooms	3
Full Baths	3
Half Baths	1
First Ceiling	8'-11'
Vaulted Ceiling	9'-11'
Max Ridge Height	31'
Roof Framing	Stick
Exterior Walls	2x4

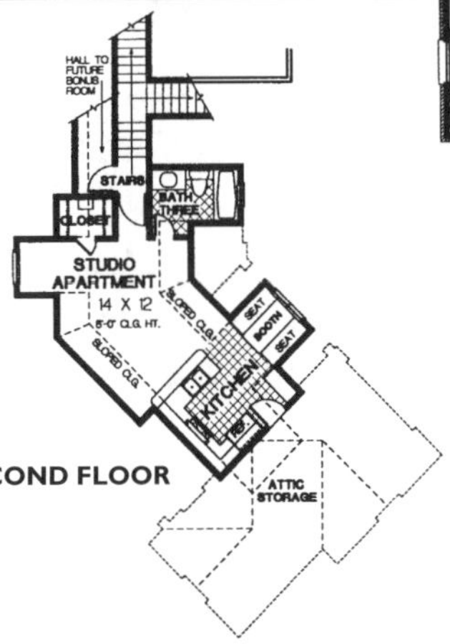

SECOND FLOOR

FIRST FLOOR

Design 94668

PHOTOGRAPHY: COURTESY OF THE DESIGNER

Please note: The photographed home may have been modified to suit homeowner preferences. If you order plans, have a builder or design professional check them against the photograph to confirm actual construction details.

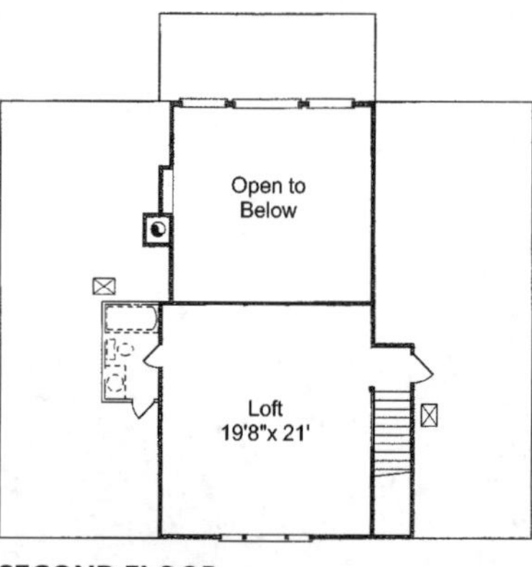

Open to Below
Loft
19'8"x 21'

SECOND FLOOR

Units	Single
Price Code	G
Total Finished	2,904 sq. ft.
First Finished	2,000 sq. ft.
Second Finished	455 sq. ft.
Lower Finished	449 sq. ft.
Deck Unfinished	452 sq. ft.
Porch Unfinished	165 sq. ft.
Dimensions	50'x60'
Foundation	Post
Bedrooms	4
Full Baths	3
Max Ridge Height	37'5"
Roof Framing	Stick
Exterior Walls	2x4

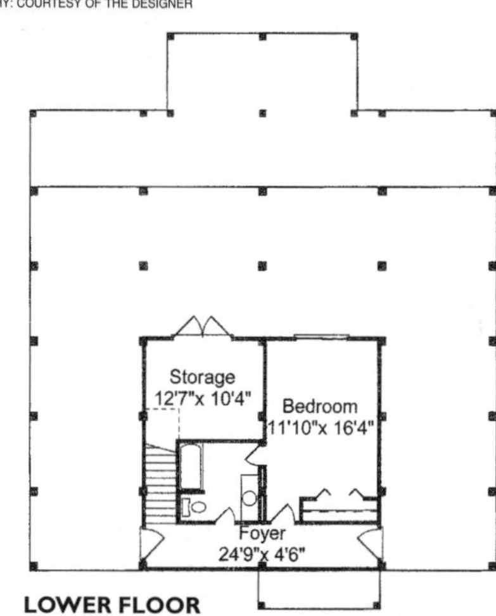

Storage
12'7"x 10'4"
Bedroom
11'10"x 16'4"
Foyer
24'9"x 4'6"

LOWER FLOOR

Deck
20'4"x 8'
Deck
14'10"x 8'
Porch
20'4"x 8'
Deck
14'10"x 8'
Bedroom
13'x 15'6"
Living
18'8"x 18'
Master Bedroom
14'8"x 20'
Breakfast
18'8"x 11'2"
Bedroom
11'10"x 12'6"
Kitchen
18'8"x 10'
Deck
13'x 4'

FIRST FLOOR

Design 99935

Ensuite W.I.C.
linen
MBR
17-6 x 14-0
Bath
Study/BR4
10-2 x 12-10
Bonus Room
11-6 x 23-6
BR2
11-8 x 12-6
Open to Below
BR3
13-6 x 13-6

SECOND FLOOR

Units	Single
Price Code	G
Total Finished	2,904 sq. ft.
First Finished	1,494 sq. ft.
Second Finished	1,410 sq. ft.
Bonus Unfinished	288 sq. ft.
Basement Unfinished	1,080 sq. ft.
Garage Unfinished	576 sq. ft.
Porch Unfinished	551 sq. ft.
Dimensions	60'x51'
Foundation	Basement
Bedrooms	4
Full Baths	2
3/4 Baths	1
First Ceiling	9'
Second Ceiling	8'
Max Ridge Height	26'6"
Roof Framing	Truss
Exterior Walls	2x6

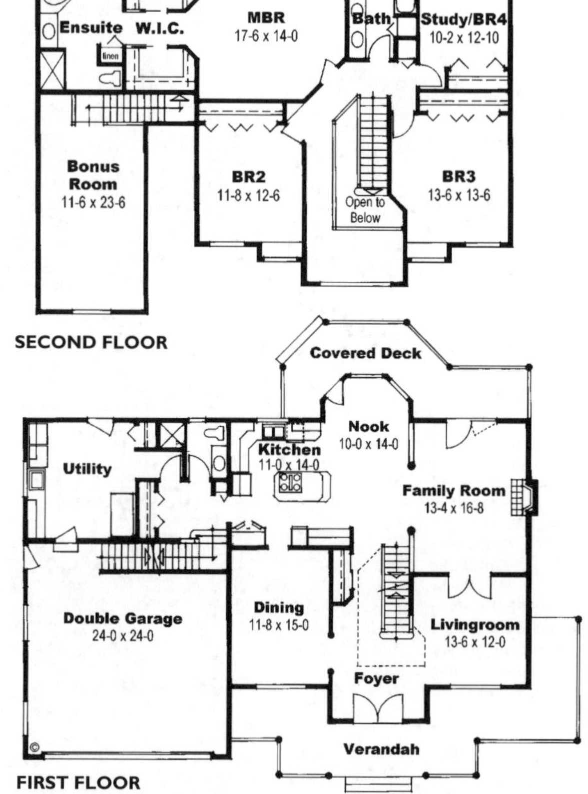

Covered Deck
Nook
10-0 x 14-0
Kitchen
11-0 x 14-0
Utility
Family Room
13-4 x 16-8
Double Garage
24-0 x 24-0
Dining
11-8 x 15-0
Livingroom
13-6 x 12-0
Foyer
Verandah

FIRST FLOOR

Design 98569

Units	Single
Price Code	G
Total Finished	2,911 sq. ft.
Main Finished	2,911 sq. ft.
Garage Unfinished	720 sq. ft.
Deck Unfinished	220 sq. ft.
Porch Unfinished	48 sq. ft.
Dimensions	78'x79'9"
Foundation	Basement Slab
Bedrooms	4
Full Baths	2
3/4 Baths	1
Half Baths	1
Main Ceiling	9'
Vaulted Ceiling	9'-12'
Max Ridge Height	30'8"
Roof Framing	Stick
Exterior Walls	2x4

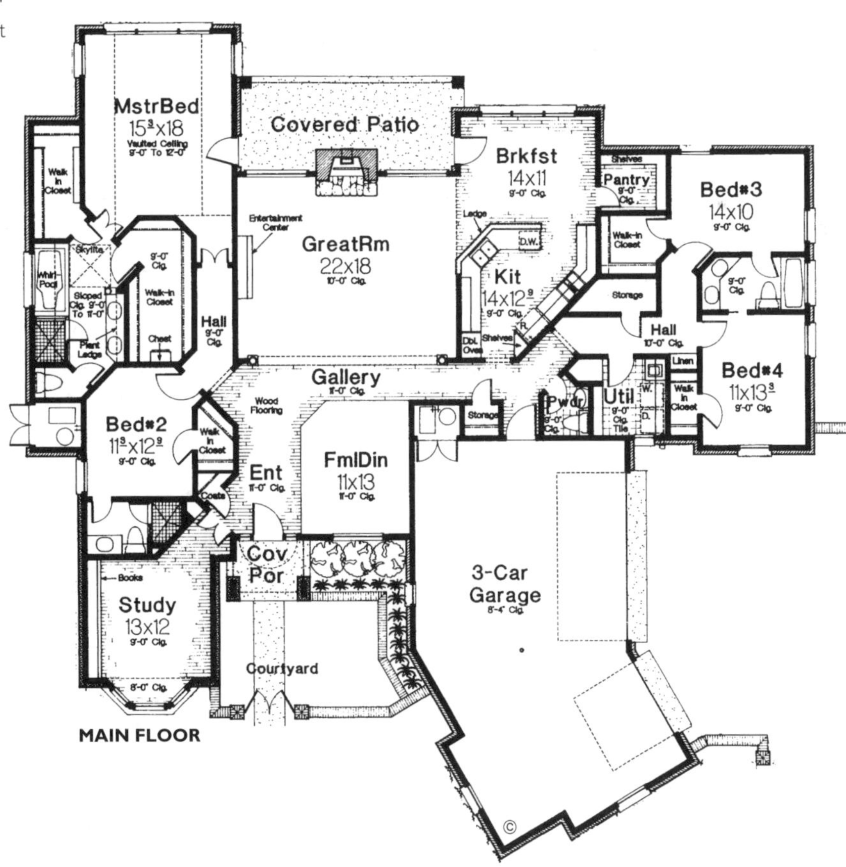
MstrBed
15³x18
Covered Patio
Brkfst
14x11
Pantry
Bed#3
14x10
GreatRm
22x18
Kit
14x12⁹
Walk-in Closet
Hall
Storage
Bed#4
11x13³
Gallery
Wood Flooring
Bed#2
11⁹x12⁹
Pwdr
Util
FmlDin
11x13
Ent
Cov Por
Study
13x12
Books
3-Car Garage
Courtyard
MAIN FLOOR

Design 98961

Units	Single
Price Code	G
Total Finished	2,911 sq. ft.
Main Finished	2,911 sq. ft.
Bonus Unfinished	512 sq. ft.
Garage Unfinished	672 sq. ft.
Deck Unfinished	928 sq. ft.
Dimensions	90'x93'
Foundation	Basement
Bedrooms	3
Full Baths	2
Half Baths	1
Main Ceiling	9'-10'
Max Ridge Height	24'
Roof Framing	Stick
Exterior Walls	2x4

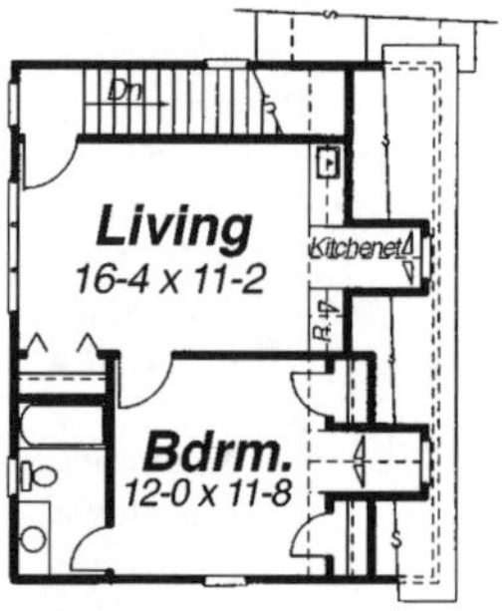

Living
16-4 x 11-2
Kitchenette
Bdrm.
12-0 x 11-8

BONUS

Keeping
15-4 x 15-6
Covered Deck
Brkfst.
8-0 x 11-6
Sundeck
Bdrm.2
13-0 x 11-0
Kit.
13-10 x 13-0
Living
19-8 x 23-6
10' Ceiling
Office/Storage
Master Bdrm.
15-4 x 17-6
Tray Ceil.
Bth.2
Butlers Pantry
Foyer
Bdrm.3
13-0 x 11-6
Lnd.
Dining
13-8 x 15-6
10' Ceiling
Study
13-8 x 15-6
10' Ceiling
M.Bath
Porch
Double Garage
23-4 x 23-4

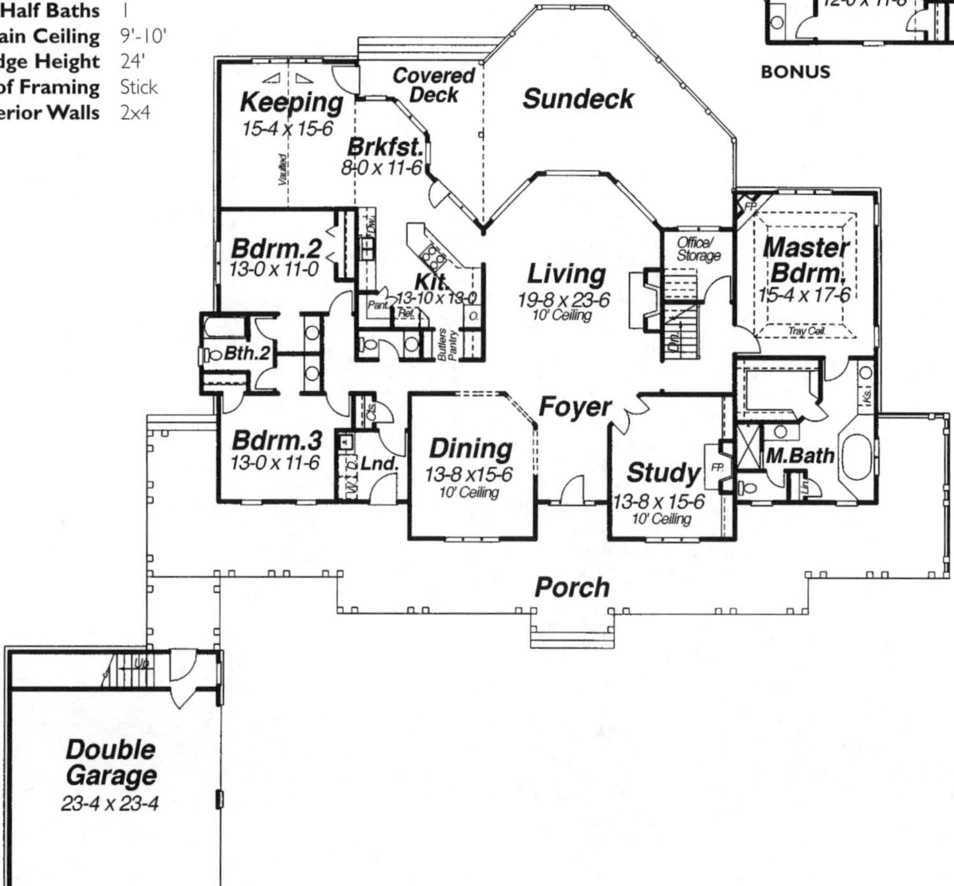

MAIN FLOOR

Design 99463

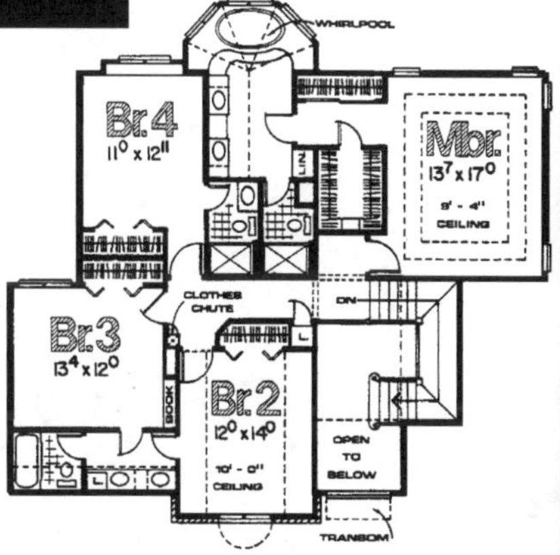

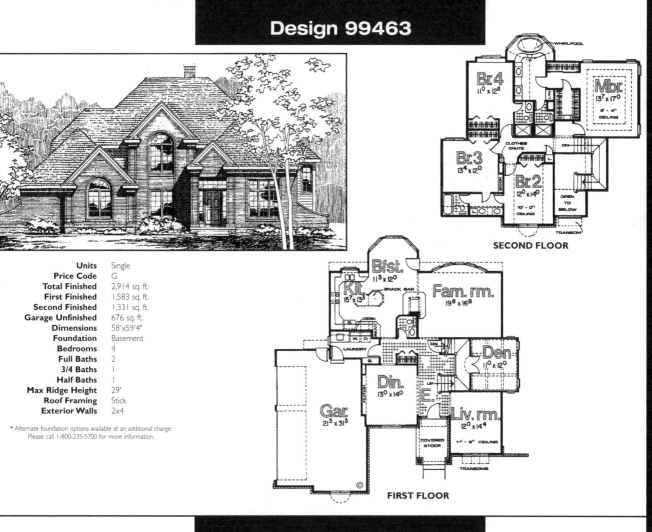

Units	Single
Price Code	G
Total Finished	2,914 sq. ft.
First Finished	1,583 sq. ft.
Second Finished	1,331 sq. ft.
Garage Unfinished	676 sq. ft.
Dimensions	58'x59'4"
Foundation	Basement
Bedrooms	4
Full Baths	2
3/4 Baths	1
Half Baths	1
Max Ridge Height	29'
Roof Framing	Stick
Exterior Walls	2x4

* Alternate foundation options available at an additional charge. Please call 1-800-235-5700 for more information.

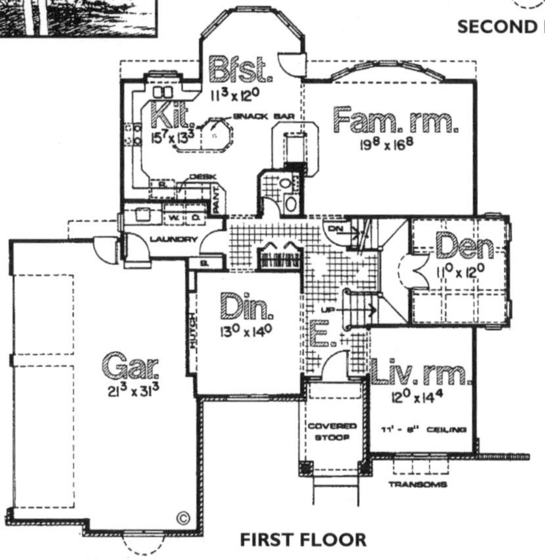

SECOND FLOOR

FIRST FLOOR

Design 65608

Units	Single
Price Code	G
Total Finished	2,918 sq. ft.
First Finished	1,884 sq. ft.
Second Finished	1,034 sq. ft.
Garage Unfinished	566 sq. ft.
Porch Unfinished	240 sq. ft.
Dimensions	49'x79'
Foundation	Slab
Bedrooms	4
Full Baths	3
Half Baths	1
First Ceiling	10'
Second Ceiling	8'
Max Ridge Height	33'
Roof Framing	Stick
Exterior Walls	2x4

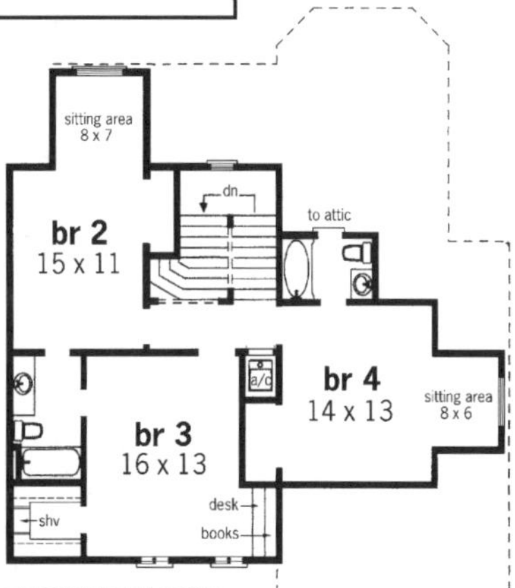

SECOND FLOOR

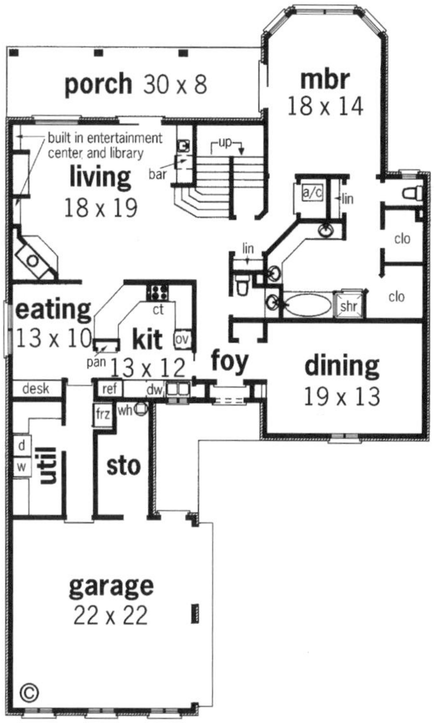

FIRST FLOOR

Design 32369

PHOTOGRAPHY: D. RANDOLPH FOULDS

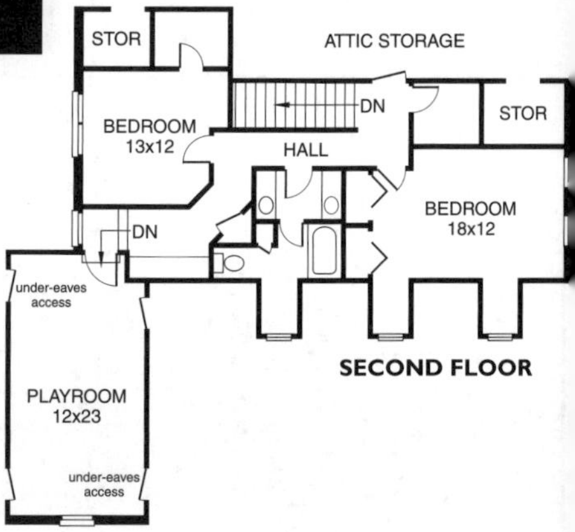

Units	Single
Price Code	D
Total Finished	2,930 sq. ft.
First Finished	1,770 sq. ft.
Second Finished	1,160 sq. ft.
Garage Unfinished	576 sq. ft.
Porch Unfinished	432 sq. ft.
Dimensions	66'x70'
Foundation	Crawlspace
Bedrooms	3
Full Baths	2
3/4 Baths	1
First Ceiling	9'
Second Ceiling	8'
Max Ridge Height	30'2"
Roof Framing	Truss
Exterior Walls	2x4

Please note: The photographed home may have been modified to suit homeowner preferences. If you order plans, have a builder or design professional check them against the photograph to confirm actual construction details.

STOR
ATTIC STORAGE
BEDROOM 13x12
DN
HALL
STOR
BEDROOM 18x12
DN
under-eaves access
PLAYROOM 12x23
under-eaves access

SECOND FLOOR

SCREEN PORCH 16x9
BRKFST 12x10
KIT 12x18
R
GREAT-ROOM 19x15
MASTER BEDROOM 13x17
BATH
CLOSET
UP
D W
DINING 13x13
ENTRY
STUDY 13x12
UP
PORCH
GARAGE 24x23

FIRST FLOOR

Design 65661

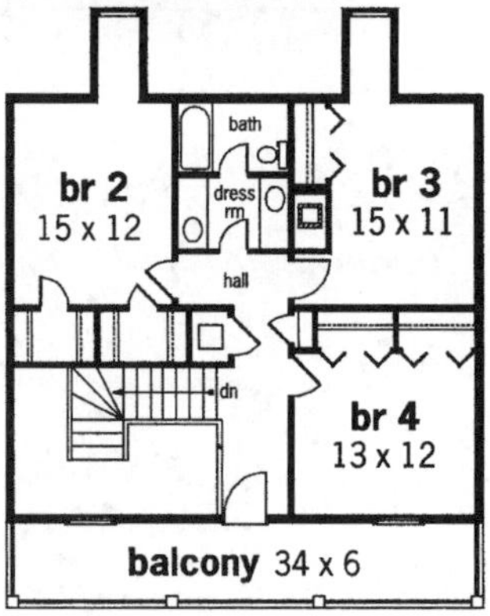

Units	Single
Price Code	G
Total Finished	2,932 sq. ft.
First Finished	2,029 sq. ft.
Second Finished	903 sq. ft.
Garage Unfinished	470 sq. ft.
Porch Unfinished	564 sq. ft.
Dimensions	77'x56'
Foundation	Basement Crawlspace Slab
Bedrooms	4
Full Baths	2
Half Baths	2
First Ceiling	9'
Second Ceiling	8'
Max Ridge Height	29'
Roof Framing	Stick
Exterior Walls	2x6

br 2 15 x 12
bath
dress rm
br 3 15 x 11
hall
dn
br 4 13 x 12
balcony 34 x 6

SECOND FLOOR

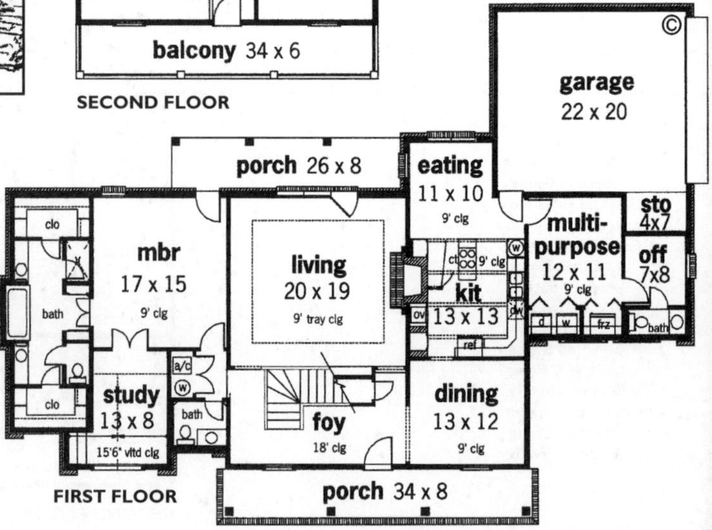

garage 22 x 20
porch 26 x 8
eating 11 x 10 9' clg
sto 4x7
clo
mbr 17 x 15 9' clg
living 20 x 19 9' tray clg
kit 13 x 13 9' clg
multi-purpose 12 x 11 9' clg
off 7x8
bath
clo
study 13 x 8 15'6" vltd clg
bath
foy 18' clg
dining 13 x 12 9' clg
porch 34 x 8

FIRST FLOOR

Design 99400

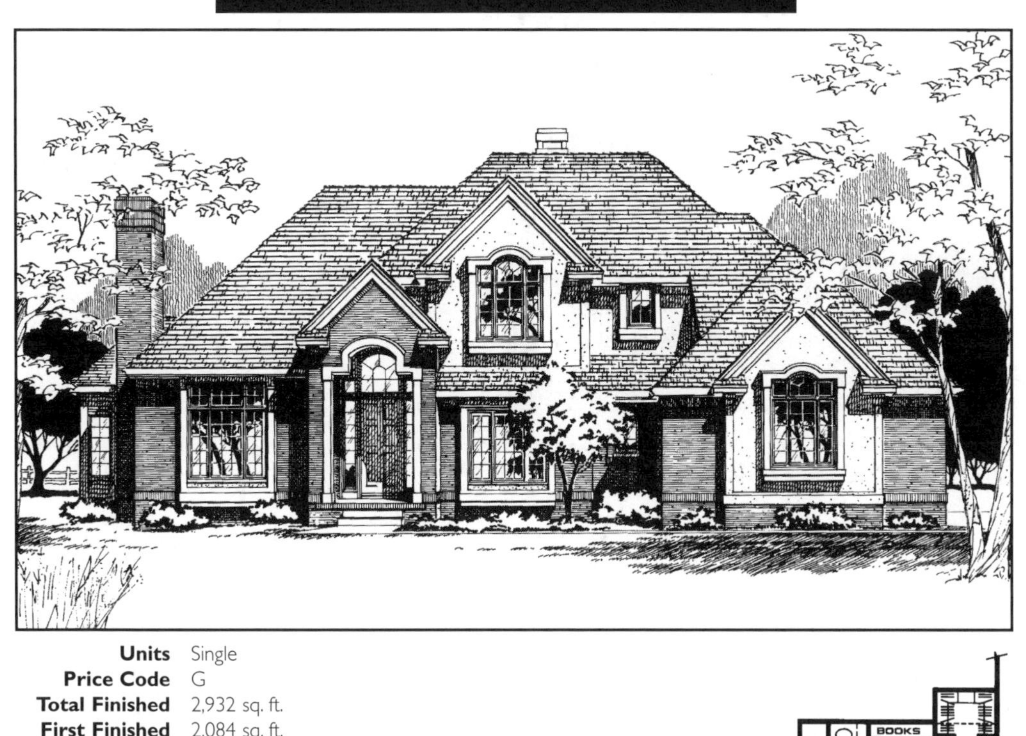

Units	Single
Price Code	G
Total Finished	2,932 sq. ft.
First Finished	2,084 sq. ft.
Second Finished	848 sq. ft.
Basement Unfinished	2,084 sq. ft.
Garage Unfinished	682 sq. ft.
Dimensions	68'8"x60'
Foundation	Basement Slab
Bedrooms	4
Full Baths	3
Half Baths	1
First Ceiling	8'
Second Ceiling	8'
Max Ridge Height	28'
Roof Framing	Stick
Exterior Walls	2x4

* Alternate foundation options available at an additional charge. Please call 1-800-235-5700 for more information.

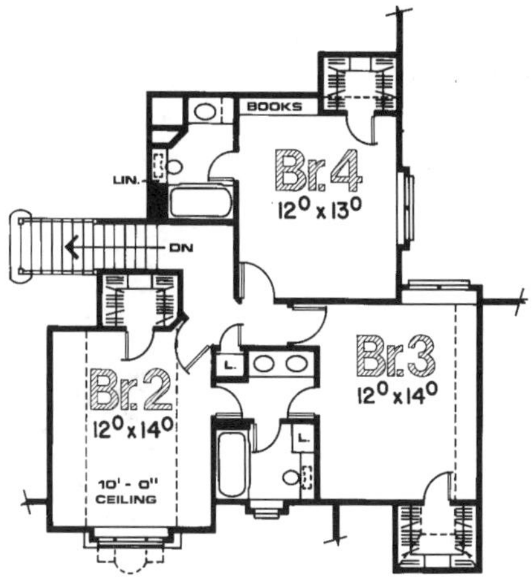

BOOKS
LIN.
DN
Br.4 12⁰ x 13⁰
Br.2 12⁰ x 14⁰
10' - 0" CEILING
Br.3 12⁰ x 14⁰

SECOND FLOOR

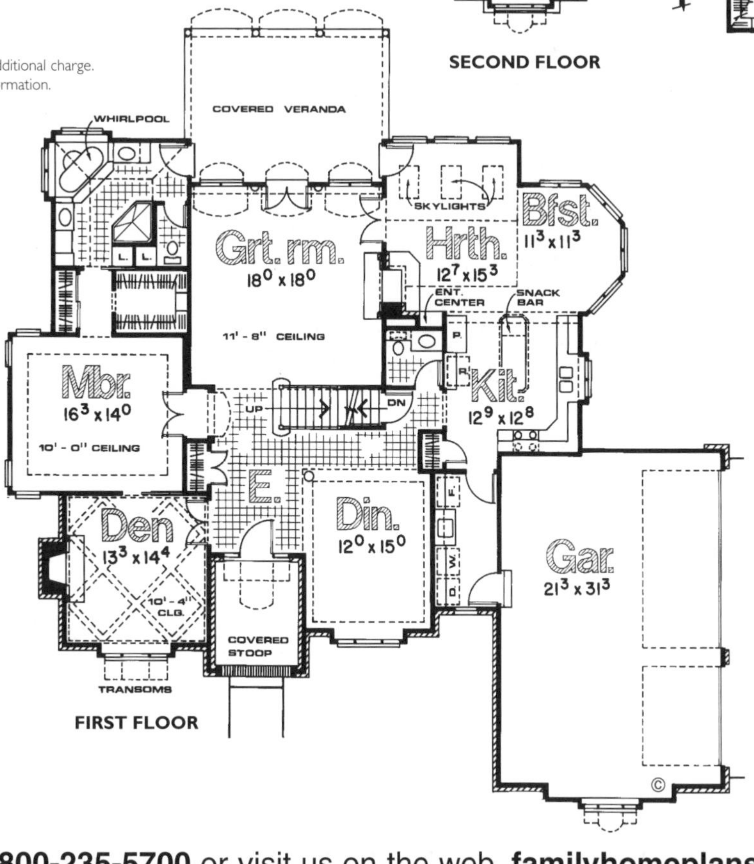

COVERED VERANDA
WHIRLPOOL
SKYLIGHTS
Bfst. 11³ x 11³
Grt. rm. 18⁰ x 18⁰
11' - 8" CEILING
Hrth. 12⁷ x 15³
ENT. CENTER
SNACK BAR
Mbr. 16³ x 14⁰
10' - 0" CEILING
UP
DN
Kit. 12⁹ x 12⁸
E.
Den 13³ x 14⁴
10' - 4" CLG.
Din. 12⁰ x 15⁰
Gar. 21³ x 31³
COVERED STOOP
TRANSOMS

FIRST FLOOR

Design 98458

CAD
FILES AVAILABLE
For more information call
800-235-5700

Units	Single
Price Code	G
Total Finished	2,940 sq. ft.
First Finished	2,044 sq. ft.
Second Finished	896 sq. ft.
Bonus Unfinished	197 sq. ft.
Basement Unfinished	2,044 sq. ft.
Garage Unfinished	544 sq. ft.
Dimensions	63'x54'
Foundation	Basement Crawlspace Slab
Bedrooms	4
Full Baths	3
Half Baths	1
First Ceiling	9'
Second Ceiling	8'
Max Ridge Height	31'4"
Roof Framing	Stick
Exterior Walls	2x4

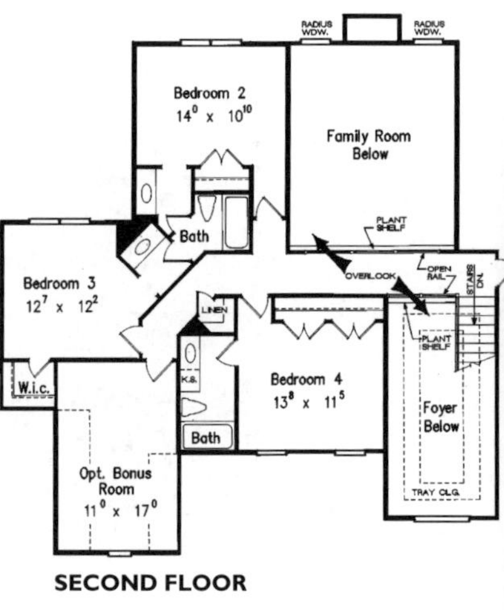

Bedroom 2
14⁰ x 10¹⁰
Family Room Below
Bath
Bedroom 3
12⁷ x 12²
Bedroom 4
13⁸ x 11⁵
Foyer Below
W.i.c.
Bath
Opt. Bonus Room
11⁰ x 17⁰

SECOND FLOOR

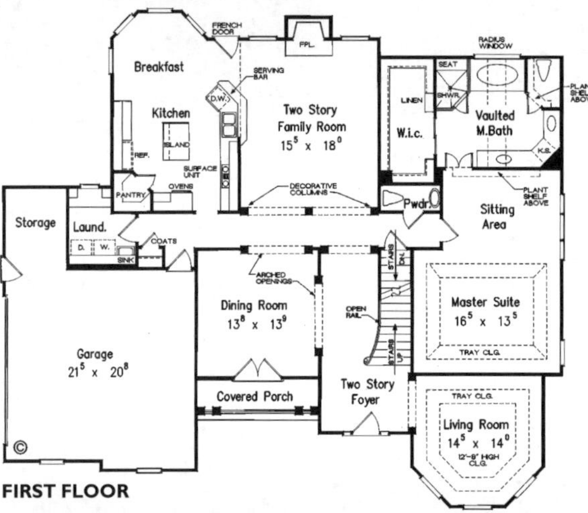

Breakfast
Kitchen
Two Story Family Room
15⁵ x 18⁰
W.i.c.
Vaulted M.Bath
Storage
Laund.
Pwdr.
Sitting Area
Dining Room
13⁸ x 13⁹
Master Suite
16⁵ x 13⁵
Garage
21⁵ x 20⁸
Covered Porch
Two Story Foyer
Living Room
14⁵ x 14⁰

FIRST FLOOR

Design 91181

Units	Single
Price Code	G
Total Finished	2,942 sq. ft.
First Finished	2,118 sq. ft.
Second Finished	824 sq. ft.
Bonus Unfinished	792 sq. ft.
Porch Unfinished	629 sq. ft.
Dimensions	62'1½"x29'6"
Foundation	Slab
Bedrooms	4
Full Baths	3
First Ceiling	9'
Second Ceiling	8'
Max Ridge Height	32'
Roof Framing	Stick
Exterior Walls	2x4

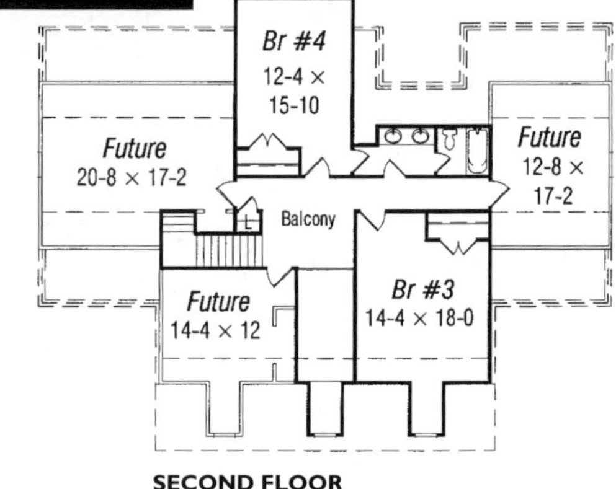

Br #4
12-4 × 15-10
Future
20-8 × 17-2
Future
12-8 × 17-2
Balcony
Future
14-4 × 12
Br #3
14-4 × 18-0

SECOND FLOOR

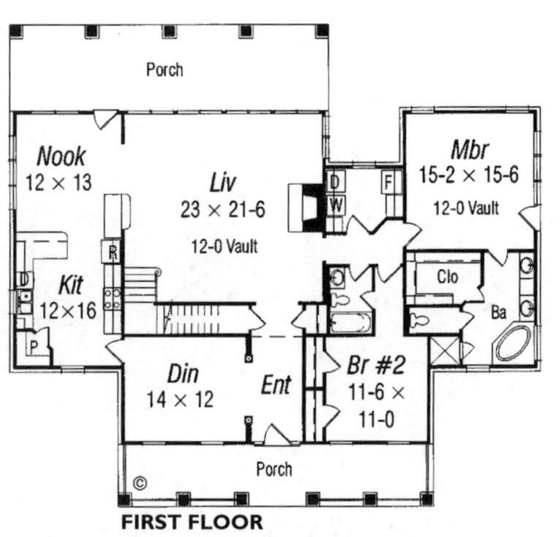

Porch
Nook
12 × 13
Liv
23 × 21-6
12-0 Vault
Mbr
15-2 × 15-6
12-0 Vault
Kit
12×16
Clo
Ba
Din
14 × 12
Ent
Br #2
11-6 × 11-0
Porch

FIRST FLOOR

Design 92452

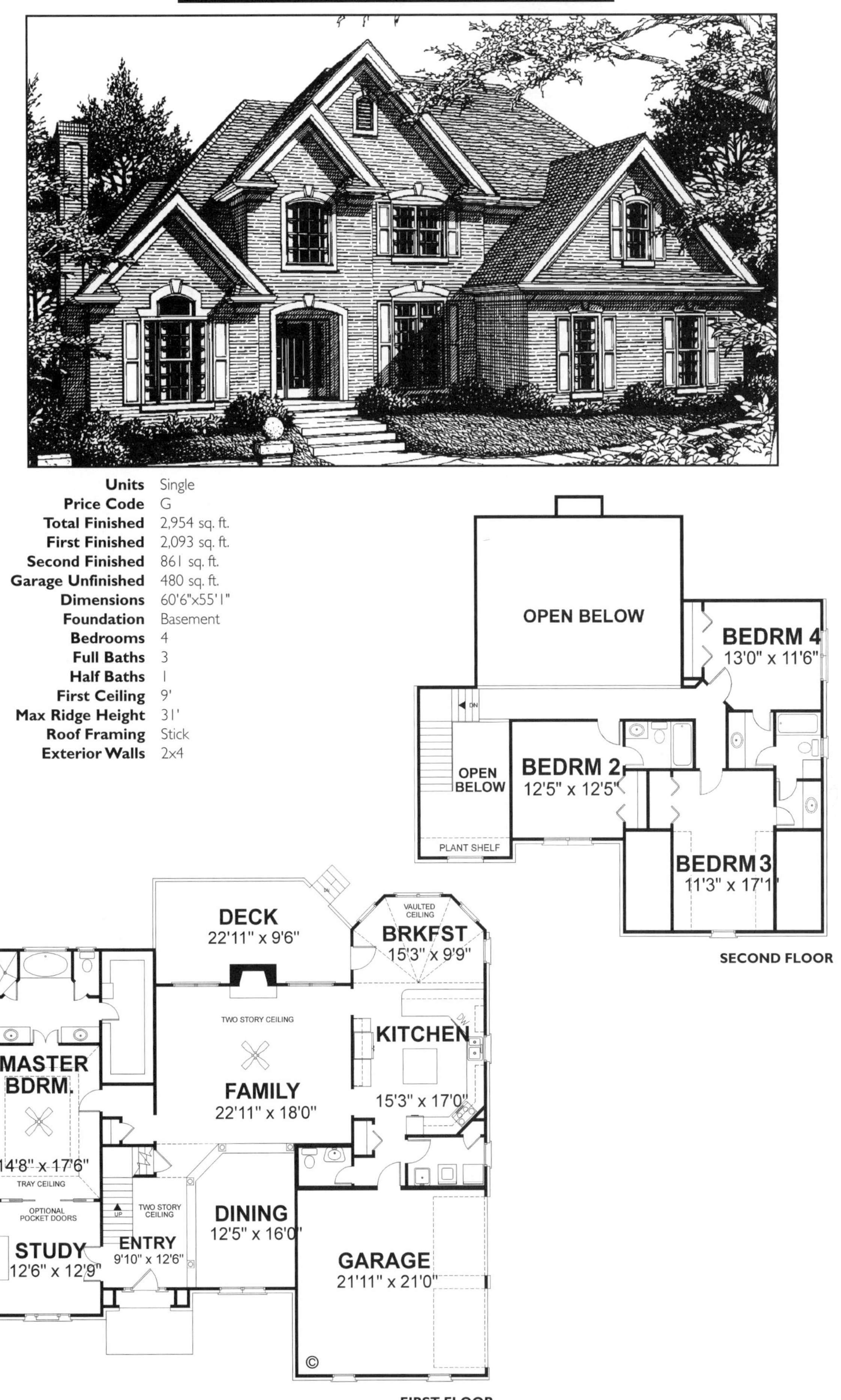
OPEN BELOW
BEDRM 4
13'0" x 11'6"
DN
OPEN
BELOW
BEDRM 2
12'5" x 12'5"
PLANT SHELF
BEDRM 3
11'3" x 17'1"
SECOND FLOOR
DECK
22'11" x 9'6"
VAULTED CEILING
BRKFST
15'3" x 9'9"
DW
TWO STORY CEILING
KITCHEN
15'3" x 17'0"
FAMILY
22'11" x 18'0"
MASTER
BDRM.
14'8" x 17'6"
TRAY CEILING
OPTIONAL POCKET DOORS
STUDY
12'6" x 12'9"
UP
TWO STORY CEILING
ENTRY
9'10" x 12'6"
DINING
12'5" x 16'0"
GARAGE
21'11" x 21'0"
©
FIRST FLOOR

Units	Single
Price Code	G
Total Finished	2,954 sq. ft.
First Finished	2,093 sq. ft.
Second Finished	861 sq. ft.
Garage Unfinished	480 sq. ft.
Dimensions	60'6"x55'1"
Foundation	Basement
Bedrooms	4
Full Baths	3
Half Baths	1
First Ceiling	9'
Max Ridge Height	31'
Roof Framing	Stick
Exterior Walls	2x4

Design 24594

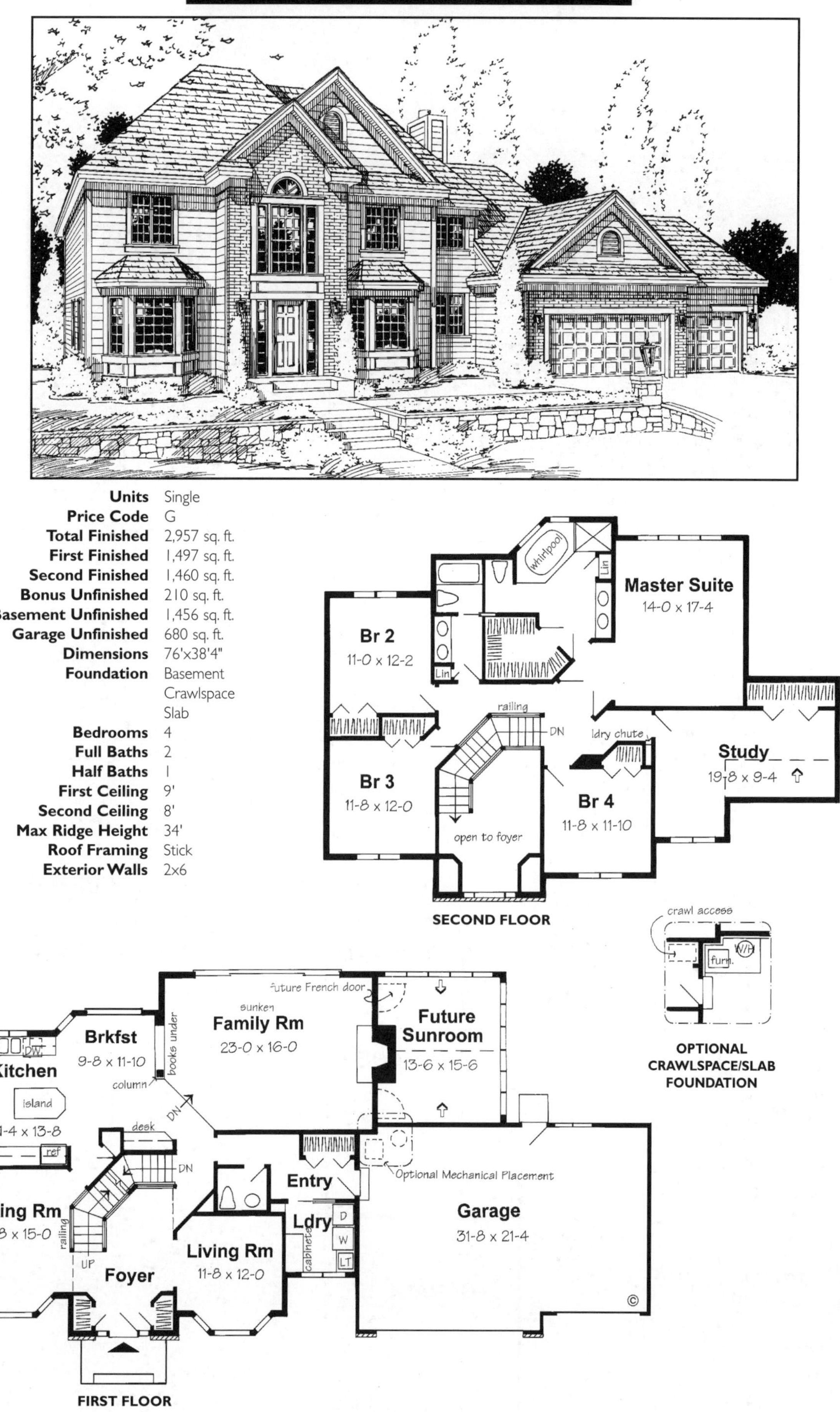

Br 2
11-0 x 12-2
Lin
whirlpool
Lin
Master Suite
14-0 x 17-4
railing
DN
ldry chute
Study
19-8 x 9-4
Br 3
11-8 x 12-0
Br 4
11-8 x 11-10
open to foyer
SECOND FLOOR
crawl access
W/H
furn.
OPTIONAL CRAWLSPACE/SLAB FOUNDATION
Future French door
sunken
Family Rm
23-0 x 16-0
books under
Future Sunroom
13-6 x 15-6
Brkfst
9-8 x 11-10
DW
Kitchen
island
column
oven
11-4 x 13-8
ref
desk
DN
DN
Entry
Optional Mechanical Placement
Garage
31-8 x 21-4
Dining Rm
11-8 x 15-0
railing
UP
Foyer
Living Rm
11-8 x 12-0
Ldry
D
W
LT
cabinets
FIRST FLOOR

Units	Single
Price Code	G
Total Finished	2,957 sq. ft.
First Finished	1,497 sq. ft.
Second Finished	1,460 sq. ft.
Bonus Unfinished	210 sq. ft.
Basement Unfinished	1,456 sq. ft.
Garage Unfinished	680 sq. ft.
Dimensions	76'x38'4"
Foundation	Basement Crawlspace Slab
Bedrooms	4
Full Baths	2
Half Baths	1
First Ceiling	9'
Second Ceiling	8'
Max Ridge Height	34'
Roof Framing	Stick
Exterior Walls	2x6

Design 94994

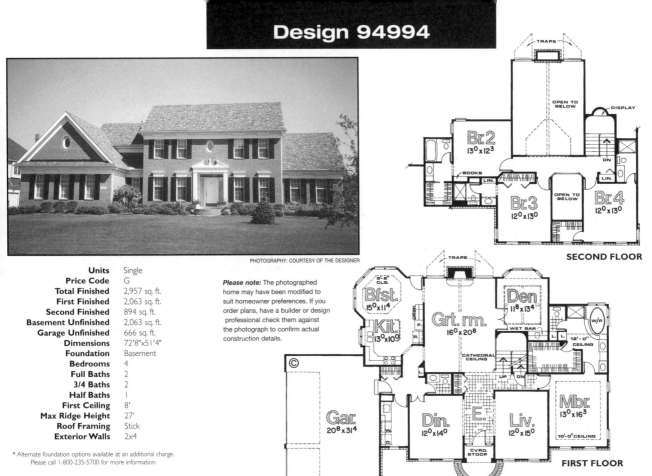

PHOTOGRAPHY: COURTESY OF THE DESIGNER

Units	Single
Price Code	G
Total Finished	2,957 sq. ft.
First Finished	2,063 sq. ft.
Second Finished	894 sq. ft.
Basement Unfinished	2,063 sq. ft.
Garage Unfinished	666 sq. ft.
Dimensions	72'8"x51'4"
Foundation	Basement
Bedrooms	4
Full Baths	2
3/4 Baths	2
Half Baths	1
First Ceiling	8'
Max Ridge Height	27'
Roof Framing	Stick
Exterior Walls	2x4

* Alternate foundation options available at an additional charge. Please call 1-800-235-5700 for more information.

Please note: The photographed home may have been modified to suit homeowner preferences. If you order plans, have a builder or design professional check them against the photograph to confirm actual construction details.

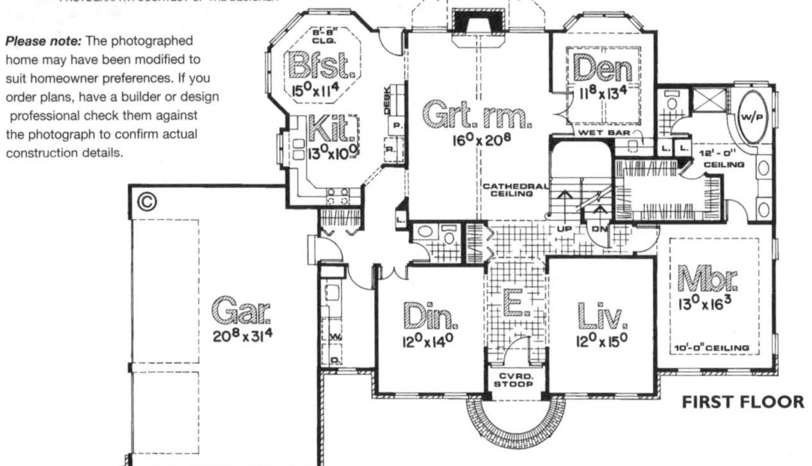

TRAPS
OPEN TO BELOW
DISPLAY
Br.2
13⁰x12³
BOOKS
LIN.
Br.3
12⁰x13⁰
OPEN TO BELOW
Br.4
12⁰x13⁰
DN
LIN.

SECOND FLOOR

TRAPS
8'-8" CLG.
Bfst.
15⁰x11⁴
Kit.
13⁰x10⁰
DESK
Grt. rm.
16⁰x20⁸
CATHEDRAL CEILING
Den
11⁸x13⁴
WET BAR
W/P
12'-0" CEILING
UP
DN
Gar.
20⁸x31⁴
Din.
12⁰x14⁰
E.
Liv.
12⁰x15⁰
Mbr.
13⁰x16³
10'-0" CEILING
CVRD. STOOP

FIRST FLOOR

Design 98534

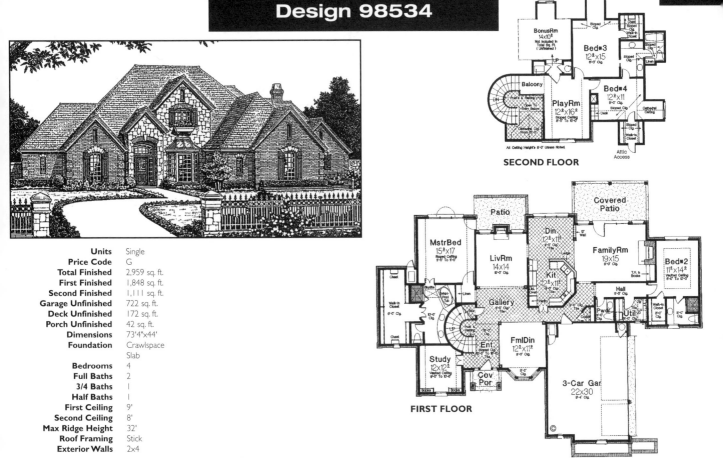

Units	Single
Price Code	G
Total Finished	2,959 sq. ft.
First Finished	1,848 sq. ft.
Second Finished	1,111 sq. ft.
Garage Unfinished	722 sq. ft.
Deck Unfinished	172 sq. ft.
Porch Unfinished	42 sq. ft.
Dimensions	73'4"x44'
Foundation	Crawlspace Slab
Bedrooms	4
Full Baths	2
3/4 Baths	1
Half Baths	1
First Ceiling	9'
Second Ceiling	8'
Max Ridge Height	32'
Roof Framing	Stick
Exterior Walls	2x4

BonusRm
14x10⁸
Bed#3
12⁸x15
Balcony
PlayRm
12⁸x16⁸
Bed#4
12⁸x11
Attic Access

SECOND FLOOR

Patio
Covered Patio
MstrBed
15⁸x17
LivRm
14x14
Din.
12⁸x11⁸
Kit
12⁸x11⁸
FamilyRm
19x15
Bed#2
11⁸x14⁸
Gallery
Hall
Pwdr
Util
Ent
FmlDin
12⁸x11⁸
Study
12x12⁸
Cov Por
3-Car Gar
22x30

FIRST FLOOR

Design 65417

Units	Single
Price Code	G
Total Finished	2,968 sq. ft.
First Finished	1,554 sq. ft.
Second Finished	1,414 sq. ft.
Basement Unfinished	765 sq. ft.
Garage Unfinished	305 sq. ft.
Porch Unfinished	98 sq. ft.
Dimensions	50'x43'
Foundation	Combo Basement/ Slab
Bedrooms	3
Full Baths	2
Half Baths	1
First Ceiling	9'
Second Ceiling	9'
Max Ridge Height	30'2"
Roof Framing	Truss
Exterior Walls	2x6

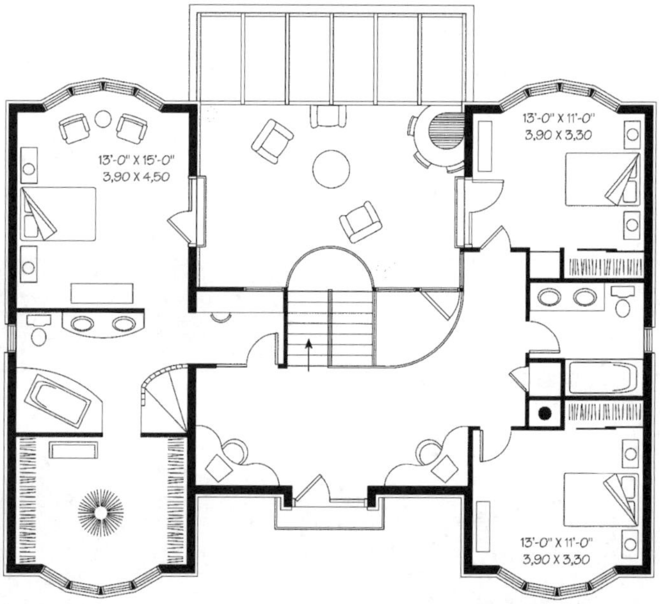

13'-0" X 15'-0"
3,90 X 4,50

13'-0" X 11'-0"
3,90 X 3,30

13'-0" X 11'-0"
3,90 X 3,30

SECOND FLOOR

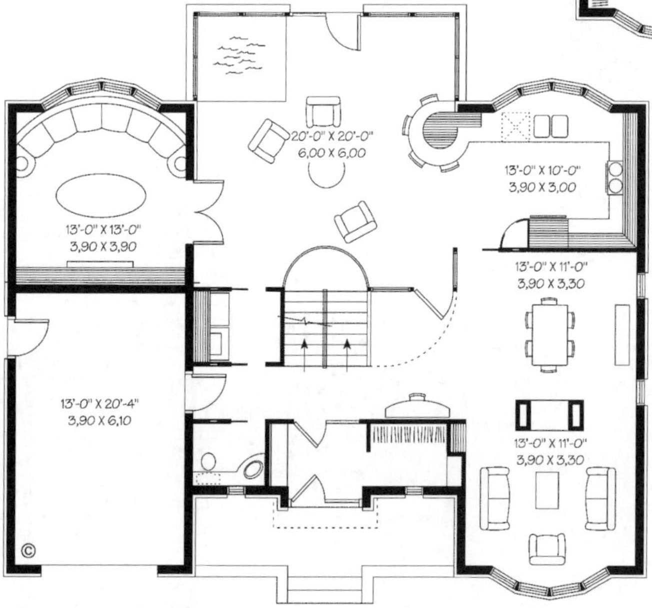

20'-0" X 20'-0"
6,00 X 6,00

13'-0" X 13'-0"
3,90 X 3,90

13'-0" X 10'-0"
3,90 X 3,00

13'-0" X 11'-0"
3,90 X 3,30

13'-0" X 20'-4"
3,90 X 6,10

13'-0" X 11'-0"
3,90 X 3,30

©

FIRST FLOOR

Design 52141

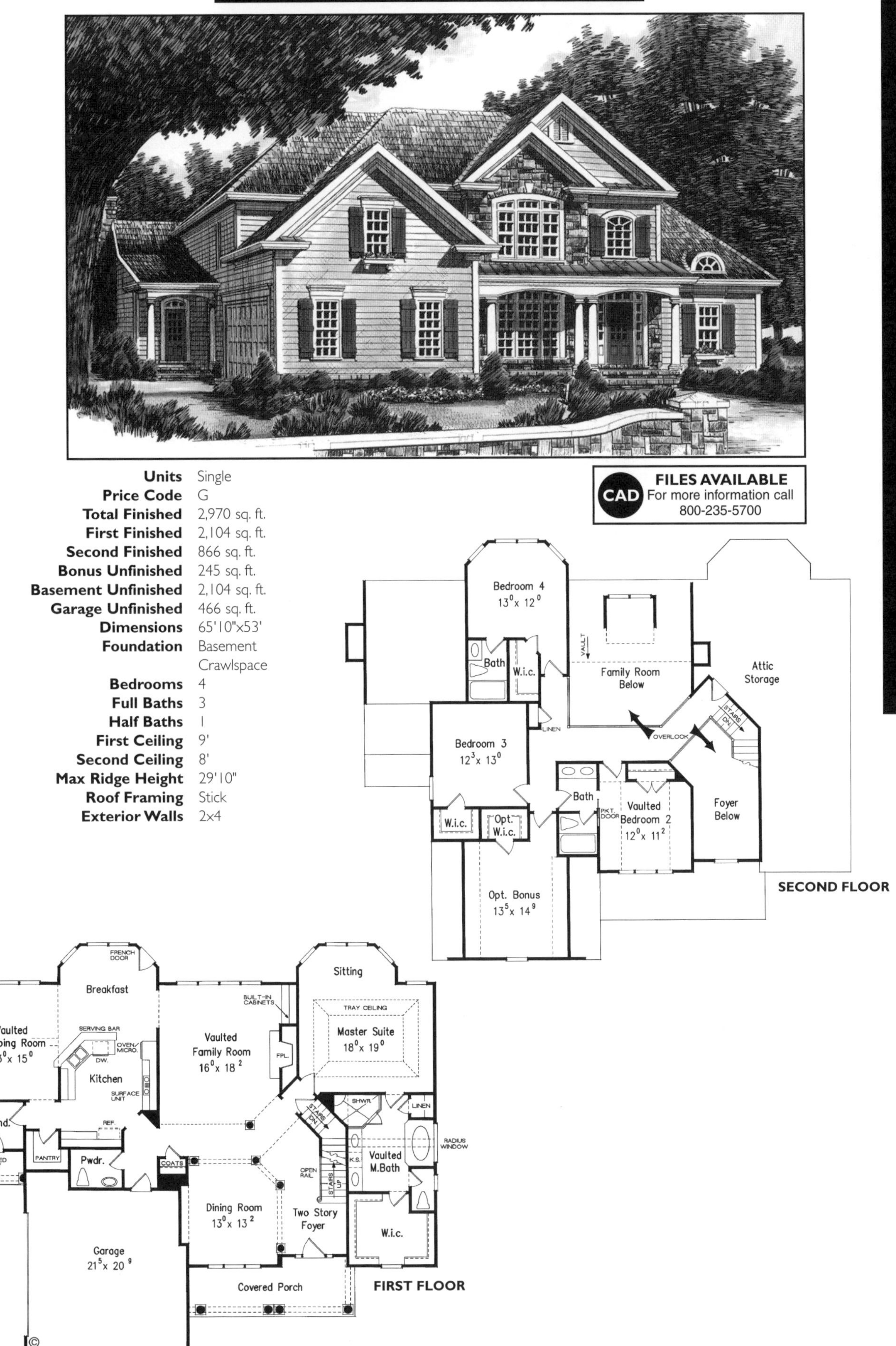

Bedroom 4
13⁰ x 12⁰
Bath
W.i.c.
VAULT
Family Room Below
Attic Storage
STAIRS DN
LINEN
OVERLOOK
Bedroom 3
12³ x 13⁰
Bath
PKT. DOOR
Vaulted Bedroom 2
12⁰ x 11²
Foyer Below
W.i.c.
Opt. W.i.c.
Opt. Bonus
13⁵ x 14⁹
SECOND FLOOR
FRENCH DOOR
Breakfast
Sitting
BUILT-IN CABINETS
TRAY CEILING
Master Suite
18⁰ x 19⁰
VAULT
Vaulted Keeping Room
13⁰ x 15⁰
FPL.
SERVING BAR
OVEN/MICRO.
DW.
Kitchen
SURFACE UNIT
Vaulted Family Room
16⁰ x 18²
FPL.
REF.
Laund.
W. D.
COVERED ENTRY
PANTRY
Pwdr.
COATS
STAIRS DN
SHWR.
LINEN
RADIUS WINDOW
K.S.
Vaulted M.Bath
OPEN RAIL
STAIRS UP
Dining Room
13⁰ x 13²
Two Story Foyer
W.i.c.
Garage
21⁵ x 20⁹
Covered Porch
FIRST FLOOR
©

Units	Single
Price Code	G
Total Finished	2,970 sq. ft.
First Finished	2,104 sq. ft.
Second Finished	866 sq. ft.
Bonus Unfinished	245 sq. ft.
Basement Unfinished	2,104 sq. ft.
Garage Unfinished	466 sq. ft.
Dimensions	65'10"x53'
Foundation	Basement Crawlspace
Bedrooms	4
Full Baths	3
Half Baths	1
First Ceiling	9'
Second Ceiling	8'
Max Ridge Height	29'10"
Roof Framing	Stick
Exterior Walls	2x4

Design 92457

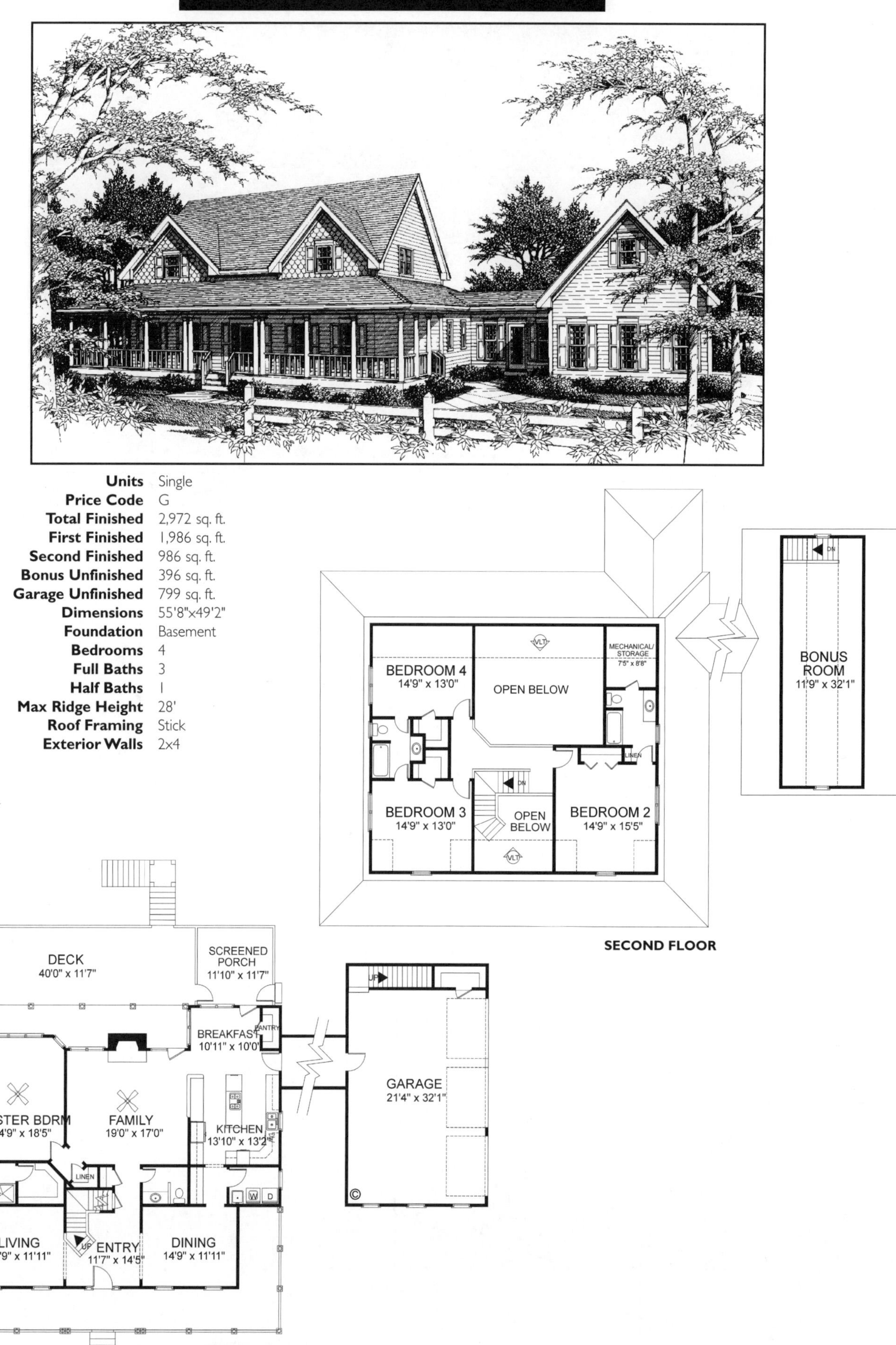
BEDROOM 4
14'9" x 13'0"
OPEN BELOW
MECHANICAL/ STORAGE
7'5" x 8'8"
LINEN
DN
BEDROOM 3
14'9" x 13'0"
OPEN BELOW
BEDROOM 2
14'9" x 15'5"
BONUS ROOM
11'9" x 32'1"
SECOND FLOOR
DECK
40'0" x 11'7"
SCREENED PORCH
11'10" x 11'7"
BREAKFAST
10'11" x 10'0"
PANTRY
MASTER BDRM
14'9" x 18'5"
FAMILY
19'0" x 17'0"
KITCHEN
13'10" x 13'2"
LINEN
GARAGE
21'4" x 32'1"
UP
W
D
LIVING
14'9" x 11'11"
ENTRY
11'7" x 14'5"
DINING
14'9" x 11'11"
FIRST FLOOR

Units	Single
Price Code	G
Total Finished	2,972 sq. ft.
First Finished	1,986 sq. ft.
Second Finished	986 sq. ft.
Bonus Unfinished	396 sq. ft.
Garage Unfinished	799 sq. ft.
Dimensions	55'8"x49'2"
Foundation	Basement
Bedrooms	4
Full Baths	3
Half Baths	1
Max Ridge Height	28'
Roof Framing	Stick
Exterior Walls	2x4

Design 32353

PHOTOGRAPHY: LAURIE BLACK

Units	Single
Price Code	G
Total Finished	2,977 sq. ft.
First Finished	2,111 sq. ft.
Second Finished	866 sq. ft.
Garage Unfinished	912 sq. ft.
Deck Unfinished	948 sq. ft.
Dimensions	76'x93'
Foundation	Crawlspace
Bedrooms	3
Full Baths	1
3/4 Baths	1
Half Baths	1
First Ceiling	8'
Second Ceiling	8'
Vaulted Ceiling	23'2
Max Ridge Height	29'6
Roof Framing	Truss
Exterior Walls	2x6

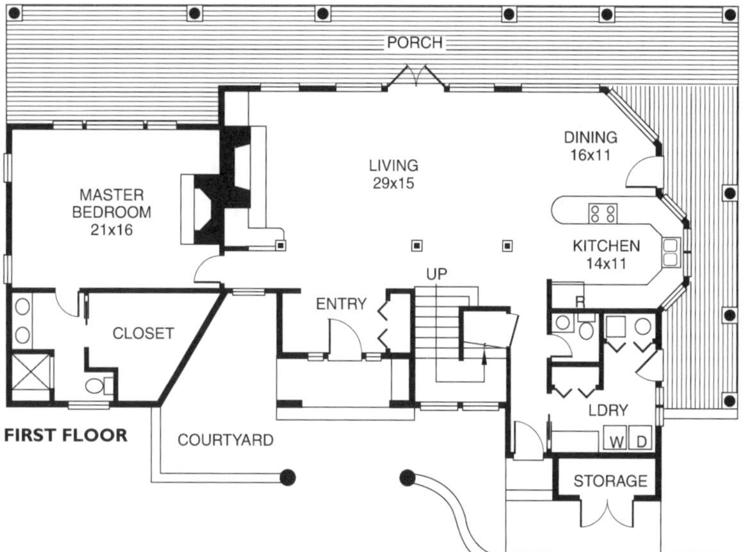

PORCH
DINING 16x11
LIVING 29x15
MASTER BEDROOM 21x16
KITCHEN 14x11
UP
ENTRY
CLOSET
LDRY
W D
COURTYARD
STORAGE
GARAGE 23x37

FIRST FLOOR

OPEN TO LIVING
BEDROOM 15x12
LOFT 13x15
DN
BEDROOM 10x12
OPEN

SECOND FLOOR

Please note: The photographed home may have been modified to suit homeowner preferences. If you order plans, have a builder or design professional check them against the photograph to confirm actual construction details.

Design 94242

Units	Single
Price Code	H
Total Finished	2,978 sq. ft.
Main Finished	2,978 sq. ft.
Garage Unfinished	702 sq. ft.
Dimensions	84'x90'
Foundation	Slab
Bedrooms	3
Full Baths	2
3/4 Baths	1
Half Baths	1
Max Ridge Height	36'6"
Roof Framing	Stick

* Alternate foundation options available at an additional charge. Please call 1-800-235-5700 for more information.

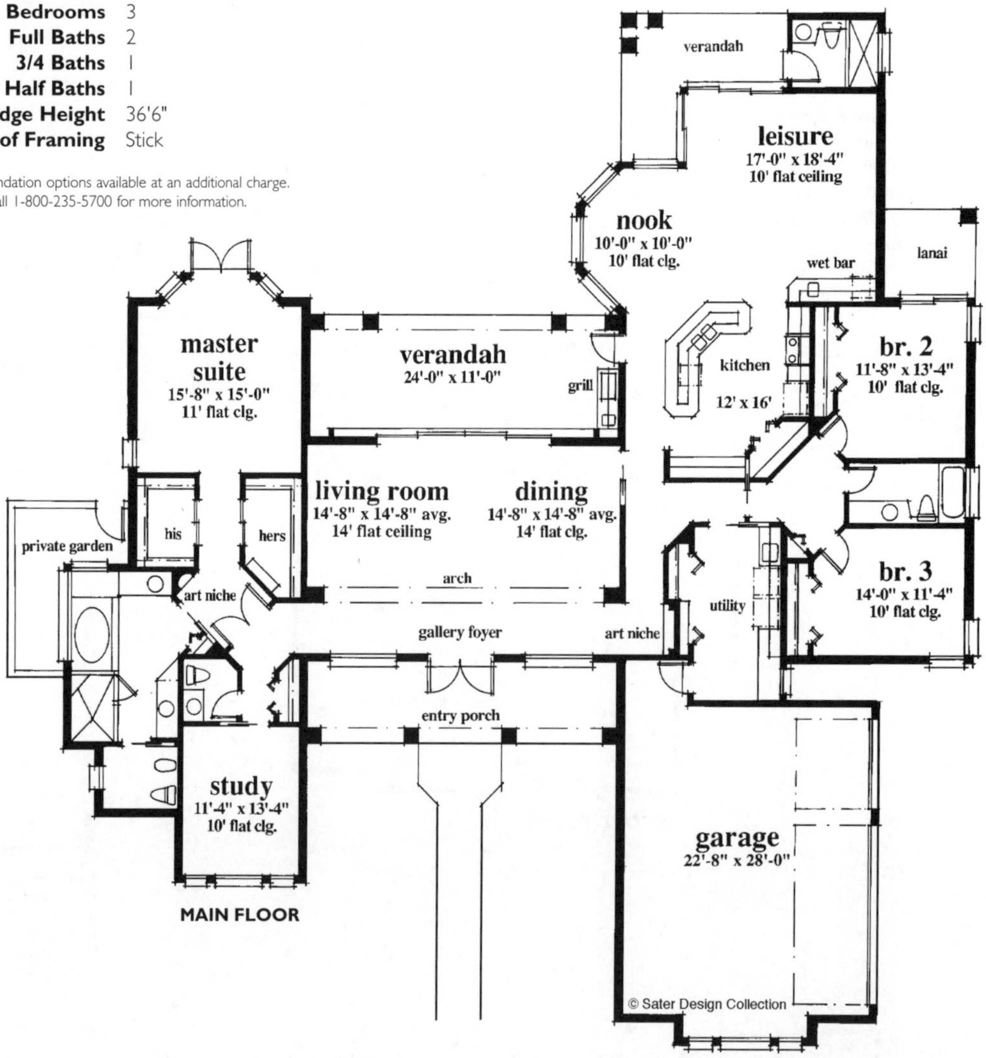

verandah

leisure
17'-0" x 18'-4"
10' flat ceiling

nook
10'-0" x 10'-0"
10' flat clg.

wet bar

lanai

master suite
15'-8" x 15'-0"
11' flat clg.

verandah
24'-0" x 11'-0"

grill

kitchen
12' x 16'

br. 2
11'-8" x 13'-4"
10' flat clg.

living room
14'-8" x 14'-8" avg.
14' flat ceiling

dining
14'-8" x 14'-8" avg.
14' flat clg.

his

hers

private garden

art niche

arch

utility

br. 3
14'-0" x 11'-4"
10' flat clg.

gallery foyer

art niche

entry porch

study
11'-4" x 13'-4"
10' flat clg.

garage
22'-8" x 28'-0"

MAIN FLOOR

Design 52095

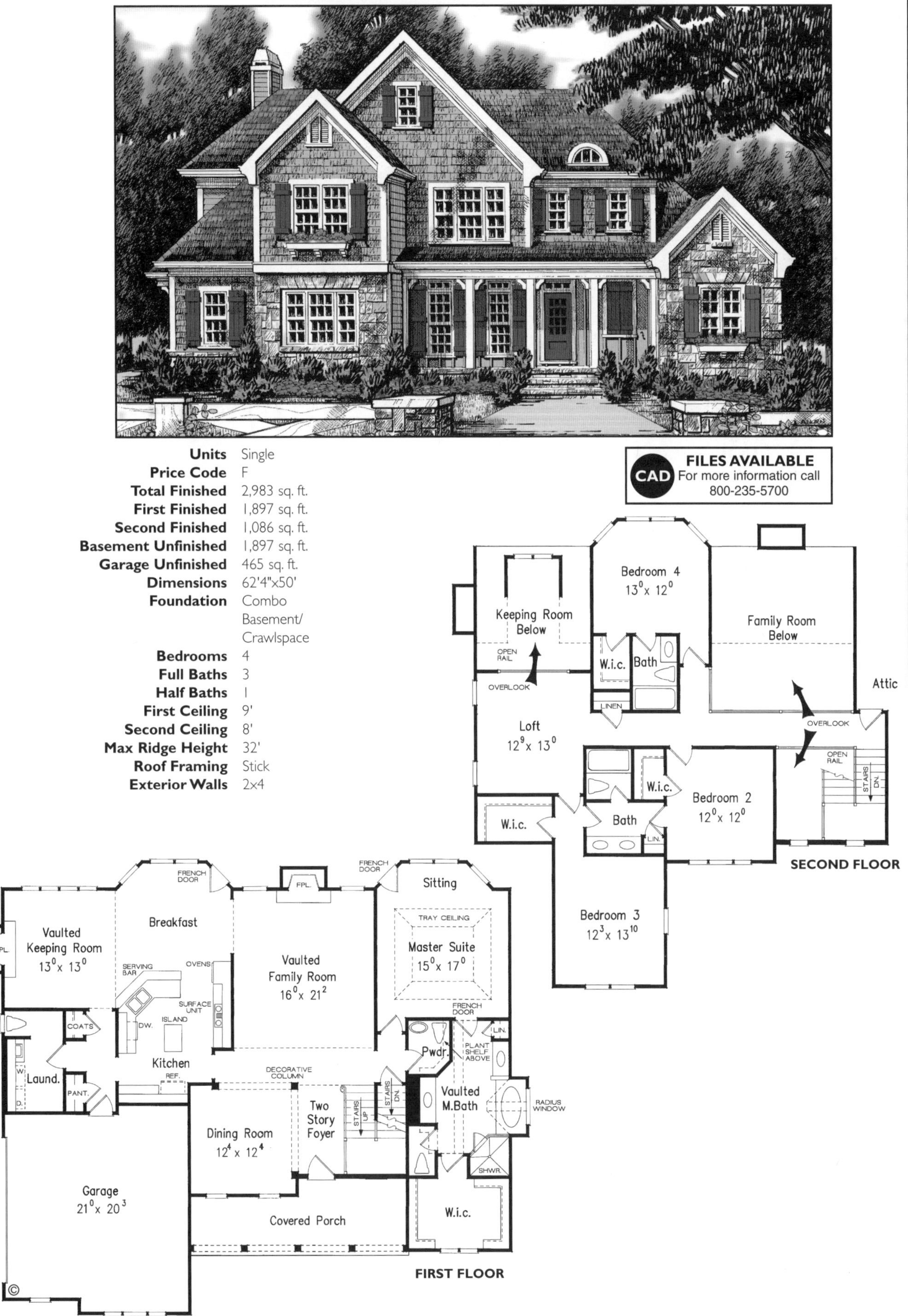

FILES AVAILABLE
CAD
For more information call
800-235-5700
Keeping Room Below
OPEN RAIL
OVERLOOK
Bedroom 4
13^0 x 12^0
W.i.c.
Bath
LINEN
Family Room Below
Attic
OVERLOOK
OPEN RAIL
STAIRS DN.
Loft
12^9 x 13^0
W.i.c.
Bath
LIN.
Bedroom 2
12^0 x 12^0
W.i.c.
Bedroom 3
12^3 x 13^{10}
SECOND FLOOR
FRENCH DOOR
Breakfast
FPL.
Vaulted Keeping Room
13^0 x 13^0
SERVING BAR
OVENS
SURFACE UNIT
DW.
ISLAND
COATS
Kitchen
REF.
Laund.
PANT.
W
D
FRENCH DOOR
FPL.
Vaulted Family Room
16^0 x 21^2
DECORATIVE COLUMN
Dining Room
12^4 x 12^4
Two Story Foyer
STAIRS UP
STAIRS DN.
Sitting
TRAY CEILING
Master Suite
15^0 x 17^0
FRENCH DOOR
LIN.
Pwdr.
PLANT SHELF ABOVE
Vaulted M.Bath
RADIUS WINDOW
SHWR.
W.i.c.
Garage
21^0 x 20^3
Covered Porch
FIRST FLOOR
©

Units	Single
Price Code	F
Total Finished	2,983 sq. ft.
First Finished	1,897 sq. ft.
Second Finished	1,086 sq. ft.
Basement Unfinished	1,897 sq. ft.
Garage Unfinished	465 sq. ft.
Dimensions	62'4"x50'
Foundation	Combo Basement/ Crawlspace
Bedrooms	4
Full Baths	3
Half Baths	1
First Ceiling	9'
Second Ceiling	8'
Max Ridge Height	32'
Roof Framing	Stick
Exterior Walls	2x4

Design 94219

Units	Single
Price Code	H
Total Finished	2,986 sq. ft.
Main Finished	2,986 sq. ft.
Garage Unfinished	574 sq. ft.
Porch Unfinished	556 sq. ft.
Dimensions	82'8"x76'4"
Foundation	Slab
Bedrooms	4
Full Baths	2
3/4 Baths	1
Half Baths	1
Main Ceiling	10'
Max Ridge Height	28'6"
Roof Framing	Stick

* Alternate foundation options available at an additional charge.
Please call 1-800-235-5700 for more information.

private garden
guest/ playroom 12'-0" x 13'-10" 10' clg.
verandah
© Sater Design Collection
leisure 17'-4" x 17'-0" 10' flat clg.
verandah 24'-0" x 12'-0" avg.
master suite 14'-0" x 16'-6" 11' stepped clg.
br. 2 13'-8" x 12'-4" 10' flat clg.
mitered glass
nook 9'-0" x 10'-0"
2 view fireplace
kitchen 14' x 13'
living 14'-0" x 14'-0" 14' stepped clg.
study 14'-2" x 12'-8" 14' stepped clg.
br. 3 11'-4" x 12'-10" 10' clg.
arch
books
gallery
books
arch
grand foyer
entry arched clg.
utility
dining 12'-8" x 15'-0" 14' tray clg.
garage 21'-4" x 24'-8"

MAIN FLOOR

Design 99784

Units	Single
Price Code	G
Total Finished	2,987 sq. ft.
Main Finished	2,987 sq. ft.
Garage Unfinished	690 sq. ft.
Dimensions	116'5"x61'
Foundation	Crawlspace
Bedrooms	4
Full Baths	2
3/4 Baths	1
Max Ridge Height	22'
Roof Framing	Truss
Exterior Walls	2x6

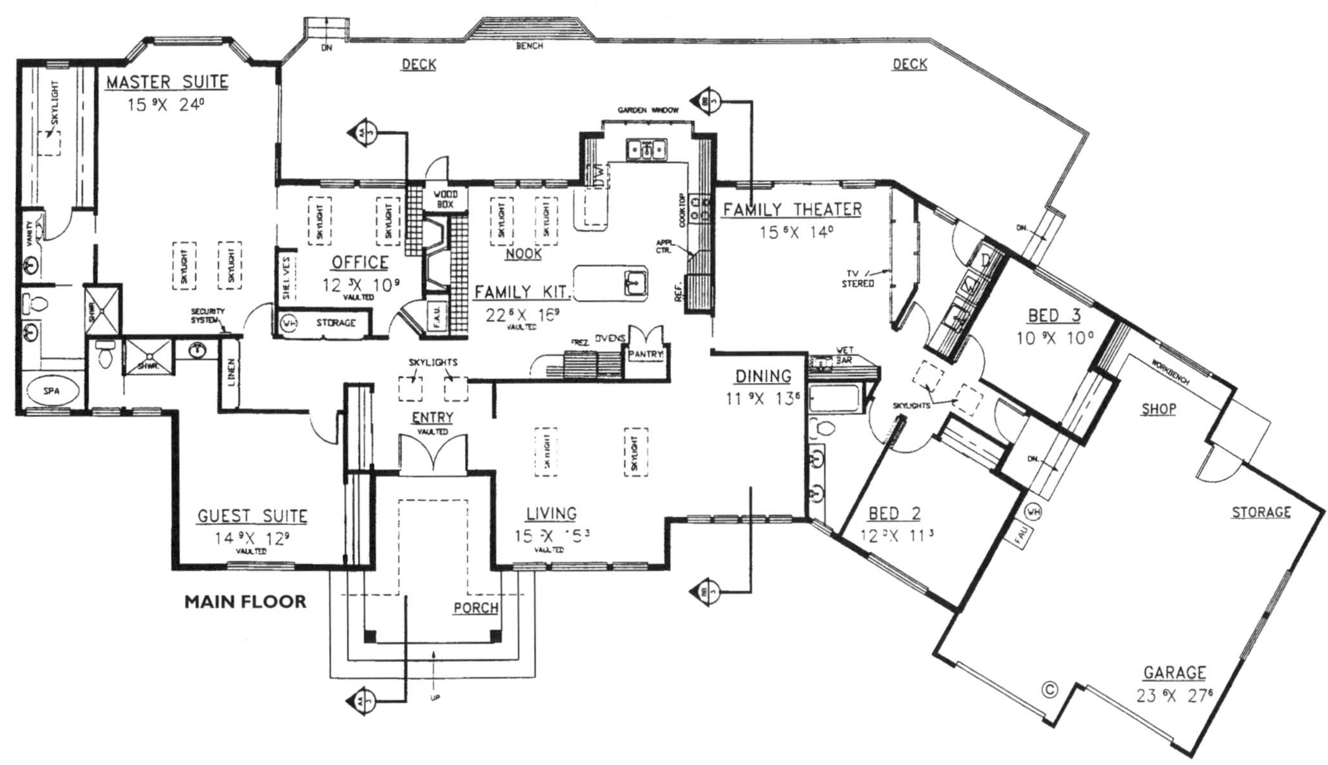
DECK
BENCH
DECK
MASTER SUITE
15^{9}X 24^{0}
SKYLIGHT
VANITY
SPA
SHWR
SECURITY SYSTEM
LINEN
GARDEN WINDOW
WOOD BOX
OFFICE
12^{3}X 10^{9}
VAULTED
SHELVES
STORAGE
NOOK
FAMILY KIT.
22^{6}X 16^{9}
VAULTED
COOKTOP
APPL. CTR.
REF.
F.A.U.
FREZ.
OVENS
PANTRY
FAMILY THEATER
15^{6}X 14^{0}
TV / STEREO
WET BAR
DINING
11^{9}X 13^{6}
SKYLIGHTS
ENTRY
VAULTED
BED 3
10^{9}X 10^{0}
WORKBENCH
SHOP
STORAGE
BED 2
12^{0}X 11^{3}
GUEST SUITE
14^{9}X 12^{9}
VAULTED
LIVING
15^{0}X 15^{3}
VAULTED
PORCH
GARAGE
23^{6}X 27^{6}
MAIN FLOOR

Design 97350

Units	Single
Price Code	G
Total Finished	2,996 sq. ft.
First Finished	2,044 sq. ft.
Second Finished	952 sq. ft.
Dimensions	76'x59'
Foundation	Basement
Bedrooms	4
Full Baths	3
Half Baths	1
Max Ridge Height	28'9"
Roof Framing	Truss
Exterior Walls	2x6

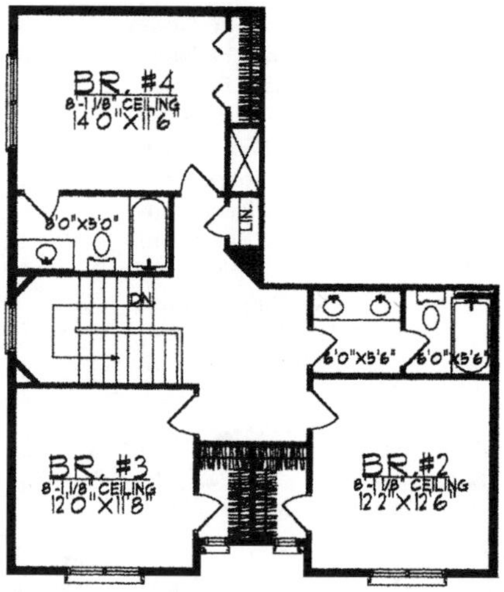

BR. #4
8'-1 1/8" CEILING
14'0"X11'6"
6'0"X5'0"
LIN.
DN.
6'0"X5'6"
6'0"X5'6"
BR. #3
8'-1 1/8" CEILING
12'0"X11'8"
BR. #2
8'-1 1/8" CEILING
12'2"X12'6"

SECOND FLOOR

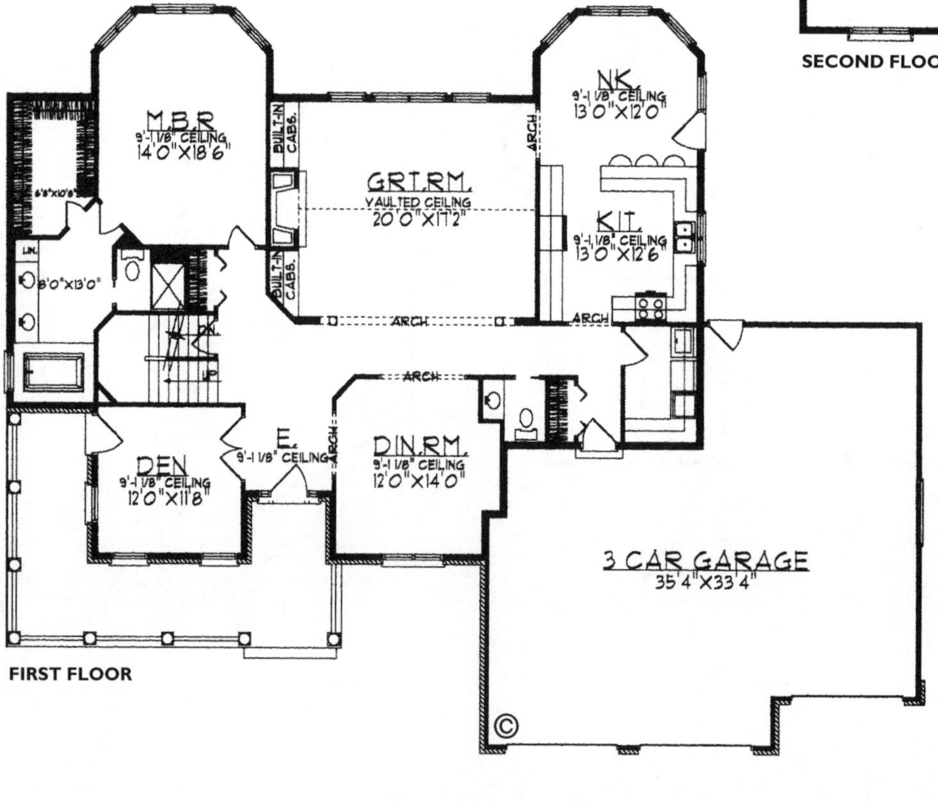

M.B.R.
9'-1 1/8" CEILING
14'0"X18'6"
6'8"X10'8"
LIN.
8'0"X13'0"
BUILT-IN CABS.
GRT.RM.
VAULTED CEILING
20'0"X17'2"
BUILT-IN CABS.
ARCH
NK.
9'-1 1/8" CEILING
13'0"X12'0"
KIT.
9'-1 1/8" CEILING
13'0"X12'6"
ARCH
ARCH
ARCH
DN.
UP
E.
9'-1 1/8" CEILING
DEN
9'-1 1/8" CEILING
12'0"X11'8"
DIN.RM.
9'-1 1/8" CEILING
12'0"X14'0"
3 CAR GARAGE
35'4"X33'4"
©

FIRST FLOOR

Design 98232

Units	Single
Price Code	G
Total Finished	2,996 sq. ft.
First Finished	1,437 sq. ft.
Second Finished	1,559 sq. ft.
Dimensions	66'x44'
Foundation	Basement
Bedrooms	4
Full Baths	3
Half Baths	1
First Ceiling	9'
Second Ceiling	8'
Tray Ceiling	11'
Max Ridge Height	33'
Roof Framing	Stick
Exterior Walls	2x4

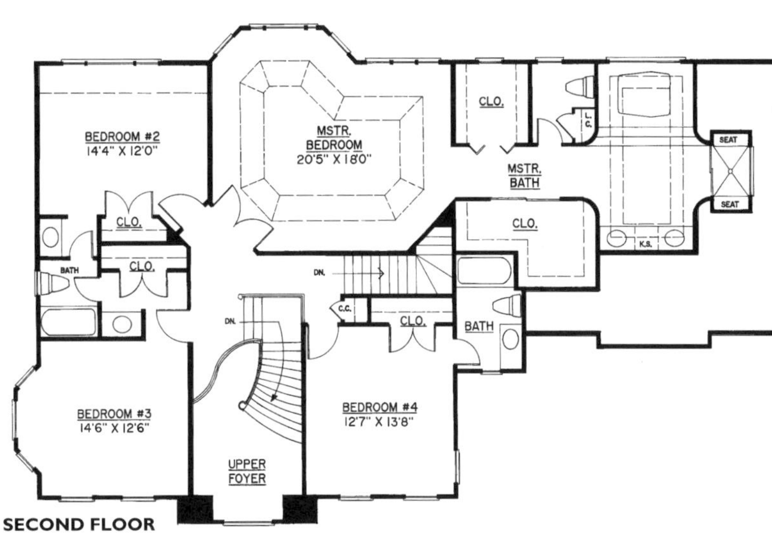
BEDROOM #2
14'4" X 12'0"
MSTR.
BEDROOM
20'5" X 18'0"
CLO.
MSTR.
BATH
SEAT
SEAT
K.S.
CLO.
CLO.
BATH
CLO.
DN.
C.C.
CLO.
BATH
DN.
BEDROOM #3
14'6" X 12'6"
BEDROOM #4
12'7" X 13'8"
UPPER
FOYER

SECOND FLOOR

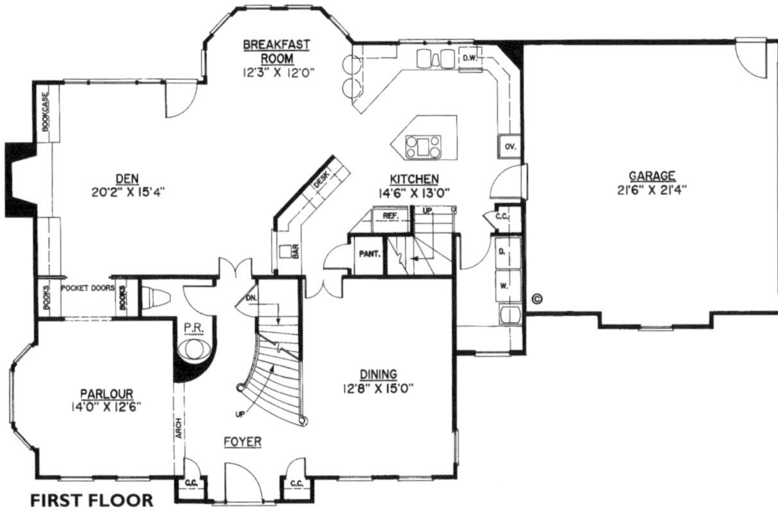
BREAKFAST
ROOM
12'3" X 12'0"
D.W.
BOOKCASE
DEN
20'2" X 15'4"
OV.
DESK
KITCHEN
14'6" X 13'0"
GARAGE
21'6" X 21'4"
REF.
UP
C.C.
BAR
PANT.
D.
W.
BOOKS
POCKET DOORS
BOOKS
DN.
P.R.
DINING
12'8" X 15'0"
PARLOUR
14'0" X 12'6"
UP
ARCH
FOYER
C.C.
C.C.

FIRST FLOOR

Design 66005

Units	Single
Price Code	H
Total Finished	3,002 sq. ft.
First Finished	2,169 sq. ft.
Second Finished	833 sq. ft.
Bonus Unfinished	272 sq. ft.
Garage Unfinished	675 sq. ft.
Deck Unfinished	352 sq. ft.
Porch Unfinished	62 sq. ft.
Dimensions	65'x67'7"
Foundation	Slab
Bedrooms	4
Full Baths	2
3/4 Baths	1
Half Baths	1
First Ceiling	10'
Second Ceiling	8'
Max Ridge Height	29'
Roof Framing	Stick
Exterior Walls	2x4

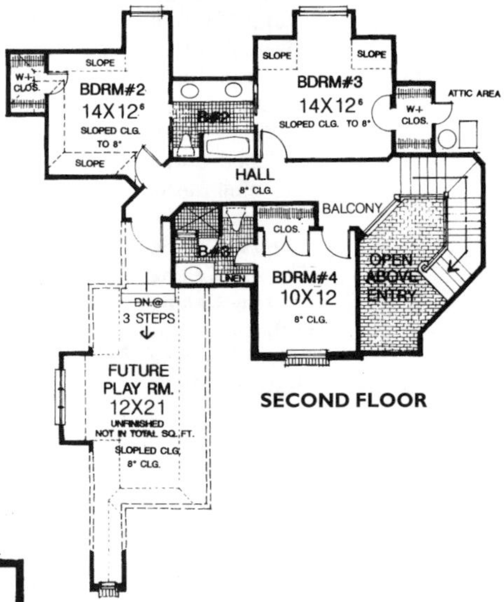

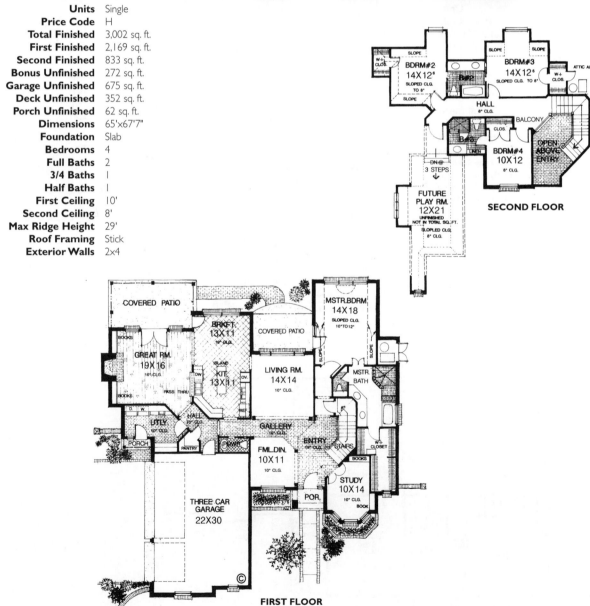

SECOND FLOOR

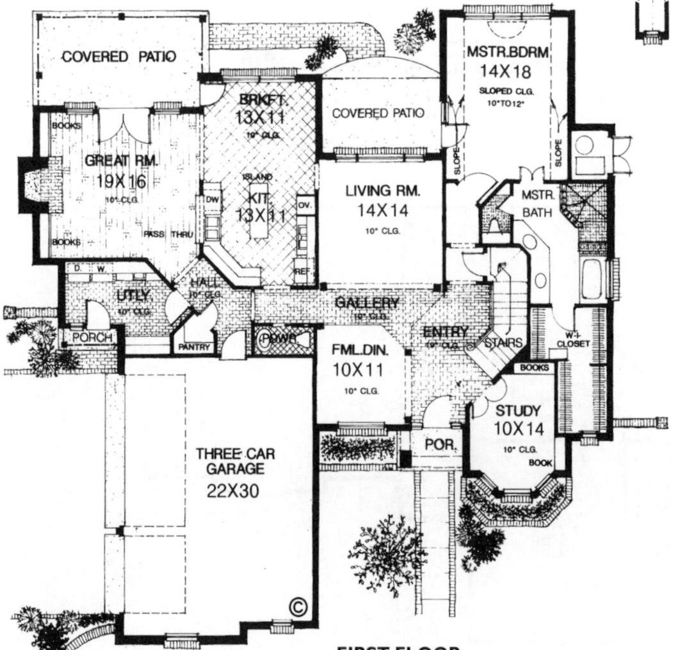

FIRST FLOOR

Design 66011

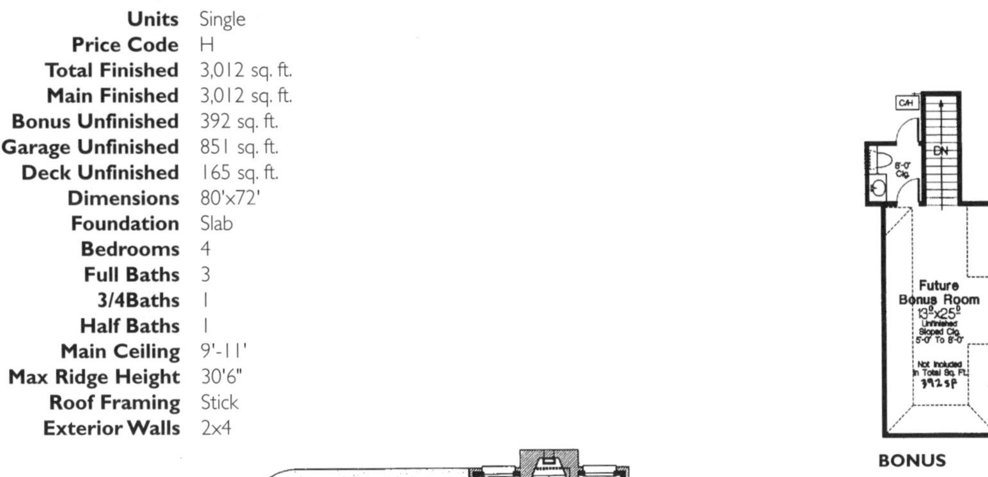

Future
Bonus Room
13⁰x25⁰
Unfinished
Sloped Clg.
5'-0" To 8'-0"
Not Included
In Total Sq. Ft.
392 SF
DN
C/H
8'-0" Clg.

Units	Single
Price Code	H
Total Finished	3,012 sq. ft.
Main Finished	3,012 sq. ft.
Bonus Unfinished	392 sq. ft.
Garage Unfinished	851 sq. ft.
Deck Unfinished	165 sq. ft.
Dimensions	80'x72'
Foundation	Slab
Bedrooms	4
Full Baths	3
3/4Baths	1
Half Baths	1
Main Ceiling	9'-11'
Max Ridge Height	30'6"
Roof Framing	Stick
Exterior Walls	2x4

BONUS

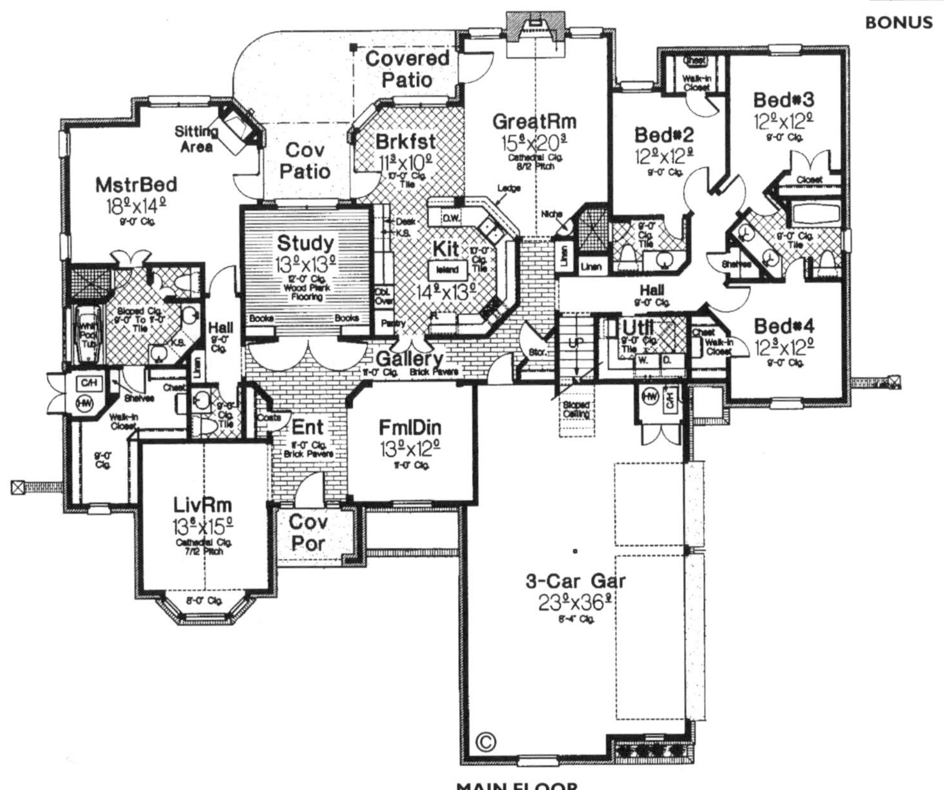

Covered
Patio
Sitting
Area
MstrBed
18⁰x14⁰
Cov
Patio
Brkfst
11⁰x10⁰
GreatRm
15⁰x20³
Cathedral Clg.
Bed#2
12⁰x12⁰
Bed#3
12⁰x12⁰
Study
13⁰x13⁰
Wood Plank
Flooring
Kit
14⁰x13⁰
Island
Hall
Utl
Bed#4
12³x12⁰
Gallery
Brick Pavers
Ent
Brick Pavers
FmlDin
13⁰x12⁰
LivRm
13⁶x15⁰
Cathedral Clg.
7/12 Pitch
Cov
Por
3-Car Gar
23⁰x36⁰

MAIN FLOOR

Design 24656

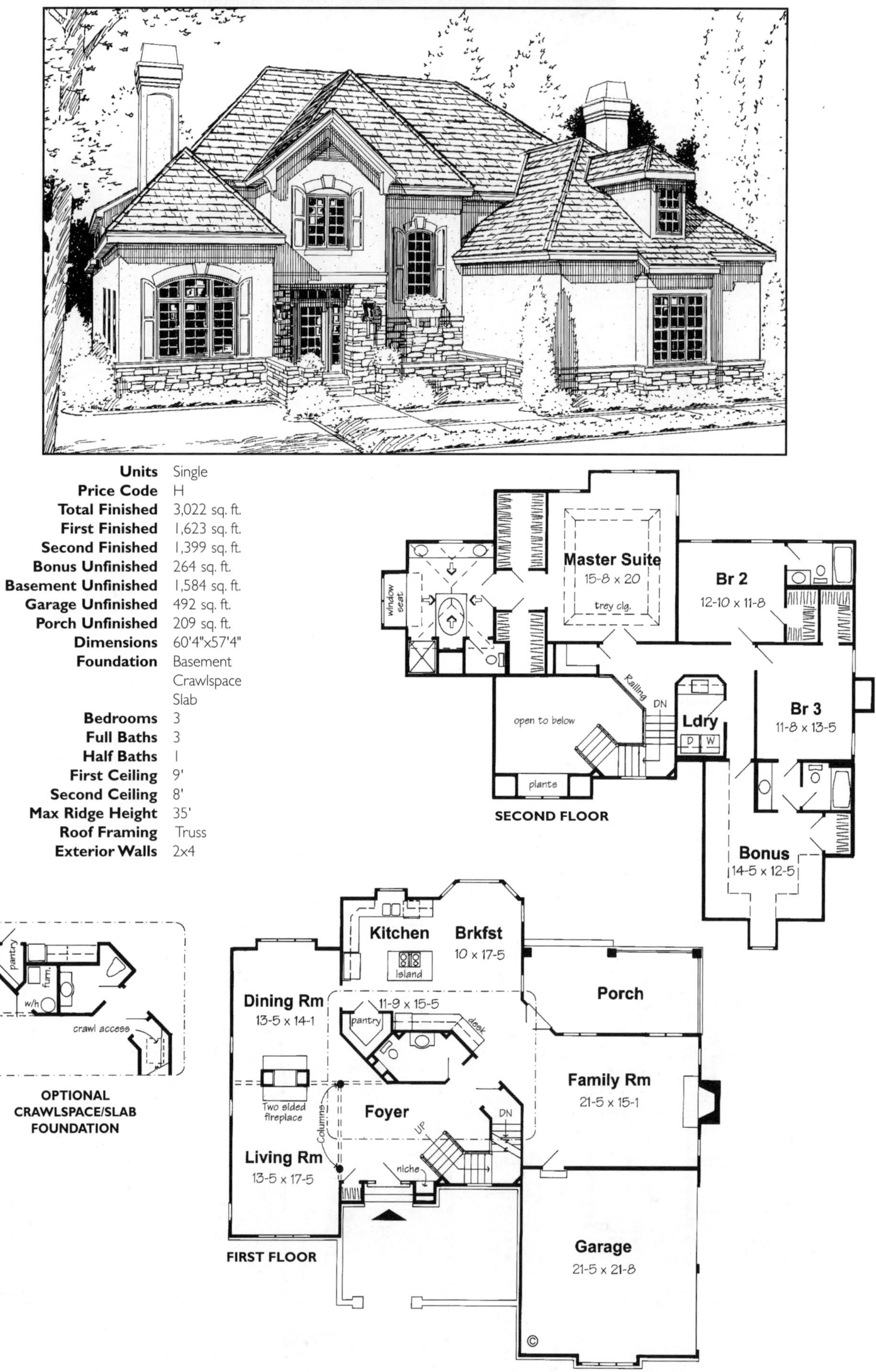

Master Suite
15-8 x 20
trey clg.
window seat
Br 2
12-10 x 11-8
Br 3
11-8 x 13-5
Railing
DN
Ldry
D W
open to below
plants
Bonus
14-5 x 12-5
SECOND FLOOR
pantry
furn.
w/h
crawl access
OPTIONAL CRAWLSPACE/SLAB FOUNDATION
Kitchen
Island
Brkfst
10 x 17-5
Dining Rm
13-5 x 14-1
11-9 x 15-5
pantry
desk
Porch
Family Rm
21-5 x 15-1
Two sided fireplace
Columns
Foyer
UP
DN
Living Rm
13-5 x 17-5
niche
Garage
21-5 x 21-8
FIRST FLOOR
©

Units	Single
Price Code	H
Total Finished	3,022 sq. ft.
First Finished	1,623 sq. ft.
Second Finished	1,399 sq. ft.
Bonus Unfinished	264 sq. ft.
Basement Unfinished	1,584 sq. ft.
Garage Unfinished	492 sq. ft.
Porch Unfinished	209 sq. ft.
Dimensions	60'4"x57'4"
Foundation	Basement Crawlspace Slab
Bedrooms	3
Full Baths	3
Half Baths	1
First Ceiling	9'
Second Ceiling	8'
Max Ridge Height	35'
Roof Framing	Truss
Exterior Walls	2x4

Design 10601

Units	Single
Price Code	H
Total Finished	3,025 sq. ft.
Main Finished	3,025 sq. ft.
Garage Unfinished	722 sq. ft.
Dimensions	98'10"x56'6"
Foundation	Slab
Bedrooms	4
Full Baths	3
Max Ridge Height	19'
Roof Framing	Stick
Exterior Walls	2x6

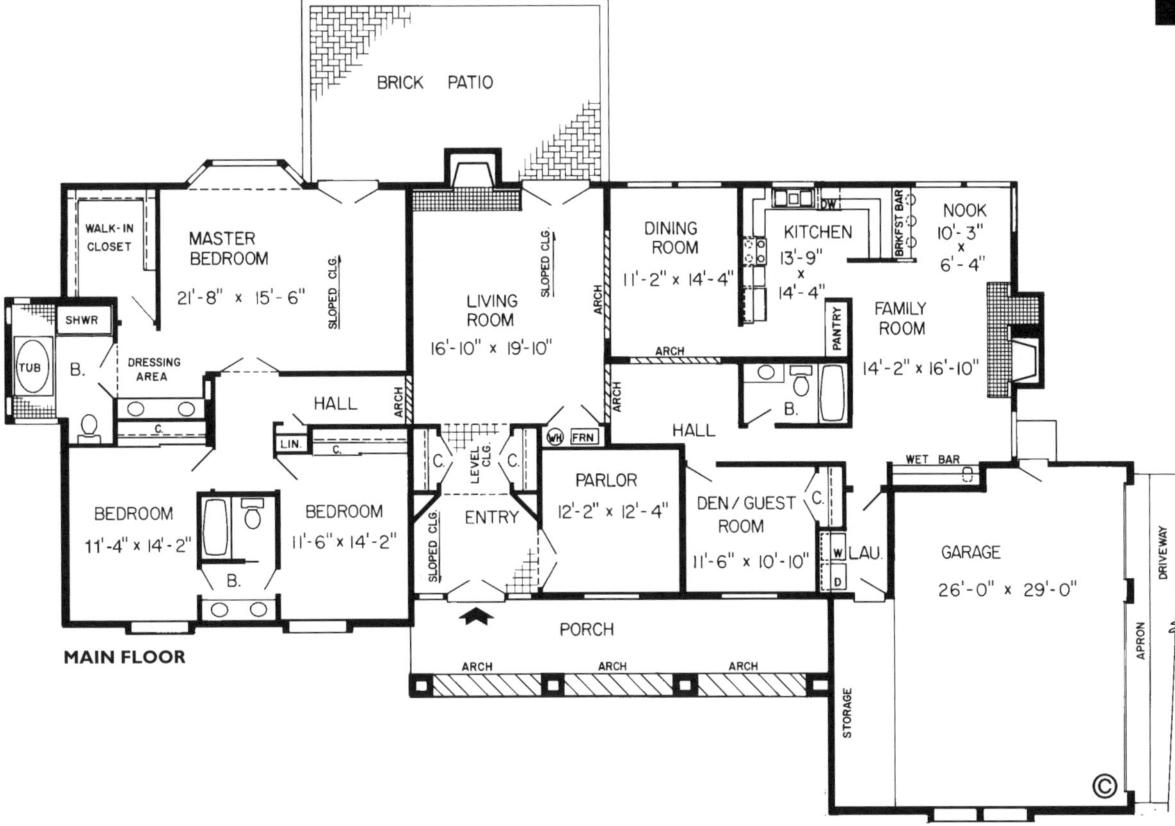
BRICK PATIO
WALK-IN CLOSET
MASTER BEDROOM
21'-8" x 15'-6"
SLOPED CLG.
SHWR
TUB
B.
DRESSING AREA
C.
HALL
ARCH
LIN.
C.
LIVING ROOM
16'-10" x 19'-10"
SLOPED CLG.
ARCH
DINING ROOM
11'-2" x 14'-4"
ARCH
KITCHEN
13'-9" x 14'-4"
DW
BRKFST BAR
NOOK
10'-3" x 6'-4"
PANTRY
FAMILY ROOM
14'-2" x 16'-10"
B.
ARCH
HALL
WH
FRN
C.
LEVEL CLG.
C.
BEDROOM
11'-4" x 14'-2"
B.
BEDROOM
11'-6" x 14'-2"
SLOPED CLG.
ENTRY
PARLOR
12'-2" x 12'-4"
DEN / GUEST ROOM
11'-6" x 10'-10"
C.
WET BAR
W
D
LAU.
GARAGE
26'-0" x 29'-0"
DRIVEWAY
APRON
PORCH
ARCH
ARCH
ARCH
STORAGE
©

MAIN FLOOR

Design 98405

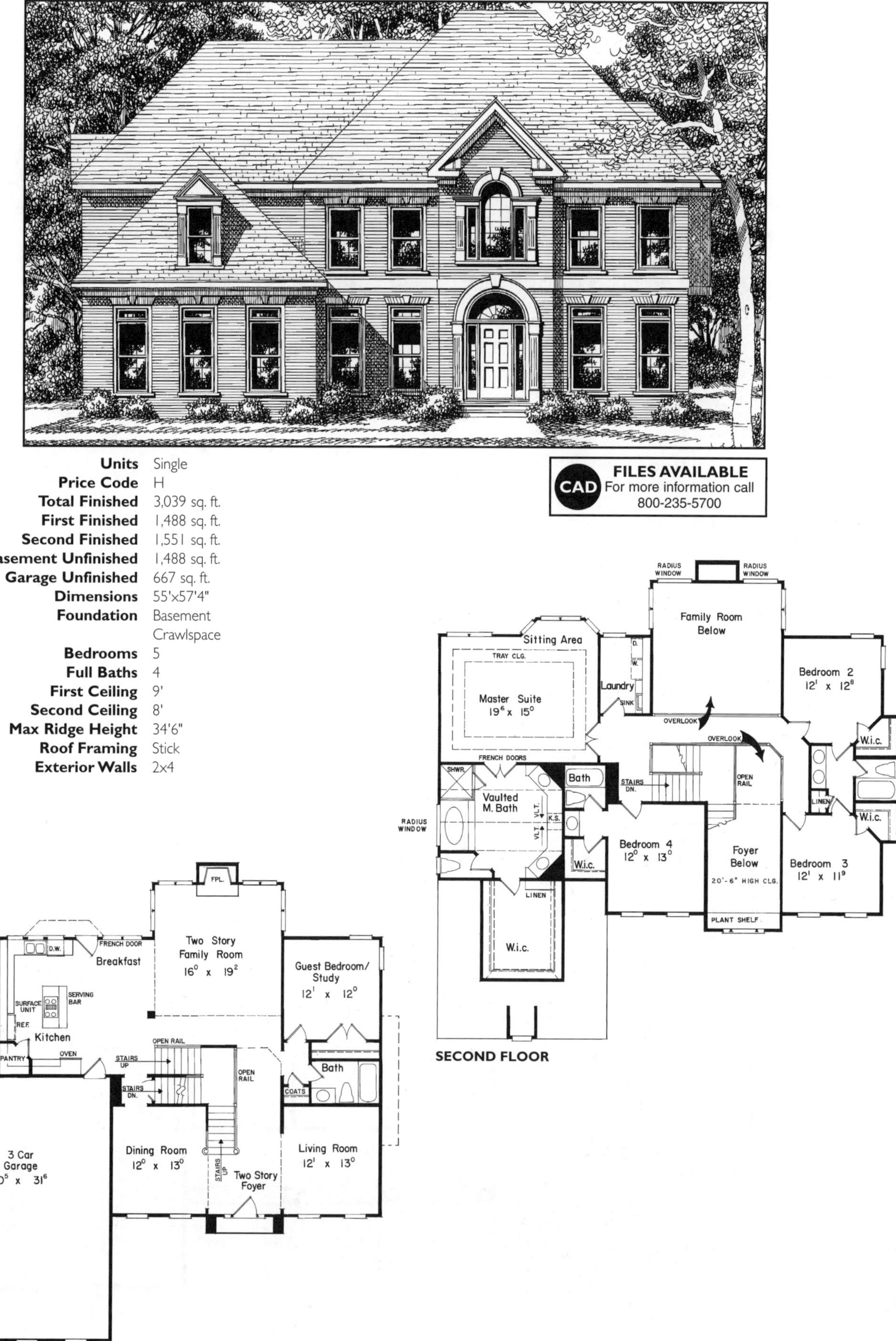

SECOND FLOOR
RADIUS WINDOW
RADIUS WINDOW
Family Room Below
Sitting Area
TRAY CLG.
Master Suite 19⁶ x 15⁰
Laundry
D.
W.
SINK
Bedroom 2 12¹ x 12⁸
OVERLOOK
OVERLOOK
W.i.c.
FRENCH DOORS
SHWR.
Vaulted M. Bath
Bath
STAIRS DN.
OPEN RAIL
LINEN
W.i.c.
RADIUS WINDOW
K.S.
Bedroom 4 12⁰ x 13⁰
Foyer Below
20'-6" HIGH CLG.
Bedroom 3 12¹ x 11⁹
W.i.c.
LINEN
PLANT SHELF
W.i.c.
FIRST FLOOR
FPL.
Two Story Family Room 16⁰ x 19²
FRENCH DOOR
D.W.
Breakfast
Storage
SURFACE UNIT
SERVING BAR
REF.
Kitchen
Guest Bedroom/ Study 12¹ x 12⁰
PANTRY
OVEN
OPEN RAIL
STAIRS UP
STAIRS DN.
OPEN RAIL
Bath
COATS
3 Car Garage 20⁵ x 31⁶
Dining Room 12⁰ x 13⁰
STAIRS UP
Two Story Foyer
Living Room 12¹ x 13⁰

Units	Single
Price Code	H
Total Finished	3,039 sq. ft.
First Finished	1,488 sq. ft.
Second Finished	1,551 sq. ft.
Basement Unfinished	1,488 sq. ft.
Garage Unfinished	667 sq. ft.
Dimensions	55'x57'4"
Foundation	Basement Crawlspace
Bedrooms	5
Full Baths	4
First Ceiling	9'
Second Ceiling	8'
Max Ridge Height	34'6"
Roof Framing	Stick
Exterior Walls	2x4

Design 60003

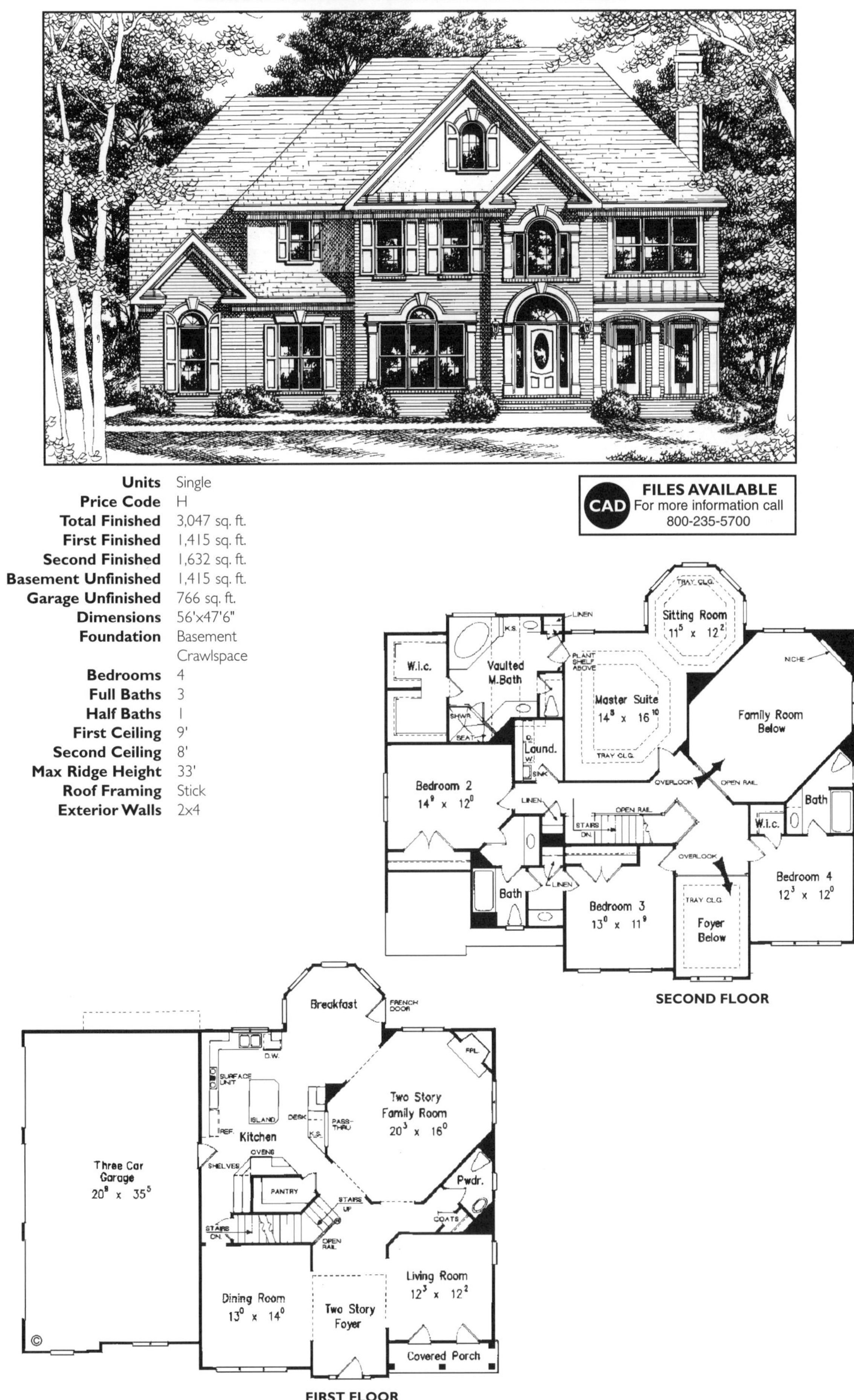
FILES AVAILABLE
CAD For more information call
800-235-5700
Sitting Room 11⁵ x 12²
TRAY CLG.
LINEN
K.S.
PLANT SHELF ABOVE
W.i.c.
Vaulted M.Bath
Master Suite 14⁸ x 16¹⁰
NICHE
Family Room Below
SHWR
SEAT
TRAY CLG.
Laund.
SINK
OVERLOOK
OPEN RAIL
Bedroom 2 14⁹ x 12⁰
LINEN
OPEN RAIL
STAIRS DN.
Bath
W.i.c.
OVERLOOK
Bedroom 4 12³ x 12⁰
Bath
LINEN
Bedroom 3 13⁰ x 11⁹
TRAY CLG.
Foyer Below
SECOND FLOOR
Breakfast
FRENCH DOOR
D.W.
FPL.
SURFACE UNIT
Two Story Family Room 20³ x 16⁰
ISLAND
DESK
PASS-THRU
REF.
Kitchen
K.S.
OVENS
Three Car Garage 20⁸ x 35⁵
SHELVES
PANTRY
Pwdr.
STAIRS UP
STAIRS DN.
COATS
OPEN RAIL
Living Room 12³ x 12²
Dining Room 13⁰ x 14⁰
Two Story Foyer
Covered Porch
©
FIRST FLOOR

Units	Single
Price Code	H
Total Finished	3,047 sq. ft.
First Finished	1,415 sq. ft.
Second Finished	1,632 sq. ft.
Basement Unfinished	1,415 sq. ft.
Garage Unfinished	766 sq. ft.
Dimensions	56'x47'6"
Foundation	Basement Crawlspace
Bedrooms	4
Full Baths	3
Half Baths	1
First Ceiling	9'
Second Ceiling	8'
Max Ridge Height	33'
Roof Framing	Stick
Exterior Walls	2x4

Design 91749

Units	Single
Price Code	H
Total Finished	3,051 sq. ft.
Main Finished	3,051 sq. ft.
Garage Unfinished	646 sq. ft.
Dimensions	90'x82'
Foundation	Crawlspace
Bedrooms	4
Full Baths	3
Half Baths	1
Max Ridge Height	22'
Roof Framing	Stick/Truss
Exterior Walls	2x6

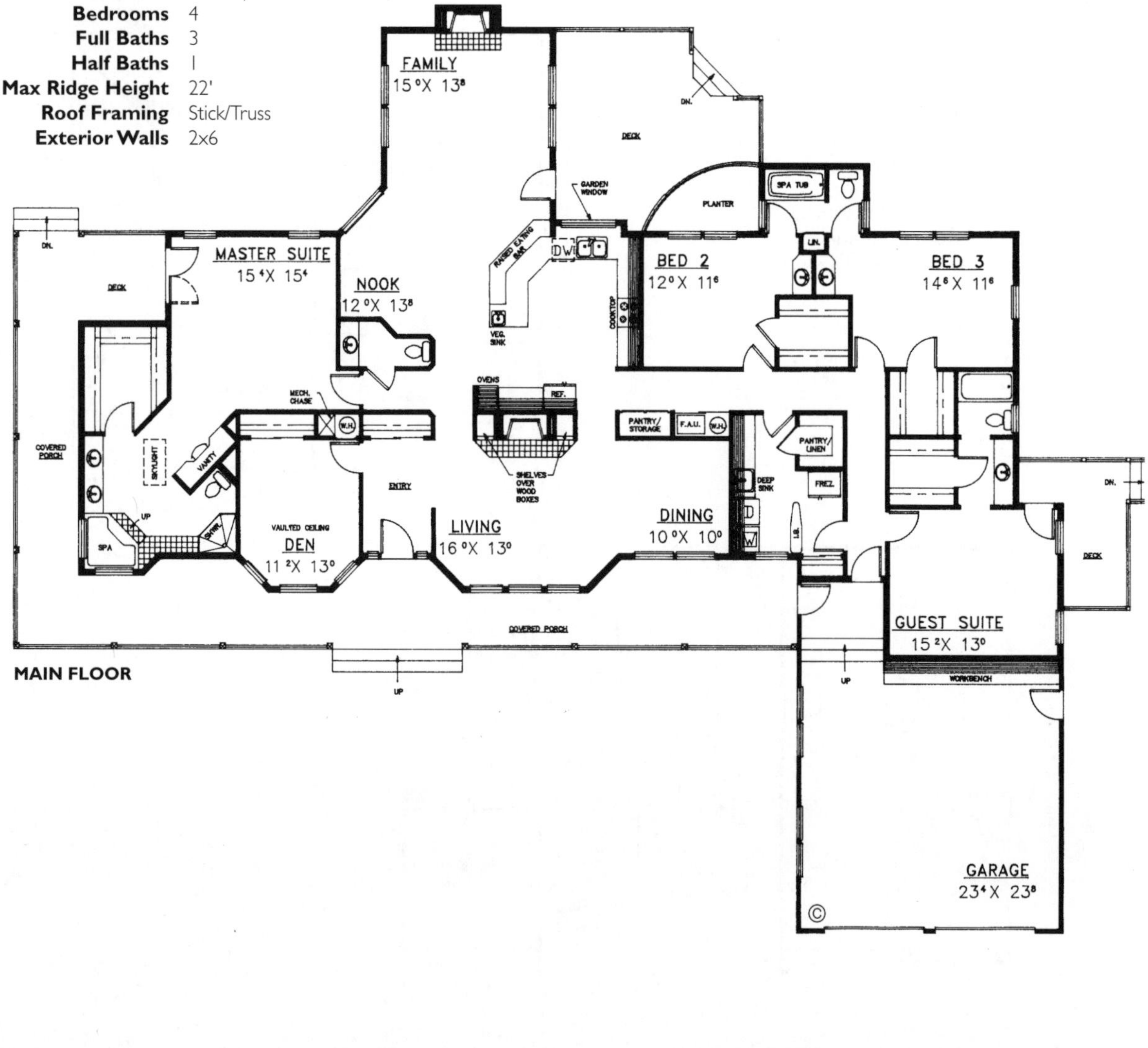

FAMILY
15^{0}X 13^{8}
DECK
DN.
GARDEN WINDOW
PLANTER
SPA TUB
LIN.
MASTER SUITE
15^{4}X 15^{4}
NOOK
12^{0}X 13^{8}
RAISED EATING BAR
DW
VEG. SINK
COOKTOP
BED 2
12^{0}X 11^{6}
BED 3
14^{6}X 11^{6}
DECK
DN.
COVERED PORCH
SKYLIGHT
VANITY
UP
SPA
SHWR.
MECH. CHASE
W.H.
OVENS
REF.
SHELVES OVER WOOD BOXES
PANTRY/ STORAGE
F.A.U.
W.H.
PANTRY/ LINEN
DEEP SINK
FREZ.
D
W
L.B.
ENTRY
VAULTED CEILING
DEN
11^{2}X 13^{0}
LIVING
16^{0}X 13^{0}
DINING
10^{0}X 10^{0}
DN.
DECK
COVERED PORCH
GUEST SUITE
15^{2}X 13^{0}
UP
UP
WORKBENCH
GARAGE
23^{4}X 23^{8}
©

MAIN FLOOR

Design 66003

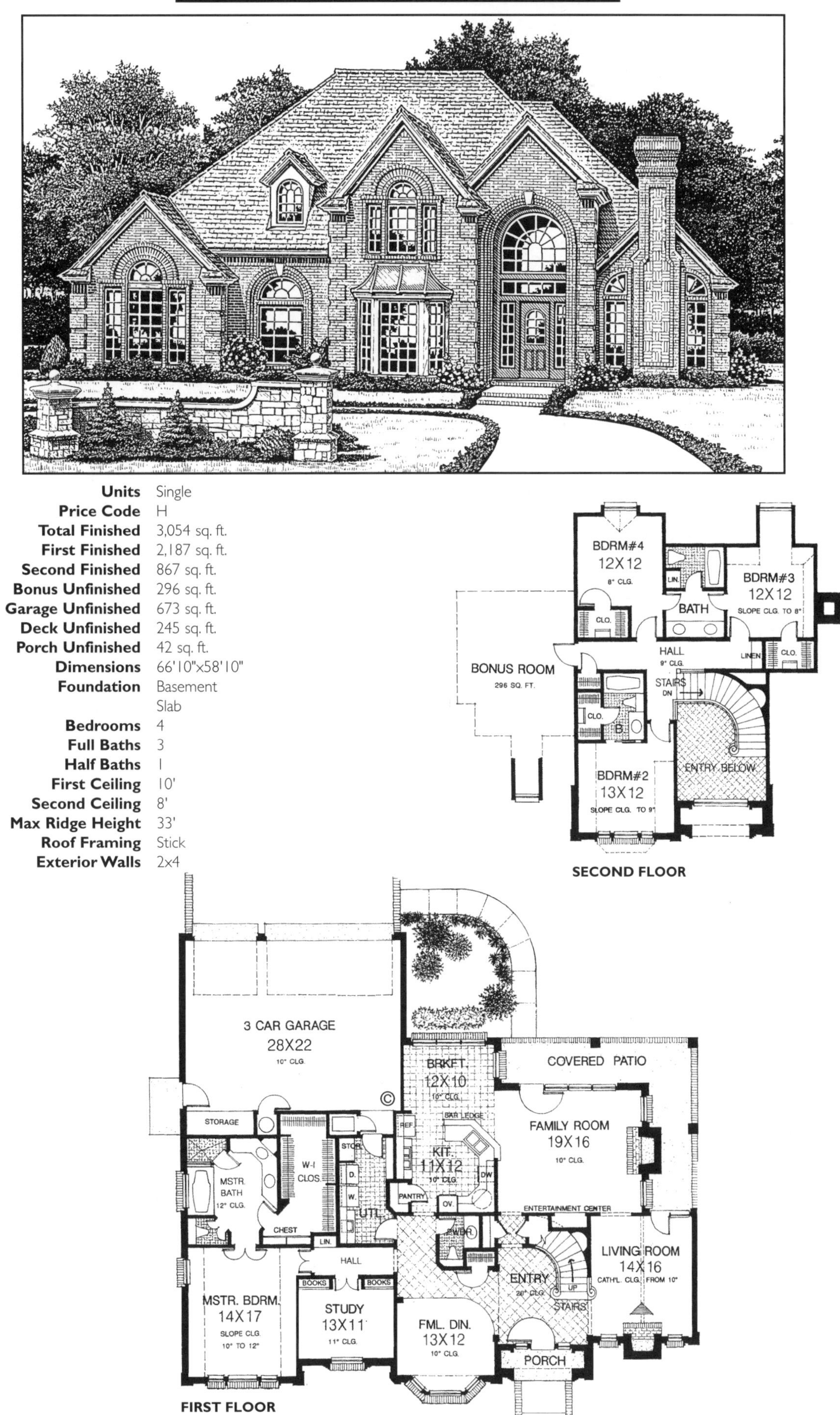
SECOND FLOOR
BDRM#4
12X12
8" CLG.
BDRM#3
12X12
SLOPE CLG. TO 8"
BATH
HALL
9" CLG.
BONUS ROOM
296 SQ. FT.
STAIRS DN
BDRM#2
13X12
SLOPE CLG. TO 9"
ENTRY BELOW
FIRST FLOOR
3 CAR GARAGE
28X22
10" CLG.
STORAGE
MSTR. BATH
12" CLG.
W-I CLOS.
CHEST
UTIL.
BRKFT.
12X10
10" CLG.
BAR LEDGE
KIT.
11X12
10" CLG.
PANTRY
COVERED PATIO
FAMILY ROOM
19X16
10" CLG.
ENTERTAINMENT CENTER
LIVING ROOM
14X16
CATH'L. CLG. FROM 10"
ENTRY
20" CLG.
STAIRS
HALL
BOOKS
BOOKS
MSTR. BDRM.
14X17
SLOPE CLG.
10" TO 12"
STUDY
13X11
11" CLG.
FML. DIN.
13X12
10" CLG.
PORCH

Units	Single
Price Code	H
Total Finished	3,054 sq. ft.
First Finished	2,187 sq. ft.
Second Finished	867 sq. ft.
Bonus Unfinished	296 sq. ft.
Garage Unfinished	673 sq. ft.
Deck Unfinished	245 sq. ft.
Porch Unfinished	42 sq. ft.
Dimensions	66'10"x58'10"
Foundation	Basement Slab
Bedrooms	4
Full Baths	3
Half Baths	1
First Ceiling	10'
Second Ceiling	8'
Max Ridge Height	33'
Roof Framing	Stick
Exterior Walls	2x4

Design 90456

Units	Single
Price Code	H
Total Finished	3,054 sq. ft.
First Finished	1,609 sq. ft.
Second Finished	1,445 sq. ft.
Basement Unfinished	1,609 sq. ft.
Garage Unfinished	527 sq. ft.
Porch Unfinished	479 sq. ft.
Dimensions	66'10"x49'6"
Foundation	Basement Crawlspace
Bedrooms	4
Full Baths	4
Max Ridge Height	38'2"
Roof Framing	Stick
Exterior Walls	2x4

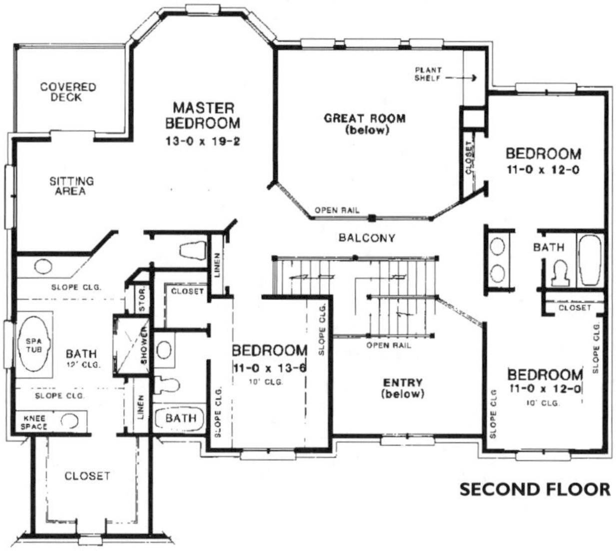

COVERED DECK
MASTER BEDROOM 13-0 x 19-2
GREAT ROOM (below)
PLANT SHELF
BEDROOM 11-0 x 12-0
CLOSET
SITTING AREA
OPEN RAIL
BALCONY
BATH
LINEN
SLOPE CLG.
CLOSET
STOR
SPA TUB
BATH 12' CLG.
SHOWER
BEDROOM 11-0 x 13-6 10' CLG.
OPEN RAIL
ENTRY (below)
BEDROOM 11-0 x 12-0 10' CLG.
KNEE SPACE
BATH
CLOSET

SECOND FLOOR

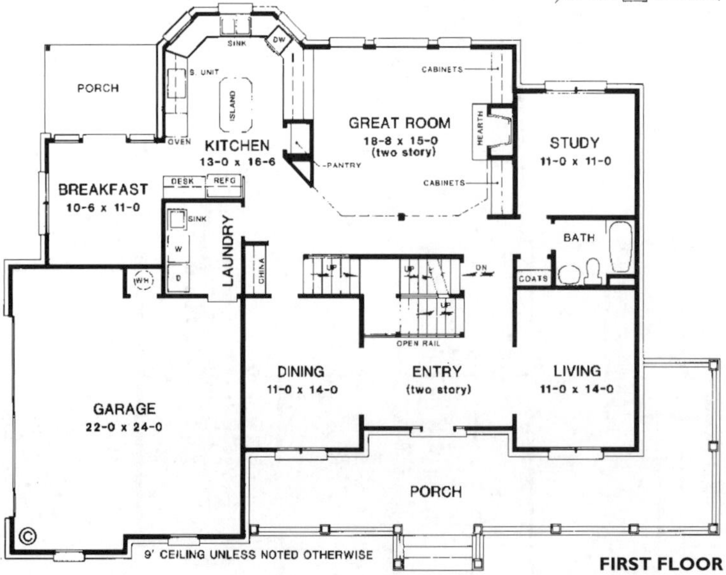

SINK
DW
PORCH
S. UNIT
ISLAND
CABINETS
GREAT ROOM 18-8 x 15-0 (two story)
HEARTH
STUDY 11-0 x 11-0
OVEN
KITCHEN 13-0 x 16-6
PANTRY
BREAKFAST 10-6 x 11-0
DESK
REFG
SINK
W
D
WH
LAUNDRY
CHINA
BATH
UP
DN
COATS
OPEN RAIL
DINING 11-0 x 14-0
ENTRY (two story)
LIVING 11-0 x 14-0
GARAGE 22-0 x 24-0
PORCH
©
9' CEILING UNLESS NOTED OTHERWISE

FIRST FLOOR

Design 98596

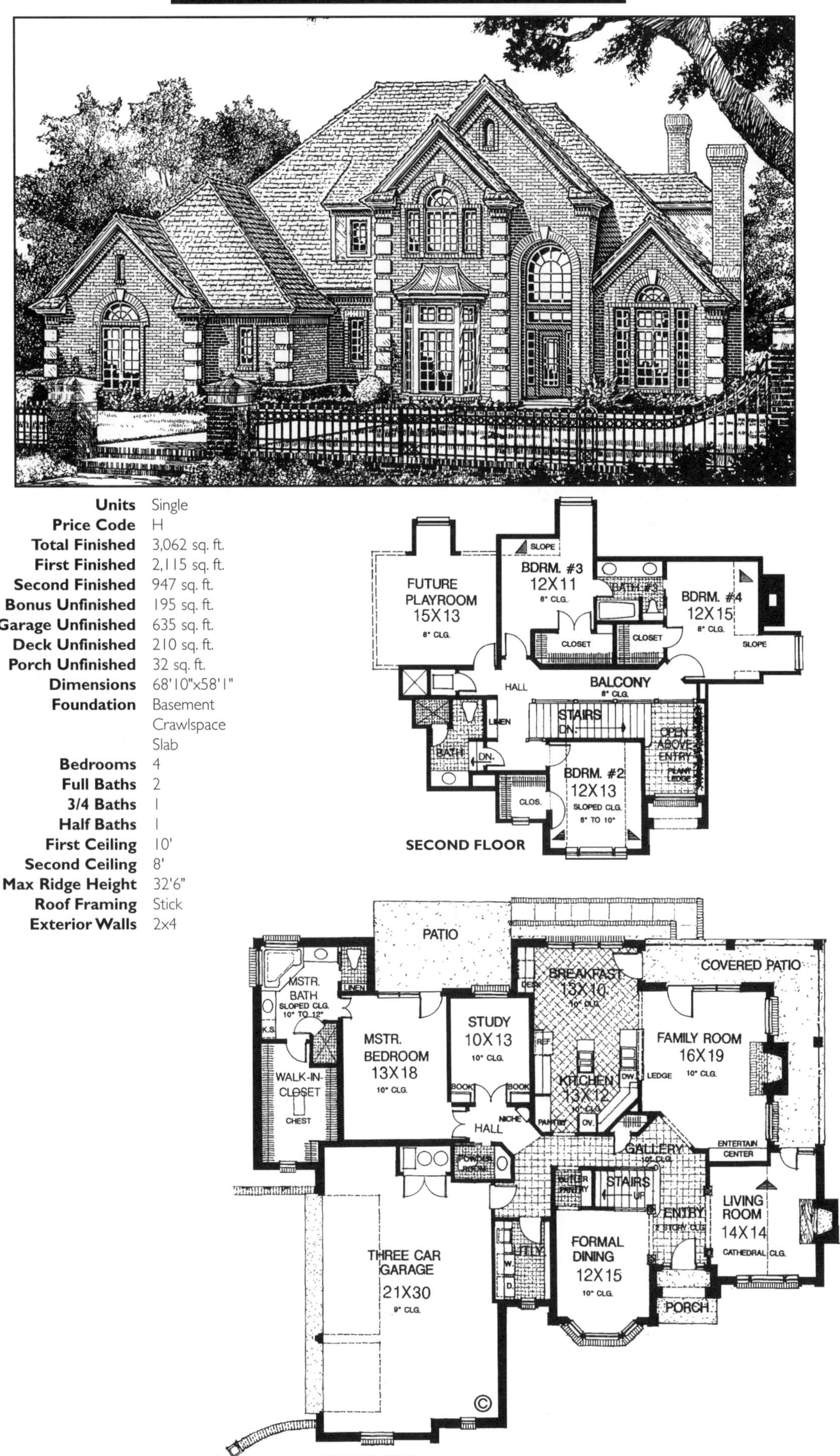
FUTURE PLAYROOM 15X13 8" CLG.
BDRM. #3 12X11 8" CLG.
SLOPE
BATH #3
BDRM. #4 12X15 8" CLG.
SLOPE
CLOSET
CLOSET
HALL
BALCONY 8" CLG.
LINEN
STAIRS DN.
BATH
DN.
OPEN ABOVE ENTRY
PLANT LEDGE
BDRM. #2 12X13 SLOPED CLG. 8" TO 10"
CLOS.
SECOND FLOOR
PATIO
COVERED PATIO
MSTR. BATH SLOPED CLG. 10" TO 12"
LINEN
K.S.
WALK-IN CLOSET
CHEST
MSTR. BEDROOM 13X18 10" CLG.
STUDY 10X13 10" CLG.
BOOK
BOOK
BREAKFAST 13X10 10" CLG.
DESK
REF.
KITCHEN 13X12 10" CLG.
DW
PANTRY
OV.
FAMILY ROOM 16X19 10" CLG.
LEDGE
HALL
NICHE
POWDER ROOM
GALLERY 10" CLG.
ENTERTAIN CENTER
BUTLER PANTRY
STAIRS UP
ENTRY 2 STORY CLG.
LIVING ROOM 14X14 CATHEDRAL CLG.
UTIL.
W.
D.
FORMAL DINING 12X15 10" CLG.
PORCH
THREE CAR GARAGE 21X30 9" CLG.
©
FIRST FLOOR

Units	Single
Price Code	H
Total Finished	3,062 sq. ft.
First Finished	2,115 sq. ft.
Second Finished	947 sq. ft.
Bonus Unfinished	195 sq. ft.
Garage Unfinished	635 sq. ft.
Deck Unfinished	210 sq. ft.
Porch Unfinished	32 sq. ft.
Dimensions	68'10"x58'1"
Foundation	Basement Crawlspace Slab
Bedrooms	4
Full Baths	2
3/4 Baths	1
Half Baths	1
First Ceiling	10'
Second Ceiling	8'
Max Ridge Height	32'6"
Roof Framing	Stick
Exterior Walls	2x4

Design 98211

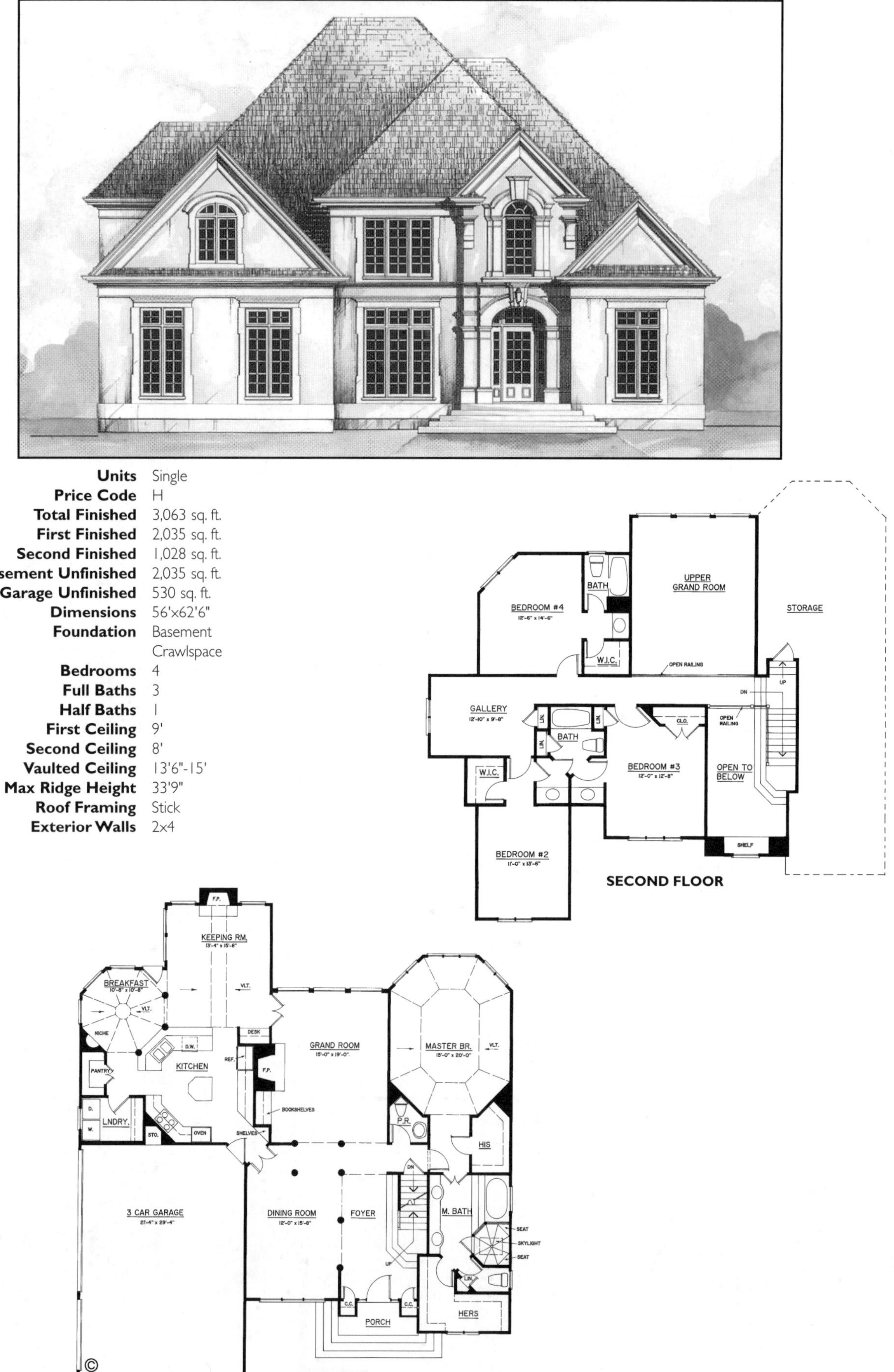
BEDROOM #4
12'-6" x 14'-6"
BATH
UPPER GRAND ROOM
STORAGE
W.I.C.
OPEN RAILING
GALLERY
12'-10" x 9'-8"
LIN.
BATH
CLO.
OPEN RAILING
DN
UP
BEDROOM #3
12'-0" x 12'-8"
OPEN TO BELOW
W.I.C.
BEDROOM #2
11'-0" x 13'-6"
SHELF
SECOND FLOOR
F.P.
KEEPING RM.
13'-4" x 15'-6"
BREAKFAST
10'-8" x 10'-8"
VLT.
NICHE
DESK
D.W.
KITCHEN
REF.
F.P.
GRAND ROOM
15'-0" x 19'-0"
MASTER BR.
15'-0" x 20'-0"
PANTRY
BOOKSHELVES
LNDRY.
STO.
OVEN
SHELVES
P.R.
HIS
3 CAR GARAGE
21'-4" x 29'-4"
DINING ROOM
12'-0" x 15'-8"
FOYER
M. BATH
SEAT
SKYLIGHT
SEAT
C.C.
PORCH
C.C.
HERS
FIRST FLOOR

Units	Single
Price Code	H
Total Finished	3,063 sq. ft.
First Finished	2,035 sq. ft.
Second Finished	1,028 sq. ft.
Basement Unfinished	2,035 sq. ft.
Garage Unfinished	530 sq. ft.
Dimensions	56'x62'6"
Foundation	Basement Crawlspace
Bedrooms	4
Full Baths	3
Half Baths	1
First Ceiling	9'
Second Ceiling	8'
Vaulted Ceiling	13'6"-15'
Max Ridge Height	33'9"
Roof Framing	Stick
Exterior Walls	2x4

Design 68181

Units	Single
Price Code	H
Total Finished	3,067 sq. ft.
First Finished	2,169 sq. ft.
Second Finished	898 sq. ft.
Basement Unfinished	2,169 sq. ft.
Garage Unfinished	699 sq. ft.
Dimensions	64'x60'8"
Foundation	Basement Combo Crawlspace/Slab
Bedrooms	4
Full Baths	2
3/4 Baths	1
Half Baths	1
First Ceiling	9'
Second Ceiling	8'
Max Ridge Height	26'8"
Roof Framing	Stick
Exterior Walls	2x4, 2x6

* Alternate foundation options available at an additional charge. Please call 1-800-235-5700 for more information.

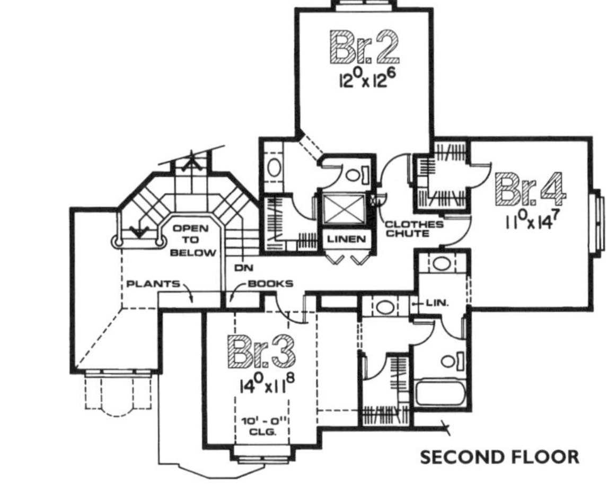
Br.2
12⁰x12⁶
Br.4
11⁰x14⁷
CLOTHES CHUTE
LINEN
OPEN TO BELOW
DN
PLANTS
BOOKS
LIN.
Br.3
14⁰x11⁸
10'-0" CLG.
SECOND FLOOR

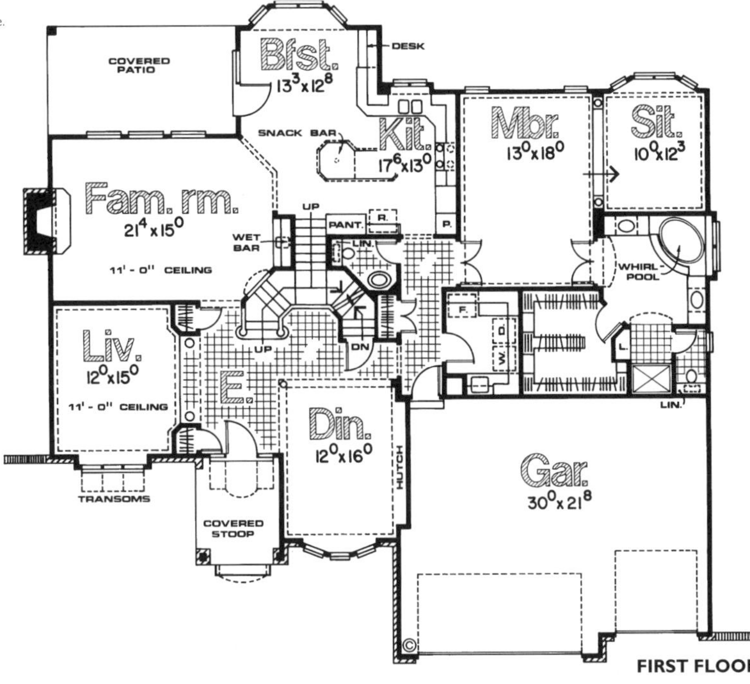
COVERED PATIO
Bfst.
13³x12⁸
DESK
SNACK BAR
Kit.
17⁶x13⁰
Mbr.
13⁰x18⁰
Sit.
10⁰x12³
Fam. rm.
21⁴x15⁰
11'-0" CEILING
UP
WET BAR
PANT.
R.
P.
LIN.
WHIRL-POOL
UP
DN
Liv.
12⁰x15⁰
11'-0" CEILING
E.
Din.
12⁰x16⁰
HUTCH
LIN.
Gar.
30⁰x21⁸
TRANSOMS
COVERED STOOP
FIRST FLOOR

Design 60138

PHOTOGRAPHY: COURTESY OF THE DESIGNER

Units	Single
Price Code	H
Total Finished	3,068 sq. ft.
First Finished	1,473 sq. ft.
Second Finished	1,595 sq. ft.
Bonus Unfinished	197 sq. ft.
Dimensions	53'x49'
Foundation	Basement Crawlspace
Bedrooms	4
Full Baths	3
Half Baths	1
First Ceiling	9'
Second Ceiling	8'
Max Ridge Height	32'6"

Please note: The photographed home may have been modified to suit homeowner preferences. If you order plans, have a builder or design professional check them against the photograph to confirm actual construction details.

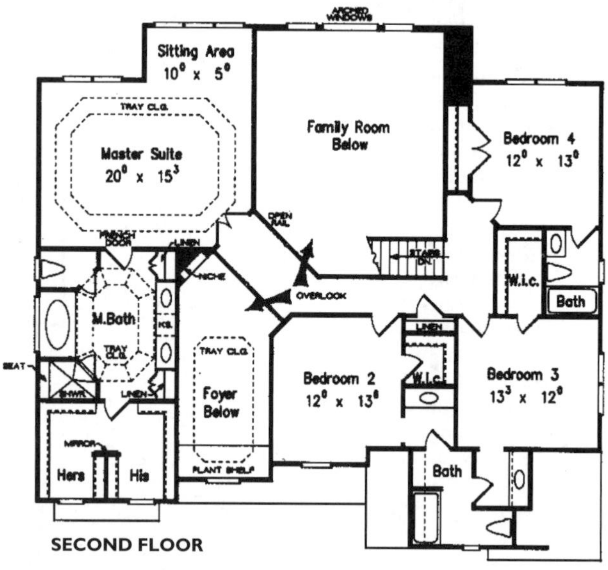
ARCHED WINDOWS
Sitting Area 10^{0} x 5^{0}
Master Suite 20^{0} x 15^{3}
TRAY CLG.
Family Room Below
Bedroom 4 12^{0} x 13^{0}
OPEN RAIL
STAIRS DN
FRENCH DOOR
LINEN
NICHE
OVERLOOK
W.I.c.
Bath
M.Bath
SEAT
Foyer Below
Bedroom 2 12^{0} x 13^{6}
Bedroom 3 13^{3} x 12^{0}
MIRROR
Hers
His
PLANT SHELF
Bath

SECOND FLOOR

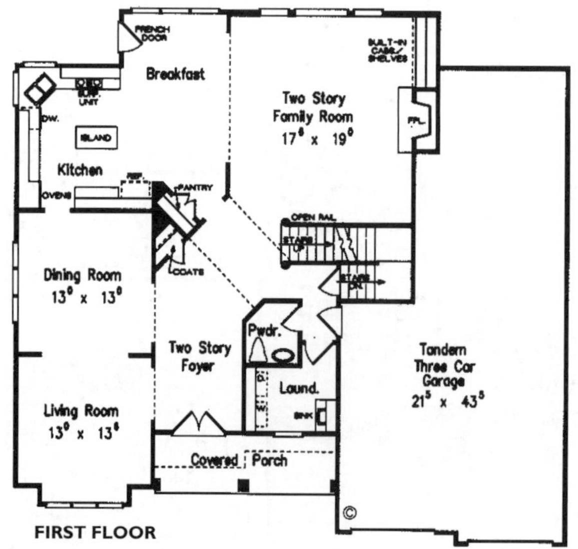
FRENCH DOOR
Breakfast
BUILT-IN CABS./ SHELVES
Two Story Family Room 17^{6} x 19^{0}
FPL.
ISLAND
Kitchen
OVENS
PANTRY
OPEN RAIL
STAIRS UP
STAIRS DN
COATS
Dining Room 13^{0} x 13^{0}
Pwdr.
Two Story Foyer
Laund.
SINK
Tandem Three Car Garage 21^{5} x 43^{5}
Living Room 13^{0} x 13^{6}
Covered Porch
©

FIRST FLOOR

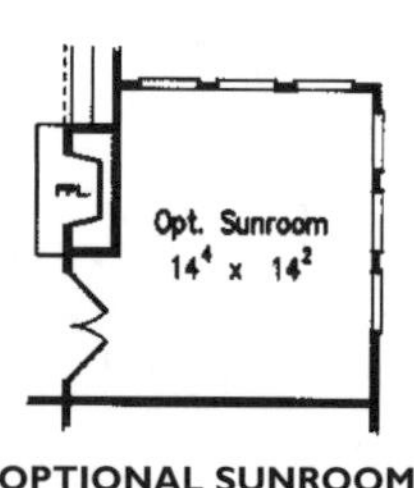
FPL.
Opt. Sunroom 14^{4} x 14^{2}

OPTIONAL SUNROOM

Design 65008

Units	Single
Price Code	H
Total Finished	3,072 sq. ft.
First Finished	1,437 sq. ft.
Second Finished	1,635 sq. ft.
Garage Unfinished	474 sq. ft.
Dimensions	36'x62'
Foundation	Slab
Bedrooms	4
Full Baths	3
First Ceiling	8'
Second Ceiling	8'
Max Ridge Height	26'6"
Roof Framing	Truss
Exterior Walls	2x6

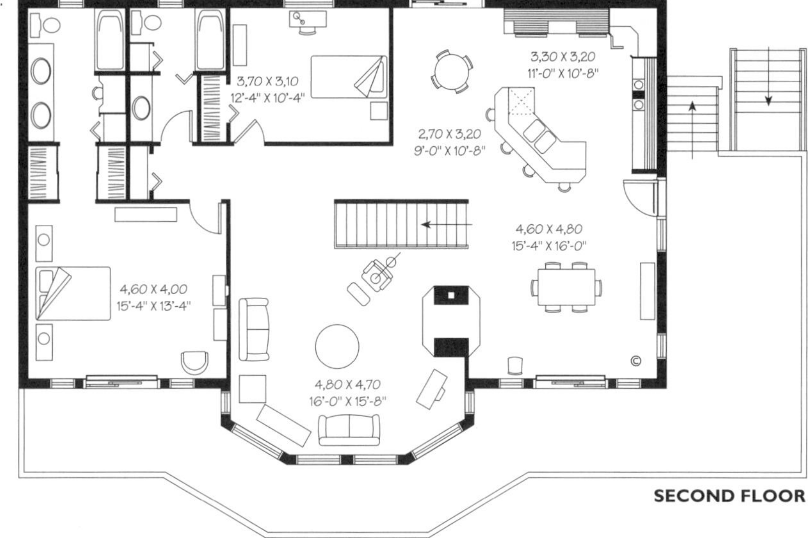
3,70 X 3,10
12'-4" X 10'-4"
3,30 X 3,20
11'-0" X 10'-8"
2,70 X 3,20
9'-0" X 10'-8"
4,60 X 4,80
15'-4" X 16'-0"
4,60 X 4,00
15'-4" X 13'-4"
4,80 X 4,70
16'-0" X 15'-8"

SECOND FLOOR

3,80 X 4,40
12'-8" X 14'-8"
3,30 X 3,30
11'-0" X 11'-0"
Bonus room
4,50 X 3,30
15'-0" X 11'-0"
3,90 X 4,00
13'-0" X 13'-4"
4,80 X 4,70
16'-0" X 15'-8"
6,20 X 6,80
20'-8" X 22'-8"

FIRST FLOOR

Design 66056

Units	Single
Price Code	G
Total Finished	3,080 sq. ft.
Main Finished	3,080 sq. ft.
Garage Unfinished	675 sq. ft.
Deck Unfinished	245 sq. ft.
Dimensions	77'x74'5"
Foundation	Slab
Bedrooms	3
Full Baths	2
Half Baths	1
Main Ceiling	9'-11'
Max Ridge Height	29'
Roof Framing	Stick
Exterior Walls	2x4

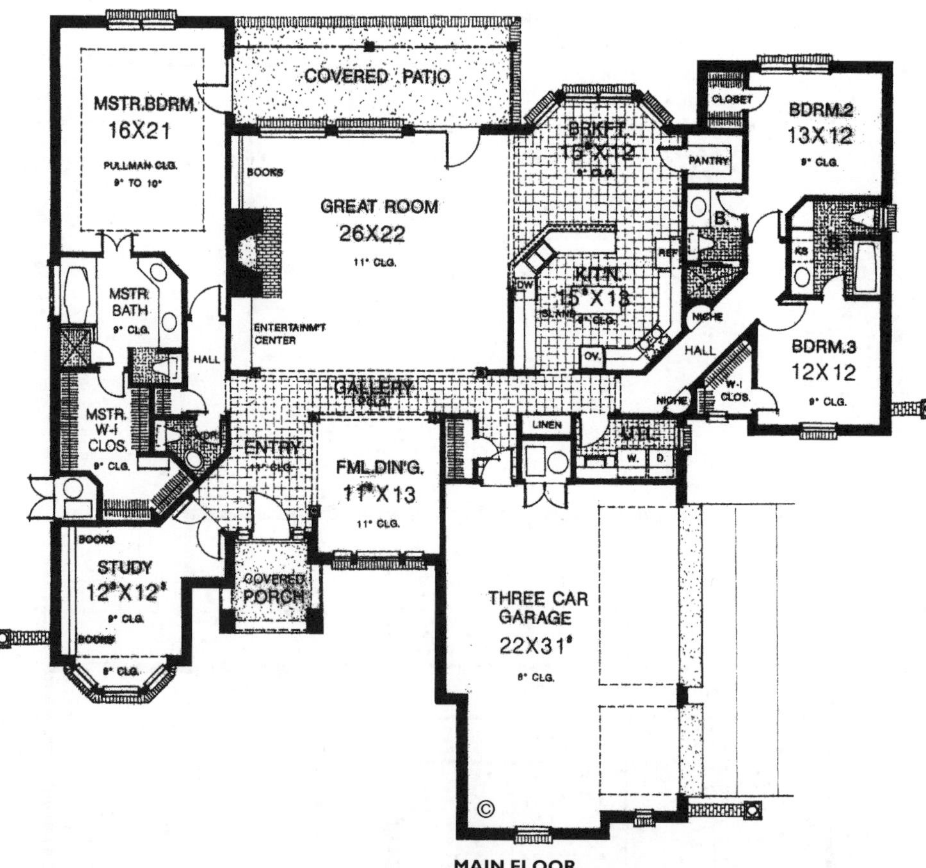
COVERED PATIO
MSTR.BDRM.
16X21
PULLMAN CLG.
9" TO 10"
BOOKS
GREAT ROOM
26X22
11" CLG.
ENTERTAINM'T CENTER
CLOSET
BDRM.2
13X12
9" CLG.
PANTRY
KIT'N.
MSTR. BATH
9" CLG.
HALL
NICHE
BDRM.3
12X12
9" CLG.
W-I CLOS.
GALLERY
MSTR. W-I CLOS.
9" CLG.
LINEN
ENTRY
FML.DIN'G.
11" CLG.
STUDY
9" CLG.
BOOKS
COVERED PORCH
THREE CAR GARAGE
22X31
8" CLG.

MAIN FLOOR

Design 98452

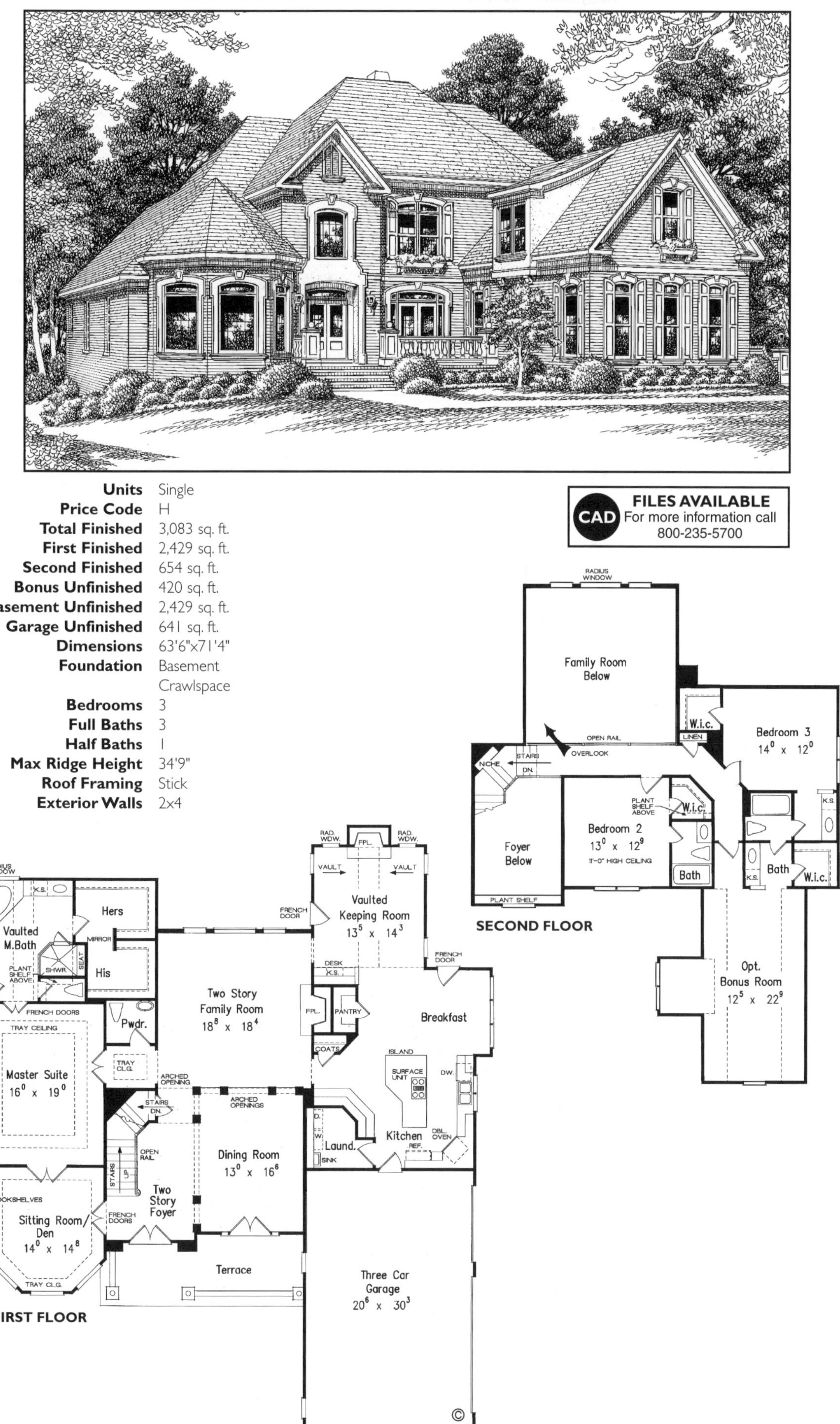
FIRST FLOOR
RADIUS WINDOW
Vaulted M.Bath
Hers
His
MIRROR
SEAT
SHWR
PLANT SHELF ABOVE
LINEN
FRENCH DOORS
TRAY CEILING
Master Suite 16⁰ x 19⁰
Pwdr.
TRAY CLG.
Sitting Room/ Den 14⁰ x 14⁸
BOOKSHELVES
TRAY CLG.
FRENCH DOORS
STAIRS DN.
STAIRS UP
OPEN RAIL
Two Story Foyer
ARCHED OPENING
ARCHED OPENINGS
Two Story Family Room 18⁸ x 18⁴
Dining Room 13⁰ x 16⁶
Terrace
RAD. WDW.
FPL.
VAULT
Vaulted Keeping Room 13⁵ x 14³
FRENCH DOOR
DESK
K.S.
PANTRY
COATS
Breakfast
ISLAND
SURFACE UNIT
DW.
DBL. OVEN
REF.
Kitchen
Laund.
SINK
Three Car Garage 20⁶ x 30³
SECOND FLOOR
Family Room Below
OPEN RAIL
OVERLOOK
NICHE
STAIRS DN.
Foyer Below
PLANT SHELF
Bedroom 2 13⁰ x 12⁹
11'-0" HIGH CEILING
PLANT SHELF ABOVE
W.i.c.
Bath
LINEN
Bedroom 3 14⁰ x 12⁰
K.S.
Opt. Bonus Room 12⁵ x 22⁹

Units	Single
Price Code	H
Total Finished	3,083 sq. ft.
First Finished	2,429 sq. ft.
Second Finished	654 sq. ft.
Bonus Unfinished	420 sq. ft.
Basement Unfinished	2,429 sq. ft.
Garage Unfinished	641 sq. ft.
Dimensions	63'6"x71'4"
Foundation	Basement Crawlspace
Bedrooms	3
Full Baths	3
Half Baths	1
Max Ridge Height	34'9"
Roof Framing	Stick
Exterior Walls	2x4

Design 96521

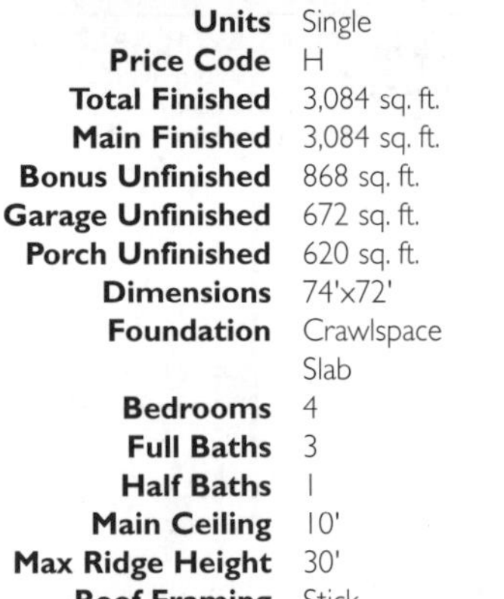

Units	Single
Price Code	H
Total Finished	3,084 sq. ft.
Main Finished	3,084 sq. ft.
Bonus Unfinished	868 sq. ft.
Garage Unfinished	672 sq. ft.
Porch Unfinished	620 sq. ft.
Dimensions	74'x72'
Foundation	Crawlspace Slab
Bedrooms	4
Full Baths	3
Half Baths	1
Main Ceiling	10'
Max Ridge Height	30'
Roof Framing	Stick
Exterior Walls	2x6

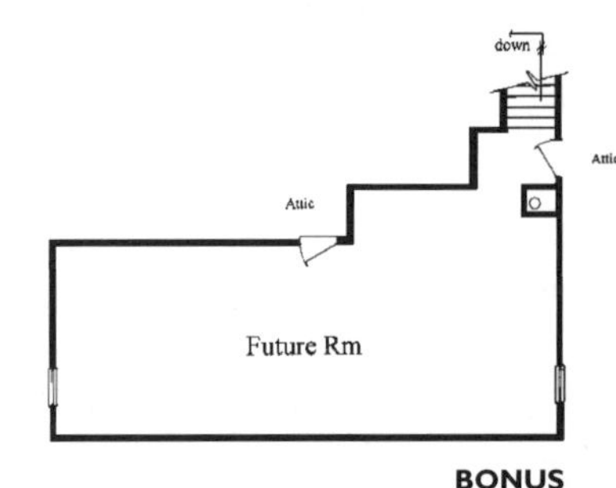

down
Attic
Attic
Future Rm

BONUS

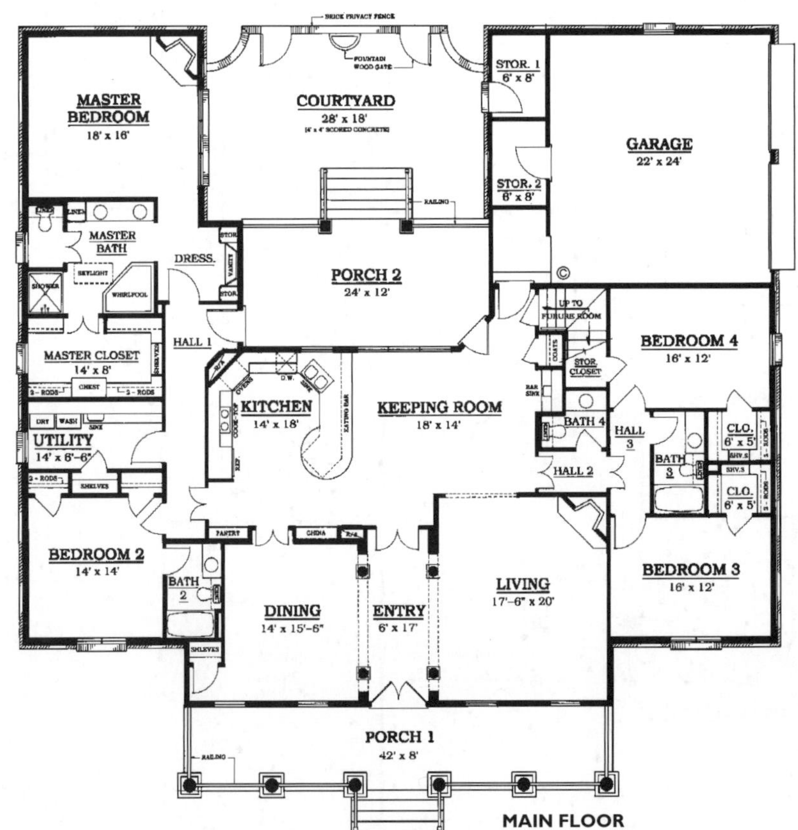

MASTER BEDROOM
18' x 16'
COURTYARD
28' x 18'
STOR. 1
6' x 8'
STOR. 2
6' x 8'
GARAGE
22' x 24'
MASTER BATH
DRESS.
PORCH 2
24' x 12'
MASTER CLOSET
14' x 8'
HALL 1
KITCHEN
14' x 18'
KEEPING ROOM
18' x 14'
UP TO FUTURE ROOM
STOR CLOSET
BEDROOM 4
16' x 12'
UTILITY
14' x 6'-6"
BATH 4
HALL 3
BATH 3
CLO.
6' x 5'
CLO.
6' x 5'
HALL 2
PANTRY
CHINA
BEDROOM 2
14' x 14'
BATH 2
DINING
14' x 15'-6"
ENTRY
6' x 17'
LIVING
17'-6" x 20'
BEDROOM 3
16' x 12'
PORCH 1
42' x 8'

MAIN FLOOR

Design 69136

Bedroom
12'4" x 10'
Bedroom
12' x 10'
Bedroom
12'4" x 10'
Bedroom
11' x 11'4"
Dn
Bedroom
12'6" x 10'8"
Study Loft
Bonus
Room
12' x 31'
SECOND FLOOR

Units	Single
Price Code	H
Total Finished	3,085 sq. ft.
First Finished	1,882 sq. ft.
Second Finished	1,203 sq. ft.
Bonus Unfinished	651 sq. ft.
Garage Unfinished	824 sq. ft.
Dimensions	102'8"x49'4"
Foundation	Crawlspace
Bedrooms	6
Full Baths	4
Half Baths	1
First Ceiling	9'
Second Ceiling	8'
Max Ridge Height	32'
Roof Framing	Truss
Exterior Walls	2x6

Patio
25' x 12'
Den
11' x 9'9"
Gathering Room
20'4" x 13'5"
Kitchen
Utility
Master
Suite
13'6" x 13'8"
Living
13'4" x 13'3"
Up
Foyer
Dining
12'8" x 13'3"
Garage
23' x 31'
Porch

FIRST FLOOR

Design 97400

Units	Single
Price Code	H
Total Finished	3,094 sq. ft.
First Finished	2,112 sq. ft.
Second Finished	982 sq. ft.
Basement Unfinished	2,112 sq. ft.
Garage Unfinished	650 sq. ft.
Dimensions	67'1"x65'10/10"
Foundation	Basement Slab
Bedrooms	4
Full Baths	3
Half Baths	1
First Ceiling	9'
Max Ridge Height	30'4"
Roof Framing	Stick
Exterior Walls	2x4

* Alternate foundation options available at an additional charge.
Please call 1-800-235-5700 for more information.

SECOND FLOOR

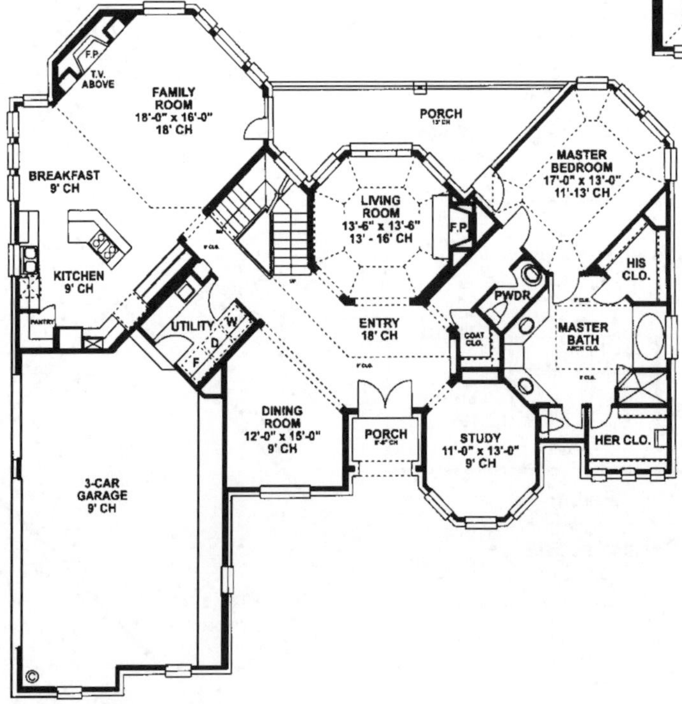

FIRST FLOOR

Design 68056

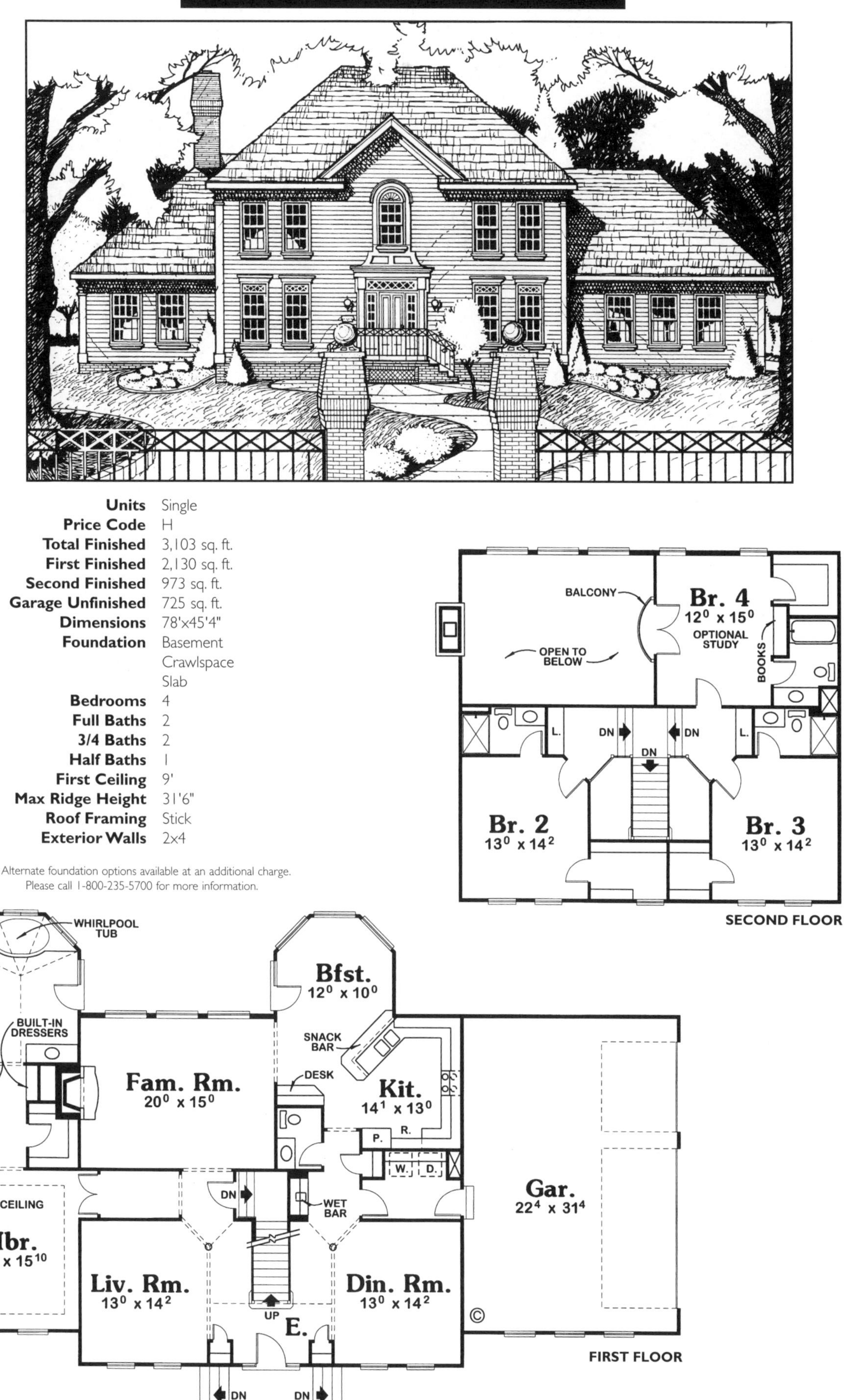
BALCONY
Br. 4
12⁰ x 15⁰
OPTIONAL STUDY
BOOKS
OPEN TO BELOW
L.
DN
DN
DN
L.
Br. 2
13⁰ x 14²
Br. 3
13⁰ x 14²
SECOND FLOOR
WHIRLPOOL TUB
PLANT SHELF
BUILT-IN DRESSERS
Bfst.
12⁰ x 10⁰
SNACK BAR
DESK
Fam. Rm.
20⁰ x 15⁰
Kit.
14¹ x 13⁰
P.
R.
W.
D.
DN
WET BAR
10'-0" CEILING
Mbr.
15⁰ x 15¹⁰
Gar.
22⁴ x 31⁴
Liv. Rm.
13⁰ x 14²
Din. Rm.
13⁰ x 14²
UP
E.
DN
DN
STOOP
FIRST FLOOR

Units	Single
Price Code	H
Total Finished	3,103 sq. ft.
First Finished	2,130 sq. ft.
Second Finished	973 sq. ft.
Garage Unfinished	725 sq. ft.
Dimensions	78'x45'4"
Foundation	Basement Crawlspace Slab
Bedrooms	4
Full Baths	2
3/4 Baths	2
Half Baths	1
First Ceiling	9'
Max Ridge Height	31'6"
Roof Framing	Stick
Exterior Walls	2x4

* Alternate foundation options available at an additional charge. Please call 1-800-235-5700 for more information.

Design 93090

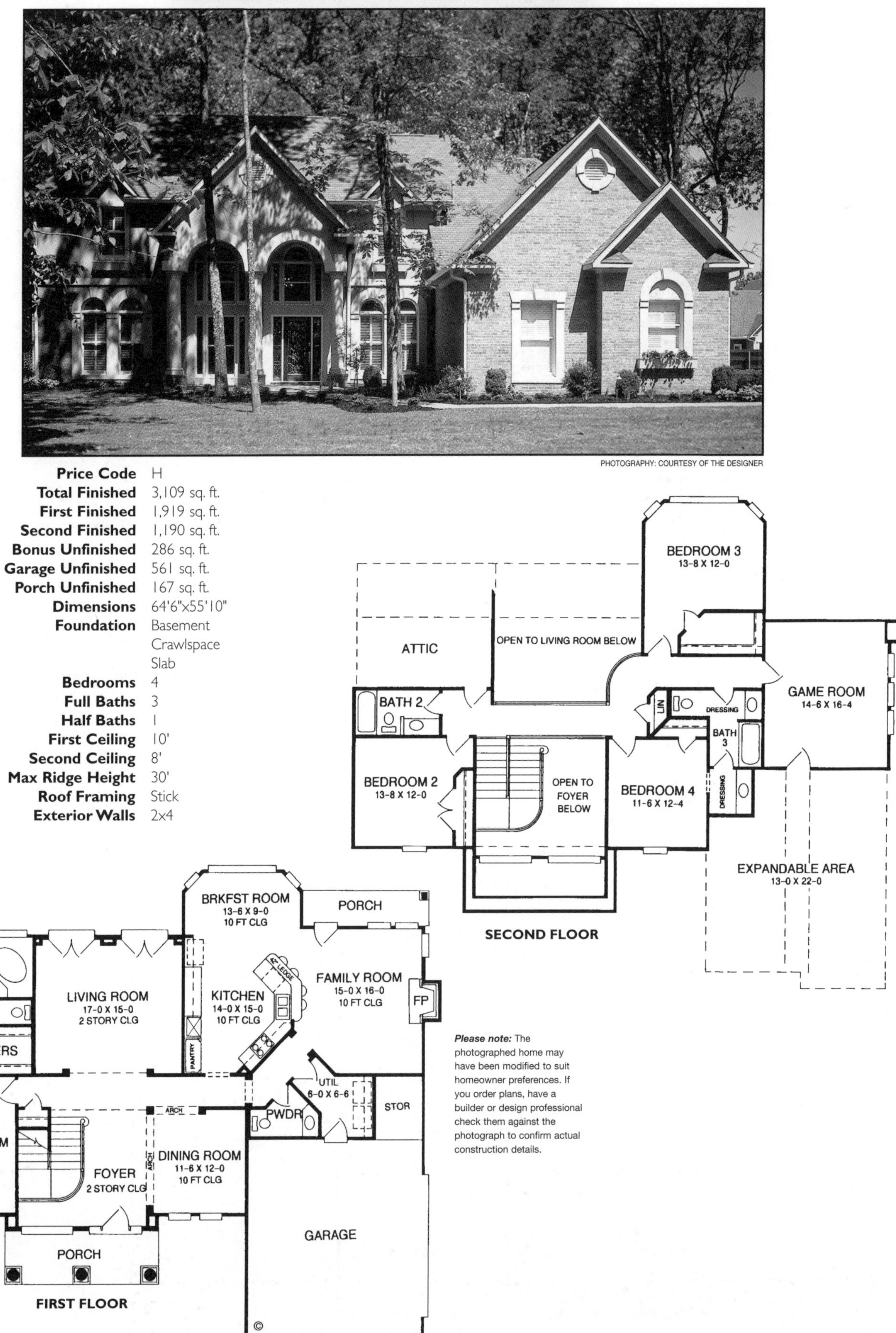
BEDROOM 3
13-8 X 12-0
ATTIC
OPEN TO LIVING ROOM BELOW
GAME ROOM
14-6 X 16-4
BATH 2
LIN
DRESSING
BATH 3
BEDROOM 2
13-8 X 12-0
OPEN TO FOYER BELOW
BEDROOM 4
11-6 X 12-4
DRESSING
EXPANDABLE AREA
13-0 X 22-0
SECOND FLOOR
BRKFST ROOM
13-6 X 9-0
10 FT CLG
PORCH
HIS
SEAT
MASTER BATH
10 FT CLG
K.S.
HERS
LIVING ROOM
17-0 X 15-0
2 STORY CLG
KITCHEN
14-0 X 15-0
10 FT CLG
42" LEDGE
FAMILY ROOM
15-0 X 16-0
10 FT CLG
FP
PANTRY
UTIL
6-0 X 6-6
STOR
PWDR
ARCH
MASTER BEDRM
13-4 X 15-6
10 FT CLG
FOYER
2 STORY CLG
ARCH
DINING ROOM
11-6 X 12-0
10 FT CLG
GARAGE
PORCH
FIRST FLOOR
©

PHOTOGRAPHY: COURTESY OF THE DESIGNER

Price Code	H
Total Finished	3,109 sq. ft.
First Finished	1,919 sq. ft.
Second Finished	1,190 sq. ft.
Bonus Unfinished	286 sq. ft.
Garage Unfinished	561 sq. ft.
Porch Unfinished	167 sq. ft.
Dimensions	64'6"x55'10"
Foundation	Basement Crawlspace Slab
Bedrooms	4
Full Baths	3
Half Baths	1
First Ceiling	10'
Second Ceiling	8'
Max Ridge Height	30'
Roof Framing	Stick
Exterior Walls	2x4

Please note: The photographed home may have been modified to suit homeowner preferences. If you order plans, have a builder or design professional check them against the photograph to confirm actual construction details.

Design 92277

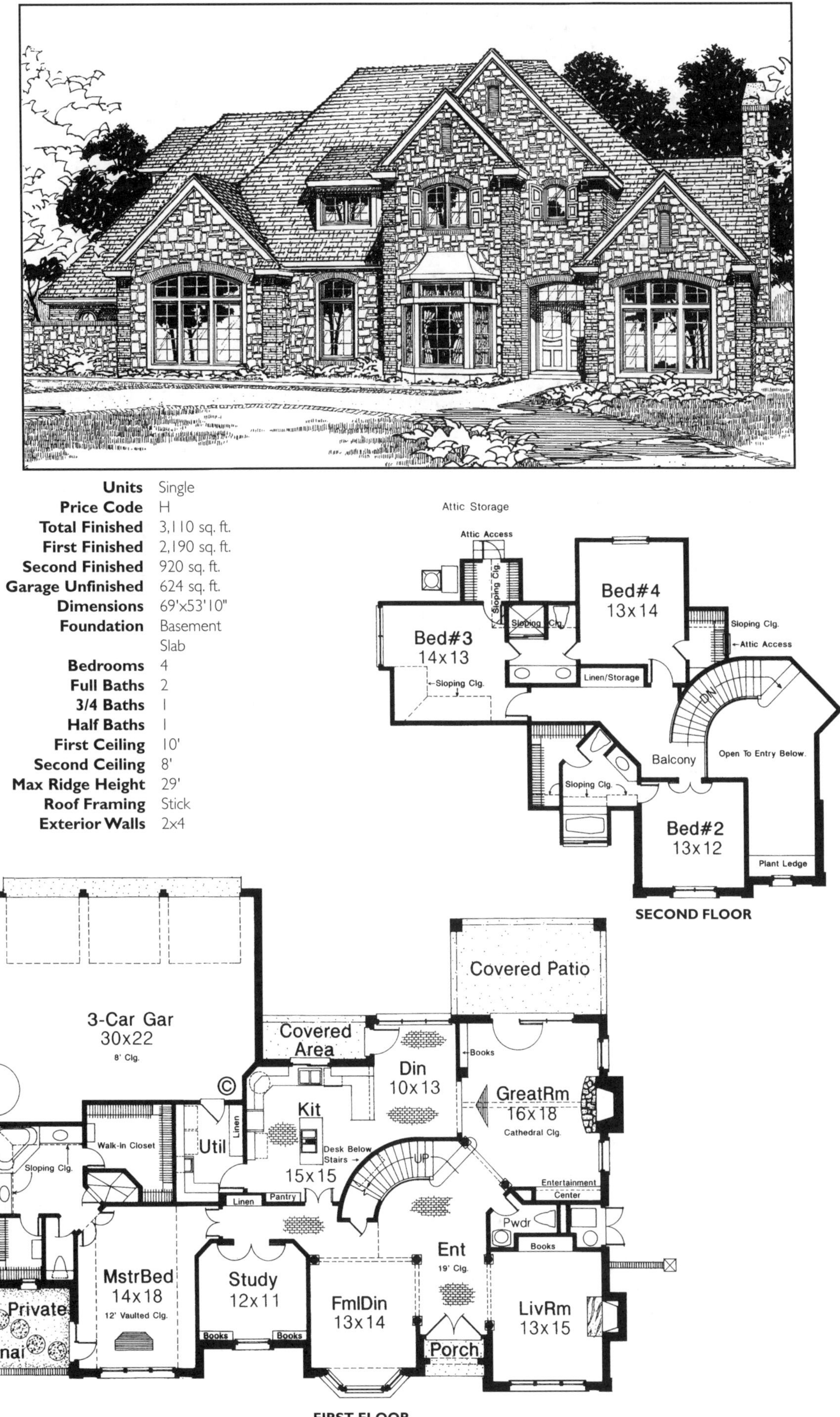
Attic Storage
Attic Access
Sloping Clg.
Bed#4
13x14
Bed#3
14x13
Sloping Clg.
Attic Access
Linen/Storage
Sloping Clg.
DN
Open To Entry Below.
Balcony
Sloping Clg.
Bed#2
13x12
Plant Ledge
SECOND FLOOR
Covered Patio
3-Car Gar
30x22
8' Clg.
Covered Area
Din
10x13
Books
GreatRm
16x18
Cathedral Clg.
Kit
15x15
Desk Below Stairs
UP
Walk-In Closet
Util
Linen
Sloping Clg.
Linen
Pantry
Entertainment Center
Pwdr
Books
Ent
19' Clg.
MstrBed
14x18
12' Vaulted Clg.
Study
12x11
FmlDin
13x14
LivRm
13x15
Private Lanai
Books
Books
Porch
FIRST FLOOR

Units	Single
Price Code	H
Total Finished	3,110 sq. ft.
First Finished	2,190 sq. ft.
Second Finished	920 sq. ft.
Garage Unfinished	624 sq. ft.
Dimensions	69'x53'10"
Foundation	Basement Slab
Bedrooms	4
Full Baths	2
3/4 Baths	1
Half Baths	1
First Ceiling	10'
Second Ceiling	8'
Max Ridge Height	29'
Roof Framing	Stick
Exterior Walls	2x4

Design 97288

Units	Single
Price Code	H
Total Finished	3,113 sq. ft.
First Finished	1,595 sq. ft.
Second Finished	1,518 sq. ft.
Basement Unfinished	1,595 sq. ft.
Garage Unfinished	475 sq. ft.
Dimensions	56'x48'
Foundation	Basement Crawlspace
Bedrooms	5
Full Baths	4
Max Ridge Height	33'6"
Roof Framing	Stick
Exterior Walls	2x4

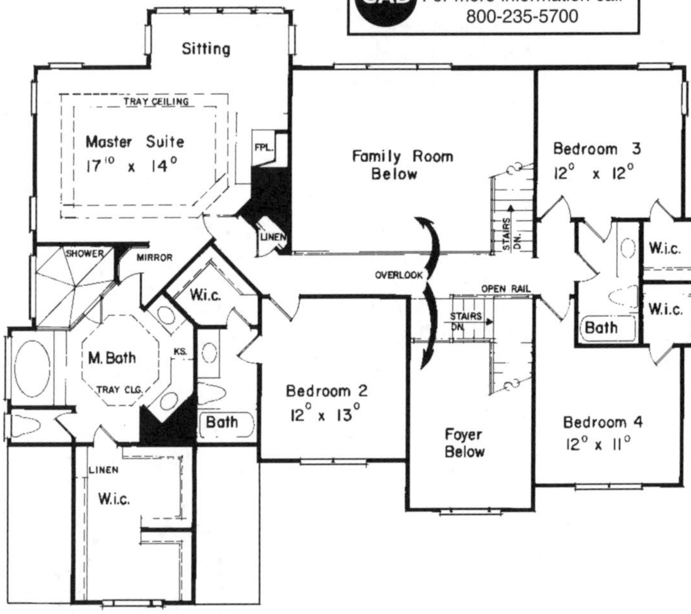

Sitting
TRAY CEILING
Master Suite
17^{10} x 14^{0}
FPL.
LINEN
Family Room
Below
Bedroom 3
12^{0} x 12^{0}
STAIRS DN.
W.i.c.
W.i.c.
SHOWER
MIRROR
W.i.c.
OVERLOOK
OPEN RAIL
STAIRS DN.
Bath
M. Bath
TRAY CLG.
KS.
Bath
Bedroom 2
12^{0} x 13^{0}
Foyer
Below
Bedroom 4
12^{0} x 11^{0}
LINEN
W.i.c.

SECOND FLOOR

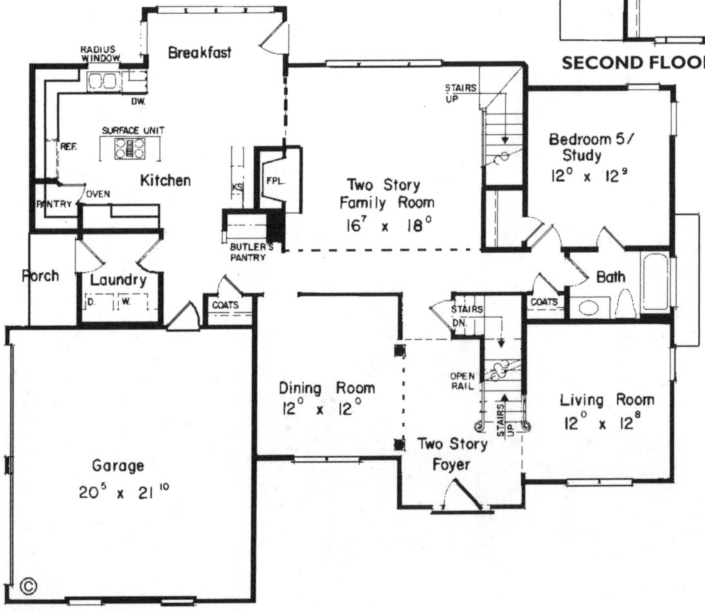

RADIUS WINDOW
Breakfast
DW.
SURFACE UNIT
REF.
Kitchen
PANTRY
OVEN
KS.
FPL.
STAIRS UP
Two Story
Family Room
16^{7} x 18^{0}
Bedroom 5/
Study
12^{0} x 12^{9}
BUTLER'S PANTRY
Porch
Laundry
D. W.
COATS
STAIRS DN.
COATS
Bath
OPEN RAIL
Dining Room
12^{0} x 12^{0}
STAIRS UP
Living Room
12^{0} x 12^{8}
Two Story
Foyer
Garage
20^{5} x 21^{10}
©

FIRST FLOOR

Design 92221

Units	Duplex
Price Code	G
Total Finished	3,121 sq. ft.
Main Finished	3,121 sq. ft.
Garage Unfinished	1,034 sq. ft.
Porch Unfinished	122 sq. ft.
Dimensions	64'x81'7"
Foundation	Slab
Bedrooms	5
Full Baths	4
Main Ceiling	8'
Max Ridge Height	22'
Roof Framing	Stick
Exterior Walls	2x4

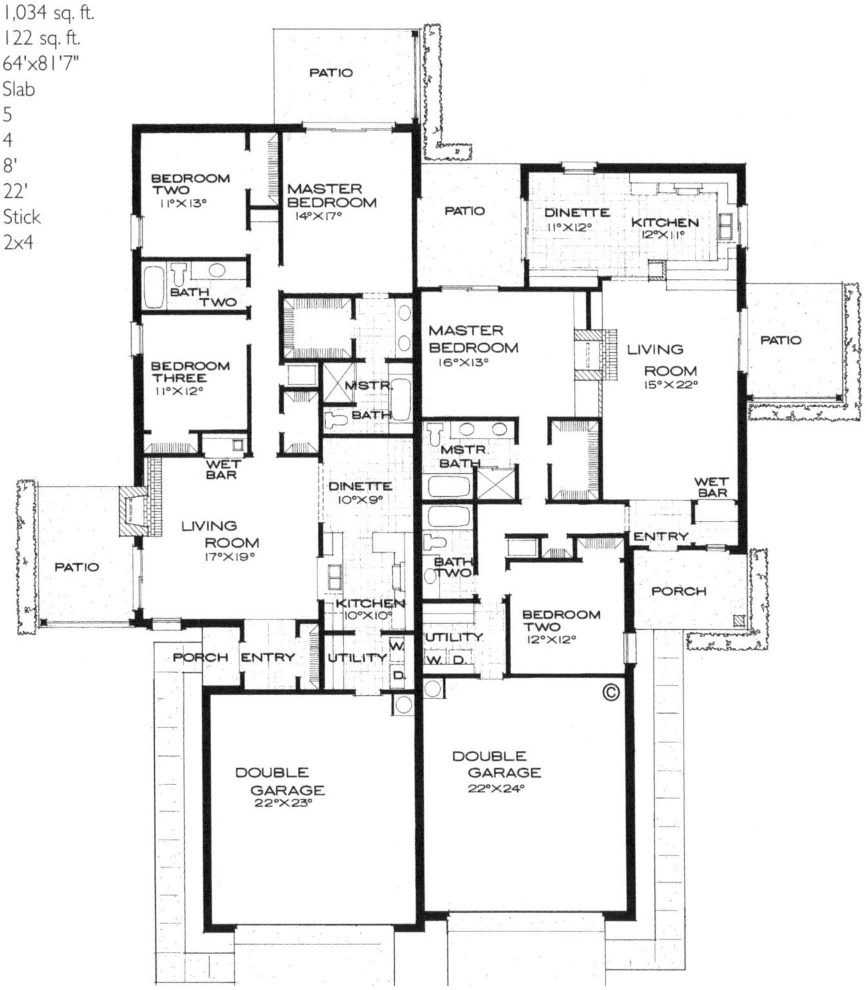

MAIN FLOOR

Design 92451

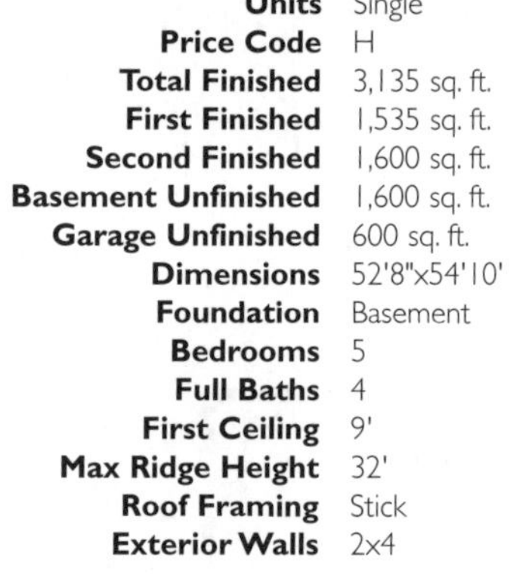

Units	Single
Price Code	H
Total Finished	3,135 sq. ft.
First Finished	1,535 sq. ft.
Second Finished	1,600 sq. ft.
Basement Unfinished	1,600 sq. ft.
Garage Unfinished	600 sq. ft.
Dimensions	52'8"x54'10'
Foundation	Basement
Bedrooms	5
Full Baths	4
First Ceiling	9'
Max Ridge Height	32'
Roof Framing	Stick
Exterior Walls	2x4

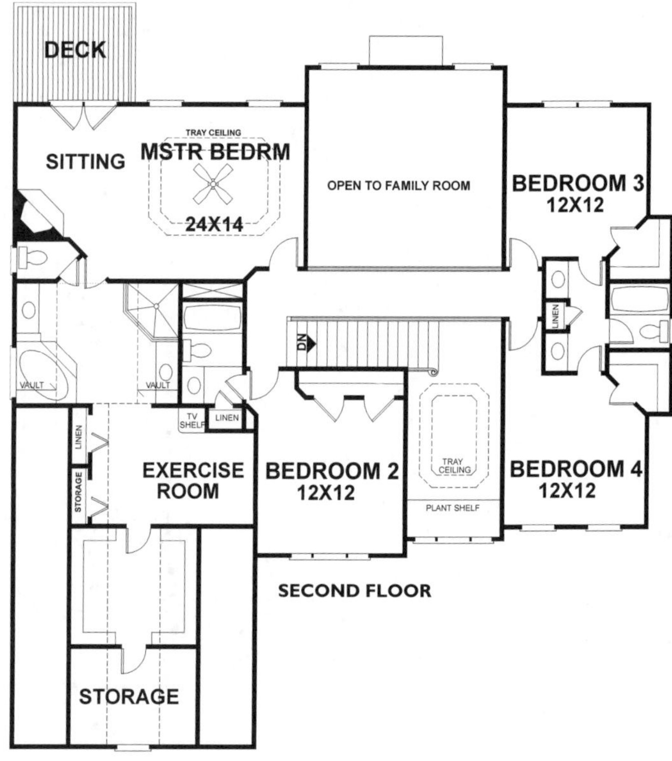

DECK
SITTING
TRAY CEILING
MSTR BEDRM
24X14
OPEN TO FAMILY ROOM
BEDROOM 3
12X12
VAULT
VAULT
DN
LINEN
TV SHELF
LINEN
LINEN
STORAGE
EXERCISE ROOM
BEDROOM 2
12X12
TRAY CEILING
PLANT SHELF
BEDROOM 4
12X12
STORAGE
SECOND FLOOR

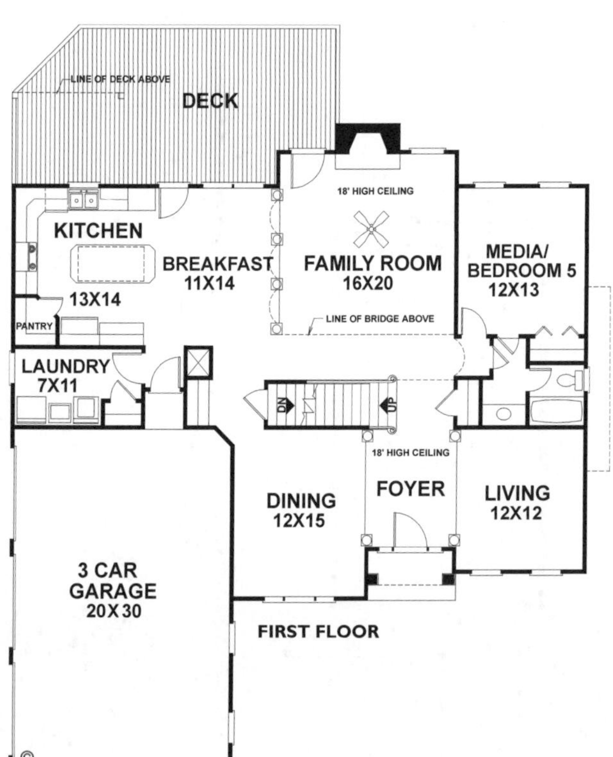

LINE OF DECK ABOVE
DECK
18' HIGH CEILING
KITCHEN
BREAKFAST
11X14
FAMILY ROOM
16X20
MEDIA/
BEDROOM 5
12X13
13X14
PANTRY
LINE OF BRIDGE ABOVE
LAUNDRY
7X11
18' HIGH CEILING
DINING
12X15
FOYER
LIVING
12X12
3 CAR
GARAGE
20X30
FIRST FLOOR

Design 69002

Units	Single
Price Code	H
Total Finished	3,144 sq. ft.
First Finished	1,724 sq. ft.
Second Finished	1,420 sq. ft.
Dimensions	77'6"x30'
Foundation	Basement
Bedrooms	4
Full Baths	3
Half Baths	1
First Ceiling	9'

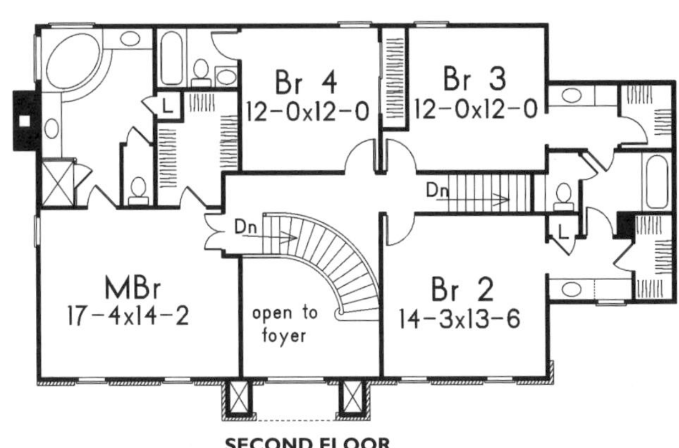
Br 4
12-0x12-0
Br 3
12-0x12-0
Dn
Dn
MBr
17-4x14-2
open to foyer
Br 2
14-3x13-6

SECOND FLOOR

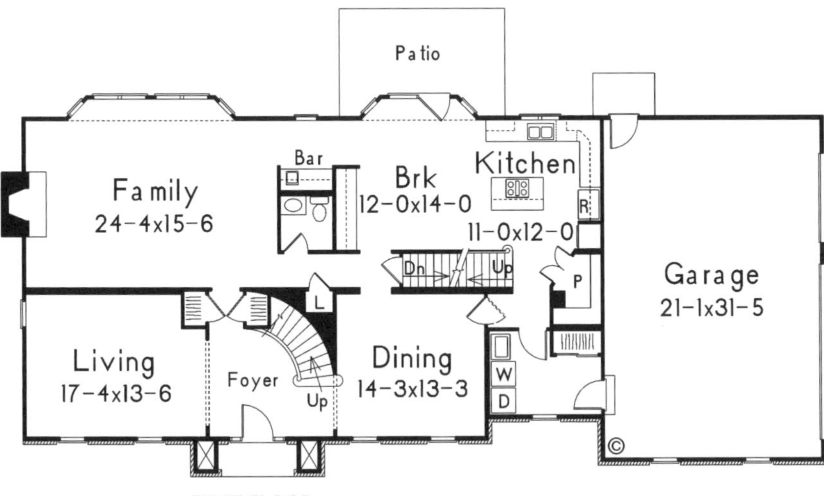
Patio
Bar
Family
24-4x15-6
Brk
12-0x14-0
Kitchen
11-0x12-0
Dn
Up
P
Garage
21-1x31-5
Living
17-4x13-6
Foyer
Up
Dining
14-3x13-3
W
D

FIRST FLOOR

Design 98493

Units	Single
Price Code	H
Total Finished	3,165 sq. ft.
First Finished	1,533 sq. ft.
Second Finished	1,632 sq. ft.
Basement Unfinished	1,583 sq. ft.
Garage Unfinished	640 sq. ft.
Dimensions	58'4"x50'
Foundation	Basement Crawlspace
Bedrooms	5
Full Baths	4
Half Baths	1
First Ceiling	9'
Second Ceiling	8'
Max Ridge Height	34'4"
Roof Framing	Stick
Exterior Walls	2x4

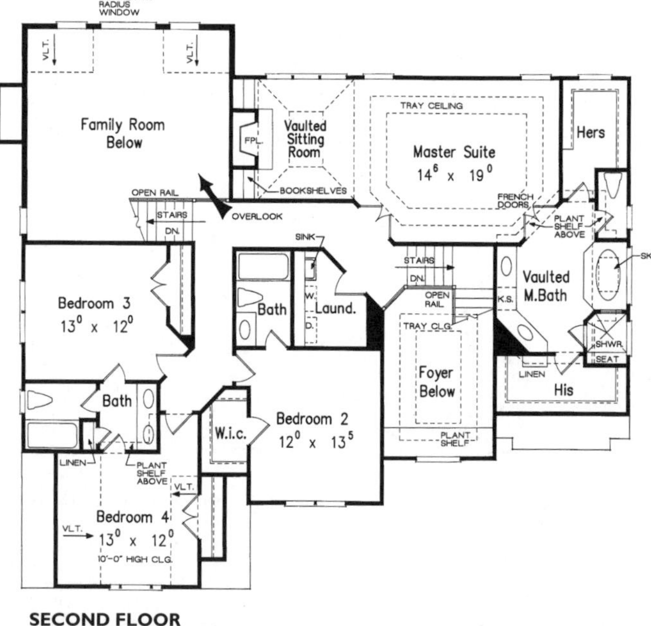

DORMER W/ RADIUS WINDOW
VLT.
Family Room Below
FPL.
Vaulted Sitting Room
BOOKSHELVES
TRAY CEILING
Master Suite 14⁶ x 19⁰
Hers
FRENCH DOORS
PLANT SHELF ABOVE
SKYLITE
OPEN RAIL
STAIRS DN.
OVERLOOK
SINK
Bedroom 3 13⁰ x 12⁰
Bath
Laund.
STAIRS DN.
OPEN RAIL
TRAY CLG.
Vaulted M.Bath
K.S.
SHWR.
SEAT
LINEN
His
Foyer Below
PLANT SHELF
Bath
W.i.c.
Bedroom 2 12⁰ x 13⁵
LINEN
PLANT SHELF ABOVE
Bedroom 4 13⁰ x 12⁰
10'-0" HIGH CLG.

SECOND FLOOR

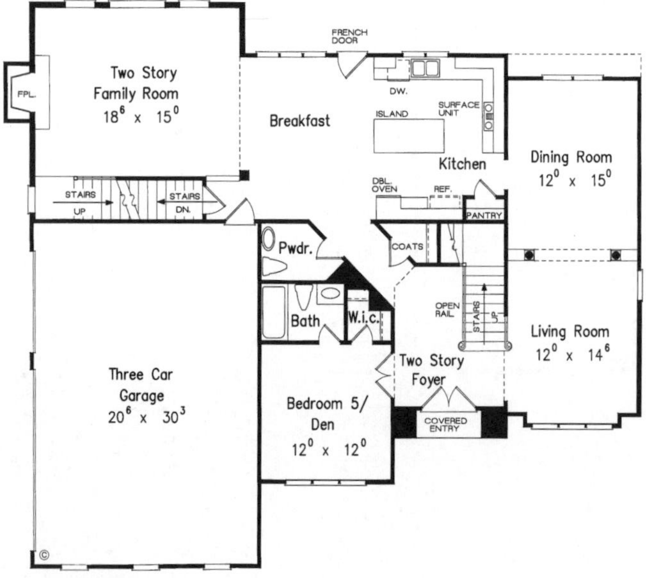

FRENCH DOOR
FPL.
Two Story Family Room 18⁶ x 15⁰
Breakfast
DW.
ISLAND
SURFACE UNIT
Kitchen
DBL. OVEN
REF.
PANTRY
Dining Room 12⁰ x 15⁰
STAIRS UP
STAIRS DN.
Pwdr.
COATS
Bath
W.i.c.
OPEN RAIL
STAIRS UP
Living Room 12⁰ x 14⁶
Three Car Garage 20⁶ x 30³
Two Story Foyer
Bedroom 5/ Den 12⁰ x 12⁰
COVERED ENTRY

FIRST FLOOR

Design 20353

Units	Single
Price Code	H
Total Finished	3,166 sq. ft.
First Finished	1,807 sq. ft.
Second Finished	1,359 sq. ft.
Basement Unfinished	1,807 sq. ft.
Garage Unfinished	840 sq. ft.
Dimensions	80'x59'
Foundation	Basement Crawlspace Slab
Bedrooms	3
Full Baths	3
Half Baths	1
Max Ridge Height	33'
Roof Framing	Stick
Exterior Walls	2x6

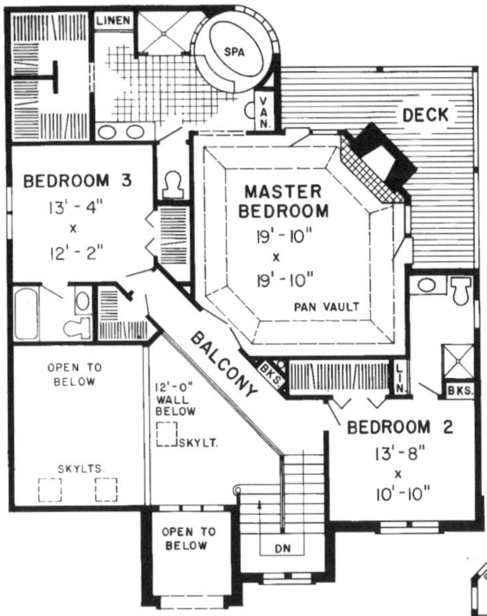

LINEN
SPA
VAN.
DECK
BEDROOM 3
13' - 4" x 12' - 2"
MASTER BEDROOM
19' - 10" x 19' - 10"
PAN VAULT
BALCONY
BKS.
LIN.
BKS.
OPEN TO BELOW
12'-0" WALL BELOW
SKYLT.
SKYLTS.
BEDROOM 2
13' - 8" x 10' - 10"
OPEN TO BELOW
DN

SECOND FLOOR

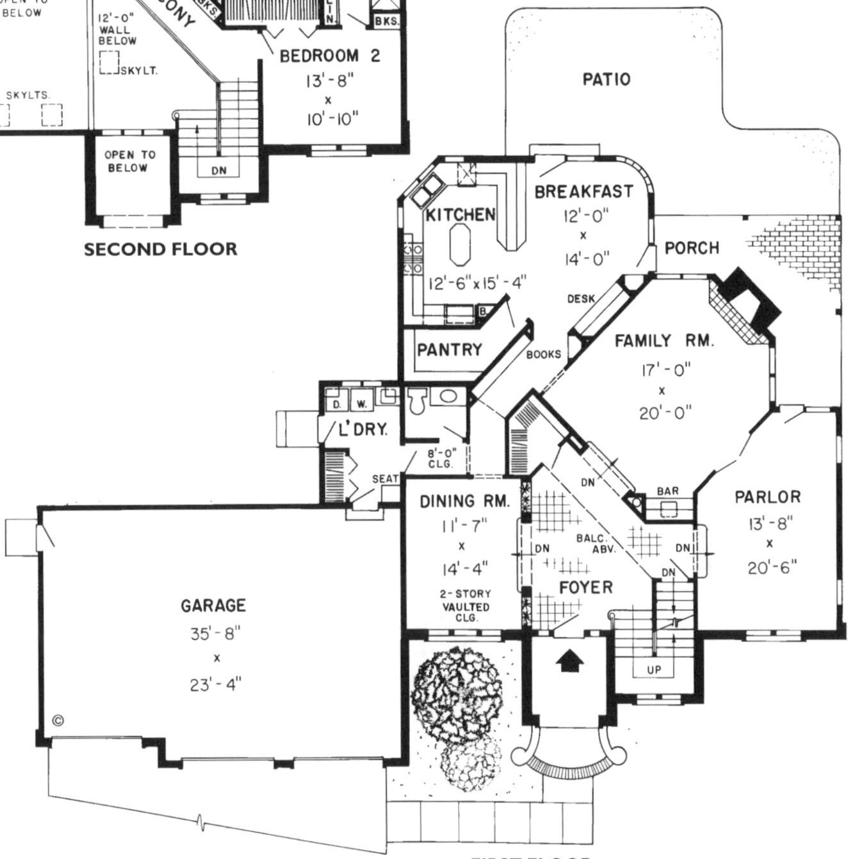

PATIO
KITCHEN
12'-6" x 15'-4"
BREAKFAST
12'-0" x 14'-0"
PORCH
DESK
PANTRY
BOOKS
FAMILY RM.
17'-0" x 20'-0"
D. W.
L'DRY.
8'-0" CLG.
SEAT
DN
BAR
PARLOR
13'-8" x 20'-6"
DINING RM.
11'-7" x 14'-4"
2-STORY VAULTED CLG.
DN
BALC. ABV.
DN
DN
FOYER
UP
GARAGE
35'-8" x 23'-4"

FIRST FLOOR

Design 92158

Units	Single
Price Code	H
Total Finished	3,168 sq. ft.
Main Finished	3,168 sq. ft.
Porch Unfinished	130 sq. ft.
Dimensions	107'10"x78'10"
Foundation	Crawlspace
Bedrooms	3
Full Baths	2
Half Baths	1
Max Ridge Height	23'
Roof Framing	Truss
Exterior Walls	2x6

Patio

*This home is not to be built in Washington State.

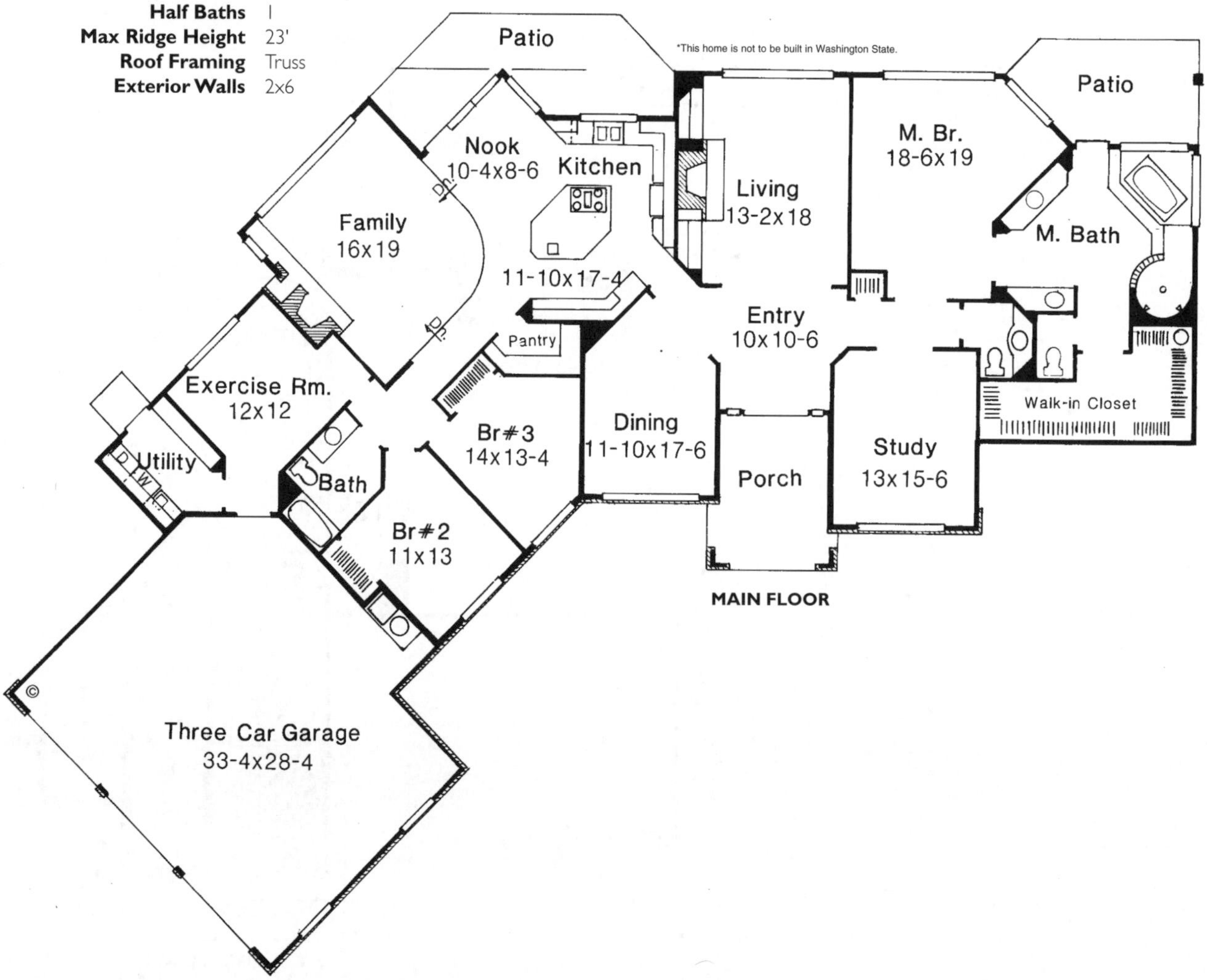

Patio

Nook
10-4x8-6

Kitchen
11-10x17-4

Family
16x19

Living
13-2x18

M. Br.
18-6x19

M. Bath

Pantry

Entry
10x10-6

Walk-in Closet

Exercise Rm.
12x12

Br#3
14x13-4

Dining
11-10x17-6

Study
13x15-6

Utility

D W

Bath

Porch

Br#2
11x13

MAIN FLOOR

Three Car Garage
33-4x28-4

Design 52130

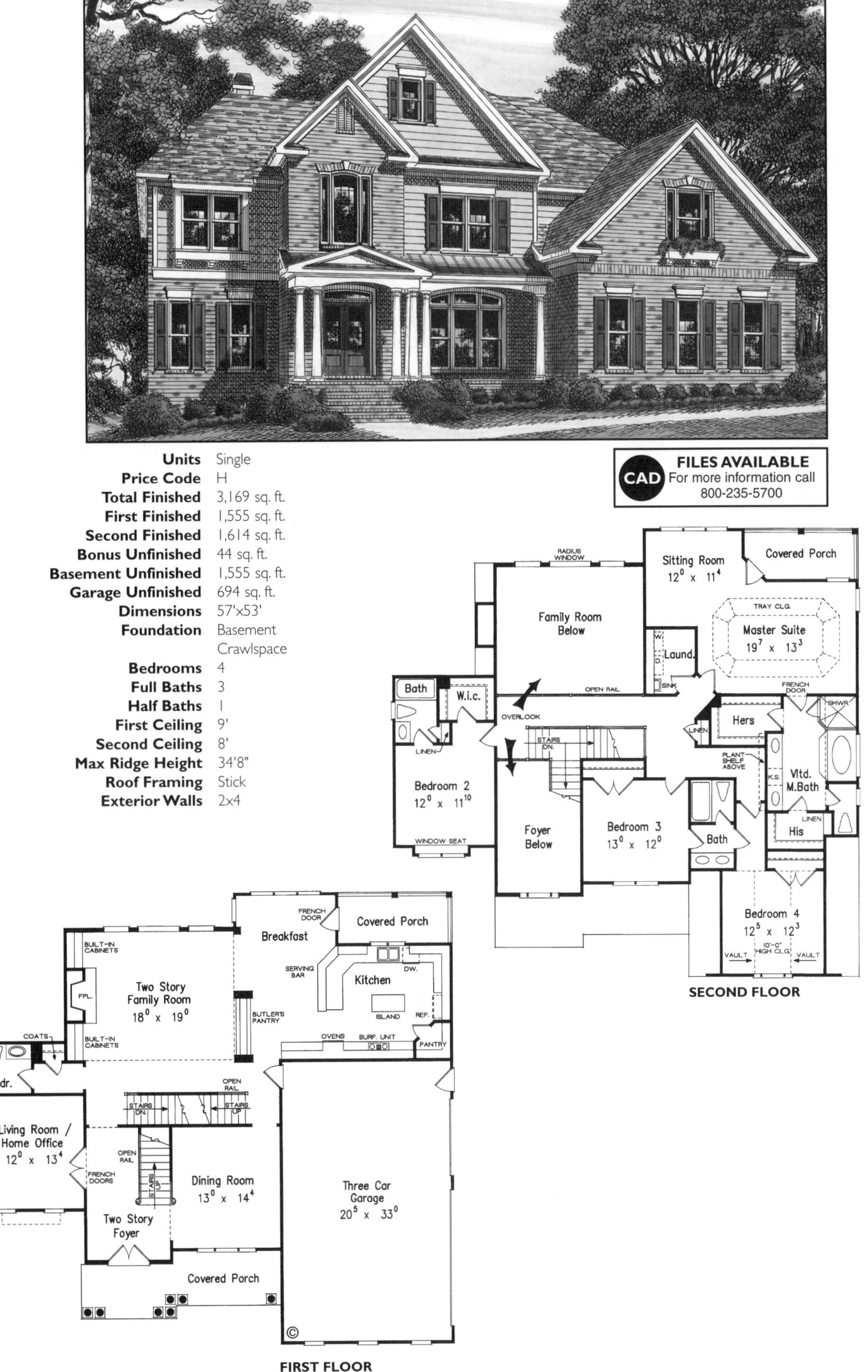
CAD
FILES AVAILABLE
For more information call
800-235-5700
Sitting Room 12⁰ x 11⁴
Covered Porch
RADIUS WINDOW
Family Room Below
TRAY CLG.
Master Suite 19⁷ x 13³
Laund.
SINK
OPEN RAIL
FRENCH DOOR
Bath
W.i.c.
OVERLOOK
STAIRS DN.
LINEN
Hers
SHWR.
PLANT SHELF ABOVE
K.S.
Vltd. M.Bath
Bedroom 2 12⁰ x 11¹⁰
WINDOW SEAT
Foyer Below
Bedroom 3 13⁰ x 12⁰
Bath
His
Bedroom 4 12⁵ x 12³
VAULT
10'-0" HIGH CLG.
SECOND FLOOR
FRENCH DOOR
Covered Porch
Breakfast
BUILT-IN CABINETS
SERVING BAR
DW.
Kitchen
FPL.
Two Story Family Room 18⁰ x 19⁰
BUTLER'S PANTRY
ISLAND
REF.
COATS
OVENS
SURF. UNIT
PANTRY
Pwdr.
OPEN RAIL
STAIRS DN.
STAIRS UP
Living Room / Home Office 12⁰ x 13⁴
FRENCH DOORS
Dining Room 13⁰ x 14⁴
Three Car Garage 20⁵ x 33⁰
Two Story Foyer
Covered Porch
©
FIRST FLOOR

Units	Single
Price Code	H
Total Finished	3,169 sq. ft.
First Finished	1,555 sq. ft.
Second Finished	1,614 sq. ft.
Bonus Unfinished	44 sq. ft.
Basement Unfinished	1,555 sq. ft.
Garage Unfinished	694 sq. ft.
Dimensions	57'x53'
Foundation	Basement Crawlspace
Bedrooms	4
Full Baths	3
Half Baths	1
First Ceiling	9'
Second Ceiling	8'
Max Ridge Height	34'8"
Roof Framing	Stick
Exterior Walls	2x4

Design 69013

Units	Single
Price Code	H
Total Finished	3,169 sq. ft.
First Finished	1,679 sq. ft.
Second Finished	1,490 sq. ft.
Dimensions	55'x49'4"
Foundation	Slab
Bedrooms	4
Full Baths	2
Half Baths	1

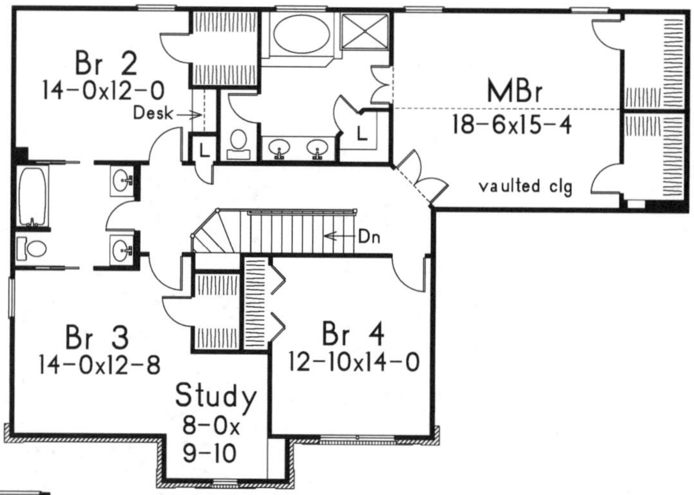

Br 2
14-0x12-0
Desk
MBr
18-6x15-4
vaulted clg
Dn
Br 3
14-0x12-8
Br 4
12-10x14-0
Study
8-0x
9-10

SECOND FLOOR

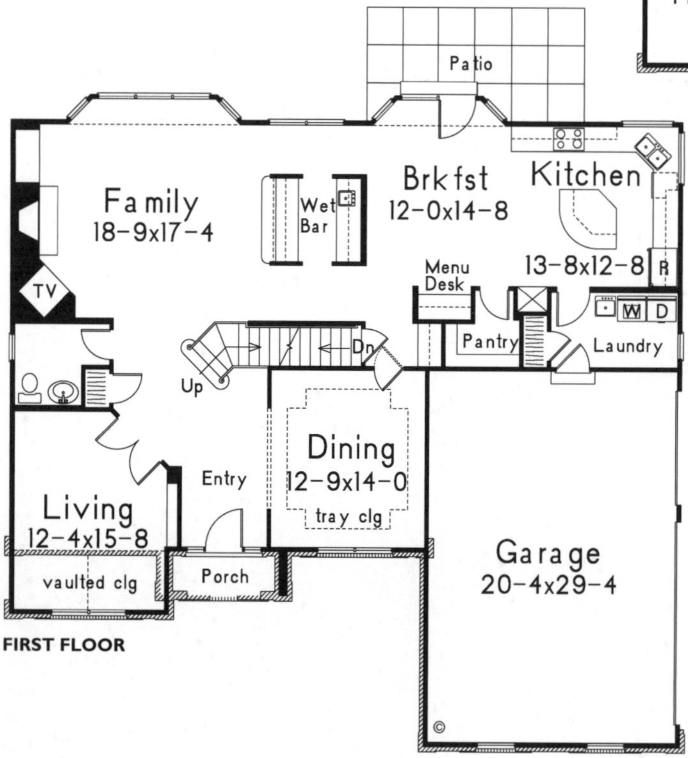

Patio
Family
18-9x17-4
Wet Bar
Brkfst
12-0x14-8
Kitchen
13-8x12-8
Menu Desk
TV
Pantry
Laundry
W D
R
Up
Dn
Entry
Dining
12-9x14-0
tray clg
Living
12-4x15-8
vaulted clg
Porch
Garage
20-4x29-4
©

FIRST FLOOR

Design 10663

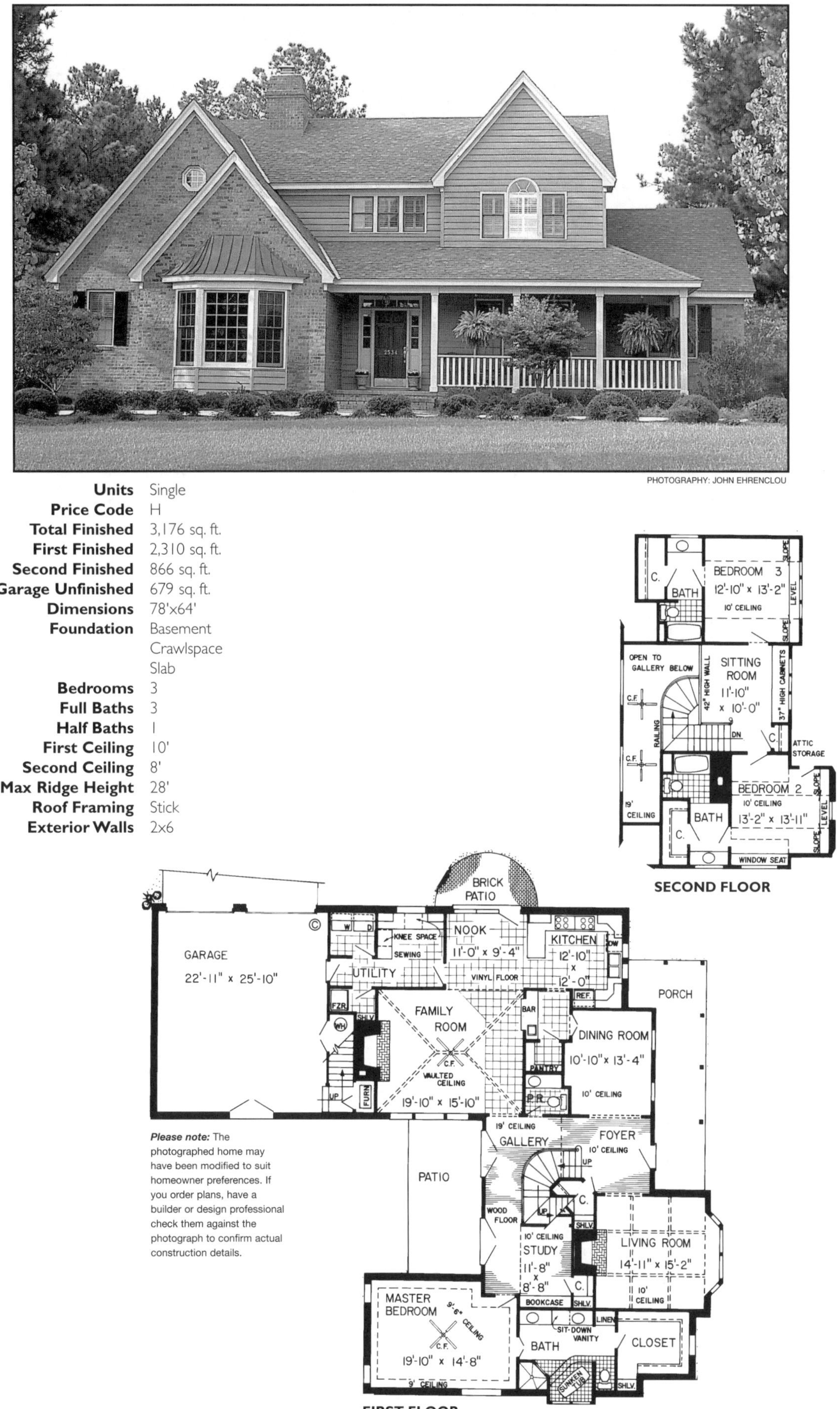
PHOTOGRAPHY: JOHN EHRENCLOU
SECOND FLOOR
BEDROOM 3
12'-10" x 13'-2"
10' CEILING
BATH
C.
SLOPE
LEVEL
OPEN TO GALLERY BELOW
42" HIGH WALL
SITTING ROOM
11'-10" x 10'-0"
37" HIGH CABINETS
C.F.
RAILING
DN
ATTIC STORAGE
BEDROOM 2
10' CEILING
13'-2" x 13'-11"
19' CEILING
WINDOW SEAT
FIRST FLOOR
BRICK PATIO
GARAGE
22'-11" x 25'-10"
KNEE SPACE
SEWING
NOOK
11'-0" x 9'-4"
KITCHEN
12'-10" x 12'-0"
UTILITY
VINYL FLOOR
REF.
PORCH
FZR
WH
SHLV
FAMILY ROOM
C.F.
VAULTED CEILING
19'-10" x 15'-10"
BAR
PANTRY
DINING ROOM
10'-10" x 13'-4"
10' CEILING
UP
FURN
P.R.
19' CEILING
GALLERY
FOYER
10' CEILING
PATIO
WOOD FLOOR
STUDY
11'-8" x 8'-8"
BOOKCASE
LIVING ROOM
14'-11" x 15'-2"
MASTER BEDROOM
9'-6" CEILING
19'-10" x 14'-8"
9' CEILING
BATH
SIT-DOWN VANITY
SUNKEN TUB
LINEN
CLOSET

Units	Single
Price Code	H
Total Finished	3,176 sq. ft.
First Finished	2,310 sq. ft.
Second Finished	866 sq. ft.
Garage Unfinished	679 sq. ft.
Dimensions	78'x64'
Foundation	Basement Crawlspace Slab
Bedrooms	3
Full Baths	3
Half Baths	1
First Ceiling	10'
Second Ceiling	8'
Max Ridge Height	28'
Roof Framing	Stick
Exterior Walls	2x6

Please note: The photographed home may have been modified to suit homeowner preferences. If you order plans, have a builder or design professional check them against the photograph to confirm actual construction details.

Design 91319

Units	Single
Price Code	H
Total Finished	3,192 sq. ft.
First Finished	1,306 sq. ft.
Second Finished	598 sq. ft.
Lower Finished	1,288 sq. ft.
Dimensions	46'x30'
Foundation	Basement
Bedrooms	3
Full Baths	1
3/4 Baths	2
Exterior Walls	2x4

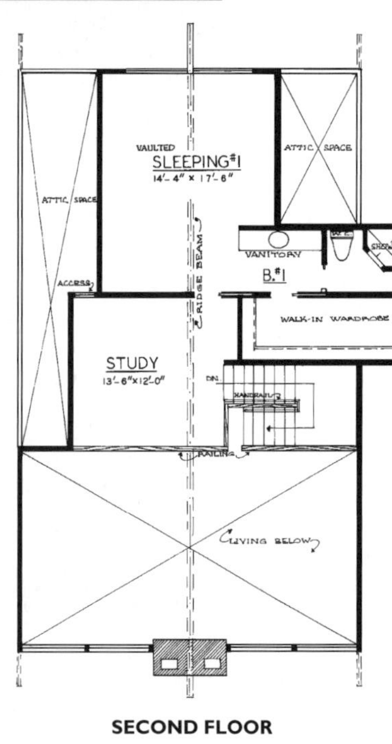
VAULTED
SLEEPING#1
14'-4" x 17'-6"
ATTIC SPACE
ATTIC SPACE
VANITORY
B.#1
WALK-IN WARDROBE
ACCESS
RIDGE BEAM
STUDY
13'-6"x12'-0"
DN.
RAILING
LIVING BELOW

SECOND FLOOR

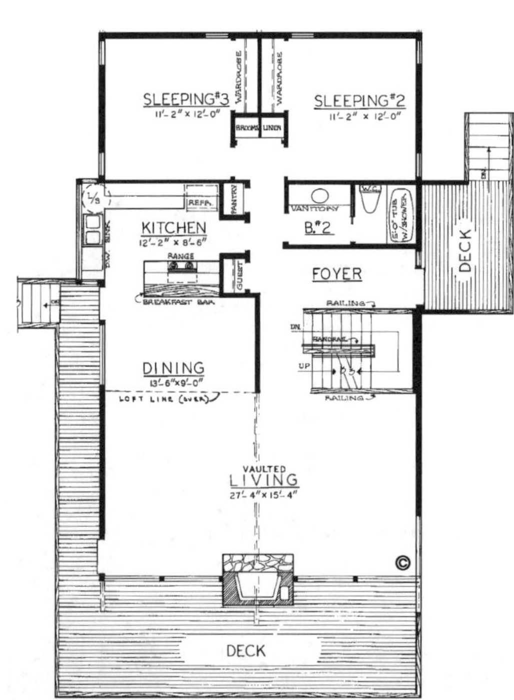
SLEEPING#3
11'-2" x 12'-0"
SLEEPING#2
11'-2" x 12'-0"
WARDROBE
WARDROBE
LINEN
PANTRY
REFR.
KITCHEN
12'-2" x 8'-6"
RANGE
BREAKFAST BAR
VANITORY
B.#2
DECK
FOYER
RAILING
DN.
UP
DINING
13'-6"x9'-0"
LOFT LINE (OVER)
VAULTED
LIVING
27'-4" x 15'-4"
DECK

FIRST FLOOR

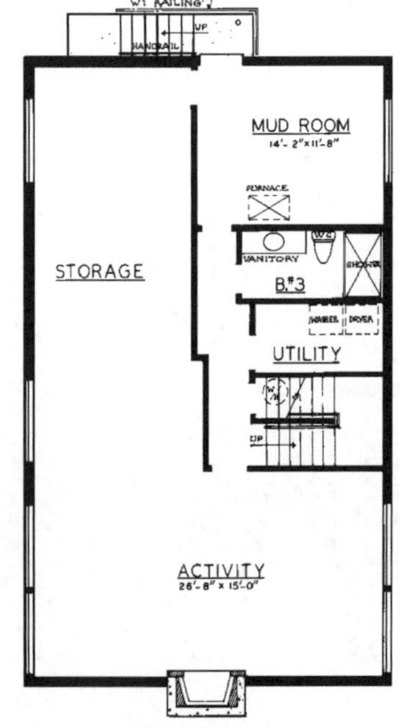
RAILING
UP
HANDRAIL
MUD ROOM
14'-2"x11'-8"
FURNACE
VANITORY
B.#3
STORAGE
WASHER
DRYER
UTILITY
UP
ACTIVITY
26'-8" x 15'-0"

LOWER FLOOR

Design 93333

M/BATH
CATH CLG
SHWR
LDY
W D
LINEN
B 2
BR 4
14-6 x 12
DN
FOYER BELOW
MBR
14 x 18-6
HALL
RAILING
BALCONY
BR 3
10 x 12(+)
ROOF
BR 2
14 x 12
ROOF
SECOND FLOOR
FLOOR ABOVE
SUN RM
13 x 12
DECK
CIRCLE-HEAD WINDOW
BOOKS
SEAT
BOOKS
DEN
14 x 13
DW
KITCHEN
13 x 14
DINETTE
12 x 11-6
SEAT
TRAY CLG
FAMILY
16 x 22
DN
OPEN ABOVE
OV
REF
LIVING
14 x 19
UP
FOYER
PAN.
B C
RAILING
DN
DINING
14 x 14
STEPPED CLG
ENTRY
P
PORCH
GARAGE
24 x 34(+)
9-FT DOORS
FIRST FLOOR

Units	Single
Price Code	H
Total Finished	3,198 sq. ft.
First Finished	1,743 sq. ft.
Second Finished	1,455 sq. ft.
Dimensions	94'6"x60'2"
Foundation	Basement
Bedrooms	4
Full Baths	2
Half Baths	1
First Ceiling	8'4½"
Second Ceiling	8'4½"
Max Ridge Height	29'
Roof Framing	Stick
Exterior Walls	2x6

Design 63066

Units	Single
Price Code	H
Total Finished	3,200 sq. ft.
First Finished	2,531 sq. ft.
Second Finished	669 sq. ft.
Garage Unfinished	656 sq. ft.
Dimensions	70'x82'4"
Foundation	Slab
Bedrooms	4
Full Baths	3
Half Baths	2
Max Ridge Height	26'10"

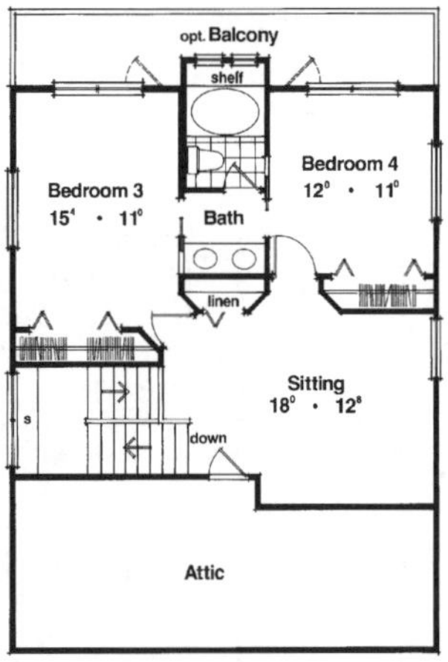

opt. Balcony
shelf
Bedroom 3
15⁴ · 11⁰
Bath
Bedroom 4
12⁰ · 11⁰
linen
Sitting
18⁰ · 12⁸
down
Attic

SECOND FLOOR

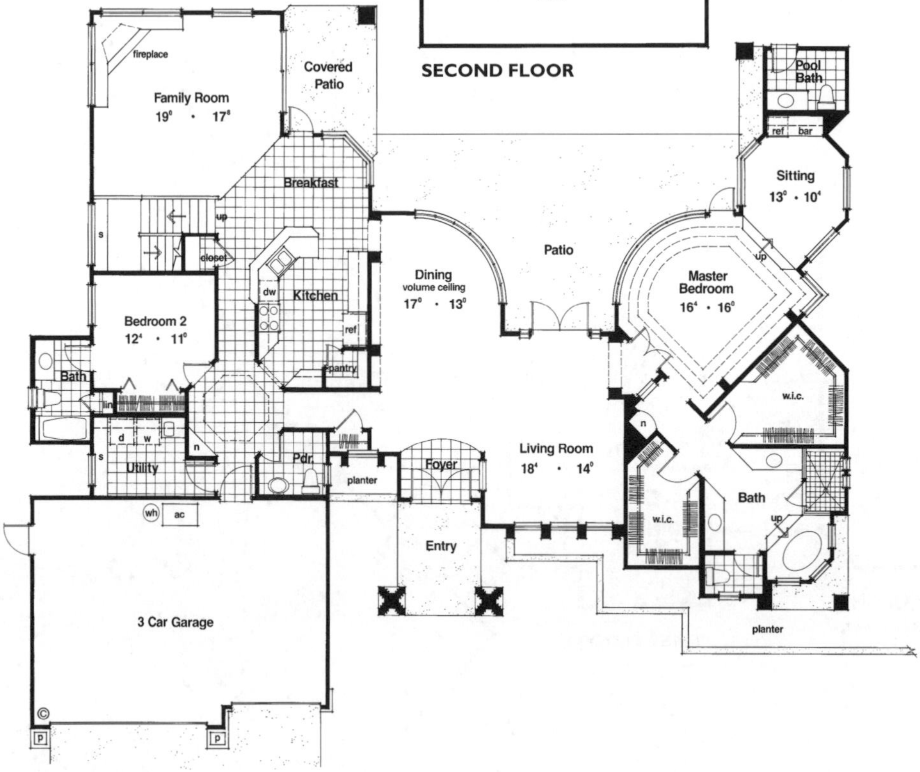

fireplace
Family Room
19⁰ · 17⁸
Covered Patio
Breakfast
up
closet
dw
Kitchen
ref
pantry
Bedroom 2
12⁴ · 11⁰
Bath
lin
d w
Utility
Pdr.
planter
Foyer
Entry
Dining
volume ceiling
17⁰ · 13⁰
Patio
Living Room
18⁴ · 14⁰
Pool Bath
ref bar
Sitting
13⁰ · 10⁴
up
Master Bedroom
16⁴ · 16⁰
w.i.c.
w.i.c.
Bath
up
planter
wh ac
3 Car Garage

FIRST FLOOR

Design 92165

Units	Single
Price Code	I
Total Finished	3,215 sq. ft.
First Finished	2,311 sq. ft.
Second Finished	904 sq. ft.
Garage Unfinished	528 sq. ft.
Dimensions	72'x78'6'
Foundation	Slab
Bedrooms	3
Full Baths	2
Half Baths	I
First Ceiling	8'1"
Second Ceiling	8'1"
Vaulted Ceiling	10'8"
Tray Ceiling	14'6"
Max Ridge Height	33'
Roof Framing	Stick/Truss
Exterior Walls	2x6

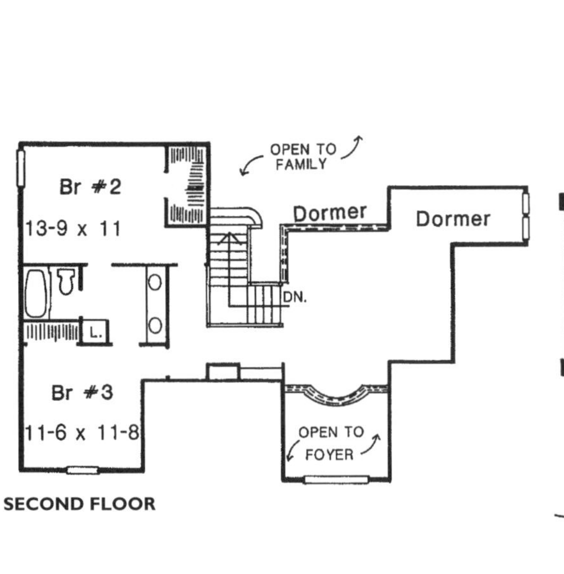

OPEN TO FAMILY
Br #2
13-9 x 11
Dormer
Dormer
DN.
L.
Br #3
11-6 x 11-8
OPEN TO FOYER

SECOND FLOOR

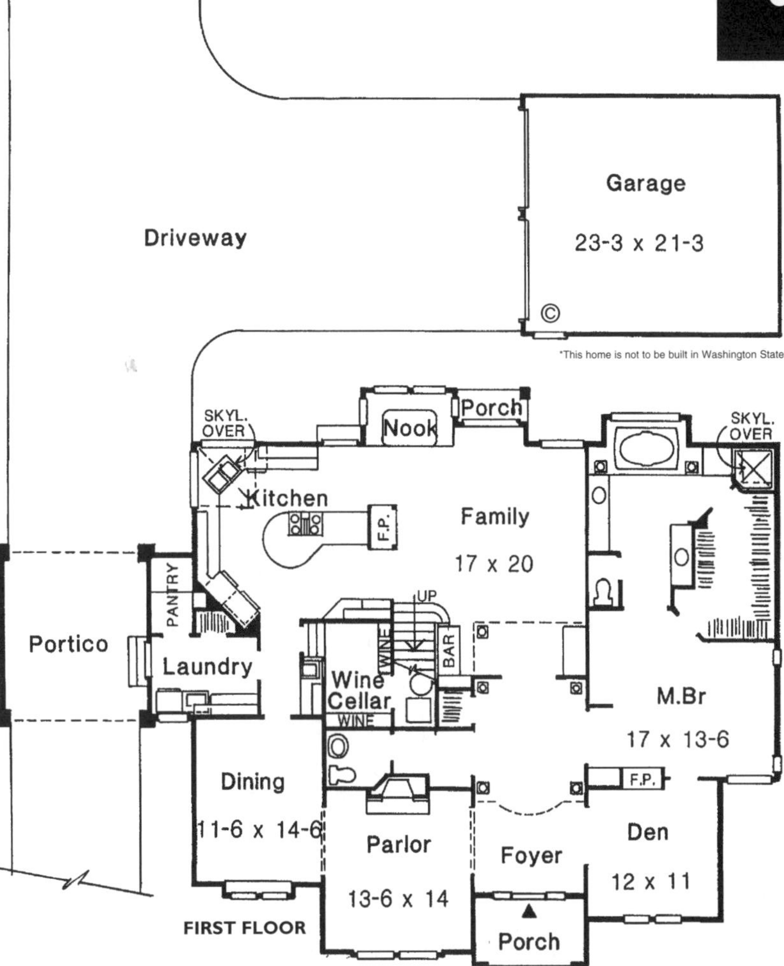

Driveway
Garage
23-3 x 21-3
©
SKYL. OVER
Nook
Porch
SKYL. OVER
Kitchen
F.P.
Family
17 x 20
PANTRY
UP
Portico
Laundry
WINE
BAR
Wine Cellar
WINE
M.Br
17 x 13-6
Dining
11-6 x 14-6
F.P.
Parlor
13-6 x 14
Foyer
Den
12 x 11
Porch

*This home is not to be built in Washington State.

FIRST FLOOR

Design 86020

Units	Single
Price Code	H
Total Finished	3,219 sq. ft.
First Finished	1,884 sq. ft.
Second Finished	1,335 sq. ft.
Basement Unfinished	1,872 sq. ft.
Garage Unfinished	753 sq. ft.
Porch Unfinished	43 sq. ft.
Dimensions	68'3"x50'8"
Foundation	Basement
Bedrooms	4
Full Baths	2
Half Baths	1
First Ceiling	9'
Second Ceiling	8'
Max Ridge Height	35'
Roof Framing	Stick
Exterior Walls	2x6

GLASS BLOCKS
SHWR
WH'POOL TUB
BEDROOM 3 12'-0"x 11'-6"
BEDROOM 2 12'-5"x 11'-6"
SHELVES
MR. BATH & DRSG
SH.
SH.
LINENS
WIC
WIC
BATH 2
DN
(OPEN TO ENTRY)
BEDROOM 4 13'-8"x 10'-5"
MR BEDROOM 13'-8"x 19'-2" (VAULTED CEILING)

SECOND FLOOR

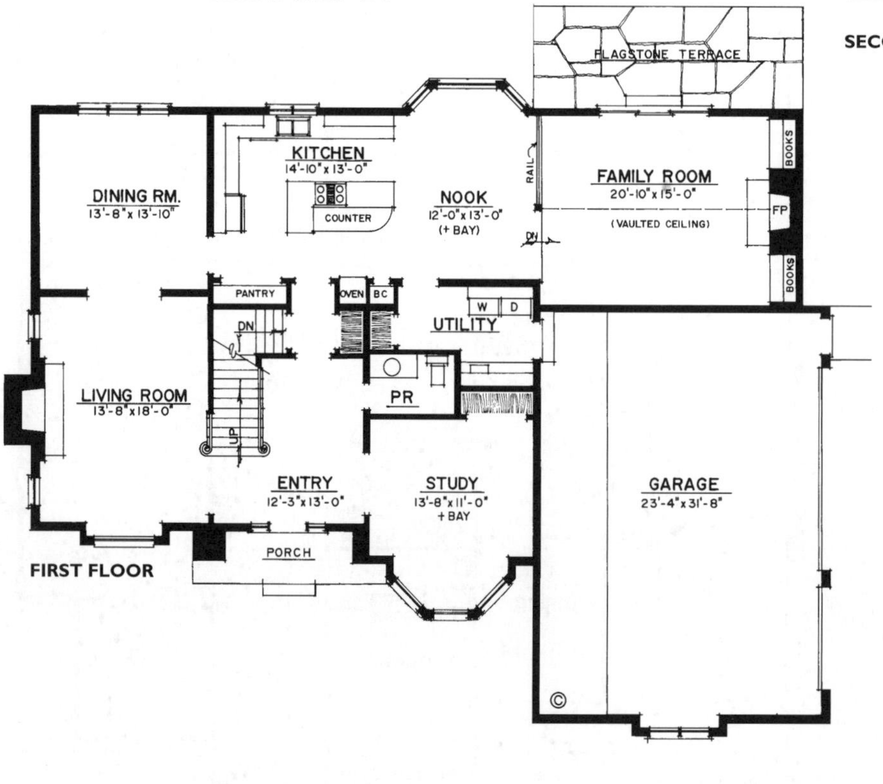

FLAGSTONE TERRACE
KITCHEN 14'-10"x 13'-0"
DINING RM. 13'-8"x 13'-10"
COUNTER
NOOK 12'-0"x 13'-0" (+ BAY)
RAIL
DN
FAMILY ROOM 20'-10"x 15'-0" (VAULTED CEILING)
BOOKS
FP
BOOKS
PANTRY
OVEN
BC
W
D
UTILITY
DN
LIVING ROOM 13'-8"x 18'-0"
UP
PR
ENTRY 12'-3"x 13'-0"
STUDY 13'-8"x 11'-0" + BAY
GARAGE 23'-4"x 31'-8"
PORCH
©

FIRST FLOOR

Design 98401

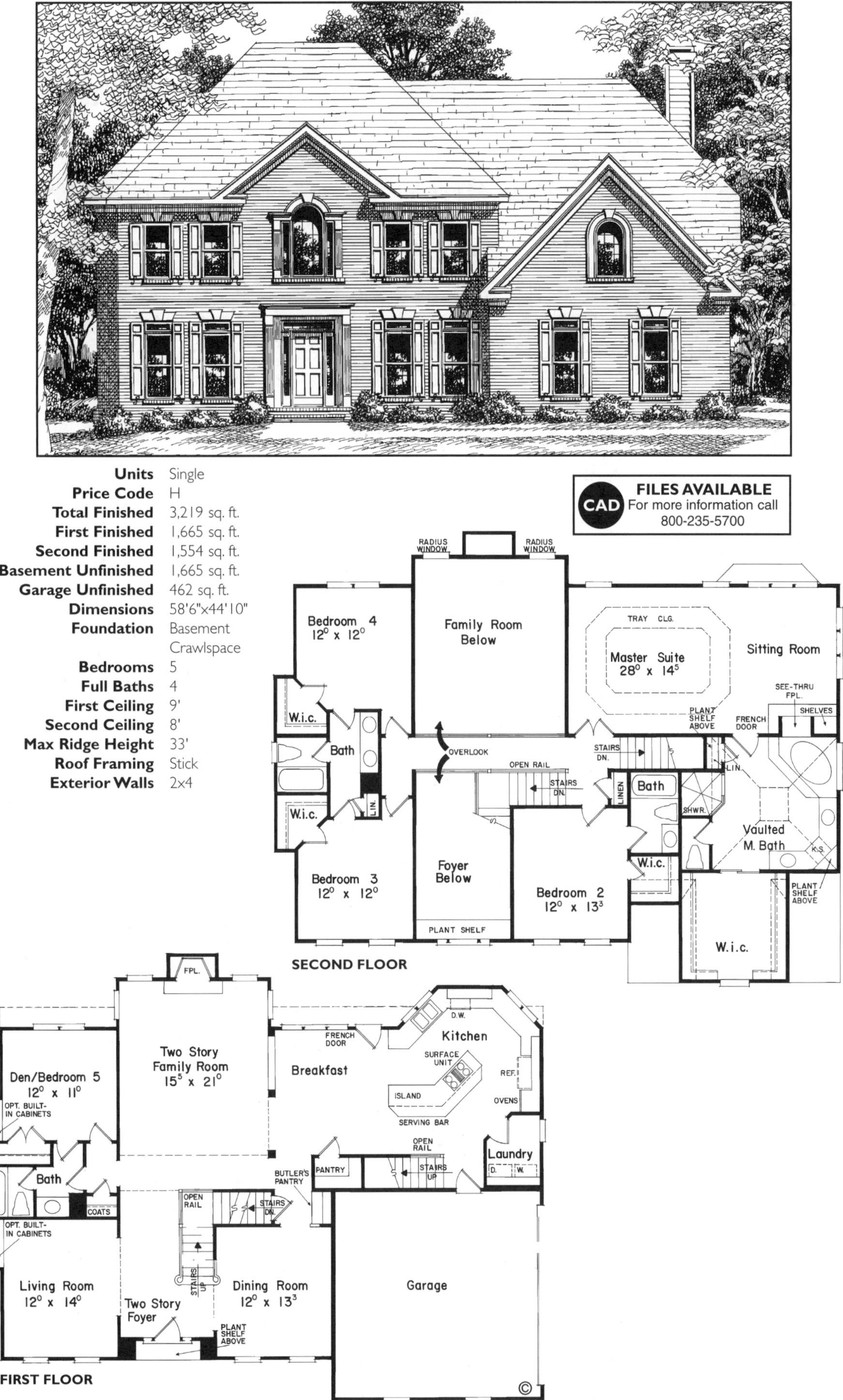
CAD FILES AVAILABLE
For more information call
800-235-5700
RADIUS WINDOW
RADIUS WINDOW
Bedroom 4
12⁰ x 12⁰
Family Room
Below
TRAY CLG.
Master Suite
28⁰ x 14⁵
Sitting Room
SEE-THRU FPL.
SHELVES
PLANT SHELF ABOVE
FRENCH DOOR
W.i.c.
Bath
OVERLOOK
OPEN RAIL
STAIRS DN.
STAIRS DN.
LIN.
LINEN
Bath
SHWR.
LIN.
W.i.c.
Vaulted
M. Bath
K.S.
W.i.c.
Bedroom 3
12⁰ x 12⁰
Foyer
Below
PLANT SHELF
Bedroom 2
12⁰ x 13³
PLANT SHELF ABOVE
W.i.c.
SECOND FLOOR
FPL.
Two Story
Family Room
15⁵ x 21⁰
Den/Bedroom 5
12⁰ x 11⁰
OPT. BUILT-IN CABINETS
FRENCH DOOR
Breakfast
D.W.
Kitchen
SURFACE UNIT
REF.
ISLAND
OVENS
SERVING BAR
OPEN RAIL
STAIRS UP
Laundry
D.
W.
PANTRY
BUTLER'S PANTRY
Bath
COATS
OPEN RAIL
STAIRS DN.
OPT. BUILT-IN CABINETS
STAIRS UP
Living Room
12⁰ x 14⁰
Two Story
Foyer
Dining Room
12⁰ x 13³
PLANT SHELF ABOVE
Garage
FIRST FLOOR
©

Units	Single
Price Code	H
Total Finished	3,219 sq. ft.
First Finished	1,665 sq. ft.
Second Finished	1,554 sq. ft.
Basement Unfinished	1,665 sq. ft.
Garage Unfinished	462 sq. ft.
Dimensions	58'6"x44'10"
Foundation	Basement Crawlspace
Bedrooms	5
Full Baths	4
First Ceiling	9'
Second Ceiling	8'
Max Ridge Height	33'
Roof Framing	Stick
Exterior Walls	2x4

Design 98588

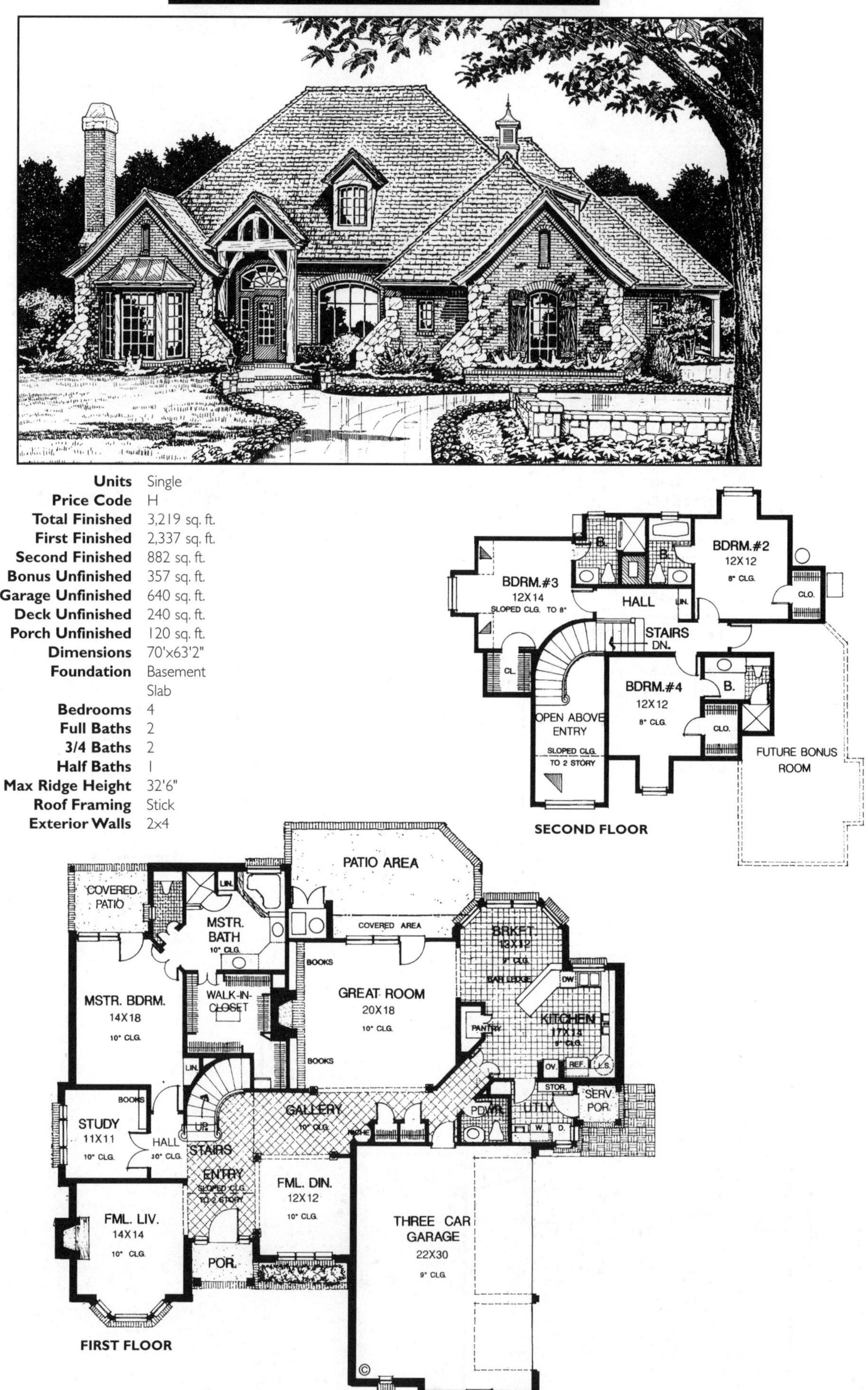

BDRM.#3
12X14
SLOPED CLG. TO 8"
CL.
B.
B.
HALL
LIN.
BDRM.#2
12X12
8" CLG.
CLO.
STAIRS
DN.
BDRM.#4
12X12
8" CLG.
CLO.
B.
OPEN ABOVE
ENTRY
SLOPED CLG.
TO 2 STORY
FUTURE BONUS
ROOM
SECOND FLOOR
PATIO AREA
COVERED PATIO
LIN.
MSTR.
BATH
10" CLG.
COVERED AREA
BRKFT.
BAR LEDGE
DW
MSTR. BDRM.
14X18
10" CLG.
WALK-IN-
CLOSET
BOOKS
GREAT ROOM
20X18
10" CLG.
BOOKS
PANTRY
KITCHEN
OV.
REF.
STOR.
SERV.
POR.
BOOKS
STUDY
11X11
10" CLG.
HALL
10" CLG.
UP
STAIRS
GALLERY
10" CLG.
NICHE
PDWR.
UTLY.
W.
D.
ENTRY
SLOPED CLG.
TO 2 STORY
FML. DIN.
12X12
10" CLG.
FML. LIV.
14X14
10" CLG.
POR.
THREE CAR
GARAGE
22X30
9" CLG.
FIRST FLOOR

Units	Single
Price Code	H
Total Finished	3,219 sq. ft.
First Finished	2,337 sq. ft.
Second Finished	882 sq. ft.
Bonus Unfinished	357 sq. ft.
Garage Unfinished	640 sq. ft.
Deck Unfinished	240 sq. ft.
Porch Unfinished	120 sq. ft.
Dimensions	70'x63'2"
Foundation	Basement Slab
Bedrooms	4
Full Baths	2
3/4 Baths	2
Half Baths	1
Max Ridge Height	32'6"
Roof Framing	Stick
Exterior Walls	2x4

Design 97513

Units	Single
Price Code	H
Total Finished	3,230 sq. ft.
Main Finished	3,230 sq. ft.
Garage Unfinished	729 sq. ft.
Porch Unfinished	212 sq. ft.
Dimensions	94'8"x88'5"
Foundation	Slab
Bedrooms	4
Full Baths	3
Max Ridge Height	30'6"
Roof Framing	Stick
Exterior Walls	2x4

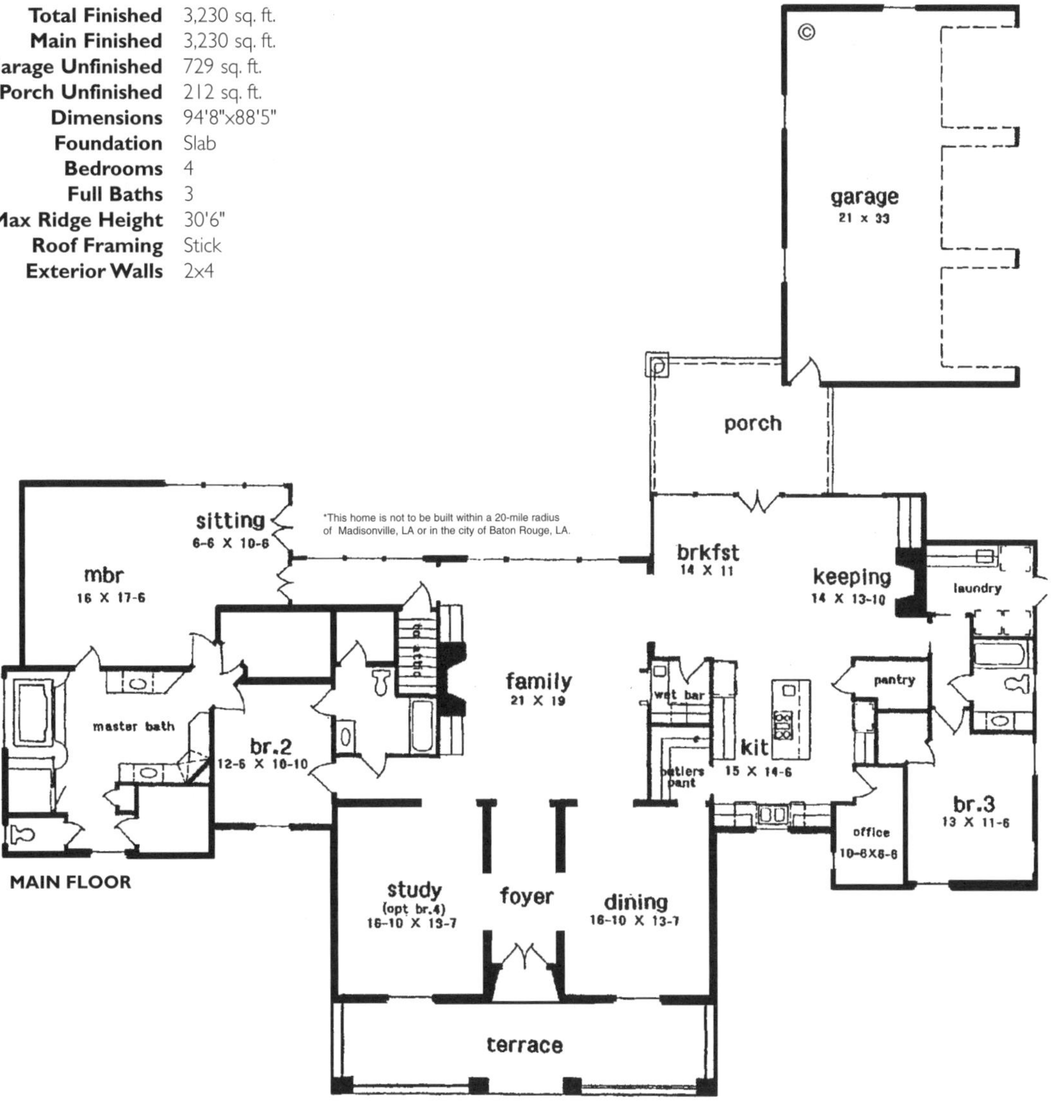

garage
21 x 33

porch

sitting
6-6 X 10-6

*This home is not to be built within a 20-mile radius of Madisonville, LA or in the city of Baton Rouge, LA.

brkfst
14 X 11

keeping
14 X 13-10

laundry

mbr
16 X 17-6

family
21 X 19

wet bar

pantry

master bath

br.2
12-6 X 10-10

kit
15 X 14-6

butlers pant

br.3
13 X 11-6

office
10-6X6-6

MAIN FLOOR

study
(opt br.4)
16-10 X 13-7

foyer

dining
16-10 X 13-7

terrace

Design 69001

Units	Single
Price Code	H
Total Finished	3,234 sq. ft.
First Finished	2,273 sq. ft.
Second Finished	961 sq. ft.
Dimensions	87'8"x46'10"
Foundation	Basement Crawlspace Slab
Bedrooms	4
Full Baths	2
3/4 Baths	1
Half Baths	1
Max Ridge Height	33'3"
Roof Framing	Stick
Exterior Walls	2x4

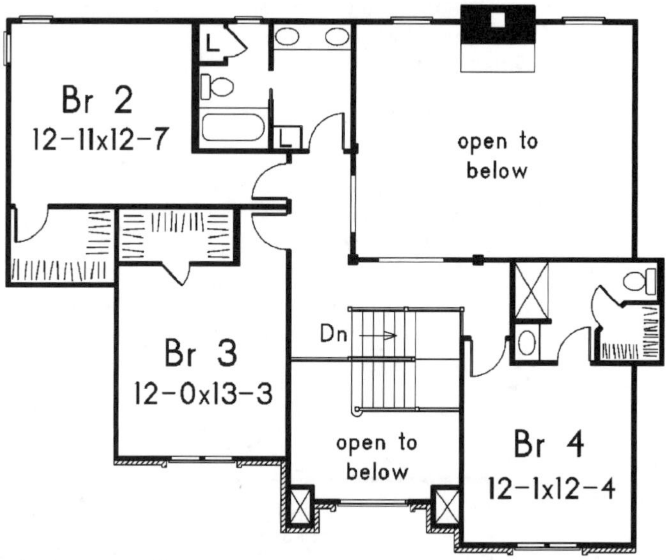

Br 2
12-11x12-7
L
L
open to below
Br 3
12-0x13-3
Dn
open to below
Br 4
12-1x12-4

SECOND FLOOR

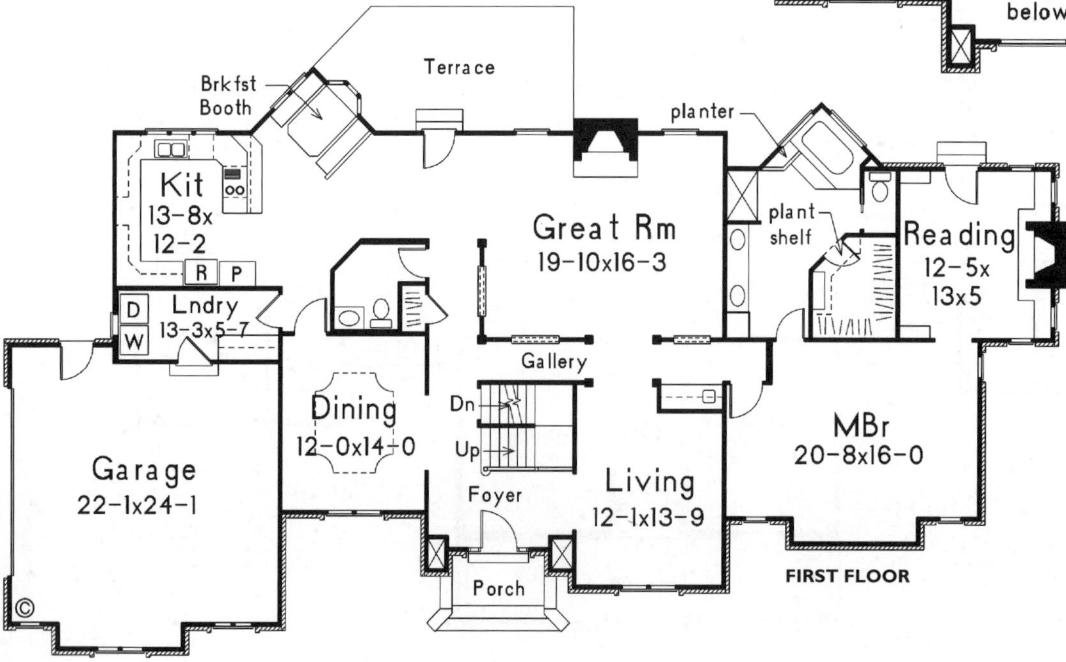

Brkfst Booth
Terrace
planter
Kit
13-8x
12-2
R P
Great Rm
19-10x16-3
plant shelf
Reading
12-5x
13x5
D W
Lndry
13-3x5-7
Gallery
Dining
12-0x14-0
Dn
Up
MBr
20-8x16-0
Garage
22-1x24-1
Foyer
Living
12-1x13-9
Porch
©

FIRST FLOOR

Design 99430

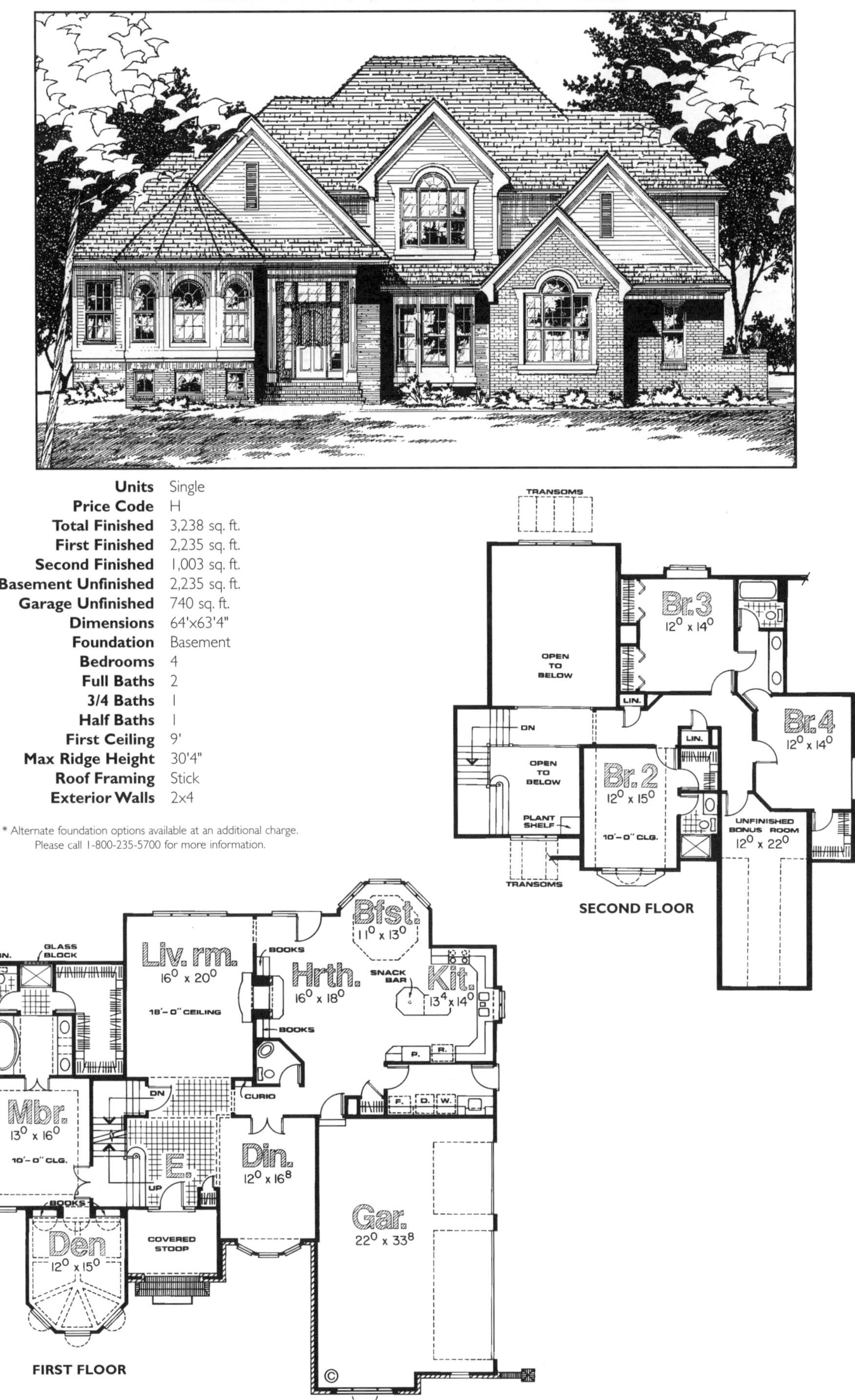
TRANSOMS
OPEN TO BELOW
Br.3
12⁰ x 14⁰
LIN.
Br.4
12⁰ x 14⁰
DN
OPEN TO BELOW
Br.2
12⁰ x 15⁰
LIN.
PLANT SHELF
10'-0" CLG.
UNFINISHED BONUS ROOM
12⁰ x 22⁰
TRANSOMS
SECOND FLOOR
Bfst.
11⁰ x 13⁰
LIN.
GLASS BLOCK
WHIRLPOOL
Liv. rm.
16⁰ x 20⁰
18'-0" CEILING
BOOKS
Hrth.
16⁰ x 18⁰
BOOKS
SNACK BAR
Kit.
13⁴ x 14⁰
P.
R.
F.
D.
W.
CURIO
DN
Mbr.
13⁰ x 16⁰
10'-0" CLG.
E.
UP
Din.
12⁰ x 16⁸
BOOKS
Den
12⁰ x 15⁰
COVERED STOOP
Gar.
22⁰ x 33⁸
FIRST FLOOR

Units	Single
Price Code	H
Total Finished	3,238 sq. ft.
First Finished	2,235 sq. ft.
Second Finished	1,003 sq. ft.
Basement Unfinished	2,235 sq. ft.
Garage Unfinished	740 sq. ft.
Dimensions	64'x63'4"
Foundation	Basement
Bedrooms	4
Full Baths	2
3/4 Baths	1
Half Baths	1
First Ceiling	9'
Max Ridge Height	30'4"
Roof Framing	Stick
Exterior Walls	2x4

* Alternate foundation options available at an additional charge.
Please call 1-800-235-5700 for more information.

Design 98598

Units	Single
Price Code	H
Total Finished	3,239 sq. ft.
Main Finished	3,239 sq. ft.
Garage Unfinished	748 sq. ft.
Deck Unfinished	184 sq. ft.
Porch Unfinished	64 sq. ft.
Dimensions	118'9"x55'1"
Foundation	Slab
Bedrooms	3
Full Baths	2
3/4 Baths	1
Main Ceiling	9'-11'
Max Ridge Height	27'
Roof Framing	Stick
Exterior Walls	2x4

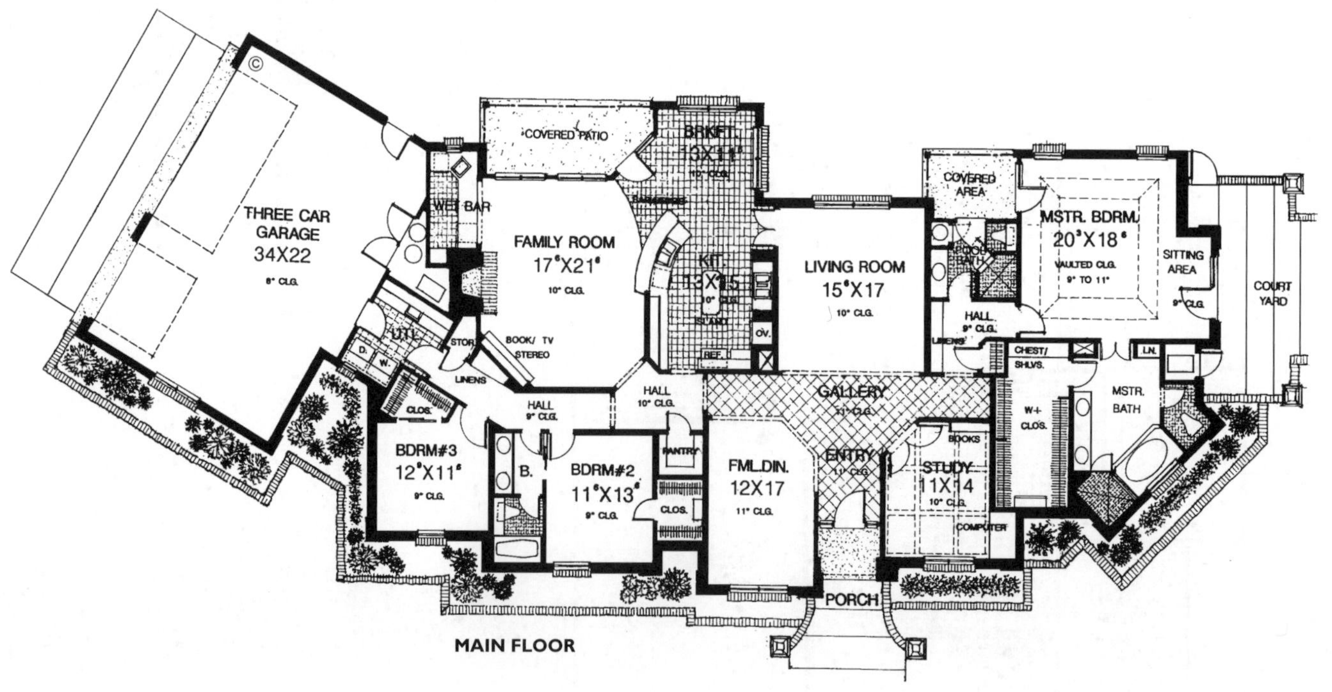
THREE CAR GARAGE
34X22
COVERED PATIO
BRKFT.
WET BAR
FAMILY ROOM
17⁶X21⁶
10" CLG.
KIT.
LIVING ROOM
15⁶X17
10" CLG.
COVERED AREA
MSTR. BDRM.
20³X18⁶
VAULTED CLG. 9" TO 11"
SITTING AREA
COURT YARD
HALL
GALLERY
MSTR. BATH
W-I-CLOS.
BDRM#3
12⁶X11⁶
9" CLG.
BDRM#2
11⁶X13⁶
9" CLG.
PANTRY
FML.DIN.
12X17
11" CLG.
ENTRY
STUDY
11X14
10" CLG.
COMPUTER
PORCH
BOOK/ TV STEREO
LINENS
UTIL.
CLOS.
MAIN FLOOR

Design 91854

Units	Single
Price Code	H
Total Finished	3,240 sq. ft.
First Finished	1,860 sq. ft.
Second Finished	1,380 sq. ft.
Bonus Unfinished	286 sq. ft.
Basement Unfinished	1,860 sq. ft.
Garage Unfinished	793 sq. ft.
Deck Unfinished	230 sq. ft.
Porch Unfinished	246 sq. ft.
Dimensions	41'x96'
Foundation	Basement Crawlspace Slab
Bedrooms	4
Full Baths	2
3/4 Baths	1
Half Baths	1
First Ceiling	9'
Second Ceiling	9'
Max Ridge Height	29'10"
Roof Framing	Truss
Exterior Walls	2x4

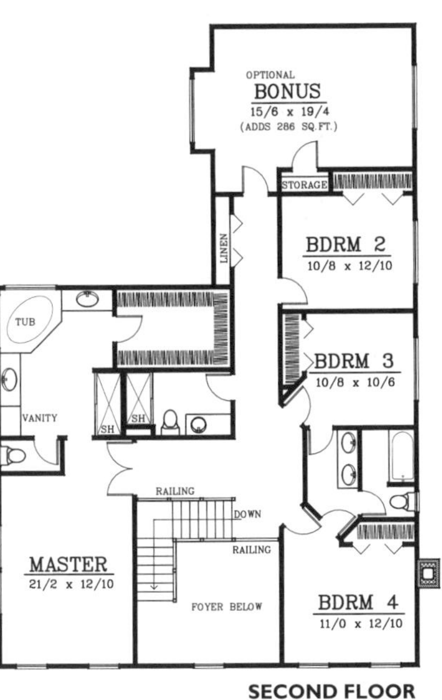
OPTIONAL
BONUS
15/6 x 19/4
(ADDS 286 SQ.FT.)
STORAGE
BDRM 2
10/8 x 12/10
LINEN
TUB
VANITY
SH
SH
BDRM 3
10/8 x 10/6
RAILING
DOWN
RAILING
MASTER
21/2 x 12/10
FOYER BELOW
BDRM 4
11/0 x 12/10

SECOND FLOOR

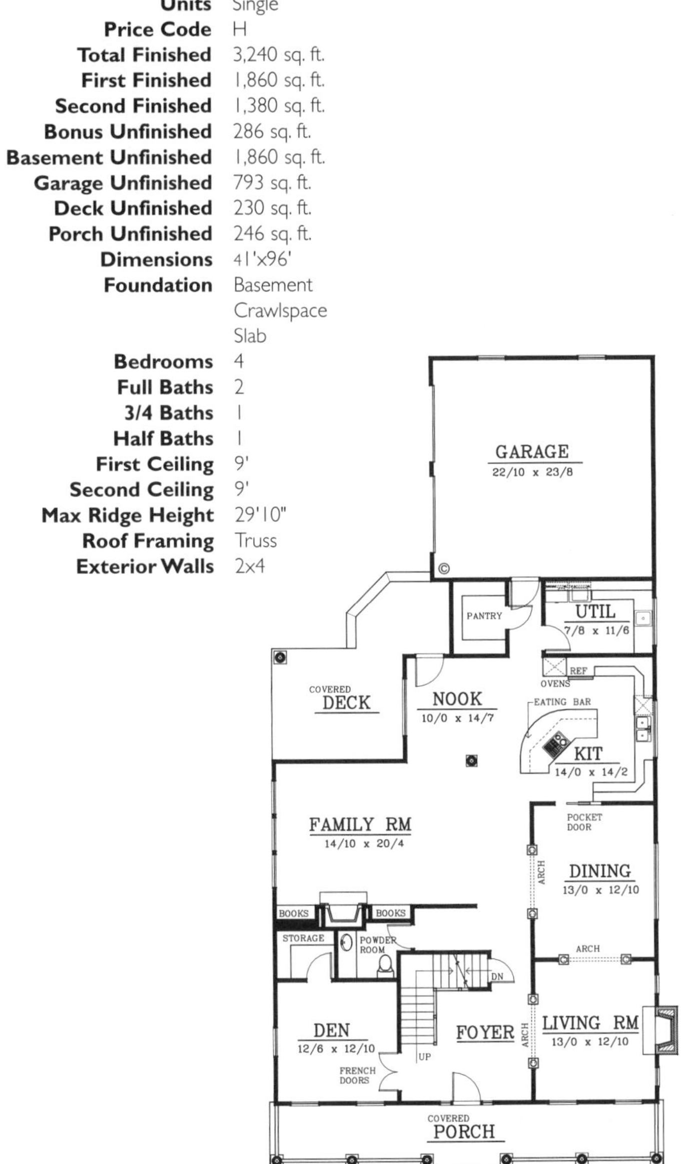
GARAGE
22/10 x 23/8
PANTRY
UTIL
7/8 x 11/6
REF
OVENS
COVERED
DECK
NOOK
10/0 x 14/7
EATING BAR
KIT
14/0 x 14/2
POCKET DOOR
FAMILY RM
14/10 x 20/4
ARCH
DINING
13/0 x 12/10
BOOKS
BOOKS
STORAGE
POWDER ROOM
ARCH
DN
DEN
12/6 x 12/10
FOYER
UP
ARCH
LIVING RM
13/0 x 12/10
FRENCH DOORS
COVERED
PORCH

FIRST FLOOR

Design 92455

Units	Single
Price Code	I
Total Finished	3,260 sq. ft.
First Finished	1,735 sq. ft.
Second Finished	1,525 sq. ft.
Basement Unfinished	1,170 sq. ft.
Dimensions	60'x46'
Foundation	Basement
Bedrooms	5
Full Baths	4
First Ceiling	9'
Exterior Walls	2x4

VAULT
VAULT
OPEN TO FAMILY ROOM
DRYER
WSHR.
BEDROOM 2 13X12
STORAGE
DN
BEDROOM 4 12X19
MASTER BEDROOM 13X17
DN
OPEN TO FOYER
BEDROOM 3 13X11
TRAY CEILING
TRAY
PLANT SHELF

SECOND FLOOR

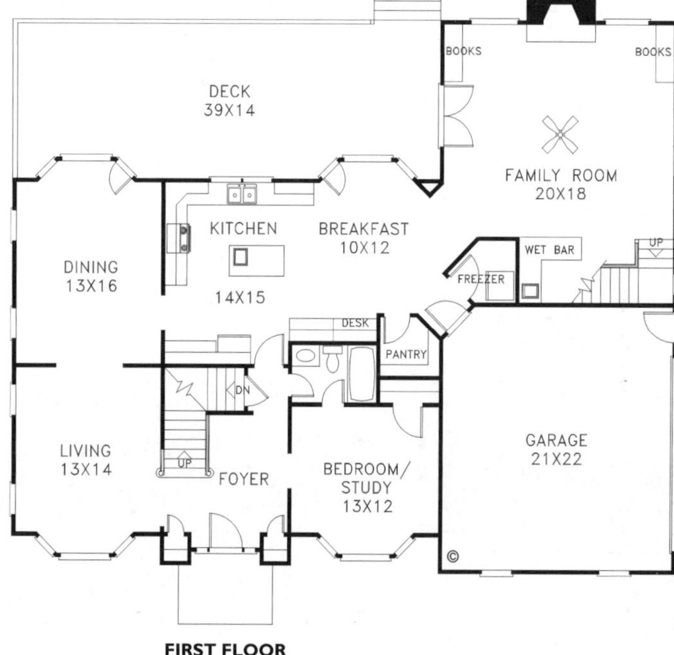
BOOKS
BOOKS
DECK 39X14
FAMILY ROOM 20X18
KITCHEN
BREAKFAST 10X12
DINING 13X16
14X15
WET BAR
UP
FREEZER
DESK
PANTRY
DN
LIVING 13X14
UP
FOYER
BEDROOM/ STUDY 13X12
GARAGE 21X22

FIRST FLOOR

Design 66013

Units	Single
Price Code	I
Total Finished	3,262 sq. ft.
Main Finished	3,262 sq. ft.
Garage Unfinished	662 sq. ft.
Deck Unfinished	172 sq. ft.
Porch Unfinished	285 sq. ft.
Dimensions	79'8"x65'4"
Foundation	Slab
Bedrooms	4
Full Baths	3
Half Baths	1
Main Ceiling	9'-10'
Max Ridge Height	31'6"
Roof Framing	Stick
Exterior Walls	2x4

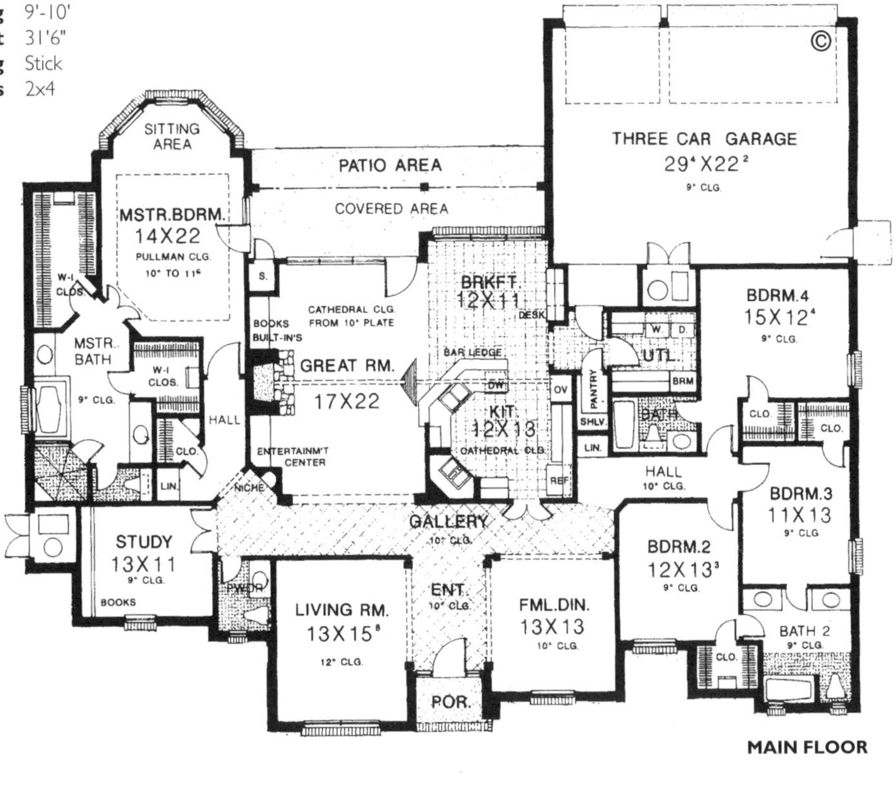

SITTING AREA
PATIO AREA
THREE CAR GARAGE 29⁴X22² 9' CLG.
©
COVERED AREA
MSTR.BDRM. 14X22 PULLMAN CLG. 10' TO 11⁶
W-I CLOS.
S.
CATHEDRAL CLG. FROM 10' PLATE
BOOKS BUILT-IN'S
BRKFT. 12X11
DESK
BDRM.4 15X12⁴ 9' CLG.
W D UTL.
MSTR. BATH 9' CLG.
W-I CLOS.
GREAT RM. 17X22
BAR LEDGE
DW
OV
PANTRY
BRM
KIT. 12X13 CATHEDRAL CLG.
SHLV.
BATH
CLO.
CLO.
HALL
CLO.
LIN.
LIN.
ENTERTAINM'T CENTER
REF
HALL 10' CLG.
BDRM.3 11X13 9' CLG.
NICHE
GALLERY 10' CLG.
STUDY 13X11 9' CLG. BOOKS
PWDR.
ENT. 10' CLG.
BDRM.2 12X13³ 9' CLG.
LIVING RM. 13X15⁸ 12' CLG.
FML.DIN. 13X13 10' CLG.
BATH 2 9' CLG.
CLO.
POR.

MAIN FLOOR

Design 94699

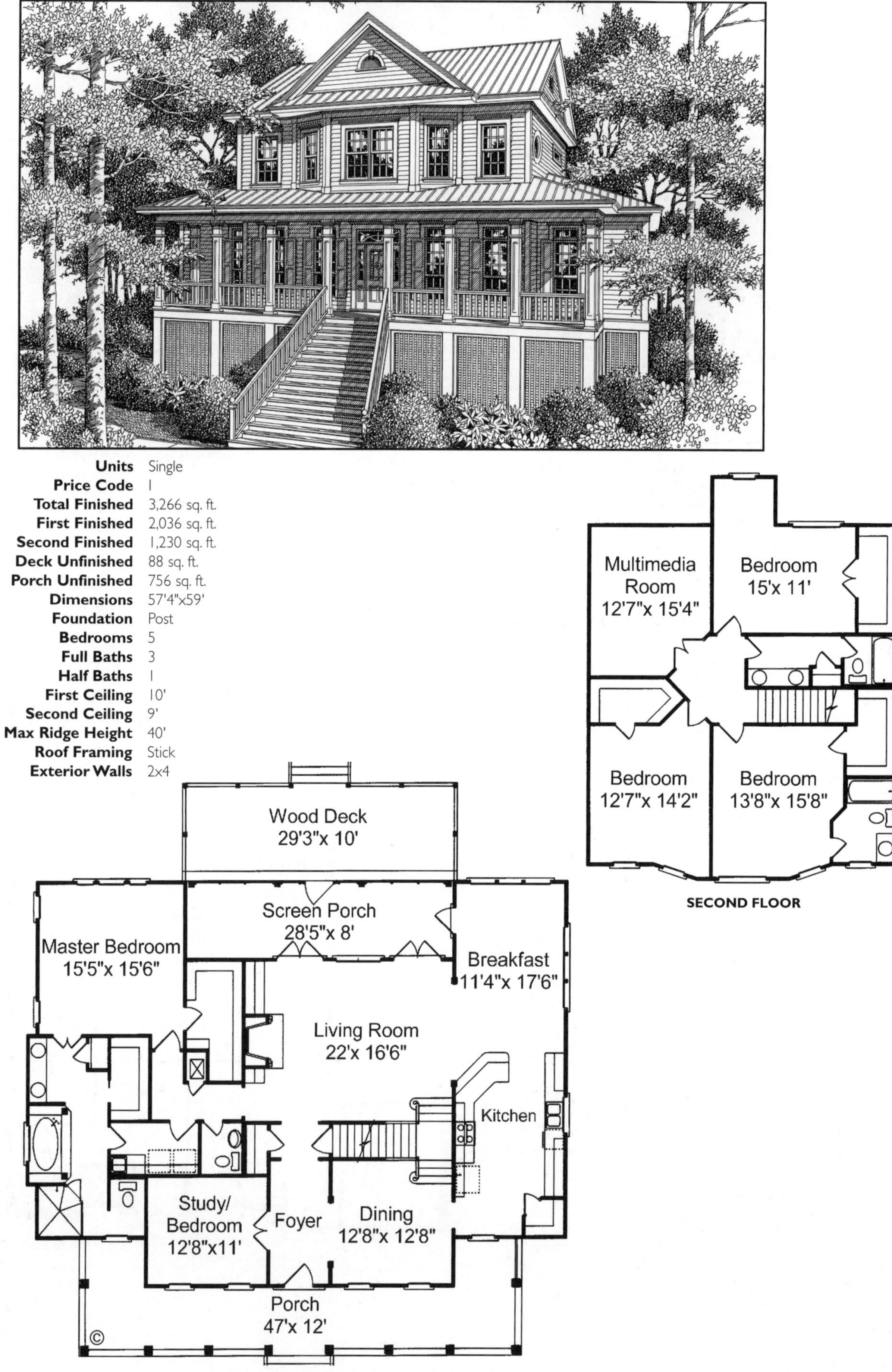

Multimedia Room
12'7"x 15'4"
Bedroom
15'x 11'
Bedroom
12'7"x 14'2"
Bedroom
13'8"x 15'8"
SECOND FLOOR
Wood Deck
29'3"x 10'
Screen Porch
28'5"x 8'
Master Bedroom
15'5"x 15'6"
Breakfast
11'4"x 17'6"
Living Room
22'x 16'6"
Kitchen
Study/
Bedroom
12'8"x11'
Foyer
Dining
12'8"x 12'8"
Porch
47'x 12'
©
FIRST FLOOR

Units	Single
Price Code	I
Total Finished	3,266 sq. ft.
First Finished	2,036 sq. ft.
Second Finished	1,230 sq. ft.
Deck Unfinished	88 sq. ft.
Porch Unfinished	756 sq. ft.
Dimensions	57'4"x59'
Foundation	Post
Bedrooms	5
Full Baths	3
Half Baths	1
First Ceiling	10'
Second Ceiling	9'
Max Ridge Height	40'
Roof Framing	Stick
Exterior Walls	2x4

Design 97633

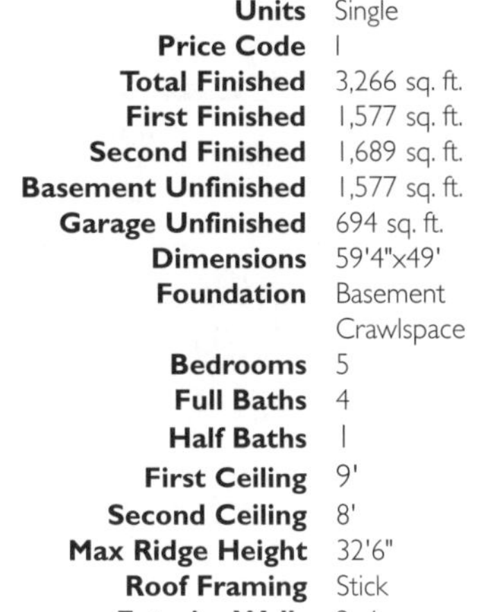

Units	Single
Price Code	I
Total Finished	3,266 sq. ft.
First Finished	1,577 sq. ft.
Second Finished	1,689 sq. ft.
Basement Unfinished	1,577 sq. ft.
Garage Unfinished	694 sq. ft.
Dimensions	59'4"x49'
Foundation	Basement Crawlspace
Bedrooms	5
Full Baths	4
Half Baths	1
First Ceiling	9'
Second Ceiling	8'
Max Ridge Height	32'6"
Roof Framing	Stick
Exterior Walls	2x4

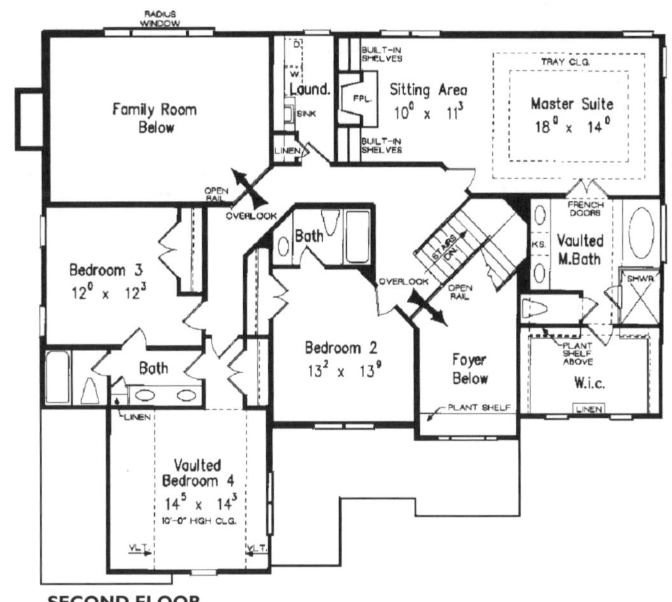
RADIUS WINDOW
Family Room Below
Laund.
SINK
LINEN
BUILT-IN SHELVES
FPL.
Sitting Area 10⁰ x 11³
TRAY CLG.
Master Suite 18⁰ x 14⁰
OPEN RAIL
OVERLOOK
Bath
FRENCH DOORS
Vaulted M.Bath
Bedroom 3 12⁰ x 12³
STAIRS DN
OVERLOOK
OPEN RAIL
SHWR.
Bedroom 2 13² x 13⁹
Foyer Below
PLANT SHELF ABOVE
W.i.c.
Bath
LINEN
PLANT SHELF
Vaulted Bedroom 4 14⁵ x 14³
10'-0" HIGH CLG.
VLT.

SECOND FLOOR

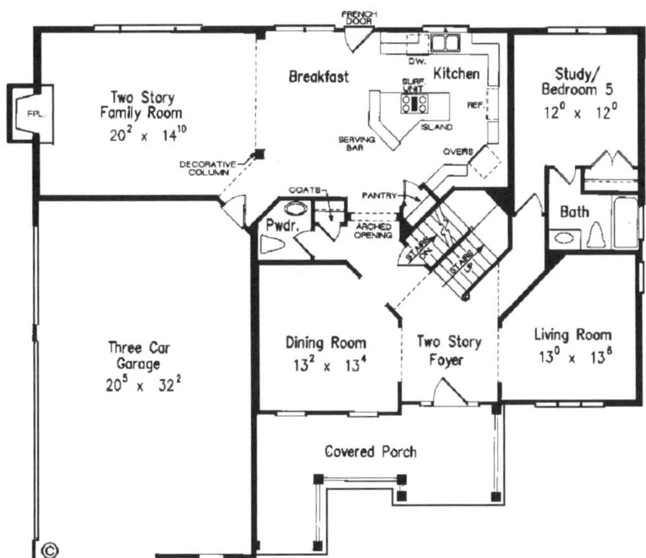
FRENCH DOOR
FPL.
Two Story Family Room 20² x 14¹⁰
Breakfast
Kitchen
SURF UNIT
REF.
ISLAND
SERVING BAR
OVENS
Study/ Bedroom 5 12⁰ x 12⁰
DECORATIVE COLUMN
COATS
PANTRY
Pwdr.
ARCHED OPENING
Bath
Three Car Garage 20⁵ x 32²
Dining Room 13² x 13⁴
Two Story Foyer
Living Room 13⁰ x 13⁸
Covered Porch

FIRST FLOOR

CAD **FILES AVAILABLE**
For more information call
800-235-5700

Design 99289

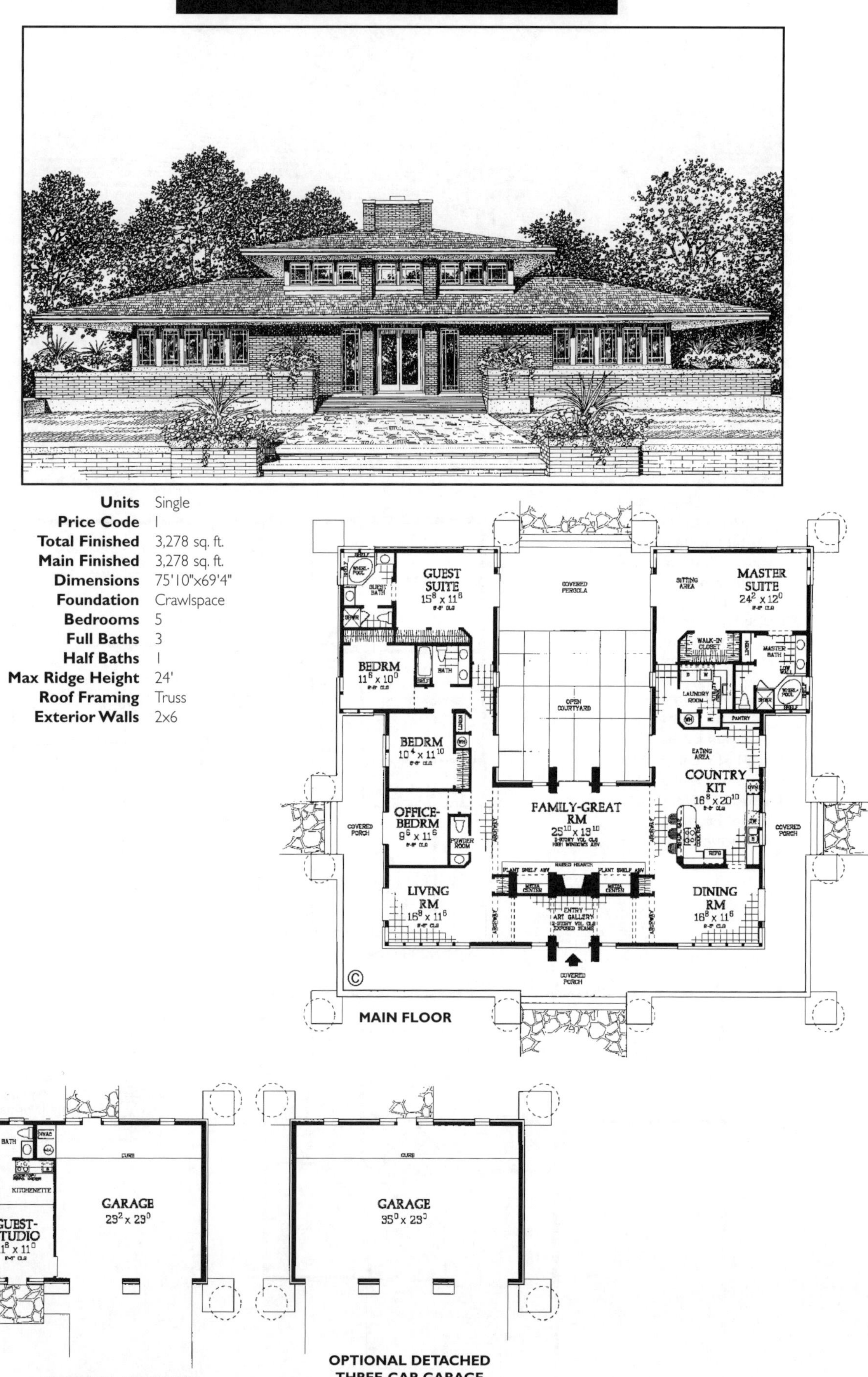

GUEST SUITE
15⁸ x 11⁸
MASTER SUITE
24² x 12⁰
COVERED PERGOLA
SITTING AREA
GUEST BATH
WALK-IN CLOSET
MASTER BATH
BEDRM
11⁶ x 10⁰
BATH
OPEN COURTYARD
LAUNDRY ROOM
PANTRY
BEDRM
10⁴ x 11¹⁰
EATING AREA
COUNTRY KIT
16⁸ x 20¹⁰
OFFICE-BEDRM
9⁶ x 11⁶
FAMILY-GREAT RM
25¹⁰ x 13¹⁰
COVERED PORCH
POWDER ROOM
RAISED HEARTH
PLANT SHELF ABV
MEDIA CENTER
LIVING RM
16⁸ x 11⁶
ENTRY ART GALLERY
DINING RM
16⁸ x 11⁶
COVERED PORCH
MAIN FLOOR
BATH
KITCHENETTE
GUEST-STUDIO
11⁸ x 11⁰
CURB
GARAGE
23² x 23⁰
GARAGE
35⁰ x 23³
OPTIONAL DETACHED TWO-CAR GARAGE WITH GUEST SUITE
OPTIONAL DETACHED THREE-CAR GARAGE

Units	Single
Price Code	I
Total Finished	3,278 sq. ft.
Main Finished	3,278 sq. ft.
Dimensions	75'10"x69'4"
Foundation	Crawlspace
Bedrooms	5
Full Baths	3
Half Baths	1
Max Ridge Height	24'
Roof Framing	Truss
Exterior Walls	2x6

Design 93630

Units	Single
Price Code	I
Total Finished	3,279 sq. ft.
First Finished	1,803 sq. ft.
Second Finished	1,476 sq. ft.
Dimensions	60'11x55'4"
Foundation	Basement Slab
Bedrooms	5
Full Baths	4

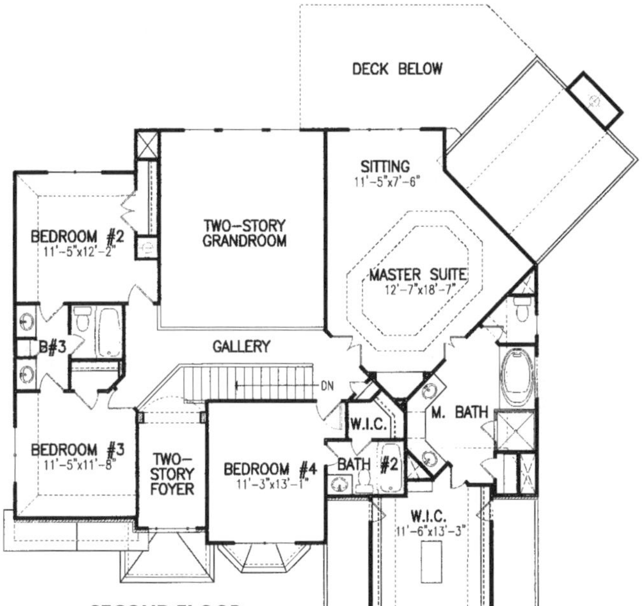

DECK BELOW
SITTING 11'-5"x7'-6"
TWO-STORY GRANDROOM
BEDROOM #2 11'-5"x12'-2"
MASTER SUITE 12'-7"x18'-7"
GALLERY
B#3
DN
BEDROOM #3 11'-5"x11'-8"
TWO-STORY FOYER
BEDROOM #4 11'-3"x13'-1"
W.I.C.
BATH #2
M. BATH
W.I.C. 11'-6"x13'-3"

SECOND FLOOR

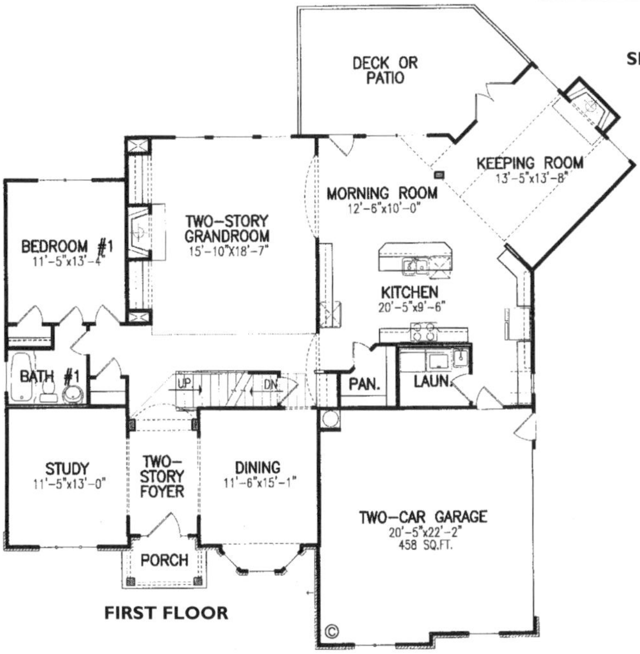

DECK OR PATIO
KEEPING ROOM 13'-5"x13'-8"
MORNING ROOM 12'-6"x10'-0"
TWO-STORY GRANDROOM 15'-10"X18'-7"
BEDROOM #1 11'-5"x13'-4"
KITCHEN 20'-5"x9'-6"
BATH #1
UP
DN
PAN.
LAUN.
STUDY 11'-5"x13'-0"
TWO-STORY FOYER
DINING 11'-6"x15'-1"
TWO-CAR GARAGE 20'-5"x22'-2" 458 SQ.FT.
PORCH

FIRST FLOOR

Design 32437

OPEN TO FAMILY
BEDROOM 13x14
BEDROOM 12x12
CLOS
DN
DN
READING LOFT 11x13
BONUS ROOM 12x13
CLOS
BEDROOM 13x14
CLOS
SECOND FLOOR
MASTER BEDROOM 14x16
FAMILY 15x18
BREAKFAST 11x11
KEEPING ROOM 16x13
UP
KITCHEN 13x12
MUD ENTRY
LDRY
D
W
DN
R
P
CLOS
CLOS
BATH
ENTRY
UP
DINING 13x13
GARAGE 21x22
FIRST FLOOR

PHOTOGRAPHY: MICHAEL PARTENIO

Units	Single
Price Code	I
Total Finished	3,330 sq. ft.
First Finished	2,021 sq. ft.
Second Finished	1,309 sq. ft.
Basement Unfinished	2,021 sq. ft.
Garage Unfinished	484 sq. ft.
Dimensions	64'6"x46'6"
Foundation	Basement
Bedrooms	4
Full Baths	2
3/4 Baths	1
Half Baths	1
First Ceiling	9'
Second Ceiling	8'
Vaulted Ceiling	18'
Max Ridge Height	30'
Roof Framing	Stick
Exterior Walls	2x6

Please note: The photographed home may have been modified to suit homeowner preferences. If you order plans, have a builder or design professional check them against the photograph to confirm actual construction details.

Design 92219

Units	Single
Price Code	I
Total Finished	3,335 sq. ft.
First Finished	2,432 sq. ft.
Second Finished	903 sq. ft.
Basement Unfinished	2,432 sq. ft.
Garage Unfinished	742 sq. ft.
Deck Unfinished	222 sq. ft.
Porch Unfinished	91 sq. ft.
Dimensions	90'x45'4"
Foundation	Basement Crawlspace Slab
Bedrooms	4
Full Baths	2
3/4 Baths	1
Half Baths	1
First Ceiling	10'
Second Ceiling	9'
Max Ridge Height	33'
Roof Framing	Stick
Exterior Walls	2x4

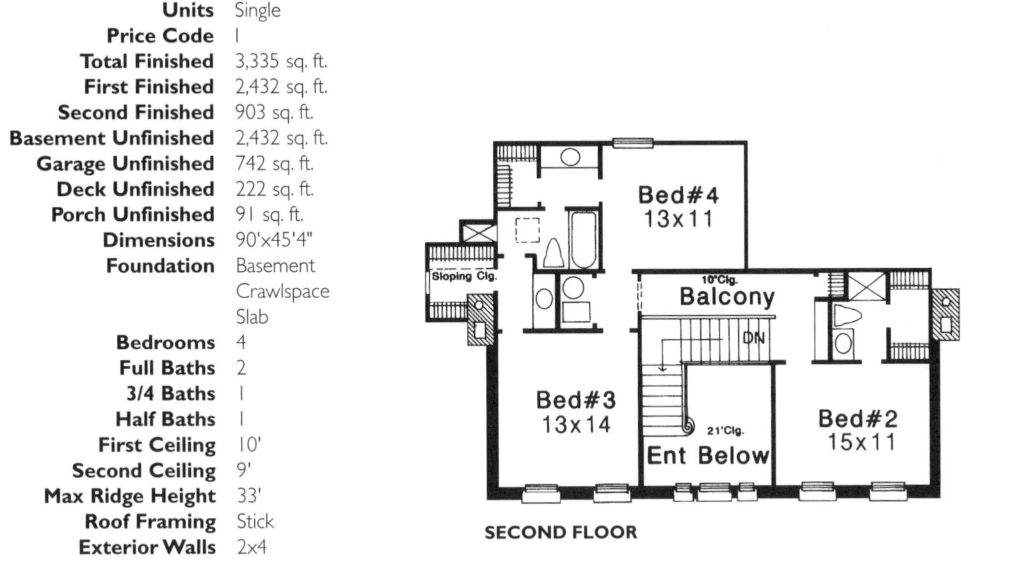
Bed#4
13x11
Sloping Clg.
10'Clg.
Balcony
DN
Bed#3
13x14
21'Clg.
Ent Below
Bed#2
15x11

SECOND FLOOR

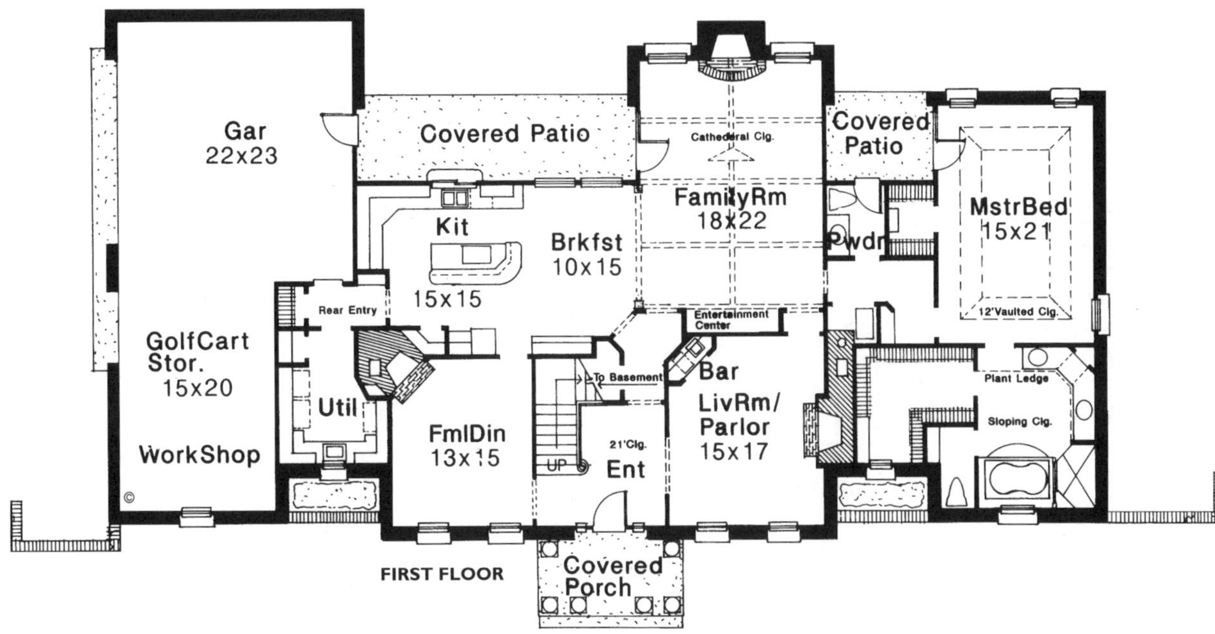
Gar
22x23
Covered Patio
Cathedral Clg.
Covered
Patio
Kit
Brkfst
10x15
FamilyRm
18x22
Pwdr
MstrBed
15x21
15x15
Rear Entry
Entertainment Center
12'Vaulted Clg.
GolfCart
Stor.
15x20
Util
To Basement
Bar
Plant Ledge
FmlDin
13x15
LivRm/
Parlor
15x17
Sloping Clg.
WorkShop
21'Clg.
UP
Ent
Covered
Porch

FIRST FLOOR

Design 92454

Units	Single
Price Code	I
Total Finished	3,358 sq. ft.
First Finished	2,144 sq. ft.
Second Finished	1,214 sq. ft.
Basement Unfinished	2,144 sq. ft.
Garage Unfinished	440 sq. ft.
Dimensions	52'x62'
Foundation	Basement
Bedrooms	4
Full Baths	3
Half Baths	1
First Ceiling	9'
Second Ceiling	8'
Exterior Walls	2x4

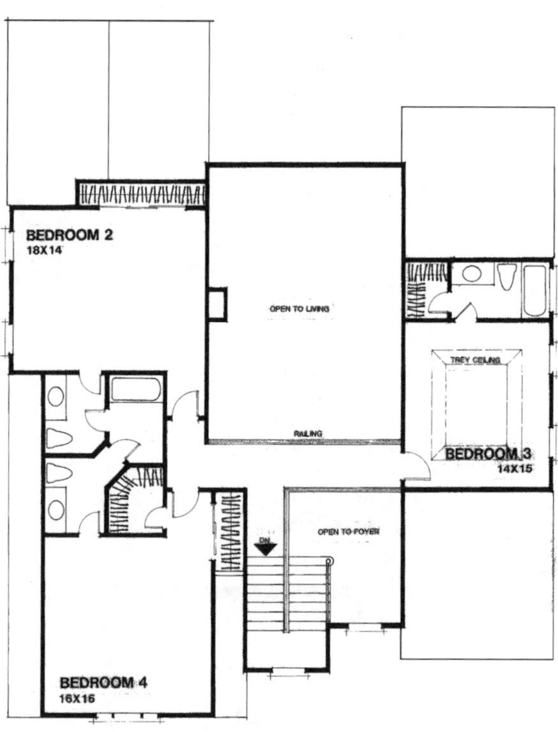
BEDROOM 2
18X14
OPEN TO LIVING
RAILING
TREY CEILING
BEDROOM 3
14X15
OPEN TO FOYER
BEDROOM 4
16X16

SECOND FLOOR

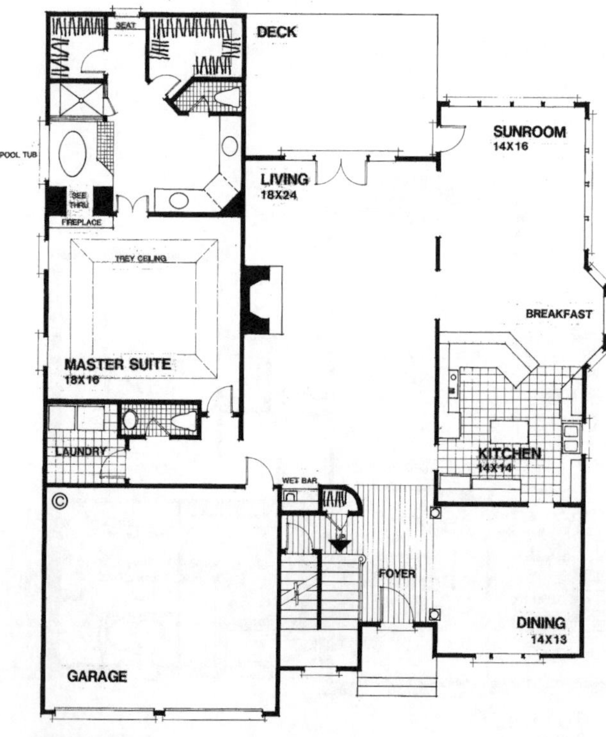
SEAT
DECK
WHIRLPOOL TUB
SUNROOM
14X16
LIVING
18X24
SEE THRU
FIREPLACE
TREY CEILING
BREAKFAST
MASTER SUITE
18X16
LAUNDRY
KITCHEN
14X14
WET BAR
FOYER
DINING
14X13
GARAGE

FIRST FLOOR

Design 91183

Units	Single
Price Code	I
Total Finished	3,363 sq. ft.
First Finished	2,201 sq. ft.
Second Finished	1,162 sq. ft.
Bonus Unfinished	343 sq. ft.
Garage Unfinished	708 sq. ft.
Porch Unfinished	34 sq. ft.
Dimensions	63'x61'2"
Foundation	Slab
Bedrooms	4
Full Baths	3
Half Baths	1
First Ceiling	9'
Second Ceiling	8'
Vaulted Ceiling	12'
Max Ridge Height	29'
Roof Framing	Stick
Exterior Walls	2x4

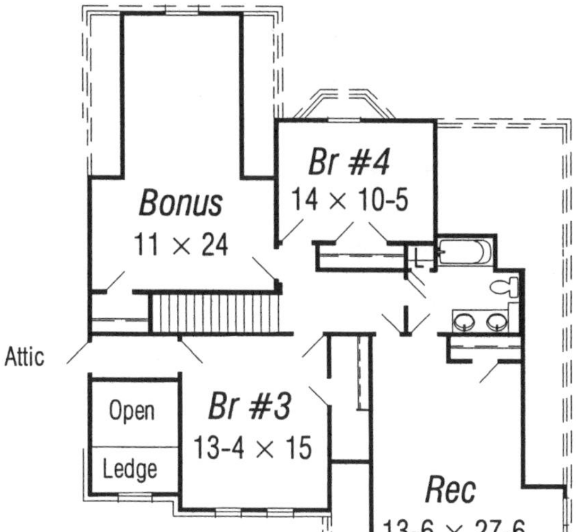

Bonus
11 × 24
Br #4
14 × 10-5
L
Attic
Open
Ledge
Br #3
13-4 × 15
Rec
13-6 × 27-6

SECOND FLOOR

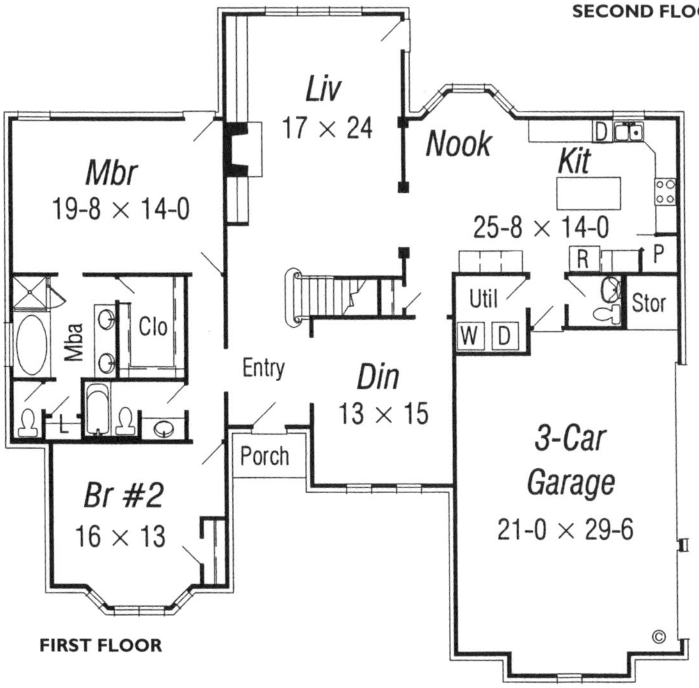

Liv
17 × 24
Nook
D
Kit
25-8 × 14-0
Mbr
19-8 × 14-0
R
P
Util
Stor
W D
Mba
Clo
Entry
Din
13 × 15
L
Porch
3-Car
Garage
21-0 × 29-6
Br #2
16 × 13
©

FIRST FLOOR

Design 50020

PHOTOGRAPHY: MARK ENGLUND

Units	Single
Price Code	I
Total Finished	3,366 sq. ft.
First Finished	1,759 sq. ft.
Second Finished	1,607 sq. ft.
Basement Unfinished	1,759 sq. ft.
Garage Unfinished	702 sq. ft.
Porch Unfinished	80 sq. ft.
Dimensions	68'8"x56'8'
Foundation	Basement
Bedrooms	5
Full Baths	4
First Ceiling	9'
Second Ceiling	9'
Max Ridge Height	34'
Roof Framing	Truss
Exterior Walls	2x4, 2x6

Master Bedroom 15'1" x 22'6"
Master Bath
walk-in closet
Great Room Below
bookshelves
walk-in closet
wood rail
Hall
stairs dn
Balcony
Bath
Bedroom 11' x 14'3"
Bedroom 11'1" x 13'1"
Bath
Bedroom 11'9" x 12'8"
walk-in closet

SECOND FLOOR

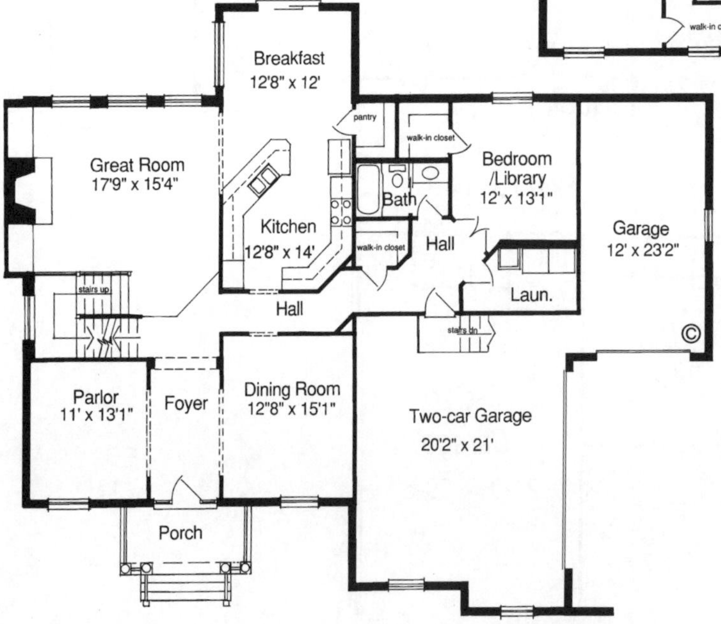

Breakfast 12'8" x 12'
pantry
walk-in closet
Great Room 17'9" x 15'4"
Bath
Bedroom /Library 12' x 13'1"
Garage 12' x 23'2"
Kitchen 12'8" x 14'
walk-in closet
Hall
Laun.
stairs up
Hall
stairs dn
©
Parlor 11' x 13'1"
Foyer
Dining Room 12'8" x 15'1"
Two-car Garage 20'2" x 21'
Porch

FIRST FLOOR

Please note: The photographed home may have been modified to suit homeowner preferences. If you order plans, have a builder or design professional check them against the photograph to confirm actual construction details.

Design 65613

Units	Single
Price Code	I
Total Finished	3,372 sq. ft.
First Finished	2,743 sq. ft.
Second Finished	629 sq. ft.
Dimensions	78'x96'
Foundation	Crawlspace
Bedrooms	4
Full Baths	4
First Ceiling	9'
Second Ceiling	8'
Max Ridge Height	30'
Roof Framing	Stick
Exterior Walls	2x6

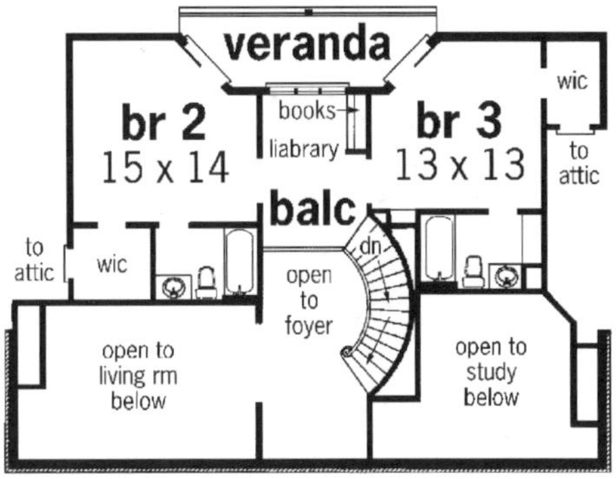

veranda
br 2
15 x 14
books
liabrary
br 3
13 x 13
wic
to attic
balc
dn
to attic
wic
open to foyer
open to living rm below
open to study below

SECOND FLOOR

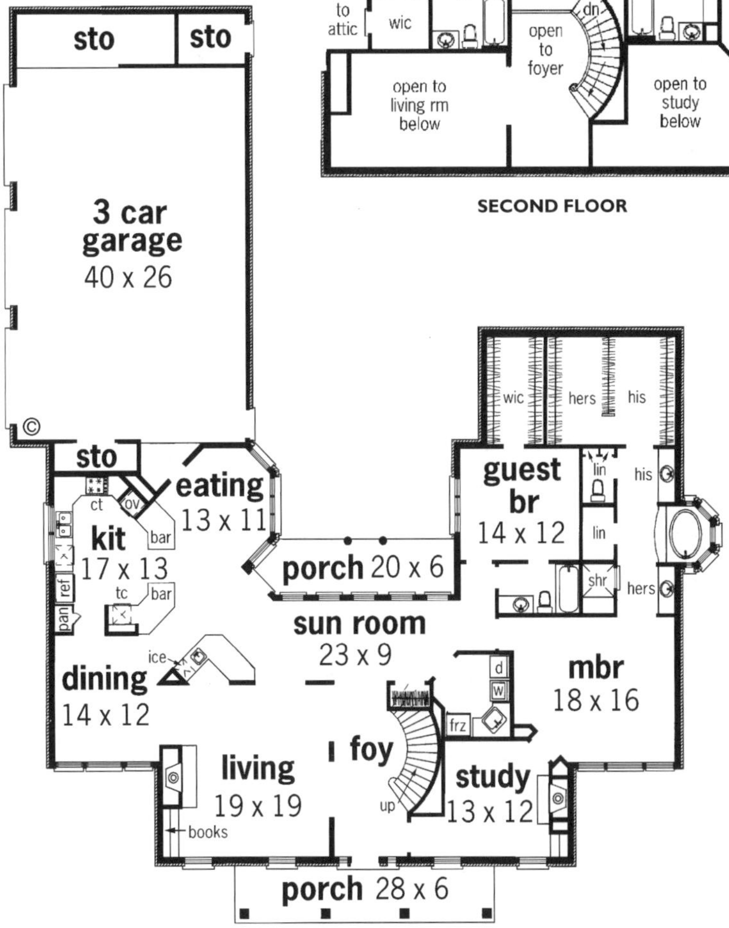

sto
sto
3 car garage
40 x 26
©
sto
eating
13 x 11
kit
17 x 13
ct
ov
bar
tc
bar
ref
pan
porch 20 x 6
sun room
23 x 9
ice
dining
14 x 12
wic
hers
his
guest br
14 x 12
lin
lin
shr
his
hers
mbr
18 x 16
d
w
frz
foy
living
19 x 19
up
study
13 x 12
books
porch 28 x 6

FIRST FLOOR

Design 98436

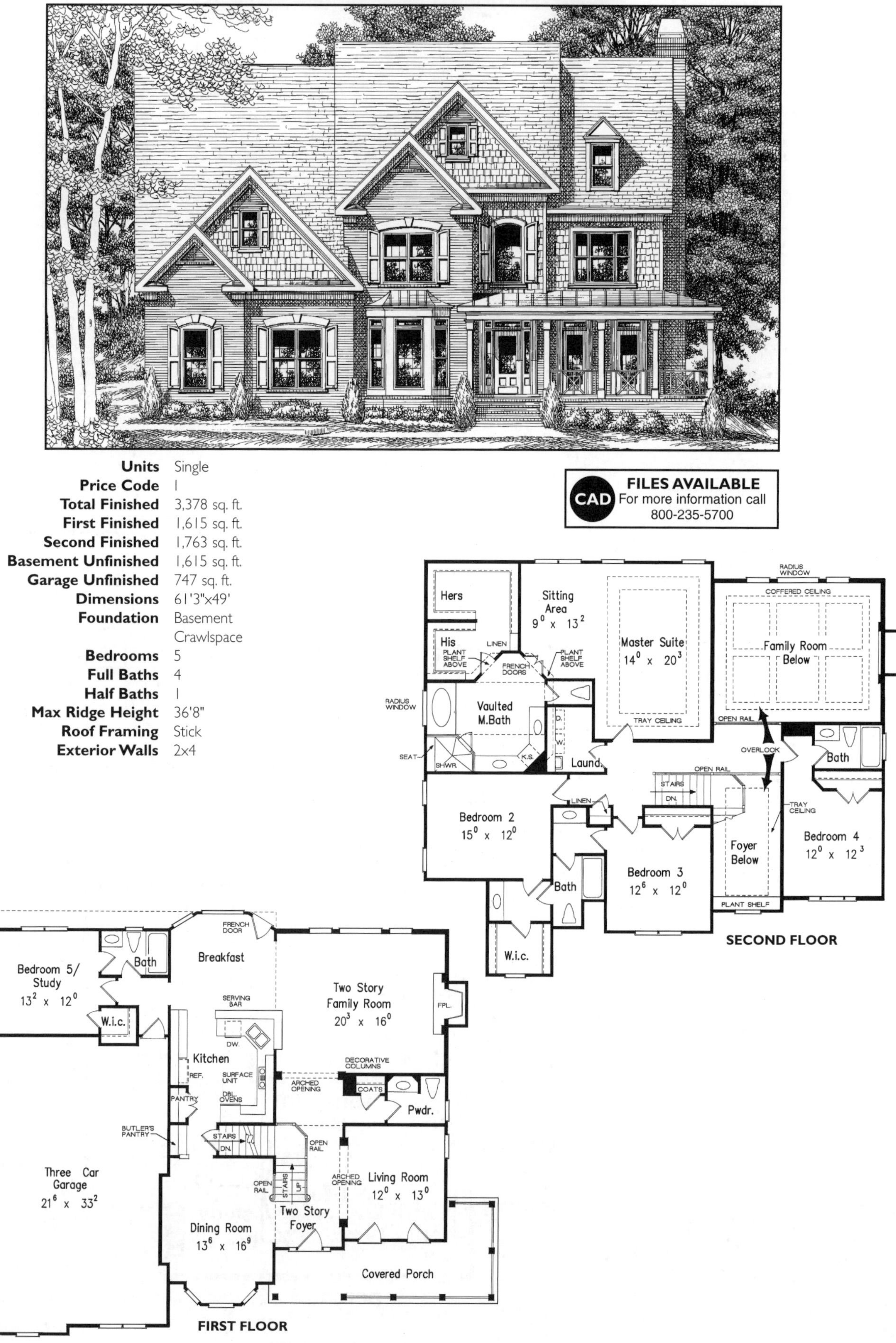

FILES AVAILABLE
CAD
For more information call
800-235-5700
Hers
His
PLANT SHELF ABOVE
LINEN
Sitting Area
9⁰ x 13²
Master Suite
14⁰ x 20³
TRAY CEILING
FRENCH DOORS
PLANT SHELF ABOVE
RADIUS WINDOW
COFFERED CEILING
Family Room Below
OPEN RAIL
OVERLOOK
Vaulted M.Bath
SEAT
SHWR.
K.S.
D.
W.
Laund.
OPEN RAIL
STAIRS
DN.
Bath
TRAY CEILING
LINEN
Bedroom 2
15⁰ x 12⁰
Bedroom 3
12⁶ x 12⁰
Foyer Below
Bedroom 4
12⁰ x 12³
Bath
PLANT SHELF
W.i.c.
SECOND FLOOR
FRENCH DOOR
Bedroom 5/ Study
13² x 12⁰
Bath
W.i.c.
Breakfast
SERVING BAR
Two Story Family Room
20³ x 16⁰
FPL.
DW.
Kitchen
REF.
SURFACE UNIT
DBL. OVENS
PANTRY
DECORATIVE COLUMNS
ARCHED OPENING
COATS
Pwdr.
BUTLER'S PANTRY
STAIRS
DN.
OPEN RAIL
OPEN RAIL
STAIRS
UP
ARCHED OPENING
Living Room
12⁰ x 13⁰
Three Car Garage
21⁶ x 33²
Dining Room
13⁶ x 16⁹
Two Story Foyer
Covered Porch
FIRST FLOOR

Units	Single
Price Code	I
Total Finished	3,378 sq. ft.
First Finished	1,615 sq. ft.
Second Finished	1,763 sq. ft.
Basement Unfinished	1,615 sq. ft.
Garage Unfinished	747 sq. ft.
Dimensions	61'3"x49'
Foundation	Basement Crawlspace
Bedrooms	5
Full Baths	4
Half Baths	1
Max Ridge Height	36'8"
Roof Framing	Stick
Exterior Walls	2x4

Design 92162

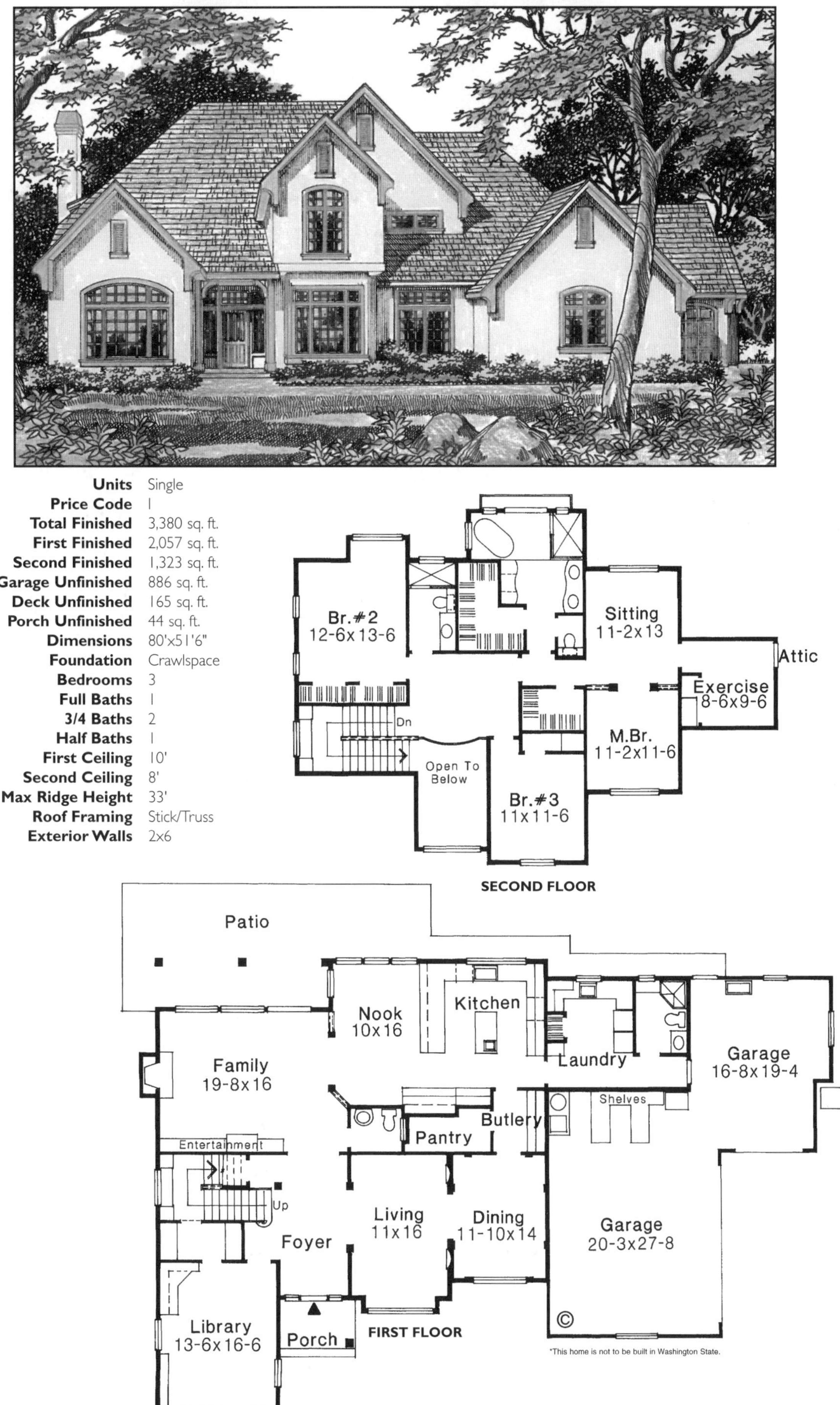
Br.#2
12-6x13-6
Sitting
11-2x13
Attic
Exercise
8-6x9-6
Dn
Open To
Below
M.Br.
11-2x11-6
Br.#3
11x11-6
SECOND FLOOR
Patio
Nook
10x16
Kitchen
Laundry
Garage
16-8x19-4
Family
19-8x16
Shelves
Butlery
Pantry
Entertainment
Up
Living
11x16
Dining
11-10x14
Foyer
Garage
20-3x27-8
Library
13-6x16-6
Porch
FIRST FLOOR
©
*This home is not to be built in Washington State.

Units	Single
Price Code	I
Total Finished	3,380 sq. ft.
First Finished	2,057 sq. ft.
Second Finished	1,323 sq. ft.
Garage Unfinished	886 sq. ft.
Deck Unfinished	165 sq. ft.
Porch Unfinished	44 sq. ft.
Dimensions	80'x51'6"
Foundation	Crawlspace
Bedrooms	3
Full Baths	1
3/4 Baths	2
Half Baths	1
First Ceiling	10'
Second Ceiling	8'
Max Ridge Height	33'
Roof Framing	Stick/Truss
Exterior Walls	2x6

Design 98514

Units	Single
Price Code	I
Total Finished	3,381 sq. ft.
First Finished	2,208 sq. ft.
Second Finished	1,173 sq. ft.
Bonus Unfinished	224 sq. ft.
Garage Unfinished	520 sq. ft.
Deck Unfinished	224 sq. ft.
Porch Unfinished	104 sq. ft.
Dimensions	72'x63'10"
Foundation	Crawlspace Slab
Bedrooms	5
Full Baths	2
3/4 Baths	1
Half Baths	1
First Ceiling	10'
Second Ceiling	9'
Max Ridge Height	33'6"
Roof Framing	Stick
Exterior Walls	2x4

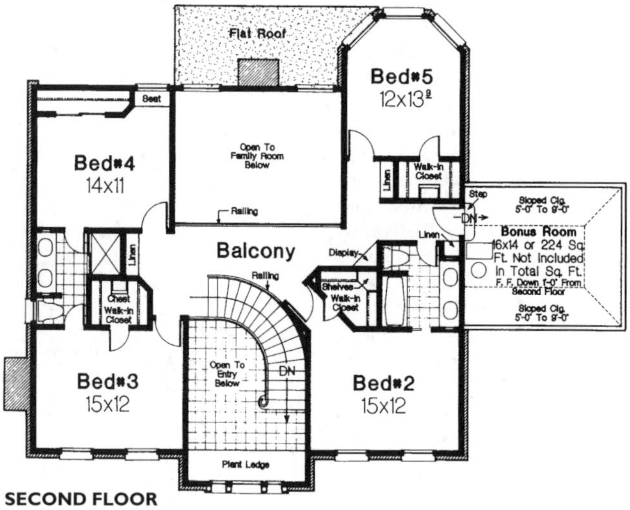

SECOND FLOOR

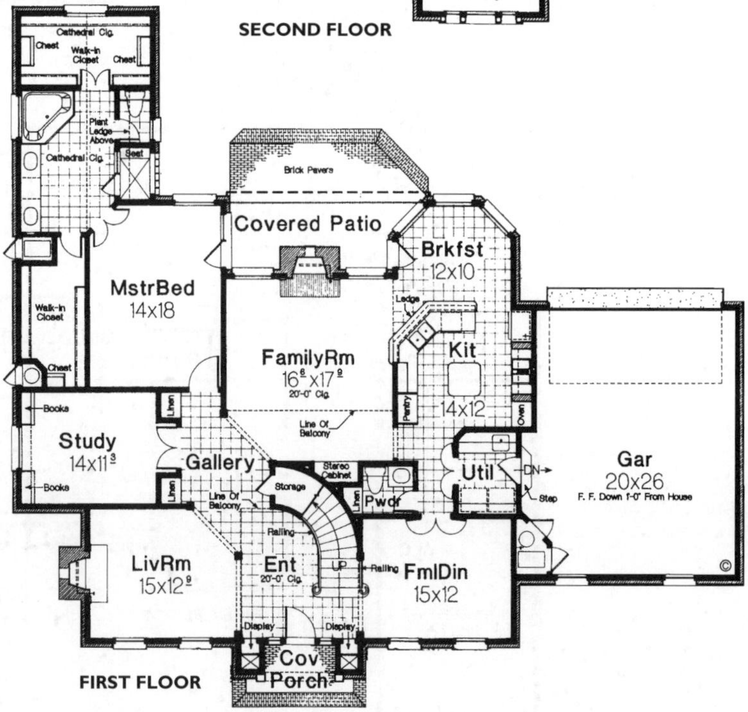

FIRST FLOOR

Design 66096

Future BonusRm
16⁸x19⁸
NOT Included In Total Sq. Ft.
Bed#3
12⁰x12⁰
Bed#4
11⁸x13⁰
Balcony
Bed#2
13⁰x13⁰
Vaulted Ceiling
SECOND FLOOR
3-CarGar
24⁰x30⁰
Pat
Util
Brkfst
14⁰x10³
Kit
14⁰x12⁰
Covered Patio
GreatRm
18⁰x21⁸
Pwdr
Pantry
Hall
Ent
Study
15⁰x13⁰
MstrBed
14⁰x17⁰
Sitting Area
11⁰x11⁸
FmlDin
13⁰x13⁰
Cov Porch
Private Lanai
FIRST FLOOR

Units	Single
Price Code	I
Total Finished	3,383 sq. ft.
First Finished	2,431 sq. ft.
Second Finished	952 sq. ft.
Garage Unfinished	692 sq. ft.
Dimensions	70'x64'3"
Foundation	Slab
Bedrooms	4
Full Baths	3
Half Baths	1
First Ceiling	9'-10'
Max Ridge Height	33'
Roof Framing	Stick
Exterior Walls	2x4

Design 69128

Units	Single
Price Code	I
Total Finished	3,384 sq. ft.
Main Finished	3,384 sq. ft.
Garage Unfinished	1,021 sq. ft.
Dimensions	122'4"x77'6"
Foundation	Crawlspace
Bedrooms	3
Full Baths	2
3/4 Baths	2
Main Ceiling	9'
Second Ceiling	10'10"
Max Ridge Height	21'6"
Roof Framing	Truss
Exterior Walls	2x6

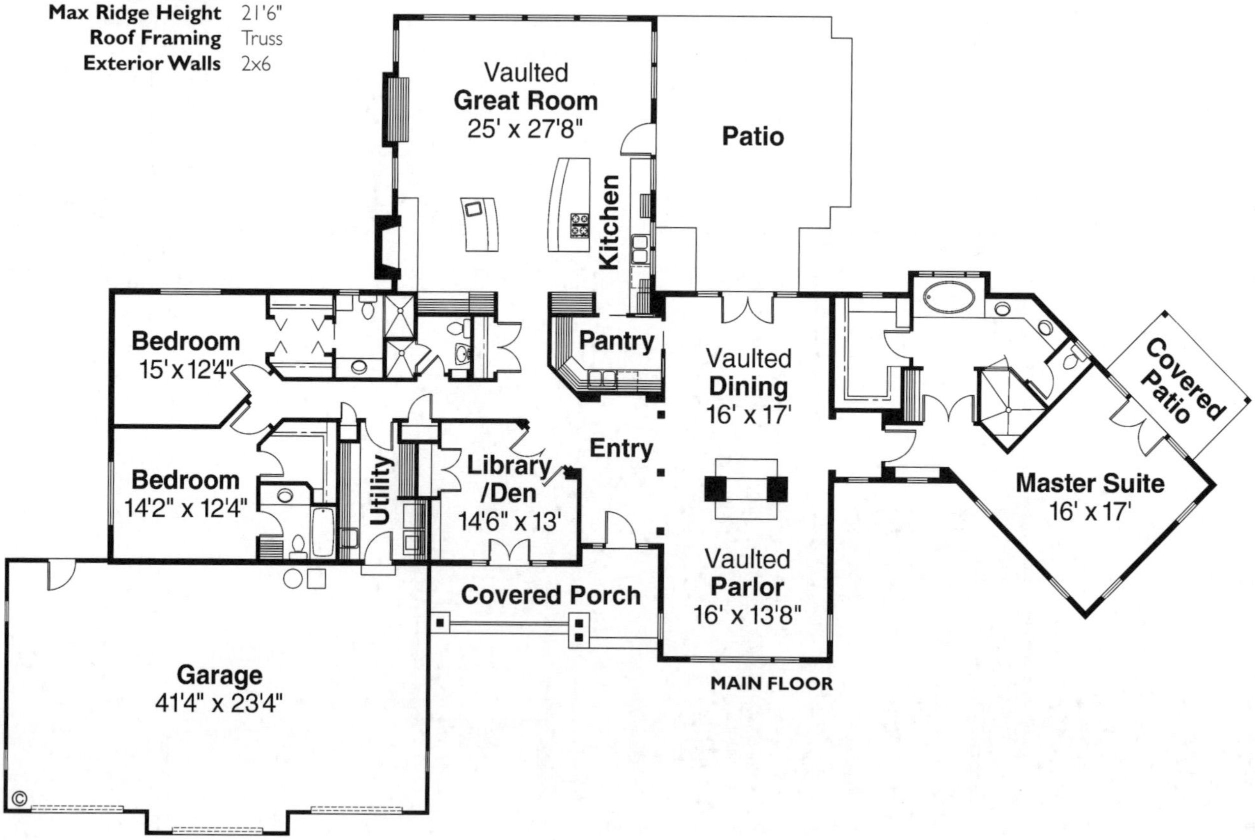

Vaulted **Great Room** 25' x 27'8"

Patio

Kitchen

Pantry

Bedroom 15' x 12'4"

Vaulted **Dining** 16' x 17'

Covered Patio

Entry

Bedroom 14'2" x 12'4"

Utility

Library /Den 14'6" x 13'

Master Suite 16' x 17'

Covered Porch

Vaulted **Parlor** 16' x 13'8"

Garage 41'4" x 23'4"

MAIN FLOOR

Design 52124

Family Room Below
Master Suite 13⁶x 20⁰
Sitting
TRAY CEILING
PKT. DOOR
SHWR.
W.
D.
Laund.
Bath
SINK
His
Vaulted M.Bath
RADIUS WINDOW
W.i.c.
OVERLOOK
STAIRS DN
LINEN
Hers
Bedroom 5 12⁰x 12⁰
Foyer Below
Bedroom 4 12⁰x 13⁸
Bath
PKT. DOOR
W.i.c.
Bedroom 3 12⁵x 14⁶
PLANT SHELF
SECOND FLOOR
BUILT-IN CABINETS
FPL.
FRENCH DOOR
Breakfast
Keeping Room 13⁶X 16⁰
BUILT-IN CABINETS
Two Story Family Room 16⁵x 24²
SERVING BAR
STAIRS UP
DW.
REF
DESK
K.S.
Bath
Kitchen
Pwdr.
STAIRS DN
OPEN RAIL
SURFACE UNIT
OVENS
PANTRY
COATS
STAIRS UP
Guest Suite 12⁰x 12⁰
Two Story Foyer
Dining Room 13⁰x 13⁹
Garage 20⁵x 24⁹
Covered Porch
FIRST FLOOR

Units	Single
Price Code	I
Total Finished	3,386 sq. ft.
First Finished	1,736 sq. ft.
Second Finished	1,650 sq. ft.
Basement Unfinished	1,736 sq. ft.
Garage Unfinished	492 sq. ft.
Dimensions	62'x56'
Foundation	Basement Crawlspace
Bedrooms	5
Full Baths	4
Half Baths	1
First Ceiling	9'
Second Ceiling	9'
Max Ridge Height	34'6"
Roof Framing	Stick
Exterior Walls	2x4

Design 93118

PHOTOGRAPHY: COURTESY OF THE DESIGNER

Units	Single
Price Code	I
Total Finished	3,397 sq. ft.
First Finished	2,385 sq. ft.
Second Finished	1,012 sq. ft.
Basement Unfinished	2,385 sq. ft.
Garage Unfinished	846 sq. ft.
Dimensions	79'x55'
Foundation	Basement
Bedrooms	4
Full Baths	3
Half Baths	1
First Ceiling	7'-9'6"
Max Ridge Height	32'
Roof Framing	Stick/Truss
Exterior Walls	2x6

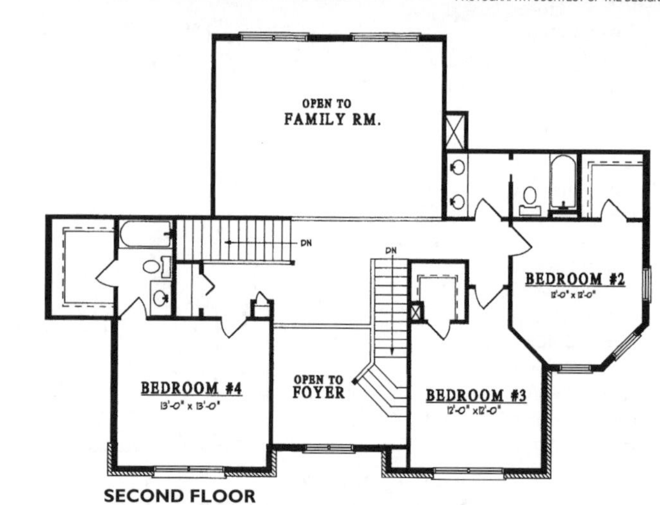

OPEN TO
FAMILY RM.
DN
DN
BEDROOM #2
12'-0" x 12'-0"
BEDROOM #4
13'-0" x 13'-0"
OPEN TO
FOYER
BEDROOM #3
12'-0" x 12'-0"

SECOND FLOOR

Please note: The photographed home may have been modified to suit homeowner preferences. If you order plans, have a builder or design professional check them against the photograph to confirm actual construction details.

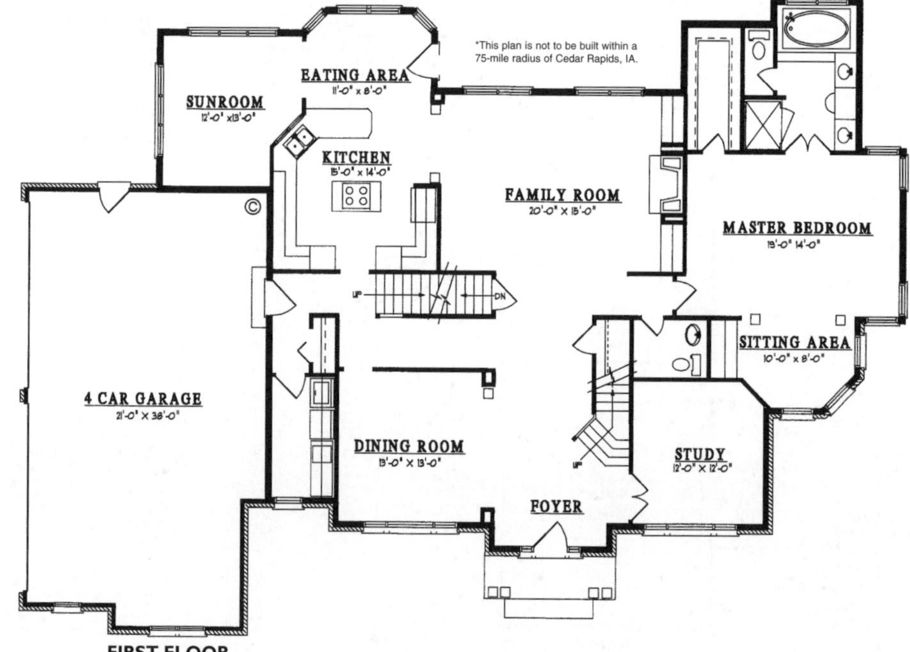

*This plan is not to be built within a 75-mile radius of Cedar Rapids, IA.
EATING AREA
11'-0" x 8'-0"
SUNROOM
12'-0" x 13'-0"
KITCHEN
15'-0" x 14'-0"
FAMILY ROOM
20'-0" x 15'-0"
MASTER BEDROOM
15'-0" x 14'-0"
UP
DN
SITTING AREA
10'-0" x 8'-0"
4 CAR GARAGE
21'-0" x 38'-0"
DINING ROOM
13'-0" x 13'-0"
STUDY
12'-0" x 12'-0"
UP
FOYER

FIRST FLOOR

Design 32036

PHOTOGRAPHY: JIM HEDRICH, HEDRICH-BLESSING

Units	Single
Price Code	I
Total Finished	3,423 sq. ft.
First Finished	1,868 sq. ft.
Second Finished	1,555 sq. ft.
Garage Unfinished	740 sq. ft.
Dimensions	67'x48'6"
Foundation	Basement
Bedrooms	4
Full Baths	2
3/4 Baths	1
Half Baths	1
First Ceiling	9'
Second Ceiling	8'
Max Ridge Height	32'
Roof Framing	Stick
Exterior Walls	2x4

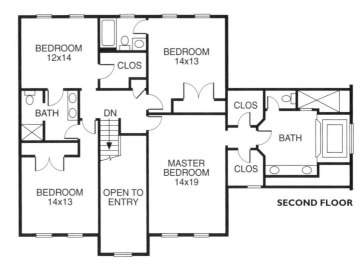

BEDROOM 12x14
CLOS
BEDROOM 14x13
BATH
DN
CLOS
BATH
MASTER BEDROOM 14x19
CLOS
BEDROOM 14x13
OPEN TO ENTRY

SECOND FLOOR

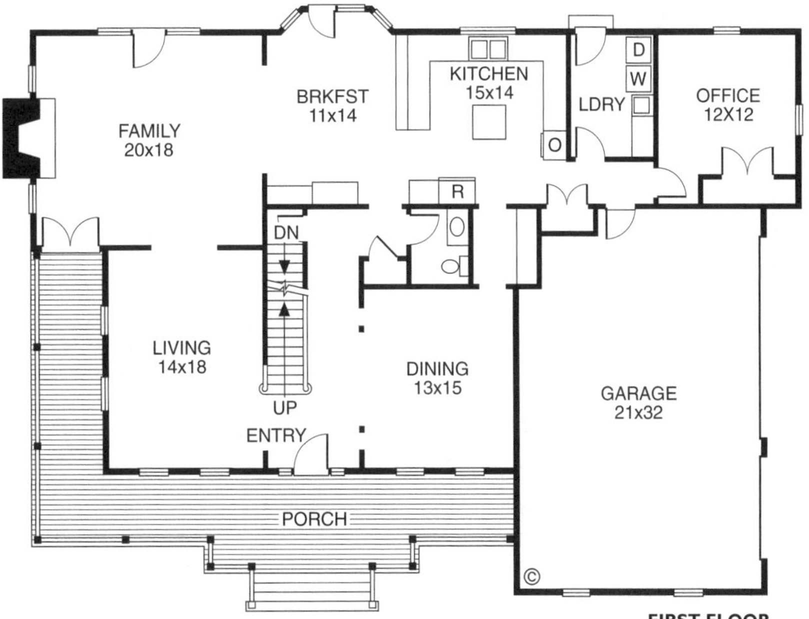

KITCHEN 15x14
D
W
BRKFST 11x14
LDRY
OFFICE 12X12
FAMILY 20x18
R
DN
LIVING 14x18
DINING 13x15
GARAGE 21x32
UP
ENTRY
PORCH

FIRST FLOOR

Please note: The photographed home may have been modified to suit homeowner preferences. If you order plans, have a builder or design professional check them against the photograph to confirm actual construction details.

Design 98536

Units	Single
Price Code	I
Total Finished	3,423 sq. ft.
First Finished	2,787 sq. ft.
Second Finished	636 sq. ft.
Garage Unfinished	832 sq. ft.
Deck Unfinished	152 sq. ft.
Porch Unfinished	212 sq. ft.
Dimensions	101'x58'8"
Foundation	Crawlspace Slab
Bedrooms	4
Full Baths	2
Half Baths	1
First Ceiling	9'
Second Ceiling	7'-9'
Max Ridge Height	28'6"
Roof Framing	Stick
Exterior Walls	2x4

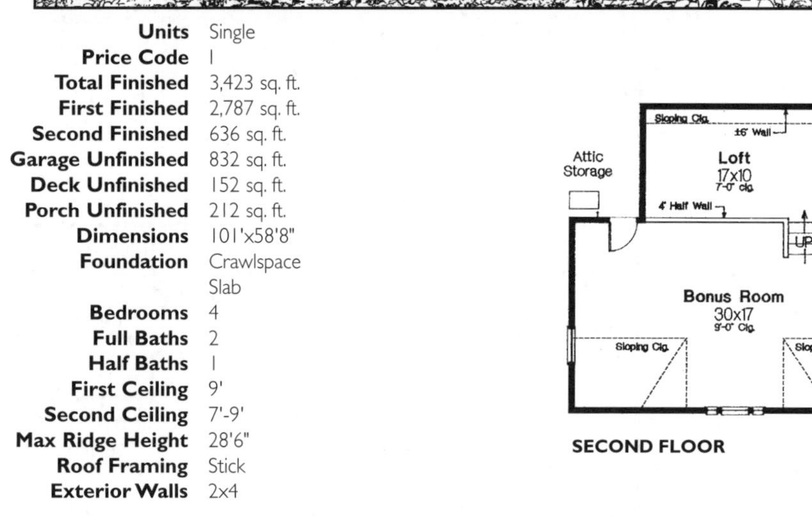

Sloping Clg.
±6' Wall
Attic Storage
Loft
17x10
7'-0" clg.
4' Half Wall
DN
UP
Bonus Room
30x17
9'-0" Clg.
Sloping Clg.
Sloping Clg.
4' Knee Wall
SECOND FLOOR

Covered Veranda
Books
FamilyRm
16x20
Covered Patio
Walk-in Closet
Shelves
Linen
Skylite
Sloping Clg. Plant Ledge
Ledge
MstrBed
18x14
Vaulted Clg. From 9'-0" To 11'-0"
LivRm
17x16
11'-0" Clg.
Skylite
UP
Brkfst
12x10
Pwdr
Broom Clos.
DN 4'
3-Car Gar
24x32
8'-0" Clg.
Bed#2
13x11
Linen
Pantry
Shelves
Sloped Clg. Below Stairs
Coats
Pantry
Oven/Microwave
Walk-in Closet
Walk-in Closet
Gallery
Sloped Clg.
Kit
17x14
Plant Ledge
Linen
Walk-in Closet
Ent
Shop Area
8'-0" Clg.
Bed#3
14x11
Util
Bed#4/Study
12x13
FmlDin
12x13
Ledge
Wall Above Plant Ledge
©
Covered Porch
Step
FIRST FLOOR

Design 63021

Units	Single
Price Code	I
Total Finished	3,434 sq. ft.
Main Finished	3,434 sq. ft.
Bonus Unfinished	512 sq. ft.
Garage Unfinished	814 sq. ft.
Dimensions	82'4"x83'8"
Foundation	Slab
Bedrooms	5
Full Baths	3
3/4 Baths	1
Main Ceiling	10'-12'
Max Ridge Height	23'5"
Roof Framing	Truss

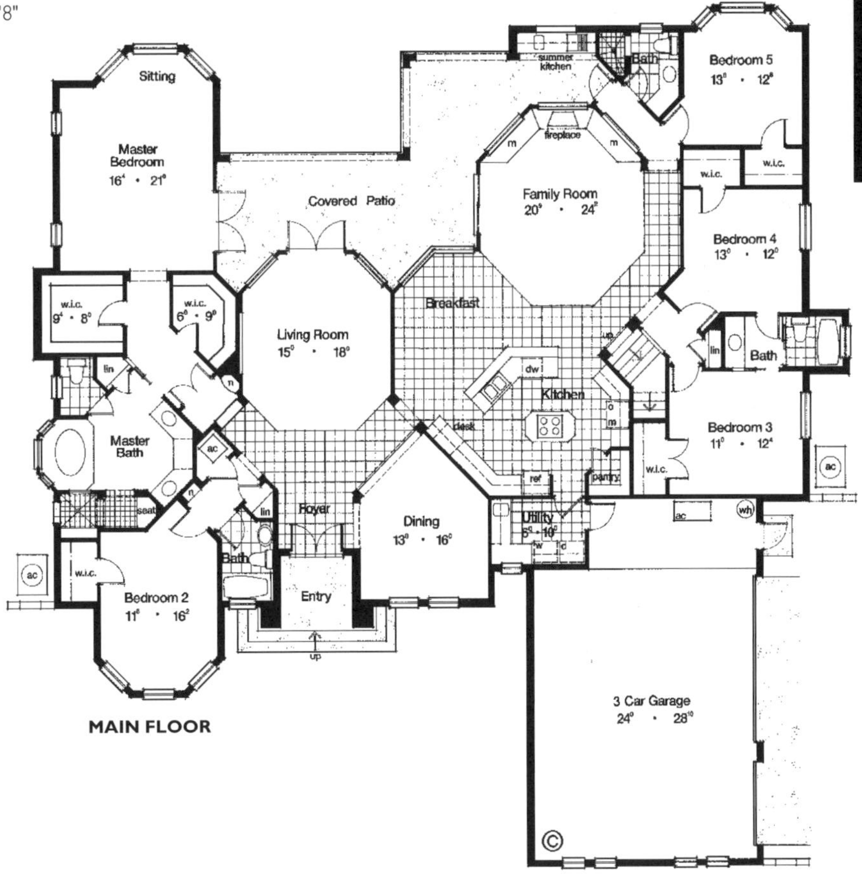

Sitting
Master Bedroom $16^4 \cdot 21^0$
Covered Patio
summer kitchen
Bath
Bedroom 5 $13^0 \cdot 12^8$
fireplace
Family Room $20^0 \cdot 24^2$
w.i.c.
w.i.c.
Bedroom 4 $13^0 \cdot 12^0$
w.i.c. $9^4 \cdot 8^0$
w.i.c. $6^0 \cdot 9^0$
Living Room $15^0 \cdot 18^0$
Breakfast
Kitchen
Bath
Bedroom 3 $11^0 \cdot 12^4$
Master Bath
Foyer
Dining $13^0 \cdot 16^0$
Utility $5^6 \cdot 10^0$
pantry
Bedroom 2 $11^0 \cdot 16^2$
Bath
Entry
3 Car Garage $24^0 \cdot 28^{10}$

MAIN FLOOR

down
Future Space $16^0 \cdot 32^0$
Balcony

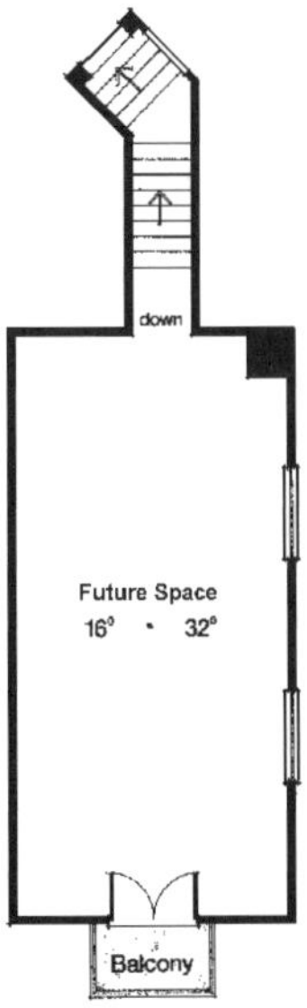

BONUS

Design 96549

Units	Single
Price Code	H
Total Finished	3,438 sq. ft.
First Finished	2,154 sq. ft.
Second Finished	1,284 sq. ft.
Garage Unfinished	778 sq. ft.
Porch Unfinished	442 sq. ft.
Dimensions	64'x75'
Foundation	Crawlspace Slab
Bedrooms	3
Full Baths	3
Half Baths	1
First Ceiling	9'
Second Ceiling	8'
Max Ridge Height	30'
Roof Framing	Stick
Exterior Walls	2x4

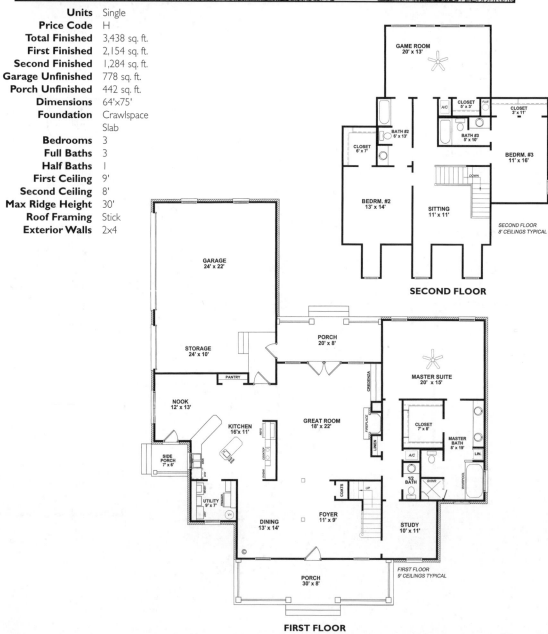

GAME ROOM 20' x 13'
BATH #2 6' x 13'
CLOSET 5' x 3'
A/C
FLUE
CLOSET 3' x 11'
BATH #3 5' x 10'
CLOSET 6' x 7'
BEDRM. #3 11' x 16'
DOWN
BEDRM. #2 13' x 14'
SITTING 11' x 11'
SECOND FLOOR 8' CEILINGS TYPICAL

SECOND FLOOR

GARAGE 24' x 22'
STORAGE 24' x 10'
PORCH 20' x 8'
PANTRY
MASTER SUITE 20' x 15'
CREDENZA
NOOK 12' x 13'
KITCHEN 16'x 11'
GREAT ROOM 18' x 22'
FIREPLACE
CLOSET 7' x 8'
MASTER BATH 8' x 19'
LINEN
SIDE PORCH 7' x 6'
A/C
LIN.
1/2 BATH
SHWR
WHIRLPOOL
COATS
UP
UTILITY 9' x 7'
FOYER 11' x 9'
DINING 13' x 14'
STUDY 10' x 11'
FIRST FLOOR 9' CEILINGS TYPICAL
PORCH 30' x 8'

FIRST FLOOR

Design 10534

PHOTOGRAPHY: JOHN EHRENCLOU

Units	Single
Price Code	I
Total Finished	3,440 sq. ft.
First Finished	2,486 sq. ft.
Second Finished	954 sq. ft.
Basement Unfinished	2,486 sq. ft.
Garage Unfinished	576 sq. ft.
Dimensions	73'4"x60'4"
Foundation	Basement Crawlspace Slab
Bedrooms	4
Full Baths	2
3/4 Baths	1
Half Baths	1
Max Ridge Height	35'
Roof Framing	Stick
Exterior Walls	2x6

LIV. ROOM BELOW
BEDROOM #4 14'-10"X13-4"
OPEN RAIL
DN.
L.
C.
B.
C.
C.
C.
FOYER BELOW
BEDROOM #2 14'-0" X 11'-0"
B.
BEDROOM #3 14'-2" X 11'-4"

SECOND FLOOR

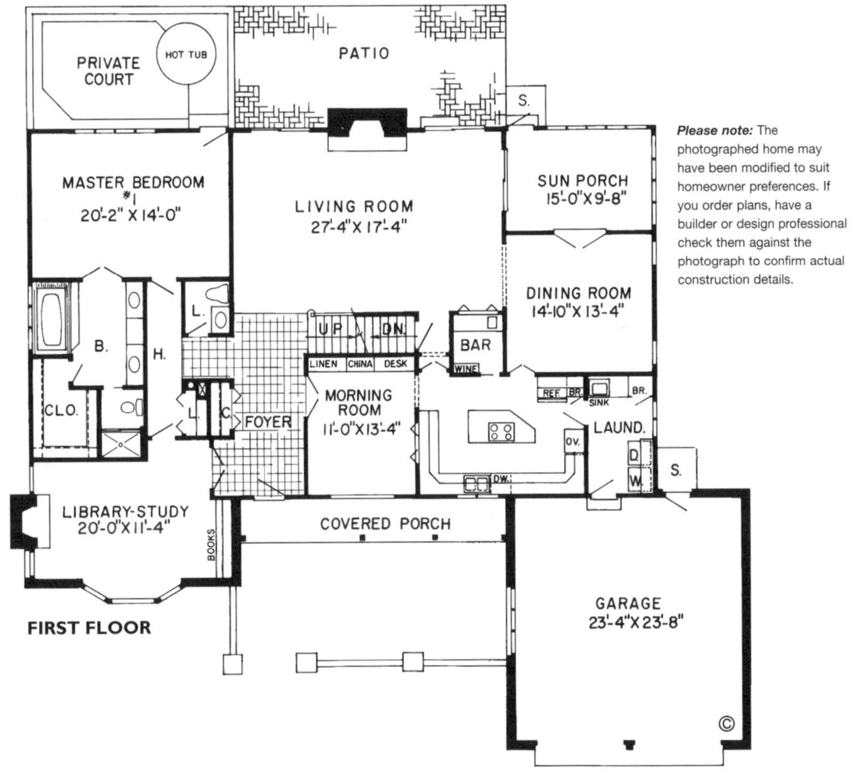
PRIVATE COURT
HOT TUB
PATIO
S.
MASTER BEDROOM #1 20'-2" X 14'-0"
LIVING ROOM 27'-4"X17'-4"
SUN PORCH 15'-0"X9'-8"
DINING ROOM 14'-10"X13'-4"
B.
H.
L.
UP
DN.
BAR
LINEN
CHINA
DESK
WINE
REF.
BR.
SINK
BR.
CLO.
L.
C.
FOYER
MORNING ROOM 11'-0"X13'-4"
OV.
LAUND.
D
W
S.
DW.
LIBRARY-STUDY 20'-0"X11'-4"
BOOKS
COVERED PORCH
GARAGE 23'-4"X23'-8"
FIRST FLOOR

Please note: The photographed home may have been modified to suit homeowner preferences. If you order plans, have a builder or design professional check them against the photograph to confirm actual construction details.

Design 68084

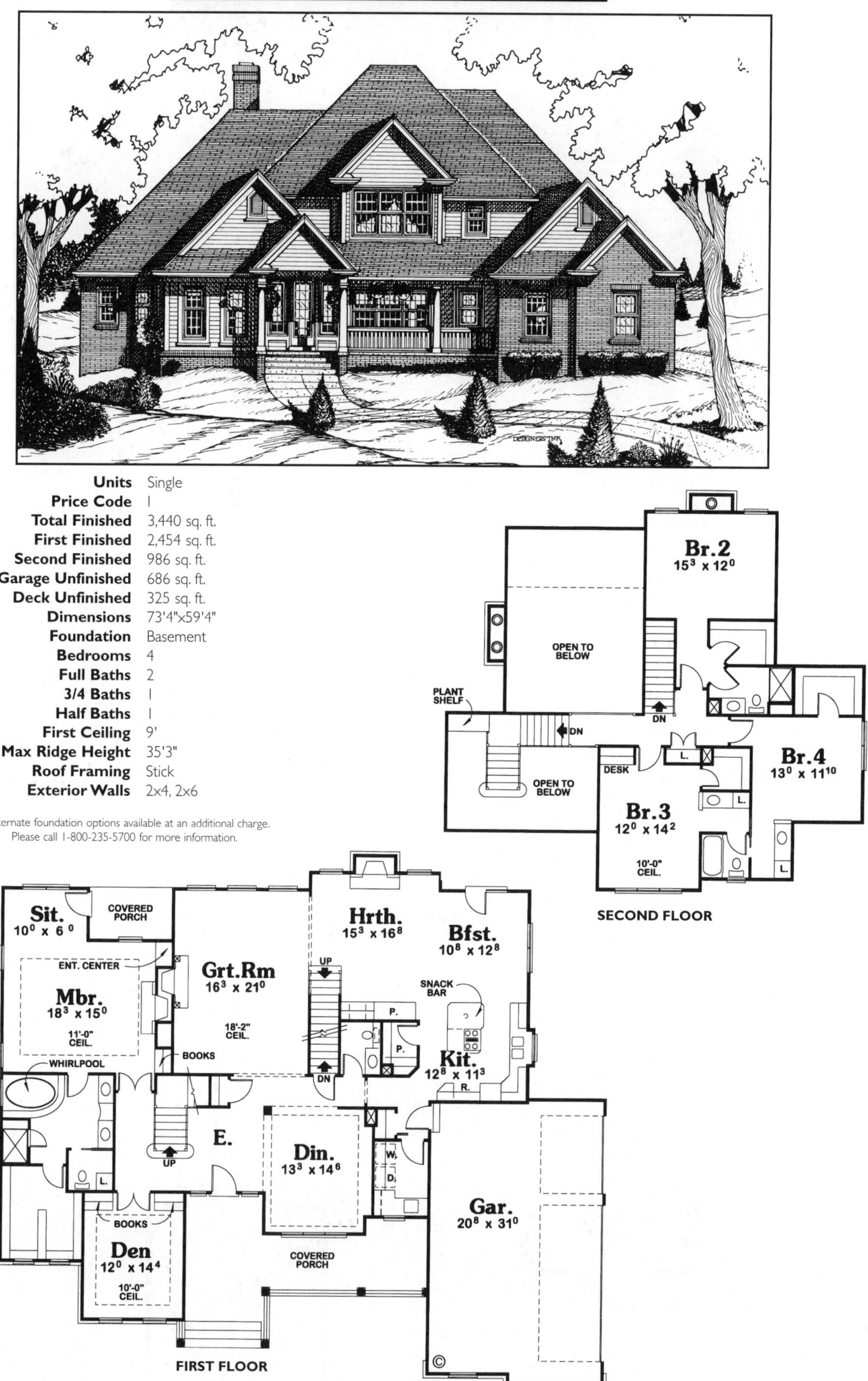

DESIGNERS THK
Br.2
15^{3} x 12^{0}
OPEN TO BELOW
PLANT SHELF
DN
DN
DESK
L.
OPEN TO BELOW
Br.3
12^{0} x 14^{2}
10'-0" CEIL.
Br.4
13^{0} x 11^{10}
L.
L.
SECOND FLOOR
Sit.
10^{0} x 6^{0}
COVERED PORCH
ENT. CENTER
Mbr.
18^{3} x 15^{0}
11'-0" CEIL.
WHIRLPOOL
Grt.Rm
16^{3} x 21^{0}
18'-2" CEIL.
BOOKS
UP
DN
Hrth.
15^{3} x 16^{8}
Bfst.
10^{8} x 12^{8}
SNACK BAR
P.
P.
Kit.
12^{8} x 11^{3}
R.
E.
UP
Din.
13^{3} x 14^{6}
W.
D.
L.
BOOKS
Den
12^{0} x 14^{4}
10'-0" CEIL.
COVERED PORCH
Gar.
20^{8} x 31^{0}
FIRST FLOOR

Units	Single
Price Code	I
Total Finished	3,440 sq. ft.
First Finished	2,454 sq. ft.
Second Finished	986 sq. ft.
Garage Unfinished	686 sq. ft.
Deck Unfinished	325 sq. ft.
Dimensions	73'4"x59'4"
Foundation	Basement
Bedrooms	4
Full Baths	2
3/4 Baths	1
Half Baths	1
First Ceiling	9'
Max Ridge Height	35'3"
Roof Framing	Stick
Exterior Walls	2x4, 2x6

* Alternate foundation options available at an additional charge. Please call 1-800-235-5700 for more information.

Design 91562

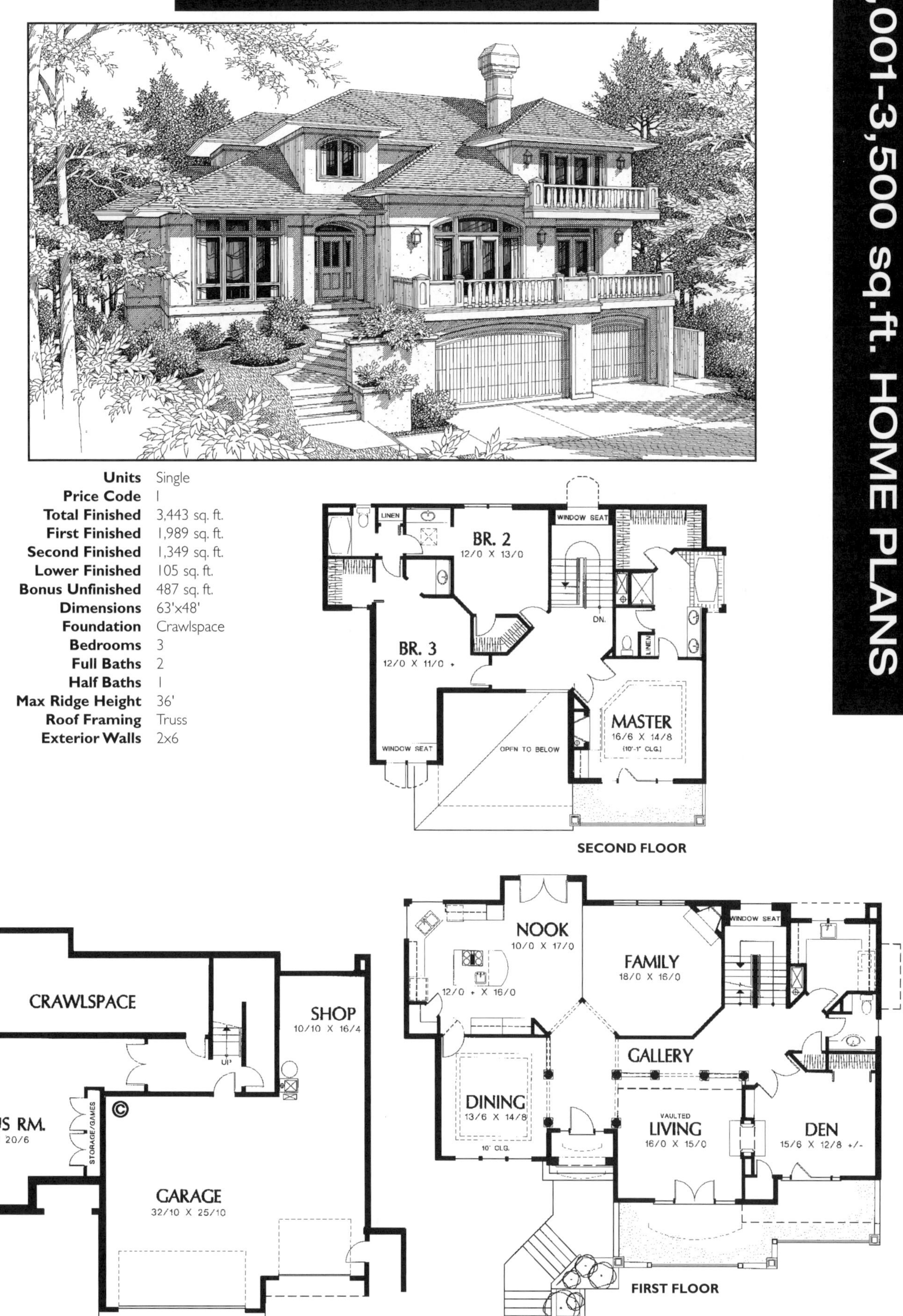
BR. 2
12/0 X 13/0
LINEN
WINDOW SEAT
DN.
BR. 3
12/0 X 11/0 +
LINEN
MASTER
16/6 X 14/8
(10'-1" CLG.)
WINDOW SEAT
OPEN TO BELOW
SECOND FLOOR
CRAWLSPACE
STORAGE
UP
SHOP
10/10 X 16/4
BONUS RM.
19/6 X 20/6
STORAGE/GAMES
GARAGE
32/10 X 25/10
LOWER FLOOR
NOOK
10/0 X 17/0
12/0 + X 16/0
FAMILY
18/0 X 16/0
WINDOW SEAT
GALLERY
DINING
13/6 X 14/8
10' CLG.
VAULTED
LIVING
16/0 X 15/0
DEN
15/6 X 12/8 +/-
FIRST FLOOR

Units	Single
Price Code	I
Total Finished	3,443 sq. ft.
First Finished	1,989 sq. ft.
Second Finished	1,349 sq. ft.
Lower Finished	105 sq. ft.
Bonus Unfinished	487 sq. ft.
Dimensions	63'x48'
Foundation	Crawlspace
Bedrooms	3
Full Baths	2
Half Baths	1
Max Ridge Height	36'
Roof Framing	Truss
Exterior Walls	2x6

Design 32606

PHOTOGRAPHY: BETH SINGER

Units	Single
Price Code	I
Total Finished	3,474 sq. ft.
First Finished	2,569 sq. ft.
Second Finished	905 sq. ft.
Bonus Unfinished	401 sq. ft.
Basement Unfinished	2,522 sq. ft.
Garage Unfinished	680 sq. ft.
Dimensions	62'10"x74'7½"
Foundation	Basement
Bedrooms	3
Full Baths	3
Half Baths	1
First Ceiling	9'
Second Ceiling	8'
Max Ridge Height	40'
Roof Framing	Truss
Exterior Walls	2x6

Please note: The photographed home may have been modified to suit homeowner preferences. If you order plans, have a builder or design professional check them against the photograph to confirm actual construction details.

OPEN TO GREAT-ROOM
CLOS
BEDROOM 13x12
CLOS
BONUS 13x19
GALLERY
OPEN
LIBRARY
CLOS
DN
OPEN TO ENTRY
BEDROOM 12x15

SECOND FLOOR

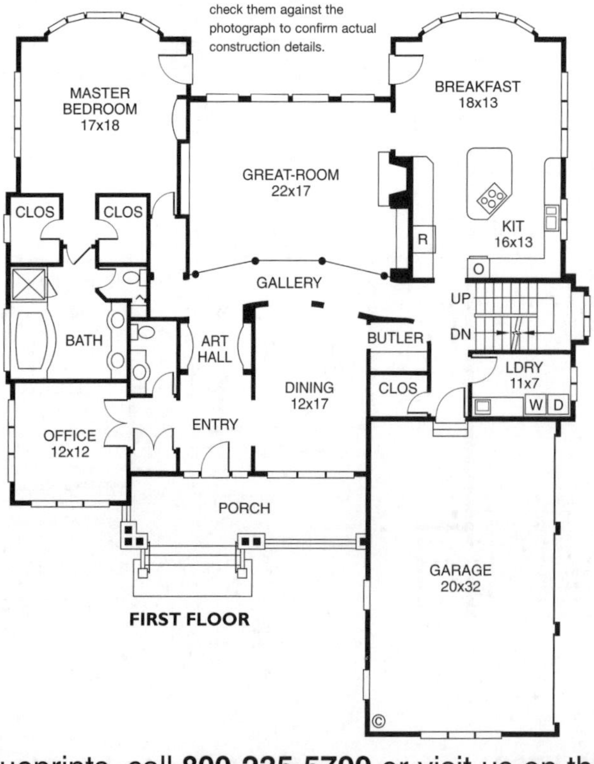

MASTER BEDROOM 17x18
BREAKFAST 18x13
GREAT-ROOM 22x17
CLOS
CLOS
KIT 16x13
R
GALLERY
UP
BATH
ART HALL
BUTLER
DN
DINING 12x17
CLOS
LDRY 11x7
W D
OFFICE 12x12
ENTRY
PORCH
GARAGE 20x32
©

FIRST FLOOR

Design 98508

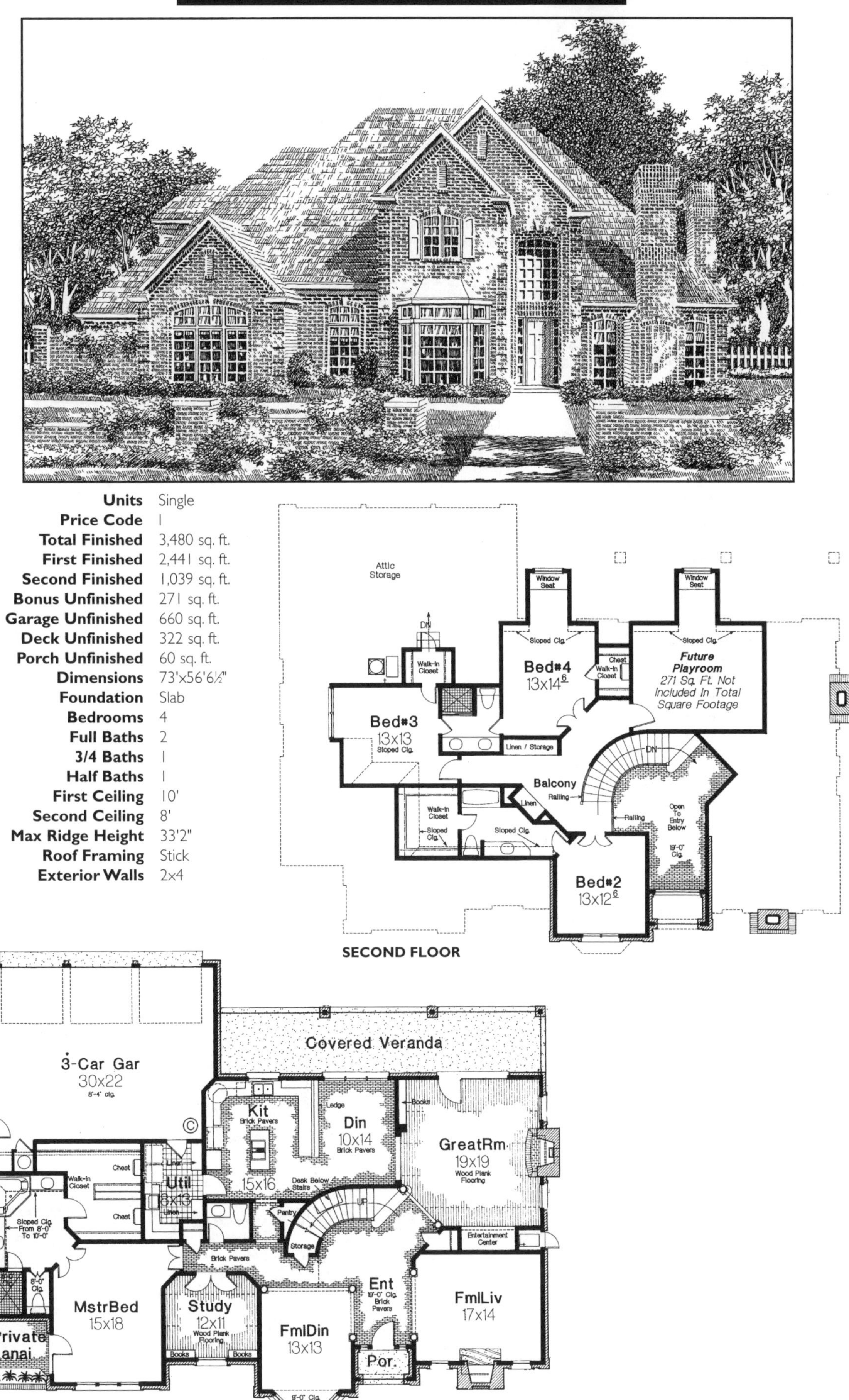
Attic Storage
Window Seat
Window Seat
Sloped Clg.
Sloped Clg.
Walk-In Closet
Bed#4
13x14⁶
Chest
Walk-In Closet
Future Playroom
271 Sq. Ft. Not Included In Total Square Footage
Bed#3
13x13
Sloped Clg.
Linen / Storage
Balcony
Railing
Linen
Railing
Open To Entry Below
19'-0" Clg.
Walk-In Closet
Sloped Clg.
Sloped Clg.
Bed#2
13x12⁶
SECOND FLOOR
3-Car Gar
30x22
8'-4" clg.
Covered Veranda
Stoop
Kit
Brick Pavers
Ledge
Din
10x14
Brick Pavers
Books
GreatRm
19x19
Wood Plank Flooring
Walk-In Closet
Chest
Chest
Util
15x16
Desk Below Stairs
Pantry
Storage
Entertainment Center
Sloped Clg. From 8'-0" To 10'-0"
Brick Pavers
Ent
19'-0" Clg.
Brick Pavers
MstrBed
15x18
Study
12x11
Wood Plank Flooring
FmlDin
13x13
FmlLiv
17x14
Private Lanai
Books
Books
Por.
9'-0" Clg.
FIRST FLOOR

Units	Single
Price Code	I
Total Finished	3,480 sq. ft.
First Finished	2,441 sq. ft.
Second Finished	1,039 sq. ft.
Bonus Unfinished	271 sq. ft.
Garage Unfinished	660 sq. ft.
Deck Unfinished	322 sq. ft.
Porch Unfinished	60 sq. ft.
Dimensions	73'x56'6½"
Foundation	Slab
Bedrooms	4
Full Baths	2
3/4 Baths	1
Half Baths	1
First Ceiling	10'
Second Ceiling	8'
Max Ridge Height	33'2"
Roof Framing	Stick
Exterior Walls	2x4

Design 66068

Units	Single
Price Code	I
Total Finished	3,494 sq. ft.
Main Finished	3,494 sq. ft.
Garage Unfinished	720 sq. ft.
Deck Unfinished	184 sq. ft.
Porch Unfinished	48 sq. ft.
Dimensions	82'8"x77'
Foundation	Slab
Bedrooms	4
Full Baths	2
3/4 Baths	1
Half Baths	1
Main Ceiling	9'-12'
Max Ridge Height	33'6"
Roof Framing	Stick
Exterior Walls	2x4

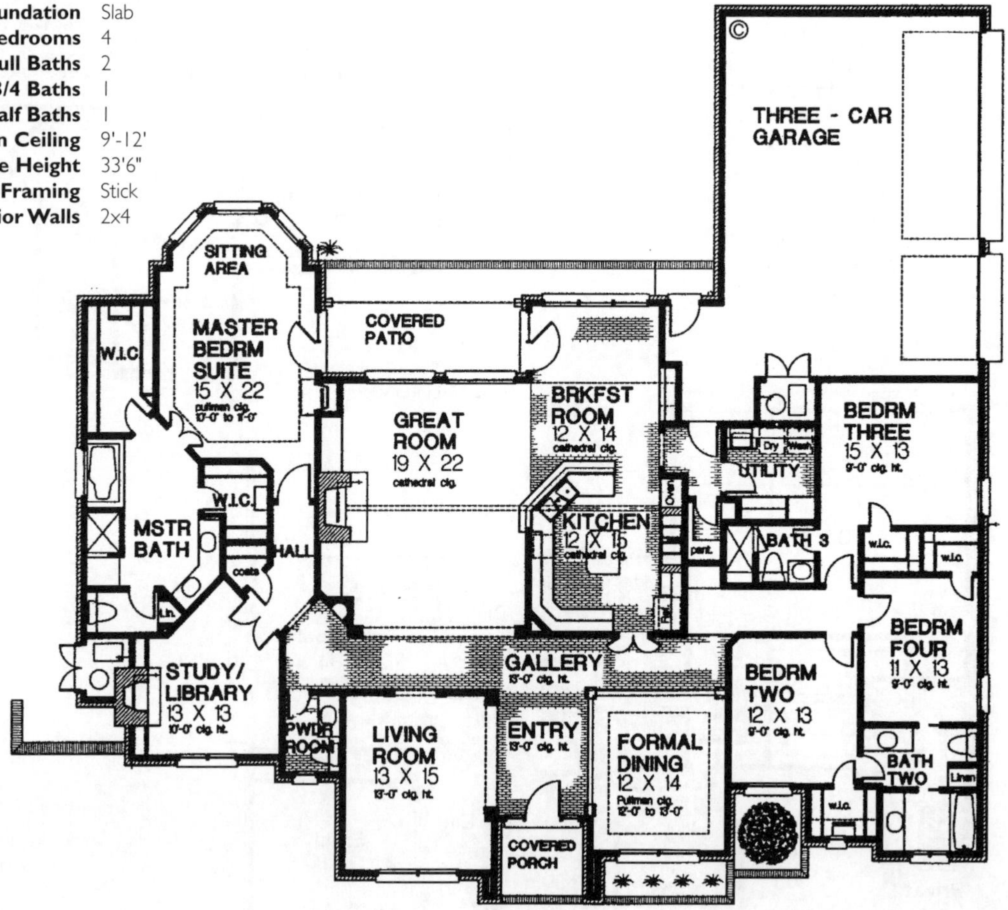

©
THREE - CAR GARAGE
SITTING AREA
MASTER BEDRM SUITE 15 X 22 pullmen clg. 10'-0" to 11'-0"
COVERED PATIO
W.I.C.
GREAT ROOM 19 X 22 cathedral clg.
BRKFST ROOM 12 X 14 cathedral clg.
UTILITY
Dry Wash
BEDRM THREE 15 X 13 9'-0" clg. ht.
W.I.C.
MSTR BATH
HALL
coats
lin.
KITCHEN 12 X 15 cathedral clg.
pant.
BATH 3
w.i.c.
w.i.c.
BEDRM FOUR 11 X 13 9'-0" clg. ht.
GALLERY 13'-0" clg. ht.
STUDY/ LIBRARY 13 X 13 10'-0" clg. ht.
PWDR ROOM
LIVING ROOM 13 X 15 13'-0" clg. ht.
ENTRY 13'-0" clg. ht.
FORMAL DINING 12 X 14 Pullmen clg. 12'-0" to 13'-0"
BEDRM TWO 12 X 13 9'-0" clg. ht.
BATH TWO
Linen
w.i.c.
COVERED PORCH

MAIN FLOOR

Design 91178

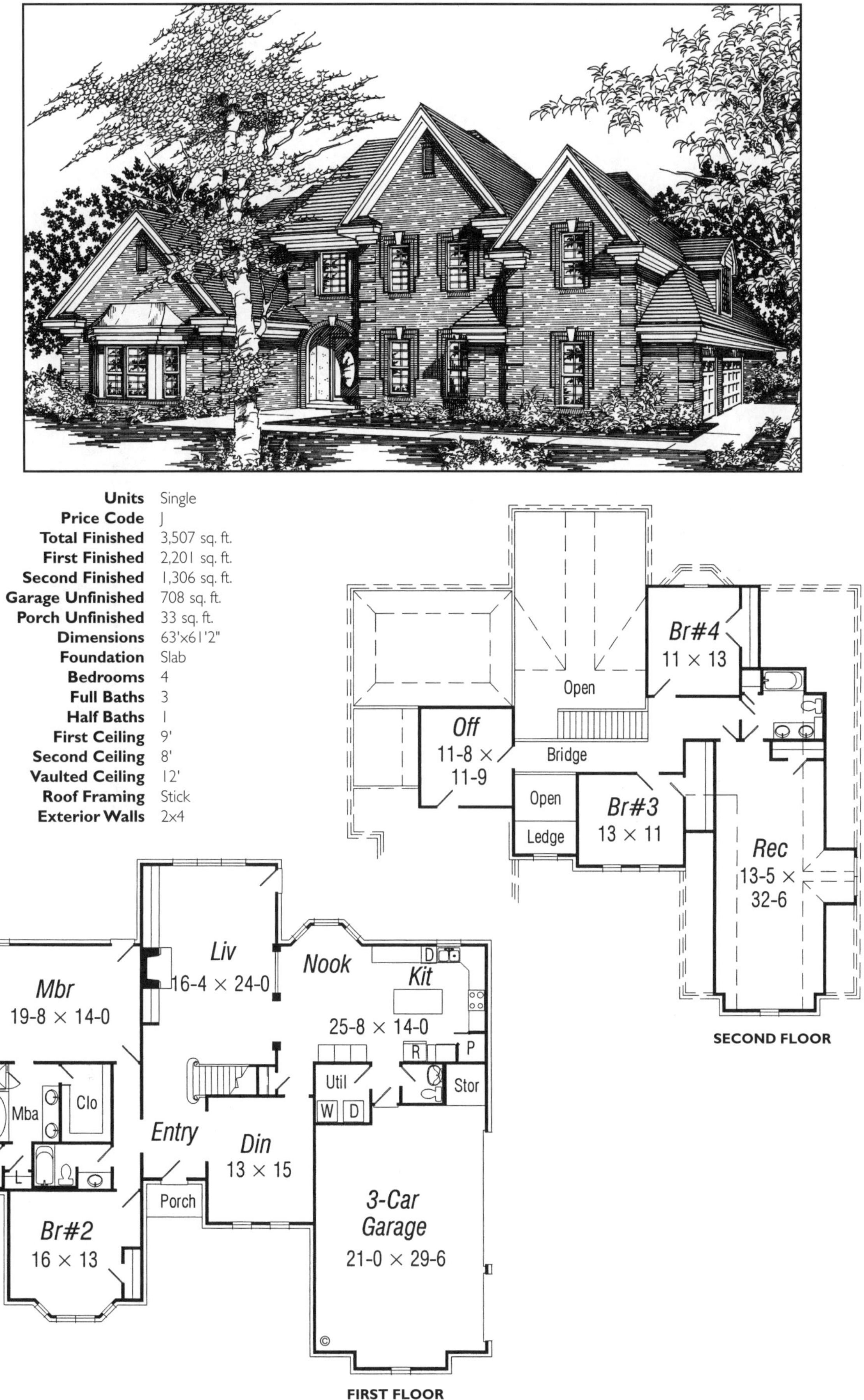
Br#4
11 × 13
Open
Off
11-8 × 11-9
Bridge
Open
Ledge
Br#3
13 × 11
Rec
13-5 × 32-6
SECOND FLOOR
Liv
16-4 × 24-0
Nook
Kit
25-8 × 14-0
Mbr
19-8 × 14-0
Mba
Clo
Util
W
D
R
P
Stor
Entry
Din
13 × 15
Porch
Br#2
16 × 13
3-Car Garage
21-0 × 29-6
FIRST FLOOR

Units	Single
Price Code	J
Total Finished	3,507 sq. ft.
First Finished	2,201 sq. ft.
Second Finished	1,306 sq. ft.
Garage Unfinished	708 sq. ft.
Porch Unfinished	33 sq. ft.
Dimensions	63'x61'2"
Foundation	Slab
Bedrooms	4
Full Baths	3
Half Baths	1
First Ceiling	9'
Second Ceiling	8'
Vaulted Ceiling	12'
Roof Framing	Stick
Exterior Walls	2x4

Design 99472

PHOTOGRAPHY: COURTESY OF THE DESIGNER

Units	Single
Price Code	J
Total Finished	3,517 sq. ft.
First Finished	2,050 sq. ft.
Second Finished	1,467 sq. ft.
Basement Unfinished	2,050 sq. ft.
Garage Unfinished	698 sq. ft.
Dimensions	62'11"x90'7"
Foundation	Basement Slab
Bedrooms	5
Full Baths	3
Half Baths	1
Max Ridge Height	34'6"
Roof Framing	Stick
Exterior Walls	2x4

* Alternate foundation options available at an additional charge. Please call 1-800-235-5700 for more information.

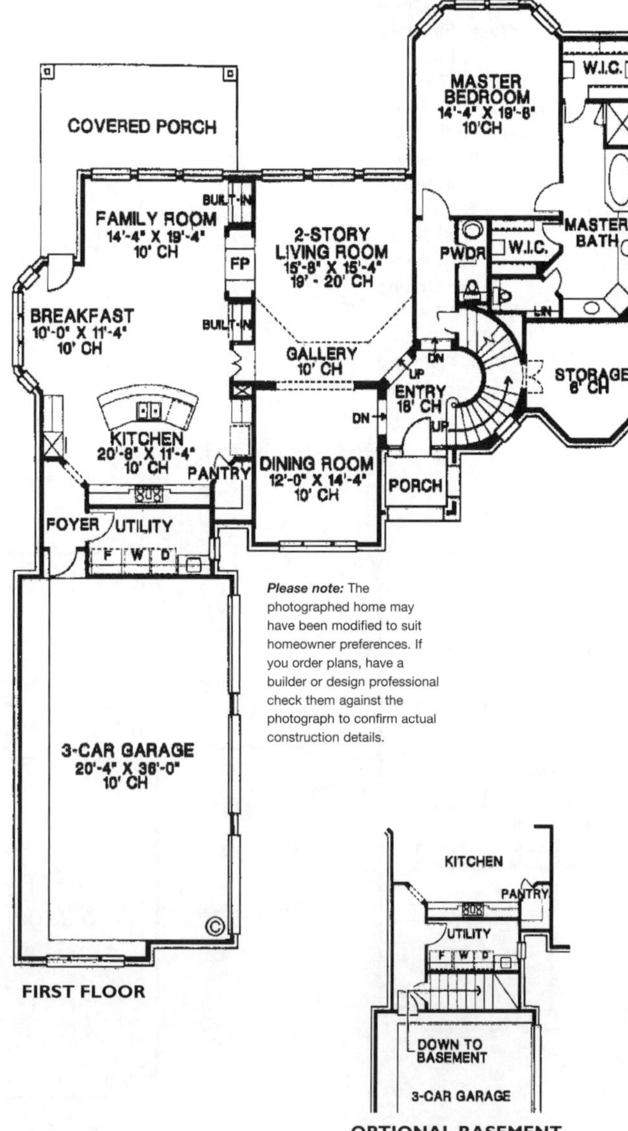
COVERED PORCH
MASTER BEDROOM 14'-4" X 19'-8" 10'CH
W.I.C.
FAMILY ROOM 14'-4" X 19'-4" 10' CH
BUILT-IN
2-STORY LIVING ROOM 15'-8" X 15'-4" 19' - 20' CH
FP
PWDR
W.I.C.
MASTER BATH
LIN
BREAKFAST 10'-0" X 11'-4" 10' CH
BUILT-IN
GALLERY 10' CH
DN
UP
STORAGE 6' CH
ENTRY 18' CH
DN
UP
KITCHEN 20'-8" X 11'-4" 10' CH
PANTRY
DINING ROOM 12'-0" X 14'-4" 10' CH
PORCH
FOYER
UTILITY
F W D
3-CAR GARAGE 20'-4" X 36'-0" 10' CH
FIRST FLOOR
KITCHEN
PANTRY
UTILITY
F W D
DOWN TO BASEMENT
3-CAR GARAGE
OPTIONAL BASEMENT STAIR LOCATION

Please note: The photographed home may have been modified to suit homeowner preferences. If you order plans, have a builder or design professional check them against the photograph to confirm actual construction details.

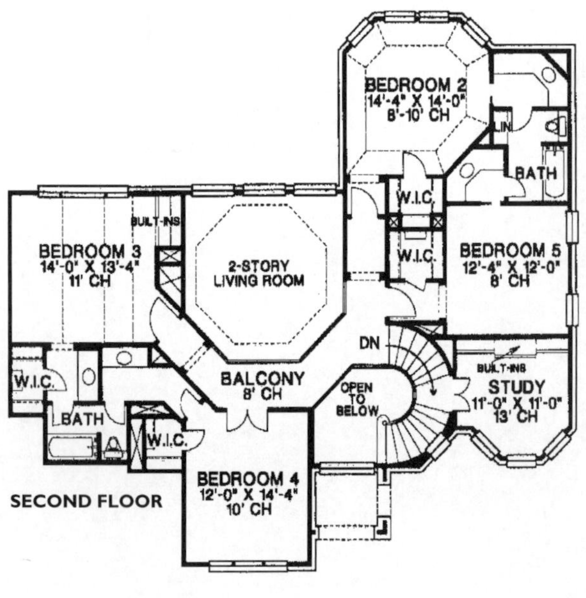
BEDROOM 2 14'-4" X 14'-0" 8'-10' CH
LIN
BATH
W.I.C.
W.I.C.
BUILT-INS
BEDROOM 3 14'-0" X 13'-4" 11' CH
2-STORY LIVING ROOM
BEDROOM 5 12'-4" X 12'-0" 8' CH
DN
W.I.C.
BALCONY 8' CH
OPEN TO BELOW
BUILT-INS
STUDY 11'-0" X 11'-0" 13' CH
BATH
W.I.C.
BEDROOM 4 12'-0" X 14'-4" 10' CH
SECOND FLOOR

Design 63068

Units	Single
Price Code	J
Total Finished	3,556 sq. ft.
Main Finished	3,556 sq. ft.
Garage Unfinished	809 sq. ft.
Dimensions	85'x85'
Foundation	Slab
Bedrooms	4
Full Baths	2
3/4 Baths	1
Half Baths	1
Main Ceiling	10'
Max Ridge Height	26'8"
Roof Framing	Truss

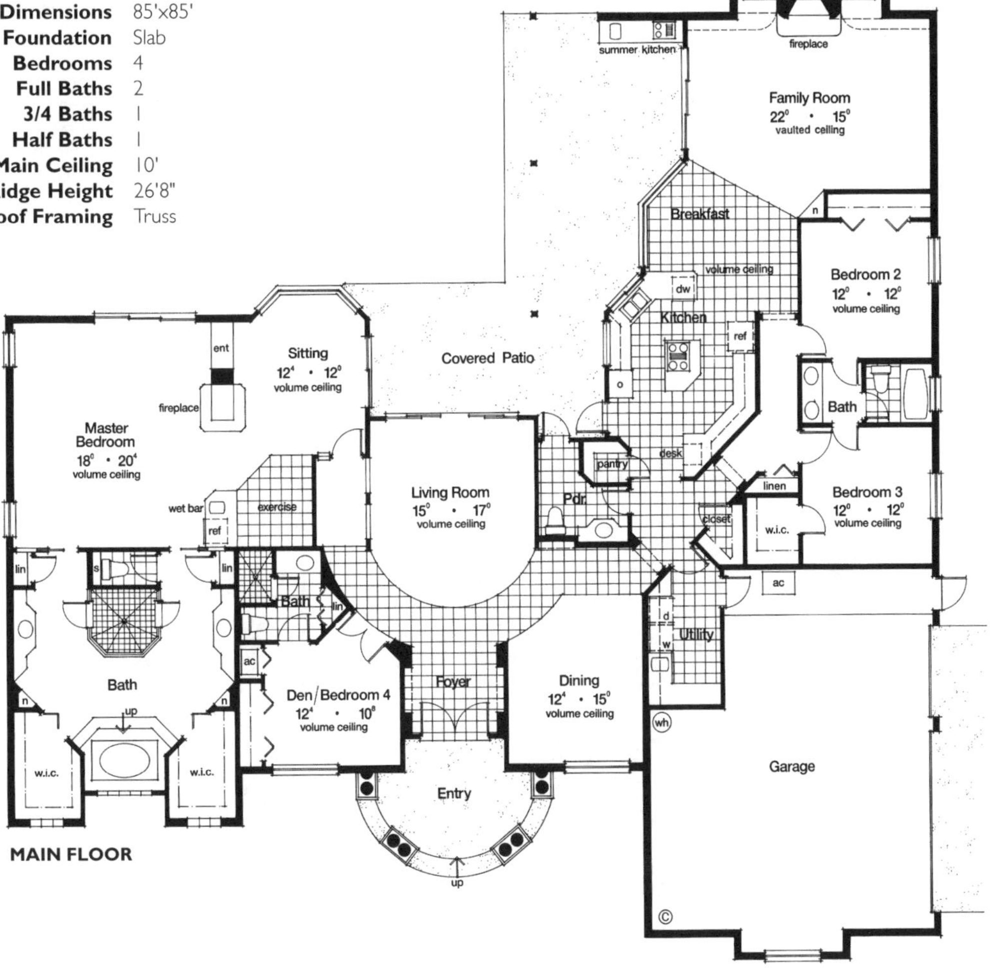

summer kitchen
fireplace
Family Room
$22^{0} \cdot 15^{0}$
vaulted ceiling
Breakfast
volume ceiling
n
Bedroom 2
$12^{0} \cdot 12^{0}$
volume ceiling
dw
Kitchen
ref
Sitting
$12^{4} \cdot 12^{0}$
volume ceiling
ent
Covered Patio
o
Bath
Master Bedroom
$18^{0} \cdot 20^{4}$
volume ceiling
fireplace
pantry
desk
linen
Bedroom 3
$12^{0} \cdot 12^{0}$
volume ceiling
wet bar
exercise
ref
Living Room
$15^{0} \cdot 17^{0}$
volume ceiling
Pdr
closet
w.i.c.
lin
s
lin
ac
Bath
lin
d
w
Utility
ac
Bath
Den/Bedroom 4
$12^{4} \cdot 10^{8}$
volume ceiling
Foyer
Dining
$12^{4} \cdot 15^{0}$
volume ceiling
wh
n
up
n
w.i.c.
w.i.c.
Garage
Entry
up

MAIN FLOOR

Units	Single
Price Code	J
Total Finished	3,556 sq. ft.
First Finished	2,555 sq. ft.
Second Finished	1,001 sq. ft.
Garage Unfinished	819 sq. ft.
Dimensions	76'x58'8"
Foundation	Basement
Bedrooms	4
Full Baths	2
3/4 Baths	1
Half Baths	2
Max Ridge Height	31'7"
Roof Framing	Stick
Exterior Walls	2x4

* Alternate foundation options available at an additional charge. Please call 1-800-235-5700 for more information.

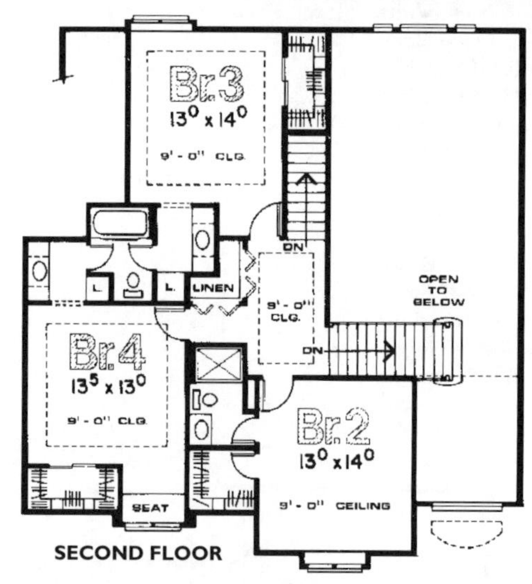
Br.3
13⁰ x 14⁰
9'-0" CLG.
LINEN
OPEN TO BELOW
DN
9'-0" CLG.
Br.4
13⁵ x 13⁰
9'-0" CLG.
Br.2
13⁰ x 14⁰
9'-0" CEILING
SEAT

SECOND FLOOR

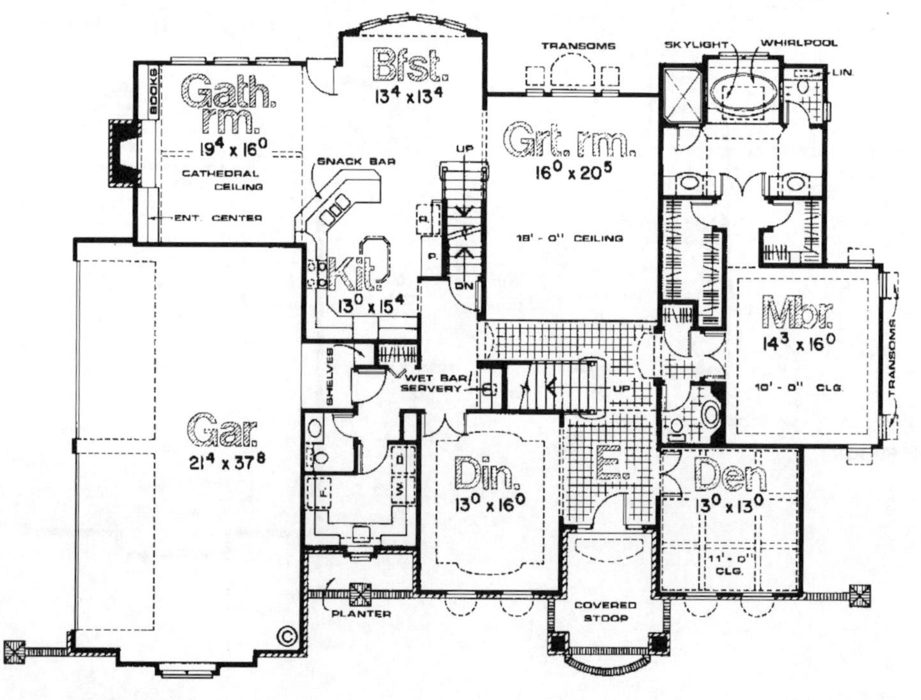
TRANSOMS
SKYLIGHT
WHIRLPOOL
LIN.
Bfst.
13⁴ x 13⁴
Gath. rm.
19⁴ x 16⁰
CATHEDRAL CEILING
BOOKS
ENT. CENTER
SNACK BAR
UP
Grt. rm.
16⁰ x 20⁵
18'-0" CEILING
Kit.
13⁰ x 15⁴
DN
Mbr.
14³ x 16⁰
10'-0" CLG.
TRANSOMS
SHELVES
WET BAR/ SERVERY
UP
Gar.
21⁴ x 37⁸
Din.
13⁰ x 16⁰
E.
Den
13⁰ x 13⁰
11'-0" CLG.
PLANTER
COVERED STOOP
©

FIRST FLOOR

Design 32076

PHOTOGRAPHY: RICK TAYLOR

Units	Single
Price Code	J
Total Finished	3,614 sq. ft.
First Finished	2,391 sq. ft.
Second Finished	1,223 sq. ft.
Basement Unfinished	2,391 sq. ft.
Garage Unfinished	484 sq. ft.
Porch Unfinished	180 sq. ft.
Dimensions	61'x68'
Foundation	Basement
Bedrooms	4
Full Baths	3
Half Baths	1
First Ceiling	9'
Second Ceiling	8'
Tray Ceiling	9'
Max Ridge Height	34'4"
Roof Framing	Truss
Exterior Walls	2x4

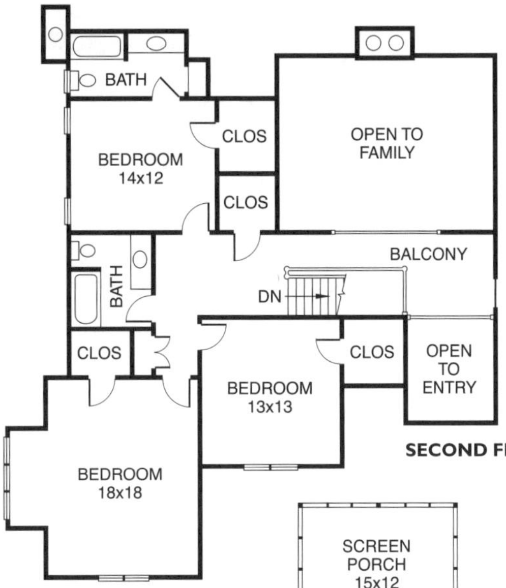

BATH
BEDROOM 14x12
CLOS
CLOS
OPEN TO FAMILY
BALCONY
BATH
DN
CLOS
BEDROOM 13x13
CLOS
OPEN TO ENTRY
BEDROOM 18x18

SECOND FLOOR

Please note: The photographed home may have been modified to suit homeowner preferences. If you order plans, have a builder or design professional check them against the photograph to confirm actual construction details.

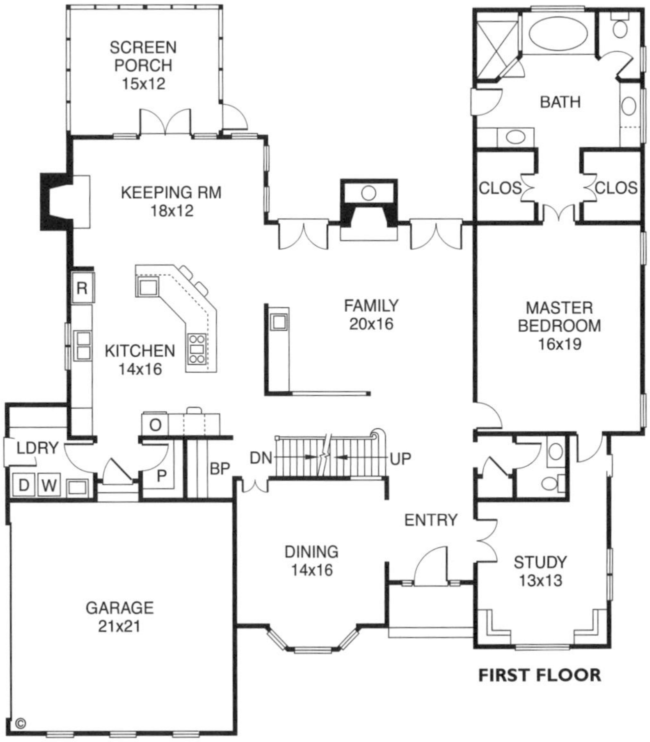

SCREEN PORCH 15x12
KEEPING RM 18x12
KITCHEN 14x16
FAMILY 20x16
BATH
CLOS
CLOS
MASTER BEDROOM 16x19
LDRY
D W
O
P
BP
DN
UP
ENTRY
DINING 14x16
STUDY 13x13
GARAGE 21x21

FIRST FLOOR

Design 93330

Units	Single
Price Code	J
Total Finished	3,620 sq. ft.
First Finished	2,093 sq. ft.
Second Finished	1,527 sq. ft.
Basement Unfinished	2,093 sq. ft.
Garage Unfinished	816 sq. ft.
Dimensions	86'x43'
Foundation	Basement
Bedrooms	4
Full Baths	2
Half Baths	1
Max Ridge Height	32'
Roof Framing	Stick
Exterior Walls	2x6

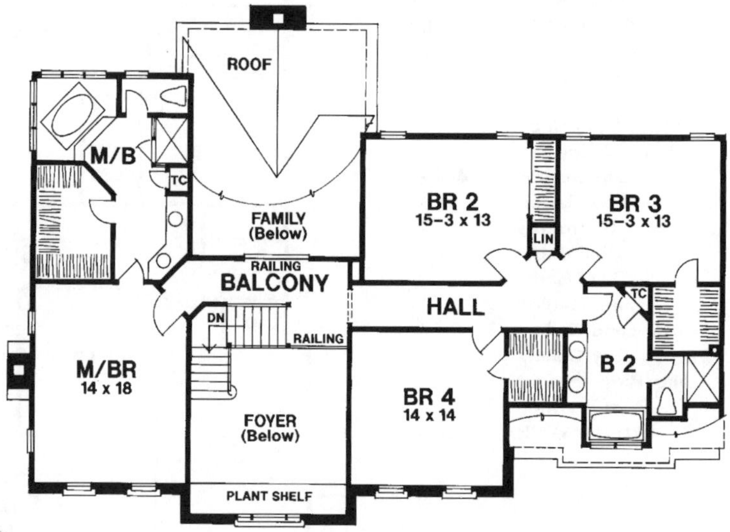

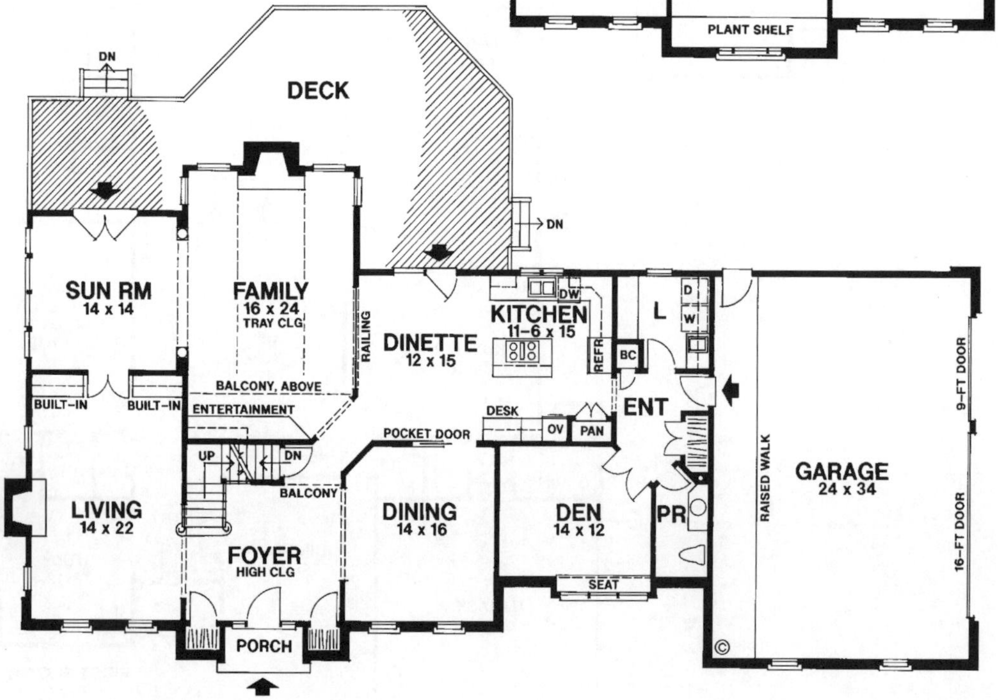

ROOF
M/B
TC
FAMILY (Below)
RAILING
BALCONY
BR 2 15-3 x 13
BR 3 15-3 x 13
LIN
HALL
TC
DN
RAILING
M/BR 14 x 18
FOYER (Below)
BR 4 14 x 14
B 2
PLANT SHELF

DN
DECK
DN
SUN RM 14 x 14
FAMILY 16 x 24 TRAY CLG
RAILING
DINETTE 12 x 15
KITCHEN 11-6 x 15
DW
REFR
D
W
L
BC
BALCONY, ABOVE
BUILT-IN
BUILT-IN
ENTERTAINMENT
DESK
OV
PAN
ENT
POCKET DOOR
UP
DN
BALCONY
LIVING 14 x 22
FOYER HIGH CLG
DINING 14 x 16
DEN 14 x 12
PR
SEAT
PORCH
RAISED WALK
GARAGE 24 x 34
9-FT DOOR
16-FT DOOR
©

Design 92164

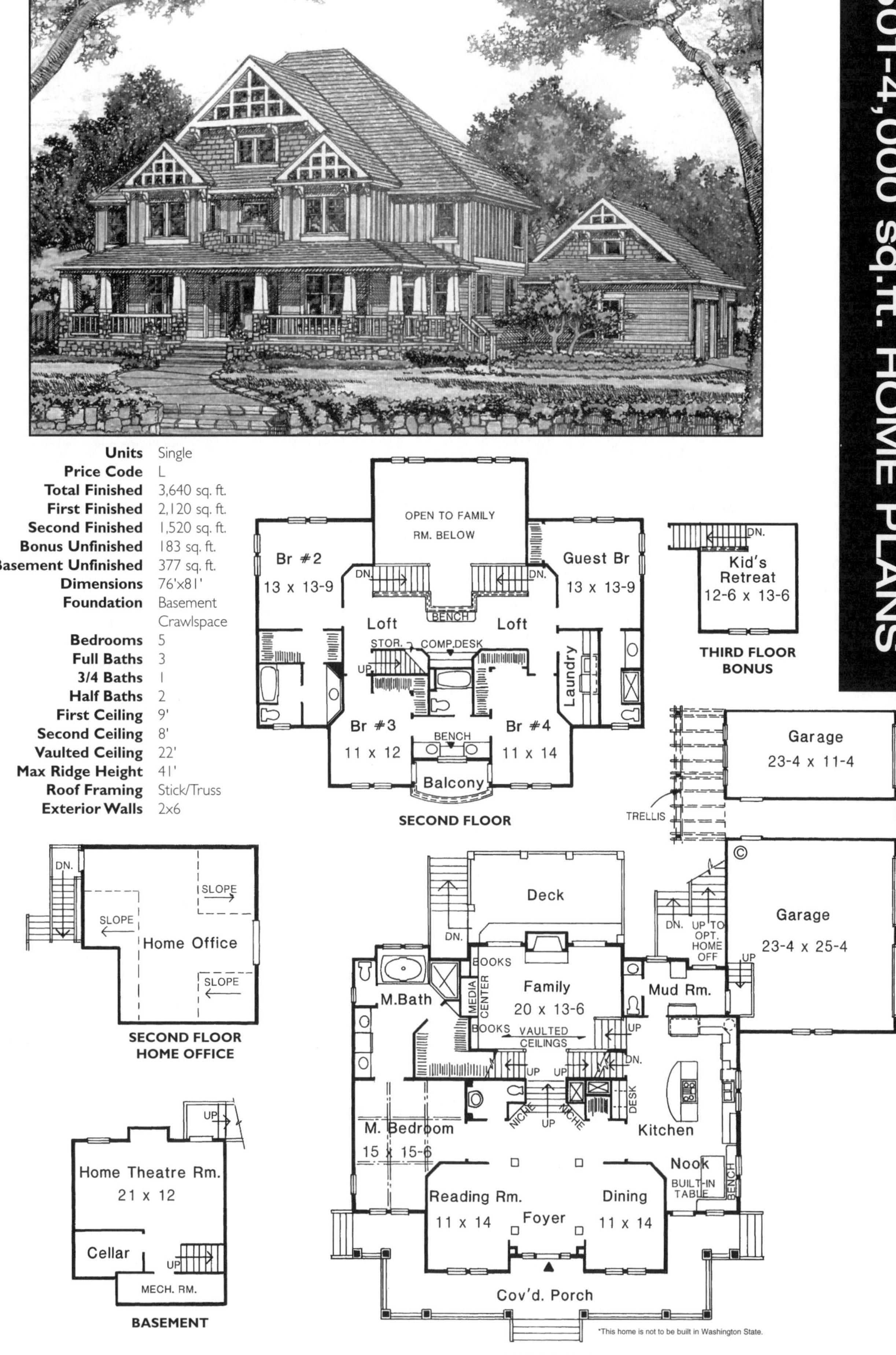
OPEN TO FAMILY RM. BELOW
Br #2
13 x 13-9
Guest Br
13 x 13-9
DN.
BENCH
Loft
Loft
STOR.
COMP.DESK
UP
Laundry
Br #3
11 x 12
Br #4
11 x 14
BENCH
Balcony
SECOND FLOOR
DN.
Kid's Retreat
12-6 x 13-6
THIRD FLOOR BONUS
Garage
23-4 x 11-4
TRELLIS
DN.
SLOPE
SLOPE
Home Office
SLOPE
SECOND FLOOR HOME OFFICE
Deck
DN.
UP TO OPT. HOME OFF
Garage
23-4 x 25-4
UP
BOOKS
MEDIA CENTER
Family
20 x 13-6
BOOKS
VAULTED CEILINGS
M.Bath
Mud Rm.
UP
DN.
UP
UP
DESK
NICHE
NICHE
UP
M. Bedroom
15 x 15-6
Kitchen
Nook
BUILT-IN TABLE
BENCH
Reading Rm.
11 x 14
Foyer
Dining
11 x 14
Cov'd. Porch
FIRST FLOOR
Home Theatre Rm.
21 x 12
Cellar
UP
MECH. RM.
BASEMENT

Units	Single
Price Code	L
Total Finished	3,640 sq. ft.
First Finished	2,120 sq. ft.
Second Finished	1,520 sq. ft.
Bonus Unfinished	183 sq. ft.
Basement Unfinished	377 sq. ft.
Dimensions	76'x81'
Foundation	Basement Crawlspace
Bedrooms	5
Full Baths	3
3/4 Baths	1
Half Baths	2
First Ceiling	9'
Second Ceiling	8'
Vaulted Ceiling	22'
Max Ridge Height	41'
Roof Framing	Stick/Truss
Exterior Walls	2x6

*This home is not to be built in Washington State.

Design 93182

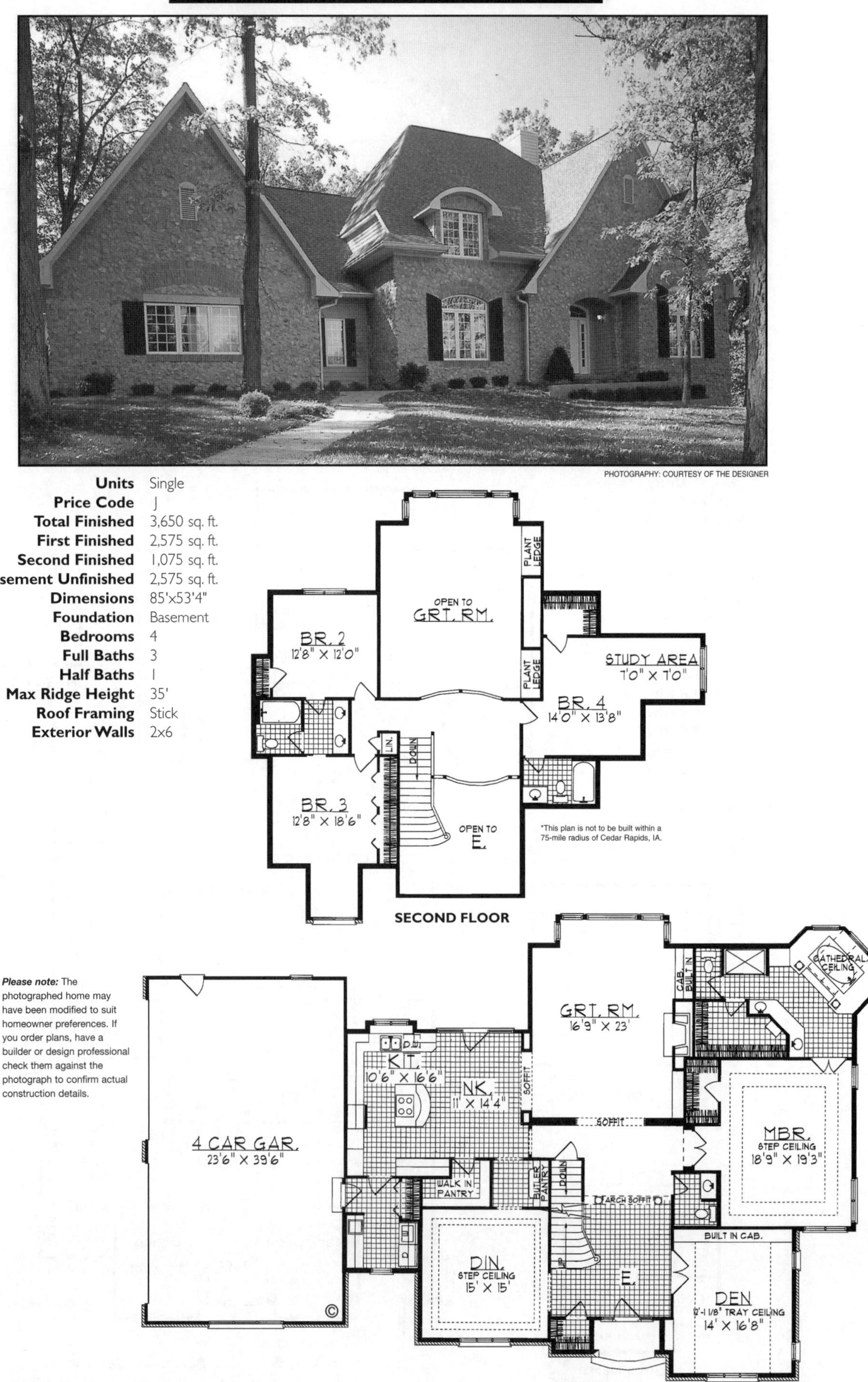
SECOND FLOOR
OPEN TO GRT. RM.
PLANT LEDGE
BR. 2
12'8" X 12'0"
STUDY AREA
7'0" X 7'0"
BR. 4
14'0" X 13'8"
LIN.
DOWN
BR. 3
12'8" X 18'6"
OPEN TO E.
FIRST FLOOR
4 CAR GAR.
23'6" X 39'6"
D/W
KT.
10'6" X 16'6"
NK.
11' X 14'4"
SOFFIT
GRT. RM.
16'9" X 23'
CAB.
BUILT IN
CATHEDRAL CEILING
MBR.
STEP CEILING
18'9" X 19'3"
WALK IN PANTRY
BUTLER PANTRY
DOWN
ARCH SOFFIT
DIN.
STEP CEILING
15' X 15'
E.
BUILT IN CAB.
DEN
12'-1 1/8" TRAY CEILING
14' X 16'8"

PHOTOGRAPHY: COURTESY OF THE DESIGNER

Units Single
Price Code J
Total Finished 3,650 sq. ft.
First Finished 2,575 sq. ft.
Second Finished 1,075 sq. ft.
Basement Unfinished 2,575 sq. ft.
Dimensions 85'x53'4"
Foundation Basement
Bedrooms 4
Full Baths 3
Half Baths 1
Max Ridge Height 35'
Roof Framing Stick
Exterior Walls 2x6

*This plan is not to be built within a 75-mile radius of Cedar Rapids, IA.

Please note: The photographed home may have been modified to suit homeowner preferences. If you order plans, have a builder or design professional check them against the photograph to confirm actual construction details.

Design 94226

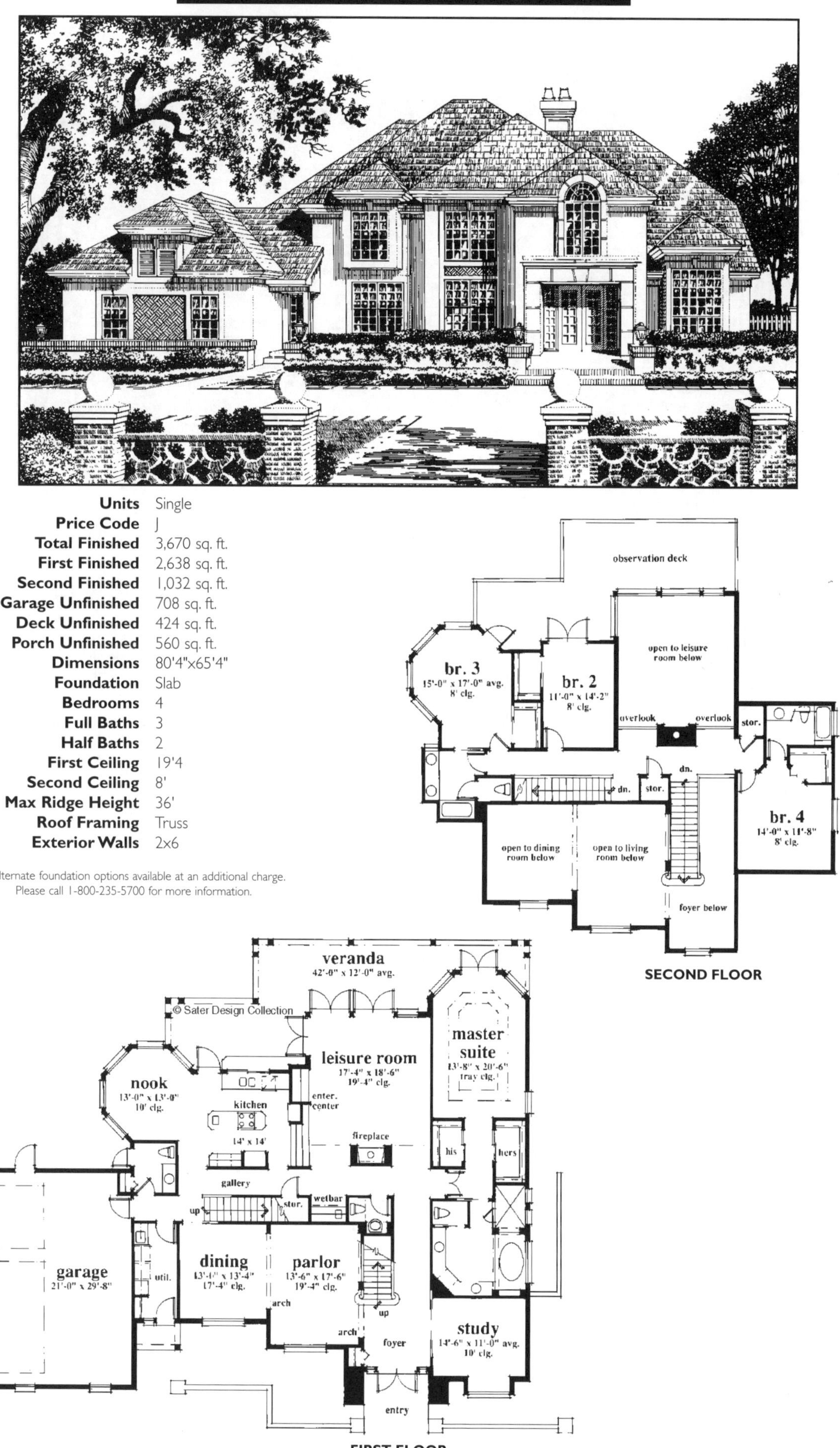
observation deck
br. 3
15'-0" x 17'-0" avg.
8' clg.
br. 2
11'-0" x 14'-2"
8' clg.
open to leisure room below
overlook
overlook
stor.
dn.
dn.
stor.
br. 4
14'-0" x 11'-8"
8' clg.
open to dining room below
open to living room below
foyer below
SECOND FLOOR
veranda
42'-0" x 12'-0" avg.
© Sater Design Collection
leisure room
17'-4" x 18'-6"
19'-4" clg.
master suite
13'-8" x 20'-6"
tray clg.
nook
13'-0" x 13'-0"
10' clg.
kitchen
14' x 14'
enter. center
fireplace
his
hers
gallery
up
stor.
wetbar
garage
21'-0" x 29'-8"
util.
dining
13'-4" x 13'-4"
17'-4" clg.
parlor
13'-6" x 17'-6"
19'-4" clg.
arch
arch
up
foyer
study
14'-6" x 11'-0" avg.
10' clg.
entry
FIRST FLOOR

Units	Single
Price Code	J
Total Finished	3,670 sq. ft.
First Finished	2,638 sq. ft.
Second Finished	1,032 sq. ft.
Garage Unfinished	708 sq. ft.
Deck Unfinished	424 sq. ft.
Porch Unfinished	560 sq. ft.
Dimensions	80'4"x65'4"
Foundation	Slab
Bedrooms	4
Full Baths	3
Half Baths	2
First Ceiling	19'4
Second Ceiling	8'
Max Ridge Height	36'
Roof Framing	Truss
Exterior Walls	2x6

* Alternate foundation options available at an additional charge. Please call 1-800-235-5700 for more information.

Design 97360

Units	Single
Price Code	J
Total Finished	3,677 sq. ft.
Main Finished	2,260 sq. ft.
Lower Finished	1,417 sq. ft.
Dimensions	83'8"x60'8"
Foundation	Crawlspace
Bedrooms	4
Full Baths	3
Main Ceiling	9'
Max Ridge Height	29'1"
Roof Framing	Truss
Exterior Walls	2x6

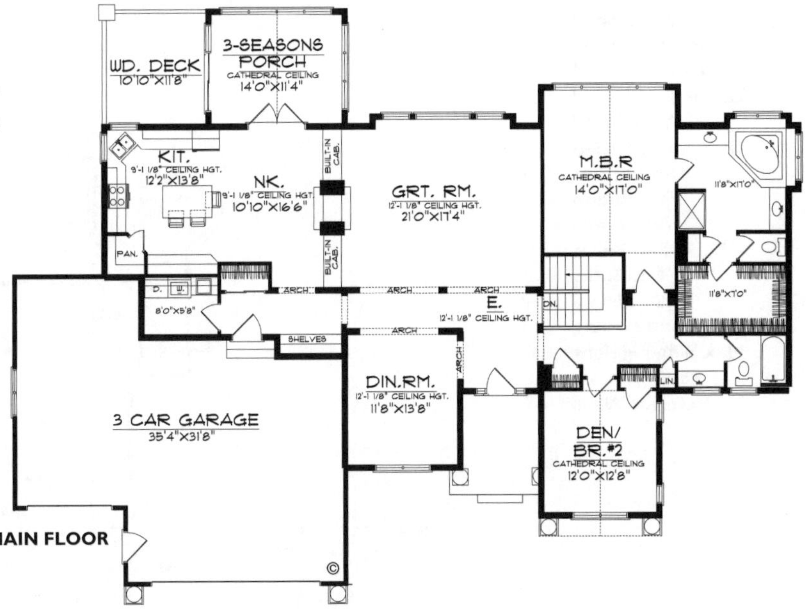

WD. DECK 10'10"X11'8"
3-SEASONS PORCH CATHEDRAL CEILING 14'0"X11'4"
KIT. 9'-1 1/8" CEILING HGT. 12'2"X13'8"
NK. 9'-1 1/8" CEILING HGT. 10'10"X16'6"
GRT. RM. 12'-1 1/8" CEILING HGT. 21'0"X17'4"
M.B.R CATHEDRAL CEILING 14'0"X17'0"
11'8"X17'0"
11'8"X7'0"
E. 12'-1 1/8" CEILING HGT.
8'0"X9'8"
DIN.RM. 12'-1 1/8" CEILING HGT. 11'8"X13'8"
DEN/ BR.#2 CATHEDRAL CEILING 12'0"X12'8"
3 CAR GARAGE 35'4"X31'8"

MAIN FLOOR

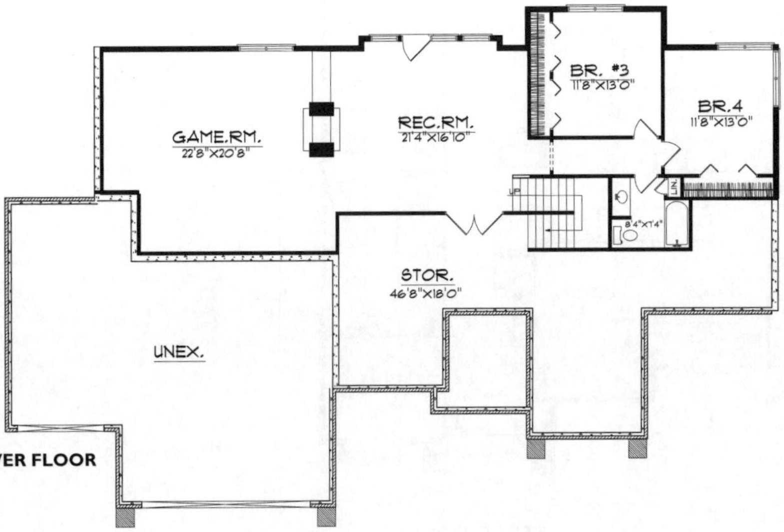

GAME.RM. 22'8"X20'8"
REC.RM. 21'4"X16'10"
BR. #3 11'8"X13'0"
BR.4 11'8"X13'0"
8'4"X7'4"
STOR. 46'8"X18'0"
UNEX.

LOWER FLOOR

Design 97199

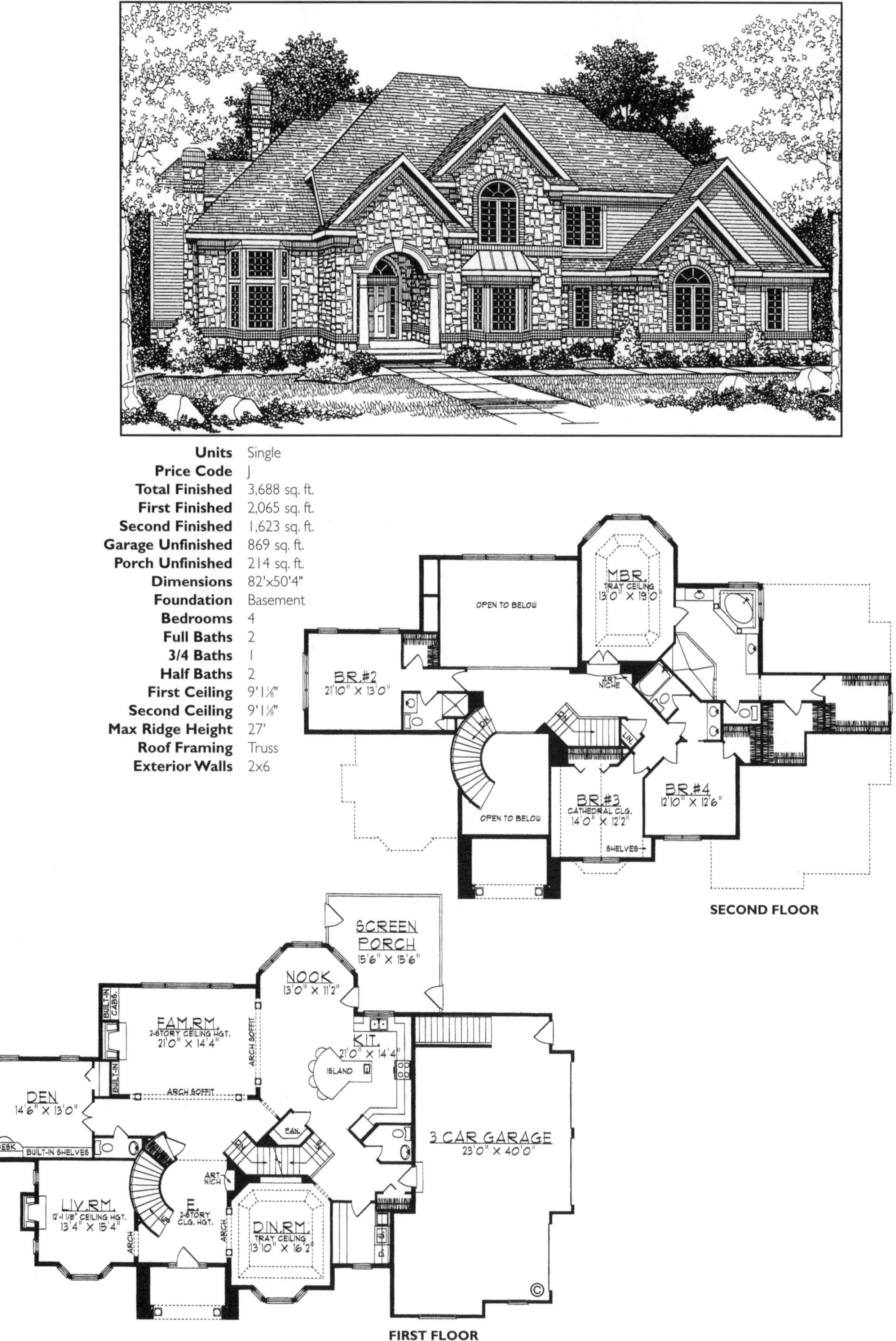
MBR.
TRAY CEILING
13'0" X 19'0"
OPEN TO BELOW
BR.#2
21'10" X 13'0"
ART NICHE
BR.#3
CATHEDRAL CLG.
14'0" X 12'2"
BR.#4
12'10" X 12'6"
SHELVES
OPEN TO BELOW
SECOND FLOOR
SCREEN PORCH
15'6" X 15'6"
NOOK
13'0" X 11'2"
FAM.RM.
2-STORY CEILING HGT.
21'0" X 14'4"
BUILT-IN CABS.
ARCH SOFFIT
KIT.
21'0" X 14'4"
ISLAND
DEN
14'6" X 13'0"
DESK
BUILT-IN SHELVES
3 CAR GARAGE
23'0" X 40'0"
LIV.RM.
12'-1 1/8" CEILING HGT.
13'4" X 15'4"
E.
2-STORY CLG. HGT.
ART NICH
DIN.RM.
TRAY CEILING
13'10" X 16'2"
FIRST FLOOR

Units	Single
Price Code	J
Total Finished	3,688 sq. ft.
First Finished	2,065 sq. ft.
Second Finished	1,623 sq. ft.
Garage Unfinished	869 sq. ft.
Porch Unfinished	214 sq. ft.
Dimensions	82'x50'4"
Foundation	Basement
Bedrooms	4
Full Baths	2
3/4 Baths	1
Half Baths	2
First Ceiling	9'1 1/8"
Second Ceiling	9'1 1/8"
Max Ridge Height	27'
Roof Framing	Truss
Exterior Walls	2x6

Design 99464

SEAT
Br. 4
12⁰x15⁵
10'-0" CEILING
Br. 2
13⁰x17⁴
LINEN
9'-0" CLG.
Br. 3
14⁰x13⁰
OPEN TO BELOW
PLANT SHELF
TRANS.

SECOND FLOOR

Units	Single
Price Code	J
Total Finished	3,689 sq. ft.
First Finished	2,617 sq. ft.
Second Finished	1,072 sq. ft.
Basement Unfinished	2,617 sq. ft.
Garage Unfinished	1,035 sq. ft.
Dimensions	83'5"x73'4"
Foundation	Basement
Bedrooms	4
Full Baths	2
3/4 Baths	2
Half Baths	1
Max Ridge Height	30'5"
Roof Framing	Stick
Exterior Walls	2x4

* Alternate foundation options available at an additional charge. Please call 1-800-235-5700 for more information.

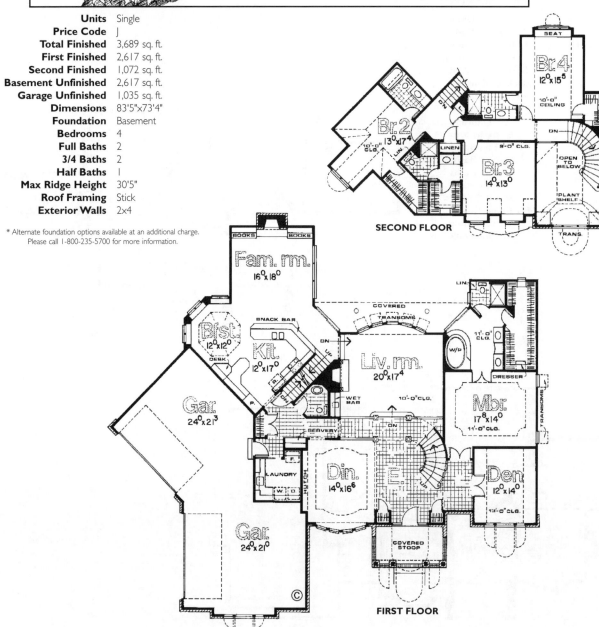

FIRST FLOOR

Design 32332

PHOTOGRAPHY: JAMES YOCHUM PHOTOGRAPHY
BEDROOM 12x13
OPEN TO LIVING
BEDROOM 12x14
LOFT 19x14
DN
BATH
LOFT 11x16
BUNK RM 12x15
CLOSET
SECOND FLOOR
COVERED PATIO
BEDROOM 12x15
MASTER BEDROOM 11x12
DEN 11x12
HALL
UP
W
D
BUNK RM 10x9
MECH
UNEXCAVATED
LOWER FLOOR
COVERED DECK
FOUR-SEASON PORCH 12x15
LIVING 23x15
KITCHEN 12x14
O
R
UP
DINING 16x14
DN
ENTRY
GARAGE 23x22
FIRST FLOOR

Units	Single
Price Code	E
Total Finished	3,705 sq. ft.
First Finished	1,311 sq. ft.
Second Finished	1,214 sq. ft.
Lower Finished	1,180 sq. ft.
Garage Unfinished	553 sq. ft.
Deck Unfinished	346 sq. ft.
Porch Unfinished	180 sq. ft.
Dimensions	38'8"x70'9"
Foundation	Basement
Bedrooms	6
Full Baths	1
3/4 Baths	2
Half Baths	1
First Ceiling	9'
Second Ceiling	8'
Max Ridge Height	35'8"
Exterior Walls	2x6

Please note: The photographed home may have been modified to suit homeowner preferences. If you order plans, have a builder or design professional check them against the photograph to confirm actual construction details.

Design 32095

PHOTOGRAPHY: STEPHEN CRIDLAND

Units	Single
Price Code	J
Total Finished	3,718 sq. ft.
First Finished	2,530 sq. ft.
Second Finished	1,188 sq. ft.
Bonus Unfinished	507 sq. ft.
Basement Unfinished	213 sq. ft.
Garage Unfinished	1,039 sq. ft.
Porch Unfinished	972 sq. ft.
Dimensions	95'x119'
Foundation	Combo Basement/ Crawlspace
Bedrooms	4
Full Baths	3
3/4 Baths	1
Half Baths	1
First Ceiling	9'
Second Ceiling	8'
Vaulted Ceiling	19'
Max Ridge Height	33'
Roof Framing	Stick
Exterior Walls	2x6

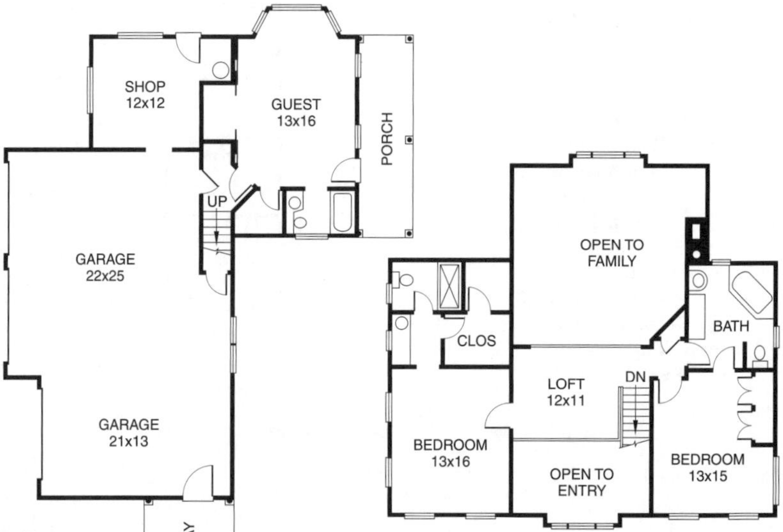

SHOP 12x12
GUEST 13x16
PORCH
UP
GARAGE 22x25
GARAGE 21x13
BREEZEWAY

Please note: The photographed home may have been modified to suit homeowner preferences. If you order plans, have a builder or design professional check them against the photograph to confirm actual construction details.

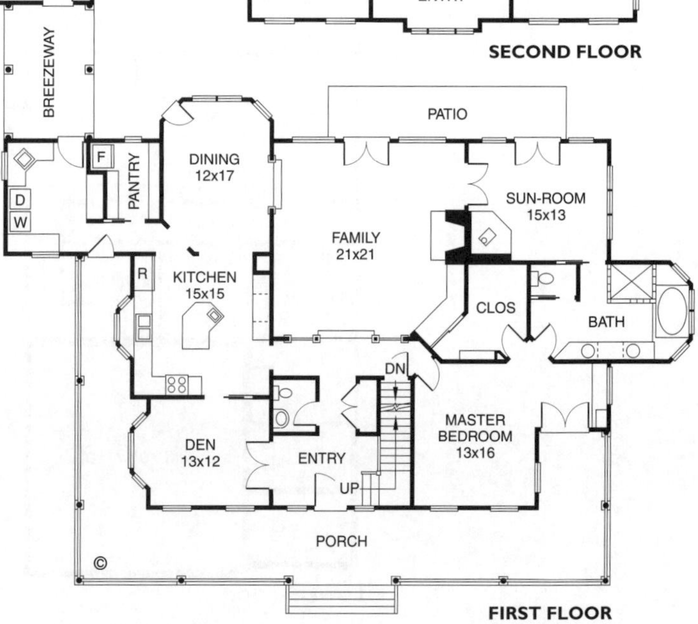

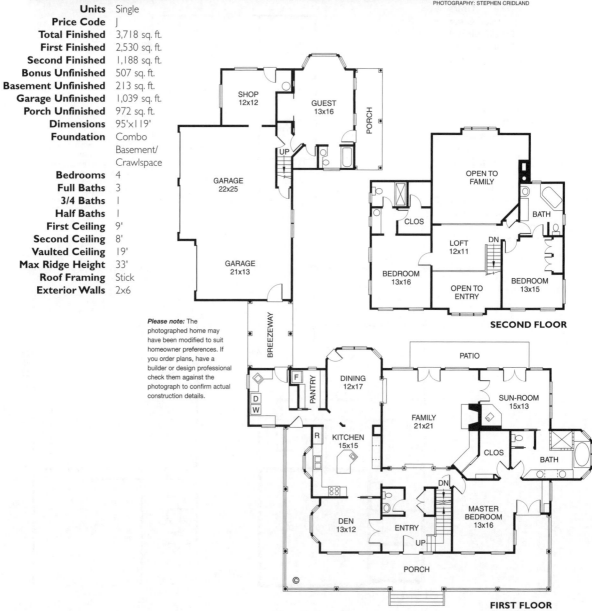

OPEN TO FAMILY
CLOS
BATH
LOFT 12x11
DN
BEDROOM 13x16
OPEN TO ENTRY
BEDROOM 13x15

SECOND FLOOR

PATIO
F
PANTRY
DINING 12x17
D
W
FAMILY 21x21
SUN-ROOM 15x13
R
KITCHEN 15x15
CLOS
BATH
DN
DEN 13x12
ENTRY
UP
MASTER BEDROOM 13x16
PORCH
©

FIRST FLOOR

Design 32337

PHOTOGRAPHY: JAMES YOCHUM PHOTOGRAPHY

Units	Single
Price Code	E
Total Finished	3,756 sq. ft.
First Finished	2,038 sq. ft.
Second Finished	1,718 sq. ft.
Basement Unfinished	1,629 sq. ft.
Porch Unfinished	144 sq. ft.
Dimensions	52'x59'4"
Foundation	Basement
Bedrooms	4
Full Baths	2
Half Baths	2
First Ceiling	9'
Second Ceiling	8'
Vaulted Ceiling	18'
Max Ridge Height	34'-6"
Roof Framing	Stick
Exterior Walls	2x4

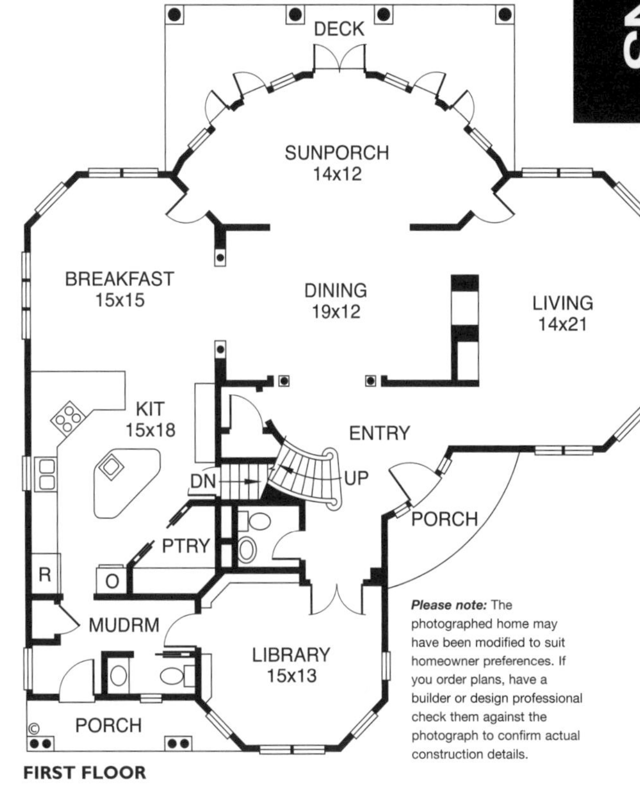
DECK
SUNPORCH
14x12
BREAKFAST
15x15
DINING
19x12
LIVING
14x21
KIT
15x18
ENTRY
DN
UP
PTRY
PORCH
R
O
MUDRM
LIBRARY
15x13
PORCH

FIRST FLOOR

Please note: The photographed home may have been modified to suit homeowner preferences. If you order plans, have a builder or design professional check them against the photograph to confirm actual construction details.

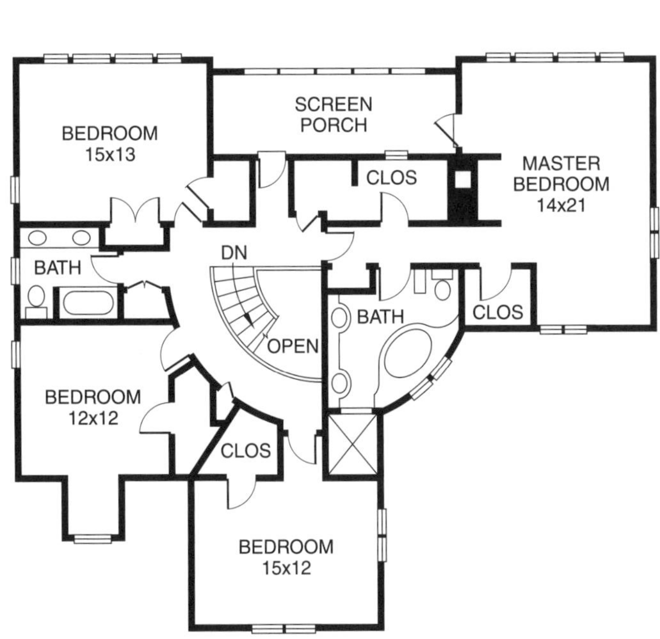
BEDROOM
15x13
SCREEN
PORCH
CLOS
MASTER
BEDROOM
14x21
DN
BATH
BATH
CLOS
OPEN
BEDROOM
12x12
CLOS
BEDROOM
15x12

SECOND FLOOR

Design 99443

Units	Single
Price Code	K
Total Finished	3,775 sq. ft.
First Finished	1,923 sq. ft.
Second Finished	1,852 sq. ft.
Basement Unfinished	1,923 sq. ft.
Garage Unfinished	726 sq. ft.
Dimensions	70'x60'
Foundation	Basement
Bedrooms	4
Full Baths	2
3/4 Baths	1
Half Baths	1
Max Ridge Height	34'
Roof Framing	Stick
Exterior Walls	2x4

* Alternate foundation options available at an additional charge.
Please call 1-800-235-5700 for more information.

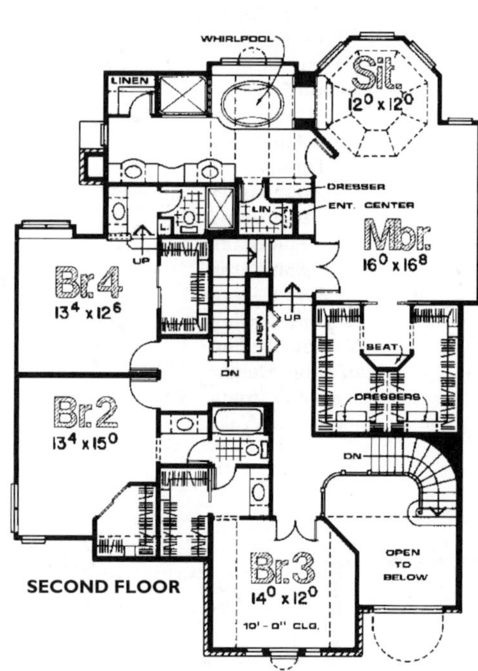

WHIRLPOOL
LINEN
Sit.
12^{0} x 12^{0}
DRESSER
ENT. CENTER
LIN
Mbr.
16^{0} x 16^{8}
UP
Br. 4
13^{4} x 12^{6}
LINEN
UP
SEAT
DN
Br. 2
13^{4} x 15^{0}
DRESSERS
DN
Br. 3
14^{0} x 12^{0}
10' - 0" CLG.
OPEN TO BELOW

SECOND FLOOR

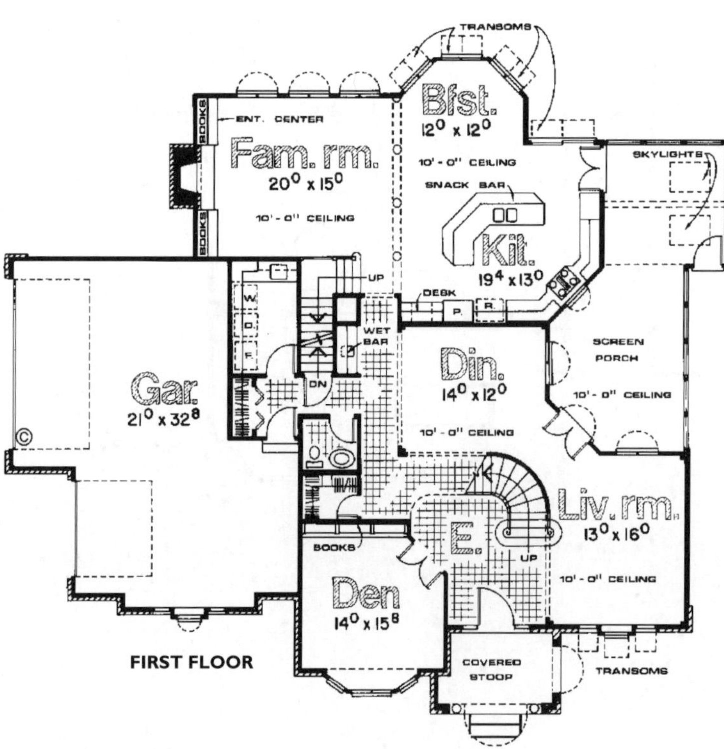

TRANSOMS
ENT. CENTER
BOOKS
Fam. rm.
20^{0} x 15^{0}
10' - 0" CEILING
BOOKS
Bfst.
12^{0} x 12^{0}
10' - 0" CEILING
SNACK BAR
SKYLIGHTS
Kit.
19^{4} x 13^{0}
UP
DESK
P.
R.
W.
D.
F.
WET BAR
DN
Gar.
21^{0} x 32^{8}
Din.
14^{0} x 12^{0}
10' - 0" CEILING
SCREEN PORCH
10' - 0" CEILING
Liv. rm.
13^{0} x 16^{0}
10' - 0" CEILING
BOOKS
E.
UP
Den
14^{0} x 15^{8}
COVERED STOOP
TRANSOMS

FIRST FLOOR

Design 32004

PHOTOGRAPHY: RICK TAYLOR

Units	Single
Price Code	K
Total Finished	3,782 sq. ft.
First Finished	2,356 sq. ft.
Second Finished	1,426 sq. ft.
Basement Unfinished	2,356 sq. ft.
Garage Unfinished	645 sq. ft.
Dimensions	102'4"x52'
Foundation	Basement
Bedrooms	4
Full Baths	3
Half Baths	1
First Ceiling	9'
Second Ceiling	8'
Max Ridge Height	34'
Roof Framing	Stick
Exterior Walls	2x4

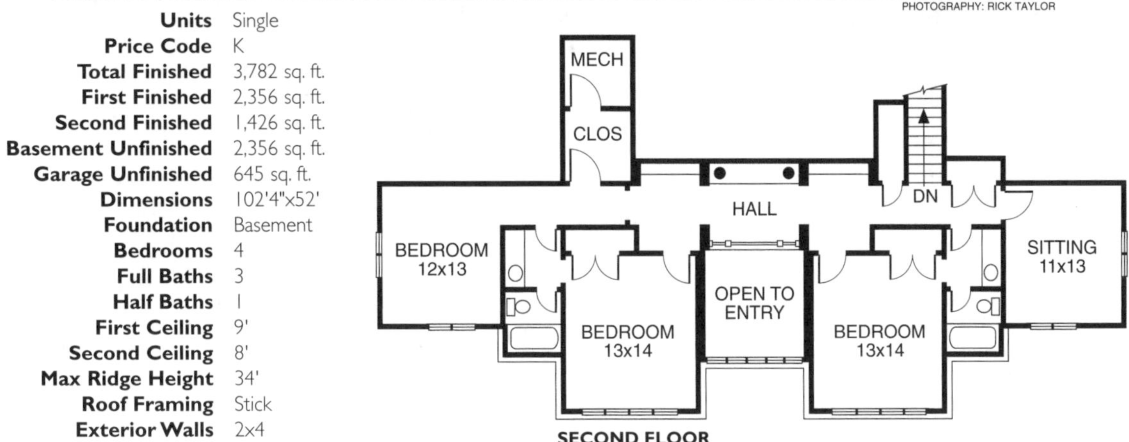
MECH
CLOS
HALL
DN
BEDROOM 12x13
BEDROOM 13x14
OPEN TO ENTRY
BEDROOM 13x14
SITTING 11x13

SECOND FLOOR

Please note: The photographed home may have been modified to suit homeowner preferences. If you order plans, have a builder or design professional check them against the photograph to confirm actual construction details.

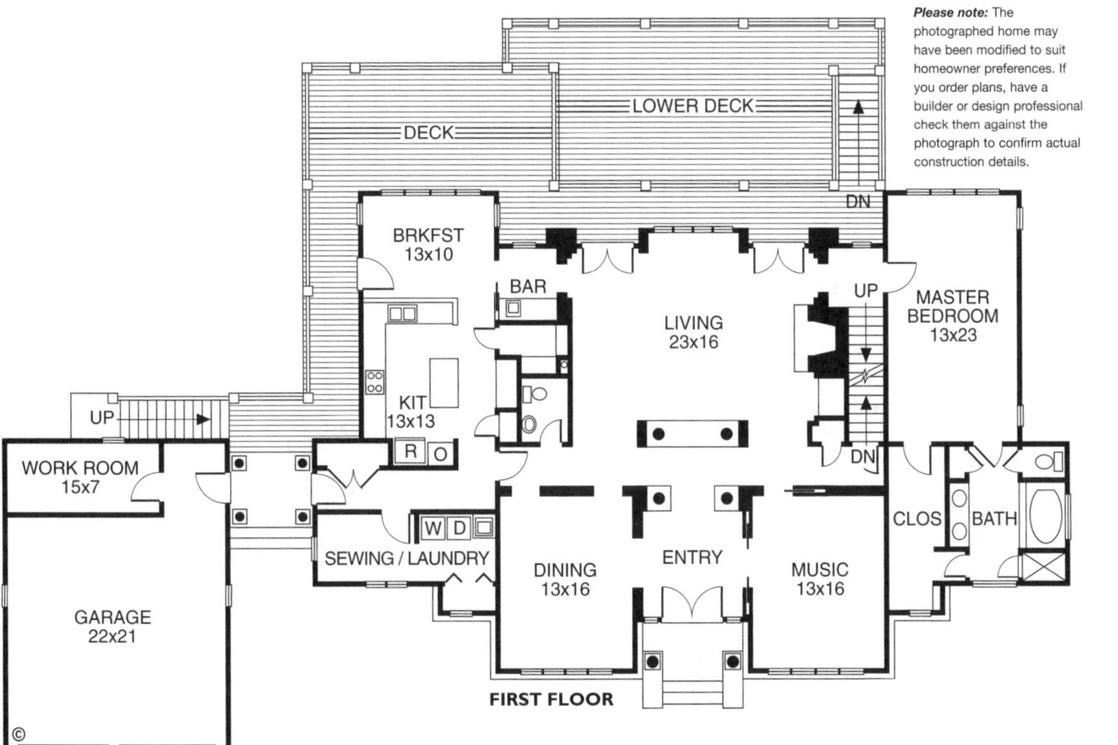
LOWER DECK
DECK
DN
BRKFST 13x10
BAR
LIVING 23x16
UP
MASTER BEDROOM 13x23
KIT 13x13
R
UP
WORK ROOM 15x7
DN
W D
CLOS
BATH
SEWING / LAUNDRY
DINING 13x16
ENTRY
MUSIC 13x16
GARAGE 22x21
©

FIRST FLOOR

Design 92237

Units	Single
Price Code	K
Total Finished	3,783 sq. ft.
First Finished	2,804 sq. ft.
Second Finished	979 sq. ft.
Basement Unfinished	2,804 sq. ft.
Garage Unfinished	802 sq. ft.
Dimensions	98'x45'10"
Foundation	Basement Slab
Bedrooms	4
Full Baths	2
3/4 Baths	1
Half Baths	1
Max Ridge Height	32'
Roof Framing	Stick
Exterior Walls	2x4

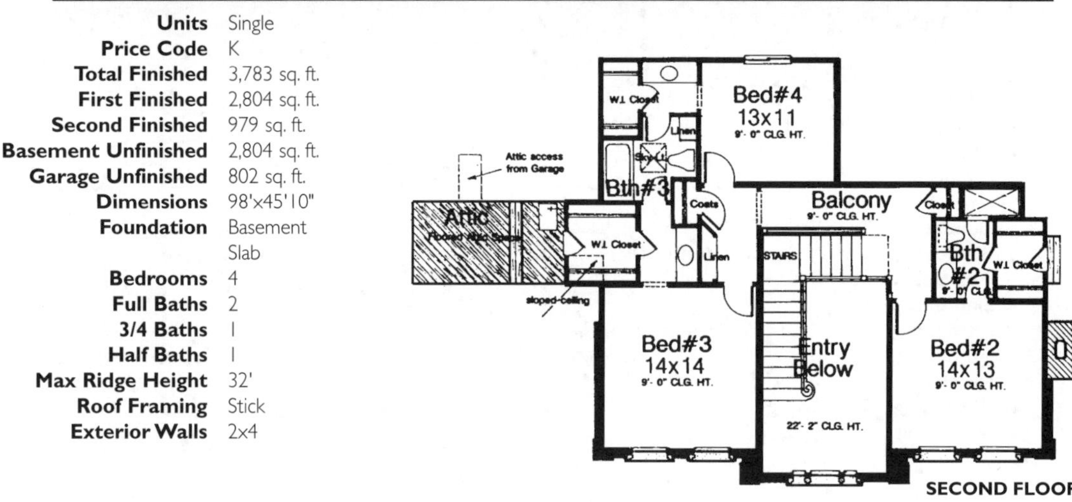
Bed#4
13x11
9'- 0" CLG. HT.
W.I. Closet
Linen
Attic access from Garage
Bth#3
Coats
Attic
W.I. Closet
Linen
sloped-ceiling
Balcony
9'- 0" CLG. HT.
Closet
STAIRS
Bth #2
W.I. Closet
Bed#3
14x14
9'- 0" CLG. HT.
Entry Below
22'- 2" CLG. HT.
Bed#2
14x13
9'- 0" CLG. HT.
SECOND FLOOR

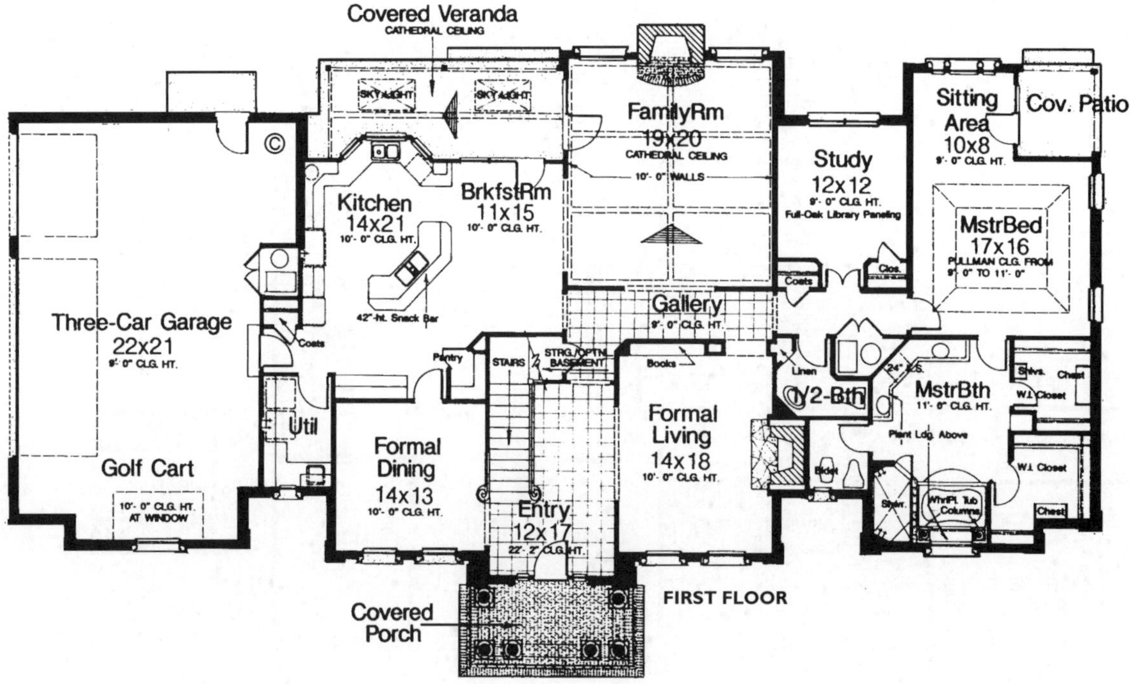
Covered Veranda
CATHEDRAL CEILING
SKYLIGHT
SKYLIGHT
FamilyRm
19x20
CATHEDRAL CEILING
10'- 0" WALLS
Sitting Area
10x8
9'- 0" CLG. HT.
Cov. Patio
Study
12x12
9'- 0" CLG. HT.
Full-Oak Library Paneling
MstrBed
17x16
PULLMAN CLG. FROM 9'- 0" TO 11'- 0"
Kitchen
14x21
10'- 0" CLG. HT.
BrkfstRm
11x15
10'- 0" CLG. HT.
42"-ht. Snack Bar
Coats
Clos.
Gallery
9'- 0" CLG. HT.
Three-Car Garage
22x21
9'- 0" CLG. HT.
Coats
Pantry
STAIRS
STRG./OPTN. BASEMENT
Books
Linen
1/2-Bth
MstrBth
11'- 0" CLG. HT.
Plant Ldg. Above
W.I. Closet
W.I. Closet
Chest
Util
Formal Dining
14x13
10'- 0" CLG. HT.
Formal Living
14x18
10'- 0" CLG. HT.
Golf Cart
10'- 0" CLG. HT. AT WINDOW
Entry
12x17
22'- 2" CLG. HT.
Whrlpl. Tub Columns
Chest
Covered Porch
FIRST FLOOR

Design 92166

Units	Single
Price Code	K
Total Finished	3,784 sq. ft.
First Finished	1,668 sq. ft.
Second Finished	2,116 sq. ft.
Basement Unfinished	911 sq. ft.
Garage Unfinished	884 sq. ft.
Dimensions	107x45'
Foundation	Combo Basement/ Crawlspace
Bedrooms	3
Full Baths	2
3/4 Baths	1
Half Baths	2
First Ceiling	9'
Second Ceiling	9'
Max Ridge Height	33.5"
Roof Framing	Stick/Truss
Exterior Walls	2x6

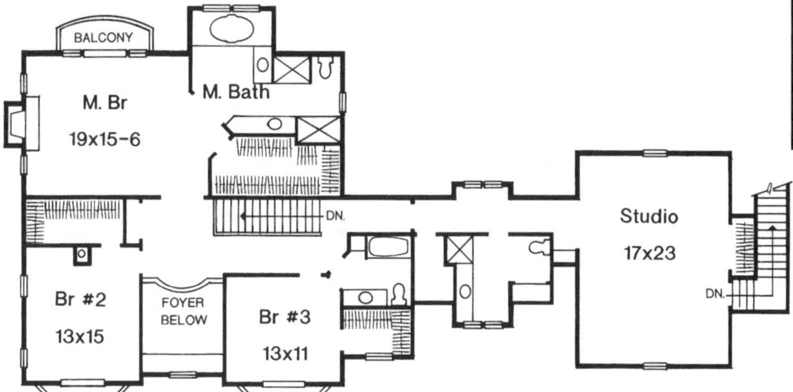

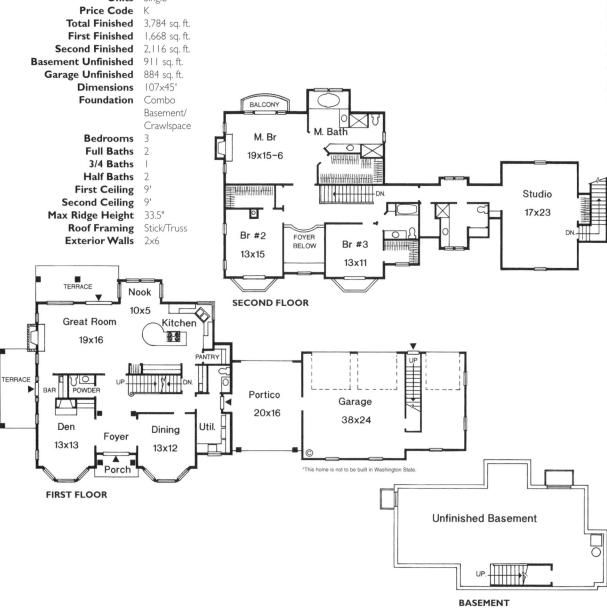

BALCONY
M. Br 19x15-6
M. Bath
DN.
Studio 17x23
DN.
Br #2 13x15
FOYER BELOW
Br #3 13x11

SECOND FLOOR

TERRACE
Nook 10x5
Great Room 19x16
Kitchen
PANTRY
TERRACE
BAR
POWDER
UP.
DN.
Portico 20x16
Garage 38x24
UP
Den 13x13
Foyer
Dining 13x12
Util.
Porch

FIRST FLOOR

*This home is not to be built in Washington State.

Unfinished Basement
UP.

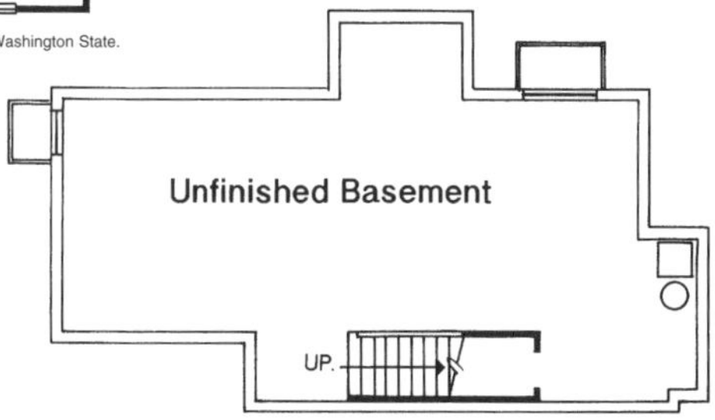

BASEMENT

Design 94246

Units Single
Price Code K
Total Finished 3,792 sq. ft.
First Finished 2,853 sq. ft.
Second Finished 627 sq. ft.
Guest House Finished 312 sq. ft.
Garage Unfinished 777 sq. ft.
Deck Unfinished 540 sq. ft.
Porch Unfinished 326 sq. ft.
Dimensions 80'x96'
Foundation Slab
Bedrooms 4
Full Baths 3
Half Baths 1
First Ceiling 10'
Second Ceiling 9'4"
Vaulted Ceiling 17'8"
Max Ridge Height 31'
Roof Framing Truss

* Alternate foundation options available at an additional charge. Please call 1-800-235-5700 for more information.

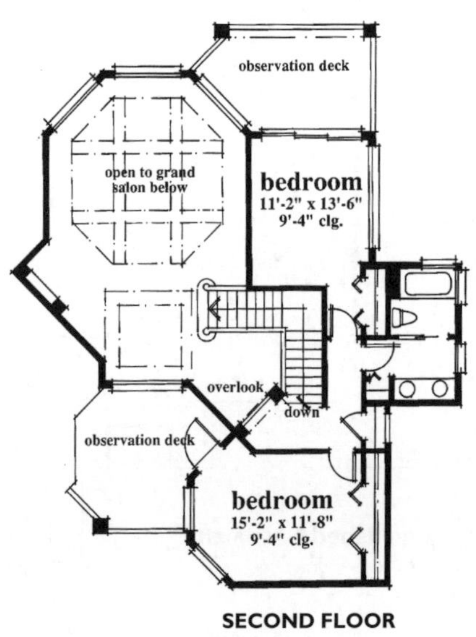

observation deck
open to grand salon below
bedroom
11'-2" x 13'-6"
9'-4" clg.
overlook
down
observation deck
bedroom
15'-2" x 11'-8"
9'-4" clg.

SECOND FLOOR

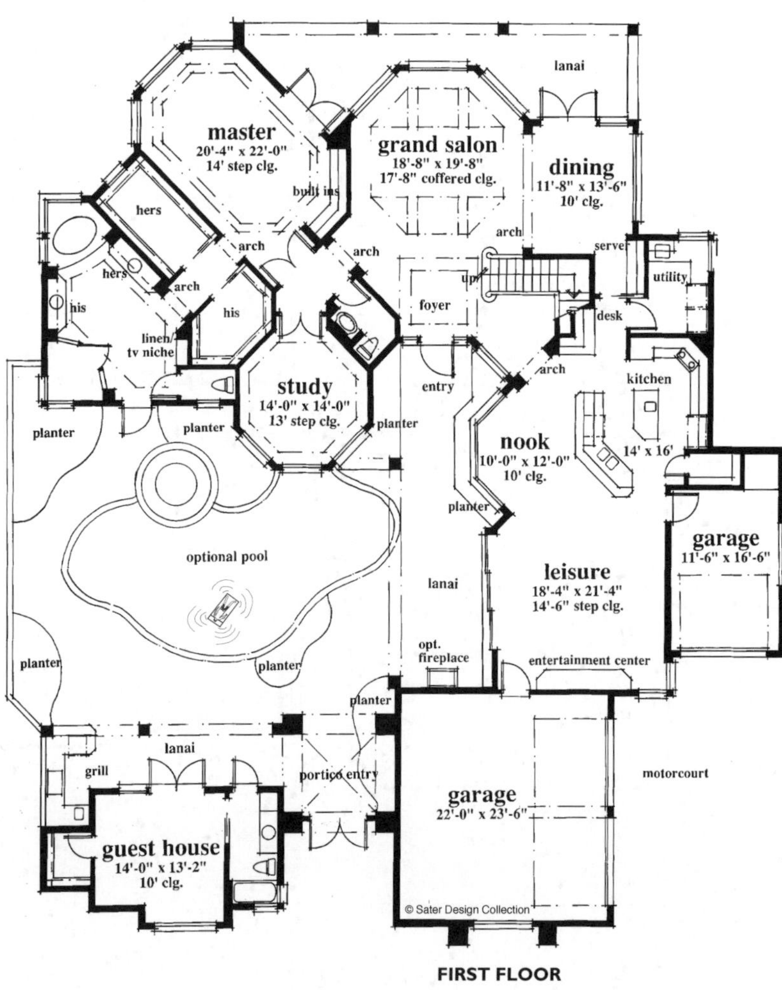

lanai
master
20'-4" x 22'-0"
14' step clg.
grand salon
18'-8" x 19'-8"
17'-8" coffered clg.
dining
11'-8" x 13'-6"
10' clg.
built ins
hers
hers
his
arch
arch
arch
arch
up
server
utility
foyer
desk
his
linen/
tv niche
study
14'-0" x 14'-0"
13' step clg.
entry
arch
kitchen
planter
planter
planter
nook
10'-0" x 12'-0"
10' clg.
14' x 16'
planter
optional pool
garage
11'-6" x 16'-6"
leisure
18'-4" x 21'-4"
14'-6" step clg.
lanai
planter
planter
opt.
fireplace
entertainment center
planter
lanai
grill
portico entry
garage
22'-0" x 23'-6"
motorcourt
guest house
14'-0" x 13'-2"
10' clg.
© Sater Design Collection

FIRST FLOOR

Design 69004

Units	Single
Price Code	K
Total Finished	3,814 sq. ft.
Main Finished	3,566 sq. ft.
Lower Finished	248 sq. ft.
Dimensions	88'x70'8"
Foundation	Basement
Bedrooms	3
Full Baths	2
Half Baths	1

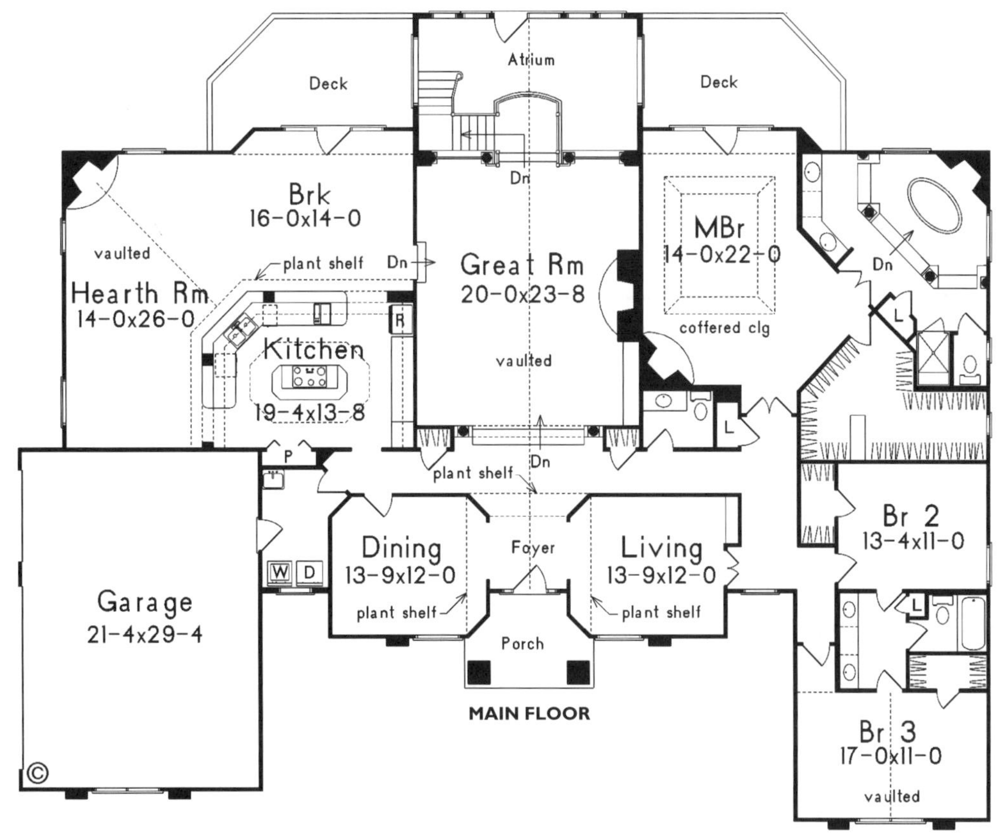
Atrium
Deck
Deck
Brk
16-0x14-0
Dn
vaulted
plant shelf
Dn
Great Rm
20-0x23-8
MBr
14-0x22-0
Dn
Hearth Rm
14-0x26-0
Kitchen
19-4x13-8
R
vaulted
coffered clg
L
L
P
plant shelf
Dn
Br 2
13-4x11-0
Dining
13-9x12-0
Foyer
Living
13-9x12-0
W
D
Garage
21-4x29-4
plant shelf
plant shelf
L
Porch
MAIN FLOOR
Br 3
17-0x11-0
vaulted
©

Design 69008

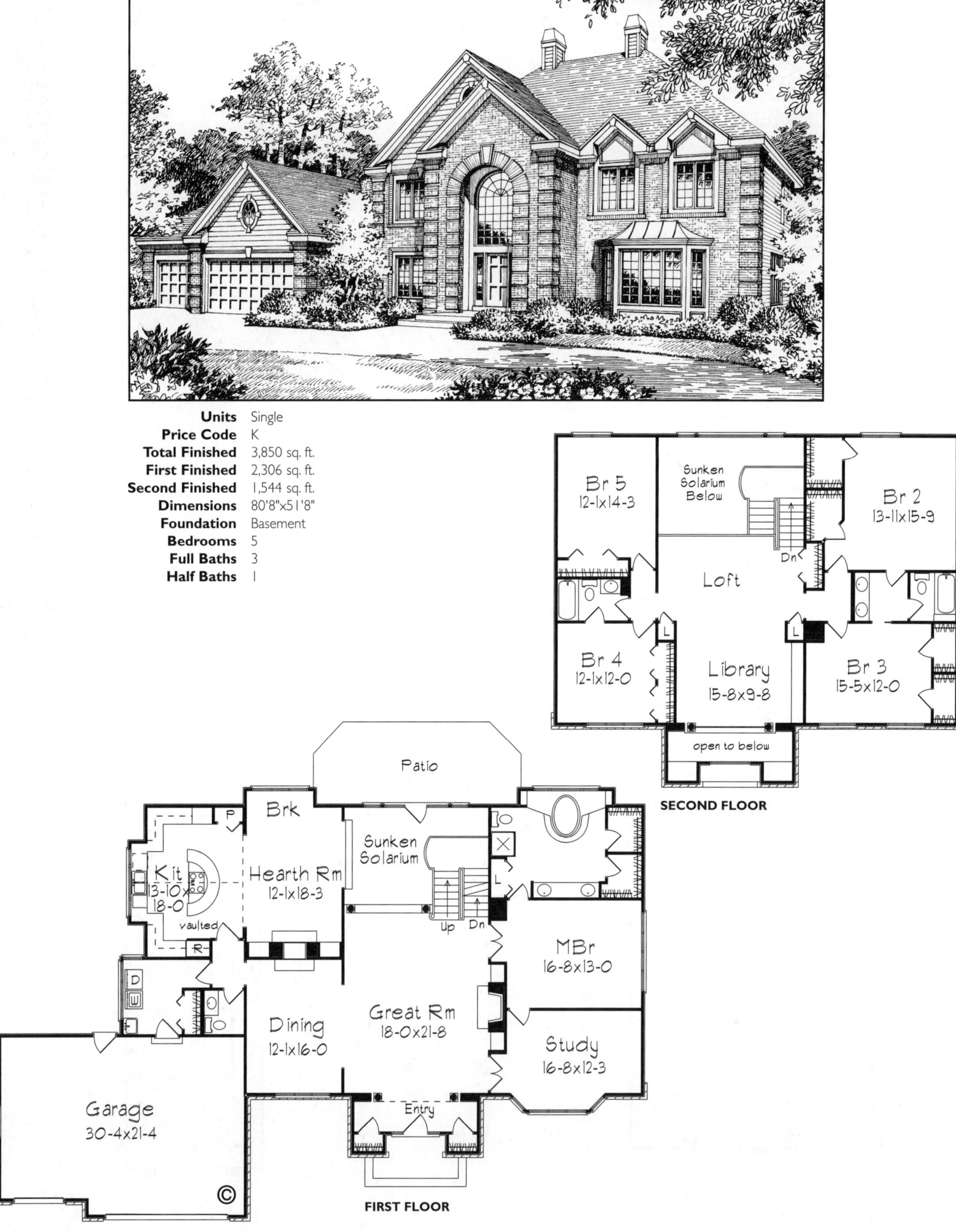

Br 5
12-1x14-3
Sunken
Solarium
Below
Br 2
13-11x15-9
Dn
Loft
L
L
Br 4
12-1x12-0
Library
15-8x9-8
Br 3
15-5x12-0
open to below
SECOND FLOOR
Patio
Brk
P
Kit
13-10x
18-0
Hearth Rm
12-1x18-3
Sunken
Solarium
L
vaulted
R
Up
Dn
MBr
16-8x13-0
D
W
Dining
12-1x16-0
Great Rm
18-0x21-8
Study
16-8x12-3
Garage
30-4x21-4
Entry
©
FIRST FLOOR

Units	Single
Price Code	K
Total Finished	3,850 sq. ft.
First Finished	2,306 sq. ft.
Second Finished	1,544 sq. ft.
Dimensions	80'8"x51'8"
Foundation	Basement
Bedrooms	5
Full Baths	3
Half Baths	1

Design 32102

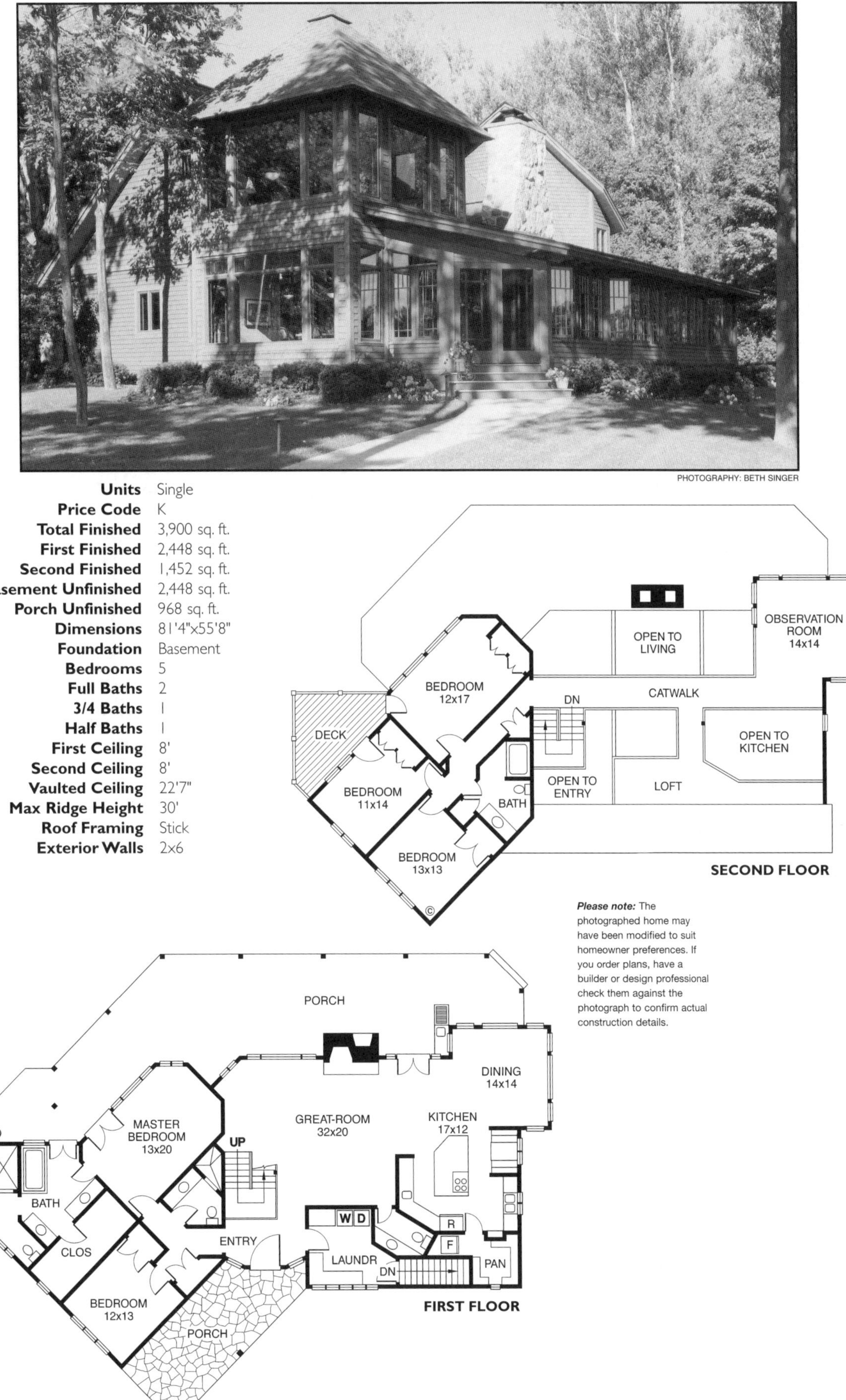
SECOND FLOOR
OBSERVATION ROOM 14x14
OPEN TO LIVING
CATWALK
DN
BEDROOM 12x17
DECK
BEDROOM 11x14
OPEN TO ENTRY
LOFT
OPEN TO KITCHEN
BATH
BEDROOM 13x13
FIRST FLOOR
PORCH
DINING 14x14
GREAT-ROOM 32x20
KITCHEN 17x12
MASTER BEDROOM 13x20
UP
BATH
CLOS
W
D
R
F
ENTRY
LAUNDR
DN
PAN
BEDROOM 12x13
PORCH

PHOTOGRAPHY: BETH SINGER

Units	Single
Price Code	K
Total Finished	3,900 sq. ft.
First Finished	2,448 sq. ft.
Second Finished	1,452 sq. ft.
Basement Unfinished	2,448 sq. ft.
Porch Unfinished	968 sq. ft.
Dimensions	81'4"x55'8"
Foundation	Basement
Bedrooms	5
Full Baths	2
3/4 Baths	1
Half Baths	1
First Ceiling	8'
Second Ceiling	8'
Vaulted Ceiling	22'7"
Max Ridge Height	30'
Roof Framing	Stick
Exterior Walls	2x6

Please note: The photographed home may have been modified to suit homeowner preferences. If you order plans, have a builder or design professional check them against the photograph to confirm actual construction details.

Design 69150

Units	Single
Price Code	K
Total Finished	3,922 sq. ft.
First Finished	2,678 sq. ft.
Second Finished	1,244 sq. ft.
Basement Unfinished	958 sq. ft.
Dimensions	74'x62'
Foundation	Crawlspace
Bedrooms	4
Full Baths	2
3/4 Baths	1
Half Baths	1
First Ceiling	10'
Second Ceiling	8'
Vaulted Ceiling	14'
Max Ridge Height	31'2"
Roof Framing	Truss
Exterior Walls	2x6

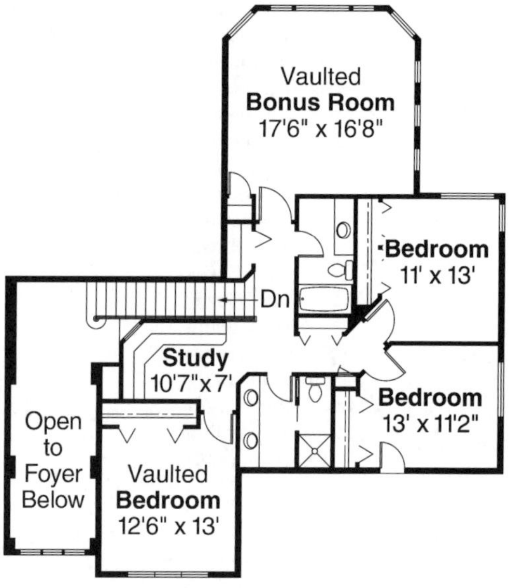

Vaulted **Bonus Room** 17'6" x 16'8"

Bedroom 11' x 13'

Dn

Study 10'7"x7'

Bedroom 13' x 11'2"

Open to Foyer Below

Vaulted **Bedroom** 12'6" x 13'

SECOND FLOOR

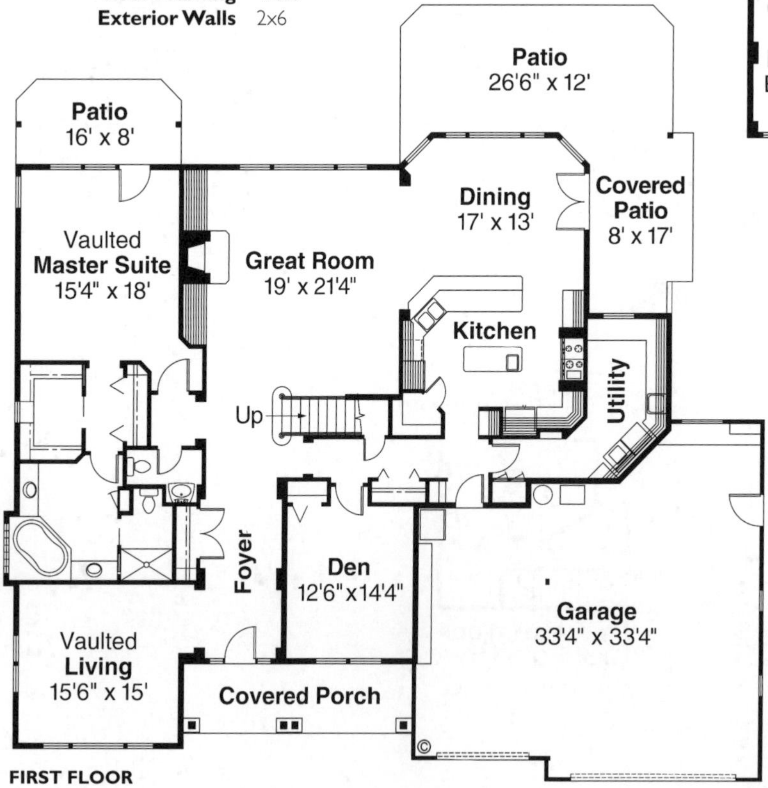

Patio 26'6" x 12'

Patio 16' x 8'

Dining 17' x 13'

Covered Patio 8' x 17'

Vaulted **Master Suite** 15'4" x 18'

Great Room 19' x 21'4"

Kitchen

Up

Utility

Foyer

Den 12'6"x14'4"

Garage 33'4" x 33'4"

Vaulted **Living** 15'6" x 15'

Covered Porch

FIRST FLOOR

Design 98539

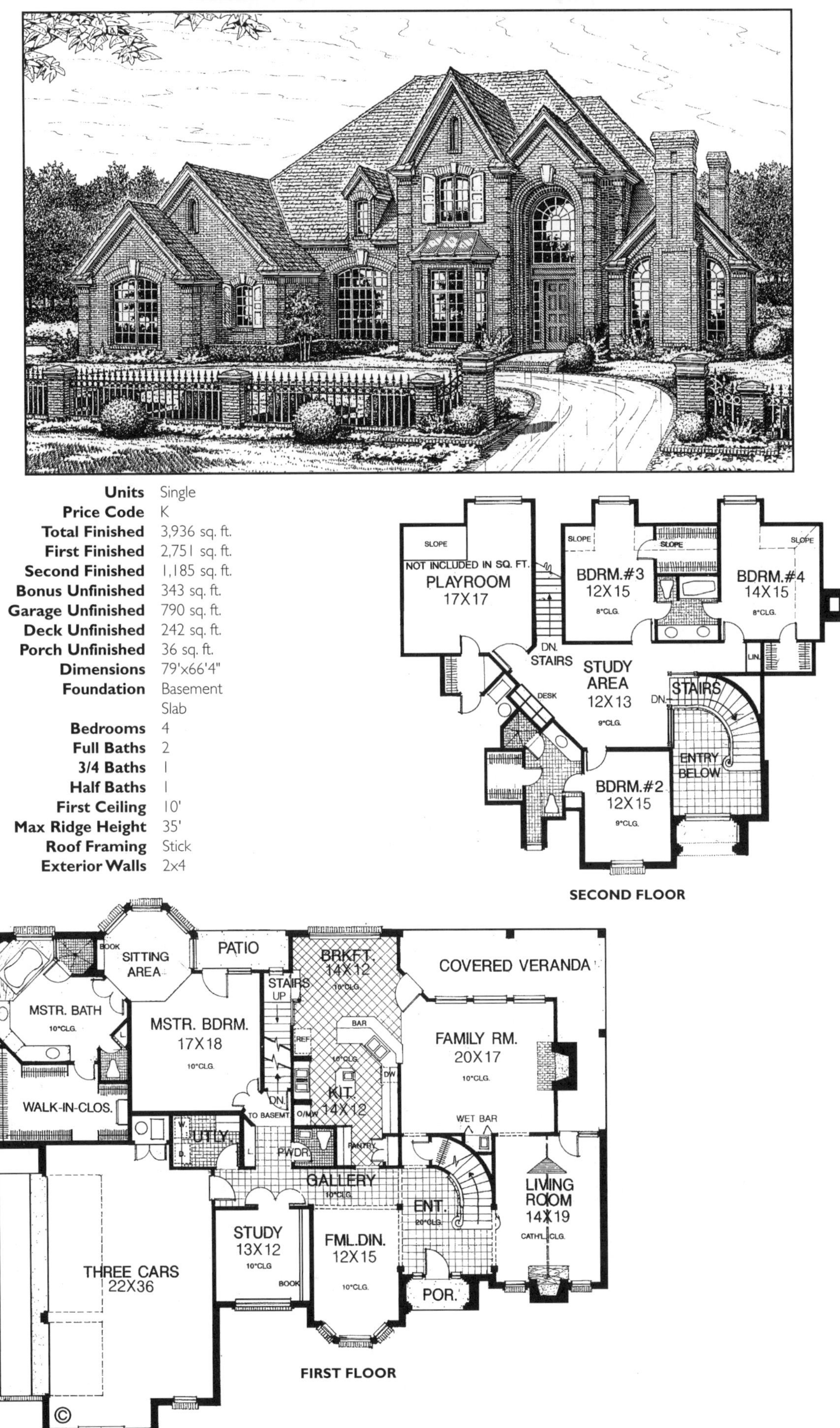
SLOPE
NOT INCLUDED IN SQ. FT.
PLAYROOM
17X17
SLOPE
BDRM.#3
12X15
8"CLG.
SLOPE
BDRM.#4
14X15
8"CLG.
SLOPE
LIN.
DN.
STAIRS
STUDY
AREA
12X13
9"CLG.
DESK
DN.
STAIRS
ENTRY
BELOW
BDRM.#2
12X15
9"CLG.
SECOND FLOOR
BOOK
SITTING
AREA
PATIO
BRKFT.
14X12
10"CLG.
COVERED VERANDA
STAIRS
UP
MSTR. BATH
10"CLG.
MSTR. BDRM.
17X18
10"CLG.
BAR
REF
FAMILY RM.
20X17
10"CLG.
DW
KIT.
14X12
WALK-IN-CLOS.
DN.
TO BASEMT
O/MW
WET BAR
UTLY.
PWDR.
PANTRY
GALLERY
10"CLG.
LIVING
ROOM
14X19
CATH'L CLG.
ENT.
20"CLG.
STUDY
13X12
10"CLG
BOOK
FML.DIN.
12X15
10"CLG.
POR.
THREE CARS
22X36
FIRST FLOOR

Units	Single
Price Code	K
Total Finished	3,936 sq. ft.
First Finished	2,751 sq. ft.
Second Finished	1,185 sq. ft.
Bonus Unfinished	343 sq. ft.
Garage Unfinished	790 sq. ft.
Deck Unfinished	242 sq. ft.
Porch Unfinished	36 sq. ft.
Dimensions	79'x66'4"
Foundation	Basement Slab
Bedrooms	4
Full Baths	2
3/4 Baths	1
Half Baths	1
First Ceiling	10'
Max Ridge Height	35'
Roof Framing	Stick
Exterior Walls	2x4

Design 66100

Units	Single
Price Code	I
Total Finished	3,942 sq. ft.
Main Finished	3,942 sq. ft.
Garage Unfinished	920 sq. ft.
Dimensions	97'x82'
Foundation	Basement Slab
Bedrooms	4
Full Baths	3
Half Baths	I
Main Ceiling	9'-11'
Max Ridge Height	33'
Roof Framing	Stick
Exterior Walls	2x4

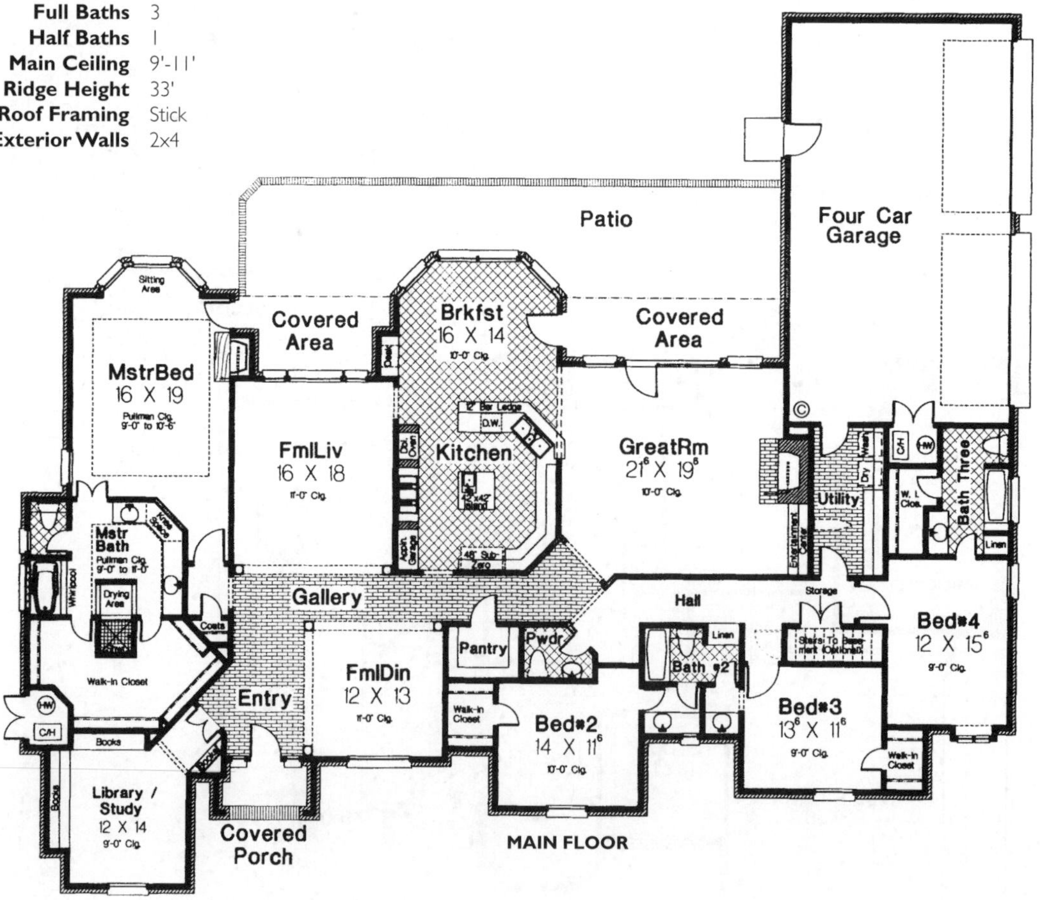

Patio

Four Car Garage

Sitting Area

Covered Area

Brkfst 16 X 14 10'-0" Clg.

Covered Area

MstrBed 16 X 19 Pullman Clg. 9'-0" to 10'-6"

FmlLiv 16 X 18 11'-0" Clg.

Kitchen

GreatRm 21⁶ X 19⁶ 10'-0" Clg.

Utility

Bath Three

Mstr Bath Pullman Clg. 9'-0" to 11'-0"

Whirlpool

Drying Area

Gallery

Hall

Storage

Bed#4 12 X 15⁶ 9'-0" Clg.

Coats

Pantry

Pwdr

Linen

Bath #2

Stairs To Basement (Optional)

Walk-in Closet

Entry

FmlDin 12 X 13 11'-0" Clg.

Bed#2 14 X 11⁶ 10'-0" Clg.

Bed#3 13⁶ X 11⁶ 9'-0" Clg.

Books

Library / Study 12 X 14 9'-0" Clg.

Covered Porch

MAIN FLOOR

Design 32041

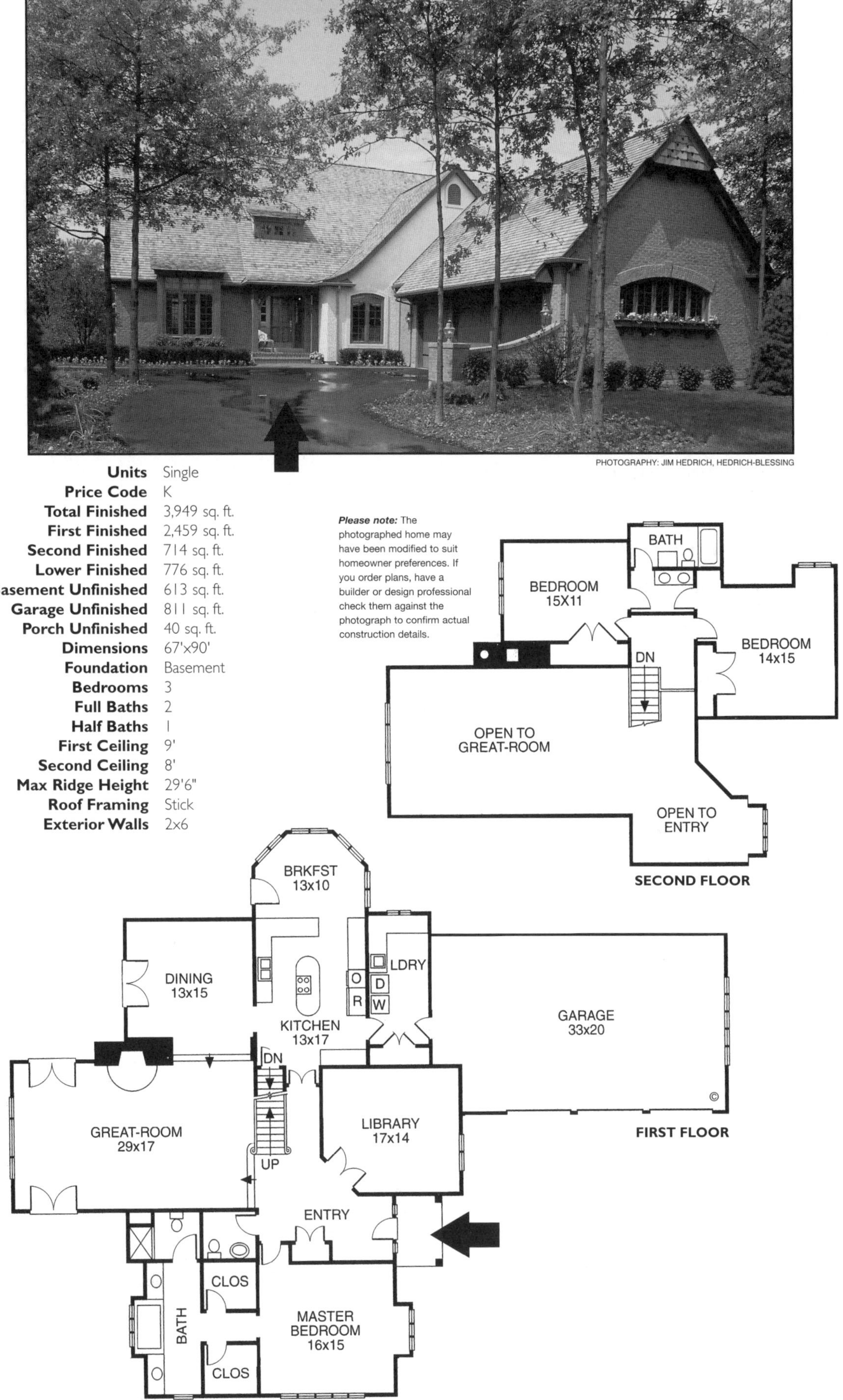
PHOTOGRAPHY: JIM HEDRICH, HEDRICH-BLESSING
BATH
BEDROOM 15X11
BEDROOM 14x15
DN
OPEN TO GREAT-ROOM
OPEN TO ENTRY
SECOND FLOOR
BRKFST 13x10
DINING 13x15
LDRY
O
R
D
W
KITCHEN 13x17
GARAGE 33x20
DN
GREAT-ROOM 29x17
LIBRARY 17x14
UP
ENTRY
CLOS
BATH
MASTER BEDROOM 16x15
CLOS
FIRST FLOOR
©

Units	Single
Price Code	K
Total Finished	3,949 sq. ft.
First Finished	2,459 sq. ft.
Second Finished	714 sq. ft.
Lower Finished	776 sq. ft.
Basement Unfinished	613 sq. ft.
Garage Unfinished	811 sq. ft.
Porch Unfinished	40 sq. ft.
Dimensions	67'x90'
Foundation	Basement
Bedrooms	3
Full Baths	2
Half Baths	1
First Ceiling	9'
Second Ceiling	8'
Max Ridge Height	29'6"
Roof Framing	Stick
Exterior Walls	2x6

Please note: The photographed home may have been modified to suit homeowner preferences. If you order plans, have a builder or design professional check them against the photograph to confirm actual construction details.

Design 10536

Units	Single
Price Code	K
Total Finished	3,972 sq. ft.
Main Finished	3,972 sq. ft.
Basement Unfinished	3,972 sq. ft.
Garage Unfinished	924 sq. ft.
Dimensions	108'8"x66'8"
Foundation	Basement
Bedrooms	4
Full Baths	4
Half Baths	1
Max Ridge Height	22'
Roof Framing	Stick
Exterior Walls	2x6

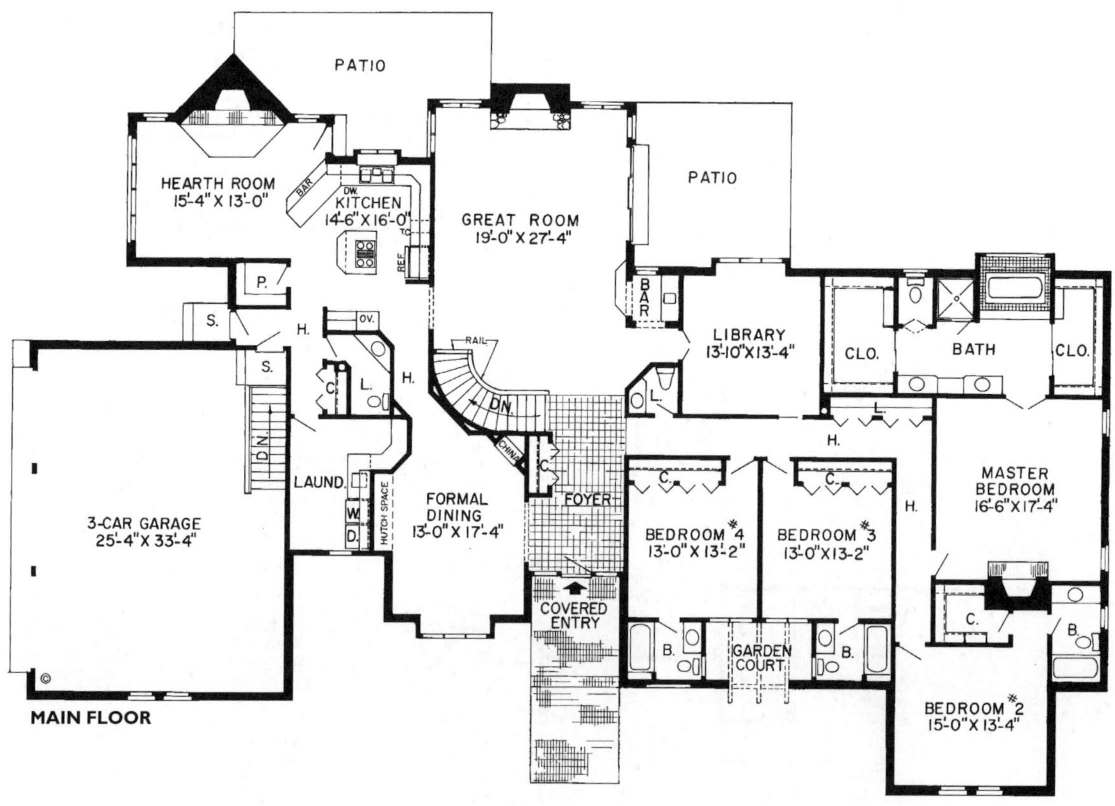
PATIO
PATIO
HEARTH ROOM
15'-4" X 13'-0"
KITCHEN
14'-6" X 16'-0"
GREAT ROOM
19'-0" X 27'-4"
LIBRARY
13'-10"X13'-4"
CLO.
BATH
CLO.
MASTER BEDROOM
16'-6"X17'-4"
3-CAR GARAGE
25'-4"X 33'-4"
LAUND.
FORMAL DINING
13'-0"X 17'-4"
FOYER
BEDROOM #4
13'-0"X 13'-2"
BEDROOM #3
13'-0"X13-2"
COVERED ENTRY
GARDEN COURT
BEDROOM #2
15'-0"X 13'-4"
MAIN FLOOR

Design 97805

Bed#3
12x15
Bed#2
13x14
Sitting Area
Balcony
Bed#4
12x12
Future Bonus Rm
SECOND FLOOR
Patio
Covered Patio
MstrBed
16x18
LivRm
15x16
Brkfst
10x11
FamRm
18x22
Kit
13x17
Gallery
Utility
Pwdr
Por
Entry
FmlDin
12x13
Walk-in Closet
Study
13x14
Gar
20x22
Gar
11x21
FIRST FLOOR

Units	Single
Price Code	L
Total Finished	4,004 sq. ft.
First Finished	2,856 sq. ft.
Second Finished	1,148 sq. ft.
Bonus Unfinished	561 sq. ft.
Garage Unfinished	650 sq. ft.
Deck Unfinished	182 sq. ft.
Porch Unfinished	48 sq. ft.
Dimensions	76'10½"x77'7"
Foundation	Slab
Bedrooms	4
Full Baths	2
3/4 Baths	2
Half Baths	1
First Ceiling	10'6"
Second Ceiling	8'-9'
Max Ridge Height	32'
Roof Framing	Stick
Exterior Walls	2x4

Design 50019

PHOTOGRAPHY: COURTESY OF THE DESIGNER

Units	Single
Price Code	E
Total Finished	4,016 sq. ft.
Main Finished	2,298 sq. ft.
Lower Finished	1,718 sq. ft.
Garage Unfinished	606 sq. ft.
Deck Unfinished	86 sq. ft.
Porch Unfinished	228 sq. ft.
Dimensions	60'x71'
Foundation	Basement
Bedrooms	3
Full Baths	2
Half Baths	2
Main Ceiling	9'
Max Ridge Height	26'
Roof Framing	Truss
Exterior Walls	2x4

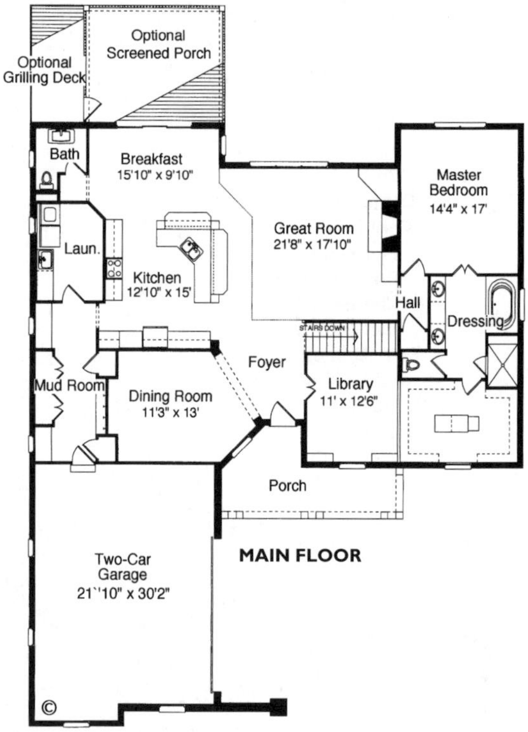

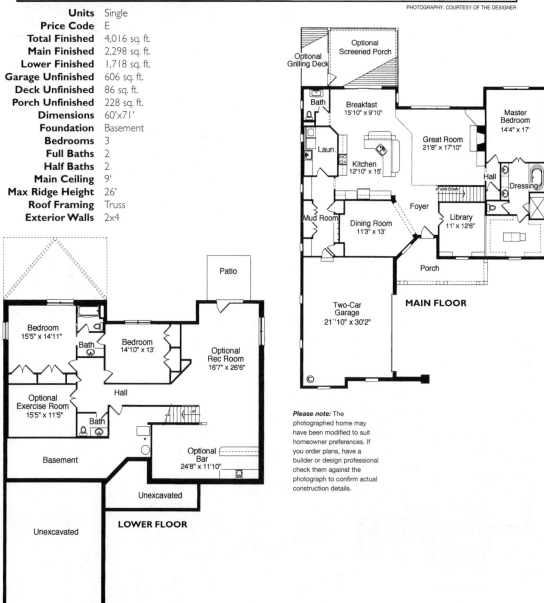

Optional Grilling Deck
Optional Screened Porch
Bath
Breakfast 15'10" x 9'10"
Master Bedroom 14'4" x 17'
Great Room 21'8" x 17'10"
Laun.
Kitchen 12'10" x 15'
Hall
Dressing
STAIRS DOWN
Foyer
Mud Room
Dining Room 11'3" x 13'
Library 11' x 12'6"
Porch
Two-Car Garage 21''10" x 30'2"
©

MAIN FLOOR

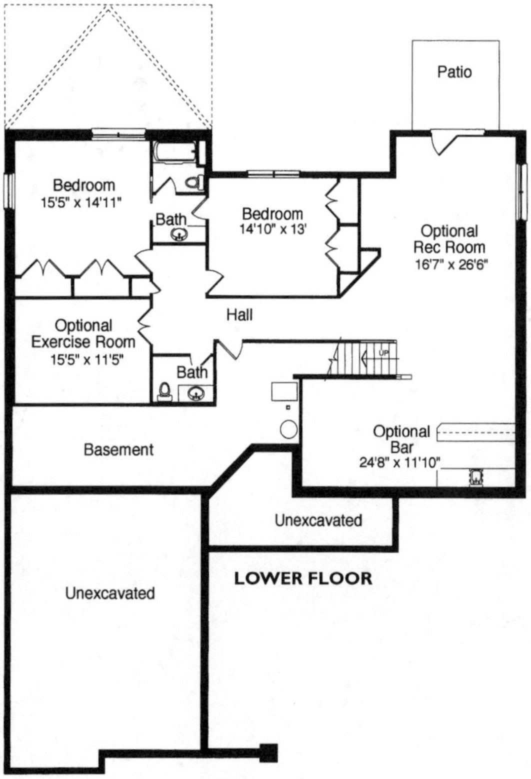

Please note: The photographed home may have been modified to suit homeowner preferences. If you order plans, have a builder or design professional check them against the photograph to confirm actual construction details.

Patio
Bedroom 15'5" x 14'11"
Bath
Bedroom 14'10" x 13'
Optional Rec Room 16'7" x 26'6"
Hall
Optional Exercise Room 15'5" x 11'5"
Bath
UP
Basement
Optional Bar 24'8" x 11'10"
Unexcavated
Unexcavated

LOWER FLOOR

Design 91182

Units	Single
Price Code	L
Total Finished	4,019 sq. ft.
First Finished	1,925 sq. ft.
Second Finished	2,094 sq. ft.
Garage Unfinished	4,761 sq. ft.
Porch Unfinished	42 sq. ft.
Dimensions	68'3½"x61'7½"
Foundation	Slab
Bedrooms	4
Full Baths	3
Half Baths	1
First Ceiling	9'1⅛"
Second Ceiling	8'1⅛"
Max Ridge Height	34'
Roof Framing	Stick
Exterior Walls	2x4

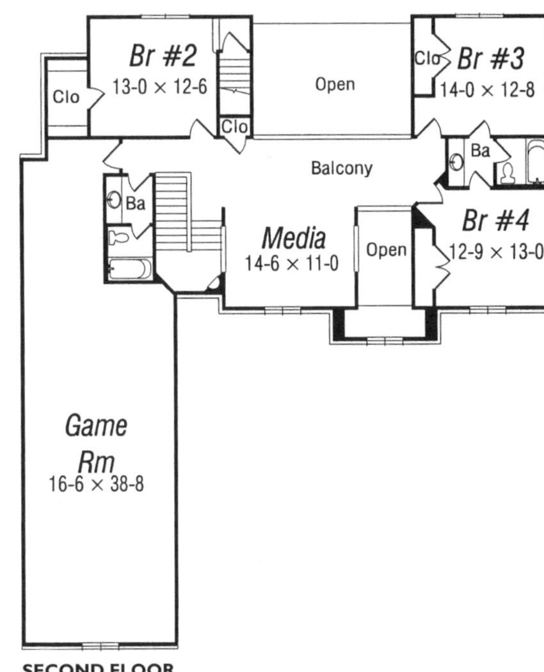
Br #2
13-0 × 12-6
Clo
Clo
Open
Clo
Br #3
14-0 × 12-8
Balcony
Ba
Ba
Media
14-6 × 11-0
Open
Br #4
12-9 × 13-0
Game
Rm
16-6 × 38-8

SECOND FLOOR

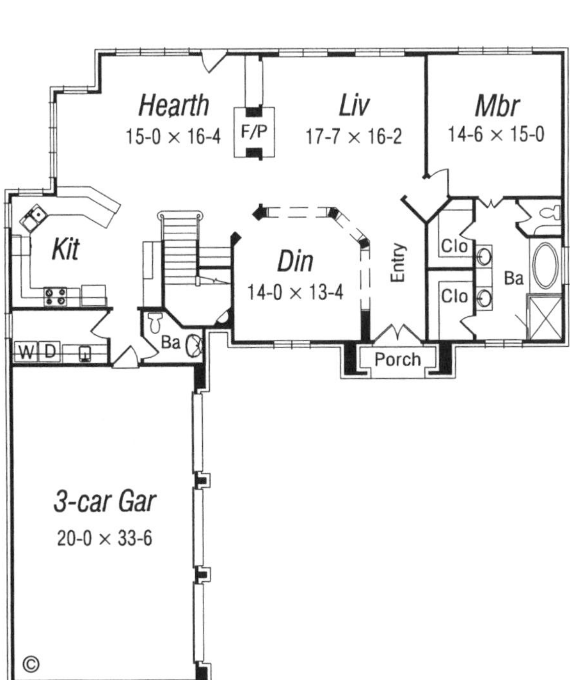
Hearth
15-0 × 16-4
F/P
Liv
17-7 × 16-2
Mbr
14-6 × 15-0
Kit
Din
14-0 × 13-4
Entry
Clo
Clo
Ba
W
D
Ba
Porch
3-car Gar
20-0 × 33-6
©

FIRST FLOOR

Design 69151

Units	Single
Price Code	L
Total Finished	4,021 sq. ft.
First Finished	3,028 sq. ft.
Second Finished	993 sq. ft.
Bonus Unfinished	539 sq. ft.
Garage Unfinished	806 sq. ft.
Dimensions	108'x66'6"
Foundation	Crawlspace
Bedrooms	3
Full Baths	1
3/4 Baths	2
Half Baths	1
First Ceiling	10'
Second Ceiling	8'
Max Ridge Height	34'
Roof Framing	Truss
Exterior Walls	2x6

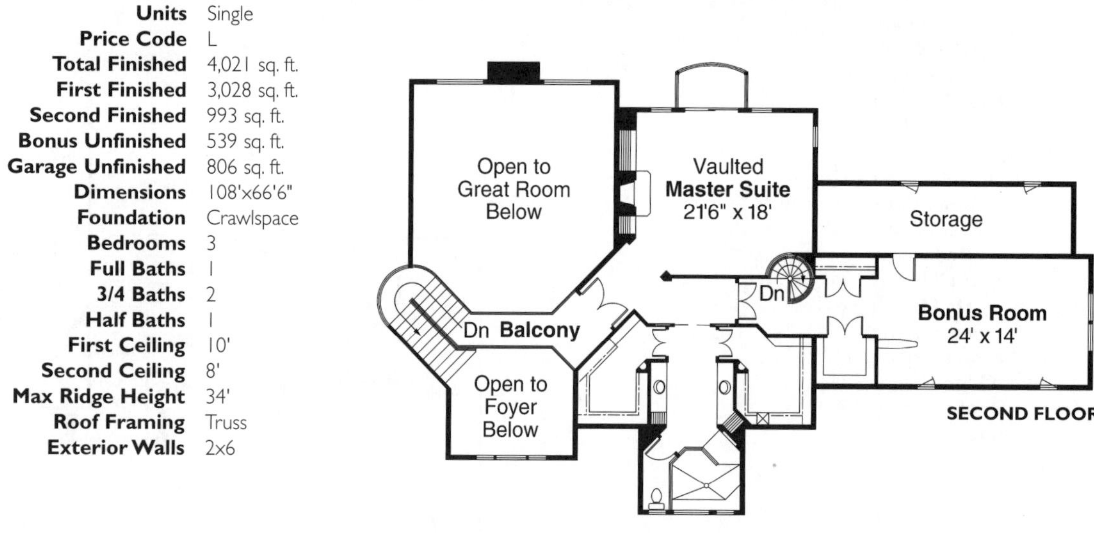
Open to
Great Room
Below
Vaulted
Master Suite
21'6" x 18'
Storage
Dn
Bonus Room
24' x 14'
Dn Balcony
Open to
Foyer
Below
SECOND FLOOR

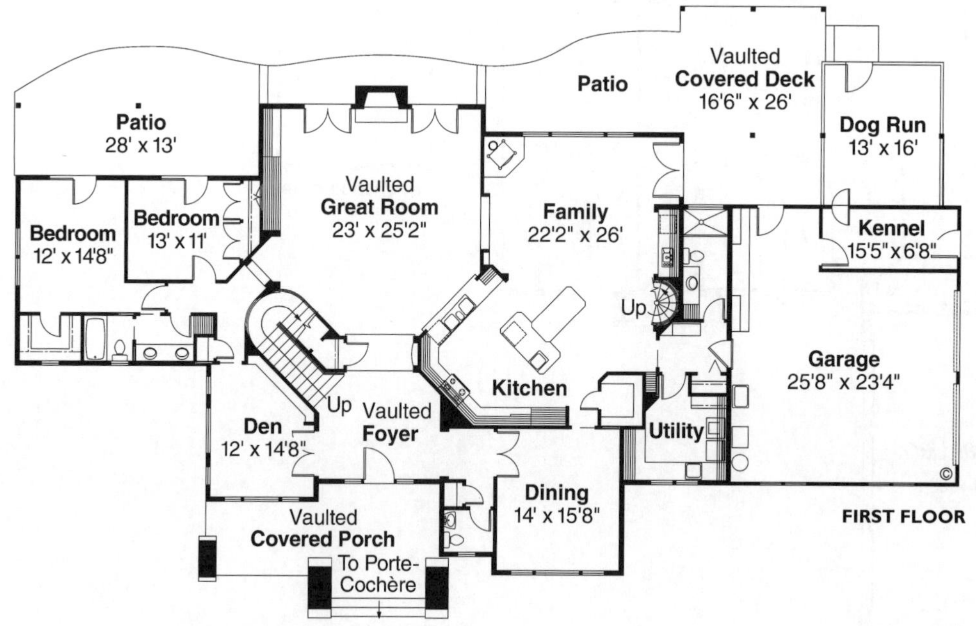
Vaulted
Covered Deck
16'6" x 26'
Patio
Patio
28' x 13'
Dog Run
13' x 16'
Vaulted
Great Room
23' x 25'2"
Family
22'2" x 26'
Kennel
15'5"x6'8"
Bedroom
12' x 14'8"
Bedroom
13' x 11'
Up
Garage
25'8" x 23'4"
Kitchen
Up
Vaulted
Foyer
Den
12' x 14'8"
Utility
Dining
14' x 15'8"
Vaulted
Covered Porch
To Porte-
Cochère
FIRST FLOOR

Design 66067

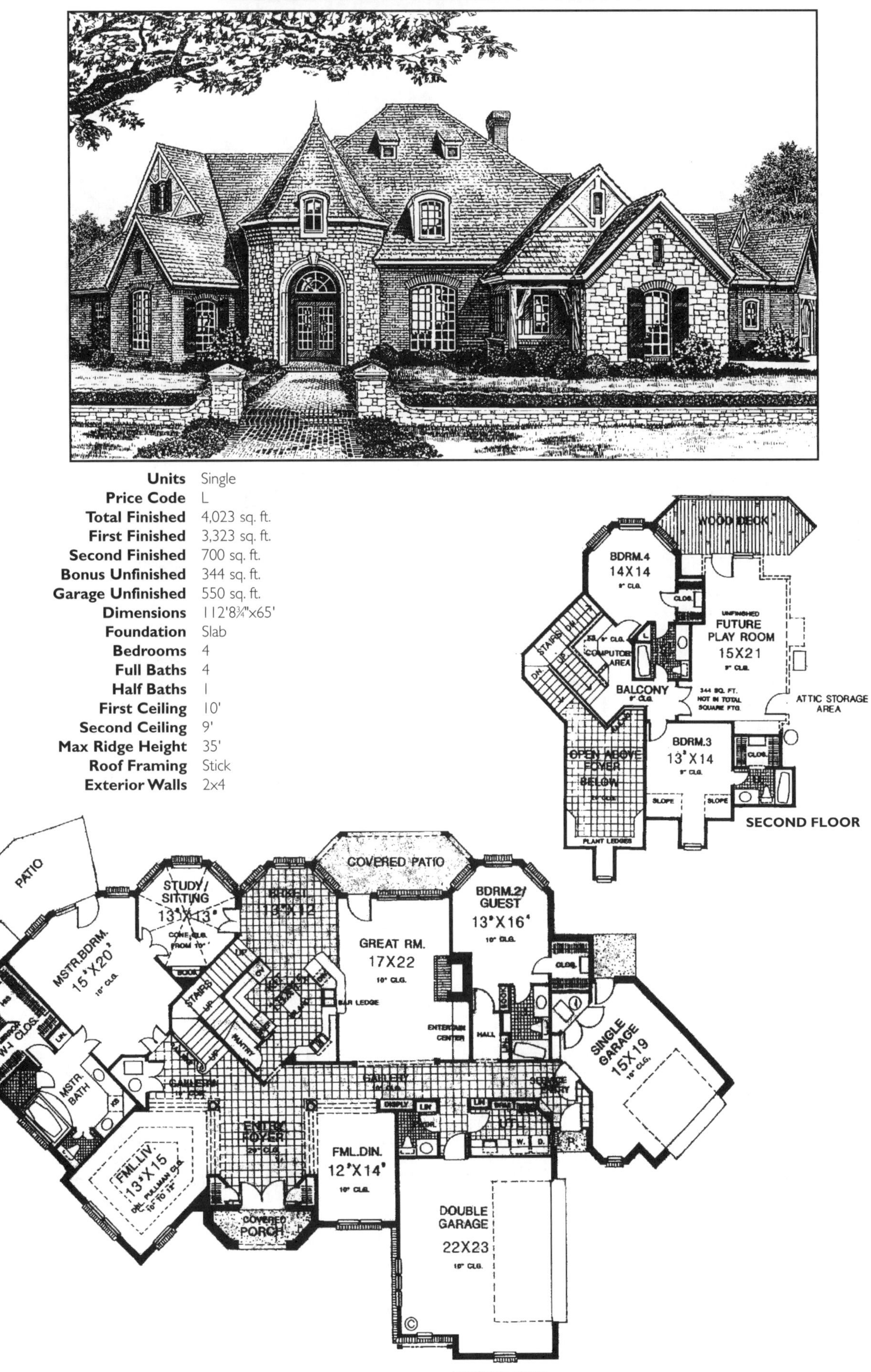
SECOND FLOOR
WOOD DECK
BDRM.4
14X14
9" CLG.
FUTURE
PLAY ROOM
15X21
9" CLG.
344 SQ. FT.
NOT IN TOTAL
SQUARE FTG.
ATTIC STORAGE
AREA
COMPUTER
AREA
BALCONY
OPEN ABOVE
FOYER
BELOW
BDRM.3
13⁶X14
9" CLG.
SLOPE
SLOPE
PLANT LEDGES
FIRST FLOOR
PATIO
STUDY/
SITTING
13⁶X13⁶
COVERED PATIO
BDRM.2/
GUEST
13⁶X16⁴
10" CLG.
MSTR.BDRM.
15⁶X20²
10" CLG.
GREAT RM.
17X22
10" CLG.
BAR LEDGE
ENTERTAIN
CENTER
HALL
SINGLE
GARAGE
15X19
10" CLG.
MSTR.
BATH
W.I CLOS.
GALLERY
ENTRY
FOYER
FML.DIN.
12⁴X14⁶
10" CLG.
FML.LIV.
13⁶X15
COVERED
PORCH
DOUBLE
GARAGE
22X23
10" CLG.

Units	Single
Price Code	L
Total Finished	4,023 sq. ft.
First Finished	3,323 sq. ft.
Second Finished	700 sq. ft.
Bonus Unfinished	344 sq. ft.
Garage Unfinished	550 sq. ft.
Dimensions	112'8¾"x65'
Foundation	Slab
Bedrooms	4
Full Baths	4
Half Baths	1
First Ceiling	10'
Second Ceiling	9'
Max Ridge Height	35'
Roof Framing	Stick
Exterior Walls	2x4

Design 92456

Units	Single
Price Code	E
Total Finished	4,028 sq. ft.
First Finished	1,696 sq. ft.
Second Finished	2,332 sq. ft.
Bonus Unfinished	412 sq. ft.
Basement Unfinished	575 sq. ft.
Dimensions	85'x46'
Foundation	Basement
Bedrooms	4
Full Baths	4
Half Baths	1
First Ceiling	9'
Second Ceiling	8'
Roof Framing	Stick
Exterior Walls	2x4

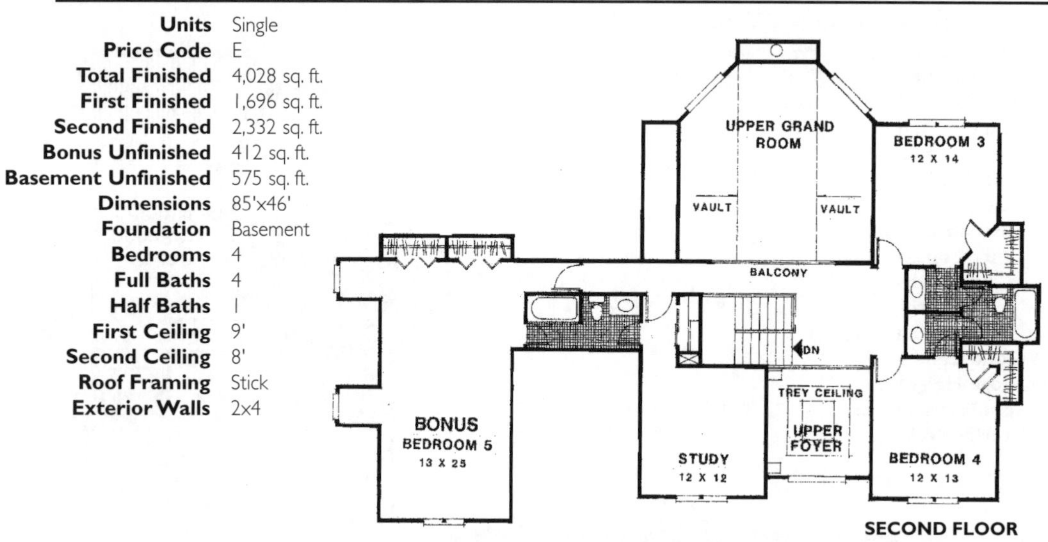
UPPER GRAND ROOM
VAULT
VAULT
BEDROOM 3
12 X 14
BALCONY
DN
TREY CEILING
UPPER FOYER
BONUS
BEDROOM 5
13 X 25
STUDY
12 X 12
BEDROOM 4
12 X 13
SECOND FLOOR

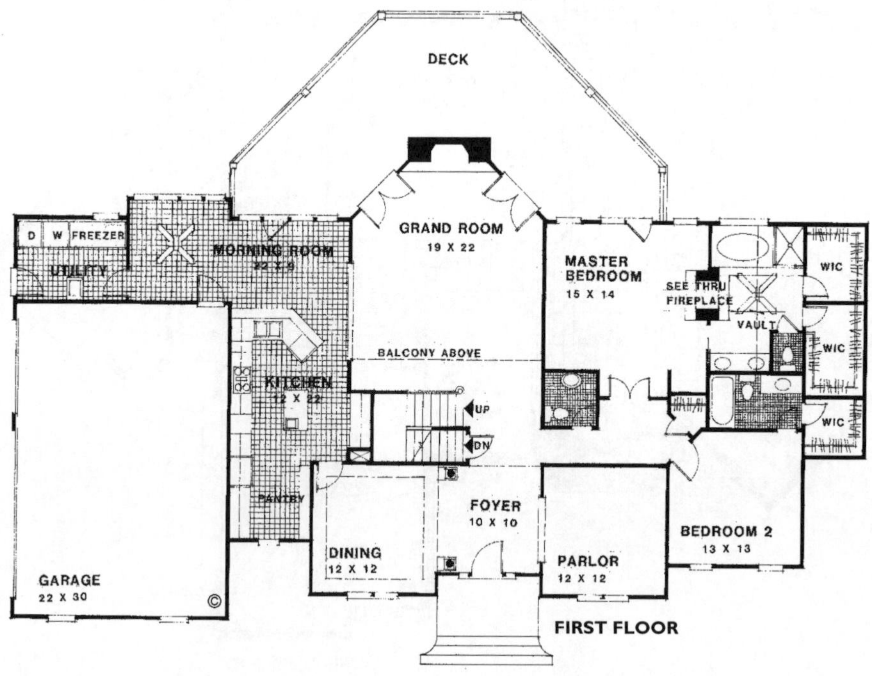
DECK
D
W
FREEZER
UTILITY
MORNING ROOM
GRAND ROOM
19 X 22
MASTER BEDROOM
15 X 14
SEE THRU FIREPLACE
VAULT
WIC
WIC
WIC
BALCONY ABOVE
KITCHEN
12 X 22
UP
DN
PANTRY
FOYER
10 X 10
DINING
12 X 12
PARLOR
12 X 12
BEDROOM 2
13 X 13
GARAGE
22 X 30
FIRST FLOOR

Design 94224

Units	Single
Price Code	L
Total Finished	4,028 sq. ft.
Main Finished	4,028 sq. ft.
Garage Unfinished	660 sq. ft.
Porch Unfinished	378 sq. ft.
Dimensions	80'x82'8"
Foundation	Slab
Bedrooms	3
Full Baths	2
3/4 Baths	1
Half Baths	1
Main Ceiling	14'
Max Ridge Height	32'6"
Roof Framing	Stick

* Alternate foundation options available at an additional charge. Please call 1-800-235-5700 for more information.

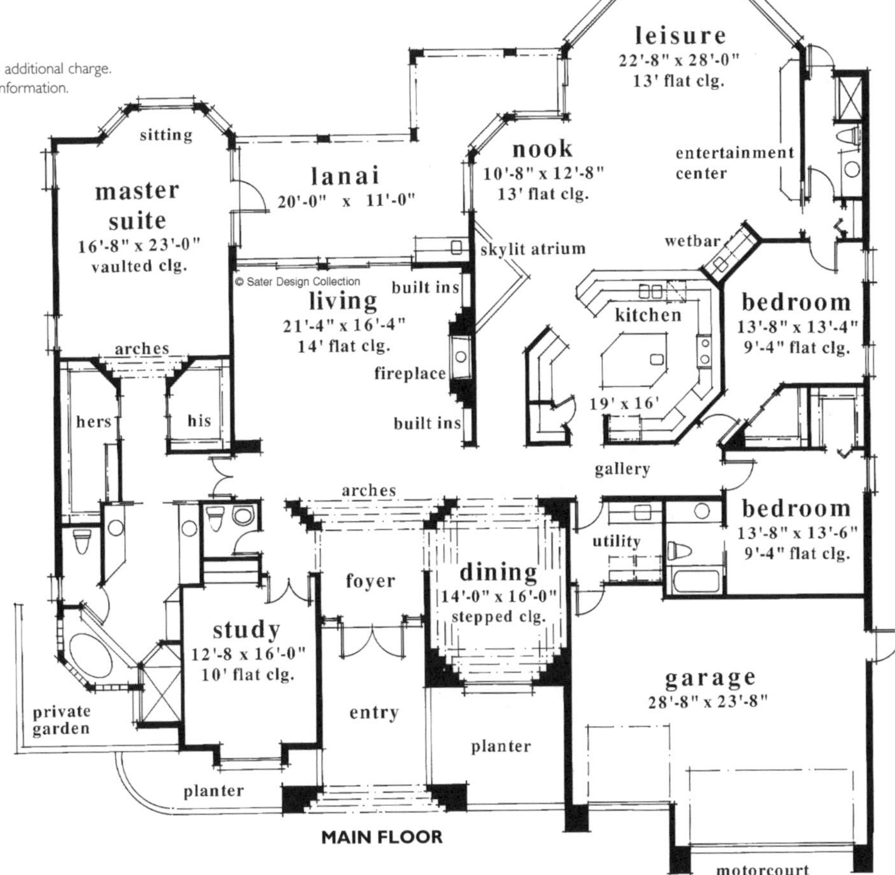
leisure
22'-8" x 28'-0"
13' flat clg.
sitting
master suite
16'-8" x 23'-0"
vaulted clg.
lanai
20'-0" x 11'-0"
nook
10'-8" x 12'-8"
13' flat clg.
entertainment center
skylit atrium
wetbar
© Sater Design Collection
built ins
living
21'-4" x 16'-4"
14' flat clg.
kitchen
19' x 16'
bedroom
13'-8" x 13'-4"
9'-4" flat clg.
fireplace
arches
hers
his
built ins
gallery
arches
utility
bedroom
13'-8" x 13'-6"
9'-4" flat clg.
foyer
dining
14'-0" x 16'-0"
stepped clg.
study
12'-8 x 16'-0"
10' flat clg.
garage
28'-8" x 23'-8"
private garden
entry
planter
planter
motorcourt

MAIN FLOOR

Design 97645

Units	Single
Price Code	L
Total Finished	4,049 sq. ft.
First Finished	2,095 sq. ft.
Second Finished	1,954 sq. ft.
Basement Unfinished	2,095 sq. ft.
Garage Unfinished	681 sq. ft.
Dimensions	56'x63'
Foundation	Basement Crawlspace
Bedrooms	5
Full Baths	4
Half Baths	1
First Ceiling	9'
Second Ceiling	9'
Max Ridge Height	36'6"
Roof Framing	Stick
Exterior Walls	2x4

CAD
FILES AVAILABLE
For more information call
800-235-5700

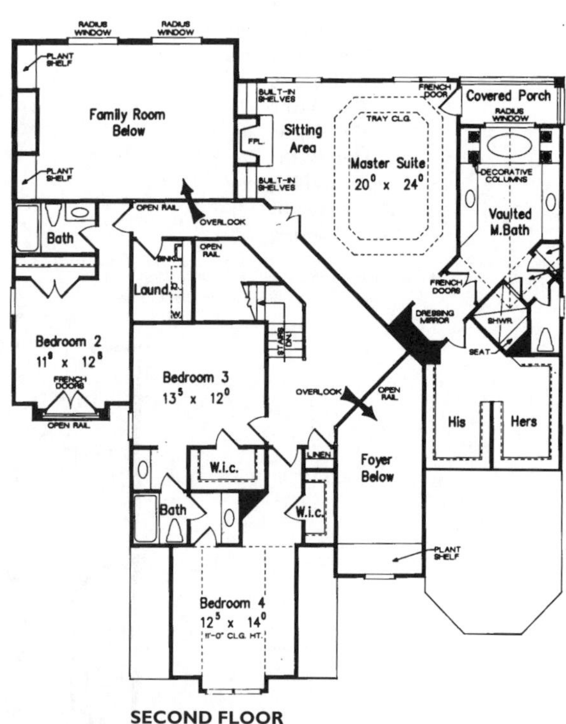
RADIUS WINDOW
RADIUS WINDOW
PLANT SHELF
Family Room Below
PLANT SHELF
BUILT-IN SHELVES
FRENCH DOOR
Covered Porch
RADIUS WINDOW
FPL.
Sitting Area
TRAY CLG.
Master Suite 20⁰ x 24⁰
BUILT-IN SHELVES
DECORATIVE COLUMNS
Vaulted M.Bath
OPEN RAIL
OVERLOOK
Bath
OPEN RAIL
Laund.
FRENCH DOORS
DRESSING MIRROR
SHWR.
SEAT
Bedroom 2 11⁹ x 12⁸
FRENCH DOORS
OPEN RAIL
Bedroom 3 13⁵ x 12⁰
OVERLOOK
OPEN RAIL
His
Hers
W.i.c.
LINEN
Foyer Below
Bath
W.i.c.
PLANT SHELF
Bedroom 4 12⁵ x 14⁰
11'-0" CLG. HT.

SECOND FLOOR

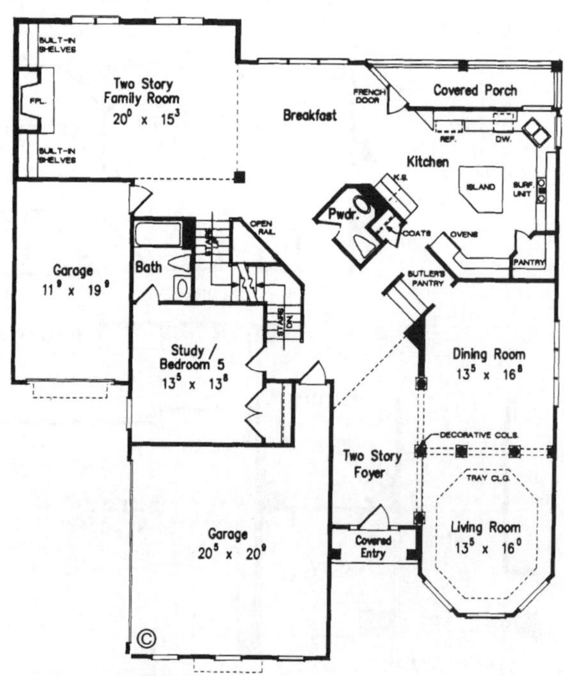
BUILT-IN SHELVES
Two Story Family Room 20⁰ x 15³
FPL.
BUILT-IN SHELVES
Breakfast
FRENCH DOOR
Covered Porch
REF.
DW.
Kitchen
ISLAND
SURF UNIT
Pwdr.
COATS
OVENS
PANTRY
OPEN RAIL
Garage 11⁹ x 19⁹
Bath
BUTLER'S PANTRY
Study / Bedroom 5 13⁵ x 13⁸
Dining Room 13⁵ x 16⁸
DECORATIVE COLS
Two Story Foyer
TRAY CLG.
Garage 20⁵ x 20⁹
Covered Entry
Living Room 13⁵ x 16⁰
©

FIRST FLOOR

Design 97860

Units	Single
Price Code	L
Total Finished	4,063 sq. ft.
First Finished	2,879 sq. ft.
Second Finished	1,184 sq. ft.
Garage Unfinished	816 sq. ft.
Deck Unfinished	207 sq. ft.
Porch Unfinished	112 sq. ft.
Dimensions	98'x49'4"
Foundation	Basement Slab
Bedrooms	5
Full Baths	3
Half Baths	1
First Ceiling	10'
Second Ceiling	9'
Max Ridge Height	30'
Roof Framing	Stick
Exterior Walls	2x4

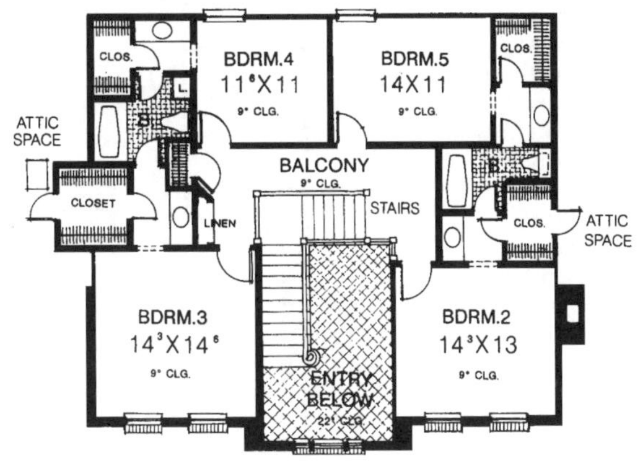

CLOS.
BDRM.4
11^6X11
9" CLG.
BDRM.5
14X11
9" CLG.
CLOS.
ATTIC SPACE
BALCONY
9" CLG.
CLOSET
LINEN
STAIRS
CLOS.
ATTIC SPACE
BDRM.3
14^3X14^6
9" CLG.
ENTRY BELOW
BDRM.2
14^3X13
9" CLG.

SECOND FLOOR

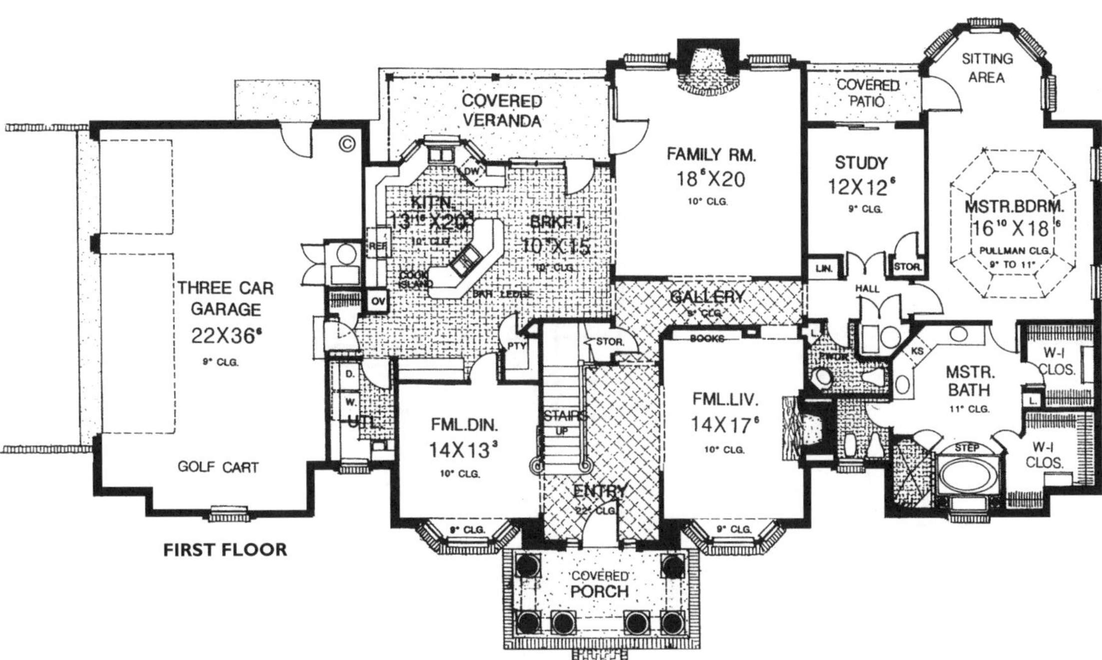

COVERED VERANDA
FAMILY RM.
18^6X20
10" CLG.
COVERED PATIO
SITTING AREA
STUDY
12X12^6
9" CLG.
MSTR.BDRM.
16^{10} X 18^6
PULLMAN CLG.
9" TO 11"
THREE CAR GARAGE
22X36^6
9" CLG.
GOLF CART
KITN.
BRKFT.
COOK ISLAND
OV
PTY
GALLERY
LIN.
STOR.
HALL
BOOKS
STOR.
MSTR. BATH
11" CLG.
W-I CLOS.
STEP
W-I CLOS.
UTL
FML.DIN.
14X13^3
10" CLG.
9" CLG.
STAIRS UP
ENTRY
FML.LIV.
14X17^6
10" CLG.
9" CLG.
COVERED PORCH

FIRST FLOOR

Design 24802

PHOTOGRAPHY: JOHN EHRENCLOU

Units	Single
Price Code	L
Total Finished	4,064 sq. ft.
Main Finished	2,466 sq. ft.
Lower Finished	1,598 sq. ft.
Basement Unfinished	876 sq. ft.
Garage Unfinished	665 sq. ft.
Deck Unfinished	144 sq. ft.
Dimensions	78'x52'4"
Foundation	Basement
Bedrooms	4
Full Baths	3
Main Ceiling	9'-11'
Second Ceiling	8'6"
Max Ridge Height	32'
Roof Framing	Stick
Exterior Walls	2x6

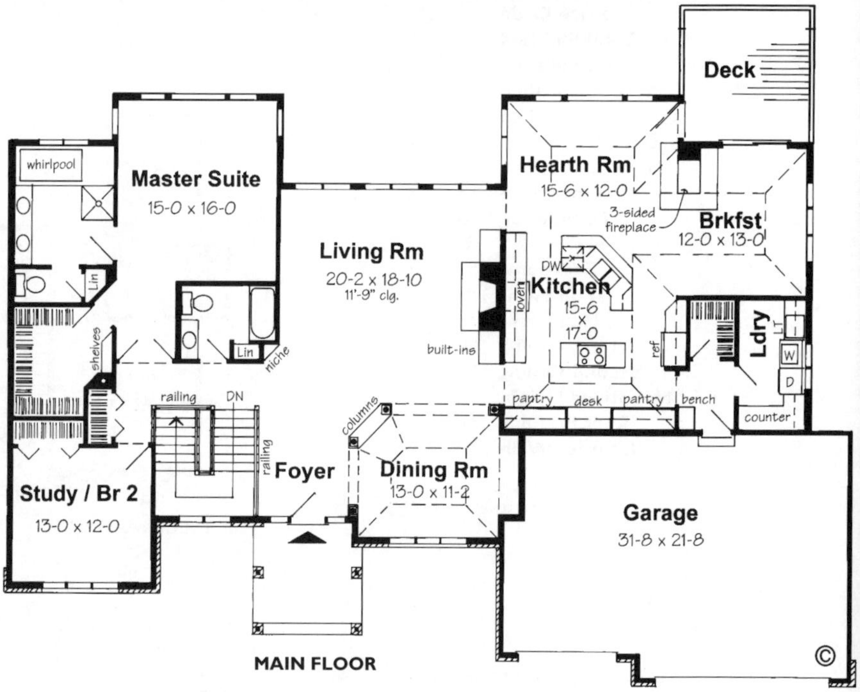

Deck
whirlpool
Master Suite
15-0 x 16-0
Lin
shelves
Lin
niche
Living Rm
20-2 x 18-10
11'-9" clg.
built-ins
Hearth Rm
15-6 x 12-0
3-sided fireplace
Brkfst
12-0 x 13-0
DW
Kitchen
15-6 x 17-0
ovens
ref
Ldry
LT
W
D
pantry
desk
pantry
bench
counter
railing
DN
railing
columns
Foyer
Dining Rm
13-0 x 11-2
Study / Br 2
13-0 x 12-0
Garage
31-8 x 21-8
©

MAIN FLOOR

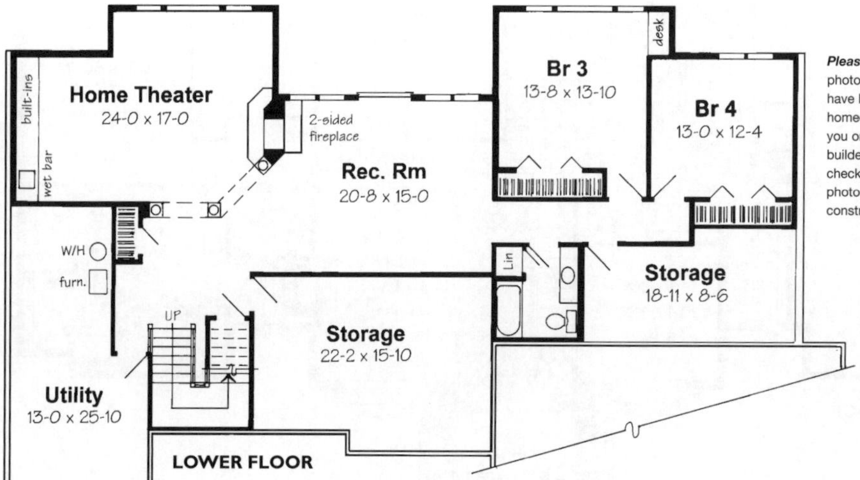

built-ins
wet bar
Home Theater
24-0 x 17-0
2-sided fireplace
Rec. Rm
20-8 x 15-0
Br 3
13-8 x 13-10
desk
Br 4
13-0 x 12-4
W/H
furn.
Lin
Storage
18-11 x 8-6
UP
Storage
22-2 x 15-10
Utility
13-0 x 25-10

LOWER FLOOR

Please note: The photographed home may have been modified to suit homeowner preferences. If you order plans, have a builder or design professional check them against the photograph to confirm actual construction details.

Design 94239

Units	Single
Price Code	L
Total Finished	4,106 sq. ft.
First Finished	3,027 sq. ft.
Second Finished	1,079 sq. ft.
Basement Unfinished	3,027 sq. ft.
Garage Unfinished	802 sq. ft.
Deck Unfinished	245 sq. ft.
Porch Unfinished	884 sq. ft.
Dimensions	87'4"x80'4"
Foundation	Basement
Bedrooms	4
Full Baths	1
3/4 Baths	2
Half Baths	1
Max Ridge Height	38'
Roof Framing	Truss
Exterior Walls	2x6

* Alternate foundation options available at an additional charge. Please call 1-800-235-5700 for more information.

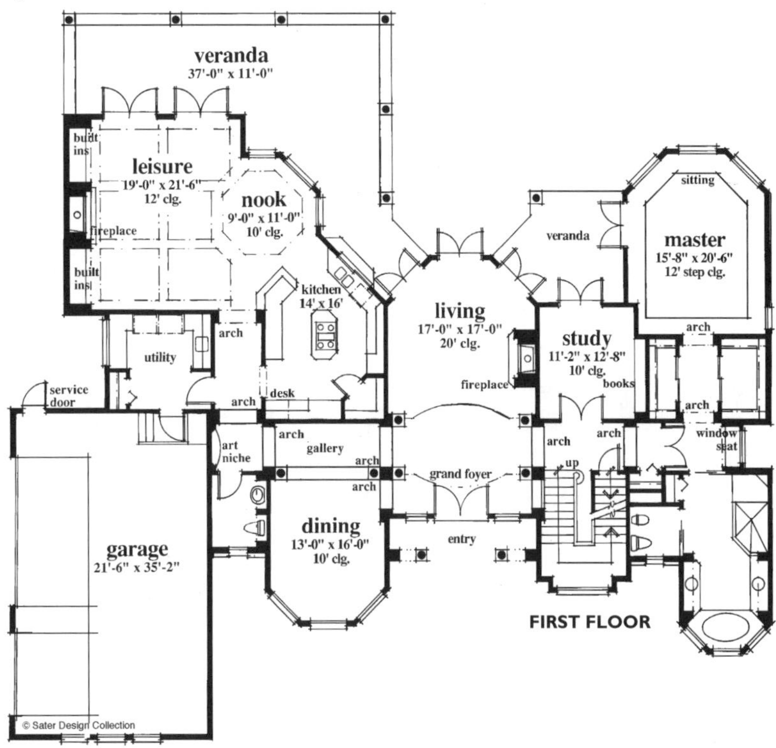
deck
deck
br. 3
13'-6" x 15'-0"
8'-8" clg.
open to living room below
guest
11'-2" x 12'-8"
8'-8" clg.
arch
art niche
down
gallery loft
arch
open to foyer below
br. 2
13'-6" x 15'-6"
8'-8" clg.
SECOND FLOOR
veranda
37'-0" x 11'-0"
built ins
leisure
19'-0" x 21'-6"
12' clg.
fireplace
built ins
nook
9'-0" x 11'-0"
10' clg.
kitchen
14' x 16'
sitting
veranda
master
15'-8" x 20'-6"
12' step clg.
living
17'-0" x 17'-0"
20' clg.
fireplace
study
11'-2" x 12'-8"
10' clg.
books
utility
arch
service door
arch
desk
arch
arch
window seat
art niche
arch
gallery
arch
arch
grand foyer
up
dining
13'-0" x 16'-0"
10' clg.
entry
garage
21'-6" x 35'-2"
FIRST FLOOR
© Sater Design Collection

Design 66097

Units	Single
Price Code	L
Total Finished	4,138 sq. ft.
First Finished	2,509 sq. ft.
Second Finished	1,629 sq. ft.
Garage Unfinished	726 sq. ft.
Dimensions	83'x56'5"
Foundation	Slab
Bedrooms	4
Full Baths	2
3/4 Baths	1
Half Baths	1
First Ceiling	10'
Second Ceiling	9'
Max Ridge Height	38'
Roof Framing	Stick
Exterior Walls	2x4

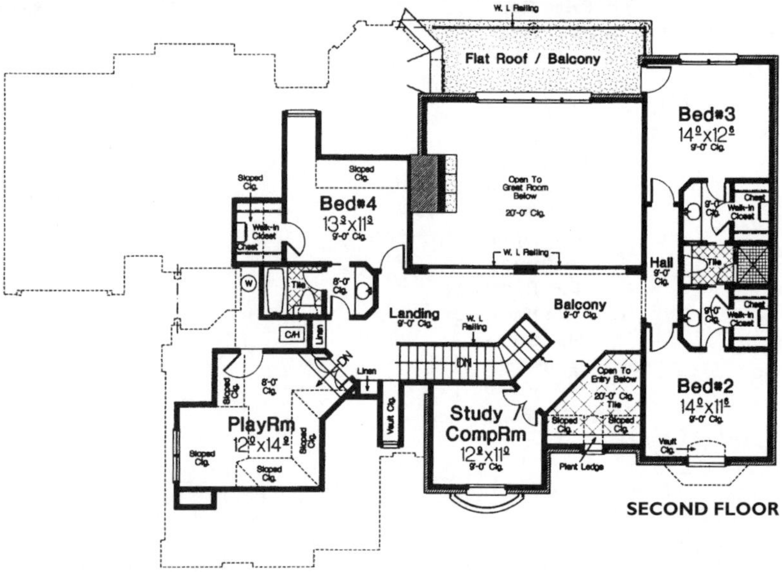

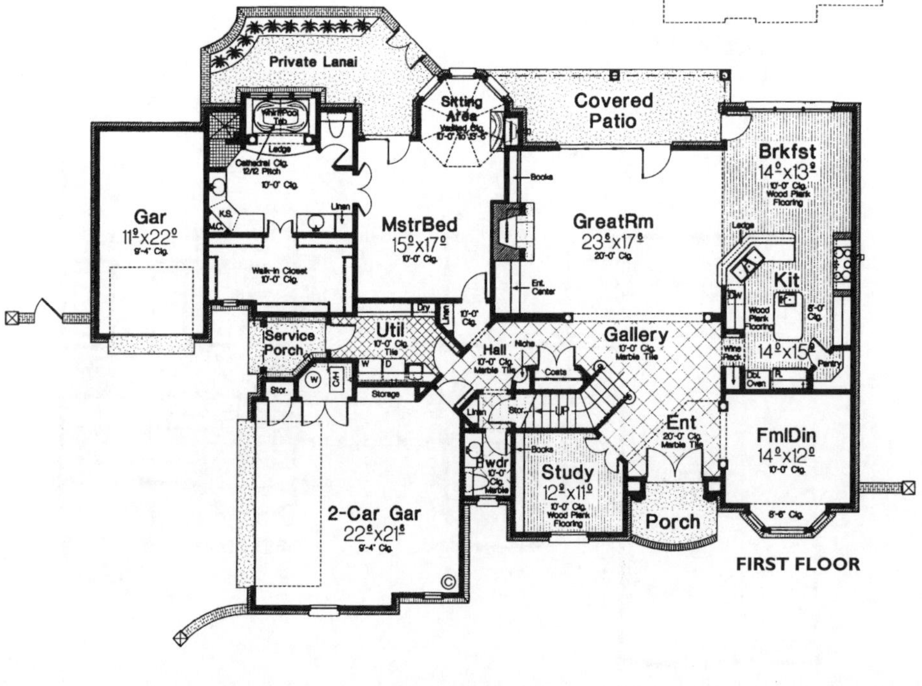

SECOND FLOOR

FIRST FLOOR

Design 69133

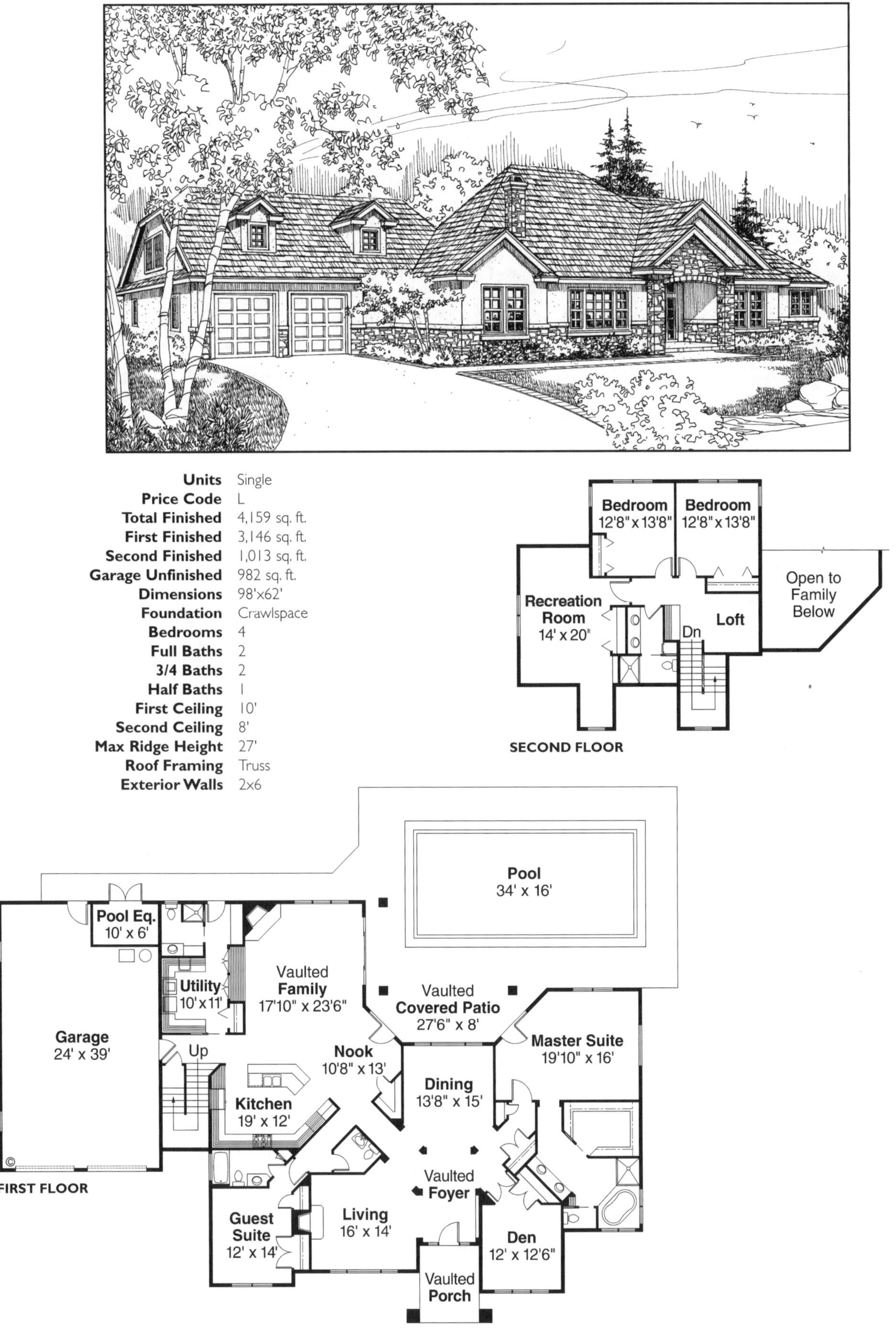
Bedroom
12'8" x 13'8"
Bedroom
12'8" x 13'8"
Open to Family Below
Recreation Room
14' x 20"
Loft
Dn
SECOND FLOOR
Pool
34' x 16'
Pool Eq.
10' x 6'
Utility
10' x 11'
Vaulted Family
17'10" x 23'6"
Vaulted Covered Patio
27'6" x 8'
Master Suite
19'10" x 16'
Garage
24' x 39'
Up
Nook
10'8" x 13'
Kitchen
19' x 12'
Dining
13'8" x 15'
Vaulted Foyer
Guest Suite
12' x 14'
Living
16' x 14'
Den
12' x 12'6"
Vaulted Porch
FIRST FLOOR

Units	Single
Price Code	L
Total Finished	4,159 sq. ft.
First Finished	3,146 sq. ft.
Second Finished	1,013 sq. ft.
Garage Unfinished	982 sq. ft.
Dimensions	98'x62'
Foundation	Crawlspace
Bedrooms	4
Full Baths	2
3/4 Baths	2
Half Baths	1
First Ceiling	10'
Second Ceiling	8'
Max Ridge Height	27'
Roof Framing	Truss
Exterior Walls	2x6

Design 98590

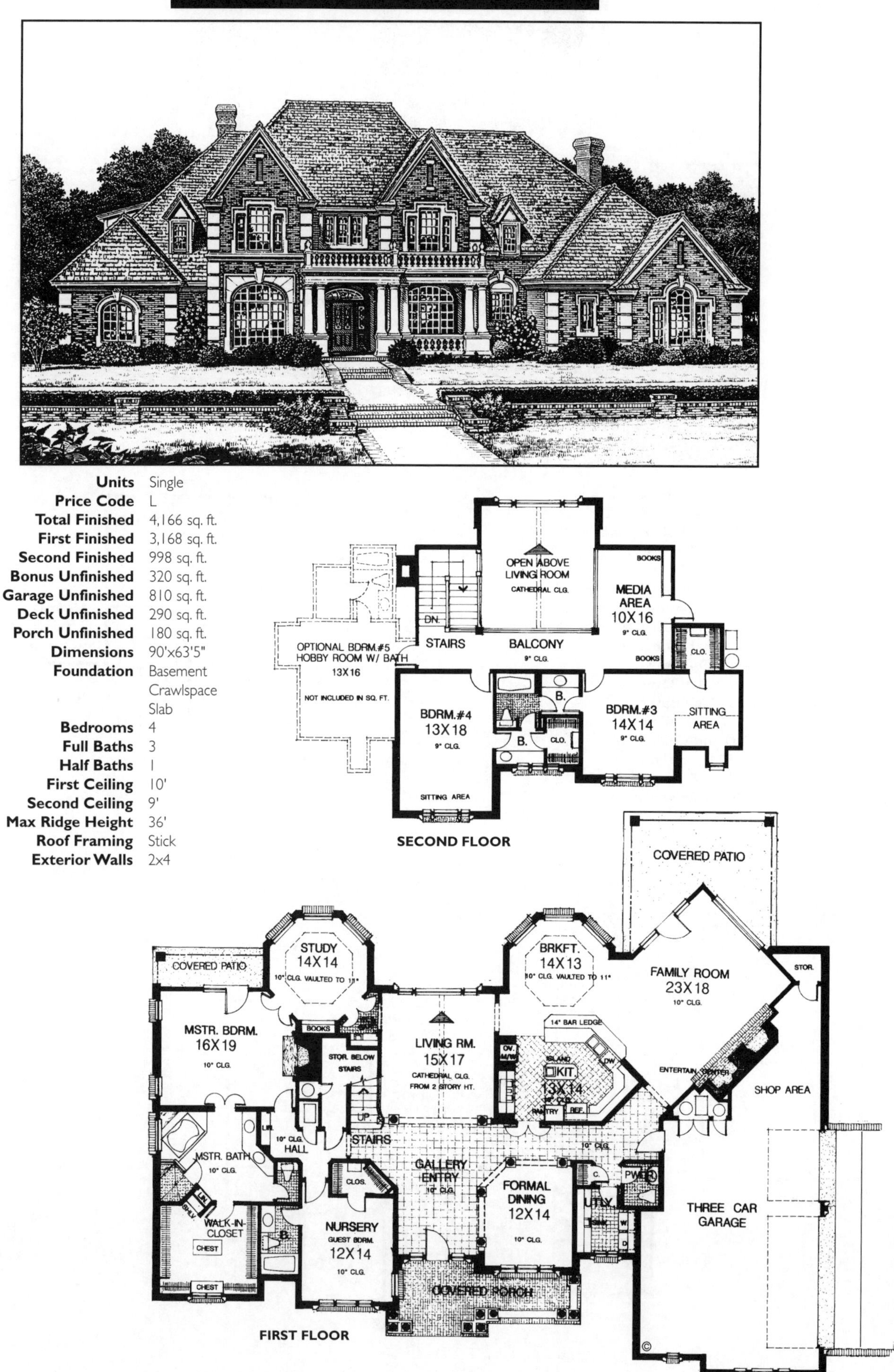
OPEN ABOVE
LIVING ROOM
CATHEDRAL CLG.
MEDIA AREA
10X16
9" CLG.
BOOKS
STAIRS
DN.
BALCONY
9" CLG.
CLO.
OPTIONAL BDRM.#5
HOBBY ROOM W/ BATH
13X16
NOT INCLUDED IN SQ. FT.
BDRM.#4
13X18
9" CLG.
SITTING AREA
B.
CLO.
BDRM.#3
14X14
9" CLG.
SITTING
AREA
SECOND FLOOR
COVERED PATIO
STUDY
14X14
10" CLG. VAULTED TO 11"
BRKFT.
14X13
10" CLG. VAULTED TO 11"
FAMILY ROOM
23X18
10" CLG.
STOR.
COVERED PATIO
MSTR. BDRM.
16X19
10" CLG.
BOOKS
STOR. BELOW
STAIRS
LIVING RM.
15X17
CATHEDRAL CLG.
FROM 2 STORY HT.
14" BAR LEDGE
ISLAND
KIT
13X14
DW
OV.
M/W
PANTRY
REF.
ENTERTAIN. CENTER
SHOP AREA
UP
STAIRS
HALL
10" CLG.
LIN.
MSTR. BATH
10" CLG.
GALLERY
ENTRY
10" CLG.
10" CLG.
FORMAL
DINING
12X14
10" CLG.
PWDR.
C.
UTLY.
W
D
CLOS.
WALK-IN-
CLOSET
CHEST
CHEST
B.
NURSERY
GUEST BDRM.
12X14
10" CLG.
COVERED PORCH
THREE CAR
GARAGE
FIRST FLOOR

Units	Single
Price Code	L
Total Finished	4,166 sq. ft.
First Finished	3,168 sq. ft.
Second Finished	998 sq. ft.
Bonus Unfinished	320 sq. ft.
Garage Unfinished	810 sq. ft.
Deck Unfinished	290 sq. ft.
Porch Unfinished	180 sq. ft.
Dimensions	90'x63'5"
Foundation	Basement Crawlspace Slab
Bedrooms	4
Full Baths	3
Half Baths	1
First Ceiling	10'
Second Ceiling	9'
Max Ridge Height	36'
Roof Framing	Stick
Exterior Walls	2x4

Design 65424

PHOTOGRAPHY: COURTESY OF THE DESIGNER

Units	Single
Price Code	L
Total Finished	4,200 sq. ft.
First Finished	1,993 sq. ft.
Second Finished	2,207 sq. ft.
Basement Unfinished	1,993 sq. ft.
Garage Unfinished	764 sq. ft.
Porch Unfinished	296 sq. ft.
Dimensions	74'6"x44'
Foundation	Basement
Bedrooms	4
Full Baths	3
Half Baths	1
First Ceiling	9'2"
Second Ceiling	8'2"
Max Ridge Height	31'
Roof Framing	Truss
Exterior Walls	2x6

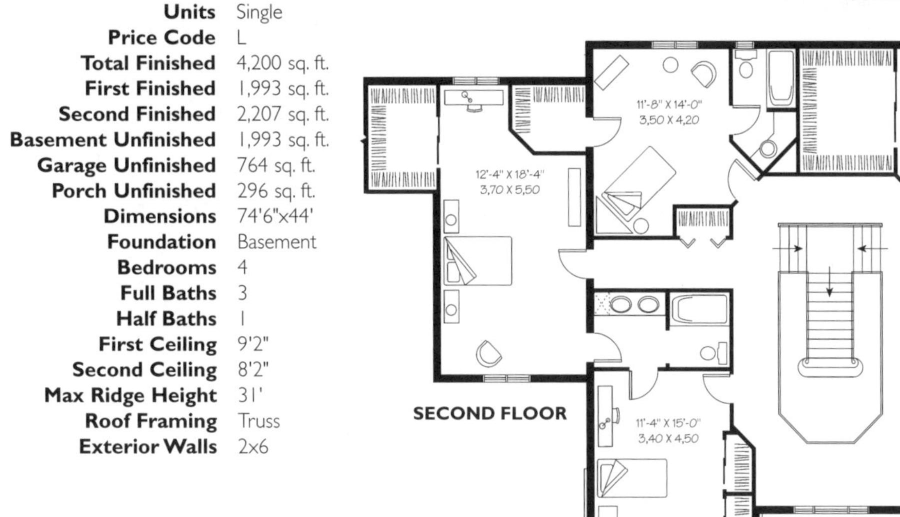
11'-8" X 14'-0"
3,50 X 4,20
18'-0" X 22'-0"
5,40 X 6,60
12'-4" X 18'-4"
3,70 X 5,50
11'-4" X 15'-0"
3,40 X 4,50

SECOND FLOOR

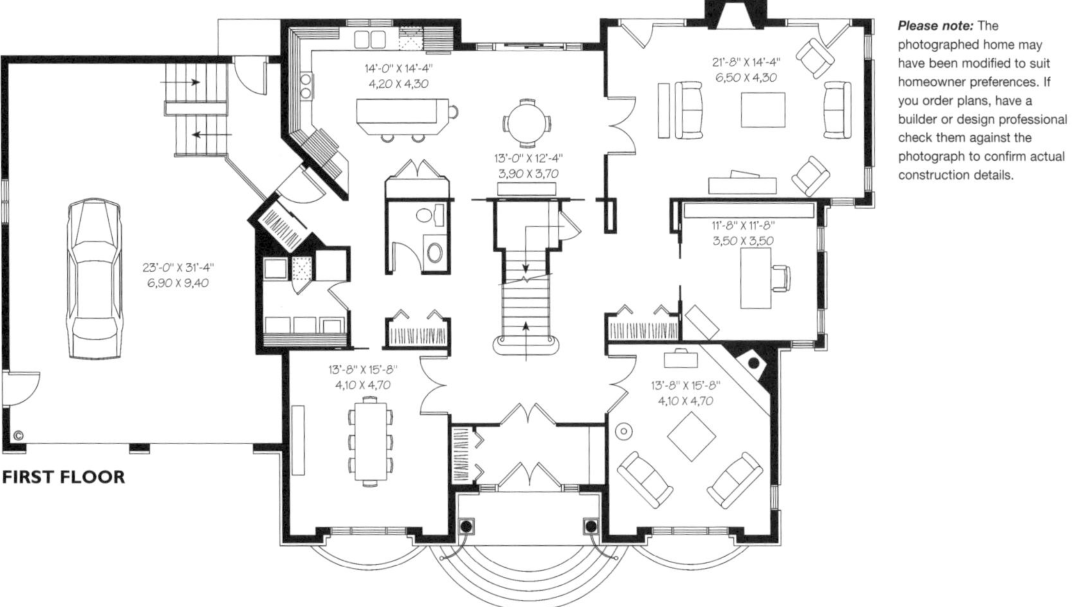
14'-0" X 14'-4"
4,20 X 4,30
21'-8" X 14'-4"
6,50 X 4,30
13'-0" X 12'-4"
3,90 X 3,70
11'-8" X 11'-8"
3,50 X 3,50
23'-0" X 31'-4"
6,90 X 9,40
13'-8" X 15'-8"
4,10 X 4,70
13'-8" X 15'-8"
4,10 X 4,70

FIRST FLOOR

Please note: The photographed home may have been modified to suit homeowner preferences. If you order plans, have a builder or design professional check them against the photograph to confirm actual construction details.

Design 32345

PHOTOGRAPHY: DAVID W. BROWN

Units	Single
Price Code	L
Total Finished	4,205 sq. ft.
First Finished	2,707 sq. ft.
Second Finished	1,498 sq. ft.
Garage Unfinished	651 sq. ft.
Deck Unfinished	848 sq. ft.
Porch Unfinished	465 sq. ft.
Dimensions	74'8"x96'
Foundation	Crawlspace
Bedrooms	4
Full Baths	4
3/4 Baths	2
First Ceiling	9'
Second Ceiling	9'
Max Ridge Height	32'
Roof Framing	Stick
Exterior Walls	2x4

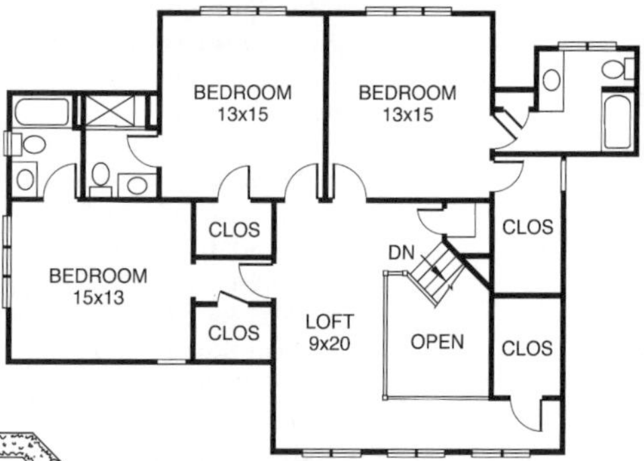

BEDROOM 13x15
BEDROOM 13x15
CLOS
CLOS
DN
BEDROOM 15x13
CLOS
LOFT 9x20
OPEN
CLOS
CLOS

SECOND FLOOR

DECK
BRKFST 12x12
GREAT-ROOM 24x16
UP
MASTER BEDROOM 15x20
R
KIT 12x19
UP
BATH
CLOSET
OFFICE
DINING 15x15
ENTRY
UP
STUDY 15x15
LDRY
D W
PORCH
GARAGE 22x27

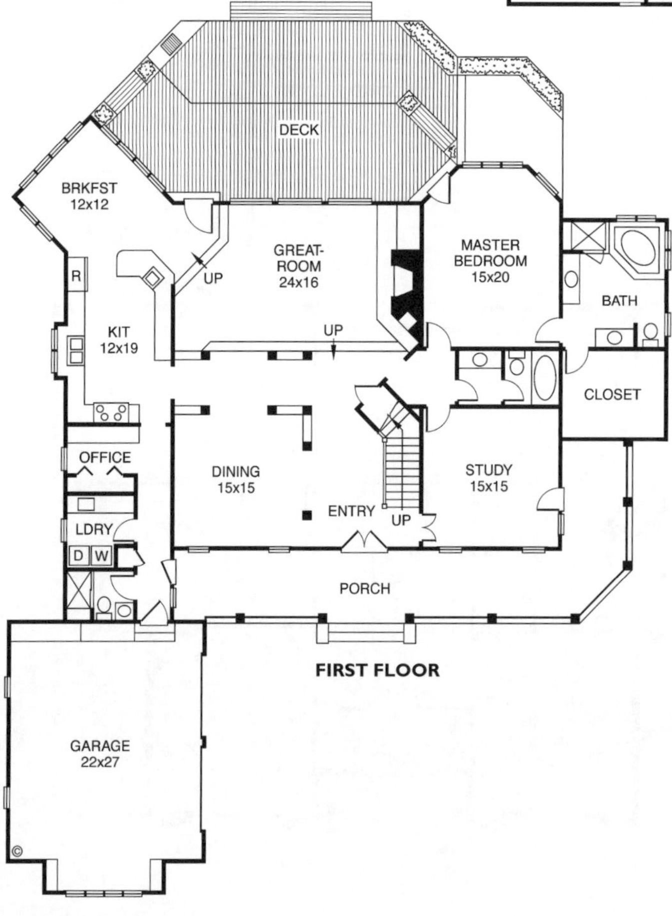

FIRST FLOOR

Please note: The photographed home may have been modified to suit homeowner preferences. If you order plans, have a builder or design professional check them against the photograph to confirm actual construction details.

Design 65614

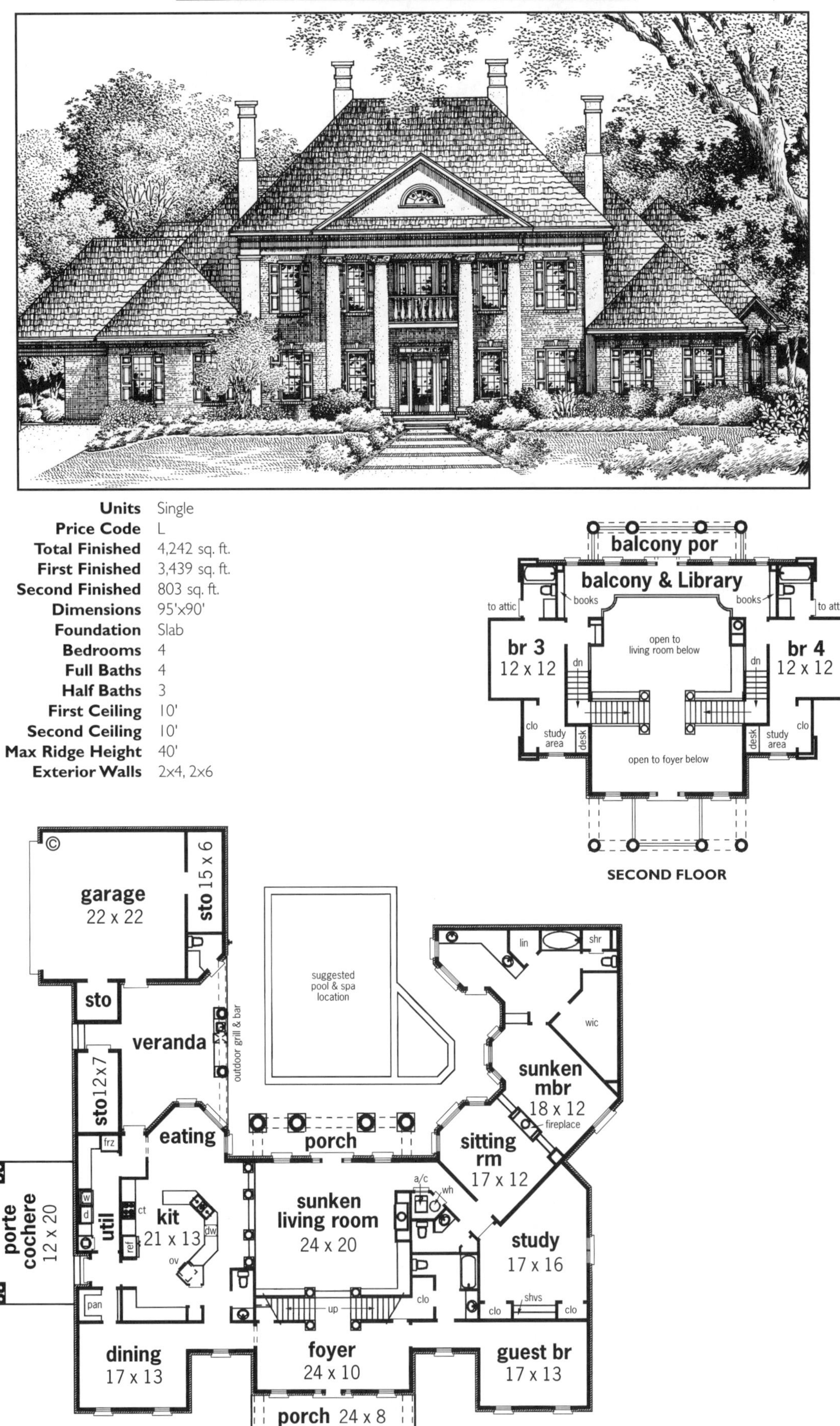
balcony por
balcony & Library
books
books
to attic
to attic
open to living room below
br 3 12 x 12
br 4 12 x 12
dn
dn
clo
clo
study area
study area
desk
desk
open to foyer below
SECOND FLOOR
garage 22 x 22
sto 15 x 6
sto
veranda
outdoor grill & bar
suggested pool & spa location
sto 12x7
frz
eating
porch
sunken mbr 18 x 12
fireplace
lin
shr
wic
sitting rm 17 x 12
porte cochere 12 x 20
util
w
d
kit 21 x 13
ct
ref
dw
ov
sunken living room 24 x 20
a/c
wh
study 17 x 16
shvs
clo
clo
clo
pan
up
dining 17 x 13
foyer 24 x 10
guest br 17 x 13
porch 24 x 8
FIRST FLOOR

Units	Single
Price Code	L
Total Finished	4,242 sq. ft.
First Finished	3,439 sq. ft.
Second Finished	803 sq. ft.
Dimensions	95'x90'
Foundation	Slab
Bedrooms	4
Full Baths	4
Half Baths	3
First Ceiling	10'
Second Ceiling	10'
Max Ridge Height	40'
Exterior Walls	2x4, 2x6

Design 96605

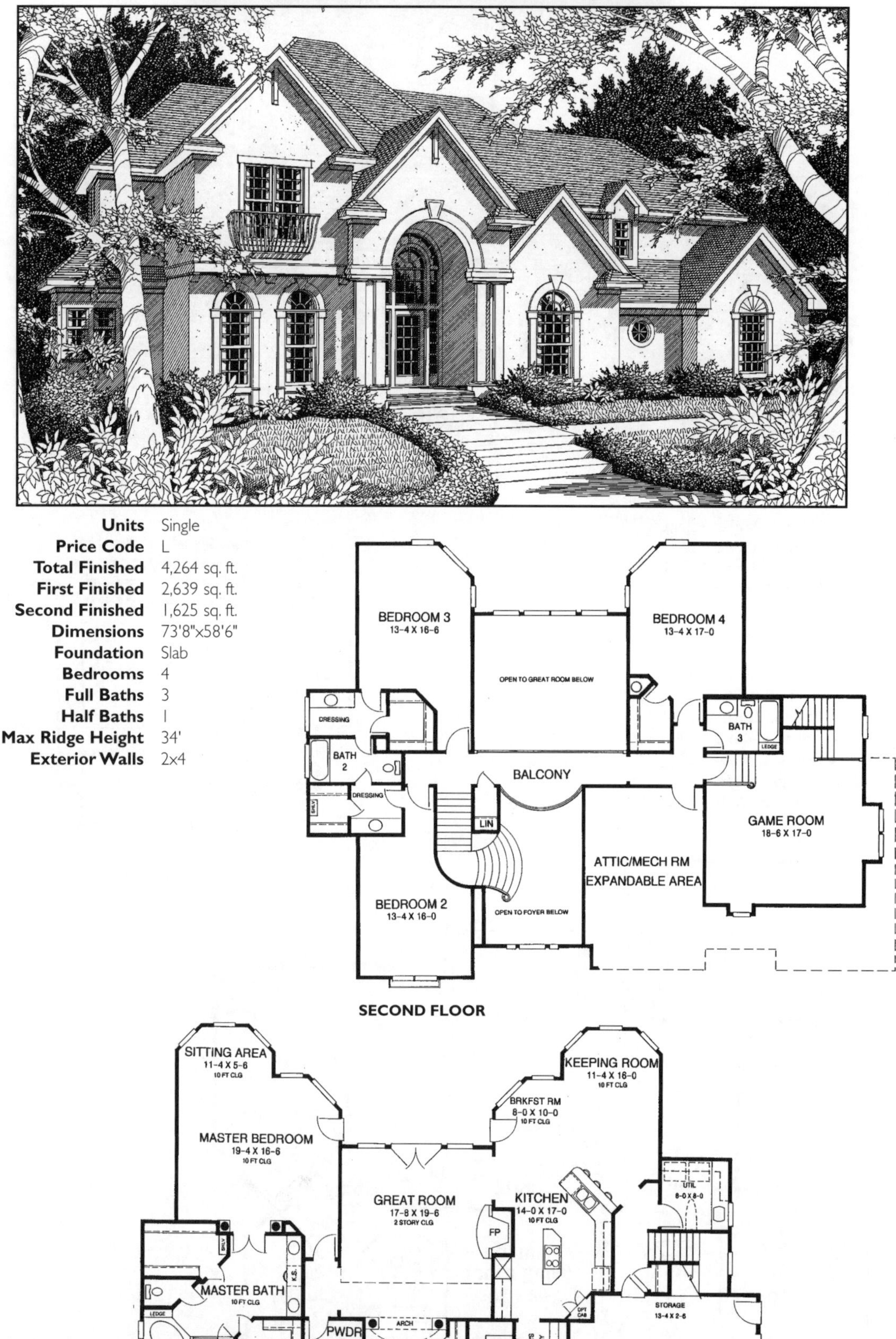

BEDROOM 3
13-4 X 16-6
OPEN TO GREAT ROOM BELOW
BEDROOM 4
13-4 X 17-0
DRESSING
BATH 2
DRESSING
BATH 3
LEDGE
BALCONY
LIN
GAME ROOM
18-6 X 17-0
ATTIC/MECH RM
EXPANDABLE AREA
BEDROOM 2
13-4 X 16-0
OPEN TO FOYER BELOW
SECOND FLOOR
SITTING AREA
11-4 X 5-6
10 FT CLG
KEEPING ROOM
11-4 X 16-0
10 FT CLG
BRKFST RM
8-0 X 10-0
10 FT CLG
MASTER BEDROOM
19-4 X 16-6
10 FT CLG
GREAT ROOM
17-8 X 19-6
2 STORY CLG
KITCHEN
14-0 X 17-0
10 FT CLG
UTIL
8-0 X 8-0
FP
MASTER BATH
10 FT CLG
LEDGE
SEAT
FLOWER BOX
PWDR
ARCH
PAN
BUTLER'S PANTRY
STORAGE
13-4 X 2-6
GARAGE
22-0 X 21-4
FOYER
2 STORY CLG
ARCH
STUDY
13-4 X 11-8
10 FT CLG
DINING ROOM
14-0 X 14-4
10 FT CLG
PORCH
FIRST FLOOR

Units	Single
Price Code	L
Total Finished	4,264 sq. ft.
First Finished	2,639 sq. ft.
Second Finished	1,625 sq. ft.
Dimensions	73'8"x58'6"
Foundation	Slab
Bedrooms	4
Full Baths	3
Half Baths	1
Max Ridge Height	34'
Exterior Walls	2x4

Design 32046

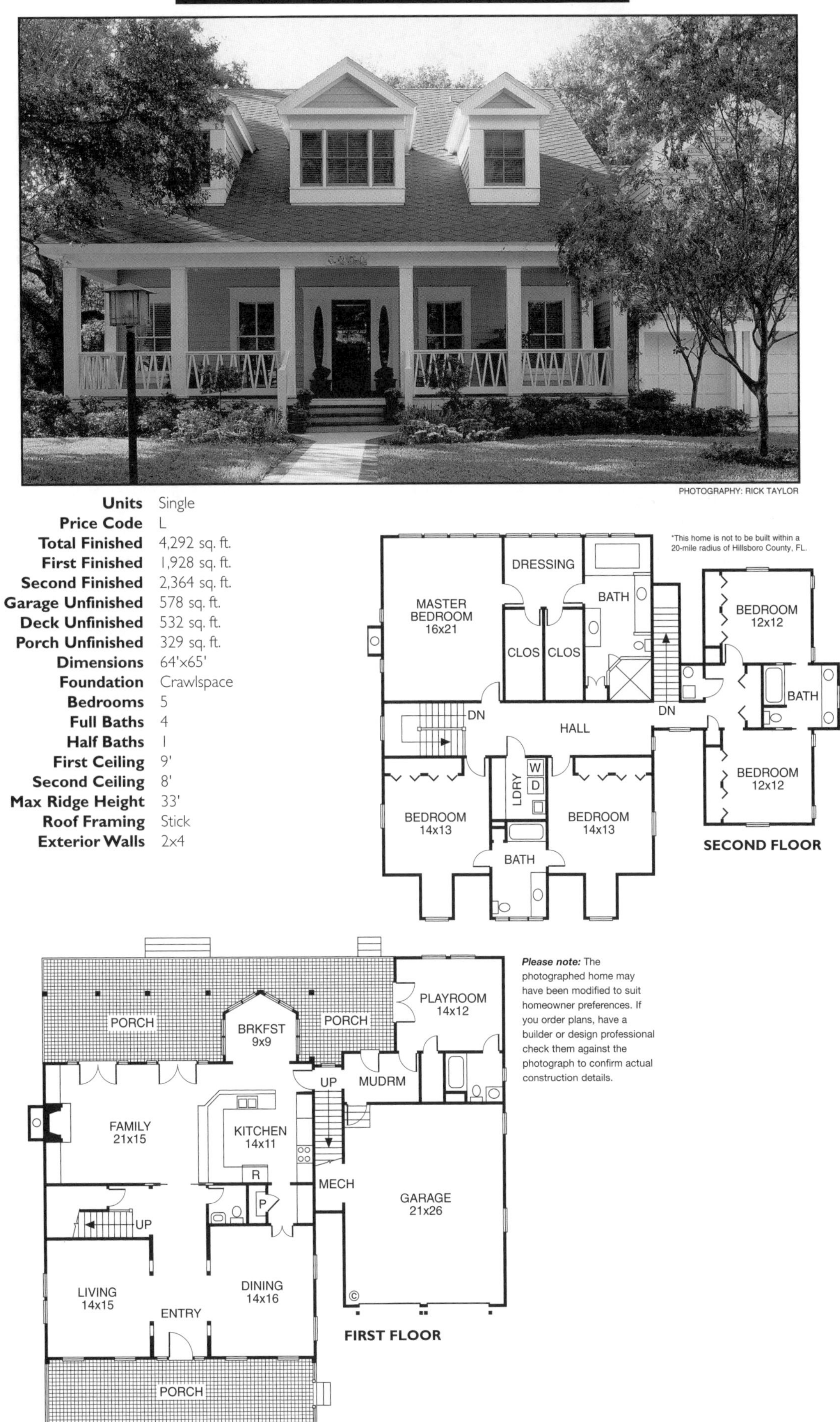
PHOTOGRAPHY: RICK TAYLOR
*This home is not to be built within a 20-mile radius of Hillsboro County, FL.
MASTER BEDROOM 16x21
DRESSING
BATH
CLOS
CLOS
DN
HALL
DN
BEDROOM 12x12
BATH
BEDROOM 12x12
LDRY
W
D
BEDROOM 14x13
BEDROOM 14x13
BATH
SECOND FLOOR
PORCH
BRKFST 9x9
PORCH
PLAYROOM 14x12
UP
MUDRM
FAMILY 21x15
KITCHEN 14x11
R
P
MECH
GARAGE 21x26
UP
LIVING 14x15
ENTRY
DINING 14x16
PORCH
FIRST FLOOR

Units	Single
Price Code	L
Total Finished	4,292 sq. ft.
First Finished	1,928 sq. ft.
Second Finished	2,364 sq. ft.
Garage Unfinished	578 sq. ft.
Deck Unfinished	532 sq. ft.
Porch Unfinished	329 sq. ft.
Dimensions	64'x65'
Foundation	Crawlspace
Bedrooms	5
Full Baths	4
Half Baths	1
First Ceiling	9'
Second Ceiling	8'
Max Ridge Height	33'
Roof Framing	Stick
Exterior Walls	2x4

Please note: The photographed home may have been modified to suit homeowner preferences. If you order plans, have a builder or design professional check them against the photograph to confirm actual construction details.

Design 97351

Units	Single
Price Code	L
Total Finished	4,303 sq. ft.
Main Finished	2,650 sq. ft.
Lower Finished	1,653 sq. ft.
Dimensions	72'4"x82'
Foundation	Basement
Bedrooms	3
Full Baths	2
3/4 Baths	1
Half Baths	1
Main Ceiling	9'
Max Ridge Height	29'
Roof Framing	Truss
Exterior Walls	2x6

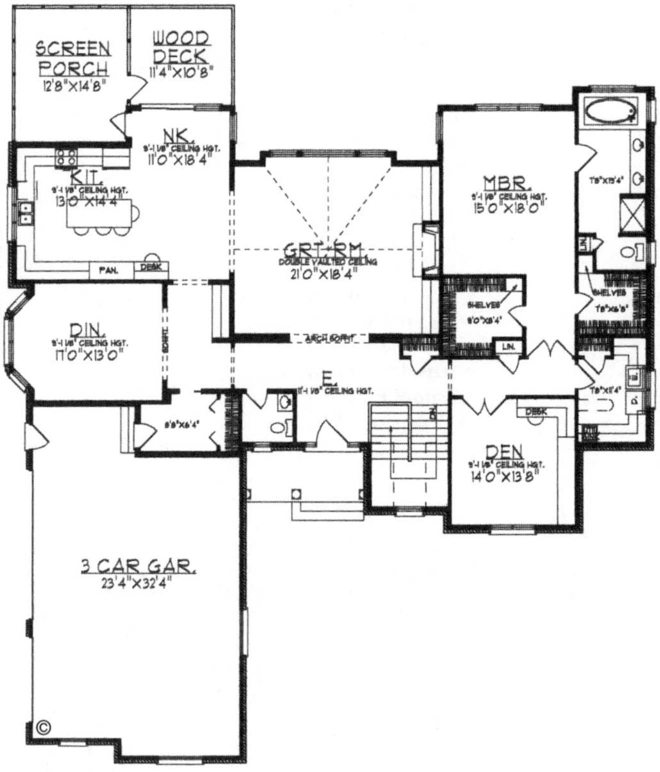

MAIN FLOOR

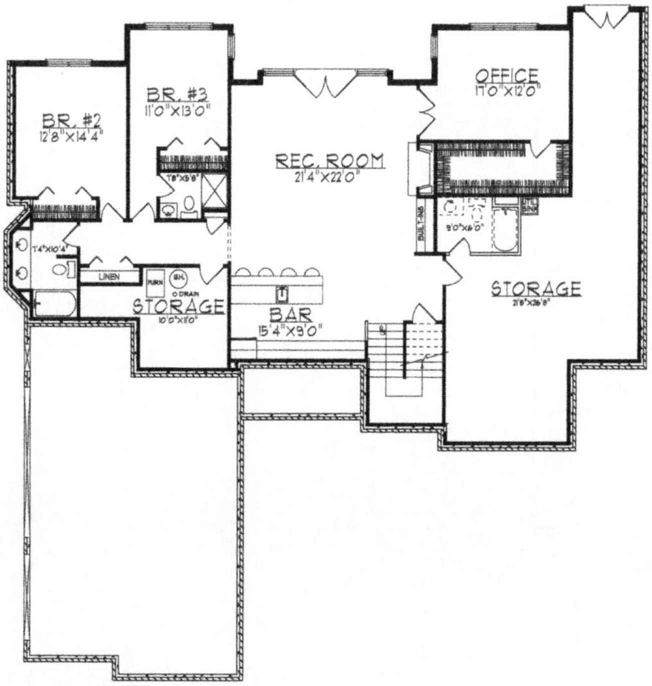

LOWER FLOOR

Design 92657

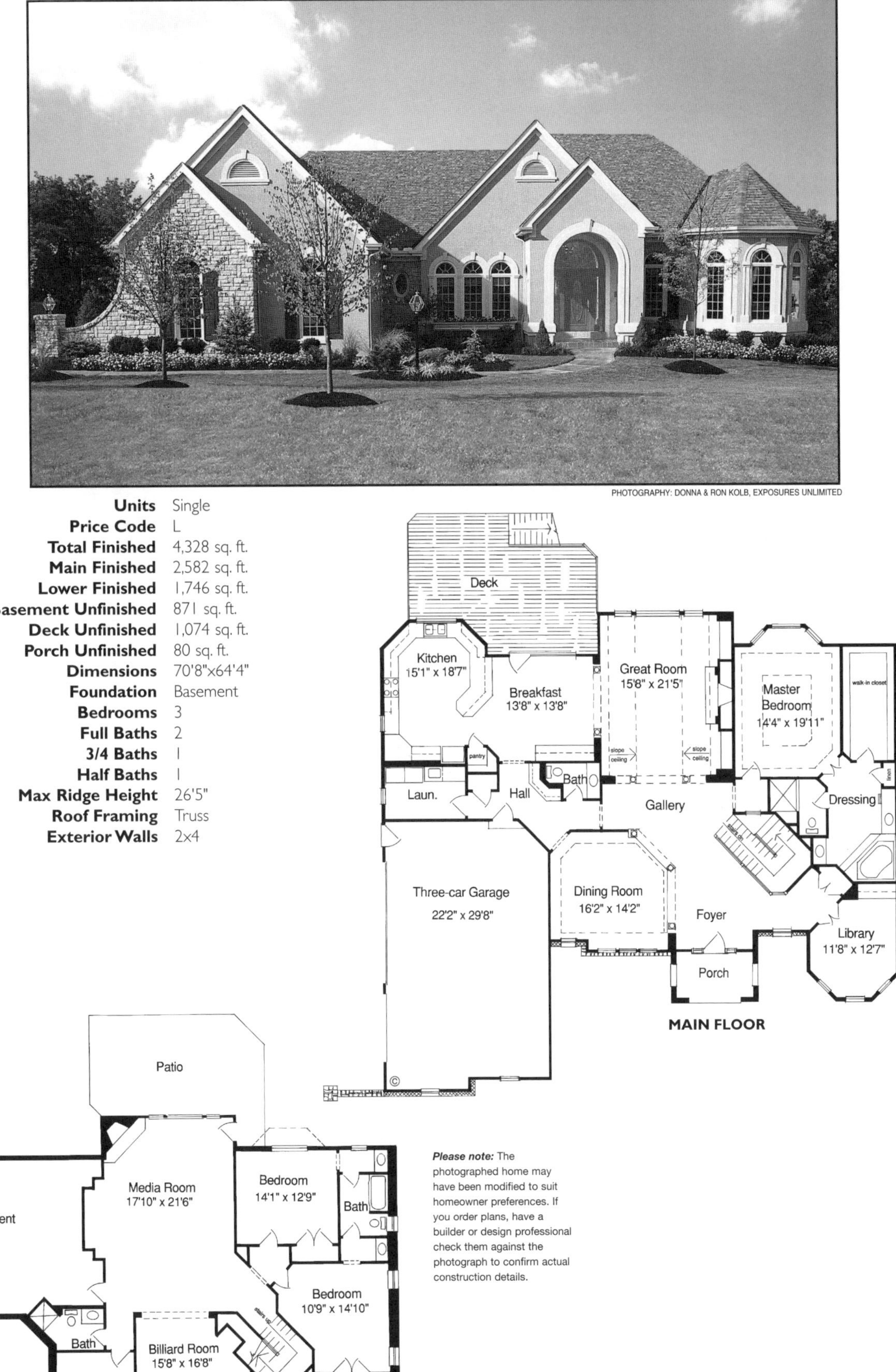
Deck
Kitchen
15'1" x 18'7"
Breakfast
13'8" x 13'8"
pantry
Great Room
15'8" x 21'5"
slope ceiling
slope ceiling
Master Bedroom
14'4" x 19'11"
walk-in closet
linen
Dressing
Laun.
Hall
Bath
Gallery
Three-car Garage
22'2" x 29'8"
Dining Room
16'2" x 14'2"
Foyer
Library
11'8" x 12'7"
Porch
MAIN FLOOR
Patio
Basement
Media Room
17'10" x 21'6"
Bedroom
14'1" x 12'9"
Bath
Bedroom
10'9" x 14'10"
Bath
Billiard Room
15'8" x 16'8"
Exercise Room
10'11" x 10'10"
Basement
LOWER FLOOR

PHOTOGRAPHY: DONNA & RON KOLB, EXPOSURES UNLIMITED

Units	Single
Price Code	L
Total Finished	4,328 sq. ft.
Main Finished	2,582 sq. ft.
Lower Finished	1,746 sq. ft.
Basement Unfinished	871 sq. ft.
Deck Unfinished	1,074 sq. ft.
Porch Unfinished	80 sq. ft.
Dimensions	70'8"x64'4"
Foundation	Basement
Bedrooms	3
Full Baths	2
3/4 Baths	1
Half Baths	1
Max Ridge Height	26'5"
Roof Framing	Truss
Exterior Walls	2x4

Please note: The photographed home may have been modified to suit homeowner preferences. If you order plans, have a builder or design professional check them against the photograph to confirm actual construction details.

Design 32112

PHOTOGRAPHY: JAMES YOCHUM PHOTOGRAPHY

Units	Single
Price Code	L
Total Finished	4,377 sq. ft.
First Finished	1,704 sq. ft.
Second Finished	1,679 sq. ft.
Lower Finished	994 sq. ft.
Basement Unfinished	710 sq. ft.
Garage Unfinished	954 sq. ft.
Deck Unfinished	153 sq. ft.
Porch Unfinished	794 sq. ft.
Dimensions	82'x70'
Foundation	Basement
Bedrooms	5
Full Baths	4
Half Baths	1
First Ceiling	9'
Second Ceiling	8'
Max Ridge Height	38'4"
Roof Framing	Stick
Exterior Walls	2x4

Please note: The photographed home may have been modified to suit homeowner preferences. If you order plans, have a builder or design professional check them against the photograph to confirm actual construction details.

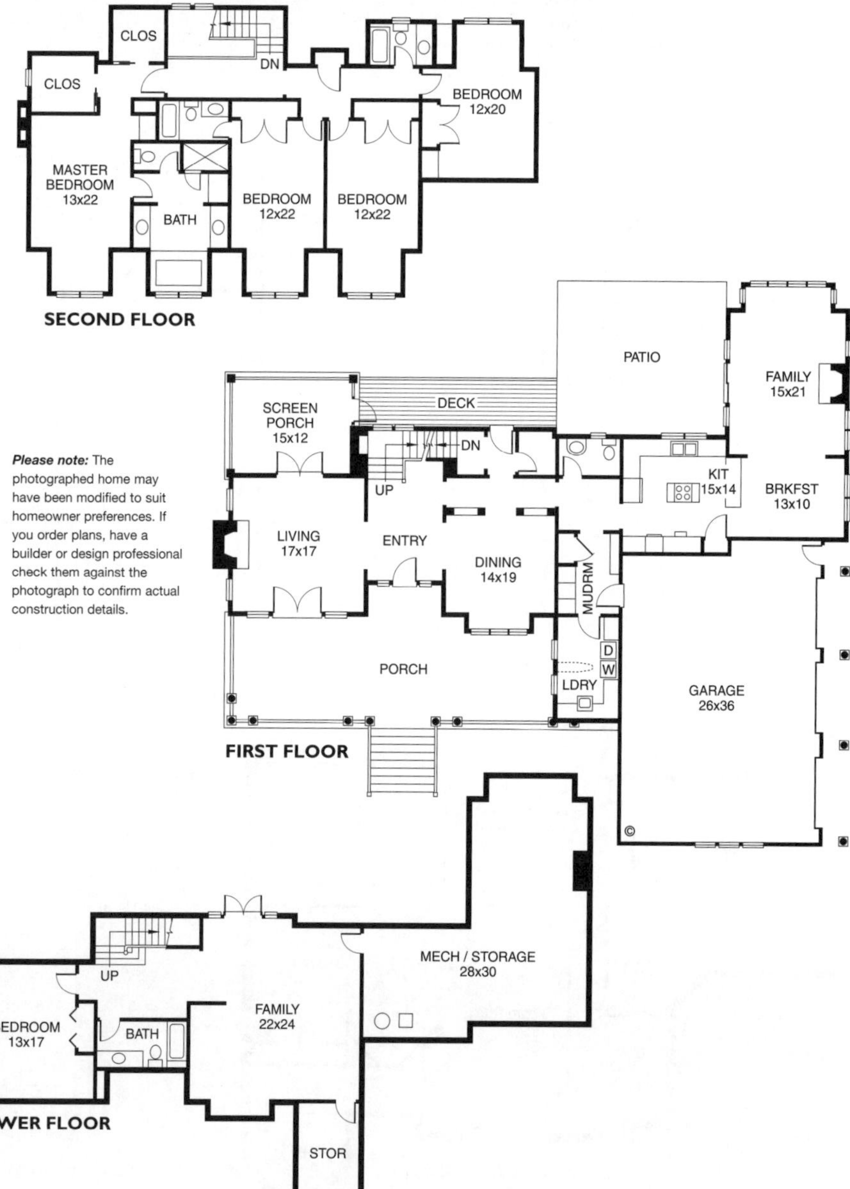

CLOS
CLOS
DN
BEDROOM 12x20
MASTER BEDROOM 13x22
BATH
BEDROOM 12x22
BEDROOM 12x22
SECOND FLOOR
PATIO
FAMILY 15x21
SCREEN PORCH 15x12
DECK
DN
UP
KIT 15x14
BRKFST 13x10
LIVING 17x17
ENTRY
DINING 14x19
MUDRM
PORCH
D W
LDRY
GARAGE 26x36
FIRST FLOOR
MECH / STORAGE 28x30
UP
FAMILY 22x24
BEDROOM 13x17
BATH
LOWER FLOOR
STOR

Design 98990

Units	Single
Price Code	L
Total Finished	4,436 sq. ft.
Main Finished	1,466 sq. ft.
Lower Finished	2,221 sq. ft.
Basement Finished	749 sq. ft.
Bonus Unfinished	388 sq. ft.
Dimensions	71'4"x67'4"
Foundation	Basement
Bedrooms	6
Full Baths	4
3/4 Baths	1
Main Ceiling	9'
Max Ridge Height	28'
Exterior Walls	2x4

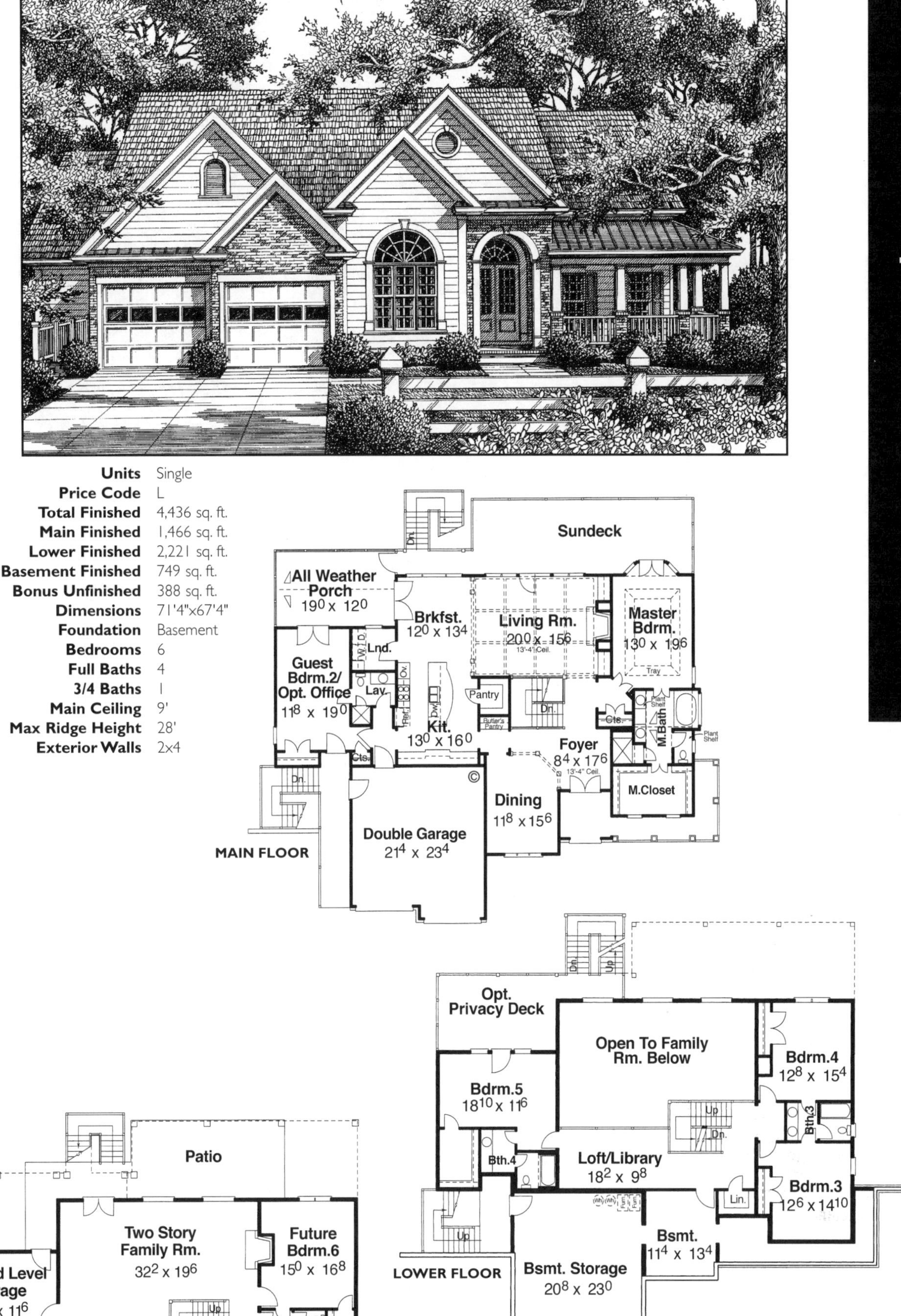
Sundeck
All Weather Porch
19^{0} x 12^{0}
Brkfst.
12^{0} x 13^{4}
Living Rm.
20^{0} x 15^{6}
13'-4" Ceil.
Master Bdrm.
13^{0} x 19^{6}
Tray
Guest Bdrm.2/ Opt. Office
11^{8} x 19^{0}
Lnd.
Lay.
Pantry
Butler's Pantry
Dn.
Cts.
M.Bath
Plant Shelf
Kit.
13^{0} x 16^{0}
Foyer
8^{4} x 17^{6}
13'-4" Ceil.
M.Closet
Dining
11^{8} x 15^{6}
Double Garage
21^{4} x 23^{4}
MAIN FLOOR
Opt. Privacy Deck
Open To Family Rm. Below
Bdrm.4
12^{8} x 15^{4}
Bdrm.5
18^{10} x 11^{6}
Bth.3
Bth.4
Loft/Library
18^{2} x 9^{8}
Lin.
Bdrm.3
12^{6} x 14^{10}
Bsmt.
11^{4} x 13^{4}
Bsmt. Storage
20^{8} x 23^{0}
Up
Dn.
LOWER FLOOR
Patio
Two Story Family Rm.
32^{2} x 19^{6}
Future Bdrm.6
15^{0} x 16^{8}
Ground Level Storage
18^{10} x 11^{6}
Stor.
Bth.5
BASEMENT

Design 98991

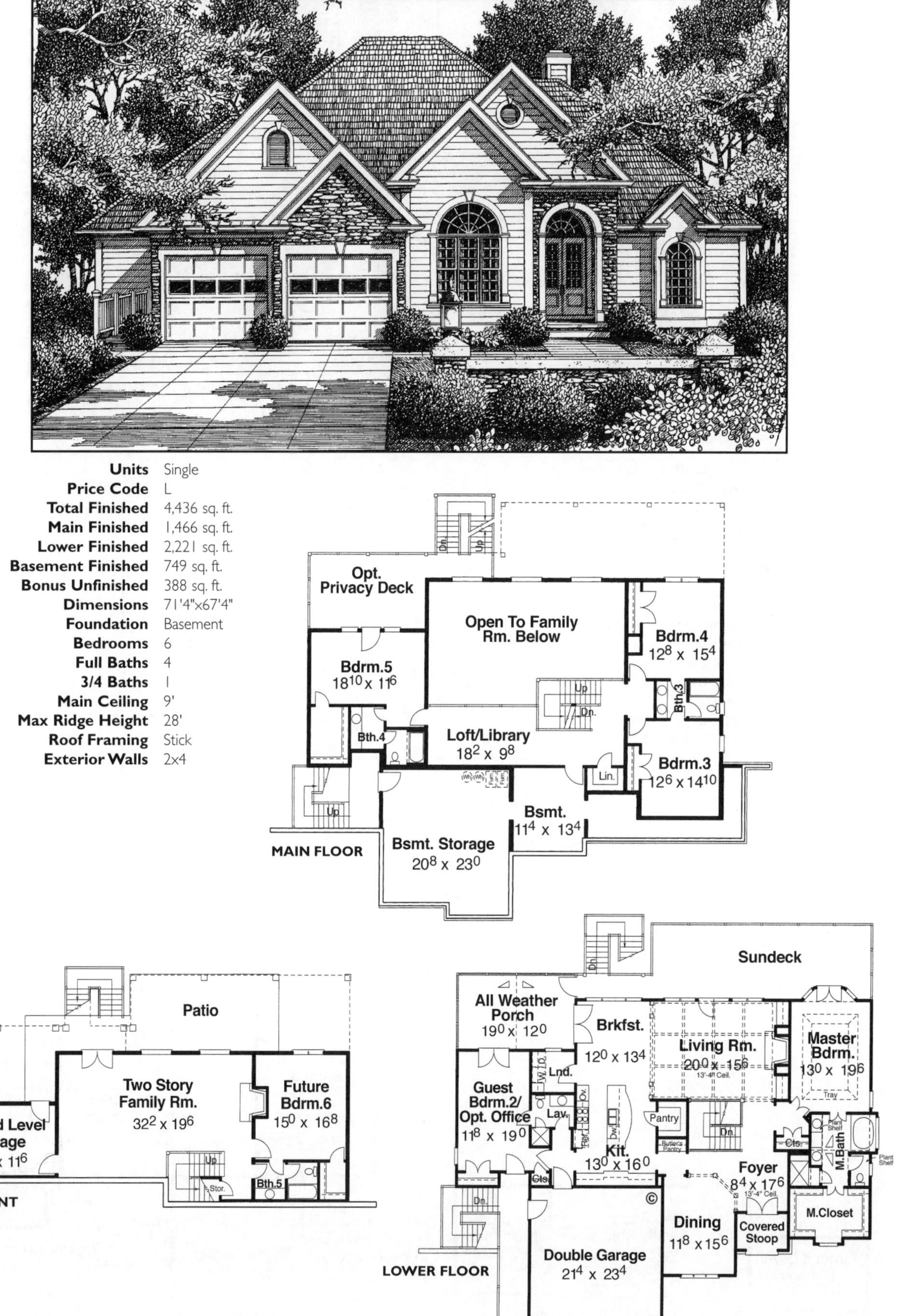

Opt. Privacy Deck
Open To Family Rm. Below
Bdrm.4
12^{8} x 15^{4}
Bdrm.5
18^{10} x 11^{6}
Bth.3
Bth.4
Loft/Library
18^{2} x 9^{8}
Bdrm.3
12^{6} x 14^{10}
Lin.
Bsmt.
11^{4} x 13^{4}
Bsmt. Storage
20^{8} x 23^{0}
MAIN FLOOR
Patio
Two Story Family Rm.
32^{2} x 19^{6}
Future Bdrm.6
15^{0} x 16^{8}
Ground Level Storage
18^{10} x 11^{6}
Bth.5
BASEMENT
Sundeck
All Weather Porch
19^{0} x 12^{0}
Brkfst.
12^{0} x 13^{4}
Living Rm.
20^{0} x 15^{6}
Master Bdrm.
13^{0} x 19^{6}
Guest Bdrm.2/ Opt. Office
11^{8} x 19^{0}
Lnd.
Lav.
Kit.
13^{0} x 16^{0}
Pantry
Foyer
8^{4} x 17^{6}
M.Bath
M.Closet
Dining
11^{8} x 15^{6}
Covered Stoop
Double Garage
21^{4} x 23^{4}
LOWER FLOOR

Units	Single
Price Code	L
Total Finished	4,436 sq. ft.
Main Finished	1,466 sq. ft.
Lower Finished	2,221 sq. ft.
Basement Finished	749 sq. ft.
Bonus Unfinished	388 sq. ft.
Dimensions	71'4"x67'4"
Foundation	Basement
Bedrooms	6
Full Baths	4
3/4 Baths	1
Main Ceiling	9'
Max Ridge Height	28'
Roof Framing	Stick
Exterior Walls	2x4

Design 65610

Units	Single
Price Code	L
Total Finished	4,440 sq. ft.
First Finished	3,465 sq. ft.
Second Finished	975 sq. ft.
Bonus Unfinished	440 sq. ft.
Garage Unfinished	808 sq. ft.
Porch Unfinished	534 sq. ft.
Dimensions	94'x92'
Foundation	Crawlspace
Bedrooms	4
Full Baths	4
Half Baths	1
First Ceiling	12'
Second Ceiling	9'
Max Ridge Height	42'
Roof Framing	Stick
Exterior Walls	2x4

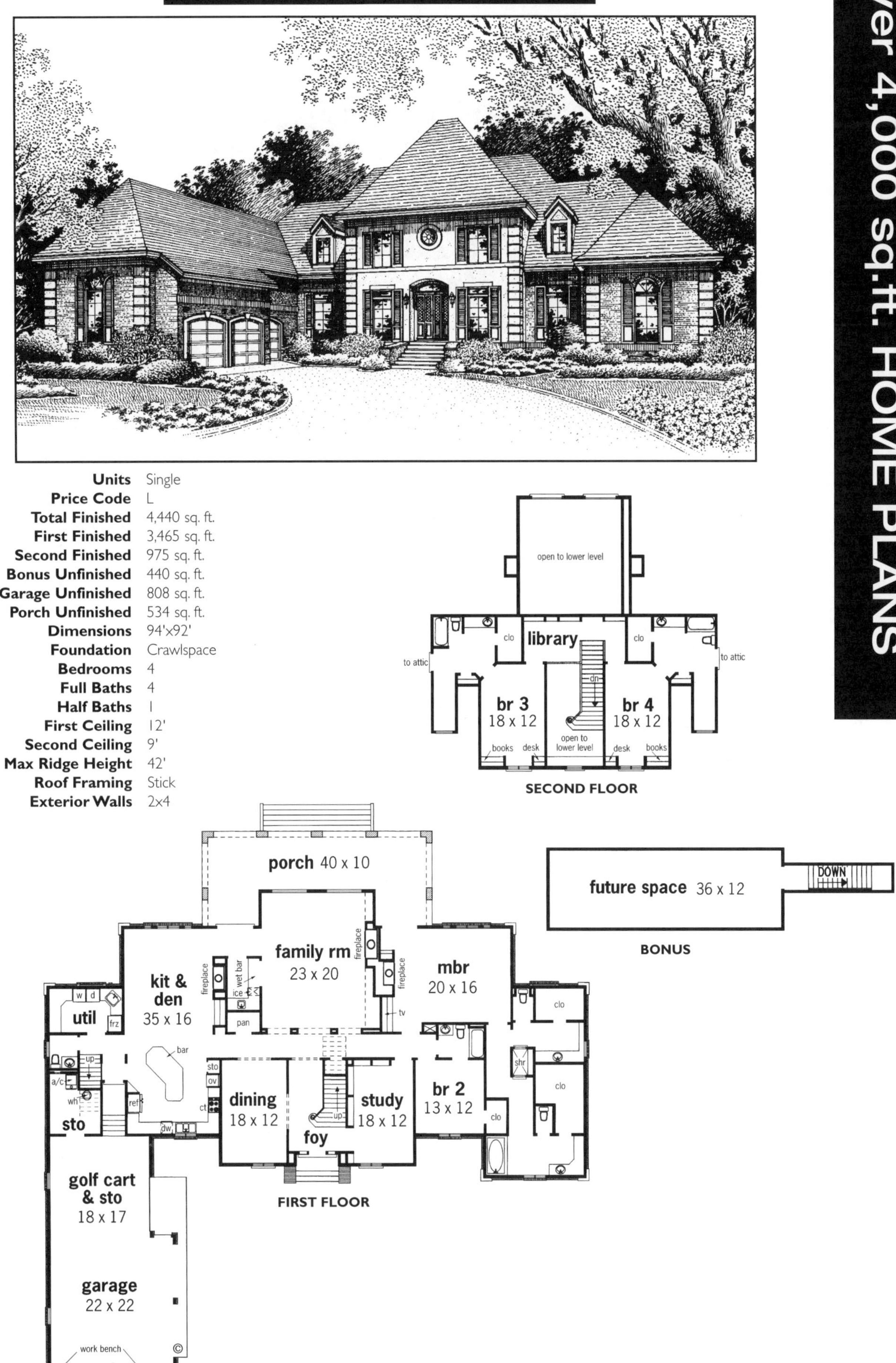
open to lower level
clo
library
clo
to attic
to attic
dn
br 3
18 x 12
br 4
18 x 12
books
desk
open to lower level
desk
books
SECOND FLOOR
porch 40 x 10
future space 36 x 12
DOWN
BONUS
family rm
23 x 20
fireplace
mbr
20 x 16
fireplace
kit & den
35 x 16
fireplace
wet bar
ice
pan
tv
w
d
util
frz
clo
bar
up
a/c
wh
ref
sto
ov
ct
dw
dining
18 x 12
up
foy
study
18 x 12
br 2
13 x 12
clo
shr
clo
sto
golf cart & sto
18 x 17
garage
22 x 22
work bench
FIRST FLOOR

Design 32033

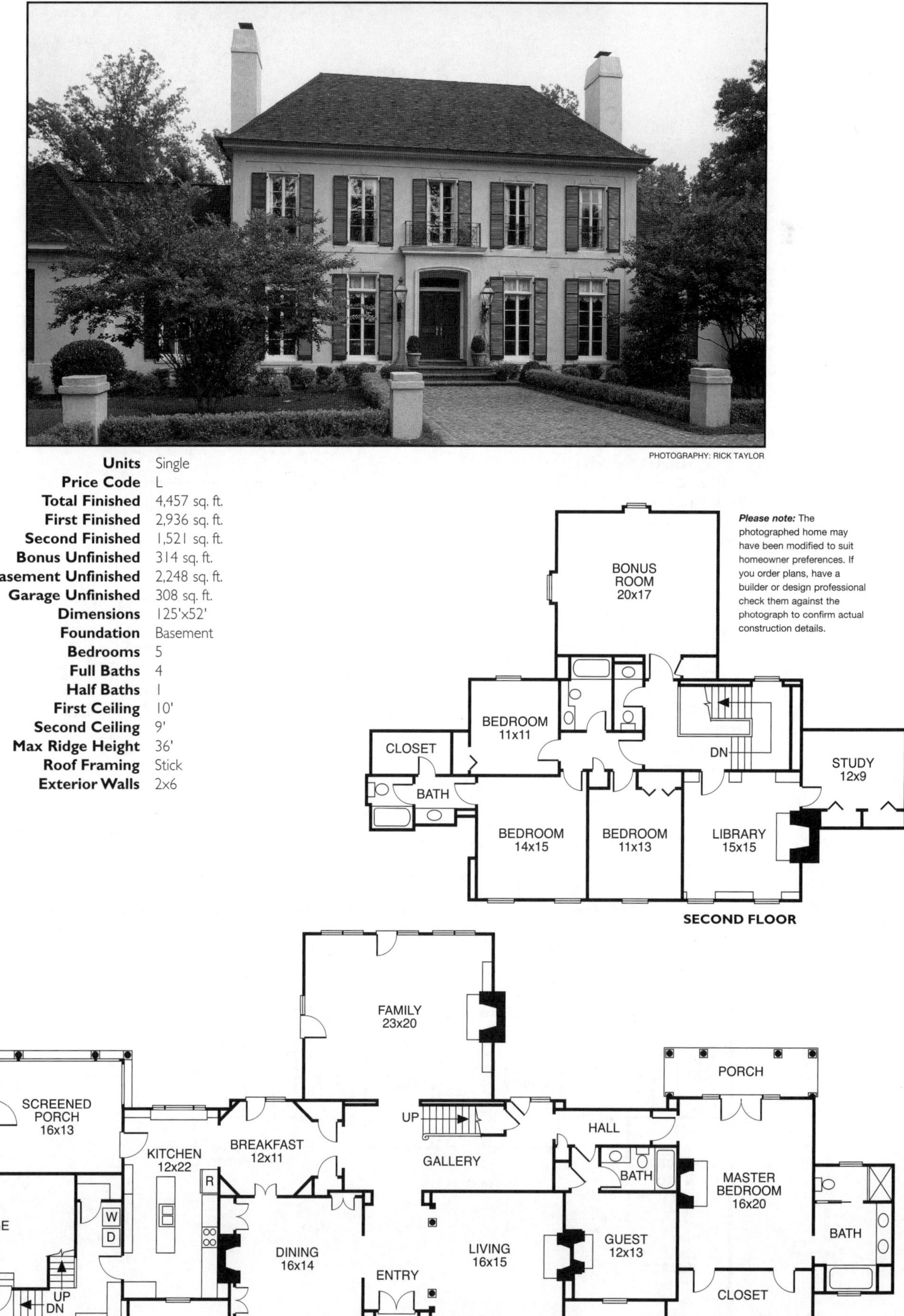
BONUS ROOM 20x17
BEDROOM 11x11
CLOSET
BATH
DN
STUDY 12x9
BEDROOM 14x15
BEDROOM 11x13
LIBRARY 15x15
SECOND FLOOR
FAMILY 23x20
SCREENED PORCH 16x13
KITCHEN 12x22
BREAKFAST 12x11
UP
GALLERY
HALL
PORCH
R
W
D
BATH
MASTER BEDROOM 16x20
GARAGE 22x14
DINING 16x14
LIVING 16x15
GUEST 12x13
BATH
ENTRY
UP
DN
CLOSET
FIRST FLOOR

PHOTOGRAPHY: RICK TAYLOR

Units	Single
Price Code	L
Total Finished	4,457 sq. ft.
First Finished	2,936 sq. ft.
Second Finished	1,521 sq. ft.
Bonus Unfinished	314 sq. ft.
Basement Unfinished	2,248 sq. ft.
Garage Unfinished	308 sq. ft.
Dimensions	125'x52'
Foundation	Basement
Bedrooms	5
Full Baths	4
Half Baths	1
First Ceiling	10'
Second Ceiling	9'
Max Ridge Height	36'
Roof Framing	Stick
Exterior Walls	2x6

Please note: The photographed home may have been modified to suit homeowner preferences. If you order plans, have a builder or design professional check them against the photograph to confirm actual construction details.

Design 63075

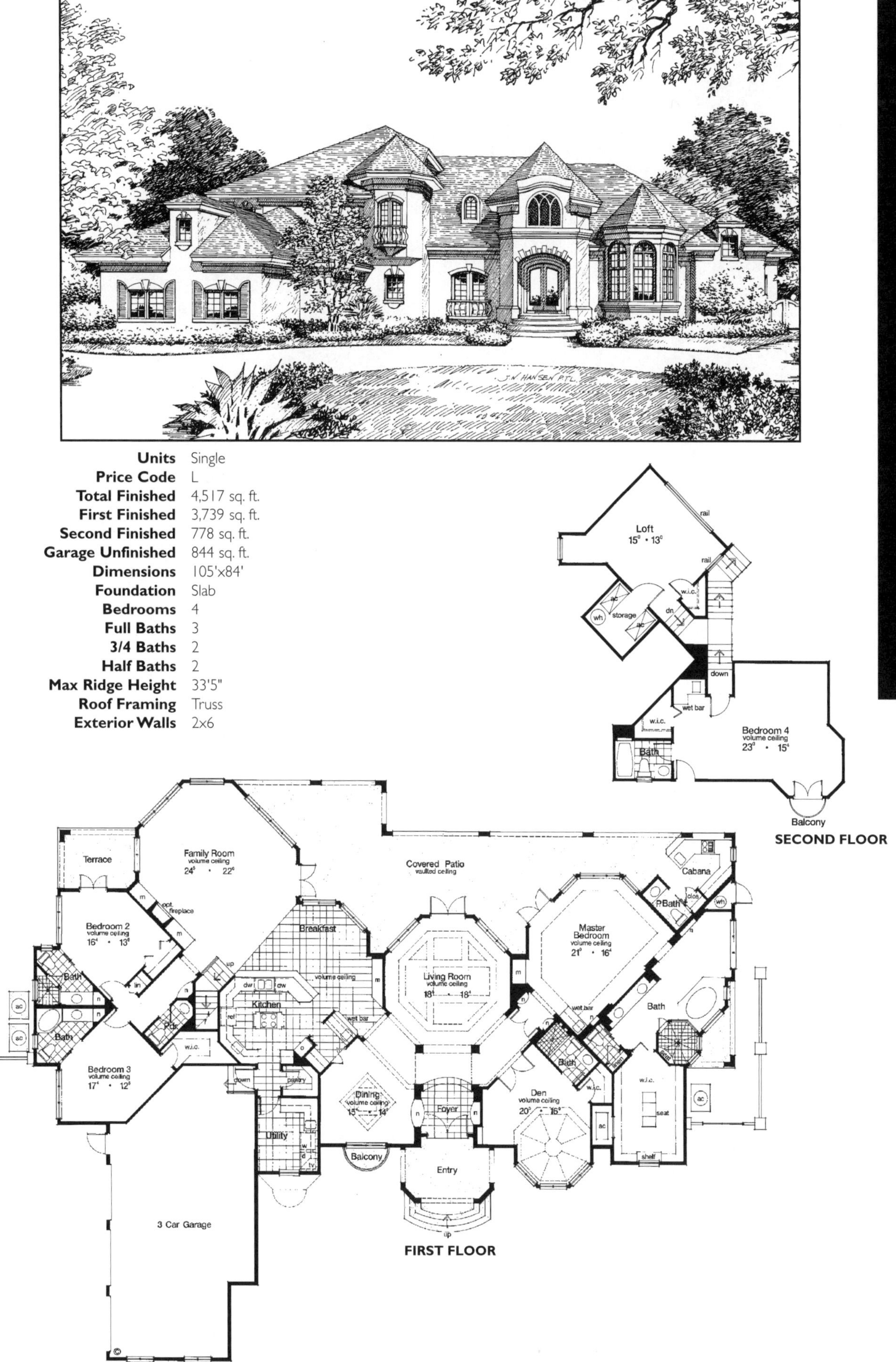
Loft
15° • 13°
rail
w.i.c.
storage
wh
ac
dn
down
wet bar
w.i.c.
Bath
Bedroom 4
volume ceiling
23° • 15'
Balcony
SECOND FLOOR
Terrace
Family Room
volume ceiling
24' • 22'
Covered Patio
vaulted ceiling
Cabana
clos.
P.Bath
wh
opt. fireplace
Bedroom 2
volume ceiling
16' • 13'
Breakfast
Master Bedroom
volume ceiling
21° • 16'
Bath
lin
up
volume ceiling
Living Room
volume ceiling
18' • 18'
Kitchen
wet bar
Bath
ac
Pdr.
Bath
Bedroom 3
volume ceiling
17' • 12'
w.i.c.
down
pantry
Dining
volume ceiling
15' • 14'
Foyer
Den
volume ceiling
20' • 16'
w.i.c.
seat
shelf
Utility
Balcony
Entry
up
3 Car Garage
FIRST FLOOR

Units	Single
Price Code	L
Total Finished	4,517 sq. ft.
First Finished	3,739 sq. ft.
Second Finished	778 sq. ft.
Garage Unfinished	844 sq. ft.
Dimensions	105'x84'
Foundation	Slab
Bedrooms	4
Full Baths	3
3/4 Baths	2
Half Baths	2
Max Ridge Height	33'5"
Roof Framing	Truss
Exterior Walls	2x6

Design 96604

COPYRIGHT LARRY E. BELK

Units	Single
Price Code	L
Total Finished	4,578 sq. ft.
First Finished	3,033 sq. ft.
Second Finished	1,545 sq. ft.
Dimensions	91'6"x63'8"
Foundation	Basement Crawlspace Slab
Bedrooms	4
Full Baths	3
Half Baths	2
Max Ridge Height	35'6"
Roof Framing	Stick
Exterior Walls	2x4

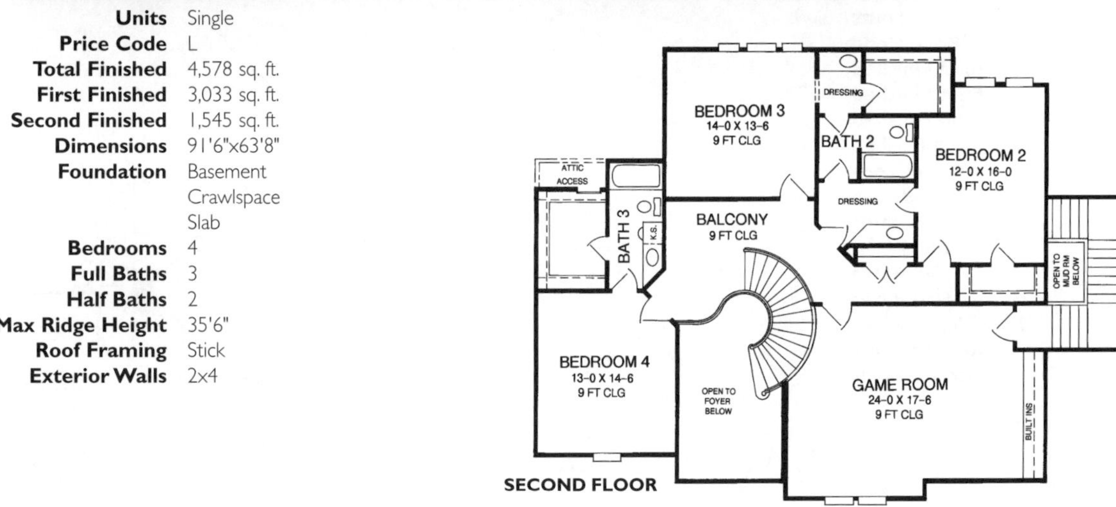
BEDROOM 3
14-0 X 13-6
9 FT CLG
DRESSING
BATH 2
BEDROOM 2
12-0 X 16-0
9 FT CLG
ATTIC ACCESS
BATH 3
K.S.
BALCONY
9 FT CLG
DRESSING
OPEN TO MUD RM BELOW
BEDROOM 4
13-0 X 14-6
9 FT CLG
OPEN TO FOYER BELOW
GAME ROOM
24-0 X 17-6
9 FT CLG
BUILT INS

SECOND FLOOR

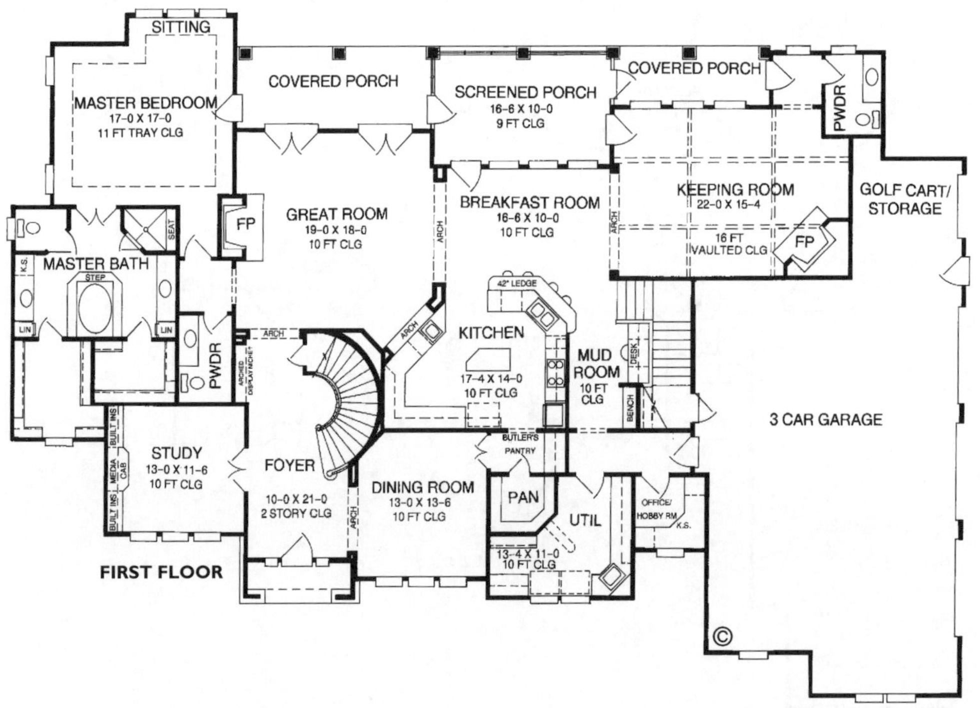
SITTING
MASTER BEDROOM
17-0 X 17-0
11 FT TRAY CLG
COVERED PORCH
SCREENED PORCH
16-6 X 10-0
9 FT CLG
COVERED PORCH
PWDR
FP
GREAT ROOM
19-0 X 18-0
10 FT CLG
BREAKFAST ROOM
16-6 X 10-0
10 FT CLG
KEEPING ROOM
22-0 X 15-4
16 FT VAULTED CLG
FP
GOLF CART/ STORAGE
MASTER BATH
STEP
SEAT
K.S.
LIN
LIN
ARCH
ARCH
ARCH
ARCH
42" LEDGE
KITCHEN
17-4 X 14-0
10 FT CLG
MUD ROOM
10 FT CLG
DESK
BENCH
PWDR
3 CAR GARAGE
STUDY
13-0 X 11-6
10 FT CLG
BUILT INS
MEDIA CAB
FOYER
10-0 X 21-0
2 STORY CLG
DINING ROOM
13-0 X 13-6
10 FT CLG
BUTLER'S PANTRY
PAN
UTIL
13-4 X 11-0
10 FT CLG
OFFICE/ HOBBY RM
K.S.
©

FIRST FLOOR

Design 91166

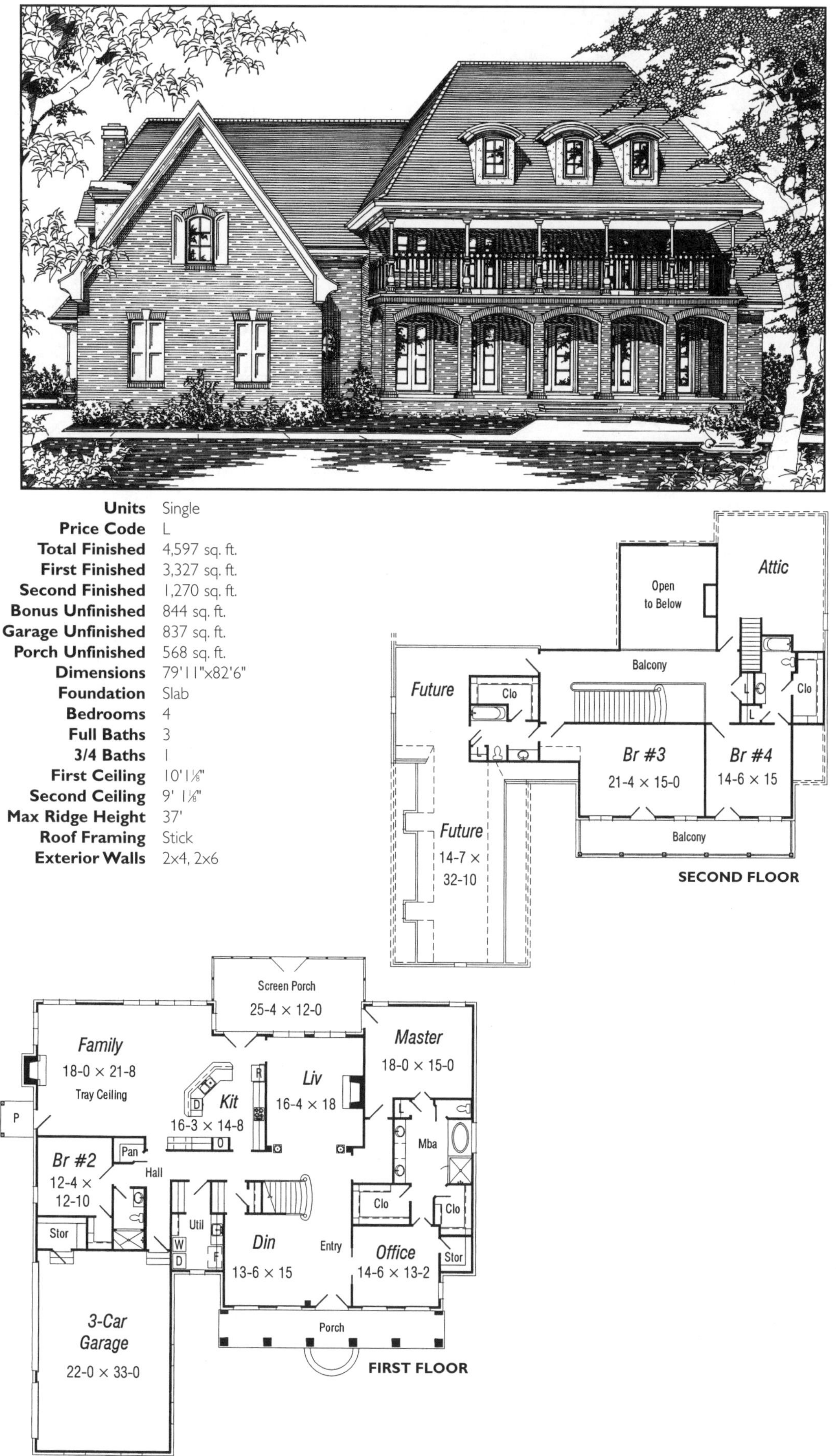
Open
to Below
Attic
Balcony
Future
Clo
Clo
Br #3
21-4 × 15-0
Br #4
14-6 × 15
Balcony
Future
14-7 ×
32-10
SECOND FLOOR
Screen Porch
25-4 × 12-0
Family
18-0 × 21-8
Tray Ceiling
Master
18-0 × 15-0
Liv
16-4 × 18
Kit
16-3 × 14-8
P
Br #2
12-4 ×
12-10
Pan
Hall
Mba
Stor
Util
Clo
Clo
Din
13-6 × 15
Entry
Office
14-6 × 13-2
Stor
3-Car
Garage
22-0 × 33-0
Porch
FIRST FLOOR

Units	Single
Price Code	L
Total Finished	4,597 sq. ft.
First Finished	3,327 sq. ft.
Second Finished	1,270 sq. ft.
Bonus Unfinished	844 sq. ft.
Garage Unfinished	837 sq. ft.
Porch Unfinished	568 sq. ft.
Dimensions	79'11"x82'6"
Foundation	Slab
Bedrooms	4
Full Baths	3
3/4 Baths	1
First Ceiling	10'1⅛"
Second Ceiling	9' 1⅛"
Max Ridge Height	37'
Roof Framing	Stick
Exterior Walls	2x4, 2x6

Design 97877

Units	Single
Price Code	L
Total Finished	4,615 sq. ft.
Main Finished	4,615 sq. ft.
Garage Unfinished	748 sq. ft.
Dimensions	113'4"x69'4"
Foundation	Slab
Bedrooms	4
Full Baths	3
3/4 Baths	1
Half Baths	1
Max Ridge Height	34'
Roof Framing	Stick
Exterior Walls	2x4

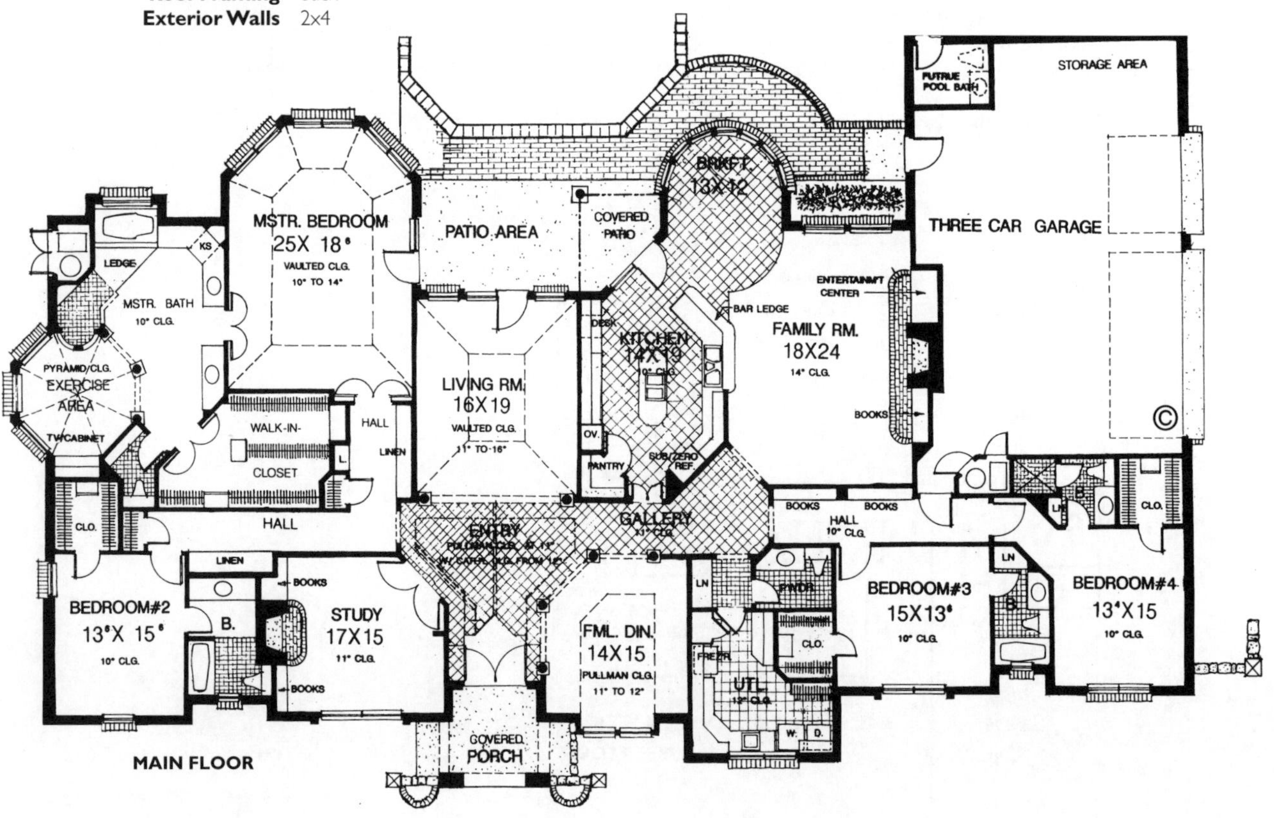

STORAGE AREA
THREE CAR GARAGE
BRKFT. 13X12
PATIO AREA
COVERED PATIO
MSTR. BEDROOM 25X 18
VAULTED CLG. 10" TO 14"
LEDGE
KS
MSTR. BATH 10" CLG.
PYRAMID CLG.
EXERCISE AREA
TV CABINET
WALK-IN-CLOSET
HALL
LINEN
LIVING RM. 16X19
VAULTED CLG. 11" TO 16"
KITCHEN 14X19
PANTRY
OV.
ENTERTAINM'T CENTER
BAR LEDGE
FAMILY RM. 18X24
14" CLG.
BOOKS
HALL 10" CLG.
ENTRY
GALLERY
CLO.
BEDROOM#2 13X 15 10" CLG.
B.
STUDY 17X15 11" CLG.
FML. DIN. 14X15 PULLMAN CLG. 11" TO 12"
PWDR.
UTL.
W. D.
BEDROOM#3 15X13 10" CLG.
BEDROOM#4 13X15 10" CLG.
LN
COVERED PORCH

MAIN FLOOR

Design 69012

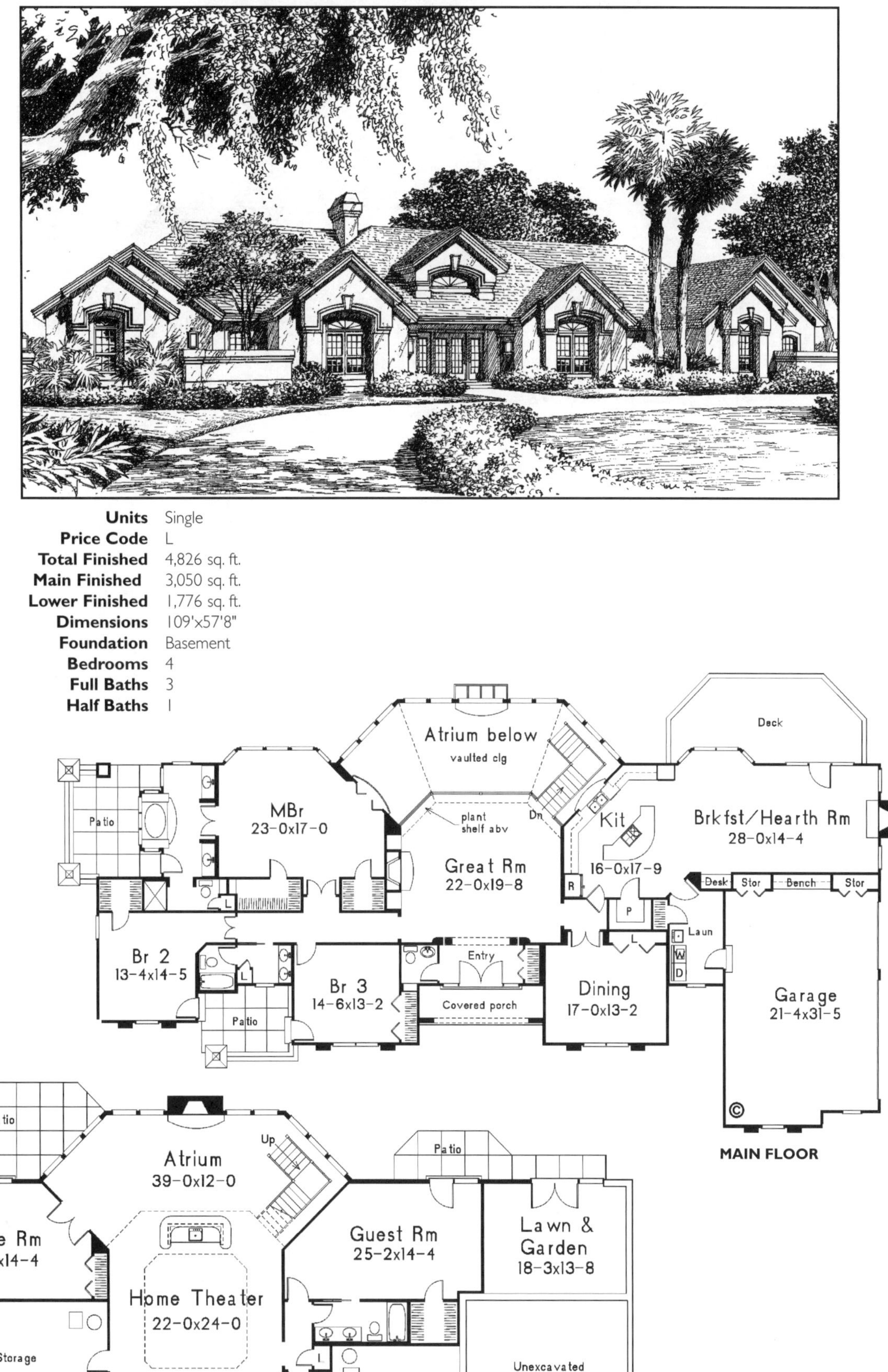
Atrium below
vaulted clg
plant shelf abv
Dn
Deck
Patio
MBr
23-0x17-0
Great Rm
22-0x19-8
Kit
16-0x17-9
Brkfst/Hearth Rm
28-0x14-4
R
P
Desk
Stor
Bench
Stor
L
Laun
W
D
Br 2
13-4x14-5
L
Patio
Br 3
14-6x13-2
Entry
Covered porch
Dining
17-0x13-2
Garage
21-4x31-5
MAIN FLOOR
Patio
Atrium
39-0x12-0
Up
Patio
Game Rm
23-0x14-4
Home Theater
22-0x24-0
screen
Guest Rm
25-2x14-4
Lawn & Garden
18-3x13-8
Mech & Storage
Mech & Storage
Unexcavated
LOWER FLOOR

Units	Single
Price Code	L
Total Finished	4,826 sq. ft.
Main Finished	3,050 sq. ft.
Lower Finished	1,776 sq. ft.
Dimensions	109'x57'8"
Foundation	Basement
Bedrooms	4
Full Baths	3
Half Baths	1

Design 92111

Units	Single
Price Code	L
Total Finished	4,866 sq. ft.
First Finished	1,888 sq. ft.
Second Finished	1,613 sq. ft.
Lower Finished	1,365 sq. ft.
Garage Unfinished	955 sq. ft.
Dimensions	76'8"x54'2"
Foundation	Basement Crawlspace
Bedrooms	5
Full Baths	2
3/4 Baths	2
Half Baths	1

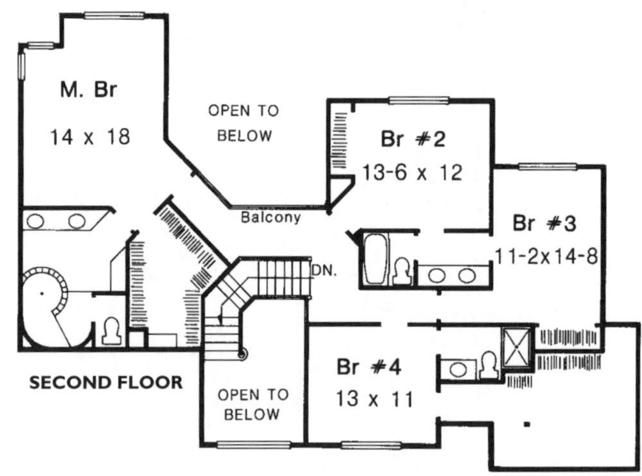

M. Br
14 x 18
OPEN TO BELOW
Br #2
13-6 x 12
Balcony
Br #3
11-2x14-8
DN.
Br #4
13 x 11
OPEN TO BELOW
SECOND FLOOR

*This home is not to be built in Washington State.

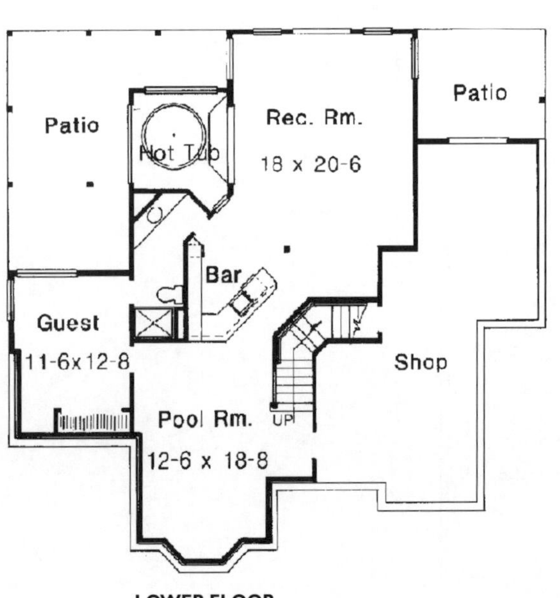

Patio
Hot Tub
Rec. Rm.
18 x 20-6
Patio
Bar
Guest
11-6x12-8
Shop
Pool Rm.
12-6 x 18-8
UP
LOWER FLOOR

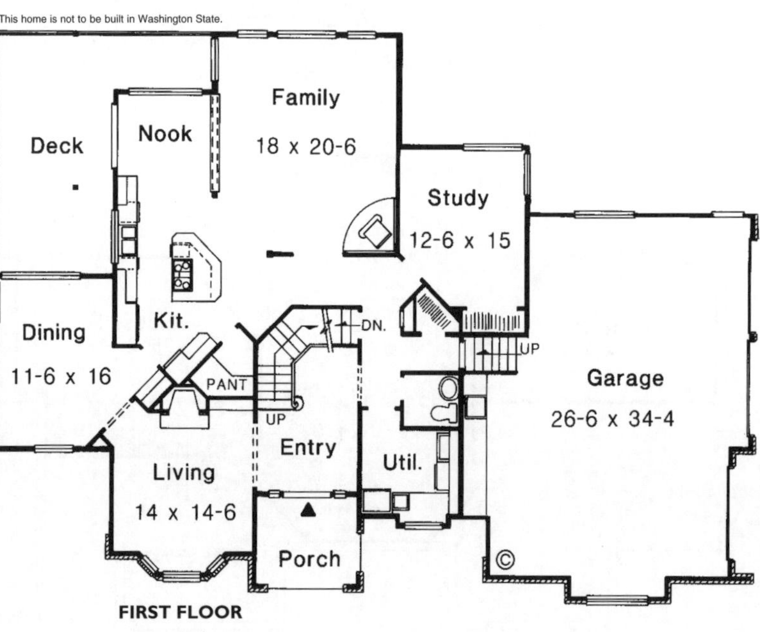

Deck
Nook
Family
18 x 20-6
Study
12-6 x 15
Dining
11-6 x 16
Kit.
DN.
UP
PANT
Garage
26-6 x 34-4
UP
Entry
Living
14 x 14-6
Util.
Porch
©
FIRST FLOOR

Design 91180

Units	Single
Price Code	L
Total Finished	4,934 sq. ft.
First Finished	3,082 sq. ft.
Second Finished	1,852 sq. ft.
Garage Unfinished	700 sq. ft.
Porch Unfinished	168 sq. ft.
Dimensions	78' 5.5"x63'11.5"
Foundation	Slab
Bedrooms	5
Full Baths	4
Half Baths	1
First Ceiling	10'1 1/8"
Second Ceiling	9' 1 1/8"
Max Ridge Height	34'
Roof Framing	Stick
Exterior Walls	2x4

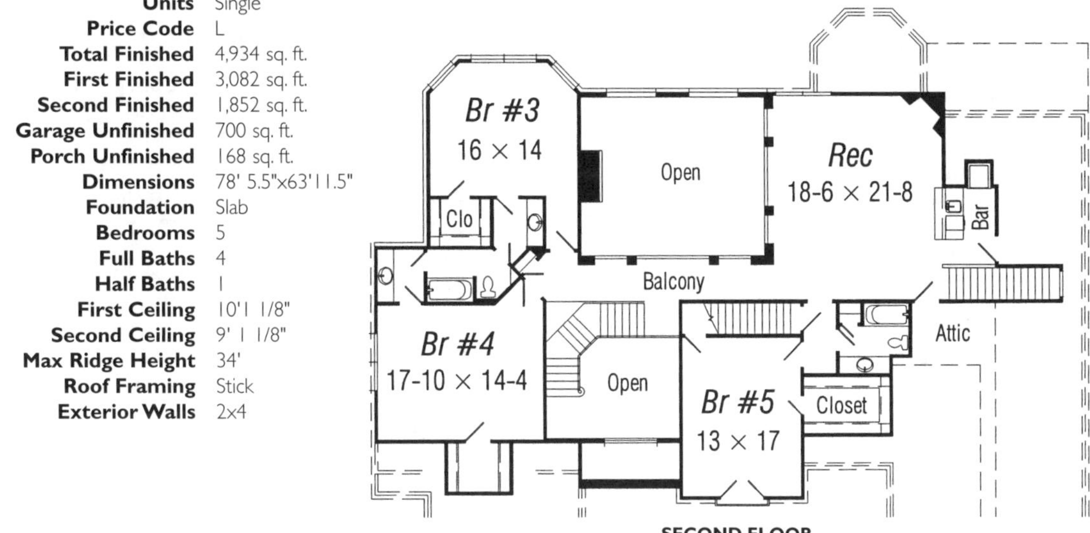
Br #3
16 × 14
Open
Rec
18-6 × 21-8
Clo
Bar
Balcony
Attic
Br #4
17-10 × 14-4
Open
Br #5
13 × 17
Closet

SECOND FLOOR

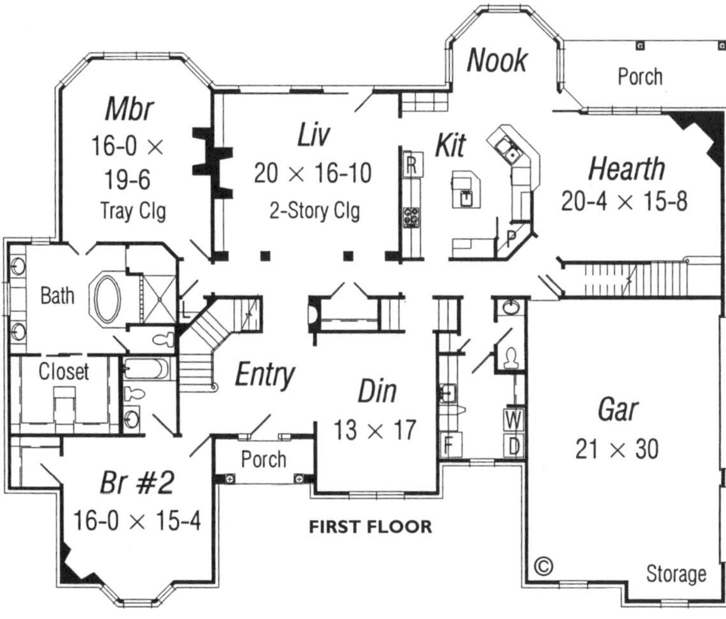
Nook
Porch
Mbr
16-0 ×
19-6
Tray Clg
Liv
20 × 16-10
2-Story Clg
Kit
Hearth
20-4 × 15-8
Bath
Closet
Entry
Din
13 × 17
Gar
21 × 30
Porch
Br #2
16-0 × 15-4
Storage

FIRST FLOOR

Design 69132

Units	Single
Price Code	L
Total Finished	4,955 sq. ft.
First Finished	3,482 sq. ft.
Second Finished	1,473 sq. ft.
Bonus Unfinished	951 sq. ft.
Garage Unfinished	1,089 sq. ft.
Dimensions	92'x79'
Foundation	Basement Crawlspace
Bedrooms	4
Full Baths	2
Half Baths	1
3/4 Baths	1
First Ceiling	10'
Second Ceiling	8'
Max Ridge Height	34'
Roof Framing	Truss
Exterior Walls	2x4

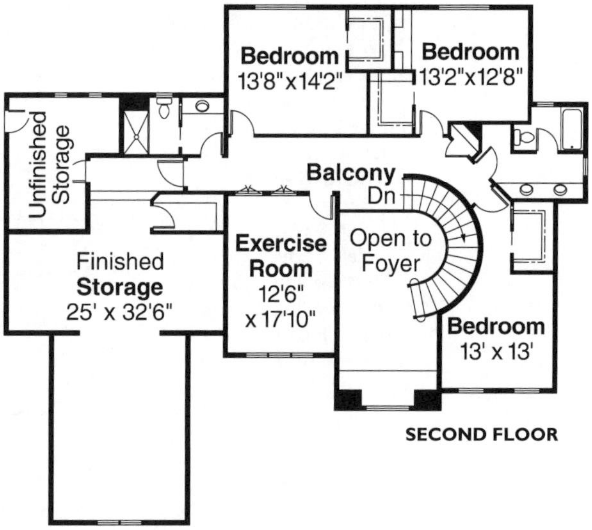

Bedroom 13'8"x14'2"
Bedroom 13'2"x12'8"
Unfinished Storage
Balcony
Dn
Exercise Room 12'6" x 17'10"
Open to Foyer
Finished Storage 25' x 32'6"
Bedroom 13' x 13'

SECOND FLOOR

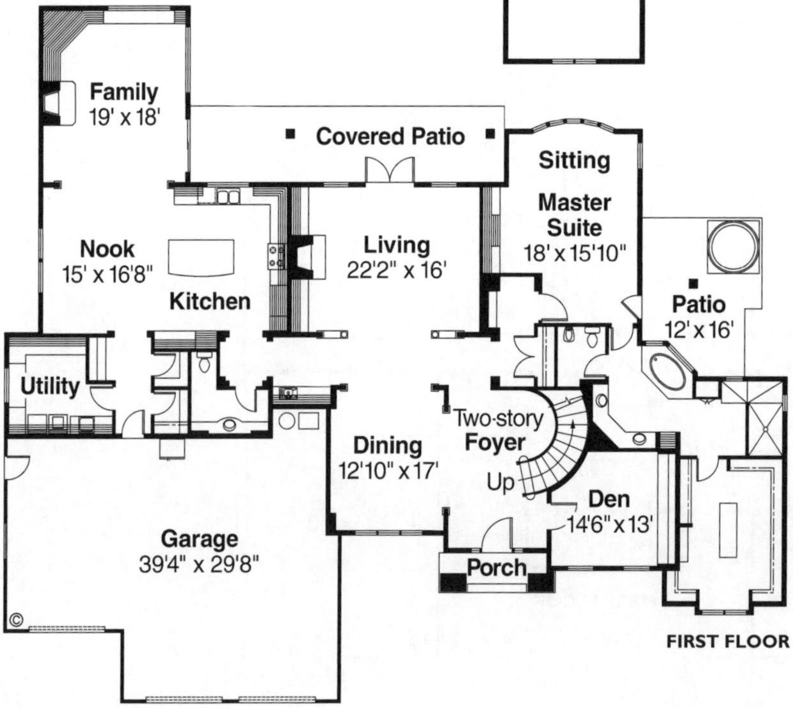

Family 19' x 18'
Covered Patio
Sitting
Master Suite 18' x 15'10"
Nook 15' x 16'8"
Living 22'2" x 16'
Kitchen
Patio 12' x 16'
Utility
Two-story Foyer
Dining 12'10" x 17'
Up
Den 14'6" x 13'
Garage 39'4" x 29'8"
Porch

FIRST FLOOR

Design 10768

Units	Single
Price Code	L
Total Finished	4,963 sq. ft.
First Finished	2,573 sq. ft.
Second Finished	2,390 sq. ft.
Bonus Unfinished	1,501 sq. ft.
Basement Unfinished	1,844 sq. ft.
Garage Unfinished	1,080 sq. ft.
Dimensions	122'x52'6"
Foundation	Combo Basement/ Crawlspace
Bedrooms	5
Full Baths	3
Half Baths	1
Max Ridge Height	38'
Roof Framing	Truss
Exterior Walls	2x6

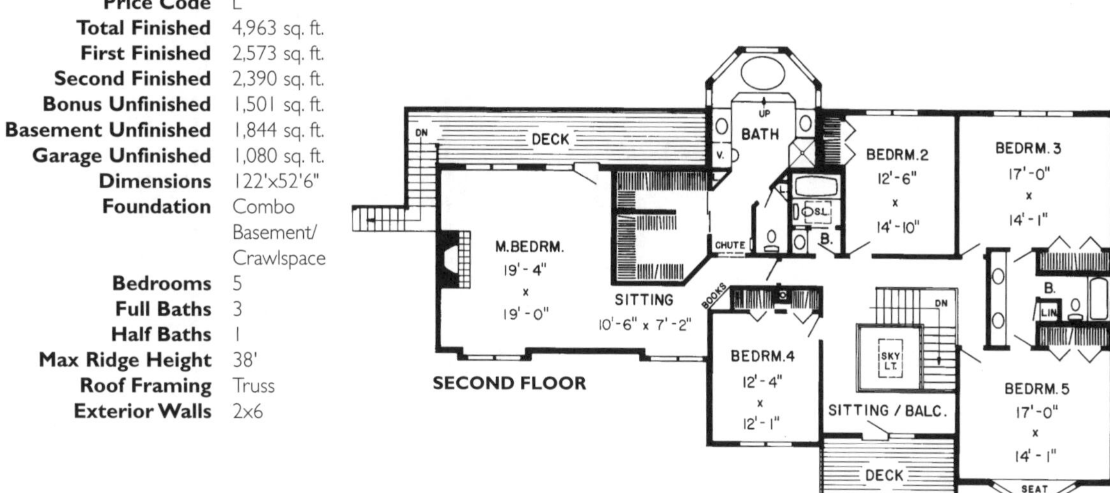
DN
DECK
UP
BATH
V.
SL.
B.
CHUTE
BEDRM.2
12'-6" x 14'-10"
BEDRM. 3
17'-0" x 14'-1"
M.BEDRM.
19'-4" x 19'-0"
SITTING
10'-6" x 7'-2"
BOOKS
B.
LIN.
DN
SKY LT.
BEDRM.4
12'-4" x 12'-1"
SITTING / BALC.
BEDRM.5
17'-0" x 14'-1"
DECK
SEAT
SECOND FLOOR

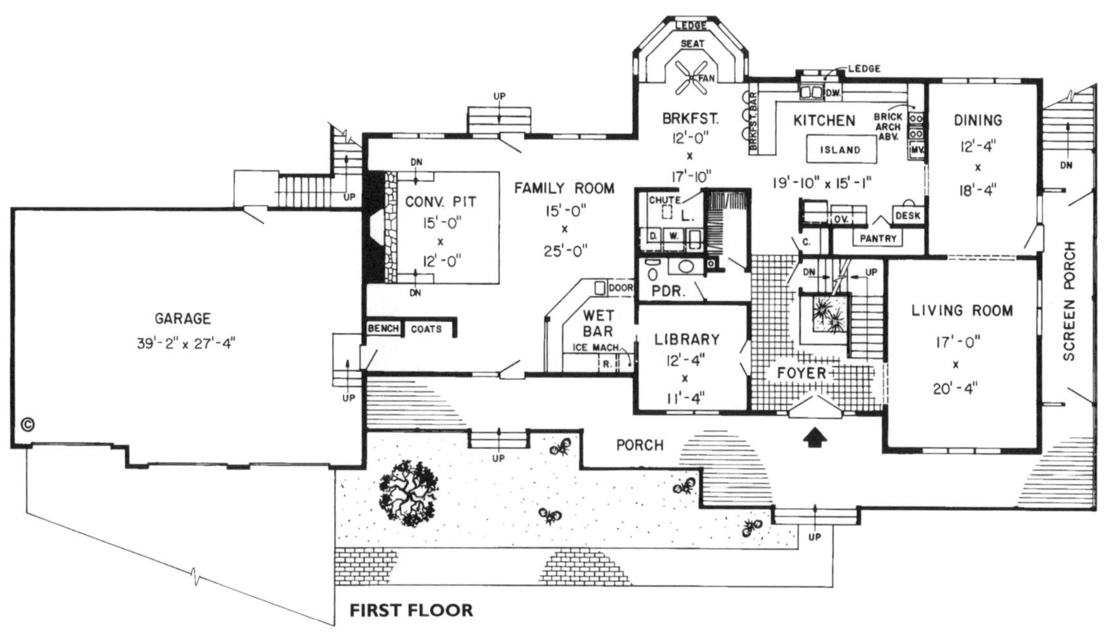
LEDGE
SEAT
FAN
LEDGE
UP
BRKFST.
12'-0" x 17'-10"
BRKFST. BAR
DW.
KITCHEN
BRICK ARCH ABV.
ISLAND
19'-10" x 15'-1"
MV.
DINING
12'-4" x 18'-4"
DN
UP
CONV. PIT
15'-0" x 12'-0"
DN
FAMILY ROOM
15'-0" x 25'-0"
CHUTE
L.
D.
W.
OV.
DESK
PANTRY
C.
DN
UP
PDR.
DOOR
WET BAR
ICE MACH.
R.
LIVING ROOM
17'-0" x 20'-4"
SCREEN PORCH
GARAGE
39'-2" x 27'-4"
BENCH
COATS
LIBRARY
12'-4" x 11'-4"
FOYER
UP
UP
PORCH
UP
©
FIRST FLOOR

Design 66086

Units	Single
Price Code	L
Total Finished	4,970 sq. ft.
First Finished	3,538 sq. ft.
Second Finished	1,432 sq. ft.
Garage Unfinished	864 sq. ft.
Deck Unfinished	20 sq. ft.
Dimensions	102'10"x77'10"
Foundation	Slab
Bedrooms	5
Full Baths	3
3/4 Baths	2
Half Baths	2
First Ceiling	10'
Second Ceiling	9'
Max Ridge Height	34'
Roof Framing	Stick
Exterior Walls	2x4

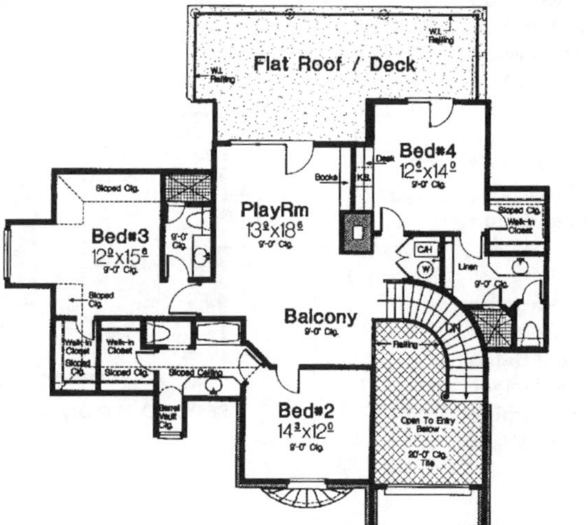

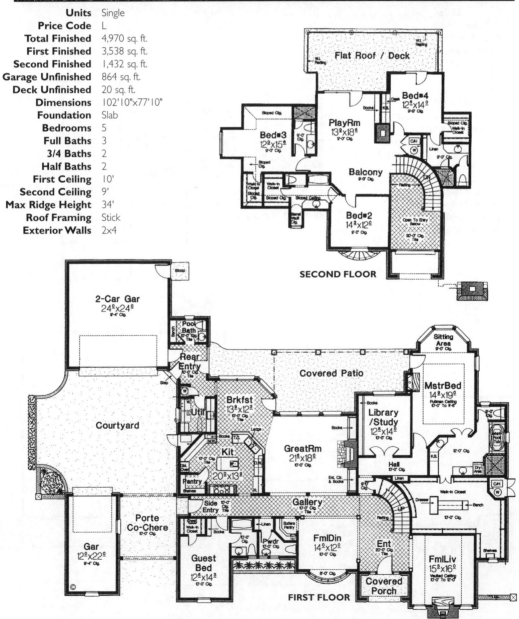

SECOND FLOOR

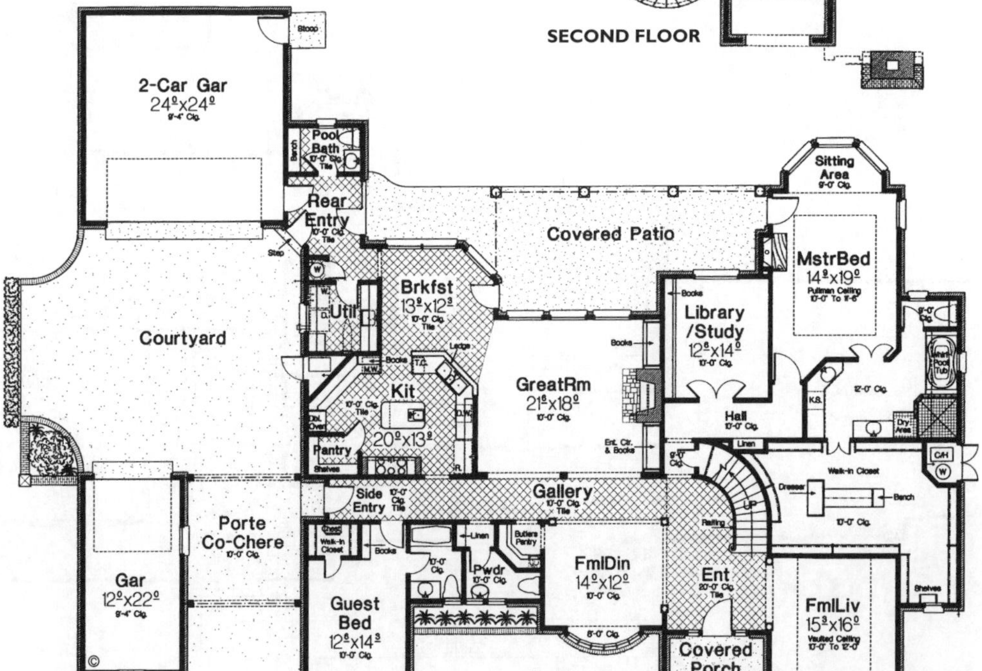

FIRST FLOOR

Design 32426

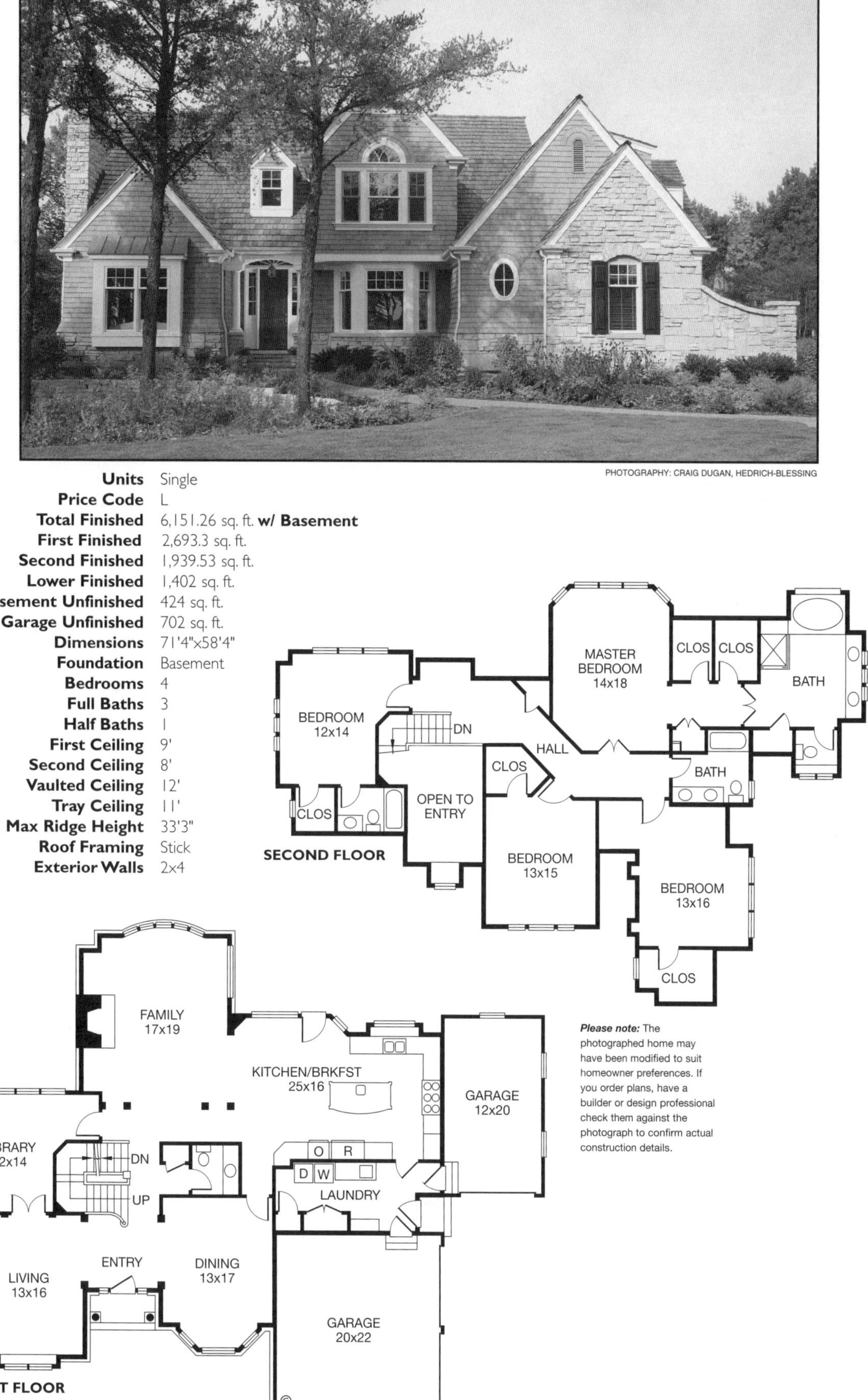
MASTER BEDROOM 14x18
CLOS
CLOS
BATH
BEDROOM 12x14
DN
HALL
CLOS
BATH
CLOS
OPEN TO ENTRY
BEDROOM 13x15
BEDROOM 13x16
CLOS
SECOND FLOOR
FAMILY 17x19
KITCHEN/BRKFST 25x16
GARAGE 12x20
LIBRARY 12x14
DN
UP
O
R
D
W
LAUNDRY
LIVING 13x16
ENTRY
DINING 13x17
GARAGE 20x22
FIRST FLOOR

PHOTOGRAPHY: CRAIG DUGAN, HEDRICH-BLESSING

Units	Single
Price Code	L
Total Finished	6,151.26 sq. ft. **w/ Basement**
First Finished	2,693.3 sq. ft.
Second Finished	1,939.53 sq. ft.
Lower Finished	1,402 sq. ft.
Basement Unfinished	424 sq. ft.
Garage Unfinished	702 sq. ft.
Dimensions	71'4"x58'4"
Foundation	Basement
Bedrooms	4
Full Baths	3
Half Baths	1
First Ceiling	9'
Second Ceiling	8'
Vaulted Ceiling	12'
Tray Ceiling	11'
Max Ridge Height	33'3"
Roof Framing	Stick
Exterior Walls	2x4

Please note: The photographed home may have been modified to suit homeowner preferences. If you order plans, have a builder or design professional check them against the photograph to confirm actual construction details.

Design 97314

Units	Single
Price Code	L
Total Finished	5,211 sq. ft.
Main Finished	3,336 sq. ft.
Lower Finished	1,875 sq. ft.
Basement Unfinished	1,470 sq. ft.
Garage Unfinished	1,377 sq. ft.
Deck Unfinished	237 sq. ft.
Dimensions	119'x57'
Foundation	Basement
Bedrooms	4
Full Baths	1
3/4 Baths	2
Half Baths	1
Max Ridge Height	33'4"
Roof Framing	Truss
Exterior wall	2x6

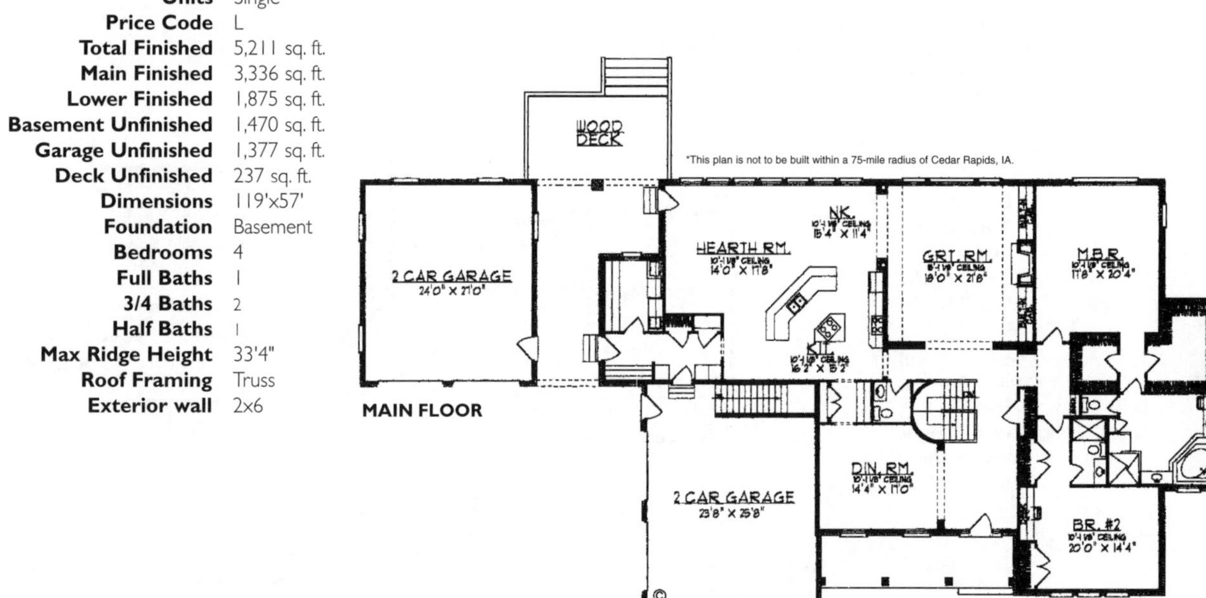
WOOD DECK
*This plan is not to be built within a 75-mile radius of Cedar Rapids, IA.
2 CAR GARAGE
24'0" X 27'0"
HEARTH RM.
14'0" X 17'8"
NK.
15'4" X 11'4"
GRT. RM.
18'0" X 21'8"
M.B.R.
17'8" X 20'4"
2 CAR GARAGE
23'8" X 25'8"
DIN. RM.
14'4" X 17'0"
BR. #2
20'0" X 14'4"

MAIN FLOOR

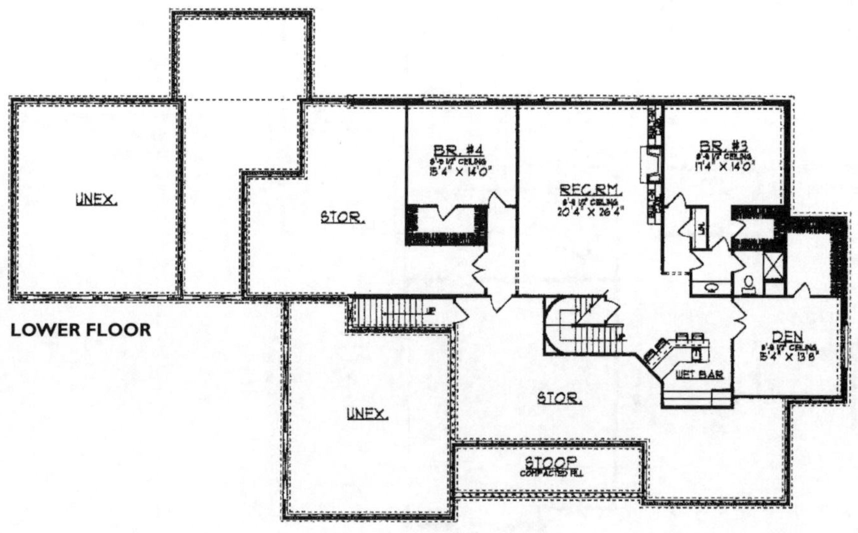
UNEX.
STOR.
BR. #4
15'4" X 14'0"
REC.RM.
20'4" X 26'4"
BR. #3
17'4" X 14'0"
DEN
15'4" X 13'8"
WET BAR
STOR.
UNEX.
STOOP
COMPACTED FILL

LOWER FLOOR

Design 69134

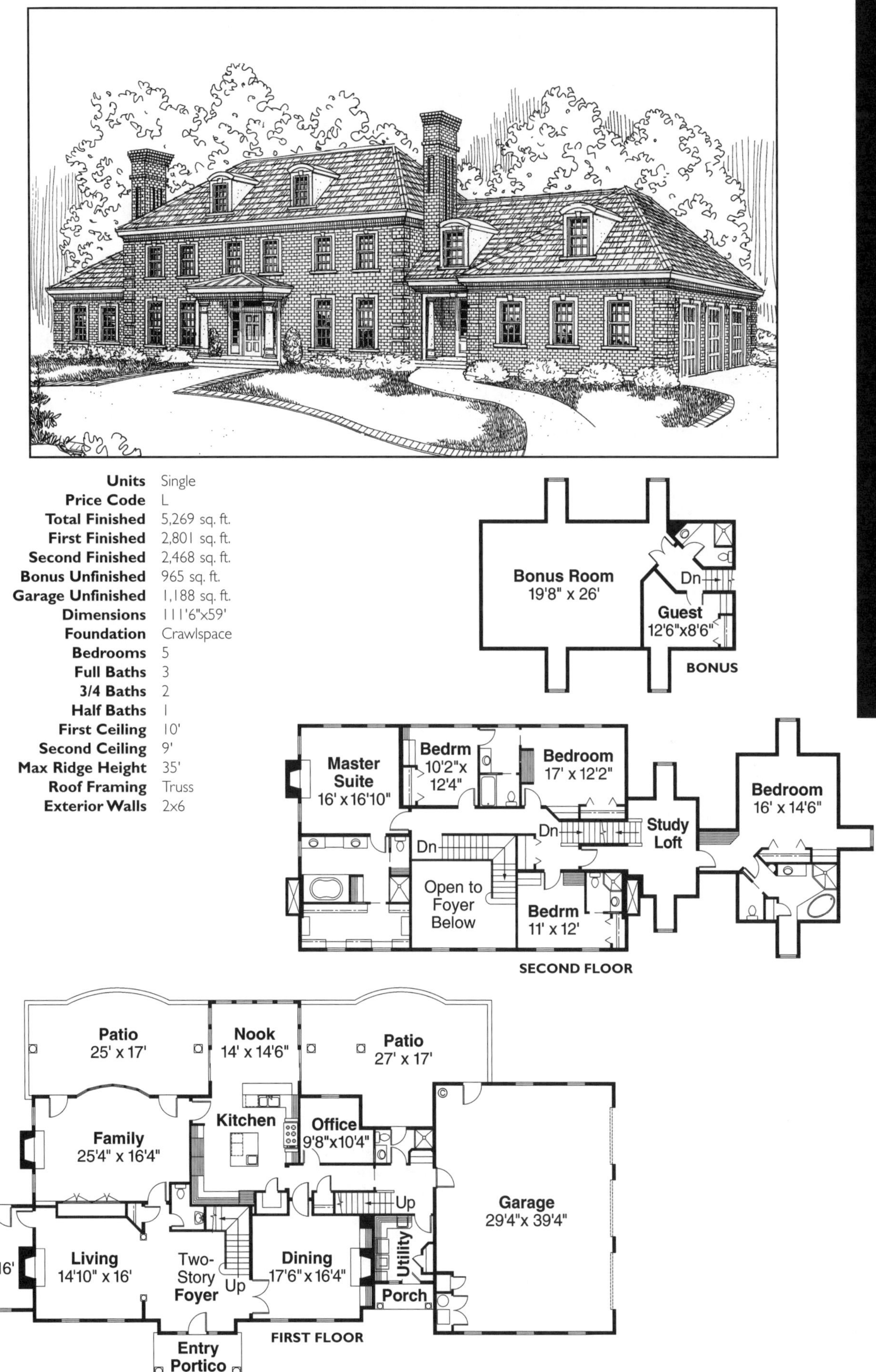
Bonus Room
19'8" x 26'
Dn
Guest
12'6"x8'6"
BONUS
Master Suite
16' x 16'10"
Bedrm
10'2"x 12'4"
Bedroom
17' x 12'2"
Dn
Study Loft
Bedroom
16' x 14'6"
Dn
Open to Foyer Below
Bedrm
11' x 12'
SECOND FLOOR
Patio
25' x 17'
Nook
14' x 14'6"
Patio
27' x 17'
Kitchen
Office
9'8"x10'4"
Family
25'4" x 16'4"
Garage
29'4"x 39'4"
Up
Den
15'6" x 16'
Living
14'10" x 16'
Two-Story Foyer
Up
Dining
17'6" x 16'4"
Utility
Porch
Entry Portico
FIRST FLOOR

Units	Single
Price Code	L
Total Finished	5,269 sq. ft.
First Finished	2,801 sq. ft.
Second Finished	2,468 sq. ft.
Bonus Unfinished	965 sq. ft.
Garage Unfinished	1,188 sq. ft.
Dimensions	111'6"x59'
Foundation	Crawlspace
Bedrooms	5
Full Baths	3
3/4 Baths	2
Half Baths	1
First Ceiling	10'
Second Ceiling	9'
Max Ridge Height	35'
Roof Framing	Truss
Exterior Walls	2x6

Design 66015

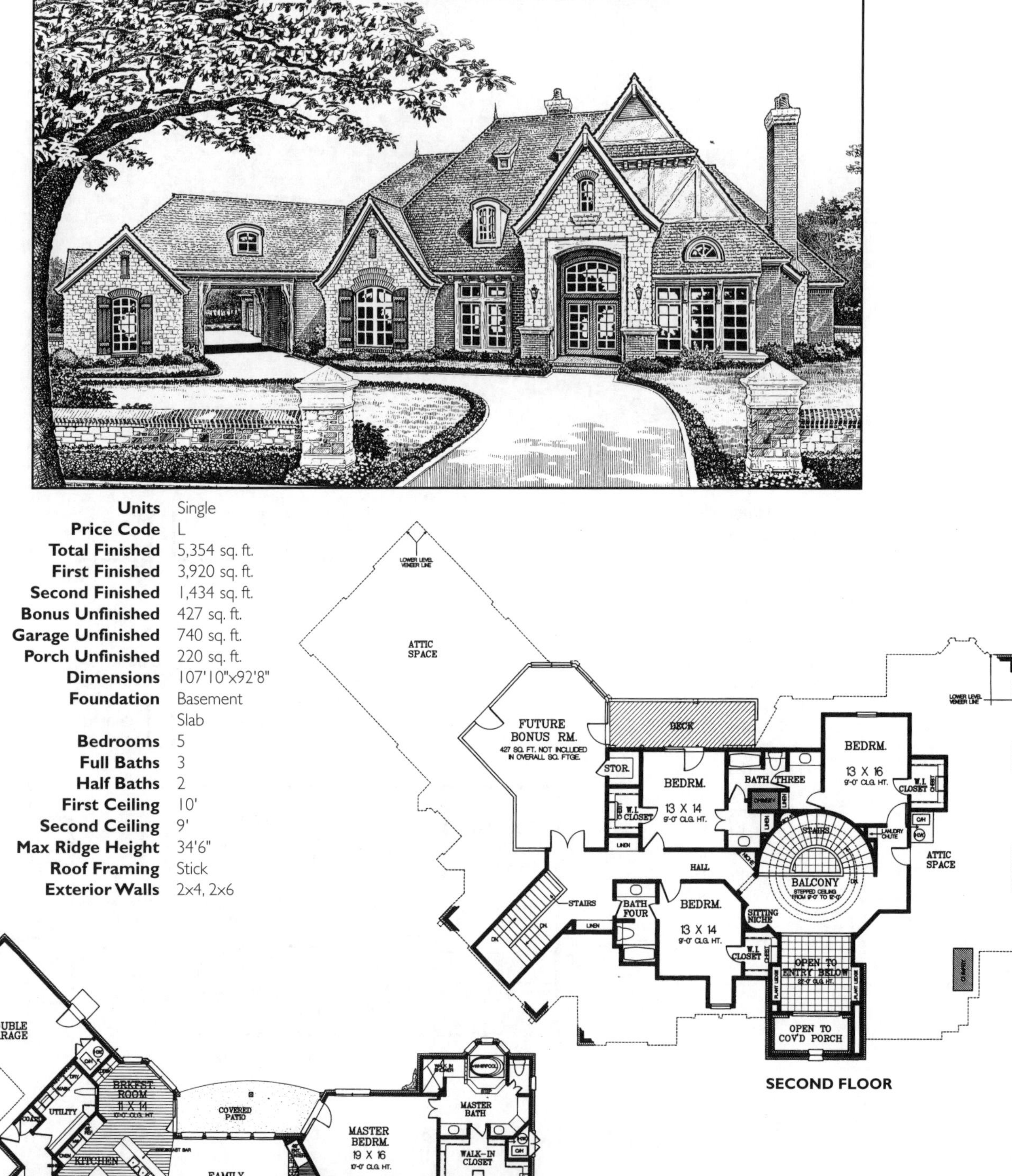
ATTIC SPACE
FUTURE BONUS RM.
427 SQ. FT. NOT INCLUDED IN OVERALL SQ. FTGE.
DECK
STOR.
BEDRM.
13 X 14
W.I. CLOSET
BATH THREE
BEDRM.
13 X 16
W.I. CLOSET
STAIRS
HALL
BALCONY
BATH FOUR
BEDRM.
13 X 14
SITTING NICHE
OPEN TO ENTRY BELOW
OPEN TO COV'D PORCH
DOUBLE GARAGE
BRKFST. ROOM
11 X 14
UTILITY
KITCHEN
REAR ENTRY
PWDR. BATH
COVERED PATIO
FAMILY ROOM
23 X 18
MASTER BEDRM.
19 X 16
MASTER BATH
WALK-IN CLOSET
STUDY
15 X 12
PANTRY
GALLERY
FORMAL DINING
15 X 14
FOYER
FORMAL LIVING
14 X 18
BEDRM.
13 X 15
BATH TWO
PORTE-COCHERE
COVERED PORCH
SINGLE GARAGE

SECOND FLOOR

FIRST FLOOR

Units	Single
Price Code	L
Total Finished	5,354 sq. ft.
First Finished	3,920 sq. ft.
Second Finished	1,434 sq. ft.
Bonus Unfinished	427 sq. ft.
Garage Unfinished	740 sq. ft.
Porch Unfinished	220 sq. ft.
Dimensions	107'10"x92'8"
Foundation	Basement Slab
Bedrooms	5
Full Baths	3
Half Baths	2
First Ceiling	10'
Second Ceiling	9'
Max Ridge Height	34'6"
Roof Framing	Stick
Exterior Walls	2x4, 2x6

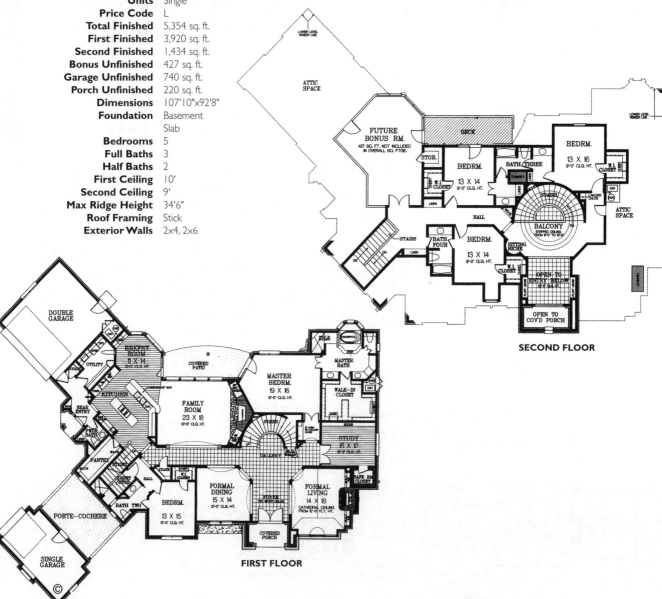

Design 66026

Units	Single
Price Code	L
Total Finished	5,389 sq. ft.
First Finished	3,746 sq. ft.
Second Finished	1,643 sq. ft.
Garage Unfinished	920 sq. ft.
Deck Unfinished	182 sq. ft.
Porch Unfinished	170 sq. ft.
Dimensions	100'x70'1"
Foundation	Slab
Bedrooms	5
Full Baths	4
Half Baths	2
First Ceiling	10'
Second Ceiling	9'
Max Ridge Height	38'
Roof Framing	Stick
Exterior Walls	2x4

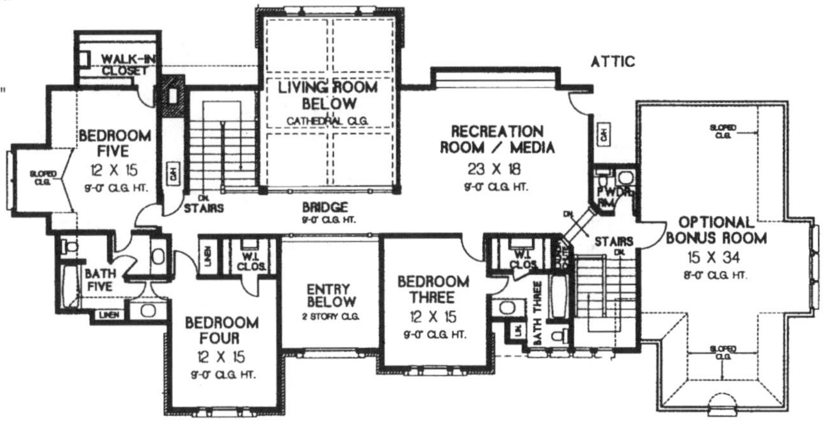

WALK-IN CLOSET
LIVING ROOM BELOW CATHEDRAL CLG.
ATTIC
BEDROOM FIVE 12 X 15 9'-0" CLG. HT.
RECREATION ROOM / MEDIA 23 X 18 9'-0" CLG. HT.
OPTIONAL BONUS ROOM 15 X 34 8'-0" CLG. HT.
STAIRS
BRIDGE 9'-0" CLG. HT.
BATH FIVE
ENTRY BELOW 2 STORY CLG.
BEDROOM THREE 12 X 15 9'-0" CLG. HT.
BATH THREE
BEDROOM FOUR 12 X 15 9'-0" CLG. HT.

SECOND FLOOR

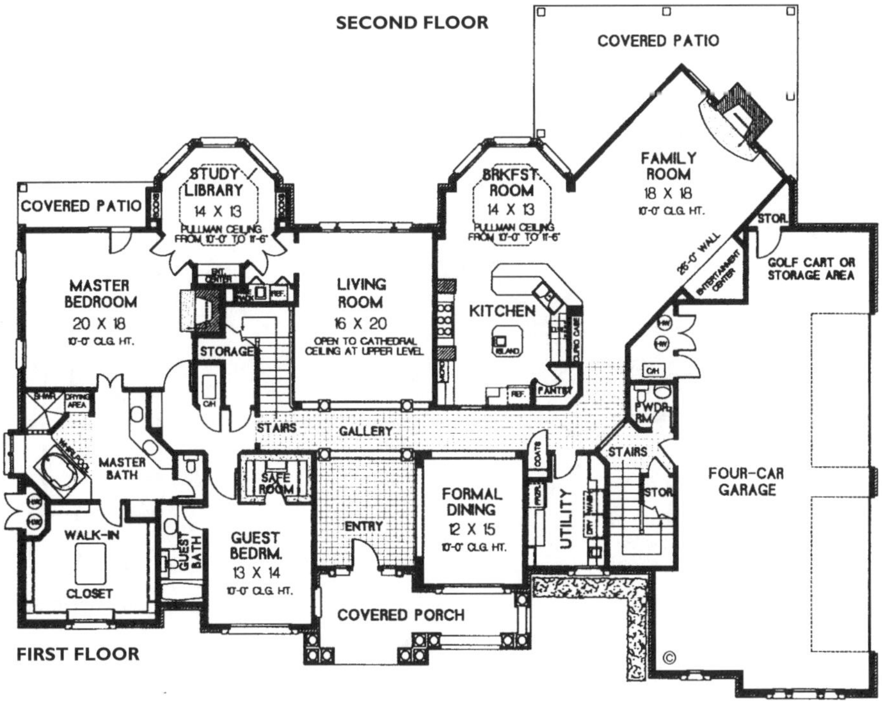

COVERED PATIO
COVERED PATIO
STUDY/LIBRARY 14 X 13 PULLMAN CEILING FROM 10'-0" TO 11'-6"
BRKFST. ROOM 14 X 13 PULLMAN CEILING FROM 10'-0" TO 11'-6"
FAMILY ROOM 18 X 18 10'-0" CLG. HT.
MASTER BEDROOM 20 X 18 10'-0" CLG. HT.
LIVING ROOM 16 X 20 OPEN TO CATHEDRAL CEILING AT UPPER LEVEL
KITCHEN
GOLF CART OR STORAGE AREA
STORAGE
STAIRS
GALLERY
MASTER BATH
SAFE ROOM
FORMAL DINING 12 X 15 10'-0" CLG. HT.
UTILITY
PWDR. RM.
FOUR-CAR GARAGE
WALK-IN CLOSET
GUEST BATH
GUEST BEDRM. 13 X 14 10'-0" CLG. HT.
ENTRY
COVERED PORCH

FIRST FLOOR

Design 97357

Units	Single
Price Code	L
Total Finished	5,500 sq. ft.
First Finished	2,670 sq. ft.
Second Finished	1,060 sq. ft.
Lower Finished	1,770 sq. ft.
Dimensions	100'4"x73'4"
Foundation	Basement
Bedrooms	4
Full Baths	2
3/4 Baths	1
Half Baths	2
First Ceiling	9'
Second Ceiling	8'
Roof Framing	Truss
Exterior Walls	2x6

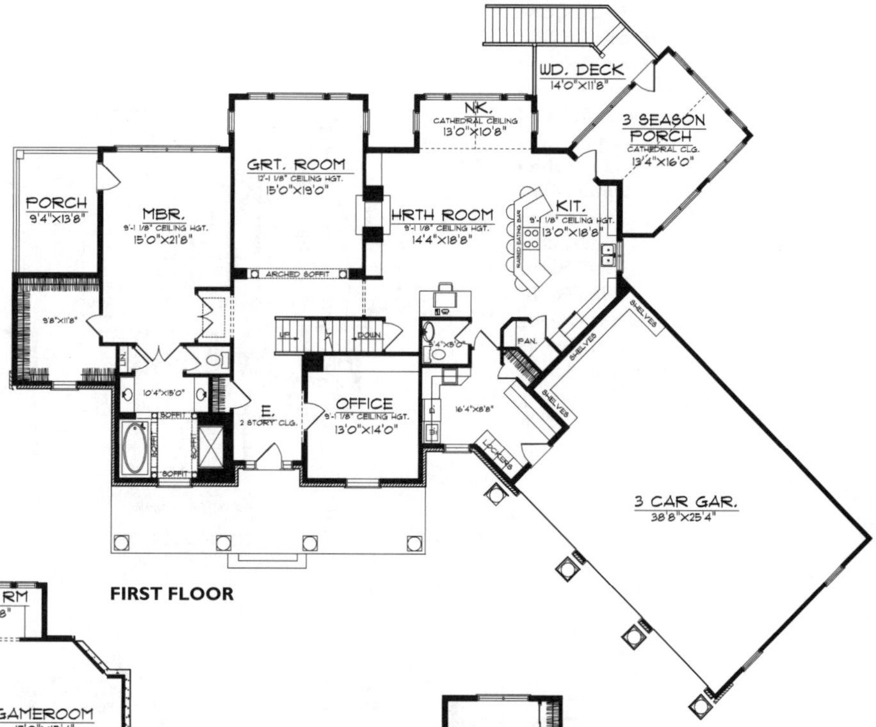

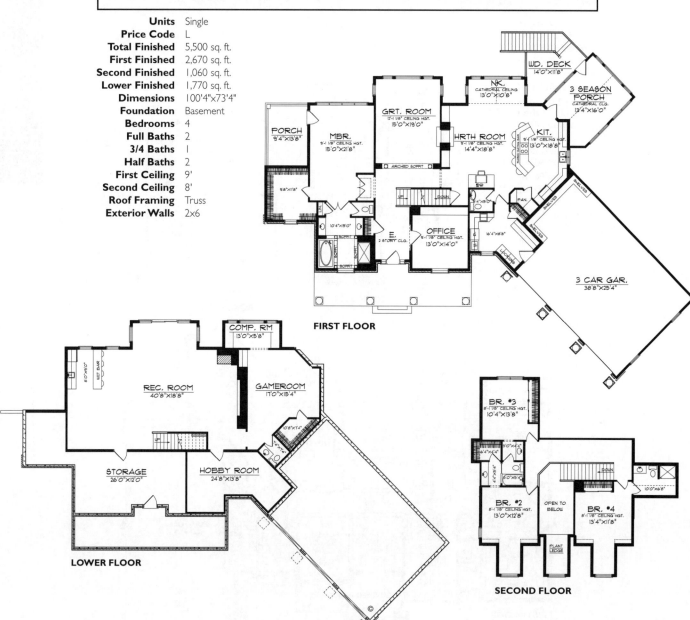

WD. DECK 14'0"X11'8"
3 SEASON PORCH CATHEDRAL CLG. 13'4"X16'0"
NK. CATHEDRAL CEILING 13'0"X10'8"
GRT. ROOM 12'-1 1/8" CEILING HGT. 15'0"X19'0"
PORCH 9'4"X13'8"
MBR. 9'-1 1/8" CEILING HGT. 15'0"X21'8"
HRTH ROOM 9'-1 1/8" CEILING HGT. 14'4"X18'8"
KIT. 9'-1 1/8" CEILING HGT. 13'0"X18'8"
OFFICE 9'-1 1/8" CEILING HGT. 13'0"X14'0"
E. 2 STORY CLG.
3 CAR GAR. 38'8"X25'4"

FIRST FLOOR

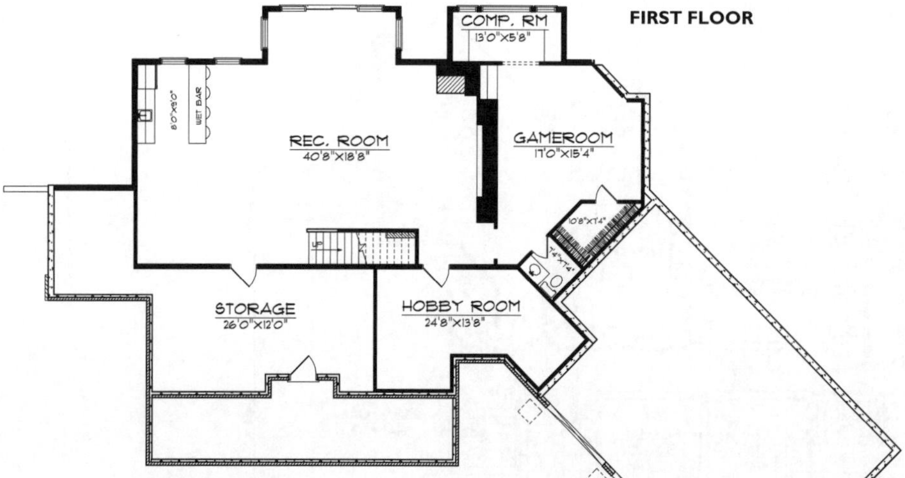

COMP. RM 13'0"X5'8"
REC. ROOM 40'8"X18'8"
GAMEROOM 17'0"X15'4"
STORAGE 26'0"X12'0"
HOBBY ROOM 24'8"X13'8"

LOWER FLOOR

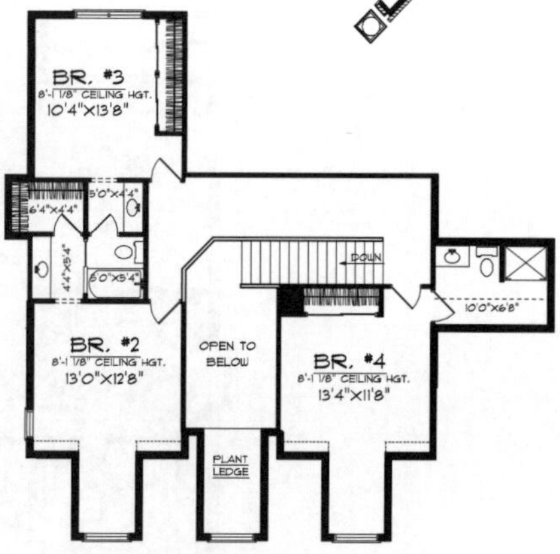

BR. #3 8'-1 1/8" CEILING HGT. 10'4"X13'8"
BR. #2 8'-1 1/8" CEILING HGT. 13'0"X12'8"
OPEN TO BELOW
PLANT LEDGE
BR. #4 8'-1 1/8" CEILING HGT. 13'4"X11'8"

SECOND FLOOR

Design 65665

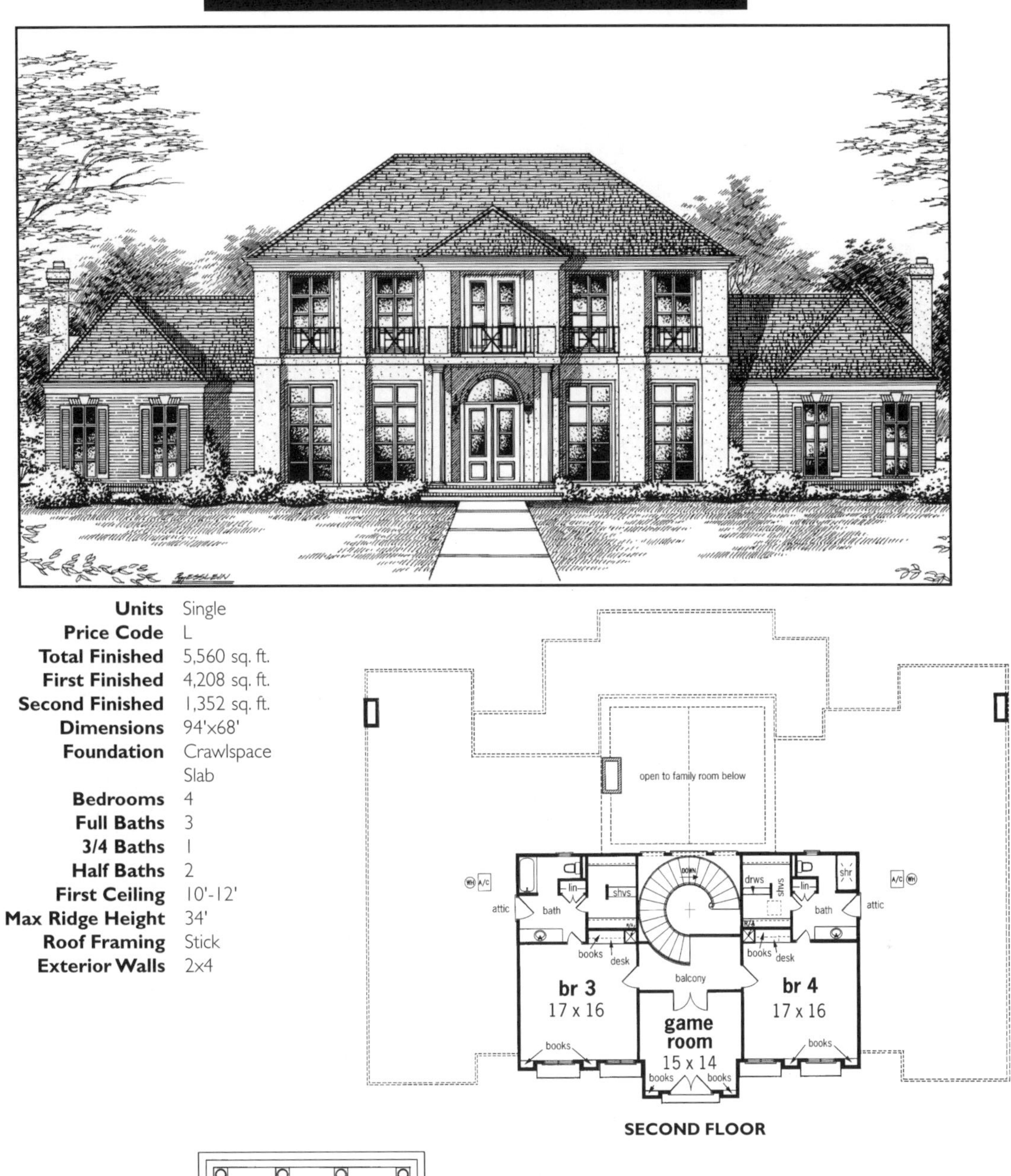
open to family room below
attic
bath
lin
shvs
down
drws
shr
books
desk
balcony
br 3
17 x 16
game room
15 x 14
br 4
17 x 16
attic

SECOND FLOOR

Units	Single
Price Code	L
Total Finished	5,560 sq. ft.
First Finished	4,208 sq. ft.
Second Finished	1,352 sq. ft.
Dimensions	94'x68'
Foundation	Crawlspace Slab
Bedrooms	4
Full Baths	3
3/4 Baths	1
Half Baths	2
First Ceiling	10'-12'
Max Ridge Height	34'
Roof Framing	Stick
Exterior Walls	2x4

veranda
sitting
16 x 13
den
16 x 12
bkfst
10 x 9
family room
26 x 22
sloped clg
entertainment ctr built-in
guest suite
14 x 13
mbr
21 x 16
util
12x12
kit
22 x 12
3 car garage
29 x 22
library
20 x 16
foy
13 x 9
dining
20 x 16
porch
sto 16 x 4

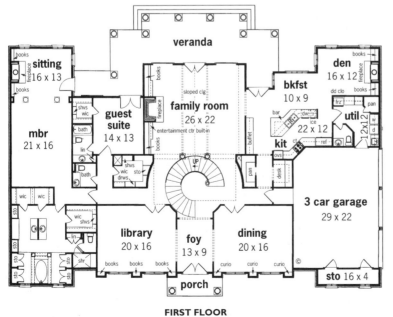

FIRST FLOOR

Design 97354

Units	Single
Price Code	L
Total Finished	5,640 sq. ft.
Main Finished	3,260 sq. ft.
Lower Finished	2,380 sq. ft.
Basement Unfinished	880 sq. ft.
Dimensions	102'5"x83'5"
Foundation	Basement
Bedrooms	4
Full Baths	2
3/4 Baths	1
Half Baths	1
Max Ridge Height	32'10"
Roof Framing	Truss
Exterior Walls	2x6

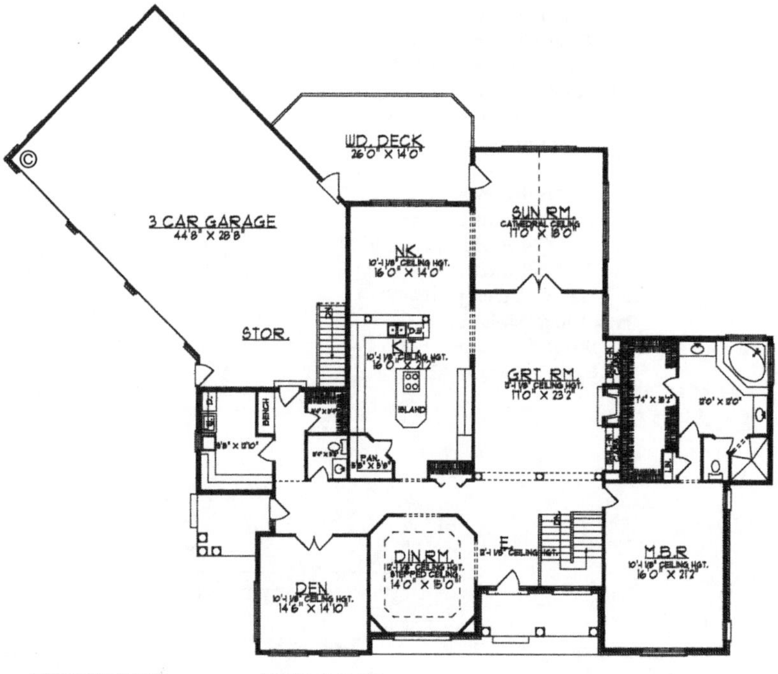

MAIN FLOOR

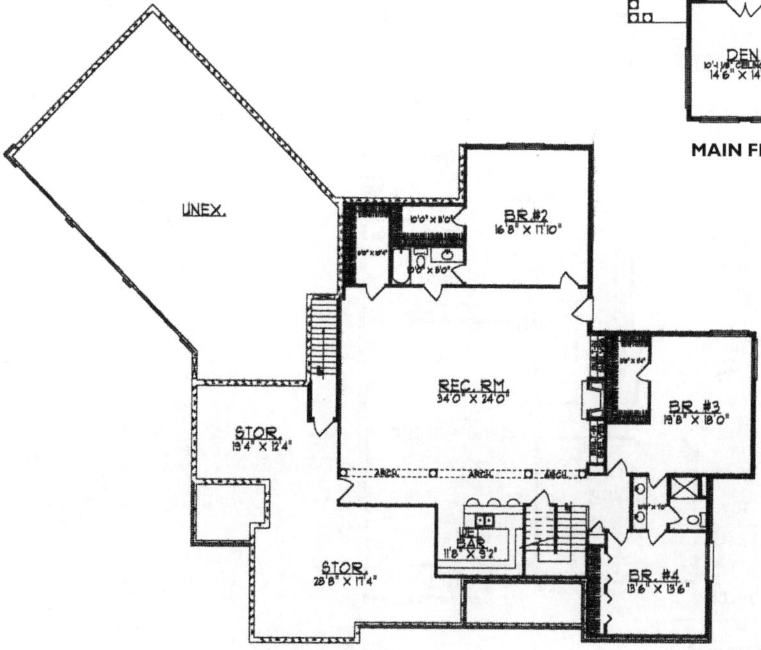

LOWER FLOOR

Design 97356

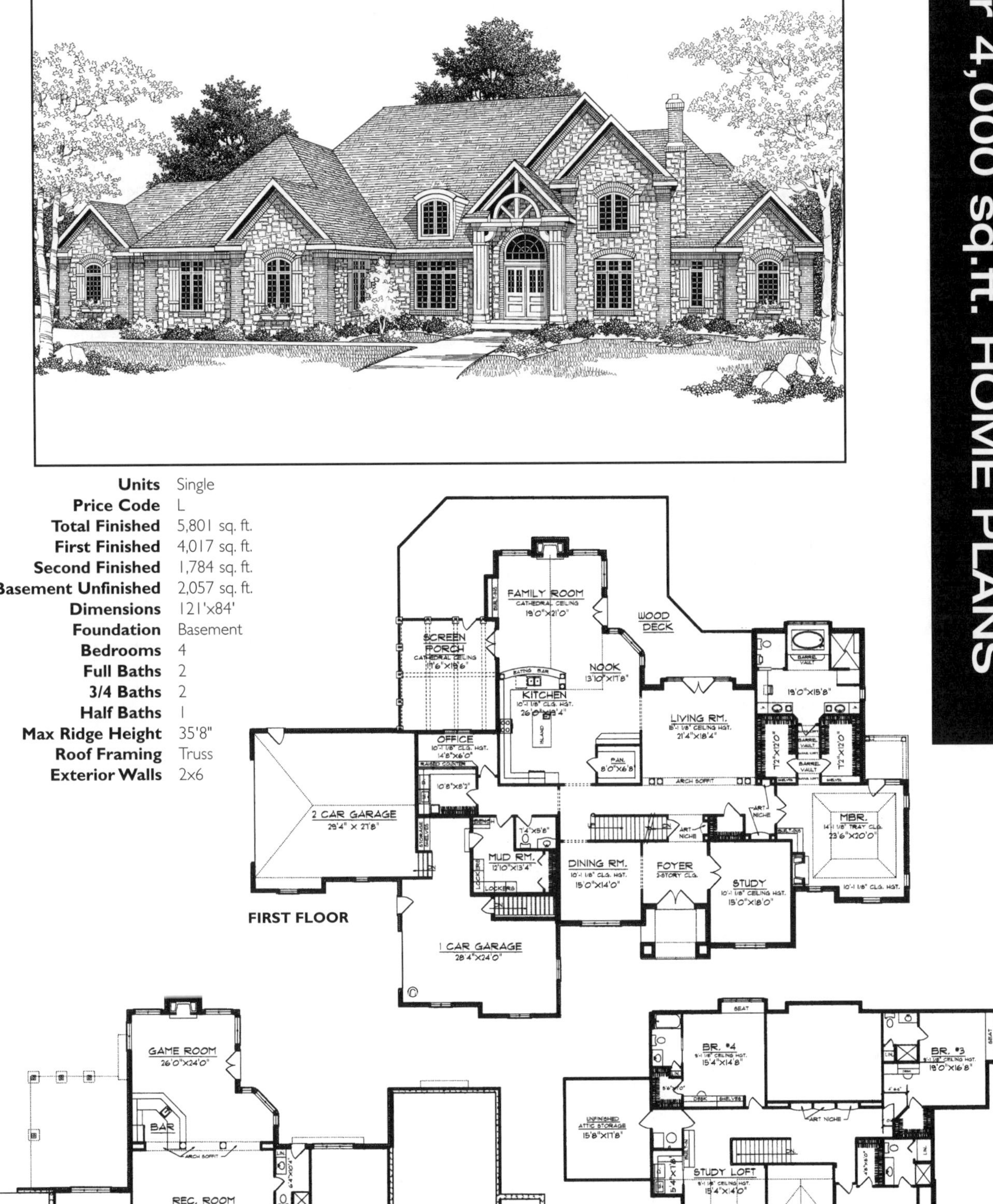
FAMILY ROOM
CATHEDRAL CEILING
19'0"X21'0"
WOOD DECK
SCREEN PORCH
NOOK
13'10"X17'8"
KITCHEN
LIVING RM.
OFFICE
14'8"X6'0"
2 CAR GARAGE
29'4" X 27'8"
MUD RM.
12'10"X13'4"
DINING RM.
15'0"X14'0"
FOYER
2-STORY CLG.
STUDY
15'0"X18'0"
MBR.
23'6"X20'0"
1 CAR GARAGE
28'4"X24'0"
FIRST FLOOR
GAME ROOM
26'0"X24'0"
BAR
REC. ROOM
26'4"X21'8"
GUEST BEDROOM
14'0"X11'4"
HOBBY ROOM
14'4"X24'0"
CAPPED GARAGE
29'8"X27'0"
CRAWL SPACE
STORAGE
STOOP
LOWER FLOOR
BR. #4
15'4"X14'8"
BR. #3
19'0"X16'8"
UNFINISHED ATTIC STORAGE
15'8"X17'8"
STUDY LOFT
15'4"X14'0"
BR. #2
15'0"X12'0"
SECOND FLOOR

Units	Single
Price Code	L
Total Finished	5,801 sq. ft.
First Finished	4,017 sq. ft.
Second Finished	1,784 sq. ft.
Basement Unfinished	2,057 sq. ft.
Dimensions	121'x84'
Foundation	Basement
Bedrooms	4
Full Baths	2
3/4 Baths	2
Half Baths	1
Max Ridge Height	35'8"
Roof Framing	Truss
Exterior Walls	2x6

Design 65651

Units	Single
Price Code	M
Total Finished	6,000 sq. ft.
First Finished	5,120 sq. ft.
Second Finished	880 sq. ft.
Dimensions	91x132
Foundation	Crawlspace
Bedrooms	5
Full Baths	5
Half Baths	1
3/4 Baths	1
First Ceiling	10
Roof Framing	Stick
Exterior Walls	2x6

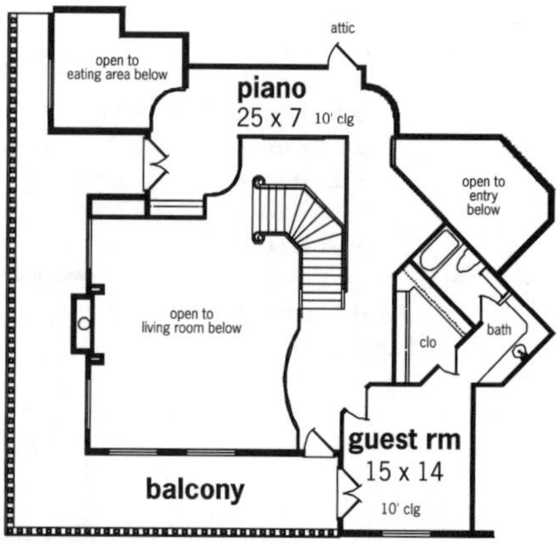

open to eating area below
attic
piano 25 x 7 10' clg
open to entry below
open to living room below
clo
bath
guest rm 15 x 14 10' clg
balcony

SECOND FLOOR

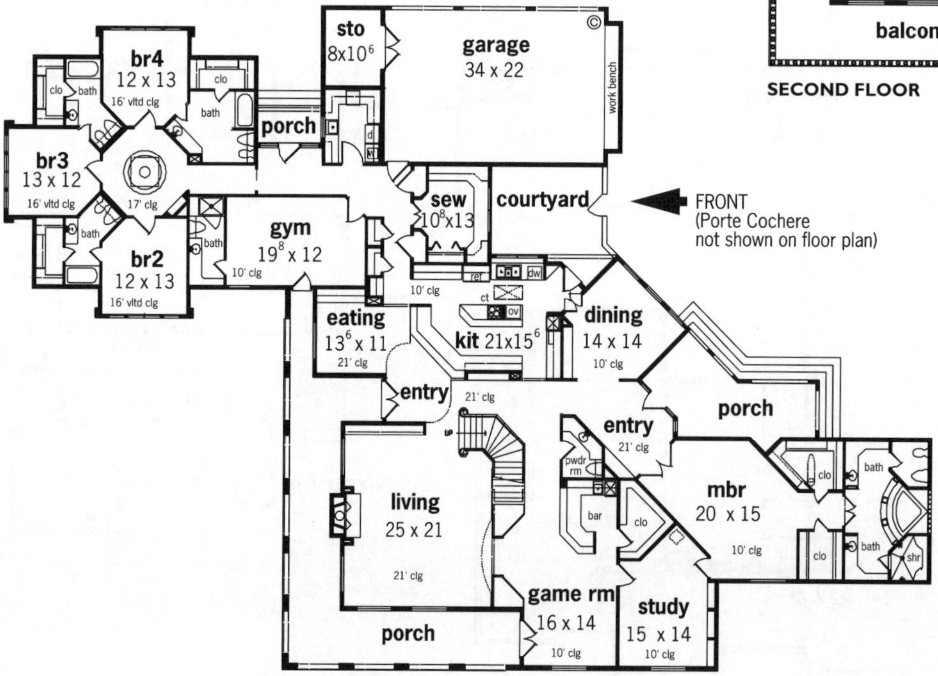

sto 8x10⁶
garage 34 x 22
work bench
br4 12 x 13 16' vltd clg
clo
bath
porch
br3 13 x 12 16' vltd clg
17' clg
sew 10⁸x13
courtyard
FRONT (Porte Cochere not shown on floor plan)
br2 12 x 13 16' vltd clg
gym 19⁸ x 12 10' clg
eating 13⁶ x 11 21' clg
kit 21x15⁶ 10' clg
dining 14 x 14 10' clg
entry 21' clg
porch
entry 21' clg
pwdr rm
bar
living 25 x 21 21' clg
mbr 20 x 15 10' clg
game rm 16 x 14 10' clg
study 15 x 14 10' clg
porch

FIRST FLOOR

 To order blueprints, call **800-235-5700** or visit us on the web, **familyhomeplans.com**

Design 32330

PHOTOGRAPHY: LAURIE BLACK

Units	Single
Price Code	L
Total Finished	6,169 sq. ft.
First Finished	3,675 sq. ft.
Second Finished	2,494 sq. ft.
Garage Unfinished	1,136 sq. ft.
Porch Unfinished	1,052 sq. ft.
Dimensions	134'4"x55'11"
Foundation	Crawlspace
Bedrooms	5
Full Baths	3
3/4 Baths	2
Half Baths	1
First Ceiling	10'
Second Ceiling	8'
Vaulted Ceiling	19'
Max Ridge Height	35'
Exterior Walls	2x6

Please note: The photographed home may have been modified to suit homeowner preferences. If you order plans, have a builder or design professional check them against the photograph to confirm actual construction details.

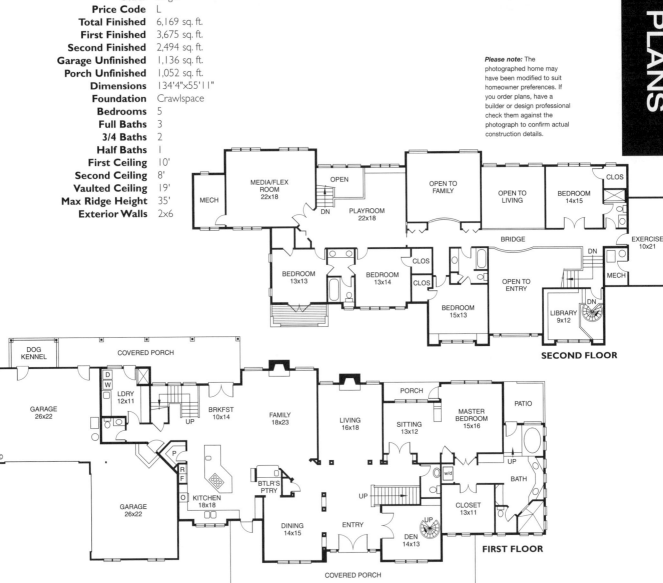

MECH
MEDIA/FLEX ROOM 22x18
OPEN
DN
PLAYROOM 22x18
OPEN TO FAMILY
OPEN TO LIVING
BEDROOM 14x15
CLOS
EXERCISE 10x21
BRIDGE
DN
MECH
BEDROOM 13x13
BEDROOM 13x14
CLOS
CLOS
BEDROOM 15x13
OPEN TO ENTRY
LIBRARY 9x12
DN

SECOND FLOOR

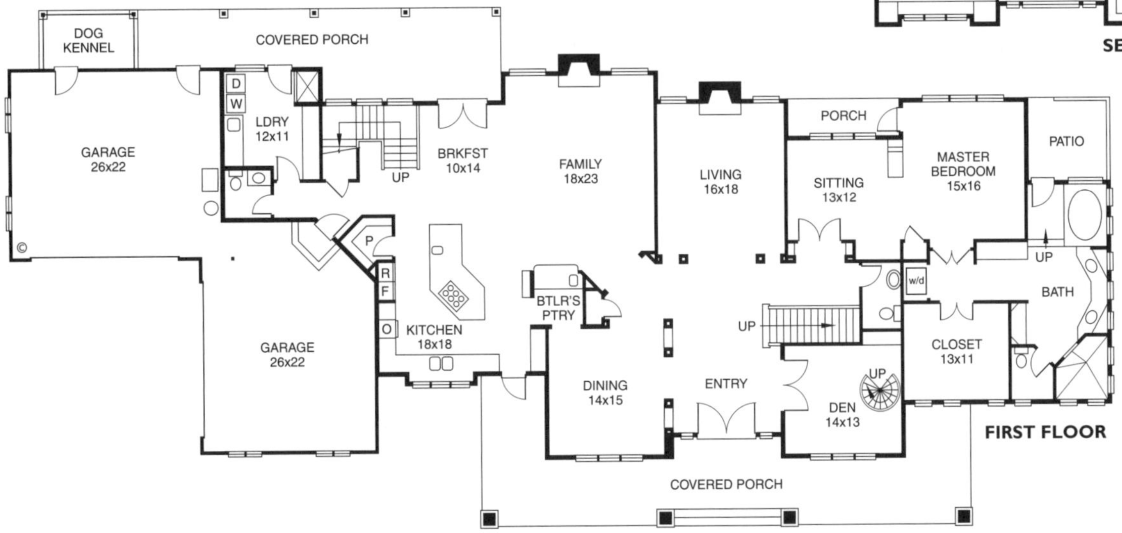

DOG KENNEL
COVERED PORCH
GARAGE 26x22
D
W
LDRY 12x11
UP
BRKFST 10x14
FAMILY 18x23
LIVING 16x18
PORCH
SITTING 13x12
MASTER BEDROOM 15x16
PATIO
P
R
F
O
KITCHEN 18x18
BTLR'S PTRY
UP
w/d
UP
BATH
GARAGE 26x22
CLOSET 13x11
DINING 14x15
ENTRY
UP
DEN 14x13
COVERED PORCH

FIRST FLOOR

Design 99934

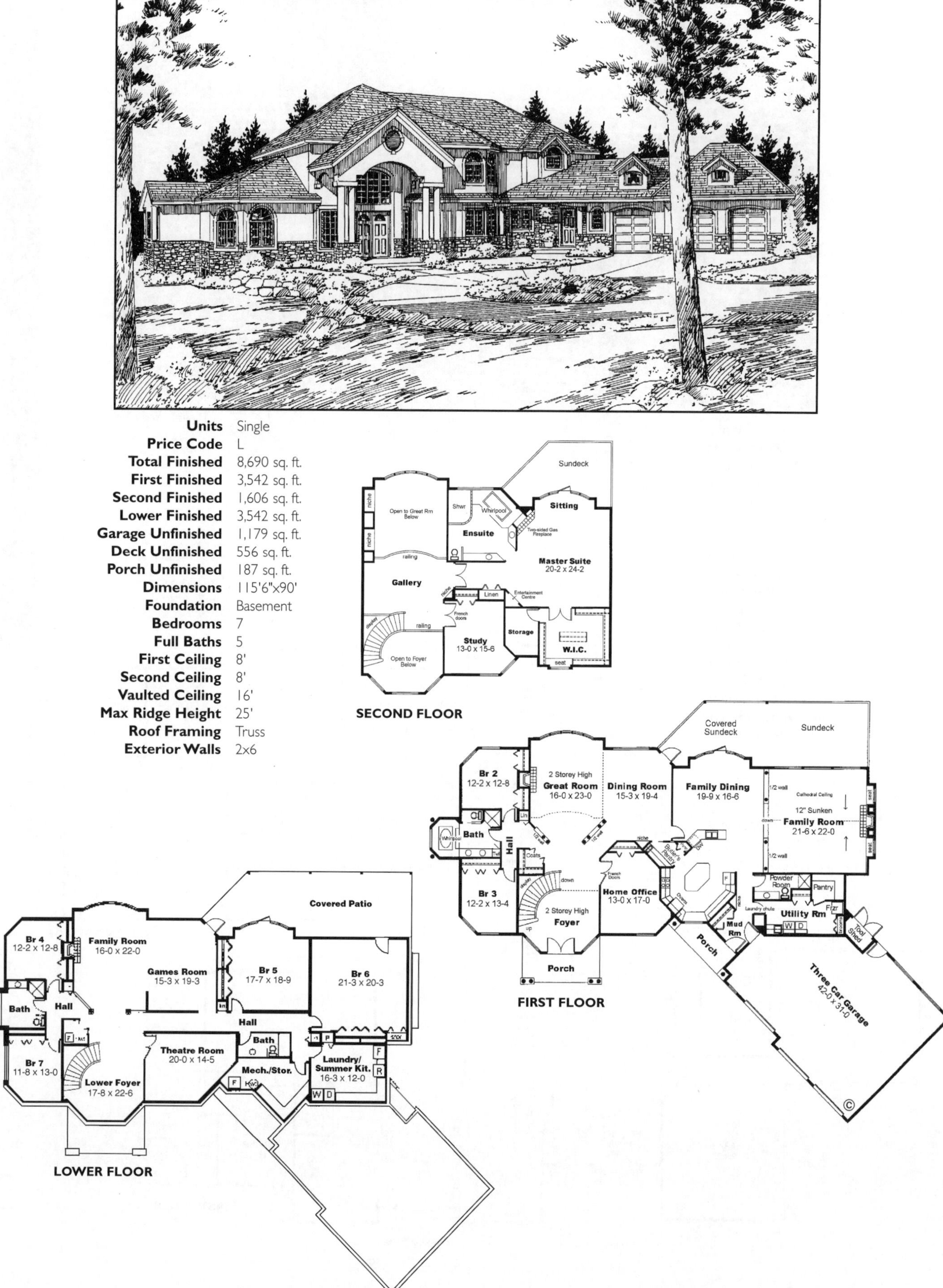

SECOND FLOOR
Sundeck
Sitting
Open to Great Rm Below
Shwr
Whirlpool
Ensuite
Two-sided Gas Fireplace
Master Suite
20-2 x 24-2
niche
railing
Gallery
Linen
Entertainment Centre
French doors
Study
13-0 x 15-6
Storage
W.I.C.
seat
Open to Foyer Below
FIRST FLOOR
Covered Sundeck
Sundeck
Br 2
12-2 x 12-8
2 Storey High
Great Room
16-0 x 23-0
Dining Room
15-3 x 19-4
Family Dining
19-9 x 16-6
1/2 wall
Cathedral Ceiling
12" Sunken
Family Room
21-6 x 22-0
Bath
Whirlpool
Hall
Coats
Butler's Pantry
Powder Room
Pantry
Br 3
12-2 x 13-4
down
2 Storey High
Foyer
Home Office
13-0 x 17-0
French Doors
Laundry chute
Utility Rm
Mud Rm
Tool Shed
Porch
Porch
Three Car Garage
42-0 x 31-0
LOWER FLOOR
Covered Patio
Br 4
12-2 x 12-8
Family Room
16-0 x 22-0
Games Room
15-3 x 19-3
Br 5
17-7 x 18-9
Br 6
21-3 x 20-3
Bath
Hall
Hall
Br 7
11-8 x 13-0
Lower Foyer
17-8 x 22-6
Theatre Room
20-0 x 14-5
Bath
Mech./Stor.
Laundry/
Summer Kit.
16-3 x 12-0

Units	Single
Price Code	L
Total Finished	8,690 sq. ft.
First Finished	3,542 sq. ft.
Second Finished	1,606 sq. ft.
Lower Finished	3,542 sq. ft.
Garage Unfinished	1,179 sq. ft.
Deck Unfinished	556 sq. ft.
Porch Unfinished	187 sq. ft.
Dimensions	115'6"x90'
Foundation	Basement
Bedrooms	7
Full Baths	5
First Ceiling	8'
Second Ceiling	8'
Vaulted Ceiling	16'
Max Ridge Height	25'
Roof Framing	Truss
Exterior Walls	2x6

Everything you Need...to Make Your Dream Come True!

Exterior Elevations

These front, rear, and sides of the home include information pertaining to the exterior finish materials, roof pitches, and exterior height dimensions.

Cabinet Plans

These plans, or in some cases elevations, will detail the layout of the kitchen and bathroom cabinets at a larger scale. Available for most plans.

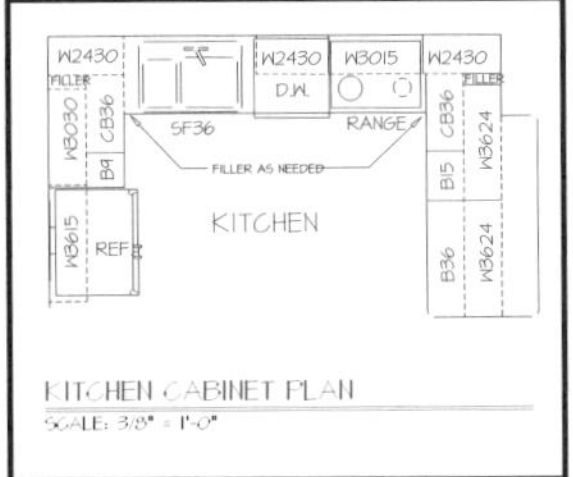
W2430
W2430
W3015
W2430
DW
RANGE
SF36
FILLER AS NEEDED
KITCHEN
REF
KITCHEN CABINET PLAN

Typical Wall Section

This section will address insulation, roof components, and interior and exterior wall finishes. Your plans will be designed with either 2x4 or 2x6 exterior walls, but if you wish, most professional contractors can easily adapt the plans to the wall thickness you require.

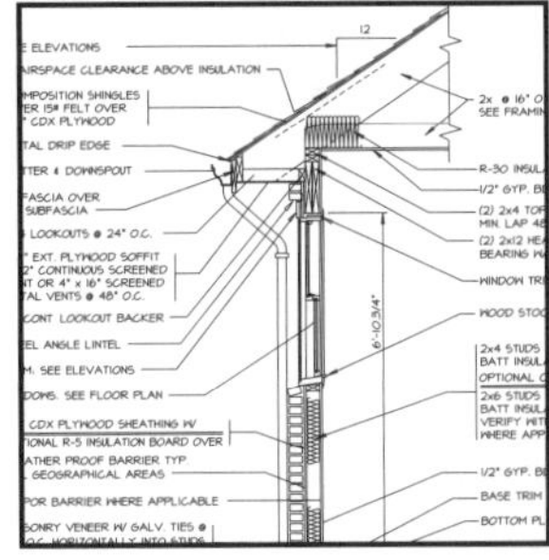

Fireplace Details

If the home you have chosen includes a fireplace, a fireplace detail will show typical methods of constructing the firebox, hearth, and flue chase for masonry units, or a wood frame chase for zero-clearance units. Available for most plans.

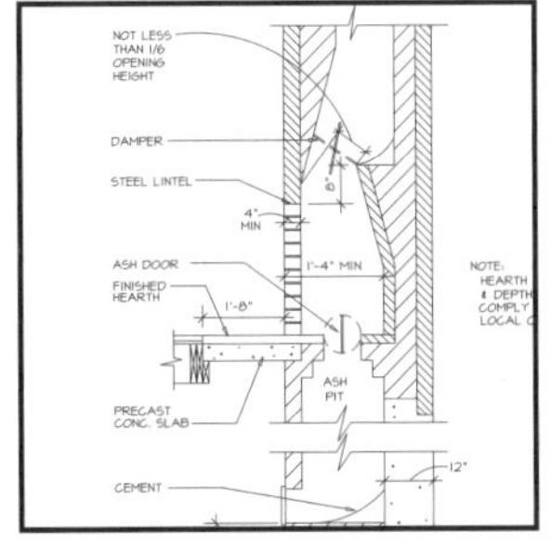
NOT LESS THAN 1/8 OPENING HEIGHT
DAMPER
STEEL LINTEL
ASH DOOR
FINISHED HEARTH
PRECAST CONC. SLAB
CEMENT
ASH PIT

Foundation Plan

These plans will accurately show the dimensions of the footprint of your home, including load-bearing points and beam placement if applicable. The foundation style will vary from plan to plan.

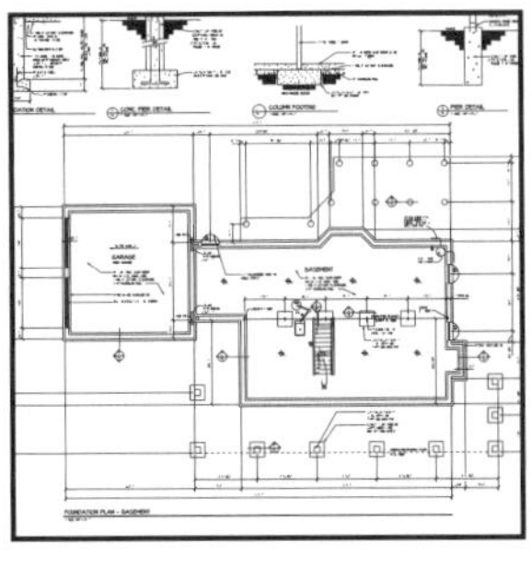

Roof Plan

The information necessary to construct the roof will be included with your home plans. Some plans will reference roof trusses, while many others contain schematic framing plans. These framing plans will indicate the lumber sizes necessary for the rafters and ridgeboards based on the designated roof loads.

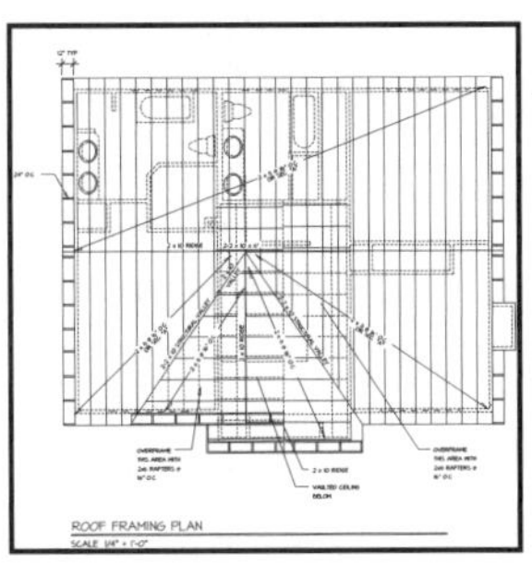
ROOF FRAMING PLAN

Typical Cross Section

A cut-away cross-section through the entire home shows your building contractor the exact correlation of construction components at all levels of the house. It will help to clarify the load bearing points from the roof all the way down to the basement. Available for most plans.

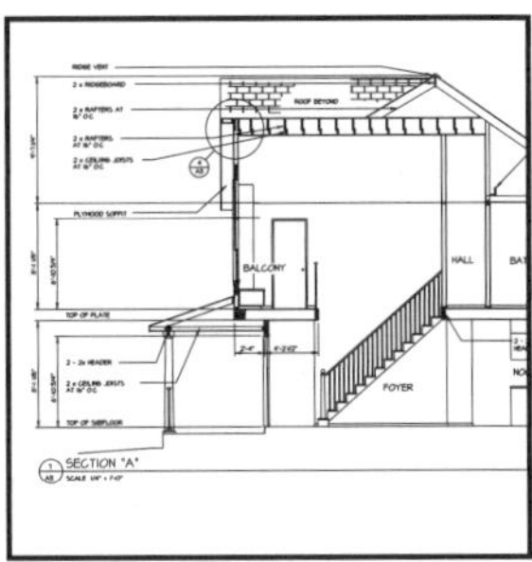
SECTION "A"
FOYER

Detailed Floor Plans

The floor plans of your home accurately depict the dimensions of the positioning of all walls, doors, windows, stairs, and permanent fixtures. They will show you the relationship and dimensions of rooms, closets, and traffic patterns. The schematic of the electrical layout may be included in the plan.

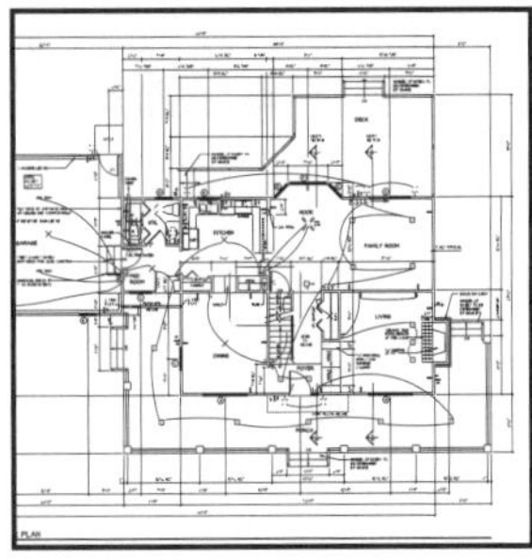

Stair Details

If the design you have chosen includes stairs, the plans will show the information that you need in order to build them—either through a stair cross section or on the floor plans.

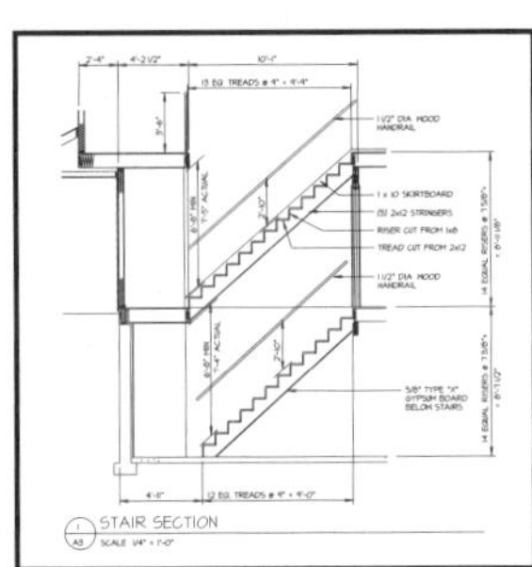
STAIR SECTION

Garlinghouse Options & Extras

Reversed Plans can Make Your Dream Home Just Right!

You could have exactly the home you want by flipping it end-for-end. Simply order your plans "reversed." We'll send you one full set of mirror-image plans (with the writing backwards) as a master guide for you and your builder.

The remaining sets of your order will come as shown in this book so the dimensions and specifications are easily read on the job site. Most plans in our collection come stamped "reversed" so there is no construction confusion.

We can only send reversed plans with multiple-set orders. There is a $50 charge for this service.

Some plans in our collection are available in "Right Reading Reverse." Right Reading Reverse plans will show your home in reverse. This easy-to-read format will save you valuable time and money. Please contact our Sales Department at 800-235-5700 to check for Right Reading Reverse availability. There is a $135 charge for this service. **RRR**

Remember to Order Your Materials List

Available at a modest additional charge, the Materials List gives the quantity, dimensions, and specifications for the major materials needed to build your home. You will get faster, more accurate bids from your contractors and building suppliers—and avoid paying for unused materials and waste. Materials Lists are available for all home plans except as otherwise indicated, but can only be ordered with a set of home plans. Due to differences in regional requirements and homeowner or builder preferences, electrical, plumbing and heating/air conditioning equipment specifications are not designed specifically for each plan. **ML**

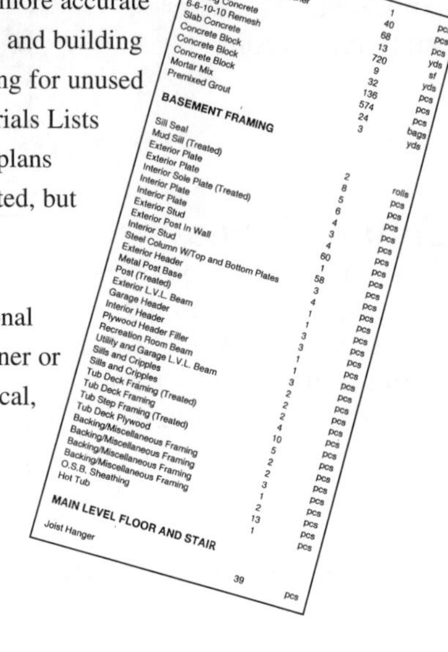
6 mil Visqueen
Anchor Bolt, Nut and Washer
#5 Rebar
Footing Concrete
6-6-10-10 Remesh
Slab Concrete
Concrete Block
Concrete Block
Concrete Block
Mortar Mix
Premixed Grout
BASEMENT FRAMING
Sill Seal
Mud Sill (Treated)
Exterior Plate
Exterior Plate
Interior Sole Plate (Treated)
Interior Plate
Interior Plate
Exterior Stud
Exterior Post In Wall
Interior Stud
Steel Column W/Top and Bottom Plates
Exterior Header
Metal Post Base
Post (Treated)
Exterior L.V.L. Beam
Garage Header
Interior Header
Plywood Header Filler
Recreation Room Beam
Utility and Garage L.V.L. Beam
Sills and Cripples
Sills and Cripples
Tub Deck Framing (Treated)
Tub Deck Framing
Tub Step Framing (Treated)
Tub Deck Plywood
Backing/Miscellaneous Framing
Backing/Miscellaneous Framing
Backing/Miscellaneous Framing
Backing/Miscellaneous Framing
O.S.B. Sheathing
Hot Tub
MAIN LEVEL FLOOR AND STAIR
Joist Hanger
1 40 68 13 720 9 32 136 574 24 3
2 8 5 6 4 3 4 60 1 58 3 4 1 1 3 3 1 1 3 2 2 2 4 10 5 2 2 3 1 2 13 1
39
pcs pcs pcs yds sf yds pcs pcs pcs bags yds
rolls pcs pcs pcs pcs pcs pcs pcs pcs pcs pcs pcs pcs pcs pcs pcs pcs pcs pcs pcs pcs pcs pcs pcs pcs pcs pcs pcs pcs pcs pcs pcs
pcs

What Garlinghouse Offers

Home Plan Blueprint Package

By purchasing a multiple-set package of blueprints or a Vellum from Garlinghouse, you not only receive the physical blueprint documents necessary for construction, but you are also granted a license to build one (and only one) home. You can also make simple modifications, including minor non-structural changes and material substitutions, to our design as long as these changes are made directly on the blueprints purchased from Garlinghouse and no additional copies are made.

Home Plan Vellums

By purchasing Vellums for one of our home plans, you receive the same construction drawings found in the blueprints, but printed on vellum paper. Vellums can be erased and are perfect for making design changes. They are also semi-transparent, making them easy to duplicate. But most importantly, the purchase of home plan Vellums comes with a broader license that allows you to make changes to the design (i.e., create a hand drawn or CAD derivative work), to make copies of the plan, and to build one home from the plan.

License to Build Additional Homes

With the purchase of a blueprint package or Vellums, you automatically receive a license to build one home and only one home. If you want to build more homes than you are licensed to build through your purchase of a plan, then additional licenses must be purchased at reasonable costs from Garlinghouse. Inquire for more information.

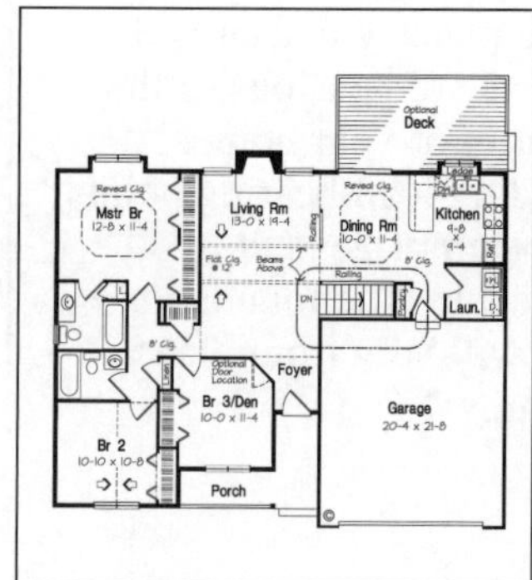
Deck
Mstr Br
12-8 x 11-4
Living Rm
13-0 x 14-4
Dining Rm
10-0 x 11-4
Kitchen
Laun.
Foyer
Br 3/Den
10-0 x 11-4
Br 2
10-10 x 10-8
Garage
20-4 x 21-8
Porch

Modifying Your Favorite Design Made Easy

MODIFICATION PRICING GUIDE

CATEGORIES	AVERAGE COST from... to
Adding or removing living space (square footage)	Quote required
Adding or removing a garage	Starting at $400
Garage: Front entry to side load or vice versa	Starting at $300
Adding a screened porch	Starting at $280
Adding a bonus room in the attic	Starting at $450
Changing full basement to crawl space or vice versa	Starting at $495
Changing full basement to slab or vice versa	Starting at $495
Changing exterior building materials	Starting at $200
Changing roof lines	Starting at $360
Adjusting ceiling height	Starting at $280
Adding, moving or removing an exterior opening	$65 per opening
Adding or removing a fireplace	Starting at $90
Modifying a non-bearing wall or room	$65 per room
Changing exterior walls from 2"x4" to 2"x6"	Starting at $200
Redesigning a bathroom or a kitchen	Starting at $120
Reverse plan right reading	Quote required
Adapting plans for local building code requirements	Quote required
Engineering and Architectural stamping and services	Quote required
Adjust plan for handicapped accessibility	Quote required
Interactive Illustrations (choices of exterior materials)	Quote required
Metric conversion of home plan	Quote required

***Please remember that figures shown are average costs. Your quote may be higher or lower depending upon your specific requirements.**

#1 Modifying Your Garlinghouse Home Plan

Simple modifications to your dream home, including minor non-structural changes and material substitutions, can be made by you and your builder by marking the changes directly on your blueprints. However, if you are considering making significant changes to your chosen design, we recommend that you use the services of The Garlinghouse Design Staff. We will help take your ideas and turn them into a reality, just the way you want. Here's our procedure:

When you place your Vellum order, you may also request a free Garlinghouse Modification Kit. In this kit, you will receive a red marking pencil, furniture cut-out sheet, ruler, a self-addressed mailing label, and a form for specifying any additional notes or drawings that will help us understand your design ideas. Mark your desired changes directly on the Vellum drawings. ***NOTE:*** Please use only a **red pencil** to mark your desired changes on the Vellum. Then, return the red-lined Vellum set in the original box to us.

Important: Please roll the Vellums for shipping—***do not fold***.

We also offer modification estimates. For a $50 fee, we will provide you with an estimate to draft your changes based on your specific modifications before you purchase the Vellums. After you receive your estimate, if you decide to have us do the changes, the $50 estimate fee will be deducted from the cost of your modifications. If, however, you choose to use a different service, the $50 estimate fee is non-refundable. (***Note:*** Personal checks cannot be accepted for the estimate.)

Within five days of receipt of your plans, you will be contacted by a member of the design staff with an estimate for the design services to draw those changes. A 50% deposit is required before we begin making the actual modifications to your plans.

Once the design changes have been completed to your Vellum plan, a representative will call to inform you that your modified Vellum plan is complete and will be shipped as soon as the final payment has been made. For additional information, call us at 1-800-235-5700. Please refer to the Modification Pricing Guide for estimated modification costs.

#2 Reproducible Vellums for Local Modification Ease

If you decide not to use Garlinghouse for your modifications, we recommend that you follow our same procedure of purchasing Vellums. You then have the option of using the services of the original designer of the plan, a local professional designer, or an architect to make the modifications.

With a Vellum copy of our plans, a design professional can alter the drawings just the way you want, then you can print as many copies of the modified plans as you need to build your house. And, since you have already started with our complete detailed plans, the cost of those expensive professional services will be significantly less than starting from scratch. Refer to the price schedule for Vellum costs.

Questions? Call our Customer Service Department at 1-800-235-5700

Ignoring Copyright Laws Can Be A $100,000 MISTAKE

U.S. copyright laws allow for statutory penalties of up to $100,000 per incident for copyright infringement involving any of the copyrighted plans found in this publication. The law can be confusing. So, for your own protection, take the time to understand what you can and cannot do when it comes to home plans.

What You Can't Do

You Cannot Duplicate Home Plans

Purchasing a set of blueprints and making additional sets by reproducing the original is illegal. If you need more than one set of a particular home plan, you must purchase them.

You Cannot Copy any Part of a Home Plan to Create Another

Creating your own plan by copying even part of a home design found in this publication without permission is called "creating a derivative work" and is illegal.

You Cannot Build a Home Without a License

You must have specific permission or a license to build a home from a copyrighted design, even if the finished home has been changed from the original plan. It is illegal to build one of the homes found in this publication without a license.

Top 5 Reasons to Visit Us On-line

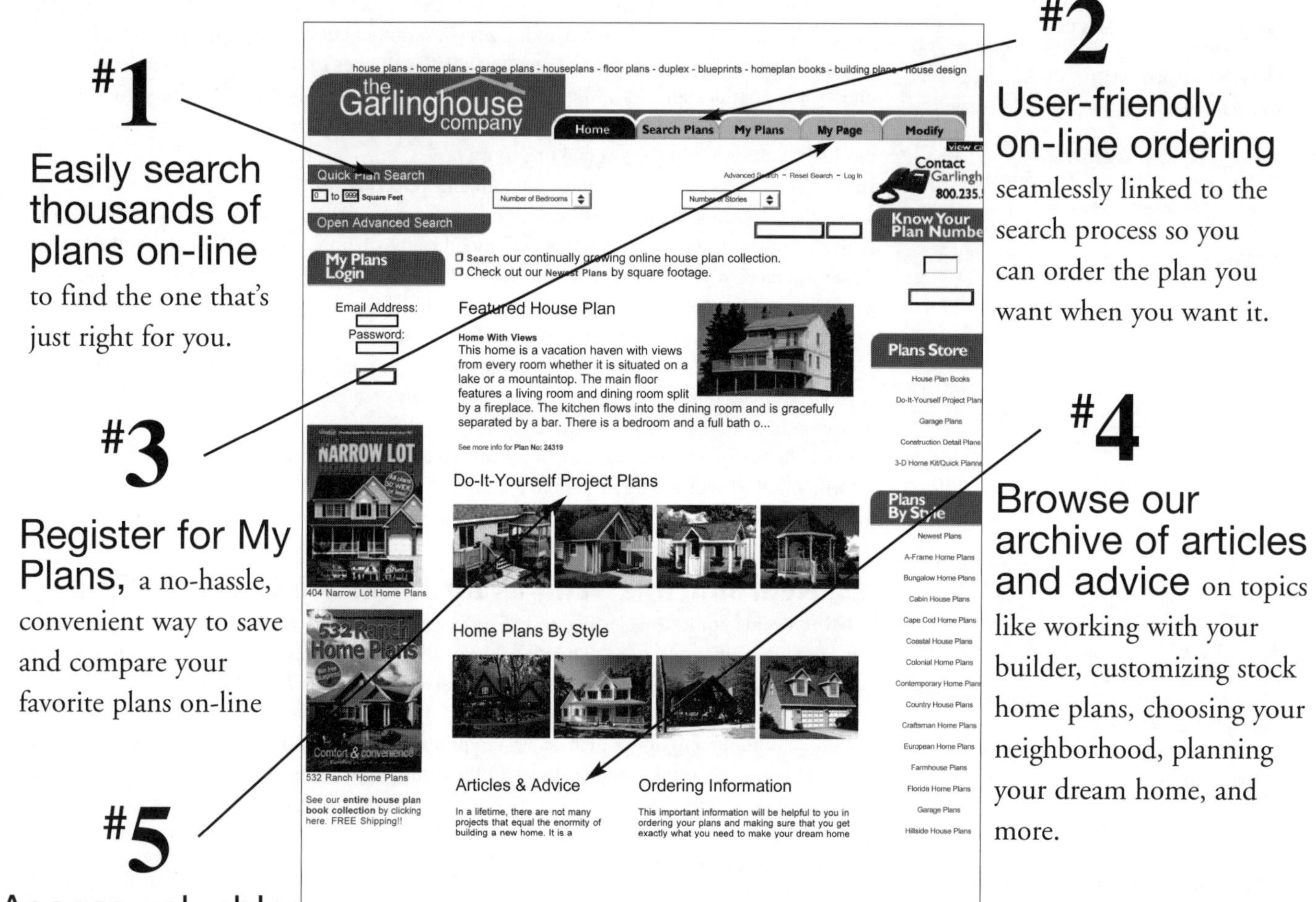
#1
Easily search thousands of plans on-line to find the one that's just right for you.
#2
User-friendly on-line ordering seamlessly linked to the search process so you can order the plan you want when you want it.
#3
Register for My Plans, a no-hassle, convenient way to save and compare your favorite plans on-line
#4
Browse our archive of articles and advice on topics like working with your builder, customizing stock home plans, choosing your neighborhood, planning your dream home, and more.
#5
Access valuable resources like mortgage calculators, helpful links, and information on buying and building stock home plans.
the Garlinghouse company
Home
Search Plans
My Plans
My Page
Modify
Quick Plan Search
Open Advanced Search
My Plans Login
Email Address:
Password:
Featured House Plan
Home With Views
This home is a vacation haven with views from every room whether it is situated on a lake or a mountaintop. The main floor features a living room and dining room split by a fireplace. The kitchen flows into the dining room and is gracefully separated by a bar. There is a bedroom and a full bath o...
Do-It-Yourself Project Plans
Home Plans By Style
Articles & Advice
Ordering Information
404 Narrow Lot Home Plans
532 Ranch Home Plans
Plans Store
Plans By Style

At Garlinghouse, we've been providing blueprints for the American dream since 1907. That's nearly 100 years of experience in providing our customers with the best, most up-to-date selection of home plans and the most comprehensive customer service available. Whether you need a large home, small home, or even just a garage, we've got your plan. Visit us on-line or give us a call at 1-800-235-5700.

www.familyhomeplans.com

From the Garlinghouse Company. Experience, Trust, and Value. Since 1907.

the Garlinghouse company **BEST PLAN VALUE IN THE INDUSTRY!**

Order Code No. **H6BHB**

Order Form

_______________ foundation

____ set(s) of blueprints for plan # __________ $______

____ Vellum __________ $______

____ Additional set(s) @ $50 each for plan # __________ $______

____ Mirror Image Reverse @ $50 each $______

____ Right Reading Reverse @ $135 each $______

____ Materials list for plan # __________ $______

____ Detail Plans @ $19.95 each

❑ Construction ❑ Plumbing ❑ Electrical $______

Shipping $______

Subtotal $______

Sales Tax (VA and SC residents add 5% sales tax. Not required for other states.) $______

TOTAL AMOUNT ENCLOSED $______

Send your check, money order, or credit card information to:
(No C.O.D.'s Please)

Please submit all United States & other nations orders to:
Garlinghouse Company
4125 Lafayette Center Drive, Suite 100
Chantilly, VA. 20151
CALL: (800) 235-5700 FAX: (703) 222-9705

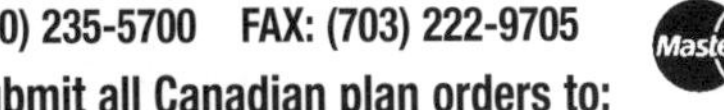

Please Submit all Canadian plan orders to:
Garlinghouse Company
102 Ellis Street
Penticton, BC V2A 4L5
CALL: (800) 361-7526 FAX: (250) 493-7526

ADDRESS INFORMATION:

NAME: ____________________

STREET: ____________________

CITY: ____________________

STATE: ____________ ZIP: ____________

DAYTIME PHONE: ____________________

E-MAIL ADDRESS: ____________________

Credit Card Information

Charge To: ❑ Visa ❑ Mastercard ❑ AMEX ❑ Discover

Card # |_|_|_|_|_|_|_|_|_|_|_|_|_|_|_|_|

Signature ____________________ Exp. ____/____

Payment must be made in U.S. funds. Foreign Mail Orders: Certified bank checks in U.S. funds only

To order your plan on-line now using our secure server, visit:
www.familyhomeplans.com

CUSTOMER SERVICE	**TO PLACE ORDERS**
Questions on existing orders?	• To order your home plans • Questions about a plan
→ **1-800-895-3715**	→ **1-800-235-5700**

Shipping

US Orders

Ground:	$20
2nd:	$35
Overnight:	$45

Canada

Overnight	$80

International 3 to 4 weeks $100

Plans ship out the following business day

Privacy Statement (please read)

Dear Valued Garlinghouse Customer,

Your privacy is extremely important to us. We'd like to take a little of your time to explain our privacy policy.

As a service to you, we would like to provide your name to companies such as the following:

- Building material manufacturers that we are affiliated with, who would like to keep you current with their product line and specials.
- Building material retailers that would like to offer you competitive prices to help you save money.
- Financing companies that would like to offer you competitive mortgage rates.

In addition, as our valued customer, we would like to send you newsletters to assist in your building experience. *We* would also appreciate *your* feedback by filling out a customer service survey aimed to improve our operations.

You have total control over the use of your contact information. You let us know exactly how you want to be contacted. Please check all boxes that apply.

Thank you.

☐ Don't mail
☐ Don't call
☐ Don't E-mail
☐ Only send Garlinghouse newsletters and customer service surveys

In closing, we hope this shows Garlinghouse's firm commitment to providing superior customer service and protection of your privacy. We thank you for your time and consideration.

Sincerely,

The Garlinghouse Company

BEFORE ORDERING, PLEASE READ ALL ORDERING INFORMATION

For Our **USA** Customers:
Order Toll Free: 1-800-235-5700
Monday-Thursday 8:00 am - 7:00 pm
Friday 8:00 am - 6:00 pm
Saturday 10:00 am - 4:00 pm Eastern Time
or FAX your Credit Card order to 1-703-222-9705

CUSTOMER SERVICE	TO PLACE ORDERS
Questions on existing orders?	• To order your home plans • Questions about a plan
➡ 1-800-895-3715	➡ 1-800-235-5700

For Our **Canadian** Customers:
Order Toll Free: 1-800-361-7526
Monday-Friday 8:00 a.m. to 5:00 p.m. Pacific Time
or FAX your Credit Card order to 1-250-493-7526
Customer Service: 1-250-493-0942

Please have ready: 1. Your credit card number 2. The plan number 3. The order code number ⇨ **H6BHB**

Garlinghouse 2006 Blueprint Price Code Schedule

**Prices subject to change without notice.*

Price Code	1 Set Study Set	4 Sets	8 sets	Vellums	CADD Files	Material List	Additional Sets
AAA	$ 385.00	$ 435.00	$ 485.00	$ 600.00	$ 1,100.00	$ 60.00	$ 40.00
AA	$ 435.00	$ 485.00	$ 535.00	$ 650.00	$ 1,150.00	$ 60.00	$ 40.00
A	$ 485.00	$ 535.00	$ 585.00	$ 700.00	$ 1,200.00	$ 60.00	$ 50.00
B	$ 515.00	$ 565.00	$ 615.00	$ 730.00	$ 1,230.00	$ 60.00	$ 50.00
C	$ 545.00	$ 595.00	$ 645.00	$ 760.00	$ 1,260.00	$ 70.00	$ 50.00
D	$ 575.00	$ 625.00	$ 675.00	$ 790.00	$ 1,290.00	$ 70.00	$ 50.00
E	$ 605.00	$ 655.00	$ 705.00	$ 820.00	$ 1,320.00	$ 70.00	$ 50.00
F	$ 635.00	$ 685.00	$ 735.00	$ 850.00	$ 1,350.00	$ 70.00	$ 50.00
G	$ 665.00	$ 715.00	$ 765.00	$ 880.00	$ 1,380.00	$ 70.00	$ 50.00
H	$ 695.00	$ 745.00	$ 795.00	$ 910.00	$ 1,410.00	$ 80.00	$ 60.00
I	$ 725.00	$ 775.00	$ 825.00	$ 940.00	$ 1,440.00	$ 80.00	$ 60.00
J	$ 755.00	$ 805.00	$ 855.00	$ 970.00	$ 1,470.00	$ 80.00	$ 60.00
K	$ 785.00	$ 835.00	$ 885.00	$ 1,000.00	$ 1,500.00	$ 80.00	$ 60.00
L	$ 845.00	$ 895.00	$ 945.00	$ 1,060.00	$ 1,560.00	$ 90.00	$ 70.00
M	$ 905.00	$ 955.00	$ 1,005.00	$ 1,120.00	$ 1,620.00	$ 90.00	$ 70.00
N	$ 965.00	$ 1,015.00	$ 1,065.00	$ 1,180.00	$ 1,680.00	$ 90.00	$ 70.00

IMPORTANT INFORMATION TO READ BEFORE YOU PLACE YOUR ORDER

How Many Sets of Plans Will You Need?

The Standard 8-Set Construction Package

*Our experience shows that you'll speed up every step of construction and avoid costly building errors by ordering enough sets to go around. Each tradesperson wants a set—the general contractor and all subcontractors: foundation, electrical, plumbing, heating/air conditioning, and framers. Don't forget your lending institution, building department, and, of course, a set for yourself. * Recommended For Construction **

The Minimum 4-Set Construction Package

*If you're comfortable with arduous follow-up, this package can save you a few dollars by giving you the option of passing down plan sets as work progresses. You might have enough copies to go around if work goes exactly as scheduled and no plans are lost or damaged by subcontractors. But for only $60 more, the 8-set package eliminates these worries. * Recommended For Bidding **

The 1 Set-Study Set

We offer this set so you can study the blueprints to plan your dream home in detail. They are stamped "study set only—not for construction" and you cannot build a home from them. In pursuant to copyright laws, it is illegal to reproduce any blueprint. 1 set-study sets cannot be ordered in a reversed format.

To Reorder, Call 800-235-5700

If you find after your initial purchase that you require additional sets of plans, a materials list, or other items, you may purchase them from us at special reorder prices (please call for pricing details) provided that you reorder within six months of your original order date. There is a $28 reorder processing fee that is charged on all reorders. For more information on reordering plans, please contact our Sales Department.

Customer Service Call 800-895-3715

If for some reason you have a question about your existing order, please call 800-895-3715. Your plans are custom printed especially for you once you place your order. For that reason we cannot accept any returns.

Important Shipping Information

Please refer to the shipping charts on the order form for service availability for your specific plan number. Our delivery service must have a street address or Rural Route Box number—never a post office box. (PLEASE NOTE: Supplying a P.O. Box number will only will delay the shipping of your order.) Use a work address if no one is home during the day. Orders being shipped to APO or FPO must go via First Class Mail. Please include the proper postage.

For our International Customers, only Certified bank checks and money orders are accepted and must be payable in U.S. currency. For speed, we ship international orders Air Parcel Post. Please refer to the chart for the correct shipping cost.

Important Canadian Shipping Information

To our friends in Canada, we have a plan design affiliate in Penticton, BC. This relationship will help you avoid the delays and charges associated with shipments from the United States. Moreover, our affiliate is familiar with the building requirements in your community and country. We prefer payments in U.S. currency. If you however are sending Canadian funds, please add 45% to the prices of the plans and shipping fees.

An Important Note About Building Code Requirements

All plans are drawn to conform to one or more of the industry's major national building standards. However, due to the variety of local building regulations, your plan may need to be modified to comply with local requirements—snow loads, energy loads, seismic zones, etc. Do check them fully and consult your local building officials.

A few states require that all building plans used be drawn by an architect registered in that state. While having your plans reviewed and stamped by such an architect may be prudent, laws requiring non-conforming plans like ours to be completely redrawn forces you to unnecessarily pay very large fees. If your state has such a law, we strongly recommend you contact your state representative to protest.

The rendering, floor plans, and technical information contained within this publication are not guaranteed to be totally accurate. Consequently, no information from this publication should be used either as a guide to constructing a home or for estimating the cost of building a home. Complete blueprints must be purchased for such purposes.

Index

Option Key

ML Materials List Available **RRR** Right Reading Reverse **DUP** Duplex

Plan	Pg.	Price	Option
10012	436	D	ML
10274	289	C	ML/RRR
10394	285	C	ML
10396	491	D	ML
10465	453	D	ML
10507	478	D	ML
10514	378	C	ML
10515	403	D	ML
10519	111	A	ML
10534	725	I	ML
10536	758	K	ML
10555	470	D	ML/RRR
10567	135	A	ML/RRR
10570	554	E	ML
10596	264	B	ML
10601	661	H	ML
10619	530	E	ML
10643	91	A	ML
10663	689	H	ML
10674	203	B	ML
10683	252	B	ML
10690	510	E	ML
10748	177	B	ML
10760	236	B	ML/RRR
10768	793	L	ML
10785	349	C	ML
10805	619	G	ML
10839	270	B	ML/RRR
19299	379	C	ML
19410	469	D	ML
19422	19	B	ML
20055	248	B	ML
20061	234	B	ML
20083	188	B	ML
20090	629	G	ML
20093	32	D	ML
20100	262	B	ML/RRR
20108	441	D	ML
20134	561	E	ML/RRR
20160	459	D	ML
20161	95	A	ML/RRR
20164	153	A	ML/RRR
20176	573	F	ML/RRR
20179	452	D	ML/RRR
20191	206	B	ML
20198	295	C	ML
20203	266	B	ML
20209	541	E	ML
20230	389	C	ML
20231	502	E	ML
20353	685	H	ML
20368	538	E	ML/RRR
22004	421	D	ML
22014	439	D	ML
24241	67	A	ML
24245	424	D	ML/RRR
24249	264	B	
24256	437	D	ML
24262	549	E	ML
24268	498	D	ML
24303	45	A	ML
24304	46	A	ML
24309	41	A	ML
24317	211	B	ML
24319	251	B	ML
24326	170	B	ML
24400	378	C	ML/RRR
24403	597	F	ML
24404	533	E	ML
24550	609	F	ML
24557	438	D	
24567	550	E	
24594	646	G	ML
24610	290	C	ML
24654	181	B	ML
24656	660	H	
24665	367	C	
24700	98	A	ML
24701	213	B	ML
24702	633	G	
24704	328	C	ML
24705	185	B	
24706	21	A	ML
24708	191	B	ML
24711	147	A	ML
24713	506	E	ML
24714	284	C	ML
24717	219	B	ML
24718	151	A	ML
24721	177	B	ML
24723	56	A	ML
24724	379	C	ML
24725	226	B	ML
24732	504	E	ML
24735	550	E	ML
24736	413	D	ML
24751	466	D	ML
24802	768	L	ML
24950	548	F	ML
24964	496	D	ML
26111	104	A	ML
26112	163	A	ML
26114	57	A	ML
32004	747	K	ML
32033	784	L	ML
32036	721	I	ML
32041	757	K	ML
32044	625	G	
32046	777	H	ML
32049	4	D	
32056	13	D	ML
32063	37	L	ML/RRR
32076	735	J	ML
32090	586	F	
32095	744	J	
32102	753	K	
32109	24	D	ML
32112	780	L	
32122	57	A	ML
32145	620	G	ML
32146	35	K	ML
32162	436	G	
32189	555	E	
32192	77	A	
32228	318	C	
32229	14	B	
32291	26	C	
~~32316~~	33	~~G~~	*Unavailable*
32321	256	B	
32323	10	A	
32330	805	L	
32332	743	E	
32337	745	E	
32345	774	L	
32353	651	G	
32358	34	I	
32369	642	D	
32399	28	A	
32426	795	L	
32437	708	I	
32606	728	I	ML
34003	62	A	ML/RRR
34011	232	B	ML/RRR
34027	374	C	ML/RRR
34029	242	B	ML/RRR
34031	314	C	ML
34043	7	B	ML/RRR
34047	600	F	ML/RRR
34049	403	D	ML/RRR
34054	128	A	ML/RRR
34055	174	B	ML/RRR
34073	607	F	ML
34077	275	C	ML
34150	165	A	ML/RRR
34600	102	A	ML/RRR
34601	133	A	ML/RRR
34602	184	B	ML
34679	388	C	ML
34705	489	D	ML/RRR
34800	289	C	ML/RRR
34825	6	D	ML
34827	497	D	ML/RRR
34851	361	C	ML/RRR
34901	25	C	ML/RRR
34926	571	F	ML/RRR
35001	207	B	ML/RRR
35007	49	A	ML
50007	202	B	
50008	582	F	
50009	311	C	
50011	271	B	
50012	553	D	
50013	245	B	
50018	579	F	
50019	760	E	
50020	712	I	
50021	22	B	
50022	578	F	
50023	525	E	
50025	294	C	
50028	572	F	
50032	332	C	
50033	574	F	
50035	109	A	
50037	452	D	
51017	9	C	ML
51018	118	A	
51020	8	A	ML
52067	548	D	
52068	631	F	
52095	653	F	
52103	529	E	ML
52124	719	I	ML
52130	687	H	ML
52141	649	G	ML
52203	556	E	ML
60003	663	H	
60013	117	A	
60020	292	C	
60052	620	G	
60066	481	D	ML
60073	350	C	
60084	158	A	
60098	363	C	
60112	64	A	
60132	250	B	
60138	670	H	
61030	471	D	
61032	161	A	
61033	161	A	
61035	164	A	
61048	297	C	
61093	43	A	
61095	449	D	
61096	455	D	
62006	605	F	
62024	129	A	
62025	149	A	
62028	233	B	ML
62053	362	C	ML
62058	205	C	ML
62062	539	E	ML
62083	455	D	
62084	306	C	ML
62086	201	B	
63001	353	C	
63018	616	G	
63021	723	I	
63027	316	C	
63028	457	D	
63045	346	C	
63046	96	A	
63047	440	D	
63048	280	B	
63049	393	C	
63050	411	D	
63052	423	E	
63054	301	C	
63055	396	C	
63056	427	C	
63066	692	H	
63068	733	J	
63072	752	K	ML
63075	785	L	
63083	194	B	
63084	187	B	
63085	418	D	
63086	282	C	
63087	284	C	
63088	184	B	
63089	187	B	
63090	276	C	
63091	214	B	
63100	490	D	
63106	585	F	
63108	545	E	
63111	287	C	
63112	307	C	
63114	336	C	
63115	338	C	
63116	341	C	
63120	417	D	
63125	399	D	
63137	58	C	
63141	348	C	
64017	213	B	ML
64128	527	H	
64132	310	G	
64165	523	H	
64171	464	H	
64173	384	H	
64194	555	H	
64196	210	G	
64500	290	C	
64504	248	D	
64508	588	F	
64508	588	F	
64513	474	D	
64515	48	C	
65000	156	A	ML
65001	159	A	ML
65003	45	A	ML
65004	31	E	ML
65005	44	A	ML
65006	12	A	ML
65008	671	H	ML
65009	30	A	ML
65012	357	C	ML
65013	20	A	ML
65014	63	A	ML
65015	113	A	ML
65036	51	A	ML
65045	40	A	ML
65048	50	A	ML
65059	139	A	ML
65073	86	A	ML
65075	67	A	ML
65078	52	A	ML
65084	74	A	ML
65091	59	A	ML
65093	54	A	ML
65095	148	A	ML
65125	401	D	ML
65131	467	D	ML/DUP
65134	95	A	
65135	427	D	
65138	36	D	
65140	84	A	
65145	513	E	ML
65149	53	A	ML
65157	355	C	ML
65161	51	A	ML
65162	38	A	ML
65173	96	A	ML
65176	109	A	ML
65179	151	A	ML
65181	144	A	ML
65198	173	B	
65207	335	C	ML
65210	377	C	ML
65234	389	E	ML
65241	16	A	ML
65259	39	A	ML
65260	47	A	ML
65263	39	A	ML
65275	165	A	ML
65284	101	A	ML
65316	526	E	ML
65366	42	A	
65376	61	A	

Index

Option Key

ML Materials List Available **RRR** Right Reading Reverse **DUP** Duplex

Index

Option Key

ML Materials List Available **RRR** Right Reading Reverse **DUP** Duplex

Plan	Pg.	Price	Option
97272	110	A	ML
97274	145	A	ML
97277	359	C	
97278	472	D	ML
97279	431	D	
97284	323	C	
97288	680	H	
97294	460	D	
97295	325	C	
97296	65	A	
97299	566	E	
97300	307	C	
97303	480	D	
97308	405	D	
97313	634	G	
97314	796	L	
97330	357	C	
97331	104	A	
97332	103	A	
97334	93	A	
97335	360	C	
97336	112	A	
97337	87	A	
97338	69	A	
97339	78	A	ML
97341	73	A	
97350	656	G	
97351	778	L	
97352	262	C	
97353	361	C	
97354	802	L	
97355	380	C	
97356	803	L	
97357	800	L	
97359	625	G	
97360	740	J	
97400	676	H	RRR
97406	411	D	ML/RRR
97408	572	F	ML/RRR
97416	321	C	ML/RRR
97427	525	E	ML/RRR
97443	146	A	ML/RRR
97455	217	B	ML
97456	276	C	ML
97462	304	B	ML
97464	191	B	ML
97466	294	C	ML
97467	70	A	ML
97470	473	D	ML
97476	94	A	
97486	570	F	
97488	446	D	ML
97489	199	B	ML
97493	136	A	ML
97494	472	D	ML
97495	212	B	ML
97503	518	E	
97504	520	E	
97505	593	F	
97506	597	F	
97507	599	F	
97513	697	H	
97604	126	A	
97609	142	A	ML
97610	300	C	
97611	309	C	
97614	91	A	
97616	333	C	
97617	242	B	ML
97618	352	C	ML
97619	408	D	
97621	521	E	
97633	705	I	
97638	120	A	
97645	766	L	ML
97652	138	A	
97678	111	A	
97707	329	C	
97708	480	D	
97710	481	D	
97712	189	B	
97719	328	C	
97731	98	A	
97737	508	E	
97740	196	B	
97755	277	C	
97757	273	B	
97759	208	B	
97760	208	B	
97762	197	B	
97763	199	B	
97764	318	C	
97773	258	B	ML
97774	492	D	
97777	333	C	
97786	190	B	
97805	759	L	
97825	475	D	
97833	509	E	
97836	77	A	
97837	576	F	
97842	557	E	
97847	477	D	
97850	500	E	
97857	526	E	
97858	488	D	
97860	767	L	
97870	354	C	
97877	788	L	
97890	441	D	
97909	329	C	
97912	391	C	
97933	257	B	ML
97946	603	F	
97978	631	G	ML
97993	369	C	ML
97999	168	A	ML
98201	577	F	
98211	668	H	
98224	271	C	
98232	657	G	
98233	524	E	
98238	360	C	
98329	492	D	
98354	143	A	ML
98361	407	D	ML
98401	695	H	ML
98405	662	H	ML
98406	204	B	ML
98407	417	D	ML
98408	330	C	ML
98409	537	E	ML
98410	543	E	ML
98413	52	A	ML
98414	190	B	ML
98415	141	A	ML
98416	211	B	ML
98418	601	F	ML
98423	231	B	ML
98424	495	D	ML
98425	323	C	ML
98426	594	F	ML
98427	416	D	ML
98430	342	C	ML
98431	235	B	ML
98432	231	B	ML
98434	107	A	ML
98435	367	C	ML
98436	714	I	ML
98441	170	B	
98443	113	A	
98444	92	A	
98445	351	C	
98447	459	D	ML
98452	673	H	ML
98454	342	C	ML
98455	530	E	ML
98456	254	B	ML
98457	603	F	ML
98458	644	G	ML
98460	178	B	
98461	68	A	
98463	200	B	
98464	286	C	ML
98466	478	D	
98467	315	C	
98468	56	A	
98469	49	A	
98470	466	D	
98472	166	A	
98474	267	B	
98476	232	B	
98478	227	B	
98485	443	D	
98486	540	E	
98488	683	H	
98493	684	H	
98493	684	H	
98497	66	A	
98498	60	A	
98505	131	A	
98508	729	I	
98511	553	E	
98512	463	D	
98514	716	I	
98517	469	D	
98518	556	E	
98519	571	F	
98534	647	G	
98536	722	I	
98539	755	K	
98544	496	D	
98548	503	E	
98549	143	A	
98554	465	D	
98555	475	D	
98557	503	E	
98559	423	D	
98560	200	B	
98561	296	C	
98569	639	G	
98571	519	E	
98572	538	E	
98580	219	B	
98583	422	D	
98588	696	H	
98589	347	C	
98590	772	L	
98593	511	E	
98594	400	D	
98596	667	H	
98598	700	H	
98714	405	D	ML
98747	89	A	ML
98807	163	A	
98812	447	D	
98912	106	A	ML
98915	75	A	ML
98924	210	B	
98925	75	A	
98931	280	C	
98946	633	G	
98956	340	C	
98957	313	C	
98958	283	C	
98959	195	B	
98960	236	B	
98961	640	G	
98968	237	B	
98970	132	A	
98980	385	C	ML
98981	254	B	ML
98982	175	B	
98983	192	B	
98984	412	B	
98984	173	B	
98985	116	A	
98986	327	C	
98987	617	G	
98988	537	E	
98989	255	C	
98990	781	L	
98991	782	L	
98992	543	G	
98993	293	C	
98994	244	B	
99045	281	C	
99055	300	C	ML
99106	167	A	
99113	349	C	
99115	368	C	RRR
99117	354	C	
99124	447	D	
99130	484	D	
99152	183	B	
99162	611	F	
99163	204	B	
99168	183	B	
99174	331	C	
99180	243	B	
99185	273	C	
99186	105	A	ML
99191	237	B	
99192	356	C	
99208	314	C	ML
99255	129	A	ML
99289	706	I	ML
99321	118	A	ML
99361	63	A	ML
99400	643	G	ML/RRR
99420	3	B	ML/RRR
99424	598	F	RRR
99427	418	G	ML/RRR/DUP
99428	78	G	ML/RRR/DUP
99430	699	H	ML
99434	325	C	ML
99437	698	H	ML
99443	746	K	ML
99446	619	G	ML
99450	604	F	ML
99457	506	E	ML
99459	501	E	ML
99463	641	G	ML
99464	742	J	ML/RRR
99467	734	J	ML/RRR
99469	573	F	ML
99472	732	J	
99473	596	F	RRR
99490	159	A	ML
99491	324	C	ML
99498	277	C	ML/RRR
99499	591	F	ML/RRR
99639	117	A	ML
99640	557	E	ML
99641	186	B	ML
99669	132	A	ML
99673	123	A	
99679	332	C	
99682	200	B	ML
99771	192	B	ML
99784	655	G	ML
99799	38	G	ML/DUP
99914	238	B	ML
99918	317	C	ML
99922	167	A	ML
99923	260	B	ML
99926	155	A	ML
99930	119	A	ML
99934	806	L	ML
99935	638	G	ML

Index

Option Key

ML Materials List Available **RRR** Right Reading Reverse **DUP** Duplex